The Complete Diary of a Cotswold Parson

The Complete Diary of a Cotswold Parson

The Diaries of the Revd. Francis Edward Witts
1783–1854
in 10 volumes

Volume 10 (Part 2)
The People and the Places

Biographical Index
H to Z
Compiled by Alan Sutton

FONTHILL

The Complete Diary of a Cotswold Parson

Volume 10

First published 2020 by
Fonthill Media Limited

www.fonthillmedia.com
office@fonthillmedia.com

ISBN 978-1-78155-800-3
(for both Part 1 and Part 2)

Front endpaper
View of Cheltenham from the roof of Pittville Pump Room,
drawn and engraved by James Fisher

15 October 1833

After breakfast accompanied my wife and son to Cheltenham ... Afterwards with Edward walked to Pittville, where we were, as non-subscribers, admitted on payment of a shilling each. The place is very well kept, the walks in excellent order, and the shrubberies much grown since I had been there; all the gardens very luxuriant. Though but a few individuals were in the splendid pump room, a small band of musicians, playing on wind instruments, performed many pleasing pieces of music.

Back endpaper
The Great Exhibition, Hyde Park

20 May 1851

Soon after passing Apsley House fell into a close line of carriages chiefly bound to the same haven as myself From Hyde Park corner along Knightsbridge, and to the entrance to the Great Exhibition, the crowd of carriages was very great: but the order quietly maintained by a line of Policemen was admirable.

Printed and bound in England

H

HADDINGTON — *see* Thomas Hamilton, 9th earl of Haddington

HADEN — George and James Haden [1]

George Haden (1788-1856) and James Haden (1790-1871), engineers. George Haden was born in Birmingham, son of a foreman of the copying machine shop at Boulton Watt & Co. He was apprenticed at Boulton Watt & Co. at their Soho manufactory in Birmingham, working on the construction of steam engines and boilers. At 21 he was sent out on the road by the firm as a travelling agent and engineer assembling, erecting, and commissioning Boulton and Watt steam engines. In 1814 he was sent by Boulton and Watt as their agent to the west of England, where there was an increasing demand for steam engines to power the machinery in the woollen mills being built in Somerset, Wiltshire, and Gloucestershire. Several mill owners in Trowbridge offered to pay him to look after their engines, which he reckoned would take less than half his time, leaving the remainder free to undertake other business. He settled in Trowbridge, where he was joined by his brother James. In 1816 they set up the firm G. and J. Haden. As well as erecting steam engines and undertaking millwright work, the firm entered the newly emerging industry of heating and ventilating with the manufacture of warm air stoves. Being a bachelor, James was the partner to travel the country supervising and taking orders for the installation of warm air stoves and expanding the firm's business. Their early clients included landed gentry, and in 1826 they installed warm air stoves at Windsor Castle for George IV.

1838: 14 Aug: *Before attending at the Turnpike meeting, I had visited the Bridewell to confer with Ford and a person named Haden, from Trowbridge, on the best method of warming the day cells on the ground floor of the prison, by an hot water apparatus.*

1839: 6 Apr: *The former accompanied me to the Bridewell, where the vis. Mag. Messrs. Lawrence and Talbot had been auditing the Quarter's accounts; glanced over the Books, and inspected the alterations which had been made by Messrs. Haden of Trowbridge for ventilating and warming the ranges of day cells with their hotwater apparatus, which is on a different and more expensive construction than is usual: but is said to answer well, and to diffuse a more wholesome warmth, combining heat with ventilation.*

HADLEY — John Joseph Hadley [2]

John Joseph Hadley (1822-1872), printer and publisher, was born at Cheltenham, son of John Joseph Allan Hadley (1789-1849) and Mary Russell (1793-1866). He was the proprietor of the *Cheltenham Journal* at Queen's Buildings, 318 High Street, Cheltenham, employing one man and two boys. He married Elizabeth (b. ±1820); they had at least 2 sons and 1 daughter:

1 Frederick William (b. ±1851)
1 Bessie Louisa (b. ±1853)
2 George Ernest Clarence (b. 1860)

1852: 16 Jan: *A bill from Hadley, proprietor and Editor of the Cheltenham Journal.*

HADSLEY — Miss Hadsley, a performer at Lady Lyttelton's musical evening

1801: 27 May: *In the Evening to a party at Lady Lyttelton's, which was musical; The Harp, Grand Piano Forte & voice; the chief performers were, Miss Hadsley, Miss Bowles, Miss Canning, Miss Kearney, the Misses Halifax, Miss Stanhope, le Compte de Montmorency &c.* 3 Jun: *Repaired in the Evening to Lady Lytteltons, where was rather a squeeze & music., Miss Guydickens's, Lady E. Lee, Mr. E. Stanhope, & a French Count & Countess &c. Miss Hadsley's played & Miss Halifax sung; Miss Bowles played, & Miss Canning sung.*

HADWEN — William Vann Hadwen [3]

William Vann Hadwen (1801-1835), surgeon, was born at Whetstone, Leicestershire, son of Thomas and Sarah Hadwen. He married, at Gloucester, 2 August 1826, Charlotte Collingwood (b. ±1805); they had at least 2 sons and 3 daughters:

1 Charlotte (b. 1827)
1 William Tidd Vann (b. 1828)
2 Julia (b. 1830)
3 Jane (b. 1831)
2 Tom (b. 1833)

Hadwen kept a detailed journal of his time as surgeon at Bridewell and recorded the high rate of venereal disease among the inmates, both male and female.

1835: 3 Feb: *In the evening, Mr. Hadwen, Surgeon to the Bridewell at Northleach, called upon me in my capacity of Visiting Magistrate. It seems, that on the evening of the 30th. Ult. the smallpox broke out again in the Bridewell, the head-turnkey being seized with the complaint, but the disease was not, as before, of a confluent character, but the eruption distinct. Three Prisoners had also caught the infection, and were in the hospital.* 24 Apr: *Townsend, the Keeper of the Bridewell at Northleach called with a set of Queries from the Prison Committee of the House of Lords which I assisted him to answer. He was also the bearer of a note from Mr. Hadwen, the surgeon of the Bridewell... proposing Mr. Lamley of Northleach or Mr. Cheatle of Burford as substitutes to discharge his duties towards the prisoners, during the period of his absence.*

HAGUE — Charles Hague [4]

Charles Hague (1769-1821), violinist, composer and professor of music, was born at Tadcaster, Yorkshire, son of Robert Hague. He was taught music and the violin by his elder brother William, and was later educated at Trinity Hall, Cambridge. In 1799 he succeeded John Randall at Trinity Hall as professor of music and in 1801 became MusD. He married, 12 November 1791, Harriet Hussey of Clapton; they had at least 3 daughters:

1 Harriet (1792-1816); became an accomplished pianist and wrote songs
2 Sophia (b. 1794)
3 Charlotte (b. 1797)

1820: 29 Jun: *I joined a musical party at Mr. Hippisley: Dr. Hague & his Daughter (he the Professor of Music at Cambridge) are the principal performers; both excellent players on the Violin.*

HAIDE — Johann Michael Friedrich Haide [5]

Johann Michael Friedrich Haide (1771-1840), actor, was born at Mainz. He is said to have been studying medicine in Duisburg when he joined the acting company of P. M. Reinberg in around 1791, originally acting under the name of Löwenfels. He followed Heinrich Vohs to Weimar. After Goethe's resignation from theatre management, Haide abandoned thoughts of retirement and remained at the Weimar stage until the end of his life. He is said to have had a very imposing appearance, which was appreciated by Witts.

1799: 12 Nov: *best Actors Vohsin, Malkolmi, Graff, Schall, Haide, Vohs & Becker.* 4 Dec., 14 Dec., 23 Dec.

1800: 30 Jan: *Representation was spoilt by the acting of Haide in the part of Seide.* 18 Feb., 3 Mar: *Extremely well acted by Haide, Vohs, Cordemann, Caspar, Graff, Spitzeder, and Teller.* 17 Mar: *well acted by Vohs, Malkolmi, Vohsin, Weyrauch, Spangler, Genast, Haide, & Becker.*

HAKE — George Hake[6]

George Hake (1783-1848), Church of England clergyman, was born in London, son of Thomas Hake of Percy Street, Bedford Square. He was educated at St John's, Cambridge. His first clerical appointment was as curate of Ellaston in 1812. He was then perpetual curate of Rocester, Staffordshire, 1820-48; vicar of Chilvers-Coton, 1829-44; and finally vicar of Ellaston, 1830-48.

---

6 Aug: *We found there, inmates of the House, Mrs. Port & her unmarried Daughter, Mrs. Ram's mother & Sister, with whom I had long ago been intimate, & Mr. Hake, the worthy and zealous Curate of Ellaston, who superintends the education of Mr. Ram's son.*

HAKEWILL — Henry Hakewill[7]

Henry Hakewill (1771-1830), architect, was the eldest son of John Hakewill (1742-1791), landscape and portrait painter, and Anna Maria Cook (1747-1818). He was the brother of James Hakewill (1778-1843). Hakewill was a pupil of John Yenn and was admitted to the Royal Academy Schools in 1790, in which year he was awarded a silver medal for a drawing of the Strand frontage of Somerset House. In 1809 Hakewill was appointed architect to Rugby School, where he designed the Gothic buildings and chapel between 1818 and 1821. He was also architect to the Radcliffe trustees at Oxford, and to the benchers of the Middle Temple, where he designed the parliament chambers (1822-24).

1827: 6 Dec: *We called at Wormington Grange. I accompanied Miss Kinloch, Mrs. Penfold and my wife in Lady Elcho's coach. We were received by Mrs. Perkins. Her father, Mr. Gist, is making large additions to the house, and employs Mr. Hakewell as an Architect, an artist of considerable reputation in his line: the plan proposed seems very suitable, and the structure will be simple and gentlemanlike, while the interior will be very commodious.*

HALDANE — John Haldane[8]

John Haldane (±1775-1857), fur trader. Haldane's career appears to have started on the Saskatchewan river in 1798 with the New North West Company. Four years later, in 1802, he joined the firm as a wintering partner. From 1805 to 1811 he was in charge of the Monontagué department to the west of Lake Nipigon, where the New North West Company conducted trade in fierce rivalry with the Hudson Bay Company. Competition sometimes became violent; in 1809, Aeneas Macdonell of New North West was killed in a clash with Hudson Bay men at Eagle Lake. When the two companies merged in 1821 under the name of Hudson Bay Company, Haldane became a chief factor and, with John Dugald Cameron, assumed command of the Columbia district. Haldane retired to Scotland, taking up residence in Haddington. In 1827 he received £2,665 from the Hudson Bay Company for his interest.

1836: 26 Jul: *With his Lordship, we found a Scotch Gentleman, Mr Haldane, an elderly man, whose early life had been spent in the inclement climate of North America, where he had passed many years as the confidential Agent of the North West Company, a situation which had exposed him to great privations at times, especially when employed in providing supplies for different expeditions of discovery in the frozen districts of the Northern parts of the New world.* 27 Jul: *Mr. Haldane had left Stanway early on his road to Town.*

HALE — Charles Henry Hale[9]

Charles Henry Hale (±1785-1864), music vendor, traded from 288 High Street before moving to 307 High Street, Cheltenham. He married Eliza Bullen (b. ±1786); they had at least 1 son and 2 daughters:

1 Maria Preston (1814-1894)
1 Edward H. (b. 1825)
2 Mary Ann (b. 182[?])

1838: 10 May: *E.F.W. had been at Stow visiting at the Rectory for some hours yesterday afternoon, and I recd. a note from him before I left Stow, brought by the person who had been conveying to Whichford the piano which my Son had bought at Hale's Music Warehouse at Cheltenham to whom, by my son's suggestion, I forwarded a cheque for the amount which he had agreed to give for the Piano.*

HALE — Robert Hale Blagden Hale and the Hale family of Alderley[10]

Robert Hale Blagden Hale (1780-1855), JP and landed proprietor, was the son of John Blagden (±1740-1808) and Anne Hale of Alderley. They married the year before Robert's birth, in 1779. John Blagden succeeded to the estate of Alderley in 1784 with the death of Matthew Hale, a lifelong bachelor. John assumed the name and arms of Hale by royal sign manual in December of that year, and was appointed high sheriff for Gloucestershire for 1790.

Robert Hale Blagden Hale was educated at Christ Church, Oxford (BA 1803). He was a JP and high sheriff for Gloucestershire in 1826. He married, 1807, Theodosia Eleanor (±1781-1845), daughter of Joseph Deane Bourke, 3rd earl of Mayo, archbishop of Tuam; they had at least 4 sons and 1 daughter:

1 Robert Blagden (1807-1883); *see below*
2 John Richard Blagden (1809-1864); educated at Christ Church, Oxford; joined the Army and rose to colonel. Married, 1848, Jane Clare (d. 1861). Two walk-on parts in the diaries: first at Stow Provident Bank, 9 October 1834; second with his sister-in-law's cousin, Robert Stayner Holford, 17 March 1852
3 Matthew (1811-1895)
4 Edward (1814-1881)
1 Theodosia Eleanor (1816-1887)

Robert Blagden Hale (1807-1883), JP, MP, and landed proprietor, was born at Alderley, son of Robert Hale Blagden Hale and Theodosia Eleanor Bourke (*above*). He was educated at Corpus Christi, Oxford (BA 1829). He was JP for Wiltshire and Gloucestershire, high sheriff for Gloucestershire in 1870, and MP for West Gloucestershire in 1836-57. He married, at Westonbirt, Gloucestershire, 6 August 1832, Ann Jane (1812-1879), daughter of Peter John Holford of Westonbirt; they had at least 2 sons and 3 daughters:

1 Ann (1832-1912); married, at Alderley, Gloucestershire, 24 November 1859, Thomas Henry Sherwood
1 Matthew Holford (1836-1912), army officer; died unmarried
2 Theodosia Hale (1839-1922); died unmarried
3 Georgiana (1846-1934); died unmarried
2 Blagden (b. 1852)

1826: 30 Mar: *Mr. Whish, the Sheriff's Chaplain & Brother in law. The Sheriff is Mr. Hale of Alderley in this County, descended from the great Sir M. Hale, the admirable and pious Judge, who possessed Alderley. The Sheriff is a man of retired habits, not generally known in the County, and residing in Wilts; he married a Lady Theodosia Bourke.* 16 Jun., 5 Aug., 15 Sep.

1829: 1 Apr.

1832: 29 Mar.

1834: 9 Oct: *To Stow, to attend my weekly duties at the Provident Bank office and in the Justice room. Messrs. Ford and Jeaffreson were my colleagues. The Dean of Gloucester looked in, but only for a short time, as usual. Other gentlemen present were Messrs. Baillie, Bowen, F. Aston, J. R. Hale, H. Rice &c.*

1835: 6 Apr.

1836: 11 Aug., 18 Oct: *None of the peers of the county present: the only M.P.'s, Codrington and Hale.*

1837: 2 Jan., 4 Jan: *The Duke of Beaufort, and R. B. Hale M.P. were on the platform.* 26 Jun: *We dined tête à tête at the Bell, as usual; but were soon joined by Dr. Cooke, who had arrived from Bristol, where he had been attending a meeting of the friends of R. B. Hale which had been called with a view to secure his reelection for the Western division of the County.* 27-28 Jun., 4 Aug.

1838: 2 Jan., 9 Apr: *The elder Hale arrived, and joined our party in the Evening at the Bell, where busied till near midnight in settling the Bridewell Accounts &c.* 10 Apr: *Breakfasted with Bathurst, Purnell and Hale at the Bell.* 15 Oct: *A sad account of R. B. Hale, MP. for the Western Division of the County, a very estimable and agreeable young man, who, on returning lately from a convivial party of his constituents, was thrown from his horse and suffered, as is believed, a concussion of the brain, by which it is understood, that his mind has been painfully affected, and that he still lies in a very precarious state, with considerable mental disturbance.* 16 Oct.

1839: 1 Jan: *There was a pretty large, though not a very full attendance of Mag. among them I saw with pleasure R B Hale, the MP. for West Gloucestershire, who looks ill and pulled down by his alarming accident, the delirium consequent upon it, and the discipline which he has undergone, but expresses himself to have now no remainder of indisposition, and to feel himself quite equal to the discharge of his usual duties.* 9-10 Apr.

1840: 30 Jun: *The Magistrates with whom, besides the two Chairmen I as most in communication were Dr. Timbrill, Ford, R B Cooper, Hale Senr. & Junr., Talbot, Waller, Barker, Ll. Baker, Canning, Crawley, Hicks &c.—The Magistrates dined together the King's Head.* 1 Jul: *The only MP. for the County present, R. Hale, proposed the address to the Queen, which was seconded by Mr. Pyrke.* 20 Oct., 5 Jan: *In the course of the evening Bathurst and I passed an hour with Robert Hale, who was obliged to seclude himself from his brother Magistrates to give rest to a bruised foot, and nothing could be more gay and even brilliant than Bathurst was in the partie quarrée of the two Hales, and our two selves.*

1842: 4 Apr: *To R B Hale MP. requesting him to use his interest with his Brother in law Holford, in Daniell's behalf, if he be the R. Holford, whom I find on the list of the Governors.* 8 Apr., 12-13 Apr.

1844: 9 Apr: *After breakfasting at the Bell, the business of the Sessions was opened in the Grand Jury room, Mr. Purnell in the Chair; besides those who were present yesterday, there were in attendance Messrs. Barker, E Viner, Mirehouse, Ford, Price, Playne, Dr. Davies, R Davies, Hartley, Hale, Hicks &c.*

1845: 26 Jan: 26 Jan: *They met with a very kind and hospitable reception, and besides some in the house, domesticated guests, Mr. Hale and Lady Theodosia, Matthew Hale, Dr. Twisleton, Mr. Huntley, Mr. Sherwood &c. they saw at the Bishop's table some of the leading people of the neighbourhood of Bristol, the Miles's, Scandrett Harfords &c.* 15 Apr., 2 Jul: *Breakfasted at the Bell—and afterwards with A Sayers, Robt. Hale, and E.F.W. visited the Church of St. Mary de Crypt, examining its many excellencies of architecture, and its antiquities, together with the extensive alterations and restorations now in progress.... The Magistrates dinner was held at the Bell—among those present were the two Hales, the MP. for West Gloucestershire and his Father.* 3-4 Jul.

1846: 1-2 Jul., 10-11 Aug., 20 Oct: *Breakfasted with Purnell. Among the leading Magistrates present were the Lord Lieutenant Lord Ducie, Sir W. C. Codrington, Sir M. H. Beech, the Hales, father and son.* 21-22 Oct.

1847: 30 Jun: *Breakfasted at the Bell with the Magistrates, Playne, Hale, Stokes, Purnell, R. Waller, E.F.W. &c.* 17 Jul., 8 Aug: *According to the latest accounts furnished in the Gloucestershire Chronicle, Grantley Berkeley, as Candidate for West Gloucestershire, is considerably ahead of Grenville Berkeley, his cousin and opponent. R B Hale's majority is far above both.* 19-20 Oct.

1848: 25 Feb: *Recd. a packet of parliamentary proceedings sent by Robert B. Hale, MP. for West Gloucestershire.* 21-22 Mar., 16-17 Oct.

1850: 15-16 Jan., 31 Dec.

1851: 9 Feb: *A note from R B Hale, MP.—requesting information as to books, published by Charles Bathurst.* 10 Feb., 18 Mar: *a thin attendance of Justices: among them were the Lord Lieutenant, Lord Moreton, Sir M. C. Boevey, R B Hale M.P.—Hale Senr.* 31 Mar., 1 Apr.

1852: 17 Mar: *The breakfast party at the Bell consisted of the Purnells, Mullings, W Playne, E.F.W, Hale—to whom flocked in Messrs. Holford, Major Hale, W. Paul, arriving to be present at an appeal against an order of Trustees for the diverting of a turnpike road, near Tetbury, a thing in itself unexceptionable, but resisted by a misguided Clergyman, the incumbent of Weston Birt, on the plea that it was a job to gratify Mr. Holford at the expence of himself and the inhabitants of his village, who might be required thereby to travel less than a hundred yards further than by the old road.* 18 Mar., 4-5 Apr., 6 Apr: *Mr. Hale, the High Sheriff, and his niece, Miss Rice, daughter of Francis Rice, a very sensible, but somewhat singular young person, were those with whom I was most in communication.*

HALE — Thomas Jacob John Hale[11]

Thomas Jacob John Hale (1789-1857), Church of England clergyman, was born at Batheaston, son of Thomas and Jane Hale. He was educated at Queen's College, Oxford (BA 1812; MA 1815; B&DD 1826). He was ordained priest on 12 June 1813 and was appointed curate of Bathampton and Bathford on 13 June 1813, and stipendiary curate of Walcot All Saints', Lansdown Place, on 3 June 1816. Hale founded a school at Lyde House, Sion Hill, Bath, but there is little information on the place. He must have given it up before his appointment as chaplain at Versailles, St Germain-en-Laye, and subsequent appointment as chaplain to the British

Embassy, Paris, 1851-57. He was married, but his wife's identity is unknown. He also had a son, probably Henry Hale whose daughter Eliza Maria married Isaac Sumsion in 1854. He had at least one other child, a daughter born in 1820.

1822: 20 Dec: *I went yesterday to Cheltenham to meet our dear Edward on his return from School for the Christmas holidays. He arrived in a Bath Coach in perfect health and spirits, the same affectionate engaging child as ever. His Master, Mr. Hale, of Lyde House, Sion Hill, Bath, who is also Curate of Lansdown Chapel, Bath, gave me by letter a very good account of the whole of our dear boy's conduct & progress.*

1823: 16 Dec: *The arrival of our dear Edward from school for the Holidays was a source of unfeigned delight to us... Our joy was not a little heightened by the excellent report, which Mr. Hale gives us of general good conduct, and proficiency in learning.*

1824: 17 Jun: *Mr. Hale writes a most satisfactory account of his progress in his learning and good behaviour.*

1825: 20 May: *These reports relate to a laxity of principle and improper heat of temper as regards Mr. Hale, indiscretion on his part in keeping under his roof an unfortunately vicious youth, his own son, and other minor charges alledged by Mr. O.P. Wathen of Woodchester, who yet does not chuse his name to be brought forward.* 11 Jun., 14 Jun: *Our conversation with Mr. Hale was long and serious; he could not deny the irregularities of his son, but urged, that they, as well as other alledged deviations from good discipline in his school, had been exaggerated: which I am very much inclined to believe; it appears from Mr. Hale's representations, that Mr. Wathen's son was the last person to cast the first stone; being a spoiled child his complaints were too hastily listened to by his parents, who were, doubtless, ignorant, that charges might have been brought against him of indelicate language & the utterance of coarse sentiments. Mr. Hale professed himself ready to follow such advice as we were disposed to give him.* 15 Jun: *At Wellington Parade I had the pleasure of being greeted by my dear son in excellent health and spirits: he had finally left Dr. Hale's school on Tuesday last, bringing with him a letter from his master a favourable report of his progress and conduct.* 2 Aug., 16 Dec.

1826: 24 Apr: *Immediately after our arrival, I walked to Dr. Hale's on Sion Hill, to see our dear boy.* 27 Apr., 30 Apr: *I went to All Saints Chapel near Lansdown Crescent, and assisted Dr. Hale, who is the stated Minister, in the performance of the duties. I took the principal part in the Communion Service, and preached. This chapel, in the parish of Walcot, is private property, like Queen's Square, Margaret's & other chapels in Bath.*

1837: 5 Feb.

HALE — police officer at Blockley

Police records for Gloucestershire only commence in 1839, so it is not known who this officer was.

1837: 23 Feb: *A letter from Mr. Pole, relating what he had done about procuring a substitute for Hale the Blockley Police man who has been discharged.* 26 Feb: *A letter from Mr. Figgures, informing me that Lord Northwick had consented to Hale's dismissal, and requesting me to write to Pole to suggest that it would be preferable that his successor should be a married man.*

HALFORD — Henry Halford[12]

Sir Henry Halford, 1st baronet (1766-1844), physician, was born Henry Vaughan, the second son of James Vaughan, a Leicester physician, and Hester, daughter of John Smalley, who had married a daughter of Sir Richard Halford. Henry was educated at Rugby School and Christ Church, Oxford (BA 1788; MB 1790; DM 1791). After studying some time at Edinburgh, Vaughan settled in London, where he was elected physician to the Middlesex Hospital in 1793. In the same year he was appointed physician-extraordinary to George III. He became a fellow of the Royal College of Physicians in 1794.

Henry inherited a large property on the death of Lady Denbigh, widow of his mother's cousin Sir Charles Halford, 7th baronet, and consequently changed his name from Vaughan to Halford by act of parliament in 1809. George III, who had a strong liking for him, created him a baronet in the same year, and he subsequently attended George IV, William IV, and Queen Victoria. He became a fellow of the Royal Society in 1810.

1830: 19 Apr: *The Physicians in attendance, Sir. H. Halford & Sir M. Tierney have issued a bulletin, from which it would appear, that the Sovereign is suffering under a bilious affection combined with a difficulty of respiration, & much languor.*

1835: 27 Feb: *The skill of Sir H. Halford and the attendance of an experienced Apothecary had assisted in enabling the lamp of life long to linger in the socket.*

HALIBURTON — Thomas Chandler Haliburton[13]

Thomas Chandler Haliburton (1796-1865), politician and writer, was born at Windsor, Nova Scotia, the only child of William Hersey Otis Haliburton (1767-1829), lawyer, MLA, and judge of the inferior court of common pleas, and Lucy Chandler Grant (d. 1797). He was educated at Windsor Grammar School, and then at the Anglican King's College in Windsor (BA 1815). Growing up, he was significantly influenced by his New England planter grandfather, William Haliburton (d. 1817), a Yankee adventurer, lawyer, and writer.

Haliburton studied law under his father and applied to be a notary public in 1819. He then moved to Annapolis Royal in 1821 to practise law. His writing career began anonymously with *A General Description of Nova Scotia* (1823). In 1835-36, in the *Novascotian*, he began publishing parts of what was to become his most successful book, *The Clockmaker, or, The Sayings and Doings of Samuel Slick, of Slickville*. It consists of humorous conversations between Sam Slick, a loquacious Yankee clock pedlar whose catchphrase 'soft sawdur and human nature' made Haliburton famous, and an Anglophile squire as they travel through Nova Scotia. It was so popular in Canada that Richard Bentley, the English publisher, decided to reprint a pirated edition in England, where it was equally successful. Upon hearing of this success, Haliburton was so flattered that he overlooked Bentley's piracy and travelled to England to offer him a sequel. A second series in 1838 was followed by a third in 1840, and two series of *The Attaché, or, Sam Slick in England* (1843-44). At the time, Haliburton's success was rivalled only by Charles Dickens.

In 1856 Haliburton sold his estate in Nova Scotia and moved to England where his public profile continued to rise. In 1858 he was awarded an honorary DCL from Oxford University. He served as MP for Launceston in Cornwall in 1859-65.

1843: 11 Aug: *Sam. Slick, the Attaché, in England, a continuation of the admirable Sayings and Doings of Sam. Slick, the Clockmaker, by Judge Haliburton, of Nova Scotia, a work replete with humour as well as with sound views of politics and society, occupied us for an hour in the evening.*

HALIFAX — the Misses Halifax, performers at Lady Lyttelton's musical evening

1801: 27 May: *In the evening to a party at Lady Lyttelton's, which was musical; The Harp, Grand Piano Forte & voice; the chief performers were, Miss Hadsley, Miss Bowles, Miss Canning, Miss Kearney, the Misses Halifax, Miss Stanhope, le Compte de Montmorency &c.* 3 Jun., 10 Jun.

HALIFAX — Miss Halifax at Mrs Travell's house in Cheltenham

1825: 20 May: *Miss Halifax joined the circle round my Aunt's tea table.*

HALKETT-CRAIGIE — *see* Craigie-Halkett

HALL — Miss Hall of Ravenflatt, Yorkshire

1834: 22 Jul: *A letter from Mr. Hartley, with minute details as to the Executorship of the late Miss Hall, and a reference to other Yorkshire business.* 28 Jul., 5 Sep., 24 Nov.

HALL — Basil Hall[14]

Basil Hall (1788-1844), naval officer and author, was the second son of Sir James Hall, 4th baronet (1761-1832), of Dunglass, Haddingtonshire, and Helen (d. 1837), second daughter of Dunbar Douglas, 4th earl of Selkirk. Hall entered the Navy in 1802, serving aboard the *Leander* (50 guns). He was present at the *Leander*'s capture of the *Ville de Milan* on 23 February 1805, and continued in the ship until the admiral's death in spring 1806. Hall was then promoted to lieutenant of the *Invincible*, and from there moved to the frigate *Endymion*. In 1808 *Endymion* was sent to Corunna to convoy reinforcements for Sir John Moore and was later ordered back to assist in re-embarking the troops. Having gone ashore, Hall witnessed the battle of Corunna on 16 January 1809.

In 1814 Hall was promoted to command the sloop *Victor*, then being built at Bombay, which he took to England in the following year. He was then appointed to the brig *Lyra* (10 guns), and ordered to China in company with the frigate *Alceste* and Lord Amherst's embassy. Following this voyage Hall wrote *An Account of a Voyage of Discovery to the West Coast of Corea and the Great Loo-Choo Islands* (1818). In 1820 he was appointed to the *Conway*, a 26-gun frigate. He sailed from England in August, and upon joining the commodore, Sir Thomas Hardy, in the River Plate, he was sent immediately to Valparaíso. He remained on the west coast of America for the next two years. The publication of Hall's *Extracts from a Journal Written on the Coasts of Chili, Peru, and Mexico* (2 volumes, 1823) met with considerable success.

1824: 2 Dec: *"Extracts from a Journal written on the coasts of Chili, Peru, and Mexico in the years 1820, 1821, 1822 by Captain Basil Hall R.N. author of a Voyage to Loo Choo. 2 Vols 8vo 3d. Edit. 1824." Captain Hall commanded the Conway frigate on the South American Station, and had many favourable opportunities of watching the progress of the cause of independence in the Countries, which he visited.*

1837: 27 Jan: *Finished reading Basil Hall's new publication, Schloss Hainfeld, a narrative of six months residence of himself, wife and children at the Country residence seat of the aged Countess Purgstall in Lower Styria.*

HALL — Charles Henry Hall[15]

Charles Henry Hall (1763-1827), Church of England clergyman, professor of divinity and dean of Christ Church, was the son of Charles Hall (1718-1774), dean of Bocking, Essex, and chaplain to Archbishop Secker, and Elizabeth, daughter of Robert Carsan, a Lambeth surgeon. He was educated at Christ Church, Oxford (BA 1783; MA 1786; BD 1794; DD 1800). He was proctor of Christ Church in 1793, tutor and censor in 1792-97, regius professor of divinity in 1807-09, sub-dean in 1805, and dean in 1809-24. In addition, he was appointed vicar of Boughton in 1794, Bampton lecturer and prebendary of Exeter in 1798, and rector of Kirk-Bramwith in 1799. He finally served as vicar of Luton, Bedfordshire, in 1807-22, and dean of Durham in 1824-27.

1803: 27 Nov: *Breakfasted with Dowell, meeting Evans. To the Church with the latter, where Dr. Hall preached.*

1806: 19 Mar: *conversed with Bright, Hall & Sir C. Pegge.* 22 Mar: *Dined in the Common Room; Rogers, Price, Dr. Cooper, Stevens & Hall.*

HALL — George William Hall[16]

George William Hall (1770-1843), Church of England clergyman, was born at Chelsea, London, son of John and Mary Hall. He was educated at Pembroke, Oxford (BA 1792; MA 1795; BD 1808; DD 1809). He served as master of Pembroke in 1809-43, rector of Taynton, Gloucestershire, in 1810-43, and vice-chancellor of Pembroke in 1820-24. Hall appears to have married Sarah Harriett.

1823: 17 Sep: *The Clerical Stewards were Dr. Timbrill, Rector of Beckford, a strong headed, intelligent, active man; a leading magistrate of this county & of Worcestershire, & Treasurer of the Clergy Charity: Mr. Selwyn, a Prebendary of Gloucester, but precluded, as I understand, by mental infirmity from attending; so that Dr. Hall, another Prebendary, Vice Chancellor of Oxford, & Master of Pembroke College, officiated in his stead.*

1826: 30 Mar.

1835: 7 Jan.

1838: 14 Dec., 28 Dec: *A letter from Dr. Hall, Prebendary of Gloucester, apprizing me that, with a view to an extended and improved popular education on religious principles in connexion with the National Society, a diocesan board of management for the Archdeaconry of Gloucester has been agreed upon, with the Sanction of the Bishop; that a public meeting at which the scheme is to be brought forward is fixed for the 8th. Jany. at the Shire Hall, and my consent is asked to act, if named an Elected Member for Stow.*

1839: 2 Jan.

HALL — George Charles Hall[17]

George Charles Hall (1811-1895), Church of England clergyman, was born in Gloucestershire, son of George William Hall and his wife, Harriet (*above*). He was educated at Pembroke College, Oxford (BA 1832; MA 1836). He became vicar of Churcham in 1837, and later appears to have succeeded his father as rector of Taynton. It is also probable that he is the magistrate referred to on 22 October 1846. Hall married, at Churcham, Gloucestershire, 9 November 1828, Harriet Toomey (1813-1865); they had at least 1 son and 3 daughters:

1 Elizabeth (1832-1905)
1 Thomas (b. 1834)
2 Mary Ann (b. 1839)
3 Jane (1843-1939)

1846: 11 Aug., 22 Oct: *Quarterly meeting: numerously attended Mr. Gambier Parry in the Chair: present, among many more, Messrs. Purnell, Hyett, Baker, Whitcomb, Hall, Avery, Cols. Cother and Hawkins, Messrs. Helps, Clarke, Worthington, Walters &c.*

1850: 7 Aug: *The two Judges of Assize, Lord Campbell, Lord Chief Justice of the Queen's Bench, and Sir Edwd. Vaughan Williams, one of the Justices of the Common Pleas, arrived in the afternoon ... they attended divine service, the Sermon being preached by the Sheriff's chaplain, the Revd. George Hall, Rector of Taynton.*

1852: 18 Mar: *Mr. Hall, the Incumbent of Churcham, came to consult me as to an alleged misconduct of Barnett, the Coroner, as to a late inquest held in his parish.* 29 Mar: *Much conversation with Mr. Hall, the Incumbent of Churcham near Gloucester, respecting the inquest held by Coroner Barnett, in his parish.* 30 Mar.

1853: 8 Jan: *Owing to a slight accident which had befallen the mail express train, the mail-train, by which I travelled, was behind its time, and we had a long pause at Didcot, where I was in conversation with George Hall of Churcham near Gloucester, and other members of Convocation.*

HALL — George Hall, carpenter, of Upper Slaughter [18]

George Hall (1817-1885), carpenter, was born at Longborough. He married Mary Cook (1805-1885), born at Little Compton; they had at least 1 son and 2 daughters:

1 Emily (b. ±1833)
2 Emy (b. ±1835)
1 Jordan (1840-1926); married, at Upper Slaughter, 10 December 1900, Ada Berry (1860-1926); 2 sons:
  1 Frederick (1900-1988)
  2 Edward Jordan (1904-1972)

1844: 16 May: *Wrote to Mr. Waller of Farmington, with particulars as to the Character and qualifications of George Hall, a parishioner, who is desirous of obtaining the situation of his carpenter.*

HALL — Henry Hall [19]

Henry Hall (1813-1878), Church of England clergyman, was the second son of John Robert Hall (1809-1893). He was educated at Christ Church, Oxford (BA 1835; MA 1837). He was curate of Warminster and rector of Semley, Dorset, 1856-78.

1830: 18 Jan: *Three youths about Edward's age came to dine with him, & slept here. ... Henry Hall, second son of my worthy acquaintance, the Rector of Batsford; a very gentlemanlike, intelligent & promising youth, second boy in the sixth form of Rugby School, and likely to do credit to the tuition of Dr. Arnold.*

1832: 11 Mar: *We then called on Henry Hall, Son of my friend the Rector of Batsford, and an Undergraduate of Christ Church, very intimate with my son; we took with him a walk on the Abingdon road, and subsequently, in Christ Church walk.*

1834: 29 Jul: *Miss Chapuset did the honours. Met the Halls, Mr. & Mrs. H. their daughter, and Henry Hall, the Colviles, Mr. and Mrs. C. with his brother Col. Colvile, Mr. Lewis, Mr. Cameron, Miss Jane Penystone, a Miss Dalton, a friend of Miss Hall, and Mr. Winter.*

1840: 9 Jul: *Accompanied Mr. Ford and his Son Frederick in their carriage to a dinner party at Capt. Leigh's at Broadway ... Henry Hall, recently ordained Deacon, a pleasant and not ill informed young man, who has improved by foreign travel.* 16 Sep: *Recd. a letter from Mr. Hall, Batsford, proposing the Revd. Mr. Annesley of Ebrington as a member of the Stow Book Society.*

HALL — John Robert Hall [20]

John Robert Hall (1765-1841), Church of England clergyman, was the eldest son of John Robert Hall of Batsford, Gloucestershire. He was educated at Christ Church, Oxford (BA 1787; MA 1790). He was prebendary of Exeter in 1807 and rector of Batsford in 1807-41. He married, at Hampstead, Middlesex, 9 April 1807, Frances (±1778-1845), daughter of John Longley (1749-1822) and Elizabeth Bond (1754-1845); they had at least 3 sons and 1 daughter:

1 John Robert (1809-1892); *see below*
1 Frances Henrietta (1810-1886)
2 Henry (1813-1878)
3 George Hall (b. 1814)

1823: 21 Mar: *We dined at Mr. Jeaffreson's at Longborough, meeting Sir C. & Lady Cockerell, Mr. & Mrs. E. Leigh, their brother & sister, Mr. & Mrs. Dumbleton, Mr. & Mrs. Hall, of Batsford, with his pupil, Mr. Tuffnell.*

1824: 26 May, 9 Nov.

1826: 19 Apr., 18 Jul., 3 Oct: *The meeting of the Stow Book Society ... Mr. Talbot presided in the room of Mr. East, who is absent from Adlestrop. The Dean of Gloucester, Messrs. E. Leigh, Malcolm, Hall, Jeaffreson, Hurd, Raine, Winter, Ford, &c.*

1827: 2 Oct.

1828: 23 Apr., 20 Aug., 7-8 Oct.

1829: 17 Jun., 18 Sep., 6 Oct., 5 Nov., 24 Nov.

1830: 18 Jan: *Three youths about Edward's age came to dine with him, & slept here. ... Henry Hall, second son of my worthy acquaintance, the Rector of Batsford.* 14 Apr.

1832: 11 Mar: *We then called on Henry Hall, Son of my friend the Rector of Batsford.* 25 Apr.

1833: 30 Oct.

1834: 29 Jul: *Miss Chapuset did the honours. Met the Halls, Mr. & Mrs. H. their daughter, and Henry Hall, the Colviles, Mr. and Mrs. C. with his brother Col. Colvile, Mr. Lewis, Mr. Cameron, Miss Jane Penystone, a Miss Dalton, a friend of Miss Hall, and Mr. Winter.* 31 Jul., 20 Aug: *Among those present at these meetings were Messrs. Hall, Western, R. Hall, Darby, Bowen, Winter, Lewes, Sadler &c.* 19 Sep.

1835: 5 Mar: *Walked to Stow, to attend at the Provident Bank, and in the Justice room. In the latter there was no business. The Gentlemen present were Messrs. Ford, Billingsley, Robt. Hall, Cameron, Winter and Vavasour.* 14 Mar: *Also to Henry Hall with a copy of the lines on Dr. Gaisford for which he applied in his note to my son mentioned yesterday.* 13 May.

1836: 27 Oct.

1837: 5 Sep: *Went in the phaeton to Shipston on Stour to view the Workhouse there; accompanied by Mr. Jeaffreson who joined me at Moreton in Marsh, where the Magistrates were holding a Justice meeting. Looked in on them, and found Messrs. Hall and Colville: the former gave a sad account of the helpless state of his wife, suffering under Rheumatic gout, which has deprived her of the use of her limbs: the latter is depressed by the recent death of a daughter, just springing into womanhood.* 13 Sep: *A letter from J. R. Hall, Junr. (Batsford) requesting from me information respecting the living of Turkdean for a friend of his, Mr. Biscoe, who is likely to succeed the late incumbent, Mr. Hornsby.* 16 Sep., 26 Sep., 6 Oct: *Of those leaning or embraced in the principles of the Evangelical school, I observed the Incumbent of Campden, Mr. Kennaway, with two friends, Hall Junr., F. Rice, Elridge, Bennet Hoskins.* 10 Oct.

1838: 19 Feb., 30 Dec.

1839: 29 Jan., 1 Feb.

1840: 9 Jul.

HALL — John Robert Hall [21]

John Robert Hall (1809-1893), Church of England clergyman, was the son of John Robert Hall and Elizabeth Bond (*above*). He was educated at Christ Church, Oxford (BA 1830; MA 1832). He served as curate of Bourton-on-the-Hill, near his father's rectory. In 1838 he was made vicar of St Mary Magdalene, Oxford, and in 1844-59 he served as vicar of Frodsham, Cheshire. He was appointed chaplain to his uncle Charles Thomas Longley (1794-1868), who was bishop of Ripon, 1836-56; bishop of Durham, 1856-60; archbishop of York, 1860-62; and archbishop of Canterbury, 1862-68. Hall continued to stay close to his uncle and benefit from his patronage. He lived in Boldon, co. Durham in 1857-63, and then, once Longley had become archbishop of Canterbury, he moved to Coulsden in Surrey, and shortly after to Hunton near Maidstone. He was appointed rural dean and honorary canon of Canterbury. He married, first, Grace Jane (b. ±1812); they had 1 son and 1 daughter:

1 George S. Hall (b. ±1847)
1 Jane S. Hall (b. ±1848)

He married, secondly, Louisa F. (b. ±1819); they had 1 daughter:

1 Frances Caroline Hall (b. ±1860)

1844: 14 Aug.

HALL — Richard Hall [22]

Richard Hall (1805-1857), barrister and poor law inspector, was born at Marylebone, London, son of Richard Hall, of Portland Place, London, and of Totteridge, Hertfordshire, and Mary Strassell. He was educated at Harrow School and East India College, Hertfordshire, and then Trinity College, Cambridge (BA 1828; MA 1831). Hall was admitted at Lincoln's Inn in 1827 and called to the bar in 1828. His various posts included special pleader on the northern circuit, poor law commissioner, and recorder of Doncaster. He held the latter post for twelve years, from 1845 to 1857. He married Susan (b. ±1817), who was born in Ireland; they had at least 1 son and 2 daughters:

1 Mary Susan (b. ±1841); born in Ireland
1 Richard S. (b. ±1843); born in Ireland
2 Katherine E. (b. ±1848)

1836: 1 Nov: *Received a letter from Stevens, announcing that the Poor Law Commrs. have removed him from his present district to complete the formation of Unions in Leicestershire, Rutlandshire, Derbyshire, and North Staffordshire, and that his place is to be supplied in Berks, Oxon, and Gloucestershire by Mr. Hall, an Asst. Commr. of longer standing than himself, and retiring on account of indifferent health from the more laborious duties which Stevens is about to undertake.* 4 Nov., 7 Nov., 10 Nov., 9 Dec: *Wrote to Hall, the Assis. P.L.C. to take his advice respecting some serious misconduct alleged against Tidmarsh, one of the Rel. Off. of the Stow Union.* 11-12 Nov., 22 Dec., 24 Dec., 31 Dec.

1837: 19 Feb: *Wrote to Mr. Hall, the Ass. Poor Law Commr. inclosing a copy of the petition which it is proposed to present to the two houses of Parliament in support of the provisions of the Poor Law Amendment Act: gave a general sketch of the state of our Union.* 23-24 Feb., 12 Mar., 9 Apr., 14 Apr., 2 May, 5 May, 25 May, 31 May, 29 Jul., 4 Aug., 18 Sep., 23 Sep., 3 Oct., 7 Nov., 9 Nov: *Finding Mr. Hall, the Asst. P.L. Commr. just arrived from C. Norton; sent back my horse, and arranged to return with him in his carriage to U Slaughter.* 10 Nov., 11 Nov: *After an early breakfast our very agreeable, amiable and well informed friend Hall left us to attend the Board of guardians at Winchcombe in his official capacity.* 4 Dec., 6-7 Dec., 12 Dec.

1838: 7 Jan., 12 Jan., 19-20 Jan., 23 Jan., 2 Feb., 7-9 Feb., 14-15 Feb., 8-9 Mar., 15 Mar., 26 Apr., 24 May: *To the Workhouse, to attend the weekly meeting of the Guardians of the Union, where informed by Mr. Pearce that Mr. Hall the Asst. P.L.C. th had arrived from C Norton, and had already inspected the establishment, with the management of which he had expressed his satisfaction.* 25 May: *Pearce called; conferred with me and Mr. Hall on various points of for Union and Workhouse management; assisted him in drawing up the minutes of yesterday's proceedings at the Board of Guardians.* 26 May: *About eleven o clock Mr. Hall left us to attend the meeting of the Guardians at Winchcomb.* 3 Sep., 6 Sep: *It was agreed to enter on the Minutes a resolution of regret that Mr. Hall was removed from the superintendance of our Union, and to express our sense of the courtesy which the Members of the Board had recd. at his hands, and of the attention he had paid to its interests.* 7 Sep., 20 Sep: *Found awaiting me a kind letter from Mr. Hall, Asst. P.L.C.—in answer to mine of the 7th. Inst. he writes from Wortley Hall, Yorkshire, where he was engaged in launching a Union, having succeeded to Mr. Gulson's district.* 6 Dec.

HALL — Richard Hall [23]

Richard Hall (b. 1806), land agent, was born at Cirencester, son of Robert Wright Hall (d. 1815), land surveyor, and his wife, Elizabeth. At one point Hall was president of the Royal Institution of Chartered Surveyors. The family lived at 8 Dollar Street, Cirencester. He married Eliza (b. ±1809), born in Monmouthshire; they had at least 2 sons and 1 daughter:

1 Robert Wright (1829-79), land surveyor; joined the freemasons' lodge at Cirencester, 13 December 1851; worked first with his father, then younger brother Richard in London
1 Mary Eliza (b. ±1838)
2 Richard (1839-79); last recorded 1871 at Teddington, Middlesex, unmarried, working as a surveyor for GWR

1839: 16 Jan.

1843: 18 Jan: *Wrote to Mr. Hall, the eminent land-surveyor of Cirencester, whom I have named as the proper person to look over the Great Risington property for which we are in treaty, both as to its value.* 25 Jan: *Also from Mr. Hall, Cirencester, that he proposes surveying the Great Risington property in a few days, and will gladly accept our invitation to Upper Slaughter.* 31 Jan: *Recd. a letter from Mr. Hall, Cirencester, intimating his intention of surveying the property at Great Risington to-day, and of arriving here in the evening to dine and sleep.* 1 Feb.

1846: 12 Aug., 23 Oct: *from Mr. Sewell, as to the Redmarley estate, that Mr. Hall would write to me his opinion as to its value as an investment; and, accordingly, Mr. Hall reports the land to be much out of order, but he considers it worth £7000 as an investment.*

HALL — Samuel Hall of Devizes

1806: 26 Aug: *Writing a Funeral Sermon upon the Death of a young man knocked on the head in a quarrel by his fellow servant.* 27 Aug: *The funeral of poor Simon Hall came on in the Evening for which at the desire of the Club I preached a funeral Sermon.*

HALL — Samuel Hall of Upper Slaughter [24]

Samuel Hall (1785-1851), carpenter, was born at Naunton, Gloucestershire. He married Elizabeth (1791-1876); they had at least 1 son and 3 daughters:

1 Job (1821-1880)
1 Maria (b. 1825)

2 Sophia (b. 1828)
3 Elizabeth (b. 1832)

1842: 15 Nov: *Making necessary arrangements for the funeral of Mrs. Backhouse on the 21st. with Samuel Hall, the Carpenter, and Mr. Bryan, the Undertaker; also giving necessary orders as to Servants mourning &c.*

HALL — Susan and Sara Hall [25]

Susan Hall (1784-1861) lived with her sister, Sara Hall (1785-1866). They were both born at Arlington, near Bibury, daughters of William and Sarah Hall. In 1851 they lived at Bourton-on-the-Water.

1828: 14 Aug: *lastly, Miss Hall, one of the Bourton quality, well meaning & sensible, I daresay, but not used to good company.*

1835: 22 May: *Mr. Daubeny, Mrs. Sampson and the two Misses Hall from Bourton on the Water (their first visit,) called upon us.*

1836: 2 Aug: *We all left our cards at Miss Halls, who are at Malvern.* 27 Sep: *Immediately after these deliberations were closed, the Members of the Book Society assembled to ballot for new members, when the following were elected: Miss Hall, Bourton on the Water; Mr. Whitmore Jones, Revd. Geo. Adams, Revd. Geo. Daubeny. Revd. H. Polson, Revd. W. Lockwood.* 14 Nov.

1837: 31 Mar: *The Misses Hall from Bourton on the Water called.* 9 May, 28 Aug: *The Misses Hall, always pushing, prayed us so earnestly to call on them, when we met them in the Village, that we did not know how to avoid the importunity, and then annoyed us by their vulgarity, and censorious gossip.*

1838: 8 Aug: *Mr. & Mrs. Morrison, of Stoneleigh, who are on a visit to the Misses Hall, at Bourton, with one of those ladies, called in the course of the day.*

1839: 4 Mar: *Left our cards for the Misses Hall, who were out taking a walk.* 3 Aug: *The Misses Hall paid a morning visit.*

1840: 15 Jul: *Drove MW. to Bourton on the Water. Called on the Polsons, whom we found at home; also on the Misses Hall, with whom we found on a visit to them their sister, a Mrs. Hinton.* 5 Aug.

1842: 8 Jan: *to Miss Hall, Bourton on the Water, informing her that I had pointed out to the Secretary of the Gloucester Infirmary the error inserted in their report as to a supposed arrear due by Miss H. of one year's subscription, and that I hoped, I had succeeded in setting the matter right.* 10 Jun: *Called on the Misses Hall, whom we found at home.* 10 Aug., 6 Sep: *The Misses Hall made a morning visit to us.*

1843: 25 Jan., 10 Aug: *In the course of the day, the Misses Hall from Bourton had called with a party; also the Hippisleys from Stow.* 6 Dec.

1844: 16 Jan., 30 Mar., 15 Apr., 16 Sep: *Called on the Misses Hall, who were from home, but whom we met afterwards in the village.*

1845: 4 Feb: *Drove with MW. to Bourton on the Water: called on the Misses Hall.* 3 Jun., 17 Jun: *The Misses Hall called in the evening.*

1846: 11 Jul: *Mrs. Dolphin had called during our absence. Also the Misses Hall from Bourton on the Water.* 15 Jul., 12 Sep.

1847: 19 Jan: *The Misses Hall paid a morning visit.* 10 Mar: *Received a letter from Mrs. Mountain, Cirencester, one of the Candidates for the office of Matron at the Gloucester Infirmary: she requests again my support, and that I would allow the Misses Hall of Bourton, who had given me their proxies to vote for whomsoever I should consider the most competent person, to vote for her.... Wrote to Miss Hall with a copy of my letter to Mrs. M.* 17 Apr: *Drove with MW. to Bourton on the Water ... called on the Misses Hall, where met Mr. Morrison and his Son.* 12 Jun., 23 Jul: *to Miss S. Hall, requesting her to give an order into the infirmary in favour of a man in the Workhouse nearly blind.* 30 Jul: *The Misses Hall and a nephew from Shropshire called in the evening.* 18 Sep: *With MW. drove to Bourton on the water. Left cards at the Misses Hall, who are absent from home.*

1848: 13-14 Jan., 25 Apr: *The ladies drove to Bourton on the Water, and called on Mrs. R. Waller, and the Misses Hall.* 25 May, 23 Aug., 25 Aug., 1 Sep., 6 Sep. *The Misses Hall made a morning visit to us.*

1850: 23 Feb., 9 Mar: *The Misses Hall from Bourton on the Water called with like enquiries; both parties sat a little time with me.* 1 Jun., 16 Jul: *Accompanied by dear Sophy and her children, drove to Bourton on the Water, and visited the Misses Hall.* 11 Sep., 18 Sep.

1851: 16 Apr: *The Misses Hall called upon me.*

1852: 26 Apr: *Met in L Slaughter the Misses Hall on their way to call on me.*

1853: 7 Apr: *George Collett, of Bourton on the Water, having called to solicit me to renew my recommendation of his son as an inpatient of the Gloucester infirmary, I wrote to Miss Hall, of Bourton, begging her to furnish a second order of admission.* 19 Apr., 25 May.

1854: 22 Mar: *The Misses Hall, from Bourton paid me a long visit.*

HALLAM — Henry Hallam [26]

Henry Hallam (1777-1859), historian, was the only son of John Hallam (d. 1812), canon of Windsor (from 1775) and dean of Bristol (1781-1800), and his wife, Eleanor (d. 1826). He was educated at Christ Church, Oxford (BA 1799; MA in 1832; DCL 1848). In 1858 Christ Church made him an honorary student in recognition of his work as a historian. Hallam's books helped materially to lay the foundations of the English historical school, and in spite of later research, they long maintained their position as standard works. His most famous work was *The Constitutional History of England from the Accession of Henry VII to the Death of George II*. He married, 1807, Julia Maria (1783-1840), eldest daughter of Sir Abraham Elton, 5th baronet (1755-1842), and Elizabeth Durbin (1756-1822). The offspring of the family were destined to die young. In thirty-three years' marriage, Henry and Julia Maria had eleven children, but only four of their progeny reached adulthood, and only one—Julia Maria Frances—outlived Hallam himself. In 1833, during a stay in Vienna, Hallam returned to his hotel after a walk about the city to find his eldest and favourite son, Arthur Henry, lying dead on a sofa. The cause is unknown. In 1850, another son, Henry Fitzmaurice, joined his father for an excursion on the Continent and was taken ill and died at Siena. Out of the eleven children, 5 sons and 2 daughters are known:

1 Arthur Henry (1811-1833); died at Vienna
2 Charles William Waterloo (b. 1815)
3 William (b. 1817)
1 Eleanor (1817-1837)
2 Julia Maria Frances (1818-1880)
4 Walter John (b. 1821)
5 Henry Fitzmaurice Hallam (1824-1850); died at Siena, Tuscany

---

1829: 27 Aug: *Mr. Hallam, author of the history of the middle ages, a talented person, with great historical acquirements, but of the Edinburgh Review school.*

1838: 29 Aug: *On the wall near this stone are two marble monuments erected to the memory of three children of Henry Hallam Esqr. the eminent Critic, and Historian, whose researches into the laws, customs, & manners of the middle ages, and whose view of the literature of Europe during & subsequent to the same period down to the commencement of the 18th. Century, together with other writings, are generally known, and, with justice, highly valued. He married a daughter of Sir Abraham Elton, and these tablets commemorate the grievous loss of a daughter and two sons.* 4 Sep: *Hallam is great authority on mediæval history, and extensively acquainted with European learning.*

HALLEWELL — Edmund Gilling Hallewell[27]

Edmund Gilling Hallewell (1796-1881), JP, MP, and landed proprietor, was the son of Revd John Hallewell, of Farnham in Yorkshire, and Ellen, daughter of Edmund Gilling of Marton-le-Moor, Yorkshire. He was educated at Ripon Grammar School. Hallewell was Conservative MP for Newry, Ireland, in 1851-52. He married Martha (1801-1846), only daughter and heir of Stroud brewer Joseph Watts of Stratford Park, Stroud, Gloucestershire; they had at least 3 sons and 8 daughters:

1 Edmund Gilling Watts (1822-1869), army officer and amateur artist; rose to commandant of the Royal Military College, Sandhurst, but best known for his series of panoramic watercolours of Bermuda (1842-47). Married Sophia Reid, daughter of Gen. Sir William Reid
2 Joseph Watts (1823-1891); educated at Sedbergh, Rugby, and Jesus College, Cambridge (BA 1846; MA 1859); appointed JP and DL for Gloucestershire, 1874; served as high sheriff until his death. Inherited Stratford Park and Stroud Brewery from maternal grandfather, 1855. Married, first, 1852, Sarah Edith, elder daughter of Robert Berrie; 1 daughter:
    1 Edith Josephine Watts (b. 1853)
    Married secondly, 1856, Mary Anne, younger daughter of Joseph Cripps of Farmhill, near Stroud; 1 daughter:
    1 Josephine Anne Watts (b. 1859)
1 Ellen (b. 1824)
2 Mary Anne (b. 1825)
3 Katherine Martha (1827-1847); died unmarried
4 Emma (1829-1900); died unmarried
5 Fanny (1830-1857); died unmarried
6 Adelaide (b. 1831)
7 Lucy Anne (1832)
3 Charles James Maynard (1833-1919)
8 Grace (1835)

Hallewell married secondly, 1855, Anne Winthrop, the third daughter of Adm. Winthrop.

1837: 4 Jan.

1838: 2-3 Jan., 10 Apr: *During the day I was much in communication with my brother Mag. Purnell, the two Hales, the Bakers, Lawrence, Ford, Archd. Timbrill, Harford, Battersby, Hallewell, Leversage, Curtis Hayward &c.* 16 Oct.

1847: 6 Jan.

1850: 1 Jul: *At the Great Western station joined by Lefroy, Mr. Halliwell, and a sister of Mr. Duncombe Pyrke.* 4 Jul: *A small party dined together at the Kings Head—Curtis Hayward, Francillon, Brickdale, R Waller, Hallewell and myself.* 7 Aug: *At the Great Western Railway Station, I met my brother Magistrate, Mr. Halliwell.* 14 Oct.

HALLFORD — Mr Hallford, a visitor to Mr Burslem in Worcestershire

1802: 3 Aug: *Rode with Mr. & Mrs. Burslem thro' the Park to Droitwich. Called upon a Mrs. Norbury. A Mr. Hallford came in the Evening.*

HALLIDAY — Mr & Mrs Halliday of Urchfont and vicinity[28]

Little is known of the Halliday family of Urchfont. Giles Halliday was a leading gentleman in the parish back in 1731, and in 1769, William Halliday married Elizabeth Hopkins at Market Lavington, a village two miles to the south-east of Urchfont. The church memorials in the village show that Ann Halliday died in 1819 and Harriet Read Halliday donated an alms dish to the church in 1845.

1807: 22 Aug: *Rode to Lavington & W. Lavington called upon Mr. Williams at the latter place with whom I agreed to do my Erchfont Duty during my approaching absence & called after there upon Mr. Halliday for his subscription to the Clergy meeting.* 12 Dec: *to W. Lavington: called on Mr. Halliday's family, our future neighbours at Wedhampton.*

1808: 4 Feb: *Rode to Wedhampton, & Rushall; called on Mr Halliday's family.* 21 Feb: *Mr. Halliday & family called & accompanied us thither.* 10 Apr: *Called on the Jaques's & Gales. Mrs. Halliday & her party called after church.*

HALLIFAX — Robert Hallifax[29]

Robert Hallifax (1760-1838), JP and Church of England clergyman, was born at Reading, Berkshire, son of Thomas Hallifax (1737-1789) and Elizabeth New (1736-1789). He was educated at both Lincoln and Magdalen College, Oxford (BA 1781; MA 1783). He was ordained deacon on 27 October 1782 and priest on 18 April 1784. Hallifax's first clerical appointment was as curate of Great Budworth, Cheshire, on 8 January 1784; on 12 October 1785 he was appointed vicar of Standish and Hardwicke in Gloucestershire. Hallifax served as a JP for the county in 1785-1838. He married, at St Martin-in-the-Fields, London, 1 May 1782, Sarah Sentence (1744-1832); they had at least 1 son and 5 daughters:

1 Charlotte (1782-1864); born at Great Budworth
2 Emma (1783-1825); born at Great Budworth
3 Louisa (b. 1785); born at Great Budworth
4 Caroline (1787-1862); born at Standish
5 Frances (1789-1847); born at Standish, twin to Thomas
1 Thomas (1789-1835); married Sarah Maria Gaze (1793-1875); 3 sons:
    1 Thomas Edward New (1819-1893)
    2 Ambrose William New (1821-1874)
    3 Augustus New (1824-1902)

1825: 29 Jul: *Mr. Jones, Curate of Upper Swell and Broadwell, who has also lately been appointed by Mr. Halifax, Rector of Standish in this county, perpetual curate of Saul, a village below Gloucester.*

HALLING — James Halling[30]

James's father, Thomas Halling (b. ±1795), was a labourer. He lived in Rutland Street, Cheltenham. Thomas Halling was convicted for assault at the 1839 sessions and imprisoned for one week. He married Mary (1797-1841); they appear to have had at least 5 sons and 2 daughters:

1 William (±1818-1852)
1 Elizabeth (b. ±1820)
2 James (±1824-1829)

3 Thomas (1825-1826)
4 John (b. 1829)
5 James (b. ±1830), butcher's boy; transported to Van Diemen's Land (Tasmania), 1848
2 Ellen (b. ±1832); married, September 1852, Henry Bowkett (b. 1827); at least 4 sons and 2 daughters

The diary entries speak for themselves. The very first case was at the assizes on 27 March 1844. James was sentenced to one month's imprisonment for stealing bread. His behaviour in prison was recorded as 'bad'. He stated his father was a chairbearer and 'goes sometimes to church'. Other comments were that his father's habits and connections were bad.

On the oath of John Jelf and another, James Halling was charged of feloniously stealing two half quartern loaves, the property of Charles Fluck, on 22 January 1845. The first sentence for transportation (seven years) was passed on 4 March 1845 at the quarter sessions. However, in 1847, having served time in prison and not yet been transported, he was released. James reoffended and a final sentence of transportation was passed at the quarter sessions of 21 March 1848. He had been imprisoned somewhere for almost three years by 5 February 1851, when the ship on which he was registered, the *Lady Kennaway*, sailed from Portsmouth. But for some reason Halling was not on board. He remained a further year in England, finally sailing for Van Diemen's Land on the *Pestonjee Bomanjee* on 16 April 1852, with a total of 297 prisoners. When the ship arrived on 31 July 1852, he was registered as 5 feet 8½ inches tall, of sallow complexion, aged 21 years, and transported for stealing lead. Due to insolence he was sentenced to four months hard labour. Unfortunately much of his prison record is difficult to read, but it appears that he finally received his 'CP' (conditional pardon) on 29 August 1854. It is not known if he remained in Australia or returned to England.

1845: 20 Mar: *Also a letter from some poor people at Cheltenham, whose son I sentenced to transportation for felony at the late Adjourned Sessions, a boy of thirteen, against whom a previous conviction had been recorded—they plead youth, poverty, and defective understanding, and entreat my interposition to procure a remission by an application to the proper authorities.* 21 Mar: *Answered the letter received yesterday from T. Hawling, Cheltenham, urging me to apply for a mitigation of the sentence passed by me at the Adjourned Sessions on his son. Refused to interfere, explained to him that the sentence was conformable to the usual course adopted in respect of previous conviction being proved against a prisoner, and that an example of severity is needed to check the prevalence of crime among the juvenile classes in the lower station at Cheltenham.* 25 Mar: *A letter from Hawling the poor man at Cheltenham, whose son I sentenced to transportation, urging me to memorialize the Home Secretary for a remission of the sentence.* 26 Mar: *Wrote to—Hawling, Cheltenham in ansr. to his letter received yesterday, explaining to him that I could not with propriety forward the proposed memorial in favour of his Son, nor would I continue any further correspondence on the subject.*

1847: 18 May: *I received a letter from one Halling of Cheltenham, a man in a humble station, whose son was trans sentenced to transportation for stealing Bread from a Baker's barrow in Cheltenham. He was tried with two other boys, his companions & accomplices, at the Gloucestershire Adjourned Sessions in 1845, and a prior conviction having been proved, sentence of transportation was passed on him, as an old offender, and the other boys were sentenced to three months imprisonment each… It is now alleged that a boy, who was the principal and most material witness against the lads convicted, has made a statement to the effect that he perjured himself.* 19 May: *Wrote to Halling, the father of the lad sentenced by me to transportation in the spring of 1845, intimating that it does not belong to me to initiate any proceedings in the matter; that it is not my duty to investigate the facts stated as to the readiness of the witness to confess that he swore falsely on the trial.* 8 Jun: *Received from the Home Office a packet from the Under Secretary, requesting a report of the evidence taken on the trial of James Halling and others at the Adjd. Sessions for Gloucestershire in 1845, at which I presided, together with memorials, correspondence &c. as to a remission of the sentence of transportation then passed on Halling, after a previous conviction for felony, on the ground that the principle witness on the trial now declares that his testimony was false.* 9 Jun: *Wrote to the Secretary of State in relation to the case of James Halling.*

1848: 26 Mar: *Wrote to Mr. Brooke Hunt, as one of the Visitors of the Gaol of Gloucester, respecting a lad from Cheltenham of the name of Halling … then followed a statement of the case by me to the Home office, and the petition of the parents was refused: but it was again urged, perhaps, with electioneering influence to support it: another correspondence passed between the Home office and myself: eventually a pardon was granted, and the lad came back to his friends in 1847: returned to his old evil habits, was tried at the late Q.S., and again sentenced to seven years transportation: it is intended to make a full statement of this case, as to which much pertinacity in applications for remission of punishment, and much manoeuvring & false statements have been exhibited, to the Home Office.* 31 Mar: *Recd. a letter from Mr. Brooke Hunt as to Halling, the convict, being a reply to my letter to him of the 27th. inst.*

HALTENHOF — Georg Friedrich Haltenhof[31]

Georg Friedrich Haltenhof (d. 1847), bass singer and composer, worked at the Weimar theatre between 1799 and 1808, making his debut on 13 April 1799. He lived in St Petersburg in 1813-16, and in 1820-30 he worked as a singing teacher in Tsarskoye Selo, a town 15 miles south of St Petersburg, where the imperial family had their residence. By the time of his death he was a teacher in Kronstadt, working under the Russianised name of Fjodor Bogdanowitsch Galtenhof.

1799: 26 Oct: *Two Songs by her inimitable Graf Almavira by Haltenhof who shewed much more Spirit & sung better than usual.*

HAMBIDGE — John Freeman Hambidge[32]

John Freeman Hambidge (1826-1895), agricultural labourer, was born at Church Icomb, son of George Hambidge (1776-1851) and Hannah Freeman. He married, 1846, Mary Ann Campin (1823-1891), born at Oddington; they had 7 sons and 1 daughter:

1 George Henry (1850-1970)
2 Thomas Valentine (1852-1920); married, at King's Norton, Worcestershire, January 1877, Clara Breakwell (b. 1851)
3 Hugo (1856-1918); married, at Stepney, Middlesex, 10 January 1886, Comfort Lumley (1857-1946)
4 Roby (1859-1931); died at Tonbridge, Kent
5 George Leonard (1861-1941)
1 Mary Ann (b. 1862)
6 Rupert (1863-1882)
7 Louis (1869-1918)

John Hambidge was committed in default of sureties on 27 December 1844 by Francis Witts and Richard Ford for refusing to find sureties to keep the peace towards Hannah Cambray for a space of twelve calendar months.

In November 1851 he was committed by coroner Joseph Lovegrove for the crime of patricide. His prison record states he was 5 feet 11½ inches tall, with brown hair, grey eyes, a long visage, fair complexion, and six moles at the back of his neck. Notable features: sunken eyes. At the trial he was convicted of manslaughter and sentenced to 14 days' solitary confinement in the common gaol. His conduct in prison was said to be 'good'.

Hambidge was again committed for trial on 17 March 1853 at the county gaol, Gloucester, for want of sureties and for using violent and offensive threats towards the Revd Francis Edward Witts at a general quarter sessions of the peace. He was sentenced to two years' imprisonment unless he could enter into sureties of £200. It is unclear what happened, but presumably he came up with the money for he was discharged 27 June 1853.

As there is a gap in the diaries between 29 June and 7 December 1853, there is no further comment on the subject. John Hambidge returned to Church Icomb and life carried on.

1838: 5 Apr: *Of the new Guardians who presented themselves with credentials from their respective parishes, were Mr. Chamberlayne, for Maugersbury, Privett, for Stow, E. Tysoe, for L Swell, J. Cooke for U Swell, Akerman for W. Rissington, Hambidge for Icomb (Glouc).*

1852: 16 Mar: *I took the opportunity, in company with Mr. Herschall, the Chaplain, to visit John Hambidge, the parricide, who is said to express contrition for his bad conduct generally, and spoke in that strain to me; my observations to him were, of course, general, as I avoided any particularly reference to the horrid crime charged upon him.* 30 Mar: *After breakfast repaired to the Crown Court, to be present at the trial of John Hambidge on the charge of murdering his father, G.H. of Icomb, on Nov. 1. 1851 ... The prisoner looked ill and mean, in his soiled everyday dress in which the offence was perpetrated, but did not exhibit any terror or marked depression, was attentive to the proceedings, & frequently communicated with his Attorney.* 1 Apr: *When I reached Stow I was met by unexpected tidings as to the issue of the trial of the wretched John Hambidge. He had been found guilty of manslaughter, the Jury having long hesitated whether they should not return a verdict of wilful murder; and Baron Platt sentenced him to fourteen days.* 10 Apr: *John Hambidge returned from prison last night—drunk and daring,——calling at the Police Station at Stow to claim his guns (the gun by which he killed his father) shot-belt &c., which were properly refused, the property of one convicted of felony being forfeited to the Crown.* 8 May: *John Hambidge has again rendered himself amenable to the law: his wife's mother from Oddington having laid an information against him.* 9 May: *Recd. a note from Superintendt. Makepeace, that J. Hambidge was arrested last evening.* 10 May: *R Waller met me at the Unicorn, where we heard the charge brought by the Campens of Oddington against John Hambidge; it was fully made out that he had, when under the influence of liquor, used the vilest provocation and most violent threats against his wife's father and mother, & brother.* 4 Nov: *Sewell assured me that he had on Tuesday had an interview with Mr. Ridler, of the County of Gloucester Bank at Cheltenham, who was stated by Mr. Du Pré to have informed him that John Hambidge had vowed to shoot me, when he was released from Gaol.*

1853: 16 Mar: *Much and anxiously engaged in conferring with Mr. Herschell, Chaplain of the Gaol, and others as to an impression prevalent in the mind of him and others, that the prisoner Hambidge, now in custody under the commitment of R. Waller and myself for want of sureties to keep the peace towards different members of his wife's family, will, on his discharge, which will take place on May 10, commit some act of violence upon me...* 17 Mar: *Went into Court, intending to hear trials: but was soon called upon to further deliberations as to Hambidge's evil designs and threats.* 19 Mar: *Drove to Bourton on the Water, where I had an interview with Mr. Wilkins, to whom I explained my position in respect of J Hambidge, as also the proceedings which I had instituted, and obtained from him information on the pecuniary affairs of JH.* 21 Mar: *Received a note from W. Wilkins, who sends me a statement of the contents of the will of the late Hambidge of Icomb, and of a deed executed by his son JH.* 22 Mar: *I also sent to Mr. B. a letter I received from J Hambidge by this day's post, in which he proposes, if I will withdraw the prosecution against him, to leave this part of the country, never to return; the words however, do not purport emigration to a foreign and distant country.* 24 Mar: *Received a letter from Mr. Burrup, in answer to that which I had written on the 22d. He is clearly of opinion that I must not shrink from pursuing against Hambidge the course on which I have entered.* 30 Mar: *From W. Wiggin I received a letter as to John Hambidge: he writes at the suggestion of Mr. Herschell, and forwards a letter addressed to JH. by his wife, in which she consents to emigrate with him, if money can be raised to accomplish that design.* 31 Mar: *To Sewell's office, where I consulted him as to the letter received by me yesterday from Wiggin, as to the project of Hambidge's emigration.* 7 Apr., 21 Apr., 26 Apr: *Mr. Tipping followed me thither, to shew me a letter which had been received at Sewell's office from Mr. Smallridge, to the effect that J Hambidge refuses to agree to the arrangements made with a view to emigration of himself and family, repudiating Mr. Herschell and Mr. Smallridge, and writing to them very offensive letters.* 24 May: *I took the opportunity of conferring with Mr. Burrup, the Archdeacon's registrar as to the proceedings to be taken against John Hambidge at the Midsummer Sessions.* 27 May, 2 Jun., 16 Jun., 22 Jun: *While at Stow I had an interview with Ex Sergeant Gallop and Constable Ford, of the Gloucestershire Police, as to their attendance at the Quarter Sessions next week, to make affidavit there, as to the vindictive language used with reference to me in my Magisterial capacity, in their hearing, by John Hambidge.* 24 Jun., 28 Jun: *Conferred with Mr. Burrup as to the proceedings to be taken to-morrow against John Hambidge.*

HAMILTON — Mrs Hamilton at Clifton

1806: 3 Jul: *In the Evening, walked alone, & with my Father & Mother, Mrs. Hamilton.*

HAMILTON — Mr Hamilton, a guest of Lady Lyttelton at Malvern

1829: 27 Aug: *Lady Lyttelton received company to-day I was introduced to a fine intelligent old Scotch gentleman, of the name of Hamilton, with whom I had much conversation on the politics of the day, and the general political relations past and present of the world.*

HAMILTON — L. C. Hamilton[33]

This is unclear. There was no Hamilton at Oxford University with these initials. They are presumably an abbreviation for lieutenant-colonel, in which case the mention *may* refer to Lt-Col Sir William Osborne Hamilton of the 1st Regiment of Foot and later the 8th Royal Veteran Battalion, who was knighted in 1815 in recognition of his services to the government of Heligoland. This is not a confident attribution.

1806: 20 Mar: *Called upon Round, walked with Dowell & Trevenen to Joh. Pullen's tree, with Trevenen to his rooms, &*

with him & Dowell to the Fencing school, where L. C. Hamilton distinguished himself.

HAMILTON — Mr Hamilton, a temporary curate at Stow-on-the-Wold

1854: 8 Jul: *A notice of a Ruridecanal meeting at Stow, and Clerical Society dinner on the 19th. Inst. issued by Mr. Hamilton, the temporary substitute for R W Hippisley, who with his family is taking a holiday.* 19 Jul: *Mr. Hamilton is locum tenens for Mr. Hippisley during a three months absence of the latter—is by dress and demeanour a manifest member of the Tractarian School, and appears to be a person of talent.* 20 Jul: *Mr. H. appears a very sensible, thoughtful person.*

HAMILTON — Anthony Hamilton [34]

Anthony Hamilton (1739-1812), Church of England clergyman, was the second son of Alexander Hamilton, solicitor, of London, and Barbara Lilley. He was educated at Harrow School and Corpus Christi, Cambridge. He was appointed rector at Hadham, Hertfordshire, and graduated DD. He served as archdeacon of Colchester, vicar of St Martin-in-the-Field, and chaplain-in-ordinary to the king. Hamilton married, 12 February 1767, Anne, daughter of Richard Terrick.

1801: 5 Jul: *Fine weather. At St. Martin's Church in the morning, where I heard an excellent Sermon preached by Dr. Hamilton, on the having one's conversation in heaven.*

HAMILTON — Charles Hamilton [35]

Charles Hamilton (b. ±1794), surgeon, lived at Claremont Cottage, Hanley Castle, Worcestershire, in 1841, before moving to the Mount in nearby Welland. He married Harriett (b. ±1800); they had at least 2 sons and 1 daughter:

1 William (b. ±1825)
1 Harriett (b. ±1829)
2 Reuben (b. ±1834)

1840: 29 May: *A letter from Miss S. Daniell from Bullingham Court, which the sisters leave for Malvern on Monday next, and propose passing three or four days with Mr. & Mrs. Mason there, purposing to be with us on Thursday or Friday in next week, the day to be fixed in a future letter: Miss S. D. sends me a letter addressed to her by Mr. Hamilton, a surgeon at Malvern Wells, who never saw my Aunt, but who has written a Monody on her decease, which he forwarded to the Daniells with a proposition to print 100 copies, the profits of the sale to be applied to the Malvern charities.* 30 May.

HAMILTON — Mr & Mrs J. Hamilton at Mrs McQueen's house in Edinburgh

1801: 1 May: *In the evening walked with George before repairing to Mrs. McQueen's, We met there Mr. J. & Mrs. Hamilton, Miss Graham, Mr. McKenzie &c.*

HAMILTON — Robert Montgomery Hamilton [36]

Lord Robert Montgomery Hamilton (1793-1868), landed proprietor and high commissioner to the General Assembly and Kirk, became 8th Baron Belhaven and Stenton in 1814. On 10 September 1831 he was created Baron Hamilton of Wishaw. He was high commissioner to the General Assembly and Kirk in 1831-41, 1847-51, 1853-57, and 1860-66. He married, 1815, Hamilton (1790-1873), a daughter of Walter Frederick Campbell of Shawfield.

1837: 22 Jul: *Very kindly recd. by his Lordship and family: a late dinner, as they were expecting Lord and Lady Belhaven from Town, who did not arrive till eleven o cl.* 23 Jul.
1839: 17 Jul.

HAMILTON — Lady Susan Hamilton — *see also* Beckford

Francis Witts was incorrect here. Beckford married Lady Margaret Gordon; his mother had been Maria Hamilton. His younger daughter, Susanna Euphemia Beckford (1786-1859), married Alexander Hamilton, 10th duke of Hamilton, and inherited Beckford's collection. The other Hamilton connection was Beckford's mother, Maria Hamilton, daughter and co-heir of George Hamilton, son of James, 6th earl of Abercorn, by Bridget Coward.

1826: 29 Apr: *Mr. Beckford by his wife, Lady Susan Hamilton (I think), had two daughters: their Mother died, when they were children, & they were educated by Lady Anne Hamilton; under their her charge I saw them at Tunbridge Wells in 1805; the younger, Miss Susan Beckford, a most lovely creature, married her relation, the Duke of Hamilton, a singular character, & much older than herself. The elder, without many personal charms, married a Col. Orde, and is since dead.*

HAMILTON — Thomas Hamilton [37]

Thomas Hamilton (1780-1858), JP, MP, and landed proprietor, was the son of Charles Hamilton, 8th earl of Haddington (1753-1828), DL, and Lady Sophia (d. 1813), daughter of John Hope, 2nd earl of Hopetoun. In 1795-1828 he was styled Lord Binning. He was educated at the University of Edinburgh and Christ Church, Oxford, before starting a career in politics. Hamilton was MP for St Germans in 1802-06, Cockermouth in 1807, Callington in 1807-12, Mitchell in 1814-18, Rochester in 1818-1826, and Yarmouth I.o.W. in 1826-27. He was lord lieutenant of Ireland in 1834-35 and first lord of the Admiralty in 1841-46. He succeeded his father as 9th earl of Haddington in 1828. He married, 1802, Maria, only surviving daughter and heir of George Parker, 4th earl of Macclesfield. There were no surviving children.

1832: 10 Apr: *These peers have carried with them several more, who voted in the majority of last October, and among them the Earl of Haddington, a great adherent of Canning.*

1833: 9 Nov: *We were in the vicinity of several seats, which I had known of old; among these Tyningham, the Earl of Haddington's, and Beanston and Amisfield, the property of the Earl of Wemyss.*

1834: 28 Dec: *Some new appointments in the Administration are announced. The Earl of Haddington is to be Lord Lieutenant of Ireland.*

1837: 8 Sep.

1842: 15 Jul: *A messenger came early from Stanway with a letter to me from Lady Wemyss, announcing the arrival of the family from town last evening; that they expected Lord and Lady Haddington on a visit to-morrow evening, and wished me to meet him.* 16 Jul: *Lord and Lady Haddington were expected to dinner, but at 7 o clock we sat down without them... The evening was passed in pleasant conversation: Lord H. is an able, practised, Statesman, agreeable and polite, not reserved, full of information, and ready to communicate it; born in 1780, we were for a few months contemporary at the University, and my old recollections of Scotland helped to make me au coulant of the conversation of a circle of Scottish nobility, while I was not unversed in those general topics which were likely to be introduced as to public proceedings, the houses of parliament, the Metropolis &c. Lady Haddington, not insensible to the position of her Lord as a Cabinet Minister, and quondam Viceroy of Ireland, looking quite as aged as he does, with a little tartness of manner, and sharpness of voice, is yet, I daresay, a very estimable person, only child of the lately deceased, aged Earl of Macclesfield, as Lord H. was also an only child.* 17 Jul: *Lord W. and Lord Haddington rode out.* 7 Nov: *Wrote to the Earl of Haddington, forwarding to his Lordship Hyett's pamphlet as to the colouring or otherwise modifying the qualities of timber by the infusion of chemical agents.*

1845: 17 May: *His object is to get a favourable introduction to Lord Haddington, as first Lord of the Admiralty.*

HAMILTON-DALRYMPLE — Janet Hamilton-Dalrymple [38]

Lady Janet Hamilton-Dalrymple, née Duff, was the wife of her cousin Sir Hew Hamilton-Dalrymple, 3rd baronet (±1746-1800), of Bargany, North Berwick, whom she married in ±1772. She was the daughter of William Duff (1701-81), of Crombie, co. Ayr, and Elizabeth Dalrymple (1713-1781). She and Hew had 3 sons and 1 daughter:

1 Hew Dalrymple-Hamilton (Hamilton-Dalrymple) (1774-1834); succeeded as 4th baronet
2 John (1780-1835), Maj.-Gen.; succeeded as 5th baronet
1 Janet (1783-1867)
3 James (d. before 1832)

1801: 18 Apr: *In the evening came (to Elcho's) Dr. & Lady F. Traill, Mr. & Mrs. Howard, Mr. & Mrs. Greathead, Lady Hamilton Dalrymple.*

HAMMERSLEY — Hugh and George Hammersley [39]

Hugh Hammersley (1774-1840), banker, was the eldest son of Thomas Hammersley (1747-1812), banker to the prince of Wales. Hugh was educated at Eton (1782-99), and it seems probable that he accompanied his younger brother George to Weimar to complete his education at the Belvedere. Hugh and George both joined their father's bank, Hammersley & Co. in Pall Mall, London, and Hugh went on to become senior partner. He was also MP for Helston in 1812-18. He married, 1822, Baroness Marie de Montolieu de St Hippolite. On his death the bank was taken over by Coutts and Company.

Of George Hammersley (1785-1835) little is known. He was a partner of Hammersley & Co., but predeceased his brother Hugh.

1799: 16 Aug: *To the "Erb Prinz" where we visited Messrs. Hammersley & W. Sloane, just arrived the younger Mr. Hammersley & Mr. S. to go to the Belvedere.*

HAMPDEN — *see* Rice

HAMPDEN — Renn Dickson Hampden [40]

Renn Dickson Hampden (1793-1868), bishop of Hereford and theologian, was the eldest son of Renn Hampden, a colonel of militia in Barbados, and Frances Raven. He was born in Barbados and sent to England with his godmother in 1798 to be educated by M. Rowlandson, vicar of Warminster, Wiltshire. He then went to Oriel College, Oxford (BA 1814; MA 1816; fellow 1814-18), and St Mary Hall (B&DD 1833). He became Bampton lecturer in 1832, principal of St Mary Hall in 1833-48, canon of Christ Church in 1836-48, regius professor of divinity in 1836-48, and bishop of Hereford in 1848-68. At Oriel College Hampden was taught by the first generation of Noetic theologians, who were active in the intellectual revival of the university and the defence of Anglicanism on the grounds of its 'reasonableness'. John Davison was Hampden's tutor; Samuel Hinds, later bishop of Norwich and also born in Barbados, was his undergraduate friend; and Thomas Arnold and Richard Whately were his contemporaries as fellows. He never abandoned his Noetic upbringing, whether as a source of controversy in the 1830s and 1840s or as a bulwark of religious orthodoxy in the 1850s and 1860s. See in particular Witts's diary entry for 14 April 1848.

Hampden married, 24 April 1816, his cousin Mary (d. 1865), the daughter of Edward Lovell; they had 2 sons and 4 daughters:

1 Augusta (1820-1838); died unmarried
2 Laura (1822-1850); died unmarried
3 Henrietta (1824-1897); died unmarried
1 Edward Renn (1826-1892); married, at Weston-under-Penyard, Herefordshire, 9 February 1876, Catherine Emma Hawkshaw
4 Cecilia (1830-1831)
2 Charles John (1832-1888)

1836: 23 Dec: *The head of Brazennose has prohibited the students of his College from attending the divinity Lectures of the Regius Professor, Dr. Hampden, under the penalty of not having their testimonials signed when applying as Candidates for Ordination.*

1837: 20 May: *Received a very satisfactory letter from Edward, containing an account of the commencement of Dr. Hampden's, the Regius Prof. of Divinity's, Course of Lectures, which he is attending.* 7 Jun: *The pamphlet is the introduction in which Dr. Hampden, the Reg. Prof. of Divinity at Oxford, has prefixed to the 2d. Ed. of his Bampton Lectures just published, and which contains his long delayed comments on the proceedings had at Oxford last Spring twelvemonth, when, as the Prof. asserts, no argument was brought against him, but his opinion were assaulted through party spirit, and in an unfair manner.* 23 Jul.

1845: 6 Feb.

1847: 13 Dec: ... *likely to be vacated by Mr. Jacobson, of Magd. Hall, formerly of Exeter Coll., of whom it is stated that he will be raised by Government to the Regius of Professorship of Divinity, about to be resigned by Dr. Hampden, when elevated to the see of Hereford.* 15 Dec., 19 Dec., 22 Dec.

1848: 13 Jan., 22 Jan., 2 Feb: *The Hampden controversy has been vigorously prosecuted.* 12 Mar., 15 Mar., 14 Apr: *Mr. Michell also is held in high consideration in the University; he was in the first instance a Member of Wadham College: he is no supporter of Ultra High Church doctrines; indeed, opposed to the Pusey and Newman party: and recently has declared himself an advocate for Dr. Hampden: so may be considered of the moderate school.*

HANBRIDGE — William Hanbridge, police superintendent at Chipping Campden [41]

William Hanbridge (1816-1891), police superintendent, was born at Dunamore, Wicklow, Ireland. Before joining the police in England he had been a farmer. He joined the new Gloucestershire Constabulary at its outset in 1839, enlisting on 1 December with warrant number 2. He was registered as 6 feet 2¾ inches in height. On 24 March 1842 he was promoted to superintendent. At the 1861 census Hanbridge was still ranked superintendent and stationed at Painswick. Afterwards he seems to have been stationed at Nailsworth and Stroud. He retired on 1 November 1878 with a superannuated pension of £129 10*s* 10*d* per year and lived at 42 Slad Road, Stroud. He married Emma (b. ±1824), born at Elrington, Gloucestershire; they had at least 3 sons and 2 daughters:

1 William Edward (1847-1913)
2 Henry (b. 1856); married Jeanette Griffiths; emigrated to Cuyahoga, Ohio, USA, 1881; 2 sons and 3 daughters:
  1 William H. (1882-1964)
  1 Emily (b. 1884)
  2 Fredrick (b. 1887)
  2 Ruby M. (1893-1969)
  3 Gertrude (b. 1897)
1 Emily Hanbridge (b. ±1857); married a Mills
3 Samuel Richtor (1863-1933); married, 16 April 1901, Annie Mabbett
2 Edith Emma (b. 1864)

1848: 30 Jun: *Called at the Police Station on Mr. Lefroy: looked over the premises with him and Keiley & Hanbridge, his deputy and chief Superintendent, with a view to enlargement.*

1852: 4 Apr: *Sergt. Gallop called ... G. is sorely vexed at this arrangement: the situation at Moreton is distasteful to him, the Police not being in good order odour there, and he not being on friendly terms with Superintendent Hanbridge of the Campden district.*

HANBURY — Frances and Henrietta Hanbury at Lady Lyttelton's accidental music[42]

Frances (1759-1818) and Henrietta (Harriet) Hanbury (1748-1827) were daughters of Capel Hanbury (1707-65), of Pontypool Park, and Jane (d. 1787), daughter of Thomas Charles, 5th Viscount Tracy. Capel and Jane had married on 7 October 1743. Frances and Henrietta both died unmarried. They had one brother, John Hanbury (1744-84), who married Jane, daughter of Morgan Lewis of St Pierre, Monmouthshire; they had 3 sons:

1 John (1775-1796); died unmarried
2 Capel (1776-1861); *see below*
3 Charles (1777-1858); married Henrietta Susanna (d. 1839), only child and heir of Henry, 8th Viscount Tracy; assumed surname and arms of Tracy; created Baron Sudeley, 1838; *see below*

Frances and Henrietta were part of the Cheltenham set and distantly related to Agnes Witts. Lady Lyttelton would have become acquainted with them at Cheltenham.

A tablet high on the south wall of St Margaret's church, Westminster (i.e. Westminster Abbey), records the burial of Henrietta and Frances Hanbury and their mother Jane of Pontypool. This was originally on the north wall. The inscription reads:

> Sacred to the memory of Henrietta and Frances Hanbury the daughters of Capel Hanbury Esq. and the Honble. Jane Hanbury formerly Tracy of Pont-y-pool Park, Monmouthshire, both of whom were interred in the vault underneath this church where the remains of their mother were also deposited on the XV [15th] of March MDCCLXXXVII [1787]. Frances Hanbury departed this life on 1 December MDCCCXVIII [1818] age LIX [59] years and was buried on the X [10th] of the same month. Henrietta Hanbury departed this life on the XVI [16th] of February MDCCCXXVII [1827] aged LXXXIX [89] years and as buried on the XXVI [26th] of the same month.

1801: 3 Jun: *Repaired in the evening to Lady Lyttelton's, where was rathe a squeeze and music. The Miss Hanbury's etc.* 9 Jun., 10 Jun: *Lady Lytteltons, accidental Music began, Miss Halifaxes sung, & Miss Morley; it was quite a squeeze: a Mr. Wood a nephew of Mr. Sheridan also sung in a very singular style. We met there the Hanbury's, Guydickens, Mrs. Scott & Miss Morley, Sir N. Dukinfield, Sir H. & Major Vavasour, Mr. Doig, Mr. Edwin Stanhope, Comte de Bruges, Miss Nevilles, Mr. & Mrs. Chambers, Miss Hungerford, &c.*

HANBURY — William Hanbury[43]

William Hanbury (1755-1798), consul of the English factory, was the son of John Hanbury (1716-1785) and his wife, Margarethe Dorothea. John Hanbury was born in El Salvador and died at Hamburg. The family were of Kelmarsh Hall, Northamptonshire.

William married Caroline Elisabeth Bohn (1758-1832), daughter of the printer and book trader Johan Carl Bohn (1712-1773). Bohn was originally from Breslau; his first wife was a daughter of the Hamburg printer Theodor Christoph Felginer, who helped him build a successful publishing business. William and Caroline had at least 1 daughter:

1 Caroline (1789-1874); married Jaques Henri de Chapeaurouge (b. 1780)

1798: *Mr. Hanbury the Consul of the English Factory here, is also a Man of much commercial as well as political Discernment and Sagacity, and in the Absence of the Minister performs the Office of British Chargé d'Affaires. To draw up the whole, altho' there are many Persons of bad Character among the Persons resident in Hamburgh, the Number of the unexceptionable is so much larger, that we forbear to dwell upon the former.*

HANBURY LEIGH — Capel Hanbury Leigh[44]

Capel Hanbury Leigh (1776-1861), JP, DL, and landed proprietor, of Pontypool Park, was the second son of John Hanbury (1744-1784) and Jane, daughter of Morgan Lewis of St Pierre, Monmouthshire. Hanbury Leigh married, first, 13 April 1797, Mary Anne (Molly), Lady Mackworth, née Miers or Myers [?] (d. 1846), widow of Sir Robert Mackworth, 2nd baronet (1764-1794), and daughter of Nathaniel Myers of Neath, Glamorganshire. She took the Gnoll estate near Neath with her to her second marriage. She had no children from either marriage.

Capel Hanbury Leigh married secondly, 1847, Emma Elizabeth Rous (1816-1888), fourth daughter of Thomas Bates Rouse of Courtyrala, Glamorganshire; they had 1 son and 2 daughters:

1 Emma Charlotte (1848-1921); married, at St George's, Hanover Square, 1878, Robert Thomas Brudenell Bruce
2 Frances Elizabeth (1850-1875); married, 12 December 1868, A. L. G. Ashley
1 John Capel (1853-1921); married, 8 January 1885, Louisa Charlotte, daughter of Col Edward Eager

---

1826: 7 Apr: *We found Mrs. Hanbury Leigh, Mrs. H. Leigh is wife to Mr. Tracy's elder brother, and was in the first instance Lady Mackworth: by the death of her first husband, this lady was left a very young widow with a splendid fortune, Sir Robt. Mackworth having made the most liberal provision for her to the impoverishment of his brother, Sir Digby Mackworth, the present baronet. Lady Mackworth was a Miss Myers of Neath, and very pretty; her Mother and other connexions, none of them in the better class of society, are thought to have manœuvred well with her weak & drunken husband in her favour. Her hand and fortune she afterwards gave to Mr. Hanbury Leigh of Pontipool Park, Monmouthshire, after the decease of his elder brother, to whom she was engaged: she has had no children by either husband, and is a very cheerful, communicative, good humoured woman of a certain age.* 10 Apr: *Our party was diminished by the departure of Mrs. Hanbury Leigh for Cheltenham.*

1827: 3 Dec: *We came to Stanway on a visit to Lady Elcho for a few days, and found there a large party ... Mr. F. Aston came to dinner; his wife called in the forenoon, as also Mr. & Mrs. Hanbury Leigh, Mrs. Tracy and Miss L. Tracy from Toddington.*

1828: 4 Oct: *I called on Lady Elcho Besides Miss Church, Mrs. Monsell & Mrs. Leigh, two widowed Sisters, Irish & Roman Catholics, are her present guests.*

HANBURY TRACY — Charles Hanbury Tracy[45]

Charles Hanbury Tracy, 1st Baron Sudeley (1778-1858), JP, MP, and landed proprietor, was the third son of John Hanbury (d. 1784), of Pontypool Park, Monmouthshire, and Jane, daughter of Morgan Lewis of St Pierre, Monmouthshire. Charles's grandfather, Capel Hanbury (1707-1765), of Pontypool Park, had married Jane Tracy (d. 1787), daughter of Thomas Charles, 5th Viscount Tracy. The family derived its wealth from its ownership of the Pontypool Ironworks.

Charles Hanbury Tracy was educated at Rugby School and Christ Church, Oxford. He married, 1798, his cousin Henrietta Susanna, daughter and heir of Henry Leigh, 8th Viscount Tracy, and Susannah Weaver; they had 6 sons and 3 daughters:

1 Henrietta (1800-1890); died unmarried
1 Thomas Charles (1801-1863); succeeded as 2nd Baron Sudeley; *see below*
2 Henry (1802-1889)
2 Frances (1806-1867)
3 John Capel (1807-1852); died unmarried
4 Capel Arthur (1809-1834); employed in HEIC civil service; married, 18 September 1833, Eliza Jane Tyler
5 William (1810-1887); employed in Madras civil service
6 Edward (1812-1887), chaplain to the embassy at Vienna (1848-56)
3 Laura Susanna (1814-1881); died unmarried

Charles Hanbury took the additional name of Tracy by royal licence on 1 January 1799, and was created Baron Sudeley on 12 July 1838. He was MP for Tewkesbury in 1807-12 and 1832-37. He was an amateur architect and rebuilt Toddington Manor between 1820 and 1835 at a cost of more than £150,000. His tastes in architecture were influenced by Uvedale Price, Richard Payne Knight, and others of the picturesque school. In 1835 Hanbury Tracy was appointed chairman of the commission to judge the designs for the new Houses of Parliament; it was largely due to his influence that Barry's plan was adopted.

The Tracy title was claimed in 1835 by Joseph Tracy (1765-1836) formerly of Geashill, King's County, Ireland, son and heir of James Tracy (1730-1794) of the same, son and heir of William Tracy of Ross, King's County, who died in 1734 at Castlebrack, Queen's County. William Tracy was alleged to be William (baptised 22 February 1693 at St Andrew's, Holborn, London), third son of the Robert Tracy (one of the justices of the court of common pleas), who died in 1735, aged 80. Robert Tracy was son of the 2nd viscount by his second wife. This petition was presented on 15 May 1835, but the claimant died on 17 March 1836. Two months after his death, his son and heir, James Tracy 'of South Street, Grosvenor Square, Esq.' (b. 14 February 1800), presented a petition which, in consequence of the attorney-general's August 1837 report, was referred to the House of Lords. He again petitioned in 1842, but the case was dismissed by the House in 1843. In both these claims the assertion was that William, the third son of the aforementioned Hon. Robert Tracy, formed an imprudent alliance in Dublin with Mary O'Brien, and was consequently disinherited by his father and family. The identity of this William was not established further than (a) by an entry in a prayer book—'married in Dublin, April 17th, 1728, William, Son of the Honourable Robert Tracy, late One of the English Judges, to Mary, Daughter of Mr James O'Brien, Merchant'; and (b) by parole evidence that there had been a tombstone at Castlebrack, with an inscription to the said William (said to have died in 1734) by the same description. Fragments of such a tombstone were indeed found later at Castlebrack and exhibited before the Committee for Privileges in 1847, but it was alleged in evidence that these had been forged in 1843. It appears probable that William, son of the Hon. Robert Tracy, baptised 22 February 1693, died an infant, as he is not mentioned in an entail of his father's lands, dated 15 December 1732.

Francis Witts, through his mother, was distantly related to the Hanbury-Tracy family. Agnes was the daughter of Anne Tracy, and her great-great-grandfather had been John Tracy, 3rd Viscount Tracy (1617-1687), who in turn was the great-great-granddaughter of the same peer.

1805: 28 Jul: *Called upon Mr. Hanbury Tracy.*

1823: 17 Sep., 11 Oct: *Mr. H. Tracy has for some years ceased to represent the borough of Tewkesbury.... Of course, as connected with the Stanway Branch by my Mother's side, I claim kindred with the Tracy's of Toddington. Mr. H. Tracy was a cadet of the Hanbury's of Monmouthshire, and assumed the name of Tracy, when he married the heiress of the last Baron of that name; the title is now extinct. Mr. & Mrs. H. Tracy have a large family, amply provided for by estates in Gloucestershire, Montgomeryshire and Somersetshire.*

1824: 1 Nov: *I went to Stanway by Lady Elcho's invitation to meet some of her neighbours at dinner.... The addition to the dinner party consisted of Mrs. Tracy with many of the younger branches of the Toddington family.* 17 Dec: *Lady Elcho has also other inmates ... Mr. Tracy and Fred. Aston joined us at dinner. Mr. Tracy is now alone at Toddington, where his splendid new house is advancing to a habitable estate. He is not now in Parliament; formerly he represented the Borough of Tewkesbury, and was also a warm oppositionist, being attached to the ultra liberalism of Sir F. Burdett &c. His manners are peculiarly polished.*

1825: 17 Sep: *The distance from Much Wenlock to Bridgnorth is about nine miles and the country very pleasing. We passed through the estate and near the mansion of Sir Edward Acton, a Roman Catholic Baronet; also at Morvill, an old fashioned seat in a pleasant vale, formerly the property of the Lords Tracy, but lately sold by Mr. Hanbury Tracy to Lord Forester.*

1826: 7 Apr: *Lady Elcho having left London and arrived at Stanway some days ago, we accepted an invitation to pass a week with her, & arrived there about three o clock. We found Mrs. Hanbury Leigh, Charles Keysall and Mr. R. Stewart her guests. Mrs. H. Leigh is wife to Mr. Tracy's elder brother.* 9 Apr: *Mr. & Mrs. Tracy and their two eldest daughters came from Toddington to dinner.* 15 Sep.

1827: 3 Dec: *We came to Stanway on a visit to Lady Elcho for a few days, and found there a large party ... as also Mr. & Mrs. Hanbury Leigh, Mrs. Tracy and Miss L. Tracy from Toddington.*

1830: 22 Jun: *Mr. Hanbury Tracy was consulted as to the architecture of the former, but his plans were not entirely followed.*

1833: 13 Oct: *Mr. John Eddy was kind enough to be our guide to see Mr. Tracy's splendid house; three years had passed since I had been there, and it is far advanced towards completion. The family still occupy apartments in what remains of the old house, but pass most of the day in the new one.*

1839: 30 Apr: *Soon after breakfast visited by two professional men, by whom I was served with the copy of an Order from the House of Lords to attend on Monday the 6th. May, before the Committee of Privileges, and to be sworn to give evidence on the petition of James Tracy Esqr. to be admitted to the title of Visct. Tracy of Rathcool, an Irish peerage, and to produce, as Vicar of Stanway, the register books of that parish from 1656 to 1800.* 6 May: *The claimant's pretensions are thus based—that Edward the 2d. Visc. Tracy who died 1662—had by his second wife, a son Robert, Judge of the Common pleas, settled at Coscomb, who died and was buried at Didbrooke in 1735 ...* 7 May: *During Mr. Prior's communication examination I was conversing with the Hon. Charles & Hen. Tracy the two elder Sons of Lord Sudely, who were present behind the bar, and in communication with the Attorney Genl.*

1840: 12 Jun: *We proceeded thence to the mansion house ... very little having been done in the way of furnishing & fitting up, but even that has been suspended since the regretted decease of Lady Sudeley about a twelvemonth ago.*

1843: 10 Jan: *Lord Sudeley has presented the benefice with its appendages, Didbrook, Hayles, Stanley Pontlarge, to my cousin, William Whalley.*

1845: 19 May: *Lord Sudeley has recently built, or rather added to, a farm house, once, probably, a manorial mansion: the additions are in the Tudor style, very substantial and well executed.*

1850: 16 Sep., 20 Sep.

1851: 4 Feb.

1852: 2 Nov.

HANBURY TRACY — **Thomas Charles Hanbury Tracy**[46]

Thomas Charles Hanbury Tracy, 2nd Baron Sudeley (1801-1863), JP, MP, and landed proprietor, was the eldest son of Charles Hanbury Tracy and Henrietta Susanna Tracy (*above*). The young Thomas took the name of Leigh by royal licence on 11 April 1806 in deference to the memory of his maternal grandfather, to whose estates in Gloucestershire, Montgomeryshire, and Shropshire he was his father's heir. He resumed the patronymic of Hanbury Tracy by royal licence on 30 March 1839. He was educated at Christ Church, Oxford and married, 1831, Emma Elizabeth Alicia, daughter and co-heir of George Hay Dawkins Pennant. Thomas and Emma had 6 sons and 7 daughters. Thomas succeeded his father as 2nd Baron Sudeley on 10 February 1858. He was MP for Wallingford in 1831-32, and died at Pau, in the south of France in February 1863. By his will he left his wife £2,000, an annuity of £3,000, and his house at Eastern Terrace, Brighton. Having settled £25,000 on each of his three married daughters, he devised the same sum to their two spinster sisters, and left £20,000 to each of his four surviving younger sons. He was succeeded in the peerage by his eldest son, Sudeley Charles George Hanbury Tracy (1837-1877), who died unmarried and was succeeded by his next brother, Charles Douglas Richard Hanbury Tracy (1840-1922). Compounding problems created by an encumbered inheritance, Charles Douglas suffered a succession of failures in business and speculation, and was twice declared bankrupt. He lost all the family estates. The children of Thomas and Emma were as follows:

1 Georgiana Henrietta Emma (1832-1921); married, 6 October 1859, Charles Henry Maude
2 Juliana Sophia Elizabeth (1833-1899)
3 Alice Augusta Gertrude (1838-1877); married, 28 May 1861, Lt-Col Charles Webber
4 Adelaide Frances Isabella (1834-1917); married, 17 May 1859, Revd Frederick Peel
1 Sudeley Charles George (1837-77); succeeded as 3rd Baron Sudeley; died unmarried
2 Charles Douglas Richard (1840-1922); succeeded as 4th Baron Sudeley; married, 1868, Ada Maria Katherine Tollemache
5 Gertrude Emily Rosamon (b. & d. 1842)
3 Algernon Cornwallis Henry (1844-1845)
6 Madeleine Emily Augusta (1845-1938); married, 30 December 1875, Revd Maurice Ponsonby
4 Alfred Francis Algernon (1846-1929); married, 21 April 1868, Agnes Jane Hoare
5 Frederic Stephen Archibald (1848-1906), MP; married, 8 September 1870, Helena Caroline Winnington
6 Hubert George Edward (1855-1940), DL and barrister; died unmarried

---

1834: 28 Jul: *Henry Tracy called with young Reginald Wynniatt on his canvass for his brother Charles Hanbury Leigh.* 31 Jul., 13 Aug: *Some of the agents told me that the election was gained by the numbers who voted at Northleach, the majority in favour of Codrington from that district considerably exceeding the calculation made of the strength of the Blue interest in that quarter. The Tory gentry had divested themselves of the blue favours, but the flags were exhibited at the various public houses engaged by the party: not a Yellow ensign was to be seen, and Mr. Tracy Leigh had betaken himself to his home to mourn over his disappointment and ponder on the probable amount of his bills.* 27 Oct: *Charles Tracy Leigh, eldest son of Mr. Hanbury Tracy, is announced as Candidate for the representation of the Eastern division of the County in opposition to Codrington, and in the Whig interest.*

1835: 4 Jan: *At Tewkesbury Mr. Dowdeswell, a conservative expects to be returned; it remains to be seen whether Mr. H. Tracy or Mr. Martin are to be ousted: they are both Whigs or Radicals.* 6 Jan: *At Tewkesbury Mr. Dowdeswell has gained his election by a majority of three: Mr. H. Tracy will be his colleague, and Martin loses his election.* 27 Jul: *Charles Tracy Leigh, eldest son of Mr. Hanbury Tracy, is announced as Candidate for the representation of the Eastern division of the County in opposition to Codrington, and in the Whig interest.* 2 Aug: *During our absence Mr. C. Hanbury Tracy Leigh left his card.*

HANCOCK — **Frederick Hancock**[46]

Frederick Hancock (1821-86), solicitor, was born at Mickleton, Gloucestershire, son of John and Hannah Maria Hancock. By the 1871 census he was a widower living with his daughter, Rebbecah Florence (1846-1903), who died unmarried. Hancock practised at Shipston-on-Stour.

1850: 5 Dec: *Mr. Hancock, Attorney of Shipston, appeared for Mr. Smith.*

HANCOCKS — **Henry Hancocks**[47]

Henry Hancocks (b. 1830), labourer, was born at Cowley, son of Thomas and Sarah Hancocks. He was referred to as Hancocks, Hancock, and Hancox, but the first seems to be correct. In the 1841 census Henry was a male servant working for John Davis, farmer, of Upper Slaughter. He then disappears from record.

1845: 19 Jan: *Conferred with J Davis on parish matters, and wrote to Mr. Pearce, desiring him to send the boy Hancox now in the Workhouse to be set to work by Mr. Humphris.*

HANCOX — **Sarah Hancocks**[48]

Sarah Hancocks (±1799-1841), pauper, was the widow of Thomas and the mother of Henry (*above*). She died at Cowley.

1840: 20 Jan: *Wrote to Mr. Humphries, Cowley, Parish Officer, respecting the out relief ordered yesterday at the meeting of our*

Guardians to S. Hancox, a parishioner of Upper Slaughter, under the special sanction of the Poor Law Commissioners. 22 Jan: *A letter from the Revd.—Smith, Rector of Cowley, addressed to the Chairman of the Stow Union, bespeaking his attention to the case of Sarah Hancox belonging to this parish, but resident at Cowley, respecting whom I wrote to Mr. Humphries on the 20th. a letter which has crossed that of Mr. Smith.* 15 May, 31 May: *The widow Handcock came from Cowley, bringing me a letter respecting her concerns from Mr. Davy, to which I replied with a donation to the poor woman from our parochial charities, as well as from my own purse.* 12 Sep: *Wrote to Mr. Humphries, a Parish Officer, at Cowley, respecting the Widow Hancox, a parishioner of Upper Slaughter, as to whom there has been a question pending with the Asst. P. L. C.—Parker, whether in her case that rule may be dispensed with, which excludes persons of her class, living beyond the limits of the Union to which they belong, from receiving out-relief.*

HANDCOCK — Anne Handcock

1840: 20 Apr: *Also to Mr. J. D. Croome, and to Anne Handcock; these letters both referred to an account in the Savings Bank at Stow, to which my attention had been drawn on the 18th. Inst. by Mr. Pain.*

HANDY — Thomas Handy[49]

Thomas Handy (1778-1853), farmer, was born at Malmesbury, Wiltshire, son of John Handy (1735-1813) and Hester Exton (1738-1812). He married, at Shipton Oliffe, 15 January 1811, Jane Ballinger (1774-1853); they had at least 3 sons:

1 Thomas (1811-1870)
2 John (1813-1899)
3 Edward (b. 1815)

1845: 7 Mar: *Went home in a Chariot from the Plough, accompanied as far as Sierford lane by Mr. Handy, an intelligent farmer, residing at Sevenhampton, who had been for the last two days foreman of the Petty Jury in my Court, and discharged his duties with great propriety.*

HANFORD — Charles Edward Hanford[50]

Charles Edward Hanford (1781-1854), landed proprietor, had an estate at Redmarley. He inherited Woollas Hall at the death of Squire Charles Hanford in 1816. He married, 1809, Elizabeth (d. 1844), daughter of James Martin of Overbury Court. Their sons died young, the last being Compton John Hanford (b. 1821). One of their daughters, Frances, married William Lloyd Flood of Farmley, co. Kilkenny, who inherited Woollas Hall and assumed the name Hanford-Flood. He had been born Lloyd, but had adopted the name Flood in 1839 by the desire of John Flood of Flood Hall Kilkenny. Frances and William had at least 1 son:

1 John Compton Hanford (1849-1911)

1823: 14 Mar: *Mr. Hanford is a Roman Catholic of an old Worcestershire family.* 23 Apr: *We left Cracomb at 11 o clock, & accompanied by Mr. Perrot repaired to Dr. Cooper's, at Bengeworth, where we met Mr. Hanford, of Woolershill, one of the Committee entrusted with the examination of the litigated accounts, & brought to a conclusion.* 17 Sep., 19 Sep: *I dined at the Ordinary at the King's Head Inn, Mr. Estcourt in the Chair, sitting between Mr. Hanford, a very agreeable Worcestershire Roman Catholic Squire, & Mr. T. Pettat.*

1825: 19 Jul: *The business at Broadway began abut 12 o clock: the tolls on the district were let for a year, and at an advanced rent; viz. from £1265 to £1596 per ann. Lord Redesdale in the chair:. Mr. E. Leigh, & a brother in the Navy, Dr. Rice, Mr. Jeaffreson, Dr. Warneford, Mr. Handford, of Woolershill, Worcestershire.*

1826: 1 Aug: *Mr. Handford's place at Wollas hill is on this side of Bredon hill.*

1829: 22 Sep.

1840: 20 Mar: *Also a letter from Mr. Price, a land surveyor, recommended to me by Mr. Handford, for public business in this Union or division.*

1845: 7 May.

1847: 22 Mar: *Considered and reported upon the proposal made at the last Sessns. by Mr. Hanford for an interchange of constabulary between the Worcestershire and Gloucestershire force, in respect of those parishes between Tewkesbury and Broadway, which alternately project into one or the other county.* 18 May: *Among them were Messrs. Hanford, Colchester, Talbot & others, with the latter of whom I travelled to Cheltenham, rain having now steadily set in for the evening.*

HANKEY — Thomas Hankey[51]

Thomas Hankey (1740-1793), banker, was born in London, son of Sir Thomas Hankey and Sarah Barnard. There is conflicting evidence regarding Thomas Hankey's wife. On his son John's birth registration she is given as Elizabeth, but another record says that she was Mary Alers, who married Thomas Hankey of Fetcham Park, Surrey. In fact, Thomas Hankey was never married to Miss Alers; according to tradition, she was a governess in the Hankey household. He married Elizabeth Weaver in 1781, ten years after the birth of his first illegitimate son.

Thomas and the governess Mary Alers had 1 son and 3 daughters:

1 William (1771-1859); bore the surname Alers, but later adopted Alers Hankey; married, 26 July 1797, Mary Martin; 6 sons and 3 daughters
1 Charlotte (1774-1816); married her cousin Sir Frederick Hankey GCMG (1744-1855); 2 daughters
2 Sarah (1776-1857); married Hugh Dillon Massey (±1768-1842); 2 daughters
3 Louisa (1779-1851); married, first, Matthew Chitty Darby; secondly, Maj.-Gen. Griffith (1772-1823) of Padworth House, Berkshire; 3 sons and 2 daughters by the latter

Thomas married, at St Martin-in-the-Fields, London, 10 November 1781, Elizabeth Weaver (±1760-1829); they had 2 sons and 1 daughter:

1 John Barnard (1784-1868); *see below*
1 Elizabeth [Eliza] (1786-1870); died unmarried at Fetcham, the family estate
2 Thomas (1791-1879); married his cousin Louisa Hankey, daughter of Thompson Hankey

In 1784 Hankey inherited the estate of his uncle, John Barnard. In 1786 he was still known to be at Southborough, Bromley. The same year he bought the lease of 18 Bedford Square, and in 1789 he purchased Fetcham Park, Surrey.

HANKEY — John Barnard Hankey — *see also* Massey *and* Griffith[52]

John Barnard Hankey (1784-1868), banker, was born in London, son of Thomas and Elizabeth Hankey. John's father was an influential banker, but he died in 1793 when John was 9 years old. The bank had been founded in 1685 and by 1783 it was known as Thomas Hankey & Co. It was sold in 1865. Presumably John had some involvement in it. Further members of the Hankey family went on to become partners, including William Alers [later William Alers Hankey], John's elder half-brother and first son of

Thomas Hankey, having joined in 1789. William became senior partner in 1830 and died in 1859. From 1804 the bank was styled Hankey, Hall, Hankey & Alers, and from 1810, Hankey & Co. In 1865 Hankey & Co. was acquired by Consolidated Bank Ltd of Manchester and London. Eventually, through subsequent owners, it became part of Royal Bank of Scotland.

John Barnard Hankey was educated at Christ Church, Oxford. He married, 1807, Catherine Elizabeth, daughter of John Blaquiere, 1st Baron de Blaquiere of Ardkill, and Eleanor Dobson; they had 8 sons and 5 daughters:

1 Mary Barnard (1808-1880)
1 George James Barnard (1809-1875)
2 William Barnard (1811-1892)
3 Frederic Barnard (1812-1896)
4 Thomas Fetcham (b. 1813)
5 Thomas Barnard (b. & d. 1814)
2 Louisa Eleanor Barnard (b. 1817)
6 John Bellingham (1817-1868)
7 Henry Barnard (1818-1880)
3 Frances Elizabeth (1820-1900)
4 Harriet Barnard (1821-1902)
5 Harriet Bellingham (b. 1822)
8 Augustus Barnard Hankey (1824-1903)

It is not known why Mrs Hankey, John, and Elizabeth [Eliza] were in Clifton, but presumably it was part of the fashionable circuit. They do not appear to have any Irish or HEIC connections; these made up the largest part of the Clifton set. They were, however, with John's sister Sarah, who had married Hugh Dillon Massey, so presumably it was a family visit.

1804: 24 Jul: *Walked with Hankey.* 25 Jul., 26 Jul: *Walked alone with Hankey & Miss Upton in the Evening... Mrs. Massey gave Tea & supper. Mr. & Mrs. Townsend, my Father & Mother & Mrs. Hankey.* 29 Jul: *A Haunch of Venison pleasant Dinner at Mr. Townsends, Mr. Baillie & Son, Mrs. Hankey & Daughter, Mrs. Pipon & ourselves.* 31 Jul: *Walked with Mrs. Massey, Hankey & Miss Upton.* 1 Aug: *An expedition in the evening to Ashton for Raspberries & Cream ending in a supper at Mrs. Massey's, consisting of Mrs. Massey, the Rawsons, Miss Monck, Miss Fortescue, Adm. & Col. Jones, Hankey & myself.* 2 Aug: *In the Evening with Mrs. Hankey, her son, Mrs. Massey, & Miss Monck. Supped at Mrs. Massey's.* 3 Aug: *Hankey & George Monck to a match between Horton's Mare & one of Mr. Sweetman's. Horton beat.* 4 Aug: *Hankey & myself strolled forth & passed the evening with El. Fortescue.* 5 Aug: *Walked with Hankey, who with his mother afterwards left us.*

1806: 19 Mar: *Called unsuccessfully upon Hankey at the Star.*

HANKINS — Thomas Frederick Paul Hankins[53]

Thomas Frederick Paul Hankins (1797-1876), Church of England clergyman, was born at Dymock, Gloucestershire, son of Thomas and Harriett Hankins. In some places he is referred to as Thomas Paul Frederick Hankins. He was educated at Queen's College, Oxford (BA 1819). He was ordained deacon on 23 April 1820 and priest on 23 December 1821. His first clerical appointment seems to have been as stipendiary curate at Notgrove, Gloucestershire, on 23 April 1820, on a stipend salary of £70 with surplice fees and ability 'to reside in the parish if a house can be procured, if not at Northleach two miles from the parish'. In 1851 he was living at Hereford with his wife, Mary Ann (b. ±1798), who was born in Cheshire. He was listed as 'clerk without a cure'. By 1861 he was chaplain of the Hereford Union Workhouse.

1824: 28 Jun: *I dined at Mr. Hurd's, the Rector of Naunton, meeting Mr. C. Keysall, Mr. Bowen, & Mr. Hankins.*

1826: 14 Sep: *Once again in the course of the morning I had occasion to visit Mr. Bankes's house, taking thither an unfortunate young lady, who was seized with epileptic fits during the performance, and whom, after being in a very distressing state for some time, we placed under the charge of a brother & sister to be conveyed to her mother in a distant part of the town in a Sedan chair; she proved to be a sister of my acquaintance Mr. Hankins, the Curate of Notgrove.*

1827: 11 Feb: *Mr. Hankins, Curate of Notgrove, served the Church here. I have engaged the assistance of this gentleman till Lady day for one duty each Sunday, in the hope, that I shall then be able to undertake the full service of my church.* 25 Feb: *Mr. Hankins read the evening service and preached, and with his assistance, I shall hope to continue for the present morning & evening service on each Sunday.* 11 Mar: *It rained so violently, when Mr. Hankins was about to set off for Notgrove, after evening Service, that we persuaded him to stay dinner.* 27 Mar: *Mr. Hankins will continue to serve the church, & by the assistance of Mr. Hurd, I trust, there will be double duty.* 4 Jul: *We had a few of our bachelor clerical neighbours to dinner to-day: Mr. Hurd, Mr. Baillie, Mr. Jones, Mr. Hankins, Mr. Winter and Mr. W. B. Pole.*

HANKS — William Hanks[54]

William Hanks (±1815-1871), farmer, was born at Naunton and farmed over 500 acres—a large farm at that time—employing fifteen labourers. He married, at Naunton, Gloucestershire, 13 February 1837, Eleanor Bullock (1816-1889); they had at least 3 sons and 2 daughters:

1 Joseph (b. 1839)
2 George (b. 1842)
1 Emma (b. 1846)
3 William Bullock (b. 1852)
2 Rosa (b. 1858)

1838: 5 Apr: *Of the former Guardians were present, Jeaffreson, Winter, Wilkins, Comely, Minchin, Smith, Hanks &c.*

1840: 5 Jun: *At half past one sat down to dinner, R Waller taking the Chair, about sixty dined, and of these eighteen or twenty were honorary Members,—Ford, Polson, Wilkins, Kendall, Welles, two Bryans, W. Smith, Palmer, T. Collett, Ransford, J Bennett, Hanks, Kimber &c.*

1850: 11 Sep: *Justice business at home; as to one case I wrote a note to Mr. Hanks, Naunton.*

HANKS — Robert Hanks[55]

Robert Hanks (b. ±1819), farmer, was born at Naunton and farmed 60 acres. Robert lived with his wife, Ann (b. ±1819). They had at least 3 sons and 3 daughters:

1 Robert (b. ±1842)
1 Sarah (b. ±1843)
2 Mary Ann (b. 1845)
2 William (b. 1847)
3 George (b. 1849)
3 Charlotte Louisa (b. 1850)

It appears that William and Robert were brothers, and that the elder brother inherited the large farm. At the time of the 1871 census Robert Hanks was a widower, living at Leckhampton at the home of his unmarried sister Margaret (b. ±1800). Margaret had been born at Moreton-in-Marsh, so it seems the family migrated from Moreton to Naunton.

1852: 26 Apr: *Justice business at home.—On one case wrote a note to Rob. Hanks of Naunton.*

HARALAND — Miss Haraland at New Park, Wiltshire

1807: 24 Jun: *Drove my Mother to call upon Mrs. Sutton at New Park. Very handsomely received by Mrs. S. & Mrs. Estcourt, found there Mrs. Shield, & Miss Haraland.*

HARBIDGE — John Harbidge, guardian at the union workhouse[56]

John Harbidge (1805-1870), farmer, was born at Todenham, son of John Harbidge (1749-1824) and Elizabeth Longford (1760-1845). He farmed 200 acres at Brookend, Chasleton, Oxfordshire. Harbidge married, at Christ Church Greyfriars, Newgate, London, 20 July 1825, Mary Sparkes (1808-1887), born at Little Rissington; they had at least 1 son and 3 daughters:

1 Robert John (1836-1864)
1 Elizabeth Eleanor (b. ±1837)
2 Norah (b. & d. 1842)
3 Barbara (b. ±1846)

1850: 6 Nov: *Mr. Davis, and Messrs. Godwin and Harbidge were the Guardians present.*

HARBORD — Edward Harbord[57]

Edward Harbord, 3rd Baron Suffield (1781-1835), MP and landed proprietor, was the second surviving son of Sir Edward Harbord, 2nd baronet of Gunton Hall, Norfolk, and Mary, daughter and co-heir of Sir Ralph Assheton, 3rd baronet of Middleton, Lancashire. He was educated at Eton, graduating in 1793, and Christ Church, Oxford, graduating in 1799. After a northern tour of Denmark, Russia, and Prussia, Harbord entered Lincoln's Inn in 1802. He was MP for Yarmouth in 1806-12 and Shaftesbury in 1820-21.

Harbord married, first, 19 September 1809, Georgiana (d. 1824), daughter of George Venables Vernon, 2nd Baron Vernon; they had 2 sons and 1 daughter. He married secondly, 12 September 1826, Emily Harriott, daughter of Evelyn Shirley and Phyllis Byam of Eatington, Warwickshire; they had 7 sons and 1 daughter. He succeeded his brother as 3rd Baron Suffield on 1 August 1821.

1830: 23 Jun: *A portrait of Lady Suffield by G. Clint is a very pleasing picture.*

1832: 17 May: *We dined to-day with Mrs. Waller at Farmington to meet Mr. & Mrs. John Shirley. This most pleasing and amiable bride, lovely and simply engaging, is the elder of the two daughters of my deceased friend and neighbour, the Revd. John Dolphin.*

HARCOURT — William Harcourt[58]

William Harcourt, 3rd Earl and 4th Viscount Harcourt (1743-1830), army officer, MP, and landed proprietor, entered the Army in 1759. In 1764 he was a lieutenant-colonel of the 31st Foot; in 1765 he went to the 4th Light Dragoons; and in 1768 he went to the 16th Light Dragoons. He was promoted to colonel in 1779 having distinguished himself in America three years earlier with his capture of Gen. Lee. He remained a colonel of the 16th Light Dragoons for the rest of his life. He was MP for Oxford in 1768-74 and master of the robes in 1808-09. He had the honour of being standard-bearer at the coronation of George IV. He married, 1778, Mary (1749-1833), widow of Thomas Lockhart and daughter of William Danby. He succeeded as 3rd Earl and 4th Viscount Harcourt in 1809.

1825: 10 May: ... *appropriation to the designs contemplated by its benevolent founder, is conveyed in trust to several Noblemen and Gentlemen, among whom Capt. Witts and myself are two: Earls Beauchamp & Harcourt, Mr. Foley, the Lord of the Manor of Great Malvern & Dr. Card, Vicar of the place, are others.* 13 May: *The Countess Harcourt, all courtly and insinuating, called in the morning & the Mesdames Campbell drank tea with us.*

HARDACRE — Alexander Hardacre[59]

Alexander Hardacre of Hellifield, Yorkshire (b. ±1780).

1838: 13 Sep: *Had an interview with a Mr. Hardacre, of Hellifield who came to speak to the respectability and responsibility of a competitor for Ravenflatt, whom we considered to have made a handsome offer, but doubted whether he had capital or energy enough to undertake the enterprize single handed.*

HARDIMAN — Joseph Hardiman[60]

Joseph Hardiman (1805-1855), agricultural labourer, was born at Broadwell, son of William and Elizabeth Hardiman. He lived with his wife, Elizabeth (b. ±1806); they had 5 sons and 3 daughters:

1 Anne (b. 1830)
2 Maria (b. 1833)
1 George (b. 1835)
2 Thomas (b. 1838)
3 William (b. 1840)
4 Joseph (b. 1842); married, at Broadwell, 19 September 1863, Eliza Scarsbrook
3 Sarah (b. 1846)
5 James (b. 1848); married, at Broadwell, 6 April 1872, Jane Pulham

---

1847: 16 Dec: ... *a charge preferred to the Poor Law Commrs. by Capt. Leigh, who complained of relief granted by the Board to a pauper of Broadwell, named Hardiman, a labourer in the employment of Mr. Beman, a man of infirm health, and with a large family, at low wages.*

HARDING — underturnkey at Northleach House of Correction[61]

The forename of this underturnkey has not been discovered. A parliamentary commission in 1843 criticised Harding for using undue force and occasional violence against inmates.

1842: 16 Oct.

HARDING — prisoner at Northleach House of Correction

1848: 14 May: *Received an impudent letter from Heneage Lupton, praying me to shorten the period of imprisonment of a poacher of the name of Harding whom I have committed to Northleach House of Correction, and whom H.L. met in that resort of bad and blackguard characters.*

HARDING — Richard Harding[62]

Richard Harding (1806-1871), butcher, was born at Northleach. He was a master butcher in Duck Bath Street, Stow. He lived with his wife, Sarah (b. ±1808); they had at least 3 sons and 2 daughters:

1 Sarah (b. ±1835)
1 William (b. ±1837)
2 Rebecca (b. ±1841); married, at Stow-on-the-Wold, 21 March 1864, Henry Barton
2 James (b. ±1843)
3 Thomas (b. 1845)

1846: 20 Jun: *Mr. Morgan, Stow, on the part of Harding, the Butcher, a request that I would recommend the latter to Mr. Morrison, to be employed by him, when he comes to reside on his Vicarage of Longborough.* 21 Jun.

1850: 1 Aug.

1851: 15 Jan: *Much occupied in the evening with taking examinations as to the embezzlement of nearly £50 of his master's money by one Forty, foreman to Harding, the Stow Butcher. He was a plausible young fellow, & well esteemed: he has gone out of the country, and possibly escaped to America.*

1852: 22 Apr: *Settling accounts for meat supplied, & cattle sold with Butcher Harding.*

HARDINGE — Henry Hardinge [63]

Henry Hardinge, Viscount Hardinge of Lahore and Kings Newton (1785-1856), MP and governor-general of India. He was MP for Durham City in 1820-30, St Germans in 1830, Newport, Cornwall, in 1830-32, and Launceston in 1832-44. He was secretary at war in 1828-30 and 1841-44, chief secretary for Ireland in July–November 1830, and again in 1834-35, and governor-general of India in 1844-48. He was created Viscount Hardinge of Lahore and Kings Newton, Derbyshire, in 1846 and field marshal in 1855.

1828: 2 Jun.

1834: 17 Dec.

HARDWICK — Charles Hardwick [64]

Charles Hardwick (1797-1874), Church of England clergyman, was born at Oxford, son of Charles Jones Hardwick and his wife, Mary. He was educated at University College, Oxford (BA 1821; MA 1823), and served as rector of St Michael and St Mary de Grace, Gloucester, 1839-74.

1846: 11 Aug.

1847: 17 Dec: *Co executors of the will of Caroline Hunt, which were administered by Mr. Hardwick, the Rector of St. Michaels Gloucester.*

1851: 29 Apr.

HARDWICKE — James Hardwicke [65]

James Hardwicke (1761-1833), Church of England clergyman, was born at Chipping Sodbury, Gloucestershire, son of George and Ann Hardwicke. He was educated at Oriel College, Oxford (BCL 1785; DCL 1790), and appointed rector of Tytherington, Gloucestershire.

1828: 18 Jul: *Among the persons present (SPCK) were Mr. R. B. Cooper, M.P., who always stands forward to support the cause of the Church and the orthodox party, Messrs. Ford, Jeaffreson, Douglas, Sayer, Hardwicke.*

HARDY — Mr & Mrs Hardy at Mrs Travell's house, Cheltenham

1804: 16 Oct: *Mr. & Mrs. Hardy & Lady Herries also drank tea.*

HARDY — Hardy & Company, newspaper agent, London

1840: 13 Apr: *I also wrote to Hardy and Co. my Newsmen in London, that notice of the death might be properly inserted in the St. James's Chronicle.*

1842: 15 Nov: *To Hardy and Co., newsvendors, London, I wrote with directions for the Insertion of Mrs. B's death in the St. James's Chronicle.*

1846: 17 Jun: ... *to Mr. Hardy, Newspaper agent, London, to forward the St. James's Chronicle to me at Upper Slaughter.*

HARDY — Louisa Georgina Hardy and Emily Georgina Hardy at the Three Choirs Festival [66]

Thomas Masterman Hardy (1769-1839), naval officer, was in command of the *Victory* at Trafalgar. In 1806 he was created a baronet, and in the same year appointed to the *Triumph*, which he commanded for three years under Sir George Cranfield Berkeley, whose daughter, Anne Louisa Emily (1788-1877), he married at Halifax, Nova Scotia, in 1807. They had 3 daughters:

1 Louisa Georgina (1808-1875)
2 Emily Georgina (1809-1887); born in Portugal; married, at St George's, Hanover Square, Westminster, July 1850, William Pollet Brown Chateris (1809-1889)
3 Mary Charlotte (1813-1896); married, at St James's, Piccadilly, 17 November 1833, John Atholl Macgregor (1810-1851); at least 5 sons and 2 daughters

---

1829: 22 Sep: ... *Lady Georgina Bathurst, two Miss Hardys, very elegant young Women, daughters of Capt. Hardy, Captain of Lord Nelson's Flagship at the battle of Trafalgar; their Mother was a daughter of Admiral & Lady Emily Berkeley.*

HARE — Richard Hare [67]

Richard Hare (1793-1876), naval officer, was the third son of Richard Hare (1747-1825), of Weston, Bath, and Anne Hornby. His parents married in 1778. Richard married, at Little Grimsby, Lincolnshire, 1835, Mary Comb Madison (1810-1879); they had 2 sons and 1 daughter:

1 Mary Hornby (1840-1875)
1 Richard Thomas (1841-1917), Lt-Col, Bengal Artillery; played a prominent part in the suppression of the Indian Mutiny during the siege of Delhi and was recommended for a VC; afterwards assisted in the relief of Lucknow and took part in the battle of Cawnpore. Married, 1868, Gertrude Adeline Spear (1838-1926); 2 daughters
2 Robert Powel (1842-1927), Lt-Col, RA; married, at St George's, Hanover Square, Westminster, July 1880, Christian Sarah Maclaine (1856-1912); 2 sons and 3 daughters

In 1851, 1861, and 1871 Richard and Mary lived at 6 Somerset Place, Walcot, Bath. Richard was listed as lieutenant in 1851, but by 1861 he was 'Commander RN retired'. Their daughter Mary lived with them. The connection leading to the friendship between Richard Hare and Thomas Welch Hunt is not known. It could not have been from school or college as Richard was eleven years older than Thomas.

1829: 22 Sep: *With Mrs. H., besides her young relations, Caroline & Maria, I found a gentleman of the name of Hare, a visitor, though accommodated with a bed out of the house. This Mr. H. is a Lieutenant in the Navy on half pay, and was the intimate friend of poor Mr. T. Hunt, of Northamptonshire, whose melancholy death by the hand of banditti .... In all this digression I seem to have started off most unceremoniously from Mr. Hare; but in truth, not without rhyme or reason, for Mr. T. W. Hunt made this friend an Executor of his will, which has necessarily brought him very much into intercourse with our friends, who have with great reason, I believe, a strong regard for, & high opinion of him. He travelled with poor Hunt on his first tour to the continent prior to his marriage, and has since, as a citizen of the world and celibataire, visited foreign parts. His father, now deceased, was a resident of Bath; there the son occasionally lives; but he is also not less at home in London, & has largely mixed in foreign circles at Paris, Brussels, Rome, Naples, Venice &c. Hence he is a conversible companion; fond of music, cheerful, & full of anecdote ...* 23 Sep., 25 Sep: *Mr. Hare proposed to remain some days longer at Mrs. Hunt's: I was pleased to make his acquaintance, having found him a gentlemanlike, well informed, and, apparently, well principled man.*

1832: 29 Mar: *When the party broke up from the Judge's lodgings, I repaired to Palace Yard, and passed an hour or more at Mrs. Hunt's: Caroline and Maria Hunt are, as usual, her inmates; to them were added Mrs. Backhouse, and Mr. Hare, an old acquaintance of mine.* 30 Mar: *Mr. Hare rode over from Gloucester, to communicate to me a letter, which he had received from his Solicitor relating to the business of his Trust; also to express, on the part of Mrs. M. Hunt, Miss C. Hunt and himself, a wish, that I would consent to become his Colleague in a new trust proposed to be created.* 7 Jun., 8 Jun: *I breakfasted at Mrs. M. Hunt's, and the early part of the forenoon was taken up in conference with her, Mr. Hare & Caroline Hunt on the unpleasant business of the Trust, to which I have before alluded.*

1834: 23 Aug: *Heard from Mr. Hare, on subjects relating to the Trust business, in which we are mutually concerned, as to the property of the late Mr. Welch Hunt.* 26 Aug.

1835: 28 Mar., 4 Apr., 21 Apr., 22 Apr: *Mr. Hare arrived from Cheltenham to dinner. In the evening much conversation with him respecting the Hunt family and their concerns.* 23 Apr., 24 Apr: *Conferred with Mr. Hare on the subject of the Wadenhoe Trust &c... Mr. H. is about to be married to a lady of the name of Madison, considerably younger than himself, without much fortune, but with expectations.* 11 May: *Received a letter from Mr. Hare, dated from Ackworth, near Pontefract, where he is on a visit to Mrs. Middleton, the widow of the learned and able Bishop of Calcutta, who is Aunt to Miss Madison, the lady to whom Mr. Hare is about to be united.* 1836: 16 Jul., 20 Jul., 9 Aug., 11 Aug: *Before breakfast received a letter from Sophia Hunt from Clifton where she joined her sisters on Tuesday, and finding that Mr. Hare was about to leave England for the continent almost directly, with the intention of being absent for two years, considered it necessary that I should be apprized of this fact.* 13 Aug., 16 Aug., 18 Aug: *A letter from Hare written on the eve of his departure from London for the continent, in reply to the one which I wrote on the 16th.* 19 Aug., 28 Aug.

1837: 25-26 Apr., 6 May, 1 Nov: *Found a letter awaiting me from Mr. Hare, who is lately returned from the Continent, and who writes on matters concerning the Wadenhoe trust.* 10 Nov.

1838: 6 Jan., 10 Jan., 8-9 Jun., 26 Sep., 28 Sep.

1839: 22 Mar., 25 Mar., 16 Apr: *When I returned to No. 5 recd. a visit from Mr. Hare, who was shortly after joined by his lady, to whom I was previously a stranger, a very pretty young woman.* 17 Apr: *Called on Mr. Hare, and sat for some time with him and his pleasing wife, admiring a landscape in oils recently executed by Mr. H. and a beautiful fancy miniature by his lady.... Mr. and Mrs. Hare, Mrs. Ballard, a widow lady, relict of an Admiral, and sister of Sir Thomas Crawley, and my old friend Charles Crawley; an aged maiden aunt of Mr. Hare, of the same name, rather an interesting and intellectual woman, who has made the best use of a protracted life, passed in good society ...* 18 Apr: *Dined with Mr. and Mrs. Hare, a family party: besides our host and hostess, Caroline & Maria H., Sophia and John Hunt, and myself.* 20 Apr., 12 Jul: *... also from Mr. Hare, dated Lyme Regis.* 15 Jul., 19 Jul.

1840: 19-20 Jun.

1842: 2 Mar., 7 Mar., 9 Jul., 11 Jul., 15 Jul., 31 Jul., 1 Aug., 5-6 Nov., 24 Nov., 27 Nov.

1843: 9 Sep., 22 Sep., 30 Sep., 2 Oct., 9 Oct., 23 Oct., 29 Oct., 25 Dec., 30 Dec.

1844: 31 Jan., 3 Feb., 1 Apr., 12 Apr., 15-21 Apr., 29-30 Apr., 1-2 May, 28 May, 30-31 May, 19 Oct., 23 Oct., 1 Nov., 5 Nov., 9 Nov., 17-18 Nov., 21-22 Nov., 7-8 Dec., 14 Dec., 18 Dec., 24 Dec., 26 Dec.

1845: 6 Jan., 9 Jan., 11 Jan., 21-22 Jan., 29 Jan., 31 Jan., 10 Feb., 14 Feb., 17 Feb., 21 Feb., 17 Mar., 23 Mar., 1 Jun.

1846: 15-16 Jun., 28 Jun., 8 Jul., 13 Jul., 21 Jul., 1 Aug., 14 Nov., 21 Nov: *received a letter from Mr. Thornton one being enclosed from Mr. Hare to Mr. T. & the latter sending me a copy of his answer to Mr. H. for my perusal. Mr. Hare refuses to concur with Mr. T & myself in the appointment of another Solicitor to the Hunt Trust in the room of Mr. Cox, so putting himself in opposition to us.*

1847: 16 Feb., 10 Mar., 18 Mar., 21 Mar., 26 Mar., 30-31 Mar., 4 Apr., 16-17 Apr., 20-21 Apr., 1 May, 3 May, 7 May, 11 May, 26 May, 28 May, 31 May: *Recd. a satisfactory letter from Mr. Hare on Hunt trust matters.* 5 Jun., 7 Jun., 10-11 Jun., 13 Jun., 15 Jun: *Recd. two letters from Mr. Hare on the interminable dispute as to Whitby's wharf: he incloses a letter he had received from Mr. Thornton.* 16 Jun., 22 Jun., 10 Jul., 14 Jul., 21 Jul., 23 Jul., 27 Jul., 2 Aug., 25 Sep., 28 Sep: *... letter from Mr. Hare, who demurs as to laying the case respecting the Wharf prepared by Messrs. Cox and Williams before Mr. Braikenridge, as Mr. Geo. Hunt's Solr: he considers that the Trustees ought first to see it.* 4 Oct., 8-9 Oct., 27 Oct., 1-2 Nov., 5 Nov: *Mr. Hare arrived from Bath before luncheon time.* 12 Nov., 26 Nov., 1 Dec., 3 Dec., 7 Dec., 26-27 Dec., 30 Dec.

1848: 1 Jan., 13 Jan., 15 Jan., 26 Jan., 2-3 Mar., 9-10 Mar., 14 Mar., 28 Mar: *Thence I went into Lincoln's Inn Fields, and called on Messrs. Cox and Williams, as Solicitors to Messrs. Hare, Thornton and myself, in our character of Trustees to the m of the late T. W. Hunt: found that the business of the Trust was conducted by the Junior partner, Mr. Williams.* 7-8 Apr., 10-11 Apr., 14-15 Apr., 17-18 Apr., 23 Apr: *Received a letter from Sophia Hunt, who forwards for my perusal two notes received by her from Mrs. Hare, announcing that Mr. Hare is very ill, and prohibited from all correspondence or attention to business.* 24 Apr., 27 Apr: *A letter from Mrs. Hare: her husband's health is improved, but is still very indifferent.* 3 May, 4 May: *Mr. Hare is much recovered from his late illness, but is still a great invalid.* 5-6 May, 9-11 May, 15 May, 20 May, 27 May, 29-30 May, 1 Jun., 17 Jun., 20 Jun., 22-23 Jun., 5 Jul., 31 Jul., 5-6 Aug., 12 Aug., 14-15 Aug., 18 Aug., 21 Aug., 28-29 Aug., 2 Sep., 5 Sep., 8-10 Sep., 15 Sep., 17-18 Sep., 22 Sep., 24 Sep., 3 Oct., 6-7 Oct., 9 Oct., 31 Oct., 4 Nov., 7 Nov., 10-12 Nov., 14-15 Nov., 17 Nov., 20 Nov.

1849: 11 Dec., 17 Dec., 21 Dec., 24 Dec., 28 Dec.

1850: 13 Jan., 16 Jan., 25 Jan., 11 Apr., 18 Apr., 21 Jun., 2 Jul., 22 Jul., 3 Aug., 9 Aug., 1 Nov.

1851: 5-6 Jan., 11 Jan., 13 Jan., 15 Jan., 17 Jan., 20 Jan., 31 Jan., 5 Feb., 14 Feb., 18-19 Feb., 26-27 Feb., 1-2 Mar., 4-5 Mar., 8 Mar., 22 Mar., 4 Apr., 3-5 May, 8 May, 10 May, 14 May, 19 May: *... the other from Mr. Hare, who, with Mrs. Hare, is on a visit to the Baron de Sternberg at his residence in George Street Portman Square, and who invites me in the Baron's name to breakfast, as affording an opportunity for us to meet and discuss matters of business.* 21 May: *Proceeded in a Cab to George Street, Portman Square, to the lodgings of Baron de Sternberg; by whom, and by his guests & visitors, Mr. & Mrs. Hare, I was kindly received. The Baron is said to be a Livonian; a portly, square, German figure and countenance betoken a vigorous constitution in advancing years;*

his manners are courteous and mild: in early life he contracted a close intimacy with the late T. W. Hunt and Mr. Hare. 24 May, 26 May: *I had an interview at my hotel with Mr. Hare on Hunt Trust concerns.* 27 May, 28 May: *I accompanied Mr. Hare to the office of Messrs. Cox and Williams ...*

1852: 16 Jan., 1 Feb: *Recd. a letter from Sophia Hunt the Hunt party at Bath much annoyed that Mr. and Mrs. Hare have broken off all acquaintance with them.* 18 Dec: *Wrote to Mr. Hare, in answer to a friendly letter received from him some weeks since.*

1854: 13 May, 15 May, 22 Jul., 21 Jul., 10 Aug.

HARENE — Edward Alexander Frederick Harene[68]

Edward Alexander Frederick Harene (1814-1853), Church of England clergyman, was the third son of Benjamin Harene and Sophia Caroline of Footscray Place, Kent. Edward married, 1841, Emily Letitia (1821-1899), fourth daughter of Capt. Charles Rooke, RA, and his wife, Emily, of Westwood House, Essex; they had 4 sons and 3 daughters:

1 Charles Edward (±1842-1903), Lt-Col, 5th Lancers and 4th Bengal Cavalry
1 Emily Frederica (b. 1843)
2 Julia (1845-1883)
3 Edith (±1846-1937)
2 Archibald Kempt (1848-1878), Lt, RN
3 Herbert Benjamin (1849-1878)
4 Alexander Berens (1850-1918)

1848: 15 Jun: *In the latter part of the evening we were joined by a Clergyman from Berks, a member of the Purton Cricket Club, and, as such, one who had been engaged in the match at Stow; he is married to one of Mr. Ford's numerous nieces; his name Harene.*

1850: 18 Sep: ... *Revd. Mr. Harene and Mrs. H. a niece of Mrs. Ford's—he is a nephew of Archd. Berens, and his curate.*

HARFORD — Charles Lloyd Harford[69]

Charles Lloyd Harford (1799-1882), JP and landed proprietor, was the son of Richard Summers Harford, ironmaster of Ebbw Vale, a collateral branch of the Bristol Harfords. In 1818 Charles and his brother Summers became involved in the family iron business, but by 1851 Charles was settled in Cheltenham as a gentleman and magistrate. He married Isabella Nicholson (b. ±1808), who was born in Ireland; they had at least 2 sons and 1 daughter:

1 Isabella Sophia (b. ±1840)
1 Charles Summers (b. ±1841)
2 Edmund (b. ±1843)

The family home was Evesham House, Pittville.

1850: 9 Aug: ... *whence I started for Cheltenham, & had for my companion Mr. C. L. Harford, a Cheltenham Magistrate.*

1851: 31 Mar: *At the Railway Station met Mr. Lovesy, and Mr. Fallon, the Barristers, Mr. Lloyd Harford and Agg, Magistrates, and others flocking to the Courts, with whom engaged in conversation in the carriage, and on the platform.*

HARFORD — John Scandrett Harford and the Harford family[70]

John Scandrett Harford (1754-1815), businessman and brassfounder, came from a Quaker family with ties to a brass company. He was both a partner in Lydney ironworks, Gloucestershire, and until his death, leading partner of Harford's Bank. In 1782 he was warden of the Bristol Merchant Venturers' Guild and in 1798 he was appointed master. He married, 1780, Mary (d. 1830), daughter of Abraham Gray of Tottenham, Middlesex; they had 2 daughters and 6 sons:

1 Mary (1782-1809)
2 Elizabeth Harford (1784-1789)
1 John Scandrett (1785-1866); *see below*
2 Abraham Gray (b. 1786); married, 11 May 1816, Elizabeth Grey, née Dundas (1794-1823); 2 sons and 2 daughters:
  1 Eleanor Dundas (1818-1884)
  1 John (1819-1875); succeeded to his uncle's estates; *see below*
  2 Mary Louisa (1821-1906)
  2 Thomas Dundas (1822-1883)
3 Charles Gray (b. 1788); died unmarried
4 Frederic (1790-1812); died unmarried
5 Alfred (1792-1856), Church of England clergyman; educated at Christ's College, Cambridge; vicar of Locking, Somerset, 1824-56; rector of Hutton, 1825-56. Married, 1852, Emily, daughter of John Taverner
6 William Henry (1793-1877); married Emily King (1807-1832); 2 sons and 2 daughters:
  1 William Henry (1829-1903)
  1 Harriet Margaret (1831-1855)
  2 Edward John (1832-1917)
  2 Emily Mary

John and Mary lived at Brunswick Square, Bristol, until 1789, when John purchased the Blaise Castle estate, near Bristol. He built a large house on the estate in 1795, and commissioned additions by John Nash, Humphry Repton, and George Stanley Repton. He commissioned John Nash to build Blaise Hamlet for the estate pensioners in 1810-11.

1804: 25 Jan: *A Beautiful morning with afternoon & Evening showers, mild & surreal. Accompanied Mrs. Dowell, Slap & Willm. On their walk thro' Westbury, afterwards with the latter thro' Mr. Harford's picturesque scenery, the Valley of Stones etc.* 4 Sep: *On the Downs, at the Brigade & Miller's & Sweet's with my Father & Mother, Mrs. Massey, S. Monck, Mr. Harford &c. very pleasant.*

HARFORD — John Scandrett Harford[71]

John Scandrett Harford (1787-1866), JP, DL, landed proprietor, banker, benefactor, abolitionist, and biographer, was the son of John Scandrett Harford (*above*). He was educated at Christ College, Cambridge. He was a staunch Quaker in his early years until his conversion to Anglicanism in 1809, and a friend of William Wilberforce.

Harford rapidly established himself as a wealthy banker in his own right. He had a sizeable property portfolio, including the Blaise Castle estate at Henbury. The estate had belonged to Thomas Farr until his bankruptcy in 1778 following the American Revolutionary War. It then changed hands a number of times until purchased by Harford's father. In 1819, he also acquired the Peterwell estate at Lampeter, buying it jointly with his younger brothers. It was previously owned by his father-in-law, Richard Hart Davis, who had built a house within its bounds in around 1812. The estate descended to his nephew John Battersby Harford, who in 1859 remodelled the house in the Italianate style, renaming it Falcondale.

Harford married, 1812, Louisa (1796-1872), daughter of Richard Hart Davis, MP for Bristol. On the death of his father in 1815, he succeeded to the family estates, and was made a magistrate and a DL for Gloucestershire and Cardiganshire. He was elected a fellow of the Royal Society in 1823. In 1862 he went blind and found employment in dictating to his wife his *Recollections of W. Wilberforce* (1864), a biography drawn from notes in his possession of Wilberforce's conversations and correspondence.

Before he lost his eyesight he was a moderately successful artist, and his oil paintings can often be found at auctions in the UK. He died childless at Blaise Castle in 1866.

Harford was succeeded by his nephew, John Battersby Harford (1819-1875), son of Abraham Gray Harford-Battersby and Elizabeth Dundas. He was educated at Balliol College, Oxford (BA 1841; MA 1846). He married, 1850, Mary Charlotte, daughter of Christian Charles Josias. He was JP and DL for Gloucestershire in 1855. He changed his name in 1850 from John Harford Battersby to John Battersby Harford.

The young layman at Clevedon National School, the friend of Revd David Clark, vicar of Yatton, is almost certainly of the same Harford family, but he has not been identified.

1832: 3 Jan: *Went to the Shire Hall ... Among the matters of chief interest was the order made for rebuilding Lawford's Gate Bridewell, near Bristol, the mob having so destroyed the prison, that it must in a great measure be a new structure. The expence is calculated at above £5000—on the Motion of Mr. Scandrett Harford, who with Mr. Newman represented the Bristol bench of magistrates, it was agreed, that the building should be made fire-proof, and that it should be so contrived, according to a plan suggested by Maj. Gen. Jackson, the Officer commanding the troops at Bristol, that a few officers within the Bridewell might be able to hold out against any tumultuary body, by which it might be assailed.*

1833: 18 Apr: *Ascended a steep hill towards Henbury: on the summit, to the right is a spacious mansion environed by a flourishing shrubbery; on the left the castellated lodge, arch and gateway, leading to Blaize Castle, the beautiful seat and demesnes of Mr. Harford, a Bristol Banker of great wealth, a magistrate of Gloucestershire, whom I have occasionally met at Gloucester, on the bench at the Quarter Sessions, a zealous conservative, a scholar and man of taste.*

1834: *During the day I was much in communication with my brother Mag. Purnell, the two Hales, the Bakers, Lawrence, Ford, Archd. Timbrill, Harford, Battersby, Hallewell, Leversage, Curtis Hayward &c.*

1837: 17 Oct.

1838: 2 Jan.

1839: 29 Aug: *A layman, by name of Harford, shortly moved the next resolution, and was seconded at great length by a young Clergyman; of the name of Clark, as I understood, and, if I mistake not, the incumbent of a neighbouring parish.*

1843: 31 Aug., 14 Sep.

1845: 26 Jan., 15 Apr.

1846: 15 Jul: *M.W. received letters from Fanny and Jane Backhouse: the latter with her sister Catherine will join their Aunt on Tuesday next, and accompany her on a visit to us: but the young ladies do not think they can be our guests for more than a week; as they are to visit the Harford Battersbys near Clifton before the end of the month.*

1850: 31 Dec: *To the Shire Hall, where at an earlier hour than usual there was a great gathering of Magistrates, including before 2 P.M. Messrs. Harford, Battersby, Mirehouse, Hughes, Fripp, George.*

HARGREAVES — Mrs Hargreaves in Hampshire

1844: 13 May: *To "the Cottage", where I met my dear children and grand-children, who had come from Stanway, to pass two days with the W. Vavasours, the elder Vavasours being absent on a visit to Mrs. Hargreaves &c. in Hants.*

HARINGTON — Henry Harington[72]

Henry Harington (1727-1816), composer and physician, was born at Kelston, Somerset, son of Henry Harington and Mary Backwell. He was educated at Queen's College, Oxford (BA 1749; MA 1752); in 1762 he returned to Oxford to study for an MB and an MD. In 1771 moved to Bath to practise medicine. He was appointed physician to the duke of York, and 'composer and physician' to the Harmonic Society of Bath in 1784.

1802: 9 Mar: *adjourned to the miscellaneous Concert. Mad. Mara & Welsh delightful. The former particularly in "Farewell ye limped Streams" "So che dovrei" &c. Also a fine Dirge on the Death of Christ by D. Harrington.*

1820: 5 Jan: *We spent the Evening at Mrs. Aston's: my old pupil Frederic A. had been with us much in the morning. We had delicious music. Mr. Aston's daughter, Mrs. Watkins, is a most superior private singer: and indulged us with several delightful songs; Italian, Handel's & others. A Mr. Harrington, Grandson of the late learned & musical & good Dr. Harrington of Bath, played on the flute & sang with taste.*

HARLAND — Christopher Harland[73]

Christopher Harland (1759-1839), surgeon of Ashbourne, Derbyshire, married Nancy (1753-1799); they had at least 1 son:

1 Christopher (1787-1860); married, St Oswald's, Ashbourne, 12 January 1808, Mary Hartshorn (1783-1865); 1 son and 1 daughter:
  - 1 Edward (1810-1890); educated at Wadham College, Oxford; vicar of Calwich, 1851
  - 1 Fanny [Frances] (1818-1892); married, 1849, George Elliott Meyrick Tapps-Gervis (1827-1896)

1802: 28 Sep: *Met Mrs. Lockhart & Miss McLeod there. Mr. Newdigate, Mainwaring, Shipley, Harland, J. Webbe, & Furnival dined & bowled at Calwich.* 6 Oct: *Mr. Furnival, Mr. Shipley, Mr. Harland, Mr. & Mrs. Bingham & Miss Edwards dined with us.*

HARPER — Samuel Charles Harper[74]

Samuel Charles Harper (±1788-1859), printer, bookseller, and stationer of 93 Winchcombe Street, Cheltenham, was born at Stepney, London, son of Thomas Harper (1763-1832) and Ann Bacon (1769-1846). He married Mary Ann Harris (1796-1854); they had 3 sons and 7 daughters:

1 Eliza (1819-1899)
2 Mary Ann (1821-1895)
1 Alfred (1823-1881)
2 Thomas (1825-1883)
3 Selina (1827-1911)
4 Emma (b. 1829)
5 Ellen (b. & d. 1831)
6 Octavia (b. 1831)
7 Ellen (1833-1860)
3 Samuel (1836-1902)

Harper was an enterprising man; as well as being a print seller, he was appointed registrar for births, marriages and deaths. By 1851 the family had moved to the more prestigious Bath Street, where they lived at no. 1.

1825: 13 Apr: *In the course of this day the Grand Jury ignored two bills successively preferred by the profligate Col. Berkley for a libel against one Harper, a print seller at Cheltenham, who had exhibited for sale a caricature of a late disgraceful assault by the Colonel on the Editor of the Cheltenham Journal.*

HARPER — Thomas Harper [75]

Thomas Harper (1786-1853), musician, was born in Worcester and sent to London at the age of ten, where he studied with Eley and played in various theatre orchestras. He was the leading trumpeter at the Drury Lane Theatre and the English Opera House. He played the slide trumpet throughout his life, and contributed to its development.

1823: 17 Sep: *The Dettingen Te Deum, the Overture to Esther, Dr. Boyce's Anthem (Charity) and W. Knyvett's new Coronation Anthem were the Musical treats for the morning. Of the vocalists, Miss Travis, Messrs. Vaughan, Bellamy, Hawes & W. Knyvett appeared; among the instrumental performers, Mr. Cramer led the band, Marshall of Oxford was second Violin, the Lindleys on the Violoncello, Harper on the Trumpet, Willman on the Clarionet etc.*

1826: 12 Sep: *Harper who has no superior in this country on the trumpet, clear, thrilling, accurate.* 25 Sep.

1829: 23 Sep: *The third part opened with Luther's hymn by Vaughan, accompanied on the Organ by Mr. C. Clarke, the Organist at Worcester, and on the Trumpet by Mr. Harper.*

HARRIS — Charles Leslie Harris [76]

Of Charles Leslie Harris (1806-1875) little is known other than his birth and death in Lower Swell. He had no children baptised at Lower Swell and presumably had sufficient income to idle by the side of the stream. He was probably related to the Harris family of Upper Swell.

1844: 22 Aug: *Returned to the Provident Bank, where met Messrs. Ford, W B Pole, Perkins, Bowen, Griffin, with whom, for the most part, adjourned to the Justice room, and there transacted various and some difficult business with Mr. Ford, as my colleague: the principal matter being a question as to a right of fishery in the parish of Lower Swell, raised by Mr. Matthews against Mr. C. Harris, claiming a right to fish by permission of Mr. Merchant: the matter left undecided.*

HARRIS — Congreve Harris [77]

Congreve Harris (1785-1837), farmer of Upper Swell, was born at Semingon Wiltshire, son of William and Ann Harris. He married, at Lower Swell, Gloucestershire, 8 April 1818, Mary Clifford (1795-1863); they had 2 sons and 3 daughters:

1 James William (1819-1855); *see below*
1 Mary (b. 1820)
2 Emma Matilda (b. 1822)
2 Congreve (1824-1863); *see below*
3 Elizabeth Anne (b. 1827)

1836: 28 Jul: *Business occupied me before breakfast, particularly, a conference, at which Stevens assisted, with Messrs. Harris and Comely, two leading guardians of the Stow Union, who, with others, felt themselves dissatisfied with the proceedings of the Board on Thursday last.* 18 Aug: *Rode to Stow, and attended a meeting of subscribers to the Police Association, which was attended by Messrs. Pole, Jeaffreson, W B Pole, Winter, Beman, Harris, Collett, Pegler, T. Collett & others.* 3 Nov: *Adjourned, after the ordinary business, with Messrs. Tombs and Harris, to the Workhouse, where inspected the house, and gave directions.*

1837: 20 Jul: *They were the Vice Chairman, Mr. Beman, Guard. for Broadwell, Mr. Tarn, G. for Stow, Mr. Wilkins, G. for Bourton on the W., Mr. Harris, G. for Upper Swell.* 21 Jul., 29 Sep: *Met Messrs. Harris, Minchin, and Gillett, and examined the Officers, and most of the adult paupers, inspected the premises &c.*

HARRIS — Congreve Harris [78]

Congreve Harris (1824-1863), farmer of 230 acres at Moreton-in-Marsh, was the son of Congreve Harris (*above*). He married, at Oxford, 14 August 1848, Mary Roff (1824-1862), born at Stow-on-the-Wold; they had 1 son and 1 daughter:

1 Mary (1853-1941)
1 William Congreve (1855-1933)

1853: 4 Jun: ... *information to Congreve Harris, of Stow, who is about to take luggage and passengers by van from Stow to Adlestrop Station, requesting him, if possible, to furnish me with a time bill. Sent this letter by my servant, who returned without finding C.H. but with the information that the trains had run to-day, and a promise that I should hear from C.H. by the post to-morrow.* 5 Jun: *A note from Congreve Harris.*

HARRIS — James William Harris [79]

James William Harris (1819-1855), farmer, was the eldest son of Congreve Harris (*above*). He farmed 604 acres and employed 21 labourers, thereby operating on a substantial scale. He married Harriet (b. 1816), born at Daylesford, Gloucestershire, daughter of Samuel and Ann Westal Dadge (±1780-1853), born at Haselemere, Surrey. James and Harriet lived at the manor house in Upper Swell. They do not appear to have had any children.

Harris took over the Vicarage Farm at Stanway from George Cook in 1843, adding about 120 acres to his existing holdings in Upper Swell. He suffered from long-term ill health and died just a few months after Francis Witts.

1843: 6 Oct: *Met Messrs. T. Cook, J Davis, and W. Harris, who had come to settle with Cook as to the entry of the latter on the farm, and to consult on the necessary arrangements, which I expect will be amicably settled, and as to which it was not my place to interfere.*

1844: 30 Jan: *Mr. Harris came between 11 & 12 o clock by appointment, accompanied by Mr. Davis from Upper Slaughter, to go over the Vicarage farm with me, and to settle as to the erection of a cart house, pig sties &c. in the farm yard, and feeding stalls on the hill:—settled that they should be built by contract; arranged the plan for advertising for tenders, the dimensions, materials &c:—fixed upon the proper sites &c:—walked over the whole farm, where Harris has already done a good deal of draining which promises to be of much service; the landlord and tenant to join in the expence.* 24 Feb., 18-19 Mar. 25 Mar: *Engaged with J W Harris in the forenoon, considering tenders sent in by tradesmen for the work on the Vicarage farm at Stanway, arranging how to curtail the expence by the substitution of less costly materials.* 1 Apr., 13 May, 15 May, 24 Aug., 14 Sep., 17 Sep., 23-24 Oct., 19 Nov: *Met my new tenant, Harris, on the Vicarage farm, and made arrangements with him as to things still necessary to be done about the farm buildings.*

1845: 12 May: *Settled half year's accounts with J W Harris, as my tenant at Stanway.* 17 May, 23 May, 29 May: *Transacted business at home with J W Harris as to a supply of water to the farm buildings and vicarage at Stanway.*

1846: 26 Jun: *Settled accounts with Harris, balancing the Lady-day rent of the Stanway Vicarage farm.*

1847: 20 Jan. 28 Feb: *Wrote to J. W. Harris for a supply of coals.*, 10 Apr., 12 Apr., 29 Jul., 8 Aug., 15 Sep: *Wrote to Mr. Westmacott with information as to J W Harris's milking cows.*, 25 Oct., 22 Nov.

1848: 4 Feb: *J W Harris called and paid up the Michs. rent for the Stanway Vicarage farm.*, 20 Apr., 15 May, 23 Jun., 20 Oct.

1850: 25 Oct., 10 Nov: *Recd. a note from J W Harris, my Stanway tenant, with an apology for not having called to see me with a view to settlement of accounts, as he had promised.* 16 Nov: *J W Harris, my tenant of the Vicarage Farm, Stanway, called to settle a long coal account. He complains much of the times, and of his inability to make his rent, asks for a deduction for the past, and a new arrangement for the future, which he proposes to make on the basis of a corn rent. I told him I would take his scheme into consideration, when he had more thoroughly developed it, showing on paper how it would work:——as to the deduction that must, I suppose, be conceded; but I have unwisely and unwarily suffered him to get into considerable arrear of rent. He is a good tenant, and it seems to be my interest not to part from him.* 23 Nov., 28 Nov., 30 Nov: *J W Harris called by appointment, with whom I came to terms as to the future occupation by him of the vicarage farm at Stanway; viz. to allow him a deduction of 10 per cent on the last three half-years.* 4 Dec., 6 Dec., 17-18 Dec.

1851: 16 Feb: *Also a letter from J W Harris, in reply to one which I had addressed to him with an order for coal, reminding him of his arrears of rent, and of his having given me reason to expect that he would have made a payment on that score before the end of last month.* 12 Apr., 17 May.

1852: 17 Jan., 23 Jan: *A letter from J W Harris, without a remittance on account of arrears of rent, and with a new proposition as to the occupation of the Vicarage farm, Stanway, which requires mature consideration, and as to which I shall probably consult Mr. Lumbert.* 24 Jan., 27 Jan., 30 Jan., 7 Feb., 17 Feb., 28 Feb., 1 Mar., 28 Apr., 7 May, 13 May: *Mr. L. had been this morning early at Stanway, with J W Harris, and had looked over the Vicarage farm at S. He was agreeably surprized at the good quality of the land, and considered it had been let at a low rate, and that I had been too liberal in my abatements to Harris, and too ready to make expensive improvements in buildings.* 16-18 May, 5 Nov.

1853: 16 May: *Having received a letter from Mr. J. W. Harris, apologizing, on account of the death of his wife's mother, that he had not called about this time to pay rent, but fixing the 23d. Inst. to wait upon me; replied that I should keep myself disengaged to received him on that day.* 23 May, 26 May, 28 May, 30-31 May, 1 Jun., 4 Jun: *Engaged during the day at intervals in superintending the work in progress for draining, and cleaning out the brook in front of my premises, with J W Harris, A Stratton, and the workmen.*

1854: 4 Feb: *Hayward gave a very indifferent account of the health of my Stanway Tenant, J. W. Harris of Upper Swell: he has been long ailing; & seems in a low condition both as to body and mind: he is much in arrear of rent, and other unsettled accounts are pending between us.* 3 Mar: *Wrote to J W Harris, urging an early settlement of accounts and arrears of rents as between him and me. He is in a very impaired state of health, without energy of body or mind.* 16 Mar., 20 Mar: *Examined J W Harris's accounts as to the drainage of the lower part of this village, and wrote to him thereon; urging him also to an early settlement of other accounts between us, he being now in arrear of rent for the Vicarage of Stanway, for a year, when Lady day comes, besides owing me more than £100 of former arrears of rent.* 22 Apr: *Recd. a note from J W Harris, in reply to one from me some time since—no remittance, promises of settlement after Stow fair, pleas of bad health. I fear proceedings must be taken to procure payment of arrears.* 23 Apr., 18 May: *Interview with Sewell: gave him instructions to apply to J W Harris, and insist on the Settlement of rent and arrears due to me on account of the Stanway Vicarage Farm.* 22 May: *Received a letter from J W Harris, who sent me a cheque for £200 in abatement of his arrears of rent for Stanway Vicarage farm—this, probably, the result of a warning letter from Sewell. He proposes to dispose of the grass-keeping on the farm by auction, and to go from home in the hope of recovering his health, wishing to continue tenant of the land.* 23 May, 1 Aug: *A letter from Mr. Francis, who has received for me from J W Harris, on account of rent due at Lady day, £54. which he has paid to my account at the Bank at Stow.*

HARRIS — James Harris, William Harris, and the Harris family of Upper Slaughter [80]

James Harris (1799-1877), carpenter of Upper Slaughter, married, at Lower Slaughter, 13 July 1821, Lucy Randle (1799-1872), born at Chadlington, Oxfordshire; they had at least 6 sons and 4 daughters:

1 Joseph (b. 1823); married, first, at Overbury, Worcestershire, 24 April 1844, Mary Anne Morris (1826-1892); 1 daughter:
  1 Mary Ann (1847-1915)
  Joseph married secondly, at Lower Slaughter, 15 November 1848, Kezia Bryan, née Clarke (1826-1892); 2 sons and 7 daughters:
  1 Sarah A. (b. 1850)
  2 Emily (1851-1914)
  3 Lucy H. (b. 1853)
  4 Fanny (1854-1930)
  1 William Clarke (b. 1855)
  5 Jane Kezia (b. 1858)
  6 Laura (1860-1949)
  2 Thomas (b. 1862)
  7 Angelina (b. 1868)
2 William (b. 1822)
3 John (b. 1825)
1 Elizabeth Harris (1828-1901)
2 Martha (b. ±1830)
3 Mary Harris (b. 1832)
4 William Harris (b. 1834), carpenter (from 1871); lived at 14 Belmont Street, London; married Annie; at least 1 daughter:
  1 Annie Clara (b. ±1857)
5 Thomas (b. ±1837)
4 Jane (b. 1839)
6 James (b. 1844)

1852: 14 Dec: *A note from Mr. Chesshyre, giving a good character of a youth of this village, who is desirous of obtaining a testimonial from me of his propriety of conduct as a recommendation of him, with a view to his obtaining the place of a porter on the Great Western Railway;—the young man (Harris) has been in Mr. Chesshyre's service as under Gamekeeper for two years.* 16 Dec: *Furnished William Harris with a testimonial of good character, to be presented by him to the authorities of the Great Western Railway, at Paddington, where he is anxious for employment as a Porter.* 28 Dec: *Walked to Eyford; called on aged & sick——Pinchin, E Norris, & James Harris who has experienced a very bad attack, in an affection of the head, requiring active depletive measures, bleeding by leeches, blisters &c. probably the result of liver derangement.*

1853: 25 Mar: *Visited Harris's, Carpenter's, house, to enquire after the health of his younger son, who has returned from service seriously ill.*

1854: 10 Jun: *Justice business at home: a case of felony, in stealing a brass furnace from J Harris of this village in January last: the thief had been apprehended at Cheltenham soon after the offence was committed, but escaped from the Constable; has been lately found and arrested in Middlesex.*

HARRIS — John Harris[81]

John Harris (±1808-1871), draper and undertaker, was born at Long Marston, Gloucestershire. He married Martha (±1809-1884); they lived at 105 Market Place, Stow-on-the-Wold. By 1861 they had moved to Worcester, where they remained.

1852: 10 Dec: *Furnished Mr. Harris Undertaker, Stow, with a certificate of the burial of A. M. Teuscher, which he had requested me yesterday to provide, being desired so to do by Mr. Paxton.*

HARRIS — Joseph Harris[82]

Joseph Harris (1792-1837), agricultural labourer and soldier, was born at Maugersbury, Stow. He married, at Upper Slaughter, 24 October 1822, Sarah Joiner; they had 1 son and 2 daughters:

1 Hannah (b. 1823)
2 Anne Mary (b. 1824)
1 James (b. 1825)

Joseph and his family lived at Hill Farm, Halford. He was buried on 24 July 1837 at Lower Swell.

1837: 21 Jul: *Rode with my son to Stow, where we parted, he going to Bourton to call on Billingsley, while I went to enquire for a parishioner, Jos. Harris, who had met with a bad accident yesterday at Stow... Hayward was present, and pointed out to me that he was in the last agony. I read the commendatory prayer to a deeply affected group, and, speaking a few words of warning and comfort to the survivors, took my leave, as the soul was just departing from the body. Harris had been for a short time a soldier many years ago, but his family had purchased his discharge. He was a good labourer, and quiet man; he leaves a widow and three or four children, mostly workers.*

HARRIS — Samuel Harris[83]

Samuel Harris (b. 1814), agricultural labourer, was born at Bledington, Gloucestershire, son of Joseph and Hannah Harris. He married Ann, born at Castle Morton, Worcestershire; they had at least 1 daughter:

1 Hannah (b. ±1840); born in Staffordshire

By 1851 the family lived at Wollaston, Worcestershire.

1834: 30 Sep: *As he was about to scale the wall on the side of the garden to get into the back lane, which led towards his master's back premises, he heard Samuel Harris coming towards the spot of the murder with a light.*

HARRIS — William Harris[84]

William Harris (b. ±1804), farmer, was born at Lower Slaughter, son of William and Hannah Harris. He farmed 262 acres in Condicote, employing seven labourers. He married Phoebe (b. ±1804); they had at least 2 sons and 1 daughter:

1 William (b. ±1834)
2 Edward (b. ±1839)
1 Anne Elizabeth (1843-1900)

1854: 11 Mar: *Mr. Hayward called upon me... He had been at Worcester to-day to consult physicians, Sir C. Hastings & Dr. Maldon, as to the cases of two patients—William Harris, & George Pearce who had accompanied him. Sir CH. does not detect much disease in Harris beyond a torpid state of the heart, and a general inertness.* 3 Aug: *Two o clock, the hour fixed for the election being passed, Mr. Francis was put in nomination by Mr. Harris (Condicote) and seconded by Mr. Johnson (Stow), and unanimously elected.*

HARRISON — Benjamin Harrison and the Harrison family[85]

Benjamin Harrison (1771-1856), hospital administrator and philanthropist, was the fourth son of Benjamin Harrison (1734-1797), treasurer of Guy's Hospital. He married Mary Pelly; they had 3 sons, the eldest of whom, another Benjamin, became archdeacon of Maidstone. There were also 6 daughters, the eldest of whom, Elizabeth, married William Cripps, MP for Cirencester (1841-48) and lord of the Treasury.

1842: 4 Apr., 8 Apr: *Recd. a letter from Wm. Cripps, MP. for Cirencester, in answer to the one I wrote to his father in favour of Edwd. Daniell on the 4th. Inst: he seems most kindly disposed to oblige me, but admits that Mr. Harrison, Treasurer of Guy's hospital has the sole disposal of the preferment, & that if he himself had really a voice, he should vote with him.* 9 Apr.

HARRISON — James Allan Harrison[86]

James Allan Harrison (±1806-1855), Church of England clergyman, was born at Ipswich, son of James Harrison (1779-1868), a captain in the Lincolnshire Militia. He was educated at Merton College and St Mary Hall, Oxford (BA 1830; MA 1831). Harrison was stipendiary assistant curate at Newnham with a 'stipend of £70 value £150 injoined to reside in the parish'. In 1832 he was curate at nearby English Bicknor. He was still residing in the vicinity of Newnham in 1840, but in 1851 he was at Leamington Priors, Warwickshire, 'without cure of souls', accompanied by his widower father. He died unmarried.

1835: 18 May: *Mr. Billingsley and his friend, Mr. Harrison dined with us.* 6 Jun: *Mr. Billingsley called to arrange with me the terms on which Mr. Harrison should be engaged to serve the Church at Upper Slaughter during our proposed excursion to the North.* 12 Jun., 20 Jun.

1836: 11 Jul: *Through Broadoak to Newnham, a dull, small town on a hill above the Severn, where is a ferry to cross to the opposite bank. Mr. Parsons, one of the editors of the Oxford edition of the Septuagint, the incumbent, Mr. Harrison, who officiated for me during my absence in Yorkshire last summer, occupying my house at U.S., was Curate of Newnham.*

HARRISON — Jane Harrison — *see also* Bragge *and* Dolphin[87]

Jane Harrison (1808-1891) was the daughter of James Goodeve Sparrow (1770-1838) of Gosfield Place, Essex. She married, 28 March 1826, Fiske Goodeve Harrison, later Fiske Goodeve Fiske-Harrison (1793-1872), heir apparent to John Haynes Harrison of Copford Hall, Essex. Their names suggest they were distant cousins. They had no children.

In 1847 Jane applied to the ecclesiastical court to have her marriage nullified on the basis of her husband's impotency. Fiske-Harrison refused to allow his private parts to be examined by a qualified person, and so the divorce appears to have been granted.

Jane married secondly, at St Marylebone, London, 13 July 1843, Thomas Pynsent (1809-1887) of Pitt House and later of Lakenham House. He was born at Hennock, Devon, son of Charles Pynsent (b. 1766) and Mary Yeo (b. 1775). How Jane managed to marry before her divorce was granted is unclear, unless it preceded the hearing in the ecclesiastical court. Another explanation may be that the 1847 publication date was a summary of several years, and that the actual hearing had been in 1843.

Jane and Thomas Pynsent had at least 3 daughters:

1 Margaret J. (1845-1920); born in Paris
2 Florence Lombe (1847-1943); born in Florence

3 Jane Augusta (1849-1902); born in Florence

Jane's elder sister Margaret (b. 1805) married, 10 November 1824, William Bragge (b. 1788), a captain in the dragoons and heir apparent to John Bragge (1764-1843) of Sadborow. William was a first cousin to Vernon Dolphin; his father, John Bragge, was the brother of Vernon's late mother, Lucy.

The reason for Jane Harrison's intimacy with Mary Ann Dolphin (née Payne) is unclear; it suggests they could have been related by blood. There may have been a Bragge connection to Mary Ann Payne as there was to Vernon Dolphin; the marriage of cousins was very common. Related or not, it is likely that Jane and Mary Ann were introduced via their links to the Bragge family, and formed a close bond over their mutual marriage problems.

1835: 24 Feb: *Accompanied Mrs. Witts to Eyford and called on Mrs. Dolphin, whom we found at home with her friend and connection, Mrs. Harrison.* 28 Feb: *Mrs. Dolphin and her friend, Mrs. Harrison called.* 4 Mar., 23 Mar: *Saw Mrs. Dolphin, her aunt, Mrs. Rowe, and Mrs. Harrison: also Lady Smith, wife of a Dorsetshire Baronet, and her invalid daughter, who, with a pretty little girl of the name of Bragge, a niece of Mrs. Harrison.* 24 May.

1836: 7 Aug., 14 Aug., 4 Sep: *Mrs. Dolphin and Mrs. Harrison called between morning and evening services, very communicative as to their recent rough voyage of nearly 24 hours by a steamer from Bristol to Ilfracombe, and of a subsequent tour in Devon.* 11 Sep., 24-25 Sep., 23 Oct., 11 Dec.

1837: 1 Jan., 14-15 Jan., 5 Feb., 7 Feb., 12-13 Feb., 21 Feb., 26 Feb., 4 Mar., 10 Mar., 12 Mar., 15 Mar., 19 Mar., 2 Apr., 9 Apr., 28 Apr., 30 Apr., 7 May, 4 Jun., 11 Jun., 18 Jun., 25 Jun., 2 Jul., 11 Jul: *Mrs. Rowe and Mrs. Harrison left Eyford this morning, for Essex.* 26 Nov: *Mrs. Payne and Mrs. Harrison called before morning service.* 10 Dec.

1838: 11 Nov., 13 Nov., 25 Nov., 9 Dec: *Mrs. Dolphin. Pain, and Mrs. Harrison called here between the services.*

1839: 27 Jan: *Mrs. Payne & Mrs. Harrison called before morning service.* 26 Feb., 7 Jul: *After morning service had a long and painful visit from Mrs. Dolphin. She is just returned from Town with her Mother and Aunt Ware; Mrs. Harrison too is at Eyford, having joined them there.* 10 Jul: *Walked with MW to Eyford to call on the ladies there; received by the four widows or widows bewitched, Mrs. Ware, Mrs. Payn, Mrs. Harrison, and Mrs. Dolphin.* 23 Feb: *With M.W. walked to Eyford, & called on Mrs. Dolphin; saw Mrs. Pain, and Mrs. Harrison.*

1840: 5 Apr., 17 Apr., 19 Apr., 16 May: *Mrs. Dolphin and Mrs. Harrison are still detained in Town.* 7 Jun., 13 Jun., 6 Jul: *Mrs. Dolphin and Mrs. Harrison are in London; the latter suing for a formal separation from her husband.* 25 Jul., 18 Sep: *Mrs. Payn and Mrs. Harrison are gone to Weymouth.* 14 Nov: *Walked with MW. to Eyford; called on the ladies; Mrs. Dolphin was out, walking: received by Mrs. Payne; Mrs Harrison is absent: it appears that the three purpose removing soon for sometime to London.*

HARRISON — Samuel Harrison [88]

Samuel Harrison (1760-1812), tenor singer, was born at Belper, Derbyshire, and sang as a boy soprano. From 1785 to 1791 he was the principal tenor of the Ancient Concerts. He married, 1790, the soprano Ann Cantelo (±1764-1831).

1801: 29 May: *The Magnificence of the band highly delighted me; every thing, which we heard was vastly superior to all I had ever seen; the following pieces pleased me particularly: the Overture by Mozart: a Concertante, Bassoon & Hautboy, Mess*[rs.] *Holmes & W. Mahon. Duetto. M*[r.] *& M*[rs.] *Harrison Gia'che mia sposa sei Sacchini.*

1826: 12 Sep: ... *to the remaining singers, who appeared at the rehearsal; suffice it to mention Vaughan, William Knyvett and Miss Travis, all remarkable for chaste execution & a faultless accuracy, combined with taste & sweetness, indicative of the genuine English school to which they belong, and which has been graced by the names & talents of Bartleman, Harrison & Greatorex.*

HARROWBY — ***see*** **Ryder**

HART — Miss Hart from Corsham

1807: 20 Jul: *Spent the Evening and supped at Mrs. Leggs. Meeting the Comptons of both families & a Miss Hart from Corsham, who played & sung not ill.* 21 Jul: *The Leggs drank tea with us with Miss Hart.*

HART — Anthony Hart [89]

Sir Anthony Hart (1757-1831), lord chancellor of Ireland, was born on 17 April 1757 on the island of St Kitts, West Indies, the fourth son of William Hart, of St Kitts, and Sarah Johnson. He followed two of his brothers to Tonbridge School, Kent, and later, in 1776, he was admitted as a student of the Middle Temple. He was called to the bar in 1781. In 1807 he was appointed a king's counsel, and in the same year he was elected a bencher of his inn. In 1816 he was made solicitor-general to Queen Charlotte, and in 1827, appointed vice-chancellor of England, succeeding Sir John Leach. In that same year he received a knighthood and, by the government of Frederick Robinson, Viscount Goderich, was appointed to succeed Thomas Manners-Sutton, 1st Baron Manners, as lord chancellor of Ireland.

1827: 2 May.

1828: 12 Feb: *Sir. A. Hart, Chancellor of Ireland, in the room of Lord Manners.*

HART DAVIS — Richard Hart Davis [90]

Richard Hart Davis (1766-1842), merchant MP and banker, was the son of Henry Davis (±1736-1802) and Mariana Hart (1744-1814). He married, 27 November 1789, Sarah, daughter of William Whittingham of Earlsmead, near Bristol; they had 3 sons and 2 daughters:

1 Hart (1791-1854); married Charlotte Dundas (1790-1861)
2 Thomas Deane (b. 1795)
1 Louisa (1796-1872); married, 1812, John Scandrett Harford (1787-1866)
3 Richard Vaughan (1797-1871)
2 Clementina (1803-1875)

In 1793 Hart Davis was recorded as consul at Bristol for the United States of America. The Davis family had been linen drapers in Bristol, but Richard Hart Davis was a more enterprising merchant than his forebears. He traded to the West Indies and from 1794 was a partner in Harford's Bank. He joined the Merchant Venturers' Society in 1803. He enjoyed early success in his commercial speculations, making £200,000 by 'getting possession of all the Spanish wool in the kingdom'. He was MP for Colchester in 1807-12 and Bristol in 1812-31.

Later in life, Hart Davis's speculations began to fail; some of them were dubiously linked to his position and influence in parliament. In May 1819 he was forced to wind up his interests in Ball, Davis, Charles & Richard Vaughan & Co., and the Bristol Brass and Copper Company. He also retired from Harford's Bank. He continued to represent Bristol in parliament until 1831.

1804: 21 Jan: *Rather too late at the first meeting of the Harmonic Society which was respectably attended & very pleasant: more than 100 persons present & 70 staid supper. The best singer Master Jones from the King's Concerts. The best songs O Nanny, Lullaby, Old Woman, O Happy Fair, Miss Bailey, Beautiful Maid, & Sir. J. Jervis President. Marriotts, Moncasters, Miles's Adams there. Conversed chiefly with John Dawkins, Smith & Hook, Hart Davis, Harriett, etc. Returned near 1 o clock.*

1808: 23 Feb: *Met several acquaintance, Hart Davis, Jas. Brougham &c.*

HARTLAND — Nathaniel Hartland[91]

Nathaniel Hartland (1791-1866), banker, corn factor, and merchant, was born at Tewkesbury of Quaker parents Nathaniel and Martha Hartland. His father was also a Tewkesbury merchant and corn factor, although in the latter he ceased his partnership with Richard Price in 1819. Two years later Price was declared bankrupt.

In records concerning the early decades of the nineteenth century it is difficult to distinguish between father and son. In 1835 Nathaniel Hartland (junior) was listed as a banker in Evesham; his brother John was agent for the Gloucestershire Banking Company. He married Eliza Dixon (b. ±1810) and later lived at Oaklands, Charlton Kings, Cheltenham.

1851: 7 Feb: *Mr. Winterbotham considers that it is now very necessary to alter this arrangement, and suggests that either Mr. Jackson Clark, Mr. Frederick Cripps, or Mr. Hartland should be appointed Treasurer.* 13 Feb: *I conferred with Mr. Clark on the retirement of Mr. R. Cripps from the Treasurership of our Union, and the appointment of Mr. Hartland to hold the office.* 14 Feb., 6 Mar: *The Poor Law Commissioner having declared the office of Treasurer of the Union vacant, Nathaniel Hartland was selected to succeed Raymond Cripps.* 10 Mar.

HARTLEY — John Hartley and the Hartley family of Settle — *see also* Dudgeon[92]

Of John Hartley (1762-1839), solicitor, little is known. He was married to Mary (1771-1811), but does not appear to have had any children. By 1822 his nephew William Hartley (±1791-1827) had become a partner in John's law firm in Settle, Yorkshire. Following John's death, his clerk George Dudgeon (1804-1865) rose to become a partner alongside William. George was born in Scotland. He married, 1841, Mary Hartley, niece of John Hartley, and changed his name to George Dudgeon Hartley in accordance to John Hartley's will.

It is clear from the diaries—and Miss Hartley's correspondence with Margaret Witts—that the connection between the Hartleys and Backhouses was of long standing. It may have been that Miss Hartley was a childhood friend of Margaret Witts, née Backhouse. The 'Mrs Hartley' in communication with Francis and Margaret Witts was, in all probability, this same Miss Hartley advanced to the status of 'Mrs', having become head of the household. If this is so, her initial is shown to be 'G'.

1808: 12 Apr: *Received a joint letter from Mr. Hartley of Settle, Mrs, Backhouse & Margaret.* 5 May: *In Queen Square most part of the morning, walking with Rowden &c. Afterwards with my Father & Mother called on the Reads, & on the Grocer Pierpoint in Argyle St. Wrote to Mr. Hartley.*

1823: 7 May: *I arrived at the Golden Lion Inn, Settle ... I passed the Evening with our Solicitor, Mr. Hartley.* 8 May, 11 May: *I called on Mr. Ingram and his family, as well as on other old acquaintances, and dined at Mr. Hartley's, meeting Mr. Woods.* 12 May.

1825: 8 Sep: *I arrived at Settle about five o clock, and my intention was to have remained at the inn. but Mr. Hartley, our Solicitor, met me, & would insist on my becoming his guest, which contributed, indeed, no small degree to my comfort.* 9 Sep: *We returned to a late dinner at Mr. Hartley's; Mr. Geldard was of the party: also a Mr. Beverley, a Solicitor of London, Mr. Hartley's agent, and formerly a Clerk in his office.* 10 Sep: *The dinner at Mr. Hartley's was at an early hour in order to allow us full time for the engagement of the evening: there was a family party, Mr. W. Hartley, nephew and partner of Mr. H. being added to the circle.* 11 Sep., 13 Sep.

1834: 22 Jul., 28 Jul., 18 Aug., 27 Aug: *Sent off by coach the Yorkshire deeds with a letter to Messrs. Hartley and Dudgeon: also the probate of Mr. Backhouses's will.* 5 Sep., 7 Sep., 13 Sep., 17 Sep., 25 Sep., 24 Nov., 26 Nov., 12 Dec.

1835: 29 Apr: Wrote ... *requesting Mr. Hartley to co-operate in our endeavours to collect evidence to support our claim, and, particularly, to procure for us copies or abstracts of the conveyances made by the Trustees of Dr. H. Moorhouse's will.* 11 May, 15 May, 4-5 Jun., 15 Jun.

1836: 15 Jul., 6 Aug., 30 Aug., 21 Oct., 30 Dec.

1837: 10 Jan., 5 Apr., 8 Apr., 15 Apr., 24 May, 21 Jun., 20-21 Jul., 21 Oct: *Having sent to Miss Hartley a letter from my wife of which I was the bearer, with a message that I would call on her and her uncle in the evening, Mr. Hartley came to us, and kindly insisted that we should become his guests during our stay, and commence our visit to him by coming to breakfast to morrow morning.* 22 Oct: *Breakfasted at Mr. Hartley's, who ordered our portmanteaus to be brought from the Inn to his house.* 23 Oct: *Borrowed a horse from Mr. Hartley and rode to Stainforth Hall by appointment, but the rain precluded me from leaving the house, and viewing any part of the farm.* 24 Oct: *Engaged with Mr. Hartley, Mr. Geldard and John Armitstead in transacting business relative to our Craven property.* 25-26 Oct., 27 Oct: *Borrowed a gig and horse of Mr. Hartley and drove with Rowden to view the Waterfalls &c.* 29 Oct.

1838: 26 Jan: *A letter to MW. from Miss Hartley brought information of the sudden decease of W. Birkbeck Senr. the Banker at Settle.* 21 Apr., 23-24 Apr., 29-30 Apr., 6-7 May, 11 Sep: *Joined by Mr. Hartley, who appears as well as when I was here last autumn, and hospitably invited me, as usual, to take up my quarters at his house, whither I accompanied him, and was most cordially received by his niece.* 13 Sep., 14 Sep., 15-17 Sep.

1839: 30 Jan., 29 Jun., 11 Jul.

1840: 28 Mar: *A letter from Mr. Dudgeon in answer to one written by me to Hartley which reached him shortly before his decease.*

1842: 14 Nov: *I was also much engaged in the evening with letters and arrangements consequent on Mrs. Backhouse's decease which I announced to E.F.W. and Sophy—to John Backhouse, to Miss Lonsdale, to Miss Gardner, to Miss Moorhouse, to Mr. Geldard, and to Mrs. G. Hartley.*

1843: 8 Nov: *MW. recd. a letter from Mrs. Hartley communicating the very recent decease of Mrs. Robinson of Settle—a worthy woman, my wife's schoolfellow and contemporary.*

HARTLEY — Joseph and Thomas Hartley, tenants of Stainforth Hall

Brothers Joseph and Thomas Hartley have not been identified; the surname was very common in Yorkshire.

1837: 25 Oct: *Arrived at the farm house, we found both the brothers Hartley, co-tenants, at home, and not unprepared to receive me as the rightful owner of the property.* 28 Oct: *After breakfast the two Hartleys from Ravenflatt came by appointment, with whom, by the advice, and with the assistance of Geldard, I entered into an agreement that they should continue tenants of their farm for another year at the same rent as they have lately paid.*

1838: 23 Jul: *Wrote to Mr. Geldard in reply to his letter, the receipt of which I named on the 20th. forwarding to him notices to quit signed by myself or Mrs. Backhouse to J. Armitstead, T. Parker, Jos. and Thos. Hartley, whose leases of Stainforth Hall, Sherwood House, and Ravenflatt will expire next Spring, with a view to the advertizing these farms to be let by tender in Sept. next, when I propose going into Craven.* 14 Sep: *After luncheon, during which I strove to conciliate the ill humour of my offgoing tenants, with tolerable success as regarded the Father and son, the former accompanied me over the higher part of the farm to Oxscar, where we parted, and I returned to Hartley's by Gigleswick Scar.*

HARTLEY — Winchcombe Henry Howard Hartley[93]

Winchcombe Henry Howard Hartley (1810-1881), JP, DL, and landed proprietor, was the son of Revd Winchcombe Henry Howard Hartley (1784-1832), of Bucklebury House, Berkshire, and Elizabeth, daughter of Samuel Watts of Williamstrip Park. Winchcombe (junior) married, 1855, Emily, daughter of Revd George Augustus Biedermann of Dauntsey, Wiltshire. They do not appear to have had any children.

Winchcombe was high sheriff for Berkshire in 1838, and for Gloucestershire in 1852; he was also colonel of the Gloucestershire Militia. He and Emily lived at Lyegrove, Gloucestershire, an Elizabethan house which had burnt down in 1833 and was then rebuilt.

1844: 2 Jan: *During the day I was principally in intercourse with Lord Bathurst, Purnell, Curtis Hayward, Ricardo, George, W. Hartley, Viner, Wintle, Sir M. H. Beach, Hicks, Playne, Sampson, Archn. Onslow, R. Onslow, Corbett Holland, Goodrich, Howell, &c.* 9 Apr: *After breakfasting at the Bell, the business of the Sessions was opened in the Grand Jury room, Mr. Purnell in the Chair; besides those who were present yesterday, there were in attendance Messrs. Barker, E Viner, Mirehouse, Ford, Price, Playne, Dr. Davies, R Davies, Hartley, Hale, Hicks &c.*

1847: 20 Oct.

1850: 2 Jan.

1852: 29 Mar: *The High Sheriff, Mr. Winchcombe Howard Hartley, of Old Sodbury, a gentleman of large fortune, having considerable landed property, both in this county, and in Berks, where also he has served as High Sheriff, appeared with a very handsome equipage, and cortége, being himself unusually resplendent in a garb of late disused by his predecessors in office, being attired in a splendid Court dress, blue velvet coat, with huge cut steel buttons, boy for the pair, embroidered waistcoat, black satin breeches, and appendages to match.*

1853: 4 Apr.

HARTOPP — Edmund Cradock Hartopp[94]

Sir Edmund Cradock Hartopp, 1st baronet (1749-1833), MP, was the only surviving son of Joseph Bunney, merchant, of Leicester, and Mary, daughter of Edmund Cradock of Knighton, Leicestershire. He was educated at University College, Oxford, and married, 8 August 1777, Anne, daughter of Joseph Hurlock and Sarah, daughter and heir of Sir John Hartopp, 4th baronet of Freathby. Sir Edmund and Anne had 5 sons and 6 daughters. He changed his name from Bunney to Cradock Hartopp by act of parliament in 1777 and succeeded his father in 1782. He was created 1st baronet on 12 May 1796. Cradock Hartopp was MP for Leicestershire in 1798-1806.

1829: 22 Sep.

1830: 23 Jun.

HARTWELL — Mrs Hartwell at Mrs Davies', London

1801: 14 Oct: *At a party in the Evening at Mrs. Davies's, where we met the Patons a large Scotch family, the father of which is going Governor to St. Helena. The young ladies are very musical & we had some good singing, & dancing of reels. We met there also Mrs. Hartwell, Mrs. Farquharson, Mr. and Mrs. Willet & family &c.*

HARTWELL — Henry Hartwell[95]

Henry Hartwell (1813-1864), whitesmith, was born at Bourton-on-the-Water, son of William Hartwell (1767-1852) and Sarah Scrivens (1767-1850). He married, at Upper Slaughter, 1 March 1836, Ann Price (1813-1879); they had at least 4 sons and 3 daughters:

1 Thomas (1837-1919); married, 1864, Elizabeth Simmons (1822-1898); no known children
2 Henry (1839-1893); married, January 1866, Jane Hayes (b. 1838); 5 sons and 4 daughters
1 Jane (b. 1841)
2 Emma (1845-1913); married, January 1875, Thomas William Barlow (b. 1847); 3 sons and 3 daughters
3 James (1848-1904); married Sarah Collett (1845-1929); 2 sons and 6 daughters
3 Mary Ann (1852-1901+); committed to Wotton Lunatic Asylum, Gloucester; died there, 1901
4 William John (1856-1928); married, March 1877, Ellen Turner (1844-1932); 1 son and 2 daughters

---

1847: 1 Oct: *Transacted Prov. Bank business with Mr. Hartwell at Bourton.*

1848: 10 Nov: *Walked to Bourton on the Water, and conferred with H. Hartwell as to the repairs and reletting of one of E.F. W's cottages there now vacant.*

HARTWELL — Sophia Hartwell — *see* Hayward *and* Job

HARVEY — Daniel Whittle Harvey[96]

Daniel Whittle Harvey (1786-1863) was MP for Colchester in 1818-20 and 1826-34, and Southwark in 1835-40.

1830: 24 Jun: ... *He is a clever, keen debater; fluent and ready, astute & quick in taking advantage of the concessions or weak arguments of an opponent; a man to be listened to with attention, but to be viewed with suspicion.*

HARVEY — John Rideout Harvey[97]

John Rideout Harvey (1808-1871), Church of England clergyman, was born at Fordington, Dorset, son of Robert Rideout Harvey, solicitor, and his wife, Susanna. He was educated at St Alban Hall, Oxford (BA 1832). Harvey was appointed vicar of Winchcombe and rector of Sudeley, 1834-71. He was chaplain of Winchcombe Union, but resigned in 1858. He was imprisoned at Gloucester Gaol in May 1858 for insolvency, and appeared before a judge two weeks later. The cost of his large family was probably a factor. He married Agnes (1811-1882), who was born in Ireland;

they had 6 sons and 4 daughters:
1 Robert (b. 1835)
2 Raymond (1837-1911), merchant mariner
3 John (1838-1841)
4 George (1840-1912)
1 Susannah Letitia (1842-1858)
2 Agnes (b. ±1843)
3 Mary Elizabeth (b. 1846)
4 Anne Catherine (1849-1937)
5 Henry Frederick (1851-1931); died at Perth, Australia
6 Julian (1853-1938)

1850: 16 Sep: *The following Clergymen were present—Mr. Head, from Aston Somerville, Mr. Covey, from Alderton; Mr. Harvey from Winchcombe; Mr. Whalley, from Toddington; Mr. Wedgewood, from Dumbleton.*

1851: 8 Mar: *Mr. Hervey, the Vicar of Winchcomb, and Mr. Du Pré, who with my Son had interceded for her, after an examination before them which proved her deficient, joined us.* 31 Mar: *Mr. Dent, with Mr. Harvey, of Winchcomb, as his Chaplain.*

HARVEY — Richard Harvey[98]

Richard Harvey (1798-1889), Church of England clergyman, was the son of Richard Harvey (1766-1814), rector of Upper Swell (1804-14) and curate of Broadwell with Adlestrop (1810-14). Richard (junior) was educated at Eton College, where he was Shelley's fag. He went on to St Catherine's College, Cambridge (BA 1818; MA 1821), and was rector of Hornsey in 1829-80 and a prebendary of St Paul's in 1843-58. He was chaplain-in-ordinary to the queen in 1847-89, canon of Gloucester in 1858-89, and chaplain to the archbishop of York in 1862-74.

1843: 21 Sep: *At the Justice room sat on the bench with Messrs. Pole, Ford, Waller, as Gloucestershire Justices, and with Mr. Whitmore Jones, acting in some Worcestershire cases: other gentlemen present at Stow with whom I was in intercourse were Messrs. Winter, Franks, W. Vavasour, Debary, Polhill, and Harvey: the latter Rector of Hornsey, Middlesex, and son of a former Rector of Upper Swell, a most estimable Clergyman, who died a few years after I succeeded to the benefice of Upper Slaughter: I had not seen the R. of Hornsey since he was a boy: being in the neighbourhood, as I understood, at Cirencester ...*

HARWARD — John Harward[99]

John Harward (1760-1855), Church of England clergyman, was born at Hartlebury, Worcestershire, son of Michael and Mary Harward. He was educated at Worcester College, Oxford (BA 1782; MA 1785), and was rector of Icomb in 1796-1855.

1842: 20 Sep: *Mr. Harward, Master of Hartlebury school, is Incumbent of Icomb, which is in the gift of the Dean and Chapter of Worcester: the living has lately been brought under the jurisdiction of the Bish. of Gloucester and Bristol, havg been formerly in the Dioc. of Worcester, as the greater part of the parish is now in that county.*

HARWARD — Richard Harward[100]

Richard Harward (±1780-1845), naval officer, landed proprietor, and JP, was promoted to lieutenant in the Royal Navy in 1801, commander in 1806, and captain on 31 July 1809. In 1808, HMS *Delphinen*, a 16-gun sloop captured at Copenhagen the year before and placed under his command, was wrecked off the Dutch coast. In 1809 he had better fortune; commanding the 10-gun HMS *Parthian*, he captured the 14-gun privateer *Nouvelle Gironde*.

Harward married, first, 11 January 1810, Julia (1789-1831), youngest daughter of Edward Pellew, 1st Viscount Exmouth, and Susannah Frowde. He married secondly, August 1834, Julia (b. ±1810), his niece by marriage and the eldest daughter of Adm. Sir Lawrence William Halsted and Emma Mary Pellew. Harward was a Gloucestershire JP. He and his second wife, Julia, lived at Maisemore Lodge. He died in Geneva in 1845.

1826: 11 Jul.

1828: 14 Oct: *I moved that a Committee of three Justices be appointed to examine and report on such rules as should be submitted for enrolment, and Archdeacon Timbrill, Captain Harward R.N. & myself were appointed such committee.*

1829: 13 Jan., 14 Jul., 22 Sep., 20 Oct.

1830: 12 Jan., 20 Apr.

1842: 12 Apr., 18 Oct.

HARWARD — Samuel Harward[101]

Samuel Harward, printer and bookseller, was from Tewkesbury, Gloucestershire. He was an enterprising man, with shops at Cheltenham and Gloucester. He also supplied a network of dealers in the area.

1801: 29 Oct: *Met Mr. Peard at Harward's.*

HARWOOD — John Harwood[102]

John Harwood (1819-1853), schoolmaster, was born at Bourton-on-the-Water, son of John Harwood (1783-1866) and Sarah Fletcher (1787-1850). He married Susan Butler (1819-1863), born at Donnington; they had at least 1 daughter:
1 Elizabeth Sarah (1842-1938)

1837: 2 Aug: *Wrote a note to the Dean of Gloucester recommending to his notice the young man Harwood whom I propose as Porter and Schoolmaster of the Workhouse.* 17 Aug: *A Porter, to perform also the duties of schoolmaster, was elected by a considerable majority, Harwood from Bourton on the Water, a young man whom I had recommended to the Board, and who brought very satisfactory testimonials as to competence and steadiness of character.*

1844: 25 Nov: *Wrote a letter to the Chairman and guardians of the Abingdon Union in favour of John Harwood, formerly Porter and Schoolmaster at our Union, who is a candidate for the situation of Porter in the Abingdon Workhouse.*

1848: 10 Sep: *Received a letter from the Clerk of the Worcester Union, who requests my opinion as to the qualifications and characters of two candidates for the office of Governor of the Workhouse of that Union ... the other Harwood, at one time Porter at our Union Workhouse.* 11 Sep.

1852: 8 Nov: *Wrote to John Harwood at Lower Guiting, Schoolmaster, formerly Porter and School master at the Stow Union Workhouse, now a candidate for the office of Rel. Off. in the Winchcomb Union, such a letter as he may shew to the Guardians, commendatory as far as my knowledge of him extends.*

HASKINS — Edmund Henry Haskins[103]

Edmund Henry Haskins (1817-1877), Church of England clergyman, was born at Oxford, son of James and Mary Ann Haskins. He was educated at Queen's College, Oxford (BA 1839; MA 1843). He served as curate of Cromwell, Nottinghamshire, curate of Naunton, and rector of Stow, Lincolnshire, 1865-77.

1854: 12 Jul: *Granted a search warrant to search the house of one Kilby, of Naunton, Father of a female servant late in the family of Palmer, Shopkeeper at Bourton, and suspected of having stolen from him a piece of silk—to discover such silk, or any part of it, and, the girl being now in the service of Mr. Haskin, Curate of Naunton, addressed a note to him, requesting him to allow a search to be made in the young woman's apartment in his house, and in her boxes, for the silk.*

HASLUCK — James George Edward Hasluck [104]

James George Edward Hasluck (1820-1901), Church of England clergyman, was born at Handsworth, Staffordshire, son of Richard and Jane Hannah Hasluck. He was educated at Pembroke College, Oxford (BA 1841; MA 1843), and was appointed rector of Little Sodbury in 1851.

1852: 29 Mar: *The High Sheriff, Mr. Winchcombe Howard Hartley, of Old Sodbury ... His chaplain, the Revd. Hasluck, has been recently presented by him to the living of Little Sodbury.*

HASTINGS — ***see*** **Rawdon Hastings**

HASTINGS WOODMAN — ***see*** **Woodman**

HASTINGS — Anna Maria Hastings [105]

Anna Maria Hastings (1747-1837) was born in Nuremberg, according to the act granting her British nationality in 1796. No date of birth is stated, but a secondary source indicates 2 February 1747. Her grandfather was Charles Chapuset de St Valentin, protestant officer in the household troops of the king of France. He was obliged to go into exile following the revocation of the Edict of Nantes in 1685. He went to Berlin as a teacher of languages and dancing, but finally settled at Altdorf, near Nuremberg. There, as a widower, he married, in 1693, Katharina Maria Müller, a clergyman's daughter; they had two sons. Another son, Johann Jakob (d. 1758), was born from a third marriage. Johann married Caroline Friederike Grundgeiger [or Krongeiger] (b. 1720) born at Karlsruhe. He died in 1758, leaving a widow and two children: Anna Maria Apollonia, the future Mrs Hastings, and Johann Paul Thomas (b. 1749).

Anna Maria was first married to Baron von Imhoff. She and her husband met Warren Hastings (1732-1818) in 1769 aboard the *Duke of Grafton*, bound for Madras. Baron von Imhoff had obtained the recommendation of Queen Charlotte, and was hoping to find employment in the forces of the HEIC; he was also hoping to find additional employment as a portrait painter, a pastime of his. Aboard the ship, an intimacy sprang up between Hastings and the baroness, no doubt fuelled by the baron's neglect and the time she and Hastings spent together when she nursed him through a severe illness. In 1773 Baron von Imhoff returned to Germany where he instituted a suit for divorce. On 8 August 1777 Warren Hastings married Anna Maria, her divorce having finally been approved by the German courts.

Warren Hastings had been appointed first British governor-general in India in 1773, controlled by a council of four. On relinquishing this position in 1785, he returned with his wife to England, together with a fortune of £80,000. In 1787 Hastings was impeached by the House of Commons for actions he had taken in India as governor-general. The impeachment was led by Edmund Burke, acting upon malicious information fed to him by Philip Francis, a council member with whom Hastings had battled during his incumbency. Around this time, Hastings bought Daylesford House, his ancestral home, located between Stow-on-the-Wold and Chipping Norton, together with 650 acres. It cost him £11,424, a sum exceeded by the costs of restoration. Mr and Mrs Hastings were acquaintances of Edward and Agnes Witts.

1825: *We dined at Mr. Ford's at Little Risington, & met Mr. Lewes, Rector of Great Barrington and Taynton, Mr. Winter, lately instituted to the Rectory of Daylesford, Worcestershire, of which he was before curate, the presentation being in Mrs. Hastings, widow of the late celebrated Governor Hastings.*

1827: 3 Sep: *We drove to make our first call on Mrs. Hastings at Daylesford. It has pleased this ancient Lady, after we have been 18 years settled here, to find us out & visit us: and though we did not particularly covet an introduction, yet we had no disinclination to accept the tardy civility.* 21 Sep., 25 Sep: *Mrs. Hastings most politely invited us this day to make up for the disappointment on Thursday last, and we reached Daylesford by six o clock.*

1828: 12 Feb: *"Die Frithioss-Sage, von Esaias Tegnér, Bischof von Wexio." Aus dem Schwedischen übersetzt von Amalie von Helvig, geborner Freiin von Imhoff. Stuttgart und Tübingen. 1826. 12mo." After a very long interval, during which I have intermitted the perusal of any German book, I have been led to recall my old familiarity with the language by the loan of Klopstock's Messias from Mrs. Hastings.* 22 Jul: *We received some of our neighbours to dinner; Mrs. Rice & two of her daughters from Oddington, Miss Chapuset (Mrs. Hastings declining dinner engagements) Mr. Ford, Mr. Winter, & Mr. W. B. Pole.* 8 Oct.

1829: 25 Jun., 27 Jun: *We dined at Mrs. Hastings's, and met a large party.* 4 Dec.

1833: 21 Jan: *Dined at Mrs. Hastings's, Daylesford House. Met nearly the same party as we did on Friday at Oddington ... Mrs. Hastings did not appear till tea time: she is much shaken and altered and aged, since I saw her.*

1834: 29 Jul: *To Daylesford, accompanied by Mr. Wellford, to dine at Mrs. Hastings's.*

1836: 31 Aug: *From Churchill we proceeded by Cornwell to Daylesford House, to call on Mrs. Hastings: she was indisposed, and confined to her dressing room.* 4 Oct.

1837: 30 Mar: *Heard of the decease of Mrs. Hastings, which took place yesterday at Daylesford House.* 26 Apr: *Sir Charles I. and Winter are gone to Town, as Executors, to prove Mrs. Hasting's will.* 15 May: *Some confidential communications from Lady I. as to the provisions of Mrs. Hastings's will.* 10 Oct: *The company consisted of Lord Redesdale and Miss Mitford, Sir C. & Lady Imhoff, a Baron Soden, who accompanied them, and who is a great nephew of the late Mrs. Hastings, an unhealthy-looking young man.*

HASTINGS — August Warren Hastings — ***see*** **Soden**

HASTINGS — Charles Hastings [106]

Sir Charles Hastings (1794-1866), physician and founder of the British Medical Association, was born at a lodging house in Ludlow, Shropshire, son of Revd James Hastings (1755-1856) and Elizabeth Paget. He was the ninth of fifteen children. In 1795 the Hastings family moved from Bitterley in Shropshire to Martley in Worcestershire. Little is known of Hastings's early education except that he attended the grammar school in Martley. In 1806 his father suffered a riding accident that rendered him permanently unfit for work, owing to physical and mental incapacity. Soon afterwards his clerical living was placed in chancery, and the Hastings family, in reduced financial circumstances, moved to Worcester.

In September 1810 Hastings began a two-year medical apprenticeship with Richard Jukes and Kenrick Watson at their practice in Stourport-on-Severn. In 1812, following a few months of further study in London, Hastings was elected house surgeon at Worcester Infirmary. Three years later he entered Edinburgh University medical school; he graduated MD in August 1818 with a doctoral thesis on blood vessels. He spent the rest of his professional life in Worcestershire.

Hastings married, 20 May 1823, Hannah (d. 1866), eldest daughter of George Woodyatt; they had 1 son and 2 daughters:

1 Mary Anne Elizabeth (b. 1824)
1 George Woodyatt (1825-1917)
2 Elizabeth Frances (b. 1827)

In 1828, while recovering from a serious accident, Hastings conceived the idea for a quarterly medical journal entitled the *Midland Medical and Surgical Reporter and Statistical Journal*. It is unclear whether it was the success of this publication, or the example of the British Association for the Advancement of Science, which provided the inspiration for the foundation of a provincial medical society; whatever the case, the new society, entitled the Provincial Medical and Surgical Association, was formally established at a meeting convened by Hastings in 1832. The PMSA was renamed the British Medical Association (BMA) in 1855, and two years later the PMSA's weekly publication, the *Provincial Medical and Surgical Journal*, became known as the *British Medical Journal*.

Hastings was knighted in 1850. He was also awarded the diploma of the Royal Medical Society in 1818 and an honorary DCL degree by Oxford University in 1852.

1854: 11 Mar: *He* [Hayward] *had been at Worcester to-day to consult physicians, Sir C. Hastings & Dr. Maldon, as to the cases of two patients—William Harris, & George Pearce who had accompanied him.*

HASTINGS — John Paget Hastings [107]

John Paget Hastings (1783-1822), Church of England clergyman, was the eldest surviving son of Revd James Hastings (1755-1856) and Elizabeth Paget. He was educated at Wadham College, Oxford (BA 1807). He was sent down in 1802 (*see* diary entry, 15 May 1802), but by 1806 he was back at Oxford, and was re-acquainted with Francis Witts.

In 1806 Revd James Hastings, John's father, fell from his horse and was eventually found, wet and confused, lying by the River Teme. He lived for another fifty years, but he never recovered and was incapable of taking any responsibility. Legal documents referred to him as 'a lunatic', and he was said to have communicated only by making animal noises. After the accident, John took charge of the parish until 1810, when he decided to become a chaplain with the HEIC. His mother Elizabeth, then aged 47 and effectively a sole parent, had no choice but to leave the rectory with nine of her fifteen children, aged 6 to 28, for rented accommodation in Worcester. Once settled, she was joined by her husband; he stayed there until his death on 10 July 1856, his 101st year and 60th year as rector.

John married Maria Leonora Neate, widow of Maj. Richard Neate who was killed in action at Corunna; they had at least 1 son:

1 Warren Hastings (1819-1838); died aged 20, Ferruckabad, Bengal

John Paget Hastings died in Bengal in 1822.

1802: 13 Feb: *Breakfasted with Mr. Edgell: meeting Alford, Hastings &c.* 14 Feb., 24 Feb: *Breakfasted with Paget, meeting Hastings, Edgell, Alford & Stevens.* 8 Mar., 13 Mar., 8 May, 15 May: *Afterwards with Williams Rashleigh & Pering in the High St. where we met Watkins & Hastings terribly drunk. Brought them home at last with difficult. At night they made a bonfire of their furniture.*

1806: 22 Mar: *Called upon Hastings, went with him in quest of a liceat first to Merton then to Worcester College.*

HATCH — Thomas Hatch [108]

Thomas Hatch (1788-1851), Church of England clergyman, was born at Windsor, son of attorney Thomas Hatch. He was educated at Eton College and King's College, Cambridge (BA 1813; MA 1817), and a fellow at King's from 1811 to 1815. He was ordained deacon on 12 June 1814 and priest on 8 January 1815. He was appointed curate of Chertsey on 24 December 1814, and vicar of Walton-on-Thames on 12 December 1816. He held the latter post until his death in Walton-on-Thames on 25 June 1851. Little did Francis Witts know that exactly one month from writing his diary entry, the vicar of Walton would be dead.

1851: 25 May: *The perpetual Curacy of Hersham is a district in the parish of Walton on the Thames, of which B. L. Witts was at one time Curate: the incumbent, by name Hatch, is an infirm invalid, and seems not friendly to my cousin. The ill will arises from a misunderstanding as to defining the boundaries of the district, which are to be finally settled by the ecclesiastical Commissioners.*

HATFIELD — Captain Alexander Hatfield of the volunteers, Twickenham [109]

Alexander Hatfield (1755-1832), landed proprietor, was born at Wakefield, Yorkshire, son of Alexander Hatfield and Barbara Sill. He married, at St Mary the Virgin, Twickenham, 12 June 1788, Mary (1757-1834), daughter of Sir Richard Perryn; they had at least 1 son and 5 daughters:

1 Mary Ann (1789-1875)
1 Alexander (1793-1794)
2 Mary (b. 1793)
3 Frances (1796-1872); married, 1826, George Brudenell Michelsen Lovibond of Hatfield Peverell, Essex
4 Jane (b. 1799)
5 Harriet Barbara (1800-1845)

1803: 19 Oct: *The general Test to day. Parade of the Volunteers at 9. Marched to Twickenham Church, sat with Capt. Hatfield.*

HATHAWAY — Abraham Sumner Hathaway [110]

Abraham Sumner Hathaway (1808-1878), farmer and police officer, was born at Lower Swell, Gloucestershire, son of Thomas and Sarah Sumner Hathaway. He married, 1835, Priscilla Roff (1813-1886); they had 2 sons and 4 daughters:

1 Thomas (1836-1843); born at Lower Swell
1 Sarah Ann (b. 1838); born at Lower Swell
2 Keturah Annie (1843-1920); born at Lower Swell; died unmarried, Cheltenham
2 James Sumner (b. 1846); born at Cheltenham
3 Kate [Kitty] Sumner (b. 1848); born at Cheltenham
4 Louisa Jane (1851-1928); married, Cheltenham, 4 July 1875, John Marshall

By 1851 they were living in Cheltenham where Abraham had joined the Gloucestershire Constabulary; however, he is not listed in the Gloucestershire Constabulary archives. By 1871 they were living at Hampnett, where Abraham was superintendent of casual tramps.

1845: 27 Jun: *to Mr. Pearce, respecting Abraham Hathaway, of Lower Swell, who had applied to me for my interest to obtain for him the situation of Porter to our Workhouse.*

HATHAWAY — Edward Penrose Hathaway [111]

Edward Penrose Hathaway (1818-1897), barrister and Church of England clergyman, was born in the parish of St Bride, Fleet Street, London, son of William Silas Hathaway and his wife, Eliza. He was educated at Queen's College, Oxford and Lincoln's Inn. He was called to the bar in 1846. Hathaway was appointed rector of St Ebbe, Oxford, in 1868, and remained in the post for five years.

1853: 14 Apr: *Mr. Hathaway, of Lincoln's Inn, an active partizan of the Anti-Gladstone interest in the University of Oxford, from whom I have previously received communication ... solicits my vote for Mr. Rowden.* 15 Apr: *to Mr. Hathaway, that I had already promised my support to Mr. Rowden, if I could possibly make it.*

HATHWAY — Daniel Gibbs Hathway [112]

Daniel Gibbs Hathway (1824-1888), beer retailer, was born at Westerleigh, Gloucestershire, son of Samuel North Hathway, farmer, and Elizabeth (Betty) Gibbs. He married, at Westerleigh, Gloucestershire, 26 April 1848, his cousin Jane Gibbs. He was remanded in custody by the coroner W. J. Ellis on 26 February 1851 for the wilful murder by poison of his wife, Jane Hathway. He was acquitted and later married secondly, at Crickhowell, Breconshire, April 1851, his mistress Caroline (±1830-1903); they had 4 sons and 3 daughters:

1 Albert (b. 1853)
1 Clara (b. ±1855)
2 Alfred Gibbs (1859-1930)
2 Margaret (b. 1861)
3 George Gibbs (b. ±1862)
4 Charles Gibbs (1866-1943)
3 Emma Gibbs (b. ±1869)

In the diary entry Francis Witts says that an illegitimate child was born prior to the murder, but this has child has not been identified.

In 1881 the family lived at Newport, Monmouthshire; Daniel Gibbs Hathway died there in 1888.

1851: 1 Apr: *a very interesting case of murder by poisoning at Chipping Sodbury, the party accused being the husband of the poor woman who suffered. Hathway, the Prisoner was a fine handsome young man, by no means of a repulsive countenance; one might suppose him to be a dissipated character, but not otherwise vicious; he possessed astonishing nerve and hardihood throughout the trial, frequently communicating with his Attorney, and having an unembarrassed air throughout.*

HAUGHTON — John Haughton [113]

John Haughton (±1802-1848), Church of England clergyman, was born at Tamlaght O'Crilly, Derry, eldest son of Revd John Haughton. He was educated at Pembroke College, Cambridge (BA 1826; MA 1830), and was president of the Union in 1824. He was appointed perpetual curate of Ainsworth, Lancashire, on 8 August 1828. He married Harriet, daughter of R. J. D. Ashworth of Manchester.

John Haughton joined the Irvingites, a religious sect named after Edward Irving (1792-1834), a deposed presbyterian minister. The sect arose from certain extraordinary 'manifestations of the spirit'—tongues, prophecies, healings, even resurrection—which were said to have taken place during Irving's ministry in London, after his deposition.

This attribution to Revd Haughton at Oddington is not given with confidence and it may be erroneous.

1846: 21 Sep., 2 Dec: *As I returned met Mr. Haughton, the Curate of Oddington, who had called and who returned with me. A strange, vain, diffuse, talking, florid Irishman, violently Anti papist, eccentric in manner.* 4 Dec.

1847: 28 Mar: *A letter from Mr. Wiggin, dated Deanery, Gloucester, who is in trouble, in consequence of a servant of his late strange curate of Oddington, Mr. Houghton, persisting in holding a cottage of which Mr. H. had the occupation.*

HAWES — Herbert Hawes [114]

Herbert Hawes (1765-1837), Church of England clergyman, was born at Wilton, near Salisbury, Wiltshire, son of Revd John Hawes and Ann Hawkins (1719-1797). He was educated at New College, Oxford (BA 1786; MA 1789; BD 1800; DD 1810). Hawes was ordained deacon on 3 June 1787 and priest on 20 September 1789. His first clerical appointment was as curate at Fugglestone with Bemerton, Wiltshire, near his family home at Wilton, from 3 June 1787. He was then appointed rector of Mellis on 27 September 1792. He remained in that post until 26 July 1802, overlapping slightly with his next appointment on 19 June 1802 as rector of Salisbury St Edmund. Hawes was later prebend of Netherbury in terra from 30 May 1812 to 21 May 1830, and then prebend of Grimston, Salisbury Cathedral, from 10 April 1830.

1804: 22 Jan., 29 Jul., 12 Aug., 26 Aug., 16 Sep., 14 Oct: *To Chapel in Dowry Square, Mr. Hawes performing indifferently.* 23 Dec., 25 Dec.

1805: 20 Feb: *At Dowry Chapel, a good Sermon by Mr. Hawes.* 24 Feb., 10 Mar: *A good funeral sermon from Mr. Hawes.*

1806: 24 Jan: *Mr. Hawes called & obligingly promised to assist my Enquiries for a Curacy.* 26 Jan., 16 Feb., 9 Mar.

1808: 27 Apr: *Attended the Clergy meeting, as Steward of the Pottern Deanry. Paid my arrears. The party at Dinner consisted of Dr. Welles, Mr. Francis, Mr. Mayo, Mr. Ledyard, Mr. Dodwell, Mr. Williams, Herbert Hawes, Mr. Seymour, & Mr. Goddard.*

HAWES — William Hawes [115]

William Hawes (1785-1846), musician, was a Chapel Royal chorister from 1795 to 1801 and then a violinist in the Covent Garden Orchestra. He also taught singing and served as deputy lay vicar at Westminster Abbey. In 1824 he was appointed musical director of the English Opera House.

1823: 17 Sep: *The Dettingen Te Deum, the Overture to Esther, Dr. Boyce's Anthem (Charity) and W. Knyvett's new Coronation Anthem were the Musical treats for the morning. Of the vocalists, Miss Travis, Messrs. Vaughan, Bellamy, Hawes & W. Knyvett appeared.* 18 Sep: *All the vocal performers distinguished themselves greatly. Mrs. Salmon, Miss Stephens, Miss Travis, Messrs. Vaughan, Bellamy & Hawes.*

HAWKINS — Ernest Hawkins [116]

Ernest Hawkins (1802-1868), secretary of the Society for the Propagation of the Gospel, was educated at Bedford School and at Balliol College, Oxford (BA 1824; MA 1827; BD 1839). He was appointed curate of Burwash, Sussex, after which he travelled on the Continent with a pupil. He returned to Oxford in 1831 as a fellow of Exeter College, and then acted as an under-librarian of the Bodleian Library and as curate at St Aldate in the city of Oxford. Having left Oxford in about 1835, he undertook the curacy of St George's, Bloomsbury, London.

In 1838 Hawkins was appointed under-secretary of the Society for the Propagation of the Gospel; in 1843 he succeeded Archibald Campbell in the secretaryship. He assisted Charles Blomfield, bishop of London, in launching the Colonial Bishoprics Council in 1841. They were supported by W. E. Gladstone, a member of the standing committee of the SPG and later a treasurer of the Colonial Bishoprics Fund, of which Hawkins himself was secretary until 1864. Hawkins married Sophia Anna Lefroy (1823-1897).

1839: 2 Jan: *The following were among the guests: Archd. Thorpe, Mr. & Mrs. Phillips, Mrs. M W. Raikes, Dr. & Mrs. Hall, Mr. G. Hall, Miss Hall, Mr. and Mrs. Hone, Mr. Hawkins, Mr. Sayers, Mr. Powell, Mr. Headlam, Mr. C. Tyre, Mr. R. Waller, Mr. Ford &c.*

1840: 22 Jul., 23 Jul: *Wrote to the Revd. C. B. Dalton, in reply to his letter received yesterday, that Mr. Hawkins's attendance at the annual meeting of the Stow Distr., Comm. S.P.G. will be very acceptable, & that I hope for the pleasure of his company at U.S.* 26-27 Jul., 30 Jul., 4 Aug., 5 Aug: *On arriving at Stow before mid-day found Messrs. Hawkins and Foley, who had driven over from Tewkesbury: they were at the Infant School, where I joined them, and with which they were much pleased.* 16 Aug: *Recd. an obliging letter from Mr. E. Hawkins, thanking me for my civilities on the 5th. Inst. and mentioning that the meeting holden at Ledbury in aid of the S.P.G. had gone off satisfactorily on the 6th.* 25 Aug.

1842: 17 Aug., 19 Aug., 5 Sep.

1844: 14-15 Sep., 11 Oct: *Recd. a letter from the Revd.— Hedley, who is about to accompany Mr. Hawkins the Secretary S.P.G. on a tour of meetings in Gloucestershire in support of the interests of that Society.*

1846: 17 Aug., 19 Aug., 22 Aug., 28 Aug.

1847: 14 Feb., 22 Aug., 24 Aug.

1848: 1 Jan., 25 Feb., 6 Sep.

1849: 28 Dec.

1850: 4 Feb., 7 Sep., 10 Sep., 16 Nov.

1851: 3 Jan.

1852: 9 Jun: *Went to the office of the Society for the Propagation of the Gospel in Foreign Parts—79 Pall Mall. Called on Mr. Vernon, the Under Secretary, from whom I learnt that his senior, Ernest Hawkins, was just gone in the Archbishop of Canterbury's carriage to the Great Western Station at Paddington.* 26 Oct., 24 Dec.

1853: 7 Mar., 17 Dec.

1854: 29 Mar.

HAWKINS — Francis Bisset Hawkins[117]

Francis Bisset Hawkins (1796-1894), physician, was educated at Eton College and Exeter College, Oxford (BA 1818; MA 1821; MB 1822; MD 1825). He was admitted as an inceptor-candidate of the College of Physicians in 1825 and as a fellow in 1826. Hawkins was appointed factory commissioner in 1833, inspector of prisons in 1836, and metropolitan commissioner in lunacy in 1842. In 1847-48 he was commissioner for the government of the model prison at Pentonville, and in 1858 he was appointed a DL of Dorset. In his report on the health and condition of the manufacturing districts, he strongly recommended the reduction of working hours for children and women, and suggested the creation of public gardens or parks in Manchester. When the government introduced the Act for the Registration of Births and Deaths, Hawkins was instrumental in securing a column for the cause of death, which included the names of diseases.

1838: 3 Feb: *Received a letter from C. Bathurst covering one written to him by Dr. Bisset Hawkins, one of the Prison Inspectors, on the state of the Gloucestershire Bridewells.* 7 Feb: *Wrote to Bathurst in reply to the letters I have lately received from him: confining myself to the questions as to the duties to be performed by the chaplain of Northleach Bridewell, and to the points of Bridewell management arising out of Dr. Bisset Hawkins's letter which he had forwarded to me, and which I returned, and leaving for a future letter the consideration of the remuneration to the Clerk of the Peace.*

1842: 18 Oct: *I shewed, as to the allegation of damp that the Bridewell, having been originally constructed with a brook flowing in a full stream through it, had so remained from the days of Sir Geo. Paul till within a few years, when that stream was diverted at the suggestion of Dr. Bissett Hawkins, the Prison Inspector, whose objection, however, was not so much against its being a cause of damp, as that it afforded by its depth to the desponding Prisoner a temptation to suicide.*

HAWKINS — John Pauncefoot Hawkins[118]

John Pauncefoot Hawkins (1784-1858), army officer, was born at Minsterworth, Gloucestershire, son of Jeremiah Hawkins and his wife, Ann. He served in the Peninsular War from June 1811 to December 1813 and was wounded at the Heights of Villares. He became a major in the 68th Foot on 17 September 1812 and brevet lieutenant-colonel on 21 June 1813; later that year took command of the regiment until early 1814. He was promoted to lieutenant-colonel sometime after 1820, and retired in July 1830. He lived in Awre, Gloucestershire. He married Bellamina (b. 1804); they had 1 son and 3 daughters:

1 John Gore (b. 1827)
1 Bellamina (b. 1828)
2 Georgiana (b. 1830)
3 Frances Winne (b. ±1832)

1846: 2 Jul: *Governors opposed to the rules now submitted by the Committee, were chiefly Mr. Avery, a Solicitor of Gloucester, a voluble speaker, one of the leaders of the old House Committee, Col. Cother, and Mr. Turner, the Treasurer—neutral, but rather leaning to the new system, Col. Hawkins, Mr. Coghlan (Rector of St. Mary de lode,) Mr. Montague, Worthington, Clark, Martin—Mr. A Wood one of the surgeons of the Institution was decidedly in favour of the amended rules.* 22 Oct.

HAWKINS — Thomas Hawkins of Edgbaston — *see also* Hunt[119]

Thomas Hawkins was the brother of Bridget Hawkins (1762-1831), who had married, 1788, Edward Hunt (1759-1822), younger brother of Rowland Hunt (1752-1811), the father of Caroline and Sophia (*below*). The uncle who had died appears to have been Thomas and Bridget's brother, Isaac Hawkins (1772-1844).

1843: 20 Sep: *Not admitted at the Rectory as Mrs. W. was preparing with for a drive with the Aitkens's, and a guest of theirs, a lady, a cousin of Mrs. A., to whom we were introduced when we called at Mr. A's, and who proved to be a connection of Mr. T. Hawkins, of Edgbaston, a cousin of Sophia Hunt, from whose house, while on a visit there, she lately wrote to me.*

1845: 7 Jan: *From Sophia Hunt on various matters relating to that family; the affairs of their uncle Hawkins lately deceased &c.*

HAYES — John Warren Hayes[120]

Sir John Warren Hayes, 3rd baronet (1799-1896), Church of England clergyman, was the second son of Sir John Macnamara

Hayes, 1st baronet. He was educated at Wadham College, Oxford (BA 1821; MA 1824). He purchased the living of Arborfield, Berkshire, in 1832 and was rector there from 1839 to 1880. He was a vicar near Bantry in south-west Ireland. He married, 1844, Ellen Beauchamp of the Priory, Beech Hill; they had at least 1 son and 1 daughter:

1 Ellen Anne (b. 1846)
1 John Beauchamp (1849-1884)

Thomas Pelham Hayes, John Warren's brother, succeeded as 2nd baronet in 1809. When he died in 1851, John Warren succeeded as 3rd baronet. The baronetcy became extinct on his death in 1896.

1827: 3 Aug: *My aunt had invited two or three persons to dinner, to which we sat down before five o clock. Besides the family quintetto from the two houses, there were Mr. Turberville, Mr. Hays & Miss Wemyss. ... Mr. Hayes is also a Clergyman, the present Curate of Malvern, but an Incumbent in Ireland, in a parish, where there is neither Church nor Parsonage, both having been suffered to go into decay. He is consequently non-resident, but maintains a Curate at £150 per ann. to perform the occasional duties among his few protestant parishioners.*

HAYNES — Alfred Haynes [121]

Alfred Haynes (b. 1827), coal dealer, was born at Ilmington, Warwickshire, son of Joseph Haynes (1805-1882), a farmer and baker, and his wife, Ann (1804-1869). He married, at Ilmington, 4 October 1849, Ann Walter (b. 1829); they had at least 3 sons and 2 daughters:

1 Elizabeth (b. ±1850)
2 Kate (b. ±1851)
1 John Jordan (1855-1894); married, at Birmingham, June 1875, Elizabeth E. Honeybourne (1855-1939)
2 Daniel Walker Henry (b. ±1856)
3 William (b. 1857); married Louisa Walker

The family lived at Front Street, Ilmington. Haynes was an enterprising young man. Ilmington lies about 8 miles from the nearest canal, at Stratford-upon-Avon; prior to the railways, this proximity enabled Haynes to supply coal at a more economical rate. By 1861 the family had moved to Redditch where Haynes had taken up his father's trade, and become a baker. Competition from railways had clearly put him out of the coal carrying trade. After 1861 the records go cold, although his sons can be traced.

1844: 3 Oct: *Wrote to Haynes, Ilmington, for a supply of coal.*
1846: 9 Aug: *Wrote to Haynes, Ilmington, to order coals for the use of the poor of this parish &c.*

HAYNES — Henry Haynes of Cheltenham, contractor for works at Northleach House of Correction [122]

Henry Haynes (±1787-1853), bricklayer, was born at Bishop's Tachbrook, Warwickshire. By 1851 he was a widower, retired, living at 4 Jersey Street, Cheltenham.

1844: 30 Dec: *The contractor, Mr. Haynes, of Cheltenham, being in attendance, and Mr. Fulljames's report being read in his presence, did not make any exception to it, said that he mainly attributed the accident to the wet season, that more concrete had been put on than necessary, at the urgency of the Clerk of the works, but that he had not remonstrated on that head with Mr. Fulljames, and he admitted that if his workmen had used precautions by putting on a tarpauling or other temporary covering over the concrete to protect it from the rain, the damage might have been avoided.*

HAYTER — Francis Hayter of Urchfont [123]

Francis Hayter (1728-1807), agricultural labourer, was born at Urchfont, Wiltshire, son of Jane Hayter. He was presumably illegitimate.

1807: 24 Dec: *Visited three sick & poor old men, John Sainsbury, William Bailey, & Francis Hayter.* 31 Dec: *Buried poor Francis Hayter.*

HAYWARD — *see* Curtis Hayward

HAYWARD — Mr Hayward of Malvern

1840: 13 Apr: *A life interest in two rooms in a cottage on the premises is further given to a cottager, named Haywood, and his wife, the latter is deceased, the former survives, blind, and at 87 years of age.* 20 May: *Consulting as to the course to be taken in respect of the interest in the property bought abo of Nibletts' devisees reserved in my Aunt's will to an old man, Hayward; it appears on the whole that the line to be adopted will be to sell the property subject to his occupation for his life of two rooms in the Cottage with a part of the garden.* 21 May: *An interview with Mr. James Walker, a respectable tradesman and farmer of Malvern on the subject of old Hayward's interest in the cottage built on the premises bought of Niblett's devisees.*

HAYWARD — George Bulley Hayward [124]

George Bulley Hayward (1811-1887), physician, was the son of Leonard Hayward (1779-1828) and Mary Bulley (1782-1866) (*below*). After completing his studies, George succeeded his father as physician/surgeon at Stow-on-the-Wold. In the interim Richard Filkins of Tetbury provided temporary cover. George appears not to have married.

1835: 13 Apr: *And now came on the trial of Edmund Jeffrey... Of the witnesses, Mr. Welch, the Surgeon, was sadly confused on his cross examination, but Hayward went through the ordeal with much steadiness.*

1837: 15 Jan., 19 Jan., 16 Mar: *Presided at the Board of Guardians: contracts made with the Med. Off. Hayward & Wells, on the same terms as last year.* 24 Apr., 3 May, 9-10 May, 20 Jun., 21 Jul: *He was immediately taken to a public house, and visited by Mr. Hayward, the Surgeon, who from the first had very slender hope of his surviving.* 3 Dec: *Attended while Hayward, who had been sent for by Polhill, the boy's Employer, placed the limb in the proper position, and assisted him in binding it up.* 16-17 Dec., 19-23 Dec., 24 Dec: *Mr. Hayward visited Mrs. Backhouse, and was detained two hours or more in consequence of her having fallen into an alarming fainting fit while he was here.* 25-31 Dec.

1838: 6 Jan: *Mr. Hayward came soon after me, and staid dinner.* 8 Jan., 12 Jan., 15 Jan., 17 Jan., 20 Jan., 24 Jan., 31 Jan., 5 Feb: *From the evidence it appeared that Anne Colin a servant of Mr. Robert Brookes had secretly delivered herself of this child in her master's house on Thursday morning early; had secreted the child between the bed and sacking; had disposed of the after birth by throwing it down the privy of her Master's premises ... it was pressed upon her by Hayward and Richd. Brookes to confess the truth.* 7 Feb., 13 Feb., 25 Jul., 31 Dec.

1839: 5 Jan., 29 May, 30 May: *Conferred with George Hayward and Mr. John Matthews, on the unpleasant dissentions between Mr. Jos. Matthews and his son.* 18 Jul., 20 Jul., 24 Jul: *Mr. Hayward called. I apprehend, he will not call again unless I send for him; he considers me well enough to engage in my usual avocations, but recommends care and abstinence.* 30 Jul., 1 Aug., 4 Aug: *before evening service Hayward called, & prescribed Salvolatile and Tincture of Henbane which corrected the hiccough which was suspended while I was officiating in Church.* 5 Aug., 8 Aug., 10 Aug., 15 Aug: *Called at Hayward's to report to him on the state of my health: he is now administering to me Quinine, with a draught combining Rhubarb, Liquor Potassi and Tincture of Taraxacum.* 19 Aug., 25 Aug.

1840: 26 Apr., 29 Apr: *It appears that a pleuritic affection was barely arrested in time to save her from a serious attack on the lungs by Mr. Hayward, who came in the Evening to see and prescribe for his patient.* 3 May, 8 May: *Mrs. Backhouse had been taken seriously ill on Tuesday ... Mr. Hayward had been called in, and was attending, his remedies had in a considerable degree been successful.* 11 May, 18 Jul., 11 Sep: *In the Evening I walked again to Eyford to visit John Palmer, a labourer, suffering under a severe injury occasioned by a heavy wall, close to which he was at work near the Eyford conservatory, falling on him yesterday morng. ... Mr. Hayward attends him.* 17 Sep., 17-18 Oct.

1841: 1 Mar.

1842: 8 Jan: 22 Jun., 3 Jul., 30-31 Jul., 1 Aug: *Mr. Hayward came early to visit Mrs. Backhouse, and reported unfavourably of her state; the remedies used had, indeed, arrested the progress of the Quinsey, but the tongue and pulse indicated low fever with tendency to inflammation, and he led us to expect wandering of mind co-existent with typhoid symptoms.* 2 Aug: *Mr Hayward considered Mrs. Backhouse as in a very dangerous state, and that her life must soon terminate.* 3-13 Aug., 15 Aug: *Mr. Hayward called: Mrs. Backhouse in nearly the same state as yesterday, feeble, wandering, irritable, and, probably, gradually & slowly sinking.* 16-24 Aug., 26-28 Aug., 29 Aug: *Mr. Hayward called, and found Mrs. Backhouse in a languid sinking state: but still likely, I think, to linger, as she takes a good deal of nourishment.* 30-31 Aug., 1-4 Sep., 6-7 Sep., 9-11 Sep., 13-17 Sep., 20-21 Sep., 23 Sep., 25 Sep., 27 Sep., 28 Sep: *Mr. Hayward called to prescribe for Broome, whose bowels are a little disordered, but in good spirits, and he looks well; a little medicine, & attention to diet will, probably, set all right soon.* 30 Sep., 3 Oct., 9 Oct., 12 Oct., 16 Oct., 22-23 Oct., 27 Oct., 29 Oct., 9 Nov., 12 Nov: *Hayward called to visit Mrs. Backhouse, and pronounced her condition to be much worse since his last attendance, so that he is of opinion that her decease cannot be very distant, or rather, may happen very soon.* 14-15 Nov., 16 Nov: *Wrote letters to Mr. Hayward, Mr. Ford, and Mr. Vavasour, inviting them to attend the funeral of Mrs. Backhouse.* 21 Nov., 26 Nov., 19 Dec.

1843: 14 Jan., 15-16 Dec.

1844: 9 Jan., 19 Apr., 26-27 Apr., 1 May, 30 Sep., 4 Nov., 8 Nov., 19 Nov.

1845: 13 May.

1846: 13-14 Jul., 31 Jul., 29 Aug., 30 Sep.

1847: 25-26 Jan., 5 Feb., 14-22 Feb., 24 Feb., 26 Feb., 28 Feb., 9 Mar., 25 Mar., 3 Jun., 30 Jul., 28 Oct: *Mr. Hayward visited our dear grandchild Freddy professionally: poor little fellow, his bowels and liver are a little out of order, and he looks pale, suffers also from toothache.* 5 Nov., 14 Nov., 18 Nov., 8-10 Dec., 15-16 Dec., 28-30 Dec.

1848: 13 Jan: *Mr. Potter addressed me in a public letter, in which he maintained his charge against Mr. Hayward, and desired to be heard on other charges against him.* 18 Mar., 18-20 Apr., 22 Apr: *Mr. Hayward called. I had slept well, but suffered much pain and weakness.* 24 Apr., 26 Apr., 2 May, 4 May, 11 May, 16 May, 23 Jun., 6 Jul., 2 Sep., 10 Oct., 29 Oct., 31 Oct., 2 Nov., 4 Nov, 7-8 Nov.

1849: 25 Dec: *Mr. Hayward visited M.W. at breakfast time, and found her much out of order.* 27 Dec., 29 Dec.

1850: 4 Jan: *Mr. Hayward called, and visited M.W. but did not find any marked improvement in her state.* 6-8 Jan., 10 Jan., 12 Jan., 15 Jan., 18-21 Jan., 23 Jan., 25 Jan., 27 Jan., 29 Jan., 31 Jan., 2 Feb., 4 Feb., 6 Feb: *Mr. Hayward called; he considers his patient in many respects to be going on favourably; the pulse, though too rapid; has almost ceased to be intermittent; there is more strength; but he admits the oedema in the lower extremities.* 8 Feb., 10 Feb., 12 Feb., 14-15 Feb., 17-18 Feb., 21 Feb., 23 Feb., 25-26 Feb., 28 Feb., 2-3 Mar., 5-6 Mar., 8-9 Mar., 10 Mar: *Mr. Hayward called, and thought M.W. weaker and more sinking.* 11-14 Mar., 16-18 Mar., 20-25 Mar., 27-28 Mar., 30-31 Mar., 2-4 Apr., 6 Apr., 8-9 Apr., 11 Apr: *Hayward called in the forenoon, and found M.W. in a very feeble and infirm state.* 12-14 Apr., 19 Apr: *Mr. Hayward preceded the corpse.* 30 Apr: *Wrote to Mr. Hayward, requesting him to send his bill for medicines and attendance.* 14 May, 17 May, 20 May, 17 Jun., 24 Jun., 25 Jul., 1 Aug., 21 Aug., 23-24 Aug., 26 Aug: *Mr. Hayward paid me a professional visit, and afterwards dined with me.* 29 Aug., 31 Aug., 2 Sep., 5 Sep., 10 Sep., 18 Sep., 28 Nov., 17 Dec.

1851: 23 Jan., 24 Jan: *Mr. Hayward called after breakfast, and visited John Griffin, prescribing for him, and bandaging his leg.* 25 Jan., 3 Mar., 27 Mar., 3 Apr.

1852: 16 Jan: *Mr. Hayward called to visit little George, who is making favourable progress in the measles.* 17 Jan., 30 Feb., 22 Mar., 24 May, 9 Dec., 13 Dec., 16 Dec.

1853: 2 Feb., 10 Feb., 19 Feb., 24 May, 8 Dec., 15 Dec., 20 Dec.

1854: 4 Feb., 5 Mar: *Sent to Hayward to come to prescribe for me—who arrived before 9 AM and remained with me till eleven o'clock——He considers that the action of the lungs is impeded by the thickening of some of the bronchial tubes.* 6 Mar., 8-9 Mar., 11 Mar: *Mr. Hayward called upon me, and seemed to think I was going on pretty well—but my breath is much impeded, there is much flatulence, and languor: and I begin to fear what I did not mention to him, dropsical symptoms shew themselves in the feet & legs.* 13 Mar: *Hayward paid me a visit; medicine, bitters, continued. He assures me there is no appearance of dropsy, or otherwise of effusion, as I had dreaded.* 21 Mar., 29 Mar., 28 Apr., 7 May, 9 May, 13 May: *To Hayward's—consulted him as to my state—the dyspeptic symptoms being on the increase, and causing much uneasiness, adding to the difficulty of respiration from other causes—He intimated more openly than before that there exists an irregular action of the heart—and examined my trunk carefully. No doubt there is a complication of disease—the stomach, the bronchial tubes, and the heart being more or less deranged—He wishes me to go with him to Worcester to see Sir C. Hastings or Dr. Malden. I am very reluctant to do so. Cui bono? On Hayward I have full reliance: I am in my 72d. Year; in the order of nature drawing nigh to the grave; ready to live or die, as pleases GOD: and not ignorant that my bodily system is very much, and, perhaps, organically disordered.* 18 May, 25 May, 29 May, 4 Jun., 8 Jun., 13 Jun., 15 Jun., 19 Jun., 22 Jun., 24 Jun., 4 Jul., 6 Jul., 13 Jul., 25-26 Jul., 31 Jul., 3 Aug: *In an interview with Hayward, he considered that I was not in need of further medical treatment at present, represented my pulse as very regular, and that I had no ground for dread as to swelling in my feet or legs.*

HAYWARD — Isaac Johnson Thomas Hayward [125]

Isaac Johnson Thomas Hayward (1778-1827), captain of the Royal South Gloster Militia, was born at Stroud, Gloucestershire, son of John Hayward (1734-1812) and Sarah Johnson (1742-1800).

He married, at St George's, Hanover Square, Westminster, Maria Elizabeth Andree, née Lemmers (1770-1823), widow of Martinus Pieter Wilten Andree, late of Surinam; they had at least 2 sons:

1 Isaac Johnson Thomas (1806-1879); married, at Chippenham, 4 February 1836, Eliza, fifth daughter of Christopher and Mary Beaven of Rowden House, Wiltshire
2 John Federick (b. 1808); married, at Beverstone, Gloucestershire, 24 March 1835, Mary Ann, only daughter of John Wigmore of Chavenage, Gloucestershire

After the death Martinus Pieter Wiltens Andree in Surinam, his widow Maria Elizabeth returned to England, where she subsequently met and married Capt. Isaac Johnson Thomas Hayward in 1805. Through this marriage, the Hayward family became involved in the slave-dependent Surinam plantations; Isaac toiled for the rest of his life to make the plantations profitable. He died there in 1827.

Clyffe Hall had been built in 1732 by a Gloucestershire man, Edward Chivers Vince. It was originally a fairly small elegant Georgian mansion, set in 20 acres of land, and approached by an avenue leading from West Lavington High Street. Edward Vince was succeeded by his son, and the house was then let for a number of years, one tenant being Capt. Hayward. At some point at the end of the first or beginning of the second decade of the nineteenth century, Clyffe Hall was bought by Duncombe Pleydell Bouverie (1780-1850), MP.

1806: 29 Aug: ... *when I repaired to W. Butchers, to meet Captn. Hayward of Cliff Hall.* 30 Aug: *Rode through Eastroft & Lavington to call upon Captn. Hayward at Cliff Hall.*

1807: 24 Jan.

1808: 3 Jan.

HAYWARD — Job Hayward [126]

Job Hayward (1812-1874), carrier, was born at Lower Slaughter, son of John and Mary Hayward. He married, at Upper Slaughter, 27 January 1853, Sophia Hartwell (1816-1888), born at Coln St Aldwyn, Gloucestershire, daughter of Elizabeth Hartwell; they had 2 daughters:

1 Elizabeth Anne (b. 1854); married, at Lower Slaughter, 24 August 1881, Albert Turner (b. 1857); 1 son and 2 daughters:
   1 Albert John (1886-1944)
   1 Emily Sophia (b. 1891); married, 1916, Joseph G. Ballard
   2 Annie Laura (1893-1963); married, at Stow-on-the-Wold, June 1919, Reginald Harraden Keck
2 Emily (1859-1904); died unmarried

1845: 2 Feb: *Wrote to Messrs. Whitcomb & Co. requesting them to forward to me the parcel of deeds concerning Hunt Turnpike Bonds by Job Hayward the Gloucester carrier, whom I had directed to call for them to-morrow.*

1850: 20 Apr: *The Housemaid, Sophia Hartwell, who has lived in the family ten years, to continue in her place, probably till she marries.*

1851: 27 Apr: *a note to be taken by Job Hayward, the Carrier, to the Bell Hotel, to order a fly to be ready on Tuesday.*

1852: 22 Dec: *Letters from M. A. Coleman, a young woman at Chadlington, who applies for my housemaid's place, which is likely to be soon vacant, as Sophia Hartwell, who has lived in my family twelve years, is shortly about to marry the man to whom she has been long engaged.*

1853: 27 Jan.

1853: 27 Jan: *Officiated at the marriage of my housemaid, Sophia Hayward, now late S. Hartwell—a worthy creature, who had lived in my family twelve years, and been a faithful attendant at the last illnesses and death-beds of my mother in law, & my dear wife—Job H. is a steady industrious man, a carrier from L Slaughter to Cheltenham and Gloucester. They enjoyed the wedding dinner in my servant's hall with their old acquaintances of my household, repairing to their home in the evening.* 31 Dec: *Made arrangements with A Stratton, & Job Hayward to the same purpose.*

HAYWARD — Leonard Hayward — *see also* Ferris [127]

Leonard Hayward (1779-1828), physician/surgeon at Stow-on-the-Wold, was the son of Leonard Hayward (1748-1819), also a physician at Stow. Before him, yet another Leonard Hayward (1715-1780), son of Robert Hayward and Mary Compere, had been a Stow physician.

There seems to be an association with the Blizard family. Thomas Blizard may have been a partner in the younger Hayward's medical practice. The will of Anthony Compere (d. 1764) named Leonard Hayward (senior) as a legatee, although Anthony's nephew, Thomas Blizard, then a minor, was his principal legatee. It may have been that Leonard Hayward (senior) was in practice with Compere, who was also recorded as a surgeon, but as seen above, the Compere and Hayward families were already connected by marriage, and this could explain the mention. Leonard married Mary Bulley (1782-1866); they had 2 sons and 2 daughters:

1 George Bulley (1811-1887); *see above*
2 Leonard (1812-1824)
1 Ann (1812-1839); married Richard J. Ferris (1802-1841) of Truro; 4 sons and 1 daughter:
   1 George (1832-1849)
   2 Richard Hayward (1835-1867); born at Penzance
   1 Mary Frediswed (1835-1857)
   3 Leonard (1838-1887)
   4 John (b. 1839)
2 Susannah M. (1817-1856)

Mary had the disappointment of losing her husband at a relatively early age, and of all her children except George predeceasing her. It seems that the orphaned grandchildren came to live with her; the 1841 census records George and Mary Ferris living with Mary Hayward in Sheep Street. In the 1851 census Mary Hayward is listed as having been born in Chadlington. Mary and Richard were still living with her. Also in the household was John Jenkins (b. ±1827), medical assistant, born at Ashby-de-la-Zouch, Leicestershire. George Ferris followed his uncle in his profession, but died young.

1825: 9 May: *We felt sorry to leave one of our Servants very ill; the Cook; the poor woman has been suffering for a fortnight under an alarming inflammation of the lungs, and Mr. Hayward, the skilful apothecary, has great apprehensions, that her disease will terminate in a decline.*

1827: 1 Jan: *This induced me on Saturday to mention my symptoms to our apothecary, Mr. Hayward, who without giving a decided opinion recommended me to go on, as I had done, taking the blue pill, and to abstain from wine and anything likely to disagree with the stomach.* 5 Jan: *The suspicions, which I entertained as to an incipient hernia, and which Dr. Shute & Mr. Hayward both considered well founded, have been confirmed by Mr. Cother, the eminent surgeon here.* 22 Jan: *Mr. Hayward resumed his visits. Dr. Shute has communicated with him by letter. Mr. Ford and other of my neighbours kindly called on me.* 16 Jun: *My servant met me with Mr. Hayward's gig & horse, and my friendly Æsculapius is disposed to spare me the latter, which seems to be very safe and steady in harness.* 25 Jun: *We took our first drive to-day in our open carriage, now returned from Gloucester and repaired, with a new horse, which I have bought from Mr. Hayward, our medical friend at Stow.*

1828: 28-29 Jul., 1 Aug., 29 Aug., 2 Sep., 7 Oct: *our skilful Apothecary, Hayward, visited her in the first instance once, but alas! the hand of death is upon him too, and he is lingering on the verge of the grave in excruciating agony from an internal complaint.* 26 Oct: *Yesterday died after lingering many days in excruciating agony, but sensible to the last, poor L. Hayward, our medical friend at Stow. He was a man of strong sense, had enjoyed the advantage of a good medical education, was firm and cool, judicious and attentive; his surgical skill was very considerable, he had much experience in the general forms of disease, and was an able accoucheur. Fond of pleasure, and of a weakly constitution, he had exhausted himself by the fatigues incident to an extensive country practice, to which he superadded in the seasons hunting, coursing, fishing and shooting; without being a polished man, he was generally acceptable to the gentry of the country.... He has left a son and two daughters; the former is now studying the medical profession at London; Mr. Filkin, with whom Hayward entered into engagements a few weeks only before his death, is to carry on the business, recieving half the profits. The remaining share is to go to Mrs. H. until her son be able to take a part in the business, which will not be for three years at least. Mr. Hayward, I imagine, was about 47 or 48 years of age.*

HEAD — George Head [128]

George Head (1822-1893), Church of England clergyman, was born at Trinity Main, near Edinburgh, the youngest son of Sir Francis Bond Head (1793-1875), colonial governor and author, and Julia Valenza Somerville (1792-1879), who happened to be a cousin to Francis Witts. He was educated at King's College, London, and Trinity College, Cambridge (BA 1845; MA 1848). He was ordained deacon in 1845 and priest in 1846. His first clerical appointment was as curate at Doncaster, Yorkshire, in 1845-46. This was followed by a curacy at Sneaton, North Yorkshire, in 1846-47, after which he became rector of Aston-Somerville, Gloucestershire, in 1847-93. There he died, unmarried.

1850: 16 Sep: *The following Clergymen were present—Mr. Head, from Aston Somerville, Mr. Covey, from Alderton.*

1851: 2 Apr: *My son & daughter arrived on horseback, being speedily followed by Laura and Constance Howell, with my dear little Grandsons, travelling in the Chariot, Mr. Head being added to the party: he, having come to Stanway to call yesterday, had been detained to dine & sleep, and, the young ladies being mightily taken with him, he had been brought on, almost vi et armis, to finish with a visit here.—He is a younger Son of the talented Sir Francis Bond Head, so well known by his interesting writings, in various public positions, and by his government in Canada, at a season of much difficulty and embarrasment. With a reserved, shy manner, the young Rector of Somervilles Aston is a clever person, of elegant pursuits.* 3 Apr: *E.F.W. and Mr. Head went out to fish, with good success.* 4 Apr: *E.F.W. and Mr. Head had been fishing ... Much music and singing, comic Irish and Irish Melodies by Mr. Head, who accompanied Sophy in many pieces.* 5 Apr.

1852: 30 Mar: *Other guests came to dinner* (Stanway); *Mr. Head from Somervilles Aston, who also slept at the Vicarage.* 1 Apr.

HEADLAM — James Garnett Headlam [129]

James Garnett Headlam (1808-1891), Church of England clergyman, was born at Bath, son of Thomas Headlam and Dorothy Brooming. He was educated at Brasenose College, Oxford (BA 1803; MA 1833). He was appointed curate of Windrush in 1833, and of St George, Liverpool, in 1838.

1834: 20 Aug: *Drove to Stow, to hold the annual meeting of the District Comm. of the Soc. for the Prop. of the Gosp. Nine members attended: Ford in the chair. Presented a report, as Secretary. One new Subscriber added to our list, the Revd.—Headlam, Curate of Windrush.* 4 Sep.

1839: 2 Jan.

HEADLEY — William Headley of Calne

1808: 21 Feb: *Proceeded in the double bodied White Lion Coach, an uneasy vehicle: roads worse & worse, as we advanced: my companions were Mr. Headley of Calne, Ned Poore, &c.* 22 Feb: *Arrived at 10 o clock in Piccadilly, & after breakfasting with Wm. Headley at Hatchett's, came to my Aunt Lady Lytteltons.*

HEATH — Charles Heath [130]

Charles Heath (1795-1868), carver and gilder, was born at Kidderminster, Worcestershire, son of John and Mary Heath. In the 1840s he worked from 27 Broad Street, Bristol, but by 1851 he was at Walton Lodge, adjacent to Montague Parade. By 1861 he was back at Broad Street, at number 32. At some point between 1851 and 1861 he married his housekeeper, Amelia Bray (b. 1823), who was born at Bristol.

1833: 9 Apr: *we went in search of an Artist, whom Mr. Riddle had recommended to us as singularly skilful in the restoration of old pictures, and of such as had sustained any injury. His shop professes to be only that of an ordinary Carver and Gilder, and his name is Heath. We found him at home and a package, which I had sent him from Upper Slaughter by the waggon, two days before we left home, had arrived. It contained my Father's picture by Romney, and a family piece by Mortimer.* 10 Apr: *After luncheon our whole party walked into Bristol, and first repaired to Mr. Heath's in Broad Street, who had unrolled my damaged altar-piece.*

HEATH — John Lardner Heath — *see also* Lardner [131]

John Lardner Heath (b. 1816), postmaster and inspector of weights and measures, was born at Moreton-in-Marsh, son of William Heath and Hannah Lardner. He married Elizabeth (b. ±1827). They appear to have moved away from Moreton, but later returned; John was listed as postmaster there in 1851. After that date the records go cold; there is a possibility that they emigrated.

1838: 30 Dec: *A letter from one Heath, Grandson, of the late Post Master of Moreton in Marsh, who died a few days ago at an advanced age.*

1839: 6 Jan., 11 Jan: *A letter from Lord Redesdale desiring information from me as to the young man Heath who had applied to him for his interest to obtain the office of Inspector of Weights and Measures.* 27-29 Jan., 1 Feb., 2 Feb: *A letter from Lord Redesdale, to explain why he has resolved to support the young man Heath, in his claim to be appointed permanently an Inspector of Weights and Measures.* 5 Feb., 12 Apr: *Wrote to Miss Lardner, Moreton, with a cheque for the amount due to her nephew, J Heath, who has resigned the office of Inspector of weights and measures for Glorshire No. 9. as he intimated to me in a letter which I recd. on the 7th. Inst. in consequence of his removal to another employment in a distant county.*

HEATHCOTE — Henry Heathcote [132]

Sir Henry Heathcote (1777-1851), naval officer, was the fourth son of Sir William Heathcote, 3rd baronet, and his wife, Frances. He married, 1799, Sarah Elizabeth Guscott; they had ten children. Heathcote made steady progress through the ranks of the Royal Navy: lieutenant, 1796; commander, 1797; captain, 1798; rear admiral, 1830; admiral of the blue, 1846; and admiral of the white, 1848. In 1821 Heathcote represented British interests in the Ionian islands and was regent of Ithaca and Cerigo. It was presumably during this period that he knew George Witts.

1823: 13 Aug: *The information comes from Mr. Pellew, Collector of the Customs at Falmouth, agreeably to the arrangement, which I made in Town with his nephew, Captain F. Pellew, and from a Capt. Heathcote, of the Ionian Service, an old acquaintance of my poor brother's, who was a passenger with him on board the Packet, and had taken a particular charge of him.* 21 Aug: *Received a letter from Captn. Heathcote containing some particulars of my poor brother, parts of which I shall transcribe.*

HEATHER — butler to Mr Chamberlayne

It is not known how long Mr Heather kept the Unicorn, but by 1861 the proprietor was Samuel Wooll.

1852: 22 Jan: *Thither I repaired by 12 o clock, it being held at the Unicorn Inn, now deprived by Death, after a lingering illness, of its aged landlord, Scarsbrook, whose bustling, active, and benevolent wife had preceded him to the grave, some months ago. The establishment is about to pass into the hands of one Heather, Butler for several years to Mr. Chamberlayne.*

HEATON — George Heaton [133]

George Heaton (1804-1893), Church of England clergyman, was born at Doncaster, son of William Stocks Heaton (1777-1834) and Mary Hornby. He was educated at St Catherine's College, Cambridge (BA 1831; MA 1835). Heaton was chaplain to the West Ham Union, Essex, in 1841-45, assistant chaplain of the county gaol, Gloucester, in 1845-51, and perpetual curate of St Mary's, Cheltenham, in 1855-57.

In 1841 Heaton and his family lived at Forest Lane, Stratford, West Ham, and in 1851 at 16 Hillfield Parade, Gloucester. In 1851 he was listed as 'Clergyman MA unemployed'. He married Jane Elizabeth Wood (1810-1886); they had 6 sons and 5 daughters:

1 George William (1833-1909); married Annette Hannah Campbell, née Ferrers (b. 1846)
2 Charles William Stocks (1835-1906); died at Guilford, Chenango, New York, USA
1 Emily Jane (1837-1927); died unmarried
2 Elizabeth (1839-1873); married, first, 14 May 1860, James Beaumont Neilson (1824-1869); secondly, 9 August 1871, Charles Holliday (b. 1830)
3 Arthur Frederick (1840-1911); married, at St Mary's, Teddington, 24 April 1884, Agnes Braby (b. 1858)
3 Augusta Mary (1842-1853)
4 Martin (1844-1933); married, at St James's Cathedral, York County, Toronto, Ontario, Canada, 16 July 1870, Mary Emily Hunter (b. 1848)
4 Rachel Stanley (1846-1920); married, in Hampshire, April 1875, Sir William Mure (1818-1885)
5 Henry (b. 1849)
5 Alice Catherine (1850-1929); married, 1872, John F. Sherwood (1844-1916); died at Guilford, Chenango, New York, USA
6 Augustus Marius (1853-1901); married, in New Zealand, 1876, Helen Marianne Norie (1846-1924)

George and Emily were born in Oakham, Rutland, which suggests that prior to West Ham, George Heaton held a curacy there. Both George William Heaton and Arthur Frederick Heaton followed their father to Cambridge and had successful careers, especially George who became a barrister and high sheriff for Vancouver, British Columbia, in 1859-60. In 1874 George Heaton became vicar of the Isle of Grain, Kent. By 1891 he was a widower, but his unmarried daughter, Emily, was living with him. Also in the house was a schoolmistress, Elizabeth Blissendon (b. ±1844), described as 'companion to above', i.e., to Emily.

1844: 9 Apr: *The Revd. Mr. Heaton was appointed Asst. Chaplain at the Gaol: there was hardly any competition for the place; and it is to be feared that the gentleman elected will not be found very well suited to the post.* 10 Apr., 31 Dec: *This excited Mr. Heaton, who rejoined in a tart and angry manner, at which the Chairman fired, and something of a scene took place ... Mr. Heaton is a sensitive person, and very likely to throw up his situation.*

1845: 19 Apr: *Read a pamphlet by Mr. Heaton, the Assistant Chaplain, Gloucester Gaol, on the education of the poor, prisons, and crime.*

1847: 11 Feb: *Wrote to the Revd. G Heaton requesting him to add my name to the list of subscribers to the forthcoming work—"The Clergyman in the Gaol."*

1848: 25 May: *Received a letter from C Bathurst, who enquires my opinion of the character of Mr. Heaton, the Assistant Chaplain of the County Gaol.* 24-25 Oct., 16-17 Nov.

1850: 29 Jul: *Recd. from Mr. Heaton, candidate for the office of Chaplain to the Gaol at Gloucester, a printed document containing divers testimonials of his fitness for the office.*

1851: 22 Feb: *Received a letter from Mr. Heaton, of Gloucester, late Assistant Chaplain at the County Gaol, but who has lost the situation, owing to the new arrangement, by which the duties of Chaplain are discharged by one Clergyman. Mr. H. is in great poverty, witht. any stated employment, burthened with a large family: his clerical neighbours and well-wishers have prepared a petition in his favour to be presented to the Archbishop of Canterbury, and he requests me to sign it.* 23 Feb., 26 Feb., 15 May.

1852: 5 Jun: *An application for further pecuniary assistance to Mr. Heaton, late Assistant chaplain at the County Gaol, Gloucester, whose large family and poverty have already made him very burdensome to charitable clergymen & magistrates.* 8 Jun.

1853: 11 Mar: *Received a call from Revd. G. Heaton, now resident as an Asst. Curate at Cheltenham, formerly Asst. Chaplain at Gloucester Goal, always in poverty, frequently taxing the charity of his brethren of the Clergy to relieve wants originating in a numerous family of children, with, no doubt, more or less of indiscretion. At present he is soliciting aid to meet extraordinary expenses in placing his son at the University of Cambridge.* 16 Mar: *Recd. a letter from Dr. Warneford, with a check for £5.5.0—as a contribution towards the present difficulties of Mr. Heaton.* 18 Mar., 21 Mar.

HEBER — Reginald Heber [134]

Reginald Heber (1783-1826), bishop of Calcutta, was born at Malpas, Cheshire, son of Reginald Heber, rector of Hodnet, Shropshire, and co-rector of Malpas, and his second wife, Mary, daughter of Revd Cuthbert Allanson. Through his father's first marriage, Reginald (junior) was half-brother to Richard (*below*).

Heber was educated at Whitchurch Grammar School, a small private school at Neasden in London, and Brasenose College, Oxford. He was ordained in 1807, and succeeded his father as rector of Hodnet. He was appointed a prebendary of St Asaph Cathedral in 1817. In 1815 he delivered the Bampton lectures at Oxford, which were subsequently published under the title *The Personality and the Office of the Christian Comforter Asserted and Explained*. In 1822 he was appointed preacher to Lincoln's Inn.

In 1823 Heber was appointed the second bishop of Calcutta—a diocese that had been established in 1814 and which then included the whole of India, southern Africa, and Australia. Heber was notable for his friendliness towards representatives of other churches, especially the non-Roman episcopal churches of the East, including the Armenians and Syrians. He came to be highly regarded by the English dissenting missionaries and the Church of Scotland ministers. In February 1826 Heber embarked upon a visitation of south India; he died suddenly at Trichinopoly, while taking a bath, on 3 April 1826.

Heber married, 14 April 1809, Amelia, third daughter of William Davies Shipley, dean of St Asaph; they had 2 daughters:

1 Emily (b. 1821); married Algernon Percy, son of the bishop of Carlisle
2 Harriet (b. 1824); married John Thornton, son of Heber's old friend

---

1826: 2 Sep: *The second Bishop of Calcutta, Dr. Heber, has fallen a victim to the laborious duties of his station: it appears, that he died by apoplexy.*
1828: 25 May, 16 Sep., 25 Oct.
1832: 25 Apr.
1840: 30 Aug., 26-27 Sep.

HEBER — Richard Heber [135]

Richard Heber (1774-1833), MP and bibliomane, was born at Westminster, the eldest son of Reginald Heber, Church of England clergyman, and his first wife, Mary Baylie. His half-brother, Reginald Heber (1783-1826) (*above*), poet and bishop of Calcutta, was the son of a second marriage.

Heber was educated at Brasenose College, Oxford (BA 1796; MA in 1797), and was MP for Oxford University in 1821-25. He was a manic book collector, with wealth to match his appetite for collecting. At his death he was estimated to have owned 150,000 books.

1826: 29 Jan: *Mr. Heber, M.P. for the University of Oxford has unexpectedly announced by letter to the heads of Colleges his intention of applying for the Chiltern Hundreds, and quite retiring from public life.... for Mr. H. is par excellence a bibliomaniac, an excellent social companion, but has not shone as a politician.... I voted for Heber: he has considerable estates in Craven, as well as in Shropshire; my wife's family had been well acquainted with his; & I felt, that in that way he had a claim upon me. His brother is the eminent Bishop of Calcutta.*

1838: 17 Sep: *... and through the village of Marton, where was the family estate of the Hebers, and where the Bibliomaniac MP. for the Univ. of Oxford, the elder brother of Bp. Reginald Heber, who lost himself towards the close of his life, resigned his seat, and died abroad, in obscurity, sometimes resided.*

HEBERT — Charles Hebert [136]

Charles Hebert (1807-1890), Church of England clergyman, was born in the parish of St Mary, Stoke Newington, London, son of Robert Hebert and his wife, Eleanor. He was educated at Middle Hill and Charterhouse, and Corpus Christi College, Cambridge. He later migrated to Trinity College (BA 1830; MA 1833; BD 1873; DD 1875). Hebert was ordained deacon on 16 June 1833 and priest on 21 December 1833. His first clerical appointment was as stipendiary curate for Longborough with Sezincote, Gloucestershire, on 16 June 1833. He became vicar of Grendon, Northamptonshire, on 16 January 1834 and held the living for just under two years, to 16 November 1835. He was curate of Cheltenham,1835-39; curate of St James's in Clapham, London, 1839-44; vicar of Lechlade, 1844-51; vicar and rural dean of Burslem, Staffordshire, 1851-58; vicar and afterwards rector of Lowestoft, Suffolk, 1862-70; and finally vicar of Ambleside, Westmorland, 1875-78.

Hebert married Elizabeth (b. ±1810); they had at least 7 sons and 3 daughters:

1 Charles Christopher (b. 1835); born at Cheltenham; died an infant
2 Robert Francis (b. 1837); born at Cheltenham; initially Charles, but the register was amended to Robert Francis
1 Grace (b. ±1838); born at Cheltenham
3 Henry Venn (b. 1840); born at Clapham
4 Martyn Carthew (b. 1841); born at Clapham
2 Elizabeth (b. 1843); born at Lechlade
3 Eleanor (b. 1845); born at Lechlade
5 Hankinson (b. 1846); born at Lechlade
6 Edward J. (b. ±1850)
7 Septimus Hebert (b. 1851); born at Burslem

1833: 25 Oct: *I was assisted during the whole sitting, from one to nearly five o'clock by Mr. Jeaffreson, and partially by Messrs. Ford and Croome. Met also Mr. Hebert, Winter, Vavasour &c.* 30 Oct: *Dined at Mr. Jeaffreson's, at Longborough, calling for Mr. Hebert by the way, and bringing him home to Stow.—Mr. H. a very pleasing, intelligent, mild and agreeable young man.*

HEDLEY — Thomas Alcock Hedley [137]

Thomas Alcock Hedley (1812-1854), Church of England clergyman, was born at Manchester, son of Matthew and Hannah Hedley. He was educated at Trinity College, Cambridge (BA 1836; MA 1839). His first clerical appointment appears to have been as a curate at Bedford, following which he was appointed curate of St Mary de Lode, Gloucester, in 1838. He was perpetual curate of St James's, Gloucester, in 1841-48[?], of Clifton, Gloucestershire, from 1850, and appointed the same of Cotham Park, Bristol, in 1854. He married Isabella (b. ±1815); they had at least 2 sons and 3 daughters:

1 Elizabeth (b. 1838); born at Bedford
2 Isabella (b. 1840); born at Gloucester
1 Arthur (b. 1841); born at Gloucester
3 Jane (b. 1843); born at Gloucester
2 William (b. 1845); born at Gloucester

1842: 9 Apr: *Received a letter from Mr. Hedley, Gloucester, Secretary to the Glouc. Distr. Comm. S. P. G. inviting me to a meeting of Treas. & Sec. of Distr. Comm. within the Archdeaconry of Glouc.* 12 Apr., 23-24 Apr.

1844: 30 Aug: *the subject of Education was urged on the meeting by the Bishop, Mr. Cooke (Wick Risington) and Mr. Hedley, incumbent of a district church near Gloucester, now secretary of the diocesan board of Education for the diocese of Gloucester, who came purposely to advocate the cause.* 14-15 Sep., 18 Sep: *The Dean of Gloucester presided: Mr. Hedley from Gloucester, ardent and busy in the cause, had come, as he said, to learn; but was an efficient aid; for he addressed the meeting in a kind of platform speech, which answered very well, and relieved the wonted evenness of our home proceedings, succeeding the report which I produced.* 11 Oct: *Revd.—Hedley, who is about to accompany Mr. Hawkins the Secretary S.P.G. on a tour of meetings in Gloucestershire in support of the interests of that Society.* 12 Oct., 31 Oct., 8 Nov., 7 Dec., 10 Dec.

1846: 1 Nov: *A circular from Gloucester, signed by Mr. Hedley, announcing a meeting of the diocesan board of education to be held at the Palace, Gloucester at which the Bishop will attend on the 4th. Inst.*

1847: 4 Feb., 18 Jul., 26 Aug., 31 Aug.

HELLIER — Thomas Shaw Hellier[138]

Thomas Shaw Hellier (1803-1888), Church of England clergyman, was born at St Aldate, Oxford, eldest son of Thomas Hellier. He was educated at Lincoln College, Oxford (BA 1824; MA 1826). He was perpetual curate at Little Compton, Warwickshire, and was later rector of Bampfylde, Somerset, in 1856-68. He married Caroline (b. ±1809), born at Fairford; they had at least 2 sons:

1 Richard (b. ±1839)
2 Samuel (b. 1844)

1844: 11 Oct.

1845: 21 Jan: *The following Clergymen came to confer with us: Mr. Helliar, Incumbent of Little Compton, who despaired of doing anything for the Society in his small and dissenterized parish, in which also he does not reside for lack of a house, and the endowment of which is very inconsiderable.* 25 Jun.

1846: 21 Sep: *those who attended were Messrs. Ford, Hippisley, Wiggin, Haughton, Pantin, Helliar, Potter, Morrison, Witts, Talmage—and the last was a stranger to the deanery—of the diocese of Oxford.*

1848: 29 Sep: *At the national Schoolroom Mr. Hellier read a long paper, carefully prepared, in a philosophical tone, shewing much research, to the purport that the almost universal belief of mankind in a future state ought to be considered as a proof of the immortality of the soul.*

HELLDORF — Karl Heinrich Anton von Helldorf — *see also* De Beist[139]

Karl Heinrich Anton von Helldorf (1767-1834), chamberlain at Weimar and lord of the manor of Schwerstedt, near Weimar, was the son of Johann Heinrich von Helldorff and his wife, Henriette Ernestine. He married Christiane Auguste Wilhelmine Helldorf.

1798: 2 Sep: *of strangers there are many. The chief are Count Marschall, the Egloffstein, Seebach, Helldorf, Luc, Lasberg, Wolfskiel, Gormar, Oldorthausen, Families &c. all of whom almost have some Office either in the Civil, Military or Immediate Court Service.*

1799: 19 Nov: *in the Evening my Father & Mother at Helldorfs.*

1800: 7 Apr: *in the Evening to a Party at Herr von Helldorfs very agreable besides Petit Jeux played a very rational Game at Boston with Fr. v. Bertel & Beist & Hauptmann v. Eggloffstein.*

HELPS — Richard Helps — *see also* Whitcombe[140]

Richard Helps (1810-1867), attorney, solicitor, and alderman, was born at Gloucester, son of Richard Helps (1770-1835) and Catherine Spry (1783-1828). He married, at Hungerford, Berkshire, 4 October 1838, Harriet Smith (1814-1899); they had 4 sons and 7 daughters:

1 Richard Sumner (1839-1888); married, at St Marylebone, Westminster, 4 April 1866, Catherine Brereton Ward
1 Catherine Frances (1841-1874); died unmarried
2 Mary Ann Emily (1843-1919); committed to Barnwood Institution for the Insane
2 Arthur Spry (1845-1908)
3 Harriet Augusta (1846-1932); died unmarried
3 Walter Bromfield (b. 1847)
4 Caroline Alice (1849-1920); died unmarried, Bath
4 Clement Stackhouse (1851-1885); died, Exeter, Devon
5 Ethel (1852-1943)
6 Florence Gertrude (1854-1942); died unmarried
7 Isabella Louisa (1856-1942); died unmarried

1835: 5 Jun: *Miss Sophia Hunt received a letter from Messrs. Whitcombe and Helps apprizing her of the result of the sales of the house and furniture &c., late Mrs. M. Hunt's, at Gloucester.* 16 Jun., 20 Jun.

1836: 6 Sep., 8 Sep., 14 Sep., 20 Oct: *I went to transact some business at the Treasurer's office and Infirmary Mr. Helps having been fully engaged both yesterday and to day, I was prevented transacting any business with him relative to my Exorship.* 24 Oct: *Received a letter from Mr. Helps, apologizing, on the score of the pressure of important business for not fixing a time when I was at Gloucester to assist me in making up my Exorship.* 31 Dec.

1837: 2 Jan., 5-6 Jan., 4 Feb., 6 Feb., 8 Mar., 11 Apr., 6-7 May, 28 Jun., 14 Jul., 20 Jul.

1839: 17-18 Mar., 10 Apr: *Transacted business relative to the Hunt family with Mr. Helps; also business at the Office of the County Treasurer; and busied in shopping.* 8 Jun., 15 Jul: *Recd. a letter from Mr. R. Helps, written in answer to a query made by me in one of the letters I had written in reference to Mr. Wood's canvass for the Office of Surgeon to the Infirmary.* 25 Aug.

1846: 11 Aug: *Of the inhabitants of Gloucester among the most conspicuous were Messrs. Whitcombe, Helps, Avery, Turner, Montague, Revd. Hardwicke, Sayers & others.* 22 Oct.

1853: 30 Dec: *from Mr. Helps, a circular, inviting me to attend a meeting of the Committee for managing the election of Sir M. H. Beach, to be held at Gloucester on Monday.* 31 Dec.

1854: 10 Feb: *To Mr. Helps, Gloucester, that it will not be in my power to be present at the dinner to be given to Sir M H Beach there to celebrate his return to Parliament on the 16th. Inst.*

HEMMING — Samuel Tyson Hemming[141]

Samuel Tyson Hemming (1767-1828), Church of England clergyman, was born at Southwark, Surrey, son of John Cheshyre Hemming (±1723-1787) and Martha Tyson (b. 1730). He was educated at St John's College, Oxford (BA 1787; MA 1791; BD 1797; DD 1801). Hemming was ordained deacon on 31 May 1790 and priest on 19 June 1791. He was appointed minister of Twickenham chapel in 1790, and served as lecturer at Isleworth in 1794-99, and rector of Fawkham, Kent, from 31 May 1797 to 3 June 1829. He was a schoolmaster at Hampton Grammar School from 13 January 1804 and rector of East Lavant, Sussex, from 17 April 1805 to his death.

Hemming married, at St Mary the Virgin, Twickenham, 3 June 1796, Elizabeth Baker (1775-1856); they had 6 sons and 4 daughters:

1 George (1798-1880), Church of England clergyman
2 Samuel (1799-1876); married, 29 September 1820, Agnes Baird (b. 1801)
3 Frederick Herbert (1800-1880)

1 Elizabeth (b. 1802)
4 Charles (b. 1805)
2 Henrietta Mary (1807-1828)
3 Maria (1807-1860)
4 Frances (1808-1886)
5 Augustus Frederick (1813-1844)
6 William (1817-1817)

1802: 29 Aug: *Heard an excellent Sermon to promote the Sunday School Charity from Mr. Hemming.*
1803: 14 Aug., 28 Aug.

HENDERSON — Mrs Henderson, daughter of Mrs Matthews at Malvern
1834: 12 Sep: *At tea the Miss Witts's, and, afterwards, their brother joined us. Mrs. Matthews returned from passing an hour or two with her daughters, Mrs. Henderson and Mrs. Fane.*

HENDERSON — Mr Henderson of Rylstone, Yorkshire
1850: 5 Jul: *A letter from Mr. Henderson, the successor of Mr. Waddilove at Rylstone, and now resident there, requesting the same privilege of preserving the game over the Scale House property, which Mr. Waddilove had enjoyed by our permission.* 6 Jul.

HENDY — Abel Dottin Hendy[142]
Abel Dottin Hendy (1782-1808), Church of England clergyman, was born at Barbados, third son of eleven children born to Dr James Hendy (d. 1794), physician to the naval hospital at Barbados and physician general to the island's militia, and Lucy Alleyne (1758-1815), of Barbados, who died at Bath. He was educated at Oriel College, Oxford (BA 1803; MA 1806), and was ordained deacon on 4 May 1807. Although he died young, he published *Three sermons on practical subjects: together with an essay on the utility of classical learning in subserviency to theological studies* (1808).

1802: 17 May: *To the Schools, where were the Examinations for Honours. Hendy of Oriel & Marriott of Christ Church the only Candidates; of whom the former by far surpassed the latter.* 18 May: *To the Schools where Hendy & Marriott were reexamined.*

HENNEY — Thomas Henney[143]
Thomas Henney (1782-1851), solicitor and JP, was born at Sudbury, Staffordshire, son of Henry and Elizabeth Henney. By 1810 he had opened a circulating library in High Street, Cheltenham, near the Plough Hotel. He was also a property developer, and in 1818 he established Sherborne Spa with Samuel Harward. Due to fall in the water table the building was dismantled and reconstructed on a site further down the Promenade, now occupied by Royscott House. Henney was primarily a Cheltenham solicitor and magistrate.
He married, at Cheltenham, 1808, Louisa Kerstine; they had at least 2 sons and 2 daughters:
1 Thomas Frederick (1810-1860)
2 William Henry (1813-1872)
1 Mary Anne (b. 1815)
2 Sarah Louise (1821-1906); married, at Leckhampton, 16 December 1841, Edmund Carrington

---

1840: 20 Oct: *The Cheltenham Mag. Messrs. Gyde, Henney, and Gale, made a strong effort to procure the appointment of one of their number conversant with house property there upon the County Rate Committee.*
1844: 30 Dec.
1845: 5 Mar., 15 Apr.
1848: 20 Mar.
1850: 14 Oct.

HENRI — servant hired in Dresden[144]
Little is known about Henri. He was hired by Agnes Witts in Dresden on 19 August 1800, and was presumably French in origin. He was hired to replace Frederick who left the family's service on 9 September 1800. He started work on around 2 September 1800, and on 21 September, his baggage was stolen while the family was *en route* to Copenhagen:

> A damp cloudy Morning, after a night of rain detain'd from setting out till near 11 tho all prepared to step into the Carriage at seven, by the misfortune of poor Henri's having had his Portmantua cut off from the Carriage in the night which of necessity occasion'd a great noise & confusion, of Town officers, searching many houses but to no purpose ...

Henri stayed with the family in Copenhagen and appears to have been evacuated with them. He remained with them in Scotland and England until at least July 1801. No further record of Henri exists after that date.

1800: 21 Sep: *The next Morning at Elsterwerda produced a disagreeable anxious scene shortly before we wished the Horses we discovered that the portmanteau with all our servants Goods were stolen: took every means, threats, promises, Amtmann, Stadtrichter visited many a hut and thus discovered a law of the Country: but all without effect.* 22 Sep: *Henry 6 Days reckoning from 1st 3: 0: 0.*
1802: 2 Jul: *We left Totteridge Park, this morning, to my great regret. I accompanied Miss Lee & my Mother in our friend's Post-chaise: my Father & Henri came by the Caterpillar.*

HENSMAN — John Hensman[145]
John Hensman (1780-1864), Church of England clergyman, was born at Bedford, son of Thomas and Anne Hensman. He was educated at Bedford Grammar School and Benet College and Corpus Christi College, Cambridge (BA 1801; MA 1804). He was ordained deacon on 12 June 1803 and priest on 24 July 1805. His first clerical appointment was as curate of Wraxall, Somerset, in 1803-09. He was then curate of Clifton in 1809-22 and Dowry chapel, Clifton, in 1822-30. Following that he was perpetual curate of Trinity, Clifton, in 1830-44, of Christ Church, Clifton, in 1844-47, and of Clifton in 1847-64. Finally he was canon of Bristol in 1858. Hensman was a noted evangelical divine. He married, 1808, Elizabeth Vaughan, sister of James Vaughan, rector of Wraxall; they had at least 1 daughter:
1 Harriet (b. 1809)

1833: 11 Apr: *In the Hotwell road there has been erected a large and handsome Chapel dedicated to the Holy Trinity, capable of containing 2000 persons. The minister, is Mr. Hensman, a very popular clergyman, was at one time the officiating & responsible Pastor of the Congregation at Clifton Church, during the absence of the incumbent, Mr. Taylor, a man of very indifferent character.* 21 Apr.

HERBERT — Frederick Herbert[146]
Frederick Herbert (1811-1878), attorney, was born at Elmbridge, Barnwood, Gloucester, son of Edward Wrenford Herbert (1786-1863) and Elizabeth Smith (1787-1844). In 1841 Frederick was listed in Northleach, practising as an attorney. He was articled, 1827, to Thomas Smith, presumably an uncle, in chancery for a

period of five years. He was gazetted in 1837. Therefore, it would seem that he was the relation of another attorney by the name of Herbert practising in the town.

Herbert married, at Charlton Kings, Gloucestershire, 8 October 1836, Sarah Skelton (b. 1813); they had at least 4 sons and 3 daughters:

1 Frederick (b. ±1835)
2 Sidney (b. ±1837)
1 Ellen Vernon (b. 1840)
3 Harry Hall (b. 1842)
2 Louisa I. (b. 1843)
4 Sydney D. (b. 1849)
3 Annie 1850-1926); died at Marrickville, New South Wales, Australia

In 1861 Herbert appears to have been resident at St Helier, Jersey.

1834: 5 Dec: *Otway having handed to me yesterday a letter he had received from Mr. Herbert, the Attorney at Northleach, requesting him to recommend a proper person from the London police establishment to be employed as a police officer for the district of Northleach and five adjacent parishes, I wrote to Mr. Herbert to intimate that the Committee superintending the Stow Association would disapprove of their officer undertaking such a responsibility.* 29 Dec: *Received a letter from Mr. Herbert of Northleach, enclosing one from Mr. Mayne, Commr. of Police; Mr. H. informs me that, after a correspondence with the Commissioners, a man has been sent down recommended by the Commrs., but who has not been in the police force. This man was the bearer of Mr. H.'s letter to me, and is a fine soldierlike person, late a Serjeant Major in the Dragoons.*

1835: 3 Jan., 16 Jan.

1837: 17 Mar.

1842: 30-31 Jan., 8-9 Feb., 18 Mar: *Called at Newmarch's offices, where only saw Clerks, G F N. being gone into Somersetshire, and Sewell to London; but heard what we were glad of, that Mr. Herbert has resigned his pretensions to the Clerkship of the Crickley Hill road trust.* 21 Mar: *Wrote to Mr. Herbert, Superintendent Registrar of the district of Northleach, to obtain information as to the population of Salperton.* 23 Mar., 25 Mar.

1845: 7 Jul: *Wrote to Mr. Price, Coln St. Dennis, requesting him to caution Herbert, the Union Clerk at Northleach, not to be behind hand with the payments to the County rates, as certain some day to be visited with the ten per Cent. penalty.*

HERBERT — Berther Vines Herbert and family, of Eyford — *see also* Lees [147]

Berther Vines Herbert (1787-1859), farmer, farmed 244 acres at Eyford. The family previously lived near Prestbury, where in 1833 a Berther Herbert was prosecuted for trespassing in pursuit of game. He married, at Cheltenham, 8 April 1821, Susan Hooker (1795-1841); they had at least 4 sons and 3 daughters:

1 Edward (b. 1823)
1 Susan Hooker (b. 1824); married, at Upper Slaughter, 11 March 1850, George Aynslie Lees; emigrated to Poland
2 Elizabeth (b. 1825)
2 Berther Kennedy (b. 1826); married, first, at Evenlode, Gloucestershire, 27 August 1862, Jane Kibble; secondly, at St Andrew's, Bordesley, Warwickshire, 25 September 1880, Elizabeth Cooper
3 Frances (±1827-1852)
3 William (1829-1881)
4 Andrew (b. 1831)

1850: 11 Mar: *Miss Herbert, daughter of an Eyford tenant, was married to-day to G. A. Lees; formerly farming bailiff to Mrs. Dolphin, and, since, holding the like situation at Cirencester Agricultural College.*

1852: 27 Apr: *Miss Herbert, daughter of the late Eyford tenant, now come to occupy the farm lately held by W. Dix—the poor girl is fast declining in a consumption; has been wasting away for six months at Eyford, and I was never aware of her being at home, or informed of her malady.* 1 May, 5 May, 7 May, 11 May, 15 May, 16 May: *Summoned in the evening to Miss Herbert's bedside, believed to be closely approaching her end—administered the Holy Communion to her, and her father—An interesting scene—the poor girl, ready to depart, amiable, gentle, in full possession of her faculties, but exceedingly feeble.* 17 May: *In the evening Mrs. Joseph Collett called upon me to announce the decease of poor Miss Herbert, which had just occurred.* 19 May, 23 May: *After evening service the funeral of Fanny Herbert.* 28 Oct: *Letter from the Commrs. Of Inland Revenue, in answer to mine addressed to them respecting the licence to Herbert for a Beerhouse,—not satisfactory.*

1853: 23 Mar: *Nominated James Cambray and Berther Herbert to be overseers of the poor.*

HERBERT — Richard Herbert [148]

Richard Herbert (±1769-1858), agricultural labourer, was born at Ampney Crucis, son of John and Anne Herbert. He married, at Turkdean, Gloucestershire, 11 October 1792, Anne Webb (1767-1858), born at Wyck Rissington; they had at least 1 son and 1 daughter:

1 John (b. 1795)
1 Kezia (1795-1860)

John and Kezia were both baptised 16 August 1795; whether they were twins, or one had been born earlier and they were baptised together, is not clear.

1850: 12 Jul: *... as to relief granted or offered to Richd. Herbert of Notgrove.* 26 Jul: *promised that R. Herbert's case should be again taken into consideration.* 24 Aug: *To Mr. Browne, in reply to a letter which I received from him by the post to-day, relating to relief refused to R Herbert of Notgrove; informed him that out-relief on a reduced scale was granted to him on the last Board-day.*

HERBERT — Thomas Herbert [149]

Thomas Herbert (±1811-1899), shoemaker, was born at Guiting Power. In 1851, Thomas was a widower living in Guiting Power with his son. By his first marriage he had 1 son:

1 Thomas (b. ±1845)

He married, secondly, Sarah (b. 1827); they had at least 2 sons:

1 George (1865-1936); married, at Northleach, January 1893, Fanny Claridge; 1 son and 1 daughter
2 Henry (b. ±1869); died unmarried

1844: 11 Jan: *the principal case brought before us being a charge of assault against T. Herbert, of Lower Guiting, for beating Constable Howell, on Dec. 25, and a charge against five others of being drunk and disorderly, aiding and abetting Herbert in such assault.*

HERDER — Johann Gottfried Herder [150]

Johann Gottfried Herder (1744-1803), philosopher and writer, was one of the most important intellectuals of the German classical period. He was a student of Kant and a pioneer of the German *Aufklärung* (Enlightenment). As a friend of Goethe he was appointed *generalsuperintendent* at Weimar, a distinguished protestant clerical position, ranked immediately below the duke. He was also a collector of folk songs, fairy tales, and legends, and gave considerable impetus to the *Sturm und Drang* romantic movement in German literature.

Johann Herder married Caroline; they had 3 sons and 1 daughter:

1 Siegmund August Wolfgang (1776-1838); born at Bückeburg; died at Dresden
2 Karl Emil Adelbert (1779-1857); born at Weimar; died at Regensburg
1 Luise Theodora Emilie (1781-1860); born at Weimar; married Gottfried Theodor Stichling
3 Emil Ernst Gottfried (1783-1855); born at Weimar; died at Erlangen

---

1798: 2 Sep: *The literary & useful Establishments here, and the College, founded by Duke William. Under the Inspection of Herder.*

HEREFORD — Lady Henrietta Charlotte Hereford — *see* Deveraux

HERRIES — John Charles Herries [151]

John Charles Herries (1778-1855), MP and president of the Board of Control, was the eldest son of Charles Herries, merchant, and Mary Ann Johnson. He was educated at Cheam School and Leipzig University. In 1798 he was appointed a junior clerk in the Treasury. By February 1801, Herries had become the private secretary of Nicholas Vansittart. Around this time he was instructed to draw up Pitt's counter-resolutions against Tierney's financial proposals. In 1810 Herries did much of the work for the budget presented by Spencer Perceval, who as prime minister appointed him secretary to the chancellor of the Irish exchequer.

Herries made his reputation by solving the problems of army supply in the Peninsular War, standing him in good stead when he entered parliament as MP for Harwich in 1823. He worked his way up in the Treasury, becoming secretary to the Treasury (1823-27), chancellor of the exchequer in Lord Goderich's government (1827-28), master of the Mint under the duke of Wellington (1828-30), president of the Board of Trade (1830), secretary at war under Sir Robert Peel (1834-35), and finally president of the Board of Control in Lord Derby's first government (1852).

It is interesting to note the extent to which Herries's early life coincided with that of the diarist—principally in the Leipzig and Vansittart connections. These connections would not have been lost on Francis Witts who had early ambitions for a diplomatic career.

1827: 7 Sep: *The great bone of contention has been the Chancellorship of the Exchequer, and the lovers of the good old ways will rejoice that his Majesty has conferred this important office on Mr. Herries, a gentleman every way suited to hold it.*

1828: 23 Jan: *Rt. Hon. J.C. Herries Master of the Mint.* 2 Jun.

1830: 6 Jun: *The bad health of Mr. V. Fitzgerald causes him to retire, & Mr. Herries in his stead is to be preside at the board of Trade.*

1834: 17 Dec: *The following ministerial appointments are announced ... Mr. Herries, Secretary at War.*

HERRIES — Robert Herries [152]

Sir Robert Herries (±1731-1815), banker, was the eldest son of William Herries of Halldykes in Dryfesdale, Dumfriesshire, and his first wife, Catherine Henderson. He had two brothers, two half-brothers, and one half-sister. Herries began his banking career in Rotterdam at the instigation of his uncles Robert and Charles. His ability was noted by the Amsterdam bankers and traders Hope & Co., but in 1754 he set himself up in Barcelona as a brandy merchant. While visiting Edinburgh in 1761 Herries was persuaded by John Coutts to become a partner in the Coutts London commission house in Jeffrey's Square. This firm became Herries, Cochrane & Co. in 1762 after a sudden loss of Coutts family interests, caused partly by their attention to the new Coutts Bank in the Strand. Robert fell out with the Coutts brothers over control at Jeffrey's Square. In January 1766, with Cochrane removed, the firm was restyled Herries & Co., with the Coutts's Edinburgh house represented by William Forbes and James Hunter. In 1769 Herries set up the London Exchange Banking Company at 16 St James's Street. He was knighted in 1774, and the Exchange Bank became known as Sir Robert Herries & Co.

By 1793 Herries was married to Catherine Ross (1762-1808), daughter of Francis Fender Foote of Charlton Place, Bishopsbourne, Kent, and widow of Col Ross. Catherine was some thirty years younger than Robert Herries, but she predeceased him. They had no children. In 1798 Herries retired from his bank, which then became known as Herries, Farquhar & Co., but not from wider business. The bank, still at 16 St James's Street, was absorbed by Lloyds Bank in 1893. In 1793 Capt. Edward James Foote, Catherine's brother, married Nina, whom Herries described in his will as 'my natural daughter by Martha Scott'. Foote divorced Nina in 1803 and remarried immediately; in the process, Herries took virtual custody of Caroline Foote, one of his three grandchildren. It is presumably Caroline who is referred to in the diaries as 'Miss Herries'.

Sir Robert Herries was a Cheltenham acquaintance of Edward and Agnes Witts and he also handled some of their financial affairs.

1801: 27 Oct: *we saw in the morning Mr. Dela Bere & Mrs. Granville, Lady Herries & Miss Hughes.* 10 Jun: *called with my Father upon Messrs. Herries, Farquhar &c.* 30 Oct: *Sir Robt. & Lady Herries, Mr. and Mrs. Whitwell, Miss Herries & Miss Whitwell & Mr. Bedell drank tea with us.* 13 Nov: *In the evening late to a great Rout at Lady Herries, or perhaps Sir Robert's.* 14 Nov: *Mrs. & Miss Wyndham & Lady Herries called in the morning.* 11 Nov: *Dined at Miss Nevilles, where we also spent the Evening, meeting our kind Granville Friends, Mrs. Bedingfield, Lady & Miss Herries &c.*

1804: 15 Oct: *Dined with Mrs. Travell at Mr. Nocsley's a Lancashire Gentleman, met Mr. Delabere Sir R. & Lady & Miss Herries, & Mr. Berrington, with more of that family in the Evening.* 16-17 Oct.

1805: 6 Jul: *For an hour at a dull party at Lady Herries's, conversed chiefly with Miss Hunt, Martha Buxton, Fowlkes &c.* 7 Jul: *Dined a family party of ten at Mrs. Travells. Sir R. & Lady Herries & a Mrs. Williams joined the Party in the Evening.* 30 Jul: *Dined at my Aunts' meeting Miss Hughes & Miss Herries & Sir R. Herries.*

HERSCHEL — William Herschel [153]

William Herschel (1738-1822), musician and astronomer, came to England from his native Hanover to escape the French occupation of that city in 1757. He became a music teacher and later took up astronomy, discovering the planet Uranus in 1781. He became the private astronomer to George III. He moved to Slough in April 1786 to be near to the royal family, who took great interest in his discoveries. The Miss Herschel mentioned in the diaries was William's sister, Caroline Lucretia Herschel (1750-1848). She was also a distinguished astronomer and, apart from assisting her brother, made many important discoveries of her own. Although remembered primarily as an astronomer, Herschel played an important role as a violinist, organist, concert manager, and composer. He was frequently at Bath, and lived there at one point. He married, 8 May 1788, Mary Pitt, the widow of his friend and neighbour John Pitt who had died in 1786; they had 1 son:

1 John Frederick William (1792-1871); created 1st baronet

1802: 6 Jan.

HERSCHELL — John Francis Israel [154]

John Francis Israel Herschell (±1821-1866), Church of England clergyman, was born in Germany and educated at Queen's College, Cambridge (BA 1840). He served as curate of Halesworth and chaplain to Wangford Union, Suffolk, in 1843-47, and curate of St Thomas's, Preston, Lancashire, in 1845-50. He was chaplain to the county gaol, Gloucester, in 1851-57, and then rector of Mainstone, Shropshire, in 1857-65. In 1861 Herschell was living in Bishop's Castle, Shropshire, with his wife, Margaret (b. ±1825), whom he had apparently met in Preston where she was born. They married in 1851 and had 1 son:

1 John Haydcock (b. ±1858)

1850: 7 Aug: *The Gentleman on whom our choice fell has the disadvantage of being born in Prussia of Jewish parents, with a very Jewish cast of countenance, but a perfect command of English, with a slight foreign tone. His name is Horschell; he, like his competitor last named, came from the diocese of Manchester with very high recommendations from the Bishop, and also from the Archbishop of Canterbury, under whose observation he had come, when he held the see of Chester.*

1852: 16 Mar: *I took the opportunity, in company with Mr. Herschall, the Chaplain, to visit John Hambidge, the parricide, who is said to express contrition for his bad conduct generally, and spoke in that strain to me; my observations to him were, of course, general, as I avoided any particularly reference to the horrid crime charged upon him.*

1853: 16 Mar: *Much and anxiously engaged in conferring with Mr. Herschell.* 30-31 Mar., 1 Apr., 5 Apr., 21 Apr., 20 Dec: *A letter from Mr. Herschell, Chaplain of our County Prison, informing me that he is about to offer himself as Candidate for another and more lucrative appointment, and requesting from me a testimonial in his favour.* 21 Dec.

HERVEY — John Rideout Harvey — *see* **Harvey**

HERVEY — William Hervey [155]

William Hervey (±1776-1863), landed proprietor, was born in the parish of St Sepulchre, Holborn, London, son of Samuel Harvey and his wife, Margaret (d. 1794). He lived at Broadwell Grove, Holwell, Oxfordshire, and was a landowner on a large scale with over 2,000 acres. He married, at Westminster, 1 September 1801, Dorothea Arabella Primrose (1779-1825); they had 1 daughter:

1 Hepzibah Happy (1811-1854); married, at Rollesby, Norfolk, 1 February 1831, John Shreeve (b. 1810); 9 sons and 2 daughters

---

1836: 30 Aug: *Capt. and Mrs. Evans, Mr. Harvey of Broadwell Grove, Mr. & Mrs. Goodlake with a party, with many others were among those whom I recognized.*

HESKETH — Charles Hesketh [156]

Charles Hesketh (1804-1876), Church of England clergyman, was born at Melling, Lancashire, a younger son of Robert and Maria Hesketh. He was educated at Trinity College, Oxford (BA 1827; MA 1830). Hesketh served as vicar of Poulton-le-Fylde, Lancashire, from 14 July 1828 to 6 October 1835, and concurrently was appointed perpetual curate of Bispham on 20 September 1831. He was then rector of North Meols, Lancashire, in 1835-76.

Hesketh married Anna Maria Alice (b. ±1808), born at Bath; they had 2 sons and 4 daughters:

1 Anna Maria Emily Fleetwood (b. 1829); born at Poulton-le-Fylde

1 Charles Fleetwood (b. 1830); born at Poulton-le-Fylde

2 Adelaide Fleetwood (b. 1831); born at Poulton-le-Fylde; married, at Manchester, 19 July 1866, John Paxton

3 Debonnaire Felixwood (b. 1833); born at Poulton-le-Fylde

2 Edward Fleetwood (b. 1834); born at Poulton-le-Fylde

4 Caroline Summer Fleetwood (b. ±1837); born at North Meols

1844: 9 Oct: *At ½ past 8 set out for Burford by the Isis, a coach going to Cheltenham, having for my fellow passengers three clergymen, who had been voting for Dr. Symons; one of whom was Mr. Hesketh, a brother of Sir Hesketh Fleetwood, a clergyman beneficed on the sea-coast of Lancashire, nephew of W. Lindow, a pleasant and estimable person.*

HESKETH-FLEETWOOD — Peter Hesketh-Fleetwood [157]

Sir Peter Hesketh-Fleetwood (1801-1866), MP and landed proprietor, was born at Wennington Hall, Lancaster, fifth son of Robert and Maria Hesketh and elder brother to Charles (*above*). He was descended through his paternal grandmother from the Fleetwood family who had owned the large Rossall estate in West Lancashire for over 200 years. His father Robert inherited the estate in 1819 on the death of his elder brother, Bold, and the family relocated to the manor house, Rossall Hall, on the Fylde coast. On Robert's death in 1824, the estate passed to Peter, his four elder brothers having predeceased him. By that time, the land extended from Heysham in the north to North Meols, near Southport, in the south, and encompassed most of the present-day Fylde peninsula. In 1831 Peter changed his name by royal licence to Peter Hesketh-Fleetwood. He served as high sheriff for Lancashire in 1830 and MP for Preston in 1832-47. He was created 1st baronet in 1838 and was responsible for the creation of the town of Fleetwood in Lancashire.

1844: 9 Oct: *At ½ past 8 set out for Burford by the Isis, a coach going to Cheltenham, having for my fellow passengers three clergymen, who had been voting for Dr. Symons; one of whom was Mr. Hesketh, a brother of Sir Hesketh Fleetwood, a clergyman beneficed on the sea-coast of Lancashire, nephew of W. Lindow, a pleasant and estimable person.*

HETLING — William Hetling at the Dowell's of Cote [158]

William Hetling (1773-1837), surgeon, was born at Bath, son of William Hetling and Eleanor Rishton. According to the account of a descendent, William (senior) had a colourful life:

> He pursued his adventurous and ruinous career of Surgeon, Distiller of Spirits [at Bath], absconder to Gretna Green with an heiress for his wife, finishing up with a seizure of the Distillery by the Excise and a Company of Light Infantry, a bankruptcy, a flight to Paris, and most probably a bloody end during the orgies of the Revolution, for when that was over Mr. William Hetling appeared to be over too, for nothing more was heard of him.

The Hetlings were of German extraction, and came to England in the train of the Georges from Hanover. William Hetling (junior) was indentured to Joseph Metford as an indoor apprentice, for which his father paid three hundred guineas. He went to Guy's and St Thomas's, and settled first at Chipping Sodbury. He came to Bristol around 1806, and resided at Colston Parade. That year, upon the death of the senior surgeon, Mr Godfrey Lowe, Hetling unsuccessfully applied for the post. The following year he had greater success: on 2 June 1807 he was elected surgeon at the Royal Bristol Infirmary. He was said to have been:

> ... a slight, thin man, not very free or communicative with his pupils; regular in his visits to the Infirmary, and he took a great deal of pains with his patients there.... He drove a close carriage and pair in his professional visits, but he sometimes walked to the Infirmary.

The physicians and surgeons were within easy call in case of emergency, and it was considered controversial when Hetling decided to move from Orchard Street to Clifton. Hetling resigned by a letter to the House Committee on 8 November 1837 and died three days later.

Hetling married, December 1794, Anne Brown, daughter of an ironmonger of Bridge Street, Bristol; they had at least 5 sons and 9 daughters:

1 Jane Rishton (1797-1867); died unmarried
2 Eleanora (b. 1798); died an infant
1 Thomas (1800-1873)
2 Henry Rishton (1801-1823)
3 Elizabeth Eleanor (1801-1887); died unmarried
4 Anne (b. 1802); died an infant
5 Harriet (1803-1815)
3 William (b. 1804); died an infant
4 William (b. 1806)
6 Anne (1806-1825)
7 Charlotte (1810-1896); died unmarried
8 Fanny (1811-1813); died an infant
5 George Hillhouse (b. 1812)
9 Mary (1813-1814); died an infant

1808: 29 Mar: *At Cote. Found my friend, very ill; Mr. & Mrs. Dowell, Mr. Hetling, Miss Webb & Mr. Jos. Hutchinson made the Evening's party, played Whist in the Evening.*

HEWITT — James Hewitt and the Hewitt family of Bristol — *see also* King *and* Leslie [159]

James Hewitt, 2nd Viscount Lifford (1750-1830), landed proprietor, was the eldest son of James Hewitt, 1st Viscount Lifford, and his first wife, Mary Rhys Williams. He was educated at Trinity College, Dublin, and Christ Church, Oxford. His second wife was Alicia Olives (d. 1845). James succeeded as 2nd Viscount Lifford in 1789.

The Hewitts of Bristol presumably refer to the family of Revd John Hewitt (1755-1804), who was educated at University College, Oxford (BA 1776), and Trinity College, Dublin (MA 1778). He was dean of Cloyne in 1779-1804 and married Jane Moore. Mrs King was Mary, née Hewitt (d. 1821), daughter of Revd John Hewitt and Jane Moore. She married, 1802, Lt-Col Sir Henry King, son of Robert King, 2nd earl of Kingston, and Caroline FitzGerald.

1804: 26 Dec: *Passed the Evening at Mrs. Hewatt's. Mrs. King a very pleasing young woman.*

1805: 4 Jan: *Passed a rational pleasant Evening of Conversation at Mrs. Hewitts': Lord & Lady Lifford very respectable, pleasing, persons: & Mrs. King as elegant & engaging as ever.* 3 Feb: *Walked from Bristol with Mr. Hewitt.* 13 Feb: *Walked with Capt. Manners, to Bristol, & with Mrs. Hewitt & Mrs. King.* 21 Feb: *Walked a little. Mrs. Hewitt & Mrs. King left us.*

HEWSON — Mr Hewson, clerk of the Fishmonger's Company [160]

David Some Hewson (1774-1851) and John Knee Hewson (1775-1842) were both wardens of the Fishmonger's Company and presumably brothers; one of them is likely to have been this clerk. They were nonconformists and were buried adjacent to each other at pieces 4000 and 4001 at Bunhill Fields Burial Ground, City Road. By coincidence, they both seem to have been associated with Broome Phillips Witts of Brunswick Square.

1832: 14 Jun: *As we passed through Maidenhead we called at the Sun Inn on a deputation of the Court of the Fishmonger's company, consisting of the Prime Warden, Mr. Mills, Mr. Hewson, a friend of Wellford's, a very worthy and amiable man, & the fat, bustling, important Clerk of this wealthy Company.*

HIBBERT — Mr Hibbert, manager of goods traffic, Oxford, Worcester, and Wolverhampton railway

1854: 24 Jun: *Mr. Hibbert, Manager of the Goods traffic; made such apologies as he could, and such promises as he thought would satisfy the complainers.*

HIBBERT — John Hibbert [161]

John Hibbert (1768-1855), JP and landed proprietor, was the second son of John Hibbert, of Jamaica, and Janet Gordon of Kingston, Jamaica. He was educated at Merchant Taylors', Eton College, and King's College, Cambridge (BA 1791; MA 1794). He married, 1800, Charlotte, daughter of Thomas Sumpter of Histon Hall, Cambridgeshire.

John Hibbert (junior) (1811-1888), barrister, was also educated at Eton and King's College, Cambridge (BA 1833; MA 1836). He was admitted to the Inner Temple in 1832, and called to the bar in 1836. He married, 1836, Charlotte Elizabeth, daughter of Lt-Gen. Charles Turner. They lived at Braywick Lodge, Maidenhead.

John Hibbert (senior) was chairman of Cookham Board of Guardians; he built a church for the poor of the Maidenhead and Cookham Union, and founded and endowed a ward in the Royal Windsor Infirmary. He was JP for Berkshire.

It is not known where the connection between Broome Phillips Witts and John Hibbert arose, but it may have been at Cookham in Berkshire that Broome had an interest in tidying the family estate of Amelia London Witts. John Hibbert, residing at nearby Bray, may also have had interests in Cookham. Broome Phillips Witts and John Hibbert were also the same age.

1830: 25 Jun: *To dinner at Mrs. Witts's, Brunswick Square—a party Messrs. Bailey, Hibbert, Bassevi, Jones, Misses Witts and Whitehouse.*

1842: 16 Mar: *An old Mr. Hibbert, whom I had met there before, a man of considerable wealth, as I apprehend, was one of the party, accompanied by his Son, a Barrister, and his Son's lady, a very agreeable, and conversible person.*

HICKES — Miss Hickes, a dinner guest of the Snow family

1801: 2 Jul: *Dinner at the Snows where we met with a hearty reception; & in the evening were joined by Mrs. Beavert, Miss Hickes, Mr. & Miss Webb, & Mr. T. Snow.*

HICKES — the Hickes family of Pedington Manor, Berkeley — *see also* Berkeley *and* Bloxsome [162]

As a general note, it appears that the Hickes/Hicks family in Gloucestershire were all related in varying degrees, descending from Baptist Hicks, 1st Viscount Campden (1551-1629), merchant and politician, who sat in the House of Commons between 1621 and 1628, when he was raised to the peerage as Viscount Campden. The name 'Baptist' persistently re-occurs in the family; whether this is from true descent or affectation has not been investigated. The Hickes of Berkeley, particularly of Pedington [Peddington] Manor Berkeley (between Berkeley and Stone), are the branch of the family most referred to in the diaries. As Thomas Dudley Fosbrooke wrote in 1821, 'the name has been indiscriminately by the family themselves spelt Hicks and Hickes'.

There are connections between Edward Jenner and the Berkeley family. The Hickes family were whigs; as associates or adherents of William Fitzhardinge Berkeley, 1st Baron Segrave, 1st Earl Fitzhardinge (1786-1857), this is hardly surprising. There was also a strong medical tradition in the family, primarily with John Heathfield Hickes.

Thomas Hickes of Pedington had at least 2 sons:

- 1 John Heathfield (1750-1808), surgeon, colleague of Edward Jenner; married, 1785, Jane Weston; at least 2 sons and 1 daughter:
  - 1 Weston (±1796-1864); *see below*
  - 1 Jane Weston (1799-1846)
  - 2 Thomas (1805-1887), road surveyor; married, at Truro, Cornwall, 1838, Grace Cox, née Blee (1812-1857); at least 4 sons:
    - 1 Thomas James (1840-1917)
    - 2 Edward (1841-1910)
    - 3 Frank (b. 1842)
    - 4 Weston (b. 1844)
- 2 Thomas (1758-1842); married Susannah [Suzannah] Elizabeth (d. 1847); at least 7 sons and 3 daughters:
  - 1 Frederick (1787-1844), Lt-Col, 2nd Bombay Grenadiers; died by cannon shot leading assault on Punella Hill Fort, Kolapore district, 27 November 1844. Married; 3 daughters and 7 sons, including the following 2 in India service:
    - 1 Frederick (1828-1856), Lt, 2nd Bombay European Light Infantry; died at Kurrachee, Lower Scinde, 20 October 1856
    - 2 Thomas William (1831-1857), Lt, 2nd Bombay Grenadiers, and A. Ajdt, 2nd Regt Scinde Irregular Horse; died at Jacobad, Upper Scinde, 28 October 1857
  - 2 Augustus Thomas (1789-1857)
  - 1 Harriet (b. 1790)
  - 2 Suzannah Elizabeth (b. 1792)
  - 3 Baptist William (1793-1871); *see below*
  - 4 Henry (b. 1795)
  - 5 John Cox (1797-1864); *see below*
  - 3 Caroline (b. 1801)
  - 6 Thomas (b. 1802); presumably died an infant
  - 7 Thomas (1806-1883); *see below*

HICKES — Baptist William Hickes [163]

Baptist William Hickes (1793-1871), wine and spirit merchant, fire office agent for Norwich Union, and cheese factor, was born at Stone, Gloucestershire, the third son of Thomas and Susanna Elizabeth Hickes (*above*). In 1841 the family lived at Long Street, Dursley; Hickes was then listed as a wine and cheese merchant. By 1851 the family lived at Woodmancote, Dursley, and Hickes was listed as 'Gentleman'. He appears to have been close to Edward Bloxsome. In 1831 a notice was posted convening a public meeting on 15 March at the Town Hall, Dursley, to consider the expediency of presenting an address to parliament approving the Reform Bill. The notice was signed by E. Bloxsome, B. W. Hickes, and E. Bloxsome (junior). Bloxsome and Hickes were both churchwardens of Dursley parish church in 1835.

Hickes married, at St Mary's, Lambeth, Surrey, 31 December 1817, Rachel (±1798-1850), daughter of Christopher Morgan; they had at least 1 son and 1 daughter:

- 1 William (b. 1818); born at Stone
- 1 Eliza (1820-1914); born at Stone; married, at Dursley, Gloucestershire, May 1852, Richard William Geldart (1821-1912); 1 son and 2 daughters

---

1845: 18 May: *one from Mr. Hickes of Dursley, a candidate for the Office of Auditor of the Poor Law district of Unions to which nearly all those in Gloucestershire appertain, written under the mistaken notion that the Stow Union will be comprized in that district:—and a letter from Mr. Bloxsome, recommending this Mr. Hickes.*

HICKES — John Hickes [164]

John Hickes was a servant boy serving the Witts family. The only diary entry which provides a clue is that of Agnes Witts on Tuesday 14 October 1806: 'Rain early in the Morning, very fine & pleasant at Noon, but hard rain in the afternoon still very busy attending the planting, & in exchange of servant Lads John Hickes leaving, & Henry Baker being his substitute.' There is no further helpful information to go on as Hickes was/is a common surname in the south Gloucestershire area.

1806: 5 Aug: Drove *John to Erchfont to make various arrangements.* 10 Aug: *Sent John back to Devizes with my horse & accepted of an invitation to a family dinner with the Jaques's.* 13 Aug: *Drove John to Erchfont, calling on Mrs. Jaques by the way.* 19 Aug: *Drove John over to Erchfont to arrange matters.* 21 Aug., 23 Aug., 25 Aug: ... *drove John over with me to Erchfont, where things were made tolerably comfortable for me.*

HICKES — Thomas Hickes [165]

Thomas Hickes (1806-1883), surgeon, was the youngest son of Thomas and Susanna Elizabeth Hickes (*above*). He lived at 4 Clarence Street, Gloucester, and was a surgeon at the Gloucester Infirmary. He married Mary Teresa; they had at least 1 son:

- 1 Thomas Harold Frederick (1845-1908); married Frances (b. ±1845), born at Plympton, Devon; at least 2 sons and 1 daughter:
  - 1 George (b. ±1873)
  - 1 Mary (b. ±1875)
  - 2 Thomas (b. ±1876)

In 1881 Thomas Hickes was a widower, at Cheddar, Somerset, staying with his son, daughter-in-law, and grandchildren.

1833: 10 Sep: *Letters from W. Howell to urge me to give my vote to Mr. Hicks at the election for Surgeons to the Infirmary at Gloucester, which I could not do, as I had sent my proxy yesterday in favour of Mr. Fletcher.*

1839: 21 Jun: *Recd. a circular from Mr. Hickes, a Surgeon at Gloucester, announcing the recent decease of Mr. Wilton, the excellent Surgeon of the County Gaol, and soliciting my vote and interest, as a Magistrate, that he may be appointed the Successor.* 2 Jul: *There were three candidates, Messrs. Hickes, A Wood, and Fletcher. The two latter seem to have neglected opportunities of rightly informing themselves, for they were uncertain whether the election would take place as on this occasion, and, therefore, had failed to collect their distant friends. Not so Mr. Hickes and his partizans: they had left no stone unturned, and consequently, he succeeded by a large majority.* 10 Jul.

HICKES — Weston Hicks [166]

Weston Hicks (±1796-1864), sub-inspector of factories, was born at Bristol, son of John Heathfield Hickes and Jane Weston. He lived at Washwell House, Cheltenham Road, Painswick. From 1824 he was a partner with John Cox of Oliver's Mill, Painswick, a cloth-making mill. He was listed as sub-inspector of factories in the 1861 census. He was unmarried.

1826: 26 Sep: *Mr. & Mrs. Hyett, from Painswick Lodge, Mr. Weston Hicks, Mr. Cother & Mr. Macleod dined there.*

1830: 20 Apr.

1834: 15 Aug.

1836: 13 Aug: *After breakfast, Mr. Weston Hicks called: he is appointed superintendant of Factories in Howell's district, who has now two subordinate officers under him, Messrs. Hicks & Webster.*

1838: 16 Oct: *Something of the matter had reached Howell thro' Weston Hicks, to whom it had been mentioned by Lord Segrave, and Howell, who is now on a Factory circuit, had desired Wintle to confer with me on the matter, the whole of which I explained to him.*

1839: 1 Jan.

1842: 6 Jan., 16 Oct: *But they had been written to, as also all other relations and connections to whom a communication was necessary, by Weston Hicks, whom I found domesticated at Prinknash, and whose services to his friend will be very valuable— Connected with him officially as Deputy Inspector of Factories, resident at Painswick, and luckily not absent on a Journey, he came on the spur of the moment, and will, in consultation with Emelyn Howell and myself, take the leading part in all the sad details of the week.* 18 Oct: *After breakfast, and an interview with poor Howell, whom I found tolerably composed, and after conferring with Emelyn and Mr. Hicks, I left Prinknash in my phaeton for Gloucester to attend the Quarter Sessions.* 19 Oct: *Hicks was absent at Stroud, and elsewhere, making arrangements with the Undertaker &c.* 20 Oct: *Walking with Howell Emelyn, William & Frederick, Hicks &c. on the Terrace in the forenoon.* 21 Oct: *Took a walk with Howell, Hicks, William & Fredk.* 22 Oct: *Good, kind, and useful, Weston Hicks continued with me to help to arrange all in the manner most likely to be satisfactory to the mourners, and to support the afflicted widower.* 13 Dec., 15 Dec.

1844: 4 Jan., 11 Apr., 13 Apr.

1853: 10 Jun: *To the family dinner party was added Mr. Weston Hicks, from Gloucestershire.*

HICKS — Henry Hicks — *see also* **Clifford, Phillimore, Purnell,** *and* **Sheppard** [167]

Henry Hicks (1757-1836), clothier of Eastington, JP, and landed proprietor, was born at Berkeley, probably the son of Nicholas Hicks. His introduction to the mill property at Eastington was probably through his brother-in-law, Nathanial Winchcombe II [later Clifford] of Frampton-on-Severn. Hicks initially leased Millend Mill in conjunction with Edward Sheppard of Uley for twenty-one years, and set about building up a substantial empire. By 1820, Hicks had been joined in the business by his two sons, James Phillimore and Henry Purnell Hicks; by this time 'H. Hicks & Sons' were adding steam engines to their three Eastington mills, and operating Bonds Mill, just over the boundary in Stonehouse parish. In 1822 they installed a 24-hp Boulton & Watt engine.

At about 1815 Hicks built 'The Leaze', now Eastington Park, to which he added a large park a short distance from his mill at Churchend. Along with this, he systematically bought up adjoining land until eventually he owned much of this area of the parish.

Hicks married, at Frampton-on-Severn, 2 November 1784, Charlotte Winchcombe (1762-1832), daughter of Nathaniel Winchcombe (1725-1766), and his second wife, Ann (1729-1791), whom he had married at Dursley, Gloucestershire, 19 June 1759. Ann was daughter of John Phillimore, of Dursley, and his wife, Elizabeth.

Nathaniel Winchcombe, a wealthy mercer, married, first, 7 June 1756, Ann Bell, ultimately the heiress to the Frampton Court estate. Ann died on 7 August 1757, leaving a son, Nathaniel Winchcombe II (±1757-1817), who inherited the family fortune and succeeded to Frampton Court. He assumed the name and arms of Clifford by royal licence in 1801.

Henry Hicks and Charlotte had at least 6 sons and 2 daughters:

1 Henry (b. & d. 1785)
2 John Phillimore (1788-1836); married Elizabeth, daughter of Humphrey Austin of Wotton-under-Edge; at least 4 daughters
1 Charlotte Winchcombe (1789-1835); married L'Estrange Southgate Austin; at least 2 sons and 3 daughters
3 Henry Purnell (1791-1862); married, first, at Aldenham, Hertfordshire, 20 August 1823, Marianne Barine Phillimore (1802-1847); secondly, at Kensington, Middlesex, 1851, Catherine
4 Charles Edward (b. 1796); died an infant
5 Purnell Thomas Baptist (1796-1825); married, at Ardingley, Sussex, 9 July 1822, Catherine Peyton (1796-1879)
6 Winchcomb Henry (1802-1824)
2 Ann Phillimore (b. 1805)

The connection with the Purnell family is interesting. Charlotte Hicks's half-brother, Nathaniel Winchcombe II, had married Mary Clifford Packer of Frampton Court, Frampton-on-Severn. In 1813, their daughter, Charlotte Anne, married Purnell Bransby Purnell (1791-1866). This does not explain how Henry Purnell Hicks was baptised with that name in 1791, so somewhere there is an earlier connection with the Purnell family of Dursley which has not yet been investigated; this, however, is beyond the scope of this work.

1823: 15 Jul., 21 Oct.

1824: 13 Jan., 31 Mar: *The hilarity of the evening was, however, exchanged for a strong feeling of gloom by a melancholy accident, which befel Mr. W. H. Hicks, son of H. Hicks of Eastington, an eminent clothier, and esteemed Magistrate, as he was setting out to ride home about nine o clock. Though he appeared quite sober, when he left the party, the outward air had the effect on a disordered stomach of making him very unsteady, & bewildered him, insomuch, that he was found on the Bristol road, a little beyond the Spa, fallen from his horse & almost dead. It appears, that he fell on his head, that a sharp stone in the road cut his temporal artery, & that he bled to death.... Winchcomb Hicks was unmarried, a young man of considerable expertness in commercial pursuits, & much beloved in his family.*

1827: 6 Jul., 12 Oct., 16 Oct.

1828: 15 Apr., 15 Jul., 14 Oct.

1829: 28 Apr.

1830: 12 Jan., 20 Apr.

1834: 12 Aug: *Conversed with the High Sheriff, Harry aller, his Brother and Chaplain, Robert; Sir W. Hicks, Mr. Hicks, Crawley and other Magistrates.* 15 Aug.

HICKS — Martha Hicks [168]

Martha Hicks (1714-1802) was born at Coberley, Gloucestershire, daughter of Revd John Browne, rector of Coberley, and Elizabeth Bourne. She married, 1739, Howe Hicks (1722-1801) of Witcombe. In her early portrait she was described as a 'little thing, with red lips and rounded shoulders and a trim waist'. Her granddaughter recalled that she 'had a beautiful complexion and lovely hands, pink inside like satin.' She was a self-possessed little lady in a white satin frock trimmed with blue, and with brown curls behind her ears.

On the death of his cousin John Baptist Hickes in 1792, Howe succeeded as 6th baronet. Howe died of a stroke in August 1801, and the event was described in detail:

> He was seventy-nine years old, and his temper had not mellowed with old age. The spring rains had burst a culvert under the road near the buildings of the Upper farm behind the church, and he rode out in the afternoon to see about it. The way the men were repairing it did not please him, and while he was saying so in forcible language, apoplexy intervened; he fell from his horse and was carried to the house across the orchards on a hurdle.

Martha continued to socialise until her own death soon after her husband's. She had recently turned 85 when she wrote the following:

> On Monday morning Mrs. Lawrence sent to enquire after me, and to say if I had no company, she wou'd come and dine with me on Tuesday, or any other day that I wou'd fix, so she came in a very friendly way yesterday, and desired I would return her visit in the same way, and very kindly wish'd that we might see each other often which was more than I expected as I think myself old and out of date.

Howe and Martha Hicks had at least 2 sons and 6 daughters:

1 Martha (1742-1826); married, at Great Witcombe, April 1766, John Pettat (1738-1811)
2 Mary (1743-1758)
3 Susannah Elizabeth (1746-1755)
4 Alice (1747-1769)
5 Anne (1749-1774)
6 Henrietta Howe (1752-1755)
1 William (1754-1834); succeeded as 7th baronet, 1801; *see below*
2 Michael (1760-1830); *see below*

1801: 7 Nov: *Lady Hickes & Mr. Delabere called in the morning, with the latter I waited upon Mr. Bedell.*

HICKS — William Hicks — *see also* Bramston [169]

Sir William Hicks, 7th baronet (1754-1834), landed proprietor, succeeded his father Sir Howe Hicks as 7th baronet in 1801. He married, first, 1784, Judith (d. 1787), third daughter and co-heir of Edward Whitcombe of Orleton, Worcestershire; they had 1 son:

1 Howe (1786-1787); died an infant

Hicks married secondly, 1793, Anne Rachel, eldest daughter of Thomas-Lobb Chute of The Vine, Hampshire; they had 1 daughter:

1 Ann-Rachael (1794-1885); married, 1816, Sir Lambert Cromie, 2nd baronet

---

1824: 18 May: *A cinerary Urn nearly entire was found near the same spot. It is on the side of the same road about four miles farther, at Whitcomb, on the property of Sir W. Hicks, that the remains of an extensive Roman Villa were found some years ago.*

1826: 11 Jul., 25 Sep.

1829: 1 Apr: *party assembled about six o clock at the Bell Inn to pay the Sheriff the compliment of dining with him, whom Among them were Sir B. W. Guise, M.P., Col. Webb, M.P., Sir W. Hicks, Mr. Hicks Beach.*

1832: 29 Mar: *The Company exceeded forty, and among others were present, the Duke of Beaufort, Lord Edward Somerset, Lord Sherborne, Hon. H. Moreton M.P. Sir B.W. Guise, M.P. & Sir W. Hicks, Bart.* 1 Apr.

1834: 12 Aug: *Conversed with the High Sheriff, Harry Waller, his Brother and Chaplain, Robert; Sir W. Hicks, Mr. Hicks, Crawley and other Magistrates.* 15 Aug: *The great attraction of the early part of the forenoon was the arrival of a procession from Cheltenham, headed by banners and emblems, with a band of musicians on a stage-coach.... the way being led by the Father of the successful Candidate, Sir Bethell Codrington, & his lady, followed by Sir William Hicks.*

HICKS — William Hicks [170]

William Hicks (1775-1866), JP and Church of England clergyman, was born in the parish of St James, Paddington, Middlesex, son of Thomas Hicks. He was educated at Peterhouse College, Cambridge (BA 1798; MA 1806). He was appointed rector of Little Braxted, Essex, in 1802, and vicar of Great Marlow, Buckinghamshire, in 1802. He later served as rector of Whittington, Gloucestershire, in 1811-66, and simultaneously as rector of Coberley in 1815-66.

Hicks married later in life, at Charlton King's, Cheltenham, 4 May 1833, Mary Grisdale (b. ±1804); they had 3 sons and 4 daughters:

1 William Grisdale (1834-1875)
2 George Grisdale (1836-1882)
1 Mary Elizabeth (b. 1838)
2 Augusta Louisa (1839-1899)
3 Harriet Anne (1841-1915)
3 Charles Philip Giffin (1846-1896)
4 Grace Emily (b. 1848)

1823: 24 Dec: *The funeral party consisted of Mr. Jervis & Mr. Davis, as officiating Clergy of the parish of Cheltenham, Mr. Hicks, Mr. Hill, & myself, as incumbents of the three livings of which Mrs. L. was Patroness.*

1826: 21 Jan: *I returned home to serve my churches. I rode by way of Crickley Hill. Near Cubberley, I noticed the new parsonage house, which my acquaintance Mr. Hicks, the Incumbent of that parish, and of Whittington is building there.*

1829: 14 Jul.

1832: 29 Mar.

1836: 10 Aug: *Of the neutrals two, W. L. Lawrence & Revd. W. Hicks were Conservatives; it seems, they had hastily all but pledged themselves to Mason, without sufficient consideration.*

1837: 7 Mar: *Those present at the discussion were the Chairman, the Archdeacon of Gloucester, Messrs. Baker, B. Baker, Martin, Purnell, Clifford, Newman, Curtis Hayward, Viner Ellis, Hicks, and Lawrence.* 8 Aug.

1838: 16 Oct.

1839: 9 Apr., 11 Apr.

1840: 30 Jun., 3 Jul., 23 Oct: *Attended the Court for an hour, and then left Gloucester for Cheltenham in a coach in which my brother Mag. Hicks was my travelling companion.*

1842: 12 Apr., 28 Jun., 30 Jun.
1843: 8 Oct: *Wrote to Mr. Hicks of Coberley.* 9 Oct.
1844: 2-3 Jan., 6-7 Mar., 9 Apr.
1845: 1 Jul.
1846: 10 Aug.
1848: 15 Apr: *From Revd. W. Hicks, Cubberley, a letter requesting me to find for him a house servant, one whom I recommended to him some years ago being on the point of leaving him.* 18-19 Apr., 22 Apr: *A letter from Mr. Hicks, that he has hired Rogers, the servant whom I had named to him.*

HICKS-BEACH — Michael Hicks-Beach [171]

Michael Hicks-Beach (1760-1830), JP, MP, and landed proprietor, was the second son of Sir Howe Hicks, 6th baronet, and Martha Browne (*above*). He was educated at Magdalen College, Oxford. Through his godfather, also named Michael Hicks, he came into a large inheritance, which included Beverstone Castle. At the time of his birth in 1760 his putative godfather made the following offer:

> I rejoice to hear of the safe Delivery of Mrs. Hicks and likewise of the additional son to your Family, and suppose he is made a Christian by this time, if not, if agreeable to yours and Mrs. Hicks Inclinations, Name Him Michael, and let somebody stand Sponsor for me.

By this somewhat random choice of an heir, an infant of four became a great landowner, exceeding his father and elder brother in wealth. Apparently Michael Hicks was also a 'well-made' man, unlike his brother William who was small, weak, unprepossessing, and afflicted by a stammer. Hicks was MP for Cirencester in 1794-1818, and high sheriff for Gloucestershire in 1791-92.

He married, 1779, Henrietta-Maria (d. 1837), only surviving daughter and heir of William Beach of Netheravon. Henrietta-Marie brought the considerable Beach wealth to the family, adding the estate of Netheravon in Wiltshire to Beverstone Castle and Williamstrip Park. Michael and Henrietta-Marie were both young—under twenty—when they married. Eleven years later in 1790, Michael took the surname and arms of Beach in addition to Hicks by royal sign manual.

Michael and Henrietta had at least 3 sons and 3 daughters:

1 Michael (1780-1815); *see below*
2 William (1783-1856); married, 1826, Jane Henrietta (d. 1831), daughter of John Browne of Salperton; *see below*
1 Anne (b. 1785)
2 Jane (b. 1786)
3 Charles Howe (b. 1786)
3 Jane Martha (1801-1882), pioneer photographer; married, 1848, Edward William St John

---

1806: 24 Oct: *After an early breakfast accompanied Compton upon horseback across the plain to Netheravon the seat of Mr. H. Beech M.P. for Cirencester, to be present at one of his Coarsing meetings. The House spacious & very pleasantly situated upon the edge of the plain. The stables and kennels in the highest perfection. Received very handsomely by Mr. Beech, his Son, Lady & Daughter.*
1807: 11 May.
1824: 13 Jan., 9 Jul: *Dr Price's dinner party—We met Mr. Hicks Beach of Williamstrip, formerly member of Parliament for Cirencester.*
1825: 18 Jul: *We dined at Mrs. Price's at Coln St. Dennis. There was a large party, but every body seemed languid and exhausted. We met Mr. Hicks Beach, his son W. Hicks Beach.*
1826: 10 Jan.
1827: 10 Jul.
1828: 15 Jan., 15 Jul.
1829: 13 Jan., 1 Apr: *party assembled about six o clock at the Bell Inn to pay the Sheriff the compliment of dining with him, whom Among them were Sir B. W. Guise, M.P., Col. Webb, M.P., Sir W. Hicks, Mr. Hicks Beach.* 2 Apr.

HICKS-BEACH — Michael Hicks Hicks-Beach [172]

Michael Hicks Hicks-Beach (1780-1815), landed proprietor, was the eldest son of Michael Hicks-Beach (*above*). He married, 1809, Caroline Jane (d. 1860), daughter of William Mount of Wasing Place, Berkshire; they had 2 sons and 1 daughter:

1 Michael (1809-1854); succeeded as 8th baronet; *see below*
2 William (1810-1844)
1 Caroline Jane (1812-1821)

1827: 7 Aug: *We dined and slept with our friends, the Browne's at Salperton. Mr. Browne has recently been much indisposed: his complaints have been of the same nature as mine, but less acute, and he is restored to tolerable health, but is incautious as to diet. Their three unmarried children, two daughters and a son are at home. Mrs. M. Hicks Beach and her two sons, fine lads, were staying at Salperton.* 21 Sep: *We dined at the Dolphins, meeting Mrs. Michael Hicks Beach, who is staying at Eyford.*
1838: 29 Sep: *We dined at Wyck Hill, meeting an old acquaintance, and very agreeable person, Mrs. Hicks Hicks Beach, who is on a visit to the Poles, also the Polsons and Billingsley.*

HICKS-BEACH — Michael Hicks Hicks-Beach [173]

Sir Michael Hicks Hicks-Beach, 8th baronet (1809-1854), MP and landed proprietor, was the eldest son of Michael Hicks Hicks-Beach (*above*). He succeeded his great-uncle William Hicks to become 8th baronet in 1834. He was MP for East Gloucestershire in 1854. He married, 1832, Harriett Vittoria (d. 1900), second daughter of John Stratton of Fathringhoe Lodge, Northamptonshire; they had at least 2 sons and 5 daughters:

1 Michael Edward (1837-1916); succeeded as 1st Earl St Aldwyn; married, at South Molton, Devon, 6 January 1864, Caroline Susan Elwes (1845-1865)
1 Caroline Julia (1840-1917)
2 William Frederick (1841-1923), JP and MP
2 Henrietta Maria (b. 1843); died an infant
3 Emily Georgiana Jane (b. 1845)
4 Alice Mary (b. 1847)
5 Henrietta Maria (b. 1849)

1829: 1 Apr: *party assembled about six o clock at the Bell Inn to pay the Sheriff the compliment of dining with him, whom Among them were Sir B. W. Guise, M.P., Col. Webb, M.P., Sir W. Hicks, Mr. Hicks Beach.*
1834: 15 Aug.
1835: 10 Jan: *The High Sheriff, H. Waller, opened the business of the day in a brief speech well delivered, and Sir Michael Hicks Beach offered himself to the meeting as the proposer of Mr. Codrington.* 13 Mar., 10 Apr.
1837: 23 Jun.
1838: 14 Aug.
1840: 1 Jul: *To the Court, where I attended until the County meeting was held which had been fixed for this day, to address the Queen and Prince Albert on occasion of their providential escape from assassination. The High Sheriff, Sir M. Hicks Beach, presided.*

1843: 16 Oct: *Recd. letters from Sir Michael H. Hicks Beach and Mr. Price, respecting the appointment of Vis. Mag. to N Leach House of Correction.* 17 Oct.

1844: 2 Jan: *During the day I was principally in intercourse with Lord Bathurst, Purnell, Curtis Hayward, Ricardo, George, W. Hartley, Viner, Wintle, Sir M. H. Beach, Hicks, Playne, Sampson, Archn. Onslow, R. Onslow, Corbett Holland, Goodrich, Howell, &c.* 31 Dec.

1845: 3 Jul., 7 Jul.

1846: 11 Aug., 20 Oct.

1847: 29 Jun.

1850: 1 Jan.

1851: 23 Jan., 18 Apr., 21 Apr., 26 Apr: *Received a friendly letter from Sir M. H. Hicks Beach in answer to mine of the 21st. Inst.*

1853: 4 Jan., 15 Mar., 8-9 Dec., 13 Dec., 14 Dec: *Drove to Wyck Hill to dinner, to meet Sir M. H. Hicks Beach, staying there.* 15 Dec., 26 Dec: *After some delay Sir Mich$^{l.}$ Hicks Beach came from Farmington, and proceeded on his canvass of the freeholders of the village ...*

HICKS-BEACH — William Hicks-Beach [174]

William Hicks-Beach (1783-1856), JP, MP, and landed proprietor, was the second son of Michael Hicks-Beach and his wife, Henrietta Marie. He was privately educated by Revd Sydney Smith in Edinburgh in 1800-03, and then at Christ Church, Oxford. He married, at Salperton, Gloucestershire, 1 February 1826, Jane Henrietta, daughter of John Brown of Salperton, Gloucestershire; they had 1 son and 2 daughters:

1 William Wither (1826-1901)
1 Mary Jane (1829-1903)
2 Henrietta Maria (b. 1835)

Hicks-Beach was MP for Malmesbury in 1812-27 and lieutenant-colonel of the North Gloucestershire Militia. He succeeded his cousin Charles Withers to the estate of Oakley Hall in Hampshire in 1832, and his mother to Keevil, Wiltshire, upon her death in 1837.

Sydney Smith said of his young pupil: 'He is, without exception, the very best and most gentlemanly young man I ever saw, and will be an ornament and comfort to his family.' He was apparently reserved, and this may account for his late marriage.

1825: 18 Oct: *I was appointed a Visiting Magistrate of the bridewell at Northleach; another gentleman was named, but the Court thought him inexperienced, and I was called on by a sort of general appeal to give my services in that capacity: I think it is about five years since I last resigned it. Mr. W.H. Beech is my present colleague, and will remain in the post till the Michas. Sessions 1826.*

1826: 6 Jan: *I met there the two Messrs. Beach, and Mr. C. Pitt. Mr. W.H. Beach is my colleague as visiting Magistrate. He is Lieutenant Colonel of one of the regiments of the Gloucester Militia, and second son of Mr. Beach of Williamstrip Park. His elder brother died some years since leaving a family. Mr. W. Beach is about to be united to Miss Browne, eldest daughter of our friends at Salperton, a very fine young woman, between whom and Mr. Lawrence there was some years since a prospect of an union, which went off after some negociation. William Beach is considerably older than the lady, but a very estimable man; the Beaches & Brownes are already nearly related. Mr. W. Beach is expected to succeed on the death of Mr. Bramstone, a relative, to a considerable landed property with a mansion in Hampshire; perhaps, also to his Mother's fortune in Wiltshire. Mr. Bramstone has given up his seat near Basingstoke to the intended bride & bridegroom.*

1829: 22 Sep., 23 Sep: *Among those immediately in my vicinity, and with whom I chiefly conversed during the concert and the ball, which followed upon it, were Col & Mrs. W. Hicks Beach, Mrs. Dolphin. Conolly, East, Mr. & Mrs. Howell, the Brownes, Dr. Cooke, Sir Edwin Stanhope, Jeaffreson, Croome &c.* 10 Oct: *dined and slept yesterday with our friends, the Browne's, at Salperton; We met a large party; Col. & Mrs. W. Hicks Beach.*

1834: 10 Oct.

1839: 11 Jun: *Very delightful weather. Rode to Salperton; called on the Brownes; saw all the family except Caroline, who is in Town. Mrs. Browne has been seriously ill, but is recovered. Met there Mr. and Mrs. Waller, from Farmington, she is convalescent: there were two Waller boys, and two sweet girls daughters of Col. Hicks Beach.*

1845: 29 Jan: *Mrs. Charles Pettat and Miss Browne called from Salperton: Col. Hicks Beach has lately promised to present Charles Pettat to the living of Ashe in Hants, and not far from his residence, now vacant by the decease of the late incumbent.*

1851: 30 Apr: *with a general feeling against Hopkinson, and much doubt as to the eligibility of Coucher Dent, it has been suggested that Col. Hicks Beach's son would be a proper person to be brought forward as a Protectionist Candidate. He is said to be a young man of good promise; he is connected with leading and respected Gloucestershire families; his Father has property in the County; and a large Estate in Hants.*

HIGFORD — *see* Parsons

HIGFORD BURR — *see* Burr

HIGGINS — Joseph Higgins [175]

Joseph Higgins (1823-1846), manservant, was born at Stow-on-the-Wold, son of John and Rachael Higgins. He was buried at Stanway by Edward Witts on 20 August 1846.

1846: 18 Aug: *A letter from E.F.W. all well at Stanway Vicarage, and our dear Sophy expecting her confinement on any day. Joseph Higgins, their late servant, whose last weeks had been passed in lodgings at a relations at Stanway, while rapidly declining by consumption, and who received much attention not only from son and his wife, but from Lord Wemyss's family while at Stanway, and from the villagers, by whom on account of his gentle and unoffending manners he was much beloved, departed this life two or three days ago.*

HIGGINSON — William Higginson [176]

William Higginson (1736-1816), Church of England clergyman, was born in the parish of St Giles-in-the-Fields, Holborn, Middlesex, son of William Higginson (1698-1775) and Sarah Stevenson (b. 1700). He was educated at University College, Oxford (BA 1759; MA 1762). He was ordained deacon on 1 June 1760 and priest on 7 March 1762. Higginson's first clerical appointment was as curate of Eltham, Kent, on 6 March 1762. He was a pluralist, becoming also vicar of Rowde, Wiltshire, from 18 September 1764, Corsham from 23 April 1765, and for a time, rector of Alvescot and vicar of Shilton. The latter two posts he appears to have relinquished to his son William Montagu.

He married, at Lacock, Wiltshire, 1 August 1764, Elizabeth Montagu (1745-1801); they had 4 sons and 1 daughter:

1 William Montagu (1766-1808)
2 James (b. 1768)
3 George (b. 1770)
4 Charles (b. 1771)
1 Arabella Montagu (b. 1781)

1806: 6 Aug: *At Erchfont, whither I rode; to arrange matters, thence through Cherrington & Patney to Dirchamstoke to call upon Mr. Mayo: called upon his Sister, him I met upon my return to Devizes, & was introduced to Mr. Higginson of Rowde.* 11 Aug: *Received a call from Mr. Higginson.*

1807: 18 Feb., 10 Aug.

HIGGS — Richard William Higgs [177]

Richard William Higgs (1815-1891), Church of England clergyman, was born at Chipping Sodbury, Gloucestershire, son of Richard and Harriet Higgs. He was educated at St John's College, Oxford (scholar and fellow 1831-35; BCL 1836; DCL 1841). He was classical tutor and librarian at King's College, London, in 1835-40, and appointed rector of Handborough, Oxfordshire, in 1854. Higgs married Catherine Day (1818-1904), daughter of Charles and Catherine Pope of Bristol; they had 2 sons and 1 daughter:

1 Kate Secretan (1856-1880)
1 Richard Philip Sainsbury (1857-1927); married, at Hardenhuish, Wiltshire, 15 April 1884, Ada Lucy Headley
2 Arthur Gerald (1858-1938); married, at Woodstock, Oxfordshire, 31 August 1898, Lucia Elizabeth Mona Hawkins

---

1854: 15 Apr: *Wrote to Dr. Higgs, Fellow of St. John's, Oxford, with an authority to attach my signature to a document now being circulated among members of Convocation.*

HIGGS — William Higgs [178]

William Higgs (1810-1890), baker and corn dealer, of 10 Barton Street, Gloucester, was born at Gloucester, son of William Higgs (1778-1865) and Elizabeth Stanger (1785-1880). William Higgs was an energetic reformer and the founder of Gloucester Choral Society. He began organising concerts in 1845 to promote the mechanics' institution, which was formally constituted in 1848. William Higgs also took a prominent part in an Evangelical Society for Young Men, established in 1839 by David Nasmith. The society had its own library. He married, at Upton St Leonards, Gloucestershire, 2 September 1835, Esther Ann Morris (1810-1834); they had 2 sons and 4 daughters:

1 John Stanger (b. & d. 1833)
1 Elizabeth (b. & d. 1834)
2 Franklin (1837-1922)
2 Emily Bowden (1838-1892)
3 Kate (1845-1925)
4 Ada Gertrude (1854-1916)

---

6 Jan: *At nine, Purnell, Bathurst, E.F.W. and myself with some others adjourned to the Shire Hall to attend a Choral Concert, arriving between the first and second part. There was a large audience, chiefly of the middle classes, professional persons, tradespeople &c.—and the performance was very creditable: perhaps 150 male & female Singers, with no other music than the occasional assistance of a piano, all under the management of one Higgs, a baker, who is a person of much musical talent, and rare powers of training and organizing, and keeping in order so large a body of musical amateurs of all ages from twelve or thirteen to five and thirty.*

HILDYARD — Horatio Samuel Hildyard [179]

Horatio Samuel Hildyard (1805-1886), Church of England clergyman, was born at Winestead, Yorkshire, fifth son of Revd William Hildyard. He was educated at Peterhouse College, Cambridge (BA 1829; MA 1832), and was a fellow there in 1831 and classical lecturer in 1836. Hildyard was ordained deacon on 17 June 1832 and priest on 8 June 1833. His first clerical appointment was as curate of Little Wilbraham, Cambridgeshire, in 1834-42, followed by rector of Loftus-in-Cleveland, Yorkshire, in 1842-86. He was also rural dean of Cleveland in 1850-80.

Hildyard married, at York, 12 June 1861, Octavia Richardson; they had at least 3 sons and 2 daughters:

1 Horatio Nelson (b. 1862)
1 Mary Louisa (b. 1863)
2 Octavia (b. 1864)
2 William Long (b. 1866)
3 Henry (b. 1868)

1832: 13 Mar: *A Mr. How, a Solicitor of Shrewsbury, with his lively and agreeable young wife, was also a guest at Mr. Wingfield's board; they were on a Tour, and on their return homeward. This gentleman is the confidential agent of my Shropshire connexion, Mr. Hunt of Boreatton, and appeared a sensible and well conducted person. A pupil of Mr. Wingfield, and a fellow of Brazennose, Mr. Hildyard, completed the party.*

HILHOUSE — Caroline Hilhouse and the Hilhouse family of Clifton — *see also* Allies [180]

Caroline Hilhouse (1781-1868) was born at Clifton, daughter of James Martin Hilhouse (1749-1822) and his wife, Mary (1755-1827), daughter of George Bush (1727-1801), West Indian merchant, and Mary Bright (1725-1787). She married, at Clifton, 16 March 1815, Revd Thomas William Allies (1785-1838); they had 1 son and 2 daughters:

1 Mary Ann (1817-1887)
1 George Hilhouse (b. & d. 1819)
2 Caroline Hilhouse (1821-1853)

The Hilhouse family of Bristol stemmed directly from Abraham Hilhouse of Artikelly, co. Derry. James Hilhouse I of Bristol (1680-1754) was the third son of Abraham. He married, 1718, at Londonderry, Mary [one other source says Rebecca] Lenox [Lennox]. They had at least 1 son, James Hilhouse II of Bristol (1721-1758). Father and son established a successful shipbuilding business in Bristol and built many ships for the Royal Navy.

There are conflicting accounts. Another source reports the following:

> James Martin's grandfather had come to Bristol from Northern Ireland. The grandfather was admitted into the liberties of the city in 1704 'for he married, Hester, daughter of John Hollister, a linen draper of that City and had taken Oath of Obedience and paid his four shillings and sixpence.' He made his way up in the world, and as generally happened with the richer men of the city, turned his attention to ship owning, joining the famous Merchant Venturers' Society, the guild which had already controlled Bristol shipping for well over a century. He became head of the Guild in 1730 when he was made Master. When he died in 1754 he left a fortune of £30,000.

This conflict apart, it seems that James Hilhouse II was sheriff of Bristol in 1756. He built Cornwallis House, Clifton. He married a Miss Martin, and they had at least 1 son, James Martin Hilhouse (1749-1822). This James married Mary [?]; they had at least 4 sons and 4 daughters:

1 George (1778-1848)
1 Marianne (b. 1780)
2 Caroline (1781-1868); *see above*
2 Martin (b. 1783)
3 Sarah (b. ±1785); died unmarried

3 Abraham (±1787-1867); served office of lord mayor of Bristol, 1822-23; lived at Sion Row, Clifton; married Phebe [Phoebe]
4 Robert (b. 1788)
4 Ellen (b. ±1794); married Mr Bush

The Hilhouses were wealthy merchants as well as shipbuilders, involved in the triangular trade, including the slave trade. The company at different times ran both the Albion and the Limekiln docks, located on opposite sides of the river close to where the SS *Great Britain* now lies. With the construction of the floating harbour in 1806, trade greatly increased. George continued to run the company after his father's death, for a time with his partner Charles Hill. The firm later became known as Hilhouse and Hill. George Hilhouse was the last active partner in Hilhouse and Hill, and he died in 1848. He had also taken an interest in the city's public affairs, having been alderman, mayor, sheriff, and chief magistrate at various times, as well as master of the Merchant Venturers' Society.

1803: 29 Dec: *A good deal of conversation with the hosts, hostesses etc, Caroline Hillhouse, Lieut. Prower Schol. of Wadham, & Capt. Becket of the Coldstream & his Brother a Barrister, who accompanied their sister & Lady Smith: both pleasant.*

1804: 28 Jan: *A most amusing Evening, during which I had much conversation with Dawkins, Smith, Hooke, Johnson, the Leyards, Hillhouses, Smiths etc. The latter formed a side table at almost Jovial Supper with Smith, Hook, Johnson & myself.*

HILL — Colonel Hill of Clifton

Nothing has been discovered about Col Hill, although he is likely to have been an HEIC army officer.

1804: 1 Oct: *To the play at Bristol in the Evening with my Mother, Lady Hunloke, Sue & Caroline Townsend & Col. Hill.* 2 Oct: *Called on the Townsends. Mr. Townsend, Col. Hill, & Miss Gregg called.*

HILL — Arthur Marcus Cecil Hill [181]

Arthur Marcus Cecil Hill, 3rd Baron Sandys (1798-1863), MP and landed proprietor, was MP for Newry in 1832-35 and Evesham in 1838-52. He served as comptroller of the household under Lord Melbourne in 1841, and under Lord John Russell in 1846-47. He was treasurer of the household under Russell in 1847-52. In 1860 he succeeded his elder brother as 3rd Baron Sandys. The following year he assumed by royal licence the surname of Sandys in lieu of Hill. He was known as Lord Marcus Hill until 1860.

1837: 25 Jul: *At Evesham the numbers were at two o cl. to day Borthwick, Conservative, 69, Rushout, Conservative, and Lord Marcus Hill, Whig, 66 each.*

HILL — Edward Grey Hill [182]

Edward Grey Hill (1796-1858), secretary to the infirmary, married Harriet Green (1806-1881); they had 2 sons and 4 daughters:

1 Harriet (b. 1826)
1 Edward Wakeman (1828-1883)
2 Robert (1833-1866)
2 Alice Grey (1836-1890)
3 Lucy Ann (1838-1924)
4 Susanna (b. 1840)

The family lived at Barnwood, where Edward is listed in the 1841 census as 'independent'. Edward Grey Hill became secretary to Gloucester Infirmary in the 1830s, but by 1849 he had been replaced by Charles Weaver.

1839: 19 Aug: *Wrote to Mr. Hill, the Secr. to the Infirmary to ascertain whether there would be a probability of his admission on Thursday next.* 21 Aug.

1840: 21 Apr.

1842: 17 Nov.

1844: 5 Jan: *I received a letter from M W. with an enclosure from Mr. E. G. Hill as to the poor little boy, who had died at the Infirmary.* 6 Jan: *Wrote to Mr. Hill, Secr. to the Gloucester Infirmary for information as to the appropriation of the clothes of little W. Phipps, lately deceased there.* 9 Jan., 29 Sep., 3 Oct: *Recd. a letter from Mr. Hill, Secretary to the Infirmary, Gloucester, in answer to my letter rece written on the 29th. Ult. stating that it is found necessary to amputate the foot of Robt. Clack of this parish, a patient in the Infirmary.* 5 Dec: *also from Mr. Hill, Secretary of the Gloucester Infirmary, addressed to the Chairman of our Union, desiring that a patient sent under the Union Subscription may be furnished with a pair of Shoes.* 6 Dec.

1845: 10 Jan., 14-15 Jan., 5-6 Mar., 24 Apr., 26 Apr.

HILL — James Hill, performer at Covent Garden and Holywell, Oxford [183]

James Hill (±1773-1817), singer and actor, was born at Kidderminster, Worcestershire. His father died when he was four and he was adopted and educated by his maternal uncle, Revd John Hale (±1706-1783), vicar of Albrighton, Shropshire. Upon the vicar's death, Hill was taken to another of his uncles in Wolverhampton; there, at sixteen, he was apprenticed to a painter. After a short visit to London, Hill went to Bristol, where he met William Dimond, manager of the theatres at Bristol and Bath. Although Dimond had no need for extra performers, Hill persuaded him to allow him to perform for a single night. This first performance was as Belville in the comic opera *Rosina* by Frances Brooke, either at Bath or Bristol. Hill so impressed Dimond on his début that he was awarded a five-year contract. With the recommendation of Ann Selina Storace, Hill studied under Mr Richards, the leader of the band at the Bath Theatre, and also under Xamenes, and finally with Venanzio Rauzzini.

After two years Hill was given permission to go to London and perform at Covent Garden for the 1798–9 season. His wage was £5 per week. His first performance in London was as Edwin in Leonard MacNally's comic opera *Robin Hood*; he went on to play more than twenty-five roles at Covent Garden over the next eight years, eventually securing a salary of £12 per week. Perhaps his most successful role was as the original Sir Edward in Thomas Knight's comic opera *The Turnpike Gate*, which was performed twenty-seven times in the 1799-1800 season. Hill's career in London finished at the end of the 1805-06 season, when he left Covent Garden following a 'fancied' injury to his pride. He was said to have gone to perform 'in the country'.

Although Hill never received great accolades as a performer, he was described as attractive, 'with a pleasing figure'. It is not known when or to whom Hill was married, but a Mr and Mrs Hill performed at Edinburgh in 1810-11; according to the *Biographical Dictionary of Actors*, James Hill was the same man who, with his wife, joined a company headed by W. Adamson in Jamaica in 1816. According to the same source, Hill took part in concerts there until his death at Mount Bay, Jamaica, on 27 June 1817.

1801: 13 Oct: *Hill in the Character of Artaxerxes was doleful except in the gentle strains of "In Infancy".*

1802: 8 Mar: *To the Music Room in the Evening, with Stevens, Evans &c. Mad. Mara, Welsh & Hill, Vicary &.*

HILL — John Hill [184]

John Hill (1786-1855), Church of England clergyman and vice-principal of St Edmund Hall, Oxford (1812-51), was born in London, son of John Hill. He was educated at St Edmund Hall, Oxford (BA 1809; MA 1812; BD 1844), and was rector of Wyke Regis, Dorset, in 1851-55. He married Sophia (1789-1849); they had at least 2 sons:

1 John (±1813-1827)
2 Henry (±1819-1837); drowned aged 18

1833: 12 Mar: *I dined with Mr. Riddle in the Hall, at Edmund Hall; the number of undergraduates now resident is small, not exceeding twelve or thirteen, well behaved and quiet youths. The class of students educated here is not of a high grade in society, and the tone of the society is supposed to be Calvinistic. Dr. Wilson, Bishop of Calcutta, was for some years the Vice Principal, and was succeeded by the present Vice Principal and Tutor, Mr. Hill, whose religious opinions are of the same tendency, perhaps, more Calvinistic than those of his predecessor.*

HILL — John Oakeley Hill [185]

John Oakeley Hill (±1803-1888), Church of England clergyman, was born at Knighton, Radnorshire, eldest son of Benjamin Hill and Sally Oakeley. He was educated at Christ Church, Oxford (BA 1824; MA 1827). Hill was ordained deacon on 6 August 1826 and priest on 10 June 1827. His first clerical appointment was as curate of Ullingswick with Little Cowarne, Herefordshire, from 6 August 1826. He was chaplain at Christ Church, Oxford, from 20 September 1827 to 19 March 1829, and headmaster of Monmouth Free Grammar School from 1829 to 1832. He was also appointed perpetual curate of Dorton, Devon, on 21 July 1829. Finally he was vicar of Bledington, Gloucestershire, in 1843-71, and rector of Little Rollright, Oxfordshire 1871-88.

Hill married, at Ascott, Oxfordshire, Anna Maria (b. ±1822); they had at least 1 son:

1 Percival Oakeley (b. ±1857)

1843: 26 Sep.

1844: 29 Aug: *Many of the clergy of the neighbouring parishes attended—Dean of Gloucester, Messrs. Wiggin, Ford, Hurd, Smith, Spring, Dolphin, Hippisley, Perkins, Twisleton, Oakley Hill, Underwood, Bowen, Pantin, and others.* 24 Sep.

1845: 25 Jun: *There were present Messrs. Aitkens, Barrow, Bowen, Biscoe, Carden, Griffin, O. Hill, Hippisley, T. Hill, Hellier, Pantin, Pole, Townsend, Underwood, Waller, Wiggin, and myself.*

1846: 24-25 Jun., 6 Aug: *To the Provident Bank, where I met Mr. O. Hill, and R. W. Hippisley.* 13 Aug., 20 Aug., 17 Sep., 29 Oct.

1847: 4 Feb., 7 Apr., 7 Jul., 5 Aug.

1848: 6 Jul: *Sat at the Justice Room with the Dean of Gloucester and R. Waller—Messrs. Polhill, W B Pole, and Oakley Hill were also present.*

1850: 5 Jul: *A letter from Mr. Oakely Hill, Bledington, bringing under my notice the case of poor Mrs. Perkins.* 6 Jul., 18 Jul., 3 Sep., 5 Sep., 18 Sep.

1853: 10 Feb: *the poor young woman is a daughter of a broken farmer, named Bagnell, a cousin of Mr. Hayward's of Stow, and a sister of the wife of Mr. O. Hill, the Vicar of Bledington.* 21 Feb: *Recd. a letter from R W Hippisley with copies of a correspondence between himself and Mr. O. Hill, as Chaplain of the Workhouse.* 24 Feb., 7 Mar., 10 Mar., 17 Mar., 19 Mar., 16 Apr: *Mr. Hill, the Workhouse Chaplain, also attended.*

1854: 10-11 Jun.

HILL — Richard Hill — *see* Richard Noel Hill

HILL — Rowland Hill [186]

Rowland Hill, 1st Viscount Hill (1772-1842), army officer, was born at Prees Hall, near Hawkstone and Shrewsbury, Shropshire, the second son and fourth of sixteen children of Sir John Hill, 3rd baronet (1740-1824), of Hawkstone, and Mary (d. 1806), daughter of Robert Chambre of Petton, Shropshire. In 1790 Sir John Hill arranged for Rowland's commission as an ensign in the 38th Foot, followed by leave to study at a military academy in Strasbourg. He was promoted to lieutenant early in 1791 and rose quickly, coming to the attention of Arthur Wellesley, later duke of Wellington, in 1805. Having distinguished himself in the Peninsular War, Hill was appointed by Wellesley in 1809 to a semi-independent command in the Portuguese region of Alentejo. On 22 February 1812, on Wellington's recommendation, Hill was made a KB. Hill was created Baron Hill of Almaraz and of Hawkstone on 17 May 1814, and granted a pension of £2,000 per annum. He was one of five generals to be honoured in this way following the Peninsular War. As he never married, Hill wanted his title and pension to pass to his nephew, and on 16 January 1816 he was granted a special remainder to the male heirs of his brother John. On his return to Shropshire he was fêted as a hero; he was honoured in Shrewsbury with a 133-foot-high memorial column, costing £6,000, inscribed with his victories. In 1828 Hill replaced Wellington, then prime minister, as commander-in-chief of the Army. At the request of William IV he abstained from voting on the Reform Bill. He continued to be influenced by Wellington, and attempted no fundamental reforms, although he did introduce reforms to reduce drunkenness in the ranks, to provide educational and recreational outlets for troops, and to curb some of the crueller forms of punishment such as flogging. In the late 1830s his health declined, and he resigned from his post on 9 August 1842. On 22 September he was created Viscount Hill with remainder to his nephew Sir Rowland Hill, Bt. He died at Hardwicke Grange on 10 December 1842.

1825: 16 Sep: *At the point, where the roads to these towns diverge, and at the extremity of the street, is one of the greatest ornaments of Shrewsbury, the column erected a few years since by public subscription of the Salopians, town & county joining in the grateful duty of doing honour to a distinguished military character, born in Shropshire, and sprung from one of its most respected families, Lord Hill.*

1828: 18 Feb: *The successor of the Duke of Wellington in the command of the army is appointed: the idea of putting the office in commission is abandoned; and Lord Hill is now the Commander of the forces. He was a distinguished chief in the Peninsular wars, where he was second in command to the Great Captain.*

1845: 10 Jul.

HILL — Thomas Stanley Hill [187]

Thomas Stanley Hill (1769-1837), landed proprietor, of Compton Scorpion, Warwickshire.

1842: 27 Jul., *A packet from Mr. Clark, Shipston on Stour, covering particulars, map, and conditions of sale of the late S. Hill's property at Compton Scorpion, and Great Risington.* 29 Apr., 3 May, 15 May: *A letter from H. D. Warter with particulars of his correspondence thus far with the Vendors of the property at Great Risington, late Stanley Hill's, which is very much what I expected: £17000 asked; £15000 suggested as nearer the mark, with a desire to know how little will be taken.* 28-30 Jun., 11 Jul., 29 Sep.,

HILL — Thomas Noel Hill — *see also* Wilson[188]

Thomas Noel Hill, 2nd Baron Berwick (1770-1832), landed proprietor, was the eldest son of Noel Hill, 1st Baron Berwick (1745-1794), and Anna Vernon. Hill married, at St Marylebone, Westminster, 8 February 1812, Sophia (1794-1875), one of the fifteen children of Swiss watch-maker John James Dubochet. Her infamous elder sister was Harriette Wilson (1786-1845).

1825: 17 Sep: *About two miles from Shrewsbury on the right was the residence of the Hon. & Revd. R. Hill: I believe, a parsonage: Belton is the name of the place. His brother's, Lord Berwick's, Seat at Attingham is on the opposite side of the Severn, near Atcham, on the Shiffnal road. His Lordship signalized himself by marrying a lady of easy virtue, one of the frail sisters of the frail and malignant chronicler Harriette Wilson.*

1826: 2 Aug: *We had a good view of Attingham Park, a deserted seat of Lord Berwick; the mansion is very extensive, and modern, but the appearance is that of a neglected place; the present peer had the indiscretion to marry his mistress, a Sophia Dubouchet, a sister of the notorious Harriette Wilson.*

HILL — Thomas Hill[189]

Thomas Hill (±1788-1875), Church of England clergyman, was educated at Trinity College, Cambridge (BA 1810; MA 1813; BD 1823). He was ordained deacon on 22 December 1811 and priest on 20 December 1812. Hill's first clerical appointment was as curate of Hungarton with Twyford and Thorpe Satchville, Leicestershire, from 22 December 1811. He next became vicar of Elmton with Cresswell, Derbyshire, from 11 February 1813 to 18 November 1822, and at the same time was stipendiary curate of Whitwell, Derbyshire, appointed 6 January 1814. Hill was a pluralist, becoming vicar of Badgeworth, Gloucestershire, from 20 December 1821 to 26 December 1835, and vicar of Chesterfield, Derbyshire, from 23 May 1822. He was also archdeacon of Derby, 1847-73; prebendary of Lichfield Cathedral, 1851-63; and perpetual curate of Hasland, Derbyshire, 1851-63.

1823: *Dr. Christie, a skilful and worthy physician of Cheltenham, a native of Scotland, and formerly a practitioner in the Island of Ceylon has been lucky enough to secure to himself the advowson of the living of Badgworth, which he intends for his eldest son, and it is now held by a Mr. Hill.* 24 Dec: *The funeral party consisted of Mr. Jervis & Mr. Davis, as officiating Clergy of the parish of Cheltenham, Mr. Hicks, Mr. Hill, & myself, as incumbents of the three livings of which Mrs. L. was Patroness.*

HILL — Thomas Hill[190]

Thomas Hill (1802-1861), Church of England clergyman, was born at Bromsberrow, near Dymock, Gloucestershire, son of Joseph and Mary Hill. He does not appear on the lists of either the Cambridge or Oxford alumni. He married Susanna (b. ±1802), born at Elkstone; they do not appear to have had any children. Hill was stipendiary curate of Hazleton and Notgrove from 25 June 1828, and on 3 February 1832 he also became curate of Compton Abdale. He held these appointments until at least 1852, and possibly longer. Thomas Hill was buried at Staunton, near Ledbury, on 25 January 1861. In in the 1861 census, Susanna is a widow living at the Rectory, Staunton (between Gloucester and Ledbury). The advowson was sold in 1861, either by Thomas Hill or his executors.

1838: 12 May: *Met Messrs. Whitmore Jones, Rawlinson, Bowen, Hill, Abr. Pole, Minett and others attending the fair.*

1844: 11 Oct: *The Dean of Gloucester, Messrs. Waller, Bowen, Perkins, Hill (Bledington) Pantin, Mangin, Wiggin, Aitkens, Barrow, Hill (Notgrove) Sadler, Hellier (Little Compton) Griffin, Underwood, W. B. Pole, and myself obeyed the summons, meeting at the Unicorn.* 5 Dec: *The following Clergymen held the pall—Messrs. Hurd, Ford, myself, Gibson, of Chedworth, Hill, Curate of Notgrove and Aston Blank, and Aston.*

1845: 26 Mar., 7 Apr: *I proceeded to Bourton Bridge, where I took up Mr. Ford, and drove with him through Aston Blank to Notgrove—roads bad—village has an air of desertion—the Curate, Mr. Hill, an estimable man, but with a slender income, and married to a farmer's widow, living in a treeless, gardenless, comfortless cottage, yet friendly and hospitable and giving us a good plain luncheon.* 25 Jun.

1846: 17 Jul.

1847: 7 Apr.

1848: 26 Apr., 7 Jun.

1852: 14 Apr: *Clergymen present were Messrs. Hippisley, Biscoe, Potter, Pantin, Wiggin, Royce, Allfree (Curate of Stow) Hill (Curate of Notgrove,) Clarke, Usher, Morrison, Talmage (Idbury) and myself.*

HILL — West Hill[191]

West Hill (±1742-1834), physician, was born in Wiltshire, son of William Hill (b. 1700) and Piercy West (1711-1804). He married, 1783, Eliza (b. 1760); they had at least 5 sons and 6 daughters:

1 Eliza (1783-1870); married, at St James's, Southbroom, Devizes, 7 September 1801, William Henry Awdry (1778-1847)
1 West Tertius (1785-1812)
2 Justly (b. 1786)
2 Arrabella (b. ±1787)
3 Clara (b. 1791)
3 John Hildebrand (b. 1793)
4 Betsy (b. 1795)
4 Henry (b. 1798)
5 Bernice (b. 1800)
6 Arabella (b. 1794)
5 Charles Thomas (1796-1877)

1807: 6 May: *Mr. Jones called in a post chaise to convey me to the Election Dinner at Devizes Mr. Smith & Mr. Estcourt being re-elected. Very pleasant & agreeably conversed with Mr. Long M.P. Estcourt, Revd. M. Wyatt, Tinker, Dr. Hill, Dr. Spalding &c.* 7 Jul: *Dr. Hill & his son called.* 10 Aug: *Drove my Mother to Devizes. Called on Mrs. Hill, & Miss Tylee.* 11 Aug: *Mrs. Poore, Mrs. Warrener & Miss Lancaster & Dr. & Mrs. Hill & their son Charles drank tea with us.* 26 Aug.

1808: 15 Jan: *called upon Mrs. Hill, & the other Tylee Family: conversed with the Miss Tylees, Charles Hill, &c.* 18 Feb: *Rode to Devizes. Conversed with Dr. Hill, Mr. Jaques, &c.* 7Mar: *Dr. Hill & his son Captn. Hill called: rode with the latter to Conock.* 11 Apr.

HILLIER — Revd Hillier present at the deanery meetings

This Revd Hillier is a mystery. The name is not mentioned among Oxford or Cambridge alumni, nor in other reference works. It is not helped that the diarist gave no initials or parish information.

1845: 26 Mar: *Of the Clergy of the Deanery there were present Revd. R. W. Ford (Rural Dean in the Chair) Messrs. Aitkens, Hill, Perkins, Biscoe, Hillier, Hodges, Todd, Hippisley, Underwood, Pantin, Barrow, Waller, Twisleton, Mangin, Griffin and myself.*

1847: 7 Apr: *These consisted of Messrs. Biscoe, Morrison, Townsend, Oakley Hill, Clarke, Dolphin, Hillier, Hill (Notgrove) Pantin, R Waller, Hunt (Curate of Great Risington) Williams (Curate of Oddington) Potter, F. E. Witts, Hutchinson (Batsford).* 7 Jul: *Then to the decanal meeting, at which the Rural Dean presided, and the following Clergymen were present—Messrs. Hutchinson, Jarratt, Mangin and Aston, not of the Deanery of Stow,—of the Deanery, R W Hippisley, Hunt, Sadler, Pantin, Hillier, Williams, Clarke, Wiggin, O. Hill, Morrison, Barrow, Turner, Biscoe, & myself.* 21 Sep: *Revd. Messrs. Ford, Wiggin, Biscoe, Williams, Hunt, Potter, Clarke, Morrison, Crompton, Hillier.*

1850: 18 Sep: *Confirmation L Ris.—Mrs. B, Miss Buller, niece of Mrs. C Pole;—Revd. Mr. Hillier.*

HILLIER — the Hillier family of Devizes — *see also* Wyatt *and* Goodman[192]

The Mrs Hillier in the diaries is Martha, née Boyes (1749-1825). She was the daughter of Revd Robert Boyes and, in 1782, became the second wife of George Hillier (1746-1794), the younger brother of Isaac Hillier. George was an eminent woollen draper in Devizes, and one of the leading citizens of the town.

George had taken for a first wife Elizabeth Periam (1744-1776); they had 3 daughters: Elizabeth (1771-1844), Sally (b. 1773), and Martha (1775-1844).

George and Martha had 1 son and 2 daughters:

1 Anne (±1784-1835), married Matthew Wyatt
2 Harriet (1785-1845)
1 George (±1790-1840), army officer; served in the Peninsular War and died a brigadier-general in Bengal

Harriot Hillier (1778-1825) (different to the Harriet above) was the daughter of Isaac Hillier (1740-1808) and Maria-Theresa Cam (1743-1783). Harriot was the younger sister of Francis Witts's favourite Clifton confidante, Elizabeth Carrick (née Hillier).

There are therefore two first cousins, both with the name Harriet/Harriot; it is not totally clear which is which in the diaries; although the presumption must be that most mentions refer to Martha's daughter.

1806: 18 Jul: *Left my cards with Mrs. Hillier & at Dr. Spaldings.* 20 Jul: *met by a Miss A. Taylor, other Company to Tea, particularly, Mrs. Hillier & her interesting Daughter nearly blind, Mrs. Carrick's cousin whom I conversed with for a long time.* 22 Jul: *To a rout at Dr. Spaldings: a large party, the Hostess more garrulous than ever; I principally conversed with Mr. Mayo & Miss H. Hillier, a very interesting creature ... Some bad music upon a worse instrument.* 25 Jul: *Passed the Evening pleasantly at Mrs. Hillier's meeting a Family party & Mr. Mayo.* 3-4 Aug., 7 Aug., 14 Aug., 22 Aug., 23 Aug: *Drank Tea & supped at Mr. J. Tylee's, walking with the party Miss Tylee, C. Tylee, Alfred Wyatt, Mrs. Hillier & Harriet, Mr. Maurice & Miss M. Gibbs. Very agreeable.* 25 Aug., 27 Aug: *Called upon my friends the Hilliers.* 4 Sep., 15 Sep., 24 Sep., 26 Sep: *called upon Mrs. Hillier, besides whom & Harriet we met Miss Gibbs.* 6 Oct: *Met & conversed with Mr. & Mrs. Tylee, Mrs. Hillier & Harriet &c.* 7 Oct., 8 Oct: *I conversed almost wholly with Harriet Hillier & felt grieved to part for perhaps a very long time from so interesting, sensible & unfortunate a young woman. Mrs. Hillier & her Daughter set out for Ireland upon Friday.*

1807: 7 Dec: *Saw & conversed with Mr. C. Tylee, his Brothers & Sisters, Mrs. & Miss Hillier, Miss Wyatts &c.* 10 Dec., 16 Dec., 18 Dec.

1808: 10 Feb: *Called on Mrs. Hillier & Harriet.* 15 Feb: *Rode to Devizes. Called upon Mrs. Hillier.* 18 Feb: *Rode to Devizes. called at Mrs. Hillier's, found her & Harriet, Susan Hughes & Mary Gibbs.* 14 Mar., 23 Mar: *Rode to Devizes. Called on Harriet Hillier & the Tylees.* 31 Mar: *Called for an instant on the Hillier's at Devizes.* 1 Apr., 11 Apr., 18 Apr., 29 Apr: *Called on Mrs. Tylee, sat with her & Harriet Hillier.*

HILLIGSBERG — Marie Louise Hilligsberg[193]

Marie Louise Hilligsberg (d. 1804). Marie Louise and her sister were dancers at the Paris Opera. They left France for England in 1792, and remained there for the rest of their lives.

1801: 2 Jun: *in the Ballet of Ken-jo & Tao, Mad. Hilligsberg & Mons. Laborie charmed me especially. The other principal dances Didelot, Madame Rose Didelot, Mad. Laborie were vastly fine, but the grace, the naiveté of Hilligsberg is surely inimitable.*

HINTON — Mrs Hinton, sister of the Miss Halls of Bourton-on-the-Water

1840: 15 Jul: *Drove M.W. to Bourton on the Water. Called on the Polsons, whom we found at home; also on the Misses Hall, with whom we found on a visit to them their sister, a Mrs. Hinton.*

HIPPISLEY — Henry Hippisley and the Hippisley family[194]

Henry Hippisley (1776-1838), Church of England clergyman and landed proprietor, was the son John Hippisley (1735-1822), rector of Stow-on-the-Wold, and Margaret Coxe (*below*). He was educated at Rugby School and Christ Church, Oxford (BA 1798; MA 1803). He was ordained deacon on 22 December 1799 and priest on 21 December 1801. He married, 1803, Anne Rollinson (1783-1855), daughter of Lock Rollinson and Mary Jones. Anne's sister, Martha, married John Walker Dolphin (1809-1859), vicar of Lower Slaughter. Anne's aunt was also named Martha (1741-1780). She married Ferdinando Tracy Travell (1740-1809), rector of Upper Slaughter and the diarist's maternal uncle. Lock Rollinson, of Chadlington, Oxfordshire, was a friend of Edward Witts back in the 1770s. They toured Ireland together in 1770-71 and went to France in 1774.

In 1804 Henry and Anne went to live at Lambourn Place, where all of their children were born; they had 3 sons and 8 daughters:

1 John (b. 1804)
1 Margaret (b. 1805)
2 Anne (b. 1807)
2 Henry (1808-1896); *see below*
3 Mary (b. 1809)
4 Frances (b. 1810)
5 Charlotte Martha (b. 1812)
6 Jane (b. 1814)
7 Emma Elizabeth (b. 1815)
3 Robert William (1818-1902); *see below*
8 Isabella Maria (b. 1820)

It is unknown how the friendship between Henry Hippisley and Richard Vavasour began, but they presumably met at Oxford where Richard Frederick Vavasour was admitted '*ad eundem*' in 1834, but he also may have been at Oxford after taking his degree at Trinity College, Dublin.

According to the will of his father, Henry was bequeathed the advowson of the church of Stow-on-the-Wold, the supervision of an almshouse, and premises in Lambourne, Sparsholt, Uffington, and East Garston (all in Berkshire) for a term of 1000 years. Through this bequest, and his friendship to Richard Vavasour, a happy combination arose.

1804: 30 Jul: *Mr. Hippisley called.* 12 Oct: *In the evening a formal freezing party at Lady E. Dundas's with good singing & harp playing by Mrs. Hippisley. Miss E. Elford, the Miss Dundasses, Foster & Davis.*

1823: 3 Apr: *I dined at Mr. Vavasour's, the Rector's of Stow, meeting his brother in law, Mr. M. Vavasour, Sir Henry & Lady Dryden, and Mr. H. Hippisley, of Lamborne Berks, the Son of my deceased venerable friend the late aged Rector of Stow.*

1829: 22 Sep.

1837: 16 Dec: *Mr. C. gives the painting; the expence of framing and fixing it and making the necessary alterations in the Chancel will be defrayed by Mr. Hippisley as Patron and Vavasour as Rector.*

1838: 4 Jun: *Recd. at Stow the information of the decease of Mr. Hippisley of Lambourne which had reached the Vavasours this morning, and had greatly shocked them, as it was wholly unexpected.* 13 Jun: *Mr. Vavasour did not join the Clerical party, his spirits being still much depressed by the recollection of the unexpected decease of his friend Mr. Hippisley.*

1843: 3 Nov: *Mr. John Dolphin and Mr. R W Hippisley called, the fomer being on a visit to the latter, probably with some reference to arrangements as to the Rectory of Stow, J.D. being co-executor with Henry Hippisley of the will of the late Henry Hippisley.*

1847: 16 Sep: *Mr. & Mrs. R W Hippisley, accompanied by his sister Jane.* 21 Sep.

1848: 7 Feb: *Drove to Stow with MW: called at the Rectory: saw Mr. and Mrs. Hippisley, & Miss Jane Hippisley.* 22 Feb.

HIPPISLEY — Henry Hippisley[195]

Henry Hippisley (1808-1896), JP, DL, and landed proprietor, was born at Lambourn, the second (but first surviving) son of Henry and Anne Hippisley (*above*). Like many in his family, he was educated at Rugby School and Exeter College, Oxford. He was a JP, DL, and high sheriff for Berkshire in 1840. Henry was the elder brother of Robert William Hippisley. Henry Hippisley inherited the family estates at Lambourn, living at Place Farm until the death of his mother, whereupon he took up residence in Lambourn Place.

He married, first, at St George's, Hanover Square, Westminster, 9 February 1839, Elizabeth Agnes Nelson (1815-1849); they had 1 son and 4 daughters:

1 Henry Nelson (1839-1894)
1 Catherine (b. 1841)
2 Agnes (b. 1845)
3 Eleanor Anne (b. 1848)
4 Beatrix (b. 1849)

Elizabeth died on 10 October 1849, just four weeks after giving birth to Beatrix, probably from complications at the birth. Hippisley married secondly, at Fulham, Middlesex, 8 May 1851, Elizabeth Mary (1817-1886), daughter of Laurence Sulivan (1783-1866), PC, deputy secretary at war, and niece of Prime Minister Henry John Temple, 3rd Viscount Palmerston. Henry and Elizabeth Mary had 2 sons and 2 daughters:

1 Emily Sulivan (1853-1889); married, 19 August 1873, Lt-Col Robert Harris Carnwath Dalzell, 11th earl of Carnwath (1847-1910)
1 Laurence Temple (1854-1892), Lt, RN; educated at St John's College, Cambridge; died unmarried
2 William Henry (1856-1908), Lt-Col; retired, 1902; married, at Wokingham, Berkshire, 16 September 1886, Flora Hargreaves
2 Gertrude Charlotte Elizabeth (b. ±1859); married, at St Martin-in-the-Fields, Westminster, 21 January 1888, Templer Lethbridge Down

---

1839: 16 Apr: *Called on Miss Rollinson, 18 Bennet Street, and passed half an hour agreeably: meeting her nephew, Mr. H. Hippisley, on a visit to her with his bride, a pleasing young person, daughter of a Berkshire clergyman, by name Nelson.* 18 Apr: *Also on Miss Rollinson, with whom I again found Mrs. H. Hippisley, and passed an hour very pleasantly.*

HIPPISLEY — John Hippisley[196]

John Hippisley (1735-1822), Church of England clergyman, was the son of Richard Hippisley (d. 1765) and Jane Edwards of Stow-on-the-Wold. He was educated at Balliol College, Oxford (BA 1756; MA 1759). John's father Richard had been bequeathed the advowson of Stow in 1756 by his cousin, Dorothy Norris, whose husband Edward Norris had been the previous rector and owner of the living.

John succeeded his father as rector of Stow in 1765, at which point he resigned the living of Cricket St Thomas, Somerset, where had been instituted as rector by his father in 1759. He married, 1769, his cousin Margaret (d. 1817), eldest daughter of John Hippisley Coxe and Mary Northleigh; they had 4 sons and 2 daughters:

1 Mary (b. 1770)
1 John William (b. & d. 1771)
2 John (b. 1772)
3 Richard (b. 1774)
4 Henry (b. 1776)
2 Frances Anne (1780-1847)

In 1795, on the death of Margaret's brother Henry Hippisley Coxe, John and Margaret inherited the Lambourn estate in Berkshire. John Hippisley was succeeded as rector by Richard Vavasour who held the living until 1844, when John's grandson, Robert William Hippisley, succeeded him.

1820: 10 Jan., 10 Feb., 3 Mar: *At dinner at Mr. Hippisley's I met among others Lord Northwick and his brother, the Rector of Burford in Shropshire.* 29 Jun: *I joined a musical party at Mr. Hippisley.* 5 Jul: *We passed the Evening at Mr. Hippisley's retreat: as he calls a Summer House situate in his plantation at the foot of Stow Hill. No wonder, that the more than Octagenerian Owner delights in these groves of his own plantation & rearing, laid out with simple and judicious taste: while the hospitality of himself and his amiable daughter makes all their acquaintances happy to visit them.*

1823: 3 Apr.

1826: 28 Jul: *We dined at Mr. Ford's: Meeting Mr. & Mrs. Vavasour & our old friend, Miss Hippisley.*

1827: 25 Jun: *We made calls at Stow on the Vavasours & Miss Hippisley, now their guest.*

1829: 12 Aug: *drank tea with Mrs. Vavasour: when I had the pleasure of meeting my old friend, Miss Hippisley, on a visit there.*

1832: 17 May: *This connection of the two parties by relationship and friendship with Lord Suffield has led to the intermarriage of Mr. Shirley and Catherine Dolphin, who are now making a tour of visits to their friends, ... with the Hippisleys, at Bath with Miss Rollinson.*

1834: 18 Sep: *Edward drove his Mother to Stow to call on Miss Hippisley at the Vavasours.* 19 Sep.

1836: 5 Sep: *Mrs. Vavasour and Miss Hippisley made a morning visit.*

1839: 16 Apr:

1838: 21 Sep: *Drove MW. to Stow; called on the Vavasours, and on Miss Hippisley, who is on a visit to them.*

1840: 12 Sep: *Called at the Rectory: received by Mrs. Vavasour; Miss Hippisley is on a visit there, whom I was glad to meet.* 15 Sep.

1847: 6 Jul: ... *a memorial painted window, by Wales of Newcastle, has been set up to record the death of Mrs. Frances Anne Hippisley, my old and worthy friend, Aunt of the present Rector.*

HIPPISLEY — Robert William Hippisley [197]

Robert William Hippisley (1818-1901), Church of England clergyman, was the third son of Henry and Anne Hippisley (*above*). He was educated at Rugby School and Exeter College, Oxford (BA 1841; MA 1845). He inherited the family property in Stow-on-the-Wold, although the advowson appears to have passed to Robert's elder brother Henry.

The fabric of Stow parish church had fallen into disrepair and Robert undertook the repairs at his own expense, but not without controversy. The restoration work was carried out in 1846-47 by John Loughborough Pearson. The two men built a rapport, for between 1856 and 1859 Pearson also built a grand Gothic mansion for Hippisley in Lower Swell called Quarwood.

One of Robert Hippisley's friends at Exeter College was Robert Raikes of Welton, Yorkshire. Hippisley married, at Welton with Melton, Yorkshire, 1 June 1841, Raikes's sister, Grace Louisa (1814-1892), daughter of Thomas Raikes and Elizabeth Armstrong; they had 2 sons and 5 daughters:

1 Grace Elizabeth Anne (b. 1844)
1 Robert Raikes (1846-1890); educated at Rugby School
2 Alice (b. 1848)
3 Gertrude (1849-1922)
2 William (1851-1922); married, at St Mary's, Plympton, Devon, Bertha Gertrude Radcliffe (1854-1922)
4 Constance (1853-1940)
5 Eva (b. 1854); married, at Stow-on-the-Wold, 16 January 1886, FitzRoy Frederick Charles Jones

Robert Hippisley's Tractarian views were unpopular and caused numerous disputes in Stow. Before Robert resigned in 1899, the townspeople had hanged his effigy.

1840: 20 Aug: *Called on the Vavasours at the Cottage, who communicated to me an approaching change in their position. Mr. W. Hippisley, youngest Son of the late H. Hippisley, and at whose option it was under family arrangements to call on Mr. V. to resign the Rectory of Stow, when he was should be in Priest's orders, but as to whom there was reason to expect that it would not be his interest to avail himself of that power, has intimated to Mr. V. that he has entered into such arrangements with his brothers, besides an engagement for an early marriage, that it is his design to take the Rectory of Stow, about next Midsummer twelvemonth. In the meantime he has arranged to become Curate to Mr. Vavasour, for a year from next Midsummer, about which time he expects to be ordained Deacon, and is to inhabit the Rectory house, putting it into repair; with a view to these arrangements the Vavasours purpose to withdraw from the Rectory at Michaelmas next to their Cottage.*

1842: 21 Jan: *to Vavasour, with a number of the British Magazine containing a bill for leasing Clerical lands, as proposed by the Bp. of London, that he might judge how far it fell in with a projected arrangement between himself and R W Hippisley.* 10 Feb: *Conferred with E.F.W. and Sophy on a new aggravation of the matters at issue between Vavasour and R W Hippisley, now brought to a sort of crisis.* 11 Feb: *Wrote a long and elaborate letter to Ford on the dispute between R W Hippisley and Vavasour, pointing out a course by which it is not improbable that matters can be set straight for the advantage of both parties, and while I decline undertaking the office of Mediator, suggesting to Ford what it seems to me he might do in the matter.* 12 Feb: *Also to Vavasour in reply to a note recd. by to day's post in which, in answer to mine to him of yesterday, he declares that he was quite unconscious of any thing having passed between R W Hippisley and himself, which could be construed as an interruption of friendly intercourse between them.* 13 Feb: *Wrote to Ford respecting the supposed variance between Hippisley and Vavasour.* 15-18 Feb., 22 Feb., 3 Mar: *Vavasour accompanied me half way home on my return—talking chiefly of the relation subsisting between him and R W Hippisley, and Ford's interference.* 5 Mar: *from Vavasour, requesting me to send him some documents which he has not seen arising out of Mr. Ford's late interference as to the matters in dispute between R W Hippisley, and himself.* 7 Mar: *A note from Vavasour, requesting me to send him a document relating to the matters at issue between him and R W Hippisley, which I had in my possession, and I forwarded it with a letter strongly urging him to maintain friendly relations, at least in appearance, with the young man, and to avoid blowing up embers of strife.* 10 Mar., 29 Apr: *Mr. R. W. Hippisley called while we were out on our drive.* 6 Jun: *Mr. R W Hippisley read prayers with a very good voice, and correctly: he was ordained, as Curate of Stow, on Trinity Sunday, and made a sad beginning on May 29. when, the Restoration Service being unusual, he became confused, and made many blunders.* 12 Jul: *Drove M W. to Stow; called at the Rectory on the Hippisleys and Miss Rollinson, now on a short visit to them, whom we saw.* 19 Jul: *Recd. a note from R W Hippisley, excusing himself from accepting our invitation to dinner for Wednesday in consequence of the death of the wife of his elder brother, John Hippisley, after childbirth.* 2 Aug., 8 Aug., 16 Aug., 31 Aug., 22 Sep., 27 Sep., 15 Nov: *Mr. R W Hippisley wrote to invite us to partake of luncheon at his house on the 23d. Inst. which is fixed for the performance of two services on occasion of the opening of the new Organ recently erected by subscription in the Church at Stow, on which occasions sermons are to be preached by the Revd. W. Villers, formerly Curate of Stow, and still borne in most favourable recollection by the parishioners.* 22 Dec.

1843: 10 Aug., 11 Aug: *It came yesterday; when it will be presented is doubtful; it was intended as a compliment on Mr. V's resignation of the Rectory of Stow to R. W. Hippisley: but it appears doubtful whether the latter will at present avail himself of that resignation, and present himself to the rectory, since by the family arrangements, and the will of his Father, it seems that he would be a loser in income by giving up an annuity to take the preferment.* 16 Aug., 19 Sep: *Mr. C. also consulted me as to the presentation of plate to Mr. Vavasour; it has hitherto been deferred, owing to the non fulfilment of the contingency in respect of which it was procured (see above Aug. 11.) it appearing now almost decided that R. W. Hippisley will not avail himself of Vavasour's proferred resignation to present himself to the Rectory of Stow.* 26 Sep., 27 Sep: *much conversation on the very awkward and unpleasant position in which both Mr. Vavasour and Mr. R. W. Hippisley are placed as to the benefice of Stow; the former still continuing to be Rector and the latter Curate; though the one is desirous to resign the preferment, and the other to present himself to it.* 27 Sep: *The impediment now arises from family disputes among the Hippisleys, as to the sense and effect of the will of the late Mr. Hippisley of Lambourne.* 29 Sep: *A note from Mr. Hippisley of Stow, in answer to mine to him respecting the parochial association to S.P.G. at Stow, which he will manage "as long as he remains there," alluding thus to the embarrassment he is under in respect of the benefice.* 30 Oct., 3 Nov: *Mr. John Dolphin and Mr. R W*

Hippisley called, the fomer being on a visit to the latter, probably with some reference to arrangements as to the Rectory of Stow, J.D. being co-executor with Henry Hippisley of the will of the late Henry Hippisley. 9 Nov: *Mr. Vavasour informed me that R W Hippisley has at last signified his intention to assume the Rectory of Stow, calling on Mr. V. to resign, which he will do on an early day: and this arrangement terminates any hope which Vavasour has entertained, sanctioned by repeated promises and pledges of RWH., of receiving during his life a pecuniary compensation for his loss in resigning the preferment, as to which it was certainly the wish and intention of the late Mr. Hippisley that he should continue to hold it for his life.* 13 Nov., 29 Nov., 21 Dec.

1844: 15-16 Feb., 29 Feb., 10 Apr: *I spent an hour, assessing Ludlow, conversing with R W Hippisley, who had arrived yesterday even. at the Deanery from Stow, to take the oaths on his institution to his living: he was accompanied to the Court by the Dean and Mr. Wiggen.* 17 Apr., 1 May: *Mrs. Hippisley and Mrs. Walters also, being young mothers and nurses, could give but little of their society in the drawing room, leaving the guests pretty much to entertain each other.* 18 May, 29-30 Aug., 15 Sep., 18 Sep., 24 Sep., 31 Oct.

1845: 7 Jan., 26 Mar: *At twelve Mr. Hippisley performed the afternoon service at the Church in presence of the assembled Clergy: who afterwards met at the National School room, where the first Decanal meeting was held.* 26 May, 17 Jun., 25 Jun., 27 Jun.

1846: 12-13 Jun., 20 Jun., 24 Jun., 27 Jun., 6 Aug., 18-19 Aug., 21 Aug: *Our dinner party went off well: our guests were Mr. Ford, Henry & Dulcy F., Mr. and Mrs. Morrison, Mr. Estcourt Clarke, Mr. Hippisley, Mr. Estcourt, and Mr. Barrow.* 3 Sep., 15 Sep., 21 Sep., 29 Sep., 5 Nov., 19 Nov., 26 Nov., 3 Dec., 10 Dec., 17 Dec., 24 Dec.

1847: 21 Jan., 28 Jan., 1 Apr., 7 Apr: *Owing to the present condition of the Church and Chancel at Stow, now in progress of being repewed, with extensive alterations and repairs, divine Service could not be performed; and, therefore, the Secretary, Mr. R W. Hippisley, read short prayers from the liturgy to the Clergy assembled in the School room.* 8 Apr: *Mr. Hippisley has not been re-elected; there is an unfavourable prejudice against him among the rate payers of Stow in certain quarters.* 26 Jun., 6-7 Jul., 19 Aug., 25-26 Aug., 16 Sep, 21 Sep., 25 Sep., 27 Sep., 7 Nov: ... *remonstrance to Mr. Hippisley, who has replied offensively, and a painful controversy is the result.* 8-9 Dec., 23 Dec.

1848: 7 Feb: *Drove to Stow with MW: called at the Rectory: saw Mr. and Mrs. Hippisley, & Miss Jane Hippisley: Mrs. H., lately confined, looked delicate.* 11 Feb, 14 Feb., 16 Feb., 18 Feb., 22 Feb., 14 Mar., 26-27 Apr., 14 May, 16 May: *It seems that Hippisley has tacitly admitted the justice of the complaints made by W. Vavasour as to the imperfect state of the roof of the chancel of Stow church; for workmen have been employed yesterday in nailing strips of wood over the interstices between the planks under the slates to shut out the air pouring through.* 16 May, 7 Jun., 20 Aug., 23-24 Aug., 16 Sep., 19-20 Sep., 26 Sep., 29 Sep.

1849: 20 Dec.

1850: 22-23 Jan., 31 Jan., 1 Feb., 23 Mar., 29 Apr., 4 May, 18 May, 30 May, 12 Jun., 8 Jul: *a sore correspondence between W B Pole and Hippisley on a question relating to the administration of baptism, in which the former, I am afraid, is wrong.* 12-13 Sep., 18-19 Sep., 24 Sep., 25 Sep: *A dinner party. My guests were Messrs. Ford, H. Ford, Chamberlayne, Vavasour, R Waller, Boggis and Hippisley.* 1 Oct., 24 Oct.

1851: 8 Feb., 10 Feb., 4 Apr., 10 Apr., 13 Apr., 18 Apr: *R W Hippisley called upon me for my advice as to the unpleasant position in which he stands relatively to the Bp. of Gloucester.* 23 Apr., 28 Apr: *Learnt, with regret, that great excitement prevails at Stow in consequence of R W Hippisley having made such disclosures to the Bishop of Jamaica respecting the character of Mr. Robinson, that his appointment as temporary Chaplain at Belize has been cancelled.* 30 Apr., 1 May, 5. May, 8 May: *Mr. Robinson left Stow to-day with his wife and her children, for Liverpool——thence to betake themselves by the first packet to the United States.... But a deep prejudice against the Rector, based on his dealing with Robinson, superadded to other causes of complaint, originating in his Tractarian tendencies and changes in the administration of the Church Services, is deeply rooted in the minds of many of his most influential parishioners.*

1852: 23 Feb., 19 Mar., 23 Mar., 2 Apr., 14 Apr., 17 May, 19-20 May, 25 May, 23 Oct., 26 Oct., 11 Nov., 2 Dec.

1853: 28 Jan., 18-19 Feb., 21 Feb: *The fact is, that RWH. is sore that Mr. Hill was elected & himself rejected.* 24-25 Feb., 3 Mar., 15 Mar., 17 Mar., 19 Mar., 21-22 Mar., 30 Mar., 24 May, 22 Jun., 10 Dec., 15 Dec.

1854: 2 Mar., 15 Mar., 23 Mar., 16 Apr., 19 Apr., 3-4 May, 24 Jun., 8 Jul.

HIRON — Samuel Hiron [198]

Samuel Hiron (1768-1845), surgeon, was born at Chipping Campden, son of John Hiron.

1853: 5 Apr: *Another interesting, but tedious, and painful trial was that of T. Cooper, charged with sending a letter demanding money with threats from Mr. Hirons, a surgeon of Campden.*

HITCH — Samuel Hitch [199]

Samuel Hitch (1800-1881), psychiatrist, was the fifth child of John and Betty Hitch. He qualified MRCS in 1822 having studied at St Bartholomew's and Paris.

The lunatic asylum in Horton Road, Gloucester, was opened in 1823, and Samuel Hitch was resident medical superintendent in 1828-45. He achieved considerable fame for his work. He was the principal founder of the Royal Medico-Psychological Association in 1841.

He severed his connection with the asylum in 1847 to open a private institution in Sandywell Park, Dowdeswell, near Cheltenham. His daughter Annie Elizabeth married F. S. Waller in 1845, and Hitch went into an architectural partnership with Thomas Fulljames the following year. Thomas Fulljames had been the architect of the Gloucester Lunatic Asylum and was also a friend of Hitch's. Between 1859 and 1861, Annie and her husband undertook the management of Sandywell Park Lunatic Asylum on behalf of Samuel Hitch, who was then living at Southwick Park, Tewkesbury. However, Hitch persistently overspent his income, and in 1864 the asylum had to be sold to meet his debts.

1828: 15 Jun: *I went to the Lunatic Asylum. A new resident Surgeon & Superintendent has recently been appointed, a Mr. Hitch, from Tewkesbury, in the place of an excellent officer, who recently resigned.*

1836: 16 Sep., 12 Dec.

1837: 14 Jul., 19 Jul., 1 Dec.

1838: 22 Jan.

1839: 7 Jun., 1 Jul: *At a late hour I accompanied Bathurst to the Lunatic Asylum, where we sat for sometime with Mr. Hitch, the skilful and humane Surgeon and Superintendent of the institution, conferring with him on several points of management relating to the Asylum.*

1842: 10 Mar: *Letters from Dr. Hitch of the Lunatic Asylum, Gloucester, to solicit my vote for his appointment as a Physician of the Gloucester Infirmary, in the room of Dr. Shute, who retires, as an individual subscriber, and as one of the Trustees of a Charity in this parish subscribing to the Infirmary.* 11-12 Mar., 18 Mar., 20-21 Mar., 30 Mar: *Wrote to Stokes that my vote for the Infirmary is promised to Dr. Hitch.* 15 Apr: *a circular from Dr. Hitch, announcing his retirement from the contest for the vacancy at the Infirmary occasioned by Dr. Shute's retirement.* 3 Sep., 6 Sep., 15 Sep.

1843: 15 Aug., 18-19 Aug., 18 Oct.

1844: 12 Jan., 23 Aug., 25-26 Aug.

1845: 4 Feb., 7-8 Feb., 10-11 Feb., 12 Mar., 2 Apr: *Dr. Hitch, the admirable resident Physician and Superintendent is much injured in health by his assiduous attention to the concerns of the Establishment, and presses for some relief.* 7 May.

1846: 25 Aug: *Dr. Hitch was allowed £300 per ann. to reside in Gloucester, but to be restricted from taking lunatic patients to reside under his care in his house: he was also bound to attend the Lunatic Asylum daily.* 31 Aug., 3 Sep.

HITCHCOCK — Miss Hitchcock

1807: 8 Feb: *Called upon Mrs. Jaques, with whom I found Miss Hitchcock.*

HITCHMAN — William Simkins Hitchman[200]

William Simkins Hitchman (1799-1881), wine merchant. The firm of Hitchman & Company was founded in 1796 by James Hitchman (1773-1830) in partnership with his brother, William Spence Hitchman, in West Street, Chipping Norton, where the Old Swan Inn formerly stood. James Hitchman had formerly been employed by Thomas Henry Kingdom who carried on business as wine merchant at the Bunch of Grapes. James married, 1796, Sarah Lock Simkins.

William Simkins Hitchman took over the business from his father, and in 1849 built the brewery and extensive malthouses in Albion Street. A supper was given on 6 April 1850 by W. S. Hitchman for sixty workmen, etc., employed in his newly erected brewery plant, which was then nearly completed. It was reported that 'they did ample justice to the good old English dishes of beef and plum pudding followed by a liberal supply of choice ale from the brewery which it was scarcely necessary to say was of excellent quality'. Hitchman was the first mayor of the borough after the corporation was formed following the Municipal Act of 1835. In addition to the business of brewer, maltster, and wine merchant, he had a farm at Chapel House, the Tally Ho Quarry at Blockley, a coal merchant's business, and was the lessee of the gas works. His mansion at Little Compton was named Kitebrook House.

1838: 26 May: *Wrote to Hitchman, Wine & Spirit Merchant at C Norton.*

1842: 14 Mar: *Mr. Hitchman, Wine and liquor merchant, Corn dealer &c at Chipping Norton, is building farm buildings, lodges, extensive hot walls &c on the road side near to Little Compton on an estate he has purchased, with the view, I suppose, of eventually erecting a mansion on the property.* 31 Dec.

1845: 6 Feb.

1847: 19 Dec.

1850: 11 Jan., 15 Jan., 25 Jun.

HOARE — Hoare's Bank[201]

C. Hoare & Company was founded in 1672 by Sir Richard Hoare. Following the early success of the bank, the foundations were consolidated by Henry Hoare II (1705-1785), known as Henry the Magnificent, who as well as being a renowned banker, was also a garden owner and designer; he laid out the gardens at Stourhead in Wiltshire, an estate bought by his father. Capability Brown, the renowned landscape gardener, carried out some of his earliest work there. Henry was succeeded by his nephew, Sir Richard Colt Hoare, 2nd baronet (1758-1838). Richard was the son of Sir Richard Hoare, 1st baronet, and his wife, Anne. He married, 1783, Hester, daughter of William Henry Lyttelton, 3rd Lord Lyttelton, baron of Frankley (1724-1808), and Mary Macartney. Hester was therefore first cousin to Thomas Lyttelton, 2nd Baron Lyttelton (the 'wicked' Lord Lyttelton), husband of Apphia, Lady Lyttelton, aunt to the diarist.

Sir Richard Colt Hoare was a fellow of the Royal Society, the Society of Antiquaries, and the Linnean Society. He succeeded to the title of 2nd Baronet Hoare, of Barn Elms, Surrey, in 1787. Richard's son, Henry Hoare (1784-1836), predeceased him and he was succeeded by his half-brother, Sir Henry Hugh Hoare (1762-1841), a partner in the bank. Henry came with his wife, Maria Acland to Stourhead, where he lived for the last three years of his life. He died in 1841, leaving Stourhead to his son, Sir Hugh Richard Hoare, 4th baronet (1787-1857).

1830: 23 Jun: *After we had passed Temple Bar, I went for a few minutes into my banker's, Messrs. Hoares, who still occupy their close, dark, dismal shop; but a more prominent edifice has been recently erected by them at the next door, into which the establishment is about to be removed, and which will be more suitable to the wealth of the firm, and the extensive range of their transactions.*

1833: 10 Sep.

1834: 23 Jul., 25 Jul., 31 Jul., 5-6 Aug., 8 Aug., 15 Nov., 27 Dec.

1835: 18 Jan., 12 Feb., 24 Apr., 3 May, 6 May, 13-15 May, 17 May, 20 May, 23 May, 10 Jun., 12 Jun.

1836: 27 Jul., 4 10 Aug., 14-15 Aug., 21 Aug., 20 Sep., 16 Nov., 12 Dec., 15 Dec.

1837: 25 Jan., 2 Feb., 7 Feb., 9 Feb., 14 Feb., 22 Mar., 29 Mar., 31 Mar., 8 May, 10 May, 21 May, 16 Aug., 19 Aug., 27 Aug., 2 Sep., 15 Sep., 17-20 Sep., 6 Oct., 8 Oct., 11 Oct., 21 Oct., 26 Oct., 7 Nov., 13 Nov., 23 Nov., 2 Dec., 4 Dec., 13-14 Dec., 16-18 Dec.

1838: 13 Jan., 22 Jan., 30 Jan., 13-14 Feb., 23-25 Feb., 23 May, 6 Jun., 8 Jun., 10 Jun., 16 Jun., 27 Jun., 30 Jun., 11-13 Jul., 15 Jul., 20-21 Jul., 24 Jul., 18 Aug., 13 Nov., 16 Nov., 21 Nov., 7 Dec., 9 Dec.

1839: 22 Jan., 24-24 Jan., 29 Jan., 5 Feb., 13-16 Feb., 19-21 Feb., 23-24 Feb., 27 Feb., 1-3 Mar., 18 Mar., 13 Jul., 20 Jul., 22-24 Jul., 7 Aug., 17 Aug., 5 Sep.

1840: 27 May, 25-27 Jun., 4 Jul., 7-9 Jul., 16-18 Jul., 24-25 Jul., 28 Jul., 12 Aug., 5-6 Nov., 8 Nov., 17 Nov., 21 Nov.

1842: 16-17 Jan., 20-21 Jan., 29 Jan., 3-7 Mar., 15 May, 8 Jul., 15 Jul., 19-21 Jul., 27 Jul., 9 Aug., 13 Aug., 20 Nov., 19-23 Dec.

1843: 14 Jan., 25 Jan., 14-15 Feb., 11 Sep., 18 Sep., 18 Nov., 5-6 Dec., 14-16 Dec., 19-20 Dec.

1844: 8 Jan., 16 Jan., 24-26 Jan., 28 Jan., 14 Feb., 14 Mar., 21 Mar., 19 May, 31 May, 2 Jun., 24 Jul., 29-31 Jul., 2-3 Sep., 8 Sep., 14 Sep., 17 Sep., 24 Oct., 31 Oct., 6 Nov., 17 Nov., 23 Dec.

1845: 2-3 Jan., 7-10 Jan., 18 Jan., 21 Jan., 24 Jan., 13 Mar., 9 May, 24 May, 31 May, 25 Aug.

1847: 1 Apr., 23-25 Apr., 25 May, 8-10 Jun., 9 Jul., 29 Sep., 1 Oct., 3 Oct., 5 Oct., 9 Oct., 1 Nov., 6 Nov., 23 Nov., 27 Nov., 3-5 Dec., 7 Dec., 10 Dec., 15-18 Dec., 24 Dec.

1848: 21-23 Jan., 26 Jan., 20 Feb., 4 Mar., 7 Mar., 25-26 Mar., 30 Mar., 11 Apr., 14 Apr., 30 May, 5 Jun., 8 Jun., 12-14 Jun., 22

Jun., 29-30 Jun., 8 Jul., 13 Jul., 20 Jul., 24 Jul., 27 Jul., 27 Sep., 30 Sep., 15 Oct., 19 Oct., 13-15 Nov.

1849: 18 Dec., 20-21 Dec., 25 Dec.

1850: 24-26 Jan., 29 Jan., 16 Feb., 19 Feb., 14-16 Mar., 26 Mar., 30 Mar., 4 Apr., 28 Apr., 13 May, 16 May, 1 Jun., 24 Jun., 3 Jul., 12 Jul., 24-26 Jul., 19 Aug., 12 Sep., 28-30 Sep., 4-6 Oct., 15 Oct., 24-26 Oct., 30 Oct., 1-2 Nov., 9 Nov., 12 Nov., 2 Dec., 8-10 Dec., 12-13 Dec., 18 Dec., 24-25 Dec.

1851: 16-18 Jan., 24 Jan., 30 Jan., 2 Feb., 21-23 Feb., 21-23 Mar., 14-16 Apr., 6-8 May, 15 Dec.

1852: 17 Jan., 21 Jan., 24 Jan., 29-31 Jan., 3 Feb., 28 Feb., 3 Mar., 26-28 Mar., 17-19 Apr., 8 May, 11 May, 9 Jun., 26-28 Oct., 3-5 Dec., 9-10 Dec., 14 Dec., 23-25 Dec., 29 Dec.

1853: 15 Jan., 18 Jan., 25 Jan., 9 Feb., 11-13 Feb., 13 Mar., 16 Mar., 26 Mar., 31 Mar., 2 Apr., 15 Apr., 24-26 May, 14 Jun., 18 Dec., 20-21 Dec., 25 Dec.

1854: 28 Jan., 3 Mar., 8 Mar., 25 Mar., 14 Apr., 28 Apr., 27 May, 28 Jun., 10 Jul., 26 Jul., 12 Aug.

HOARE — Samuel Hoare [202]

Samuel Hoare (1751-1825), banker, was a wealthy Quaker merchant and abolitionist born in Stoke Newington. He was one of the twelve founding members of the Society for the Abolition of the Slave Trade. He was a partner in the Bank of Hoare, Barnett & Company.

1820: 5 Jan: *Mr. Hoare the Banker of Lombard Street, a very intelligent and cheerful man is one of the little circle round Col. Barry's chair before breakfast.—I often enjoy mixing in the conversation.*

1825: 19 Jul: *I observe in the newspapers the death of Mr. Hoare, the head of the banking firm of Hoares, Barnett & Co. Lombard Street. This worthy and very intelligent old man had long banished the exterior of a Quaker, but was connected with all the opulent and leading members of the Society of Friends. I became acquainted with him at Bath, whither he resorted every winter. His conversation was full of anecdote; he was shrewd, discerning & fond of society. In early life he was distinguished as a leading abolitionist in the question of the slave trade, and was in latter life prominent in all public charities.*

1838: 13 Nov: *Wrote to Messrs. Hoare desiring them to pay to Barnett Hoare & Co. to be placed in the acct. of Lawrence and Newmarch with the Co. of Glouc. Bank at Cirencester the sum of £100, in further liquidation of what still remains due by me to those Attorneys on their bill of charges for business done chiefly in the prosecution of our claim to the property of the late Dr. H. Moorhouse.*

HOARE — Samuel Hoare [203]

Samuel Hoare III (1783-1847), banker, was the son of Samuel (*above*). He married Louisa Gurney (1784-1836), and thereby became brother-in-law of Elizabeth Fry (1780-1845). Samuel was a Quaker banker and chaired the Society for the Improvement of Prison Discipline.

1835: 5 May: *Wrote to Saml. Hoare Esqr., Chairman of the Committee of the Society for the improvement of Prison Discipline, in answer to a printed letter from him addressed to the Keeper of Northleach Bridewell.*

HOBBS — Henry Hobbs [204]

Henry Hobbs (b. ±1807), slater and plasterer, was born at Longborough, Gloucestershire. He married, at Bourton-on-the-Water, 28 February 1832, Jane Fletcher (1806-1879); they had 4 sons and 4 daughters:

1 Anne Mary (b. 1832)
2 Elizabeth (b. 1834)
1 George (1836-1910), plasterer; married Emma (b. ±1842), born at Marlborough, Wiltshire; lived at Chelsea, 1891
2 William (b. 1838), carpenter; married Emma; lived at Willesden, Middlesex
3 Emma (b. 1841)
4 Margaret Jane (b. 1845)
3 John (1848-1933), plasterer; married, 1875, Laura, born at Hoten, Suffolk; lived at Willesden, 1911
4 Sydney Charles (b. 1851); unmarried and lived with brother William at Willesden, 1881

After Jane Hobbs's death, Henry went to live with his son William at Willesden.

1853: 11 May: *A note from Mrs. Griffin, of Hyde Farm, Lessee of the Eyford Slate quarries as to 5500 slates with which I have been supplied, requesting me to retain in my hands for her the price which may be charged for them by H. Hobbs, of Bourton, the Slater, who ordered them on my account.*

HOBDELL — Henry Bashard Hobdell, goldsmith, of Oxford [205]

Henry Bashard Hobdell (1800-1849), goldsmith, was born in the parish of St Paul's Churchyard, London, son of Henry Hobdell, goldsmith. He married Emily Fisher (1808-1880), born at Oxford, and moved to Oxford; they had at least 2 sons and 7 daughters:

1 Emily (b. & d. 1830); born and died in parish of St Bride, Fleet Street, London
2 Emily Rachael (1832-1909); born at Oxford; died unmarried
3 Fanny (b. 1834)
4 Ann (b. 1835)
5 Eliza Mary (1837-1915); married, at Long Ashton, Somerset, 4 March 1862, Israel Maynard Froud
6 Selina (1839-1891); married, at St Mark, Notting Hill, Kensington, 31 December 1867, Thomas Kempson Gray
1 Alfred Fisher (1840-1841)
2 John Bashard (1842-1928), surveyor and auctioneer; married, at Woodstock, Oxfordshire, 9 April 1865, Sarah Evans (b. 1846); joined the freemasons' lodge at Oxford, 1875
7 Lucy (1844-1885); died unmarried

Following Henry's death, Emily continued trading at 128 High Street, Oxford, referring to herself as a silversmith.

1845: 20 Feb: *Also to Hobdell, a jeweller, of Oxford, of whom I bought, when there, a signet ring, which he had promised to send early in this week, but wh. has not yet arrived.* 21 Feb., 22 Feb: *Wrote to Hobdell, Oxford, that I had recd. the ring.*

HOBHOUSE — Henry Hobhouse [206]

Henry Hobhouse (1776-1854), archivist, lawyer, and civil servant, was born at Clifton, only son of Henry Hobhouse and Sarah Jenkyns of Hadspen House, Somerset. He was educated at Eton and Brasenose College, Oxford (BA 1797; MA 1799; DCL 1827). In 1801 he was called to the bar at the Middle Temple. He was solicitor to His Majesty's Customs from 1806 to 1812, and then became solicitor to the Treasury. He was appointed permanent under-secretary of state for the home department in 1817, and held that office until July 1827.

1829: 26 Feb: *Dr. Jenkins, Master of Balliol, who, probably, is prevented from supporting Inglis, by his intimacy with &*

relationship to the Right Hon. H. Hobhouse, for so many years undersecretary of the Home department, and, therefore, high in the confidence of Mr. Peel and the government.

HOBHOUSE — John Cam Hobhouse[207]

John Cam Hobhouse, 1st Baron Broughton (1786-1869), politician, was born at Redland, Bristol, the eldest child of Sir Benjamin Hobhouse, 1st baronet (1757-1831), politician and financier, and his first wife, Charlotte (d. 1791), daughter and heir of Samuel Cam of Chantry House, Bradford-on-Avon, Wiltshire. He was educated at Westminster School and at Trinity College, Cambridge. At Trinity he became friends with Lord Byron, and accompanied him on his journeys in Greece. In 1816 he was with Byron after the latter's separation from his wife, and contributed notes to the fourth canto of *Childe Harold*, which Byron dedicated to Hobhouse. He was a political radical, and wrote various pamphlets, for one of which he was imprisoned in Newgate in 1819. In 1820, he entered parliament, sitting for Westminster.

Hobhouse served under Lord Grey as secretary at war in 1832-33, as chief secretary for Ireland in 1833, and as first commissioner of woods and forests in 1834. He was president of the Board of Control under Lord Melbourne in 1835-41, and under Lord John Russell in 1846-52. He was made a privy counsellor in 1832 and created Baron Broughton in 1851.

Hobhouse married, 28 July 1828, Julia Tomlinson (1795-1835), daughter of George Hay, 7th marquess of Tweedale (1753-1804), and Hannah Charlotte Maitland (1762-1804); they had 3 daughters:

1 Julia (1829-1849); died of cholera
2 Charlotte (b. 1831)
3 Sophia (b. 1832)

1828: 12 Feb: *Mr. Hobhouse in the Commons moved that the thanks of the house should be given to Sir. E. Codrington and the officers and men under his command in the battle of Navarino, but withdrew his motion, after very able speeches by Messrs. Huskisson & Peel.*

1835: 7 Jan: *I was able to communicate the intelligence that, in all probability, Bristol would return two Conservatives, Sir. R. Vyvyan and Mr. Miles being at the head of the first day's poll, and far in advance of the coalesced yellow Candidates Col. Baillie and Sir J. C. Hobhouse.* 19 Apr.

HODGES — Richard Hodges[208]

Richard Hodges (±1784-1866), Church of England clergyman, was born at Woolhope, Herefordshire, son of Richard Hodges. He was educated at Brasenose College, Oxford (BA 1806; MA 1810). He was ordained deacon on 12 June 1808 and priest on 15 October 1809. His first clerical appointment was as curate of Pixley, Herefordshire, from 12 June 1808. He was then curate to his father at Fownhope with Woolhope, from 8 January 1813. He was made stipendiary curate of Eastington, Gloucestershire, on 3 January 1822, and nearby Stonehouse, Gloucestershire, on 22 June 1826. He became vicar of Little Barrington in 1841, where he remained until his death.

Hodges married Anne Mary; they had 3 sons and 6 daughters:

1 Mary Anne (b. 1811)
2 Caroline (b. 1813)
3 Elizabeth (b. 1815)
1 William (b. 1817)
4 Charlotte (b. 1820)
2 Richard (b. ±1821), barrister of the Middle Temple; succeeded father as vicar of Little Barrington
5 Ann Elizabeth Mary (b. ±1822); born at Frocester, Gloucestershire
6 Eliza Mary (b. 1823)
3 John (b. ±1826)

1844: 15 Sep: *A letter from Mr. Hodges, Little Barrington, in reply to a circular from me, intimating that he has become a subscriber to the Burford Distr. Comm. S.P.G. and, therefore, declines joining that at Stow.*

1845: 26 Mar.

1853: 24 May.

HODGKINS — pauper at the Stow Union Workhouse

1836: 22 Dec., 29 Dec.

HODGSON — John Hodgson[209]

John Hodgson (1795-1870), Church of England clergyman, was born in the parish of St George the Martyr, Southwark, Surrey, son of John Hodgson and Sarah, daughter of George Harris, 1st Baron Harris. He was educated at Trinity College, Cambridge (BA 1818; MA 1822). He was ordained deacon on 25 May 1816 and priest on 1 June 1817. His first clerical appointment was as curate of Tunstall with Hartlip, Kent, from 1818. He was perpetual curate of Oare in 1818-26, vicar of Kennington in 1821-35, vicar of Sittingbourne in 1826-35, and vicar of St Peter's-in-Thanet in 1835-57. Hodgson was rural dean of Westbere in 1852-56, and secretary to the Clergy Mutual Assurance Society in 1857-70. At the time of his death he was living at 3 Broad Sanctuary, Westminster.

1839: 12 Jan: *Having noticed in the Ecclesiastical Gazette an advertisement to incumbents by the Revd. Hodgson, Secr. to the Clergy Mutual Assurance Society ... I employed half an hour in supplying the information as to my Uncle and myself as past and present incumbents of this benefice.*

HODGSON — William Hodgson[210]

William Hodgson (1805-1873), Church of England clergyman, was born at Wakefield, Yorkshire, son of Robert and Rebecca Hodgson. He was educated at Queen's College, Oxford (BA 1826; MA 1829). In 1841 he was the priest in charge at Monkton Combe, Somerset, and he served as curate of St Peter's, Cheltenham, in 1845-66.

Hodgson married Cecilia (±1800-1873), born in Cornwall; they had 1 daughter:

1 Frances (b. 1833)

The family lived at North Cottage, North Place, Cheltenham.

1850: 3 May: *Finding that the keys are kept at an Infant Schoolroom not far distant, I repaired thither to procure them, and found a spacious building, and the work of teaching conducted by two mistresses—one of whom went in search of the keys, and returned with answer that Mr. Hodson would soon come with them. He proved to be the Minister of the Church, a very obliging, courteous person, and with him I visited this somewhat singular structure.*

HODSON — Charles Hodson, solicitor, of Pershore[211]

Charles Hodson was an attorney and solicitor at Pershore. He was originally in partnership with Obadiah Burgess Rogers, but this was dissolved by mutual consent on 1 September 1827. Shortly after, on 25 October 1827, an advertisement was published in the *Worcester Journal* saying that Mr Lees was to hold an auction for 'the whole of the substantial household furniture, crockery etc., belonging to Mr. Charles Hodson, at his Residence in Pershore, who leaving the County ...' etc. However, despite this departure from the county, in 1834 Roger Hall, of Great James Street, Bedford Row, was recorded as being assigned (presumably as an articled clerk) to Charles Hodson of Pershore, Worcestershire. This does not add up. Dates of birth or death have also proved to be elusive.

1823: 14 Mar: *The business proposed was to examine the Attorneys Bills ... which on a first view appeared exorbitant. The three Solicitors had been desired to produce their bill; one of them, Mr. Hodson of Pershore, refused to sign the bill produced by the two others, Mr. Phelps of Evesham, and Mr. Griffiths of Broadway, stating, that he considered some of the charges unreasonable.*

HODSON — John Johnston Hodson [212]

John Johnston Hodson (1790-1869), Church of England clergyman, was born at Wigan, Lancashire, son of James Hodson and Jane Johns[t]on. He was educated at St Mary Hall, Oxford (BA 1820; MA 1823), and served as rector of Yelvertoft, Northamptonshire, in 1828-69. His brother, James Alexander Hodson, was MP for Wigan in 1820-31.

1825: 17 Aug: *dined at Mrs. Rice's at Bourton on the water. Mr. & Mrs. Boudier accompanied by a gentleman of the name of Hodson, a clergyman, & brother of the present member for Wigan.*

HOFJÄGER — Anton Georg Hauptmann Hofjäger [213]

Anton Georg Hauptmann Hofjäger (1735-1803), architect and builder, was responsible for many of the buildings in classical Weimar, including Schiller's house.

1798: 2 Sep: *The Original Purpose of this building is for the accomodation of the States of the Duchy of Weimar which are astablished sembled every Year, tho' it is now the temporary dwelling of the Ducal Family, during the rebuilding of the Castle ... It was built by a man of the name of Hauptmann Hofjäger who besides this Edifice & the Theatre built several other Houses in the Town & Neighbourhood with little Elegance & less durability.*

1800: 17 Jan: *Concert at the Hofjägers. About 40 People present a young man of the name of Bubier playing extremely well on the Piano-Forte.*

HOGG — master of the brig *George and Mary*

1798: 5 Aug: *We embarked on board the George and Mary Merchant Brig, Captn. J. Hogg Master.* 7 Aug: *our Commodore hailing Captn. Hogg requested him to take in Tow the Bacchus, a very heavy Hulk.* 13 Aug: *After dining with the Captain on Board, we left the Vessel in a Shore Boat, and landed on a Place called the Foresaddle Back.*

HOLDEN — George Holden [214]

George Holden (1815-1842), Church of England clergyman, was born at Giggleswick, son of Robert and Ann Holden. He was educated at Giggleswick School and St John's College, Cambridge. He was perpetual curate at Maghull, Liverpool. He died at Nice on 24 July 1842.

1838: 11 Sep: *Mr. Christ. Geldard was also at home: and a Clergyman a friend of the family, the Revd. Geo. Holden, had arrived very unexpectedly on a visit, shortly before I came.*

HOLDERS — Miss Holders at Clifton

1804: 11 Jan: *The principal belles were Miss Tringhams, Miss Castle, Miss Holder's, Miss S. Gibbons &c. &c. I danced with most of these & on the whole was thoroughly amused.*

HOLDSHIP — Josiah Holdship [215]

Josiah Holdship (1770-1835), glover, was born at Worcester, son of Josiah Holdship (b. 1747) and grandson of Richard Holdship, glover, and his wife, Betty. They were all Quakers. Richard Holdship was a prominent man in Worcester trade and an early investor in the Worcester porcelain factory; in the partnership agreement dated from 4 June 1751, he is shown to have subscribed £562 10*s*. Josiah (junior) moved to Cheltenham, where he married Ann Wood (b. 1769), born at Maidstone, Kent; they had at least 1 son:

1 Edwin Henry (1815-1888)

In November 1819, Josiah Holdship, glover dealer and chapman, was declared bankrupt in *The London Gazette*. By 1830 he was listed at 'Spa', but not under any trade, living at 'Royal Wells'. In the 1851 census, Ann is listed as a widow aged 80, keeper of the meeting house. They were both buried in the Friend's Burial Grove Street cemetery, also known as Grove Street Burial Ground, Cheltenham.

1808: 29 Mar: *Set off between two & three for Bristol, the lower road, took up Holdship the Cheltenham Quaker Glover.*

HOLFORD — George Peter Holford [216]

George Peter Holford (1767-1839), MP and landed proprietor, was born in the parish of St Giles-in-the-Fields, Holborn, London, second son of Peter Holford (1719-1803), master in chancery, of Lincoln's Inn Fields, and Anne Nutt. He was educated at Harrow School and St John's College, Cambridge (BA 1788; MA 1791). He was admitted at Lincoln's Inn in 1788 and called to the bar in 1791. He served as MP for Bossiney, Cornwall, in 1803-6, Lostwithiel in 1807-12, Dungannon, Tyrone, in 1812-18, Hastings in 1818-20, and Queenborough, Kent, in 1820-26. He was secretary to the Board of Control in 1804-06 and 1807-10. He married, 1802, Anne Daniell of Lifford, Donegal; they had at least 3 sons and 3 daughters:

1 Mary Anne (b. 1804); born at Horsted-Keynes, Sussex
1 Robert Stayner (1808-1892); born at Westminster; *see below*
2 Anne Jane (1812-1879); born at Westminster; married, at Westonbirt, Gloucestershire, 6 August 1832, Robert Hale Blagden Hale (1807-1882), son of Robert Hale Blagden Hale and Theodosia Eleanor Bourke; at least 2 sons and 3 daughters
2 James (b. 1813); born at Westminster
3 Emily Elizabeth (1815-1871); born at Westonbirt; married, 26 February 1836, Sir George Joseph Palmer, 3rd Baronet Hudson (1811-1866), of Wanlip Hall, Leicestershire; 2 sons and 1 daughter
3 George Stewart (1818-1819); born at Westminster; died an infant

The Holfords had owned Westonbirt Manor since 1666 when a Holford married the heiress Sarah Crew; George Peter Holford inherited the estate from his father in 1803. George demolished the Elizabethan house in 1818 and built a new mansion in 1823.

Holford came from an extremely wealthy family; at the death of his brother Robert (1758-1838) the estates were said to be worth over £1 million. His professional career began at the bar, keeping chambers at Lincoln's Inn, while his parliamentary career commenced in 1803; Lord Liverpool thought highly of him and arranged his Dungannon seat in 1812. Holford was instrumental in proposing prison reform: he promoted a bill to abolish gaol fees and soon afterwards moved that the House reconsider the condition of prison hulks, for which he was successful. In February 1817 he presented an individual's petition for the abolition of capital punishment except for those convicted of murder. Holford's attention to the subjects of prison discipline and the reformation of juvenile offenders continued unabated. He retired from parliament in 1826.

Holford was one of Castlereagh's executors and also one of Liverpool's. He was frequently in Ireland, his wife's native country, but was not hopeful of good results from Catholic relief, nor did he have any faith in parliamentary reform. He followed his father in 1804 as governor of the New River Company.

1822: 15 Oct: *Among the leading Magistrates were the Duke of Beaufort, Mr. Holford, M.P. for Queenborough, a great authority on all matters relating to Prisons.*

1823: 14 Oct: *my colleagues are Mr. Holford M.P. Mr. Byles, Mr. T. Baker, Mr. Cheston, Mr. Goldney, Mr. C. Cranley.*

1824: 13 Jan.

1829: 22 Sep., 24 Sep.

1832: 29 Mar: *Of the Stewards Mr. Holford, Son of George Holford Esqr. of Weston Birt, an old and valiant valued acquaintance of mine, attended.*

HOLFORD — Margaret Holford[217]

Margaret Holford (1778-1852), novelist, was the eldest of four daughters of Allen Holford, of Davenham, Cheshire, and Margaret, daughter of William Wrench of Chester. Her mother was a poet, Minerva Press novelist, and playwright, and sufficiently prolific for her works to be repeatedly confused with those of her daughter. The younger Margaret's first published work, a lengthy metrical romance called *Wallace*, or, *The Fight of Falkirk* (1809), published anonymously, was a contemporary success in the wake of Walter Scott's *Marmion* (1808). She married, at South Kirkby, Yorkshire, 16 October 1826, Revd Septimus Hodson (1768-1833), Church of England clergyman and author; they had no known children.

1806: 21 Jan: *I contrived to reach a dance at Lady Teresa Dease's, before ten o clock, where I danced with a Miss Holford from Cheshire in obedience to Lady Teresa's Commands.* 25 Feb: *Conversed with the Salters, Ryan, Tyler, Gould & Gillibrand party, Robin, Miss Holford, the Poetess, the Roberts's &c.*

HOLFORD — Robert Stayner Holford[218]

Robert Stayner Holford (1808-1892), MP, JP, DL, and landed proprietor, was the only surviving son of George Peter Holford (1767-1839) and Anne Daniell (*above*). He was educated at Oriel College, Oxford (BA 1829), and served as high sheriff for Gloucestershire in 1843, and MP for East Gloucestershire in 1854-72.

In 1838 Holford inherited the fortune of his uncle, Robert (1758-1838), said to be worth over £1 million. He was a lover of art and literature and, with his inheritance, began collecting paintings and books for what was to become known as the 'Holford Collection'. He built Dorchester House in Park Lane, London, between 1851 and 1853, to accommodate his collection, employing Lewis Vulliamy as his architect.

Holford married, 1854, Mary Anne Lindsay (1829-1901), the daughter of Lt-Gen. James Lindsay; they had 1 son and 3 daughters:

1 Margaret (1855-1908); married, at St George's, Hanover Square, 17 June 1876, Albert Edmund Parker, 3rd earl of Morley (1843-1905); 3 sons and 1 daughter

2 Evelyn (b. 1857-1943); married, at St George's, Hanover Square, September 1887, Robert Henry Benson (1850-1929); 3 sons and 2 daughters

3 Alice (1858-1944); married, 1887, Albert Henry George Grey, 4th Earl Grey (1851-1917); 1 son and 4 daughters

1 George Lindsay (1860-1926), Lt-Col; knighted; married late, 1912, widow, Susannah Menzies, née Wilson (1865-1943); no children

Between 1863 and 1870 Robert Holford built the present Westonbirt House to display his many art treasures. He also developed extensive pleasure grounds and a huge arboretum for his collection of trees.

1829: 24 Sep: *and a new half dozen of Stewards are ready to take the field in 1832: the Hon. J. F. Mitford, son of Lord Redesdale, the eldest son of G. P. Holford Esqr. and the eldest son of Sir Bethel Codrington are the proposed Lay stewards.*

1832: 29 Mar: *Of the Stewards Mr. Holford, Son of George Holford Esqr. of Weston Birt, an old and valiant valued acquaintance of mine, attended.*

1838: 16 Oct.

1842: 4 Apr., 8 Apr.

1851: 23 Jan.

1852: 17 Mar: ... *to whom flocked in Messrs. Holford, Major Hale, W. Paul, arriving to be present at an appeal against an order of Trustees for the diverting of a turnpike road, near Tetbury, a thing in itself unexceptionable, but resisted by a misguided Clergyman, the incumbent of Weston Birt, on the plea that it was a job to gratify Mr. Holford at the expence of himself and the inhabitants of his village, who might be required thereby to travel less than a hundred yards further than by the old road.*

HOLLAND — 3rd Baron Holland — *see* Vassall-Fox

HOLLAND — Edward Holland[219]

Edward Holland (1806-1876), MP and landed proprietor, was a son of Swinton Colthurst Holland (1777-1827), a London banker, and Anna Willetts. His father bought Dumbleton Hall, Evesham, in 1827. Edward's paternal grandparents were Samuel Holland and Anne Swinton. They had had at least three sons and four daughters, the fourth of whom, Elizabeth, Edward's aunt, married William Stevenson, a Unitarian minister. Their daughter, Elizabeth Cleghorn Stevenson (1810-1865), married, at Knutsford, Cheshire, 30 August 1832, another Unitarian minister, William Gaskell. She became Mrs Gaskell, and under that name published such famous novels as *Mary Barton* (1848), *Cranford* (1851-53), *Ruth* (1853), and *North and South* (1854-55). Elizabeth was a frequent visitor to her cousin Edward Holland, staying with him at his house in Park Lane, London, and at Dumbleton. He made investments on behalf of the Gaskells, and in a letter dated 13 January 1849, Elizabeth thanked her cousin for his 'very kind & advantageous advice'.

Holland was MP for Evesham in 1855-65 and was involved in the founding of the Royal Agricultural College at Cirencester. He married, 1832, Sophia Isaac (1813-1851)—the same year that Elizabeth married William Gaskell. Edward and Sophia had at least 4 sons and 5 daughters:

1 Harriet Sophia (b. 1834)

1 Edward Thurston (1836-1884); married, at Manchester, July 1866, his cousin Marianne Gaskell

2 Frederic Whitmore (1837-1880), vicar and rural dean of Evesham; married, 1870, Penelope Martin

2 Anna Caroline (b. 1840)

3 Swinton Colthurst (1844-1922), Adm., RN; married, at Plymouth, 1881, Eva Amy Williams
3 Frances Margaret (b. 1846)
4 Edgar Swinton (1847-1896); managing director of Santa Barbara and Pintangui gold mining companies (45 Drury Buildings, 21 Water Street); murdered by revolver shot, 29 October 1896, by Catherine Kemspshall, whom he had jilted. Kemspshall was sentenced to hang, but was removed instead to Broadmoor where she died, aged 88, in 1953
4 Lucy Georgina (b. 1848)
5 Jessie Clara (b. 1850)

In 1830 Holland commissioned the architect G. S. Repton to build the new Dumbleton Hall. It was constructed of stone from the Temple Guiting quarries, and of brick. Holland carried out many improvements to the village, including the rebuilding of some of the farmhouses and the construction of a number of semi-detached cottages. For this purpose he established a brickyard to the north of the village.

Edward was Charles Darwin's second cousin. In Darwin family correspondence of 1832, Erasmus Darwin reported that Mrs Holland was 'vulgar and sulky ... she is not only stupid herself, but makes other people stupid'. Catherine Darwin was also disparaging of the family; she dismissed Edward Holland as 'awfully pompous' and was not impressed by the grand ceremony of laying the first stone on the new Dumbleton Hall.

Edward Witts was a near neighbour to Edward Holland, and the two men, similar in age, got on well, notwithstanding their political differences. It was Edward Holland who strongly advocated Edward Witts's appointment as a county magistrate.

Edward Holland was first cousin to Henry Holland (*below*) through both his mother and father—Henry Holland's father, Peter Holland (1766-1855), physician, having married Mary Willits (1766-1803).

1836: 27 Oct: *Some of their own connections, of the Clutton, Holland and Isaacs families from Worcestershire were staying in the house.*

1837: 1 Mar: *Mrs. Isaacs and Miss Louisa Holland, sisters of Mr. Holland, were the other ladies, and with them we returned to the house, over which I was conducted.... I was not quite a stranger to some of them, having met Mrs. Holland and her sister, Miss Isaacs, at Chastleton; they are nearly connected with the Whitmore Jones's.*

1843: 4 Oct: *We all went to call at Dumbleton, on Mr. and Mrs. Holland: MW & Broome with me in my open carriage—E.F.W. driving Sophy.*

1844: 21 Feb., 4 Oct., 18 Oct: *My son communicated that his neighbour, Mr. Holland, had notified to him that it is his intention to urge Lord Fitzhardinge, as Lord Lieutenant of Gloucestershire, very strongly to put E.F.W. into the Commission for this County, a Magistrate being greatly wanted in the vale, to act with Dr. Timbrill and Mr. Holland in the Winchcomb Division, and both are very desirous that my son should be appointed.* 28 Nov., 16 Dec: *Recd. a letter from E.F.W. covering two others, one from Mr. Holland to himself, another from Lord Ellenborough to Mr. Holland, from which it appears that Lord Fitzhardinge has at last surrendered to a whole broadside of letters from Holland, and reluctantly consented to propose the addition of my Son's name to the commission of the Peace for this County.*

1845: 31 Mar: *Besides, he was unwilling to leave Sophy three days running, and he feels it necessary to attend to-morrow at Winchcomb a dinner given by the Guardians of that Union in compliment to Mr. Holland, and is further engaged on the following day in public business at Winchcomb.*

1846: 25 Aug: *By this train I travelled to Cheltenham in the same coach with Mr. Holland, who was returning to Dumbleton from Cirencester, where he had been visiting the Agricultural College, of which he is one of the most active managers.* 12 Oct.

1847: 7-8 Jul., 17 Jul: *Mr. Holland retires from the contest for East Gloucestershire.*

1848: 15 Feb., 6 Oct: *Lord Ellenborough and Mr. Holland justly complimented my Son for the ability & talent and sound principles which he had developed.* 17 Oct.

1850: 24 Apr., 16 Sep: *Soon after the confirmation the Bishop and Mr. Browne departed, his Lordship renewing the assurance of his perfect satisfaction. He proceeded to Dumbleton to be the guest of Mr. and Mrs. Holland.*

1851: 9 Jan: *My son rode to Stanway, where he learnt the sad intelligence, of which a rumour had reached us, what Mrs. Holland, of Dumbleton, had died after a short illness, on Saturday last—She leaves a numerous family of young children, to whom and to her husband she will be a great loss; her frame was delicate, and her constitution exhausted: she had been seized with bronchitis, which turned to pleurisy.* 29 Apr.

1852: 7 Apr: *At half past 3 P.M. I drove, accompanied by my dear Freddy, to Mr. Holland's at Dumbleton, to meet my grandson Broome, coming home for the Easter holidays. He was to be conveyed to D. by Mr. Holland, who had driven to Park Hall to bring home his little schoolboy, Broome's school fellow. They arrived soon after we reached D: but I did not see Mr. H., who had sent the boys in the carriage, and left them on the road to visit his farm.... Remained a short time after Broome came, while my carriage was being sent round from the stable, with a troop of H's children—his eldest daughter, a pleasing delicate girl of seventeen, his eldest son a well-mannered lad, an Etonian, & two or three little girls—all to be pitied as having lost their mother about a twelvemonth since. Their grandmother, Mrs. Isaacs, and a maiden sister of Mr. H. reside at Dumbleton House, but I did not see them.* 4 Jun: *While we were there, Mrs. Isaacs, mother of the late Mrs. Holland, and residing with him and his children at Dumbleton, called with two of Holland's daughters, children of twelve and thirteen years of age.*

1854: 28 Jan: *Letter received from Holland, who returns me Purnell's letter on his return to the Chair, which I had forwarded to him.* 30 Jan., 2 Feb., 4 Feb., 6 Feb., 11 Feb., 14 Feb., 21 Feb., 23 Feb., 12 Mar., 14 Mar., 19 Mar., 22 Mar., 31 Mar., 27 Apr: *Edwd. Holland has unluckily broken his leg in playing with his children.* 7 Jun.

HOLLAND — Francis Dermot Holland — *see also* **Corbett Holland Corbett** [220]

Francis Dermot Holland (1828-1907), JP and landed proprietor, was the son of Francis Holland Corbett (1796-1878) and Jane Warry (±1792-1851). He was educated at Christchurch College, Oxford, and was a student at the Inner Temple. He lived at Cropthorne Hall, Worcestershire.

Holland married, at Bolton, Lancashire, 1850, Ann Fletcher (1832-1920); they had 3 sons and 4 daughters:

1 Francis Corbett (1852-1925)
2 Ellis Charles Fletcher (±1855-1920)
1 Annie Jane (b. ±1856)
2 Alice Beatrice (1858-1908)
3 Louisa Charlotte (b. 1860)
4 Mary Blanche (b. ±1862)
3 Walter Dermott (1865-1912)

Francis Dermot Holland was the nephew of Corbett Holland Corbett (1792-1872), who took by royal licence, on 2 May 1839, the additional surname of Corbett in compliance of the will of his late maternal uncle Michael Corbett (1759-1839) of Admington House. It must be presumed that Francis's father, Francis Holland Corbett, had done likewise.

1851: 12 May: *Called on the Vavasours at "the Cottage", and partook of luncheon there with Mr. & Mrs. Vavasour, Mr. and Mrs. W. Vavasour, and Mr. Holland of Cropthorne, a Worcestershire Squire, and acquaintance of the Vavasours.*

1852: 4 Mar: *Mr. Holland of Cropthorn, Worcestershire, called during my absence.* 12 May: *Received a note from E.F.W. brought by Mr. Holland (Cropthorne) from Stanway.* 23 Dec: *Mr. Holland, of Cropthorne, called when I was at Stow, he being now staying at the Unicorn Stow, to hunt with Lord Redesdale's foxhounds.*

1854: 7 May: *Received a letter from Mr. Holland (Cropthorn) The account he gives of Thomas Day, as to a tendency to indulge occasionally in habits of intoxication, is such as to determine me not to take him into my service.*

HOLLAND — Henry Holland[221]

Sir Henry Holland, 1st baronet (1788-1873), physician, was born at Knutsford, Cheshire, son of Peter Holland (1766-1855), physician, and Mary Willits (1766-1803). He was therefore first cousin to Edward Holland (*above*), through both his mother and his father—Edward Holland's father, Swinton Colthurst Holland (1777-1827), banker, having married Anna Willits.

Henry Holland began his medical studies in Edinburgh, but he broke off in 1812 to undertake an eighteen-month journey through Portugal, Spain, Greece, and Turkey. It was the time of the Peninsular War and Henry spent three months at a military hospital in Portugal, helping to treat the wounded. His experiences in Europe and the Near East came as a novelty at a time when the Napoleonic Wars had restricted travel for several years; on his return to London, he rapidly gained acceptance among the highest reaches of London society. He became friendly with Lord Lansdowne, Lord Aberdeen, and Lord Holland, and frequently met Lord Byron and Sir Humphrey Davy, among others. His new social contacts led to an invitation to attend the princess of Wales as her physician at her intended residence on the Continent.

He married, 1822, Margaret Emma Caldwell (1795-1830); they had 2 sons and 2 daughters:

1 Henry (1825-1914); created 1st Viscount Knutsford
2 Francis James (1828-1907)
1 Emily Mary (1824-1908)
2 Elinor Anne (1826-1829)

Emma died in 1830 and Henry later married Saba, daughter of the celebrated Sydney Smith. Henry and Saba had 2 daughters:

1 Caroline (1834-1909)
2 Gertrude (1840-1898)

In 1816 Holland became a licentiate of the Royal College of Physicians and a fellow of the Royal Society. In 1828 he became a fellow of the Royal College of Physicians. His first practice was in Berkeley Square; he then moved to Brook Street, Grosvenor Square.

1853: 7 May: *I regret to say that more frequent recurrence of headache with indisposition in the intervals between the attacks, has led my children to the prudent determination of going to London in the week after next to take the advice of an eminent Physician, Sir H. Holland. It appears that a sister in law of Mrs. W.B. Pole, Mrs. Richard Pole, has been a sufferer from headaches in the same manner as dear Sophy, & from the same cause—concussion of the brain. Mrs. R.P., after consulting other Medical authorities with little advantage, has desired great benefit from Sir H. H's treatment. He is a cousin and friend of Mr. Holland of Dumbleton, who will introduce Edward & Sophy to him, so as to secure his attentive consideration of the case.* 19 May: *Letter from E.F.W., on the whole satisfactory: written after a long interview with Sir H. Holland, who entered fully into Sophy's case, and pronounced that there is no organic mischief, no injury of the brain, the headaches arising from something wrong with a superficial nerve: in fact, neuralgia is the complaint, and likely in time to wear off.*

1854: 14 Jun: *Last week they spent 47 hours in Town, that Sophy might consult Sir Henry Holland, who considered that, as regards the neuralgic affection to which she is subject, there is no change for the worse, and that the same palliatives and course of treatment already observed ought to be persevered in.*

HOLLIS — Amy Hollis, lady's maid to Margaret Witts

1848: 10 Jul: *Arrived at the Plough Hotel, Cheltenham at 11 o cl. where we were joined by Elizabeth Simmons, a young person from Stanway, who comes into our service as Lady's maid instead of Amy Hollins, who leaves us.* 27 Sep: *A letter from a Major Kennedy of Cheltenham, enquiring the character of our late servant Amy Hollis.* 28 Sep: *Wrote to Major Kennedy with a character of Amy Hollis.*

HOLLIS — Frances Hollis, servant of Margaret Witts

1825: 9 May: *At Tewkesbury we remained half an hour, while we sought & at last found, in a neat Cottage, an estimable person, late a Servant of Margaret's, Frances Hollis; her father is an Excise man.* 19 May: *We had a delightful drive to Tewkesbury, where we were obliged to wait at Fanny Hollis's for two hours, that Mrs. F. Witts might see an aspirant for the place of cook in our family.*

HOLLIS — William Hollis[222]

William Hollis (1799-1867), gun maker, was born in the parish of St Philip, Birmingham, son of William and Jane Hollis. He was in trade as a gun maker at 407 High Street, Cheltenham, employing three men. In 1851 he lived at 89 High Street with his wife, Elizabeth (b. ±1799). By 1861 he was retired and living at Badgeworth.

1842: 18 Oct: *The moving power in that quarter, it would seem, is a tradesman, by name Hollis, a gunmaker, remarkable for his ultraism in politics; being an avowed Chartist, and delegate of those inhabitants of Cheltenham, who entertain such extreme opinions, to the so-called conventions of that revolutionary party, held in the Metropolis, Birmingham and the other great towns, where their strength lies.*

HOLME — Frederick William Holme[223]

Frederick William Holme (1771-1853), Church of England clergyman, was born at Upholland, Lancashire, son of Thomas Holland. He was educated at Corpus Christi College, Oxford (BA 1792; MA 1796; BD 1804; fellow until 1812), and served as rector of Meysey Hampton, Gloucestershire, in 1809-53. He married Mary Elizabeth Pigott (b. 1783); they had at least 3 sons and 1 daughter:

1 Mary Elizabeth (b. ±1811)
1 Frederick (b. 1812)
2 Frederick William (b. 1815)
3 Meyrick (b. 1815)

1804: *With him to Church. Morn. & afternoon at the former Dr. Lawrence's 2nd Bampton Lecture very moderate, at the latter Mr. Holme of C. C. C. at St. Peter's, eccentric.*

HOLMES — *see* À Court

HOLMES — the Holmes family at Clifton

Nothing has been discovered about Mr Holmes and J. Holmes, but they seem to be connected with John Ryan of Montserrat, of St Croix in the West Indies, and of Copenhagen, Denmark. He may possibly be John Holmes (1763-1836), of Jamaica, but this is too tentative to qualify as an attribution; *see* UCL—Legacies of British Slave-ownership.

1804: 23 Aug: *Walked with my Father & Mother, Mr. Ryan, Mr. Holmes, Capt. Ross &c.* 30 Aug., 31 Aug: *Walked in the Evening with Mr. Holmes & Ryan.* 2 Sep: *Walked with Holmes, Ryan, Manners, Napier &c.* 6-7 Sep., 15 Sep., 30 Sep., 4 Oct., 11 Oct: *Walked with Mr. J. Holmes, & Miss White, Russel Manners &c. Called at Cote.* 28 Dec: *Left my card at Mr. Parris's. Walked with Mr. J Holmes &c.*

1805: 11 Jan: *Walked with Holmes, Mrs. Townsend, the Newnhams &c.*

HOLMES — Mrs Holmes, servant of Mr Deane

1852: 18 Feb: *A packet from Mrs. Deane; my advice & assistance wanted as to obtaining the money & property forfeited to the Crown on the conviction of Eliz. Davies for felony, which the Lords of the Treasury, on a memorial from Mrs. Wynch, have consented to give up to her old servant, Mrs. Holmes, whom, no doubt, E.D. had robbed at Mr. Deane's house.* 19-20 Feb., 25 Feb.

HOLOSWORTH — Captain Holosworth, a guest of the Dowell family at Cote

1804: 24 Jan: *Dined & slept at the former's House at Cote, where I experienced a friendly reception, & was extremely pleased. Besides the family & Slap, the party consisted of Mr. & Mrs. Foster, the Lamottes, Capt. Holosworth, Col. Coke, Mr. & Mrs. John Alleyne.*

HOLT — Thomas Holt[224]

Thomas Holt (1796-1876), registrar and secretary to the bishop of Gloucester, solicitor, and notary public, was born at Peterborough, and was married to Anne (±1794-1860), also born at Peterborough. Little has been found on Holt. He was a practising solicitor and his Gloucester professional address was 'cloisters'. He wrote a treatise on the act of parliament in relation to clergy holding more than one benefice: *Act 1 & 2 Vict. c. 106 (holding benefices in plurality and making better provision for clergy residence), with analysis, some practical notes, and a copious index*'. In 1861 he lived at 'The Elms', London Road, Gloucester.

It seems likely that Thomas Holt assisted Francis Witts and may have influenced the bishop in relation to Frederick Aston's presentation to the living of Northleach. The entry for 30 November 1838 details this conversation which had probably been held on 18 October 1837. When a subscription was raised for the presentation of silver plate to Holt, Witts subscribed £1, but he did not go to the actual presentation. In 1847, when Edward Witts hoped to acquire the living of Stanton from Edward Bloxsome, his relationship with Holt was less cordial, although Francis Witts did not appear to think that Holt influenced the bishop in his decision.

Thomas appears to have had a son with him in his practice, presumably William James Holt. William first appears on the scene on 7 March 1845, when he was a candidate for the poor law district auditorship.

1832: 7 Jun: *In the course of the forenoon I called on the Bishop's Secretary, Mr. Holt, with the Papers of my neighbour, Mr. Pitcher, who is about to be ordained Priest, early in the next month.*

1837: 18 Oct: *Called on Mr. Holt, the Bishop's secretary, to advise with him as to the documents which my Son will have to transmit to the Bishop preparatory to the Ordination.* 28 Nov., 30 Nov.

1838: 3 Jan: *He met me with a very cordial assurance of his entire satisfaction with the Examination which my Son had recently passed, and his Secretary Holt, told me the Bishop had been greatly pleased with him.* 8 May, 10-11 May, 13 May: *A letter from Mr. Holt, intimating that Dr. Maddy and himself will be ready to receive E.F. W. at Gloucester to-morrow, that he may be resworn to the affidavit on which the Marriage Licence has been issued, and that the latter may be duly corrected.* 23 Oct., 30 Nov.

1839: 2 Jan., 10 Apr: *Missed seeing Holt, the Bishop's Secretary, who was engaged at the Palace; wrote to him for information as to the papers necessary to be forwarded by my son to the Bishop in order to obtain a licence as Curate of Stanway: subsequently recd. an answer from Mr. Holt.*

1840: 21 Jun., 20 Aug.

1844: 5 Nov., 22 Nov: *Also from the Comm. of Clergymen, chiefly in the neighbourhood of Gloucester, who have associated themselves to raise a subscription to present a Testimonial of respect and regard to Mr. Holt, the Bishop of Glouc. and Bristol's private Secretary—a very good man, a very attentive man, a very judicious man, very well read in Ecclesiastical law, and deserving much esteem.* 23 Nov: *to the Revd. H. A. S. Attwood Vicar of Ashleworth, enclosing £1. 0. 0 as my subscription to the Holt testimonial.* 26 Nov.

1845: 23 Feb: *A circular fixing a meeting at Gloucester for the 27th. Inst. when the Subscribers to the proposed testimonial of respect and esteem to be presented to Mr. Holt, Secretary to the Bishop of Gloucester and Bristol, and Registrar, are to agree on what price or pieces of plate shall be selected for his acceptance.* 7 March: *Letters awaited me from Mr. Estlin, a candidate for the Poor Law District Auditorship, from Mr. W. J. Holt, also a like Candidate.* 11 Apr: *A circular from the Revd. Attwood announces that the plate procured by a subscription of clergymen, to which I have contributed, will be presented at a dinner to be given at the Bell Hotel, Gloucester, on the 17th. Inst. to Mr. Holt, the respected secretary of the Bishop of Gloucester.* 12 Apr.

1847: 11 Jan., 12 Oct., 19 Oct., 9 Nov., 16 Nov: *Recd. a letter from Mr. Sewell, who has had an interview with the Bishop's Secretary, Mr. Holt.... Mr. Holt observed that it would be both unwise and improper, either that E.F.W. or myself should communicate on the matter with himself or the Bishop.*

1850: 15 Jul: *I have already intimated my intention to support him: his competitors are Mr. Septimus Pruen, Attorney, Cheltenham, Mr. Holt, Junr. Attorney, Gloucester.* 17 Jul: *By a circular received from Mr. W. Holt, Gloucester, it appears that he has retired from the contest for the vacant Coronership in favour of Mr. Lovegrove.*

1853: 9 Feb., 12 Feb.

1854: 8 May: *Wrote to Mr. Holt, the Bp's Secretary, requesting him to send me a form of nomination to be used as to the appointment of E. Clifford as Curate, and his being licensed.* 11 May.

HONE — Joseph Frederick Hone[225]

Joseph Frederick Hone (1801-1888), Church of England clergyman, was born in the parish of St Marylebone, Westminster, eldest son of Joseph Terry Hone and Augusta Sinclair. He was educated at University College, Oxford (BA 1825; MA 1829). He was ordained deacon on 21 September 1825 and priest on 18 June

1826. His first clerical appointment was as stipendiary curate of Churchdown, starting on 21 September 1825; he was then presented with the living of Tirley on 15 May 1827, where he served as vicar until 1888. The term 'Chosen' is a Gloucestershire form of slang for Churchdown, as in 'Chosen Hill'. He was married to Anne Grimshaw (b. ±1806), who was born in Lancashire. There do not appear to have been any children.

1826: 25 Jan: *Mr. Fred. Hone, recently ordained, is Curate of Chosen Church, near Gloucester.*

1839: 2 Jan: *The following were among the guests: Archd. Thorpe, Mr. & Mrs. Phillips, Mrs. M W. Raikes, Dr. & Mrs. Hall, Mr. G. Hall, Miss Hall, Mr. and Mrs. Hone.*

HONE — Joseph Terry Hone[226]

Joseph Terry Hone (1776-1831), JP and barrister-at-law, was the son of Brindley Hone and Sarah Strong. He married, at St Paul's, Covent Garden, Westminster, 5 November 1799, Augusta Sinclair; they had 3 sons and 3 daughters:

1 Joseph Frederick (1801-1888), Church of England clergyman; *see above*
2 Richard Brindley (1805-1881), Church of England clergyman
1 Augusta Maria (1807-1820)
3 Harry Ridley (1809-1828)
2 Sarah Albinia Elizabeth (b. 1812)
3 Anna Maria (b. 1814)

By 1818 Hone was living in Gloucester, but later he apparently lived at Faringdon.

1826: 25 Jan: *We dined at our old friend's Mrs. M. Hunt's in Palace Yard: besides Miss Caroline & Miss Maria Hunt, Mr. & Mrs. Hone & their Son, Mr. F. Hone, One or two others came in the Evening. Mr. Hone is a barrister from the Sister Island, who has long resided at Gloucester, picking up a little business, chiefly in working bankruptcies, but never overdone with briefs at the Sessions or Assizes: indeed Othello's occupation is every day lessening since Mr. Philpotts, a quondam Solicitor here, a man of considerable talent, experience, and address, has taken his place at the bar.*

HONOR — Mrs Honor at Clifton

1804: 10 Sep: *Set out after an early breakfast, in two Sociables, & myself on horseback. Mrs. Honor & Miss Pigott, Mrs. Bates, my Father & Mother.*

HONYWOOD — *see* Barne[227]

Mary Anne Elizabeth Barne, née Honywood (b. 1809), was the daughter of Sir John Courtenay Honywood, 5th baronet (1787-1832), and his wife, Mary Anne, and the sister of Sir John Edward Honywood, 6th baronet (1812-1884). She married Frederick Barne (1801-1886), MP and landed proprietor.

1835: 3 Feb: *Mr. Barne is a sportsman, & has engaged Maugersbury House as a hunting seat. He is eldest Son of a gentleman of large fortune in Suffolk, and, before the Reform Act passed, the represented in Parliament the Borough of Dunwich, which has now been disfranchised. He was from home: but we see saw his lady, an elegant young woman, sister of Sir J. Honywood, a Kentish Baronet.*

HOOK — Mr Hook at Clifton

1804: 21 Jan: *Conversed chiefly with John Dawkins, Smith & Hook, Hart Davis, Harriett, etc. Returned near 1 o clock.* 12 Aug: *Walked in the Evening; with Hook.* 28 Jan: *A most amusing Evening, during which I had much conversation with Dawkins, Smith, Hooke, Johnson, the Leyards, Hillhouses, Smiths etc. The latter formed a side table at almost Jovial Supper with Smith, Hook, Johnson & myself.*

HOOK — James Hook[228]

James Hook (±1771-1828), Church of England clergyman, was born in the parish of St Giles-in-the-Fields, Holborn, London, son of James Hook (1746-1827) and Elizabeth Jane Madden. He was brother of Theodore (*below*). He was educated at St Mary Hall, Oxford (BA & MA 1799; BCL 1804; DCL 1806). Hook served as vicar of Mickleton, Gloucestershire, chaplain to the prince of Wales and to the king, prebendary of Winchester in 1807, archdeacon of Huntingdon in 1817, rector of Whippingham, Isle of Wight, and Preston Candover, Hampshire, in 1817, dean of Worcester in 1825, and vicar of Bromsgrove and of Stone, Worcestershire, in 1826.

1825: 16 May: *The Deanery of Worcester will it is said fall to the lot of Dr. Hook, Archdeacon of Huntingdon and prebendary of Winchester, whom I had occasion to mention lately.*

1828: 25 Mar: *Dr. Hook, his predecessor (as Dean of Worcester?), Archdeacon of Huntingdon, Rector of Bromsgrove & Stone in Worcestershire, died lately, as it is said, in very embarrassed circumstances. He was a very expensive man, & had been much in the King's Society in early life; he was considered a man of talent, which was evinced in an occasional Sermon or charge, which I have seen.*

HOOK — Theodore Edward Hook[229]

Theodore Edward Hook (1788-1841), writer, hoaxer, and accountant-general and treasurer of Mauritius, was born in the parish of St George, Bloomsbury, Camden, Middlesex, son of James Hook (1746-1827) and Elizabeth Jane Madden. He was younger brother of James (*above*). Theodore's father, James, was the composer of numerous popular songs; with his father, Theodore achieved much success at the age of 16 with *The Soldier's Return*, a comic opera.

The prince regent was charmed by Hook's talent, and appointed him accountant-general and treasurer of Mauritius with a salary of £2,000 a year—in spite of his total ignorance of accounting. For five delightful years Hook was the life and soul of the island, but in 1817, a serious deficiency was discovered in the treasury accounts; he was arrested and brought to England on a criminal charge. During the audit board's tardy investigations Hook lived obscurely and maintained himself by writing for magazines and newspapers. In 1820 he launched the newspaper *John Bull*, the champion of high toryism and virulent detractor of Queen Caroline. Witty, incisive criticism and pitiless invective secured it a large circulation, and from this source alone Hook derived, for the first year at least, an income of £2,000. He was, however, arrested for a second time on account of his debt to the state, which he had made no effort to defray. In the debtor's prison he wrote the nine volumes of stories collected afterwards under the title, *Sayings and Doings* (1824-28).

1825: 26 Apr: *"Sayings and doings. A series of sketches from life. 4th. Ed. 3. Vols. 12mo Lond. 1824". This has been a very popular book, and not undeservedly so. The tales present a succession of views of life, particularly fashionable life, of manners, prejudices, errors, and vices with their results, and the narrative is spirited, racy, witty and well concocted... The supposed writer is Mr. Theodore Hook, who is known to possess considerable talents,*

& suspected of employing them in the service of the bold and ably written newspaper, John Bull. He had a civil employment in the island of Mauritius, where, through carelessness or worse, his accounts got into confusion, & his payments to government in an arrear, which led to judicial investigation. I do not recollect, what was the issue. His brother Dr. Hook, a man of talent, is a Prebendary of Winchester and Archdeacon of Huntingdon.

HOOK — Walter Farquhar Hook [230]

Walter Farquhar Hook (1798-1875), Church of England clergyman, was the son of James Hook (*above*). He was educated at Christ Church, Oxford (BA 1821; MA 1824; B&DD 1837). He served as chaplain-in-ordinary to the king in 1827, and the queen in 1839-75; he was also dean of Chichester in 1859-75, and vicar of Leeds in 1837-59.

1829: 22 Aug: *"Friendly and seasonable advice to the Roman Catholics of England. Fourth Edition: with an appendix & notes by the Revd. Walter Farquhar Hook MA Chaplain in Ordinary to the King &c. Lond. 1829. 12mo." Mr. Hook is son of the late Dean of Worcester, a young divine of considerable talents, and acquirements. He is now beneficed in Coventry, a Crown living in that populous city having been lately given him.*

1837: 28 Jun., 8 Jul.

1838: 2 Sep: *Read a Sermon preached before the Queen by Dr. Hook, as her Chaplain, which has been supposed to have given great offence at Court and to Ministers.*

1842: 30 Oct: *Also a note from Col. & Mrs. Dawkins, Over-Norton, inviting us to a luncheon, which they propose to give at the Town Hall, Chipping Norton, on Nov. 15; to such of their friends and acquaintances as shall attend at the service to be performed at the Church there, on Nov. 15. when a sermon is to be preached by the eminent Dr. Hook, Vicar of Leeds.* 13 Nov:

1845: 13 Feb.

1847: 26 Jun., 6 Jul.

HOOKHAM — Clara Hookham, candidate for the position of nurse at Stow Union Workhouse

1847: 15 Jul: *Also Charlotte Wilkins was chosen as nurse by a bare majority over her competitor, Clara Hookham.*

HOOPER — Thomas Poole Hooper [231]

Thomas Poole Hooper (1773-1837), Church of England clergyman, was the son of John Hooper, linen draper in Oxford Street, London. Hooper inherited an estate from Thomas Poole in Shoreham, which presumably included the living. He is not listed as a curate at the Oxford chapel [later known as Marylebone chapel], which was just off Oxford Street, but presumably he was on some temporary clerical duty near his home in London, having returned from his initial curacy in the wilds of the Isle of Man. He was educated at Pembroke College, Oxford (BA 1797; MA 1800). He was curate of Kirk Patrick, Isle of Man, in 1797, vicar of Shoreham, Sussex, in 1801-15, vicar of Kingston-by-the-Sea in 1809, and vicar of Sompting in 1815-37.

1801: 16 Aug: *In the afternoon to Oxford Chapel very neatly fitted up: a Mr. Hooper officiated very well.* 23 Aug: *Went twice to Oxford Chapel, where Mr. Hooper read prayers & preached well both times.* 30 Aug., 6 Sep., 4 Oct: *Went twice to Oxford Chapel, the first time Mr. Hooper officiated extremely well.* 11 Oct: *To Oxford Chapel both morning & Afternoon, where Mr. Hooper officiated, as usual, well.* 17 Oct.

HOOPER — William Hooper [232]

William Hooper (1798-1869), confectioner, was born at Cheltenham. He married Mary (b. ±1805), born in Norfolk; they had at least 1 daughter:

1 Sarah (b. ±1840)

Hooper traded from 369-370 High Street, Cheltenham.

1848: 22 Sep: *Had luncheon at Hooper's, the Pastry cook, where excellent mutton chops may be had.*

1850: 26 Oct: *Wrote to Hooper, Cook and Confectioner, Cheltenham, with an order for game & confectionery for dinner parties.* 23 Nov: *Wrote to Hooper, Confectioner, Cheltenham, with an order for game for dinner on Wednesday.*

1852: 7 Nov: *Wrote a note to Hooper, Confectioner, Cheltenham, to send me a pheasant, or some other game bird or birds, for my dinner party on Friday.*

HOOPER — Miss Hooper of Moreton-in-Marsh

1845: 23 Jan: *I wrote to the party, Miss Hooper of Moreton in Marsh, explaining the views of the Trustees & Managers, and suggesting that the deposits of herself and different members of her family should be withdrawn.* 29 Jan.

HOPE — Anne Hope, inmate at Stow Union Workhouse [233]

Anne Hope (1782-1846) was born at Upper Slaughter, the daughter of Thomas and Anne Hope. She has not been found in the 1841 census and it appears she died unmarried.

1846: 14 Dec: *Funeral of Anne Hope, from the Workhouse.*

HOPE — Henry Thomas Hope [234]

Henry Thomas Hope (1807-1862), MP and patron of the arts, was the eldest son of Thomas Hope (1769-1831) and Louisa de la Poer Beresford (*below*). He became estranged from his brothers when he inherited his father's art collection, wealth, and property, and that of his uncle's, Henry Phillip Hope (d. 1839).

Hope was educated at Eton College and Trinity College, Cambridge (MA 1829). He inherited the estate of Deepdene, Surrey, and Trenant Park, Cornwall. He subsequently sold Trenant Park and bought Castle Blayney in Ireland. He was MP for East Looe, Cornwall, in 1829-32, and for Gloucester in 1833-52. He married, 1851, Anne Adele, daughter of Joseph Bichat.

1833: 13 Apr: *Mr. Hope, thus foiled at Gloucester, had in the mean time stood a contest for the borough of Mary le bone, and though he was considerably ahead of the government candidate, a Mr. Murray, he was inferior in strength to a Sir. S. Whalley, a man of ultra liberal politics, who now sits for that modern borough in the room of Mr. Portman.*

1835: 4 Jan: *For Gloucester City four candidates start: Messrs. Hope and Cother on the Tory Interest, and Mr. Philpotts and Captain Berkeley on the Whig Interest.* 5 Jan: *Our progress was somewhat impeded by the noises around us; at the Shire Hall, the nomination of Candidates for the representation of the City was going ... the four candidates, Hope, Cother, Berkeley, and Philpotts, were duly proposed and seconded.* 6-7 Jan., 8 Jan: *Several of our colleagues were engaged at the election dinners of Messrs. Hope & Berkeley: the friends of the former being assembled at the Bell, and those of the latter at the Kings Head. The chairing of the city members had taken place to-day: they paraded the streets in open carriages.*

1837: 25 Jul: *At Gloucester Hope, a Conservative, has been returned, and Philpotts, a Liberal has ousted Frederick Berkeley.*

1838: 3 Jul: *The town much crowded and in a great bustle from the afternoon till late in the Evening in consequence of a visit to his constituents by Hope the representative of the City.*

1853: 4 Jan: *The seat is contested by a Conservative committee, bringing forward Mr. Hope, a former representative of the city unseated at the election last summer, when W P Price was returned as Admiral Berkeley's colleague.* 5 Jan: *The Election for the City of Gloucester was proceeding throughout the day with much noise and acrimony—The Conservatives headed the poll for Mr. Hope, during the first hour, but the Whig Radical party, favouring Adm Berkeley, soon gained & maintained an ascendancy, obtaining the victory by a majority of 93 votes.*

HOPE — John and Hugh Hope[235]

Sir John Hope, 11th baronet (1781-1853), and Hugh Hope (1782-1823) were both sons of Sir Archibald Hope of Craighall, 9th baronet (1735-1794), by his second marriage to Elizabeth Patoun. Sir John Hope married, 17 June 1805, Anne, daughter of John Wedderburn and Alice Dundas; they had 8 sons. Hugh Hope married, 1819, Isabella Gray Mackay, daughter of Capt. Æneas Mackay of Scottstoun; they had 1 son and 1 daughter. Hugh Hope was a member of the Bengal Civil Service and died in 1823.

The Hope brothers were students at the Belvedere, Weimar; they feature more extensively in the diaries of Agnes Witts. The brothers appear to have arrived in Weimar on 21 September 1798 accompanied by a tutor, Mr Walker. They remained there until early 1800.

1800: 27 Jan: *In the Evening. Mr. Walker & the two Mr Hops & Mademoiselle d'Outel. Played at Pope Joan.*

HOPE — Thomas Hope[236]

Thomas Hope (1769-1831), art collector and connoisseur, was born in Amsterdam, the eldest of the three sons of John Hope (1737-1784) and Philippina Barbara van der Hoeven (±1738-1789). Hope was a member of an immensely wealthy and prestigious family of Amsterdam merchants of Scottish descent, and was a partner in their highly successful firm, Hope & Co. In 1784 he shared his father's fortune with his brothers Adrian Elias (b. 1772) and Henry Philip (1774-1839). Instead of following in the family business he took up the study of classical architecture and civilisation; from 1787, apart from short periods in Amsterdam, he spent eight years travelling and studying architecture in countries bordering the Mediterranean. The austere simplicity of classicism impressed Hope greatly, but he was also infused with the romanticism of Mediterranean culture; in Turkey, for example, he adopted local dress and abandoned his Christianity. His romantic novel, *Anastasius* (1819), first published in French but subsequently in four languages and thirteen editions, was based on the experience of these travels.

During the French occupation of Amsterdam in 1795, Hope, like most of his family, settled in London, living in Duchess Street from 1799, and there winning recognition as a scholar, collector, writer, proponent of neo-classicism, and enlightened patron of young and promising artists and craftsmen. He married, 16 April 1806, Louisa (1786-1851), the beautiful daughter of William de la Poer Beresford, archbishop of Tuam and later 1st Baron Decies, and niece of the 1st marquess of Waterford. They had at least 4 sons and 1 daughter:

1 Henry Thomas (1807-1862); *see above*
2 Charles William (1808-1884)
1 Louisa Elizabeth (b. 1810)
3 Adrian John (1811-1863); married, in London, 21 July 1836, Emilie Melanie Mathilda Rapp
4 Alexander James Beresford (1820-1887)

1801: 10 Oct: *walked in the Evening for an Hour or two to see the general Illumination, the Houses which were most ornamented were those of Mr. Hope in Cavendish Square, & of Mr. Otto in Hereford Street.* 12 Oct.

HOPEGOOD — Mr Hopegood of Barnet

1802: 11 Jan: *Walked with Fiott to Barnet; meeting Mr. Hopegood.* 13 Jan: *Mr. Hopegood made a morning visit.*

HOPKINSON — Edmund Hopkinson[237]

Edmund Hopkinson (1787-1869), JP, DL, and landed proprietor, was a son of George Caesar Hopkinson (1738-1825) and Elizabeth Field (1743-1841) of Wotton Court, Gloucester. He purchased Edgeworth Manor in around 1820, and married Octavia Burton (1786-1846). Edmund and Octavia died childless and Edgeworth descended to Edmund's great nephew, George Henry Hopkinson (1842-1919). Edmund was a JP and high sheriff for Gloucestershire in 1845-46.

1835: 6 Apr: *The Gentlemen present this Evening at the Bell, and who took part in these deliberations were, Messrs. Codrington M.P., Bathurst, Goodrich, R. B. Cooper, Sampson, Savage, Fripp, Hopkinson, Hale, Miller, Gist, Goldney, Revd. Messrs. Crawley, Pettat, Witts &c.*

1836: 14 Sep: *The Mag. present were, R. B. Cooper, in the chair, Lord Ellenborough, Mr. Seale Evans, Fulwar Craven, Col. Carrington Smith, and Edmund Hopkinson, who like myself came to watch the proceedings against the swindling horse dealer and stealer.*

1837: 2 Jan.

1842: 12 Apr: *The Magistrates who had given Notice of a motion for the diminution of the force were Sir J. Guise, H. P. Jones, Hopkinson, Canning, and Harward, mostly men of ultra-Whig politics—all, indeed, with the exception of the Tory, Hopkinson, who had unwisely mixed himself in the affair, was greatly annoyed at his position, and knew not how to extricate himself cleverly.* 18 Oct.,

1844: 8 Apr., 1 May.

1845: 24 Mar., 2 Apr: *Soon after I reached the Bell, the new High Sheriff, Mr. Hopkinson, of Edgeworth, arrived in his carriage from his sister's house at Wootton, escorted by a long cortége of farmers from hill and vale.* 4 Apr.

1846: 11 Aug: *Dined at the annual Infirmary dinner at the Kings Head, at which about twenty five were present, and the Chair was filled by Mr. Hopkinson, the Sheriff of last year. Though under great anxiety in consequence of the dangerous and declining state of Mrs. H.'s health, the Ex sheriff abounded as usual in all manner, of jokes and anecdotes.*

1847: 5 Apr.

1851: 18 Apr: *the Farmers of the Cirencester and Fairford Country are eager to nominate Hopkinson, of Edgworth House, as a protectionist candidate in opposition to Lord Moreton, or any other free trader who might be put forward. Beach approves of the choice, and reports that H. consents to stand if guaranteed against any expence.* 24 Apr: *It appeared that the peremptory requirements of Hopkinson as to being returned free of expence had been distasteful to those who had deliberated together at Cirencester.* 30 Apr.

HOPKINSON — Elizabeth Hopkinson[238]

Elizabeth Hopkinson, née Field (1743-1841), was the widow of George Caesar Hopkinson (1738-1825). She lived at Wotton Court, Gloucester.

1804: 20 Sep: *I accompanied Mrs. Hopkinson & Miss Lang, Mr. Townsend & his six daughters (Mrs. Munro, Susan, Charl., Carol, Jane & Sophia) in Mrs. H's coach & a Sociable to the New Passage 10 miles.* 24 Sep: *To Bristol & the Earthen Ware Manufactory with Mrs. Townsend, Mrs. Monro, Mrs. Lang, & Mrs. Hopkinson.*

1828: 18 Mar: *We dined at Wotton, at Mrs. Hopkinson's. This hospitable old lady is widow of the late Colonel Hopkinson, who closed a long life two or three years ago; in middle life he had been Army agent and Banker, and subsequently an active magistrate for the County, till advanced life and increasing infirmities caused him to withdraw from active public engagements.* 21 Mar: *Mrs. Lydia Plumtre dined at Mrs. Hunt's; Mrs. and Miss Hopkinson and Mrs. Gregory joined the evening party.*

1832: 29 Mar: *I accompanied Mrs. Backhouse and my wife to Gloucester, where the former was going to visit her friends Mrs. M. Hunt, Mrs. Jones and Mrs. Hopkinson.*

HOPPNER — Henry Parkyns Hoppner[239]

Henry Parkyns Hoppner (1795-1833), naval officer, explorer, and painter, was born in London, the fourth of five children of John Hoppner, artist, and Phoebe Wright. Henry was an officer in the Royal Navy, an Arctic explorer, and in continuance of the family tradition, a draughtsman and an artist. His career included two ill-fated voyages culminating in the loss of HMS *Alceste* in 1816 and HMS *Fury* in 1825. He died unmarried in Lisbon.

1825: 20 Oct: *It appears by the newspapers, that Captain Parry is again returned from his northwest expedition without accomplishing his object. His vessel, the Hecla, has brought back the crew of the Fury, her consort, commanded by Lieut. Hoppner, that vessel having been so dreadfully damaged by ice bergs, that it was absolutely necessary to abandon her.*

HOPTON — John Hopton — *see also* Parsons[240]

John Hopton (1782-1870), Church of England clergyman, was born at Chacely, Worcestershire, son of Revd William Parsons [later Hopton]. He was educated at Brasenose College, Oxford (BA 1805; MA 1807) (recorded as Parsons). He served as vicar of Canon Frome, Herefordshire, in 1808-70, and prebendary of Hereford in 1832. John Parsons/Hopton was a contemporary of Francis Witts at Oxford, although there only appears to be one fleeting mention of him in the diaries. It seems likely that Francis Witts did not recall that this Revd Hopton was a Brasenose alumnus.

1805: 16 Nov: *Afterwards upon the Hill with Parsons etc.*

1844: 14 Nov: *Recd. a letter from Mr. Hopton of Canon Frome Court near Ledbury, proprietor of an estate in Icomb, Gloucestershire, probably written at the suggestion of Mr. Pole, deprecating a union of the two Icombs under one rate, and one set of Parish Officers, and requesting my interposition to prevent such a measure.* 15 Nov.

HORN — Thomas Horn[241]

Thomas Horn (1800-1874), Church of England clergyman, was born at Westminster, son of Thomas and Sarah Horn. He was educated at St Edmund Hall, Oxford (BA 1826; MA 1829). He was ordained deacon on 21 May 1826 and priest on 10 June 1827. His first clerical appointment was as curate of Peterborough from 21 May 1826. He was then appointed stipendiary curate of St Mary's, Islington, on 10 October 1828, and later served as rector of Mursley-cum-Salden, Buckinghamshire, in 1832-51, and of Haverfordwest in 1851-66.

Horn married Eleanor (b. ±1800); they had at least 2 sons and 1 daughter:

1 George Thomas (b. 1832)
1 Maria (b. ±1834)
2 Edward (b. ±1836)

1847: 18 May: *I received a letter from Howell, announcing the very unexpected intelligence that Emmeline had, at her place of seclusion, Mursley, in Buckinghamshire, where she is residing with a Clergyman named Horne, whose wife is sister to Mrs. Parsons, late of Upton St. Leonards, formed a connection with a medical Gentleman, named Wynter, practising at Winslow, a widower of 40 years of age, of respectable character, well spoken of by Mrs. Parsons and her Sister.*

HORNBY — Messrs Hornby & Roughsedge

1825: 13 Sep: *one place was pointed out to me as Little Kirkham, built for the accommodation of the labourers at the Mills of Messrs. Hornby & Roughsedge: the former gentleman is of a family connected with the Langtons and settled at Kirkham in Lancashire.*

HORNE — Edward Horne[242]

Edward Horne (1781-1825), solicitor, was the son of Thomas Horne (1737-1824) of Chiswick. Horne was admitted to Lincoln's Inn entitled to practise as a solicitor. It appears that Edward Horne was working on two fronts: first in association with the problems of George Witts; secondly on the marriage settlement of Francis Witts and Margaret Backhouse. If not this *young* Edward Horne, it was another Edward of the same family. The evidence comes from the diaries of Agnes Witts. On Tuesday 30 August 1808 Agnes was at Cheltenham and wrote: 'saw no one during the Morning, but Sr. C. Pegge & a very unexpected call from Mr. Horne the solicitor.' On Wednesday 15 February 1815 she wrote: 'rec'd Letters from Mrs. V. Snow & Mr. Edward Horne, interesting enough.' On Friday 25 September 1817 Agnes was staying near Ware in Hertfordshire, and wrote: 'M^rs^. Horne & her Brother in law a M^r^. Bold made an early call, no going out until Miss Hatton & myself went to dine at M^r^. Smiths at the Parsonage in the Villiage, where we met the Horne Family.' On 2 October 1817 she wrote: 'Miss Hatton & I dined at Mr. Hornes at Epping Green a dull place in the Parish of L. Berkhamstead, meeting only Mr. & Mrs. Davison, good entertainment but rather dull, altogether.' The property belonged to Sir William Horne (1774-1860), barrister and politician, the second son of Revd Thomas Horne, of Chiswick, and therefore the elder brother to Edward Horne. It also seems that Revd Dr Thomas Horne was a college contemporary of Agnes's brother, Ferdinand Tracy Travell, and the connection may have come from this source. From all of this it may be deduced that Edward and Agnes Witts had been long-standing friends of the Horne family, and that they patronised the services of young Edward Horne after he had recently qualified. No doubt a young solicitor was also less expensive. They used his services to extract George Witts from his embarrassing financial circumstances in Edinburgh, and after that he drafted the marriage settlement for Francis Witts and Margaret Backhouse.

Edward married, 1800, Barbara Julia Paine; they had 4 sons and 2 daughters:

1 Julia Barbara (b. 1801)
1 Edward (b. 1802)
2 James Thomas (b. 1803)
3 Henry (b. ±1805)
4 John (b. 1806)
2 Julia (b. ±1807)

1806: 21 Jan: *Wrote upon business to Mr. Edwd. Horne the Solicitor.* 30 Jan., 7 Feb., 21 Feb., 23 Feb., 26-28 Feb., 3 Mar., 25 Jul: *Wrote in my Father's name to Sir John Callander, & to Mr. Horne & Mr. Adamson.* 31 Jul., 4 Aug., 15 Oct: *Wrote letters upon business to Mr. Adamson & to Horne.* 6-7 Nov., 15 Dec., 19 Dec., 23 Dec.

1807: 2 Jan: *Wrote letters upon business to Mr. Travell & Mr. Horne.* 30 Jan., 10-11 Feb., 17 Feb., 16 Mar., 20 Mar., 23 Mar., 6 May, 9 May, 15 May, 10 Jun., 26 Jun., 10 Jul., 12 Jul., 15 Jul., 29 Jul., 6 Aug: *A Gentleman from Mr. Horne brought us various deeds to sign.* 8 Aug., 13-14 Aug., 20 Aug., 26 Aug., 29 Aug.

1808: 18 Jan., 23 Jan., 25 Jan., 7 Feb., 18 Feb., 23 Feb: *Called on Horne & conversed with him for two hours on the Marriage Settlement business. Dined with him afterwards & even supped, meeting his Brother Mr. John Horne, & a Mr. Baines, a pleasant party.* 26 Feb., 15 Mar., 26 Mar., 7 Apr., 20 Apr., 24 Apr: *Received a Parcel of Deeds from Horne being the rough Draft of the proposed Marriage Settlement.* 25 Apr.

HORNE — Thomas Horne[243]

Thomas Horne (1784-1861), grocer and wine merchant, was born at Moreton-in-Marsh, a son of Joseph Horne (1744-1814) and Ann Attwood (1746-1823). He married, first, at Stow-on-the-Wold, 6 August 1808, Rebecca Clifford (1787-1824); they had at least 2 sons and 3 daughters:

1 Selina (b. 1812)
2 Louisa (b. 1815)
1 Thomas (1817-1896)
2 James (b. 1820)
3 Maria (b. 1822)

Thomas Horne married secondly, 1827, Elizabeth Tombs (1806-1865); they had at least 2 sons and 7 daughters:

1 Charles (b. 1829)
1 Anne (b. ±1830)
2 Maria (b. 1832)
3 Emma (b. ±1833)
4 Lucella (b. 1834)
2 Frederic (b. 1835)
5 Rebecca (1840-1925)
6 Frances (b. ±1845)
7 Lucy (b. ±1848)

1844: 29 Oct: *Wrote to Mr. Mason, Govr, of Gloucester gaol, in favour of Jas Miles, of Moreton, servant to Mr. Horne, Grocer, who applied to me yesterday to promote an application made by him to the Trustees of the County prison charity, a year having elapsed since his discharge from gaol, where he had suffered imprisonment for a long term on a charge of sending a threatening letter, and he having kept his place with one master with credit, as certified in a memorial signed by several principal inhabitants of Moreton.* 4 Nov., 9 Nov.

1846: 1 Aug., 5-6 Nov.

HORNE TOOK — John Horne Tooke[244]

John Horne Tooke (1736-1812), Church of England clergyman and politician, was born at Soho, Middlesex, third son of John Horne, poulterer, of Newport Street, Soho, and his wife, Elizabeth. He was educated at Soho Square Academy, Westminster School, Eton College, and St John's College, Cambridge. He was admitted to the Inner Temple in 1756, but instead of practising law, he took holy orders and was ordained priest on 23 November. He served as perpetual curate of St Lawrence, New Brentford, in 1760-73.

Horne took up the cause of John Wilkes, supporting him in the famous parliamentary election in Middlesex. Drawn into the vortex of political controversy and engaged in a long dispute with Wilkes, he broke away, and formed the Constitutional Society in 1771. In that year he became unpopular and was burnt in effigy by the mob. He changed course once more; resigning his benefice, he returned to law studies in 1773. He was fined and imprisoned for libel in connection with an appeal to raise a subscription for widows and orphans of American colonists in 1778.

Having been refused admission to the bar, and on inheriting some money, Horne lived in London, giving famous suppers and engaging in political discussions. He assumed the additional name of Tooke when he became heir to his friend Mr William Tooke in 1782. As a supporter of parliamentary reform he unsuccessfully contested Westminster in 1790, and again in 1796. He was arrested on a charge of high treason, and committed to the Tower; he was tried and acquitted in 1794. Having succeeded to the estate of William Tooke, at Purley, Surrey, John took up his residence there in 1803, and received the benefit of much society, including visits from Thurlow, Erskine, Bentham, Coleridge, and Godwin. He is said to have been a complex personality, who rendered unquestionable service to the cause of public justice and popular rights. His undoubted consistency was the chief reason for his unpopularity with time-serving politicians. He was MP for Old Sarum in 1801-02 and it was in this context that Francis Witts saw him in the House of Commons. He died, unmarried, at Wimbledon.

1801: 8 Jun: *Mr. Grey appeared by far the greatest orator on the opposition side: the other speakers, were, Mr. Martin, Horne Tooke, Tinney, W. Smith, Sir F. Jones Burdett, Dr. Lawrence, & Mr. Whitbread.*

HORNER — Leonard Horner[245]

Leonard Horner (1785-1864), geologist and factory inspector, was the youngest son John Horner, a linen merchant in Edinburgh. Leonard's elder brother Francis (1778-1817) became an MP and statesman.

Horner entered the University of Edinburgh in 1799. There in the course of the next four years he studied chemistry and mineralogy, and became fascinated by geology. At the age of 19 he became a partner in a branch of his father's business, and went to London. In 1808 he joined the newly formed Geological Society and two years later was elected one of its secretaries. He was elected a fellow of the Royal Society in 1813. In 1815 he returned to Edinburgh to take personal superintendence of his business, and while there (1821) he was instrumental in founding the Edinburgh School of Arts for the instruction of mechanics. He was also one of the founders of the Edinburgh Academy. In 1827 he was invited to London to become warden of the London University, an office which he held for four years. In 1833 he was appointed one of the commissioners to inquire into the employment of children in the factories of Great Britain, and he was subsequently selected as one of the inspectors.

1825: 17 May: *Here the structure of the rocks is clearly discernible to the Geologist, & on this subject an able essay has been written by an old schoolfellow of mine at Edinburgh High School,*

Mr. L. Horner, younger brother of the distinguished opposition Statesman & political economist, Francis Horner, whose early death some years since, in Italy, was so generally deplored.

HORNSBY — George Hornsby and the Hornsby family of Turkdean[246]

George Hornsby (1781-1837), Church of England clergyman, was born at Oxford, son of Thomas Hornsby (1733-1810) (*below*), professor of astronomy, and his wife, Ann (d. 1812). He was educated at Christ Church, Oxford (BA 1803; MA 1805). He was ordained deacon on 27 May 1804 and priest on 9 June 1805. Hornsby's first clerical appointment was as curate of Culworth, Northamptonshire, from 18 April 1806. He then became curate of Aldsworth on 8 April 1807, and finally vicar of Turkdean on 8 May 1807.

Hornsby married, 1808, Cordelia Emma Astley (1783-1857); they had at least 3 sons and 5 daughters:

1 Eliza Cordelia (1810-1843)
2 Harriet (b. 1812)
3 Emma Isabella (b. 1814)
4 Georgina Mary (b. 1815)
1 Frederic John (1817-1881)
5 Mary Hay (1822-1899); died unmarried
2 John William (b. 1822)
3 George Henry (b. 1825); married, 1855, Emily Banks (b. 1830)

In 1851 Mary was living at Weeping Cross, Stafford, with her widowed mother, Cordelia Emma Hornsby, née Astley (b. ±1782), and nephews William Ainslie (b. ±1845) and John Astley (b. ±1847). There may have been carelessness on the part of the census gatherer for these last two names. By 1861 Mary was listed as an annuitant and living at Fullbrook Cottage, Staunton, with one female servant. She died at Newent in 1899.

1828: 14 Oct.

1834: 11 Aug.

1835: 13 Mar.

1837: 17 Mar., 31 Aug: *Heard of the death of a neighbouring Clergyman, with whom, however, my acquaintance has been only slight: the Incumbent of Turkdean, Hornsby, a contemporary of mine at the University, and Son of a former Prof. of Astronomy at Oxford.* 13 Sep.

1842: 26 Feb: *we adjourned to Bourton Rectory, and visited Mrs. R. Waller; her guest Miss Hornsby, daughter of the late Rector of Turkdean, a very pleasing young person.*

1845: 28 Feb: *I walked with R Waller to the Rectory at Bourton, where I partook of luncheon, with him, Mrs. R.W. and their agreeable guest, Harriet Hornsby.* 11 Mar., 31 Mar., 1 Apr., 4 Apr: *At Cheltenham received a note from MW:—met and conversed with Mrs. and Miss H. Hornsby.*

1846: 7 Jul: *Called at R. Waller's, who is recovering from an indisposition which has hung upon him for some time past. He gave a favourable account of his lady and her infant. Harriet Hornsby is on a visit there, cheerful as usual.* 15 Jul., 28 Jul.

1847: 22 Jun: *Called at the Rectory, where I saw Mrs. R. Waller, and Harriet Hornsby.*

1848: 19 Jan: *dined at Mr. Ford's: met Mr. & Mrs. John Scott from Banksfee; Mr. and Mrs. R. Waller; Mrs. and Miss Mary Hornsby, now on a visit to the R. Wallers; Mr. Albert Boudier, Mr. Hunt, and Mr. Terry.* 1 Feb: *Called at the Rectory; saw Robert Waller, Mrs. W., and Miss M. Hornsby.*

HORNSBY — George Hornsby, schoolmaster at Stow Union Workhouse[247]

George Hornsby (1793-1853), workhouse schoolmaster, was born at Stow-on-the-Wold, son of George and Elizabeth Hornsby. The Hornsby family of Stow were tailors, but it appears that this member of the family was unable to hold a needle.

1847: 22 Apr: *Accompanied him in visiting the house: his principal enquiries were as to the Schools, with a view to ascertain the competency of the present Schoolmaster; this ended in the provisional appointment of Hornsby, to be made permanent, if, at the expiration of a few months, he acquires greater proficiency in arithmetic.* 19 May: *Mr. Pearce ... and as to the provisional appointment of Hornsby as School-master in the Workhouse.*

1850: 6 Nov: *fixed for an examination of the boys of the Union School, Mr. Jelinger Symons, the Government Inspector having reported unfavourably of the qualifications of the Schoolmaster, Hornsby, and of the progress made by the boys, of which Mr. V., as Chaplain, had spoken with commendation in his journal.*

1851: 15 Mar: *it appeared that Hornby, the Workhouse Schoolmaster, a miserably helpless cripple from rheumatic gout, insomuch that he needed help for dressing himself, and had been waited on by a female pauper, had taken such liberties with her, that the woman became pregnant (whether by him or someone else may be doubted,) and having left the establishment some weeks ago, was brought in last night, in labour. H. admits great indiscretion, and the course to be taken is clearly to suspend him from the office, and report such suspension to the Guardians, and eventually to the Poor Law Commissioners, with a view to his removal from the situation.* 19 Mar: *Received a letter from Mr. Pearce, whence it appears that the worthless Workhouse Schoolmaster, Hornsby, has resigned his situation, thus anticipating a dismissal.*

HORNSBY — Thomas Hornsby[248]

Thomas Hornsby (1733-1810), Sedleian professor of natural philosophy, was born at Durham, a son of Thomas Hornsby. He was educated at Corpus Christi College, Oxford (BA 1753; MA 1757; DD 1785). He was Savilian professor of astronomy and professor of experimental philosophy in 1763-1810, Sedleian professor of natural philosophy in 1782-1810, Radcliffe observer in 1772-1810, and Radcliffe librarian in 1783-1810.

1804: 13 Nov: *At Hornsby's Lecture on Electricity with Evans.* 14 Nov: *At Hornsby's Lecture on Electricity.*

HORROCKS — Miss Horrocks of Preston

Miss Horrocks was a daughter of Samuel Horrocks (1766-1842) and Alice Duckworth (d. 1804). Horrocks was MP for Preston in 1804-26. He and Alice had eight children; they were all under the age of 14 when Alice died in 1804. Samuel was wealthy cotton manufacturer.

1824: 9 Jul: *Dr Price's dinner party Miss Horrocks, daughter of the Member for Preston, & niece to Mrs. C. Pitt.*

1830: 10 May: *By his wife, who was a schoolfellow of my wife, at Preston & in Lancashire, and sister to Mr. Horrocks, a great manufacturer there, who also represented that borough, Mr. C. Pitt has a family; she is now deceased, and the father & son are on better terms.*

HORSLEY-BERESFORD — John Horsley-Beresford — *see also* Thomas Hope *and* Henry Thomas Hope[249]

John Horsley-Beresford, 2nd Baron Decies (1774-1855), Church of Ireland clergyman, was born in Dublin, fourth but first surviving heir of William Beresford, 1st Baron Decies, and Elizabeth FitzGibbon. He was educated at Emmanuel College, Cambridge (BA; MA 1809; DD), and was sometime rector of Tuam. He succeeded as 2nd Baron Decies in 1819. He married, 26 July 1810, Charlotte Philadelphia (d. 1852), only daughter and heir of Robert Horsley of Bolam House, Northumberland. Upon his marriage, John assumed the additional surname of Horsley.

John Horsley-Beresford was a first cousin of Henry Thomas Hope, MP for Gloucester.

1829: 22 Sep: *Lord Calthorpe, the Hon. G. Rice Trevor; the Dean of Gloucester & Mrs. Rice, three or four Miss Rices, & their brother Henry Rice; Hon. Henry and Mrs. Moreton; Viscount Chetwynd, Lord Decies.*

HORTON — William Horton and the Horton family at Clifton[250]

William Horton (1783-1853) was born in the parish of St Philip and St Jacob, Bristol, the second son of Edward and Jane Horton. It is not clear who Capt. Horton was; it could have been William's father, Edward, in which case he may have been in the volunteers. Edward Horton (b. 1756) married, at Bristol, 25 December 1780, Jane Morgan. William had two siblings; George (b. 1781) and Susannah (b. 1787). This attribution to William Horton and his family is tentative due to insufficient evidence.

1804: 7 Jan: *Passed a dull evening crowned with a supper at Mrs. Moncasters, which would have been intolerable, had I not played speculation, making Bank with Miss Adam. Captns. Smith & Horton, Mr. Port, Harriet & Miss Leyard, Miss Duce's etc. there.* 8 Jan: *Partook of a hearty luncheon at Mr. Marriotts: & afterwards walked with the Mesdemoiselles of that party, Misses Horton & Purvis, Captn. Horton & Prower on the Downs.* 10 Jan: *A very pleasant ball of about 120 persons. Danced also with Misses Port & Horton. A little bustle about a man in the Bedford & Horton's sister, which I hope will end in nothing. I believe the Bedfordian to be a coward as well as Blackguard. Poor Horton had not a friend in the room to stand by him but myself. Half a dozen people frightened out of their wits about it.* 14 Jan., 17 Jan: *Sat mournfully enough at home till time to go to the York House Ball, which the thin was pleasant enough; danced with H. Marriott, Misses Horton & Adair. Some pleasant men there Horton, Dawkins, Smith, Lear etc. etc.* 18 Jan., 21 Jan: *Walked with Harriett on the Downs afterwards with her sisters & the Miles's & with Edgell. Dined with Horton & met Benson.* 22 Jan: *Called on Horton.* 26 Jan: *Met Prower, Horton etc. And called on Mr. McBride.* 21 Jul: *At a party at Ashton in the Evening, the Taylors, Miss Vanderhorst, Manners's, Weir, Horton &c.* 27 Jul: *Walked back with Horton.* 3 Aug: *Hankey & George Monck to a match between Horton's Mare & one of Mr. Sweetman's. Horton beat.*

HOSKINS — James Williams Hoskins[251]

James Williams Hoskins (1759-1844), Church of England clergyman, was born at Witney, Oxfordshire, son of Charles Hoskins. He was educated at Jesus College and Magdalen College, Oxford (BA 1778; MA 1781; BD 1794; DD 1797), and was a fellow there from 1792 to 1803. He was prebendary of Wells (combe) in 1813, and rector of Appleton, Berkshire, in 1802. He married, at St George's, Hanover Square, Westminster, 28 May 1803, Frances Jane Taylor.

1802: 19 Mar: *Heard from Dr. Hoskins.* 8 Jul: *Called on Dr. Hoskins.*

HOSKYNS — Bennet Hoskyns — *see* Reade[252]

Bennet Hoskyns (1781-1843), Church of England clergyman, was born at Harewood, Herefordshire, younger son of Hungerford Hoskyns and Catherine, daughter of Edwyn Francis Stanhope and Catherine Brydges. Bennet Hoskyns was the brother of Sir Hungerford Hoskyns (*below*). He was educated at Balliol College, Oxford (BA 1806; MA 1808), and ordained deacon on 18 December 1808, but it was ten years until his first clerical appointment as rector of Bacton, Herefordshire. He served in that post from 5 December 1818 to 28 August 1834. He was then vicar of Montacute, Somerset, in 1838-43. He married, 1815, Amelia, daughter of Adm. Chamberlain. Lady Reade was Bennet Hoskyns's aunt; she was born as Jane Hoskyns, the only daughter of Sir Chandos Hoskyns. Bennet and Amelia had no children.

1837: 27 Sep: *Her nephew, the Revd. Bennet Hoskins, an old schoolfellow and college acquaintance of mine, and brother of the Herefordshire Baronet, with his wife, are staying with Lady R.* 30 Sep: *Returning home, I found Mr. & Mrs. Bennet Hoskins paying a morning visit, having driven over from Oddington.* 6 Oct.

1838: 14 Aug., 3 Oct: *Rode with E.F.W. to Broadwell; called on Mr. Leopold Dryden, met there Mr. & Mrs. Bennet Hoskins.* 6 Oct.

HOSKYNS — Hungerford Hoskyns — *see* Reade[253]

Sir Hungerford Hoskyns, 7th baronet (1776-1862), JP, DL, and landed proprietor, was born at Harewood, Herefordshire, eldest son of Hungerford Hoskyns and Catherine, daughter of Edwyn Francis Stanhope and Catherine Brydges. He succeeded as 7th baronet in 1802 and was high sheriff for Herefordshire in 1814. He married, 1803, Sarah (1779-1860), youngest daughter of John Philips of Bank Hall, near Stockport; they had at least 3 sons and 4 daughters:

1 Hungerford (1804-1877); succeeded as 8th baronet
1 Catherine-Sarah (1806-1814)
2 Sarah (1808-1869)
3 Caroline-Anne (1810-1872)
2 Chandos Wren (1812-1876)
4 Catherine Mary Jane (1815-1911)
3 John Leigh Hoskyns (1817-1911), Church of England clergyman; succeeded as 9th baronet

---

1829: 22 Sep., 23 Sep: *near us were Messrs. Ll. Baker, Clifford, Twisleton, Sir H. Hoskins, Sir E. Stanhope &c.*

1830: 22 Apr.

1834: 23 Jul: *Mr. Arkwright is one of the Sons of the celebrated inventor of improved machinery in the cotton factories, who realized in that trade a princely fortune, and resides in Herefordshire on his estates at Hampton Court, a very ancient mansion, which he is now restoring in the taste of the times in which it was originally erected. He married a great niece of Lady Reade's, a very pleasing young person, one of the daughters of Sir Hungerford Hoskins, a Herefordshire Baronet.*

HOSTE — Harriet Hoste[254]

Harriet Hoste, née Walpole (±1783-1875) was the daughter of Horatio Walpole, 7th earl of Orford (1752-1822), and Sophia Churchill. She married, 1817, Capt. Sir William Hoste, 1st baronet (1780-1828), son of Revd Dixon Hoste and Margaret Stanforth; they had at least 1 son and 2 daughters:

1 William Legge George Hoste (1818-1868); succeeded as 2nd baronet; married Caroline Dorothea Prideaux-Brune
1 Caroline Harriet Clementina (b. 1820); married David Kay
2 Priscilla Ann (1823-1854); married [unclear] Francis Jack Needham, 2nd earl of Kilmorey (1787-1880). Lord Kilmorey scandalised Victorian society by eloping with his ward, Priscilla Anne Hoste, when he was in his late fifties and she was 20. A year after their elopement, in July 1844, they had a child, Charles, who Lord Kilmorey acknowledged as his son and to whom he gave his surname. He set up his mistress in an adjoining house with an underground tunnel between the two

---

1853: 16 Jun: *there; visited the ancient and, with all its anomalies of architecture, truly royal palace. Mrs. B.L.W. called on one of its inmates, Lady Harriet Hoste, a sister of the Earl of Orford, and Widow of an eminent naval officer, Admiral Hoste, to whom very enjoyable apartments are assigned, and by whom, a very courteous lady, and her daughter, we were graciously received. Lady Harriet is Sister of Lady Georgina, the wife of the strange and adventurous Missionary, Wolff.*

HOUGH — Charles Hough of Hough's, booksellers, Gloucester[255]

In 1801 the firm Hough, booksellers, Gloucester, was run by John James Hough, a bookseller, stationer, and freeman of the City of Gloucester. By 1811 the firm was listed as John Hough and Son, the son being James, who was married to Sarah. They had at least two sons: a younger son, George Hough (1787-1867), was educated at Pembroke College, Oxford, and emigrated to South Africa to serve in the Church. By 1825 the firm was run by Charles Hough (b. 1782), but he appears to have left Gloucester in around 1831. By 1849 the name had ceased to be listed.

1826: 16 Sep: *I was busy in making arrangements respecting the Collection & produce of the sale of tickets at the bankers, and at Mr. Hough's, the booksellers.*

HOUGHTON — George Murray Houghton[256]

George Murray Houghton (1820-1847), Church of England clergyman, was born at Lutterworth, Leicestershire, son of George Houghton and Chailoth Elizabeth Cheatle or Chittle [?].

Houghton was educated at Lincoln College, Oxford (BA 1843; MA 1845). He was ordained deacon on 3 March 1844, but his clerical career is hard to follow; indeed, there is no precise evidence to prove he was the Revd Houghton at Oddington, but no other Oxford or Cambridge cleric fits, so it is more probable that this is the correct person. He married at Leicester in the second quarter of 1847, but the name of his spouse is not clear. He died in the last quarter of the same year; cause unknown. It appears that he fathered a child during his brief marriage:

1 Charlotte Elizabeth (b. 1848); married Allen MacDonogh of Athgarven Lodge, The Curragh, co. Kildare

It seems that George's mother was Irish, and indeed Irish connections continued. It would be interesting to know what Francis Witts meant by his comment 'late strange curate of Oddington, Mr. Houghton'.

1846: 26 Aug: *The Dean of Gloucester presided. Messrs. Ford, Waller, Hurd, Wiggin, Barrow, Pantin, Morrison, Smith, Potter, Houghton, Clarke, Estcourt, Winter, Hutchinson & myself were the Clergy present.*

1847: 28 Mar: *A letter from Mr. Wiggin, dated Deanery, Gloucester, who is in trouble, in consequence of a servant of his late strange curate of Oddington, Mr. Houghton, persisting in holding a cottage of which Mr. H. had the occupation as Curate, to the great inconvenience of Mr. Williams, the present Curate, and annoyance of the Dean and Wiggin.* 5 Apr: *The latter was returning from Oddington to the Deanery at Gloucester; he had managed to obtain possession of the cottage, respecting which he had communicated with me; Mr. Houghton's female servant had given up the Key, and left the house, and the property of Mr. H. had been removed.* 6 Apr.

HOULDEY — Lewis Houldey[257]

Lewis Houldey (1805-1871), manservant and blacksmith, was born at Lassington, two miles north-west of Gloucester. Houldey gave up his attempts to re-enter service and began a business as a blacksmith at Whaddon near Gloucester. He lived with his wife, Ann (b. ±1798), born in Elmore; they had at least 2 sons and 1 daughter:

1 John Charles (1836-1910)
1 Harriett (1839-1903)
2 Henry (b. 1842)

Lewis appears to have lived in Gloucester in the 1820s and 1830s when John was born. By 1871 the family had moved to Pitchcombe, near Painswick, and Lewis died in July of that year.

1846: 22 Aug: *To Stow, where I answered a letter from Lewis Houldey, a Servant out of place, who had by offered to live with me, that I purposed being at Gloucester on Tuesday next, and would meet him there at the Bell Hotel.* 25 Aug: *Proceeded to Gloucester by the Railway, and at the Bell Hotel, met Lewis Houldey, the servant who had offered himself as successor to John Bateman. His age, near 50, is against him, but I left it open whether I would engage him, subject to my interview with George Baldwin or others.* 29 Aug: *Wrote to George Baldwin to come into our service on Sept. 10: and to Lewis Holdey, to inform him that I have engaged another Servant, and so cannot take him into my place.*

HOUSTON — George Augustus Frederick Houston, a dinner guest of Thomas Jones Howell[258]

Sir George Augustus Frederick Houston-Boswall, 2nd baronet (1809-1876), army officer, was the eldest son of Gen. Sir William Houston, 1st baronet (1766-1842), and Jane (1769-1833), the fourth daughter of James Maitland, 7th earl of Lauderdale and widow of Samuel Long, who had married 5 November 1808.

Sir William Houston had been governor of Gibraltar from 8 April 1831 to 28 February 1835, and this is where Thomas Jones Howell would have met his son, George.

George Augustus Frederick Houston married Euphemia (1819-1882), daughter of Thomas Boswall of Blackadder, and they had 5 sons and 1 daughter:

1 George Lauderdale (1847-1908), succeeded as 3rd baronet
2 William (1849-1885)
3 Thomas Alford (1850-1918)
4 Robert (1853-1913)
5 Alfred (1854-1920)
1 Evelyn (1854-1932)

1851: 22 May: *The dinner party (Howell) was large ... Mr. Houston and Son—the former an old Artillery officer known to Howell, when he was Judge Advocate at Gibraltar, is now, by marriage with an heiress, possessed of considerable landed property near Belfast.*

1853: 7 Jun: *Mr. Houston, a large landed proprietor near Belfast, whom I had met here before, with an agreeable and well informed Captain Mack.* 12 Jun: *At dinner in the evening two guests, Mr. Houston & M. Matthews: both of them previously known to me: the former embued with strong Protestant principles and Anti-catholic prejudices, as cosistent with a residence in the Presbyterian regions of Belfast, the latter an ardent Roman Catholic Barrister, talented and sensitive: Mr. H not knowing, or not discovering the religious opinions of the younger guest, and being of an outspoken John Bullish temperament, made certain allusions as to the Catholic priesthood, and the necessity of making a law for the inspections of nunneries, which led to a sharp and not unamusing collision.*

HOW — Mr How, solicitor, of Shrewsbury

1832: 14 Mar: *A Mr. How, a Solicitor of Shrewsbury, with his lively and agreeable young wife, was also a guest at Mr. Wingfield's board; they were on a Tour, and on their return homeward. This gentleman is the confidential agent of my Shropshire connexion, Mr. Hunt of Boreatton, and appeared a sensible and well conducted person.*

HOWARD — Charles John Howard [259]

Charles John Howard, 17th earl of Suffolk and 10th earl of Berkshire (1805-1876), landed proprietor, was the son of Thomas Howard, 16th earl of Suffolk, and Elizabeth Jane, daughter of James Dutton, 1st Baron Sherborne. Charles was styled Viscount Andover between 1820 and 1851. He married his kinswoman Isabella Catherine, daughter of Henry Thomas Howard-Molyneux-Howard.

1829: 22 Sep: *Lord & Lady Andover; she is a bride, not handsome, daughter of the late Lord H. Molyneux Howard, brother to the Duke of Norfolk and formerly MP for the City of Gloucester.*

HOWARD — Howard de Walden — *see* Griffin

HOWARD — George Howard [260]

George Howard, 7th earl of Carlisle (1802-1864), politician, was the eldest son of Francis Howard, 6th earl of Carlisle. He was educated at Eton College and Christ Church, Oxford. On the death of his grandfather in September 1825 he was granted the courtesy title, Lord Morpeth. In 1826, his father arranged for him to be elected MP for the constituency of Morpeth, one of the boroughs under his control. He was a whig and took a particular interest in removing all religious forms of discrimination. In his maiden speech he seconded Sir Francis Burdett in his attempt to bring an end to Catholic disabilities. The following year he was active in the campaign to repeal Jewish disabilities. A supporter of reform, George Howard left the pocket borough of Morpeth and became one of the whig candidates for Yorkshire. In the general election in August 1830, Lord Morpeth headed the poll. In the debate on the Reform Act in March 1831, he called the proposed measure 'a safe, wise, honest, and glorious measure'. He succeeded his father as 7th earl of Carlisle in 1858.

1835: 19 Apr: *The newspapers announce the near completion of a Whig Ministry under Lord Melbourne as Premier... Lord Mulgrave to be Lord Lieutenant of Ireland, with Lord Morpeth as his Secretary.* 11 May.

1837: 27 Jul: *Recd. a letter from Settle, written by direction of the local Committee organised there to support the Conservative Candidate for the West riding of Yorkshire, the Hon. Mr. Stuart Wortley, son of Lord Wharncliffe, who opposes the Secretary for Ireland, Lord Morpeth, on this occasion, as he did at the last general election.* 29 Jul.

1839: 6 May: *Various political rumours were floating in the atmosphere of the House of Lords, and its purlieus; among others that Lord Melbourne and John Russel were about to retire from the administration, the former to be replaced in the post of Premier by the Marquis of Normanby, and the latter by Lord Morpeth at the Home Office.*

HOWARD — Julia Howard — Lady Suffolk [261]

Julia, née Gaskarth (1741-1819), widow of Stanwix Nevinson, married, 1774, John Howard, 15th earl of Suffolk (1739-1820). Their eldest son, Charles Nevison Howard (1775-1800), was accidentally killed by a discharge of his gun. His young widow was Jane Elizabeth (1777-1863), daughter of Thomas William Coke, 1st earl of Leicester (1754-1842), and Jane, sister of James Dutton, 1st Baron Sherborne (1744-1820). Jane Elizabeth was granddaughter of James Lennox Dutton, formerly Naper of Loughcrew, co. Meath. As such she was the niece of William Naper (1749-1791), the husband of Jane Naper, née Travell, Francis Witts's first cousin.

To make matters more complicated, James Dutton had married Elizabeth, sister of Thomas William Coke, 1st earl of Leicester. Elizabeth (d. 1824) died at Ruscombe House, Berkshire, indicating connections with the Howard de Walden family; *see* Griffin and the diary entry for 8 July 1801.

The earl of Suffolk had been an influential resident of Cheltenham for a long time. In 1808 he bought the land around what is now called Suffolk Square from the De la Bere family of Southam. Lady Suffolk was on very friendly terms with Agnes Witts.

1804: 19 Oct: *Lady Suffolk, Lady C. Howard & Fanny Dutton called.*

HOWARD — Elizabeth Jane Howard — Lady Suffolk [262]

Elizabeth Jane Howard (1775-1836) was the daughter of James Dutton, 1st Baron Sherborne (1744-1820), and of Elizabeth, sister of Thomas William Coke, 1st earl of Leicester. Elizabeth married, 1803, Thomas Howard (1776-1851). He succeeded as 16th earl of Suffolk in 1820.

1826: 15 Sep: *And this seems the proper place for inserting a list of some of the leading families & individuals, whose presence on this occasion served so many good purposes; benefiting the charity ... two Ladies Howard...*

HOWELL — Constable Howell [263]

There were two constables with the name of Howell in the Gloucestershire Constabulary at this time: officer 335, Mark, and officer 521, John. Mark Howell enlisted on 24 June 1841, aged 22, and is registered as a shoemaker from Sedbury (Forest of Dean), 5 feet 8 inches in height. He was later dismissed for allowing a prisoner to escape from Stroud. John Howell enlisted on 26 September 1842, aged 19, and is registered as 5 feet 8¾ inches in height, a tailor from Horsley, Nailsworth. He was later dismissed for drunkenness.

1844: 11 Jan: *the principal case brought before us being a charge of assault against T. Herbert, of Lower Guiting, for beating Constable Howell, on Dec. 25, and a charge against five others of being drunk and disorderly, aiding and abetting Herbert in such assault.*

HOWELL — Thomas Jones Howell[264]

Thomas Jones Howell (1793-1858), barrister, legal writer, and inspector of factories, was the son of Thomas Bayly Howell (1768-1815), of Jamaica, and Lucy Anne, daughter of Robert Long. Through his marriage to Lucy Long in 1790, Thomas Bayly Howell became a joint owner of Longville estate in Clarendon, Jamaica.

It has been suggested that Thomas Jones was the same Thomas Howell who matriculated at Christ's College, Cambridge, in 1814. He was admitted in 1814 to Lincoln's Inn and called to the bar on 15 May 1822. He succeeded his father as editor of *State Trials*. These had been commenced in 1809 through the auspices of William Cobbett, who first commissioned Thomas Bayly Howell, a lawyer, to edit the work. He edited volumes 1 (1809) to 21 (1814); his son, Thomas Jones Howell, completed the remaining twelve volumes, finishing the work in 1826.

Thomas Jones Howell inherited Prinknash Park in 1815 on the death of his father. The estate had been bought by his grandfather, John Howell (d. 1803), in 1770 on his return from Jamaica.

Thomas Jones served as judge advocate of the forces and admiralty court in Gibraltar in 1822, secretary of the Commission for Colonial Enquiry in 1830, and commissioner for the West India Islands Relief in 1832. His final post, which he held for twenty-five years until his death, was as inspector of factories under the Factories Regulation Act of 1833. He married, in London, 1818, Susanna Maria, eldest daughter of Alexander Hume Macleod of Harris, Inverness; they had 7 sons and 3 daughters:

1 William Charles (1818-1914), Church of England clergyman; educated at Brasenose College, Oxford (BA 1840; MA 1843); served as chaplain at Havre, curate at Tysoe, Warwickshire, 1847, and vicar of Holy Trinity, Tottenham, 1861-1904. He married, at Hayes, Middlesex, 23 December 1846, Mary Augusta (1827-1911), daughter of Richard Willan (1802-1847), of Bloomsbury, London, and Sarah Catherine Toosey (1804-1886); they had at least 1 son and 1 daughter:

  1 Frederick Francis (b. 1848); cannot be traced after the 1871 census

  1 Mary Emmeline Cordelia (1852-1940); born at Great Walthingfield, Suffolk; died unmarred.

'Emmeline' was the name of William's sister, whom he appears to have been closest to. The family lived at Rose Villa, Philip Lane. William fell out with his father in 1845 and the diary entries for 22 October 1846 and 7 August 1848 provide useful background. Francis Witts considered William to be eccentric. He lived to the age of 96

2 Frederick Donald (1820-1846); studied medicine and entered the Army as a surgeon officer; killed in South Africa when attacked by Hottentots at the Kei river. ('1st Bn. engaged near Kei River [1st Kaffir War]; Capt. Gibson and Assist.-Surg. Howell killed'—*The Rifle Brigade Chronicle*.) The diary entry by Francis Witts for 6 April 1847 provides the melancholy detail

1 Emmeline Jane (1821-1865). The diary entry for 26 September 1826 tells that Emmeline accompanied her parents to Gibraltar: 'the little girl, a nice child of five or six years old, will accompany them'. Following her mother's death Emmeline took over the running of the household at Prinknash. In 1845 an unknown event occurred involving William and Emmeline which upset the household. (Edward Witts seems to have had some involvement if the supposition was correct that he was responsible for the loss of the diaries for this period.) The diary entry for 22 October 1846 is enigmatic, referring to 'the misconduct of Emmeline, William's eccentricities'. The misconduct remains mysterious, but the suspicion is that it was a flirtation with someone her father disapproved of, or perhaps an affair. It appears that William stood up for his sister, causing further disturbance. On 18 May 1847 Francis Witts received a letter from Thomas Howell: 'I received a letter from Howell, announcing the very unexpected intelligence that Emmeline had, at her place of seclusion, Mursley, in Buckinghamshire, where she is residing with a Clergyman named Horne, whose wife is sister to Mrs. Parsons, late of Upton St. Leonards, formed a connection with a medical Gentleman, named Wynter, practising at Winslow, a widower of 40 years of age, of respectable character, well spoken of by Mrs. Parsons and her Sister—Howell had gone down to see the parties, had given his consent to their marriage in July, and congratulates himself that this event will relieve him from much embarrasment, and solve difficulties.' The diary entry of 7 August 1848 also provides interesting background on Emmeline and William. Emmeline married John Wynter (b. ±1808) and the couple lived at Buckingham Road, Winslow. There do not appear to have been any children from the marriage, and Emmeline died in April 1865

2= Constance (b. 1826), twin of Laura. She the last person in the Howell family that Francis Witts communicated with; he sent her a letter on 14 August 1854, just four days before he died. Constance disappears from the census, and she was not living with her step-mother and half-brother and half-sister at 6 West Eaton Place in 1871. The most likely explanation is that she married and appears under another name. In 1888 a novel, *A More Excellent Way*, by Constance Howell was published by Sonnenschein & Company, and received excellent reviews. It is tempting to see this by 'our' Constance

2= Laura (1826-1882), twin of Constance. In the diaries she is not usually differentiated from her sister Constance, except for the entry for 29 October 1850: 'the daughters are much improved by a London residence; Laura a talented, somewhat romantic and imaginative person: Constance more commonplace than her sister, an accomplished singer...' Laura married, 1852, Hubert Engels (1824-1891), a German music director. *See* diary entries for 11 March and 17 and 27 April 1852

3 Edward (b. 1828); born at Gibraltar. Little is known of him. He was first referred to (unnamed) in the diary entry of 15 July 1829, and first named in the entry of 22 August 1834. He then appears in brief snatches until 30 June 1845: 'and that he has settled to send his son Edward to be pupil to a French Protestant Clergyman, married to an English lady, a Miss Trye, at Nismes, until he be required to join the regiment, in which he has obtained a commission.' On 25 July 1846 we learn that 'Edward has safely joined his regiment at Chambly in Canada'. Edward was back in England in 1851; on 31 May 1853 we learn that his regiment was the 23rd Rifles in Canada. No further records have been found for him in the census or in births, marriages, and deaths

4 Henry Hyett (1830-1915), Francis Witts's godson. He receives only bit-part entries in the diaries. The best snatch is in the entry for 18 April 1853: 'Agreeably surprized by a visit from Henry Howell, who has been stationed for a short time at Blockley, conducting the Geological Survey of the country of which it is a centre: he is on the point of removing to Nuneaton to pursue the survey in the coal field of North Warwickshire. I found him an agreeable, conversible, well informed, intelligent, and open-hearted young man.' Henry had a distinguished career as a geologist. In the 1881 census he is listed as 'District Surveyor Geological Survey of England,

Department of Science and Art'. He married Julia (b. ±1842), born in Ireland; they had 2 sons and 1 daughter:

1 Willoughby John (1865-1938+), Church of England clergyman; minister of St Bartholomew's episcopal church, Greenock, in the 1920s
2 Edward Thomas (b. 1870)
3 Ellen (b. ±1875); baptised 1878

The family lived at Darlington. By 1891 they had moved to Edinburgh where Henry was the director of the Geological Survey. His career appears as follows in the records of the Darwin Project: assistant geologist with the Geological Survey of Great Britain, 1850; geologist, 1857; district surveyor, 1872; director for Scotland, 1882; director for Great Britain, 1888-99

5 Willoughby Wintle (1833-1861); appears in the diaries in snatched mentions until 22 October 1846: 'He had left London by a midday train, and came in good spirits, leading in his son Willougby, in his naval uniform, blue jacket, trousers, navy buttons, gold laced cap, and cutlass, as a naval cadet, having passed at Portsmouth, and being appointed by Lord Auckland to the Rattlesnake, surveying ship, which is going out under the command of an eminent and scientific officer, Capt. Stanley, son of the Bishop of Norwich, to survey Torres Straits, the coast of Carpentaria &c.' More information on the voyage was given on the 8 June 1850 entry. He was promoted to lieutenant on 4 February 1854. Willoughby died at the Royal Naval Hospital at Plymouth on 7 February 1861

6 John 'Johnny' Davis (1837-1895); educated at St Catherine's College, Cambridge (BA 1860; MA 1864). In the 1881 census John D. Howell, born at Prinknash Park, is listed as a merchant's clerk. He lived at 14 North Road, Kingston-on-Thames, and was married to Lucilla, born in Ireland; they had 1 son and 1 daughter:

1 Beatrice (b. 1871)
1 Francis (b. ±1869)

7 Francis Weston Macleod (1842-1851); his complicated birth caused his mother's death. His death is recorded in the diary entry for 12 March 1851: 'Received a letter from Howell. He informs me of the death of his youngest child—poor Macleod—in consequence of a violent attack of epileptic fits. Born in affliction, for his poor mother died in giving him birth, he has always been a tender plant, subject to fits; a singular but clever boy, and by his very infirmity, with the watchfulness rendered necessary by it, and never having left home even for a school, his education having been conducted chiefly by his sister Laura, he had become specially dear and, as it were, necessary to his Father and sisters. The latter, particularly Laura, are much distressed.'

Thomas Jones Howell was probably Francis Witts's closest friend. Their bond was such that upon the death of his wife Susanna in childbirth, Thomas dashed off a few lines 'written in deep distress' to summon his friend to his side. Witts then stayed at Prinknash for several days, baptising the infant and giving support to Thomas until after the funeral. It even appears that Macleod was christened 'Francis Weston Macleod', indicating further closeness.

Howell sold Prinknash in 1846 and went to live in London. On 6 August 1851 he married Ellen (1818-1902), daughter of Thomas Ffooks, a solicitor. Thomas and Ellen had 1 son and 1 daughter:

1 Alan George Ferrers (1855-1928); born when his father was 62 years old; educated at Eton College and Trinity College, Cambridge (LLB 1879; LLM 1882); admitted to the Inner Temple, 1877, and called to the bar, 1881. Howell was a classical scholar and in 1906 published *Fransican Days*, based on the writings of St Francis of Assisi; he also translated other works including a version of Dante from Latin. By 1901 he lived at Southlands, Heavitree, Devon, with his wife Anne (b. ±1860) and mother Ellen

1 Gertrude Lucy (1858-1914); married, 24 February 1886, Richard Frencis Steele Biddulph

After Thomas's death, Ellen went to the Ffooks family home in Sherborne, Dorset; she was there at the time of the 1861 census. She and her children later returned to 6 West Eaton Place; she was still living there in 1891 with Alan and his wife, Anne. Some time after that, she sold the London house and moved with Alan and Anne to Devon.

Thomas Jones Howell enjoyed considerable wealth. In addition to his inheritance from his father and the income earned from his formal positions, he was bequeathed £5,000 in his grandfather John's will of 1803. He formed friendships with people of high rank, and particularly with those interested in travel. He took pleasure in very long, solitary pedestrian tours; it seems that many of his factory inspection tours were undertaken on foot with nothing more than a shoulder bag. Twenty miles or more at a time seemed nothing to him, whereas others of his rank would have travelled on horseback.

Despite Francis Witts's friendship to Thomas Jones Howell, he made frequent comments about his attitudes and his devotion to the worldly life. Notwithstanding this, there was a deep bond between the two. Francis Witts enjoyed cultivated conversation and it is clear that his friend had a magnetic character. Perhaps the best quote from the diaries which gets to the nub of their common interest is that of 13 June 1825: 'While resident on his estate, he was an ornament of the bench of Magistrates, his legal acquirements being very extensive, to which he adds considerable literary acquirements, with a great store of anecdote, and a felicity of expression, which renders him a peculiarly agreeable companion.' This was reinforced in the entry for 15 October 1829:

> Our friends, the Howells, from Prinknash Park, arrived, to pass a few days with us... His store of anecdote, high spirits, and good sense, with an inexhaustible fund of varied information, make him a most agreeable companion, and conversation never flags, for lack of more interlocutors.

1825: 13 Jun: *Prinknash Park, the seat of my friend, T. Howell, is a pleasing object adjacent to the road. The venerable old fashioned mansion, within which I have enjoyed the hospitality of its talented owner, resembles Stanway House in its arrangements and architecture, & like it was of ecclesiastical origin; Stanway having belonged to the Abbots of Tewkesbury, as Prinknash did to those of Gloucester. Mr. Howell's father was editor of the State trials, & the same valuable publication is continued by his son, who was, like his father, bred to the bar, at which, however, he does not practice, but at present holds the important situation of Judge Advocate at Gibraltar, to which is annexed another judicial post. While resident on his estate, he was an ornament of the bench of Magistrates, his legal acquirements being very extensive, to which he adds considerable literary acquirements, with a great store of anecdote, and a felicity of expression, which renders him a peculiarly agreeable companion.* 19 Oct: *Among the magistrates attending the Sessions to-day was Mr. Howell of Prinknash Park, who is returned from Gibraltar on leave of absence for a twelvemonth. It gave me great pleasure to resume my intimacy with this talented person, whom, indeed, I had to thank for great civility and friendliness towards my poor brother, whom, out of regard for me, he wished to have taken to his house at Gibraltar, while the packet, on board of which he was, remained there; but George's distressing state of extreme debility both of mind and body precluded his landing.*

1826: 27 Jan: *I left my family in Wellington Parade this afternoon, being engaged to dine at my friend Mr. Howell's at Prinknash Park, whither I went in a post chaise.* 16 Jun., 11 Jul., 6 Aug: *Being strongly pressed by my friend Howell, who had sent a horse for me in the morning, I rode out to dinner at Prinknash Park.* 14 Sep., 26 Sep: *Margaret & myself dined at Prinknash Park. The Howells are soon to return to Gibraltar, where he after more than a year's leave of absence is about to resume the duties of his official situations of Judge Advocate and civil Judge. Mrs. Howell has recently been confined of twins, little girls, whom she must leave behind her; it would be too hazardous to expose to the dangers of the voyage, an inclement season, & a change of climate, such tender infants. Two little boys will also be left at school at Bromley in Kent: the little girl, a nice child of five or six years old, will accompany them.*

1828: 15 Apr.

1829: 13 Jan., 28 Apr., 14 Jul., 15 Jul: *I accepted an invitation from my friend Mr. Howell, who has been returned from Gibraltar for some weeks, to dine en famille and sleep at Prinknash Park ... Another narrow escape was experienced by my friends last summer. They were occupying a cottage on the sea coast, just without the lines, and on Spanish ground, and, as they were walking together in the evening, were suddenly attacked by some ill looking vagabonds, who with knives brandished soon overpowered and brought to the ground both Mr. & Mrs. Howell, robbing them of their watches, money, rings, &c. Providentially, Mrs. Howell, though in an advanced state of pregnancy, was not materially hurt, though greatly alarmed, and, judicious measures having been promptly taken, one of the highwaymen was apprehended the next day in the town of Algesiras, when he was offering Howell's gold watch and appendages for sale, and the ferocious fellow has since been sentenced to the gallies. My friends are now surrounded by their little people; the two boys, who were left at school in England, the twins, who remained behind, when they last sailed for Gibraltar, then just born, now pretty little things nearly three years of age, an infant born at Gibraltar last summer, and a sweet little girl of six or seven years of age. No other guest but myself dined at Prinknash, but in the evening Mr. & Mrs. Ferrers came from Cheltenham, where they had been passing the day. Mrs. F. is Mrs. Howell's younger sister, and her husband, an agreeable, well informed man, I believe, a Stock-broker in Town.* 22-23 Sep., 15 Oct: *Our friends, the Howells, from Prinknash Park, arrived, to pass a few days with us; they reached this place to dinner; the country, beyond Andoversford, was quite new to them. His store of anecdote, high spirits, and good sense, with an inexhaustible fund of varied information, make him a most agreeable companion, and conversation never flags, for lack of more interlocutors.* 16-17 Oct., 19-20 Oct.

1830: 12 Jan., 20 Apr., 24 Jun: *On our return to our hotel from our most enjoyable drive & visit to the Zoological gardens we found our friend Howell waiting for us; he returned to Town from Prinknash Park yesterday, after a few days absence. His time is now fully taken up in the important duties of his temporary office, as Secretary to the Commission now sitting on the details of our colonial establishments.*

1833: 10 Sep., 14 Oct: *Received a letter from Howell, from Prinknash; he returns to London to-morrow, and shortly enters on his Western tour to visit the Manufacturers, in his new character of Inspector of Factories.* 15 Oct., 19 Oct., 23 Oct., 30 Oct., 1-3 Nov.

1834: 12 Mar., 6 Aug., 10 Aug., 11 Aug: *to Prinknash, where we arrived at half past four, and were kindly welcomed by our excellent friends, Mr. and Mrs. Howell, whom we found surrounded by their fine family of children, but no other guests besides ourselves.* 12-13 Aug., 14 Aug: *Strolled about with Howell and his family in the grounds at home, except that we took a sauntering walk through the beech woods to the beautifully situate village of Cranham.* 15 Aug: *Mrs. Howell, Emmeline and William set out before breakfast to pass the day at Cheltenham with some friends, and attend a concert by some distinguished vocalists, Grisi, Tamburini and Ivanhoff, with Puzzi on the horn.* 16 Aug., 22 Aug: *While they were with us arrived our friends from Prinknash Park, Mr. & Mrs. Howell, Emmeline, Edward and my Son, in a fly, and William on horseback. They remained with us more or less during the forenoon, and returned to Prinknash to dinner.* 23 Aug: *one o clock arrived the Prinknash party, Mr. & Mrs. Howell, Emmeline, Laura, Constance, and Edward in a fly, and William on his poney, whom we accompanied to a temporary circus to witness an exhibition of horsemanship and the like.* 28 Aug., 14 Sep: *Received a letter from Howell mentioning that Mrs. H. had been seriously ill, in consequence of a miscarriage, and was now recovering; proposing a visit to us on the 22d. Inst. provided she be sufficiently recovered to leave home, or, should that not be the case, that Edward should come to him on that day, and accompany him on a circuit to visit the Factories under his superintendence.* 16 Sep., 18 Sep., 22 Sep: *On our return home we found our friends Mr. and Mrs. Howell and Emmeline arrived from Prinknash Park: Mrs. H. looking in delicate health, but convalescent.* 25-26 Sep., 29 Sep: *About mid-day our friends the Howells left us for Prinknash Park, their usual conveyance, a fly from Painswick, having come to fetch them.* 13 Oct., 17 Oct: *I could not extricate myself from the Court till half past three o'clock, when I left Gloucester in a fly for Prinknash Park, where I arrived to dinner, and passed the evening enjoyably with my kind friends and their delightful family. Edward, of course, was one of the party.* 18 Oct., 28 Oct., 30 Oct., 14 Nov., 2 Dec., 17 Dec.

1835: 6 Jan: *I breakfasted with Bathurst and Baker at the Bell, and went down with the Chairman to open the Court. My son joined me there, and afterwards went to Prinknash Park on foot, to visit the Howells, returning to dinner.* 14 Jan., 25 Feb., 27 Feb., 3 Mar: *My Son rode to Prinknash Park to pass a day or two with the Howells.* 4 Apr., 7 Apr., 9 Apr., 13 Apr: *Edward shortly afterwards left Gloucester for Prinknash Park in conformity with a note from our friend Howell.* 15 Apr: *the rest of the day and slept under the roof of our valuable friends the Howells, in their domestic circle.* 7-8 May, 12 May: *My Son left us in the Phaeton this forenoon for Cheltenham on his way to Prinknash Park, to be ready to accompany Howell on his factory circuit and into North Wales.* 13 May, 16 May, 20-23 May, 26 May, 28 May, 20 Jun.

1836: 22 Jul., 30 Jul., 1 Aug., 7 Aug., 11 Aug: *arrived by 5 o cl. at the house of my excellent friends, the Howells.* 12 Aug: *Between breakfast and dinner whiled away the time with Howell in walking through Pope's wood, and over Painswick Hill to call on Hyett.* 13 Aug: *After breakfast, Mr. Weston Hicks called: he is appointed superintendant of Factories in Howell's district, who has now two subordinate officers under him, Messrs. Hicks & Webster.* 15 Aug: *After breakfast with Mrs. W. accompanied Howell and E.F.W. in the phaeton as far as L. Slaughter Turnpike Gate: they proceeded to visit a Factory at C. Norton; we walked home.* 16-19 Aug., 20 Aug: *Howell left us for Prinknash Park.* 26 Aug., 30 Aug., 23 Dec., 26 Dec: *Wrote to Howell, and conveyed to him my thoughts respecting the prudence of his persevering in the intention of sending his son to Brazennose.*

1837: 5 Jan., 7 Jan: *After breakfast, an hour or two of conversation with Howell, partly on the terrace, partly in his study, and lastly on the roadside while waiting, near the Park gate, for the arrival of the Bath Coach, which arrived came between 12 & 1 o cl., and conveyed me to Cheltenham.* 10 Mar: *A letter from Howell, who writes on the point of taking his eldest son to be entered at Brazen Nose.* 16 Mar., 18 Mar: *Wrote to Howell, declining on the part of my son the invitation to visit Prinknash at the latter end of next week, but pressing Howell and William to pass some days here, either at the beginning or latter end of Easter week: advising on many points as to William Howell's outfit for college.* 21 Mar., 27 Mar., 12 Apr: *Fredk. Howell rode from Prinknash Park with a note from his father, pressing me to come thither, when I left Gloucester, which I declined, as I had settled to return home today.* 8 May, 11 May, 26 Aug., 4 Sep., 12 Sep: *Met. Howell and his son Frederick; he was returning from a Northern Factory Circuit in which the latter had accompanied his Father, and were, now when we met them, just arrived by the Bath coach from Birmingham, which was to set them down at Prinknash Park gate.* 27 Nov., 12 Dec., 15 Dec.

1838: 2 Jan., 4 Jan., 5 Jan: *Walked with Howell and his Son Frederick to Painswick Lodge to call on Hyett.* 7 Mar., 20 Mar., 18 May, 9 Jun., 11 Jun., 17 Jun: *Recd. a letter from Howell, announcing that he will be with us to-morrow.* 18 Jun: *Towards mid-day our friend Howell arrived from Prinknash Park, having come by the Novelty Northampton Coach thro' Stow, C Norton, Banbury &c.—from Cheltenham.* 19 Jun., 20 Jun: *A very wet day with little intermission, which confined Howell and me entirely to the house.... Towards four o cl. Frederick Howell arrived on horseback from Prinknash, in obedience to a summons sent in a letter from his Father by yesterday's post.* 21 Jun: *Howell, pére, accompanied me in the open carriage to Stow, whence he proceeded on foot to Chipping Norton to visit a mill there, and returned chiefly on foot, but partly by the Novelty coach to Stow, arriving as soon as my business was over, and accompanying me home to dinner in the phaeton... Frederick Howell rode to Whichford to call on E.F.W. and returned in the evening, having found the Curate and Sophy quite well; our young friend much pleased with the reception he met with, with the place &c.* 22 Jun: *Frederick remained with us till after dinner that he might enjoy a few hours fishing ... and left us about 7 P.M. on his horse to join his father at Broadway.* 2 Jul., 3 Jul: *Learnt from Hyett that Howell had been hurried up to Town in consequence of a cause in which he is deeply interested, an appeal from a decision of the Scotch Courts of law to the H. of Lords coming on this week unexpectedly: consequently my intended visit to Prinknash Park will not take place.* 4-5 Jul., 24 Jul., 16 Oct., 21 Nov., 2 Dec: *from Howell, a long, kind, clever, gossiping letter from Prinknash Park.*

1839: 1 Jan: *William Howell came from Prinknash Park with a friendly note from his Father, pressing me to come to pass a couple of days there before the week closed, which I promised to do.* 3 Jan: *Left Glouc. about half past three o cl. in a chariot for Prinknash Park, where most kindly and cordially recd., as usual, by my valued friends, Mr. & Mrs. Howell, surrounded by all their children with the exception of Frederick who is studying surgery and medicine at the King's College, London.* 4 Jan., 5 Jan: *Emmeline Howell prepared for me an early breakfast, before I had concluded, her father appeared, and accompanied me to the Park gate to meet the Stroud Coach on its way to Cheltenham.* 16 Feb., 21 Feb., 11 Apr: *He was accompanied by William Howell, who has been passing two or three days at Stanway: W. Vavasour also met him here.* 5 Jun: *I called on Mr. and Mrs. Riddle at their lodgings: also on W. Howell at Brazennose.* 12 Jun: *returned thro' Stow to Upper Slaughter, expecting Howell, who had come up by the Novelty Coach, and having sent his carpet bag from Eyford, had on passing through Stow to Chipping Norton, sent a message from the Unicorn that he would be with us to dine, and sleep ... Pleasant chat with Howell in the Evening.* 13 Jun., 2-3 Jul., 4 Jul: *Passed a pleasant, cheerful evening with Howell, and his family; Emmeline, William &c.* 5 Jul: *Emmeline Howell most kindly rose to make my breakfast at seven o clock.*

1840: 19 Mar., 21 Mar., 24 Mar., 26-28 Mar., 13 Apr: *Met and conversed with Howell, whose family is removing from their temporary residence at Cheltenham to Prinknash Park.* 25 Aug., 26 Aug: *Walked to Eyford to meet Howell coming by the Novelty coach about mid-day.* 27 Aug: *Rode to Stow. Howell accompanied me to and fro on foot.* 28 Aug: *Before luncheon sauntering with Howell and Capt. Witts, superintending the removal of Capt. W's broken carriage, which had been brought from Naunton Inn to Stow to be repaired, &c.* 4 Sep., 16 Sep., 18-19 Sep., 21 Sep., 29 Sep., 23 Oct., 8 Nov.

1842: 6 Jan: *Cordially welcomed by the Howells; they were all at home except Frederick, who is diligently pursuing his studies in surgery in London.... Emmeline is in better health than she has been lately, but still not quite well, and looking delicate.... William has a prospect of a title for orders next summer at Uxbridge.* 7 Jan: *After breakfast I took leave of the Howells and Moores, Howell walking with me to meet the Stroud and Cheltenham coach, by which I travelled to the latter place, where I arrived about 11 o clock.* 26 Jan., 31 Jan., 6-7 Feb., 5 Mar., 15 Mar., 5 Apr., 8 Apr., 12 Apr., 14 Apr: *Dressed at Prinknash, and having detained the Fly, accompanied Howell, William and Emmelyn, to dinner at Saintsbridge at Mr. Wintle's, where a large party was assembled.* 18 Apr., 13 May, 20 May, 22 May, 27 May, 31 May: *William Howell lately ordained by the Bishop of London, and now officiating as Curate of Uxbridge.* 6-7 Jun., 11 Jun: *Received a letter from Howell, who readily consents that his name should be substituted for that of J Backhouse in our Marriage Settlement as a Trustee.* 14 Jun., 16 Jun., 19 Jun., 23 Jun., 25 Jun., 29 Jun., 24 Aug., 18 Sep., 20 Sep., 22 Sep., 30 Sep., 3 Oct., 7 Oct., 10 Oct., 14 Oct., 16 Oct: *Sad news awaited me on getting up, an express having arrived from Prinknash Park with a few lines written in deep distress by my poor friend Howell intimating the death of his excellent wife.... Poor Howell was very grievously affected at meeting me in his bedroom, where I found him with his children Emmeline and Edward, the latter having been fetched from his Tutor's, Mr. Moore's at Brimpsfield.... The two eldest sons only were absent—William at his Curacy at Uxbridge—Frederick studying medicine at the London Hospital.... In the evening poor H. braced himself to meet his daughters Constance & Laura, and retired more calm and composed to his chamber than might have been expected.* 17 Oct: *Devoted the whole day to my poor friend Howell, endeavouring to support his spirits, and divert his thoughts from anxious and harrowing topics.... William Howell arrived in the evening, having received this morning the melancholy intelligence of his poor Mother's decease, and hastened down by the Great Western railway.* 18 Oct: *After breakfast, and an interview with poor Howell, whom I found tolerably composed, and after conferring with Emelyn and Mr. Hicks.... In the course of the day I wrote to E.F.W. requesting him and Sophy, at the solicitation of poor Howell to be sponsors to the poor babe at Prinknash, whose entrance on life occasioned a parent's departure: I have ventured to assure my widowed friend of their ready acquiescence.* 19 Oct: *I remained in Court till 1 P.M. when I left Gloucester to return to Prinknash, where I found Fredk. Howell, who had arrived from Town yesterday afternoon ...* 20 Oct: *Walking with Howell*

Emelyn, William & Frederick, Hicks &c. on the Terrace in the forenoon... It was a trying scene; the mourning father, with nine children (Fredk. only was absent, not being aware that the rite was then to be performed, and having gone for a walk), William & Constance were proxies for E.F.W. and Sophy, as sponsors to the babe: Hicks answered in person; and Francis Weston Macleod, were the Christian names given: the first name as borne by my son and myself, the second by Hicks, the last being the poor little infant's mother's maiden name.... Much serious conversation with my poor friend, as to family arrangements rendered necessary by the decease of his wife, and I consented to be nominated in the new will which he is about to make Executor, Guardian, and Trustee, in conjunction with his friend John Davis, of Brunswick Square, London. 21 Oct: *Took a walk with Howell, Hicks, William & Fredk.—by Cranham Wood to Prinknash Rough Park.* 22 Oct: *As soon as the arrangements could be completed the mournful procession moved towards the Church, a distance of more than a mile; a mourning coach conveyed Messrs. Parsons, Fendall, and Wollen; and the hearse was followed by another Mourning coach, of ample dimensions, containing poor Howell, his two eldest sons, Ferrers, Hicks, and myself. It was on my arm that the grieving and agitated widower heavily rested, as he descended from his chamber to the carriage.* 26 Oct: *Wrote to my poor friend Howell.* 30 Oct: *A letter from poor Howell reached me written in tolerable spirits—but there is no prospect of his soon visiting us.* 2 Nov., 5 Nov., 8-9 Nov., 12 Nov., 14 Nov., 21 Nov., 25 Nov: *Recd. from B. P. Witts a letter of condolence on the death of Mrs. Backhouse ... also a letter from Howell very kindly inviting MW. and me to Prinknash Park.* 26 Nov., 29 Nov., 30 Nov: *Recd. a letter from Howell, written in a dejected tone, pressing us to come to Prinknash on a visit on the 12th Dec.* 6 Dec., 7 Dec: *Emmeline Howell paid us a morning visit, having been driven into Cheltenham for a few hours by Mr. Fendall.* 8-9 Dec., 12 Dec: *We arrived at Prinknash by half past three P.M. and were kindly welcomed by Howell, Emmelyn, and the other children at home; William and Frederick being, the former at his Curacy, the latter at his hospital, and Laura, with Constance on a visit to the Hyett's.* 13 Dec., 15 Dec: *My godson, Henry Howell, came home today from School for the Christmas holidays.* 16 Dec., 23 Dec.

1843: 3 Jan: *Edward and Henry Howell rode to Gloucester to bring me a letter from their father, who engages to meet me at Cheltenham on Thursday at the Plough, with Edward, and to accompany me to Upper Slaughter.* 4 Jan: *Wrote to E.F.W. to inform him that Howell and his son Edward were to visit us at Upper Slaughter, that my son might fix a day on which we might dine and sleep at the Vicarage, Stanway.* 5 Jan: *Howell with his son Edward, arrived from Prinknash, to meet, and accompany me to U. Slaughter.* 6 Jan., 7 Jan: *Howell & his son Edward accompanied me in a drive to Stow.* 8-9 Jan., 10 Jan: *Howell and myself with E. Howell walked to Church Stanway, where we went over the Church, house, and grounds, in all which my friend took much interest.* 11 Jan: *After breakfast Howell and his son left us in a fly for Cheltenham and Prinknash.* 14 Jan., 6 Feb., 17 Feb., 10 Aug., 11 Aug: *My wife, Emmeline Howell, and myself bent our course in the same direction in our phaeton.* 12 Aug: *Our dear children and Grandchild left us after luncheon for Stanway, and we felt lonely without them, yet retained the amiable, sensible and affectionate Emmeline Howell.* 14-16 Aug: *Emelyn Howell, much indisposed with a cough and cold, left us to-day, being conveyed by MW. in our phaeton to Andoversford, where her father's carriage met her, Willoughby coming to accompany his sister home.* 19 Aug., 23 Aug., 2 Sep: *MW. heard from Emmeline Howell, who has recovered from her cough, and all at Prinknash are well—poor Emmeline had a sad alarm the other day; driving out of Cheltenham in the open carriage with Laura, in the open carriage, the mare being frightened and starting, a poor deaf and paralytic man fell beneath the wheel of their carriage, while confused in trying to avoid it and two others; no bones were broken, but the poor fellow bruised; no blame attached to the Howell's servant, but no wonder that poor Emmeline was much hurried and distressed.* 7 Sep: *Letters had come—one from William Howell, requesting me to apply to F. Aston for his interest as connected with the Grammar school at Northleach in favour of a youth who is candidate for Townsend's exhibition to Pembroke College, Oxford, being a son of Mr. Price, the Incumbent of Uxbridge, whose curate William Howell is.* 8 Sep, 13 Sep., 30 Sep., 5 Oct., 11 Oct: *a letter from Howell, who purposes visiting us with Constance and Willoughby in the week after the Sessions.* 12 Oct., 17 Oct: 23 Oct: *Howell arrived from Prinknash with his two children, Constance and Willoughby, and were not long followed by our dear children and grandchild from Stanway.* 24 Oct., 25 Oct: *Howell and I, with Willoughby & Constance drove to Stow in H's open carriage, followed by E.F.W., Sophy, and our darling Broome to "the Cottage", where took luncheon with the Vavasours.* 26-28 Oct., 23-24 Nov., 27 Dec., 29 Dec: *to Howell in reply to his note recd. on the 27th. that, if tolerably well, I would leave Gloucester for Prinknash on Thursday, dine and sleep at P. and return home on Friday in next week.*

1844: 2 Jan., 4 Jan: *I left Gloucestershire with the Chief Constable, and we were as usual cordially greeted by the Howells, all of whom were well.* 24 Jan., 26 Feb., 3 Apr: *MW. Recd. a letter from Emmeline Howell expressing a wish that we should visit Prinknash Park next week.* 8 Apr., 9 Apr: *My servant came from Prinknash with notes from MW. who arrived safely there yesterday, and from Howell, pressing me to leave Gloucester to-morrow, and join a dinner party at Prinknash, which I promised to do.* 10 Apr: *All the children were at home, excepting William and Frederick, the former at his Curacy at Uxbridge, the latter pursuing his medical studies at Paris... There came to dinner Mr. and Mrs. Charles Pettatt from Whitcomb—also Mr. and Mrs. Clements, with Miss Clements, and Mr. E. Mansfield from Upton: and there were staying in the house two fine lads, Turner and Swayne, pupils of Mr. Moore, of Brimpsfield, and so Schoolfellows of Edward Howell, passing the Easter holidays with him.* 11 Apr: *After breakfast till luncheon, wandering about home with Howell, till joined by Weston Hicks, who followed the boys, who had set out earlier to prepare for a game at cricket.* 12 Apr: *Strolled a little in the grounds with Howell before luncheon, but kept close by the fire side in conversation afterwards.* 13 Apr: *Busily engaged in shopping till 1 P.M. when we repaired to Mr. Lefroy's domicile at the Belle Vue Hotel, who kindly entertained us at luncheon, where we were joined by Emmeline, Constance, and Laura Howell, who had driven in from Prinknash to accompany MW. and me to a morning concert at the Assembly rooms.* 11 May, 7-8 Aug., 12-13 Aug., 4 Sep: *Wrote to Howell, inviting him, Frederick and Laura to visit us next week.* 8 Sep: *A letter to me from Emelyn Howell, writing for her father, who is too much immersed in factory papers to reply to my letter: he is going on a factory tour, so cannot come to us: Frederick declines, being absorbed in medical studies; and it is proposed that Constance and Laura shall come to Slaughter on a visit on the 17th. Inst.* 17 Sep: *Laura and Constance Howell came from Prinknash Park on a visit.* 18 Sep., 25 Sep., 26 Sep: *Our amiable guests, Constance and Laura Howell, left us to return home, much pleased with their visit; they are good, affectionate, and estimable.* 19 Nov: *Wrote to Emelyn Howell, so answering a letter she had lately written to MW, and one I had recd. from her many weeks since, saying also that we hoped if her father visited us before Xmas, that she would accompany him.* 9 Dec., 13 Dec., 27 Dec., 31 Dec: *During the morning I was called out to Emmeline & Laura Howell who had driven to Gloucester, and who engaged me to dine to-morrow and sleep at Prinknash with their Father, who would be alone as the young people are invited to a ball near Stroud.*

1845: 2 Jan: *After a cheerful breakfast with my friendly host and his children, left Prinknash in Howell's carriage, accompanied by his son Frederick, who was about to spend the day at Gloucester with an acquaintance, but who remained with me till I had seated him in court.* 15 Apr., 26 Apr., 27 Apr: *Wrote to Howell that MW. and myself would have much pleasure in visiting him next week: that we proposed arriving there on Monday, and remaining till Friday.* 30 Apr., 5 May: *MW. and I left home on a visit to the Howells.* 7-8 May, 12 May, 24 May, 31 May: *MW. received a letter from Emmeline Howell who with her father proposes to visit us on June 9.* 7 Jun: *Recd. a letter from Maria Witts with an account of the sayings and doings of Laura and Constance Howell while guests in Brunswick Square, where they have been passing a fortnight with Mrs. W. and her daughters: the first visit of the girls from Prinknash to the metropolis, and so sights and wonders crowding on them, wch. the young ladies whom they went to visit exhibited con amore.* 8 Jun., 9 Jun: *Howell arrived, accompanied by Emmeline and Willoughby, in their open carriage from Prinknash: passed a cheerful evening together.* 10-11 Jun., 12 Jun: *Drove to Stow; Howell and his son Willoughby accompanied me, and went in my carriage to Blockley, to inspect silk-mills, joining me on their return at the Justice room.* 13 Jun., 17 Jun: *E.F.W. proposes to go to Prinknash to-morrow to be present at a cricket party, and great gathering at the Howells.* 30 Jun: *Howell looked in for a short time, chiefly to communicate to me that his son Frederick had obtained an appointment in the Rifle Corps, as army surgeon and that he has settled to send his son Edward to be pupil to a French Protestant Clergyman, married to an English lady, a Miss Trye, at Nismes, until he be required to join the regiment, in which he has obtained a commission.* 9 Jul: *from Howell, whose son Frederick, as an Army Surgeon, has joined the depot of his regiment at Dublin——the regiment is stationed in the Ionian Isles.*

1846: 25 Jul: *Recd. a letter from Howell, he asks me to come to Prinknash—when I go to the Assizes at Gloucester: informs me that many enquiries are made as to his place now on sale, and to be put up to Auction in Town on Aug. 14: that his son Frederick is about to leave the Ionian Islands with his regiment for Jamaica: that Edward has safely joined his regiment at Chambly in Canada.* 3 Aug: *Received a letter from Howell, inviting me to Prinknash, while I am at Gloucester at the Assizes. His place is to be offered for sale by auction on the 15th. Inst. in London: many parties have applied, and looked over the property, with a view, no doubt, to its purchase. Frederick Howell's regiment is ordered from the Ionian Islands to the Cape of Good hope, which is the seat of harassing incursions by the Caffres.* 4 Aug., 6 Aug: *to Howell that my visiting Prinknash next week is quite out of the question.* 2 Sep., 6 Sep: *A letter from Howell: Prinknash Park is not yet sold; but he anticipates parting with it by private contract very shortly. A change has occurred in his plans. Owing to the illness of Mad. Frossard, the lady at Nismes to whose care Emmeline Howell was to have been consigned, that destination has been altered, and she is to reside with a Clergyman and his wife who are settled in Bucks or Bedfordshire; the lady of the Clergyman being sister to Mrs. Parsons, late of Upton St. Leonards.* 9 Oct., 13 Oct., 17 Oct: *from Howell that he shall not reach home (Prinknash) till Wednesday next, being delayed in town in consequence of having obtained a naval cadetship for his son Willoughby, on board the Rattlesnake, a vessel to be employed on surveying service in the Torres Straits.* 21 Oct., 22 Oct: *left Gloucester in a fly for Prinknash Park, where we arrived about half an hour before its master, and we were very cordially and gladly received by Laura and Constance Howell. Emmeline is still in Devon, now on a visit to an old Gibraltar friend at Exeter. William had paid a hurried visit to his sisters yesterday: both he and Emmeline are, not without cause, aliens from the paternal home; yet it cannot be said that the Father is free from blame, though more sinned against than sinning. He had left London by a midday train, and came in good spirits, leading in his son Willougby, in his naval uniform, blue jacket, trousers, navy buttons, gold laced cap, and cutlass, as a naval cadet, having passed at Portsmouth, and being appointed by Lord Auckland to the Rattlesnake, surveying ship, which is going out under the command of an eminent and scientific officer, Capt. Stanley, son of the Bishop of Norwich, to survey Torres Straits, the coast of Carpentaria &c. Howell has also the promise of a naval Cadetship from Sir. C. Adam, one of the Lords of the Admiralty, for his next son, Johnny..... the coming sale of his Upton property, the purchase of a house in Town, &c. but observing a deep silence as to the painful events of last winters, the misconduct of Emmeline, William's eccentricities, and approaching marriage, the affair with the Widow Caldwell &c. My poor friend has an uncommon buoyancy of spirit, a great power of putting aside painful reflections, and, alas! Too entire a sympathy with this world and its engagements and pursuits, to the exclusion of the unseen world, and the fitting preparation of futurity. But much of this is the result of circumstances, the force of habit, and the constitutional tendency of the mind. One mourns that there is so much of levity, apparently so little of deep feeling on the eve of surrendering to others his parental property. The step is prudent, no doubt; for the events of last winter and spring have made the residence distasteful; his irritated temper has separated him from old friends and neighbours, without sufficient offence given by them; and a London life will be more congenial to his temperament, and, probably, suit better his views in furthering placing out his sons yet unemployed: but more of seriousness, more of feeling, would have been more becoming. My son, who had been so greatly mixed up with the sad scenes of last spring, and so much interested in the position of Laura and Constance, was naturally impressed with deep emotion on this visit to Prinknash. We were both likely to feel acutely this, probably, the last visit we should pay to a place which for many years had been so familiar to us.* 27 Nov: *Received a letter from Howell: he has purchased a house in Kensington garden terrace; to which he talks of removing from Prinknash Park from about Christmas.* 12 Dec., 28 Dec: *A letter from Howell; the conveyance to Mr. Ackers of Prinknash Park will not be completed for some weeks: he Howell will Keep up his establishment there till shortly before he yields possession: at the last will have a sale of furniture; before that wishes us to receive Constance, Laura and Macleod, till he has prepared for them a lodging in Town, near Wilton Place West, where he has bought a house, which will not be ready for him before the end of March.* 29 Dec.

1847: 7 Jan: *A letter from Howell, whose Prinknash Property will not be conveyed to Mr. Ackers till towards the end of February: he writes to me for information as to the Assessment of Prinknash to the County rate: does not mention when the twins and Mc.Leod are to visit us.* 8 Jan., 11 Jan., 4 Mar: *Recd. a letter from Howell: his establishment at Prinknash is not likely to be broken up till towards the end of the month, at which time, I suppose, Laura & Constance, with Macleod will be our guests.* 6 Mar., 16

Mar: *A letter from Howell, to say that his daughters, Laura and Constance, will be with us for a visit on the 3d. April, bringing McLeod & his attendant.* 17 Mar., 3 Apr: *Laura, Constance, and Macleod Howell arrived on a visit to us; having finally left Prinknash Park this morning, as also their Father, who is gone to Town, to furnish his new house to receive them at the end of the month.* 4 Apr: *Received a distressing letter from poor Howell, stating that on his arrival yesterday in Town, he had met with a letter from his friend, Major Sandham, communicating to him that a strong rumour prevailed that three Officers had been killed in an affray with the Kaffirs in South America, Africa of whom one was Frederick Howell, Surgeon in the Rifles, lately arrived in the Colony of the Cape of Good Hope.* 5 Apr., 6 Apr: *Here I received a letter from MW. informing me that Howell had written to his poor daughters, confirming the evil tidings he had communicated in his letter received on Sunday, and which, indeed, had been noticed in the London paper which I had seen at Gloucester this morning: the facts appear to be that on the Kei river in the Kaffir country, and beyond the limits of the Colony, a small military detachment had been stationed; Fred. Howell had charge of the sick and wounded there; with him was a Capt. Gibson, like himself of the Rifles; also an Hon.—Chetwynd, a son of Lord Chetywnd, an officer of another regiment: that these three had gone out to procure cattle, to increase their store of provisions; that they had advanced beyond the main body of their party, with four or five Hottentots; had met with a lot of cattle, perhaps, purposely placed as a decoy; had proceeded to drive this small herd, in the direction of their quarters: had so fallen into an ambush of savages; that poor Fredk. Howell's horse was shot dead; himself killed & his two brother officers with two Hottentots, fighting in his rescue, were also massacred before the main body of their party which was a mile or two in the rear, and heard the firing, could come to their aid.... It was nearly seven o clock when I reached home: of course it was a melancholy evening of forced conversation, Laura and Constance being greatly overpowered.* 8 Apr: *Two letters from Howell, with further details as to the death of poor Frederick.* 10 Apr., 13-15 Apr., 23 Apr: *this packet I sent by the Servant with the open carriage, which conveyed little Macleod Howell and his attendant to pass the morning with the children at Stanway, & to return accompanied by his sisters.* 26 Apr: *Walked with Laura and Constance Howell to Bourton on the Water and back.* 27-30 Apr., 3 May: *Our young friends, Laura and Constance Howell, with their little brother, left us, after an early breakfast, to join their Father at his new house in Town; travelling to Oxford in a fly to the foot of Stow hill, thence by the coach to Oxford Station, and thence by railway.* 5 May, 8 May, 14-15 May, 18 May: *I received a letter from Howell, announcing the very unexpected intelligence that Emmeline had, at her place of seclusion, Mursley, in Buckinghamshire, where she is residing with a Clergyman named Horne, whose wife is sister to Mrs. Parsons, late of Upton St. Leonards, formed a connection with a medical Gentleman, named Wynter, practising at Winslow, a widower of 40 years of age, of respectable character, well spoken of by Mrs. Parsons and her Sister—Howell had gone down to see the parties, had given his consent to their marriage in July, and congratulates himself that this event will relieve him from much embarrasment, and solve difficulties.* 20 May: *Wrote to Howell, congratulating him on the prospect of Emmeline's marriage, not as an event likely to give unmixed satisfaction, but as likely to relieve the family from much difficulty and anxiety.* 29-30 May, 11 Jun., 17 Jun., 19 Jun: *Received a letter from Howell; Emmeline is to be married to Mr. Wynter, Medical practitioner at Winslow, on the 29th. Inst.—Johnny Howell has brought back from school at Gosport the measles, which his sisters and Macleod are likely to catch.* 21 Jun., 24 Jun., 30 Jun., 2 Jul: *A letter from Howell—Emmeline was married on Tuesday last:—Constance and Macleod have caught the measles, likely to be communicated to Laura and Henry.* 12 Jul., 19 Jul., 18 Aug: *A letter from Howell, from Dawlish, whither he has gone with Laura, Constance, and Macleod.* 23 Aug., 27-28 Aug., 26 Sep: *Cards sent by the post announce the marriage of Wm. Howell to Miss Willan. It has been a long engagement, and not very likely to end in prosperity: the lady is the daughter of a man who lived extravagantly, and was in latter years hardly sane. W.H. is eccentric, and alienated from his Father, who does little for him—He has recently undertaken the curacy of Tysoe in Warwickshire, where the new married will reside.* 26 Dec.

1848: 31 Jan., 2 Feb., 12 Mar., 17 Mar., 28 Mar: *My next object was to call on Laura and Constance Howell in Eaton place West: I knew that their father was absent from Town on a factory circuit. Walked part of the way, and took a cab for the rest. The young ladies were gone out for the day.* 29 Mar: *Received a note from Laura Howell before I was dressed, which I answered, and promised to call in Eaton Place West to-morrow.* 30 Mar: *My next movement was to the "far west,"—to Eaton Place West, to call on Laura and Constance Howell, partly on foot, partly in a cab:—received with kind warmth by the young ladies—Macleod improved in appearance.* 24 Apr., 30 May, 6 Jul: *Howell announces that he has had a severe illness, having suffered from inflammation of the bowels and liver; but is now convalescent, and planning to betake himself with part of his family to the sea side.* 14 Jul., 21 Jul: *Also a letter from Howell, who with his daughters, Laura & Constance, Macleod &c. proposes to visit Weymouth very shortly.* 7 Aug: *My son has engaged to go on Wednesday next to Tysoe in Warwickshire, returning home on Thursday, to be present at the christening of the first born child of William Howell, who is now residing there as Curate. His marriage to Miss Willan has been the result of a long attachment, but the lady brought him little fortune, and his father, very blameably, as I think, makes no pecuniary provision for him. It is true that William has displeased his father by his violence and eagerness of temper, particularly at the time of his sister Emmeline's strange misconduct, or derangement, whichever it might be; but the young man's general deportment is free from reproach, and it may be that mental infirmity would account both in him and in his eldest sister, for much that gives the parent just uneasiness & displeasure. Yet he never made a proper allowance to his son, and has, I grieve to say, failed generally in the paternal duties; turning his back, as it were, and leaving his eldest son and daughter without due countenance and provision; and not making himself beloved by his younger daughters. E.F.W. is invited to be Godfather to W. Howell's infant.* 13 Sep., 17 Sep., 10 Oct., 22 Oct: *from Howell as to placing his son John at Carshalton, a preparatory school from which the pupils, if found sufficiently prepared, proceed to Woolwich academy, there to receive a military education preparatory to their being appointed to commissions in the Artillery or in the Corps of Engineers H. has received this appointment for his son from the Marquis of Anglesey, Master General of the Ordnance.*

1849: 23 Dec: *Received a letter from T. J. Howell, family intelligence and political gossip. By a new arrangement of the Factory office, he is to superintend the factories in Ireland with a small, and, as H. thinks, inadequate increase of salary.*

1850: 9 Jan., 14 Mar., 29 Mar., 5 Apr., 8 Apr., 17 Apr., 16 May: *Wrote to Howell in answer to his letter of condolence on the death.* 8 Jun: *Recd. a letter from Howell, who incloses for my perusal a letter he has had from his son Willoughby, dated Sydney in Australia, containing an account of the voyage made in parts of the Pacific Ocean, on the coasts of New Guinea and Louisiade, by the Ship on board of which he is serving as a midshipman under Capt. Stanley, who is engaged on a scientific survey of the Torres Straits and other little known parts in that quarter.* 24 Jun., 29 Aug., 7 Sep., 13 Sep: *Received a letter from Howell. He and his family may, probably, pass a week here; when they leave Leamington at the end of October. Sad levity and devotion to the world characterize his letter.* 24-25 Sep., 9 Oct: *Henry Howell has got an appointment on the Geological survey now carried on by a Government body of engineers &c. under the direction of Sir H. Delabeche.* 20 Oct., 25 Oct., 29 Oct: *Mr. Howell, with his son Edward, and his daughters, Laura and Constance, arrived on a visit.... the daughters are much improved by a London residence; Laura a talented, somewhat romantic and imaginative person: Constance more commonplace than her sister, an accomplished singer... Willoughby, the midshipman, is reported as just arrived in the Rattlesnake, from a voyage of discovery, on a surveying course for the last four years in the seas between New South Wales and the Eastern Archipelago, the Torres Straits, coasts of New Guinea &c.* 30-31 Oct., 1 Nov: *Walked with Howell, and his children to Eyford, & back by a circuitous route.* 2 Nov., 4-5 Nov., 14 Nov., 19 Nov., 22 Nov., 29 Nov.

1851: 21 Jan., 6 Mar., 7 Mar: *Laura and Constance Howell did not arrive, as expected, yesterday. Macleod having been taken ill, their Father had suddenly recalled them.* 10 Mar., 12 Mar: *Received a letter from Howell. He informs me of the death of his youngest child—poor Macleod—in consequence of a violent attack of epileptic fits. Born in affliction, for his poor mother died in giving him birth, he has always been a tender plant, subject to fits; a singular but clever boy, and by his very infirmity, with the watchfulness rendered necessary by it, and never having left home even for a school, his education having been conducted chiefly by his sister Laura, he had become specially dear and, as it were, necessary to his Father and sisters. The latter, particularly Laura, are much distressed, and Howell intimates to me that it would be very acceptable to him if E.F.W. and Sophy would now invite them to pass a few days at Stanway.* 16 Mar., 2 Apr: *my son & daughter arrived on horseback, being speedily followed by Laura and Constance Howell.* 4 Apr: *Constance Howell executed many of her songs in a finished style, but with no very high quality of voice.* 5 Apr., 22 Apr., 25 Apr., 14 May: *A letter from Howell who invites me to dinner on the 19th. Inst. the day on which it is my intention to go up to Town: he invites me to occupy his bedroom in 6 Eaton Place West between the 26th. and the 31st. Inst. during which interval Factory Business will take him into Wales—He desires me to hold myself engaged to dine with him every day during my visit to the Metropolis, on which I may not be otherwise engaged.* 19 May: *I hastened to keep my dinner engagement with the Howells in Eaton Place West. There I found a large party not yet having gone down to dinner——Howell and his daughters, Constance and Laura.* 20 May: *After breakfast repaired in a cab to the Crystal Palace, to keep an appointment I had made with Laura Howell ... This was the trysting place agreed upon between me and my fair and very intelligent guide, Laura Howell, who soon came, accompanied by a Lady acquaintance, Mrs. Lewis, and under Laura's auspices I entered on my first and cursory survey of the wondrous scene.* 21 May, 22 May: *At the usual late hour I repaired to a dinner party at the Howells ... The dinner party was large, the entertainment handsome, and conversation, varied and cheerful. Music, instrumental and vocal, in the Evening.* 23 May: *Dined at no. 6. Eaton place West, and the two Howell girls, made up a not unpleasant, almost domestic party.* 26-27 May,

1852: 11 Mar: *H. touches lightly on Laura's misadventure, as he calls it: she will, probably, be married to Hubert Engels about the middle of next month, & depart with him for his home at Bonn.* 24 Mar., 17 Apr: *he brought a short note from E.F.W., accompanying two letters he had found awaiting their return; one to Sophy from Laura Howell was written on the day before her intended union to the German Musician, Hubert Engels, in which it is pretty plain that she repents of the rash engagement she had formed, and reproaches herself, but too late, for contracting such an engagement without her father's approval: yet she speaks of the affair as settled, as to take place on the morrow, and as likely to lead to her future happiness in wedded life; sending to Sophy her address at Bonn whither the new married couple are to proceed on the day after their wedding to take up their abode with Engel's mother:——but from the other letter addressed by Howell to E.F.W. from Town, a day later than that the date of Laura's letter, it would seem that the ill omened marriage did not take place on the day proposed, being postponed for a week, but on what grounds does not appear. It is altogether a lamentable affair, whatever be the issue.* 27 Apr: *Laura Howell is married to Hubert Engels, and has departed with him to take up her residence with his mother at Bonn.* 8 Jun., 9 Jun: *Wrote to Howell, accepting his invitation to pass next week at Eaton Place West; intimated my intention to return home on Saturday to discharge my clerical duties, and to travel back to Town on Monday next.* 2 Nov., 22 Nov: *also a letter from Henry Howell, thanking me for my introduction to J W Martin, and mentioning that in the prosecution of his employment in the Geological survey, he is about to leave Tewkesbury, and to remove to Broadway, or Campden.* 23 Nov., 15 Dec.

1853: 18 Apr: *Agreeably surprized by a visit from Henry Howell, who has been stationed for a short time at Blockley, conducting the Geological Survey of the country of which it is a centre: he is on the point of removing to Nuneaton to pursue the survey in the coal field of North Warwickshire. I found him an agreeable, conversible, well informed, intelligent, and open-hearted young man.* 19 Apr., 20 Apr: *Wrote to Howell, mentioning the pleasure I had felt in a visit from his son Henry.* 23 Apr., 7 May: *Wrote to Mrs. Howell, accepting the invitation conveyed in a letter lately received from her to pay a visit.* 17 May, 25 May, 27 May, 31 May: *Capt. B. is a very plain, cheerful, unaffected, and, apparently, sensible young officer, now at home on leave of absence, his regiment, the 23ᵈ· Rifles, being quartered in Canada, whither he is about shortly to return: this is the regiment in which Edward Howell has a commission.* 6 Jun: *To 6 Eaton Place West—very kindly received by the Howells, with whom on a visit Mr. and Mrs. W. Ffookes he Mrs. H's brother, and Clerk of the Peace for Glouces Dorsetshire, she born a Pickard: her Father has assumed the name of Cambridge, as Heir of old Mr. Cambridge of Whitminster.* 7 Jun: *Took a short walk with Howell before luncheon Conversation with him.* 11-12 Jun., 19 Jun: *Recd. a letter from Howell, informing me that his son Henry is settled for a time at Ashby de la Zouch on the Geological Survey; and requesting me to give him an introduction to Marmaduke Vavasour.* 20 Jun.

1854: 1 Jan., 8 Feb., 3 Apr., 7 Apr: *From Mrs. Howell a very friendly letter with a pressing invitation to me not to fail to visit at Eaton Place West this spring.* 25 Apr., 27 Apr., 1 May: *Wrote to Mrs. Howell, explaining that I felt obliged to forego the proposed visit to Town, partly as my health had rather given way, since I settled to leave home, and also to the unsettled state of my family, and the mental condition of my in-door Servant's wife.* 4 May: *Received a letter from Howell, expressing in his light tone his thoughts as to my declining to visit him in consequence partly of my domestic discomforts, but not noticing that I considered myself less well than some time ago: and so regarding my visit as only postponed.* 13 May: *Received a long letter from Constance Howell, with an account of the musical service at St. Paul's on the bicentenary festival of the Sons of the Clergy. She had gone with Miss Ffoolks, and Johnny Howell, Mrs. Howell not liking to leave her husband for so long a time, as he is confined to the house with the relics of influenza, and very deaf.* 16 May, 2 Jun: *A letter from Mrs. Howell—her husband barely recovered from the influenza, and poor Constance fallen into weak health—a decline may be dreaded, and great seclusion from gaiety enjoined.* 13 Jun., 6 Aug: *Received a pleasant letter from Constance Howell, now on a visit to friends at Newport, Isle of Wight: she seems to enjoy a better state of health than in the Spring, and gives pleasant details of excursions in the island. Her father and Mrs. H. are now in Ireland.* 14 Aug: *Wrote to Constance Howell.*

HOWLEY — William Howley[265]

William Howley (1766-1848), archbishop of Canterbury, was born at Ropley, Hampshire, only son of William Howley, vicar of Bishop's Sutton and Ropley, and Mary, daughter of John Gauntlett, a Winchester wine merchant. He was educated at Winchester College and New College, Oxford (BA 1787; MA 1791). In 1794 he was elected fellow of Winchester College, and he succeeded his father as vicar of Bishop's Sutton in 1796. He became vicar of Andover on 22 January 1802, and on 23 May 1811, he was appointed vicar of Bradford Peverell. Both were Winchester College livings. In 1804 he was made canon of Christ Church, Oxford, and in 1809 he was appointed regius professor of divinity there. He was offered the see of London by the prime minister, Lord Liverpool, in August 1813 after the death of John Randolph. He was consecrated on 10 October 1813 at Lambeth Palace. Howley was an active freemason, having joined the Royal York Lodge, Bristol, in 1791, and served the lodge regularly until his appointment as bishop of London.

Howley's translation to Canterbury in July 1828 after the death of Charles Manners Sutton was widely anticipated. Wellington fought shy of appointing him because of his strong opposition to Catholic emancipation, but there were few other feasible candidates. Howley was archbishop during the repeal of the Test and Corporation Acts (1828), the Emancipation of the Catholics (1829), and the passing of the Great Reform Act (1832). The bench of bishops was generally opposed to all three measures. As archbishop, Howley was their spokesman and his heart-felt opposition to the Great Reform Act led to his carriage being attacked in the streets of Canterbury.

Howley married Mary Frances (d. 1860), eldest daughter of John Belli, of Southampton and the HEIC service, on 29 August 1805; they had 2 sons and 3 daughters:

1 Mary Anne (b. 1806)
2 Anne Jane (b. 1808)
1 William Hamilton (b. 1810)
3 Harriet Elizabeth (b. 1812)
2 George Gordon (b. 1814)

1826: 11 Oct: *"Bishop of London's charge to the Clergy of his Diocese 1826." An excellent, moderate, temperate address: the distinguished prelate speaks very decidedly, but calmly on the subject of Roman Catholic pretensions.*

1828: 2 Aug: *It was always surmised, that on the death of Archbishop Sutton, Dr. Howley, Bishop of London, would be raised to the metropolitan See, and the expectation was well founded.... But to return to Dr. Howley; he is a Winchester man, was a fellow of New College, and rose through his own merits, not by early & powerful patronage: it is to be regretted, that he is an indifferent speaker in the House of Lords.*

1838: 26 Mar: *This is the creation of the poet Wordsworth who resided for some time near his friend the late Baronet, and converted an old stone quarry into this little paradise; of whom and of the present Archbishop of Canterbury, whose daughter, now deceased, married the present owner of Cole Orton.*

1839: 7 Feb.

1840: 26 Jul., 22 Nov.

1842: 21 Aug.

1844: 23 May, 17 Dec.

1845: 8 May.

1848: 13 Feb: *The papers announce the death of the venerable, aged and excellent Arbp. of Canterbury, Dr. Howley.*

HOWMAN — George Ernest Howman, later Little[266]

George Ernest Howman (±1797-1878), Church of England clergyman, was born at Burstow, Surrey, son of Arthur and Louisa Howman. He was educated at Balliol College, Oxford (BA 1818; MA 1821), and lived at Newbold Pacey Hall, Warwickshire. Howman was master of St Nicholas's Hospital, Salisbury, in 1824; perhaps he was the model for Septimus Harding in Anthony Trollope's *The Warden*. Howman was later vicar of Sonning, Berkshire, in 1822-41, and rector of Barnsley, Gloucestershire, in 1841-74. He assumed the name of Little after inheriting the estate of Newbold Pacey from William Little, a relation by marriage, in 1834.

1848: 24 Aug: *the first lesson was read by Mr. Howman, the Rector of Barnsley, and Rural dean of Fairford Deanery, who is also Honorary Canon of Bristol.*

HOWSE — Mr Howse

1835: 2 Apr: *Rode to Stow, to attend at the Provident Bank and Justice room. At the former met Messrs. Jeaffreson, Ford, and Cameron. At the latter Ford and Jeaffreson sat with me as Magistrates: Messrs. Price of Coln St. Dennis, his neighbour, Mr. Howse, Messrs. Winter, Vavasour and E. F. Witts were also present.*

HUDDLESTON — John Walter Huddleston[267]

Sir John Walter Huddleston (1815-1890), MP, barrister, and judge, was born in Dublin, eldest son of Thomas Huddleston, captain in the merchant service, and Alethea, daughter of H. Hichens of St Ives, Cornwall. He was educated at Trinity College, Dublin. He entered Gray's Inn in 1836, and was called to the bar in 1839. Huddleston went on the Oxford circuit, and attended the Worcester and Staffordshire sessions. He also practised at the Middlesex sessions, where he chiefly argued poor-law cases, and at the Old Bailey. There and on circuit he gradually acquired an extensive criminal practice. He appeared for the prosecution in the trial of William Palmer, 'the Rugeley poisoner', in 1856, and was engaged in many other *causes célèbres*, in which he distinguished himself in cross-examination and by the lucidity with which he presented his points to the jury. Huddleston was MP for Canterbury in 1865-68, and Norwich in 1874. He was knighted in 1875.

1851: 1 Apr: *Mr. Skinner and Mr. Pigott were counsel for the prosecution (of Hathway); Sergeant Allen, and Mr. Huddleston for the defence: the number of witnesses for the prosecution was great.*

1852: 30 Mar: *Mr. Smallridge of Gloucester was the Attorney for the defence (of Hambidge), and Messrs. Huddlestone & Powell were his counsel.*

1853: 6 Apr: *The case for the Prisoner was admirably pleaded by Huddleston, solemnly and eloquently urging the Jury not to find a verdict of guilty of murder, only of manslaughter.*

HUDSON — John Hudson [268]

John Hudson (1795-1869), gentleman farmer, was born at Grimston, Norfolk. In 1822 he and his father took on the tenancy of two farms, Lodge Farm and Manor Farm, at Castle Acre, Norfolk, from Thomas William Coke of Holkham. Combined, the farms amounted to 1,441 acres. Hudson soon became a leading figure among the farmers on the Holkham estate. He married Anne Rebecca and continued managing the farms until his father's death in 1840, when he moved to Cirencester. He died at 'The Beeches' in 1869.

1845: 22 Apr: *Recd. a letter from Mr. Sewell about putting down a beer house at Lower Swell: the Atkins Wright property there has been purchased by his Father in law, Mr. Hudson, an eminent Agriculturist in Norfolk, and the Beer house is one of the houses on the Estate.*

1846: 15 Aug: *Mr. Sewell came to breakfast from Lower Swell, where he had left Mrs. Sewell on a visit to her brother, now residing at the Bowle farm—Mr. Hudson, Mrs. Sewell's father, has recently purchased the considerable estate, late belonging to the Atkyns Wright family, in Lower Swell, and is occupying that position of it, which was leased for many years by Jos. Clifford, placing one of his sons there to manage it. Mr. H. is a very eminent agriculturist, a Norfolk farmer, and tenant formerly to Mr. Coke, afterwards Earl Leicester—he now resides at or near Castle acre, having a large business there, but intends to keep in hand the farm at Lower Swell, having a strong opinion that a better style of farming will show that the Cotswold land is more productive than is generally believed.*

1847: 7 Sep., 23 Oct., 9 Nov.

1851: 15 May: *Already handsome contributions have been pledged by Mr. and Mrs. Royce, Mr. Hudson, Mr. Sewell &c.*

HUDSON — Richard Hudson [269]

Richard Hudson (1773-1850), JP and landed proprietor, was born at Pershore, Worcestershire, son of Richard and Eleanor Hudson. He lived at of Wick House, Pershore, and was succeeded by his son, also Richard (1811-1854).

1823: 14 Mar: *The Gentlemen, whom we met, were Messrs. Hudsons (Brothers) & Hanford from the Pershore Trust.* 25 Apr: *We were very hospitably received by M^r. & M^rs. Perrot, & met D^r. Cooper, of Bengeworth, M^r. Hudson, of Pershore, two of the Gentlemen, with whom we had been transacting business in the morning.*

1826: 1 Aug: *The immediate vicinity of Pershore is very pretty; the ground undulating, the meadows rich, an abundance of foliage; at Wick, are the elegant seats of two brothers of the name of Hudson.*

HUDSON — Stephen Hudson [270]

Stephen Hudson (±1808-1867), acting governor of Millbank Prison, was born at Lambeth, Surrey, son of Stephen Hudson (1771-1843) and Susannah Sewell, née Wight (1793-1837). In 1843 he was recommended for the position of deputy governor of Stafford House of Correction, but he does not seem to have gained the post; perhaps it was just as well as the Millbank position was to prove more lucrative. He married Frances (b. ±1808); they had at least 3 sons and 1 daughter:

1 Stephen (b. ±1833)
2 George (±1835-1880)
1 Frances Sarah (b. ±1837)
3 John Thomas (1841-1873)

It appears that Frances died young; in the 1851 census Hudson lived at Cheriton, Kent, with his wife Elizabeth (b. ±1807) and the same three children. He died at Portsea, Hampshire.

1847: 18 May: *S. Hudson, Supervisor at the Millbank Penitentiary, was provided with excellent testimonials.*

HUDSON — Thomas Hudson [271]

Thomas Hudson (1772-1852), MP and landed proprietor, was born at Wigton, Cumberland, third but only surviving son of Thomas Hudson (d. 1807) and Ann, daughter of William Dodgson of Wigton. Hudson was MP for Evesham in 1832-34. He married Frances, daughter of Robert Bamford Hesketh of Bamford, Lancashire, and Gwyrch Castle, Denbighshire.

1835: 7 Jan: *Mr. Kinsey, who as an Ultra Whig, Tory and Ultra-High-Church-man, has made himself conspicuous for some years at Cheltenham, where he is Minister of St. John's Church, was very full upon the Tory victory lately gained at Evesham, where the Whig Representative, Hudson, has been supplanted by the Tory, Borthwick, whose Colleague will be our amphibious neighbour, Sir. C. Cockerell.*

HUGHES — Mrs Hughes of Long Compton

There are numerous families with the name of Hughes in Long Compton, and this Mrs Hughes cannot be identified with confidence.

1847: 20 Oct: *Wrote to Mrs. Hughes, Long Compton, the result of my conversation on Monday with G. Cooper, that he agreed to pay through Mr. Baughan, Churchwarden of Long Compton, 25/ each Christmas towards the Schooling of his illegitimate child, and that he would do more as the child grew older, advised her not to irritate him by writing angry letters.* 27 Oct., 28 Dec.

1848: 14 Jan., 16 Jan: *A letter from one Baughan, Churchwarden of Long Compton, who writes to inform me that Mrs. Hughes of that place had made a false statement to me as to the alleged neglect of George Cooper.* 18 Jan.

HUGHES — David Hughes, a guest at Stanway

1822: 30 Sep: *I dined and slept at Lady Elcho's at Stanway, meeting, besides Miss Church and my Mother, the Gist family from Wormington Grange, and from Toddington Mr. Eddy & his son, and Mr. David Hughes.*

HUGHES — Edward Hughes [272]

Edward Hughes (1786-1864), librarian, was born at Amlwych, Anglesey, son of William Hughes. He was educated at Jesus College, Oxford (BA 1808; MA 1810; BD 1818). He was fellow until 1833, vice-principal, and librarian in 1823.

1824: 9 Jul: *Dr Price's dinner party Miss Horrocks, daughter of the Member for Preston, & niece to Mrs. C. Pitt, Mr. Whitehead of the East Indian Company's naval Service, nephew to Mrs. C. Pitt, Mr. E. Hughes, a fellow of Jesus Coll. Oxford.*

HUGHES — John Hughes [273]

John Hughes (1790-1857), author, scholar, and linguist, was born at Putney, Surrey, the only child of Thomas Hughes (1756-1833), clerk of the closet to George III and George IV, vicar of

Uffington, Berkshire, and canon of St Paul's Cathedral, and his wife, Mary Anne (1770-1853), daughter of Revd George Watts, vicar of Uffington. Mary Anne was an early friend of Sir Walter Scott, whom she visited with her husband in 1824.

John Hughes was educated at Oriel College, Oxford (BA 1812; MA 1815), and lived at Donnington Priory, Berkshire. He married, in Suffolk, 14 December 1820, Margaret Elizabeth (1797-1887), daughter of Thomas Wilkinson of Stokesley Castle, Yorkshire; they had 7 sons and 1 daughter:

1 George (1821-1872)
2 Thomas (1822-1896), author of *Tom Brown's School Days* (1857) and *The Scouring of the White Horse, or, The Long Vacation Ramble of a London Clerk* (1859); married, at St Thomas, Devon, July 1847, Anne Frances Ford (1826-1910); 5 sons and 3 daughters
3 John (1824-1895), Church of England clergyman
4 Walter Scott (1826-1846)
1 Jane Elizabeth (1828-1877)
5 William Hastings (1833-1909)
6 Henry Salusbury (1836-1862)
7 Arthur Octavius (1840-1867)

Apart from his travel book on the Rhône, Hughes wrote *Boscobel Tracts*. In around 1820 he went to live at Uffington, where most of his children were born. On the death of his father in 1833, Hughes moved to Donnington Priory, Berkshire.

1824: 1 Jun: *"An itinerary of Provence and the Rhone, made during the year 1819. By John Hughes AM. Oriel College Oxford. Lond 1822. 8vo" This is a very spirited account of the author's tour from Paris to Lyons; thence by Vienne, Valence, Orange to Avignon, along the course of the Rhone; to Montpellier & Nismes on the one side; to Marseilles, Toulon, Frejus, Antibes, Nice on the other, ending with his entrance into Italy by the Col di Tende... The lively cheerful style of the book is very attractive, and while it is quite full enough to gratify the stay-at-home traveller, it is well adapted both as to size and matter to serve as an excellent itinerary to those, who have leisure to pursue their travels beyond the limits of their own country.*

1829: 1 Feb: *"A letter to John Hughes Esqr. MA Oriel College, Oxford, one of His Majesty's Justices of the Peace for the County of Berks, on the Systems of Education proposed by the popular parties. By the Revd. John Philips Potter MA Oriel College, Oxford. 3d. Ed. Lond. 1828." ... He addresses Mr. Hughes, a gentleman, who some years since was held in just consideration as fellow of that richly talented Society of Oriel, a successful versifier, a good tourist, as his little publication descriptive of an excursion on the Rhone & in the adjacent country testified, and now an active & useful country gentleman and magistrate.*

HUGHES — John Hughes, magistrate of Downend[274]

John Hughes (1800-1859), JP and landed proprietor, was born at Newcastle Emlyn, Carmarthenshire, son of Samuel Hughes (1760-1827) and his wife, Ruth. He married, at Bedminster, Somerset, 7 June 1834, Louisa Cockin (b. 1810).

1848: 27 Jun: *Several new magistrates qualified——Mr. Hughes, of Downend near Bristol.*

1850: 31 Dec.

HUGHES — Juliana, Lady Hughes[275]

Juliana Hughes was the wife of Sir Richard Hughes, 2nd baronet (1729-1812), of East Bergholt Lodge, Suffolk. She was the daughter of William Sloane, of South Stoneham, Hampshire, a nephew of Sir Hans Sloane. This attribution is tentative, as there was also an Elizabeth, Lady Hughes (±1769-1839), wife of Sir Bulkeley Hughes, of Plascoch, Anglesey, but she is less likely to have been on the Cheltenham and Wells circuit.

1804: 5 Sep: *Lady Hughes called in the forenoon.* 5 Oct., 9 Oct.

HUGHES — Susan Hughes at Stert and Devizes[276]

Susan [Susanna] Hughes (1786-1869) was born at Devizes, a daughter of William and Sarah Hughes. By 1851 she was deaf, and living at 18 Brook Street, Bath, with her sister, Mary (1790-1860). She and her sister died unmarried.

1807: 10 Dec: *Called upon Miss Hillier, where I met Miss C. Wyatt, Miss S. Hughes, & Miss H. Tylee.*

1808: 17 Jan: *visited Mrs. Jaques, where I found the Miss Hughes's; pleasant young women.* 18 Feb: *Rode to Devizes. Called at Mrs. Hillier's, found her & Harriet, Susan Hughes & Mary Gibbs.*

HUGHES — Thomas Hughes and the Hughes family of Cheltenham[277]

Thomas Hughes (1732-1794), attorney, was a son of Robert Hughes, of an old Monmouthshire family, and Jane, sole daughter and heir of John Roydon of Roydon Hall, Denbighshire. In 1732 another Thomas Hughes was born at Coberley, Gloucestershire, son of William Hughes; this is a strange coincidence considering that our Thomas's younger son, Robert, was to write a novel entitled *Coberley Hall: a Gloucestershire Tale of the 14th Century* (1824).

Hughes moved to Cheltenham in 1749 and was articled to John de la Bere, the steward of the manor. He married, 1763, Elizabeth Bridges (1728-1786), of Keynsham Abbey, Somerset, a wealthy heiress. Hughes set up his own practice as a solicitor in 1772, and bought for his residence Powers Court house and estate. This gave him a large area of land stretching from the High Street along the west side of the present Rodney Road to Oriel Terrace. This included 'a walled garden, a moat, orchard and fishponds, a meadow together with the Ball Room and its garden'. On the site of this primitive ballroom he built his new assembly rooms which were opened in 1783. They became the centre for Cheltenham's most fashionable assemblies. He was under-sheriff of Gloucestershire in 1772. Thomas and Elizabeth had 3 sons and 1 daughter:

1 Thomas Bridges (1765-1815); married, at Cheltenham, 11 April 1809, Marianne Elizabeth Anne (1781-1869), daughter of Robert St John Lucas and his wife, Mariana; 1 son and 1 daughter:
  1 James Roydon (1810-1894), rector of Long Ditton (1874)
  1 Elizabeth (1811-1879); married Revd Thomas Francis Penrose Hart-Davies
1 Elizabeth (1768-1850); died unmarried
2 John Roydon (1770-1771); died an infant
3 Robert (1771-1827); married Elizabeth Price (1784-1813), who died of consumption; 1 son:
  1 Charles Robert (1809-1810); died an infant

The two sons were in partnership as solicitors. Robert Hughes was a whig, an attorney, and a local landowner responsible for founding the Cheltenham Masonic Lodge in 1818. By June 1824 Hughes was in financial difficulties and therefore placed one of his properties, 13 Portland Street, on the market. In 1827, just after his death, it was advertised by the *Cheltenham Journal* as 'A Very substantial Stone-built DWELLING-HOUSE, being No. 13, Portland Street.'

According to a newscutting, a Miss Tanner was related to the Hughes family on her maternal side, although the precise connection is not known. Robert Tregoze Tanner was the illegitimate son of Robert Hughes and joined the Hughes's practice as a clerk; he finally took over on Robert Hughes's' death in 1827. By 1850 the firm had ceased to exist.

It may be of no connection, but the incumbent (or perpetual curate as he was listed) of St Mary's, Cheltenham, between 1778 and 1789, was Revd Hugh Hughes. He features in the diaries of Agnes Witts and the *Torrington Diaries*. He is recorded in Agnes Witts's diary on 28 March 1789:

> Miserable cold Day with flying storms of snow & turn'd out very hard rain in the afternoon. Mr Witts & I went to dine at my Sisters meeting Mr Hugh Hughes who was very conversible; Mr Bridges Hughes, his Brother & Sister.

The fact that Revd Hugh Hughes and the children of Thomas Hughes were all guests at Mrs Travell's suggests there was a family link. He is last recorded in Agnes Witts's diary on 21 September 1789. The diary entries by Francis Witts dated 2 and 13 November 1801 are enigmatic.

One of Agnes Witts's closest friends was Elizabeth Hughes (1768-1850). By 1830 she was living at Roydon Cottage, which she obviously named after the family connection.

1801: 27 Oct: *we saw in the morning Mr. Dela Bere & Mrs. Granville, Lady Harries & Miss Hughes.* 28 Oct: *I accompanied, the two Mr. Hughes & their Sister to Mrs. Myers Ball.* 31 Oct., 2 Nov: *Dined at Mr. Granville's, meeting Mr. H. Hughes. Mr., Mrs. & Miss Markham & in the Evening Mrs. & Miss Boswells.* 3 Nov., 6 Nov: *Waited also on Miss Hughes, who played & sang to me. Dr. & Mrs. Jenner, the inventor of the Vaccine Pox, & Miss Hughes rendered our Evening very agreeable.* 9-12 Nov., 13 Nov: *Dined at Mr. Markham's, his lady's birth-day feast: pleasant, because the Granvilles were there. Besides them, Mr. H. Hughes, Mr. Foulkes, Captn. Fotheringham, Mr. Nettleship &c.* 14-16 Nov., 19 Nov., 20 Nov: *Dined at Mr. Granville's, meeting Mr. & Mrs. Newell, & Mr. & Miss Hughes.* 22 Nov: *Called upon the Hughes. Dined with them.* 23 Nov., 25 Nov.

1802: 19 Jan: *Called upon the Guydickens, upon Mr. B & Mr E. Witts upon Mr. B. Hughes &c.* 5 Aug., 13 Aug., 31 Aug., 5 Sep., 14 Oct: *Mr. & Miss Hughes came Mr. Wheler & Mr. Cotton dined at Calwich.*

1803: 27 Dec: *Went in the Evening to a card party at a Miss Price's with her & our friend a Miss Hughes in Richmond place, which the presence of three lively Miss Marriotts rendered agreeable to my Brother & myself.* 28 Dec: *Accompanied my Brother in the Evening to Sir Ed. Williams's Club for half an hour; which was rendered less intolerable by Miss Hughes & Mrs. Port being there.* 30-31 Dec.

1805: 7 Jul. 13 Jul: *A sad constrained dinner at Mrs. Travells, the family party broken by Miss Hughes & in the Evening by Mrs. Bates & her Party.* 20 Jul., 22 Jul: *In the Evening for an hour at a sombre party at Miss Hughes's: conversed with Miss Hunt & Miss Buxton.* 30 Jul., 31 Jul: *A party in the Evening & supper at Miss Hughes's: less unpleasant then usual.*

1825: 9 Jun: *We dined at my Aunt Travell's, & met Miss Hughes.* 15 Mar: *Mr. Eddy and Mr. Perkins left Stanway, and Miss Hughes arrived from Cheltenham.*

HUGHES — Thomas Smart Hughes [278]

Thomas Smart Hughes (1786-1847), historian, was born at Nuneaton, Warwickshire, the eldest surviving son of Hugh Hughes, curate of Nuneaton and rector of Hardwick, Northamptonshire. He was educated at Shrewsbury School and St John's College, Cambridge. He was a friend of John Lee, of the Lee and Fiott family, well known to Francis Witts in his youth. Hughes named his son Thomas Fiott Hughes. In 1832 he was presented by the dean and chapter of Peterborough to the rectory of Fiskerton, Lincolnshire, and in the same year succeeded to the family living of Hardwick. His chief work, the continuation of the *History of England from the accession of George III* by David Hume and Tobias Smollett, was undertaken in 1834. In May 1846 he was presented to the perpetual curacy of Edgware, Middlesex, by Lee, but he died there the following year.

1847: 13 Aug: *One topic of condolence and regret was the sudden death at Edgware, of which parish he was the Incumbent, of Mr. Hughes, a Canon of Peterborough, who had lately left the place in apparently good health, but had died with but short notice of his approaching end, from disease of the heart. He was brother of Mrs. Monk the wife of the Bishop of Gloucester.*

HUGHES — William Hughes Hughes [279]

William Hughes Hughes (1792-1874), politician and barrister, was the eldest son of John Hewitt (d. 1821), of St Anne, Westminster, and Sophia, daughter of William Hughes of Clapham. He was educated Lincoln's Inn in 1822, and called to the bar in 1827. He married, 23 August 1814, Maria, daughter of Richard Field of Brixton Rise, Surrey; they had 2 sons and 6 daughters.

William took the name of Hughes by royal licence on 25 May 1825 in compliance with the will of his grandfather, William Hughes, and styled himself Hughes Hughes. A whig, he was narrowly defeated for a seat in 1826, but finally succeeded; he was MP for Oxford in 1830-32, and again from 18 March 1833 to 1837.

1826: 16 Jun: *two Candidates courted the favour of the freemen ... the other a novus homo, a Mr. Hughes, who happened at the juncture to be visiting some personal friends at Oxford: availing himself of being on the spot, being also very full of money, acquired, it has been whispered, in the obscure trade of pawn-broking ... Langston, discomfited as he was at Woodstock, had sufficient spirit and purse long enough to comply with the solicitations of his friends at Oxford, and immediately on starting was placed at the head of the poll, a situation, which he maintained to the close, when he was brought in triumphantly, with Mr. Lockhart, to the exclusion of Mr. Hughes, whose money had been lavished in vain in sesquipedalian advertisements.*

1833: 12 Mar: *I left Edmund Hall for my quarters at the Angel Inn at ten o' clock, and after looking into the papers of the day retired to my chamber; but not to sleep, for the arrival & departure of coaches for some hours kept me awa* Hülssner *ke: to this was added the disturbance arising from the excited state of the city in consequence of a decision of a committee of the House of Commons on a petition presented by Mr Hughes, one of the unsuccessful candidates at the late Election, against the return of Mr Stonor, who has been unseated on the ground of treating.*

HUGHES-CHAMBERLAIN — Edward Hughes-Chamberlain — *see also* Kirby *and* Knight [280]

Edward Hughes-Chamberlain (1805-1892), barrister-at-law, was born at Wardington, Oxfordshire, the eldest son of Revd Thomas Chamberlain Hughes-Chamberlain. He was educated at University College, Oxford (BA 1827; MA 1830), and admitted to the Middle Temple in 1831. By 1835 he was practising on the midland circuit.

Hughes-Chamberlain married, October 1832, Emma Knight (1793-1861+), who was some eleven or twelve years his senior. There were no children of the marriage.

Edward and Emma were living at 6 Norfolk Street in both the 1841 and 1861 census. At the time of the former, Caroline Knight (1799-1856) was also with them; Mary Anne Dolphin's half brother, George Hutchinson, married Charlotte Knight (1798-1879).

In 1892, by the terms of Edward Hughes-Chamberlain's will, the arms in the second and third quarters are those of Hughes and were granted to a relative, Robert Edward Hughes. He was also given the name Chamberlain in addition to Hughes in order to comply with the terms of the will.

1840: 18 Sep: *Walked to Eyford to visit John Palmer, whom I found restless and in low spirits. At his cottage met Mrs. Dolphin, and her connections and guests, Mrs. Chamberlain and Miss Knight.* 25 Sep., 27 Sep: *With MW. walked to Eyford; visited at the Mansion house: Mr. Hutchinson and Mr. Chamberlayne, now with his lady staying there, were out: we were received by Mrs. Dolphin Mrs. Payn, Mrs. Hutchinson, and Mrs. Chamberlayne.*

1844: 27 Sep., 28 Sep: *Mr. Hutchinson and Mr. Chamberlayne called.* 8 Oct: *those with whom I was brought into contact, were ... Mr. Chamberlain, a barrister, lately on a visit at Eyford.*

1852: 9 Mar: *A long letter from Mrs. Dolphin ... very enthusiastic in the expressions of love & sympathy for all the connections around her—for Staveley, Hutchinson, Mrs. H., Mr. and Mrs. Chamberlayne.*

HÜLSSNER — actor/singer at Weimar [281]

Mozart's opera (really more of a singspiel) *Die Entführung aus dem Serail* which premiered in Vienna on 16 July 1782 is one of two singspiels that are still continually performed in opera houses around the world. The opera follows Belmonte as he travels to Turkey to free his beloved Konstanze from the grasps of the Pasha Selim. He encounters Osmin, the Pasha's servant, who ignores his requests. Eventually, with the help of his servant Pedrillo, Belmonte manages to get into the palace....

The performance at Weimar on 8 February 1800 included Hülssner, a new singer; others must have shared Francis Witts's view, for poor Hülssner's name was not recorded for posterity—he has not been found in any references. Agnes Witts wrote that the theatre was full due to the presence of a new actor: 'Mr. Witts & myself went to the Opera which was renderd fuller from the appearance of a new Actor, who was no great thing.'

1800: 8 Feb: *To the Opera Die Entführung aus dem Serail my Father & Mother a new Actor by name Hülssner who acted the Character of Osmin but poorly.*

HUME — Henrietta Hume or Mary Anne Hume at Clifton [282]

Henrietta Hume (b. 1759) was the eldest daughter of John Hume (±1704-1782), bishop of Bristol, dean of St Paul's (1758-66), bishop of Oxford (1758-66), and bishop of Salisbury (1766-82), and his wife, Lady Mary (±1723-1805), youngest daughter of George Henry Hay, 8th earl of Kinnoull (1689-1758). They had married on 5 August 1758. Mary Anne (b. 1760) was their second daughter, after Henrietta.

There were two Miss Humes in Bristol at this time with their mother, Lady Mary: Henrietta, called in the diaries 'Miss Hume', and Lucy (b. 1761), a third daughter, who is called by her forename in the diaries of Agnes Witts, presumably to differentiate her. It is not clear which out of the two elder daughters this Miss Hume is.

1806: 19 Jun: *Called upon Miss Hume & I walked with W. Deacon &c.*

HUME — Joseph Hume [283]

Joseph Hume (1777-1855), surgeon and politician, was educated at Montrose Academy, Edinburgh University, and Aberdeen University. He qualified MD in 1799, and entered the service of the HEIC as an assistant surgeon. He was an able administrator and rose rapidly in the Company. He returned to England in 1808 with a fortune of £40,000. Hume championed radical causes and based his outlook on the principles of Bentham and Mill. He was MP for Weymouth and Melcombe Regis in 1812, Aberdeen Burghs in 1813-30, Middlesex in 1830-37, Kilkenny in 1837-41, and Montrose Burghs in 1842-55.

1823: 21 Jul: *On points relating to the public expenditure, ministers have shewn themselves active in promoting its curtailment, while the unwearied M^r. Hume sometimes right, more generally misinformed & vexatious, has, as usual, practically prolonged the Sessions by his motions for papers. The country is little aware of the expence incurred by these motions.*

1825: 2 Apr: *We shall, probably, experience the fate of others of our brethren, the Clerical petitions have been uniformly met with the sneers and sarcasm of certain members of both houses. Lord King distinguishes himself thus discreditably in the Upper house ... Mr. Hume has been his Lordship's imitator in the Commons.* 7 Sep: *The trade of this populous town and its vicinity is chiefly in woollen stuffs, and there has subsisted for many weeks a variance between the Master Manufacturers and a certain class of their workmen, or, as they are termed in the new fangled jargon of modern times, the operatives. The old fashioned term of labourer is now well nigh exploded; and in these unsettling times, when Messrs. Brougham, Birkbeck, Hume &c. with their Mechanic Institutes, their schemes for giving the lower orders lectures in political economy, and teaching them all the sciences and all the ologies.*

1826: 18 Dec: *M^r. Brougham, with almost rival but very different eloquence, responded on behalf of his party to the call of the Foreign Secretary. M^r. Hume, nearly alone, demurred & was———scouted.*

1828: 2 Jun.

1830: 23 Jun.

1832: 6 Jun.

1833: 13 Mar.

1837: 4 Aug: *Breakfasted with a conservative party of Magistrates and Grand Jurors at the Bell, where we mutually congratulated ourselves on the triumph of sound principles in the County of Middlesex, where Hume has been rejected by a large majority: one seat is thus rescued from the Radical party.* 10 Aug: *O'Connel with one of his party has been returned for the County City of Dublin, and Hume is likely to be returned for Kilkenny vice O'Connel: that city being thus made the refuge of the destitute.*

HUME — Robert Hume [284]

Robert Hume (±1810-1868+), army officer, JP, and landed proprietor, was born in the 'British Colonies'; his wife, Jane (b. ±1812), was born at Maidstone, Kent. Hume lived in Main Street, Marshfield, and is listed as a landed proprietor and magistrate.

1848: 27 Jun: *Several new magistrates qualified ... lastly, a Mr. Hume, of Marshfield, formerly in the Army.*

HUMFREY — William Green Humfrey[285]

William Green Humfrey (1771-1812), Church of England clergyman, was the son of William and Ann Humfrey of Dorset. He was educated at Eton College and Peterhouse, Cambridge (LLB 1796). Humfrey was appointed curate of Clevedon in 1795, and served as precentor of Bristol Cathedral in 1803-12 and vicar of Rumney, Monmouthshire, in 1804-12. The spelling of his name varies, even on the Clergy of the Church of England database. It seems probable that this was the same 'Humphrey' who performed the service at Clifton on 22 March 1806; the initials 'J. W.' given by Francis Witts are confusing and likely to be an error. No other clergyman of that name or with those initials is listed. There is a possibility that the John Humfrey (1764-1857[?]) on the Cambridge alumni was a brother, in which case he *could* have been visiting and performed the service, but this is a postulation only and highly speculative.

1804: 1 Jan: *Accompanied the family to Dowry Square Chapel where we were greeted with an excellent sermon from a Mr. Humphries.* 15 Jul., 22 Jul., 24 Jul: *At the Cathedral Service & Sir E. Williams's Burial. Foster & Humphries performing.* 5 Aug., 19 Aug., 23 Sep: *To Chapel in Dowry Square Mr. Humphries preaching admirably.* 7 Oct: *At Dowry Square Chapel an excellent sermon & service performed by Mr. Humphries.* 30 Dec.

1805: 26 Jan., 10 Nov.

1806: 19 Jan., 2 Feb: *At Dowry Square Chapel Mr. Humphries preached with great eloquence.* 9 Feb., 23 Feb: *Dowry Chapel: Mr. Humphries officiated, & preached a very fine Sermon.* 2 Mar., 22 Mar: *Accompanied my Mother to Clifton Church, where J. W. Humprey officiated.*

HUMPHRIES — parish officer at Cowley

1840: 12 Sep: *Wrote to Mr. Humphries, a Parish Officer, at Cowley, respecting the Widow Hancox, a parishioner of Upper Slaughter.* 20 Nov., 22 Nov.

HUMPHRIES/HUMPHRIS/HUMPHREYS family of Kineton, Temple Guiting, Gloucestershire and vicinity

It seems that few if any of this family of predominantly agricultural labourers could read or write. If they were challenged by a new curate or other clergyman new to the village on the matter of how they spelt their name, it may be conjectured that they would be hard put to answer.

As far back as 1608, when John Smith compiled *Men and Armour for Gloucestershire*, there was a John Humphries in Temple Guiting, recorded as a servant to John Wood. It therefore seems that these are all members of the same family—if somewhat distant cousins—and that the variation of spelling was merely at the whim of the officiating clergyman. In the case of the family of Richard Humphreys/Humphries (1764-1840), the rector of Upper Slaughter, Ferdinand Tracy Travell, uncle of the diarist, seems to have taken it upon himself to simplify the family name to Humphris.

HUMPHRIES — John Humphries[286]

John Humphris (1817-1870), carter, was born at Kineton, Temple Guiting, Gloucestershire, son of Thomas and Mary Humphries. He married, at Upper Slaughter, 15 August 1843, Emma (1824-1878), daughter of Samuel Jones (1797-1878) and Elizabeth Betterton (1794-1828) of Upper Slaughter. It appears that it was a hasty wedding as the first-born, Henry, made his appearance in December. From the wedding certificate it is clear that neither could read nor write; both they and their two witnesses put a cross for their mark. John and Emma had 3 sons and 5 daughters:

1 Henry (1843-1872)
1 Emily (b. 1845)
2 Elizabeth (b. 1849)
2 George (1852-1872)
3 Eliza (b. 1855)
3 James (b. 1858)
4 Mary Ann (b. 1860)
5 Ellen (b. 1862)

From the diaries it appears that John tried his hand at farming a small-holding at Eyford. The reason for not continuing is not clear, but it may have proved that the cost was against him. At the time of the 1861 census, John was a carter living at Lower Slaughter.

1843: 15 Aug: *Officiated at the marriage of John Humphris and Emma Jones.*

1845: 18 Jan: *Wrote a note to, and received an answer from Mr. Humphris, Eyford, as to his employing a poor boy of this parish.* 19 Jan: *Conferred with J Davis on parish matters, and wrote to Mr. Pearce, desiring him to send the boy Hancox now in the Workhouse to be set to work by Mr. Humphris.* 20 Jan: *Called on Mr. Humphris, the Eyford farmer, but who is not expected to continue the occupation of the farm. He & his young wife appear to be well conditioned respectable people, frequent in their attendance at Church and I shall regret their removal. I called respecting a lad belonging to this parish, but long an inmate of the Workhouse, whom Mr. H. is about to take into his employment, and as to whom I had received to-day a note from Mr. Pearce.* 22 Apr: *Also to Mrs. Dolphin urging upon her to name a person to be appointed Overseer of Eyford: both her tenants, Humphris and Moor, have left their farms, and have no successors.*

HUMPHRIS — Louisa Humphris[287]

Louisa Humphris cannot be accurately placed with the other Humphris families, but she was probably related. Her daughter was Mary Anne, who had 1 illegitimate daughter:

1 Elizabeth (b. 1850)

1849: 16 Dec: *Visited a sick parishioner, Louisa Humphris, who appears in a very suffering state, from chronic internal disease: her step-daughter too in a bad state from unhallowed pregnancy.* 17-18 Dec.

1852: 11 Feb: *Visiting a young woman, M. Humphris, of doubtful character, returned from her place of service in bad health.*

HUMPHRIS — Richard Humphris and the Humphris family of Upper Slaughter[288]

Richard Humphris (1764-1840), agricultural labourer, was born at Temple Guiting, son of Edmund and Anne Humphreys. His baptismal record states his surname as Humphreys. He married, at Upper Slaughter, 12 June 1797, Betty [Elizabeth] Insull; they had at least 4 sons and 4 daughters:

1 Sarah (b. 1798)
2 Elizabeth (1801-1838); married, 8 February 1831, widower Samuel Jones
1 Robert (1803-1882); *see below*
3 Eliza (b. 1805); married, May 1830, Job Betterton
4 Sophia (b. 1807); married, at Upper Slaughter, 29 November 1832, John Dix of Charlton Kings
2 Job (b. 1809)
3 John (1812-1839); died at the union workhouse, Stow, aged 27. It must be presumed that he had a serious illness and that hospital was not possible due to expense
4 William (b. 1814)

1835: 18 Apr: *Wrote to Sarah Cuss, in London, in behalf of my parishioner, Richard Humphries.*

1840: 17 Sep: *I left early to return to the funeral of my old parishioner, R. Humphris.*

HUMPHRIS — Robert Humphris[289]

Robert Humphries (1803-1882), pig dealer, married, at Upper Slaughter, 28 October 1830, Lucy Betterton,
(1807-1901); they had 2 sons and 5 daughters:

1 Anne (1831-1833)
2 Emma (b. 1832)
3 Helen (b. 1835)
1 George (b. 1838)
2 William Insol (b. 1841)
4 Eliza (1843-1874)
5 Helen [Ellen] (1846-1862)

1836: 31 Jul: *A letter from Mr. Trenfield on the subject of a fraud perpetrated at Winchcomb Fair on Thursday on two parishioners of mine, G. Collett and R. Humphries, by giving a £10 note of a Gloucester Bank which stopped payment many years ago in payment for a poney.*

1847: 2 Oct: *Walked to Bourton on the Water to consult with Mr. Kendal as to proceedings to be taken against Henry Collett, son of J. B. Collett, of this parish, a very turbulent, ill-conditioned young man, who had attempted pound breach yesterday morning, when George Lea, by order of his Father, as Road Surveyor, had impounded a cow belonging to Farmer Price, and a horse the property of R. Humphris, which were found straying on the village green.*

1851: 16 Apr: *Visited R Humphris's daughter, who has come home from Service, ill.* 19 Apr.

1852: 25 Nov: *Mr. Turney returned to sleep at Bourton, meaning to travel back to Town tomorrow morning, after an interview with his tenant Robert Humphris, whom I directed to call on him early to-morrow morning.*

1853: 10 Jan: *Transacted business with George Lea and Robt. Humphris as to the rent due from the latter to Lord Sherborne for a month's occupation of late John Blandford's Cottage, in the interval between his decease, and the conveyance of the property to me.* 17 May: *Overlooking masons and carpenter now at work at Robt. Humphris's cottage.* 26 May: Much engaged in superintending workmen at R Humphris's cottage. 1 Jun.

HUNGERFORD — Miss Hungerford at Lady Lyttelton's music evening

1801: 10 Jun: *Lady Lytteltons, accidental Music began, Miss Halifaxes sung, & Miss Morley; it was quite a squeeze: a Mr. Wood a nephew of Mr. Sheridan also sung in a very singular style. We met there the Hanbury's, Guydickens ... Miss Hungerford, &c.*

HUNLOKE — Margaret Hunloke[290]

Margaret Hunloke, née Coke (±1754-1824), was the sister (possibly twin sister) of Thomas William Coke (1754-1842), 1st earl of Leicester. She married, 1769, Sir Henry Hunloke, 4th baronet (1724-1806), of Wingerworth, Chesterfield, Derbyshire; they had 7 daughters and 2 sons:

1 Margaret Elizabeth (1772-1855)
2 Charlotte Susanna (1774-1862); became countess of Albemarle
3 Marina (1777-1793)
4 Georgina (1779-1805)
5 Ann Sophia (1781-1803)
1 James (1784-1856); succeeded as 5th baronet
6 Louisa (1786-1790)
2 Marmaduke Cuthbert (1787-1804)
7 Dame Anne Sophia (1788-1872)

1804: 12 Sep: *Called on Lady Hunloke.* 23 Sep: *with Lady Hunloke & my Father & Mother.* 27 Sep: *pleasant party at Lady Fingals Singing moderately by Mrs. Menton & Mrs. Legeete. Lady Hunloke amazing.* 1 Oct: *To the play at Bristol in the Evening with my Mother, Lady Hunloke, Sue & Caroline Townsend & Col. Hill.* 6-7 Oct., 10 Oct., 13-14 Oct., 21 Dec: *Accompanied my mother on visits to the Mr. Rennie's & their sisters, an agreeable Scotch family, to Miss Hunloke, handsome, elegant and clever.*

1805: 12 Jan., 10 Feb: *Poor Georgina Hunloke died.* 13 Feb: *My Mother passed the day & my Father the Evening with Miss Hunloke.*

HUNT — the Hunt family of Boreatton, Salop, and Stoke Doyle, Northants. — *see also* Ward Hunt[291]

The Hunt family are dealt with extensively in volume 1, *The Nomad*, pages 133-142. The following is a slightly truncated version.

In 1664, Rowland Hunt of Shrewsbury bought the Boreatton estate from the Harris family and built Boreatton Hall. Much of this was pulled down in Victorian times and rebuilt as Boreatton Park, completed in 1857. The Wadenhoe estate in Northamptonshire, owned by the collateral side of the family, was equally impressive. The earl of Westmorland oversaw the construction of the house in 1617. A hundred years later the estate passed into the ownership of Sir Edward Ward, whose daughter Jane married Thomas Hunt, and the estate devolved to the Hunts (H1, *below*). Our interest starts with Thomas Hunt (H4), who married Sarah Witts, daughter of Edward Witts (1676-1736), sister to Broome Witts (1713-1768), and therefore aunt to Edward Witts (1746-1816) and great-aunt to Francis, our diarist.

The first four pedigrees show only those who reached adulthood. After that all children have been listed until we get to the generation following our period of interest; this generation has been omitted. To make sense of 'who was who', each has been given a numbering in ascending sequence starting with 'H1'.

PEDIGREE 1

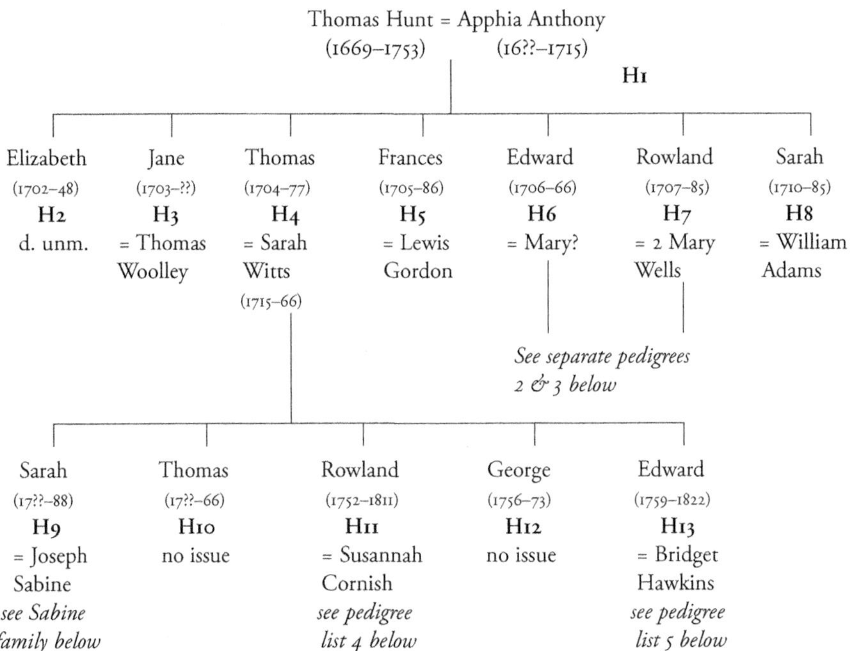

PEDIGREE 2

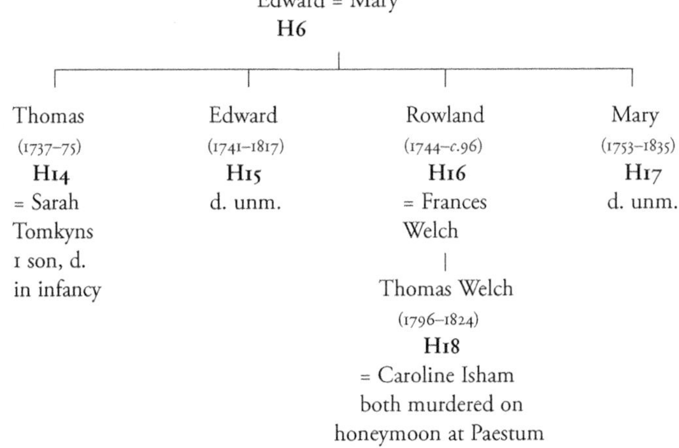

PEDIGREE 3

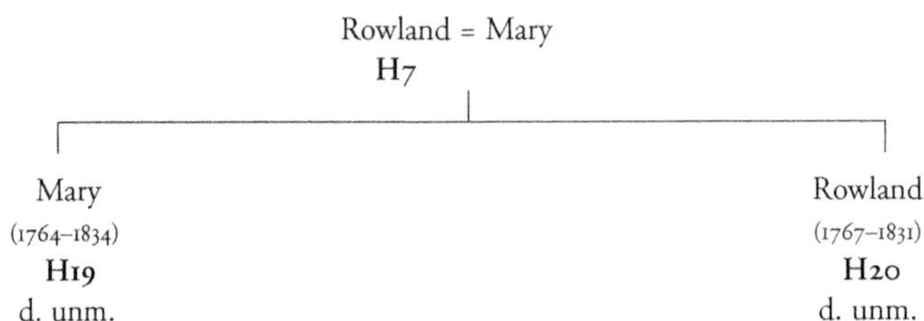

This next generation, the generation contemporary to Francis Witts, demonstrated surprising fecundity, so much so that traditional pedigree tables would require paper of exceptional width; therefore the families have simply been listed.

Pedigree list 4
Susanna, H21 (1782-1866); died unmarried
Rowland, H22 (1784-1835) = Mary Lloyd
Annabella Eliza, H23 (b. 1826); Charlotte Frances, H24 (b. 1827); Rowland, H25 (1828-1878); Thomas Edward Lloyd, H26 (1830-1853)
George, H27 (1786-1853) = Emma Gardiner
Emma Sophia, H28 (1819-1831); Mary, H29 (b. 1821); Eliza Frances, H30 (1822-1861); Julia, H31 (1824-1831); George Ward, H32 (1825-1877); Jane Emelia, H33 (b. 1827); Edward Vernon, H34 (1829-1832); Emma, H35 (1831-1832); Julia Henrietta, H36 (b. 1832); Emily Ellen, H37 (b. 1834); Matilda Selina, H38 (b. 1836); Ellen, H39 (b. 1838); Laura, H40 (b. 1841)
Thomas, H41 (1786-1860) = Jane Harding
Edward, H42 (b. & d. 1823); Frances Elizabeth, H43 (b. & d. 1824); Harriet Susanna Anne, H44 (b. 1825); Thomas Henry, H45 (b. 1826); Charles John, H46 (1828-1857); Jane, H47 (1831-1837); Frances Sophia, H48 (1832-1836); Emily, H49 (b. & d. 1833); Caroline Emma, H50 (b. 1834); William Cornish, H51 (b 1835)
Edward, H52 (1788-1808); died unmarried
John, H53 (1789-1806); died unmarried
Sarah, H54 (1791-1825); died unmarried

Pedigree list 5
Sarah, H55 (b. 1790); died unmarried
Thomas, H56 (b. 1791); died unmarried
Mary Caroline, H57 (1792-1847); died unmarried
Edward, H58; baptised and buried in infancy, with no year given
Sophia Bridget, H59 (b. 1796); died unmarried
Frances Harriet, H60 (1797-1857); died unmarried
Maria Anne, H61 (b. 1799); died unmarried
William, H62; baptised and buried in 1804
Edward, H63 (1801-1854); died unmarried
John, H64 (b. 1806)

The heart of the problem with the executorship (*see below*) lay in the surprising failure of two lines of the family. Despite commendable breeding on the part of Edward Hunt (H6), his line failed when his son Thomas Welch Hunt and daughter-in-law Caroline, née Isham (1801-1824), were murdered on their honeymoon by brigands in Italy—amazingly, the two of them were killed by a single bullet. That the second line failed was even more unexpected due to the strong demonstration of fecundity by Edward Hunt (H13) and his wife Bridget. They had ten children, eight of whom survived infancy, but none of whom married. Francis Witts hinted at their unattractiveness. This complete line failed—but in truth, due to the unusual will of T. W. Hunt, the failure of the line made little difference to the complexity of the trust.

Before going to Italy on his honeymoon, Thomas Welch Hunt made his will. In the (seemingly unlikely) event of his death, the life interest in the estate was to pass to his closest surviving relation, his aunt Miss Mary Hunt of Palace Yard, Gloucester (H17); on her death it was to pass to Mary Caroline Hunt (H57), and on her death to George Hunt (H27). In this way, Thomas Welch Hunt was initially ignoring the elder branch of the family—presumably on the basis that they were already comfortable enough with the Boreatton estate—and instead benefiting the junior line, but why he chose Mary Caroline above her brother, and why after her death it was to bounce back to a collateral line, is a mystery. In the end, the life interest in the estate went to George Hunt, a difficult and suspicious man, and the leading representative of the second branch of the Boreatton side of the family.

George had been educated at University College, Oxford (BA 1807; MA 1810), and was a student of Lincoln's Inn in 1806. He served as rector of Barningham, Suffolk, in 1818-50, and of Boughton, Norfolk, in 1820-53. He had been an Oxford contemporary of Francis Witts.

The Hunts were a wealthy family with extensive landholdings. Mrs Hunt (H17) (really 'Miss'—a maiden lady) was not a blood relation of the Wittses; Sarah Witts had been her aunt, but only by marriage. Francis first met 'Mrs Hunt' in November 1801 when she called at his family's lodgings in Cheltenham. In 1804, while at Oxford, he struck up an acquaintance with Rowland Hunt (H22) of Brasenose College; Rowland was Francis's second cousin. In July 1805, at Cheltenham, the Hunt family were involved in what Francis considered an 'irksome' family meeting; they were obviously considered to be close enough to the family core to take part in discussions of such important things as Francis's future: 'Saturday 6 July 1805: During the forenoon, had the meeting, more or less irksome, with various relations & connections, Lady Lyttelton, Whalleys, Buxtons, Hunts &c. ...' Which of the Hunts were present and why they were in Cheltenham is not made clear.

There are occasional references to the Hunt family in Agnes Witts's diaries, but little is heard in Francis's diaries until 21 January 1823, when he met Mrs Hunt, then living in Palace Yard, Gloucester. Six months later Francis met other cousins at Palace Yard and helpfully attached a family tree:

> Friday 17 October 1823: We passed the evening at Mrs. M. Hunt's in palace yard. We met her guests, two Miss Hunts, daughters of the late Revd. Edwd. Hunt, a Northamptonshire Clergyman & Mr. T. Hunt, High Sheriff of the same County, nephew to Mrs. M. Hunt, an intelligent young man educated at Christ Church Oxford, and who has travelled abroad. I am related to all these Hunts, as also to those of Boreatton in Shropshire.

In the diary a pedigree appears. Francis Witts did, therefore, meet Thomas Welch Hunt on one occasion prior to his murder. He was to have many more dealings with the two Misses Hunt in later years, in his role as executor.

During the mid-to-late 1820s Francis built up a close relationship with Mrs Hunt and her family, dining with them frequently. When Lady Lyttelton was in Gloucester, she was also of the party, as she remained close to the Hunt family generally.

> Monday April 27. 1829: ... Mr. T. Hunt is Rector of West-Felton in that county, and youngest brother of Mr. Hunt of Boreatton Park. He was of Westminster School, & of Christ Church, Oxford, and married a Warwickshire Lady, Miss Harding, a very pretty and elegant woman, by whom he has three children. I never saw him but once before; when, as a school boy, he accompanied his father to call on me at Wadham College, when I was an undergraduate; he is a few years, therefore, my junior, and appears a very estimable, conversible, intelligent man. He spoke in kind and favourable terms of our dear Edward, who receives many friendly civilities from all the branches of the Hunt family.

This Thomas is H41 in our pedigree. West Felton is a village 4 miles south-east of Oswestry. Edward Witts, Francis's son, was a frequent visitor at West Felton parsonage when he was at school in Shrewsbury. (See the diary entry for 24 February 1835.)

> Tuesday Aug. 4. 1829: Our friends the Hunts from Gloucester passed some hours with us to-day ... They were very full of the recent festivities in Shropshire, at Boreatton Park, on occasion of the christening of the Son & heir of my relation, Mr. Hunt. Like his father, he delights in parade, and had made splendid preparations. My Aunt, Lady Lyttelton, was god-mother to the infant Rowland, and in her 87th year, with all her extraordinary energy, was one of the most conspicuous personages at the fête, which was protracted several days, at very considerable expence, not only the intimate friends, relations & neighbours being most hospitably entertained, but on successive days the tenantry, tradespeople, benefit societies, villagers &c. Music &c. Marquees, dancing & speechifying, the planting an oak in commemoration of the event, and the distribution of presents signalized the event. At a former christening in the family my son had been a guest from Shrewsbury, and, probably, would have been again invited, if the festivities had not been fixed for the period of the holidays: but then it was a daughter, and less ceremony was considered requisite. After all, were I a squire of high degree, I hope, I should avoid so much ostentation.

The ostentatious father was Rowland (H22), whom Francis had met as an undergraduate on 29 February 1804 when he was at Wadham and Rowland was at Brasenose. The son, also Rowland, is H25. This Rowland, when he reached his majority, took down much of Boreatton Hall to replace it with the Victorian gothic Boreatton Park.

> Tuesday 22 September 1829: With Mrs. H., besides her young relations, Caroline & Maria, I found a gentleman of the name of Hare, a visitor, though accommodated with a bed out of the house. This Mr. H. is a Lieutenant in the Navy on half pay, and was the intimate friend of poor Mr. T. Hunt, of Northamptonshire, whose melancholy death by the hand of banditti, near Pæstum, as he was returning to Naples, with his young wife, also killed by the same shot, I have had before occasion to mention. I have, however, omitted to name, that he had made a disposition of his property before he left England for the Continent, in which, contemplating the possibility of his own death & his wife's without having any issue, he left his estates to this Aunt, Mrs. M. Hunt, for her life, then to his cousin, Miss Caroline Hunt for her life, & ultimately to Mr. George Hunt, brother to Mr. Hunt of Boreatton ...

This detailed entry when read in full spells out the relationship in detail. Mr Hare had a long involvement with Francis for the next twenty-five years in relation to the tangled web of the estate.

> Monday Feb. 27. 1832: ... Mrs. F. Witts returned to Upper Slaughter; and I proceeded to Gloucester, to Mrs. Hunts', to transact business with Miss Hunts as Executor for their deceased Mother. Took up my abode in Palace Yard, at Mrs. Hunts'.

The deceased mother was Bridget, the widow of Revd Edward Hunt (H13), who had died in 1822. He had been educated at Pembroke College, Oxford (BA 1781; MA 1784), and served as rector of Stoke Doyle in 1786-1822, and Bennifield in 1807-22. Bridget died on 4 December 1831, and it appears from this entry that Francis had taken on the executorship of the mother, although her affairs were probably straightforward. This is different to the troublesome executorship referred to above; for the beginning of the matter, see the following entry:

> Thursday Mar. 29. 1832: I repaired to Palace Yard, and passed an hour or more at Mrs. Hunt's: Caroline and Maria Hunt are, as usual, her inmates; to them were added Mrs. Backhouse, and Mr. Hare, an old acquaintance of mine, and Trustee of the Northamptonshire property, which has devolved on Mrs. Hunt for her life, on Caroline Hunt after Mrs. M. H's decease, for her life, and at her decease on Mr. Geo. Hunt and his family in perpetuity.—Misconduct, amounting, almost, if not altogether, to fraud, on the part of Mr. Hare's Co-Trustee, has involved the parties in considerable uneasiness, and some pecuniary loss, and a new arrangement of the Trust is at present in contemplation. The affairs have been for some time communicated confidentially to me.
>
> Saturday Mar. 31. 1832: Mr. Hare rode over from Gloucester, to communicate to me a letter, which he had received from his Solicitor relating to the business of his Trust; also to express, on the part of Mrs. M. Hunt, Miss C. Hunt and himself, a wish, that I would consent to become his Colleague in a new trust proposed to be created, with some third person to be nominated by Mr. Geo. Hunt. I declined giving an immediate answer to the proposition, but at the same time I felt, that it would be difficult to refuse my assent, and if Mr. Geo. Hunt acquiesces in the arrangement suggested, I shall, probably, consent to act in the Trust, on certain conditions, which I named to Mr. Hare.

This seems to have been the vital, but as it turned out, wrong decision. Why he should have felt it was difficult to refuse is unclear, but he might have wanted to please his aunt, Lady Lyttelton, who remained close to the Hunt family. The trust was complicated, not local, and muddled by its previous arrangement and the involvement of a less than honest trustee. He received £105 for the duty, but it was probably the hardest £105 he ever earned.

> Thursday June 7. 1832: After breakfast at Mrs. M. Hunt's I had a long conversation with Mr. T. Hunt on business of importance to Mrs. M. Hunt and Caroline, arising out of the Trust created by the late Mr. T. W. Hunt, to which I have before alluded. The view taken of this matter by Mr. George Hunt is calculated to give considerable uneasiness to Mrs. M. Hunt, Caroline & Mr. Hare, one of the Trustees under Mr. T. W. Hunt's will, and was by no means unimportant to myself as one of the Trustees proposed for a new management of the property real and personal. We were pleased to find, that Mr. T. Hunt concurred in the view we had taken of the subject, although unfavourable to his brother; it was desirable, that certain explanations should be made to put Mr. G. H's family in possession of the real facts of the case, which were strangely misapprehended by Mr. G. Hunt.

Thomas (H41) was George's younger (and the youngest surviving) sibling. He had nothing to gain or lose from the trust. His cousin Caroline was next in line to receive the benefits, before they devolved on George.

> After tea retired with Sophia Hunt, who placed in my hands the Will of our departed friend with other documents. We had a long and anxious conversation as to the arrangements of the funeral, which is fixed for Thursday, the contents of the will, the prospects of Caroline, the condition and resources of the Stoke Doyle branch of the family, and other interesting matters. My first care was to make myself fully conversant with the disposition which Mrs. M.

Hunt had made of her private fortune, as contained in her will and two Codicils. I found myself, as I had always understood to be her intention, left sole Executor, and, besides, that the personalty of which she had the disposal was much larger than I had anticipated; amounting, in all probability, to more than £16000 ...

The will is dated May 20th. 1833—the codicils 19th. Sept. and 8th. Oct. in the same year. The effect of the latter is decidedly unfavourable to Caroline ... Late in the evening arrived Mr. Geo. Hunt from London to attend the funeral of his deceased relative. We had not met for many years, and the handsome young man was become a singular looking senior. His conversation and habits are not particularly clerical, but I believe there is as little real harm about him, as there is much which is repulsive and abrupt. In temperament he is warm, in appearance selfish & scheming, yet there is not much of disguise ...

Thursday Mar. 26: Soon after breakfast arrived from Stoke Doyle Mr. Thomas Hunt, the only brother of the Misses Hunt resident in England; the two other sons are in the military service of the East India Company abroad. Mr. Thomas Hunt was originally a Clerk in the Victualling office ... he has resided with his sisters, a lounger, ever since. His appearance is feeble and unprepossessing, his address embarrassed, and his apprehension seems to be slow.

This Thomas Hunt (H56) was the second child of the brood and the elder brother to Caroline.

'Saturday May 27. 1837: A letter from Sophia Hunt, chiefly to announce the arrival of her brother John from India.' John (H64) was the youngest of the ten brothers and sisters.

Tuesday Nov. 28. 1837: A gloomy, rainy, raw day. Much trying conversation with Mrs. Backhouse, in the course of which it was elicited from her, that the late Mrs. Mary Hunt had many years since imparted to her in confidence that there was a fear of hereditary derangement in my family; for that my Grand mother Witts had been more than once deranged; and that Mrs. M.H. mentioned this under an apprehension that I might be overpowered as to my mind, if I engaged too much in the transaction of public business, or other engrossing and agitating pursuits. This intimation so long withheld fell on me like a thunderbolt ...

For a little while after the receipt of this intelligence, Francis was extremely anxious, demonstrating a terror of mental illness. He communicated with all members of the family who, he thought, might have had information on the subject. During this time, in fact from 1836 through 1838, he was extremely involved in trust matters, none of which seem to have been successfully resolved. His own death in 1854 occurred before these matters were settled; what happened to the trust after his death remains a mystery.

In 1843 Francis met George Hunt by accident at Brighton, and took the opportunity to go over trust business with him, seemingly in a civil, businesslike manner. In 1844 there was much correspondence involving disputed turnpike securities; again, like so much involving this tedious matter, nothing seems to have been resolved:

Friday 8 March 1844: Recd. letters from the Revds. Geo Hunt and W J Thornton on the vexatæ questio of the Hunt Turnpike Securities ... Friday 15 Mar 1844: To Sophia Hunt on the wearisome subject of the Hunt Turnpike bonds. ...

Nothing of substance and no interesting family revelations appear in the diaries regarding the trust, merely the tedious exchange of letters going nowhere. The turnpike securities issue rumbled on until June 1846. In 1847 there was an unusual event: the visit by Francis and his wife to Wadenhoe. A mere three months later Caroline died at Clifton. Other trust matters kept going until Francis Witts's death in August 1854; the last related diary entry was made on Thursday 10 August, and he died on 18 August.

Because of the large number of diary entries for the Hunt family, code numbers have been adopted to ease the identification of family members; for instance, Sophia Hunt is 'H59'. When the diary entry contains sufficient narrative to indicate clearly the person referred to, a code number is not used. The same applies if the entry is vague or refers merely to the Hunt family, if the identity of a particular family member is uncertain, or if the reference is simply related to business regarding the executorship.

1802: 2 Feb: *Miss Hunt called.*

1804: 29 Feb: *Mr. Hunt of Brazennose called on me.* 4 Mar: *Called on Mr. Hunt at Braznose.* 10 Nov: *In the evening at Hunt's of Univ. a pleasant party where I met James, Trevenen, Mr. Scott B. &c. &c.* 16 Nov: *Dined with Mr. Travell at the King's Arms. The Hunts joined us in the evening.*

1805: 6 Jul: *For an hour at a dull party at Lady Herries's, conversed chiefly with Miss Hunt, Martha Buxton, Fowlkes &c.* 12 Jul: *Mrs. Bates & Miss E. Elliston & drank Tea very pleasantly at Mrs. Hunts'.* 22 Jul: *In the Evening for an hour at a sombre party at Miss Hughes's: conversed with Miss Hunt & Miss Buxton.*

1823: 21 Jan: *Spent the Evening at Mrs. M. Hunt's, an old resident in Gloucester, and a distant relation on my Father's side.* 9 Apr: *I paid my respects this morning at Mrs. M. Hunt's to a hitherto unknown cousin, Mrs. Baring Goold, who with her daughter was on a visit to Mrs. Hunt, & about to leave Gloucester to-day on a visit of a short duration to my Aunt Lady Lyttelton at Pickham Grove. Mrs. B. Goold is daughter of the late Mr. & Mrs. Sabine. Mrs. S. was Sister to Mrs. Hunt, of Boreatton in Shropshire & consequently cousin to my Father; the late Mr. Hunt's Mother having been a Witts, Sister to my Grandfather.* 17 Oct: *We passed the evening at Mrs. M. Hunt's in palace yard. We met her guests, two Miss Hunts, daughters of the late Revd. Edwd. Hunt, a Northamptonshire Clergyman & Mr. T. Hunt, High Sheriff of the same County, nephew to Mrs. M. Hunt, an intelligent young man educated at Christ Church Oxford, and who has travelled abroad.*

1824: 14 Jul: *I spent an hour at Mrs. M. Hunt's in the evening to meet Lady Lyttelton, Mrs. Backhouse, & Miss Witts's.* 28 Sep: *Mrs. Backhouse arrived from Gloucester on a visit to us; she was accompanied by our distant connections, Mrs. M. Hunt, of Gloucester, and Misses Sophia & Caroline Hunt, daughters of the late Revd. Edward Hunt.* 4 Oct: *The Hunts left us, returning to Gloucester; the older lady is agreeable, well informed and conversible; the younger ladies amiable & pleasing.* 19 Oct: *I called on Mrs. M. Hunt. She had kindly copied for me a pedigree in her possession illustrative of the connection of the families of Arnold, Anthony, Skynner, Hunt, Witts &c. which throws considerable light on the family descent, of which before as relates to my Grandmother Witts & her connexions, I had but vague ideas.* 29 Dec: *A very melancholy event has happened to Mr. T. Welsh Hunt, late High Sheriff for Northamptonshire, and his wife, one of the Northamptonshire Ishams. Mr. T. W. Hunt is a distant relation of mine, a very respectable young man, of good fortune, and only married about half a year ago.... Mr. Hunt's carriage was attacked by three brigands, to whom he surrendered an inconsiderable sum of money, protesting he had no more abut him, and even asking for some small coins back to pay necessary demands on his return to Naples. The banditti persisted, that he had more money in his possession, and required him to deliver it up, with a threat of firing at him; he rejoined, that they dared not shoot, as it was in the day light; scarcely had he uttered the words, when a shot was fired, & the contents of the piece lodged in the heart of Mr. Hunt, & in the lungs of his wife.*

1825: 28 Jan: *Mrs. M. Hunt with her relations Miss C. & Miss M. Hunt dined with Mrs. Backhouse.* 2 Feb: H17, 16 Sep: *There is an unfortunate hereditary mental malady in the Hunts, supposed to have crept in by an intermarriage with a daughter of a Lord Chief Justice Ward; where this melancholy tendency has not been fully developed, eccentricity of character has sometimes discovered itself, and in the late Mr. Hunt assumed an useful, though at times amusing type.... Rowland Hunt, the present head of the house, was my cotemporary at Oxford, & of Brazennose College: he was married a few years since to a Miss Lloyd of Shropshire; he is a respectable, worthy man, of weak health, & limited powers of mind. He has two brothers, both in the Church.* 2 Nov: *I found a letter from Mr. Hunt of Boreatton, announcing to me the death of his younger sister Miss Eliza Hunt.*

1826: 25 Jan: *We dined at our old friend's Mrs. M. Hunt's in Palace Yard: besides Miss Caroline & Miss Maria Hunt.* 27 Feb: H17-H57-H61, 30-31 Mar: H17, 15 Jun: H17-H57-H61, 2 Aug: *He gave me a letter left in his charge by my relation, Mr. Hunt of Boreatton, who had been informed of our intended visit to Shrewsbury and its object, and most obligingly invited us to spend some days at Boreatton.* 8 Aug: H17-H57-H61, 31 Aug: H17-H61, 16 Sep: H17, 27 Sep: H57.

1827: 16 Jan: *Mrs. M. Hunt with her two inmates, Miss Caroline & Miss Sophia Hunt, drank tea with us.* 23 Apr: H17.

1828: 17-18 Jan: H17, 17 Mar: H17-H57-H61, 20-22 Mar: H17, 14 Apr: H17, 16 Jun: H22, 26 Aug: *Our friends, Mrs. M. Hunt, Misses Caroline & Maria Hunt arrived from Gloucester to pass a few days.* 29-30 Aug: H57-H61, 2 Sep: *Mrs. Hunt and the young ladies left us this forenoon to pursue their journey into Northamptonshire.*

1829: 12 Jan: H17-H57-H61, 15 Jan: H17, 2 Apr: *About nine o clock, when the party separated, I repaired for an hour to Mrs. M. Hunt's in Palace Yard, where my wife and Mrs. Backhouse had dined; three of the Miss Hunts are staying with her, Caroline, Fanny & Sophia. Our old friend is but in indifferent health.* 27 Apr: *In the evening I called on Mrs. Hunt, to pay my respects to my relations, Mr. and Mrs. T. Hunt, who had arrived there from Shropshire on a visit two days since. Mr. T. Hunt is Rector of West-Felton in that county, and youngest brother of Mr. Hunt of Boreatton Park. He was of Westminster School, & of Christ Church, Oxford, and married a Warwickshire Lady, Miss Harding, a very pretty and elegant woman, by whom he has three children. I never saw him but once before; when, as a school boy, he accompanied his father to call on me at Wadham College, when I was an undergraduate; he is a few years, therefore, my junior, and appears a very estimable, conversible, intelligent man.* 1-2 May: H60, 30 May: H17, 14 Jul: H17, 4 Aug: *Our friends the Hunts from Gloucester passed some hours with us to-day, taking an early dinner en passant, as they were on a journey, first to Leamington, and from thence to Northamptonshire. Mrs. M. Hunt is accompanied by Misses Caroline & Maria Hunt. They were very full of the recent festivities in Shropshire, at Boreatton Park, on occasion of the christening of the Son & heir of my relation, Mr. Hunt. Like his father, he delights in parade, and had made splendid preparations. My Aunt, Lady Lyttelton, was god-mother to the infant Rowland, and in her 87th year, with all her extraordinary energy, was one of the most conspicuous personages at the fête, which was protracted several days, at very considerable expence.* 22 Sep: *I have, however, omitted to name, that he had made a disposition of his property before he left England for the Continent, in which, contemplating the possibility of his own death & his wife's without having any issue, he left his estates to this Aunt, Mrs. M. Hunt, for her life, then to his cousin, Miss Caroline Hunt for her life, & ultimately to Mr. George Hunt, brother to Mr. Hunt of Boreatton. The property is situate chiefly at Wadenhoe and Oundle in Northamptonshire; there is a good residence at the former, & at the latter a sort of jointure house at the edge of the Town. The total value of the property amounted, I believe, at his decease, to nearly £3000 per ann. but has probably not been let for so much since, and it was a good deal clogged with jointures & bequests. Of the former there were two, viz. to Mrs. Rowland Hunt, the Widowed Mother of the poor Testator himself, and to another widow, Mrs. Hunt, the widow of his Uncle, who resided in the house at Oundle, but has since died. To Mr. Rowland Hunt, formerly of Lincoln's Inn, & now, having retired from the profession of the law, a resident at Exeter, Mr. T. W. Hunt left, I believe, £500 per ann. for his life—and Mrs. M. Hunt, with an honourable feeling wishing to do what would be agreeable to her nephew, if he could know it, has added some hundreds a year to the jointure of his mother. The consequence is, that our old friend has never reaped a larger benefit from the succession to the parental property, thus late in her life, than a few hundreds per annum; but she has had the good sense not materially to enlarge her style of living, continually residing in her old & not expensive house at Gloucester, except when taking a little tour, or repairing on an annual visit to Northamptonshire, where the Mansion houses are let, and she visits Mrs. E. Hunt and her family at Stoke Doyle. This gives her an opportunity of transacting business with her Steward.* 24-25 Sep: H17, 20 Oct: H17-H57-H61.

1830: 12 Jan: H17-H57-H61, 14 Jan: H17, 21 Jan: H17, 8 Mar: H17, 21 Apr: H17-H57-H61, 22-23 Apr: H17.

1832: 27 Feb: *Mrs. F. Witts returned to Upper Slaughter; and I proceeded to Gloucester, to Mrs. Hunts', to transact business with Miss Hunts as Executor for their deceased Mother. Took up my abode in Palace Yard, at Mrs. Hunts'.* 28 Feb: H17, 14 Mar: H22, 29-30 Mar: H17-H57-H61, 31 Mar: *Mr. Hare rode over from Gloucester, to communicate to me a letter, which he had received from his Solicitor relating to the business of his Trust; also to express, on the part of Mrs. M. Hunt, Miss C. Hunt and himself, a wish, that I would consent to become his Colleague in a new trust proposed to be created.* 6 Jun: H17, H41, 7 Jun: *After breakfast at Mrs. M. Hunt's I had a long conversation with Mr. T. Hunt on business of importance to Mrs. M. Hunt and Caroline, arising out of the Trust created by the late Mr. T. W. Hunt.* 8 Jun: H57.

1833: 1 Apr: H17, 13 Apr: H17.

1834: 3-10 Mar: H17-H57-H61, 12-14 Mar: H17, 23 Aug: *Heard from Mr. Hare, on subjects relating to the Trust business, in which we are mutually concerned, as to the property of the late Mr. Welch Hunt.* 13 Oct., 23 Dec: *Received a letter from Miss Sophia Hunt, containing a very indifferent account of the health of Mrs. Mary Hunt and Caroline. The latter had been alarmingly ill in Autumn, and is still in a delicate and nervous state. The former is very much shaken, & has been compelled, from inability to travel, to forego her intention of removing from Wadenhoe to Gloucester for the winter. But the main object of the letter is to request my advice as to the manner in which a letter shall be answered, which has been written to Caroline by Mr. Cother, adapted to give her great embarrassment and uneasiness, and wholly unworthy of the writer as a man of sense and proper feeling. The letter in question was enclosed to me in Sophia's letter: and the object seems to be to induce Caroline again to enter into correspondence with the writer, though she more than a twelvemonth since closed all communication with him, and broke off a matrimonial engagement which she had unadvisedly entered into.* 25 Dec: *Wrote to Miss Sophia Hunt, returning the letter from Mr. Cother which she had forwarded to me, and giving the best counsel I could under the circumstances, with a sketch of a reply to Mr. Cother, to be written by Miss S.H. with the sanction of her sister, and calculated to discourage him from again intruding similar letters upon Caroline.*

1835: 24 Feb: *Received a letter from Miss Hunt, from Ruyton, announcing the decease of her eldest Brother, Rowland Hunt Esqr. of Boreatton. He had, I believe, attained to the age of fifty, struggling through life with a very weakly constitution, and in mind not much stronger than in body. In former years I had been his contemporary at Oxford, and acquainted with him as not a distant connexion of my Father's family... He has left three or four children by his widow, who was a Miss Lloyd, who, with Mr. Slaney, lately representative for Shrewsbury, and Miss Hunt, is left guardian of the infant family.* 25 Feb: *Wrote to Miss Hunt, a letter of condolence in reply to the letter received from her yesterday.* 3 Mar: *From Miss Sophia Hunt I received a letter giving a very deplorable account of the declining state of Mrs. Mary Hunt, who cannot, in all probability, long survive.* 4 Mar: H59, 7 Mar: H59, 21 Mar: *Received a letter from Miss Sophia Hunt, apprizing me of the decease of our aged friend and relative, Mrs. Mary Hunt on the morning of the 19th. Inst. and begging me lose no time in coming to Wadenhoe.* 24 Mar: H57, H59, H61, 25 Mar: *At eleven o clock the preparations for the funeral of our deceased friend were nearly completed. Mrs. M. Hunt had desired to be buried in an unostentatious manner.* 26 Mar: H56,-H27-H57, 27 Mar: *Accompanied Mr. George Hunt and Mr. Tebbutt in a walk over parts of the Wadenhoe property.* 29-30 Mar: H59-H41, 31 Mar., 1 Apr., 4-5 Apr: H17, 6 Apr: *Leaving the Court, I proceeded to Palace Yard to the house of the late Mrs. M. Hunt, to give directions to the person left in charge there.* 7-9 Apr: H17, 11 Apr: *Wrote to Miss Sophia Hunt on my Executorship business.* 14-15 Apr: H59, 22 Apr: *Mr. Hare arrived from Cheltenham to dinner. In the evening much conversation with him respecting the Hunt family and their concerns.* 23-24 Apr: H59, 29-30 Apr: H17, 3 May: H17, 6 May: *Received a letter from Miss Sophia Hunt, who, with her sisters Caroline and Maria, are arrived safe at Clifton from Wadenhoe.* 4 May, 8-9 May: H17, 10 May: *Received a letter from Sophia Hunt with a very unfavourable account of the state of her sister, Caroline's mind and health. Dr. Prichard, an eminent Physician, whose studies have been directed to the subject of mental alienation, and who has published an approved work on diseases of the mind, has been called in.* 16 May: H57-H59, 18 May: H59, 21 May: H59, 23 May: H17, 25 May: H17, 28 May: H59, 31 May: H17, 1 Jun: *I drove in the phaeton to Andoversford, where I met Miss Sophia Hunt.* 2 Jun: *Much deliberation with Sophia Hunt on family affairs.* 3-7 Jun: H59, 14 Jun., 18 Jun: *A letter from Sophia Hunt from Clifton with an indifferent account of Caroline.* 19-20 Jun: H59.

1836: 16 Jul: H59, 19 Jul: H59, 23 Jul: H59, 28 Jul: *We lingered at Stow till the arrival of the Northampton coach in expectation of the arrival of Miss Sophia Hunt whom we expected from Stoke Doyle, but who did not make her appearance.* 29 Jul: *When we reached home we found Sophia Hunt arrived; it seems she had reached Northampton yesterday a few minutes too late for the Cheltenham coach: had proceeded by coach to Oxford, where she slept.* 30 Jul., 1 Aug: *A conference with Sophia Hunt on Wadenhoe affairs was interrupted by the arrival of Mr. Pole, who remained for an hour or more.* 2 Aug: *Engaged with Sophia Hunt in discussions on Wadenhoe affairs.* 5 Aug: *Engaged with Sophia Hunt in conversation on business, nearly from breakfast time till dinner time with the interruption of an hour at mid-day.* 6 Aug: H59, 9 Aug., 11 Aug: *Before breakfast received a letter from Sophia Hunt from Clifton where she joined her sisters on Tuesday, and finding that Mr. Hare was about to leave England for the continent almost directly, with the intention of being absent for two years, considered it necessary that I should be apprized of this fact.* 16 Aug., 18-19 Aug: H59, 22-23 Aug: H59, 26 Aug: H59, 28 Aug: *In consequence of my having hinted in my letter that E.F.W. was on the eve of an excursion into Devon, Caroline H. sends a very kind invitation to him to spend a little time with them at Ilfracomb, taking a bed at their house, and making excursions with them to objects of curiosity and interest in that part of N. Devon.* 3 Sep: *Wrote to Sophia Hunt a letter not on business, but to acknowledge the kindness of Caroline H. in inviting my son to her house at Ilfracombe, explaining the route he was taking &c.* 6-8 Sep., 14 Sep., 15 Sep: H57, 20 Sep: H57, 15-16 Oct., 31 Oct: H59, 3 Nov: H59., 20 Dec: *A letter from Sophia Hunt, from Clifton on business; she and Fanny have been great invalids: Caroline pretty well.* 21 Dec: H59, 27 Dec.

1837: 2 Jan., 6 Jan., 18 Jan: *Received a letter from Sophia Hunt, from Bath, with details of that family, and on Northamptonshire & other business.* 4 Feb., 6 Feb., 17 Feb: *Also a letter from Sophia Hunt with a very sad account of the health of herself and most of her sisters, with some details of business.* 22 Feb: H59, 3 Mar., 8 Mar., 13 Apr., 25 Apr., 6 May: H59, 11 May: H59, 24-25 May, 27 May: *A letter from Sophia Hunt chiefly to announce the arrival of her brother John from India.* 28-29 May, 4 Jun., 7 Jun., 14 Jun: H59, 28 Jun., 1 Jul: H59, 11 Jul: H59, 12 Jul., 14 Jul., 20 Jul., 22 Jul: H59, 18 Aug: H59, 3 Sep., 9 Sep: H59, 14 Sep: H59, 4-5 Oct: H59, 5 Oct: H59, 6 Nov: H59, 11 Nov: H59, 28 Nov: *Much trying conversation with Mrs. Backhouse, in the course of which it was elicited from her, that the late Mrs. Mary Hunt had many years since imparted to her in confidence that there was a fear of hereditary derangement in my family; for that my Grand mother Witts had been more than once deranged; and that Mrs. M.H. mentioned this under an apprehension that I might be overpowered as to my mind, if I engaged too much in the transaction of public business, or other engrossing and agitating pursuits.* 1 Dec: H59, 18 Dec: H59.

1838: 18 Jan: H59, 25 Apr., 1 May, 9 May: H59, 27 May: *Recd. a letter from Sophia Hunt, now on a visit at Gloucester, in answer to one written by me sometime since, congratulating us on my Son's marriage.* 28 May: *A letter from Miss Hunt of Ruyton, very kindly expressed, to congratulate us on my son's marriage.* 29 May: H21, 10 Jul: *Also a letter from Messrs. Crawfurd and Co. London, acquainting me that they hold Lieut. E. Hunt's legacy receipt for the £200 bequeathed to him by Mrs. M Hunt, and desiring to know where they may receive the amount on surrendering the document.* 11 Jul: H63-H59, 13 Jul: H63, 15 Jul., 20 Jul: H59, 30 Aug: *Recd. a letter from Sophia Hunt, written partly from Southampton and partly from Ryde, whither she has gone from Northamptonshire to stay with Caroline in the Isle of Wight.* 2 Nov: H59, 14 Nov: H59, 7 Dec: *There was also a letter from Sophia Hunt dated from Clifton, where she is staying with Caroline, after removing the rest of the family for the winter from Stoke Doyle to Bath; so that the sisterhood will, as last winter, be partly at Clifton, and partly at Bath.* 10 Dec: *Also to Messrs. Yorke, Bankers, Oundle directing them out of the monies in their hands standing to my credit, as*

Exor. of the late Mrs. M. Hunt, to pay to Messrs. Coutts £700 to be by them equally divided, & the shares placed to the accounts of Misses, S B H.—F.H.H.—MAH. 22 Dec., 24 Dec: H59.

1839: 18 Jan: *A letter from Miss Hunt of Ruyton acquainting me with the death of her aged Mother on the 14th. Inst.* 19 Jan: H21, 17 Mar., 25 Mar., 29 Mar: H59, 1 Apr: H59, 7 Apr: H59, 10 Apr.,15 Apr: *Caroline Hunt is at Bath for a fortnight from Clifton, in lodgings in Marlborough Street, with her Sisters Sarah and Maria ... Received by Fanny Hunt, who looks and is very delicate; we were soon joined by Sophia H. and at dinner by their brothers Thomas, and John, an officer at home on leave of absence from his corps, a native regiment in the E. India Company's Service.* 16 Apr: *Dined with Caroline Hunt, entirely a family party—myself with the six brothers and sisters: there are off seven; one, Edward, in the East India company's military service, is abroad; the rest all collected at one table—a rare contingency in any family.* 17 Apr: H57-H59, 18 Apr: *A long conference with Sophia, Fanny, and Maria Hunt on the affairs of my Executorship, in which I exhibited to them accounts and documents; also on Wadenhoe matters, and the concerns of Caroline Hunt... Dined with Mr. and Mrs. Hare, a family party: besides our host and hostess, Caroline & Maria H., Sophia and John Hunt, and myself.* 20 Apr: *Breakfasted with Mr. J. Hunt at 7 o cl. A.M. and accompanied him to the top of Milsom Street, where we parted; he by a coach from the York House to London, whither he is going to consult a physician, whether his health is sufficiently reestablished to allow of his return to the East Indies in Sept. to rejoin his regiment, or whether it be advisable to solicit the authorities at home for a prolonged leave of absence.* 24 Apr: H27, 21 May: *Wrote to Sophia Hunt to inform her that Lady Elizabeth Dutton and Mr. Cambridge had promised to give votes in favour of the deaf and dumb boy, whose admission into the asylum in Town is advocated by Mr. and Mrs. George Hunt.* 15 Jun: *A letter also from Capt. Hunt, dated Malvern, apologizing for not coming over to see us from Cheltenham, while staying there lately under Dr. Baron's care, who had recommended his removal to Malvern, on an attack of fever; which fell on him when he was meditating a visit to Slaughter; Malvern has restored him, and he is about to leave it to see his Shropshire relations, in the expectation of being sufficiently well to return to India this autumn.* 27 Jun: H59, 19 Jul: H59.

1840: 29 Mar: H59, 4 Apr: H59, 13 Apr: H57, 16 Apr: H59, 18 Apr: H59, 25 Apr: H57, 27 Apr: *Also from Miss Sophia Hunt, now visiting friends at Gloucester with her sister Maria in indifferent health.* 3-4 Jun: H59, 22 Jun: *Caroline Hunt is keeping house here, chiefly induced by a hope that the Malvern air will be beneficial to the health of her sister Maria; Fanny and Thos. Hunt are also staying with her; Sophia left her on Friday last, having been staying here for a short time lately with Maria before Caroline's arrival.* 23 Jun: *Called on the Hunts, who were from home, but whom we met, and they walked back with us to the Foley Arms, where they rested for some time in our apartment, and we attended them to their lodgings.* 24 Jun., 21 Aug: H59.

1842: 11 Jan: H59, 3 Mar: H59, 7 Mar., 30 Apr: H59, 6 Jun: H59, 9 Jul., 10 Jul: H59, 15 Jul., 31 Jul., 15 Nov: H59, 20 Nov: H59, 23 Nov: *Recd. a letter from Miss Hunt of Boreatton respecting some error made by Messrs. Coutts the Bankers as to some dividends placed to her account, but which, no doubt, should have been placed to the credit of one of her cousins, the daughters of Mr. Edwd. Hunt—for whom I am a Trustee—or they may have made a mistake as to some of the Wadenhoe personal property which should have gone to the credit of Caroline Hunt.* 24 Nov., 27 Nov., 29 Nov., 1 Dec., 28 Dec: H59, 31 Dec: H59.

1843: 11 Jan., 13 Jan: H59, 23 Aug: *A letter from Sophia Hunt in answer to mine on the proposed plan for settling the question as to the Hunt Turnpike Bonds, written in some what of a litigious spirit: it is dated from some place in the Highlands, where, not far from Loch Lomond, she is touring with her sister Fanny, and brother Thomas.* 24 Aug: H59, 26 Aug: *As we were walking in the forenoon towards and near the railway station we met Mr. and Mrs. George Hunt, who have been staying here with an invalid daughter, and were leaving the place, but had missed their train.* 27 Aug: H59, 30 Aug: *Called on Mrs. Geo. Hunt, who returned to Brighton on Monday; her invalid daughter with a younger girl, and her youngest with her: the invalid and her little sister elegant and handsome, and pleasing; but the elder seems a martyr to rheumatic gout; which is benefited by the use of Bath water, but apparently aggravated here.* 31 Aug: *Wrote to Sophia Hunt the particulars of my conversation with Mr. George Hunt on Saturday last.* 6 Sep: H59, 9 Sep: *Drove to call on Mrs. Hunt, by whom and her eldest daughter we were received: the young lady still a great sufferer: they leave Brighton on Monday or Tuesday.* 20 Sep: H59, 22 Sep: H27, 2 Oct., 9 Oct., 18 Oct., 23 Oct., 29 Oct., 25 Dec: *A letter from Mr. Hare on the interminable topic of the Hunt Turnpike Bond Securities.* 23 Dec: H59, 30 Dec: H59.

1844: 8 Jan: H59, 11-12 Jan: H59, 20 Jan H59, 22-23 Jan: H59, 27 Jan., 9-11 Mar: H27, 13-15 Mar: H59, 18 Mar: *Recd. a strange letter from Mr. Geo Hunt on the Hunt Turnpike bonds.* 25 Mar: *Letters from Mr. George Hunt Hunt, and Mr. Thornton on the Hunt Turnpike bonds; the two former write very lengthily, as is their wont, with one-sided views, and bitterness of feeling, making an arrangement of the matters in dispute very difficult.* 27 Mar: H59, 28 Mar: H27, 30 Mar: H27, 1 Apr: *A letter from Mr. Hare as to Hunt Turnpike concerns.* 3 Apr: H59, 4 Apr., 5 Apr: *A letter, in somewhat better tone, from Mr. Geo. Hunt, respecting T. P. Bonds.* 6-7 Apr: H27, 10 Apr: H59, 12 Apr., 14 Apr., 15 Apr: *Recd. a troublesome letter from Sophia Hunt about the Turnpike bonds.* 16 Apr: H27, 18 Apr: H27, 20 Apr: H59, 21 Apr: H27, 24 Apr., 26-27 Apr: H27, 29-30 Apr: H27, 1 May, 4 May: H27, 8 May, 28 May, 30 May, 1 Jun: H27, 3 Jun: H27, 26 Jul., 27 Jul: H59, 4 Aug: H59, 2 Oct: H59, 19 Oct., 23 Oct: H59, 27 Oct: H59, 2 Nov: H59, 5 Nov., 8 Nov., 9 Nov: H59, 17 Nov., 20 Nov., 22 Nov: H59, 24 Nov: H59, 30 Nov., 1-2 Dec: H59, 4 Dec., 7 Dec., 8 Dec: H59, 10 Dec., 18 Dec., 24 Dec: H27-H59, 26 Dec., 28 Dec: H27.

1845: 1 Jan: H59, 2 Jan., 6 Jan., 7 Jan: *From Sophia Hunt on various matters relating to that family; the affairs of their uncle Hawkins lately deceased &c... The Stoke Doyle part of the family are now on a visit to Caroline at Clifton, and going, as usual to Bath for a residence of some months.* 9 Jan., 13 Jan: H59, 21 Jan., 25 Jan., 26 Jan: *they saw a good deal at Bristol, the Hotwells, and Clifton, which was new and interesting to Sophy (Witts), and called to take luncheon at Caroline Hunt's in the Mall.* 28-29 Jan: H27, 31 Jan., 2 Feb., 4-5 Feb., 6 Feb: H27, 10-11 Feb., 14 Feb., 17-18 Feb: H27, 7 Mar: H59, 10 Mar: H59, 14 Mar: H59, 16-17 Mar: H59, 23 Mar: *Received a letter from Mr. Hare, who entirely relinquishes all claim to any share in the Hunt Turnpike money, except as to one third of a fourth share, which he is entitled to as Executor of the Widow, Mrs. F. Hunt, who was entitled to it as her thirds, under Administration to her husband's estate.* 12 Apr: *To Sophia Hunt expressing surprize that I had not heard of her taking measures to obtain from Mr. Briggs a share of the expences payable to the attorneys in respect of the Hunt Turnpike Securities affair.* 13 Apr: H59, 15-17 May: H59, 3 Jun: *A letter from Sophia Hunt giving a very poor account of the health of her sister Caroline.* 4 Jun: H59, 8 Jun: *MW. Recd. a letter from*

Sophia Hunt with a very indifferent report as to the health of her sister Caroline: she has been visited by the eminent physician, Sir C. Clarke, whose fee was Fifty Guineas, coming by the Oxford Commemoration from his seat in Leicestershire, I believe. 9 Jun., 26 Jun., 27 Jun: H59, 29 Jun: H27, 5 Jul: H59, 9 Jul: *In the heart of these hills to the East of Stretton, three or four miles distant, is the parish and village of Cardington, of which my Uncle John Witts was for many years the Incumbent, having been presented to the living by his cousin, Hunt of Boreatton.* 10 Jul: *On my reaching Claremont Bank I found there Mr. Thomas Hunt from West Felton, calling to welcome us into Shropshire—cheerful, gentlemanlike, handsome, and conversible, very grey headed… Wrote a note to Miss Hunt, proposing to drive to Boreatton and pay our respects to her on Monday next.* 11 Jul: H59.

1846: 22-23 May: H59, 6 Jul: H59, 8 Jul: H27-H59, 14 Jul: H59, 21 Jul: *from Sophia Hunt as to the appointment of a Solicitor to the Wadenhoe Trust; S.B.H. and two of her sisters meditate an excursion up the Rhine.* 9 Aug: *Recd. from Mr. Thornton a letter on the appointment of a Solicitor to the Wadenhoe trust: he forwarded to me a copy of a letter on that subject which had been written by Mr. Geo. Hunt to Caroline Hunt.* 17 Aug: *With M.W, Sophia and Fanny Hunt drove out to visit Polebrook, where there is a farm belonging to the Wadenhoe Estate.* 7 Oct: *M.W. recd. a letter from Sophia Hunt, who with her brother Thomas, and sisters Maria and Fanny are lately returned from a tour on the Rhine, and in Switzerland. She gives hurried but ample details of their adventures.* 13 Oct: H27, 14 Oct: H59, 23 Oct: H27,

1847: 10 Feb: H59, 16 Feb: H59, 26 Feb: H59, 4 Apr., 12 Apr: H59, 16 Apr: H27, 17 Apr., 20 Apr: H59, 22 Apr: H27, 23 Apr., 24 Apr: H27, 3 May, 5 May, 7 May H27, 11 May, 25 May: H27, 26 May, 28 May: H27, 31 May, 5-7 Jun., 10-12 Jun: H27, 13 Jun: H59, 14 Jun., 15 Jun: H59, 16 Jun., 17-19 Jun., 21-22 Jun: H59, 7 Jul., 13 Jul., 18 Jul: H59, 24 Jul: H59, 31 Jul: *from Sophia Hunt, accepting our proposed visit to Stoke Doyle.* H27, 2 Aug: H27, 9 Aug: *we were most kindly received by the Hunt family—Sarah, Sophia, Fanny and Thomas.* 10 Aug: *After luncheon we drove, M.W., Sophia & Fanny Hunt, and myself, in a comfortable carriage.* 11 Aug: *Drove with M.W., Sophia, and Fanny Hunt, to Wadenhoe, distant between two and three miles.——Met there Mr. Tebbutt, the Steward of the estate, and with him and Sophia looked at many improvements.* 13 Aug: *with M.W. Sophia and Fanny Hunt, on an excursion for some hours to Peterborough.* 14 Aug: *With Sophia Hunt and her brother Thomas drove out in the hired Clarence with a pair of horses, our first point being Thrapston distant six or seven miles.* 15 Aug: *The Stoke Doyle property has, indeed, been alienated; but the Wadenhoe, and Oundle and other property once possessed by Sir E.W. form the bulk of the estate now held for life by Caroline Hunt.* 16 Aug: H59, 17 Aug: *we returned to Polebrook, and rejoined our party at the Parsonage, being politely received by the aged Rector and his lady. Here in a comfortable small house, in a pretty small garden, Mr. Isham shewed us portraits of his lamented daughter and son in law, Mr. and Mrs. T. Welch Hunt.* 7 Sep., 3 Oct: *a letter from Sophia Hunt, dated Clifton, giving a very alarming account of the health of her sister Caroline.* 9 Oct: *Mr. George Hunt manifests a lamentable wrong-headedness, is impetuous, overbearing, dictating, and deluded: he seems unmanageable, and cannot view things calmly; one fears over excitement.* 10 Oct: *M.W. received a letter from Sophia Hunt, from Clifton with a very indifferent account of the health of her sister Caroline.* 25 Oct: *M.W. received a letter from Sophia Hunt, with a very alarming account of the declining state of her sister Caroline.* 30 Oct: H59, 31 Oct: *A letter from Sophia Hunt communicates a much worse account of the state of her sister Caroline, who may have already departed this life, and cannot, it would seem, last many days.* 1 Nov: *Received from Sophia Hunt a letter announcing the death of her sister Caroline which took place on Saturday night; she summons me to Clifton.* 2 Nov: *All the property of which Caroline died possessed after payment of debts, funeral and testamentary expences, and a few legacies, is to be equally divided between her brothers and Sisters,——Thomas, Edward, Sarah, Sophia, Fanny, and Maria in equal proportions: but the portion coming to Edwd. is to be in trust, to be invested in the public funds or on real securities, the interest to be paid to E.H. during his life, and the principal, after his decease, to all and any of his children; failing such, to all and every his brother and sisters then living, and to the issue of those who shall have died. (This Edward is a weak man, who was, for some misconduct into which he fell, or was led by bad example or advice, reduced from the East India Company's military service, with a small pension, on which he subsists at or near Bombay, living, it is believed, with a native woman. His family have had little or no intercourse with him by letter for several years past: all attempts to extricate him from his degraded position have been ineffectual.)* 2 Nov: *The small freehold cottage belonging to her at Wadenhoe is to be sold, the refusal of it to be given to the Owner of the Estate——now George Hunt, who, by Caroline's decease, succeeds to the whole life interest which she held, and is to enjoy in perpetuity under T. W. Hunt's will the Northamptonshire estates, together with the personalty which is considerable; as to the whole Mr. Hare, Mr. Thornton and I are in trust.* 3 Nov: *Conferring with Sophia Hunt on Exorship concerns.* 4 Nov: *Constant conference with Sophia Hunt and her sisters as to our Executorship.* 5 Nov: *Mr. George Hunt having intimated by letter to Sophia Hunt that the indisposition of one of his children (apprehended measles) will prevent his attending the funeral at Wadenhoe on Tuesday next, Mr. Hare was invited to be present. Mr. Ward Hunt, now of Christ Church, Oxford, Son of George Hunt, has been requested to attend… to Edward Hunt, at Bombay, explaining to him the disposition made in his favour by his sister Caroline, how he will now be affected by a division of the £2000 in which she had a life interest under Mrs. Mary Hunt's will, which is to be distributed between her Brothers and Sisters, and desiring instructions from him as to payments to be made to him.* 10 Nov: H59, 12 Nov: *Mr. Hare attended; also Mr. Ward Hunt:—Thomas Hunt of Stoke was present, but hardly equal to encounter the exertion.... S.H. incloses for my perusal a note from Mrs. Hunt, stating that her husband, George Hunt, had fallen into a depressed and dejected state of mood, since Caroline's decease.* 20 Nov: *Received a letter from Sophia Hunt from Stoke Doyle, on Exorship matters: she proposed to return to Clifton next week.* 22 Nov: H59, 24 Nov: H59, 26-27 Nov: H59, 30 Nov: H59, 3 Dec: H59, 6 Dec: H59, 10-11 Dec: H59, 14 Dec: *A letter from Sophia Hunt engaging to meet me at Mr. Whitcombe's office at Gloucester.* 17 Dec: H59, 24 Dec: *a letter from Sophia Hunt of Hunt Trust and Executorship matters. Sarah Hunt is in a very weak, perhaps a declining state, and her brother Thomas an invalid.* 27 Dec: H59, 30 Dec: H59.

1848: 2 Jan: H59, 8 Jan: H59, 10-11 Jan: H59, 18-19 Jan: H59, 8 Feb: H59, 13 Feb: H59, 15 Feb: *At the desire of Sophia Hunt, to whom the measure has been suggested by a Col. Ottey, of the E.I. Company's service, I wrote, as Exor of M C Hunt, to Major Rowley, Superintendent of Pensioners, Bombay, as to Edward Hunt.* 19 Feb: H59, 23 Feb: H59, 27-28 Feb: H59, 7 Mar: H59, 10 Mar: H59, 15 Mar: H59, 23 Mar: *Received a letter from Mr. George Hunt, a disagreeable one, as usual.* 25 Mar: H27-H59,

28 Mar: *With this valuable document betook myself to the Banking office of the Messrs. Coutts, in the Strand, where I paid it to the account of myself and Sophia Hunt as the Executors of her sister Caroline.* 30 Mar: H59 ... *Thence I proceeded to Bartlett's Buildings, Holborn, to the office of Mr. Braikenridge, Mr. George Hunt's Solicitor, with whom I had a long and confidential interview.* 4-5 Apr: H59, 8 Apr: H59, 12 Apr: H59, 14 Apr: H59, 15 Apr: *From Mr. Hare a letter, with extracts from letters of Mr. Braikenridge, and of Messrs. Cox & Williams, as to transfering to Mr. Geo. Hunt the personal estate of the late T. W. Hunt.... From Sophia Hunt, on Hunt Trust and Executorship affairs, chiefly as to Mr. George Hunt's claim of the watch given many years ago by Mrs. Rowland Hunt to Mr. Hare.* 18-20 Apr: H59, 23 Apr: *Received a letter from Sophia Hunt, who forwards for my perusal two notes received by her from Mrs. Hare, announcing that Mr. Hare is very ill, and prohibited from all correspondence or attention to business.* 24 Apr: H59, 3 May: *Recd. a letter from Sophia Hunt in Trust and Executorship business: she forwards for my perusal letters from Mr. Hare & Geo. Hunt.* 12-13 May: H59, 14 May: *Received a letter from Mr. Thornton with enclosures on the Hunt Trust concerns: he has transmitted to Mr. Braikenridge the bills, which I forwarded to him, that he may examine them on the part of his Client, Mr. Hunt.* 15 May: *It is proposed that the Stock standing in our names as Trustees be transfered into the name of Mr. Geo. Hunt, a small portion being reserved to meet any expences to which the Trustees may be put by any adverse proceedings which Mr. G.H. may be advised to take, and which may be chargeable to the corpus of the estate: and the title-deeds of the landed property are also to be handed over to Mr. G.H.* 17 May: *Stock held by the Trustees to Mr. Geo. Hunt, and to deliver up the title deeds to Mr. Braikenridge as his agent.* 18 May: H59, 23 May: H59, 26 May: H27, 26 May: *to Messrs. Coutts, desiring them to transfer to the account of Captain John Hunt one seventh share.* 27 May, 29 May, 30 May: *Recd. a letter from Mr. Boye, Paymaster of the Bombay Pensioners, with a full account of the present circumstances of Mr. Edward Hunt. This letter is a reply to one written by me on Feb. 15. last to Major Rowley Superintendent of Pensioners, Bombay establishment.* 1 Jun: *A letter from Sophia Hunt, who forwards to me copies of a letter on Trust business which she had received from one of Mr. G. Hunt's daughters, written by his desire, and of the answer she (S.H.) had sent in reply, which is not calculated to smoothe matters.* 8 Jun: *from Mr. Thornton, who returns to me the copies of the correspondence between Miss M. Hunt H. and Mr. Geo. Hunt.* 9 Jun: *Received a letter from Sophia Hunt, who forwards for my perusal a letter received by her from her Brother Edward in India——I also received a letter addressed to me by E.H. writing from Daprolee Camp, near Bombay, where he resides—a pensioner on the Bombay pension list.* 10 Jun: *M.W. had received a letter from Fanny Hunt who is now with Maria on a visit at Gloucester: Sophia remains with Thomas and Sarah at Clifton, the latter in so declining a state that no attempt can be made at present to remove her to Stoke Doyle.* 16 Jun: *The account which she gives of her eldest Sister, Sarah, is very unfavourable: it will not be possible, apparently, to remove her alive to Stoke Doyle—Her death seems near at hand.* 20 Jun: *A letter from Sophia Hunt on Executorship business, accompanying one from Fanny Hunt to M.W.—the latter contained a very bad account of the fast-sinking state of Sarah Hunt.* 20 Jun: H59, 23 Jun: H59, 29 Jun: *Her report of the declining state of her sister Sarah leads me to think that her life must soon close ... when I went to the Bell, to meet Sophia Hunt, who had arrived with a day ticket from Bristol.* 4 Jul: H59, 7 Jul: *A letter from Sophia Hunt brought the intelligence of the death of her sister Sarah, which took place at Clifton.* 8 Jul: H59, 16 Jul: *A letter from Sophia Hunt, dated from Stoke Doyle, with particulars as to the funeral of her sister Sarah—of her will—and other matters, relating to the Hunt family, especially as to her brother Edward.* 17 Jul: *Wrote letters to Messrs. Coutts, desiring them to remit to Mr. Edwd. Hunt at Dapoolee near Bombay.* 18 Jul: H59, 25 Jul: *We found that visitors had sought us out yesterday: Mrs. Hunt had been so obliging as to drive over with her family from her residence at Glangwnna, between Caernarvon and Llanberis; she had been informed of the circumstance that we were staying at Beaumaris by Miss S. Hunt. This was an unexpected civility and compliment, as we had no personal acquaintance with this very distant relative, who is the widow of the late Rowland Hunt of Boreatton: she resides in North Wales at a place near which we had passed this morning, not knowing that we were in its vicinity, with her two sons and daughter. The elder son will soon attain his majority, and come into possession of his Shropshire estates. Whether Glangwnna belongs to the Hunt family, or to the Lloyds, a Shrewsbury family, Bankers, Mrs. Hunt having been a Miss Lloyd, I am not sure... My son, as a schoolboy at Shrewsbury, had experienced much kind civility, from the Hunts, being a frequent guest at Boreatton, at West Felton, the residence of Mr. Thos. Hunt, who is incumbent of that parish, and brother of Rowland Hunt the elder, and George Hunt, and at Ruyton, where the widow Mrs. Hunt, grandmother of the present possessor of Boreatton, resided with her daughter, Miss Hunt.* 28 Jul: *to Mrs. Hunt of Glangwnna, apologizing for not returning her visit, and acknowledging her politeness in calling upon us.* 8 Aug: H59, 12 Aug: H59, 13 Aug: H59, 31 Aug: H59, 4 Sep: *Wrote very fully to Sophia Hunt on the questions at issue with Mr. Geo. Hunt.* 8 Sep: *Received from Sophia Hunt a very strange, ill-judged, and fretful letter.* 12 Sep: H59, 15 Sep: H59, 19 Sep: H59, 23 Sep: H59, 27 Sep: *From Sophia Hunt received a formal letter addressed to the three Hunt trustees, in which she declines personal communication on the matters in dispute with them individually, and desires that any proposition they may have to make be forwarded to Mr. Whitcombe as the Solicitor employed by her family: this accompanies a private letter to me, in which she details transactions with Mr. George Hunt as to the furniture at Wadenhoe, its sale by auction &c.——I cannot but lament and feel annoyed at the temper in which the family at Stoke Doyle conduct the controversy as far as they are concerned, respecting the Hunt succession & their claims as conflicting with those of Mr. Hunt. It is ungrateful, unjust, and irritating to treat the Trustees with suspicion and distrust: but S.H. has conceived a prejudice, which is wholly unfounded, and persists in upholding her own false impressions, as if they were infallibly just, and her own angry views as if they were undeniably well grounded.* 28 Sep: *From Mr. Hunt a strange letter, in which he calls upon me to give up the £1000. 3 Pr. Ct. Cons. which the Hunt Trustees have retained to await the final settlement of the matters in debate, expressing himself as if the above mentioned reserve were wholly and solely my act: he wants the money, he says, to invest it in the purchase of land, and pledges himself to make it good when called upon so to do. It is impossible to avoid the conclusion that Mr. H., with ungovernable ill-temper, and rooted false prejudice on the whole points in dispute, and a most grasping disposition pursues the end he aims at in a spirit calculated to lead one to suspect his sanity.* 30 Sep: *Wrote to Mr. G. Hunt in reply to his letter received on Thursday; stating that I should communicate its contents to my co-trustees.* 2-4 Oct: H59, 5 Oct: *letter from Mr. Thornton: he rather leans to assenting to the request of Mr. Hunt.* 6 Oct: *Mr. Hare agrees with*

me that, under the sanction of the opinion given to us by Mr. Turner & Mr. Bates, we ought not to consent to Mr. Hunt's demand. 14 Oct: *A letter from Sophia Hunt from Hastings, whither she and her sisters have betaken themselves on a short excursion.* 23 Oct: H59, 1 Nov: *A letter from Mr. E. Hunt from India in reply to one written by me to him from Beaumaris, and as to remittances to be made to him, his position under the Company's service &c.* 3 Nov: *To Miss S. B. Hunt, forwarding to her the letter I had received from her brother Edward.* 5 Nov: *A letter from Sophia Hunt, as to the inscription proposed for the monument in memory of Caroline Hunt.* 7 Nov: H59, 9 Nov: H59.

1849: 11 Dec: H59, 15 Dec: *Letter from Sophia Hunt on Hunt Trust and Executorship concerns in the wonted flighty and unsatisfactory style.* 19 Dec: H59, 29 Dec.

1850: 5 Jan., 18 Jan: *Miss Sophia Hunt wrote a letter of kind enquiry, not mixed up with business.* 29 Jan: H59, 6 Feb: H59, 7 Mar: H59, 9 Mar: H59, 16 Mar: *Letters from S. B. Hunt, who writes very kindly as to MW's painful state.* 23 Mar: H59, 24 Mar: *Received a letter from Sophia Hunt, announcing that she and Mr. Geo. H. have agreed on an arbitration.* 25 Mar: H59, 27 Mar: H59, 1 Apr: H59, 12 Apr: H59, 18 Apr: *Several letters were received in answer to those written by E.F.W. to announce his poor mother's decease ... Miss S. B. Hunt.* 20 Apr: *I received a very welcome & affecting note from Mrs. George Hunt, with expressions of kind sympathy, written by her husband's bedside, at his earnest desire, in the warmest terms of friendly condolence. As the tenor of our correspondence on Hunt Trust matters has latterly been very unpleasant, he labouring under a false and exaggerated view of his position, and charging the Hunt Trustees with injuring him, not scrupling to write with a most uncontrolled asperity, and in offensive and unjustifiable language, I could not but feel satisfaction in this altered tone.* 3 May: *A kind letter from Sophia Hunt; nothing as to business has transpired: Mr. George Hunt has been able to take a carriage airing.* 6 May: H59, 28 Jun: *A letter from Miss S. B. Hunt on Hunt trust and Executorship affairs dated from Malvern.* 29 Jun: H59, 3 Jul: H59, 6 Jul: *Wrote to Miss S. Hunt in answer to her letter received by me at Gloucester, in which she invited me to pass a day with her family at Malvern.* 19 Jul: H59, 29 Jul: H59, 6 Aug: H59, 16 Aug: H59, 22 Aug: H59, 31 Aug: H59, 6 Sep: H59, 10 Sep: H59, 24 Sep: H59: *A long, rambling, and not very coherent letter from Sophia Hunt on Hunt Trust.* 5 Oct: H59, 19 Oct: *from Mr. Ward Hunt, and Mr. Thornton on Hunt Trust business.* 21 Oct: *Also a letter from Miss Sophia Hunt, on Hunt trust and executorship business, and general topics, dated from Exmouth, where she, with her brother and sisters, has been making a short sojourn.* 28 Oct: H59.

1851: 18 Feb: *Recd. from Mr. Hare, for my signature, the conveyance of the Red Lion Wharf, Thames Street, to Mr. Geo. Hunt.* 20 Feb: H27, 16 Apr: H59, 1 May: *I received an angry letter from Sophia Hunt, who is very angry indignant with Mr. Hare.* 3 May: H59, 7 May: H59, 11 May: *Received a letter from Sophia Hunt, who writes in a needlessly angry and irritable tone.* 14 May: *A letter from Sophia Hunt written in a sore, unbusiness like, and rambling style, and not conveying a reply to my late letter respecting the Hunt Trust accounts.* 23 May: H59

1852: 19 Jan: H59, 1 Feb: *Recd. a letter from Sophia Hunt—delicate health of her sister Fanny—details of Boreatton Hunts—the young head of the house, jilted by a lady, to whom he was about to be married, has set off on a tour to the East Indies—the Hunt party at Bath much annoyed that Mr. and Mrs. Hare have broken off all acquaintance with them.* 6 Feb: *A letter from Miss S. Hunt, who forwards to me a correspondence between herself and Mr. Hare.* 14 Feb: H59, 29 Mar: *Mr. G. W. Hunt left his card for me at the Bell, and I made myself known to him in the Court. He has been lately called to the Bar, and this is his first circuit. He is a fine, intelligent looking young man, of good address; and we met on cordial terms, each apparently well disposed to entertain friendly feelings for the other, and not to retain any uncomfortable recollections of past transactions. For myself, I can have no desire but to forget and forgive the harsh judgments, the unfounded surmises, and the unwarrantable asperities of his prejudiced father, exhibited for years past during the subsistence of the Hunt Trust, now, it is to be hoped, finally closed.* 30 Mar: *In one case, in which I had requested R. Brookes to give a brief to Mr. Ward Hunt, I was pleased to see that he acquitted himself with great readiness, good judgment, and in a businesslike and unaffected manner.* 1 Dec: *A cheerful, gossiping letter from Sophia Hunt.* 6 Dec: H59.

1853: 11 Mar: *Recd. a letter from Mr. Thornton, announcing to me the decease on Monday last, of George Hunt: he had passed a tranquil winter in comfortable health and calm spirits; but was carried off in a few days after an attack of erysipelas. To Mr. Thornton & me, who have had reason to complain for poor Mr. H's violent prejudices angrily expressed and acted upon, the death of this irascible being, at times hardly responsible for what he said or did, gives room for much serious and some painful reflection. To his family his removal will be a source of pain, for he was an attached parent and husband, and all, both wife & children, were assiduous in soothing him & calming his aspirates, but, if his affairs are left in a well ordered state, his removal will be less to be deplored than if he had been of a less wayward temperament.* 12 Mar: *A letter from Sophia Hunt, with information as to the death of George Hunt, of which she supposed I might not otherwise have received an early account.* 18 Mar: *Wrote to Sophia Hunt in answer to her letter, announcing to me the death of George Hunt.* 14 May: H59, 20 May: H59.

1854: 22 Jul: H59, 29 Jul: H59.

HUNT — Charles Brooke Hunt[292]

Charles Brooke Hunt (±1794-1888), JP, DL, and landed proprietor, was born at Nottingham. By 1851 he lived at Bowden Hall, Upton St Leonards. Brooke Hunt held a senior position in the ordnance office in the Tower of London, and in the 1861 census he was listed as JP, DL of Gloucestershire, and on the civil superannuation list of the Ordnance Department. He married Louisa Maria Newcomb, who was twenty-one years his junior; they had at least 4 sons and 2 daughters:

1 William Henry (b. 1828)
1 Louisa Maria Jane (1842-1915)
2 Charles George Brooke (b. 1844), Lt, RN
3 Robert Henry Brooke (1846-1939)
2 Mary Harriet Louisa (b. 1850)
4 Arthur Ernest Brooke (1854-1915)

Robert and Arthur adopted the surname Brooke-Hunt. Their father sold Bowden Hall to Dearman Birchall in 1868 and moved to Piers Court, Stinchcombe, Gloucestershire.

1842: 15 Dec: *Returned to Prinknash, where Weston Hicks called, as also Mr. Brooke Hunt, the new resident at Bowden Hall.* 1845: 8 May.

1847: 16 Mar: *Reached the asylum by 11 AM. where were assembled Curtis Hayward, Purnell, Dr. Timbrill, Mr. Brooke Hunt, Clifford and Hyett.* 28 Jun.

1848: 3 Jan., 20 Mar., 26 Mar: *Wrote to Mr. Brooke Hunt, as one of the Visitors of the Gaol of Gloucester, respecting a lad from*

Cheltenham of the name of Halling, respecting as to whom I had a correspondence some time back with the authorities. 31 Mar: *Recd. a letter from Mr. Brooke Hunt as to Halling, the convict, being a reply to my letter to him of the 27th. inst.* 16 Oct.

1849: 31 Dec.

1850: 28 Jan., 1 Jul., 7 Aug., 30 Dec: *passing & auditing the county accounts, by myself, Messrs. Baker, Brooke Hunt, Curtis Hayward, Lysons &c.*

1851: 17 Mar: *Committee of accounts present were ... Brooke Hunt.*

1852: 13 Mar.

1853: 3 Jan., 27-28 Jun.

HUNT — Dodington Hunt — *see also* William Hunt Prinn [293]

Dodington Hunt (±1743-1803), barrister-at-law, was born at Pauncefoot, Somerset, son of Revd Dodington Hunt (1707-1750) and Susannah Webb. He was educated at Brasenose College, Oxford (DCL 1773). He was a barrister-at-law of the Inner Temple in 1768. He married, at Charlton Kings, Gloucestershire, 7 August 1770, Elizabeth Prinn (d. 1772); she died giving birth to their son:

1 William Hunt Prinn (1772-1821)

In 1784, Dodington's father-in-law, William Prinn, died, and he inherited the estate, presumably under an entail. In 1788 he hosted a visit by George III. He married secondly, 1797, Anna Nettleship, the daughter of a Cheltenham attorney and a friend of Agnes Witts.

1801: 2 Nov: *Mr. Delebere & Mrs. Hunt called in the morning.* 5 Nov: *Called with my Mother upon Mr. & Mrs. Hunt at Charlton & Miss Jones.* 9 Nov: *Dined & spent the Evening with the Granvilles meeting Mr. & Mrs. Hunt.* 19 Nov: *walked with my Mother, Mrs. Granville & Fanny to Charlton called upon the Hunts, returning thro' their beautiful park to Sandford & home.*

1802: 19 Aug: *Called on the Hunts at Charlton & Ansley's at Sandford.*

HUNT — Frederick Hunt, curate of Great Rissington [294]

Frederick Hunt (1820-1895), Church of England clergyman, was born at Lechlade, Gloucestershire, son of Revd Thomas Maxwell Hunt (b. 1790) and his wife, Elizabeth. He was educated at Queen's College, Oxford. He married, first, a Miss Angus [first name unknown]; they had 1 son and 1 daughter:

1 Emma (b. ±1848); born at Tirlemont, Belgium

1 Frederick W. (1850-1929); born at Koblenz, Rheinland-Pfalz, Germany

His first wife must have died young for in the 1861 census he was living at Oulton, Norfolk, with his parents, assisting his father as curate. He married secondly, at Roydon, Norfolk, 25 June 1861, Charlotte Emma Baynes (1820-1898); they had no known children.

Nothing specific or conclusive has been found to identify this clergyman, so this attribution to Frederick is tentative. He did not remain in Great Rissington very long, probably not beyond 1848.

1847: 7 Apr., 17 Apr: *made a first call on Mr. and Mrs. Hunt, and Mrs. Angus, now occupying the house lately inhabited by Mr. and Mrs. Aitkens: Mrs. Angus, a lady from Liverpool, mother of Mrs. H., has taken the house for six months, until after her daughter's confinement, and until Mr. and Mrs. H. remove into a very small house at Gt. Risington lately built by the Dean of Gloucester, and assigned by him for the residence of his curate.* 21 Apr: *Mr. Hunt from Bourton on the Water called.* 8 May, 4 Jun: *Mr. Ford, R Waller, Mr. Turner, Mr. Hunt (Gt. Risington) Messrs. Bryan, Bennet, &c. were of the number of honorary members.* 8 Sep., 18 Sep: *drove to Bourton on the water. Called on the Hunts. Mrs. H. was out; received by Mr. H. and Mrs. Angus, Mrs. Hunt's mother.* 21 Sep.

1848: 19 Jan., 26 Apr.

HUNT — George Ward Hunt — *see* Ward Hunt

HUNT — James Hunt, poor law district auditor [295]

James Hunt (b. 1799), accountant, was born at Kingham, Oxfordshire, son of James Hunt and Mary Beman (b. 1756). By 1851 he was a widower, and listed in the census as a land and house proprietor. In 1830 Hunt had business premises in High Street, Oxford. He became the poor law district auditor in 1845 and was a thorn in the side of Francis Witts. Little has been discovered about him, and this attribution is tentative.

1844: 2 Oct: *A letter from Mr. Hunt, accountant, Oxford, soliciting my interest, as chairman of the Stow on the Wold union in his favour as candidate for an Audit district under the Poor Law further amendment Act.* 20 Nov: *a letter from Mr. Hunt, of Oxford, candidate for a Poor Law Union Auditorship with a printed copy of his very good testimonials.* 22 Nov: *Recd. a letter from the Revd. W. Bricknell canvassing me in favour of Mr. Hunt, the persevering candidate for a Poor Law Union Auditorship.* 16 Dec: *Perkins called, accompanied by Mr. Hunt, of Oxford, Accountant, and a candidate for the Auditorship of the District of Unions in which Stow on the Wold Union is likely to be included: a sensible, well-conducted man, in middle life, thoroughly conversant with business, and furnished with excellent testimonials; they remained to luncheon.*

1845: 6 Jun., 28 Jun., 11 Jul: *from Mr. Austin, the Asst. P.L. Commr., announcing that Messrs. Hunt, Knott, and Draper, candidates for the situation of Auditor of the Oxfordshire and Warwickshire Poor Law Audit district, had obtained a majority of votes of Chairmen and Vice Chairmen within the district, and that, consequently, the selection must be made from these three, Chairmen and Vice Chairmen now giving a second vote, as they might see fit.*

1846: 25 Jun: *To the Workhouse, where I had a conference with Mr. Hunt, the District Auditor, who is now holding his audit there.* 13 Jul., 10 Dec.

1847: 19 May: *Mr. P also laid before me a private letter recd. by him from Mr. Hunt, the Auditor of the Union, together with a letter addressed to the Chairman & Guardians of the Union, which, coupled with a former private letter addressed to Pearce, and the tone of conversation in his intercourse with the officers held by Mr. H., require careful consideration.* 20 May: *I brought forward the correspondence of Mr. Hunt, the Auditor, with a view to challenge him to an explicit statement in a formal manner of his imputations against the Clerk and Governor, and Relieving & Medical Officers, and of his censure on the guardians as to the general management of their business.* 21 May: *Wrote to Mr. Hunt, as stated in the Diary of yesterday.* 22 May, 24 May: *Drove to Lower Swell: called on the Perkins's: much conversation with him as to Mr. Hunt, the Auditor, with whom he has been long acquainted, and whose appointment he warmly advocated, but whose present proceedings as to this Union he wholly disapproves, and mentioned some passages of Mr. H's early life which were discreditable, and lessen one's surprize at his present overbearing and offensive tone and conduct.* 1 Jun: *Recd. a letter from Mr. Hunt the Auditor of our Union in reply to mine of May 21. he disclaims dictating to the Guardians as to their manner of conducting the business of the Union; but persists in his allegations and imputations against the competency, integrity, or diligence of the Clerk and Governor.* 2 Jun., 3 Jun., 5 Jun., 8 Jun., 17 Jun., 15 Jul: *The Poor Law Commissioners have at length replied to the communications made to them from the Guardians respecting the imputations thrown out by the District Auditor against the Clerk and Governor, Medical Officers &c.—The Commrs. express an opinion that Mr. Hunt has not exceeded the line of his duties, remind the Guardians that it is to be expected that in the discharge of his functions the Auditor is likely to make comments unpalatable to Guardians and their officers, trust that the Guardians will reconsider the matter, and thus the Commissioners seem disposed to uphold the Auditor, and let the question drop.* 8 Aug., 17 Aug., 18 Nov: *Mr. Auditor Hunt has been at Stow for some days, auditing the Union Accounts for two past quarters ... his manner is unbending, he shews a great disposition to find fault, and harrasses the officers by his minute and captious examination into the accounts, giving great trouble and annoyance to all parties.* 25 Nov: *The Auditor has left Stow, having made himself very disagreeable, and shewn his ill-temper by disallowing several items of the Unicorn accounts for very trifling errors, none of them involving any real loss to the institution, or damaging any person, parish or party.* 3 Nov: *From Mr. Hunt, the Auditor, disagreeable letters had been addressed to the Officers.*

1848: 18 May: *Laid before the Board a letter addressed to me as Chairman from the P. L. Commrs.—(like letters having been addressed by them to Mr. R. Cripps, as Treasurer of the Union, and to Pearce, as the Clerk) purporting that they had confirmed the surcharge made by Auditor Hunt on Mr. Pearce. At the same time it should be observed that the offence imputed to him, at the utmost, only amounted to an irregularity, or technical error in the management, he having committed no moral offence, nor done any injury to the Union at large, or to any parish, or any individual.* 24 Feb., 9 Mar., 16 Mar., 25 Mar., 3 Jun., 9 Jul: *Received a letter from Mr. Hunt, the District Auditor, addressed to the Chairman and Guardians of our Union, who makes few observations on the management, and no complaint. He completed his audit last week in two days, in an amicable temper, avoiding controversy.* 17 Jul.

1852: 20 Jan: *Much interrupted during the day by persons calling with their parish rate books for correction, according to a new rule laid down by the Auditor of our Union, which appears to savour more of form than of substance, but which he would defend as a literal observance of a statute; and yet it is not strictly to the letter after all: but Mr. Hunt gives offence by over strictness, and needless demands.* 2 Dec: *To the Workhouse to attend a Committee of Guardians appointed to investigate the charges preferred by Mr. Hunt the Auditor, against Mr. Pearce, in his capacity of Master of the Workhouse.* 6 Dec.

1853: 3 May: *In the Evening, quite late, received a formal letter from Mr. Hunt, the Auditor of our Union, apprizing me that he proposed to surcharge me, as Chairman, in the amount of an order made, as he contends, illegally, for the payment of £43 and upwards to Messrs. Wilkins and Kendall, for costs of proceedings touching a paper lunatic from Bledington, as to whom the expences were incurred in procuring an adjudication as to settlement, and maintenance in the Gloucester Lunatic Asylum. Mr. Hunt fixes to-morrow at 3 P.M. as the hour on which, if so disposed, I may appear before him to shew cause, why I should not be so surcharged.* 4 May: *Thus armed, & having received a note from Mr. Wilkins, to the effect that Mr. Hunt's ground of surcharge was what I have intimated above, and that he (Wilkins) wished to accompany me to be present at the conference with the Auditor, I drove to Bourton on the Water, and took up Mr. W. explaining to him by the way the line of argument I proposed taking, and the new light thrown on the matter by the recent decision in Reg. v. Leonard's Shoreditch.—On arriving at the Board Room, Stow, we found Mr. Hunt very confident in the accuracy of his views, & somewhat slow to be convinced that he was in error: at length he yielded to the argument, upheld as it was by Lord Campbell's recent decision, and expressed his satisfaction at not being under the necessity of making the surcharge.*

HUNT — William Hunt

1852: 12 Dec: *Letter from the Adjutant of the 14th. Reg. Stationed at Limerick, intimating an expectation that W. Hunt, whose furlough expires this day, is likely to desert, and requesting that he may be apprehended, as such, if seen at or near Stow after to-day. The Adjutant writes to me, as I had occasion some time since to write to the Captain of W. H's company, at the desire of the soldier, for a remittance of pay. W.H. is a fellow of very bad character.* 13 Dec: *Wrote to Superintendent Makepeace, forwarding to him the letter I recd. yesterday from the Adjutant of the 14th Reg.*

HUNTER — Mr W. Hunter in the Temple

It seems likely that this was William Hunter, a barrister of the Inner Temple. (Harcourt's Buildings are in the Inner Temple.) This was a time when Francis Witts was giving serious consideration to his future, and a career in the law was probably one of the options. It seems that Hunter was an acquaintance of the family, and may have been a son of Sir James and Lady Jane Hunter-Blair (*below*).

1801: 17 May: *We called upon Mr. Talbot, Lady Hereford, Lady Lyttelton, Mr. Drummond, Col. Robertson, Mr. Hunter, but did not find them at home.... Mr. Hunter's Chambers are No. 10 Harcourts Buildings.* 4 Jun: *Sat for a long time with Mr. W. Hunter in the Temple.*

HUNTER-BLAIR — David Hunter-Blair [296]

Sir David Hunter-Blair, 3rd baronet of Dunskey (1778-1857), was the fourth, but second surviving, son of Sir James Hunter, later Hunter-Blair, 1st baronet of Dunskey (1741-1787), and Jane Blair (d. 1817) (*below*). He succeeded his elder brother James (d. 1800) as 3rd baronet. He married, first, 2 July 1813, Dorothea Hay-Mackenzie (d. 1820); and secondly, January 1825, Elizabeth Hay (d. 1859). David and Elizabeth had 1 daughter:

1 Mary Elizabeth (1830-1870); died at Naples

1801: 3 Apr: *Sir D. H. Blair came to welcome us to Edinburgh, with his usual affability & cordiality.* 27 Apr: *went to supper at Lady H. Blair's, where our reception was as usual hearty & obliging.*

HUNTER-BLAIR — Jean Hunter-Blair [297]

Jane Hunter-Blair (d. 1817), or Jean in some references, was the daughter of John Blair of Dunskey, co. Wigton. She married, 1770, James Hunter (1741-1787), son of an Ayr merchant. James became a banker in Sir William Forbes's company, and acquired the estate of Robertland. He adopted the name Hunter-Blair when Jane inherited her father's estate in 1777, and he was created 1st baronet in 1786. He was an enthusiastic freemason and an acquaintance of Robert Burns. He and Jane had fourteen children.

Agnes Witts was a good friend of Jane Hunter-Blair's during her years in Edinburgh, and she spent much time in her company between 1795 and 1798.

1801: 3 May: *After dinner my Mother & myself called upon Lady Hunter Blair.*

HUNTINGFORD — George Isaac Huntingford [298]

George Isaac Huntingford (1748-1832), bishop of Gloucester and later Hereford, was born at Winchester, son of James Huntingford (1724-1772). He was educated at Winchester College and New College, Oxford (BA 1773; MA 1776; B&DD 1793). Huntingford was curate of Compton, Hampshire, before he became a master at Winchester College; he served as warden there from 1780 until his death. During this time there was considerable disorder in the school, including two rebellions. Through his friendship with Henry Addington, whom he had taught at Winchester, Huntingford became bishop of Gloucester for 1802-15, and bishop of Hereford for 1815-32. He continued to live at the school, in the comfortable warden's lodgings.

1824: 25 Apr.

1825: 6 Jun: *Accompanied by F. Aston, I dined at Mr. Twisleton's at Adlestrop. This polite and agreeable young man has recently become Rector.... The venerable prelate, Dr. Huntingford, was now passing a day or two with him, and Mr. Twisleton pressed me to meet him, his Lordship having mentioned me with esteem as one of his old clergy, with whom he should like to renew his acquaintance.* 20 Sep.

1826: 5 Jun: *I dined at Mr. Twisleton's at Adlestrop, & there met the amiable old Bishop of Hereford, Dr. Huntingford, returning from Hereford to Winchester.*

1827: 14 Jan: *Mr. Sandby has never been in Gloucestershire since I have held the curacy, to which Bp. Huntingford appointed me in 1813, the living being then sequestered.*

1832: 2 May: *The death of the Bishop of Hereford is announced. Dr. G. I. Huntingford was in the 84th or 85th year of his age, and held the Wardenship of Winchester College with the Bishoprick... He was raised to the Episcopal Bench during the Premier-Ship of Lord Sidmouth.*

1840: 24 Jan: *The appointment is most useful, as well as gratifying, to Twisleton with his numerous and motherless young family. It was an unanimous election; and, while the vacant stall has been conferred by his brother dignitaries on a man of estimable character, the ruling motive seems to have been a desire to carry into effect the wishes of Twisleton's venerated deceased patron, the late Bishop Huntingford.*

HUNTINGFORD — Henry Huntingford [299]

Henry Huntingford (1787-1867), Church of England clergyman, brother of Thomas (*below*), was born at Warminster, Wiltshire, a younger son of Thomas and Mary Huntingford. He was educated at New College, Oxford (BCL 1814), and served as rector of Bishop's Hampton, Herefordshire.

1829: 22 Sep: *Revd. W. L. Bowles, Revd. W. M. Prosser, Revd. J. Rowden, Revd. T. Huntingford & family, Revd. H. Huntingford.*

HUNTINGFORD — Thomas Huntingford [300]

Thomas Huntingford (1783-1855), Church of England clergyman, brother of Henry (*above*), was born at Warminster, Wiltshire, a son of Thomas and Mary Huntingford. He was educated at New College, Oxford (BA 1805; MA 1809), and served as vicar of Kempsford, Gloucestershire, in 1810, precentor of Hereford in 1817, and rector of Weston-under-Penyard, Herefordshire, in 1831-55.

1829: 22 Sep: *Revd. W. L. Bowles, Revd. W. M. Prosser, Revd. J. Rowden, Revd. T. Huntingford & family, Revd. H. Huntingford.*

HUNTLEY — Richard Webster Huntley — *see also* Mills [301]

Richard Webster Huntley (1793-1857), Church of England clergyman, was born at Boxwell, Gloucestershire, eldest son of Richard Huntley (1766-1831) and Anne Webster of Boxwell Court. He was educated at Oriel College, Oxford (BA 1815; MA 1819), and served as vicar of Alderbury, Shropshire, in 1829, and rector of Boxwell in 1831. He was the author of *A Glossary of the Cotswold Dialect*. Richard was the nephew of Wadham Huntley (*below*) and brother to Clara Jane (1799-1874), who married, at Boxwell, 5 June 1817, William Mills (b. 1780) of Saxham Hall, Suffolk.

1845: 26 Jan.

1848: 2 Feb: *These vehement men are Mr. Powell, the Incumbent of Cirencester, Mr. Huntley, of Boxwell, both in this diocese, and both very estimable, but over strenuous Clergymen, with whom I have been long acquainted, and Mr. Jebb, an incumbent of the Diocese of Hereford.*

HUNTLEY — Wadham Huntley [302]

Wadham Huntley (1771-1844), Church of England clergyman, was born at Boxwell, Gloucestershire, son of Revd Richard Huntley (1721-1794) and Anne Beaker (1734-1782). He was educated at Merton College, Oxford (BA 1791; MA 1794), and served as vicar of Aston Blank in 1802-44.

1823: 17 Sep: *The Clerical Stewards were ... & the Revd. Wadham Huntley, Rector of Eastington & Aston Blank, also absent & represented by the Revd. T. Pettal of Southrop, brother to Mrs. Browne of Salperton.*

1826: 15 Sep.

1827: 16 Nov: *Having received intimation by the post yesterday, that my poor Uncle's funeral is fixed for to-morrow, & having secured the promise of Mr. Huntley's assistance on Sunday, for the service of the church.*

1828: 23 Apr.

1829: 20 May.

1830: 10 May.

1837: 16 Jan.

1842: 11 Jan: *Recd. a note from Mr. Huntley, with his annual subscription to the Soc. for the Prop. of the Gosp. which I acknowledged by a reply.* 30 Dec., 31 Dec.

1843: 29 Dec: *A note from Mr. Huntley with his annual subscription to the S.P.G. doubled for this time in consequence of the appeal made by the Bishop to his Clergy in the increased demands for aid preferred to the Society, and the insufficiency of its resources.*

1844: 28 Nov: *Learnt the decease of my old neighbour, Huntley, V. of Aston Blank, aged 73, having been Incumbent 42 years.* 30 Nov., 1 Dec: *Wrote to Mr. Ford to inform him that I had accepted the invitation to attend the late Mr. Huntley's remains to the grave, and offering him (Ford) on that occasion the accommodation of my carriage.* 3 Dec., 5 Dec.

HURD — John Hurd [303]

John Hurd (±1783-1866), Church of England clergyman, was born at Shifnal, Shropshire. It seems likely that he was related to the unmarried Richard Hurd (1720-1808), bishop of Worcester, as there is an Emmanuel College connection. He was educated at Derby and Emmanuel College, Cambridge (BA 1804; MA 1807).

Hurd was ordained deacon on 22 December 1805 and priest on 21 December 1806. He was appointed rector of Naunton on 16 April 1807, and remained there until his retirement in 1860. He was also appointed stipendiary curate of Condicote on 3 July 1816. He appears to have married quite late in life; his wife, Emma (±1802-1860), was some twenty years his junior. Emma was the daughter of Ambrose Mainwaring and Charlotte Hurd, and was therefore a cousin in some degree to John Hurd. John and Emma had 1 son:

1 John Ambrose (1832-1917)

By 1861, Hurd was staying with his son and daughter-in-law Mary at St Briavels in the Forest of Dean. His son was listed as a fund holder, while he was listed as a widower and clerk in holy order without cure of souls. This was presumably just a visit to St Briavels, for his death was registered at Stow-on-the-Wold. He presumably retained a residence near or at Naunton. His son's wife Mary presumably died shortly after the census, for John (junior) later married Charlotte Bull. Both were still alive in 1911, living at Hailsham in Sussex.

John Hurd was a neighbour and friend of Francis Witts for several decades, but although he was mentioned very frequently in the diaries, there was no particular closeness between them, or at least it dissipated. In the earlier years the men frequently dined with each other, but as the years passed this ceased. It is particularly surprising that he is not mentioned in the diaries between 1829 and 1836.

1810: 17 Oct: Letter to Margaret Witts: *Our Greenhouse looks very nice and full. The fireguards are come from Stanway and suit well. Mr. Hurd officiated last Sunday. The window Curtains in the dining room were put up before I came.*

1812: 3 Aug: *Mr. Hurd, of Naunton took charge of my Church. August to November.*

1820: 28 Feb. 11 Apr.

1823: 18 Nov: *We had a dinner party. Mr. Ford, Mr. Croome, Mr. Hurd, Mr. Jones, Mr. F. Aston were our guests.* 18 Dec.

1824: 8 Apr: *Mr. Hurd dined with us.* 22 Jun: *Our neighbour, Mr. Hurd, the Rector of Naunton, calling about dinner time, gave us his company for the rest of the day.* 28 Jun: *I dined at Mr. Hurd's, the Rector of Naunton, meeting Mr. Wynniatt, Mr. R. Wynniatt, Mr. C. Keysall.* 3 Jul., 11 Oct.

1825: 8 Jan: *I therefore sent back my Servant and horses, whom my dear wife had dispatched for me, and fortunately hearing, that my neighbour, Mr. Hurd, the Rector of Naunton, was in the town, I had an interview with him, when he kindly promised to undertake my duty at Upper Slaughter & Lower Swell to-morrow.*

1826: 2 Feb: *Mr. Hurd, was in Gloucester, & about to return home in his gig, I requested him to drive me thither.* 31 Mar., 19 Apr., 21-22 Apr: *I dined at my neighbour Hurd's at Naunton. The other guests were Messrs. Talbot, Browne, R. Wynniatt.* 23 May: *Mr. Hurd and Mr. Winter joined our party at dinner.* 6 Aug.

1827: 1 Jan: *I had agreed to meet Mr. Hurd to-day on public business at Stow, but felt so ill, that instead of riding thither, I sent for Mr. Hayward... Mr. Hurd, who had learnt at Stow, that Hayward had been sent for, kindly came to enquire after me, & we detained him to our family dinner. He is so good as to promise to take my duty here on Sunday next.* 4 Feb: *My obliging neighbour, Mr. Hurd was kind enough to serve the Church here.* 9 Mar: *Mr. Hurd called late in the morning, and staid to dine with us.* 27 Mar: *Mr. Hankins will continue to serve the church, & by the assistance of Mr. Hurd, I trust, there will be double duty.* 4 Jul: *We had a few of our bachelor clerical neighbours to dinner to-day: Mr. Hurd, Mr. Baillie, Mr. Jones, Mr. Hankins, Mr. Winter and Mr. W.B. Pole, one of the Sons of Mr. Pole of Wyck Hill, who has lately taken Deacon's orders, and is the Curate of Oddington.* 24 Aug., 25 Aug: *Mr. Hurd called and joined our family party at dinner.* 26 Aug: *I went to officiate at Longborough in the room of Mr. Hurd; who was engaged to assist Mr. Jeaffreson, now absent on a tour to Paris. Mr. Hurd secured my services yesterday, that he might himself be at liberty to take Mr. R. Wynniatt's duties at Staunton and Snowshill, Mr. W. being at present indisposed.* 2 Oct., 18 Dec.

1828: 15 Apr., 23 Apr.

1829: 24 Nov.

1836: 23 Jul: *Near Naunton Inn we met Mr. Hurd and his little boy.*

1838: 31 Dec: *As I passed Naunton Inn left a note which I had written to Mr. Hurd yesterday, to apprize him that the Curacy of Whichford will be vacant at Lady Day, in case a brother in law of Mr. H's, who is looking out for a Curacy, should wish to apply for it.*

1839: 1 May.

1840: 25 May: *About sixteen partook of an excellent dinner at the Unicorn ...* 13 Aug: *Met and parleyed with Mr. Hurd.* 20 Aug.

1842: 25 Feb., 5 Mar., 8 Mar: *At Naunton kindly received by Mr. Hurd, who is a great invalid: visited his church, which has ample accommodation for the inhabitants, especially since Mr. H. has rearranged and increased the number of the Pews, and enlarged the North Aisle at his own expence last year.* 23 May, 2 Jul.

1843: 13 Feb: *While I was engaged in taking the examination of an invalid female pauper, with a view to a suspended order of removal, my wife remained with Mrs. Griffin at the Mill, where we met and conversed with Miss Davies, Mr. Hurd's niece.* 14 Aug: *Very different is the spirit in which Mr. Hurd wrote to me this day, inclosing £1. 15. as the annual subscription to the S.P.G. of himself, his wife, and their son, with an assurance of a further remittance.* 15 Aug.

1844: 15 Jan: *I called on Bowen; who appeared considerably better than when I saw him last; I found Messrs. Ford and Hurd calling on him.* 29 Aug., 5 Dec: *The following Clergymen held the pall—Messrs. Hurd, Ford, myself, Gibson, of Chedworth, Hill, Curate of Notgrove and Aston Blank, and Aston.* 28 Dec.

1845: 10 Feb., 26 May.

1846: 20 Aug., 5 Nov., 3 Dec.

1847: 20 May, 14 Oct.

1848: 26 Apr., 16 May, 22 Aug., 12 Nov: *Mr. Hurd and Mr. Billingsley, as well as Mr. Ford, have been unvaried in acts of kindness towards the dying man.* (Bowen).

1850: 26 Jan: *Mr. and Mrs. Hurd very kindly sent their son to call on me with friendly enquiries as to Mrs. W.'s health.* 18 Sep., 17 Oct., 6 Nov., 8 Nov., 11 Nov., 9 Dec.

1851: 10 Apr: *I expressed an opinion that Mr. Hurd's interference was very objectionable. True, he was included as Commr. in the Name Act, but he had ceased to act for many years past either as Commr. or Mag.—He professed that he considered such secular engagements inconsistent with his spiritual character, but in truth had retired because certain transactions of his connected with the Prov. Bank many years since had excluded himself from taking a share with the Gentlemen of the District in public business—and that now to revive himself into activity, and dictate to those who had borne the burden and heat of the day was indecent and intolerable.* 16 Apr.

1852: 23 Jan., 26 Jan., 17 May, 23 Dec.

1853: 12 Jan: *A letter from Mr. Hurd, as to a mistake made by him in sending a pauper to the Workhouse, and in answer to a letter I had addressed to him on that subject, last Thursday week.* 16 May, 21 May, 31 May.

1854: 19 Jul: *Mr. Hurd called to obtain information as to the charges against H. Kilby, and advice whether it is desirable to retain counsel in her case for the defence.* 10 Aug.

HURST — Miss Hurst, evacuated from Denmark [304]

The only information available regarding Miss Hurst is from an entry in Agnes Witts's diary dated 22 March 1801:

> Captain Hammond gave us a very polite reception, his Cabin large & elegantly fitted up, here we were soon joind by many other passengers, among the most agreable were M^rs. Chapman & her Friend Miss Hurst, our apparent satisfaction in being safe on board was soon check'd by the doleful intelligence that 2 of our Trunks with some of Mr Drummonds had reach'd the Frigate too late to be taken in, after an excellent Dinner, we came in sight of the Grand Fleet, thro which we sail'd & went so near as to be within hearing of Sir Hyde Parkers order to our Captain, after this I knew little of what pass'd beginning to be intensely sick, & pass'd a most wretched night on the floor on a Mattress, with nothing to alleviate my sufferings but the kind attention of Miss Hurst.

1801: 6 Apr: *to dinner in Mr. Chapman's Apartments. The party were the same as formerly with the addition of Mr. & Mrs. Fletcher both of whom pleased me much. Miss Hurst was very unwell: yet we staid till late & supped with them comfortably upon oysters &c. Captn. Digby also joined our party rendering it very agreable.* 15 May, 27 May, 1 Jun: *Miss Hurst breakfasted with us.* 17 Aug: *Miss Hurst called in the forenoon.* 26 Aug: *Miss Hurst dined and drank Tea with us, whom I accompanied home to Bedford Row, my Father & Mother going part of the way.*

HUSCHKE — Wilhelm Ernst Christian Huschke [305]

Wilhelm Ernst Christian Huschke (1760-1828), Weimar doctor, privy councillor, and personal physician, was the family doctor of Goethe, Herder, and Wieland.

1799: 27 Nov: *Also a very fine day, my Mother, Dukinfield and myself walked a little in the Gardens but returned in time to meet the Hof Medicus Huschke whom we had called in to my Father.*

HUSKISSON — William Huskisson [306]

William Huskisson (1770-1830), politician, was born at Birtsmorton Court, Worcestershire, the eldest of four sons of William Huskisson (1743-1790) and his first wife, Elizabeth Rotton (±1743-1774). In 1783, Huskisson was sent to Paris to live with his great-uncle Dr Richard Gem, physician to the British Embassy. He remained in Paris until 1792, and his experience as an eyewitness of the French Revolution gave him a life-long interest in politics. Huskisson became a protégé of the marquess of Stafford, and returned to London with him. He soon gained two more powerful political patrons: Henry Dundas, the home secretary, and William Pitt, the prime minister. He served as MP for Morpeth in 1796-1802, Liskeard in 1804-07, Harwich in 1807-12, Chichester in 1812-23, and Liverpool in 1823-30. After a distinguished career in a variety of offices he became treasurer of the Navy for 1823-27, president of the Board of Trade for 1823-27, and secretary of state for the colonies for 1827-28; he also received a seat in the cabinet. In 1823 he was returned for Liverpool as Canning's successor, and as the only man who could reconcile the tory merchants to a free trade policy. After Canning's death in the same year, Huskisson accepted the secretaryship of the colonies under Lord Goderich; he continued to hold this office in the new cabinet formed by the duke of Wellington the following year. After succeeding with great difficulty in inducing the cabinet to agree to a compromise on the corn laws, Huskisson finally resigned office in May 1828 over the disfranchisement of East Retford.

While attending the opening of the Liverpool and Manchester Railway on 15 September 1830, Huskisson rode down the line in the same train as the duke of Wellington. At Parkside railway station, close to Newton-le-Willows in Lancashire, the train stopped to observe a cavalcade on the adjacent line. Several members of the duke's party stepped onto the trackside to observe more closely. Huskisson went forward to greet the duke. As he was exiting his car, the locomotive *Rocket* approached on the parallel track. As the train drew close he held on to the open carriage door, but the door was wider than the gap between the two trains and the *Rocket* struck it, forcing Huskisson off balance and under its wheels; he died a few hours later.

1827: 11 Feb: *Many persons of distinction are represented in the public papers as suffering in health from the same cause; among them the Duke of Sussex, Mr. Canning, & Mr. Huskisson.* 14 Apr., 2 May, 7 Sep: *The great bone of contention has been the Chancellorship of the Exchequer ... Mr. Huskisson was talked of, but his health is not sufficient for the fatigues of the post .... this Mr. Huskisson has taken; having been recalled on the death of his friend Canning from the continent, where he was travelling to recruit his greatly impaired health.*

1828: 23 Jan., 12 Feb: *after very able speeches by Messrs. Huskisson & Peel, who declared, that the present government had not the slightest intention to find fault with the gallant admiral ...* 17 May: *Roman Catholic Emancipation has been agitated in the House of Commons.* 28 May: *Disunion reigns in the cabinet; for it is announced, that Mr. Huskisson and Lord Palmerston have resigned their offices ... I own, I cannot feel much regret at the resignations of Huskisson and Lord Palmerston; the former I have long been led, to consider as a politic & able but dangerous statesman, the latter of an inferior order, both as to talent & principle.* 30 May: *and it is understood, that Mr. Huskisson has expressed his resolution of retiring entirely into private life: his age & ill health.* 2 Jun.

HUTCHINSON — Frances Hutchinson [307]

Frances Hutchinson, née Goodwyn (1753-1835), daughter of Henry and Frances Goodwyn, married, at St Andrew's, Enfield, Middlesex, Revd Julius Hutchinson (1750-1811) of Woodhall Park, Hertfordshire; they had at least 4 sons and 7 daughters:

1 Frances (b. 1775)
2 Cassandra (b. 1777)
3 Elizabeth (1779-1851); married Sir Henry Edward Leigh Dryden, 3rd baronet (1787-1837)
1 Julius (b. 1780)
4 Mary Anne (b. 1782)
2 Henry (b. 1784)
3 Charles (b. 1786)
4 Charles (b. 1789)
5 Emma (b. 1792)
6 Henrietta Mary Clarissa (b. 1793)
7 Julia (b. 1795)

1834: 7 Mar: *Met the Egerton Leighs; he just arrived from High Leigh, she from Broadwell to meet him; they go home tomorrow. Walked with them to Beauchamp Square, where they were going to their friends, Mrs. & Miss Hutchinsons, the mother & sisters of Lady Dryden.*

HUTCHINSON — Cyril George Hutchinson [308]

Cyril George Hutchinson (1800-1887), Church of England clergyman, was born in Manchester, son of George and Elizabeth Hutchinson. He was educated at Christ Church College, Oxford (BA 1822; MA 1824), and was perpetual curate of Hawkhurst, Kent, in 1832, rector of Batsford, Gloucestershire, in 1842, and honorary canon of Gloucester in 1852. Hutchinson was married to Ellen (b. ±1828), a much younger woman, who was born in Holyhead, Anglesey. There do not appear to have been any children.

1844: 14 Aug: *We dined at Mr. Poles;—a sumptuous entertainment—Met Mr. Hutchinson and two sisters: he is the successor of the late Mr. Hall in the Rectory of Batsford.*

1845: 7 Jan: *The Revd. Cyril Hutchinson, Rector of Batsford, was elected a Member of the Book Society.*
13 Feb: *My fellow travellers were Messrs. Perkins, Debary, Wheeler (Wadh. Coll) Rector of Gt. Wolford, Underwood, Hutchinson, Rector of Batsford.* 26 Mar.

1846: 24 Jun: *The reunion was agreeable enough: Mr. Hutchinson, late Student of Christ Church, nephew or great nephew of Cyril Jackson, the able Dean of Christ Church in my youth, and, I believe, the possessor of his library, is a man of considerable talent and research.* 26 Aug., 29 Sep., 10 Dec.

1847: 7 Apr., 6-7 Jul., 28 Sep.

1848: 26 Apr., 15 Jun., 26 Sep.

1850: 30 Jan: *To Mr. Hutchinson, Batsford, in answer to a letter received from him to-day, in which he asks for information from me, as far as I can give it, as to the movements of the deputation of the S.P.G.* 31 Jan., 21 Mar., 18 Sep: *Dressed for dinner at the Unicorn, and then went to the Rectory to meet the Bishop of Gloucester, Mr. & two Misses Hutchinson, Captain Leigh.* 19 Sep: *Confirmation L Ris. Revd. R W Hippisley and Mrs. H.—Revd. W. Wiggin;—the Hon. the Misses Rice, and Mrs. J. T. Rice:—Revd. C Hutchinson, his younger sister, and Miss Chapman, a lady staying with them.* 1 Oct., 8 Nov.

1851: 23 Apr: *one shrank from appending one's name to a document, which, though signed by Clergymen in whom one has confidence (Cyril Hutchinson, for instance) was mainly subscribed by others of little discretion and of extreme opinions in various and distant localities.* 20 May: *Held a long talk with Hutchinson, the Rector of Batsford, discussing, amid the wonders surrounding us, the sad state of things at Stow as relates to the indiscretion of its Rector.*

1853: 24 May: *Hutchinson, the Rural Dean of Campden, attended, as being probably so engaged to-morrow as to be unable to meet the Archdeacon at Campden.* 28 May: *I received a visit from Mr. Hutchinson, the Rector of Batsford, who sought counsel from me as to matters which appear to worry him exceedingly.* 30 May: *Wrote to Mr. Hutchinson as to his dispute with the Road Surveyor of Batsford, and the proceedings to be taken in that matter at the Moreton in Marsh Petty Sessions.* 2 Jun: *Received a satisfactory letter from Mr. Hutchinson as to the dispute regarding the entry into his fields to dig for materials by the Surveyor of the Highways of Batsford.* 6 Jun., 8 Jun.

1854: 3 May: *Hutchinson has been very ill during the winter, is in better health; but seems uneasy still in his position at Batsford, to which he is returned, as it were, on trial.* 19 Jul.

HUTCHINSON — George Hutchinson — *see also* Dolphin, Knight, *and* Staveley [309]

George Hutchinson (1797-1852), JP and landed proprietor, was the son of Michael Hutchinson, doctor of physic, and Mary Tanfield. His father died relatively young and his mother Mary married, secondly, Thomas Payne (±1745-1815) of Edstaston Hall, Shropshire, and Brook Street, Grosvenor Square, London. George was half brother of Mary Anne Dolphin, née Payne. His elder brother was Thomas Kitchingman Staveley (±1792-1860) of Old Sleningford, North Stainley-cum-Sleningford, Yorkshire. Thomas was born Hutchinson, but adopted the name Staveley by royal licence in 1815 to accept the inheritance of a cousin, Gen. Miles Staveley.

George married, 1824, Charlotte Smith (1798-1879) of Strathfield House, Lillington, Warwickshire. He appears to have inherited Edstaston Hall, a red brick house built in 1807.

1824: 19 Feb: *Dolphin's dinner party—Miss Browne of Salperton, Mr. G. Hutchinson, half brother to Mrs. Dolphin, a well informed conversible travelled man.*

1838: 1 Jul: *Mrs. Dolphin called between the services, accompanied by Mrs. Hutchinson, a very agreeable woman, wife of Mr. H. Mrs. D's half-brother.*

1840: 22 Sep: *Mr. Hutchinson, Mrs. Dolphin's half-brother had called during my absence.* 23 Sep: *Mr. G. Hutchinson called, his business being to lay an information against a young farmer of Naunton for a trespass in the pursuit of game on the manor at Aylworth.* 24 Sep: *I repaired to the Justice room, where much and some difficult business was transacted ... The young farmer whom Mr. Hutchinson prosecuted for a trespass in pursuit of game was fined.*

1844: 15 Sep: *Mrs. Dolphin and Mrs. Hutchinson, now with her husband visiting at Eyford, called before afternoon Service.* 27 Sep: *With MW. walked to Eyford; visited at the Mansion house: Mr. Hutchinson and Mr. Chamberlayne, now with his lady staying there, were out: we were received by Mrs. Dolphin Mrs. Payn, Mrs. Hutchinson, and Mrs. Chamberlayne.* 28 Sep., 13 Oct.

1848: 19 Apr: *Mrs. Dolphin called on us, accompanied by her brother, Mr. Hutchinson and her friend Miss Walmesley.* 3 Jun: *Walked with MW. to Eyford: called on Mrs. Dolphin, and Mrs. Hutchinson, wife to Mrs. D's brother, who, with her sister, Miss C Knight, is now on a visit at Eyford.* 11 Jun: *Encountered Mrs. Hutchinson and Miss C Knight, with whom conversed as to the agitating affair of Vernon Dolphin's visit to Mr. Polhill at Broadwell.*

1850: 13 Jan: *Miss C Knight writes from Tanfield, Mr. Hutchinson's, in answer to a letter from me.*

1851: 20 May: *Met with Mr. and Mrs. Hutchinson, Mrs. Dolphin's half-brother & his wife; but only joined in a general conversation with them, and learned as particulars as to Mrs. D.*

1852: 9 Mar: *A long letter from Mrs. Dolphin, written from the residence of her brother Mr. Staveley, near Ripon, whither she has hurried to the bedside of her brother, poor Mr. Hutchinson, who, from her account, appears to be very near his end, sinking under a heart disease.* 12 Mar: *From Mrs. Kirby, of Cheltenham, who writes by Mrs. Dolphin's desire to inform me of the death of Mr. Hutchinson on Tuesday morning.* 14 Mar: *A letter from Mrs. Dolphin, with an interesting account of the death of her half brother, Mr. Hutchinson: there being no prospect of her immediate return to Eyford.*

HUTCHINSON — Joseph Hutchinson

1808: 29 Mar: *At Cote. Found my friend, very ill; Mr. & Mrs. Dowell, Mr. Hetling, Miss Webb & Mr. Jos. Hutchinson made the Evening's party, played Whist in the Evening.*

HUTTON — medical student at Edinburgh

1801: 3 Apr: *We dined in company with the Chapmans, Avison, & a young Medical Student of the name of Hutton at Mr. Fletcher's the Advocate.* 10 Apr: *I staid the greater part of the morning at home, going out only to call upon Mr. Hutton.* 13 Apr: *Mr. Hutton after sitting with me for half an hour, walked two or three turns in Princes Street.* 18 Apr: *Called upon Dr. Hill, Mr. Hutton &c. Walked with Mr. H. Brougham.*

HUXLEY— James Edmund Huxley [310]

James Edmund Huxley (1820-1907), physician, was born at Ealing, son of George Huxley (1780-1855) and Rachel Withers (1786-1852). He was educated at St Andrew's University and Charing Cross Hospital, London, where as a student in 1843 he won a prize for 'Diligence and Good Conduct'. He made the acquaintance of the director of the lunatic asylum at Wotton, Gloucester, and as a very young man was given the post of dispenser or 'apothecary'. He conducted himself so satisfactorily in the position that he was promised it would be held for him should he go to London for two years to complete his medical training. James had a remarkable younger brother, Thomas Henry Huxley (1825-95); both brothers looked to obtaining the free scholarships offered by the Charing Cross Hospital to students whose parents were unable to pay for their education. Testimonials as to the position and general education of the candidates were required, and one of the persons applied to succeeded in getting both young men admitted. The authorities stated that 'although it is not usual to receive two members of the same family at the same time, the officers, taking into consideration the age of Mr Huxley, sen., the numerous and satisfactory testimonials of his respectability, and of the good conduct and merits of the candidates, have decided upon admitting Mr J. E. and Mr T. Huxley on this occasion.'

James returned to Gloucester where he was duly appointed to a senior position. He qualified MRCS, and moved to Maidstone, Kent, where he remained a resident until his death. He married, first, at St Mary de Lode, Gloucester, 24 Jun 1845, Mary Rosser, born at Tewkesbury; they had at least 1 son and 1 daughter:

1 Katherine (b. 1847)
1 James Henry (b. 1851)

It seems probable that his wife Mary died young. In the 1861 census Katherine was recored as a 14-year-old scholar residing at North Bank, Marylebone, London, with her uncle and aunt George and and Mary Anne Huxley, who seemed to be childless. George was a wealthy and successful barrister.

James Huxley married, secondly, Mary Ann Coleman (1836-1873); they had at least 1 son and 5 daughters:

1 Rose Mary (b. 1861)
2 Ellen (b. 1862)
3 Mary Ann (b. 1863)
4 Harriet (b. 1865)
1 George Edward (b. 1869)
5 Violet (b. 1871)

James's younger brother Thomas Henry was to have a distinguished career. He was a biologist specialising in comparative anatomy and became known as 'Darwin's Bulldog' for his advocacy of Charles Darwin's theory of evolution. Thomas's famous debate in 1860 with Samuel Wilberforce was a key moment in the wider acceptance of evolution and in his own career. He had been planning to leave Oxford on the previous day, but after an encounter with Robert Chambers, author of *Vestiges*, he changed his mind and decided to join the debate. Wilberforce was coached by Richard Owen, against whom Thomas Huxley also debated about whether humans were closely related to apes. Almost entirely self-educated, Huxley became an authority in anatomy and palaeontology, and after the discovery of the archaeopteryx, he was the first to suggest that birds had evolved from dinosaurs. He was also a keen promoter of scientific education and strove to make science a paid profession, not dependent on patronage or wealth. Interestingly, Thomas Huxley also coined the word 'agnostic' and was the grandfather of the writer, novelist, and philosopher Aldous Leonard Huxley (1894-1963).

1842: 6 Sep: *Recd. a letter from Mr. Huxley, secretary to the Lunatic Asylum Gloucester, in reply to my letter to Dr. Hitch of the 3d. Inst.*

1846: 25 Aug: *the place of resident Superintendent being now, & having been for some weeks, vacant by the removal of Dr. Huxley to a like post at the Lunatic Asylum at Maidstone for Kent.*

HUXTABLE — Anthony Huxtable [311]

Anthony Huxtable (1808-1883), Church of England clergyman, was born at Williton, Somerset, son of Anthony Huxtable, surgeon, of 3 King's Square, Bristol. He was educated at Trinity College, Cambridge (BA 1833; MA 1836). Huxtable was rector of Sutton Waldron, Dorset, in 1835-71, prebendary of Salisbury in 1854, rural dean of Shaftesbury, and archdeacon of Dorset in 1862. While rector of Sutton Waldron, Huxtable carried out agricultural experiments, which attracted the interest of many visitors; his primary object was to provide profitable work for the unemployed. He married, 16 July 1840, Maria Sarah (b. 1799), daughter of John and Sarah Langston of Sarsden, Oxfordshire. There do not appear to have been any children of the marriage.

1847: 14 Sep: *clergymen present were Messrs. Barter, W. Vavasour, Huxtable, Jarratt, Winter, Clarke, Berridge.... Mr. Beman, after some sensible agricultural comments, proposed the health of the Revd. Mr. Huxtable, whose acknowledgment of the compliment was the speech of the Evening. This Gentleman, who married Miss Langston, a good deal his Senior, with her large fortune, is beneficed, I believe, but, at all events, settled near Blandford in Dorsetshire, and has of late years devoted himself to Agriculture & Agricultural Chemistry.*

HYDE — *see* East for Hyde East

HYDE — John Hyde [312]

John Hyde (1763-1843), agricultural labourer, lived at Vine House, Stow-on-the-Wold, with Rebecca Butler (1797-1850), presumably his wife; they had 2 sons and 1 daughter:

1 Solomon (1823-1895); married, first, at Stow-on-the-Wold, 12 October 1844, Eliza Humphries (1822-1864); secondly, at Stow-on-the-Wold, 16 May 1865, Susannah Hitchman; at least 2 daughters and 1 son from his first marriage:
    1 Sarah A. (b. ±1849)
    1 Alfred (b. ±1852)
    2 Harriet (b. ±1844)
2 Joshua (1828-1910); married, at Stow-on-the-Wold, 23 September 1856, Sarah Ann Dixon (1830-1891); 3 sons and 4 daughters:
    1 Mary (b. 1851)
    2 Elizabeth (b. 1859)
    1 John (b. 1862)
    3 Emma (b. 1863)
    2 Frederick (b. 1866)
    3 Albert (1869-1951)
    4 Ellen (b. 1872)
1 Ruth (b. ±1833)

1834: 18 Jul: *A close and anxious enquiry as to the statements made by W. Rogers to John Hide on May 29. Rogers suppressed the truth, equivocated and shewed callous indifference... evidence of his daughter, Martha, who detailed some facts of a very suspicious description, implicating her Father, and proving that the conversation held by him with Hide was deeply impressed on his mind, though he swore to us that it had entirely passed off his memory.*

HYETT — Benjamin Hyett[313]

Benjamin Hyett (1741-1810), landed proprietor, was the son of Nicholas Hyett (d. 1777). He was educated at Oriel College, Oxford (MA 1762), and was a student of Lincoln's Inn. He married Sarah Adams (1746-1804), a friend and correspondent of Samuel Johnson. The Hyetts were on friendly terms with the diarist's mother and father, Agnes and Edward Witts.

In 1733 Charles Hyett bought the Herrings from the Adey family and built a gentleman's residence on the site of the farmhouse. From Charles (d. 1738) the estate passed in turn to his sons Benjamin (d. 1762) and Nicholas (d. 1777), and then to Nicholas's son Benjamin.

1801: 28 May: *made unsuccessful calls at Lord Balgonie's & at Mr. Hyett's.*

HYETT — William Henry Hyett[314]

William Henry Hyett (1795-1877), MP, JP, DL, and landed proprietor, was the son of Revd Henry Cay Adams (1762-1808) and Frances Marston (1732[?]-1828). It seems impossible that Frances could have been thirty years her husband's senior, and have borne children at the age of 63 plus. This is clearly an error, and it is probable that she was the same age as her husband.

The younger Benjamin Hyett (d. 1810) (*above*), devised Painswick House with the land adjoining to his wife's cousin Mrs Frances Adams (d. 1828) for life, with reversion to her son William Henry, who assumed the surname Hyett in 1813.

William was educated at Westminster and Christ Church, Oxford. He was a JP and DL, and MP for Stroud in 1832-34. He married, 1821, Anne Jane, second daughter of Joseph Seymour Biscoe of Hempsted Court, Gloucester.

William inherited the Painswick property from Benjamin Hyett (d. 1810), the husband of his mother's first cousin. In point of fact the property had been bequeathed to his mother, but William appears to have entered onto it immediately, changing his name to Hyett in 1813. It seems that he lived to begin with at Painswick Lodge, and this may indicate that his mother was in residence in the main house. William's father, Henry Cay Adams, died at Painswick House in 1808, so it appears the family were in residence prior to Benjamin Hyett's death in 1810.

Hyett was made a fellow of the Royal Society for his work in agricultural science, and took an active part in local affairs at Painswick, particularly in educational matters.

William and Anne Hyett had 4 sons and 6 daughters:

1 Henry Adams (b. & d. 1823)
1 Frances Stephana (1824-1893)
2 William Henry Adams (1825-1850)
2 Josephine (1828-1854)
3 Mary Clementina (1832-1905)
3 John Biscoe (1835-1837)
4 Annie Grace (b. 1837)
5 Sarah Jane (1840-1862)
6 Stephana Inglis (b. 1842)
4 Francis Adams (1844-1941)

1824: 10 Mar., 27 Apr.

1826: 26 Sep: *Mr. & Mrs. Hyett, from Painswick Lodge, Mr. Weston Hicks, Mr. Cother & Mr. Macleod dined there.*

1829: 28 Apr., 14 Jul., 22 Sep.

1830: 20 Apr.

1834: 13 Oct., 21 Dec: *The Gloucestershire Chronicle announces that Mr. Hyett has withdrawn from the representation of the Borough of Stroud. He declares that he is induced so to do solely on private grounds, and I think it probable that, with a large young family and moderate fortune, he is acting prudently.* 28 Dec.

1835: 6 Jan., 13 May.

1836: 12 Aug: *Between breakfast and dinner whiled away the time with Howell in walking through Pope's wood, and over Painswick Hill to call on Hyett... Passed a couple of hours very agreeably in conversation with [Hyett] and Howell, on the proceedings at Gloucester relative to the appointment of a Governor of the Gaol, when it appeared that Hyett, had his health allowed him to attend, would have voted against Mason, on principle, on a suit for defamation likely to be tried at the Assizes.* 13 Sep.

1837: 6 Jan: *Hyett had come in from Painswick two or three hours before, agreeably to an arrangement made between us on Wednesday, to take me to dine and sleep at Prinknash Park, and having packed up my carpet bag, I started with him from Gloucester about half past three, in his dog cart; an hour brought us to our friend's house, whom we found in is usual fine flow of spirits, though, I regret to say, Mrs. H. was unable to appear, being under the influence of a severe cold, which, in her case, always requires great care and seclusion, as her constitution, like that of her family generally, is sadly inclinable to pulmonary mischief.*

1838: 5 Jan: *Walked with Howell and his Son Frederick to Painswick Lodge to call on Hyett, who is suffering from a bad attack of gout, which, however, does not impair his natural energy.* 19 Jan., 3-4 Jul., 11 Jul.

1839: 4 Jan: *In the evening Hyett joined us after dinner, and the three gentlemen for the rest of the Evening discussed many of the forgoing topics, with the Poor Law matters, Lunatic Asylum, Emigration &c. Hyett had brought his lady and children, to whom were added the young people from Upton, children of Mr. Parsons, who with the Howell tribe made up a nice little domestic circle of dancers, who enjoyed themselves till summoned to a pretty early supper in the school room, after which the youngsters parted, and before 11 o cl. the Seniors repaired to their Chambers.* 1-2 Jul.

1842: 6 Jan: *After dinner the party was increased by the addition of the Hyett family, and Weston Hicks.* 14 Jan., 15 Jan: *Wrote to Hyett in reply to his letter recd. yesterday that I did not understand him to have said any thing reflecting on Mr. Cox, as having misconducted the late election, but that I understood him to refer to a remark made by that gentleman before the Election, that his health would not permit him to undertake the management of it single-handed.* 28 Jan: *A letter to announce that Messrs. Adamson had dispatched by the Carrier a dozen of Whisky according to orders they had received to that effect from Mr. Hyett; I had requested the latter to order some for me when I met him at Prinknash.* 1 Nov., 7 Nov.

1844: 11 Apr: *Mrs. and Miss Clements, Mr. and Mrs. Parsons, several Misses Hyett, and other ladies graced the gathering, but it was cold, raw, and comfortless.*

1845: 2 Apr., 30 Jun.

1846: 25 Aug., 22 Oct., 18 Nov.

1847: 16 Mar., 18 Mar., 5 Apr.

1848: 3 Jan.

I

IBBETSON — Henry Carr Ibbetson [1]

Sir Henry Carr Ibbetson, 3rd baronet (1769-1825), army officer, was the son Sir James Ibbetson, 2nd baronet, and Jane Caygill. He married, 14 November 1803, Alicia Mary, daughter of William Fenton Scott. There were no children of the marriage.

Ibbetson served as a captain in the 3rd Dragoon Guards in Flanders under the duke of York in 1794. It is surprising that Francis Witts does not mention having known Ibbetson at Weimar. He is also not mentioned in his diary of 1798, but he does appear in Agnes Witts's diary on 15 December 1798: 'Sr. Thos. Tancred, Mr. Mills, Mr. Walker & Mr. Ibbetson here before they went to the Opera.' It is possible that the Ibbetson at Weimar was a brother, Charles Ibbetson (1779-1837), or a cousin, and not Henry himself.

1802: 4 Jan: *Talked much with our friends with Mr. Barnewall Countess D'Alton, Sir H. Ibbetson &c. &c. At home between one & two.* 6 Jan: *Called in the morning upon the Granvilles, & afterwards without success upon Mr. Barnewall & Sir H. Ibbetson: the latter of whom I met in the Pump Room as also the Granvilles, Fanny &c.*

IBBOTSON'S HOTEL [2]

Ibbotson's Hotel at 3 Vere Street, Cavendish Square, had been a fashionable hotel for the wealthy since the eighteenth century. In 1807 it was run by John Ibbotson and his son, also John.

1839: 4 May: *At the Paddington Station the Coach is met by a pair of horses, the Passengers resume their seats, and your journey is continued by the Edgware Road &c. to Oxford Street &c. I took a coach at the Green Man, and proceeded to Ibbotson's Hotel, Vere Street, where I had formerly been staying, a quiet, orderly, place, with good quiet sleeping rooms.* 5-9 May,

1842: 9 Mar: *Wrote to the proprietor of Ibbetson's hotel to secure beds for myself and my son on Monday next.* 14 Mar: *At the Paddington station again all hurry-skurry and bustle; a cab soon found conveyed my son and me to our quarters, Ibbotson's Hotel, Vere Street, where we found comfortable rooms already allotted to us, and afterwards a good beef steak solaced us in the coffee room.*

IFFLAND — August Wilhelm Iffland [3]

August Wilhelm Iffland (1759-1814), actor, playwright, and theatre director, was born at Hanover. His father had intended him for the Church, but Iffland preferred the stage; at 18 he ran away to Gotha to prepare himself for a theatrical career. He made his debut at Gotha in one of Engel's comedies, in which he took the part of an old Jew. In 1779 he joined the theatrical company at Mannheim, and was the leading actor there when, in the latter part of 1781, Schiller gave him the manuscript for the *Robbers*. The play was produced the following January, with Iffland in the part of Franz Moor; its success brought Schiller into notice and confirmed the reputation of Iffland. The latter remained in Mannheim till 1796, when he assumed the direction of the National Theatre of Berlin. He was also director of the National Theatre of Prussia, and in 1811, he was made general director of all presentations before royalty. Iffland produced the classical works of Goethe and Schiller and his best-known plays are *Die Jäger, Dienstpflicht, Die Advokaten, Die Mündel*, and *Die Hagstolzen.*

1800: 17 Mar: *In the Even. to the Play in five Acts by Iffland.* 19 Mar: *my Father and Dukinfield at the Comedy das Herbsttag by Iffland.* 31 Mar: *afterwards with Dukinfield with the latter in the Evening to the Play Die Advokaten by Iffland: the Characters acted by Malkolmi, Graff & Spangler extremely well done.* 21 Apr: *at my usual Employment till the Play: Der Fremde by Iffland extremely well performed.*

ILIFF — Frederick Iliff [4]

Frederick Iliff (1799-1869), Church of England clergyman, was born at Nottingham, a younger son of William Tiffin Iliff (1772-1830). He was educated at St Paul's School, Christ's Hospital, London, and Trinity College, Cambridge (BA 1823; MA 1826; DD 1838). He was ordained deacon in 1823 and priest in 1824. He was appointed assistant master at Shrewsbury School and perpetual curate of St Julian, Shrewsbury, in 1826. He became headmaster of the Royal Institution's School, Liverpool, and served as perpetual curate of St Philip's, Liverpool, in 1844-46, master of the Grange School, Bishop Wearmouth, Durham, in 1856-62, and perpetual curate of Gateforth, Yorkshire, in 1862-68.

Iliff married, at St Anne's, Soho, Westminster, 23 December 1825, Sarah Cheyne; they had at least 8 sons and 3 daughters:

1 Frederick (b. 1828)
1 Sarah (b. 1830)
2 Robert Sanfield (b. 1831)
3 George (b. 1832)
4 Edward (b. 1835)
5= Frederick (b. 1836)
5= Richard (b. 1836)
2 Caroline (b. 1838)
7 Arthur (b. 1841)
3 Margaret (b. 1843)
8 Charles (b. 1845)

1828: 2 Mar: *We have good accounts of him from Shrewsbury; he took three places at the examination, which followed on their return to school, and has begun a play of Euripides, the Phoenissæ, with his tutor, Mr. Iliff.*

1830: 17 Jun: *He notices an affectation of singularity: this, I think, is a mistaken view, taken up from a measured & rather pompous tone of reading, which Edward has acquired, and which is particularly disliked by his Tutor, Mr. Iliff, at the head of whose class he is.*

ILLES — Alexander Illes [5]

Alexander Illes (1792-1856), physician, was the son of Daniel Illes, yeoman farmer, of Kempsford. He had worked in asylums in London and saw an opportunity in the Fairford area, where his father owned some land called Curtis Piece on Milton Street. Illes obtained a licence for ten patients in 1823, and took them into his own house. In 1827 he had thirteen patients. In 1834 the Poor Law Amendment Act increased the intake of pauper admissions, and Alexander quickly started to build to accommodate them. From forty patients in 1829, he had over 119 patients according to the 1841 census. By 1844 there were 140 patients, of whom 119 were paupers.

Charles Cornwall was the first physician at Illes's asylum in Fairford. His apprentice John Hitchman married Mary Ann

Illes, probably a sister of Alexander. After qualifying in London, Hitchman became head of a new model asylum in Derbyshire, and his experience may have helped with the policy of non-restraint adopted at Fairford.

Alexander Illes was married to Mary [Marianne]; they had at least 3 sons:

1 Daniel (b. 1819); married Susan; at least 3 sons:
  1 Richard Tovey (b. ±1844)
  2 Alexander Hitchman (1844-1897); married, at Fairford, 22 July 1879, his first cousin, Alice
  3 Albert William (b. 1850)
2 Albert (b. 1821)
3 Alexander (b. 1823); married Caroline; at least 1 son and 4 daughters:
  1 Alice (b. 1851); married, at Fairford, 22 July 1879, her first cousin, Alexander
  2 Louise Caroline (b. 1851); married, at Fairford, 25 September 1873, Daniel Arkell
  3 Mary Anne (b. 1854); married, at Fairford, 21 September 1875, Henry Arkell
  4 Katherine Eliza (b. 1856)
  1 Alexander (b. 1859)

In 1856 Alexander Illes died and left everything to Daniel, his eldest son.

1847: 10 Apr: *Wrote to Dr. Williams, Superintendent, Gloucester Lunatic Asylum, and Mr. Illes of the Fairford Lunatic Asylum, to ascertain whether Moses Roff of Bourton could be admitted into either of these asylums, he having relapsed into a state of insanity.* 13 Apr: *from Mr. Illes, Fairford Lunatic Asylum, that they would receive M. Roff at 12/- per week.* 20 Aug: *Wrote to Mr. Illes, Lunatic Retreat, Fairford on behalf of Roff, of Bourton, who called on me for advice as to his son, a patient in confinement there, and the future arrangements necessary in the event of the fund being exhausted which is now applied to the poor man's maintenance.* 23 Aug., 27 Aug: *A letter from Mr. Illes, Fairford Lunatic Retreat, as to the condition of his patient, Moses Roff.*

ILLES — Elizabeth Illes[6]

Elizabeth Illes (1756-1846) was a parishioner of Upper Slaughter and lived with her son, John Illes (±1781-1850), and daughter-in-law, Sarah (1776-1848).

1844: 30 Sep: *Administered the holy Sacrament privately to old Mrs. Illes, in tolerable health both of body and mind, though upwards of ninety years of age.*

1846: 12 Dec: *Visited at John Illes, whose aged mother seems to approach to her end.* 13 Dec: *Old Widow Illes died last night.* 16 Dec: *The funeral of Mrs. Illes, aged 90 years.*

ILLES — John Illes[7]

John Illes (±1781-1850), agricultural labourer, was the son of Elizabeth (*above*). He lived at Upper Slaughter. He married, at Upper Slaughter, 11 October 1819, Sarah (1776-1848), daughter of Samuel and Anne Collett.

1848: 23 Feb: *Called at J. Illes's.*

1850: 26 Feb: *John Illes met with a bad hurt in falling from the top of a waggon load of wood at Eyford, working for me in bringing home faggots & poles I had bought there at the Wood Sale. I dispatched the groom to bring Mr. Hayward to see him, who found that the poor old man had fractured his right blade-bone.* 27 Feb: *Visited John Illes, whom I found as well as could be expected.* 1 Mar: *Visited John Illes, who is going on as well as can be expected after his late accident.* 2-3 May, 5 May, 6 Mar: *I attended by the dying bed of John Illes, whose life cannot, it would seem, be long protracted, and administered the Holy Communion to him, two brothers Collett, and his sister Restall from Naunton.* 7 Mar: *Poor John Illes breathed his last about midnight.* 9 Mar: *Officiated at the funeral of John Illes.*

ILLES — Sarah Illes[8]

Sarah Illes (1776-1848) was a parishioner of Upper Slaughter, the daughter of Samuel and Anne Collett, and daughter-in-law of Elizabeth Illes (*above*).

1848: 7 Feb: *In the evening I was called to visit Sarah Illes, who was seized with an alarming attack.* 8 Feb: *Visited S. Illes, who is very ill, but apparently not in immediate danger.* 9-12 Feb., 15 Feb., 22 Feb: *My parishioner, Sarah Illes, died to-day rather suddenly.* 25 Feb: *Officiated at the funeral of Sarah Illes.*

IMHOFF — Charles Imhoff[9]

Charles Imhoff (1766-1853), army officer and landed proprietor, was born at Nuremburg, the second son of Christophe Adam Karl, Baron von Imhoff (1734-1788), and Anna Maria Apollonia (1747-1837), daughter of Baron von Chapuset.

The Imhoffs and their two sons, Charles (1766-1853) and Julius (1768-1799), moved to England in 1768 through the good offices of Elizabeth Schwellenberg, Queen Charlotte's mistress of the robes. The baron soon obtained a cadetship in the HEIC's Madras Army; as an accomplished miniature portraitist, he no doubt also saw a market for his artistic skills in India. Early in 1769, accompanied by his wife and eldest son Charles, he embarked for Madras in the *Duke of Grafton*. Among the passengers was Warren Hastings (1732-1818), then a widower of 37, who was returning to India. The baroness took Hastings under her care when he fell ill and a shipboard romance blossomed.

Baron von Imhoff lived in Madras with his wife until the latter part of 1770, when having resigned his army commission, he moved to Calcutta in search of a wider clientele for his portraits. His wife remained in Madras, a resident—for part of the time at least—in Hastings's house. She joined her husband in Calcutta in October 1771. Hastings followed in February 1772 upon accepting his new appointment as governor of Bengal. In a letter from the Company dated 25 March 1772, the baron was ordered to return to Europe for declining his military service. He arrived back in September 1773 and, presumably, started divorce proceedings. Four years later, Anna [Marian] married Warren Hastings.

Hastings undertook to adopt the Imhoffs' two boys Charles and Julius and almost certainly made funds available for legal and other expenses. Relations between their father, Baron von Imhoff, and both his former wife and Hastings remained amicable during and after the divorce proceedings. The baron returned to Germany in 1775 and married Frances Louise Sophia von Schardt (1750-1803), the youngest sister of Charlotte von Stein, Goethe's close friend. He and Frances had sixteen children, the eldest of whom was Anna Amalie von Imhoff (1776-1831), named after her godmother, the dowager duchess of Weimar.

Julius Imhoff died in 1799. He had three illegitimate sons—William, Charles, and John—whom he left in the care of Calcutta banker John Palmer. Their story is of interest. The boys would in time possess 'handsome fortunes for a middling condition in life'. Worried about the 'declining state of public instruction' in

Calcutta, Palmer consulted Hastings, who had long since retired as governor-general, on how best to secure 'their permanent or ultimate happiness'. He explained that an English education would be suitable only for William and Charles, the two eldest boys, as John was considered too dark-skinned to thrive in England. As it happened, Charles was 'snatched away' in March 1802 under mysterious circumstances. Some accounts say that he and his ayah (nurse) drowned in a well, but Palmer describes a distressing last illness 'apparently of an hereditary nature'. Later that year, Palmer gave Hastings further particulars of William, who was then about 7: 'He is fairer than the ordinary run of these children, but is still discernible in his complexion to be of a native mother.' Palmer thought his capacity was probably good, but found it difficult to judge as he had not been well taught. As for John, who was 'dull and idle' as well as dark, he concluded that 'it can never be advisable that this child should go home'; he recommended that he should be educated in 'our Mughal schools'. Thus, at the age of 3 or 4, John's fate was sealed by the colour of his skin.

In 1804, William, known by the surname Fitzjulius rather than Imhoff, entered the household of Mr and Mrs Warren Hastings at Daylesford House, where he was fitted out with a blue coat and pantaloons. At first all went well. Hastings told his surviving stepson Charles Imhoff that 'Little Fitz ... has made himself a great favourite at Over Norton'. The boy was sent to a small school run by a clergyman, but he acquired there only 'a strong disinclination to every species of application and restraint'. In 1805 Hastings asked his friend David Anderson of Edinburgh to suggest a Scottish school which would apply more rigorous control. The terms in which he recommended William are significant: 'I have mentioned his complexion, as liable to objection, but I must qualify it by saying that I have seen children of English parentage to the full as dark. To counteract this defect, the boy is handsome, lively, wonderfully active, and good-tempered; and before he went to school, showed as forward a disposition to learn, as he has now, or seems to have, an aversion to it.'

As William got older his personality defects became more apparent; Warren and Marian Hastings refused to have him come home to Daylesford during the holidays and clearly found him an 'embarrassment'. Hastings admitted to his stepson Charles in 1809 that to have the lad to stay 'would prove a torment and discredit to us and this would be the more unfortunate, as we expect much company during all the time that he would be with us'. It seems evident that William felt unwanted. There is a letter in his best copperplate handwriting saying how happy he was to hear that he was to go back to his 'native country', and only wished 'that the time was come'. Nevertheless, he hoped to have the pleasure of seeing his grandparents and uncle before leaving England.

Upon his arrival at Calcutta, the young William Fitzjulius met with John Palmer, his old guardian, who found him a job 'in the indigo line' at Semalbarree. When he got there, William described it as 'nothing but a jungly place, where we see nothing but Tigers and other whild [*sic*] animals'. For over a year he endured this lonely existence out of temptation's way, receiving few letters from his Hastings and Imhoff families and, by his own account, spending 'almost all day out in the sun' and contracting fevers. He then took himself back to Calcutta where, once again, John Palmer found him. The lad had not apparently been 'seduced into any extravagant or vicious habits', but he showed every sign of 'natural indolence' as well as 'diffidence and timidity'. Late in 1813, Palmer had still not been able to place his ward in another job, but he assured Hastings that he would not neglect him. William seems to have stopped writing to Hastings at this point, so it is difficult to establish whether he ever did find useful employment. Legal records show that he and his brother successfully challenged their father's will to establish their legitimate rights; but William did not enjoy any benefits, for he died in 1824 aged 29.

William's uncle, Charles Imhoff was educated at Harrow School and later at Westminster School, followed by Magdalen College, Oxford. He joined the Army in 1783 as an ensign in the 49th Foot. He was on half-pay from 1783 to 1799, during which time he served in one of the prince of Waldeck's regiments, where he was appointed on the recommendation of Queen Charlotte. He was later in the Berkshire Militia. He was a lieutenant in the 1st Life Guards, promoted to captain in 1799, and became a major in the 4th Foot in 1801. He was promoted to lieutenant-colonel in 1802, and served in the 4th Garrison Battalion in 1807; he was in command at Jersey in 1809-12. He was promoted to colonel in 1811, and major-general in 1814. In 1807, by royal warrant of King George III, Charles Imhoff was created a knight grand commander of the Order of Saint Joachim.

Warren Hastings died at Daylesford in 1818. In accordance with a settlement of 1798, he left the property to his wife Marian for her life with reversion to Charles Imhoff. Mrs Hastings died in 1837, and Sir Charles Imhoff subsequently remained in possession of the manor until 1853.

Charles Imhoff married, 1801, Charlotte (±1772-1847), daughter of Sir Charles William Blunt, 3rd baronet, and Elizabeth Peers. His half-sister, Anna Amalie von Imhoff (1776-1831), married Gen. von Helvig (*see* diary entry, 12 February 1828); presumably the 'young Imhoff' mentioned on 21 March 1800 was a half-brother.

1800: 21 Mar: *Mr. Mills left Weimar proceeding to England by Hamburgh, as far as Capel with young Imhoff.*

1823: 8 Jan: *Dined at Oddington with Lady Reade and Sir John. The usual showy display, & well lighted cheer. A large party as of old, Sir H. & Lady Dryden, Sir C. & Lady Imhoff, Mr. & Mrs. Lechmere, the Penystones &c.*

1824: 19 Feb: *Dolphin's dinner party—Miss Browne of Salperton, Mr. G. Hutchinson, half brother to Mrs. Dolphin, a well informed conversible travelled man, Mr. Willan & the Revd. Mr. Bragge, Cousin to Mr. Dolphin (the two latter of the sporting genus) and Mr. Bowen, were inmates at Eyford. Sir Charles & Lady Imhoff, and Miss Chabuzet, with ourselves, formed the party. Sir C. Imhoff, a Major Genl. in our Service, is of German Origin, being son of Mrs. Hastings, the wife of the Governor General of India, by her first husband Baron d'Imhoff, whose second wife & family by the Second Couche I knew intimately in my early days at Weimar.*

1826: 2 Nov.

1827: 3 Sep: *We drove to make our first call on Mrs. Hastings at Daylesford .... retaining her children, one of whom, Sir Charles Imhoff, still lives, a Major General in our Service.*

1828: 12 Feb: *"Die Frithioss-Sage, von Esaias Tegnér, Bischof von Wexio." Aus dem Schwedischen übersetzt von Amalie von Helvig, geborner Freiin von Imhoff. Stuttgart und Tübingen. 1826. 12mo." After a very long interval, during which I have intermitted the perusal of any German book, I have been led to recall my old familiarity with the language by the loan of Klopstock's Messias from Mrs. Hastings, & now by the less bulky work just named, which her son, Sir Charles Imhoff, has been so good as communicate to me. The fair translator is his half sister, daughter of his father by his second wife, married after he had divorced himself from Mrs. Hastings. I had the pleasure of her acquaintance during our residence at Weimar in 1798, and the two following years. She was then young, accomplished, talented, elegant, possessed of considerable literary attainments, & filled the post of demoiselle d'honneur to that most estimable and gifted Princess, the reigning Duchess of Weimar. Mademoiselle d'Imhoff even then was called by her friends the Sappho of Germany, lived in the Society of Goethe, Schiller, Kotzebue, at the Athens of Germany.... Amalie von Imhoff married an Officer of Rank, Gen. von Helvig, a Swede & originally in the Swedish Service, in the Artillery, I fancy, but her husband now holds rank in the Prussian service, & Berlin is their residence.* 19 Dec.

1829: 21 Jan: *We had a party of our friends to dinner. Sir C. Imhoff and Miss Chapuset.*

1833: 18 Jan., 1 Feb.

1835: 29 Jan., 21 Feb: *Mr. Perrot and Sir Charles Imhoff paid us a morning visit.*

1837: 2 Feb: *I omitted to mention yesterday a note which I had written to Lady Imhoff, accompanying one of the Lithograph prints of Lady Lyttelton, of which I requested her acceptance, as a memorial of an old friend of her mother, Lady Blunt.* 16 Feb., 30 Mar., 8 Apr., 26 Apr., 15 May: *Sir C. and Lady Imhoff called upon us.* 5 Jul: *Drove MW. to call at Daylesford House, where we found Sir Chas. and Lady Imhoff at home, and took luncheon.* 14 Jul., 26 Jul., 10 Aug: *Sir C. Imhoff looked in upon us.* 14 Aug., 16 Aug., 21 Sep: *Met a large party: there were staying in the house Miss Blunt, an elderly unmarried sister of Lady Imhoff's, in former years very intimate with my late cousin, Mrs. Naper, afterwards Rycroft—and so, well acquainted with my mother, Mrs. Whalley, my Aunt Travell &c.—as on my Father's side with Lady Lyttelton.* 23 Sep., 26 Sep., 10 Oct: *The company consisted of Lord Redesdale and Miss Mitford, Sir C. & Lady Imhoff, a Baron Soden, who accompanied them, and who is a great nephew of the late Mrs. Hastings, an unhealthy-looking young man, speaking only German, my little remaining skill in that language being brought into play to converse with him.*

1838: 7 Sep: *Sir Charles and Lady Imhoff brought with them a very agreeable & well informed man, now on a visit to them, Colonel Chesney, the Commander of what is called the Euphrates expedition.* 9 Sep: *As she mentioned that Miss Blunt, sister to Lady Imhoff, had called at Peach Field Lodge, much mortified that she could not be admitted, and had expressed an anxious wish to possess one of the lithograph prints of my Aunt, I packed one up, and wrote with it a few lines to Lady Imhoff, requesting her to present it from me to her sister.* 28 Sep: *Accompanied MW. in the phaeton to call at Daylesford House, where we found Sir Charles and Lady Imhoff at home, and a visitor with them, Capt. Boyce R.N.* 19 Nov: *An invitation came from Sir. C. & Lady Imhoff to us to dine at Daylesford next week.* 1 Dec: *Sir Charles and Lady Imhoff made a morning visit to us.*

1840: 26 Jun., 18 Nov: *We had a rough drive to and from the Rectory at Daylesford, whither we went to dine with the Winters; meeting Sir Charles and Lady Imhoff, the Dean of Gloucester, Emma and John Talbot Rice, Compton & Clara Reade, and Mr. Lewes. A pleasant party.*

1842: 23-24 Aug., 26-27 Aug., 27 Sep.

1843: 15 Feb., 14 Oct., 2 Nov: *Met and parleyed with Sir C. & Lady Imhoff.* 29 Nov: *Sir Chas. and Lady Imhoff called.*

1844: 1-2 May, 4 May, 24 Sep.

1847: 17 Mar: *Heard of the recent decease of our old acquaintance Lady Imhoff, at an advanced age, in Town.* 20 Mar., 20 Apr., 11 Sep., 27 Sep: *Received a visit from Sir Charles Imhoff, and his half sister, the Baroness von Klock—Poor Sir C. is heart-whole, but very feeble; yet he has accomplished during the summer a tour up the Rhine into Germany.* 20 Apr: *Saw Mrs. W. & Sir C. who is much aged, and infirm, but in comfortable health and spirits, having revived greatly since the death of Lady I. and his removal into the country.*

1848: 11 Feb.

1850: 11 Jan., 29 May: *Sir Charles Imhoff and Mrs. Winter called upon me: the former was too feeble to get out of his carriage.* 31 May: *we were admitted to pay our compliments to poor old Sir Charles Imhoff, whom we found out of spirits.* 25 Jun: *After luncheon sallied forth in the Winter's family four-wheel, with its sturdy and safe poney—first to Daylesford House, now only occupied by servants, Sir Charles Imhoff being now resident at his house in town.* 1 Aug.

1851: 22 May: *During part of the time I joined Mr. and Mrs. Winter, who arrived in Town with Sir Charles Imhoff yesterday or the day before, and are staying with him in Portugal Street.*

1853: 15 Feb: *Heard of the death of Sir. C. Imhoff, at Daylesford, at a very advanced age: he has long been in a very feeble state both of body and mind.* 17 Feb.

IMPEY — Elijah Impey and the Impey family [10]

Warren Hastings had been on friendly terms with Elijah Impey (1732-1809) at Westminster School; it seems that when he was in a position of influence, Hastings invited his friend to Calcutta, presumably to offer him a position under his patronage.

Impey had been educated at Trinity College, Cambridge, and at Lincoln's Inn. He was called to the bar in 1756 and practised for seventeen years on the western circuit. Impey married, 1768, Mary, daughter of Sir John Reade of Shipton Court, Oxfordshire; they had 5 sons and 2 daughters.

In 1773 the East India Regulating Act established the Bengal supreme council and a supreme court; Hastings was appointed governor-general and Impey chief justice. In the *Hastings's Memoirs*, Gleig says: 'Hastings had another associate at Westminster of whom we shall have occasion to make frequent mention, Elijah Impey. We know little about their school days. But, we think, we may safely venture to guess that, whenever Hastings wished to play any trick more than usually naughty, he hired Impey with a tart or a ball to act as fag in the worst part of the prank.'

Impey's son was also Elijah (±1779-1849). He was educated at Christ Church, Oxford (BA 1803; MA 1806). It is not clear which of the sons and daughters are referred to in the diaries.

1837: 29 May: *Drove MW. to call on Lady Reade at Oddington: she seemed in tolerable health and spirits: but is, as we were informed by the friend staying with her, her granddaughter, Miss Reade, Miss Impey, and Miss Grainger, much agitated when her daughter's death is adverted to.*

1838: 28 Sep: *Called at Oddington on Lady Reade, whom we found at home, in good health and spirits, having with her two friends, and former acquaintances of ours, Mrs. Roberts and Miss Impey.*

1842: 27 Sep: *The party consisted of Mr. Franks, Sir C. Imhoff, who was accompanied by Mr. Impey, and Mr. Hastings Woodman.*

INCLEDON — Charles Incledon [11]

Charles Incledon (1763-1826), singer, was born in Cornwall, the son of a surgeon. He joined the Navy as a seaman and served in the latter stages of the American Revolutionary War; his officers were said to have encouraged his singing. In 1784 he was paid off and made his first stage appearance at Southampton with Collins's company; he played Alphonso in Arnold's *The Castle of Andalusia*. He later said that he knew what it was to be a strolling player earning half a guinea a week. In 1785 he reached Bath, where he appeared as Belville in Shield's *Rosina*. He was taught by the retired castrato Venanzio Rauzzini, who presented him in concerts at Bath and Bristol. He continued to appear at Bath through the late 1780s, and also sang each summer from 1786 at Vauxhall, performing mainly patriotic songs. He made his London stage début at Covent Garden on 17 September 1790 as Dermot in Shield's *The Poor Soldier*, and appeared there almost every season until 1815.

Incledon was quickly recognised as the finest English tenor of his day, able to hold his own with ease opposite Mrs Billington in Arne's virtuoso opera Artaxerxes. The taste of the time, however, required him to sing in ballad operas such as Bates's The Woodman and (as Macheath) The Beggar's Opera, besides many farces. In concert his repertory included sailor songs and patriotic pieces, but he was most famous for the songs 'Black-ey'd Susan' and his standby, 'The Storm', a dramatic work said to have astonished Talma, the great French tragedian. Haydn noted in 1791, 'a good voice and quite a good style, but he uses the falsetto to excess'.

1801: 30 May: *Mr. Incledon objected to sing Old Towler, which after all he did not finish.* 13 Oct: *Incledon, whose voice is vastly fine, is, at the same time, so vulgar, as to be much inferior, I think, even to Townshend.*

1805: 4 Mar: *Mr. J. Delabere dined with us; we all went to the Play together, taking Miss Ford. Incledon as Lionel in Clarissa, & as steady in the Quaker, & Mallinson as Solomon in the latter, inimitable, were the only attractions.* 11 Mar: *Dined at Gloucester House with Mr. Delabere, met Mr. Parsons. Accompanied Delabere to the Play. Incledon excelling in Don Carlos in the Duenna, & Patrick in the Poor Soldier, & unrivalled in the storm.*

1806: 20 Jan: *The Duenna was represented; Don Carlos by Incledon, whose vulgarity quite subdues the effect his Notes might produce.*

INGLEBY — the Ingleby family of Austwick

Charles Ingleby, Ellen Ingleby (Miss Ingleby), Agnes Ingleby, and Isabel Clapham, née Ingleby, were the offspring of Richard Hodgson Ingleby of Westhouse and Austwick.

1823: 12 May: *Dined at Mr. Peart's, a Banker in Settle, & formerly practising as a Solicitor, meeting a large party, and others came in the evening: among the guests were Mr. Wiglesworth, Rector of Slaidburn, and his second wife, Mrs. Clapham & Miss Gurnall, the Robinsons; the Ingrams, Mr. Rycroft, Mr. & Mrs. C. Ingleby &c.*

1825: 13 Sep: *I took an early dinner at Giggleswick with Mrs. Bolland, where I met Mrs. A. Currer, Miss A. Ingleby, of Austwick.*

1828: 25 Jul: *agreeably surprized by the unexpected arrival of an old Yorkshire acquaintance, Miss Ellen Ingleby, a stout and enterprising elderly spinster, who arrived from Cheltenham in a hired Phaeton to pass the day with us. This lady had accompanied a friend to Leamington, and leaving her there for a day or two, had come to Cheltenham yesterday by the coach; there she had perambulated the town, visited the undress ball at the Rotunda, and set off to take the chance of finding us at home & disengaged. She came fraught with Craven news.*

1837: 27 Oct: *There were Mr. & Mrs. C. Ingleby, and Miss Ellen Ingleby from Austwick, Mr. Dawson, and Mr. Robert Geldard, besides the members of the Cappleside family, who were at home.*

INGLIS — Robert Harry Inglis[12]

Sir Robert Harry Inglis, 2nd baronet (1786-1855), politician, was the only son of Sir Hugh Inglis, 1st baronet (1744-1820), MP for Ashburton (1802-06) and director and three-times chairman of the HEIC. Robert was educated at Winchester College and Christ Church, Oxford (BA 1806; MA 1809; DCL 1826). He married, 1807, Mary (1787-1872). He succeeded his father as 2nd baronet in 1820. Inglis was at the coronation of George IV in 1821 and deputed by the government to perform the delicate task of meeting Queen Caroline at the door of Westminster Abbey to inform her that she was to be denied admission to the ceremony. Inglis was MP for Dundalk in 1824-26, Ripon in 1828-29, and Oxford University in 1829-54.

He was opposed to measures that weakened the Anglican Church. Naturally, he strenuously opposed the Catholic Relief Bill; its passing left him politically disorientated. For the rest of his career he avoided firm party commitments. When Robert Grant petitioned for Jewish relief in 1830, Inglis was violently opposed, alleging that the Jews were an alien people with no allegiance to England. He denounced the Reform Bill and Wellington's attempt at a compromise solution in May 1832, and in 1833 he protested against the Irish Church Temporalities Act. He was only slightly disappointed when Peel did not invite him to join his short-lived first ministry in 1834. In 1845 he broke with Sir Robert Peel, his longterm friend and college contemporary, over the Maynooth grant, which would have granted a yearly £26,000 subsidy to the Catholic Maynooth seminary.

1828: 17 May.

1829: 18 Feb: *They have put in nomination Sir Robt. Harry Inglis M.A. of Christ Church, the present member for Rippon, and who, for several past Sessions has distinguished himself as the able, learned, eloquent, and argumentative opponent of the Roman Catholic pretensions, who fought the battle well last Sessions against the successful advocates for the repeal of the corporation and test acts, who has invariable shewn himself alive to the interests of the establishment, and has on the present momentous occasion stood firm, where others have stumbled and fallen.* 26 Feb., 1 Mar: *A note from Winter, who returned last evening from Oxford, and from Mr. Croome, who also left the University after the final close of the poll yesterday, agree in the numbers, by which Sir R. H. Inglis's election was carried triumphantly by the staunch friends of Protestant ascendancy.* 7 Mar.

1830: 21 Jun.

1832: 27 Mar: *Great talent has been shewn on both sides of the house, but the preponderance of weight eloquence and judgment and acuteness appears to me to have been on the side of the Anti-reformers—Sir Robert Peel, Mr. Croker, Sir R. Inglis, Sir E. Sugden, Sir C. Wetherell, Mr. Praed, Lord Mahon, Lord Porchester and many others spoke with great force and convincingness.*

1833: 15 Feb.

1854: 23 Jun: *Received a notification from Mr. Griffiths, Wadham College, that it is intended to raise subscriptions for a testimonial to the good, and talented Sir R H. Inglis, late MP. for the University for very many years.*

INGRAM — Mrs Ingram, a dinner guest at Calwich Abbey

1802: 5 Oct: *Mrs. Gilbert, Mrs. Ingram, Mrs. Palmer, Mrs. Lockhart, Mr. Baker & Mr. Bennet dined with us.*

INGRAM — James Ingram[13]

James Ingram (1774-1850), scholar and antiquary, was born at Codford St Mary, near Salisbury, Wiltshire, son of John Ingram (1714-1785) and his wife, Elizabeth (1735-1814). He was educated at Warminster School, Winchester College, and Trinity College,

Oxford (BA 1796; MA 1800; BD 1808; DA 1824). From 1799 to 1803 Ingram was an assistant master at Winchester; he became a fellow of Trinity College on 6 June 1803, and acted as tutor there. He was Rawlinsonian professor of Anglo-Saxon in 1803-08, keeper of the archives in 1815-18, and rector of Rotherfield Greys in 1816-24; he was appointed president of Trinity in 1824, and became rector of Garsington, near Oxford, by virtue of his presidency.

Ingram was a notable archaeologist. His edition of the *Saxon Chronicle* (1823) was a great advance on Gibson's 1692 edition, particularly for its thorough exploration of the Cottonian manuscripts in the British Museum. He also published an edition of *Quintilian* (1809), but he was best known for his *Memorials of Oxford*, with a hundred plates by Le Keux, which appeared in three volumes between 1832 and 1837, and was reissued in two volumes in 1847. He was married but had no family and survived his wife.

1829: 18 Feb: *Two Committees were promptly formed in Oxford, one of men, who considered Peel unworthy of being re-elected, the other who were anxious to continue him in the representation of the University. Among the opponents of the Minister we find Dr. Ingram President of Trin. Coll.* 26 Feb: *Dr. Ingram, President of Trinity rose, when Dr. Marsham ceased, on finding it impossible to gain a patient hearing, but the new Orator, although prepared to advocate the cause of Inglis, was not more successful than his brother dignitary.*

INGRAM — John Richard Ingram [14]

John Richard Ingram (1783-1854), Church of England clergyman, was born at Claines, Worcestershire, son of Richard and Mary Ingram. He was educated at Pembroke College, Oxford (BA 1805; MA 1808), and was a JP for Worcestershire and rector of Droitwich, 1810-54.

Ingram was married to Mary (b. ±1793), born at Warwick; they had at least 3 sons and 2 daughters:

1 Richard Hunt (1816-1877)
1 Mary (1818-1892)
2 Edward Russell (1820-1856), attorney and solicitor
3 Matthew Lisle (Lyle) (1825-1897)
2 Alice Susannah Elizabeth (b. 1833)

1804: 6 Mar: *Drank wine with Trevenen, Messrs. Ingram, Plymly, Crawley, Yeomans &c.*

INGRAM — Rowland Ingram [15]

Rowland Ingram (1765-1848), grammar school headmaster, was born at Wormingford, Essex, son of Revd Robert Ingram (1726-1804) and Katherine Acklom (1727-1809). He was educated at Sidney College, Cambridge (BA 1786; MA 1789; BD 1796). Ingram was headmaster of Ipswich Grammar School in 1798-1800, and of Giggleswick School in 1800-44. He married, at St John's, Newcastle-upon-Tyne, 28 May 1797, Mary (1769-1838), daughter of Sir Cuthbert Shafto; they had at least 2 sons and 3 daughters:

1 Sarah (1799-1844)
2 Mary (1800-1870)
1 Rowland (1803-1880), Church of England clergyman; *see below*
3 Catherine Matilda (1805-1870)
2 Francis (1808-1832)

1823: 11 May: *Attended divine service twice at Giggleswick Church. Mr. Clapham, the Vicar, read prayers, and Mr. Ingram, the Curate, and Head Master of the Grammar School at Giggleswick, preached. The school is in high repute, and frequented from all parts of the North, as well as by the young people of the immediately surrounding neighbourhood. After church I called on Mr. Ingram and his family.*

1825: 11 Sep: *I twice attended church at Giggleswick. Mr. Clapham, the Vicar read prayers in the forenoon, Mr. Ingram, his curate, preached. In the evening, Mr. Ingram read prayers. I dined at a late hour with Mr. Ingram at the School house at Giggleswick. This amiable and worthy man continues to preside over the large and flourishing establishment, which was endowed by the excellent Dean Nowell in the Reign of Edward 6. The income is very good, better than £500 per ann. to the head master.*

1837: 24 Oct.

1838: 16 Sep: *Before evening church called on Mr. Ingram Senr.*

INGRAM — Rowland Ingram [16]

Rowland Ingram (1803-1880), Church of England clergyman, was born at Giggleswick, Yorkshire, son of Rowland and Mary (*above*). He was educated at Giggleswick School and Pembroke and Trinity Colleges, Cambridge (BA 1826; MA 1830). He was appointed rector of Wickenby, Lincolnshire, in 1832, and served as curate of Giggleswick in 1834-39, and vicar in 1839-53. He was perpetual curate of Walsham-le-Willows, Suffolk, in 1859-60, rector of Great and Little Ellingham, Norfolk, in 1860-72, and chaplain to the earl of Carnwath. Ingram married, at St Martin's, Leicester, 28 October 1830, Maria (1805-1873), only daughter of Samuel Alston of Leicester; they had 2 sons and 6 daughters:

1 Maria (1831-1917)
2 Catharine (1833-1888)
3 Frances (1834-1834)
4 Henrietta (1835-1928)
1 Samuel Alston (1837-1915)
5 Anna (1838-1852)
2 Delaval Shafto (1840-1920), Church of England clergyman
6 Sarah (1844-1928)

By 1861 the family were living at Little Ellingham, Norfolk; Maria, Henrietta, and Sarah were still at home, unmarried.

1837: 5 Apr: *Received a letter from Mr. Rowland Ingram, informing me of the progress made towards the erection and endowment of a church at Great Stainforth, and applying to us for support of the scheme, as possessed of property at Little Stainforth.* 8 Apr., 22 Oct.

1838: 16 Sep: *Officiated at Gigleswick church by reading the morning service for Mr. R. Ingram, who with his father had called on me yesterday.*

1840: 28 Mar., 14 May: *a letter from Mr. Geldard on the subject of the new claim set up for tithes by Mr. R. Ingram, the new Vicar of Giggleswick, and which the proprietors in that parish are prepared to resist.* 28 May, 12 Jun: *Found a letter from Geldard on the subject of Rowland Ingram's claim for tithe in the parish of Gigleswick. It seems that he has taken proceedings against nearly fifty occupiers of land in the parish, and among them against our tenant, Maudsley, and Mr. Geldard has instructed Mr. Robinson for himself and us to defend the action.*

1841: 2 Mar: *Wrote to Mr. Geldard respecting our right to the pews in the Stainforth Aisle of Giggleswick Church, with copies of various documents referring to them, shewing that we have a prescriptive, if not a possessory, right. This necessary, as Mr. Geldard, in a late letter to M.W. names that the Vicar, R. Ingram, is not unlikely to claim the right of appropriating such of them as may become at any time vacant.*

1847: 25 May: *Wrote to Rowland Ingram, Vicar of Giggleswick, with a check on Messrs. Alcock, Birkbecks & Co. for £3. 3. 0 as my subscription towards the fund for assisting the poor inhabitants not receiving parochial relief resident in the townships of Giggleswick & Settle to purchase the necessaries of life in this season of scarcity.* 30 May.

1850: 25 May.

1853: 10 Jun: *He further names that the Vicar of Giggleswick, Mr. Ingram, having received notice that he is expected very shortly to resign his preferment to the Clergyman for whom he has been holding it, the schemes for rearranging the sittings, & restoring the Chancel of the Church, are postponed if not abandoned.*

INNES — George Innes [17]

George Innes (1760-1842), Church of England clergyman and schoolmaster, was born at Devizes, Wiltshire, son of Revd Edward Innes (1721-1788), record of Devizes, and his wife, Elizabeth (1728-1809). He was educated at Magdalen College, Oxford (BA 1782; MA 1785), and was a fellow there from 1788 to 1793. Innes was assistant master at Rugby School in 1783-92, master of the King's School, Warwick, in 1792, and rector of Hilperton, Wiltshire, in 1798-1842.

1828: 14 Aug: *Set out with my wife and Mrs. Backhouse to dine with Mrs. Rice, we met rather a motley party: Mr. Innes, a Clergyman & Master of the King's School at Warwick, a man full of anecdote, which he has accumulated during a life of seventy years, & pours forth without parsimony.*

INVERARDI — Italian musician and singer at Weimar [18]

Messrs Giordani, Folchini, and Inverardi appear to have been a travelling team. They performed in Stockholm on 17 June and 19 July 1798, and in January 1801 they were recorded performing in Hamburg. At other times they were cited at Leipzig.

1799: 24 Aug: *To a Concert in the Play house performed by three Italian strangers, assisted by the usual orchestra. M. Giordani played on the Viola Anglaise, a species of improved & ornamented Hurdy Gurdy M. Folchini and Inverardi sung, the former also played on the Guitarre and Mandolin, the latter on the lute.*

IRELAND — George Ireland [19]

George Ireland (1791-1847), Church of England clergyman, was the son of George Ireland, a hatter in Leeds. He is not recorded at Oxford or Cambridge, but he entered the Church, and in 1817 was at Ossett, presumably as curate, where he married Ann Bentley. In April 1832 he was curate at West Harptree in Somerset, with a stipend of £75 a year, but something untoward must have happened. On 17 December 1833 the bishop of Bath and Wells took the severe action of revoking his licence: 'George Henry Bp. of B. & W. To George Ireland, Clerk, Greeting — Whereas We did on Nineteenth day of April 1832 grant you our Licence .... to perform Office of Curate in ... West Harptry Now by virtue .... for sufficient causes ... We do ... revoke ... said Licence And we do hereby dismiss you ... from performing Office of Curate in Par. Ch. afsd.' The *Clergy List* for 1841 records a George Ireland at nearby Bitton in Gloucestershire; he may have obtained a temporary curacy there. He was later in Malmesbury, but in what capacity is unknown. He left a wife and seven children, who in 1847 were still living at or near Malmesbury.

1847: 30 Jan: *Heard of the miserable end of Mr. Ireland, Chaplain to the House of Correction, Northleach, who committed suicide on Wednesday night. He was elected at the Michs. Sessns. came into duty early in December, was understood to be a person of doubtful character: but this not known till after his election; he had brought good testimonials. He was an elderly man, with a wife & children, not resident at Northleach, but at or near Malmsbury, where he had held a Curacy, or chaplaincy of a Workhouse, is said to have a son at University: probably, poverty unsettled his mind, and led to the sad catastrophe.* 23 Mar.

IRELAND — Thomas Ireland [20]

Thomas Ireland (1743-1816), Church of England clergyman, a son of Thomas Ireland of Hereford, was educated at Brasenose and Queen's College, Oxford (BA 1764; MA 1767; B&DD 1779). He was ordained deacon on 21 December 1765 and priest on 13 October 1767. Ireland's first clerical appointment was as curate of Ledbury, beginning on 18 October 1767. He was a prebendary of Wells Cathedral, prebend of Combe from 26 December 1780 to 11 July 1792, and then prebend of Whitelackington from 27 December 1791 up to his death. He was also rector of Christ Church with St Ewen, Bristol, from 10 June 1785, and rector of Bourton-on-the-Water from 9 July 1793; he held both livings up to his death. He died at Bristol.

1829: 1 Mar: *Mr. Cassan is an energetic writer; almost an angry polemic. He resides, I believe, as Curate, at Mere in Wilts, and married a niece of my old and now many years departed neighbour, Dr. Ireland, Rector of Bourton on the Water.*

1837: 18 Aug.

IRVINE — Charles Chamberlayne Irvine — *see also* Reade [21]

Charles Chamberlayne Irvine (1771-1856), naval officer and landed proprietor, was the fourth son of Samuel Irvine (d. 1778) and Lydia Catharine (b. 1737), daughter of Edmund Chamberlayne (1706-1774) and Elizabeth Atkyns (±1706-±1778). His parents married in 1763. Charles Irvine married, at Gloucester, 17 September 1821, Susan, daughter of Thomas Reade and Catherine Hill, and niece of Sir John Reade; they had 1 son:

1 Charles Reade (1822-1850); born in Paris

Charles Irvine entered the Royal Navy in 1789, presumably as midshipman. He was promoted to lieutenant in 1799, commander in 1808, and retired in 1840 with the rank of captain. The family lived in Paris, and his son Charles was baptised in April 1823 at the British Embassy chapel there. The family later lived at Brussels.

1824: 27 Oct: *I accepted the office of Trustee to a Settlement made by Mr. Reade of Bath in favour of his children with his eldest son & a Mr. Batchellor of Bath. Though not highly valuing the father, by whom the request was made, yet I was anxious to serve his wife & family, who have suffered in many respects from the want of sense and prudence, which is but too notorious in him. Besides I am already in trust for his eldest daughter Mrs. Irvine, who married a relation of the Chamberlaynes of Maugersbury, a Commander in the Royal Navy. Mr. Reade is the surviving brother of the late Sir John Reade, & uncle of the present Baronet.*

1829: 25 Jun: *We dined at Lady Reade's. Lady Reade has been very ill, but her health appears almost entirely reestablished. Mrs. Reade & her two daughters from Bath are staying at Oddington; the health of the former has declined greatly, especially since the decease of her daughter Lucy, some time since; the lot of this respectable lady has been painful; a husband fond of low company, and deficient in sense; a Son talented and a small poet, but without useful practical abilities; a daughter married to Captain Irvine, in bad health, and not in flourishing circumstances.*

1837: 13 Mar: *The boy is at school at Brussels, where, as I infer, Capt. and Mrs Irvine reside.* 14 Mar: *A letter from Capt. Irvine, accompanying a power of Attorney to be signed by me as a Trustee of his marriage Settlement, empowering Messrs. Child and Co. to receive the dividends on some stock, which comes to his wife as a division of property on the decease of her Father, Mr. Reade.* 15 Mar., 18 Mar., 20 Mar., 1 Apr., 14-15 Apr., 17 Apr.

1838: 16 Aug: *Called at the Unicorn Inn, on the Misses Irvine, who had expressed a wish to see me and to introduce to me their nephew, the only son of Capt. Irvine. R.N. by his wife, late Miss Reade, daughter of Mr. Reade of Bath, now deceased.*

1839: 17 Apr: *More came in the evening to tea, till the drawing room was oppressively hot—there were the two spinsters, Irvines, my old acquaintances, one of whom is an original; a lady of 70 years of age, with a bare neck, a bright coquelicot dress, a belt of unutterable materials and patters to match, cum multis aliis qua nunce perscribere longum est.* 14 May: *Before breakfast arrived Capt. Irvine, who had travelled from London by a night coach to Moreton, whence he had walked by Stow.... We had not met for many years; not to communicate with each other since his ill-starred marriage to Miss Reade, cousin of Sir J. Reade, in 1821.*

1840: 19 Mar: *Received a letter from Capt. Irvine, dated from Darmstadt, and relating to the transaction which has recently taken place as to the funded property standing in the names of Mr. John Reade & myself, as Trustees of Mrs. Irvine's marriage Settlements.* 26-27 May.

1842: 18 Mar: *A letter from Miss Emily Reade, now staying with her Aunt at Oddington, and accompanying a document signed by her, and requiring my signature as Trustee to the Marriage Settlement of Capt. and Mrs. Irvine.*

1848: 19 Oct: *Received a letter from Mrs. Matthews, late Emily Reade, residing with her husband near Shepton Mallet, who forwards a letter addressed to me by her sister, Mrs. Irvine, long resident at Brussels ... She entreats my influence in her favour, addressing me as a Trustee of her marriage settlement: but I have no intercourse with Capt. Irvine or his son, and, if I had, should be very unwise to interfere in family quarrels, where blame, no doubt, attaches to both parties, and on one side at least there is a strangeness bordering on insanity.* 27 Oct: *Received a letter from Mrs. Matthews, who forwards to me the address of her sister, Mrs. Irvine, at Brussels. I suppose I must write to the latter, thought I have no inclination so to do.* 28 Oct: *Wrote to Mrs. Irvine, at Brussels; declined to interfere in her disputes with her husband and son.*

1850: 24 Jan: *Capt. Irvine R.N. called upon me at the Workhouse, and expressed his intention of paying me a visit on Saturday, to confer with me respecting the terms on which he is with his wife, and the trust in which I am concerned as to the settlement made twenty seven years ago on his marriage with Miss Reade:—he is feeble & deaf, as may be expected at nearly fourscore, but energetic, and now staying for a short time at his relation's, Mr. Chamberlayne's house at Maugersbury, for change of air.* 26 Jan: *Captain Irvine also called upon me, and joined our party at luncheon, after an interview with me on the subject of his marriage Settlement, his dissentions with his wife, his grievances, his Son's past life and future prospects, and relations subsisting between him and his wife &c.—The conclusion forced upon me, and corresponding with the impression conveyed by a former conference several years ago, is that the poor man labours under a strange delusion as to his intercourse with his wife, amounting to a monomania—that the match was most unhappy,—that on both sides there have been bad temper, and unsoundness of mind, and on the lady's part want of principle and extravagant notions as to the rights of women, with a rooted dislike of & contempt for her husband: she has used him and her son ill; and deserves the annoyances which her own strange course have in great measure brought upon her. Feeble, & deaf, and strange in manner, barring the delusions under which he labours, the old man has a sort of talent, information, and observation, rendering him not an unpleasant companion when abstracted from the matters which irritate his mind.* 21 Jun., 26 Jun: *Mrs. Irvine writes to me a long and very complaining letter.*

1853: 10 Dec: *The procession from Cheltenham not yet arrived, but Mr. Chamberlayne, Captain Irvine, Capt. Leigh, Mr. Wiggin & Mr. Hippisley were in waiting at the Unicorn.*

ISAAC — Harriet Isaac — *see also* Holland[22]

Harriet Isaac, née Whitmore (1786-1867), was born at Quatt, Shropshire, fifth daughter of William Whitmore (1745-1816) and Frances Barbara Lyster (1750-1792). She married, at Quatt, 2 April 1807, Elias Isaac (1776-1841); they had 5 sons and 2 daughters:

1 John Whitmore (1808-1884)
2 William Lister (1808-1878), Church of England clergyman
1 Harriet Barbara (b. 1810)
2 Sophia (1813-1851); married, 1832, Edward Holland (1806-1876), MP and landed proprietor
3 Henry Edward (b. 1816)
4 Frederick Neville (b. 1820)
5 Charles Powys (1831-1917), Church of England clergyman

1836: 27 Oct: *Some of their own connections, of the Clutton, Holland and Isaacs families from Worcestershire were staying in the house.*

1837: 1 Mar: *I was not quite a stranger to some of them, having met Mrs. Holland and her sister, Miss Isaacs, at Chastleton; they are nearly connected with the Whitmore Jones's... Mrs. Isaacs and Miss Louisa Holland, sisters of Mr. Holland, were the other ladies, and with them we returned to the house, over which I was conducted.*

1852: 7 Apr., 4 Jun: *While we were there, Mrs. Isaacs, mother of the late Mrs. Holland, and residing with him and his children at Dumbleton, called with two of Holland's daughters, children of twelve and thirteen years of age.*

ISHAM — Charles Euseby Isham[23]

Charles Euseby Isham (1776-1862), Church of England clergyman, was born at Lamport, Northamptonshire, son of Euseby and Diana Isham. He was educated at Christ Church, Oxford (BA 1795; MA 1798), and ordained deacon on 3 June 1798. His first clerical appointment was as rector of Polebrooke, Northamptonshire, which he held from 1 July 1800 to 1862, a remarkably long span. He was also appointed vicar of Oundle with Ashton on 9 February 1807, and stipendiary curate of Yaverland on 31 October 1829.

Isham married, at Stockton-on-Tees, Durham, 12 September 1801, Caroline Johnson (1772-1856); they had at least 4 daughters:

1 Caroline (1801-1824); married, 9 February 1824, Thomas Welch Hunt (1796-1824); both murdered in Italy
2 Diana Elizabeth (b. 1803)
3 Isabella Mary (b. 1805)
4 Charlotte (1808-1885)

1835: 25 Mar: *Mrs. M. Hunt had desired to be buried in an unostentatious manner ... Besides George Hunt, Thomas Hunt, and myself, who attended as Mourners, four gentlemen of the neighbourhood had been invited. Mr. Yorke of Thrapstone ... Mr. Isham from Polebrooke... Mr. Thos. Welch Hunt was in the flower of his age, and had married Caroline, daughter of the Revd. C. H. Isham, Rector of Polebrook near Oundle.*

1847: 12 Aug: *Mr. Isham, a fine old Clergyman, but very deaf, father of the late Mrs. T. W. Hunt, Rector of Polebrook, and formerly Vicar of Oundle: he was accompanied by his daughter, Mrs. Currie, the wife of a Clergyman, an agreeable woman.* 17 Aug: *we returned to Polebrook, and rejoined our party at the Parsonage, being politely received by the aged Rector and his lady. Here in a comfortable small house, in a pretty small garden, Mr. Isham shewed us portraits of his lamented daughter and son in law, Mr. and Mrs. T. Welch Hunt.*

J

JACKSON — Miss Jackson at the Master of the Ceremonies Ball at Cheltenham

1802: 9 Aug: *To the Master of the Ceremonies Ball in the Evening with my mother. Danced with Miss Jackson & Miss Wardlaw. A poor ball in all conscience.*

JACKSON — Major-General Jackson at Bristol

1832: 3 Jan: *Among the matters of chief interest was the order made for rebuilding Lawford's Gate Bridewell, near Bristol, the mob having so destroyed the prison, that it must in a great measure be a new structure. The expence is calculated at above £5000—on the Motion of Mr. Scandrett Harford, who with Mr. Newman represented the Bristol bench of magistrates, it was agreed, that the building should be made fire-proof, and that it should be so contrived, according to a plan suggested by Maj. Gen. Jackson, the Officer commanding the troops at Bristol.*

JACKSON — toll renter of Lower Slaughter turnpike

1853: 25 Jan: *Having been informed that W. Edgeworth and his wife, toll-takers at Lower Slaughter Turnpike gate, have received from Jackson, the renter, notice to quit on an early day, I wrote to Mr. Stokes, recommending W.E. to him as a fit person to be employed by the trustees as Toll-taker at any gate which may be kept in hand.*

JACKSON — Alfred Jackson, solicitor at Dursley [1]

Alfred Jackson (1805-1866), solicitor, was born at Dursley, son of William Jackson. He was a solicitor practising in Long Street, Dursley, and at one time was a partner of Edward Bloxsome. He appears to have lived at Woodmancote, Dursley, in 1844. He married, at St Lawrence's, Stroud, 30 October 1838, Rebecca Biddle Bennett, of Stratford Abbey, Stroud, daughter of William Bennett, tutor at Stroud; they had at least 1 son and 1 daughter:

1 Rebecca (1839-1902); died unmarried at Hastings, Sussex, where she had lived from the 1860s
1 Alfred William (b. 1843)

By 1861 Jackson was clerk to the union workhouse in Dursley, and the local registrar. He appears to have died at Henley, Oxfordshire, in 1866, but there is surprisingly little information about him or his family.

1837: 16 Oct: *Saw Mr. Goodrich, and the usual County Functionaries, Bloxsome, Wilton, Jackson &c.*

1845: 12 Mar: *The County Chairman has sent Mr. Riddiford to investigate the matter at the Bridewell, procure evidence, arrange documents, and watch the case, with the assistance of Mr. Jackson, Mr. Bloxsome's partner.* 14 Apr: *Mr. Jackson and Mr. Riddiford havinge been watching the proceedings on the part of the County, the Vis. Justices, and the Officers of the Bridewell, making notes of the evidence, tendering witnesses, endeavouring, as far as the Coroner will allow, so to cross examine the parties giving testimony as to elicit the truth.* 7 May: *The enquiry will have cost the County a large sum of money: Mr. Jackson (partner to Mr. Bloxsome,) and Mr. Riddiford were in frequent attendance at the Inquest.*

1846: 2 Jul: *While I was at Gloucester, I asked Mr. Jackson, Mr. Bloxsome's partner, whether it was in contemplation to part with the advowson or next presentation of the Rectory of Stanton, which belong to Mr. B's clergyman son, who is now in a very dangerous state of health, and, it is believed, cannot long survive.*

1847: 25 Aug., 31 Aug., 28 Oct: *Received a letter from Sewell, who was not able to meet either of the Messrs. Bloxsome at Dursley yesterday, but had an interview with Mr. A. Jackson, their partner.*

JACKSON — John Jackson, solicitor and Conservative agent at Settle

1843: 16 Sep: *From Mr. Jackson, a Solicitor and Conservative agent at Settle, I received a letter enquiring whether, under the late Registration Act, I meditated selecting any other place than Settle, where to poll at a county election.* 18 Sep.

JACOB — schoolmaster at Malvern

1840: 24 Apr: *five domestics, viz. Abraham and Sarah Gibbs, Mr. Jacob, formerly Gardener to my Aunt, and now Schoolmaster at the principal parochial school at Malvern, Mary Good, the under female Servant, and Miss. Niblett, the nurse.* 24 Jun: *Engaged early with J. and MA Jacob, legatees under my Aunt's will, paying the amount due to them.*

JACOBSON — William Jacobson [2]

William Jacobson (1803-1884), Church of England clergyman and professor of divinity, was born at Great Yarmouth, Norfolk, only son of William Jacobson (d. 1803) and Judith Clarke. He was educated at St Edmund Hall and Lincoln College, Oxford (BA 1827). Further to that, he was a fellow at Exeter College in 1829-36 (MA 1829), librarian in 1830, and an honorary fellow in 1882-84. He was canon of Christ Church in 1848-65 (DD 1848), public orator in 1842-48, and regius professor of divinity in 1848-65. He was also vice-principal of Magdalen Hall in 1832-48. Jacobson was perpetual curate of Iffley in 1839-40, rector of Ewelme in 1848-65, and bishop of Chester in 1865-84. He married, at Great Yarmouth, 23 June 1836, Eleanor Jane Turner (1811-1895); they had 5 sons and 5 daughters:

1 Mary (1839-1855)
1 William Bowstead Richards (1840-1880), Church of England clergyman
2 Ellen Hannah (1841-1873)
3 Hester Sterling (1843-1933)
4 Grace Matilda (1845-1855)
2 Walter Hamilton Acland (1847-1924)
3 Edward Burton (1848-1856)
5 Katharine Mary (1850-1917)
4 Charles Longley (1852-1897)
5 Robert Clerke (1856-1894)

1833: 13 Mar: *Dr. Macbride added, that, with one or two exceptions, the Undergraduate Members of his Hall were respectable and well conducted; that he had great confidence in the Vice Principal, Mr. Jacobson, fellow of Exeter College, & formerly of St. Edmund Hall, a man of decided talent, and thoroughly fitted for the duties of Tutor.*

1836: 31 Oct: *Received a long and satisfactory letter from Edward, giving an account of his studies, and, particularly, the outline of the scheme of reading, which, with the advice of Messrs. Jacobson and Cockey, he has formed with a view to obtaining the honours of a Class at his second examination before taking his Bachelor's degree.* 15 Nov: *My son doubts whether these lectures will be concluded by the time when his six weeks residence at Magd. Hall are expired, and he even contemplates the prolonging his stay at Oxford to take some private tuition in Aristotle from Mr. Jacobson, the Tutor of the Hall.*

1838: 20 Aug: *It was agreed that Jacobson, the V. Principal of Magd. Hall, late fellow of Exeter, should set off for Oban to take measures for the removal of the body, which there is reason to suppose is yet unburied, to Oxford for interment.*

1842: 19 Nov: *Mr. Jacobson, Vice Principal of Magd. Hall, who has been some little time in the field, and has, probably, thereby obtained a decided advantage over any competitor, and, as far as I am concerned, my vote would be neutralized by my son's, as he would, of course, support a tutor and acquaintance of his own Society.*

1847: 13 Dec: *Mr. Jacobson, of Magd. Hall, formerly of Exeter Coll., of whom it is stated that he will be raised by Government to the Regius of Professorship of Divinity, about to be resigned by Dr. Hampden, when elevated to the see of Hereford.*

1848: 14 Apr.

JAGEMANN — Henriette Karoline Friederike Jagemann [3]

Henriette Karoline Friederike Jagemann (1777-1848), opera singer, was born at Weimar, daughter of the scholar and librarian Christian Joseph Jagemann (1735-1804) and sister of the painter Ferdinand Jagemann (1780-1820). The dowager duchess, Anna Amalia, had her trained as a singer at Mannheim, where she was very successful. She was a mistress of Duke Karl August and bore him 2 sons and 1 daughter:

1 Karl von Wolfgang (1806-1895)
2 August von Heygendorff (1810-1874)
1 Mariana von Heygendorff (1812-1836); married, 15 October 1835, Daniel, Baron Tindal

Henriette's predecessor was Luise Rudorf (1777-1852), who bore the duke a son in 1796. It is not known when Henriette became his mistress, but presumably after 1800 as it is almost inconceivable that the duchess, Luise, would have allowed her to sing at court at her birthday celebrations had she known the true circumstances.

In 1809 Henriette was granted a patent of nobility, with the title of Frau von Heygendorf. In 1828, after the death of Duke Karl August, she was retired on a pension and moved to Dresden, where she died in 1848.

1798: 2 Sep: *Mademoiselle Jagemann the chief singer in the Opera is the greatest ornament of this Stage, with a little figure, but with an enchanting Voice tho' not high enough for several parts, equally adapted for Tragedy or Comedy which she shines as much in as in the opera, she is the admiration of every Stranger, who is astonished to see her paid the greatest Notice to even by the Duke & his Family; but her lively, easy manner enchants everyone, & to see her without wishing to be acquainted with her were impossible.*

1799: 26 Oct: *Mademoiselle Jagemann charming as Rosina.* 27 Oct: *Mademoiselle Jagemann made her debut for this Year in two charming Italian Songs.* 3 Nov: *To Don Juan in the Evening, pretty well amused. Mad. Jagemann acted well.* 16 Nov: *The Costume of Mad. Jagemann bad, her singing very good.* 17 Nov: *Jagemann sung charmingly.* 30 Nov: *Mad. Jagemann as Oberon excellent all the rest acted miserably indeed besides.* 7 Dec: *The best performers were Jagemann, Matiegzeck, Weyrauch, & Spitzeder.* 14 Dec: *dined all at Court, Mad Jagemann sung very finely & a beautiful Symphonie composed & played by Destouches.* 20 Dec: *Mademoiselle Jagemann as Sertus perfectly good: none of the rest equall to their Parts.* 25 Dec: *Mademoiselle Jagemann sung very finely: also her younger Sister who sung a Duett with her shewed a fine voice & considerable Abilities in Singing.*

1800: 12 Jan: *Mademoiselle Jagemann singing delightfully Court Party &c.* 30 Jan., 2 Feb: *in the Evening to Court which being the Duchesses Birthday was very splendid. Mademoiselle Jagemann sung finely, & the Concert was very pretty.* 8 Mar., 22 Mar: *In the evening with my Brother to Tarare an Opera which I had before seen & which was tolerably acted particularly by Jagemann and Weyrauch, without whom indeed few Operas here are tolerable.* 29 Mar., 5-6 Apr., 13 Apr: *to a very numerous Court; where in the Concert a Simphonie and a beautiful Air both by Destouches were played and charmingly sung by Mademoiselle Jagemann &c.* 20 Apr: *in the Evening at Court, a beautiful Concert tho' the Jagemann did not sing.*

JAMES — managing clerk at Williams, Deacon and Company

1851: 28 May: *The accounts have been kept with Messrs. Cox & Williams, and Messrs. Williams, Deacon and Co., Bankers ... Mr. Williams seems heartily tired of the affair, and pleaded an important engagement for leaving us with a Gentleman of the name of James, who appeared pretty conversant with the business, and a very well educated and intelligent young man: he, probably, will ere long be admitted into the firm.*

JAMES — Miss James, a dinner guest of Thomas Howell

1853: 7 Jun: *A Baroness Ollenstein, a young English lady married to a German nobleman, and her sister—a Miss James, an elderly young lady of good fortune.*

JAMES — Charles James [4]

Charles James (1804-1857), Church of England clergyman, was born at Longborough, Gloucestershire, son of William and Ann James. He was educated at Christ's College, Cambridge (BA 1828). He was ordained deacon on 21 December 1828 and priest on 28 December 1829. His first clerical appointment was as stipendiary curate of Woodchester, Gloucestershire, from 21 December 1828. He then served as rector of Evenlode, Worcestershire, in 1830-57. He married, first, Esther (d. 1836), daughter of Nathaniel Dimock (1766-1809) and Priscilla Coatts (1764-1796) of Bridgend House, Stonehouse, Gloucestershire; they had at least 1 daughter:

1 Ann (b. ±1836)

It seems likely that Esther died in childbirth. Charles James married, secondly, Mary Christina; they had 1 daughter:

1 Mary Christina (b. 1843)

1834: 26 Jul.

1836: 26 Aug: *I also wrote to Mr. James, the Incumbent of Evenlode, to explain to him the purport and effect of the resolutions passed yesterday in relation to the prevalence of small-pox within his parish.* 27 Oct., 1 Dec: *At a subordinate meeting of the Book Society, which I was unable to attend, being engaged at the Board of Guardians, the Revd. Mr. James of Evenlode, was elected a member.* 22 Dec: *The allegations were stated by me with reference to a document on which they were founded, to a letter exculpatory of the Officer, which I received this day from Mr. James, the Clergyman of Evenlode.*

1837: 5 Mar: *Mr. James, the Rector of Evenlode, wrote to me for the character of my late servant, Geo. Bowles.*

1838: 14 Dec.

1843: 24 Nov., 30 Nov: *A conference with Mr. James, the Rector of Evenlode, as to the inquest lately held there.*

1844: 3 Feb., 7 Feb., 29 Feb., 7 Apr: *Wrote to Mr. James, Evenlode, asking his permission to have the use of a bull of his now let for the season to Edginton of Maugersbury.* 11 Apr: *Recd. a note from Mr. James, Evenlode, in answer to one I had written to him; he permits me to use his bull now let out to Mr. Edginton, Maugersbury, on payment of two guineas for each cow I may send.* 25 Oct., 27 Oct.

1847: 29 Jan: *also to Revd. C. James, Evenlode, acknowledging a letter I had received from him yesterday respecting an application for relief made by one of his Parishioners, explaining the principle on which relief, in a certain way had been accorded to one, & denied to another.* 30 Jan., 1 Feb., 8 Feb., 11 Feb., 19 Mar.

1850: 1 Oct: *A letter from Whitmore Jones as to the readmission of Mr. James of Evenlode as a member of the Stow Book Society.*

1851: 3 Mar: *Also Mr. Hayward to bring under my notice a charge of negligence and unskilful treatment of a pauper at Evenlode alleged against him by Mr. James, the Incumbent of that parish.* 3 Apr.

1854: 2 Feb: *Justice business at Mr. Brookes's office with Mr. James of Evenlode.* 4 Feb: *On my return home found awaiting me the Police with a prisoner apprehended under my warrant on a charge of obtaining goods under false pretences from the Revd. C. James, Evenlode.* 5 Feb.

JAMES — George and Sarah James[5]

George James (1801-1857), agricultural labourer, was born at Upper Slaughter, son of Thomas James (1757-1823) and his wife, Mary (1765-1850). He married, at Upper Slaughter, 4 February 1822, Sarah (1780-1851), born at Upper Slaughter, daughter of William Sly (1753-1828), of Harford Hill, Naunton, and his wife, Mary (d. 1786). Sarah was therefore some twenty-one years George's senior. Edward Witts's sloppy entry in the Upper Slaughter burial register for 1857 states George to be 47 not 57, but this is incorrect; Ferdinand Travell, Edward's great-uncle, clearly records the baptism on 1 March 1801. Nevertheless, it seems strange that a young man aged 21 should wish to take a bride aged 42. There do not appear to have been any children. Sarah had at least one brother, John (1783-1805), and one sister, Elizabeth (b. & d. 1785). William Sly appears to have married again, to another Mary, who died in 1806.

1851: 14 Feb: *Visited an aged parishioner, Sarah James, who has been struck with paralysis, and is lying senseless.* 17, Feb., 19 Feb., 21 Feb., 28 Feb., 10 Mar., 22 Mar., 5 Apr., 12 Apr., 19 Apr., 26 Apr: *Visited my parishioner, George James, who is confined to the house by illness—He & his aged wife are in a pitiable condition.* 2 May: *Visiting parishioners—the Dunfords, Townsends, G. & S. James, and Widow Wilcox.* 6 May, 16 May: *Visited sick and aged parishioners, Townsends, G. James.*

JAMES — James James of Lower Guiting[6]

James James (1815-1892), farm labourer, was born at Guiting Power. In 1851 he lived at Guiting Grange as a servant and farm labourer. By 1861 he was married to Mary (b. ±1816) and was listed in the census as a farm bailey (bailiff [?]). It may be presumed that Mary died, for in 1871 he was married to Harriet (1830-1890), born at Guiting Power; they had 1 son:

1 William (b. 1870)

Harriet was either a widow or the mother of an illegitimate child, as her son, James Lovesey (1856-1914), was also living in the house. On 17 December 1869, James was sentenced as a juvenile offender to ten days' hard labour for stealing a quantity of tobacco.

1844: 18 Jan: *I joined Messrs. Ford and R. Waller at the Justice room, where the principal business was the conviction of James James for an assault at Lower Guiting on the Constables (see Jan. 12) he was fined £5.*

JAMES — John Thomas James[7]

John Thomas James (1786-1828), bishop of Calcutta and writer on art, was born at Rugby, Warwickshire, eldest son of Dr Thomas James (1748-1804), headmaster of Rugby School, and his second wife, Arabella Caldecott (d. 1828). He was educated at Rugby School, Charterhouse, and Christ Church, Oxford (BA 1808; MA 1810). In 1813 he toured northern Europe with Sir James Riddell, and published, in 1816, his *Journal of a Tour in Germany, Sweden, Russia, and Poland, during 1813 and 1814*. Also in 1816, James visited Italy, and studied painting at Rome and Naples. On his return to England he entered the Church, and was appointed vicar of Flitton-cum-Silsoe, Bedfordshire. He married, 1823, Marianne Jane, fourth daughter of Frederick Reeves of East Sheen, Surrey, and formerly of Mangalore, Bombay presidency; they had at least 1 son:

1 John Acland James (1825-1896), Church of England clergyman

Following the death of Bishop Heber, James was appointed to the bishopric of Calcutta. He resigned his vicarage in April 1827; the University of Oxford gave him the degree of DD by diploma on 10 May, and on Whitsunday, 3 June, he was consecrated at Lambeth. He landed at Calcutta on 18 January 1828, and was installed in the cathedral on the following Sunday, the 20th. After a reorganisation of the parishes, James commenced a tour of the western provinces of his diocese on 20 June. He was taken ill *en route*, and upon returning to Calcutta was ordered to take a sea voyage for the sake of his health. He sailed for China on 9 August, but died during the voyage on 22 August 1828.

1805: 18 Mar: *Adjoined to the Music Room, which was well attended; joined Trevenen, James &c. the Performer, Mrs. Mountain, Morelli, Signor Lanza & Mr. Fitzsimmons.*

1827: 5 Apr: *It has transpired, that the See of Calcutta is to be filled by the Revd. J.T. James, Incumbent of Flitton in Bedfordshire. It is many years since I have met with him; when undergraduates at Oxford, we were well acquainted. He is a Son of the late Dr. James, Head Master of Rugby School, and Prebendary of Worcester.* 13 May: *This work is by the new Bishop of Calcutta, and has been very generally read.* 16 Dec.

1828: 20 Jan.

1829: 21 Feb.

1832: 25 Apr.

JAMES — John and Wintle James of Newnham-on-Severn[8]

John and Wintle James were solicitors at Newnham-on-Severn.

1845: 9 Apr: *Mr. James of Newnham, a Solicitor, called to search my parish registers.*

JAMES — Thomas James[9]

Thomas James (1805-1885), gardener's labourer, was born at Upper Slaughter, younger son of Thomas James (1757-1823) and his wife, Mary (1765-1850), and younger brother to George (*above*). He married, at Upper Slaughter, 19 April 1826, Martha Williams; they had 5 daughters and 1 son:

1 Eliza Jane (1827-1834)
2 Anne (b. 1831)
3 Mary Elizabeth (b. 1833)
4 Elizabeth (b. 1835)

5 Emily (b. 1838)
1 Thomas (b. 1842)

1850: 21 Oct: *Visited sick parishioners——Mrs. Rogers, and the Widow Townsend, with whom I prayed: also a daughter of Thomas James, who has been afflicted with fever, and Widow Wilcox.*

JAMES — Thomas and Mary James of Upper Slaughter [10]

Thomas James (1757-1823), agricultural labourer, was married to Mary (1765-1850); they had at least 6 sons and 1 daughter:

1 William (1789-1838); married, at Upper Slaughter, 31 July 1817, Elizabeth Williams (±1778-1834)
2 John (d. 1802)
3 Charles (d. 1796)
4 Charles (1797-1861); died in Stow Union Workhouse
5 George (1801-1857); *see above*
6 Thomas (1805-1881); *see above*
1 Hannah (1808-1809)

1838: 7 Jul: *Visiting my poor parishioner W. James, dying by inches by a cancer in the throat.* 28 Aug: *W. James dead, and buried on Sunday.*

1846: 13 Dec: *Conferring with Churchwarden &c. as to the state of the Widow James & her son, living together—the former very old and deranged: the latter infirm in body and mind; a very difficult case to be dealt with.*

1850: 5 Feb: *visited Mrs. Collett, Widows Gardner, E. Wilcox's wife, and Mrs. Dix for Mary James.* 17 Dec: *Called on my parishioners, the Dixes, for information as to what clothing would be most wanted by their relations Mary and Charles James, of whom the one is insane, and the other of feeble intellect.*

1851: 3 Jan: *Attended the funeral of an aged parishioner, Mary James.*

JAMES — William James [11]

William James (1771-1837), lawyer, land agent, engineer, and surveyor, was a member of the Stratford Canal management committee during its final stages. He was also briefly employed as clerk to the Stratford & Moreton Tramway. He had originally intended for Stratford-upon-Avon to feature on a rail route, powered by George Stephenson's steam locomotives, between the Midlands and London, via Oxford. James had interests in collieries around the Midlands and wanted to establish new transport links to reach new markets for coal; he surveyed the route of the Liverpool & Manchester Railway in 1822 and a good many other potential railway routes around the country—often at his own expense. In 1823 James was declared bankrupt and sent to debtor's prison in London. He spent his time there productively, formulating what was effectively a national network of railways. His plan for the Stratford and Moreton line, called 'Plan of the lines of the Central Junction Railway or Tram-road', included a connection to London. William James, a pioneering promoter of the railways, was an expansive thinker.

1824: 6 May: *At a meeting of the Commissioners of the Foss and Cross Turnpike roads to-day, at which I presided, a proposition was made by Mr. James, Engineer of the Stratford & Moreton Railway, for diverting a portion of the Turnpike road, near Moreton, as a mutual accommodation. At the same time this gentleman communicated much information on the subject of rail roads, with which he is connected, either in progress or in agitation.* 27 Aug.

JAMES — William James [12]

William James (1787-1861), Church of England clergyman, was born at Rugby, Warwickshire, younger son of Dr Thomas James (1748-1804), headmaster of Rugby School, and his second wife, Arabella Caldecott (d. 1828). He was brother of John (*above*). James was educated at Oriel College, Oxford (BA 1807; MA 1810), where he was a fellow until 1837 and proctor in 1821. He served as vicar of Cobham, Surrey, and rector of Bilton, Warwickshire, in 1853-61. He married, January 1854, Anna Parker (1802-1878), daughter of Sir Grey Skipwith, 8th baronet, and Harriet Townsend. Anna was a widow, and William was her second husband. Her sister, Selina (±1790-1880), married James Lenox William Naper (1791-1868), first cousin once removed to the diarist Francis Witts.

1827: 5 Apr: *A brother of Mr. James is or was a tutor of Oriel: a sister was married to Mr. Robt. Morris, late banker here with Messrs. Turners; who was removed from the partnership shortly before the concern stopped payment, a catastrophè, to which Mr. Morris's indiscreet speculations are believed to have materially contributed.*

JAQUES — George Jaques [13]

George Jaques (±1748-1822), Church of England clergyman, was the son of George Jaques (1718-1773), vicar of Urchfont. George was not an alumnus of Oxford or Cambridge and information on his career is scarce. He was rector of Haselbury in 1783-1822, and curate at All Cannings and Etchilhampton. He and his wife were helpful and friendly to Francis Witts, although there is a sense that they were homely rather than worldly acquaintances. Francis appears to have particularly appreciated the company of Mrs Jaques; he visited her frequently, writing notes in his diary such as, 'Called upon Mrs. Jaques, as usual.'

1806: 29 Jun: *Received with politeness by Mrs. Jaques, Miss Gale &c.* 6 Jul., 17 Jul: *Rode to Erchfont; met & conversed with the Revd. G. Jacques by the way.* 18 Jul: *Rode to Stert Cottage & walked from thence with Mr. & Mrs. Jacques four miles to Stoke to dine with Mr. Mayo.* 19-20 Jul., 21 Jul: *Dined with the Jacques's at Stert Cottage, meeting Mr. Compton of Erchfont & Newbury, an honest, plain man, his wife & sister. A good plain dinner, wine, beer, pipes of tobacco.* 22 Jul: *Rode to Erchfont in hopes of arranging matters with Smith but a sudden dispute made one quickly return, & occasioned two letters to & from him to me & one to & from Jaques.* 26 Jul: *Rode over to Erchfont to settle matters with Smith, from whom I parted without regret, as he set off for Andover. Conversed a little with Jaques, upon the road.* 27-28 Jul., 3 Aug: *called upon Mrs. Jaques as usual.* 8 Aug., 10 Aug: *Sent John back to Devizes with my horse & accepted of an invitation to a family dinner with the Jaques's.* 13 Aug., 16-17 Aug., 20 Aug: *Mr. Jaques paid me a visit.* 21 Aug., 23-24 Aug., 26 Aug., 31 Aug., 1 Sep., 6-7 Sep., 11 Sep: *Walked in the Evening over to Jaques & smoked, drank tea, & supped with him.* 14 Sep., 17 Sep., 21 Sep., 28 Sep., 30 Sep: *Called upon the Jaques's & rode with Mr. Jaques through Ashlington to All Cannings where we called upon Mr. Davis & Mr. & Mrs. Newman.* 5 Oct., 10 Oct., 12-13 Oct., 15 Oct., 19 Oct: *administered at Erchfont Church by Jaques, I took his duty at All Cannings & Ashlington.* 20 Oct., 26 Oct: *Jaques undertook the Sacrament duty at Stert & the afternoon duty at Erchfont, in consequence of which I took his duty at Allcannings & Ashlington .... Returned to a late dinner & found Mr. & Mrs. Jaques & their neice dining at the Vicarage. Not sorry when they took their departure.* 27 Oct., 1-2 Nov., 4 Nov., 9 Nov: *calling of course upon Mrs. Jaques.* 11 Nov., 14 Dec., 18 Dec., 21 Dec., 28-29 Dec.

1807: 4 Jan: *Undertook Jaques's Duties, as he performed the Sacrament duty at Erchfont.* 5 Jan: *Drove my Mother to call upon Mrs. Jaques & Miss Gales.* 18 Jan., 25-27 Jan., 30 Jan., 1 Feb., 8 Feb., 15 Feb., 17-18 Feb., 8 Mar., 12 Mar., 15 Mar., 22 Mar., 27 Mar., 29 Mar., 5-6 Apr., 12 Apr., 19-20 Apr., 24 Apr., 26 Apr., 10-11 May, 17 May, 28 Jun., 5 Jul., 9 Jul., 12 Jul., 14 Jul: *Drove my Father to dine at Jaques's. Met the Comptons of Erchfont & Eastcott.* 17 Jul., 19 Jul., 24-26 Jul., 2 Aug: *Called upon Mrs. Jaques, as usual.* 8 Aug., 13 Aug., 16 Aug., 20 Aug., 23 Aug., 29 Aug., 6 Dec., 10 Dec: *Called on Mr. & Mrs. Jaques, walked with the latter into town.* 13 Dec., 18 Dec., 22-23 Dec., 25 Dec., 30 Dec: *Jaques called. Rode with him part of his way home.*

1808: 1 Jan: *Dined at Jaques's meeting Miss A. Gale & Miss M. Gabriel; very unpleasant & dull.* 3 Jan., 9 Jan., 22 Jan., 24 Jan., 31 Jan., 7 Feb., 10 Feb., 14-15 Feb: *Called upon the Jaques's Drank tea, played commerce, & supped at the Legg's, meeting the Butchers.* 17-18 Feb., 13 Mar., 20 Mar., 27 Mar., 31 Mar., 1 Apr., 2-3 Apr., 8 Apr., 10 Apr., 12 Apr., 15-16 Apr., 20 Apr., 24 Apr., 29 Apr., 1 May.

JARRATT — Robert Jarratt [14]

Robert Jarratt (1801-1882), Church of England clergyman, was born at Wellington, Somerset, son of Revd Robert Jarratt (±1765-1843), rector of Wellington. He was educated at St John's College, Cambridge (BA 1822; MA 1825). His first clerical appointment was as curate of Combe St Nicholas, Somerset, from 1823. He was vicar of Lockington, Leicestershire, in 1825-29, curate of Halifax in 1829-34, perpetual curate of Ripponden and Luddenden, Yorkshire, in 1834-38, curate of Bourton-on-the-Hill, Gloucestershire, in 1838-55, and rector of Bourton-on-the-Hill with Moreton-in-Marsh, in 1855-82. Jarratt was married to Caroline (b. ±1807); they had at least 1 son and 1 daughter:

1 Francis Robert (1840-1870)
1 Margaret Penelope (1841-1859)

1840: 6 Jun: *Received a letter from Newmarch, proposing that he and Mrs. N. should visit us on Thursday next, on which day he has business with Dr. Warneford, and Mrs. N. wishes to accompany him, to renew an early acquaintance with Mrs. Jarrett, the wife of the Curate of Bourton on the Hill, and to be introduced to my wife, and sleep at Upper Slaughter, on the road back to Cirencester.*

1844: 27 Jan., 29 Feb.

1847: 27 Jan., 6 Jul., 7 Jul: *Then to the decanal meeting, at which the Rural Dean presided, and the following Clergymen were present—Messrs. Hutchinson, Jarratt, Mangin and Aston, not of the Deanery of Stow.* 14 Sep.

1850: 10 Jan., 7 Mar.

1851: 24 Apr.

1853: 20 Jan.

JARVIS — John Jarvis and the Jarvis family of Upper Slaughter — *see also* Dix [15]

John Jarvis (±1795-1879), agricultural labourer, married, at Upper Slaughter, 15 May 1815, Rachel (1799-1822), daughter of Joshua Dix (1769-1847) and Hannah Williams (1774-1818). It was a hasty marriage; their firstborn, William, was baptised on 21 July of that same year. Rachel died in 1822, after which John and young William disappeared from records.

JARVIS — Joseph Jarvis [16]

Joseph Jarvis (±1795-1879), agricultural labourer, was presumably a brother to John (*above*). The 1861 census states that he was born at Upper Slaughter, but there are no baptismal records to confirm this, nor is it known when he married Hannah (1790-1842). They had 3 sons and 4 daughters:

1 Ann (b. 1818)
1 David (1819-1860)
2 George (b. 1822-1879)
3 Emanuel [Emmanuel] (b. 1824)
2 Selina [Salina] (b. 1827)
3 Rachel (b. 1830-1834)
4 Elizabeth (1834-1879); in domestic service at Bourton by 1851; died unmarried

Joseph married secondly, 23 February 1859, Hannah (b. 1830), daughter of Thomas Collett of Little Rissington. She married secondly, at Blockley, 25 December 1880, Charles Webb (b. ±1817).

Joseph and two of his children, George and Elizabeth, were all buried within six days of each other, between 18 and 24 June 1879.

1837: 3 Dec: *Between services much engrossed with attendance on a boy of 14 years, whose leg was broken this morning by a kick from a cart horse. He is the son of a labourer, Jarvis, of this village. Attended while Hayward, who had been sent for by Polhill, the boy's Employer, placed the limb in the proper position, and assisted him in binding it up. It is a compound fracture.*

1842: 13 Sep: *A funeral in the evening—poor Hannah Jarvis.*

JEAFFRESON — Christopher William Baldrey Jeaffreson [17]

Christopher William Baldrey Jeaffreson (1769-1846), Church of England clergyman, was the eldest son of Revd Christopher Jeaffreson (1729-1789), of Tunstall, Suffolk, and Mary Syer (b. 1742). He was educated at Pembroke College, Cambridge (BA 1792; MA 1799). Jeaffreson's first clerical appointment was as curate of Tunstall and Iken, Suffolk, from 1792. He was then appointed vicar of Longborough and Sezincote, Gloucestershire, in 1813, thanks to the patronage of Sir Charles Cockerell. He served in this post until 1846. He was also a JP at Moreton-in-Marsh. He married, first, 1796, Elizabeth Syer (1765-1813), presumably a cousin; they had 3 sons and 1 daughter:

1 Christopher Jeaffreson (±1794-1870); *see below*
2 William Jeaffreson (±1798-1865[?]), noted oculist; *see below*
1 Eliza Mary (b. 1806); married, at Longborough, 16 October 1827, Arthur Clark Kemball
3 Samuel John Jeaffreson (±1811-1870); *see below*

Jeaffreson married, secondly, a woman surnamed Baldrey, whose name he took in addition to his own, as is explained in the account below, which provides several interesting details about his life.

> Christopher William Jeaffreson was a tall man with a handsome face and slightly aquiline profile, and his elegant figure offered no striking indications of the Herculean strength which was one of his physical endowments. Possessing the amount of classical scholarship to be looked for in a gentleman of academic training, he was also a musician of uncommon ability. But he was chiefly admirable for his conversational address, his lively humour and his perfect mastery of the noble art of self-defence. When he reflected, in his mature age, on his youthful career at Cambridge, he recalled with complacency how he had distinguished himself as one of the younger 'Pitt's body-guard' during the election that made that statesman Member of Parliament for the University. It may be declared boldly that, from the year of his ordination to the death of George III, he was the smartest pugilist of the clerical profession. Sparring with a skill and energy that were applauded by every ring he entered, he befriended the professors of an art

that even in George III's time was decried by many people as inhuman and brutalizing. On falling 'into trouble,' prize-fighters of repute hastened to him for sympathy and material assistance. He was known to have entertained unfortunate pugilists at his Suffolk parsonage; and instead of crying 'Shame!' on their Rector for opening his doors to the "ornaments of the ring" in their moments of distress, the parishioners of Tunstall extolled him for doing what was right to 'men of merit.'

There were occasions when this clergyman of an old school fought without the gloves. He had attained to middle age and was walking with his eldest son (at that time a Cambridge undergraduate), from their London lodgings to the theatre, when he was rudely accosted by an able-bodied ruffian, who derided him for being 'a parson.' A crowd came about the able-bodied ruffian and encouraged him with cheers to persist in his disorderly behaviour. As the encouragement incited the able-bodied ruffian to be guilty of still wilder outrages, the Suffolk rector remarked, in his softest tone, 'My good fellow, if you go on in this way, I shall be forced to punish you.' 'Oho, oho!' retorted the ruffian, putting up his fists and springing about in a style that showed him to have some acquaintance with the noble art, 'so you mean to punish me, do you? Then, if that's your game, just punish me at once. Just please, parson, be good enough to punish me at once.' He had his prayer. 'The mill' was over in five minutes. The able-bodied ruffian was still lying upon the pavement, when the gentle-mannered parson went onwards to the theatre, without a scratch on his face or any serious disarrangement of his dress.

By the many sportsmen of his acquaintance, the rector of Tunstall and the other parishes was regarded as the best partridge-shot in East Suffolk; and there was something curious in his way of shooting partridges. It was his practice when he went out with his gun and pointer to wear a waistcoat whose right-hand pocket was lined with tinfoil and charged with snuff. As soon as his dog had pointed and he saw the covey on the point of rising, he laid his gun upon his left hand, forced the fingers of his right hand into his snuff-pouch and took a pinch of snuff before he fired with deadly effect at the birds upon the wing. To persons who enquired whether he snuffed in this eccentric manner at a critical moment, in order to clear his vision and steady his nerves, he would answer, 'No, but I am so nervous and excitable that I am apt to fire before the birds have fairly risen and to miss them by firing over their heads, unless I check my impetuosity by taking a hasty pinch.'

The rector of Tunstall and the other places was a superlatively patriotic person. In 1803-4, when the volunteers were revived and every ploughman of the Eastern Counties glowed with martial ardour, the rector raised a strong company of volunteers. Consisting for the most part of the young farmers and labourers of Tunstall and the adjoining parishes, the corps was commanded by the rector himself, who, as the duly commissioned Captain of the force, used to drill his men on Sundays. At the beginning of the 19th Century it was the fashion for officers of the Army to wear their uniform at all places and hours of the day, and in his military fervour, the handsome rector wore his red coat at dinner parties and dances. It was even alleged that he wore it in church under cover of his canonical habiliments. Whilst he was wearing his red coat as his usual dress, the Rector was invited by his Bishop to pass two nights at the Palace of Norwich. On his return from the cathedral city the rector spoke and had reason to speak with complacence of the civilities which the bishop had lavished upon him. But inferences were drawn by the rector's neighbours from the fact that he henceforth forbore to wear his military costume when he was not on duty with his soldiers.

In his later time, when he had become the rector of Longhborough-cum-Seasoncote, co. Gloucester, this handsome clergyman rarely visited Suffolk, unless he was in attendance upon the Marquis of Hertford at Sudbourne, in the shooting season. Taking for his second wife a considerable heiress, whose surname Baldrey he assumed, in accordance with her father's will, though no one of his multitudinous friends ever called him by it, he was rich enough to keep house in London and follow the pleasures of the town, where he was known to 'all the world' and was on equally good terms with the great people of Mayfair and the comparatively insignificant people (including such Jews as the Disraelis and the Lindos), who gathered about his brother, John Jeaffreson—the Islington surgeon. He died at his residence in Connaught Terrace, Hyde Park, after a very long and severe illness.

Jeaffreson was an unusual man for a cleric, but Francis Witts, who knew him well, seems to have held him in high esteem. The date of his first marriage was likely 1793, given that his eldest son appears to have been born in 1794. Details of his connection to Sir Charles Cockerell are unknown, but it was probably of a military or sporting context. Jeaffreson's portrait, a watercolour on ivory, was painted in 1810 by John Smart and sold in recent years by Sotheby's.

1820: 29 Jun: *I joined a musical party at Mr. Hippisley: Dr. Hague & his Daughter (he the Professor of Music at Cambridge) are the principal performers; both excellent players on the Violin; Mr. Jeaffreson, Sir H. Dryden, also on the Violin; Miss Hippisley on the Violoncello; Mrs. & Miss Jeaffreson on the Pianoforte.*

1823: 21 Mar: *We dined at Mr. Jeaffreson's at Longborough, meeting Sir C. & Lady Cockerell.* 22 Mar: *We dined at Mr. E. Leigh's at Broadwell, meeting the Jeaffresons, the Dumbletons & Mr. Vavasour.* 23 Apr., 8 Oct., 21 Oct., 25 Nov: *I dined and slept at Dr. Warneford's, meeting Lords Redesdale and Northwick, Mr. Pole, Mr. Jeaffreson, Mr. Ford, Mr. Saumarez and Mr. Eyre.*

1824: 18 Oct: *I left home for Gloucester to attend the quarter Sessions. I accompanied my neighbour. Mr. Jeaffreson, Rector of Longborough, who, having been recently put on the Commission of the peace for this county, was about to qualify .... Mr. Jeaffreson and myself spent a pleasant evening together at Wellington Parade.* 19 Oct: *Mr. Jeaffreson was prevented from qualifying, owing to an error in the spelling of his name, which will require correction by the Chancellor. The same circumstance occurred to myself, when I was about to qualify; my Christian name of Edward being omitted in the Dedimus protestatem.*

1825: 5 Apr: *We had a dinner party. Mr. & Mrs. Jeaffreson and Miss E. Jeaffreson, Dr. Warneford, Mr. Croome & Mr. C. Keysall.* 19 Jul., 25 Sep., 3 Nov., 15 Dec.

1826: 19 Apr., 22 Apr: *I dined at my neighbour Hurd's at Naunton. The other guests were Messrs. Talbot, Browne, R. Wynniatt, Bowen & Jeaffreson: an agreeable party, but late.* 5 Jul: *We dined at Mr. Jeaffreson's at Longborough meeting Dr. Warneford, Mr. & Mrs. Ford, Mr. Twisleton & with him a Mr. Brownlow Layard, born at Ceylon, and grandson of a former Dean of Bristol, Mr. Bowen, Mr. Malcolm & Mr. Jones.* 11 Jul., 18 Jul., 23 Aug: *We had some of our friends to dinner. Our party consisted of the Egerton Leighs, Mr. & Mrs. Jeaffreson, Mr. & Mrs. Dolphin, & their guest, Miss Oliver, & Miss E. Jeaffreson.* 8 Sep., 17 Oct., 20 Oct.

1827: 24 Apr., 5 Jun: *We dined at Mr. Jeaffreson's at Longborough, ... and two neices of Mr. Jeaffreson, daughters to an eminent surgeon at Islington; the elder a very elegant looking girl with much expression of countenance and the look of intellect & talent, is engaged to Christopher Jeaffreson Junr. an East India Chaplain: the Miss Jeaffresons of Longborough and their youngest brother formed the party.* 9 Jul., 11 Jul., 26 Aug: *I went to officiate at Longborough in the room of Mr. Hurd; who was engaged to assist Mr. Jeaffreson, now absent on a tour to Paris. Mr. Hurd secured my services yesterday, that he might himself be at liberty to take Mr. R. Wynniatt's duties at Staunton and Snowshill, Mr. W. being at present indisposed.* 2 Oct., 12 Oct: *Mr. Jeaffreson came by appointment to breakfast with us, and accompanied me to the Petty Sessions at Northleach Bridewell.*

1828: 12 Feb., 14 Apr: *I left home in the phaeton accompanied by my friend Mr. Jeaffreson for Gloucester.* 15 Apr., 17 Apr., 18 Apr: *Mr. Jeaffreson hurried home to Longborough, it being announced to him, that his Son, a Chaplain in the East India Company's service, was just arrived on leave of absence. His return at this time, with a view to form a matrimonial connection with a cousin, who won his heart before he repaired to India seven years ago, was anticipated. Mr. Chr. Jeaffreson was at one time curate of Moreton, & relinquished that situation in consequence of his evangelical bias, strongly contrasted with the opinions of his Rector, Dr. Warneford.* 15 Jul., 17-18 Jul., 27 Sep., 1 Oct., 8 Oct: *My wife and I dined at Mrs. Hastings's, meeting a large party, Mr. & Mrs. Jeaffreson, and their youngest son.* 17 Dec.

1829: 12 Aug., 18-19 Sep., 22-23 Sep., 6 Oct., 5 Nov., 13 Nov: *We dined at Mr. Jeaffreson's at Longborough and met Mr. & Miss Villers, now visiting there.*

1830: 18 Jan: *One of the hardest frosts & coldest days of this severe winter. Three youths about Edward's age came to dine with him, & slept here. Mr. S. Jeaffreson, son of my friend, the Rector of Longborough, & private pupil to Mr. Dean of Collwall, Herefordshire.... Capt. Witts, & I was accessory to the placing of young Jeaffreson under his tuition.* 10 May, 26 May: *We entertained some of our neighbours at dinner today—Mrs. & Miss Leigh from Broadwell (Mr. E. Leigh was absent in London;) Mr. & Mrs. Jeaffreson; Mr. & Mrs. M. Vavasour & Mr. Winter.*

1831: 11 Dec.

1833: 17 Oct: *To Stow; attended at the Provident Bank, and in the Justice Room: Mr. Jeaffreson my Colleague on the bench.* 25 Oct: *I was assisted during the whole sitting, from one to nearly five o'clock by Mr. Jeaffreson.* 30 Oct: *Dined at Mr. Jeaffreson's, at Longborough.* 31 Oct.

1834: 16 Jul: *Rode to Stow to confer with Messrs. Pole, Jeaffreson and Wilkins on some propositions made by the inhabitants of Bourton on the Water and the adjacent villages for the establishment of a police association for that district.* 17 Jul., 18 Jul: *Rode to Stow through very heavy thunder rain to meet Messrs. Ford, Jeaffreson and Pole, and examine evidence in the matter of the pros. against Clifford and Cox for the robbery and murder of F. J. Rens.* 21 Jul: *With Mr. Jeaffreson at Mr. Brooke's pursuing the investigation into the murder of poor Rens.* 24 Jul., 26 Jul., 31 Jul., 7-9 Aug., 19 Aug., 21 Aug., 28 Aug., 13 Sep: *On the 9th Inst. after our departure for Peach Field Lodge, the Clerk of Mr. Croad, the Attorney of Gloucester, who was employed for the defence of Clifford and Cox, the prisoners committed by myself and other Magistrates on suspicion of the murder of the late F. J. Rens, called to deliver a notice of action against Messrs. Ford, Jeaffreson and myself for false imprisonment, with a letter from Mr. Croad.* 18-19 Sep., 22 Sep: *Mr. Jeaffreson arrived here to breakfast, in order to accompany me to Bourton on the Water, by appointment, to confer with Mr. Ford respecting the prosecution threatened against us by Mr. Croad as Attorney for Clifford.* 30 Sep., 2 Oct., 9 Oct., 19 Oct: *A note from Vavasour to inform me that formal notices on Croad to discontinue the Prosecution against Ford, Jeaffreson and myself had been signed by Cox and Clifford and forwarded to Gloucester by the Post yesterday.* 23 Oct: *Rode to Stow to attend to the business of the Provident Bank, and in the Justice room. Messrs. Pole, Ford and the Dean of Gloucester met me; much business was transacted. Jeaffreson detained at home by indisposition; I had a letter from him on the subject of the Prosecution menaced by Croad, and on other matters.* 27 Oct., 30 Oct., 6 Nov., 11 Nov: *Received a letter from Mr. Jeaffreson, written on behalf of the bench of Magistrates at Moreton.* 13 Nov., 20 Nov., 27 Nov., 4 Dec: *Walked to Stow, to attend to my weekly duties there in the Provident Bank Office, and Justice room. In the latter Mr. Jeaffreson was my only colleague.* 18 Dec., 20 Dec., 24 Dec: *A note arrived from Mr. Baillie couched in rounded terms of general assurance that he had not meant in what he had said any imputation against my honour or integrity ... I submitted the note to Mr. Pole, W. B. Pole, Billingsley and Jeaffreson.* 26 Dec.

1835: 1 Jan: *At a later hour, Mr. Talbot and Winter laid on the table in the Prov. Bank office a paper to which they affixed their signature, and which, subsequently, was signed by Mr. Jeaffreson, to the effect that, having read with attention a correspondence between Messrs. Witts and Baillie ...* 15 Jan., 17 Jan: *I subsequently ascertained, that, after what had passed between Mr. Ford and myself on Thursday last, which had been, doubtless, reported to him, he had consulted Mr. Jeaffreson, who had given it as his opinion that Baillie must tender the most ample apology.* 22 Jan: *I received, while at Stow, a long letter from Mr. Jeaffreson, who is detained at Longborough by indisposition, in which he enters into the detail of various correspondence and interviews between himself, Messrs. Ford and Baillie on the subject of the late unpleasant controversy.* 23 Jan., 31 Jan., 2 Feb., 19 Mar., 22-23 Mar., 2 Apr., 4 Apr., 23 Apr., 7 May, 13 May, 21 May, 28 May, 4 Jun., 6 Jun., 17 Jun., 18 Jun.

1836: 28 Jul., 4 Aug., 21 Aug: *Wrote to Mr. Jeaffreson, soliciting him to use his interest with his son, now visiting him, to give his advice as an Oculist, in which capacity he had a high reputation in the East Indies, in the case of my poor parishioner, Benj. Casey, who, within these few days, has been so seriously attacked by an inflammation in his only remaining eye.* 29 Sep., 6 Oct., 3 Nov., 10 Nov., 17 Nov., 22-24 Nov., 28 Nov., 1 Dec., 5 Dec., 8-9 Dec., 15 Dec., 22 Dec.

1837: 16 Jan., 19 Jan., 10 Feb: *A letter from Jeaffreson, brought by the Clerk of Longborough, inclosing two letters having reference to a charge of misconduct preferred against W. Bennett, our subordinate Policeman, in respect of certain discreditable transactions of his in London, before he was detached to Stow.* 11 Feb., 12 Feb: *I was obliged to omit Evening Prayers at Slaughter, that I might assist poor Mr. Jeaffreson at Longborough, whither I drove in the open carriage.* 6 Apr., 13 Apr., 19 Apr., 21 Apr., 24 Aug: *To the Savings Bank and to Brookes's office: at the former met Jeaffreson, recently returned to Longborough, in poor health, and very anxious about his wife, who is in a declining state.* 31 Aug., 5 Sep., 14 Sep., 21 Sep., 26 Sep., 26-28 Sep., 12 Oct., 9 Nov., 16 Nov., 9 Dec., 12 Dec: *A note from Mr. Jeaffreson in answer to mine of the 9th. Inst. from which it appears doubtful whether his state of health will allow him to meet Mr. Ford & me to-morrow.*

1838: 18 Jan., 28 Jan., 1 Feb., 5 Feb., 8 Feb., 14-15 Feb., 19 Feb., 22 Feb., 1 Mar., 8 Mar., 15 Mar., 29 Mar., 29 Mar., 5 Apr., 25 Apr: *A very indifferent account of the health of our friend Jeaffreson, who had been in considerable danger, in so much that Dr. Baron was called in from Cheltenham, though he was attended by his son, Dr. S.J. and Roberts the Apothecary at Moreton.* 27 Jul., 31 Aug: *The engagements of Mr. Pole, the only other Mag. in the division, for Mr. Jeaffreson's increasing ill health almost wholly incapacitates him from attendance, preclude me from having any supporter or moderator on whose attendance I could rely.* 26 Sep., 24-25 Dec.

1839: 17 Jan., 27 May: *Rode to Longborough to call on Mr. and Mrs. Jeaffreson, who are returned after a long protracted absence. Found them both, and, especially Mr. J. great invalids, he is suffering under severe inward spasmodic attacks, which at near three score and ten medicine will not controul or subdue: it remains to be proved whether the mischief is functional or organic: he is weak in strength, and depressed in spirits.* 28 Jun: *To Mr. Jeaffreson, to request to be informed of the address of his son, the Oculist, that I might communicate it to Capt. Witts; poor Mrs. W., almost dark, still hoping against hope, and, though, from general ill health, almost unequal to be moved, clinging to the delusion that relief may still be had by consulting some new practitioner, of whom men speak favourably.* 6 Jul: *Recd. a letter from Jeaffreson in reply to mine addressed to him on the 28th. Ult. He and Mrs. J. are now at Cheltenham, vainly, I fear, seeking for renovation of health and strength. His Son, the East India Chaplain, is just returned to England, on the retiring allowance, and will, probably, discharge those clerical duties at Longborough, which, for a long time past, thro' the long indisposition of the Vicar, and partly through his failure in appointing a permanent substitute during his absence, have been sadly neglected.* 7 Jul.

1840: 1 Aug: *thence to Longborough Vicarage, to call on the Curate and his Lady, who came to reside there six weeks ago: his name is Bushnell; Mr. Jeaffreson gave him a title for Deacon's orders, but he appears much above 23 years of age, and has a child of more than three years old. He appears a sensible man with collected manner; his lady, being indisposed, did not appear. The Jeaffresons are travelling about, and now, I believe, with their youngest son, the Physician, at Grantham. From Mr. B's account, as from others, it would seem that Mr. and Mrs. J. are both in very declining health, and the former never likely to be equal to any kind of active duty.* 2 Oct: *Wrote to Mr. Jeaffreson, addressing him at his son's, Dr. Jeaffreson's, at Grantham, where, I believe, he and Mrs. J. are, in bad health, suggesting to him that, if, as is expected, Mr. Bushnell should relinquish the Curacy of Longborough, on the plea that the place does not agree with his wife, Mr. Massie would be an eligible successor to Mr. B.* 13 Oct: *Recd. a letter from Mr. Jeaffreson in reply to one which I wrote to him on the 2d. Inst. It is dated from a place in Suffolk, where he and Mrs. J. are staying: both invalids, her mind as well as body decaying. It appears that he has made an arrangement as to the service of the church at Longborough, which may last for some months; afterwards all is uncertain, but at a future time the curacy may suit Massie, if he be disengaged and disposed to take it.* 18 Oct.

1842: 4 Mar: *To Jeaffreson, who had written to Vavasour to ask me in his name to dine with him on Tuesday next, to excuse myself, as Apphia Witts will be our guest at that time; to apologize, on the ground of having been without horses, for not having called upon him since his return to Longborough; and to express the regret I have felt at his uneasiness with respect to his relations towards his Curate, parishioners, servant & others, causing much strife and angry feeling, and advising him, in consideration of his impaired health and spirits, to come to some fixed and definite arrangements, whereby he might avoid the responsibility of parochial engagements, and live at ease.* 29 Mar: *Rode to Longborough; called on Mr. Jeaffreson, whom I found in a low, nervous, hypochondriac state, with weakness incident to his advanced age, and suffering from indigestion.* 27 Apr: *Of these all were of the dinner party, except Mr. Ross.—Mr. Wollaston, of Farmington, presided, Mr. Ford, Mr. Malcolm, Mr. Lewis, Mr. Winter, Mr. Bowen, Mr. Perkins, Mr. Billingsley, Mr. Underwood, Dr. Twisleton, Mr. Griffin, Mr. Jeaffreson, Mr. Vavasour and myself made up the party.* 6 Jun: *Mr. and Mrs. Franks, with their children, Dr. Twisleton & his children, and Mrs. Kemball (daughter of Mr. Jeaffreson) were with ourselves the occupants of Mrs. Clark's windows.* 26 Jul., 27 Aug: *A letter from Mr. Jeaffreson, now at Grantham, in reference to a candidate for the vacant place of Rel. Off. of our Union.*

1844: 23 Apr: *Went out with Bowen in the phaeton to call on Mr. Jeaffreson at Longborough.* 19 Aug: *Mr. Shelton called to ask me to visit Mr. Jeaffreson before he leaves Longborough for town; he expresses a desire to see me on business relating to his living in Suffolk, but, probably, desires to confer with me about the controversy between him and his curate, which has been brought under the notice of the Bishop, and, by his directions, investigated by the Rural dean.* 20 Aug: *Drove to Longborough—called on Mr. Jeaffreson,—a wreck of his former self, greatly worn out, a valetudinarian, wanting firmness and decision, to whom all is a burden, yet retaining his faculties, and acutely feeling what disturbs him.* 5 Sep., 7 Sep: *From Mr. Griffin a very long, strange, bitter, sweet, canting, complaining letter, representing his case, or, at least, his view of the controversy between himself and his vicar, and the injuries done to him by the Vicar and the Rural dean, bespeaking my interference to restore peace, as it would seem, by prevailing on Jeaffreson to leave Longborough for ever, and Griffin in sole charge of the Parish—I shall not interfere, and shall state as much to him in reply to his letter.* 11 Sep., 27 Sep: *Wrote to Mr. Jeaffreson, now in town, to acknowledge, in the name of our Book Society, and as its Secretary, a compliment paid by his son William, an oculist, of some note, practising in London, in sending a copy of a work lately published by him on the eye, to remain on the standing list of the Society.* 11 Oct., 17 Oct., 22 Oct., 24 Oct., 28 Oct., 5 Nov: *Recd. a letter from Mr. Griffin in answer to my last to him, but not a reply to the question proposed: rather an attempt to induce me to interpose in the matters at issue between him and Mr. Jeaffreson, with a request that I would meet him to-morrow at the Chancellor's visitation at Stow to be present at an interview which he expects to have with Mr. Holt, the Bishop's Secretary.*

1845: 20 Mar: *there is a probability that, on the decease of Mr. Jeaffreson, an arrangement may be made by the concurrence of Lord Leigh, between Mr. Dryden, and Mr. Morrison, to whom it is arranged that Longborough shall be presented when it becomes vacant*

JEAFFRESON — Christopher Jeaffreson [18]

Christopher Jeaffreson (±1794-1870), Church of England clergyman, son of Christopher Baldrey Jeaffreson (*above*), was educated, like his father, at Pembroke College, Cambridge (BA 1816; MA 1828). He was a chaplain to the HEIC, serving at Quilon in 1821-28, Kamptee in 1829-37, Jaulnah in 1837-38, and Cannanore in 1838-39. He retired from the HEIC in 1839, and served as chaplain to Edmonton Union, Middlesex, in 1842-70.

1839: 6 Jul: *Recd. a letter from Jeaffreson in reply to mine addressed to him on the 28th. Ult. He and Mrs. J. are now at Cheltenham, vainly, I fear, seeking for renovation of health and strength. His Son, the East India Chaplain, is just returned to England, on the retiring allowance, and will, probably, discharge those clerical duties at Longborough, which, for a long time past, thro' the long indisposition of the Vicar, and partly through his failure in appointing a permanent substitute during his absence, have been sadly neglected.*

JEAFFRESON — Samuel John Jeaffreson [19]

Samuel John Jeaffreson (±1811-1870), physician, was the youngest son of Christopher Baldrey Jeaffreson (*above*). He was also educated at Pembroke College, Cambridge (MB 1835; Med. Lic. 1836; MD 1865; LRCP 1838; FRCP 1848). He was senior physician to the Chelsea, Brompton, and Belgrave dispensaries, and practised in Half Moon Street, Piccadilly, in 1845, and at Leamington in 1850-70. He married, 1838, Sophia Kenney.

1834: 8 Aug: *Examined two new witnesses, Lane and his housekeeper, whose testimony strengthens the case; saw others of the witnesses, arranged the order of the evidence, and decided on those who should be taken to Gloucester for the prosecution, amounting in all to forty two. Messrs. Vavasour, S. Jeaffreson, Winter and H. Rice were also present.* 21 Aug., 19 Sep.

1837: 14 Sep., 26-27 Sep., 23 Dec: *Dr. Jeaffreson and the men Servants of his Father & Mr. Scott attended to substantiate the case against them.* 28 Dec.

1838: 25 Apr: *A very indifferent account of the health of our friend Jeaffreson, who had been in considerable danger, in so much that Dr. Baron was called in from Cheltenham, though he was attended by his son, Dr. S.J. and Roberts the Apothecary at Moreton.* 24 Dec: *Mr. & Mrs. J. are now in town—his youngest Son, Dr. Jeaffreson, lately settled as a Physician at Gainsborough or Grantham, with fair prospects, is just married to a poor Miss Kenny, a daughter of a literary man, author of some dramatic pieces: the young lady was Governess in Chandos Leigh's family abroad, when S. Jeaffreson travelled with him as domestic Physician.*

1840: 1 Aug: *thence to Longborough Vicarage, to call on the Curate and his Lady, who came to reside there six weeks ago: his name is Bushnell; Mr. Jeaffreson gave him a title for Deacon's orders, but he appears much above 23 years of age, and has a child of more than three years old. He appears a sensible man with collected manner; his lady, being indisposed, did not appear. The Jeaffresons are travelling about, and now, I believe, with their youngest son, the Physician, at Grantham. From Mr. B's account, as from others, it would seem that Mr. and Mrs. J. are both in very declining health, and the former never likely to be equal to any kind of active duty.* 2 Oct: *Wrote to Mr. Jeaffreson, addressing him at his son's, Dr. Jeaffreson's, at Grantham, where, I believe, he and Mrs. J. are, in bad health, suggesting to him that, if, as is expected, Mr. Bushnell should relinquish the Curacy of Longborough, on the plea that the place does not agree with his wife, Mr. Massie would be an eligible successor to Mr. B.*

JEAFFRESON — William Jeaffreson [20]

William Jeaffreson (±1798-1865), physician, was the second son of Christopher Baldrey Jeaffreson (*above*). He was ophthalmic surgeon to the HEIC on their Bombay, Malabar, and China establishments. From January 1824 to October 1834 he was presented with 53,359 cases of every class of opthalmia. Of these cases, 8,680 he did not treat, having classified them as incurable; 36,564 he restored to perfect sight by operation and other treatment; 8,108 he restored to a useful degree of sight, or relieved; and only seven of this vast number died of fungus haematoides. The number included 67 cases of persons born blind, and many others who had suffered blindness from the ages of 5 to 20 years. In addition to these cases, Jeaffreson oversaw the successful or partially successful treatment of 2,300 people for deafness, and the treatment, by operation or otherwise, of 37,500 cases of other diseases. In recognition of his services, the natives presented him with a service of plate worth 300 guineas.

In 1851 Jeaffreson was no longer practising and by 1861 he was retired and living as a lodger at 21 South Audley Street, London.

1837: 12 Feb: *Such is the opinion of her son William, a Surgeon, now at Longborough.*

1839: 16 Jul: *Wrote to Capt. Witts, giving him the address of Mr. W. Jeaffreson, the Oculist, and adverting to matters mentioned in his Sister's letter to MW. recd. on the 14th.*

1844: 27 Sep: *Wrote to Mr. Jeaffreson, now in town, to acknowledge, in the name of our Book Society, and as its Secretary, a compliment paid by his son William, an oculist, of some note, practising in London, in sending a copy of a work lately published by him on the eye, to remain on the standing list of the Society.*

JEBB — John Jebb [21]

John Jebb (1805-1886), Church of England clergyman and writer on church music, was born in Dublin, the eldest son of Mr Justice Richard Jebb and Jane Louisa Finlay. He was nephew of John Jebb, bishop of Limerick. Jebb was educated at Winchester College and Trinity College, Dublin (MA 1829). Following a brief spell as rector of Dunerlin in Ireland, he became a prebendary of Limerick Cathedral in 1832. He then became rector of Peterstow, Herefordshire, in 1843, a prebendary of Hereford Cathedral in 1858, and a canon residentiary in 1870. He married, September 1831, Frances (d. 1866), daughter of Gen. Sir Richard Bourke.

Jebb was a leading authority on the Anglican choral tradition and a significant figure in the English choral revival. When in 1841 Walter Hook, vicar of Leeds, proposed to reinstate choral services and a surpliced choir at Leeds parish church, it was to his friend Jebb that he looked for advice. With his cathedral background, Jebb argued that in churches with a choir, the desired musical effect should not be marred by 'the roar of the congregation'. Jebb's policy was first made public in *Three Lectures on the Cathedral Service* (1841). Two years later he published a more scholarly and definitive treatment of the topic, entitled, *The Choral Service of the United Church of England and Ireland* (1843), an enquiry into the low state of service and music provision in cathedrals and collegiate churches.

Jebb funded the building costs of the new rectory at Peterstow and oversaw the restoration of St Peter's church alongside architect Sir George Gilbert Scott. The restoration was completed on 2 July 1866. It also appears that Jebb might have had some involvement in the Hampden controversy; a highly detailed book published in 1849 entitled *A Report of the Case of the Right Rev. R. D. Hampden, D.D.* was written by a Lincoln's Inn barrister named Richard George Webb (1808-1878). It seems likely that Richard was related to John.

1848: 2 Feb: *The Hampden controversy has been vigorously prosecuted.... and Mr. Jebb, an incumbent of the Diocese of Hereford.*

1852: 27 Nov: *To Revd. J. Jebb, Rector of Peterstow near Ross, to ascertain whether in 1849 he had privately baptized and registered a child of Samuel and Elizabeth Grove or Groves now inhabiting this parish, who have applied to me to admit this child into the Church, & to baptize two of their younger children.* 5 Dec.

JEBB — Joshua Jebb[22]

Joshua Jebb (1793-1863), army officer, was born at Walton, Derbyshire. He was commissioned as a 2nd lieutenant in the Royal Engineers in 1812 and served in Canada and the West Indies. In 1838 he was appointed to advise the Home Office on the building of prisons. Parkhurst, a military hospital on the Isle of Wight, was one of the first conversions he supervised; it was turned into a juvenile prison. In 1839 he was made a visitor at Parkhurst. In September of that year Jebb's secondment to the Home Office was put on a more permanent footing; he was relieved of his remaining military duties but retained his rank, and was promoted to major in 1841 and lieutenant-colonel in 1847. Much of Jebb's early work for the Home Office concerned the construction of Pentonville, a new penitentiary which opened in 1842. Upon completion, he was appointed as one of its commissioners. Two years later Jebb was appointed to the newly created position of surveyor-general of prisons, which came with a wide remit. He was responsible for the conversion and construction of government prisons, and was consulted thereon by local authorities; in this regard he published *Modern Prisons: their Construction and Ventilation*. His position also carried some responsibility for prison administration. Local authorities also sought his advice on much wider issues of punishment.

1843: 9 Oct: *The object of the Committee meeting to day, was to examine the plans for the enlargement of the County Gaol, its improvement, and the enlargement and improvement of the Houses of correction, so as to make them suitable for the new systems and rules of prison discipline, so urgently pressed by the Government,—those plans being prepared by Mr. Fuljames, and approved by Major Jebb, an officer of Engineers employed by Government in superintending the construction or adaptation of prisons.* 17 Oct.

1844: 2 Jan., 30 Dec.

1847: 18 May.

JEENS — Henry Morland Jeens[23]

Henry Morland Jeens (1807-1872), clothier, was born at Uley, Gloucestershire, son of Joseph William Jeens
(1781-1838) and Mary Hodges (1781-1824). Jeens weathered the difficult times that had seen the downfall of the prosperous Uley clothier Edward Sheppard, but he finally succumbed to the continued downturn in trade; on 8 February 1842, he was registered as insolvent. By 1851 he had been appointed clerk to the county prison. The diarist in his comment is being unfair and showing his tory colours; the whigs supported Jeens in his appointment. Bearing in mind his own father's misfortunes, the term 'broken' might have been replaced with a kinder word.

Jeens married Maria Hinton (1809-1854); they had at least 5 sons and 3 daughters, but some are missing from the following list:

1 Mary M. (b. ±1830)
2 Hannah M. (b. ±1832)
3 Emily C. (b. ±1835)
1 John William (1838-1910)
2 Thomas Edward (b. 1839)
3 Octavius Brown (b. 1842)
4 William (b. 1842)
5 George Frederick (b. 1843)

1847: 18 May: *But as to the appointment of Clerk and Deputy Governor of Gloucester Gaol there was no such unanimity: the Lord Lieut. and his tail were bent on bringing in a broken Clothier of Uley, one Jeens, who was supported by a long list of sponsors, testifying to his talent, integrity, familiarity with accounts &c.* 29 May, 28 Jun.

JEFFERIS — Mr Jefferis, a guest of B. P. Witts at Champion Hill

1801: 15 May: *I had the pleasure of being introduced to Mr Jefferis, a very well informed & public spirited man, with his wife, son, & two daughters.*

JEFFERSON — Anna Mervynia Dunnington Jefferson[24]

Anna Mervynia Dunnington Jefferson, née Vavasour (1812-1898) was the daughter of Lt-Gen. Sir Henry Maghull Mervyn Vavasour, 2nd baronet. Anna married, 1839, Joseph Dunnington Jefferson (1807-1880), vicar of Thorganby, 1832-80. He was born Dunnington, but assumed the additional surname by royal licence in 1841. He became a prebendary of York in 1852, and was responsible for building Thicket Priory in the 1840s and developing its 150-acre park. He controlled 7,278 acres with a combined rental of nearly £11,000. In addition, he held over 500 acres in the West Riding which drew in over £1,000.

1847: 13 Jul: *To Maugersbury House, where found the W. Vavasours at home, with Emma, who is lately returned from visits to Lady Styles at Chester, and Mrs. Donnington Jefferson in Yorkshire.*

1853: 20 Mar: *She has heard from her Brother, Sir Henry Vavasour, that, as to her share of the old Vavasour estate at Spaldington, Mrs. Campbell has left to him one moiety, and the other equally divided between his three sisters, Mrs. Jefferson, Mrs. W. Vavasour, &c. Mrs. Whitehall Dod.*

JEFFREY — Edwin Jeffrey[25]

Edwin Jeffrey (±1814-1835), carter at Stow-on-the-Wold. Little is known of Edwin Jeffrey and his brother John. A John Jeffrey, probably the father of the two brothers, died at Stow-on-the-Wold in 1838. John Jeffrey (junior) may have died in 1849 or 1851 as there are death records at Stow-on-the-Wold in both years for a person of that name.

Edwin was employed as a carter by Stow butcher Richard Ellis (±1798-1873). He was executed on 15 April 1835 for the murder of François J. Rens, an immigrant from the Low Countries who had been living at Stow-on-the-Wold since December 1828. Francis Witts had been introduced to Mr Rens by Charles Pole, who also had Dutch family connections. Witts made an error in 1835, writing 'Edmund' instead of 'Edwin'.

1834: 26 Sep: *Mr. Pole had set the Police Officers in motion, & they had secured one Edwin Jeffrey, Carter to Mr. Ellis, Butcher of Stow, the person who had on Friday the 19th taken Rens's watch, which was now fully identified by Mr. Pain, to Thornton, with whom on Sunday the 21st. he had exchanged it for a trumpery old Pinchbeck watch, not worth ten shillings.* 29 Sep: *I wrote to the Dean of Gloucester to apprize him what had been done as to Edwin Jeffrey, to mention that the reexamination would probably take place on Wednesday, and to request him to attend upon that occasion.* 30 Sep: *It appears that Mr. Ford, actuated by curiosity, and, perhaps, wishing to extract something from the Prisoner, had gone yesterday to the Bridewell & sent for him. In the presence of the Keeper he asked him whether he had any communication to make, to which at first he made no reply, but on Ford's repeating the question, guarding him at the same time against saying anything to prejudice himself, and telling him that he could not hold out any promise of favour or benefit to him, the prisoner trembled exceedingly, and before Ford could procure writing materials to take down his words burst forth—"Please, Sir, I murdered the poor Gentleman".* 1 Oct: *Wrote to Mr. Bloxsome ... Related to him the apprehension and committal of Edwin Jeffrey.* 8 Oct.

1835: 13 Feb., 18 Feb., 23 Feb., 20 Mar., 2 Apr., 4-5 Apr., 8-9 Apr., 13 Apr: *With Edmund Jeffrey was arraigned a person of the name of Forbes, late an architect at Cheltenham charged with forgery. He pleaded not guilty: not so Edmund Jeffrey.* 14 Apr: *Repaired before breakfast to the Gaol to confer with the Chaplain on the importance of ascertaining from Edmund Jeffrey, whether he really had any accomplice in the murder of poor Rens ... I immediately went to Sir. J. T. Coleridge, communicated with him on the subject, and obtained his written authority that the poor mother and her daughter should have access to the cell of their guilty, but, let us hope, penitent relative.* 15 Apr: *The Execution of poor Edmund Jeffrey took place this forenoon.* 23 Apr: *The bookseller at Stow has published a little pamphlet containing a narrative of the murder of poor Rens, of the consequent investigations, and of the trial and execution of E. Jeffrey.*

JEFFRIES — Miss Jeffries

1834: 8 Mar: *Calls from Miss Jeffreys, and Miss C. Hunt before we left our lodgings in a phaeton for Warwick to return the call of Mr. & Mrs. Boudier.*

1835: 8 Apr: *Engaged afterwards in the transaction of business relating to my Executorship, which took me to call on Miss Jeffries, a lady intimate with Mrs. M. Hunt, and who had lately transacted some matters of minor business for her.* 14 Apr: *Thence I accompanied Mr. Whitcombe to my lodgings, where the Commission for proving the late Mrs. M. Hunt's will was held. Mr. Kempthorne as Vicar of St. Michael's, the parish in which I was a temporary resident, was Commissioner; and, owing to the circumstance that the codicils to the will were not witnessed, it was necessary to prove the handwriting of the Testatrix; this was done by Mr. Whitcombe and Miss Jefferies making affidavit to that effect.* 15 Apr.

JEFFRIES — Mr Jeffries, a friend of Broome Witts, Francis Witts's uncle

1805: 17 Jul: *Tea & a Party at my Aunts dull & tiresome. The Berringtons, Louisa Jones, Mr. Welford & Mr. Jeffries, Fowlkes &c.* 19 Jul: *Mr. Welford & Mr. Jeffry called. Walked with the latter a little.*

JEFFS — Anne Jeffs, housemaid at Eyford House[26]

Anne Jeffs (1824-1883), servant and laundress, was born at Oddington and was in service at Eyford. By 1861 she was living with her widower father, Richard Jeffs, back in her native village. In 1881 she was registered as a laundress, unmarried, living with her brother, Samuel (b. ±1825), an agricultural labourer. She died unmarried.

1850: 26 Oct: *I administered to her, with her housekeeper and personal attendant, the holy communion, and afterwards witnessed her signature of a second codicil to her will, Anne Jeffs, housemaid, of an Oddington family, being the other witness.*

JELLICOE — Emma Carter Jellicoe — *see also* Jodrell[27]

Emma Carter Jellicoe (1806-1869) was born in London, daughter of Joseph Jellicoe (1769-1851), of Finchley, Middlesex, and Charlotte (1781-1823), daughter of Egerton Leigh and Elizabeth Jodrell. She married, at Holy Trinity church, Marylebone, Westminster, 26 March 1836, Thomas Maltby (1794-1866); they had 1 son and 1 daughter:

1 Henrietta Emma (1848-1918)
1 Thomas Crichton Maltby (1850-1924)

In 1851 the family lived at 84 Acre Lane, Brixton, with two infant children. Thomas was listed as secretary of Royal Copper Mines. In 1861 the family lived at 2 Brunswick Terrace, Lambeth. Thomas (junior) emigrated to New Zealand in 1874.

1829: 5 Nov: *We dined at Mr. Leigh's at Broadwell, meeting Mr. & Mrs. Ford, Mr. & Mrs. Jeaffreson, & Mr. Hall. Mrs. Ford brought three of her daughters, too young yet to join the party at the dinner table. A niece of Mr. Leigh's, daughter of his deceased sister, Mrs. Jellicoe, is staying at Broadwell.*

JENKINS — John Edwin Jenkins[28]

John Edwin Jenkins (1828-1892), medical assistant, surgeon, and general practitioner, was born at Ashy-de-la-Zouch, Leicestershire. He lodged at Sheep Street, Stow-on-the-Wold, with Mary Hayward, mother of physician George Bulley Hayward. He married, at Stow-on-the-Wold, 6 February 1853, Alice Arthurs (b. 1832); they had 3 sons and 3 daughters:

1 Elizabeth Barker (b. 1855)
1 John Edwin (b. 1856)
2 Wilfred Bosworth (1857-1936)
2 Alice Editha (b. 1858)
3 Annie Cordelia (b. 1860)
3 Wilton Bernard (b. & d. 1861)

Jenkins left Stow at some point after 1861, and by 1871 he was a surgeon and general practitioner at Hunslet, Leeds.

1852: 30 Feb: *Police Constables Ford and Coates, were the most material witnesses: Mr. Jenkins, Mr. Hayward's assistant, gave evidence as to the wound and as to the cause of death.*

JENKINS — Stivard Jenkins — *see also* Beale Browne[29]

Stivard Jenkins (1766-1842), Church of England clergyman, was born at Berkeley, Gloucestershire, son of John Jenkins. He was educated at Trinity College, Oxford (BCL 1793), and was ordained deacon on 25 September 1792 and priest on 1 June 1794. His first clerical appointment was as curate of Laverstoke, Hampshire, from 5 March 1792. He was later appointed stipendiary curate at Weston-super-Mare, Somerset, on 17 March 1814, and assistant stipendiary curate of Congresbury, Somerset, on 3 November 1826. He finally served as vicar of Locking, Somerset, in 1833-42.

1840: 20 Nov: *Rode to Salperton to call on the Browne family. Received by Mrs. Browne, by whom I was introduced to her daughter in law, Mrs. Beale Browne, a very pleasing, elegant, well looking and agreeable young person. Tom has, apparently, been fortunate in the connection he has made: the lady had a pretty fortune, and is well connected, being a daughter of a Gentleman of the name of Sullivan, resident at Wilbury in Wilts. Her Mother was a Miss Jenkins, daughter of the Revd. Stiverd Jenkins of Locking, Somerset, and was at one time greatly admired by my poor deceased friend Dowell, then Vicar of Locking.*

JENKINS — William Jenkins[30]

William Jenkins (±1783-1856), Church of England clergyman, was born at Sidbury, Devon, son of Revd William Jenkins (1749-1821) and Mary Pearse (1765-1826). He was educated at Oriel College, Oxford (BA 1805; MA 1808), and ordained deacon on 20 December 1806 and priest on 20 December 1807. His first recorded clerical appointment was as curate of Salcombe Regis, Devon, from

13 December 1816. He was then vicar of Sidmouth in 1821-56. He married Mary Banger (b. 1794); they had at least 1 daughter: 1Eleaner Elizabeth (1834-1891)

1804: 29 Jan: *Rode on the outside of the mail as far as Fairford: no company except from Bath to Tetbury, Burge, who from thence proceeded with Jenkins of Oriel in a Post Chaise.*

1806: 19 Mar: *Conversed with Sir. J. Riddell, Priest, More, Trevenen, Micklem, Jenkins.*

JENKINSON — double drum player at the Three Choirs Festival, September 1826

1826: 25 Sep: *I shall set down the terms, on which the principal performers were engaged ... Jenkinson ... £24. 3. 0.*

JENKINSON — John Banks Jenkinson [31]

John Banks Jenkinson (1781-1840), bishop of St David's, was born at Winchester, second son of John Jenkinson (±1734-1805) and Frances (d. 1811), daughter of Rear Adm. John Barker of Guildford. John Jenkinson (senior) was a brother of Charles Jenkinson, 1st earl of Liverpool. He was a colonel in the Army, joint secretary for Ireland, and gentleman usher to Queen Charlotte.

John Banks Jenkinson was educated at Winchester College and Christ Church, Oxford (BA 1804; MA 1807; DD 1817). His advancement in the Church was assisted by his cousin, Prime Minister Robert Banks Jenkinson, 2nd earl of Liverpool. He became prebendary of Worcester on 30 August 1808, rector of Leverington, Cambridgeshire, on 8 July 1812, dean of Worcester on 28 November 1817, and master of St Oswalds, Worcester, on 8 January 1818. He married, 8 April 1813, Frances Augusta (1790-1860), daughter of Augustus Pechell of Berkhamsted, Hertfordshire; they had at least 2 sons and 2 daughters:

1 Frances Sarah (1815-1877); married, at Claines, Worcestershire, 5 July 1849, Henry Brooke Boothby (1818-1893)
1 George Samuel (1817-1892); succeeded his uncle, Sir Charles, as 11th baronet (1855); married, 31 July 1845, Emily Sophia Lyster (d. 1892)
2 John Henry (1823-1914)
2 Augusta Mary Frederica (1826-1910); married, at Great Malvern, Worcestershire, April 1855, Arthur Tower (1817-1877)

1825: 16 May: *Here I learnt the clerical arrangements consequent on the demise of the late Bishop of Salisbury. Dr. Jenkinson, the worthy Dean of Worcester, is promoted to the See of St. David's, vacant by the translation of its bishop Dr. Burgess to that of Salisbury. Dr. Jenkinson is a relative of the Earl of Liverpool: he was educated at Winchester College, & was fellow of New College Xt. Church Oxford, where he was my cotemporary; and where I frequently met him at New College in the Society of my old acquaintance, now deceased, the Revd. R. Odell.*

JENKINSON — Robert Banks Jenkinson [32]

Robert Banks Jenkinson, 2nd earl of Liverpool (1770-1828), prime minister, was the eldest son of Charles Jenkinson, 1st earl of Liverpool (1729-1808), MP, and his first wife, Amelia (1750/51-1770), daughter of William Watts, governor of Fort William and president in council at Bengal.

Jenkinson was styled Lord Hawkesbury in 1796-1803, and was summoned to the House of Lords in his father's barony of Hawkesbury in 1803. He succeeded his father as 2nd earl of Liverpool in 1808. He was MP for Rye in 1790-1803, secretary of state for foreign affairs in 1801-04, for home affairs in 1804-06 and 1807-09, and for war and colonies in 1809-12, and prime minister in 1812-27.

Jenkinson married, first, 25 March 1795, Lady Theodosia Louisa (1767-1821), third daughter of Frederick Augustus Hervey, 4th earl of Bristol. He married secondly, 24 September 1822, Mary (1777-1846), sixth daughter of Revd Charles Chester and niece of Lord Bagot. There were no children of either marriage.

1801: 8 Jun: *on the Ministerial side Mr. Wilberforce seemed to me the best orator: Mr. Abbot, Mr. Addington, Mr. Baker, Mr. Yorke, Mr. Windham, Mr. O'Hare & Lord Hawkesbury chiefly arrested my attention.*

1827: 21 Feb: *The newspapers convey an account of a great public calamity, which has visited the nation in the dangerous illness of the excellent Premier, the Earl of Liverpool. His Lordship was seized with a fit, partly apoplectic & partly paralytic, on Saturday morning last, and though he survives, yet there is little prospect of his recovering sufficiently to hold the high station, which he now occupies in the cabinet. Lord Liverpool has long been delicate in his health, and generally has derived benefit from occasional visits to Bath, whence he has recently returned, and seemed equal to the fatigues of parliament and the busy season of politics.* 14 Apr.

1828: 1 Feb., 6 Dec: *On Thursday Lord Liverpool died, having lingered in a melancholy condition His Lordship was born in 1770; he has left no children, and is succeeded in his title by his half-brother, the Hon. Cecil Jenkinson.*

1836: 12 Jul.

1844: 4 Jun.

JENKYNS — Richard Jenkyns [33]

Richard Jenkyns (1782-1854), Church of England clergyman and master of Balliol College, was born at Evercreech, Somerset, son of Revd John Jenkyns (1753-1824) and Jane Banister (d. 1825). He was educated at Balliol College, Oxford (BA 1804; MA 1806; B&DD 1819), where he was a fellow until 1819, tutor in 1813, bursar in 1814, master of the school in 1819, and master of the college in 1819-54. Jenkyns was ordained deacon on 2 December 1805 and priest on 21 December 1806. He was vicar of Evercreech with Chesterblade from 2 January 1822 to 16 July 1825. He was also prebendary of Wells Cathedral, prebend of Dinder (appointed 20 August 1824), and dean of Wells in 1845.

Richard Jenkyns married, at Clifton, Gloucestershire, 23 April 1835, Troth Grove (1791-1857). There do not appear to have been any children.

1832: 14 Mar: *A miserably wet day, raining and snowing from the forenoon till night. Breakfasted with my son in his rooms, and proceeded after writing a letter or two to pay a morning visit to my old acquaintance, Dr. Jenkyns, the Master of Balliol College.*

JENNER — Mr Jenner, a guest of Mrs Auriol

1806: 4 Feb: *Supped at Mrs. J. Auriol's; besides ourselves, the Lady & her Husband, Gillisbrand, the notorious Mr. Stackpole & his wife & a Mr. Jenner formed the party.*

JENNER — Edward Jenner [34]

Edward Anthony Jenner (1749-1823), surgeon and pioneer of smallpox vaccination, was born at the vicarage, Berkeley, Gloucestershire, the fourth son and eighth of nine children of Revd Stephen Jenner (1702-1754), vicar of Berkeley, and Sarah

(1709-1754), daughter of Revd Henry Head and his wife, Mary, of Berkeley. He was educated at Wotton-under-Edge and Cirencester Grammar School. From 1763 his education turned towards medicine when he began training with Daniel Ludlow, an apothecary in Chipping Sodbury; in August the following year he was apprenticed to George Hardwicke of Sodbury. John Hunter (1728-1793) was the greatest influence on Jenner's career; he trained with him as a private pupil and student at St George's Hospital, London, in 1770-72. In addition to receiving invaluable training there, Jenner made important contacts at St George's with the likes of Joseph Banks, later president of the Royal Society, Everard Home, and Henry Cline. On his return to Berkeley in 1772, he set up in general practice, living first with his brother Stephen. He married, 1788, Catherine (1761-1815), daughter of Robert Fitzhardinge Kingscote of Kingscote, near Dursley; they had 2 sons and 1 daughter:

1 Edward (1789-1810)
1 Catherine (1794-1833)
2 Robert Fitzhardinge (1797-1854); *see below*

Jenner had a modest private income and was well connected, belonging to the minor landed gentry. His contacts through Lord Berkeley and the Kingscote family strengthened his social position in his immediate neighbourhood, while Hunter and Banks provided contacts in London and Cheltenham. His qualifications and status ensured him a distinguished clientele, inclusive of numerous members of the aristocracy. He fitted well into fashionable life in Cheltenham, where he was founder and first president of the Cheltenham Literary and Philosophical Society.

Before Jenner introduced vaccination, smallpox could be prevented by variolation, the deliberate inoculation of matter from smallpox pustules into the skin in the hope that a mild but protective infection would result. Jenner, an experienced variolator, had unpleasant memories of his own variolation and became interested in safer alternatives. He knew that in rural areas it was commonly believed that those who recovered from cowpox, a mild, localised disease, were rendered immune to natural and inoculated smallpox. In 1789 he and another doctor, John Hickes, inoculated some individuals, including the infant Edward Jenner, with a sample of the disease variously described as swinepox, pigpox, and cowpox.

From 1795 Jenner established a second home in Cheltenham where well-to-do patients of his London colleagues could consult him when they visited the fashionable spa. He performed the first documented cowpox inoculation on 14 May 1796, and very shortly afterwards he inoculated 8-year-old James Phipps with cowpox material taken from a dairymaid. The boy recovered uneventfully, and successfully resisted variolation six weeks later. Jenner was tempted to publish his data at this stage, but was advised informally by the Royal Society that it would harm his reputation to publish such slender evidence. He collected more epidemiological information and conducted more vaccinations, and in 1798 published his results privately in his famous *Inquiry into the causes and effects of the variolae vaccinae a disease ... known by the name of the cow-pox*. The extra vaccinations were the important addition, but their total is not known; Jenner named only ten, though more were performed. He showed that cowpox could be transferred serially by arm-to-arm inoculation, and that the first and last in the series resisted variolation, though as with Phipps, the challenge was made after only a few weeks. At first 'cowpox inoculation' and 'vaccine inoculation' (from *vacca*, 'cow') were used to describe the process, but 'vaccination' soon became the generally accepted term.

Jenner maintained a house in London, but only spent short periods there. He corresponded with and was received by George III, Queen Charlotte, and the prince of Wales. He was received in London by the tsar and the king of Prussia, and corresponded with Napoleon. During the wars with France, letters from Jenner to Napoleon secured the release of English prisoners. He received honours, testimonials, and diplomas from all over the world; shortly before his 72nd birthday, he was made physician-extraordinary to George IV, a purely honorary title.

Jenner served terms as mayor of Berkeley and commissioner of Cheltenham, and as magistrate in both places. He was a freemason by 1804 and served some official role in a Berkeley lodge in 1811. His enjoyment of his new-found fame and social mobility was marred by his increasing concern over his wife's illness. Catherine Jenner died from tuberculosis in 1815 and Jenner spent his remaining years in Berkeley. He had a minor stroke in 1821 but still continued to see patients occasionally, until just before his death.

From a historical perspective, along with Goethe, Edward Jenner was one of the most famous and influential people that Francis Witts knew.

1801: 6 Nov: *Waited also on Miss Hughes, who played & sang to me. Dr. & Mrs. Jenner, the inventor of the Vaccine Pox, & Miss Hughes rendered our Evening very agreeable.* 8 Nov: *In the morning for two Hours with the beneficent Dr. Jenner, inoculating various patients, & receiving a complete lecture upon the subject.* 12 Nov: *Mr. & Mrs. & Miss Markham & Dr. Jenner dined with us upon a Haunch of Venison.* 13 Nov: *In the evening late to a great Rout at Lady Herries, or perhaps Sir Robert's. Conversed much with Dr. Jenner, the Jones's &c.* 15 Nov: *Between Churches at Dr. Jenners inoculations, at Mr. Granvilles, & walking with their party.* 16 Nov: *Conversed much with Jenner.* 18-19 Nov.

1802: 5 Feb: *Called upon Dr. Jenner.*

1804: 18 Oct: *Walked with Cressy Jones, Louisa, Dr. Jenner, &c. &c.*

1823: 28 Jan: *Learnt the news of the sudden death of the eminent Dr. Jenner, the discoverer of vaccination, which happened at Berkley on the 26th. Apoplexy was the malady, which quickly terminated his useful life at the age of 74. He was a man of distinguished talents, an original thinker, some times rather eccentric, but always kind hearted. I had known him for more than twenty years, and had frequently benefited by his intelligent and instructive conversation.*

1825: 9 Nov: *Mr. Sievier is the Sculptor employed to design and execute the two monuments now erecting in the Cathedral to Sir G. Paul & Dr. Jenner. He was, I am told, bred up an engraver, & has only of late turned his talents to the art of sculpture.*

1826: 31 Aug: *Between the Inn and the castle is the house of the late Dr. Jenner, the Benefactor of mankind, who began & closed his career in this place; it is now the occasional residence of his son, a dissipated man, who has left all the baneful influence of the contiguity to the Castle & its unprincipled owner.... I noticed also a miniature of Dr. Jenner, an excellent likeness.*

JENNER — Robert Fitzhardinge Jenner[35]

Robert Fitzhardinge Jenner (1797-1854), JP and landed proprietor, was the second son of Edward Anthony Jenner and Catherine Kingscote (*above*). In 1818 he was made a freeman of the City of Gloucester. He was a Gloucestershire JP and gained the rank of lieutenant-colonel in the Gloucestershire Militia. He does not appear to have married nor had any children.

1824: 27 Apr.

1826: 31 Aug: *Between the Inn and the castle is the house of the late Dr. Jenner, the Benefactor of mankind, who began & closed his career in this place; it is now the occasional residence of his son, a dissipated man, who has left all the baneful influence of the contiguity to the Castle & its unprincipled owner.*

1829: 13 Jan.

1834: 14 Oct: *An attempt was made to cut down the salary of the Chaplain of the Gaol on the motion of Mr. Jenner seconded by the Revd. Mr. Dunsford, but, the sense of the Court being against the proposition, it was abandoned by the mover after consultation with Lord Segrave, who, probably, had put forward his underlings.*

1837: 17 Oct: *Jenner was selected to advocate the Whig Scheme, which he did lamely, being ill-seconded by Grantley Berkeley, MP. for the Western division.*

1839: 1 Jan.

1840: 20 Oct.

1845: 3 Apr.

1847: 5 Jan., 23 Mar: *It was feared that a party would be made to support the man, but the case was too gross, the Peer threw the Keeper overboard, and Jenner contented himself with not voting for his dismissal.*

JENNER-FUST — **Herbert Jenner-Fust** [36]

Sir Herbert Jenner-Fust (1778-1852), lawyer, was the second son of Robert Jenner, of Chislehurst, Kent, by his second wife, Ann, eldest daughter of Peter Birt of Wenvoe Castle, Glamorganshire. He was educated at Trinity Hall, Cambridge (LLB 1798; LLD 1803), and called to the bar in 1800. He was admitted as an advocate in the ecclesiastical and admiralty courts and as a fellow of the College of Doctors of Law in 1803. In 1828, on the same day, he was both appointed king's advocate-general and knighted by George IV at St James's Palace. He became vicar-general to the archbishop of Canterbury in 1832. He resigned that post and that of advocate-general on 21 October 1834, upon his appointment as official principal of the arches and judge of the prerogative court of Canterbury. On 29 October his name was added to the list of privy counsellors. He assumed the additional surname of Fust in 1842 on succeeding to Hill Court, Gloucestershire, and Capenor Court, Somersetshire, which had belonged to his deceased cousin, Sir John Fust. He married, 1803, Elizabeth (1784-1828), daughter of Lt-Gen. Francis Lascelles.

There were accusations of nepotism and bias involving the Jenner-Fust family. Several of the officers, judges and practitioners in Doctors' Commons were related by family ties. A comment in *The Times* of February 1848 refers to Doctors' Commons as 'an oyster bed where every oyster is called Jenner'.

1830: 31 Jan.

1839: 1 Aug.

1840: 5 May: *I proceeded, accompanied by Messrs. Thrupp and Fielder to Drs. Commons, where we found the Court sitting, Sir Herbert Jenner presiding as Judge, and Dr. Dodson pleading, a quiet, still, family like party, without spectators.*

1850: 10 Jan: *The subject is suggested by the proceedings now before the High Court of appeal (the Privy Council) instituted by the Revd. Gorham against the judgment of the ecclesiastical Judge, Sir H. Jenner Fust, in a case brought before him as to the legality of a decision come to by the Bishop of Exeter, who, having declined to institute Mr. Gorham to a benefice in his diocese.*

JENNINGS — **Joseph Jennings** — *see also* **John Rogers** [37]

Joseph Jennings (1806-1889), architect and agent, was born in Fenchurch Street, London, second son of David Jennings (1753-1819), draper, and Rebecca (1777-1860), daughter of John Rogers and Mary Neal. He was admitted a freeman of the City of London on 28 February 1828.

Joseph Jennings acted for Francis Witts as surveyor and agent for his London properties. He had London offices in Essex Street and a separate residence in Hawkhurst, Kent, as well as a London home at 14 King Street, Portman Square, just off Baker Street. Joseph was married to Elizabeth (1810-1898), daughter of Stephen Wilson and Sarah Lea; they had at least 4 sons and 4 daughters:

1 Julia Rebecca (b. 1838)
1 Newton Edward (1840-1902); married, at St Peter's, Islington, 9 November 1870, Kate Hannah Turker; died at Kensington, Victoria, Australia
2 Cecilia Elizabeth (b. 1842)
2 Herbert John (1844-1917)
3 Arthur (1846-1930); married Lavinia Killigrew Raymond
3 Emily (1847-1929); married Revd Henry Stern
4 Clara Agnes (1850-1913); died unmarried at Sydney, Australia
4 Cecil Frederick (b. 1855)

It is likely that Jennings inherited a family estate in Hawkhurst. His father, David Jennings (d. 1819), wrote *Hawkhurst, a Sketch of its History, &c.* (1792), while his grandfather, also Joseph, had married a daughter of Daniel Neal and Elizabeth Lardner. Elizabeth was the sister of Nathaniel Lardner (1684-1768), a nonconformist divine and biblical and patristic scholar, who was born at The Hall House, Hawkhurst, Kent, on 6 June 1684. Joseph's paternal great-grandfather was David Jennings (1691-1762), a dissenting minister and tutor and the author of *Jewish Antiquities*.

By 1881 Joseph and Elizabeth lived at 2 Grove Hill, Tunbridge Wells, a fashionable part of town. It is not known how Jennings was introduced to Francis Witts. He was first mentioned on 5 August 1834, but there are various gaps in the diaries between 1830 and 1834; he must have started acting as Witts's surveyor during the period covered by one of the missing diaries. However, a tenuous social connection existed before they were introduced. On 2 May 1837 Witts referred to Mr Rogers as Joseph Jennings's uncle, a brother of his mother, Rebecca. This Mr Rogers was a close friend of Francis Witts's late uncle, Broome Witts, and clearly on friendly terms with Broome's sister, Apphia, Lady Lyttelton.

1834: 5 Aug: *Received a letter from Hoares, announcing that Mr. Jennings had paid to my account with them the London Mids. rents.* 6 Aug., 20 Aug: *A letter from Jennings on the subject of a new lease to be granted to Mr. Dixon for the premises which he holds of me in Fenchurch Street.* 31 Aug., 1 Sep: *Wrote to Mr. Jennings, desiring him to confer again with Mr. Dixon, and to intimate to him, that I was not indisposed to extend his lease for three years from Midsummer 1836, on fair terms.* 15 Nov., 17 Nov.

1835: 3 Feb: *Wrote to Mr. Jennings, requesting him out of our London rents payable about this time, to discharge the Tenths of the Rectory of Upper Slaughter, and a bill due to our Fishmongers.* 12-13 Feb., 13-15 May, 9 Jun: *Called at Mr. Jennings' office in Essex Street, Strand, to confer with him about our London houses.* 10 Jun., 21 Aug., 23-24 Aug.

1836: 16 Nov: *A letter from Mr. Jennings with a statement of our Michas. rents from our City Tenants, and apprizing me that he had paid to my acct. with Messrs. Hoare £147. 9. 11.* 8 Dec: *Received a letter from Jennings, who reports to me that the storm of the 29th. Ult., which was peculiarly violent in and about the Metropolis, had injured one of our houses in Fenchurch Street, but not to any considerable extent.* 10 Dec., 23-24 Dec.

1837: 7 Jan., 14 Feb., 16 Feb., 19 Feb., 8 Mar., 10 Mar: *Wrote to Jennings to assent to the proposal of letting to Mr. Dixon the premises now occupied by him from year to year in Fenchurch Street at £180 on an agreement for a lease for four years from the expiration of his late lease.* 2 May: *Wrote to Mr. Rogers to apologise for not having before sent to him and Mrs. R. a copy of the lithograph of Lady L. and to request their acceptance of one which I propose forwarding to Mr. Jennings to be conveyed by him to his Uncle.* 3 May: *Wrote to Mr. Jennings requesting him to forward to Mr. Rogers the two copies of the lithograph of Lady Lyttelton which I had addressed to him.* 21 May, 5 Jun., 16 Aug., 1-2 Sep., 6 Oct., 1 Nov., 23-24 Nov.

1838: 14 Feb., 24 Feb., 26 Feb., 28 Apr., 5 May: *Recd. a letter from Jennings in reply to mine of the 28th. respecting the account with the Newspaper agent, and announcing that one of the London Tenants, Gilson, was backward in paying his rent.* 7 May, 23 May, 25 May, 18 Aug., 25 Aug., 9 Sep: *Recd. a letter from Mr. Jennings acquainting me that our tenant Clarke wishes to transfer the remaining 6½ years of his lease in the house at in Bucklesbury to a Mr. Richardson, who is willing to pay the present rent £100 per ann. for the remainder of the lease, provided he can get a further lease of 21 or 23½ years from the expiration of the present term at £90 per ann.* 28-29 Sep., 7-8 Oct., 10 Oct., 21 Nov., 24 Nov., 26 Nov., 30 Dec: *Recd. a letter from Mr. Jennings, apprizing me that a sewer is being made in Fenchurch Street, and suggesting to me whether it be not expedient that drains be made into it from our two houses in that street.*

1839: 23 Feb., 2 Mar., 4 Mar., 20 Mar: *A letter from Mr. Jennings, inclosing one from Mr. Dixon tenant of one of our houses in Fenchurch Street, who wishes an extension of his lease which ends at Michms. 1840, and a reduction of rent from £180 to £150.* 22-23 Mar., 6 May: *After breakfast called upon Mr. Jennings, whom I find residing in one of the side streets leading out of Baker Street, and was introduced to his wife, late a Miss Wilson.* 8 May: *After breakfast I called on Mr. Jennings, and conferred with him on various points as to our London property.* 8 Jun., 5 Jul: *Recd. a letter from Mr. Jennings with information and advice how to act in respect of Mr. Richardson, one of our tenants in Bucklersbury, who has fallen into embarrassments by over-speculation, and fails in making good the payment of three quarters rent now due. The question is whether to distrain, or to take a warrant of Attorney, or to agree to receive the rent in arrear by monthly instalments. On the whole Mr. Jennings recommends the last course.* 6 Jul., 7 Aug., 14 Aug: *Recd. a letter from Mr. Jennings with a statement of rents recd. from our London Tenants, advice as to the letting of the premises in Fenchurch Street occupied by Mr. Dixon's under-tenants, and as to the arrears owing by Richardson.* 17 Aug.

1840: 20-21 Mar., 31 Mar: *Recd. a letter from Mr. Jennings with the particulars of an agreement he has entered into with a Mr. Paruther for a lease to of the premises No. 50 Fenchurch Street, for 21 years from Midsr. next at £190.* 4 Apr: *Wrote to Mr. Jennings in reply to his letter received on the 31st. Ult., sending up for Mr. Warter's references, and at his desire, the old lease of No. 50 Fenchurch Street to Mr. Dixon, and the existing lease under which Mr. Oliver holds No. 49.* 5 May: *Called on Mr. Jennings, from whom I received satisfactory information respecting our London Tenants.* 27 May, 29 May, 1 Jun., 9 Jun., 12 Aug., 16-17 Aug., 20 Aug., 21 Aug: *To Mr. Jennings requesting him maturely to consider and to give me his full opinion upon any proposition that might be made by the Clothworker's Company for the purchase of our property in Fenchurch Street.* 25 Aug., 27 Aug., 29 Aug., 31 Aug., 23 Oct: *A letter awaited me from Mr. Jennings, to apprize me that one of our London Tenants, Richardson, who is somewhat in arrear of rent, had proposed to his creditors a composition at 5/ in the pound, and requesting to know whether I would come into those terms.* 26 Oct., 21 Nov., 26 Nov., 29 Nov: *Received a letter from Mr. Jennings, inclosing copies of letters from Mr. Perring, Agent to the Clothworkers Company, to Messrs. Parker and Warter, and of the latter to Mr. Jennings; by which it appears that the Clothworkers offer £8100 for our premises in Fenchurch Street.* 1 Dec.

1842: 12 Feb., 1-2 Mar., 15 Mar: *From thence to Mr. Jennings, with whom held a long conference as to the investment of the money to be paid by the Clothworkers company for our houses in Fenchurch Street.* 17 Mar: ... *Jennings was examined as to the Rents of the houses having always been paid to me since my Aunt's decease, also that the sum to be given for the houses in Fenchurch St. by the Clothworkers was so considerable as to make the proposed arrangement very advantageous to the parties interested under my Uncle's will; also that the clauses proposed for giving power to grant longer leases of the Bucklersbury houses would be very beneficial.* 9 Apr., 16 Apr., 19 Apr., 15 May, 22 May, 25 May, 13 Aug., 20 Aug., 22 Aug., 30 Oct., 20 Nov., 22 Nov., 7 Dec: *Received a letter from Mr. Jennings about our London Tenants, one of whom, Gilson, occupying Nos. 5 & 6 Bucklersbury, as a Tavern and Coffee House, is become a bankrupt.* 12 Dec: *also a letter from a Mr. Sole, Solicitor to the Assignees of Mr. Gilson, Tenant of Nos. 5 & 6 Bucklersbury, making certain propositions with reference to G's bankruptcy, and the occupation of those premises, to which I replied.*

1843: 5 Jan: *Recd. a letter from Jennings about the premises in Bucklersbury tenanted by the Bankrupt, Gilson.* 6 Jan., 11 Jan., 14 Jan., 14-15 Feb., 18 Feb: *Also to Mr. Jennings in answer to his letter recd. on the 14th. Recd. from Mr. Warter a letter, accompanying the lease of 5 & 6 Bucklersbury, the London Hotel, occupied by Gilson, now a Bankrupt, and relet to a Mr. Thomas, as tenant to be responsible for the rent, but by whom the premises are underlet to Mr. Gilson, who has obtained his certificate—this lease is sent for my signature, as also a receipt in the matter of Gilson's bankruptcy to be signed by me.* 31 Aug., 1 Sep., 18 Nov., 6 Dec., 8 Dec.

1844: 9 Jan., 14 Feb., 27-28 Feb., 1 Mar., 3-4 Mar., 19 May, 3 Jun., 3 Sep., 11 Sep., 14 Sep., 17 Sep., 17 Nov.

1845: 11 Mar., 13-14 Mar., 19 Mar., 9-10 May, 26 Jun.

1846: 6 Jun., 9 Jun: *Wrote to Mr. Jennings in answer to his letter received on the 6th. Inst. pressing him to look out for an investment in good freehold houses, or ground rents in or near London, for the £9000, the produce of the sale of our houses in Fenchurch Street, now that the treaty for the purchase of the estate at Great Risington is broken off.* 21 Jun: *Recd. a letter from Mr. Jennings as to the purchase of houses or ground rents in or near the Metropolis.* 22 Jun., 25 Aug., 2 Oct., 5 Oct., 2-3 Nov., 11-12 Dec.

1847: 3 Feb: *A letter from Mr. Jennings, as to certain ground rents offered to us for purchase; suggesting that I should come to Town to see and judge of the fitness of any of those which have been offered.* 4 Feb., 5 Feb., 6 Feb: *A letter from Mr. Jennings in answer to mine of Friday last, with some particulars as to other ground rents at Chelsea, and houses, near the Blackwall terminus on sale.* 8 Feb., 10 Feb., 22 Feb: *Wrote to Mr. Jennings expressing my approval of, and concurrence in all that had been arranged as to the purchase of ground rents &c.—between him, my son, and Mr. Warter.* 5-6 Mar., 13 Apr., 17 May: *Wrote to Mr. Warter in answer to his letter received yesterday, desiring him, with the assistance of Mr. Jennings, to endeavour to procure another suitable investment in ground rents or houses, in or near the Metropolis, for the money to be laid out in a purchase to replace the property sold by us in Fenchurch Street.* 19 May: *Received a letter from Mr. Warter, who mentioned that no further correspondence had taken place between him and the Solicitor for the Vendors of the Chelsea ground rents, the price demanded by the latter being higher than Mr. Jennings considered the true value; also that he was not aware whether any thing more had been done as to the houses near the terminus of the Blackwall railway; he talks of again advertizing for ground rents; suggests whether some of our settled Yorkshire property might not be sold to serve as an investment for the produce of the sale of the Fenchurch Street houses &c.* 25 May, 14 Jul., 16 Jul., 23-24 Jul., 28-29 Aug., 1 Sep: *Recd. a letter from Mr. Jennings, announcing that he has, together with Mr. Warter, entered into an agreement on my part for the purchase of the Ground rents in St. George's in the East.* 2-3 Sep., 23 Nov.

1848: 24 Jan., 3-4 Feb., 20 Feb., 24 Mar., 27 Mar., 29 Mar: *Soon after 11 o cl. Mr. Jennings called to accompany me to the "far East," to shew me the property lately purchased in St. Georges in the East. We journeyed thither on foot and in an Omnibus.* 30 Mar: *Wrote to Mr. Jennings, requesting him to colour a plan of the Estate of Mr. Furze in Ground rents in St. George's in the East, as lithographed with the particulars of the property offered for sale by auction, that I might be able to distinguish the portion bought for us, and keep it as a memorandum for reference.* 28 Apr., 29 Jun., 6 Jul., 8 Jul., 30 Sep., 22-23 Oct.

1850: 26 Mar., 9-10 Apr., 18 Sep., 20 Sep., 25 Sep., 28 Sep., 5 Oct., 24 Dec.

1851: 18 Jan., 8 Feb., 10 Feb.

1852: 24 Apr., 30 Apr., 1 May, 8 Jun: *Walked to King Street, Portman Square, & left my card for Mr. Jennings.* 9 Jun: *Mr. Jennings called upon me.* 29 Dec.,

1853: 1 Jan., 6 Jan., 8 Jan., 11 Jan., 26 Mar., 31 May, 4 Jun: *Received from Mr. Jennings, a letter with balance sheets of London rents received; he will be ready to meet me in Town on any day I may appoint next week; and kindly wishes me to visit him and Mrs. Jennings at Hawkhurst in the week following.* 8 Jun: *After breakfast to Mr. Jennings, 14 King Street, Portman Square.* 13 Jun: *Mr. Jennings's open carriage with a servant met me at Etchingham, the distance being four miles and a half to Hawkhurst. The weather was now clearing up, and I could see all the beauty of a well wooded fertile, undulating, populous district. We arrived at our destination by 3 P.M. and I was most hospitably received by Mr. and Mrs. Jennings, who had arrived from Town this morning; rejoining their children and governess; five children were here; one, a boy, is at the King's College School, London; and the eldest daughter at school at Ipswich.—Mr. J. occupies a tasteful cottage on his own property in that part of the parish of Hawkhurst which is called Highgate, being the principal part of the village, at least as to continuity of houses, the Rye turnpike road passing through it. Mr. J's residence is of recent creation; rather too near the road, But from the principal apartments commanding a lovely view, over his own grounds, and estate of between two and three hundred acres.* 14-15 Jun.

1854: 11 Feb., 25 Feb., 7 Mar: *Recd. a letter from Mr. Jennings, who is a candidate for the office of Surveyor to the Merchant Tailor's Company; now vacant, and is anxious that I should use in his favour any influence I may have with Mr. Thrupp, the London Solicitor, who is a member of the Court of that company, and so is one of the parties entitled to vote for the candidates.* 16 Mar., 17 Mar: *To Mr. Jennings a letter testifying to his skill, experience and business habits as Surveyor conversant with London house property—such as he may produce to the Court of the Merchant Tailors Company, at whose hands he seeks the Office of Surveyor.* 27 Mar., 30 Jun., 3 Jul.

JEPHSON — Henry Jephson [38]

Henry Jephson (1798-1878), physician, was born at Sutton-in-Ashfield, Nottinghamshire. He practised at 7 York Terrace, Leamington, and lived at Beech Lawn. He was a popular and celebrated physician locally with a national reputation; he promoted the virtues of Leamington's spa waters and was a generous benefactor to the town. He came to Leamington in 1819 to assist a Dr Chambers, and stayed there for the remainder of his life. In 1847 his health broke down and the following year he went blind; he retired and lived on for a further 31 years. Among his most famous patients were Princess Victoria, the duchess of Kent, George IV, Florence Nightingale, W. E. Gladstone, and John Ruskin.

1840: 17 Jul: *Miss Browne continues a great invalid under the care of the celebrated Dr. Jephson of Leamington.* 20 Nov.

1842: 15 Dec: *Mrs. Browne also is greatly indisposed, and is now at Leamington, consulting the celebrated Dr. Jephson, the idolized of many, the distrusted and depreciated of others, and of no small portion of his own profession—but, doubtless, an able, talented practitioner, albeit somewhat irregular in the arts of killing and curing.*

1843: 20 Jan.

1845: 6 Jan.

1847: 20 May, 12 Aug.

JERRAM — Charles Jerram [39]

Charles Jerram (±1770-1853), Church of England clergyman, was born at Blidworth, Nottinghamshire, son of Charles Jerram (b. 1734) and Mary Knutter. He was educated at Magdalen College, Cambridge (BA 1797; MA 1800). He was curate of Long Sutton, Lincolnshire, in 1797-1805, curate of Chobham, Surrey, in 1805-10, and vicar there in 1810-34. He was then vicar of St John's chapel, Bedford Row, in 1824-26, and finally rector of Witney, Oxfordshire, in 1834-53.

Jerram married, at Tydd St Mary, Lincolnshire, 24 April 1798, Ann Stanger (1775-1864); they had at least 2 sons and 1 daughter:

1 Charles Stanger (1803-1824)
2 Samuel John (1815-1887); married, at Witney, 16 June 1851, Grace de Vere Hunt (1825-1909)
1 Elizabeth Harriet (b. & d. 1817)

1834: 24 Sep: *He spoke in terms of great praise of Mr. Jerram, the new Incumbent of Witney a very zealous, able and devoted Clergyman.*

JERVIS — Charles Jervis [40]

Charles Jervis (1782-1826), Church of England clergyman, was born in Birmingham, son of Charles Jervis (b. 1749) and Sukey Heycocke (b. 1749). He was educated at Trinity College, Oxford (BA 1805; MA 1808), and afterwards served as chaplain to the duke of Cambridge, rector of Luddenham, Kent, in 1813, and perpetual curate of Cheltenham in 1816-26.

Jervis married, at St George's, Hanover Square, 25 April 1817, Maria Grape (1782-1840); they had at least 1 son and 2 daughters:

1 Henry Harcourt (1820-1852); married, at Claines, Worcester, 13 March 1845, Prudence Sill (1814-1870)
1 Mary Frances Elizabeth (1821-1895)
2 Anna Maria (b. 1824)

1823: 4 Nov: *The Bishop of Gloucester this day consecrated the new church dedicated to the Holy Trinity, at Cheltenham: it is in the Gothic Style; the funds for its erection have been, I am told, chiefly supplied by Lord Sherborne; the duty will be performed by Mr. Jervis, the Vicar of Cheltenham, & his curates.* 24 Dec.

1824: 29 Mar: *"Statement of facts and copies of and extracts from letters in reference to the refusal of the Hon. and Right Revd. H. Ryder D.D., late Lord Bishop of Gloucester, and now Bp. of Lichfield and Coventry to licence the Revd. Geo. Bonner L.L.B. as assistant Minister of Trinity Church, Cheltenham. In a letter to a member of the congregation. Cheltenham. 1824." Such is the title of a pamphlet, which has excited much attention in the populous & fashionable town of Cheltenham, where elegant critics of all ages and both sexes are keenly engaged in canvassing the merits of the dispute between Mr. Bonner, Mr. Jervis the Incumbent of the Church, & their late Diocesan.*

1825: 20 May: *This induced him to sell the Advowson, and it fell into the hands of Mr. Simeon and others of Evangelical principles, who faithful to their scheme of placing in public situations clergymen of congenial sentiments to their own fixed at Cheltenham the present incumbent, Mr. Jervis.*

JERVIS-WHITE-JERVIS — John Jervis-White-Jervis [41]

Sir John Jervis-White-Jervis (1765-1830), barrister, was born at Bally Ellis, co. Wexford. He was a barrister in Dublin and in 1793 took the name of Jervis after his own surname by royal licence. He raised a corps of riflemen in 1796 to support the government and was created a baronet in 1797. He subsequently raised a like corps in Somerset in 1803. He married, 1789, Jane, eldest daughter of Henry and Elizabeth Nisbett of Aghmore, co. Longford. He married secondly, 1828, Mary Bradford of Sandbach, Cheshire. The Jervises were part of the large Irish community in Clifton at this time. There were at least 4 sons:

1 John (d. 1803)
2 Humphrey (d. 1813)
3 Henry Meredyth (1793-1869), Cdr, RN; knighted
4 Thomas (1797-1879)

1802: 5 Sep: *Drank tea at Lady Jervis's meeting Mrs. Lindsay & Miss Stafford.* 7 Sep: *Wrote to George. At Lady Jervis's in the Evening.*

1804: 21 Jan: *Rather too late at the first meeting of the Harmonic Society which was respectably attended & very pleasant: more than 100 persons present & 70 staid supper. The best singer Master Jones from the King's Concerts. The best songs O Nanny, Lullaby, Old Woman, O Happy Fair, Miss Bailey, Beautiful Maid, & Sir. J. Jervis President.* 30 Jul: *At a party at Lady Jervis's: conversed chiefly with Miss Monck & Miss Fortescue: played at Commerce.* 3 Aug., 17 Aug: *A grand Rout & Supper at Mr. J. Jervis's.* 5 Sep: *To the fair at Bristol, with Lady Jervis & Miss White.* 3 Oct: *The Westbury & Clifton Vols. the Sea Fensibles & Sir J.J. W. Jervis's Rifle Corps.* 5-6 Oct., 12-13 Oct.

1805: 11 Mar: *Called at Mr. Townsend's & Sir John Jervis's.*

1806: 1 Mar: *a party of Savoyards playing German Tunes, who had fixed themselves in Sr. J. J. W. Jervis's Hall called me forth for an hour's Walk by moonlight.*

JESSOP — William Jessop [42]

William Jessop (1746-1814), civil engineer, lived and worked in Newark, where he served twice as mayor. He had seven sons, four of whom became engineers, and one daughter. At the time of his death in 1814, the family home was Butterley Hall, Derbyshire. Jessop had been summoned to provide a solution to the inadequacy of Bristol's docks; he came up with the successful floating harbour scheme, which cost £600,000. It is not known which of his sons these following entries relate to.

1806: 18 Feb: *Dined at Dr. Carrick's to meet Mr. Jessop, a very ingenious & pleasing young man, superintendant of the improvements upon the harbour, Son of the celebrated Engineer. Our trio & quartette in the Evening as pleasant & instructive, as it must always be in such refined Society.* 6 Mar: *Walked ... to view the Mechanism of the Pumps & Steam Engine with Mr. Jessop.* 10 Mar., 20 Mar., 23 Jun: *After dinner, joined a party at the Goolds for Ashton, the usual set, R. Adair excepted, with the addition of Jessop & Captn. Fallon.*

JESSOP — Charles Hale Jessop [43]

Charles Hale Jessop (1798-1859), gardener, was born at Cheltenham, son of local solicitor Walter Hilton Jessop (1769-1820) and Elizabeth Hale (1777-1850). In Alstone, Cheltenham, he designed and planted a botanical garden of approximately 20 acres, standing on a gentle rise from the River Chelt, which ran along the bottom of the garden. It was open to the public and contained several attractions, including hothouses, greenhouses, parterres, aviaries, pagodas, rustic fowl houses, and a broad gravelled path leading to Bayshill. Such a lovely and gracious amenity located in the centre of town could not fail to please, and St James Square gradually grew up alongside it.

Befitting their location within a spa town, the nursery gardens were also laid out to attract visitors, boasting a pond stocked with fish, a vinery, hothouses, beehives, and a warehouse selling seeds, bulbs, and tools. Rustic arbours, rose walks, and rockwork grottos encouraged loitering, as did the fancy breeds of rabbit and exotic birds on display. In 1843 Josiah Jessop, Charles's eldest brother, set up The Aviaries, a separate but connected establishment next door. He was subsequently joined at The Aviaries by his younger brother Jesse, and by 1851 they employed five men and three boys. In 1845 some of the land belonging to Jessop's nursery was sold to GWR for the building of a railway station at St James Square. Another of Charles Jessop's brothers, Walter, was a shareholder in GWR and there may have been some family cooperation in the deal. It precipitated the sale of 1,100 fruit trees, 400 grape vines, 1,600 roses, and 600 Italian cypress tress, as well as other trees and shrubs. Subsequently, a 150-yard stretch of a new sewer connecting to the Chelt was built through the nursery, necessitating the disposal of further nursery stock.

In July 1855, after two days of continual rain, the sewer failed and the Chelt broke its banks, inundating the nursery. It never fully recovered from the disaster and Charles Hale Jessop was declared bankrupt in 1858. His sons continued to develop The Aviaries as a menagerie, and later added a maze, but the popularity of Cheltenham as a spa destination was on the decline, and their innovations were not a commercial success. By 1872, The Aviaries had closed.

1839: 17 Jun: *We returned through the extensive nursery grounds of Jessop the principal gardener, an enterprizing character, and one of the leaders of the Cheltenham Tea totallers.*

1842: 15 Dec: *A letter from Jessop, Nurseryman, Cheltenham, with particulars of trees sent to Upper Slaughter four for our orchard and pleasure ground.*

1843: 7 Dec: *A letter from Jessop, the Cheltenham Nurseryman, with an invoice of goods sent.*

1852: 18 Apr: *Recd. a letter from the Brothers Jessop, nurserymen at Cheltenham, craving permission to add my name to the list of patrons of an exhibition of poultry fixed for June 3. at Cheltenham.* 19 Apr., 2 May, 1 Jun: *Having received from Messrs. Jessop, Cheltenham, four tickets of admission to the Poultry shew at Cheltenham on Thursday, inclosed them in an envelope, and forwarded them to my daughter at Stanway.*

JEUNE — Francis Jeune[44]

Francis Jeune (±1806-1868), Church of England clergyman and master of Pembroke College, was born at St Helier, Jersey, eldest son of Francis Jeune. He was educated at Pembroke College, Oxford (BA 1827; MA 1830; B&DCL 1834), and was ordained deacon on 17 June 1832 and priest on 2 June 1833. He was appointed headmaster of King Edward VI Grammar School, Birmingham, on 3 September 1834, and served as master of Pembroke College in 1843-64.

1848: 13 Jan: *Dr. Jeune, Master of Pembroke College, Oxford, and Canon of Gloucester, a personal friend, and strong partizan of Dr. Hampden, also a scion and pillar of Evangelicalism, moved the amendment or counter resolution in a speech of great ability, vigour, and tact.* 18 Jan., 22 Jan.

JOCELYN — Robert Jocelyn[45]

Robert Jocelyn, 3rd earl of Roden (1788-1870), politician and religious leader, was born at Brockley Park, Queen's County, Ireland, eldest son of Robert Jocelyn, 2nd earl of Roden (d. 1820), and Frances Theodosia, eldest daughter of Robert Bligh, dean of Elphin. He was educated at Harrow School between 1801 and 1805. In 1806 he was returned as MP for co. Louth, but being a minor, his seat was occupied by his uncle until 1810, at which date Viscount Jocelyn, as he was styled during his father's lifetime, took his seat in the Commons. In 1820 he succeeded his father as 3rd earl of Roden. (Here, for clarity, he will continue to be referred to as Jocelyn). In parliament he demonstrated strong tory views, and regularly voted against Roman Catholic relief.

Jocelyn married, 9 January 1813, Maria Frances Catherine (1794-1861), second daughter of Thomas Stapleton, Lord le Despencer; they had 3 sons and 3 daughters.

Jocelyn and his wife became staunch adherents of the Evangelical movement in the Church of Ireland. Their home at Tollymore Park, co. Down, was run on strongly spiritual lines, with the earl himself regularly leading services in his private chapel and teaching in Sunday schools on his estates. Tollymore became something of a haven for his co-religionists.

Jocelyn took a prominent role in the network of societies which promoted the 'Second Reformation' in Ireland. He saw his devotional and religious life as the mainspring of his political endeavours. His faith was also reflected in his conscientiousness as a landlord, which inspired affection among both his Catholic and protestant tenants. He was a vigorous critic of absentee Irish proprietors.

Jocelyn held several appointments in the royal household: as treasurer in 1812, vice-chamberlain in 1812-21, and as a lord of the bedchamber in 1828-31. Despite his piety, he got on well with George IV, who at his coronation in 1821 created him Baron Clanbrassill in the peerage of the United Kingdom.

In the House of Lords, Jocelyn became a leader of the Irish tory peers, a position confirmed in 1831 by his election as president of the Irish Protestant Conservative Society. During the 1830s he played a central role in mobilising protestant opinion on both sides of the Irish Sea to defend the Church of Ireland, notably through great public meetings in 1834 and 1837. He was also instrumental in the Conservative leadership's maintenance of a robustly anti-Catholic stance.

1827: 8 Mar.

1833: 8 Feb: *In the Lords, Lord Aberdeen and the Duke of Wellington attacked the foreign policy of the Government, especially as regards the question between Belgium and Holland, Lord Roden was full on Irish matters, as the advocate of the Protestant interests.* 11 Mar.

JODRELL — Frances Maria Jodrell — *see also* Leigh and Stratton[46]

Frances Maria Stratton, née Jodrell (1782-1850), daughter of John Bower Jodrell, married, 1809, John Stratton (1781-1819); they had 1 son and 4 daughters:

1 Georgina Maria (1812-1892)
2 Harriett Vittoria (1813-1900)
3 Elizabeth Julia (1815-1885)
4 Emily Ann (1816-1883)
1 John Locke (1818-1903)

Elizabeth Jodrell (d. 1807), of Cheshire, had married, 21 September 1778, Egerton Leigh (1751-1833); therefore the Miss Strattons would have been first cousins once removed to Egerton Leigh (1779-1865).

1829: 15 May: *We dined with the Egerton Leighs at Broadwell, meeting the two Miss Strattons, nieces of Mrs. E. Leigh, on a visit at Broadwell. They are daughters of her younger brother, John Stratton, a Captain in the Oxfordshire Militia, now deceased. I was well acquainted with him; his widow survives him, she was a Miss Joddrel of Cheshire, and a connection of Egerton Leigh. These young ladies are handsome & elegant, surpassing in beauty their cousin Miss Leigh, who yet is a well looking girl.*

JOHNS — David Johns, burglar, of Stow-on-the Wold[47]

David Johns (b. ±1786), burglar and chimney sweep, was from Stow-on-the Wold. His presumed wife, Rosanna Johns (b. ±1787), is listed as 'convict's wife (goes to field work)' in at least two censuses. In 1851 she lived at '52 Behind Noon', Maugersbury, Stow, with her daughter, Emma (b. ±1828), who also 'went to field work', and a son, Shadrach (±1829-1906), an agricultural labourer. Rosanna was born at Swateley, Oxfordshire, and Emma was born at Whichford, Warwickshire; Shadrach was born at Maugersbury, showing that David and Rosanna had moved to Stow at some time around 1828. With them lived a grandson, George (b. ±1847). The other son, who was presumably convicted with his father, was Thomas (b. ±1827). Shadrach married Rachel, ten years his junior, and they had a family. By 1901 Rachel had died, but Shadrach, aged 74, was still working as a road labourer.

1840: 20 Aug: *To the Justice room, where there was a good deal of business to be transacted by Messrs. Pole, R. Waller, and myself: Mr. Dickens of Cherrington in Warwickshire, a leading Mag. in the Shipston on Stour district, and acting also for Worcestershire and Gloucestershire, attended to be present at the reexamination of the Chimney Sweeper Johns, who is supposed to be connected with a Whichford gang, by some of whom a serious house robbery has lately been committed at Sutton under Brailes, and two persons are already in custody on suspicion: nothing particular transpired to-day to implicate Johns, who was committed to for trial at the Michs. Glouc. Sess. for stealing a sack the property of Mr. R. Field.* 21 Oct: *After the preliminary business had been gone through, I passed an hour in Purnell's court, attending the trial of three prisoners from Stow and Bledington, whom I had committed, Johns, Bolter, and Clark, of whom Johns was strangely acquitted by the jury.*

1844: 24 Oct: *Transacted Justice business in the Board room of the Workhouse, chiefly as to a charge against a Chimney sweeper, D. Johns, an old offender, at Stow, for breaking open a barn at Paxford, near Blockley, and stealing a considerable quantity of wheat and beans—remanded him for a few days, that the evidence against him may be collected.* 28 Oct: *Drove to Stow, where a long sitting at the Unicorn, ending in the Commitment of David Johns and his son, who had been remanded on the 24th. Inst. on a charge of felony.*

1850: 8 Feb: *Having recd. a note from Jackson Clark, accompanying a letter addressed to John Pegler by Sergt. Banning, of the Constabulary, by which it appeared that he had not as yet benefited in any way by the subscription raised for him, as a testimony of approval of his courage and good conduct in apprehending the burglar, David Johns, at a great personal risk, wrote to my Son, forwarding him the letter so written.*

JOHNSON — Mr Johnson of Stow-on-the-Wold, guardian of the union workhouse

1852: 2 Dec.

1853: 23 Mar., 16 Apr.

1854: 8 Jun., 3 Aug: *Two o clock, the hour fixed for the election being passed, Mr. Francis was put in nomination by Mr. Harris (Condicote) and seconded by Mr. Johnson (Stow), and unanimously elected.*

JOHNSON — Mr Johnson of Hersham

1853: 17 Jun: *The guests, besides Woodroffe and myself were Sir Richard Frederick, and his brother, Capt Frederick, Major Macdonald with a friend on a visit to him, the Revd. Mr. Jones, I believe from Barnet,—Mr. Locker, Mr. Johnson, and Mr. Middleton, all, with the exception of Mr. Jones, inhabitants of Hersham.*

JOHNSTON — Mr Johnston of the Royal Wiltshire Militia

1804: 2 Jan: *took a second very late breakfast with Prower & Mr. Johnston.* 12 Jan: *Walked up to Clifton with Johnston of the Wiltshire.* 13 Jan., 14 Jan: *Went late to Bristol where I met several of the Wilts. Officers particularly Prower & Johnson.* 16 Jan., 24 Jan., 28 Jan.

JOHNSTON — Miss Johnston, sister of Mrs Olivia Greene

1851: 7 Mar: *Deviated from the road to pay a morning visit to Mr. and Mrs. Greene at Lower Guiting. Mr. G. was not at home, but I was received by Mrs. G. and her sister, Miss Johnston, very pleasing young persons.*

JOHNSTONE — George Frederic Johnstone[48]

Sir George Frederic Johnstone, 7th baronet of Westerhall (1810-1841), JP, MP, and landed proprietor, was the son of Sir John Lowther Johnstone, 6th baronet of Westerhall, Westerkirk, Dumfriesshire, and Charlotte Gordon (±1785-1845) of Cluny, Aberdeenshire. Johnstone was MP for Weymouth in 1832-35. His great-uncle was Sir William Johnstone Pulteney, 5th baronet, lawyer, property developer, and politician, who became one of the richest men in Britain. Sir William amassed a huge fortune in America, and was a property developer in Britain, America, and the West Indies. His magnificent wealth was partly due to his marriage to Frances (±1728-1782), daughter and heir of Daniel Pulteney (1682-1731) MP. Sir William bought the borough of Weymouth and sat in seven successive parliaments. His only child married Sir James Murray in 1794; she inherited the Pulteney estates and was created countess of Bath. Sir William Johnstone Pulteney died 1805. His baronetcy, the Westerhall estate in Scotland, the borough of Weymouth ('a source both of wealth and of political influence'), and the extensive lands in America, were inherited by his nephew, Sir John Lowther Johnstone.

Sir George Frederic Johnstone married, at Auchincruive, St Quivox, Ayrshire, 24 October 1840, Maria (1815-1858), daughter of William Craven, earl of Craven (1770-1825), and Louisa, countess of Craven, née Brunton (1785-1860); they had 2 sons (twins):

1= Frederick John William (1841-1913); succeeded as 8th baronet; married Laura Caroline Russell

1= George Charles Keppel (b. 1841), Col; married Agnes Caroline Chamberlayne (1845-1925)

Sir George Frederic Johnstone was killed in a riding accident. His son, Sir Frederick John William Johnstone, 8th baronet, was, like his father, a racehorse owner and Conservative MP for Weymouth and Melcombe Regis. He served in that post from 1874 to 1885.

1828: 20 Oct: *In the Evening my wife and myself dined at Farmington Lodge, at the Wallers. We met the Fords, Mrs. Boudier, Sir Frederick Johnstone, a pleasing young man, who on attaining his majority will come into possession of a very large property.*

JOLLIFFE — Mr Jolliffe of Ashton, Wiltshire

1806: 9 Oct: *met in Devizes, a Mr. Jollife of Ashton, whom I accompanied upon his journey to Conock Gate whence I returned to Wedhampton with Mrs. Poore & Mrs. Warrener.*

JONES — Admiral and Colonel Jones at Clifton

No admiral by the name of Jones is listed in 1804. The colonel was likely to have been with either the HEIC—many East India Company officers favoured Clifton—or of one of the local militias formed to counter the French threat.

1804: 1 Aug: *to Ashton for Raspberries & Cream ending in a supper at Mrs. Massey's, consisting of Mrs. Massey, the Rawsons, Miss Monck, Miss Fortescue, Adm. & Col. Jones, Hankey & myself.*

JONES — Dr Jones, a dinner guest at the house of Broome Phillips Witts in Brunswick Square, London

1830: 25 Jun: *To dinner at Mrs. Witts's, Brunswick Square—a party Messrs. Bailey, Hibbert, Bassevi, Jones, Misses Witts and Whitehouse (then afterwards a Capt. Orange, Messrs. Rodicks x 3) & Mr. H. Warter.*

1835: 11 Jun: *The bridal party on their return to Brunswick Square were joined by other friends, relatives and connections. Of the five or six and twenty present, there was not anyone who was not related to the Witts or Lake family. Besides those already mentioned, there were Mr. and Mrs. Bassevi. Dr. Jones and his Son, two Messrs. Rodicks, a Mr. Fleming and a Mr. Whitehouse.*

JONES — Lieutenant-Colonel Jones of the Royal Engineers at Dover Castle

1844: 31 May: *He obligingly allowed me to use the order given which was signed by Lt. Col. Jones, Commanding officer of Engineers, either to-day or to-morrow.* 3 Jun: *A guard of honour from the castle was drawn up within the terminus to receive her, where also were the Commandant of the Garrison, Col. Jones, of the Engineers, a fine looking old soldier.*

JONES — Mr Jones of Hay Hill

The Jones family of Naas and Hay Hill had resided in the vicinity of Lydney for several centuries. This member of the family is likely to have been related to Henry Prowse Jones, possibly a nephew.

1845: 30 May: *Another Gloucestersh. Magistrate, Mr. Jones, the younger, of Hay Hill, is also a candidate.*

JONES — Revd Mr Jones of Enford

Unusually, no information has been found on this clergyman. He does not appear to have been curate or vicar of Enford.

1806: 17 Sep: *Jaques & a Mr. Jones of Enford, Steward for the Widows & Orphans of the Clergy.*

1807: 29 Apr: *To Devizes. To the Clergy meeting. Conversed with Mr. Jones, Mr. Brereton &c.* 7 Aug: *Visitation at Lavington found Archb. Danberry with many Clergymen, Messrs. Key, Spencer, Smith, Prince, Jones, Basset, Richards, Dr. Skinner, Williams, Rogers &c. &c.*

1808: 9 Mar: *Rode to Enford to make enquiries of the Revd. Jones respecting the Clergy Fund. Saw his Lady.* 30 Apr.

JONES — Mr A. G. Jones, secretary to the Gloucestershire Agricultural Society

1852: 29 Jan: *Wrote to Mr. A. G. Jones, Secr. to the Glouc. Agricultural Society, requesting him to put down my name as a subscriber of £2. to the fund raised to insure the meeting of the Royal Agricultural Society being held at Gloucester in 1853.* 5 Apr.

JONES — Mr D. Jones of Conock, Wiltshire

1807: 17 Mar: *Mr. D. Jones of Conock called upon us.* 28 Mar., 14 Apr., 25 Apr., 4 May, 6 May, 11 May, 24 May, 26 Jun., 16 Aug: *Sundry Parishioners drank tea with us, Mrs. M. Giddings, Mr. Jones's wife the Widow Jones, C. Giddings' Wife & Daughters.* 20 Aug., 26 Aug: *Drove my Mother to Conock & Stoke, called upon Mrs. Warrener, Mrs. Jones, Mrs. & Miss L. Mayo.* 30 Dec: *then thro' Wedhampton to Conock; & called upon Jones & his Aunt Warriner.*

1808: 7 Mar: *called upon Mr. Jones & Mrs. Warriner; rode with Jones & Hill to Devizes.*

JONES — Mr E. J. Jones, manager of the Hereford County Bank

1838: 25 Aug: *Wrote to a Mr. Jones, Manager of the Hereford County Bank, for information as to the decision alleged to have been made by Mag. or Commrs. of Turnpike roads in respect of drills being exempt from toll as implements of husbandry.* 28 Aug: *Recd. a letter from Mr. E. J. Jones, of Hereford, in reply to that which I wrote to him on Saturday last.* 30 Aug.

JONES — Edward Jones, chaplain of Gloucester County Gaol[49]

Edward Jones (1755-1828), Church of England clergyman, was educated at Pembroke College, Oxford (BA 1777; MA 1780). He was vicar of Corse in 1795 and rector of Rudford in 1804. Jones was also a Gloucestershire JP and canon of Gloucester Cathedral. He was married and had at least 1 son:

1 Richard Jones (±1795-1836); *see below*

1822: 15 Oct: *The most important business before us was a charge of misconduct & cruelty brought by Mr. Jones, Chaplain of the County Gaol, against Mr. Cunningham, the Governor. The Chaplain, who had held the Station more than thirty years, and had been a Magistrate of the County for many years, alledged several serious charges against the Governor.*

1823: 14 Jan: *Letters addressed to the Chairman, Dr. Cooke & Mr. Cripps, and to Dr. Timbrell, by Mr. Jones, the late Chaplain, written in angry & intemperate terms.* 8 Apr: *Much interest was occasioned by the reading of various important letters on the same subject, which has now for six months agitated the county, namely, the charges brought by Mr. Jones, the late Chaplain, against the Governor of the Gaol, and the consequent dismissal of Mr. Jones from his office.*

JONES — Edward Jones[50]

Edward Jones (1772-1847), Church of England clergyman, was born at Hay Hill, Newnham-on-Severn, Gloucestershire, eldest son of Roynon Jones (junior) (d. 1815), a famous sportsman. He was the elder brother of Henry Prowse Jones (*below*). Jones was educated at Worcester College, Oxford (BA 1795; MA 1798), and ordained deacon on 30 November 1795 and priest on 12 March 1797. He was appointed curate of Awre, Gloucestershire, on 30 November 1795. The family wealth had originally devolved from William Jones, a founder of the Haberdashers' Company in London. In the early eighteenth century the Joneses upgraded the interior of Naas House, Lydney, installing panelling in a number of rooms. Edward Jones lived at Naas House, although due to a family tragedy, he grew up elsewhere. In 1771 Mary Jones, a daughter of the family, was murdered on her way home from a dinner at the rectory at Lydney. Soon after this the family moved to another house, Hay Hill, near Newnham-on-Severn, built by Roynon Jones (senior) in 1771.

Edward Jones was married to Elizabeth, daughter of Revd Edward Owen of Ty Gwyn, Merioneths; they had 1 son:

1 Edward Owen Jones (1808-1872), Church of England clergyman; married, 14 October 1840, Catherine Sophia, daughter of John Fortescue Brickdale of Newland, Gloucestershire

---

1826: 31 Aug: *Some of my old schoolfellows are among my intimate acquaintance in the County, & sitting on the same bench with me as Magistrates, Genl. Guise, Mr. Edwd. Jones, Col. Webb, M.P. for Gloucester, Charles Crawley &c.* 15 Sep: *And this seems the proper place for inserting a list of some of the leading families & individuals, whose presence on this occasion served so many good purposes; benefiting the charity ... Revd. E. Jones & family.*

1829: 22 Sep.

1838: 4 Jan: *Mr. P. was a Clergyman in Huntingdonshire, and Son of a late Prebendary of Peterborough, formerly of Elmore, where among many others of Gloucestershire connections, Sir John Guise, E. Jones, C. Crawley &c.*

JONES — Elias Jones[51]

Elias Jones (±1801-1866).

1846: 27 Oct: *Wrote to Mr. Marshall, Snowshill in respect of a poor man, late his servant.* 30 Oct: *Letter from Mr. Marshall, Snowshill, in answer to my note to him as to Elias Jones; he declines interfering in his favour.*

JONES — Emma Jones[52]

Emma Jones (1824-1878) was the daughter of Samuel Jones (below). She married, at Upper Slaughter, 15 August 1843, John Humphris (1817-1870).

1843: 15 Aug: *Officiated at the marriage of John Humphris and Emma Jones.*

JONES — Henry Prowse Jones[53]

Henry Prowse Jones (1781-1864), Church of England clergyman, was born at Hay Hill, Newnham-on-Severn, a younger son of Roynon Jones (junior) of Naas House, Lydney, and Hay Hill,

Newnham-on-Severn, Gloucestershire. He was younger brother to Edward Jones (*above*). Henry was educated at Corpus Christi, Cambridge (BA 1802; MA 1837). He was rector of Llanvihangel Torymynnidd, Monmouth, in 1809, curate of Micheldean, curate of Awre and Blakeney in 1810, curate of Newnham and Littledean in 1812, rector of Edgeworth in 1820-64, vicar of Berkeley in 1837-39, and rector of Hazleton with Yanworth in 1840-64. He married, at Doncaster, 18 May 1805, Sarah Huffey, younger daughter of Sir Cuthbert Shafto of Barington Hill, Northumberland. By 1841 he was a widower.

1829: 17 Jun., 22 Sep., 9 Dec.

1834: 15 Aug., 17 Dec.

1836: 24 Aug., 13 Sep: *But Prouse Jones, one of Mason's uncles on the bench, and himself but recently appointed, stood forward in a set speech to advocate his nephew's claims, to disparage Rowan, and make insinuations against the proceedings of those by whom he was brought forwards.*

1837: 16 Jan.

1842: 12 Apr: *The Magistrates who had given Notice of a motion for the diminution of the force were Sir J. Guise, H. P. Jones, Hopkinson, Canning, and Harward, mostly men of ultra-Whig politics.* 18 Oct.

1844: 8 Apr., 10 Apr.

1846: 11 Aug.

1847: 29 Jun: *Mr. Prowse Jones (Uncle of Mason, the Governor) commenced a fierce attack upon the County Chairman, second Chairman, and myself, on the ground that we, backed by the board of Visitors, were prejudiced against the Governor, depreciated his merits, sought to supersede him, or to fetter and dictate to him, grounding the charge on inferences drawn from our speeches on May 18.*

JONES — John Jones and the Jones family at Cheltenham [54]

Frustratingly little has been discovered about this family. In the 1791 *Universal British Directory* for Cheltenham, John Jones is listed as a gentleman and a freeholder. He was reported to have a 'truly elegant house'. Miss C. Jones (who in the entry of 16 October 1804 was referred to as 'Cressy', presumably Cressida), Sophia, and Louisa Jones are likely to be the daughters of John. In Agnes Witts's diary on 17 November she mentions there being four 'Miss Jones's'. The Joneses appear frequently in the diaries of Agnes Witts, and they seem to have been permanent residents at Cheltenham.

1801: 3 Nov: *Walked in the morning with Miss C. Jones.* 4 Nov: *Mr. Beddell & Miss C. Jones dined with us, the former modest & well informed the latter forward & absurd.* 5 Nov., 12 Nov., 13 Nov: *In the evening late to a great Rout at Lady Herries, or perhaps Sir Robert's. Conversed much with Dr. Jenner, the Jones's &c. With the latter walked home.* 14 Nov: *Miss Sophia & Miss Louisa Jones dined with us, the former, repairing with us to tea & Cards at Mr. Rooke's, where her powers of attraction fell before the unassuming preeminence of the amiable Fanny, who with the Granvilles, Mrs. Newell, & Miss Markham were also there.* 16 Nov: *In the Evening at a Rout at Miss Hughes: conversed chiefly with Miss C. Jones; all the Town there.* 17 Nov., 20 Nov: *Called upon Mr. & Mrs. Myers, & Miss Jones's, who played & sang to me ... Walked with the Granville party & with Miss C. Jones.* 23 Nov: *Called on Miss Hughes who played & sung to me. Mrs. Newell & Miss Jones dined with us, the latter sang.*

1802: 5 Aug: *Called upon & walked with Miss Hughes. Afterwards with my Mother upon Mrs. Jordan, & the Miss Jones's.* 28 Aug: *Walked in the Evening with Mr. Fotheringham & Miss C. Jones.* 31 Aug., 6 Sep.

1804: 16 Oct: *Walked towards the Well & with Cressy Jones.* 17 Oct: *Called on the Jones's. Music &c. from them. Mr. Delabere, Mr. & Mrs. Worsley & Mr. Wilmot called. Dined alone. In the evening Mr. Wilmot & Lady Herries. Aunt C. worse. Late to a rout & singing by Miss Griglietti a pupil of Rasiggini at Mrs. Grays: pleasant enough. Baillies, Jones's, O'Callaghans &c. &c.* 18 Oct: *Walked with Cressy Jones, Louisa, Dr. Jenner, &c. &c.*

1805: 17 Jul: *Tea & a Party at my Aunts dull & tiresome. The Berringtons, Louisa Jones, Mr. Welford & Mr. Jeffries, Fowlkes &c.* 18 Jul., 22 Jul., 26 Jul.

JONES — John Collier Jones [55]

John Collier Jones (1770-1838), Church of England clergyman, was born at Plympton Erle, Devon, son of Richard and Maria Jones. He was educated at Exeter College, Oxford (BA 1792; MA 1796; BD 1807; DD 1819), and was a fellow of the college in 1792-99, rector in 1819-38, and vice-chancellor in 1828-32.

1829: 7 Feb: .... *at this convocation the Vice Chancellor, Dr. Jones, Rector of Exeter College, communicated to the Members a letter addressed to him by Peel, in which he tendered his resignation of his seat for the University.* 26 Feb.

1838: 20 Aug: *Recounted to us the strange particulars of the death of Dr. Jones, Rector of Exeter Coll., who was stepfather to Mrs. P., having married her mother, then a widow.*

JONES — John Fowell Jones [56]

John Fowell Jones (1790-1877), Church of England clergyman, was born at Longney, Gloucestershire, son of Benjamin Jones (d. 1830) and Catherine Watts, a descendent of the Fowell family of Devon. He was educated at Balliol College, Oxford (BA 1813; MA 1817), before embarking on a career in the Church. He was appointed perpetual curate of Saul and, in 1825, vicar; he remained in the post until his death in 1877. He was also stipendiary curate of Broadwell in 1818-29 and curate of Upper Swell in 1825. From the latter position he collected an annual salary of £100 and was allowed to reside in the parsonage house of Upper Swell. In addition to his vicarship at Saul, Jones was vicar of Moreton Valence in 1830-77, and following the death of his father in 1831, he served as rector of Gwernesney until 1871. He married Elizabeth Greenham (b. 1799); it is not known if there were any children.

1823: 23 Apr: *first meeting of the Stow Clerical Society for this year: Mr. Jones, the Secretary, Curate of Upper Swell & Broadwell.* 18 Nov: *We had a dinner party. Mr. Ford, Mr. Croome, Mr. Hurd, Mr. Jones, Mr. F. Aston were our guests.*

1825: 22 Jun: *Prayers were read by Mr. Jones, Curate of Broadwell & Upper Swell.* 29 Jul: *We dined at Mr. Ford's at Little Risington, & met Mr. Lewes, and Mr. Jones, Curate of Upper Swell and Broadwell, who has also lately been appointed by Mr. Halifax, Rector of Standish in this county, perpetual curate of Saul, a village below Gloucester.* 23 Aug., 26 Oct., 3 Nov: *I dined at Mr. Jones's at Upper Swell; meeting Messrs. Jeaffreson, Bowen, Winter & Baillie.*

1826: 3 Jan: *Mr. Baillie, the worthy little curate of Great Risington came to pass a day or two with us, and the Messrs. Jones, from Upper Swell joined our party at dinner. The younger brother has relinquished his views in the army, as a Lieutenant of Artillery, to enter into the church, and is preparing himself for holy orders at Cambridge; a quick, intelligent respectable young man.* 3 Mar., 19 Apr., 5 Jun., 5 Jul., 9 Nov.

1827: 21 Feb: *The effect of this will be Mr. Jones taking leave of the curacy of Broadwell, as now held by him.* 5 Jun: *There were also at the Symposium of our host & hostess, the Egerton Leighs and his brother, the Revd. Peter Leigh, Mr. Jones & his dandy pupil, Mr. Winter.* 4 Jul: *We had a few of our bachelor clerical neighbours to dinner to-day: Mr. Hurd, Mr. Baillie, Mr. Jones, Mr. Hankins, Mr. Winter and Mr. W.B. Pole, one of the Sons of Mr. Pole of Wyck Hill.* 20 Jul., 24 Aug., 2 Oct.

1828: 18 Jan., 23 Apr., 4 Jun., 2 Jul., 20 Aug., 29 Aug: *Mr. Jones & Mr. Baillie dined with us, & the latter slept here.* 27 Sep: *I dined and slept at Mr. M. Vavasour's at Broadwell, The party was given as a farewell to Mr. Jones, who has resigned the Curacy of Broadwell, and accepted one at Sevenoaks in Kent. He had for some time considered it desirable to move nearer the Metropolis, where he hoped to be more in the way of preferment, at least more likely to increase his income by tuition, &, I suspect, did not find himself quite comfortable with his Rector, Mr. Twisleton, though there was no serious cause of complaint; the rector, perhaps, wishing unnecessarily to interfere in the parish, and the Curate being a little too prone to take offence.*

1839: 17 Jan: *He covers a letter from J. Fowell Jones, formerly settled in this neighbourhood as Curate of U Swell and Broadwell, but now incumbent of Moreton Valence & Saul, villages in the Vale of the Severn, who is endeavouring by the raising of subscriptions to provide a fund for the enlargement of his church at Saul.*

1840: 13 Apr.

1842: 15-16 May.

1844: 1-2 Aug., 6 Aug., 18 Sep: *Five Pounds from the funds of the Society were voted on my suggestion to aid the fund for building a parsonage house at Saul, both from regard for such a good work, and from a friendly recollection of the Incumbent, Fowell Jones, formerly Curate of Broadwell &c. and for several years Secretary to the Stow Clerical Society.* 19 Sep., 22 Sep.

1845: 16 Feb., 19 Feb.

1850: 8 Nov: *We repaired at mid-day to the Cathedral library, where already many Clergymen were congregated; many of my personal friends and acquaintances, such as Canons Crawley and Morgan, Messrs. Moore, Sayers, Fowell Jones, Lysons, Riddle &c.*

JONES — John Jones [57]

John Jones (1821-1895), agricultural labourer at Upper Slaughter, was the eldest son of Samuel Jones (*below*). He married Elizabeth Benfield (b. ±1824), possibly a daughter of James Benfield.

1846: 23 Dec: *John Jones and Elizabeth Benfield were married.*

JONES — Margaret Jones and the Jones family at Gloucester — *see also* Poyner *and* Turner [58]

Margaret Jones (±1769-1847), friend of Mary Hunt and Jane Backhouse, was widowed in 1817. Her husband, John Jones, had been the rector of Foy, Herefordshire. Upon his death he was succeeded as rector by his and Margaret's son, John (1792-1869). Of their daughters Charlotte and Caroline, Caroline inherited £100 in 1825 from her godfather, Thomas Hardwick.

Mrs Margaret Jones lived at Palace Yard, Gloucester. By 1838 (if not slightly before) she had 'inherited' Robert Poyner, who had formerly been manservant to Francis Witts. Poyner had married in December 1833, and presumably sought a post where his family could be with him; Margaret Jones provided a house for his wife and (at that time) two young daughters.

1829: 2 May: *Mrs. Backhouse remaining behind us in our lodgings till Monday, when she goes to visit Mrs. Jones.* 30 May: *She is come back in pretty good health & excellent spirits; accompanied by Miss Charlotte Jones, daughter of Mrs. Jones, with whom Mrs. B. has been staying. Her father was a Clergyman & Rector of Foy in Herefordshire, of which parish her Brother is now the incumbent. There is a large family; three sisters are married; one of them to Mr. T. Turner, late Banker at Gloucester, in partnership with his Father & Mr. R. Morris, whose affairs proved so disastrous at the time of the late panic. Mr. T. Turner is generally esteemed & pitied. Miss C. Jones is a pleasing, mild young woman.* 18 Jun., 22 Sep.

1830: 8 Mar., 21 Apr: *I had the pleasure of finding the three ladies in Palace Yard pretty well, and before repairing to court, paid a short visit to their neighbour & Mrs. Backhouse's kind friend, Mrs. Jones, whom with her daughter Caroline I found at home.*

1832: 29 Mar: *I accompanied Mrs. Backhouse and my wife to Gloucester, where the former was going to visit her friends Mrs. M. Hunt, Mrs. Jones and Mrs. Hopkinson.* 6 Jun: *Mrs. Backhouse was to meet her daughter at Cheltenham, to return with her to Upper Slaughter, after so long an absence, during which her time had chiefly been divided between Mrs. M. Hunt, and Mrs. Jones.* 7 Jun.

1834: 12 Aug: *Called at the Jones's in Palace Yard.*

1842: 17 Nov: *Communicated intelligence of the same event to Mrs. Jones, and Miss Davies, of Gloucester.* 23 Nov.

JONES — Richard Jones [59]

Richard Jones (1756-1816), Church of England clergyman, was rector of Charfield in 1790-1816 and Dodington in 1803-16. He was married and had at least 1 son and 1 daughter:

1 Richard Prankerd (1792-1853), Church of England clergyman; rector of Charfield, 1816; vicar of Compton, Berkshire, 1829 until his death on 4 October 1853

1 Harriot; married, 1816, Henry Hawes Fox

In the Cambridge Alumni entry for Henry Hawes Fox, his father-in-law Richard Jones is referred to as 'One of the best "whips" in the country'. Regarding the diary entry of 27 December 1801, it seems likely that Richard and Thomas Jones were brothers, and that Richard was standing in for Thomas on this day.

1801: 27 Dec: *To Nibley Church early, where Mr. Jones of Charville officiated well.*

JONES — Richard Jones [60]

Richard Jones (±1795-1836), Church of England clergyman, was the son of Edward Jones of Gloucester. He was educated at Worcester College, Oxford (BA 1818), and served as perpetual curate of Norton, Gloucester.

1825: 15 Jul: *The Revd. R. Jones, one of the Minor Canons of the Cathedral, read the report of the proceedings of that as well as of the other branches established in the different quarters of the diocese.*

JONES — Samuel Jones of Upper Slaughter — *see also* John Humphries [61]

Samuel Jones (1797-1878), agricultural labourer, was born at Winchcombe. He married, first, at Upper Slaughter, 25 October 1819, Elizabeth Betterton (1794-1828); they had at least 4 sons and 2 daughters:

1 John (1820-1895)

1 Anne (b. 1822)

2 William (b. & d 1823)

2 Emma (1824-1878); married, at Upper Slaughter, 15 August 1843, John Humphris (1817-1870)

3 William (1826-1900)

4 George (b. & d. 1828)

Samuel Jones married secondly, 8 February 1831, Elizabeth Humphris (1801-1838); they had 1 son:

1 Samuel Insol (b. & d. 1838)

Samuel was twice a widower; both of his wives died in childbirth with the child also dying. In 1851 he lived with his son at Upper Slaughter.

1847: 30 Aug: *Wrote to Mr. Morgan, Stow, as Secretary of the Stow & C Norton agricultural Association with a certificate to procure for my parishioner Samuel Jones, a premium at the approaching annual meeting of the Association, on the score of thirty years service on one farm in this parish under three successive tenants, all of the same family.* 11 Sep: *A letter from Mr. Morgan, that the Committee of the Stow and Chipping Norton Agricultural Association had awarded to my parishioner, Saml. Jones, £1. on account of thirty years service.*

1851: 4 Jan: *Visited Edward Lea on parish matters—Also Widows Townsend and Wilcox, and Saml. Jones.*

JONES — Thomas Jones [62]

Thomas Jones (1745-1832), Church of England clergyman, was vicar of Kilmeston, Wiltshire, and perpetual curate of North Nibley from 1785 to 1832.

1801: 29 Nov: *Walked to the Village Church, which is large, handsome, & clean: tho' nearly empty, large as the Parish is, not very cold. The Clergyman Mr. Jones, Welch, but serious, & his Sermon good, but I fear only intelligible to ourselves.* 6 Dec: *In the Afternoon to Nibley Church hearing Mr. Jones who preached a good Sermon.* 13 Dec: *To Nibley Church in the morning, where the Service was performed as usual by Mr. Jones.*

JONES — Thomas Jones [63]

Thomas Jones (±1800-1867), Church of England clergyman, was the third son of Samuel Jones of Gloucester. He was educated at Wadham College, Oxford (BA 1822; MA 1827), and served as rector of Hempstead in 1826-67.

1826: 31 Jul: *A Mr. Jones, Son to an Alderman & Brushmaker of Gloucester, is the new incumbent, having bought the next presentation of the heirs of the late Duchess of Norfolk.*

1848: 25 Feb.

JONES — Valentine Jones, later Valentine Jones Graeme [64]

Valentine Jones (1783-1833), army officer, was the son of Edward Jones of Northop, Flintshire. He was educated at Eton College and Jesus College, Oxford, where he was a contemporary of Francis Witts. From his letter to Francis, received on 8 November 1805, it appears that Valentine was aware of the latter's search for a curacy. Francis later sent a letter on the subject to Valentine's father. In 1822 Valentine inherited from his uncle, Thomas Graeme, the splendid property of Oldbury Court, near Frenchay, 3.5 miles from the centre of Bristol. The grounds of this property had been designed by Humphry Repton. Valentine became an army officer and rose to lieutenant-colonel; he served in the Peninsular War with the 18th Hussars.

The attribution to Valentine Jones is tentative, but likely. One doubt springs from the diary entry of 29 November 1805, where Francis Witts refers to 'V. Jones junior', implying that there was a 'V. Jones senior'. However, if the early entries are ambiguous, the latter entries definitely refer to Valentine. In support of the attribution is the entry dated 1 April 1829, in which Col Graeme was referred to in terms of being either an 'acquaintance' or an 'old friend'.

1805: 8 Nov: *Received a letter from V. Jones Esqe. which I answered & wrote one to Matthews & another to Dove.* 28 Nov: *Heard from Mr. Jones.* 29 Nov: Wrote letters recommending Mr. V. Jones Junr. to Messrs. Schmidt & Böttiger.

1806: 20 Feb: *Received a very polite amusing letter from Mr. V. Jones Junr. from Dresden.*

1826: 16 Jun: *On the right hand side were Messrs. Estcourt, Browne, Goodrich, Beach, Lord John Somerset, Dr. Cooke, Messrs. Howell, Wintle, Worrall, Lawrence, Trye, Pettat, Codrington, Niblett &c. on the left the Hon. H. Morton, Messrs. Pyrke, Webb, Kingscote, T. Kingscote, Adey, Jones, R. Canning, E. Sheppard.* 17 Oct: *Among the magistrates present were Mr. Bathurst, Mr. Cooper M.P. Mr. Goodrich, the Archd. of Gloucester, Mr. Davies, Dr. Davies, Mr. Goldney, Mr. Newman, Major Jones Graeme, Mr. Baker, his Son, &c. &c.*

1829: 1 Apr: *A large party assembled about six o clock at the Bell Inn to pay the Sheriff the compliment of dining with him, whom I joined, and passed a very pleasant evening; almost every one present being of my acquaintance, & many old friends. Among them were Sir B. W. Guise, M.P., Col. Webb, M.P., Sir W. Hicks, Mr. Hicks Beach, Mr. Browne, Mr. Goodrich, Dr. Cooke, Archdeacon Timbrill, Col. Graeme, Mr. Pettat, Messrs. Baker, Hale, Clifford, Niblett, Lawrence, Paul, Newman, R. Canning, &c.* 14 Jul.

JONES — William Jones of the Gloucestershire Constabulary [65]

William Jones (b. ±1818), police officer, enlisted in the Gloucestershire Constabulary on 1 January 1844, warrant number 640. He was registered as a shoemaker from Upleadon, Gloucestershire, 5 feet 8½ inches in height. He was promoted to sergeant on 1 July 1845 and resigned from the force on 18 July 1848.

1847: 30 Jan: *A letter from Sergt. Jones, P.C. stationed at Combe Hill, near Tewkesbury, soliciting from me a recommendation to aid him as a Candidate for the office of Inspector of Borough Police Tewkesbury.* 31 Jan., 11 Feb: *from Sergt. Jones, Glouc. Const. thanking me and other Magistrates for our recommendation, but the vacancy expected in the Inspectorship of Police at Tewkesbury, which he hoped to obtain, did not occur.*

JONES — William Jones of the Gloucestershire Constabulary [66]

William Jones (b. ±1823), police officer, enlisted in the Gloucestershire Constabulary on 9 June 1847, warrant number 888. He was registered as a tailor from Poulton, Wiltshire, 5 feet 10½ inches in height. He later resigned from the force.

1845: 4 Feb: *Wrote to Lord Redesdale, soliciting his interest for Police Constable W. Jones, who is desirous, to obtain a place in the Excise.* 8 Feb., 20 Feb., 12 Feb: *To Mr. Makepeace respecting Jones's application to Lord Redesdale for a place in the Excise, enclosing Lord R's letter to me on the subject.* 18 Feb: *To Lord Redesdale, expressing a hope that he would, though at a distant period, promote Constable W. Jones's wish of being made an Excise man.* 26 Feb.

1848: 11 Jan: *Constable W. Jones, Glorshire Constabulary, stationed at Marshfield.* 12 Jan: *Wrote to Const. W. Jones in answer to his letter received yesterday.*

JONES — Willoughby Jones[67]

Willoughby Jones (1820-1884), MP, JP, DL, and landed proprietor, was the second son of Maj.-Gen. John Thomas Jones, a veteran of the Peninsular War, and Catherine Lawrence. He was educated at Eton and Trinity College, Cambridge (BA 1843). The Jones baronetcy was created in 1831 for his father, who died in 1843. Willoughby inherited the baronetcy from his brother Lawrence, who was murdered in Turkey in 1845. In July 1847 he won the seat of Cheltenham by a majority of 108, but he was unseated by petition in May the following year. He was a member of the Canterbury Association from 27 March 1848. He lived at Cranmer Hall near Fakenham in Norfolk, and was high sheriff for Norfolk in 1851. He married, 1856, his cousin Emily, daughter of Henry Taylor-Jones (1790-1860), his father's half-brother.

1847: 17 Jul: *There is an opposition made to the return of Mr. Craven Berkeley for Cheltenham: offence has been taken at some incautious remarks made by him as to the salubrity of the place, and his re-election is opposed by some of his supporters of old, and by those who have always been adverse to him. A Sir Willoughby Jones, a resident at Cheltenham, is brought forward to compete with him.* 29 Dec.

1848: 29 Jun: *Sir Willoughby Jones, the member elected on the conservative interest at the general election, has been unseated by a Committee on a petition charging treating and bribery ...*

JORDAN — Dorothy Jordan[68]

Dorothy Jordan (1761-1816), actress and royal mistress, was born in the neighbourhood of Leicester Square and Covent Garden, Westminster, one of reputedly nine children of Francis Bland and Grace Phillips. She began her acting career with a touring Dublin company, and soon became mistress to its manager, Richard Daly. The couple had one child, Francis Daly. Dorothy was later recommended to Richard Sheridan, and afterwards appeared at the Theatre Royal in Drury Lane. There she found a protector in Richard Ford (1758-1806), the son of a court physician and a major shareholder at Drury Lane. She lived with Ford as his wife at 5 Gower Street and had three children by him—two daughters and a son who died at birth. Ford appears to have intended to marry her, but he never did.

By 1790 Prince William Henry, duke of Clarence [later William IV], had admired Dorothy Jordan at Drury Lane for about a year. When he learned she was unmarried, he took her to live with him at Clarence Lodge, Roehampton. She was allowed an annuity of £1,200 and an equipage. Provision was also made for her children. Despite this income, Jordan continued to work at Drury Lane and Covent Garden, as well as a vast number of provincial theatres which she visited on lengthy tours. She shared the money she made with the duke. In January 1797, Clarence was appointed ranger of Bushy Park, which included the use of Bushy House; to there he and Jordan repaired. She was mother to ten of the duke's children, all surnamed FitzClarence.

On 2 October 1811, Jordan was touring at the Cheltenham theatre when she received a letter from Clarence asking her to meet him at Maidenhead; there he stipulated that they must part. Debts were mounting, and his priority was to find a rich and eligible woman to marry. In a deed of settlement drawn up in November, Jordan was to receive £4,400; she would look after the duke's daughters, to whom he was to have free access, until they reached the age of 13.

Jordan made her provincial tours primarily for financial reasons. In 1788 John Boles Watson I invited her to the Cheltenham theatre on the occasion of a visit by George III and Queen Charlotte. So great was her popularity in the spa town that a commemorative medal depicting the comic muse was struck. Henry Thornton was another manager in whose playhouses Jordan performed; she appeared at the first season of the newly built Reading theatre in 1788, and from that time made regular visits on the circuit along the Bath and Portsmouth roads. After her break with Clarence she relied on Thornton and others for work; in 1812 and 1813 she performed at his and Thomas Collins's theatres at Gosport, Southampton, Ryde, and Portsmouth, in spite of her dismay at the rowdiness of the seafaring audiences. After retiring from the theatre she moved to France, where she died, at Paris, in 1816.

Agnes Witts was a visitor to Mrs Jordan and her name appears several times in her diaries.

1802: 5 Aug: *Miss Stone called on us. Called upon & walked with Miss Hughes. Afterwards with my Mother upon Mrs. Jordan, & the Miss Jones's.*

1803: 29 Aug: *to the Play at Richmond in the Evening with my Father & mother, where Mrs. Jordan performed the part of the Widow Bellmour in the Way to keep him in a masterly style.*

JOSEPH — Ellis William Joseph[69]

Ellis William Joseph (1794-1859), landed proprietor, was the son of Samuel and Leah Joseph. He married, at St Marylebone, Westminster, 15 March 1832, Amelia Hurdis Orme (1807-1890); they had at least 1 son and 1 daughter:

1 William Ellis Hurdis (b. 1833)
1 Amelia Sophia Sarah (b. 1834)

In 1841 the family was residing at North View House, Newchurch, Ryde, Isle of Wight. Whether they lived there at the time or were on holiday is not known. In the 1851 census, the family lived at 9 Park Place, Cheltenham. It is presumed that this is the same family who initially lived near Deerhurst, where the children were baptised.

1834: 15 Oct: *At the Palace a large party assembled to dinner. The Bishop and Mrs. Monk very courteous. I believe there were eleven ladies and as many gentlemen ... a Mr. & Mrs. Joseph, residing at or near Deerhurst.*

1847: 6 Nov: *travelling in the same coach with Mr. Josephs, an intelligent resident at Cheltenham, an acquaintance of some years standing.*

JOYNER Ellis — *see* Ellis

JUSTICE — John Justice

John Justice was a barrister, but he is not recorded among the lists of Oxford or Cambridge alumni.

1828: 17 Oct.

1830: 22 Apr.

1834: 16 Oct: *Conversations with Dr. Timbrill, Ford, and John Justice, the Barrister, and leader of the Sessions bar, about the prosecution threatened by Croad, who has not yet served on Mr. Bloxsome the writ. Dr. T. has ascertained that Croad is plotting to entangle Cox in the affair, by getting him into employment here, and bringing the action in his name only, the Cliffords abandoning it. Mr. B. furnished Brookes with a copy of notice to discontinue the action to be brought signed by Clifford and Cox and served on Croad: Brookes to get this signed by the parties—Justice cautioned me in the most friendly terms to be on my guard against any insidious proceeding of Croad or others acting for him, not to act personally in the affair, but to refer all to Bloxsome.*

K

KALKBRENNER — Friedrich Wilhelm Michael Kalkbrenner [1]

Friedrich Wilhelm Michael Kalkbrenner (1785-1849), pianist, composer, piano teacher, and piano manufacturer, was born in Germany, son of Christian Kalkbrenner. From a young age he studied at the Paris Conservatoire, and later in life he settled in Paris. He died there in 1849. Before the advent of Frédéric Chopin, Sigismond Thalberg, and Franz Liszt, Kalkbrenner was considered by many to be the foremost pianist in France and England, even Europe.

1820: 19 Jan: *In the second act also, Mr. Kalkbrenner a masterly performer on the Pianoforte played a beautiful Fantasia.*

KARR — *see* Seton-Karr

KAY-SHUTTLEWORTH — James Phillips Kay-Shuttleworth [2]

Sir James Phillips Kay-Shuttleworth, 1st baronet (1804-1877), civil servant and educationist, was born James Phillips Kay at Rochdale, Lancashire, the eldest of six children of Robert Kay, cotton merchant, and Hannah Phillips. He studied medicine and joined the Royal Medical Society, becoming its senior president for the 1825-26 session. In Edinburgh he worked at the New Town Dispensary which provided medicine and medical assistance on its premises and in the homes of the poor. His experience there, particularly during an outbreak of typhoid fever, gave him a rare insight into the lives of Edinburgh's poor; he was shocked by the conditions in which they lived and the extent of their suffering. It shaped his belief that poverty, disease, and misery were not caused—as many of his contemporaries insisted—by the individual failings of the poor, but were the consequences of broader social issues.

Kay believed that the workhouse schools were producing a new generation of young felons and thereby perpetuating the evils society identified in their parents. He became convinced that education held the secret to society's regeneration and began involving himself in the education of pauper children. In 1839 Lord Melbourne's whig administration established the committee of the privy council on education to better administer the government grant to education which had existed since 1833. Kay was appointed the committee's assistant secretary, effectively its senior bureaucrat; during his nine years in that office, he laid the foundations of the British public elementary school system. He was created 1st baronet in 1849.

1839: 2 Sep: *Recd. a packet forwarded "on her Majesty's Service"—free, from the Committee of Privy Council charged with superintending national education, containing three pamphlets on the subject, viz the substance of the two speeches made during the last session on this difficult question by the Marquess of Lansdowne, and Lord John Russell; and another entitled "Recent measures for the promotion of Education in England"—which may have been drawn up by Dr. Kay, late an Assistant Poor Law Commr. and now Secretary of the Comm. of Privy Council for the direction of a system of National Education.*

KAYAT — Assaad Yakub Kayat [3]

Assaad Yakub Kayat, also As'ad Khayyat or Assaad Jacoob Kayat (b. 1811), lecturer, translator, and surgeon, was born in Beirut, Lebanon. He was a Greek Orthodox Christian and taught at convents in Syria; he also studied and lectured in Britain, where he served as an emissary to the Persian princes Reeza Koolee Meerza, Najaf Koolee Meerza, and Taymoor Meerza. He had been visiting Syrian schools in the 1840s, helping the poor and distributing copies of the Holy Scripture. During this period, Syria was of particular interest to the Church of England given its proximity to the Holy Land. Kayat eventually earned a surgeon's degree and returned to the Middle East to practise.

Kayat learned English from American missionaries Issac Bird and Pliny Fisk, whom he met in 1823 in Syria when he was 12. Fisk had embarked on the first American mission to the Near East in 1819, with the primary aim of converting the Jews of Palestine. He died in Beirut in 1825, having nearly completed an Arab/English dictionary.

Kayat went on several lecture circuits. He wrote several books including *A Voice from Lebanon: With the Life and Travels of Assaad Y. Kayat*, published in 1847. He was certainly in England as early as 1836 when he acted as interpreter to the three princes of Meerza, who were members of the freemasons' lodge. He was married to Martha; they had at least 1 daughter:

1 Angelina Amelia Victoria Kayat (1844-1923+); recorded as living in Kensington, 1923

Kayat last comes to notice in 1865, acting for the British vice-consul in Jaffa.

1843: 31 Aug: *At three o'clock we went to the Town hall to attend the first of two lectures to be delivered by the Syrian Assaad Y. Kayat, to whom I had been introduced last spring in Town by the Witts's of Brunswick Square.* 1 Sep: *To Assaad's second lecture.*

KAYE — John Kaye [4]

John Kaye (1783-1853), bishop of Lincoln, was born in London, the only son of Abraham Kaye, a linen draper. He was educated at Christ's College, Cambridge (BA 1804; MA 1807; BD 1814; DD 1815). He was a fellow of the college in 1804, and a tutor and praelector. He was master in 1814-30, vice-chancellor in 1815-16, and regius professor of divinity in 1816-27. Kaye was elevated to the bishopric of Bristol in 1820 and served in that post until 1827; he was then translated as bishop of Lincoln and remained there until his death in 1853. Kaye was inducted as a fellow of the Royal Society in 1848, and made president of the Philosophical Society in 1827. He married, 1815, Eliza, eldest daughter of John Mortlock, banker, of Cambridge.

1823: 6 Feb.

1827: 17 Feb: *Dr. Kaye, Regius Professor of Divinity at Cambridge, and Head of Christ's College, is to be translated from the see of Bristol to that of Lincoln. There is some reason to hope, that Bishop Kaye may find an opportunity of providing in the Church for my friend F. Aston; there being an old family acquaintance, which Mr. Aston Senr. has diligently kept alive.*

1829: 11 Jul: *As I returned from Stanway in the carriage I read the excellent primary charge of the Bishop of Lincoln to his clergy delivered in 1828.*

1830: 31 Jan.

1832: 10 Apr.

1835: 6 Feb: *It appears that government has issued a Commission to enquire into the Reforms of which our Church establishment is susceptible, particularly, as refers to the equalization of the duties and revenues of the Bishops ... On this Commission are appointed the Archb. of Canterbury and York, the Bishops of Lincoln & Gloucester, the Bishop of London, the principal Ministers of State, Lord Harrowby, and certain eminent Civilians.*

KAYE — **William Kaye** — *see also* **Daubeny**[5]

William Kaye (1795-1864), barrister-at-law, JP, and landed proprietor, was born at Dulwich, Surrey, son of Joseph and Sarah Kaye. He was educated at Christ Church College, Oxford (BA 1819; MA 1821), and in 1821 was registered as a barrister-at-law of the Middle Temple. Kaye appears to have lived at Dowdeswell, near Cheltenham, and then at adjacent Sandywell, but these references from baptismal records may refer to the same home. By 1851 he lived at Ampney Park with his wife, Mary Cecilia (b. ±1799), who was born in Scotland. They had at least 3 sons and 4 daughters:

1 Ann (b. ±1826)
1 Joseph (1827-1901); educated at Eton College and Merton College, Oxford; barrister-at-law at the Middle Temple; a master of common pleas, 1869-75
2 Cecilia (b. ±1829); married Thomas Daubeny (1825-1887), son of Revd Edward Andrew Daubeny (1785-1877) and Jane Croome (1787-1860)
2 James (±1831-1886); educated at University College, Oxford; barrister-at-law of the Middle Temple
3 Ellen (b. ±1834)
4 Alice (b. ±1841)
3 Arthur (1843-1911), Church of England clergyman; educated at Magdalen College, Oxford; vicar of St Paul's, Middlesborough, 1875-84, and of Hessle, Yorkshire, 1884

By 1861 the family was living at Tetworth Hall, Huntingdonshire.

1845: 2 Apr: *The Gentlemen of the County, and personal friends of the High Sheriff, soon began to congregate—Mr. Daubeny (Ampney) Lyon (Miserden) Kaye (late of Sandywell Park, now of Ampney) Smith (Southrop) Col. Fendall (Sevenhampton) Henry, Frederick, and Raymond Cripps, C Pettatt, and several others.*

KEAN — **Edmund Kean**[6]

Edmund Kean (1789-1833), actor, was probably the most famous actor of his day; an extensive biography exists in the *DNB*. He married, at Stroud, 1808, Mary Chambers (1779-1849). Both Edmund and Mary performed on the Gloucester circuit, and later the Cheltenham circuit.

1820: 7 Jan: *In the Evening we went to the Theatre to see Kean in the character of Shylock, and it was truly well performed.* 21 Jan: *An anecdote of Kean, the actor, worth preserving, was mentioned by Lady Saumarez. While he was labouring in his vocation in an itinerant company of performers, he visited Guernsey, where, having engaged in the instruction of one or two young persons in reading and elocution, he had serious thoughts of setting up a school, if he could have been secure of a limited number of pupils, and so totally abandoning the stage. Disappointment in this scheme proved advantageous by throwing him eventually in the way of judges of his merit as an actor. It is said, that Dr. Drury of Harrow School first pointed him out to Mr. Arnold, when manager of Drury Lane, as worthy of an engagement.*

KEARNEY — **Henry John Kearney of White Waltham** — *see also* **Doyne**[7]

Henry John Kearney (1748-1827), JP, landed proprietor, and lieutenant-colonel in the 2nd Berkshire Militia, was the eldest son of Revd John Kearney and Henrietta, daughter of Revd Henry Brydges and niece of James Brydges, 1st duke of Chandos. He married, first, 20 January 1778, his second cousin, Augusta Brydges, daughter of Henry, 2nd duke of Chandos, and his only child by his second wife, Anne Jeffreys. Kearney was therefore great-nephew to the 1st duke of Chandos and son-in-law to the 2nd. Lady Augusta died without issue little more than a year after the marriage. Henry Kearney married secondly, at Walton, 29 November 1784, Anne (d. 1814), daughter and heir of Joseph Banks, of Revesby Abbey, Lincolnshire, sometime MP of Sheffield, of Lincoln's Inn, and chancellor of York; Anne and Henry had 3 daughters:

1 Caroline Mary Anne (1785-1854); married, at White Waltham, Berkshire, 23 September 1828, Bury Doyne (1794-1865), son of Charles Powlett Doyne and Eliza Jane Vicars
2 Henrietta Sophia (1787-1820); married, 2 December 1815, Tristram Cary (b. 1786) of White Castle, co. Donegal and The Casino, Derry; three children
3 Frances Elizabeth (1790-1874); died unmarried

Kearney was a keen military officer and served under Gen. Elliot at the siege of Gibraltar.

1801: 27 May: *In the evening to a party at Lady Lyttelton's, which was musical; The Harp, Grand Piano Forte & voice; the chief performers were, Miss Hadsley, Miss Bowles, Miss Canning, Miss Kearney, the Misses Halifax, Miss Stanhope, le Compte de Montmorency &c.* 13 Jul: *Walked with my Father to White Waltham to visit Col. Kearney. The Road leads through the Villages of Lawrence Waltham & Shottisbrook. We found Mr. and Mrs. Kearney at home, with Mr. Cartwright, her brother.* 15 Jul: *Mrs. & Miss Kearnies made a morning visit, when we had some music.* 8 May: *Received a letter from Mrs. Doyne, of White Waltham, near Maidenhead, soliciting a further examination of our title deeds of the Beck House property, in the hope that something may be discovered to elucidate the descent of the Banks family, formerly, as to one branch, possessed of Beck House, and in respect of whom I have been in correspondence with Miss Cooper, and Mrs. Williams. Mrs. D. is the party moving to substantiate a claim, as heir to one Revd. Moses Banks, who died many years ago at Brentford, leaving personalty, and whose heirs are now advertized for. Mrs. Doyne's mother was a Banks; her Father, the late Lt. Col. Kearney, formerly commanded, I believe, the Cambridgeshire Militia, and was known to my Father and Mother in my boyhood at Edinburgh.*

KEARSEY — **John Kearsey**[8]

John Kearsey (±1794-1842), Stow Union Workhouse relieving officer, was a failed corn and coal merchant before he accepted the position of relieving officer at the union workhouse. He took advantage of the law for insolvent debtors to make a fresh start in life. His wife, Frances (1789-1868), was the schoolmistress at Stow-on-the-Wold. In 1841 there were two children on the census:

1 Frances (1823-1891); died unmarried
2 Emily (b. ±1825)

By 1851 Frances was listed as a widow living at 126 Sheep Street. One reference states that the school was actually run by both John and Frances prior to his death, so it may have been that the post of relieving officer was not a full-time commitment.

1837: 8 Jun: *It soon appeared that three of these had no chance, and the competition rested between Kearsey, Milbourn, and J. P. Reynolds.*

1838: 22 Nov: *While these matters were going on, Kearsey the R.O. Dist. 2. was arrested by a Sheriff's officer in the hall of the*

W.H. at the suit of a Creditor for a private debt incurred before his appointment as R.O.; and was carried away to Glouc. gaol. 29 Nov., 17 Dec: *Recd. and ansd. a note from Pearce, accompanying a letter arrived this morning from the P.L.C. approving the resolutions to which our board had come as to the appointment of Coll. of Poor Rates; recommending that Kearsey the unfortunate Rel. Off. should be advised to resign, in failure of which the P.L.C. propose to discharge him as incompetent to hold office in consequence of his Insolvency.* 20 Dec: *The Guardians had been also summoned to hear the letter of the PLC. on the subject of the appointment of Collectors of Poor Rates, & the arrest of the Rel. Officer of Distr. 2. as mentioned by me on the 17th. when the Board acceded to a proposition which I made, that a Committee should be formed to collect facts as to the arrest of J. Kearsey in order to ascertain the correctness of the general impression that he had been ill-used by the Creditor at whose suit he is thrown into prison.* 27 Dec.

1839: 10 Jan: *I recd. an answer to the effect that the P.L.C. had sanctioned the Board's retaining Kearsey in the office which he holds, when he shall be discharged at the next sitting of the Insolvent Debtors Court at Gloucester.* 21 Mar: *Kearsey the R.O. resumed his duties, having been discharged a few days since from Gloucester Gaol by the Commrs. of the Insolvent debtors Court, without further stain on his character.* 2 May: *Kearsey desired time for consideration.*

1842: *To Kearsey, R. O. of our Union, requesting him to procure for me the valuation for parochial purposes of the hamlet of Clapton.* 28 Jul: *His colleague, Kearsey, was put in charge of Distr. 1. late Tidmarsh's, for the remainder of this quarter, and to ascertain, by experience, whether the business of out-relief &c for the whole union could be conducted properly by one Officer.* 15 Aug: *A note from Mr. Wilkins, brought by a candidate for the situation of Rel. Off., announced to me the decease of poor Kearsey, who was taken ill after the meeting of the Guardians on Thursday, and died this morning; a great loss, for he was an honest, punctual, well-meaning man.* 18 Aug.

KEATING — Henry Singer Keating[9]

Sir Henry Singer Keating (1804-1888), MP, judge, and solicitor-general for England and Wales, was born in Dublin, the third son of Lt-Gen. Sir Henry Sheehy Keating KCB and Mary Anne, eldest daughter of James Singer of Annandale, co. Dublin. He was educated at Trinity College, Dublin, and the Inner Temple. He practised on the Oxford circuit, at the Oxford and Gloucester sessions. Keating was MP for Reading in 1852-60, and solicitor-general for England and Wales in 1857-58 and 1859. He was knighted in 1857.

1840: 21 Sep: *At the Unicorn met and parleyed with Mr. Keating, one of the Revising Barristers for East Gloucestershire, now on a circuit with a colleague for the purpose of revising the registration lists of County Voters. Mr. K. is a sound lawyer, and talented man, who attends our Quarter Sessions. He is an Irishman.*

1843: 23 Sep., 27 Sep., 2 Oct.

1845: 4 Jul: *With Curtis Hayward, Hale, and other Magistrates, held a conference with the leading and Senior counsel, Greaves, Keatinge, and Francillon, as to the rule respecting fees to Counsel which they consider objectionable.*

1846: 11 Aug.

1847: 5 Apr: *Left home after breakfast for Gloucester; to Cheltenham in the phaeton: thence to Gloucester by the railway; travelling with Mr. Keating, the Barrister, and Mr. Wiggin.*

1848: 22 Nov.

1852: 30 Mar: *Agreeably to what had been arranged between myself and Mr. Brookes, who was Attorney for the prosecution, Mr. Keating, Q.C., had been retained as Senior.*

KEBLE — John Keble[10]

John Keble (1792-1866), Church of England clergyman, was born at Fairford, Gloucestershire, son of John Keble (1745-1834), vicar of Coln St Aldwyn. He was educated at Corpus Christi, Oxford, and later became a fellow of Oriel College. Keble was asked to stand for the Oxford chair of poetry in 1821, but he declined. On the death of his mother in 1823 he became curate at Southrop to be nearer to his father at Fairford. He remained a fellow of Oriel, although he seldom visited the college. He did, however, retain links with Oxford, and pupils occasionally joined him for reading parties at Southrop in the vacation.

During his time at Southrop Keble wrote *The Christian Year*, which appeared in 1827 and was probably the widest selling book of poetry in the nineteenth century. Its diverse readership went well beyond the high-church element within the Church of England, and beyond the Church of England itself. Published anonymously in July 1827, a first edition of 500 copies was soon followed by a second edition in November. Six additional poems were added to the third edition in 1828. By 1837 there had been sixteen editions, and ninety-five by Keble's death in 1866. When copyright expired in 1873 there were 158 editions and copyright sales stood at 379,000. The phenomenal success of the book distressed its reticent author, who devoted the profits to the restoration of Hursley church, where he had been appointed vicar in 1835. He remained vicar of Hursley for thirty years until his death.

It was from the relative—although somewhat 'cultivated'—obscurity of the country parish that Keble achieved his fame both as a poet and a protagonist in the ecclesiastical events of his day. His active interest in church affairs never abated. He visited Oxford or London when necessary and published forceful tracts and letters on doctrinal issues and matters of church and state. At Hursley, Keble endeavoured to implement Tractarian pastoral ideals in a quiet yet firm manner, working under the watchful eye of his patron, the Tractarian squire at Hursley Park, who ensured that no dissenting tenants rented land in the village. New churches were built for the outlying hamlets of Ampfield and Otterbourne; Hursley church was completely rebuilt and daily services were introduced. Being out of Oxford, Keble could give little active support to the events unfolding there.

Keble contributed nine of the *Tracts for the Times* and was joint author with Newman and Pusey from 1836 of *The Library of the Fathers*. Keble was not the man to marshal Tractarian sympathisers shaken by Newman's secession. Nevertheless he did not withdraw from public controversy, and sought to reassure those who, like himself, felt it impossible to desert the Church of England. He helped Pusey in opposing Hampden's elevation to the bishopric of Hereford in 1847, and threw himself into the controversy relating to the Gorham judgment in 1850.

1827: 16 Dec: *Among them stand preeminent Davison, Bishop, Whately, Keble, James, Hawkins, Tyler &c. most of whom have striven to rival each other in publications on points of Divinity or metaphysical Science; and their works have always excited attention and respect.*

1838: 5 Jan: *Enjoyed two or three hours of conversation on all manner of topics ... the opinions entertained by Newman, Pusey, Keble &c.*

1844: 8 Oct: *The greater number of the non placets were young men; Dr. Pusey did not appear, Newman & J. Keble were present.*

KEBLE — Thomas Keble [11]

Thomas Keble (1793-1875), Church of England clergyman, was the younger son of John Keble, vicar of Coln St Aldwyns, and the brother of John Keble (*above*). Thomas was educated entirely by his father up to his election as Gloucestershire scholar of Corpus Christi, Oxford (BA 1811; BD 1822). He served as curate of Sherborne with Windrush in 1817-18. He married, 1824, Elizabeth Jane (1804-1870), elder daughter of Revd George Clarke, rector of Meysey Hampton, near Cirencester, and an old family friend. In 1827 Keble was instituted to the living of Bisley, which he served for forty-six years, adopting Tractarian views. He published four of the *Tracts for the Times*, numbers 12, 22, 43, and 84. The last was completed by Prevost.

1839: 2 Jan: *Of the Clergy there were present Dr. Hall, Prebendary, the Archd. of Bristol, Sir Geo. Prevost (*b. ±1807*), Messrs. Phillips, Parsons, Powell, Trye, Ford, Waller, Christie, Dowling, Winchester, Davies, Keble, and many others: Also a good many ladies, Mrs. Monk, Mrs. Phillips &c.*

KEEN — George Keen [12]

George Keen (±1802-1874), toll gate collector, lived at Stow-on-the-Wold in 1841. By 1851 he had moved to Warwick, where he was registered as a toll gate collector. He lived with his wife Hannah (b. ±1807); they had at least 2 sons and 1 daughter:

1 George (b. ±1827)
2 Edward (b. ±1833)
1 Hannah (b. ±1837)

There was another George Keen (b. ±1798) at Stow, and therefore this attribution is somewhat tentative. However, this George Keen was closer in age to Cox and Clifford, and is likely to have been in the same social circle.

1834: 18 Jul: *Rode to Stow through very heavy thunder rain to meet Messrs. Ford, Jeaffreson and Pole, and examine evidence in the matter of the pros. against Clifford and Cox for the robbery and murder of F. J. Rens... The evidence of George Keen, as corrected by that of J. D. Charles, goes far to prove the existence of a jealous feeling on the part of Cox.*

1837: 29 May: *A letter from Mr. Pole, who returned to Town this morning on Police matters, with papers annexed, and to inform me that the Lords of the Treasury have consented to pay £20 towards the expences incurred by the Mag. in prosecuting the estreat of the recognizances of R. Clifford, Keen and Marshall.*

KEETCH — William Keetch of Urchfont, Wiltshire [13]

William Keetch (1779-1844), gentleman farmer, was born at Urchfont, son of William Keetch (1751-1806) and Judith Compton (1759-1847). She married her husband in 1778 'with the consent of her parents'.

1806: 28 Oct: *Met a party to Tea & Supper at Mr. Compton's, the Legg's, Butchers, Mr. W. Keetch & ourselves.*

1807: 24 Jan: *After breakfast rode to meet Mr. Edwards's Foxhounds with Butcher & Keetch.* 20 Apr.

KEILEY — Charles Keiley [14]

Charles Keiley (b. 1812), deputy chief constable of Gloucestershire, was married to Maryann (b. ±1815). They had at least eight children, including the following 2 sons and 1 daughter:

1 Mary (b. ±1834)
1 Charles (b. ±1837)
2 Samuel (b. ±1840)

In 1841 the family lived at 6 St George's Place, Cheltenham, and by 1851 at 54 St George's Place. Keiley joined the Gloucestershire Constabulary on 1 December 1839, and was promoted to superintendent on 12 December 1839. He became the first deputy chief constable in July 1840. On 21 June 1853 he absconded with the Tewkesbury and Cheltenham divisions' wages, amounting to £485. The following day Chief Constable Anthony Lefroy, assuming that Keiley and his family planned to leave the country, telegraphed the information to Southampton, Bristol, Liverpool, London, and Birmingham. He then advised Purnell, the chairman of the quarter sessions, on what had happened. Purnell told him to also telegraph Hull, Holyhead, and Glasgow, adding, 'If you have no policeman of sufficient acuteness in your own town you had better employ a London detective officer as you are responsible for the deficit.' The quarter sessions agreed to offer a reward of £100 for Keiley's apprehension, but despite continual surveillance of his address and numerous other investigations, he disappeared without trace.

1840: 29 Jun: *We devoted the evening, and till nearly midnight, to the auditing of accounts, chiefly to the examination of the Constabulary Accounts for the Quarter, Mr. Keiley, the Superintendent of the Cheltenham district, and very efficient subordinate to the Chief Constable, attending upon us in the absence of Mr. Lefroy.*

1842: 7 Jan: *Repaired to the Station House, where passed some time in conferring with Lefroy, and his deputy, Keiley, on Rural Police affairs.* 11-12 Apr., 15 Apr., 27 Jun., 22 Oct., 17 Nov: *Mr. Keiley, Deputy Chief Constable, waited on me to solicit me for a recommendation to the Staffordshire Magistrates, he being one of the Candidates for the office of Chief Constable in that county.* 18 Nov., 7 Dec: *Mr. Keiley has not succeeded in his application for the office of Chief Constable of Rural Police in Staffordshire.*

1843: 2 Jan., 16 Oct.

1844: 1 Jan., 8 Mar., 14 Oct., 30 Dec: *A complaint against the High Constable is expected to-morrow in consequence of his having dismissed Russel, the acting, thief-taking, and clever Superintendent at Cheltenham: Keiley his Co-Superintendent being principally engaged in duties of Deputy Chief Constable and in keeping the books and accounts of the force.*

1845: 17 Apr., 30 Jun: *The Magistrates present took into consideration a very unpleasant affair connected with the Constabulary, a charge of assault with intent to commit a rape having been brought before the Cheltenham Magistrates against Mr. Keiley, the Deputy Chief Constable, by a girl, the daughter of a police-man who lived as nurse to Keiley's children, in the Cheltenham station house, where Mr. & Mrs. K. with their family have apartments.* 1 Jul., 5 Jul: *... on the 22d., on which day the investigation into the charge against Keiley is to be undertaken.*

1847: 22 Mar., 28 Jun., 18 Oct.

1848: 3 Jan., 20 Mar., 26 Jun., 30 Jun: *Called at the Police Station on Mr. Lefroy: looked over the premises with him and Keiley & Hambidge, his deputy and chief Superintendent, with a view to enlargement.* 16 Oct., 19 Oct.

1849: 31 Dec.

1850: 28 Jan., 3 May, 14 May, 1 Jul., 5 Jul., 14 Oct., 19 Oct., 30 Dec.

1851: 17 Mar.

1852: 16 Mar.

1853: 3 Jan., 25 Jun: *Lefroy drove from Cheltenham and arrived while I was at breakfast; he came with a heavy heart, and sad countenance. All things he said were against him: Mrs. L. was very ill, having miscarried; and his Deputy, Keiley, had absconded with more than £400 of the County money, on Thursday night. L. had only discovered the delinquency on Friday forenoon—the money had been remitted to him by the County Treasurer, under Lefroy's authority, to pay the Constables of the Cheltenham and Tewkesbury districts, over which K. was Superintendent, together with other demands on the Constabulary for rents of Station houses, coals, &c. supplied.... He had unbounded confidence in Keiley: so, indeed, had most who knew him either in his public or private capacity: he was considered a good, active, intelligent officer, and excellent accountant & Clerk: but, no doubt, he has fallen into pecuniary embarrassment, through the burden of a large family,—a wife and eight children—and perhaps, a taste for betting, card playing or billiards. K. is an Irishman, & came with Lefroy in 1839, when our Rural Police was first established: he held from the first the office of Deputy Chief Constable, and one habitually looked on the pair as Robinson Crusoe and his man Friday: giving the man credit for more abilities than the master.* 27 Jun: *Mr. Boodle, probably, with a hope that proceedings might not be taken against K. if the money taken by him were restored, intimated to Lefroy and me, that, if the Deputy Chief Constable had not been guilty of embezzlement or larceny, his friends would make good the amount taken to the extent of £500. Possibly, too, this communication might be made in order to gain time for the offender's escape by checking prompt measures for his apprehension....*

KELLY — Mr Kelly at Clifton — *see also* Sheridan *and* de Mauny

The entry for Kelly and Sheridan is enigmatic. Nothing has been found to identify them conclusively, but presumably Kelly was of the Clifton Irish set. Sheridan was almost certainly Charles Francis Sheridan (1750-1806), elder brother to Richard Brinsley Sheridan.

Given the Sheridan connection, there is a chance that Mr Kelly was Michael Kelly (1762-1826), Irish singer, composer, and theatrical manager, who made a significant international career. A close associate of Richard Brinsley Sheridan, Michael Kelly was one of the leading figures in British musical theatre around the turn of the nineteenth century, and a friend of Mozart and Paisiello. With his friend Nancy Storace, he was one of the first singers of the age from Ireland or Britain to make a front-rank reputation in Italy and Austria. In Italy he was also known as O'Kelly or even Signor Ochelli.

It would not be at all surprising for him to be in Bristol or Clifton at this time, but even so, this attribution should be treated as tentative.

1806: 26 Feb: *Walked with Robins, the Ch. de Mauny, Mr. Kelly, Mr. Sheridan, all of whom I ought to avoid.* 3 Mar: *To Bristol: to the Fair etc: joined Mr. Kelly.*

KELLY — the Kelly family of Acton, Middlesex

1836: 29 Aug: *A party of friends arrived from Cheltenham: three Roman Catholic ladies, a mother and two daughters, of the name of Kelly, Irish, but residing near London.* 30 Aug: *While we had been rambling about Langstone's premises, the ladies had been driving to Miss Langstone's Cottage in Sarsgrove, and the whole party assembled to luncheon, after which a new arrangement for the amusement of his guests was made by Barter, ever studious to make his guests them enjoy a visit to his hospitable house. While the married ladies with the younger of the Misses Barter, Miss Louisa Kelly, and the Governess went partly on foot, and partly in an open carriage to the Mansion and grounds of Mr. L., Mr. Barter and I accompanied by the eldest Miss B., a very pleasing and well informed, though not handsome, girl, and Miss Adelaide Kelly took a long ride.* 31 Aug: *Shortly after breakfast Mrs. Kelly and her daughter departed for their residence at Acton.*

KEMBALL — Eliza Mary Kemball, daughter of Christopher Jeaffreson

Eliza Mary Kemball, née Jeaffreson (b. 1806), married at Longborough, 16 October 1827, Arthur Clark Kemball.

1842: 6 Jun.

KEMBLE — Charles Kemble[15]

Charles Kemble (1775-1854), actor, was born at Brecon, a younger brother of John Philip Kemble, Stephen Kemble, and Sarah Siddons. He was educated at Douai in France. His first London stage appearance was in 1794, as Malcolm to his brother's Macbeth. In comedy he was ably supported by his wife, Marie Therese, née De Camp, whom he had married in 1806. His visit to America with his daughter Fanny in 1832-34 aroused much enthusiasm. The later part of his career was beset by money troubles in connection with his joint proprietorship of Covent Garden Theatre. He formally retired from the stage in December 1836.

Maria Theresa Kemble, née De Camp (1777-1838), actress, was born in Vienna on 17 January 1777, the eldest of the six children of George Lewis De Camp, a musician, and Jeanne Adrienne Dufour, a dancer. She was brought to England as a child, and at the age of 8 appeared at the King's Theatre as Cupid in the ballet *Noverre*. She was later secured for Drury Lane, where, as Miss De Camp, on 24 October 1786, she played Julie in Burgoyne's *Richard Coeur de Lion*. After a lengthy courtship—and some delay given the disapproval of his family—Maria Theresa De Camp married Charles Kemble on 2 July 1806 at St George's, Bloomsbury. She then accompanied him, and the rest of the Kemble clan, to Covent Garden, where she made her first appearance as Maria in *The Citizen*. She remained at Covent Garden for the rest of her acting career. Charles and Maria had numerous children; those surviving were John Mitchell, Henry Vincent James (1812-1857), Frances [Fanny], and Adelaide.

1808: 25 Feb: *In the Evening to Covent Garden Theatre, where I was much amused by a very interesting Drama a Swedish Fable, entitled the Wanderer, or the Rights of Hospitality. Miss Smith very great, Charles Kemble excellent as the Hero. This was followed by a capital new Farce the Widow's Choice by Allingham, very humorous, much applauded, musical: Miss Decamp, Fawcett, Munden, excellent.*

KEMP — Mr Kemp, editor of the *Gloucestershire Chronicle*

1835: 26 Apr: *Received a private circular from Mr. Kemp, the Editor of the Gloucestershire Chronicle.* 7 May: *Wrote to Mr. Kemp, the editor of the Gloucestershire Chronicle.*

1837: 4 Jan.

KEMPTHORNE — John Kempthorne[16]

John Kempthorne (1775-1838), Church of England clergyman, was born at Plymouth, son of Adm. James Kempthorne (1737-1808) and Eleanor (1747-1817), daughter of Revd Sampson Sandys, rector of Landewednack and Ruan Minor, Cornwall. He was educated at St John's College, Cambridge (BA 1796; MA 1799; BD 1807). He was a fellow of the college in 1796-1802, and ordained deacon on 25 April 1802 and priest on 19 December 1802. His first clerical appointment, from 13 May 1808, was as curate of Claybrooke with Wibtoft, straddling the boundaries of Warwickshire and

Leicestershire. He was then domestic chaplain to Henry Ryder (1777-1836), bishop of Gloucester, and later bishop of Lichfield and Coventry. He served as vicar of Northleach, Gloucestershire, in 1816-38, vicar of Preston in 1817-20, and rector of St Michael's and St Mary-de-Grace, Gloucester, in 1825-38.

Kempthorne married, 8 June 1802, Eliza (1739-1823), daughter of Revd Richard Whish, rector of Northwold, Norfolk; they had at least 1 son and 2 daughters:

1 Sampson (1809-1873); married, at St Stephen's, Coleman Street, City of London, 18 January 1838, Marianne Pratt
1 Mary Buchanan (1810-1892); died unmarried
2 Elizabeth (1812-1830); died unmarried

1826: 15 Jun: *Nine penitents are now accommodated in the house, and there are accommodations for eleven; the Matron appears a very respectable person; Messrs. Kempthorne and Whish are prominent persons in the Committee.*

1828: 18 Jul.

1835: 14 Apr: *Mr. Kempthorne as Vicar of St. Michael's, the parish in which I was a temporary resident, was Commissioner.*

1838: 1 Dec: *Northleach is vacant by the recent decease of Mr. Kempthorne, a very pious and talented divine, of the Evangelical School, who held also the living of St. Michael's, Gloucester.*

KENDALL — Edward Kendall — *see also* Nurse *and* Symons [17]

[George] Edward Kendall (1789-1872), JP and landed proprietor, was the son of Edward Kendall (b. 1750), of Austrey, Warwickshire, and Elizabeth Irton (b. 1767). He married Anna Maria Darling (d. 1831); they had at least 3 daughters:

1 Georgiana (±1820-1888); married, 1845, John Sobieski Stolberg Stuart [real name John Carter Allen] (±1795-1872), who claimed to be the heir of Charles Edward Stuart, the Young Chevalier; no children
2 Rose (±1821-1899); married, at Cheltenham, 14 March 1844, William Nurse (1814-1866) of Barbados
3 Angelina (±1824-1913); married, at St James's, Paddington, 16 June 1845, Jelinger Cookson Symons (1809-1860)

1852: 18 Mar: *Mr. Kendall, an agreeable & sensible man, with whom as a Magistrate I had long been acquainted, not now resident at Cheltenham, but possessing a house there, and visiting his Son in law, and daughter, Mr. and Mrs. Nourse, who were of the Lefroy's Guests, the gentleman less attractive than the lady, who is pretty and pleasing. Another daughter of Mr. Kendal is married to Mr. Jelinger Symons, the Barrister.*

KENDALL — William Kendall [18]

William Kendall (±1794-1877), solicitor at Bourton-on-the-Water, was in partnership with John North Wilkins (±1788-1854). He was born in the parish of St James, Westminster, son of William and Amelia Kendall, and married, at Bourton-on-the-Water, April 1825, his business partner's half-sister, Letitia (b. 1803). She was the daughter of Baptists Revd William Wilkins and his second wife, Letitia, daughter of John Field and Anne Cromwell. William and Letitia Kendall had at least 2 sons and 5 daughters:

1 William Hubert (1825-1880); in both 1851 and 1861 he resided in lodgings, and was listed in the latter census as 'imbecile'; presumably died unmarried
1 Letitia Amelia (1826-1855); married, at Kemnay, Aberdeenshire, 2 September 1849, Alexander George Burnett, 6th laird of Kemnay (1816-1908); 2 sons and 2 daughters
2 Harriet Edith (b. 1828)
3 Frances Harriet (b. 1829)
2 Edmund (1831-1839)
4 Isabella (1834-1909); died unmarried at Hastings
5 Harriet (±1835-1921); died unmarried at Hastings

By 1881 Harriet and Isabella, both unmarried, lived together at 3 Quarry Terrace, Hastings, Sussex.

1828: 20 Oct: *I went by appointment to the Office of Messrs. Wilkins & Kendal, Solicitors, Bourton on the Water, to complete a purchase, which we had recently made of Mr. Dolphin.*

1830: 22 Apr.

1834: 22 Sep., 15 Nov: *Walked with E.F.W. to Bourton to Messrs. Wilkins & Kendal's office, where I met Mr. Ford, and held a bed of justice.*

1835: 6 Jan., 18 Mar: *Engaged at home and at the office of Messrs. Wilkins & Kendal, Bourton, transacting parochial business, in the matter of Jacob Parker, a man of very questionable character.* 15 May, 28 May, 1 Jun: Messrs. *Wilkins and Kendal called in the Evening to confer with me about the proceedings of Mr. Ackerley, the letter to Lord Melbourne &c.*

1836: 25 Aug., 24 Oct.

1837: 6 Feb: *Rode to Bourton to call at Messrs. Wilkins & Kendal's office to make affidavit before one of them as an extra master in Chancery in a matter arising out of my Hunt Exorship.* 8 Apr., 14 Apr., 31 May, 1 Jun., 10 Jun., 30 Sep., 18 Nov., 13 Dec: *Suggested the propriety of our putting in an appearance and of employing Wilkins and Kendal as our Attornies.* 14 Dec: *Arranged with the Dean of Gloucester that Messrs. Wilkins & Kendall should be employed by us to defend the action brought against us by Mr. D'Oyley.*

1838: 2 Feb., 14 Feb., 4 May, 7 May, 1 Jun., 16 Jun., 19-20 Jun., 24 Jun., 30 Jun: *In the evening Messrs. Wilkins and Kendal called, and conferred with me on parochial business.* 24 Jul., 11 Aug., 14 Aug.

1839: 17 May.

1840: 15 May, 30 May, 5 Jun., 5-6 Aug., 10 Sep.

1842: 21 Jan., 11 Feb: *Wrote to Messrs. Wilkins and Kendal, soliciting them to give their advice as to a difficult point as to the course which should be taken by a good old parishioner of mine.* 12 Feb., 14 Feb., 25-26 Feb., 13 Mar., 28 May, 3 Jun.

1843: 27 Jan., 18 Aug., 30 Sep., 27 Oct., 27 Nov., 4 Dec., 12 Dec.

1844: 16 Feb., 10 Aug., 4 Oct.

1845: 6 Jun.

1846: 28 Jul: *Talked with Mr. K. as to the land in Lower Slaughter, which Prosser has unwarily contracted to buy, and which he has asked me to purchase. Mr. K assured me that if I were disposed to become the owner, the money for the purchase should be advanced by himself and partner to me without mortgage, on my note, to be repaid as might suit my convenience.* 5 Sep.

1847: 25 Jun., 30 Sep., 2 Oct.

1848: 11 Jun.

1851: 14 Feb., 15 Mar.

1852: 3 Apr., 8 Jun.

1854: 13 Jul.

KENDRICK — John Kendrick and the Kendrick family at Toddington and Stanway [19]

John Kendrick (b. 1763), innkeeper and chapman, was imprisoned in 1823. Nothing unrelated to his bankruptcy and imprisonment has been discovered about his unfortunate wife or sons.

1823: 29 Apr: *Frederick Aston very unexpectedly came to dinner. He had been induced to ride over to communicate a very distressing event, which had happened at Stanway this morning, the suicide of one of the parishioners, a married woman, of the name of Kendrick, about sixty years of age, who drowned herself in the canal, a piece of water in the pleasure grounds of Stanway House. Kendrick, the husband, has resided at Stanway for some years, since he became bankrupt as an Innkeeper at Toddington; he is now committed to gaol, for refusing to answer questions put to him by the Commissioners of his second bankruptcy, his affairs being again involved Kendrick &, I fear, his sons, are most unprincipled persons: the want of sound religious principle, uncontrolled passionateness of feeling, and dread of poverty and accumulated distress, have no doubt brought on the temporary insanity, under the influence of which the wretched woman has sought a watery grave.*

1840: 9 Sep: *Also a letter from F. Aston accompanying a report of the London Orphan Asylum Institution, followed by a list of subscribers, to be looked over with a view to aid the cause of Eliza Kendrick, the orphan niece on whose behalf E. Chidley wrote to me yesterday.* 12 Sep., 15 Sep: *Wrote to F. Aston, returning to him the list of subscribers to the London Orphan Asylum, and reporting what I had done to forward the interest of Eliza Kendrick.* 16 Sep., 20-21 Sep., 29 Sep., 2 Oct.

KENNAWAY — Charles Edward Kennaway [20]

Charles Edward Kennaway (1800-1875), Church of England clergyman, was born at Talaton, Devon, the second son Sir John Henry Kennaway, 1st baronet (1758-1836), and Charlotte Amyatt (1775-1845). He was educated at Harrow School and St John's College, Cambridge. He served as vicar of Chipping Campden, Gloucestershire, in 1832-73, perpetual curate of Christ Church, Cheltenham, in 1840-43, and perpetual curate of Holy Trinity chapel, Brighton, in 1843-47. Charles married, first, 17 June 1830, Emma (1810-1843), fourth daughter of Revd Gerard Thomas Noel. He married secondly, at St Margaret's, Westminster, 30 December 1845, Olivia (1816-1888), daughter of Revd Lewis Way of Stansted Park, Sussex; they had 1 son and 2 daughters:

1 Charles Louis (1847-1940)
1 Agnes Olivia (1849-1936)
2 Mariona (1850-1929)

1837: 6 Oct: *Of those leaning or embraced in the principles of the Evangelical school, I observed the Incumbent of Campden, Mr. Kennaway.*

1838: 19 Feb.

1840: 3 Jul: *At the former admired the exceedingly beautiful new Church lately erected and consecrated, of which Mr. Kennaway, the Vicar of Campden, is minister.* 27 Oct: *The sermon was preached by the Revd. —Kennaway, a very estimable and zealous Clergyman, who has taken a leading part in the arrangements for the erection of this new church. I had formed his acquaintance some time ago at the table of Lord Northwick: he is a brother of a Devonshire Baronet, himself a builder and restorer of Churches, and Vicar of Campden, where he was highly esteemed during the time of his residence there, as also in the neighbourhood; but he has removed to Cheltenham, to be the minister of the new Church built at Bays Hill, which was consecrated last winter, and where he is looked upon as a very good preacher by many. I apprehend that he should be classed as of the Evangelical party in the Church, zealous and serious.*

1843: 27 Aug: *The stated minister of this chapel since the decease of one of the brothers Anderson, Clergymen held in high esteem at Brighton, is Mr. Kennaway, the Incumbent of Campden, and lately Minister of St. Paul's, Cheltenham, from which he retired some time since.*

1848: 13 Jan: *Mr. Estcourt was seconded by Kennaway, Vicar of Campden, also bred in the Low Church School, well known in Cheltenham and Brighton, as a preacher, and the writer of theological and devotional publications, but having likewise imbibed some of the inclinations of the Tractarian party.* 22 May.

1850: 1 Oct., 8 Nov: ... *Mr. Kennaway, always ambitious to speak, always fluent, never deep, followed ably, enforcing and enlarging upon what had fallen from the preceding speakers.* 17-18 Nov.

KENNEDY — Charles Pratt Kennedy [21]

Charles Pratt Kennedy (±1790-1875), HEIC army officer, was born in Ireland, son of John Kennedy and Elizabeth Cole (d. 1828). He married Charlotte Unett (±1822-1903). Kennedy was in the Bengal Artillery, and later the Royal Artillery, from 1808 to 1865. He is considered to be the founder of Shimla, summer capital of the British Raj and current capital of Himachal Pradesh. The couple lived at 13 Lansdown Crescent, Cheltenham. There do not appear to have been any children.

1848: 27 Sep: *A letter from a Major Kennedy of Cheltenham, enquiring the character of our late servant Amy Hollis.* 28 Sep.

KENNEY — Sophia Kenney — *see* Samuel John Jeaffreson

KENNY — Matthias Kenny — *see also* Richard Vavasour *and* Pollard [22]

Matthias Kenny (±1788-1874), army officer, JP, and doctor of medicine, was born at Treanmanagh, Ballyclancahill, Kilfenora, Ireland, the eldest son of David Kenny and Mary O'Gorman. He studied at Ennis College and Edinburgh University, where he graduated with a medical degree in 1810. He joined the Army as an assistant surgeon in 1810, and later served in the Royal Artillery in the Peninsular War and the battle of Waterloo. He retired on half pay in 1819 and became a licentiate of the College of Physicians on 25 July 1819; he is included on their roll of eminent physicians. He married, in 1836, Anna Maria Pollard, of Castle Pollard, a first cousin to Richard Vavasour—Maria's mother Sophia was the younger sister of Anne Vavasour, née Bull, who was Richard's mother. There were no children of the marriage. The couple lived at Clifton Terrace in Monkstown, Dublin, and in the village of Castle Pollard.

1845: 19 Feb: *A medical gentleman, Dr. Kenny, from Ireland, who had been many years back the professional attendant of the Vavasours, and of their connections, the Pollards, and who, some few years ago, married Miss Pollard, happened very opportunely to have lately arrived at Cheltenham after a sojourn abroad, and to have taken a house there; though in very bad health, he and Mrs. Kenny kindly offered to receive Mr. and Mrs. Dryden into their house.* 21 Feb., 24 Feb., 3 Mar: *I called afterwards at the house in Oriel Place occupied by the Kennys and Drydens, but was not admitted further than the vestibule where I had a few moments interview with Mrs. Vavasour, who was sadly agitated, and cast down.* 22 Mar., 30 May, 2 Jun: *E.F.W. walked over with his fishing rod; Sophy and the children had driven by Stow, having called at "the Cottage" on Dr. and Mrs. Kenny, who are on a visit to the Vavasours.* 4 Jun.

1846: 19 Oct.

KENT — the duchess of Kent — *see* Saxe-Coburg-Saalfeld

KENT — John Kent of Upton-on-Severn[23]

John Kent, liquor merchant, of Buryfield House, Upton-on-Severn.

1837: 17 Feb: *Wrote to Mr. Kent of Upton on Severn for the character of the person whom Gibbs has recommended to me as a Servant.* 20 Feb., 23 Feb.

KENYON — George Kenyon[24]

George Kenyon, 2nd Baron Kenyon (1776-1855), barrister-at-law, was born in the parish of St Giles-in-the-Fields, Middlesex, the second but first surviving son of cousins Lloyd Kenyon (1732-1802) and Mary Kenyon (1741-1808). He was educated at Christ Church, Oxford (BA 1797; MA 1801; DCL 1814). Kenyon was called to the bar at the Middle Temple. He succeeded as 2nd Baron Kenyon in 1802.

1828: 2 May: *Lord Kenyon, unable to attend in his place in consequence of the decease of his daughter.*

1832: 15 Mar., 6 Jun.

KERSLAKE — Thomas Kerslake[25]

Thomas Kerslake (1813-1891), bookseller, lived at Westbury-on-Trym. His bookshop was at 3 Park Street, Bristol.

1852: 16 Jan., 31 Jan: *Wrote to Kerslake, Bookseller, Bristol, with an order for a book on the County History of Gloucestershire, Bigland's Glouc., which appears to be on sale in one of his catalogues.* 5 Feb., 12 Apr., 15 Apr., 24 Apr., 28-29 Apr., 2 May, 4 May, 7 May, 24 Nov., 27 Nov., 4 Dec., 8 Dec, 13 Dec., 16 Dec.

1853: 16 Feb., 18 Feb., 26 Feb., 1 Mar., 7 May: *Wrote to Kerslake, Bookseller, Bristol, desiring him to send the copies of Lyson's Illustrations of Gloucestershire and Woodchester, to meet me next Monday or Tuesday at Gloucester.* 3 Jun., 29 Dec.

KEY — John Key[26]

Sir John Key, 1st baronet (1794-1858), MP and lord mayor of London, was born at Denmark Hill, Surrey, the eldest son of John Key. He entered his father's wholesale stationery business in 1818. He was elected alderman for the ward of Langbourn in 1823, and served as sheriff of London and Middlesex in 1824. He was then master of the Stationers' Company in 1830, and in the same year was elected lord mayor. He was one of the leading supporters of the Reform Bill in the City, and received the unusual honour of re-election to the mayoralty in 1831. William Key was created a baronet by William IV in 1831. He was elected MP for the City in 1832 but retired in August 1833. He supported the immediate abolition of slavery, the introduction of the ballot and triennial parliaments, and the repeal of the corn laws.

1832: 17 May: *The Lord Mayor, Key, who has always lent himself to the violent reformers, purchasing ephemeral popularity, the éclat of a second Mayoralty, and a Baronetcy, by throwing himself into the arms of the Ministry and Ultra Whigs, was deeply culpable, in not providing a sufficient force of police to put down the disgraceful riot at St. Bride's.*

1850: 1 Jan: *Three new Magistrates qualified, Sir John Key (ci-devant Lord Mayor of London).*

KEYSALL — Charles Woodcock Keysall[27]

Charles Woodcock Keysall (1785-1829), Church of England clergyman, was the son of John Keysall (1760-1836) and (Anna) Eleanora Woodcock (*below*). He was educated at University College, Oxford (BA 1808; MA 1813). He married, at St Nicholas's, Worcester, 13 July 1822, Penelope (1801-1823), fifth daughter of George Woodyatt, medical practitioner; she died in December 1823, a few months after giving birth. They had 1 daughter:

1 Mary Elizabeth (1823-1914); married, at Hatfield, 1845, William Bathurst Bradford (1807-1864); 4 sons

Charles was appointed curate of Stanway on 3 December 1809 by the bishop of Gloucester, George Isaac Huntingford. In 1813 when Francis Witts acquired the living, he also acquired Keysall *in situ*; Keysall remained as curate to Witts until his resignation in October 1822.

The entries below include Charles, his daughter Mary Elizabeth (b. 1823), and his step-mother Elizabeth Keysall, née Colton, his father's second wife.

1822: 15 Oct.

1823: 8 Apr., 15 Jul., 11 Oct: *I rode to Bredon in Worcestershire to dine & sleep at the Revd. John Keysall's, Rector of that parish ... The parsonage house at Bredon is a very old, long, rambling house, which has been greatly improved into a most comfortable residence by Mr. Keysall; the grounds attached are however of small extent. The Rectory is exempt from Archidiaconal Visitations, and the Rector holds his own visitation with the authority of Archdeacon. Land is allotted in lieu of tithes. Mr. Keysall is one of the King's Chaplains, & an acting Magistrate for Worcestershire & Gloucestershire. I have known him for many years, his Son the Revd. C. Keysall having been curate of Stanway for several years both previous to & since my incumbency. On his resignation of the Curacy I appointed F. Aston, who is also Curate of Mr. Keysall at Cutsdean. With C. Keysall we have long been on very intimate terms. I had now great regret on finding him in deep affliction watching the death bed of his young wife, to whom he has been married about 15 months. She was a daughter of Dr. Woodgate, a Physician in considerable practice at Worcester, & having given birth to a daughter about 4 months since, has been rapidly declining ever since.* 28 Oct: *Received the news of the decease of poor Mrs. C. Keysall, who died at Bredon on Thursday last.*

1824: 6 Apr: *Our friend, Mr. C. Keysall, arrived from Bredon, on a short visit.* 12 Apr., 28 Jun., 2 Jul., 3 Jul: *Mr. C. Keysall came to us from Bredon. He has for some weeks past assisted Dr. Rice in the duty at Oddington, during the absence of the latter with his family in town.* 5 Jul., 13 Jul., 12 Aug: *Our friend Charles Keysall unexpectedly gave us the pleasure of his company to-day, dining and sleeping here.* 13 Aug: *Mr. C. Keysall returned to Bredon. He has taken the Curacies of Bretforton and Somerville's Aston; the former in Worcestershire, the latter in Gloucestershire: both places are near Evesham.* 19 Oct., 1 Nov., 17-18 Dec., 29 Dec.

1825: 1 Jan: *The Stanway party is greatly reduced by the departure of the Stewards. C. Keysall left it this morning. I returned home to dinner.* 16 Mar., 4 Apr: *Mr. C. Keysall came from his residence, Knowl Hill, near Evesham, to pass a few days with us.* 5 Apr: *We had a dinner party. Mr. & Mrs. Jeaffreson and Miss E. Jeaffreson, Dr. Warneford, Mr. Croome & Mr. C. Keysall.* 6 Apr., 9 Apr., 28 Apr: *Mr. C. Keysall dined and slept here.* 29 Apr., 9 May: *We divided our first stage to Tewkesbury by baiting for an hour at F. Aston's, at Wood Stanway, where we accidentally met Mr. C. Keysall, and had a cheerful luncheon to supply the place of dinner.* 24 May: *I set out to dine and sleep at my friend Charles Keysall's at Knowl hill near Evesham.... On the whole it is affords a tolerable accommodation for C. Keysall, who could not get a house in either of his curacies, Bretforton or Aston Somerville.*

He is within a mile from Evesham, three miles from the nearest of his churches, and they are at a greater distance still from each other. 23 Aug: *We had a dinner party: Mr. & Mrs. Egerton Leigh, Mr. & Mrs. Ford, their son, Mr. Croome, Mr. Bowen, Mr. Jones and Mr. C. Keysall. The latter came to-day on a short visit.* 24 Aug., 26 Aug., 17 Sep., 18 Oct., 15 Dec., 17 Dec.

1826: 8 Feb., 30-31 Mar., 7-8 Apr., 11 Apr., 13 Apr., 17 Jun: *Charles Keysall was at the bottom of the table; Lady Rossmore is still with her mother, & Miss Church made up the circle.* 26 Jun., 28-29 Jun., 25 Jul: *Mr. C. Keysall arrived from Bredon to pass some days with us.* 29 Jul., 14 Sep: *I strolled about with my friends, Howell & Charles Keysall.*

1827: 31 Jul: *My principal inducement in thus deviating from the customary road by Tewkesbury, was to call on my poor friend Charles Keysall, whom, I lament to say, I thought looked very ill.... I saw for the first time my friend's delicate child, a nice, quick, little girl of four years of age. Mrs. Colton, Mrs. Keysall's mother, made up the family party.*

1828: 15 Jan., 12 Mar: *I drove to Bredon, distant thirteen miles, to see my poor invalid friend Mr. Charles Keysall. I found him very reduced in appearance.* 16 Jun: *I reached Tewkesbury by three o clock, where I found the Archdeacon of Gloucester and Mr. Keysall busy in the Administration of Justice; from the latter I lamented to hear a melancholy account of the state of my poor friend Charles, who is again putting himself, but with little, if any hope, under the care of Dr. Shute.* 15 Jul., 14 Oct.

1829: 13 Jan., 19 May: *I was informed of the death of our poor friend, Charles Keysall, who sunk into the grave, quite worn out, on Thursday last at his Father's house at Bredon. Many years of intimacy and frequent intercourse cause a deep regret for the departure of one, to whom death was a the release of a merciful Providence. Our departed friend, with his share of the defects ever adhering to our fallen nature, had many estimable qualities: and his nearest friends, particularly, his father, must be in some measure reconciled to his loss, when he considers the lingering & hopeless state of decline, which preceded his dissolution. He has been two years and a half wearing away; and nearly all that time nursed under the paternal roof, and watched by his excellent Stepmother, herself a great invalid. His only child, between six & seven years of age, a delicate little girl, survives him; but this tender flower is not very likely to be brought to maturity. Charles Keysall's Grandfather purchased the advowson of Bredon, which on his Father's decease, now the Rector, would have devolved to my poor friend, had he survived his parent: but the old Banker entailed it in default of male heirs in the family of his son, and now it will go into another family, namely to the descendants of Mr. Keysall Senr.'s married daughter; for the Rector of Bredon, though twice married, had only one child, & that by his first wife, my poor friend now at rest.* 14 Jul: *The Magistrates: T. Wintle, H. W. Newman Esq., Revd. J. B. Cherton, J. Keysall, H. Campbell.* 20 Oct.

1830: 12 Jan.

1844: 13 Apr: *Before we went to it, M W. and I received a short visit from good Mrs. Keysall, whose house is opposite to the Belle Vue Hotel, and having seen us enter, followed to greet us, and to introduce Miss K. the daughter of our old friend C Keysall, now so long deceased.* 13 Aug.

KEYSALL — John Keysall — *see also* Colton[28]

John Keysall (1760-1836), Church of England clergyman, was born at Holborn, London, son of John Keysall (1735-1813) and Mary Browne (1736-1769). He was educated at Brasenose College, Oxford (BA 1783; MA 1785). He was ordained deacon on 25 September 1785 and priest on 18 December 1785. His first clerical appointment was as rector of Groton, Suffolk, from 19 December 1785 to 1806. He was then presented to the living of Bredon, Worcestershire, in 1806 by John Keysall, Esq.—presumably his father—who bought it on his behalf. As well as serving as rector of Bredon, Keysall was chaplain-in-ordinary to King George IV.

Keysall married, at Heston, Middlesex, 28 August 1782, Anne Eleanora Woodcock; they had at least 1 son:

1 Charles Woodcock (1785-1829); *see above*

Anne appears to have died young. John Keysall married, secondly, Elizabeth Colton (1776-1864).

1823: 8 Apr., 15 Jul., 11 Oct: *I rode to Bredon in Worcestershire to dine & sleep at the Revd. John Keysall's, Rector of that parish ...*

1844: 13 Apr: *Before we went to it, M W. and I received a short visit from good Mrs. Keysall, whose house is opposite to the Belle Vue Hotel, and having seen us enter, followed to greet us, and to introduce Miss K. the daughter of our old friend C Keysall, now so long deceased.* 13 Aug.

1845: 5 Jul: *Found M W. at the Plough, who had arrived there yesterday, and had dined & spent yesterday evening with Mrs. Keysall,—with whom also we breakfasted to-day, and engaged her to come on a short visit to Upper Slaughter on the 22d.*

1847: 22 Mar., 1 Jun: *Afterwards repaired to the house of our good old friend Mrs. Keysall, with whom we passed some hours pleasantly, taking an early dinner & tea with her.* 20 Sep: *Also to Mrs. Keysall, offering the Curacy of Stanway, should my Son vacate it, to Mr. Bradford, a respectable Clergyman, who married Mary Keysall, daughter of my old friend and Curate Charles Keysall.* 24 Sep.

1848: 24 Aug.

1850: 5 Jul: *At Cheltenham busy in shopping and paying bills.—Called at good Mrs. Keysall's, with whom I partook of a mutton chop, which the kind old friend insisted on providing for me.*

KIDD — John Kidd[29]

John Kidd (1775-1851), physician, was born in the parish St James, Westminster, son of John Kidd, captain of the *Swallow*, a merchant ship, and Beatrice, daughter of Samuel Burslem, vicar of Etwall, near Derby. After attending school at Bury St Edmunds, Kidd obtained a king's scholarship at Westminster School in 1789. His academic abilities attracted the attention of the headmaster, Dr William Vincent, and earned him a place at Oxford upon the 'golden election' (BA 1797; MA 1800). He then embarked upon a four-year medicine course at Guy's Hospital, London, as a pupil of Sir Astley Cooper. In 1801 he returned to Oxford and graduated BM; he took up a lectureship in chemistry and remained at Oxford for the rest of his life.

Kidd's most enduring legacy was his contribution to science education. Appointed first Aldrichian professor of chemistry at Oxford in 1803, he took an active part in defining a role for the natural sciences at a time when they being marginalised by the priorities of examination reforms.

1802: 18 Mar: *To the Chemistry Lecture with Mr. Gehegan of Christ Church. Kidd is very uninteresting.* 6 May, 8 May.

1832: 15 Mar: *The worthy Professor is a fellow of Magd. Coll. but his residence at the Museum is unique: he occupies a range of soutterains beneath the apartments containing the Ashmolean treasures, where Dr. Kidd, a former Chemical Professor, some years before was the first to inhabit.*

KILBY — William Kilby and Hannah Kilby [30]

William Kilby (1796-1884), agricultural labourer, was born at Naunton, son of John and Hester Kilby. He lived with his wife, Elizabeth Crook (1806-1896); they had at least 4 sons and 2 daughters:

1 William (1829-1921); married, at Naunton, 12 October 1859, Rhoda Preston (1834-1906); died at Lenox, Taylor County, Iowa, USA
1 Hannah (b. 1831); *see below*
2 Elizabeth (1838-1933)
2 Thomas (1844-1917)
3 George (1840-1845)
4 George (±1848-1933)

At the time of the 1851 census Hannah was in service with Edward and Elizabeth Lea of the Manor House, Upper Slaughter. She was committed to prison for theft on 18 July 1854 and discharged after six months on 18 November. We know from prison records that she was 5 feet 3 inches in height and had a scar inside the left thumb and a mole beneath her right ear. It is not known what happened to her after her release.

1854: 12 Jul: *Granted a search warrant to search the house of one Kilby, of Naunton, Father of a female servant late in the family of Palmer, Shopkeeper at Bourton, and suspected of having stolen from him a piece of silk—to discover such silk, or any part of it, and, the girl being now in the service of Mr. Harkin, Curate of Naunton, addressed a note to him, requesting him to allow a search to be made in the young woman's apartment in his house, and in her boxes, for the silk.* 17 Jul: *With R. Waller, as my colleague, at Mr. Palmer's house, took the evidence of himself and his daughter, and P.C. Evans, as to a wholesale robbery committed on his premises of his property by his late Servant, Hannah Kilby, in whose possession, on a Search made, were found almost numberless articles of dress table linen, baby linen, and small miscellaneous property, plundered by the girl from the shop, warehouse, and dwelling house of her Master.* 18 Jul: *Mrs. E Lea called on me to confer with me as to giving evidence in favour of H Kilby at the trial now close at hand.* 19 Jul., 10 Aug: *A note from Mr. Hurd, as to the clothes of H. Kilby, lately convicted of felony at Gloucester Assizes, which the parents of the wretched girl are anxious to recover, that they may be available at the expiration of her sentence.*

KILWARDEN — Lord Kilwarden — *see* Wolfe

KIMBER — James Kimber, clerk at the Stow branch of the Gloucestershire Banking Company [31]

James Kimber (1825-1858), banker's clerk, was born at Withington, Gloucestershire, son of Thomas and Martha Kimber. In 1851 he was unmarried, living with his parents and his sister Emma at Sheep Street, Stow-on-the-Wold. He appears to have died unmarried, and relatively young.

1852: 31 May: *J.C. being indisposed the reply came from Kimber, one of the Clerks of the Establishment.* 17 Mar: *Mr. Kimber, Clerk at the Stow Branch of the Gloucestershire Banking Company, had been waiting for my return some time, being desirous of conferring with me as to the office of Treasurer of the United district of Stow and Moreton.* 18 Mar., 21 Mar., 24 Mar: *At the office of the Gloucestershire Bankg. Company conferred with Mr. Kimber as to the Treasurership of the Stow and Moreton United Turnpike Trust: he has received great encouragement in his canvass of Trustees.*

1853: 7 Apr: *Mr. Kimber, having taken offence at a preference given by the directors to another clerk, Cox, appointed by them to reside on the Bank premises as principal Clerk, a position which Kimber thinks himself entitled to. This would affect the appointment of Kimber as Treasurer of our United Turnpike trust.* 9 Apr., 12 Apr., 23 Apr: *Mr. Kimber, late Clerk in the Branch bank of Gloucestershire Banking Company at Stow, called to apprize me that his connection with that firm had ceased, & that, consequently, he had no claim now to the office of Treasurer of our United Turnpike Trust.*

KIMBER — Mary Kimber of Sapperton — *see also* Playne [32]

Mary Moore, née Kimber (1819-1852), was the daughter of William Kimber and Hester Playne. Her parents had married at Minchinhampton on 5 January 1805. She married, at Sapperton, Gloucestershire, 16 April 1844, Henry Moore, son of Revd Thomas Ottiwell or O'Hiwell [?] Moore (1777-1854) and Rachel Colles (1779-1864). Mary and Henry had 2 sons and 1 daughter:

1 Ottiwell Henry (1845-1892)
2 William Allen (1846-1929)
1 Mary Catherine (b. 1848)

1844: 21 Apr: *Mr. H. Moore, the young Irish tenant on the Dolphin property at the Parks farm, having brought home his bride, late Miss Kimber, the daughter of a respectable Yeoman at Sapperton, and niece of my acquaintance and brother Magistrate, Mr. Playne.*

KIMBER — William Kimber [33]

William Kimber (1788-1874[?]), farmer, was born at North Cerney, Gloucestershire, son of William Kimber (b. 1767) and Rebecca Kendall (b. 1764). Kimber lived with his wife, Mary (b. ±1790), and farmed at Bourton-on-the-Water. No reliable records have been found, but one William Kimber of the same age died in Warwickshire in 1874. There do not appear to have been any children.

1836: 23 Nov.
1837: 16 Jun., 20 Jun., 11 Aug.
1838: 4 May, 1 Jun.
1839: 17 May, 7 Jun.
1840: 15 May, 5 Jun., 31 Aug: *Met and rode home with Mr. Kimber.*
1842: 3 Jun.
1843: 16 Nov: *To the Office of the Glostershire Bkg Co. conferred with J. Clark as to his and Kimber's witnessing the execution of the deeds of conveyance by Forty on Monday next.*
1849: 21 Dec: *Mr. Kimber, of Bourton on the Water, called respecting a fine imposed on him for not attending according to his summons as a Grand Juror at the last Sessions at Gloucester; much conversation with him as to Mrs. Dolphin.* 24 Dec.
1850: 9 Feb: *Justice business at home with Mr. Kimber.*

KING — Mr King, a connection of Baroness Grey de Ruthyn [34]

This Mr King is not known, but following the logic of the diary entry, he was a relation of Barbara Rawdon Hastings, née Yelverton (1810-1858), who was in her own right Baroness Grey de Ruthyn.

1838: 26 Mar: *A hunting whip in her hand, a long blue cloth habit, a boa of foxes brushes, blue trowsers which she was at no pains to keep out of view, a golden spur on one heel, a cap on her head, she vaulted into her saddle, and rode off to covert, attended by a Cavaliere servente, a connexion of her own, a handsome, fashionable looking, Mr. King.*

KING — Isabella Lettice King [35]

Isabella Lettice King (1772-1845) was born in Dublin, third daughter and sixth of the seven children of Edward King, 1st earl of Kingston (1726-1797). By 1803 she was living at 7 Great Bedford Street, Bath, a fashionable area behind the Royal Crescent, and socialising among the city's élite. At an evening party held at her home in January 1805, a discussion arose about what could best be done to benefit the city. This led to Isabella's collaboration with Bath's leading male philanthropists to establish the Bath Society for the Suppression of Vagrants, Street Beggars and Impostors, Relief of Occasional Distress, and Encouragement of Industry.

Isabella's most ambitious project and the one closest to her heart was the Ladies Association, established 'for the benefit of gentlewomen of good family, reduced in fortune below the state of comfort to which they have been accustomed'. In 1821 she moved to Cornwallis House in Clifton, Bristol; from there, initially, the association flourished, but Isabella began to feel alienated from her friends and support network in Bath. By 1833, the association was in decline; Cornwallis House was sold in 1837, and the funds were devoted to religious and charitable endeavours in Bristol.

1833: 11 Apr: *We passed under the establishment of Lady Isabella King, which occupies a large mansion, the residence of a widow Lady during the period of my former acquaintance with Clifton.*

KING — Mary King — *see also* Hewitt *and* Leslie [36]

Mary King, née Hewitt (±1781-1821), daughter of Revd John Hewitt (d. 1804) and Jane Moore (d. 1848), married, 1802, Lt-Col Sir Henry King, son of Robert King, 2nd earl of Kingston, and Caroline FitzGerald; they had 2 sons and 1 daughter:

1 Louisa Mary (1803-1883)
1 John Wingfield (1807-1868)
2 Edward Richard (1808-1879)

1804: 7 Oct., 26 Dec: *Passed the Evening at Mrs. Hewatt's. Mrs. King a very pleasing young woman.*

1805: 4 Jan: *Passed a rational pleasant Evening of Conversation at Mrs. Hewitts': Lord & Lady Lifford very respectable, pleasing, persons: & Mrs. King as elegant & engaging as ever.* 3 Feb: *Walked from Bristol with Mr. Hewitt.* 13 Feb: *Walked with Capt. Manners, to Bristol, & with Mrs. Hewitt & Mrs. King.* 18 Feb: *Mrs King passed the Evening with us.* 21 Feb: *Walked a little. Mrs. Hewitt & Mrs. King left us.*

KING — Isaac King [37]

Isaac King (1804-1865), Church of England clergyman, was born at Lee, Buckinghamshire, son of Revd Isaac King (1779-1832). He was educated at Christ Church, Oxford (BA 1826; MA 1829), and ordained deacon on 10 June 1827 and priest on 1 June 1828. King's first clerical appointment was as stipendiary curate for his father at West Wycombe, Buckinghamshire, from 10 June 1827. He became perpetual curate of Lee, Buckinghamshire, on 1 March 1832, and succeeded his father as rector of Bradenham, Buckinghamshire, on 15 June 1832. He served in that post until his death in 1865.

King married Maria Golding (b. ±1812); they had at least 3 sons and 4 daughters:

1 Isaac (b. 1834)
2 Charles Rickford (b. 1835)
1 Elizabeth Maria (b. 1837)
2 Edith Harriette (b. 1840)
3 William (b. ±1839)
3 Catherine (b. ±1842)
4 Sarah (b. ±1844)

1850: 13 Aug: *Morning visitors were the Revd.——King, the Clergyman of the adjacent village of Bradenham, and Mrs. Naish, the lady of the present Mayor of High Wycomb.*

KINGSCOTE — Robert Kingscote [38]

Robert Kingscote (1754-1840), JP and landed proprietor, was the eldest son of Robert Fitzhardinge Kingscote and Mary Hammond. Kingscote was a colonel in the Gloucestershire Militia and a whig; he was related to the Berkeley family and shared many pastimes with Lord Fitzhardinge. He was a keen sportsman, but he himself was hounded during the disturbances of 1825 when poachers gathered in a force forty strong to terrorise him in his home while their comrades went shooting on his private estate. He died unmarried and was succeeded by his nephew, Thomas Henry Kingscote (1799-1861), son of his younger brother Thomas Kingscote and Harriet Peyton (*below*).

1804: 13 Dec: *Proceeding on our Walk, we came to Kingscote, a Chapelry, to Beverstone, which has lately acquired a celebrity of a very different kind from that once enjoyed by the Village we had just left. On the right hand of the Road, the White Posts fixed at equal distances in the level turf, the leaping Bar, the Stand & other appendages of a Race Course apprized us, whose domain we were approaching, Col. Kingscote, Colonel of the North Glocester Militia has an Estate & handsome place in the Hamlet, which bears his name, & being much attached to the Pleasures of the Turf, has instituted a Club, on the Model of that held at Bibury.*

1806: 21 Jan: *Mounted a hackney between four & five to repair to Capt. Webb's at Stoke, where a large & pleasant party were assembled, & most hospitably & handsomely entertained. His dinner excellent; his Madeira & Claret delicious. Besides my excellent friend Dowell, whom I had infinite pleasure in again seeing, we had Col. Kingscote, Sir Will. Guise, & Sir Henry Lippincott, Major Durbin, Capt. Cooke, Mr. Probyn, Messrs. P & J. Baillie, & Mr. Foster.*

1823: 15 Jul., 17 Sep.

1825: 12 Jul.

1826: 16 Jun

KINGSCOTE — (Robert) Nigel Fitzhardinge Kingscote [39]

Sir (Robert) Nigel Fitzhardinge Kingscote (1830-1908), MP and landed proprietor, was the second son of Col Thomas Henry Kingscote (*below*) and his first wife, Lady Isabella Anne Frances Somerset (1808-1831). His mother died when he was less than a year old. He was educated at a school in Weymouth before going abroad with a tutor. He returned aged 16, and through the influence of his maternal great-uncle, Lord Fitzroy Somerset (afterwards Lord Raglan), obtained a commission in the Scots Fusilier Guards. In 1854 he went out to the Crimea as aide-de-camp to Lord Raglan, whose body he escorted back to England in 1855. He was made brevet major on 12 December 1854, and subsequently lieutenant-colonel and CB.

Kingscote sold out of the guards in 1856, and thereafter lived a retired life in the country. On the death of his father on 19 December 1861, he inherited the Kingscote estate; he kept up the family traditions as a squire, breeder of pedigree livestock, and follower of the hounds. He was Liberal MP for West Gloucestershire in 1852-85, and in 1885 was made a commissioner of woods and forests by Gladstone. He remained in the post for ten years.

Kingscote married, first, at Petworth, Sussex, 13 March 1851, Caroline Sophia (1830-1852), daughter of George Wyndham, 1st Baron Leconfield. He married secondly, at Market Bosworth, Leicestershire, 5 February 1856, Emily Marie (1836-1910), daughter of Richard Curzon, 1st Earl Howe; they had 2 sons and 2 daughters:

1 Nigel R. Fitzhardinge (1857-1921)
1 Harriet Maude Isabella (1860-1906)
2 Winifred Ida (1862-1938)
2 Albert Edward Leicester Fitzhardinge (b. & d. 1865)

From 1859 to 1866 Kingscote was parliamentary groom in waiting to Queen Victoria; thus began a lifelong intimacy with the royal family. In May 1864 he was appointed superintendent of the prince of Wales's stables, a post which he held until 1885. He was a member of council of the prince of Wales from 1886, and receiver-general of the duchy of Cornwall from 1888. He was appointed extra equerry to the prince in 1867, and was made extra equerry to the king and paymaster-general of the royal household on Edward VII's accession. Kingscote was an authority on agriculture and an active member of the Royal Agricultural Society from 1854 to 1906. He was chairman of the finance committee in 1875-1906, and president of the society at Bristol in 1878.

1853: 4 Jan: *There was a numerous assemblage of the magistracy;—the Lord Lieutenant, the Marquis of Worcester, MP. Nigel Kingscote, MP., R J Mullings MP., O Ricardo MP.—Sir M. H. Beach, Hon. Gustavus Talbot &c.* 4 Apr., 27 Jun.

KINGSCOTE — **Thomas Henry Kingscote**[40]

Thomas Henry Kingscote (1799-1861), army officer, JP, and landed proprietor, was the son of Thomas Kingscote and Harriet Peyton. He was also nephew of Robert Kingscote (*above*). He married, first, 1828, Lady Isabella Anne Frances (1808-1831), daughter of Henry Charles Somerset, 6th duke of Beaufort, and Lady Charlotte Sophia Leveson-Gower; they had 1 son:

1 Robert Nigel Fitzhardinge (1830-1908); *see above*

Kingscote married secondly, 1833, Harriott Mary Anne, daughter of Lt-Gen. Benjamin Bloomfield, 1st Baron Bloomfield, of Oakhampton and Redwood, and Harriott Douglas. Col Thomas Henry Kingscote was JP for Gloucestershire and high sheriff for the county in 1841.

1826: 16 Jun., 15 Sep.

1829: 22 Sep: *The Stewards resorted to their posts near the great Western entrance, Messrs. Estcourt, Junr. MP. for Downton, who had taken the principal charge of the arrangements for the meeting, Mr. T. Kingscote, and Mr. Waller ... First then we must name the Lord Lieutenant, the Duke of Beaufort, with two unmarried daughters; his married daughter, Lady Isabella Kingscote, with her husband, one of the Stewards; Col. Kingscote, his Uncle.* 20 Oct.

1832: 29 Mar.

1833: 16 Oct: *When I was last there a most unjustifiable attack on the Clerical Magistrates was made by that hot headed, ill conditioned veteran Whig, Colonel Kingscote.* 23 Oct., 28 Oct: *Replied to Baker's letter received on the 23d that I could not yet persuade myself that Col. Kingscote's insinuation against the Clerical magistrates did not call for animadversion.*

1835: 7 Feb: *Mr. Baker, in his own peculiar, dry manner, reported to Bathurst, with a desire that it might be communicated to me, a conversation which had incidentally passed between himself, Col. Kingscote & Mr. Sheppard. The latter gentlemen, ever prone to find fault, prejudiced men, & sour Whigs, seized an opportunity of cavilling at the proceedings of the Quarter Sessions, the attempted reforms of the Committee of accounts.* 11 Mar: *Wrote to T. J. Ll. Baker, forwarding to him his memorable letter, reporting the conversation between himself, Col. Kingscote, and Mr. Sheppard.*

1840: 1 Jul.

1841: 6 Apr.

1848: 21 Oct.

1850: 1 Jan., 30-31 Dec.

KINLOCH — **Miss Kinloch of Gilmerton**[41]

Miss Kinloch was a daughter of Sir David Kinloch, 5th baronet (±1710-1795). In 1795, two months after he had succeeded to the title, David's eldest son, Sir Francis Kinloch, 6th baronet (±1747-1795), was murdered on the front stairs by his deranged brother Archibald Gordon Kinloch, whose health had declined after service in the West Indies. Sir Archibald was not hanged after his trial but released into the care of his family. It was to prove a very controversial plea and one of the earliest recorded defences on grounds of insanity. Sir Archibald died five years later and was buried in Greyfriars Church in Edinburgh. Miss Kinloch's sister, Harriet, married Sir Foster Cunliffe.

1827: 31 Oct: *I went to pass a day or two with Lady Elcho at Stanway. I found Miss Kinlock and the Miss Guydickens's her Ladyship's guests. Miss Church, as usual, is demoiselle d'honneur. Miss Kinlock is aunt to a Scotch Baronet, whose seat is at Gilmerston in East Lothian; there in my younger days a dismal tragedy was enacted: a younger brother in a moment of exasperation having killed his brother; both were brothers of Miss Kinlock: the murderer was tried, and insanity successfully set up as a plea in his defence; but it was generally believed, that the madness of vindictive & malignant passions alone prompted the horrible crime. The wretched man remained till his death under surveillance. Miss K. is a sensible old Lady, resident at Chester. A sister of hers is married to Sir Foster Cunliffe.* 3 Dec: *We came to Stanway on a visit to Lady Elcho for a few days, and found there a large party ... The there is Miss Kinloch, an excellent old maiden lady of a good Scottish family, an adept at all games of cards; she is an old and respected acquaintance of ours.* 6 Dec.

1828: 5 Aug.

KINSEY — **William Morgan Kinsey**[42]

William Morgan Kinsey (1788-1851), Church of England clergyman, was born at Abergavenny, son of Robert Kinsey. He was educated at Trinity College, Oxford (BA 1809; MA 1813; BD 1822). He was a fellow of the college in 1815-44, dean in 1822, vice-president in 1823, bursar in 1824, and proctor in 1821. He was curate of St John's, Cheltenham, at least during the years 1830-42; thereafter he was rector of Rotherfield Greys, Oxfordshire, in 1843-51.

1835: 7 Jan: *Mr. Kinsey, who as an Ultra Whig, Tory and Ultra-High-Church-man, has made himself conspicuous for some years at Cheltenham, where he is Minister of St. John's Church, was very full upon the Tory victory lately gained at Evesham ... The Bishop and Mrs. Monk had apologized for not asking us to join their dinner party to-day, their table being full, but insisted on our spending the Evening with them. We arrived as the Ladies were retiring from the dining room, and my son and myself joined the Bishop and the Gentlemen of his party over their wine. We found there Sir Robert Ricketts, an admiral, who resides at Cheltenham, Dr. Hall, one of the Prebendaries of the Cathedral, the Revd. Mr. Kinsey of Cheltenham, Mr. Dowdeswell of Down House, and several others.*

1842: 4 Feb: *The Bp. does not approve of the proposed address, and does approve of his Clergy withholding their signatures from it: it emanates from hot-headed parties, as Kinsey, who have come into personal collision with "Tractarians".*

KIRBY — Mary Anne Kirby — *see also* Chamberlain Hughes-Chamberlain, Hutchinson, *and* Knight[43]

Mary Anne Kirby, née Knight (1792-1861), was the daughter of John Knight (1758-1822), of Dodington, Whitchurch, Shropshire, and Mary Smith (1758-1832). She married Thomas Cox Kirby (1783-1850), a lieutenant-colonel of the 54th and 80th Foot. He was commissioned as ensign in the 54th in 1800 and was wounded during the landing at Alexandria in 1801. He commanded a company at the battle of Waterloo. Kirby retired on half pay from the 80th Foot on 25 May 1822, and died at Cheltenham in 1850. Mary died in 1861 at Derry, near Ross Carbery, co. Cork. They had at least 1 son and 2 daughters:

1 Mary Susannah (b. 1832)
1 Franklin Knight (1835-1855); educated in Cheltenham; entered the Army and appointed ensign without purchase in 1854; became lieutenant, 93rd Highlanders; died of typhus in the Crimea, 16 February 1855
2 Caroline Georgina (±1840-1873); married, 1862, Richard Charles Webb (d. 1867) of Belmont Castle, Essex, Brockworth, Gloucestershire, and later of Holt Lodge, Norfolk

Marry Anne Kirby had three younger sisters: Emma Hughes-Chamberlain (b. 1793), Charlotte Hutchinson (1798-1879), and Caroline Knight (1799-1856), who died unmarried. The connection with Mary Anne Dolphin pertains to her half-brother, George Hutchinson, who married Charlotte Hutchinson, née Knight.

1828: 5 Nov: *We dined at Eyford. The Dolphins have a large party in their house; Mrs. & three Miss Knights.*

1845: 6 Jul.

1849: 14 Dec: *Went to Eyford by appointment, where I found Mrs. and Miss Kirby (Miss Knight's sister and niece) from Cheltenham, who had been passing a day or two with Mrs. Dolphin.*

1850: 15 Jan., 10 Mar: *A short interview with two Misses Kirby, connections of Mrs. Dolphin, now staying at Eyford.* 7 Jun: *passed a few minutes with the younger Miss Kirby who is on a visit to her.* 10 Jun: *In the evening Mrs. Dolphin paid me a visit, accompanied by Miss C. Kirby now visiting her.* 24 Jun., 30 Jun., 4 Nov: *Visited Miss C. Knight and her nieces, the Misses Kirby.* 9 Nov: *Met Miss Knight and Miss Car-Kirby at Eyford, who returned with me to near the village of U Slaughter. The elder Miss K. is an invalid.* 27 Nov: *Miss C Knight has left her, to join her sister, Mrs. Kirby, at Cheltenham, whose husband Col. K. died rather suddenly on last Monday week: he had been in very bad health.* 13 Dec., 20-21 Dec.

1852: 12 Mar: *From Mrs. Kirby, of Cheltenham, who writes by Mrs. Dolphin's desire to inform me of the death of Mr. Hutchinson on Tuesday morning.* 13 Mar., 2 Apr: *Called at Eyford on Mrs. Dolphin, who returned home on Monday last, and with whom I found Mrs. Kirby and Miss Caroline Kirby on a visit.* 8 May, 11 May, 14 May, 19 May: *Miss Kirby called on me with Mrs. D's note, who with Miss K. accepts my invitation, and I urged that Mr. Staveley, if then at Eyford, as is rather expected, should accompany them.* 26 May, 28 May, 31 May, 2 Jun.

KIRCHGESSNER — Maria Anna Eva Theresia Kirchgessner[44]

Maria Anna Eva Theresia Kirchgessner (1769-1808), glass harmonica player, was blind from the age of 4. She made numerous successful concert tours, visiting Munich, Salzburg, and Vienna. Mozart heard her in Vienna and composed the Adagio and Rondo (k617) and the Fantasie (kAnh92/616*a*) for glass harmonica, flute, oboe, viola, and cello, and the Adagio (k356/617*a*) for glass harmonica. In 1799 she retired to Gohlis, near Leipzig, but later made several concert tours. She also visited Goethe.

1799: 2 Nov: *went to Mr. Schmids My Mother & Mr. Dukinfield to a Concert by a Demoiselle Kirschgessner: on the Musical Glasses. The accompaniment spoilt the whole Effect of her good Play.*

KIRWAN — Miss Kirwan at Bath — *see also* Blake[45]

The Blake and Kirwan families were related. Mark Blake (d. ±1810) was the son of Marcus Blake and Sibilla French. He married, January 1777, Christian, daughter of Martin Kirwan. Mark Blake lived at Ballinafad, Drum, co. Mayo, Ireland. Mark and Christian had at least 4 sons and 1 daughter:

1 Maurice (d. 1852)
2 Martin
3 Mark
4 Joseph
1 Mary

Miss Kirwan was possibly Margaret Kirwan, daughter of Martin Kirwan (d. 1752), of Kilfinny, co. Galway, who married his cousin Elizabeth Kirwan. Margaret's brother Andrew married, at St Mary's, Dublin, 19 September 1787, Mary Margaret Blake, daughter of Maurice Blake; they had four sons. Therefore these Kirwans and Blakes were all cousins to some degree, and the two families appear to have continued intermarrying.

The Kirwans descended from Edmund Airgid Kirwan, son of Patrick Kirwan who died in 1608. Edmund married Anastasia Blake. Their son, Edmund's successor, Alexander Kirwan, was father of Edmond Kirwan, whose son, Martin Kirwan, of Dalgin, co. Mayo, had six sons.

1802: 6 Jan: *Dined at Lady Riddell's with my Father & Mother meeting Countess D'Alton, & in the Evening with her party to one of Rauzzini's grand Choral Concerts. Miss Kirwen & two Miss Blakes were of her party at tea & in the Concert, which is held in the great Room of the upper Rooms, & is to me a finer sight than even the Master of the Ceremonies Ball.*

KITE — John Kite of Urchfont, Wiltshire

1807: 10 Aug: *Had previously called at Erchfont on poor John Kite.* 12 Aug., 15 Aug.

KLOCH — Luise Concordia Henriette, Baroness Kloch — *see also* Imhoff[46]

Luise Concordia Henriette, Baroness Kloch (1787-1848), was the youngest of the six children born to Christophe Adam Karl, Baron von Imhoff (1734-1788), and his second wife, Luise Franziska Sophie von Schardt (1750-1803), whom he married on 2 February 1775. She was the widow of Regierungsrat Leopold Otto Ferdinand Freiherr von Kloch (1791-1839).

1847: 11 Sep: *We also drove to Daylesford House, and left our cards for Sir Charles Imhoff, and Baroness Klock, who had driven out. The aged General has accomplished, since we met him at Mr. Winter's in the Spring, soon after the decease of Lady Imhoff, a voyage and Journey into the Interior of Germany, to visit his connections there, and, in spite of old age and infirmities, has borne the fatigue and excitement well; bringing back with him on a visit his half sister, a widowed Baroness Klock, the daughter of his father Baron Imhoff, by his second wife, whom he married after his divorce from his first wife, afterwards Mrs. Hastings—Baroness Klock was, I believe, the youngest child by the second marriage: the elder daughters & a Son of Baron Imhoff, as also his widow, were resident at Weimar, when my Father & Mother, with my Brother and myself passed two Winters there in 1798 & 1799: we were much acquainted with them; the elder, Amalia von Imhoff, was already an accomplished writer, a poetess; Demoiselle d'honneur to the Reigning Duchess of Weimar: this lady afterwards married a Swedish officer, Von Helwig, who died a General of Artillery in the Prussian service; Mad. de Helwig is also deceased; she maintained her literary reputation by many works of poetry and fiction.— The second daughter died a widow, the Son was an Officer in the service of the Duke of Weimar; Mad. de Klock has a daughter now Demoiselle d'honneur to the present Reigning Duchess of Weimar.* 27 Sep: *Received a visit from Sir Charles Imhoff, and his half sister, the Baroness von Klock—Poor Sir C. is heart-whole, but very feeble; yet he has accomplished during the summer a tour up the Rhine into Germany, to visit his family connections, and has brought back with him a sexagenarian widowed Baroness, daughter of his father by his second wife, whom in my youth I knew well at Weimar. I believe this lady had not then emerged from the Nursery.* 23 Dec.

KNATCHBULL — **Edward Knatchbull**[47]

Sir Edward Knatchbull, 9th baronet (1781-1849), MP and paymaster-general, was the son of Sir Edward Knatchbull, 8th baronet (1758-1819), MP, and Mary, daughter of William Western Hugessen. He was educated at Winchester College, Christ Church, Oxford, and Lincoln's Inn. He married, 1806, Annabella Christina Honeywood.

Edward Knatchbull was MP for Kent in 1819-31, and Kent East in 1832-45. He was also privy counsellor in 1834 and paymaster-general in 1834-35 and 1841-45. He succeeded his father as 9th baronet in 1819.

1827: 7 May: *In the House of Commons Mr. Canning utterly lost his temper, and exhibited an exacerbation quite unsuitable to his station; his opponents were the vehement Mr. Dawson, Mr. Peel, who was received with constant cheering, & Sir E. Knatchbull, the representative of the Country Gentry.*

1829: 7 Feb: *In the house of Commons the Marquis of Chandos, Sir John Knatchbull, Mr. Moore, Mr. B. Cooper, Col. Rochfort and others remain unmoved in their old position.*

1834: 17 Dec: *The following ministerial appointments are announced ... Sir Edward Knatchbull, Pay-master of the Forces.*

KNEBEL — **Henriette Magdalene von Knebel**[48]

Henriette Magdalene von Knebel (1755-1813) was a governess. In 1791 she took on the education of 5-year-old Caroline, only daughter of the ducal couple in Weimar. She was recommended for this position by her pronounced musicianship (she composed and was an excellent pianist) and her literary knowledge. She became sister-in-law to Luise Ulrica Dorothea Emilia von Knebel (1777-1852), daughter of Capt. Rudorf of the Preussisch-Bellingschen Hussar Regiment.

Luise arrived at Weimar in 1791 with her widowed mother. She was said to be an adorable, youthful creature gifted with a clear soprano, trained in the school of the famous Franz Benda. Caroline Jagemann writes in her memoirs that she was 'slender and supple like a birch in the wind, with a long, mobile neck, not without a few graceful twists and turns, the red-bobbed head, which, however, cannot be denied beauty and expression'. After a short rehearsal, Kapellmeister Wolf appointed the young singer to be a member of the opera. After three years Luise left the opera and was appointed to the household of the dowager duchess, Anna Amalia, where she caught the eye of the duke, Karl Augustus (1757-1828). In the summer of 1795 Luise had to confess to the duchess that she was expecting the duke's child:

1 Karl Wilhelm [later] von Knebel (1796-1861)

In 1798 Carl Ludwig von Knebel (1744-1834), although more than thirty years her senior, married Luise to provide her with some respectability. Her son Karl Wilhelm adopted the name von Knebel.

1798: 5 Aug: [sub-section] Weimar: *The Princess, between 14 & 15 years of age, small in stature is a Brunette, lively, & clever, extremely fortunate in her Governess, a Mademoiselle de Knebel.*

KNIGHT — **Caroline Knight** — *see also* **Kirby**[49]

Caroline Knight (1799-1856) was the third daughter of John Knight, of Dodington, Whitchurch, Shropshire, and Mary Smith. She died unmarried at Hastings, Sussex, and was buried there.

1828: 5 Nov: *We dined at Eyford. The Dolphins have a large party in their house; Mrs. & three Miss Knights.*

1840: 18 Sep: *Walked to Eyford to visit John Palmer, whom I found restless and in low spirits. At his cottage met Mrs. Dolphin, and her connections and guests, Mrs. Chamberlain and Miss Knight.* 25 Sep.

1843: 15 Oct: *Morning prayers; after which Mrs. Dolphin's friend, Miss Knight, a pleasing and sensible person, called, with whom conferred on the unpleasant investigations to which the misconduct of Mrs. Dolphins bailiff and gardener have has led, and as to which I have been made a party; indeed was obliged twice to-day to see on the subject one of the labourers, the second time in the presence of Miss Knight.*

1844: 27 Jul: *Mrs. Dolphin and Miss. C. Knight called on us in the evening.* 29 Jul., 6 Aug: *With the Astons and Mrs. W. walked to Eyford, the latter being desirous of reviving her recollections of a place, where she had visited her parents more than thirty years ago;—Mrs. Dolphin being indisposed, kept her room: we saw Mrs. Payne and Miss C. Knight, the latter accompanying us to the Conservatory, garden &c.* 18 Aug., 25 Aug., 1 Sep.

1845: 18 Feb: *Walked to Eyford, called at Mrs. Dolphin's, whom I saw; also Mrs. Payn, and Miss C. Knight.* 8 Mar., 30-31 Mar., 9 Apr., 12 Apr., 18 Apr: *Walked to Eyford: read prayers with Mrs. Payne, who is very languid & ill—Mrs. Dolphin and Miss C Knight joined in this chamber service: the latter returned with me as far as the Village, anxious about the condition of Mrs. P. and the Eyford affairs.* 25 Apr., 11 May, 13 May, 16 May, 6 Jul: *Miss Knight, accompanied by her niece, Miss Kirby, called after Evening service.*

1846: 27 Jun., 7 Jul: *Miss C. Knight had called on us in the forenoon, to take leave of us before her departure from Eyford to-morrow.*

1847: 19 May: *While with us, we all walked to Eyford to call on Mrs. Dolphin, who was so much of an invalid as to be unable to receive us; but we visited her friend, Miss C Knight, who arrived on a visit, a few days since; and we met there Miss Browne from Salperton.* 29-31 May, 6 Jun., 21 Dec.

1848: 23 May, 28 May, 3 Jun: *Walked with M.W. to Eyford: called on Mrs. Dolphin, and Mrs. Hutchinson, wife to Mrs. D's brother, who, with her sister, Miss C Knight, is now on a visit at Eyford.* 11 Jun., 15 Jun., 17 Jun.

1849: 14 Dec: *M.W. received a letter from Miss Knight, who wishes to hear my opinion as to the real state of Mrs. Dolphin's health.* 15 Dec.

1850: 13 Jan: *Miss C Knight writes from Tanfield, Mr. Hutchinson's, in answer to a letter from me respecting the state ... it seems that Mrs. D. in correspondence, or by her amanuensis, Mary Anne Ryan, has exaggerated expressions which have fallen from me in my interviews with Mrs. D., making it appear that I greatly blame Capt. Frobisher and Miss Knight as to certain transactions of the one, and assumed neglect on the part of the other. Miss K. writes to explain.* 14 Jan., 24 Jan., 22 Oct: *Walked to Eyford, and called at Mrs. Dolphin's, whom I saw;—also her guests, Miss Walmsley, and Miss Car-Knight, who arrived there yesterday.* 27 Oct., 4 Nov: *Visited Miss C. Knight and her nieces, the Misses Kirby.* 6 Nov., 9 Nov., 27 Nov., 13 Dec.

1852: 18 Jan: *Miss Knight called on us after the morning service.* 25 Jan., 30 Jan., 14 Feb: *Mrs. Dolphin and Miss C. Knight have both left Eyford for Bath.* 5 May, 19 May: *A letter from Miss Caroline Knight, arising from the circumstance of my having sent by Miss Walmsley to her a contribution to the fund for relief of the wives and children of soldiers now serving in the East: much is said by her as to regrets for the misunderstanding with Mrs. Dolphin, which prevents her visiting Eyford; there is an assurance that I should judge her favourably, and censure Mrs. D.—what I do know of the difference leads me to exonerate Miss K. & her sisters, and to blame Mrs. D.*

1854: 24 May.

KNIGHT — Francis Knight[50]

Francis Knight (±1767-1837), Church of England clergyman, was born in the parish of St James, Westminster, son of Francis and Catherine Knight. He was educated at Magdalen Hall, Oxford (BA 1802; MA 1819; B&DD 1819).

1833: 21 Apr: *We attended divine service at Clifton Church in the afternoon... The Sermon was preached by an old divine, I believe, a Dr. Knight, whose articulation was very imperfect and indistinct.*

KNIGHT — Thomas John Knight[51]

Thomas John Knight (1805-1870), barrister and attorney-general in Tasmania, was born in the parish of St James, Westminster, son of William Young Knight (1753-1836) and Elizabeth Claridge. He was educated at Westminster School and Trinity College, Cambridge (BA 1828; MA 1831). Knight was admitted to the Middle Temple in 1826 and called to the bar in 1831. He served on the Hampshire circuit and quarter sessions, and was special pleader QC, chairman of quarter sessions in Jamaica in 1841-44, and judge of common pleas. He went to Hobart, Tasmania, where he practised from 1845 to 1857. He was a member of the House of Assembly in 1856-61, solicitor-general in 1857-60, and attorney-general in 1860-61. He returned home in 1865.

Knight married, at St John's, Weston-super-Mare, Somerset, 5 May 1841, Margaret Ward (1813-1899); they had 2 sons and 3 daughters:

1 Amelia Elizabeth (b. 1847)
2 Matilda (b. 1848)
1 Henry Palmer (1850-1911)
3 Julia Anne (b. 1852)
2 Charles Frederick (1856-1919)

1836: 23 Jul: *It would seem that Mr. Knight, the great Chancery Barrister, acquiesces in the principle which was laid down by Mr. Parry, another Chancery lawyer of considerable repute, whose opinion on the case we had taken.* 29 Jul., 6 Aug., 14 Nov.

KNIGHTLY — Mrs Knightly at London

1801: 19 Oct: *to Mrs. Beaver's in the evening, where were a numerous party Mrs. Knightly, Mrs. Gillies, Mrs. Noel, Mrs. Arnold &c.*

KNOLLIS — James Knollis[52]

James Knollis (1776-1860), Church of England clergyman, was born at Burford, Oxfordshire, son of Francis Knollis. He was educated at Trinity College, Oxford (BA 1798; MA 1801; BD 1809), and was a fellow of Lincoln College in 1798-1815. He later served as vicar of Penn, Buckinghamshire, in 1823, and perpetual curate of Maidenhead, Berkshire, in 1819-60.

1825: 4 Jul: *Maidenhead is partly in the parish of Cookham & partly in that of Bray, one side of the street belonging to these parishes respectively, according to their relative position. There is, however, a corporation at Maidenhead, who present to this chapel, and the Revd. Mr. Knollis is the present Incumbent, but resides at Penn in Bucks. A Curate performs the duty. Mr. Knollis is son of the aged rector of Burford, in Oxfordshire, who is of that family, which lays claim to the Banbury peerage.*

KNOLLYS — William Frederick Erskine Knollys[53]

William Frederick Erskine Knollys (1816-1898), Church of England clergyman, was born at St Germain-en-Laye, France, third son of William Knollys. He was educated at Merton College, Oxford (BA 1837; MA 1840). Knollys served as rector of Quedgeley in 1842-61, perpetual curate of Aldborough Hatch in 1862-65 and Holy Trinity, Twickenham, in 1867-69, rector of Saltwood, Kent, in 1869-79, honorary canon of Canterbury in 1876, and rector of Wrotham, Kent, in 1879-83. Knollys married, at Cheltenham, 13 October 1840, Caroline Augusta North (1816-1878); they had 6 sons and 1 daughter:

1 Constance Rachel (1841-1924)
1 Erskine William (±1842-1923)
2 William Edward (±1843-1910)
3 Dudley Robert (1844-1846)
4 Edward Francis (1846-1859)
5 Louis Edward Hartley (±1846-1922)
6 Clement Courtenay (±1848-1905); married, at All Saints', Headley, Surrey, 6 May 1874, Ellen May Delamotte

---

1851: 29 Apr: *Archdeacon Thorpe, Sir George Prevost, Alexr. Watson, Powell, Erskine Knollys, Canon Banks, ... The sermon was preached by Mr. Knollys, the excellent and talented Rector of Quedgley, who selected for his text Is. 33. 20, 21. He delivered an eloquent, heart stirring & powerful discourse, in which he vindicated the outlay of wealth in the costly structure of temples dedicated to the glory and worship of GOD.*

KNOTT — William Knott[54]

William Knott (1812-1888), poor law auditor, was born at Hallow, Worcestershire. By 1861 he had eventually succeeded in becoming a poor law auditor. He was registered as living at Lower

Wick, St John's, Worcester. He married, first, Sarah; they had 3 sons and 4 daughters:

1 Ambrose William (1836-1912)
1 Eliza Harriet (b. 1837)
2 Samuel Brookes (1840-1860)
2 Sarah Ann (1842-1921)
3 Henry Nicholl (1844-1880)
3 Ellen Louisa (1846-1852)
4 Milbro Anna (1849-1917)

Knott married, secondly, Anne (1819-1910); they had 3 sons and 2 daughters:

1 John Reginald Stanhope (1853-1883)
1 Elina Millicent (1854-1919)
2 Arthur Richard Walter (b. 1855)
3 Gerald Stephen Leonard (b. 1857)
2 Clara Louisa (1859-1935)

1844: 25 Aug: *A letter from a Mr. Knott, Auditor of the Pershore Union, with testimonials annexed, soliciting my interest for his appointment as Auditor, in the event of the Stow Union being included in the same Audit-district with that of Pershore.* 19 Oct: *Mr. Knott, of Birlingham, Worcestershire, auditor of the Pershore Union, waited on me to solicit my support in his behalf as Auditor of a projected district of about 17 Unions, including that of Stow, covering an area, of which the four corners may be stated as Rugby, Droitwich, Shipston on Stour, and Witney.*

1845: 22 Apr., 5 Jun., 26 Jun: *Wrote to Mr. Austin, Asst. Poor Low Commr., nominating Mr. Knott as Auditor of our Poor Law Union District.* 27 Jun: *Should Mr. Knott, therefore, eventually not have the greatest number of votes, I should be at liberty to vote for Mr. H.* 11 Jul.

1848: 11 Sep., 16 Sep.

KNOUR — the Knour family at Clifton

1806: 25 Jun: *Afterwards walked with the Goolds. & the Knours & Miss Ford.*

KNOWLES — James Sheridan Knowles[55]

James Sheridan Knowles (1784-1862), playwright and actor, was born at Cork, son of James Knowles (1759-1840), a lexicographer. Richard Brinsley Sheridan was his father's first cousin. At the age of 6, Knowles was placed in his father's school at Cork, but in 1793 he moved with the family to London. There he was befriended by William Hazlitt, an acquaintance of the family, who introduced him to Samuel Taylor Coleridge and Charles Lamb. After his education, Knowles settled down to life as a schoolmaster in Glasgow, but also indulged his interest as a playwright.

In 1820 Knowles wrote *Virginius*, which was performed with success in Glasgow. John Tait, a friend of William Charles Macready, saw the play and urged Macready to read it. This marked the beginning of a tumultuous relationship between Macready and Knowles which would last over twenty years and see the production of seven of Knowles's plays. *Virginius*, performed at Covent Garden on 17 May 1820 with Macready in the title role, was the first. Excited reviewers wrote of a dramatic renaissance, recognising in Knowles's mixture of Roman grandiloquence and English domesticity a new and distinctive voice.

The Hunchback was initially accepted by the authorities at Drury Lane, but Macready asked for changes; his hesitation over the revised text caused a breach between him and Knowles. The latter demanded the return of his manuscript, and took it to Charles Kemble at Covent Garden. It was produced there on 5 April 1832, with Knowles himself in the part of Master Walter. *The Hunchback* was a great success and enjoyed an almost uninterrupted run until the end of the season, although Knowles's acting did not meet with much approval. However, on taking *The Hunchback* to Glasgow and Edinburgh, he was received with enthusiasm by former friends and pupils. When his next important play, *The Wife*, was brought out at Covent Garden on 24 April 1833, Charles Lamb wrote both the prologue and epilogue. In his prime, Knowles was recognised as the leading dramatist of the day.

1836: 13 Sep: *Two younger Goodrich's, who are in the army, did not dine with us, having an engagement in Gloucester, at the Theatre, to be present at the representation of the Hunchback, a popular play by Sheridan Knowles, himself both author of the drama and acting the principal character.*

KNYVETT — Charles Knyvett[56]

Charles Knyvett (1752-1822), musician and singer, was born in the parish of St Margaret's, Westminster, son of Charles Knyvett (1710-1782) and Jane Jordan (1714-1785). Knyvett was educated at Westminster School and was a boy chorister at Westminster Abbey under Benjamin Cooke. He was appointed joint organist at the abbey in November 1770. In 1772 he married Rose Alleway (1750-1807) from Sonning in Berkshire, where Knyvett later acquired property. They had 3 sons:

1 Charles (1773-1852)
2 Henry (1774-1848)
3 William (1779-1856); *see below*

Knyvett performed occasionally at the theatre: in May 1775 he was paid for fourteen nights' harpsichord playing at Drury Lane, and in June 1790 he accompanied Mrs Billington when she sang Purcell's 'Mad Bess' in character as Ophelia in *Hamlet*. He was an organist in the oratorios at Covent Garden from 1789 to 1792, sang in the Chapel Royal choir from 1786, and was appointed organist there in 1796. Knyvett was also a principal alto at the Handel commemoration concerts from 1784.

The 'Two Master Knyvetts' in the 1784 choir were Knyvett's sons Charles and Henry, the latter of whom became an army officer. A third son, William, born in 1779, was a singer and composer. Between 1785 and 1799 Charles Knyvett (senior) sang at the annual Concerts of Ancient Music. He played the organ at the Three Choirs meeting in 1780 and sang at the Cambridge Festival during the 1780s. With the tenor Samuel Harrison, he founded the Vocal Concerts, a fashionable subscription series which ran each spring from 1792 to 1795. Knyvett appeared as singer and piano accompanist in these concerts, which featured English songs and glees. He sang for the Noblemen's and Gentlemen's Catch Club, the Je ne sais quoi Club, and the Anacreontic Society. The younger Charles and William performed with their father, and a number of three-part glees were published as sung by the Messrs Knyvett.

1804: 5 Nov: *First Subscription Concert. Very fully attended. Bartleman Knyvett & Miss Parke & Lindley.* 6 Nov: *Dined with Davis at the Music Room. Lindley Miss Parke & Knyvett charming. Poor Bartleman very ill: had a great deal of conversation with him.*

KNYVETT — William Knyvett — *see also* Travis[57]

William Knyvett (1779-1856), singer and composer, was born in London, the third son of Charles Knyvett (1752-1822) and Rose Alleway (1750-1807). He was educated by his father and glee composer Samuel Webbe, as well as Giambattista Cimador. In 1788 he sang in the treble chorus at the Concerts of Ancient Music, and in 1795 he appeared there as the principal alto. In 1797 he became a gentleman of the Chapel Royal, and shortly afterwards, a lay clerk at Westminster Abbey. He was appointed composer of the Chapel Royal in 1808, succeeding his father.

Knyvett helped his father run the Vocal Concerts at Willis's Rooms, and in 1811, with his brother Charles and Thomas Vaughan, he established the Vocal Subscription Concerts, which continued until 1822. From 1832 to 1840 he conducted the Concerts of Ancient Music; he also conducted at the Birmingham festivals from 1831 to 1843, and the York Festival in 1835.

One of the finest alto singers of his day, Knyvett sang in London and at provincial festivals, and formed a trio with Samuel Harrison and James Bartleman. The glee 'With sighs, sweet rose' was composed for him by John Wall Callcott. Knyvett was a popular songwriter, and his songs and glees included 'My love is like the red, red rose' (1803), 'The Bells of St Michael's Tower' (1810), 'The Boatie Rows' (1810), and 'As it fell upon a day' (1812). His glee 'When the fair rose' was awarded the Prince of Wales prize at the Harmonic Society in 1800.

Knyvett was married twice. His second wife, whom he married in 1826, was Deborah Travis (1797-1876), singer, of Shaw, near Oldham, Lancashire. She was one of the Lancashire chorus singers at the Concerts of Ancient Music from 1813 to 1815, and appeared as a principal from 1815. She was much in demand, especially as an oratorio singer, until her retirement in 1843. Knyvett died in poverty on 17 November 1856 at Clarges House, Ryde, Isle of Wight.

1823: 17 Sep: *The Dettingen Te Deum, the Overture to Esther, Dr. Boyce's Anthem (Charity) and W. Knyvett's new Coronation Anthem were the Musical treats for the morning. Of the vocalists, Miss Travis, Messrs. Vaughan, Bellamy, Hawes & W. Knyvett appeared.*

1826: 12 Sep: *to the remaining singers, who appeared at the rehearsal; suffice it to mention Vaughan, William Knyvett and Miss Travis, all remarkable for chaste execution & a faultless accuracy, combined with taste & sweetness, indicative of the genuine English school to which they belong, and which has been graced by the names & talents of Bartleman, Harrison & Greatorex.* 25 Sep.

1829: 22 Sep: *Not pretending to particularize all the pieces, but chiefly those, by which I was most struck, I could not notice, with others, the great improvement in Mrs. W. Knyvett's singing. As Miss Travis, and such she was at the last Gloucester Music Meeting, she was a very correct, chaste and elegant performer, of the second grade, peculiarly useful, & very successful in Handel's music, but since her marriage with W. Knyvett, so good a judge and able a professor of his art, she has made a great advance in taste & delicacy. Her song "Bid me not forget thy smile," composed by Knyvett, was a very elegant and feeling morçeau ... Vaughan and Braham & Knyvett have kept their ground these thirty years or nearly; and the same may be remarked of instrumental performers, F. Cramer, Lindley &c.* 23 Sep: Knyvett 290923 *Mrs. Knyvett sang with great correctness and pathos the beautiful recitative and air by Handel, "what tho' I trace".*

KOHLHOFF — Christian Samuel Kohlhoff[58]

Christian Samuel Kohlhoff (1815-1881), missionary, was born at Tanjore, the son of Revd J. C. Kohlhoff, of the SPCK Mission, and grandson of Revd J. B. Kohlhoff of the Royal Danish Mission. He was educated at Bishop's College, Calcutta, and ordained deacon in 1839 and priest in 1840 by the bishop of Madras. He died at Tranquebar in 1881. His principal work was at Erungalore, where his father founded a mission and built a church. He worked there from 1858 until his death.

1854: 20 Mar: *Received a note from Mr. Vernon, dated on Saturday, at Cirencester, from which I learn that he and Mr. Kohlhoff assent to the arrangements sketched out by me for the S.P.G. meeting on Thursday.* 23 Mar: *Mr. Vernon and Mr. Kohlhoff, the deputation from S.P.G. having arrived from Bibury, where a meeting was held yesterday evening; found their way to Mr. Hippisley's, where I went to meet them, and made necessary .... Mr. Kohlhoff then was called on to speak, and in a hesitating and monotonous tone, quite in contrast with the fluency, almost volubility of his companion, Vernon, entered into very pertinent details of Missionary life in Southern India.* 24 Mar: *My guests, Mr. Vernon and Mr. Kohlhoff, left us at 11 AM. for Cirencester, thence to proceed to hold an evening meeting in aid of S.P.G. at Cricklade.*

KOTZEBUE — August Friedrich Ferdinand von Kotzebue[59]

August Friedrich Ferdinand von Kotzebue (1761-1819), dramatist and writer, was born at Weimar to a respected merchant family. He was educated at Wilhelm-Ernst-Gymnasium in Weimar, where his uncle, the writer and critic Johann Karl August Musäus, was among his teachers. He spent a great deal of his life in St Petersburg, where he was a civil servant from 1781 through to 1795. After that, he spent several years in Vienna, working in the theatre; however, he was obliged to resign over disagreements with the actors with whom he worked. He returned to Weimar, his native town, but his position there was not comfortable; he was on bad terms with the powerful Goethe, whose characteristic romantic style he had openly attacked.

In 1798 Kotzebue decided to return to St Petersburg, but at the frontier he was arrested on an unknown charge and transported to Siberia. Fortunately, before his arrest, he had written a comedy which flattered the vanity of Emperor Paul I of Russia; he was quickly brought back from Siberia and presented with an estate from the crown lands of Livonia. He was also made director of the German theatre in St Petersburg.

When Tsar Paul died, Kotzebue returned to Germany, and settled again in Weimar, and then Berlin. In association with Garlieb Merkel (1769-1850), he edited *Der Freimutige* (Free Courage) from 1803 to 1807, and began his *Almanach dramatischer Spiele* in 1803, which was published posthumously in 1820. Towards the end of 1806, Kotzebue was once more in Russia; from the security of his estate in Livonia, he wrote many satirical articles against Napoleon Bonaparte in his journals *Die Biene* and *Die Grille*. As counsellor of state in 1816, he was attached to the department for foreign affairs in St Petersburg; in 1817 he went to Germany to report to Russia on German affairs. He was murdered in Mannheim by Karl Ludwig Sand, a student and 'Burschenschaftler', who viewed Kotzebue as a reactionary spy.

1800: 6 Jan: *in the Evening with my Mother to the Comedy, new, by Kotzebue Gusta Vasa, a Drama in 5 Acts. It is hardly to be called a play 'tis like the Henry's &c. of Shakespeare: more an History thrown into the form of a Drama. The Action is of nearly a years length & the Author professedly has no design of keeping a single unity.* 15 Jan: *to the Play Die Corsen von Kotzebue. a very interesting tho' in some places tedious play.* 22 Jan: *To the Wildfang by Kotzebue in the Evening my Mother & Dukinfield.* 3 Mar: *In the Evening to the play Die Sonnen Jungfrau von Kotzebue.* 5 Apr: *with my Mother to a new Play by Kotzebue Bayard: the Famous French Chevalier Sans peur et sans reproche, a fine interesting Piece tho' as most of the Plays of this Author without the Unities.* 10 Apr: *walked both morning and afternoon met Seckendorff, going in full Parade on his Cream coloured Nag to Leipzig: attending thither August von Kotzebue & his Family, who were going to Livonia.* 12 Mar: *in the Evening with my Mother to a new Comedy by Mad. de Kotzebue translated from the French of the unfortunate Fabre d'Englantine.* 24 Mar: *my Father & Dukinfield at the Hofmeister: Mad. de Kotzebue translation from Fabre d'Eglantine.*

KRANZ — Johan Friedrich Kranz [60]

Johann Friedrich Kranz (1752-1810), conductor, composer, and violinist, was the son of court wigmaker Georg Kranz. He was a precociously talented violinist who studied music with chamber musician C. G. Göpfert and Hofkapellmeister E. W. Wolf. He was given a place in the Weimar court orchestra as early as 1766, and became a chamber musician in 1778. He undertook extended journeys between 1780 and 1787.

1798: 2 Sep: *The Orchestra is extremely good. Concertmeister Kranz, though not a good Player, leads a Band very well, Destouches, without being a very great Composer, plays extremely well on the Harpsichord, & some violins & German Flutes are well executed.*

KRATTER — Franz Kratter [61]

Franz Kratter (1758-1830), writer and set designer, was born at Oberndorf am Lech. He studied philosophy and theology at the University of Dillingen, and then went to Vienna where he studied law. Having completed his education he was employed as a private secretary. In 1786, guided by a love of theatre and writing, he moved to Lviv, where he took an active interest in the local theatre. In 1795 he became the director of the Lviv stage. Under his management, the theatre's repertoire was modelled on the Viennese repertoire, and was said to have had a timeless character. His dramas were played throughout Germany; *The Maid of Mairenburg*, his most famous play, was published in 1798.

1799: 23 Dec: *in the Afternoon to the Comedie Das Mädchen von Marienburg, as it were the fellow piece of Der Friede am Pruth: both containing the same Characters in part & written by Kratter. the piece is very interesting & well written: force of imagination could not have much room for work, the subject being taken out of the real History of the Czar Peter the Great.*

KRAUS — Georg Melchior Kraus [62]

Georg Melchior Kraus (1737-1806), painter, was born in Frankfurt, son of Johann Georg Kraus and Cornelia Paulsen. His parents ran the 'Zur weissen Schlangen' hotel in the Sandgasse in Frankfurt. He was 8 years old when his father remarried after his mother's death.

From 1759 to 1762 Kraus trained in the studio of court painter Johann Heinrich Tischbein the elder at the court of Landgraf Frederick II of Hesse-Kassel. In November 1762 he travelled to Paris to study under Johann Georg Wille, the best-known copper-engraver of the time. In Paris he also came into contact with the genre painter Jean-Baptiste Greuze, and soon became 'genre painter familiar to His Holiness the prince bishop of Wirsbourg'. In 1766 Kraus returned to Frankfurt, where he initially worked as a private tutor and genre painter. His pupils included Sophie von La Roche, Friedrich Heinrich Jacobi, and Johann Wolfgang Goethe, with whom he formed a lasting friendship. Kraus later moved to Weimar, and in 1776, with private secretary to the duke, Friedrich Justin Bertuch (1747-1822), he co-founded the Fürstliche freie Zeichenschule Weimar, an art and literature educational establishment. It was financed by Carl Augustus, grand duke of Saxe-Weimar-Eisenach, and heavily promoted by Goethe, who also taught there. Among its pupils were Carl Augustus's future mistress, Karoline Jagemann.

1800: 8 Apr: *in the Evening to Mr. Gore's after a pleasant Turn in the Garden: several people there chiefly French a beautiful set of Drawings: taken by Rath Kraus on his Journey with Mr. Gore, thro' part of Germany, the Tirol and Italy: very beautiful.* 2 Sep: *The Drawing Academy here is under the direction of the well known Counsellor Kraus, whose Execution is well known to exceed his taste, Messrs. Femler, Müller, Herdig & Hornÿ, Keinert &c. give also Instructions, in every Branch of Painting and Drawing.*

L

LABORIE — Monsieur and Madame Laborie on the London stage[1]

Monsieur and Madame Laborie were dancers. They had appeared before in London in 1794 when they were paid £800 at the King's Theatre. At the same time Madame Hilligsberg and Didelot were each paid £1,000. M. and Mme Laborie were frequent performers at opera houses; along with Mrs Billington, Naldi, *et al*, they were stars of the day.

1801: 2 Jun: *in the Ballet of Ken-jo & Tao, Mad. Hilligsberg & Mons. Laborie charmed me especially. The other principal dances Didelot, Madame Rose Didelot, Mad. Laborie were vastly fine, but the grace, the naiveté of Hilligsberg is surely inimitable.*

LAIGHT — John Laight of Winson[2]

John Laight (1804-1880), agricultural labourer, was born at Winson, Gloucestershire. He was tried for sheep stealing at Gloucester on 5 April 1835 and acquitted. He was married to Margaret (b. ±1809), born at Coln St Dennis; they had at least 5 daughters:

1 Ann (b. ±1837)
2 Elisabeth (b. ±1838)
3 Mary (b. ±1843)
4 Harriet (b. ±1845)
5 Jane (b. ±1848)

1834: 4 Oct: *Drove to Northleach, accompanied by Otway, to assist Mr. Price in the examination of witnesses against a man named John Laight, of Winson, charged on suspicion of stealing five sheep on the 16th Sept. from W. Bryan, Lower Slaughter.* 10 Oct: *I rode to Northleach to attend at the Petty Sessions at the Bridewell preparatory to the Quarter Sessions. Met Messrs. Barker and Hicks Beach, Messrs. Ford and Price, Magistrates, Mr. Bowen was also present. With Price finally committed to Gloucester Gaol for trial on a charge of sheep stealing John Laight, the man whom we had under examination and had remanded on Saturday last.*

LAIRD — James Laird at Tunbridge[3]

James Laird was an old acquaintance of the Witts family in Edinburgh. He later seems to have settled at Great Malvern, where he was a benefactor to the church. Laird was also a frequent visitor at fashionable places in Bristol and Cheltenham. There is a possibility that there was more than one James Laird, but the tenor of the extracts from the diaries of Agnes Witts suggests that the various mentions refer to the same person. He may have been a doctor of medicine. He died at some point before 1817.

1805: 28 Aug: *Mr. James Laird, coming by accident to the Inn gave us the pleasure of his company in the Evening.*

LAIT — Richard Lait and the Lait family of Eyford[4]

Richard Lait (1758-1846), shepherd, married Ann Page (1766-1832); they had at least 4 sons and 5 daughters:

1 Mary (b. 1788); born at Prestbury, Gloucestershire; was in service with Jane Backhouse at Gloucester
2 Sarah (b. 1791); born at Prestbury; married, 30 April 1809, George Mills of Lower Swell
1 John (1793-1881); born at Colesborne, Gloucestershire; died at Witney, Oxfordshire
3 Elizabeth (1794-1873); married, at Upper Slaughter, 11 January 1814, William Banting (1791-1845); 4 sons and 3 daughters:
    1 James (b. & d. 1816)
    1 Hannah (1817-1818)
    2 William (1818-1895)
    2 Eleanor (1821-1884)
    3 Elizabeth (1823-1851)
    3 Henry (1825-1896)
    4 George (1830-1917)
2 Joseph (b. 1796); born at Colesborne; died at Witney, Oxfordshire; married Esther; at least 5 daughters:
    1 Anne Davis (b. 1826)
    2 Mary (b. 1828)
    3 Ellen (b. 1832)
    4 Amelia (b. 1834)
    5 Sarah Anne (b. 1838)
4 Hannah (b. 1798); born at South Cerney, Gloucestershire; married, at Upper Slaughter, 14 October 1822, Henry Calton of Donnington, Herefordfordshire
3 Richard (1802-1873), mason; born at Colesbourne; died at Strand, London; married Mary (d. 1825); at least 4 sons and 4 daughters:
    1 William (1811-1813)
    1 Mary (1812-1813)
    2 William (b. 1814)
    2 Mary Anne (1815-1817)
    3 Elizabeth (b. 1816)
    3 John Bradley (1818-1825)
    4 Ester Mary (1822-1823)
    4 Richard (b. 1824)
5 Ann (1805-1869); born at Colesborne
4 James (1808-1877); married Anne Southern (b. ±1811); at least 3 sons and 2 daughters:
    1 George William (b. & d. 1831)
    1 Anne Elizabeth (b. 1832)
    2 William (b. 1834)
    2 Jemima (1837-1906); married, first, at Liverpool, 5 May 1861, James Totty (1836-1863); secondly, at Liverpool, 1865, Samuel Arnold (1840-1901)
    3 George (1838-1862)

The Lait who wanted to join the Gloucestershire Constabulary was most likely James; his age, 38, was probably the reason he was deemed ineligible. Most of the family appear to have moved away from Eyford as no burials were recorded after Richard's death in 1846.

1826: 10 Feb: *Nor is it without suspicion, that the other Servant, Mary Lait, from Eyford, is regarded: her appearance indicates pregnancy, but she has complaints, which often cause an enlargement of the body; & she solemnly denies the charge. She also has been as long the Servant of Mrs. B., who brought them both with her from Upper Slaughter, when she went to take up her residence at Gloucester in 1821. Both have had the credit of being excellent servants, but I suspect, they have lived sad lives during Mrs. Backhouse's absence from home with us last year.* 27 Feb: *The suspicions entertained respecting Mrs. Backhouse's other servant, Mary Lait, were too well founded; & from several quarters during the last week, she received information, that left no doubt of the miserable woman's guilty pregnancy. Her crime is enhanced by her bold and impudent hypocrisy: the partner of her iniquity is a mere boy compared to herself, as she is approaching forty years of age.... This woman has also lived nearby five years in her present service, was considered a valuable servant, though ill health made her unequal to fatigue or much hurry, & had the exterior of modesty even amounting to prudery. She is the daughter of an old Shepherd at Eyford.*

1846: 1 Nov: *Wrote to Mr. Lefroy, respecting J. Lait, who solicited me yesterday to procure for him a situation in the Constabulary force.* 4 Nov: *Recd. a letter from Mr. Lefroy, intimating that he does not consider James Lait eligible to be a Constable.*

LAKE — John James Lake[5]

John James Lake (1781-1809), Church of England clergyman, was born at Lanivet, Cornwall, son of Revd John Lake. He was educated at Exeter College, Oxford (BA 1802; MA 1805), and fellow from 1805 to 1809.

1802: 7 Mar: *sitting first a couple of Hours in Stevens's Rooms, meeting Alford & Lake.* 21 Mar: *Spent the Evening with Stevens & Lake, & with Paget to St. John's College Chapel.*

LAKE — William Charles Lake — *see also* Bashford, Broome Phillips Witts, *and* Lowe[6]

William Charles Lake (1753-1836), merchant and landed proprietor, was born in Berkeley County, South Carolina, and presumably returned to England as a loyalist. He established himself as a successful Liverpool merchant. He lived at Birkenhead Priory, before the town of Birkenhead was built, when the Benedictine priory was surrounded by only a few houses. Lake married, 1777, Ann Orange (1758-1810). Ann had been born in Virginia, and she died at Birkenhead Priory. The couple had at least 6 sons and 12 daughters:

1 Richard (b. 1778)
1 Mary (1779-1865); married, at St Anne's, Liverpool, 12 November 1798, William Whitehouse (1770-1844); 5 sons and 5 daughters
2 Barbara (1780-1861); died unmarried at Lower Bebington, Birkenhead, Cheshire
2 William (1781-1856); died unmarried at Lower Bebington, Birkenhead, Cheshire
3 Sophia (1782-1822); married, 1809, at Birkenhead Priory, Capt. James Bashford, RN (1777-1832)
3 Thomas (1783-1805)
4 Ann (b. 1784)
4 Charles (1786-1870); Capt., 2nd Bn, 3rd Foot (Royal Scots), Lt-Col Sir Alexander Gordon's Company; wounded at Waterloo and thereafter lived in retirement. In a letter from Brussels to his father dated 19 June, he gave details of his injuries and a brief resumé of the battle, and asked to be remembered to Mr Witts. Married, 1816, Anna Louisa, youngest daughter of Henry Halsey of Henley Park, Surrey; at least 1 son:
  1 William Charles (1817-1897); *see below*
5 Jane (1787-1853); married, at Liverpool, 2 May 1809, Broome Phillips Witts (1767-1845)
6 Frances Elizabeth (1788-1864); died unmarried at Lower Bebington, Birkenhead, Cheshire
7 Clarissa (1789-1848); died unmarried at Lower Bebington, Birkenhead, Cheshire
8 Harriet (1790-1860); married, at St Mary's, Birkenhead, 3 October 1816, Revd James Aspinall (1795-1861)
9 Agnes (1792-1838); died unmarried at Gloucester
10 Isabella Orange (1793-1866); died unmarried at Lower Bebington, Birkenhead, Cheshire
11 Charlotte (1794-1861); married, by brother-in-law Revd James Aspinall, at Painswick, 12 September 1826, Robert Atwell Lowe of Cheltenham; 1 daughter:
  1 Emmelina; married, 4 October 1859, Sir Robert Cavendish Spencer Clifford (1815-1892)
5 John Orange (1796-1797); died an infant
12 Eliza Esther (1797-1856); died unmarried at Lower Bebington, Birkenhead, Cheshire
6 Alexander (1800-1833); died at Port of Islay, Peru

Some time shortly after 1819 William Charles Lake moved to Castle Godwyn, Painswick, Gloucestershire.

The Whitehouse family married extensively into the Lake and Townsend families. H. W. Townsend, of Rugby, married, at Bebington, Cheshire, 8 August 1833, Elizabeth Anne, eldest daughter of William Whitehouse. At the same time, James Thomas Lake Whitehouse married Esther Louise, youngest daughter of Revd Richard Lowndes Salmon, vicar of Sandbach.

1825: 13 Jun: *At Castle Godwin, a small place perched among the beech woods adorning the upland valley contiguous to Painswick resides a Mr. Lake, formerly of Liverpool, & father to the wife of Mr. B.P. Witts, of Brunswick Square, my second cousin, an opulent merchant largely engaged in the silk trade.* 9 Nov: *We drove this forenoon to pay a visit at Castle Godwin, near Painswick, to Mr. & the Miss Lakes, who reside there. We found some of the young ladies at home, but Mr. Lake & his daughter, Mrs. B.P. Witts, who has been making a long visit to her friends, were absent at Cheltenham.*

1835: 10 Jun: *The bridegroom and Mr. Taylor came in the evening: the Settlements were read over, to which I was only a party by being called upon to witness the signatures of different parties. Mr. Bassevi, a Barrister connected by marriage with the Lake family, and young Broome Witts are Trustees on behalf of the Bride.* 11 Jun: ... *They were followed by Mr. and Mrs. Lowe with their only child, a pretty little bridesmaid, scarcely six years old, two Misses Lake, and Mr. Blackford. Mrs. Lowe and the Misses Lake are sisters of Mrs. Witts.*

1839: 5 May: *At my cousin's table I met two nieces of Mrs. W. the Misses Aspinall, daughters of a Liverpool Clergyman, who married one of the Misses Lake, and who is known to the public by some volumes of sermons which he has published.*

1840: 4 Aug: *B. L. Witts, being obliged to pursue his journey towards Liverpool this evening, and having taken an early dinner, accompanied MW. and myself in the Chariot to Stow, where at six P.M. he took a place on the Novelty Coach for Cheltenham, meaning to proceed from thence to Gloucester, where his maternal Aunts, the Misses Lake, reside.*

1842: 16 Mar: *There was also at table Miss Bromhead, a connection of the Lake family.*

1844: 12 Sep: *With Mr. Duncan drove to Stow; he made enquiries there as to the coach to Cheltenham, which on Thursdays passes through Stow from Banbury about 6 P.M. and by which he proposed travelling, to proceed later in the evening from the Cheltenham station by rail to Ashchurch, and thence to visit the Ruddles, connections of the Lakes, Whitehouses, Duncans, Martins*

&c., at Walton House near Tewkesbury; proposing to proceed to Liverpool by way of Wrexham.

LAKE — William Charles Lake — ***see also*** **Broome Phillips Witts**[7]

William Charles Lake (1817-1897), dean of Durham, was the eldest son of Capt. Charles Lake, an officer in the Scots Fusilier Guards, who was wounded at the battle of Waterloo, and his wife, Anna Louisa, youngest daughter of Henry Halsey of Henley Park, Surrey. He was grandson of William Charles Lake (*above*). Some of Lake's childhood was spent in France and the Channel Islands before the family settled in Rugby, where he attended Rugby School as a day boy under Dr Wooll and Dr Arnold. After Rugby, Lake went to Balliol College, Oxford (BA 1838; MA 1841), where he was fellow in 1838-59, tutor in 1842-57, proctor in 1852-52, and public examiner in 1853. He served as rector of Huntspill, Somerset, in 1858-69, prebendary of Wells in 1860-69, and dean of Durham in 1869-97. He became a doctor of divinity in 1869.

Late in life, Lake married, 2 June 1881, Katherine, daughter of John Neilson Gladstone, brother of the prime minister. There were no children of the marriage.

1853: 8 Jan: *At ten minutes before 12 o cl. I left Oxford Station in a train for Didcot, to meet the mail train travelling down: the platform was crowded by members of convocation returning from the poll. I travelled in the same carriage with two men of some Oxford notoriety—Mr. Lake, of Balliol Coll, Tutor & late Senr. Proctor, a relation of the Broom Lake Witts's, being a nephew of Mrs. B.P.W., a man of considerable talent, a favourite pupil of Dr. Arnold, late Head Master of Rugby.*

LAMARTINE — Alphonse Marie Louis de Prat de Lamartine[8]

Alphonse Marie Louis de Prat de Lamartine (1790-1869), writer, poet, and politician, was born in Mâcon, Burgundy, where his family were members of the provincial nobility. He is famous for his partly autobiographical poem, *Le Lac*, which describes, in retrospect, the fervent love shared by a couple from the point of view of the bereaved man. He wrote *Histoire des Girondins* in 1847 in praise of the Girondists. He worked for the French Embassy in Italy from 1825 to 1828, and in 1829 he was elected a member of the Académie Française. He was elected a 'député' in 1833, and was briefly in charge of the government during the turbulence of 1848. He was minister of foreign affairs from 24 February to 11 May 1848, and then a member of the executive commission, the political body which served as France's joint head of state.

Lamartine was instrumental in the founding of the Second Republic of France, having met with republican deputies and journalists in the Hôtel de Ville in Paris to agree upon the composition of its provisional government. Lamartine himself was chosen to declare formally the Republic in traditional form from the balcony of the Hôtel de Ville.

1848: 19 May: *France has just passed through, or is passing through, the horrors of the second revolution within the short space of three months. On the assembly of the National Convention, the Provisional Government resigned their authority into the hands of that body. Thus Lamartine and his Associates, motley men of various grades and shades of democracy, abdicated their power; but only to resume it in another modification of parties; for, a Commission of government being appointed by the National Assembly to exercise the functions of government until the new Constitution should have been settled and decreed, the same parties as before, with a few exceptions, and especially Lamartine and Ledra Rollin, have been nominated to carry on the public service.* 29 Jun: *Lamartine may be considered as the type of the Conservative section among them, Ledru Rollin, Louis Blanc and others, as the representatives of the Jacobinism of the old Revolution fifty years ago.*

LAMB — William Lamb[9]

William Lamb, 2nd Viscount Melbourne (1779-1848), prime minister, was the supposed son of Peniston Lamb, 1st Viscount Melbourne (1745-1828), and Elizabeth Milbanke, but there is a strong possibility that his true father was George O'Brien, 3rd Earl Egremont (1751-1837). Lamb was educated at Eton College and Trinity College, Cambridge, and in his youth fell in with a set of radicals that included Shelley and Byron. In 1805 he succeeded his elder brother as heir to his father's title and married Caroline Ponsonby. In January 1806 he became MP for Leominster, and at the election of that same summer he took the seat of Haddington Burghs. He was subsequently MP for Portarlington in 1807-12, Peterborough in 1816-19, Hertfordshire in 1819-26, Newport IoW in 1827, and Bletchingley in 1827-28. He succeeded his father in July 1828 as 2nd Viscount Melbourne. Lord Melbourne was secretary of state for home affairs from November 1830 to July 1834, and prime minister from July to November 1834, and April 1835 to September 1841.

Melbourne was unfortunate in having to face two public scandals during his career. The first, his wife Lady Caroline Lamb's affair with Lord Byron, was the talk of the town in 1812. She coined Byron's famous characterisation, 'mad, bad, and dangerous to know'. Melbourne and his wife were eventually reconciled, although they separated in 1825. Still, her death in 1828 affected him considerably. In the second scandal, Melbourne was the victim of an attempted blackmail by the husband of a close friend, the society beauty and author Caroline Norton. Having refused to pay a demanded sum of £1,400, Melbourne was publicly accused by the husband of having an affair with his wife, Lady Norton. It is a measure of the respect contemporaries had for his integrity that Melbourne's government did not fall; both the king and the duke of Wellington urged him to stay on as prime minister. After Norton failed in court, Melbourne was vindicated, but he did stop seeing Lady Norton.

Lord Melbourne is perhaps best known for his successful mentoring of Queen Victoria after her accession in 1837. Barely 18, Victoria was only just breaking free from the domineering influence of her mother, the duchess of Kent, and her mother's advisor, John Conroy. Over the next four years Melbourne trained her in the art of politics and the two became friends; Victoria was quoted as saying she considered him like a father. He was given a private apartment at Windsor Castle. Tutoring Victoria was possibly the climax of Melbourne's career; he spent four to five hours a day visiting and writing to her, and she responded enthusiastically. Even after Lord Melbourne had stepped down as prime minister in 1841, Victoria continued writing to him. Their correspondence, however, came to be seen as inappropriate and eventually it ceased; instead of Melbourne, Victoria came to rely on her new husband Prince Albert, and on herself.

1827: 2 May.

1828: 28 May: *Disunion reigns in the cabinet; for it is announced, that Mr. Huskisson and Lord Palmerston have resigned their offices, & it is surmised, that the rest of the liberal party in the administration, Mr. C. Grant, Mr. Lamb, Lord Dudley &c. will also retire.* 28 Jun: *Lord Francis Leveson Gower, is appointed Secretary for Ireland in the room of Mr. Lamb, who has resigned.*

1832: 10 Apr: *Lord Melbourn was calm and gentlemanly in his advocacy of the bill, Lord Durham, provoked by the intemperate comments of the Bishop of Exeter, was bitter and personal against that ill judging prelate, who also received a merited rebuke from the Premier.*

1834: 16 Nov: *The newspapers announce the dissolution of Lord Melbourne's administration, an event not generally expected.*

1835: 9 Apr: *Breakfasted at the Bell Hotel, where the worthy conservatives learnt with pain what they must have anticipated, that Sir Robert Peel has resigned his post of Premier, and that his administration is dissolved. He will, doubtless, be succeeded by a rifaccimento of the Melbourne Administration.* 19 Apr: *The newspapers announce the near completion of a Whig Ministry under Lord Melbourne as Premier...* 15-16 May, 20-21 May, 28 May: *The Chairman then put the question as to the adoption of the motion made by me, which was carried unanimously in the affirmative, and fifty six signatures were forthwith attached to it the letter to Lord Melbourne.* 1 Jun., 4 Jun: *Mr. R. Brookes produced the letter to Lord Melbourne with more than 220 signatures attached. Gave directions that it should be forwarded to his Lordship by to-morrow's post.*

1837: 10 Aug: *On the whole the Melbourne parliament is likely to be less favourable to his government than the late Peel parliament.*

1839: 6 May: *Various political rumours were floating in the atmosphere of the House of Lords, and its purlieus; among others that Lord Melbourne and John Russel were about to retire from the administration.* 10 May: *Recd. a letter from Round acquainting me that there was every prospect that a firm Conservative government would be formed: that at the suggestion of Lord Melbourne, the Queen had sent for the D. of Wellington, who had advised her to call on Sir Robt. Peel, to take measures for forming an administration: that the Queen had recd. Sir R.P. in a very satisfactory manner, that everything was likely to be arranged smoothly, that he was busily employed in constructing the Cabinet, that as to its members thus much only had transpired, that he was to hold the rank of Premier, with the offices of First Lord of the Treasury, & Chanc. of the Exch.*

LAMBERT — young Lambert at Stert

1807: 12 Apr: *Walked to Stert, found Mrs. Newman, Miss & Master Newman, Mr. F. Gibbs, & young Lambert, with Mrs. Jaques.*

LAMBERT — Miss Lambert at Giggleswick

1837: 24 Oct: *After dinner Miss Hartley, Rowden and myself went to pass the evening with Mr. and Mrs. Robinson where we met Miss Lambert and Miss Robinson.*

1838: 15 Sep: *Mr. & Mrs. Robinson—Miss Lambert,—John and Mary Swale.*

LAMBERT — Mrs S. Lambert at Clifton [10]

This Lambert family has not been identified conclusively. In the 1841 census, widow Frances Lambert (±1755-1846) lived at 20 the Mall, Clifton. In 1830 Richard Lambert (±1765-1851), landed proprietor and merchant, born in Dublin, lived at Park Place, Clifton. By the 1841 census he lived at Frederick Place, Clifton, with his wife, Hester Goodman Lambert (±1769-1847); they had at least 5 sons and 3 daughters, including:

1 Esther Davis (b. 1791-1870); died unmarried at Clifton
2 Caroline (1798-1883); died unmarried at Clifton
3 Ann (b. ±1799)
1 Henry (b. ±1809), merchant
2 Richard Joseph Farran (±1810-1877), clergyman

Whether or not Frances and Hester were the 'two Mrs Lamberts' received in visits by Agnes Witts is not clear. Although Agnes Witts mentions Mr and Mrs Lambert from Clifton (at Clifton and in Cheltenham), at no point does she mention Mr Lambert being a general. No general of the name of Lambert appears to have been in either the British Army or the HEIC Army at this time. On 7 December 1815 Agnes recorded receiving a letter from Sabina Lambert, and mentioned curtly the following day, 'wrote to Lambert'. Of course, this Sabina Lambert may not have been related to the Clifton Lamberts.

1804: 17 Jul: *Walked alone in Leigh Woods in the Evening. My Father & Mother being at Mrs. Gen. S. Lambert's.*

1805: 14 Jan: *Passed the Evening alone, my Father & Mother being at Mrs. Lamberts.* 4 Feb., 9 Mar., 7 Nov.

LAMLEY — Charles Lamley, surgeon at Northleach [11]

Charles Lamley (±1787-1841), surgeon, was a physician/surgeon at Northleach for more than twenty years. In the 1841 census he was at Worcester Street, Gloucester, where he died a few months later. He was buried in the same grave as Charles Robert Gibbs (1814-1840). One might have supposed this was Charles Lamley's son, but apparently Charles Robert Gibbs Lamley was the son of William and Hannah Lamley, and was therefore presumably a nephew.

1835: 24 Apr: *Townsend, the Keeper of the Bridewell at Northleach called with a set of Queries from the Prison Committee of the House of Lords which I assisted him to answer. He was also the bearer of a note from Mr. Hadwen, the surgeon of the Bridewell... proposing Mr. Lamley of Northleach or Mr. Cheatle of Burford as substitutes to discharge his duties towards the prisoners, during the period of his absence.*

LAMOTTE — the Lamotte family at Cote

The Lamotte family has not been identified.

1804: 24 Jan: *Dined & slept at the former's House at Cote, where I experienced a friendly reception, & was extremely pleased. Besides the family & Slap, the party consisted of Mr. & Mrs. Foster, the Lamottes, Capt. Holosworth, Col. Coke, Mr. & Mrs. John Alleyne.*

LANCASTER — Daniel Lancaster of Patney, Wiltshire [12]

Daniel Lancaster (1761-1814), Church of England clergyman, was born at Dean, Cumberland, son of Daniel Lancaster and Martha Grayson. He was educated at Queen's College, Oxford (BA 1787). Lancaster was ordained deacon on 12 March 1786 and priest on 3 June 1787. He was appointed rector of Patney, Wiltshire, in 1804-14. He married, at Bridekirk, Cumberland, 10 June 1787, Mary Winn (b. ±1751); they had at least 2 sons and 1 daughter:

1 Elizabeth (1788-1869)
1 Jonathan (b. 1790)
2 Daniel (b. 1793)

1806: 12 Sep: *Rode to Easticott, to the dwelling House of the late Mr. Axford to join the cavalcade upon occasion of his burial. The gentlemen assembled were Messrs. Lancaster, Bruges, Smith, Sainsbury... Lancaster dined with me.*

1807: 18 Feb: *Rode forth to get Erchfont served during my absence & a testimonial to shew the Bp. Accomplished the former by calling upon Mr. Lancaster at Patney.* 29 Jun: *In the Evening drove my Mother to drink tea at Mrs. C. Mayo's at Beeching Stoke;*

met Mrs. J. Gent, Miss H. Tylee, Mr. & Mrs. Lancaster. 11 Aug: *Mrs. Poore, Mrs. Warrener & Miss Lancaster & Dr. & Mrs. Hill & their son Charles drank tea with us.*

LANCEY — William Lancey [13]

William Lancey (1799-1866), army officer, was born at Greenwich, Kent. When a lieutenant in the Royal Engineers he was engaged in work on the ordnance survey in England and Ireland. He wrote a comprehensive illustrated memoir of his time in Donegal in 1835, and published it as *Ordnance Survey Memoirs of Ireland Parishes of County Donegal.* Playwright Brian Friel turned the publication into a successful play in Ireland called *Translations*, in which Capt. Lancey and Lt Yolland were included as characters.

Lancey was a director of the Naval, Military, East India and General Life Assurance Society for more than twenty years. He commenced his army career as a cadet, and was promoted to 2nd lieutenant in 1816, 1st lieutenant in 1825, captain in 1838, and major in 1854. He died at Newtown Limavady.

1825: 12 Mar: *We dined at Mr. Ford's, at Little Risington, There were also of the party two officers of the Engineers, Messrs. White & Lancey: these gentlemen with a third, of the name of Gosset, have been stationed for some time at Stow to survey this district for the grand trigonometrical map, which is in a course of publication under the direction of the board of Ordnance.*

LANCHBURY — James Lanchbury [14]

James Lanchbury (1788-1853), agricultural labourer, was born at Fifield, Oxfordshire. He lived at Upper Slaughter with his widowed mother Mary (1749-1836) and wife Sarah, née Eden (1781-1864); they had at least 1 son and 2 daughters:

- 1 Richard (1815-1862); married Elizabeth Evans (1826-1879); at least 5 sons and 2 daughters:
  - 1 Joseph (b. & d. 1844)
  - 2 William (1845-1846)
  - 3 George (1848-1926)
  - 1 Anne Mary (b. 1852)
  - 4 James (b. & d. 1855)
  - 2 Elizabeth (1856-1886)
  - 5 Richard (1860-1929)
- 1 Mary (1818-1895); died unmarried
- 2 Elizabeth (1821-1832)

1851: 4 Mar: *Visited poor parishioners Sarah James, James Townsend, Widow Wilcox, James Lanchbury.*

1852: 10 Feb: *Visited E. Wilcox & wife—Betterton's wife—Lanchburys—all aged infirm, or sick parishioners.* 21 Feb., 10 Dec.

1853: 16 Mar: *Wrote to Dr. Williams, Superintendent of the County Lunatic Asylum, requesting information as to the health, both bodily and mental, of James Lanchbury—Recd. an answer to the effect that he was gradually sinking, and could not long survive.* 17 Mar: *Recd. a note from Dr. Williams, informing me that poor James Lanchbury, of U. Slaughter, had died at the Lunatic Asylum this morning.* 18 Mar: *To Dr. Williams, Superintendent of the Lunatic Asylum, Gloucester, with an intimation that the remains of Jas. Lanchbury, of this parish, must be interred in the grave-yard of that Institution.* 6 May.

1854: 28 Feb., 15 Apr., 11 Jul.

LANDON — James Landon [15]

James Landon (1764-1850), Church of England clergyman, was born at Tedstone Delamere, Hereford, son of John Landon (1722-1782) and Elizabeth Higgins (1729-1802). He was educated at Worcester College, Oxford (BA 1787), and then Oriel College, Oxford (MA 1789; BD 1799), where he was a fellow and, in 1798, proctor. He served as vicar of St Mary the Virgin, Oxford, in 1797, of Aymestrey with Leinthall-Earls, Herefordshire, in 1797, and of Aberford, Yorkshire, in 1805. He married, at Aberford, Yorkshire, 7 June 1808, Anne Bainbridge (1783-1861); they had at least 1 son and 8 daughters:

- 1 Anne (1809-1876)
- 2 Mary Elizabeth (1810-1897)
- 3 Lucy (b. 1813)
- 4 Caroline (1813-1883)
- 5 Dorothy Snell (1814-1885)
- 1 James Timothy Bainbridge (1816-1890)
- 6 Barbara (1820-1895)
- 7 Julia (1825-1903)
- 8 Isabella Jane (1827-1911)

1804: 4 Mar: *St. Mary's assize sermon by Mr. Landon of Oriel with an inaudible voice.*

LANE — Edmund Lane [16]

Edmund Lane (b. 1816), Church of England clergyman and schoolmaster, was born at Stratford-on-Avon, Warwickshire, son of John and Catherine Lane. He was educated at Magdalen Hall, Oxford (BA 1839; MA; BCL 1850). He does not appear to have remained at Gloucester very long. He was rector of St Mary, Manchester, in 1844-56, and until 1871 he was a private chaplain living at Charlcombe, Bath, Somerset. He then moved to Scotland where he became episcopalian incumbent of St John's, Selkirk, 1872. He was married to Selina (b. ±1826); they had at least 1 son and 4 daughters:

- 1 Flora Diana (b. 1855); born at Manchester
- 2 Selina Louisa Greatbed (b. ±1857)
- 3 Maud Hartwell (b. ±1861)
- 4 Elizabeth F. (b. ±1863)
- 1 Edward D. (b. ±1866)

1842: 14 Apr., 27 Apr: *At three o clock an appointment was made for a meeting of the Clergy of the Deanery, to take into consideration a letter from the Revd. Mr. Lane, Clerical Principal of the Diocesan School at Gloucester, and Secretary of the Diocesan Board of National Education.* 26 Nov: *Recd. a note from Mr. Lane, Principal of the Diocesan National School, Gloucester, announcing a meeting of the Comm. for the 28th Inst.*

1844: 29 Jan: *A note from Mr. Lane, the Master of the Diocesan School at Gloucester, summoning for Feb. 1. a meeting of the Diocesan Education Comm. to deliberate on the combination of the Gloucester and Bristol boards of National Education.* 30 Jan., 9 Feb.

LANE — Richard James Lane [17]

Richard James Lane (1800-1872), lithographer and sculptor, was born at Berkeley Castle, Gloucestershire, the second son of Revd Theophilus Lane (1764-1814), prebendary of Hereford Cathedral, and Sophia Gardiner, the niece of painter Thomas Gainsborough. At the age of 16 he was apprenticed to the line engraver Charles Heath. In 1827, having completed his apprenticeship and become an engraver, he produced a fine print after Sir Thomas Lawrence's 'Red Riding Hood'. By this time Lane had become dissatisfied with the commercialisation of engraving; he abandoned it for lithography, a process Heath had pioneered in Britain. Lane's earliest lithographs date from 1824, when his skills were recognised by the leading lithographic printer Charles Hullmandel. Lane first exhibited at the Royal Academy in 1824 and continued exhibiting there regularly, and occasionally at the Suffolk Street Gallery, until his death. He was elected an associate member of the Royal Academy in 1827. Lane worked mainly as a reproductive lithographer and produced several sets of lithographs which were much praised at the time. He married, 1825, Sophia Hodges; they had 2 sons and 3 daughters.

1836: 22 Jul: *I wrote to an engraver of the name of Lane in the Regent's Park, who has successfully lithographed several paintings of private characters, with a view to ascertain the expence and the best method of procuring a plate of a picture of Lady L. Two portraits of her have been taken within these two years: one in her own possession, a three quarterlength figure, another on a smaller scale in the possession of Mrs. Walker. It is proposed that the latter be lithographed, either by the subscription of her numerous connections, or by selling each print at a fixed price. Both the portraits are excellent likenesses, and taken by a Worcester artist of the name of Cole.* 31 Jul: *A letter from Mr. Lane, the Artist to whom I wrote on the 22d. for particulars as to the expence of a lithographic portrait of Lady Lyttelton.* 15 Aug.

LANE — Richard Weight Lane [18]

Richard Weight Lane (1794-1872), printer, was born at Cirencester, son of John and Ann Lane. He lived at Mount Pleasant, Maugersbury, Stow-on-the-Wold. He was unmarried, and by 1861 he was retired from business.

1834: 8 Aug: *Examined two new witnesses, Lane and his housekeeper, whose testimony strengthens the case.*

1839: 30 May.

1840: 8 Aug: *Rode to Stow: arranged with the Printer, Lane, about printing 200 Copies of the report of the Stow Distr. Comm. S.P.G. presented to me at the meeting on the 5th.* 18 Oct., 21 Oct., 24 Oct.

1842: 12 Sep: *Wrote to ... Mr. Lane, Bookseller, Stow, to order abstracts of the Acts of Parliament during the last two Sessions.* 4 Nov: *Wrote to Lane, Bookseller, Stow, as to a publication to be procured for the Book Society.*

1844: 5 Oct: *Wrote to ... Mr. Lane, Printer, Stow, to print certain forms of certificate for the Poor Law Union.*

1846: 14 Dec: *Busy in correcting for the press the Book Society catalogue; writing to Lane, the Printer, therewith.*

1847: 6 Aug: *To Mr. Lane, printer, desiring him to print some notices of the Annual meeting of the Stow district Committee. S.P.G.* 8 Dec: *with Mr. Morgan and Churchwarden Lane.*

1850: 21 Jan: *Wrote to Lane, printer, Stow, to prepare him to be ready to execute some printing to-morrow.*

1853: 12 Feb: *Wrote to Lane, Printer, Stow, with directions to him to print handbills and notes announcing a special meeting S.P.G. at Stow on Mar. 2.* 15 Feb.

LANG — the Lang family at Clifton

This family has not been identified although there was a Robert Lang who was prominent in Bristol society at this time, probably as a merchant or banker.

1804: 20 Sep: *the whole party at Mr. Townsend's, I accompanied Mrs. Hopkinson & Miss Lang, Mr. Townsend & his six daughters, (Mrs. Munro, Susan, Charl., Carol, Jane & Sophia) in Mrs. H's coach & a Sociable to the New Passage 10 miles.* 22 Sep: *Dined with Mr. Townsend meeting the same party & Mrs. Lang & Mrs. Garraway, & late joined a party at Mrs. Massey's.* 24 Sep: *To Bristol & the Earthen Ware Manufactory with Mrs. Townsend, Mrs. Monro, Mrs. Lang, & Mrs. Hopkinson.*

LANGHAM — Mrs Langham at Clifton

1804: 17 Aug: *Called on Mrs. Langhams, Mrs. Bates & Mrs. Carrick.*

LANGSTON — James Haughton Langston — *see also* Barter [19]

James Haughton Langston (1796-1863), JP, MP, and landed proprietor, was born and baptised in the parish of St James, Westminster, son of John Langston (±1758-1812), MP, and Sarah, daughter of John Goddard of Woodford Hall, Essex. He was educated at Eton College and Christ Church, Oxford (DCL 1819), and served as high sheriff for Oxfordshire in 1819. He was MP for Woodstock in 1820-26, and Oxford in 1826-35 and 1841-63.

The family's wealth had been generated by James's grandfather, James Haughton Langston (d. 1795), a merchant banker and wine merchant, who had bought Sarsden and the neighbouring estates in 1792. His son, John, our James's father, having inherited his father's property and fortune, summoned Humphry Repton (1752-1818) to Sarsden in 1795. In March 1796 Repton produced a red book containing his proposals for the park and pleasure grounds in text and watercolours; they appear to have been largely carried out over a period of decades. Following John's death, his son, James (d. 1863), employed Humphry Repton's son, George Stanley Repton, from around 1817 to continue the improvements to the estate, including the erection of various picturesque buildings.

In 1817 James's sister, Elizabeth, married Revd Charles Barter, and lands were obtained adjacent to the north end of Sarsden Park, on which George Repton subsequently built a new rectory, Sarsden Glebe. The glebe's grounds were probably laid out by William Smith, a local surveyor who was subsequently influential in establishing the science of geology.

James Haughton Langston married, 1824, Julia Frances (1805-1869), daughter of Thomas, 1st Earl Ducie; they had 1 daughter:

1 Julia (1827-1895); married, 24 May 1849, her cousin Henry John Reynolds-Moreton, 3rd Earl Ducie (1827-1921)

1824: 27 Aug.

1826: 16 Jun: *Mr. Hughes, therefore, and Mr. Lockhart were expected to walk over the course, & the latter had taken no peculiar pains, nor even begun a canvass, when a large body of respectable freemen, indignant at having a perfect stranger forced on them in the person of this Mr. Hughes, resolved to offer their services & interest to Mr. Langston of Sarsden, a very estimable & wealthy gentleman of large fortune & estate in the County, who had just lost his election for Woodstock, which place he had represented in the last parliament, being unable to withstand the influence of the rising sun of Blenheim, the Marquis of Blandford.* 15 Sep.

1827: 4 Dec.

1829: 24 Nov.

1833: 12 Mar.

1836: 29 Aug: *The village of Churchill greatly improved by its very handsome Gothic Church built by Mr. Langstone some years since at a great expence.* 30 Aug: *Two Misses Langstone ordinarily reside here; but have been long absent in the Metropolis, chiefly on account of the ill health of Miss Henrietta Langstone, who is under the care of the Homoeopathic Dr. Dunsford, in whom and his system all the branches of this family place so much confidence*

... *Mr. L. who has been sailing with Capt. Berkeley, who married another daughter of Lord D., and who now commands a man of war forming part of a fleet lately sent to the Mediterranean, is expected at Chipping Norton tomorrow, to preside at the weekly meeting of the Board of Guardians of that Union.* 31 Aug: *Soon after we had sat down to breakfast Mr. Langstone came in, having travelled by the Mail from London, whither he had gone from Falmouth, where he landed on his return from a cruize in the fleet.* 11 Dec: *A circular addressed to Mrs. W. & signed by Miss Langstone gives information of a scheme for providing a more sound and useful education of the daughters of farmers and tradesmen to supersede the superficial market town Boarding schools, where little solid is taught, and the time engrossed in acquiring a smattering of French, music, and drawing.* 30 Dec: *Wrote to Mr. Langstone, Chairman of the Chipping Norton Union in favour of Mr. T. Crump, a candidate for the office of Governor to the Workhouse there.*

1837: 4 Sep.

1838: 12 May: *Had a long conversation with Mr. Langstone, the Chairman of the C Norton Union, on the working of the new Poor Law, and the management of our respective unions.*

1844: 16 May: *I received a letter from Mr. Langston, of Sarsden, reporting favourably of the character of the parish Clerk of Churchhill, who appeared before us as drunk and disorderly, having assaulted the Constables, and behaved at the fair in a most outrageous manner, very inconsistent with the testimonial kindly given to him.* 17 May.

1845: 12 May, 10 Jun: *Great latitude is allowed to him by the Guardians, and their Chairman, Mr. Langston, is his warm supporter.*

1847: 14 Sep: *On the shew-ground I had also much intercourse, with Lord Redesdale, Sir W. Codrington, the Dean of Gloucester, Messrs. Jarratt, Westmacott, Clarke, Polhill, Winter, W. Vavasour, Langston, Barter see Huxtable.*

1850: 31 Oct.

LANGTON — Jane Langton at Stanway[20]

Jane Langton (1776-1854) was the second daughter of Bennet Langton (±1736-1801) and Mary, countess of Rothes, née Lloyd (1743-1820). She died unmarried at Richmond, Surrey, on 12 August 1854—just six days before the diarist Francis Witts's own death. It was said (*The Gentleman's Magazine*) that she always wore a 'beautiful miniature' of her godfather, Samuel Johnson.

Bennet Langton was a son of Revd Bennet Langton (1696-1769) and Diana, daughter of Edmund Turner of Stoke Rochford, Lincolnshire. Langton matriculated from Trinity College, Oxford, where he became friendly with Topham Beauclerk. The two youths took Johnson for his famous 'frisk' to Billingsgate. Johnson later visited the Langtons' home, and there declined the offer of a good living from Langton's father. In another recorded instance, Johnson was provoked to the laughter which echoed from Fleet Ditch to Temple Bar by Langton's will in 1773, and soon afterwards caused a quarrel, which apparently lasted for some months, by censuring Langton for introducing religious questions in a mixed company.

Langton married, 24 May 1770, Mary (1743-1820), daughter of Gresham Lloyd and widow of John Leslie, 10th earl of Rothes (1698-1767); they had 4 sons and 5 daughters, including:

1 George (1772-1819); succeeded to the estate
1 Diana (b. 1774)
2 Jane (1776-1854); goddaughter of Dr Samuel Johnson; died unmarried, 12 August 1854
3 Elizabeth (b. 1777)
2 Peregrine (1780-1856); married Miss Massingberd, of Gunby, and took her name

Johnson once requested Langton to tell him what in his life was faulty, and was greatly irritated when Langton brought him some texts enjoining mildness of speech. Johnson's permanent feeling, however, was expressed in the words, 'Sit anima mea cum Langtono' ('May my soul be with Langton'). During Johnson's last illness Langton came to attend his friend; Johnson left him a book, and Langton undertook to pay an annuity to Francis Barber, Johnson's black servant, in consideration of a sum of £750 left in his hands.

Langton was famous for his Greek scholarship, but wrote nothing except some anecdotes about Johnson, published by Boswell in his *Life* under the year 1780. Johnson and Boswell frequently discussed Langton's incapacity for properly managing his estates. He was too indolent, it appears, to keep accounts, in spite of the exhortations of his mentor. Langton was very tall and thin, and his gentle and amiable nature made him universally popular. According to Sir William Jones, Langton's conservative political opinions made him 'vehement against the lovers of freedom in all countries', while Hester Thrale confirmed that he was 'a Tory and a high Churchman up to the Eyes'. He was an original member of the Literary Club (about 1764), and was appointed in April 1788 to succeed Johnson as professor of ancient literature at the Royal Academy.

1823: 22 Jul: *We left home on a short visit to Lady Elcho at Stanway. We found my mother & Miss Church her inmates, and Miss Langton arrived from Cheltenham soon after us. This Lady is daughter of the late Mr. Bennet Langton & the Countess of Rothes: her father was the intimate of Dr. Johnson.*

LANGTON — Thomas Langton and the Langton family — *see also* **Currer** *and* **Dunsford**[21]

Thomas Langton (1770-1838), merchant, was the fifth son of Thomas Langton (1724-1794), flax merchant, of Kirkham, and Jane Leyland (±1731-1774). In 1787, aged 17, he was sent to Riga, then in Russia, on behalf of Messrs. Thorley, Morrison and Co., with the promise—not entirely fulfilled—of a partnership when he reached his majority. He remained in Riga for fifteen years, only visiting England once during this period. In about 1802 he returned to England and married Ellen (1766-1846), daughter of Revd William Currer, rector of St James the Apostle parish church in Clapham, Yorkshire. The Currers were a well-known Yorkshire family with connections to the literary Brontës. Ellen and her sister Alice were presumably first cousins to Margaret Witts, whose grandmother's maiden name was Margeret Currer; she was the daughter of Henry Currer. Revd William Currer was brother to Margaret Moorhouse, née Currer.

Thomas and Ellen rented a home at Farfield, in the parish of Addingham, West Riding of Yorkshire; they had 3 sons and 1 daughter:

1 William (1803-1881); *see below*
1 Anne (1804-1893); died unmarried at Sturgeon Lake, near Fenelon Falls, Ontario, Canada; *see below*
2 Thomas (1806-1812)
3 John (1808-1894); *see below*

In 1804 Langton purchased Blythe Hall, in the parish of Ormskirk, Lancashire, and in 1807 became DL of Lancashire. Between the years 1815-21 he travelled with his family around Europe, mainly in Switzerland, Italy, Germany, and France. In 1826 there was a commercial crisis which resulted in the winding up of his affairs, including the sale of Blythe Hall. He next moved to Bootle in Lancashire. In 1837 Langton departed from Liverpool for Canada to join his younger son, John, at his farm property on Sturgeon Lake, near Fenelon Falls. He travelled there via New York with his wife, Ellen, his daughter, Anne, and his wife's unmarried sister, Alice Currer (1770-1846).

William Langton (1803-1881), eldest son of Thomas and Ellen, remained in England. He became a successful banker in Manchester and the manager of Williams Deacon Bank; he was also a prominent social reformer and connoisseur of the arts. He married, in 1831, Margaret Hornby, a wealthy heiress from a noted Lancashire family; they had nine children. William, Margaret, and their family kept in close correspondence with the 'Canadian' Langtons.

Anne Langton (1804-1893), second child and only daughter of Thomas and Ellen, was an accomplished gentlewoman artist in the genres of miniature portrait painting and landscape. With her parents and aunt Alice, she became a pioneer settler in 1837 at her brother John's farm on Sturgeon Lake. She travelled widely and returned to England several times for extended visits.

John Langton (1808-1894), the youngest of the family, was educated at Midhurst, Sussex, and Trinity College, Cambridge (BA 1830; MA 1833). He immigrated to Canada and settled on Sturgeon Lake, near Fenelon Falls, first in a log cabin in 1833, and then in a large log cabin house in 1841, which he named Blythe House. He married Lydia Dunsford in 1845; they had eight children. John became a politician and rose to senior positions in the Canadian government; by 1865 he was auditor of the provinces of Canada. In 1867, John and Lydia Langton spent part of the year in England when, in his capacity as auditor, John was required to be in London for negotiations between the Canadian and British governments, leading up to the declaration of confederation. Post-confederation, John Langton became the deputy minister of finance and inspector of Her Majesty's prisons in Canada.

1825: 10 Sep: *Mr. Langton is one of the Trustees of our Marriage Settlement. He is a very intelligent man, and of a literary turn; his long residence in Germany has given him a foreign air and foreign habits. He has two sons and a daughter: of the former, the elder is educating in commercial pursuits, and the younger preparing for the University.* 13 Sep: *one place was pointed out to me as Little Kirkham, built for the accommodation of the labourers at the Mills of Messrs. Hornby & Roughsedge: the former gentleman is of a family connected with the Langtons and settled at Kirkham in Lancashire.*

1837: 8 Apr: *Also a letter from Mr. Langton one of the Trustees of our Marriage Settlt. and related to my wife by marriage, stating that as he was about to leave the Kingdom, probably, for life, he wished to resign his trust, and requested me to ascertain by examination of the deed whether any act on his part was necessary to divest himself of the trust, and communicate to him the result of such examination.* 9 Apr: *Wrote to Mr. Langton under cover to Mr. Backhouse at the Foreign Office.* 12 Apr: *By a letter which M.W. had received from Mrs. A. Currer it appears that the destination of the Langtons is U. Canada, and that Mrs. A.C. accompanies her Brother in law, sister, and niece, without any prospect of returning to England.* 15 Apr., 10 May, 26 May: *MW. received a letter from Mrs. A. Currer, written on the very eve of her sailing from Liverpool to New York with Mr. and Mrs. Langton and their daughter, on their way to join their youngest son at his farm of Blythe on Sturgeon Lake in Upper Canada; professedly to end their days there.*

1838: 15 Feb: *MW. had received a letter from A. Currer, dated from Blythe, in the Back Settlements of Upper Canada, on the edge of the interminable forest, detailing particulars of the Voyage and journey through the United States of the adventurous Quartetto, Mr. & Mrs. Langton and their daughter, and A.C. their reception by John Langton, their abode, their mode of living, the cold of the winter, the fineness of the Canadian winter &c.* 1 Jul: *A letter to Mrs. Backhouse from Liverpool brought information of the death of Mr. Langton in Upper Canada, but without particulars as to the time or circumstances of his decease... It remains to be seen whether the elder ladies, advanced in life, and in delicate health will persist in continuing exiles from their native land, or will seek a home in the vicinity of Mr. W. Langton, the eldest son, who is a Banker in affluent circumstances residing at or near Manchester.* 4 Jul: *MW. has recd. a letter from Alice Currer by which it appears that Mr. Langton died on May 4.*

1844: 31 Aug: *MW. received a letter from Mrs. A. Currer from Canada, with good accounts of herself and the Langtons.*

1846: 29 Aug: *MW. received a letter from Mrs. A. Currer, from Canada, announcing the death of her sister, Mrs. Langton, at 80 years of age. The illness was short, and very trying to A.C. who feels her last tie to earth unloosed. One would suppose that she will pass her few remaining months or years, for she is between 70 & 80, in the distant land whither she accompanied her sister: the niece, Miss Langton, was suffering from an illness when her Mother died: the brother John Langton, was from home, in attendance on his wife, who had lately been confined at her father's house at Peterborough, a colonial town, forty miles distance from Blythe, the location of the Langtons—the infant had died. It is to be hoped that the aged Aunt will be kindly treated by her nephew and nieces, and sink peacefully into a far-off grave.*

LANZA — Francesco Lanza[22]

Francesco Lanza (1783-1862), composer and concert artist, was born at Naples and taken to England by his father Gesualdo Lanza (±1750-1812+). He began teaching the piano and later became a successful concert artist. In 1808 he returned to Naples where he opened a private piano school and gave lessons at court.

1805: 18 Mar: *Drank wine with Dowell, meeting Prower, adjoined to the Music Room, which was well attended; joined Trevenen, James &c. the Performer, Mrs. Mountain, Morelli, Signor Lanza & Mr. Fitzsimmons: the two former great as usual, the latter moderate.*

LAPPER — John Lapper[23]

John Lapper (±1816-1869), quarryman, died at Northleach. There was another John Lapper (±1824-1893), an agricultural labourer, recorded living at Stow-on-the-Wold. However, as the diary entry states that Lapper had lost both hands 'in consequence of an accident in blasting a rock', we can be confident of the attribution.

1850: 12 Oct: *Wrote also to Mr. Rideout, the Post office Inspector for the district, in recommendation of a man named Lapper, a pauper of this Union, whose hands have been amputated in consequence of an accident in blasting a rock, but who thinks himself able to perform the work of a walking postman from Andoversford to Hampen, Salperton, Turkdean &c. and seeks the office.* 22 Oct., 23 Oct: *A letter from Mr. Rideout, Post Office Inspector for the district who places at my disposal the place of walking postman to and from some of the villages in the neighbourhood of Northleach, respecting the appointment to which I had solicited him in favour of one John Lapper.* 25 Nov: *J Lapper came by appointment to whom I named that I had procured for him the place of walking postman, and I wrote to Mr.*

Rideout, forwarding his name, and acceptance of the office. 28 Nov: *Received a letter from Mr. Rideout, Post Office Surveyor, who considers it likely that J. Lapper, having lost both his hands, is disqualified for the office of a Rural Post messenger.* 29 Nov: *Interview with J Lapper, and wrote to Mr. Rideout, that it seems to me probable that the man, with a mechanical contrivance to supply the want of one hand, will be equal to the duties required of a rural post messenger.*

1851: 20 Apr: *Wrote to Tipping, the Postmaster at Stow, requesting him to find out Lapper, and to send him to meet Mr. Forrest at Northleach.*

LARDNER — John Lardner and the Lardner family of Moreton-in-Marsh — *see also* Heath [24]

John Lardner (1770-1838), postmaster and inspector of weights and measures, lived at Moreton-in-Marsh. He married Sabrina Heath (±1768-1855); they had at least 1 son and 1 daughter:

1 Hannah (1798-1877); married, at a very young age, her cousin William Heath; he appears to have died relatively young; she married secondly, at Moreton-in-Marsh, 9 March 1824, Isaac Jelfs (1797-1853); she had 3 sons and 4 daughters by Jelfs and at least 1 son, the following, by William Heath:
  1 John Lardner (b. 1816)

1 John (1808-1886), carpenter and joiner; succeeded his father as part-time inspector of weights and measures; married, at Cheltenham, 3 September 1838, Ann Matthews (1807-1879); at least 1 son and 5 daughters:
  1 Elizabeth Matthews (1839-1906)
  2 Sarah Ann (1840-1920)
  3 Ellen Louisa (1842-1856)
  4 Sabina Maria (1844-1899)
  1 William Collett (1846-1862)
  5 Clara Emma (1847-1906)

By the time of the 1861 census the family had moved back to Moreton-in-Marsh from Bourton-on-the-Water, and William (1846-1862) had become a solicitor's clerk. By 1881 John, father of William and five other children, was a widower and listed as 'retired land agent and carpenter'. He was living with his widowed daughter, Sabina Robinson, at the post office, Barton-on-the-Heath, Warwickshire, not far from Moreton-in-Marsh. John appears to have died at Bakewell, Derbyshire, but this final attribution is uncertain.

It is unclear if William Lardner (b. ±1820), of Moreton, is related, but a connection is likely. His early career is unknown, but by 1891 he was living in London, a single man working as a groom stable man. The diarist's comment relating to the 'wreck of the property of Lardner, Moreton' (14 February 1842) is enigmatic; no further clues were given.

1836: 28 Dec: *Walked as far as the Lower Slaughter Turnpike gate: the letter bag had arrived: Mr. Lardner, the Postmaster sent a line to say that no mail from London had reached his office since Sunday.*

1838: 16 Apr: *Also to Mr. Lardner, Inspector of Weights and Measures for the Moreton District, with whom I had been in correspondence since my return from the Sessns. on the subject of his allowances.* 29 Jun., 6 Jul: *Wrote to Lardner, Moreton in Marsh, with a cheque on Messrs. Cripps, for the amount of his fees at the Easter and Trinity Sessns as County Inspector of Weights and Measures, which I had received for him.* 30 Dec.

1839: 6 Jan: *Wrote to J. Heath, Moreton in Marsh, forwarding a cheque for the amount of fees due to the estate of his late Grandfather Lardner as Inspector of Weights and Measures.* 5 Feb., 12 Apr: *I had recd. from the County Treas. the balance due on his acct.; and I also forwarded the Order appointing his Uncle, J. Lardner, to be his successor in office, whom I had proposed to the Court at Glor., and who was elected by a majority of votes over one Staines of Campden proposed by Mr. Lawrence.* 13 Apr: *A letter from J Lardner, Moreton, acknowledging my note to his sister yesterday with its contents, and thanking me for proposing him as Inspector of Weights and Measures.* 30 Jun., 6 Jul.

1840: 6 Apr., 12 Apr., 4 Jul., 6 Jul.

1842: 10 Jan: *wrote to Lardner, Bourton on the W. Inspector of Weights and Measures that the Court of Sessions continued him in that office though he had changed his residence from Moreton in Marsh to Bourton, and that I would pay him the small balance due to him for this quarter from the County the first time I came to Bourton.* 14 Feb: *recd. a note from Mr. Kendall as to the arrangements made to secure a small sum out of the wreck of the property of Lardner, Moreton, for A Gardner.* 16 Aug: *Recd. a letter from Mr. W. Lardner, Moreton in Marsh, offering his services as Relieving Officer.* 27 Oct.

1843: 20-21 Oct., 24 Oct.

1844: 14 Apr.

1846: 7 Jul.

1850: 12 Jan: *J Lardner, Inspector of Weights and measures, called to solicit a testimonial from me as a candidate for the vacant place of Relieving Officer in the Chipping Norton Union.*

LARGE — John Large, Charles Large, and the Large family of Kencot, Broadwell, Oxfordshire [25]

John Large (±1795-1854), farmer and landed proprietor, acquired Kencot Manor with the Manor Farm, a malthouse, and three cottages. He was from a local yeoman family and later styled himself a gentleman. He married Mary (b. ±1800); they had at least three children, including Charles Edward and Elizabeth (b. ±1807). Large initially lived in Kencot Manor and farmed the estate himself—together with 130 acres leased from another owner—but between 1840 and 1852 he sold over half his land to his relation Charles Large (b. ±1798), a major landowner in Broadwell, whose successors sold it in 1889.

By 1852 Kencot Manor was let to John's relative, William Large, and another house to the prominent Kencot farmer Thomas Wakefield. Of Large's remaining land, around 92 acres were farmed by Thomas Tuckwell, presumably a relative of the previous owner. After John Large's death in 1854, his younger son Charles Edward bought out his co-heirs. The precise relationships are unclear, and there is little to be found on the family at all.

John's relation Charles Large (b. ±1798), landed proprietor, of Broadwell, was married to Mary (±1801-1889). He may have been a brother or cousin of John, but there is no conclusive evidence. In 1851 he farmed 698 acres in Kencot, Broadwell, Oxfordshire, and employed twenty-four men, three women, and six boys. Charles does not appear to have had children. It is unclear whether it was John or his relation Charles who was the 'eminent agriculturist' referred to by the diarist; in fact, given their relative youth in 1820, it may have been their father or uncle.

1820: 12 May: *At Stow Fair this day Mr. Large of Broadwell Oxfordshire, an eminent agriculturist, whose assistance I had called in as Land Surveyor here and at Stanway pointed my attention to a sheep bred by him & killed by a butcher of the place.*

1823: 24 Apr: *After the ordinary business of the day at Stow, I proceeded to Bourton on the Hill, where I dined & slept at Dr.*

Warneford's, meeting only Mr. Large of Broadwell, Oxfordshire, an eminent land surveyor. 29 Apr: *Mr. Large is a very considerable farmer & sheep breeder:—his stock has long been in the highest repute, & the size, to which he brings his fat sheep & rams, is surprizing: I have seen a prize sheep of his slaughtered, & weighing about 70 lbs per quarter. His prices for letting rams for the season are from seven to ten & fifteen guineas; the bone remarkably small, & the wool of the finest quality. He is very largely employed, in this & the neighbouring counties, as land surveyor, steward, & arbitrator; is skilful & intelligent in his profession; a very cool headed and well conducted man.* 30 Apr., 16 Aug: *Mr. Large dined here. The future & the actual tenants of the Vicarage farm at Stanway met him in the morning to settle the conditions of leaving and entering on the land.* 15 Sep., 24 Oct.

LARKING — Georgina and Juliana Larking and the Larking family of East Malling, Kent — *see also* Waller[26]

Georgina Matilda Larking (1806-1858) was the daughter of John Larking (1754-1838) and Dorothy Style (1770-1840), of Clare House, East Malling, Kent, and the sister of Caroline Elizabeth Waller, née Larking (1800-1840). Another of her sisters was Juliana Elizabeth (1815-1898). Her brothers included Lambert Blackwall Larking (1797-1868), antiquary, and John Wingfield Larking (1802-1891), governor of Alexandria, Egypt.

John Larking (senior) died at Boulogne; it is likely that he was in France to evade creditors.

1827: 6 Jul: *Mr. Waller seems a very promising young man. I have known him from boyhood,.... He has married a young Lady, whom he met at Boulogne, well connected, accomplished, pleasing, elegant & handsome, but with little fortune; her name, Larkins, and an elder sister is now on a visit to them.*

1840: 2 Oct: *Dined at the Wallers at Farmington Lodge, a very agreeable party—meeting our good old friend, Miss Rollinson, who is staying there, Mr. Browne, Mr. and Mrs. Pole, and W. B. Pole, James Dutton, and Mr. Wollaston. Two agreeable unmarried sisters of Mrs. W.,—Misses Larkin, are on a visit at Farmington.*

1842: 8 Jul: *It was the first time we had visited Farmington Grove since the lamented decease of Mrs. H. W.—her sister, Miss Larken, sits at the head of her Brother in law's table, and appears domiciliated there; all the Children, eight motherless orphans, the eldest under fourteen, the youngest under two years of age, are at home.*

1843: 13 Oct: *Met Miss Browne and Miss Larken calling there from Salperton.*

1846: 4 Dec: *went to dine with the Wallers at Bourton; meeting Harry Waller, two Misses Larkin, Captain Pettatt, Mr. Wollaston, Mr. and Mrs. Winter.*

1850: 19 Jul.

1853: 3 Jun: *Drove to the Rectory, where I was kindly received by Robert Waller & his wife, and their guest, one of the Misses Larkin.*

1854: 19 May: *Mrs. R. Waller and Miss Juliana Larkin, now on a visit at Bourton Rectory, called on me.* 7 Jun: *Drove after luncheon with E Clifford to Bourton on the Water, to call upon the Wallers, whom, with Miss J Larkin, we found at home.*

LASBERG — Friedrich August Ludwig von Lasberg[27]

Friedrich August Ludwig von Lasberg (1751-1815), military officer, was the son of Maximilian Johann Albrecht von Lasberg (1711-1788), commander of the guard at Weimar. Friedrich rose to the rank of captain.

1798: 2 Sep: *of strangers there are many. The chief are Count Marschall, the Egloffstein, Seebach, Helldorf, Luc, Lasberg, Wolfskiel, Gormar, Oldorthausen, Families &c. all of whom almost have some Office either in the Civil, Military or Immediate Court Service.*

LASCELLES — Arthur Lascelles[28]

Arthur Lascelles (1807-1880) was born at Harewood, Yorkshire, fourth surviving son of Henry Lascelles, 2nd earl of Harewood (1767-1841), and Henrietta Saunders, née Sebright (1770-1840). He married, 18 November 1834, Caroline Frances Brooke (1813-1895); they had 3 sons and 7 daughters.

1842: 15 Oct: *Recd. a letter from Mr. Chr. Geldard to solicit my vote and attendance at Wakefield in favour of the Hon. A. Lascelles, a son of the late Lord Harewood, who is a candidate for the Office of Registrar of deeds for the West Riding of Yorkshire, just vacant by the decease of the late occupant, Mr. Fenton Lister Scott.* 15 Nov., 18-19 Nov.

LATCHAM — Charles Arthur Latcham and his son Charles Latcham[29]

Charles Arthur Latcham (1788-1857), solicitor, was born at Stapleton, son of Charles Latcham (1760-1822) and Mary Parkes (1759-1818). He married Maria Haythorne (1795-1865); they had at least 1 son and 6 daughters:

- 1 Mary Haythorne (b. 1815)
- 2 Maria Haythorne (1815-1889)
- 1 Charles (1821-1899); married Mary Washbourn (1828-1915); 1 son and 4 daughters:
  - 1 Maria Jane (b. 1849)
  - 2 Mary (b. 1851)
  - 3 Elizabeth Margaret (1858-1947)
  - 4 Susannah Haythorne (1865-1953)
  - 1 Charles Haythorne (1866-1886)
- 3 Elizabeth Haythorne (b. 1823)
- 4 Susan Haythorne (1826-1893)
- 5 Louisa El. Haythorne (b. 1830)
- 6 Henrietta Mutlow Haythorne (1836-1925)

Latcham practised at 4 Stokes Croft, Bristol, and lived at Gloster Row, Clifton. His son, Charles, was a solicitor and farmer. He lived at Cherry Rock Farm, Filton, where he employed two men on the farm.

1848: 8 Nov: *A letter from Mr. Latcham, Clerk to the magistrates appointed Visitors of the private madhouses.* 16 Nov., 22 Nov: *Mr. Latcham, Bristol, Solr. the stated Clerk to the Visitors of the private madhouses near Bristol in Gloucestershire, with his son, and Mr. Riddiford.*

LATHAM — an inmate of Stow Union Workhouse

1847: 30 Jul: *Wrote to Mr. Pearce, desiring him to ascertain whether Mr. Hayward recommends one Latham to be sent to Gloucester Infirmary on account of defective sight.*

LATHAM — John Latham[30]

John Latham (1787-1853), JP and landed proprietor, was born at Oxford, the eldest son of John Latham (1761-1843) and Mary Mayer, eldest daughter and co-heir of Revd Peter Mayer, vicar of Prestbury, Cheshire. His parents had married on 12 April 1784. Latham (senior) was president of the Royal College of Physicians and updated their *Pharmacopoeia*. He bought the Bradwall estate.

John Latham (junior) was educated at Brasenose College, Oxford (BCL 1810; DCL 1815), and was a fellow of All Souls' College until 1821. He married, 24 May 1821, Elizabeth-Anne (d. 1839), eldest daughter of Sir Henry Dampier, one of the justices of the king's bench; they had 3 sons and 1 daughter:

1 John Henry (1823-1843); died unmarried
1 Mary-Frances; married Revd Ambrose Jones, incumbent of Elworth, Cheshire
2 George William (1827-1886), barrister-at-law and MP; married, at West Dean, Chichester, Sussex, 21 August 1856, Elizabeth Sarah Luttman [or Johnson]
3 Francis-Law (1837-1923), advocate-general of Bombay (1882-93); married, at Ramsgate, Kent, 15 August 1893, Clara Eliza Gilbert Maitland

---

1806: 18 Mar: *Dined at Dr. Price's, meeting Stevens, Round, & a Mr. Latham of B.N.C.*

LAURENCE — French Laurence [31]

French Laurence (1757-1809), MP and regius professor of civil law, was born at Bath, son of Richard Laurence (1729-1773), watchmaker, and Elizabeth (1727-1808), daughter of John French, clothier, of Warminster, Wiltshire. He was educated at Winchester College and Corpus Christi, Oxford (BA 1777; MA 1781; DCL 1787), and the Inner Temple (1785). Laurence was MP for Peterborough in 1796-1809 and regius professor of civil law at Oxford University in 1796-1809. He died unmarried.

1801: 8 Jun: *On the Ministerial side Mr. Wilberforce seemed to me the best orator: Mr. Abbot, Mr. Addington, Mr. Baker, Mr. Yorke, Mr. Windham, Mr. O'Hare & Lord Hawkesbury chiefly arrested my attention. Mr. Grey appeared by far the greatest orator on the opposition side: the other speakers, were, Mr. Martin, Horne Tooke, Tinney, W. Smith, Sir F. Jones Burdett, Dr. Lawrence, & Mr. Whitbread.*

1804: 4 Mar: *St. Mary's assize sermon by Mr. Landon of Oriel with an inaudible voice. Justice Lawrence & Sir Simon Le Blanc.*

LAURENCE — Richard Laurence [32]

Richard Laurence (1760-1838), Church of England clergyman, regius professor of Hebrew at Oxford, and archbishop of Cashel, was born at Bath, son of Richard Laurence (1729-1773), watchmaker, and Elizabeth (1727-1808), daughter of John French, clothier, of Warminster, Wiltshire. Like his brother French (*above*), he was educated at Corpus Christi, Oxford (BA 1782; MA 1785; DCL 1794). Laurence was later appointed rector of Rolleston, Wiltshire, and of Mersham, Kent, in 1805. He was deputy professor of civil law at Oxford University in 1796, Bampton lecturer in 1804, regius professor of Hebrew and a canon of Christ Church in 1814-22, and archbishop of Cashel in 1822-38.

1804: 11 Mar: *At St. Mary's. Dr. Lawrence Bampton Lecturer read his introductory sermon.* 18 Mar: *With him to Church. Morn. & afternoon at the former Dr. Lawrence's 2nd Bampton Lecture very moderate.*

LAURENT — the Laurent family, visitors of the Royces of Lower Swell

1851: 6 Feb: *also met Mr. Royce, who, on the part of himself, his wife, and her half-sister, Miss Laurent.* 12 Feb: *Mr. and Mrs. Royce, with Miss Laurent, Mrs. Royce's half-sister, Mr. and Mrs. R. Waller, and Mr. and Mrs. Potter, dined with me.* 21 Feb.

1852: 9 Mar: *Mr. and Mrs. Royce, and Miss Laurent, called on me.* 9 Mar., 24 Mar., 20 May: *Dressed at the Unicorn for dinner at Mr. Royce's, where found Mr. Laurent, (not Lawrence,) Mrs. Royce's step-father.*

LAW — Edward Law [33]

Edward Law, 1st Viscount Southam and earl of Ellenborough (1790-1871), politician and governor-general of India, was born at Bloomsbury, Middlesex, the eldest son of Edward Law (1750-1818), who made his name at the bar as counsel for the defence at Warren Hastings' impeachment, and his wife, Anne (d. 1843), daughter of Capt. George Phillips Towry, RN. He was educated at Eton College and St John's, Cambridge (MA 1809). Law was MP for St Michael's, Cornwall, in 1813-18, and succeeded his father as 2nd Baron Ellenborough on 13 December 1818. He was lord privy seal and privy counsellor in 1828, a member of the Board of Control for India in 1828-30, and president of the same in 1828-30, 1834-35, and 1841. He was made a lord of the Treasury in 1834, chief clerk of the pleas in 1837, and governor-general of India in 1841. Law was responsible for the annexation of Scinde in 1843 and the subjugation of Gwalior in 1844. He was recalled that year and created Viscount Southam and earl of Ellenborough, and made a knight of the Grand Cross (GCB). He was first lord of the Admiralty in 1846.

Law married, first, 1813, Octavia Stewart (1792-1819), youngest daughter of Robert, 1st marquess of Londonderry, and secondly, 1824, Jane Elizabeth, daughter of Rear Adm. Henry Digby. In 1830 he divorced his second wife by act of parliament for her adultery with Prince Schwartzenberg in 1828.

Edward Law died at his Gloucestershire seat, Southam House, Southam Delabere, on 22 December 1871, and was buried at nearby Oxenton church. He left three illegitimate children from a liaison that followed his divorce. There was no heir to the earldom, but his nephew Charles Law succeeded as the 3rd baron.

1827: 4 May: *Lord Ellenborough and Lord Mansfield spoke openly & warmly in disparagement of the new administration, announcing their intention to oppose it.* 7 May.

1828: 23 Jan., 2 Jun., 22 Sep.

1832: 10 Apr: *While every meeting of reformers in the Country were urging the creation of a sufficient number of new Peers for the express purpose of carrying the Bill, counter addresses, earnestly imploring the King not to exercise his prerogative in that way, were sent up from all quarters: and it could not be denied, that these addresses spoke the convictions of a large proportion of the influential classes, the Gentry, and the land owners. Such an address went up from Gloucestershire, in moderate language, drawn up by Lord Ellenborough.* 9 May, 6 Jun.

1834: 15 Aug: *Many were the county gentlemen, nobles and clergy, yeomen &c. with whom I mingled in conversation—among them Lords Ellenborough, Edward & John Somerset, the handsome hero of the day, of whom it were to be wished that his talent and habits of business equalled the enthusiasm of his adherents.* 13 Sep., 14 Oct: *Much other miscellaneous business was transacted, and much that ought to have been done was postponed to the close of the Sessions. It was half past seven before we sat down to dinner at the Bell, where a large party assembled. Mr. Codrington, the new representative for the Eastern district was present; also Lord Ellenborough, Hon. James Dutton &c.* 17 Dec.

1835: 1 Jan: *The effect of this would be a return of two Tories and two Whigs for the County without a contest. A rumour prevails, but, I hope, an ill-founded one, that this arrangement has been effected by a compromise made by four Peers who met in London for the purpose: viz. Lords Sherborne, and Segrave, Whigs, and Lord Ellenborough and Earl Bathurst, Tories. If this be true, Gloucestershire, in the teeth of the Reform bill, becomes two close boroughs in the nomination of influential Peers.*

1836: 6 Sep: *Besides the leading farmers of the neighbourhood, I noticed a host of gentlemen interested in agriculture, Lord Macclesfield, Lord Ellenborough, Lord Edwd. Somerset, James Dutton, Browne, Waller, Elwes, Barker, Messrs. Barnsby and Phillips from Herefordshire, E. Cripps, A. Pole, with many others.* 14 Sep.

1837: 5 Jul: *At Northleach, Abingdon, Newent, Winchcomb, and elsewhere such public entertainments have been lately given to Messrs. Waller, Dodson, Ricardo, Lord Ellenborough &c.* 17 Oct: *I was in communication through the day with most of the leading Magistrates, and many personal friends, Bathurst, Dr. Cooke, Crawley, Baker, Purnell, Lawrence, Lord Ellenborough, Lord Redesdale, &c. &c.* 30 Nov: *It is also probable that Lord Ellenborough, at whose house the Bp. has met Aston, may have influenced him the Bp. in his favour.*

1840: 20 Oct: *A very large attendance of Magistrates; among them, and among those with whom I was especially in intercourse, were Prothero, MP. for Halifax, Baker Senr., H. Waller, R Waller, R W Ford, Lord Ellenborough...* 6 Nov: *Edward has an engagement to morrow at Winchcombe, to meet the patrons of the agricultural institutions formed within that Union under the direction & sanction of Lord Ellenborough, to reward agricultural servants for long and faithful services, independence, and exertions in bringing up large families of children.*

1842: 3 Dec: *At Southam we got out of our carriage, and walked across a field or two to reach a point, where we had an excellent view of the front of Lord Ellenborough's most striking and interesting old mansion, the ancient seat of the Delaberes, since his purchase of which his Lordship has enlarged and repaired the house, and improved the grounds in the very best taste.*

1844: 16 Dec: *Recd. a letter from E.F.W. covering two others, one from Mr. Holland to himself, another from Lord Ellenborough to Mr. Holland, from which it appears that Lord Fitzhardinge has at last surrendered to a whole broadside of letters from Holland, and reluctantly consented to propose the addition of my Son's name to the commission of the Peace for this County.*

1848: 6 Jan., 4 Oct: *Received a letter from E.F.W: all well at Stanway Vicarage; my son details the particulars of past engagements in which he has been in the society of Lord Ellenborough the Messrs. Dent &c.* 6 Oct: *Lord Ellenborough and Mr. Holland justly complimented my Son for the ability & talent and sound principles which he had developed.* 16 Oct: *To Cheltenham in my phaeton, and thence by the Great Western line to Gloucester in the same carriage with Lord Ellenborough, who was travelling to London.*

1850: 1 Jan., 15 Oct: *To the Shire Hall, where attended to the County business in a full, but not a crowded court. The Lord Lieutenant and Lord Ellenborough were present.* 31 Dec.

LAW — George Henry Law[34]

George Henry Law (1761-1845), bishop of Bath and Wells, was born at Cambridge, seventh son of Edmund Law (1703-1787), bishop of Carlisle, and Mary (1722-1762), daughter of John Christian. He was educated at Charterhouse School and Queen's College, Cambridge (BA 1781; MA 1784; DD 1804), where he was a fellow from 1781 to 1784. He was later prebendary of Carlisle in 1785, vicar of Torpenhow, Cumberland, in 1787-91, rector of Kelshall, Hertfordshire, in 1791-1802, vicar of Carleton, Lincolnshire, in 1797-1845, rector of Willingham, Cambridgeshire, in 1804-12, bishop of Chester in 1812-24, and bishop of Bath and Wells in 1824-45. Law was a staunch Conservative in ecclesiastical matters; he vigorously opposed the Test and Corporation Acts and other measures of reform. He married, 1784, Jane (1764-1826), eldest daughter of Gen. Adeane, MP for Cambridgeshire; they had at least 4 sons and 5 daughters:

1 Joanna (1784-1848)
2 Anna (1786-1832)
3 Augusta (1789-1822)
1 James Thomas (1790-1876), Church of England clergyman
2 George (1794-1811)
3 Henry (1797-1884), Church of England clergyman; born at Kelshall Rectory, Hertfordshire
4 Robert Vanbrugh (1800-1884), Church of England clergyman
4 Jane Waugh (1801-1843)
5 Margaret (1803-1838)

1824: 8 May: *The two sees of Bath and Wells and Chichester are again filled, the former by the Translation of Bishop Law, from Chester ... Dr. Law stands very high in the esteem of the Orthodox members of the Church, and is a man of very sound talent and extensive theological learning.* 14 May. 27 Jun: *The sophistry & false reasoning of the Unitarians were most ably exposed by Bishop in Law in a speech worthy of his own Dr. Paley.*

1825: 15 Sep: *The eldest daughter, Lady Charlotte Grey, very early married a Son of Revd. Law, the present Bishop of Bath & Wells, who is Chancellor of Lichfield, as I believe.*

LAWLER — Thomas Lawler, bass vocalist at Exeter Hall, Oxford[35]

Thomas Lawler (1818-1893), bass vocalist, was born at Cowes, Isle of Wight. In 1851 he lived at Lorrimore Road, Lambeth, with his parents, John (b. ±1783), registered as blind and born in Ireland, and Grace (b. ±1787), born at Shapwick, Somerset. Lawler himself was registered as a professor of music. He was married to Helen (b. ±1824), born at Sheffield, Yorkshire; they had at least 3 sons and 2 daughters:

1 Thomas (b. ±1844)
1 Julia (b. ±1846); listed in the 1881 census as a lunatic
2 Ellen (b. ±1848)
2 Charles (b. ±1853), banker and accountant; a widower by 1891, caring for 2 sons and 3 daughters with his mother
3 Ernest (b. ±1854), wine merchant

By 1871 the family lived at 26 Lambeth Terrace, and by 1881 at 126 Lambeth Road (probably the same house renumbered).

Lawler studied under Bianchi Taylor and established the City Glee Club in 1853; on his retirement in 1886, he was presented with a testimonial. He was for many years a gentleman of the Chapel Royal, and resigned on a pension early in 1887. He sang in oratorio in London and the provinces, and appeared on the stage, but it was for singing glees and old English songs that he was most celebrated. He died in London on 16 May 1893.

1852: 7 Jun: *The immense audience were witnesses to the excellences of the performance, and the sublimity of the music. The chorus parts were magnificently given—The principal vocalists were Messrs. Sims Reeves—Herr Staudigl—Mr. Lawler, in the absence of Herr Formes,—suffering from hoarseness.*

LAWLEY — Francis Lawley[36]

Sir Francis Lawley, 7th baronet (1782-1851), JP, MP, and landed proprietor, was born at Spoonhill, Much Wenlock, Shropshire, second son of Sir Robert Lawley, 5th baronet of Spoonhill

(1736-1793), and Jane Thompson (1742-1816). He was educated at Christ Church, Oxford (BCL 1808; DCL 1813), and was MP for Warwickshire in 1820-32. Francis succeeded his elder brother Robert (1768-1834) as 7th baronet, and married, at St Marylebone, Westminster, 18 May 1815, Mary Anne Talbot (1789-1851); there were no children of the marriage.

1833: 6 Nov: *We had previously passed a seat of Lord Middleton's, which is now and has long been occupied by Mr. F. Lawley, late MP. for Warwickshire and Son in Law of our neighbour Mr. Talbot. He is a truly estimable man.*

1835: 21 May: *It amounts to this; that Mr. Talbot, brother to a brother in law of the Duke of Beaufort, and brother to the widow of the late Mr. Chamberlayne, who is herself since deceased, in conjunction with his Co-trustees under the late E. J. Chamberlayne's will, Sir Francis Lawley, and the Dean of Gloucester, found themselves under the necessity of placing their trust in Chancery, in order to obtain the judgment of that court as to the due execution of their trust, owing to certain indiscretions on the part of the present Mr. Chamberlayne & his brother Ackerley.*

LAWRENCE — Miss Lawrence at Littleton, Wiltshire

Miss Lawrence appears to have been a friend or connection of the Tinker family of Littleton.

1808: 19 Feb: *Mrs. Tinker, Miss Tinkers, & Miss Lawrence called.*

LAWRENCE — Charles Lawrence [37]

Charles Lawrence (1794-1881), farmer and solicitor, was born at Cirencester, son of William Lawrence (1753-1837), surgeon of Cirencester, and Judith, second daughter of William Wood of Tetbury, Gloucestershire. The surgeon Sir William Lawrence was his eldest brother. Charles married, 1818, Lydia, youngest daughter of Devereux Bowly of Chesterton House, Cirencester. Lawrence took a leading part in establishing the Royal Agricultural College at Cirencester between 1842 and 1845. For many years he owned an adjoining farm where he experimented on improving agricultural machinery to maximise the fertility of the land. Many visitors, among them Baron Liebig, came to inspect the farm, and it was always open to students from the college.

The Lawrence family lived at the Querns, Cirencester. As well as being an innovative farmer, Charles was also one of Cirencester's leading solicitors, and was in partnership with George Newmarch (1791-1857) for more than ten years.

1826: 6 May: *Near Cirencester on the right hand, opposite Lord Bathurst's park wall, Mr. Lawrence, an Attorney, & partner to Mr. Newmarch, is building an expensive house, but well designed, in the style of twisted chimneys, gable ends, billett windows, oriels & returns: when the place is planted & the gardens & pleasure ground begin to flourish, it will be very pretty.* 7 Aug: *I called as I went down Westgate Street on Mr. Newmarch, who with his partner Lawrence conducts the case for the prosecution.* 28 Aug., 5 Sep: *Lord Sherborne was in the chair, & had sent a very fine haunch of venison. Mr. Browne, Mr. Pettatt, Mr. Ford, Mr. Price, Mr. Croome, Mr. Lewis, the Dean of Gloucester, Mr. Lawrence & Mr. Newmarch were of the party.*

1835: 18 Jan.

1837: 29 Mar., 31 Mar., 31 May, 21 Jun., 28 Jun., 10 Jul., 13 Sep., 21 Oct., 26 Oct.

1838: 23 Feb., 25 Feb., 29 Apr., 1 Nov: *He communicates to me in confidence that his partnership with Mr. Lawrence will expire at Christmas next, and that it is not intended to renew it for a longer term.* 13 Nov., 16 Nov.

1839: 27 Feb: *Wrote to Messrs. Hoare to pay on my a/c to Messrs. Masterman to the a/c of Mr. Newmarch with Messrs. Cripps, Bankers, Cirencester, £119. 7. 6. which closes my account with Messrs. Lawrence and Newmarch for business done in the prosecution of our claims on the Estate of the late Dr. H. Moorhouse, and other business of less magnitude.*

LAWRENCE — James Henry Lawrence and the Lawrence brothers in Germany [38]

Sir James Henry Lawrence, knight of Malta (known as Chevalier Lawrence) (1773-1840), writer, was the eldest son of Richard James Lawrence (1745-1830), of Fairfield, Jamaica, whose ancestor, John, younger son of Henry Lawrence (1600-1664), had settled in that island in 1676, and of Mary, daughter of Thomas Hall of Kirkpatrick and Worcester, Jamaica. He was grandson of Col James Lawrence (±1709-1756), *custos* of St James.

Lawrence was educated at Eton College, where he was Montem poet in 1790, and afterwards at the University of Göttingen in Germany. A precocious author, he produced in 1791 a poem entitled 'The Bosom Friend', 'which,' said the *Monthly Review* of April 1792, 'instead of being a panegyric on friendship, is written in praise of a modern article of a lady's dress'. In 1793 his essay on the heterodox customs of the Nairs of Malabar, with respect to marriage and inheritance, was inserted by Wieland in his *Der Teutsche Merkur*. In 1800 at Schiller's behest, Lawrence completed a romance on the subject, also in German, which was published in the *Journal der Romane* for the following year under the title *Das Paradies der Liebe*, and reprinted as *Das Reich der Nairen*. The book was subsequently translated into French and English by the author himself, and published in both languages; the English version, entitled *The Empire of the Nairs*, was published in four volumes in 1811 by Thomas Hookham. On 17 August 1812 Percy Shelley wrote to Lawrence, 'Your *Empire of the Nairs*, which I read this Spring, succeeded in making me a perfect convert to its doctrines'. Shelley met with Lawrence in London the following year. In 1801 a German version of Lawrence's poem 'Love: an Allegory' appeared in *Irene*, a German magazine. The original was published in London in the following year and was attacked in 1803 by the *Anti-Jacobin Review*, which dismissed it as 'a dull and licentious publication'.

In 1803, when in France with his father, Lawrence was arrested along with other English residents and tourists. For several years he was detained at Verdun, until eventually he effected his escape by passing himself off as a German. Having returned to London he published a prose account of his captivity entitled *A Picture of Verdun* or *The English Detained in France* (2 vols, 1810), and in 1813 a drama in five acts entitled *The Englishman at Versailles* or *The Prisoner of Peace*.

After his long internment, Lawrence led a roving life, chiefly in Europe. He was apparently never at a loss for money; this was presumably due to the profits generated by the family's sugar plantation at Fairfield, Jamaica, which was worked by slave labour. Having been made, as he asserted, a knight of Malta, Lawrence assumed the title of Sir James Lawrence, and was frequently known as Chevalier Lawrence. In 1824 he published *On the Nobility of the British Gentry*, in which he intended to establish the proposition that an English gentleman, according to his sense of the term, is the equal of a foreign nobleman. In 1828 he brought together most of his early writings, with others of a similar description, in a collection entitled *The Etonian Out of Bounds*. He died unmarried on 26 September 1840, and was interred with his father in the burial ground of St John's Wood chapel. By the time of his death, his *Nobility of the British Gentry* had reached four editions, and it was republished posthumously in 1842 under the title, *British and Continental Titles of Honour*.

James's younger brother was Charles Lawrence (1776-1853), merchant, who was born in Albemarle Street, London (one source disputes this, saying he was born in Liverpool), and died in 1853 at Mossley Hall, Liverpool. He was awarded a share of the compensation for the Fairfield estate in St James, Jamaica, and was almost certainly the recipient of part of the compensation for the retirement estate in Westmoreland. He married, 1800, Rose D'Aguilar (1780-1857); they had 3 sons:

1 George Hall (1803-1869)
2 Arthur Johnstone (1809-1892)
3 Charles Washington (b. 1805)

Charles Lawrence was mayor of Liverpool in 1823-24, and was registered as a 'merchant of Fairfield and Mossley Hill near Liverpool'. He left a fortune of £70,000 on his death.

There were also two younger brothers. The diaries indicate that at one point there were three Lawrence brothers in Germany; the third brother was either Henry (1779-1864) or Frederick Augustus (1780-1840). The Witts family met two Lawrence brothers in Göttingen in 1799. According to the diary of Agnes Witts, these two Mr Lawrences arrived in Weimar on 30 March 1799, accompanied by Augustus John Foster (1780-1848). They are mentioned again in her diary entries of 1 April and 5 April 1799. They then left Weimar, but on 8 December a third brother arrived in Weimar in the company of Joseph Charles Mellish (1769-1823).

1799: 8 Dec: *Rather drier had been a Frost; walked out to the Concert at Court in the Evening, where many people. a Stranger Mr. Lawrence Brother of the two who were at Göttingen, a Knight of Malta then also Mr. Mellish.* 9 Dec: *Messrs. Mellish and Lawrence called on us in the morning went to fetch a walk.* 10 Dec: *Took my fourth Musical Lesson; called on Messrs. Martin and Lawrence.*

1800: 20 Jan: *Called on Mr. Lawrence walked with my Father in the Gardens and on the Belvedere Road.* 19 Feb: *A Charming day walked in the Morning after having been at the Academy & Library and after having called on Mr Lawrence.* 21 Feb., 3 Aug: *After dinner on the 3d. August: we took leave of our friend M. Lawrence, and of the Joys of Leipsic to proceed on our Route.*

LAWRENCE — Walter Lawrence Lawrence — *see also* Lightbourne *and* Timbrell [39]

Walter Lawrence Lawrence (1799-1877), JP, DL, and landed proprietor, was born Walter Lawrence Morris, but assumed the patronymic Lawrence by desire of his maternal grandfather, Walter Lawrence (d. 1810). He was the son of William Morris (d. 1834) and Mary Lawrence (d. 1839) (married, 1796), and grandson of Walter Lawrence (d. 1810), of Sevenhampton, and Mary Hayward (married, 1766). His uncle on his father's side was Robert Morris (d. 1816), MP for Gloucester in 1805-16.

Walter Lawrence Lawrence was educated at Magdalen College, Oxford, and in 1821 he was a student of Lincoln's Inn. He married, 24 July 1824, Mary (1806-1889), only daughter of Christian Splidt of Stratford, Essex; they had at least 3 sons and 3 daughters:

1 Mary Elizabeth (1826-1907)
2 Alice (1828-1919)
3 Agatha (1830-1904)
1 Walter (b. 1834)
2 Christian William (1836-1920)
3 Anthony Cocks (1843-1904), Church of England clergyman; born at Bonfalls, Belgium

Lawrence was a Gloucestershire JP and DL. He inherited the Sandywell estate from the Timbrell sisters and with it the advowson of Whittington, which by 1846 belonged to Richard Janion. In a similar manner, he sold the advowson of Upper Slaughter to Francis Witts. In 1839, on the death of his mother, Walter also inherited the manor of Sevenhampton. The background to his inheritance of the Sandywell estate was as follows: Thomas Tracy, MP for Gloucestershire, died in 1770, and his estates were retained by his widow Mary until her death in 1799. Mary Tracy died intestate and litigation over her estate lasted until 1807. Three sisters, Rebecca Lightbourne, Patience Timbrell, and Judith Timbrell, were then declared heirs to the bulk of it, and in 1809 had a conveyance from Mary Tracy's surviving trustees, Charles Hanbury Tracy and his wife Henrietta. Other claimants were compensated with land at Upper Slaughter or with cash; Rebecca's estranged husband, Thomas Lightbourne, surrendered his rights in return for an annuity. Judith died in 1812 and Patience in 1814, both devising their shares to Rebecca, who died in 1823, leaving her estate to Walter Lawrence Lawrence. Attempts by other claimants to upset Rebecca's will, partly on the grounds of undue influence by Walter's father, William Morris, who had managed her affairs, failed.

In 1838 Walter Lawrence Lawrence's estate in Dowdeswell parish comprised 328 acres, including Sandywell house and park, and at Andoversford, Home Farm and the village inn.

1823: 24 Dec: *It had been for some time pretty well known, that the bulk of the fortune would centre in the family of Mr. W. Morris, brother of the late banker at & member for Gloucester, who by his marriage with the heiress of the Lawrence's, a yeoman's family at Sevenhampton, possessed a good estate in that parish, and whose son has assumed the name of Lawrence, with the immediate enjoyment of some of his grandfather's property, since coming of age. The young man has been well educated, & was gentleman-commoner of Magdalen Coll. Oxford, but is said to be of expensive habits. He was some time since engaged to the eldest Miss Browne of Salperton; but a little display of temper on the part of the Gentleman, some difficulties as to a settlement, & a want of gentility on the side of the Lover—brought the affair to a close, which had not been anticipated.* 24 Dec: *In an adjoining room were the chief mourners and their friends: Mr. W. Morris, Mr. R. Morris of the Gloucester bank, now resident at Cheltenham to superintend the branch of the establishment there, his cousin Walter Lawrence... Mr. Lawrence, Mrs. Lightbourne's heir, has not been idle since the old lady's decease: he is about to make Sandywell Park his residence, and is employing many people there in altering & modernizing the house, in enlarging the Park as far as the new line of road, & in planting. It is said, that he is about to marry some rich heiress.*

1825: 17 Oct: *Mr. Lawrence has built rather a shewy apparatus of gates & lodges into his park, which he has extended in this direction as far as the new road.*

1826: 6 Jan: *Mr. W. Beach is about to be united to Miss Browne, eldest daughter of our friends at Salperton, a very fine young woman, between whom and Mr. Lawrence there was some years since a prospect of an union, which went off after some negociation.* 30 Mar., 15 Jun: *Mr. Lawrence of Sandiwell park, who had heard of the accident accosted me with great kindness.* 16 Jun., 15 Sep.,

1829: 19 Feb: *I went alone to dine with the Brownes at Salperton: Mr. & Mrs. Lawrence of Sandywell Park, and T.*

Pettat, Mrs. Browne's nephew, a young dragoon officer. We had a cheerful party. Mr. Lawrence, I presume, has now every prospect of retaining undisturbed possession of the property left to him by Mrs. Lightbourn; the attorneys, who espoused Mrs. Freeman's cause have long ceased to litigate his right, whether they considered their cause hopeless, or whether they were moved induced to desist by valuable consideration received. 1 Apr., 22 Sep., 6 Oct.

1832: 27 Mar: *Communicated to Mr. Newmarch, my Solicitor, and Steward of Lord Sherborne, that the sum of £310 had been paid by my bankers in London to his account, in fulfilment of the purchase by me of the Pleasure ground before the Rectory house at Upper Slaughter... it was important, that I should purchase the freehold, as I am now the owner of the advowson of the Rectory itself. The latter I acquired by purchase of Mr. Lawrence of Sandywell Park, in December last, and it cost me £1016. 5.* 29 Mar.

1834: 15 Aug.

1836: 10 Aug: *Of the neutrals two, W. L. Lawrence & Revd. W. Hicks were Conservatives; it seems, they had hastily all but pledged themselves to Mason, without sufficient consideration.* 11 Aug: *Breakfasted with a party of conservative Mag. at the Bell Hotel, conversing with Cooke, Hale, Phelps, W L Lawrence, Purnell &c.* 29 Nov: *Mr. Lawrence, Sandywell Park, was the Steward.*

1837: 7 Mar., 17-18 Oct.

1838: 2 Jan., 8 Jan., 5 Feb., 10 Apr., 29 Jun: *Rode to N. Leach with the intention of being present at the Quarterly meeting of Mag. usual holden on the Friday before each quarter Sessns. to audit the accounts of the Bridewell there: but found that to accommodate the Visiting Mag. Ford & Lawrence, the meeting had been deferred till to-morrow.* 3 Jul., 16 Oct.

1839: 1 Jan., 6 Apr., 9 Apr., 12 Apr.

1840: 25 Mar: *A letter from the Secretary of the Union Life Assurance Office, requesting confidential information as to the health of Mr. Lawrence of Sandywell Park, who is about to make an assurance of his life in that office. Mr. Rogers being Chairman of the Directors, and B. P. Witts, one of the Board, accounts for this private application being made to me.*

LAWRENCE — William Lawrence [40]

Sir William Lawrence, 1st baronet (1783-1867), surgeon, was the eldest of the four sons of William Lawrence (1753-1837), a prominent surgeon of Cirencester, and elder brother of Charles Lawrence (*above*). He was educated at a school at Elmore, near Gloucester, and in 1799 was apprenticed to John Abernethy, assistant surgeon to St Bartholomew's Hospital in London. In 1805 Lawrence became a member of the Royal College of Surgeons, and in 1813 an assistant surgeon at St Bartholomew's. In the same year he was elected a fellow of the Royal Society. Alongside his work at St Bart's, Lawrence obtained posts in some of the more specialised medical establishments: for example, from 1814 he was surgeon to the London Infirmary for Diseases of the Eye. In 1833 he published his *Treatise on Diseases of the Eye*. Lawrence was appointed sergeant-surgeon to Queen Victoria in 1857, and in 1867 he received a baronetcy.

1836: 20 Nov: *It seems that since last spring, when he had an attack of influenza, he has suffered more or less from tenderness and soreness of the throat, which for several weeks has teazed him so much that he has resorted to the advice of an eminent London Surgeon, Copeland, by which he has not been benefited, and is now gone to consult Brodie or Vance, or Lawrence.*

LAWRENCE — William Edwards Lawrence [41]

William Edwards Lawrence (1814-1857), JP, DL, and landed proprietor, was born at Cowley, Gloucestershire, son of William Lawrence (d. 1817) and Harriet Martin (1777-1857). He was educated at Brasenose College, Oxford, where he matriculated on 5 April 1832, aged 18, but he does not appear to have taken a degree. His father was listed as William Lawrence, of Wotton-under-Edge, a distant cousin to Walter Lawrence Lawrence of Sandywell. In the 1851 census, William Edwards Lawrence lived at Greenway House with his mother, Harriet Blackman (b. ±1777)—presumably she had remarried and was widowed once more. Ten years earlier, at the time of the 1841 census, he was not present at Greenway House, but in addition to Harriet there were three independent ladies: an aunt, Kitty Martin (b. ±1762); Ann Seward (b. ±1805); and Mary Seward (b. ±1810). The Lawrence family eventually sold the estate in 1854. Lawrence died unmarried. He had one sister:

1 Harriett (1816-1891); married, at Badgeworth, Gloucestershire, 12 October 1841, Henry Bull Strangways (1808-1884); at least 1 son:
  1 Edmund Lawrence (1842-1870)

1837: 28 Sep: *In addition to the entire family circle met Mrs. Blackman, widow of the late Mr. Lawrence of Shurdington, and now widow of her second husband, Dr. Blackman, who resides at the Greenway, Shurdington, with her son Wm. Lawrence, a young man of good fortune, but of no great calibre of mind, a Mag. for the County and a conservative. He was also a guest at Salperton, as was his sister, Miss Lawrence, a very lovely young woman, whom I had never met before, but with whose beauty, amiable temper, good sense, and unaffected manners I was greatly pleased. There was also a Mr. W. Elwell, a young man of pleasing manners, though of low politics, who had accompanied the Lawrences on this visit to Salperton, being an old schoolfellow of W. Lawrence & T. Browne. He is brother of the MP. for Andover.*

1851: 17 Mar.

LAYARD — Brownlow Villiers Layard — *see also* Port *and* Granville [42]

Brownlow Villiers Layard (1779-1861), army officer and Church of England clergyman, was the son of Charles Peter Layard (1749-1803), dean of Bristol, and Elizabeth Ward (±1758-1796). He was educated at St John's College, Cambridge. He gained a commission as lieutenant in the 7th Foot (Royal Fusiliers) in 1795, and became ADC to the duke of Kent. Layard then changed career; he was ordained deacon at St Asaph on 11 September 1803 and priest on 21 September 1803. He served as rector of Uffington, Lincolnshire, in 1803-61, with a dispensation from the archbishop to hold the vicarage of Tallington from 1820 until his death in 1861. In 1810 he received an MA at Lambeth.

Layard married, first, 6 October 1803, Louisa (1778-1817), daughter of John Port (d. 1807), born John Sparrow, and Mary (Pauline) D'Ewes (1745-1814); they had 6 sons:

1 Brownlow Villiers (1804-1853); died at Riversdale, Dublin, Ireland
2 George Henry (1806-1848); married, at St Pancras, Middlesex, 14 July 1828, Eliza Matilda Hughes
3 John Beville (1809-1846), Lt, 22nd Madras Native Infantry; died in India
4 Bernard Granville (1813-1872), Bt Lt-Col; died at Beverley, Yorkshire
5 Louis [Lewis] Frederick (1815-1883)
6 Charles Clement (1817-1895); died at Bath

Brownlow Villiers Layard married secondly, 1821, Sarah Jane, daughter of Thomas Margary of Clapham; they had at least 2 sons and 3 daughters:

1 John Thomas (1821-1885); died at Smallburgh, Norfolk
1 Louisa Jane (b. 1823)
2 Augustus Villiers (1824-1848), Lt, 23rd Madras Native Infantry; died at Kamptoe, India
2 Caroline Mary (1827-1848); died unmarried
3 Sarah Frances (1830-1914); died unmarried

These entries are interesting as they show connection with the Ports, close connections of the Granvilles.

1803: 30 Dec: *Accompanied my Mother & George to call upon Mr. & Mrs. Leyard who with Mr. Port, & their farmer's sister we met at home. Louisa looking ill but kind & pleasant as ever.*

1804: 1 Jan: *Repaired afterwards to Mr. Adams's, in a large party—Leyard, the Marriott's & ourselves. Walked with the latter up the Hill. Called on Mr. Marshall, walked with Miss Upton, & with my mother & George visited Lady Francis Flood & the Leyards.* 4 Jan: *Called on the Ports, sitting some time with Miss Leyard, Harriet, & her Father. Poor Leyard afterwards was taken terribly ill.* 7 Jan., 11 Jan., 28 Jan: *A most amusing Evening, during which I had much conversation with Dawkins, Smith, Hooke, Johnson, the Leyards, Hillhouses, Smiths etc.*

LAYARD — Brownlow Edward Layard[43]

Brownlow Edward Layard (1811-1890), army officer, was born Kalatura, Ceylon, son of Charles Edward Layard (1786-1852), born in the parish of St Martin-in-the-Fields, London, and Barbara Bridgetina Mooyaart (1789-1845), born in Jaffna, Ceylon. He was the nephew of Brownlow Villiers Layard (*above*). He had twenty siblings. He married, first, 18 June 1839, Emily (1812-1840), born at Tidenham, Gloucestershire; daughter of John Powley Kensington; they had 1 daughter:

1 Emily (1840-1841)

Layard married secondly, 18 October 1842, Caroline Maria (1825-1848), born at Corsham, Wiltshire, daughter of Capt. Thomas Charles Fenton and Harriette Rooke; they had 2 daughters:

1 Caroline Emily (1844-1895); married, 18 July 1867, Revd John Shepherd; died at Sainte-Luc, Switzerland
2 Agnes Maria (1845-1881); married, 9 July 1872, Revd Henry Francis Limpus

Layard married thirdly, 10 January 1854, Louise Henrietta (1820-1898), daughter of Revd Thomas Carter; they had 2 sons and 2 daughters:

1 Ernest Brownlow (1856-1934), Church of England clergyman
2 Cyril (b. & d. 1861)
1 Ethel Mary (±1862-1935); died unmarried
2 Evelyn Mary (1864-1878)

1826: 5 Jul: *We dined at Mr. Jeaffreson's at Longborough meeting Dr. Warneford, Mr. & Mrs. Ford, Mr. Twisleton & with him a Mr. Brownlow Layard, born at Ceylon, and grandson of a former Dean of Bristol.*

LE BLANC — Simon Le Blanc[44]

Simon Le Blanc (1748/9-1816), judge, was the second son of Thomas Le Blanc (1704-1765), of Charterhouse Square, London, and Ann Tully. His father, a wealthy merchant and a director of the South Sea Company, was descended from a Huguenot family of Rouen. Simon Le Blanc was educated at Trinity Hall, Cambridge, and afterwards admitted to the Inner Temple in 1771 and called to the bar in February 1773. He graduated LLB from Cambridge in 1773 and was a fellow of Trinity Hall from 1779 to 1799. Le Blanc joined the Norfolk circuit and by February 1787 was sufficiently eminent in the profession to be created serjeant-at-law. He was then made king's serjeant on 4 March 1795, and was treasurer of Serjeants' Inn from 1798 to 1799. One of the most successful advocates of his generation, in the year 1790 Le Blanc made 271 appearances in the court of common pleas; only one other barrister made more.

Le Blanc was selected as one of the judges charged particularly with the suppression of Luddism. During the initial phase of machine-breaking in the midlands and the north, some of the justices on the assize circuit had directed or encouraged acquittals in spite of the scale of disturbances. Le Blanc sat with Sir Alexander Thomson at both Lancaster and York, at which twenty-five prisoners were executed in all. At York he tried the murderers of the woollen manufacturer William Horsfall, whose conviction was critical. The judges advised the prosecuting counsel, James Alan Park and Henry Hobhouse, the Treasury solicitor, that moving the executions of the three condemned men to Huddersfield would be unwise as it would entail a respite, raising hopes of mercy. They were hanged at York two days after trial. Before the next convictions took place, Le Blanc conferred with Park on the advantages of early hangings, as had been adopted at the Lancaster special commission. The judges also agreed to accept no applications for mercy but to leave the entire discretion with the secretary of state. Le Blanc and Thomson recommended mercy for only one of the seventeen sentenced to death.

1804: 4 Mar: *St. Mary's assize sermon by Mr. Landon of Oriel with an inaudible voice. Justice Lawrence & Sir Simon Le Blanc.*

LE MARCHANT — William Hirzel Le Marchant[45]

William Hirzel Le Marchant (1814-1906), Church of England clergyman, was born in Guernsey. He was educated at Elizabeth College, Guernsey, in 1825-31 and Trinity College, Dublin (BD & DD 1864). He succeeded E. H. Niblett as vicar of Haresfield in 1853 and remained in that post until 1890, when he retired to Weston-super-Mare. He married, at St John's, Notting-Hill, Middlesex, 12 June 1855, Anna Catherina Rickards, daughter of Hugh Hovell Farmar (1822-1890), JP, and Meliora Rickards Mynors; they had at least 3 daughters:

1 Mary Matina (b. 1857)
2 Eleanor Jane (b. 1859)
3 Emily (b. 1863)

1846: 18 Nov: *We were kindly received by the pleasing Mrs. Hayward, and in due time the party was increased by the arrival of Mr. Lysons, with two ladies, from his house at Hempstead, connections of his, a mother and daughter, whose names I did not catch, and a Mr. Le Marchant, Curate of Hardwick.*

LEA — Edward Lea and the Lea family of Upper Slaughter[46]

Edward Lea (1795-1858), farmer, was born at Crudwell, son of Thomas Lea (1761-1821), later of Kirkham Farm, Upper Slaughter, and Esther [or Hester] Burford (1757-1827). He seems to have come to Upper Slaughter at an early period. It appears from the diary entry for 24 December 1823 that one Lea, presumably Edward's father, had a claim to the Manor Farm, which was successful. Edward had at least one brother, William (1792-1838), who farmed Kirkham Farm after the death of their father (*below*).

Edward married, 8 June 1820, Elizabeth (1802-1879), daughter of Thomas Smith and Alley Pearce of Weston-sub-Edge. Elizabeth was the sister of Sophia Arkell and Harriett Tysoe, both née Smith. Edward and Elizabeth lived at the manor house in Upper Slaughter, where Edward farmed 560 acres, employing nineteen men and four boys and women; he was a farmer on a substantial scale. The couple had at least twelve children; 7 sons and 5 daughters:

1 William Smith (1821-1822)
2 George Edward (b. 1823); married Mary Gillett (b. 1838); at least 1 daughter:
  1 Edith Emma Lea (1861-1947)
3 Thomas (b. 1825); married, at Parramatta, New South Wales, Australia, 25 August 1859, Ann Norris (Annie) Griffith (b. 1838); at least 1 son:
  1 Edward Tysoe (1870-1944)
1 Susan Elizabeth (1827-1887); married, at Stow-on-the-Wold, 26 January 1860, Samuel Boyce (1809-1875); 5 sons:
  1 Arthur Edward (1861-1881)
  2 Sydney Thomas (1862-1945)
  3 William Tysoe (1864-1951)
  4 Joseph Henry (1867-1932)
  5 Frank Lea (1870-1887)
2 Emily Ann (1829-1848); died unmarried
4 William Henry (b. 1831); emigrated to Australia
3 Lucy Anna (b. ±1833); married, at Adlestrop, 8 December 1870, William Bryan (1823-1893)
5 Samuel Smith (1837-1905); married, at Ashendon, Buckinghamshire, 18 December 1866, Catherine Hannah Shield (1837-1918); died at Tacoma, Pierce, Washington, USA; 4 daughters:
  1 Emily J. (b. 1870)
  2 Catherine E. (b. 1873)
  3 Laura E. (b. 1876)
  4 Bessie E. (b. 1882)
4 Eliza (1839-1906); married, at Upper Slaughter, 31 July 1867, James Gillett (1842-1875); at least 1 son and 1 daughter:
  1 Emily Elizabeth (b. 1869)
  1 Edward Lea (1871-1872)
6 Joseph (1842-1924); married Rose Emily Foster [?] (1853-1924)
7 Edward (1845-1917); married, at Cold Aston, 15 April 1873, Rebecca Acock (1847-1929); 3 sons and 7 daughters:
  1 Amy Elizabeth (1874-1954)
  2 Emily Kate (1875-1964)
  3 Mary Louise (1877-1956)
  4 Alice May (1877-1950)
  1 Edgar Joseph (1879-1965)
  5 Mabel Helen (1880-1970)
  2 Arthur Henry (1882-1969)
  6 Rosa Ann (1884-1884)
  3 William Reginald (1887-1936)
  7 Gladys Ethel (1892-1974)
5 Emily Sophia (b. 1848); married, at Aberystwyth, 12 September 1871, her second cousin, William George Smith (b. 1848); 3 daughters:
  1 Ada Elizabeth (1872-1953)
  2 Emily Blanche (b. 1875)
  3 Mary Sophia (b. 1877)

Thomas and William immigrated to Australia in 1850, although one source states that William died at Camberwell, London, in 1899. This may be an incorrect attribution, or it is possible that William returned to England. By 1871, Elizabeth was living at Adlestrop Farm House with three children, Joseph, Edward, and Emily.

1823: 24 Dec: *In the interval between 1805 and 1808 a decree of court put them in possession of the Estates in litigation, with the exception of the Manor and land at Upper Slaughter, which they were advised to give up to two claimants Williams & Lea, whose pretensions were plausible, and their supporters active. As a continuance of litigation was much to be deprecated by the Timbrells, now advancing in years, an arrangement was adopted for terminating the cause by relinquishing in favour of Lea & Williams the Slaughter property, but when the Advowson of the Rectory was also demanded, the sisters said nay; they had promised the next presentation, and they would keep their word.*

1824: 17 Nov: *The principal farmers of Upper Slaughter, Messrs. Cook, Collett, E Lea, & Davis, dined with us.*

1827: 2 Nov: *The farmers dined with us: Mr. R. Collett of Bourton on the Water, long a resident here, but now a miller at Bourton; Mr. Cook, Mr. E. Lea & Mr. Davis.*

1828: 24 Sep: *The principal farmers in the Village, according to our annual custom, dined with us to-day; Messrs. Cook, E. Lea, & Davis formed the party.*

1829: 22 Dec: *The three farmers of the village, Messrs. Cook, E. Lea, & Davis, who are accustomed to dine with us towards the close of the year, were our guests to-day.*

1836: 27 Aug., 12 Sep: *The majority approved of modifying the rate, but Lea, the principal paymaster, being in the minority, I suggested that a case be laid before Counsel, and an opinion taken as to the point of law: each party to be bound by the opinion, and, in the meantime, the present rate to be made on the old Assessment.*

1837: 22 Jan: *Rather a more unfavourable report of Mr. Smith; his son in law E. Lea seriously ill with the prevailing epidemic.* 23 Jan: *In my ride called to enquire after Mr. Smith, who is better, as also E. Lea, who is, however, much indisposed.* 20 Mar: *Attended a parish meeting when it was settled that Davis should be the new Guardian of U. Slaughter instead of Lea.* 20 Jun: *I joined, at the Rectory, the Committee appointed to draw up rules for the proposed Friendly Society, meeting Robt. Waller, Ford, Billingsley, Wilkins, Kendall, Kimber, E. Lea, Collett, Ashwin.* 19 Sep., 10 Nov., 15 Nov: *Engaged with Edwd. Lea, assisting him in preparing a memorial to the Commrs. of Excise to deprecate any penalty which he may have incurred by an unintentional breach of the excise laws which is alleged against him.*

1838: 2 Mar: *Received a letter from the Australian Emigration Agent attached to the Colonial Office, with a number of printed documents respecting emigration to New South Wales & Van Dieman's land, which were sent in reply to my letter to the Colonial Secretary on the 26th. Ult. and which I communicated to my neighbour E. Lea, that they might be available to the Smith family.* 16 Aug: *My neighbour, Edward Lea, very dangerously ill, probably, from inflammation of the bowels.* 17 Aug: *E Lea in a very dangerous and precarious state.* 18 Aug: *My parishioner Edward Lea considered in very imminent danger.* 19 Aug: *Edward Lea believed to be a shade better to-day; but continues in a very precarious state.* 20 Aug: *Visited my parishioner E. Lea, whose disease has taken a favourable turn, so that hopes are entertained of his final recovery.* 21 Aug: *Visited my neighbour, E Lea, who continues to gain ground.* 28 Aug: *Mr. E. Lea recovering.* 31 Oct.

1839: 7 Jun: *besides a considerable party of ordinary members and musicians about fifteen dined on very good and well cooked viands at the high table, being Trustees & Honorary members—Waller, Polson, Wilkins, Kimber, W. Smith, E. Lea, J. Bennett, Ransford, T. Collett, W. & Jos. Bryan, C. Barton &c.*

1840: 1 Apr: *In the meeting evening a Vestry meeting was held in my study. Messrs. Davis, Lea, Gregory, and Jos. Price attended.*

1842: 31 Jan: *Visited Mrs Smith who continues in a very precarious way. Privately administered to her the holy Communion, also to her three daughters Mrs. Lea, Mrs. E. Tysoe, and Mrs. Arkell.* 2 Apr., 5 Apr: *Churched my parishioner Mrs. Lea, and christened her infant.* 2 Apr., 3 Jun.

1843: 4 Dec: *In the evening Messrs. Lea, J B Collett, Davis, and Gregory, came by appointment to settle with me as to the poor parishioners among whom should be distributed 18½ pairs of blankets purchased out of the funds of the Church and Charity Estate.*

1844: 26 Sep: *Administered the Sacrament of the Lord's supper to J. B. Collett's eldest daughter, now lying apparently on her death-bed, her parents and Aunt Lea communicating with her.* 10 Dec., 16 Dec.

1845: 25 Mar: *A vestry meeting was held in my study—Messrs. Lea, Davis, J B Collett, and Gregory attended.* 2 Apr., 25 Apr: *Privately baptized the infant child of Mr. & Mrs. Lea.* 29 May, 6 Jun., 30 Jun: *Early in the morning, before leaving home, transacted business with J Davis and George Lea.*

1846: 8 Jul: *Called at Mr. Lea's on parish business.* 6 Oct., 27 Oct: *Parish business with the Overseer, on whom I called (E Lea).* 3 Nov: *Mr. Lea called with a letter from Mr. Croome, Land Surveyor, of Tewkesbury, as to the terms on which he would undertake the valuation of this parish. Assisted Mr. L. in writing a reply to this letter.* 10 Nov: *Visited Mr. E Lea, who is suffering from rheumatism on Parish business.* 11 Nov., 14 Nov., 19 Dec.

1847: 22 Jan: *transacting business with E Lea &c. as to Land Tax & parish trust concerns.* 30 Jan., 6 Feb., 22 Feb., 6 Mar., 8-9 Mar., 20 Mar: *Called on E Lea, and conferred with him on various parish matters.* 1 Apr., 7 Apr., 20 Apr., 28 May, 9 Jun., 15 Jun., 25 Jun., 14 Jul., 19 Aug., 5 Oct., 2 Oct: *Walked to Bourton on the Water to consult with Mr. Kendal as to proceedings to be taken against Henry Collett, son of J. B. Collett, of this parish, a very turbulent, ill-conditioned young man, who had attempted pound breach yesterday morning, when George Lea, by order of his Father, as Road Surveyor, had impounded a cow belonging to Farmer Price, and a horse the property of R. Humphris, which were found straying on the village green.* 5 Oct., 8 Nov., 11 Nov: *Visited Mr. E Lea's family; his second daughter, a very lovely, interesting, amiable girl of eighteen, is rapidly declining to the grave: nor is this the only calamity apprehended: the second son is suffering from defective vision, and fears are entertained that his lungs, like his sister's are affected with disease.* 15 Nov: *Mrs. Lea called and gave us a very unfavourable report of the health of her children——the second daughter fast sinking under a decline; the second son with symptons of a tendency to consumption, and moreover with very impaired vision.* 15 Dec., 22 Dec: *Visited poor Emily Lea, far gone in consumption, and whose days are numbered: prayed with her an interesting and lovely girl of eighteen: her parents and her Aunt Tysoe were present.* 27 Dec.

1848: 1 Jan: *Visited the Lea family: prayed with Emily Lea in presence of her parents and Sister.* 10 Jan., 12 Jan: *A note from Mr. Lee, bookseller, Cheltenham, who has sent a packet of Bibles and Prayer books, from which Emily Lea may select such as she may wish to present to her brothers.* 15 Jan: *But death has arrested her career; she has not lived to present her pious and affectionate momento to those she loved. She died at 7 P.M. this evening: and the Brothers will receive from another hand the parting token of her love and concern for their welfare.* 18 Jan: *Visited the Lea family: the anxiety and grief attendant on the death of his daughter has deranged the health of her father.* 21 Jan: *Poor Emily Anne Lea was buried to-day: I preceeded the corpse from the house to the Church: her Father suffering from rheumatism, but able to attend.* 23 Jan: *All the mourners, & connections of the Lea family, who had attended on Friday at the interment of Emily Lea, were present.* 26 Jan., 9 Feb: *Much illness at E. Lea's.* 15 Feb., 23 Feb: *Visited the Lea family: still does sickness prevail among them: the second Son has visited Dr. Baron, at Cheltenham.* 18 Mar., 25 Mar., 1 Apr., 5 Apr., 22 Apr: *Called a on my parishioners, the Leas: illness still lingers in that family.* 26 Aug., 11 Sep: *I called on E. Lea's family as to the funeral of his niece, who died yesterday at Rendcomb.* 12 Sep., 15 Sep: *Officiated at the funeral of Miss Sarah Gregory Lea.* 5 Oct., 27 Oct: *Called on parish business at Edwd. Lea's and William Gregory's; illness in both families.*

1849: 17 Dec: *Visited E Lea on parish business, which also brought W. Gregory and W. Bateman to me in the Evening.* 28 Dec.

1850: 5 Feb., 20 Feb., 26 Feb: *Engaged in the forenoon with Mrs. Lea and W. Gregory in distributing to my poor parishioners.* 27 Feb: *Making extracts from the Register as to the baptisms of the two sons of E. Lea who are about to emigrate to Australia, and preparing commendatory letters addressed to Colonial Bishops and others, which they may produce at the place of their destination in proof that they are members of the Church of England, bearing good characters.* 15 Mar., 29 Apr., 2 May, 15 Jun., 21 Jun: *Attended a vestry meeting for two hours, with Mr. Lea, Mr. Gregory, and Mr. J. B. Collett.* 10 Jul., 22 Jul., 19 Aug: *Transacting business as to school charities with Mrs. Lea, who called upon me.* 31 Aug., 14 Sep: *Mrs. Lea attended with her son and daughter.* 7 Oct: *After breakfast an interview with Mrs. Lea as to parish charities & other matters.* 22 Oct: *Mrs. Lea called on parish matters ... She consulted me also as to the best method of remitting money to Sydney and in New South Wales for two sons who are soon to sail for that colony, whither they are about to emigrate, and where two Uncles and another relation, settlers of some years standing, and, it would appear, in pretty good circumstances, will receive them. This scheme has been long in agitation.* 22 Oct., 24 Oct., 25 Oct: *Conferred twice with Mr. and Mrs. E. Lea as to the remittances to be made for the use of their Sons about to emigrate, to Sydney, New South Wales. It is arranged that each shall have £200 over and above the expence of their passage out, outfit and other incidental outlay—a very liberal provision, considering that the parents have a very numerous family. Mr. E. Lea gave me a cheque for £400 in return for which I wrote to Messrs. Hoare, directing them to procure for the young men respectively a letter of credit each for £200 payable to them at Sydney.* 30 Oct., 2 Nov., 4 Nov: *Visited the Lea family to leave for the young men about to leave quit their native homes to-morrow, to seek their fortunes in Australia, as a mark of my good will, and trust that they will lead virtuous and religious lives, each a copy of that excellent book, the New Manual of Devotions.* 16 Nov., 10 Dec., 13 Dec., 16 Dec., 18 Dec: *Conferring with George Lea, son of the Churchwarden, on parish matters, charities, and accounts.* 20 Dec.

1851: 4 Jan., 22 Jan., 28 Jan., 7 Feb: *Attended a vestry meeting. E Lea & J. B. Collett met me on the business to be transacted.* 18-19 Feb., 21 Feb., 24 Feb., 3 Mar., 11 Mar., 14 Mar., 21 Mar., 24 Mar: *Attended a vestry meeting—E Lea, J B Collett, S. Collett, W Dix, & Jos. Price were present.* 28 Mar., 11 Apr., 25 Apr., 30 Apr., 2 May: *Parish business with George Lea.* 7 May, 10 May, 17 May.

1852: 31 Jan., 4 Feb: *Engaged with George Lea on parish business.* 20 Feb., 5 Mar., 24 Mar., 2 Apr., 3 Apr: *Transacted business with George Lea.* 12 Apr., 17 Apr., 4 May, 8 May, 15 May, 17 May: *After breakfast drove to Stow, taking with me my*

Churchwarden, Lea. 25 May, 5 Jun., 23 Oct: *Transacting parish trust business &c. with George Lea.* 24 Oct., 28-30 Oct., 8 Nov: *Transacting parish business with George Lea.* 4 Dec., 15 Dec: *Called on W. Lea, Churchwarden, & Trustee of the Church estate, to arrange with him and his wife as to distribution of clothing & bedding out of our charity funds.* 17 Dec., 21 Dec: *Transacted business with George Lea as to the village charities.* 23 Dec., 29 Dec., 31 Dec: *Engaged in the afternoon with Mrs. lea at the School room in distributing bedding and clothing to the amount of more than £10. among poor parishioners, from the funds of the parish Church and Charity Estate.*

1853: 10 Jan: *Transacted business with George Lea and Robt. Humphris as to the rent due from the latter to Lord Sherborne for a ye month's occupation of late John Blandford's Cottage, in the interval between his decease, and the conveyance of the property to me.* 19 Jan., 26 Jan., 5 Feb., 14 Feb., 12 Mar., 23 Mar: *The two Churchwardens, Lea and Stratton, were the only rate-payers present.... I nominated Lea as Guardian of the Parish—George Lea was set down to serve the office of Parish Constable.* 2 Apr., 23 Apr., 2 May, 4 May, 17 May: *With George Lea going through the accounts of the Parish Church and Charity Estate.* 18 May, 7 Dec., 15-16 Dec., 28 Dec: *Brought home in my carriage Miss Lea, the daughter of my Church Warden, who, being at Stow, was glad to be saved a walk in the snow.* 31 Dec.

1854: 6 Feb., 3 Mar., 15 Mar., 18 Mar., 22 Mar., 27 Mar., 30 Mar., 28 Apr., 16 May: *Mrs. Lea called to make deposits in the Prov. Bank for her younger children, the little accumulation of Christmas and Birthday presents &c.* 19-20 May, 19 Jun., 21 Jun., 27 Jun., 10 Jul: *Transacting parish business with George Lea.* 18 Jul., 28 Jul: *Called at E. Lea's to inform him that he & Stratton are appointed Surveyors of the Highways. He was on his farm; saw and chatted with Mrs. Lea.*

LEA — William Lea — *see also* Gregory [47]

William Lea (1792-1838), farmer, was born at Crudwell, son of Thomas Lea (1761-1821) and Esther Burford (1757-1827), and elder brother to Edward (*above*). He married, first, at Lower Slaughter, 21 September 1818, Sarah Gregory (1800-1828). Sarah's name is not recorded in either of the Lower or Upper Slaughter registers. At her marriage the witnesses were Anna Maria Gregory, William Gregory, and Martha Gregory. Anna Maria is not known, but William and Martha are probably the two known children of Thomas and Sarah Gregory. If this is so, then Sarah could possibly have been a younger sibling who was either not baptised, or possibly baptised at a nonconformist chapel. William and Sarah had 3 sons and 2 daughters:

1 Sarah Gregory (1819-1848)
1 William (1821-1890)
2 Thomas (b. 1823)
2 Ann Elizabeth (1824-1881)
3 Edwin (b. & d. 1828)

William married secondly, at St Mary's, Cheltenham, 10 August 1836, Martha (1796-1884), daughter of Thomas and Sarah Gregory; they had 1 daughter:

1 Ellen Margaretta Letitia (1836-1919)

As stated above, it seems possible that William's first wife, Sarah, may have been his second wife Martha's sister. This seems odd as such a union was considered unlawful until 1907, when the Deceased Wife's Sister's Marriage Act was passed, legalising marriage between a man and the sister of his deceased wife. It is therefore more probable that Sarah was a cousin to some degree.

In her younger years Martha was a personal servant to Jane Backhouse and brought disgrace to the Upper Slaughter rectory by bearing an illegitimate child. It seems unlikely that the child survived and there is no record of burial or baptism. Martha presumably left the village and went into service elsewhere, probably at Cheltenham.

1826: 10 Feb: *A day of much confusion & anxiety, owing to the shameful Misconduct of Mrs. Backhouse's confidential Servant, Martha Gregory, sister of Will. Gregory, my late tenant. At a very early hour in the morning she was taken ill; not a soul, except her fellow servant, indeed, suspected the cause of her indisposition, and at six o clock she was brought to bed of a seven months child.*

1838: 30 Mar: *Officiated at the interment of William Lea, Farmer, of Upper Swell, formerly, of Kirkham Farm in this parish.*

1854: 6 Apr: *Called on Mrs. Gregory to enquire as to a letter from the lunatic Wakelam written to Martha Lea, and forwarded through Mr. Pearce for my judgment & perusal. It refers to his confinement in the Lunatic private asylum at Hook Norton.*

LEAKE — Charles Leake

There were two solicitors in Witney in 1852, Charles Leake and James Leake. This reference is likely to have been regarding the former.

1836: 19 Aug: *Howell and my son returned to dinner, they learnt at Witney that Stevens had been for a third time baffled in his attempt to obtain a conviction, before the Oxford bench of Mag. on Saturday last, against Leake, the volunteer and unpaid Clerk of the Witney Union. Gardner's Directory of Oxfordshire, 1852.*

LEAR — Mr Lear at Clifton

1804: 17 Jan: *Sat mournfully enough at home till time to go to the York House Ball, which the thin was pleasant enough; danced with H. Marriott, Misses Horton & Adair. Some pleasant men there Horton, Dawkins, Smith, Lear etc. etc.* 18 Jan: *Called on the Marriott's. Walked with Lear to Bristol. & with him & Horton... I accompanied Horton & Lear to the Queen's Ball at Bristol; full, gay, amusing: the Marriotts, Moncasters etc. there; great fun with Dowell, Horton, Smith, Lear, Susan Gibbons, The Marriott's, Smiths, Prower, Eagles etc. etc. etc.* 20 Jan: *Edgell called afterwards. Then with H. & C Marriott & Lear on the Downs, & at the Marriotts.* 28 Jan: *Called & took leave of Mr. & Mrs. Adams & of my dear friends the Marriotts, who confided to me the proposals made by Lear to my lovely sister Harriet.*

LECHMERE — Anthony Lechmere — *see also* Berwick [48]

Sir Anthony Lechmere, 1st baronet (1762-1849), landed proprietor, was born at Hanley Castle, Worcestershire, son of Edmund Lechmere (1710-1805), MP, and Elizabeth Whitmore (b. 1740). He married, first, at Hanley Castle, Worcester, 15 May 1787, Mary Berwick (1767-1820); they had 2 sons and 6 daughters:

1 Sarah (1788-1864)
2 Eliza Anne (1789-1875)
3 Frances (1791-1847)
1 Edmund Hungerford (1792-1856); succeeded as 2nd baronet
4 Mary Foley (1799-1803)
2 Anthony Berwick (1802-1878), canon of Worcester; *see below*
5 Georgiana Felicia (1806-1886)
6 Emma Catherine (1809-1885)

Lechmere was created 1st Baronet Lechmere in 1818. He married secondly, at St Mary's, Gloucester, 8 September 1823, Eleanor (1808-1857), daughter of Bayley Villiers; they had 1 son:

1 William Henry (1825-1857); died unmarried

In the detailed and interesting diary entry for 16 May 1825, Francis Witts is in error; the sister of Lady Reade was the wife of Sir Anthony's son (*below*).

1825: 16 May: *Our first point was to the Rhydd, the Seat of Sir Anthony Lechmere Bart. The road lay sometimes across the common skirted by orchards & bordered by scattered sketchy cottages, sometimes through lanes between flourishing meadows & cornfields, chiefly planted with rows of fine pear and apple trees. The Rhydd is a hamlet on the banks of the Severn, and there are two or three enjoyable gentlemens seats besides that of Sir Anthony Lechmere. The Baronet is advanced in years, a wealthy and prosperous banker at Worcester and Tewkesbury, a successful speculator and experienced agriculturist, in a word gifted with much worldly wisdom. He has ceased to make his delightful mansion here his home, but keeps it up as a residence for his unmarried daughters & their brother by his first wife, with whom he had a considerable fortune. The reason of this arrangement is, that the charms of a fair bar-maid at Worcester had made such an impression on the susceptible heart of the baronet, that after vainly tempting the damsel to engage in an illicit connexion by the most promising offers of settlement, he was fain at last to make her his wedded wife, or forego the prize. This young person's name was Villers, more remarkable for good sense and conduct than for beauty; she is a native of Gloucester, where her father followed the occupation of a little schoolmaster, while her mother superintended a shop for the sale of cordials, pickles, ham, gin & bitters; a specious dame, who kept also a servants register office, and was bustling and active in her vocation. Of late she has ceased to vend glasses of spirits to passers by, but continues her trade in made wines, pickles, hams & tongues. Such being the new Lady Lechmere's parentage, she shewed much discretion in inducing her spouse to resign the Rhydd to his daughters, who were not likely to acquiesce with satisfaction in the ... connexion formed by their father ... and how a handsome house in Worcester is the stated residence of the married pair. The propriety of Lady L's conduct, however, had been such, that after her marriage there was no hesitation on the part of persons of consequence and respectability in Worcester and its vicinity, to visit her in her new capacity, nor have I heard, that she comports herself less becomingly in the drawing room, than she did at the bar.... Mrs. Lechmere (first) having been sister to the late admirable Lady Reade, whose death a few years since was so just a cause of affliction to Sir John Reade of Shipton, whom she left with a family of young children. We were most obligingly received by two of the Miss Lechmeres, and greatly admired the prospect from the house.*

LECHMERE — Anthony Berwick Lechmere — *see also* Darell[49]

Anthony Berwick Lechmere (1802-1878), Church of England clergyman, was born at Hanley Castle, Worcestershire, the second son of Sir Anthony Lechmere, 1st baronet (1762-1849), and Mary Berwick (1767-1820). He was educated at Christ Church, Oxford (BA 1824; MA 1826), and was appointed vicar of Eldersfield, Worcestershire, in 1826. He later served as vicar of Welland, Worcestershire, in 1828-76 and Hanley Castle, Worcestershire, in 1839-78. He married, at Upton-on-Severn, Worcestershire, 11 October 1842, Emily Mary (1810-1869), daughter of Sir Harry Verelst Darell, 2nd baronet (1768-1828), and Amelia Mary Anne Beecher (1789-1878), and elder sister to Sir Lionel Darell, 4th baronet of Fretherne, Gloucestershire.

1834: 10 Sep: *Again a large dinner party: 17 sat down to table. Besides the inmates of Peach Field Lodge, and my cousin John, there were Mr. Turbervile, Rector of Hanley, Dr. Card and Mr. Thrupp, two Miss Lechmere's, the daughters of Sir Anthony L., with their brother, Mr. Berwick Lechmere, a beneficed Clergyman in this neighbourhood.*

1840: 13 Apr: *It was settled that the following Gentlemen should be invited to attend as Officiating Clergymen, at Medical Attendant, and Pall Bearers; the Revd. Dr. Card, and Revd. Mr. Simms, Vicar and Curate of the parish; Mrs. Addison; Revd. Messrs. B. Lechmere, Plumtre, Philpot, Dean, Thrupp.* 24 Apr: *The other Gentlemen were the Revd. Berwick Lechmere, Incumbent of Hanley Castle and Welland, Son of Sir Anthony Lechmere, of the Rhydd, Rural Dean of Powick Deanery, with whom I had a previous acquaintance: he succeeded to Hanley on the decease of George Turberville.*

1845: 21 Mar: *A letter from G. Siers, requesting me to recommend him to Mr. Berwick Lechmere as a fit person to fill the office of Hall Keeper, now vacant at the County Courts, Worcester.* 22 Mar: *Wrote to Mr. Berwick Lechmere, speaking favourable by G. Siers, but explaining that his wife's levity and misconduct had caused me to dismiss him from my service.—To George Siers, that I had so written to Mr. B.L.* 25 Mar: *A letter from Mr. A B Lechmere in answer to mine respecting George Siers, whom, of course, he does not encourage, after what I stated as to the character of his wife to offer himself as a candidate for the situation of hall-keeper at Worcester.* 8 Jul.

1847: 20 Oct: *Met an old acquaintance Barwick Lechmere, the Rector of Hanley Castle, Worcestershire, son of Sir A. Lechmere, and Brother of Mr. Lechmere, the Banker, of Worcester and Malvern.*

LECHMERE — Edmund Hungerford Lechmere — *see also* David Murray[50]

Sir Edmund Hungerford Lechmere, 2nd baronet (1792-1856), banker, was born at Worcester, eldest son of Sir Anthony Lechmere, 1st baronet (1762-1849), and Mary Berwick (1767-1820). He was educated at Worcester College, Oxford (BA 1813; MA 1816), and succeeded as 2nd baronet in 1849. He married, at St James's, Westminster, 22 June 1819, Maria Clara (1788-1865), daughter of David Murray and sister of Louisa, Lady Reade, née Murray; they had 1 son and 2 daughters:

1 Mary Clara Elizabeth (1824-1894)
1 Edmund Anthony Harley (1826-1894), MP; succeeded as 3rd baronet
2 Louisa Augusta (1829-1906)

1820: 3 Mar.

1823: 8 Jan: *Dined at Oddington with Lady Reade and Sir John. The usual showy display, & well lighted cheer. A large party as of old, Sir H. & Lady Dryden, Sir C. & Lady Imhoff, Mr. & Mrs. Lechmere, the Penystones &c.*

1825: 17 May: *Sir Anthony's Son and heir resides chiefly in London and its vicinity: he is a very well informed man, who has profited much by foreign travel, and married Miss Murray, a niece of Lord Elibank and maid of honour to Queen Charlotte, a very pleasing woman, but without much fortune. I have met them both in society in our own neighbourhood.*

1847: 20 Oct: *Met an old acquaintance Barwick Lechmere, the Rector of Hanley Castle, Worcestershire, son of Sir A. Lechmere, and Brother of Mr. Lechmere, the Banker, of Worcester and Malvern. He informed me of a sad grief in his family, the conversion of a young girl, his brother's daughter, to the Church of Rome. She is first cousin of Compton Reade, and his sisters, having lost her Aunt, the wife of Sir John Reade, who, with her sister, Mrs. Lechmere, was a Miss Murray, of the Elibank family.*

LEDIARD — James Lediard[51]

James Lediard (±1758-1833), Church of England clergyman, was the son of Thomas Lediard of Bristol. The family were friends with Charles Wesley. He was educated at Balliol College, Oxford (BA 1781), and in 1788 took up the post of curate to Edward Innes, the rector of Devizes, Wiltshire. On the death of Innes, Lediard became rector, and remained so from 1789 to 1833.

1806: 24 Sep: *Rode to the Clergy meeting at Devizes for the purpose of raising a fund for the orphans & widows of the Clergy of the County of Wilts, to which I subscribed my quota. Conversed chiefly with Ward of Bradford Dr. Skinner, Ledyard, C. Mayo, &c. met Mrs. Hillier &c.* 13 Oct: *Upon my return met Jaques & walked with him & with Lediard.*

1807: 30 Jan: *Called upon Miss Tylee. Conversed with Mr. Ledyard &c.* 18 Feb: *Rode forth to get Erchfont served during my absence & a testimonial to shew the Bp. Accomplished the former by calling upon Mr. Lancaster at Patney, the latter by waiting upon Jaques, Lediard, & Higginson.* 16 Mar: *Called upon Mr. Ledyard & Mr. John Tylee.* 25 May, 18 Dec: *Called upon Mr. Lediard.*

1808: 10 Feb: *Called on Mrs. Hillier & Harriet. Met Lediard with them.* 27 Apr: *Attended the Clergy meeting, as Steward of the Pottern Deanry. Paid my arrears. The party at Dinner consisted of Dr. Welles, Mr. Francis, Mr. Mayo, Mr. Ledyard, Mr. Dodwell, Mr. Williams, Herbert Hawes, Mr. Seymour, & Mr. Goddard. A very good dinner, & wine tolerable. Some quarreling ensued & much folly was uttered.*

LEE — Elizabeth Lee[52]

Elizabeth Lee, née Harcourt (1739-1811), was the daughter of Simon, 1st Earl Harcourt. She married, 1763, Sir William Lee, 4th baronet (1726-1799), of Hartwell, Buckinghamshire. Lee was first cousin to William Lee (1726-1778) of Totteridge.

1801: 19-20 May, 22 May, 3 Jun: *Lady E. Lee ; Repaired in the Evening to Lady Lytteltons, where was rather a squeeze & music., Miss Guydickens's, Lady E. Lee, Mr. E. Stanhope, & a French Count & Countess &c. Miss Hadsley's played & Miss Halifax sung; Miss Bowles played, & Miss Canning sung.*

LEE — Harry Lee[53]

Harry Lee (1765-1838), Church of England clergyman, was born at Winchester, son of Revd Harry Lee and Caroline Michel. He was educated at New College, Oxford (BA 1785; MA 1789), and was a fellow of the college in 1782-89. He was a fellow of Winchester in 1789, vicar of Hound with Bursledon, Hampshire, in 1812, perpetual curate of Hamble in 1815, and prebendary of Hereford in 1821-38. He married, at St Michael's, near Winchester, Hampshire, 8 May 1790, Philippa Blackstone (b. ±1769); they had at least 2 sons:

1 William Blackstone (1794-1874)
2 Harry (1795-1880)

1826: 5 Jun: *I dined at Mr. Twisleton's at Adlestrop, & there met the amiable old Bishop of Hereford, Dr. Huntingford, returning from Hereford to Winchester; his Lordship seems to enjoy as firm health as he did last year. He was accompanied by a Mr. Lee, I believe, a Master of Winchester College, and connected by marriage with the present Bishop of Gloucester, a quick agreeable man.*

LEE — John Lee — *see* John Fiott

LEE — John Lee, Roman Catholic priest at Hatherop[54]

John Lee (1768-1839), Roman Catholic priest, was born in London and educated at Douay. He served at Hatherop and then moved to the Bavarian chapel, London. He died in 1839.

1823: 10 Jan: *Attended the quarterly Petty Sessions at Northleach Bridewell, after which I went to dine and sleep at Mr. Price's, the Rector of Coln St. Dennis. Met there among others a Mr. Lee, a Roman Catholic Priest, residing at Hatherop in this County, where he has a chapel.*

LEE — John Edward Lee[55]

John Edward Lee (1808-1887), antiquary and geologist, was born at Newland, Kingston-upon-Hull. His early interest in science was fostered by Hull's Literary and Philosophical Society, founded in 1822, and by the society's museum.

For several years Lee travelled for the benefit of his health, visiting Norway and Sweden, and later Russia and other parts of the Continent. During that period he learned French and German, and made sketches. On his return to Britain he joined the staff of J. J. Cordes & Co. (ironworks) at Monmouth. In leisure hours he turned to geology and the Roman archaeology of Caerleon. He was a founder of the Monmouth and Caerleon Antiquarian Society and a frequent contributor to the society's *Proceedings*. In connection with his geological interest, Lee accumulated a vast collection of fossils, exchanging specimens and corresponding with other collectors in Europe and America. He presented his fossils, comprising over 21,000 specimens contained in thirty-one cabinets, to the British Museum in 1885. He married, 1846, Anne Graveley (1809-1885).

1843: 15 Oct: *Recd. a letter from E.F.W: all well at Stanway, he comes into this neighbourhood on Wednesday and Thursday, on a geological excursion with three other naturalists, the Revd.— Brodie of Hatherley, Mr. E. Lees of Worcester, and Mr. Buckman of Cheltenham.* 19 Oct: *As I approached Harford Bridge, stumbled on my Son, with Messrs. Brodie, Lee & Buckman, busy with their geological hammers; they had devoted yesterday and today to observations on geology, botany, and ecclesiastical architecture on Kineton hill among the Stonesfield slate quarries, at Swell, Stow, Upper Slaughter &c. sleeping last night at Stow.*

LEE — John Lee, bookseller and librarian, of Cheltenham[56]

John Lee (1787-1859), bookseller and librarian, was born at Chepping Wycombe, Buckinghamshire, a son of John Lee and Mary Vickers. He was married to Mary Anne (±1786-1847); they had at least 2 daughters and 1 son:

1 Matilda (b. ±1821)
1 Lewis/Louis (b. ±1822)
2 Elizabeth (b. ±1824)

The family lived at 384 High Street, Cheltenham, where John Lee also had his trading premises. By 1851 John was a widower, retired, and living at Grosvenor Place, Cheltenham, in lodgings with his daughter Elizabeth, a governess.

1840: 10 Oct: *a note from Lea, the Bookseller of Cheltenham, requesting directions as to the binding of a set of Books which I had left with him, when we were last at Cheltenham.* 15 Oct: *I omitted to mention on Tuesday a letter which I wrote to Mr. Lee, Bookseller, Cheltenham in reply to his which reached me on the 10th. Inst.*

1844: 25 Jul: *wrote to Mr. Lee, bookseller, Cheltenham, desiring to know the price of a church bible and prayer book, bound in rough calf, folio or quarto.* 29 Jul., 3 Aug: *Wrote to Mr. Lee, Bookseller, Cheltenham, with an order for a Church Bible and prayer book, such as have been selected by the Churchwardens for type and price.*

1848: 10 Jan: *Wrote to Mr. Lea, Bookseller, Cheltenham, requesting him to send me a parcel of Bibles.* 12 Jan: *A note from Mr. Lee, bookseller, Cheltenham, who has sent a packet of Bibles and Prayer books, from which Emily Lea may select such as she may wish to present to her brothers.* 15 Jan: *Wrote to Mr. Lee, Bookseller, Cheltenham, returning to him the parcel of Bibles and Prayer books which he had sent, that Emily Lea might select two of each for a dying present to her elder brothers.*

LEE — Louisa Lee and the Lee family of Totteridge Park — *see also* Arrowsmith *and* Fiott [57]

Louisa Lee (1766-1840) was the daughter of William Lee (1726-1778) and Philadelphia Dyke (±1729-1799). Louisa married, 1802, Edward Arrowsmith (1742-1827), a retired coal merchant. They lived at Totteridge Park in Hertfordshire, where Louisa's mother, Philadelphia Lee, ruled as head of the household.

Louisa Lee was one of Agnes Witts's closest friends, and is mentioned 272 times in her diaries, mostly in relation to letters received and sent. It is not known for certain when their friendship began. The first reference in the Witts family papers is in Agnes Witts' diary for 17 November 1789:

> After 10 o'clock it began being very violent hard rain & so continued the whole of the Day. Mr. Witts was again obliged to go to Town in the hope of completing his bussiness but in vain, & join'd me at Totteridge Park at Dinner in a Hired Post Chaise, I found the road good thro Harrow on the Hill, Stanmore, & Edgeware about 16 miles, & the country seem'd to abound in many beauties if the weather would have permitted me a sight of them; met with a very polite reception from Mrs. Lee & a real friendly one from her Daughters; a large handsome old House & place, with many comforts in & about it, Mr. & Mrs. Fiott (another Daughter) & a Miss Lygett a Lady with them dined & supt at Totteridge, & a Mr. Arrowsmith was staying in the House, a lively pleasant middle aged Man, a very handsome Dinner & everything quite in a stile of hospitality; a Table at Whist & Cribbage I play'd at the former.

From this entry it appears that Agnes was already well acquainted with Louisa Lee and Harriet Fiott, but was meeting Mrs Philadelphia Lee and Mr Arrowsmith for the first time.

Philadelphia Lee was the daughter of Sir Thomas Dyke, 2nd baronet, and Anne Bluet, née Hart, widow of John Bluet, of Holcomb Regis, Devon, and heiress of Percival Hart of Lullingstone, Kent. Philadelphia's husband, William Lee (1726-1778), was the son of Sir William Lee (1688-1754), of Hartwell, and his first wife, Ann Goodwin. Sir William was MP for Hartwell in 1727-30, a justice of the king's bench in 1730, and lord chief justice of England and Wales from 1737 until his sudden death in 1754. In that year he was also appointed chancellor of the exchequer as a temporary expedient. His son, William Lee, of Totteridge, had a first cousin also named William Lee (1726-1799); he was made a 4th baronet (*see above,* Elizabeth Lee). William and Philadelphia, of Totteridge, had at least 1 son and 4 daughters:

1 Philadelphia (1762-1836); died unmarried
2 Harriet (1763-1794); married, 19 July 1782, John Fiott (1749-1797)
1 William (1764-1815), MP; *see below*
3 Louisa (1766-1840); married, 1802, Edward Arrowsmith
4 Sophia (1768-1812); died unmarried

Louisa's sister, Harriet, married John Fiott, merchant, of London, who was descended from an old Burgundian family of Dijon. This family later settled in Jersey and John Fiott ended up in Totteridge where he became acquainted with the Lee family. There is a detailed account under the entry for Fiott. Louisa's other sisters, Philadelphia (d. 1836) and Sophia (d. 1812), both died unmarried. She had one brother, William Lee Antonie (1764-1815), MP (*below*). He lived on the other family estate of Colworth, Bedfordshire.

1801: 1 May: *with Miss Lee's of Totteridge Park, near Barnet.* 29 May: *The three Miss Lee's breakfasted & spent the whole forenoon with us.* 2 Jun: *my Father, Mother & myself left Town accompanied by Miss Lee's, who obligingly came to carry us to their seat. It is situated 10 miles from the Metropolis, near Barnet.* 6 Jun: *While Miss Lee took my Father & Mother to North Mims, the seat of Mr. Browne, I accompanied Miss Louisa &c to call upon Genl. Maitland a most singular antique; who resides here with a wife & two Daughters: his Son, whom we had known in Scotland is now at Totteridge.* 13 Aug: *Miss Lees, Mr. Fiott & Miss Fiott breakfasted and dined with us. We walked in the morning with these kind friends, who shewed us seperately the greatest friendship.* 14 Aug: *Wrote Letters from Dresden & to Mr. Debrett: also to Miss L. Lee.* 30 Jun., 2 Jul., 11 Sep: *Miss Lees called here.* 12 Oct: *Miss Lees came soon after breakfast, & staid till three o'clock.*

1802: 8 Jan., 11 Jan: *A Ball in the Evening at Mr. Ellill's; Geo. also there: very animated & agreable. Danced with Miss Lee, 'Miss Rivington', Miss Guysom, Miss Nicholson, P. Fiott, &c.* 5 Feb: *The dear Miss Lee's spent the morning in Town & I was much with them.* 16 Mar: *Wrote to Miss L. Lee.*

1803: 5 Oct: *Left Montpellier Row in the forenoon with my Father & Mother for Lee, Arrowsmith & Co. at Totteridge Park.* 11 Oct: *Rode with Miss S. Lee to Southgate & to see Nicholas Fiott.*

1836: 4 Nov: *Totteridge was once, many years ago, well known to me, as I visited there with my Parents the family of the Lees of Totteridge Park, three Sisters, one of whom, subsequently, married Mr. Arrowsmith, whom she survived, and still resides at Totteridge, the only one of the sisters remaining.*

LEE ANTONIE — William Lee Antonie [58]

William Lee Antonie (1764-1815), MP and landed proprietor, was born at Totteridge, the only son of William Lee (1726-1778) and Philadelphia Dyke (1733-1799). He was educated at Westminster School and succeeded his distant cousin Richard Antonie, of Colworth, in 1771, taking the additional surname of Antonie. He succeeded his father in 1778. Lee Antonie was a major of the Bedfordshire Volunteers in 1803, and MP for Great Marlow in 1790-96 and Bedford in 1802-12.

On the death of his father, Lee Antonie was entrusted to the care of his father's first cousin, Sir William Lee, of Hartwell, whose superintendence was fussily assisted by John Fiott (1749-1797), husband of his sister, Harriet. In 1781 the Buckinghamshire estates of Little Marlow and Medmenham were purchased on Lee Antonie's behalf; according to a local resident the interest deriving from them, 'with proper attention and management, would always command a seat' for Great Marlow. However, to Fiott's exasperation, his brother-in-law proved a reluctant and lazy politician from the outset. When, in 1786, the former was negotiating on the latter's behalf for the acquisition of additional property in the borough, Lee Antonie was touring the Continent with his mistress. Two years later, when a dissolution was expected, he was cajoled into making a brief visit to Marlow to declare his intention of standing. However, Lee Antonie preferred his Colworth estate to Little Marlow and began to establish himself in the whig society of Bedfordshire and London.

John Fiott continued to look with dismay on Lee Antonie's flaunted and 'unhappy connexion' with his mistress, and on other things besides. On the eve of the general election of 1790, he wrote despairingly to his brother-in-law's guardian, Sir William Lee, of Hartwell, of Lee Antonie's persistent neglect of the electors, which threatened to ruin his chances, and his 'continued want of attention towards his best friends, and disregard of what is meant for his good'. Lee Antonie was nevertheless returned unopposed, although he abandoned the borough in 1796. At the request of some of his supporters he permitted Fiott to contest it on his interest, but after Fiott's heavy defeat he concerned himself no further with Marlow, and he sold his Buckinghamshire estates in 1810.

Lee Antonie's friendship with his Bedfordshire neighbour, the younger Samuel Whitbread, was strengthened by their joint formation, with the 5th duke of Bedford, of the Oakley Hunt in 1798, of which William Lee Antonie was the first master. It was Whitbread who recommended him to the 6th duke when he was casting round for a candidate for Bedford in 1802. Considerable blandishment from Whitbread was necessary, however, before Lee Antonie consented to become his colleague. Bedford told Lord Holland on 1 March 1810 that Whitbread 'generally takes care of' Lee Antonie, and he trailed somewhat half-heartedly in his friend's political wake for the rest of his parliamentary career. William Lee Antonie remained a loyal whig in opposition, but began to withdraw from county affairs in 1809 when he gave up mastership of the Oakley Hunt. By the summer of 1811, under pressure from the duke, he had decided to retire from parliament, and did so at the dissolution of 1812. He died unmarried in 1815.

1801: 13 Jun: *Mr. Lee Anthony spent the day a most handsome wellbred gentleman.*

1802: 20 Jan: *Walked down to Highgate & thence drove myself conveniently hither in a Taxed Cart. Met here at dinner Mr. Lee, Mr. & Mrs. Pugett, Mrs Garrow & Mr. Marsham. Played at Commerce.* 21 Jan: *Jno. Fiott left us, accompanying Mr. Lee to his Seat of Colworth in Beds.*

LEE — Rachel Fanny Antonina— *see also* the Gordon brothers[59]

Rachel Fanny Antonina Lee (±1774-1829), wealthy and outlandish female eccentric, was the illegitimate daughter of Sir Francis Dashwood, 11th Baron le Despencer (1708-1781), rake and politician, chancellor of the exchequer, and founder of the Hellfire Club. He adopted his daughter five years after his long-suffering wife had died, and upon his own death, he left the infant handsomely provided for.

Rachel was 20 years old when, in 1794, she eloped with Matthew Allen Lee, whom she subsequently married. 'Handsome Lee,' he was called, having apparently nothing to boast of besides his face and fortune; a year and a half sufficed for her to tire of the one and run through a considerable portion of the other. They separated, and a settlement of £1,000 was added to Rachel's already large income. Henceforth, she was independent (her mother had committed suicide not long before).

In 1796 Rachel Lee was at Manchester, where she visited the house of Thomas De Quincey's guardian at Greenhay. There she caused a profound commotion, not only by her impromptu performances on the organ, but also by her agnostic views and dangerous powers of disputation, in which she showed herself more than a match for the local clergymen. Her encounter with De Quincey's guardian 'presented,' recalled the writer, 'the distressing spectacle of an old, toothless, mumbling mastiff, fighting for the household to which he owed allegiance against a young leopardess fresh from the forests.' But the principal sufferer was De Quincey's mother, who had a serious nervous attack at discovering (for the first time, apparently) that a person could deny Christianity, and at the thought of the havoc which her visitor's handsome footman might cause in the tender consciences of the female element in the servants' hall. De Quincey preserved a vivid recollection of the episode, and, years after, embodied it in Chapter IV of his *Autobiographical Sketches*—'The Female Infidel'.

For the next few years, the Honourable Mrs Lee (as she now called herself) flitted about the country, changing her residence and her friends with dizzying frequency, and enlivening an otherwise solitary life with a succession of unnecessary quarrels. She was not, of course, without her admirers. These included a young Oxonian named Loudon Gordon, who spent a good deal of his time on her doorstep. On 15 January 1804, he sent her a pathetic message ('Only see me, and treat me like a dog') that secured him an invitation to dinner. With him he brought his brother, the Revd Lockhart Gordon, who despite being a married clergyman had similar appetites to Loudon. The next thing that the Honourable Mrs Lee realised was that she was bowling along the Oxford Road in a postchaise, with her importunate lover and his clerical brother. She resisted all blandishments until a certain point, when she drew from her bosom a gold locket containing a camphor-bag, at which she gazed fondly. 'This,' she said, 'has hitherto preserved my virtue.' The window was providentially open, and she threw it out. 'Now welcome, pleasure!' she said.

They were overtaken two stages out of Oxford. The two young men were arrested on a charge of abduction, and brought up for trial at the Lenten assizes. De Quincey was in court, with many other undergraduates, for old association's sake, and noted that all those in academic costume had their caps smashed in by the staves of the constables (in ordinary life bargemen, and happy to have the chance of avenging past insults with impunity). Mrs Lee, under pressure from her husband, was so unwise as to go into the box to give evidence, but her examination was stopped when she intimated her disbelief in Christianity. In consequence, the Gordon brothers were acquitted, though severely censured, while their 'victim' was mobbed by the irate citizens.

Rachel Lee continued her infamous life until she died, in 1829, leaving behind her an obituary in *The Gentleman's Magazine*, and an enduring claim to a place in the illustrious roll of English female eccentrics.

1804: 6 Mar: *to the Assizes to attend Mr. Lees famous Prosecution of the Gordons, who were acquitted.*

LEE WARNER — Daniel Henry Lee Warner — *see also* Wynniatt[60]

Daniel Henry Lee Warner (1776-1858), landed proprietor, was born at Boxwell, Gloucestershire, son of Henry Lee Warner, formerly Woodward (1752-1835), and Margaret Haworth (1751-1831). His paternal grandparents were Daniel and Mary Woodward; she was the daughter of the Revd Richard Huntley, of Boxwell, Gloucestershire, and Anne, daughter of Col Henry Lee of Donjon, Kent. Daniel Henry Lee Warner's father, Henry, assumed the name Lee Warner upon inheriting the Lee estate.

Lee Warner married, 1806 [one other source says 1808], Anne Henrietta (1788-1868), eldest daughter and co-heir of Francis William Thomas Brydges of Tyberton Court. Her sister,

Catherine, wife of Revd Reginald Wynniatt, of Guiting Grange, Gloucestershire, was her father's other heir. Daniel and Anne had at least 9 sons and 3 daughters:

1 Henry James (1809-1886)
2 Francis Henry (b. 1810)
3 George Brydges (1812-1880)
4 Charles Henry (1816-1870)
5 John (b. 1817)
6 Septimus Henry (1820-1870)
1 Margaret Anna Maria (1822-1903)
7 Robert Henry (1823-1895)
8 William Henry (1826-1896)
9 Thomas Henry (1827-1890)
2 Ann Henrietta (±1829-1903)
3 Mary Isabella (1831-1906)

1845: 14 Mar: *Besides the members of the Wynniatt family there were Mr. Guise, eldest son of the Baronet with his young wife, a niece of Mrs. Wynniatt, and daughter of Mr. Lee Warne.*

1846: 8 Dec: *Dined at Mr. Wynniatt's, Guiting Grange, meeting Mr. and Mrs. Lee Warner, with two daughters, on a visit there.*

1847: 3 Jul: *Wynniatt, with Susan W.,—accompanied by Mr. Lee Warner, Junr. and his lately married lady, called upon us.*

LEES — George Aynslie Lees — *see also* Herbert[61]

George Aynslie Lees, agricultural bailiff, married, at Upper Slaughter, 11 March 1850, Susan Hooker (b. 1824), eldest daughter of Berther Vines Herbert (1787-1859) and Susan Hooker (1795-1841). The couple emigrated to Poland.

1850: 11 Mar: *Miss Herbert, daughter of an Eyford tenant, was married to-day to G. A. Lees; formerly farming bailiff to Mrs. Dolphin, and, since, holding the like situation at Cirencester Agricultural College——a Scotchman, and clever, enterprizing person, as the destination of the couple shews; for they will shortly embark for Hamburgh, whence they will proceed to Warsaw, Lees being engaged to superintend the farming concerns of a Polish nobleman and great landed proprietor, whose son has been for some time studying agriculture at the Cirencester College, and who has already, I believe, sent English labourers and live stock &c. with a view to introduce English systems into his country.*

LEES — Henry Lees — *see also* Lydia Smith *and* Walmesley[62]

Henry Lees (1813-1872), physician, apparently had a wife and large family before he married Lydia Bosworth (1808-1876), daughter of Sir John Wyldbore Smith, 2nd baronet (1770-1852), and Elizabeth Anne Marriott (1770-1847). The name Bosworth came from Lydia's maternal grandfather. One source states that Lydia Bosworth graduated with an MD.

In the 1851 census Sir John Wyldbore Smith was at Blandford St Mary with his son John James (b. ±1800) and daughters Frances (b. ±1803) and Lydia. Henry Lees was a visitor and listed in the census as married. Presumably he obtained a divorce, or perhaps his first wife died; the details are sadly lacking. His marriage to Lydia Bosworth took place in Edinburgh on 4 April 1855.

1852: 27 Dec: *Heard at "the Cottage" that Miss Lydia Smith has taken the fatal plunge which rumour had represented her as having already perpetrated: she is said, on Miss Walmsley's authority, to have gone off last week with Dr. Lees—a physician of Blanford,—a married man with eight or nine children. This is stated to have been a heavy blow to Mrs. Dolphin—What are accomplishments? What are talents? What is fascination of manner, unattended by virtue, and piety, and sound religious principle?*

LEFEVER — Richard Lefever[63]

Richard Lefever (±1777-1861), land agent and steward, was born at Shoreditch, London. He married, first, at St Andrew Undershaft or St Alphage's, London Wall [there are two records for the same marriage, same day, at different churches], 5 May 1805, Ann Halladay (1776-1836); they had at least 1 daughter:

1 Sophia Elizabeth (b. 1808)

He married secondly, at Todenham, Gloucestershire, 12 December 1846, a widow, Frances Lightfoot (b. ±1812).

1834: 7 Aug: *To Stow, to attend at the Provident Bank, and in the Justice room; at the former George Payn took his seat for the first time as book-keeper, with the assistance of Mr. Lefevre, Steward of Mr. Abraham Pole, who since the murder of poor Rens has been engaged as a temporary book-keeper.*

1847: 20 Mar: *Received a letter from Mr. Lefevre as to the valuation of the parish of Toddenham, for the country rate.* 6 Aug: *to Mr. Lefevre, Toddenham, with information which he had requested yesterday as to the County rate Act, and Parochial Assessments act, and proceedings as to valuation of parishes.* 19 Aug., 23 Dec.

1848: 12 Oct: *To the Provident Bank, where Mr. Lefevre acted as sole Clerk, Mr. Pain being confined to his bed.*

LEFFLER — Adam Leffler[64]

Adam Leffler (1808-1857), bass vocalist. Leffler performed at the Three Choirs in 1829 and 1839.

1829: 22 Sep: *The finale of the first act was an admirable piece from Don Giovanni—by Mozart—"Venite pur avante" sung by all the principal performers with the exception of Mrs. W. Knyvett. I have already named them separately, omitting only a Mr. Leffler, who, I believe, comes from Bath & Wells, who seems to have been brought here as a make-weight, a convenient personage, as yet without pretension or fame, but giving promise of future excellence.* 23 Sep.

LEFROY — Anthony Thomas Lefroy[65]

Anthony Thomas Lefroy (1802-1890), chief constable of Gloucestershire (1839-65), was the son of Anthony Thomas Lefroy, born at Limerick, who served as a captain at Gibraltar and the Cape of Good Hope. Anthony Lefroy joined the Irish Police in 1823, and by 1839 he had attained the position of chief constable for co. Wicklow.

At a general quarter sessions for Gloucestershire on 4 November 1839, a discussion took place regarding the formation of a county constabulary and the appointment of a chief constable. Lord Ellenborough said that the magistrates should apply to Col MacGregor at the inspectorate of constabulary in Ireland to see if he had anyone serving under him who would be suitable for the post. He was eager to ensure that there was 'no chance of its being supposed that the office of chief constable was given by acquaintances, by connection with the County, by private intimacy on the part of the magistrates or otherwise than by the appointment of the very best man.' Col MacGregor recommended Lefroy, and on 18 November 1839 he was appointed chief constable of Gloucestershire.

Francis Witts quickly became acquainted with Anthony Lefroy upon his arrival in Gloucestershire; the two men became friends, and were on equally good terms with Thomas Howell (*above*). Lefroy was a frequent overnight guest at Upper Slaughter rectory, and on 30 October 1846, he attended the christening of Francis Witts's grandson, George Backhouse Witts. In the last year of his life, Witts considered that the chief constable had somewhat overstepped his position and the friendship cooled slightly.

1840: 22 Apr: *Met Mr. Lefroy, with whom I conferred on Constabulary business, and whom I accompanied to the Police Station House, where I looked over the arrangements of the office, saw the manner of keeping the accounts, & correspondence, and making the returns, the internal arrangements as relates to the accommodation of the men in barracks, their mess room &c.* 29 Jun., 30 Jun: *Engaged in auditing accounts till the hour for breakfast, at which Bathurst, Purnell and myself were joined by Mr. Lefroy, the Chief Constable.* 30 Jul., 1 Aug., 4 Aug., 25 Aug: *Met with Mr. Lefroy, the Chief Constable of the County of Gloucester, who had called at Upper Slaughter on his road from Northleach.* 19 Oct., 5 Nov: *Mr. Lefroy attended at the meeting, being on a circuit of the Police Stations in this part of the County. He declined my invitation to dine and sleep at Upper Slaughter.*

1842: 7 Jan: *Repaired to the Station House, where passed some time in conferring with Lefroy, and his deputy, Keiley, on Rural Police affairs, advising them as to the Report to be presented to the Easter Sessions, and as to the line to be followed in the present state of public opinion respecting the force.* 11 Mar., 19 Mar: *recd. a letter from Lefroy, who is very uneasy as to his position, expecting that the Police may be broken up, or reduced; and much displeased with the Lord Lieutenant, with whom he has had a recent and unpleasant interview.* 22 Mar: *To Lefroy, on the Constabulary question in answer to his letter, received on the 19th.* 25-26 Mar., 11 Apr., 15 Apr., 1 Jun: *Wrote to A. T. Lefroy about the annexation of the Lower Guiting Police Station to the Stow district, shewing the inconvenience of the Stow Superintendent being required to attend the Petty Sessions at Winchcomb.* 14 Jun., 16 Jun., 17 Jun: *Mr. Lefroy arrived, and dined and slept here.* 18 Jun., 20 Jun., 27 Jun: *I proceeded from Cheltenham by railway to Gloucester, travelling with Lefroy and Keiley.* 22 Jul., 23 Sep: *Called upon and took luncheon with Mr. Lefroy.*, 4 Oct: *Mr. Lefroy also called, and, with C H F., took luncheon here: the Chief Constable was on his survey of Police Stations in this neighbourhood.* 14 Oct., 18 Oct., 7 Nov., 12 Nov., 29 Nov., 1 Dec., 6-7 Dec., 12 Dec: *Before we set out Mr. Lefroy called upon us.* 15 Dec: *A. T. Lefroy joined our party at dinner.* 17 Dec.

1843: 2 Jan., 5 Jan: *Afterwards went with the Howells to Lefroy's lodgings to eat luncheon.* 7 Jan: *When we returned home we found Lefroy, who had arrived from Cheltenham by invitation to stay with us till Monday.* 8-9 Jan., 12 Jan., 1-2 Feb., 16-17 Oct., 19 Oct., 22 Nov: *Mr. Lefroy arrived from Cheltenham on a round of visits to his Constabulary stations.* 23 Nov: *After breakfast Lefroy drove me in his open carriage to Stow, where he visited his Station, and whence he proceeded to Moreton, Blockley, and Campden.* 2 Dec.

1844: 1 Jan., 4 Jan: *At that hour Mr. Lefroy came over in a gig, agreeable to a promise made by him on Tuesday to drive me to Prinknash Park to dine and sleep there.* 5 Jan., 8 Mar., 8 Apr., 13 Apr: *Busily engaged in shopping till 1 P.M. when we repaired to Mr. Lefroy's domicile at the Belle Vue Hotel, who kindly entertained us at luncheon, where we were joined by Emelyn, Constance, and Laura Howell, who had driven in from Prinknash to accompany M W. and me to a morning concert at the Assembly rooms.* 20 Apr: *Mr. Lefroy arrived to pass a day or two with us.* 21-22 Apr., 16 Aug., 14 Oct., 18-19 Oct., 22 Oct: *Mr. Lefroy came from Cheltenham to dine and sleep here.* 23 Oct., 7 Nov., 8 Dec., 16 Dec., 30-31 Dec.

1845: 3 Mar., 7 Mar., 14 Apr., 17 Apr., 8-9 May, 26 May: *Wrote to Mr. Lefroy to invite him to visit us on the 4th. and 5th. June.* 29 May, 4-6 Jun., 30 Jun., 1 Jul: *The affair as to Mr. Keiley was laid before the Court and referred to a committee of enquiry as arranged yesterday. We are to sit after the Shrewsbury agricultural meeting is over: Curtis Hayward and myself being engaged there, and no earlier time could be fixed, so as to allow evidence to be prepared, and due notice given to the Girl and her parents. In the mean time Mr Lefroy will suspend Keiley from the duties of his office.* 8 Jul., 14 Aug: *Mr. Lefroy arrived on one of his Constabulary circuits: he dined and slept here.*

1846: 25 Aug., 19 Oct., 30 Oct: *Mr. Ashworth, an uncle of my dear Sophy's, being the husband of her mother's sister, was represented by Mr. Lefroy.* 1 Nov., 4 Nov.

1847: 4 Jan., 22 Mar., 19 Apr: *Mr. Lefroy came about mid-day, and, having ridden on to Stow and Moreton, to visit the Police Stations there, returned to dine and sleep here.* 20 Apr., 5 May, 15 May: *Mr. Lefroy left us for Cheltenham, making a tour of Stations by Stow, Moreton, Campden &c.* 18 May, 29 May, 28 Jun., 9 Aug., 28 Aug: *Mr. Lefroy called and partook of luncheon with us.* 18 Oct., 23 Oct: *Mr. Lefroy arrived from Cheltenham to pass a day or two with us.* 25 Oct.

1848: 3 Jan., 17 Jan., 20 Jan., 20 Mar., 31 Mar., 26 Apr., 30 Jun: *Called at the Police Station on Mr. Lefroy: looked over the premises with him and Keiley & Hambidge, his deputy and chief Superintendent, with a view to enlargement.* 7 Jul., 14 Sep: *Lefroy returned home with me in my open carriage, sending his horse to my stable by a policeman.* 15 Sep., 16 Oct., 19 Oct.

1849: 10 Dec: *Lefroy left us after breakfast for Cheltenham.* 31 Dec.

1850: 24-25 Jan., 28 Jan., 1-2 Feb., 7 Feb., 8 Mar: *Mr. Lefroy called here on a circuit to visit his police Stations, and partook of luncheon with.* 19 Apr., 3 May, 4 Jun: *Mr. Lefroy came on a visit, and dined & slept here: he accompanied me in my open carriage to Stow.* 5 Jun., 1 Jul., 8 Jul., 14 Oct., 19 Oct: *Called at the Police Station, where I saw Mr. Keiley, and left a message with him, inviting Mr. Lefroy to visit me on Nov. 2, when I expected the Howells to be my guests.* 21 Oct., 2 Nov., 30 Dec.

1851: 29 Jan: *Mr. Lefroy also calling, and with the intention of dining and sleeping here, I persuaded F.A. to remain and meet the Chief Constable, sending to Northleach to bring a change of clothes for the young man from the Vicarage, and inform his family that he would return tomorrow.* 30 Jan., 8 Mar: *Mr. Lefroy also arrived, whom my Son had invited to pass two days, in the expectation of meeting there Laura and Constance Howell.* 17 Mar., 20 Mar: *Partook of Luncheon at Lefroy's lodgings, who had sought me out.* 25 Mar: *Received a letter from Lefroy, announcing his approaching marriage with Miss Elliott, a young lady of Cheltenham, twenty years his junior, to whom he has been attached for four years.* 26 Mar., 26 Apr: *Wrote to congratulate Lefroy on his approaching union with Miss Elliott; all preliminaries are settled.* 30 Apr: *Received a letter from Lefroy in answer to mine of congratulation: he is to be married on May 12th.* 14 May: *Mr. & Mrs. Lefroy having been married on the 12th. Inst. I received from them today the compliment of cards and a wedge of wedding cake.* 19 May: *The Lefroys are passing the honeymoon at Leamington.*

1852: 18 Feb: *Lefroy called on me, being on his round of visiting stations, but would not stay for the night.* 15 Mar., 16

Mar: *Having received a note of invitation from Mrs. Lefroy, to dine and sleep at Swindon on Thursday and Friday, told L. that I would accept his hospitality for Thursday, but must return home on the following day.* 18-19 Mar., 20 May, 20 Dec: *Mr. Lefroy came from Cheltenham, to dine & sleep here.* 21 Dec., 28 Dec: *Received a kind note of invitation from Mrs. Lefroy, urging me to come to them at Swindon on Thursday the 6th. from the Quarter Sessions at Gloucester, and to stay till Saturday.* 29 Dec.

1853: 3 Jan., 6 Jan: *Lefroy met me in his open carriage at the Cheltenham Station, I betook myself with Lefroy to Swindon, where I had a very kind reception from Mrs. L. and was introduced to Miss Whittle, a niece of Lefroy's, now on a visit to him, and whose residence is with her parents at Helmsley in Yorkshire.— The Lefroy's infant girl of six months old, is a healthy and pretty baby.* 7 Jan., 15 Jan., 20 Jan., 14 Mar., 6 May, 10 May: *letter from Mrs. Lefroy announced that she is afraid to accept my invitation to visit me with her husband, owing to her baby being a little indisposed with teething, and the coldness of the weather deterring her from bringing the infant.* 10 May, 11 May: *Mr. Lefroy, anxious that his wife should join our party, drove to Cheltenham and back between eleven in the forenoon, and six o clock in the afternoon, and returned accompanied by Mrs. Lefroy.... A dinner party—entertained Mr. and Mrs. Winter, Mr. and Mrs. R Waller, Mr. and Mrs. Lefroy, Mrs. W. V ... Mrs. Lefroy performing very well on the Piano.* 12 May, 22 Jun., 25 Jun: *Lefroy drove from Cheltenham and arrived while I was at breakfast; he came with a heavy heart, and sad countenance. All things he said were against him: Mrs. L. was very ill, having miscarried; and his Deputy, Keiley, had absconded with more than £400 of the County money, on Thursday night.* 27 Jun.

1854: 7 Feb: *Wrote to Purnell in answer to his last letter, and with special reference to the course now taken by the Chief Constable, shewing that he considers the vote of the majority at the Epiphany Sessns. to have rescinded all the orders made at the previous Sessions in respect of the Constabulary; and so to have annihilated the Police Committee, to have absolved him from the necessity of finding security for £1000, to have brought down the increased pay of the force to its former standard, and, in a word, to have placed him and the Constabulary on the same footing as before the Michs. Sessions.* 14 Feb: *After an early breakfast drove to Cheltenham in my close carriage, and proceeded thence by rail to Gloucester, travelling with Talbot and Lefroy to a meeting of the Police Committee.... It appears also that the Lord Lieutenant had an interview with Talbot and Lefroy yesterday, and that the latter is advised to address a letter to the Chairman of the Police Committee apologizing for the wrong construction of the Epiph. Sessns. order on which he had acted.* 22 Mar: *The Chief Constable to find Security for the public money passing through his hands. The districts of Cheltenham & Tewkesbury to be thrown into one with two Superintendents resident at Cheltenham; the Accounts to be kept as formerly by Lefroy and his deputy Chief Constable— in a word, Lefroy to be reinstated on the old footing as before Keiley's defalcation, & the Clerk to be dismissed. Thus all the plans and alterations projected by Purnell and those who acted with him in Committee, or nearly all, are negatived, and Lefroy and his partizans, headed by the Lord Lieutenant & Talbot, gain a signal victory.* 23 Mar: *A letter from E.F.W. with an account of what passed at the Quarter Sessions on Thursday especially as to Purnell's resumption of the County Chair, on the motion of Lord Fitzhardinge, seconded by Talbot. Every point for which Purnell and his friends had struggled as to the Police arrangements, is by P. conceded: so that Lefroy and his partizans ride triumphant, and Purnell goes back without power to contest any proposition advocated by the dominant party.* 1 May, 6 May: *A note from Mr. Lefroy in answer to mine of the 1st. Inst.; he will admit G. Bantin into the Police Force on production of the Certificate of his marriage with M. A. Coleman.*

LEGATE — Mrs Legate at Clifton

The diarist gives two versions of this lady's name: Leogate and Legeete. Agnes Witts mentioned her just once, on 25 September 1804, using the name Legate. All three mentions occurred over the short date span of 25 to 27 September 1804. It seems likely that she was a visitor for a short period to one of the Clifton Irish set.

1804: 26 Sep: *In the evening, walked with Mrs. Townsend, Mrs. Brenton & Mrs. Leogate.* 27 Sep: *pleasant party at Lady Fingals Singing moderately by Mrs. Menton & Mrs. Legeete. Lady Hunloke amazing.*

LEGG — Richard Legg, Joseph Legg, and the Legg or Legge family of Market Lavington [66]

The Legge family farmed Grove Farm, which consisted of about 300 acres. A probable relation, John Legg, lived in Market Lavington from around 1755 to 1802. In 1780 he wrote a book on the migration of birds, which uncovered several previously unknown facts; it was published anonymously under the sobriquet, 'a naturalist'. John was a bachelor, but the Legg family who entertained Francis Witts were presumably relations.

Among the beneficiaries of Edith Pope's will, published in 1791, were Jane Legg, Mary Legg, and Elizabeth Legg ('the Leggs of Market Lavington, Spinsters'); the executor was named as 'Richard Legg of Market Lavington, Gentleman'. In 1840 Grove Farm was owned by Elizabeth Ford Legge.

1806: 21 Sep., 22 Oct: *Mrs. Butcher in the Evening gave a rout & supper, at which were present our family the Comptons & Legges: not very unpleasant.* 23 Oct: *Drank tea, played cards, & supped at Mrs. Legges, meeting the Butchers & Comptons & played at Commerce, not wholly disagreeable.* 28 Oct: *Met a party to Tea & Supper at Mr. Compton's, the Legg's, Butchers, Mr. W. Keetch & ourselves. Played at Commerce, not unpleasantly.* 31 Oct: *Mrs. Compton's, Mrs. Butcher's & Mrs. Legg's families met at the Vicarage to tea, cards & supper; not unpleasant.* 15 Dec., 19 Dec: *Drank tea plaid cards & supped at Butcher's: Mrs. & Miss Legg, Miss Smith.* 23 Dec: *Mr. Butcher, his wife, brother Charles & Miss Smith, met Mrs. & Miss Legg to tea, cards & supper at the Vicarage.*

1807: 18 Jan., 13 Apr., 13 May, 22 May, 3 Jun: *Wrote to Mr. Walsh of Oxford. Poor Joseph Legg died.* 8 Jun: *Attending poor Joseph Legg's funeral M. Lavington 1 Hearse 11 Coach. Mr. Smith. Apoth. the Father Brother & myself. Mr. Williams met us at the Church yard wicket.* 16 Jul., 20-21 Jul., 24 Jul., 18 Aug: *Mr. & Mrs. Legg & Miss Trusler, Mr. & Mrs. Butcher drank tea— cards.* 20 Aug., 30 Aug., 2 Sep: *Mrs. Legg & her family party, viz Braham, Strace, her Mother, visited me after dinner.* 17 Dec.

1808: 19 Jan: *Mrs. Legg called in the morning.* 15 Feb., 15 Mar., 20 Mar., 16 Apr., 25 Apr: *Drank tea at the Legg's. Met Mrs. Butcher.* 30 Apr: *Walked in the fields, with Mesdames Butcher & Legg. Dined at home, drank tea & supped at the Legg's, meeting Butcher & his wife & M. Giddings & his wife.*

LEGGE — Edward Legge [67]

Edward Legge (1767-1827), bishop of Oxford, was born at Westminster, seventh son William George Legge, 2nd earl of

Dartmouth (1731-1801), and Frances Catherine Nicoll (1733-1805). He was educated at Rugby School and Christ Church, Oxford (BA 1788). He migrated to All Soul's College (BCL 1791; DCL 1805), where he was fellow in 1789 and warden in 1817-27. He served as vicar of Lewisham, Kent, in 1797-1827, prebendary of Winchester in 1795 and Canterbury in 1797, canon of Windsor in 1802 and dean in 1805, and bishop of Oxford in 1815-27.

Henry Reeve, editor of *The Greville Memoirs*, wrote in a footnote, 'The *Musæ Cateatonenses*, a burlesque narrative of a supposed expedition of Mr George Legge to Cateaton Street in search of a Swiss chapel. Nothing can be more droll. The only copy I have seen is still at Saltram. This *jeu d'esprit* (which fills a volume) was composed by Canning and his friends one Easter recess they spent at Ashbourne.' It is therefore unclear whether the subject of the *jeu d'esprit* was George or Edward Legge.

1826: 9 Apr: *It had always been surmised, that Dr. Legge, the present Bishop of Oxford would be Dr. Barrington's successor: & his Lordship has for many years performed many episcopal functions for the late Prelate of Durham; such as consecration, confirmation &c: but the interest of the Dartmouth family is not such as in the late King's reign, & Dr. Legge, though an amiable & very respectable man, is not a luminary of the Church.*

1844: 22 Aug: *In the evening Mr. B. read to us from a MS. a lively jeu d'esprit of considerable length, entitled Musæ Cateatonenses, being a satire on the Earl of Morley and Dr. Legge, Bishop of Oxford, in their early days, on occasion of a visit to Cateaton Street, in search of a supposed Swiss Preacher holding forth in some chapel there, the authors being Canning, Lord Seaford, his brother and a Mr. Sneyd.*

LEGGE — George Augustus Legge[68]

George Augustus Legge (1801-1826), Church of England clergyman, was born at Wonston, Hampshire, son of Augustus George Legge (1773-1828) and Honora Bagot (1775-1863). He was educated at Christ Church, Oxford (BA 1824), and served as vicar of Bray in 1825-26. He married, at Bray, 23 August 1825, Frances Augusta Bowyer.

1824: 12 Sep: *Shortly after Mr. Wellford became Curate of Bray, near Maidenhead, where his sentiments & opinions were all congenial: the Vicar, Mr. Townsend, an excellent man, was like himself serious; and similar religious views prevailed in the parish & neighbourhood: there M. Wellford has now for several years resided, much respected & beloved; but is likely to be removed ere long, as the former Vicar being dead, the living is now held for a short term by a non-resident, who will resign it to a nephew of the Bishop of Oxford, as soon as he shall be of age to take Priest's orders. Mr. Legge, however, is not yet Deacon.*

1825: 4 Jul: *At Mr. Wellford's we met Mr. & Mrs. Bowyer Atkins of Braywick, and their daughter a very fine young woman, who is on the point of marriage to the Revd. Mr. Legge, who was also of the party, a very pleasing young man. He is son of the Hon. & Revd. Mr. Legge, a Prebendary of Winchester & brother of the late Earl Dartmouth, & of the present Bishop of Oxford... When Mr. Legge, who is a Student of Christ Church, entered into Deacon's Orders, he came to Bray, as assistant Curate to Wellford, in order to gain an acquaintance, with the parish, which was soon to be placed under his care; & although Mr. Legge & Mr. Wellford have not been brought up in exactly the same school of divinity, yet such has been the right feeling, such the good sense, and just appreciation of merit as belonging to each, that on the approaching institution of Mr. L. to the vicarage, the connexion, as between Vicar and Curate, is not to cease.*

1827: 12 Jun: *Mr. G. Wellford drove over from Bray to tea and spent an hour with us. He looked ill, and has been indisposed. He retains the Curacy of that parish under the new Vicar Mr. Levett, who succeeded about a twelvemonth since to the living, on the decease of the late amiable young Incumbent, Mr. Legge, whom I met two years since at my friend Wellfords' lodgings in the Hospital at Bray.*

LEGGE — William Legge[69]

William Legge, 4th earl of Dartmouth (1784-1853), MP and landed proprietor, was the eldest son of George Legge, 3rd earl of Dartmouth (1755-1810). He was educated at Eton College and Christ Church, Oxford (BA 1805; DCL 1834), and was MP for Milborne Port in 1810. He married, first, 1821, Frances Charlotte (1801-1823), daughter of Charles Chetwynd, 2nd Earl Talbot. He married secondly, 1828, Frances (1802-1849), second daughter of George Barrington, 5th Viscount Barrington. William Legge succeeded his father as 4th earl of Dartmouth in 1810.

1805: 29 Mar: *At an Examination, where Lord Lewisham distinguished himself.*

LEIGH — Chandos Leigh — *see also* East[70]

Chandos Leigh, 1st Baron Leigh (1791-1850), poet and literary patron, was born in London, the only child of James Henry Leigh (1765-1823), MP, of Adlestrop, Gloucestershire, and Julia Judith Twisleton (d. 1843), daughter of Thomas Fiennes, 13th Baron Saye and Sele. Chandos's father inherited the Leigh family seat at Stoneleigh Abbey, Stoneleigh, Warwickshire, following the death of his distant cousin Edward Leigh, 5th Baron Leigh. His grandfather was the 2nd duke of Chandos.

Leigh had four sisters: Julia (d. 1871), who married, 1836, Gen. Henry Robert Colvile (d. 1875) of Kempsey House; Caroline Eliza (d. 1870), who married, 27 June 1822, Sir James Buller East, 2nd baronet; Mary (d. 1871), who married, 1817, Frederick Charles Acton Colvile (d. 1872) of Barton House; and Augusta Elizabeth (d. 1877), who married, 1827, Grenville Charles Lennox Berkeley (d. 1896). He was educated at Harrow School, where he was a friend of Byron, and Christ Church, Oxford. He dined with Byron the evening before the poet left England for Europe in April 1816. Leigh Hunt was also a close friend and confidant, and Jane Austen was one of his cousins. She visited Stoneleigh Abbey in 1806 and there is good evidence that it was on Stoneleigh that she based the chapel of Sotherton Court in *Mansfield Park*. Despite illustrious contemporaries, Leigh was to prove himself an author and poet of some repute in his own right.

Chandos Leigh married, 7 June 1819, Margarette (1798-1860), daughter of Revd William Shippen Willes, of Astrop House, Northamptonshire, by his second wife, Margaret (d. 1831), daughter of John Williams of Panthowell, Carmarthenshire. Margarette's parents married on 27 February 1797. Chandos and Margarette had 3 sons and 7 daughters:

1 Julia Anne Eliza (1820-1887); married, at Warwick, 28 July 1842, Charles Bowyer Adderley (1814-1905)

2 Emma Margarette (1822-1892); died unmarried at Hanover Square, Westminster

1 William Henry (1824-1905); succeeded as 2nd Baron Leigh of Stoneleigh; *see below*

3 Augusta (1825-1898); died unmarried at Scarborough, Yorkshire

4 Louisa Georgina (1829-1907)
5 Caroline (1825-1909)
6 Mary (1826-1906); married, 1848, Henry Pitt Cholmondeley, son of Thomas Cholmondeley, 1st Baron Delamere of Vale Royal and Henrietta Elizabeth Williams-Wynn
2 Edward Chandos (1832-1915)
7 Sophia (1838-1926)
3 James Wentworth (1838-1923)

Chandos Leigh inherited his father's 12,000-acre Stoneleigh Park estate in 1823. He was keenly interested in political and social issues with leanings towards the Liberal cause. He was high sheriff for Warwickshire in 1825 and created 1st Baron Leigh in 1839.

All of the Leigh families were related, although going back several generations. Sir Thomas Leigh, of Stoneleigh, married Mary, daughter of Sir Thomas Egerton back in 1615. (*See below*, Egerton Leigh.)

1823: 17 Sep: *Chandos Leigh is an eccentric mortal, possessed of talent, & studious in an odd way. He has been a warm admirer of theatrical performances, & performers male & female; a poet in a small way; one of his earlier productions, "the Pleasures of Love," was by the prudence of his friends suppressed; another little volume has been lauded by the Edinburgh Reviewers; perhaps, not so much for the poetry as the politics of the poet, who with pretensions to hereditary toryism has on more than one occasion betrayed a strong bias to whiggism. He is married to a daughter of the late Mr. Willes of Alstrop, & resides much at Adlestrop, but without taking a share in the public business of the County or neighbourhood.*

1829: 4 Dec: *We dined at Mrs. Hastings's at Daylesford House, meeting a very pleasant party. There were five from Adlestrop; Mr. & Mrs. East, her Mother, the Hon. Mrs. Leigh, (sister of Lord Say and Sele, and widow of the late J. H. Leigh Esqr., of Stoneleigh MP. for Winchester) a person of considerable talent and of an active mind; her son Chandos Leigh Esqr.—the possessor of Stoneleigh Abbey, an eccentric person, but clever in an odd way, and master of a princely fortune; more at ease, now that the vexatious suit is dismissed from the House of Lords, in which a claimant of the dormant barony of Leigh of Stoneley strove by a tissue of fictions, as I verily believe, and some of them calculated to throw great discredit on the Hon. Mrs. Leigh, to establish a claim not only to that dignity, but to the ample estates now in Chandos Leigh's possession. Then there was Miss Leigh, the unmarried sister of Mrs. East, Mrs. Colville & Mrs. Granville Berkeley*

1834: 13 Mar: *To our left were the groves embosoming Mr. Leigh's noble mansion of Stoneleigh Abbey, of which we had a distant and imperfect view.* 18 Jul: *Wrote to Chandos Leigh to solicit his subscription to the Police Assoc. for Stow.* 24 Jul: *A letter from Chandos Leigh, covering his subscription to the Police Association, in answer to the letter I had written on the 18th.*

1835: 25 Feb: *With Mrs. Witts & my Son dined at Adlestrop at Mr. Perrots; a very agreeable party. We met the Revd. Mr. & Mrs. Way of Glympton Park, Oxon, Captain Leigh, and Mr. & Mrs. Whitmore Jones.*

1838: 16 Jan: *Met Leopold Dryden, who had recd. this morning from Chandos Leigh the promise of the presentation to the vacant living of Leek Wotton near Warwick, lately held by Leopold's brother, and my old acquaintance, Sir H. Dryden.* 22 Aug: *several ladies were present—Capt. Leigh with his two nieces—Mrs. Leigh, of Stoneleigh Abbey with a daughter, who had been confirmed—my Son and daughter who were greeted by Bp. Monk with the utmost cordiality and kindness—Mrs. Ford with two daughters. Mrs. and Miss Cameron &c.* 24 Dec: *Mr. & Mrs. J. are now in town—his youngest Son, Dr. Jeaffreson, lately settled as a Physician at Gainsborough or Grantham, with fair prospects, is just married to a poor Miss Kenny, a daughter of a literary man, author of some dramatic pieces: the young lady was Governess in Chandos Leigh's family abroad, when S. Jeaffreson travelled with him as domestic Physician.*

1839: 10 Jul., 14 Jul.

1840: 16 Sep., 2 Oct.

1842: 1 Nov: *The Drydens had reached Stanway yesterday: they are now resident at Leamington; he having resigned the vicarage of Leek Wooton in favour of the eldest Son of Mr. Colville of Barton, a nephew of Lord Leigh's, and accepted from his kinsman and patron, the same noble Lord, the Rectory of Whitnash, of nearly equal value with Leek Wotton, situate little more than a mile from Leamington, and not having a habitable Parsonage house.*

1844: 11 Dec.

1845: 16 Jan: *This line is not objected to by Lord Leigh, but much opposed by Lord Redesdale, for it will so interfere with his hunting country, dissevering it, cutting through, or bordering on coverts, as to make it worthless.* 14 Mar: *A letter from Lord Leigh recommending to my favourable notice Mr. E. Draper, of Kenilworth, Solr. and heretofore Clerk of the Warwick Poor Law Union, who is a candidate for the Oxfordshire and Warwickshire districts of Unions.* 17 Mar., 20 Mar: *There had been much hesitation as to the place of sepulcture: Cheltenham was repugnant to the deceased: Whitnash was distant, and, besides, there is a probability that, on the decease of Mr. Jeaffreson, an arrangement may be made by the concurrence of Lord Leigh, between Mr. Dryden, and Mr. Morrison, to whom it is arranged that Longborough shall be presented when it becomes vacant, so that Mr. D. will exchange Whitnash with Mr. M. for Longborough: Adlestrop was thought of, on account of the relationship between Mr. Dryden and Lord Leigh; but at length Broadwell was chosen, for the like reason, and because Mr. D. had held the curacy of that parish, in which also Mr. Vavasour's residence is situate.* 22 Mar: *Dr. Twisleton, as a Connection of Mr. Dryden, came shortly after my son to attend the funeral, and was soon followed by Lord Leigh, who, out of respect and regard for his connection Mr. Dryden, had made a point of being present, leaving Stoneleigh park Abbey this morning, and proposing to return this evening.*

1846: 17 Dec: *much needless labour was caused to-day by revision of the pauper list of the parish of Longborough, owing to an ill judged, but well meant interference on the part of Lady Leigh, (a lady bountiful) who, in charitable visits to the Cottagers of that parish, in which Lord L. has property, has been imposed upon by artful and untrue tales of destitution. It appeared that the complaints of insufficient relief alledged by her ladyship were almost; if not altogether, groundless.* 18 Dec.

1849: 28 Dec: *A packet from Stanway, containing a letter to M.W. from Sophy; the boy was sent on purpose, in consequence of a note having been received this morning addressed Mrs. Witts, Stanway, Stow on the Wold, being an invitation to dinner to-morrow at Adlestrop House from Mr. and Lady Caroline Leigh, inviting also E.F.W. and Sophy, if they are at home, evidently written in a strange ignorance and misapprehension of our localities, which, indeed, they have shewn before. I dispatched a servant immediately with a note to Mr. Leigh, calculated to undeceive him and his lady as to the places of residence of ourselves, and our children, explaining why Lady C.L's note had not been sooner answered, and declining the invitation in consequence of M.W's health being now so indifferent that it precluded our go.*

1850: 3 Aug: *Having received a note of invitation to dine at Mr. and Lady Caroline Leigh's, at Adlestrop, on Monday next, replied in the affirmative.* 5 Aug: *At half past six set out in my chariot to dine at Adlestrop with Mr. and Lady Caroline Leigh ... Lady Caroline is a ladylike, quiet, unaffected, pleasing person, but not particularly well-looking.* 1 Oct: *The Chair should have been filled by the Hon. W H Leigh, but he has suddenly succeeded to the titles borne by his father, Lord Leigh, who died a few days since at Bonn, on the Rhine, as he was returning from a visit to some of the German baths. These had been of no benefit to his broken and feeble constitution, and he seems to have sunk in his 60th. year under repeated attacks from which he had not strength to rally. His son and Lady Caroline Leigh had been summoned to the bed side of their dying parent.*

LEIGH — Egerton Leigh [71]

Egerton Leigh (1752-1833), JP and landed proprietor, was born at West Hall, High Legh, Cheshire, son of Revd Peter Leigh (1725-1758), rector of Lyme, Cheshire, and Mary Doughty (1727-1811). He was educated at Sidney College, Cambridge (BA 1775). He married, at Rosthern, 21 September 1778, Elizabeth (±1755-1807), daughter and co-heir of Francis Joddrell (1723-1756) and Jane Butterworth (1723-1775) of Yeardsley and Twemlow, Cheshire; they had 4 sons and 6 daughters:

1 Egerton (1779-1865); *see below*
1 Mary Anne (1780-1874); married, at Marylebone, 14 June 1802, James Abercromby, 1st Baron Dunfermline (1776-1858), barrister, MP, and speaker of the House of Commons (1835-39); at least 1 son:
  1 Ralph (1803-1868); succeeded as 2nd Baron Dunfermline
2 Charlotte (1781-1823); married, at St George's, Hanover Square, Joseph Jellicoe; died at Rome; at least 1 son and 1 daughter:
  1 Emma Carter (1806-1869); married, at Holy Trinity Church, Marylebone, Westminster, 26 March 1836, Thomas Maltby (1794-1866); 1 son and 1 daughter:
    1 Henrietta Emma (1848-1918)
    1 Thomas Crichton Maltby (1850-1924)
  1 William Edward (1814-1890)
2 Peter (1782-1841), Church of England clergyman; educated at Rugby School and Trinity College, Cambridge; rector of Lymm, Cheshire, 1806-25; married Mary, daughter of Sir J. Blackburne
3 Emma (1783-1851); married, at Sandbach, Cheshire, 1 May 1811, John Smith, MP, of Dale Park, Sussex
4 Augusta (1784-1851); married, 1821, Thomas Dumbleton (b. 1783)
5 Caroline (1786-1856)
3 Jodrell (1790-1863), Vice Adm., RN; *see below*
4 Timothy (unknown)
6 Harriet (1795-1809)

1825: 15 Sep: *to the right of the road: & farther off in the same direction is High Leigh, where are two Mansions of Leighs, but of different families, and as to which is the veritable Amphitryon, which Squire represents the oldest family, which is the genuine Leigh of High Leigh, ad huc sub judicialis est. Of the contesting Kings of Brentford, one, who married the heiress of the Leighs of Twemlow, in this County, and who has been building and endowing a chapel at High Leigh, a respectable gentleman, now far advanced in life, is father to my neighbour & brother Justice in Gloucestershire, Egerton Leigh of Broadwell; who will in proper season succeeded to the paternal estates in Cheshire & Gloucestershire.*

LEIGH — Egerton Leigh and the Leigh family at Broadwell — ***see also*** **Dumbleton** ***and*** **Stratton** [72]

Egerton Leigh (1779-1865), JP and landed proprietor, was born at Davenport, Cheshire, eldest son of Egerton Leigh (*above*). Leigh married, at Charlbury, Oxfordshire, 26 December 1809, Wilhelmina Sarah Stratton (1785-1849); they had at least 1 son and 6 daughters:

1 Eleanor Agnes (1811-1837)
2 Anna Elizabeth (1812-1879)
3 Beatrice Julia (1813-1891); married, first, 1844, John Oliver Hopkins (1810-1853); secondly, 1859, Robert Lingen Burton (1803-1887)
1 Egerton Leigh (1815-1876); *see below*
4 Caroline (±1817-1898); married, 1858, Richard Morris
5 Emma (d. 1819); died in infancy
6 Augusta (1826-1903); married, 1852, Charles Gresley (1817-1900)

Following his father's death in 1833, Egerton Leigh appears to have taken up residence at West Hall in High Legh and at Jodrell Hall. He was high sheriff for 1836. His younger brother, Vice Adm. Jodrell Leigh (*below*), later lived at Broadwell Manor in Gloucestershire.

1812: 6 Aug: *Mr. & Mrs. Egerton Leigh, of Broadwell, our acquaintance & neighbours in Gloucestershire, arrived unexpectedly on a visit of a few days in the Evening.*

1820: 10 Feb., 11 Apr.

1823: 21 Mar: *We dined at Mr. Jeaffreson's at Longborough, meeting Sir C. & Lady Cockerell, Mr. & Mrs. E. Leigh, their brother & sister, Mr. & Mrs. Dumbleton.* 22 Mar: *We dined at Mr. E. Leigh's at Broadwell, meeting the Jeaffresons, the Dumbletons & Mr. Vavasour.* 8 Aug: *We dined at Mr. Ford's, the Rector of Little Risington, meeting Mr. & Mrs. E. Leigh.*

1824: 17 Feb: *The alienation between Mr. Dolphin and myself had subsisted unaltered up to this time. We rarely met by accident, never in private society, and in public only at the Music meeting, where no recognition of each other occurred. On Friday last, however, an effort was made by two neighbours, men of honourable & benevolent principles, to effect a renewal of the interrupted intercourse between us. This interference on the part of Mr. Egerton Leigh, & Mr. Vavasour was unsolicited on either side.* 6 Apr: *We had a dinner party; Lady & Miss Reade, Mr. & Mrs. Egerton Leigh, Mr. R. Wynniatt, Mr. Bowen.* 26 May: *We dined at Mr. E. Leigh's at Broadwell.* 6 Aug., 17 Sep., 9 Nov.

1825: 19 Jul., 23 August: *We had a dinner party: Mr. & Mrs. Egerton Leigh, Mr. & Mrs. Ford, their son, Mr. Croome, Mr. Bowen, Mr. Jones and Mr. C. Keysall.* 15 Sep: *to the right of the road: & farther off in the same direction is High Leigh, where are two Mansions of Leighs, but of different families, and as to which is the veritable Amphitryon, which Squire represents the oldest family, which is the genuine Leigh of High Leigh, ad huc sub judicialis est. Of the contesting Kings of Brentford, one, who married the heiress of the Leighs of Twemlow, in this County, and who has been building and endowing a chapel at High Leigh, a respectable gentleman, now far advanced in life, is father to my neighbour & brother Justice in Gloucestershire, Egerton Leigh of Broadwell; who will in proper season succeeded to the paternal estates in Cheshire & Gloucestershire, for a mansion house and estate at Broadwell came by marriage into the Leigh family; he, like his father, has a large family, chiefly of daughters, by a daughter of the late Mr. Stratton of Great Tew, a very sensible, well informed woman. Of her husband, formerly in the Dragoons, I will say, that he is a sensible, well educated man, with high principle and honourable feelings; but withal captious, haughty, apt to take offence, and unconciliating.*

1826: 3 Mar: *We dined at Mr. E. Leigh's at Broadwell ... & Capt. Leigh, E. Leigh's brother, a naval Officer.* 23 Aug: *We had some of our friends to dinner. Our party consisted of the Egerton Leighs, Mr. & Mrs. Jeaffreson, Mr. & Mrs. Dolphin, & their guest, Miss Oliver, & Miss E. Jeaffreson.* 15 Sep., 2 Nov., 13 Dec., 18 Dec: *I dined and slept at Lord Redesdale's. The old Peer is, as usual, full of talk and information, very communicative, confidential & kind. Mr. Mitford was not at home. His Sister and Aunt were at Batsford. We had a very handsome dinner; the guests were Lord Northwick, his Sister (Mrs. Rushout) Sir C. & Lady Cockerell, Col. Belli, a relation of Sir C. C. & brother to the Lady of the Bish. of London, Mr. & Mrs. E. Leigh, Mr. Ford.*

1827: 28 Apr., 5 Jun: *We dined at Mr. Jeaffreson's at Longborough ... There were also at the Symposium of our host & hostess, the Egerton Leighs and his brother, the Revd. Peter Leigh, Mr. Jones & his dandy pupil, Mr. Winter.* 12 Nov: *We dined at Mr. Egerton Leigh's at Broadwell .... This is the last visit, which we shall pay to the Egerton Leighs for some time, as they are going to France for some months for the education of their girls.*

1829: 21 Jan: *We had a party of our friends to dinner. Mr. & Mrs. E. Leigh and Miss Leigh; Mr. Ford.* 15 May: *We dined with the Egerton Leighs at Broadwell, meeting the Dean of Gloucester, his son Francis, & his ... These young ladies are handsome & elegant, surpassing in beauty their cousin Miss Leigh, who yet is a well looking girl.* 6 Oct., 16 Oct: *a dinner party in the evening; Mr. & Mrs. E. Leigh & Miss Leigh, Mr. & Miss Croome, Mr. & Mrs. Twisleton, & Mr. Winter.* 5 Nov: *We dined at Mr. Leigh's at Broadwell, meeting Mr. & Mrs. Ford, Mr. & Mrs. Jeaffreson, & Mr. Hall. Mrs. Ford brought three of her daughters, too young yet to join the party at the dinner table. A niece of Mr. Leigh's, daughter of his deceased sister, Mrs. Jellicoe, is staying at Broadwell.*

1830: 26 May: *We entertained some of our neighbours at dinner today—Mrs. & Miss Leigh from Broadwell, (Mr. E. Leigh was absent in London;) Mr. & Mrs. Jeaffreson; Mr. & Mrs. M. Vavasour & Mr. Winter.* 22 Jun: *Mr. Egerton Leigh, when he was in town lately, had made enquiries for us at several hotels, and found their terms much on the same footing.*

1832: 17 May.

1833: 1 Feb: *We dined at Mr. Leighs's at Broadwell, and met Sir Chas. and Lady Imhoff, Miss Chapuset, Mr. & Mrs. Vavasour of Stow, Messrs. W. B. and Mundy Pole: with the family party we sat down fifteen to dinner.* 17 Oct., 25 Oct., 26 Oct: *The Misses Leigh from Broadwell rode over to request me to come to their Mother, who was anxious to advise with me on a matter of importance. Accompanied them to Broadwell, where I found Mrs. Leigh in distress arising out of the increasing feebleness of her aged mother, Mrs. Stratton.*

1834: 7 Mar: *walked back to Leamington, where before dinner I walked for an hour as Cavaliere Servente of my friend Mrs. E. Leigh: & subsequently joined the Hunts, with whom we drank tea in the evening.*

1835: 5 Apr: *Received a letter from Egerton Leigh Esqr. from High Leigh, inclosing a deposit of £10, to be made for a Servant of his in our Provident Bank.* 9 Apr., 15 Jun: *to E Leigh to offer a visit of a day at High Leigh.* 12 Jun: *I was struck with a full length portrait of Mrs. Leigh of High Leigh, Cheshire; not the Mrs. Leigh with whom we have been so long intimate, but her of the West East-hall.*

1838: 30 Jun: *M W. proceeded to call at Maugersbury on Mrs. Chamberlayne, but particularly, on her guests, Beatrice and Caroline Leigh, two of the daughters of Egerton Leigh, who are on a visit there.* 13 Jul: *Mr. Ford, W. Ford, and Miss Caroline Leigh called.* 10 Aug: *Entertained a large party at dinner ... Capt. Leigh & his two nieces, Beatrice and Caroline, with E.F. W. made up the party.*

1845: 6 Jul: *Recd. a letter from Egerton Leigh, dated from Joddrell Hall.*

LEIGH — Egerton Leigh [73]

Egerton Leigh (1815-1876), JP, DL, MP, and landed proprietor, was born at Broadwell, Gloucestershire, son of Egerton Leigh (*above*). He was educated at Eton College, and in April 1833 became a cornet in the 2nd Dragoon Guards (Queen's Bays); he was promoted to lieutenant in 1835, and to captain in 1840. In 1843 he retired from the Army and joined the 1st Cheshire Militia, which he left in 1870 with the rank of honorary colonel. Leigh was high sheriff for Cheshire in 1872, and MP for Mid Cheshire in 1873-76.

Leigh married, at St George's, Hanover Square, 20 September 1842, Lydia Rachel (1813-1893), daughter and co-heir of John Smith Wright of Balcote Lodge, Nottinghamshire; they had 5 sons and 1 daughter:

1 Egerton (1843-1928); married, at St George's, Hanover Square, 5 August 1874, Elizabeth Mary Gore Hedges-White (1847-1880)
2 John Jodrell Egerton (1845-1860); died a pupil at Eton College
1 Eleanor Sophia Egerton (1847-1898); married, at High Legh, Cheshire, July 1869, Sir Robert Alfred Cunliffe (1839-1905)
3 Edward Egerton (1851-1913); married, at St John the Baptist, Halifax, Yorkshire, Laura Maude Edwards (1850-1924)
4 Neville Egerton (1852-1929), Church of England clergyman; died unmarried
5 Arthur Egerton (1853-1914); married, at West Ashford, Kent, July 1882, Mary Louisa Hay Murray (1858-1922)

Apart from his military and political interests, Leigh was a keen antiquary with a thorough knowledge of Cheshire's history. His special interests were archaeology, local ballads and folklore, and the Cheshire dialect. He published several works, the most important of which were *Ballads and Legends of Cheshire* (1867) and *A Glossary of Words used in the Dialect of Cheshire* (1877).

1830: 18 Jan: *Three youths about Edward's age came to dine with him, & slept here ... Lastly Egerton Leigh, younger than any of the rest, only son of my friend, the Squire of Broadwell, a nice quick boy, an Etonian.*

1838: 26 Apr: *Met Mr Chamberlayne and young Egerton Leigh, our host's nephew, and the only son of our friend at Joddrel Hall, whom I had not seen since he went into the Dragoons. He is a fine, amiable, well informed young man, holding the rank of Lieutenant, and has seen no foreign Service, having been chiefly quartered in English Cavalry Stations, and in Ireland; his regiment being now at Kilkenny, and he having at present leave of absence. He is on his way home into Cheshire.*

LEIGH — Emma Leigh — *see* Jellicoe

LEIGH — Jodrell Leigh [74]

Jodrell Leigh (1790-1863), JP, farmer, and Royal Navy vice admiral, was born at Jodrell Hall, Cheshire, the third son and sixth child of Egerton Leigh (1752-1833) and Elizabeth Jodrell (±1755-1807). Leigh entered the Navy as a cadet midshipman in 1801 at the age of 10 or 11. He was promoted to lieutenant in 1808, commander in 1820, captain in 1829, and vice admiral on 19 May 1862.

Jodrell Leigh lived on an estate in Broadwell, Gloucestershire, which seems to have been inherited by his nephew, Egerton (1815-1876) (*above*), when Jodrell's elder brother, Egerton (1779-1865), succeeded to the Cheshire estates. Jodrell Leigh bought Broadwell Farm (also referred to as Redhill Farm in 1849), and in the 1861 census he was listed as rear admiral, farming 170 acres, and employing five men. He died unmarried on 27 October 1863 at West Hall, High Legh, Cheshire, where presumably he had gone to stay with close family when his health was failing.

'Capt. Leigh' is one of the most frequently mentioned characters in the diaries. He first came to notice in 1834 and was often in conflict with his farming neighbours—a constant theme running down the years. He was a Gloucestershire JP and took a leading part in local business matters. Leigh was clearly eccentric; he accused the rector and churchwardens of misappropriating the rates, had a long and unsuccessful struggle with the vestry and the villagers for diversions of the roads, and quarrelled with the rector over changes in the church. One of his antagonists was the equally eccentric Capt. William Polhill (±1800-1868), a veteran of Waterloo (where he was a cornet of only 14 or 15 years of age), who celebrated the victory annually in his garden at Millbrook. Broadwell notables of greater national but less local renown were the vice admiral's nephew, Egerton Leigh (1815-1876) (*above*), writer on dialect, who owned the manor house but lived there little, if at all.

1834: 30 Sep: *This busy day concluded with the annual meeting and dinner of the Stow Book Society. Mr. Pole took the chair in the absence of Mr. Talbot, who is now in a declining state of health at Brighton. Captain Leigh, Mr. F. W. Rice and Mr. Cameron were elected members. Capt. Leigh was nominated Chairman for the next year.* 27 Oct., 21 Nov: *A dinner party. Mr. and Mrs. Pole, W. B. Pole and Capt. Pole—Capt. Leigh—Winter—Mr. & Mrs. and the two Misses Vavasour were our guests.*

1835: 28 Jan: *Captain Leigh called, and concurred in the view I had taken as to this extraordinary measure of Mr. Baillie.* 29 Jan: *Dressed at the Unicorn Inn, and proceeded from thence in a chaise with my son to dine at Capt. Leigh's at Broadwell.* 13 Feb: *Robert Waller came to dine and sleep here. We had a gentleman's dinner party. Captn. Leigh, Messrs. Winter and Daubeny dined with us.* 25 Feb: *With Mrs. Witts & my Son dined at Adlestrop at Mr. Perrots; a very agreeable party. We met the Revd. Mr. & Mrs. Way of Glympton Park, Oxon, Captain Leigh, and Mr. & Mrs. Whitmore Jones.* 26 Feb., 24 Apr: *Captain Leigh and the two Messrs. Daubeny called.* 7 May.

1836: 3 Aug., 5 Aug., 27 Sep.

1837: 17 Apr., 21 Apr: *M.W. and myself dined at Capt. Leigh's at Broadwell, meeting Mr. and Mrs. Colville, Mr. & Mrs. Ford, Miss D. Ford, Mr. & Mrs. Twisleton, Mr. Lockwood, and Miss Leigh, a maiden sister of the Leighs, now on a visit to her brother.* 28 Apr., 2 May, 6 May, 14 Jul: *Entertained a party of our neighbours at dinner.—Mr. and Mrs. Barter with their daughter, from Sarsden. Mr. Lockwood, from Kingham;—Sir C. and Lady Imhoff, Mr. Winter and Miss Chapuset, from Daylesford;—Mr. Leopold Dryden, Capt. Leigh & Capt. Crole from Broadwell.* 31 Aug., 5 Sep., 26 Sep., 10 Oct., 16 Nov.

1838: 8 Mar., 20 Mar: *A long visit of three hours from Capt. Leigh, who came to advise with me on his position at Broadwell: owing to the violent feuds in that parish, all the Farmers being united against him, and annoying him in all possible ways.* 20 Apr: *Engaged in the forenoon with Mass Matthews, a farmer of L Swell and Capt. Leigh.* 24 Apr: *Capt. Leigh called to invite me to dine with him on Thursday.* 26 Apr: *Accompanied Ford to Broadwell, he taking me thither in his carriage, to Capt. Leigh's where we dined, & I slept.* 27 Apr., 30 Apr., 16-17 May, 9 Aug., 10 Aug: *Entertained a large party at dinner; Mr. Ford, with his lady & eldest daughter, his sister, Mrs. Ekins, an agreeable person, Widow of a late Canon of Salisbury, and his niece Miss Rooke, daughter of Capt. Rooke—Mr. & Mrs R. Waller—Capt. Leigh & his two nieces, Beatrice and Caroline, with E.F.W. made up the party.* 13 Aug: *We took Emily V., with us to Broadwell, to dine at Capt. Leigh's, where we met Mr. and Mrs. Ford, Miss D: Ford, Miss E. Rooke, Mr. and Mrs. Cameron, Vavasour and Edward, who had followed us in V's open Carriage.* 16 Aug., 22-23 Aug., 25 Sep., 8 Nov., 22 Nov.

1839: 21 Feb., 7 Mar., 4 Apr., 15 May, 13 Aug.

1840: 27 Mar: *Capt. Leigh paid me a long morning visit, as usual at variance with his Broadwell neighbours.* 28 Mar: *took luncheon with Capt. Leigh; examined the Award of the parish of Broadwell; and gave him my opinion as to the points in dispute respecting a church path between him and his neighbours.* 30 Mar., 31 Mar: *Wrote to Mr. Beman on the matters in dispute between Capt. Leigh, and his Broadwell neighbours, and to Capt. Leigh, sending him a copy of my letter to Beman.* 3 Apr., 7 Apr: *A long visit from Capt. Leigh, who took luncheon with us, and engaged me in long discussions as to his dissensions with his neighbours at Broadwell.* 6 Jul: *Capt. Leigh called and paid a long morning visit: he is very excited on the subject of his differences with the Broadwell farmers, and even expects a personal assault and insult.* 9 Jul: *Accompanied Mr. Ford and his Son Frederick in their carriage to a dinner party at Capt. Leigh's at Broadway: a pleasant evening.* 10 Jul., 13 Aug., 21 Aug., 27 Aug., 29 Sep., 7 Oct: *Received a party at dinner—Miss Rollinson, who arrived to stay two days with us from Farmington Lodge, Mr. & Mrs. R. Waller, Mr. & Mrs. Cameron, Mr. and Mrs. Polson, and Capt. Leigh.—All went off pleasantly.*

1842: 2 Feb: *Capt. Leigh called, followed, and overtook me, full of parish troubles; he rode home with me & concluded a visit begun on horseback.* 12 May, 14 May: *Reached home after 3 P.M. and found Capt. Leigh awaiting me; having made an appointment to meet Ford here, to advise with me as to a grievance at Broadwell, one of those which perpetually worry him, arising out of suspicion on his part that some work undertaken by the Road Surveyor there has been entered upon with a view to his annoyance.* 19 May, 28 May, 30 May, 1 Jun., 26 Jul., 27 Sep., 28 Dec.

1843: 18-19 Aug., 28 Aug., 2 Sep: *A letter from E.F.W: all well at Stanway and Upper Slaughter: lively and agreeable details of our childrens visits to the Wallers and Capt. Leigh, who gave a very elegant entertainment to all the neighbourhood.* 26 Sep., 16-17 Nov., 24-25 Dec., 28 Dec.

1844: 22 Feb: *Attended a meeting of the Trustees of the road from Stow to Burford at which Capt. Leigh presided.* 29 Mar., 1-5 Apr., 6 May, 25 Jul., 29 Jul., 23 Aug: *A dinner party ... and Capt. Leigh.* 24 Sep., 31 Oct.

1845: 6 Feb., 2 Apr., 29 May, 1 Jun., 4 Jun: *We received a party to dinner to-day ... Capt. Leigh.*

1846: 29 Sep., 5 Nov., 9 Dec.

1847: 11 May: *My son and daughter rode to Broadwell to lunch with Capt. Leigh, and meeting his niece Anna, who is visiting there.* 19 Aug: *With the Dean of Gloucester and Mr. Ford sat in the justice room, hearing cases. Capt. Leigh was present, making an application as to a Broadwell grievance, as to which we had no jurisdiction.* 25 Nov., 9 Dec., 16 Dec: *a charge preferred to the Poor Law Commrs. by Capt. Leigh, who complained of relief granted by the Board to a pauper of Broadwell, named Hardiman, a labourer in the employment of Mr. Beman, a man of infirm health, and with a large family, at low wages. Captain Leigh, Mr. Polhill, and Mr. Potter were present.* 20 Dec.

1848: 17 Aug: *Mr. and Mrs. C Pole entertain very handsomely; much good cheer, and a well appointed table—the guests, besides ourselves, were Mr. & Mrs. C. R. Pole, their two sons and two daughters, Mr. and Mrs. J. T. Rice, Mr. and Mrs. Winter, Captain Leigh, and Mr. Lewes.* 26 Sep., 2 Nov.

1849: 12 Dec.

1850: 28 Feb: *Conferred with Mr. Vavasour and Mr. Wilkins as to the claim made by W. Vavasour for payment from Mr. Chamberlayne for extra manure laid on the lands late in W.V's occupation——It seems that Captain Leigh, one of the parties to whom Mr. Chamberlayne had proposed that the question might be referred, has decided it in favour of W.V.* 21 Mar: *At "the Cottage" I also saw Mr. and Mrs. Vavasour, Capt. Leigh, Mr. Hutchinson and Mr. Winter.* 18 Sep., 1 Oct., 7 Oct., 26-28 Dec.

1851: 3 Jan: *Received a letter from Capt. Leigh, written in civil terms of acknowledgment of my letter.* 30 Jan., 3 Feb: *Capt. Leigh called to apply for a summons to Mr. Rose of Broadwell to shew cause why he should not be fined for wilful trespass and damage done to a public stone quarry in the parish of Broadwell, which is set out in the award for getting stone for the repair of the Highways—he having dug and carted away stone from thence for his own private purposes.* 13 Feb: *At Sewell's office discussed the same subject with him, and looked at it the opinion given by Mr. Pigott as to the case submitted to him by Sewell on behalf of Capt. Leigh, respecting the Broadwell Stone quarries.* 24 Apr.

1852: 3 Feb., 22 Mar., 7 Nov., 9-12 Nov., 2 Dec.

1853: 3 Mar., 31 Mar., 7 Apr., 11 May: *A dinner party—entertained Mr. and Mrs. Winter, Mr. and Mrs. R Waller, Mr. and Mrs. Lefroy, Mrs. W. Vavasour, and Mr. Ball, with Capt. Leigh.* 8 Dec: *Met there Captain Leigh, who supports Sir M.H.H.B.* 10 Dec., 14-15 Dec.

1854: 10 Apr: *Captain Leigh and Mr. Potter called to consult me as to diversion of a road and footpath at Broadwell, a measure which has been heretofore attempted, and failed, but which it is believed can be now carried out.* 14 Apr., 20 Apr., 20 Apr., 29 Apr: *Engaged for two hours with Capt. Leigh, who called respecting the diversion of roads in his village of Broadwell ... He remained to partake of luncheon with E Clifford and me.* 7 Jun., 10 Jun: *Capt. Leigh called on the matter of the diversion of highways in Broadwell; mortified that he has not accomplished all he wished at the Vestry meeting on Thursday.* 12 Jun., 28 Jul., 30 Jul: *Received a note from Capt. Leigh, who accepts my invitation to dinner on Friday next.* 4 Aug: *I entertained besides our home party, Mr. and Mrs. W. G. Clarke, Mr. and Mrs. W. Vavasour, Mr. Ball and Captain Leigh.*

LEIGH — John Smith Leigh [75]

John Smith Leigh (1759-1813), lieutenant-colonel of the Somerset Militia, JP, and landed proprietor of Combe Hay, Bath, Somerset, was the only son of John Smith (±1727-1775), MP for Bath (1766-75), and Anne, daughter of Thomas Charles Tracy, 5th Viscount Tracy. His parents married in 1757. His father was the eldest son of Robert Smith, of Foxcote and Stony Littleton, Somerset, who was educated at Oriel College, Oxford. His father succeeded to Combe Hay Manor in 1755, and later extended it.

John Smith Leigh married, 2 April 1782, Mary (1754-1822), youngest daughter of George Shirley of Lower Ettington, Warwickshire. He was high sheriff for Somerset in 1811, and grand master of the freemasons in Somerset. In 1802 he changed his name by sign manual from John Smith to John Smith Leigh.

Agnes Witts was third cousin to John Smith Leigh; they had a common great-great-grandfather in John Tracy, 3rd Viscount Tracy (1617-1687), of Rathcoole. It was via this connection that Agnes hoped to forward Francis's accession to the curacy of Foxcote and Combe Hay, assisting the elderly incumbent, Francis Merewether (±1737-1806). Unfortunately, Merewether had the discourtesy to die shortly after Francis's appointment, leaving his burial as his new curate's first and final task. Thus ended Francis Witts's exceedingly brief first clerical appointment.

1806: 13 Mar: *Assisted my Mother in writing to Col. Leigh, the Patron of Coombe Hay, requesting his sanction in my Treaty with Mr. Merewether.*

LEIGH — Thomas Leigh [76]

Thomas Leigh (1734-1813), Church of England clergyman, was born at Adlestrop, Gloucestershire, a younger son of William Leigh (1691-1757) and Mary Lord (1694-1756). He was educated at Balliol College and Magdalen College, Oxford (BA 1755; MA 1758; BCL 1763). He was ordained deacon on 21 May 1758 and priest on 1 June 1760.

Leigh's first clerical appointment was as vicar of Longborough with Sezincote, starting on 12 August 1762, a position he retained to his death in 1813. He was also appointed rector of Broadwell with Adlestrop on 24 March 1763, rural dean of Stow in August 1768, and domestic chaplain to James Brydges, 3rd duke of Chandos (1731-1789), on 29 December 1771. Leigh was a younger brother to James Leigh (1724-1774), of Adlestrop and Longborough, and uncle to James Henry Leigh (1765-1823), of Adlestrop, Longborough, and Stoneleigh, who married, 1786, Julia Judith (d. 1843), daughter of Thomas Twisleton, 13th Lord Saye and Sele. Thomas Leigh was therefore great-uncle to Chandos Leigh, 1st Lord of Stoneleigh (1791-1850).

Leigh married, at Oxford, 3 November 1762, his first cousin, Mary (1731-1797), daughter of Theophilus Leigh (1691-1785), master of Balliol College, Oxford, and Ann (b. 1702), only daughter of Edward Bee of Beckley Park, Oxfordshire. The couple remained childless. Mary Leigh was a friend of Frances Guydickens, née Tracy, and Agnes Witts, and is mentioned numerous times in the latter's diaries. On 12 August 1789 Agnes wrote, '... sat down 11 to Dinner, rather formal but Mrs. Leigh is always pleasant & agreeable'.

Leigh was a cousin of Jane Austen, who stayed with her Leigh cousins at Adlestrop several times and kept in constant touch with events there by letter. It was in Gloucestershire that she witnessed first-hand how the eighteenth-century craze for improvements transformed the village landscape. It is probable that Adlestrop Park and the parsonage house inspired fictional places such as Thornton Lacey in *Mansfield Park*. The colourful lives and inheritance problems of the Leigh family influenced many of the plot lines in Jane Austen's books.

1801: 29 Oct: *The Honble. & Revd. Ed. Lyse, Mr. Delabere, Mrs. Leigh &c. called.*

LEIGH — Thomas Charles Leigh — *see also* Hanbury Tracy

Thomas Charles Leigh (1801-1863) was the eldest son of Charles Hanbury Tracy and Henrietta Susanna, daughter and heir of Henry Tracy, 8th Viscount Tracy. Thomas adopted the name of Leigh by royal licence on 11 April 1806, when he was about 5 years old, in deference to the memory of his maternal grandfather, to whose estates in Gloucestershire, Montgomeryshire, and Shropshire, he was his father's heir. He resumed the patronymic of Hanbury Tracy by royal licence on 30 March 1839.

LEIGH — William Leigh[77]

William Leigh (1752-1809), Church of England clergyman, was the son of John Burridge Leigh (d. 1774) of Rushall, Staffordshire, and Olympia Broughton. He was educated at University College, Oxford, and Trinity College and Corpus Christi College, Cambridge. He married, 1790, a widow, Elizabeth Perceval, daughter of Stratford Canning and first cousin of George Canning, prime minister, 1827; they had 2 daughters:

1 Elizabeth (±1791-±1850); married a Mellish
2 Frances Harriet (±1793-±1854); married, 26 November 1813, Alexander Campbell (Sinclair) Sinclair, 13th earl of Caithness

This attribution is tentative, but no relevant clergyman by the name of Lee (as the diarist spells it) has been found, and both Francis and his mother Agnes alternated between 'Lee' and 'Leigh' on several occasions in their diaries during their September 1802 visit to Calwich Abbey. The most telling entry in Agnes's diary regarding the alternative spelling is for 22 September 1802: 'Wensday Sepr. 22nd: Mrs. Leigh, her two Daughters & Sister Miss Canning dined here ...'

1802: 16 Sep: *Mr. & Mrs. Lee & Miss Canning. Dined at Calwich.* 19 Sep: *At Ellaston Church in the morning. Mr. Webb officiated in reading Mr. Lee preached an excellent discourse.*

LEIGH — William Henry Leigh

William Henry Leigh, 2nd Baron Leigh of Stoneleigh (1824-1905), JP and landed proprietor, was born at Adlestrop, Gloucestershire, son of Chandos Leigh, 1st Baron Leigh of Stoneleigh (1791-1850), and Margarette (1798-1860), daughter of Revd William Shippen Willes. His parents married on 7 June 1819. Leigh was educated at Harrow School and Trinity College, Cambridge, and he succeeded as 2nd Baron Leigh of Stoneleigh on 27 September 1850. Leigh was lord-lieutenant of Warwickshire in 1856-1905 and a colonel in the 3rd Battalion, Warwickshire Regiment. He married, 22 August 1848, Caroline Amelia, daughter of Richard Grosvenor, 2nd marquess of Westminster, and Elizabeth Mary Leveson-Gower; they had 4 sons and 3 daughters:

1 Margaret Elizabeth (1849-1945); married, 19 September 1872, Victor Albert George Child-Villiers, 7th earl of the Island of Jersey
1 Gilbert Henry Chandos (1851-1884); died unmarried
2 Agnes Eleanor (1853-1942); died unmarried
2 Francis Dudley (1855-1938); succeeded as 3rd Baron Leigh of Stoneleigh; married, first, 29 November 1890, Frances Hélène Forbes Beckwith; secondly, 2 October 1923, Marie Campbell
3 Rupert Leigh (1856-1919); married, 14 July 1906, Beatrice Mary, daughter of Dudley Robert Smith
4 Rowland Charles Frederick (1859-1943); married, 31 October 1898, Mabel, daughter of Gen. William Washington Gordon
3 Mary Cordelia Emily (1866-1956); died unmarried

1846: 28 Nov: *Our dear children left us for Maugersbury House on a visit to the W. Vavasours, to remain till Wednesday next, and on the Tuesday to join the assembled neighbourhood at Stow Ball, revived under the stewardship of the Hon. Henry Leigh, eldest son of the Lord Leigh, now and for some time past resident at their seat at Adlestrop, which has been an engrossing topic with the young and gay.*

1850: 16 Jul: *Mr. W. H. Leigh, of Adlestrop, called on the fruitless errand of canvassing me in favour of Mr. Pruen, the candidate for the vacant Coronership. He is supported by the Whig, Radical, and Berkeley interest.* 18 Jul: *In the Justice room Messrs. Ford, Pole, W. H. Leigh & myself sat as Magistrates, and much business was brought before us.* 1 Aug., 3 Aug: *Having received a note of invitation to dine at Mr. and Lady Caroline Leigh's, at Adlestrop, on Monday next, replied in the affirmative.* 5 Aug: *At half past six set out in my chariot to dine at Adlestrop with Mr. and Lady Caroline Leigh.* 1 Oct: *The Chair should have been filled by the Hon. W H Leigh, but he has suddenly succeeded to the titles borne by his father, Lord Leigh, who died a few days since at Bonn, on the Rhine, as he was returning from a visit to some of the German baths. These had been of no benefit to his broken and feeble constitution, and he seems to have sunk in his 60th. year under repeated attacks from which he had not strength to rally. His son and Lady Caroline Leigh had been summoned to the bed side of their dying parent.*

1851: 14 May: *Lord Leigh, accompanied by his Brother in law, Mr. Cholmondeley, had attended, before I reached Broadwell, to sign the School deed, as a principal contributor—Mr. Cholmondeley is not unlikely to become the Rector of Broadwell with Adlestrop, at an early period, on the resignation of Lord Saye and Sele: ... Lord Leigh has lately purchased from his Father's Executors and Trustees the ancient family estate at Longborough, which the late Lord had directed by his will to be sold to pay the fortunes of younger children. By this arrangement Lord L. preserves in the family the greater part of an ancient Leigh property, and is enabled to accommodate his neighbour, Sir Charles Rushout; whose Sesincote estate will be greatly enlarged and improved by the addition of six hundred acres of the Longborough land which, being the property of the Leighs, so closely hemmed in the Sesincote grounds as to be almost indispensable to the comfort of the proprietors of the latter.*

1852: 9 Jun: *Made a long visit to the Exhibition of the Royal Academy. Met there Mr. Ansley Robinson, Lord Leigh &c.—The latter kindly promised to procure me an order to see the gallery of his Father in law the Marquis of Westminster.*

LEITH — Miss Leiths from Kensington visiting the Dukinfields at Standlake

1801: 8 Jul: *Two Miss Leiths arrived from Kensington to spend this holidays here. Music & Dancing in the Evening.*

LEMAN — James Leman[78]

James Leman (1795-1876), solicitor, was born in Bristol, son of Thomas Curtis Leman (1768-1831) and Ann Shapland Jones (1770-1825). He was married to Caroline Cecilia Morgan (1812-1885); they had 5 sons and 4 daughters:

1 James Curtis (1833-1897)
1 Caroline Gertrude (1835-1913)
2 Julia Lucy (1837-1878)
2 George Downton (1838-1906)
3 Philip Ernest (1839-1900)
4 Frederick William (1841-1865)
3 Mary Katherine (1842-1886)
5 Robert Edward (1844-1927)
4 Edith Grace (1846-1937)

Leman was a partner with William Vizard, of Dursley, in the firm Vizard and Leman, of 51 Lincoln's Inn Fields, but this partnership ended on 31 December 1852. He had a hand in assets resulting from slavery—possibly through his Bristol connections—and was awarded part of the compensation for Lord Holland's estates Sweet River and Friendship Pen in Westmoreland, Jamaica, almost certainly as trustee with Benjamin Curry.

1840: 5 Aug: *I found poor Mrs. Dolphin awaiting my arrival, in great distress and agitation.... by Messrs. Leman and Bowen, as Trustees of the Eyford property.* 6 Aug: *Mrs. D. proposes to go to London to-morrow to consult her legal friend, Mr. Leman, on the predicament in which she and her mother are now placed.*

1847: 23 Jan: *A letter from the Office of Messrs. Vizard & Leman Solrs.—London, addressed to me by error: should have been addressed to E.F.W; as one of the Exors. of the late Lady Burdett ...*

1852: 28 May: *... and the affair ended, so far as this preliminary step is concerned, by my paying the Bailiff £2.—to prevent his carrying away the farming stock (probably, a cow,) which he had seized; this being done, professedly, against Mrs. D's will, to prevent the publicity incident to a removal of the animal taken in execution—Mrs. D., of course, repaid me the £2. 0. 0. and would state all that had passed to her Solicitor and Trustee, Mr. Leman, in London, who must do what is further needful in the matter ...*

1854: 30 Jun: *Received a letter from Revd. J. Dolphin, from Autingham, in Norfolk, asking for information as to the sale of the Eyford estates, now advertised for public competition at an early date. He has been led to suppose that he has a contingent interest in the property, though assured by Mr. Leman, the Trustee and Solicitor, that it is not so.*

LENNARD — *see* Barrett-Lennard

LENNOX — Lady William Lenox — *see* Paton

LEONARD — Henry Leonard[79]

Henry Leonard was a furnishing ironmonger and cutler, trading from 395 High Street, Cheltenham. His partnership had been dissolved by 1846, and by 1848 he was a bankrupt.

1838: 2 Jun: *Also to Leonard, Cutler, Cheltenham, with a remittance for the amount of his bill for articles supplied to E.F.W. and for the payment of the sacramental Service which I presented to the Stow Union on the 31st. Ult.* 5 Jun.

1846: 8 Jul: *from Mr. Leonard, Cheltenham, Hardwareman, with a bill.* 6 Dec: *A letter from an official assignee at Bristol as to a small sum owing by me to ____ Leonard, of Cheltenham, an Ironmonger, a Bankrupt.* 7 Dec.

1847: 15 Jan., 18 Jan: *Remitted to E M Miller, Official Assignee, Bristol, 2/9 in postage stamps, in payment of a debt due by me to the estate of H Leonard, late Ironmonger, Cheltenham, now a Bankrupt.*

LESLIE — Alexander Leslie[80]

Alexander Leslie, 9th earl of Leven (1749-1820), comptroller of the customs, was born in Edinburgh, son of David Leslie Melville, 6th earl of Leven (1722-1802), and Wilhelmina Nisbet (±1724-1798). Leslie was styled Lord Balgonie between 1754 and 1802, during which time he succeeded as 9th earl of Leven. He was comptroller of the customs from 1786 until his death, and was created DL of Fife in 1794. Why Francis Witts was trying to see him is unknown, but it is likely to have been in relation to his career as he was actively job-hunting at the time. Lord Balgonie was an acquaintance of Edward and Agnes Witts; they were first introduced to him on 5 October 1796 and there are frequent references in Agnes's diary to the Leslie family in Edinburgh.

Alexander Leslie married, 1784, Jane Thornton (1757-1818). He succeeded as 9th earl of Leven in 1802.

1801: 28 May: *made unsuccessful calls at Lord Balgonie's & at Mr. Hyett's.*

1805: 7 Jul: *Called upon Lady Leven & Miss Hughes.* 31 Jul: *Mr. Vansittart & Lord Leven called & sat some time with me.*

LESLIE — Charles Powell Leslie — *see also* Madden[81]

Charles Powell Leslie (1769-1831), MP and landed proprietor, was born at Glasslough, co. Monaghan, eldest son of Charles Powell Leslie, MP for co. Monaghan, and his first wife, Prudence Penelope, daughter of Arthur Hill Trevor, 1st Viscount Dungannon. He was educated at Christ Church, Oxford, and was MP for co. Monaghan in 1801-26, and New Ross in 1830-31. He married, first, 1791, Anne (d. 1813), daughter of Dudley Charles Ryder; they had 3 daughters:

1 Alicia Maria
2 Charlotte; died unmarried
3 Anne; married John Gurdon of Assington, Suffolk

Leslie married secondly, 24 May 1819, Christiana, daughter of George Fosberry of Clorane, co. Limerick; they had 3 sons and 4 daughters:

1 Charles Powell
2 John
3 Thomas
1 Christiana; married, 1843, Revd Lord John Beresford
2 Prundentia Penelope
3 Julia
4 Emily

Charles Powell Leslie was sheriff for co. Monaghan in 1788-89, governor in 1802, and colonel of the Monaghan Militia in 1797-1831. He was the elder brother of John Powell Leslie (*below*).

1826: 17 Jun: *I found poor Lady Rossmore under considerable agitation and uneasiness, owing to letters received from Ireland, intimating, that her step-son, Mr. Westenra, who has, contrary to my surmises, succeeded in securing his return for the County of Monaghan, on the popular, that is, the Roman Catholic interest, turning out his old colleague, Colonel Leslie, has been wounded in a duel, arising out of the contest, with a Col. Madden, nephew of Colonel Leslie. Very strong, & what we in England should call very unjustifiable measures, have been resorted to both at the Monaghan.*

LESLIE — John Powell Leslie — *see also* Hewitt, King, *and* Lifford[82]

John Powell Leslie (1772-1854), Church of Ireland clergyman, was born at Glasslough, co. Monaghan, second son of Charles Powell Leslie, MP for co. Monaghan, and his first wife, Prudence Penelope, daughter of Arthur Hill Trevor, 1st Viscount Dungannon. This attribution is not certain, but there seem to have been connections among this Irish set in Clifton. John Powell Leslie's son, Charles Leslie (1810-1870), was later to marry, first, 8 April 1834, Frances (d. 1835), daughter of Gen. Robert Edward King, 1st Viscount Lorton of Boyle, and Lady Frances, née Parsons. He married secondly, 22 August 1837, Louisa Mary, daughter of Lt-Col Sir Henry King and Mary Hewitt.

John Powell Leslie was bishop of Dromore from 1812 to 1820, when he was translated to the See of Elphin. In 1841 he became the first bishop of the united diocese of Kilmore, Elphin, and Ardagh.

If the mention in the diary does not, in fact, refer to John Powell Leslie, it may refer instead to his elder brother, Charles Powell Leslie (1769-1831) (*above*). There was also a Miss Leslie in Clifton, frequently mentioned in Agnes Witts's diaries, who was occasionally in the company of Mrs King.

1806: 12 Feb: *I presided at supper at one of the Tables, where the Goold party, the Adairs & Cecilia made my office very pleasant.*

Formed a little quiet Circle after the Ladies were gone, Gillibrand, Geo. Gould, Mr. Leslie, Mr. Adair, Napier & myself. Kept up the dancing till four o clock in the Morning.

LEVERSAGE — Peter Leversage [83]

Peter Leversage (1805-1864), JP, landed proprietor, barrister, and businessman, was born at Middle Lypiatt, Gloucestershire, the only son of Peter Leversage. He was educated at Harrow School, Jesus College, Cambridge, and the Middle Temple, where he was called to the bar on 21 November 1845.

There is surprisingly little information on Leversage. He inherited Middle Lypiatt estate, which entailed about 347 acres, and presumably also shares in the Stroud Brewery, which his father had founded in 1793. However, there is a chance that his father's business partner, Joseph Watts of Stratford Park, had taken ownership of the whole brewery before it was to pass to Leversage. By 1826 Leversage's father had died, and by the 1830s he was living at Eastington. In 1845 he sold the Lypiatt estate to Henry Wyatt, of Farmhill Park, and then appears to have moved to nearby Ebley.

Leversage married, first, at St Marylebone, Westminster, 25 August 1829, Mary (1802-1831), eldest daughter of R. Holden, but she died young and was buried at Eastington. He married secondly, ±1832, Margaret Ann (1816-1906), daughter of Donald MacLean, of Stanley House, Gloucestershire, and Jane, daughter of George Brown of London; they had 3 sons and 2 daughters:

1 Peter (1833-1898)
1 Mary (1837-1906)
2 Edward Howard (1840-1913); married, at Greenwich, Kent, 18 November 1863, Catherine Williams (b. ±1841)
2 Ellen (b. 1855)
3 Cecil de Worthe (1855-1944)

By 1861 the family was living at 32 Clarendon Villas, Kentish Town, London. Margaret remained in London following her husband's death.

1838: 10 Apr: *During the day I was much in communication with my brother Mag. Purnell, the two Hales, the Bakers, Lawrence, Ford, Archd. Timbrill, Harford, Battersby, Hallewell, Leversage, Curtis Hayward &c.*

1842: 1 Jul: *from Mr. Leversage, a Glostershire Mag. residing at Ebley, a letter containing references to certain adjudged cases, which he had promised to send me.*

LEVESON-GOWER — Francis Leveson-Gower [84]

Francis Leveson-Gower, later Egerton, 1st earl of Ellesmere (1800-1857), politician and poet, was born at 21 Arlington Street, Piccadilly, London, the younger son of George Granville Leveson-Gower, 2nd marquess of Stafford (1758-1833), politician and art patron, created duke of Sutherland in 1833, and Elizabeth, countess of Sutherland, only daughter of William Sutherland, 18th earl of Sutherland. He was educated at Eton College and Christ Church, Oxford. On 6 August 1819 he became a lieutenant in the Staffordshire Regiment of Yeomanry, and was promoted to captain on 27 September in the same year. He was elected MP for Bletchingley on 19 February 1822, and commenced his public career. He also began his literary career around this time with the publication of his translations of Goethe's *Faust* and Schiller's *Song of the Bell* (1823). Leveson-Gower married, 18 June 1822, Harriet Catherine (1800-1866), only daughter of Charles Greville and Charlotte, eldest daughter of William, 3rd duke of Portland; they had 5 sons and 2 daughters.

As a liberal Conservative of the Canning school, Leveson-Gower spoke eloquently on behalf of free trade well before it became a fashionable cause. He carried in the House of Commons a motion for the endowment of the Catholic clergy, and warmly supported the project of the founding of London University. On 26 June 1826 he became MP for Sutherland, was re-elected for that county in 1830, and afterwards sat for South Lancashire in the parliaments of 1835, 1837, and 1841 until July 1846. In the meantime he held office as a lord of the Treasury (April to September 1827), under-secretary of state for the colonies (January to May 1828), chief secretary to the marquess of Anglesey, lord lieutenant of Ireland (21 June 1828 to 30 July 1830), and secretary for war (30 July to 30 November 1830). He was sworn of the privy council on 28 June 1828, and likewise for Ireland on 9 August 1828.

On the death of his father in 1833 he assumed the surname and arms of Egerton in place of his patronymic, Leveson-Gower. Under the will of Francis Egerton, 3rd duke of Bridgewater, he became the owner of estates estimated at £90,000 per annum. At the commemoration at Oxford on 10 June 1834 he was created DCL, and in October 1838 he became rector of King's College, Aberdeen. He spent the winter of 1839 in the East, voyaging in his own yacht to the Mediterranean and the Holy Land. He recorded his observations in *Mediterranean Sketches*, published in 1843.

1828: 28 Jun: *Lord Francis Leveson Gower, a very promising young nobleman, Son of the Marquis of Stafford, a literary character, and translator of Goethe's Faust, is appointed Secretary for Ireland in the room of Mr. Lamb, who has resigned.*

LEVETT — Walter Levett [85]

Walter Levett (1784-1860), Church of England clergyman, was born at Stafford, son of Richard and Lucy Levett. He was educated at Westminster School and Christ Church, Oxford (BA 1806; MA 1808). He served as vicar of Carleton, Yorkshire, in 1816-49, vicar of Bray, Berkshire, in 1823-25 and 1826, and sub-dean of York in 1827. It appears from the diaries that Walter Levett continued his connection with Bray. He married, 1823, at Halifax, Miss Susanna Sheepshanks.

1825: 4 Jul: *The Vicarage of Bray is in the gift of this very respectable prelate, who on the decease of a late worthy vicar, the Revd. Mr. Townsend, gave the living to the Revd. Mr. Levett, Incumbent of Carlton near Skipton, Yorkshire, & late Tutor of Christ Church, to hold till his nephew should be in priest's orders.*

1827: 12 Jun: *Mr. G. Wellford drove over from Bray to tea and spent an hour with us. He looked ill, and has been indisposed. He retains the Curacy of that parish under the new Vicar Mr. Levett, who succeeded about a twelvemonth since to the living, on the decease of the late amiable young Incumbent, Mr. Legge, whom I met two years since at my friend Wellfords' lodgings in the Hospital at Bray.*

1832: 12 Jun: *Mr. Levett, the Vicar, was at this time absent from home, on a visit to his preferment and friends in Craven; where he is Vicar of Carlton near Skipton; he married a Miss Sheepshanks, a lady of good fortune, nearly related to Mrs. Lister Marsden, the wife of Mr. L. M. the Vicar of Gargrave in Craven, at whose house Mr. & Mrs. Levett are now staying.*

1842: 21 Jul: *He is a very pious, devoted Christian; adheres strictly to the Puritan school, has a great horror of the opinions and writings of the so called Puseyite school, and generally disapproves what are styled high Church principles; but lives on terms of friendship with some who hold them, as with his Vicar (Levett) and myself.*

LEWES — Thomas Lewes[86]

Thomas Lewes (1793-1873), JP and Church of England clergyman, was born at Llysnewydd, Carmarthenshire, son of William Lewes. He was educated at Eton College and Brasenose, Oxford (BA 1815; MA 1817). He was ordained deacon on 15 June 1816 and priest on 21 December 1817. He was given his first clerical appointment as stipendiary curate at Llanfihangel-ar-Arth on 21 December 1817, and was later made vicar on 14 March 1818. He then served as rector of Taynton, Oxfordshire, from 3 December 1819, and vicar of Great Barrington, Oxfordshire, from 1820 to 1873.

Thomas Lewes was a Gloucestershire JP. He lived at Taynton and died unmarried. His brother, Price Lewes (±1795-1878), was also educated at Eton College and Brasenose, Oxford; he became a barrister at Lincoln's Inn in 1826. Price Lewes lived at lodgings in 4 Suffolk Place, St Martin-in-the-Fields, and also died unmarried. On some occasions the diarist inadvertently wrote 'Lewis' instead of 'Lewes'.

1825: 29 Jul: *We dined at Mr. Ford's at Little Risington, & met Mr. Lewes, Rector of Great Barrington and Taynton.*

1826: 5 Sep.

1827: 20 Jul: *We dined at Mr. Ford's at Little Risington, and met Mr. Phillimore, Rector of Shipton under Wychwood, Mr. Lewis, Rector of Little Barrington in this county & Incumbent of Taynton in Oxfordshire.* 2 Oct.

1828: 8 Oct.

1829: 6 Oct.

1832: 25 Apr: *The first meeting for the year of the Stow Clerical Society, which I attended. About twelve members dined at the White Hart Inn, Mr. Lewes, the Incumbent of Taynton in Oxfordshire, and Great Barrington in Gloucestershire, being in the Chair.*

1834: 29 Jul., 1 Aug: *On the Blue side, James Dutton, Lord Sherborne's eldest son was conspicuous, maintaining a cause opposite to that espoused by his Father. Of the same party there were presents Messrs. Ford, Pitt, Newell, Bowen, Hornsby, Cresswell, Pantin, Lewes &c.* 20 Aug.

1835: 13 Jan., 12 Feb., 12 May, 17 Jun.

1836: 22 Aug: *Soon after our return my son and I went in our open carriage to dine with Winter at Daylesford. Met Bowen, Lewes, Barter and his son, and Mr. Lockwood.* 24 Aug., 27 Sep: *A cheerful party assembled at an excellent dinner at the Unicorn.* 21 Dec.

1837: 17 Mar., 19 Apr., 28 Apr: *At the Fords I met Capt. Leigh & his sister, Bowen, Lewes, and Polson.* 16 May, 23 Nov.

1838: 25 Sep.

1839: 6 Apr., 20 Jun: *I dressed at Stow, and M W. called for me in the chariot to dine at Daylesford parsonage with the Winters. We had a pleasant party, meeting Mr. & Mrs. Pole, Mr. and Mrs. Lockwood, and Mr. Lewes.* 15 Aug: *A good deal of justice business transacted with the Dean of Gloucester, Ford, and R. Waller as my colleagues: present also Messrs. Winter, Vavasour, Bowen, Lewes, and his brother, Price Lewes.* 23 Aug.

1840: 26 Mar., 29 Apr., 17 Jun., 30 Jul., 20 Aug., 29 Sep., 12 Nov: *A full bench of magistrates—the Dean of Gloucester, Messrs. Pole, Ford, R. Waller and myself, assisted by Messrs. C. R. Pole, E. Rudge, W B. Pole, Baillie, Winter, Lewes.* 18 Nov: *We had a rough drive to and from the Rectory at Daylesford, whither we went to dine with the Winters; meeting Sir Charles and Lady Imhoff, the Dean of Gloucester, Emma and John Talbot Rice, Compton & Clara Reade, and Mr. Lewes. A pleasant party.* 22 Nov: *A letter from Mr. Lewes on the same subject, naming a young man of his parish, Barrington, likely to suit me, but with the fault of being older than I wish.* 23 Nov.

1842: 28 Jan: *At Bourton met and conversed with Mr. Lewes.* 3 Mar., 24 Mar., 31 Mar., 21 Apr., 27 Apr., 7 Jul., 27 Sep., 6 Oct.

1843: 26 Sep., 16 Nov., 7 Dec.

1844: 29 Feb., 20 May: *There we awaited the arrival of the Wonder coach for the Farringdon station, in which we proceeded having a sensible and well-informed fellow passenger inside, apparently of London, and a commercial gentleman; at Burford we took up our agreeable acquaintance, Mr. Lewes, who was travelling to town, and from whom we did not part till we reached the Paddington station.* 25 Jul., 11 Dec.

1845: 23 Jan., 25 Jun.

1846: 10 Sep., 15 Oct., 12 Nov.

1847: 11 Mar., 24 Jun., 29 Jul., 5 Aug: *To the Justice room, where R. Waller attended as my Colleage, and we heard and settled several cases. Mr. Perkins, Mr. W. B. Pole, Mr. Lewes, and Mr. Price Lewes were our assessors.* 16 Sep., 14 Oct., 23 Dec.

1848: 9 Mar., 13 Apr., 16 May, 15 Jun., 17 Aug., 23 Aug.

1850: 24 Jan., 7 Mar., 28 Mar., 24 Jun: *Most cordially and kindly received by my friends at Daylesford Parsonage. Mr. Lewes, of Taynton, and Mr. Beck, Curate of Cornwell, joined us at dinner.* 12 Sep., 24 Oct., 8 Nov: *Other Clergymen, like ourselves, proceeding by rail to Gloucester, among them Messrs. Hurd, Scott, Greene, Hutchinson, Lewes &c. Joined Hutchinson & Lewes, who, with Vavasour and myself, were occupied for the hour which preceded mid-day, the time fixed for the Archi-diaconal meeting in inspecting the Shire Hall and the County Prison, with both of which, especially the latter, my neighbours were much struck and greatly interested.*

1851: 9 Jan., 19 Feb., 4 Nov., 2 Dec.

1853: 3 Mar., 18 Jun: *Much hurry and confusion in the transfer of passengers and luggage from the Great Western to the Oxford, Worcester and Wolverhampton line.——Here I met Winter and Lewes returning, like myself, from Town.*

1854: 2 Feb., 9 Feb., 22 Jun.

LEWIS — Arthur G. Lewis — *see also* Westenra[87]

Arthur G. Lewis (d. 1869), lieutenant-colonel and land agent, was born in Ireland. He acted as agent for William Warner Westenra, 2nd Lord Rossmore (1765-1842) of Monaghan. Warner Westenra's son, Richard Westenra (1796-1838) married Henrietta (d. 1860), daughter of Henry Owen Scott of Scotstown, co. Monaghan; the couple had at least 3 daughters. In 1841, three years after Richard Westenra's premature death, Arthur G. Lewis married Richard's widow, Henrietta, apparently with the blessing of his employer.

1840: 13 Sep: *When the Service was over, and at the Churchyard gate, I was accosted in a friendly manner by Mr. Gist, who explained that his lady was absent from being slightly indisposed: and a middle aged gentleman, Irish from his accent, whom I understand to be a Mr. Lewis, and a relation of Lord Rossmore, addressed me in his Lordship's name in set phrase of politeness and thanks, requesting me to call on Lord R. when I came to Cheltenham.* 22 Sep: *Two Gentlemen, to whom I was introduced by his Lordship, were sitting with him: the name of one, a Clergyman, escaped my; the other, I believe, was Mr. Lewis, but not the gentleman of that name whom I saw at Stanway; and who is a connection of Lord R., and his agent in Ireland.*

LEWIS — George Lewis[88]

George Lewis (1806-1868), sculptor and monumental mason, was born at Gloucester. At the time of the 1851 census he was at 14 Clarence Street, Cheltenham, but he later moved to number

7, Clarence Street, Rose & Crown passage, Cheltenham. He was married to Frances (±1809-1851); they had 1 son and 7 daughters:

1 Frances (b. ±1830)
2 Hannah (b. ±1833)
1 George (1835-1867); married, at Coventry, 25 August 1858, Sarah Maria French (b. ±1837)
3 Ann (b. ±1842)
4 Louisa C. (b. ±1843)
5 Adelaide (b. ±1844)
6 Ellen H (b. ±1847)
7 Kate Clara (b. 1849)

1842: 3 Dec: *We afterwards visited the Shop of Geo. Lewis, the Sculptor, who executed the monument erected at Stanway in memory of Lady Rossmore, and who has just completed a very handsome marble monument in memory of the late Sir W. B. Burdett, to be placed in St. Philip's Church, Leckhampton.* 9 Dec: *Lewis the Sculptor, called by appointment, and we fixed upon a monumental tablet to be erected to the memory of Mrs. Backhouse in the Chancel of Upper Slaughter Church.*

1843: 5 Jan., 10 Jan., 10-11 Feb.

1845: 10 May: *Wrote to Dryden, enclosing a note which I had received at Cheltenham from Lewis, the Sculptor there, as to his charge for a tablet, similar to the one erected in this Church in memory of Mrs. Backhouse, with a view to the raising one like it at Broadwell in remembrance of Mrs. Dryden.* 29-30 May, 4 Jun., 8 Jun., 27-28 Jun.

LEWIS — John Lewis Hampton Lewis [89]

John Lewis Hampton Lewis (1798-1871) was born at Henllys, Llanfaes, Anglesey, son of John Hampton Hampton Lewis (1775-1843) and Mary (1774-1842), daughter of Richard Chambers of Whitbourn Court and Cradley Hall, Herefordshire. By 1830 his father had assumed by royal licence the additional surname and arms of Lewis.

John Lewis Hampton Lewis married, 1833, Elizabeth Frances [Frances Elizabeth] Anson (1815-1878), only child and heir of Thomas I'Anson of Prior House, Richmond; they had 2 sons and 2 daughters:

1 Thomas Lewis Hampton (1834-1912); *see below*
2 John Vivian Hampton (1835-1890); married, 1868, Laura Elizabeth Phipps
1 Fanny Mary Hampton (b. 1838)
2 Mary Freeman Grace Hampton (b. 1842)

Thomas Lewis Hampton Lewis (1834-1912) was educated at Sandhurst and entered the Army in 1852. He served in the Crimean War in 1854-56 and was at Balaclava, Inkerman, Tchernaya, and Sebastopol.

1848: 13 Jul: *Between it and Beaumaris are the parkish grounds & fine woods of Baron Hill, the seat of Sir R. Bulkeley, and very near to Llanfaes, overlooking it, the well placed mansion of Mr. Hampton Lewis, which, however, he does not himself occupy, residing at or near York. This gentleman is a first cousin of Mrs. Aston, being the son of a sister of her father, Mr. Chambers.* 16 Jul: *After the service was concluded, I followed the main stream of the congregation to Beaumaris by a different road from that which I had come. The new line led, below Mr. Hampton Lewis's house, and near to Baron Hill, through well wooded pastures, and hayfields, commanding magnificent views of the Caernarvonshire mountain range, of the Bay, and Strait, with a striking prospect of the old Castle and Church, and town of Beaumaris.*

LEWIS — Thomas Frankland Lewis [90]

Thomas Frankland Lewis (1780-1855), MP and landed proprietor, was the son of John Lewis, of Harpton Court, Radnorshire, and Anne, daughter of Adm. Sir Thomas Frankland, 5th baronet. He was educated at Eton College and Christ Church, Oxford. He married, first, 1805, Harriet (d. 1838), daughter of Sir George Cornewall, 2nd baronet, and Jane Naper. He married secondly, 1839, Mary Anne Ashton.

Thomas Frankland Lewis was MP for Beaumaris in 1812-26, Ennis in 1826-28, Radnorshire in 1828-34, and New Radnor Boroughs in 1847-55. He held various government posts including that of commissioner of revenue in 1822-25. Jane, Lady Cornewall was the first cousin once removed of the diarist, Francis Witts.

1825: 25 Jan: *besides Mrs. Whalley we met Mrs. Charles Whalley and her two agreeable daughters; also her eldest Son, Mr. Henry Whalley, who is a clerk in the Comptroller's Office, Whitehall, of which his Uncle Frederick is the Secretary, & also acts as private Secretary to another Uncle, Mr. Frankland Lewis, who is at the head of an important commission, which is engaged in enquiries as to the Revenue department in Ireland, with a view of consolidating some of the Offices, remodelling others, limiting the expences incident to the collection of the Revenue, and generally improving the System.*

LEWTON — Edward Lewton [91]

Edward Lewton (±1769-1830), Church of England clergyman and professor of classical and general literature, was born at Bristol, son of Edward Lewton. He was educated at Wadham College, Oxford (BA 1792; MA 1794), and ordained deacon on 30 November 1792 and priest on 22 December 1793. He was chaplain of the East India College, Haileybury, in 1812-13, and also professor of classical and general literature, librarian, and registrar.

1802: 14 Jul: *Dined in the Common Room with Williams, meeting the Honbl. & Revd. Mr. Meade, Dr. Lewton, Mr. Carrington & Brown.*

1804: 12 Feb: *Evans breakfasted with me. Accompanied him to hear Lewton at St. Mary's.*

LIDDELL — Robert Liddell [92]

Robert Liddell (1808-1888), Church of England clergyman, was the fifth son of Thomas Henry Liddell, 1st Baron Ravensworth (1775-1855), and Maria Susannah Simpson (1773-1845). His parents married on 26 March 1796. Robert Liddell was educated at Christ Church, Oxford (BA 1829; MA 1834). He was vicar of Barking, Essex, in 1836-51, and then vicar of St Paul, Knightsbridge, in 1851-81. He married Emily Ann Charlotte (1803-1876), daughter of Gerald Wellesley, granddaughter of Garret Wesley, 1st earl of Mornington, and great-niece to Arthur Wellesley, 1st duke of Wellington; they had 3 sons and 1 daughter:

1 Georgiana Maria (b. 1836)
1 Arthur Thomas (1837-1919); succeeded as 5th Baron Ravensworth
2 Gerald George (1839-1897)
3 Charles John (1843-1931)

1853: 12 Jun: *Accompanied the Howells & Mrs. W. Ffooks to St. Paul's Church, Knightsbridge, where I obtained a seat in Mrs. Backhouse's pew:—a very full and polished congregation:—the service very well performed, with chanting &c.: and an excellent sermon preached by Mr. Liddell, the Incumbent.*

LIDDIARD — John V. Liddiard[93]

John V. Liddiard (±1794-1870), stationer and clerk, was born in Bristol and is listed in the 1861 census as a solicitor's managing clerk. He appears to have settled in Chipping Norton early on in his life.

1842: 22 Dec: *In a case of affiliation, Mr. Lediard, of Chipping Norton, Defendant's Attorney, took an objection on a point of form, which was probably, valid, and is likely to defeat the present application for an order: the point was reserved for further consideration.*

1843: 16 Feb: *Much business respecting the medical arrangements of the Union, the Settlement case of R. Fox, and other difficult matters, occupied me till 3 P.M. when I joined Messrs. Ford and Waller at the Justice Room, where again I had to encounter heavy and rather difficult work in an order of bastardy (the party charged being defended by Lediard, an Atty. from Chipping Norton,) a suspended order of removal—a charge of sheep stealing not made out &c.*

1851: 8 May: *A person from Salford, Baughan by name, summoned to our Petty Sessions as putative father of a bastard, with a view to an order of filiation being made on him, called with a letter addressed to me by Mr. Leddiard, Managing Clerk of Mr. Aplin of Chipping Norton, requesting that the hearing may be postponed, as he had only recently been instructed in the case, to defend Baughan.... Among the cases brought before us was the order of filiation respecting which I had received a note from Mr. Leddiard this morning—the case was heard—the order made.* 16 May.

LIFFORD — *see* Hewitt

LIGHT — Captain Light, candidate for the position of gaoler at Gloucester

1836: 16 Jul: *A printed letter from Capt. Light, one of the candidates for the vacant situation of Gaoler at Gloucester.* 23 Jul: *A letter from Mr. Pye, Incumbent of Cirencester and Preb. of Worcester, bespeaking my favourable attention to the claims of Capt. Light, one of the Candidates for the vacancy caused by the decease of Cunningham the Gaoler at Gloucester.* 10 Aug: *Consequently, it was necessary to throw overboard two other candidates otherwise very likely to discharge the duties of the office satisfactorily, Capt. Light, and Corporal Major Swinley of the Horse Guards.*

LIGHTBOURNE — Rebecca Lightbourne— *see also* Timbrell[94]

Rebecca Lightbourne, née Timbrell (1749-1823), was born in London, the youngest daughter of William Timbrell (1705-1774) and Patience Gleadow (b. 1711). She married, at St Marylebone, Westminster, 27 November 1780, Thomas Lightbourne (1750-1813).

Francis Witts made a surprising error in calling Rebecca Judith in reference to her funeral. In her will Rebecca Lightbourne desired that her coffin should be laid in the family vault at Bunhill Fields, London, alongside her maiden sisters, Patience and Judith.

The detailed entry for 24 December 1823 is worth reading in full for the history behind the Timbrell sisters' success in acquiring the Sandywell estate. It was through these sisters that Francis Witts acquired the living of Upper Slaughter. The full entry for 7 August 1826 is also of interest.

1823: 23 Dec: *Very early in the morning, before I rose, I received a letter from my wife, inclosing a card of invitation to attend the funeral of Mrs. Judith Lightbourne. She had rightly judged, that I should consider this mark of respect indispensable.* 24 Dec: *I resorted at the early hour of ½ past eight in a mourning coach to the residence of the late M*[rs.] *Lightbourne in a small street near the bottom of the town, where with her sisters, now deceased, she had resided since first their claim to the estates and fortune of the late Mrs. Travell Tracy of Sandy well Park was made.*

1826: 7 Aug: *when Mrs. Lightbourne died in the close of 1823, mentioned the disposition, which she made of her property in favour of Mr. Walter Lawrence, superseding a former will made in favour of her former legal adviser, Mr. Thompson of London. By that older will, besides the bequest to Mr. Thompson, a tenement in Whittington & £10000 were bequeathed to a man named Freeman, a Cheltenham Apothecary, and who attended Mrs. Lightbourne professionally. This person is dead, leaving a widow & family in great distress, and Mr. Newmarch, considering himself under some obligations to the poor woman, has been a great friend to her.*

1832: 27 Mar: *Some hesitation might have arisen also as to Mr. Lawrence's title to the Advowson in a person not well acquainted with the manner, in which he has hitherto maintained his ground against the impugners of the validity of Mrs. Lightbourne's will, under which Mr. Lawrence holds. But an abortive attempt having already been made to set aside that will, it is not very likely, at the interval of some years, that another like attempt should be made.*

LINDLEY — Robert Lindley[95]

Robert Lindley (1776-1855), cellist, was born at Rotherham, Yorkshire, son of Shirley Linley, a proficient cellist, of Masbrough. He began to teach his son the violin when he was 5 and the cello when he was 9. In 1792 Robert became a pupil of James Cervetto, the outstanding cellist of his day, who having heard him play, gave him free tuition.

In 1794, having moved to the south of England, Robert succeeded Sperati as principal cello at the Italian Opera in London—a post he held until 1851—and at all the major concerts. Domenico Dragonetti, the great double bass virtuoso, joined the opera orchestra in the same year as Lindley, and a close friendship developed between them, lasting fifty-two years.

Robert Lindley was generally considered to be the greatest English cellist of his time. Perhaps his most celebrated achievement was his elaborate and ornamental accompaniment of recitative. His exceptional technique, using a firm hand and brilliant full tone complemented by deep artistic feeling, was widely recognised. Robert Lindley was appointed one of the first professors of the Royal Academy of Music upon its formation in 1822.

1801: 29 May: *Violin & Violoncello Mr. Seamus & Mr. Lindley.*

1803: 21 Nov: *Evans sat with me in the Evening, when we adjourned to the Music Room where heard a delicious Concert, in which Miss Parke & Lindley were the principal performers.* 22 Nov: *Miss Parke & Lindley performed beautifully.*

1804: 5 Nov: *First Subscription Concert. Very fully attended. Bartleman Knyvett & Miss Parke & Lindley.* 6 Nov: *Dined with Davis at the Music Room. Lindley Miss Parke & Knyvett charming.*

1805: 29 Nov: *The Concert above the mediocre, Mrs. Ashe very sweet in Se ty ti perdo & th Sweet Bird, Morelli—& eccentric as ever. Lindley surprising & fascinating upon his Violoncello in a less animated Concerto than usual.*

1806: 19 Mar: *Accompanied Round & Burney to the Music Room, where the sorry attractions of Mr. Miller, Mrs. Salmon & a Mr. FitzMaurice on a vile squeaking Union Pipe, had collected a tolerably full room. Lindley great as usual, the others not above mediocrity.*

1826: 12 Sep: *Pass we over the heavy looking, but scientific Lindley, unequalled on the Violoncello, Dragonetti superior to all other artists, on what Voss in his Luise, a poem much admired by me in my Juvenile days of reading German poetry, called the mächtige brum-bass.* 13 Sep., 25 Sep.

1829: 17 Sep: *Nor was the Instrumental treat less rich: with such compositions as Haydn's, Rossini's, Mozart's, Cherubini's, Bach, Paer's, Clarke Whitfields's Bishop's, Calcott's & Attwood's, & such masters & such masters in execution as Cramer, Lindley, Marshall, Nicholson on the Flute, Willman on the Clarionet, Bochsa on the harp, it was impossible not to be delighted.* 22 Sep: *Vaughan was chaste, elegant and correct in that beautiful cantata, "See, from the silent grove Alexis flies", which he delights to sing, and amateurs of good taste and feeling equally delight to hear; the music is by Pepusch, and he was admirably accompanied on the Violoncello by Lindley.... Vaughan and Braham & Knyvett have kept their ground these thirty years or nearly; and the same may be remarked of instrumental performers, F. Cramer, Lindley &c.* 23 Sep: *Vaughan's first air was from Judas Maccabaeus, in which he was accompanied on the Violoncello by Lindley with unrivalled skill.*

LINDOW — Charles Thomas Lindow [96]

Charles Thomas Lindow (1827-1864), fund holder, was born at Lower Slaughter, Gloucestershire, the second son of Henry Lindow Rawlinson Lindow (1777-1848) and Charlotte Elizabeth Barnard (1794-1847) (*below*). In 1851 he was listed in the census for Charlbury and Walcot as a fund holder; Charlbury was the home of his uncle, Abram Rawlinson, and he was presumably living at one one of the previous family homes. In 1861 Charles was unmarried, and a boarder at the Three Cocks, Aberllunvey, Breconshire. He died at Chipping Norton, Oxfordshire, presumably at Charlbury.

1846: 6 Aug: *In the Justice room R Waller, the Dean of Gloucester, and myself sat as magistrates; we were assessed by W. B. Pole, Winter, Clarke and two young Lindows.* 17 Sep., 5 Nov.

1850: 7 Feb., 29 Aug.

1852: 1 Apr.

1853: 21 Apr., 5 May, 15 Dec.

LINDOW — Henry Lindow Rawlinson Lindow [97]

Henry Lindow Rawlinson Lindow (1777-1848), landed proprietor, was born Henry Rawlinson. He and his twin brother Abram were the sons of Henry Rawlinson of Grassyard Hall, Caton-with-Littledale, Lancashire. Abram was the elder by some twenty minutes and he inherited the Grassyard Hall estate, but he later moved to Charlbury, near Chipping Norton, Oxfordshire (*see* Rawlinson). Henry inherited the wealth of his uncle, William Lindow (d. 1786), a prosperous West India merchant who had resided in Lancaster with his wife Abigail (1740-1790). Henry was educated at Rugby School and Christ Church, Oxford, where he matriculated in 1795. He assumed the name Lindow by licence in 1792. He married, 1819, Charlotte Elizabeth (1794-1847), daughter of Robert-Cary Barnard, rector of Withersfield, Suffolk, and Elizabeth, daughter of Robert-Cary Elwes of Throcking, Hertfordshire; they had 2 sons and 1 daughter:

1 Henry William (1824-1887); became a first-class cricketer and played for the MCC; *see below*

2 Charles Thomas (1827-1864); died unmarried

1 Louisa Elizabeth (1831-1902); married, 1856, Charles Paget Fitzhardinge Berkeley, 3rd Baron Fitzhardinge of Bristol (1830-1916), son of Adm. Maurice Frederick Fitzhardinge Berkeley, 1st Baron Fitzhardinge of Bristol, and Lady Charlotte Lennox

Henry and Charlotte Lindow appear to have had two London homes over the years: the first was in Hanover Square, and the second was in Cambridge Terrace, Hyde Park, where Charlotte died in 1847. It is unclear when and why Henry left Lancashire for Chadlington, Oxfordshire, but it appears that his twin brother, Abram, was living there. Before 1821 Henry moved to Lower Slaughter, Gloucestershire, where he remained the remainder of his life. It is likely that he took a long tenancy of the Lower Slaughter manor house from the Whitmore family.

1834: 11 Aug.

1835: 13 Jan., 28 May, 4 Jun.

1836: 9 Aug: *Rode with E.F.W. by L. Slaughter, Hyde Mill, Lower Swell and Eyford: Mr. Lindow rode part of the way with us.* 27 Sep: *A cheerful party assembled at an excellent dinner at the Unicorn.*

1838: 10 Feb: *In my walk to the L. Slaughter Turnpike gate met Mr. Lindow, who joined me & with whom I went over the history of the unpleasant controversy now subsisting as to the appointment of a Chaplain to the W.H.* 22 Feb., 25 Sep.

1839: 26 Apr: *Wrote a note to Mr. Lindow with an opinion as to a question put by him to me yesterday, respecting the punishment of persons leaving carriages and horses without persons to guide the horses in highways.* 11 May, 27 Jun.

1840: 30 Apr., 14 May, 11 Jun: *Rode to Stow with Mr. Lindow, whom I met in the Coppice Lane.* 29 Jul: *As I returned home, rode from L Slaughter home with Mr. Lindow, engaged in general conversation.* 24 Oct: *At Mr. Brookes's office held a bed of justice with R. Waller as my colleague, Messrs. Lindow & his brother in law, Barnard, Whitmore Jones and Winter being present.*

1841: 4 Mar.

1842: 20 Jan., 27 Jan., 10 Feb., 17 Feb., 28 Jul., 4 Aug., 11 Aug., 22 Sep., 29 Sep., 6 Oct., 13 Oct.

1843: 20 Aug.

1844: 25 Jul: *Gentlemen present were Mr. Reade, Mr. Chamberlayne, Capt. Leigh, Mr. Winter, Mr. Lewes, Mr. Perkins, a young Lindow, Mr. Bowen &c.* 9 Oct: *At ½ past 8 set out for Burford by the Isis, a coach going to Cheltenham, having for my fellow passengers three clergymen, who had been voting for Dr. Symons; one of whom was Mr. Hesketh, a brother of Sir Hesketh Fleetwood, a clergyman beneficed on the sea-coast of Lancashire, nephew of Mr. Lindow, a pleasant and estimable person.* 23 Dec: *Going and returning for my letters between Lower Slaughter and the Turnpike Gate, met and parleyed with Mr. Lindow.*

1845: 4 Apr.

1846: 26 Jul: *Wrote to Mr. H. Lindow inviting him to dinner on that day.* 23 Aug: *A letter from Geo. Baldwin, who is about to leave Mr. Lindow's service, and would be glad to come into mine. He is now with Mr. L's family at Cheltenham, where Mrs. L is in a poor state of health.* 26 Aug: *Wrote to Mr. Lindow for the character of George Baldwin, and to George Baldwin, that I will take him into my service, if the character be satisfactory. Mr. Lindow and the ladies of his family are now at Cheltenham; for medical advice, Mrs. Lindow being much indisposed.* 28 Aug: *A letter from Lindow with a fair character of George Baldwin.* 18 Sep: *As I walked to and from the turnpike gate at Lower Slaughter, had a long parley with Mr. Lindow.*

1847: 29 Jan: *Learnt the death of poor Mrs. Lindow in Town, of a disease in the womb: she had been considered for some time in a hopeless state.* 11 Mar: *Returned to the Provident Bank, where I met Messrs. Winter, Lewes, W. Vavsour, and H. Lindow.—The latter gave a very bad account of his father's state, who was seized on Tuesday night with an attack of Paralysis, not unaccompanied by Apoplexy. His speech is inarticulate, he has lost the use of one side, and the best hope is a partial recovery, and that very doubtful.* 30 Mar: *A very bad account of the state of our neighbour Mr. Lindow, who is said to have experienced another apoplectic or paralytic attack.*

1848: 12 May: *Informed today that Henry Lindow is likely to be appointed a Magistrate for the County of Gloucester—His father continues miserably infirm and incapacitated by paralysis, a wreck in body and mind, so that the charge of the parent & his concerns has devolved on the Son, who is nowise deficient in ability, but is less steady, sober, and settled in habits than might be wished. As to politics he, like his father, professes Whiggism.* 19 Jun: *Met and chatted with Mrs. W. Vavasour and Emma V. who were driving to call on Miss Lindow.*

1850: 25 Oct: *Other letters and notes received by me were from Winter, excusing himself and wife from dining with me on Wednesday, because Miss Lindow is their guest, who is an invalid, and reluctant to accept invitations to dinner. As I learnt that she was to accompany the Winter's to dine with the Chamberlaynes on Tuesday, I replied to Winter's note by inviting him, Mrs. W. and Miss L. to dinner on Friday in next week;—tho' I met W. we parted without my getting an answer from him.* 27 Oct: *A letter from Winter, who with Mrs. Winter and Miss Lindow decline my invitation for Friday.*

LINDOW — Henry William Lindow[98]

Henry William Lindow (1824-1887), JP, cricketer, and stockbroker, was the eldest son of Henry Lindow Rawlinson Lindow and Charlotte Elizabeth Barnard (*above*). Like his father, he was educated at Rugby School and Oriel College, Oxford. Henry was appointed, by purchase, cornet in the 17th Lancers in July 1844. He spent much of his time in London and was a keen cricketer, playing for the MCC in 1849. By 1851 he had qualified as a Gloucestershire JP, but at the time of the census he was living as a bachelor at 28 Harrington Square, St Pancras, London. Henry married, at Westminster, Middlesex, 24 August 1867, Eliza Mitchell (1840-1905), who was born in Dublin. In 1871 the couple were living at 11 West Cromwell Road, Chelsea, where Henry was listed as a stockbroker. No records have been found regarding children, but the couple were separated in 1883 and Henry petitioned for divorce.

Francis Witts on more than one occasion recorded him as H. L. Lindow. This was probably a slip of the pen.

1842: 8 Jul: *Among the players were Messrs. Colville, Harry Waller, R Waller, T. Wynniatt, Guise, Stenson, H. Lindow, W. Vavasour, Aitkins, W Bryan, Winter, W. B. Pole, E. F. W.* 4 Aug., 29 Sep.

1843: 19 Jan: *At the Unicorn I found the Dean of Gloucester and Mr. Ford, (Magistrates) also Messrs. Winter, W B Pole, and H. Lindow.* 28 Sep.

1844: 4 Apr.

1846: 29 Jul: *A dinner party: the Dean of Gloucester, Mr. and Mrs. Wiggin, J. T. Rice, Mr. and Mrs. W. Vavasour, Miss Vavasour, and Henry Lindow made up our party.* 17 Aug: *Received from Craven two boxes with two brace of grouse in each: the one being sent by Christ. Geldard, the other by Henry Lindow.*

1847: 11 Mar: *Returned to the Provident Bank, where I met Messrs. Winter, Lewes, W. Vavasour, and H. Lindow.—The latter gave a very bad account of his father's state, who was seized on Tuesday night with an attack of Paralysis, not unaccompanied by Apoplexy. His speech is inarticulate, he has lost the use of one side, and the best hope is a partial recovery, and that very doubtful.* 12 May, 24 Sep.

1848: 3 Feb., 12 May: *Informed today that Henry Lindow is likely to be appointed a Magistrate for the County of Gloucester—— His father continues miserably infirm and incapacitated by paralysis, a wreck in body and mind, so that the charge of the parent & his concerns has devolved on the Son, who is nowise deficient in ability, but is less steady, sober, and settled in habits than might be wished. As to politics he, like his father, professes Whiggism, and so has been noticed by Lord Fitzhardinge, whose hunt he has joined, & the Peer enlists him for his own & his party, by proposing to call him to the bench on an early cold seal being issued.*

1850: 26 Sep., 7 Nov: *The result of the meeting is that the Dean of Gloucester, Pole Senr. Ford, R Waller, Witts, Lindow, and Hurd are qualified to act as Commrs. of Land and Assessed taxes.*

1851: 10 Apr: *Ford privately urged upon me the same course, to whom I repeated what I had said to Brookes, with my opinion that the proposition would be repudiated. F. regards this matter as personal, and likely to lead to a quarrel. I argued against any such antagonism as need end in a collision. He protested against the vote of H Lindow being allowed.* 17 Apr.

1852: 25 Mar: *A petty Sessions, at which I presided: Ford, R Waller, & H Lindow being my colleagues, W B Pole, Winter &c. bystanders. Had not met Lindow since his frightful accident last year: he is in a great measure restored to health, but strangely altered in appearance.—His faculties, however, now unimpaired; and he is about to fit up rooms for his future residence at Gawcomb farm, his property, which he proposes to keep in his own hands, and adopt the life of a country gentleman; which will be desirable as withdrawing him from the dissipations and entanglements of a London life, though one cannot expect him to turn the occupation of farmer to a profit. He is decidedly fond of country business, as Magistrate, Commissioner of taxes, and turnpike trusts &c.—and in these departments may be very useful in the neighbourhood.* 27 Mar: *Drove to Stow by appointment to transact Justice business with H L Lindow.* 8 Apr., 22 Apr., 20 May, 1 Dec: *After breakfast drove to Stow, to attend a meeting of Commissioners on an appeal to the assessments to the Property and income tax. Mr. Lindow met me and we were engaged till past three o'clock, having begun soon after eleven.* 2 Dec: *Mr. H W. Lindow, and the Revd.——Saunders were unanimously elected Members of the Stow Book Society.* 16 Dec., 23 Dec.

1853: 13 Jan., 20 Jan., 21 Jan: *Having learnt in a conversation with H. W. Lindow yesterday, that certain impressions of an unfavourable nature had been made on his mind as to the management of our Union concerns, and particularly, as to the employment of Mr. Wilkins in a late parish settlement & lunatic case, and to the Union of the offices of Clerk and Guardian in one person, Mr. Pearce, Exparte views on this subject having been conveyed by John Pegler, who is a busy critic of Union management, ill disposed towards Wilkins, & desirous of change, especially if it should result in a discomfiture of Dissenters, wrote to HWL. At considerable length, pointing out to him the real facts of the matters complained of, and shewing that there is another side of the affairs, different from that which has been presented to him.* 25 Jan: *A very proper letter from H. W. Lindow in answer to that which I lately addressed to him.* 24 Feb., 10 Mar., 24 Mar: *To the Unicorn to hold a Petty Sessions, H W Lindow being my Colleague on the Bench.* 7 Apr., 21 Apr., 5 May, 13 May: *Having failed of meeting H.L.Lindow, whom I had expected to meet at the Board of Guardians, and to whom my son had desired me to give a letter in respect of a coming match at Cricket, and having received from my son at a late hour another letter respecting the same game to be communicated to HLL. I wrote to him a few lines from Stow.* 19

May, 26 May: *H L Lindow attending for the first time as Ex Off. Guardian.* 23 Jun., 15 Dec.

1854: 2 Feb., 9 Feb., 23 Feb., 2 Mar., 23 Mar., 30 Mar: *With H W Lindow held a petty Sessions, to pass the accounts of the Surveyors of Highways for the division, &c.* 13 Apr: *Much may be said for, and something against Lindow—He is a man of pleasure, and apt to be absent from home; but he is a considerable land owner and large occupier, a magistrate, with considerable tact, talent, firmness and discernment; likely to master the details of business, and generally regarded as very clear headed and intelligent.* 20 Apr., 27 Apr: *This I did because I believed the Guardians generally wished to see him in the V. Chair with precedence; because I expected it would lead to his being named Chairman on my retirement; and because I thought he ought not to turn his back on the Church party of Guardians who had proposed him, and would be ready to support him.* 4 May, 11 May, 18 May, 25 May: *... on the Board; at which H. W. Lindow had presided with clearness, steadiness, & good judgment, as far as I could learn by inspection of the minutes, and his own and others representations. I had purposely abstained from attendance to make way for HWL's conducting the business as Vice-Chairman.* 5 Jun., 7-8 Jun., 12 Jun., 15 Jun., 22 Jun., 6 Jul., 13 Jul., 20 Jul., 27 Jul., 3 Aug.

LINDSAY — Mr Lindsay, a dinner guest of Mrs Witts at Champion Hill

1801: 21 Sep: *Mrs. Pages, Mr. Rogers, all very agreeable & a Mr. Lindsay dined with Mrs. Witts.*

LINDSAY — Mrs Lindsay, a guest of Lady Jervis at Clifton

No definite connection has been found, but it is quite possible that Mrs Lindsay was the sister of Lady Jervis (Jane Jervis, née Nisbett). One of Lady Jervis's grandsons was Thomas Lindsay Jervis-White-Jervis (1852-1885), which indicates a Lindsay connection to the family.

1802: 5 Sep: *Drank tea at Lady Jervis's meeting Mrs. Lindsay & Miss Stafford.* 8 Sep: *Walked with Mrs. Lindsay & Miss Stafford Jones &c.*

LING — Miss Ling of Southampton

1835: 14 Jan: *Mr. and Mrs. Dolphin returned together to Eyford on the 8th Inst. an arrangement having been made between them which will suspend, if it does not supersede, the articles of separation to which they agreed some time ago, in consequence of the great misconduct of Mr. Dolphin in attaching himself to Miss Ling of Southampton.*

1847: 21 Jun: *It would seem that V.D. has never left England, but lived in obscurity in some retired place on the allowance furnished by his wife, but of late with-held, as is supposed, from a sense that his bad habits are still persevered in, and that he lives with a mistress; not Miss Ling, who is married.*

LING — William Ling [99]

William Ling (b. 1775), composer and oboist, was the son of Thomas Ling (b. ±1750), a performer on the violin, bassoon, and oboe. His younger brother, also Thomas (1787-1851), was an oboe reed maker, well known for the high quality of his workmanship. As a composer and oboist, Ling was active in London between 1790 and 1831. He remained virtually unknown until the discovery by Egbert Ennulat of the University of Georgia of an extensive manuscript in the Deutsche Staatsbibliotek, Berlin. This manuscript, which lists Ling's significant compositions, states that Ling was organist at St Dunstan in the West.

1826: 25 Sep: *I shall set down the terms, on which the principal performers were engaged ... Ling—(oboe)—(1 other) 31.10.*

LINTON — Mr Linton, a Whitby trader

1801: 11 May: *On entering the Coach, we found a Gentleman & Lady a Mr. Linton, a Whitby trader, a civil young man, & a well looking young woman a Miss DeBrau, both going to London.*

LIPPINCOTT — see also Cann Lippincott

LIPPINCOTT — Henry Cann Lippincott — *see also* Ludlow [100]

Sir Henry Cann Lippincott, 2nd baronet (1776-1829), JP and landed proprietor, was the son of Henry Lippincott (1737-1780) and Catherine Jeffries. He succeeded as 2nd baronet when still a minor. He was educated at Oriel College, Oxford, and became a Gloucestershire JP. The Stoke property came via his mother; when the previous owner, Robert Cann-Jeffries, died in 1773, the whole estate passed to Cann-Jeffries' sister, Catherine, who married Henry Lippincott in 1774. Henry Cann Lippincot died unmarried in Portman Square, Marylebone.

Henry Cann Lippincott had an illegitimate son, Robert (b. 1819), who adopted the name Cann Lippincott by royal licence in 1831. Robert's first wife was Margaret Agnes (d. 1845), daughter of Sgt Ebenezer Ludlow, who interestingly had been one of Robert's trustees in 1832, when he was a boy of 12. Robert and Margaret had four children. He married secondly, at Compton-Greenfield, Gloucestershire, 18 July 1854, Julia Sullivan (b. ±1825), daughter of John Francis Davis.

1804: 4 Sep: *Walked round Sir H. Lippincott's &c. before breakfast.*

1806: 21 Jan: *Besides my excellent friend Dowell, whom I had infinite pleasure in again seeing, we had Col. Kingscote, Sir Will. Guise, & Sir Henry Lippincott, Major Durbin, Capt. Cooke, Mr. Probyn, Messrs. P & J. Baillie, & Mr. Foster.*

1833: 18 Apr: *nearer to Durdham Down, is the old-fashioned & formal but handsome mansion of the late Sir H. C. Lippincott, with whom I had been acquainted in former years, as a Magistrate of Gloucestershire, High Sheriff for the County, & Officer in its Militia. I know not who succeeded to the property of this unhappy man, who with a capacity for better things yeilded to the force of his passions, & so disgraced himself by criminal sensuality, & dishonourable conduct dictated by depraved desires, that his reputation was grievously stained, and debauchery led to a miserable alienation of mind, and prostration of his bodily powers, ending in premature death.*

1845: 30 Jun: *Mr. Bloxsome having received a hurried letter from Mr. Sergeant Ludlow, dated Harrowgate, naming that he had been summoned hastily to that place to the death-bed of his daughter, Mrs. Lippincott, and that her decease would prevent him from presiding in Court at this Sessions.*

LIPSCOMB — Christopher Lipscomb [101]

Christopher Lipscomb (1781-1843), bishop of Jamaica, was the son of William Lipscomb, writer, and Margaret Cooke. He was educated at New College, Oxford (BA 1804; MA 1811; BD 1825; DD 1825). He served as vicar of Sutton Benger, Wiltshire, in 1818-24, and was appointed the first bishop of Jamaica in 1824. He took up the post in 1825.

1824: 19 Jun: *The ministerial arrangements consequent on the formation of the new sees not being concluded, Bp. Lipscomb and Bp. Coleridge have not yet sailed for those colonies, where, it is to be hoped, they will be able gradually to effect much good by concentrating the interests, zeal & intelligence of the Episcopal Clergy, by spreading abroad a spirit of rational piety, by fostering, improving & giving a right direction to education, by ameliorating the tone of morality, and watching over the progress of true religion.*

LISTON — Mr Liston of London

Nothing is known of this person, but he was probably somebody who had been approached, this time by Newbigging (senior), in relation to a position for Francis Witts.

1802: 29 Jan: *Heard from Newbigging, enclosing a letter from his father to Mr. Liston.* 5 Feb: *Wrote to Mr. Liston. Called upon Dr. Jenner.* 8 Feb: *Called upon Mr. Liston, & Mr. B. Witts.*

LITCHFIELD — Harriett Litchfield [102]

Harriett Litchfield, née Sylvester Hay (1777-1854), actress, was daughter of John Sylvester Hay (±1750-±1787), surgeon of the East Indiaman *Nassau* and later head surgeon of the Royal Hospital, Calcutta. He died in Calcutta when his daughter was 9 years old.

Harriett made her first appearance at Richmond in the summer of 1792 as Julia in Colman's *The Surrender of Calais*. She was encouraged by Dorothy Jordan and Robert Burns, but her next engagement, under Francis Aickin at Liverpool, proved unsatisfactory. He allowed her only two parts: Sophia in Thomas Holcroft's *The Road to Ruin* and Edward in Elizabeth Inchbald's *Everyone has his Fault*. On 27 May 1796 Harriett appeared in London at Covent Garden 'as a young Lady' for the benefit of Mary Ann Davenport, playing her Liverpool role of Edward.

Harriett married, 1796, John Litchfield (1774-1858), and briefly left the stage, but reappeared during 1797 for benefit performances at the Haymarket. Her reception at these performances gained her engagements for the following season.

By 1800 Harriett Litchfield was a well-established actress, but after 1806 she appears to have mostly retired from the stage. She played for six nights at Bath in May 1810 as Lady Clermont in Dimond's Adrian and Orilla, and performed in a monodrama by Matthew Gregory Lewis which had been written especially for her. On 8 October 1812 she appeared at the Haymarket as Emilia in Othello, one of her best characters. This was announced as her first appearance on the stage for six years, and it seems to have been her last.

1802: 28 Aug: *To the Play in the Ram's box. the Heir at Law: Mrs. Litchfield reciting Dryden's Alexander's Feast. Field singing a comic Song. Cunningham appearing as Harlequin.*

LITTLEDALE — Joseph Littledale [103]

Sir Joseph Littledale (1767-1842), judge, was the eldest son of Henry Littledale, mercer and draper, of Eton House, Lancashire, and Mary, daughter of Isaac Wilkinson of Whitehaven. He was educated at St John's College, Cambridge (BA 1787; MA 1790), where he was fellow from 1789 to 1821. He was admitted at Lincoln's Inn in 1786, but migrated to Gray's Inn in 1793. He was called to the bar in 1798. Littledale was a special pleader on the northern circuit in 1813 and a bencher in 1821; he became a serjeant-at-law in 1824, and was a judge of the king's bench from 1824 to 1841.

Joseph Littledale married, 1821, Hannah Timberlake. He was knighted in 1824 and became a privy counsellor in 1841.

1830: 20 Apr: *I looked into the Court; Baron Bolland, a new judge, was engaged in nearly the last trial; his Colleague, Mr. Justice Littledale having finished the business at Nisi Prius, had left the town.*

1832: 29 Mar: *... proceeded to the Shire Hall, where I took my place in the Crown Court. The judges were Sir W. E. Taunton and Sir Jos. Littledale.*

1836: 10 Aug: *The Judges, Littledale and Patteson, had arrived at about 6 o clock.*

LITTLEHALES — Joseph Gascoyne Littlehales [104]

Joseph Gascoyne Littlehales (1775-1854), Church of England clergyman, was born at Clerkenwell, London, the son of Revd Joseph Laurentious Littlehales (1741-1804) and Margaret Vernon Gascoigne (1738-1819), who had married at St Andrew's, Holborn, London, on 6 December 1770.

Littlehales was educated at Brasenose College, Oxford (BA 1797; MA 1800), and was ordained deacon on 31 December 1797 and priest on 17 February 1799. He was appointed rector of Condicote, Gloucestershire, on 19 February 1799 and served in the post until 1840. His other appointments were as vicar of Little Bishop's Langham, Norfolk, in 1814, rector of Shalstone, Buckinghamshire, in 1821-54, and rector of Lillingstone Dayrell, Buckinghamshire, in 1848-54.

Littlehales married, at Bicester, Oxfordshire, 13 August 1798, Elizabeth Davis (1780-1863); they had 9 sons and 3 daughters:

1 Margaret (1799-1828)
1 Thomas (1800-1849); *see below*
2 Marie (1802-1827)
2 Charles (1804-1806); died an infant
3 Edward John (1806-1821)
4 Baker Joseph (1807-1895); married, at St Pancras, London, 24 August 1842, Catherine Risdon
5 William Benjamin (1809-1853); died at Boulogne, France
6 George Gascoyne (1811-1871); married, October 1839, Elizabeth Powell
3 Elizabeth Maria (1813-1832)
7 Lee Henry (b. 1815)
8 John Laurentius (b. 1818)
9 Frederick Gascoyne (1821-1903); married, 31 March 1857, Sarah Maria Hall

---

1840: 22 Nov: *Recd. a note from W. B. Pole, inclosing forms of testimonial in his favour for my signature; addressed to the Archb. of Canterbury and Bp. of Glouc. & Bristol; they are to pave the way for his institution to the Rectory of Condicote, to be held by dispensation with that of Upper Swell. The living of Condicote is vacant by the cession of Mr. Littlehales, who has accepted a better piece of preferment in Bucks; and, I presume, Mr. Pole has purchased the advowson of Condicote, that the two livings of Condicote and U. Swell, being small adjacent parishes, may henceforth be held together.*

LITTLEHALES — Thomas Littlehales [105]

Thomas Littlehales (1800-1849), Church of England clergyman, was born at Ambrosden, Oxfordshire, son of Joseph Gascoyne Littlehales (1775-1854) and Elizabeth Davis (1780-1863). He was educated at Westminster School and Christ Church, Oxford (BA 1823; MA 1826). Littlehales was ordained deacon on 13 June 1824 and priest on 28 May 1826. His first clerical appointment was as curate of Charlbury with Shorthampton, Oxfordshire, which also included Chadlington chapel, beginning on 4 January 1825. In 1829 he sailed from Gravesend to Bermuda on HMS *Winchester*; whether he was working as a naval chaplain is not clear, but he remained in Bermuda until at least the end of 1831. By 1834 he was back in England, and on 21 May of that year he was appointed vicar of Butlers Marston, Warwickshire, where he remained until 1843. In parallel he was also rector of Sheering, Essex, in 1834-49. He does not appear to have married.

1827: 16 Aug: *We met the Wynniatts from Guiting Grange, Messrs. Waller, Bowen, Winter, Littlehales. The latter is, I believe, Curate of Chadlington, and Son of a Buckinghamshire Clergyman, who is incumbent of Condicote, but does not reside there.*

1829: 24 Nov.

LIVETT — solicitors of Bristol [106]

The firm of Livett occupied Albion Chambers, Broad Street, Bristol, and was composed of A. J., H., and James Livett.

1848: 22 Nov: *On behalf of Dr. Jos. Bompas, the party whose management was impeached, appeared that rising and eminent counsel, Keatinge, well known to most of the Magistrates, as leader of the Sessions bar at Gloucester, a man of much legal knowledge, strictly honourable, gentlemanlike and judicious, instructed by Messrs. Livett, Solrs. Bristol, advisers of the Bompas family.*

LLEWELLYN — a dinner guest of the Dowells at Cote

This is likely to be Richard Llewellyn of Westbury-upon-Trym, but the attribution is tentative.

1805: 21 Jan: *Dined with the Dowells & slept at Cote, my Father accompanied me part of the way thither. Llewellyn, Slade Baker, Edw. Webb & his sister, & F. Daubeny dined with us.*

LLOYD — Mr Lloyd, a pupil of Mr Boudier's

1837: 22 Aug: *We also met Mrs. & Miss Wynniatt, Mr. Escott, and Geo. Daubeny: with a Mr. Lloyd, a pupil of Mr. Boudier's.*

LLOYD — Miss Lloyd of Birmingham — *see also* Birkbeck

1839: 8 May: *By his first wife, a Miss Lloyd, of Birmingham, a friend, he has a Son, a Barrister.*

LLOYD — Charles Lloyd [107]

Charles Lloyd (1784-1829), regius professor of divinity and bishop of Oxford, was the second son of Thomas Lloyd, rector of Aston-sub-Edge, Gloucestershire, who also ran a school at Great Missenden. Lloyd was educated at Eton College and Christ Church, Oxford (BA 1806; MA 1809; BD 1818; DD 1821). He was curate of Drayton in 1810 and Binsey in 1818, both near Oxford. In June 1819, under Peel's influence, he was appointed to the preachership of Lincoln's Inn, which he held until February 1822, when he was appointed regius professor of divinity on the nomination of Lord Liverpool. Attached to this post was a canonry at Christ Church and the rectory of Ewelme. Lloyd was consecrated bishop of Oxford in 1827, and died two years later. He married, 1822, Mary Harriet Stapleton (1787-1857); they had 1 son and 3 daughters:

1 Charles (1823-1862)
1 Charlotte (b. 1825)
2 Martha (b. 1826)
3 Isabel (b. 1827)

1827: 17 Feb: *The new arrangements consequent on the decease of the Bishops of Oxford and Lincoln are now declared. Dr. Lloyd, Regius Professor of Divinity at Oxford, is to succeed Bishop Legge. This distinguished Divine is understood to come on the bench by the friendship of Mr. Peel; and the University has reason to gratulate herself on seeing him on the Episcopal chair of Oxford, as she will thus retain his valuable services as Professor, and he will still chiefly reside in the bosom of Alma Mater. Dr. Lloyd was Preacher at Lincoln's Inn, if I mistake not, before he succeeded to the professorship.*

1829: 3 Jun: *Dr. Lloyd, Bishop of Oxford, is deceased; I understand, that he had for some time been considered in a precarious state of health. This prelate would have departed into another life with greater reputation, if he had been removed prior to the late concessions made to the Roman Catholics. His tergiversation and sophistry on that occasion had exposed him to severe and just strictures.*

LLOYD — Daniel and Nathaniel Lloyd — *see also* Lloyd Baker [108]

It is likely that Francis Witts was confusing Uley with Wotton-under-Edge. Daniel Lloyd (d. 1850) and Nathaniel Lloyd (d. 1853) leased Dauncey's Mill in 1811 from (presumably) their relation, Revd William Lloyd Baker (*below*) for a period of twenty-one years. They also owned Angeston Workshops in Uley and Upper Cam Mill. Daniel and Nathaniel became bankrupt in 1826 and thereafter little is heard of them. Nathaniel's daughter, Elizabeth Head Lloyd (b. 1787), married, 1831, Edward Dalton of Dunkirk Manor House, Nailsworth. A Daniel Lloyd is listed in Pigot's 1842 directory as manager of the National & Provincial Bank, Long Street, Wotton-under-Edge; it is likely that this was the same Daniel, taking a sideways career to earn a living.

1826: 31 Jan: *the worst cases now will receive two years incarceration in one of the Houses of Correction. An attempt has been made in their favour by instituting a prosecution against Messrs. Lloyd's, Manufacturers at Wotton under edge, who found it necessary to fire upon the mob, whose hostilities seemed mainly directed against their security and property. But the Grand Jury, judging them to have been justified in this measure have ignored the bill against them.*

LLOYD — Francis Sackville Lloyd — *see also* William Way [109]

Francis Sackville Lloyd (1762-1812), son of Mary Lloyd (d. 1803), married Elizabeth (1765-1846), eldest daughter and co-heir of Maximilian Western of Cokethorpe, Oxfordshire. Glympton Manor estate in Oxfordshire was bought by Sackville Lloyd's grandfather, Sir Jacob Wheate, in around 1765 for his daughters Sarah Wheate (d. 1805), Anne Wheate (d. 1807), and Mary Lloyd (d. 1803). They held the property jointly. They were succeeded by Mary's son, Francis Sackville Lloyd, who assumed the additional surname Wheate. After his death in 1812, his widow Elizabeth and her second husband William Way held Glympton until Elizabeth's death in 1846.

1835: 25 Feb: *With Mrs. Witts & my Son dined at Adlestrop at Mr. Perrots; a very agreeable party. We met the Revd. Mr. & Mrs. Way of Glympton Park, Oxon, Captain Leigh, and Mr. & Mrs. Whitmore Jones. Mrs. Way was widow of Mr. Lloyd, nephew and heir of Misses Wheate, singular old maiden ladies, proprietors of the Glympton Estate.*

LLOYD — Samuel Lloyd [110]

Samuel Lloyd (±1793-1863), Church of England clergyman, was the son of Nathaniel Lloyd (1757-1808), of Uley, and Elizabeth Hopkins (d. 1807). They married at Arrow, Warwickshire, on 7 August 1778, and were nonconformists. Samuel was educated at Magdalen College, Oxford (BA 1819; MA 1822). He was a student at Lincoln's Inn in 1817, but turned his back on law to enter the Church. He was vicar of Horsley in 1825-49.

He married, first, at St George's, Cam, Gloucestershire, 29 July 1824, Mary Ankers (1796-1829). He married secondly, at St Martin's, Horsley, Gloucestershire, 26 January 1832, Eliza Young (1812-1873); they had at least 1 son:

1 William Henry (1833-1896), Church of England clergyman

1837: 17 Sep: *A circular from Mr. Lloyd, Incumbent of Horsley praying for a subscription in aid of the fund for rebuilding the parish church, which now can only accommodate 500 out of a population of 4000 inhabitants, and is much out of repair.*

LLOYD BAKER — Thomas John Lloyd Baker and the Lloyd Baker family [111]

Thomas Baker (1693-1755) was a Church of England clergyman. He served as vicar of Bibury. He married, first, Anne, who died on 16 March 1734, and secondly, Mary (1710-1785), daughter of William Lloyd, chancellor of Worcester, and sister of Revd John Lloyd of Ryton, co. Durham. Through Baker's second wife, Mary, the 'Lloyd' name was brought into the family. Their son, Revd William Lloyd Baker (1752-1830), bought Stoutshill, Uley, in 1785, and Hardwicke Court in 1816. He married his cousin Mary (1749-1819), daughter of Revd John Lloyd of Ryton, co. Durham. This reverend was the last of the male line of Lloyd and grandson of William Lloyd, bishop of St Asaph, Lichfield, Coventry, and Worcester. William and Mary had 1 son, Thomas John Lloyd Baker (1777-1841), and 2 daughters.

The two marriages across two generations brought considerable wealth to the Baker family from the Lloyd estate at Clerkenwell, London. The two following generations were headed by Thomas John Lloyd Baker (1777-1841) and his son Thomas Barwick Lloyd Baker (1807-1886).

Thomas John Lloyd Baker (1777-1841) married, first, May 1800, Mary (±1777-1812), only child of William Sharp (1729-1810), of Fulham, Middlesex—reported to have acted as surgeon to King George III—and Catherine (d. 1814), fifth daughter and heir of Thomas Barwick; they had 1 son and 2 daughters:

1 Catherine (1801-1882); born at Fulham, Middlesex, married, 4 February 1834, Revd Thomas Murray Brown, vicar of Standish, Gloucestershire, and later Almondsbury, Gloucestershire; 5 sons:
    1 Thomas Lloyd Murray (b. ±1839)
    2 Charles Chapman (b. 1841), Church of England clergyman
    3 Walter Raleigh (b. 1842)
    4 James Henry Granville (b. 1844)
    5 William Bevil Browne (1845-1928), Church of England clergyman

1 Thomas Barwick Lloyd (1807-1886); married, 10 March 1840, Mary (1815-1905), daughter of Nicholas Lewis Fenwick (1779-1844), of Besford Court, Worcestershire, and Mary Anne (1779-1854), daughter of Sir John Saunders Sebright, 7th baronet (1767-1846); 2 sons:
    1 Granville Edwin Lloyd (1841-1924); married, 30 December 1868, Catherine (1843-1890), daughter of Arthur Lascelles (1807-1880), of Norley, Cheshire, and Caroline Frances Brooke (b. 1814); at least 2 sons and 5 daughters
    2 Henry Orde Lloyd (1842-1909); died unmarried

2 Mary Anne (1804-1882); born at Fulham, Middlesex; married, 25 March 1832, Col Benjamin Chapman Brown (1779-1853), formerly of the 9th Lancers; resided at Stoutshill, Uley; 3 sons and 1 daughter:
    1 Arrabella Maria (1833-1907); died unmarried at Uley, Gloucestershire
    1 William Lloyd (1835-1915), officer of the 5th Lancers; married, 1863, Charlotte Elizabeth Orde (1842-1901); 1 daughter
    2 Charles Orde (1838-1900); married, first, at Monkstown, Dublin, 8 August 1861, Wilhelmina Frances Reeves (1838-1863); secondly, at Eastry, Kent, 20 August 1866, Annie Maria Michell (1844-1917); 1 son and 6 daughters
    3 Benjamin Chapman (1839-1917); married, at St James's, Benwell, Northumberland, 9 February 1861, Ann Atkinson (1838-1929); 4 sons and 4 daughters

Thomas John Lloyd Baker married secondly, at Maulden, Bedfordshire, 27 September 1814, Annabella (1795-1856), daughter of Revd William Ralfe (1743-1825), rector of Maulden, Bedfordshire, and his wife, Annabella (d. 1830). There do not appear to have been any children of this marriage.

Francis Witts first met the Baker family at Stoutshill on 19 December 1801 when he accompanied his uncle Broome Witts on a ride from North Nibley; many years later he became a good friend of Thomas John Lloyd Baker. Thomas's son, Thomas Barwick, was also known to Francis Witts. He was a noted pioneer in the prison service and an early member of the Howard League for Penal Reform. He served as an officer in the Gloucestershire Yeomanry Cavalry in 1835-65 and was instrumental in the founding of the Social Science Congress. He was also a leading figure in the movement of the reform school, and established the Hardwicke Reform School in 1852. He was appointed high sheriff in 1847.

Since his visit to Stoutshill in 1801, Francis Witts is unlikely to have come into further contact with the Lloyd Bakers until his appointment as a magistrate for Gloucestershire in 1811; thereafter he would have met them every quarter at the sessions. The first diary entry to refer to them is that of 15 October 1822; the 'Messrs. Baker' would have been William and his son Thomas John. Interestingly, the entry for April 1828 refers to the Bakers (father and son) of Stoutshill, seeming to indicate that they were not in residence at Hardwicke at that particular time.

Witts's friendship with Thomas John Lloyd Baker grew, and in 1836 the latter stayed at Upper Slaughter for a few days to take advantage of a nearby agricultural sale—agricultural improvement was one of his interests. This was probably the high point of the friendship between the two men. Shortly afterwards, Lloyd Baker retired from the committee of accounts pleading ill health, but he still attended the sessions alongside his son Thomas Barwick until his death in 1841. Surprisingly his death was not recorded in the surviving diaries, but there is a gap in which entries for January and February 1841 are missing.

Thomas John Lloyd Baker's son, Thomas Barwick, was on the prison committee and took great interest in the county gaol in Gloucestershire; he was especially active during the building works in 1844, and in 1845 he joined the committee of accounts, taking up a role once held by his father. He was also a member of the committee attached to the lunatic asylum.

Thomas Barwick Lloyd Baker took a hard view on how to deal with troublesome youths. Reformatories were to be reserved only for recidivistic youths and designed to deter further delinquency by the use of severe measures. At Hardwicke the inmates were compelled to carry out heavy spade work on the clay soil of the farm and were punished by beating or confinement in cells for any disobedience. Lloyd Baker was sure that hard labour in the countryside away from the corruption of cities would condition minds and bodies to habitual labour, induce mental tranquillity, and (incidentally) roughen and callous hands deliberately kept tender and nimble for pickpocketing or till raiding. There were night classes in reading, writing, and arithmetic, but classroom education took second place to labour, and the inmates slept in hammocks in dormitories. Lloyd Baker kept the young offenders for much shorter periods than reformatories run on the nurturing/interactive model—only two years on average—and always released them on licence, often to work for local farmers. The regime depended on a marks system, whereby compliance earned amelioration of severity; it was this model of deterrent, pioneered at Hardwicke and other places, which prevailed in the reformatories that spread across Britain. Lloyd Baker was convinced that his severe model hugely reduced crime by general deterrence and the habituation of the inmates to labour and obedience.

1801: 19 Dec: *Rode with my Uncle over to Mr. Cooper's at Dursley. Walked with that Gentleman & his two Boys to Mr. Baker's at Stout's Hill near Uley, & scaited there for some hours. Mr. Baker's House is in the Gothic stile & beautifully wooded. The Tea was very good. Mrs. Cooper her daughter & her Governess with whom we walked back to Dursley, joined the party on the tea. As also Mrs. H. Baker.*

1822: 15 Oct: *Mr. R. B. Cooper, M.P. for the city of Gloucester, Sir W. Guise, member for the County, Messrs. Baker, father & son.*

1823: 8 Apr., 15 Jul., 17 Sep: *The Ordinary for Gentlemen ... was at the King's Head ... I sat agreeably, between Dr. Cooke, the Chairman of the Quarter Sessions, and Mr. Baker of Hardwick Court.* 14 Oct.

1824: 13 Jan., 10 Mar., 31 Mar: *The new High Sheriff is my friend Thomas John Lloyd Baker, of Hardwick Court, a very worthy, intelligent country Gentleman & Magistrate, whose deserved popularity was sufficiently evinced by the very numerous party, upwards of seventy gentlemen, including the first names in the County, who dined with him.*

1825: 18 Oct.

1826: 10 Jan., 11 Jul., 31 Aug: *we passed Hardwick Court, the mansion of my friend T. J. Lloyd Baker, a magistrate, & lately High Sheriff, of the County: the estate was purchased of Lord Hardwick, who derives his tithe from hence; before it passed by purchase into that noble family, it was for nearly three centuries the property of the Trye's, a family of Norman extraction.* 17 Oct.

1827: 15 Apr., 24 Apr., 10 Jul., 16 Oct.

1828: 15 Jan., 15 Apr., 17 Apr: *Messrs. Baker, of Stouts Hill.* 14 Oct.

1829: 13 Jan., 1-2 Apr: *We were much crowded at table, but had a good dinner and pleasant party. I sat near the head of the table between my friends Dr. Cooke & T. J. L. Baker.* 28 Apr., 14 Jul., 22-23 Sep., 20 Oct., 27 Oct: *The ardour, with which Granville Sharp espoused the principles of the American revolters, made it a point of honour with him to relinquish the subordinate situation, which he held in a department of the State ... another brother was an eminent surgeon, & resided during his latter years at Chiswick, whose daughter, and only child, was the first wife of my acquaintance, T. J. LL. Baker, of Hardwick Court.*

1830: 12 Jan.

1832: 29 Mar.

1833: 23 Oct: *Another letter arrived from that worthy, kind-hearted man, Baker, of Hardwick Court, who endeavours to shake my supposed resolution to absent myself from the Sessions.* 28 Oct., 1 Nov.

1834: 13-14 Oct., 17 Oct., 5 Nov., 15 Dec., 22-23 Dec., 25 Dec.

1835: 4-7 Jan., *Received a letter from Mr. Bathurst, enclosing one to him from T. J. Ll. Baker ...The latter was a gem of its kind. Mr. Baker, in his own peculiar, dry manner, reported to Bathurst, with a desire that it might be communicated to me, a conversation which had incidentally passed between himself, Col. Kingscote & Mr. Sheppard.* 21 Feb., 23 Feb., 26-27 Feb: *Received a letter from Mr. Baker, inviting me to his house at Hardwicke Court on Monday next to meet Mr. Bathurst.* 10 Mar., 13 Mar., 21 Mar., 13 Apr.

1836: 15 Jul., 10 Aug., 30 Aug: *Engaged before breakfast in writing letters: to T. J. Ll. Baker, reminding him of the great agricultural sale of the Stock &c. of the late Mr. Talbot.* 1 Sep: *Recd. a letter from Baker, offering to come to stay with us two or three days in the beginning of next week.* 5-8 Sep: *Mr. Baker, accompanied by his elève, young Waldron, arrived to dinner, and to pass some days with us.* 12 Sep: *I left home in my open carriage for Hardwick Court, to visit the Bakers, and dine and sleep there, and thence to return tomorrow to Gloucester.... Mr. and Mrs. Baker, Mr. & Mrs. Rolfe (Mr. R. being a brother of Mrs. Baker) Mr. Phelps, Mr. Clifford and his Son, Mr. Walrond, and, when the first course was finished, Barwick Baker, who had been at a drill of the yeomanry Cavalry in which he holds a commission ... The library and dining room contain some good family portraits: an excellent resemblance of my old acquaintance, now deceased, the Revd. Mr. Baker, of Stout's-hill, Father of my host: a good portrait of himself in a shooting dress.* 13 Sep: *Barwick Baker was bound for Gloucester, and thence on a visit to Lord Edwd. Somerset at Ampney, near Cirencester; his conveyance a Phaeton with fly away steeds.* 1 Oct., 17 Oct., 20 Oct.

1837: 2 Jan., 4 Jan: *... if Baker insisted on retiring on account of increasing infirmity, we ought not to oppose it.* 6 Mar: *Then joined Bathurst, Baker, and Purnell, at the Bell, with whom debating the difficult question of remodelling the Prison Regulations for this county.* 7 Mar., 8 Apr: *Received a letter from T. J. Ll. Baker, to state that he was suffering so severely from indisposition that he could not attend to the business of he Comm. of accounts on Monday next preparatory to the Sessns.* 10 Apr: *... Purnell, who had arrived from Stancomb Park, and whom it is proposed to place on the Committee of accounts in the room of Baker, who retires on account of increasing ill health.* 11 Apr., 27 Jun., 13 Sep: *A letter from T. J. Ll. Baker, desiring me to procure for him from Berman, four bushels of his six-eared Chevalier Wheat.* 15 Sep., 17 Oct., 2 Dec., 6 Dec., 9 Dec., 11 Dec.

1838: 1 Jan: *Bad accounts of the health of our friend & former colleague on the Comm. of accts. Baker, who has lately had a bad plunge; Barwick Baker too has had an attack of small pox rather severe, but mitigated as all such cases are by his having been vaccinated in infancy.* 3 Jan., 8 Jan., 19 Feb., 21 Feb., 10 Apr., 16 Jun., 18 Jun., 3 Jul., 5 Jul., 16 Oct.

1839: 1 Jan., 23 Mar., 10 Apr., 2 Jul.

1840: 20 Jan.

1842: 12 Jan., 18 Jan., 13 Apr.

1844: 6-7 Mar., 8 Apr., 10 Apr., 14 Oct: *Messrs. Baker, Col. Browne, Sampson, Brickdale, and Sayers, attended to receive the County Surveyor's report as to the progress of the works at the County Gaol, and to receive and report upon tenders for £8000 to be advanced on loan.* 30 Dec.

1845: 17 Jan., 20 Jan., 29 Jan., 31 Jan., 5-6 Mar., 3 Apr., 14-15 Apr., 6-7 May., 30 Jun., 2 Jul., 4 Jul.

1846: 29-30 Jun: 2 Jul., 11 Aug., 25 Aug., 19 Oct: *Dinner at the Bell: Messrs. Purnell, C Hayward, Goodrich, Baker, Witts.* 20 Oct., 22 Oct., 18 Nov.

1847: 4 Jan., 22 Mar: *There were present Purnell, Curtis Hayward, Baker, (now hors de combat, as being High Sheriff.)* 5 Apr: *The High Sheriff, Baker, came, attended by his Under Sheriffs, Wilton and Burrup, to take possession of his Gaol, according to custom: he had come in from Hardwick Court with a large cortege of horsemen, yeomen &c. whom he had feasted at his mansion, and again regaled at Gloucester.* 28 Jun: *Baker, who, as High Sheriff, is precluded from acting as a magistrate, came in and assisted his friend Parry.* 13 Aug.

1848: 20-21 Mar., 26 Jun., 16 Oct.

1849: 31 Dec.

1850: 1 Jan., 8 Nov: *I repaired to the Railway station, being joined on the road thither by Barwick Baker, who was full of communications as to County matters, a projected County meeting to address the Queen on the Papal aggression &c.* 9 Nov: *Wrote to Barwick Baker, to whom I returned his paper of propositions for alterations in the Prison Rules, with an assurance that I would give his suggestions due weight.*

1851: 17 Mar., 29 Apr.

1852: 15 Mar., 17 Mar.

1853: 3 Jan., 5 Jan: *Late in the Evening ... Messrs. Purnell, father & son, Barwick Baker, myself & Broome, thus enjoyed a Selection from the Messiah.* 14 Mar., 27-28 Jun.

LOCK — a pauper inmate of Stow Union Workhouse

1845: 26 Jun: *Lock, a female pauper inmate, admitted that she was pregnant, but denied that Ellens was the Father of the child.*

LOCK — R. Lock of Bourton-on-the-Water

1837: 15 Jun: *As to R. Lock the Foreman of the Pseudo-jury at Bourton, we bound him in his own recogn. in £10 to keep the peace &c. considering him as a deluded ignorant person, a catspaw & tool in the Agitator's hands.*

LOCKER — Mr Locker of Hersham

1853: 17 Jun: *The guests, besides Woodroffe and myself were Sir Richard Frederick, and his brother, Capt Frederick, Major Macdonald with a friend on a visit to him, the Revd. Mr. Jones, I believe from Barnet,—Mr. Locker, Mr. Johnson, and Mr. Middleton, all, with the exception of Mr. Jones, inhabitants of Hersham.*

LOCKEY — Charles Lockey [112]

Charles Lockey (1820-1901), singer, was born at Thatcham, near Newbury, Berkshire, son of Angel Lockey of Oxford. He was a chorister at Magdalen College, Oxford, from 1828 to 1836, and then studied singing with Edward Harris at Bath. In 1842 he became a pupil of George Smart. Lockey sang in the choirs of St George's chapel, Windsor, and Eton College chapel. In 1843 he became a vicar-choral of St Paul's Cathedral. His first public appearance in oratorio was in October 1842, when he sang in Rossini's *Stabat mater* for the Melophonic Society. He performed in the Ancient Concerts in 1846, at the Three Choirs Festivals in 1846-56, and at the concerts of the Sacred Harmonic Society. He married, 1853, Martha Williams, a contralto, who died in 1897. The couple had one son.

1850: 2 Jan: *This really enjoyable treat was afforded by the Gloucester Choral Society aided by four professional singers—— Machin, a Bass, and Lockey, a tenor: with two Misses Williams, the one having a contralto, the other a soprano voice.... Lockey, a delightful tenor, and good musician, sang very well in the music appropriated to Obadiah; I liked him still better when I heard him on a like occasion, at the Michs. Sessions, in the Creation.*

LOCKHART — Mrs Lockhart at Cotton, Staffordshire

1802: 28 Sep., 5 Oct: *Mrs. Gilbert, Mrs. Ingram, Mrs. Palmer, Mrs. Lockhart, Mr. Baker & Mr. Bennet dined with us.*

LOCKHART — Mr Lockhart, mortgagee in Buckinghamshire

Nothing has been found in relation to this Mr Lockart. It seems that Francis Witts never actually met him; the business between them was handled by Sewell and Newmarch, solicitors. The only fragments of information handed out are that the mortgage sum was £4,300 and that the estate was in Buckinghamshire. Francis Witts did not have sufficient funds at the time to complete the mortgage and Sewell and Newmarch lent him the required balance, presumably secured on a second mortgage. The mortgage was increased to £5,300 in July 1846.

1843: 16 Dec: *Wrote to Messrs. Hoare for my annual balance sheet, desiring them to pay on my account £100 to the account of Messrs. Sewell and Newmarch with the Gloucestershire Banking Company at Cirencester; and to G. F. Newmarch advising him that I had so done in part liquidation of my debt to him and his partner for money advanced on Mortgage by me to Mr. Lockhart.* 20 Dec: *Received a letter from G. F. Newmarch acknowledging the receipt of £100 on acct. of the money advanced to me by him and his partner towards making up the sum lent on mortgage to Mr. Lockhart.*

1844: 22 Jan., 26 Jan., 31 Jan., 1 Feb., 6 Feb., 24 Jul: *Wrote to Mr. G. F. Newmarch, forwarding a receipt for the Interest lately paid by Mr. Lockhart on the money lent by us on mortgage of property in Bucks.* 29 Jul.

1845: 17-18 Jan., 21 Jan., 4 Jul., 6 Jul.

1846: 8 Jun., 11-12 Jun., 20 Jun., 22 Jun., 9-10 Jul., 14 Jul., 18 Jul: *Mr. Sewell called by appointment after breakfast, bringing with him the deed securing repayment of the additional £1000 lent by us to Mr. Lockhart on mortgage of his estates in Bucks.*

1847: 8 Jan., 28-29 Sep., 20 Oct.

1848: 18 Jan., 8-9 Aug.

1851: 25 Feb., 7 May: *A letter from G. F. Newmarch confirms what I had learnt from Sewell was in contemplation; viz. that Mr. Lockhart proposes to sell his landed property in Bucks on which I have a mortgage for £4300.* 8 May.

1853: 8 Jan: *from Mr. Sewell a letter acquainting me that having nearly wound up Mr. Lockhart's affairs, he & his partner propose to pay off £2300 part of my principal sum of £5300 lent on mortgage of that property, leaving £3000 still on the security till the final arrangement of the concern, the eventual value of the funds being estimated at £4000.* 13 Jan., 27 Jan: *They proved to be conveyances of the Bucks Estate of the late Mr. Lockhart to purchasers, the amount being payable to me on account of my mortgage to the extent of £3000; the balance of the money lent by me, £2300, I am shortly to receive from Sewell and Newmarch, to be invested with other money, which I am to provide, on mortgage of Wynniatt's estate &c. at Stanton.*

LOCKHART — John Ingram Lockhart [113]

John Ingram Lockhart (1765-1835), MP and barrister, was a younger son of James Lockhart, merchant banker, of St Dunstan's, London, and Melchett Park, Wiltshire, and Mary Harriot Gray of St Benet and St Peter, Paul's Wharf, London. He was educated at Eton College (1779-83) and University College, Oxford (1783). He entered Lincoln's Inn in 1783 and was called to the bar in 1790. He was MP for Oxford in 1807-18 and 1820-30. Lockhart married, 14 January 1804, Mary (d. 1831), daughter and heir of Francis Wastie of Cowley and Haseley. He took the name of Wastie by act of parliament on 23 May 1832 to hold estates for life following the death of his wife.

1826: 16 Jun: *The city of Oxford also exhibits a curious instance of the changes and chances of elections. The old Members were the Solicitor General, and Sir Charles Wetherell, and Mr. Lockhart, formerly at the bar, a man of wealth and talent and popularity.*

LOCKHART ROSS — *see* ROSS

LOCKEY — Ralph Lockey — *see also* Phillipps *and* Wynniatt [114]

Ralph Lockey (±1770-1834), Church of England clergyman, was born at Cam, Gloucestershire, the son of Revd Richard Lockey, curate of St George's, Upper Cam. He was educated at Gloucester and Peterhouse College, Cambridge (BA 1792; MA 1796). He was ordained deacon on 24 February 1793 and priest on 12 October 1794. Lockey's first clerical appointment was as curate of Stinchcombe from 25 February 1793; this was followed by curacies at the nearby parishes of Uley, from 12 October 1794, and Owlpen, from 31 December 1810, which he served alongside Lasborough. He was then vicar of Much Dewchurch, Herefordshire, from 21 October 1812 to 7 March 1834, with the curacy of Much Birch. He ended his clerical career as rector of Llanwarne, 1818-34.

Lockey married, at Lugwardine, Herefordshire, 22 May 1817, Mary (b. 1795), daughter of James Phillipps and Mary Beachcroft. Mary's aunt was Frances Wynniatt, née Phillipps. She was a cousin of Catherine Phillipps.

Ralph Lockey and Mary had at least 2 sons and 3 daughters:

1 Mary (b. 1820)
1 Samuel Ralph (1820-1880)
2 James (b. 1822)
2 Frances (b. 1825)
3 Catherine Ann (1825-1872)

1827: 24 May: *We met a party from Herefordshire, a Mr. & Mrs. Lockie, the Lady a relative of the Wynniatts, Mr. Wynniatt of Stanton, Miss C. Phillips, & Mr. Bowen; a pleasant visit, and I did not find myself much fatigued.*

LOCKWOOD — John William Lockwood [115]

John William Lockwood (1800-1879), Church of England clergyman, was born at Yoxford, Suffolk, son of Revd John Lockwood. He was educated at Christ Church College, Oxford (BA 1821; MA 1823), and was appointed vicar of Chalgrove, Oxfordshire, in 1832, rector of Chelsea in 1836, and rector of Kingham, Oxfordshire, in 1836. He married, 1832, Alicia Davis (±1811-1884); they had at least 6 sons and 1 daughter:

1 John (b. 1834)
2 Edward Dowdeswell (b. 1834)
1 Matilda (b. 1837)
3 Henry Boileau (1840-1919)
4 Samuel Davis (b. 1842)
5 Richard Bernard (1844-1879)
6 Charles Vernon (1847-1882)

1836: 22 Aug: *Soon after our return my son and I went in our open carriage to dine with Winter at Daylesford. Met Bowen, Lewes, Barter and his son, and Mr. Lockwood, the new Rector of Kingham, lately Rector of St. Luke's, Chelsea, a pleasing, well informed man.* 30 Aug: *Mr. Lockwood and Mr. Barker joined the home circle at dinner. Mrs. L. was prevented coming by a slight indisposition.* 27 Sep., 27 Oct: *The Lockwoods from Kingham, with Miss Barter, and Miss Davis, Mrs. Lockwood's Sister.* 11 Dec.

1837: 21 Apr., 6 May: *Drove M W. to make a first call on the Lockwoods at Kingham.* 13 Jun: *Edward rode to Kingham to call on Mr. Curtis, the Naturalist, to whom he had been introduced at Oxford, and who is visiting Mr. Lockwood, and being invited to dine & sleep there, sent Mr. L.'s servant for a change of dress.* 14 Jun., 14 Jul: *Entertained a party of our neighbours at dinner.—Mr. and Mrs. Barter with their daughter, from Sarsden. Mr. Lockwood, from Kingham.*

1839: 21 May: *Rode to Stow; called at the Library, where I met and conversed with Mr. Lockwood.* 20 Jun.

1840: 5 Aug.

1842: 8 Jul., 27 Sep.

1843: 26 Sep.

1845: 16 Jan: *Winter & W. B. Pole were present; as also Mr. Debary, late Curate of Icomb, now returned from a long foreign Tour, and at present affording temporary clerical assistance to Mr. Lockwood at Kingham.* 26 Mar.

1847: 26 Mar., 6 Jul., 28 Sep.

1850: 1 Oct.

LODER — John David Loder [116]

John David Loder (1788-1846), violinist, was born at Bath, son of John Loder (d. 1795), a musician. His family were long residents of Bath and well known for their musical talent. After initially playing in concert orchestras, John David Loder appeared as the first violin in a string quartet at the New Assembly Rooms on 4 April 1800. From 1799 to 1836 he was a member, and for most of that time leader, of the orchestra of the Theatre Royal. Famous musicians from London often attended his annual benefit night at the theatre. On 7 October 182 Angelica Catalani, the celebrated Italian soprano, appeared with him at a concert; it is reported that she returned her fee 'as a small tribute of regard for [Loder's] private worth, and high professional skill'. He left the theatre in 1836 after a disagreement, but returned in 1840-41.

Among other engagements, Loder appeared as leader of the Yorkshire music festival on 15 September 1825 alongside Franz Cramer, Mori, and Kiesewetter, soloist at the Gloucester music festival in 1826, and leader at the Three Choirs Festival in 1826-45. On 12 May 1817 he became the first Englishman to lead the orchestra at the Philharmonic Society of London, which, according to Temperley, he appears to have done at least once a year since then. He also performed in the Ancient Concerts, succeeding Cramer as leader in 1845.

Loder's business as a music publisher and seller of musical instruments operated from 46 Milsom Street, Bath, from around 1820 to 1835. He subsequently resided in London and, in 1840, became professor of violin at the Royal Academy of Music. He married Rosamund Charles Mills (1791-1867), stepdaughter of the comic actor John Fawcett; they had 5 sons and 2 daughters, including:

1 Edward James (1809-1865), composer and conductor
2 John Fawcett (1809-1853), violinist and viola player, music teacher and concert director in Bath. He was a member of various London orchestras and played viola in Blagrove and Dando's Quartet Concerts from 1842 until his death. He was Edward's twin
3 William Sowerby (1812-1851); studied the cello at the Royal Academy of Music and later played in Bath
4 George (1814-1815); died at 3 months

1826: 12 Sep: *Loder, who is to lead on the second & third evenings, tells me, she has much to unlearn, namely, what Velluti has taught her.* 14 Sep: *Cramer withdrew from his post of leader to make room for Loder, who acquitted himself in an admirable manner. I cannot praise him equally with Cramer, but he is an excellent performer.* 15 Sep: *Miss Cann maintained the credit, she had gained on the first evening, by her variations on Rule Britannia, & Mr. Loder's fantasia was graceful and rich, while it displayed great skill and execution.* 25 Sep.

LODERS — **Mr Loders at the turnpike meeting**

1837: 18 Aug: *The Turnpike meeting was attended by Mr. Brown who took the chair, Messrs. Waller, Talbot, Price, Ford, Pitt, Loders, Ansell and Pettat.*

LODGE — **Edmund Lodge** [117]

Edmund Lodge (1792-1866), farmer, was born at Hawling, son of Edmund and Mary Lodge. He was unmarried and farmed 235 acres at Naunton, employing seven labourers. His sister, Ann (b. ±1811), was also unmarried, and lived with him. In the 1841 census Ann had been living in Hawling, the village of her birth, with, it appears, her twin sister Sarah.

1853: 16 May: *I conferred with the Rel. Off. on cases of Lunacy and other Poor Law matters, and was consulted at Mr. Hurd's suggestion by a farmer Lodge of Naunton, whose sister has become deranged.*

LONG — **Richard Godolphin Long** [118]

Richard Godolphin Long (1761-1835), banker and MP, was born at West Lavington, Wiltshire, son of Richard Long and his wife, Meliora, a descendant of Sir John Lambe. Long was a partner in the Melksham Bank together with John Awdry, Thomas Bruges, and his younger brother, John Long. In 1799 he purchased Steeple Ashton manor house and farm, and in 1808 he commissioned architect Jeffry Wyattville to build Rood Ashton House. Long was MP for Wiltshire in 1806-18, although he had few qualifications to recommend him to the post, other than belonging to an ancient family of the county. He was a fox-hunting country squire, often drunk on rent day, and considered to be a man of inferior knowledge. Only one speech is reported of him in parliament. He married, 27 March 1786, Florentina, third daughter of Sir Bourchier Wrey, 6th baronet; they had 2 sons and 4 daughters. His second daughter, Florentina, was a frequent visitor of Jane Austen, who she referred to as 'cousin', although the exact relationship is unknown. His eldest son, Walter, was MP for North Wiltshire (*below*).

1807: 6 May: *Mr. Jones called in a post chaise to convey me to the Election Dinner at Devizes Mr. Smith & Mr. Estcourt being re-elected. Very pleasant & agreeably conversed with Mr. Long M.P. Estcourt, Revd. M. Wyatt, Tinker, Dr. Hill, Dr. Spalding &c.* 11 May: *Drove Mr. Jones to the nomination of his cousin Rich Long, & H. P. Windham Esq., for the County at Devizes. Conversed with Jaques, Mr. Richards, Mr. H. Beech, J. Tylee, &c.*

LONG — **Walter Long** [119]

Walter Long (1793-1867), JP, DL, MP, and landed proprietor, was the eldest son of Richard Godolphin Long (*above*). He was educated at Winchester College and Christ Church, Oxford (MA 1812). Long was MP for North Wiltshire in 1835-65, DL for Somerset, Montgomeryshire, and Wiltshire, and JP for Wiltshire. He married, 1819, Mary Anne Colquhoun.

1837: 4 Aug., 10 Aug: *There learnt that the Conservative Sir F. Burdett has been returned at the head of the Poll by a large majority for North Wilts, his competitors being Long and Methuen, the old Whig members, of whom, I believe, the latter is excluded from the representation.* 14 Aug: *A few lines from Ford, inclosing a letter he had recd. from his niece, Miss Rooke, narrating how, at the declaration of the poll at Devizes, on occasion of the success of Burdett and Long, Ackerley had created a disturbance, by haranguing the mob out of his gig.*

LONGHURST — **Edward Alexander Longhurst** [120]

Edward Longhurst (±1811-1880), supervisor for the excise office, was born at Dover, Kent. He married, 1839, Anna Sweetlove (1806-1856); they had 4 sons and 1 daughter:

1 James (b. 1840)
2 Henry (b. & d. 1842)
3 Sidney (1844-1911)
4 Charles (b. 1846)
1 Anna Maria (1849-1898)

Edward Longhurst was an accountant; in 1840 his office was at the Queens Head, High Street, Maidstone, where he was supervisor for the excise office. By the census of 1851, Edward and his family had left the village of Donnington and were living in nearby Sheep Street, Stow-on-the-Wold. By 1861 Edward was a widower living at Chorlton-upon-Medlock, near Manchester, where he was a clerk in the tax office. By this time, the only child at home was Anna. It is unknown why he was dismissed from his post in Gloucestershire, but the diary entry for 21 November 1846 demonstrates that he was unwisely making enemies among influential county magistrates.

1844: 27 Dec: *Mr. Brookes Senr. having been superannuated as Surveyor of Taxes, his place is filled by a young man from Kent, by name Longhurst, who appears quiet, steady, intelligent, and conversant with his business.*

1846: 21 Nov: *To Mr. Morgan, Stow, returning to him with my comments thereon, a letter addressed by him to him on Tax business by Mr. Longhurst, the Surveyor of Taxes, who, as it appeared to me & other Commissioners, had taken a liberty in seeming to dictate to us.*

1847: 20 May: *Had an interview on Tax business for a parishioner with Mr. Longhurst, surveyor of taxes.*

1849: 20 Dec: *To the Unicorn Inn by 11 AM. to a meeting of Income Tax Commissioners, where I was joined by Mr. Ford, and Mr. Waller, who sat with me hearing appeals under Sched D. of the Income Tax act as to trade, professions &c.—with a few cases under Schedules A & B. as owners and occupiers. Mr. Credland attended as Surveyor of the District in the room of Mr. Longhurst, dismissed.*

1850: 20 Jul: *In the evening received a letter from the wretched man Longhurst, formerly Surveyor of Taxes for this district, but reduced to poverty by dissipation and improvidence, having been dismissed from his situation; he lives now at Donnington, and appeared before the Magistrates on Thursday last with one of his children, not seven years of age, apprehended stealing pease from a field near the cottage where the family now live, having, doubtless, been sent out for the purpose by one or both of his parents.* 27 Aug: *From Mr. Longhurst a letter soliciting the appointment of Clerk to the Commissioners of Taxes lately held by Morgan. But this is quite out of the question; his utterly lost character and dissolute habits prevent me doing anything for him.* 29 Aug.

LONGSTREET — **Thomas Longstreet** [121]

Thomas Longstreet (b. ±1808), police officer and schoolmaster, was born at Berkeley. By 1851 he lived at Hersham with his wife, Drusilla Wall (1810-1893), who was from Dursley; they had 2 sons and 1 daughter:

1 Isabella (b. ±1839)
1 Daniel (b. ±1840)
2 Thomas (b. ±1847)

Thomas and Drusilla were schoolmaster and schoolmistress at Hersham, but by 1861 Drusilla was listed in the census as a married housekeeper in London. By 1871 she was still listed as married, but living at St Helier, Jersey, with her son Daniel and his family. Thomas's whereabouts are unknown after 1851.

1851: 25 May: *Nearly opposite the Church and parsonage are the school buildings, comprizing apartments for the Master and his family. In the former I recognized an old Gloucestershire Policeman, who was stationed at Stow when the Constabulary was first instituted; by name Longstreet, from Berkeley or Thornbury—he remained some time in the force, and was esteemed a good and respectable officer; and he gives satisfaction in his present occupation to my cousin.*

LONSDALE — Jane Lonsdale and the Lonsdale family at Skipton — *see also* Cooper [122]

Jane Lonsdale (±1784-1862) was born at Skipton, Yorkshire, daughter of Thomas Lonsdale and Mary Chamberlain. She was a cousin of some degree to Margaret Witts, née Backhouse. She lived with her mother in Embsay, Yorkshire. By 1861 she was living in the same village, at Primrose Cottage with her unmarried nieces Jane and Sarah Cooper.

James Lonsdale, druggist of Market Place, Skipton, is listed in *Pigot's Directory* and may have been Jane's brother. It seems likely that the Lonsdales were on the maternal, 'Currer' side of Margaret Witts's family, her grandmother having been Margaret Currer.

1823: 7 May: *The coach stopped for half an hour at Skipton, which enabled me to pay a short visit to Mrs. & Miss Lonsdale, relations of my wife.* 13 May: *I left this hospitable neighbourhood for Skipton, 16 miles, where I arrived to an early dinner with Mrs. & Miss Lonsdale. In spite of boisterous wind, I walked in the Evening to Bow Bridge, about a mile out of the Town, to look at a house, into which she & her Mother are about to remove. It is at the extremity of the Village of Embsay, in a direction behind Skipton Castle and church.* 14 May: *I borrowed a horse of Mr. Cooper, brother in law of Miss Lonsdale, & rode to look over Mrs. Backhouse's farm at Seale House, about four miles from Skipton ... I returned again to the hospitable roof of Mrs. & Miss Lonsdale, with the latter of whom I transacted business, it being my intention to travel homeward on the following day.*

1825: 7 Sep: *I determined, contrary to my first intention, to proceed no farther by the coach to-day, but to dedicate the afternoon to a visit to Mrs, Backhouse's tenant at Scale House. Accordingly after calling on Mrs. Lonsdale & Mrs. Cooper, distant relations of my wife.* 8 Sep: *I passed the forenoon with Miss Lonsdale, an esteemed relative of my wife. She resides with her Mother, who is now visiting her other daughter, Mrs. Cooper, at Skipton, at Mill Holm, abut a mile & half from the town, in the direction of Embsay.*

1837: 21 Oct: *Returned to Skipton between 12 and 1 o clock, and called on the Lonsdales. Mrs. Lonsdale & her daughter fully as well as when we visited them last, and heartily glad to see me, being full of friendly enquiries after my wife and her mother, as also my son. Met two Misses Cooper there, pleasing young women, who, like their Grandmother and Aunt Lonsdale, are, in nearer or remoter degrees, cousins of my wife.*

1838: 14 Sep: *Wrote to MW.... and to Miss Lonsdale to acquaint her that I proposed being at Skipton on Monday next.* 17 Sep: *I was enabled to fulfil my intention of leaving Settle this forenoon, and, mounting on the roof, arrived at Skipton between one and two o'clock.—Called on Mrs. and Miss Lonsdale, and partook of some refreshment there: Mrs. L. looking well, considering her very advanced age, 85 years; Miss L. looking thin and ill.*

1842: 14 Nov.

1847: 2 Oct: *MW. received a letter from Jane Lonsdale: her nephew, Thomas Cooper, died lately of consumption.*

1850: 19 Mar: *Wrote letters conveying a report of MW's health to Miss Lonsdale.* 23 Mar: *MW. received a very kind and proper letter from Jane Lonsdale, in reply to the letter I had written.* 27 Apr: *From Miss Lonsdale a very proper letter of sympathy addressed to me...* 1 May: *Wrote to Miss Lonsdale, in reply to her kind letter of condolence on my late severe loss, and forwarded to her a cheque on Messrs. Alcock, Birkbecks & Co. for £5.; my dear wife, in a memorandum signed by her some weeks ago, as to her wishes in respect of things to be done by me after her decease, having desired me to present her cousin with that sum as a token of remembrance.* 8 May, 8 Jun: *Wrote to Miss Lonsdale with a cheque on the Craven Bank for £27. the amount of interest for a twelve-month due to her at this season.*

1852: 5 Jun: *Wrote to Miss Lonsdale, with a cheque on the Craven Bank for £27—a year's interest for £600 which I hold of hers.* 9 Jun: *Received a letter from Miss Cooper, written by the desire of Miss Lonsdale, and acknowledging the receipt of my letter to Miss L. together with the cheque for £27.*

1853: 7 Apr: *Received a letter from a Mr. Robinson, of Croft House, Skipton, written on behalf of Miss Lonsdale, who is represented to be in delicate health, and, desirous to avoid Legacy duty & probate charges, wishes that the note of hand I have given her for £600 should be cancelled, on my giving another to the same amount to her nieces, the Misses Cooper.* 8 Apr., 29 May, 2 Jun.

1854: 9 Jun: *Letters from Miss S. Cooper, with a receipt for the £27. Interest which I had forwarded to her on the 3d. Inst. The Coopers, and, I believe, Jane Lonsdale, now live at Embsay, near Skipton.—J.L. is very unwell.*

LONSDALE — John Lonsdale [123]

John Lonsdale (1788-1867), bishop of Lichfield, was born at at New Miller Dam, near Wakefield, Yorkshire, the eldest son of Revd John Lonsdale (1736-1807) and Elizabeth Steer, heir of the Gylby family. He was educated at Eton College and King's College, Cambridge (BA 1811; MA 1814; BD 1824; DD 1844). Lonsdale occupied several posts during his career: he was chaplain to Archbishop Manners-Sutton, rector of Mersham, Kent, in 1822-27, prebendary of Lincoln in 1827-28, precentor of Lichfield in 1828-31, rector of St George's, Bloomsbury, in 1828-34, prebendary of St Paul's in 1831-43, rector of Southfleet, Kent, in 1836-43, principal of King's College, London, in 1839, archdeacon of Middlesex in 1842, and bishop of Lichfield in 1843-67.

1853: 12 Jun: *To the afternoon Service at the Temple Church, with tickets from Mr. Butt, Q.C. as Bencher: accompanied Mr. and Mrs. W. Ffooks and Constance, going and returning in Cabs, at least for the greater part of the distance.——The service chanting and anthem very enjoyable: an excellent Sermon preached by Bishop Lonsdale of Lichfield.*

LOOKER — Mrs Looker of Banbury

1853: 9 Jan: *Wrote to Mrs. Looker, Banbury for the character of M. A. Coleman, who has offered herself as my housemaid.* 11 Jan: *Recd. a letter from Mrs. Looker, Banbury, with a favourable character of her late servant M. A. Coleman, to whom I wrote, desiring her to come into my service on the 22d. Inst.*

LOUDON — John Claudius Loudon [124]

John Claudius Loudon (1783-1843), landscape gardener and horticultural writer, was born at Cambuslang, Lanarkshire, the eldest son of William Loudon (d. 1809), farmer, of Kerse Hall, Lothian, and Agnes Somers (d. 1831). At the age of 11 he began working part-time as an assistant to John Mawer, a nurseryman and landscape gardener at Dalry. On Mawer's death in 1798 he became a part-time apprentice to Dickson and Shade, nurserymen at Leith Walk, Edinburgh. At the same time he entered the University of Edinburgh, where he studied agriculture, and attended classes in botany and chemistry. As well as having exhibited as a painter at the Royal Academy, Loudon wrote several treatises on agriculture at a young age.

In 1807 Loudon published a pamphlet, *An Immediate and Effectual Mode of Raising the Rental of the Landed Property of England*, and in consequence was invited by Gen. George F. Stratton to appraise his property at Great Tew, Oxfordshire. Loudon took over the tenancy of Tew Lodge Farm hoping to double its rental value. In 1809 he established a small agricultural college at Tew, and in 1811 he published *Designs for Laying out Farms and Farm-Buildings, in the Scotch Style*, celebrating his accomplishments there. Gen. Stratton bought back the lease in February 1811, but the strain placed on agriculture by the Napoleonic Wars meant that his expected profits did not materialise.

Loudon moved to London, living at 42 Pall Mall, having amassed a fortune of £15,000 at Tew. In 1812 he published *Hints on the Formation of Gardens and Pleasure Grounds*, which included designs for formal gardens as well as informal landscapes. He journeyed though the south of England, and in 1813-14, he travelled on the Continent, visiting Germany, Latvia, St Petersburg, Moscow, and central Europe. When he returned to England he found that his banker had mishandled his finances and his fortune was gone.

In 1817 Loudon published *Remarks on the Construction of Hot-Houses*, and the next year, *A Comparative View of the Common and Curvilinear Mode of Roofing Hot-Houses and Sketches of Curvilinear Hot-Houses*. Loudon invented a glazing bar in wrought iron that could be made in curvilinear sections.

In 1819 Loudon visited France, Italy, Switzerland, and the Low Countries to gather material for a proposed *Encyclopaedia of Gardening*. The book was published in 1822 as an octavo of nearly 1,500 pages, covering plant culture, botany, garden design, and an international survey and history of gardening. It went through six editions, with varying degrees of revision and expansion during Loudon's lifetime. Posthumous editions continued to appear into the 1870s.

In 1826 Loudon began publishing *Gardener's Magazine*, first as a quarterly, but then from 1827 as a bi-monthly, and from 1831 as a monthly. Loudon's magazine, which reached nineteen volumes before it ceased at the time of his death, was soon imitated by magazines edited by Joseph Paxton and others. As well as writing numerous books, he was at one point editing five monthly publications. His most famous publication was *Arboretum et fruticetum Brittanicum* (8 vols, 1838).

Loudon had a major influence on domestic architecture and the London landscape. Despite his extraordinary energies, he suffered greatly with poor health. He was a man widely respected for his distinguished career and it is not known why Francis Witts was so rude about his work and achievements.

1826: 16 Jun: *Hence an active opposition has been organized against Ashurst, and a requisition very numerously signed has been presented to Mr. Stratton, formerly possessor of Great Tew in Oxfordshire, to come forward as their candidate. The requisitionists make up in number what they want in weight: hardly a country gentleman or clergyman is to be found in the list, but hosts of attorneys, innkeepers, little farmers, shopkeepers, dissenters &c. To call Stratton the farmer's friend is exceedingly absurd: blessed with a noble fortune, he dissipated it many years since in idle speculations; one was the inviting to farm his fine estate a Scotch adventurer of the name of Loudon with strange wild notions of improvement which consisted only in indiscriminately overturning all established principles and practices of the country, and endinged in the ruin of himself and his Patron, the would-be farmer's friend, who to admit this charlatan had turned out a large and most respectable tenantry.*

LOUIS — Louis XVIII of France [125]

Louis-Stanislas-Xavier, comte de Provence (1755-1824), king of France and of Navarre, was the fourth son of the dauphin Louis, son of Louis XV. He received the title comte de Provence at his birth, and after the death of his two elder brothers and the accession of his remaining elder brother as Louis XVI in 1774, he became heir presumptive. The birth of two sons to Louis XVI, however, put a temporary stop to his royal ambitions.

When the French Revolution broke out in 1789, he remained in Paris, possibly to exploit the situation as a royal candidate; but he fled the country in June 1791. With little concern for the safety of Louis XVI and Marie-Antoinette, who were held captive in Paris, the comte de Provence issued uncompromising counter-revolutionary manifestos, organised émigré associations, and sought the support of other monarchs in the fight against the Revolution. When the king and queen were executed in 1793, he declared himself regent for his young nephew, Louis XVII; at his nephew's death in June 1795, the comte de Provence proclaimed himself Louis XVIII.

Louis XVIII spent twenty-three years in exile, from 1791 to 1814, and again in 1815, for 100 days, upon the return of Napoleon from Elba. While in exile, he lived in Prussia, the United Kingdom, and Russia. When the allies captured Paris in 1814, Louis XVIII was restored and ruled as king for a little less than a decade, during the Bourbon Restoration period. Louis XVIII's royal prerogative was reduced substantially by the charter of 1814, France's new constitution. He had no children, and upon his death the crown passed to his younger brother, Charles, comte d'Artois.

1824: 17 Sep: *It appears from the newspapers, that the King of France, Louis 18. has paid the debt of nature. His dissolution has been for some time anticipated, as likely soon to occur. After a very chequered life of troubles, dangers, and disappointments, and the accomplishment of hopes so long deferred, that they were well-nigh abandoned, this aged head of the Bourbon family, oppressed with a load of fleshly infirmity, so that protracted life must have been burdensome, transmits his crown to his brother Monsieur, the former Count d'Artois.*

LOUIS PHILIPPE — Louis Philippe of France — *see also* D'Orleans [126]

Louis-Philippe, duc d'Orléans (1773-1850), king of France, was the eldest son of Louis-Philippe Joseph de Bourbon-Orléans, duc de Chartres, and Adélaïde de Bourbon-Penthièvre. At the outbreak of the French Revolution in 1789, Louis-Philippe joined the group of progressive nobles who supported the revolutionary government. He became a member of the Jacobin Club in 1790, and when France went to war with Austria in April 1792, he joined the Army of the North. His father, meanwhile, had changed his name to Philippe Égalité and had been elected to the National Convention in Paris. After Neerwinden, Louis-Philippe associated himself with Dumouriez by deserting the revolutionary cause and coming to terms with the Austrians. However, he did not put his services at the disposal of the enemies of France. Instead, he went to Switzerland, where he joined his sister Adélaïde, who had earlier gone there from Tournai. Despite the fact that he had voted for the execution of Louis XVI in January 1793, the elder Louis-Philippe was arrested in Paris after his son's desertion.

The execution of Philippe Égalité in November 1793 made Louis-Philippe duc d'Orléans. He became the centre of the Orleanist intrigues, but he refused to countenance any plan to set himself up as king in France, possibly because he was negotiating with the revolutionaries for the release of his two brothers, duc de Montpensier and comte de Beaujolais, who had been arrested at the same time as their father.

Louis-Philippe travelled in Scandinavia for about a year (1795-96), and then sailed to the United States and settled in Philadelphia, where in February 1797 he was joined by his brothers. They spent more than two years in America, until, on hearing of Napoleon Bonaparte's coup of November 1799, the three brothers decided to return to Europe. By the time they reached England early in 1800, the power of the first consul was so well established that there was no hope of intervening in France. Instead, the house of Orléans became reconciled with the elder branch of the Bourbon family. Even so, Louis-Philippe never took up arms to fight with émigré forces for the royalist cause against other Frenchmen as the princes of Condé had done. Perhaps Louis XVIII mistrusted Philippe Égalité's son too much to allow him any close contact with French troops, or perhaps Louis-Philippe himself merely preferred to remain in England with his brothers, who had both developed tuberculosis (Montpensier died in 1807, Beaujolais in 1808).

In 1809, after a long residence at Twickenham in Middlesex, England, Louis-Philippe went to join the Neapolitan royal family at Palermo in Sicily, where on 25 November he married Marie-Amélie, a daughter of King Ferdinand IV of Naples and Maria Carolina of Austria. Louis-Philippe returned to France at the First Restoration in 1814. Although Louis XVIII refused to grant Louis-Philippe the style of royal highness (later allowed to him by Charles X), the king did grant him the dignities traditionally held by the head of his family. During the Hundred Days (1815) he returned to England instead of following the court to Ghent.

Under the Second Restoration, the duc d'Orléans was a steady and more or less open adherent of the liberal opposition, entertaining its most prominent deputies and journalists at the Palais Royal and giving open patronage to the opposition newspaper *Le Constitutionnel*, as well as tacit support to the more radical and Orleanist organ *Le National* (founded in January 1830).

In 1830 Charles X's attempt to enforce repressive ordinances touched off a rebellion (27-30 July) that gave Louis-Philippe his long-awaited opportunity to gain power. Following the abdication of Charles X the provisional government of deputies and peers present in Paris declared the throne vacant, and Louis-Philippe was proclaimed king on 9 August 1830.

The revolution of 1848 by those desiring parliamentary reform swept through Europe and caused Louis-Philippe to abdicate on 24 February 1848 in favour of his grandson, the comte de Paris. With Queen Marie-Amélie he escaped to Honfleur and thence to England. Incognito, as the comte and comtesse de Neuilly, they settled at Claremont, an estate in Surrey placed at their disposal by Queen Victoria. It was there that Louis-Philippe died in August 1850. He was the last king to rule France.

1843: 5 Sep: *The rumour of the Queen's arrival here to-day proved to be incorrect: it appears that her Majesty is visiting the King of the French at the Chateau d'Eu, and may be looked for here on Thursday.*

1844: 8 Oct: *It is stated on good authority that the Duke of Wellington expressed great indignation at the resistance to his nomination, looking on it as an act of insubordination, and himself having discovered that suffrage was not contemplated in the statute: his Grace expressed not only a readiness, but an anxiety, to come and preside, and appoint, in person, though it would be very inconvenient, as he was required to meet the King of the French on his landing at Portsmouth to-day, on a visit to the Queen.*

1848: 5 Mar: *The newspapers announce the arrival at Newhaven on the Sussex coast of Louis Philippe, and his Queen, with two or three attendants. They were picked up at sea by a steamer, and taken on board from a French fishing boat. Great have been the perils and anxieties of these aged victims of a successful rebellion. Flying from Paris, without preparation, with hardly any money or clothes, in the most obscure vehicles, by highways & byways, in disguise, and under feigned names, making for the coast, forced to rely for succour and concealment to on persons of humble means and humble station, concealed near Harfleur, and in communication with the British Consul at Havre, Mr. Featherstonehaugh, the persecuted ex Sovereigns, lately esteemed so puissant & so secure, under the assumed name of Smith, in a blouse and a peasant's cap, as regards Louis, and in a humble mourning gown & bonnet, as regards the Queen, landed, almost literally without a change of clothes, with one carpet bag, or portmanteau: forced to remain at the humble inn of the obscure port till clothing could be procured from London.*

LOVEGROVE — Joseph Lovegrove [127]

Joseph Lovegrove (1780-1857), potter and timber dealer, was born at Gloucester, son of Joseph Lovegrove, sometime coroner for the City of Gloucester and known as the 'Honest Lawyer', and his wife, Sarah Gardener. They had married at Old Sodbury in 1773. Another source states Joseph's parents to be Thomas Lovegrove (1733-1808) and Frances Wicks (b. 1751).

Joseph bought a pottery at Cranham that had been set up by John Weeks. By 1851 he had sold it on to William Moulton, who worked the pottery and claimed the patronage of Queen Adelaide (d. 1849).

Joseph Lovegrove married, 1807, Elizabeth Burdock (1786-1862); they had at least 7 sons and 2 daughters:

1 George (b. 1808)
2 John (1810-1848)
1 Mary Ellen (1811-1846)
3 Samuel (1812-1881)
4 Edwin (1814-1847)
2 Elizabeth (b. 1817)
5 Cornelius (b. 1820)
6 Joseph (1822-1883); *see below*
7 George Hymeneus (1827-1861)

1834: 14 Aug: *Looked into one of the potteries, where the process was going forward: rude turning lathes at work. The master and his men bore striking marks of the practical zeal with which the blue interest had been supported: black eyes and a broken nose disfigured the potters, master and man. Mr. Lovegrove, the potter, acted as our Cicerone to the Church.*

LOVEGROVE — Joseph Lovegrove [128]

Joseph Lovegrove (1822-1883), solicitor, county coroner, and city coroner, was born at Cranham, the sixth son of Joseph and

Elizabeth Lovegrove (*above*). Joseph followed his grandfather into the law, and like him, became a coroner. In 1861 he lived at Barton Street, Gloucester, with his sister Elizabeth. By 1871 he still lived at Barton Street, and had married Margaret Du-Pré (1824-1878) of Berkhamstead. He married, secondly, Mary Elizabeth (Natalie) Tayler (1834-1885). There were no children of either marriage. By 1881 Joseph had retired to 'Fortfield', Weston-super-Mare, where he was listed as a landowner. He died at Hotel d'Oasis, Algiers. What took him there is unclear, but his body was brought back to England and he was buried at Cranham. Natalie died in London.

Details of the contest between Pruen and Lovegrove in 1851 are not given by the diarist, but it seems clear that Lovegrove managed to unseat Pruen.

1848: 26 Jun: *Mr. Barnett, the Coroner, and Mr. Lovegrove, Asst. Coroner waited on us with reference to their bills.* 2 Aug: *from Mr. Lovegrove, of Gloucester, deputy coroner, a circular.* 28 Aug: *On my way fell in with Mr. Lovegrove, deputy coroner, who had been calling at Upper Slaughter ... Yet it behoves Mr. L. to press his claims, seeing that others are canvassing for the office—— Mr. Pruen, Solr. Cheltenham, and a Mr. Smith of Winchcombe. I promised to support Mr. Lovegrove.*

1850: 15 Jul: *From Mr. Lovegrove, Gloucester, a circular announcing that he is a candidate for the Coronership for the Northern division of this County, vacant by the decease of Mr. Cooke. Mr. L. is Coroner for the city of Gloucester, an attorney resident there, and for two years acted as Mr. Cooke's deputy, giving much satisfaction.* 18 Jul., 26 Jul., 29 Jul: *Mr. Lovegrove, the Candidate for the Coronership, called to request me to second his nomination at Cheltenham to-morrow: he is to be proposed by Lord Campden. I declined on the score of indisposition, and being afraid to encounter a crowded assembly.* 1 Aug: *thither, being freeholders, to record their votes in favour of Mr. Lovegrove,... Great concourse of conveyances of all sorts and sizes in the interest of, and provided by the rival candidates, the Conservative Lovegrove, and the Whig Pruen.* 3 Aug: *It is stated that the majority of votes at the close of the poll in the three polling places yesterday was in favour of Mr. Pruen, so that Lovegrove has been defeated.* 11 Oct: *At the junction station near Gloucester, while awaiting the arrival of the train from London, I had ten minutes conversation with Mr. Lovegrove, the late unsuccessful candidate for the Coronership of the Northern division of our County, who shewed me counsel's opinion lately procured, which is very favourable to him, and encourages the expectation that the rival, Mr. Pruen, maybe ousted by a Quo Warranto. The contest has already cost Mr. Lovegrove £1200; but it is very desirable, if funds can be raised, that Mr. Pruen be removed.* 28 Oct., 31 Oct.

1852: 30 Mar.

1853: 2 Mar: *Coroner Lovegrove has held his inquest on the dead body of the infant found in Naunton Brook to-day and has committed the wretched mother, Susan Barnett, for trial on the charge of child murder.*

LOVEGROVE — William Lovegrove [129]

William Lovegrove (1778-1816), actor, was born at Shoreham, Sussex, and was apprenticed to his father. After playing Hamlet as an amateur at a private theatre in Tottenham Court Road, London, he made his first professional appearance at the Richmond Theatre in June 1799. From there he went to Dublin, where he appeared as Anhalt in Lovers' Vows, an adaptation from the German by Elizabeth Inchbald. He made his first appearance at Bath in November 1802 in the part of Lazarillo in Robert Jephson's farce Two Strings to your Bow. During the season he played other roles, including Edgar in King Lear, and gained some popularity. When John Edwin left Bath for Dublin, a large range of comic characters fell to Lovegrove; his name appeared in Bath and Bristol in numerous roles. Lovegrove appeared in London on 3 October 1810 at the Lyceum, the temporary home of the Drury Lane company, and he played original parts in dramas by Dimond, Masters, Millingen, Arnold, and other writers. His Lopez in Kiss, an alteration of Beaumont and Fletcher's The Spanish Curate, won him much applause. Lovegrove remained with the company in the new Drury Lane Theatre until his retirement, and rose to be one of the principal supports of the house.

1806: 10 Mar: *At six o clock went to the Play; joined the Goold & Gillibrand party, sat by Mrs. Gillibrand & her humorous Spose: conversed much with them all & with Jessop: amused with the play. Shakespear's Twelfth Night; some characters infamously represented, Sir Andrew Aguecheek by Mallinson, Malvolio By Lovegrove, Viola by Miss Fisher passably well acted.*

LOVESY — Conway Whithorne Lovesy [130]

Conway Whithorne Lovesy (1818-1885), judge, was born at Charlton Kings, Gloucestershire, son of Conway Whithorne Lovesy and his wife, Margaret. He was educated at Queen's College, Oxford (BA 1841; MA 1874). Lovesy was a student of the Middle Temple in 1839, and was called to the bar in 1845. He married, 1847, Colin Campbell, née Lloyd. Conway Lovesy was a Gloucestershire JP, a police magistrate in Trinidad (1871-73), a puisne judge in British Guiana (1873-78), and a captain of the South Gloucestershire Militia (1855-61).

1851: 31 Mar: *At the Railway Station met Mr. Lovesy, and Mr. Fallon, the Barristers.*

1852: 29 Mar: *At the railway station met Mr. Ansley Robinson, Mr and Mrs. Lovesy, and others of my acquaintance.*

1853: 4 Apr.

LOWDER — John Lowder [131]

John Lowder (1781-1829), architect, was born at Southampton, son of John Lowder (1740-1810) and Ann Glass (1746-1821). He married, at St George's, Hanover Square, Westminster, 17 May 1804, Mary D'Oyley (1780-1837); they had 3 sons and 3 daughters:

1 Louisa Ann (b. 1805)
1 Charles D'Oyley John (1806-1878)
2 Mary Henrietta (1807-1854)
2 John Thomas (b. 1808)
3 Anne Glass (b. 1810)
3 John (1811-1849), episcopal chaplain at Shanghai, China; drowned 24 September 1849 while bathing at Poo Too, China. Married, 1840, Lucy (1812-1899), daughter of J. W. Windsor of Bath; at least 1 daughter:
    1 Amy Henrietta (1847-1924)

John Lowder was an architect and surveyor working in Bath, Somerset. He was appointed as the Bath City surveyor in 1817, and remained in the post until 1823. The first design submitted for the building of the Holy Trinity church recalled Ancient Greece, but Gothic was considered more fitting. Lowder was so conscientious in his work on the project that his health broke down, and he died in 1829, at the age of 48. He gave all his profit to the church he had designed. Nikolaus Pevsner refers to the building as an 'irregular fanciful composition', but to the untutored eyes of Bathonians who remembered it before the air raids of 1942, it had a friendly and pleasing character. The city of Bath was bombed in April

1942—one of the Baedeker raids—and Holy Trinity was hit by a high explosive shell; it was badly damaged, and in a subsequent raid it was destroyed by fire. The church was finally demolished in 1957.

1826: 29 Apr: *In the lower part of the Town we were struck with the exterior of a new church built a few years since in the parish of Walcot, not far from Green Park Place. The architect is Mr. Lowder of Bath; the workmanship and execution of the Gothic ornaments are very beautiful, but the whole has an eccentric appearance. Perhaps, Mr. Lowder was cramped for room, & so fell into errors of taste; perhaps, too, he was limited as to expence.*

LOWE — Mrs Lowe at Lady Lyttelton's musical party

1801: 23 Oct: *to a very pleasant Musical party at Lady Lyttelton's, where were the Pattons, Mrs. Davies. the Morley's, Mrs. Lowe, the Guydickens's, Vicomte De Bruges & Comte de Gourmand, Mr. Wood & the like.*

LOWE — Robert Atwell Lowe [132]

Robert Atwell Lowe (±1780-±1758) was an HEIC judge. He married, at Painswick, Gloucestershire, 12 September 1826, Charlotte (1794-1861), daughter of William Charles Lake (1753-1836) of Castle Godwyn, Painswick, formerly of Liverpool and Birkenhead (*above*). The marriage was conducted by Charlotte's brother-in-law, James Aspinall. They had 1 daughter:

1 Emmelina; married, 4 October 1859, Sir Robert Cavendish Spencer Clifford (1815-1892)

1835: 11 Jun: ... *They were followed by Mr. and Mrs. Lowe with their only child, a pretty little bridesmaid, scarcely six years old, two Misses Lake, and Mr. Blackford. Mrs. Lowe and the Misses Lake are sisters of Mrs. Witts.*

LOWE — George Lowe [133]

George Lowe (1793-1876), silversmith and jeweller of Westgate Street, Gloucester, was born at Chester. He married, at St Peter's, Bolton-le-Moors, Lancashire, 5 November 1817, Elizabeth Jackson (b. 1794); they had 2 sons and 4 daughters:

1 Mary Cawley (1820-1908)
1 George Cliff (1821-1872)
2 Elizabeth (1823-1893)
2 Edward Jackson (1825-1893); married, at Kensington, 1860, Mary Wainright (1840-1880)
3 Charlotte (1827-1923)
4 Sophia (1828-1861); died on the Hereford and Shrewsbury Railway, 4 January 1861; whether by suicide or accident is not clear

In the 1841 census George Lowe is listed as a goldsmith, living with his wife and four of their children at Westgate Street, Gloucester.

1842: 18 Apr: *Wrote to Lowe, a Silversmith at Gloucester, declining to purchase an article I had cheapened at his shop.*

LÖWENSTEIN — Herr von Löwenstein and Mademoiselle de Löwenstein at Weimar

1799: 25 Dec: *Mademoiselle de Löwenstein presented a Mademoiselle Weber played very well on the Harp: but the Room was too large and the Harp but a bad Instrument.*

1800: 26 Jan: *In the Evening the Piano Forte which was too small for the Salle, belonged to Herr von Löwenstein properly made at Dresden.*

LOWNDES — Richard Lowndes [134]

Richard Lowndes (1771-1828), Church of England clergyman, was a younger son of William Lowndes (afterwards Lowndes Selby), of Winslow, and Mary, daughter and co-heir of Thomas Goostrey of London and Great Missenden Abbey, Buckinghamshire. He was educated at Merton College, Oxford (BA 1794; MA 1799), and served as rector of Gamlingay, Cambridge, and of Farley, Surrey, in 1814-28.

In the Sheppard tomb at Thornton crypt lie the remains of Maria Lowndes, née Sheppard (1776-1798), wife of William Lowndes, of Whaddon Hall, Buckinghamshire, who died on 14 December 1798, aged 22 years. This was probably Richard Lowndes's sister-in-law, a Sheppard by birth and sister to Sir Thomas Cotton Sheppard (1785-1848) of Crakemarsh Hall, Staffordshire. Maria Selby Lowndes was the daughter of Maria Sheppard and William Lowndes.

William Lowndes (±1767-1840) was MP for Buckinghamshire in 1810-20. He married secondly, 1806, Ann Eleanor Isabella Hanmer. His first marriage is not mentioned in *History of Parliament*.

1812: 5 Aug: *We found Mr. & Mrs. Dewes of Wellesbourne with their Son, Mr. Granville's guests: he is Mr. G's elder Brother. Miss Louisa Port, Mr. G's great niece, resides with them. Two daughters of Mr. Wheler of Crakemarsh were also on a visit at Calwich. Mr. Cotton Shepherd & Mr. Wheler, both well known to me of old, were added to our dinner party. Miss Shepherd accompanied the former, as also the Revd. Lownds, Brother to the Member for Bucks.*

LOWNDES-STONE — William Charles Lowndes-Stone — *see also* Wynniatt [135]

William Charles Lowndes-Stone (1812-1845), JP and landed proprietor, was the son of William Francis Lowndes-Stone (1783-1858), of Brightwell House, Oxfordshire, and Caroline Strickland (1782-1867). He was educated at Eton College and Christ Church, Oxford. He married, at Lower Guiting, 5 May 1840, Catherine Wynniatt (1814-1850); they had 1 son, who died in infancy, and 2 daughters:

1 Catherine Charlotte (1841-1882); married, 1862, Capt. Robert Thomas Norton, later Lowndes-Stone-Norton (d. 1895)
2 Margaret Susan (1845-1932); married, 1871, Henry John Elwes (1846-1922)

See the diary entry for 26 April 1845. Catherine died in April 1850.

1840: 27 May: *Drove M.W. to Guiting Grange to call on the Wynniatt family on occasion of the recent marriage of Miss. C.W. to Mr. Lowndes, eldest Son of Mr. Lowndes Stone, an Oxfordshire Gentleman, whose estate and place at Brightwell adjoin Watlington.* 17 Jul: *On our return home called at Guiting Grange to pay our respects to Mr. and Mrs. W. Lowndes, now visiting the Wyniatts, for the first time after their Union. Saw Mrs. Wynniatt, her son Tom, and eldest daughter, also the Bride and Bridegroom.*

1842: 17 May: *Soon after twelve M.W. and I went in the Phaeton to Stanway, making a morning call at Guiting Grange, where we saw Mrs. Wynniatt and two of her daughters, her son Thomas, and her Son in law Lowndes Stone.* 20 Jul: *A dinner party; we were favoured with the company of Mr. and Mrs. Pole, Watson Pole, Mr. Wynniatt with his daughter Harriet, and son in law, W. Lowndes, Mr. and Mrs. Winter, and J. T. Rice; the evening passed off pleasantly.*

1844: 15 May: *M.W. and I drove to Stanway: as we passed by Guiting Grange, we met and parleyed with Mr. Wynniatt and*

Mr. & Mrs. W Lowndes Stone; accepted an invitation to dine at the Grange on Friday next. 17 May: *dined at Guiting Grange, meeting Mr. and Mrs. Robt. Phillips from Herefordshire, agreeable people with whom we were already acquainted, Mr. and Mrs. W. Lowndes Stone, a Miss Gordon, and the many young ladies of the house, with F. Wynniatt—A pleasant and conversible evening.*

1845: 26 Apr: *His second daughter, married to Mr. Lowndes Stone, of Oxfordshire, has lately been confined in London of a daughter, having already two children, a son and daughter. Mr. W.L.S. left her in town for his Father's seat in Oxfordshire, intending to return to accompany her thither in a few days: he took with him his little boy: somewhere he caught a contagious disease, and in two days, I believe, was a corpse; the poor little boy died on the day following;—of course the widow & both families, at Guiting Grange and Brightwell, plunged in the deepest grief: the widow barely recovering after her accouchement.* 16 May, 20 May.

LOWTHER — John Henry Lowther [135]

Sir John Henry Lowther, 2nd baronet (1793-1868), JP, MP, and landed proprietor, was the eldest son of Sir John Lowther, 1st baronet (1759-1844), and Elizabeth (d. 1844), daughter of John Fane, 9th earl of Westmorland. He was educated at Westminster School and Trinity College, Cambridge (MA 1814). Lowther was MP for Cockermouth in 1816-26 and 1831-32, Wigtown Burghs in 1826-31, and York in 1835-47. He succeeded his father as 2nd baronet in 1844. He was lieutenant-colonel of the 1st West Riding Yorkshire Militia in 1830-52, and high sheriff in 1852. He died unmarried.

1833: 7 Nov: *Our street was very noisy: an adjoining Inn was the head quarter of Mr. Lowther, of Stillington in this county, who has been nominated as opponent to Mr. Dundas, eldest Son of Lord Dundas, the candidate for the representation of the city in the room of Mr. Bayntun, recently deceased, a gentleman of very equivocal character.*

LOWTHER — William Lowther [136]

William Lowther, 2nd earl of Lonsdale (1787-1872), JP, MP, and landed proprietor, was the eldest son of Sir William Lowther, 2nd baronet. Lowther was educated at Harrow School and Trinity College, Cambridge (MA 1808). He was styled Viscount Lowther in 1807-44. In 1810 he was made a fellow of both the Society of Antiquaries and the Royal Society. He was MP for Cockermouth in 1808-13, for Westmorland in 1813, 1818, 1820, 1826, and 1832-41, and for Dunwich in 1831. He was junior lord of the Admiralty in 1809-10, commissioner for affairs of India in 1810-18, lord of the Treasury in 1813-27, and privy counsellor in 1828. These posts were followed by his appointment as first commissioner of woods and forests in 1828-30, treasurer of the Navy in 1834-5, vice-president of the Board of Trade in 1834-35, and postmaster-general in 1841-45. He was lieutenant-colonel of the Westmorland Militia in 1835, lord lieutenant and custos rotulorum for Cumberland and Westmorland in 1844-68, lord president of the council in 1852, and first commissioner to enquire into laws respecting pilots in 1835. Lowther succeeded his father as 2nd earl of Lonsdale in 1844. He was the character of 'Lord Eskdale' in Disraeli's *Coningsby*. He died unmarried.

1827: 14 Apr: *In addition to these may be named some of the subordinate members of government, whose resignation indicates the sentiments of those, with whom they are connected: thus Lord Granville Somerset & Lord Lowther relinquish their seats at the Treasury.*

1828: 2 Jun.

1834: 21 Dec: *Further intelligence is communicated in the newspapers as to the Ministerial appointments. The Earl of Aberdeen holds the Office of Colonial Secretary, while Earl De Grey is to preside at the Admiralty; Earl Maryborough is to be Post-master General; Lord Lowther, Treasurer of the Navy and Vice President of the Board of Trade.*

LUC DE LIGNAC — Louis François Luc de Lignac [137]

Louis François Luc de Lignac (1740-1809). Louis François Luc is best known for his book *Physical view of man and woman in a state of marriage*, published in England in 1798. It was printed on the Continent, but most of the copies imported were seized by customs owing to the alleged indecency of the plates. The book was originally published in 1772 at Lille, France, as *De l'homme et de la femme ... dans l'état du mariage*.

It would not be surprising if M. de Luc was in Weimar in 1798; it would be a natural place for him to migrate to, especially with the upheaval in Paris. In his book, *Proofs of a Conspiracy Against all the Religions and Governments of Europe Carried on in the Secret Meetings of Free Masons, Illuminati and Reading Societies*, a supposed exposé of the illuminati, Robison said:

> M. de Luc, a very eminent naturalist, has shewn, in a letter to the Chevalier Dr. Zimmermann (published, I think, about the year 1790) how very scanty the knowledge of these observers has been, and how precipitate have been their conclusions. For my own part, I think the affair is of little consequence. Moses writes the history, not of this globe, but of the race of Adam.

Francis Witts states in his diary that Weimar was a home for the illuminati thanks to the duke's influence: 'Of his Connection with the Illuminati so often imputed to him, I shall not venture to mention: particularly as I had no Opportunity of knowing the Opinion of his Highness in Philosophical or Political Concerns.' Having said this, this attribution, although likely, has to be considered as speculative.

1798: 2 Sep: *of strangers there are many. The chief are Count Marschall, the Egloffstein, Seebach, Helldorf, Luc, Lasberg, Wolfskiel, Gormar, Oldorthausen, Families &c. all of whom almost have some Office either in the Civil, Military or Immediate Court Service.*

LUCAS — Charles Lucas [138]

Charles Lucas (1769-1854), Church of England clergyman and author, was the son of William Lucas of Daventry. He was educated at Harrow School and Oriel College, Oxford. He was curate of Huish Episcopi, Somerset, in 1792, and stipendiary curate of Avebury with Winterborne Monkton, Wiltshire, in 1814, although according to *DNB* he was curate at Avebury from 1791. At Avebury he devoted himself to writing religious poems and novels, such as *A Descriptive Account in Blank Verse of the Old Serpentine Temple of the Druids at Avebury* (1795), *The Castle of St Donat's* or *The History of Jack Smith* (1798), and *The Infernal Quixote: a Tale of the Day* (1801). He married, 1803, Sarah Ann Williams, sister of Revd H. Williams; they had a large family. Lucas continued to write, producing a novel entitled *The Abissinian Reformer* or *The Bible and the Sabre* in 1808, and *Joseph* in 1810, a religious poem in two volumes. Lucas left Avebury in 1816 and settled at Devizes, where he died in 1854.

1806: 18 Jul: *Dinner at Mr Mayo's.—The party consisted besides ourselves of Revd. Mr. Lucas, Mrs. Mayo, three Miss Hilliers, & a Miss Ferrals.* 4 Nov: *In pursuance of an invitation dined with the Mayor & Corporation of Devizes upon occasion of the Election of Members for the Town; Mr. Smith & Mr. Estcourt being re-elected. Met a very large & select party & dined at ½ past four in the Town Hall. Conversed chiefly with the Mr. Salmons, F. Merewether, Mr. Estcourt, Mr. C. Lucas, Compton, Jaques &c.*

LUDLOW — Ebenezer Ludlow — *see also* Lippincott[139]

Ebenezer Ludlow (1777-1851), barrister, was the son of Ebenezer Ludlow, a Chipping Sodbury apothecary and former employer of Edward Jenner of smallpox vaccination fame. He was educated at Oriel College, Oxford (BA 1795; MA 1821). He was a lieutenant of the provincial cavalry in 1798 and, in 1803, a cornet in the Winterbourne Horse. He studied at Gray's Inn and was called to the bar in 1805. He was a serjeant-at-law in 1827 and then QC. His further appointments included that of town clerk of Bristol in 1819-36, commissioner of the court of bankruptcy for Liverpool district in 1842, and for Bristol district in 1849-51, and chairman of Gloucestershire quarter sessions in 1842-49. He married Jane (1784-1861) in around 1804.

1826: 7 Aug: *Serjeant Wilde had been retained, & was expected every moment from the Western circuit; he had been paid his three hundred guineas, he was to come from Wells, he had written within a few days to the Attorneys on the management of the cause, but he was not come. They could not go to trial without him: Messrs. Curwood, Ludlow & C. Phillips without him, would be as chaff before the wind; able men as they are, before Mr. Scarlett, supported by Messrs. Campbell, Russel, Talfoard and Justice.*

1827: 19 Apr: *The counsel on both sides, Messrs. Ludlow & Twiss, conducted the business with great talent & judgment and Mr. Baron Vaughan charged the Jury with much impartiality and distinctness; perhaps, went over the ground rather too often, incurring the risk of confounding the Jury in the desire of leaving nothing unsaid.*

1829: 3 Apr: *Mr. Serjeant Ludlow, my old acquaintance, a very acute & able lawyer, but hasty in manner, yet of a kind, cheerful disposition.*

1830: 20 Apr: *The Calendar had contained the appalling list of nearly 220 prisoners, and the learned Baron had been assisted in his duties by Mr. Serjeant Ludlow, who had been trying prisoners in the Grand Jury-room.*

1834: 30 Sep: *He also threw out the question whether it were expedient to retain Messrs. Ludlow and Talfourd.* 14 Oct: *Mr. Bloxsome is of opinion that it will be impossible for the prosecutors to prosucceed in the action, and that our conduct in the business is unimpeachable: he recommended our going on steadily, and, if the writ be served, that we should retain Mr. Serjeant Ludlow, and, perhaps, Mr. Alexander as Junior Counsel.*

1835: 8 Apr: *They were ably defended by Sergt. Ludlow, but all, with the exception of one individual, were found guilty, and sentence of death recorded against them.* 13 Apr: *Before, however, taking the case of murder, that of Forgery was selected for trial, in order to release Serjeant Ludlow who was retained for the defence of Forbes.*

1839: 5 May: *Mr. Serjeant Ludlow, endeavoured to persuade a beadle to find me room, but without success; so like many others I must have stood during all the service, had I not obtained a hassock which furnished me with a lowly seat.*

1842: 18 Jan: *It is thrown out, whether Sergt. Ludlow would not be a fit Chairman, if he cease to go on the Oxford Circuit.* 19 Jan., 6 Feb: *A letter from Howell, from London; he had seen Sergeant Ludlow, who is not indisposed to accept the chair of our Quarter Sessions, but sees no reason why it should be incompatible with his engagements on the Circuit.* 21 Feb: *A letter from Codrington informing me that Serjt. Ludlow had consented to take the situation of Chairman of the Quarter Sessions for this County with certain stipulations.* 12 Apr: *When the Lord Lieutenant arrived, he took the Chair, and in a very proper and carefully measured speech suggested what had been arranged among the leaders on county matters of both political parties,—that henceforth there should be two joint Chairmen of equal authority and rank, of whom one, Serjeant Ludlow, should preside in the hearing of appeals and trying of prisoners, and the other, Purnell, should preside in County business.* 13 Apr: *Sergeant Ludlow, who had arrived from his residence near Bristol yesterday evening, joined us, and was cordially received as Judicial Chairman.* 29-30 Jun., 19 Oct.

1843: 3 Jan: *Nor will those be wanting who may fancy that he resigns the chair of Assistant for trials, from some prejudice against his colleague Sergt. Ludlow.* 4 Jan: *Went into Court, where Sergt. Ludlow presided, to whom Purnell announced his intention of vacating the second chair, which, as I had anticipated, was not quite palatable to the learned Chairman.* 18 Oct: *Attended at the opening of the Court by Mr. Sergt. Ludlow, who arrived last Evening from his residence near Manchester, in good health and spirits.* 19 Oct.

1844: 3 Jan: *After breakfast went down to the Court, and attended more or less throughout the day in that which was presided over by Sergeant Ludlow, who arrived from Cheshire yesterday evening.* 29 Feb., 1-2 Mar., 9 Apr: *The party at dinner at the Bell was not very numerous, but pleasant.—I was very kindly complimented for my late services as Chairman in the absence of Serg. Ludlow at the Adjd. Sessns.* 10 Apr., 16 Oct., 18 Oct., 31 Dec.

1845: 1-2 Jan., 27 Jan., 15-16 Apr., 29 Apr., 30 Jun: *Mr. Bloxsome having received a hurried letter from Mr. Sergeant Ludlow, dated Harrowgate, naming that he had been summoned hastily to that place to the death-bed of his daughter, Mrs. Lippincott, and that her decease would prevent him from presiding in Court at this Sessions.* 1 Jul.

1846: 30 Jun: *Mr. Bloxsome received a note from Serjeant Ludlow, which made it doubtful whether he could attend to-morrow to preside in the Crown Court on the appeals & trials of Prisoners.* 1 Jul., 21-22 Oct.

1847: 6-7 Jan., 30 Jun: *To the Court, where joined Sergeant Ludlow, who presided at the trial of appeals, which lasted nearly all day: only two or three prisoners being tried in the evening.* 1 Jul., 20-21 Oct.

1848: 5 Jan: *Attended till noon in the Court in which Sergt. Ludlow presided.* 22-23 Mar., 28 Jun: *Thence to the Court Shire Hall where I remained in Sergeant Ludlow's Court.* 18 Oct.

1850: 1 Jan: *The Lord Lieutenant, adverting to the retirement of Sergeant Ludlow.*

1851: 31 Mar: *I arrived in Court just after Talfourd had finished his charge to the Grand Jury, which he very gracefully, eloquently, and properly closed with a well considered and pertinent tribute of admiration and esteem to the memory of Sergeant Ludlow, for many years his rival and Competitor on this Circuit.*

LUDLOW WALKER — Charles Ludlow Walker[140]

Charles Ludlow Walker (1787-1856), JP, DL, banker, and businessman, was born at Harborne, Worcestershire, son of Capt.

Thomas Walker (1756-1805) and Harriet Ludlow (b. 1763). He married, at Kings Areley, Worcestershire, 16 November 1816, Mary Anne (1794-1869), daughter of Revd Reginald Pyndar, of Hadsor, Worcestershire, and Kempley, Gloucestershire, and cousin of the 1st Earl Beauchamp; they had 2 sons and 2 daughters:

1 Charles Pyndar Beauchamp (1817-1894), Gen.; saw service in North America, the Crimea, and the Indian Mutiny of 1857; married Georgiana, daughter of Capt. Richard Armstrong, 100th Foot; 1 son and 1 daughter
1 Mary Anne (1821-1857)
2 Charles (b. 1831)
2 Elizabeth (1838-1907)

Charles Ludlow Walker was a JP and DL of Gloucestershire, sheriff for Bristol in 1824 and 1828, and mayor in 1833. He and his family lived at Redland, near Bristol. He was involved in local business and gave evidence during the reading of the Great Western Railway Bill. As a representative of the Bristol Municipal Corporation, he was a member of the Bristol committee for the GWR Company. He was also a partner in Harfords & Bristol Brass & Copper Company. By 1836 the company was no longer a manufacturing concern, and it leased its premises at Baptist Mills to Ludlow Walker at a rental of £500 per annum. Ludlow Walker then started building a new plant at Keynsham designed to operate, it is thought, on steam rather than water power.

1822: 15 Oct.

1827: 16 Oct: *The Quarter Sessions commenced; Sir B.W. Guise, Mr. Cooper, Mr. Goodrich, Messrs. Baker, Mr. Ludlow Walker, Mr. Talbot, Mr. Phelps, Mr Purnell, Mr. Clifford, Revd. Messrs. Ford, Archdeacon Timbrell, Hicks and Campbell were present.*

1830: 12 Jan.

1847: 5 Apr: *The magistrates with whom I was most in communication during the evening were Purnell, Curtis Hayward, Niblett, Wallington, D Pyrke, Ludlow Walker, Sir M B. Crawley, John Browne, W H Hyett, Hopkinson, Crawley, R. Onslow &c.*

LUMBERT — Richard Collett Lumbert[141]

Richard Collett Lumbert (±1791-1853), land agent, was born at Wyck Rissington and came from an old Gloucestershire family. His mother was a Collett from Upper Slaughter. He lived at Scrubs, Burghfield Hill, Berkshire, with his wife, Mary Stephens (b. ±1792), who was born at Tetbury; they had at least 1 daughter:

1 Mary (±1825-1845)

Lumbert was regularly employed in Berkshire and Hampshire and had been involved in enclosure assessments.

1842: 30 Jan: *letter from Lumbert as to the arrears due from J W Harris, to whom he will apply for a settlement.* 2 Apr: *She had married a Methodist Preacher, and was resident at Edgbaston, near Birmingham, whence her corpse was brought by her nephew, Richard Collett Lumbert, of Burghfields, Berks, a very worthy, sensible man, following the business of Land Surveyor, and Farmer, and possessor of a small estate here, the ancient patrimony of the Colletts.*

1844: 6 Nov: *To Mr. Lumbert with a cheque on Hoare in payment of Thos. Andrew's rent.* 10 Nov., 12 Nov: *Wrote to Mr. Lumbert in answer to his letter recd. on Sunday, explaining to him the charities of Upper Slaughter, whence arising, how dispensed.* 17 Nov:*—from Mr. Lumbert in answer to my late letter to him on the Upper Slaughter charities: he kindly promises to give me £1. 0. 0. every Christmas to be distributed in charity among our poor people.*

1845: 11 Feb: *To Mr. Lumbert, explaining to him how I had distributed among poor old people here the Sovereign he sent to me before Christmas.* 8 Apr: *Recd. from Mr. Lumbert, now at Wyck Hill, as Mr. Pole's agent, a note as to Justice business, to which I replied, adding a few lines of condolence, on understanding that he had recently lost his only daughter.*

1847: 25 Jan., 31 May: *At a later hour Mr. Turner called; and after him Mr. Lumbert, whom I saw rep respecting digging stone on his land to erect a wall to mound out the road in my rectory fields, Pease Hill & Short Riff Hill, on the way to the Cheltenham turnpike road.* 14 Jul: *Wrote to Mr. Lumbert, enquiring whither the report is true that he meditates selling his property at Upper Slaughter: explained to him how I am circumstanced as to the investment in lands or other freeholds of the proceeds of the sale of our houses in Fenchurch Street; and that I should be prepared to buy his farm here on reasonable terms, if the price and title be such as would be approved in the Court of Chancery.* 22 Jul: *A letter from Mr. Lumbert, who acknowledges the receipt of mine of the 14th. Inst: he does mean to sell his farm at Upper Slaughter, but not unless for a higher price than I should be at liberty to give for property purchased under sanction of the Court of Chancery.*

1848: 13 Jan: *Mr. R. C. Lumbert called, and left in my hands the very liberal donation of Three Pounds.* 19 Mar.

1850: 3 Jan: *Good Mr. Lumbert sends me a cheque for three pounds as his liberal gift to the poor of the parish.* 16 Feb.

1851: 1 Mar., 26 Apr: *Wrote to Mr. R. C. Lumbert, requesting him to value and let my rectory farm & other lands held by John Davis.* 29-30 Apr., 13 May: *Mr. Lumbert called on me early by appointment.* 14 May: *Also a letter from Mr. Lumbert, which was accompanied by his valuation of my Rectory farm, which he calculates to be worth at the present price of agricultural produce £180.* 15 May, 18 May: *A letter from Lumbert announces that he has let my rectory Farm to A Stratton from year to year at the rent of £180.* 20 May: *Wrote to Mr. Lumbert that I accepted A. Stratton as my tenant of the Rectory farm from Michaelmas next.* 22 May.

1852: 22 Jan., 24 Jan., 27-28 Jan., 31 Jan., 7 Feb., 17-18 Feb., 1 Mar., 3 Mar., 14 Apr: *Mr. Lumbert called on me by appointment, after having gone over my farm here, with A Stratton. He reported well of S's management, and approved my outlay.* 28 Apr: *From Mr. Lumbert, fixing the 13th. of May for a visit with J W Harris to the Vicarage farm at Stanway, and to meet me at Stow afterwards to report to me thereon.* 29 Apr., 2 May, 10 May, 13 May: *at the Library with Mr. Lumbert, at which Sir H. Vavasour was present during part of the time; but L. could not recommend to him such a person as he required.... Mr. L. had been this morning early at Stanway, with J W Harris, and had looked over the Vicarage farm at S. He was agreeably surprized at the good quality of the land, and considered it had been let at a low rate, and that I had been too liberal in my abatements to Harris, and too ready to make expensive improvements in buildings.—He also considered the farm to be well cultivated, and told me that H. had promised to pay up his arrears of rent shortly.* 15 Nov., 18 Nov.

1853: 17 Feb: *Heard also, with great regret, of the sudden death of R C Lumbert, which occurred a few days since. It was only on Thursday last that he sent me by Mr. Pole's bailiff his usual annual charity of three sovereigns to be distributed among the poor of my parish. He was an honest, sensible, worthy man, and most useful man of business, as Land agent: I shall miss him, Pole miss him greatly.* 17 May: *Had an interview with Mr. Paice, Executor to the late R.C. Lumbert, who had arrived to look over his property in this village & parish, which is to be sold ... The worthy deceased has left a full provision for his invalid widow, his mother and sister, near relations beyond them he has none; distant kindred he has not forgotten in his will: and in charities to religious societies, infirmaries &c. he has been very liberal.*

1854: 23 Mar: *To Sewell's office; signed the transfer &c. of the mortgage I have hitherto held on the property of Mr. Davis of Cricklade, the amount of which will go towards the payment for the Lumbert property at Upper Slaughter.*

LUMLEY — William Golden Lumley [142]

William Golden Lumley (1802-1878), barrister, was born at Sidmouth Street, London, the eldest son of William Lumley and Elizabeth Saunders. He was educated at Trinity College and Trinity Hall, Cambridge (LLB 1825; LLM 1859), and was a fellow of Trinity Hall in 1825-40. He was admitted to the Middle Temple in 1823 and called to the bar in 1827. Lumley was on the Oxford circuit and, in 1832, became a revising barrister under the Reform Act. He became QC in 1868, and was professor of English Law at the University of London in 1834-38. In 1835 he reported for the *Law Journal*. In addition, he was assistant secretary to the poor law commission in 1839-72, counsel to the committee of the privy council on education in 1840, and counsel to the local government board in 1874. He married Elizabeth Ann, daughter of George Johnson and widow of Joseph Oswald Lumley, solicitor, presumably William's cousin.

1842: 5 Apr: *Cases with reference to the Administration of the Poor Law: Collected by Mr. Lumley, a Barrister, employed in the P. L. C. office as an Asst. Secretary.* 30 May, 14 Jun., 24 Aug., 29 Aug.

LUMSDEN — Hugh Lumsden [143]

Hugh Lumsden (1783-1859), JP, DL, and landed proprietor, was the son of Harry Lumsden (d. 1833), of Pitcaple House, Aberdeen, and Catherine, daughter of Hugh McVeagh and Margaret Lumsden, who had married in 1781. Hugh Lumsden was educated at Wadham College, Oxford, and became a JP, DL, and sheriff for Sutherland. He married, first, 30 April 1813, Frances, second daughter of Alexander Brebner of Learney; they had 1 daughter:

1 Christina (d. 1891); married Revd George Bain

Hugh Lumsden married secondly, 1824, Isabella (d. 1888), fourth daughter of Walter Fergus of Strathone, Fife; they had 2 sons and 4 daughters:

1 Henry (1825-1918), Col, London Scottish Rifle Volunteers; inherited Pitcaple Castle
2 Walter (1834-1872); employed by the HEIC; died in Rome
1 Charlotte Fergus
2 Catherine Edith; married her cousin Lt-Col H. W. Lumsden, RA
3 Isabella
4 Elizabeth; married Revd Robert Lovett (d. 1859)

1803: 16 Nov: *Newbigging & Odell dined with me; Dowell & Lumsden joined the party.* 24 Nov: *In the Evening at a party at Mr. Lumsden's.* 1 Dec: *Called on Lumsden. Wrote to George. Evans & Lumsden sat with me in the Evening.* 4 Dec: *Passed the Evening with Evans, meeting Lumsden.*

1804: 5 Feb., 13 Feb., 27 Feb., 12 Mar: *Passed a very dull Evening at a party at Lumsdens.*

LUPTON — Charles Lupton and Heneage Lupton of Stow-on-the-Wold [144]

Charles Lupton (b. ±1829), teenage army deserter, and Heneage Lupton (±1825-±1855), grocer-cum-policeman-cum-soldier, were born at Chailey, Sussex, sons of William Lupton (b. ±1790), land agent, and Frances Mansell [?] (±1792-1854), who died at Stow-on-the-Wold. Charles and Heneage appear to have been two of six children; 3 sons and 3 daughters:

1 Heneage (±1825-±1855)
1 Frances Lupton (b. ±1826)
2 William Mansell (b. ±1824-1901); died at Hastings, Sussex
3 Charles Lupton (b. ±1829)
2 Mary Lupton (b. ±1830)
3 Caroline (b. ±1832); unmarried in 1861 and a housekeeper at Greenwich

Enumerators for the 1841 census tended to round up or down to the nearest 5 years, and therefore some of the dates above are quite arbitrary; those for Heneage, Charles, and Caroline, however, are more accurate as they have been confirmed by other sources.

At the time of the 1841 census, Heneage, aged 16, and Caroline, aged 8, were living with Anne Mansell (b. ±1805), the post mistress at Stow-on-the-Wold. William (b. ±1824) had the second name of Mansell, so it is likely that Anne was Frances's sister and the children's aunt. The remainder of the family were living at Chailey in 1841. References are sparse and little is known for certain, but it seems that this family's story was a sad one.

Charles Lupton, aged 17, was committed to Northleach House of Correction for 6 months' hard labour by Francis Witts on 5 December 1846 for the use of 'threatening language'. He was certainly resident at Northleach House of Correction on 19 March 1847. The prison records state that he could read and write well. It appears he had enlisted in the Army at the very early age, probably 15.

Heneage Lupton (b. ±1825) married, at Stow-on-the-Wold, 1 June 1846, Susanne Fletcher (b. ±1824), daughter of Richard Verney, veterinary surgeon; they had at least 1 daughter:

1 Frances Miriam (1847-1848)

Susanne died young, and was buried at Stow on 26 June 1848. Heneage married secondly, at St Mary's, Cheltenham, 14 April 1849, Sarah (b. ±1826), daughter of Robert Turner, farmer or labourer, of Upper Rissington or Westcote, Gloucestershire. Acting as witnesses at the marriage were his brother Charles and his sister-in-law from his first marriage, Elizabeth Verney. On the marriage certificate Heneage stated that he was a policeman, but there is no person of his name recorded in the Gloucestershire Constabulary records. A census record for 1851, however, shows him as a constable in the Metropolitan Police in London, living with Sarah at 40 Skinner Street in the parish of St Botolph without Bishopsgate.

From the diary entry for 14 May 1848, it appears that Heneage had also enjoyed the comforts of Northleach House of Correction, but no prisoner record appears to exist for him. It seems surprising that within just months of incarceration for assaulting a police constable he should manage to find a position within the Metropolitan Police; we may presume that during his application he was economical with the truth regarding his past. In 1851 he and Sarah had 1 son:

1 Robert Heneage (1850-1918); born at Plaistow, Essex; married, at St Barnabas's, Oxford, 8 August 1875, Ann Eleanor Bayliss; died at Stow-on-the-Wold (probably Westcote, but registered at Stow)

Heneage apparently left the police in 1851 and served in the Royal Marines at Woolwich. On his son Robert's marriage certificate, his occupation was given as 'soldier'. Robert was baptised later in life, on 16 January 1868, at his mother's parish church of Westcote. He became a smallholder farmer. In the 1861 census he was registered as living with his mother and stepfather, John Sandell, cordwainer [shoemaker] at Westcote; from this it may be presumed that Heneage had died at some time between his discharge from the marines and 1861, alternatively it is possible that he was a casualty of the Crimean War.

As for Charles Lupton, no further records have been discovered. It is possible that he emigrated to Canada or Australia, or perhaps he succumbed to the Californian Gold Rush.

1846: 15 Aug: *Recd. from the War Office a letter about C. Lupton, a deserter.* 7 Dec: *Conferred with R G K Brookes as to Justice business; an unpleasant interview—there is a probability that the commitment of Charles Lupton on Thursday last for want of sureties will be called in question, Mr. Griffiths, Solr., Campden, having applied to Brookes for a copy of the examinations.* 8 Dec: *to Mr. Brookes's office, to meet the parties who had laid informations against Charles Lupton, to reduce their evidence into formal examinations, that copies may be forwarded to Mr. Griffiths, Campden.*

1848: 14 May: *Received an impudent letter from Heneage Lupton, praying me to shorten the period of imprisonment of a poacher of the name of Harding whom I have committed to Northleach House of Correction, and whom H.L. met in that resort of bad and blackguard characters. It is amusing that the Prisoner committed for an assault on a Police Constable should intercede with the Committing Magistrate on behalf of a brother prisoner suffering the punishment adjudged to him by the same Magistrate!*

LUSHINGTON — Mrs Lushington at Lady Call's party, Clifton

It seems likely that Lady Call (née Philadelphia Batty) and Mrs Lushington were related, but nothing specific has been discovered. The Call family had strong HEIC connections; Lady Call's husband, Sir John Call, 1st baronet (1731-1801), had been the chief engineer and captain-general of artillery in one of the Company's settlements, possibly Madras, and had eventually gained a seat on the governor's council. He was strongly recommended by Robert Clive for the governorship of Madras, but he had had to return to England on the death of his father on 31 December 1766. Sir Stephen Lushington, 1st baronet (1744-1807), was chairman of the HEIC between 1790 and 1791.

One potential attribution is to Anne Elizabeth Lushington, née Harris (d. 1856), who married, 1797, Stephen Rumbold Lushington (1776-1868) of Norton Court, near Faversham, Kent. Stephen had been a writer for the HEIC, and returned to England in 1803. As the couple would have been young and Clifton was a popular resort for HEIC officers, this would seem to fit. But this attribution is highly speculative, and the diary mention could refer to any one of several members of the Lushington family connected to the 1st baronet.

1804: 21 Dec: *Accompanied my mother and to Lady Call's Family: Lady Aylmer, a pretty little woman: Mrs. Lushington also there, the handsome wife of a formal handsome man.* 22 Dec: *To be a large & handsome party at Lady Call's. Mrs. Lushington played with great science on the Piano.*

LUSHINGTON — Stephen Lushington[145]

Stephen Lushington (1782-1873), MP and judge, was educated at Christ Church, Oxford (BA 1802; MA 1806). Lushington was an advocate of Doctors' Commons in 1808, a judge of the consistory court in 1828-38, and a judge of the court of Admiralty in 1838-67. He was MP for Ilchester in 1820-26 and 1831, Tregony in 1826-30, Winchelsea in 1831, Tower Hamlets in 1832-41, and Yarmouth, Norfolk, in 1866-68. He was also a privy counsellor in 1838.

1840: 7 May: *I was resworn in open Court, before Dr. Addams: Dr. Lushington was the Presiding Judge, the question under litigation was cognizable before him in the capacity of Judge of the Admiralty, I believe, being with reference to seamens wages, and, as I understood, one of intricacy in respect of jurisdiction, the parties claiming being Spanish sailors on board a Russian vessel.*

LUXMOORE — Charles Scott Luxmoore[146]

Charles Scott Luxmoore (1792-1854), Church of England clergyman, was the eldest son of John Luxmoore, bishop of Hereford. He was educated at Eton College and St John's, Cambridge (BA 1815; MA 1818). He served as rector of Bromyard, Herefordshire, in 1815-54, prebendary of Hereford in 1815-54, rector of Cradley in 1816-54, rector of Darowen, Montgomeryshire, in 1819-54, prebendary of St Asaph in 1819, dean of St Asaph in 1826-54, and chancellor of St Asaph. He married, 1829, Catherine, daughter of Sir John Nicholl, dean of the Arches, of Merthyr Mawr, Glamorganshire.

1826: 14 Sep: *At ten in the forenoon I attended a meeting of Subscribers to the Triennial festivals ... For some time no one was present but his Grace of Beaufort & myself; subsequently, the Archdeacon of Gloucester, the Archdeacon of Hereford (Wetherell) the Dean of St.Asaph (Luxmoore) Dr. Cooke, Mr. Russel, of Powick near Worcester, Mr. Phelps and one or two more attended.*

1830: 27 Jan: *His eldest Son, Mr. Luxmoore, is Dean of St. Asaph; he was appointed on the decease of Dean Shipley, more than three years ago; that valuable preferment is in the gift of the Bishop; another son has a stall in the Cathedral of St. Asaph.*

1840: 20 May.

LUXMOORE — John Luxmoore[147]

John Luxmoore (±1757-1830), bishop of Bristol, Hereford, and St Asaph and father of Charles (*above*), was educated at Eton College and King's College, Cambridge (BA 1780; MA 1783), where he was fellow from 1779 to 1782. He became tutor to the earl of Dalkeith and was rector of St George's, Bloomsbury, London, in 1782-1806. He was also prebendary of Canterbury in 1793, dean of Gloucester in 1800-08, rector of Taynton, Gloucestershire, in 1800, rector of St Andrew's, Holborn, in 1806-15, and archdeacon and chancellor of the diocese of St Asaph. He served as bishop of Bristol in 1807-08, of Hereford in 1808-15, and of St Asaph in 1815-30. He married Elizabeth, daughter of Thomas Barnard of Eton College.

1830: 27 Jan: *The newspapers announce the decease of the respectable & aged Bishop of St. Asaph, Dr. Luxmoore. His eldest Son, Mr. Luxmoore, is Dean of St. Asaph; he was appointed on the decease of Dean Shipley, more than three years ago; that valuable preferment is in the gift of the Bishop; another son has a stall in the Cathedral of St. Asaph.* 17 Feb: *The Episcopal arrangements consequent on the decease of Bishop Luxmoore are partially, perhaps, entirely concluded: thus far is certain, that Dr. Carey is to be translated from Exeter to St. Asaph, & Dr. Bethell from Gloucester to Exeter.*

LYDIATT — Mrs Lydiatt at Clifton

1804: 16 Sep: *Walked with my Father & Mother, Mrs. Bruston, Mrs. Lydiatt & Miss Martin.*

LYE — Henry Lye

1823: 22 Aug: *I received this day a letter from Mr. H. Lye, Surgeon of the Camden Packet, giving a long & minute report of my poor brother's case.*

LYGON —Edward Pyndar Lygon[148]

Edward Pyndar Lygon (1786-1860), army officer and MP, was the fourth son of William Lygon (1747-1816), 1st Earl Beauchamp. He was educated at Westminster School until 1802. Lygon was a cornet in the 2nd Life Guards in 1803 and was promoted to lieutenant in 1805. He then became captain in 1808, major in 1815, lieutenant-colonel in 1818, colonel in 1822, and major-general in 1837. He later joined the 13th Dragoons, where he was colonel in 1845-60, lieutenant-general in 1846, and general in 1854. In conjunction with his army career, Lygon was MP for Callington in 1818-20. He died unmarried.

1827: 2 Aug: *His brother Edward is of the same rank in the army, & commands the other regiment of Life guards; Edward is unmarried, his elder brother is united to a daughter of Earl St. Germains; these brothers, with a sister, Lady Louisa Lygon, live in great harmony, but, I apprehend, are not on the pleasantest terms with the present Earl Beauchamp.*

1844: 8 Oct: *After a very early breakfast, set out for Oxford—to the foot of Stow hill in E.F.W.'s carriage—there met the "Wonder" Coach—to Oxford with Genl. E. Lygon, Mr. Pole, and J. Perkins inside.*

LYGON — Henry Beauchamp Lygon[149]

Sir Henry Beauchamp Lygon, 4th Earl Beauchamp (1784-1863), army officer and MP, was the third son of William Lygon (1747-1816), 1st Earl Beauchamp. He was educated at Westminster School and Christ Church, Oxford. Lygon was MP for Worcestershire in 1816-31, and Worcestershire West in 1832-53. He succeeded his brother John Reginald Pyndar as 4th Earl Beauchamp in 1853.

Lygon was a cornet in the 13th Dragoons in 1803 and lieutenant in 1804. He then went to the 16th Dragoons where he was captain in 1807, major in 1812, and brevet lieutenant-colonel in 1815. He was a major in the 1st Life Guards in 1815, lieutenant-colonel in 1821-27, brevet colonel in 1822, and major-general in 1837. He was a colonel in the 10th Hussars in 1843-63, lieutenant-general in 1846, and general in 1854. Lastly, he became a colonel in the 2nd Life Guards and Gold Stick in 1863.

Lygon married, at St George's, Hanover Square, Westminster, 8 July 1824, Susan Caroline (1797-1835), daughter of William Eliot, 2nd earl of St Germains, and Georgiana Augusta Leveson-Gower; they had 4 sons and 3 daughters:

1 Felicia Susan (1825-1848); married, at St George's, Hanover Square, Westminster, 26 October 1847, Charles William Cavendish (1822-1890)
2 Georgiana Harriet (1826-1827); died an infant
3 Georgina (1832-1865); married, 25 September 1856, Richard Henry FitzRoy Somerset, 2nd Baron Raglan (1817-1884)
1 William (1828-1834); died an infant
2 Henry (1829-1866); succeeded as 5th Earl Beauchamp; died unmarried, from tuberculosis
3 Frederick (1830-1891); succeeded as 6th Earl Beauchamp; married, first, at St George's, Hanover Square, Westminster, 18 February 1868, Mary Catherine Stanhope (1844-1876); secondly, at Perlethorpe, Nottinghamshire, 24 September 1878, Emily Annora Charlotte Pierrepont (1853-1935)
4 Reginald (b. & d. 1834); died shortly after birth

1827: 2 Aug: *The old hall is a lofty apartment, there are two fine pictures by Opie, ... among the rest a very striking likeness of Col. H. Lygon, brother of Lord Beauchamp, commanding one of the Regt. of life guards, and representative for Worcestershire: he resides at Spring-hill near Broadway, which he purchased from Lord Coventry's family; living in our neighbourhood, I have had the pleasure of his acquaintance for several years, & lament to learn, that he is now indisposed.*

1844: 29 Feb: *Satisfactory letters of acquiescence and support were read from Lord Dynevor, Genl. Lygon, Sir J. Cathcart, the Dean of Gloucester, Mr. Pole, Mr. Chamberlayne &c.*

LYGON — John Reginald Lygon, later Pyndar, 3rd Earl Beauchamp — *see* Pyndar

LYNE — Mr Lyne, auctioneer, of Kingham, Oxfordshire

1838: 1 Mar: *Conferred with Lyne, Auctioneer, on the subject of laying in necessary furniture for E.F.W. at Whichford.* 19 Mar.

1842: 28 Jan: *A circular from Lyne the Auctioneer to state that he had united himself in partnership with Mr. Cocker of Middle Aston.*

1848: 24 Jan: *Wrote to Mr. Lyne, Auctioneer, forwarding a cheque in payment of poles and faggots.* 28 Jan., 16 Mar., 18 Mar.

1850: 31 Oct.

1853: 19 Mar., 9 Dec.

LYON — Gilbert Lyon[150]

Gilbert Lyon was a Bristol physician and lived at 1 Lansdown Place.

1848: 22 Nov: *The Medical Visitor, Dr. Lyon, a Scotch Physician, resident at Bristol, was also in attendance.*

LYON — James Wittit Lyon[151]

James Wittit Lyon (±1787-1861), JP and London banker, was the eldest son of Benjamin Lyon (1750-1792) and Rebeckah Wittit (1760-1797), who were married at St George's, Bloomsbury, in 1785. Lyon bought the Miserden Park estate from Revd Edward Reed in 1839. He married, 1825, Emma Dalton (1801-1873), daughter of Mrs Edwards, of Regent Street, London, and Rheola, Glamorganshire; they had 4 sons and 2 daughters:

1 Henry Dalton (b. 1826)
2 Arthur James (1827-1843)
3 Nash Edwards Vaughan (1829-1866)
1 Juliana Lucy Sarah (1831-1853)
4 Frederick Lee Hopkinson (1833-1905)
2 Emmeline Sarah (1836-1910)

Lyon died at Boulogne-sur-Mer, France, where he had presumably gone to evade his creditors. In 1862 the Miserden Park estate was seized and sold by his mortgagors.

1842: 12 Jan: *I named Chamberlayne, Compton Reade, Whitmore Jones, E. Maddy.—Lyon, Gambier Parry,—Baker Esqrs. the Revds. W B Pole, E. F. Witts, Aston, T M Browne, C. Pettat.* 18 Jan.

1845: 2 Apr: *The Gentlemen of the County, and personal friends of the High Sheriff, soon began to congregate—Mr. Daubeny (Ampney) Lyon (Miserden) Kaye (late of Sandywell Park, now of Ampney) Smith (Southrop) Col. Fendall (Sevenhampton) Henry, Frederick, and Raymond Cripps, C Pettatt, and several others.*

LYSONS — Daniel Lysons[152]

Daniel Lysons (1762-1834), Church of England clergyman and topographer, was the elder son of Samuel Lysons (1730-1804), rector of Rodmarton and Cherrington, and Mary (1734-1791), daughter of Samuel Peach of Chalford. He was educated at Bath

Grammar School and St Mary Hall, Oxford (BA 1782; MA 1785). He was assistant curate of Mortlake from 1784 to 1789 and curate of Putney from 1789 to 1800. At this time he began work on his *Environs of London* (4 volumes, 1792-96), a topographical account of the parishes within 12 miles of London.

Horace Walpole was a close friend of both Daniel and his younger brother Samuel (1763-1819). The brothers had other well-placed friends and connections; their correspondence with Thomas Lawrence, who painted them both, and Mrs Piozzi survives.

On the death of his uncle, the physician Daniel Lysons (1727-1800), Daniel inherited Hempsted Court and the family estates in Gloucestershire. He married, first, 1801, Sarah (1780-1808), eldest daughter of Lt-Col Thomas Carteret Hardy of the York Fusiliers; they had 2 sons and 2 daughters:

1 Sarah (1802-1833); married John Haygarth
1 Daniel (1804-1814); died as a child
2 Samuel (1806-1877); succeeded to the family living of Rodmarton (*below*)
2 Charlotte (1807-1848); married James Carnegie

Lysons married secondly, 1813, Josepha Catherine Susanna (1781-1868), daughter of John Gilbert Cooper of Thurgarton Priory, Nottinghamshire; they had 1 son:

1 Daniel (1816-1898); appointed GCB and constable of the Tower

Daniel Lysons collaborated with his brother Samuel on *Magna Britannia*, a concise topographical account of the counties of Great Britain. It was intended to fill the gap between large-scale county histories and *Camden's Britannia*, and was even more ambitious than the *Beauties of England and Wales*, on which work had recently begun. The first volume of *Magna Britannia*, covering Bedfordshire, Berkshire, and Buckinghamshire, appeared in 1806; further volumes covering Cambridgeshire, Cheshire, Cornwall, Cumberland, Derbyshire, and Devon were published by 1822, when the work ended. The decision to curtail the project was taken upon Samuel's death in 1819; Daniel, who was extremely fond of his brother and dependent on his archaeological expertise, declared: 'I cannot go on without my fellow labourer. Our lives wd not have sufficed to the completion had they been protracted even to old age. It is as well to give up now'.

1823: 17 Sep: *I was introduced to Mr. Bowles by Mr. Lysons, the eminent antiquary, Rector of Rodmarton in this Diocese, an old acquaintance of mine on the Magisterial bench.*

1826: 31 Aug: *They occupy for the summer apartments in a cottage, close to the grounds of the Mansion house, which is the seat of the Lysons family. The Revd. Daniel Lysons, the antiquary, is the present proprietor, having succeeded to it on the death of his brother, the still more distinguished Antiquary ... Mr. D. Lysons Rector of Rodmarton near Cirencester, an elderly man, now abroad with his family.*

1828: 15 Apr., 15 Jul.

1829: 16 Jul., 22 Sep., 20 Oct.

LYSONS — Samuel Lysons [153]

Samuel Lysons (1806-1877), Church of England clergyman, antiquary, and philanthropist, was the second son of Daniel Lysons (1762-1834) (*above*), rector of Rodmarton. He was educated at Exeter College, Oxford (BA 1830; MA 1836). He was ordained deacon on 3 October 1830 and priest on 5 June 1831. On his ordination as deacon he became stipendiary curate to his father at Rodmarton, and following his father's death he succeeded as rector, a living in the gift of the family. He married, first, 1 January 1834, Eliza Sophia Theresa Henrietta (d. 1846), eldest daughter of Maj.-Gen. Sir Lorenzo Moore; they had 4 sons and 2 daughters:

1 Alice Elizabeth (b. 1834); married, at Kingsthorpe, Northamptonshire, 19 December 1861, George Hacker
1 Arthur Charles (1836-1855); became a gentleman cadet in religious instruction at Sandhurst, 1852
2 Lorenzo George (1839-1917); married Victoria Richards; died at Plymouth
2 Clementina Agnes (1840-1917); married, at Tor Mohun, Devon, 25 August 1864, Revd Francis John Atwood
3 Edmund Hicks-Beach (1842-1916); married, at St George's, Camden Hill, December 1869, Honora Mary Jervis
4 Daniel George (1844-1929); married Katherine Anne Eyton (1845-1913)

Lysons married secondly, 1847, Lucy (d. 1872), daughter of Revd John Adey Curtis-Hayward; there were no recorded children of the marriage. He married thirdly, 1872, Gertrude Savery (1836-1912), second daughter of Simon Adams Beck of Cheam, Surrey; they had 1 son and 1 daughter:

1 Gertrude Teresa (1874-1942); married, at Kensington, 1899, Joseph Alfred Pattinson (1861-1919); died at Paddington, New South Wales, Australia
1 Nigel Lucius Samuel (1877-1914), Maj.; killed in action and buried at Comines-Warneton, Hainaut, Belgium

Two days after Lysons' first marriage, his father died and he succeeded to the family estates, which comprised Hempsted Court and other lands in Gloucestershire. Samuel Lysons built a church at Hempsted and furnished it with an endowment of £1,000. Schools were erected, charitable clubs were organised, and a scripture reader was provided at his expense. Altogether he spent between £5,000 and £6,000 on the district, which rapidly improved.

From 1865 to 1876 Samuel Lysons was rural dean of Gloucester. In 1867 he became honorary canon of Gloucester.

1838: 3 Jan: *This is to be built by my acquaintance Lysons, with aid from the Association, he himself to be the Minister, which appointment will enable him to reside at his own mansion at Hempstead, and to be non-resident as to his benefice at Rodmarton the climate of which he considers to be prejudicial to his health.*

1839: 5 Jun: *I omitted to name that in the convocation house I shook hands with many old acquaintances—Billingsley, Rowden, Lysons &c.* 11-12 Jul.

1843: 15 Sep: *On the platform we met Mr. and Mrs. Lysons, returning from the Bavarian baths of Kissingen, with whom we held brief parley: they were on their road into Gloucestershire.* 9 Oct., 16 Oct: *To the Shire Hall where engaged with Messrs. C. Hayward and Lysons in auditing County Accounts till past six in the Evening.* 17 Oct.

1844: 1 Jan., 6 Mar., 8 Apr., 10 Apr: *There appeared at this meeting the Dean of Gloucester, the Archdeacon of Gloucester, Messrs. Purnell, Jones, Goodrich, Baker, Lysons, Sayers, Fulljames, and myself, Curtis Hayward leaving his court, and joining us for a short time.* 13 Apr., 10 May: *On my way to Stow, met and chatted with Mr. & Mrs. Lysons, travelling in an open carriage.* 15 Aug., 14 Oct: *To the Shire Hall, where I met the County Chairman, and my colleagues on the Committee of accounts, Curtis Hayward and Lysons; but, the latter being indisposed, retired.* 7 Dec: *A letter from R P. B. Purnell, announcing that Mr. Lysons, from ill-health, was about to leave Hempstead for a time, and, therefore, resigned his place as Member of the County Committee of Accounts.* 11 Dec., 30 Dec: *I met Lysons at the Railway Station at Cheltenham on his way to Worcester; he was looking ill, and complained of serious indisposition: he has left Hempstead and his clerical duties at his Church, near the Spa, for a season, and, I believe, means to pass the winter with his family at Dover, where his mother resides.*

1846: 20 Jun: *at Swindon we stopped for ten minutes, and took some refreshment: there our party was increased by the addition of Mr. Lysons with a school-boy son, whom he had travelled from Hempstead to meet this morning at Reading, on his way home from school near Winchester for the holidays.—Much lively conversation with L.* 10 Aug: *At the Judges lodgings I had sat by Lysons and Stoughton, had seen much of Curtis Hayward, Newman & others.* 20 Oct., 18 Nov: *We were kindly received by the pleasing Mrs. Hayward, and in due time the party was increased by the arrival of Mr. Lysons, with two ladies, from his house at Hempstead, connections of his, a mother and daughter, whose names I did not catch, and a Mr. Le Marchant, Curate of Hardwick. A Miss Nisbet, a niece of CH's was also one of the party staying in the house. We passed a pleasant evening, with music, and looking at portfolios, especially those brought by Lysons containing a valuable collection of engravings of antiquities, especially of tesselated pavements, both from Italy, Spain, & France, & from England. These had been acquired by his Uncle and Father, the celebrated Antiquarians, and were now produced in consequence of Purnell's having lately discovered the remains of a Roman Villa on his property at Stancombe.*

1847: 29 May., 29 Jun: *Mr. & Mrs. Lysons (his second and lately married wife, sister of Curtis Hayward,) his five children by his first wife, Sir Michael H. Beach, and his friend Mr. Smith of Southerop, a very agreeable travelled man, and a distant relation of the Vavasours of Rochdale, i.e. of Marmaduke V., Mrs. V. of "the Cottage" &c.—Mr. Winston Hayward, a Clergyman, Brother of Curtis Hayward, lately married to a Miss Phelps of Chavenage, a nice couple, Mr. Gambier Parry and myself made up a party of eight: not reckoning the children.* 17 Aug: *A letter from P. B. Purnell, inviting me to his house on the 24th. Inst. to meet Mr. and Mrs. Curtis Hayward, and Mr. and Mrs. Lysons, at dinner and to sleep, and on the following day to view the site of the Roman Villa which he has been disinterring on his grounds at Stancombe Park.* 18 Oct.

1848: 3 Jan., 16 Feb., 20 Mar., 22 Mar., 26-27 Jun., 20 Sep., 16-17 Oct., 18 Oct: *E.F.W., he and I dressed for dinner, having accepted an invitation to the Lysons's at Hempstead Court.... to which, after dinner, having just arrived by the Railway train, was added Capt. Lysons, brother of our host, recently returned from Canada, where his regiment is stationed, and on leave of absence.*

1849: 31 Dec.

1850: 28 Jan., 1 Jul., 14 Oct., 8 Nov., 30 Dec.

1851: 17 Mar., 29 Apr.

1852: 16 Mar: *Before dinner, with the two Purnells, Lysons and my son, visited the Docks.*

1853: 3 Jan., 14 Mar., 4 Apr: *The evening being moist or rainy, most of the party from the Bell went in an Omnibus, or by a Fly; Lysons and E.F.W. accompanied me in the latter conveyance.* 27-28 Jun.

LYTTELTON — Apphia Lyttelton

A very full account of the life of Apphia, Lady Lyttelton, née Witts (1743-1840) is given in volume 1, pages 105-120. Apphia sailed to India in 1769 to marry her cousin, Richard Witts, only to find on her arrival that he had died. They had not seen each other since his departure for India in 1763l. However, within a matter of months of arriving in India she had found a husband. Col Joseph Peach had a distinguished career behind him; he had been in the Army since 1746 and had fought in the Canada campaign of 1754-55. They married in 1770, but the union was short-lived; within six months Joseph was dead. Apphia returned to England, a rich young widow.

With her new-found wealth and a decided taste for rural life in splendid surroundings, Apphia bought Leasowes, near Hagley, Shropshire, and soon became acquainted with her neighbours, the Lytteltons. It was not long before word of Apphia Peach's fortune of £28,000 reached the ears of Thomas Lyttelton. Although he could be charming, Thomas already had a formidable reputation as a profligate, a gambler, and a rake. Quite how Apphia was taken in by him is a mystery, but in a whirlwind romance, seemingly cynical on his part and sincere on hers, the couple gained the blessing of George, 1st Baron Lyttelton, and married on 26 June 1772. The marriage lasted only eight months. In February 1773 a separation was agreed, and Thomas went to live with his mistress and illegitimate child.

Lord Lyttelton had a close relationship with his daughter-in-law and took it upon himself to support her. The pair seem to have got on remarkably well; the London season suited them both, with the elderly lord at his brightest for years and Apphia also enjoying herself. The Queen told him that she 'had made a new acquaintance with a relative of his which gave her pleasure, as Mrs. Lyttelton had a universal good character'. Unfortunately, Lord Lyttelton's protection did not last long; he died on 22 August 1773.

Apphia's husband, Thomas, known as 'the wicked Lord Lyttelton', died in strange circumstances on 27 November 1779. Thereafter, Apphia lived in some comfort on a settlement of £1,000 a year. She lived at Southall Park in the 1790s, but by 1801 she had moved to London, to a house in Berkeley Street [now Upper Berkeley Street]. At some time around 1808, she sold up in London and moved to Malvern, Worcestershire, where she lived for the remainder of her life.

Apphia was eccentric, but cultivated, and moved in an interesting blue-stocking circle of literati. She remained an influential person throughout her long life. Francis Witts ensured that he kept well in with his aunt—even though she appears to have disliked his wife, Margaret. Most importantly, he ensured that he was not out-manoeuvred in her affections by his cousins John, Apphia, and Anne. His assiduous work paid off, and on Lady Lyttelton's death her estate passed to Francis's son, Edward.

Francis had known his aunt but briefly before 1801. As a child he had met her a few times between 1783 and 1793, the last time being on 24 January 1793, when he was 9 years old. The family then moved to Edinburgh, and from there, in 1798, to Weimar, and then to Copenhagen in 1800; Francis did not return to Britain until April 1801. When he next saw his aunt on 13 May 1801, he was a well-educated 18-year-old. Apphia seems to have taken to her nephew on their first meeting, while Francis clearly realised from just a short time in her company that she had an eccentric character.

1800: 4 Mar: *finished a letter to Lady Lyttelton.*

1801: 1 May, 12 May: *Upon landing at the Glocester Coffeehouse Piccadilly, we did not find my Father & Brother in their apartment; they were dining at Lady Lytteltons, but kindly returned soon to welcome us to Town.* 13 May: *We visited Lady Lyttelton, in Berkley Street, but were not happy enough to find her at home. Miss Eycott, nevertheless received us very handsomely. Her house is good & well furnished, but neither overgrown nor gaudy.... Lady Lytteltons universal kindness was extreme I assisted as Landlord, & she behaved to me with the greatest affection: in a kind aunt some little eccentricities may be forgiven.* 15 May,

16 May: *I called, but without success upon Mr. Talbot No. 13. Bentinck Street, & afterwards attended Lady Lyttelton to the Royal Institution, Albermarle Street.* 17-20 May, 21 May: *We sallied early out with Lady Lyttelton & Miss Eycott to visit St. Paul's, where the Anniversary meeting of the Charity Schools took place this day.* 25 May, 26 May: *I accompanied Miss Snow & my Mother to Lady Lyttelton's, whose Tuesday was peculiarly dull.* 27 May: *In the Evening to a party at Lady Lyttelton's, which was musical.* 28 May, 30 May, 1 Jun., 3 Jun: *Repaired in the Evening to Lady Lytteltons, where was rather a squeeze & music.* 6-7 Jun., 8 Jun: *Afterwards attended my Mother, Lady Lyttelton &c to the Panorama of Constantinople, Leicester Square, which by far exceeded my expectations, it being a perfect circle.* 9-10 Jun., 2-4 Jul., 21 Jul., 28 Jul., 31 Jul: *Dined with Lady Lyttelton.* 7 Aug: *Dined at Lady Lyttelton's; walked with her in the Evening in Portman Square.* 9 Aug: *Went to Portman Chapel with Lady Lyttelton & Miss Eycott.* 14 Aug., 20 Aug: *dined with Lady Lyttelton.* 24 Aug., 29 Aug., 30 Aug: *Drank tea & spent the Evening at Lady Lytteltons, where we met Miss Stone & Mrs. Schrader.* 31 Aug: *Dined with my Father & Mother at Lady Lyttelton's.* 1 Sep., 5 Sep: *Dined with Lady Lyttelton, and spent the Evening there.* 13 Sep., 15-16 Sep., 24 Sep: *Dined with Lady Lyttelton, meeting there Mrs. Witts of Champion Hill, whose sons came up in the Evening.* 29-30 Sep., 7 Oct., 9-10 Oct., 15-16 Oct., 20 Oct., 23 Oct: *to a very pleasant Musical party at Lady Lyttelton's, where were the Pattons, Mrs. Davies. the Morley's, Mrs. Lowe, the Guydickens's, Vicomte De Bruges & Comte de Gourmand, Mr. Wood & the like.* 25 Oct.

1802: 19 Jan: *Breakfasted again with Lady Lyttelton.* 29 Jan: *Early in the morning to Town, by way of Colney Hatch in the Leeds Mail. Breakfasted with Lady Lyttelton.* 4 Feb., 7 Feb: *Our dear George with us dined at Lady Lyttelton's.* 10 Jun., 3 Oct.

1803: 29-30 Sep.

1804: 6 Oct., 10 Oct. *Wrote to Lady Lyttelton.*

1805: 6 Jul: *During the forenoon, had the meeting, more or less irksome, with various relations & connections, Lady Lyttelton, Whalleys, Buxtons, Hunts &c.*

1806: 19 Jun: *Wrote to Lady Lyttelton.*

1808: 18 Feb: *Wrote to Lady Lyttelton & Horne.* 22 Feb: *came to my Aunt Lady Lyttletons, whom I found economising but not comfortably.* 24 Feb: *Wrote to my Parents; dined with Lady Lyttelton.* 26 Feb: *After an early dinner at Lady Lyttelton's repaired to Hatchett's; took my place in the Bath (Pickwick's) Post Coach.*

1820: 13 Jun: *My Mother arrived to-day on her customary summer visit, last from Cheltenham, where she had been spending a few days with my Aunt Mrs. Travell: as she had been before for a month with Lady Lyttelton near Malvern.*

1822: 8 Oct.

1824: 10 Jul: *My Aunt Lady Lyttelton arrived from Cookham to stay a day or two here. At the age of eighty one, she had been making a long and fatiguing tour, particularly, after a severe illness in the winter & spring, by which she been greatly debilitated. Among other places, she had formed one of the many guests at Stowe, the Seat of the Duke of Buckingham, on occasion of the Christening of the Marquis of Chandos's eldest Son, the heir of the Dukedom, which was celebrated with great and expensive festivities. The ancient alliance between the Grenvilles & Lytteltons entitled my Aunt to appear, as on a former occasion, among the family friends of the Temples & Chandos's. She is now on her return to her house near Malvern.* 13 Jul., 14 Jul: *After dining at the King's Head Inn with my brother Magistrates, as usual, I spent an hour at Mrs. M. Hunt's in the evening to meet Lady Lyttelton, Mrs. Backhouse, & Miss Witts's.*

1825: 29 Mar: *My cousin, Captain Witts, arrived to pass a day or two with us …They have lately been residing at Pickham Grove, in Great Malvern, where my Aunt, Lady Lyttelton, lived for many years, before she removed to the house, she has lately built in the immediate vicinity; but they are about to leave that place, and make an excursion into the Highlands of Scotland.* 9 May: *We left home on a long talked of visit to my Aunt Lady Lyttelton at Malvern.* 10 May: *The day being very fine we rambled about all the morning. Twice we explored the Lilliputian domain at Pickham Grove, the creation of my good Aunt's contriving turn; a tasty cottage in its earlier days of better repair, but in the holes and corners appropriated to domestic uses, at all times sadly devoid of comfort.* 14 May, 16 May: *We made an excursion to Worcester with Lady Lyttelton and Miss Witts in a barouche procured at Malvern, an extremely comfortable conveyance.* 18 May: *Lady Lyttelton gave a dejeuné a la fourchette to her Malvern acquaintance. The day was very fine & the company strolled in the garden or amused themselves in conversation in the drawing room. The arrangements were very suitable, but it seemed unnecessary at 82 to undergo so much fatigue about the entertainment of persons, the majority of whom were mere strangers. There were about 25, besides the family party. This is the style of society, which Lady L. prefers; she has been accustomed during the Malvern season to have a weekly day for receiving her acquaintance: and at some times, there has been, in the newspaper phraseology, a brilliant display of rank & fashion.* 5 Jul: *We drove to Dropmore, the seat of the distinguished statesman, Lord Grenville. Private as well as public considerations ever make me respect this nobleman; as a minister his talents, judgment, eloquence, and extensive range of constitutional knowledge secure to him general admiration and esteem … As a private individual, Lord Grenville merited my gratitude and support, by the friendly assistance, which, at the request of Lady Lyttelton, and as a connexion of that family, he gave to my brother, when he wished to enter into the Artillery.*

1826: 11 Sep: *In the Evening I called on my Aunt, Lady Lyttelton, who had just arrived from Malvern at lodgings, which her neices, the Miss Witts's, had engaged for her, & who, at 83 years of age, had spirit and strength enough to propose to herself to go through the musical fatigues of the week: a festival of this nature is to my good aunt a new scene; though resident for so many years at Malvern, she has never yet visited those at Worcester, & I am much indebted to her for the present tax on her strength and spirits and purse, which, I really believe, nothing would have moved her to submit to, but the wish of testifying her regard for me.* 12 Sep: *Before the musical treat was over, we withdrew to Mrs. Backhouse's to dinner; Lady Lyttelton & Miss Witts's dined at Wellington parade, en famille.* 14 Sep: *My wife, cautious of fatigue, absented herself, & Mrs. Backhouse had determined not to undergo the labour of attending any of the concerts: Lady Lyttelton & Miss Witts's, however, were there.* 16 Sep: *I called on my good Aunt, Lady Lyttelton, who seems to rise in strength and spirits, as the fatigue increased, and was so pleased with her sejour at Gloucester as to determine on passing several days longer.* 27 Sep: *we passed the Evening with Lady Lyttelton, who still lingers on in her lodgings at Gloucester, but leaves them in a day or two. Besides Miss Witts's, we met Miss Caroline Hunt.* 21 Oct: *My good Aunt has been very active in her proceedings since we saw her at Gloucester, having set to work to build two additional rooms, a second drawing room, and a bed room, which will considerably extend the size and accommodations of her cottage residence; the shell of the rooms is already nearly complete; before she came to Gloucester, not the slightest preparations had been made; but brick & mortar, contract work, and money in advance make quick progress.* 1 Nov: *they will occupy the house contiguous to Lady Lyttelton's, which my Aunt has rented for more than a twelve month passed, hoping to let it to select tenants, & so prevent the neighbourhood of objectionable persons. The scheme, however, has failed; for the only tenant she has had turned out to be a ruined, swaggering, broken down gentleman, with a houseful of children & grandchildren; he was a troublesome, officious and intruding person, paid none of the tradesmen, and gave bills not worth the paper on which they were written in payment of his rent; ate good dinners at Lady L's, and poilt the furniture of the house; shuffled and bullied, and at last found his way into Worcester gaol. At last my Lady has given notice to quit the house, and should never have taken it; it was against my advice & Captain Witts's, and had I not drawn up a cautious agreement for her, she would have been much more out of pocket than she even now is, by embarking in the concern.*

1827: 11 Jul: *They have recently been on a visit to Lady Lyttelton & Captain Witts, at Malvern, and have brought a very pressing invitation from Lady L. to Edward & myself, to pay a visit there before the former returns to school.* 31 Jul: *we arrived at Peachfield lodge, for such is the name, which my good Aunt has at last given to her singular abode; a name recalling to her memory her earlier matrimonial connection, the more auspicious of the two, that which subsisted between herself, and a respectable Colonel Peach, of the East India Company's service, much her Senior in years, who paid his addresses to her in that distant clime, whither she had gone to fulfil an engagement with a cousin, an Edward Witts, in the company's service, but who had died previously to her arrival at Madras. Death soon removed the worthy colonel, and his young widow, a sincere mourner, returned to her native land with twenty thousand pounds, which he had left her, and many romantic ideas. She in an evil hour accepted the addresses of the profligate, selfish, unprincipled Mr. Lyttelton; he deserted her, she took refuge in the protection of his excellent Father, who then lived. The solid good of her Indian thousands was commuted for a settlement of £1000 per ann. on the Hagley Property. But this is not the place to give a history of Lady L's life; return we to Peachfield lodge, which, since we were here in 1825, and ndeed, during the past autumn, has been enlarged by the addition of two excellent rooms, with their appendages, tending greatly to the improvement and comfort of the house; they are hardly finished, and unfurnished.* 2 Aug: *Our family party were assembled at dinner at my Aunt's but adjourned for tea to Captain Witts's; a Mrs. Walker, residing at Pickham Grove, my Aunt's late abode, a near neighbour on the common, joined our circle.* 3 Aug., 14 Nov: *Of my Father's brothers and sisters, only Lady Lyttelton & Mrs. Stone survive, the former nearly 84 the latter 82 years of age, I believe.—On reference to my pedigree I find, I am right in the ages of my Uncle & Aunts.* 17 Nov.

1828: 16 Jun: *Of the contiguous houses, Peachfield Lodge & Hayes Bank Cottage, my domicile this time was to be the latter, but it was with a very kindly reluctance that Lady Lyttelton ceded me to Captain & Mrs. J. Witts. My Aunt joined the family circle at tea, which was completed by the presence of my Cousins, the Miss Witts's.* 17 Jun: *With my good Aunt we found a fair and pretty young Quaker, Miss Atkins, from Chipping Norton.* 18 Jun: *A very rainy day, so that we scarcely could leave the house. I passed an hour with my Aunt.* 19 Jun., 24 Sep: *We received this evening, to pass a day or two with us, my aunt Lady Lyttelton, who with wonderful energy had accepted of an invitation to Stanway from Lady Elcho, and had arrived there on Saturday last. We had written to intreat her to prolong her journey hither, if it were only for a day or two, and begged her to bring her friend and companion at Stanway, Lady Juliana Annesley, half sister to Earl Mount-norris, sister to Lady John Somerset, &c. This elegant young woman, a connection of the Lyttelton family, is a frequent and favoured guest at Peachfield Lodge; but being very acceptable to the circle at Stanway she was detained there, & could not accept our invitation. I thought my Aunt stouter than when I parted from her in the summer at Malvern.* 26 Sep: *Lady Lyttelton left us after breakfast to conclude her visit at Stanway, proposing to return to Peachfield Lodge to-morrow. She continued very tolerably well during her short visit, but her energy and spirits much exceed her bodily strength.*

1829: 24 Aug: *Nearly one o'clock had arrived, when, after taking a light repast, we left home, accompanied by Mrs. Backhouse, in our close carriage, for my Aunt, Lady Lyttelton's at Peach-Field lodge, to pass a few days with her ... We found my aunt in good health and spirits, & not deficient in her wonted energy, after all her fatigues, her spring campaign in London, her visit to Shrewsbury and Boreatton, not to mention others to Lacey Green, Cookham Grove &c. During her absence her house has been enlarged & much improved by the addition of two new rooms, intended for a bedroom for herself and her female attendant.* 25 Aug: *Lady Lyttelton will now, I presume, make an endowment to each of these schools, as well as to that at Great Malvern, the Sunday School of her institution, being better able to do so, by the windfall, which has so unexpectedly poured into her lap and into that of Mrs. Stone, a sum of £2000 each, being the proceeds of the personal estate of their cousin Mr. R. P. Witts.* 28 Aug: *Lady Lyttelton, having ordered post horses, accompanied my ladies & my cousin Apphia to Great Malvern.* 29 Aug.

1830: 19 Apr: *They gave us but an indifferent account of my Aunt, Lady Lyttelton, who has been failing for some time, but will, I trust, rally again, as a more genial season advances; she complains of bodily weakness, which, at her very advanced age, is not to be wondered at; the mind also seems occasionally, as they have remarked, less accurate than usual.*

1833: 10 Sep: *After breakfast left Upper Slaughter with Mrs. Witts and Mrs. Backhouse in our close carriage to visit my Aunt Lady Lyttelton at Peachfield Lodge, Great ... Lady L's feebleness much increased.* 11 Sep., 13 Sep.

1834: 9 Mar., 28 Jul., 18 Aug., 23-24 Aug., 8 Sep: *At seven o'clock, set out in the phaeton with Edward and my servant for Peach Field lodge to visit Lady Lyttelton.* 9 Sep., 10 Sep: *Assisted in unpacking a portrait of my Aunt recently painted.* 11-13 Sep., 25 Sep., 6 Oct., 22 Oct., 7 Dec.

1835: 1 Apr., 19 May, 24 May.

1836: 17 Jun., 18 Jul: *After breakfast, accompanied by E.F.W., set out for Peach Field Lodge on a visit to my Aunt, Lady Lyttelton.* 19-20 Jul., 21 Jul: *A large dinner party at Lady L's followed; eighteen sat down to table.* 22 Jul., 23 Jul: *whither it shall please GOD that I may see again my aged Aunt, or my cousin John's feeble wife, may well be doubted; the life of both seems to hang on a thread.* 31 Jul., 1 Aug., 15 Aug., 28 Sep: *From our Malvern relatives we hear that Lady Lyttelton is in her ordinary health.* 3 Oct: *Wrote to Miss Daniell, enclosing a cheque on my Bankers for £5. 5. the amount of my contribution towards the Lithograph print of Lady Lyttelton.* 21 Oct., 28 Oct., 1 Nov., 15 Nov., 18 Nov., 24 Nov., 3 Dec, 6 Dec., 9 Dec., 19-20 Dec., 22 Dec., 25 Dec: *M. W. Recd. a letter from Miss Witts, from Malvern; the account of my Aunt Lyttelton is not very favourable: she had been suffering from a bilious attack which had debilitated her a good deal, but has rallied: yet the medical Attendant does not seem to consider her as quite safe; indeed, at her great age, in severe seasons, life must be held by a thread.*

1837: 7 Jan: *We reached home by five o clock: found several letters which had arrived during my absence: one from Miss Daniell, by to-day's post, brought the unwelcome tidings that my aged Aunt Lyttelton was seized on the 4th. Inst. with a paralytic attack, which had partially taken away the use of one side, and that she had lost the sight of one eye, while that of the other was much impaired.* 8 Jan., 10-11 Jan., 21 Jan: *From Miss Daniell, giving a pretty comfortable account of Lady Lyttelton, but suggesting that it might be well if I made an unannounced visit at Peach Field Lodge shortly, in the same manner as John Witts has done, who is now staying for a few days with his sisters, having come from Salop.* 31 Jan: *Left home at a little after seven A.M. in the phaeton for Cheltenham on my way to visit my Aunt Lyttelton.* 1 Feb: *Lady L. rather more alive to what passed around her than yesterday, and had an enjoyed a good night's rest.* 2-3 Feb., 9 Feb., 16 Feb., 12 Mar: *A letter from Eliza Daniell, giving a very indifferent account of Lady Lyttelton, whom she represents as having been fast sinking within the last fortnight, both in debility of body and mind.* 19 Mar., 20 Apr: *M W. had received a letter from A. Witts, with an account of my Aunt Lyttelton, who continues in nearly the same state of slow and gradual decay, the strength of her constitution resisting the malady dreaded but sure at last to carry her off—paralysis.* 26 Apr: *Received a letter from Eliza Daniell, giving a sad account of our Aunt Lyttelton, who was seized on Friday last with a second paralytic stroke, which appears to have reduced her to a state of infantine weakness of mind and body: her memory quite gone for persons and things; yet cheerful, placid, and contented, without apparent pain, or any irritability.* 2-3 May, 12 May: *M W. received a letter from A. Witts, conveying a more favourable account of the state of our aunt Lyttelton than could have been expected.* 20 May, 26 May, 10 Jun., 2 Jul., 8 Aug., 3 Sep., 21 Sep., 5 Nov., 28 Dec., 29 Dec: *Recd. a letter from Miss Witts, with a pretty good account of Lady Lyttelton, who continues in the same state.*

1838: 7 Apr: *M W. Recd. a friendly letter from Miss Witts, who gives a pretty good account of the state of Lady Lyttelton, and reports favourably of the rest of the family colony at Malvern.* 17 Apr., 22 Apr: *He mentions that he found Lady Lyttelton on his arrival on Thursday in good health considering her extraordinary age, though very sadly broken as to memory; but that on Friday she experienced another slight paralytic seizure, from which, however, she had rallied when he wrote yesterday.* 23 Apr., 15 May: *I omitted to mention on Sunday that E.F. W. had recd. a letter from Miss Witts, full of kindness, covering a remittance for £30. as a wedding present from Lady Lyttelton to her great nephew.* 14 Jun., 16 Jul., 17 Jul: *When my poor Aunt was ready to admit me and her other relations to her apartment, I found her seated in her chair, looking much as when I parted from her some eighteen months since, placid and contented; but her mind very much gone.* 18 Jul., 20 Jul: *The rest of the morning passed in conversation with my many cousins, and by my aged and imbecile Aunt's arm-chair.* 10 Aug., 14 Aug., 9 Sep., 19 Sep: *Between eight and nine o clock, I proceeded in a fly to breakfast at Peach Field Lodge, being anxious to pass a few hours with my relatives there, and take, perhaps, a last look at my aged and feeble Aunt Lyttelton.* 20 Oct., 9 Dec: *M W. had a letter from A. Witts with a very sad report of Lady L. in the beginning of last week she had suffered from fainting, vomiting &c. but had rallied.* 24 Dec., 28 Dec.

1839: 27 Jan., 20 Mar., 1 May: *M W. Recd. a letter from Anne Witts, who reports of our connections at Malvern, that my poor aunt continues in the same helpless and hopeless state of vegetation, almost without consciousness, sitting up for an hour or two daily, but enjoying sound sleep, and rarely excited; suffering little pain, and rarely any derangement of the bodily functions.* 19 Jun., 14 Jul., 5 Aug.

1840: 18 Mar., 1 Apr: *A letter from J. Witts, mentioning that our poor Aunt Lyttelton continues to sink but very slowly, and that her end must shortly be looked for, but how soon cannot be anticipated.* 8 Apr., 12 Apr: *In the afternoon a messenger arrived from Malvern dispatched by Captain Witts with a letter to announce to me the decease of our aged Aunt, Lady Lyttelton, which took place about 4 o cl. P.M. yesterday.* 13 Apr: *Of the last hours of my aged Aunt, who would have completed her 97th. year, if she had survived till May the 8th., I learnt that towards the last her sufferings appeared very great in struggling for breath; that her form had been wasted to a shadow, and the symptoms those of a person dying of a deep decline. She had not spoken for a month, and yet it was thought that towards the last moment she recognized all the relatives and attendants about her, and bade farewell of to each with an expressive glance.* 14-15 Apr., 18 Apr., 20 Apr., 22-25 Apr., 28 Apr., 30 Apr., 1 May: *Wrote to E.F. W. a long letter with reference to concerns at Peach Field Lodge, Lady Lyttelton's will &c.* 2-3 May, 5-10 May, 14 May, 16 May, 20-22 May, 28-30 May, 11 Jun., 22 Jun, 24 Jun., 27-28 Jun., 12 Jul., 30 Jul., 5 Aug., 27 Oct., 24 Nov.

1841: 1 Mar: *Wrote to Sophy Daniell, requesting her to desire Mrs. Shard to burn any letters of my Father's, Mothers, Brother's, or mine, which might be found among Lady Lyttelton's papers.* 5 Mar.

1842: 7 Jan., 11 Jan., 17 Jan., 22 Jan., 24 Jan., 18-19 Feb., 15 Mar.

1844: 16 Sep: *In the evening looking over old correspondence, illustrative of the early life of Lady Lyttelton.*

1845: 11 Jul.

LYTTELTON — George William Lyttelton[154]

George William Lyttelton, 4th Baron Lyttelton and 4th Baron Westcote (1817-1876), landed proprietor and politician, was first cousin once removed to Thomas Lyttelton (1743-1779), 'the wicked Lord Lyttelton', husband of Apphia Witts. Following Thomas's early death in 1779, the Hagley estate passed to his uncle, William Henry Lyttelton (1725-1808), who was succeeded by his son George Fulke Lyttelton (1763-1808), who died childless. George was succeeded by his half-brother, William Henry Lyttelton (1782-1837), who in turn was succeeded by his son, George William Lyttelton (1817-1876).

Lyttelton was educated at Eton College and Trinity College, Cambridge. In 1837, while still at Cambridge, his father died and he succeeded to the peerage. He was lord lieutenant of Worcestershire in 1839-76, under secretary for the colonies in 1846, and privy counsellor in 1869. He was made KCMG in 1869 and received a DCL from Oxford 1870.

Lyttelton became acquainted with Mary (1813-1857), younger daughter of Sir Stephen Richard Glynne, 8th baronet of Hawarden Glynne, when he was 18. She was a year younger than her sister, Catherine, and they were devoted to each other. A double wedding took place at Hawarden in July 1839 between Mary and George Lyttelton and Catherine and William Gladstone.

William Ewart Gladstone admired his new brother-in-law for his brilliant scholarship and his wit. In 1861 the two men published a volume of Greek translations of part of Milton's *Comus* and Tennyson's *Lotos-Eaters*, and Latin translations of Goldsmith's *The Deserted Village* and Gray's *Ode to Adversity* (work on the volume was intended by Gladstone to be a distraction for Lyttelton following the death of his wife). The Glynnes evolved a private language, Glynnese, which an outsider would not readily have understood. Lyttelton compiled a *Glossary of the Glynne Language*, which was privately printed in 1851.

Lyttelton and Mary had 8 sons and 4 daughters:

1 Meriel Sarah (1840-1925); married John Gilbert Talbot
2 Lucy Caroline (1841-1925); married Lord Frederick Cavendish
1 Charles (1842-1922); succeeded his father as 5th Baron Lyttelton and (1889) his distant relative Richard Temple-Nugent-Brydges-Chandos-Grenville, 3rd duke of Buckingham and Chandos, as 8th Baron and Viscount Cobham; married, 1878, Mary Susan Caroline, daughter of William George Cavendish, 2nd Baron Chesham
2 Albert Victor (1844-1928), headmaster of St Andrew's School, Bloemfontein (1884-85)
3 Neville Gerald (1845-1931), Gen.
4 George William Spencer (1847-1913), private secretary to Gladstone
3 Lavinia (1849-1939); married Revd Edward Stuart Talbot
4 May (1850-1875)
5 Arthur Temple Lyttelton (1852-1903), bishop of Southampton
6 Robert Henry (1854-1939)
7 Edward (1855-1942), headmaster of Eton College
8 Alfred (1857-1913)

Lyttelton married secondly, 1869, Sybella Harriet, widow of Humphrey Francis Mildmay and daughter of George Clive, MP; they had 3 daughters:

1 Sarah Kathleen (1870-1942); married, 26 April 1900, John Bailey
2 Sybil (1873-1934); married, 16 July 1895, Sir Lionel Cust
3 Margaret (1874-1958); married, 5 April 1904, Revd Cyril Argentine Alington

Lyttelton requested Gladstone to grant him an earldom in November 1873 as he disliked the possibility of inheriting the title of Viscount Cobham from his distant cousin, the duke of Buckingham and Chandos, but this was refused. Increasingly he became subject to fits of depression; in 1876 he was accompanied by his family to Italy for the sake of his health. On his return to London, he was placed under close medical supervision, but on Easter Tuesday, 19 April 1876, he managed to elude his attendant and threw himself over the balusters of the staircase in the family house, 18 Park Crescent, Portman Place, London. He died the same day. He was succeeded by his eldest son Charles, who also, in 1889, succeeded as 8th Viscount Cobham.

1840: 13 Apr: *Busy till a late hour in writing letters—to M. W.—to E.F. W.—to the following connexions or friends to apprize them of my Aunt's death—the Lord Lyttelton—Miss M. C. Hunt:—Miss Hunt of Boreatton Park—the Bishop of Gloucester and Bristol—Mrs. Guydickens.* 27 Jun: *Recd. a letter from B P Witts requesting a copy of the lithograph of Lady Lyttelton, which he wishes to present to Lord Lyttelton.*

1842: 19 Feb: *An unexpected visit from E.F. W. who rode over to communicate to, and advise with me upon, a letter he had yesterday received from Lord Lyttelton, Lord Lieutenant of Worcestershire, desiring him to allow himself to be put on the Commission for Worcestershire, as his services were likely to be very useful, especially as regarded the parish of Broadway, where a Magistrate was needed.*

1843: 6 Sep: *Returning to Brighton we met the Royal children proceeding on their accustomed airing, attended by their governess, Lady Lyttelton and nurses: we could not catch a glimpse of them, though they were in an open barouche, drawn by four horses, preceded by an outrider, two grooms or footmen in the rumble behind.*

M

MACBRIDE — John MacBride[1]

John MacBride (1735-1800), Royal Navy officer and MP for Plymouth (1784-90), was born in Scotland, the son of Revd Robert Macbride (1687-1739) and Jane Laing (b. 1690). He rose to the rank of admiral. MacBride married, Ursula (b. 1731), daughter of William Folkes and Ursula Taylor on 14 July 1774, and they had 1 son and 2 daughters:

1 Charlotte (1775-1836), married, 19 May 1795, Admiral Sir Willoughby Thomas Lake

1 John David (1778-1868), college head, born at Plympton St Maurice, Devon, educated at Cheam School and Exeter College, Oxford (BA 1799; BCL & DCL 1811). He married, 1805, Mary (1771-1862), second daughter of Sir Joseph Radcliffe; they had 1 daughter:

  1 Frances (1806-1878); born at Colchester; died unmarried at Oxford

2 Mary Anne (1777-1855), buried in Bath Abbey

John David MacBride interested himself in oriental literature, and in 1813 was appointed lord almoner's reader in Arabic, becoming professor in 1862. In 1813 he appointed principal of Magdalen Hall, succeeding Henry Ford in both this and the readership. He retained these Oxford appointments until his death. He held several other university offices, being a perpetual delegate of privileges from 1813, a perpetual delegate of the university press from 1814, a commissioner of sewers (1823-45), and of the market (1825-66). He published three volumes of his theology lectures, and a few other articles and speeches, but his principal work was *The Mohammedan Religion Explained*, 1857.

It seems reasonably certain that John David MacBride was of the same McBride family, of Clifton, the son of Admiral MacBride, with whom the Wittses socialised between 1802 and 1806. Mary Anne became a close friend to Agnes Witts; they met frequently at Clifton and Cheltenham. In all there are 96 references to the Macbride family in Agnes's diaries, the very last being on 12 May 1818 at Cheltenham. Agnes's reference for Friday 27 June 1806 particularly appears to clinch the attribution: 'I walk'd a little & call'd on Mrs. Auriol & Miss Macbride to wish her joy of her new Niece ...' Frances Macbride was born in 1806, and this entry dovetails with the known facts. Also, Francis Witts's entry for 16 March 1805 refers to both men taking the journey together to Oxford.

1802: 29 Apr: *Called upon Mrs. Barnewall, Mr. McBride, Mrs. Stewart, Mrs. Bates.*

1803: 31 Dec: *Made several visits with George: to the adorable Misses Price & Hughes; the sensible Jnr. Mc.Brides: the good assured Smiths; fulsome Mrs. Pennington: & the pleasant family of Mrs. Moncaster.*

1804: 26-27 Jan., 5 Sep: *Called on the Mc. Bride's.* 7 Sep: *with McBride, Ryan, Mrs. McMahon & Miss Briscoe to the Jewish Synagogue.* 13 Sep: *Called on McBride & Mrs. McMahon.* 23 Sep., 24 Dec.

1805: 23 Jan: *To Bristol & called on McBride.* 26 Jan: *walked with Mc.Bride.* 31 Jan., 21 Feb., 8 Mar:
Called on my friend Mrs. Carrick & on McBride. 16 Mar: *Left Bristol at ½ past 7 by the Oxford Mail. McBride was Campagnon De Voyage. Breakfasted at Bath. Dined at Cirencester.*

1806: 17 Jan: *called upon the agreable Miss Macbride.* 12 Feb: *Walked with my Father & Mother, Miss Macbride, Col. Napier &c.* 4 Jul: *the band playing & with Miss Macbride.*

1829: 18 Feb: *On the part of Mr. Peel, the chairman of the Oxford Committee is Dr. Marsham, Warden of Merton, a Barrister, and a Commissioner of Charities, Dr. Shuttleworth, the learned Warden of New College, a frequent and favoured visitor at Holland House, Dr. Macbride, Head of Magdalen Hall &c.*

1833: 13 Mar: *After some deliberation it was agreed that Mr. Riddle should wait on the Principal of Magdalen Hall, and state the circumstances of the case to him, with a view to Edward's admission into that Society. I did not accompany Mr. Riddle from motives as well of personal feeling, as of delicacy. Dr. Macbride was an old acquaintance of mine, although we had not kept up any intercourse for several years; had I gone, I should have in some measure dwelt upon my former acquaintance with him.*

1839: 7 Feb.

1848: 14 Apr.

McCAUSLAND — Theodosia McCausland and the McCausland family at Clifton— ***see also*** **Tyndall**[2]

Theodosia McCausland, née Mahon (±1746-1822), was the daughter of Thomas Mahon, of Strokestown, Roscommon, and Jane Brandon, daughter of Maurice, Lord Brandon. Theodosia married, 1778, Conolly McCausland (1754-1827) of Fruit Hill Drenagh, co. Derry. This marriage was apparently lucrative for Conolly. Theodosia and Conolly had 3 sons and 4 daughters:

1 Jane (1778-1822); married Gustavus Hamilton

1 Marcus (1787-1862); *see below*

2 Conolly Robert (1789 1817); died in Poona, India

3 Frederick Hervey (1793-1817)

2 Elizabeth; married J. Ross of Newtownlimavady

3 Theodosia (d. 1825); married Charles, son of Thomas Tyndall of the Fort, Bristol

4 Eleanor (d. 1818); died unmarried

Marcus McCausland (1787-1862), DL for co. Derry, was the eldest son of Connolly McCausland and Theodosia Mahon. He was educated at Christ Church, Oxford, and married, 1815, Marianne, daughter of Thomas Tynall of the Fort, Bristol. The couple had eight children.

There was a strong Tyndall/Bristol connection with the McCauslands. This link had been forged by Marcus but was strengthened by his sister, Theodosia, who married Marianne Tynall's brother, Charles, brother-in-law to Marcus. The connection was strengthened further in 1827 when Marcus's cousin, Conolly Gage, married Henrietta, his wife's sister.

The Irish set in Clifton was numerous, even predominant. The other definable set was the HEIC contingent, and occasionally the families included both connections—East India Company *and* Ireland.

1803: 31 Dec: *the rest of the party being gone before to Mrs. McCausland's Rout of 90 persons great & small; a wondrous collection of Masters & Misses.*

1804: 3 Jan: *In the Evening late to the M.C's magnificent & crowded Ball. The Duchess of Devonshire with a large party there from Bath.* 19 Jul: *In the Evening a party at Mrs.*

McCausland's. 19 Aug: *Miss Dunne & Mr. McCausland called.* 26 Aug: *to a hum drum conversation & music with Count Bosuwlaski at Mr. McCausland's.* 26 Sep.

1805: 10 Jan., 11 Nov.

1806: 27 Jan: *to a Rout & dance given by Mrs. M. Causland, which would have been more pleasant, if I had known more of her guests & there had been fewer children.* 19 Mar: *Called unsuccessfully upon Hankey at the Star & upon McCausland in Peckwater.*

1808: 30 Mar: *Rode to Clifton. Called upon Mrs. Carrick & Mr. Garden; walked with Marcus Maccausland*

MACCLESFIELD — the earl of Macclesfield — ***see*** **Parker**

MACDONALD — Captain Macdonald, a guest of Brooke Lake Witts at Hersham

1853: 17 Jun: *The guests, besides Woodroffe and myself were Sir Richard Frederick, and his brother, Capt Frederick, Major Macdonald with a friend on a visit to him, the Revd. Mr. Jones, I believe from Barnet,—Mr. Locker, Mr. Johnson, and Mr. Middleton, all, with the exception of Mr. Jones, inhabitants of Hersham.*

MACDONNELL — Miss Macdonnell, a guest of the Howell family at Eaton Place West

1851: 22 May: *The guests were Miss Macdonnell, a Roman Catholic young lady, daughter of a Monmouthshire Gentleman, whose acquaintance Laura and Constance Howell had made at Cheltenham.* 24 May, 27 May.

MACE — William Mace of Wyck Rissington[3]

William Mace (1803-1859), labourer, was born at Wyck Rissington. He married, at Stow-on-the-Wold, Maria, née Bown. He died at Cirencester.

1834: 24 Dec: *There was also a long and worrying assault case, the defendant, W. Mace of Wick Risington, demeaning himself with great impropriety, and being not only fined for the assault, but bound in sureties to be of the good behaviour towards the Magistrates meeting at Stow.*

MACEY — H. Macey

1854: 24 Apr: *Took the examination of H. Macey, a Prisoner under my warrant of commitment for Vagrancy in deserting his family of children, so that they are chargeable to Stow & Bledington, in order to removing them from the former to the latter parish; so far as regards two now chargeable to the parish of Stow in the Union Workhouse, that the cost of maintaining them be laid on Bledington.*

MACFARLAN — Miss Macfarlan, of Edinburgh, in London[4]

Miss Macfarlan was a close acquaintance of the Witts family. She was from Edinburgh and first appeared in Agnes Witts's diary on 19 May 1795.

1801: 11 Apr: *Called with my Mother on Mrs. Fletcher, & afterwards with my Father upon Miss McFarlans.* 15 Apr: *Miss McFarlan called in the forenoon.* 18 Apr: *We afterwards repaired to Miss McFarlan's, where we met M. Riddel, Mr. & Mrs. Dewar.* 25 Apr: *Miss McFarlans & Mr. McKenzie called in the forenoon.* 4 May: *In the Evening drank tea with the well-meaning Miss Mc.Farlans & took a very unwilling leave of the Browns, like leaving near relations.*

MACFARLANE — Mr Macfarlane at Devizes

1808: 14 Jan: *Accompanied my Father & Mother in a Chaise to Devizes Assembly. Conversed with the Tylee family, the Salmons, the Tinkers, the Spaldings, Mr. Rogers, Mr. Banvis, W. Wood, Eldridge, Macfarlane, Brabant, H. Merewether, Miss F. Goodman &c.*

McGREAL — assistant medical officer at Stow Union Workhouse

1846: 15 Oct: *To the Workhouse, where I had a long and somewhat disagreeable investigation as to the manner in which Mr. Hayward's assistant, Mr. McGreal, had conducted himself generally in his intercourse with the officers, nurses & paupers, and particularly as to two cases, which appeared on his Medical report book.* 13 Nov.

MACHEN — Edward Tomkins Machen[5]

Edward Tomkins Machen (1783-1862), JP, DL, and landed proprietor, was born at Eastbach Court, Gloucestershire, eldest son of James Machen (b. 1743) and Lucy, daughter of John Dighton of Ascot, Oxfordshire. His parents married in 1781. Edward married, 6 July 1816, Sophia (1796-1825), daughter of Richard Dighton of the Wilderness, Gloucestershire; she was presumably a cousin. They had 3 sons and 2 daughters:

1 Edward (1817-1893), Church of England clergyman; married, 10 November 1847, Sophia (1826-1893), daughter of Revd James Lister Dighton; 3 sons and 10 daughters
1 Lucy Anne (1819-1833)
2 Charles Vaughan (1821-1847), officer of the 75th Regt.
3 James Davies (dates unknown); died unmarried
2 Henrietta Maria (±1825-1874); died unmarried at English Bicknor, Gloucestershire

Edward Tomkins Machen, of Eastbach Court and Whitemead Park, was deputy surveyor of the Forest of Dean from 1805 to 1855. He was instrumental in quelling the Forest riots of 1831 and in bringing the foresters' leader, Warren James (1792-1841), to justice. In June 1831, Machen confronted James at Park Hill enclosure, between Parkend and Bream, but James, at the head of a group of over 100 foresters, proceeded to demolish the fences there. Machen, with only about fifty unarmed crown officers, was powerless to intervene. He returned to Parkend and sent for troops. On the Friday, a party of fifty soldiers arrived from Monmouth, but by now the number of foresters had grown to over 2,000, and the soldiers returned to their barracks. By Saturday night, there was scarcely a mile of unbroken fence in the forest. The next day a squadron of heavily armed soldiers arrived from Doncaster, and they were met the day after by another 180 infantrymen arrived from Plymouth. The foresters' resistance soon crumbled. Most melted away into the forest and returned home. Warren James was arrested, and committed to trial at Gloucester assizes on Monday, 13 August 1831. He was sentenced to transportation.

1836: 14 Jul: *here and there a bare and turfy hill-side, with miner's cottages, approachable by winding tracks and paths: the common over which we passed planted with young oaks of a few years growth, though unprotected by a fence, such being the system adopted by Mr. Machen, of Whitemead Park, the Deputy Surveyor under the Crown, to keep up the supply of young timber.*

1846: 11 Aug.

1850: 10 Oct: *Dinner followed, at which Mr. Machen and his sister, Miss Davies, from Whitemead Park, very estimable persons, were guests.*

MACHIN — William Machin[6]

William Machin (1798-1870), bass singer, was born at Birmingham in 1798. He began his singing career as a chorister in Lichfield Cathedral, and on Sir Robert Peel's recommendation, he was appointed to the Chapel Royal, London. Machin later sang at the Temple Church and St Paul's Cathedral. He sang at the Birmingham Festivals from 1834 to 1849.

1850: 2 Jan: *This really enjoyable treat was afforded by the Gloucester Choral Society aided by four professional singers— Machin, a Bass, and Lockey, a tenor: with two Misses Williams, the one having a contralto, the other a soprano voice.* 3 Jan.

McINTYRE — Andrew McIntyre, constable in the rural police[7]

Andrew McIntyre (b. 1809), police constable, was one of the very first officers in the newly formed Gloucestershire Constabulary. He enlisted in December 1839 with warrant number 6. He was registered as a shoemaker from co. Antrim, standing 5 feet 9½ inches in height. He later resigned, but no reason was recorded.

1840: 25 Jun: *it appeared to me very suspicious and a culpable neglect on the part of McIntyre, the Constable in charge, that the occurrence was in no way noticed in the Diary kept by him.* 30 Jul: *A letter from Const. A. Mc.Intyre requesting myself and other Mag. to send to Chief Const. Lefroy a certificate of his (Mc.Intyre's) good conduct while stationed at Stow.* 1 Aug: *Wrote to Mr. Lefroy on the subject of Const. Mc.Intyre's conduct while he was stationed at Stow: this was in consequence of the letter recd. from Mc.Intyre on the 30th. Ult.*

MACKEY — Phipps and Mackey, attorneys of Shepton Mallet

1850: 3 Jul: *Messrs. Phipps and Mackey, attornies, Shepton Mallet, write to desire me to search my parish Registers.* 6 Jul., 10 Jul., 13 Jul.

MACKECHNIE — Somersall Richards Mackechnie[8]

Somersall Richards Mackechnie (1791-1844), Church of England clergyman, was born at St Kitts, son of Claude Mackechnie. He was educated at Glasgow University and St John's College, Cambridge (BA 1829). He was appointed curate of Portland, Jamaica, in 1831, but he returned to England and died at Hoxton, London, in 1844. Somersall must have looked older than his years, for Francis Witts considered him to be above forty.

1824: 7 May: *I rode to Stanway, and dined with my friend F. Aston, meeting M. Wynniatt & Mr. Mackechnie. The latter Gentleman is a native of the Island of St. Christopher's, who at the mature age of 40 is desirous of preparing himself for holy orders, with a view of exercising his ministry in some of the West Indian Colonies; for this purpose he has placed himself for some months under the tuition of my Curate; he seems a well disposed intelligent man, but, I fear, Greek, after forty, will be a difficult enterprize both to Tutor and pupil.*

MACKENZIE — Henry Mackenzie[9]

Henry Mackenzie (1745-1831), writer, was born in Edinburgh, son of Joshua Mackenzie, a prosperous physician, and Margaret Rose, of Kilravock, eldest daughter of the 16th baron of Kilravock. He was a direct descendent of the 8th baron of Kintail, chief of clan Mackenzie. Henry Mackenzie was educated at Edinburgh High School and, between 1758 and 1761, at the University of Edinburgh. He left for London in 1765 to complete his studies in English exchequer practice, which having been regulated by the Act of Union was also the law of the exchequer of Scotland. Mackenzie returned to Scotland in 1768 and went into partnership with George Inglis. Around this time he began writing his sentimental novel *The Man of Feeling*; it was published anonymously in 1771 and became the most popular novel of the decade.

Mackenzie married, 1776, Penuel Grant, daughter of Sir Ludovick Grant, of Grant, and granddaughter of the earl of Findlater and Seafield. They had eleven children. From 1789 Mackenzie was active in the Highland Society of Scotland; he became one of its directors and edited its 'Transactions'. In 1797 he was asked to convene and chair a committee within the society to be charged with inquiring into the authenticity of the poems of Ossian, 'translated' by James Macpherson.

Mackenzie occupied a unique position in Edinburgh society and exercised great influence in all matters literary; his prominence coincided with Edinburgh's cultural and intellectual heyday in the final quarter of the eighteenth and first two decades of the nineteenth century. His 1831 obituary in *The Edinburgh Evening Courant* observed, 'We cannot but with feelings of regret, notice the departure of almost the last of that eminent class of literary men, who, about fifty years ago, cast such a lustre on our city ... there have been few authors more distinguished'.

1801: 15 Apr., 20 Apr: *Mr. McKenzie, Miss Graham & Miss Monypenny called in the forenoon.* 25 Apr: *Miss McFarlans & Mr. McKenzie called in the forenoon.* 1 May, 9 May: *The Situation of Durham upon a hill surrounded on three sides by the River Were is charming. The view of the Cathedral & Bishop's Palace is delicious. Durham is 15 miles distant from Newcastle. We had the pleasure of meeting Miss M. McKenzie, a daughter of the Man of Feeling.*

1833: 10 Nov: *Here too was the house of the talented author of the Man of Feeling, Mackenzie.*

MACKENZIE — William Lyon Mackenzie[10]

William Lyon Mackenzie (1795-1861), rebel leader, was raised in Scotland by his widowed mother. Together they ran a general store, but sometime after 1814 the business went bankrupt and Mackenzie left Scotland to find work. He spent time in London before sailing west in 1820 and settling in Upper Canada. In May 1824 Mackenzie published the first issue of the *Colonial Advocate*, which immediately became a leading voice of the new reform movement, advocating for responsible government and opposing the colonial regime ruling Upper Canada at the time. To be closer to the provincial parliament, Mackenzie moved his operation to York [Toronto] in the autumn of 1824. His forthright manner and ardent denunciation of the Family Compact contributed to his popularity, and in 1828 he was elected to the House of Assembly for York County.

In 1832 Mackenzie visited England to present the grievances of his political supporters before the imperial government; the sympathetic hearing he received outraged Upper Canadian conservatives. In 1834, when the reformers won a majority on the newly created Toronto city council, Mackenzie was elected its first mayor, and at the end of the year, he was elected once again to the provincial parliament. However, he was defeated at the polls in 1836, and by late autumn the following year, he began to turn his mind to the option of armed revolt.

On 5 December 1837, convinced that he would gain spontaneous support, Mackenzie led an erratic expedition down Yonge Street towards Toronto. The rebels planned to march to the house of Lt-Gov. Sir Francis Bond Head and perhaps to City Hall, but they were let down by disorganised leadership and a lack of discipline. As the rebels neared Toronto they were dispersed by a few shots from loyalist guards. On 7 December, loyalist troops under Lt-Gov. Head marched north to Montgomery's Tavern and easily defeated the rebels. Mackenzie fled to the US and attempted to continue the rebellion from Navy Island in the Niagara river. He declared a provisional government and issued a proclamation calling for American-style democratic reform. Canadian militia bombarded the island and sank the rebel supply ship *Caroline*. Fellow rebels Samuel Lount and Peter Matthews were captured and executed for treason after pleading guilty to participating in the rebellion, but Mackenzie managed to escape. He went to New York where he founded *Mackenzie's Gazette*, but he was soon convicted of violating US neutrality laws and imprisoned for a year. He spent the next ten years in the US, eventually finding employment as a correspondent for the *New York Daily Tribune*.

Mackenzie returned to Canada in 1849 following a government pardon. Undaunted, he quickly resumed both his journalistic and his political careers, serving with characteristic energy as a member of the legislative assembly for Haldimand and occasionally publishing a political squib, usually entitled *Mackenzie's Weekly Message*. He retired in 1857. The fiery and principled Scot died at his home on Bond Street, now one of Toronto's historic museums.

1838: 15 Feb: *The alarm had, however, subsided on the defeat and evasion of the Rebel Mackenzie.*

MACKENZIE-FRASER — *see* **Fraser**

MACKESY — William Philip Mackesy, of Airton, in Craven and Brimscombe, Gloucestershire [11]

William Philip Mackesy (±1815-1894), Church of England clergyman, was born at Waterford, Ireland. He was possibly one of the sons of Thomas Lewis Mackesy (1789-1869), a doctor of repute of co. Kilkenny, whose daughter, Mary Elizabeth, married, 1856, Joseph Birkbeck (b. 1830) of Settle. In documents dating from 1856, Elizabeth is referred to as 'of Langcliffe', which is an outlier of Settle.

William Philip Mackesy was curate of Kirkby Malhamdale, near Settle, Yorkshire, and in 1854 he became the incumbent. By 1891 he had moved south and become the incumbent of the new church of Holy Trinity, Brimscombe, Stroud, Gloucestershire, which was consecrated on 7 April 1840. He was married to Jane Anne (b. ±1822). He died at Brimscombe in 1894.

1850: 21 Mar: *Received a letter from Mr. Mackersy the Incumbent of Kirkby Malhamdale, soliciting a subscription to a Sunday School room which it is in contemplation to build at Airton, a township in his parish; his claim on us being that part of the Ravenflatt property is in that Township.* 22 Mar: *Wrote to Mr. Mackesy, Incumbent of Kirkby Malhamdale, promising a contribution of Five pounds.*

1851: 5 Apr: *Received a letter from the Revd. Mackesy, of Airton in Craven, who claims a promised subscription of £5 towards the erection of a School-house in that township, in which part of our Ravenflatt property is situate.*

MACKINLAY — Mrs Mackinlay at Clifton

1805: 21 Nov: *Called upon an afflicted Scotch Lady Mrs. Mackinlay in the evening recommended by B. P. Witts in sad distress.*

MACKINTOSH — John Mackintosh [12]

John Mackintosh (1767-1844) was a bassoonist. Nothing is known of his early career, but by 1794 he was recommended for membership in the Royal Society of Musicians by Samuel Okell, who reported him to be a violinist as well as a bassoonist. Beginning in 1795, John played bassoon regularly in concerts at St Paul's, sponsored by the society. By 1800 he was a governor of the Royal Society of Musicians, and in later years he served on the court of assistants and the house committee. He was celebrated 'for the excellence of his tone and style' and known as one of the finest performers of his day. He had two musical sons, Alphonso Mackintosh and John William Macintosh.

1826: 25 Sep: *I shall set down the terms, on which the principal performers were engaged ... Mackintosh (Bassoon) (1 other) 31.10.*

1829: 22 Sep: *He was accompanied in this song by old Mackintosh on the Bassoon, doing wonders on an apparently most impracticable instrument.* 23 Sep: *and accompanied on the Bassoon Obligato by Mackintosh.*

MACKWORTH — Mary Anne [Molly] Mackworth — *see also* **Capel Hanbury Leigh** [13]

Mary Anne [Molly] Mackworth, née Miers (d. 1846), was the widow of Sir Robert Mackworth, 2nd baronet (1764-1794). Mary married, secondly, Capel Hanbury Leigh (1776-1861), of Pontypool Park, taking the Gnoll estate, near Neath, with her into her second marriage. She had no children from either marriage.

1826: 7 Apr: *We found Mrs. Hanbury Leigh, Charles Keysall and Mr. R. Stewart her guests. Mrs. H. Leigh is wife to Mr. Tracy's elder brother, and was in the first instance Lady Mackworth: by the death of her first husband, this lady was left a very young widow with a splendid fortune, Sir Robt. Mackworth having made the most liberal provision for her to the impoverishment of his brother, Sir Digby Mackworth, the present baronet.*

MACKWORTH-PRAED — *see* **Praed**

MACLEAN — Donald Maclean [14]

Donald Maclean (±1772-1853), JP and clothier, was born in Argylleshire. He married Jeane (b. ±1788), who was born in Leith. In 1851 they were living at 37 Brunswick Square, London, with their son, Charles Edward (b. ±1826), and daughter, Catherine (b. ±1830). Both Charles and Catherine had been born in Kings Stanley, Gloucestershire. In the 1851 census, Charles was listed as an 'engineer' and his father Donald was listed as a 'general merchant'; he appears to have been a London woollen merchant, buying wool and selling cloth. In 1813, in association with George Harris, Donald bought Stanley Mill from Joseph Wathen. Donald and George completely rebuilt the mill in brick, erecting dye-houses, wool-lofts, stoves, cloth-rooms, and a workshop. In around 1821 they were joined in partnership by Charles Stephens, and in 1827 George Harris left the partnership. In 1833 Maclean claimed that the mill gave employment to 800–900 people, including the outdoor weavers. He sold his share of the business to Charles Stephens in 1839.

1834: 29 Aug: *Wrote to Mr. Maclean of Stanley House, near Stroud, an eminent Clothier, and lately placed on the bench of Magistrates for this county, a sensible Scotchman and man of business, who, at the Assizes, had requested me to furnish him with the details of our Police Association.* 13 Sep.

MACLEAN — Donald Maclean [15]

Donald Maclean (1800-1874), barrister and MP, was the second son of Sir Fitzroy Maclean, of Barbados, West Indies, chief of Clan Maclean and representative of the Lords of Duart. Maclean was educated at Eton College, Balliol College, Oxford (BA 1823; MA 1827; DCL 1844), and Lincoln's Inn (1827), and became a barrister-at-law. He was MP for Oxford from 1835 to 1847.

1833: 12 Mar: *they have succeeded in pressing into their cause a talented and spirited young Barrister of my acquaintance, Mr. Maclean of the Oxford circuit, who practises at the Gloucester Sessions, to stand forward as the champion of old institutions.*

1834: 13 Aug: *Subsequently from a conversation with Byles and Maclean I ascertained pretty accurately what had passed in the Grand Jury room.*

1837: 25 Jul: *At Oxford Maclean, the Conservative, keeps his seat, but Hughes, who generally votes with the Conservatives, has been replaced by Erle, a liberal Barrister on the Northern Circuit.*

MACLEOD — Miss MacLeod at Mrs Gilbert's house at Cotton, Staffordshire

1802: 28 Sep: *Met Mrs. Lockhart & Miss McLeod there.*

MACLEOD — Alexander Norman MacLeod — *see also* Howell [16]

Alexander Norman MacLeod III of Harris (1790-1834), JP and landed proprietor, was the eldest son of Alexander Hume MacLeod II of Harris, Inverness, and grandson of Capt. Alexander MacLeod of Harris (d. 1790). He was the brother of Donald Hume MacLeod (1806-1861), Susan Maria Howell (d. 1842), Lavinia Ferrers (d. 1831), John William (±1792-1829), William Hume, and Charles Murray Hume (d. 1835). Alexander Norman MacLeod III was the head of MacLeod family and had a colourful life. Although the diary entries do not specifically mention him, this entry is given due to the importance of the Howell family in the life of Francis Witts. The Howells were linked to the MacLeods via Susan Maria Howell, Alexander's sister.

Alexander MacLeod was born at Madula, India, and educated at Christ Church, Oxford. He married, at Uphall, West Lothian, 1817, Richmond Margaret Inglis (1800-1866); they had 2 sons and 5 daughters, including:

1 Donald John (1818-1858); became involved in the Indian Mutiny and died in India very shortly afterwards
1 Unknown (b. 1820)
2 William (1821-1822); born in Paris
2 Agrippina (b. 1824); married, at New York, Jose Maria Magallon Y. Campuzano of Madrid
3 Emmeline Sophia (1826-1857); born at Florence, Tuscany; married James Mandeville Carlisle (1814-1877), born in Alexandria, Virginia; the couple lived at Washington DC

Following MacLeod's death, his widow, Richmond Margaret, went to Washington to live with her daughter, whom she survived by nine years. She was buried at Washington.

MacLeod succeeded his father in 1811 as Alexander Norman MacLeod III of Harris, but was an absentee landlord, being a magistrate in Jamaica for a time. The family estate was prosperous, drawing most of its income from kelp, but by 1830 MacLeod was deeply in debt. He died a bankrupt, and in 1834 his trustees sold Harris to Lord Dunmore for £60,000, a sum that hardly met MacLeod's debts. His widow, Richmond Margaret, was granted a small pension by Lord Dunmore.

The MacLeod connection with Harris began in 1779. Alexander MacLeod, an East Indiaman captain, was a proprietor of Harris and attempted to make it an important location for the herring industry. He was a son of Donald MacLeod (1692-1781), 'The Old Trojan', famous in Clan MacLeod history for fathering twenty-nine children with three different wives. Having made his fortune as captain of the *Lord Mansfield* East Indiaman, Alexander MacLeod purchased Harris in the summer of 1779 from his cousin Norman MacLeod, of Dunvegan. In later life MacLeod married a woman named Hume; their son Alexander Hume MacLeod became the II of Harris. Having spent much of his life in India working for the Nizam of Hyderabad, Alexander Hume MacLeod returned in 1802, but found the climate at Rodel uncongenial and lived in England.

MACLEOD — Arthur James Lyttelton MacLeod — *see also* Annesley [17]

Arthur James Lyttelton MacLeod (1803-1882), landed proprietor, was the son of Maj.-Gen. Norman MacLeod (d. 1830) and Hester Annabella Annesley (d. 1844), daughter of Arthur Annesley, 9th Viscount Valentia, Baron Mountnorris (1744-1816), and his first wife, Lucy Fortescue Lyttelton. Arthur was educated at Rugby School and matriculated at Cambridge, but kept no terms. He assumed the name of Annesley in lieu of McLeod by royal licence on 31 October 1844. He married, 1835, Mary, daughter of John Bradley of Colborne Hall, Staffordshire.

1825: 17 May: *Mr. D. superintends the education of several private pupils. Among them were two promising youths of the name of McLeod, sons of Col. and Lady Arabella McLeod: this Lady being a sister of Earl Mountnorris, a near connexion of the Lyttelton family, with whom & his mother & sisters my Aunt has retained an intimacy, these youths are frequently guests at her cottage.*

1840: 14 Apr: *To Lord Mountnorris, and to Arthur Macleod Esqr. his nephew, and relations of my Aunt's second husband, with this branch of whose family connections she had kept up an intimacy, I wrote to announce her decease.* 22 Apr., 27 Apr: *Wrote to Mr. McLeod of Broadwas Court in reply to his letter recd. on the 22d. and offering to attend at the funeral, with an explanation that the invitations were limited to six Clergymen, Pallbearers, and that had they been extended to lay men, it would have been difficult to draw the line without giving offence.*

MACLEOD — Donald Hume MacLeod — *see also* Howell [18]

Donald Hume MacLeod (1806-1861), army officer, was the son of Alexander Hume MacLeod II of Harris, Inverness, and grandson of Capt. Alexander MacLeod of Harris (d. 1790). He was the brother of Alexander Norman MacLeod III (*above*), Susan Maria Howell (d. 1842), Lavinia Ferrers (d. 1831), John William (±1792-1829), William Hume, and Charles Murray Hume (d. 1835). He appears to have lost out badly in his brother Alexander Norman's financial affairs.

In 1827 Donald was appointed as an ensign in the 63rd Regiment, and in 1829 he was recorded in Tasmania. He bought a small estate in Australia which he later sold. Donald appears to have married, in South Africa, Selina Mackenzie (b. ±1826). In 1861 they were living at 24 Strand, Dawlish, Devon, where Donald was recorded as a retired army captain. They had at least 3 daughters:

1 Louise (b. ±1845)
2 Lavinia (b. ±1847)
3 Frances Anne Mackenzie (b. ±1849); married, 1877, John Dalrymple Dundas

Louise had been born at Herne, Kent, but Lavinia and Frances were both born in Scotland. Donald was buried in the Wedderburn grave in the churchyard of St John and St Cuthbert in Edinburgh, where there were Mackenzie connections.

1835: 15 Apr: *Passed the rest of the day and slept under the roof of our valuable friends the Howells, in their domestic circle. Besides my Son I found there, Mr. Donald Hume Macleod, a brother of Mrs. Howell, an Officer in the Army.*

MACLEOD — John William MacLeod — *see also* Howell [19]

John William MacLeod (±1792-1829), barrister, was the son of Alexander Hume MacLeod II of Harris, Inverness, and grandson of Capt. Alexander MacLeod of Harris (d. 1790). He was the brother of Alexander Norman MacLeod III (*above*), Donald Hume MacLeod (*above*), Susan Maria Howell (d. 1842), Lavinia Ferrers (d. 1831), William Hume, and Charles Murray Hume (d. 1835). He was born in Dingigal, India, and educated at University College, Oxford, and Lincoln's Inn.

1826: 27 Jan: *I left my family in Wellington Parade this afternoon, being engaged to dine at my friend Mr. Howell's at Prinknash Park, whither I went in a post chaise... Mr. Macleod, Mrs. H's brother, a barrister, but not engaged in the active duties of his profession, owing to his indifferent health.* 6 Aug: *Being strongly pressed by my friend Howell, who had sent a horse for me in the morning, I rode out to dinner at Prinknash Park, where I met Mr. Wintle, Mr. Macleod, & Mr. Monro.* 26 Sep: *A Miss Bearcroft was staying in the house (Howells, Prinknash). Mr. & Mrs. Hyett, from Painswick Lodge, Mr. Weston Hicks, Mr. Cother & Mr. Macleod dined there.*

McMAHON — the McMahon family at Clifton [20]

The following attribution is tentative due to insufficient evidence, but Witts's description of Mrs McMahon as the 'lady of the mansion' indicates a family of some affluence. Only one family fits that description, the McMahons of Hollymount, Carlow, Queen's County [co. Laois].

Charles Moore McMahon (1757-1830), of Hollymount, married, 1784, Isabella Clarges (1764-1811); they had at least 1 son:

1 Alexander St Leger (1790-1866), Maj.; married Catherine Fishburne (1802-1865); 3 sons and 1 daughter:
  - 1 Alexander Ruxton (1829-1899), Capt., 80th Regt, Madras Native Infantry; married, first, 1856, Horatia Anna, daughter of Capt. Davies, RN; 1 daughter: Horatia. He married secondly, 1862, Jemima Fanny, daughter of Gen. Morden Carthew of Denton Lodge, Norfolk; 3 daughters: Ethel, Mary, and Violet
  - 2 Robert Moore (1831-1915)
  - 3 Charles Joseph (b. 1833-1903), Lt-Gen., RA; married, Mary Louisa, daughter of Richard Lewis of Hobart, Tasmania
  - 1 Isabella

Charles Moore McMahon was a country gentleman and a lieutenant in the Garryhunden cavalry and infantry in co. Carlow, Queen's County. According to the tone of the diary entries, he was not present at Clifton, but the family would have had Irish acquaintances there, and it is not surprising that his wife and son should have been there for the holiday season. Given their later service in India, the McMahon family emphasises the dual influence at Clifton of the Irish and HEIC sets.

It seems that the 21-year-old Francis Witts was somewhat smitten by Mrs McMahon; he seems to have taken it upon himself to be a Clifton Cicerone. She would have been only 40 years old, and presumably she had retained her charms. That Francis Witts should also have volunteered to entertain her 14-year-old son is also not out of character. Interestingly, the McMahons were never mentioned in the diaries of Agnes Witts.

1804: 26 Aug: *Called on Mrs. McMahon.* 27 Aug: *Walked in the Evening with Mrs. McMahon &c.* 28 Aug., 2 Sep: *In the Evening on the Promenade with Ryan, Mrs. McMahon, Manners &c.* 5 Sep: *To the fair at Bristol, with Lady Jervis & Miss White, Mrs. McMahon, Ryan.* 7 Sep: *with McBride, Ryan, Mrs. McMahon & Miss Briscoe to the Jewish Synagogue.* 13 Sep: *Called on McBride & Mrs. McMahon. Mrs. Bates called.* 14 Sep., 25 Sep: *Afterwards to a large party at Mrs. McMahon's where the Lady of the mansion & two Miss Mosses sung tolerably: thence to the Ball then, but not unpleasant: danced with Miss White & Caroline Townsend.* 27 Sep: *In the evening with McMahon & finished by a pleasant party at Lady Fingals.* 4 Oct: *Walked with Ryan, McMahon, Holmes &c.* 21 Dec: *Left my card for the McMahon party at Sion House.*

1805: 7 Feb: *Called upon Mrs. McMahon.*

MACONOCHIE — candidate for the position of clerk and deputy governor of Gloucester Prison

1847: 18 May: *Of these one Maconochie, had been in the Scotch Fusilier Guards, Inspector of Police on the Eastern Counties railway, and for four years a Wardsman at the Pentonville Prison: he was strongly commended by Major Jebb, Surveyor of Prisons.*

McPHERSON — Mr McPherson at Edinburgh

This person has not been identified, but he was a past friend of the Witts family during their Edinburgh years.

1801: 8 Apr: *On returning to Edinburgh, I strolled about with Mr. McPherson, of the death of whose brother I was much hurt to hear.* 12 Apr., 14 Apr.

MACQUEEN — Elizabeth MacQueen [21]

Elizabeth MacQueen, née Ord (d. 1820), was the second wife of Robert MacQueen (1722-1799). In 1776 Robert MacQueen became a judge, and was created Lord Braxfield. He was often referred to as 'the hanging judge'; his statement 'let them bring me prisoners, and I will find them law' encapsulated his legal theory. In 1788 MacQueen was promoted to lord justice clerk. It has been suggested that he was the inspiration for the character Lord Weir in Robert Louis Stevenson's unfinished novel *Weir of Hermiston*. Agnes and Edward Witts were on friendly terms with the MacQueens in Edinburgh.

Robert MacQueen married Elizabeth in 1792, having wooed her in inimitable fashion: 'Lizzy, I am looking out for a wife, and I thought you just the person that would suit me. Let me have your answer, off or on, the morn, and nae mair aboot it'. In her he seems to have met his match. When his butler resigned on the grounds that he could no longer stand her continual scolding, MacQueen retorted: 'Lord! ye've little to complain o'; ye may be thankfu' ye're no married to her'. They had no children, although there were four children from Robert MacQueen's first marriage. The family lived at 13 George Square, Edinburgh, and at two houses in Lanarkshire: Hardington and Braxfield.

1801: 13 Apr: *I was already too late on returning to town, where I went to Mrs. McQueen's par bienséance.* 23 Apr., 27 Apr: *Mrs. McQueen called before dinner.* 1 May.

1833: 10 Nov: *Here too resided the acute, broad Scottish, and very learned Judge, Macqueen of Branxfield, near Lanark, Lord Chief Justice Clerk, with whom our family was in intimacy, and whom we visited at his country seat.*

MADAN — George Madan [22]

George Madan (1807-1891), Church of England clergyman, was born at Birmingham, son of Spencer Madan (1758-1836) and Henrietta Inge (1770-1816). He was baptised at Lichfield Cathedral and was educated at Christ Church, Oxford (BA 1830; MA 1832). Madan was vicar of Cam, Gloucestershire, in 1838-52, and St Mary Redcliffe, Bristol, in 1852-65. He was rector of Dursley, Gloucestershire, in 1865-87, and was made an honorary canon of Bristol in 1851. He married, at Seal, Leicestershire, 8 August 1837, Harriet Gresley (1813-1905); they had 5 sons and 2 daughters:

1 Henry George (1838-1901)
2 James Russell (1841-1905)
1 Mary (1844-1940)
3 Arthur Cornwallis (1846-1917)
4 William Nigel (1848-1919)
5 Falconer (1851-1935)
2 Edith Harriet (1855-1946)

1851: 29 Apr: *Darell, Hardwick, Madan, G. Escott, &c.*

MADDEN — John Madden — *see also* Leslie [23]

John Madden (1782-1844), landed proprietor, was the son of Col Samuel Madden, of Hilton Park, co. Monaghan, a spendthrift who died in 1814. With the help of his grandfather Revd Charles Dudley Ryder, of Leicestershire, John Madden restored order to the family fortunes and brought the estate back under control. He was a successful breeder of hackney horses, and his particular strain was much in demand long after his death. He participated warmly in the 1826 elections, which led to the duel mentioned by Francis Witts.

1826: 17 Jun: *I found poor Lady Rossmore under considerable agitation and uneasiness, owing to letters received from Ireland, intimating, that her step-son, Mr. Westenra, who has, contrary to my surmises, succeeded in securing his return for the County of Monaghan, on the popular, that is, the Roman Catholic interest, turning out his old colleague, Colonel Leslie, has been wounded in a duel, arising out of the contest, with a Col. Madden, nephew of Colonel Leslie.*

MADDY — Edwin Maddy [24]

Edwin Maddy (1795-1867), barrister-at-law, was the only son of Philo Maddy, leather merchant, of Gloucester, and Betty Byard Price (1757-1842). He was educated at Pembroke College, Cambridge (BA 1816; MA 1819), and Brasenose College, Oxford (BCL 1835; DCL 1835). He was admitted to Lincoln's Inn in 1816, and called to the bar in 1821. Maddy was deputy chancellor of the diocese of Gloucester and mayor of Gloucester in 1837-38. He married, at St Mary de Crypt, Gloucester, 18 January 1827, Maria Elizabeth Wood (1798-1878), daughter of Sir Matthew Wood, 1st baronet (1768-1843), MP, of Hatherley House; they had 2 sons and 5 daughters, including:

1 Edwin Davis (1828-1899); barrister; served as first class clerk in the charity commission, 1853-99, and private secretary to the chief charity commissioner, 1876-84
2 Henry (1829-1909), Church of England clergyman; curate of Nuthurst, Warwickshire, 1852-54; curate of St Briavels, Gloucestershire, 1855-56; rector of Down Hatherley, Gloucestershire, 1856-1907; rural dean of Winchcombe, 1892-1902; and honorary canon of Gloucester Cathedral, 1889-1909
1 Elizabeth (b. 1831)
2 Maria D. (b. 1833)
3 May (b. 1835)

By 1851 the family had moved back to London and was living at Paddington.

1826: 27 Jan: *I left my family in Wellington Parade this afternoon, being engaged to dine at my friend Mr. Howell's at Prinknash Park, whither I went in a post chaise... lastly Mr. Maddy, a barrister, whose father is a resident at Gloucester, to which place, the Son, a very well informed man, has removed as a Provincial, from the Metropolis.*

1838: 3 Jan: *A series of resolutions were moved and seconded by Archd. Timbrill, Sir Geo. Prevost, the Mayor of Gloucester (Dr. Maddy), the Revd. Messrs. Ford, Trye, Parsons, Dr. Claxson, Spencer Phillips, Powell, myself and others.* 10 May: *Finding now by my letter that Ford is from home, he advises that the licence and affidavit be procured from his house, where, if not forwarded, it would be found, and that my son should come to Gloucester to be resworn before Dr. Maddy, the Chief Surrogate, that the necessary correction might be made by due authority.* 13 May, 22 Aug., 23 Oct: *Drove MW. to Stow, where I had occasion to consult Dr. Maddy, the official representative of the Chancellor of the Diocese, who was holding a visitation of this deanery.* 31 Oct.

1839: 6 Jan.

1842: 8 Jan., 12 Jan., 14 Apr: *Dressed at Prinknash, and having detained the Fly, accompanied Howell, William and Emmelyn, to dinner at Saintsbridge at Mr. Wintle's, where a large party was assembled—Mr. and Mrs. W. with their son, a young Solicitor, just establishing himself at Gloucester, their daughter, Mr. & Mrs. Viner Ellis, Dr. and Mrs. Maddy, with the party from Prinknash, made up the circle at dinner.*

MADEGAN — George Madegan, builder, of Cheltenham [25]

George Madegan (±1766-1834), developer, was buried at Prestbury, Gloucestershire, on 10 April 1834.

1825: 7 Jun: *We received an unexpected visit this morning from Mrs. Phillips of Cheltenham, widow of the late Capt. Phillips, to who the house, No. 2 Bellevue Place, occupied by my poor mother, belongs. She was accompanied by Mr. Madegon, who erected the house, and granted the lease of it to my Father.*

MADISON — Mary Comb Madison — *see* Hare

MAGGS — Sarah Maggs [26]

Sarah Maggs (±1773-1846), linen and woollen draper, was in partnership with her sons Thomas and James as linen and woollen drapers at 344 High Street, Cheltenham. The partnership was dissolved in January 1830. Sarah died in 1846 and was buried at Winchcombe.

1828: 13 Oct: *We soon reached Cheltenham, and without much difficulty found suitable & commodious lodgings in the High Street, at Mrs. Maggs's, No. 345, below the Town Hall, close to the Churchyard.*

MAHON — *see* Stanhope

MAINWARING — Mr Mainwaring, a quondam protégé of Miss Witts

1846: 14 Jun: *from a Mr. Mainwaring, a quondam protegé of Miss Witts, whom we long since saw for one day at Brecon, and who has been, I believe, in the East Indies, going out as a schoolmaster: he wishes to learn my cousin's address.* 15 Jun: *to Mr. Mainwaring, informing him of the death of my cousin, Anne Witts, and giving him the address of Captn. Witts, and his sister Apphia.*

MAINWARING — Charles Kynaston Mainwaring[27]

Charles Kynaston Mainwaring (1803-1861), JP, DL, and landed proprietor, was born at Oteley Park, Shropshire, the eldest son of Revd Charles Mainwaring (1768-1807) and Sarah Susannah, daughter of John Townshend of Hem House, Denbighshire. His parents had married on 24 June 1800. Mainwaring was educated at Brasenose College, Oxford, and became high sheriff for Shropshire in 1829. He owned Oteley Park, Shropshire, and Bromborough Hall, Cheshire. He married, 2 October 1832, Frances, second daughter and co-heir of John Lloyd Salusbury; they had at least 1 son:

1 Salusbury Kynaston (1844-1895)

1827: 3 Dec: *We came to Stanway on a visit to Lady Elcho for a few days ... Miss Kinloch, an excellent old maiden lady of a good Scottish family, an adept at all games of cards; she is an old and respected acquaintance of ours: a Mr. Mainwaring, her protégé, a young man of fortune from Shropshire, a staid gentleman, and thinks himself very witty.* 5 Dec: *Mr. Mainwaring left Stanway for Cheltenham. On farther acquaintance he seemed to be a well principled young man; his property near Ellesmere is considerable.*

MAINWARING — James Eyton Mainwaring[28]

James Eyton Mainwaring (1750-1808), Church of England clergyman, was the fifth son of Edward Mainwaring, of Whitmore Hall, Staffordshire, and Sarah Bunbury. He was educated at Repton School and Magdalen College, Cambridge (BA 1774). Mainwaring was vicar of Ellaston, Staffordshire, from 1783 to 1808, and rector of Whitmore, Staffordshire, until 1808. His owned Boden Hall and Millgate in Cranage, Cheshire. He married, first, 1784, Anne, daughter and heir of Thomas Vawdrey of Cranage, Cheshire, and secondly, Anna, daughter of T. Bridge of Cheshire.

1802: 12 Sep: *To Ellaston Church where a Mr. Webb performed. B. Port left us. Called on Mr. Mainwaring.* 23 Sep: *returned to Ellaston after Dinner where I joined our party at Mr. Mainwaring's.* 25 Sep: *Mrs. Allen & Miss Mainwaring dined at Calwich.* 26 Sep., 28 Sep: *Mr. Newdigate, Mainwaring, Shipley, Harland, J. Webbe, & Furnival dined & bowled at Calwich.* 3 Oct.

1812: 6 Aug: *The Parsonage House is tenanted by Mr. & Miss Manwarings, Son & Daughters of the late incumbent.*

MAITLAND — Alexander Maitland[29]

Sir Alexander Maitland, 1st baronet (1728-1820), army officer, joined the 1st Foot Guards as captain in 1756 and was made colonel in 1762. In 1768 he joined the 49th Foot. He was promoted to major-general and lieutenant-general in the same year, 1777, and general in 1793. He married, at St George's, Hanover Square, Westminster, 6 July 1754, Penelope Madan (1730-1805); they had at least 5 sons and 3 daughters:

1 Alexander Charles (1755-1848); succeeded as 2nd baronet
2 William (1757-1781)
3 James Martin (1759-1778)
1 Penelope Judith (1759-1846); married, 21 October 1802, Thomas Cope Marsham (1761-1818)
4 Augustus (1761-1797)
5 Frederick (1763-1848)
2 Harriotte (1765-1853)
3 Charlotte Mary (1767-1853)

Gen. Maitland was created 1st Baronet Maitland, of Clifton, Midlothian, on 30 November 1818.

1801: 6 Jun: *I accompanied Miss Louisa &c to call upon Genl. Maitland a most singular antique; who resides here with a wife & two Daughters: his Son, whom we had known in Scotland is now at Totteridge.* 20 Jun.

1802: 17 Jan: *Called with Jno. Fiott upon the Mannings, Genl. Maitland & Mr. Marsham.*

MAITLAND — James Maitland[30]

James Maitland, 8th earl of Lauderdale (1759-1839), Scottish politician and economic writer, was born at Hatton [Haulton] House, Ratho parish, Midlothian, the eldest son and heir of James Maitland, 7th earl of Lauderdale, whom he succeeded in 1789. He was educated at Trinity College, Oxford, and at Glasgow, Edinburgh, and Paris. Maitland was MP for Newport in 1780-84, and Malmesbury in 1784-89. He was created Baron Lauderdale of Thirlestaine in 1806. He married, 1782, Eleanor Todd (±1762-1856).

1801: 13 Apr: *repairing to Lord Elcho's, we found a large party assembled. At supper I remarked among the most predominant personnages Mr. & Mrs. & Mr. B. Greathead. Mr. & Lady G. Douglas, Lady Lauderdale &c.*

1827: 3 Mar: *the Peers are all land owners: and there is a strong party in that house adverse to any innovation; amongst them the most earnest are Lord Lauderdale, Lord Stanhope & Lord Redesdale.*

MAITLAND — Samuel Roffey Maitland[31]

Samuel Roffey Maitland (1792-1866), Church of England clergyman and religious controversialist, was born at King's Road, Bedford Row, London, son of Alexander Maitland, a merchant and nonconformist of Scottish descent, and Caroline Busby, a descendent of the seventeenth-century headmaster of Westminster School, Dr Richard Busby. Upon their marriage, Caroline provided her husband Alexander with a Gloucestershire estate.

Maitland was educated at St John's College and Trinity College, Cambridge, and at the Inner Temple. He was called to the bar in 1816. He was made a fellow of the Royal Society in 1839 and of the Society of Antiquaries in 1841. He was conferred a Lambeth DD in 1848. Maitland was curate of St Edmund's, Norwich, in 1821-23, and perpetual curate of Christ Church, Gloucester, in 1823-27. He then travelled abroad, studying conditions on the Continent. He was the author of a monograph on the Albigenses and Waldenses, published in 1832, and became librarian and keeper of the manuscripts at Lambeth in 1838. From 1839 to 1849 he was editor of the *British Magazine*.

Maitland married, 1816, Selina, daughter of Christopher Stephenson, vicar of Olney; they had 1 son:

1 John Gorham (1817-1863)

Maitland outlived his wife and son and died at Spa Road, Gloucester.

1823: 21 Jan: *Looked into the new Church at the Spa ... The Revd. Mr. Maitland is, I believe, to be the Minister.*

1837: 4 Jan.

1847: 25 Jan: *Wrote to Mr. Maitland, librarian to the Apr Arbp. of Canterbury, in answer to his circular to the Clergy requesting information as to ancient printed books contained in old church or school libraries, that I knew of none in this neighbourhood; I named two such collections which had come under my observation, one at Ashby de la Zouch, one at Skipton.*

MAKEPEACE — Henry Makepeace [32]

Henry Makepeace (1804-1871), superintendent of police at Stow-on-the-Wold, was born in the parish of St Paul's, Bristol, son of Henry Makepeace (b. 1767) and Anne Flower (1773-1836). He joined the Gloucestershire Constabulary as a constable on 17 February 1840, and was promoted to superintendent on 1 July 1840. He retired on a police pension in 1868, and became postmaster at Chipping Campden. Makepeace married, at St Paul's, Bristol, 18 February 1832, Mary Small (1804-1887); they had 5 sons and 5 daughters:

1 Mary Deloris (1832-1913)
2 Anne (1834-1913)
1 Henry William (1835-1916)
2 William Henry (1837-1891)
3 Emma (b. 1839)
3 Edward Henry (1841-1911)
4 Frances Ann (1842-1919)
4 James Henry (1844-1924)
5 Frederick Henry (1845-1890)
5 Eliza (1849-1934)

1840: 14 Jul: *Mr. Makepeace, the newly appointed Superintendent of the rural constabulary for this division called, by directions of the Chief Constable, to report to me his arrival at his post.*

1842: 24 Jan: *Mr. Makepeace called to take my advice to preparing certain returns as to the Rural Police.* 29 Jan., 8 Feb., 12 May, 3 Jun: *At a late hour I was called on by Superintendent Makepeace to give directions as to two prisoners apprehended on a charge of highway robbery in Oxfordshire.* 23 Aug., 25 Aug: *with Mr. Pole, R. Waller, and Mr. Makepeace, on matters relating to the Police, and on the riotous conduct of the disorderly at Stow on Monday night, which had ended in a fight, and the death of one of the combatants.* 1 Sep., 14 Oct., 18 Oct: *also a note from Mr. Lefroy, informing me that he had exonerated Mr. Makepeace from the charges brought against him by Peter Hemus, and had dismissed the latter from the Constabulary: also a letter from Makepeace, expressive of gratitude to me for my interference with Mr. Lefroy in his favour.*

1843: 7 Jan., 21 Jan., 8 Oct., 24 Oct., 18 Nov., 27 Dec.

1844: 14 Feb., 5 Mar., 9 Mar., 25 Mar: *An interview with Mr. Makepeace, chiefly as to a mistake which has occurred as to the holding of an inquest at Lower Swell.* 15 Apr: *Mr. Makepeace called in the Evening for a summons against a man who had caused a bad accident to him — the man had left his horse and cart at the side of the road, while he went for refreshmt. into a public house; M. road by; the horse in the cart took fright, ran away, rode overtook M., rushed against him so as to throw down the horse and rider in one direction, and with the cart to be upset in another: M. much hurt.* 18 Apr.

1845: 12 Feb., 24 Feb.

1846: 21 Jul., 8 Dec.

1847: 30 Jan., 24 Feb., 27 Feb., 19 Mar.

1848: 14 Jan., 3 Feb., 22 May: *Gave directions to Superintendent Makepeace as to apprehending and searching trampers.* 2 Sep., 4 Nov.

1850: 9 Feb., 25 Feb: *Mr. Makepeace came with a case of felony committed at Burford.* 15 Mar., 12 Sep., 12 Oct., 28 Dec.

1851: 25 Mar: *I sent my groom with a note to Mr. Makepeace, & the warrant, directing that it should be promptly executed.* 13 Apr: *Mr. Makepeace having come to inform me that he had under his charge at the Station house at Stow numerous prisoners for various offences, I sent him to Bourton on the Water to request R Waller.*

1852: 28 Jan., 13 Mar., 8-9 May, 13 Dec.

1853: 1 Jan.

MALCOLM — Gilbert Malcolm [33]

Gilbert Malcolm (1775-1855), Church of England clergyman, was the sixth son of George Malcolm (1729-1803), of Burnfoot, Langholm, Dumfriesshire, and Margaret (1742-1811), daughter of James Pasley. He was educated at Edinburgh and Trinity College, Cambridge (BA 1796; MA 1799), and was ordained deacon on 21 December 1800 and priest on 13 December 1801. Malcolm's first clerical appointment was as vicar of Aysgarth, Yorkshire, where he was incumbent from 1806 to 1812. He was also curate of Toppesfield. He then served as rector of Todenham, Gloucestershire, from 1812 to 1855, and honorary canon of Gloucester.

Gilbert Malcolm married, 1806, Helen (1775-1863), daughter of Matthew Little of Langholm; they had at least 4 sons and 3 daughters:

1 Helen (1807-1808); died an infant
1 George Hailesbury (b. & d. 1810)
2 Matthew (1811-1905), land steward; married, at St Andrew's, Clifton, 27 January 1857, Catherine Lyons Walcott (b. 1823); at least 1 daughter:
  1 Amy Helen (b. 1860)
3 Gilbert Hailesbury (1813-1834); employed by the HEIC on the Bombay station; died at sea, 30 June 1834
4 Archibald (1813-1873); educated at Shrewsbury and Trinity College, Cambridge (BA 1838; MA 1842); served as curate of Wellesbourne, Warwickshire, 1838-41, and vicar of Duns Tew, Oxfordshire, 1841-73; married, at Cherington, Warwickshire, 6 September 1866, Georgina Dickins (1826-1918)
2 Grace (1815-1877); died unmarried
3 Agnes (1816-1836)

Following Gilbert's death, his widow Helen went to live at nearby Batsford with their daughter Grace.

1823: 23 Apr: *first meeting of the Stow Clerical Society for this year: Mr. Malcolm, Rector of Todenham (Brother to Sir John Malcolm eminent for his Military & diplomatic transactions in the East, & author of some valuable works on Oriental subjects, also to Sir Pultney Malcolm, a distinguished Admiral, who served at St. Helena during the early part of Bonaparte's imprisonment.*

1824: 7 Apr: *The first dinner this season of the Stow Clerical Society. Mr. Malcolm was in the chair.* 9 Jun., 4 Aug.

1826: 19 Apr., 5 Jul., 18 Jul., 31 Aug: *My excellent friend, Malcolm, Rector of Toddenham in Gloucestershire, a highly talented person, an admirable scholar, a pious & laborious parish priest, and a most judicious character, brother to the above mentioned gifted men, has told me, that Telford first came up as a mason to London about 1782 to work at the Adelphi, then building. His talent & scientific turn of mind, with the patronage of powerful & discerning men, among whom was Sir James Pulteney, who employed him largely on his estates and collieries, canals &c. in Shropshire, have gradually advanced him to the very summit of his profession.* 8 Sep.

1827: 24 Aug: *The following friends dined with us; Mr. Malcolm, Rector of Todenham, the first time, that he has visited us; though the distance be so considerable, at least ten miles, he could not be persuaded to sleep here, Mrs. Malcolm, being unwell.* 2 Oct.

1828: 22 Feb: *"Sketches of Persia, from the Journals of a Traveller in the East. 2 Vols. A new edition. Lond. 1728. 12mo."*

These very informing and entertaining little volumes are ascribed and, I believe, correctly, to the pen of the distinguished Sir John Malcolm, who now occupies the high post of Governor of Bombay, and who twice visited the Court of Persia in the capacity of Envoy from the Governor General of India. 23 Apr., 20 Aug.

1829: 11 Sep: *I understand from my friend, his Brother, that the admirable Governor of Bombay is now engaged in writing a life of Lord Clive, the family documents having been entrusted with to him by Earl Powis.* 18 Sep., 6 Oct.

1830: 14 Apr.

1833: 30 Oct: *A letter from Mr. Malcolm communicating to me the information he had obtained through a friend at Edinburgh as to gentlemen there taking private pupils; of whom two only are named, a Preacher of the Scotch Church, on very moderate terms, and Mr. Terrot.* 4 Nov.

1834: 19 Sep., 30 Sep.

1836: 26 Oct: *The Colvilles from Bacton; with Miss Malcolm.*

1837: 19 Apr., 14 Jun.

1838: 14 Feb., 19 Feb., 25 Apr., 13 Jun., 25 Sep., 17 Nov., 7 Dec.

1839: 1 May.

1840: 17 Jun., 9 Jul: *The rest of the party were Whitmore Jones, rattling and dashing at every subject with his usual volubility and good humour, Cameron, Henry Hall, recently ordained Deacon, a pleasant and not ill informed young man, who has improved by foreign travel, and a Son of Mr. Malcolm's, a very pleasing young man, who has been in India, I believe, in the Company's civil service, but has returned home in bad health, having, if I am not mistaken, retired from his public employment.* 29 Sep., 27 Oct., 1 Nov: *I wrote to Mr. Malcolm, as Rural Dean of Campden Deanery, to give an account of Sunday and Day Schools at Stanway... I wrote in consequence of a conversation on Tuesday last with Mr. Malcolm, who named to me that he had summoned a meeting of the Clergy of his deanery for Tuesday next to consider the propriety of bringing the village and other schools into connection with the Diocesan Board of National Education.*

1842: 8 Mar: *Hospitably received with a luncheon by Bowen, at which I met my son, who rode from Stanway, also Mr. Matthew Malcolm.* 27 Apr., 7 May, 16 Jun., 21 Jun., 29 Aug., 27 Sep.

1843: 26 Sep.

1845: 26 Mar., 19 May: *Accompanied E.F.W. to Church Stanway, to meet Mr. Malcolm, the Rural Dean, now on a tour through his deanery, visiting the churches under his charge.* 25 Jun.

1846: 24 Jun., 8 Aug.

1847: 27 Jan., 31 Aug., 1 Sep., 28 Sep.

1850: 3 Jan: *Mr. Sadler writes to know whether I should like to possess a lithograph portrait of my old friend Mr. Malcolm, the Rector of Toddenham, & late Rural dean of Campden deanery. It seems that his nephew has prevailed upon him to sit for his portrait, and that it is proposed to engrave a lithographic print to be a memorial of so good a man.* 8 Jan: *Wrote to Mr. Sader, Sadler expressing the satisfaction it would give me to be allowed to possess myself of a copy of the lithograph portrait of the excellent Mr. Malcolm.* 7 Mar., 26 May, 30 May: *Called at the Rectory ... and received the lithographic portrait of Mr. Malcolm, entrusted to Mr. RWH's care for me, which is an admirable likeness of that good man.* 3 Jul., 6 Jul.

1851: 24 Apr.

MALCOLM — Pulteney Malcolm [34]

Sir Pulteney Malcolm (1768-1838), naval officer, was the third son of George Malcolm (1729-1803), of Burnfoot, Langholm, Dumfriesshire, and Margaret Pasley (1742-1811). He was an elder brother of Gilbert Malcolm (*above*). Pulteney had a distinguished naval career and was knighted in 1815. In 1816-17 he commanded the St Helena station, where he was ordered to enforce a rigid blockade of the island and keep a close guard on Napoleon, who was imprisoned there. Malcolm and his wife became on friendly terms with the former emperor.

1823: 23 Apr: *first meeting of the Stow Clerical Society for this year: Mr. Malcolm, Rector of Todenham (Brother to Sir John Malcolm eminent for his Military & diplomatic transactions in the East, & author of some valuable works on Oriental subjects, also to Sir Pultney Malcolm, a distinguished Admiral, who served at St. Helena during the early part of Bonaparte's imprisonment.*

1829: 7 Feb: *A large and imposing French expedition, under the command of Genl. Maison, sent with the concurrence of our government, and co-operating with our squadron, now placed under the command of Sir Pulteney Malcolm, landed during last summer in the Morea.*

MALDEN — Jonas Malden [35]

Jonas Malden (1792-1860), physician, was born at Putney, Middlesex, son of Jonas Malden (1752-1805) and Mary Barlow (1768-1850). He married, 1816, Frances Lucas (1796-1872); they had at least 5 sons and 3 daughters:

1 Robert Hurd Dillon (1818-1831)
2 Henry John Woodyatt (1819-1893); married, at Leatherhead, Surrey, 7 July 1843, Georgiana Augusta Drinkwater
1 Frances Charlotte (1820-1893); married, at St James's, Westminster, 21 July 1846, John Biggs
2 Mary Ann (dates unknown)
3 Francis Charles (1825-1857)
4 Martin Fitzwilliam (±1828-1897); married, at Berrington, Shropshire, 13 October 1852, Emily Harriet Quicke
5 Alexander Lloyd (1829-1852)
3 Susan Emily (d. 1836)

Malden died at Cheltenham.

1854: 11 Mar: *He had been at Worcester to-day to consult physicians, Sir C. Hastings & Dr. Maldon, as to the cases of two patients—William Harris, & George Pearce who had accompanied him.*

MALIBRAN — Maria Felicia Malibran [36]

Maria Felicia Malibran (1808-1836), mezzo-soprano, was born at 3 rue de Condé, Paris, the second child of the Spanish tenor Manuel García (1775-1832) and Maria Joaquina Sitchès (1780-1854). Her elder brother, Manuel Patricio García (1805-1906), a teacher of singing, founded the English branch of this musical family, while her younger sister, Pauline Viardot (1821-1910), also became a famous singer.

Having been trained by her father, Maria made her London début in 1825 at the King's Theatre in Rossini's *Il barbiere di Siviglia*. In October of that year García took his family and other singers to New York. Maria was the prima donna, performing operas mainly by Rossini. In 1826 she married a naturalised American merchant, Eugène Malibran (1781-1836), who was twenty-seven years her senior. In 1827 she returned to France alone.

In Paris, for the next four years, she was prima donna at the Théâtre Italien, and enjoyed great success; her influence on the Romantic generation—particularly on writers—was considerable. As Rossini's Desdemona she became a Romantic icon. Maria also sang frequently in England, where she was acclaimed as an outstanding singer, although she never generated quite the same adoration there as she did in France and, later, in Italy.

In 1829 Maria fell in love with the Belgian violinist Charles de Bériot (1802-1870). She succeeded in obtaining a civil annulment of her marriage in 1835, and married Bériot on 29 March 1836.

From 1832 until her death, Maria sang in Italy and England. In Italy she became the supreme interpreter of Bellini's music, and her final season at La Scala (1835-36) marked the apogee of her career. She spent the summer of 1836 in London, and on 5 July, while riding in Regent's Park with Lord William Lennox, she fell from her horse. She died two months later, but not before giving a sensational final performance at the Manchester festival.

Francis Witts, a competent judge of music, was enthralled by her performances. His detailed diary entries provide much further information.

1829: 22 Sep: *Place aux Dames! and stand forward Madame Malibran Garcia, Prima Donna, and prime favourite with all Miss Paton is charming; but on the same day "Oh! no! we never mention her": the quality of Malibran's voice is infinitely richer, the compass greater; the facility of utterance wonderful; while Lady William Lenox labours; you see the working of the machinery & hear the heaving of the bellows, if you sit near the Orchestra; but Malibran's strains proceed as if there were no exertion.*

1829: 23 Sep: *Madame Malibran and Mr. Vaughan performed a delightful duet by Marcello – "Qual anelante cervo."... She was also delightfully liquid and moving in an Air by Guglielmi.* 24 Sep: *I cannot persuade myself, that my friend, the Dean of Gloucester, or his family received any damage to day from acts of hospitality towards Malibran, Miss Paton, Vaughan &c.; nor that other unprofessional guests of the Rice's, Lords Redesdale & Chetwynd, Lady Sherborne, Hon. Mrs. Moreton, Lady E. Dutton, the Talbots, Mrs. M. Beach, ourselves &c. were at all contaminated by taking luncheon at the same table with them in the Deanery.*

1836: 27 Oct: *A kind of temporary interest was raised in most minds by remembering how lately she had been witness to the unexpected last illness and death, at the Manchester Musical Festival, of Malibran, the Queen of song.*

MALKOLMI — Karl Friedrich Malkolmi [37]

Karl Friedrich Malkolmi [or Malcolmi] (d. 1819), actor, tended to play the roles of crusty old gentlemen, old peasants, and comic or noble fathers. He performed in the Weimar company from 1788 to 1817, frequently alongside his two daughters, Anna Amalie Christiane (1780-1851) and Franziska. He was a widower for many years. His daughter Anna Amalie was married to Heinrich Becker (1770-1822), whom she divorced. She later married Goethe's favourite pupil, Pius Alexander Wolff, who performed at the Weimar theatre between 1803 and 1816.

1798: 2 Sep: *For low Comedy Becker is very good besides those I have mentioned, Malkolmi, Spangler, Haide, Cordeman &c. are very tolerable Performers, among the actresses, Malkolmi, Göbe, &c. hardly deserve mention.*

1799: 7 Nov: *To the Play Die Versöhnung by Kotzebue a pretty interesting piece a Comedy where Becker, Madame Beck, Malkolmi, Vohsin & Weyrauch played very well.* 12 Nov: *best Actors Vohsin, Malkolmi, Graff, Schall, Haide, Vohs & Becker.* 20 Nov: *The best Actors were General von Horstwall by Graff, his Son by Vohs. Graf Wernau by Malkolmi, his daughter Linora by Vohsin. Baron Rahming by Schall, his wife by Beck.* 4 Dec: *best actors Graff, Malkolmi, Schlanzovsky, Vohs, Becker, Genast, Haide, Weyrauch.* 16 Dec., 23 Dec.

1800: 15 Jan., 12 Feb., 18 Feb., 12 Mar: *well acted by Vohs, Teller, Beckin, Metzner, Becker, Casper, d. j., Cordemann & Malkolmi.* 17 Mar: *well acted by Vohs, Malkolmi, Vohsin, Weyrauch, Spangler, Genast, Haide, & Becker.* 31 Mar., 2 Apr.

MALLAM — Richard Mallam [38]

Richard Mallam (1811-1889) was a surgeon (qualified MRCS), general practitioner, and the proprietor of the Hook Norton private asylum, which he took over from Henry Tilsley in 1843. He married, 1843, Catherine Liddell (1820-1850); they had 3 sons and 2 daughters:

1 Robert (1844-1892)
1 Kate (b. 1845)
2 William Prior (1846-1928), medical practitioner; married, at St Luke's, Shepherds Bush, Middlesex, 28 August 1877, Jessie Helen Dodd; died at Adelaide, Australia
3 Richard Freeborn (1848-1943), Church of England clergyman; married, at Bloxham, Oxfordshire, 2 April 1891, Ida Aline Launitz; died at Cheltenham
2 Mary Catherine (1850-1902)

It is likely that Catherine died giving birth to Mary, or soon after.

1848: 19 Jun: *Wrote to Dr. Williams, Superintendent of the Lunatic Asylum at Gloucester, respecting a pauper lunatic of the parish of Condicote,, who is confined at Mr. Mallam's private Madhouse at Hooknorton, and of whom it is reported that she is sufficiently recovered to return home.* 6 Oct: *I called and introduced myself to Mr. Mallam, the Superintendent and proprietor.*

1853: 14 Dec: *To Mr. Waller's at Bourton, and there, having obtained the opinion of Mr. Moore as to the insanity of W. Wakelam, whom we personally examined at the Police Station, made an order for his conveyance to-morrow by the Rel. Officer, to the licenced house for reception of Lunatics at Hook Norton, kept by Mr. Mallam.*

1854: 29 Apr: *Mr. Mallam, the proprietor of the Hook Norton House has taken some offence at the management of our Lunatic Asylum, in selecting cases to be admitted there, and handing over chronic or possibly incurable cases to private establishments, and positively refused to receive the patient, whom the Rel. Off. accordingly brought back to Lower Swell, and placed him under proper care there.*

MALLINSON — Joseph Mallinson [39]

Joseph Mallinson (1777-1853) was a comic actor and singer. Information about his life is surprisingly scarce, and what does exist is scattered thinly across a variety of sources. He married, at Bristol, 1810, Ann Gelson (±1783-1878), of New Bond Street, London. In 1841 they were living at Oxford Row, Walcot, Bath, with one female servant. Joseph was listed in the census as 'comedian', and elsewhere he was described as 'of the Bath and Bristol Theatres and one of the managers of the Tenby theatre'. He and Ann appear to have had at least four children, one of whom was Lucinda.

Having achieved success in Bath and Bristol, Mallinson made his London debut in 1811. His performance was reviewed as follows: 'Mr Mallinson, from the Theatre Royal, Bath, made his first appearance on the London boards, in the character of *Ralph*. He possesses a good comic countenance, and is evidently well acquainted with the business of the stage; he exhibited a great portion of rich comic humour, totally divested of buffoonery. His song, "*What's a Woman like?*" received a general encore.'

One of Mallinson's colleagues, Abbott, was a talented actor who subsequently became a London manager. In 1810 he eloped to Gretna Green with a Bath lady. The previous year, during the summer season, he conducted a theatrical performance at a venue at Tenby with Joseph Mallinson and so far interested the inhabitants that it was proposed to build a theatre for them by subscription, but nothing came of this.

Mallinson was a leading vocalist in the west of England for more than thirty years. He appeared at Vauxhall Gardens, London, in 1823, 1824, 1825, and 1844, and on 24 September 1821 a benefit concert was held in his honour at the Theatre Royal in Birmingham. He died at Bath and was buried there at Weston All Saints'. By 1861 Ann was living at Woodford Green, Essex, with her much younger unmarried sisters, Mary Gelson (b. ±1803) and Susannah (b. ±1807), who were dressmakers. She died in 1878 at the grand age of 95.

1804: 1 Oct: *To the play at Bristol in the Evening with my Mother, Lady Hunloke, Sue & Caroline Townsend & Col. Hill. The Child of Nature, the Farm House & my Grandmother. The Actors very indifferent. Egerton, a Miss Jameson, her first appearance, Mrs. Windsor, & Mr. Mallinson, the best.*

1805: 4 Mar: *Mr. J. Delabere dined with us; we all went to the Play together, taking Miss Ford. Incledon as Lionel in Lionel in Clarissa, & as steady in the Quaker, & Mallinson as Solomon in the latter, inimitable, were the only attractions.* 11 Mar: *Accompanied Delabere to the Play. Incledon excelling in Don Carlos in the Duenna, & Patrick in the Poor Soldier, & unrivalled in the storm. Mallinson, Lovegrove, Blisset, Webber & Mrs. Windsor above mediocrity.*

1806: 10 Mar: *amused with the play. Shakespear's Twelfth Night; some characters infamously represented, Sir Andrew Aguecheek by Mallinson, Malvolio By Lovegrove, Viola by Miss Fisher passably well acted.*

MALLORY — Robert Mallory[40]

Robert Mallory (1809-1889), ironmonger, was born at Hackney, Middlesex, son of Daniel Mallory. He married, at St Mary's, Cheltenham, 29 January 1835, Caroline Bubb (1799-1884); they had 1 son and 2 daughters:

1 Elizabeth (b. 1836)
2 Emma (1838-1863)
1 Daniel (1840-1911)

In 1861 Elizabeth and Emma were both unmarried and living with their parents.

Mallory had been in partnership with William Churchill (b. ±1792) as Churchill and Mallory, but in 1837 there was a legal dispute, which led to the dissolution of the partnership. By 1858 Mallory was trading as Robert & Henry Mallory of 395 High Street, Cheltenham, employing twelve men and boys. Henry (b. ±1804) was probably Robert Mallory's brother. The family lived at Painswick Lodge, Leckhampton.

1840: 16 Apr: *Letters awaited me from Messrs. Churchill and Mallory, Ironmongers, Cheltenham, respecting grates and a stove to be erected at the Workhouse at Stow.*

1850: 2 Feb: *Letters from Mallory, Cheltenham, Ironmonger, as to a Joyces's Stove, which he has sent me.* 5 Apr: *An envelope containing a bill from Mr. Mallory, the Cheltenham Ironmonger.*

1851: 8 Jan: *Wrote to Mallory, Iron-monger, Cheltenham, to complain of a deficiency in measure of some prepared fuel which he supplied me to be used in a Stove.* 11 Jan.

1852: 7 Nov: *To Mallory, Ironmonger, Cheltenham, for a supply of prepared fuel for Joyce's stove.*

1854: 15 May: *To Mallory, Ironmonger, Cheltenham, to send a workman to take directions as to a new kitchen grate, and boiler: those now in use being much out of order.* 2 Jun: *A letter from Messrs. Mallory, Cheltenham, as to hot-plate, and kitchen range, respecting which I sought information in vain on Wednesday.* 8 Jul: *Wrote to Messrs. Mallory, ironmongers, respecting the kitchen range ordered by me, and which has not been put up, as I had expected, before this time, desiring that the work be not delayed.* 15 Jul., 18 Jul., 20 Jul., 27 Jul., 11 Aug: *Wrote a note to Messrs. Mallory, Cheltenham, as to the long expected kitchen range, for which I am about to send to-morrow, hoping that it will be put up in next week.*

MALTBY — Edward Maltby[41]

Edward Maltby (1770-1859), bishop of Durham, was born in the Norwich parish of St George Tombland, the fourth son of George Maltby (1731-1794), master weaver and merchant, and Mary Fearman (1738-1804). He was educated at Norwich, Winchester, and Pembroke College, Cambridge (BA 1792; MA 1794; BD 1801; DD 1806). In 1784 Maltby's cousin Elizabeth Maltby married George Pretyman, later George Pretyman Tomline, bishop of Lincoln (from 1787) and confidant to Pitt the Younger. It was through Pretyman's influence that Maltby entered Pembroke College in 1789.

Maltby was ordained deacon on 26 May 1793 and priest on 6 April 1794. His first clerical appointment was as curate of Buckden, Huntingdonshire, from 26 May 1793. After this, his career progressed as follows: vicar of Holbeach, Lincolnshire, 1794-1831; vicar of Buckden, Huntingdonshire, 1794-1823; vicar of Leighton Buzzard and preacher at Lincoln's Inn, 1824-33; prebendary of Lincoln; bishop of Chichester, 1831-36; and bishop of Durham, 1836-56. He was the author of *Lexicon Graeco-prosodiacum*, published in 1815.

Edward Maltby was a controversial character, as is shown in the detailed *DNB* entry. His retirement from the bishopric of Durham on a pension of £4,500 a year was referred to by Gladstone as 'simony'.

Maltby married, first, at Norfolk, 10 July 1794, Mary (1776-1825), daughter of Jeremiah Ives Harvey of Catton, Norfolk; they had 5 sons and 1 daughter:

1 George Rivers (1796-1820)
2 Edward Harvey (1798-1867)
3 Charles Henry (1801-1873)
1 Mary Lydia (1803-1883)
4 Frederick William (1805-1868)
5 Henry Joseph (±1812-1863)

He married secondly, 31 August 1826, Margaret Green.

The maiden sister mentioned by Francis Witts at Cheltenham in 1823 was Sophia (1774-1849), who died at 53 Upper Portman Street, Berkeley Square, London.

1823: 12 Sep: *Mrs. Travell's tea table in the Evening was surrounded by a small party. Among them was Mrs. Maltby, the maiden Sister of Dr. Maltby, recently appointed Preacher at Lincoln's Inn, on the resignation of Bp. Heber. Dr. Maltby is a literary man, & excellent Grecian; his Sermons recently published exhibit a deficiency in the inculcation of the peculiar doctrines of Christianity almost enough to induce a suspicion, that they are not deeply imprinted on the heart of the Preacher.*

MAMMATT — John Simmonds Mammatt[42]

John Simmonds Mammatt (1805-1851), banker, was the son of Edward Mammatt (b. 1776) and Eliza Simmonds (b. 1785). He was the managing partner of the bank at Ashby-de-la-Zouch and steward of the marquis of Hastings.

1838: 25 Mar: *In the course of the afternoon with Mrs. M.V. and Mr. J.V… took a walk in the environs of the town, by the ruins of the ancient castle, the modern mansion lately erected within its precincts, belonging to the Marquis of Hastings, and occupied by his steward, Mr. Mammot.*

MANCE — John Mance[43]

John Mance (1792-1857), governor of Petworth Prison, was born at Datchet in Buckinghamshire. He served as a sergeant in the 84th Regiment of Foot from 1808 to 1819. He was a Bow Street runner from 1820 to 1824, and governor of Petworth Prison from 1824 to 1856.

1836: 10 Aug: *Mance, Keeper of Petworth H. of C. was highly recommended by the D. of Richmond, E. Egremont, and other Sussex Mag., had been a Sergeant in the army, and a valuable officer in the Metrop. Police; but there is a coxcombry about the man which operated in his disfavour, and as an enthusiast on certain points in prison discipline, particularly, as to the construction of tread-wheels, and inventions for calculating the rate of labour, it was feared that if so wide a sphere was assigned to him as a County Gaol, he would ride his hobby at full speed.*

MANGIN — Edward Nangreave Mangin[44]

Edward Mangin (1817-1879), Church of England clergyman, was the eldest son of Dublin-born writer, translator, and Church of Ireland cleric Edward Mangin (1772-1852), of Bathwick, and Mary (1791-1845), an illegitimate daughter of Col Nangreave. He was educated at Wadham College, Oxford (BA 1839; MA 1842). After serving as curate of South Cerney, he was appointed vicar of Horsley in 1849, and held the living until 1861. He was then rector of Howick, Northumberland, 1862-65, and vicar of Woodhorn, 1865-79. He married, at Dorchester Abbey, Oxfordshire, 1852, Lucy Fountaine Addison (b. ±1818); they had at least 3 sons and 2 daughters:

1 Edward Addison (1854-1925); educated at Gonville & Caius College, Cambridge; died at Ripon, North Yorkshire
2 William Nangreave (1856-1915); married, 1881, Constance Wilhelmina Baker Cressell
1 Lucy Mary (1858-1930)
2 Emily (1859-1927)
3 Robert Rattray (1863-1944)

1844: 25 Apr: *We subsequently dined at Mr. Fords — M W.— E.F. W.—Sophy and myself: the only other guests were two young Clergymen, brothers, the Messrs. Mangin; one we had met before last year at South Cerney, where he is Ford's Curate.* 9 May, 16 May, 18 Sep., 24 Sep., 11 Oct., 21 Oct., 19 Dec.

1845: 7 Jan., 7 Mar., 11 Mar., 13 Mar., 26 Mar., 22 May, 22 May: *Mr. Hippisley was elected Secretary in the room of Mangin, who has left the Deanery.*

1847: 6 Jul., 7 Jul.

1848: 24 Aug: *The services of the day were read by Mr. Mangin, the Curate of South Cerney, a very estimable and useful Clergyman.* 14 Sep.

1850: 10 Jan: *Mr. Ford had also given me a short printed address, which he delivered some time ago at South Cerney, on occasion of presenting the Revd. E. N. Mangin, his late curate there, with a service of plate (tea and coffee &c.) subscribed for by the parishioners. Mr. Mangin has been lately presented by the Bishop of Gloucester to the very populous and important, but inadequately endowed benefice of Horsley in this diocese.* 17-19 Sep.

MANGIN — Samuel Wareing Mangin[45]

Samuel Wareing Mangin (1821-1906), Church of England clergyman, was the second son of Edward Mangin (1772-1852), of Bathwick, and Mary (1791-1845), an illegitimate daughter of Col Nangreave. He was the younger brother of Edward (*above*). He was educated at Wadham College, Oxford (BA 1843), and afterwards entered the Church. He was curate of Icomb; perpetual curate of St Matthias, Stoke Newington, 1854-58; perpetual curate of Headington Quarry, Oxfordshire, 1858-63; vicar of St Columba, Kingsland Road, London, 1863-73; rector of St Martin, Sarum, 1873-79; and vicar of Bramshaw Hampshire, appointed 1874.

Mangin married, at Bovey Tracey, Devon, 1854, Rosamond Fountaine Addison (1823-1893), sister to his brother Edward's wife, Lucy; they had 3 sons and 3 daughters:

1 Rosamond (±1856-1916)
1 Joseph Wareing (1858-1907)
2 Samuel Henry (1860-1928)
2 Dorothea (b. 1862)
3 Alban Rattray (1863-1936)
3 Mary E. (b. 1867)

1844: 25 Apr: *We subsequently dined at Mr. Fords—M W.— E.F. W.—Sophy and myself: the only other guests were two young Clergymen, brothers, the Messrs. Mangin; one we had met before last year at South Cerney, where he is Ford's Curate; the younger, ordained on Sunday last, is the new curate of Icomb, in the room of Mr. Debary, and appears to be a talented and well informed young man.* 18 Sep., 27 Sep: *To Messrs. S. Mangin and Barrow, inviting them to dinner on Oct 4., the former to sleep here.* 2 Oct: *A note from Mr. Saml. Mangin, in which he accepts an invitation to dine here on Friday next.* 4 Oct: *Mr. S. Mangin, the Curate of Icomb, and Mr. Barrow, the Curate of Wick Risington, dined with us; pleasant, well informed young men; an agreeable evening.*

1845: 11 Mar., 28 Mar: *Mr. S. Mangin called.*

MANNERS — Robert Manners and the Manners family at Clifton[46]

Robert Manners (1743-1810), of Grantham, Lincolnshire, was possibly one of the illegitimate children of Lord William Manners and Corbetta Smith. He married, at Christ Church, Spitalfields, 6 November 1784, Elizabeth White (1749-1817); they had at least 3 sons and 2 daughters:

1 Louisa Ann (1772-1848); lived at Millbrook, Hampshire, with her brother Russell; died unmarried
1 Russell (1775-1850); *see below*
2 William Henry (1782-1820); born at Sarratt, Hertfordshire
3 Henry Herbert (1786-1843) army officer; born at Sarratt; became lieutenant-colonel of the 37th (North Hampshire) Regt of Foot on 28 June 1838
2 Maria Wilhelmina (1788-1855); born at Sarratt; died unmarried

Robert and Elizabeth's marriage date of November 1784 is troublesome as it post-dates the birth of three of their children. The only logical explanation is that Elizabeth White was a second wife, and that Robert Manners had previously married another Elizabeth who had died.

Russell Manners (1775-1850), army officer, was born in Charles Street, Holborn, London, and baptised on 30 January 1775 at St Andrew's church, Holborn. He served in India from 1791, and was promoted to lieutenant on 9 June 1794. He was present at the sieges of Seringapatam and Pondicherry. He was promoted to captain on 3 May 1801, and major in the 74th Foot on 11 March 1808. He was next promoted to brevet lieutenant-colonel on 6

February 1812. He served in the Peninsular War in two separate stages from February 1810 to February 1813, and again from January to April 1814. He was present at many battles, including the second siege of Badajoz, Ciudad Rodrigo (for which he was mentioned in despatches), Salamanca, Tarbes, and Toulouse. Manners retired as a lieutenant-general on 18 April 1822 and was appointed CB for his service. He does not appear to have married; the only surviving sibling at the time of his death was his youngest sister, Maria Wilhelmina, to whom he left everything in his will.

This Russell Manners is not to be confused with his cousin Russell Manners (1771-1840), MP, of Clewer Lodge, Berkshire. It was initially difficult to know which of the two Russell Manners these diary entries referred to. The answer was provided in the diaries of Agnes Witts who mentioned 'Captain Manners' and 'the 5 young Manners'. Francis Witts's mention of 'Miss Augusta Manners' in his entry for 23 August 1804 poses a difficulty as she has not been identified, but she may have been a previously unrecorded sister.

As the diary entries are somewhat discursive, the whole chronological sequence of references is listed below; the references are not arranged according to individual family members.

1804: 14 Jul: *In the evening walked with my Father & Mother towards Bristol, alone in Bristol & on the Rocks & with H. Manners.* 15 Jul: *Walked with them, alone, & with Hen. Manners till dark.* 16 Jul., 18 Jul., 21 Jul: *At a party at Ashton in the Evening, the Taylors, Miss Vanderhorst, Manners's, Weir, Horton &c.* 19 Jul., 21 Jul: *Walked Miss Upton & Hen. Manners and his brother.* 22 Jul: *In the Evening walked with my Father & Mother, the Townsends & Capt. & H. Manners &c.* 23 Jul: *Walked in the Evening with my Father & Mother, Mr. Ryan, the Manners's &c.* 24 Jul: *Walked with Hen. Manners before breakfast to Pen Park Hole beyond Westbury.* 27 Jul: *The Miss Manners's sat with us great part of the Evening.* 28 Jul: *To Bristol, & walked with the Manners's.* 5 Aug: *Called on Miss Port, & the Manners's.* 5 Aug: *Walked with H. Manners.* 6 Aug: *Walked in the Evening with my Father & Mother, Miss Upton, the Manners's.* 7 Aug: *Walked with Manners.* 8 Aug., 10 Aug: *Walked with Russl. Manners.* 14 Aug: *Walked with Manners.*, 19 Aug: *Walked in the Evening with my Father & Mother, & the Manners's.* 20 Aug: *Walked with Miss Manners's & their brothers.* 21 Aug: *Walked with Col. Griffiths, Geo Monck, Manners's &c.* 22 Aug., 23 Aug: *A Promenade & Ball very fully attended & hot at York House for the Benefit of the little Polish Count Bosuwlaski. Great deal of Conversation with many people. Danced with Miss Warre & Miss Augusta Manners.* 24 Aug., 26 Aug: *In the Evening for a short time with the Manners's on the Downs with the Devon Band.* 27-28 Aug., 30 Aug., 1 Sep., 2 Sep., 4 Sep., 7 Sep., 8 Sep., 12 Sep., 13 Sep: *In the Evening accompanied two of the Miss Townsends & the Miss Manners's to Mrs. Van Der Horsts in the Garrison Parade in Queen Square.* 17 Sep., 23-24 Sep. 1 Oct: *Walked to Bristol & with H. Manners before breakfast.* 2 Oct., 5-6 Oct., 9 Oct., 11-13 Oct., 22 Dec: *Called upon the Townsends and Uptons & walked a little way with Capt. Manners.*

1805: 13 Feb: *Walked with Capt. Manners, to Bristol.* 17 Feb., 28 Nov: *Walked with Miss A. Manners. Heard from Mr. Jones.*

MANNERS-SUTTON — Charles Manners-Sutton and the Manners-Sutton family — *see also* Peart[47]

Charles Manners-Sutton (±1760-1828), archbishop of Canterbury, was the fourth son of Lord George Manners-Sutton (1723-1783), third son of John Manners, 3rd duke of Rutland. His younger brother was Thomas Manners-Sutton, 1st Baron Manners, lord chancellor of Ireland. His father, Lord George, assumed the additional surname of Sutton in 1762 upon inheriting, from his elder brother Lord Robert, the estates of his maternal grandfather Robert Sutton, 2nd Baron Lexington. Lord George married secondly, 6 February 1783, Mary, daughter of Joshua Peart of Settle; they had 1 daughter.

Charles Manners-Sutton was educated at Charterhouse and Cambridge University. He married his cousin Mary Thoroton at the age of 23, probably having eloped with her. In 1785 Manners-Sutton was appointed to the family living at Averham with Kelham, in Nottinghamshire, and in 1791 he became dean of Peterborough. He was consecrated bishop of Norwich in 1792, and two years later was appointed dean of Windsor *in commendam*. In 1805 Manners-Sutton was chosen to succeed John Moore as archbishop of Canterbury.

1826: 26 Jan: *We passed the evening in a friendly way with Lady George Sutton & her sisters, the Mrs. Pearts, who reside near Mrs. Backhouse, being also old acquaintances of my poor Mother's. Lady George Sutton, a most pleasing and respectable old lady is step-mother to the Archbishop of Canterbury, having been the second wife of Lord George Sutton, younger brother of the celebrated Marquis of Granby.*

1828: 22 Jul: The Archbishop of Canterbury, Dr. Manners Sutton has just paid the debt of nature. He has long been in a declining state of health, but had been able to discharge the various public duties of his high station, till within a few days of his decease.

MANNERS-SUTTON — Charles Manners-Sutton[48]

Charles Manners-Sutton, Viscount Canterbury (1780-1845), speaker of the House of Commons, was the eldest son of Charles Manners-Sutton, archbishop of Canterbury. He was also related to the Manners family (*above*). He was educated at Eton College, Trinity College, Cambridge, and Lincoln's Inn, and was MP for Scarborough in 1806-32 and for Cambridge University in 1832-35. He was speaker of the House of Commons from 1817 to 1834.

1826: 22 Nov: *Parliament assembled on the 15th. but the week has been consumed in swearing in the new Members; Mr. Manners Sutton being re-elected Speaker.*

1833: 1 Feb: *The Reform Parliament assembled on Tuesday. Mr. Manners Sutton was re-elected Speaker.*

1835: 20 Feb: *News was brought by my son, who rode out, that on the opening of the Sessions of Parliament yesterday the Commons elected Mr. Abercromby Speaker by a majority of ten over Sir. C. M. Sutton.*

MANNERS-SUTTON — Thomas Manners-Sutton[49]

Thomas Manners-Sutton, Baron Manners (1756-1842), lord chancellor of Ireland, was the uncle of Charles Manners-Sutton (*above*) and related to the Manners family (*above*). He was educated at Charterhouse, Emmanuel College, Cambridge, and Lincoln's Inn. He was created Baron Manners in 1807 and was lord chancellor of Ireland from 1807 to 1827.

1828: 12 Feb: *Sir. A. Hart, Chancellor of Ireland, in the room of Lord Manners.*

MANNING — tenant of the Hunt family at Wadenhoe

1835: 30 Mar: *Wrote also to Messrs. Manning and Nicholls, tenants on the estate who are in arrears of rent.*

MANNING — William Manning — *see also* John Ryan[50]

William Manning (1763-1835), MP and slave plantation owner, was the son of William Manning (d. 1791), a West India merchant, and Elizabeth Ryan of St Kitts and Santa Cruz [St Croix, Danish West Indies]. He was the owner of two large slave plantations at what was commonly called Negro Bay in St Croix, which had descended from the Ryan family. He joined his father's firm and took it over when his father died in 1791. He also inherited two-thirds of the Ryan estates on Santa Cruz from his mother, and purchased the remaining third.

Manning married, first, 1786, Mary, daughter of Abel Smith, banker, of Nottingham; they had two daughters. He married secondly, 1792, Mary, daughter of Henry Lannoy Hunter, barrister; they had four sons and four daughters. The family lived at Copped Hall, Totteridge. Manning was MP for Plymton Earle in 1794-96, Lymington in 1796-1806, Evesham in 1806-18, Lymington again in 1818-20 and 1820-26, and finally Penryn in 1826-30. He was director of the Bank of England in 1792-1810 and 1814-31, and deputy-governor in 1810-12. Manning was also appointed captain of the Bank of England volunteers in 1798, major in 1801, and lieutenant-colonel in 1803. His third son by his second wife, Henry Edward Manning (1808-1892), was an English Roman Catholic who became a cardinal and archbishop of Westminster.

1802: 16 Jan: *Dined & spent the Evening, very pleasantly at Mrs. Manning's, our own Party alone there & a Miss Wilder a friend of Mrs. Manning's.* 17 Jan: *Called with Jno. Fiott upon the Mannings, Genl. Maitland & Mr. Marsham.* 21 Jun: *Mr. & Mrs. Manning, Mr. Bosanquet & Mr. Peyett, called afterwards.*

1803: 16 Oct: *Called on Taylor's, Mannings, Garrow & Ellill.*

MANNING — William Manning[51]

William Manning (±1798-1855), goldsmith and jeweller, was born at Thetford, Norfolk, son of Thomas Manning (1745-1836) and Ann Shackle. He married Mary Ann Spooner (b. ±1800); they had 4 sons and 4 daughters:

1 William Thomas (1822-1888)
1 Mary Spooner (1823-1854)
2 Louisa (1824-1875)
2 Henry (1826-1905)
3 Frederick (b. 1828)
3 Emily (1830-1911)
4 Jesse Emma (b. 1834)
4 Alfred (b. 1837)

At the 1851 census Manning was listed as a goldsmith, living with his wife Mary and son Frederick, who was also a goldsmith. He died at Guernsey. Although in trade, Manning seems to have been part of the Worcester gentry.

1840: 27 Apr: *Mr. Bentley, the Auctioneer and Appraiser arrived from Worcester, accompanied by Mr. Manning, a Jeweller & Silversmith.*

MANSELL — Ann Mansell[52]

Ann Mansell (±1789-1859) was postmistress at Stow-on-the-Wold. By 1851 she had retired and was living as a lodger at 32 Sheep Street with Richard and Hannah Gardner. Ann had been postmistress since before 1830. She died unmarried.

1839: 1 Sep: *Wrote to Miss Mansell, Postmistress, Stow, with directions as to forwarding our letters.*

1843: 11 Sep: *Wrote to ... and to Miss Mansell to cease forwarding our letters hither.*

1846: 30 May: *Wrote to Miss Mansell, Postmistress, Stow, to desire her to forward our letters to Ventnor.*

MANSFIELD — Edward Mansfield — *see also* Clements[53]

Edward Mansfield (±1819-1889), Church of England clergyman, was the son of Edward Mansfield (±1778-1826), vicar of Bisley, and Hesther (1790-1870), only daughter of Joseph Grazebrook, a Stroud banker, of Farhill, Oxfordshire. His sister Susannah was married to Jacob Clements. Mansfield was educated at Exeter College, Oxford (BA 1842). He held numerous curacies, including that of Dursley in Gloucestershire; by 1851 he had been selected by Thomas Gambier Parry to become the perpetual curate of the new church at Highnam.

Mansfield married, at Upton St Leonard, Gloucestershire, 22 February 1848, Margaret Eliza (±1826-1874), born at Lower Clapton, Middlesex, the daughter of James Crooke Clements and Mary Jubb. She appears to have been the sister of Jacob Clements, husband to Edward Mansfield's sister Susannah. Edward and Margaret Eliza had at least 3 sons and 8 daughters:

1 Edward (b. ±1849)
1 Emily (b. ±1850)
2 Margaret Isabel (b. 1852)
3 Blanche Hester (b. 1853)
4 Katharine Julia (1855-1934); died unmarried; buried at Highnam
5 Amy Rachel (b. 1856)
2 William (b. ±1857)
6 Helen Millicent (b. 1858)
7 Ethel (b. ±1859)
3 Cyril James (1861-1916)
8 Evelyn (b. 1862)

Having given birth to at least eleven children, it is hardly surprising that Margaret Eliza died at a relatively young age.

By 1881 Edward Mansfield had left Highnam, and was incumbent at Broadwater, near Worthing, Sussex. He married secondly, Caroline (b. ± 1850). She had been born in India, and was thirty-one years Mansfield's junior. The only other member of the family with them at Broadwater was his unmarried daughter, Helen Millicent. Edward Mansfield died in Sussex in 1889, and was buried at Highnam.

1844: 10 Apr: *Mr. Clements is curate of Upton: his lady a daughter of a former Rector of Bisley, Mr. Mansfield, whose son, Mr. E. Mansfield, is Curate of Dursley, and going to-morrow to present himself to the Bishop at Gloucester for examination previous to ordination as Priest on Sunday next.*

1851: 29 Apr: *The service was chiefly performed by Mr. Mansfield, a young man of much promise, and highly esteemed, whom Parry has selected for his first pastor.*

MANT — Richard Mant[54]

Richard Mant (±1776-1848), bishop of Down and Connor and bishop of Dromore, was born at Southampton, eldest son and fifth child of Richard Mant (1745-1817), master of King Edward's Grammar School and rector of All Saints', Southampton, and Elizabeth Roe (1746-1826). Mant was educated by his father and then at Winchester College and Trinity College, Oxford (BA 1797; MA 1800; B&DD 1815), where he was lecturer in 1812. He was ordained deacon in 1802, and having acted as curate to his father, he took a travelling tutorship. He was detained in France during the war in 1802–03.

Mant was appointed vicar of Great Coggeshall, Essex, in 1810, and took pupils there. In 1811 he was elected Bampton lecturer, and chose as his topic a vindication of the evangelical character of Anglican preaching against the allegations of Methodists. The lectures attracted notice. Charles Manners-Sutton, archbishop of Canterbury, made Mant his domestic chaplain in 1813, and Mant resigned Coggeshall in order to reside at Lambeth. In 1815 he was made rector of St Botolph without Bishopsgate, and in 1818 he was presented to the rectory of East Horsley, Surrey, which he held with St Botolph's. He was bishop of Killaloe in 1820-23, vicar of Mountsea and rector of Killaloe in 1821, bishop of Down and Connor in 1823-48, and bishop of Drömore in 1842-48.

Mant married, 22 December 1804, Elizabeth (1777-1846), daughter of William Wood [or Woods] of Chidham, Sussex; they had 3 sons and 1 daughter:

1 Agatha (1806-1875)
1 Walter Bishop (1807-1869)
2 Frederick W. (1809-1893)
3 Richard Edward (b. & d. 1813)

Mant was a prolific writer. His most enduring work is his *History of the Church of Ireland from the Reformation to the Revolution* (2 vols, 1840).

1826: 5 Feb: *The orthodox prelate points out, that latitudinarianism is contrary to the apostolical precepts.*

1840: 20 Sep: *The Gloucestershire Chronicle announces the death of my good old friend, Dr. Cooke, Rector of Tortworth and late Chairman of the Quarter Sessions for this county ... among his pupils were ... the Bishop of Down and Connor, Mant.*

MARA — Gertrud Elisabeth Mara [55]

Gertrud Elisabeth Mara, née Schmeling (1749-1833), soprano, was born at Kassel, Germany. She was neglected as a child and suffered rickets, from which she never fully recovered; the condition marred her stage appearance later in life, and she was never considered a good actress. Her father, a violinist, exhibited her as a prodigy in Vienna. In 1759 she was taken to London where she played before the queen and was urged to take up singing in preference to the violin. In 1771 Frederick the Great, who had been prejudiced against German singers, was converted by her arias. He opposed her marriage to Johann Baptist Mara (1746-1808), 'an idle drunken man, and bad player on the violoncello,' according to Lord Mount-Edgcumbe, with whom she had become involved, and arrested the couple when they attempted to escape. However, the king consented to the marriage on condition that Gertrud remained permanently in the Berlin opera. In 1779 she succeeded in escaping, and he released her from her obligation.

In 1780 Gertrud toured the Continent. She failed to impress Mozart, but nonetheless, at the height of her career she displayed a high-handedness typical of prima donnas. In 1783 she engaged in a fierce rivalry with Luiza Todi in Paris, and in 1784 she moved to London. She was outstandingly successful there in 1787 as Cleopatra in Handel's *Giulio Cesare*. Gertrud sang in Venice and Turin in 1788, and then returned to London, where she was praised for her performances in the oratorios of Handel and Joseph Haydn. She finally left London in 1802, taking with her her lover, the flautist and composer Charles Florio (she had separated from Johann Baptist Mara several years before). The pair toured France and Germany, settling in Moscow until the destruction of the city in 1812. In 1819 she returned to London, but by this time her voice had gone. Her last years were spent in Tallinn, where she gave music lessons.

1802: 8 Mar: *To the Music Room in the Evening, with Stevens, Evans &c. Mad. Mara, Welsh & Hill, Vicary & Slatter. Judas Maccabeus. Mad. Mara sung charmingly "Pious orgies Pious Airs". Father of Heaven &c.—"Lovely Peace" also well sung.* 9 Mar: *adjourned to the miscellaneous Concert. Mad. Mara & Welsh delightful. The former particularly in "Farewell ye limped Streams" "So che dovrei" &c.*

MARDENBOROUGH — George Wright Mardenborough [56]

George Wright Mardenborough (±1781-1848), barrister-at-law, was the fifth son of Christopher Mardenborough (1734-1806), of St Kitts, West Indies, by his second wife, Rhoda Fryers. He was educated at St John's College, Oxford, but appears not to have taken his degree. In the newspapers reporting on the marriage of his only daughter, Margaret Christiana, to Edward Dixon on 15 June 1841, he was recorded as a barrister-at-law of the island of St Christopher [St Kitts]. Further information is scant. He died in Freetown, Sierra Leone, leaving a modest estate of £50 to his daughter, Margaret Christian[a] Dixon.

1803: 5 Nov: *Dined famously with Newbigging at St. John's Gandy, Messrs. Glead, Frith, Brodwen, Wynne & Mardenburgh made up the party; barring a short dispute, the Evening passed pleasantly enough.*

MARIOTTI — Antonio Mariotti [57]

Antonio Mariotti (1757-1843), trombonist, was born at Bologna and began learning the cello and singing at the age of 10. He found an old trombone in his uncle's house and was so delighted with it that he soon mastered it. He arrived in London in 1792 and was immediately engaged for the Ancient Concerts and the opera. He played in London for a period of forty years.

1826: 25 Sep: *I shall set down the terms, on which the principal performers were engaged... Marriotti—(Trombone) (1 other) 18.18.*

MARJORIBANKS — John Marjoribanks [58]

Sir John Marjoribanks, 1st baronet (1763-1833), army officer and MP, came from an Edinburgh family. He entered the Army in 1779 as an ensign in the 18th Foot, and became an ensign in the 1st Foot Guards in 1780. He was promoted to colonel in 1785 and retired in 1792. He was MP for Buteshire in 1812-18 and Berwickshire in 1818-26. He was created a baronet in 1815 and was lord provost of Edinburgh in 1814-15 and 1825-26.

This attribution is tentative as there were other candidates named 'Capt. Marjoribanks'. There was a Campbell Marjoribanks, for instance, who was captain of the *Arniston* East Indiaman from 1795 to 1797.

1801: 16 Oct: *Called upon Mrs. Davies, & the Patons No. 40 Manchester Street Manchester Square; where we met Col. & Mrs. Brooke & Capt. Majoribanks.*

MARKHAM — Elizabeth Markham and the Markham family of Cheltenham — *see also* Nettleship [59]

Alexander Markham (1716-1767), Church of England clergyman, was born at Winslow, Buckinghamshire, son of John Markham. He was educated at Lincoln College, Oxford (BA 1736; MA 1739), and was ordained deacon on 23 September 1739 and priest on 24 May 1741. His first clerical appointment was as curate of Oving from 24 September 1739. In 1741 Markham was presented by Viscount Fermanagh to the livings of Steeple Claydon and East Claydon, adjoining parishes in Buckinghamshire.

Alexander Markham married, at Charlton Kings, Gloucestershire, 18 August 1752, Elizabeth (b. 1731), daughter of Thomas Nettleship; they had 3 sons and 1 daughter:

1 John (1753-1811); *see below*
2 Thomas (1755-1824), attorney at Cheltenham; *see below*
1 Elizabeth (1757-1826); died unmarried
3 Henry (1762-1799); *see below*

In his will, Revd Alexander Markham stipulated that, according to the terms of his marriage settlement, his 'estate' in Yorkshire would descend to his eldest son. To the rest of his children he gave, as 'tenants in common and not joint tenants', his messuage in London, near Temple Bar, and his property near St Albans, which he had inherited from his great-grandmother, Elizabeth Simpson. Markham also died possessed of the advowson of the parish church of Emberton, Buckinghamshire, which he desired to be sold for the benefit of his family. His wife and her two brothers were his executors and the guardians of his children.

The Nettleship marriage brought the Markham family in touch with Cheltenham, and their connections with the town lasted up to the death of Revd Markham's daughter, Elizabeth. Elizabeth's uncles were connected with the cloth industry, one being a mercer of Cheltenham and the other a 'warehouseman' in Cheapside. One uncle, Thomas Nettleship (1733-1820), was a leading attorney at Cheltenham.

Henry Markham (1762-1799), Alexander and Elizabeth's youngest son, was indentured in 1780 as an apprentice to his elder brother Thomas. By 1791 he was a practising attorney, and by 1795 he was taking apprentices himself. He was later in partnership with Theodore Gwinnett. He appears to have died unmarried. In his will he left Gwinnett his law books, and the remainder to his siblings John and Elizabeth, but not to Thomas.

John Markham (1753-1811), the eldest son, was a Church of England clergyman. He was born at East Claydon, Buckinghamshire, and was educated at Brasenose College, Oxford (BA 1774; MA 1777). He was instituted perpetual curate of Northill, near Biggleswade, which he held until his death in 1811. He died possessed of a considerable fortune, which he left to his surviving brother Thomas and his only sister Elizabeth.

Thomas Markham (1755-1824), the second of the three sons of Revd Alexander Markham, also resided at Cheltenham. In 1773 he was indentured to John de la Bere, attorney, of Cheltenham. In the 1791 census he was listed as a practising attorney. He married, at Llysworney, Glamorganshire, 1798, Eleanor (1769-1842), the only surviving child of Revd John Carne, lord of the manor of Nash. Thomas and Eleanor resided at her ancestral home, and in 1805 he became high sheriff for Glamorganshire. There were no children of the marriage.

By his will, dated 26 March 1819, Thomas Markham bequeathed to his wife Eleanor his entire property, with the exception of the house in North Street, Cheltenham, and a sum of £300 to his only sister, Elizabeth. His estate was sworn under £9,000. Although their main home was at Llysworney, we know from the diaries of Agnes Witts that Thomas and Eleanor were frequently at Cheltenham. They may have maintained a residence there, perhaps the named property at North Street—there is no North Street in Cheltenham, but there is one at nearby Winchcombe.

Elizabeth Markham (1757-1826), Alexander and Elizabeth's only daughter, remained single. In her will she did not mention any Markham relations, but made specific bequests to some of her mother's family (the Nettleships), and left a legacy of £50 to her sister-in-law, Mrs Eleanor Markham. Agnes Witts was a close friend of 'Miss Markham' right up to the time of her own death in 1825. There are many references to Miss Markham and the family in the diaries of Agnes Witts, although they are often fleeting, for instance: 3 August 1788: 'the Markham family dined here'; 25 July 1805: 'breakfasted very agreeably with Miss Markham, no one there but her Brother & Sister'; 26 January 1813: 'I made a long consoling visit to poor Miss Markham'; 22 April 1820: 'drank Tea with Mrs. Roberts meeting Misses Markham'; 23 April 1824: 'we dined at Mr. Rosenhagens, meeting Mr. & Mrs. Wall, & Mr., Mrs. & Miss Markham'.

It seems that the Markham family were ignorant of their heritage, for on 1 June 1783, Revd Charles Markham, of Shangton, Leicestershire, wrote the following lines to Thomas Markham, attorney, at Cheltenham:

> Sir, I recd. Yours relating to the pedigree of the Markhams. I have never studied that matter, therefore am incapable of assisting you in the Completion of your Genealogical Table. The estate at St. Albans now enjoyed by your family, and also that part possessed by my late Father (who died Twenty years since) as appears by Deed of Conveyance, was purchased in 1661 by Mrs. Eliz: Markham who was my late father's Grandmother who was then a Widow. My Grandfather Markham lived at Staines in Middlesex, as I have heard, was a silk throwster, my father was born at Staines ...

This lack of a pedigree was rectified in 1913 by the publication of the 2-volume *Markham Memorials*.

1801: 29 Oct., 2 Nov: *Dined at Mr. Granville's, meeting Mr. H. Hughes. Mr., Mrs. & Miss Markham & in the Evening Mrs. & Miss Boswells.* 12 Nov: *Mr. & Mrs. & Miss Markham & Dr. Jenner dined with us upon a Haunch of Venison.* 13 Nov: *Dined at Mr. Markham's, his lady's birth-day feast: pleasant, because the Granvilles were there. Besides them, Mr. H. Hughes, Mr. Foulkes, Captn. Fotheringham, Mr. Nettleship &c.* 14 Nov: *Miss Sophia & Miss Louisa Jones dined with us, the former, repairing with us to tea & Cards at Mr. Rooke's, where her powers of attraction fell before the unassuming preeminence of the amiable Fanny, who with the Granvilles, Mrs. Newell, & Miss Markham were also there.* 20 Nov: *Miss Markham called in the morning.* 21 Nov: *Breakfasted at Miss Markhams.*

1802: 27 Aug: *Drank tea at Mr. Nevilles, meeting Miss Markham, Dr. Sanders, Mr. Cruickshanks, Captn. Rogers.*

1805: 14 Jul: *Between Churches Mrs. Travell & Jane Napier called & Miss Markham.* 25 Jul: *Breakfasted at Miss Markham's en famille, meeting her brother & his wife.* 30 Jul: *Mrs. & Miss Markham joined the party in the Evening.* 31 Jul.

1823: 24 Dec: *The Attorneys, Welles, Gwynnett & Newmarch, who succeeded to the office in Cheltenham of Mrs. Tracy's Steward, Mr. Markham, took up and prosecuted at their own expence and hazard the cause of these sisters, and after much research, many difficulties, and great anxiety, established their claim in such a manner, as to leave little doubt of their ultimate success. At this juncture, in 1805, it occurred to my Father and Mother to make themselves known to the three sisters, and to solicit their patronage for me on the decease of my uncle Ferdinand Travell, the Rector of Upper Slaughter.*

MARLBOROUGH — *see* Spencer-Churchill

MARLEN — the Marlen family of Urchfont

1807: 15 Apr: *Calling upon Mrs. Crook & praying with John Marlen's wife.* 17-18 Apr., 20 Apr: *Called to pray with Marlen's Wife.* 22 Apr., 24 Apr: *Giving the sacrament to John Marlen's Wife &c.*

MARLING — Nathaniel Samuel Marling — *see also* Playne[60]

Nathaniel Samuel Marling (1797-1861), clothier, was the son of William Marling (1776-1859) and Sarah Hillman (±1772-1856). He was baptised at the Calvinistic chapel at Rodborough, and married, at St Gregory's by St Paul's, City of London, 15 July 1824, Lucina (1792-1880); they had 2 sons and 2 daughters:

1 Lucina Maria (1826-1905); married, 1848, Henry Lund (1813-1873)
1 Henry Hotspur (1827-1865); educated at Magdalen Hall, Oxford (BA 1852; MA 1858); married, 1862, Adrianna Johanna; 1 son:
  1 Henry Hotspur (±1864-1874)
2 Nathanial Summers (1830-1857)
2 Sarah Sophia (1833-1895)

In 1841 the family was living at Stanley Mills and Nathaniel was recorded as being a cloth merchant. By 1851 they were living at Stanley House and Nathaniel stated that he employed 116 men, 107 women, 107 boys, and 107 girls. By 1861 Nathaniel had recently died, and the family was living at Stonehouse Court.

Nathaniel Samuel Marling came from a clothier family and was successful in business, buying many mills in the Stroud region, some to work himself and others apparently for speculation. When he died, his brothers acted as his executors; four years later, they also acted as the executors for his son Henry Hotspur. After Henry's death, the management of the family business was taken over by Nathaniel's brother (Henry's uncle), Samuel Stephens Marling of Stanley Park, Stroud.

Thomas Marling (1803-1876) was another off Nathaniel's brothers. He married, secondly, Catherine Anne Playne (d. 1863), presumably a daughter of William Playne (1804-1885) of Longford's, Avening; they had 1 son:

1 William Playne (1863-1895); died unmarried

1838: 16 Oct: *Messrs. Hale, Holford Junr., Paul, Col. Drummond, Goodrich, Bakers Senr. and Junr. Cooper, Phelps, Dr. Timbrill and Davies, R. Davies, Mirehouse, Ford, Lawrence, Hicks, Playne, Marling, Overbury, Col. Browne, Halliwell, Carruthers, Onslow, Pye, Newman, cum multis aliis.*

1839: 1 Jan.

1847: 5 Oct: *Mr. N. Marling is the party to whom the temporary advance of £1000 is to be made: he is a clothier near Stroud.*

1848: 31 Mar: *Messrs. Sewell and Newmarch notify that Mr. Marling will repay with interest the temporary loan made by me of £200: on Apr. 16. S & N offer me an investment on Mortgage for £1000.* 1 Apr., 15 Apr.

1853: 27 Jun.

MARLOW — Michael Marlow[61]

Michael Marlow (1757-1828), Church of England clergyman, was born in the parish of St Leonard's, London, the son of Michael Marlow, vicar of Nazing, Essex, and his wife, Sarah. He was educated at the Merchant Taylors' school and St John's College, Oxford (BA 1780; MA 1784; BD 1789; DD 1795), where he matriculated as a scholar 1776 and was elected a fellow in 1779. He was president of St John's from 1795 to 1828, vice-chancellor from 1798 to 1802, and select preacher in 1805 and 1817. He served as rector of White Staunton, Somerset, from 1789 to 1793, and was appointed vicar of St Giles, Oxford, in 1789, and rector of Hand-borough in 1795. He was canon of Canterbury from 1808 until his death.

1802: 11 Feb: *Breakfasted in College with Mr. Mitchell & a Mr. Dunsford, a Scholar, who accompanied us whi to Dr. Marlow's, the Head of St. John's, the Vice Chancellor of the University: in whose Lodgings I was matriculated & took the customary Oaths.*

1828: 25 Mar: *A Prebend of Canterbury void by the decease of Dr. Marlow, President of St. John's College, Oxford, has been given to a very excellent man, Rector of Mary-le-bone, Dr Spry.*

MARRIOTT — Harvey Marriott[62]

Harvey Marriott (1781-1865), Church of England clergyman, was the third son of William Marriott, of Dorking, Surrey, and Jane, daughter of Peter Capper of Redland, Bristol. His father was of the HEIC service, and his parents married at Bath in 1774. He was educated at Worcester College, Oxford, and Corpus Christi, Cambridge. He was curate of Marston, Worcestershire, in 1807, rector of Claverton, Bath, in 1808-46, vicar of Loddiswell, Devon, in 1847-62, and vicar of Wellington, Somerset, in 1862-65. He married, 1825, Caroline (b. ±1795), daughter of William Paterson of Jamaica; they had at least 4 sons and 4 daughters:

1 Caroline (b. 1827)
2 Sophia (b. ±1828)
1 Harvey (1830-1904)
2 William [Peter in the census] (1831-1902)
3 George Herbert (1832-1918); married, first, 1865, his cousin Cordelia Isabella Paterson (d. 1866); secondly, Angelina Elizabeth Berry (1846-1910)
4 Randolph (1835-1920)
3 Charlotte (b. ±1836)
4 Cordelia (b. ±1837)

Harvey was the nephew of Randolph Marriott (*below*) and first cousin to the Marriott girls, Charlotte, Elizabeth, and Harriett, who were friends of Francis Witts at Clifton. Witts does not appear to have been acquainted with Harvey Marriott at Clifton.

1839: 29 Aug: *The first resolution was briefly moved by the Vicar of Clevedon, and seconded at considerable length by the Revd. Harvey Marriott, Incumbent of Claverton, near Bath, a Clergyman advanced in years, and not unpractised in public speaking; a good and pious man, but with a strong leaning to Calvinistic opinions.* 1 Sep: *The prayers were read, and well read, by Mr. Harvey Marriott.*

MARRIOTT — John Marriott[63]

John Marriott (1780-1825), poet and Church of England clergyman, was born at Cotesbach Hall, Cotesbach, near Lutterworth, Leicestershire, the third and youngest son of Robert Marriott (d. 1808), rector of Cotesbach and Gilmorton, and Elizabeth (d. 1819), daughter and only child of George Stow of Walthamstow, Essex. He was educated at Rugby School and Christ Church College, Oxford (BA 1802; MA 1806). Marriott went to Dalkeith, Scotland, in 1804 to become tutor to George Henry, Lord Scott, brother of the 5th duke of Buccleuch. By 1805 he was describing himself as 'half a Scotchman'. Robert Southey, meeting him then, was impressed by his ability to 'tell by the track what horse has past [*sic*] and how long ago'. His naturalisation was attested to by his neighbour Sir Walter Scott, who dedicated to his friend the introduction to the second canto of *Marmion* (1808), celebrating their mutual enjoyment of hunting and poetry. Intervals 'between each merry chase' were free from dullness.

A pulmonary disorder forced Marriott to resign his post as a tutor and retreat to Penzance in Cornwall. On 28 April 1807 he became rector of Church Lawford and Newnham Chapelry in Warwickshire, a benefice in the gift of the Buccleuch family. He married, 19 April 1808, Mary Anne (d. 1821), daughter of Rugby solicitor Thomas Harris and Ann Harrison; they had 4 sons and 1 daughter:

1 John (b. ±1809)
2 Thomas (b. & d. 1810)
3 Charles (1811-1858)
4 George
1 Mary Ann

Mary's poor health caused the family to move to Devon, where Marriott served as curate of St James, Exeter, St Lawrence, Exeter, and Broadclyst. Marriott collected and published his sermons in 1818, and after his death his sons John and Charles edited another volume of them in 1838. His sympathies were with the low church party. In the summer of 1824, having been diagnosed with 'ossification of the brain', Marriott moved to London for medical treatment and died there on 31 March 1825.

1802: 17 May: *To the Schools, where were the Examinations for Honours. Hendy of Oriel & Marriott of Christ Church the only Candidates; of whom the former by far surpassed the latter.* 18 May: *To the Schools where Hendy & Marriott were reexamined.*

MARRIOTT — Randolph Marriott and the Marriott family at Clifton — *see also* Smyth[64]

Randolph Marriott (1736-1807), army officer (HEIC), was born at Emberton, Buckinghamshire, son Randolph Marriott (1699-1782) and Lady Diana Feilding (1706-1756). As with so many families at Clifton, the Marriotts had East India Company connections; Randolph Marriott, of Lease Hall, Bedale, Yorkshire, served under Robert Clive with distinction at the battle of Plassey in 1757. Fascinating papers relating to his family are held in Nottingham University Library.

Randolph married, 4 December 1769, Elizabeth (1747-1821), second daughter of Christopher Wilson (1715-1792), bishop of Bristol (1783-92); they had 6 sons and 8 daughters:

1 Randolph (1770-1821)
2 Christopher (1772-1830)
3 Thomas Marriott (1773-1847), Lt-Gen., HEIC, and JP for Worcestershire; served in Mysore under Lord Cornwallis and was present at the siege of Seringapatam, 1792; married, 1811, his first cousin, Anne Beckett (d. 1867); at least 2 sons, including:
  2 Edward John Beckett (1817-1882), JP for Gloucestershire and Worcestershire and DL for Worcestershire; educated at Trinity College, Oxford
1 Frances (1774-1794)
4 George (1776-1801)
5 Richard (1777-1805)
2 Ann Yeoman (1778-1802); married Capt. John Yeoman, who died significantly in debt, the son of Col Henry Yeoman of Redcar. Randolph Marriott wrote to Col Henry Yeoman in 1798 seeking to clarify whether he would assist his son; Yeoman responded that he had effectively disowned him on account of his 'uniformly imprudent' and 'highly offensive' conduct. The correspondence between Marriot and Col Yeoman ran on in detail for several years
3 Diana (1780-1780)
6 Charles (1781-1848)
4 Harriott (1782-1843)
5 Charlotte (1783-1804)
6 Elizabeth Hester (1785-1844)
7 Jemima (1786-1787)
8 Georgiana (1790-1813)

The family estate was later at Avonbank, Pershore, Worcestershire. One daughter appears to have had a mental affliction, and three others are mentioned in the diaries: Harriett, Charlotte, and Bessy (presumably Elizabeth). It appears that Francis Witts had some affection, attachment, or partiality for Harriett, but did not—or could not—pursue it. The month of January 1804 was an intense period in the diarist's life, but thereafter there is hardly a mention of the Marriott family. Charlotte died in July 1804, seemingly at Lyme Regis.

Martha (1791-1822) was another of the Marriott family; she married, 1809, Jonathan Sweeting (b. 1788). Thomas Marriott and his sisters were first cousins to Harvey Marriott (*above*). The Ashton Court connection derives from Elizabeth's sister, Margaret Wilson (d. 1819), the fifth daughter of Christopher Wilson, who married, 1797, Sir Hugh Smyth, 3rd baronet (1772-1824) of Ashton Court.

1803: 29 Dec: *Merry & pleasant Ball—with two of the pleasant unaffected Miss Marriott's.* 30 Dec: *Called with my Brother on Marriott's, where we met Father & Daughter Charlotte at Home as well as a sad object an idiot Sister.*

1804: 1 Jan: *Repaired afterwards to Mr. Adams's, in a large party — Leyard, the Marriott's & ourselves.* 3 Jan: *Little dancing tho' not home till three o'clock. Exhibited with Miss Adams, Miss Beckett, & Miss Marriott. Drank Tea with Lady Smith's party, & passed the Evening very pleasantly.* 4 Jan: *Accompanied Harriet & Betsy Marriott to Lady Smith's at Upton Court: Miss Beckett & her aunt were both at home & Lord Stourton & his two sons called while we were there.* 5 Jan., 6 Jan: *At a small but lively party at Mrs. Marriott's, where the Young Folks, played speculation. I made Bank & won with Harriett Marriott.* 7 Jan: *Called on the Marriotts. Passed a dull evening crowned with a supper at Mrs. Moncasters, which would have been intolerable, had I not played speculation, making Bank with Miss Adam. Captns. Smith & Horton, Mr. Port, Harriet & Miss Leyard, Miss Duce's etc. there.* 8 Jan: *Dowry Square Chapel, whence accompanied Prower & C. Marriott up the Hill afterwards.* 9-11 Jan., 13-14 Jan., 16-18 Jan., 20 Jan: *Then with H. & C Marriott & Lear on the Downs, & at the Marriotts.* 21-22 Jan., 23 Jan: *Called on & accompanied Harriett & Bessy on a fruitless call to Mrs. Dowell at Cote, while Willm. was as it happened here. No wonder thus I liked my morning's amusement & contentedly passed the Evening at home.* 27 Jan: *Called on the Marriott's. To Bristol, met & walked with Frank Adams, took my place for Sunday in the Oxford Mail. My Father & mother having gone before accompanied the Marriotts to Mrs. Ames's grand route, crowded with fine people & princely refreshments beautiful hothouse plants, jewels etc. etc. Yet would have been dull as I did not play at a stupid sound? if the lovely Harriett have not been of the party. Conversed chiefly with her & Bessy, poor Charlotte being ill at home.* 28 Jan: *Called & took leave of Mr. & Mrs. Adams & of my dear friends the Marriotts, who confided to me the proposals made by Lear to my lovely sister Harriet.*

1826: 1 Aug: *The immediate vicinity of Pershore is very pretty; the ground undulating, the meadows rich, an abundance of foliage; at Wick, are the elegant seats of two brothers of the name of Hudson, & of General Marriott; the former I have met on Turnpike business at Evesham; the latter is son of an East Indian Gentleman, with whom many years since & with his amiable family I was intimate at Clifton.*

1836: 27 Oct: *Mr. Marriott, an Oxonian, Son of Genl. Marriott; there were others whose names have escaped me, or whom I did not know.*

1839: 27 Aug: *In days long since gone by, when an Undergraduate at the University, and occasionally resident with my parents at Clifton, I sometimes visited the Lady Smith of that generation with her relations the Marriotts, and more than 33 years ago, very soon after going into Orders, I officiated on one occasion in the ancient parish church of Long Ashton.*

MARSCHALL — Count Marschall[65]

Ernst Friedrich, Baron von Brenn was the seventh (illegitimate) child, and third son, of Ernst August I (1688-1748), duke of Saxe-Weimar, and Friederike von Marschall. Ernst married, 1773, Beate Helene Bormann (d. 1819); the couple had seven children, but this line had died out by 1849. Whether or not Count Marschall was connected with Friederike is unknown as there is insufficient information.

1798: 2 Sep: *of strangers there are many. The chief are Count Marschall, the Egloffstein, Seebach, Helldorf, Luc, Lasberg, Wolfskiel, Gormar, Oldorthausen, Families &c. all of whom almost have some Office either in the Civil, Military or Immediate Court Service.*

1800: 21 Mar: *We were all much hurt by the death of the Countess Marshall whose loss will be severely felt by a very numerous Body of people.*

MARSDEN — Anthony Marsden — *see also* Pudsey Dawson[66]

Anthony Marsden (1777-1852), Church of England clergyman, was born at Giggleswick, Yorkshire, as Anthony Lister, son of Anthony Lister (1744-1814) and Alice Carr (1742-1796). In 1827 he changed his surname by royal licence to Marsden to inherit Wennington Hall, in accordance to the will of his distant cousin John Marsden. However, the legacy was subject to two legal challenges, and he eventually failed on the second point.

After John Marsden's death in 1826, his steward George Wright was to retain control of Wennington Hall until Anthony Lister succeeded. The will was contested by Adm. Sandford Tatham, a first cousin to John Marsden. The first trial took place at York in 1830 and resulted in favour of the will. Another trial in 1833, at Lancaster, resulted in a verdict for Tatham. The validity of the will was again tried at Lancaster in 1834 and approved by the jury. At another trial, in 1836, the verdict was for Tatham, and a similar decision afterwards made in the Queen's Bench was finally confirmed by the House of Lords in 1838. Adm. Tatham died in 1840 and was succeeded by his kinsman Pudsey Dawson.

Marsden [Lister] was educated at Clare College and Emmanuel College, Cambridge (BA 1800; MA 1803). He was ordained deacon on 21 September 1800 and priest on 2 May 1802. His first clerical appointment was as curate of Hornby, after which he was vicar of Gargrave, Yorkshire in 1806-52, and vicar of Tatham, Lancashire, in 1809-23. He married, 4 October 1807, Mary (1781-1846), only daughter of William York; they had at least 2 sons and 1 daughter:

1 Mary Elizabeth (b. 1808)
1 Charles John (1815-1903), Church of England clergyman
2 Anthony Lister (1821-1873); educated at Trinity College, Cambridge; admitted at Lincoln's Inn, 12 November 1842; called to the bar, 8 June 1847, and served on the Oxford Circuit; married, 17 June 1854, Nancy Copley, née Mackenzie (1827-1905)

1834: 31 Jul: *A letter from my old acquaintance, Mr. Marsden, Rector of Gargrave, requesting us to accommodate him by allowing him to produce the title deeds of the Ravenflat estate, bought by Dr. H. Moorhouse of the late Mr. Marsden of Hornby Castle, on the impending trial at Lancaster.* 1 Aug., 7 Sep: *The great will-cause has been decided at Lancaster in favour of Mr. Marsden; ten days were occupied in the hearing. While it was in progress, two or three days previously to the decision, poor Mrs. Marsden, who has been a great invalid for some months past, departed this life.*

1838: 11 Sep: *Was waited upon by Mr. Dawson, who came to receive my felicitations on the favourable issue of the great Hornby Castle Will cause, which after having been litigated repeatedly in various courts was finally settled on an appeal to the H. of Lords this Sessions, whereby the will of the late John Marsden was set aside.*

1850: 3 Jan: *The Revd. A. Marsden, Vicar of Gargrave, writes to solicit a subscription towards the rebuilding of his church, which is in a very decayed condition.* 7 Jan., 12 Jan., 14 Jan: *Wrote to Mr. Marsden with a cheque on the Craven Bank for £5.* 20 Jan: *From Mr. Marsden an acknowledgment of my cheque for £5. as our contribution towards the rebuilding of the Church at Gargrave; he seems well satisfied with what we have done.*

MARSDEN — Thomas Marsden[67]

Thomas Marsden (1810-1890), Church of England clergyman, was born at Wigan, Lancashire, son of John Marsden (1769-1835), a pawnbroker, and Ann Leyland (1790-1828). He was educated at Corpus Christi, Cambridge (BA 1834). He was curate of Standish, Lancashire, in 1834-38, and of Bengeworth, Worcestershire, in 1838-43. He was vicar of Childswickham, Gloucestershire, in 1843-55, rector of Burstow, Surrey, in 1855-74, and rector of St John's, Horselydown, in 1874-81. Marsden married, at St Wilfrid's, Standish, Lancashire, 13 September 1854, Margery (1833-1902), daughter of Richard Fisher of Bradley Hall, Lancashire; they had 6 sons and 2 daughters:

1 Ann Eliza (b. 1855)
1 John Edward (1856-1936), Church of England clergyman
2 Thomas Fisher (b. 1858)
3 William Henry (1860-1908)
4 James Aspinall (1861-1932)
5 Richard Leyland (b. 1864); died in India
2 Clara Alice Margery (b. 1868)
6 Benjamin Anderton (1872-1933)

Thomas Marsden was the author of *Sacred Steps of Creation* and other theological works.

1850: 16 Sep: *The following Clergymen were present ... Mr. Marsden from Childs Wickam.*

MARSH — Edward Garrard Marsh[68]

Edward Garrard Marsh (1783-1862), Church of England clergyman, was born at Salisbury, Wiltshire, son of John Marsh (b. 1753) and Elizabeth Catherine Brown. He was educated at Wadham College, Oxford (BA 1804; MA 1807), and was a fellow of Oriel College from 1804 to 1814. He was Bampton lecturer in 1848. Marsh was ordained deacon on 20 December 1807 and priest on 18 December 1808. He was curate of Nuneham Courtenay from 1813 until at least June 1821. He was appointed perpetual curate of North Hinksey, Oxfordshire, on 15 August 1820, minister of Hampstead on 12 December 1820, and canon of Southwell Minster and prebend of Woodborough on 2 August 1821. He later served as vicar of Sandon, Hertfordshire, from 6 June 1828 to 20 January 1829, and vicar of Ardeley, Hertfordshire, from 18 December 1828 to 5 February 1835. He was then appointed rector of Waltham on 6 October 1834, and finally, vicar of Aylesford, Kent, in 1841.

Marsh married, at Southwell, Nottinghamshire, 7 July 1813, Lydia Williams (1788-1859); they had at least 1 son and 6 daughters:

1 Edward Sydney (1814-1876)
1 Elizabeth Lydia (b. 1816)

2 Mary Sophia (b. 1817)
3 Catherine Rebecca (b. 1818)
4 Anne Caroline (b. 1820)
5 Frances Louisa (b. 1829)
6 Jane Emma (b. 1832)

1802: 21 Feb: *Spent the Evening with Paget, meeting Alford, Marsh, Gamlin of Baliol.* 6 Mar., 13 Mar., 15 Mar: *Fine weather. Breakfasted with Marsh.* 18 Mar: *Paget Stevens & Marsh in my Rooms.*

1806: 21 Mar: *A very large male Party to Cards & Supper at the Knights: I played three rubbers unsuccessfully; of the party were Stevens & his Wife, Matthias of B.N.C., Budd of C.C.C., Marsh, Marshall of Ball. Dr. Price, Michel, Simmons, Round, Dr. Cooper, Mr. Jebb, Mr. Davis &c.*

MARSH — Thomas Marsh[69]

Thomas Marsh, hotel keeper, Southgate Street, Gloucester, died between 1830 and 1841. His widow Susannah Marsh (±1783-1851) continued the business, assisted by her daughter Martha (b. ±1816).

1836: 15 Jul: *I proceeded without delay in a Chariot from the Bell, which Mr. Marsh agreed to my taking at the same price as a fly.*

1842: 29 Jun: *In consequence we all returned to the Bell, where Mr. Marsh soon sent us up a nice little dinner.*

1843: 29 Dec.

1844: 11 Oct., 27 Dec.

1845: 28 Feb., 11 Apr., 27 Jun.

1846: 26 Jun: *to Mrs. Marsh, Bell Hotel, Gloucester, that a bed may be reserved for me next week at the Sessions.* 6 Aug., 16 Oct.

1847: 1 Jan: *to Mrs. Marsh to reserve a comfortable bed for me next week at the Bell at Gloucester.* 2 Apr.

1851: 3 Jan: *left a pair of boots at the Bell at Gloucester, wrote to Mrs. Marsh, to beg that they might be forwarded.* 7 Jan: *A note from Miss Marsh as to the boots respecting which I had written to her mother.*

MARSHALL — the Marshall family at Clifton[70]

There is frustratingly little information on the Marshall family mentioned in the diaries. They were clearly influential, most likely the Marshall family of Bath, although there is no firm evidence for this. The head of this family appears to have been James Marshall (±1737-1822). He was married to Mary, and they had at least 3 sons and 1 daughter:

1 Jane Margaret (1774-1854); lived at 1 Royal Crescent in 1841; died unmarried and was buried in Bath Abbey cemetery
1 James Ford (1775-1791)
2 William (±1778-1847), Church of England clergyman; *see below*
3 Charles Henry Marshall (1779-1861), master of ceremonies at Bath, Cheltenham, and Tunbridge Wells; born at Bath; retired as captain (and paymaster) of the 81st Regt; married Eliza Lucas [maiden name unknown but probably Johnson] (b. ±1794), born in Dublin; lived at at Hawthorn Cottage, Newport Road, Cowes, Isle of Wight (1851), and 3 Horton Terrace, Kensington (1861); at least 1 son and 3 daughters (all born at Bath):
  1 Frances Henrietta (b. 1815)
  1 Henry Johnson (1817-1875)
  2 Emma (b. ±1822)
  3 Jane A. (b. ±1825)

James Marshall owned an exclusive circulating library at 23 Milsom Street, which opened in 1787. Originally it was jointly owned by Marshall and Samuel Jackson Pratt, but by 1793 Marshall was the sole proprietor. The list of his subscribers read like an extended extract from *Who's Who*. Of royalty and nobility it included two princes (the prince of Wales and Frederick, prince of Orange), five dukes, four duchesses, seven earls, fourteen countesses, and forty-three knights; professional customers numbered three admirals, four generals, twenty-six majors, and seventy-one captains; and ecclesiastics included one archbishop, six bishops, and 114 clerics.

Marshall's library flourished between 1793 and 1799, but the rise in the price of books—up to 100 per cent—was a serious threat to the business in general. Marshall increased his rates by 25 per cent, but ultimately, following a decline in the number of his subscribers, he could not save himself from being declared bankrupt in 1800. His son, probably Charles Henry, joined him that year and together they managed to revive the library, stocking up to 25,000 books, until it was bought by Henry Godwin in 1808.

1804: 1 Jan: *Called on Mr. Marshall, walked with Miss Upton, & with my mother & George visited Lady Francis Flood & the Leyards.* 9 Jan: *In the Evening first at a party at Mr. Marshall's where I did not stay sufficiently to decide on the dullness or agreeableness of it.* 10 Jan: *In the Evening to Glocester House Ball taking down Miss Jane Marshall & H. Port.* 22 Jan: *Walked with the Marriotts, & Miles's, Marshal etc.*

MARSHALL — Chapman Marshall[71]

Sir Chapman Marshall (1788-1862), lord mayor of London, was born at Peterborough, the only son of Anthony Marshall. He established a wholesale grocery business at 179 Upper Thames Street, London. As a tory he was sheriff in 1830, alderman for the ward of Bridge Within in 1832-59, and lord mayor in 1839-40. He was also a member of the Haberdashers' Company. Marshall was knighted at St James's Palace on 9 March 1831.

1847: 13 Aug: *At 4 P.M. we started homeward from the Peterborough Station, travelling in the same carriage with a communicative Alderman of London, Sir Chapman Marshall.*

MARSHALL — Charles Marshall[72]

Charles Marshall (±1775-1854), farmer and steward, was born at Sedgeberrow, Worcestershire, and lived at Snowshill, where he farmed 747 acres, employing twenty-five labourers. His married Susanna Mary (±1777-1851); they had at least 3 sons and 4 daughters:

1 Charles (±1798-1854); *see below*
2 John (b. ±1799-1857); educated at Worcester College, Oxford (BA 1825; MA 1827); *see below*
1 Susanna (1803-1851)
3 Russell William Richard (1807-1841)
2 Letitia Durham (1807-1851)
3 Ann (1813-1841)
4 Lucretia (1818-1881)

1823: 25 Jul: *Mr. C. Marshall of Snowshill, a respectable farmer of the higher class, and Steward of Lord Wemyss, dined with us.*

1824: 27 Sep: *I dined and slept at Lady Elcho's; meeting, besides my mother and Miss Church, Genl. & Mrs. Fuller, Mr. C. Keysall, Mr. F. Aston & Mr. Marshall, Lord Wemyss's Steward.*

1825: 15 Mar: *Besides her, Mr. & Mrs. S. Gist were added to the dinner party, with Mr. W. Gist: as also Mr. Marshall & his daughter, and F. Aston.* 16 Mar., 25 May: *From Broadway I followed the beautiful valley below Middle Hill, & crept up to the retired Village of Snowshill, perched near the summit of a ridge sloping from the Cotswold into the vale: a romantic little place. There is a good old fashioned Mansion house, where Mr. C. Marshall, Lord Wemyss's Steward, resides.*

1826: 13 Apr: *Mr. Marshall of Snowshill, and his son dined with Lady Elcho. The latter is recently ordained, having been educated at Worcester College, Oxford, and is one of Mr. Stafford Smith's Curates, doing the duty at the Chapelries annexed to the living of Fladbury.* 27 Jun.

1834: 15 Jul: *His Lordship gone out with his Steward, Mr. Marshall, to view some part of the estates.*

1835: 27 Feb: *My Son rode to Snowshill to carry to Mr. Marshall, the steward of the Stanway property a letter from Mr. Stewart addressed to him by mistake at Upper Slaughter.* 3 Mar: *Mr. Marshall Junr., by the desire of his Father, called to consult me about some of the details of the funeral of Lady Elcho.*

1836: 26 Jul: *He appears highly pleased with the state of his Gloucestershire property, and the management of his Steward, Mr. C. Marshall.*

1837: 28 Feb., 17 Jul.

1839: 9 Jul: *I had recommended my son to consult Mr C. Marshall, Lord Wemyss's steward, as to the difference in value between produce sold to be consumed on or off the premises.*

1840: 18 Jul: *To the Mansion House to call on the Earl of Wemyss and family. Met with his Lordship on the point of riding out with his steward, Mr. C. Marshall, to look at his plantations and improvements.*

1842: 22 Feb: *I wrote to C Bathurst in answer to his letter recd. yesterday, and to Mr. Marshall, Snowshill, requesting him to procure me information respecting the unfortunate lunatic believed to be improperly confined at Stanton.* 25-26 Feb., 1-2 Mar., 10-12 Mar., 18 Mar., 16 Jul.

1846: 27 Oct., 30 Oct: *Letter from Mr. Marshall, Snowshill, in answer to my note to him as to Elias Jones; he declines interfering in his favour.*

MARSHALL — Charles Marshall[73]

Charles Marshall (±1798-1854), farmer, was born at Broadway, Worcestershire, son of Charles Marshall (*above*). He farmed 69 acres at Stanton, employing two labourers. He was married to Mary (b. ±1806), who was born at Manchester.

1835: 3 Mar: *Mr. Marshall Junr., by the desire of his Father, called to consult me about some of the details of the funeral of Lady Elcho.*

1839: 22 Feb: *Also as to a cottage for my Son's servant; on this subject, conferred with Mr. Cook, on whom I called, and met his son and Mr. Marshall of Stanton.*

1854: 2 Mar: *Charles Marshall of Stanton died yesterday morning; worn out; brain fever, says one report.*

MARSHALL — James Marshall[74]

James Marshall (1770-1832), cellist, was born at Olney, Buckinghamshire, and studied violin, cello, pianoforte, and the organ under an unnamed 'master' at Oxford. He gained the patronage of the earl of Dartmouth, and was sent to London to study under John Ashley, the assistant conductor at the Westminster Abbey meetings. At London Marshall learned to play the viola and double bass; he was engaged, through Ashley, to play double bass at the Abbey meeting in 1790. Ashley also helped Marshall secure engagements at provincial meetings, including one at Worcester.

Marshall lived at Worcester for about a year and then moved to Northampton, where he married Mary. After three and a half years he moved to Rugby, where he was appointed church organist, a post he held until 1801, when he was offered the position of organist at St Mary's in Warwick. Marshall remained at Warwick, though he regularly attended the meetings of the three choirs—Gloucester, Hereford, and Worcester. He and Mary had 2 sons and 2 daughters, including:

1 Frederick (b. 1791)
1 Mary (b. 1801); born at Northampton
2 Jane (b. 1803); born at Rugby

The elder son, Frederick, became an organist and pianist. He was appointed organist of the chapel at Rugby School, and composed a number of hymns and preludes.

The diary entry for 9 March 1834 raises some doubt regarding this attribution; if not James Marshall, the 'Mr. Marshall' in question would appear to have been a brother of James.

1823: 17 Sep: *Mr. Cramer led the band, Marshall of Oxford was second Violin, the Lindleys on the Violoncello, Harper on the Trumpet, Willman on the Clarionet etc.... & such masters in execution as Cramer, Lindley, Marshall, Nicholson on the Flute, Willman on the Clarionet, Bochsa on the harp, it was impossible not to be delighted.*

1834: 9 Mar: *There is a small organ played by Mr. Marshall, Son of the late Violoncello performer at Warwick, & nephew of the able violinist of Oxford.*

MARSHALL — John Marshall[75]

John Marshall (±1799-1857), Church of England clergyman, was born at Broadway, Worcestershire, the second son of Charles Marshall (*above*). He was educated at Worcester College, Oxford (BA 1825; MA 1827), and was ordained deacon on 12 August 1821 and priest on 1 September 1822. Marshall's first clerical appointment was as curate of Lawhitton, Cornwall, from 1 September 1822. He was then perpetual curate of St Sidwell, Exeter, Devon, from 28 September 1825 to 27 November 1828. He was the final vicar of All Saints' with St Lawrence, Evesham, to which parish he was appointed on 18 August 1827. He was married to Fanny (±1808-1879); it is not known if they had any children.

1840: 27 Oct: *Several Clergy of my acquaintance were there, Billingsley accompanied by his wife, Mr. Malcolm of Toddington, and his son, who is curate of Wellesbourne in Warwickshire, Mr. Marshall of Evesham, Mr. John Eddy, Mr. Prosser of Moreton, Mr. Coyle of Blockley &c.*

MARSHALL — William Marshall[76]

William Marshall (±1774-1864), Church of England clergyman, was born at Totnes, Devon, son of William Marshall (b. 1737) and Dorothy Chadder (b. 1742). He was educated at Corpus Christi (BA 1795) and Balliol College, Oxford (MA 1797; BD 1807). He was a fellow of Balliol from 1797 to 1816, and proctor in 1806. Marshall was ordained deacon on 11 June 1797 and priest on 2 December 1798. His first clerical appointment was as curate of Putney, Middlesex, from 6 March 1801, and he appears to have been a curate at Bath Abbey at some point. He was rector of Chickerell, Dorset, from 18 December 1830 to his death in 1864. He married Isabella Caroline Clarke Perry Ogilvie (±1792-1833); they had at least 5 daughters:

1 Clementina (1819-1905); died unmarried
2 Caroline M. (b. 1820)
3 Emily Jane (1822-1895); died unmarried

4 Blanche (b. ±1825)
5 Isabella (b. 1827)

1806: 21 Mar: *A very large male Party to Cards & Supper at the Knights: I played three rubbers unsuccessfully; of the party were Stevens & his Wife, Matthias of B.N.C., Budd of C.C.C., Marsh, Marshall of Ball. Dr. Price, Michel, Simmons, Round, Dr. Cooper, Mr. Jebb, Mr. Davis &c.*

MARSHALL — William Marshall [77]

William Marshall (±1778-1847), Church of England clergyman, was born at Bath, Somerset, son of James Marshall (*above*). He was educated at Corpus Christi, Oxford (BA 1799; MA 1803), and was ordained deacon in 1801 and priest on 19 December 1802. His first clerical appointment was as curate of Chalton, Hampshire, from 1801, followed by the curacy of St Peter and St Paul, Bath (Bath Abbey), in 1803. It is unknown when he acquired the living at Weston Zoyland, but he died there in 1847. Marshall married, at Bath, 21 January 1808, Caroline (±1785-1831), youngest daughter of Benjamin Cole of Bath; they had at least 4 sons and 5 daughters:

1 Caroline (1809-1830)
2 Louisa (b. & d. 1810)
1 Peter Charles (1812-1864), Church of England clergyman; became curate of St John's, Weston, Bath
2 George Albert (b. 1814)
3 Stirling Frederic (b. 1816)
4 Henry James (1818-1881), Church of England clergyman; curate of Weston Zoyland, 1842-46; vicar of Weston Zoyland, 1846-54; married, at Bridgwater, 16 June 1846, Emma Lovell Sealy
3 Martha Maria (1819-1832)
4 Harriet Louisa (b. 1822)
5 Emily (b. 1826); married, at West Chickerell, Dorset, 11 December 1845, Stenning Johnson

---

1820: 23 Jan: *In the Evening, Mr. Marshall, Curate of the Abbey Church, preached.* 30 Jan: *Mr. Marshall, the Curate, going thro' the ordinary duty for Septuagesima Sunday.*
1826: 25 Sep.

MARSHAM — Robert Bullock Marsham [78]

Robert Bullock Marsham (1786-1880), barrister-at-law and warden of Merton College, was born at Thurnham, Kent, son of Jacob Marsham (1759-1840) and Amelia Frances Bullock (1762-1836). He was educated at Christ Church and Merton College, Oxford (BA 1814; MA 1814; DCL 1826), and Lincoln's Inn (1817). He was dean of Merton College in 1824, and warden of the college from 1826 to his death in 1880. Marsham married, at Edinburgh, 27 March 1828, Janet Dewar (1793-1881); they had 3 sons and 2 daughters:

1 Charles Jacob Bullock (1829-1901)
1 Mary Amelia Frances (1830-1861)
2 Jessie Elizabeth Bullock (1832-1922)
2 Robert Henry Bullock (1833-1913)
3 Cloudesley Dewar Bullock (1835-1915)

1829: 18 Feb: *On the part of Mr. Peel, the chairman of the Oxford Committee is Dr. Marsham, Warden of Merton, a Barrister, and a Commissioner of Charities.* 26 Feb: *Dr. Routh, nominated Sir R. H. Inglis, and Dr. Marsham, Warden of Merton College, Mr. Peel.*

MARSHAM — Thomas Cope Marsham [79]

Thomas Cope Marsham (1761-1818), Church of England clergyman, was born at Peterborough, son of Thomas and Eliza Marsham. He was educated at Eton College and King's College, Cambridge (BA 1784; MA 1787), where he was a scholar, and a fellow from 1783 to 1801. He was ordained deacon on 6 June 1784 and priest on 19 December 1784. Marsham's first clerical appointment was as vicar of Kew with Petersham, Surrey, from 13 March 1801 to his death. He was also curate of Bishop's Hatfield, Totteridge chapel (appointed 10 August 1803), and chaplain to the duke of York and the prince of Wales. He married, 21 October 1802, Penelope Judith, eldest daughter of Sir Alexander Maitland, 1st baronet.

Although Marsham was not appointed to Totteridge until 1803, it is clear from the diary entries that he had resided there and officiated at the church since an earlier date.

1801: 14 Jun: *Cold weather: went to Church, a small neat Chapel, where Mr. Marsham officiated, & where we saw many of the neighbouring Gentry.* 16 Jun., 20-23 Jun., 28-29 Jun.
1802: 10 Jan: *To Church in the forenoon, hearing a good Sermon from Mr. Marsham.* 17 Jan., 20 Jan: *Met here at dinner Mr. Lee, Mr. & Mrs. Pugett, Mrs Garrow & Mr. Marsham.* 23 Jan., 25 Jan: *Walked out & called on Mr. Marsham. Dined at Mr. Ellill's, our own party, & Mr. Marsham.* 26-27 Jan.
1803: 6 Oct: *Walked with my Father to Marsham's, whom with his Wife we found at home.* 7 Oct., 9 Oct., 16 Oct.

MARTER — Miss Marter at Bath

Miss Marter was a pupil of Gertrud Elisabeth Schmeling Mara (1749-1833).

1802: 6 Jan: *The Overture in Esther, a fine piece of Handel's was followed by a song by Mara's pupil Miss Marter, whose execution I cannot help thinking is far superior to her voice.*

MARTIN — Miss Martin at Clifton

1804: 21 Aug: *Miss Martin called.* 10 Sep: *Set out after an early breakfast, in two Sociables, & myself on horseback. Mrs. Honor & Miss Pigott, Mrs. Bates, my Father & Mother, Mrs. Parry Price, Miss Martin, Mr. C. & Mrs. C. & Mrs. Doyle.* 16 Sep: *Walked with my Father & Mother, Mrs. Bruston, Mrs. Lydiatt & Miss Martin.*

MARTIN — Messrs Martin, newsagents at 9 Cornhill

1834: 7 Mar: *My newspaper having failed, wrote to Martins, 9 Cornhill.*
1837: 23 Feb: *Wrote to Martin and Co. to complain that my London paper had not reached me yesterday.* 2-3 Mar. 11 Oct: *Recd. a letter from one Allnatt, stating himself to be a partner in the house of Martin & Co. which has supplied me with London newspapers for many years; and claiming an arrear of £12. 0. 10. alleged to be due by me on a balance of accounts: the fact being that I have punctually paid my bills yearly by a cheque on Hoare.* 14 Oct: *A letter from J B Allnatt in answer to mine of the 11th. Inst. giving me credit for the assertion that I had punctually paid the bills forwarded to me from the house of Martin & Co. and explaining that they have been robbed by a Clerk who intercepted the letters containing remittances, and applied the contents dishonestly.*
1838: 7 May.

MARTIN — Messrs Martin & Co., jewellers [80]

Martin, Basket & Martin, 4 Imperial Circus, Promenade.

1850: 18 Jul: From Messrs. Martin & Co. Jewellers, Cheltenham, a registered packet by the post, containing a mourning ring, which I had ordered in memory of my dear wife, to be worn by myself, in which a small lock of her hair is inserted. 24 Aug: Also from Messrs. Martin and Baskett, Cheltenham, a packet, containing my mourning ring with my poor wife's hair.

MARTIN — Mr Martin, a traveller to Messrs. Garaway & Co.

1852: 31 Dec: *Wrote to Mr. Martin, traveller to Messrs. Garaway & Co. with a cheque on the Gloucestershire Bankg. Co. at Stow, for £1. 8. 6 - the amount of my bill.*

1853: 7 Jan.

MARTIN — Charles Herbert Martin [81]

Charles Herbert Martin (1794-1865), Church of England clergyman, was born at Chester, son of Lt-Col Charles Martin (1759-1827) and Elizabeth Williams (d. 1854), daughter of Solomon Williams of Dublin. He was the grandson of Joseph Martin (±1725-1776), banker of Lombard Street and MP for Tewkesbury, and Eleanor, daughter of Sir John Torriano. He was educated at Exeter College, Oxford (BA 1817; MA 1820), and was ordained deacon on 25 January 1818 and priest on 25 April 1819. Martin's first clerical appointment was as assistant curate of St John the Baptist, Gloucester, from 25 January 1818. He was then appointed as curate for Whimple, Devon, on 14 November 1819. He became rector of both St Martin's, Exeter, and Winkleigh, Devon, from 18 June 1825 to 13 October 1827. He became perpetual curate of Maisemore, Gloucestershire, on 30 July 1829.

Martin married, first, at Rockbeare, Devon, 29 December 1818, Eliza Porter (1795-1845), second daughter of William Sloane of Tobago; they had 1 son and 3 daughters:

1 Henrietta Ann Bidgood (1820-1855); married, 3 August 1843, Samuel White Baker, eldest son of Samuel Baker of Lypiatt Park, Gloucestershire
2 Eliza Heberden (b. 1825); married, 3 August 1843, John Garland Baker, second son of the aforesaid Samuel Baker
1 Charles (b. 1825)
3 Charlotte Louisa (b. 1831)

Martin married secondly, at Glandford Brigg, Lincolnshire, April 1849, Frances Anne Goodwin (b. 1821); they had 1 daughter:

1 Gertrude (b. 1861)

1834: 15 Oct: *The Bishop and Mrs. Monk very courteous .... and Mr. Martin and his wife; he being the incumbent of Maisemore.*

1837: 7 Mar.

MARTIN — Humphrey Martin — *see also* Samuel Favell [82]

Humphrey Martin (1771-1810), merchant, was born in Prince Rupert's Land, Canada (probably at Fort Albany in what is now Cochrane District, Ontario), the illegitimate son of John Favell (1740-1784). His father had been born in Southwark in or just before 1740, and emigrated to Canada in 1754 at the age of 14 or 15. Samuel Favell (1760-1830) was John's younger brother and Humphrey Martin's uncle. In about 1769 John entered into a form of marriage with an Indian woman named Titameg [Whitefish in English], a member of the Swampy Cree nation. Although she was known as Favell's 'Country Wife', their relationship cannot be classified as a marriage according to English law. John and Titameg had 2 sons and 2 daughters—Jane, Humphrey Martin, Mary, and Thomas; unlike Samuel's children who died without issue, there are many descendants of John and Titameg's children in Canada today.

On 22 August 1775 John Favell wrote to the governor of the Hudson Bay Company: 'I have a son in this Country, which as is natural for a Parent, I am solicitous to [have] him brought up in a virtuous manner. He is now of a proper Age to receive any Instructions, and I would be infinitely obliged to your Honours to permit the Captain to receive him on board your ship next year.' This request seems to have been granted, for Favell wrote again on 8 September 1776: 'I return Thanks for the notice taken of my request concerning the child, but should it seem pleasing to you, should be extremely glad if my request was Complied with before my return to England, on Account of his Age, he being now above 4 years Old, and I could sincerely wish (as is my Duty) to have him in England where he might be well educated.' John Favell died on 2 November 1784. He left a will in which he made provision for his Indian wife and his 'four natural children'.

Humphrey Martin was named after a factor of the Hudson Bay Company who was with John Favell at Moose Fort and Albany Fort. The two men, John and Humphrey Martin, seem to have been posted at the same fort at the time of Humphrey's birth in 1771. Humphrey married Jenny Jane, née Pawpitch (b. ±1773), daughter of Questach Cree and an unknown mother; they had 3 sons and 3 daughters:

1 Thomas (± 1790)
2 Humphrey (±1794-1850)
1 Mary (1795-1876)
3 John (b. ±1800)
2 Nancy (b. ±1808)
3 Harriet Charlotte (b. ±1810); born at Fort Garry, Red River Settlement, Manitoba

Interestingly all of the children and their descendants carried the surname Favell [or Favel] and not Martin.

1801: 27 Jul: *Mrs. Favell, Mr. Martin an American, the Revd. Mr. Winter with his wife & Daughter & the two gentlemen dined with us.*

MARTIN — Mr Martin — James Martin [?] — at Weimar [83]

Mr Martin has proved to be enigmatic. He was introduced to Edward and Agnes Witts in Hamburg by Mr J. Blair on 22 August 1798. Whether Mr Blair was a new acquaintance of the Wittses in Hamburg or one of the Edinburgh Blairs is not clear, but the latter seems most likely. Agnes Witts initially referred to him as Mr Blair (22-23 & 25-26 August), before switching to call him Mr Hunter on 27 August and thereafter. She was almost certainly referring to the same man. It can hardly have been a coincidence that, on 24 August, Agnes wrote a letter to her friend, Lady Hunter-Blair—probably to say that she had fallen into company with her ladyship's son on her journey south.

Lady Hunter-Blair had eight sons, but three had already died by 1798. Out of the five survivors, only one had an initial 'J'; this was James Hunter-Blair (±1780-1822), MP and army officer, of Dunskey and Robertland. He was the third son of Sir James Hunter-Blair, 1st baronet of Dunskey, and Jane, daughter and heiress of John Blair of Dunskey. He succeeded his father to the maternal estate of Dunskey and Robertland in 1787. He was MP for Wigtownshire from 1816 to 1822 and died unmarried, ranked lieutenant-colonel, in 1822. His obituary in the *Gentleman's* Magazine stated that he 'spoke with fluency the French, Italian and German languages'.

There is no firm evidence to account for the identity of Mr Martin, but certain assumptions can be made about him. It seems likely that he was at M. Mounier's Academy at the Belvedere, Weimar. It may further be assumed that he was roughly the same age as his friend James Hunter-Blair (b. ±1780), and that they had been at school together. This would make him about two or three years older than Francis Witts. Mr Martin was mentioned very frequently in the diaries of Agnes Witts from 22 August 1798 to 8 March 1799; he was often accompanied by 'Mr Hunter', and the two were usually referred to as 'our young friends'. On 8 March Messrs Hunter and Martin left Weimar: 'At 5 o'clock in the afternoon Mess[rs.] Hunter & Martin came to take their leave being going away the next Day.' Mr Martin returned to Weimar on 13 October 1799, but after November he was no longer mentioned in either the diaries of Agnes or Francis Witts. The frequent mentions in Agnes Witts's diaries are not recorded here; the index entries below relate solely to Francis Witts.

Taking into account all that is known, it is possible that this Mr Martin was James Martin (1778-1870), third son of James Martin (1738-1810) of the banking family of Overbury Court, Worcestershire, and Lombard Street, London. He married, 20 September 1819, Julia Vignoles (1792-1866) of Portarlington, Queen's County, Ireland. The Martins became very friendly with Elizabeth Moulton-Barrett [Elizabeth Barrett Barrett] (1806-1861), who became, in 1846, Elizabeth Barrett Browning. Their Hertfordshire estate, Old Colwall, adjoined the Hope End estate of the Moulton-Barret family, and their house was about three-quarters of a mile from that of the Moulton-Barretts as the crow flies, and 1½ miles by road. Elizabeth Moulton-Barrett reported that Mr Martin had once said his house was 'built for posterity'; it is still standing.

There was a close neighbourly connection between the Moulton-Barretts and the Martins. Julia Martin was a longterm friend and correspondent of Elizabeth Moulton-Barrett [Barrett Browning]. However, during the Hope End years, Elizabeth was in two minds about the Martins. They, like most other people in the locality, failed to satisfy her yearning for intellectual companionship. She wrote in her diary (p. 51): 'They have not the key of my mind. They are superior & feeling people; and yet I can neither think nor feel aloud when they are present.' She also wrote (p. 74): 'How very very odd it is, that Mrs Martin, who, I think, likes me, & I, who, I am sure, like Mrs Martin, should be oil & water together.' On two other occasions (pp. 57 and 120 of her diary), Elizabeth wrote that she and Mrs Martin didn't 'amalgamate'. Despite these reservations, after the Moulton-Barretts' removal from Hope End in 1832, a correspondence sprang up between Elizabeth and Mrs Martin that did not end until Elizabeth's death in 1861. Her diary included frequent mention of visits back and forth, of her husband going shooting with Mr Martin (pp. 142 and 166), and of Martin's playing cricket at Hope End (p. 51). He and Elizabeth were on close terms, and she enjoyed talking with him on various subjects, including Lord Byron (p. 39) and 'the pleasure of writing letters' (p. 139). She mentioned him breakfasting at Hope End (p. 75) and of him reading from 'his journal in & out of Africa' (p. 74) during a visit by the younger Moulton-Barretts to Old Colwall. It is possible that James Martin had travelled to Africa as an extension of his European travels; this also lends credence to a connection between himself and James Hunter-Blair.

1798: 27 Aug: *The Doubts, which from the Information we obtained at Hamburgh relative to the Town which should be our Winter Quarters and terminate our first Journey were settled by an Introduction to Mr. Martin a Gentleman who had resided some time in Weimar, and whose Opinion with Respect to that Town decided our Choice. The Advantage also of our Accompanying Mr. Martin on his Return who well understood the Mode of Travelling and the German Language were great Encouragements to us who were so compleatly Novices in these Points.*

1799: 6 Nov: *Very cold. walked in the Morning. with Martin. at my usual Business.* 18 Nov: *Maj Seckendorff & Martin.—to Mr. Schmids at my usual Employments.* 19 Nov: *A Charming clear fine day: walked in the Gardens with Martin.* 10 Dec: *called on Messrs. Martin and Lawrence.*

MARTIN — John Martin — *see also* Mr Martin at Weimar[84]

John Martin (1774-1832), banker, was born at Ledbury, Herefordshire, the eldest son of James Martin (1738-1810) and Penelope (1740-1830), daughter of John Skipp. His brother was James Martin (1778-1870). He was the chief beneficiary of his father's considerable estate; his share included the title to the banking house at 68 Lombard Street, known as the 'Grasshopper'. John Martin joined his father in partnership in the 1790s after an apprenticeship at the Grasshopper. On his father's retirement in 1807 he became the bank's senior partner, a position he held until 1830. He was MP for Tewkesbury in 1812-32, and successfully steered the bank through the financial crisis of 1825-26.

John Martin married, 1803, Frances (1770-1862), daughter of Richard Stone, a partner in the Grasshopper; they had 5 sons and 3 daughters, including:

1 John (1805-1880), MP for Tewkesbury (1832-34 & 1837-59); married, 1837, Mary Morse (d. 1843); became a partner in Martin, Stone, and Co., a director of the Guardian Assurance Co., and an East India stock proprietor
2 James (1807-1878)
3 Robert (1808-1897)

All three sons listed above became partners in the Grasshopper, ensuring a close family connection with the bank as it progressed into the later nineteenth century. John Martin lived in Lombard Street and Downing Street, before moving to Camden Place, Chislehurst, in Kent.

1823: 12 Oct: *Mr. Martin of Overbury is the other representative. He calls himself a Whig.*
1835: 4 Jan., 6 Jan.
1837: 26 Jul.

MARTIN — John Martin[85]

John Martin (1789-1854), artist, was born at East Land Ends, Haydon Bridge, Northumberland, the thirteenth and youngest child of William Fenwick Martin and Isabella, daughter of Richard Thompson of Lowland's End, Haydon Bridge. Only five of William and Isabella's children, one of them a daughter, survived childhood. William held several occupations, including publican, coach builder, fencing master, and tanner. His son John was apprenticed to a coach-painter in Newcastle-upon-Tyne, but moved to London in 1805 and made a living painting china and glass. In 1809 he married Susan Garnett.

John Martin first exhibited at the Royal Academy in 1811. His painting, *The Fall of Babylon*, exhibited in 1819 at the British Institution, was a panorama reduced to respectable proportions. Cycloramic in its vasty architecture and wide horizons, it shows diminutive troops swarming past the Tower of Babel and across the Euphrates to the ramparts and hanging gardens of the palace where the impious Belshazzar reigns. Later, in *Belshazzar's Feast*, 1820, panic sets in as God's writing flares on the wall of the immense banqueting hall. This sequel won Martin a £200 premium at the Royal Academy exhibition of 1821.

1825: 5 Aug: *I took the opportunity of seeing a picture, which is now exhibiting at Cheltenham. The name of the Artist is Mr. J. Martin, and it was rewarded by the directors of the Royal Institution for the encouragement of painting with their highest prize some few years since. The subject is Belshazzar's feast; a subject, worthily handled by the poet Milman, and poetically painted by the present artist.*

MARTIN — John Martin [86]

John Martin (1816-1891), Church of England clergyman, was born at Saffron Walden, Essex, the second son of John Letch Martin, DL for Essex (appointed 1814), and Mary Anne Elizabeth. He was educated at Sidney College, Cambridge (BA 1839; MA 1842). His first clerical appointment was as curate of Dursley, Gloucestershire, from 1839. Martin was later curate of Dawlish, Devon, from 1855 to 1858, and vicar of St Andrew-the-Great, Cambridge, from 1858 to 1885. He married, 1842[?], Sarah Jane Rodd, born at St Just, Cornwall; they had at least 1 daughter:

1 Mary Ellen Rodd (b. ±1857); born at Dawlish

This attribution is not certain, but it is the only Martin that fits. It seems logical that he could have remained in the diocese of Gloucester after leaving Dursley. It also seems likely that after leaving Dursley he entered into numerous relatively short-term curacies before settling at Dawlish for three years, where his daughter was born. He appears to have left Rissington in 1843.

1842: 5 Feb: *Rode to Stow: left my card at the lodgings of Messrs. Martin and Debary, Curates of Wick Risington, and Icomb, on whom I had not yet called: they were from home.* 8 Feb: *Messrs. Martin and Debary, the two young Clergymen on whom I lately called, returned the Compliment: they appear well conducted men; Mr. Martin the older and more prepossessing of the two.* 10 Mar., 20 Apr., 27 Apr., 26 May: *Wrote notes of invitation to Messrs. Martin, Debary, Underwood &c.* 1 Jun: *A dinner party: our Guests being Mr. & Mrs. Perkins, Mr. Underwood (Curate of Broadwell,) Mr. Martin (Wick R.) Mr. Debary (Icomb)—Mr. Aitkens (Bourton) with his Father, a lame, gouty-looking old Gentleman, Incumbent of Hanley, one of the Overgrown parishes in the Staffordshire Potteries.* 7 Jul., 15 Jul: *Walked with Wellford to Wick Risington, and called on Mrs. Martin, whom we found at home.* 6 Aug: *A kind note from Mr. J. Martin, Wick Risington, who had heard of my Mother-in-Law's serious illness, and offered to assist me in the duties of to-morrow.* 11 Aug: *I left the Guardians before the relief lists were gone through to join the Magistrates at the Unicorn Inn, where met Mr. Pole, Mr. Ford, Mr. R. Waller, Mr. L. Pole, Mr. W B Pole, Mr. Lindow, Mr. J. Martin.* 16 Aug., 20 Aug: *Mr. C. Pole called, also Mr. Martin.* 23 Aug., 31 Aug., 27 Sep., 28 Dec.

1843: 26 Jan., 28 Jan., 8 Feb: *Wrote to invite Mr. Martin to join a party at dinner here on Wednesday next.* 9 Feb., 15 Feb.

MARTIN — John Williams Martin [87]

John Williams Martin (1795-1859), JP and landed proprietor, was born at Chester, son of Charles Martin (1759-1827) and Elizabeth Williams (1770-1854), who was born in Dublin. He married, first, at Upton-on-Severn, Worcestershire, 14 April 1817, Jane Clarke (d. 1839); and secondly, at Ashchurch, Gloucestershire, 17 July 1841, Sophia Bashford Whitehouse (1809-1887), who was born at Liverpool. John and Sophia had 1 son:

1 Charles Stanhope (1845-1886)

Martin owned considerable property in the area, including Fleet Farm and Freemans Court, and had other property interests in Worcestershire and London. He lived at Showberrow House, Twyning, Gloucestershire, and was a JP for Gloucestershire and Worcestershire. He lived with his wife Sophia, his son Charles Stanhope, and his mother Elizabeth.

In 1828 a complex legal case was determined in chancery—'Farmer *v.* Martin'—in which John Williams Martin and Sir Anthony Lechmere were named as potential beneficiaries, but the relationship between these families has not been explored.

1837: 27 Jun: *In the course of the day, I was in communication with many old friends and acquaintance, Dr. Cook, Dr. Timbrill, Ford, Crawley, Cooper, Baker, Waller, J. W. Martin, Codrington, Hale, Purnell, Goodrich, Playne &c.*

1839: 9 Apr: *Of those present I will name, Purnell, R. B. Cooper, Lawrence, Hon. G. C. Talbot, Ford, Price, Dr. Timbrill, Dean of Gloucester, Hale, Dr. Davies, J. W. Martin, Mirehouse, Viner, Hicks, Clifford, Sayers, Davies, R Waller &c.*

1845: 15 Apr.

1846: 2 Jul.

1847: 16 Mar: *at the railroad Station met and parleyed with J W Martin &c.*

1848: 31 Mar: *walked about with Lefroy and J. W. Martin.*

MARTIN — Richard Martin [88]

Richard Martin (1754-1834) was MP for co. Galway, 1801-12 and 1818-27.

1801: *Mr. Grey appeared by far the greatest orator on the opposition side: the other speakers, were, Mr. Martin, Horne Tooke, Tinney, W. Smith, Sir F. Jones Burdett, Dr. Lawrence, & Mr. Whitbread.*

MASON — Mr Mason, curate at South Cerney

It is unusual not to find information on a clergyman, especially when so many curacies are known, but this curate has proven to be an exception. There are many of the name 'Mason' among the Cambridge and Oxford alumni, but no one stands out to match this individual.

1850: 18 Jun: *The only addition to the party was Mr. Mason, Mr. Ford's Curate at South Cerney, a gentlemanlike person, who had been curate of Dr. Card at Malvern, to Mr. Powell at Cirencester, and, I believe, Mr. Snow at Bibury: he is also a traveller, having visited Syria and Jerusalem &c.—a gentlemanly, well informed man.* 20 Jun., 31 Jul.,

MASON — Mrs Mason and daughters, relations and guests of the Howells at West Eaton Place

1851: 22 May: *The dinner party was large, the entertainment handsome, and conversation, varied and cheerful. Music, instrumental and vocal, in the Evening.—The guests were Mrs. and two Misses Mason, relations of the Howells, visitors.*

MASON — George Henry Mason of Gloucester [89]

George Henry Mason (±1758-1837), army officer (HEIC), was a captain in the 102nd Foot (Royal Madras Fusiliers), raised by the East India Company. He was promoted to major in 1795 and lieutenant-colonel in 1801. In 1789, Mason travelled to Canton, one of only two cities in China that outsiders could legally visit at the time; he later relished providing 'partial instruction and general amusement' about an 'exotic' foreign land to a fascinated but parochial audience of armchair tourists in England. He wrote two influential works, *The Costume of China* (1800) and *The*

Punishments of China (1801). Mason was married to Susannah Jones [?] (1767-1830).

1823: 20 Feb: *A party and music at Col. Mason's.*

MASON — George Henry Mason [90]

George Henry Mason (±1800-1880), governor of Gloucester Prison and colonel of the South Gloucestershire Militia (8th Gloucestershire Militia), was born at Newnham-on-Severn, Gloucestershire, son of George Henry Mason (1755-1837) (*above*) and Susannah Jones [?] (1767-1830). He married, at St Mary de Lode's, Gloucester, 25 September 1833, Mary (±1811-1851), of Barnwood, Gloucester, born at Felton, Herefordshire, third daughter of Henry Apperley of Hereford; they had at least 3 sons and 7 daughters:

1 Mary Ann Adeline Apperley (±1834-1918)
2 Henrietta Louisa (±1836-1913)
1 George Henry (b. ±1837)
3 Hebe (b. ±1838)
4 Frances Emily (1840-1910)
5 Edith Caroline (b. 1841)
2 Herbert Apperley (b. ±1842)
6 Alice (b. ± 1844)
3 Richard Bingham (b. ±1846)
7 Florence (b. ±1847)

George Mason was appointed governor of Gloucester Prison on 26 September 1836, with a salary of £400. Francis Witts did not like Mason and was against his appointment from the outset. During 1847 there were attempts to oust him which failed; thereafter Witts was somewhat silent on the subject of the governor.

1836: 10 Aug: I *found from Bathurst, Goodrich and others, that on deliberation yesterday and mature consideration of the Testimonials of the different Candidates for the Governorship of the Goal, it had been deemed advisable ... to oppose Mason.* 12 Aug: *Passed a couple of hours very agreeably in conversation with [Hyett] and Howell, on the proceedings at Gloucester relative to the appointment of a Governor of the Gaol, when it appeared that Hyett, had his health allowed him to attend, would have voted against Mason, on principle, on a suit for defamation likely to be tried at the Assizes.* 27 Aug: *On my road to Stow found a letter from Bathurst respecting the appointment of a Gaoler. It appears that Capt. Rowan is disposed to withdraw from the contest on the plea that he is unwilling to stand in the way of a gentleman connected with the County who has a family, and to whom the income of the place is a matter of much importance ... there are many Mag. very desirous of appointing an experienced officer in contradistinction to Mason, an untried man.* 6 Sep., 13 Sep: *Mason, then, was vigorously supported.*

1837: 26 Jun: *The Sheriff examined a host of witnesses, and the general bearing of the evidence certainly is that the Executioner did not show any indecent levity or coarseness, but performed his duties in the ordinary manner, soberly, actively & properly: at the same time to several present within the walls of the Prison his actions conveyed a different impression; and, particularly, to the Governor, Mason, whose hasty and incautious comments to a friend oozing out in conversation led to the wide dissemination of his evidently erroneous impressions.*

1842: 13 May: *Desired Mason to confer on the subject with the Visiting Magistrates and Surgeon, and to report to me the result.* 10 Jun: *Wrote to H Mason requesting a reply to the letter I had written to him on May 13. the parties having again applied to me on the subject.* 15 Jun: *A letter from H. Mason in answer to mine of the 10th. Inst. signifying that the Visiting Mag. of Gloucester Gaol do not consider the case of Campion one to be recommended to the Secretary of State for remission of the remaining term of his imprisonment.* 27 Jun.

1843: 16 Oct., 1 Dec: *To the Shire Hall, where was subsequently joined by P B Purnell, his Father, J C Hayward, Mr. Crawley Boevey, Mr. Sayers, members of the Prison rules and Gaol Committee; also Mr. Fuljames, the County Surveyor, Mr. Riddiford from the office of the Clerk of the Peace, Mr. Mason, the Governor; and Mr. R Cooper, the Chaplain of the Gaol — deliberated till nearly three o'clock, on various points referred to us by the last Sessions, examined and went over the plans and estimates of enlargement at the Gaol and Bridewells, and agreed to a report to be presented at the Epiphany Sessions.*

1844: 1 Jan., 22 Feb., 8 Apr: *A very full, and sometimes noisy and eager, but not contentious discussion took place, and the proposed arrangements were fully examined and agreed upon, to be submitted to the Court to-morrow — Messrs. Fulljames, Mason, and Riddiford were in attendance.* 10 Apr., 25 Apr., 10 Oct: *A letter from Mr. Mason, Govr. Gloucester Gaol, intimating that my attendance at the Gaol on the 11th. Oct. at a meeting of the Board of Vis. Justices, was not considered necessary.* 14 Oct., 29 Oct., 2 Nov.

1847: 23 Mar: *left the Court between three and four P.M. and before another case came on of much interest — a charge against the Clerk and deputy Governor of the County Prison, who had charged the Governor with a total disobedience of the rules laid down for the management of the prison, speaking of them as dead letter & not to be regarded &c.... The result of Moore's probable dismissal is utter confusion in the Prison Management, and the full exposure of Mason's incompetency.* 18 May: *From the speeches made by the Chairman, Curtis Hayward, and myself Capt. Sinclair inferred that we considered the Governor, Mason, incompetent; and this seemed in certain quarters to give great offence.* 29 May: *Mr. Mason hesitated as to nominating a Deputy Governor to-day, saying that he did not consider Jeens as yet sufficiently acquainted with the duties of the place, but fully expected he would in time be fit for it: but, being pressed, he did nominate Jeens.* 28 Jun: *A very important meeting of the Visiting Justices of the Gaol ... who determined on a report to be made to the Quarter Sessions to-morrow, embodying the views and resolutions entertained by the Board of Visiting Justices on May 29. with but little change, which we to-day communicated to the Governor, Mason, and his Clerk, Jeens.* 29 Jun: *Mr. Prowse Jones (Uncle of Mason, the Governor) commenced a fierce attack upon the County Chairman, second Chairman, and myself, on the ground that we, backed by the board of Visitors, were prejudiced against the Governor.*

1852: 13 Mar: *A letter from C Bathurst as to the Subscription raised to relieve Mr. Mason, the Governor of the County Prison, from pressing pecuniary difficulties.* 20 Mar: *Also a letter from C. Bathurst, asking me to write to Mr. Mullings to beg him to subscribe to the fund now being raised to relieve Mason the Governor of Gloucester Gaol.*

1853: 16-17 Mar.

MASON — George Mason [91]

George Mason (1800-1876) was a farmer and farm bailiff. This attribution is tentative, but a George Mason was born at Stow-on-the-Wold, son of William and Elizabeth Mason. He married Mary (b. ±1792), and secondly, Ann (b. ±1823), who was born at Lacock, Wiltshire.

1852: 8 Apr: *With Mr. Davis and Mr. Mason, as Guardians & Members of the House Committee, inspected the boys yard.*

1853: 23 Mar., 16 Apr: *Other Guardians who met Mr. J.S. were Mr. Wilkins, Mr. J Pegler, Mr. Johnson and Mr. Mason.* 15 Dec.

MASON — James Mason, Oliver Mason, and the Mason family of Great Malvern[92]

The Mason family inherited the Grange estate, which comprised the former monastic land south of the Priory gatehouse at Great Malvern. The property owned by James Mason was sold in 1846, following his death. It included his house, known as The Grange, 'Spa Villa', and the Chalybeate spring. Also included was the adjacent Swan Pool and 180 acres of land in South Field. In *Pigot's Directory* for 1835, James Mason is not mentioned, but among the gentry was Oliver Mason, presumably James's son; it was Oliver who oversaw the land and property sale of 1846.

1833: 11 Sep: *Accompanied Mrs. Backhouse to Malvern in Capt. Witts's open carriage—he drove—not much incommoded by the rain—while Mrs. B. called on some Gloucester acquaintance now at Malvern, John & I strolled to the Chalybeate Spa and Pump room, where we took shelter during a heavy shower. A pretty public garden and promenade of moderate size—the property of a Mr. Mason, who is building two or three villas on his ground adjoining in the Tudor style.*

1840: 24 Apr: *The Carriages were, I believe, those of the Countess of Haddington, a dowager lady resident at Malvern, Sir A. Lechmere, Mrs J. Walker, Mr. Essington, Mr. Woodyares, Revd.—Biddulph, Mr. Allen (of the Rhydd), Mrs. Stratton (widow of Geo. Fred. Stratton, now residing at Barnards Green) Mr. Mason's, Col. Parker's, Miss Mosleys', and perhaps one or two more.* 22 May: *Wrote a note to the Misses Daniell, who are expected from their cousins at Bullingham, where they have been sojourning since they left Peach Field Lodge, on a visit of a few days to Mr. and Mrs. Mason at the Priory, Great Malvern.* 29 May: *A letter from Miss S. Daniell from Bullingham Court, which the sisters leave for Malvern on Monday next, and propose passing three or four days with Mr. & Mrs. Mason there.* 3 Jun.

MASSEY — Hugh Dillon Massey — *see also* Hankey[93]

Sir Hugh Dillon Massey, 2nd baronet (1767-1842), MP and landed proprietor, was the eldest son of Sir Hugh Massey, 1st baronet (d. 1807), and Elizabeth, daughter of George Stacpoole of Annagh, co. Clare. He was educated at Trinity College, Dublin. In 1797 he was elected to the Irish House of Commons as MP for Clare, and sat for the seat until its abolition under the Acts of Union 1800. He was returned to the House of Commons of the United Kingdom as the MP for Clare in 1801, but lost his seat in the general election of 1802. On 29 April 1807 he succeeded to his father's baronetcy.

Massey married, 14 May 1796, Sarah (1778-1858), daughter of Thomas Hankey (1740-1793), banker, of Fetcham Park, Surrey, and Mary Wyver; they had at least 2 daughters:

1 Susannah (1816-1861)
2 Charlotte Elizabeth

1804: 16 Jul: *The little Masseys dined with us.* 24 Jul: *Called on Mrs. Massey. Walked with Hankey.* 26 Jul: *Mrs. Massey gave Tea & supper.* 27-29 Jul., 31 Jul., 1 Aug: *to Ashton for Raspberries & Cream ending in a supper at Mrs. Massey's, consisting of Mrs. Massey, the Rawsons, Miss Monck, Miss Fortescue, Adm. & Col. Jones, Hankey & myself.* 2-4 Aug., 7-12 Aug., 14 Aug., 16 Aug., 20 Aug., 25 Aug: *Passed the rest of the Even. tete a tete with Mrs. Massey.* 1 Sep: *Walked with my Father & Mother & C. Massey & Miss Upton before dinner.* 4 Sep: *On the Downs, at the Brigade & Miller's & Sweet's with my Father & Mother, Mrs. Massey, S. Monck, Mr. Harford &c. very pleasant.* 10 Sep., 22 Sep: *& late joined a party at Mrs. Massey's.* 30 Sep., 1 Oct: *With Mrs. Massey at Bristol for nearly five hours.* 2-3 Oct., 14 Oct.

MASSIE — Edward Massie[94]

Edward Massie (1805-1893), Church of England clergyman, was born at Chester, the ninth son of Revd Richard Massie (1771-1854) and Hester Lee, daughter of Edward Venables Townshend of Wincham Hall, Cheshire. His father, Richard, was the only son of Thomas Massie, of Coddington, Cheshire, and Elizabeth, daughter of Nathaniel Marriot of Cheshunt, Hertfordshire. Richard and Hester had a total of twenty-two children, eighteen of whom survived to maturity.

Massie was educated at Magdalene Hall, Cambridge, and then Wadham College, Oxford (BA 1830; MA 1834), where he was a fellow and chaplain from 1840 to 1845. He was also a fellow and tutor of University College, Durham, from 1841 to 1845. He married, at Macclesfield, 1845, Sophia (b. ±1806), daughter of Revd Charles Thornycroft of Thornycroft Hall, Cheshire.

In 1851 Massie was curate of Gawsworth, Cheshire, where he lived with his wife, Sophia. By 1881 he was a widower living at Nutwood, East Broughton, Lancashire, with his niece Henrietta, who acted as his housekeeper. He was listed in the census as 'clergyman without a cure'.

1840: 28 Jun: *The bequest made to him by his aunt Lyttelton enables him to take this indulgence, and by an arrangement with Mr. Cockey he has secured assistance in his clerical duties of a satisfactory kind. Mr. Massie of Wadham College, who has distinguished himself as a scholar, will reside at the Vicarage, with two pupils, who are reading with him preparatory to examination for their degrees.* 18-19 Jul., 20 Jul: *on my way home called on Mr. Massie at the Vicarage. While I was with him a Mr. Fowle, an old College intimate, called on him, coming from Bredon, where he is fixed as Mr. Strickland's Curate.* 2 Aug: *Wrote to Mr. Massie to invite him and the gentleman who is reading with him at Stanway to pay us a visit on Tuesday and Wednesday the 11th. and 12th. Inst.* 5-6 Aug., 9 Aug., 11 Aug: *Mr. Massie arrived on foot from Stanway to dinner accompanied by the two young Oxonians who are reading with him for honours.* 12 Aug., 19 Aug., 4 Sep., 11 Sep: *A letter from Massie declining our invitation to himself and young men to visit us on Saturday (to-morrow) previously to Massie's undertaking my duties on Sunday.* 13 Sep., 14 Sep: *I sauntered with Billingsley over his minute village, containing less than eighty inhabitants, and his pretty, antique church; and set off for Stanway Vicarage, where I staid for half an hour, and took luncheon with Massie and Darnell.* 21 Sep., 25-26 Sep., 29-30 Sep., 2 Oct., 8 Oct., 13 Oct., 18 Oct.

1845: 13 Feb: *I counted about 40 at the different tables; with a few only was I acquainted, chiefly with the two Griffiths, the two Foleys, Cockey, Brancker, Wheeler, and Massey.* 14 Feb: *Breakfasted at the Vice Chancellor's, Mrs. Symons, her husband, Massey, and myself— M. had slept at the Warden's lodgings.*

MASTER — *see* Chester-Master

MASTERMAN — Masterman, Peters, Mildred, Masterman & Co.[95]

The bank began as the partnership Mildred & Walker in 1779. Masterman joined in 1780 and the bank operated from 35 Nicholas Lane from 1823, when it became known as Masterman, Peters, Mildred & Masterman. It was formed into Agra & Masterman's Bank in 1865, and failed the following year. Masterman acted as a London clearing agent for many provincial banks.

1836: 10 Nov: *On arriving at Stow, found at Cripps's bank a letter from Raymond Cripps announcing that Messrs. Masterman had received and sent to them Exch. Bills, value £4200.* 8 Dec.

1837: 8 May: *Wrote to Hoares to direct them to pay £100 at Mastermans to my account with Messrs. Cripps, and to Howell.* 10 May, 6 Oct., 8 Oct.

1838: 6 Jun: *Wrote to Messrs. Hoare, directing them to pay £200 for me to Mastermans & Co. to be placed to the a/c of Mr. Skinner with Clinch and Co. Bankers, Witney.* 8 Jun.

1839: 27 Feb., 1 Mar.

1843: 28 Sep.

1844: 28 Jan., 14 Sep.

MATHIAS — Daniell Mathias[96]

Daniel[l] Mathias (±1767-1837), Church of England clergyman, was born at Warrington, Lancashire, son of John Mathias. He was educated at Brasenose College, Oxford (BA 1789; MA 1792), where he was a fellow from 1793 to 1810. Mathias was ordained deacon on 26 May 1793 and priest on 22 December of the same year. His first clerical appointment was as stipendiary curate of Chesterton, Warwickshire, from 27 May 1793. He was appointed curate of Warrington (St Helens), Lancashire, on 12 September 1795, and served as rector of St Mary's, Whitechapel, from 1807 to 1837.

1806: 21 Mar: *A very large male Party to Cards & Supper at the Knights: I played three rubbers unsuccessfully; of the party were Stevens & his Wife, Matthias of B.N.C., Budd of C.C.C., Marsh, Marshall of Ball. Dr. Price, Michel, Simmons, Round, Dr. Cooper, Mr. Jebb, Mr. Davis &c.*

MATHIAS — Thomas James Mathias[97]

Thomas James Mathias (1754-1835), satirist and Italian scholar, was the eldest son of Vincent Mathias (±1711-1782), sub-treasurer in the queen's household, and Marianne (1724-1799), daughter of Alured Popple, secretary to the Board of Trade and governor of Bermuda. Mathias's uncle Gabriel was an artist and held a post in the office of the keeper of the privy purse. Another uncle, James, was a Hamburg merchant, well-known amateur singer, and minor enemy of Mrs Thrale. Mathias's brother George, queen's messenger from 1792, was a long-standing friend of Charlotte Burney, who found him 'excessive comical'. Andrew, the other brother, became surgeon-extraordinary to the queen. The family lived in Middle Scotland Yard.

Mathias was educated at Eton College and Trinity College, Cambridge, where he became intimate with Spencer Perceval, apparently acting as a kind of private tutor to him. His father died in 1782 and Mathias left Cambridge to become successively sub-treasurer to the queen, vice-treasurer, and treasurer of the accounts of the queen's household. The wide range of Mathias's interests and connections is indicated by his election as fellow of the Society of Antiquaries in January 1795 and of the Royal Society in March of the same year. According to Fanny Burney, he was 'particularly agreeable & pleasant as well as cultivated and sensible' in social circles.

Mathias was known as a satirist and Italian scholar; he wrote numerous works and moved in the best literary and social circles; it is not surprising that both Agnes and Francis Witts were pleased to meet him. The *DNB* entry provides interesting detail on his life. In her diary, Agnes Witts noted: 'Wet & disagreable till after noon, w.ch made it quite confining till Frank & I accompanied Mrs. Doig to Covent Garden Theatre to hear Mrs. Bellington in Mandane, the party Mrs. Scott, Mrs. Walter Riddell & her Daughter, Miss Eycott & the celebrated Mr. Mathias.' The opera being performed was *Artaxerxes* by Thomas Arne. Mandane is actually a character in the opera, the daughter of Artaxerxes.

1801: 13 Oct: *My Mother as well as myself were in Mrs. Doig's box, very agreeably: the remaining Company consisted of Mrs. Scott & Mrs. Eycott, & two most agreeable persons, the former of whom I had long wished to know, & the latter I had formerly seen much of at Edinburgh. Mr. Matthias, & Mrs. W. Riddell. I conversed chiefly with them, who had a real taste for what was passing.*

MATHIR — M. Mathir at Weimar

1798: 2 Sep: *Mr. du Vaux as a Mathematician, du Stuat as natural philosopher, and M. Mathir as Linguist, are all able Professors, & from their age are rather the Steady Companions, than the Preceptors of their Pupils.*

MATIEGZECK — Franziska Maximiliane Matiegzeck [Maticzeck][98]

Franziska Maximiliane Matiegzeck (17[??]-1823) was a sängerin und schauspielerin (singer and actress). She was in Weimar between 1794 and 1801, before moving to Hamburg. She then moved to Kassel in 1802 and Naumburg in 1803. From 1804 onwards she was in Dresden.

1799: 16 Nov: *the best Performers were Benda Matiegzeck & Genast.* 7 Dec: *The best performers were Jagemann, Matiegzeck, Weyrauch, & Spitzeder.*

MATTHEWS — Mr Matthews, solicitor

It is uncertain who this Mr Matthews was, but he may have been the same Mr Matthews whom Agnes Witts met at Lady Lyttelton's on 6 June 1801. If so, there may also have been a connection between Mary Matthews (*below*) and Miss Eycott. If this was the case it is likely that Mr Matthews married a sister of Miss Eycott's. Why Francis Witts was corresponding with him is unknown, but it is possible that he may have been considering a career in the law.

1802: 4 Jun: *Wrote to George, Mr. Matthews, & Mr. Granville.* 1 Aug.

1805: 12 Feb: *Wrote to Mr. Matthews.* 15 Feb: *Heard from Mr. Matthews.* 2 Mar., 14 Mar., 8 Nov.

1806: 31 Jan., 5 Feb: *Wrote to Matthews, the Solicitor, upon business.* 22 Feb., 27 Feb., 18 Jun., 9 Sep.

MATTHEWS — Mrs Matthews at Malvern

Nothing has been discovered of the enigmatic Mrs Matthews. The tone of the diary entries suggests that she was long acquainted with the Witts family.

1834: 8 Sep: *The Bishop of Gloucester, Mrs. Monk, and three lovely children, daughters, were my Aunt's guests, also her frequent companion, Mrs. Matthews, the widow of a Worcestershire Clergyman, whom I had not seen for many years, if ever before.* 11 Sep: *Entirely confined to the house till an hour before dinner, except that I spent an hour at John Witts's. Conversing with my Aunt and Mrs. Matthews, with Mrs. Monk &c. till there was a possibility of getting out on the common, when the Bishop and myself contrived to get an hour's exercise.* 12 Sep: *Mrs. Matthews returned from passing an hour or two with her daughters, Mrs. Henderson and Mrs. Fane.*

1839: 5 Sep: *Anne and Apphia think of repairing to Clifton, there to join their old acquaintance Mrs. Matthews, who happens to be staying there.*

1840: 5 Jul: *On a former occasion she had visited him in company with Mrs. Matthews, and settled matters on a proper footing, when his inability to take care of himself became known to his daughters, who, at a still earlier period, had joined him on the continent, and made an excursion with him along the Rhine, in Flanders, Germany &c.*

MATTHEWS — Emily Jane Matthews — *see also* Irvine *and* Reade[99]

Emily Jane Matthews, née Reade (±1795-1856), was the daughter of Thomas Reade (1762-1837) and Catherine (d. 1830), daughter of Sir John Hill. Thomas was the twin brother of Sir John Reade (1762-1789). Emily had one brother, John Edmund Reade (1800-1870), who married, 1847, his cousin Maria Louisa (d. 1866), daughter of George Compton Reade (1788-1866). Susan, one of Emily's sisters, married Charles Chamberlayne Irvine (±1775-1856), and there was another sister who has not been identified. In 1842 Emily lived at 6 Daniel Street, Bath.

Emily Jane Reade married, at Bedminster, Somerset, 19 June 1843, William Edward Matthews (1810-1893). William was born at Cold Harbour Farm, Cranmore, Somerset, and was a widower, having married, 1836, Fanny Stockford (1811-1838). After Emily's death in 1856, William married for a third time, 1857, Elizabeth Frances Blanch (1821-1901). He died in Missouri. Elizabeth, his widow, died at Des Moines, Iowa.

1846: 2 Sep: *Drove with MW. to Oddington; called at Lady Reade's: she had not left her room. We were received by Mrs. Matthews, late Miss Emily Reade of Bath, now the wife of a gentleman resident on his property in Somersetshire, without any profession, not far from Wincanton.*

1848: 20 Oct: *Received a letter from Mrs. Matthews, late Emily Reade, residing with her husband near Shepton Mallet, who forwards a letter addressed to me by her sister, Mrs. Irvine, long resident at Brussels... Wrote to Mrs. Matthews, Alham House, near Shepton Mallet.* 27 Oct.

MATTHEWS — Henry Matthews[100]

Henry Matthews (1826-1913), home secretary, was the only son of Henry Matthews (1789-1828), a puisne judge in Ceylon, and his wife, Emma (d. 1861). His father, a son of John Matthews, of Belmont, Herefordshire, was of Welsh descent, while is mother, the daughter of William Blount, of Orleton, Herefordshire, came from an old Catholic family. After his father's death, Henry's mother took him, aged 6, to live in Paris. He attended a school run by a German protestant, but was brought up in the Roman Catholic faith, to which he remained conspicuously loyal. Debarred by his religion from Oxford and Cambridge, he graduated at the Sorbonne as bachelier-ès-lettres before proceeding in 1845 to University College, London. He was called to the bar at Lincoln's Inn in 1850. After a distinguished legal career, Henry Matthews became MP for the Irish borough of Dungarvon in 1868. Disraeli offered him the prospect of office as solicitor-general, but he lost Dungarvon in the general election of 1874, and failed to regain a seat until the general election of 1886, when he was returned for East Birmingham, becoming the first Conservative to represent that city. A display of Matthews' ability in a celebrated case persuaded Lord Randolph Churchill to secure his unexpected appointment as home secretary in Lord Salisbury's first administration. He was the first Roman Catholic since the reign of James II to become a minister of the crown. In 1895 he was raised to the peerage as Viscount Llandaff. He died unmarried.

1851: 22 May: *The guests were Mrs. and two Misses Mason, relations of the Howells, Mr. Matthews, a young and talented Roman Catholic barrister, of a Herefordshire family, son of the author of an interesting book descriptive of the West Indian Islands—"The Diary of an Invalid."*

1853: 12 Jun: *At dinner in the evening two guests, Mr. Houston & H. Matthews: both of them previously known to me: the former embued with strong Protestant principles and Anti-catholic prejudices, as consistent with a residence in the Presbyterian regions of Belfast, the latter an ardent Roman Catholic Barrister, talented and sensitive: Mr. H not knowing, or not discovering the religious opinions of the younger guest, and being of an outspoken John Bullish temperament, made certain allusions as to the Catholic priesthood, and the necessity of making a law for the inspections of nunneries, which led to a sharp and not unamusing collision, of which Howell, W. Ffooks & myself succeeded in preventing a serious result.*

MATTHEWS — John Matthews of Lower Swell[101]

John Matthews (b. ±1780), farmer, of Lower Swell, was a guardian of the Union Workhouse at Stow-on-the-Wold, representing the parish of Lower Swell. In the 1841 census his name is spelt 'Mathews', but this is likely to be an error. He was married to Martha (b. ±1785).

1838: 20 Apr: *Engaged in the forenoon with Matthews, a farmer of L Swell and Capt. Leigh.*

1843: 2 Nov: *With the House Committee inspected the workhouse. Present Messrs. Privett, Cook, Matthews.* 16 Nov: *To the Workhouse, to meet the Members of the Visiting Comm. Messrs. Rose, Privett, Matthews, Cook, Gillett, with Mr. Pearce: inspected the whole establishment, conferred on several points, examined correspondence, gave directions for necessary work &c.*

1844: 22 Aug: *adjourned to the Justice room, and there transacted various and some difficult business with Mr. Ford, as my colleague: the principal matter being a question as to a right of fishery in the parish of Lower Swell, raised by Mr. Matthews against Mr. C. Harris, claiming a right to fish by permission of Mr. Merchant: the matter left undecided, to be made subject of litigation elsewhere, as it is supposed.*

1845: 20 Mar: *To the Workhouse, where I sat with Messrs. Davis and Matthews, Guardians, on a Committee for auditing the Tradesmens bills &c. for the Quarter.*

1851: 15 Apr.

MATTHEWS — Joseph and John Matthews of Stow-on-the-Wold

1839: 29 May: *Wrote to Mr. Hayward on the dissentions between the two Matthews's, his relations, living at Stow, Father and Son. Their feuds are to be brought before the Magistrates to-morrow.* 30 May: *at the Unicorn, where the painful and very discreditable family disputes between the Messrs. Matthews, Father & Son, were to be heard before us: we made the sitting private, except as to Messrs. Chamberlayne, Vavasour, Hayward, Winter,*

Lane, Minchin—The younger Matthews was found guilty of, and fined for, a rash assault he had made under strong excitement upon the younger sister of a profligate woman, who has gained a sad ascendancy over his Father—Jos. Matthews—who is shamefully engrossed by this worthless woman, and addicted to hard drinking, which brings him into a state bordering on insanity… Conferred with George Hayward and Mr. John Matthews, on the unpleasant dissentions between Mr. Jos. Matthews and his son.

MATTHEWS — **Mary Matthews, niece to Miss Eycott**

1808: 22 Feb: *Miss Eycott & her neice, Mary Matthews, her inmates.*

MAUDSLEY — **Thomas Maudsley** [102]

Thomas Maudsley (1798-1880), farmer, was the son of Thomas Maudsley and Jennet Proctor. He married Mary Bateson (±1805-1845) and lived at Stainforth Hall, a farm of 313 acres, where he was a tenant of Francis Witts. Thomas and Mary had at least 5 sons and 1 daughter:

1 Thomas (±1829-1899)
2 John (b. ±1830)
1 Jennett (b. ±1832)
3 Henry (b. ±1834)
4 William (b. ±1836)
5 Christopher Bateson (b. ±1842)

By 1861 Thomas had left Stainforth Hall and was farming at Rome, Giggleswick, a smaller farm of 87 acres, where he employed one boy. Farming with him was his youngest son, Christopher. Another son, William, was living at home with his parents, but was employed as a chemist and druggist. By 1871, Christopher, by then a widower, was listed as head of the family. The farm had grown to 200 acres. Mary had died but Thomas was still alive and lived with his son. He was listed as a land owner. He died in October 1880.

1838: 17 Sep: *At first it appeared to me in consultation with Hartley and Geldard, that it would be desirable that I should postpone my intended departure, and that Gorral, the farmer who had made a tender of £330 per ann., should be requested to meet on the following morning with a view to the acceptance of his offer, and to the signing of agreements: but on going out into the fair, I met Mr. Geldard's brother from Rathmell, who had been conversing with T. Maudsley, the person by whom £320 per ann. had been offered, who had said, he would adhere to his tender, provided it were promptly accepted; but would recede from it, if it were so that the farm was offered to any other bidder in the expectation of a higher rent.*

1840: 12 Jun: *Found a letter from Geldard on the subject of Rowland Ingram's claim for tithe in the parish of Gigleswick. It seems that he has taken proceedings against nearly fifty occupiers of land in the parish, and among them against our tenant, Maudsley, and Mr. Geldard has instructed Mr. Robinson for himself and us to defend the action.* 1 Aug.

MAULE — **William Henry Maule** [103]

Sir William Henry Maule (1788-1858), MP, barrister, and judge, was born at Edmonton, Middlesex, son of Henry Maule, a medical practitioner, and Hannah Rawson, a Quaker from Leeds. He was educated at Trinity College, Cambridge (BA 1810; MA 1813), where he was made a fellow in 1811. He was admitted at Lincoln's Inn in 1810 and called to the bar in 1814. He was appointed king's council in 1833, after which he was on the Oxford circuit. Maule was MP for Carlow in 1837-99, counsel to the Bank of England in 1835, and baron of the exchequer in 1839. He was knighted in 1839 and became justice of the court of common pleas in 1840. He retained that post until 1855, and died unmarried in 1858.

1842: 13 Apr: *Mr. Justice Taunton, Lord Campbell, & Mr. Baron Maule, were leading Counsel at the Sessions Bar.*

1843: 4 Dec: *Baron Rolfe is expected to attend; Baron Maule is joined with him in the commission.*

1846: 10 Aug: *The business of the Assizes was begun—Maule presided in the Crown Court, the Lord Chief Baron of Common Pleas. Maule was suffering from Asthmatic affection, and seemed greatly indisposed. He exhibited lassitude, languor, and something closely akin to carelessness in the trials of prisoners: one might almost suppose that early and long indulgence in immoral habits had rendered him indifferent to virtuous principle, and tender to vice.*

1847: 5 Apr: *Mr. Sergt. Gaselee preceded Mr. Justice Maule, who arrived at a later hour from Monmouth.* 6 Apr: *Mr. Sergt. Gaselee only was present: his brother Maule not appearing, probably excusing himself on the score of bad health.*

MAXWELL — **Major Maxwell**

1804: 13 Sep: *In the Evening accompanied two of the Miss Townsends & the Miss Manners's to Mrs. Van Der Horsts in the Garrison Parade in Queen Square. Genl. Fisher & Maj. Maxwell met us.*

MAY — **the May family at Malvern and Richmond**

There was a connection between the May, Dillon, Tonkins, and Todd families that has not yet been unravelled. Mrs Todd appears to have been a Tonkins; her sisters were Sophia and Charlotte. How the May and Dillon families were connected is not clear, but they were at Malvern and Richmond together.

1802: 28 Jul: *At Malvern dined. Was introduced to the May's &c. &c. but particularly to the lovely Charlotte Tonkins. Mr. Dillon & Miss Tonkin, sung Italian.* 29 Jul: *Walked on the Malvern Hills. Conversed with Mr. Dillon, Miss Tonkins, May &c. A Dance in the Evening where I danced with Misses Burt, May, Raikes & the divine Charlotte who sung after supper Italian finer than I had ever heard off the Stage with Dillon.*

1803: 12 Sep: *Rowed my Father & Mother to Richmond & back, calling on the charming Mrs. Todd, & Mr. & Mrs. May.*

MAYER — **Samuel Mayer** — *see also* **Lovegrove** [104]

Samuel Mayer (±1810-1871), solicitor, was born at Gloucester, probably a son of nonconformists Samuel and Elizabeth Mayer. He lived and practised at 11 Worcester Street, Gloucester. In addition to his solicitor's practice, Mayer held public offices, including that of clerk to the board of guardians of Gloucester Union Workhouse. He was married to Mary (±1811-1890); given that one of their sons was named 'Lovegrove', she may have been a relation of Joseph Lovegrove. Mary and Samuel had at least 3 sons and 2 daughters:

1 Catherine E. W. (b. ±1835)
1 Charles M. (b. ±1836)
2 Samuel Ralph Townshend (1841-1880); *see below*
2 Frances Hannah Cargill (b. ±1842); married, 1872, Alfred Alexander De Lessert (1847-1907)
3 Lovegrove Griffin Hubert (1849-1904)

By 1861 only Samuel (junior) and Lovegrove were still living at home. Samuel, rather pretentiously for a 20-year-old, was listed in the census as 'author, general literature'; this youngster had an interesting career. As he grew up he was said to have borne a remarkable resemblance to the poet Keats, not least in regards to his poor health. He was for several years a frequent contributor to the Gloucester newspapers, and to many serial publications. In 1859 he published a novelette, *Amy Fairfax*. Moving to London, he founded the Free and Open Church Association, advocating for the abolition of pew rents. He was secretary of the association from 1866 to February 1872. Samuel edited the *Churchman's Shilling Magazine*, the *Illustrated Review* (from January to June 1871), and the *Free and Open Church Advocate* (3 volumes). He was also proprietor and editor of the *St James's Magazine* for a short period in 1875.

1847: 19 Jan: *A letter from Mr. Mayer, Clerk to the Gloucester Union acknowledging my late remittance to Mr. Newton on account of the maintenance of Moses Roff in the Gloucester Lunatic Asylum.*

1850: 1 Jul., 30 Dec: *County officers in attendance, Messrs. Wilton, Bloxsome, Riddiford, Lefroy, Keily, Fulljames, Mayer.*

1851: 17 Mar.

1852: 14 Feb: *Recd. a letter from Mr. Mayer, Gloucester, with the intelligence that he has gained by a large majority his election to the office of Clerk to the Gloucester Infirmary.*

1853: 3 Jan., 8 Apr., 27 Jun.

1854: 27 Apr: *A note from Mr. Mayer, Clerk to the Gloucester Infirmary, informing me that W. Lawrence, the patient I lately sent thither, had refused to keep his bed, as required by the Med. Attendant, and had left the Infirmary.* 5 May: *To Mr. Mayer, Clerk to the Infirmary, Gloucester, expressing a hope that I should not forfeit my privilege of sending an In-patient to the Institution in consequence of the bad conduct of W. Lawrence refusing to submit to the orders of his medical Attendant, and leaving the Infirmary very shortly after I had sent him thither.* 9 May.

MAYNARD — Jane Maynard [105]

Jane Maynard (1739-1826) was the daughter of John Maynard (1704-1747) and Anne, daughter of Thomas Bayly of Devizes. She was the granddaughter of Jacob Maynard (1681-1719) and Jane (1678-1751), daughter of John Mayo (d. 1692) and Joan Hayes (1746/7-1719). She was therefore a first cousin once removed to Charles Mayo (*below*).

By 1806, when Francis Witts mentioned her in his diary, Jane had just one sibling still alive, Anne (1735-1816); her seven brothers and one other sister had all died before the entry was written. A Miss Maynard was mentioned numerous times in the diaries of Agnes Witts from 26 February 1802 (Agnes's beloved son's nineteenth birthday) onwards. Miss Maynard had been introduced to Agnes by their mutual acquaintance, Lady Riddell: 'Quite a beautiful Spring day, mild like April, & charming dry walking, blest the sun that shone so bright on my Franks natal day, had an early visit from a Miss Maynard one of Lady Riddells introduced acquaintance, a well behaved Woman of a certain age styled a blue stocking ...' It is difficult to be sure which of the sisters this was, but it is presumed it was Anne. Agnes met Miss Maynard on more than twenty occasions at Clifton between 1802 and 1806, before finally meeting her on her home ground at Devizes on 29 July 1806: 'I had a visit from Mrs. & Miss Spalding who went with me to call on Miss Maynards at their pretty little retreat at the Brow the end of the Town, who received me in the most obliging manner & the situation & view from the place is infinitely pretty ...' Here it is noticeable that she referred to the Miss Maynards in the plural.

The original Brow Cottage was built in 1766 by the sisters' uncle, James Maynard (1707-1786), who 'built a villa or "summer house" to the designs of Thomas Collins Overton'. It was situated on the north side of the Bath road, Devizes, and called the Brow or Browfort. Before 1835 it was a small squat house of two storeys and three bays. Following Jane's death, the house passed to her kinsfolk, the Mayo family, and in particular to Revd Joseph Mayo (1764-1851), rector of Ozleworth, Gloucestershire.

1806: 11 Aug: *In the Evening walked with the Ladies & Mrs. J. Maynard to the very pretty Gardens of the latter at the Brow.*

MAYO — Charles Mayo [106]

Charles Mayo (1750-1829), Church of England clergyman, was born at Beechingstoke, Wiltshire, the fifth child and fourth son of John Mayo (1713-1779) and Barbara [probably Stevens] (±1718-1796). He was educated at Queen's College, Oxford (BA 1771; MA 1774; BCL 1779), and was ordained deacon on 7 March 1773 and priest on 9 April 1775. Mayo's first clerical appointment was as curate of Wilton with Netherhampton, Ditchampton, and Bulbridge, Wiltshire, from 8 March 1773. He was then appointed rector of Huish, near Marlborough, in 1775, and in 1779 he succeeded his father as rector of Beechingstoke (Stoke); he held both livings until his death. It was at 'Stoke', only 2 miles from Urchfont, that Francis Witts met and dined with him.

Charles Mayo was said to have been a man of great simplicity, and was thought to bear a considerable resemblance to Dr Syntax. He was so absent-minded that, so the story goes, a friend met him one day, deep in thought, walking from Devizes to Beechingstoke with his horse's bridle hung over his arm; to his friend's surprise, he was unaware that his horse, which he had been leading, had rid itself of the bridle and escaped.

Charles Mayo lived with his sister Lucy (1744-1812); they both died unmarried. Lucy is the sister mentioned in the diary extracts; she was referred to as 'Mrs.' on 23 and 26 April 1807, a convention at that time.

1806: 18 Jul: *Mr. Mayo called in the forenoon... Rode to Stert Cottage & walked from thence with Mr. & Mrs. Jacques four miles to Stoke to dine with Mr. Mayo.* 25 Jul: *Passed the Evening pleasantly at Mrs. Hillier's meeting a Family party & Mr. Mayo.* 6 Aug., 11 Aug: *Dined at Dr. Spalding's, Mr. Spalding his Brother an elegant & agreeable man. The Dr. & his wife highly ridiculous. Mr. Gaisford, & Mr. C. Mayo made up the party.* 15 Aug: *Dined with the J. Tylee's a very pleasant party Mr. C. Mayo & his Sister, Mrs Newman Mr. Neat, Mrs. C. Tylee, Mr. & Mrs. Gent & Mrs. Hillier, & Mr. Thomas.* 11 Sep: *Busy in the House & Gardens &c. Mr. Mayo called upon me.* 24 Sep., 25 Oct., 27 Oct., 29 Oct: *Dr. & Mrs. & Miss Spalding called upon us & we proceeded together to dine at Mr. C. Mayo's at Stoke, where we made a very agreeable visit.* 7 Nov.

1807: 23 Apr: *Drove my Mother to visit Mrs. L. Mayo, whom with her brother we found at home.* 26 Apr: *Mrs. L. Mayo among my Congregation.* 4 May: *In the Evening Mrs. Warrener & Mrs. L. Mayo, Mr. Mayo & Mrs. Jones visited us to tea.* 29 Jun: *In the Evening drove my Mother to drink tea at Mr. C. Mayo's at Beeching Stoke.* 23 Jul., 25 Jul., 26 Aug: *Drove my Mother to Conock & Stoke, called upon Mrs. Warrener, Mrs. Jones, Mr. & Miss L. Mayo: Met at the two Houses Dr. Hill & Mrs. Collins.*

1808: 9 Jan: *Rode to Beching Stoke: called on Mr. Mayo & his sister.* 21 Jan: *dined agreeably at Mr. Mayo's of Beching Stoke; met Mr. Dyke, Mrs. Dyke Poore, Mr. W. Dyke.* 27-28 Apr.

MEADE — Peirce Meade [107]

Peirce Meade (1776-1834), Church of Ireland clergyman, was born at Ballintober, Castlemagner [Ballymartle], co. Cork, a younger son of John Meade, 1st earl of Clanwilliam (1744-1800), and Theodosia Hawkins-Magill (1743-1817). He was educated at St John's and Wadham College, Oxford (BA 1799; MA 1802), and was archdeacon of Dromore from 1810 to 1832. He married, at Dromore parish, co. Down, 6 April 1801, Elizabeth Percy (1780-1823); they had at least 1 son and 1 daughter:

1 Theodosia Barbara (1804-1890)
1 Edward Richard (1805-1890)

1802: 14 Jul: *Dined in the Common Room with Williams, meeting the Honbl. & Revd. Mr. Meade, Dr. Lewton, Mr. Carrington & Brown.*

MEADE — Richard Meade — *see also* Stone *and* Grub [108]

Richard Meade (1782-1844), Church of England clergyman, was born at Cripplegate, Middlesex, son of Edward Meade (1734-1783) and Anne Sampey (1761-1785). He was educated at St Paul's School and Wadham College, Oxford (BA 1805), and was ordained deacon on 22 December 1805 and priest on 21 September 1806. His first clerical appointment was as curate of Princes Risborough and Horsenden, Buckinghamshire, from 22 December 1805. He then became rector at Horsenden on 27 March 1811, and was elevated at the same time as perpetual curate of Prince's Risborough. Meade married, at Islington, Middlesex, 22 May 1811, Frances Aldwin Soames (1786-1871); they had at least 2 sons:

1 John (b. 1813)
2 Edward (b. 1816)

It seems surprising that Richard Meade was at the same college as Francis Witts, matriculating a mere eight months before him, and yet is not mentioned in the diaries of 1802 to 1805. He may have rarely stayed at Wadham. The connection between the Stones and the Meades was via Richard Meade's grandparents, Thomas Meade (1703-1770) and Elizabeth Stone (1709-1772), who married, at Chesham, Buckinghamshire, on 18 September 1727. Elizabeth Stone's parents were Edward Stone (d. 1751) and Elizabeth Grubb (1670-1751), who had married on 23 April 1707. Her half-brother was Edward 'Edmund' Stone (1702-1768), father-in-law to Sarah Stone, née Witts (1745-1834), the diarist's aunt.

1850: 12 Aug: *Called on Mr. Charles Gray, the Perpetual Curate, a connection of Mrs. Shard's by the father's side. Mr. Stone, Mrs. S's father, had been, in his day, the incumbent of this place, and was succeeded by a Mr. Meade; also a connection of the Stones.*

MEAGHER — Thomas Francis Meagher [109]

Thomas Francis Meagher (1823-1867), Irish nationalist, was leader of the Young Irelanders in the rebellion of 1848. Having been convicted of sedition, he was sentenced to death, but received transportation for life to Van Diemen's Land in Australia. In 1852 he escaped and made his way to the United States, where he settled in New York City. There Meagher studied law, worked as a journalist, and travelled to present lectures on the Irish cause. At the beginning of the Civil War, Meagher joined the Union Army and rose to the rank of brigadier general. He was most notable for recruiting and leading the Irish Brigade, and for encouraging support for the Union among Irish immigrants. Following the war, Meagher was appointed acting governor of the Montana Territory. In 1867, he drowned in the Missouri River after falling accidentally from a steamboat at Fort Benton.

1848: 24 Mar: *In Ireland the uncompromising, undisguised, open & prominent talkers and publishers of sedition, Smith O'Brien, Meagher, and Mitchell, have been bound by recognizance to answer the offences.* 19 May: *In Ireland Smith O'Brien, and Meagher, have been indicted for sedition, but it has proved impossible to obtain a conviction against them.*

MELLERSH — William Peachey Mellersh [110]

William Peachey Mellersh (1808-1892), Church of England clergyman, was born at Godalming, Surrey, son of Thomas G. Mellersh (b. ±1780) and his wife, Martha J. (b. ±1780). He was educated at St John's College, Cambridge (BA 1833; MA 1836). He was curate of Hambleton, Lancashire, 1834; domestic chaplain to the earl of Winterton, 1835-78; curate of Shipton-Sollars, Gloucestershire, 1837-62; perpetual curate of Compton Abdale, 1837-47; and vicar of Cold Salperton, 1840-84.

Mellersh was married to Jane M. Pou[l]ter (±1806-1884), born at Dunsfold, Surrey; they had at least 3 sons and 4 daughters:

1 George (1836-1910)
1 Mary [Martha] Jane (1840-1865)
2 Thomas George (1840-1926)
2 Emily Mary (b. & d. 1842)
3 William Henry (1844-1931)
3 Isabella Sarah (b. 1847)
4 Fanny [Frances?] (1849-1899)

1840: 25 May.

1842: 25 Feb., 11-12 Mar., 21 Mar: *Rode to Salperton to visit the Church there; met the Perp. Curate, Mr. Mellersh, by appointment; transacted with him what was necessary under the Commission issued by the Bp.*

1845: 26 May: *Many retired before the dinner; among them Messrs. Griffin, Perkins, Mellersh, Biscoe, Newport, W. B. Pole &c.*

1853: 24 May: *Many Clergy who attended the Visitation, and with whom I was in conversation, returned home after divine service & the charge.—Messrs. Todd, R Waller, Cholmondeley, Dean of Gloucester, Ball, Hodges, Mellersh &c.*

MELLISH — Joseph Charles Mellish [111]

Joseph Charles Mellish (1769-1823), poet, linguist, and translator, was the son of Charles Mellish (1737-1797), of Blyth, Nottinghamshire, and Judith Stapleton (d. 1806). His father was a barrister at Lincoln's Inn. Joseph was educated at Eton College, Trinity College, Cambridge, and Lincoln's Inn (1787), but does not appear to have continued with a legal career. In Charles Mellish's will, made in 1794, Joseph was bequeathed £1,000, compared to £9,000 for each of his two sisters. The Blyth estate was entailed upon his younger brother Henry Francis Mellish and his heirs, with remainder to the two sisters; Joseph was disinherited by his father on account of his extravagance and gambling.

Joseph Charles Mellish married a German baroness, Karolina Ernestina Friederike Sophia von Stein (1777-1824), of Nord-und Ostheim, and had a house in Weimar itself, as well as a schloss at Dornburg. He appears to have been on friendly terms with the ducal family. Karolina was a relation of Charlotte von Stein, Goethe's close friend. To enable the marriage, the duke gave Mellish the title of a Prussian Kammerherr (chamberlain). Quite why he needed to 'enable' the union is unclear, but it shows that Mellish was well regarded in Weimar.

Mellish was the grandson of Joseph Mellish and Dorothy Gore, the sister of the director of the Hamburg Company. Both the Mellish and Gore families were London merchants. Charles

Gore (1729-1807) and Joseph Charles Mellish were cousins of one degree or another, which may have been a factor in Gore's decision to settle in Weimar. Although disinherited, it appears that Mellish's family still supported him; in 1802 Friedrich Schiller bought Joseph's Weimar house and messuage to the esplanade for 4,200 Taler. Mellish did not remain permanently in Germany. He attained the post of consul in Louisiana in 1809, and then in Palermo and Hamburg. He later became HMB chargé d'affaires and consul-general for the circle of Lower Saxony from 1814 to 1823.

Mellish was an accomplished linguist and wrote and translated poetry and plays in German, English, and Latin. He translated Friedrich Schiller's *Mary Stuart* into English and was on very friendly terms with both Schiller and Goethe in Weimar. It may have been that his wife's family relationship to Charlotte von Stein brought him further into the Goethe circle; Goethe became godfather to Mellish's son, Richard. Schiller said that Mellish combined 'alle Liebenswürdigkeiten eines Deutschen und eines Engländers' (all the most agreeable features of a German and an Englishman). Some twenty years later, Goethe wrote a poem in his honour, *An Freund Mellish*. (For the full poem see vol. 1, page 355.) Joseph Charles Mellish is buried at Twickenham.

Joseph and Karolina had at least 3 sons and 3 daughters:

- 1 Amalie (1799-1872); married August Ferdinand Theodor Count Marschall von Burgholzhausen (1791-1867), royal Prussian erb-marshal in the landgraviate of Thuringia, royal Saxon chamberlain, and chief forestry master to Moritzburg, the son of August Dietrich Marshal (1750-1824)
- 1 Richard Charles (±1801-1865); born at Weimar; educated at St John's School, Hamburg, and Trinity College, Cambridge (BA 1825); married Mary (b. ±1811); at least 1 son and 3 daughters:
  - 1 Ursula (1844-1903); married, at St George's, Hanover Square, Westminster, 3 June 1865, Frederick Henry Fergusson Dundas (1832-1875); 2 sons
  - 2 Caroline (b. ± 1845)
  - 1 Lancelot A. H. (b. ± 1848)
  - 3 Sophia (b. ± 1848)
- 2 Caroline Eliza (1810-1845)
- 3 Wilhelmina Anne Catherine (1811-1884); married, at St Lawrence's, Morden, Surrey, 18 June 1844, Robert Joseph Ignatius Monteith (1812-1884); 2 sons and 3 daughters:
  - 1 Mary Frances Cameron von Stein (1846-1916)
  - 2 Christina C. (b. 1849)
  - 2 Caroline (1850-1854)
  - 1 Henry (1851-1875)
  - 2 Joseph Francis Stanislaus Robert von Stein Cameron (1852-1911)
- 2 Edward (b. 1814); born at Twickenham
- 3 D. A. G. Mellish (dates unknown), Capt.; fought in India, 1842

The diary entry for 16 May 1801 is enigmatic. The property at Albemarle Street had been owned by William Mellish, a cousin, or at least a close relation, of Joseph Charles Mellish. Whether or not Joseph owned part of 20 or 21 Albemarle Street prior to 1801 is not known, and why Mr Mellish should have been considered 'unhappy' has not been investigated; whether this relates to William or Joseph is also unknown.

1799: 24 Jul: *Paying a visit for some days to our Country man, & friend Mr. Mellish, at Dornburg Castle, three German, fifteen English Miles, from Weimar, we continued on the Jena Road, as far as Kötschau… The old Castle, inhabited by a Rent Commissary, is at the one extremity of that side of the Rock, which faces the beautiful Vale below, thro' which runs the Chaussée from Jena to Naumburg. The Age of this Building, is not ascertained.—The Centre is occupied by the new Castle, a handsome building, inhabited by M. Mellish and farther beyond is a well looking ancient House, the property of a rich farmer…. A steep Wood of seven or eight acres in size, which Mr. Mellish has caused to be intersected by various walks, adds much to the agrèment of the place, and to the Convenience, not only of himself, but also of his Neighbours, to whom he has generously given the permission of walking in it.* (This entry is not dated in the diary, and is included in Francis Witts's 'Tour of Germany', WFP F154, vol. 1, p. 289. The actual date has been ascertained from the diary of Agnes Witts, WFP F197.)

1799: 25 Aug: *You will give me much pleasure in telling me what one thinks among you other Britons of the Poem entitled Herrman & Dorothea one of my friends has translated it into English, in Iambics, that will appear soon, but I no longer remember the name of the bookseller Printer. I have read it in Manuscript, but I would like to know if public opinion agrees with mine which is perhaps a little prejudiced. The same Monsieur must translate the two Tragedies of Schiller, the author of the Voleurs & of Don Carlos &c, that is to say, Wallenstein & Marie Reine des Escosses on which he works at present. One will give them well in London the coming winter, where I doubt not but that the beautiful imagination & the beautiful Thoughts of Schiller will be much applauded. M. Mellish who must translate this & other very interesting things, is of a good English family. He is attached by the Bonds of friendship to the Duke of Weimar, in a Chateau of whom he lives in the Country, he is attached to Germany by a very happy marriage. Without being his friend, one only needs to know him in order to esteem him: but unhappily you have never seen him, and in making his just Praises, I paint, the author, the scholar, but not a virtuous man of the sort in which you can be interested.* (This entry is the English translation of Francis Witts's letter in French to his friend 'Monsieur R. Newbigging'.)

1799: 11 Nov: *Dry above wet on the Ground walked a little in the Gardens, being Mellishes Christening & all the Ducal Family were gone to Dornburg.* 8 Dec: *Rather drier had been a Frost; walked out to the Concert at Court in the Evening, where many people. a Stranger Mr. Lawrence Brother of the two who were at Göttingen, a Knight of Malta then also Mr. Mellish.* 9 Dec: *Messrs. Mellish and Lawrence called on us in the morning went to fetch a walk.*

1801: 16 May: *This house formerly belonged to the unhappy Mr Mellish.*

MELLON — Alfred Mellon [112]

Alfred Mellon (1820-1867), conductor and composer, was probably born in London, although his early years were spent in Birmingham, his parents' home town. He became a violinist and played in the opera and other orchestras, and was later appointed leader of the orchestra at the Royal Italian Opera, Covent Garden. He then held the post of music director at the Haymarket and Adelphi theatres, and afterwards at the Pyne and Harrison English opera company, which produced his opera *Victorine* at Covent Garden in 1859. He was conductor of the Musical Society and Promenade Concerts, which for several seasons were given under his name at Covent Garden. In September 1865 he became conductor of the Liverpool Philharmonic Society. Among his compositions were the opera *The Irish Dragoon* (1845), the glee *Crown'd with clusters of the vine* (1850), and numerous songs for farces and plays, and ballads and piano pieces.

1851: 21 May: *Herr Moligne played exquisitely in duets with his daughter, who accompanied him on the Piano-forte and quartetts of surpassing excellence were performed by him with Herr Schmid, and Mr. Mellon, on the Violin and Viola, and Signor Piatti, a capital Viollincellist.*

MELVILLE — Mrs M. A. Melville of Stow [113]

M. A. Melville was probably Mary Anne Melville, although no details of her life have been found. She probably hailed from Brighton as Francis Witts was enquiring of her about that place. One Mary Anne Melville died in Brighton in 1847, and it may be that she returned to her home town in her later years.

1836: 11 Nov: *Also to Mrs. Melville, a retired housekeeper of the Lindows, in reply to a note I had received from her on Prov. Bank business, and forwarded to her the amount of a recall I had made and received for her.*

1837: 14 Jun: *Recd. a letter from Sophia Hunt on business relating to the concerns of that family: also from M. A. Melville, acknowledging the receipt of money forwarded by me from the Savings Bank.*

1843: 20 Aug: *Wrote to Mrs. Melville, Stow, thanking her for information as to Brighton.*

MENTON — Mrs Menton, a guest at Lady Fingal's party

1804: 27 Sep: *In the evening with McMahon & finished by a pleasant party at Lady Fingals Singing moderately by Mrs. Menton & Mrs. Legeete.*

MERCER — Cavalié Alexander Mercer, the strange boy at a Bourton-on-the-Water dinner party [114]

Cavalié Alexander Mercer (1817-1882), surgeon, was the second, but only surviving, child of Alexander Cavalié Mercer (1783-1868) and Fanny [Frances] (1793-1817), sister of Edward Rice, dean of Gloucester. His mother died just three days after his birth. Mercer became a member of the Royal College of Surgeons in 1843 and served in Triploi, Syria, in 1875. It is not known if he married. He is overshadowed by his famous father, whose memoirs he successfully edited and published in 1870.

Alexander Cavalié Mercer (1783-1868) was a British artillery officer. He is well-known due to his command of G Troop Royal Horse Artillery at the battle of Waterloo and his subsequent memoir of the campaign, *Journal of the Waterloo Campaign* (1870). Mercer's six-gun horse artillery troop arrived too late to take part in the battle of Quatre Bras, but it fought with the cavalry rearguard, covering the Army's retreat to Waterloo. The troop fought on the extreme right wing of Wellington's army at Waterloo, before being moved into the thick of the fighting nearer the centre of the line. There it beat off repeated charges by French heavy cavalry, disobeying orders to abandon the guns and retire inside nearby infantry squares as the enemy closed. The location of this action is marked by a memorial on the Waterloo battlefield. After the battle, Mercer's troop marched on Paris with the Allied armies, and formed part of the army of occupation. Mercer's *Journal* is an important source for historians of the Waterloo campaign; it also gives a detailed description of the landscape and people of Belgium and France in the early nineteenth century. It is one of the few accounts of the period written by an artillery officer.

Mercer remained in the peacetime army, twice serving in Canada. He was a painter of some merit, and a number of his watercolours of Canadian landscapes were purchased by the National Gallery of Canada in the 1980s. The rest of the family has not received so much recognition. Alexander Cavalié Mercer's father, Alexander Mercer (±1739-1816), had a distinguished career in the Royal Engineers, rising ultimately to become a general and colonel commandant. Joining the Army in 1759 he saw service in the Seven Years' War in France and the Mediterranean, in the American War of Independence, in the West Indies, at Guernsey, and in England. Alexander Mercer (senior) and his wife Thedosia Dickson had five children who survived to adulthood, of whom all four sons served in the armed forces, while their daughter married a naval captain.

Alexander Cavalié Mercer married Frances [or Fanny] Rice on 10 November 1813 at Bourton-on-the-Water, Gloucestershire, while he was stationed in Woodbridge, Suffolk. She travelled with him to France after his leave in November 1815. They lived in Berkshire at the time of the Waterloo campaign, but in later life Mercer lived at Cowley Hill near Exeter. He died there on 9 November 1868, and is buried at St David's Church, Exeter.

1828: 14 Aug: *Morrison's pretty children & Major Mercer's strange boy completed the circle.*

MERCER — Samuel Mercer [115]

Samuel Mercer (1809-1878), naval officer, was born at Deal, Kent, son of John and Elizabeth Mercer. He was promoted commander in 1838, and by 1858 he was on the retired list. In 1843 and 1844 he was stationed at Dover, conducting the packet service. By 1861 he was living in Devon. Mercer married, at Worth, Kent, 20 February 1839, Eliza Mary Dornford (1814-1880); they had 5 sons and 5 daughters:

1 Mary Frances (b. ±1843)
1 Henry Dornford (b. ±1845)
2 Frank Aubrey (b. ±1846)
2 Charlotte Elizabeth (1849-1899)
3 Eliza Mary (b. ±1850)
3 Cecil John (1851-1921)
4 Emma Annette (1852-1914)
4 Joseph Dornford (b. ±1855)
5 Eliza (dates unknown)
5 George Dornford (b. 1842)

1844: 3 Jun: *A guard of honour from the castle was drawn up within the terminus to receive her, where also were the Commandant of the Garrison, Col. Jones, of the Engineers, a fine looking old soldier, Captain Mercer R.N. at the head of the Packet department, the Mayor of Dover, and other officials.*

MERCHANT — James Merchant [116]

James Merchant (1812-1889), farmer, was the son of James Merchant. He continued with the tenancy of Lower Swell Farm, a considerable undertaking. The farm was comprised of 400 acres and employed sixteen labourers. He married, 1840, Anna Mary (±1819-1888), daughter of George Pain (±1793-1871), jeweller of Stow-on-the-Wold, and Mary Knowles (±1795-1875); they had at least 2 sons and 2 daughters:

1 James (b. ±1843); at school in Stow at the 1851 census
1 Ann Mary (b. ±1847)
2 William Henry Archer (1854-1876)
2 Katherine Elizabeth (1857-1893)

James Merchant (senior) and his wife had disappeared from the records by 1841. It seems likely that the diary entry for 1833 refers to the elder James Merchant.

1833: 14 Jan: *Mr. Perkins had been engaged in the forenoon, looking over the Vicarial land at Lower Swell, and endeavouring to come to an arrangement with the old tenant, J. Merchant, as to its future occupation by him: but no definite agreement was made.*

1837: 15 Feb: *Walked to Lower Swell; paid a visit of condolence to my old parishioners, the Merchants, their respectable mother having lately died.* 13 Sep.

1844: 22 Feb., 24 Feb., 22 Aug.

1846: 14 Jul: *Hayward considered him quite competent to make such will, signed Davis's name by his direction, and witnessed the will with Mr. James Merchant and myself.*

1847: 27 Dec: *he furnishes a correction of his valuation of this parish, as relates to lands held by Mrs. Dolphin and James Merchant.* 30 Dec.

1850: 11 Jun: *Having received a notification of the sale by auction at Stow on Thursday of four acres of standing clover on the Vicarage farm, Lower Swell, wrote a note to James Merchant, requesting him to try and purchase it for me: took my note to Lower Swell in the event of my not finding JM. at home, which proved to be the case.* 26 Jul., 30 Aug: *Drove Mr. Royce to Lower Swell, and formally inducted him to the Benefice—Called with him on Merchant, the Churchwarden, and assisted at a conference as to the temporalities of the Vicarage, particularly, with reference to the numerous allotment tenants now in occupation of the greater part of the glebe.* 31 Oct.

1854: 24 Jun.

MEREWETHER — Francis Merewether [117]

Francis Merewether (1737-1806), Church of England clergyman, was born at Chippenham, Wiltshire, son of Dr John Merewether (1686-1774) and Mary Selby (1706-1756) of Cirencester. He was educated at St John's College, Oxford (BCL 1776), and was appointed rector of Foxcote with Combe Hay, Somerset. He married, at Easton Royal, Wiltshire, 19 January 1784, Ann Neale. It is not known if there were any children.

Col Leigh was distantly related to Agnes Witts, which was the reason she wrote to him on her son Francis's behalf.

1806: 12 Mar: *so he (Smith) obligingly accompanied me on a visit to the Rector, Mr. Merewether, Walcot Parade.* 13 Mar: *Assisted my Mother in writing to Col. Leigh, the Patron of Coombe Hay, requesting his sanction in my Treaty with Mr. Merewether.* 17 Mar: *Instead of breakfasting at Bath visited Mr. Mereweather respecting the Curacy & Parsonage of Coombe Hay; he is not disinclined to treat with us, & I delegated the whole business to my Father, whom I led him to expect in a few days.*

1824: 25 Apr: *In the year 1806 I was ordained Deacon by letters dimissory from Bishop Beadon to Bp. Porteus, then holding the See of London, my nomination being given by the Revd. Mr. Merewether, Rector of Combhay and Foscote, in Somersetshire. I was to reside in the Parsonage at the former place, near Bath: but the death of the incumbent, which took place between my ordination at London, and my arrival at Bath a very few days after, put an end to the engagement after I had once or twice officiated: new incumbents, by whom my services were not required, being quickly appointed to both parishes. In the course of the summer of the same year, I was appointed Curate of the united Vicarage of Erchfont & Stert, near Devizes, where I resided in the former till I removed into Gloucestershire, on being presented to the living of Upper Slaughter in the autumn of 1808. The Revd. G. Smith was Vicar of Erchfont, & ceased to reside on my taking charge of his parishes.*

MEREWETHER — Francis Merewether [118]

Francis Merewether (1784-1864), Church of England clergyman, was born at Calne, Wiltshire, son of Henry Merewether (1735-1803) and Mary White (1752-1828); it seems likely that he was related to Francis Merewether (*above*). He was educated at Christ Church, Oxford (BA 1805), and St John's College, Cambridge (MA 1809). He was vicar of Haverhill, Suffolk, in 1808-15, rector of Cole-Orton, Leicestershire, in 1815-64, and vicar of Whitwick in 1819-64. He was also chaplain to the marquess of Lansdowne.

Merewether married, at Great Yeldham, Essex, 24 April 1810, Frances Elizabeth, daughter of Charles John Way, rector of Boreham, Essex; they had at least 2 sons and 1 daughter:

1 Emily (1818-1874); married, at Ashby-de-la-Zouch, Leicestershire, October 1864, George Currey (1817-1885), master of Charterhouse; 3 daughters
1 Charles George (1822-1884), recorder of Leicester and MP for Northampton
2 Lewis (1824-1842)

It seems probable that Francis Witts and Francis Merewether were acquainted at Oxford, although Merewether is not mentioned in any of the earlier diaries.

1806: 25 Aug: *Had a visit from F. Mereweather from Calne, who called with me upon Gaisford &c.* 9 Oct: *Set out after an early breakfast to call upon Frank Merewether at Calne.* 4 Nov: *Conversed chiefly with the Mr. Salmons, F. Merewether, Mr. Estcourt, Mr. C. Lucas, Compton, Jaques &c.*

1838: 24 Mar: *Renewed a long interrupted acquaintance with my contemporary the Revd. F. Merewether, Incumbent of Cole Orton and Whitwick, villages in the vicinity of Ashby.* 26 Mar: *The worthy Mr. Merewether was not at home, being engaged in professional duty in some one of the farm houses or cottages which are grouped round his residence; for Cole Orton contains no continuous village, the houses being scattered here & there.*

MEREWETHER — Henry Alworth Merewether [119]

Henry Alworth Merewether (1782-1864), attorney-general to the queen dowager, was born at Calne, Wiltshire, the son of Henry Merewether (1735-1803) and Mary White (1752-1828). He was elder brother to Francis (*above*). After his education at Oxford, Merewether entered a career in the law. He was a barrister at the Inner Temple in 1809, serjeant-at-law in 1827, king's serjeant in 1832, attorney-general to the queen dowager, and town clerk of London from 1842 to 1859.

Merewether married, first, at Plymouth, Devon, 12 February 1809, Elizabeth Maria Lockyer (1791-1837); they had 12 sons and 2 daughters:

1 Henry Alworth (1812-1877), barrister QC
2 Francis White (1814-1832), naval officer; served on HMS *Rainbow*; died 20 September 1832 at Port Royal, Kingston, Jamaica
3 John Lockyer (b. & d. 1814)
4 Edmund Robert (b. & d. 1814)
5 Herbert Walton (1816-1843); died, 6 July 1843, at Ardres, Pas-de-Calais, France
1 Eliza Mary Ann (1817-1900)
6 John Robert (1818-1841); drowned at Table Bay, Cape of Good Hope, South Africa
7 Edward Christopher (1820-1893)
2 Lucy Eleanor (1821-1898)
8 Richard Thomas (1823-1834)
9 William Lockyer (1825-1880); appointed KCSI and CB; became a member of council of India

10 Alworth (1827-1861)
11 Edmund Robert (b. & d. 1834)
12 John Lockyer (b. & d. 1834)

Merewether married secondly, at St Marylebone, Westminster, 5 December 1838, Cealia Maria Hadow (1806-1874); they had 1 daughter:

1 Ethel Lucy (1850-1921)

1808: 14 Jan: *Conversed with the Tylee family, the Salmons, the Tinkers, the Spaldings, Mr. Rogers, Mr. Banvis, W. Wood, Eldridge, Macfarlane, Brabant, H. Merewether, Miss F. Goodman &c. On the whole a pleasant meeting.*

MERRETT — John Merrett [120]

John Merrett (1780-1856), tailor, was born at Churchdown, Gloucestershire. He was listed in the 1830 directory as being at 396 High Street, Cheltenham. In 1841 Merrett was living on the High Street premises with three children at home. He was a widower, with at least 3 sons and 1 daughter:

1 Eliza (b. ±1816)
1 Edwin (b. ±1825)
2 Henry (b. ±1825)
3 Charles (b. ±1830); listed, 1851, as a grocer at 89 High Street, and a grocer's clerk in 1881

By 1851 Merrett was at 439 High Street, and listed as a woollen draper. With him were Eliza, who was unmarried, and one son, Henry.

1842: 15 Nov: *I wrote to Merrett, tailor, Cheltenham, respecting mourning for our two men-servants.*

1846: 3 Jul: *also from Merrett, tailor, Cheltenham, announcing his removal to another shop.* 6 Jul: *from Merrett, tailor, Cheltenham, with patterns for trowsers.*

1848: 4 Nov: *Wrote to Merrett, tailor, Cheltenham, to order some clothes.*

1853: 13 Mar: *Wrote a note to Merrett, Tailor, Cheltenham, with a cheque for £14. in payment of his bill.*

METZ — Johann Martin Metz [121]

Johann Martin Metz (±1730-1800), painter, was born at Bonn and died in London in 1800, probably very soon after his return from Dresden. Little is known about him, but he drew the original design for the engraving 'Autumn', published in James Thomson's *The Seasons*. The two diary entries are enigmatic, but Agnes Witts throws a little more light on the subject in her diary entry for 13 September 1800: 'Lady Webb made an early call here after which Mr Witts & I join'd Frank in the Gallery for the purpose of being introduced to an English artist Friend of his Mr Metz.' Considering Francis Witts's life-long passion for art, it is not surprising that he should have been interested in Johann Metz and his work. Presumably in 1801 he was paying a call to his widow.

Metz was a kurkölnisch court painter in Bonn. In 1771 he opened a painting school in Cologne for 'figures, landscapes, flowers and embroidery'. Metz was employed at an early stage of his career at the court of Clemens August, prince elector of Cologne. Clemens August was an enthusiastic builder and employed Metz for his decorative and elegant still life compositions. Metz's work was to be found in all of the palaces owned by the prince elector; he was considered the most important artist working on the interior decorative schemes of this last great prince of the Church of Germany. Metz later worked for Karl Theodor, prince elector of Palatinate.

Johann Metz settled permanently in London in 1781 and distinguished himself as a painter of genre scenes and still lifes, particularly flower arrangements. His wife is unknown, but he had at least 1 son and 1 daughter:

1 Konrad Martin (1755-1827); trained in London as an engraver under Bartolozzi; took the engraving, completed in twelve large sheets between 1801 and 1808, of the 'Last Judgment' by Michelangelo in the Sistine Chapel in Rome
1 Caroline (d. 1794); came to London with her father; began exhibiting her paintings at the Royal Academy in 1773 and was a frequent exhibitor there until 1794; her work included portraits, landscapes, and still lifes

---

1800: 3 Aug: *Two old pictures of Francobigio: the St. Sebastian exists in the original Drawing in the Collection of Mr. Metz in England, one of the valuable Artists I know, and a worthy excellent Friend.*

1801: 14 Aug: *Called upon Lady Lyttelton & Mrs. Metz No. 9 Great Marylebone Street.*

MEYLER — William Meyler of Bath — *see also* David Walker [122]

William Meyler (±1755-1821), JP, printer, publisher, bookseller, and poet, was born at Bath. He was, for a period, in partnership with Joseph Sheldon. Meyler was a printer and bookseller on a large scale and an influential Bath citizen. He was a magistrate and member of the common council, and famed for his circulating library in the Grove (Orange Grove). He became a freemason of the Perfect Friendship Lodge, Bath, on 22 April 1783. Meyler was also proprietor of the *Bath Herald* and a minor poet. In 1777 he published his *Ode to Health—Poetical Amusement on the Journey of Life; consisting of Various Pieces in verse: serious, theatric, epigrammatic and miscellaneous.*

William Meyler married, at Minchinhampton, Gloucestershire, Alice Hyatt [Hyett, Hiatt] (±1753-1827), possibly a relation of the Hyatt family of Painswick.; they had at least 2 sons and 2 daughters:

1 William Morgan (1788-1862); *see below*
1 Mary (b. 1792)
2 Margaret (b. 1793)
2 John George (1794-1802)

The diary entry almost implies that Meyler was a coachmaker, but it was probably the case that a Bath coachmaker recommended calling at Mr Meyler's as he knew he had a gig for sale.

1806: 30 Jun: *Mrs. Bates gave us a very handsome breakfast, after which my Father & myself explored the different Coachmakers for Gigs, respecting one of which we called upon Mr. Meyler in the Grove.*

MEYLER — William Morgan Meyler [123]

William Morgan Meyler (1788-1862), surgeon, was born at Bath, the eldest son of William Meyler (±1755-1821) and Alice Hyatt (±1753-1827) (*above*). He married, at St Mary de Crypt, Gloucester, 10 September 1827, Eleanor Maria Mowbray, née Walker (1802-1865), the daughter of David Walker, a Hereford printer who had bought the *Gloucester Journal* and presumably also the printing interests from the Raikes family in 1802. The marriage united two of the region's major newspaper families.

William and Eleanor had at least 1 son and 3 daughters:

1 Elizabeth Eleanor (1829-1905)
1 Thomas (1830-1897)
2 Margaret Alice (1832-1833)
3 Alice (b. 1834)

In 1841 Meyler lived at Eastgate Street with wife Eleanor and children Eleanor, Thomas, and Alice. By 1849 he had moved his practice to Clarence Street.

1827: 18 Oct: *There were, no doubt, several younger practitioners anxious for the appointment, as a step in their profession, as an opportunity of gaining greater experience, and as qualifying them to take pupils with considerable premiums; Messrs. J. Wilton, Shrapnell, Meyler, Heane &, I believe, one or two more, were candidates, if an increase were resolved on.*

1847: 16 Mar: *Mr. Meyler represented the interests of the City of Gloucester.*

MEYRICK — Meyrick & Cox solicitors

1835: 9 Jun: *Called on Mr. Cox in Red Lion Square, junior partner in the house of Meyrick & Cox, Solicitors, and held a conversation with him on the business of the Wadenhoe Trust.*

MICHELL — Edward Thomas Michell[124]

Edward Thomas Michell (1786-1841) was the son of John Michell, of Huish Champflower, Somerset, and brother of John Michell and William Michell (*below*). He entered the Royal Military Academy, Woolwich, on 27 January 1802, and passed out as second lieutenant in the Royal Artillery on 8 September 1803. Michell served with distinction during the Peninsular War.

In 1840, with the local rank of brigadier-general, Michell was dispatched to Syria to command the Royal Artillery detachments and sappers and miners of Adm. Stafford's fleet. Their objective was to assist the Turks in driving the Egyptian Army out of Syria. With the other British officers, Michell accompanied the Turks, under Gen. Jochmus, in their advance from Jaffa towards Gaza, and was present at the battle of Medjdel on 15 January 1841, which compelled the Egyptians to retreat. The British advised the immediate seizure of Gaza, 6 miles distant. Jochmus prevaricated over the bad state of the roads, and two days later news arrived of the convention concluded by Napier at Alexandria, ending the war.

Michell, who was appointed CB on 19 July 1838 and was in receipt of £300 a year for wounds, was popular with his fellow officers and his men. He was described as an open-hearted, frank old soldier, small in stature, with a stoop from the effects of an old wound and a keen, clear eye. He died on 24 January 1841 of fever caused by sleeping in wet clothes the night after the battle of Medjdel.

1826: 27 Jan: *Then there was Major Michell, Son of the Prebendary, Dr. Michell, an Artillery Officer, who has seen much foreign Service, & was grievously wounded at Bergen op Zoom.*

1827: 11 Jul: *I dined at the Palace; the Bishop looks ill; and was much indisposed, when in town. He entertained a small party, the Archdeacon, Messrs. Ford & Jeaffreson, myself, Major J. Michell, & the Revd. Mr. Michell. The two latter are sons of Dr. Michell, one of the Prebendaries of Gloucester & constantly residing at his house in the College. Major Michell is in the Artillery, and another brother, Edward, with whom I am acquainted, bears the same rank in the same service; the latter being in the Horse Artillery. The Clerical brother is an Incumbent in Glamorganshire*

MICHELL — John Michell[125]

John Michell (1750-1828), Church of England clergyman, was born at Huish Champflower, Somerset, son of John Michell. He was educated at Exeter College, Oxford (BCL 1797; DCL 1814), and was appointed prebendary of Gloucester in 1798 and vicar of Fairford in 1810.

1825: 15 Jul: *the Sermon a collection was made at the door of the Cathedral: Dr. Michell, Prebendary of Gloucester, the Archdeacon, Mr. Ford and myself, held the plates: the sum of £25. 8 was collected.*

1826: 17 Jun: *The plates at the door were held by the Bishop, the Archdeacon, Dr. Michell, Prebendary of the cathedral.*

1828: 18 Jul: *afterwards the Bishop, Dr. Michell the Prebendary in residence, the Archdeacon & myself held boxes for the contribution of the congregation.*

1829: 4 Feb: *F. Rice formed the party; the latter recently admitted to Priest's orders, & presented by his father, the Dean of Gloucester, to the Vicarage of Fairford, vacant by the decease of Dr. Michell, late Prebendary of Gloucester.*

MICHELL — John Michell[126]

Sir John Michell (±1781-1866), army officer, was the eldest son of John Michell. He was the brother of Edward Michell (*above*) and William Michell (*below*). He rose to the rank of brigadier-general and was appointed KCB. He married Jane Elizabeth Breedon (±1786-1869); they had at least 2 sons and 3 daughters:

1 Maria (±1815-1890); born at Jersey
2 Jane Eliza (b. 1816)
1 William (1817); born at Woolwich, Kent
3 Julia Mary (1818-1896); born at Woolwich, Kent
2 John Edward (±1827-1883), Maj.-Gen.; appointed CB; lived at Huish House, Langport, Somerset; married, December 1874, Caroline Anne Stisted (1832-1910)

1827: 11 Jul: *I dined at the Palace; the Bishop looks ill; and was much indisposed, when in town. He entertained a small party, the Archdeacon, Messrs. Ford & Jeaffreson, myself, Major J. Michell, & the Revd. Mr. Michell. The two latter are sons of Dr. Michell, one of the Prebendaries of Gloucester & constantly residing at his house in the College. Major Michell is in the Artillery, and another brother, Edward, with whom I am acquainted, bears the same rank in the same service; the latter being in the Horse Artillery. The Clerical brother is an Incumbent in Glamorganshire*

MICHELL — Richard Michell[127]

Richard Michell (1766-1826), Church of England clergyman, was born at Totnes, Devon, son of John Michell (1732/33-1811) and Elizabeth Cranch (b. 1743). He was educated at Wadham College, Oxford (BA 1788; MA 1793; BD 1804; DD 1811), where he was a fellow from 1793 to 1812 and proctor in 1803. Michell was rector of Fryerning and appointed vicar of Eastwood, Essex, in 1811. He married, at Totnes, Devon, 18 September 1763, Martha Burrel (b. ±1766).

1802: 10 Feb: *Breakfasted with the Revd. Mr. Mitchell Subwarden & Tutor of Wadh. Coll.* 11 Feb: *Breakfasted in College with Mr. Mitchell & a Mr. Dunsford, a Scholar, who accompanied us to Dr. Marlow's, the Head of St. John's, the Vice Chancellor of the University: in whose Lodgings I was matriculated & took the customary Oaths.* 12 Feb: *I underwent an Examination by Mr. Michell in Sallust, Xenophon, Thycidides, Virgil & Homer.* 15 Feb., 17 Feb., 20 Feb., 14 May, 17 May: *With Alford in the Evening, meeting Williams, Edgell, & Evans. To the Music Room with all but Edgell, conversed chiefly with Michell.* 6 Jul.

1803: 9 Nov.

1804: 30 Jan., 21 Oct., 25 Oct., 6 Nov., 11-13 Nov., 16-17 Nov.

1805: 18 Mar: *Called on Michell. Virgil & Tacitus.*

1806: 18-19 Mar., 21 Mar: *of the party were Stevens & his Wife, Matthias of B.N.C., Budd of C.C.C., Marsh, Marshall of Ball. Dr. Price, Michel, Simmons, Round, Dr. Cooper, Mr. Jebb, Mr. Davis.* 22 Mar: *Walked with Round: with Michell round the Parks.*

MICHELL — Richard Michell[128]

Richard Michell (1805-1877), college head, was born in Bruton, Somerset, the third son of Edward Michell, of Bruton, and Ann Clements (1773-1843) of Wyke Champflower, Somerset. He was a cousin to some degree of the Michells (*above*), and a nephew of Richard Michell (*above*). He was educated at Bruton Grammar School, Wadham College, Oxford (BA 1824; MA 1827)—where his uncle Dr Richard Michell (1766-1826) was a fellow—and Lincoln College, Oxford (BD 1836). At Lincoln Michell was a fellow from 1830 to 1842, bursar in 1832, public examiner in 1829-30 and 1833-37, tutor in 1834-48, claviger in 1835, praelector of logic in 1839-49, public orator in 1848-77, and Bampton lecturer in 1849. He was appointed rector of South Moreton, Berkshire, in 1856, and was vice-principal of Magdalen Hall, Oxford, in 1848-68, where he was awarded his DD in 1868. Michell was principal of Magdalen in 1868-74, and was appointed first principal of Hertford College in 1874. He remained in that post until his death in 1877.

Michell was a leading manager of the tory party in Oxford, which may have been a reason why the Witts family supported him. Regarding religion, he was more or less of the evangelical school. He married, at Holy Trinity, Marylebone, Westminster, 4 July 1841, Amelia (1811-1896), youngest daughter of Thomas Blair; they had 6 sons and 2 daughters:

1 Edward Blair (1842-1896)
1 Eliza Maria (b. 1844)
2 Richard Brooke (1845-1915)
3 Rowland Lyons Nosworthy (1847-1931)
2 Mary Caroline (1848-1912); married, first, her cousin Arthur Kindersley Blair (d. 1883); secondly, at Dunedin, Florida, USA, 4 March 1889, George Granville William Sutherland Leveson-Gower (1828-1892)
4 Herbert William Creswell (1851-1909)
5 Arthur Tompson (1852-1923)
6 Walter Gordon (1854-1925)

1839: 28 May: *Wrote to Cockey, and promised him to go to Oxford on the 5. June to vote for Mr. Michell.* 31 May, 4-5 Jun.

1847: 13-14 Dec.

1848: 14 Apr: *Recd. a circular from the Revd. Mr. Michell, of Lincoln College, Oxford, thanking me for my promised vote, to assist in his election as Public Orator of the University.* 22 Apr: *Recd. a letter from the Revd. Griffith, Wadh. Coll. announcing that Mr. Michell had been elected Public Orator.*

1854: 3 Jul: *Sent to Mr. Michell, Magd. Hall, Oxford, the paper forwarded to me yesterday, which I had signed; Mr. M. being one of those to whom communications were directed to be made.*

MICHELL — William Michell[129]

William Michell (±1783-1828), Church of England clergyman, was the son of John Michell (*above*) and brother of John Michell and Edward Michell (*above*). He was educated at Exeter College, Oxford (BA 1806), and Queen's College, Cambridge (BA 1819; MA 1819). Michell was ordained deacon on 25 July 1806 and priest on 31 March 1807. His first clerical appointment was as curate of Compton Dundon, Somerset, from 25 July 1806. He was rector of Barwick, Somerset, in 1824-27, and vicar of Compton-Dundon, Somerset, in 1822-28.

It is not known why Francis Witts should have thought that William Michell was an incumbent in Glamorganshire; no records suggest that this was the case. Records are sparse and it is not known if he was married.

1827: 11 Jul: *I dined at the Palace; the Bishop looks ill; and was much indisposed, when in town. He entertained a small party, the Archdeacon, Messrs. Ford & Jeaffreson, myself, Major J. Michell, & the Revd. Mr. Michell. The two latter are sons of Dr. Michell, one of the Prebendaries of Gloucester & constantly residing at his house in the College. Major Michell is in the Artillery, and another brother, Edward, with whom I am acquainted, bears the same rank in the same service; the latter being in the Horse Artillery. The Clerical brother is an Incumbent in Glamorganshire*

MIDDLETON — Mr Middleton of Hersham

1851: 25 May: *Returning through the village, and through retired lanes, by one or two villa residences, we arrived at a house of more pretensions than the other, the residence of a Mr. Middleton, at which we called, that I might see the flower garden, and dressed ground attached to the house.*

1853: 17 Jun.

MIDDLETON — the Middleton family visiting Turkdean — *see also* Biscoe *and* Davies[130]

Diana Middleton [later Davies] (1820-1880) was the daughter of Capt. Robert Gambier Middleton, RN (1774-1837) and Susanna Maria Martin Leake (1778-1830). Robert was the son of George Middleton (1724-1794), former comptroller of customs for the port of Leith, and Elizabeth Wilson. His elder brother was Sir Charles Middleton. In 1795 Capt. Middleton commanded HMS *Lowestoffe*, a 32-gun fifth-rate frigate, famous for being the ship in which the young Horatio Nelson served shortly after passing his lieutenant's examination.

Robert and Susanna married at St Marylebone's, Westminster, on 11 December 1802. They had 4 sons and 3 daughters:

1 Charles John (1809-1894)
1 Diana (1811-1880); born at Chelsea; married, 15 August 1854, Revd Edward Reed Davies (±1828-1876), a young curate at Aldsworth; (*see* Davies)
2 Alexander (1814-1846), twin of William
3 William (b. 1814), twin of Alexander
2 Mary Susannah (1815-1904); born at Chelsea; married, 1 December 1837, Frederick Biscoe (1808-1880)
4 John George (1817-1878)
3 Helen (b. & d. 1819)

1843: 19 Aug: *Mr. and Mrs. Biscoe, and Miss Middleton called while we were from home.*

1845: 23 Apr., 14 May, 4 Jun: *We received a party to dinner to-day: Mr. and Mrs. Biscoe, Miss Middleton, a Mr. Middleton, brother of Mrs. Biscoe and Miss M.*

1846: 8 Sep: *Accompanied M.W. on a drive to call on the Biscoes at Turkdean: when we arrived within a mile of the village, we met Mr. B. Miss Middleton, and a brother of hers on a visit to the Biscoes going to call on the Astons at Northleach.* 18 Sep., 26 Nov.

1847: 31 Aug.

1848: 24 Aug.

1854: 26 Jun: *Miss Middleton, Mrs. B's agreeable sister, who has lived with the Biscoe's since their marriage, is on the eve of marriage with a young Curate of Aldsworth (Mr. Davies?) said to be 26 years of age, and 16 years younger than Miss M.—She seemed in high spirits.* 15 Aug: *Early dinner, to suit E. Clifford, who went to Turkdean in the evening, to join a party at Biscoe's, closing with gaiety the wedding day of Mrs. Biscoe's sister, Miss Middleton, for many years an inmate of the parsonage at Turkdean, now married to a Mr. Davis, Curate of Aldsworth.*

MILBANKE — *see* Arthur Moore

MILES — James Miles of Moreton-in-Marsh

1844: 29 Oct: *Wrote to Mr. Mason, Govr, of Gloucester gaol, in favour of W Jas Miles, of Moreton, servant to Mr. Horne, Grocer, who applied to me yesterday to promote an application made by him to the Trustees of the County prison charity, a year having elapsed since his discharge from gaol, where he had suffered imprisonment for a long term on a charge of sending a threatening letter, and he having kept his place with one master with credit, as certified in a memorial signed by several principal inhabitants of Moreton.* 2 Nov., 4 Nov., 9 Nov.

MILES — Philip John Miles and the Miles family of Leigh Court [131]

Philip John Miles (1774-1845), MP, banker, slave-owner, and merchant, was the son of William Miles (1727-1803) and Sarah Ann Berrow (1745-1823). His father was a Bristol merchant who went to Jamaica as a young man and acquired a fortune. Upon his return, William Miles became one of Bristol's leading merchants; he was also a landowner in Somerset and a banker of enormous wealth. He was sheriff for Bristol in 1766 and mayor in 1780.

Philip John Miles was MP for Corfe Castle in 1820-32 and Bristol in 1835-37. He married, first, at Clifton, 13 June 1795, Maria Whetham (1776-1811), daughter of Arthur Whetham; they had 2 sons and 7 daughters:

1 William (1797-1878); educated at Christ Church, Oxford, and Lincoln's Inn; MP for Chippenham (1818-20) Romeny (1830-32) and East Somerset (1834-65); created 1st baronet of Leigh Court; married, 12 September 1823, Catherine (1798-1869), daughter of John Gordon; 5 sons and 7 daughters
1 Sarah Agatha (1799-1830)
2 Elizabeth (b. 1801)
2 William (1801-1878)
3 Maria (b. 1804)
4 Millicent (1806-1861)
5 Charlotte Louisa (b. 1807)
6 Agatha (b. 1808)
7 Milly (b. 1810)

Miles married secondly, at Tockington [Olveston], Gloucestershire, 11 May 1813, Clarissa (1790-1868), daughter of Samuel Peach Peach and Clarissa Partridge; they had 7 sons and 4 daughters:

1 Clara Philippa (1814-1892)
1 John William (1816-1878); educated at Christ Church, Oxford; MP for Bristol (April–June 1868)
2 Philip William Skynner (1816-1881); educated at Christ Church, Oxford; MP for Bristol (1837-52)
3 Robert Henry William (1819-1883); educated at Christ Church, Oxford; rector of Bingham, Nottinghamshire (1845-83)
2 Ellen Octavia (1821-1907)
4 Charles William (1823-1892)
5 George Frederick William (1823-1886)
3 Sybella Mary (1827-1889)
6 Edward Peach William (1829-1889); married Olivia Cave, granddaughter of John Cave; became a partner in the firm Kington, Miles and Co., which did extensive trade in New Zealand *c.* 1850-1900
4 Marianne Adelaide (1834-1921)
7 Henry Cruger William (1834-1888); educated at Eton College and Christ Church, Oxford

Philip John Miles bought the Kings Weston property in 1833 from the executors of Edward Southwell IV. He also purchased Leigh Court estate in 1811 and several art collections, including that of Richard Hart Davis. Miles demolished the house at Leigh Court, which was in a state of disrepair, and in 1814 rebuilt it a quarter of a mile further north-east. It was rebuilt according to Thomas Hopper's designs for Pythouse in Wiltshire.

Philip Miles died in 1845, leaving Leigh Court to his eldest son, William Miles, for whom the Miles baronetcy of Leigh Court, Somerset, was created in 1859. The mansion eventually housed a collection of over a hundred paintings representing many old masters—Domenichino, Titian, Poussin, Michelangelo, Raphael, Rubens, Claude Lorrain, and Van Dyke—as well as numerous family portraits. The majority of the more famous paintings were sold between 1884 and 1898. In 1884 the 2nd baronet, Sir Philip Miles, entertained the Prince of Wales, later Edward VII, at Leigh Court.

1806: 11 Mar: *Dined in a large, dashing party at Gillibrand's the Adair family, Lords Kilwarden & Ruthven; Major Cochrane & P.J. Miles, formed the party.*

1827: 26 Jul: *At Bristol, Miles, Conservative, and Berkeley, Liberal.*

1833: 18 Apr: *On the Somersetshire bank of the Avon was the village of Leigh, with its tall Church Tower rising out of a grove; lower down the Park and Mansion, the drest grounds and woods of Leigh Court, the seat of P. J. Miles Esqr., an opulent proprietor and Bristol Banker.*

1835: 7 Jan: *I was able to communicate the intelligence that, in all probability, Bristol would return two Conservatives, Sir. R. Vyvyan and Mr. Miles being at the head of the first day's poll, and far in advance of the coalesced yellow Candidates Col. Baillie and Sir J. C. Hobhouse.* 8 Jan: *Mr. Newman arrived this Evening from Bristol, whither he had gone in the morning to vote for the Conservative Candidates. The Election had closed, before he set out on his return to Gloucester, and he reported the triumphant success of Sir. R. Vyvyan and Mr. Miles, who were returned by a large Majority.*

1839: 27 Aug: *On our right stretched Country down to the course of the Avon, and its embouchure, the village of Abbots Leigh, Leigh Court, the handsome seat of the rich Bristol Merchant and Banker, Mr. Miles. MP. for East Somerset.*

1845: 26 Jan: *They met with a very kind and hospitable reception, and besides some in the house, domesticated guests, Mr. Hale and Lady Theodosia, Matthew Hale, Dr. Twisleton, Mr. Huntley, Mr. Sherwood &c. they saw at the Bishop's table some of the leading people of the neighbourhood of Bristol, the Miles's, Scandrett Harfords &c.*

1846: 29 Oct: *Letter from Sewell: the Longbands and Applehurst farm was sold on Tuesday last for £8200 to Fergus O'Connor the Chartist: Mr. Miles of Bristol being his competitor.*

1848: 8 Jan: *In consequence of a letter received from Sophia Hunt, I wrote to Messrs. Miles, Bankers, Bristol.*

MILES — William Miles and the Miles family of Bristol [132]

William Miles (1727-1803), merchant and banker, was born at Ledbury, Herefordshire, son of Robert Miles (1700-1737) and Sarah Hatton (1700-1766). He lived in Jamaica and then at 61 Queen

Square [now renumbered 69/70/71], Bristol. The house became the headquarters of his family's extensive business interests. William Miles was sheriff for Bristol in 1766 and mayor in 1780. He was also warden of the Merchant Venturers.

Miles married, at Bristol, 23 April 1766, Sarah Ann Berrow (1745-1823); they had 4 sons and 7 daughters:

1 Ann (1739-1816)
1 William (1767-1790)
2 Sarah (1769-1785)
2 Philip John (1774-1845); *see above*
3 Charlotte (1774-1844)
3 John Robert (1777-1780)
4 Millicent (1778-1855)
5 Milborough (b. & d. 1780)
4 Robert John (1781-1797)
6 Elizabeth (1783-1800)
7 Molly (1785-1855)

William had two brothers: Philip (1735-1823) and John (1737-1812). Philip married Elizabeth Peachy and they had two children:

1 Eliza (d. 1862)
1 William (1791-1844)

John married, 1777, Milly, daughter of Revd Richard Hallings; there is no record of any children.

The diary entries are a little enigmatic. The Caroline of 9 October 1804 probably refers to Caroline Townsend.

1804: 21 Jan., 21 Jan: *Walked with Harriett on the Downs afterwards with her sisters & the Miles's & with Edgell.* 22 Jan: *Walked with the Marriotts, & Miles's, Marshal etc.* 26 Jan: *Passed the Evening away ennuié at Lady J. Floods conversing chiefly with Sarah Miles.* 31 Jul: *To the Ball. Danced with Miss Sarah Miles & Miss Fortescue.* 28 Aug: *Danced two Dances with Miss S. Miles, conversed with Townsends, Manners's, Miss Adair &c. Not very full nor unpleasant.* 9 Oct: *Danced with Caroline & Sara Miles.* 22 Dec: *To a large & handsome party at Lady Call's.... Conversed with the Miss Miles's Deace &c.*

1805: 9 Jan: *Danced with Miss Gould, whom I thought very pleasing, the gentle Miss Dundas, & Sarah Miles.*

MILL — Lady Mill at Charlton

1805: 25 Jul: *Walked with my Mother to Charlton. Called on Lady Mill.*

MILLAR — Robert Millar [133]

Robert Millar (1789-1865) was a union pipe player. The union pipes, also known as the uilleann pipes, are the national bagpipes of Ireland. They are named after their method of inflation, 'uilleann' being a partial translation of the Irish-language term píoba uilleann (literally, 'pipes of the elbow'). Robert Millar was one of the key union pipe players in Scotland and northern England. The Highland Society of London, 1788-1822, included the performers Richard Fitzmaurice, Patrick O'Farrell, John Murphy, John MacGregor, Dennis Courtney, Malcolm MacGregor, and James McDonnell. It is reasonably likely that this performance attended by Francis Witts at Oxford was by the society, which on this occasion included Robert Millar, one of the key exponents of the pipes.

1806: 19 Mar: *Accompanied Round & Burney to the Music Room, where the sorry attractions of Mr. Miller, Mrs. Salmon & a Mr. FitzMaurice on a vile squeaking Union Pipe, had collected a tolerably full room ... & the piper, thanks to good taste, fairly hissed off the field.*

MILLER — John Miller [134]

Sweet & Miller was a firm of nurserymen at Durdham Down, co-founded in 1786 by John Sweet (d. 1822) and John Miller. John Claudius Loudon called them 'the most extensive garden tradesmen in the West if England'.

1804: 3 Sep., 4 Sep: *On the Downs, at the Brigade & Miller's & Sweet's with my Father & Mother, Mrs. Massey, S. Monck, Mr. Harford &c. very pleasant.*

1834: 28 Nov: *Wrote to Miller, the Bristol nurseryman, to send some garden seeds.*

1835: 26 Jan: *Wrote to Miller, Seedsman, Bristol, for a supply of garden seeds.* 11 Feb.

1836: 15 Dec: *Wrote to Miller, Seedsman, Bristol, respecting some seeds which had been ordered, but had not been sent.*

1837: 20 Jan: *A letter from a Mr. Garaway, announcing himself as acting under the Assignee of Miller the Bankrupt Nurseryman near Bristol in the management of that extensive concern.* 14 Feb: *Wrote to Garaway, the Manager for the Assignee of Miller, the nurseryman on Durdham Downs, to order the usual bundle of garden seeds &c.*

1838: 11 Dec: *Wrote to Garaway the manager of Miller's Nursery, Bristol, to order a supply of garden seeds.*

1839: 22 Feb: *also from the Manager of the Nursery, late Miller's, on Durdham Down, with an invoice of garden seeds &c. sent by the waggon.*

MILLER — Robert Marratt Miller [135]

Robert Marratt Miller (1786-1839), Church of England clergyman, was born at Warwick, the son of Robert Miller. He was educated at Wadham College, Oxford (BA 1810; MA 1813; B&DD 1826), and was resident chaplain at Lisbon from 1811 to 1818, and vicar of Dedham, Essex, from 1819 to 1839. He married, 1819, Mary Nanison; they had at least 1 son and 1 daughter:

1 John Harrison (b. 1821)
1 Mary Marratt (1824-1869); born in Scotland; married Samuel Charles Alston Swinton (1820-1920)

1829: 26 Feb: *I sat by the sub-warden, & next to me was an agreeable man, Dr. Miller, Vicar of Dedham, Essex, a member of the College, & formerly for many years British Chaplain at Lisbon.*

1832: 15 Mar: *I conversed chiefly with the Warden, and with Dr. Miller, whom I had previously met on similar occasions.*

MILLER — William Miller [136]

William Miller (1782-1848), JP and landed proprietor, was born at Newington Bagpath, son of Richard Miller and Esther Parslowe. He lived at Ozleworth Park, Gloucestershire, which is also referred to as Sheep Court in one document. Miller married, first, 1809, Frances (1789-1870), daughter of Charles Wyndham, 2nd earl of Egremont. By 1822 they were separated, and later they divorced. Frances went to live in Paris; she subsequently married, 1847, Augustin Denis Pinon Duclos, 2nd vicomte de Valmer. William married, secondly, Melicent Amelia (1803-1890), daughter of John Redman (1775-1843) and Elizabeth Ellen Smith (b. 1778) of Spine, Wiltshire; they had at least 6 sons and 3 daughters:

1 William Redman Ponsford (1822-1906); died at Richmond, Melbourne, Australia
1 Amelia Millicent (1824-1851); married James Edward Taylor
2 George Barnes (1826-1911); married, first, Elizabeth Ann Turner; secondly, Sarah Jones
3 Henry Richard (1827-1907); died at Castlemaine, Victoria, Australia

2 Charlotte Augusta Willkins (1832-1902)
4 Charles Tangier (1835-1906); married Kate Dudley; died at Melbourne, Australia
5 Richmond Augustus (1837-1908)
6 Culloden Robert (1839-1858); drowned at sea near Bonny, Nigeria
3 Georgiana (1840-1853)

William Miller was a Gloucestershire JP and high sheriff for Gloucestershire (1821). His widow, Melicent Amelia, who had been born at Salisbury, Wiltshire, married secondly, at St Modwen, Burton-on-Trent, Staffordshire, 13 November 1856, John Kieves Pountney (1815-1888).

1832: 29 Mar.

1835: 6 Apr: *The Gentlemen present this Evening at the Bell, and who took part in these deliberations were, Messrs. Codrington MP, Bathurst, Goodrich, R. B. Cooper, Sampson, Savage, Fripp, Hopkinson, Hale, Miller, Gist, Goldney, Revd. Messrs. Crawley, Pettat, Witts &c.*

MILLINGTON — George Millington [137]

George Millington (1807-1875), police officer, was born at Lambeth, Surrey. In the 1841 census he was registered as a police officer living at 16 Upper Crown Street, London. He later retired to his home parish of Lambeth, where he died unmarried.

1834: 26 Sep: *While we were examining this man, Millington went to Broadwell in search of his brother John, who had lived creditably for several years in the service of Mr. Vavasour and Mr. E. Leigh.*

1835: 1 Jan: *A meeting was held of the Stow Police Association... All the gentlemen present, consisting of the leading farmers of the district, spoke in most cordial terms of the benefits derivable from the plan adopted, and of the manner in which the duties of Police-officers had been discharged by Otway and Millington.* 19 Mar.

1839: 6 Jan: *Otway and Millington came about midday, that the latter might obtain from me a letter in his favour to the Metropolitan Commrs. of Police.*

1850: 23 Sep: *Wrote to Millington, formerly of the Metropolitan Police, and stationed at Stow under Otway, informing him of a vacancy in the office of outer door keeper at Gloucester Gaol, which is likely to suit him, if he is a married man. When lately at Stow, he asked me to procure him a situation, if I had an opportunity.* 27 Sep: *Received a letter from Geo. Millington, who, being single, and having temporary employment under the Metropolitan Police Commissioners, cannot offer himself as a Candidate for the situation of outer lodge officer at Gloucester Gaol.*

MILLS — Mrs Mills, daughter of Thomas Paxton, Eyford land agent

1846: 25 Sep: *We found with Mrs. D. A Mrs. Mills, daughter of the Agent, Mr. Paxton, who was also at Eyford.*

MILLS — Henry Mills [138]

Henry Mills (1815-1906), JP and Church of England clergyman, was born at Barford, Warwickshire, son of Revd Francis Mills (1759-1851), rector of Barford, and Catherine Mordaunt (1776-1852). He was educated at Balliol College, Oxford (BA 1837; MA 1840), and succeeded his father as vicar of Pillerton Hersey, Warwickshire. He married, 1841, Mary Hippisley (1809-1892); they had at least 1 son and 2 daughters:

1 Francis (1844-1916), Church of England clergyman; married, 27 December 1877, Selina Mary Knightley; succeeded his father as vicar of Pillerton Hersey
1 Catherine (1847-1895); married, 20 April 1882, Revd Alfred Freeman
2 Fanny (b. ±1851); died unmarried

1844: 1 May: *The latter a pleasing young lady, sister to R W Hippisley, and married to a young Clergyman without preferment, lately a Curate in Somersetshire, and now on their way to reside at a Curacy in Warwickshire, at Pillerton Hersey, a living of a Mr. Mills, who married another Miss Hippisley.*

MILLS — Thomas Mills — *see also* Dyer [139]

Thomas Mills (1794-1873) was the son of Job Mills (1771-1831) and Unity Fisher (1773-1859). He married, at Fairford, Gloucestershire, 7 August 1820, Sarah Smith (1789-1856); they had at least 1 son:

1 Thomas (1823-1891); married, at Bristol, 31 December 1848, Mary Ann Coventry (1826-1916); 4 sons and 1 daughter

Thomas Mills (senior) died at Victoria, Australia. The family was from Yate, Gloucestershire—where Thomas (junior) died—so the appellation of 'the Wickwar Gang' is a little misleading. The brothers Dyer—John Dyer (1795-1827) and Mark Dyer (1797-1827)—were hanged on 28 April 1827. Francis Witts was in error: the 'accomplice Mills' was Job Mills, of Yate, with his wife Unity; they were tried at the August 1826 assizes and found not guilty.

1827: 19 Apr: *I attended the Crown Court, and heard a very interesting trial for maliciously shooting with intent to murder &c. the indictment laid under Lord Ellenborough's Act. The two prisoners, Brothers of the name of Dyer, had been charged by an accomplice, Thomas Mills, with burglary, and being tried at the last assizes, were aquitted, there being no collateral evidence to support the testimony of the approver. All belonged to what has received the appellation of the Wickwar gang. Malice is presumed to have actuated the Dyers; a shot was fired into a cottage, in which the approver with his wife & several other members of his family were sitting one evening round a bright fire; the content of the gun, evidently directed at Thos. Mills, came in contact with the back of a chair close by where he sat on a low stool & lodged in the left side of his wife, who providentially survived the shot.*

MILLS — William Mills — *see* Foster, Huntley, Ibbetson, *and* Tancred 140

William Mills (1780-1865), JP, DL, and landed proprietor, was born in the parish of St Olave, London, the eldest son of Thomas Mills (1749-1834) and Susanna (1760-1833), daughter of Christopher Harris of Bellevue, Plymstock, Devon. He was educated at Eton College and the Mounier Academy at the Belvedere in Weimar, Thuringia, Germany. Mills married, at Boxwell with Leighterton, Gloucestershire, 5 June 1817, Clara Jane (1799-1874), daughter of Revd Richard Huntley (1766-1831) and Anne Webster (1773-1855); they had 2 sons and 6 daughters:

1 Thomas Richard (1818-1884), Lt, 1st Dragoons, and high sheriff for Suffolk (1871); born at Bath, Somerset; married, at Chambly, near Montreal, Canada, 31 May 1843, Emily, third, but only surviving, daughter of Samuel Hall, seignior of Chambly; 2 sons and 1 daughter:
    1 William (b. 1844)
    1 Emily Matilda (b. 1849); born in Canada; registered as living with her widower father at Exeter in 1871
    2 Thomas Richard (b. 1854); born at Exeter; also registered as living with his widower father (and sister Emily) at Exeter in 1871

1 Clara Mary Anne (1820-1905); married, at Great Saxham, 27 May 1845, her cousin Revd Wadham Huntley Skrine, second son of Henry Skrine of Stubbings House
2 Susanna Caroline (1822-1890)
3 Ann Harriet (1822-1877); married, 17 May 1853, Sholto James Douglas (1820-1868), son of Gen. Sir James Dawes Douglas and Marianne Bullock
2 William (b. 1823)
4 Julia Jane (1826-1898); married, at Thingoe, Suffolk, July 1852, Theodore Thring (1816-1891)
5 Catherine Mary (b. ±1830); married, 1854, George James Edward Brown of Tostock Place
6 Elizabeth Georgina (±1837-1912); married, 11 August 1863, Revd Henry Kwyworth Creed

William's father, Thomas Mills, had bought the grounds of the Elizabethan Nutmeg Hall at Great Saxham, Suffolk, from the trustees in bankruptcy of Hutchison Mure shortly after 1793. Great Saxham Hall and its estate were originally part of the estates of Bury St Edmunds abbey.

The estate of Great Saxham in Suffolk was acquired by Sir Richard Long after the dissolution of the monasteries and subsequently sold to John Eldred, a Levant merchant, for £3,000. The house that he built was known appropriately as 'Nutmeg Hall'. The Eldreds sold the property to Hutchinson Mure in 1754. Mure's wealth was derived from his West Indian sugar plantations; in 1762 he commissioned Robert Adam to design a new Palladian-style house. Nothing was done at the time, but in 1774 the old house was demolished and a new D-plan house in an Adamesque castle-style was begun. Between 1774 and 1776 Adam produced designs for certain interior features, ceilings, etc., though he may not have been responsible for the design of the whole building. This fantasy castle was destroyed by fire in 1779. Adam provided designs for a new classical-style house in 1780, but these were rejected in favour of Mure's own designs for converting the stables into a new house. Work progressed slowly. Mure was declared bankrupt in 1793 and died the following year.

Thomas Mills bought the unfinished house and its estate for £32,000. He employed the architect Joseph Patience to redesign and complete the house between 1797 and 1806. He also employed Capability Brown to landscape the grounds. Further alterations were undertaken by William Mills in the early Victorian period, including an extensive new service wing.

William Mills was a co-student with Sir Thomas Tancred (1780-1844), Augustus Foster (1780-1848), and others at M. Mounier's Academy at Weimar. The Witts family knew them in Weimar, and they are mentioned together in the diaries of Agnes Witts for 15 December 1798: 'Sr. Thos. Tancred, Mr. Mills, Mr. Walker & Mr. Ibbetson here before they went to the Opera. ... 8 August 1799: ... Sr. Thos. Tancred, Mr. Mills Mr. Oakely, Mr. Hope Mr. Foster & Mr. Ibbetson drank Tea here ...'

Little is known of William Mills after he returned from Weimar; he does not appear to have gone to Cambridge or Oxford. The diary entries for 1801 suggest that he was studying for the law. In later life he was nominated as sheriff for Suffolk in 1845 and 1847, but was excused on the basis of ill health.

1799: 18 Aug: *To Dinner at Court to Mr. Mills's Lodgings where read Pizarro Mr. Sheridan's last Play.*

1800: 20 Mar: *Mr. Mills called to take his leave previous to going to England.* 21 Mar: *Mr. Mills left Weimar proceeding to England by Hamburgh, as far as Capel with young Imhoff.*

1801: 29 May: *Accompanied my Father & Mother in the Evening to Mr. Lee's Concert, King's Theatre Great Concert Room ... I had the pleasure of meeting Mr. Mills.* 2 Jun: *afterwards with Mr. Mills No. 2. Tanfield Court Inner Temple.* 7 Jun: *Meeting Mr. W. Mills, I walked with him in Hyde Park & Kensington Gardens.*

MILLS — William Mills[141]

William Mills (±1793-1834), professor of moral philosophy, was born at Deddington, Oxfordshire, son of Moses Mills. He was educated at Lincoln College (BA 1813; MA 1816) and Magdalen College, Oxford (BD 1823). He was a fellow at Magdalen from 1820 to 1834. He was then appointed senior dean of arts at the college in 1822, bursar in 1823, vice-president in 1827, tutor in 1829, and dean of divinity in 1830. Finally he was Whyte's professor of moral philosophy from 1829 to his death in 1834.

1833: 28 Jan: *"Lecture on the Theory of Moral obligation, being the first of a course of Lectures delivered before the University of Oxford in Lent Term 1830. By William Mills B.D. Fellow of Magd. Coll.—Professor of Moral Philosophy. Oxford 1830." A very well written & able introductory lecture by the talented Professor of Moral Philosophy. The professorship is lately revived in his person.*

MILMAN — Henry Hart Milman[142]

Henry Hart Milman (1791-1868), poet, historian, and dean of St Paul's, was born in London, the third son of Sir Francis Milman, 1st baronet (1746-1821), physician to George III, and Frances (1754/5-1836), daughter of William Hart of Stapleton, Gloucestershire. He was educated at Eton College and Brasenose College, Oxford (BA 1814; MA 1816; B&DD 1849), where he was Bampton lecturer in 1827.

Having taken orders, Milman was presented to the living of St Mary's, Reading, in 1818, but he continued for some time to be known principally as a poet. His first poetical publication was a verse drama, *Fazio*, written for the stage but published in book form in 1815. *Fazio* was later successfully performed on the stage at Covent Garden and abroad. His next publication was *Samor, the Lord of the Bright City* (1818), a poem about the Saxon invasion of Britain. 'The bright city' was Gloucester. Milman also published *The Fall of Jerusalem* (1820), *The Martyr of Antioch* (1822), and *Belshazzar* (1822), dramatic poems that demonstrated a more authoritative touch. In 1821 he was elected professor of poetry at Oxford. *Anne Boleyn* (1826) ended his career as a dramatist. In 1831 he was succeeded as professor of poetry by John Keble.

Milman married, 1824, Mary Ann (1804-1871), daughter of Lt-Gen. William Cockell; they had 4 sons and 2 daughters:

1 Louisa Harriett (1827-1842)
1 William Henry (1824-1908)
2 Arthur (1829-1913); married, at St Michael's, Highgate, Camden, 6 April 1872, Frances Mary Tatham
2 Augusta Frances (1830-1839)
3 Archibald (1834-1902)
4 Charles Louis Hart (1845-1849)

Milman was a prolific contributor to the *Quarterly Review*, writing at least 65 articles. His *History of the Jews* (3 vols, 1830) shocked contemporaries by its depiction of the Jews as an oriental people. With *The history of Christianity from the birth of Christ to the Abolition of Paganism in the Roman Empire* (3 vols, 1840) Milman widened his scope from national to epochal history: 'the story of the Jews was that of a nation, the history of Christianity is that of a Religion'. *The History of Latin Christianity* (6 vols, 1854-5) showed development during a 'mythic period, when poetry and history are inseparable'. Milman's work produced predictable protests from high churchmen and Tractarians.

Robert Peel made Milman canon of Westminster and rector of St Margaret's, Westminster, in 1835. In November 1849 Lord John Russell appointed him dean of St Paul's (the first dean for a century who was not also a diocesan bishop). Milman set the cathedral's business on a sound footing and introduced evening services under the dome in 1858. He also wrote the cathedral's history in *Annals of St. Paul's Cathedral* (1868).

1829: 26 Feb: *The convocation house being now less crowded, we had space to notice the various characters moving within it, persons of note for learning or station; among the former Milman the poet, and Davison the Prebendary of Worcester; both voted for Peel.*

1832: 15 Mar: *Among these were several people of note both lay and clerical; of the former Lord Kenyon, Rt. Hon. Charles W. Wynne, Hon. W. Bathurst, East MP for Winchester &c.; of the latter, the Hon. and Revd. the Dean of Hereford, brother to the Premier, Archdeacon Barnes, Dr. Spry, Rector of St. Mary le bone, Dr. Dibdin, the Bibliomaniac, Minister of one of the district churches of Mary le bone, the poet Milman, the well known Coryphaeus of the Evangelical party, Danl. Wilson, who, it is reported has declined going out to India as Bishop of Calcutta &c.*

MILNERS — Miss Milners at Standlake

1801: 17 Jul: *Miss Milners arrived, pleasant woman of a certain age.*

MILWARD — George Milward [143]

George Milward (±1808-1871), JP and barrister, was born in London. He married, 1835, Sarah Grace (1815-1892); they had 4 sons and 4 daughters:

1 Sarah Grace (1836-1915); died unmarried
2 Mary Ann Grace (b. ±1838); married Revd James George Tetley
3 Catherine Grace (1841-1861); died unmarried
1 George (1843-1930), JP; educated at Rugby School and Magdalen College, Oxford; succeeded his father at Lechlade; married, at Lechlade, 11 January 1866, Augusta Susanna (d. 1891), daughter of Thomas Shaen Carter and Maria Susan Tilson; at least 1 son:
    1 George Harold Shaen (1866-1949); married, at St Stephen's, Kensington, Middlesex, 14 January 1892, Edith Sophia Marian Chowen (1865-1959)
2 Henry Anderson (1845-1871); died at Reading, Berkshire
3 Hardwick Browning (1847-1927); married, at Holy Trinity, Bessborough Gardens, Middlesex, 28 July 1869, Laura Rachel Willcox
4 Frances Grace (±1850-1939); married William Stancomb (1850-1941)
4 Arthur Prendergast (1852-1879); married, at Holy Trinity, Worcester, 20 September 1876, Edith Marion Bellers

At some point prior to 1841 the Milward family moved from Clapham to Lechlade, where, in 1830, George Milward's grandfather George Milward had been lord of the manor. They resided at the manor house.

1848: 22 Nov: *Magistrates present were Purnell, Curtis Hayward, Gambier Parry, W P. Price, Gyde, Milward, Fripp, Battersby, and Mirehouse. The last three are from the neighbourhood of Bristol, ... Mr. Milward, a barrister and magistrate, residing near Lechlade, and Mr. Gyde, of Cheltenham, might be regarded as partizans of Dr. Bompas.*

MINCHIN — Henry Minchin [144]

Henry Minchin (b. ±1804), schoolmaster, was born at Stow-on-the-Wold. He was married to Elizabeth (b. ±1789), who was born at Gosport, Hampshire; she was some fourteen years his senior. By 1851 the couple were living at Twerton, Bath, where Henry was a schoolmaster. By 1861 they had moved to Halstead, Essex, where Henry was a schoolmaster at the workhouse.

1835: 19 Mar: *To-day, in the Justice room, and in Ackerley's presence, who came purposely to attend the hearing, Smith came forward to claim justice at our hands for a calumny which had been raised against him by Henry Minchin, who was present, as were also Otway and Millington.* 21 May: *A copy of this circular fell into the hands of Henry Minchin, who, as will appear on reference to my diary of Mar. 19., had just cause of offence against Mr. Ackerley.*

1836: 27 Oct: *I had not time to attend at the Justice meeting, where I understood that a serious and unpleasant fracas occurred between H. Minchin and C. Ackerley.* 17 Nov: *H. Minchin saying something to Rousham expressive of his surprize at his preferring the charge, I gave him a severe rebuke for intruding a remark as a bystander, and without being called upon to speak.*

MINCHIN — Richard Minchin [145]

Richard Minchin (1791-1842), farmer and a guardian of the Union Workhouse, was married to Hannah (b. ±1795). They had at least 2 sons and 1 daughter:

1 Thomas (b. ±1822)
2 Joseph (±1828-1894)
1 Emma (b. ±1835)

1837: 29 Sep: *Met Messrs. Harris, Minchin, and Gillett, and examined the Officers, and most of the adult paupers, inspected the premises &c.* 20 Nov: *Rode to Stow by appointment to meet the Visiting Committee of the Workhouse: only Messrs. Minchin and Gillett attended besides myself.* 24 Nov.

1838: 5 Feb: *Visited the Workhouse with the Med. Off. Hayward and Rd. Minchin, one of the Stow Guardians.* 22 Feb: *The only case ready for hearing was R. Minchin against the Maugersbury Assessment, grounded on the inequality and unfairness of the Rate made on him as compared with others occupying lands of greater value to occupy.* 5 Apr., 30 Apr: *Visited the W.H. with Vavasour; gave some directions to Mr. Pearce, and advised with Richd. Minchin, the Guardn. of Stow on different matters regarding the workhouse premises.*, 19 May, 8-9 Aug.,

1839: 30 May.

1840: 17 Sep., 14 Nov: *Recd. a letter from the P. L. Commr., addressed to me jointly with Messrs. Beman and Minchin.*

MINET — Charles William Minet — *see also* Pole [146]

Charles William Minet (1803-1874), landed proprietor, was the son of Isaac Minet (1767-1839) and Susannah Van Notten Pole (1779-1869), only sister of Sir Peter Pole and Charles Van Notten Pole. He married, at York, 26 March 1830, Leah Fortrie (1805-1871), daughter of Col Gossip of Thorp Arch, Yorkshire; they had 7 daughters:

1 Fanny Cecilia (1831-1891)
2 Susan Millicent (1834-1918); married Charles William Dunbar Staveley (1817-1896)
3 Gertrude (1837-1872)
4 Sophia Louisa (1839-1855)
5 Geraldine Helena (1842-1931)
6 Georgina Emma (1846-1918); married Henry Bethune Patton
7 Delia Jane Adelia (1849-1900)

1838: 12 May: *Met Messrs. Whitmore Jones, Rawlinson, Bowen, Hill, Abr. Pole, Minett and others attending the fair.* 17 May: *Mr. V. and Emily, with her fiancé Leopold Dryden, Mr. and Mrs. M. Vavasour, Capt. Leigh & Billingsley were our guests: to whom are to be added Mr. and Mrs. Chamberlayne, accompanied by Mr. Minett, a Gentleman visiting at Maugersbury, an agreeable young man, a nephew of Mr. Pole's, who is often staying with his Uncle Abraham Pole at Toddenham, to Join in the sports of the field, and whose conversation is lively and instructive, as having roamed far and wide in foreign travel.*

1840: 12 Sep: *I had on Thursday endeavoured to forward the cause of the poor orphan by speaking in her behalf to Pole & Ford: to the former that he might influence Mrs. Pole, Mr. W. Pole, Mr. L. Pole, Mrs. Rudge & Miss Minett, and to the latter that he might apply to his Brother C. B. Ford.*

MINORS — Elizabeth Minors [or Mynors] [147]

Elizabeth Minors (b. ±1819), nurse, was born at Winchcombe, Gloucestershire. In 1851 she was a nurse in the household of Edward and Sophia Witts. Nothing further has been found.

1850: 12 Sep: *when the Servant came for me he brought word that my two younger grandchildren with an attendant had arrived at Upper Slaughter, bringing a note from E.F. W, by which it appeared that their valuable servant, Elizabeth Mynors, had been taken ill, and, therefore, for precaution the little boys had been sent to me: it remains to be proved whether the attack will prove turn out one of the endemic fever, under which two others of my son's female servants have sunk.* 14 Sep: *also a letter to inform me that the apprehensions as to Elizabeth Mynors were groundless, that her transient indisposition was the effect of over fatigue and anxiety, and that the Medical attendant pronounces her to be without fever.* 16 Sep: *Elizabeth Mynors in better health and spirits, and equal to much exertion.* 21 Sep: *Recd. a short letter from E.F. W, notifying the safe arrival of himself and family at Brighton, where they were fixed in lodgings in a convenient situation: Sophy, the children, and E Mynors all well.*

1854: 28 Jan: *Georgie with Eliz. Minors in my chariot.* 31 May, 7 Aug: *Mr. Shipton Curate of Toddington, an old schoolfellow of E. Clifford and J Purnell, came to visit us: we accommodated him with a bed, by coupling Georgie with Elizth. Minors.*

MINORS — William Minors [or Mynors]

William Minors (b. ±1815), manservant, was probably the brother of Elizabeth Minors (*above*). Surprisingly little has been discovered about this family.

1842: 11 Aug: *Wrote to W. Mynors, my son's servant, to announce that I should officiate at Stanway on Sunday next.*

MIREHOUSE — William Squire Mirehouse [148]

William Squire Mirehouse (1790-1864), JP and Church of England clergyman, was born at Castle Martin in Pembrokeshire, the son of John Mirehouse (1753-1823) and Mary Edwards (1767-1856). He was educated at Harrow School and Clare College, Cambridge (BA 1814; MA 1817). He was vicar of Sandhurst, Gloucestershire, in 1817-21, perpetual curate of St John's, Fishponds, Gloucestershire, in 1821-64, and rector of Colsterworth, Lincolnshire, in 1826-64. He also served as honorary chaplain to HRH Princess Sophia.

William married, at St Mary's, Cheltenham, 2 February 1832, Eliza Brunetta (1816-1874), daughter of George Arthur Herbert of Glan-Hafren, Montgomeryshire; they had at least 2 sons and 4 daughters:

1 Georgina Eliza (1836-1925)
2 Milicent Mary (b. ±1837)
1 John (1839-1911)
3 Mary Cornelia Brunetta (1841-1930)
4 Esther Avarina (1843-1932)
2 William Edward (1844-1925); married, at Reigate, Surrey, 1903, Ethel Annie Shearly (1880-1957)

The family lived at Hambrook Grove, Winterbourne, Gloucestershire. William Mirehouse was JP for Gloucestershire and Pembrokeshire.

1834: 25 Dec: *Received from Bristol, with Mr. Mirehouse's compliments, a printed table of a scale of fees to Petty Sessions Clerks proposed to be submitted to the Court of Quarter Sessions at Gloucester on Jan 6.*

1835: 6 Jan: *Mr. Mirehouse addressed the Court in a set and formal maiden speech, delivered in a pompous and declamatory manner.*

1838: 10 Apr: *A very long discussion conducted on the part of one of the Mag. residing near Bristol, the Revd. Mr. Mirehouse, with much warmth and excitement: he made a long, vehement, oratorical speech, and was calmly, judiciously, and pertinently answered by the Chairman.* 16 Oct.

1839: 1 Jan., 9 Apr.

1840: 20 Oct.

1842: 29 Jun: *From the Station, whither I had accompanied them, I repaired to the Kings Head, and joined the Magistrates at tea, Serjt. Ludlow, Purnell & Son, Ford, Archd. Timbrill, Mirehouse, Sayer, Waller &c.*

1844: 3 Jan: *I was much in communication during the day with Messrs. Ludlow, Curtis Hayward, George, Sayers, Mirehouse, Waller, Hicks, Viner, Ricardo, Steel, Dr. Greaves, &c.* 9 Apr.

1845: 15 Apr.

1846: 30 Jun., 20 Oct.

1847: 29-30 Jun.

1848: 6 Jan., 22 Mar: *The dinner at the Bell was attended by Ludlow, Purnell, Curtis Hayward, Mirehouse, Lysons, Hale, Brickdale, George, J. Purnell, E.F. W., myself &c.* 27 Jun: *Of the Vis. Justices one only, Mr. Mirehouse was present, his Colleagues, Mr. Fripp and Mr. Battersby, were absent.* 28 Jun., 22 Nov.

1850: 31 Dec.

MITCHEL — John Mitchel [149]

John Mitchel (1815-1875), Irish nationalist, was born at Camnish, near Dungiven, Londonderry, the first surviving son of John Mitchel (d. 1840), a presbyterian minister, and Mary Haslett (1786-1865). He became a leading member of both Young Ireland and the Irish Confederation.

The first edition of the *United Irishman* appeared on 12 February 1848. In the prospectus it was announced that the paper would be edited by John Mitchel, aided by Thomas Devin Reilly and John Martin, of Loughorne, and other competent contributors.

Mitchel was charged with 'Treason Felony' and transported to Ireland Island, Bermuda. He escaped from the colony in 1853 and settled in America, where he edited Mangan and Davis's collections of poetry and established the radical Irish nationalist newspaper *The Citizen in New York*, a mouthpiece for radical Irish-American anti-British opinion. The paper was controversial for its defence of slavery, highlighting the hypocrisy of the abolitionists in the debate. Mitchel felt that slaves in the southern United States were better cared for and fed than Irish cottiers or industrial workers in English cities like Manchester. He was a critic of international capitalism, which he blamed for both the pending Civil War and the Great Hunger.

Mitchel resigned from *The Citizen in New York* and toured as a spokesman for the South, founding a new paper, the *Southern Citizen*. He was the first to claim that slavery and abolition were not the causes of the conflict in the United States, but a pretence. Two of his sons died in the war, and a third lost an arm. Mitchel equated the Confederacy with Ireland, regarding both as agricultural economies tied into an unjust union.

After the Civil War Mitchel returned his focus to the issue of Ireland. He founded his third American newspaper, the *Irish Citizen*, but it failed to attract readers and folded in 1872. Mitchel returned to Ireland, and was elected in a by-election in 1875 as MP for Tipperary. His election was invalidated on the grounds that he was a convicted felon. He contested the seat again in the resulting by-election, and was again elected, this time with a greater majority. A constitutional crisis was only averted by his sudden death. Mitchel's opponent was returned unopposed in the third by-election.

1848: 24 Mar: *In Ireland the uncompromising, undisguised, open & prominent talkers and publishers of sedition, Smith O'Brien, Meagher, and Mitchell, have been bound by recognizance to answer the offences.* 19 May: *This is alarming, and such a state of things is calculated to encourage the Repealers, whether the moral force men whom O'Connel leads, rather by the Prestige of his Father's name than by his own waning influence, and who will probably soon dwindle into insignificance, or the Physical force Confederates, excited by such violent spirits as Smith O'Brien, Meagher, Dillon, O'Gorman, Doheny & others, who, in fact, are little better than openly revolutionary. Among them stands preeminent one Mitchell, a publisher of undisguised sedition in his most outrageous Journal.* 30 May: *John Mitchell, the Editor of "United Irishman", a Dublin inflammatory newspaper, having been indicted for a treasonable felony under a recent act for the security of the Queen's person, throne, and dignity, has been found guilty, and sentenced to fourteen years transportation.*

MITCHELL — Thomas Livingston Mitchell [150]

Sir Thomas Livingston Mitchell (1792-1855), surveyor and explorer in Australia, was born in the parish of Falkirk, Stirlingshire, Scotland, the eldest of the four children of John Mitchell and Janet Wilson. He was educated at Grangemouth School and the University of Edinburgh, and in 1811 he joined the Army in Spain and Portugal as a lieutenant in the 95th Regiment. He took part in the storming of Ciudad Rodrigo, Badajoz, and to a lesser extent, Salamanca. After the war, having been given a permanent posting on the quartermaster-general's staff, he was sent back to Spain and Portugal to survey the battlefields and record the positions of the armies. This work lasted from 1814 to 1819, and continued afterwards at Sandhurst.

Mitchell married, 1818, Mary Thomson Blunt (1800-1883), eldest daughter of Lt-Gen. Richard Blunt. The couple had eleven children. Mitchell was promoted to captain in 1822 and major in 1826, but was then put on half pay. In 1827 he published *Outline of a System of Surveying for Geographical and Military Purposes*. In the same year he was appointed deputy surveyor-general of New South Wales, a post he held until his death.

Mitchell arrived in Sydney in September 1827. He and the greater part of the survey staff were engaged on *The Map of the Colony of New South Wales* for more than six years; it was published in 1834 and has scarcely been equalled since then. It was said to be Mitchell's greatest achievement. Further expeditions followed, during which colleagues were attacked and killed by aborigines.

Sir Thomas Livingston Mitchell was professionally greatly accomplished, but he was also a man of culture and wide interests; his translation of the Portuguese classic *Lusiad of Luis de Camoens*, published in 1854, and his patenting of a new 'Boomerang' screw propeller for steamships are just two examples of his achievements beyond his profession. His detailed article in *DNB* is worth reading in full. He was knighted in 1839, and died at his home, Carthona, at Darling Point, Sydney, on 5 October 1855. Francis Witts met Mitchell at a dinner party given by his friend Thomas Jones Howell.

1853: 7 Jun: *Home to dress for a dinner party, a pleasant reunion——Sir. T. Mitchell, Surveyor General of Australia, author of travels in New South Wales, and now bringing out a project in navigation of a screw propeller, on the principle of the savages of Australia war engine, the boomerang: an enthusiastic projector, a clever talker, with an intellectual countenance & Scotch twang, very full of thought and anecdote on savage life in New South Wales &c.*

MITCHELL — William Mitchell [151]

William Mitchell (1786-1855), cartographer and surveyor, was born at Stanway. He married, 1811, Sarah (1785-1875), daughter of James Hopkins and Elizabeth Tye; they had at least 4 sons and 2 daughters:

1 Sarah (b. ±1815)
1 John (±1816-1841)
2 Charles (b. ±1820)
3 Henry (±1821-1907)
4 Joseph (±1826-1871)
2 Ann (±1827-1851)

1846: 12 Nov: *To Mitchell of Cutsdean, measurer and mapper, to desire him to call here on one of the three days named, to measure and map this parish previous to valuation.* 14 Nov: *Engaged with Mr. Lea, Overseer, in giving directions to W. Mitchell as to measuring.* 21 Nov: *to Mr. Alder, Stationer &c. Cheltenham, to order paper to be mounted for the map to be made by Mitchell of this parish.*

1847: 9 Mar: *Engaged in the forenoon at the School room with Mitchell and his son, who produced the map of the parish which they had made, that the owners and occupiers of land might give information as to the ownership and occupancy, and name of each parcel of land, house, cottage &c.* 19 Mar: *Mitchell has brought the map of the Parish, with its measurement and reference book of owners and occupiers.* 9 Apr: *Transacting business ... with W. Mitchell, the Measurer and Mapper, in whose favour I wrote a commendatory letter to Mr. Dent, Sudeley Castle.* 30 Dec: *Conferred with Mitchell, the land measurer, as to the map he has made of this parish.*

MITFORD — John Freeman-Mitford [152]

John Freeman-Mitford, 1st Baron Redesdale (1748-1830), speaker of the House of Commons, was born the younger son of John Mitford (d. 1761), barrister, of Exbury Park, Hampshire, and Philadelphia (d. 1797), daughter of Willey Reveley of Newby Wiske, Yorkshire; his elder brother William (*below*) was a Greek historian. John took the additional name of Freeman in 1809 on succeeding to the estates of Thomas Edwards Freeman.

In 1772 Mitford was admitted a student of the Inner Temple and was called to the bar in 1777. He rapidly acquired a large chancery practice and took silk in July 1789. Having been elected a bencher of Inner Temple in November 1789, he was appointed second justice of the Carmarthen circuit and chancellor of Durham. Other honours came his way, and his success in practice enabled him to purchase the Redesdale estate in Northumberland, the ancestral lands of the Anglo-Norman Mitford family. He entered parliament in December 1788 as MP for the borough of Bere Alston, Devon, 1788-99, after which he was MP for East Looe, 1799-1802. An ultra-conservative, he believed that the principle of equality was inconsistent with well-constituted government. He became solicitor-general on 13 February 1793, and was knighted two days later.

John Mitford succeeded Addington as speaker of the House of Commons in 1801, and was admitted to the privy council a week later. The following year he was appointed lord chancellor of Ireland and created a peer of the United Kingdom with the title of Baron Redesdale of Redesdale in the county of Northumberland.

John Mitford was described by Sir Egerton Brydges as 'a sallow man, with round face and blunt features, of a middle height, thickly and heavily built ... with a heavy, drawling, tedious manner of speech'. He was noted for his stiff manner and lack of a sense of humour, which made him easy prey for the wits of the Irish bar. He was a bitter opponent of Catholic emancipation, and deeply distrustful of the Catholic priesthood in Ireland, whom he regarded as intolerant agitators constantly plotting to weaken the union. He worked closely with Philip Yorke, the lord lieutenant, to establish a degree of independence for the Irish government under the new constitutional arrangements. At the same time he clearly felt that they were not getting sufficient support from London; Mitford was often angered by the government's dilatoriness and indifference regarding Irish affairs. But it was his views on Catholic emancipation and the Irish Catholic Church, underlined by the controversy in the early months of 1806 surrounding the application of Valentine Lawless, 2nd Baron Cloncurry, for magisterial appointment, that led to his recall. The 'ministry of all the talents', which took office in February 1806, was intent on conciliating Catholic opinion in Ireland, and one of their first actions was to replace Mitford. He never took office again, but took an active, if largely ineffective, part in parliamentary debates, and sat frequently to hear appeals and peerage claims. Mitford's principal achievement was to obtain some relief for insolvent debtors through legislation enacted in 1813 and 1814; it was later described in his obituary in *The Times* as 'a lasting monument to the philanthropy of Lord Redesdale'.

John Mitford married, 1803, Frances (1767-1817), seventh daughter of John Perceval, 2nd earl of Egmont, and sister of Spencer Perceval, prime minister (1809-12). They had 1 son and 2 daughters:

1 John Thomas (1805-1886); created 1st earl of Redesdale; *see below*
1 Frances Elizabeth (1804-1866)
2 Catherine (1807-1811)

1822: 27 Sep., 1 Oct.

1823: 17 Sep., 7 Oct., 8 Oct: *I dined and slept at Batsford Park, the seat of Lord Redesdale. The venerable Peer at the age of 75 retains great activity of mind and body, and is now making considerable improvements on a large scale. He has been enabled by the late inclosure at Bourton on the Hill to make new approaches to his place, which before was inconvenient of access. The house itself is an excellent Mansion, situate in a well wooded park. The suite of apartments appropriated for company is very handsome, and furnished with some very good paintings, his Lordship being not only a connoisseur, but himself an artist. The library contains busts of W. Pitt & Spencer Perceval, the latter of whom was brother of the late Lady Redesdale; who so much resembled him, that she sat to the artist after his assassination to enable him to put the finishing strokes to his work.... These made up the party with Lord Redesdale's Son & daughter, both pleasing young persons. Mr. Mitford has lately left Eton, and is about to become a member of the University of Oxford, and of New College.* 23 Oct: *We dined at Mr. Pole's at Wick Hill, meeting Miss Mitford (Lord Redesdale's daughter).* 25 Nov.

1824: 28 Jul., 27 Aug: *When the meeting broke up Mr. Rice and myself rode back by engagement with Lord Redesdale to Batsford, where we dined and slept. Besides Mr. John Mitford, and his Sister, we met a nephew of Lord R's. Mr. Bertram Mitford, with his wife and daughter, all very pleasant persons, on a visit at Batsford. Mr. B. Mitford has a place under the Irish Government, & resides near Dublin. Of course this was procured for him by his Uncle, when Chancellor.* 15 Sep.

1825: 19 Jul., 22 Sep: *I rode to Batsford to dine and sleep at Lord Redesdales. There I met Lord Northwick, Mr. & Mrs. Pole of Wick Hill, three Miss Selwyns, elderly young ladies, daughters of a former Incumbent of Blockley, who have for many years resided in the village of Batsford; also Mr. John Mitford and his sister.* 23 Sep.

1826: 18 Jul., 2 Sep., 8 Sep., 15 Sep: *And this seems the proper place for inserting a list of some of the leading families & individuals, whose presence on this occasion served so many good purposes; benefiting the charity ... Lord Redesdale, Hon. John & Miss Mitford.* 3 Oct., 18 Dec: *I dined and slept at Lord Redesdale's. The old Peer is, as usual, full of talk and information, very communicative, confidential & kind. Mr. Mitford was not at home. His Sister and Aunt were at Batsford.*

1827: 3 Mar., 15 Jun., 12 Dec.

1828: 2 May, 20 Aug: *Lord Redesdale presided at both, and evinced wonderful activity, spirit, accuracy & energy at fourscore years of age; his eightieth birth day comes before this month elapses. His Lordship is equally ready with his pen, as in conversation.* 23 Aug: *I dined at Batsford at Lord Redesdale's, returning home at night.* 1 Oct., 7 Oct., 17 Oct., 17 Dec.

1829: 7 Feb., 25 Mar., 18 Sep: *The Commissioners met under the presidency of Lord Redesdale, who seemed to continue to enjoy the vigorous & green old age, which enables him still to be so serviceable in Parliament & elsewhere.* 22 Sep., 6 Oct.

1830: 17 Jan: *The news reached me to day of the decease of poor Lord Redesdale, which occurred at Batsford Park yesterday afternoon. The event had been anticipated for a fortnight or three weeks past, and his Lordship's suffering and precarious state had excited much concern among his friends and neighbours. He had throughout the autumn experienced considerable uneasiness, occasioned, as he supposed, by rheumatic affections & sciatica, causing great pain in his back & loins. Extensive as his knowledge was on almost all subjects, he seems to have been but little conversant with the medical art, and slenderly versed in the knowledge of those ills, which flesh is heir to.... Thus has departed from this life, a man, to whom his country is deeply indebted, one, who was a kind of connecteding link between an almost worn out race of statesmen, and the new lights, which, with what are called more liberal opinions, illumine & direct the age.*

MITFORD — John Thomas Freeman-Mitford[153]

John Thomas Freeman-Mitford, 1st earl of Redesdale (1805-1886), politician and author, was a son of John Freeman-Mitford, 1st Baron Redesdale (1748-1830) (*above*) and Frances Perceval (1767-1817). He was born at Port Rush, co. Antrim, and educated at Eton College (1818-23) and New College, Oxford (BA 1825; MA 1828; DCL 1853).

On the death of his father, Freeman-Mitford succeeded as 2nd Baron Redesdale, but he took little part in the debates in the House of Lords until 1837, when he began to interest himself in the wording and detail of parliamentary bills. Wellington recommended him to study the private business of the house to qualify himself for the chairmanship of committees; in 1851, with inter-party support, he succeeded Lord Shaftesbury as lord chairman. Freeman-Mitford served as chairman until his death, becoming especially known for his domination of private bill legislation. His handling of this did much to assert the Lords' prominence over the Commons with respect to the large volume of private bills. His shrewdness and independence of judgement enabled him to detect the artifices of attorneys and agents, while his dictatorial manner was proverbial. Although he regarded all things, great and small, with a genuine conservatism, he never allowed his peculiar views to warp his decisions. He was also a frequent speaker on general topics, especially when innovation was suggested. He passionately opposed the repeal of the corn laws in 1846, and during the debates on reform in 1867, he opposed Earl Grey's amendment for the disfranchisement of certain boroughs, arguing that the matter was beyond the proper jurisdiction of the peers, and that it was a mistake to make the franchise a party question. On the *Alabama* affair Freeman-Mitford maintained in 1872 that the United States had no claims to compensation because the Southerners had re-entered the Union at the close of the war.

Freeman-Mitford's interests lay chiefly in religious topics, on which he assumed a pronouncedly protestant and orthodox attitude. He published in 1849 *Reflections on the Doctrine of Regeneration and its Connection with both Sacraments*, and in 1850, *Observations on the Gorham Judgment*. In 1853 he was one of the revivers of convocation. He refused to sign the report of the royal commission on the law of divorce on the grounds that the dissolution of the marriage tie was contrary to scripture, justifying his views in a pamphlet entitled *The Law of Scripture Against Divorce* (1856).

In 1873, on Disraeli's recommendation, Freeman-Mitford was created earl of Redesdale; this was despite Disraeli's view that he was 'narrow-minded, prejudiced, and utterly unconscious of what is going on in the country'. To the end of his days the earl wore the old-fashioned tailcoat and brass buttons of the previous generation. He died unmarried in London, and was buried at Batsford Park. The peerage became extinct, but Algernon Bertram Mitford (1837-1916), great-grandson of William Mitford (*below*), was created Baron Redesdale in 1902.

1823: 17 Sep., 8 Oct: *These made up the party with Lord Redesdale's Son & daughter, both pleasing young persons. Mr. Mitford has lately left Eton, and is about to become a member of the University of Oxford, and of New College.* 23 Oct: *We dined at Mr. Pole's at Wick Hill, meeting Miss Mitford (Lord Redesdale's daughter).*

1824: 27 Aug: *When the meeting broke up Mr. Rice and myself rode back by engagement with Lord Redesdale to Batsford, where we dined and slept. Besides Mr. John Mitford, and his Sister, we met a nephew of Lord R's. Mr. Bertram Mitford, with his wife and daughter, all very pleasant persons, on a visit at Batsford. Mr. B. Mitford has a place under the Irish Government, & resides near Dublin. Of course this was procured for him by his Uncle, when Chancellor.*

1825: 22 Sep: *I rode to Batsford to dine and sleep at Lord Redesdales. There I met Lord Northwick, Mr. & Mrs. Pole of Wick Hill, three Miss Selwyns, elderly young ladies, daughters of a former Incumbent of Blockley, who have for many years resided in the village of Batsford; also Mr. John Mitford and his sister.*

1826: 15 Sep: *And this seems the proper place for inserting a list of some of the leading families & individuals, whose presence on this occasion served so many good purposes; benefiting the charity ... Lord Redesdale, Hon. John & Miss Mitford.* 18 Dec: *I dined and slept at Lord Redesdale's. The old Peer is, as usual, full of talk and information, very communicative, confidential & kind. Mr. Mitford was not at home. His Sister and Aunt were at Batsford.*

1829: 18 Feb., 22 Sep., 23 Sep: *The fare was excellent; plenty of Venison & game, & a very handsome desert afterwards. Waller presided in a very unaffected gentlemanlike manner; but at the bottom of the table, where Moreton, Mitford, and other exuberant spirits were congregated, the noise and boisterous merriment were unrestrained.* 24 Sep: *and a new half dozen of Stewards are ready to take the field in 1832: the Hon. J. F. Mitford, son of Lord Redesdale, the eldest son of G. P. Holford Esqr. and the eldest son of Sir Bethel Codrington are the proposed Lay stewards.*

1832: 29 Mar.

1836: 30 Aug: *Mr. Langstone is the Manager of the Heythrop foxhounds, to which he and Lord Redesdale are the principal subscribers, since the pack was remodelled, when the Duke of Beaufort relinquished hunting in this part of the Country.* 7 Sep., 13 Sep., 1 Oct., 27 Oct.

1837: 16 Feb., 21 Feb., 23-24 Feb., 24 Jun., 16 Aug: *On the way met and had a long conference with Lord Redesdale, on a measure about to be put forward by the Conservative party in East Gloucestershire, the appointment of several additional polling places, as Stow, Winchcombe, Fairford &c. with a view to the diminution of expences to the Conservative Contests Candidate on future contests which may be now pretty surely anticipated.* 10 Oct: *The company consisted of Lord Redesdale and Miss Mitford, Sir C. & Lady Imhoff.* 17 Oct., 25 Nov: *A letter from Lord Redesdale, now in Town, since the meeting of Parliament on the 15th. Inst. written in confidence to obtain my advice and assistance in organizing a committee for registration and other election purposes at Stow, now that it is about to become the centre of a polling district.* 27 Nov: *Wrote to Lord Redesdale a confidential letter in reply to the one received from his Lordship on Saturday.* 29 Nov., 1 Dec., 14 Dec: *Wrote to Lord Redesdale in consequence of a communication made to me yesterday by Mr. Ford, that he had submitted to several Conservative Gentlemen at the Ball on Tuesday night a scheme for the Establishment of a Registration Committee at Stow, professing to be under his Lordship's sanction, though Mr. F. had held no communication with him on the subject, but only presumed that it would be approved by him.* 16 Dec: *A very satisfactory letter from Lord Redesdale in reply to mine of the 14th.* 26 Dec: *A letter from Lord Redesdale, now at Batsford, communicating to me the purport of a letter recd. by him from Mr. Ford, on the subject of a Registration committee at Stow.* 27 Dec: *While we were absent Ford called with the intention of shewing me the letter which he had recd. from Lord Redesdale.* 28 Dec: *Ford did not shew me the letter he had recd. from Ld. Redesdale, but on my naming the subject, entered briefly into its contents, and I expect that he will allow the scheme of a registration Comm. at Stow to die a natural death, as far as he is concerned, now that he finds it unpalatable to Lord R.* 29 Dec., 31 Dec.

1838: 8 Jan: *Recd. a letter from Lord Redesdale, informing me of a letter he had recd. from Ford, on the old subject of Registration Committees.* 5 Feb., 30 Dec.

1839: 11 Jan., 27 Jan., 2 Feb.

1842: 18 Jan., 15 Mar., 17 Mar.

1843: 19 Jan., 14 Dec.

1844: 22 Jan: *Walked with M W. to Eyford: we fell in with Lord Redesdale's hounds at the close of a long chase; an exhilirating, cheerful, sight, in the valley by Eyford, and in the coppices: recognised Lord R., Sir C. Cockerell, Franks, W. Vavasour, Polhill &c. among the sportsmen.* 27 Jan., 22-23 Feb., 28-29 Feb., 1 Mar., 8 Mar., 28 Nov., 17 Dec.

1845: 16 Jan., 20 Jan., 4 Feb., 8 Feb., 12 Feb., 18 Feb., 20 Feb., 26 Feb., 27 Mar: *This project is very distasteful to Lord Redesdale, who will oppose it to the utmost, as interfering with his property, and injuring his country as Master of a pack of fox hounds.*

1846: 26 Aug.

1847: 27 Jan., 25 Mar: *Lord Redesdale has written a long letter, promises to present our petition for an abolition of the law of settlement.* 19 Jun: *Lord Redesdale has brought in a bill to relieve parishes from a burden entailed on them by the operation of the Act for securing the irremovability of the Poor who have resided five years in any parish ...* 26 Aug., 14 Sep., 28 Oct.

1848: 28 Mar: *Met Lord Redesdale, and, under his auspices, were admitted into the interior part of the chamber, where the peers sit, so as to have a full view of the whole.* 23 Jun., 30 Oct., 6 Nov., 11 Nov., 13 Nov., 17 Nov.

1850: 10 Jan., 31 Oct., 14 Nov., 21 Nov.

1851: 23 Jan., 22 Mar., 25 Mar., 18-19 Apr., 24 Apr., 26 Apr., 7 May, 11 May.

1852: 22 Jan., 15 Apr., 9 Jun.

1853: 20 Jan., 18 Mar., 21 Mar., 9 Apr., 12 Apr., 25 Apr., 28 May.

1854: 9 Feb.

MITFORD — William Mitford[154]

William Mitford (1744-1827), historian of ancient Greece, was born in London, the first son of John Mitford (d. 1761), barrister, of Exbury House, Hampshire, and Philadelphia, daughter of Willey Reveley of Newton Underwood and Throphill, Northumberland. He was the elder brother of John Freeman-Mitford (1748-1830) (*above*). He was educated at Queen's College, Oxford, and the Middle Temple, and succeeded to the property at Exbury in 1761. He married, 1766, Frances (d. 1776), daughter of James Molloy, of Dublin, and his wife, Anne.

In 1774 Mitford published *An Essay on the Harmony of Language*, dealing with English prosody. Following the death of his wife in 1776, he travelled to France, where he met the Greek scholars J. B. G. d'Ansse de Villoison and the baron de Sainte-Croix. In 1784 he published the first volume of his principal work, the *History of Greece*, covering events from early times to the end of the Persian Wars (479 BC); the detail of his research was on an unprecedented scale. After Gibbon's death in 1794, there ensued a lively contest between Mitford and John Gillies, author of a complete *History of Greece* (2 volumes, 1786), to succeed Gibbon as professor of ancient history at the Royal Academy. In the event the post was left unfilled until Mitford finally took it up in 1818. In 1797 he published the third volume of his *History*, covering the period from the oligarchic coup of the Thirty Tyrants in Athens at the end of the Peloponnesian War to the peace of Antalcidas in 386 BC. In 1808 the fourth volume was published, covering events up to the battle of Chaeronea in 338 BC. In 1816 a *History of the Mahometan Empire in Spain* by John Shakespear and T. H. Horne was published with an introductory chapter entitled 'Review of the Early History of the Arabs'. The chapter was attributed to 'the Historian of Greece'; this was probably Mitford rather than Gillies. The fifth and final volume of Mitford's *History* was published in 1818.

1801: 21 May: *Returning home with Lady Lyttelton & Miss Eycott, we called upon Miss Forrest, I afterwards dined with her Ladyship. In the Evening I again repaired there & met chiefly a blue stocking party; blind Dr Moyne, the two Grecian Historians, Gillies & Mitford, Mrs. Goodenough, Miss Fords, Miss Guydickens's, &c. I had much conversation with the latter, as also with Dr. Gillies & a very agreable young man, Mr. Holford.*

1804: 15 Mar: *Read Mitford in the Evening.*

MOFFAT — Mary Moffat, personal attendant to Lady Elcho

1835: 27 Feb: *Received a letter from the Hon. Edward Stewart, Chairman of the Board of Customs, and Son in law of Lady Elcho, to announce to me the decease of our venerable and excellent friend, in her 92d. year, on the Evening of the 25th. Inst... She had been nursed by her faithful friend and companion, Miss Church, and by her admirable personal attendant, Mary Moffat...*

MOLIGNE — Němec Vilém Moligne[155]

Surprisingly little is known of the violinist Herr Moligne (d. 1869). He played alongside Paganini, with the former playing on a Joseph Guarnerius while Moligne was on a Stradivarius. He does not appear in *Grove* or the other usual reference books. It is likely that he was a certain Němec Vilém Moligne, in which case he appears to have been either Polish or Czech, or at least from the east of Europe.

1851: 21 May: *The concert was of that character now called "Chamber music"—one of a series given by a celebrated German violinist, Herr Moligne, at the Beethoven rooms in Queen Anne Street West... The performance was chiefly instrumental, and of first rate character—Herr Moligne played exquisitely in duets with his daughter, who accompanied him on the Piano-forte.*

MONCASTER — Elizabeth Moncaster — *see also* Dale[156]

Elizabeth Moncaster, née Dale (±1748-1834), was born at Newcastle-upon-Tyne or its vicinity. Her brother was Shallett Dale (1740-1800), attorney and wine merchant, of Mosley Street, Newcastle-upon-Tyne; he married, 1775, Barbara Sadler (1749-1822). Elizabeth married, at Wallsend, Northumberland, 22 September 1767, James Moncaster (1717-1797), son of James Moncaster (d. 1739), merchant, and Isabel Burdon (d. 1764). Her husband was a much older man, but wealthy thanks to his career as a merchant adventurer.

Elizabeth does not appear to have had any children, but she looked after at least three of her nieces, daughters of her brother, Shallett Dale. She lived at the Mall in Clifton, presumably in some comfort, having had her own carriage. She was probably the same Elizabeth Moncaster who died at Withycombe Raleigh, Devon [now part of Exmouth]; in the 1851 census, two of her nieces, Jemima and Eliza, were listed as widows residing at nearby Wear, Topsham, Devon, which shows a connection with that county.

1803: 27 Dec: *Could hardly continue to make with my Brother a pleasant long visit at Mrs. Moncaster's.* 31 Dec.

1804: 7 Jan: *Passed a dull evening crowned with a supper at Mrs. Moncasters, which would have been intolerable, had I not played speculation, making Bank with Miss Adam.* 11 Jan., 18 Jan., 19 Jan., 21 Jan., 28 Jan., 17 Jul., 20 Jul.

1806: 12 Mar: *Called upon Mrs. Moncaster.*

MONCK — George Monck and the Monck Family at Clifton [157]

George Monck (1777-1846), Church of England clergyman, was born at of Walcot, Bath, son of John Monck (1734-1809) and Emilia Snee (1745-1795). He was a younger brother of John Bligh Monck, of Coley Park, Berkshire, and a member of a cadet branch to the earls of Rathdowne. He had one sister, Emilia (1778-1849), who married, at All Saints', Laleham, Surrey, 6 May 1802, Charles Vaughan (1774-1851).

Monck was educated at Pembroke College, Oxford (BA 1801), and was ordained deacon on 31 May 1801 and priest on 11 December 1802. His first clerical appointment was as curate of Westfield, Sussex, 1802-05. He married, at Brighton, Sussex, 13 April 1809, Sarah (1775-1849), who was born in Ireland, the eldest daughter of Gustavus Hamilton, 5th Viscount Boyne (1749-1816), and Martha Matilda Somerville. George and Sarah had at least 1 son:

1 George Gustavus (1815-1885); married Harriet Horne (b. 1811)

It appears that the family lived later at Corston, Somerset, where George (senior) died. In the 1841 census, instead of being listed as 'clergyman', he was registered as 'independent'.

Francis Witts's statement in his diary that he 'Danced with El. & Sarah Monck' could be interpreted in two ways. He may have danced with both Elizabeth Monck and Sarah Monck, or alternatively, given his closeness with Elizabeth Fortescue, he may have danced with her and Sarah Monck.

1804: 23 Dec: *At Dowry Chapel & Mr. Hawes read prayers & Mr. Monck preached a vague sermon.* 25 Dec: *Dowry Chapel, where Mr. Monck & Mr. Hawes officiated.*

MONCK — George Monck/Moncke [158]

Little is known of George Moncke (d. 1806) and the Monck/Moncke family. The family was related to Lady Frances Flood (*The Monthly Review*, volume 97, 1822, p. 187), but this connection may go back several generations on the Cavendish side. There are some hints pointing to a connection with the Massey family; Elizabeth and Sarah were possibly sisters or cousins of George Moncke. It is known from the diaries of Agnes Witts that he died in 1806; she wrote on 10 June 1806, 'walk'd a little while on the Promenade in the evening the Band playing but our minds were little tuned to harmony from having learnt the melancholy Deaths of Col: Velley & poor George Moncke.' Thomas Velley (1748-1806), botanist, fellow of the Linnean Society, and lieutenant-colonel of the Oxford Militia, died on 6 June 1806 when jumping from a runaway stage-coach at Reading. It may well be that George Moncke was a fellow passenger in the stagecoach and suffered the same demise.

1804: 28 Jul: *A party at Mrs. Masseys's with a supper. Pleasant conversation with Miss Monk.* 29 Jul., 30 Jul: *In the Evening walked with Mr. & Miss Stewart. At a party at Lady Jervis's: conversed chiefly with Miss Monck & Miss Fortescue: played at Commerce.* 1 Aug: *to Ashton for Raspberries & Cream ending in a supper at Mrs. Massey's, consisting of Mrs. Massey, the Rawsons, Miss Monck, Miss Fortescue, Adm. & Col. Jones, Hankey & myself.* 2 Aug: *Walked with Hankey & Miss Upton —In the Evening with Mrs. Hankey, her son, Mrs. Massey, & Miss Monck. Supped at Mrs. Massey's.* 3 Aug: *Rode with Miss Fortescue, Hankey & George Monck to a match between Horton's Mare & one of Mr. Sweetman's. Horton beat.* 4 Aug: *Dined with Mrs. Massey to meet Miss Monck who left us in the evening & Mr. Port joined the party.* 10 Aug: *Walked with Russl. Manners. In the Evening with El. Fortescue & G. Monck.* 14 Aug: *To the Ball. Danced with El. & Sarah Monck. Conversed & drank tea with Mrs. Waddington.* 17 Aug: *A grand Rout & Supper at Mr. J. Jervis's: Count Bonnelarhi of the party: pleasant on the whole long & interesting conversation with Eliz. & the Ports, Brandrams, Monck's, Cadairs, Jenny Upton &c. &c.* 21 Aug: *Walked with Col. Griffiths, Geo Monck, Manners's &c.* 22 Aug: *Walked before breakfast with G. Monck &c.* 4 Sep: *On the Downs, at the Brigade & Miller's & Sweet's with my Father & Mother, Mrs. Massey, S. Monck, Mr. Harford &c. very pleasant.* 7 Sep., 21 Dec.

1806: 3 Feb: *Conversed with Mrs. Dowell, E. Webb, G. Monck, &c.*

MONCRIEFF — Miss D. Moncrieff at Edinburgh

1801: 3 May: *The Evening we spent with the Browns, we supped there also & met Miss D. Moncrieff.*

MONK — James Henry Monk [159]

James Henry Monk (1784-1856), classical scholar and bishop of Gloucester and Bristol, was born at Buntingford, Hertfordshire, the only son of Charles Monk (1753-1785), an officer of the 40th Regiment, and Sarah (1747-1848), daughter of Joshua Waddington, vicar of Harworth, Nottinghamshire. He was educated at Trinity College, Cambridge (BA 1804; MA 1807; BD 1818; DD 1822), where he was elected a fellow in 1805 and became an assistant tutor in 1807. In January 1809 he was elected regius professor of Greek.

Monk was an influential college tutor. His work was chiefly on Euripides, and his editions of *Hippolytus* (1811) and *Alcestis* (1816) were regularly reprinted. He was ordained deacon in 1809 and priest in 1810. As Whitehall preacher in 1812 he attracted the attention of Lord Liverpool, who appointed him to the deanery of Peterborough in 1822; being unable to continue his professorship, Monk began a life of service to the Church. In right of his deanery, he nominated himself to the rectory of Fiskerton, Lincolnshire, in 1822, and afterwards held the rectory of Peakirk-cum-Glinton, Northamptonshire, from 1829. In 1830 he was given a canonry at Westminster and in the same year was consecrated bishop of Gloucester. In 1836 the see was amalgamated with Bristol.

Monk married, 1823, Jane Smart, only daughter of Revd Hugh Hughes, rector of Hardwick, Northamptonshire; they had 1 son and 3 daughters:

1 Jane Emily (1823-1917)
1 Charles James (1824-1900), author of the Revenue Officers' Disabilities Removal Act (1868); elected MP for Gloucester in 1859, but unseated on petition; re-elected for Gloucester in 1865 and held the seat until 1885; married, 1853, Julia Pandia (d. 1870), daughter of Pantia Stephen Ralli
2 Mary (1826-1917)
3 Penelope Anna (1829-1917)

James Henry Monk was an old-fashioned conservative, equally suspicious of nonconformity and Tractarianism, and hostile to reform. Within his own diocese he was troubled by the increasing influence of evangelicals, particularly in Bristol, Cheltenham, and Clifton, but he supported the demand of the Bristol Church Union for the revival of convocation. He gave considerable sums of money to charities, contributing part of his income towards the restoration of churches, the augmentation of clergy stipends, and the building of parsonages and church schools. For some years before his death Monk suffered from partial blindness, although it did not stop him from producing new editions of Euripides's *Iphigeneia in Aulis* (1840) and *Iphigeneia in Tauris* (1845).

1823: 6 Feb: *"A letter to the Right Revd. John (Kaye) Lord Bishop of Bristol, respecting an additional Examination of Students in the University of Cambridge and the different plans proposed for that purpose. By Philograntus. Lond. 1822".—Is not this pamphlet the production of Dr. Monk the Greek Professor at Cambridge, and Dean of Peterborough? It is a sensible recommendation of a material improvement much wanted in Cambridge.*

1830: 17 Feb: *It is said, that Dr. Monk, Dean of Peterborough, is to be our new Bishop.* 14 Apr: *His successor, Dr. Monk, Dean of Peterborough, has not yet been elected, but his elevation to the episcopal bench will, doubtless, soon take place.* 10 May: *Dr. Monck has not yet been gazetted for Gloucester, and Dr. Bethell is still entitled to sign himself Chr. Gloucester.* 13 Jun: *Dr. Monk, the Dean of Peterborough, is at last gazetted as Bishop of Gloucester, and as the Congé d'elire has at length been issued, he will, probably, ere long take up his residence in his diocese.*

1832: 10 Apr: *Dr. Monk is not devoid of firmness, and while he spoke with feeling as to the discrepancy of his views from those of some of his brethren, to whom he was united in the bonds of strict intimacy and personal regard, he vindicated his own views with judgment, and answered with much spirit and force a very unwarrantable and intemperate attack.* 9 May.

1834: 23 Aug: *A letter from John Witts, expressing a wish on the part of Lady Lyttelton, that the proposed visit of Edward and myself should be postponed till Sept. 8. at which time the Bishop of Monk and his lady will be her guests.* 8 Sep: *The Bishop of Gloucester, Mrs. Monk, and three lovely children, daughters, were my Aunt's guests.* 9 Sep: *Morning visitors arrived, and protracted the hour for taking exercise till the Bishop and myself could only accomplish a walk to within a short distance of Great Malvern, instead of reaching the well, as we had proposed.* 10 Sep: *In conference with the Bishop on ecclesiastical matters relating to his diocese.* 11 Sep: *Conversing with my Aunt and Mrs. Matthews, with Mrs. Monk &c. till there was a possibility of getting out on the common, when the Bishop and myself contrived to get an hour's exercise.* 12 Sep., 14 Sep., 25 Sep: *A letter from the Bishop of Monk, in very friendly terms, acknowledging the receipt of my packet to him on the subject of garden allotments, and mentioning that he had left Lady Lyttelton well on his departure from Malvern a few days previous to the date of his letter.* 15 Oct: *At the Palace a large party assembled to dinner. The Bishop and Mrs. Monk very courteous.*

1835: 5 Jan: *Mrs. Backhouse visited some of her old acquaintances, and Edward found his way to the Palace, and was very kindly received by Mrs. Monk.* 6 Jan: *On returning to the Spa Hotel I found that Mrs. Monk had kindly sent her carriage to take my Son with her party to Barnwood.* 7 Jan: *Called at the Palace on the Bishop of Gloucester and Mrs. Monk: sat for sometime with the Lady, and afterwards with his Lordship in his Study.* 8 Jan., 9 Jan: *Edward had ridden to Prinknash in the forenoon to call on the Howells, and had afterwards gone to dine en famille at the Palace, from whence he accompanied Mrs. Monk and the ladies of her party to the Ball given this Evening at the Bell Hotel.* 16 Jan: *My son went to Cheltenham in the phaeton in the afternoon, to be present at a ball to be given by the Hon. Mrs. Godsal in the Rotunda.... Mrs. Monk had kindly procured for my son an invitation to this party.* 6 Feb., 12 Jun., 3 Sep., 20 Oct., 15 Nov., 18 Nov., 23 Nov., 19-20 Dec.

1837: 2 Jan: *I called at the Palace on the Bishop, and Mrs. Monk: saw his Lordship for a few minutes, who was much engrossed with the meeting to be held to-morrow for establishing the Diocesan Association for building churches and chapels.* 4 Jan: *The Bishop took the chair, and in a long speech dilated on the objects of the institution, with frequent pauses, and a hesitating manner: vindicating himself, perhaps, with unnecessary earnestness, from some calumny which had been aimed at him in a public journal in which his sentiments as delivered at the late meeting at Bristol had been misrepresented.* 17 Feb., 7 Mar: *A note from the Bish. of Gl: & Bristol and Mrs. Monk to invite me to dinner at the Palace to-morrow.* 8 Mar., 10-11 Apr., 4 Aug., 8-9 Aug., 17 Sep., 18 Oct., 28 Nov., 30 Nov., 6 Dec., 24 Dec., 31 Dec.

1838: 2 Jan: *I went to leave my card at the Palace, but the Bp. was so much engaged that he could not be spoken with.* 3-4 Jan., 13 Jan., 7 Feb., 9 Feb: *Wrote to Bp. Monk, soliciting him to permit my Son to resign this Curacy, in order to accept the Curacy of Whichford, stating the grounds on which the application was made, my son's engagement with Sophy Vavasour, the wish on all sides that their Union should not be long deferred &c.* 11 Feb: *Recd. a letter from Bp. Monk in reply to mine of the 9th. couched in kind and cordial terms as to myself and my son, with congratulations on his intended marriage, but expresses a reluctance to any arrangement which might take him out of his diocese, as likely to create a precedent which might be quoted upon himself, and giving to my Son's late ordination the appearance of having been a mere accommodation and matter of convenience.* 12 Feb: *Wrote to Bp. Monk in reply to his letter recd. yesterday, and to the purport which suggested itself to my mind on receiving his letter.* 14 Feb: *Recd. a letter from the Bp. of Glouc. and Bristol in reply to mine of the 12th. Inst. in which he concedes the point as to my Son's acceptance of the Curacy of Whichford, still trusting that even now, if an opportunity should occur, a situation in this diocese may be obtained.* 26 Feb., 14 Apr., 25 Jun., 10 Jul., 22 Aug: *The Bishop shortly after arrived from Campden, where he had confirmed and visited yesterday, complaining of fatigue and over-exertion, and suffering both bodily and mentally from the continued, &, it is to be feared, increasing infirmity of his eyesight.* 16 Oct., 21 Oct., 26 Oct., 30 Nov., 1 Dec: *To the Bp. of Gloucester; expressed my satisfaction at the intimation given me that he was about to present F. Aston to the living of Northleach; ventured to say that such notice taken of a respectable curate of long standing in the diocese was in strict conformity with his Lordship's disinterestedness, and regard for the principles most conducive to the welfare of the Church.* 3-4 Dec., 5 Dec: *Wrote to the Bp. of Glouc. that at Whichford I had to combat with the unwillingness of my son and his wife to relinquish a residence to which they were attached.* 7 Dec., 9 Dec., 12 Dec: *Wrote to the Bp. of Glouc. & Bristol to acquaint him that my son had accepted the Curacy of Stanway; the reasons which had caused hesitation I explained more fully.* 14 Dec., 15 Dec: *Recd. a letter from the Bp. of Gloucester in answer to mine of the 12th. expressing his satisfaction that E.F.W. had accepted the Curacy of Stanway.* 16 Dec., 28 Dec.

1839: 1 Jan: *In the course of the day I absented myself for half an hour from the Court, to pay my respects at the Palace, where I did not see the Bp. who was engaged in the institution of a Clergyman, but was admitted by Mrs. Monk, who recd. me with wonted hos cordiality, and engaged me to dine at the Palace to meet a large party to morrow.* 2 Jan., 13 Jan., 15 Jan., 17 Jan., 9 Feb., 11 Feb., 15 Feb., 1 Mar., 3 Apr., 10 Apr., 12 Apr., 29-30 Apr., 1 May.

1840: 13 Apr., 22 Apr: *The Bp. of Gloucester acknowledged in a very proper manner the letter I addressed to him on the 13th. Inst.* 29 Apr., 22 Nov.

1842: 14 Jan., 18 Jan., 22 Jan., 31 Jan., 1 Feb: *Wrote to Mr. Murray Browne, the Bishop of Gloucester's Chaplain to learn something as to the proposed address to his Lordship touching the Tract Controversy, from whom it emanates, and whether it would be acceptable to his Lordship that his Clergy keeping the via media should attach their signatures to it.* 4 Feb: *The Bp. does not approve of the proposed address, and does approve of his Clergy withholding their signatures from it: it emanates from hot-headed parties, as Kinsey, who have come into personal collision with "Tractarians", and Ultra Protestants, as the Cheltenham Clergy.* 5 Feb., 8 Feb., 10-11 Feb., 13 Feb., 22 Feb., 24 Feb., 21 Mar., 26 Mar., 7 Apr., 27 Apr., 7-8 May, 23 May, 20 Sep.

1843: 4 Jan: *I called at the Palace, but the Bishop was from home.* 12 Dec., 29 Dec.

1844: 16 Jan., 9-10 Apr., 15 Aug., 19 Aug., 29 Aug: *The sitting closed at 3 P.M. on the arrival of the Bishop of Gloucester, from Moreton in Marsh, where he had been holding a confirmation, as upon his circuit of confirmations and visitation.* 30 Aug: *Left home at 11 AM. to attend the Visitation at Stow: met Mr. Francis by appointment at L Slaughter Turnpike gate, who took a place in my carriage, but I did not bring him back, as he did not stay to dine with the Bishop and Clergy, walking home after the Visitation.* 5 Sep., 18 Sep., 11 Oct., 7 Nov., 12 Nov., 22 Nov., 30 Nov., 4 Dec., 7 Dec., 18 Dec.

1845: 7 Jan., 13 Jan: *MW. recd. a letter from Mrs. Monk inviting us to visit the Bishop of Gloucester and herself at the Palace at Stapleton, at dinner, on Wednesday next, and to remain till Saturday. It seems they have also invited my Son and daughter, but had not received their reply, which is accounted for, probably, by their absence at Leamington at the close of last week. The time, being short, precluded communication with Stanway; the trouble and expence with uncertainty whether our children would accept the invitation, and my wife not being very well, determined us to decline this invitation on the plea that I had a particular engagement on business on the 16th.* 18 Jan: *A note came from E.F.W—the housemaid at Stanway Vicarage has been taken so ill, that they are obliged to send her to her friends, and they ask that our Gardener's daughter may be sent to them as a temporary substitute: they wish us also to spare Anne (my wife's made) to wait on Sophy in the visit they are about to pay to the Bishop of Glouc. and his family.* 21 Jan., 25 Jan., 26 Jan: *A letter from E.F.W. with a very pleasant account of his and Sophy's visit last week to the Bp. of Gloucester & Bristol and Mrs. Monk, and family at Stapleton palace near Bristol.* 23 Feb., 12 Mar., 16 Mar., 11 Apr.

1846: 8 Aug: *Gloucester, the Bp. began by nominating Dr. Warneford first, as the great Church Benefactor; next Murray Browne, his Lordship's Chaplain was appointed; then Malcolm, a recently appointed Rural Dean; but it so happens that Bp. Monk was admitted of Trin. Coll. Camb. under M. as Tutor; and now, greatly to his satisfaction, Ford is selected.*

1847: 7 Apr., 23 Jun., 25 Jun., 27 Jun: *Recd. a letter from the Bishop of Gloucester, who cordially accepts our invitation to visit us at the time of the visitation, if he should be prevented going to Little Risington, by Mrs. Ford's illness, or otherwise.* 8 Aug., 13 Aug., 25 Aug: *I joined the Bishop, his Chaplain, Murray Browne, and others of the Clergy, at the Rectory, Stow ... The dinner over, I hastened in my carriage homeward to receive the Bishop and Murray Browne, and they followed very closely on my steps. The party whom we had invited to meet his Lordship were Mr. Ford with his daughters Dulcy and Sophia, my son and his wife, who had arrived from Stanway this afternoon with the baby, and who slept here, Mr. and Mrs. Hippisley, who were accompanied by their Visitors, Miss Digby, and Mr. Raikes, a young brother of Mrs. Hippisley; Mr. and Mrs. W. B. Pole, who brought with them Mrs. Vavasour; Messrs. Perkins and Potter, whom I brought in my carriage from Stow, Messrs. Hunt, Turner and Clarke—Tea and Coffee, with a cold supper at 9 P.M., with conversation, were the arrangments of our Episcopal soirée.* 26 Aug: *After breakfast the Bishop and his Chaplain took leave of us, and went to Stow to the Confirmation.* 31 Aug., 12 Oct: *His Lordship cautions him not to be hasty in resigning his preferment: trusts that he is not so dangerously ill as he apprehends; hopes he may recover; suggests that he had better not personally confer with him on the subject, but delegate some friend to apply to him, or through his secretary, Mr. Holt.* 9 Nov: *Mr. Holt readily explained that his Lordship peremptorily refused to accept the tendered resignation, because he considered the transaction, as respects the Incumbent and Vendor, to have been conducted in too open and undisguised a manner, to have been publicly divulged by him, so that the Bishop was informed of the intention as long ago as on his visitation at Campden, when it was intimated to him by a third party that he intended to keep the advowson, but to sell the next presentation with the assurance of an early avoidance, which of course would greatly increase the value, and this the Bp. regards, I apprehend, as a culpable trafficking.* 16 Nov: *Mr. Holt observed that it would be both unwise and improper, either that E.F.W. or myself should communicate on the matter with himself or the Bishop.*

1848: 24 Aug.

1850: 8 Jul: *The Bishop proposes to hold a confirmation at Stow in the second week of September,—also, to gratify Ford, at Little Risington.* 19 Jul., 10 Aug: *My son tells me that he has received a letter from the Bishop, in reply to one written by him to place his Vicarage at his disposal at the time of the proposed confirmation at Stanway, to the effect that the Stewards of the music meeting at Gloucester having fixed for that festival the same week which he had fixe chosen for his confirmations in the deaneries of Stow and Campden, he is disposed to postpone confirming in those deaneries until his visitation next year, unless his Clergy press for the administration of the rite this year. This betrays sad vacillation, and indifference: and those to whom this has been made known justly censure such conduct. Perhaps he may be induced to hold the Confirmations still, though evidently desirous of shirking. A missionary bishop would not act so.* 16 Sep: *About half past two the Bishop of Gloucester, and his chaplain, Murray Browne, arrived from Gloucester, and joined the party at table: his Lordship accosting all present in his usual courteous manner, and expressing himself much pleased with all which was done...* 18 Sep: *To the Rectory, where I met the Bishop and his chaplain, Murray Browne, just arrived from Moreton in Marsh, where he had been holding a confirmation in the forenoon, having confirmed at Campden yesterday.*

1851: 18 Apr., 29 Apr: *It was eleven o clock before the Bishop arrived from the palace at Gloucester, looking ill, and complaining of having been seriously indisposed for some time past with chest complaints.* 16 May: *It is said that Bp. Monk is in very impaired health, and very sensitive as to any movement tending to the separation of Gloucester and Bristol, assuming that mooting the question conveys a tacit censure of himself; and it seems to be settled that active proceedings in this direction should be suspended for the present: yet so far kept alive as that the sentiments of Clergy and Laity should be collected, with a view to prompt action at a proper time.* 20 May: *Many were the acquaintances whom I met in the crowd; among them was the Bishop of Gloucester, with Mrs. Monk and his three daughters: his Lordship seemed to be, and said that he was, in better health than when I saw him at the consecration of Highnam Church; he proposes going abroad for a few weeks for the recovery of his health; his destination being the Rhine district, and one or more of the German Baths.*

1852: 29 Apr.

1854: 13 May, 17 May: *Received a letter from the Bishop of Gloucester and Bristol, from whom also Edd. Clifford received one; both related to his being licensed to this curacy curacy, and both were written in an obliging tone. My nomination is accepted, and the Bishop considers the selection I have made of a curate fortunate — having a favourable opinion of E.C.*

MONK — William Garrow Monk [160]

William Garrow Monk (1785-1859), HEIC writer, was the son of William Monk and Jane Garrow. He rose in the HEIC service to become assistant under-secretary to government in the revenue and judicial department. He married, 20 June 1832, Eliza Ann Archer (b. 1812); they had 4 sons and 2 daughters:

1 William (1832-1877); married Ellen Keell
1 Eliza Garrow (b. 1837); married, 1863, Charles Morgan
2 Francis Tebbut (1838-1904)
3 Henry Haden (1840-1925)
4 John Gordon Archer (1843-1931); married, 1873, Eliza Trevelyan, née Deacon
2 Mary Louisa (b. 1848); married, 1868, Francis Frederick Archer

---

1851: 25 May: *I had an opportunity of judging that B.L.W. and his wife stand very well with the more opulent residents in the Village: those whom we met expressed much interest in his state of health; particularly solicitous was one kind hearted elderly East Indian, a species of the genus Paul Pry, who was perpetually looking in, and planning and considering what arrangements ought to be made, and how he could aid and assist during my cousin's intended absence from home.... the ubiquitous Mr. Monk.* 26 May: *Mr. Monk looked in at our breakfast, for the last adieux, and kindly guided me to the line of footpath along which I was to walk to the Walton Station; a fly bringing my cousins and their children with the nurse.*

MONSELL — Margaret Monsell, a guest of Lady Elcho [161]

Margaret Monsell (±1748-1828) was buried at Charlton Kings, Gloucestershire, on 27 December 1828; she was recorded at her death as being 'about 80 years of age'. Agnes Witts mentioned her fifty-six times in her diaries between 1804 and 1824, spelling her name 'Moncell'. There appears to have been a connection with Lady Elcho—Stanway and Bryanstone Square—but nothing in particular has been discovered.

1825: 14 Mar: *We found Mrs. Moncell from Cheltenham an inmate, and the circle at dinner was increased by the addition of Mr. Eddy, the Rector of Toddington & his daughter, Mr. Perkins, Curate of Broadway, & Mr. F. Aston.*

1828: 4 Oct: *I called on Lady Elcho Besides Miss Church, Mrs. Monsell & Mrs. Leigh, two widowed Sisters, Irish & Roman Catholics, are her present guests.*

MONTAGU — Emily Montagu [162]

Emily Montagu, Viscountess Abingdon, née Gage (1776-1838), was the youngest daughter of Gen. Thomas Gage. She was the sister of Henry, 3rd Viscount Gage. She married, 1807, Robert, 5th earl of Abingdon (1784-1854).

1826: 15 Sep: Present at the Three Choirs Festival, Gloucester.

MONTAGUE — William Montague [163]

William Montague (±1770-1847), ironmaster, was a partner in John Coles's ironmongery business early in his career. He came to Gloucester from Wokingham, and in 1794, took on the contract for digging the first section of the Gloucester & Berkeley Canal south from the basin at Gloucester. He established an iron foundry on the Island in Gloucester in 1802. In the late 1820s the foundry was producing castings of a high quality, using Forest of Dean iron from works at Cinderford and Parkend, in which Montague had an interest.

In 1824 Moses Teague formed the Forest of Dean Iron Company with William Montague and Benjamin Whitehouse of Monmouth and Redbrook. John James joined shortly after. Using a furnace at Parkend, the company planned to exploit Teague's discovery of a method of making good iron with coke made from local coal. The furnace had been bought by John Protheroe, of Bristol, in 1807, and in 1824 he sold it to his nephew Edward Protheroe of Newnham.

In 1825 William Montague and John James purchased equal shares (undivided moieties), claiming through or under George Stephens, a free miner. Whether this Stephens was a relation of Montague's wife Mary, née Stephens, is not clear. From 1826 Montague and James were the only partners, but Montague also continued to trade as a wholesale ironmonger in partnership with Charles Church. After Montague's death in 1847, John James bought out his interest at Parkend, but the foundry was continued by Charles Montague, William's son, until its closure in 1865.

William Montague lived at Constitution House, Gloucester, and married, 1806, Mary (±1784-1857), daughter of Merrett Stephens, banker of Gloucester, who died suddenly in 1815 while singing at a dinner celebrating the nomination of the new mayor. William and Mary had at least 1 son and 3 daughters:

1 Charles (±1815-1887); married, at Clifton, 16 April 1850, Maria Haythorne Latcham; at least 1 son:
    1 Charles Arthur Haythorne (b. 1852)
1 Emily (1822-1885)
2 Constance (±1825-1845); died unmarried
3 Clara (±1827-1910); died unmarried

At the time of the 1851 census Mary was living at 1 Sion Row, Clifton, with her unmarried daughter Clara. This was presumably to be close to her son Charles, later commissioner of taxes, who was living at Leigh Woods, just across the suspension bridge.

1825: 20 May: *Mrs. Backhouse came over from Gloucester to pass part of the morning with us. She was brought in an open carriage by Mr. & Mrs. Montague of Gloucester: he is an active intelligent person, who has large concerns in the Iron trade He was desirous of some conversation with me respecting some unpleasant rumours prevalent as to Mr. Hale's School, where he has two sons.* 13 Jun: *I reached the York House at Bath where I found Mr. Montague from Gloucester, and we were soon joined by Mr. Croome from Bourton on the Water, who also has a son at Mr. Hale's school.* 14 Jun., 9 Nov: *I dined with Mr. Montague, meeting, besides his own family, Mrs. Church, the wife of his partner in the extensive Ironworks, Mr. Sievier, and the Revd. J. Bishop.*

1826: 17 Jan: *The parties, with whom they are about, in March, to unite, are Mr. Gladstone, MP for Woodstock, a very eminent Liverpool Merchant, of Scotch extraction, who has been residing of late at Gloucester Spa, in consequence of the indisposition of one of his family, a gentleman of great practical experience; Mr. Montague, our acquaintance, the great Ironmaster here and a Mr. Nicholls.* 22 Feb: *The proposed union of Messrs. Turner with Messrs. Gladstone, Montague & Nicholls will not take effect.* 30 Apr: *Service being over I called at Lyde House, and was accompanied from thence by my dear Edward, and three of his companions, two Montagues, sons of Mr. Montague of Gloucester, & Charles Croome, younger son of Mr. Croome of Bourton on the Water. They all dined and passed the Evening with us.*

1827: 23 Apr: *I borrowed Mr. Montague's phaeton, and drove my new horse, Mrs. F. W. accompanying me, as far as Brockthorp on the Stroud road.*

1837: 4 Jan.

1846: 2 Jul., 11 Aug.

MONTMORENCY — Mathieu Paul Louis de Montmorency-Laval [164]

Mathieu Paul Louis de Montmorency-Laval (1748-1809), French aristocrat, was the son of Guy André Pierre de Montmorency-Laval (1723-1798) and Jacqueline Marie Hortense de Bullion (1720-1795). He married, December 1765, Catherine Jeanne Tavernier de Boullongne (1749-1838). They were were divorced by 1790, but had 2 sons:

1 Mathieu Bouchard Jean Félicité (1767-1826); married Pauline Hortense d'Albert de Luynes (b. 1774); 1 daughter:
   1 Elisabeth (1790-1843); married Sosthène de La Rochefoucauld, 2nd duc de Doudeauville (1785-1864)
2 Ann Pierre (1769-1794); died at the guillotine

With his son Mathieu Jean Félicité, Montmorency-Laval fought on the rebel side in the American Revolutionary War. He returned to France as colonel of the Auvergne Infantry Regiment, and became brigadier in the army of the king in 1784, and governor of Compiègne. It seems that he fled at some point to England, but later returned to France and fought for Napoleon as a member of his elite guard, commanding a corps of cavalry volunteers known as the Gendarmes. He was promoted to brigadier on 28 October 1808 and died the following year.

Montmorency-Laval's elder son, Mathieu Jean Félicité, was appointed, like his father, governor of Compiègne when he was elected as a deputy for the noblesse to the Estates General in 1789. At the beginning of the French Revolution he joined the Third Estate and sat on the left side of the National Assembly. After the storming of the Tuileries Palace in August 1792, he abandoned his idealism and fled first to Switzerland, and then to England. In 1795, he returned to Paris but took no part in politics under the Directory, Consulate, or Empire, and appears to have soon gone back to London. At the beginning of the Bourbon restoration, Mathieu Jean Félicité was promoted to the rank of maréchal de camp; he accompanied Louis XVIII to Ghent during the Hundred Days. After the battle of Waterloo and the final defeat of Napoleon in 1815, he was made a peer of France and received the title of vicomte de Montmorency-Laval. He became the minister of foreign affairs under Jean-Baptiste Guillaume Joseph, comte de Villèle, in December 1821. At the Congress of Verona in October 1822 he recommended armed intervention in Spain to restore Ferdinand VII, but he resigned his post in December, being compensated by the title of duc de Montmorency-Laval and, soon after, the cross of the Legion of Honour.

1801: 27 May: *In the Evening to a party at Lady Lyttelton's, which was musical; The Harp, Grand Piano Forte & voice; the chief performers were, Miss Hadsley, Miss Bowles, Miss Canning, Miss Kearney, the Misses Halifax, Miss Stanhope, le Compte de Montmorency &c.*

MONTPENSIER — *see* **d'Orleans** *and* **Louis Philippe of France**

MONYPENNY — Miss Monypenny at Edinburgh

1801: 20 Apr: *Mr. McKenzie, Miss Graham & Miss Monypenny called in the forenoon.*

MOORE — Arthur Moore [165]

Arthur Moore (1804-1853), Church of England clergyman, was born at Dublin, the son of Arthur Moore (1764-1846), of Queen's County, and Frances Stoney (1768-1854). His grandfather was John Moore (1730-1805), archbishop of Canterbury, and his father was a judge of the common pleas in Ireland. He was educated at University College, Oxford (BA 1825; MA 1832), and was ordained deacon on 8 July 1827 and priest on 15 June 1828. His first clerical appointment was as stipendiary curate to Revd Richard Ford at South Cerney from 8 July 1827. He was later appointed stipendiary curate at Stratton on 6 November 1833. He does not appear in the *Clergy List* for 1841, so he presumably retired from the Church.

Moore married, at St Mary's, Southampton, 2 May 1825, Anna Maria (1805-1876), daughter of Sir John Peniston Milbanke, 7th baronet (1776-1850), and a cousin of Lord Melbourne. Arthur and Anna had 2 sons and 1 daughter:

1 Arthur Peniston (1827-1891)
2 Lewis James (1828-1881), Rear Adm.
1 Louisa Frances Lumley (1833-1920)

1826: 28 Jul: *We dined at Mr. Ford's: Meeting Mr. & Mrs. Vavasour & our old friend, Miss Hippisley, Mr. Twisleton, Mr. Baillie & his sister, Mr. Watson Pole & a young man of the name of Moore, a grandson of the late Archbishop of Canterbury, now a pupil at Mr. Boudier's at Farmington. Edward accompanied us.*

1837: 22 Aug: *There were staying in the House Mrs. and Miss Niblett from Haresfield, and the Revd. Mr. Moore and Lady from Stratton near Cirencester, where he is, I believe, Curate. He was formerly curate to Ford at South Cerney, and married to a pleasing young person, a daughter of Sir John Milbanke. Mr. Moore is a fine performer on the flute, and indulged us with several beautifully executed pieces.*

MOORE — George Ogle Moore [166]

George Ogle Moore (1778-1847), MP and landed proprietor, was born in Dublin, the fifth, but fourth surviving, son of John Moore (d. 1799), of Summerhill, co. Dublin, and Mary Anne [Ogle?]. He was educated at Trinity College, Dublin (BA 1797; LLD 1808), Gray's Inn (1798), and King's Inns (1800), and was called to the bar in 1800. Moore was MP for Dublin in 1826-31, and succeeded his uncle George Ogle to Belview, Enniscorthy, co. Wexford, in 1814. He married Elizabeth Armstrong, and they had 4 sons and 2 daughters:

1 William Ogle (1801-1874), Church of England clergyman; married, at Ely Place, Dublin, 23 April 1833, Anna Casey (1809-1882), daughter of Thomas Casey, MP of Kilamallock, and Anna de Cloise; eleven children
2 John (b. ±1802); married, before 1837, Elizabeth Jones; emigrated to Australia, 1852
3 James Moore (1807-1895), lawyer, pastoralist, and banker; emigrated to Australia
4 Lorenzo (1808-1894); died at Nelson, New Zealand
1 Mary Anne Jane (dates unknown)
2 Elizabeth (dates unknown); married, 1833, Edward Beauman

George Ogle Moore was a descendant of Garrett, 1st Viscount Moore of Drogheda, whose ancestry traced from the union of John of Gaunt and Katherine Swynford.

1827: 8 Mar: ... *ably supported the Protestant cause; among them Mr. Bankes, & Mr. G. Moore, MP for Dublin.*
1828: 17 May,
1829: 7 Feb.

MOORE — George Moore [167]

George Moore (1808-1889), surgeon, was born at Tewkesbury, son of Charles Moore (d. 1811) and Rebekah Sandlands. He married, at Ashchurch, Gloucestershire, 17 March 1831, Eliza New (1804-1872); they had 2 sons and 8 daughters:

1 Eliza (b. 1832)
2 Frances A. (b. 1834)
3 Mary Anna (b. 1837)
4 Ellen (b. 1839)
5 Norah (b. 1840)
1 John New (1842-1904); married, at Moreton-in-Marsh, 30 April 1872, Ann Shirley
6 Margaret (b. 1843)
2 William (b. 1845)
7 Lucy Mary (b. 1846)
8 Penelope Blanche (b. 1851)

1834: 19 Sep: *Met at Dr. Warnefords Messrs. Colvile, Moore (Surgeon at Moreton in Marsh,) Capt. Collier, and S. Jeaffreson, laymen; also Revd. Messrs. Hall, Malcolm, Coyle, Jeaffreson and Robt. Hall.*

1843: 7 Oct: *When I got to day's letter went to Bourton, I took Lower Slaughter Turnpike in my way, where I found a letter from Mr. Moore, surgeon, Moreton in Marsh, requesting my advice as to obtaining for a person there in indifferent health exemption from serving as a Juror at the coming Quarter Sessions at Gloucester.* 8 Oct., 14 Oct., 18 Oct.

1846: 3 Oct: *During my absence from home, Mr. Moore, the Med. Off. of Distr. 3. of this Union called.* 2 Dec: *His object being to urge me to adopt his views ... as to obtaining from the Guardians of our Union a vote of extraordinary remuneration for one year to Mr. Moore, the Med. Off. of Great Risington district, in consideration of his good services & extraordinary expence in attending on the poor of Great Risington, during a late period of epidemic typhoid fever there.* 3 Dec., 21 Dec., 28 Dec.

1847: 11 Jan: *Recd. a note from Mr. Moore, Med. Off. of a district of the Stow Union, craving my advice as to certain points in the discharge of his official functions.* 12 Jan., 22 Feb., 3 Jun: *Mr. Moore, having accompanied poor Bowen yesterday on his journey to Brentford, was not present.* 4 Jun: *Good tidings had reached Bourton, through Mr. Moore, the Med. attendant, as to the success which had attended the operation for the Stone, by crushing, which had been performed on Bowen by Dr. Costello at Brentford yesterday.* 17 Jun: *Met and conferred with Mr. Moore, the Surgeon of Bourton on the Water, who read to me a letter he had just received from Dr. Costello.* 22 Jun., 25 Jun., 13 Nov: *From Mr. Moore, Med. Off. of one of the districts of our Union, a note suggesting that measures should be taken by the Guardians to improve the sanitary state of the villages, under the probability that Asiatic Cholera.* 14 Nov., 18-19 Nov., 1 Dec.

1848: 15 Apr., 5 Jun., 6 Sep., 16 Sep., 18 Sep: *Mr. Moore called; with whom I conferred on the sanitary state of the district.* 26 Sep., 7 Nov.

1852: 2 Feb., 12 Apr.

1853: 15-16 Jan., 19 Feb., 23 Feb., 10 May, 14 Dec.

MOORE — Henry Moore, a tenant of Mrs Dolphin at Eyford [168]

Henry Moore (1822-1876), farmer, was born in co. Wexford, Ireland, son of Thomas O'Hiwell Moore (1777-1854) and Rachael Colles (1779-1864). He married, first, 16 April 1844, Mary (b. ±1820), daughter of William Kimber of Sapperton; they had 2 sons and 1 daughter:

1 Ottiwell Henry (1845-1892)
2 William Allen (b. 1846)
1 Mary Catherine (b. 1848)

Henry married secondly, 2 September 1854, Jane Frances Hull (d. 1877); they had 3 sons and 5 daughters:

1 Emily Frances (b. 1855)
1 Edmund Notley (1858-1922)
2 Henry Burton (b. 1860)
3 Frederick Thomas (b. 1862)
2 Esther (b. 1863)
3 Margaret Sophie (b. 1866)
4 Caroline Lucy (b. 1869)
5 Annie (b. 1871)

Henry and Jane emigrated to Australia; all of the children of Henry's second marriage were born in Victoria.

1844: 21 *Apr: Mr. H. Moore, the young Irish tenant on the Dolphin property at the Parks farm, having brought home his bride, late Miss Kimber, the daughter of a respectable Yeoman at Sapperton, and niece of my acquaintance and brother Magistrate, Mr. Playne.* 28 Apr: *Among the congregation was the Revd. R. Moore, brother of the tenant of "the Parks" farm, Eyford, an Irish Clergyman.* 29 Apr: *Wrote a note to Mr. H. Moore, Eyford, offering to his brother, should he remain his visitor on Sunday next, the use of my pulpit.* 30 Apr: *Recd. a note from Mr. H. Moore: he tells me that his brother has already left Eyford, but that he expects his father to be his visitor on Sunday next, and that it would please him greatly to have an opportunity of hearing him preach: replied that I should have great satisfaction in acceding to his wish.* 5 May: *Before morning service Mr. Moore, from the Parks, Eyford, called to introduce his father to me, who is a very fine old clergyman, beneficed in the County Wexford, conversible, gentlemanly, and apparently of a very good school.* 10 Sep: *Wrote to Mr. Moore, Eyford, to correct an error into which he had fallen as to the Jury List for that place.* 12 Sep.

1845: 26 Mar: *Recd. from Mr. Moore a note as to the time of christening his new-born infant, to which I replied.* 28 Mar: *Christened the infant child of Mr. and Mrs. Moore of Eyford at the Church.* 22 Apr: *Also to Mrs. Dolphin urging upon her to name a person to be appointed Overseer of Eyford: both her tenants, Humphris and Moor, have left their farms, and have no successors.*

1848: 7 Aug: ... *making extensive repairs, additions and alterations to the mansion house at Eyford; as resolved to dismantle, and even pull down, the farm house at the Parks, erected only a few years ago for the residence of Mr. Polhill, and since occupied by W. Smith, Moore &c.*

MOORE — James Moore [169]

James Moore (1768-1845), Church of England clergyman, was the son of James Moore of London. He was educated at Merchant Taylors' School, Magdalene College, Cambridge, and St John's College, Oxford (DCL 1817). He was admitted at the Inner Temple in 1792, but had a change of heart and entered the Church. He was ordained on 1 January 1795 and appointed curate of Latton, Wiltshire, on the same day. He was later rector of Sutton-on-Derwent, Yorkshire, in 1809-14, and vicar of St Pancras Church, Euston Road, London, in 1814-45. He also held the lectureship of St Clement Danes and was preacher of Portman and Bedford chapels and evening preacher at the Foundling Hospital.

James Moore married, first, 1795, Agnes (1774-1839); they had 1 son and 1 daughter:

1 John Rush (1799-1857)
2 Caroline Anne (b. 1812)

Moore married secondly, at the parish chapel, St Pancras, Middlesex, 27 February 1840, Caroline Anna White (1795-1863).

1801: 6 Jun: ... *we repaired to Lady Lyttelton's, where we met a most agreable emphatic & clever clergyman, Mr. More.* 7 Jun: ... *to the Foundling Hospital, where was a general baptism & an excellent Sermon was preached on the occasion by our acquaintance Mr. More.*

1835: 11 Jun: *The Rector of St. Pancras, Dr. Moore, an elderly man, who succeeded Bishop Middleton in the incumbency of the Parish, and who in his early days was a very popular preacher, came into the Church, and introduced himself to me: at his request I introduced him to Mr. Duncan.*

MOORE — John Moore, later Moore-Stevens [170]

John Moore (1784-1865), Church of England clergyman, was born at Torrington, Devon, son of Revd Thomas Moore (1740-1802) and Lady Christian Stevens (1743-1828). He was educated at Exeter College, Oxford (BA 1806; MA 1808), where he was a fellow from 1806 to 1811. He was rector of Langtree, Devon, in 1810-22, and vicar of Otterton, Devon, in 1822-65. He was also appointed prebendary of Exeter in 1821, archdeacon in 1828, and canon in 1842. He assumed the additional surname Stevens.

Moore-Stevens married, at Eton, Buckinghamshire, 31 December 1817, Ann Eleanor Roberts (1790-1849); they had 1 son and 2 daughters:

1 John Curzon (1818-1903), Capt., Devon Hussars; became JP, DL, and MP
1 Anne Eleanor (1820-1897)
2 Louisa Julia (1823-1856)

1804: 5 Mar: *At the Assizes: not within the Bar. With G. Cabbell & J. Moore.*

1805: 21 Mar: *At an Examination at the Schools, where Round & Moore of Exeter very much distinguished themselves.* 26 Mar: *Met Messrs. Fort, J. Dunne, Gravenell, Barton, Vashon, Wilson, Moore & Leech: a pleasant party enough.*

MOORE — Thomas Moore [171]

Thomas Moore (1779-1852), poet, was born at 12 Aungier Street, Dublin, the only son and eldest child of John Moore (1741-1825), grocer and wine merchant, and Anastasia Codd (1749-1832). Moore's first school was conducted by a Mr Malone, and his second by Samuel Whyte, who years earlier had taught the playwright R. B. Sheridan. Whyte was deeply involved in Dublin's theatrical life and encouraged Moore's talents as an elocutionist. Moore was further educated at Trinity College, Dublin, where he became a sound classical scholar; he published his translations of Anacreon, the Greek lyric poet, in 1800.

In 1799 Moore moved to London and entered the Middle Temple with a view to a legal career. He thrived socially, and his songs were in great demand at the parties he attended. This popularity encouraged him to publish his songs and poems; his *Poetical Works of the Late Thomas Little* (1801) was a commercial success, although its mildly erotic flavour eventually caused him some embarrassment.

In 1803 Moore was appointed as registrar of the naval prize court in Bermuda. While there he made a notable contribution to the colony's social life but saw little future in the business of the prize court. Having come to this conclusion he appointed a deputy, and spent five months travelling in North America. He found the United States barbarous and disorderly. He returned to London where he soon noticed that a reviewer of one of his works had referred to him as 'the most licentious of modern versifiers', and his book as 'a public nuisance'. Moore challenged the reviewer to a duel, but the contest was interrupted by police officers who took both men into custody. After the embarrassment of the duel, Moore withdrew to Dublin, where he spent the winter of 1806–07.

In Dublin Moore was approached by William and James Power to take part in a venture that was to prove astonishingly successful. They asked him to write words for characteristic Irish airs arranged by Sir John Stevenson, forming what became known as the *Irish Melodies* (1808–34). Moore's splendid performances were more than enough to recommend the songs to fashionable society. Moore also enjoyed some success in the theatre. He delivered a vivacious performance as David in Sheridan's *The Rivals*, and used his familiarity with the theatre to good effect in his own musical comedy, *MP, or, The Blue-Stocking*. It was performed in London's Lyceum Theatre in September 1811 and well received.

By 1812 Moore's standing soared as a leading literary partisan of the whig opposition. His status was reinforced by the close friendship he developed with Lord Byron, whom he had met for the first time in November 1811. For many years Moore contributed his lively and accomplished verses to the *Morning Chronicle*, and for a while *The Times*. It was a useful source of income; *The Times* paid him £400 in 1826 and 1827, and £200 thereafter. Then there was the £500 a year he received from James Power for the continued publication of new numbers of *Irish Melodies*.

Moore's most famous early publication was *Lalla Rookh* (1817), which he sold to Longman for £3,000. His next work, *The Fudge Family in Paris* (1818), was a satirical set of verse epistles attributed to writers ranging from a servile creature of the tories to a passionate champion of Ireland, with some light relief from Miss Biddy Fudge, a young lady of fashion. This also enjoyed considerable success, but nonetheless, Moore found himself in serious financial difficulties. His deputy in Bermuda absconded, leaving him responsible for a debt of £6,000. As he could not possibly pay this sum, he went abroad to avoid arrest, spending three years in France and Italy. It was an unproductive time for him; he only wrote a pedestrian continuation of the Fudge family travels, later published as *Rhymes on the Road* (1823). When in Italy, Moore visited Byron, who presented him with the manuscript of his memoirs, a gift that was to prove troublesome for Moore, but which eventually led him to write a biography of the poet. In 1821 a friend arranged for his debts to be paid and he returned to England. There he continued to exploit his talent for exotic sensuousness in *The Loves of the Angels* (1823). He then embarked on a new career as a biographer in his *Memoirs of the Life of the Right Honourable Richard Brinsley Sheridan* (1825). His last major work was *Letters and Journals of Lord Byron* (1830).

Francis Witts first met Thomas Moore in 1805 at Tunbridge Wells when the poet was staying there with his mother and sisters. This was after his return from the United States.

Moore married, at St Martin's, Kilkenny, 25 March 1811, Elizabeth Dyke (1796-1865)—Bessy, as he always called her. They had 2 sons and 3 daughters:

1 Ann Jane Barbara (1812-1817)
2 Anastasia Mary (1813-1829)

3 Olivia Byron (1814-1815); died an infant
1 Thomas Lansdowne Parr (1818-1849); died at Algiers
2 John Russell (1823-1842), Lt, HEIC; died at his parents' home at Bromham, Wiltshire, after returning from India in poor health

---

1805: 25 Sep: *at a party at Miss Windhams, which turned out a lively pleasant dance of six couple, some singing & music & a supper. Danced with Miss Bicknall & Miss Moore three nice girls & with a Mrs. Moore.* 1 Oct: *A party at Mrs. Moore's of about twenty very pleasant, Miss Windham, the Bucknalls, O'Callaghan, Tickells etc.* 4 Oct: *Walked with the Moore's Drewes, O'Callaghan etc.*

1826: 20 May: *"Memoirs of the life of the Right Honourable R.B. Sheridan. By Thomas Moore. London 1825. 2 Vols 8vo." This is a work, which has excited much attention.* 14 Sep: *After a hasty & scrambling dinner, I retired to Wellington Parade to dress for the Concert: it was after I left the room, that the poet Moore's health was given, which he acknowledged in a light jocose manner, but which was not cordially received by some rigid professors in morals & politics: some, it was said, refused to fill their glass to the toast; & truly the laxity of the poet's morality, his bitter party spirit, his acrimonious and insidious political publications, and, above all, his atrocious attack on the king, aggravated by gross and wilful misrepresentation, in the life of Sheridan, are enough to excite a prejudice against him in the hearts of those, who desire to promote the cause of religion, virtue & loyalty.... His companion, Tommy Moore, is a short dapper, spruce, little man, without anything very striking in his countenance: he is much altered since I saw him in 1805, when we both lodged in the same house at Tunbridge Wells.*

1830: 23 Jun: *There are several pictures by the late Sir Thos. Lawrence ... a portrait of the Poet & Biographer, Moore, a most marvellous likeness, impossible to be mistaken; these will remain strongly impressed on my memory.*

MOORE — Thomas Moore[172]

Thomas Moore (1807-1882), master of Worcester Union Workhouse and clerk, was born at Dursley, Gloucestershire. Having been dismissed from the post of deputy governor of Gloucester Prison, Moore was appointed master of Worcester Union Workhouse. His wife Selina (b. ±1809), also born at Dursley, became matron. He later became a clerk in Liverpool, where he died.

1847: 23 Mar: ... *left the Court between three and four P.M. and before another case came on of much interest — a charge against the Clerk and deputy Governor of the County Prison, who had charged the Governor with a total disobedience of the rules laid down for the management of the prison, speaking of them as dead letter & not to be regarded &c. But this serious charge Moore, when required to substantiate it, failed to make good: so that it seems likely that he must be dismissed, though, in fact, the charge made by him is to all intents and purposes correct, though, probably, not capable of being proved by direct evidence, though the Governor is notoriously inefficient, and his deputy an active and effective officer.* 6 Apr.

1848: 10 Sep: *Received a letter from the Clerk of the Worcester Union, who requests my opinion as to the qualifications and characters of two candidates for the office of Governor of the Workhouse of that Union, both of whom are known to me: one is Moore, late Clerk of the County Gaol, Gloucester.* 11 Sep., 16 Sep: *From Mr. Knott, Clerk to the Worcester Union, a letter to acquaint me that Mr. Moore, late Clerk to the County Gaol, Gloucester, has been elected Governor of the Workhouse of the Worcester Union.*

MOORE — William Moore[173]

William Moore (1798-1879), Church of England clergyman, was born at Bisley, Gloucestershire, son of Revd William Moore (1764-1834) and Elizabeth Warner (1770-1818). He was educated at Pembroke College, Oxford (BA 1814; MA 1817), and was rector of Brimpsfield for fifty years, from 1829 to his death in 1879. Moore married, at Bath, 9 July 1823, Sarah Eliza Emily Worthington (1798-1852); they had at least 5 sons and 1 daughter:

1 Charles Caulfield (1825-1882)
2 William Worthington (1829-1871)
3 Arthur Godfrey (1832-1841)
1 Clara Maria (1833-1911)
4 Clement Feudal (1839-1840)
5 Ferdinand Pettal (1845-1928)

Interestingly, at the time of the census, Edward, Laura, and Constance Howell from Prinknash were at the vicarage, where William Moore was running a small school.

1834: 14 Aug: *The living is in the gift of Mrs. Pitt of Gloucester; it is held with the adjoining benefice of Brimpsfield in the same patronage: a Mr. Moore is the present incumbent.*

1842: 6 Jan: *Mr. and Mrs. Moore, from Brimpsfield with some children, and a pupil, staying in the house.* 7 Jan. 16 Oct: *Poor Howell was very grievously affected at meeting me in his bedroom, where I found him with his children Emelyn and Edward, the latter having been fetched from his Tutor's, Mr. Moore's at Brimpsfield.* 13 Dec.

1844: 10 Apr: ... *and there were staying in the house two fine lads, Turner and Swayne, pupils of Mr. Moore, of Brimpsfield, and so Schoolfellows of Edward Howell, passing the Easter holidays with him.* 11 Apr.

1845: 16 May: *Wrote to Mr. Moore, Brimpsfield, for particulars as to the date of the marriage of James Curtis to his first wife, which was solemnized at Cranham: this with a view to the removal of J.C. now chargeable to our parish.* 23 May: *A letter from Mr. Moore, Brimpsfield, as to the first marriage of the pauper, James Curtis, and his settlement at Cranham.*

1847: 5 May.

1850: 8 Nov: *We repaired at mid-day to the Cathedral library, where already many Clergymen were congregated; many of my personal friends and acquaintances, such as Canons Crawley and Morgan, Messrs. Moore, Sayers, Fowell Jones, Lysons, Riddle &c.*

MOORHOUSE — William Moorhouse and the Moorhouse family[174]

William Moorhouse (1731-1813), physician, married, 1754, Margaret (1731-1799), the daughter of Henry Curry. They had 2 sons and 1 daughter:

1 Edward (b. 1755)
1 Jane (1757-1842); married Thomas Backhouse
2 Henry (1759-1794); qualified MD, 1785; married, 1790, Anne (d. 1834), daughter of William Clayton of Newcastle-upon-Tyne; 1 son and 1 daughter:
    1 William Henry; died in infancy
    1 Margaret; died in infancy

It is unclear how Alice and Elizabeth Moorhouse come into the picture, but they were presumably unmarried daughters of Edward Moorhouse, and therefore first cousins to Margaret Witts. Most of the diary entries refer to the claim on the estate of Henry Moorhouse (1834 and 1835) and the bi-annual payment to Elizabeth Moorhouse.

The Moorhouse siblings, presumed children of Edward Moorhouse (b. 1755), were born in Gargrave; there were at least four of them—William, Thomas, Elizabeth, and Alice—all of whom appear to have remained single. It is commonly known that the 1841 census (the first of its kind) was unreliable in that birth years were often rounded to the nearest 5. In 1841 William was listed as '55', Alice as '55', and Thomas and Elizabeth both as '50'. By 1851 William and Alice had disappeared—William died in 1843 and Alice in 1847—while Thomas was listed as '60' and Elizabeth as '62'. Elizabeth appears to have survived beyond 1871. The censuses indicate that the siblings all lived in the village of Long Preston from at least 1841 to their deaths.

1823: 12 May: *Very much engaged in business, with Messrs. Hartley, Geldard, Moorhouse, Slingsby & others till twelve o clock, then rode to Stainforth Hall, and accompanied by our tenant & his Father to the higher parts of our Estate there.*

1833: 8 Nov: *the want of a good night's rest precluded any endeavour to seek out Mrs Moorhouse, Widow of my Mother in law's brother, formerly a Physician at Newcastle, who still resides in the place. Indeed, we have never met, and friendly intercourse is only maintained by letter. She is advanced in years, but, I believe, enjoys firm health: on her decease the estate of the late Dr. Moorhouse, at Ravenflat near Skipton will devolve to my wife.*

1834: 15 Jul: *A letter from Mr. Newmarch, fixing to come to U Slaughter on Saturday to consult about the measures necessary in respect of the property at Ravenflatt and Cracoe, lately devolved to my wife on the decease of the life-tenant, Mrs. Moorhouse.* 19-20 Jul., 31 Jul., 6 Aug., 7 Sep., 11 Oct., 18 Oct., 11-12 Nov., 17 Nov.

1835: 14 Feb., 21 Feb., 7-8 Apr., 29 Apr.

1836: 23 Jul., 29 Jul., 4 Aug., 26 Aug., 30 Aug., 21 Oct: *MW. had also received a letter from the Moorhouses at Long Preston soliciting my interference with Mr. Hartley to obtain for them a small farm on the property of Mr. Yorke, which Hartley has to let, and to which, they say, a Stewardship is annexed.* 4 Nov.

1837: 5 Mar., 10 Jul., 18 Aug: *By this arrangement, Ravenflatt will be made over to us with the Rents from last May day: Cracoe is yeilded by us to Mr. Walters: the rents recd. from Ravenflat since Mrs. Moorhouse's decease are to be retained by Mr. Walters as an equivalent to the Rent charge of £500 to the late Mrs. Moorhouse under her husband Dr. H. Moorhouse's will, and a further sum exceeding £420 is to be paid by us in liquidation of certain claims under the Trust created by Dr. H.M's will, which we cannot dispute.* 13 Sep., 12 Nov.

1838: 16 Feb: *On a cursory survey it appears that the sum of nearly £1000 will have been expended by us in this litigation, of which about £430 has been on account of claims made by Mr. Walters under the will of Dr. H. Moorhouse, and admitted by us, and about £5. are to be deducted from the law charges as being the amount of the conveyance of the Bourton Rectory land-tax; so that about £565 have been spent in law.* 18 May: *MW. recd. a painful letter from Miss Moorhouse of Long Preston, begging for £5 to enable her to pay half a year's rent.* 12 Sep., 17 Sep: *... a handsome place, where I have formerly paid a morning visit: there having been an intimacy between bygone generations of that house, and Dr. Moorhouse and Mrs. Backhouse.* 28 Sep., 13 Nov.

1839: 27 Feb.

1840: 8 Jun: *Wrote to Miss E. Moorhouse, in MW's name, in answer to a begging letter, which she had addressed to my wife, and which arrived on Saturday, that she and her sister must rest contented with the pecuniary assistance already rendered to them by Mrs. Backhouse, and as to which Mrs. W. had pledged herself that it shall be continued after her mother's decease, provided she be not harrassed by their continual importunity.*

1842: 14 Nov: *I was also much engaged in the evening with letters and arrangements consequent on Mrs. Backhouse's decease which I announced to E.F.W. and Sophy—to John Backhouse, to Miss Lonsdale, to Miss Gardner, to Miss Moorhouse, to Mr. Geldard, and to Mrs. G. Hartley.* 21 Nov., 26 Nov.

1843: 16 Aug: *I recd. a melancholy letter from Miss E. Moorhouse, Long Preston, a relation of my wife's, announcing the decease of her brother William, of, as she styles it, a frightful disorder, and praying for pecuniary relief.* 17 Aug. 12 Nov., 24 Nov: *To Miss E. Moorhouse in reply to a letter recd. from her by MW. yesterday, soliciting further supplies of pecuniary aid, with a strong picture of the distress of herself and sister, written immediately after our half-yearly remittance of £5, which we have promised to make punctually, as long as their necessities require it; so fulfilling Mrs. Backhouse's wishes to their full extent.*

1844: 7 May, 17 Sep.

1845: 3 May.

1846: 10-11 Jul., 9 Nov: *Also to Miss Moorhouse, with a remittance for £5.* 28 Dec.

1847: 7 May: *Wrote to Miss Moorhouse, forwarding a cheque on the Craven Bank for £7. in her favour; viz. £5., the half yearly aid afforded to the Misses M. by MW., with £2. extra in consideration of their plea of bad health.* 8 Nov: *Wrote to E Moorhouse, Longpreston, with a cheque on Alcock & Birkbecks, for the sum which we usually give to this fallen branch of MW's family at this season: £5. 0. 0.* 6 Dec: *Wrote to E. Moorhouse, forwarding a cheque on Messrs. Alcock and Co. for £3. to assist her in meeting the expence of the funeral of her sister Alice.* 28 Oct: *Recd. a letter from Chr. Geldard; information is required as to the date of the decease of Mrs. Moorhouse, of Newcastle, and her children, as to the payment of the legacies left in Dr. Henry Moorhouse's will, and as to the date and place of my wife's baptism: all this with reference to the sale of a portion of the Ravenflatt estate to the directors of the Railway Company.*

1848: 23 Sep.

1850: 25 Apr., 8 May: *Also to Miss E. Moorhouse to the same effect, and sent her a cheque on the Craven Bank for £5. the amount of her half yearly allowance due about this time.* 19 May: *A letter from Miss E Moorhouse, who acknowledges the receipt of my remittance, and begs for some of my poor wife's clothes, as she is too poor to replenish her wardrobe.* 21 May: *Wrote to Miss E. Moorhouse in answer to her note received on Sunday: explained that all my dear wife's wardrobe, as regarded the commoner articles of dress, had been, by her desire, appropriated to her attendant, Elizabeth Simmons.* 20 Jun: *Received a letter from Miss E Moorhouse begging for pecuniary assistance, which I must refuse to so persevering a petitioner.* 21 Jun., 10 Oct: *A letter from Miss E. Moorhouse, pleading great distress and illness of herself and brother, and begging that the allowance I make to her in November may be anticipated.—Answered her letter, and sent a cheque in her favour on Messrs. Alcock & Co., Settle, for Five Pounds.* 15 Dec: *Received a begging letter from E Moorhouse.* 16 Dec: *Wrote to Miss E Moorhouse, sending her, on account of her alleged urgent distress, a cheque on Alcocks, Birbecks & Co. for £2—but warned her that for the future, let the circumstances pleaded be ever so bad, I should strictly limit myself to the payment of £10 per ann. to which I am pledged.*

1851: 9 Apr: *A letter from Elizth. Moorhouse, pleading, as usual, great distress, and soliciting me to anticipate the payment which I should make to her in May.—Acceded to this request and wrote to her in reply, forwarding a cheque for £5. on the Craven Bank.*

1852: 4 Feb: *Recd. a letter from Miss Moorhouse, pleading sickness and distress, as usual, and soliciting aid. — I am resolved to adhere to what I have said, not to afford further assistance than the £10 a year, to which I am pledged, and not to answer the letter.* 4 May, 29-30 Oct.

1853: 22 Feb., 2 May.

1854: 27 Feb: *A letter from Elizth. Moorhouse, requesting me to forestal by a few days the customary remittance of £5 paid in May. To this I replied by forwarding a cheque for the amount.*

MOORSOM — William Scarth Moorsom[175]

William Scarth Moorsom (1804-1863), civil engineer and soldier, was born at Upper Stakesby, near Whitby, Yorkshire, the youngest of the four children of Adm. Sir Robert Moorsom (1760-1835) and Eleanor (1765-1828), daughter of Thomas Scarth of Stakesby. William entered the Royal Military College, Sandhurst, in 1819, where he distinguished himself, particularly in fortification and military surveying. After serving as an ensign in Ireland, he was transferred to Nova Scotia where he found himself in his element, surveying the province.

Moorsom met his wife, Isabella Ann Morris (d. 1860), in Nova Scotia, where her father, the judge Lewis Wilkins, was head of the supreme court. William and Isabella married and had 6 sons and 3 daughters. On their return to England Moorsom bought his release from the Army, and at the end of 1833 he was asked to survey the route for a proposed Birmingham and Gloucester Railway by Messrs Sturge, corn merchants of Gloucester and Birmingham. The railway directors were almost exclusively concerned with trade between Birmingham and Gloucester, and Moorsom was instructed to survey the most direct route. Unfortunately this route bypassed many of the main towns and included the severe Lickey incline near Bromsgrove. The directors accepted Moorsom's report, believing it was the cheapest option. In 1835–36, while the scheme was promoted, Moorsom toured railway and canal works in progress, and assisted Robert Stephenson on work associated with the London and Birmingham Railway. He surveyed the line of the Cheltenham, Oxford, and London and Birmingham Union Railway in 1835, and gave evidence against the rival Cheltenham scheme of the Great Western Railway in 1836. Work began on the Birmingham and Gloucester line in 1836 and was completed in 1841—not without overcoming severe problems brought by the steepness of the Lickey incline.

In 1840 Moorsom began work on several railway surveys in Cornwall, including the Cornwall and West Cornwall railways. In both these cases he was eventually replaced as engineer by I. K. Brunel. In the railway mania period Moorsom was engineer for a large number of schemes, often in association with Robert Stephenson or Sir John Macneill.

1837: 1 Nov: *Travelled as far as Droitwich in company with two well informed persons, one of whom proved to be Capt. Moorsom, an eminent civil engineer, who is engaged in constructing the railway from Gloucester to Birmingham, which is in progress.*

MORE — the Mores at Oxford

1806: 19 Mar: *Conversed with Sir. J. Riddell, Priest, More, Trevenen, Micklem, Jenkins.* 20 Mar: *Conversed with Stacie, the More's,•Darke, Burney, Marsh, Priest, Cabbell &c.*

MORELLI — Giovanni Morelli[176]

Giovanni Morelli (*floruit* 1787-1815) was a buffo bass singer who settled in London in 1787 and performed at the King's Theatre between 1787 and 1807. He was considered one of the best comic singers of his time, with an astonishing depth of tone and a voice of great power and quality.

1805: 18 Mar: *to the Music Room, which was well attended; joined Trevenen, James &c. the Performer, Mrs. Mountain, Morelli, Signor Lanza & Mr. Fitzsimmons: the two former great as usual, the latter moderate.* 19 Mar: *Adjourned to the Music Room, an Orchestra Song by Morelli, an Aria of Paisiella, some of Handel's Airs, & just like love by Mrs. Mountain very good.* 29 Nov: *The Concert above the mediocre, Mrs. Ashe very sweet in Se ty ti perdo & the Sweet Bird, Morelli —— & eccentric as ever.*

MORETON — Augustus Henry Moreton[177]

Augustus Henry Moreton (1804-1862), MP and landed proprietor, was a younger son of Thomas Reynolds-Moreton, 1st earl of Ducie (1776-1840), and Frances (1775-1830), daughter of Henry Herbert, 1st earl of Carnarvon. Henry Reynolds-Moreton, 2nd earl of Ducie (*below*), was his elder brother. Augustus was MP for West Gloucestershire in 1832-35 and East Gloucestershire in 1835-41. He was also a campaigner for homeopathy. In 1836 he published *Civilisation, or, a Brief Analysis of the Natural Laws that Regulate the Numbers and Condition of Mankind.* He married, 1837, Mary Jane (d. 1851), daughter of Sir Charles Macdonald-Lockhart, 2nd baronet. The couple had at least 1 son and 4 daughters:

1 Emelia (b. ±1841)
2 Mary (b. ±1842)
3 Julia (b. ±1844)
4 Jane G. (b. ±1845)
1 Augustus H. (b. ±1848)

Augustus (senior) later assumed the surname Macdonald in lieu of his patronymic Moreton. He rebuilt Largie Castle on a new site at Tayinloan.

1829: 20 Mar: *We dined at Lady Reade's at Oddington, ... The Easts were there; the Colville's; Miss Chapuset; Messrs. Barter, Hon. — Morton (a son of Lord Ducie's).*

1835: 1 Jan: *It transpired to-day that the Hon. H. Morton and his brother, the Hon. Aug. Morton, had resigned their seats in parliament for the Eastern and Western divisions of this County. This retirement of the two Whig Brothers was unexpected, and time will shew its motives and results. It is suspected that Augustus Morton will offer himself as the Whig Candidate for the Eastern division to sit as colleague of Codrington, and so to leave the field open in the Western division to the Marquis of Worcester, the Tory Candidate.* 4 Jan: *From the Gloucestershire Chronicle it appears that Saturday next is fixed for the nomination and election of the representatives for the Eastern division of the County at Gloucester. The Hon. Aug. Moreton offers himself in the place of his brother Henry, who retires. No other Candidate will present himself, and thus a contest will be avoided. The retirement of Augustus Moreton from the Western division makes room for the Marquis of Worcester as colleague of Grantley Berkeley without a contest.* 10 Jan: *Mr. Aug. Moreton was ushered in by his friends, and the Shire Hall was by degrees filled, but not crowded. It was, however, very observable that the majority present were decorated with blue favours.*

1837: 30 Jul: *The Gloucestershire Chronicle announces that at the nomination of members yesterday for the Eastern division of the County the former representatives, Codrington and Aug. Moreton were alone proposed; so that the Election took place forthwith, and all struggle of parties is obviated.*

MORETON — Francis Reynolds-Moreton [178]

Francis Reynolds-Moreton, 3rd Baron Ducie of Tortworth (1739-1808), naval officer and landed proprietor, was the son of Francis Reynolds, MP for Lancaster (1745-73), of Strangways, Manchester, and Elizabeth, sister of Matthew Ducie Moreton, 1st Baron Ducie. Reynolds-Moreton joined the Royal Navy and was a post-captain by 1762. He commanded HMS *Monarch* in Adm. Rodney's victory over the French in 1782.

Reynolds-Moreton married, first, at St George's, Hanover Square, Westminster, 10 October 1774, Mary, daughter and co-heir of Thomas Provis of Charlton, near Shepton Mallet, Somerset. She died young in 1789 in Portman Square, Marylebone. Francis and Mary had at least 1 son:

1 Thomas (1776-1840); *see below*

Reynolds-Moreton married secondly, at St George's, Hanover Square, Westminster, 18 January 1791, Sarah Child, née Jodrell, daughter of Gilbert Jodrell, of Ankerwycke, by his first wife, Mary (1741-1793), daughter of William Craddock of Hartforth, Gilling, Yorkshire. Sarah was the widow of Robert Child (1739-1782) of Osterley Park, Middlesex.

1801: 28 Dec: *Rode with my Uncle to Lord Ducie's at Tortworth; whom we did not find at home. Tortworth lies low, but agreably: In the garden is a Chestnut Tree which was famous for its size at the time of King Stephen.*

1804: 7 Jan: *Passed a dull evening crowned with a supper at Mrs. Moncasters, which would have been intolerable, had I not played speculation, making Bank with Miss Adam. Captns. Smith & Horton, Mr. Port, Harriet & Miss Leyard, Miss Duce's etc. there.*

MORETON — Henry Reynolds-Moreton [179]

Henry Reynolds-Moreton, 2nd earl of Ducie (1802-1853), MP and landed proprietor, was the first son and heir of Thomas Reynolds-Moreton, 4th Baron Ducie of Tortworth and 1st earl of Ducie, and Frances, only daughter of Henry Herbert, 1st earl of Carnarvon, and Elizabeth Alicia Maria Wyndham (1775-1830). Reynolds-Moreton was educated at Eton College and Trinity College, Cambridge, and was styled Lord Moreton from 1837 to 1850. He was MP for Gloucestershire in 1831-32 and East Gloucestershire in 1832-35. He succeeded as 5th Baron Ducie of Tortworth and 2nd earl of Ducie in 1840. He married, 1826, Elizabeth (1807-1865), eldest daughter of John Dutton, 2nd Baron Sherborne; they had 10 sons and 4 daughters:

1 Henry John (1827-1921); succeeded as 3rd earl of Ducie; *see below*
2 Herbert Augustus (1828-1863)
3 Algernon Thomas (1829-1880)
1 Georgina Mary Louisa (1830-1867)
4 Berkeley Basil Moreton (1834-1924)
5 Reynolds (1835-1919)
6 Howard (1837-1856)
7 Wyndham Percy (1839-1877)
8 Seymour (1841-1905)
2 Alice (1843-1922)
3 Eleanor (1845-1925)
9 Richard Charles (1846-1928)
10 Matthew Henry (1847-1909)
4 Evelyn (1850-1945)

1823: 17 Sep: *My colleagues will be the Hon. Mr. Moreton, eldest son of Lord Ducie.*

1824: 13 Jan., 1 Apr., 19 Oct: *Among the Magistrates present were, Lords Dynevor, Ducie, Sherborne & Apsley: the Hon. H. Morton.*

1826: 10 Jan: *The Epiphany Quarter Sessions commenced. There was a very large attendance of Magistrates: the Lord Lieutenant, Lords Sherborne & Ducie, Hon. H. Morton.* 31 Mar: *It was not long before the deliberations about the Music meeting commenced, & were protracted for nearly three hours. Of the Stewards the Hon. Mr. Moreton & Mr. Bankes were absent; the former having been detained in Leicestershire by fox-hunting had written his ideas on the subject to Mr. Dolphin... Our colleagues, at least the Lay Stewards are young and otherwise engaged: two of them are in election for matrimony, Henry Moreton, Lord Ducie's eldest Son, being engaged to Miss Dutton, Lord Sherborne's daughter, & James Dutton to his cousin, Lord Suffolk's daughter, the Lady Elizabeth Howard.* 16 Jun., 13 Sep: *I repaired to the Ordinary at the Bell Inn, which was not very numerously attended, but all the leading people were present. Mr. Dutton presided, and Mr. Moreton acted as Vice President.* 15 Sep: *From the Chapter room we adjourned to the Ordinary at the Bell, which was fully attended. Mr. Moreton presided, flanked on each side by a goodly row of grandees. The successful results of the meeting, as regarded the charity, were warmly greeted and most hearty acclammations followed on the health of the Stewards being given. Moreton returned thanks on our behalf: "the Company", he said, "were very kind in so handsomely acknowledging the endeavours of the Stewards to promote the interest, hilarity and harmony of the week; but the compliment, he added, ought not to be equally distributed; to Mr. Bankes was due all the merit of hospitality, Mr. Bowles was the Poet Laureate, and Mr. Witts deserved all the credit for the arrangements of the Music, and the details of the festival, which seemed to have given such general satisfaction.*

1828: 15 Apr.

1829: 28 Apr., 14 Jul., 22 Sep., 23 Sep: *Waller presided in a very unaffected gentlemanlike manner; but at the bottom of the table, where Moreton, Mitford, and other exuberant spirits were congregated, the noise and boisterous merriment were unrestrained.*

1831: 11 Dec.

1832: 29 Mar.

1833: 8 Apr: *Henry Moreton, Lord Ducie's eldest son, who at the preceding election had been brought in by the Reformers to the exclusion of Lord Edwd. Somerset, and whose violent principles as a politician make him a very unfit representative of a county.*

1835: 1 Jan: *It transpired to-day that the Hon. H. Morton and his brother, the Hon. Aug. Morton, had resigned their seats in parliament for the Eastern and Western divisions of this County. This retirement of the two Whig Brothers was unexpected, and time will shew its motives and results. It is suspected that Augustus Morton will offer himself as the Whig Candidate for the Eastern division to sit as colleague of Codrington, and so to leave the field open in the Western division to the Marquis of Worcester, the Tory Candidate.*

1836: 30 Aug: *A picture of Mrs. Langstone and her infant daughter by Say, in the dining room is a fine portrait. She is a daughter of Lord Ducie, and in very lingering ill health, now treated under the Homoeopathic System by Dr. Dunsford of London, where she at present is, but is expected in a day or two.*

1846: 20 Oct: *Breakfasted with Purnell. Among the leading Magistrates present were the Lord Lieutenant Lord Ducie, Sir W. C. Codrington, Sir M. H. Beech, the Hales, father and son, Archdeacon Timbrill.*

MORETON — Henry John Reynolds-Moreton [180]

Henry John Reynolds-Moreton, 3rd earl of Ducie (1827-1921), MP and landed proprietor, was the first son and heir of Henry

George Francis Reynolds-Moreton, 2nd earl of Ducie (1802-1853), and Elizabeth Dutton (1807-1865). He succeeded as 6th Baron Ducie of Tortworth and 3rd earl of Ducie in 1853. He was educated at Eton College and styled Lord Moreton from 1840 to 1853. He was MP for Stroud in 1852-53. He married, 1849, his cousin Julia Langston (1829-1895), only daughter of James Haughton Langston of Sarsden House, Oxfordshire; they had 2 sons and 1 daughter:

1 Richard Charles (1846-1928)
1 Constance Emily (1850-1929)
2 Henry Haughton (1857-1920)

1851: 23 Jan: *Lord Moreton, son of Earl Ducie, it is understood, will be brought forward on the first vacancy, on the Radical and Dissenting Interest.* 18 Mar: ... *a thin attendance of Justices: among them were the Lord Lieutenant, Lord Moreton, Sir M. C. Boevey, R B Hale MP — Hale Senr.* 31 Mar.

MORETON — Thomas Reynolds-Moreton [181]

Thomas Reynolds-Moreton, 4th Baron Ducie of Tortworth and 1st earl of Ducie (1776-1840), landed proprietor, was the eldest son and heir of Francis Reynolds-Moreton, 3rd Baron Ducie of Tortworth (1739-1808) (*above*). He was educated at Eton College and Exeter College, Oxford. He married, 5 December 1797, Frances, only daughter of Henry Herbert, 1st earl of Carnarvon, and Elizabeth Alicia Maria Wyndham (1775-1830); they had 3 sons and 4 daughters:

1 Mary Elizabeth Kitty (1798-1842); married, at Woodchester, Gloucestershire, 8 May 1822, William Basil Percy Feilding, 7th earl of Denbigh (1796-1865)
1 Henry George Francis (1802-1853); succeeded as 2nd earl of Ducie; *see above*
2 Augustus Henry MacDonald (1804-1862); married, 15 September 1837, Mary Jane MacDonald-Lockhart (1821-1851)
2 Julia Frances (b. 1805)
3 Charlotte (1806-1881); married, at Woodchester, Gloucestershire, 30 September 1834, Adm. Maurice Frederick Fitzhardinge Berkeley, 1st Baron Fitzhardinge (1788-1867)
3 Percy (1808-1886); married, at St George's, Hanover Square, Westminster, 28 April 1846, Jane Frances Price (1819-1903)
4 Emily (1810-1900); married Adm. Sir James Whitley-Deans-Dundas (1785-1862)

1824: 13 Jan., 19 Oct: *Among the Magistrates present were, Lords Dynevor, Ducie, Sherborne & Apsley: the Hon. H. Morton.*

1826: 10 Jan: *The Epiphany Quarter Sessions commenced. There was a very large attendance of Magistrates: the Lord Lieutenant, Lords Sherborne & Ducie, Hon. H. Morton.*

1826: 15 Sep., 24 Nov.

MORGAN — Arthur Charles Llewyllin Morgan [182]

Arthur Charles Llewyllin Morgan (±1814-1850), solicitor, of Icomb, near Stow-on-the-Wold, was probably a son of Morgan Walter Morgan (*below*). He was admitted as an attorney in Trinity Term, 1838. In the 1841 census he was listed as a solicitor and appears to have been unmarried. He was a clerk in the office of attorney Miles Brookes Tarn, and appears to have taken over the practice at the surprisingly young age of 25. Francis Witts referred frequently to Morgan, but with little comment; he seems to have regarded him as a perfunctory clerk, undertaking basic legal duties. In fact Arthur Morgan was a busy man of business in the locality, and was trying to build something for himself. He was involved in numerous concerns, including the Stow & Chipping Norton Agricultural Association, of which he was secretary. The diary entry for 21 August 1850 tells us a little more. He married, but had no children. He was buried at Stow-on-the-Wold on 26 August 1850.

1837: 26 Sep: *Thence to Mr. Tarn's office, where advised with A. Morgan, his clerk, the Clerk to the Commr. of Taxes, respecting the course to be pursued in respect of the Land Tax of the Rectory of Bourton on the Water.*

1838: 1 Sep: *Arthur Morgan, Mr. Tarn's Clerk, having taken the Complainant Hilling, the owner of the drill for which exemption from toll was claimed, to his principal, with a view to them proceeding to an appeal.*

1842: 20-21 Jun, 23 Jun: *Mr. Morgan appeared for the defence, and acted with good sense and right feeling in not pressing the inaccuracy of the warrant under which his Client was apprehended; forbearing to bring an action for the error.* 4 Jul: *Engaged with Mr. Morgan, Clerk to the Commrs. of Taxes for this district, at home, in considering the working of the new Property Tax Act.* 8 Jul., 15 Aug., 25 Aug., 31 Aug., 20-21 Sep., 3-4 Nov.

1843: 7-9 Jan., 12 Jan: *I sent my groom to Stow, with a note to Mr. Morgan on Property Tax business.* 15 Oct., 2 Nov., 3 Nov: *Mr. Morgan called on me with some documents found by him among Mr. Tarn's papers, referring to Forty's purchase from T. Arkell, one of which I retained, and forwarded by post to G F Newmarch with a letter on the subject.* 17 Nov: *Mr. Morgan called on Tax business.* 19-20 Nov., 29 Nov.

1844: 17 Feb., 22 Feb., 24-25 Feb: *Wrote to Mr. Morgan on the business of the proposed agricultural protection Society.* 27 Feb: *Called at Mr. Morgan's office—he was absent: looked over the communications he had received as to the Agricultural meeting, and left for him a letter of hints.* 29 Feb., 12-14 Mar., 2-3 Apr., 22 Aug., 2 Oct., 4 Oct., 22-23 Oct., 26 Dec.

1845: 9 Jan., 30 Jan: *Attended at Mr. Morgan's office with a poor man from Bourton on the Water, claiming exemption from the income tax.* 27 Feb., 27 Mar., 10 Jun., 26 Jun.,

1846: 20 Jun., 26 Aug., 19 Sep., 24 Sep., 29 Oct., 5 Nov., 12 Nov., 21 Nov., 24 Dec.

1847: 21 Jan., 4 Feb: *had an interview with Mr. Morgan on Tax matters.* 15 Apr., 21 Apr., 10 Jun., 24 Jun., 7-8 Jul., 5-6 Aug., 30 Aug., 2 Sep., 11 Sep., 8 Dec., 14 Dec.

1848: 2 Mar., 31 Aug.

1850: 27 Mar., 17-19 Jul., 26 Jul., 6 Aug., 21 Aug: *The servant brought back the intelligence of the death at midday of Mr. Morgan, the Attorney, who has been sinking for nearly a fortnight past from brain fever ending in confirmed typhus. He had been slightly injured in the head by falling from his horse, and shaken by a second fall——Of a very full habit of body, he has of late been much fatigued and excited by the canvassing for Lovegrove, the Candidate for the Coronership, and the election to that office; and the unhandsome treatment he experienced from Mr. Pruen was, probably, very trying to him. He leaves a young widow, but no child.* 29 Aug.

MORGAN — Charles Henry Morgan [183]

Charles Henry Morgan (±1782-1861), Church of England clergyman and JP, was born at Shepton Mallet, Somerset, the son of Walter Morgan. He was educated at Trinity College, Oxford (BA 1806; MA 1810), and was ordained deacon on 28 June 1807 and priest on 28 June 1809. His first clerical appointment was as stipendiary curate of Roggiet with Ifton, Monmouthshire. He was later stipendiary curate of Portskewett with St Pierre and

Sudbrooke, Monmouthshire, and from there moved a few miles east to Tidenham, Gloucestershire, where he was stipendiary curate from 1833 to 1853. He was appointed canon of Bristol in 1853, and was vicar of Abbot's Leigh from 1852 to 1861. Morgan married, first, Frances Susanna Williams (±1790-1831); they had at least 2 sons and 1 daughter, including:

1 Thomas Henry (±1818-1884)
2 Charles James (+1819-1899); educated at Lincoln College, Oxford

Morgan married secondly, 1839, Maria Christiana Brice.

1836: 12 Jul: *The Mag. who met him were Mr. Ormerod, the Historian of Cheshire, who resides near Chepstow, Mr. Morgan, the Incumbent of Tidenham.* 13 Jul: *conversed with Mrs. B. till nearly the hour for luncheon, when Charles Crawley arrived on a visit, and Bathurst made his appearance. Mr. Morgan and his daughter from Tidenham made a morning visit.*

1840: 20 Oct: *A very large attendance of Magistrates; among them, and among those with whom I was especially in intercourse, were Prothero, MP. for Halifax, Baker Senr., H. Waller, R Waller, R W Ford, Lord Ellenborough, Hale, R B Hale, MP., Archd. Timbrill, R. B. Cooper, Crawley, Capper, Sir J. Guise, Maj. Jenner, George, Straton, Newman, M Mirehouse, Fulljames, Morgan &c.*

1850: 1 Jan: *Mr. Morgan played the organ, doing all that could be accomplished by an excellent instrument, but such a noble work as the Elijah is but very inadequately rendered in the absence of a full accompaniment of wind & stringed instruments.* 8 Nov: *We repaired at mid-day to the Cathedral library, where already many Clergymen were congregated; many of my personal friends and acquaintances, such as Canons Crawley and Morgan, Messrs. Moore, Sayers, Fowell Jones, Lysons, Riddle &c.*

MORGAN — Frederick Morgan[184]

Frederick Morgan (1791-1863), Church of England clergyman, was the son of Francis Morgan (1734-1812) and Mercy Rogers (b. 1744), of Shepton Mallet, Somerset, and therefore was probably a cousin of some degree to Charles Henry Morgan (*above*). He was educated at Balliol and at Worcester College, Oxford (BCL 1817), and was appointed curate of Fairford in 1820. He married, 1820, Harriet Taylor of Frenchay, Gloucestershire. In 1851 census he was recorded as a visitor at Reeves Hotel, Weston-super-Mare, a widower and a clergyman without a cure. He died at Cheltenham in 1863. It is difficult to work out when Frederick Morgan left Fairford, but it was possibly not until 1828; the Church of England database has no record of him between his appointment as curate and Francis Rice's accession as vicar in 1828.

1823: 23 Apr: ... *first meeting of the Stow Clerical Society for this year: Mr. Morgan, curate of Fairford.*

1840: 13 Apr: *As far as Tewkesbury I had an old acquaintance by me on the coach, the Revd. Mr. Morgan, formerly curate of Fairford, a school and College friend of the J. F. Jones, now Incumbent of Saul and Moreton Valence, and for some time Curate of Broadwell and Upper Swell. Mr. Morgan, having been frequently on visits to Jones, and a member of the Stow Clerical Society, was well known to most of the Clergy in our neighbourhood. He has now neither Clerical duty, nor fixed residence.*

MORGAN — Morgan Walter Morgan[185]

Morgan Walter Morgan (b. ±1783), Church of England clergyman and chaplain at the Stow Union Workhouse, was ordained deacon on 28 June 1809. His first clerical appointment was as curate of Machen, Caerphilly, from 1809 on a sitpend of £30, and then at Icomb in 1812. He was presumably the father of Arthur Charles Llewyllin Morgan (*above*). The entries from 1826 to 1829 are presumed to relate to Morgan Walter Morgan, but they may equally relate to Frederick Morgan (*above*). At the time of the 1841 census, Morgan Walter Morgan was living at Icomb with his wife Amelia (b. ±1781). He had either moved or died by 1845 or 1846, as William Grasett Clarke (1821-1893) was the new curate of Icomb by at least August 1846.

1826: 19 Apr.

1828: 23 Apr.

1829: 12 Aug.

1838: 2 Apr: *Mr. Morgan, of Icomb, called before breakfast, to intimate to me his intention of offering himself as a candidate for the office of Chaplain to the Workhouse.* 5 Apr., 14 Apr: *Passed by the Workhouse to speak with Mr. Pearce, who shewed me a letter from the Bishop of Glouc. and Bristol, conveying his sanction to the appointment of Mr. Morgan as Chaplain of the W.H.*

1840: 25 May: *About sixteen partook of an excellent dinner at the Unicorn including the Archdeacon, and his official assessor, Mr. Burrup. Among the Clergy present on the occasion were ... Morgan.*

MORGAN-CLIFFORD — *see* Clifford

MORLAND — Benjamin Morland and the Morland family of Abingdon — *see also* Buckland *and* Pegge[186]

Benjamin Morland (1768-1833), solicitor, was a member of the West Ilsley brewing family. He became wealthy during the Napoleonic Wars and took an active interest in local politics. He was also deeply involved in the Forest of Dean coal mines and the promotion of canals. He married Harriet Baster (1777-1799); they had at least 1 daughter:

1 Mary (1797-1857), geological artist and curator; married William Buckland (1784-1856)

Mary's mother Harriet died just over a year after her birth, and it was her father who first aroused in her an interest in geology. She was educated at Southampton but developed a close relationship with the childless regius professor of anatomy at Oxford, Sir Christopher Pegge (1764/5-1822). She spent some of her childhood with him and his wife at Oxford. Pegge had been an early advocate for teaching geology at Oxford, and had given a number of private lectures on mineralogy. In his will he made a bequest to Mary Morland of 'his mineral cabinets and all the minerals and fossils contained in them at the time of my decease and all my books of natural history and comparative anatomy as a mark of my esteem and regard for her'.

Mary met William Buckland on a coach trip to Dorset on which they were both, by coincidence, reading Cuvier's latest work.

1805: 22 Mar: *Joined the Pegge & Morland Party. Walked back at ½ past 9 getting to College by 11.*

MORLEY — the Morley family at Berkeley Street, Mayfair[187]

Nothing has been discovered in relation to the Morley family, but they were clearly part of the Mayfair set. They were acquaintances of Lady Lyttelton and the Snows. There is a possibility that they might have been related to James Morley (1742-1798), senior Bombay merchant of the HEIC.

1801: 10 Jun: *Lady Lytteltons, accidental Music began, Miss Halifaxes sung, & Miss Morley; it was quite a squeeze: a Mr. Wood a nephew of Mr. Sheridan also sung in a very singular style. We met there the Hanbury's, Guydickens, Mrs. Scott & Miss Morley, Sir N. Dukinfield, Sir H. & Major Vavasour, Mr. Doig, Mr. Edwin Stanhope, Comte de Bruges, Miss Nevilles, Mr. & Mrs. Chambers, Miss Hungerford, &c.* 15 Sep: *Drank Tea & spent the evening in Berkely Street, meeting Mrs. Doig, & Miss Morley.* 18 Sep: *Called at Mrs. Morley's, whom I saw, as also Miss Morley & Miss Ann. Very bad accounts of Tom Snow.* 9 Oct: *Evening at Mrs. Doig's where met Lady Lytt, Mr. and Miss Morley, Mrs. Campbell, Mr. & Miss Wilkins.* 23 Oct: *to a very pleasant Musical party at Lady Lyttelton's, where were the Pattons, Mrs. Davies. the Morley's, Mrs. Lowe, the Guydickens's, Vicomte De Bruges & Comte de Gourmand, Mr. Wood & the like.* 25 Oct: *Called with my Mother upon the Guydickens, Lady Lyttleton, the Pattons, & the Morleys.*

MORRIS — Charles Morris [188]

Charles Morris (1768-1844), businessman and philanthropist, was the son of James Morris, high sheriff (1764) and DL for Surrey, and Mary Magdalene Mathew. He was married to Sarah Haldimand (1772-1841), daughter of Anthony Francis Haldimand, merchant, and sister of Gen. Sir Frederick Haldimand, governor of Quebec. William Haldimand, a director of the Bank of England, was her nephew. Charles and Sarah had 4 sons and 2 daughters:

1 James (1795-1882)
1 Jane (1796-1869); died unmarried
2 Charles (1799-1856); died unmarried
2 Emma (d. 1832)
3 Francis Anthony (d. 1842)
4 Frederick (d. 1821)

The son and daughter mentioned by Francis Witts were the eldest children, Jane and Charles. From the 1830s the family spent the summer months in Malvern, where Charles Morris (senior) was a considerable benefactor; he paid, for example, for the building and running of the National School. Francis Witts clearly disliked him. Charles (junior) and Jane contributed greatly to the building of Holy Trinity church at North Hill, Link Top, Malvern, in 1851.

1834: 10 Sep: *Again a large dinner party: 17 sat down to table. Besides the inmates of Peach Field Lodge, and my cousin John, there were Mr. Turbervile, Rector of Hanley, Dr. Card and Mr. Thrupp, two Miss Lechmere's, the daughters of Sir Anthony L., with their brother, Mr. Berwick Lechmere, a beneficed Clergyman in this neighbourhood, and a family of Morris's now visiting Malvern, persons of opulence, consisting of a Father and Mother with a Son and daughter, the latter being a cheerful, agreeable person. In the evening several more visitors, gentlemen and ladies from Malvern.*

1836: 21 Jul: *Then the family of Morris: father, mother, son and daughter: nouveaux riches, and frequent resorters to Malvern, very liberal in their charities, and, as such, great favourites with Lady L. but I should say shallow, purse-proud & presuming: the daughter more pleasing than the rest of her family.*

1838: 18 Jul: *Drove with Capt. Witts to Malvern, to the North Hill, where I inspected a well constructed tank built at the expence of a wealthy visitor from Town, Mr. C. Morris, whom with others of his family I have met at my Aunt's, to detain and distribute a fine spring of water, for the convenience of the population at this end of the parish, where not an inconsiderable hamlet has sprung up.*

MORRIS — William Morris — *see also* Lawrence *and* Turner [189]

William Morris (1767-1834), banker, was the younger son of John Morris, of Barnwood, Gloucester, and brother of Robert Morris (d. 1816), MP for Gloucester (1805-16). He married, at Cheltenham, 6 December 1796, Mary (1768-1839), daughter of Walter Lawrence (1729-1810) and Mary Hayward (1732-1804); they had 1 son:

1 Walter Lawrence (1800-1877); married, 24 July 1824, Mary Spildt (1806-1889); at least 3 sons and 3 daughters

The Morris family owned 720 acres in Barnwood which fell to the lot of Robert Morris, William's brother. William inherited 64 acres at Wotton, a suburb of Gloucester and valuable land for building. He was high sheriff for Gloucestershire in 1816 and a partner in a Gloucester bank with Thomas Turner, John Turner, and his nephew Robert Morris. The bank failed in 1825 and William Morris was declared bankrupt in 1829.

William and Mary's son Walter was born Walter Lawrence Morris, but assumed the patronymic Lawrence in accordance to the wishes of his maternal grandfather Walter Lawrence (1729-1810) of Sevenhampton, Gloucestershire. He inherited a substantial estate which was once coveted by Francis Witts.

1823: 24 Dec: *It had been for some time pretty well known, that the bulk of the fortune would centre in the family of Mr. W. Morris, brother of the late banker at & member for Gloucester, who by his marriage with the heiress of the Lawrence's, a yeoman's family at Sevenhampton, possessed a good estate in that parish, and whose son has assumed the name of Lawrence, with the immediate enjoyment of some of his grandfather's property, since coming of age. The young man has been well educated, & was gentleman-commoner of Magdalen Coll. Oxford, but is said to be of expensive habits... In an adjoining room were the chief mourners and their friends: Mr. W. Morris, Mr. R. Morris of the Gloucester bank now resident at Cheltenham to superintend the branch of the branch of the establishment there.*

1826: 17 Jan: *The Messrs. Turner are about to embark in a new concern at Gloucester; they have entirely separated themselves from their partner Mr. Morris, whose indiscretions, it is alledged, have principally contributed to the suspension of their payments.* 7 Aug: *when Mrs. Lightbourne died in the close of 1823, mentioned the disposition, which she made of her property in favour of Mr. Walter Lawrence, superseding a former will made in favour of her former legal adviser ... her strange habits, her proneness to indulge in spirituous liquors, her falling into the hands of Mr. W. Morris, his manoeuvres to get himself or his son made her heir.*

1829: 1 May: *drank tea with our friends, the Davies's, in Wellington Parade, meeting Mrs. Wood (Mrs. Davies's married daughter from Tetbury), Miss F. Hunt, Mr. Morris & Miss S. Pearce.*

1842: 25 Nov.

MORRISON — Archibald Charles Henry Morrison — *see also* Scott [190]

Archibald Charles Henry Morrison (±1794-1866), Church of England clergyman, was born at Marylebone, Middlesex, son of Archibald and Mary Louisa Morrison. He was educated at Wadham College, Oxford (BA 1815; MA 1820), and was ordained deacon on 5 January 1817. His first clerical appointment was as curate of St Mary's, Warwick, from 25 July 1818. He was then appointed stipendiary curate of Stoneleigh, Warwickshire, on 10 October 1820, and later rector of Sezincote and vicar of Longborough. He married, at St Nicholas's, Warwick, 13 July 1820, Frances Mary (1799-1879), born at Upper Swell, the daughter of William Wilton. Archibald and Frances had 4 sons and 5 daughters:

1 Caroline Frances (1822-1909); married, 18 August 1847, Richard Ashley Scott (±1796-1860)
1 Archibald (1823-1823)

2 Mary (1824-1914)
2 Henry (1826-1826)
3 Archibald Frederick (b. & d. 1827)
3 Frances (1830-1849)
4 William (1832-1895); educated at Christ Church, Oxford (BA 1856; MA 1858); served as chaplain of the college, 1856-68; curate of South Hincksey and Woolton, Berkshire, for seven years; vicar of Midsomer Norton, Somerset, appointed 1867
4 Emily Charlotte (1834-1860); married Thomas Commeline (1821-1890)
5 Julia Judith Anne (1839-1922)

1824: 3 Aug: *We dined at Mrs. Rice's, Bourton on the Water, who spends some summer months at her house there every year; at other times she resides with her protegé Mr. Morrison and his wife, also a former protegée, at Stoneleigh, in Warwickshire, where he is Curate, & takes pupils.*

1825: 9 Aug: *Croome party: Mrs. Rice. brought a large party to Mr. Croome's table: among them were the Revd Mr. Wilton and his wife; he is Curate of Blakeney and Awre, and son of a former Incumbent of Upper Swell, who died in 1804, leaving a large and distressed family, for whom bountiful subscriptions were raised. A sister of his, Now Mrs. Morrison, was a protegée of Mrs. Rice, and with her husband, who also owes his education to the same benevolent lady, was a guest at Mr. Croome's feast. Mr. Morrison is of Wadham College, and Curate of Stoneleigh in Warwickshire; he takes pupils; two of these are with him now; inmates of Mrs. Rice's roomy mansion.* 17 Aug: *dined at Mrs. Rice's at Bourton on the water. There was a large party. Mr. & Mrs. Morrison; Mr. Torrens, & Mr. Wilson, Mr. Morrison's pupils.* 26 Aug.

1827: 29 Aug: *Mr. & Mrs. Morrison & Mrs. Rice, & Mrs. Waller & Miss Rollinson were also our visitors at different hours this morning.*

1828: 14 Aug: *to dine with Mrs. Rice, we met rather a motley party: Mr. & Mrs. Morrison, from Stoneleigh,. Morrison's pretty children & Major Mercer's strange boy completed the circle. The Morrisons & Miss Boys gave us some middling music.* 27 Aug.

1829: 26 Feb: *and after being tightly wedged in with Mr. Morrison, the Curate of Stoneleigh, an old acquaintance, by me, to beguile by conversation the tediousness of the operation, I was admitted within the barrier to give my vote.*

1834: 10 Mar: *On my return to our lodgings we had a visit from Mr. & Mrs. Morrison.* 13 Mar: *The parish is extensive, and the population amounts to 1200 souls. We were soon arrived at the Parsonage House, a small, and not very comfortable house, adjoining the Church, where the worthy Curate, Morrison, and his pleasing wife, received us hospitably, with whom we passed a pleasant hour.* 17 Jul: *Wrote to Morrison, now staying at Mrs. Rice's at Bourton to request him to bury a corpse for me to-morrow. Received his answer in the affirmative.* 18 Jul., 29 Jul., 1 Aug., 19 Dec: *Drove Mrs. Witts to Bourton on the Water to call on Mr. & Mrs. Morrison, who leave that place to-morrow; Mr. M. & his wife having been there since a day or two before the decease of Mrs. Rice, by whom they had been both educated, and who regarded them as her adopted children.*

1838: 16 Feb: *Recd. a letter from Morrison, the Curate of Stoneleigh, soliciting me to recommend pupils to be placed under his charge.* 17 Feb: *Wrote to Mr. Morrison in reply to his letter recd. yesterday, promising to embrace any opportunity to recommend pupils to be placed with him.* 8 Aug: *Mr. & Mrs. Morrison, of Stoneleigh, who are on a visit to the Misses Hall, at Bourton, with one of those ladies, called in the course of the day.*

1845: 20 Mar: *There had been much hesitation as to the place of sepulcture: Cheltenham was repugnant to the deceased: Whitnash was distant, and, besides, there is a probability that, on the decease of Mr. Jeaffreson, an arrangement may be made by the concurrence of Lord Leigh, between Mr. Dryden, and Mr. Morrison, to whom it is arranged that Longborough shall be presented when it becomes vacant.*

1846: 20 Jun: *from Mr. Morgan, Stow, on the part of Harding, the Butcher, a request that I would recommend the latter to Mr. Morrison, to be employed by him, when he comes to reside on his Vicarage of Longborough.* 21 Jun., 15 Aug: *At Longborough called at the Vicarage to pay our respects to our old acquaintances, Mr. and Mrs. Morrison, now lately fixed there, on his preferment to the Vicarage by the favour of Lord Leigh.* 18 Aug., 21 Aug., 26 Aug., 18 Sep: *We dined at the Fords, We met also, Mr. and Mrs. Morrison, and their eldest daughter.* 28 Sep: *Mr. Morrison walked over from Longborough, accompanied by his son, a fine lad of fourteen, and a pupil of the same age.* 29 Sep., 7 Oct: *MW. did not feel sufficiently well to accompany me to dine at Longborough with Mr. and Mrs. Morrison: I had a very stormy drive thither and back: they had been disappointed of some expected guests: those who came, besides myself were Mr. Ford, Henry and Dulcy F. and Mr. Clarke. The Misses Morrison are very pleasing girls, and musical.* 18 Oct., 9-10 Dec., 18 Dec., 29 Dec: *Recd. letters from Morrison ... announces the engagement and approaching marriage of his eldest daughter to Mr. Scott, of Banksfee, with which he and Mrs. M. are greatly pleased: she is a fine, well looking, well educated young woman; her intended must be a good deal her Senior, and is a strange looking, unprepossessing man, almost unknown in the neighbourhood, but, I daresay, sensible, and well informed, hitherto chiefly residing in town: M. speaks very favourably of him from personal observation, and the report of others: at all events, it will be what is called a good match, the Lady's fortune being I suppose, nil, and the Gentleman son & heir of an old lady of good property and Estate.* 30 Dec.

1847: 28 Jan., 4 Feb., 5 Mar: *Mr. Morrison paid us a morning visit.* 18 Mar., 25 Mar., 1 Apr., 7 Apr., 15 Apr., 17 Apr., 29-30 Apr., 13 May, 27 May, 7 Jun., 10 Jun., 24 Jun., 6-8 Jul., 15 Jul., 22 Jul., 29 Jul., 5 Aug., 19 Aug: *Informed of the marriage of Mr. Scott of Banksfee to Miss Morrison, eldest daughter of the Vicar of Longborough.* 8 Sep., 14 Sep., 16 Sep., 21 Sep., 23 Sep., 28 Sep., 14 Oct., 11 Nov., 27 Nov: *Mr. Morrison and his son called on us. They walked from Longborough.* 8-9 Dec.

1848: 20 Jan., 3 Feb., 10 Feb., 2 Mar., 9 Mar., 16 Mar., 6 Apr., 13 Apr., 26 Apr., 16 May: *Met and conversed with Mr. and Mrs. W B Pole, Mr. and Mrs. and Miss Morrison, and Mrs. R A Scott.* 18 May, 1 Jun., 7 Jun., 20 Jun: *Mr. and Mrs. J Scott and Mrs. Morrison called when we were absent from home.* 23 Aug., 11 Sep., 14 Sep., 26 Sep., 12 Oct., 8-9 Nov.

1849: 12 Dec., 27 Dec.

1850: 31 Jan., 7 Feb., 14 Feb., 21 Feb., 25 Feb: *Mrs. R. W. Scott and Miss Morrison very kindly drove from Longborough to make enquiries after my wife.* 7 Mar., 9 Mar., 14 Mar., 21 Mar., 28 Mar., 11 Apr., 20 Apr: *A kind letter of condolence from Capt. Witts. — A friendly note to the same effect from Mr. Morrison.* 29 Apr., 30 May, 4 Jun., 12 Jun., 20 Jun., 11 Jul., 18 Jul., 20 Jul., 1 Aug., 18 Sep: *Confirmation L Ris. Mr. F. Niblett, Architect, by whom the plan for enlargement of the Church at Little Risington was furnished:—the Misses Hall;—Revd. A. C. H. Morrison & Mrs. M.* 18 Sep., 24 Sep., 1 Oct., 24 Oct., 14 Nov., 19 Nov: *Also invitations to Mr. and Mrs. Scott, and Mr. Mrs. and the Misses Morrison.* 21 Nov., 27 Nov: *A dinner party. Mr. & Mrs. J. T. Rice, Mr. Wiggin, Mr. & Mrs. and Miss Morrison, Mrs. R. A. Scott, and*

Mr. Ogle were our guests, added to our home party. 6 Dec: *Mrs. R. Scott, and her sister, Miss Morrison, kindly called upon me, but near the village the pretty poney drawing their little carriage strained some joint, and suddenly became dead lame; so that they were obliged to leave both carriage & poney, and returned home in my carriage.* 11 Dec., 26 Dec.

1851: 16 Jan., 6 Feb., 13 Feb., 20 Feb., 27 Feb., 13 Mar., 10 Apr., 23 Apr., 1 May, 8 May.

1852: 22 Jan., 29 Jan., 12 Feb., 4 Mar., 25 Mar., 8 Apr., 14 Apr., 22 Apr., 29 Apr., 6 May, 12 May, 17 May, 20 May, 29 May: *Recd. a note from Mr. Morrison requesting me to sign a testimonial to enable his son William to obtain an exhibition from the Mercer's Company, London, to assist in the expence of maintaining him at College, he being a Bible Clerk of Christ Church: the value is £20 per ann: the allegation made is that such are the circumstances of the family that such aid is much required for his support at the University.* 28 Oct., 4 Nov., 9 Nov: *Mrs. R. A. Scott & Miss Morrison were guests, passing the morning with Mrs. W. Vavasour and her sister. Mrs. W. Dod appeared in high spirits as a bride, and looked well.* 18 Nov., 2 Dec., 16 Dec., 22 Dec., 30 Dec.

1853: 20 Jan., 3 Feb., 17 Feb., 4 Mar: *I replied to a note I Recd. in the evening from Morrison, who begged my signature to a certificate to forward an appeal he is now preferring to the Trustees of the Cholmondeley Charity to poor Clergymen; he solicits an exhibition of £40 per ann. — for his son William, now a Servitor of Christ Church. I hope he may succeed: he is a worthy man, deserving a better position as to this world's goods than he enjoys.* 10 Mar., 30 Mar., 7 Apr., 14 Apr., 28 Apr., 19 May, 24 May, 26 May, 2 Jun., 22 Jun., 8 Dec., 15 Dec., 22 Dec., 29 Dec.

1854: 2 Feb., 16 Feb., 23 Feb., 2 Mar., 9 Mar., 11 Mar., 15-16 Mar., 23 Mar., 25 Mar: *M. has kindly written to a friend in Warwickshire to enquire whether he knows of any person in orders, or of an age to take orders, who might be recommended for my assistant curate.* 27 Mar., 30 Mar., 6 Apr., 8 Apr., 13 Apr., 20 Apr., 25 Apr: *To Morrison a note of condolence on the death of the aged Mrs. Scott, of Banksfee, who departed this life suddenly two or three days ago. Mr. and Mrs. R. Scott (nee Morrison) will now become possessed of the Bankfee property and Mansion.*28 Apr., 3 May, 11 May, 18 May, 24-25 May, 10 Jun: *Drove with E. Clifford to call at Banksfee on Mr. and Mrs. Scott, now possessed of that residence and property by the recent decease of Mr. S's mother. Found them at home, with a large family party of Morrisons collected in the grounds at Banksfee to welcome W. Morrison, who had availed himself of the facility afforded by the Railway to come from Oxford for the day to see his friends.* 15 Jun., 20 Jun: *On my return received a visit from Mr. and Mrs. Scott, Miss Morrison, and a lady, a friend of theirs.* 22 Jun., 29 Jun., 19-20 Jul., 27 Jul., 3 Aug., 17 Aug.

MORSE — Miss M. Morse at Clifton

1806: 27 Jan: *to a Rout & dance given by Mrs. M. Causland, which would have been more pleasant, if I had known more of her guests & there had been fewer children. We were accompanied by Mrs. C. Roberts. I danced with Miss M. Morse, Mrs. J. Auriol, Mrs. Parris & Miss Binden.*

MOSLEY — Mr Mosley at Mayfair

1801: 6 Jun: *to Mrs. Doig's, where we found neither a very numerous, nor a very pleasant party. Mr. Mosley &c. Sir D. Carnegie, Mrs. Scott, Major Vavasour &c.*

MOSS — the Miss Mosses at Clifton

1804: 25 Sep: *Afterwards to a large party at Mrs. McMahon's where the Lady of the mansion & two Miss Mosses sung tolerably.*

MOSSON — Joseph Mosson

1835: 28 Jan: *Walked with my son to Wick Risington to visit old Joseph Mosson, who for many years was employed by me as a mason; his son now works for me.*

MOTHERWOOD — Mrs Motherwood of Fernihough, Staffordshire

1802: 9 Oct: *Walked under Norbury Bank, & to Fernihough with the party. Mrs. Motherwood her Son an artist musical.*

MOULD & GORE — solicitors of Melksham

1853: 23 Feb: *it seems that her sister, not being able to bring Mrs. Dolphin to a settlement of the affair, and to surrender to her as Administratrix the money & clothes &c., has placed the matter in the hands of Messrs. Mould and Gore, Soltr. at Melksham, who, having in vain urged Mrs. D. and her agent, Paxton, to an arrangement, are prepared to bring the affair before the County Court at Stow.*

MOULD — *see* Royce

MOUNIER — Jean Joseph Mounier [191]

Jean Joseph Mounier (1758-1806), politician, judge, and college master, was born at Grenoble. He studied law, and in 1783 obtained a judgeship at Grenoble. He took part in the struggle between the parlements and the court in 1788, and promoted the meeting of the estates of Dauphiné at Vizille on the eve of the French Revolution. He was secretary of the Assembly, and drafted its notebooks of grievances and remonstrances that were presented to King Louis XVI. Thus brought into prominence, Mounier was unanimously elected deputy of the Third Estate to the Estates General of 1789; he also founded the Monarchiens party in August 1789. Mounier was an active participant in the French Revolution; he proposed the Tennis Court Oath and helped frame the Declaration of the Rights of Man. On 28 September 1789 he was elected president of the Constituent Assembly. Being unable, however, to approve the proceedings that followed, Mounier withdrew to Dauphiné and resigned as deputy. He then took refuge in Switzerland in 1790.

By the late 1790s Mounier surfaced at Weimar. At Duke Carl Friedrich's behest he maintained an academy at the Baroque Schloss Belvedere, designed primarily for the education of young Englishmen of good family. Among the tutors were Böttiger, Melos, and Eckermann, and the duke's own son received some of his education there. The academy closed in 1801, and Mounier returned to France. He was named by Napoleon Bonaparte prefect of the department of Ille-et-Vilaine. He reorganised the department, and in 1805 was appointed councillor of state. He died in Paris.

Mounier married Marie-Philippine Borel (1762-1795); they had at least 1 son:

1 Claude-Philibert-Édouard (1784-1843); born at Grenoble; married, 11 May 1810, Wilhelmine Lightone; 2 sons and 1 daughter:
   1 Philippine (1811-1891)
   1 Victorine Louise Albertine (1814-1860)
   2 Edouard (1820-1895)

Claude-Philibert-Édouard followed his father into exile at Weimar, where he was employed in a government post in 1808. In 1809 he was appointed secretary of cabinet of the Emperor Napoleon and remained in that post until Napoleon's abdication.

1798: 2 Sep: *It was built for a Summer Residence of the Dukel Family, tho' now appropriated by the Dukes Beneficence, to an Academy kept by Mr. Mounier, a Frenchman of the highest & worthiest Character, a Protestant, a liberal & well informed man, bold & steady in his Conduct, & beloved by all the worthy who know him intimately of every age. No man was ever better adapted to be the Head of an Institute, than Mr. Mounier, & there are few places on the Continent, where young Persons could be placed with more safety: for in Weimar you can enjoy the Privileges, Politeness, & Good manners without the vices, attending Society, in a great Town.*

1799: 6 Nov: *to Mr. Gore's where met Messrs. Foster, Mounier, Schöndorf, de Manion, de Vaux &c.*

1828: 28 Jun: *one of the Country Seats within two miles of Weimar was appropriated by him, as an institution for the Education of young men of the higher ranks under the superintendance of M. Mounier, a celebrated French man, who played a prominent character on the political stage in the early part of the French revolution; he was assisted by able Tutors; & many English were under his care, having constant opportunities of mingling in the Court circles; some of these youths, my contemporaries & acquaintance, have moved since in important stations, among them Lord Heytesbury, better known as yet by his former title of Sir. W. A'Court.*

MOUNTAIN — Mrs Mountain, of Cirencester, candidate for housekeeper at the infirmary

1847: 14 Feb: *A letter from Mrs. Mountain, a candidate for the vacant situation of Housekeeper to the Gloucester Infirmary.* 20 Jan., 10 Mar: *Received a letter from Mrs. Mountain, Cirencester, one of the Candidates for the office of Matron at the Gloucester Infirmary: she requests again my support, and that I would allow the Misses Hall of Bourton, who had given me their proxies to vote for whomsoever I should consider the most competent person, to vote for her. Wrote in answer that I should beg those ladies to vote as seemed them best: but that I should not vote for her, as her age, 54, as compared with that of two other candidates with equally good testimonials, was against her.*

MOUNTAIN — Rosemund Mountain [192]

Rosemund Mountain, née Wilkinson (±1768-1841), singer and actress, was born in London. Her father, whose name was Wilkinson, was a tightrope walker and maker of theatrical wigs; her mother was a minor actress and theatrical dresser. Charles Dibdin taught Rosemund to sing, and she first appeared at the Haymarket Theatre in 1782. After accompanying her parents to the north of England, she was offered a two-year contract by Thomas Harris of Covent Garden. She made her Covent Garden début as Fidelia in *The Foundling* on 4 October 1786, and was to remain mainly at Covent Garden until 1798.

In Liverpool Rosemund met an Irish violinist, John Mountain; they married in 1787 and had one son. John Mountain led the orchestra at Vauxhall Gardens from about 1792, and was leader of the band at Covent Garden from about 1794. After a quarrel with Harris in 1798, Rosemund left Covent Garden and toured the provinces and Ireland for two years. While performing at Bristol she studied with Venanzio Rauzzini at Bath.

In 1800 Rosemund returned to the London stage, initially at the Haymarket, but thereafter at Drury Lane. In addition to her work in the theatre, she sang in oratorios and at Vauxhall Gardens; during the summer seasons she performed in Edinburgh, Dublin, and the provinces. Her farewell performance was at the King's Theatre on 4 May 1815.

1802: 17 May: *To the Music Room with all but Edgell, being Choral night, when Mrs. Mountain & Denman sung, Mountain on the Violin & Wipperton the Harp, Mrs. Mountain lovely in "Pity kind Gentlemen "Ye Gloomy thoughts "Nel bel volto "Not mine the Narrow Soul.* 18 May: *Went to the Music Room. Same Performers. Mrs. Mountain lovely, next best to Billington, & like her in stile. Charming in "Again my absent love to meet", in "O Lovely Peace" with Denman; & in "What tho' fate".*

1805: 18 Mar: *To the Music Room, which was well attended; joined Trevenen, James &c. the Performer, Mrs. Mountain, Morelli, Signor Lanza & Mr. Fitzsimmons: the two former great as usual, the latter moderate.* 19 Mar: *Adjourned to the Music Room, an Orchestra Song by Morelli, an Aria of Paisiella, some of Handel's Airs, & just like love by Mrs. Mountain very good.*

1808: 22 Feb: *The other best performers were my friend Storau, Mrs. Mountain, Bannister &c.*

MOUNTAIN — Joseph Mountain [193]

Joseph Mountain (±1774-1839), attorney and coroner, lived at Cecily Hill, Cirencester. He was married to Susanna [Cosburn/Cosbourne?], and had seven children, of whom 3 sons and 2 daughters are known:

1 Rosana [Roseanna?] Cosbourne (b. 1815)
2 Susanna (b. 1816)
1 John Cosburn (b. 1818)
2 John (b. 1821)
3 Alfred (b. 1830)

According to *The Gentleman's Magazine*, he left his wife and children 'almost in a state of destitution'.

1835: 16 Jan: *Wrote to Mr. F. Herbert, Attorney at Northleach, inclosing to him a copy of the depositions taken at the Coroner's inquest held at Northleach on the body of the infant child of Eliz. Day (Dec 1. 1834) which had been forwarded to me yesterday by Mr. Mountain.*

1837: 17 Jun: *Held a conference with Mountain, the Coroner, who had just concluded holding his inquest on the body of the prisoner, who strangled himself in the lock-up-house on Thursday: a verdict of Felo de se was returned.*

1838: 5 Feb.

MOUNTSTEPHEN — Miss Mountstephen, a dinner guest of the Howells

1853: 6 Jun: *... with Constance Howell, and a Miss Mount Stephen, who dined with us, went to the Opera.*

MOURHEAD — Captain Mourhead of the South Devon Militia

1804: 3 Sep: *Military Funeral Procession of the late Capt. Mourhead of the S. Devon Militia.*

MUDGE — William Mudge [194]

William Mudge (1762-1820), surveyor, was born at Plymouth, the ninth of twenty children born to Dr John Mudge (±1721-1793) and his second wife. His grandfather was the Revd Zachariah Mudge, and he was half-brother to another Zachary Mudge, the naval officer. The Mudges were a notable scientific family; William's father was a physician and his uncle Thomas Mudge (1715/16-1794) was a horologist. William's godfather was Dr Johnson. The family also had important artistic connections, most notably with Sir Joshua Reynolds. William's upbringing led him to appreciate both the scientific and the artistic aspects of map making.

William Mudge entered the Royal Military Academy at Woolwich in 1777. In 1779 he was commissioned second lieutenant in the Royal Artillery, and was sent to South Carolina to fight in the American Revolutionary War. On his return home he was stationed at the Tower of London. He became an excellent mathematician and, on Hutton's recommendation, he was appointed in 1791 to the Ordnance Trigonometrical Survey.

Mudge took a great interest in scientific work and greatly advanced surveying techniques. As well as developing the Ordnance Board's trigonometric survey, Mudge was responsible for the interior or topographic survey, which resulted in the publication of topographical maps at a scale of one inch to a mile. The first was of Kent, published by William Faden in 1801. Finding that such maps were costly to produce, Mudge carried through changes in the organisation of the Survey, showing a good grasp of management and budgeting. He recruited engravers to the drawing office, and helped establish the Ordnance Survey as a map publisher and eventually a map seller. While head of the Survey he lived first at the Tower of London and then, from his marriage in 1808 to his death in 1820, at 4 Holles Street, London.

Mudge was one of the most important men in the history of the Ordnance Survey; he laid its scientific and structural foundations, and by promoting Thomas Colby to succeed him, helped shape its later development.

1817: 1 Sep: *Carrying the Eye to the West, a line of mountains connect the Fells above named with Black Comb, an enormous round hill in the County of Cumberland, and in the direction of Ravenglass, between the estuary called the Duddon sands, & the Irish sea: the height of Black Comb is estimated in the Trigonometrical survey of Col. Mudge at 1919 feet.* 8 Sep.

MULGRAVE — *see* Phipps

MULLINGS — Joseph Randolph Mullings [195]

Joseph Randolph Mullings (1792-1859), solicitor, JP, and MP, was born at Devizes, the son of Richard Mullings of Estcourt House, Malmesbury, Wiltshire. He was admitted an attorney-at-law in 1820 and practised at Cirencester. After retiring from the law he entered parliament and was MP for Cirencester in 1848-59. He was also JP for Gloucestershire and Wiltshire and DL for Gloucestershire in 1852. He married, 1823, Margaret Anne (1797-1878), only daughter of Richard Gregory of Cirencester; they had at least 2 sons and 5 daughters:

1 Margrette Anne (1826-1850)
2 Caroline (1828-1895)
3 Agnes (1829-1911)
4 Jane (1830-1920)
5 Emily Mary (b. 1833)
1 Joseph (b. 1837)
2 Arthur Randolph (1839-1885); died at Queens County, New York

Joseph Mullings died suddenly at Montpellier, France, on 18 October 1859.

1850: 15 Jan: *Received a letter from Mr. Mullings, informing me that the 31st. Inst. will suit him and Mr. Winterbotham for a meeting of the Committee of accounts.* 28 Jan., 14 Feb: *Mr. Mullings has sent me a copy of the Bill brought into the House of Commons for the appointment of County Financial Boards, to consist of Magistrates, one for each Union elected by the Ex officio Guardians of that Union, and elected Guardians, one from each Union to be chosen by the elected members.* 16 Feb., 21 Feb., 7 Jun: *Wrote to Mr. Mullings, requesting him to send me a copy of the bill for newly adjusting the law as to Savings Banks.* 11 Jun., 14 Jun., 19 Jun., 2 Jul., 4 Jul., 8 Dec., 10 Dec., 14 Dec., 18 Dec., 28 Dec., 30-31 Dec.

1851: 9 Feb: *Recd. from Mr. Mullings, MP. a printed copy of notice of forthcoming motions and orders in the House of Commons, shewing that he is about to move for returns as to Salaries and emoluments of Clerks of the Peace.* 11 Feb., 31 Mar., 1 Apr., 10-11 Apr., 30 Apr.

1852: 9 Mar., 12 Mar., 15-16 Mar., 17 Mar: *Mullings has been solicited to take office under Lord Derby, and to fill the important post of Chief Secretary to the Poor Law Commission, but peremptorily declined on various grounds —— a wish to appear and to be strictly independent — an apprehension that his health might suffer from the labours of a heavy working place —— a strong feeling on the Protection of agricultural produce, and on the refusal of the Maynooth grant, in which he might probably come to a different judgment from the premier —— and a disinclination to be wholly withdrawn from the habits of domestic life, appear to have operated with him in determining not to accept a post in which he might have done eminent service.* 18 Mar.

1853: 4 Jan.

MUNDEN — Joseph Shepherd Munden [196]

Joseph Shepherd Munden (1758-1832), actor, was born in the parish of St Andrew's, Holborn, London, the son of Joseph Munden, a poulterer of Brook's Market, Leather Lane, Holborn, and his wife, Alice. At the age of 12, Joseph (junior) was apprenticed to an apothecary, but his fine handwriting obtained him a situation with a law stationer in Chancery Lane. He took an interest in the theatre and appeared from 1779 to 1780 in private performances at the Haymarket Theatre. When the low comedian in Austin and Whitlock's circuit died, Munden successfully applied to replace him. He appeared thereafter at Chester, Whitehaven, Newcastle-upon-Tyne, Manchester, Preston, and Liverpool. He eventually became a shareholder in the circuit of theatres that included both Newcastle and Chester, but sold his shares in 1790 when he was invited to Covent Garden to replace the recently deceased comedian John Edwin.

Joseph Munden had a long and successful career on the stage. His range was limited, but he was versatile; if he played three drunken parts on the same night he would be fresh in each. He was able to portray serious old men, such as Old Dornton, and comic ones like Sir Francis Gripe. Moreover, he could appear kind-hearted or testy; not surprisingly, Sir Anthony Absolute was a character he frequently played. Thomas Gilliland praised his portrayals of sailors and cunning rustics, and his Shakespearian roles included Launce, Autolycus, Menenius, Dogberry, and Polonius (to the Hamlets of both John Philip Kemble and Kean).

Munden married, 1789, Frances Butler (d. 1837), a young actress. They had two sons, one of whom died in infancy.

1801: 13 Oct: *Incledon, whose voice is vastly fine, is, at the same time, so vulgar, as to be much inferior, I think, even to Townshend. The farce was the Irishman in London; replete with farcical humour: Munden & Fawcett, are inimitable.*

1808: 25 Feb: *In the Evening to Covent Garden Theatre, where I was much amused by a very interesting Drama a Swedish Fable, entitled the Wanderer, or the Rights of Hospitality. Miss Smith very great, Charles Kemble excellent as the Hero. This was followed by a capital new Farce the Widow's Choice by Allingham, very humorous, much applauded, musical: Miss Decamp, Fawcett, Munden, excellent.*

MUNDY — Thomas Mundy[197]

Thomas Mundy (b. ±1803), baker, lived and worked at 13 Green Street, Bath. He employed seven men and was married to Ann (b. ±1804). They had at least 2 sons:

1 Edward (b. ±1837)
2 Frederick (b. ±1839)

1844: 26 Jan: *Wrote to the Dean of Gloucester with the address of a biscuit baker at Bath—by whom we are supplied with that article.*

1850; 18 Aug: *Wrote a note to the Biscuit Baker at Bath for a fresh supply of biscuits.*

1851: 14 Mar: *Wrote to Mundy, Biscuit Baker, Bath, with payment of his bill for Biscuits supplied.*

1853: 29 May: *Wrote to the Biscuit Baker, Bath, with an order for biscuits.*

MUNRO — Elizabeth Munro of Richmond Terrace, Clifton — *see also* **Townsend** *and* **Newnham**[198]

Elizabeth Munro, née Townsend (±1774-1818), was born at Belmont estate, Grenada, West Indies, an elder daughter—possibly the eldest—of Thomas Townsend (d. 1824), the owner of sugar plantations in Grenada. Upon returning to England Townsend bought Poyle Park in Tongham, near Aldershot, Surrey. He also owned property at Godmanchester in Huntingdonshire and Pickwick House in Corsham, Wiltshire, but the family seem to have preferred living at Clifton; at some point Townsend purchased nos. 3 and 4 Rodney Place, although this was not necessarily the family's residence in 1804-06.

Elizabeth had at least five sisters: Sophia (1777-1853), Caroline (1784-1858), Charlotte, Jane, and Susanna. Susanna married William Moore Newnham; her dates and those of Charlotte and Jane are unknown. Elizabeth married, probably in Grenada and probably in 1793 or 1794, Matthew Munro (1761-1797); they had 1 son and 2 daughters:

1 Matthew (1795-1866); married, at Edmondsham, Dorset, 16 February 1822, Philadelphia Jane Caroline Monro (1800-1867); 1 daughter:
   1 Caroline Harriet (1823-1897)
1 Elizabeth Barbara (b. 1796[?]); married, at Southampton, 14 December 1821, Robert Aitchison
2 Charlotte Isabella (b. 1797); born at Poyle Park, Surrey, on 31 March 1797; probably died young

Matthew Munro arrived in Grenada in the spring of 1772 as the new clerk for Houstoun & Paterson. He rose to become a member of the island's assembly by the late 1780s. In 1792 he was granted a 500-acre plantation named Edinburgh on the coast of Berbice. He was also in partnership with William Macfarlane and James Blair, both of Grenada, and Lambert Blair, of Berbice, trading as Lambert Blair & Co.

Matthew Munro died in England in February 1797, aged 36, and was buried in Bath Abbey. His will, proved on 15 February 1797, showed him to be late of the town of St George in the Island of Grenada, and of West Horsley, Surrey, at the time of his death. The will included a legacy of £750 to his wife Elizabeth. One of his executors was Thomas Townsend of Poyle Park, Surrey, late of the Island of Grenada.

Elizabeth and her infant children lived at Richmond Terrace, Clifton. She died at Bath in 1818 having appointed her father and her son Matthew as her executors. She bequeathed £12,000 to her daughter Elizabeth Barbara Munro, but there was no mention of Charlotte Isabella; she had presumably died young.

Matthew (junior) joined the Royal Navy. By 1846 he was a half-pay lieutenant. He married, 1822, Phildelphia Jane Caroline, eldest daughter of Lt-Gen. William Hector Monro (b. 1742), of Edmonsham House, Dorset, and Philadelphia Bower (b. ±1770). This marriage hints at a connection between the Munro and Monro families, presumably going back several generations.

The following diary entries written by Agnes Witts throw some more light on the picture: 27 February 1804: '... had visits from Lord Mayo, Mrs. & Miss Venours & Mrs. Blackburn after visiting Mr. Townshend just returnd home & bringing his Daughter Mrs. Monro with him...'; 15 March 1804: 'Mrs. Monro & Sophie Townsend, & Mrs. Upton here before I went to Mrs. J. Ram...'; 22 November 1804: 'Mr. Townshend here early to inform us of the marriage that Morning of his eldest Daughter to Mr. Newnham...'; 29 November 1804: 'took shelter in a violent storm of rain at Mrs. Monros at Richmond Terrace...'; 4 January 1805: '... but had visitors in abundance, Mrs. Monro, Mrs. Newnham, & Miss Jane Townsend...'

1804: 15 Sep: *accompanied Mrs. Monro, Misses S. C. & Car. Townsend, Mrs. Nuneham & Matthew on a walk.* 16 Sep: *Downy Square Chapel with Mrs. Monro, S. Townsend where Mr. Hawes officiated.* 24 Sep: *To Bristol & the Earthen Ware Manufactory with Mrs. Townsend, Mrs. Monro, Mrs. Lang, & Mrs. Hopkinson.*

1805: 9 Nov: *Called on Mrs. Townsend etc. & Mrs. Monro etc. & on Mrs. Upton.* 10 Nov: *walked with Miss Upton, Mrs. & Miss Anson, Mr. & Mrs. Newnham & Mrs. Monro etc.* 14 Nov: *Called on Matthew Monro at Sayer's School.* 20 Nov: *Called on Mrs. Monro & Mrs. Newnham.* 29 Nov: *Walked with my Mother. Called on Mrs. Monro.*

1806: 14 Jan: *Called upon the good Mrs. Monro & Mrs. Newnham.*

MUNRO — William Munro[199]

William Munro (±1781-1856), plantation and slave owner and JP, was born in Scotland. He had an estate at St Ann, Jamaica, called Charlton Kings, and was awarded £794 *9s 6d* on 24 October 1836 for the emancipation of fifty-five slaves. He was a Gloucestershire JP and lived at Druids Stoke, Westbury-in-Trym, Gloucestershire. He married Mary Ann Barnett (d. 1847) and together they had at least 1 son and 6 daughters:

1 William (1818-1880), Gen.; became a noted botanist
1 Mary Ann (b. ±1819)
2 Emily (b. ±1821)
3 Louisa (b. ±1822)
4 Sophia (b. ± 1827)
5 Fanny (b. ±1829)
6 Janet (b. ±1831)

In his will William Munro (senior) stated that before his marriage, while he was in Jamaica, he had had two children with Mary Ann Cleghorne. The children's names were Sarah Munro and Mary Ann Munro. By 1850 they were both living in England, at Pentonville and Kensington respectively, both having trained as milliners and dress-makers.

1826: 6 Aug: *Being strongly pressed by my friend Howell, who had sent a horse for me in the morning, I rode out to dinner at Prinknash Park, where I met Mr. Wintle, Mr. Macleod, & Mr. Monro, besides two ladies visitors of Mrs. Howell. We passed a very agreeable afternoon, and Mr. Monro was kind enough to bring me home in his gig. He is a West Indian Gentleman, who has purchased Stoke, near Bristol, formerly the Seat of Mr. Webb, the representative for Gloucester. Mr. Monro has been for some years a Magistrate for the county, & Mr. Wintle also has lately been placed in the commission.*

1833: 18 Apr: *When we had indulged ourselves by lingering long on the splendid prospect from Pen Pole Point, we returned to our carriage & pursued the road to Clifton by Stoke: it is a short but hilly drive, through delightfully undulating ground; to our right were Sneyd Park, the Seat of G. W. Hall Esqr., a celebrated Agriculturist, and Stoke, formerly the property of my old school-fellow & acquaintance, Edward Webb Esqr., for many years representative of the City of Gloucester, whose hospitality in by-gone years I had here enjoyed, but now it has passed by purchase into the hands of — Munro Esqr., a gentleman of Scotch extraction, who made his fortune in the West Indies.* 19 Apr: *Edward deviated to explore the beauties of Blaize Castle; and I went to leave my card with Mr. Monro at Stoke; after which I pursued a retired path to Cote, returning to Clifton across Durdham Down. We all met again at dinner.*

MUNTZ — George Frederick Muntz [200]

George Frederick Muntz (1794-1857), political reformer and industrialist, was born in Great Charles Street, Birmingham, the eldest son of Philip Frederick Muntz (d. 1811) and Catherine Purden, who had married on 26 November 1794. George Frederick had Polish ancestors who had been driven by persecution to France; his grandfather, an aristocratic landowner, had been born in a country château near Soulz sur la Forêt. During the French Revolution the family was broken up, and Philip Frederick Muntz, George's father, travelled extensively; after moving to England, he finally settled in Birmingham where he bought shares in a metalwork factory.

George Frederick joined the family metalwork business, taking it over following his father's death in 1811. He made a large fortune from the manufacture and extended application of what became known as 'Muntz metal'. He married, 1818, Eliza, daughter of Revd John Pryce and Mary Devereux; they had 7 sons and 2 daughters.

From his youth Muntz had been fascinated by politics, especially the 'currency question'. As a follower of Thomas Attwood's high tory radical currency reform he wrote a famous series of letters in 1829 to the duke of Wellington, urging a change of policy. He was associated with Attwood again in helping to repeal the Test and Corporation Acts, and in advocating Catholic emancipation and reform of parliament. Muntz's unpolished oratory and thorough contempt for all convention made him a favourite with the people, and an acceptable speaker at meetings of the working class. On 24 May 1840 Muntz was elected MP for Birmingham, and he held the seat until his death. Muntz's brand of tory radicalism fitted no accepted mould and his fierce political independence infuriated potential allies. Although opposed to universal suffrage, he voted for the Charter and was elected an honorary Chartist deputy for Birmingham. Hostile to sanitation standards and environmental controls, he nevertheless supported factory reform. He was a free-trader who yet often spoke up for protection. As a parliamentary speaker he was often obscure and epigrammatic.

1842: 15 Mar: *Among the members of the lower house I noticed no remarkable person except the eccentric Radical representative for Birmingham, Muntz, whom nature made a fine handsome man, but who has disfigured himself strangely by nourishing an immense growth of beard descending like a huge bird's nest to his chest.*

MURCHISON — Roderick Impey Murchison [201]

Sir Roderick Impey Murchison, baronet (1792-1871), geologist and geographer, was born at Tarradale in Easter Ross, the elder son of Kenneth Murchison and Barbara, the daughter of Roderick Mackenzie of Fairburn. The Murchisons were a highland clan who had lost their ancestral lands for participating in the rebellions of 1715 and 1745. Roderick's father Kenneth Murchison was educated for the medical profession. He went out to India in 1769 and amassed a fortune as a surgeon in the service of the East India Company. After seventeen years he returned to Scotland and purchased Tarradale. He married in 1791.

After the birth of Roderick's younger brother Kenneth in 1794, their father's health began to fail. He died at Bath in 1796, and his widow settled in Edinburgh with her two boys. Before long she married Col Robert Macgregor Murray, a friend of her late husband.

After a military career including service in the Peninsular War, Roderick Murchison took up the study of geology. In 1825 he was admitted a fellow of the Geological Society. His publications were very numerous; Francis Witts would have been made aware of his influence by his son Edward, who was greatly interested in geology.

1845: 9 Jul: *All this country, including Ludlow and its immediate vicinity is very interesting to the Geologist, what Murchison, I believe, has designated the Silurian System of rocks being largely developed, of which a beautiful publication by him furnishes ample account, with drawings, outlines, sections &c.*

MURE — Katherine Mure and the Mure family at Edinburgh [202]

Katherine Mure, née Graham (1734-1820), was the daughter of James Graham, Lord Easdale, and Anne Stewart, daughter of Sir James Stewart, baronet of Coltness. Her parents married in 1711. Katherine married, 1758, William Mure, Baron Mure (1718-1776), of Glanderston and Caldwell. He was appointed baron of the exchequer in 1761. They had at least 2 sons and 3 daughters, including:

1 William (1758-1831), Col; fought in the American Revolutionary War during which he was wounded, taken prisoner, and exchanged; present at the British surrender at Yorktown, 1781; returned to Scotland and appointed colonel of the Renfrew Militia, vice-lieutenant of Renfrewshire, and Lord Rector of Glasgow University, 1793-94; married, 1791, Anne (d. 1854), eldest daughter of Sir James Hunter Blair, 1st baronet (1741-1787) of Dunskey, Wigtownshire; at least 3 sons and 7 daughters, including:
    1 William (1799-1860), Col
2 James (1760-1848), barrister-at-law; educated at Lincoln's Inn (1784) and Gray's Inn (1799); lived at Cecil Lodge, London; married, 8 November 1790, Frederica Sophia (d. 1834), daughter of Christopher Metcalf of Halsted, Suffolk; 3 sons and 4 daughters, including:
    1 Catherine
    2 Margaret
    3 Elizabeth
    4 Anne (1764-1854)

Mrs Mure was a friend of Agnes Witts in Edinburgh; she was mentioned eighty-four times in her diaries.

1795: 4 Sep: *We here met Miss E. Mure who with her brother & sister were going the same tour as ourselves.* 6 Sep: *We dined at the inn with Mr. Mure's party, after having fatigued the Ladies with a walk to Lord Breadalbane's burying place, which was by no means worth seeing, & delayed our setting out for Kenmore to a later hour than proper.*

1801: 6 Apr: *Mrs. Mure looking younger, if possible & the Spiers's all arrayed in black.*

MURRAY — David Rodney Murray [203]

David Rodney Murray (±1790-1878), Church of England clergyman, was born at Marylebone, Westminster, son of David Murray (1748-1794), MP, and Elizabeth Harley (1764-1824). He was educated at Christ Church, Oxford (BA 1814), and was ordained deacon on 22 December 1816 and priest on 20 December 1818. His first clerical appointment was as curate of Silchester, Hampshire, from 30 December 1816; this was followed by several other curacies. He was later rector of Cusop and Brampton Bryan, Herefordshire, from 1826 to his death in 1878, and vicar of Beedon, Berkshire, from 1828 to 1874. He married, 4 December 1828, Frances Portal (1807-1892); they had 3 sons and 1 daughter:

1 David Mortimer (1832-1881), Maj.
2 Elibank Harley (1833-1901), Vice Adm.
3 Alexander William (1836-1857); died at Delhi, India, presumably during the Indian Mutiny
1 Agnes (b. 1842)

David Rodney Murray had at least two sisters: Maria Clara, who married Edmund Hungerford Lechmere, and Louisa, Lady Reade (d. 1821), who had married, 1811, Sir John Chandos Reade, 7th baronet (1785-1868).

1828: 19 Dec: *We dined at Oddington, at Lady Reade's, and met a large party. Mr. & Mrs. Murray were staying in the house; he is a Clergyman & incumbent of Brampton Brian in Herefordshire; they are a newly married couple; he brother to the late Lady Reade too early lost to her family.*

MURRAY — George Murray [204]

Sir George Murray (1772-1846), army officer and politician, was born in the old house of Ochtertyre, Crieff, Perthshire, the younger son of Sir William Murray, 5th baronet (1746-1800), of Ochtertyre, and Lady Augusta Mackenzie (1746-1809), youngest daughter of George, 3rd earl of Cromarty. He was educated at Edinburgh High School and Edinburgh University before being sent to Geneva to learn French. In March 1789 he was commissioned ensign in the 71st Foot. He had a long and distinguished military career; he received several foreign honours and in 1813 he was knighted KB.

Murray entered politics and was elected MP for Perth County in the Dundas interest in 1824. He held the seat until 1830. He succeeded Viscount Beresford as lieutenant-general of the ordnance in 1824, and was commander-in-chief in Ireland from 1825 to 1828. In 1828, on Huskisson's resignation as secretary of state for the colonies, Wellington offered Murray the vacant post.

Though an uninspiring speaker in the House, as colonial secretary Murray was a conscientious administrator. He supported Catholic emancipation and opposed parliamentary reform. He left office on the fall of the Wellington government in November 1830 and was defeated in the 1832 general election, but was re-elected for Perthshire in a by-election in 1834. He stood unsuccessfully for Westminster in 1837 and for Manchester in 1839. He was master-general of the ordnance in Peel's brief ministry of 1834-35, and again, but without a seat in cabinet, in Peel's ministry of 1841 to June 1846.

Murray married, 1825, Lady Louisa Erskine (1777-1842), sister of the 1st marquess of Anglesey and widow of Lt-Gen. Sir James Erskine, who had died during their divorce proceedings.

1828: 2 Jun: *Colonial Sec. Sir George Murray is a Lieut. Gen.; a man very highly esteemed, and distinguished as an officer, having seen much service, & been engaged in many important public transactions: latterly, he has been Commander in the Forces in Ireland.*

1834: 17 Dec: *The following ministerial appointments are announced ... Sir George Murray, Master Genl. of the Ordnance.*

MURRAY — George Murray [205]

George Murray (1784-1860), bishop of Sodor and Man and bishop of Rochester, was educated at Christ Church, Oxford (BA 1806; MA 1810; DD 1814). He served as bishop of Sodor and Man from 1814 to 1827 and bishop of Rochester from 1827 to his death in 1860. Murray married, 1811, Sarah, second daughter of Robert Hay-Drummond, 10th earl of Kinnoull; they had 5 sons and 6 daughters.

1827: 30 Oct: *the papers, with every appearance of its being a fact, that the vacant Bishopric of Rochester is intended for the Bishop of Sodor and Man, who will thus be elevated to the Episcopal bench in the House of Lords. Dr. Murray, the present Manks Bishop, is a nephew of the Duke of Athol, being son to the late Lord George Murray, who was Bishop, I think, of Llandaff, and who died soon after his accession to his See.*

1828: 25 Mar: *The vacant preferments in the Church have at last after considerable delay been disposed of. The Bishop of Rochester, Dr. Murray, obtains the valuable Deanery of Worcester as a Commendam.*

MURRAY — Maria Clara Murray — ***see* Edmund Hungerford Lechmere**

MURRAY BROWNE — ***see* Browne**

MUSGRAVE — James Musgrave [206]

Sir James Musgrave, 9th baronet (1785-1858), landed proprietor, of Barnsley Park, Barnsley, near Cirencester, was the eldest son of Sir James Musgrave, 8th baronet (1752-1814), and Clarissa Blackall (d. 1823). He was educated at Eton College and Christ Church, Oxford (BA 1807), and succeeded as 9th baronet in 1814. Musgrave was high sheriff of Gloucestershire in 1825-26. He died unmarried.

1825: 18 Jul: *We dined at Mrs. Price's at Coln St. Dennis. There was a large party, but every body seemed languid and exhausted. We met Mr. Beach, his son W. Beach, lately appointed Lieut Col. of the North Gloucester Militia, and once MP. for Shaftesbury, Sir James Musgrove of Barnsley park, High Sheriff for the County.*

1829: 24 Nov.

1842: 18 Mar: *I do not suppose that we went more than a mile out of our way; but we were obliged to go at a foot's pace through very deep and wet village cross roads, partly under Sir James Musgrave's park wall to Foss Cross.*

MUSTO — Thomas Musto [207]

Thomas Musto (b. ±1813), labourer, was born at Brockhampton, Gloucestershire, and later lived at Guiting Power, Gloucestershire. He was sentenced for larceny at the assizes of 29 March 1848 and served a nine-month sentence. He was committed for larceny a second time on 15 November 1852. Following this later committal he was sentenced to seven years' transportation. It has not been discovered if he ever returned to England.

1852: 10 Nov: *Much engaged all the forenoon in taking evidence on a case of burglary, which occurred in this village last night; a notorious bad character from Lower Guiting having been detected in the act of plundering the village shop into which he had broken. A young man of the place, returning early in the morning from Stow, found the marauder in the act of robbery, & with good judgement having called up assistance, secured the evil-doer—Committed the thief to Gloucester jail for trail at the Lent Assizes.* 12 Nov: 12 Nov: *Justice business at home;—more burglaries imputed to Thos. Musto by a Worcestershire policeman.* 13 Nov: *Much engaged in the forenoon with another burglary case against Thomas Musto, whom I remanded on Wednesday, that the Police might make the needful enquiries. I to-day committed him to the County Prison, on this new charge—he having broken open a shop at Aston Blank on the night of the 21st. October.*

1853: 5 Apr: *The first trial was that of T. Musto, whom I had committed for burglaries at Cold Aston and Upper Slaughter: the Aston case was the only one tried, and the prisoner, being found guilty, was sentenced to seven years transportation.*

MUTLOW — **William Mutlow** [208]

William Mutlow (±1760-1832), cathedral organist, was a chorister in Gloucester Cathedral and went on to become organist in 1782. He married, 1788, Mary Maria Wilton; they had at least 1 son:

1 William Wilton (1790-1865); educated at Pembroke College, Oxford (BA 1812; MA 1815); a minor canon of Gloucester Cathedral, 1815; vicar of Brookthorpe, 1816; rector of Rudford, 1828

In his long career Mutlow was much involved with the Three Choirs Festival; Francis Witts must have been aware that he was dealing with a safe pair of hands.

1826: 31 Mar: *It was not long before the deliberations about the Music meeting commenced, & were protracted for nearly three hours. Of the Stewards the Hon. Mr. Moreton & Mr. Bankes were absent; the former having been detained in Leicestershire by fox-hunting had written his ideas on the subject to Mr. Dolphin, the latter excused himself from taking any part in the arrangements till he came to residence in the Cathedral early in August. The Hon. James Dutton, Mr. Dolphin & Mr. Bowles attended, & Mr. Mutlow the Organist of the Cathedral was called to our counsel.* 29 Apr., 22 May: *Mr. Mutlow, Organist of Gloucester Cathedral, and conductor of the Music Meeting, came hither for a conference on the arrangements necessary for the celebration now approaching.* 15 Jun., 13 Jul: *Engaged till nearly twelve o clock with Mr. Mutlow, the Conductor of the Music meeting in various arrangements.* 5 Aug: *After service, I was obliged to go to Mr. Mutlow's to hold a consultation on matters relative to the approaching Music-meeting. I met there Mr. Cramer, the celebrated Violinist, and leader of the Orchestra.* 13 Sep: *... there was some misunderstanding with Miss Stephens about this song, and an unpleasant conversation occurred; the genus irritabile was somewhat excited, in so much, that Mr. Mutlow & myself had some difficulty in pacifying Miss Stephen's brother, who deemed his sister ill-used.* 13 Sep: *The Cathedral service was performed by Mr. Mutlow, Son of the conductor, who is Precentor of the Cathedral, and Incumbent of St. Mary de Lode.* 25 Sep... *As to Mr. Mutlow, I will acknowledge, that he takes great pains, that he labours hard to engage the performers on moderate terms, and does his best to curtail incidental expences, but he is advanced in years, inactive, not calculated for business, slow in correspondence, and altogether not a quick, ready person out of his professional walk; there I believe, he is a very respectable musician of the old school, & a good teacher.*

1827: 8 Apr: *The service was performed and a sermon preached by the incumbent Mr. W. Mutlow, Precentor of the Cathedral, and Son of the Organist. He is a pretty good reader, without much unction or earnestness of manner, & his discourse (on the Lord's supper,) was too rapidly and somewhat carelessly delivered. He is now rather under a cloud as to his pecuniary affairs, having been led into expences beyond his means by social indulgences, fondness for company, good living and the card table.*

1832: 29 Mar: *The new Organist of the Cathedral, Mr. Amott, successor to Mr. Mutlow, who died about Christmas last, attended on this occasion to communicate with and receive instructions from the Stewards. He was a pupil of Mutlow, is considered a scientific Musician, and was highly esteemed at Shrewsbury.*

MYERS — **Simeon Hart Myers** [209]

Simeon Hart Myers (1765-1803), merchant, was born in New York, the younger son of Naphtali Hart Myers (1711-1788) and Hester Moses. His parents were married in London in 1754, as reported in the *London Daily Advertiser* of Saturday, 9 March of that year: 'Last Wednesday Mr Naphtali Hart Myers, of New York, Merchant, was married to Miss Hetty Moses, daughter of Mr. Simon Jacobus Moses, of Bury-Street, Merchant; a young Lady, with a genteel Fortune, and possessed of every Qualification that can add Happiness to the Matrimonial State.'

Simeon Myers was from a Jewish family. He entered Clement's Inn in 1794, one of the lesser inns of chancery in that era, but he cannot have regarded it as a step towards entering the bar as such a profession was not available to Jews until the 1830s. In the fire insurance records Simeon is recorded as still being at the Inn in 1796, but the extent of his training and career is not known. He married (in a Christian ceremony), 10 November 1796, a widow, Catherine Peard, née Winsloe (±1764-1848); they had 1 son:

1 John Powell Matthew (1801-1869); born at Cheltenham; married, at St Nicholas's, Brighton, 6 December 1826, Mary Anne Duncan (1798-1874); died at Tours, France; 6 sons and 3 daughters

The Myers family tenanted 'Grove Cottage'. A sale advertisement in *The Times* of January 1805 reads: 'so well known ... consisting of a dining and drawing-room, 24 feet by 18, boudoir, 3 best bed-rooms, 3 servants ditto, with offices of various descriptions, coach-house, stables and kitchen garden, with 6 acres or thereabouts of meadow-land, held for a term, whereof five years were unexpired, at Michaelmas last'. The family did not stay at Cheltenham. Simeon died at Twickenham.

1801: 28 Oct: *I accompanied, the two Mr. Hughes & their Sister to Mrs. Myers Ball; the house is at the Top of the Wellwalk; the meeting was agreeable, tho' the Company not very select. I danced three dances with Fanny Port, a charming girl, & three with a Miss Berrington; we returned by one o'clock.* 29-30 Oct., 11 Nov: *Mr. Rawlinson dined with us & repaired with us in the Evening to Mrs. Hughes, where I enjoyed a most pleasant evening supping there. The Granvilles, Fanny &c. were among the most agreeable, beside them were Mr. & Mrs. Myers, Mr. & Mrs. Brown of Sapperton, Mr. & Mrs. Delabere &c.* 14 Nov: *Walked with Mr. Myers &c. Called upon the Granville's.* 16 Nov., 24 Nov.

MYNORS — *see* **Minors**

MYTTON — **Miss Mytton at Clifton**

1804: 29 Jul: *Walked alone; with Mrs. Carrick & Miss Mytton.*

MYTTON — **John Mytton** [210]

John Mytton (1796-1834), sportsman and eccentric, was born at Halston, Shropshire, the only son of John Mytton (1768-1798), landowner, of Halston, and Sarah Harriet (1774-1853), a younger daughter of William Mostyn Owen of Woodhouse, near Halston. Mytton was educated at Westminster School from 1807, where he spent twice his £400 yearly allowance and was expelled in 1811. By 1813 he was referred to as being from Harrow School, but he was later placed with a private tutor, whom he knocked down. He entered at both Oxford and Cambridge, but matriculated at neither, though he sent 339 gallons of port to Cambridge to await his arrival. Always impervious to advice, Mytton read only the *Racing Calendar and Stud Book*. At the age of 18 he toured the Continent, and on 30 May 1816 he became a cornet in the 7th Hussars, part of the army of occupation in France. He left the Army the following year but continued in the North Shropshire Yeomanry Cavalry (captain 1812, major 1822) until his death. He was sheriff for Merioneth in 1821 and for Shropshire in 1823.

Jack Mytton (as he was known) married, 21 May 1818, Harriet Emma, eldest daughter of Sir Thomas Jones, 1st baronet, of Stanley Hall, Shropshire; they had 1 daughter:

1 Harriet Emma Charlotte (1819-1885); married, 26 June 1841, Clement Delves, fifth son of Col John Hill of Hawkstone

Following the death of his first wife in 1820 after the birth of his daughter, Mytton married secondly, 29 October 1821, Caroline Mallet, sixth daughter of Thomas Giffard of Chillington, Staffordshire; they had 4 sons and 1 daughter:

1 Barbara Augusta (b. 1822); married, 1847, Col Poulett George Henry Somerset, son of Lord Charles Henry Somerset, a younger brother of the 6th duke of Beaufort
1 John Fox Fitz-Giffard (1823-1875)
2 Charles Orville (1825-1834); died young
3 Euphrates Henry (1826-1834); died young
4 William Harper (1827-1854)

Caroline separated from her husband in 1828. It would seem that the Eton boy in the diaries was John Fox Fitz-Giffard Mytton. He entered the Army, but also had problems, being gaoled in 1856 for a tavern debt of £1,500. He married and had family, most of whom appear to have emigrated to Australia and Canada.

As master of foxhounds from 1818 to 1821 Jack Mytton hunted a vast country extending from Halston into Staffordshire, including what was later the country of the Albrighton hunt. He flouted many established hunting conventions when hunting around Halston with new hounds and harriers. He was on the turf from 1817 to 1830, and though he kept a large racing stable he never bred a good horse.

Mytton had a pleasing countenance rather than a handsome face. He was a man of great physical strength and foolhardy courage, with a taste for practical jokes. He was a splendid shot and a daring horseman, and there are numberless stories of his recklessness. He is said to have galloped at full speed over a rabbit warren just to see if his horse would fall—it did, and rolled over him too. Again, for a wager he drove a tandem at night across country, surmounting a sunk fence 3 yards wide, a broad deep drain, and two stiff quickset hedges. He would sometimes strip to his shirt to follow wildfowl in hard weather, and is said once to have stripped naked to follow some duck over the ice. One night he even set fire to his nightshirt to frighten away the hiccups. Inordinately convivial, Mytton drank from four to six bottles of port a day, beginning in the morning while shaving; he eventually lived in a 'nearly constant state of intoxication'.

Mytton inherited, before he was two years old, an estate worth £10,000 per annum plus £60,000 in cash. He squandered it all, but gave people something to talk about; he spent his money on hounds and horses, gambling, reckless generosity and insensate conviviality, as well as on the satisfaction of the most outlandish whims and endless practical jokes which earned him his place among the English eccentrics. He eventually went into hiding from his creditors at Calais and died of delirium tremens in the King's Bench prison. In his short description of 'the late Mr Mytton', Francis Witts was certainly not exaggerating.

1836: 21 Jul: *A large dinner party at Lady L's followed; eighteen sat down to table. Besides our own party there were three of the name of Mytton, a lady like and sensible Miss M. far advanced in life, with a great nephew, an Eton boy, and a niece: the latter are the children of the late Mr. Mytton of Halsted in Shropshire, notorious for the extravagance and irregularities of his life; a bad husband, a violent politician, a noted sportsman on the turf, and a spendthrift.*

N

NALDI — Giuseppe Naldi[1]

Giuseppe Naldi (1770-1820), singer and composer, was born at Bologna, the only son of Giuseppe Naldi, of the same city, who held a high government appointment. He was educated in the universities of Bologna and Pavia, where he made very rapid progress in his studies for the law, his chosen profession, but finding this uncongenial he obtained, at the personal request of the Marchese Litta, a secretary's place in a government department. However, the Italian Revolution put an end to his career in this direction, and he left the country.

Naldi next appeared at Milan, where he achieved his first success on the stage. He appeared at Rome in 1789, then at Naples, and next at Venice and Turin. In 1796 and 1797 he reappeared at Milan. In London he made his début at the King's Theatre on 15 April 1806 in Guglielmi's *Le due nozza ed un sol marito*. He continued to sing at the King's Theatre for every subsequent season up to and including 1819. He sung principally in *Le Cantatrici Villane*, *Così fan tutte* and *Il Fanatico per la musica*, demonstrating his skill as a cellist as well as a singer in the latter.

Lord Mount Edgcumbe described Naldi's voice as 'weak and uncertain', while another critic called it 'sonorous and powerful' with the exception of his performance as Sancho in the *Villeggiatori bizarri*. Naldi rather foolishly excused this poor performance on the plea that he was 'too much the gentleman to play the clown' (*Monthly Mirror*). All critics agreed, however, that Naldi was extremely clever and able to write fair verses and compose very tolerable music. He had an accurate ear, could play the piano and cello proficiently, and read at sight with perfect ease and intonation. As an actor, he was excellent, and played with 'irresistible humour, effect, judgment, and truth'. A good portrait-sketch of him as Figaro in *Le Nozze*, 'Drawn and Etched expressly for the *British Stage*', appeared in February 1818.

In 1819 Naldi was engaged at Paris, where he made his début in *Così fan tutte*; but his powers were much faded. He returned once more to London. On 16 December 1820, when at Paris, he met an untimely death. He had been to dinner, with his daughter and wife, at the apartments of his friend Manuel García to witness the trial of a newly invented pressure cooker. The trial was just about finished, when Naldi, examining the cooking pot in the fireplace, decided—seemingly out of curiosity—to stop up the conduit of the steam using the fireplace pincers; the heat, with the help of the compression, built to such a point that with a sudden explosion, the cover of the cooker struck Naldi in the forehead, opening his skull and leaving him dead at the feet of his daughter.

Naldi's daughter Caroline (1809-1876) was also a celebrated singer. She appeared in operas by Rossini and Bellini in Paris between 1819 and 1824. When she retired upon marrying Conte di Sparre in 1824, it was said to be a great loss for the stage.

1820: 5 Jan: *We spent the Evening at Mrs. Aston's: my old pupil Frederic A. had been with us much in the morning. We had delicious music. Mr. Aston's daughter, Mrs. Watkins, is a most superior private singer: and indulged us with several delightful songs; Italian, Handel's & others. A Mr. Harrington, Grandson of the late learned & musical & good Dr. Harrington of Bath, played on the flute & sang with taste. Naldi, one of the first singers & teachers in England, Mrs. Watkins's old Master, was also there: his Physionomy Italian of the worst order, his skill & powers wonderful. A duet with his daughter, the subject a Music Master and his pupil, is a charming buffa. Madam Naldi is an interesting girl, and lovely singer; unceasing tuition and practice have produced the perfection of the science, that simplicity & apparent ease, which is truly difficult.* 19 Jan: *Attended the concert, when an unusual style of performance was presented, namely, a little comic opera, made up of selections, chiefly from Il Fanatico per la Musica, the Music by Mayer. Naldi and his daughter performed admirably; the other vocalists were two Miss Ashes, a Signor Vercellin, a Mr. O Callaghan, and a Mr. Cole. The Comic acting of Naldi is excellent, his daughter moves with grace & ease, and in the second act executed a beautiful air by Rossini.*

1829: 22 Sep: *The subject, an enthusiastic composer instructing an orchestra at the first rehearsal of his new composition. I rather think, I heard it performed several years ago at Bath by Naldi, a celebrated Buffo now deceased.*

NAPER — Jane Naper and the Naper family of Loughcrew — ***see also* Cornewall, Rycroft, *and* Travell**[2]

Jane Naper [later Rycroft], née Travell (1765-1797), was the daughter of Ferdinando Tracy Travell (1740-1809) and Martha Rollinson (1741-1780), and first cousin to Francis Witts. She married, first, William Naper (1749-1791); they had 1 son and 1 daughter:

1 James Lenox William (1791-1868); *see below*

1 Jane (1792-1853); married, 1815, Sir George Cornewall (1774-1835)

The Naper family was long-established in co. Meath; at their peak, the Naper holdings measured 180,000 acres in north Meath, Westmeath, and Cavan, but by 1870 they had reduced to 18,863 acres—still a very considerable estate.

Jane married, secondly, 1794, Henry Rycroft (1776-1846). Jane and Henry did not have any children, and Jane died in April 1797 'in the 32nd year of her age'. She was buried in Cuckfield church, East Sussex.

James Lennox William Naper (1791-1868), writer and landed proprietor, was orphaned when his mother died in 1797; it is not clear who brought him up, but his grandfather must have taken much of the responsibility. He was educated at Eton College and Christ Church, Oxford, and was MP for Weobley in 1813-18. He married, 3 May 1824, Selina Skipwith (±1790-1880), daughter of Sir Grey Skipwith, 8th baronet of Hovington Hall, Warwickshire; they had 2 sons and 2 daughters, including:

1 Lelia Jane (d. 1879)

1 James Lenox (1825-1901)

2 William Dutton Naper (1830-1915), JP and DL for co. Meath; his son, James Lenox Naper, a major in the Meath Militia, served as high sheriff and endured the first major fire at Loughcrew House in 1888; another son, William Lenox Naper, was awarded the Military Cross for services in the Royal Horse Guard during the First World War, but died without issue

The family lived at Loughcrew, Oldcastle, co. Meath, Ireland. James Naper (senior) commissioned the building of Loughcrew House by Charles Cockerell in 1821. He served as chairman of the poor law guardians during the famine years in the 1830s, when he subsidised the emigration of his tenants to Canada. Following the death of William Lenox Naper, grandson of James Lennox William Naper, the estate passed to another branch of the family. Loughcrew House was finally destroyed by fire in 1964. The Naper family sold the estate in 2008.

James Lennox William Naper featured, under the name of Napier, in the memoirs of the courtesan Harriette Wilson as a 'long-backed' foxhunting dandy worth £20,000 a year. She coaxed him into a liaison with her unfortunate friend Julia Johnstone. With a fine indifference she reported in 1813:

> Napier came sneaking and grinning into the room, and informed us, that either Lord Bath or Lord Bathurst, I forget which, was bringing him into Parliament. 'More shame for you, you ought not to have given up your independence for millions', said I. 'You cannot now vote against the man who give [*sic*] you a seat.'

In this Harriette Wilson was perhaps right. Naper, brought in by Lord Bath on a vacancy, gave his first known vote for Catholic relief on 30 May 1815, but revised it on 21 May 1816 and did not vote the following year. He voted with ministers on the regent's expenditure on 31 May 1815, but against them, with the majority, on the duke of Cumberland's establishment bill of 3 July. He was in the government minority on the property tax bill of 18 March 1816, and, after a month's leave from 24 April, again sided with the government on the public revenue bill of 17 and 20 June. He supported the suspension of habeas corpus and its modus operandi on 23 June 1817 and 10 and 11 February 1818. No speech of his is known and he did not seek re-election until 1831, when he was defeated for Meath.

See volume 1 for further information on the Naper family.

1801: 14 May: *I sallied along Oxford Street, which, if regular, would be the finest range of buildings in the world, to No. 14 Great Cumberland Street, where I had the satisfaction of being kindly received by my Uncle Ferdinand who was sitting with Master Naper in Mrs. Eeles's No. 14 Great Cumberland Street.* 15 May: *At three o'clock I set out with my Uncle Travell & Mast. Naper in a coach to Mr. B. Witts's at Champion hill.* 1 Jun: *My Mother & myself afterwards called at Mrs. Kearney's & Lady Lyttelton, whom we did not find at home; & upon our little cousin Miss Napier, at Mad. Renouard's Boarding School, a fine little girl.*

1805: 14 Jul: *Between Churches Mrs. Travell & Jane Napier called & Miss Markham.*

1822: 20 Dec: *Miss Buxton together with her Brother-in-law, Mr. F. Whalley, who is Secretary to the Comptroller's Office, & her Cousin Mr. Naper, has lately discharged an act of duty and affection to the memory of their deceased Grandfather by causing to be erected in the Chancel of my Church a very elegant monument, designed by Mr. Naper himself.*

1837: 21 Sep: *Met a large party: there were staying in the house Miss Blunt, an elderly unmarried sister of Lady Imhoff's, in former years very intimate with my late cousin, Mrs. Naper, afterwards Rycroft—and so, well acquainted with my mother, Mrs. Whalley, my Aunt Travell &c.*

1850: 19 Jun.

NAPIER — Charles James Napier [3]

Sir Charles James Napier (1782-1853), army officer, was born in Whitehall, London, the eldest of the eight children of Col George Napier (1751-1804), son of the 6th Lord Napier and his second wife Sarah Bunbury, née Lennox (1745-1826), daughter of the 2nd duke of Richmond (*below*). The family moved to Celbridge, 10 miles from Dublin, in 1785. At the age of 12, Charles Napier was commissioned as an ensign in the 33rd Regiment. He transferred a few months later to the 89th, in which his father was assistant quartermaster-general. When the 89th was sent to Ostend, Napier was transferred to the 4th, but instead of joining the regiment he was sent to the grammar school at Celbridge, where he was one of few protestant pupils. Aged 16, in the Irish uprising of 1798, he helped his father defend the family estate against the rioting peasants; even then he was conscious of the oppression that had led them to rebel. As he put it later, the starving Irish were 'obedient to the laws of man, instead of adopting God's law of self-preservation'.

Napier distinguished himself in the Peninsular campaign (for more detail about him being 'presumed dead' *see* the Napier family entry below) before being sent to Bermuda in 1812 during the Anglo-American War, where he commanded a brigade with orders to harass the American coast. He devised a plan for defeating the Americans by raising an army of slaves—who outnumbered the white inhabitants in the south—officered by the British and under his overall command. This army was to march on Washington and dictate peace, the terms of which would include the freedom of slaves in America. Napier alleged that his superiors ignored his plan because of the effect the liberation of the American slaves would have on those in the British West Indies. His regiment was sent to Nova Scotia, but hoping for further action in the Peninsular campaign he transferred in September 1813 to the 50th Regiment. By the time he reached England the war with France was over.

In 1821 Napier was appointed to a new post in the Ionian Islands where he remained until 1838. In 1841 he was appointed to a Bombay command at Poona, and in August 1842 he was made commander of the British forces in Sind. There, in 1843, Napier achieved his greatest military success, establishing his mythic reputation. In a dramatic move on 5 January he took a force of 350 men to seize the great desert fortress of Imamgarh. To his surprise he found the fortress deserted, and news soon arrived of an attack on the British residency. Napier moved swiftly, engaging the combined forces of the amirs on 17 February at the Fuleli river at Miani with around 2,200 men, mostly sepoys, against roughly 20,000. In the ensuing battle, British casualties amounted to about 300, while the amirs reportedly lost in the region of 6,000 men. With reinforcements from Bombay, Napier continued to hound his enemies. At Dabo, 8 miles from Hyderabad, on 24 March, Napier's force, then numbering 5,000, attacked the amir of Mirpur's ragtag army of 25,000 men. Napier lost 270 men while the amir lost 5,000. The amir escaped, but after another defeat on 14 June, all organised opposition to British power in Sind was over. In August 1843 the annexation of Sind was announced.

The majority of the diary entries (i.e. those of 1805-06) which almost certainly refer to Charles James Napier have been placed in the Napier family section below.

1848: 4 Oct: *Lord E. has procured for him admission to a dinner at which his Lordship is shortly to preside at Cheltenham, and which is to be given by the East Indian Officers now resident there, to the gallant hero of Scinde, Sir Charles Napier, whom my son has lately met with a large party of East Indians at Southam; Sir C.N. being a visitor at Cheltenham to recruit his health.*

NAPIER — George Napier and the Napier family at Clifton [4]

George Napier (1751-1804), army officer, was born in Edinburgh, the eldest son of Francis Scott [later Napier], 6th Lord Napier (1705-1773), of Merchistoun, and his second wife, Henrietta Maria (1733-1795). He was appointed ensign in the 25th Foot and became a lieutenant in 1771. He married, 1775, Elizabeth (d. 1780), daughter of Capt Robert Pollock; they had an unknown number of children. Napier served in the American Revolutionary War and was present at the siege of Charleston, South Carolina, in 1780. His wife and all his children—except for one daughter, Louisa Mary (1776-1856)—died of yellow fever; he himself was put on board a ship unconscious and dying, but he recovered on the voyage.

George Napier married secondly, 1781, Sarah Bunbury, née Lennox, fourth daughter of Charles Lennox, 2nd duke of Richmond and Lennox (1701-1750), a descendant of one of Charles II's bastards by a French woman. Her previous husband, the well-known racing baronet and MP Sir Charles Thomas Bunbury (1740-1821), finally divorced her for desertion in 1776 after she had left him in 1769 for Lord William Gordon. George and Sarah had 5 sons and 4 daughters:

1 Charles James (1782-1853); *see above and below*
1 Emily Louisa Augusta (1783-1863); married, at Pau, France, 22 September 1830, Lt-Gen. Sir Henry Edward Bunbury, 7th baronet
2 George Thomas (1784-1855), Lt-Gen.; died at Geneva
3 William Francis Patrick (1785-1860), author of *The Life and Opinions of General Sir Charles James Napier, GCB* (1857)
4 Richard (1787-1868); married, 1817, Anne Louisa Stewart (1781-1867)
2 Anne (1788-1866)
5 Henry Edward (1789-1853), historian; born in Italy; became a midshipman in the Royal Navy
3 Caroline (1790-1810)
4 Cecilia (1791-1808)

Napier rose to the rank of lieutenant-colonel in 1794 and distinguished himself during the Irish Rebellion in 1798. He became brevet colonel in 1800 and moved to Clifton for the benefit of his health. He died of consumption at Clifton on 13 October 1804.

The diary references of 1805 and 1806 to 'Colonel Napier' are confusing. It is believed they refer to George's eldest son, Charles James Napier; in 1805 he was a captain, but there is the possibility that he was a colonel in one of the local volunteer regiments. It is known that Charles Napier was in Clifton and Gloucestershire at this time; following his father's death he accepted Lord Bathurst's invitation to Cirencester and spent several weeks there. But it is surprising that in his diary entry for 4 October 1848, Francis Witts did not mention his previous acquaintance with the Napier family.

The diary fragment that seems to confirm the attribution to Charles is provided by Agnes Witts, dated 25 January 1809. At Corunna on 16 January of that year, Charles Napier was wounded five times: his leg was broken by a musket shot; he received a sabre wound to the head, a bayonet wound in the back, and severe contusions from the butt end of a musket; and his ribs were broken by a gunshot. Eventually he was taken prisoner; his name was returned among the killed, but his life was saved by a French drummer. Agnes Witts recorded in her diary on 25 January 1809, 'my spirits much oppressed by the miserable account contain'd in the Gazette, which confirm'd the Death of poor Colonel Napier.' On 26 January she wrote, 'A miserable day of perpetual showers with strong wind, but the air mild, dirt in the streets dreadful but I went out merely to call on the poor Napiers'. The *London Gazette* stated 'Majors Napier and Stanhope, 50th Regiment, killed'.

Napier was taken to Marshal Soult's quarters, where he received every attention. Marshal Ney, who succeeded Soult as commander, was particularly kind. On 20 March, having discovered that Napier's mother was a blind widow, he set Napier at liberty, on parole and not to serve again until exchanged. It was not until January 1810 that an exchange was put into effect and Napier was able to rejoin his regiment.

According to William Francis Patrick Napier, George Napier's widow and four daughters were in a poor financial position until the prime minister, William Pitt, hearing of their situation, provided them with a pension.

1804: 21 Aug., 1 Sep: *At an entertaining Party at Mrs Waddington's, Mr. & Mrs. A. Thompson Mr. & Mrs. Ball, Mrs. & Miss Buikstocks, Napier's &c. much literary conversation.* 2 Sep: *Walked with Holmes, Ryan, Manners, Napier &c.* 3 Sep: *Walked back & at the Fair with Richd. Napier & Clements.*

1805: 22 Nov: *With the Miss Napiers on the Downs etc.* 28 Nov.

1806: 2 Feb: *Joined Col. Napier, to whom I was introduced, & his Sisters, & walked with them to the Wells.* 3 Feb: *Called upon Col. Napier, but found only his Mother & elder sister at home.* 4 Feb: *Called upon my excellent friend Mrs. Carrick, where Col. & the Miss Napiers paid a short visit.* 9 Feb: *Walked a little before Chapel & after with Col. & Miss A. Napier.* 11 Feb: *Dined with Lieut. Col. Napier at his Mother's in St. Vincent's Parade, the young Ladies & Major Patton formed our party, which was pleasant enough.* 12 Feb: *Walked with my Father & Mother, Miss Macbride, Col. Napier &c. About nine o clock repaired to Mrs. Salter's, carrying Col. & Miss Ann Napier.* 13 Feb: *I walked with Col. Napier & Major Patton upon the hill.* 14 Feb., 27 Feb., 28 Feb: *Col. Napier called upon us. I visited, with him the Wolseley family.* 6 Mar: *Had a letter from Napier to excuse his visiting Lady Wolseley.* 12 Mar: *Called upon Mrs. Napier, the Colonel, & the young Ladies.*

NAPLETON — Lucy Napleton, a dinner guest of Lady Lyttelton [5]

Lucy Napleton (±1742-1822) was the daughter of John Napleton (d. 1760) and Elizabeth Pococke (b. 1701). Her brother was the Revd John Napleton (1737-1817), educational reformer and canon residentiary of Hereford Cathedral. Lucy died unmarried at Hereford, but it appears that much earlier in her life she had come miraculously close to an untimely death. On 13 March 1790, John Coakley Lettsom wrote the following paragraph to a correspondent: 'I do not know whether thou art acquainted with the nature of the Humane Society for the Recovery of Drowned Persons; but I may add, that I have the honour to be an active member of it. What I mean to observe is, that last week we had the wonderful success of restoring a lady, whom we learnt had been one whole hour under water, and appeared as lifeless as this paper. This is Miss Lucy Napleton. Our Anniversary is on the 30th, when about 300 of us dine together; after which her wonderful recovery will be published.' Sadly the facts relating to this letter have not been discovered.

1801: 5 Sep: *Dined with Lady Lyttelton, and spent the Evening there, where we met Mrs. Napleton.* 7 Sep: *Drank Tea and spent the evening at Mrs. Beavers, where we met Mrs. Noel, Napleton, extremely dull.* 14 Oct.

NAPOLEON — *see* Bonaparte

NARES — Edward Nares [6]

Edward Nares (1762-1841), Church of England clergyman, historian, and writer, was born in London, the third and youngest son of Sir George Nares (1716-1786), justice of the court of common pleas, of Warbrook House, Eversley, Hampshire, and Mary (1726-1782), daughter of Sir John Strange, master of the rolls. He was educated at Westminster School and Christ Church, Oxford (BA 1783; MA 1789).

Nares married, first, at Henley-on-Thames, 16 April 1797, Georgina Charlotte (1770-1802), third daughter of George Spencer, 4th duke of Marlborough (1739-1817), and Caroline (1743-1811), daughter of John Russell, 4th duke of Bedford. Her parents were opposed to the match and Nares and his wife were never invited to Blenheim again. Edward and Georgina had at least 1 son and 1 daughter:

1 Henry Robert Bateman (b. & d. 1799)
1 Charlotte Maria (1800-1803)

Nares married, secondly, Cordelia (1781-1856), second daughter of Thomas Adams (d. 1807) of Swift's Place, Cranbrook, Kent; they had at least 1 son and 1 daughter:

1 Edward Robert (1804-1865), rector of Newchurch
1 Mary Anne Rolls (1808-1811)

Nares was an accomplished scholar with expertise in several areas. He was rector of Biddenden, Kent, from 1798 to his death in 1841, Bampton lecturer in 1805, and regius professor of modern history from 1813 to his death.

1805: 17 Mar: *A vague Discourse at St. Mary's by Mr. Nares of Morton, Bampton Lecturer.* 31 Mar: *At St. Mary's, Mr. Nares preached a good Lecture.*

1832: 10 Mar: *Memoirs of the life and administration of William Cecil, Lord Burghley ... By the Revd. Edwd. Nares, D.D. Reg. Prof. of Modern History in the Univ. of Oxford.—3 Vols. 4to. Lond 1831.—" Such is the date, at least, of the Third Volume; for the three have been published at distant intervals. I have perused them all attentively, and they deserve and reward attention and perseverance.*

1850: 26 Jul: *Mrs. Pole also kindly called, whom I received: she was accompanied by her niece, Miss Buller, and her friends, Mrs. Nares, widow of Dr. Nares, of Biddendon, Kent.*

NAYLER — Richard Nayler[7]

Richard Nayler (1759-1816), surgeon at the Gloucester Infirmary, was born at Stonehouse, Gloucestershire, son of George Nayler (1724-1780) and Sarah Park (1724-1802). He was an alderman and twice mayor of Gloucester. He published *A Cursory View of the Treatment of Ulcers* (1800). Nayler married, at Huntley, 8 December 1796, Frances Blunt (1770-1805) of Huntley Court, Gloucestershire; they had 4 sons:

1 Charles (1797-1877)
2 Thomas (1799-1873), Church of England clergyman
3 Richard Francis (1800-1801)
4 George Richard (1804-1871)

1832: 14 Mar: *My son and myself dined and passed the evening at Mr. Wingfield's. He is a Shrewsbury man by birth, was a pupil of the late Mr. Nayler, an eminent Surgeon at Gloucester.*

NEATE — Arthur Neate[8]

Arthur Neate (1803-1870), Church of England clergyman, was born at Podington, Bedfordshire, eldest son of Revd Thomas Neate (1774-1856) and Catherine Church (b. 1775). He was educated at Harrow School and Trinity College, Cambridge (BA 1827), and incorporated at Oxford in 1828 (MA 1829). Neate succeeded his father as rector of Alvescot with Shilton, Oxfordshire, in 1829, and remained incumbent until his death in 1870. He married, at Witney, Oxfordshire, October 1844, Eleanor Burnaby (1827-1906); they had 3 sons and 1 daughter:

1 Thomas Arthur (b. 1845)
2 Charles Burnaby (1846-1916), Cdr
3 Walter (1852-1917), Church of England clergyman
1 Eleanor (b. 1859)

1836: 30 Nov: *We had a call from the Revd. Mr. Neate, of Alvescot, Oxon, a friend of the Polsons, and now staying with him.*

1838: 9 May: *Called at Billingsley's, who was from home, but I met him at the Polsons, where I also called, & met besides Mr. & Mrs. & Miss P.—Mr. Neate and Geo. Daubeny.*

1840: 5 Aug: *Of Clergy there were the Revd. Messrs. Ford, Vavasour, Bowen, R Waller, A. Neate, Polson, Billingsley, Lockwood, Tocker, Allen, Wollaston, Baillie, Ekins &c.... The meeting was less fully attended than could have been wished; perhaps, above 60 persons were present; the half of them ladies, or at least females—Mrs. Vavasour, the Misses Ford, the Misses Hall, Miss Neate, Miss Wilcox were of the number.*

1852: 20 Apr: *Mrs. R. Waller, attended by three of her boys, called on me to request me to vote in convocation at Oxford on the 29th. Inst. in favour of a Mr. Neate, a candidate for the Professorship of Political Economy: he is a brother of Mr. Neate of Alvescot, a friend of the Polsons ...—of the candidate himself I know nothing; his brother very slightly.*

NEAVE — Richard Digby Neave[9]

Sir Richard Digby Neave, 3rd baronet (1793-1868), artist and author, was the son of Sir Thomas Neave, 2nd baronet of Dagnam Park, Essex, and Frances Caroline Digby. He was educated at St Mary Hall, Oxford, and Lincoln's Inn. He married, 7 August 1827, Mary Arundell (d. 1849), daughter of James Everard Arundell, 9th Baron Arundell of Wardour, and Mary Jones; they had 7 sons and 5 daughters:

1 Arundell (1829-1877); succeeded as 4th baronet; married Gwyn Gertrude Hughes, daughter of William Hughes, 1st Baron Dinorben
2 Edward Digby (1830-1858); served in the Bombay civil service
1 Mary Blanche (1833-1916); married, 1860, John Richard Westgarth Hale [later Hildyard], barrister
3 Kenelm (±1833-1861), officer, Bombay Army; died at Ghoona
4 Wyndham (1834-1858), officer, 71st Highlanders; died in action in Morar, Gwalior, on 16 June during the Central Indian campaign of 1858
5 Reginald (b. & d 1836); died an infant
2 Eleanor Frances (b. 1837)
3 Venetia (1838-1901); married, 1860, Revd John Whitaker Maitland
4 Cicely (b. 1839); married, 1863, Wyndham Slade, barrister
6 Ednowain Reginald (±1842-1874); educated at Trinity Hall, Cambridge (BA 1865); died in Colorado
5 Mariquita (±1847-1938); married, 1874, her second cousin, Alexander George Middleton
7 Edgar (1848-1849); died an infant

Neave acted as the first assistant poor law commissioner in the Chester area from January 1836. He was a friend of John Constable, and visited his London studio on 21 May 1819. In 1825 Constable painted portraits of Neave and his brother Sheffield, and in the same year Neave became godfather to Constable's daughter Emily. Constable stayed with Neave at Pitt Place in Epsom in 1831, when Neave was leasing it from Rowland Stephenson. He and other family members later bought it at auction in 1840.

Neave was a landscape painter and exhibited at the Royal Academy *A Scene in the New Forest*. Two of his landscapes were engraved by David Lucas. *Four Days in Connemara* (1852), a pamphlet by Neave focusing on workhouses and places of correction, was called 'more polemical than topographical' by *The Athenaeum*. In 1861 he was elected a member of the Royal Geographical Society.

1838: 6 Dec: *When our business was nearly half over we were visited by an Assist. P.L. Commr. Mr. Neave, to whose charge has been consigned the district lately superintended by Hall, with the addition of Bucks, and some Unions in Northamptonshire, Worcestershire, and Warwickshire.*

1839: 30 Jan: *A note from J Pegler, the Veterinary Surgeon, to tell me that an Asst. P.L.C. (probably Neave) is to dine to-day at Sir Geo. Phillipps at Weston Park after visiting C Norton Union, and means to visit the Stow Board of Guardians tomorrow.* 31 Jan: *Drove in the phaeton to Stow, where met Mr. Neave, the Asst. P.L.C., a gentlemanly, sensible and pleasant person.* 11 Apr., 14 Apr., 2 May: *It was announced from headquarters that Mr. Neave retires from the superintendence of the district in which our Union is included, and he is to be succeeded by Mr. Asst. Comm. Parker.*

NETTLESHIP — Thomas Nettleship — *see also* Dodington Hunt, Markham, *and* Prinn [10]

Thomas Nettleship (±1685-1762) married, at Staverton, Gloucestershire, 23 February 1731, Mary Buckle (d. 1784); they appear to have had at least 4 sons and 5 daughters:

1 Elizabeth (b. 1731); married, at Charlton Kings, Gloucestershire, 18 August 1752, Revd Alexander Markham (1716-1767)
1 Thomas (1733-1819), attorney at Cheltenham; *see below*
2 Mary (±1734-1769)
2 Henry (b. 1737), merchant and clerk of the Grocers' Company; married, at St Mary Le Bow, City of London, 12 January 1760, Hester Bridgman, at least 4 sons and 1 daughter:
  1 Henry Bridgman (b. 1763)
  2 Samuel (1766-1850); awarded the Freedom of the City of London, 12 February 1806; lived at North Cray Place, Kent, where he had taken a lease.
  3 Thomas (d. 1840), attorney, king's bench, and clerk of the Grocers' Company; lived at North Cray; died at his home in Lower Seymour Street, Portman Square, Middlesex
  4 William (±1772-1826); lived at Cheltenham; married, at St Giles's [presumably London], 25 November 1823, Mary, daughter of John Best; 1 daughter:
    1 Mary Anne (1824-1887); married, 1842, William Angerstein (1811-1897), of Weeting Hall, youngest son but eventual heir of John Angerstein (1773-1858) and his wife, Amelia; 3 sons and 3 daughters
  1 Anne [Anna] (±1770-1846); lived at Warfield Hall, Berkshire; appears to have lived her last days with her brother Samuel at North Cray Place, Kent, where she died unmarried and was buried
3 Ann (1739-1746)
3 William (1741-1821); *see below*
4 Katherine/Catherine (b. 1744); married, at Cheltenham, 7 July 1794, Revd John Hunt (±1748-1816), rector of Pitcombe, Somerset
4 John (1747-1810)
5 Anna (1749-1813); married, at Charlton Kings, 9 November 1797, a widower, Dodington Hunt (±1744-1803)

The family of the attorney Thomas Nettleship, eldest son of Thomas Nettleship (senior), remains unclear. There are no records of a marriage or any births or deaths, so it may be that he remained unmarried. In his will he appointed his brother William as executor; his nephews, nieces, and his brother William were the main beneficiaries.

William Nettleship followed his brother to the grave two years later. He likewise appears to have been childless. In his will he mentioned his nephews Samuel, Thomas, and William, of Grocer's Hall, London, 'sons of his late brother Henry'; they, along with Anne, were the main beneficiaries.

On 13 March 1824 Agnes Witts mentioned that she was '... meeting Mr and Mrs Nettleship'. This was probably William and Mary. On 28 May 1824 she wrote, 'went in the evening to a small party at Mrs. W. Nettleshipps, their House excellent.' She mentioned a Miss Nettleship on 14 April 1822, probably Anne [Anna], the unmarried daughter of Henry. A Mrs Mary Nettleship was registered as a Cheltenham resident in 1830, living at 1 Sandford Place; where she fits into the picture remains unclear.

1801: 13 Nov: *Dined at Mr. Markham's, his lady's birth-day feast: pleasant, because the Granvilles were there. Besides them, Mr. H. Hughes, Mr. Foulkes, Captn. Fotheringham, Mr. Nettleship &c.*

NEVILLE — the Miss Nevilles of Cheltenham [11]

Nothing has been found in relation to the Miss Nevilles. They were acquaintances of Agnes Witts and moved in the higher Cheltenham set, mixing with the Delaberes, Herries, Hughes, and Markham families among others. The Miss Nevilles met the Witts family in Edinburgh in September 1794 following a tour of the Highlands. Anne Neville was referred to as Mrs Neville, but whether she was really married and the mother of the Miss Nevilles is unclear; the prefix may simply have been due to the usual courtesy of giving the elder of a group of maiden sisters the title of 'Mrs'. In Agnes Witts's diaries there are other references: one to a Charles Neville in 1815 and numerous others to visits and general socialising. There also appears to have been a connection between the Neville and Watts families, but this has not been investigated with any success. There is a possibility that the Nevilles were related to the Nevilles of the Braybrooke barony.

1801: 22 May, 10 Jun: *Lady Lytteltons, accidental Music began, Miss Halifaxes sung, & Miss Morley; it was quite a squeeze: a Mr. Wood a nephew of Mr. Sheridan also sung in a very singular style. We met there the Hanbury's, Guydickens, Mrs. Scott & Miss Morley, Sir N. Dukinfield, Sir H. & Major Vavasour, Mr. Doig, Mr. Edwin Stanhope, Comte de Bruges, Miss Nevilles, Mr. & Mrs. Chambers, Miss Hungerford, &c.* 28 Oct: *Mr. and Mrs. Granville, & Miss Delabere, who looks ghostly, & Miss Nevilles, came in the evening.* 31 Oct: *Called upon Miss Hughes, Miss Neville &c.* 18 Nov: *Dined at Miss Nevilles, where we also spent the Evening, meeting our kind Granville Friends, Mrs. Bedingfield, Lady & Miss Herries &c.*

1802: 5 Aug: *Walked in the Even. with my Parents & Mrs. Nevilles on the Well Walk.* 15 Aug: *At a party at Miss Nevilles in the Evening.* 24 Aug., 27 Aug: *Drank tea at Mr. Nevilles, meeting Miss Markham, Dr. Sanders, Mr. Cruickshanks, Captn. Rogers.* 29-30 Aug., 1-3 Sep.

1804: 19 Oct: *In the forenoon called on Nevilles, Sheldons &c.*

1806: 27 Jun: *To a large, pleasant party at Lady Ford's; the Miss Nevilles & Mary Ford playing, conversed with the Goolds, Adairs, Salters, Cox, Miss Ford &c.*

NEVILLE — Louisa Anne Neville — *see also* Henry Vavasour [12]

Louisa Anne Neville (±1823-1889) was the daughter of Richard Griffin, 3rd Baron Braybrooke (1783-1858), and Jane Cornwallis (1799-1857), daughter of Charles Cornwallis, 2nd Marquess Cornwallis. Her father was known as Richard Neville until 1797 and as Richard Griffin between 1797 and 1825. He married Jane Cornwallis in 1819 and together they had 5 sons and 3 daughters. Richard Neville succeeded as 3rd Baron Braybrooke in 1825.

Louisa married Sir Henry Mervin Vavasour, 3rd baronet (1814-1912); they had 1 daughter:

1 Constance (±1856-1927)

1853: 1 May: *She communicated to me, but not before I had received the intelligence from another quarter, that her brother Sir. Henry is engaged to marry the Hon. Louisa Neville, a younger daughter of Lord Braybrooke: reported to be pleasing, 31 years of age, and with a fortune of £10,000: he is 38 years old, and the connection is altogether suitable: the recent windfall by Mrs. Campbell's decease places him in easy, though not in affluent circumstances.*

NEWBIGGING — Robert Newbigging [13]

Robert Dundas Newbigging (1782-1823), legal writer, was born in the parish of St Cuthbert's, Edinburgh, son of James Newbigging (d. 1814), Edinburgh sheriff's clerk, of Whitehouse, Bruntsfield Links, Edinburgh, and Mary Mirtle. He had at least four sisters: Mary (b. 1775), Agnes (b. ±1784), Henrietta (b. ±1784), and Harriet, the last of whom married, 1825, Archibald Gibson. Robert Newbigging presumably went to the high school in Edinburgh; he was a schoolfriend of long-standing with Francis Witts. They were also at Oxford together; Robert was at St John's College, but took his degrees late (BA 1813; MA 1814). He appears to have entered the legal profession and become a legal writer, publishing, as early as 1807, a work entitled *Disput. jurid. ad Tit. 7 Lib. xii Digest: De condictione sine causa.* In 1816 he was appointed to the office of sheriff substitute of the upper ward of the county of Lanark. He died there in 1823. It is unfortunate that so little has been found relating to this old friend of Francis Witts.

1799: 25 Aug: *Finished a letter to R Newbigging.*

1801: 2 Apr: *I met, some I instantly renewed: & with pleasure enjoyed the conversation of Newbigging &c.* 8 Apr: *Mrs. Riddell called early in the morning, as did Mr. Newbigging, with whom I walked round the Calton hill & to Leith & back again.* 13 Apr: *Mr. Brougham &c. Mr. Hutton after sitting with me for half an hour, walked two or three turns in Princes Street; accompanying me afterwards as far as Georges Square on my Road to Mr. Newbigging's at Whitehouse, Bruntsfield Links, where I was invited to dinner. I arrived earlier than the rest of the party, but spent my time pleasantly with Mr. R. Newbigging.* 17 Apr., 20 Apr., 24 Apr., 28 Apr: *Called on Mrs. Halkett Craigie, & upon Mr. Newbigging &c. at Whitehouse.* 2 May: *I dined quite en'famille at Mr. Newbigging's, where I was kindly received.* 12 May, 1 Jul.

1802: 15-16 Jan., 29 Jan: *Heard from Newbigging, enclosing a letter from his father to Mr. Liston.* 16 Feb.

1803: 1 Oct: *Received a very old Letter from Newbigging, whom to my surprize I shortly afterwards met, a Gentleman commoner of St. Johns, tho' not till after I had answered his Letter. Walked with Edgell & Rashleigh & with Newbigging.* 2 Oct., 2 Nov: *Newbigging dined with me & Dowell joined us in the Evening.* 4 Nov: *Walked before breakfast with Dowell & Price. Afterwards with Dowell & Newbigging.* 5 Nov: *Dined famously with Newbigging at St. John's Gaudy, Messrs. Glead, Frith, Prower, Wynne & Mardenburgh made up the party; barring a short dispute, the Evening passed pleasantly enough.* 7 Nov., 12 Nov., 16 Nov: *Newbigging & Odell dined with me; Dowell & Lumsden joined the party.* 27 Nov., 3 Dec.

1804: 12 Feb: *Called on Newbigging & Odell on me.* 26 Feb: *With Newbigging greater part of the Evening.* 6 Mar: *With Brown, Paget, Newbigging &c. Drank wine with Trevenen, Mess*[rs.] *Ingram, Plymly, Crawley, Yeomans &c.*

NEWCOMBE — Catherine Newcombe — *see also* Twisleton [14]

Catherine Newcombe, née Wingfield (1797-1855), was the eldest daughter of Richard Wingfield, 4th Viscount Powerscourt (1762-1809), and his second wife, Isabella Brownlow (±1775-1848). She married, 12 July 1833, Revd Arthur Newcombe (1787-±1837), of Abbeyleix, Queen's County, son of William Newcombe and Elizabeth Bradell; they had at least 1 son and 1 daughter:

1 William Wingfield (1834-1857); died unmarried
1 Isabella (1836-1921); married, 18 September 1861, Sir John Christopher Guise VC (b. 1826), of the 90th Light Infantry, who fought at Crimea and during the Indian Mutiny; 2 sons and 2 daughters:
  1 Catherine Isabella (d. 1936)
  2 Mary Emily (d. 1948)
  1 John Henry (1865-1899)
  2 Arthur St Valery Beauchamp (1868-1928)

1838: 16 Aug: *Thence to the Rectory, where I met Twisleton with all his fine family of motherless children, and their maternal Aunt, Mrs. Newcome, the widow of an Irish Clergyman, and sister of the late Lord Powerscourt.*

NEWDIGATE — Francis Parker Newdigate — *see also* Parker *and* Sneyd [15]

Francis Parker Newdigate (1774-1862), landed proprietor, was the son of Francis Newdigate (±1752-1835) and Frances (1750-1809), daughter of Ralph Sneyd (1723-1793) and Barbara Bagot (1725-1796) of Ashcombe Park, Leek, Staffordshire. His paternal grandfather was William Parker.

Francis Parker Newdigate became lord of the manor of Kirk Hallam, near Ilkeston, Derbyshire, where there is a memorial window dedicated to his memory in the parish church. He was also lord of the manor of neighbouring West Hallam.

Most sources state that Francis Parker Newdigate was born Francis Parker, and that he changed his name to Newdigate on inheriting estates at Arbury and Harefield upon the death of his distant cousin Sir Roger Newdigate, 5th baronet. There is some confusion here; the *Oxford Alumni* states that it was his father Francis Newdigate (±1752-1835) who changed his name. Whatever the truth may be, after inheriting in 1806, Francis (junior) lived at Arbury Hall, Warwickshire. He was also a grandnephew of Sir Richard Newdigate, 3rd baronet. He married, 1820, Barbara Maria, daughter of George Legge, 3rd earl of Dartmouth; they had 9 sons and 2 daughters:

1 Francis William (1822-1893); married, first, Charlotte Elizabeth Agnes Sophia Woodford
1 Frances Barbara (1823-1897)
2 Charles John (±1823-1876), Church of England clergyman
3 William Henry (b. ±1824)
4 Edward Newdigate (1825-1902); appointed KCB
5 George (b. ±1826)
6 Alfred (1829-1923)

2 Caroline (b. ±1830)
7 Henry Richard Legge (b. ±1832)
8 Albert (b. ±1839)
9 Daniel (b. & d. 1840)

Newdigate is associated with the novels of Mary Anne Evans (George Eliot). Her father, Robert Evans, was born in 1773 at Roston, a hamlet lying close to Ellastone. The following is an extract from the *Gentleman's Magazine*:

> In 1796, Robert being twenty-three years of age, a gentleman named Mr. Francis Newdigate came to reside temporarily at Wootton Hall, near Ellastone, pending settlement upon a prospective inheritance at Kirk Hallam in Derbyshire. About this time Robert moved from Roston to Ellastone, and there opened a carpenter's shop on his own account. His industry and sound common sense attracted the attention of Mr. Newdigate, and when the latter went to Kirk Hallam in 1799 he appointed Robert his agent.

Mary Anne Evans apparently modelled part of the character of Adam Bede on her father during this period of his life. Sketches of Newdigate are also apparently included in her texts. Another version of the link between Robert Evans and Francis Newdigate goes as follows:

> In 1806, upon the death of Sir Roger Newdigate, Francis Newdigate inherited a life interest in the Arbury estate in Warwickshire, and Evans accompanied him thither in his old capacity. Colonel Newdigate, son of Francis, was much impressed by the merits of his father's agent, and through the colonel's influence Evans became agent to various other great landowners in the district. As became his position, Robert Evans was a sturdy Tory.

The dates given in the above extract do not completely match; Newdigate was still at Wootton in 1802. It is also unclear who Mrs Newdigate was; Newdigate's mother would have born with the name Parker. Agnes Witts's diaries add to the confusion. On 4 November 1791 she wrote, 'A beautifull clear Day & the sun quite warm, Miss Snows went away after Breakfast to Mr. Harts for a week, we took a charming walk dined at Mr. Newdigates at Wooton Hall no one but their own family, play'd both at Commerce & Vingt'un at each of which I was successfull.' On 1 January 1802 she wrote, '... dined at Mr. Granvilles, meeting Baron Wolff & to Tea & Cards Mr. & Mrs. Newdigate & Miss Parker, all went to Tysons Ball at the Upper rooms, immense crowd & therefore not pleasant.' Taking into account that Francis Parker Newdigate (1774-1862) inherited from his great-uncle, it seems logical to conclude that the Mr and Mrs Newdigate at Wootton Hall were either his parents or grandparents, and that the Miss Parker mentioned in Agnes Witts's diary was his sister. It appears, therefore, that most of the mentions in Francis Witts's diary refer to the elder Francis Newdigate, while the entry of 27 September refers to his son, Francis Parker Newdigate. The very first entry of 4 January 1802 was written at Bath, while the others were written at Calwich, Staffordshire.

1802: 4 Jan: *At the Pump Room, where I was agreably surprized by some very fine pieces of music by Handel, Corelli &c. Conversed there with Mr. Barrett, Mr. Granville &c. Dined in Alfred St. meeting Sir Pomposo Plausible or Baron Wolff a man like Rademaker. We all repaired together at nine to Tyson's, the Master of the Ceremonies Ball, Mr. & Mrs. Newdigate & a Miss Parker having joined our party.* 17 Sep: *Rode with Mrs. Granville & Fanny to the summit of Wever, Mrs. Newdigate came in the afternoon.* 20 Sep., 27 Sep: *With Mr. Granville, my Father, & Fanny to dine with F. Newdigate at Wootton.* 28 Sep: *Met Mrs. Lockhart & Miss McLeod there. Mr. Newdigate, Mainwaring, Shipley, Harland, J. Webbe, & Furnival dined & bowled at Calwich.* 1 Oct: *Miss Sneyd, Mr. Newdigate & Mrs Palmer dined at Calwich.* 4 Oct: *Walked & rowed. Mr. Newdigate dined with us.*

NEWELL — Thomas Newell [16]

Thomas Newell (±1765-1836), physician and JP, was a renowned doctor of medicine in the area. In 1820 he published an open letter to the *Literary Gazette* on the 'Misrepresentations contained in a Pamphlet recently published by Dr. Neale, upon the Subject of the Cheltenham Waters, Cheltenham.' In S. Y. Griffith's *Cheltenham* (1826), Newell was listed as 'T. B. Newell M.D., Surgeon Extraordinary to the King, 5 St. George's Place'. This was probably the same person that Francis Witts referred to as 'the great Cheltenham Apothecary' in his diary entry of 1801.

Thomas Newell was married to Lucretia (±1767-1839), and together they had at least 1 son:

1 Thomas Blackman (±1793-1850); *see below*

1801: 10 Nov: *adjourned to a party at Mr. Newell's, the great Cheltenham Apothecary, where I was against my desire forced to play at Cards, & could not enjoy the Conversation of Fanny or of any of the friends, whom I met there.* 14 Nov: *Miss Sophia & Miss Louisa Jones dined with us, the former, repairing with us to tea & Cards at Mr. Rooke's, where her powers of attraction fell before the unassuming preeminence of the amiable Fanny, who with the Granvilles, Mrs. Newell, & Miss Markham were also there.* 20 Nov: *Dined at Mr. Granville's, meeting Mr. & Mrs. Newell, & Mr. & Miss Hughes. Of course most agreeable; the Evening we spent there also, Fanny playing us, & dressed in blue ribbands looking charmingly.* 21 Nov: *At Mrs. Newell's in the Evening, to a great rout, as disagreable as such things always are, particularly so the Granvilles not being there.* 23 Nov., 25 Nov.

1802: 4 Sep.

1825: 11 Apr: *I found my aged relative confined to her sofa by a wound on the leg, which has afflicted her now for a month, and at her very advanced age, 86, there is certainly reason for apprehension. Her spirits appear good, but she is thinner & more feeble. The hurt was not occasioned by any accident, but came of itself, and the inflammation, now removed, was considerable, so that great fears were at first entertained. Under the advice of Dr. Newell, and Mr. Seager, an eminent Surgeon of Cheltenham, the wound is kept open.*

1826: 8 Feb.

1829: 22 Sep.

NEWELL — Thomas Blackman Newell [17]

Thomas Blackman Newell (±1793-1850), Church of England clergyman, was the son of Thomas and Lucretia Newell (*above*). He was educated at Christ Church, Oxford (BA 1815; MA 1817), and served as perpetual curate of Cold Salperton, Gloucestershire, from 1823 to his death in 1850. He married, at St Nicholas's, Worcester, 15 December 1831, Catherine Crane (±1805-1874); they do not appear to have had any children. The 'F. Newell' mentioned by Francis Witts in his diary entry of 30 March 1824 was probably Thomas Blackman Newell—the 'F' being a transcription error due to the similarity of the diarist's capital 'F' and 'T'.

1824: 30 Mar: *I left for Cheltenham on horseback, and at my Mother's met Mr. F. Newell, who acted as Commissioner to administer to my Mother an oath, as to the amount of my late poor brother's effects.*

1826: 8 Feb.

1828: 18 Oct: *The project was taken up by a Committee of Subscribers, and, I believe, some difficulties and disagreements have arisen; Dr. Newell, who was very earnest in the business, designed this Church as a provision for his son, who is Perpetual Curate of Salperton, an estimable man, but an invalid, & not well calculated for the situation, to which his Father destined him.*

1829: 20 May, 22 Sep.

1830: 10 May.

NEWMAN — the Newman family of All Cannings, Wiltshire

1806: 15 Aug., 30 Sep: *Called upon the Jaques's & rode with Mr. Jaques through Ashlington to All Cannings where we called upon Mr. Davis & Mr. & Mrs. Newman.* 26 Oct: *Called upon Mr. Newman's pleasant family at Cannings.*

1807: 4 Jan: *Called upon Mr. Newman's family at Cannings.* 12 Apr: *Walked to Stert, found Mrs. Newman, Miss & Master Newman, Mr. F. Gibbs, & young Lambert, with Mrs. Jaques.* 31 May, 6 Dec.

1808: 22 Jan: *Called at Wedhampton on Jacob Giddings, & on the Newmans at Cannings.*

NEWMAN — Mr Newman, undertaker, of Chipping Norton

1825: 17 Jan: *Mr. Newman, the Undertaker, an unobtrusive and respectable person, was the fourth in the mourning coach, which followed the hearse.*

NEWMAN — Abram Newman — Davison, Newman and Co. [18]

Abram Newman (1736-1799), grocer, was a partner in one of the leading grocers of eighteenth-century London, importing a wide range of produce including tea, coffee, sugar, and spices. Newman was born at Mount Bures, Essex, in 1736, and moved to London to begin his career as a grocer. In 1759 he married Mary Davison (1720-1783), the sister of Monkhouse Davison, a partner in the firm Rawlinson & Davison, 'dealers in coffee, tea, chocolate, snuff, etc.' The firm, situated 'at the sign of the three sugar loaves and crown' at 14 Creechurch Lane, Leadenhall Street, had been founded in 1650 as grocers and importers of West-Indian produce. Two years after his marriage, Newman was made a freeman of the Grocer's Company, and in 1764 he joined Rawlinson & Davison as a third partner. In 1771 the senior partner Thomas Rawlinson died, and the company became known as Davison, Newman and Co. In 1790, Newman purchased the manor of Mount Bures. Monkhouse Davison died three years later, and shortly afterwards Newman retired. He died in 1799 at his house in Fenchurch Street.

Davison, Newman and Co. is probably best known today for its tea chests being among those thrown into Boston Harbour during the Boston Tea Party in 1774. The company sought compensation from George III amounting to £480 for the loss of its tea. It was bought up by the West-Indian Produce Association Limited on 1 January 1911, but products branded with the company name are still being sold today, over 360 years after its foundation. Francis Witts used Davison, Newman and Co. for his basic grocery supplies from 1835 onwards.

1835: 1 Apr: *Wrote to Messrs. Davison, Newman & Co. our London Grocers.* 22 Apr., 24 Apr.

1836: 29 Aug.

1837: 7 Feb., 22 Jul.

1838: 26 Jan., 28 Jan., 5 May, 8 May, 23 Jun.

1839: 7 Jan.

1840: 9 Sep., 11 Sep.

1841: 5 Mar.

1842: 7 Jun., 10 Jun., 22 Aug., 24 Aug.

1844: 2 Mar., 30 Nov., 4 Dec.

1847: 16 Apr., 18 Apr.

NEWMAN — Edmund Lambert Newman [19]

Edmund Lambert Newman (1793-1874), solicitor, was born at Calne, Wiltshire, son of Mitchell Newman and Susan Mary. Articles of partnership in a firm of solicitors between Edmund Lambert Newman and William Henry Gwinnett (±1809-1891), both of Cheltenham, were raised in 1832. They were later joined in partnership by Rowland Ticehurst. Newman lived at 1 Pittville Lawn, Cheltenham. He had left the partnership by 1858.

1845: 8 Feb: *Mr. Ticehurst, a Partner in the house of Gwinnett, Newman, and Ticehurst, Solrs. Cheltenham, arrived from Stow, where he had been on a similar errand to Mr. Vavasour, with the will of the late Lady Burdett — as Vicar of Stanway, and Commr. I administered the oaths to my son as one of the Exors. of the late Lady Burdett's will.*

NEWMAN — Henry Wenman Newman [20]

Henry Wenman Newman (1788-1865), DL, JP, landed proprietor, and amateur naturalist, was born at Thornbury Park, Gloucestershire, son of Richard Newman-Toll and Grizel Pardy. He married, 1846, Frances Margaret Goodenough (1813-1904); they had at least 3 sons:

1 Henry Ashburnham Toll (b. 1847)
2 George William (b. 1850)
3 Richard Goodenough (1851-1852)

Henry Wenman Newman succeeded to the Thornbury Park estate on the death of his father in September 1829, but the family lived at Clifton. He was a lieutenant-colonel in the Royal North Gloucester Militia and was appointed DL in 1822. He was also a Gloucestershire JP and appointed high sheriff for Gloucestershire in 1835. The Newman family sold the Thornbury Park estate to the Howard family in 1850.

Newman was an amateur naturalist and published a short note in the 15 October 1861 issue of the *Journal of Horticulture*. It brought an enquiry by Charles Darwin: 'Would Col. Newman, who has so carefully attended to the habits of humble bees, have the kindness to state whether the queen humble bees are fertilised in the air or on the ground? I have a special reason for wishing to know this little fact, and whether the fertilisation does not often take place as late as in September?—C. DARWIN.'

There are numerous references to Newman in the diaries, but most merely note his presence at the assizes or sessions.

1823: 8 Apr., 14 Oct.

1824: 13 Jan., 27 Apr., 13 Jul., 19 Oct.

1825: 18 Oct.

1826: 10 Jan., 17 Oct.

1827: 24 Apr., 10 Jul.

1829: 13 Jan., 1 Apr., 28 Apr., 14 Jul., 22 Sep.

1830: 12 Jan., 20 Apr.

1832: 3 Jan: *Dr. Cooke presiding as Chairman. Among the matters of chief interest was the order made for rebuilding Lawford's Gate Bridewell, near Bristol, the mob having so destroyed the prison, that it must in a great measure be a new structure. The expence is calculated at above £5000—on the Motion of Mr. Scandrett Harford, who with Mr. Newman represented the Bristol bench of magistrates, it was agreed, that the building should be made fire-proof, and that it should be so contrived, according to a plan suggested by Maj. Gen. Jackson, the Officer commanding the troops at Bristol, that a few officers within the Bridewell might be able to hold out against any tumultuary body, by which it might be assailed.*

1834: 5 Nov: *Wrote to Mr. Newman, a Magistrate for the County resident at Clifton, with a detail of our Police arrangements, agreeably to a request which he had made to me at the last Sessions.* 26 Nov., 14 Dec:
Received a letter from Mr. Newman, who requests me to forward to the Clerk of Petty Sessions at Bristol a copy of the regulations of the Stow Police Association, and informs me that in consequence of my letter to him (Newman) on Nov. 5. which he communicated to Mr. E. Welby, the representative in Parliament for Grantham, our system of police has been adopted and is in force in that borough.

1835: 8 Jan: *Mr. Newman arrived this Evening from Bristol, whither he had gone in the morning to vote for the Conservative Candidates.* 6 Apr: *Went into Court. Sir. J. T. Coleridge, recently appointed to the Judicial bench presided at the Crown Bar; Sir. J. A. Parke sat at Nisi Prius... H. W. Newman Esqr. was the High Sheriff.*

1837: 7 Mar.

1838: 3 Jul., 16 Oct.

1839: 1 Jan.

1840: 20 Oct.

1846: 10 Aug: *At the Judges lodgings I had sat by Lysons and Stoughton, had seen much of Curtis Hayward, Newman & others.*

1853: 4 Apr: *Besides the Lord Lieutenant, there were present Col. Kingscote, Major Newman, and others holding commissions in the two Gloucestershire Regiments, Purnell & several others on the Grand Jury &c.*

NEWMAN — John Henry Newman[21]

John Henry Newman (1801-1890), theologian and cardinal, was born at 80 Old Broad Street in the City of London, the eldest son of John Newman (d. 1824), banker, and Jemima Fourdrinier (d. 1836). He was educated at Trinity College (BA 1820) and Oriel College, Oxford (MA 1823; BD 1836), and Lincoln's Inn (1819). He was a fellow at Oriel from 1822 to 1845, a tutor from 1826 to 1831, treasurer in 1828, dean in 1833, and vice-principal of St Alban Hall in 1825. He was vicar of St Mary the Virgin, Oxford, from 1828 to 1843, and seceded to Rome in 1845. He was raised to cardinal in 1879 and was instrumental in the founding of the Catholic University of Ireland. This evolved into University College, Dublin, which today is the largest university in Ireland. Newman was also a literary figure of note. His major writings include his autobiography *Apologia Pro Vita Sua* (1865-66), the *Grammar of Assent* (1870), and the poem *The Dream of Gerontius* (1865), which was set to music in 1900 by Edward Elgar as an oratorio.

The Oxford movement and Rome's growing popularity among the English clergy were serious concerns for the Anglican Church in the period towards the end of Francis Witts's life; they were themes to which he frequently returned in his diaries.

1837: 3 Jun: *I omitted to mention yesterday that I finished the perusal of Newman's 'Lectures on the prophetical office of the Church, viewed relatively to Romanism and Popular Protestantism', a very deep and interesting work, embodying the views of the pious and learned writer, and his school of divinity, now attracting so much attention, especially in the University of Oxford.* 4 Dec: *This sermon had been mentioned to me by Hall, the Ass. P.L. Commr., when he visited us, as a most bold, uncommon, and powerful discourse, and was followed in the same church, an on the same day, by another equally startling and vigorous sermon by Newman.*

1838: 5 Jan: *Enjoyed two or three hours of conversation on all manner of topics, many very interesting ... the opinions entertained by Newman, Pusey, Keble &c.* 19 Feb: *There was much general conversation, on politics, all being conservatives, and besides touching on topics of a local nature, the state of parties in and the interests of the Church were discussed, as well generally, as more privately between myself and Mr. Kennaway, who is apparently a very amiable, pious man bred up among the Evangelical Clergy, but moderate, and now disposed, I should say, to keep a middle course between that party and the High Church section owning Pusey and Newman as their leaders, and at present exercising no small influence, probably, to good, in the Church.*

1839: 27 Feb: *Concluded to-day the 4th. Vol. of "Newman's Sermons," not long since published: pious, impressive, subtle, eloquent, deep.* 11 Mar., 5 May: *The subject of his discourse was very interesting; the opinions held by the eminent Oxford divines and others who have attached themselves to the school of Newman, Pusey &c.*

1840: 22 Sep: *I also called on Mr. and Mrs. Riddell, at their lodgings near the new Church at Leckhampton, by whom I was obligingly received, but had not time to stay long: his manner continues to be hurried and abrupt, and he is still vehement in any view he takes of opinions and persons; especially bitter, at present, in his censure of those who adhere to the opinions of Dr. Pusey and Mr. Newman, whom, by a vulgar error, unworthy of a scholar, he designates as Papists.*

1842: 21 Jan: *Thus outvoters will be spared a journey to Oxford next week at a very ungenial season; and a momentous point, which has greatly agitated the public mind, has been settled; namely, that the opinions of the disciples of Newman, Pusey &c are not predominant among Members of the Convocation, but that about two fifths only were prepared to support, in his claim to Academical distinction as a Professor, an avowed adherent of the Newman School.* 22 Jan: *"A letter to the Bp. of Oxford on occasion of No. 90 In the series called "The Tracts for the Times. By J. H. Newman BD. Vicar of St. Mary's Oxford. Oxf. 1841."* 31 Jan., 4 Feb.

1844: 5 Apr., 26 Sep., 8 Oct: *The greater number of the non placets were young men; Dr. Pusey did not appear, Newman & J. Keble were present.*

1845: 13 Feb., 2 Jun: *My son reported to me the purport of a conversation he lately had with Mr. Copeland, the surgeon, at Cheltenham, whose brother was Curate to Newman, and, with himself, far advanced in Tractarian error.*

1847: 10 Jul: *"From Oxford to Rome," — a recent publication, partly narrative, and fiction, partly grounded on events of notoriety as to what has been called the Oxford movement, shewing the steps by which an able, pious, enthusiastic student, trained by Newman, entered into the Church of England, ministered as Curate, and passed over to the Church of Rome: intended also, it would seem, to shew that such a step is not necessary in point of conscience, for that the Anglican Church principles and practices, fully carried out, suffice to meet the utmost longings of the pious, and satisfy the demands of those who aspire to carry out the principles of the Catholic Church: — a fascinating book, and therefore to be distrusted ...*

NEWMAN — R. Newman, Stow Workhouse inmate

1837: 9 Nov: *The case of R. Newman, who has been detected in a presumed attempt to starve himself, secreting his food, actuated by mixed motives, partly from remorse, partly from a hope of exciting pity and alarm among the Guardians, and so inducing them to discharge him, and partly from dread of some punishment for escaping from the W.H. which he dreaded & hoped by this course to avert, engaged attention and occupied considerable time.*

NEWMAN — Thomas Newman [22]

Thomas Newman (1812-1882), surgeon, was the son of William Ireland Newman (1785-1849) and Margaret Lovesy (1791-1850). He was born at Norton House, Gloucestershire, and qualified MRCS. He married, first, Mary Ann Goode (1813-1862); they had at least 2 sons and 4 daughters:

1 Mary Louisa (1844-1919)
1 Ashwin Conway (1846-1907)
2 Mary (b. 1850)
3 Margaret (b. 1851)
4 Emily Rowlina (b. 1852)
2 Thomas Whithorn (b. 1854)

He married, secondly, Caroline Griffin (1832-1925); they had 1 daughter:

1 Blanche Caroline (1865-1933); married, at Islington, Middlesex, 31 March 1888, Goodrich Lardner Cook (1863-1949)

In the 1871 census Newman was registered as living in the High Street, Winchcombe, with his second wife Caroline and several of his children, including Blanche Caroline from his second marriage.

1844: 11 Jan: *The parties charged were defended by Mr. Smith, Attorney, Winchcomb, and Mr. Newman, Surgeon of the same place, came to give evidence as to the severe wound of the head which T. Herbert had recd. in the scuffle.* 29 Jan.

1848: 4 Jul: *In a short time Mr. Newman, the Surgeon, from Winchcomb, who had been sent for arrived, and remained with poor Sophy from 6 P.M. yesterday till 11 AM. to-day. GOD be thanked, the remedies used have been so far successful! Consciousness is now restored, and there is no head ache now when the patient is perfectly still.*

NEWMAN — Thomas Newman [23]

Thomas Newman (b. ±1822), farmer and grocer, was born at Great Rissington. He farmed 130 acres at Home Farm, Maugersbury, Stow-on-the-Wold, employing seven labourers. He was unmarried in 1851 and living with his sister Jane (b. ±1828). He married, June 1856, Alice Francome (b. 1836); they had at least 2 sons and 3 daughters:

1 Mark Francome (1859-1917); died at Omoana, Taranaki, New Zealand
2 John Paul Francome (±1859-1935); died at Ashburton, New Zealand
1 Alice Francome (1862-1875)
2 Emma (b. 1865)
3 Fanny (b. 1868)

Newman moved to Cricklade and later to Hullavington, Wiltshire, by which time he had given up farming and had become a grocer.

1854 11 May: ... *very few [guardians] present H W Lindow, R Comely, J. N. Wilkins, Newman (Maugersbury).*

NEWMARCH — Charles Newmarch [24]

Charles Newmarch (1782-1823), solicitor, was born at Halifax, Yorkshire, son of Joseph Newmarch (1755-1823) and Honor Ward (1757-1820). He was in partnership as an attorney with Theodore Gwinnett and Francis Welles at Cheltenham. Gwinnett became a bankrupt in 1813 and the partnership was wound up. Newmarch married, 21 August 1809, Carolyne Welles (1785-1867) of Marsh Hill, Prestbury; they had at least 1 son:

1 Charles Francis (1811-1878)

In 1811 Charles Newmarch was clerk to the Gloucester and Cheltenham Railway (a horse tram), and his brother George (*below*) was a tenant of the same company at Wotton, Gloucester. By 1820 Charles lived at Priory Cottage, High Street.

1823: 24 Dec: *The Attorneys, Welles, Gwynnett & Newmarch, who succeeded to the office in Cheltenham of Mrs. Tracy's Steward, Mr. Markham, took up and prosecuted at their own expence and hazard the cause of these sisters, and after much research, many difficulties, and great anxiety, established their claim in such a manner, as to leave little doubt of their ultimate success. At this juncture, in 1805, it occurred to my Father and Mother to make themselves known to the three sisters, and to solicit their patronage for me on the decease of my uncle Ferdinand Travell, the Rector of Upper Slaughter ...*

NEWMARCH — Charles Henry Newmarch [25]

Charles Henry Newmarch (1824-1903), Church of England clergyman and author, was born at Burford, Oxfordshire, the second son of George Newmarch and his wife, Mary (*below*). He was educated at Rugby School and Corpus Christi College, Cambridge. He spent time in the merchant navy in his younger years, and published in 1847 *Five Years in the East* under the pseudonym R. N. Hutton. The book attracted favourable reviews, and was followed in 1848 by *Recollections of Rugby, by an Old Rugbeian*, and a novel, *Jealousy*. Settling in his home town of Cirencester, Newmarch demonstrated a keen interest in local antiquities; in 1850 he wrote with James Buckman (1814-1884) *Illustrations of the Remains of Roman Art in Cirencester*. In 1851 he was instrumental in the founding of the *Cirencester and Swindon Express*, which was soon amalgamated with the *Wilts and Gloucester Standard*. Newmarch was joint editor of the paper and, until the end of his life, a regular contributor under the name of Rambler. In 1868 he published with his brother an account of the Newmarch pedigree.

Charles Henry Newmarch married, at Cheltenham, 6 February 1855, Anne Straford (1832-1910) of Cheltenham and Charlton Kings; they had 2 sons and 3 daughters:

1 Ernest Charles (1855-1897)
1 Emily Mary (1857-1882)
2 Bernard (1858-1896)
2 Geraldine (1862-1885)
3 Clara Judith (1863-1956)

After his ordination, Newmarch was appointed rector of Wardley-cum-Belton, Rutland, in 1856. He held the living until 1893, and also served as rural dean of the district for ten years from 1857. He was greatly interested in agricultural matters, and was a frequent contributor on the subject to *Bell's Life*. Newmarch championed the cause of village labourers, who in turn defended him against the attacks of Joseph Arch, when Arch visited Belton on his tour of the village districts in 1872.

1837: 10 Jul: *Mrs. N. a civil and respectable person: the elder son, Frederick, a fine, intelligent, well conducted young man, in his Father's office; the younger son, a school boy, now in delicate health.*

1840: 26 Sep: *In the evening Mr. and Mrs. Newmarch, accompanied by their younger son, who has left Rugby, and is now in his father's office, arrived in their open carriage from Cirencester, to pass a day or two with us. Mr. N. suffering much, as usual, from his arm. This was Mrs. N's first visit to us: she is a lady like woman; the son a nice, reserved lad.*

1847: 25 Nov: *A letter from the elder Newmarch, who informs me that his younger Son, having been obliged in consequence of ill health to relinquish his profession as a sailor,—an officer on board an East Indian Trader,—has employed himself, not unprofitably, in telling his tale of what he had seen in his voyages to and from India and China, in a publication which has lately appeared, entitled, "Five years in the East by R. N. Hutton".* 26 Nov., 1 Dec: *Received letters from the elder Mr. Newmarch and his son Charles with reference to the book published by the latter, and the copy which he had promised to send to me by the carrier, but which, by some mistake, has not been forwarded.* 7 Dec: *The promised book, "Five years in the East" by Hutton als. Charles Newmarch came to-day.—It appears to be written in a pleasant light, gossiping style, & gives much, but not deep, information on the many countries visited, mixed with personal narrative.*

1850: 22 Jun: ... *the other from the Messrs. Bailey, publishers of the work by Newmarch and Buckman on the Roman remains at Cirencester, announcing that it is ready for distribution.*

NEWMARCH — George Newmarch — *see also* Sewell[26]

George Newmarch (1791-1857), solicitor, was born at York, the third son of Joseph Newmarch (1755-1823) and Honor Ward (1757-1820). He married, 1815, Mary Hardy (1792-1851); they had 2 sons:

1 George Frederick (1817-1891)

2 Charles Henry (1824-1903); *see above*

In the 1841 census, George was listed as living with his sons, George Frederick, listed as a solicitor, and Charles, listed as a solicitor's clerk. It is unclear what had brought him to Gloucestershire, but it was probably something to do with his elder brother Charles (*above*).

Until the 1840s all Francis Witts's legal matters were handled by George Newmarch (senior). By the 1840s Joseph Sewell entered the partnership and eventually took a senior position; the firm was then renamed Sewell and Newmarch. By that stage George's eldest son George Frederick had also joined the firm.

References to the firm from the early 1840s onwards are to be found under George Newmarch (junior), while those from June 1848 are listed under the entry for Sewell and Newmarch.

1823: 15 Dec: *Mr. Newmarch, the Solicitor of Burford, dined and slept here; transacted some business with him.*

1824: 13 Sep: *Mr. G. Newmarch, the Attorney, dined here, having come on business relating to the money, which under our marriage settlement is on mortgage of an estate at Ilmer in Bucks. Mr. N. is about to leave Burford for Cirencester, where he is to go into partnership with Mr. Lawrence.*

1825: 9 Jul: *In passing through Burford, I called at the office of Messrs. Newmarch & Price to ascertain whether some business of ours entrusted to them had been brought to a conclusion this day, as was proposed.* 22 Oct: *I went by coach to Burford, where I had business with my attorney, Mr. Newmarch, relative to the administration to my poor Mother's effects.*

1826: 24 Apr: *We travelled post by the accustomed road through Cirencester; at that place we waited half an hour, while I called on Mr. Newmarch, our Solicitor.* 4 Aug., 7 Aug., 28 Aug., 5 Sep.

1828: 20 Oct.

1829: 2-3 Apr.

1832: 27 Mar: *Communicated to Mr. Newmarch, my Solicitor, and Steward of Lord Sherborne, that the sum of £310 had been paid by my bankers in London to his account, in fulfilment of the purchase by me of the Pleasure ground before the Rectory house at Upper Slaughter... it was important, that I should purchase the freehold, as I am now the owner of the advowson of the Rectory itself. The latter I acquired by purchase of Mr. Lawrence of Sandywell Park, in December last, and it cost me £1016. 5. the sum fixed by Mr. Fulljames, after a survey made by him as an arbitrator mutually fixed on by Mr. Lawrence and myself.*

1834: 15 Jul: *A letter from Mr. Newmarch, fixing to come to U Slaughter on Saturday to consult about the measures necessary in respect of the property at Ravenflatt and Cracoe, lately devolved to my wife on the decease of the life-tenant, Mrs. Moorhouse.* 19 Jul: *Newmarch arrived here from Cirencester on horseback before breakfast.* 25 Jul., 29 Jul., 1 Aug., 5-6 Aug., 23 Sep., 27 Sep., 9 Oct., 11 Oct: *Mr. Newmarch arrived before dinner, intending to stay with us till Monday morning. Conferred with him on the difficulty raised by Mr. Walters as to the Cracoe property.* 12 Oct: *Much conversation on business and otherwise with Newmarch, whose calm, judicious good sense and information on other points as well as professional make him a very agreeable acquaintance.* 18 Oct., 20 Oct., 23 Oct., 25 Oct: *Heard from Newmarch stating that he might leave Dublin earlier than he had expected.* 11-12 Nov., 14 Nov., 17 Nov., 21 Nov., 13 Dec.

1835: 12 Jan., 18 Jan., 20-21 Jan., 14 Feb: *A letter from Mr. Newmarch, covering one which he had received from Mr. Walters on the business relating to Ravenflat & Cracoe. Mr. W. has sent a mass of papers, abstracts of title deeds &c. to Mr. N. who will examine them carefully and be prepared to report upon them to us some days hence, when he proposes to come hither to consult with us as to the measures proper to be adopted for the establishment of our claims. Mr. N. insinuates that we shall find that Dr. H. Moorhouse died possessed of leasehold property only.* 18 Feb., 21 Feb: *Mr. Newmarch arrived to dinner with a Mass of Papers, abstracts of title &c. forwarded to him by Mr. Walters from Newcastle, all bearing upon our claim to the late Dr. H. Moorhouse's Estates at Ravenflat and Cracoe. Conferred on their content and determined upon submitting a case to Mr. Wilbraham of the Chancery Bar for his opinion.* 22-24 Feb., 3 Mar., 5 Mar., 13 Mar: *Received a letter from Mr. Newmarch, explaining that the case to be submitted to Counsel as to the Ravenflat and Cracoe business had not yet been forwarded, owing to a domestic affliction which he had experienced in the sudden death of a brother.* 21 Mar., 26 Mar., 1 Apr., 4 Apr., 7 Apr: *From Mr. Newmarch also I received a letter and parcel containing Mr. Wilbraham's opinion on the case submitted to him as to our claim under Dr. H. Moorhouse's will to the Estates at Ravenflat and Cracoe. As far as I can judge ... Mr. Wilbraham is of opinion that our claim to the freehold is unquestionable, that as to the leasehold we have a claim to as much thereof as shall be a full equivalent for the value of the ... but that owing to the great difficulty... he would recommend a compromise between ourselves and Mr. Walters.* 8 Apr., 11-12 Apr., 18 Apr., 26 Apr., 29 Apr., 2 May: *Mr. Newmarch arrived to dinner, and slept here.* 3 May: *Before breakfast conferred further with Newmarch on the Ravenflat business.* 11 May, 15 May, 23 May, 5 Jun., 15 Jun., 17 Jun: *Mr. Newmarch & Son came to breakfast.*

1836: 23-24 Jul., 29 Jul: *Mr. Newmarch had reached Northleach from Cheltenham before us. He laid before us two opinions which he had taken from Knight and Parry, Chancery Barristers, on our claim to the Rilston, Cracoe and Ravenflat estates.* 4 Aug., 6 Aug., 13 Aug., 15 Aug., 23 Aug., 26 Aug: *Between two and three o'clock Stevens left us for Shipston on Stour, in preparation for an attendance at the weekly meeting of the Guardians of that Union to-morrow: and not long after his departure arrived Mr. Newmarch and his eldest Son from Sherborne to dine and sleep with us. The object of this visit was that we might confer on the proper steps to be taken in consequence of Mr. R. Walters's peremptory refusal to recognize our claim to the Ravenflat and Cracoe properties.* 27 Aug., 30 Aug., 7 Sep., 12 Sep., 25 Sep., 21 Oct., 4 Nov: *Received a letter from Newmarch, announcing that Mr. Parry of the Chancery bar had prepared the Bill which we are about to file against the Trustees of the late Dr. H. Moorhouse & that Newmarch had carefully examined it, and returned it to Town to be forwarded as quickly as the forms of the Court will admit.* 14 Nov: *A letter from Newmarch communicates that our bill against Mr. Walters and his son has been put upon the file of the Court of Chancery, and Mr. Knight retained as leader in the Cause.* 13 Dec: *Received a letter from Newmarch who is returned from Ireland, and proposes to come to us to dine & sleep on Friday next.* 16 Dec.

1837: 7 Jan., 10 Jan., 17 Jan., 21 Jan., 29 Jan: *A letter from Newmarch to the effect that the time had expired within which Mr. Walters should have put in his answer to the bill we had filed in Chancery, but that he had not done so, and, consequently, was liable to an attachment. Mr. W.'s agent had, however, applied for ten days delay, which N. considered it prudent to grant.* 5 Mar: *A letter from Newmarch, who has been very seriously indisposed in Town.* 12 Mar: *Received a letter from Newmarch accompanying two opinions given by Mr. Parry, our counsel, on the answer put in by Messrs. Walters to the bill we have filed against them: pointing out the course to be now pursued.* 13 Mar., 16-17 Mar., 22 Mar., 28-29 Mar., 31 Mar., 15 Apr., 19 Apr., 2 May, 9 May, 11 May: *Recd. a letter from Newmarch in answer to the one I wrote to him on Tuesday about his horse, in which he mentioned that Mr. Walters's counsel has been suggesting to our Counsel, Mr. Parry, that, perhaps, a compromise might be effected between Walters and us: it does not clearly appear from Newmarch's letter what the proposition hinted at is; but the intimation well deserves to be followed up.* 13 May, 15 May, 20-21 May, 24 May, 31 May: *A letter from Newmarch with a correspondence on the proposed compromise between Mr. Walters and ourselves, which had passed between Walters's professional agent in London, and the agent of Messrs. Lawrence and Newmarch.* 2 Jun: *Newmarch came before breakfast from Cirencester, with whom we had a long conference respecting our chancery suit, and the conditions on which it would be right to compromise with Walter.* 10 Jun., 20 Jun., 21 Jun: *Wrote to Messrs. Newmarch and Lawrence (N. being gone to the Isle of Wight) to offer £525 for the Bourton land tax.* 28 Jun., 30 Jun: *Recd. a letter from Newmarch, who is in the Isle of Wight, conveying to me Mr. Walters's comments on the proposition made by us for a compromise, which he rejects, but makes another offer, which Mr. Parry considers it would be wise in us to close with.* 7 Jul., 9 Jul: *Recd. a letter from Newmarch, apprizing me of his return to Cirencester from an excursion yesterday, and that he will be ready to confer with me there to-morrow, though much engaged, unless I should prefer Tuesday; he proposed that my Son and myself should drive over to-morrow Evening, & sleep at his house.* 10 Jul: *Arrived there at ½ past 10 o cl. and had an hour's conference with Newmarch at his office on our Ravenflat affair, when we agreed to accept the terms of compromise last proposed by Mr. Walters.* 22 Jul., 8-10 Aug., 16 Aug., 18 Aug., 26 Aug., 1-2 Sep., 5 Sep., 13 Sep., 19 Sep., 29 Sep., 3 Oct., 5 Oct., 15 Oct., 18 Oct., 21 Oct: *There settled ourselves at the Golden Lion, and found a letter from M.W. with a good account from home, conveying two letters from Newmarch which she had forwarded, and which purported that he had met Mr. R. Walters in town, who had executed the conveyance to us of the Ravenflat property.* 26 Oct., 10 Nov., 12-13 Nov., 16 Nov., 21 Nov., 25 Nov., 28 Nov.

1838: 13 Jan., 16 Feb., 18 Feb., 23 Feb., 25 Feb., 28 Feb., 10 Mar., 12-13 Mar., 14 Mar: *Mr. Newmarch arrived to dine and sleep here from Dr. Warneford's, whither he had gone on business in the morning.* 15 Mar., 17 Mar., 22 Mar., 31 Mar., 4 Apr: *A letter from Mr. Newmarch appointing Saturday at 2 P.M. for an interview with Mr. Vavasour and myself on the proposed Marriage Settlements.* 5 Apr., 7 Apr., 24 Apr., 29-30 Apr., 2-3 May, 6-8 May, 15 May, 27 Jul., 14 Aug., 5 Oct: *Recd. a letter from Mr. Newmarch offering to pass to-morrow evening with us on his return from Bourton on the Hill, to sleep here, and to leave us after morning service on Sunday.* 23 Oct., 26 Oct., 29-30 Oct., 1 Nov., 11 Nov., 13-14 Nov., 16 Nov., 3 Dec., 7 Dec.

1839: 5 Jan., 8 Jan., 12 Jan., 16 Jan: *Newmarch arrived from Cirencester and Northleach in the evening to tea, and slept here.* 17 Jan., 21 Jan., 2 Feb., 4-10 Feb., 13-14 Feb., 19-21 Feb., 26 Feb: *A letter from Newmarch left at L Slaughter Turnpike, as he passed through to Bourton on the Hill this morning announcing his intention of being with us by dinner time.* 27 Feb: *Mr. Newmarch left us for Cirencester before breakfast.* 22 Mar., 30 Mar., 6 Apr., 8 Jul., 19 Jul., 21 Jul., 3 Aug., 8-9 Aug.

1840: 24-25 Mar., 6 Jun., 7 Jun: *Wrote to Newmarch that we shall be prevented having the pleasure of receiving him & his wife on Thursday next, as our only spare double bed will be occupied by the Daniells; but that if any circumstance should prevent Mrs. N. from accompanying him to Bourton on the Hill, a Bachelor's bed should be at his service.* 4 Sep., 9 Sep., 15 Sep: *Wrote to Newmarch in answer to his letter recd. on the 9th. Inst. that we should be glad to see him, Mrs. N., and his youngest son on the 26th. to pass two days with us.* 24 Sep., 26 Sep: *In the evening Mr. and Mrs. Newmarch, accompanied by their younger son, who has left Rugby, and is now in his father's office, arrived in their open carriage from Cirencester, to pass a day or two with us. Mr. N. suffering much, as usual, from his arm. This was Mrs. N's first visit to us: she is a lady like woman; the son a nice, reserved lad.* 28 Sep: *The Newmarches left us after an early breakfast to return to Cirencester. Mr. N's professional engagements did not allow of their being prevented by the bad weather from proceeding homewards.*

1842: 12 Jan: *Received a letter from G Newmarch, dated from York, announcing to me his retirement from the duties of his profession and all its engagements, of which I had already been apprized by his son.* 14-15 Jan., 18 Mar: *Heard but an indifferent account of the elder Newmarch, in respect of his health: called at his house, but not admitted, neither was Mrs. Newmarch at home.* 1 Sep., 25 Oct., 30-31 Oct.

1843: 7 Feb., 19 Aug., 25 Sep., 2 Oct., 1 Nov., 25 Nov., 30 Nov., 2 Dec., 5 Dec., 16 Dec.

1844: 28 Jan., 25-26 Mar., 29 Mar., 1 Apr., 4 Apr., 29 Jul: *Wrote to Mr. Newmarch, to name that I should direct Messrs. Hoare to pay £100 to the account of himself and his partner with the Gloucestershire Banking Company at Cirencester, in part payment of the sum advanced to me by them to make up the amount lent on mortgage to Mr. Lockhart.* 31 Jul., 1 Aug: *Recd. a letter from Mr. Newmarch, accompanying a copy of my cash account with himself and partner.*

1845: 21 Jan., 8 Feb., 26 May.

1847: 4 Jun: *Recd. a letter from Newmarch Senr., or, rather, copies of a correspondence between him and Lord Sherborne relative to the disagreement between them as principal and agent, which have been existing for some years past—N. considers himself aggrieved, and, probably is so: his desire seems to be that his and his Son's clients should be in possession of his case against Lord S. and his L'ship's evading to do him justice.* 25 Nov: *A letter from the elder Newmarch, who informs me that his younger Son, having been obliged in consequence of ill health to relinquish his profession as a sailor,—an officer on board an East Indian Trader,—has employed himself, not unprofitably, in telling his tale of what he had seen in his voyages to and from India and China, in a publication which has lately appeared, entitled, "Five years in the East by J. N. Hutton".* 26 Nov.

1854: 29 Jun: *Conferred on business to come before the Petty Sessions with Mr. Newmarch, attending for Sewell, who is gone with his family to the sea in Norfolk.*

NEWMARCH — George Frederick Newmarch[27]

George Frederick Newmarch (1817-1891), solicitor, was educated at Rugby School. He followed in his father's footsteps, becoming a solicitor and joining the family's legal firm. He lived at 55 Sheep Street, Cirencester, and remained unmarried.

1837: 10 Jul: *Frederick, a fine, intelligent, well conducted young man, in his Father's office; the younger son, a school boy, now in delicate health.*

1838: 30 Apr: *Wrote to Newmarch on the same subject; also on my son's concerns, that since it appeared necessary that there should be additional Trustees to his marriage Settlt. it was probable that on the lady's side Sir H. Vavasour would be appointed, and that Edwd. would take it as a favour, if Frederick Newmarch would consent to act in that capacity.* 2 May.

1842: 15 Jan., 19 Jan., 21 Jan., 24 Jan., 26 Jan: *A letter from F. Newmarch, stating that, in consequence of Mr. Price of Burford having commenced a canvass on his behalf in the neighbourhood of Witney and Burford for the Clerkship of the Crickley Hill district of Turnpike Roads, he had determined to sally forth as to day to solicit votes for himself, and proposed to dine and sleep here.* 27 Jan., 31 Jan., 2 Feb., 6 Feb., 8 Feb., 12 Feb., 22 Feb., 28 Feb., 3-4 Mar., 12 Mar., 18 Mar: *Called at Newmarch's offices, where only saw Clerks, G F N. being gone into Somersetshire, and Sewell to London.* 22 Mar., 23 Mar: *G F Newmarch was appointed to the office in lieu of his Father, being proposed by Mr. Elwes, and seconded by me.* 25 May, 26 Aug., 30 Aug., 26 Sep., 29 Sep., 29 Nov., 30 Nov: *A letter from G. F. Newmarch, fixing Friday as the day on which he will visit us here.* 2 Dec., 7 Dec., 18 Dec., 20 Dec: *After breakfast, Mr. G. F. Newmarch came on his road from Cirencester to Bourton on the Hill, to wait on Dr. Warneford, and fixed half past 3 PM. as the hour at which he proposed to return to transact his business here.* 21 Dec., 23 Dec.

1843: 6 Jan., 14 Jan., 17 Jan., 10 Feb., 18 Aug., 27-28 Sep., 3-4 Oct., 8 Oct., 10 Oct., 13 Oct., 20 Oct., 22-23 Oct., 26-27 Oct., 3 Nov., 5-6 Nov., 13-15 Nov., 8 Dec., 20 Dec.

1844: 22 Jan., 25-26 Jan., 31 Jan., 1-2 Feb., 6 Feb., 13 Feb., 16 Feb., 27 Feb., 8 Mar., 19 Mar., 24 Jul.

1845: 18 Jan., 25 Jan., 28 Jan., 10 Feb., 22 Feb., 12 Mar., 20 May, 4 Jul., 7 Jul., 11 Jul.

1846: 8 Jun: *... also to G. F. Newmarch, explaining to him that I should not be able to pay £500, part of the money to be advanced on mortgage to Mr. Lockhart, till after the 6th. July, when the sale of Stock could be effected: that I would desire Messrs. Hoare to remit to him £250 prior to the 23d. Inst. in part of the sum to be lent to Mr. L: that I should rely on his providing temporarily £750 to make up the £1000 — of which I should pay £500, when the Stock was sold, and the residue as soon as my accounts with my bankers would permit.*

1847: 5 Jun: *Wrote to G. F. Newmarch with reference to the documents forwarded to me which arrived yesterday, as to late correspondence between Lord Sherborne and his Father, regretting that it was not more satisfactory, and expressing my good will to N. and persuasion of his integrity.* 6 Oct.

1848: 18 Jan., 10 Feb., 11 Feb., 19 Mar.

1850: 14 Feb., 19 Mar.

1851: 13 Feb., 21 Feb., 23 Mar., 7 May, 22 May.

1852: 10-11 Feb., 14 Feb., 30 Mar.

NEWNHAM — William Moore Newnham — *see also* Townsend[28]

William Moore Newnham (1755-1832), Church of England clergyman, was the son of William Moore Newnham (d. 1796) of Ash, Surrey. He was educated at Corpus Christi College, Oxford (BA 1775; MA 1779). He married, 22 November 1804, at Clifton, Susan [Susanna] (1775-1853), born at Grenada in the West Indies, the daughter of Thomas Townsend. Elizabeth Munro and Caroline, Charlotte, Sophie, and Jane Townsend were her sisters.

William Newnham was rector of Bassingham, Lincolnshire, a living within the gift of Corpus Christi College. He also held the living of Midsomer Norton, Somerset. He and his wife Susan had at least 1 son and 1 daughter:

1 George William (1806-1893)

1 Sophia Elizabeth (1808-1876); married, at Midsomer Norton, 9 September 1831, William Batchellor (1808-1876) of Holcombe, Somerset; lived at Walcot, Bath

The following extracts from the diaries of Agnes Witts throw a fraction more light on the picture: 27 February 1804: '... had visits from Lord Mayo, Mrs. & Miss Venours & Mrs. Blackburn after visiting Mr. Townshend just returnd home & bringing his Daughter Mrs. Monro with him ...'; 15 March 1804: 'Mrs. Monro & Sophie Townsend, & Mrs. Upton here before I went to Mrs. J. Ram....'; 22 November 1804: 'Mr. Townshend here early to inform us of the marriage that Morning of his eldest Daughter to Mr. Newnham....'; 29 November 1804: 'took shelter in a violent storm of rain at Mrs. Monros at Richmond Terrace'; 4 January 1805: '... but had visitors in abundance, Mrs. Monro, Mrs. Newnham, & Miss Jane Townsend ...' No further information has yet been uncovered.

1804: 11 Sep: *Mr. Nuneham &c. Mr. Port & Mr. Townsend called.* 12 Sep., 15 Sep: *accompanied Mrs. Monro, Misses S. C. & Car. Townsend, Mrs. Nuneham & Matthew on a walk.* 23 Dec: *Walked to Clifton with the Newnham party, called with them upon the Townsend's. Found Mr. Newnham's conversation very instructive.* 24 Dec: *... called upon Mrs. Russell, a very obliging woman, & Mr. Newnham.* 28 Dec: *... party at Mr. Townsends & music; conversed much with my agreeable friend Mrs. Newnham.* 31 Dec.

1805: 1 Jan: *Conversed chiefly with Mrs. Newnham.* 4 Jan: *Called upon the agreeable Mr. Rennie, & Mr. & Mrs. Newnham.* 6 Jan., 11-12 Jan., 14 Jan., 18 Jan., 26 Jan., 31 Jan., 3 Feb., 5 Feb., 6 Feb: *Walked to Bristol, with Mr. Newnham, & the Townsend Family.* 8 Feb., 15 Feb., 28 Feb., 10 Nov., 14 Nov., 20 Nov., 26-27 Nov.

1806: 14 Jan: *Called upon the good Mrs. Monro & Mrs. Newnham.* 17 Jan., 19-20 Jan., 22 Jan., 9 Feb: *For a long time in very interesting Conversation with Mr. Newnham.* 10 Feb., 16 Feb., 21 Feb., 4 Mar.

NEWPORT — John Newport[29]

John Newport (±1783-1868), Church of England clergyman, was born at Frome, Somerset. He was a contemporary of Francis Witts at Oxford, but the two men do not seem to have known each other there. He was educated at St Alban Hall and Worcester College, Oxford (MA 1808). He was ordained deacon on 18 December 1808 and priest on 17 December 1809. His first clerical appointment was as curate of Haversham, Buckinghamshire, from 18 December 1808. He was then appointed curate of Bitton, Gloucestershire, on 9 September 1811, and by 30 December 1824 he was stipendiary curate of Elmore and Longney, Gloucestershire. He was finally appointed stipendiary curate of Hawling, Gloucestershire, on 27 August 1835. Newport did not have access to family patronage and his clerical appointments appear to have been lowly and poorly paid; the diarist alluded to this on 9 March 1842.

John Newport married Fanny (b. ±1784); they had at least 3 sons and 4 daughters:

1 Henry (1823-1890); educated at Cambridge; had a successful career as a headmaster and cleric
1 Amelia (b. & d. 1825)
2 Maria (b. 1826)
2 Theodore (1828-1900)
3 Frederick (1830-1848); buried at Hazleton where his father was a curate; the funeral was conducted by Revd John Walker Dolphin (1818-1859), later vicar of Lower Guiting, only son of George Dolphin of Hallow, Worcestershire
3 Fanny Amelia (b. 1832)
4 Lucy (b. 1834)

In the census of 1841 John Newport was registered as living with his wife Fanny (b. ±1784) and daughters Maria and Lucy. By 1851 he was a widower, retired, and living at Sevenhampton with his sister, Amelia Childs.

1842: 25 Feb., 2 Mar: *A letter from Bowen with a return as to the state of his Church and parish, and an appointment that I should visit the Church on the 8th. Inst. also from Mr. Newport with a like return as to Hawling, and a proposal that I should visit that church on the 10th. Inst.* 3 Mar., 9 Mar: *Kindly received by Mr. Newport, the Curate, a gentleman of worth, but oppressed with poverty, and a large family.*

1845: 26 May.

1846: 17 Jul.

NEWTON — Augustus Newton[30]

Augustus Newton (1802-1875), barrister and gambler, was born at Woodstock, Oxfordshire, son of John Frank Newton, of St Christopher, West Indies, and Cornelia Collins. He married, 1828, Letitia Frances, daughter of Adm. Sir Robert-Tristram Ricketts, baronet, and Rebecca Gumbleton of the Elms, near Cheltenham; they had 2 sons and 1 daughter:

1 Frank Robert (1829-1890)
2 William (b. ±1830)
1 Caroline (b. ±1838); married Dr Eichbaum

In 1851 the family was living at Wandsworth, and ten years later they were at 58 Curzon Street, Westminster. By 1871 Augustus had retired and he and Letitia were living at Battersea. It seems that he spent time in debtors' prison having accumulated gaming debts. In 1835 a case was made against him for £304 9*s* 6*d*. Another case was made in 1840:

> ... Plea that before the recovering of the said judgment in the declaration mentioned to wit on &c at a certain house then used as a common gaming house the said Augustus Newton did play at a certain game of cards called écarte other than with or for ready money with one Edward Claude Musack and the said E. C. Musack did then and there win of the said Newton at one time divers sums of money amounting together to the sum of £125 and the said sums having been so lost and won as aforesaid the said Newton did not pay down the same at the time when he so lost the same and for securing the payment thereof....

Finally Augustus Newton appeared in January 1856 at the court for relief of insolvent debtors. He was named in the court as follows: '... Augustus Newton, formerly of Heathfield, Wandsworth Common, Surrey, and also of No. 19, Manchester Buildings, Westminster, and afterwards also of No. 34, Essex Street, Strand, Barrister-at-Law, afterwards of No. 58, Curzon Street, Mayfair, and also of the Great Northern Hotel, King's-cross, all in Middlesex, Agent to a Mining Proprietor.' It would appear that the property listed was either in trust, or in his wife's name. Whatever the circumstance, Augustus Newton led a colourful life.

1843: 17 Oct: *Much time was taken up in going through the Gaol and Bridewell accounts, and in matter arising out of them and the different prison Journals; but nothing final could be settled on various points brought forward, owing to the uncertainty as to the Prison rules now pending before the Secretary of State, and the plans for improvement and enlargement which are equally unsettled: the result was that various points were reserved to be submitted to the Prison rules Committee, among them a long petition as to the arrangements of the debtors prison, emanating from the notorious Augustus Newton, Barrister, now confined there.*

1845: 1 Jan: *The interesting matter of the day was a fracas between the Chairman and the notorious Aug. Newton, Barrister.*

NEWTON — John Newton at Swerford

1805: 25 Mar: *Our party early interrupted by the arrival of Miss Anne Wheaton & her dear Champion, Mr. John Newton, in an Equipage fifty years old at least, in every part a great entertainment to us young people, who were more inclined to laugh at than to admire the Spinster & her favourite.*

NEWTON — Lord Newton — *see* Butler *and* Brinsley Butler

NEWTON — William Newton[31]

William Newton (b. ±1785), landed proprietor, was born at Lichfield, Staffordshire. He lived at Northfield House, Wotton, Gloucester, with his wife Joyce (±1783-1861), who was born at Gloucester.

1846: 10 Jul: *Wrote to W. Newton, Guardian of the Hamlet of Wotton near Gloucester, with a remittance for the maintenance of Moses Roff, chargeable to that place, having received the amount from his Father.* 29 Oct.

1847: 16 Jan.

NIBLETT — Miss Niblett, nurse at Malvern

1840: 24 Apr: *five domestics, viz. Abraham and Sarah Gibbs, Mr. Jacob, formerly Sch Gardener to my Aunt, and now Schoolmaster at the principal parochial school at Malvern, Mary Good, the under female Servant, and Miss. Niblett, the nurse.* 20-21 May.

NIBLETT — Daniel John Niblett and the Niblett family of Haresfield [32]

Daniel John Niblett (1785-1877), JP, DL, and landed proprietor, was the son of John Niblett and Catherine Whitcombe, daughter of Edward Whitcombe of Eastham, Worcestershire. He was educated at Trinity College, Cambridge. Niblett was a major in the Gloucestershire Militia and a JP and DL for Gloucestershire. He was also high sheriff for the county in 1816. He married, 1808, Emma Catherine (d. 1879), eldest daughter of Revd Thomas Drake, vicar of Rochdale; they had at least 5 sons and 3 daughters, including:

1 John Daniel Thomas (1809-1883), JP; succeeded his father as lord of the manor at Haresfield; married, 1849, Caroline Saunders; no children; appears in the diaries from 1845 onwards

2 Edward Henry (1810-1881); educated at Exeter College, Oxford; appointed vicar at both Redmarley d'Abitot and Haresfield; married, at St Andrew's, Clifton, 2 November 1848, Margaret Anne Stewart (b. 1824); 2 sons:

  1 Arthur Edward (1852-1904); married, at Christ Church, Lancaster Gate, London, 5 December 1883, Grace Ursula Cotgrave Farmer (1860-1958); 4 daughters

  2 Henry Morton (1854-1941); married, 1887, Marian; 2 daughters

3 Francis (1814-1883), architect; designed numerous buildings in Gloucester and Bristol; made alterations to Haresfield church and the manor house; married, 1853, Matilda Court; 1 son:

  1 John Morton (1854-1894); died childless

1 Katherine (1814-1867)

4 William (1815-1849)

5 Robert (1816-1860)

2 Elizabeth (b. 1821)

The family estates, including Harescombe, were bought by Catherine Whitcombe, Daniel's mother, in 1804, and passed to Daniel. He purchased Haresfield Manor in 1808 and increased the family holdings at Haresfield and Harescombe, eventually amassing about 1,000 acres.

Francis Niblett was chosen by Edward Witts to design the Witts memorial chapel at St Peter's, Upper Slaughter. The introduction almost certainly came about via Edmund Clifford, curate to Francis Witts. Edmund was related to the Niblett family and a friend of both Francis Niblett and Edward Witts. Francis Witts was incorrect in his diary entry for 31 August 1847; the architect was Francis, not Edward.

It is uncertain how Sophia Hunt became friendly with Mrs Niblett, née Whitcombe. Sophia's solicitor at Gloucester was a Whitcombe, and may have been Catherine's brother, which could explain it. This would also make a Gloucester connection for the Niblett family.

1824: 13 Jan.

1826: 16 Jun., 11 Jul.

1827: 10 Jul.

1828: 15 Jul., 14 Oct.

1829: 1 Apr., 14 Jul., 22 Sep., 20 Oct.

1830: 12 Jan.

1832: 29 Mar.

1835: 7 Jun: *Preparing for my journey to London to-morrow; and engaged in writing and conversation with Miss Sophia Hunt as to my Executorship. It is proposed that Mrs. Witts take Sophia as far as Cheltenham on Tuesday, from whence she will proceed to Gloucester, spend a day or two with Mrs. Niblett at Haresfield.*

1836: 7 Sep., 13 Sep: *I accompanied Bathurst, Baker and Niblett to the Gaol with Mason, some business requiring the presence of two or three Mag.*

1837: 22 Aug: *There were staying in the House Mrs. and Miss Niblett from Haresfield, and the Revd. Mr. Moore and Lady from Stratton near Cirencester, where he is, I believe, Curate.*

1840: 3 Jun: *Wrote to Sophia Hunt in answer to her letter received on the 27th. Ult. directing to her at the Niblett's at Haresfield, where I understood she was to arrive to-morrow—but sent for my letter back again from the Turnpike Gate, on receiving one from her from which it appeared that the visit to Haresfield was given up; Miss S.H. writes with details of a charge made by Whitcombe for business done in the business of the Turnpike securities belonging to the Hunt family.* 16 Oct: *The Misses Ford with Miss Niblett had called during our absence.*

1842: 30 Jun: *Far from well with a disordered stomach, but recovered in great measure before I started from the Railway Station for Cheltenham with Ford and his daughter Sophia, whom he had brought from home to pass the Session days with her friend Miss Niblett at Haresfield.*

1845: 6 Mar: *Opened my Court at 9 AM. and sat till 6 P.M — Messrs. Baker, J Niblett, Clutterbuck, Sayers, Dr. Davies &c. assisted me.* 7 Mar: *I was assisted by Messrs. Sayers, J. Niblett and others, and had tried 10 prisoners by 2 P.M. when I broke up, leaving another hour or two of work to be finished by C Hayward.* 15 Apr., 7 May.

1846: 18 Nov: *representing the County of Gloucester there were present Messrs. Curtis Hayward, in the chair, Purnell, Baker, Clifford, Timbrill, Viner, Baker, Sayers, Walters, J. Niblett & myself; Mr. Hyett represented the Subscribers.*

1847: 22 Mar: *There were present Purnell, Curtis Hayward, Baker (now hors de combat, as being High Sheriff,) Raymond Barker, Danl. John, T. Niblett, with the usual officials, Bloxsome, Riddiford, Wilton, Whitehead, Lefroy, Keiley &c.* 5 Apr., 31 Aug: *consecration of the district church of St. Mark's, built near the Kingsholm Turnpike ... Mr. Edward Niblett, son of Mr. N., the Magistrate, my old acquaintance, is the Architect.*

1848: 26 Jun.

1850: 19 Jun: *The work is well done under the directions of Mr. F. Niblett, Architect.* 18 Sep., 17 Oct., 18 Oct: *An excursion to Berkeley Castle, in two carriages—Mrs. Purnell, Mrs. Niblett, and Miss E. Purnell in a brougham——Mrs. Niblett, Miss Niblett, John and Fanny Purnell in Barouchette, driven by Purnell.* 19 Oct: *After breakfast, at 11 AM. I took leave of John Purnell and his amiable sisters, and proceeded in Purnell's carriage, which he drove, and which conveyed also Mrs. P. with Mrs. and Miss Niblett, to the Berkeley Road Station.*

1854: 16 Aug: *E. Clifford returned to dinner, having gone from Turkdean, where was a very hilarious party of dancers numerous, and ill arranged, as it would appear, to sleep at Salperton House, now rented by Mr. Peel, formerly of Broadstone, Oxon, and family. The late Mrs. Peel was sister of Mrs. Niblet of Haresfield, and, as such, the Peels known to the Cliffords, between whom and the Nibletts there is a close intimacy.*

NICHOLL — John Nicholl [33]

Sir John Nicholl (1759-1838), MP and landed proprietor, was born at Llanmaes, Glamorganshire, the second son of John Nicholl and Elizabeth Havard. He was educated at Bristol Grammar School, St John's College, Oxford (BCL 1780; DCL 1785), and Lincoln's Inn (1775). He married, 1787, Judy, daughter of Peter Birt of Wenvoe Castle, Glamorganshire. Nicholl was MP for Penryn in 1802-06, Hastings in 1806-07, and Great Bedwyn in 1807-21 and 1822-32.

1826: 29 Jan., 4 Feb: *Sir John Nicholl does not offer himself as a candidate on this occasion, having pledged himself, that he*

will not a second time during the same Parliament turn his back on his Constituents at Bedwin.
1830: 31 Jan.

NICHOLLS — Mr Nicholls, tenant on the Hunt estates

1835: 30 Mar: *also to Messrs. Manning and Nicholls, tenants on the estate who are in arrears of rent.*

1836: 11 Oct: *Wrote to Mr. Archbould at Thrapston as to the Market Harborough Turnpike bonds, and for information as to the measures taken with regard to Nicholls's arrears.*

NICHOLLS — George Nicholls [34]

Sir George Nicholls (1781-1865), poor law reformer and administrator, was born at Trenithen, Cornwall, the eldest son of Solomon Nicholls (1755/6-1793) and his wife, Jane (1760/61-1849). After an early education at the parish school at St Kevern and the grammar school at Helstone, Nicholls eagerly accepted from his uncle an offer of maritime service with the East India Company. Upon completing the necessary lessons in geometry, trigonometry, and navigation at Mr Weatherdon's school in Newton Abbot (1796-97), Nicholls went to sea in 1797 as a midshipman aboard a Company ship bound for Bombay and China. He rose rapidly through the ranks and prospered financially, becoming a captain in 1808 at the age of 27. He married, 1813, Harriet (d. 1869), daughter of Brough Maltby of Southwell, Nottinghamshire; they had 1 son and 6 daughters.

In 1815 a fire on board Nicholls' ship the *Bengal* resulted in the loss of several lives and the destruction of the vessel and its uninsured cargo. Though acquitted of all blame by the Company's directors, Nicholls suffered severe financial losses in consequence of the tragedy and resigned his post. He settled with his wife at Southwell, where he resolved to take an active part in the operation of the poor laws and to became an overseer of the poor. He was appointed by the Revd J. T. Becher, who had been involved for a number of years in reforming poor relief at the local level. The two men held similar views on the need for more stringent administration of poor relief, although Becher was to prove more open to ameliorative policies towards the poor.

In 1823 Nicholls moved to Gloucester to plan, together with Thomas Telford, the construction of a canal linking the English Channel and Bristol Channel. The financial crisis of 1826 rendered this project untenable, but another scheme, the Gloucester Canal, which Nicholls undertook shortly afterwards, was brought into operation in 1827. Nicholls was next engaged in an attempt to rescue a financially distressed bank of considerable regional importance. While unsuccessful, his efforts impressed the directors of the Bank of England, who offered him the post of manager of their newly opened Birmingham branch.

The poor laws royal commission, appointed in 1832, sent its investigators throughout the country to report at first hand on the prevailing system. John Cowell, the assistant commissioner for Nottinghamshire, was directed to Nicholls on undertaking an inquiry at Southwell. In his subsequent report Cowell praised the Southwell reformers; the report was widely circulated, and contributed to Nicholls' selection as one of the three commissioners created by the Poor Law Amendment Act of 1834. Nicholls went on to have a distinguished career and was knighted in 1851.

1826: 17 Jan: *The parties, with whom they are about, in March, to unite, are Mr. Gladstone, M.P. for Woodstock, a very eminent Liverpool Merchant, of Scotch extraction, who has been residing of late at Gloucester Spa, in consequence of the indisposition of one of his family, a gentleman of great practical experience; Mr. Montague, our acquaintance, the great Ironmaster here and a Mr. Nicholls.* 22 Feb: *The proposed union of Messrs. Turner with Messrs. Gladstone, Montague & Nicholls will not take effect.*

1836: 25 Aug: *It seems that Wilkins had an audience of Mr. Nicholls, one of the Commrs. and eventually succeeded in prevailing on him to replace the Stow on the Wold Union on the list of those unions, which are to receive accommodation from the Exch. Bill Loan Commrs.*

1838: 3 Sep: *I understood a short time ago, that Mr. Earle, the Asst. Commr. who had charge of the district comprizing Warwickshire and Northamptonshire, was about to be moved to Ireland, where, under the direction of Mr. Nicholls, the P.L.C., the system, modified to suit the condition of that country, is about to be introduced under an Act of Parlt. passed during the last Sess., and that Hall was likely to be transferred from our district to Mr. Earle's.* 7 Sep: *Mr. Nicholls is to be the resident Commr. at Dublin.*

NICHOLSON — Miss Nicholson at Totteridge

1802: 10 Jan: *Skaited with George & Fiott; Mr. Bowzer's family & Miss Nicholson's as Spectators.* 11 Jan: *Danced with Miss Lee, 'Miss Rivington', Miss Guysom, Miss Nicholson, P. Fiott, &c.*

NICHOLSON — Charles Nicholson [35]

Charles Nicholson (1795-1837), flautist, was born at Liverpool, the son of Charles Nicholson, also a flautist. He was taught by his father and, when quite young, went to London, where he became principal flute at Drury Lane. He then moved to Covent Garden, and from about 1832, was principal flute to the Royal Italian Opera. Nicholson played at the Philharmonic Society's concerts, where several of his compositions for the flute were performed between 1823 and 1842. Upon the foundation of the Royal Academy of Music in 1822, he was appointed professor of the flute.

Nicholson was the most celebrated flautist of his day. His father was probably the first to enlarge the finger and mouth holes on the instrument in order to increase its tone, and Nicholson had his flutes made this way. He was noted for his powerful sound and technical brilliance, although his hard tone was not universally admired. He experimented with new types of vibrato and advocated the use of alternative fingerings. He was the first to introduce glissando, which up to that point had been considered impossible on the flute.

1823: 17 Sep: *Nor was the Instrumental treat less rich: with such compositions as Haydn's, Rossini's, Mozart's, Cherubini's, Bach, Paer's, Clarke Whitfields's Bishop's, Calcott's & Attwood's, & such masters in execution as Cramer, Lindley, Marshall, Nicholson on the Flute, Willman on the Clarionet, Bochsa on the harp, it was impossible not to be delighted.*

1826: 12 Sep: *Nicholson, one of the sweetest performers on the flute.* 13 Sep: *Miss Travis sung in a most correct & tasteful manner "Lo! here the gentle lark" and was accompanied by Nichols on the flute.* 25 Sep.

1829: 23 Sep: *Two delightful pieces of instrumental music were introduced, a fantasia on the flute by that excellent performer Nicholson, & a concerto on the Violoncello by the unrivalled Lindley.*

NIELD — Jonathan Nield [36]

Jonathan Nield (±1768-1843), singer, was a celebrated tenor at the principal concerts and music meetings. Little is known of him, but he appeared at the Three Choirs at Gloucester in 1793 as a 'soft voice'. Having been appointed a gentleman of the Chapel Royal, he was made a singer of the King's Chapel. Nield often sang in concerts in London in the 1790s, and was particularly appreciated for his renditions of Handel's music, both in London and in Bath, where he was Rauzzini's principal male singer during the 1790s. When in London he frequently deputised for the organist and singing teacher R. J. S. Stevens.

1802: 6 Jun: *The first act consisted of a Requiem composed by Rauzzini sameness seemed to mark his Composition, tho' the Exquisite Mara Miss Sharpe, & Nield sung well in it, & one or two Chorus's were amazingly fine.*

NIND — Benjamin Ireland Nind, apothecary at Berkeley and Cheltenham [37]

Benjamin Ireland Nind (1802-1871), apothecary, was born at Tewkebury, the son of John Pitt Nind (1768-1839) and Charlotte (1767-1841), daughter of John Ireland (1743-1828) and Elizabeth Phelps (1742-1833). The family was related to the Ninds of Overbury, Gloucestershire [now Worcestershire]. Benjamin's paternal grandmother was Sarah Pitt, daughter of John Pitt of Gloucester. His grandfather was Issac Nind.

Benjamin Nind was in partnership with Charles Harris, apothecary and chemist, of Cheltenham. The *London Gazette* reads as follows: 'Nind, Benjamin Ireland, formerly of High-Street, Cheltenham, Gloucestershire, Surgeon and Apothecary, next of Great Dover-Road, Southwark, Surrey, Medical Student, and lastly of Cheltenham aforesaid, carrying on business in "Copartnership" with Charles Harris, as Chemist and Druggist'. This partnership was dissolved on 23 November 1825, and Nind appears to have been made bankrupt in 1826.

Later in his life Nind was faced with imprisonment. It is not clear what his misdemeanour was, but the following lines were recorded at the Epiphany sessions of 1835: 'Articles of the Peace was exihibited by the Right Hon. Lord Segrave. Nind was ordered to be imprisoned for two years, unless in the meantime he could find sureties, and enter into recognizance himself in one hundred pounds, and two sufficient sureties in fifty pounds each.'

By the time of the 1841 census Nind was listed as 'surgeon', but incarcerated in the lunatic asylum at Wotton, Gloucester, where he remained until his death thirty years later. He was unmarried.

1835: 9 Jan: *Attended in Court; busily engaged all day. Lord Segrave was present to prefer articles of the Peace against a miserable Apothecary of the name of Nind, formerly in practice at Berkeley, who had greatly annoyed his Lordship by irritating conduct for several years past.*

NIND — Esther Nind [38]

Esther Nind (±1835) was born at Hailes, Gloucestershire, the daughter of Charles Nind (1790-1854) and Esther Baylis (1796-1888). She married, at Stanway, 28 October 1854, John Henry Richardson (b. 1831); they had 2 sons and 2 daughters:

1 Charles Henry (1855-1870)
2 Samuel Baylis (1857-1927)
1 Mary Ellen (1859-1905)
2 Edith Jane (1862-1930)

1852: 14 Nov: *I departed for Stanway in my phaeton, arriving there shortly before 11 o clock. I sent my carriage, servant and horses to the Vicarage, remaining at the mansion house in the interval between the morning & afternoon Services. The musical parts of the service were conducted very nicely by Miss Nind, daughter of a gentleman farmer, who takes her turn at the Organ with Mrs. E. F. Witts.*

NISBET — Miss Nisbet, niece of Curtis Hayward and daughter of Harry and Anne Nisbet [39]

Harry Nisbet (±1794-1890), landed proprietor, was born at Nevis, West Indies, the son of Walter Nisbet (1745-1797), of Mount Pleasant, Nevis, and Grafton Street, London, and Anne (1752-1819), daughter of Robert Parry of Plas Newydd, Denbighshire. Walter Nisbet was born and died at Nevis, while his wife Anne died at Bath on 2 December 1819, aged 67. Her will shows that she was consumed with anxiety for her daughter Caroline, who she feared would be left destitute after her death. She also wrote that she had nothing to leave to her dear sons. In a subsequent note attached to the will, she recorded that some support had been provided for her and her daughter by her sons, one of them being Harry Nisbet.

By the 1820s Harry Nisbet was living at Walcot, Bath, where he may have moved prior to his mother's death. He married, at Quedgeley, 19 February 1828, Anne Curtis Hayward; they had 2 sons and 4 daughters:

1 Anne (1828-1923); born at Brenzett, Calcutta, India
1 Harry Curtis (1830-1907); born at Fettehgurgh, Bengal, India
2 Emelia (b. 1832); born at Brenzett, Calcutta, India
3 Mary Ellen (1837-1913); born at Wynberg, Cape of Good Hope, South Africa
4 Harriet Elizabeth (1842-1923); born at Newland, Gloucestershire
2 Josiah (1844-1869); born at Highgate, Middlesex

It appears that Nisbet was in the service of the HEIC. By 1851 the family was living at Cookham, Berkshire. The niece mentioned by Francis Witts was probably Harry Nisbet's eldest daughter, Anne.

1846: 18 Nov: *We were kindly received by the pleasing Mrs. Hayward, and in due time the party was increased by the arrival of Mr. Lysons, with two ladies, from his house at Hempstead, connections of his, a mother and daughter, whose names I did not catch, and a Mr. Le Marchant, Curate of Hardwick. A Miss Nisbet, a niece of CH's was also one of the party staying in the house.*

NOEL — Mrs Noel at Mrs Beaver's, London

1801: 7 Sep: *Drank Tea and spent the evening at Mrs. Beavers, where we met Mrs. Noel.* 19 Oct: *to Mrs. Beaver's in the evening, where were a numerous party Mrs. Knightly, Mrs. Gillies, Mrs. Noel, Mrs. Arnold &c.*

NOEL — Baptist Wriothesley Noel [40]

Baptist Wriothesley Noel (1799-1873), Church of England clergyman, was the eleventh son of Sir Gerard Noel Noel, 2nd baronet, and Diana Middleton, Baroness Barham. He was educated at Trinity College, Cambridge (MA 1821), and was admitted to Lincoln's Inn in 1821. Following an appointment as curate of Cossington, Leicestershire, Noel served as minister of St John's chapel, Bedford Row, London, from 1827 to 1848. There he became a leading evangelical preacher. He was chaplain-in-ordinary to the queen from 1841 to 1849, but then resigned from the Church of England. He was baptised by immersion in John Street Baptist chapel, where he subsequently served as Baptist minister from 1849 to 1868. He was president of the Baptist Union in 1855 and 1867. Noel gave vigorous support to the North in the American Civil War. He married, 1826, Jane, eldest daughter of Peter Baillie of Dochfour, Inverness-shire.

1839: 5 May: *the principal, and by many much admired minister, who preached this evening, is the Hon. Baptist Noel, brother of Lord Barham, and of another popular divine of the same school, Gerard Noel.*

NOEL — **Charles George Noel**[41]

Charles George Noel, 8th earl of Gainsborough (1818-1881), landed proprietor, was the son of Charles Noel Noel, 7th earl of Gainsborough, and Elizabeth (d. 1818), daughter of Sir George Grey, 1st baronet. His parents married in 1817. He was styled Viscount Campden between 1841 and 1866, and was MP for Rutland in 1840-41. He married, 1 November 1841, Adelaide Harriet Augusta (1821-1867), eldest daughter of William George Hay, earl of Erroll, and Elizabeth FitzClarence, the illegitimate daughter of William Henry, duke of Clarence, afterwards William IV. Charles George Noel succeeded his father as the 8th earl of Gainsborough in 1866.

1848: 17 Oct: *Several gentlemen qualified as magistrates to-day; among them was Lord Campden, eldest son of the Earl of Gainsborough, and now residing on the paternal property near Campden.*

NOEL — **Charles Noel Noel**[42]

Charles Noel Noel, 7th earl of Gainsborough (1781-1866), MP and landed proprietor, was known as Charles Edwardes until 1798, Charles Noel between 1798 and 1823, and as the Lord Barham between 1823 and 1841. He was the eldest son of Sir Gerard Noel, 2nd baronet, and Diana, daughter of Adm. Charles Middleton, 1st Baron Barham. His paternal grandfather was Gerard Anne Edwardes, illegitimate son of Lord Anne Hamilton, younger son of James Hamilton, 4th duke of Hamilton, and his paternal grandmother was Lady Jane, daughter of Baptist Noel, 4th earl of Gainsborough. Charles's father, Sir Gerard Noel, succeeded his father-in-law, Adm. Charles Middleton, as 2nd baronet of the Navy in 1838, while his mother succeeded the admiral, her father, as 2nd Baroness Barham in 1823, both according to special remainders in the letters patent.

In 1798, on the death of his kinsman Henry Noel, 6th earl of Gainsborough (on whose death the earldom became extinct), Charles and the rest of the family assumed by royal licence the surname of Noel in lieu of his patronymic, becoming, therefore, Charles Noel Noel. He succeeded his father as MP for Rutland in 1808, and held the seat until 1814. In 1823 he succeeded his mother in the barony of Barham and entered the House of Lords. In 1838 he succeeded his father in the baronetcy. In 1841 the family's earldom was revived when Charles was created 7th earl of Gainsborough.

Charles Noel Noel was married four times. He married, first, 1809, Elizabeth (d. 1811), daughter of Thomas Welman; there were no children from this marriage. He married secondly, 1817, Elizabeth (d. 1818), daughter of Sir George Grey, 1st baronet; they had 1 son:

1 Charles George Noel (1818-1881); *see above*

Charles married thirdly, 1820, Arabella (d. 1829), daughter of Sir James Hamlyn-Williams, 2nd baronet; they had 2 sons and 2 daughters. He married fourthly, 1833, Frances, daughter of Robert Jocelyn, 3rd earl of Roden; they had 2 sons.

1825: 21 Jun: *The Rector of Campden read prayers, the Hon. & Revd. Leland Noel, brother of Lord Barham, a very delicate looking young man with a weak voice.*

1839: 5 May: *the Hon. Baptist Noel, brother of Lord Barham.*

NOEL — **Gerard Thomas Noel**[43]

Gerard Thomas Noel (1782-1851), Church of England clergyman, was the second son of Sir Gerard Noel Noel, 2nd baronet, and Diana Middleton, Baroness Barham. He was younger brother to Charles Noel Noel (*above*). Gerard was educated at Trinity College, Cambridge (BA 1805; MA 1808), and was admitted to Lincoln's Inn in 1798. He entered the Church, and following an appointment as curate of Radwell, Hertfordshire, he served as vicar of Rainham, Kent, in 1807-26, prebendary of Winchester in 1834-51, and vicar of Romsey, Hampshire, in 1840-51. He married, first, 1806, Charlotte Sophia O'Brien, daughter of Sir Lucius O'Brien, 3rd baronet, and Anne Ffrench. He married secondly, 1841, Susan Kennaway, daughter of Sir John Kennaway, 1st baronet.

1839: 5 May: *the principal, and by many much admired minister, who preached this evening, is the Hon. Baptist Noel, brother of Lord Barham, and of another popular divine of the same school, Gerard Noel.*

NOEL — **Leland Noel Noel**[44]

Leland Noel Noel (1797-1870), Church of England clergyman, was the tenth son of Sir Gerard Noel Noel, 2nd baronet, and Diana Middleton, Baroness Barham. He was younger brother to both Charles Noel Noel and Gerard Thomas Noel (*above*). Leyland was educated at Westminster School and Trinity College, Cambridge (MA 1821). He was vicar of Chipping Campden in 1824-32 and vicar of both Lavendon with Brayfield, Buckinghamshire, and Exton with Horn, Rutland, in 1832-70. He was also canon of Peterborough in 1850-70. Leland married, 1824, Mary Arabella, daughter of John Savile Foljambe of Nottinghamshire; they had 1 daughter:

1 Mary Penelope (d. 1859)

1825: 21 Jun: *I attended the Bishop of Gloucester's primary visitation at Campden, as Vicar of Stanway....The Rector of Campden read prayers, the Hon. & Revd. Leland Noel, brother of Lord Barham, a very delicate looking young man with a weak voice. He is understood to be of the Evangelical party.*

NOEL — **William Middleton Noel**[45]

William Middleton Noel (1789-1859), MP and landed proprietor, was the fifth son of Sir Gerard Noel Noel, 2nd baronet, and Diana Middleton, Baroness Barham. He was younger brother to both Charles Noel Noel and Gerard Thomas Noel (*above*). He married, 1817, Anne, daughter of Joseph Yates. He was MP for Rutland in 1838-40.

1853: 15 Mar: *New Magistrates who qualified were the Hon. Middleton Noel, and his nephew, from the Forest division.*

NORFORD — **Charles Norford**[46]

Charles Norford (1777-1867), Church of England clergyman, was said to be the 26th child of William Norford (1715-1793), physician and surgeon, of Bury St Edmunds. He was educated at Caius College, Cambridge (BA 1800; MA 1803), and was appointed curate of Leyton, Essex, in 1800. He then served as rector of Westonbirt, Gloucestershire, from 1803 to 1867.

1852: 17 Mar: *Mr. Norford was obstinate and ill judged, and tho' as good a fight was made for him by his Counsel as circumstances would admit, when the case came on after Curtis Hayward's court opened, the order of trustees was confirmed with a strong feeling on the part of the court that the appeal was frivolous and vexatious.*

NORMAN — George Bethune Norman[47]

George Bethune Norman (1817-1876), Church of England clergyman, was born in the parish of St George's, Holborn, London, the son of James Ormond Norman (1774-1838), of Holborn and Cuckfield, Sussex, and Mary Bethune (1788-1851). He was educated at St John's and Trinity College, Cambridge (BA 1841; MA 1845), and was admitted *ad eundem* to Oxford in 1850. Norman was curate of Prescot, Lancashire, in 1842-43, assistant minister of St Mary de Crypt, Gloucester, in 1846, minister of St Mary Magdalen chapel in 1846, and minister of St Margaret chapel, Gloucester, in 1847-50. He married, at Langham, Westminster, 26 April 1842, Ann Elizabeth, daughter of John Manship Ewart of Broome, Surrey; they had at least 1 son and 1 daughter:

1 Elizabeth Catherine (b. 1845)

1 Basil John Augustine (1846-1877)

Ann must have died young as George Norman married secondly, at Dover, 1858, Marie Joseph Lucie Sophie Blaquiere. He died in Italy.

1846: 18 Nov: *Daily morning and evening service is performed here by the incumbent, a Mr. Norman, once Curate of St. Mary de Crypt church: a weekly Sacrament in also administered, and a miscellaneous congregation from different parts of Gloucester and its suburbs are collected.*

NORRIS — Mary Norris[48]

Mary Norris (±1767-1857) was born at Winson. She was listed in the census as a pauper widow.

1850: 7 Jun: *Visited Pinchin and Norris, aged inhabitants of Eyford.*

1851: 6 Jan.

1852: 23 Jan., 2 Feb., 28 Apr., 14 May.

NORTH — Matthew North of Urchfont, Wiltshire, and his wife

1807: 10 Feb: *Visited in the forenoon Dame North.* 1 Aug: *Visited Matt. North & his Dame.* 17 Dec., 26 Dec.

1808: 12 Jan., 19 Feb., 19 Apr.

NOTT — George Frederick Nott[49]

George Frederick Nott (1767-1841), Church of England clergyman, was born (presumably) at Westminster, the son of Samuel Nott (1740-1793) and Augusta Hawkins (1746-1813). He was baptised at St James, Westminster. Nott was educated at Christ Church, Oxford (BA 1788; MA 1792; BD 1802; DD 1807), where he was proctor in 1801 and Bampton lecturer in 1802. He was appointed perpetual curate of Stoke Canon, Devon, in 1807. He was then appointed vicar of Broadwinsor, Dorset, and in 1810, prebendary of Winchester. He was finally rector of Harrietsham and Woodchurch, Kent, from 1812 to 1841. He died at the Close, Winchester.

1802: 28 Mar: *To hear an excellent Lecture on Enthusiasm from the Bampton Lecturer Nott of All Souls.* 2 May, 9 May, 23 May: *At St. Mary's heard a fine Sermon from Nott of all Souls.* 20 Jun.

NOTT — John Nott[50]

John Nott (1751-1825), physician and classical scholar, was born at Worcester, the son of Samuel Nott (d. 1775) and Elizabeth Hodgetts (d. 1771). His father was of German origin and had held an appointment in George III's household. Nott acquired a taste for classical poetry at an early age and made some translations from the Latin classics while at school; he never gave up his study of classical texts, but he was destined for a career primarily in medicine. He studied surgery in Birmingham under Edmund Hector and in London under Sir Caesar Hawkins; he also studied in Paris. In about 1775 he went to the Continent with an invalid gentleman and returned to London two years later. In 1783 he travelled to China as a surgeon on board an East India Company vessel. During his three years abroad he learned Persian, and later demonstrated his proficiency for the language in a faithful translation of *Select Odes from the Persian Poet Hafez* (1787). Soon after returning to England he accompanied his brother and his family on another journey abroad, this time for the benefit of his and his brother's health.

On his return in 1788, Nott was urged to graduate by Dr Richard Warren, the king's physician. This he duly did—although it is not known where—and on 8 October 1789 he became an extra-licentiate of the Royal College of Physicians. On Warren's recommendation he was appointed physician to Georgiana, duchess of Devonshire, and her sister, Lady Duncannon, on their tour of the Continent. While in Italy Nott investigated the medicinal properties of the thermal waters at Pisa and the springs at Asciano. He published his findings in 1792. He remained the duchess's physician until 1793, when he settled at the Hotwells in Bristol. There Nott continued to practise medicine. He published two further works, one on the Hotwells and one on a local outbreak of influenza in 1803.

During the last eight years of his life Nott suffered from hemiplegia which confined him to his house, but he continued his classical studies nonetheless; at his death he had just finished a complete translation of Petrarch. He died unmarried in a boarding house in Dowry Square, Clifton. His nephew and heir, the Revd Dr George Frederick Nott (*above*) conducted the funeral service.

1806: 24 Jun: *In the Evening accompanied Mrs. Carrick, Dr. Nott, & Captn. Bradshaw to Miss Bethells, where we met Miss M. Boycott & drank Tea, with a Sullabub & strawberries & cream in Dr. Nott's Hayfield afterwards.*

NOVELLO — Clara Novello[51]

Clara Anastasia Novello (1818-1908), soprano, was born at 240 Oxford Street, London, the fourth daughter of the music publisher Vincent Novello (1781-1861) and Mary Sabilla Hehl (1789-1854). Clara revealed her musical talent at an early age. Her first official music lessons were at York with John Robinson, organist of the city's Catholic chapel, where her brother (Joseph) Alfred Novello was already serving as an apprentice. On the recommendation of François-Joseph Fétis, she was placed in Alexandre Choron's prestigious singing class at the Institution Royale de Musique Classique et Religieuse in Paris. During this period Clara made the acquaintance of Rossini, who was impressed by her talents; in later years he frequently requested her to perform his music.

Clara made her public début in England on 22 October 1832 at a benefit concert at the Theatre Royal, Windsor. By 1833 she had regular public engagements, notably at the Three Choirs Festival and the Philharmonic Society concerts. She followed this with an extensive and successful tour of European cities, including Berlin, Vienna, Dresden, and Weimar. In 1838 she went to Milan to study operatic technique with the cavaliere de Micheroux; she made her Italian opera début in Rossini's *Semiramide* at Padua on 6 July 1841. Rossini also selected her to perform in the Italian première of his Stabat Mater. In 1842, during her engagement to sing in the Italian city of Fermo, she met Count Giovanni Baptista Gigliucci, whom she married in London on 22 November 1843. They had 2 sons and 2 daughters:

1 Giovanni (1844-1906)
1 Porzia (1845-1938)
2 Mario (1847-1937)
2 Valeria (1849-1945)

Clara discontinued her career after her marriage. She went to live with the count in Italy, where she raised her family and assisted her husband in the fight for Italian independence. The count lost his property during the uprisings of 1848, and Clara willingly resumed her professional career on the stage.

Clara Novello's career in England was based largely on her performances of oratorio, which continued its general popularity over opera. She appeared at large choral festivals, including, again, the Three Choirs festival and the reopening of the Crystal Palace in 1854. She also sang before Queen Victoria in 1852 and on various other occasions. Her final appearance was on 21 November 1860 at St James's Hall, London. The concert included selections from oratorio as well as opera, and boasted an orchestra and choir of 250 performers.

Clara and her husband retired to Rome and Fermo. Count Gigliucci died on 29 March 1893 and Clara died at Rome on 12 March 1908.

1836: 27 Oct: *We had not till now visited them, but had accepted this invitation, of a hospitable and open hearted pair, who wished that all their neighbours and acquaintance should participate in the pleasure of hearing the fine singing of that very rising vocalist, Clara Novello, who is staying at their house.*

1837: 10 Jun: *About half past six my son arrived from Oxford, rather tired with a week of bustle, during which he had mingled with his studies much of gaiety in the society of different parties of acquaintance congregated during the Commemoration week; Mad. Schroeder Devrient and Clara Novello as Vocalists had attracted him at a Concert.*

1850: 26 Jun: *Called in on Mr. & Mrs. Whitmore Jones, whom we found at home, with two of their daughters, also Mrs. & Miss Rawlinson, wife and daughter of Mr. A Rawlinson, Solr., Chipping Norton I had only once before visited Chastleton House, many years ago, when its hospitable owners, now rather confined in their means, from large outgoings, and a numerous family, unable too to relieve themselves by family arrangements contemplated on the eldest Son's coming of age, gave a large party and concert, Clara Novello, the accomplished public singer, being the principal performer.*

1852: 7 Jun: *The immense audience were witnesses to the excellences of the performance, and the sublimity of the music.... Clara Novello at first rather disappointed me, but came out well in the wonderful conclusion of the piece — I had heard her formerly, when she first entered into the profession, in a private concert at Whitmore Jones's at Chastleton.* 9 Jun.

NOYES — **Maria Noyes**[52]

Maria Noyes (1777-1861) was a domestic servant. In the 1844 *Pigot's Directory* and the 1847 *Hunt's Directory* she was registered as living at 5 Bath Place, Cheltenham. She was buried at St Mary's, Cheltenham.

1834: 30 Nov: *Wrote to M. Noyes, an old servant at Cheltenham, about her Provident Bank concerns, in answer to a letter received from her.*

1850: 8 Jul: *Received a letter from Maria Noyes, an old Servant living at Cheltenham, who wishes to return into my servantice as Cook.* 9 Jul: *Wrote to Maria Noyes, intimating that I had no occasion for her services.*

NUGENT — **Percy Fitzgerald Nugent**[53]

Sir Percy Fitzgerald Nugent, 1st baronet (1797-1874), MP and landed proprietor, was MP for Westmeath in 1847-52. He was made a baronet of Donore, co. Westmeath, on 30 September 1831.

1851: 28 May: *Though I had caught cold and was suffering from cough, I sat up in the Coffee room at the Queen's Hotel with a party of the habitués, chiefly Irish Members, dropping in after the debate in the Commons, Sir Percy Nugent, Mr. Sullivan &c.—amusing, fluent talkers,—Irish all over, clever & abounding in humour.*

NURSE — **William Nurse** — *see also* Kendall[54]

William Nurse (1814-1866), landed proprietor, was born at Ashbury, Barbados, the second son of John Henry Nurse. He married Rosa Juliana Harriet (1821-1899), second daughter of Edward Kendall; they had 1 daughter:

1 Ada (b. 1867)

Nurse died at his estate of Villa Nova, Barbados. Rosa returned to England and died at Cheltenham.

1852: 18 Mar: *Mr. Kendall, an agreeable & sensible man, with whom as a Magistrate I had long been acquainted, not now resident at Cheltenham, but possessing a house there, and visiting his Son in law, and daughter, Mr. and Mrs. Nourse, who were of the Lefroy's Guests, the gentleman less attractive than the lady, who is pretty and pleasing. Another daughter of Mr. Kendal is married to Mr. Jelinger Symons, the Barrister.*

NUTT — **Revd Nutt, candidate for chaplain at Stow Union Workhouse**

1838: 5 Apr: *The main business of the day was the appointment of a Chaplain: three Candidates offered themselves; two of whom were present; Messrs. Morgan and Bowstead; the third, Mr. Nutt, did not appear, and was, indeed, wholly ineligible, being a very singular, eccentric character, a peripatetic, advanced in life, and of penurious habits, not known by residence in the neighbourhood, and associating with low people; in short, a harmless, useless, half crazy, wandering being.*

O

O'BRIEN — William Smith O'Brien[1]

William Smith O'Brien (1803-1864), Irish nationalist and leader of the Young Ireland movement, was born at Dromoland, Newmarket on Fergus, co. Clare, the second son of Sir Edward O'Brien, 4th baronet, of Dromoland Castle, and Charlotte Smith. He was a descendant of the eleventh-century Ard Rí (high king of Ireland) Brian Boru. He took the additional surname Smith upon inheriting a property called Cahirmoyle in co. Limerick from his maternal grandfather. He lived at Cahermoyle House, a mile from Ardagh, co. Limerick.

William Smith O'Brien was educated at Harrow School and Trinity College, Cambridge. He studied law at King's Inns in Dublin and Lincoln's Inn in London, and was MP for Ennis in 1828-31, and for Limerick County in 1835-48. O'Brien was convicted of sedition for his part in the Young Irelander Rebellion of 1848, but his sentence was commuted from death to deportation to Van Diemen's Land. In 1854 he was released on the condition of exile from Ireland. He lived in Brussels for two years, but in 1856 he received a pardon and returned to Ireland. He was never active again in politics.

1848: 24 Mar., 19 May: *In Ireland Smith O'Brien, and Meagher, have been indicted for sedition, but it has proved impossible to obtain a conviction against them.* 2 Aug: *Apparently, a decisive blow has been struck at an obscure place in Tipperary, where Smith O'Brien, with other leaders, at the head of a large body of insurgents, collected among the collieries, came into a contact with a small force of police, not exceeding sixty: these being judiciously posted in a house on a common which was strongly built, detached from others, and containing several apartments, sustained a sort of siege, firing from the windows, killing a few, and wounding more of the mob.* 9 Aug: *Smith O'Brien has been arrested by a Railway guard at the Thurles Railway Station; he was taking a ticket for Limerick, when apprehended; worn in appearance, exhausted, looking miserably, as one hunted down.* 20 Aug., 12 Oct: *Smith O'Brien, after a long trial at Clonmel, has been found guilty of high Treason.*

O'CALLAGHAN — the O'Callaghan family at Cheltenham and Clifton[2]

Nothing tangible has been discovered about the O'Callaghan family, but it appears that they lived at Cheltenham and were visiting Clifton, where they joined the fashionable circle. There is a clear connection to the Goold family of Clifton (*see* 14 January 1804 and the diaries of Agnes Witts). Catherine Goold, née O'Callaghan (b. 1750+), was the daughter of Donatt O'Callaghan of Kilgoorey, co. Clare. She married, 1777, Henry Michael Francis Goold (1757-1786), son of George Goold (1720-1789) and Marie Catherine Gallwey (1725-1805). It has not been ascertained whether Catherine had any siblings, but whether or not they were immediate relations, the O'Callaghan family of Cheltenham appear to have been family to some degree.

Interestingly, the name Cornelius recurred in the family of Catherine O'Callaghan [later Goold]. Although recorded many years later, Capt. Henry B. Savile, RA, third son of the late Albany Savile, of the Oaklands, Devon, married, at Clifton, 1848, Mary, eldest daughter of the late Cornelius O'Callaghan of Ballynahinch, co. Clare. In 1844, Frances, widow of the late Cornelius O'Callaghan, married, at Filton, Gloucestershire, Lord William Somerset, canon of Bristol. In that same decade, W. Shaw Bond, of Devonshire Place, Cavendish Square, married, at Cheltenham, France Jane, daughter of the late Cornelius O'Callaghan of Ballynahich, co. Clare. There is also the possibility that these O'Callaghans were related to Cornelius O'Callaghan, 1st Viscount Lismore (*below*).

1804: 15 Oct: *At a numerous dressey Ball danced with a daughter of Sir Alexander Grant. Conversed with Delabere, Mrs. O'Callaghan, Baillie &c.* 16 Oct: *Walked with my aunt, Mrs. Worsley & Mrs. Reid. Called on Mrs. Delabere & Mrs. O'Callaghan.* 17 Oct: *Called on Mrs. Delabere & Mrs. O'Callaghan.*

1806: 14 Jan: *Found Mrs. Gould's family at home with the beautiful Miss O'Callaghan of Cheltenham, & made an agreeable visit.* 17 Jan: *Had much Conversation with Captn Webb, Mrs. O Callaghan the beautiful Mother, her sweet Daughter.* 19 Jan., 25 Jan., 29 Jan., 12 Feb., 14 Feb: *Walked with Col. Napier & Major Patton, in Town, & upon the Hill, also with the beautiful Miss OCallaghan.* 28 Feb: *Walked with Miss O Callaghan & Miss Goold on Richmond Terrace.* 2 Mar., 8 Mar., 15 Mar: *Miss Ford upon the Piano, Miss M. Stables upon the Harp in a very superior style, & Miss O Callaghan very moderately singing.*

O'CALLAGHAN — Mr O'Callaghan, vocalist at Bath

1820: 19 Jan: *Attended the concert, when an unusual style of performance was presented, namely, a little comic opera, made up of selections, chiefly from Il Fanatico per la Musica, the Music by Mayer. Naldi and his daughter performed admirably; the other vocalists were two Miss Ashes, a Signor Vercellin, a Mr. O Callaghan, and a Mr. Cole.*

O'CALLAGHAN — Cornelius O'Callaghan[3]

Cornelius O'Callaghan, 1st Viscount Lismore (1775-1857), MP and landed proprietor, was the son of Cornelius O'Callaghan, 1st Baron Lismore (1741-1797), and Frances Ponsonby (1757-1827). He lived with his mother at Tunbridge Wells and was created Viscount Lismore in 1806. He married, 1808, Eleanor Butler.

1805: 29 Sep: *Walked with the Hon. Mr. O'Callaghan, & Mr. Abbott.* 30 Sep: *At the Wells before breakfast & on the walks & library with O'Callaghan in the forenoon.* 1 Oct: *A party at Mrs. Moore's of about twenty very pleasant, Miss Windham, the Bucknalls, O'Callaghan, Tickells etc.* 4 Oct.

O'CONNELL — Daniel O'Connell[4]

Daniel O'Connell (1775-1847), Irish nationalist leader, was born near Carhen, Cahirciveen, co. Kerry, the eldest of the ten children of Morgan O'Connell (1739-1809) and Catherine O'Mullane (1752-1817). Being a Catholic, O'Connell was unable to go to Trinity College and instead went to France to complete his education. In 1794, after France, he went to London to study the law, passing at least one term at Gray's Inn. Following the Catholic Relief Act of 1793, he was, in 1798, one of the first Catholics to be called to the Irish bar. O'Connell enjoyed great success practising as a barrister for over twenty-three years. He became a wealthy man, and by

1828, the year of Francis Witts's first serious reference to him in his diaries, his emoluments exceeded £8,000 and he only went to court for a special fee, when his visits were made the occasion of public rejoicings. His professional reputation was outstanding, and at cross-examination he was said to have been unrivalled.

O'Connell's historic struggle for Ireland and for Catholic emancipation started with a public speech in January 1800 at the Royal Exchange; for the next twenty-eight years he worked assiduously for the cause against prodigious opposition. In 1815 he was challenged to a duel by D'Esterre, one of the guild of merchants who took offence to O'Connell's reference to the corporation of Dublin as 'beggarly'. The duel resulted in D'Esterre's death, but O'Connell was spared prosecution by the courtesy of D'Esterre's second, Sir Edward Stanley. For his part, O'Connell behaved with thoughtful generosity to his opponent's family. The result of the duel was highly satisfactory to O'Connell's friends, particularly as the patching up of a previous matter of honour between him and a fellow barrister had given his enemies cause to sneer at his courage.

A few months after D'Esterre's death, O'Connell was challenged once again, this time by Robert Peel. O'Connell accepted the challenge, but to avoid legal implications the duel was set to take place on the Continent. Peel crossed to Ostend to await his opponent, but on his way O'Connell was arrested in the Strand and bound over in heavy penalties to keep the peace. Ten years later, after the second reading of the Catholic Relief Bill, O'Connell tendered a full apology to Peel, acknowledging himself to have been in the wrong in their dispute a decade earlier.

O'Connell's aim in life was to rescue the Irish peasantry from the malice of their enemies and consequences of their own poverty and crime. In 1823 he proposed the formation of a Catholic Association, inviting Catholic gentlemen to join with an annual subscription of one guinea. The initial result was discouraging, but when O'Connell allowed membership to be bought for a penny a month or a shilling a year, the peasantry responded with vigour and membership of the so-called Catholic Rent snowballed. Before long branches of the association had sprung up in most parishes, becoming a focus for Irish nationalism. In June 1828 O'Connell successfully contested the parliamentary seat of co. Clare, defeating William Vesey Fitzgerald. Parliament rose in July and removed the opportunity for O'Connell to take his seat. Although it was generally assumed that he was legally debarred as a Catholic, O'Connell himself believed that in the absence of any direct prohibition in the Act of Union, no legal obstacle could prevent a duly elected Catholic from taking his seat. On 16 November Wellington proposed to concede to the Catholics the right to sit in Parliament, but the king was strongly against the concession. Pressure and a new administration finally prevailed, and on 13 April 1829 the king gave way; the Catholic Emancipation Act received the royal assent.

O'Connell presented himself at the bar of the House of Commons on 16 May, but was ordered by the speaker to withdraw when he declined to take the oath of supremacy tendered him. On the motion of Brougham that his explanation for his refusal should be heard, O'Connell addressed the House three days later from the bar. Although he made a great impression, his claim to sit was rejected by 190 votes to 116.

On 4 February the following year O'Connell successfully took his seat and soon established a reputation as one of the most useful members of the House. He never entirely overcame the prejudices of his audience, but the tendency to snub him was eroded gradually by the incontrovertible good sense of his arguments. Francis Witts displayed this same prejudice in his diaries; his opinions were probably shaped by the constant barrage of anti-O'Connell articles in *The Times*—over three hundred in total—which undoubtedly set the tone adopted by most of the tory gentry and clerical classes.

O'Connell laboured long and hard against the union of Ireland with Great Britain. The king's speech of 1834 condemned 'the continuance of attempts to excite the people of Ireland to demand a repeal of the legislative union'. In the debates that followed, O'Connell spoke for five hours, and although defeated he succeeded in creating a more conciliatory disposition towards Ireland in the House of Commons. On behalf of the Irish government Edward Littleton went so far as to promise O'Connell that when the Coercion Act came up for renewal, the political clauses within it would be abandoned if he in turn would promise that the agitation would cease. O'Connell agreed, but unfortunately the prime minister had not been consulted; the result was that the agreement was reneged upon. O'Connell made the affair public and following dissensions in the cabinet, Lord Grey resigned his office and the administration of Lord Melbourne came into power. As the whigs and tories were nearly equal, O'Connell held the balance of power and the Melbourne administration played into his hands. From this time onwards his influence in both Ireland and England placed him at the forefront of political life.

Following the success of the 1843 'monster meetings', the Irish government, in panic, arraigned O'Connell and succeeded in securing a conviction with a twelve-month sentence. Having served four months his sentence was quashed by the House of Lords and O'Connell returned to Ireland in triumph. Owing to the failure of the potato crop in 1846, O'Connell called the attention of the House of Commons to the prevalence of famine and disease in Ireland. He made his last appearance in February 1847, appealing to the House to save his country: 'She is in your hands — in your power. If you do not save her, she cannot save herself.'

1825: 7 Feb: *Mr. O'Connel, a Roman Catholic Barrister, of considerable talents, and powerful in oratory, is the Coryphæus of this dangerous assembly, and the unlucky Mr. Plunkett, the Irish Attorney General, has lately in vain arraigned him for an inflammatory tirade uttered in one of the sittings of this body; but the Jury would not find him guilty.* 2 Apr: *A strong effort was made, that the Roman Catholic Associators might be heard by counsel at the Bar of the Houses of Parliament, and a deputation, headed by Lord Killeen, eldest Son of Lord Fingal, and Messrs. O Connel, Shiell, Brice &c. as advocates, repaired to London, but were not allowed to plead their cause.* 20 May.

1827: 8 Mar.

1828: 9 Jul: *Mr. O'Connell, the Irish Barrister, and chief Roman Catholic agitator, announces his intention to stand. Although the exclusion of Papists from Parliament has been for years the topic of complaint, and the object of petition, yet all at once Daniel O'Connell professes himself convinced, that not any law exists to prevent his being elected & sitting in Parliament.*

1829: 7 Feb: *The election of the popular demagogue O'Connel for the County of Clare, who never attempted to take his seat in the house, has given fresh impetus to the cause, and emissaries of the Catholic Association traversed the Country, working upon the feelings of the People.* 13 Feb: *The Coryphæus of the Catholic association, the new member for Clare, O'Connel, is in London, and resting on his oars: he does not attempt to force his way into the house, as he expects the doors will ere long open to him spontaneously.* 26 Jun: *By the act no person could sit in the House without taking the oaths required before its passing, if his election had occurred previously: the act has a prospective, not a retrospective force: and this seems to have been especially aimed at O'Connel, the Member for the County of Clare.*

1830: 23 Jun: *The Peer was very diffuse on his own exertions in Ireland as a Protestant leader in the great cause of emancipation; he hinted, that O'Connel & the Catholic Agitators were jealous of him, & therefore thwarted him; that he was as bold, uncompromising & determined as the best man among them, till the great point was carried, but then ceased from troubling & made it a point of honour to be at rest; while O'Connel, once his dear friend and admired demagogue, by persevering in agitation from motives of base personal ambition & aggrandisement, had with others of the same class, fallen deservedly in the public estimation & were sinking into well merited contempt.* 24 Jun: *There was a very full house, & the gallery had been much crowded, but many were dropping off, who had been listening to the debates in the early part of the evening, which had not been uninteresting, as an altercation had taken place between Mr. Doherty, the Irish Solicitor General, a man of talent, & O'Connel. A personal quarrel exists between these gentlemen ... O'Connel was this evening justly charged & reprobated for his conduct in this matter. And there he sat, silent and sulky, as it seemed to me, on the Opposition side of the house, but as the attack on him had passed, & he did not join in the debate, which followed, I had no opportunity of hearing the Milesian Agitator.*

1832: 6 Jun.

1833: 8 Feb: *The King's Speech was delivered by his Majesty in person on Tuesday last. The part referring to the disorganized and disturbed state of Ireland, and declaratory of the determination of the Government to put down by force the nascent and almost open rebellion there, excited the bitterest and most furious opposition on the part of O'Connel and his partizans, causing the adjournment of the debate on the address in the House of Commons, where the Irish question engrossed the whole attention of the House.* 15 Feb: *Ministers have brought forward their scheme of Church reform in Ireland, and a sweeping measure it is.... O'Connel professed his gratitude and delight.* 29 Feb., 11 Mar., 13 Mar.

1835: 4 Apr., 19 Apr: *The Conservative Journals assert that a compact has been made with O'Connel, to whom has been conceded, as the price of his support of the new administration, a veto on the Irish appointments.*

1837: 4 Aug., 10 Aug: *O'Connel with one of his party has been returned for the County City of Dublin, and Hume is likely to be returned for Kilkenny vice O'Connel: that city being thus made the refuge of the destitute.*

1848: 19 May.

O'CONNOR — Feargus Edward O'Connor[5]

Feargus Edward O'Connor (±1796-1855), Chartist leader, was born at Connorville, co. Cork, son of Roger O'Connor (1762-1834) and his second wife, Wilhelmina Bowen of Connorville. In around 1819 he was admitted to King's Inns, Dublin, and in 1826 he joined Gray's Inn, London; he was called to the Irish bar in 1830, but he practised law only briefly.

Feargus O'Connor inherited the estate of Fort Robert, co. Cork, from his uncle Robert Conner in around 1820. He was a reforming landlord and later claimed to have taken part in Whiteboy activities. After the passing of the Reform Bill, O'Connor stormed the country organising the registration of the new electorate. In the general election of December 1832 he was returned as a repealer at the head of the poll for co. Cork, and as a member of Daniel O'Connell's repeal party he was an outspoken critic of the whig government's policies in both Ireland and England. He soon allied himself with London's popular radicals and was involved in various radical campaigns, including those for press freedom and the return of the transported Dorchester labourers. In summer 1833 O'Connor clashed with O'Connell over the 'Liberator's' refusal to move a motion for the repeal of the union.

As an independent agitator O'Connor did more than any other leader to lay the groundwork for Chartism. He was the chief figure at the Chartist convention which assembled on 4 February 1839, when he declared that body to be 'the only constituted authority representing the people of this country'. On 17 March 1840 O'Connor was found guilty at York assizes of seditious libel for speeches—his own and those of others—published in the *Northern Star*, and on 11 May was sentenced to eighteen months' imprisonment in York Castle.

In 1848, inspired in part by the revolution in France and bolstered by co-operation with Irish nationalists, the Chartists again mobilised large numbers with O'Connor at their head. A third national petition was organised and a convention sat to co-ordinate Chartist strategy. O'Connor presided at the great Kennington Common demonstration on 10 April 1848, when he managed to persuade the people to abandon the proposed procession to the House of Commons to present the petition, thus avoiding a violent confrontation with government troops, police, and a large middle-class force enrolled as special constables. That evening O'Connor presented the national petition to the Commons, claiming that it contained 5,706,000 signatures; he was greatly embarrassed when the committee on petitions reported that the total came to 1,975,496, a figure that included many bogus signatures.

O'Connor never married, although in the 1830s it was rumoured that he and Louisa Nisbett, a celebrated actress, were lovers. He fathered several illegitimate children. Through much of his Chartist career he lived in Hammersmith, having leased his Irish estate. He died a poor man; his claim that he exhausted his personal wealth in the cause of radicalism was probably true.

1846: 29 Oct: *Letter from Sewell: the Longbands and Applehurst farm was sold on Tuesday last for £8200 to Fergus O'Connor the Chartist: Mr. Miles of Bristol being his competitor; this was £1000 above the reserved bidding, and £1200 above Mr. Hale's valuation to me.* 2 Nov: *... to H D Warter, enclosing the last letter from S. & N. with particulars as to the sale of the Redmarley farm to Fergus O'Connor, that I had declined treating for the Swell Wold farm, and that he and Mr. Jennings might now look out for an investment in ground rents or houses in or near London.*

1848: 12 May: *... he was a very useful person, and not long ago had signalized himself by a strong, but well merited censure and castigation of Feargus O Connor, the Representative of Nottingham, and dangerous Chartist leader.*

O'HALLORAN — Laurence Hynes O'Halloran[6]

Laurence Hynes O'Halloran (1765-1831), pioneer schoolteacher and journalist, was born in co. Meath and orphaned at a young age. He was educated at Christ's Hospital and appears eventually to have been awarded a doctorate in divinity from King's College, Aberdeen. He never achieved the Anglican ordination he so craved, so he assumed it—with considerable success—for most of his life.

In 1783 as a young naval midshipman, O'Halloran was jailed for stabbing and killing a colleague. Although acquitted shortly afterwards, he was later to become embroiled in a number of duels and in numerous disputes. He married in 1784 and ran private classical schools near and in Exeter and Alphington for some twelve years, during which period he achieved recognition as a skilled and accomplished educator despite also being charged with immorality. While living in Exeter he married Mary ['Polly'] Boutcher, a Catholic lady ten years his senior, by whom he had six children. His sister's illegitimate daughter Anna, who was twelve years younger than him, also posed as his spouse later in his life; they had twelve children together.

In 1796, due to insolvency, O'Halloran managed to rejoin the Navy by posing as a chaplain. He was additionally appointed as secretary to Lord Northesk, third-in-command at the battle of Trafalgar. *The Trafalgar Roll* confirms the presence of 'Revd L. H. Halloran, DD' at the battle, as chaplain on board Northesk's flagship *Britannia*. The 'Reverend Dr.' was appointed chaplain to HM forces in the Cape, sailing to South Africa in 1807 with the added brief that he would 'receive 12 young gentlemen as pupils'. The position seemed promising but O'Halloran's behaviour, which included libellous conduct, disobeying orders, and pecuniary irregularities, soon led to severe disagreements with the commander-in-chief Gen. Grey. By 1810 O'Halloran had been found guilty of defamatory libel and was fined heavily. He was expelled from the colony. Back in England his colourful past was catching up with him, and after several years spent trying to rebuild his social standing, O'Halloran was caught trying to forge accreditation for himself as a curate. He was transported to Australia for seven years, arriving in Sydney in June 1819.

Sydney offered fresh opportunities. With the aid of friends and the support of Governor Macquarie (who was later to call him'the best and most admired instructor of youth in the Colony'), O'Halloran was soon able to open his 'establishment for liberal education', also known as 'Sydney Free Public Grammar School'. He was joined by his second family and his niece, acting as his wife, in 1822. She died following the birth of their twelfth child, and in August 1824 he married, probably bigamously, Elizabeth Turnbull, aged 17, who was to bear him four more children.

O'Halloran appears by general consent to have been an inspiring teacher, but among other faults, he had an obsessive sense of persecution, a weakness for indulging in litigation, a poor sense of financial management, and a penchant for writing libellous tracts.

1826: 18 Sep: *I have heard it mentioned, that his only classical tutor was the well known Dr. O'Halloran, now an exile in New South Wales, where he keeps a large Academy, & who, after a series of swindling transactions, was transported for forging the name of Mr. Justice Garrow to a frank, when he was in parliament. O'Halloran, though not in orders, officiated as Curate, under another name, both in Worcestershire & Gloucestershire for a considerable length of time. He was Curate of Dursley & Lechlade. Previous to his settling as a teacher at Exeter, he had been tried for his life there; having stabbed a Midshipman on board a man of war, in which he served as purser's clerk, or in some other subordinate station; by a skilful cross-examination of the principal witness against him, the Surgeon, who spoke of the wound inflicted by him on the youth, he made it appear, that the blow or stab was unpremeditated, at least might be so thought, and thus obtained a verdict, which negatived the capital office.*

OAKELEY — Charles Oakeley [7]

Sir Charles Oakeley, 2nd baronet (1778-1829), diplomat and landed proprietor, was born at Madras, the son of Sir Charles Oakeley, 1st baronet (1751-1826), administrator in India, and Helena (d. 1839), only daughter of Robert Beatson of Kilrie, Fife. He was educated at Rugby School, followed by a short spell at M. Mounier's Academy in Weimar, where he met the Witts family. He was secretary of legation and chargé d'affaires in Bavaria, Sweden, and the United States, where he succeeded Augustus Foster in 1809.

Charles Oakeley succeeded his father as 2nd baronet in 1826. He married, 1820, Charlotte Francoise Auguste Gisberte (1803-1850), only child of Ramadier, Baron de Lormet, of Meysenbrock, Netherlands. It is not known if there were any children, but certainly no male heir survived him as he was succeeded as 3rd baronet by his younger brother Sir Herbert Oakeley (1791-1845).

Francis Witts was incorrect in his assertion of 28 June 1828. It had been reported by gossips that Sir Charles Oakley had become 'devoted' to Elizabeth Patterson while he was in Washington serving at the legation. He apparently already had a scandalous past, having reportedly eloped with the queen of Prussia's sister, then a married woman. All of Baltimore—according to a contemporary account—was making bets on whether Oakley 'will offer [and] if so, whether she will accept or decline.' Even Bishop John Carroll relayed to his sister the intriguing news that Oakley had 'transferred his attentions to Madame Bonaparte', and wondered whether they would be married. As it turned out, Elizabeth Patterson rejected Oakley. Her brother Joseph assumed she had merely 'made use of O' to get Napoleon and Turreau to agree to her demands for an annuity.

The gossip seems to have persisted; numerous publications recorded Charles Oakeley's marriage to Elizabeth Patterson in 1810. An entry in the *Gentleman's Magazine* stated that Charles Oakeley had married Miss Patterson: 'Lately, the lady of Jerome Buonaparte, ci-devant Miss Patterson, to Charles Oakley Esq., and son of Sir Charles O. bart. of Shrewsbury'. Clearly this had stuck in the minds of many people—including Francis Witts.

1828: 28 Jun: *Another pupil of M. Mounier was Mr. Foster, also of the Diplomatic body, and, I believe, an Envoy at one of the Italian Courts, having long held a like Station at Copenhagen; Mr. Oakley, subsequently, Chargé des Affaires in America, where he married the repudiated wife of Jerome Bonaparte; he is now Sir Charles Oakley.*

OAKELEY — Frederick Oakeley [8]

Frederick Oakeley (1802-1880), Roman Catholic convert, priest, and author, was born at the Abbey House, Shrewsbury, the eleventh and youngest child of Sir Charles Oakeley, 1st baronet (1751-1826), and youngest brother of Sir Charles Oakeley, 2nd baronet (*above*). He was educated at Christ Church, Oxford (BA 1824; MA 1827), and was a fellow of Balliol College. He was a tutor at Balliol in 1831-37 and senior dean in 1834. Oakeley was the incumbent of Margaret chapel, Margaret Street, London, in 1839-45. He seceded to Rome, and was Roman Catholic canon of Westminster in 1852.

1845: 13 Feb: *Mr. Ward occupied the rostrum to the left hand of the Vice Chancellor, and was assisted by his friend the Revd. Frederick Oakely, also a Fellow of Ball. Coll. holding kindred views with Mr. Ward, a clergyman with preferment in London, formerly Fellow Tutor of his College, and a prominent person in the Tractarian ranks.*

OAKLEY — Jane Oakley [9]

Jane Oakley (dates unknown) lived at 13 Brunswick Square, Gloucester, and was listed in directories for 1830 and 1849.

1836: 6 Aug: *I accompanied Sophia: in a short time Edwd. brought our carriage, and conveyed our friend to Naunton Inn, where she took a fly and proceeded to Cheltenham in the expectation of reaching Miss Oakley's at Gloucester tonight.*

OAKLEY HILL — *see* Hill *and* John Oakley Hill

OATRIDGE — John Oatridge [10]

John Oatridge (1787-1835) was governor of Lawford's Gate House of Correction. Little is known about him, but he was governor by at least 1824.

1833: 23 Apr: *Lawford's Gate bridewell is adjacent to the Church. This was the scene of some of the worst tumults during the disgraceful Bristol riots in 1831.—Many of the vagabonds, who were concerned in those scandalous excesses, were well acquainted with the interior of this prison, or connected with its inmates: revenge cooperated with their love of mischief and mad frenzy, so that having assailed the Bristol Gaol with success, it is not wonderful that their fury was next directed hitherward. The Keeper, Oatridge, was not deficient in courage, though in leaving his prison to place in security the Journals & account books &c. under his charge, he acted with bad judgment, and received a reprimand from the Court of Sessions at Gloucester.*

ODELL — Richard Odell [11]

Richard Odell (±1782-1825), Church of England clergyman, was born at Ardmore, co. Waterford, Ireland, son of John Odell. The Odells had a long connection with Ardmore; the family had been in co. Waterford for two centuries. The Ardmore property (until its sale in 1888) comprised Ballinamertina, Curragh, Duffcarrick, Dysert, and Farrengarret. Richard Odell was educated at New College, Oxford (BA 1804; MA 1808), and was a fellow there until 1825. He was ordained deacon on 2 December 1805 and priest on 4 May 1807. He was curate of Barnham Overy and of Hockham, Norfolk, and chaplain to the duke of Sussex.

1803: 13 Nov: *Odell called upon & dined with Dowell, meeting Evans & a Mr. Trevannon.* 16 Nov: *Newbigging & Odell dined with me; Dowell & Lumsden joined the party.* 4 Dec: *Evans & Odell breakfasted with me.* 8 Dec: *Dined & passed the Evening very pleasantly in the New College Common Room with Odell.*

1804: 30 Jan: *called on Mr. Michele & on Odell, & D. Robison.* 12 Feb., 16 Feb., 21 Oct: *Called on & walked with Odell in the forenoon.*

1805: 20 Mar: *Breakfasted with Odell, meeting Adams & Bathurst.*

1825: 16 May: *Dr. Jenkinson is a relative of the Earl of Liverpool: he was educated at Winchester College, & was fellow of New College Xt. Church Oxford, where he was my cotemporary; and where I frequently met him at New College in the Society of my old acquaintance, now deceased, the Revd. R. Odell.*

OFFLEY — Charles Offley [12]

Charles Offley (1757-1830), port merchant, was the son of William Offley. He continued in the family business as a partner in the Porto firm of Offley, Forrester and Webber, port and Madeira exporters/importers. Charles succeeded his father in 1786, and became one of the foremost wine purchasers and exporters of his day. During one very busy season in 1785, the firm purchased 6,085 pipes in the Douro and Gaia. Until 1801, Offley ranked consistently among the leading exporters; that year's 5,278 pipes was one of the firm's four totals above 5,000 since 1781. In 1803 it was reported that Offley possessed Porto wine and property worth around £70,000. Offley himself had more or less retired by 1810, but the firm continued.

The situation was very different in 1811 following the disruption caused by the Peninsular War, but the firm held on. From 1825 to 1828 Offley, Forrester and Webber ranked third among exporters. They advanced to second in 1829 and 1830, and in 1831, the year after Charles Offley's death, they gained first place.

Offley returned to England in about 1810 and bought Upfield Lodge in Stroud. He married, 1825, Arabella Theresa, youngest daughter of Thomas Martin, previously of the HEIC's Bengal Army. There do not appear to have been any children, and none were mentioned in Offley's will. After Charles Offley's death, Arabella became an extremely wealthy widow. She married secondly, 1832, John Fitzjames James.

1828: 16 Oct: *A Portrait by Vandyke, from the collection of Mr. Offley, a gentleman of fortune residing near Stroud, and married to a pretty young woman, with Hindoo blood & complexion, the natural daughter of a former neighbour and acquaintance of Mrs. Backhouse on Wellington Parade, Blind Captain Martin, of the family settled in Cambridgeshire, and connected with those of Overbury and Ham Court.*

OGILVIE — Charles Atmore Ogilvie [13]

Charles Atmore Ogilvie (1793-1873), Church of England clergyman, was born at Whitehaven, Cumberland, son of John Ogilvie (d. 1839) and Catharine Curwen of the Isle of Man. He was educated at Balliol College, Oxford (BA 1815; MA 1818; B&DD 1842), where he was a fellow from 1816 to 1834, tutor from 1819 to 1830, bursar and senior dean, and regius professor of pastoral theology in 1842. He was vicar of Ross-on-Wye, Herefordshire, from 1839 to his death in 1873. Ogilvie married, at Dinder, Somerset, 18 April 1838, Mary Anne Gurnell Armstrong (1807-1875); they had 2 daughters:

1 Catherine (b. 1839)
2 Mary Anne (1842-1931)

1833: 12 Mar: *I joined my kind friend and judicious adviser at his rooms, whence he sallied to take counsel with the excellent Mr. Ogilvie, fellow of Balliol, but was disappointed, as that gentleman, it appeared, was absent from Oxford.*

OGILVIE — George Shadforth Ogilvie [14]

George Shadforth Ogilvie (±1792-1868), surgeon, lived at Calne, Wiltshire, where he was listed as a surgeon and apothecary. He was also a land tax commissioner. He married, 1 December 1820, Bridget Mary Bishop.

At Calne Ogilvie opened a small house in 1833 for the reception of patients. From one female patient the numbers increased only slowly, never rising above seven. The inspectors appointed by the justices registered a complaint in 1844 about 'boarders'—i.e. people who were not certified patients—residing in this house. The house closed before the 1846 publication of the first report of the commissioners in lunacy. In fact Ogilvie had a troubled career with mental hospitals; in 1851 he was refused a licence for an establishment at Turnham Green, London.

1848: 17 Oct.

1849: 22 Dec: *Received a letter from the County Chairman, who sends me a printed copy of his report made at the Michaelmas Quarter Sessions on the Lunatic asylums near Bristol, chiefly as to those under the management of Mr. Ogilvie, and the Bompas family.*

1850: 1 Jan: *Mr. Ogilvie has made no movement towards a renewal of the licence heretofore granted to the Ridgway House private asylum, and, so doing, has tacitly admitted the justice of the censures passed on his establishment in the County Chairman's reports.*

OGLE — Esther Jane Ogle [15]

Esther Jane Ogle (1776-1817) was the daughter of Revd Newton Ogle and Susanna Thomas. She married, 27 April 1795, as his second wife, Richard Brinsley Sheridan (1751-1816); they had 1 son:

1 Charles Brinsley Sheridan (1796-1843)

1826: 20 May: *In a daughter of Dean Ogle of Winchester, Sheridan some years after found a young and amiable partner, who survived her husband but a short time.*

OGLE — James Ambrose Ogle [16]

James Ambrose Ogle (1825-1900), Church of England clergyman, was the eldest son of James Adey Ogle of Oxford. He was educated at Brasenose College, Oxford (BA 1846; MA 1849), and began a career in the Church. He was curate of Icomb in 1848-51, vicar of Sedgeford, Norfolk, in 1858-74, and appointed rector of Southmere with Sedgeford in 1874. He married, 1856, Henrietta Agneta (1826-1920), daughter of George Pellew and Frances Addington. Henrietta was the granddaughter of Viscount Sidmouth, prime minister (1801-04).

1848: 21 Sep: *While I was at Stow Mr. Clarke had called to take leave of us: he has resigned the curacy of Icomb, and goes to Town: he is to be succeeded by Mr. Ogle, a son of an Oxford Physician, who is already known in the neighbourhood as a cricketer.*

1849: 12 Dec., 20 Dec.

1850: 25 Feb: *Mr. Ogle called to enquire after MW., being on his way to Stanway.* 28 Feb., 28 Mar., 28 May, 5 Jun: *Mr. Ogle joined the party at dinner, being the only guest unconnected with me.* 6 Jun: *After breakfast my dear Son and daughter left me for Stanway, accompanied by Mr. Ogle, whom they had invited to accompany them, and who staid here for half an hour before their departure.* 19-20 Jun., 17-18 Sep., 22 Sep: *Purnell's promised neck of venison having arrived this morning, wrote notes of invitation to dinner on Wednesday next to Mr. Ford, R Waller, Vavasour, Chamberlayne, and Ogle.* 24 Sep., 23 Nov: *Wrote to Mr. Ogle, inviting him to dinner on that day.* 26 Nov., 27 Nov: *Mr. & Mrs. J. T. Rice, Mr. Wiggin, Mr. & Mrs. and Miss Morrison, Mrs. R. A. Scott, and Mr. Ogle were our guests, added to our home party.*

1851: 25 Jan: *Mr. Ogle called to take leave of me: he goes to Writtle, near Chelmsford, to take the place of Mr. Clarke, as Curate of that parish, under the aged and resident Rector, Dr. Penrose—The stipend is considerably larger than that which he receives as Curate of Icomb, but the duties far heavier, and more responsible. Mr. Clarke is desirous of resuming his old position at Icomb, but it seems doubtful whether he can permanently fix himself there as Curate. What private motives influence either of these young men is not certainly known.*

1853: 11 Jun: *Met and conversed with Mr. Ambrose Ogle.*

OLIVER — Miss Oliver, a friend of John Dolphin

1826: 23 Aug: *We had some of our friends to dinner. Our party consisted of the Egerton Leighs, Mr. & Mrs. Jeaffreson, Mr. & Mrs. Dolphin, & their guest, Miss Oliver, & Miss E. Jeaffreson.* 7 Sep: *I dined at Mr. Dolphin's at Eyford, and met the Dean of Gloucester with Mrs. & two Miss Rices, Mr. & Mrs. Browne, and Mr. & Mrs. John Dolphin, who with their two daughters & a Miss Oliver are guests staying at Eyford.*

OLIVER — James Oliver, tenant of Francis Witts, Fenchurch Street, London [17]

James Oliver, carpenter and builder, operated from 49 Fenchurch Street.

1837: 23 Nov: *Oliver had failed to pay his half year's rent.*

1840: 31 Mar: *Recd. a letter from Mr. Jennings with the particulars of an agreement he has entered into with a Mr. Paruther for a lease to of the premises No. 50 Fenchurch Street, for 21 years from Midsr. next at £190. I am to enter into a bond with covenants to let to him the premises No. 49 at the expiration of Mr. Oliver's lease for 21 years.* 4 Apr: *Wrote to Mr. Jennings in reply to his letter received on the 31st. Ult., sending up for Mr. Warter's references, and at his desire, the old lease of No. 50 Fenchurch Street to Mr. Dixon, and the existing lease under which Mr. Oliver holds No. 49.*

OLLNEY — John Harvey Ollney [18]

John Harvey Ollney (1759-1836), JP, DL, and lieutenant-colonel of the Royal South Gloucestershire Militia, was born in the parish of St Sepulchre, Holborn, London, the son of John Ollney (1711-1776) and Ann Harvey (1715-1788). He married, 1798, Joanna (d. 1838), one of the four daughters and co-heirs-at-law of Revd Gervas Powell (±1723-1795), of Llanharan, Glamorganshire, and his wife, Margaret (±1736-1798). According to one source, Richard Brinsley Sheridan's immortal comic character Mrs Malaprop was modelled on Joanna's mother, Margaret Powell; the following malapropism may well have referred to Llanharan House: 'A turpentine walk through a scrubbery is a very nice reproach to a house'. It was said that Margaret Powell's children inherited her trait; one of her daughters reportedly told a friend that her husband had added a crocodile to his will. Margaret Powell's first language was Welsh, and Sheridan may well have been intrigued by her Breconshire accent and possibly by her unwillingness or shyness to speak fluent English in polite Bath society. Both the Powell and Sheridan families were frequently at Bath.

In 1802 John Harvey Ollney bought a commission as ensign in the 85th Regiment of Foot. By 1805 he was on half-pay as a lieutenant in the 9th Foot, and was in the same situation as late as 1824. He was also in the Royal South Gloucestershire Militia, and a captain as early as 1794, having been promoted from his previous rank of captain-lieutenant. He rose to become a lieutenant-colonel in the militia. Ollney was an active alderman and councillor at Gloucester where his occupation was somewhat surprisingly given as a 'woolstapler'; this may have been a business he had inherited from his father.

Ollney and his wife Joanna appear to have been childless, and little is known of Ollney's family. A sister, Anne, married, 1879, Revd William Allen, chaplain of the 93rd Foot. By 1823 Ollney and his wife appear to have lived at Cheltenham, where Mrs Ollney was mentioned three times in the diaries of Agnes Witts, including on 24 April 1823: 'went at Night to a large Rout at Mrs. Ollneys House so handsome & large there was no heat from the Crowd'. The house was Cambray Pavilion, 'an elegant mansion house', newly built on Cambray meadow in 1805.

The source of Ollney's vast wealth has not yet been discovered. In modern day (2018) terms it was approaching the equivalent of £80 million. On his death, apart from provisions made for his wife, Ollney gave his fortune to various charities (many still in existence), as detailed in the *Gentleman's Magazine*:

> The following charities are bequeathed by the late Colonel Ollney:—for the Corporation of Gloucester £8,000 to found almshouses at Gloucester for ten poor men and eight poor women; to the Clergyman and Churchwardens of Cheltenham £8,000; to the Corporation of Tewkesbury £8,000 and to the Minister and Churchwardens of Winchcombe £8,000 to found almshouses in those respective places; to the Gloucester Infirmary £1,000; to the School of Industry at Cheltenham £500; and to

the towns of Berkeley £300; Bisley £300; Chipping Camden £200; Cirencester £300; Coleford £200; Dursley £300; Fairford £200; Horsley £300; Lechlade £200; Minchinhampton £300; Mitcheldean £200; Marshfield £200; Newnham £300; Newent £200; Northleach £200; Painswick £300; Leonard Stanley £200; Sodbury £300; Stow-on-the-Wold £200; Tetbury £300; Thornbury £300; Wickwar £300; Wotton-under-Edge £300; to the village of Llanbarren in Glamorganshire £200; and to Brighton £500; all these sums (amounting in the whole to the sum of forty thousand pounds) to be placed out at interest, and the proceeds to be applied at Christmas, yearly, in the purchase of coals and blankets for the deserving poor of the several towns enumerated.

1829: 13 Jan: *The Quarter Sessions commenced. Howell, Clifford, D. Ricardo, Col. Berkeley, Lieut. Col. Olney ...*

ONLEY — Samuel Onley [19]

Samuel Onley (±1787-1868) was a builder and collector of taxes. In 1830 he was listed as a carpenter and joiner at 64 High Street, Cheltenham. By 1844 he had moved to Hewletts Road, and by 1851 he and his family lived at St John's Cottage, Carlton Street. By this stage he had changed his profession and become a tax collector. He was married to Sarah (±1782-1858), born at Hartpury, Gloucestershire; they had at least 2 sons:

1 Samuel (b. ±1815)
2 John (b. ±1820)

1848: 27 Mar: *Immediately a Gentleman on horseback, Mr. Only, took out of his pocket a sheet of paper, from which he read a long address to his Lordship, purporting to emanate from inhabitants of Cheltenham, recounting in complimentary terms the great benefits which it was alleged had been conferred upon the town by his Lordship having for so many years made it his residence during part of the winter, and for several months in each season the head quarters of his hunting establishment.*

ONSLOW — Richard Foley Onslow [20]

Richard Foley Onslow (1802-1879), landed proprietor, was the son of Richard Francis Onslow (*below*). He was educated at Christ Church, Oxford (BA 1825), and lived at Stardens Newent. He was lord of the manor of Newent and a major landowner. Onslow owned many of the mineral rights in the area and therefore benefited from coal mining. He also appears to have been involved in unscrupulous dealings; he was accused of wronging or taking advantage of many farmers in the area. He married, 5 July 1826, Catherine, daughter of Latham Blacker; they had 4 sons and 5 daughters:

1 Catherine Harriett (1827-1829); died an infant
1 Andrew George (1830-1894); married, at Taynton, 13 June 1861, Mary Owen (1834-1892)
2 Mary Charlotte (1834-1910); died unmarried
3 Anne Theodosia (1834-1907); married, at Newent, 2 October 1866, William Charles Hill ((1831-1910)
2 Richard (1836-1872); married, at Victoria, Australia, 28 July 1865, Elizabeth Anne Troutbeck (1829-1900)
3 William Arthur (1837-1903); married, at Preston Bagot, Warwickshire, 19 August 1880, Mary Elizabeth Cartwright (1847-1931)
4 George (1839-1880)
4 Caroline (1841-1918); married, at Oxenhall, 11 October 1868, Robert Burroughes
5 Emma Frances (1844-1931); died unmarried

1838: 3 Jul: *Among those present, naming the Gentlemen with whom I was most in communication were Crawley, Ford, Hyett, Sir W. B. Burdett, Newman, Baker, Ford, Archd. Timbrill and Onslow, R. Onslow, R B Cooper, W L Lawrence, &c.*
1844: 2 Jan.
1845: 15 Apr.
1847: 5 Apr.

ONSLOW — Richard Francis Onslow — *see also* Thomas Commeline [21]

Richard Francis Onslow (1776-1849), Church of England clergyman, was the son of Revd Arthur Onslow (1746-1817), of Reading, Berkshire, and Frances Phipps. He was educated at Christ Church, Oxford (BA 1797; MA 1800), and began a career in the Church. Onslow was domestic chaplain to the bishop of Worcester and vicar of Kidderminster, Worcestershire, from 1801 to 1834. He was also appointed rector of Newent, Gloucestershire, in 1804, archdeacon of Worcester in 1815, prebend of Salisbury in 1823, and rector of Stoke Edith in 1834. He married, 7 July 1801, Harriet Mary (1779-1860), daughter of Andrew Foley and Elizabeth Tomlinson; they had 3 sons and 5 daughters:

1 Richard Foley (1802-1879)
1 Harriet Frances (1803-1857); married, at Newent, 12 December 1833, Thomas Commeline (1796-1842)
2 Constantia (1806-1879)
3 Anna Cecilia (1808-1856)
4 Elizabeth (1810-1879)
5 Frances (1811-1887)
2 Arthur Andrew (1815-1864)
3 Thomas Phipps (1818-1850)

1823: 14 Jan: *The bench was very much crowded. The Lord Lieutenant, Lord Apsley MP. for Cirencester, Mr. Pitt, MP. for Cricklade, Messrs. Pye, Browne, Archdeacon Sandiford (Wells) Archdeacon Onslow, (Worcester) Archdeacon Probyn (Landaff) Dr. Timbrell &c.*
1825: 2 Aug., 17 Sep: *My acquaintance Archd. Onslow is Rector of Kidderminster & obtained the preferment by intermarriage with the Foley family, who have the advowson. He is a most respectable, obliging, right judging man, of the old school of divinity, and greatly esteemed by a large circle of friends and acquaintance. I am often in the habit of meeting him on the bench of Magistrates at Gloucester, as he resides a good deal at Newent in the forest of Dean, of which place he is the incumbent. His Archdeaconry is Worcester, of which Cathedral his father was Dean, and also Archdeacon of Berks.*
1829: 17 Jul., 20 Oct.
1830: 12 Jan., 20 Apr.
1832: 29 Mar: *The Company exceeded forty, and among others were present, the Duke of Beaufort, Lord Edward Somerset, Lord Sherborne, Hon. H. Moreton M.P. Sir B.W. Guise, M.P. & Sir W. Hicks, Bart., Archdeacons Wetherell and Onslow, Revd. Drs. Cooke & Davis, Messrs. Goodrich, Browne, Cooper, T. Kingscote, Lawrence, Hale, R. F. Onslow, Davis, Webbe M.P., Miller, Purnell, Baker, Niblett, Revd. Messrs. Hicks Ford, &c. I sat near the head of the table between Archd. Wetherell & Mr. Cooper.*
1834: 12 Aug: *We were at the Bell in conversation with Lord John Somerset, Dr. Cooke, Archd. Onslow and other anxious blues.* 15 Aug.
1838: 3 Jul., 16 Oct.
1839: 1 Jan.
1842: 15 Nov.
1844: 2 Jan., 29 Oct., 31 Dec.
1847: 29 Jun., 19 Oct.

ORANGE — John Edward Orange, a family guest at Mrs Witts's of Brunswick Square[22]

John Edward Orange (1805-1871), army officer, was born at Stafford, the son of William Orange (1764-1815) and Eliza Wright Burton Phillipson (1764-1806). As the Orange family was related to the Witts family by marriage, some extra detail has been provided.

William Orange was born at Norfolk, Virginia, and presumably departed from America as a loyalist (or at least his parents presumably departed as loyalists). After his education he entered the Army, and at the time of his marriage to Eliza Wright Burton Phillipson, at St John's, Peterborough, 23 October 1796, he was a captain in the 86th Regiment of Foot. Eliza was the daughter of Revd Burton Wright Phillipson; she and William had 5 sons and 1 daughter:

1 William Nesbitt (1797-1859); married, at Gretna Green, Scotland, 11 July 1836, Juliana Vittoria Yates (1819-1888); died at Vichy, Allier, Auvergne, France; 2 sons:
  1 Francis Xavier De Coucy (1836-1864)
  2 Frederick Bradshaw (1843-1866)
2 Charles Burton (1799-1820); born in South Africa; died unmarried, a young man
3 Augustus Richard (1800-1816); died unmarried, a young man, at Hooghly River, West Bengal, India
4 Frederick Lake (1803-1808); died young
5 John Edward (1805-1871); joined the Army as an ensign in the 34th Regiment of Foot, 10 April 1825; promoted lieutenant, 15 October 1827; captain, 27 December 1833; and major, 9 November 1846; fought in the Burma war, 1825, and placed on half-pay, 30 July 1844. He married, at Eckington, Derbyshire, 14 July 1835, Mary Crawford Bromehead (1808-1884); 2 sons and 2 daughters:
  1 Mary Louisa (1837-1912)
  2 Elizabeth Agnes (1839-1914)
  1 William Alexander Wildman (1839-1870)
  2 John Edward Bromehead (1842-1919)
1 Louisa Eliza (1806-1885); married, at Hartlebury, Worcestershire, 27 December 1824, Nathaniel Basevi (1792-1869), son of George Bas[s]evi (b. 1770) and his wife, Bathsheba

Mrs Witts (1787-1853) was born Jane Lake, the daughter of William Charles Lake (1753-1836) and Ann Orange (1758-1810). She was elder sister to William Orange (*above*), and John Edward Orange was therefore her first cousin once removed. She married Broome Phillips Witts.

Jane Witts's great-grandfather was Gilbert Orange (1691-1740), who was born at Coventry, Warwickshire, to an unknown Orange and Ann Winter (1650-1700), possibly a de Winter of Dutch origin. Gilbert's father may also have been of Dutch origin. Interestingly these family roots echo those of the Witts family; it is not beyond possibility that the families had been known to one another ever since they had arrived in England.

Gilbert's son was William Orange (1721-1789), who was born at Newcastle-upon-Tyne and died at Liverpool. He married Mary Malbone Kenner (1719-1783); they had 1 son and 3 daughters:

1 Ann (1758-1810); married William Charles Lake (1753-1836)
2 Elizabeth Winter (1759-1790)
3 Mary (1760-1792)
1 William (1764-1815); *see above*

1830: 25 Jun: *To dinner at Mrs. Witts's, Brunswick Square—a party Messrs. Bailey, Hibbert, Bassevi, Jones, Misses Witts and Whitehouse (then afterwards a Capt. Orange, Messrs. Rodicks x 3) & Mr. H. Warter.*

ORGAN — William Brewer Organ[23]

William Brewer Organ (±1802-1876), governor of Lawford's Gate House of Correction, was born at Brockworth, Gloucestershire. He married, at St Botolph's, London, 1831, Kezia Stringer (b. ±1802) of Thornhill, Yorkshire. It is likely that he received his police training in the Metropolitan Police. His wife Kezia became matron at Lawford's Gate.

1845: 15 Apr: *Sergeant Organ of the County Constabulary was appointed Governor of the Bridewell at Lawford's gate in the room of the deceased governor.*

ORLEANS— ***see*** **D'ORLEANS — Louis Antoine Philippe d'Orléans —** ***and*** **Louis Philippe of France**

ORMEROD — George Ormerod[24]

George Ormerod (1785-1873), JP, DL, and Cheshire county historian, was born in High Street, Manchester, the only son of George Ormerod (1757-1785), of Bury, Lancashire, and Elizabeth (1752-1822), daughter of Thomas Johnson, of Manchester and Tyldesley, and Susanna Wareing of Bury. His father died thirteen days before his birth.

Ormerod was educated at King's School, Chester, and Brasenose College, Oxford (BA 1806; MA 1807). On his twenty-first birthday he came into his inheritance, which included extensive estates in south Lancashire left by both his paternal grandparents and his mother's family. He married, 1808, Sarah (1784-1860), daughter of John Latham and Mary Mayer. The following year he and Sarah moved to Great Missenden, Buckinghamshire.

By 1809 Ormerod was involved in extensive research for his history of Cheshire. To facilitate the task, he decided to move back north, and in 1811 he bought the 83-acre Chorlton House estate, 4 miles from Chester. The family spent summers there from then until 1817, and winters in London so that Ormerod could conduct his research in the British Museum. The resulting work was entitled *The History of the County Palatine and City of Chester.* It appeared in ten parts, forming three volumes, between 1816 and 1819.

Having completed his work in the autumn of 1817, Ormerod left Cheshire immediately and never again lived in the north of England. He sold Chorlton House in 1823, and in the same year inherited important property and mining and financial interests from his uncle Thomas Johnson. With this increased wealth he was able, in 1825, to buy the 208-acre Barnesville estate at Sedbury, Gloucestershire, on the narrow peninsula between the Severn and Wye estuaries. He renamed the property Sedbury Park, and lived there from 1828 until his death. Ormerod was appointed a JP for Gloucestershire in 1827 and for Monmouthshire in 1830. He served as DL for Gloucestershire in 1861.

1836 : 12 Jul: *Rose early, wrote and read before breakfast, which meal I took tête a tête with Mrs. Bathurst; Bathurst, according to custom, rising late, and not making his appearance till it was time for him to repair to Lidney to attend a Justice meeting, which was followed by a Forest Court, at which as Verderer he administers justice under a special act of Parliament to the inhabitants of that district. The Mag. who met him were Mr. Ormerod, the Historian of Cheshire, who resides near Chepstow.*

OSWALD — Alexander Oswald Emmott[25]

Alexander Oswald Emmott (b. 1764), draper, was born at Dunnikier, Fife, the eldest son of James Townsend Oswald (1748-1814), MP, and Janet Grey (d. 1843) of Skibo, co. Sutherland. He had several siblings, including Gen. Sir John Oswald (1771-1840) and Elizabeth, second wife of the 7th earl of Elgin and 11th of Kincardine. He married, 17 April 1805, his cousin Eleanor [Ellen] Susannah Grey (1768-1829) of Upper Harley Street, Cavendish Square. She owned substantial estates in Rawdon and Guisley in Yorkshire.

Oswald ran a clothing business at 51 Dean Street under the name of Alexander Oswald & Co., in partnership with George Howell and W. H. Palmer; the partnership was dissolved in 1811. Alexander and Eleanor added the surname of Emmott by royal licence in 1821.

A case heard in the House of Lords on 11, 13 and 17 May 1841 and 8 March 1842 throws some light on Oswald's business activities:

> *Appellant:* William Parrot Carter, Esq., *Respondent:* Sir William Henry Palmer, Bart.
>
> In 1809, Alexander Oswald and George Howell, then carrying on the business of army clothiers, on Ormond Quay in Dublin, and in Dean Street, Soho, London, under the name of Oswald & Company, proposed to the Respondent, that if he would procure for their house the clothing of the regiments in the King's service in Ireland, by his influence with the colonels, a percentage should be allowed him upon the profits they would derive from such contracts as should be obtained through him. The Respondent acceded to their proposal, obtained several contracts for them, and his connexion with them in that way continued for three or four years. The firm of Oswald & Co. became embarrassed within that time; and Oswald then residing in London, or elsewhere abroad, Howell alone was declared a *bankrupt* in *Ireland.*

It seems likely that Francis Witts knew Alexander Oswald in Edinburgh, but there is no reference to the surname 'Oswald' in the diaries of Agnes Witts.

1803: 4 Sep: *Met Mr. A. Oswald No. 51 Dean St. Soho.*

OTTER — William Otter [26]

William Otter (1768-1840), bishop of Chichester, was born at Cuckney, Nottinghamshire, the fourth son of Revd Edward Otter, vicar of Cuckney. He was educated at Jesus College, Cambridge (BA 1790; MA 1793), where he was a fellow from 1796 to 1804.

Otter was curate of Helston, Cornwall, and master of the grammar school there in 1791-96. He travelled with his friend Thomas Robert Malthus in northern Europe in 1799. He was rector of Colmworth, Huntingdonshire, in 1804-10, of Sturmer, Essex, in 1810, and of Chetwynd, Shropshire, in 1811-22. He was also a private tutor in Oxford in 1822 and rector of St Mark's, Kennington, in 1825. Otter became the first principal of King's College, London, in 1830, and remained in the post until 1836, when he was appointed bishop of Chichester. He held the see until his death in 1840.

William Otter married, 3 July 1804, Mary Sadleir (1784-1860), daughter of William Bruère, governor of Bengal, of Ashtead, Surrey; they had 3 sons and 5 daughters:

1 William Bruere (1805-1876), archdeacon of Chichester; married, at the British consulate, Den Haag, S-Gravenhage, Zuid-Holland, Netherlands, 8 May 1837, Elizabeth Melvil (1814-1892)
1 Sophia Marian Frances (1807-1889); married, at St James's, Westminster, 16 June 1836, Revd Henry Malthus (1805-1882), son of William Otter's friend Thomas Robert Malthus
2 Caroline Charlotte (1809-1856); married, at St Mark's, Kennington, London, 22 October 1833, John Romilly, 1st Baron Romilly (1802-1874)
3 Jacqueline Elizabeth (1811-1849); married, at St James's, Westminster, 16 June 1836, Alexander Trotter (1804-1865)
4 Maria (1814-1891); married, at St James's, Westminster, 4 August 1836, Sir William Milbourn James (1807-1881), lord justice
2 Alfred William (1815-1866); married, at Wembury Cottage, Stanley, Huron, Ontario, Canada, 15 September 1842, Anna Louisa de la Hooke (1824-1907)
5 Amelia [Emily] Harriet (1817-1890); married, at St James's, Westminster, 28 March 1837, Edward Strutt, 1st Baron Belper (1801-1880), MP
3 Reginald William Ongley (1826-1862)

1829: 24 Jul: *"The Life and remains of Edward Daniel Clarke, Professor of Mineralogy in the University of Cambridge. By the Revd. W. Otter M.A. 2 Vols. 8vo. Lond. 1825." A very interesting piece of biography. Mr. Otter was the intimate friend of Dr. Clarke from early days, himself a talented man, and has had free access to all the papers of the deceased Traveller. Mr. Otter, like Mr. Clarke, was of Jesus College, Cambridge, and since he retired upon preferment from his college took pupils, chiefly the sons of leading men among the Whigs.*

OTTO — Louis-Guillaume Otto [27]

Louis-Guillaume Otto (1754-1817), diplomat, began his career in 1779 as private secretary to the chevalier de La Luzerne on an embassy to the United States of America. In May 1785, while in the USA, he succeeded François Barbé-Marbois as secretary of the legation. He then served as chargé d'affaires. George Washington and the main members of Congress honoured him with their friendship.

Otto returned to France at the end of 1792 and was appointed head of the first political division for foreign affairs by the committee of public safety. However, the fall of the Girondins in May 1793 led to his dismissal and arrest. He came close to being guillotined, but was spared. Released from custody, he followed Emmanuel-Joseph Sieyès to Berlin as secretary to the legation. He stayed there as chargé d'affaires when Sieyès was elected director. In 1800 he was moved to London, at first as commissioner for the exchange of prisoners of war, and then as minister plenipotentiary. In 1801 he negotiated with the British the preliminaries of the peace of Amiens.

In 1803 Otto was posted to the court of Maximilian, prince-elector of Bavaria, in Munich. His influence on the elector impressed Napoleon, who appointed him in 1805 to the conseil d'état, and made him a grand officer of the légion d'honneur. In 1810 he was made ambassador to Vienna, where he negotiated the conditions for Napoleon's second marriage to Archduchess Marie Louise. Napoleon thanked him by making him comte de Mosloy.

1801: 10 Oct: *walked in the Evening for an Hour or two to see the general Illumination, the Houses which were most ornamented were those of Mr. Hope in Cavendish Square, & of Mr. Otto in Hereford Street.*

OTWAY — James Otway [28]

James Otway (1803-1875), police officer and workhouse master, was born at Carshalton, Surrey. He presumably began his career in the Metropolitan Police, as it was usually from that force that local police associations drew their personnel. Otway moved to Stow-on-the-Wold and took lodgings in the Market Place. He married Elizabeth (b. 1815), a born-and-bred Stow resident; they had at least 4 sons and 3 daughters, including:

1 Henry Charles (±1836-1896); married, at St Peter's, Notting Hill, Kensington and Chelsea, 2 October 1859, Isabella Melita Robinson (b. 1839); 1 son and 2 daughters
2 John (b. 1838)
1 Mary Jane (b. 1840)
3 Robert (1841-1918), carpenter; married Catherine (b. ±1841); died at Dorking, Surrey
4 George (1846-1918), clerk; admitted to Southwark Workhouse, 1915; died three years later
2 Elizabeth Barnard (1848-1907); married, at Heston, Middlesex, 14 March 1868, Edward Regan (b. 1831); 1 son and 1 daughter

By 1871 James Otway was master of the Woodstock Union Workhouse and his wife Elizabeth was matron.

1834: 16 Jul., 26 Jul: *The evening proved very rainy, and it was between ten and eleven when my Son and myself returned home, enveloped in borrowed garments, myself in a waterproof cloak lent me by Otway, & Edward in a great coat furnished by Brookes.* 9 Aug., 30 Sep: *In a few minutes Otway was seen driving his wretched Prisoner in a gig at a rapid pace into the Town: an immediate rush took place among the mob; but it had been arranged to take the culprit in the first to Otway's lodgings in the Market place, for some refreshment; the other Police Officers ran by the gig to keep the mob aloof—but no attempt to insult the poor wretch was made, though with eager curiosity they crowded round the door of Otway's lodgings. After a short interval Otway conveyed Jeffrey by a back passage, unmolested by the crowd to the Unicorn, where we held our Sitting in the Ballroom, which had been arranged for the purpose.* 4 Oct., 16 Oct: *Nothing very interesting, except, as far as I was concerned, the trial of Teal, of Stow, for an assault on Otway, by savagely biting his thumb, when in the discharge of his duty as a constable. Teal found guilty, and sentenced to four months imprisonment, to hard labour.* 5 Nov., 24 Dec., 29 Dec.

1835: 1 Jan., 23 Feb., 19 Mar: *On this Ackerley again folded up my letter, saying, he would not read it, except in the presence of those men: I intimated, that the sooner he himself withdrew, the better; and, taking the hint, he flung out of the room in a towering wrath. The provocation was great, and We were taken by surprize: but, on reflection, I regret that I did not myself observe greater calmness towards a man in whom mischief and mental malady are nearly equally balanced; nor ought I to blame severely the warmth into which Otway was betrayed, when I found it so difficult to restrain my own temper.* 13 Apr: *And now came on the trial of Edmund Jeffrey... The confession taken down by Mr. Ford was then read in evidence, and Otway was put into the witness box to testify to the further admissions made by Jeffrey to himself.* 27 Apr., 5 Jun.

1836: 30 Jul., 8 Aug., 19 Oct., 7 Nov., 25 Nov: *A long interview with Otway, on Police Management, the organization of a Constabulary force on a new basis &c., preparatory to a report which I am preparing to be transmitted to the Constabulary Force Commrs.* 5 Dec.

1837: 10 Feb., 16 Feb., 30 Apr., 31 May, 3 Jun., 25 Aug., 9 Oct., 4 Nov., 12-15 Dec.

1838: 5 Feb., 28 Jun., 27 Jul., 3 Aug., 6 Aug., 9 Aug: *Otway in a manly, feeling, way rebutted the charge of neglect of duty, declared his anxious with to act up to his views of duty, and to the directions of his Employers, but claimed a discretionary power in the exercise of his office, without which he could not fulfil the objects of his appointment.* 1 Sep., 26 Dec., 29 Dec.

1839: 2 Jan., 6 Jan., 12 Feb., 15-16 May, 21 Jun., 26 Jun., 29 Jun., 9 Aug., 12 Aug: *Had a long interview with Otway on the subject of Rural police, the regulations to be recommended for its government, &c.* 17 Aug.

1840: 26 Mar: *W B Pole informed me that he had learnt from his Father that there was another change in Otway's views: that he had resigned the office of Superintendent of in the Essex Constabulary to accept that of Porter at the principal lodge at Blenheim Park, to which he had been recommended by the Metropolitan Commissr. of Police, who had been requested by the new Duke of Marlborough to send him a proper person: it appears that the perquisites and privileges of that place are likely to insure to him a larger income than a post in Essex Constabulary would supply; and that without labour, risk or responsibility.*

1844: 19 Apr: *Wrote to Otway, the Porter at Blenheim Palace, and old Stow Policeman, to thank him for a grateful mark of attention and respect to his old patron and Justice, in the present of a brace of fine tench which arrived some days since.* 18 May: *A packet from Otway with a document circulated by the D. of Marlborough.*

1848: 3 Mar.

1853: 21 Mar: *Received a visit from Otway, our worthy Constable of Stow and its district in bygone years, before a Constabulary was organized for the County, and now Porter at Blenheim Palace Gate. This grateful and attached person had accompanied a tradesman of Woodstock to a sale of farming stock in this neighbourhood, and took the opportunity of calling on me.*

1854: 14 Aug: *Visited by G. Cooper, the Wardsman of the Penitentiary at Gloucester, Ex Policeman at Bourton on the Water, accompanied by the eldest son of Otway the Porter at Blenheim. The young man is 19 years of age, and is looking out for employment as a Clerk, but not in a law office. His Father wished to bring him under my notice, and sent him to call on me with Cooper, who, being on leave of absence from Gloucester Gaol, has been visiting Otway.*

OTWAY — Robert Waller Otway [29]

Sir Robert Waller Otway, 1st baronet (1770-1846), vice admiral, was born in Ireland, the son of Cooke Otway (1728-1800) and Elizabeth Waller (1747-1807). His father intended him for an army career, but he entered the Royal Navy as a midshipman in 1784; by August 1793 he was promoted into the brig *Falcon* as lieutenant. In December 1793 he was appointed to the 98-gun *Impregnable*, and in January 1795 he was promoted to command the sloop *Thorn*. In April of that year Otway captured *La Belle Créole*, a large schooner sent from Guadeloupe by Victor Hugues (who had been sent to capture Guadeloupe by the French Jacobin government). The schooner was sent to raze St Pierre on the island of Martinique, whose royalist inhabitants gratefully presented Otway with a gold-hilted sword valued at 200 guineas.

After six years of distinguished service in the West Indies, Otway returned to England in November 1800. Sir Hyde Parker took him as his flag captain in the *Royal George*, and in February 1801, in the *London*, when Parker took command of the fleet sent to break the armed neutrality of the Baltic powers. During the ensuing battle, when the commander-in-chief determined to hoist the signal to 'discontinue the action', Otway, opposing the signal, obtained permission to go to Adm. Nelson to ascertain his situation. He was sent home with dispatches. In August 1801 Otway was appointed to the *Edgar*, serving in the Baltic, the English Channel, and the West Indies. He returned to England in July 1802.

In late 1801 Otway married Clementina Holloway (1782-1851), daughter of Adm. John Holloway; they had 5 sons and 5 daughters:

1 Elizabeth (1803-1828)
2 Clementina Matilda (1805-1877)
3 Frances Augusta (1808-1881)
1 Robert Waller Otway (1813-1840), Capt., RN

2 Charles Cooke (1815-1842)
3 George Graham (1816-1881), Adm.; succeeded as 2nd Baronet Otway of Brighton; died at Villa Rone, Naples, Italy
4 Caroline Letitia (1817-1891)
5 Adelaide Louisa (1819-1837)
4 Arthur John Otway (1822-1912); succeeded as 3rd Baron Otway of Brighthelmstone
5 Edward John Otway (1824-1881)

Otway's later career was as eventful and successful as his earlier years. He was promoted to vice admiral and created a baronet on 15 September 1831. He was appointed groom of the bedchamber to both William IV and Victoria, and was promoted to admiral on 23 November 1841. He was appointed GCB on 8 May 1845.

This attribution of 'Captain Otway' to Robert Waller Otway is tentative but likely. The Clifton Irish community is one factor; also it appears that he was at home on leave during early 1806. Otway's daughter Clementina was born and brought up at nearby Wells in Somerset, making another local connection. It seems likely that there was a family connection with the Salters, but despite considerable research nothing has transpired.

1806: 25 Jan: *A very small party; only Lady & Miss Ford, Capt. & Mrs. Otway and another Gentleman besides ourselves. Played at Loo.* 5 Feb: *Called upon the Salters, and made a pleasant visit to the young Ladies, Mrs. Salter not being returned from Bath; met at their house Capt. and Mrs. Otway.* 8 Mar: *at Mrs. Salters, meeting the Hon. Mrs. Yorke & Miss Bradby, Lady Ford & Miss Ford, Mrs. Otway, & Mr. Cox.*

OVERBURY — Joseph Overbury[30]

Joseph Overbury (±1780-1844), JP and land tax commissioner, was born at Tetbury, the son of Nathaniel Overbury (1730-1805), a prominent Tetbury Baptist, and Mary Roper (1740-1815). As a young man he was a captain in the Tetbury volunteers. The family was involved in the local clothing industry and was relatively wealthy. In 1806, after the death of their father, Joseph and his brother Anthony continued in the family trade as woolstaplers, but with the decline of trade in the area—not helped by the Napoleonic Wars—they wound up the business. By 11 May 1806 they had dissolved their partnership.

Joseph Overbury married, at Hankerton, Wiltshire, 15 February 1807, Elizabeth Pike (1782-1832); they had 5 sons and 2 daughters:

1 John (1807-1866); educated at Mill Hill; married, at Battersea, Surrey, 1 June 1832, Mary Ann Lee (1808-1842); 1 son and 1 daughter
2 Joseph (b. 1808)
3 Anthony (b. 1811)
4 Nathaniel (1811-1868)
5 Edward (b. 1812)
1 Helen Elizabeth (1817-1873)
2 Maria Louisa (1820-1858)

On 28 June 1831 Overbury was appointed feoffee of Tetbury, a position he held until his death. He was a nonconformist, and held strong religious views. He became involved in a notorious case, dubbed the 'Last Trial by Jury for Atheism in England', in which he argued controversially and unequivocally that to spread any form of anti-religious opinion was tantamount to a breach of the peace. George Jacob Holyoake, a socialist lecturer, wrote the following about his trial:

> On the morning after my apprehension I was taken before the Rev. Dr. Newell, R. Capper, and J. Overbury, Esquires, magistrates of Cheltenham ... Mr. Overbury said he considered the case satisfactorily proved, and added, "Whether you are of no religion is of very little consequence to us, but your attempt to propagate the infamous sentiment that there is no God, is calculated to produce disorder and confusion, and is a breach of the peace."

The decision was to be overturned two decades later; the judge described Overbury's conduct as 'unnecessarily harsh'.

Overbury was a wealthy man and keen to increase his financial resources. On 7 March 1837 he purchased fifteen shares worth £750 in the new 'Grand Connection Railway' [also known as the Worcester and Wolverhampton Railway] and thirty shares at £1,500 in the 'London and Blackwall Railway and Steam Navigation Company'. By 1833 Overbury had moved to 10 Pittville Parade, Cheltenham, and by 1836 he had become a JP. He served as a land tax commissioner for Cheltenham in 1838.

Overbury died aged 64 and was buried at Tetbury. His will, running to a lengthy five pages, made considerable bequests to his family and friends, including over £20,000 to his children and £3,000 to all his living grandchildren. He made no bequests, however, to his church or the poor.

1838: 16 Oct.
1839: 11 Apr: *The Mag. present on the bench, and usually acting for the district were Messrs. Trye, C. Trye, Capt. Sinclair, Viner Ellis, Overbury and Whittuck.*

OXFORD — Edward Oxford[31]

Edward Oxford (1822-1900), would-be assassin, was born in Birmingham in 1822, the son of George Oxford and Hannah Marklew. On 4 May 1840, he bought a pair of pistols for £2, and a gunpowder flask, and began practising target shooting in various shooting galleries in Leicester Square, the Strand, and the West End. A week before his planned attack, he visited a Lambeth shop owned by a former schoolmate named Gray. He bought fifty copper percussion caps and enquired where he could buy some bullets and thrupence of gunpowder.

At about 4:00 p.m. on 10 June 1840, Oxford took up a position on a footpath at Constitution Hill, near Buckingham Palace. The queen, who was four months pregnant with her first child, was accustomed to riding out in a phaeton, a low, open horse-drawn carriage, with her husband, Prince Albert, in the late afternoon or early evening. She took with her only two outriders as her escort. Oxford shot twice at the couple, missing both times. He was seized by onlookers, arrested and tried at the Old Bailey in July 1840. He was acquitted on the grounds of insanity and sent to Bethlem Royal Hospital, where he remained until the institution's criminal patients were transferred to Broadmoor Hospital in 1864. Three years later, Oxford was offered a discharge if he would agree to leave the country. He lived out the rest of his life in Melbourne, Australia, under the name John Freeman.

1840: 21 June: *On this day was read for the first time in the congregations of the Church the form of thanksgiving, and prayer for Unity, enjoined by public authority in grateful acknowledgment of the goodness of divine Providence in the deliverance of the Queen and Prince Albert on the 10th. Inst., when, as they were passing in an open carriage from Buckingham Palace in the direction of Hyde Park for an evening drive, two pistol shots were fired at them by a youth named Edward Oxford, a native of Birmingham, but of late years employed as a servant in public houses in and about London.* 12 Jul: *Edward Oxford, the youth who fired two loaded pistols at the Queen & Prince Albert has been acquitted of treason on the ground of insanity; ample evidence was adduced of his own insanity derived from his father and grandfather.*

P

PABST — a Dutch family at the Weimar Court

1799: 1 Sep: *dined drank Tea & supped at Court—where many strangers particularly a Dutch Family Pabst. Father, son & daughters.*

PAGET — Henry William Paget [1]

Henry William Paget [born Bayly], 1st marquess of Anglesey (1768-1854), army officer and politician, was born in London, probably at Uxbridge House, Burlington Gardens. He was the eldest of the twelve children of Henry Bayly (1744-1812) and Jane (d. 1817), daughter of Arthur Champagne, dean of Clonmacnoise, Ireland, and his wife, Marianne. Via a tortuous line of descent starting from William, 1st Baron Paget (1505-1563), Henry Bayly became, in 1770, the 10th Baron Paget (taking by royal licence the name Paget in place of Bayly) and, in 1784, the first earl of Uxbridge of the second creation.

Paget had a long and successful military career, serving with particular distinction in the Peninsular War. In 1808, when Sir John Moore was given command of a 20,000-strong expeditionary force to Spain, Paget obtained command of the cavalry within Sir David Baird's 19,000-strong force, which had been sent to Corunna to join Moore's army marching up from Lisbon. However, news of Napoleon's rapid advance and complete overthrow of the Spanish armies Moore was to have succoured precipitated an immediate change to the British strategy. Baird began retreating to Corunna while Moore retreated to Lisbon. Meantime, Napoleon, believing Moore and Baird to be in full flight, decided to march on Madrid, leaving only Marshal Soult's 18,000 men in the north-west. Paget succeeded in joining the two British armies at Mayorga on 20 December 1808; so successful was he in masking the junction that Soult was quite unaware that it had taken place. Next morning there followed what Charles Oman described as 'perhaps the most brilliant exploit of the British cavalry during the whole six years of the [Peninsular] war'.

Paget had a colourful life. On his return to England he was fêted a hero. He became embroiled in a famous scandal involving an elopement, a divorce, a duel, and a second marriage; *DNB* offers a detailed account. Besides his military career, Paget was MP for Caernarvon Boroughs in 1790-96 and Milborne Port in 1796-1804 and 1806-10. He served as master general of ordnance in 1827-28 and 1846-52, and lord lieutenant of Ireland in 1828-29 and 1830-33. He was known as Lord Paget from 1784 to 1812, and succeeded as 2nd earl of Uxbridge in 1812 and marquess of Anglesey in 1815.

1827: 20 Apr: *Mr. Canning proceeds slowly in the organization of his Ministry. The Master-generalship of the Ordnance is assigned to the Marquis of Anglesey, a brave & gallant soldier.* 2 May.

1829: 7 Feb: *Lord Anglesey, formerly a vigorous opponent of Emancipation, is now its sanguine advocate.*

1848: 25 Jul: *On the opposite shore of the strait we had a view of Plas Newydd, the seat of the Marquis of Anglesey.*

PAGET — Thomas Bradley Paget — *see also* Alford [2]

Thomas Bradley Paget (1782-1846), Church of England clergyman, was born at Tamworth, Staffordshire, the son of Thomas Bradley Paget (1760-1817) and Mary Warren (b. 1746). He was educated at Wadham College, Oxford (BA 1804; MA 1809), and was ordained deacon on 21 December 1806 and priest on 20 December 1807. Paget's first clerical appointment was as stipendiary curate of Grendon, Northamptonshire, from 18 January 1811. He was later appointed incumbent of Long Acre episcopal chapel and vicar of Evington, Leicestershire, in 1842. He held the Evington living for four years until 1846. Paget married, first, at Rock, Worcestershire, 7 September 1809, Elizabeth Watkins (1788-1815); they had 1 son 2 daughters:

1 Elizabeth (b. 1810)
1 Thomas Bradley Paget (1812-1893)
2 Mary (b. 1813)

Also in 1809, Henry Alford, Paget's close college friend, married his sister Sarah Paget. Paget married secondly, at Lenton, Nottinghamshire, 20 April 1819, Charlotte Dorothy Evans (b. 1789).

Francis Witts was close to Thomas Paget during his first year at Oxford, and then they drifted apart. He made no reference to him in his diaries later in life.

1802: 21 Feb: *Spent the Evening with Paget, meeting Alford, Marsh, Gamlin of Baliol.* 22 Feb., 24 Feb: *Breakfasted with Paget, meeting Hastings, Edgell, Alford & Stevens.* 28 Feb: *Walked with Stevens, Paget, Alford, Gamlin, Williams & Rashleigh, to Headington.* 2 Mar., 6 Mar., 9-10 Mar., 13 Mar: *Spent the Evening with Paget, meeting a Gentleman of Worcester College, a Mr. Alworthy.* 14 Mar., 18 Mar., 20-21 Mar., 1-2 May, 4 May: *Accompanied Evans, Edgell, Paget, Alford, Edwards, & Williams to Nuneham Lord Harcourt's place six miles down river.* 5-7 May, 14 May, 16 May, 19-20 May, 3 Jun., 13-14 Jun.

1804: 6 Mar.

1806: 18 Mar: *Called upon Round; walked a little with Alford & Paget; visited the Bodleian.*

PAICE — Mr Paice, surveyor, of Basingstoke

1853: 23 Mar: *Recd. a letter from Mr. Paice of Basingstoke, Executor of the late R.C. Lumbert.* 26 Mar., 17 May: *Had an interview with Mr. Paice, Executor to the late R.C. Lumbert, who had arrived to look over his property in this village & parish.* 9 Dec.

PAIN — George Pain — *see also* Merchant [3]

George Pain (±1793-1871), jeweller, was born at Stow-on-the-Wold, possibly a son of Alexander Pain (1763-1837), draper, who went bankrupt in about 1805. He married, 1818, at St Cross, Oxford, Mary (±1795-1875), daughter of Thomas Knowles (1754-1826) and Sarah Clements (1760-1846); they had 1 son and 1 daughter:

1 Anna Mary (±1819-1888); married James Merchant (1812-1889), farmer, of Lower Swell
1 George Archer (1821-1892), Bank of England clerk; married Catherine Dorothea (b. ±1830), born at Chelsea, Middlesex; lived at Gravesend in 1861 and 1871, according to censuses; had retired to Finstock House, Oxfordshire, by 1891 with his second wife, Harriet (b. ±1838), born at Upper Clapton, Middlesex. His death was registered at Chipping Norton

The Pain family lived at Market Place, Stow-on-the-Wold, where George Pain was a respected tradesman. He ran a watchmaking shop, but more importantly to Francis Witts, he was actuary of the savings bank and oversaw the book society and other local organisations. Witts, who liked and respected George Pain, used his premises to hold meetings and even once changed for dinner at his house (31 December 1852). Pain's employee Henry Stone (b. ±1803) boarded with with him and his wife Mary until as late as 1871. In the census for that year Stone was listed as 'librarian', presumably having taken over the Stow book society librarianship from George Pain.

1834: 7 Aug: *To Stow, to attend at the Provident Bank, and in the Justice room; at the former George Payn took his seat for the first time as book- keeper, with the assistance of Mr. Lefevre, Steward of Mr. Abraham Pole, who since the murder of poor Rens has been engaged as a temporary book-keeper.* 26 Sep: *While so engaged, Henry Stone, Shopman to Mr. Pain, Watchmaker, Stow, came with notes from Mr. Pole and Mr. Winter, to inform me, that yesterday one Thornton of Stow, Tailor, and repairer of watches, had brought to Pain's shop a part of the gold repeater of the late unfortunate Mr. Rens. That in his Master's absence, who was engaged as Actuary at the Savings Bank, Henry, who observed to Thornton that he had seen the watch before, desired the man to bring all the watch to Mr. Pain the next morning, which he did, accounting for the manner, in which it came into his possession.* 30 Sep.

1835: 27 Feb: *Wrote to George Pain, Actuary of the Provident Bank, with directions for entries to be made by him in the minutes of that institution.* 23 Mar., 13 Apr.

1836: 22 Nov., 10 Dec., 21 Dec: *Certain modifications of the Regulations were agreed to; among others that the Clerk, Mr. Geo. Pain, be paid a gratuity of £20 for his diligent services of the past year; and that his salary for the future be raised from £52. 10. 0. to £80. per ann.*

1837: 11 Jan., 17 Jan: *Wrote to Newmarch to make enquiries respecting a Clergyman near Cirencester, to whose care Geo. Pain, the Watchmaker and Clerk to our Provident Bank, thinks of consigning his son, for a year's instruction in a sound course of English grammar, Arithmetic and writing, with a view to his being qualified to hold the situation of a Clerk in the bank of England, to which he hopes to obtain an appointment thro' the interest of Mr. Pole.* 24 Jan., 6 Jun., 4 Nov., 17 Nov., 30 Dec.

1838: 28 Mar: *Then joined my son at G. Pain's with whom he was consulting as to purchases of furniture at a sale about to take place in the town to day, and at which Pain was to bid for E.F.W.* 6 Apr., 6 Nov., 12 Nov., 30 Nov.

1839: 12 Mar., 25 Jun., 27 Jun., 11 Jul: *A meeting of the Committee appointed on June 27. had been appoin fixed for to-day, to consider the accommodation for the Prov. Bank, Book Society, and Distr. Comm. of the Soc. for prom. Xtian Knowl., which might be provided under George Pain's roof.* 5 Aug.

1840: 11 Apr., 18 Apr., 20 Apr., 14 May, 10 Jun., 9 Jul., 21 Jul., 25 Aug., 10 Sep., 12 Sep., 21 Sep., 29 Sep.

1842: 5 Feb., 12 Jul., 12 Sep., 5 Oct., 19 Dec., 28 Dec: *The services of the Actuary, Mr. Pain, were justly commended.* 29 Dec.

1843: 12 Jan., 26 Sep., 15 Dec., 22 Dec.

1844: 6 May: *As we returned through Stow, I called at the Workhouse, and conferred with Mr. Pearce on Union matters: also at Mr. G. Pain's, and conversed with him on the projected change in the law as to Savings Banks.* 10 May, 17 May, 30 May, 30 Sep: *At the Library conferred with Mr. Pain, who is also an invalid from derangement of the biliary organs.* 7 Oct., 15 Nov., 12 Dec.

1845: 7 Jan: *Mr. Pain, as Actuary, had prepared a draft of amended resolutions for our consideration in a manner most creditable to him.* 27 Jan., 6-7 Feb., 17 Feb., 24 Feb., 1 Mar., 15 Mar., 22 Mar., 30 Mar: *George Pain from Stow called in the evening to consult me whether he must obey a subpoena to attend at the Assizes at Gloucester as a witness in a cause of money lent & not repaid: the lender having withdrawn the money from the Prov. Bank to accommodate the Borrower, and Mr. Pain's evidence being required, as Actuary of the Prov. B., to prove such withdrawal.* 2 Apr: *Mr. Pain came from Stow to accompany me in the phaeton to Cheltenham, where he would pass the day with friends, and whence he would proceed to-morrow to Gloucester, to give evidence in a cause to be tried at the Assizes.* 28 Jun: *Mr. Pain came from Stow with some gold watches for my inspection: selected one, which he recommended — so superseding, ere long, my old fashioned companion of seven & thirty years, who is, indeed, like myself, the worse for wear.*

1846: 6 Jul., 11 Jul., 26 Aug., 26 Sep., 13 Nov.

1847: 21 Mar., 26 Mar., 20 May: *Attended at the Prov. Bank, where I regretted to find Mr. Pain very unwell.* 24 May: *Called at the library: Mr. Pain is a great invalid, but slowly recovering.* 29 May, 2 Jul., 16 Jul., 8 Aug: *also to Mr. Pain, desiring him to come or send Henry Stone to rectify a time piece which is out of order.* 10 Sep., 28 Sep., 12 Nov., 23 Dec.

1848: 21 Jan., 25 Mar: *also wrote to Mr. Pain to send me my watch, which he had undertaken to repair.* 20 Apr., 25-26 Apr., 19 May, 22 May, 29 May, 12 Oct: *To the Provident Bank, ... Mr. Pain being confined to his bed by a fit of the gout.* 27 Oct., 10 Nov.

1849: 30 Dec., 31 May, 6 Jun., 17-18 Jun., 24 Jun., 26 Jun., 8 Jul., 23 Jul., 18 Sep., 1 Oct., 6 Oct., 12 Oct., 25 Oct., 9 Nov., 16 Nov: *Wrote a note to G. Pain, Stow, as to repairing a time-piece which I sent to his shop, as it is out of order.* 19 Dec.

1851: 2 Jan., 20 Jan., 20 Feb., 7 Mar., 23 Apr., 2 May, 5 May.

1852: 23 Jan: *On my return found Mr. G. Pain, who had been regulating and restoring to active service my time-piece; he advised with me as to the assessment to the Poor Rate of Stow, charged on him for his house.* 12 Feb., 1 Mar., 14 Mar., 18 Nov: *To the Provident Bank, where I met Mr. Pole, and Mr. Morrison. George Pain suffering sadly from gout.* 25 Nov., 6 Dec., 31 Dec: *Having dressed at G. Pain's, and the Carriage having come from U.S. bringing Mr. Ball, who had been taken up at Lower Slaughter Turnpike Gate, I went to dine with Mr. and Mrs. W.B. Pole at Upper Swell.*

1853: 16 May, 19 May, 14 Dec., 17 Dec: *To Mr. Pain, Stow, with my watch, which is out of order, and as to which I begged him to examine it, and advise Brookes the watchmaker as to its repair.*

1854: 30 Jan., 3 Mar., 4 Apr., 3 May, 26 May: *Wrote to Mr. Burrup, to get him, as Under Sheriff, to relieve G. Pain, Stow, of a fine imposed on him for non attendance as Juror at the last Q.S: the case being that I had written to Curtis Hayward to excuse the fine, as G.P. is above 60 years of age.* 2 Jun.

PAINE — William Paine[4]

William Paine (±1801-1874), farmer, was born at Cheltenham, probably a son of William and Hannah Paine. He was married to Ann (b. ±1803), who had been born at Willesden, Middlesex and they had 2 sons and 3 daughters:

1 Charlotte Nicoll (b. ±1833), born at Chesham, Buckinghamshire

1 Richard (b. ±1841), born at Saunderton, Buckinghamshire

2 Charles (b. ±1845), born at Saunderton

2 Ann (b. ±1846), born at Saunderton

3 Sarah (b. ±1847), born at Princes Risborough, Buckinghamshire

Based on the birth places of the children, William Paine moved to Buckinghamshire and farmed at Chesham, Saunderton, and

Princes Risborough before taking a tenancy on a farm owned by Sarah Shard of 180 acres. He did not remain Lacey Green very long, for by the time of the 1861 census he was farming 232 acres at Botley Hill Farm, Titsey, Surrey. By 1871 he had retired and was living with his son Charles, who became a butcher at Ealing, Middlesex. He died at Ealing.

William had at least one brother, Joseph (1812-1867), a carpenter by trade, who followed him to Buckinghamshire. He was married to Eliza (b. ±1824), born at Great Missenden, Buckinghamshire, and they lived in High Street, Great Missenden which is about 5 miles from Lacey Green. There were no children of the marriage.

1850: 14 Aug: *In the evening, Mrs. Shard's tenant, Payne, came to renew an old acquaintance with me. In 1814, when I succeeded to the Vicarage of Stanway, his family held the Paper-mill farm in that parish. He seemed a cheerful, well informed man of his class.*

PAINTER — Elizabeth Painter — *see* Paynter & Pugh

PAKINGTON — John Somerset Russell Pakington — *see also* Thomas Henry Hastings Davies[5]

John Somerset Russell Pakington [born Russell], 1st Baron Hampton (1799-1880), politician, was born at Slaughter's Court, Powick, Worcestershire, the second son of William Russell (d. 1812) and Elizabeth (d. 1813), daughter of Sir Herbert Perrott Pakington, 7th baronet. Elizabeth was the sister and heir of Sir John Pakington, 8th and last baronet Pakington, of Aylesbury.

Russell [later Pakington] was educated at Eton College and Oriel College, Oxford. In 1830, upon inheriting the estates of his maternal uncle, he assumed by royal licence the surname Pakington. Among these estates was Westwood House in Worcestershire, where he moved in 1832. Pakington was MP for Droitwich in 1837-74. He was given office by Sir Robert Peel in 1841 and created, 1846, 1st Baronet Pakington of the second creation, of Westwood, Worcestershire. He next served under Lord Derby in 1852 as secretary of state for war and the colonies. He again held office under Lord Derby as first lord of the Admiralty in 1858-59, after which he was appointed GCB, and in 1866-67. As first lord he commissioned the first ironclad warship, HMS *Warrior*, launched in 1860. Under Derby and his successor, Benjamin Disraeli, Pakington was secretary of state for war in 1867-68. He was elevated to the peerage in 1874 as Baron Hampton of Hampton Lovett and Westwood in the county of Worcester.

Pakington married, first, at Lichfield Cathedral, 14 August 1822, Mary (1799-1843), only child of Moreton Aglionby Slaney (1765-1817), of Shifnal, Shropshire, and Mary (1771-1818), daughter of Richard Prince Corbet of High Hatton; they had 1 son:

1 John Slaney (1826-1893); succeeded as 2nd Baron Hampton, 1880

Pakington married secondly, 4 June 1844, Augusta Anne (1817-1848), third daughter of Revd George Murray, bishop of Rochester, and Sarah Maria Hay-Drummond; they had 1 son and 1 daughter:

1 Herbert Perrott Murray (1846-1901); succeeded as 3rd Baron Hampton, 1893
1 Edith (b. & d. 1845)

Pakington married thirdly, 5 June 1851, Augusta Davies, née Champion-de Crespigny (1799-1892), widow of Col Thomas Henry Hastings Davies (1789-1846), MP, of Elmley Castle, Worcestershire.

1825: 16 May: *Beyond is the village of Powick; the situation of the Church, grouping with trees and rural buildings on a high bank, is very striking. Here———is a seat of Mr. Russel, nephew of Sir John Packington, who has a fine old place, in the style of a French chateau, near Droitwich.*

1826: 14 Sep: *At ten in the forenoon I attended a meeting of Subscribers to the Triennial festivals ... For some time no one was present but his Grace of Beaufort & myself; subsequently, the Archdeacon of Gloucester, the Archdeacon of Hereford (Wetherell) the Dean of St.Asaph (Luxmoore) Dr. Cooke, Mr. Russel, of Powick near Worcester, Mr. Phelps and one or two more attended.*

1844: 20 Dec: *Wrote to Mr. Pakington, Chairman of the Worcestershire Quarter Sessions respecting a county rate charged on Icomb (late Worcestershire) for this Quarter, as if it remained a part of that County, whereas early in the Quarter it was attached to Gloucestershire by a late Act of Parlt. and has been assessed to the County rate for this County—urged that the Worcestershire claim is unfair, and, probably, untenable in law.* 23 Dec: *A letter from Mr. Pakington, Chairman of the QS. for Worcestershire in answer to mine of the 20th. Inst. as to the claim made on Icomb for County rate to Worcestershire: Mr. P. will recommend that no claim made by his County shall be enforced.*

1850: 27 Feb: *The Conservative party now in the ascendant; Lord Derby Prime Minister, Disraeli Chancellor of the Exchequer, Messrs. Walpole, Lord Malmesbury, and Sir John Pakington, Secretaries of State for the Home, Foreign & Colonial Departments—Duke of Northumberland, First Lord of the Admiralty, Mr. Henley at the Board of Trade, Sir E. Sugden, Lord Chancellor &c.*

PALEY — Edmund Paley[6]

Edmund Paley (1782-1850), Church of England clergyman, was born at Carlisle, second son of William Paley, archdeacon of Carlisle (1743-1805) (*below*) and Jane Hewitt (1744-1791). He was educated at Carlisle Grammar School and Queen's College, Oxford. Paley was ordained deacon on 7 February 1808 and priest on 14 August 1808. He was vicar of Cawthorne, Yorkshire, in 1809-22, vicar of Easingwold, in 1812-37, and rector of Gretford, Lincolnshire, in 1837-50. He married, at St Andrew's the Great, Cambridge, 14 October 1812, Sarah Apthorp (1788-1864); they had 7 sons and 3 daughters:

1 Anne (1813-1872)
1 Frederick Apthorp (1815-1888), professor of classics
2 William (1816-1911), MD, JP, and alderman of the City of London
2 Jessey (1818-1866)
3 Catherine (1819-1880)
3 Edmund (1821-1840)
4 Edward Graham (1823-1895)
5 Temple Chevallier (1825-1910), surgeon
6 Francis Henry (1826-1909), Church of England clergyman
7 John Hewitt (1830-1857)

1833: 8 Nov: *The benefice [Easingwold] is in the patronage of the Archbishop of York, and the present incumbent is Mr. Edmund Paley, a Son of the late eminent Archdeacon Paley: Mr. E.P. was formerly of Queen's College, Oxford, and my contemporary.*

PALEY — James Paley[7]

James Paley (1783-1863), Church of England clergyman, was born at Carlisle, the third son of William Paley, archdeacon of Carlisle (1743-1805) (*below*) and Jane Hewitt (1744-1791). He was educated at Carlisle Grammar School, Queen's College, Oxford, and Magdalen College, Cambridge (BA 1813). Paley was ordained deacon on 20 September 1812 and priest on 20 December 1812.

His first clerical appointment was as curate of St John the Baptist, Devizes, Wiltshire, from 20 September 1812. He was then appointed vicar of Lacock, Wiltshire, on 19 April 1814. He married, at Bury, Lancashire, 10 July 1810, Alice Hutchinson (1780-1855); they had 4 sons and 3 daughters:

1 William (b. 1811)
1 Sarah (1815-1865)
2 John (1816-1899); educated at Sherborne School and Peterhouse College, Cambridge (BA 1838); served as curate of Lacock, Wiltshire, 1840-43; vicar of Hook, Yorkshire, 1843-59; vicar of Codsall, Staffordshire, 1859-67; vicar of Longstone, Derbyshire, 1867-72; and vicar of Lacock, Wiltshire, 1878-95; married, 1843, Emily Anne, eldest daughter of Capt. F. W. Rooke, RN, of Lackham House, Wiltshire; resided at Bath, 1898
2 Alice (1817-1838)
3 James (1818-1870)
4 Charles Edward (1822-1897)
3 Mary Jane (1823-1872)

1843: 14 Oct: ... *also Mr. and Mrs. Ford, accompanied by Mr. and Mrs. Paley. Mrs. P. we had known as Miss Rooke, daughter of Captn. Rooke of Lackham; she has lately married a Clergyman of small fortune, beneficed in the East riding of York, grandson of Archdeacon Paley, son of James Paley, the youngest of the sons of the Archdeacon, formerly well known to my wife and me at Giggleswick in days long passed: he had been, perhaps, still is beneficed at Laycock, near Chippenham, but in declining health, and now resident with his son and daughter in law.*

PALEY — William Paley[8]

William Paley (1743-1805), Church of England clergyman, was born at Peterborough, Northamptonshire, son of Canon William Paley (1711-1799), vicar of Helpston, near Peterborough, and headmaster of Giggleswick, and Elizabeth Clapham (1712-1796) of Stackhouse. He was educated at Christ's College, Cambridge (BA 1763; MA 1766; DD 1795), and was a pluralist in grand style. He was rector of Musgrave, Westmorland, 1775-1805; vicar of Dalston, 1776-93; vicar of Appleby, 1777-89; prebendary of Carlisle, 1780-95; archdeacon of Carlisle, 1782-1805; rector of Great Salkeld, Cumberland; chancellor of Carlisle, 1782-95; vicar of Addingham, 1792-95; vicar of Stanwix, Cumberland, 1793-95; prebendary of St Paul's Cathedral, 1794; sub-dean of Lincoln, 1795-1805; and rector of Bishop Wearmouth, Durham, 1795-1805. Paley married, first, at St Mary's, Carlisle, Cumberland, 6 June 1776, Jane Hewitt (1744-1791), daughter of a Carlisle spirit merchant; they had 4 sons and 4 daughters:

1 Jane (1777-1826)
1 William (1779-1817), chancery barrister; educated at Pembroke College, Cambridge, and Lincoln's Inn
2 Elizabeth (1781-1838)
2 Edmund (1782-1850); *see above*
3 James (1783-1863); *see above*
3 Mary (1787-1851)
3 Edward (1788-1833)
4 Anne (1789-1876)
4 John (b. & d. 1790)

Paley married secondly, at Carlisle, Cumberland, Catherine Dobinson of Carlisle.

1824: 27 Jun.
1825: 30 May.
1843: 14 Oct.

PALMER — Mr Palmer, dinner guest at Calwich Abbey

1802: 1 Oct: *Miss Sneyd, Mr. Newdigate & Mrs Palmer dined at Calwich.* 5 Oct: *Mrs. Gilbert, Mrs. Ingram, Mr. Palmer, Mrs. Lockhart, Mr. Baker & Mr. Bennet dined with us.*

PALMER — John Palmer[9]

John Palmer (1805-1884), gardener, was born at Poole, Dorset, the son of Thomas Palmer. He married, at Upper Slaughter, 14 May 1840, a widow, Anne Johnson, née Lait (1805-1869), born at Colesbourne, the daughter of Richard Lait. John and Anne had 2 sons and 2 daughters:

1 Mary Ann (b. 1841)
2 Elizabeth (b. 1842)
1 James (1845-1928); married, 1872, Sarah Maria Ricks (1847-1890); 3 daughters:
   1 Edith Ann (1878-1930)
   2 Elizabeth (b. 1882)
   3 Eliza Mary (b. 1885)
2 Joseph Lait (1848-1912), lodging house keeper; lived at Leamington Priors, Warwickshire, with his wife, Emma Elizabeth (b. ±1844), born at Sidlesham, Sussex; at least 1 son and 2 daughters:
   1 Florence (b. ±1875)
   1 Arthur (b. 1880)
   2 Daisy (b. ±1883)

The family appears to have lived at Eyford and worked across three generations as gardeners for the Dolphin family and their successors.

1840: 11 Sep: *In the Evening I walked again to Eyford to visit John Palmer, a labourer, suffering under a severe injury occasioned by a heavy wall, close to which he was at work near the Eyford conservatory, falling on him yesterday morng. He was buried in the ruins, and nearly a quarter of an hour elapsed before he was extricated: I found him very much bruised, his face greatly excoriated; no serious internal injury is apprehended, but he seems to have a broken thigh, which cannot yet be meddled with in consequence of the swelling. The same limb had been broken many years ago, and ill set, causing lameness. Mr. Hayward attends him. It is a mercy that the man was not killed outright, the stones falling first against a bank, the force of the fall was somewhat broken.* 12 Sep: *Rode home by Eyford that I might enquire after John Palmer, who is reported to be going on pretty well: there is less fever and swelling, and the injured limb has been placed in a proper position.* 18 Sep: *Walked to Eyford to visit John Palmer, whom I found restless and in low spirits. At his cottage met Mrs. Dolphin, and her connections and guests, Mrs. Chamberlain and Miss Knight.* 10 Oct: *Visited J. Palmer of Eyford.*

1851: 6 Jan: *Walked to Eyford: called on John Palmer, who is recovering from a serious illness.* 22 Apr: *Walked to Eyford— Visited poor inhabitants there — Pinchin, Watts, Palmer.*

1852: 31 Dec: *I meant to have sent the groom with this note, but substituted J Palmer as I found the former to be suffering from a bad feverish cold.*

1854: 28 Apr: *My upper Servants had considered how best the inconvenience could be remedied. Charles Clift undertook to drive the phaeton, while John Palmer should take the stable work.*

PALMER — Joseph Palmer[10]

Joseph Palmer (b. ±1799), butcher, of Withington, Gloucestershire, was committed on 2 May 1820 by Francis Witts on suspicion of felony, for stealing seven teg sheep, valued at £14, the property of

Edward Baker of Bourton-on-the-Water. He was tried at Gloucester on 9 August 1820 and sentenced to death. His sentence was commuted to transportation for life, and he sailed on 26 March 1821 for New South Wales on the *Adamant*. The medical journal of the *Adamant*, convict ship from 10 March to 12 September 1821 by James Hamilton, surgeon superintendent reports: Folio 2: Struck one iron off the following men— ... ... Joseph Palmer, butcher....

It is known that he arrived alive in New South Wales on 8 September, 1821, but nothing more has been discovered about him.

1820: 21 Aug: *At the latter (Gaol) I had an interview with Jos. Palmer, a Sheep Stealer, whom I had committed & who had been tried, sentenced & left for execution: tho' found guilty on the clearest & most direct evidence, this hardened young man, persisted in denying his crime, & at the same time, that he had every reason to believe, that he would be hanged on the following Saturday: nor did my admonitions appear to affect him more than other exhortations, which had been addressed to him.*

PALMER — Robert Palmer [11]

Robert Palmer (1793-1872), JP, MP, and landed proprietor, of Holme Park, Sonning, Berkshire, and 6 Charles Street, Berkeley Square, London, was the eldest son of Richard Palmer, of Hurst and Holme Park, and Jane, daughter of Oldfield Bowles of North Aston, Oxfordshire. He was educated at Eton College and Trinity College, Cambridge. He was MP for Berkshire in 1825-31 and 1832-59, and high sheriff for the same county in 1818-19.

1832: 13 Jun: *In politics, a moderate Tory, he has recently stood forward to support Mr. Palmer, the newly elected representative for Berkshire, who was opposed by the veteran Radical, Mr. Hallett, backed by the interest of the Political Unionists of Birmingham, Bristol &c., the thorough reformers of this County, and the radical press, especially the Times journal, one of the leading editors of which, a Mr. Walter, has considerable influence in Berks.*

1839: 4 May: *The coach in which I travelled held only myself and Mr. Palmer of Holme Park, MP. for Berkshire, a very pleasant, gentlemanly person.*

PALMER — Thomas Palmer of Eyford [12]

Thomas Palmer (±1767-1839), gardener, was most likely the father of John Palmer (*above*). John was born at Poole, Dorset, and from an early point in the nineteenth century his father was probably employed by the Dorset connections of the Dolphin family as a gardener, later relocating from Dorset to Gloucestershire. John succeeded his father as gardener at Eyford and his son James succeeded him; for a continual span of over eighty years the Palmers were the estate's gardeners.

Thomas Palmer appears to have also had a daughter, Mary Anne, who married, at Upper Slaughter, 25 June 1827, Richard Williams, a widower from Naunton.

1839: 28 Jul: *Between the services I went to Eyford to administer the Sacrament to T. Palmer, whom I had promised to visit for that purpose tomorrow; but I was summoned under the impression that the poor man was not likely to survive many hours: a painful and fatiguing duty.* 2 Aug: *Officiated in the evening at the funeral of Thomas Palmer of Eyford.*

PALMER — Thomas Palmer of Bourton [13]

Thomas Palmer (1799-1856), draper, was born at Bourton-on-the-Water, the son of Baptists Samuel Palmer (1762-1851) and Elizabeth Wilkins (d. 1829). He ran a general store of drapery and grocery and was also sub-postmaster and agent to Hand in Hand Fire & Life Insurance Society, founded in 1696. It seems that his general store was the largest shop in the area. He married, at Chaceley, Worcestershire, 1835, Mary Anne (1812-1854[?]), born in Cheltenham, the daughter of William and Amelia Stone; they had 2 sons and 5 daughters:

1 Ellen Amelia (b. 1837)
2 Louisa (1840-1919); married, at Mangotsfield, Gloucestershire, 23 October 1859, John Stiddard (1839-1909)
1 Alfred John (1841)
3 Fanny (b. 1845)
4 Laura Jane (1846-1908); married, at St George's, Hanover Square, Westminster, 2 August 1871, Joseph Sotham (1840-1897); died at Toronto, Canada; 1 son and 5 daughters
5 Mary Edith (1849-1936); married, at Holy Trinity, Upper Tooting, Wandsworth, Surrey, 18 July 1887, Edward Sampson (b. ±1835)
2 William Stone (b. 1851)

By the time of the 1861 census the family had left Bourton and apparently spread out. In 1861, Fanny was a 'visitor' at the home of 49-year-old cattle dealer Robert Miller. Alfred was registered as a grocer at Burford, Oxfordshire; it seems that he was living with a previously unknown sister, who was 18 and a schoolmistress. The census taker was very sloppy in listing her as a 'daughter' when really she was a boarder, like her brother Alfred. Her initials seem to be A. M., and she was said to have been born in 'Oxon, Bourton', another obvious error. In the same household, listed as a scholar, was 14-year-old Margaret Miller from Lechlade. This seems too much of a coincidence; the Millers were most likely related to the Palmers. Mary Edith, Thomas Palmer's youngest daughter, was listed as an 11-year-old 'scholar' living with her uncle, William Lane, farmer, and her aunt Edith, presumably née Stone, who was born at Cheltenham. Apart from this little has been found.

1837: 11 Aug: *We met Messrs. Ford, Waller, Daubeny, Dr. Stenson, Stenson Junr., Coles, Kimber, Palmer, Ransford, W. Smith, Jos. Bryan, Kendall, Wells &c.*

1838: 1 Jun.

1839: 25 Mar.

1840: 5 Jun.

1842: 3 Jun.

1844: 30 Sep: *Before I left the W.H. Mr. and Mrs. Palmer of Bourton, who are connected with Mrs. P., arrived.*

1848: 2 Jun.

1851: 29 Mar: *Drove to Bourton on the Water to Palmer's shop to give directions as to the outfit for these emigrants.* 30 Mar: *Wrote to Palmer, Bourton on the Water, with a cheque for £2. 16. 0 in payment of charge for Insurance in the Union fire office, which I had forgotten to leave with him yesterday.* 2 Apr., 8-9 Apr., 12 Apr., 21 Apr., 3 May, 17 May: *Wrote to Mr. Palmer, Bourton on the Water, with a cheque for the amount of his bill for the outfit of the Emigrant Smiths. Received an acknowledgment of the receipt of the cheque.* 18 May.

1852: 21 Mar: *To Mr. Palmer, Bourton on the Water, with a cheque for years insurance for this house &c.* 23 Mar.

1853: 3 Jun: *Few Honorary Members were present — R Waller in the Chair, myself, Boggis & Ball, Stenson, two Bryans, Palmer, two Colletts (Wick Risington, and Lower Slaughter) Healths drunk, and speeches made, secundum usum, discussion as to Rules, songs by W. Bryan, and Stenson, a comic story or two by T. Palmer, &c.*

1854: 1 Apr: *parleyed with RW. and after transacting a little business at Palmer's shop, proceeded to Little Risington.* 24

Jun., 12 Jul: *Granted a search warrant to search the house of one Kilby, of Naunton, Father of a female servant late in the family of Palmer, Shopkeeper at Bourton, and suspected of having stolen from him a piece of silk.* 13 Jul: *The young woman charged on suspicion of stealing silk from Palmer, brought before us, some child bed linen, the property of the Palmers having been found in her possession.* 17 Jul: *With R. Waller, as my colleague, at Mr. Palmer's house, took the evidence of himself and his daughter, and P.C. Evans, as to a wholesale robbery committed on his premises of his property by his late Servant, Hannah Kilby.* 18 Jul.

PALMER — William Jocelyn Palmer [14]

William Jocelyn Palmer (1777-1853), Church of England clergyman, was born at Mixbury, Oxfordshire, the son of William Palmer (1737-1821) and Mary Horsley (1747-1824). He was educated at Brasenose College, Oxford (BA 1799; MA 1802; BD 1811), and was appointed rector of Mixbury, Oxfordshire, in 1802, and of Finmere in 1814. Palmer married, at York, 10 September 1810, Dorothea (1792-1867), third and youngest daughter of Revd William Roundell (1746-1821), of Gledstone and Screven, and Mary (1752-1818), youngest daughter of Revd Henry Richardson (1711-1778), rector of Thornton. Her parents had married in 1775. William and Dorothea had 6 sons and 5 daughters:

1 William (1811-1879), Church of England clergyman
2 Henry Roundell Palmer (1812-1895); created 1st earl of Selborne
3 Thomas (1814-1823)
4 Henry Roundell (1816-1834)
1 Mary Richardson (1818-1859)
2 Eleanor (1820-1873)
5 George Horsley (1822-1890)
6 Edwin (1824-1895)
3 Emma (1827-1874)
4 Dorothea (1829-1852)
5 Emily Frances (1831-1906)

1838: 24 Nov: *A letter addressed to the Chairman of the Stow Union from the Revd. Mr. Palmer of Mixbury, Oxon.* 29-30 Nov.

PALMERSTON — Viscount Palmerston — *see* Henry Temple

PANTIN — Thomas Pinder Pantin [15]

Thomas Pinder [Pindar] Pantin (1792-1866), theologian, was born at West Smithfield, London, the son of Thomas Pantin (1762-1820), brushmaker, and Elizabeth Lidgould (d. 1828). He was educated at Queen's College, Oxford (BA 1821; MA 1827), and was ordained deacon on 26 September 1824 and priest on 25 September 1825. Pantin's first clerical appointment was as stipendiary curate of Swinford, Leicestershire, from 26 September 1824. He was appointed curate of Stratford-upon-Avon, Warwickshire, on 1 January 1825, and then rector of Westcote, Gloucestershire, on 25 September 1828, where he remained until his death. His son, John Wickliffe, succeeded him as rector of Westcote.

Pantin wrote several small polemical works against Roman Catholic claims, including *Observations on certain passages in Dr Arnold's Christian duty of granting the Roman Catholic claims* (1829), *The Novelty of Popery in Matters of Faith and Practice* (1837), and *The Church of England, apostolical in its origin, episcopal in its government, and scriptural in its belief* (1849). He also edited, with additional notes, Bishop Stillingfleet's *Origines Britannicae* (2 vols, 1842) and Bishop Bull's *Corruptions of the Church of Rome* (1836), adding a preface.

Pantin married, first, Ann (surname unknown); they had at least 1 son and 1 daughter:

1 Unknown daughter; died an infant
1 Thomas Pinder Pantin (±1817-±1850), ensign; married, at Islington, Middlesex, 26 November 1839, Sophia Maria Farmer Woodruffe (b. 1819). She remarried, as a widow, at St Peter's, Walworth, Surrey, 3 December 1856, William Edward Style (b. ±1826), wood sawyer, son of Edward Style, timber dealer

Pantin married secondly, at St George the Martyr, Holborn, London, 25 January 1822, Hannah Godfrey (1793-1882), born at East Hendred, Berkshire; they had at least 1 son:

1 John Wickliffe (1829-1902), Church of England clergyman; born at Lutterworth, Leicestershire; married, at Upper Hollway, Middlesex, Caroline (b. ±1850)

1829: 30 Aug: *"Observations on certain passages in Dr. Arnold's Christian duty of granting the Roman Catholic Claims", relating to the supremacy of the Bishop, and the idolatry of the Church of Rome; the probability of reformation in the churches of England & Rome; the persecuting doctrines maintained by the two churches; and the origin and independence of the ancient British Church. By the Rev. Thos. P. Pantin MA of Queen's College, Oxf. Curate of Stanford & Swinford, near Lutterworth, Leicestershire. ... as to Mr. Pantin himself, who is Rector of Westcot, in this neighbourhood, & is soon coming to reside among us. He is not of gentle blood, being the son of a certain London brushmaker, originally from Charlbury; but that would not have been a bar to his propitious introduction into our clerical society, if his conduct in early life had been discreet; but when yet a layman, & studying for Orders, he became known at Stow by taking lodgings there, and living with a female Servant, whom he has since married, in a very ambiguous manner. A report made to the Bishop by the rural Dean on this subject, together with something approximating to a simoniacal engagement between Mr. P. and the gentleman holding the living of Westcote for him, has retarded his coming to reside in this deanery, but, I believe, he is soon expected at Westcote, and although I do not think he is likely to be received with cordiality by his clerical neighbours, I trust, he has now for several years lived with such propriety, that his early irregularity may be, as much as is consistent with propriety, a sense of duty consigned to oblivion.*

1830: 10 May.

1834: 11 Aug.

1837: 23 Jan: *Engaged in Justice business, which ended in my writing a letter to the Revd. Mr. Pantin, Incumbent of Westcote.* 24 Jan.

1840: 25 May, 15 Oct: *From the Workhouse I went to the Justice meeting, where I found the Dean of Gloucester, Messrs. Ford and Waller, and Mr. Winter, with Mr. Pantin, who had come on some matter relating to his parish of Westcote were also present.*

1844: 16 May: *Walked down Stow Hill in conversation with Mr. Pantin, the Rector of Westcote.* 29 Aug., 12-13 Sep., 18 Sep: *Mention having been made by me and Mr. Hedley of the newly appointed Bishop of Newfoundland, and the wants of his diocese; this was followed by a private letter explanatory of his position and the state of his cure, produced by Mr. Pantin, the Rector of Westcote, and led to an extra contribution for the Diocese of Newfoundland, which amounted to £6 or £7.* 3 Oct., 8 Oct., 11 Oct., 7 Nov., 5 Dec.

1845: 21 Jan: The following Clergymen came to confer with us ... *Pantin from Westcote, pompous and full of pretensions, big with clerical talk, and testy because in a paragraph which I had caused to be inserted in the Gloucestershire Chronicle last year, I had omitted his name in a list of clergymen, who had taken part in the proceedings of the Annual meeting of the Stow District Comm.* 26 Mar., 25 Jun.

1846: 24 Jun., 26 Aug., 3 Sep., 21 Sep., 29 Sep., 4 Oct: *Wrote to Mr. Pantin, inclosing a recommendation of Thos. Cook of Westcote to the Gloucester infirmary.* 11 Nov: *Wrote to Mr. Pantin, thanking him for the loan of a volume of Stillingfleet's works.*

1847: 18 Jan: *Wrote to Mr. Pantin requesting him to take measures to remove from the Gloucester infirmary Thos. Cook, whom I had caused to be admitted there on his recommendation.* 22 Jan: *Recd. letters from Mr. J. W. Pantin, on behalf of his father, who is ill, acknowledging my letter to him as to a patient in the Gloucester infirmary.* 7 Apr., 7 Jul., 8 Sep., 28 Sep.

1848: 22 Feb., 27 Oct.

1849: 13 Dec.

1850: 12 Jun: *Mr. Pantin had also addressed to the Rural Dean a very voluminous letter to be laid before the meeting, in which he followed up the remarks made by him at the last decanal meeting on the topic of Baptismal regeneration, protesting against the opinion of the rest of the Clergy then present, and upholding low views by a catena of quotations from low church divines, and by arguments drawn from the recent publications &, argumentations which the Gorham controversy has elicited.* 12 Nov.

1852: 3 Apr: *Received a letter from Mr. Pantin, addressed to me as Chairman of the Union; the Revd. gentleman is displeased at a notification from the Rel. Off. of an alleged nuisance in that the Village of Westcote, in a public pool said to be filthy & offensive, and likely to be prejudicial to health.* 5 Apr., 8 Apr., 14 Apr., 17 May, 22 Oct: *Wrote at more length to two of the number Revds. T. P. Pantin and S. F. Sadler, than to the others.* 28 Oct: *Letter from Mr. Pantin in reply to my note to him as to his subscriptions to the S.P.G. from which it appears that he has punctually paid the amount to Ford, who, it would seem, has omitted to pay me one year's subscription.* 5 Nov., 10 Nov., 17 Nov.

1853: 18 Jan., 21 Jan: *Also a letter from Mr. Pantin. My appeal to him decided him to go to Oxford at the eleventh hour to record his vote for Mr. Perceval.* 3 Mar: *We were joined by Mr. Potter, and Mr. Pantin Junior; but as to audience the aspect of the room was most freezing.* 30 Mar., 24 May.

1854: 2 Feb: ... *but left the Board to attend a meeting of Commissioners of Taxes, to hear a few appeals, and especially to rehear Mr. Pantin's case as to the liability to pay House tax for his parsonage, from which he was relieved on the production by a party appearing on his behalf of the poor rate assessment of the parish of Westcote, shewing that the rateable value is under £20 per ann. As the irritable Rector did not attend in person, nor Mr. Ford, who had interfered in this business unbecomingly, the business affair was conducted without recrimination or asperity.* 19 Jul.

PAOLI — Pasquale Filippo Antonio Paoli [Pascal Paoli] [16]

Pascal Paoli (1725-1807), Corsican general and patriot, was born in the hamlet of Stretta di Morosaglia in the pieve (canton) of Rostino, Corsica. He was the younger son of Giacinto Paoli and Dionisia Valentini, and had one brother, Clemente, and two sisters, Maria Francesca and Maria Chiara.

In 1738, when a French force was sent to assist the Genoese in maintaining their grip on Corsica, Paoli went into exile with his father to Naples, where he studied in a military academy. Having excelled at the academy he was appointed lieutenant, then colonel, in the Neapolitan cavalry. When the French evacuated Corsica in 1752, Paoli returned to fight against the Genoese. In 1755 a gathering of Corsican local chiefs proclaimed him their 'Generalissimo' and asked him to govern the island.

The Genoese once more turned to France, and in 1764 another invasion took place. In 1768, realising their position was impossible without French support, the Genoese ceded Corsica to France. Paoli led a guerrilla resistance against the French rulers, but after a major battle in 1769, the rebellion was suppressed. Paoli and a few hundred supporters were evacuated by a British frigate to Tuscany, where they were treated as heroes. Paoli then came to England where he was visited by many dignitaries and introduced to King George III.

Paoli went to Paris following the French Revolution, and in April 1790 appeared at the bar of the National Assembly, where he was received with enthusiasm. He delivered an address promising fidelity to the new order of things in France and was appointed lieutenant-general and military commandant of Corsica by King Louis XVI. Returning to the island he re-established his paternal rule, but he was rapidly estranged from the republican government in Paris, and the execution of the king made him despair. He turned his hopes to independence for Corsica by bringing the island under British protection.

Paoli had known Napoleon Bonaparte since autumn 1791, when he had told the future emperor, 'You were cast in an antique mould; you are one of Plutarch's men. The whole world will talk of you.' The powerful Bonaparte family was directly opposed to any course of action that favoured the British; they advocated instead for amalgamation with France. Paoli ordered their summary arrest and expulsion, and the family fled from Calvi to Marseilles. Paoli then asked for British assistance in driving out the remaining French garrisons in Corsica, which was achieved with the aid of Adm. Samuel Hood and Gen. Sir David Dundas, with the French surrendering on 10 June 1794. Meanwhile a deputation had been dispatched to England offering the sovereignty of the island to George III. The king's acceptance of this offer was announced on 17 June. Paoli himself came to England in 1795, urging his compatriots to remain firm in their allegiance to the British crown; however, by 1796 anti-British feeling had risen to such an extent that the British were forced to evacuate the island. Corsica then became united with France.

Paoli lived in Edgware Road, London, until his death in 1807. Notwithstanding his family's deep-seated antagonism towards Paoli, Napoleon was reported to have written with regret at St Helena towards the end of his life that he 'had never been able, in the midst of all his preoccupations with great affairs, to summon Paoli to his side, to consult with him, when, as emperor and king, he was virtually master of Europe.'

Paoli was probably one of the most important and distinguished men that Francis Witts ever met. They met at a party given by Lady Lyttelton in Berkeley Street. Paoli had known George III, Louis XVI, Napoleon, and countless others. He had been visited in Corsica by Dr Johnson who wrote in admiration of him. He was a giant of his time. Unfortunately the diarist did not offer any description of Paoli at the party, nor did he mention whether or not he spoke with him. Francis's mother Agnes was more fortunate; Gen. Paoli visited Clifton in December 1802–January 1803, and she reacquainted herself with him. Agnes played whist with him on 1 November 1802, and met him again on the 5th, 12th and 17th of November 1802, and the 7th and 9th of January 1803.

1801: 13 May: *We returned home after dinner & prepared to attend a party there at 8 o'clock. I cannot say, it was any thing very charming, but I was highly delighted by the kind & friendly manner, in which Principal Gordon met us. General Paoli was also there. We were introduced to Mr Boldero the Banker.*

PARISH — Jane Parish

Jane Parish married Richard Witts (1705-1755) and they had at least one son, Richard Parish Witts (1748-1828). Richard Witts was the diarist's great-uncle, therefore Richard Parish Witts was his first cousin once removed. Nothing has been discovered in relation to the Parish family.

1838: 14 Jun: *These silver cups bear an inscription purporting that they were presented to Richard Parish Witts in 1750 by his Uncle and Aunt Parish.*

PARK — James Alan Park [17]

Sir James Alan Park (1763-1838), judge, was born at Edinburgh, the son of James Park, an Edinburgh surgeon. His father took up a practice at Newington, Surrey, and James was brought up in England. He was educated at Northampton Grammar School, and later became a student at Lincoln's Inn. He was called to the bar in 1784. James Park married, 1791, Lucy, daughter of Richard Atherton, a woollen draper, of Preston, and one of the original partners of Preston Old Bank. In the same year Park was appointed vice-chancellor of the duchy of Lancaster. In 1795 he was appointed recorder of Preston, and in Trinity vacation 1799, a king's counsel. This was followed in 1802 by his appointment as recorder of Durham, and in 1811 as attorney-general of Lancaster. When Edward Law, later Lord Ellenborough, left the northern circuit in 1802 to become attorney-general, Park obtained the lead of the circuit. In 1816 he was promoted to the bench of the common pleas and was knighted.

1824: 31 Mar: *The commission of Assize for the County was opened this afternoon by Sir James Allan Park, whose colleague, Sir E. Garrow, following ed him from Monmouth.* 1 Apr.

1829: 1 Apr: *Sir James Allan Park, and Mr. Justice Parke, the new Judge, are on the Oxford circuit. The present is the first circuit since the appointment of the latter; there is likely to be a puzzle between two Judges, whose names sound alike, when pronounced, and vary so little, when written: but the bar has settled the difficulty by giving to the old stager, who is a very religious and worthy, though particular and fretful man, the name of St. James's Park, and to the new debutant, that of the Green Park.* 2 Apr: *Sir J. A. Park is in the Common Pleas. The Oxford circuit almost invariably falls to the lot of the Junior Judge, as being the most laborious; the gaols at Stafford and Gloucester are usually so crowded, that the fatigue of presiding at the Criminal bar in those Counties is great*

1835: 6 Apr: *Went into Court. Sir. J. T. Coleridge, recently appointed to the Judicial bench presided at the Crown Bar; Sir. J. A. Parke sat at Nisi Prius...*

PARKE — James Parke [18]

James Parke, 1st Baron Wensleydale (1782-1868), judge, was born at Highfield, near Liverpool, the ninth son of Thomas Parke (d. 1819), merchant, of Liverpool, and Anne, daughter of William Preston. He was educated at Macclesfield Grammar School and Trinity College, Cambridge. He studied under a special pleader before being called to the bar at the Inner Temple in 1813. He was appointed to the court of the king's bench in 1828 and was made a privy councillor in 1833. A year later he was made a baron of the exchequer. Angered by the passing of the Common Law Procedure Acts he resigned his post in 1855, but was recalled by the government and given a peerage—making him Baron Wensleydale of Walton—to allow him to undertake the judicial functions of the House of Lords. He married, at St Olave's, York, 8 April 1817, Cecilia (1793-1879), daughter of Samuel F. Barlow of Middlethorpe, Yorkshire; they had 3 sons and 3 daughters, including:

1 Cecilia Anne (1821-1845)
2 Mary Priscilla Harriet (1822-1843)
3 Charlotte Alice (1828-1908); married, 1853, William Lowther (1821-1912)

1826: 30 Mar: *The Courts opened soon after my arrival, and I attended for the greater part of the day in the Crown Court; in this Mr. Baron Garrow presided, as Mr. Justice Park at Nisi Prius.*

1829: 1 Apr: *Sir James Allan Park, and Mr. Justice Parke, the new Judge, are on the Oxford circuit. The present is the first circuit since the appointment of the latter; there is likely to be a puzzle between two Judges, whose names sound alike, when pronounced, and vary so little, when written: but the bar has settled the difficulty by giving to the old stager, who is a very religious and worthy, though particular and fretful man, the name of St. James's Park, and to the new debutant, that of the Green Park.* 3 Apr: *The Judge too shewed some indications of his peculiarities, petty fretfulness, and fidgetty temper, which are oddly mingled with sterling excellencies, a fine, honourable, pious, charitable heart, and much learning combined with good sense.*

PARKE — Maria Frances Parke [19]

Maria Frances Parke (1772-1822), musician, was the eldest daughter of John Parke (1745-1829), oboist. She was born in London and given a musical education by her father. Her earliest known public performance was at her father's benefit concert in 1781, where she played the harpsichord. Her first public appearance as both a vocalist and pianist was at her father's benefit concert in April 1782. She sang at the Handel commemoration concerts in 1784, and on 11 March 1785 she played in a concerto during the interval of a performance of Handel's *Samson* at Drury Lane. In 1790 she performed at the Three Choirs Festival in Gloucester as second soloist, and in 1794-97 and 1807 she appeared as principal soprano. Parke was heard at many London concerts, oratorios, and provincial festivals, but not in opera. Her family's associations with Haydn led to the composer presiding at the pianoforte at her benefit concert in Hanover Square rooms on 19 May 1794. Other published works included three grand sonatas in 1799, two further grand sonatas in or after 1800, a 'Divertimento and Military Rondo', probably in 1807, and two duets. Parke was a fine musician, scientific and accurate in her singing; she retired from the profession on her marriage to John Beardmore, of Queen Street, Mayfair, in 1815.

1803: 21 Nov: *Evans sat with me in the Evening, when we adjourned to the Music Room where heard a delicious Concert, in which Miss Parke & Lindley were the principal performers.* 22 Nov: *Went with Dowell, Evans etc to the Music Room. Joined Trevennen. Very pleasant. Miss Parke & Lindley performed beautifully.*

1804: 5 Nov: *First Subscription Concert. Very fully attended. Bartleman Knyvett & Miss Parke & Lindley.* 6 Nov.

PARKER — Charles Frederick Parker [29]

Charles Frederick Parker (1787-1870), Church of England clergyman, was the son of Thomas Parker of Churcham, Gloucestershire. He was educated at Pembroke College, Oxford (BA 1806; MA 1809), where he was a fellow until 1819. Parker served as rector of Ringshall, Suffolk, from 1819 until his death in 1870.

1834: 15 Aug: *A clergyman of the name of Parker, a friend of Mr. Wintle, and incumbent of a Pembroke Coll. living in Suffolk, near Ipswich, called before breakfast, to ask leave to see the house, and prospect from the terrace. He appeared a worthy man, strongly bitten with a taste for antiquarian and architectural research. Howell obligingly detained him to breakfast, and I offered to drive him to Saintbridge or Gloucester.*

1853: 7 Jan: *Betook myself to the Angel Hotel, where I was very comfortably accommodated, and spent the evening in the Coffee room where were many members of convocation—among them——Mr. Parker, a Suffolk Clergyman, now residing at Torquay, formerly Fellow of Pembroke Coll.*

PARKER — Francis Parker Newdigate — *see* Newdigate

PARKER — George Parker [21]

George Parker, 7th [in some sources 4th] earl of Macclesfield (1755-1842), was the eldest son of Thomas Parker, 6th [3rd] earl of Macclesfield (1723-1795), and Mary (1726-1812), eldest daughter of Sir William Heathcote, 1st baronet. He was educated at Eton College and Exeter College, Oxford. He succeeded as 7th earl of Macclesfield in 1795.

Parker was MP for Woodstock in 1777-84 and Minehead in 1790-95; he was DCL of Oxford in 1797 and lord lieutenant of Oxfordshire in 1817-42. He married, 25 May 1780, Mary Frances (1761-1823), second daughter and co-heir of Revd Thomas Drake, rector of Amersham, and Elizabeth, daughter of Isaac Whittington of Orford, Suffolk. George and Mary had only one surviving child, a daughter:

1 Maria (1781-1861); married, 13 November 1802, Thomas Hamilton, 9th earl of Haddington

On his death George Parker was succeeded in the earldom by his brother Thomas (1762-1850).

1836: 6 Sep: *Besides the leading farmers of the neighbourhood, I noticed a host of gentlemen interested in agriculture, Lord Macclesfield, Lord Ellenborough, Lord Edwd. Somerset, James Dutton, Browne, Waller, Elwes, Barker, Messrs. Barnsby and Phillips from Herefordshire, E. Cripps, A. Pole, with many others.*

1837: 3 Aug.

PARKER — Henry Walter Parker [22]

Henry Walter Parker (1808-1874), barrister of Gray's Inn, was the third son of Thomas Parker, barrister-at-law, of Gray's Inn. He was admitted to Gray's Inn in June 1827. Parker first came to public notice in 1833 through the publication of a work entitled *The Rise, Progress, and Present State of Van Diemen's Land; with Advice to Emigrants, and a Chapter on Convicts.* In 1838 he was assistant secretary to the poor law commission, and in 1839 he was appointed as an assistant poor law commissioner. Parker was severely criticised regarding the scandal of the Andover Workhouse in 1846. He lived at Highgate, London, but at some point after the scandal he left for South Australia, where he seems to have had family connections. He lived at Wattlebury, near Mitcham, in a house he built in 1865. He did not hide from publicity and rose to become South Australia's first judge.

1839: 2 May: *It was announced from headquarters that Mr. Neave retires from the superintendence of the district in which our Union is included, and he is to be succeeded by Mr. Asst. Comm. Parker.* 24 Jul: *Mr. Pearce called, accompanied by his connection, Mr. Stone, a retired Cheltenham tradesman, to inform me that Mr. Parker, the Asst. Poor Law Commr. in charge of this district, called at the Workhouse yesterday evening, and had promised shortly to attend a Board meeting, and take measures to readjust the averages.* 18 Aug., 22 Aug: *To the Workhouse, where I met Mr. Parker, the Asst. Commr. who has the charge of this district, with whom I had a private conference on some points of Poor Law management. He appears to be a sensible, agreeable, and gentlemanly person.*

1840: 13 Jun: *Wrote at great length to Mr. Parker, Ass. P.L. Commr., on the disputed question as to the contribution required of Daylesford by the guardians of our Union, detailing particulars, and urging his attendance on the 25th.* 22 Jun., 25 Jun: *I bent my steps to meet Mr. Parker, the Assistant Poor Law Commr.—who had arrived last night, in conformity with the letter I received from him on the 21st. Inst.—He expressed an opinion that the Guardians of our Union were quite in order as to the point in dispute between them and Mr. Winter on the part of Daylesford; that our proceedings had been all correct.* 26 Jun., 12 Sep., 8 Oct., 15 Oct.

1842: 17 Feb: *Mr. Parker announces that Stow ceases to be one of the Unions under his particular charge, as there has been a new arrangement of districts among the Asst. Commrs.*

PARKER — Jacob Parker — *see also* Collett [23]

Jacob Parker (1795-1860), labourer, was born at Winchcombe, the son of William Parker (1761-1843) and Martha Rastall (1759-1828). He married, at Upper Slaughter, 15 February 1815, Keziah (1797-1825), daughter of Henry Collett (1751-1828) and Margaret Brain (1762-1827); they had 1 son and 2 daughters:

1 Mary (b. 1816)
1 Harry (b. 1816)
2 Caroline (b. 1820)

Parker died at Cirencester.

1835: 18 Mar: *Engaged at home and at the office of Messrs. Wilkins & Kendal, Bourton, transacting parochial business, in the matter of Jacob Parker, a man of very questionable character, but a clever, scheming, unprincipled fellow, who had left his children for some years, during which he has not been heard of, chargeable to this parish. He is now come to claim some money, to which he is entitled in right of his first wife, Kezia Collett, and which is chargeable on the property of her brother, John B. Collett.* 20-22 Mar.,

PARKER — John Fleming Parker [24]

John Fleming Parker (1782-1862), Church of England clergyman, was born at Mackfield Settle, Yorkshire, a younger son of John Parker (1755-1797) and Beatrix Lister (1749-1807). He was educated at Brasenose College, Oxford (BA 1803; MA 1807), and entered the Church. He was appointed prebendary of Llandaff, perpetual curate of Waddington, Yorkshire, in 1818, and rector of Bentham, Yorkshire, in 1825. He married, December 1817, his cousin Catherine Day, née Lister (1793-1873), widow of James Skurr Day and daughter of Thomas Lister, 1st Baron Ribblesdale (1752-1826), and Rebecca (1773-1816), daughter of Joseph Fielding. John and Catherine had at least 2 sons and 1 daughter:

1 John (d. 1845)
1 Catherine (1827-1841)
2 Frederick (1834-1841)

1825: 13 Sep: *The living of Bentham has recently fallen to Mr. John Parker, son of the late Mrs. Parker of Marshfield, Settle, and widow of Mr. Parker of Browsholme, in Lancashire. Mrs. Parker's eldest son has been blessed or cursed with taste: his pursuit of the elegant, the rare, the uncommon, has led him into vast expence, and driven him to the sale of his fine estate and mansion. John, the second another son, married the daughter of his maternal uncle, Lord Ribblesdale, the widow of a Somersetshire gentleman of the name of Day, and has been for some years incumbent of Waddington, near Clitheroe, from whence he is now removing to Bentham. He is also a prebendary of Llandaff. Mr. John Parker, and his respectable Mother were well known to me in former days, when we used to visit Beck House, before Mrs. Backhouse removed to Gloucester.*

PARKER — Joseph and John Parker, booksellers, of Oxford[25]

Joseph Parker (±1774-1850) and John Henry Parker (1806-1884) were Oxford booksellers. The firm of Parker was founded by James Fletcher, the former partner of James Rivington of St Paul's Churchyard. Fletcher came from Salisbury to Oxford, and established his bookselling business in Turl Street in 1731, taking his son-in-law into partnership to form a new firm, Fletcher & Hanwell. In 1797, after Fletcher's death, Hanwell went into partnership with Joseph Parker, who had served his apprenticeship in the book trade with Daniel Prince, and whose great-uncle, Sackville Parker, had already established a bookshop at 88 High Street, Oxford.

Joseph Parker (a direct descendant of Samuel Parker, bishop of Oxford 1686-88) matriculated at the University of Oxford as a 'bibliopola' on 27 January 1798. In 1817 he was recorded as occupying property both to the east and south of 26 Broad Street; these properties were No. 27 Broad Street and Fletcher's old Turl Street shop, a tiny house measuring 16 feet squared, just inside the city wall. It appears that Parker ran his bookshop in Broad Street and lived in the little Turl Street house. One of Joseph Parker's sons became a vicar and the other a surgeon, so the book business went to his London-born nephew, John Henry Parker. John Henry passed it on to his son, James Parker. In 1937 the shop was expanded into No. 26 Broad Street, next door. Both buildings were demolished and rebuilt in 1964.

1832: 15 Mar: *After breakfast, Dr. Daubeny introduced Mr. Croome and myself into the Senior reading room, a recent establishment in the Turl, whither the Dons, as the young men denominate their seniors, congregate to read the newspapers, reviews, magazines and modern publications, mingling conversation with their lighter studies. The room is on the ground floor of the house of Mr. Parker, the principal Bookseller in the University.*

1840: 21 Jun: *Recd. circulars from Parker, the Oxford Bookseller, announcing a new series of Theological publications of old Church of England divines.*

PARKER — Thomas Parker, of Cheshire, at Malvern — *see also* Henry Pitt Cholmondeley[26]

Thomas Parker (±1766-1840), army officer, was probably born at Astle Hall, Cheshire, the son of Revd John Parker (d. 1795) and Jane, daughter of Robert Gartside of Manchester. He was educated at Eton College. Parker married, at Stanmore, Middlesex, 12 [or 14] September 1795, Dorothy (b. 1776), daughter of Thomas Cholmondeley, of Vale Royal, and sister of Thomas, 1st Baron Delamere; they had 1 daughter:

1 Jane; died young

Thomas Parker was promoted to lieutenant in the Worcestershire Militia on 24 July 1812. After his death his wife Dorothy remained in Malvern; in the 1851 census she was listed as a lodger living at Laburnam Cottage. Dorothy Parker was the aunt of Henry Pitt Cholmondeley.

This attribution is likely but uncertain. Col Parker may also have been John Parker, who was promoted to major in the 2nd Ceylon Regiment on 10 February 1810. Malvern, like Cheltenham, was a popular place for retired HEIC officers and officials.

1829: 24 Nov.

1834: 9 Sep: *Besides the inmates of the house we had Dr. Card, the Vicar of Great Malvern, Mr. Thrupp, the Curate, Col. and Mrs. Parker, from Cheshire, people of fortune and highly connected, well bred and agreeable.*

1840: 24 Apr: *The Carriages were, I believe, those of the Countess of Haddington, a dowager lady resident at Malvern, Sir A. Lechmere, Mrs J. Walker, Mr. Essington, Mr. Woodyares, Revd. — Biddulph, Mr. Allen (of the Rhydd), Mrs. Stratton (widow of Geo. Fred. Stratton, now residing at Barnards Green) Mr. Mason's, Col. Parker's, Miss Mosleys', and perhaps one or two more.*

PARKER — Thomas Lister Parker[27]

Thomas Lister Parker (1779-1858), landed proprietor, antiquary, and collector, was born at Browsholme Hall, Yorkshire [now in Lancashire], the eldest of the eight sons of John Parker (1755-1797) and Beatrix (1749-1807), daughter of Thomas Lister of Gisburne Park, Yorkshire. He was elder brother to John Fleming Parker (*above*).

Thomas Parker was educated at Clitheroe Royal Grammar School and Christ's College, Cambridge. He succeeded to the Browsholme estate in 1797. He was elected a fellow of the Society of Antiquaries in 1801, and later a fellow of the Royal Society. He was appointed high sheriff for Lancashire in 1804. Interestingly, he held the sinecure of 'Trumpeter to the Queen', and also claimed the hereditary office of 'Bowbearer of the Forest of Bowland' in Lancashire.

In 1804 and 1805 Parker made alterations to the sixteenth-century Browsholme Hall, rebuilding the west wing. Later on he made additions under the superintendence of Sir Jeffrey Wyatville. Parker had a taste for landscape gardening, and between 1797 and 1810 he spent large sums on laying out his grounds. In the house he displayed a collection of antiquities and pictures, many of which were his own acquisitions. He was a liberal patron of artists, but his expenditure brought him into difficulties later in life. In 1824 he sold the Browsholme estate, with the mansion, to his cousin Thomas Parker of Alkincoats, Lancashire.

1837: 27 Oct: *Pursued our route to Sherwood House, where I passed a few minutes with our tenant Thos. Parker.*

1838: 23 Jul: *Wrote to Mr. Geldard in reply to his letter, the receipt of which I named on the 20th. forwarding to him notices to quit signed by myself or Mrs. Backhouse to J. Armitstead, T. Parker, Jos. and Thos. Hartley, whose leases of Stainforth Hall, Sherwood House, and Ravenflatt will expire next Spring, with a view to the advertizing these farms to be let by tender in Sept. next, when I propose going into Craven.* 13 Sep., 17 Sep.

PARKER — William Parker of Parker & Warter, solicitors — *see also* Warter[28]

William Parker and Henry Degory Warter were solicitors with premises at 1 Carey Street, London.

1840: 29 Nov: *Received a letter from Mr. Jennings, inclosing copies of letters from Mr. Perring, Agent to the Clothworkers Company, to Messrs. Parker and Warter.*

1842: 15 Mar: *Then with E.F.W. in a cab to Carey Street to the offices of Messrs. Parker and Warter where we found an assemblage of persons whose attendance was required at the house of Lords on the "Witts's Estate Bill"—to be sworn to-day.*

PARKES — manufacturer of iron machinery, mills & c.

1836: 7 Nov: *Wrote to one Parkes, a Manufacturer of Iron Machinery, Mills &c. mentioned by Mr. Hall, the Asst. Commr., to make enquiries as to Iron or steel flour mills to be worked by a crank, suited for paupers in Workhouses.*

PARR — Samuel Parr [29]

Samuel Parr (1747-1825), Church of England clergyman and schoolmaster, was born at Harrow-on-the-Hill, the elder of the two children of Samuel Parr (1712-1766), surgeon and apothecary, and his first wife, Anne (±1712-1762), daughter of Leonard and Elizabeth Mignard. He was educated at Harrow School and Emmanuel College, Cambridge (MA 1772; LL.D).

Parr's educational appointments were as follows: assistant master at Harrow School, 1767-71; headmaster of Colchester Grammar School, 1776-79; and headmaster of Norwich Grammar School, 1779-85. His first clerical appointment was as curate of Willesden with Kingsbury, Middlesex, from 1769. This was followed by the following appointments: curate of Holy Trinity, Colchester, 1778-79; curate of St George's Colegate and St Saviour's, Norwich, 1779; rector of Asterby, Lincolnshire, 1780-83; perpetual curate of Hatton, Warwickshire, 1783-1825; prebendary of St Paul's, 1783-1825; rector of Wadenhoe, Northamptonshire, 1792-1825; and rector of Graffham, Huntingdonshire, 1802-25.

Parr married, first, 1771, Jane, only daughter of Zachariah Masingale of Carleton, Yorkshire. The marriage was said to have produced little 'connubial felicity'; his wife had a caustic tongue and delighting in 'exposing her husband's foibles and ridiculing his peculiarities in the presence of others. He was kept in a constant state of irritation.' Porson, who visited Samuel Parr at Hatton, said, 'Parr would have been a great man but for three things—his trade, his wife, and his politics.' According to his wife, Parr was 'born in a whirlwind and bred a tyrant'. She died in 1810. He married secondly, 1816, Mary, daughter of John Eyre of Coventry.

1825: 16 Sep: *He was a intimate friend of the learned and eccentric Dr. Parr; and when that singular man died, he preached his funeral sermon, agreeably to the wish of the deceased. It was a difficult task, where, amidst so much to extol in point of high talent & great acquirements, there was so much to disapprove in temper, and moral perversity in many respects; but Dr. Butler discharged his task with delicacy; fulfilling what was due to his departed friend without trespassing on the demands of Christian morality and principle by extenuating what was culpable & indefensible.* 29 Nov: *"A Letter to the Revd. Dr. Milner occasioned by some passages contained in his book entitled "The End of religious controversy" By the late Revd. S. Parr. LLD. Lond. 1825. 8vo" This pamphlet is a posthumous work of that learned and singular man, who was remarkable for pomp of diction, depth of erudition, simplicity and ignorance of the world in some points, vanity, an overbearing temper, & dictatorial assumption on many occasions; who was a whig in politics and a low churchman in religion; yet at all times a remarkable man, whether his vast learning, or powerful intellect, or extensive acquaintance with men of talent and knowledge though a long life be considered. It is published by his grandson the Revd. Mr. Lynes, of Elmley Lovett near Worcester.*

PARRIS — David Parris and the Parris family at Clifton [30]

David Parris (d. ±1808), sugar merchant, shipowner, and plantation owner, married a Miss Carrington, the daughter of the owner of Carrington plantation in Barbados; they had at least 1 son and 1 daughter:

1 Paul Carrington (±1789-1813); *see below*
1 Anna Maria; married, 1809, George Carrington (b. 1782), of Bengal, probably her cousin

David Parris was a major plantation owner and sugar merchant in Barbados in the last quarter of the eighteenth century; as such, he would have occasionally been in Bristol due to the concentration of sugar refineries there. His parentage, however, is uncertain.

Another David Parris died in 1796, probably the younger David Parris's father; there may have been two, or even three generations with the same name. Agnes Witts frequently mentioned in her diaries a Mr and Mrs Parris after 1796; for example, on Monday 7 April 1806, she wrote, 'I did not go out & had no other company but Mr. Parris to take leave previous to his going to the West Indies'. However, the UCL-Slave record states the following: 'the David Parris whose will was proved in 1796 was David Parris the younger, son of David Parris of Barbados, and half-brother or step-brother of Anna Maria Carrington nee Parris ...' This appears to be incorrect; at her marriage Anna Maria was referred to as 'the daughter of the late David Parris of Barbados'. Furthermore, the Carrington plantation accounts (1810-55) held at the University of Texas Library seem to imply that David Parris had been recently involved in the management of the Carrington plantations.

Paul Carrington Parris matriculated at Christ Church, Oxford, in 1808, but did not take his degree. This might have had something to do with the death of his father around this time. Paul died at Belgrave Terrace, Pimlico, only five years later, at the early age of 24. The sugar business devolved to his sister Anna Maria and her husband, George Carrington, who was most likely of HEIC service.

1804: 11 Jan., 22 Jan., 28 Jan: *Accompanied in the Evening my Father & Mother Miss Upton & Mrs. Barton to the meeting of the Harmonic Society at Gloster House, which was very respectably attended & well managed under the Presidency of Mr. Parris.* 19 Jul., 8 Aug., 2 Sep., 14 Oct., 28 Dec.

1805: 5 Feb: *Called on the Townsend's & Pennington's. Walked with Newnham & Mr. Parris.* 15 Feb: *A dull very large Rout at Mrs. Parris's by no means agreeable, some playing & singing & a little dancing.* 1 Mar., 23 Nov.

1806: 24 Jan: *Mr. Parris calling upon my Father & Mother, conversing agreeably.* 27 Jan.,

PARROTT — Ann Parrott and the Parrott family — *see also* Burgoyne, Thrupp, *and* Witts [31]

Ann Witts, née Parrot (1783-1865), was the daughter of Richard Parrott (1755-1807), banker, of Quebec Street, London, and Ruth Fuller (b. 1755), who married at Salford, Oxfordshire, on 20 June 1776. Ann had an elder sister, Ruth (1779-1837), who married, at St George's, Hanover Square, Westminster, 20 July 1803, Thomas John Burgoyne (1775-1847). She also had an elder brother, Richard (1777-1835), who married, at Marylebone, 22 May 1806, Charlotte Burgoyne (1782-1857). The entry has been placed here as it would become lost in the detailed Witts index entries. Little is known of Ann's early life; for more on the background to the Parrot family, see George Parrott (*below*).

Ann married Edward London Witts in July 1838. At the time of the 1861 census Ann was visiting her cousin John Burgoyne at 14 Upper Harley Street. She died at Champion Hill in January 1865.

1801: 1 June: *accompanied her Ladyship to call upon Mr. & Mrs. Parrott's. Quebec Street.*

1833: 10 Sep: *Lady L's feebleness much increased... Miss Parrott her guest—an elderly maiden lady—sister of Mr. P., a partner in Sir C. Scott's banking house, London.* 11 Sep: *At the School, our place of rendezvous, Miss Parrott, who had walked to the village to see her friends, met us and returned with us.* 12 Sep.

1838: 16 Jul: *I wrote to Mr. E. L. Witts, Champion Hill, congratulating him on his marriage with Miss Parrott which took place on the 12th. Inst. an event of the early accomplishment of which we had been apprized by Miss Witts. E.L.W. is an old Bachelor of seventy: the lady a Spinster of fifty five; both have comfortable fortunes. While the Mother of Mr. E L W. lived, and she was nearly 100 when she died, her son devoted himself wholly to his aged parent; now that he feels the want of female society, he unites himself with a person long known to him, and all his connections, and to me also as having passed some years since a few days in her company when she was visiting Lady Lyttelton. She is a good tempered, cheerful person, daughter of a confidential friend of my aunt, who in early life, went with her to India in the capacity of lady's maid, and on her return united herself to a respectable tradesman. They prospered in life, and the late Mr. Parrot, brother of Mrs. E.L.W., who died not long since, was acting partner in the banking house of Sir Claude Scott and Co., a person of great respectability. My cousin Edward and his lady have probably done wisely in coming together, tho' one is apt to smile at a union of snow topped 70 with mature 55.*

1840: 13-14 Apr.

1842: 17 Mar: *We proceeded towards our hotel, shopping by the way, and reached it before six o clock in time to dress for dinner with Mr. and Mrs. Thrupp at their private residence in Upper Brook Street, where we met Mrs. E. L. Witts, and were joined in the evening by her nephew and Mrs. Thrupp's cousin, Mr. Geo. Parrot, a young man connected, either as a Junior partner or Clerk, with Sir Claude Scott's bank, of which his late Father was the resident and managing partner.*

PARROTT — George Parrott — *see also* Burgoyne *and* Thrupp [32]

George Parrott (1817-1858), banker, was the son of Richard Parrott (1777-1835) and Charlotte Burgoyne (1782-1857), and grandson of Richard Parrott (d. 1807), banker, of Quebec Street, London. He lived at 1 Cavendish Square and became principal manager of Sir Claude Scott's bank. He married, at Dover, Kent, 16 June 1849, Caroline Louisa (±1824-1906), daughter of Henry Joseph Da Silva, Baron de Lagos, an attaché to the Portuguese legation; they had at least 3 sons and 2 daughters:

1 Rosa Charlotte (1850-1905)
2 Jessie Louisa (b. 1851)
1 Richard (1853-1891); married, at Kensington, January 1878, Clara Hotchkin (1856-1925); 2 sons and 2 daughters:
  1 Mabel Rosa (1879-1963)
  1 Harold George (b. 1880)
  2 Ruth Annie (b. 1881)
  2 Douglas Annesley (1885-1965)
2 George Leonard (b. 1855); married, at Christ Church, Lancaster Gate, Westminster, 18 December 1888, Eleanor Kathleen Harrington (1865-1946); 3 daughters:
  1 Eleanor Sybil (1895-1938)
  2 Violet Irene (b. 1897)
  3 Kathleen Marjory (b. 1899)
3 Walter (1857-1938); married, at St James's, Paddington, Westminster, 11 November 1896, Annie Turner Howard (1864-1904), born at Barnes, Surrey; 1 daughter:
  1 Annie Howard (1898-1956)

George Parrott's cousin, Maria Burgoyne (b. ±1813), was visiting the Parrott family at 1 Cavendish Square at the time of the 1851 census.

George's grandmother, Ruth Parrott, née Fuller, had accompanied Apphia Witts [later Lady Lyttelton] to India in 1769 as her lady's maid. A Hannah Parrott died at Chadlington, Oxfordshire, aged 84, and was buried on 24 August 1824; she would therefore have been born in around 1740. Given that Chadlington is only 3 miles south of Chipping Norton and features no less than fourteen times in the diaries of Agnes Witts, one might suspect that the Parrott family lived there at one time.

George Parrott's aunt was Ann Parrott (*above*). Late in life she married Edward London Witts, cousin of the diarist.

1840: 7 May: *Called on Mr. Thrupp by appointment, who introduced me to his partner, Mr. Burgoyne, an elderly gentleman, who married a Sister of the late Mr. Parrot, a partner in Sir Claude Scotts' house, and son of a very worthy person, who originally went out to India with my Aunt Lyttelton, as her servant. Miss Parrot, who has married my cousin E L Witts was her daughter. Mr. Burgoyne is Father to Mrs. Jos. Thrupp.*

1842: 17 Mar: *We proceeded towards our hotel, shopping by the way, and reached it before six o clock in time to dress for dinner with Mr. and Mrs. Thrupp at their private residence in Upper Brook Street, where we met Mrs. E. L. Witts, and were joined in the evening by her nephew and Mrs. Thrupp's cousin, Mr. Geo.Parrot, a young man connected, either as a Junior partner or Clerk, with Sir Claude Scott's bank, of which his late Father was the resident and managing partner.*

PARRY — junior counsel at the chancery bar

Despite research, no information has been found regarding this barrister.

1836: 23 Jul: *It would seem that Mr. Knight, the great Chancery Barrister, acquiesces in the principle which was laid down by Mr. Parry, another Chancery lawyer of considerable repute, whose opinion on the case we had taken.* 29 Jul., 6 Aug., 26 Aug., 7 Sep: *Found a letter from Newmarch, who, without going to Town, had an interview with Mr. Parry of the Chancery Bar, who was visiting near Cirencester, and who retains the same view of our case as against Mr. Walters, which he did before & will draw the Bill accordingly.*

1836: 4 Nov: *Received a letter from Newmarch, announcing that Mr. Parry of the Chancery bar had prepared the Bill which we are about to file against the Trustees of the late Dr. H. Moorhouse & that Newmarch had carefully examined it, and returned it to Town to be forwarded as quickly as the forms of the Court will admit.*

1837: 5 Mar: *The answer will be laid before our Junior Counsel, Mr. Parry, for his consideration, & to report thereon.* 12 Mar., 11 May, 20 May, 24 May. 10 Jun., 30 Jun., 10 Jul: *In agreeing to these terms of compromise we are actuated by a desire to escape from protracted and doubtful litigation, and follows the advice of our counsel, Mr. Parry, who recommends accepting Mr. Walters's terms, expressing an opinion that it would be advisable for us to make even greater sacrifices, rather than not bring the suit to a termination.*

PARRY — Charles Henry Parry [33]

Charles Henry Parry (1779-1860), physician, was born at Broadgates, Gloucester Street, Cirencester, the eldest son of Caleb Hillier Parry (1755-1822) and his wife, Sarah (1749-1831), a sister of Edward Rigby (1747-1821) of Norwich. He was educated at Bath Grammar School and Göttingen, where he studied medicine. In 1799 he was one of Samuel Taylor Coleridge's companions in the Harz mountains, and later he travelled in Scandinavia with Clement Carlyon. On 24 June 1804 Parry graduated MD at

Edinburgh, where he became acquainted with Henry Brougham. He was admitted licentiate of the Royal College of Physicians on 22 December 1806, and elected a fellow of the Royal Society in 1812. From 1807 to 1815 Parry practised at Cheltenham, where he was befriended by Edward Jenner.

Charles Henry Parry married, 17 July 1809, Emma Mary Bedford (±1788-1872), born at Sutton Coldfield, Warwickshire; they had at least 3 daughters:

1 Augusta Bertie (1817-1871); died unmarried
2 Laura E. W. (b. 1819); probably died unmarried
3 Sarah Louisa (1820-1842)

In 1815 Parry moved to Bath, where the following year he took over his father's practice. He was physician to the general hospital at Bath from 1818 to 1822, and in 1825 he published the *Collections from the Unpublished Medical Writings of the Late Caleb Hillier Parry*, to which he added an introductory volume. He retired to Brighton in 1849, and died there in 1860. At the time of the 1861 census his widow and two unmarried daughters were lodging at Belle Vue Place, Southampton.

1808: 6 May: *Walked with Charles Parry &c.—Dined at home. Dressed for a party at Mr. Worthingtons in the Evening. Many assembled to Conversation & Music: Mr. Richards & his Daughter, professional performers, the young Miss Worthingtons &c.*

1823: 9 Apr.

1829: 2 Apr.

PARRY — Thomas Gambier Parry [34]

Thomas Gambier Parry (1816-1888), JP, DL, landed proprietor, benefactor, and art collector, was born at Belgravia, London, the only child of Richard Parry (1776-1817) and Mary (d. 1821), daughter of Samuel Gambier and niece of James, Adm. Lord Gambier. His father and grandfather, Thomas Parry, of Banstead, Surrey, were wealthy directors of the East India Company. Parry was brought up by two maiden Gambier aunts and educated at Eton College and Trinity College, Cambridge (BA 1837; MA 1848). He purchased the 1,811-acre estate at Highnam Court in 1838, and established a pinetum there in 1844, having been encouraged to do so by the collector and arboriculturist Robert Stayner Holford of Westonbirt. Parry was a JP and DL for Gloucestershire, and high sheriff for the county in 1850.

Parry married, first, 1839, Anna Maria Isabella Fynes-Clinton (1816-1848); they had 4 sons and 1 daughter:

1 Charles Clinton (1840-83); married, at Sutton Courtenay, Berkshire, 14 August 1865, Florence Caroline Hinde (b. 1845); 2 sons and 2 daughters
1 Lucy Anna (±1841-1861); died unmarried
2 Francis Gambier (b. & d. 1843)
3 Edward Clement Hervey (1844-1845)
4 Charles Hubert Hastings (1848-1918), composer; knighted; married, at London, 25 June 1872, Elizabeth Maude Herbert (1851-1933); 2 daughters

Anna Maria died in 1848, presumably at childbirth or soon after, and in her memory Parry commissioned Henry Woodyer to design the church of the Holy Innocents at Highnam in the decorated Gothic style. Parry paid for and endowed the church, the school, the church lodge, and the rectory.

Parry married secondly, 1851, Ethelinda (1827-1896), daughter of Francis Lear, dean of Salisbury; they had 2 sons and 4 daughters:

1 Linda Isabel (1852-1936); died unmarried
1 Ernest Gambier (1853-1936); married, at London, 1882, Evelyn Elizabeth Palk (1854-1935); 1 son
2 Mary Beatrice (1855-1934); died unmarried
3 Ethel Geraldine (1858-1943); married, 1887, Oxley Durant Parker
2 Sidney Gambier (1859-1948); married, at London, 6 November 1890, Grace Denman (1859-1935); 2 sons and 1 daughter
4 Hilda Katherine (1866-1953); married, 1902, Egerton Tymewell Cripps

Thomas Gambier Parry devoted his inherited wealth to good works. He adopted the principles of the Oxford movement and was a prominent member of the Ecclesiological Society. He was also a notable collector of medieval and renaissance art; the Courtauld Institute of Art later acquired his collection. He was a philanthropist, founding a children's hospital, an orphanage, and a college of science and art at Gloucester. He also provided a school for his tenants at Highnam. His son Ernest became the family archivist and was a noted writer.

1842: 12 Jan.

1846: 2 Jul: *Mr. Gambier Parry, of Highnam Court, presided as a Vice-chairman.* 11 Aug: *The Chair was taken and well filled by Mr. Gambier Parry, as Vice President, and the Committee room was very much crowded.* 22 Oct: *Quarterly meeting: numerously attended Mr. Gambier Parry in the Chair.*

1847: 28 Jun: *Mr. Gambier Parry, of Highnam Court, recently appointed a magistrate, and member of the Committee of accounts, was initiated into that business: Curtis Hayward and Goodrich were the other colleagues with whom and the Chairman I worked: Baker, who, as High Sheriff, is precluded from acting as a magistrate, came in and assisted his friend Parry.* 29 Jun., 31 Aug., 18 Oct.

1848: 26 Jun., 16 Oct., 17 Oct: *Twenty magistrates dined together at the Bell, Purnell presiding ... Gambier Parry.* 22 Nov.

1849: 31 Dec.

1850: 28 Jan.

1851: 17 Mar., 17 Apr: *Received a card of invitation to the Consecration of the beautiful new Church recently built and endowed by T. Gambier Parry at Highnam—a kind mark of friendly attention on his part.* 1851., 26 Apr: *Having received a note from Gambier Parry with two tickets of admission into his Church on Tuesday next, the day fixed for the consecration, I wrote a few lines to E. F. W, sending him one of those tickets.* 29 Apr: *we drove to the mansion of Gambier Parry, whither carriages were resorting from all quarters ... Parry's spacious mansion stands on a gentle eminence overlooking the vale of Gloucester, and bounded by the Cotswold range on the opposite side of the Severn, backed by the hills extending in an almost uninterrupted range from the Malvern heights to the eminences passing through the Forest of Dean to the Wye.... We entered a spacious hall, leading into an inner apartment of the same character in which are beautiful specimens of art in vases, statuettes &c.—Thence we proceeded to a large billiard room, where I noticed a choice collection of modern Water colour paintings.*

1853: 3 Jan., 27 Jun.

1854: 14 Feb.

PARRY — William Edward Parry [35]

Sir William Edward Parry (1790-1855), naval officer and Arctic explorer, was the fourth son of Caleb Hillier Parry and the younger brother of Charles Henry Parry (*above*). He entered the Royal Navy in 1803 on board Adm. Cornwallis's flagship, the *Ville de Paris*. In 1810 he was promoted to the rank of lieutenant and appointed to the frigate *Alexandria*, which was employed for the next three years in protecting the Spitsbergen whaling fleet.

In June 1813 Parry joined the 74-gun *La Hogue* at Halifax, Nova Scotia, and continued in *La Hogue* and other ships on the North American station until 1817, when he returned to England on hearing that his father had suffered a stroke. He was at home on half pay when appointed in 1818 to command the *Alexander*, a hired brig, under the orders of Capt. John Ross in his expedition to the Arctic seas in search of a north-west passage to the Pacific. The expedition followed the coast of Baffin Bay without making any new discoveries, and Parry was back in England early the following year. In 1819 Parry was appointed to the *Hecla* in command of a new expedition to discover the passage. He sailed from Deptford in May, with the brig *Griper* in company. The expedition was unsuccessful due to blocked ice, but the two ships returned safely, arriving into the Thames in November 1820 having collected valuable scientific material. Parry's dispatches, sent in advance by a whaler, had reached the Admiralty on 4 November, on which date he was promoted to the rank of commander. He received the freedom of his native city and many other honours; in the following February he was elected a fellow of the Royal Society and, alongside the officers and men of the expedition, he received a parliamentary grant offered as a reward for those who should first pass the meridian of 110° W within the Arctic circle.

In May 1821 Parry sailed again for the Arctic commanding HMS *Fury* accompanied by HMS *Hecla* under George Francis Lyon. Through the summers of 1822 and 1823 he and his crew continued to examine the long-sought-after passage, but blocked by ice and with symptoms of scurvy beginning to appear, Parry judged it inadvisable to attempt a third winter in the Arctic. The ships returned to Britain and were paid off at Deptford on 14 November 1823. Parry by this time had been promoted to the rank of post captain. In 1824 he went on a third expedition, again in the *Hecla*, accompanied by Henry Hoppner in the *Fury*, but the north-west passage still proved elusive and he returned to England in November 1825.

Parry married, first, at Alderley, Cheshire, 23 October 1826, Isabella Louisa (1801-1839), daughter of John Thomas Stanley, 1st Baron Stanley of Alderley; they had 3 sons and 4 daughters:

1 Stanley (b. ±1827); born at Alderley, Cheshire
1 Isabella (1830-1837); born in New South Wales
2 Edward (1830-1890), Church of England clergyman; born at St Philip's, Sydney, New South Wales; became suffragan bishop of Dover; married, ±1858, Matilda Williams (1831-1902); 4 sons and 3 daughters
2 Lucy (1832-1906); born at St Philip's, Sydney, New South Wales; married, at Lewisham, Kent, 14 February 1854, Adm. Robert Coote (1820-1898); 1 son and 1 daughter
3 Charles (1833-1868), Cdr; born at Hexham, Newcastle, New South Wales; died at Naples
3 Emmeline Louisa (1836-1837)
4 Caroline (1837-1927), Church of England clergyman; married, at Tonbridge, Kent, July 1861, John Hugh Way (1835-1912); 3 sons and 1 daughter

Parry was knighted in 1829. He then spent four years in Australia as commissioner of the Australian Agricultural Company. His first wife died in 1839, and he married secondly, 1841, Catharine Edwards (1808-1896), daughter of Revd Robert Hankinson and widow of Samuel Hoare. They had 1 son and 2 daughters:

1= Elizabeth (1844-1906)
1= Katharine (1844-1929)
1 William Edward (1845-1861); died at Harrow School

1823: 9 Apr: *Much anxiety begins to be felt for news of the Arctic navigators; I saw Captn. Parry at Bath, shortly before his last departure, & was introduced to him by his excellent & highly talented brother, my valued acquaintance, Dr. C.W. Parry, of Bath. It was a most pleasing spectacle, when Captn. P. received the freedom of the Corporation of his native city, Bath, accompanied with an gold oaken box made of a fragment of the Vessel, in which he explored the icy seas, & ornamented with a medallion in gold, representing one of the Icebergs of the frozen ocean, and the discovery ships, as pourtrayed on one of the plates engraved for the narrative of the Voyage. It is impossible to see & know Captn. Parry without admiring him as a model of the intrepid, cool, collected, intelligent, cheerful, friendly British Sailor; to these qualities science & courage & judgment of the highest order are united. Nor do I here introduce him merely in a parenthesis; as he is likely, should Providence bring him home from his hazardous enterprize; to unite himself with Miss Browne, another of my Sabine connexions.* 19 Oct: *The papers announce the unexpected return of Captains Parry & Lyon with their crews from the Northern Seas, bringing home their vessels in safety: and having lost four or five men from accident, and organic complaints.* 1 Nov: *The development of the unfortunate rupture between Captn. Parry & Miss Emily Browne has arrived sooner than I expected, in a copy of a letter on the subject from Miss Sabine (Aunt to the young Lady,) to Mrs. M. Hunt, and by her transmitted to us. It seems, that this Miss Browne is the same, who in early days was guilty of a juvenile indiscretion & elopement with a boy gardener at North Mims; of this I had heard before, and of the speedy separation of the silly fugitives on being pursued. When Captn. Parry paid his addresses, Mr. Browne honourably told him her whole history: and then surely he should have retracted his offer, if he considered the past misconduct a bar to his prospect of happiness: nor could he then have been blamed. But during his late absence Parry's family has come to the knowledge of this transaction, which has so set them against the connection, that on Captn. Parry's return to England, & subsequent to his waiting on Mr. Browne who was in Town, & writing very affectionately to Miss Browne in Worcestershire, they imparted to him the information they had collected coupled with the dying request of his Father, the late Dr. Parry of Bath, whom on departing for his last voyage he had left in the last stage of paralysis, that this union should not be carried into effect.*

1824: 26 Oct.

1825: 20 Oct: *It appears by the newspapers, that Captain Parry is again returned from his northwest expedition without accomplishing his object.*

1829: 2 Apr.

PARSONS — Henry Parsons [36]

Henry Parsons (±1797-1878), Church of England clergyman, was born at Elmore, Gloucestershire, son of Joseph Parsons (1762-1829), of Peterborough, and Laetitia Catherine Patteson (1764-1829). His father had been Francis Witts's old schoolmaster (*see below*, Joseph Parsons). Parsons was educated at Balliol College, Oxford (BA 1820; MA 1823), and was ordained deacon on 21 December 1820 and priest on 2 June 1822. His first clerical appointment was as curate of Stoke Doyle, Northamptonshire, from 21 December 1820; to this was adjoined other curacies. He remained in Northamptonshire until he accepted the appointment at Upton St Leonards on 23 April 1833, where he remained until 1846. After a four-year gap, presumably abroad, he then became perpetual curate of Sandhurst, Berkshire, in 1850, and remained so until his death in 1878.

Parsons married, at Peterborough, Northamptonshire, 3 April 1821, Anne (1796-1887), daughter of Francis Hopkinson (1758-1816) and Sarah Whitsed (1777-1834); they had at least 1 son and 4 daughters:

1 Louisa Catherine (1821-1873)
2 Caroline (1823-1903)
1 John Tourney (1825-1878), Church of England clergyman; married, at Begbroke, Oxfordshire, 31 December 1850, Mary Adair Coulson (1815-1890); 1 daughter
3 Jane (1829-1881)
4 Laura (1830-1866)

1838: 3 Jan., 4 Jan: *Mr. & Mrs. Parsons from Upton, and a Mr. C. Parsons came to dinner.... Mr. P. was a Clergyman in Huntingdonshire, and Son of a late Prebendary of Peterborough, formerly of Elmore, where among many others of Gloucestershire connections, Sir John Guise, E. Jones, C. Crawley &c. I was his pupil. He and a brother in law, Patterson, had a very respectable school at Elmore for many years.*

1839: 2 Jan., 3 Jan: *An assistant Curate to Mr. Parsons at Upton St. Leonards, dined and slept at Prinknash, by name Winchester, recently ordained, a Xt. Ch. man, said to have distinguished himself at the Univ: he resides with his widowed Mother at Glouc. and appears amiable, but shy and reserved: and no wonder, for I understand that his Father, the late Alderman Winchester, of London, having fallen into embarrassment, terminated his days by suicide.* 4 Jan: *In the evening Hyett joined us after dinner, and the three gentlemen for the rest of the Evening discussed many of the forgoing topics, with the Poor Law matters, Lunatic Asylum, Emigration &c. Hyett had brought his lady and children, to whom were added the young people from Upton, children of Mr. Parsons, who with the Howell tribe made up a nice little domestic circle of dancers, who enjoyed themselves till summoned to a pretty early supper in the school room, after which the youngsters parted, and before 11 o cl. the Seniors repaired to their Chambers.* 6-7 Jan.

1840: 4 Sep: *Wrote to Howell respecting the Curacy of Upton St. Leonards, which he had mentioned to me when here, and which I named yesterday to Massie. As it may possibly suit the latter, when his engagement with my son terminates, I made enquiries of Mr. Parsons, who is leaving Upton to reside for some time abroad for his health.* 25 Sep.

1842: 18 Oct: *Called by the way on Mr. Parsons, the Incumbent of Upton St. Leonards, at his elegant Tudor Villa, St. Leonards, to inform him that the funeral of poor Mrs. Howell is fixed for Saturday.* 21-22 Oct., 12 Dec: *A Miss Dowell was on a visit, a middle aged single lady, pleasing, quiet, sensible, well-informed, and well-bred, the sister of a Clergyman, who had been Curate of Upton St. Leonards, occupying Mr. Parsons's residence during his absence with his family on the Continent.*

1844: 11 Apr: *Mr. Lefroy, Mr. W. Hicks, Mr. Clements, Mr. T. Parsons, and a Son of Prebendary Banks, joined the game, and the numbers were augmented by Servants and village lads.*

1845: 8 May: *The day closed by a dinner party; at which were present Mr. & Mrs. Pearson, the purchasers of, and resident at the Villa erected by Mr. Parsons at the foot of Upton Hill.*

1846: 6 Sep.

1847: 18 May.

PARSONS — James Parsons[37]

James Parsons (1762-1847), Church of England clergyman, was born at Cirencester, son of James Parsons and Jane Hayes. He was educated at Wadham College (BA 1781; MA 1786) and St Alban Hall, Oxford (BD 1815). Parsons was ordained deacon on 31 October 1784 and priest on 18 May 1788. He was appointed perpetual curate of Newnham and Littledean on 12 July 1800 and held the position until his death in 1847.

1836: 11 Jul: *Through Broadoak to Newnham, a dull, small town on a hill above the Severn, where is a ferry to cross to the opposite bank. Mr. Parsons, one of the editors of the Oxford edition of the Septuagint, the incumbent, Mr. Harrison, who officiated for me during my absence in Yorkshire last summer, occupying my house at U.S., was Curate of Newnham.*

PARSONS — John Parsons[38]

John Parsons (1771-1852), landed proprietor, was born at Toddington, Gloucestershire, the son of John Parsons and Agnes, daughter of James Higford (d. 1742) of Dixton, Gloucestershire. He lived at Newark House, Hempsted, near Gloucester, which he rebuilt in the 1830s.

1826: 8 Mar: *The property of the Duchess of Norfolk, who lived separate from her husband in a state of derangement at the Mansion of Hom Lacy, and survived him some years, having died without issue, came eventually to be divided, between her three nearest of kin, Sir Edwyn Stanhope, son of an Admiral and himself a captain in the royal navy & a baronet, General Burr, and Mr. Parsons, of the family formerly possessed of Dixton Estate & Manor in Gloucestershire, whose father was Rector of Toddington and who has recently assumed the name of Higford. Sir E. Stanhope had married a relation of poor Dowell's, a daughter of Major Dowell, his uncle, of the East India company's service, & thus he was induced to exercise his patronage as to the Vicarage of Hom Lacy in favour of my friend.* 20 Mar.

PARSONS — John Parsons — *see also* Hopton

John Parsons (1782-1870) and his father Revd William Parsons both changed their name to Hopton prior to 1807, presumably upon his father inheriting the Canon Frome estate in Herefordshire.

PARSONS — Joseph Parsons[39]

Joseph Parsons (1762-1829), Church of England clergyman and schoolmaster, was born at Oxford, son of Joseph Parsons (1720-1797) and Mary Kirby. He was educated at Trinity College, Oxford (BA 1782; MA 1785), and entered the Church. Parsons was rector of Caldecote, Hertfordshire, in 1806-16 and of Holwell, Bedfordshire, in 1810. He was appointed prebendary of Peterborough in 1815 and was finally rector of Glinton with Peykirk, Northamptonshire, in 1816-29. There is a fine marble memorial to Joseph and his wife in Peterborough Cathedral.

Parsons married, 1788, Laetitia Catherine Patteson (1764-1829); they had 1 son and 3 daughters:

1 Letitia (1791-1856)
2 Catherine (1792-1824)
3 Elizabeth (b. 1795)
1 Henry (1797-1878), *see above*

It seems probable that Laetitia Catherine was the younger sister of Edward Patteson. A deed in Oxfordshire Record Office signed by both Edward Patteson and his son Edward Patteson, as well as Joseph and Laetitia Parsons, seems to indicate that this was a Patteson family affair. Joseph ran a school at Elmore Court with his presumed brother-in-law Edward Patteson.

1802: 2 Oct: *Wrote to Fletcher & Parsons & Thomas Dodd.* 1805: 20 Feb: *Walked, with Mr. Parsons.* 11 Mar: *Dined at Gloucester House with Mr. Delabere, met Mr. Parsons.*

1826: 31 Aug: *distant view of Elmore court, the place, where I first went to school, on an eminence not far from the Severn. It is a deserted mansion of Sir W. Guise's: in 1793, when I was an inmate within its walls, & left it on my parents removal to Scotland, incident on my Father's reverse of fortune, a highly respectable academy was kept there by Messrs. Parsons & Patteson, Clergymen and brothers-in-law, both, I believe, still living, and enjoying a competence well earned by their industry; some of my old schoolfellows are among my intimate acquaintance in the County, & sitting on the same bench with me as Magistrates, Genl. Guise, Mr. Edwd. Jones, Col. Webb, M.P. for Gloucester, Charles Crawley &c.: Others, as the Raikes's, are now removed from the County.*

1838: 4 Jan.

PARTIS — Ann Partis[40]

Fletcher Partis (1760-1820), lawyer, was born in the parish of St James, Westminster, son of Fletcher Partis and his wife, Ann. He married another Ann (1758-1846), and upon Fletcher's retirement as a lawyer and conveyancer, the couple moved to Bath. Ann and Fletcher shared a concern for women left in reduced circumstances, which in those days often meant the death of a male relative upon whom they were dependent. Life for such gentlewomen could be very distressing, and there was little help available to them. Together Fletcher and Ann Partis recognised a need and had the determination and means to do something about it.

Fletcher Partis purchased a plot in 1820 for the what was to become known as Partis College, a collection of almshouses for women left in reduced circumstances. He died only six weeks later, but his widow continued the work as both founder and benefactor, taking an active interest in all aspects of the building of the houses. The college was founded in 1825 and continues to this day, providing accommodation in thirty terraced houses.

There is a marble memorial in Bath Abbey to Fletcher Partis, depicting him as the Good Samaritan. When Ann died in 1846 she was buried in the abbey cemetery, where she is commemorated by an impressive Greek revival tomb.

1839: 17 Apr: *Descending to the Upper Bristol Road, we directed our steps homewards by the Weston road and Park; pausing, as we went, to view Partis College .... The institution is governed by certain regulations, and Mrs. Partis is, as might be supposed, Lady paramount... The house which we viewed, was a model of comfort and neatness; the nest of a nice old maid.*

PARUTHER — Paruther and Fisher, solicitors, Fenchurch Street

The partners Paruther and Fisher were solicitors at 50 Fenchurch Street.

1840: 31 Mar: *Recd. a letter from Mr. Jennings with the particulars of an agreement he has entered into with a Mr. Paruther for a lease to of the premises No. 50 Fenchurch Street, for 21 years from Midsr. next at £190.* 5 May: *The Mr. Paruther, who has taken our houses in Fenchurch Street, is a respectable Solicitor, who is about to remove from his house of business in that neighbourhood in consequence of its being in the line of the Blackwall railway: he purposes to occupy the principal part of the premises himself, and to let the remainder.* 24 Jun., 27 Jun., 3 Jul., 17 Aug., 20 Aug.

PASHLEY — William Pashley[41]

William Pashley (1793-1858), Church of England clergyman, was the son of William Pashley (1756-1816) and Priscilla Thompson (d. 1793). He was educated at St John's College, Cambridge (BA 1823; MA 1842), and was ordained deacon on 23 February 1822 and priest on 25 May 1823. Pashley's first clerical appointment was as stipendiary curate of Newland from 24 February 1822, to which was added the curacy of Longhope, Gloucestershire, on 29 October 1822. He was curate of Sedgeberrow, Worcestershire, in 1847-59, and rector of Aston-Somerville, Gloucestershire, in 1841-59. He died at Welling, Kent.

1843: 4 Oct: *Without, the church yard is rough, and rude, and unneat; adjacent is a paltry, neglected, modern parsonage house, and garden: inhabited, I believe, by a Mr. Pashley, Incumbent or Curate, a person of penurious habits, without some of those attainments, or qualities of heart or mind, which most adorn the Country parish priest.*

PATON — Mary Ann Paton[42]

Mary Ann Paton (1802-1864), singer, was born in Edinburgh, the eldest daughter of George Paton, a writing-master and amateur violinist, and his wife, N. N. Crawford, of Cameron Bank, also an amateur musician. As a child she studied the harp, the violin, and the piano, and began making an appearance in 1810 as a singer, also playing the harp and piano, and reciting. The family settled in London in 1811, and Mary Ann sang at the Noblemen's Subscription Concerts, but then withdrew on the grounds of her health. In 1822 she joined the Haymarket company, where her performances included Susanna in *The Marriage of Figaro* and Rosina in *The Barber of Seville*. Her reputation was greatly enhanced when she sang Agathe in the first English version of Weber's *Der Freischütz* at the Lyceum on 22 July 1824. A still greater triumph followed with her rendition of the character Reiza in the première of Weber's *Oberon*, conducted by him on 12 April 1826. 'Miss Paton is a singer of the very first rank, and will sing Reiza divinely,' Weber wrote, but he later complained when rehearsals were interrupted by the death of her child. Weber also found that she, like others, was a poor actress, and he deplored her ornamentation of his music.

At her father's insistence, Mary Ann broke off her engagement to a young doctor named Blood, who acted for a short time under the name of Davis. Afterwards, in 1824, she became the wife of Lord William Pitt Lennox (1799-1881). In 1831 she divorced her husband in the Scottish court of session, and in the same year married the tenor named Joseph Wood (1801-1890). She and her husband Joseph had a son in 1838. In 1831 she was engaged at the King's Theatre, where she sang in Rossini's *La Cenerentola* and other Italian operas. She then returned to Drury Lane, where she sang Alice in Henry Bishop's version of Meyerbeer's *Robert le diable*. She and her husband moved to Woolley Moor, Yorkshire, in 1833, though she later made three successful tours of America. She retired to a convent for a year, but reappeared at the Princess's Theatre and at several concerts in which her husband was also engaged to perform. The couple finally settled at Bulcliffe Hall, near Chapelthorpe.

1829: 22 Sep: *Miss Paton was new to me, and new to Gloucester; but her reputation is great and very deservedly so. Her voice and science are almost of the first order: her popularity great both on the stage & in the orchestra; her history singular, and her situation ambiguous. In her profession she is Miss Paton; out of it Lady William Lenox; for she is now the acknowledged wife of a younger brother of the Duke of Richmond, to whom the revenue to be derived from her talents is very acceptable. It is understood, that the ladies of his Lordship's family recognize her and receive her in their domestic society; & he accompanies her on her professional tours, being now, indeed, with her at Gloucester.* 23 Sep: *The kind soothings of Lady W. Lenox could hardly keep her with the assistance of the usual restoratives from fainting away at one moment, and at another from falling into strong hysterics, and as soon as she was able to remove from the orchestra she retired to her lodgings. But her strong emotions did not prevent her doing full justice to the beautiful Air by Cimarosa "Ah! parlate"... The principal performers were regaled to-day at the Palace, where Miss Paton desired Mr. Waller to introduce her by her proper name, as Lady W. Lenox. She observed to the Bishop, that if Lord William had been able to accompany her, he would have presented her in her proper character &c. The good Bishop's unpremeditated answer was not amiss: "I am obliged to you Lady William; you have relieved me from a dilemma." If Miss Paton, she was Lord W's mistress, and as such not fit to be received at a Bishop's board; but it was otherwise, if Lord W. L. had made her his wife.* 24 Sep.

PATTEN — Thomas Patten — *see* Wilson-Patten

PATTESON — Edward Patteson [43]

Edward Patteson (±1762-1845), Church of England clergyman and schoolmaster, was the son of Edward and Elizabeth Patteson of Smethwick, Staffordshire. He was brother-in-law to Joseph Parsons; a deed in the Oxfordshire Record Office signed by both Edward Pattesons (senior and junior) and Joseph and Laetitia Parsons seems to indicate that Laetitia was Edward's younger sister.

Patteson was educated at Trinity College, Oxford (BA 1784; MA 1787), and was curate for a short while at Weston-on-Trent, Derbyshire. He then joined his brother-in-law Edward Parsons in setting up a school at Elmore Court, Gloucestershire. He lived for the remainder of his life at Richmond, Surrey. From May to December 1814 he was vicar at Weston, Hertfordshire, near Stevenage. He died at East Sheen, near Richmond.

Patteson was married to Sarah (1760-1829); they had at least 3 sons:

1 Unknown
2 Edward (1801-1871), Church of England clergyman; educated at Balliol College, Oxford, and Queen's College Cambridge (BA 1826); rector of Gedding, Suffolk, 1831-71; married Mary (b. ±1801); at least 1 son and 1 daughter:
    1 Samuel (b. ±1832)
    1 Mary (b. ±1833)
3 Henry (1804-1834)

Edward Patteson was fortunate in having a 1603 edition of Florio's *Montaigne*, said to contain a genuine autograph of William Shakespeare. He sold the book in 1838 for £140. He published, 1804, *A General and Classical Atlas* at a price of 3 guineas.

1803: 20 Aug: *Walked with my Mother in the forenoon to Richmond & called upon the Revd. Mr. & Mrs Patteson, the former my old Elmore School Master.* 9 Sep., 28 Sep., 29 Sep: *Dined with Mr. Patteson at Marsh Gate Richmond.* 9 Nov., 15 Nov., 20 Nov.

1805: 6 Jul: *Wrote about schools to Mr. Burslem & Mr. Patteson.* 11 Jul., 26 Jul.

1826: 31 Aug: *distant view of Elmore court, the place, where I first went to school, on an eminence not far from the Severn. It is a deserted mansion of Sir W. Guise's: in 1793, when I was an inmate within its walls, & left it on my parents removal to Scotland, incident on my Father's reverse of fortune, a highly respectable academy was kept there by Messrs. Parsons & Patteson.*

1838: 4 Jan.

PATTESON — John Patteson [44]

Sir John Patteson (1790-1861), judge, was born at Coney Weston, Suffolk, second son of the Revd Henry Patteson, of Drinkstone, Suffolk, and Sophia, daughter of Richard Ayton Lee, a London banker. He was educated at Eton College and King's College, Cambridge (BA 1813; MA 1816). Patteson was unsure whether to study medicine, law, or divinity, but chose in the end to pursue a career in law, and joined the Middle Temple in London. In 1815 he went on the midland circuit as marshal to Mr Justice Chambre, and read in the chambers of Godfrey Sykes, an eminent pleader, and Joseph Littledale, later a judge.

Patteson married, first, 23 February 1818, his cousin Elizabeth (d. 1820), daughter of George Lee of Dickleburgh, Norfolk; 1 daughter:

1 Joanna Elizabeth (1819-1884); died unmarried

He married secondly, 22 April 1824, Frances Duke (1796-1842), daughter of Capt. James Coleridge, of Ottery St Mary, Devon, and sister of Sir John Taylor Coleridge; they had at least 3 sons and 2 daughters:

1 Frances Sophia Coleridge (1825-1913); died unmarried at Rome
1 John Coleridge (1827-1871), bishop of Melanesia
2 James H. Patteson (1828-1904); married, at Honiton, Devon, Elizabeth Anne Walker (1836-1879); 2 sons and 2 daughters
2 Elizabeth A. (b. ±1835)
3 Francis George (b. 1830)

In 1821 Patteson began to practise as a special pleader, and was called to the bar. He joined the northern circuit, and began to attract attention through his skill in pleading. He became assistant to Littledale as counsel to the Treasury and was one of the legal commissioners on the reform of the Welsh judicature, which led to the act of 1830, by which three additional judges were appointed—one in each the king's bench, common pleas, and exchequer. In November 1830 Lord Lyndhurst appointed him to the new judgeship in the court of king's bench, and he was knighted. For over twenty years Patteson was considered to be one of the most practical and learned judges in that court; he was praised for his memory, clarity of expression, courtesy, and erudition. Deafness forced Patteson to resign at the end of January 1852.

1836: 8 Apr., 10 Aug: *The Judges, Littledale and Patteson, had arrived at about 6 o clock.* 11 Aug., 19 Oct.,

1848: 2 Feb.

1851: 31 Mar: *Mr. Justice Patteson presided at Nisi Prius ... Mr. Justice Patteson is still the exceedingly deaf person he has long been; but with a mechanical contrivance beneath his wig the misfortune is much mitigated, and he is cheerful and quite alive to what is passing.*

PATTON — Andrew Patton [45]

Andrew Patton (1771-1838), army officer, was born at Clatto, near St Andrews, co. Fife. When he was at school in France he received a commission as ensign in the 6th Regiment, of which his father was a colonel. In 1794 he was appointed lieutenant in the 10th Regiment, and in 1798 captain in the 92nd, or Gordon Highlanders; in the same year he was also made ADC to the marquess of Huntley, later duke of Gordon. In 1809 Patton received promotion as major in the 45th, but interestingly he carried the rank of major in the *Army List* as early as 1805.

Patton took part in putting down the Irish Rebellion of 1798. He served in Holland under Sir Ralph Abercrombie and the duke of York in 1799, and fought at the battles of Helder, Bergen, and Alkmaar. He assisted in quelling the insurrection in Jamaica, and afterwards served once again under Sir Ralph Abercrombie, this time in the Egyptian campaign of 1801. In 1807 Patton was with Lord Cathcart's army, in the division commanded by Sir Arthur Wellesley, at the attack on Copenhagen. In 1808 he was in Spain under Sir John Moore, where he endured the hardships of the retreat in midwinter.

After the Peninsular War Patton retired from active military life. He emigrated to Canada in 1816, and settled on a farm in the township of Adolphustown, on the bay of Quinte; however, by 1820 he had accepted the position of ordnance storekeeper at Fort Wellington, Prescott. He was the first registrar of the county of Grenville. In 1829 he was offered the barrackmastership at York [now Toronto]; he held the appointment until 1836. Patton married Elizabeth Simpson (d. 1868), of Derby, and had six children.

1806: 11 Feb: *Dined with Lieut. Col. Napier at his Mother's in St. Vincent's Parade, the young Ladies & Major Patton formed our party, which was pleasant enough.* 13 Feb: *I walked with Col. Napier & Major Patton upon the hill.* 14 Feb: *Walked with Col. Napier & Major Patton, in Town, & upon the Hill Walked with Col. Napier & Major Patton, in Town, & upon the Hill.*

PATTON — Robert Patton[46]

Robert Patton (1742-1812), army officer (HEIC), was a younger son of Philip Patton (1709-1794), collector of customs at Kirkcaldy, Fife, and Annas Loch (b. 1708). He was the younger brother of Philip and Charles Patton, and a friend and admirer of Warren Hastings.

Patton married, at Calcutta, 31 July 1772, Constantia Adriana Sally (1756-1811), daughter of Revd Robert Mapletoft (1722 1756) and Sarah Beale (1728-1792); they had 6 sons and 11 daughters:

1 Constantia Sarah (1773-1822)
2 Anna (1774-1813)
1 Robert (1775-1837), Maj.-Gen.; married Sophia Brown; 1 son:
  1 James Patton (1797-1841)
3 Isabella (b. 1779)
2 James (1780-1811); arrived in India, 21 December 1798, married, at Berhampore, India, 5 October 1802, Isabella Hardwicke (d. 1821); 1 son and 2 daughters:
  1 Isabella Sarah (1803-1863)
  1 James Hardwicke (1803-1870)
  2 Anna (1807-1856)
4 Sarah (1781-1863)
3 Charles (b. 1783)
5 Eleanora (b. 1784)
6 Eliza (1785-1863)
7 Jenny [Jessy?] (1787-1879)
8 Margaret (b. 1788)
4 Philip Eyles (1789-1870)
5 Hugh Inglis (1791-1864), Adm.
9 Selina (1793-1872)
6 John Wogan (1794-1833)
10 Frances Jean (1799-1891)
11 Ann Maria (d. 1852)

Between 1776 and 1779 Patton lived either in Thistle Street, Edinburgh, at Grange, near Burntisland, or at Pitliven, near Dunfermline. In September 1797 he was based at Edinburgh Castle. Patton published *An Historical Review of the Monarchy and Republic of Rome (*1797) and *Principles of Asiatic Monarchies Politically and Historically Investigated* (1803). He later became governor of St Helena. He died at Wallington, Hampshire, on 14 January 1812, a fortnight after the death of his wife, Constantia.

1801: 14 Oct: *At a party in the Evening at Mrs. Davies's, where we met the Patons a large Scotch family, the father of which is going Governor to St. Helena. The young ladies are very musical & we had some good singing, & dancing of reels.* 16 Oct: *Called upon Mrs. Davies, & the Patons No. 40 Manchester Street Manchester Square.* 23 Oct: *to a very pleasant Musical party at Lady Lyttelton's, where were the Pattons, Mrs. Davies. the Morley's, Mrs. Lowe, the Guydickens's, Vicomte De Bruges & Comte de Gourmand, Mr. Wood & the like.* 25 Oct.

PAUL — George Onesiphorus Paul[47]

Sir George Onesiphorus Paul, 2nd baronet (1746-1820), prison reformer and philanthropist, was born at Woodchester, Gloucestershire, son of Sir Onesiphorus Paul, 1st baronet (±1706-1774), a successful woollen manufacturer, and his first wife, Jane (±1707-1748), daughter of Francis Blackburn of Richmond, Yorkshire. He was baptised Onesiphorus but used the additional forename George from about 1780.

Paul was educated at St John's College, Oxford (BA 1766), after which he spent two years travelling in Germany, Austria, and Italy. On his return he led a leisured life, entering his horses at local race meetings, visiting London, Bath, and Weymouth, and frequenting gaming clubs. After his father's death in September 1774 he inherited the family business and property, including Hill House, at Rodborough, near Woodchester. The cloth mill was let, and Paul lived on the rent of a modest-sized estate. In 1780 he entered into the public affairs of the county, and by his administrative ability and tireless energy came to dominate. He was high sheriff for the year 1780-81, and on at least two occasions he contemplated standing for election as MP for Gloucestershire.

Influenced by the writings of John Howard, Paul chose to dedicate himself to prison reform. He was also greatly motivated by the appalling condition of Gloucestershire's county gaol, which was then located in what remained of the keep of Gloucester Castle. He studied the subject of prison reform in depth, and probably corresponded with John Howard—who visited Gloucestershire's county gaol in 1777 and 1784—although it is not known whether the two men ever met. In 1783 Paul launched his campaign among his fellow magistrates of the Gloucestershire bench, and at the county's March assizes they passed a series of resolutions committing themselves to reform the county prisons. At the following assizes in August and at a general meeting of the county a few months later, Paul presented his ideas in detail; in 1785, a committee under his direction secured an act of parliament for the building of a new gaol at Gloucester and four houses of correction in other parts of the county. Paul's scheme, having been brought to a successful conclusion, provided a model for the magistrates of other counties, who benefitted from his printed addresses on the subject and his detailed list of rules and regulations for the Gloucestershire prisons, published in the first of several editions in 1790.

As the leading magistrate in his home area, the Stroud valleys, Paul brought the same meticulous attention to petty sessional business, to minor matters of the government of Rodborough parish, to local charity schools (for which he set himself to improve the quality of masters and introduce Andrew Bell's monitorial system), and to Stroud's pauper dispensary. During a severe slump in the cloth industry in 1784, Paul headed up efforts to combat distress among the weavers and was the leading subscriber to their relief. He was also, in 1783, a promoter of a new Gloucester to Bath turnpike road, which was constructed along the Woodchester valley below his house. At his own cost he built a substantial coaching inn to service the road users. When George III (then staying at Cheltenham) visited the area in 1788, Paul organised proceedings, taking pains to ensure that people turned out in suitable numbers to line the route, and entertaining the royal party at Hill House.

Sir George Onesiphorus Paul died at Hill House in 1820. He never married and left as his heir a nephew, Robert Snow, who took the name and arms of Paul. The baronetcy came to an end at his death, but a new one was created in 1821 for a cousin, John Dean Paul.

Paul was a friend and acquaintance of Edward and Agnes Witts, particularly in the years 1791 to 1793, when the Witts family lived at Rodborough. Anne Snow, who lived at London, was Agnes's particular friend. She was the daughter of Elizabeth Snow, née Paul, and George Snow, and therefore niece to Sir George.

1801: 7 Jun: *I then accompanied Sir G. Paul, M. R. Snow, & Mr. D. Paul to Mr. Townly's in Westminster.*

1824: 11 Jul: *The lingering affair of the monument to Sir G.O. Paul was again brought forward. It is now proposed to employ a rising young artist, by name Sevier, who is to execute the monument in memory of Dr. Jenner, now in progress, and also to be erected by subscription.... The difficulty of making a good resemblance of Sir G. Paul is great: the only guide, which Mr. Sevier had to follow in a bust exhibited this day was a small medallion in wax, the production of Lady Denbigh, Lord Ducie's daughter, many years ago, & though Mr. S.'s bust was very creditable to his talents, and represented a fine, stern, prominent featured, intelligent man, it was not a likeness of Sir G.P. This will, however, it is to be hoped, be remedied in another attempt, my old Schoolfellow & brother magistrate, the Revd. G. Crawley, having great skill in drawing likenesses, has furnished from memory a sketch of the departed Baronet, which in the principal features is a great resemblance, and which he has given to Mr. Sevier as an aid for the modelling his bust.* 19 Oct.

1825: 18 Oct: *In the Evening, though not originally a member of the Committee for the erection of a monument to the memory of Sir G.O Paul, I was requested by the gentlemen forming it to assist them in their deliberations.* 9 Nov.

1842: 18 Oct.

PAUL — John Dean Paul [48]

Sir John Dean Paul, 1st baronet (1775-1852), banker, was the son of cousins John Paul and Frances (1755-1794), daughter of Robert Snow and Valentina Paul, sister to George Snow (1745-1822). His parents had married in January 1775. Paul was created a baronet in 1821 and inherited the Rodborough and Woodchester estate following the death of his kinsman, Robert Snow Paul (*below*).

The Hill House estate in Rodborough had been bought in 1757 by Onesiphorus Paul, a successful Woodchester clothier. He built a mansion there and was made a baronet in 1762. He was succeeded on his death in 1774 by his son Sir [George] Onesiphorus Paul, 2nd baronet (*above*). Sir George devised the Hill House estate and the manor of Rodborough, which he had purchased in 1806, to his nephew Robert Snow (1768-1849), who changed his name to Robert Snow Paul. In 1847 he in turn conveyed the estate to his kinsman Sir John Dean Paul.

John Dean Paul married, first, 1799, Frances Eleanor (1776-1833), daughter of John Simpson (1740-1802) and Anne Lyon (1747-1821); they had 3 sons and 4 daughters:

1 Anne Frances (1801-1863)
1 John Dean (1802-1868), banker and convicted fraudster; succeeded as 2nd baronet; married, 10 October 1826, Georgiana, daughter of Charles George Beauclerk and Emily Charlotte Ogilvie; 1 son:
  1 Aubrey John Dean (1827-1890); succeeded as 3rd baronet
2 George Robert (1803-1880); married Louisa Harriet Bevan (1804-1870)
2 Eleanor Maria (1804-1885); died unmarried
3 Maria Horatia (1805-1866); married, 20 December 1825, Charles Bankhead (1797-1870)
4 Jane (1807-1891); married, at Harrow, Middlesex, 25 October 1827, Capt. Edward Fox FitzGerald (1794-1863); at least 1 daughter:
  1 Pamela Françoise Lucie Augusta Charlotte (1830-1907)
3 William Wentworth (1812-1852)

Sir John Dean Paul, 2nd baronet, sold the estate to Thomas Marling in 1854.

1801: 22 May: *We dined with the Miss Snows; Major & Mrs. Campbell, the new married Couple, returned from Epsom races to meet us; in the Evening, the tea table was encreased by Miss Turner, Mr. D. Paul, Mr. R. Snow jun &c.* 1 Jun: *The Evening we spent as usual most agreeably at Mr. Snow's. Mr. Snow, Mr. D. Paul, Miss Webb, Col. & Mrs. Clithero &c.* 7 Jun: *I then accompanied Sir G. Paul, M. R. Snow, & Mr. D. Paul to Mr. Townly's in Westminster.*

1842: 18 Oct.

1844: 14 Oct: *The lender is Sir John Deane Paul, Banker, Strand, a Magistrate of the County, a very wealthy person, who has recently succeeded to a large property.*

1846: 11 Aug: *I may enumerate as County gentlemen, Sir M. H. Beach, Mr. Crawley Boevy, Sir J. D. Paul, Messrs. Hopkinson, Purnell, Curtis Hayward, Baker, Machin, Bernard, Goodrich, Stanton, Vizards, Colchester.*

PAUL — Robert Snow Paul — *see also* Anne Snow [49]

Robert Snow Paul (1768-1849), banker, was born at Minchinhampton, Gloucestershire, son of George Snow (1745-1822) and Elizabeth (d. 1772), daughter of Sir Onesiphorus Paul, 1st baronet, and sister to Sir George Onesiphorus Paul, 2nd baronet (*above*). He was the grandson of Robert Snow (1720-1772) and Valentina Paul, who had married in 1742.

Robert Snow married, at Langton, Long Blandford, Dorset, 23 September 1795, Charlotte Ellis (d. 1838). There were no children of the marriage. Robert inherited the Rodborough and Woodchester estate following the death of his cousin and uncle, Sir George Onesiphorus Paul. He changed his name to Paul by royal licence.

1826: 15 Sep: *And this seems the proper place for inserting a list of some of the leading families & individuals, whose presence on this occasion served so many good purposes; benefiting the charity ... Mr. Paul & family...*

1829: 1 Apr.

1838: 16 Oct.

PAXTON — Thomas Paxton [50]

Thomas Paxton (±1804-1896), land agent and farmer, was born at Woburn, Bedfordshire, son of William Paxton (1783-1859) and Mary Anne Pitkin (1781-1864). Paxton was land agent for Mary Ann Dolphin at Eyford. By 1871 he was living at Langford, Bicester, where he was listed as a widower. He married, 1873, Mary (b.

±1830), his second wife. By 1881 he was farming 369 acres and employing eight men and three boys. He died at Langford at the age of 91.

1846: 25 Sep: *We found with Mrs. D. A Mrs. Mills, daughter of the Agent, Mr. Paxton, who was also at Eyford.*

1850: 15 Jan: *Walked to Eyford, to call on Mrs. Dolphin; but, finding that Mrs. Kirby and her daughter were there, and also the steward, Mr. Paxton, with a gentleman on business.*

1852: 11 May: *Poor Mrs. D. Miss Lydia Smith sat at the head of her table, the other guests, besides the Vavasours and myself, were James Wynniatt, Miss Kirby, and Mr. Paxton, Mrs. Dolphin's Steward.* 10 Dec., 22 Dec., 31 Dec.

1853: 2 Mar.

1854: 9 Jul., 23 Jul.

PAYNE — Mary Payne — *see also* **Dolphin, Harrison, Hutchinson, Kirby, Knight, Polhill, Staveley,** ***and*** **Walmesley** [51]

Mary Payne, née Tanfield (1763-1846), was the third daughter of John Tanfield (b. ±1719), of Carthorpe, Yorkshire, and Catherine (b. 1722), daughter and co-heir of William Beckwith of Lamb Hill. Her paternal grandparents were Kerby [or Kirby] John Tanfield (b. 1691) and Susanna Staveley (b. 1699). Mary had four known sisters: Katherine (b. 1757), Martha (b. 1762), Dorothy (1767-1840), and Ann (1769-1847). Dorothy married, 22 June 1793, as his second wife, Revd Basil Bury Beridge (1737-1808). Ann is known to have died unmarried.

Mary married, first, at Burneston, Yorkshire, 17 November 1785, Michael Hutchinson (1738-1785), doctor of physic; they had 2 sons:

1. Thomas Kitchingman (1786-1860); later changed his surname from Hutchinson to Staveley
2. George (1797-1852)

Michael died young and Mary married, secondly, Thomas Payne (±1745-1815) of Edstaston Hall, Shropshire, and Brook Street, Grosvenor Square, London; they had 1 daughter:

1. Mary Anne (1803-1857); married, 1822, Vernon Dolphin (1800-1890)

1826: 17 Apr.

1828: 5 Nov: *We dined at Eyford. The Dolphins have a large party in their house; Mrs. & Miss Knights, Mrs. Payne.*

1829: 10 Jun: *We had a party of friends & neighbours to dinner. From Eyford Mrs. Payne & Mr. Polhill.*

1835: 26 Apr: *Miss Spurrier called before morning service, and informed us that Mrs. Dolphin had been hurried away this morning to Cheltenham on intelligence received yesterday of the alarming state of the health of her mother, Mrs. Payne.* 28 Apr: *Mrs. Payne is declared out of danger.* 23 May.

1836: 10 Dec: *Mrs. Witts accompanied me in the phaeton to Stow, and returned, driven by the servant, to Slaughter, whence Mrs. Backhouse accompanied her to call on Mrs. Dolphin at Eyford, where Mrs. Payn, her mother, is now staying.*

1837: 9 Mar: *Admitted, saw her and Mrs. Payn; walked to the Great Pool, Conservatory, Hothouse &c.* 28 Apr: *I called at Eyford on Mrs. Payn now staying with her daughter.* 4 Jul., 11 Jul., 26 Nov.

1838: 15 Jan: *Accompanied Mrs. D. home, and called on Mrs. Payne, who is somewhat of an invalid.* 13 Apr., 4 May, 13 May, 22 Jul., 21 Oct., 9 Dec: *Mrs. Dolphin. Pain, and Mrs. Harrison called here between the services.*

1839: 27 Jan., 23 Feb: *With M.W. walked to Eyford, & called on Mrs. Dolphin; saw Mrs. Pain, and Mrs. Harrison.* 26 Feb., 10 Jul: *Walked with MW to Eyford to call on the ladies there; received by the four widows or widows bewitched, Mrs. Ware, Mrs. Payn, Mrs. Harrison, and Mrs. Dolphin.* 28 Jul., 19 Aug., 23 Aug., 25 Aug.

1840: 3 May, 16 May, 24 May, 31 May, 13 Jun., 6 Jul., 25 Jul., 5 Aug., 6 Aug: *On my way homeward, deviated to Eyford, at the request of Mrs. Payne, from whom I had received a message while I was at Stow, to confer with her and Mrs. Dolphin on the contents of the reply written by Mr. Burrup to my letter written last night, and dispatched to Gloucester this morning.* 12 Aug: *Mrs. Payne called to advise with me under the painful circumstances which at present exist at Eyford. Mrs. Dolphin gone to Gloucester to consult Burrup, the Under Sheriff, as to the execution now on the premises. Mrs. Payne was on her road to Bourton to the Attorneys there.* 23 Aug: *Mrs. Payne and Mrs. Dolphin called after the evening service. They are still harrassed with bailiffs in the house, and intricate pecuniary difficulties environ them.* 18 Sep: *Mrs. Payn and Mrs. Harrison are gone to Weymouth.* 14 Nov.

1842: 4 Apr., 26 Jun: *Mrs. Pain called before morning service.* 5 Jul., 12 Jul., 29 Jul., 6 Sep., 4 Oct., 9 Oct., 12 Oct., 26 Oct., 20 Dec., 23 Dec: *Drove MW. To Eyford to call on Mrs. Dolphin, whom we saw: Mrs. Payn indisposed.* 31 Dec: *Called at Eyford on Mrs. Dolphin and Mrs. Payne; the latter recovering from a bad cough.*

1843: 16 Jan., 23 Jan., 29 Sep., 13 Oct: *Mrs. Payn has been seriously ill, but is now better.* 3 Nov: *Called with MW. at Eyford House: saw Mrs. Dolphin and Mrs. Payn; the latter much indisposed.* 11 Nov: *Called, as we returned at Eyford House, where saw Mrs. Payn, in better health.* 9 Dec.

1844: 8-9 Jan., 12 Jan., 15 Jan., 1 Feb: *Mrs. Payn has rejoined her daughter from Cheltenham.* 3 Feb: *Mrs. Dolphin still a great invalid, but not confined to her room, Mrs. Payn returned from Cheltenham in consequence of her daughter's indisposition.* 10 Feb., 16 Feb. *Mrs. Payn engaged with Mr. Kendal.* 28 Feb., 19 Mar., 27 Mar., 26 Apr., 30 Apr., 7 May: *With MW. called on Mrs. Payn at Eyford, whom we found at home, with her visitors, Mrs. and Miss Algar: the former is Mrs. P's niece, and widow of a Clergyman, who was incumbent of a church at Frome.* 11 May: *As I returned met and parlyed with Mrs. Payn, and her lady guests, who had been visiting MW.* 24 Jul: *I called at Eyford on Mrs. Dolphin and Mrs. Payne: the latter seems in a precarious state of health.* 29 Jul., 6 Aug., 9 Aug., 13 Sep., 27 Sep: *With MW. walked to Eyford; visited at the Mansion house: Mr. Hutchinson and Mr. Chamberlayne, now with his lady staying there, were out: we were received by Mrs. Dolphin Mrs. Payn, Mrs. Hutchinson, and Mrs. Chamberlayne; — the usual amount of anxiety arising out of embarrassed affairs to be detailed and descanted upon.* 22 Oct: *Walked with MW. and the Daniells to call on Mrs. Dolphin &c. at Eyford; saw Mrs. Dolphin. Pynsent, and Mrs. Payn, who is again much indisposed.* 4 Nov: *I called at Eyford; saw Mrs. Dolphin, and Mr. and Mrs. Pynsent: Mrs. Payn confined to her room, greatly indisposed, with one of her usual serious attacks on the chest, besides other complaints; attended by Mr. Hayward; but considered to be better than yesterday.* 8 Nov: *Mr. Bowen called from Eyford, and announced that Mrs. Payn was in a very alarming state, suffering from a violent attack on the chest, which impeded her breathing, and might end in suffocation.* 9 Nov: *Visited Mrs. Payn, in whose state a very favourable change has taken place, and to whom I administered the Lord's supper, with Mrs. Dolphin. Pynsent, and two female attendants.* 12 Nov: *Mrs. Payn still a great invalid and apprehensions entertained as to the issue; being then asleep I was not admitted to her chamber.* 15 Nov: *Walked to Eyford; called on Mrs. Payn, whom I found in her bed-room, sitting up, and slowly recovering from her late indisposition; saw also Mrs. Pynsent; Mrs. Dolphin was from home walking with Mr. Stavely, her brother who came from Yorkshire on Tuesday last, to visit his Mother, in consequence of the bad account he had recd. of her health: he leaves Eyford for the North to-morrow, or the next day.* 22 Nov., 10 Dec., 20 Dec.

1845: 20 Jan., 18 Feb., 8 Mar., 24 Mar: *Mrs. Payn also confined to her room, having experienced an attack of her usual complaint.* 30 Mar: *Mrs. Payn is very ill with an attack of an inflammatory kind, such as she commonly experiences.* 31 Mar: *Administered the sacrament privately at Eyford to Mrs. Payn, Mrs. Dolphin, and Miss C. Knight.* 9 Apr: *Called on the ladies there: Mrs. Payn seriously ill.* 12 Apr: *Mrs. Payn too languid and ill to admit me to pray by her.* 18 Apr: *Walked to Eyford: read prayers with Mrs. Payne, who is very languid & ill.* 25 Apr., 10 May, 13 May, 23 May, 30 May, 4 Jun., 24 Jun.

1847: 11 Jan: *I doubt whether her malady is so serious as she apprehends; loneliness, having just now no visitor, recurrence to the loss of her mother at this season last year, vexations and embarrassments, unwise resort to sedatives.*

1852: *Mr. Price, Solicitor, Burford, called upon me for the copy of the Registry of the death of the late Mrs. Payne, Mrs. Dolphin's Mother, which he supposed had taken place at Eyford, and that she had been buried here. It is wanted with reference to proceedings pendant in the Court of Chancery respecting a mortgage to Mr. Geo. Bennett of Westcote, in connection with the Clapton property—More trouble for Mrs. D.—Explained to him that Mrs. P. had died at Cheltenham, but forgot at the time to name that she had been buried at Edstaston, Salop.*

PAYNTER — Paynter of Bourton-on-the-Water

1842: 21 Jan: *Walked to Bourton on the Water and back. To the Office of Messrs. Wilkins and Kendall, where executed, as Trustee, a deed of conveyance of two cottages at Bourton to my son from one Paynter, bringing back the same and a deed corroborative of the title, &c.*

PAYNTER — Elizabeth Paynter — *see* Pugh

PEACH — Henry Peach [52]

Henry Peach (1765-1786), scholar, was the son of Henry Peach, of Twickenham, and nephew of Apphia, Lady Lyttelton's first husband, Col Joseph Peach. Apphia adopted the boy and apparently doted on him. He was educated at Kington, Herefordshire, and matriculated at Pembroke College, Oxford, in 1783. He died on 27 April 1786. He was buried at Cardington, Shropshire, a living held by John Witts, Apphia's younger brother. Apphia, Lady Lyttelton was eccentric, and on some unfathomable whim, she had his remains disinterred and brought to Malvern.

1840: 13 Apr: *The Memorandum accompanying the will provides that she shall be interned in a vault which she caused to be made very many years ago in Jesus Chapel, in Great Malvern Church, and whither she caused to be removed the remains of her adopted son, Henry Peach, Nephew of her first husband, Col Peach, a youth to whom she had greatly attached herself, and who, dying young, had been buried at Cardington in Shropshire, the parish of which my Uncle John was the incumbent.*

PEARCE — George Pearce [53]

George Pearce (1800-1857), clerk to the guardians, superintendent registrar, and master of the workhouse, was born at Aston Somerville. George married Sarah Anne (1811-1844), and together they had at least 3 daughters:

1 Caroline (b. ±1835)
2 Emma (1838-1906)
3 Amelia (1841-1842)

Following Sarah's death, George's maiden sister Mary (b. ±1816) became matron of the workhouse, and his niece, Anne Pearce (b. ±1822), born at Poplar, Middlesex, became schoolmistress there.

Francis Witts regularly spent hours with Pearce drawing up the minutes of workhouse board of guardians; it appears from the diary entries that he very much dictated what Pearce wrote. The meeting of 22 April 1837 is a typical entry: 'Mr. Pearce came, with whom I prepared the minutes of the meeting of the Guardians on Thursday, and talked over various points of Poor Law management'. Occasionally a whole morning would be set aside to getting these minutes in good order.

1836: 16 Jul: *After breakfast engaged with Pearce, in examining the draft minutes of the Transactions of the B. of Guardians on Thursday last, making an abstract of them.* 25 Jul., 39 Jul., 2 Aug., 6 Aug., 15-17 Sep., 23 Sep., 26-27 Sep., 30 Sep., 8 Oct., 12 Oct., 14-15 Oct., 22 Oct., 29 Oct., 4 Nov., 7 Nov., 12 Nov., 19 Nov., 22 Nov., 26 Nov., 5 Dec., 10 Dec., 23 Dec., 30 Dec.

1837: 4 Jan., 9 Jan., 13 Jan., 16 Nov., 19-20 Jan., 27 Jan., 6 Feb., 10 Feb., 14 Feb., 17 Feb., 24 Feb., 3 Mar., 10 Mar., 18 Mar., 25 Mar., 31 Mar., 8 Apr., 14 Apr., 22 Apr., 29 Apr., 5 May, 19 May, 27 May, 3 Jun., 9 Jun., 13-14 Jun., 16 Jun., 23-24 Jun., 30 Jun., 4 Jul., 8 Jul., 12 Jul., 15 Jul., 19 Jul., 21 Jul., 26 Jul., 28 Jul., 7 Aug., 9 Aug., 11 Aug., 16 Aug., 19 Aug., 26 Aug., 29 Aug., 1 Sep., 7 Sep: *Conferred with Mr. and Mrs. Pearce on many points relating to the domestic economy of the Establishment, with the Clerk of the Works, and Contractors, as to points relating to the finishing of different parts of the building, and with several of the paupers of whom there are between 25 and 30 in all.* 9 Sep., 15 Sep., 22 Sep: *I returned to the Workhouse, where I transacted business with Mr. Pearce in his double capacity of Clerk and Governor, with his wife as Matron, and with other persons who sought me out to advise with me respecting points connected with the administration of the Poor Law.* 2 Oct., 7 Oct., 13 Oct., 23-24 Oct., 3 Nov., 11 Nov., 17 Nov., 24-25 Nov., 27 Nov., 29 Nov., 5 Dec., 7-8 Dec., 16 Dec., 22-23 Dec., 30 Dec.

1838: 10 Jan., 12 Jan., 20 Jan., 24 Jan: *Mr. Pearce called to consult me on the course requisite to be taken in consequence of a letter having been found on the Workhouse premises (anonymous) imputing to the porter an improper intimacy with a female pauper.* 27 Jan., 29 Jan., 2 Feb., 5 Feb: *Visited the Workhouse with the Med. Off. Hayward and Rd. Minchin, one of the Stow Guardians: found Pearce absent, gone to Evesham to visit a sick brother: Mrs. Pearce much indisposed: the house in confusion, owing to the insanity of a female pauper now removed to the custody of her relatives; and the dangerous illness of another female pauper, who from a state of gonorrhoea has passed into that of Typhus fever, which creates much anxiety on the part of the Med. Off.—Matron &c. the more so as there is a case of recent confinement, the pauper confined being of a delicate constitution.* 13-14 Feb., 21-22 Feb., 27 Feb., 3 Mar., 6 Mar., 9 Mar., 17 Mar., 6 Apr., 14 Apr., 17 Apr., 21 Apr., 25 Apr: *Pearce's surviving child is recovering from its dangerous illness.* 27 Apr., 30 Apr., 8 May, 12 May, 15 May, 19 May, 24-25 May, 4 Jun., 6 Jun., 12 Jun., 27 Jun., 30 Jun., 10 Jul., 25 Jul., 10 Aug: *Mr. Pearce called to report to me the escape from the Workhouse of a pauper, A. Waring, who has repeatedly evaded the observation of the officers, and got off.* 11 Aug., 15 Aug.,

18 Aug: *In the Evening, Mr. Pearce called to inform me that Jane Waring had found her way back to Stow, after wandering over the Country by Cheltenham, Gloucester, N. Leach &c. and was lodged in the W. House.* 20-21 Aug., 31 Aug., 3 Sep., 21 Sep., 1 Oct., 3 Oct., 6 Oct., 12-13 Oct., 23 Oct., 31 Oct., 3 Nov., 7 Nov., 9 Nov., 17 Nov., 22-23 Nov., 30 Nov., 15 Dec., 17 Dec., 22 Dec., 29 Dec.

1839: 10 Jan., 14 Jan., 25 Jan., 28 Jan., 2 Feb., 12 Feb., 15 Feb., 25 Feb., 12 Mar., 18-19 Mar., 26 Mar., 3 Apr., 12 Apr., 14 Apr., 22 Apr., 29 Apr., 3 May, 11 May, 13 May, 21 May, 25 May, 31 May, 7 Jun., 15 Jun., 8 Jul., 15 Jul., 18 Jul., 20 Jul., 24 Jul., 5 Aug., 9 Aug., 18 Aug., 21 Aug., 24 Aug.

1840: 20-21 Mar., 25 Mar., 28 Mar., 6 Apr., 8 Apr., 11 Apr., 18 Apr., 21 Apr., 2 May, 12 May, 16 May, 25 May, 3 Jun., 8 Jun., 10-11 Jun., 15 Jun., 17 Jun., 22 Jun., 27 Jun., 7 Jul., 10 Jul., 21 Jul., 27 Jul., 6 Aug., 20 Aug., 25 Aug., 31 Aug., 3 Sep., 12 Sep., 17 Sep., 21 Sep., 23 Sep., 29 Sep., 1 Oct., 3 Oct., 6 Oct., 10 Oct., 12 Oct., 15 Oct., 29 Oct., 9 Nov: *Visited the workhouse; inspected the wards: the Governor and Matron were absent for the day on private business.* 12 Nov: *Visited the Workhouse: conferred with Mr. Pearce on many points of management, visited the men's ward, looked over the correspondence of the week.* 24 Nov: *I visited the Workhouse and conferred with Mr. and Mrs. Pearce on various matters relating to the Management of the Union and Poorhouse.* 26 Nov: *I went to the Workhouse; no meeting of the Guardians to-day; but I consulted with Mr. Pearce on various points of Union and Workhouse management.* 1 Dec: *Finishing a document respecting Union Management, which I had been preparing, and forwarded it to Mr. Pearce with a note by the Post.*

1841: 27 Feb., 4 Mar.

1842: 24 Jan., 27 Jan: *To the Workhouse; conferred on Union business with Mr. Pearce, and the Matron, visited the paupers in their different wards and apartments, present, when dinner was served out to the paupers—114—now in the house.* 10 Feb., 18 Feb., 1 Mar., 9-10 Mar., 24 Mar., 28 Mar., 1 Apr., 7 Apr., 10 Apr., 16 Apr., 18 Apr: *at the Library, at the office of the Gloucestershire Banking Company, at some shops, and at the Workhouse where I conferred with Mr. & Mrs. Pearce on matters of Union management, and chiefly on the threatened proposition for a reduction of the stipend of Governor and Matron.* 20-21 Apr., 27 Apr: *To the Workhouse, where only remained a short time, as I learnt that Mr. and Mrs. Pearce had last evening lost their youngest child rather suddenly: it was, therefore, out of the question to discuss with him matters of business.* 2 May: *Mr. Pearce came, with whom engaged for two hours in considering and arranging the proper course to be taken as to his situation, and the change in it to be canvassed at the meeting of the Guardians on Thursday next.* 3 May: *A letter from Pearce on the charge made against the Matron by the Porter of the Workhouse, which had been named to him by Mr. Shelton.* 5 May, 9 May: *A long sitting with Mr. Pearce who came by appointment—drawing up minutes, and wording resolutions, expressive of the investigations made by the Guardians on Thursday last, and their results.* 19 May: *Mr. Pearce submitted to the Guardians other documents justificatory of himself and Matron, disproving the charge of wastefulness alleged against them by the late porters.* 31 May, 2 Jun: *Presided at the fortnightly meeting of the Guardians of our Union; a full board, at which the Shoemaker was reproved for misconduct, and given to understand that any future misbehaviour would be immediately visited with dismissal: the question of baking bread in the workhouse was resumed; and Mr. Pearce produced documents and calculations which satisfied the Guardians that the plan could not be adopted in this Union without entailing a heavy expence: in fact, the competition for baking by contract is so lively, and the bakers employed are content with so small a profit, that the Guardians would lose by entering into competition with them.* 7 Jun., 20-21 Jun., 4 Jul., 7 Jul., 12 Jul., 21 Jul., 25-27 Jul., 9 Aug., 13 Aug., 15-16 Aug., 18 Aug., 23 Aug., 29 Aug., 31 Aug., 1 Sep., 8 Sep., 13 Sep., 15 Sep., 22 Sep., 5-6 Oct., 11 Oct., 31 Oct., 1 Nov., 3 Nov., 5 Nov., 24 Dec., 27 Dec., 29 Dec.

1843: 7 Jan., 30 Jan: *Conferred on Poor Law matters with Mrs. Pearce, her husband being from home.* 9 Feb., 15 Feb., 29-30 Aug., 19 Sep., 21 Sep., 23 Sep., 24 Oct., 2 Nov., 13 Nov., 16 Nov., 5 Dec., 14-15 Dec., 22 Dec., 28 Dec.

1844: 13 Jan., 25 Jan., 12-13 Feb., 17 Feb., 19 Feb., 27 Feb., 4 Mar., 16-17 Mar., 20 Mar., 23 Mar., 6 Apr., 6 May, 16 May, 23 Jul., 25 Jul., 7-8 Aug., 12 Aug., 14 Aug., 20 Aug., 22 Aug., 5 Sep., 19 Sep: *To the Workhouse, where I found cause for uneasiness, Mr. and Mrs. Pearce being both seriously indisposed, the former with acute rheumatism, the latter with Jaundice; Mr. P, confined to his bed, his wife, better than a few days since, attending to the duties of the establishment, but very unequal to the task.* 20 Sep., 21 Sep: *A very indifferent account of Mr. Pearce's health was given to me by Mrs. Pearce; the former still confined to his bed, but not considered worse: the latter hardly equal to the duties to be performed, but still going about them.* 24 Sep: *I visited the Workhouse; superintended, and gave directions there; Mr. and Mrs. Pearce continue very ill, both confined to their bed chamber.* 26 Sep: *To the Workhouse—Mr. and Mrs. Pearce still quite incapable of discharging their duties, as Clerk, Governor and Matron, confined to their bed-chamber, and attended by their medical friend.* 28 Sep., 30 Sep: *Mr. Pearce still helpless in body from rheumatic fever, confined to his bed: his wife considered by Mr. Hayward to be in danger, suffering greatly from disease of the liver, bed-ridden; and the visit to the two sufferers very distressing.* 1 Oct., 3 Oct., 5 Oct., 7 Oct: *To the Workhouse, where found Mr. Pearce still a great invalid, and his wife in an alarming state, wandering in mind, and confined to her bed.* 9 Oct., 11 Oct: *Repaired to the Workhouse, where I transacted business, but did not see Mr. Pearce; his poor wife died last night.* 21 Oct: *to the Workhouse; conferred with Mr. Pearce, whom I found in better health and spirits than I had expected, considering his severe attack of disease, now gradually leaving him, and the loss of his wife.* 22-23 Oct., 24 Oct: *Conferred with Mr. Pearce at the latter place on Union business: he is slowly recovering, but more alive to the loneliness and gloom consequent on his poor wife's decease.* 25 Oct: *Fourteen or fifteen guardians present, who unanimously approved of the arrangement which I had proposed as to the vacancy of Matron, concurring with me in opinion that the appointment of Mr. Pearce's sister would be most advantageous to the Union, as well as most satisfactory to his feelings, whose long judicious, and diligent services merited our esteem, and dictated to us that his comfort should be consulted.* 26 Oct., 28-29 Oct., 31 Oct., 7 Nov: *Mr. Pearce's sister was unanimously approved as Matron, to be formally appointed on the 21st. Inst. and to enter on her office on that day.* 8 Nov., 14-15 Nov., 20-21 Nov., 25 Nov: *I went to the Workhouse, where I was engaged with Mr. Pearce in auditing bills, settling minutes &c.—MW. joined me there, went over some of the wards with Mr. P. and the Matron.* 28 Nov., 3 Dec., 12 Dec., 21 Dec., 26-27 Dec.

1845: 4 Jan., 7 Jan., 9 Jan., 19-21 Jan., 3 Feb., 6 Feb., 8 Feb., 12 Feb., 20 Feb., 1 Mar., 10 Mar., 13 Mar., 15 Mar., 27 Mar: *To the Workhouse — found Mr. Pearce very much indisposed, and hardly equal to the discharge of his duty; the Rel. officer also is ill, and could not attend.* 5 Apr., 8 Apr., 11 Apr., 1 May, 3 May, 5 May, 15 May, 21 May, 29 May, 10 Jun., 12 Jun., 13 Jun: *Wrote to Pearce a letter which I desired him to lay before the Guardians at their next meeting, pointing out various matters in respect of the management and arrangements of the Workhouse in which alterations ought to be made, with a view to more scrupulous order, discipline and cleanliness—most of the changes being suggested by what I had observed at the Chipping Norton Workhouse.* 14 Jun., 18 Jun: *From Mr. Pearce in answer to my letter finding fault with the management of the Workhouse at Stow, admitting the accuracy of many of my observations, and fairly enough exculpating himself on some points, in which from the construction of the building, and the economizing spirit of the guardians, he cannot compete with the Master of the Chipping Norton Workhouse.* 19-20 Jun., 22-24 Jun., 26-29 Jun., 1 Jul., 3 Jul., 5-7 Jul.

1846: 20 May, 30 May, 6 Jun., 9 Jun., 22 Jun., 25-27 Jun., 9-10 Jul., 13 Jul., 17 Jul., 23 Jul., 28 Jul., 4 Aug., 22 Aug., 26 Aug., 28 Aug., 3 Sep., 7 Sep., 9 Sep., 17 Sep., 25 Sep., 29 Sep., 14 Oct., 29 Oct., 1 Nov., 12 Nov., 13 Nov: *Took down in writing the complaint of John Wilkins, the pauper who is endeavouring to ruin Mr. and Miss. Pearce by charging them with malversation and irregularities in the management of the establishment.* 14 Nov: *Recd. a packet from Mr. Pearce: with his answers to the charges made yesterday by John Wilkins, a note from himself on that subject.* 16 Nov., 19 Nov: *Entered on & went through with the charges preferred against the Governor and Matron by the pauper John Wilkins, with the defence and answers of Mr. Pearce, a statement prepared by me.* 20 Nov., 26 Nov., 4 Dec., 8 Dec., 10-12 Dec., 18 Dec., 21 Dec.

1847: 9 Jan., 12 Jan., 18 Jan., 27 Jan., 3 Feb., 8 Feb., 12 Feb., 17 Feb., 20 Feb., 24 Feb., 1 Mar., 3 Mar., 8 Mar., 26 Mar., 13 Apr., 15 Apr., 27-30 Apr., 12 May, 19 May, 22 May: *Mr. Pearce called, with further documents to exculpate himself from the blame cast on him by Mr. Hunt, the Auditor, and with a letter, a circular, received from the P.L.C. referring to the scarcity of wheat and other grain, and suggesting for the consideration of the Guardians some arrangement whereby relief may be given with bread of a wholesome, but inferior sort.* 27-28 May, 2 Jun: *Wrote to Mr. Pearce, informing him that I had received a letter from Mr. Hunt, the Auditor, and what was its tenor.* 3 Jun., 5 Jun., 24 Jun., 26 Jun., 7 Jul., 13 Jul., 15 Jul: *A schoolmistress was elected—Ann Pearce, niece of the Clerk and Governor, by a majority of three or four voices above her competitor Sarah Walker, a young person from Banbury.* 19 Jul., 30 Jul., 5 Aug., 8 Aug., 17 Aug., 19 Aug., 16 Sep., 28 Sep., 11 Oct., 14 Oct., 25 Oct., 8 Nov., 12-15 Nov., 18 Nov., 25 Nov., 29-30 Nov., 1 Dec., 8-10 Dec., 13 Dec., 16 Dec., 20 Dec., 23 Dec., 29 Dec., 31 Dec.

1848: 20 Jan., 24 Jan., 3 Feb., 7 Feb., 17 Feb., 22 Feb., 2 Mar., 6 Mar., 16 Mar: *Mr. Pearce being gone to meet Mr. Hunt, the District Auditor, at Chipping Norton.* 25 Mar., 20 Apr., 27 Apr., 16 May, 18 May, 22 May, 25 May, 29 May, 3 Jun., 6 Jun., 8 Jun., 22 Jun., 1 Jul., 7 Jul., 9 Jul., 17 Jul., 16-17 Aug., 22-23 Aug., 31 Aug., 6 Sep., 14 Sep., 12 Oct., 15 Oct., 24 Oct., 26 Oct., 8-9 Nov.

1850: 11 Jan., 18 Jan., 7 Mar., 10 Apr., 27 Apr: *From Mr. Pearce, written in his capacity of Clerk to the Stow on the Wold Union, with a copy of a very proper and kind resolution expressive of sympathy and condolence at my great affliction, passed by the Guardians.* 29 Apr., 15 May, 17 May, 27-28 May, 2 Jun., 6-7 Jun., 11 Jun., 17 Jun., 20 Jun., 26 Jun., 6 Jul., 18 Jul., 25-26 Jul., 6 Aug., 17 Aug., 21-22 Aug., 5 Sep., 10 Sep., 25 Oct., 21 Nov., 23 Nov., 5-7 Dec., 9 Dec.

1851: 22 Jan., 27 Jan., 8 Feb., 10 Feb., 10 Feb., 14 Feb., 19 Feb., 27 Feb., 8 Mar., 11 Mar., 13 Mar., 15 Mar., 19 Mar., 21 Mar., 27 Mar., 8 Apr., 22 Apr., 13-14 May, 17 May.

1852: 22 Jan., 28 Jan., 10 Feb., 12 Feb., 23 Feb., 2 Mar., 8 Mar., 10 Mar., 22 Mar., 25 Mar., 3 Apr., 8 Apr., 21-22 Apr., 26 Apr., 30 Apr., 6 May, 12 May, 20 May, 25 May, 3 Jun., 5 Jun., 25 Oct., 4 Nov., 18 Nov., 23 Nov., 27 Nov., 29 Nov., 2 Dec: *To the Workhouse to attend a Committee of Guardians appointed to investigate the charges preferred by Mr. Hunt the Auditor, against Mr. Pearce, in his capacity of Master of the Workhouse, the complaints having been laid before the P.L.C. and by them remitted to Mr. P. for his answer thereon.* 3 Dec: *Received a letter from Mr. Pearce, as to the charges preferred against him by Mr. Auditor Hunt.* 6 Dec: *Called at the Workhouse, found Mr. Pearce much indisposed, and greatly worried by a letter from the Poor Law Board pointing out to him errors alleged against him by Auditor Hunt as committed in the making up of the ledger in his capacity of Clerk of the Union —The complaint is as to form, and not as to substance—misapprehension as to the manner of entry, not false entries. Truly, this Auditor is a vindictive persecutor, and may hunt down his prey by persevering in frivolous charges.* 9 Dec: *To the Workhouse, where presided for between two and three hours at the fortnightly meeting of the Guardians. The report of the Committee held on Thursday last as to the alleged charges against Mr. Pearce was adopted by the board, and ordered to be forwarded to the P.L.C.* 11 Dec., 14 Dec., 16 Dec., 22 Dec., 27 Dec., 30 Dec.

1853: 13 Jan., 21 Jan., 28 Jan., 10 Feb., 24 Feb., 10 Mar., 19-21 Mar., 24 Mar., 26 Mar., 28 Mar., 1 Apr., 7 Apr., 11 Apr., 20 Apr., 26 Apr., 29 Apr., 4-5 May, 16 May, 19 May, 30 May, 2 Jun., 10 Jun., 21 Jun., 25 Jun.

1854: 17 Jan., 2 Feb., 8 Feb., 2 Mar., 9 Mar., 11 Mar: *He had been at Worcester to-day to consult physicians, Sir C. Hastings & Dr. Maldon, as to the cases of two patients—William Harris, & George Pearce who had accompanied him. Sir CH. does not detect much disease in Harris beyond a torpid state of the heart, and a general inertness—likely to end unfavourably. Dr. M has a bad opinion of Pearce's condition; believes the heart to be affected, and that spasmodic attacks may be fatal.* 13 Mar: *Mr. Pearce came, looking very ill, and suffering much from difficulty in breathing and other complaints akin to those by which I am afflicted.* 16-17 Mar., 30 Mar: *Mr. Pearce prevented by illness from attendance; I visited him in his apartment. His state very precarious; Hayward now pronounces his complaint to be Angina Pectoris.* 6 Apr., 7 Apr: *Entered into some discussion with W. as to the declining state of Pearce's health the probabilities of his death, the arrangements consequent on such an event &c.* 13 Apr: *Mr. Pearce attended as Clerk, but looked miserably ill, and Hayward tells me there is no improvement in his condition.* 15 Apr., 20 Apr: *To the Workhouse, where conferred with Pearce and his family on Union matters. He appears in a very precarious state.* 27 Apr: *Mr. Pearce was too ill to attend the Board, which is very inconvenient.* 29 Apr., 3 May: *Heard that Pearce had gone to London for medical advice, & was detained there for a few days.* 8 May, 9 May: *There saw Pearce, who returned from Town yesterday. Dr. Williams, a physician eminent for chest complaints, pronounces that he has an enlargement of the heart, with other unfavourable symptoms; but that the disease may be mitigated by due care & medicine and the fatal issue deferred. He bore his journey well, and is certainly improved in health of late.* 13 May, 20 May, 24-25 May, 27 May, 3 Jun: *From Miss A Pearce, niece to G. Pearce and School mistress at the Workhouse, naming that it is in the contemplation of certain Guardians, at the next board-day, to raise the question as to Pearce's ability, in his present bad state of health, to discharge the duties of either or both his offices of Clerk of the Union, and Governor of the Workhouse, with a view to his being induced to resign. Replied to this letter, that the question of resignation is one for the consideration of Mr. P. and his family: that admitting that the duties of governor may be tolerably performed by him with the assistance of his sister, the Matron, and the other members of his family, the duties of Clerk require constant attendance at Board Meetings, with cognizance of all proceedings, so as to advise, and check where error creeps in: are, therefore, of a personal nature, capable only of being eased by the aid of a person acting solely as amanuensis. Thus I allowed it to be seen that my impression is that the Clerkship should be resigned, and the office of Governor may be kept.* 5 Jun: *Had an interview with Pearce in his apartment; little, if any improvement in his condition: did not broach the matter as to resignation, but allowed him to observe that I considered his malady very serious, the main evil being only capable of mitigation, not of care.* 15 Jun: *He reported to me that Pearce has been very ill, but, with his family, struggles against a removal from either of his offices, and purposes to go to London to obtain further advice and opinion from Dr. Williams.* 20 Jun: *A note from Mr. Pearce to me, accompanying a copy of a letter written by him to Messrs. Comely and West, and to be brought before the Guardians on Thursday, in which he endeavours to shew that no parts of his duties as Clerk & Master of the Workhouse have been neglected in consequence of his illness, and that the proposition made to him to resign the office of Clerk is harsh and unreasonable, and must originate from bad feeling.* 22 Jun: *The main business was the receiving a report from Mr. Comely and Mr. West of the interview between them, and Mr. Pearce, who professed to consider himself ill used by the suggestion that a resignation of the office of Clerk would be the proper course for him to adopt.* 23 Jun., 24 Jun: *From Pearce I received a letter, explaining that he did not mean in his letter addressed to Messrs. Comely and West, to impute to me or any other guardian severity, unkindness, or injustice, and had no notion that the suggestion made emanated from me.* 26 Jun., 5 Jul., 6 Jul: *Pearce appears to have in some degree rallied, but was much exhausted before the business closed.* 10 Jul., 19-20 Jul., 3 Aug: *There is no doubt that the new Clerk and Mr. Pearce, in his capacity of Master of the Workhouse, will work well together.* 10 Aug., 14 Aug., 17 Aug.

PEARCE — William Pearce [54]

William Pearce (1771-1825), Church of England clergyman, was the son of William Pearce of Boddington, Gloucestershire. He was educated at Worcester College, Oxford (BA 1792; MA 1795), and was ordained deacon on 25 July 1795 and priest on 24 August 1796. His first clerical appointment was as curate of Aston Cantlow, Warwickshire, from 24 August 1796. He was then perpetual curate of Cold Salperton from 19 August 1808 to 10 December 1813, and of Sevenhampton from the same date to his death in 1825. He was also vicar of Leigh from 28 December 1813 to his death. Pearce died at Staverton House, indicating a close relationship to William Prothero Pearce (*below*).

1823: 22 Jan: *Rode on the Tewkesbury road as far as the Village of Leigh. My acquaintance Mr. Pierce is Incumbent of this Church, which is situate half a mile from the road to the left, about five miles from Gloucester.* 23 Apr: *First meeting of the Stow Clerical Society for this year: Mr. Pierce Incumbent of the Leigh, & perpetual curate of Sevenhampton.*

PEARCE — William Prothero Pearce [55]

William Prothero Pearce (1789-1871), JP and landed proprietor, was born at Cheltenham, the son of Joseph Pearce (d. 1807) and Elizabeth Lewis (d. 1836). He lived at Staverton House, Staverton and Ffrwgrech, Brecknockshire, but was also occasionally resident in Cheltenham, where he had been born. Pearce married, first, at Usk, Monmouthshire, 12 May 1826, Rhoda Prothero (1790-1837); there do not appear to have been any children. He married secondly, at Brecknock, 23 October 1838, Mary Church Morrice (1801-1868), born at Cardiff; they had 1 son:

1 John Church (b. 1839)

In 1861 Pearce was living at Fauconberg House with his wife, Mary. He was, by this stage, a retired lieutenant-colonel and a major commander in the 2nd Battalion, Gloucestershire Rifle Volunteers. He was high sheriff for Brecknockshire in 1849.

1835: 6 Jan: *Several Gentlemen took the oaths as Magistrates, some who had never before qualified, although they had been long on the Commission, others who had been recently appointed under a cold seal. Among them were Capt. Frederick Berkeley, the Hon. Grantley Berkeley, Messrs. Probyn, Surman, Agg, Clutterbuck, W. Pitt and Lt. Col. Pearce.*

1838: 9 Apr: *Went to several shops at Cheltenham, whence I proceeded by a Coach, travelling with Lt. Col. Pearce, a Brother Mag.*

PEARD — Mr Peard of Cheltenham

1801: 29 Oct: *Met Mr. Peard at Harward's. Read in the Evening Bourgoing's Travels in Spain.*

PEARD — Emily Peard [56]

Emily Peard (1818-1862) was a servant at Upper Slaughter rectory. In the 1841 census she was registered as 25 years old, but ages were generally rounded for that census to a somewhat arbitrary nearest five years. At her death in Cheltenham, late February, or very early March 1862, she was stated to be 43, so her year of birth was probably 1818. Her place of birth is unknown, but it was not Gloucestershire.

1842: 13 Nov: *This was the condition of the sufferer, when we retired to our bed rooms at night, leaving her in charge of two confidential females, Emily Peard, my wife's maid, an attentive nurse, and M. Bateman an experienced person, the worthy Village Schoolmistress.* 14 Nov., 12 Dec: *Settled our accounts with the landlady of our lodgings, which we quitted for Prinknash Park about 2 P.M. leaving Peard with her friends at Cheltenham, and George Siers to visit some connections in the neighbourhood, both to return to U.S. Peard with us at the close of the week.* 17 Dec.

1850: 19 Aug: *Received a visit in the evening from Emily Peard, an old servant, now living at Cheltenham with her friends, and a great invalid: she is on a visit to her former fellow servant, Mrs. Yearp, wife of the shoemaker at L Slaughter.*

1852: 15 May: *A grateful note from Emily Peard, acknowledging a present I had sent her in consideration of her feeble state of health and consequent impoverishment. She was a faithful servant for many years, and very attentive to my poor wife and her mother.* 1 Jun: *Called at Mrs. T. Yearp's to speak with her as to Emily Peard.*

1853: *Walked to Lower Slaughter to make enquiries of Mrs. T. Yearp as to Emily Peard, stated to be in a very impaired health, and straitened circumstances, at Cheltenham left with Mrs. Y. a Sovereign to be remitted by her to E.P., as a distressed and deserving old Servant.* 27 Jan: *A letter from E. Peard, thanking me for the present of a sovereign, which I had sent to her, and intimating that I may soon hear from her again, when she has applied for relief to the Union of Cheltenham, that I may make some interest with a member of the Board to obtain for her out relief from that Union.*

1854: 3 Jul: *Received a note from E Peard complaining of illness and poverty.* 4 Jul: *Wrote to E. Peard, to whom I sent ten shillings, to help her to pay her rent.*

PEARSON — Thomas Aylmer Pearson[57]

Thomas Aylmer Pearson (±1811-1890), army officer, was the son of Lt-Gen. Sir Thomas Pearson (1781-1847) and Ann Eliza Coffin (1788-1859), a Canadian. His maternal grandfather was an army officer who found fame for his defence of Canada against the Americans in the War of 1812. Thomas Aylmer was born in New Brunswick.

On 19 July 1812, only a day after the United States had declared war on Britain, Lt-Col Pearson (as he was then), his wife, and infant son, Thomas, were on board the small British schooner, *Mary Ann*, bound for Quebec from Halifax with 350 barrels of tar. They were intercepted and captured by an American privateer, *Buckskin*. The American master, Israel Bray, put a prize crew on board and made for Salem, Massachusetts. The schooner was just a few miles from her destination when she was recaptured by His Majesty's frigate *Maidstone*, which escorted the *Mary Ann* back to Halifax.

Thomas Aylmer Pearson became an ensign in the 90th Foot, and was promoted to captain in the rifle brigade. He married, 1841, Frances Armstrong; they had at least 3 sons and 1 daughter:

1 Thomas Horner (1843-1937)
1 Frances Edith (1844-1916)
2 John Armstrong (1846-1942)
3 Aylmer Charles (1850-1938)

1845: 8 May: *The day closed by a dinner party; at which were present Mr. & Mrs. Pearson, the purchasers of, and resident at the Villa erected by Mr. Parsons at the foot of Upton Hill.*

1850: 7 Aug.

1851: 19 May: *At the Swindon and Paddington stations, met and chatted with many Gloucestershire people, and others my acquaintance, repairing to the Metropolis ... Capt. Pearson ....*

1853: 17 Mar.

PEART — John Peart and the Peart family of Giggleswick and Settle — *see also* Birkbeck[58]

John Peart (1764-1846), solicitor and banker, was born in the Settle/Giggleswick area. He was a founder in 1791 of the Craven Bank at Settle with partners William and John Birkbeck, young Quaker merchants, and William Alcock. Peart married, at Giggleswick, Yorkshire, 23 March 1785, Ellen Clapham; they had at least 1 son and 2 daughters, including:

1 Jane (1786-1843); married her cousin William Robinson
1 William (±1801-1827); *see below*

William Robinson succeeded his father-in-law as a partner in the Craven Bank in 1835. It was absorbed by the Bank of Liverpool in 1906, and eventually became part of Martins Bank 'the Grasshopper'. It is now part of Barclays Bank.

John Peart was probably the nephew (or otherwise close relation) of Eleanor, Mary, and at least one other unknown sister—all daughters of Joshua Peart. Mary Peart married, 6 February 1768, as his second wife, Lord George Manners-Sutton (1723-1783); they had at least 1 daughter. The Mrs Peart referred to on 26 October 1837 was in reality Miss Peart.

1823: 12 May: *Dined at Mr. Peart's, a Banker in Settle, & formerly practising as a Solicitor, meeting a large party, and others came in the evening: among the guests were Mr. Wiglesworth, Rector of Slaidburn, and his second wife, Mrs. Clapham & Miss Gurnall, the Robinsons; the Ingrams, Mr. Rycroft, Mr. & Mrs. C. Ingleby &c.*

1825: 10 May: *Called on different acquaintances at Giggleswick & Settle, & dined at the former place with Mrs. Bolland, meeting the Pearts, Robinsons & Geldards, and Mr. Rycroft.* 13 Sep: *I took an early dinner at Giggleswick with Mrs. Bolland, where I met Mrs. A. Currer, Miss A. Ingleby, of Austwick, Mrs. Willis, & Mr. Robinson, a very respectable young Solicitor, settled at Settle, and married to Miss Peart.*

1826: 26 Jan: *We passed the evening in a friendly way with Lady George Sutton & her sisters, the Mrs. Pearts, who reside near Mrs. Backhouse, being also old acquaintances of my poor Mother's.*

1837: 26 Oct: *Called on Mrs. Peart.*

PEART — William Peart[59]

William Peart (1802-1827), Church of England clergyman, was born at Giggleswick, the son of John Peart and Ellen Clapham. He was educated at Giggleswick School and St John's College, Cambridge (BA 1824). He was ordained deacon on 29 May 1825 and priest on 24 September 1826. Peart was appointed stipendiary curate of St Mary's, Bedford, on 24 September 1826. He married, that same year, Isabella, second daughter of James Dunlop of Sydenham, Kent. He died of tuberculosis at Settle.

1826: 28 Sep: *As we were sitting at tea, we were agreeably surprized by the entrance of a gentleman, Son to one of Mrs. Backhouse's old neighbours at Settle, Mr. Peart, at whose hospitable house we have often received so much civility. Mr. W. Peart is in orders, recently ordained priest; and his curacy is in the town of Bedford; he is now on a little tour, for recovering strength after an illness, but seems very delicate, & I should fear, consumptive. He consulted us about his progress, wishing to see Chepstow Castle, Tintern Abbey, Bath & Bristol &c. in the few days, which he can allow himself; he had been for two days at Cheltenham.* 29 Sep: *I passed the morning in shewing our young friend the principal sights of Gloucester, the Cathedral, Jail, Shire hall, Spa &c. and he afterwards dined & spent the evening with us at Wellington Parade. He seemed much to enjoy his day, we talked of Yorkshire, his acquaintances & connexions; & he was greatly pleased with what he saw. He seems an estimable, well intentioned young man; we had not seen him since he was a school boy at Giggleswick.*

1827: 3 Mar: *To-day, I hear of the decease of an only son, doubtless, as tenderly cherished by his parents, as ours by us. Poor W. Peart, whose visit to Gloucester I mentioned above, in September last, whose then consumptive appearance I noticed, has sunk into the grave. He went to Settle, & died among his own people: a rapid decline carried him off: he has followed a sister, who was removed by the same complaint; & his surviving sister, Mrs. Robinson, is in a very precarious state.*

PECK — Kenrick Peck[60]

Kenrick Peck (±1769-1837), Church of England clergyman, was the son of Kenrick Peck (1729-1802), of London, and possibly of Cornish Hall, Holt, Denbighshire, and Sarah Humphreys (1732-1802). He was a cousin of the sculptor Joseph Nollekens (1737-1823), of London, generally considered to be the finest British sculptor of the late eighteenth century.

Peck was educated at Oriel College, Oxford (BA 1794; MA 1798), and was ordained deacon on 1 March 1795. His first clerical appointment was as curate of Greatham, Hampshire, from 3 March 1795. He was later appointed stipendiary curate of Rushall, Wiltshire, on 25 November 1814, and of Manningford Bruce, Wiltshire, on 8 November 1816. He later served as rector of Ightfield, Shropshire, from 1820 to 1827.

Peck married, at St Swithin's, Walcot, Bath, 18 October 1798, Mary (±1769-1849), daughter of Philip Ditcher (1720-1781), of

Bath, and Mary 'Polly' (1735-1783), daughter of the novelist Samuel Richardson. Kenrick and Mary had at least 6 sons and 3 daughters:

1 Sarah (d. 1802); died an infant
1 Kenrick (1800-1817)
2 Philip Richardson (1802-1858)
3 Jasper William (1803-1804); died an infant
4 Jasper (1805-1853), Church of England clergyman
5 Samuel Richardson (1806-1819); died a minor
2 Beatrice (b. & d. 1807)
3 Mary (1809-1852)
6 William Peck (1810-1826); died a minor

Kenrick Peck and his wife seem to have been very well regarded in Rushall; although he left the living in 1820, a tablet dedicated to him and his family was placed in the church some seventeen years later. There is also a tablet in the church to their daughter Sarah (d. 1802).

1806: 25 Oct: *The Revd. Mr. Peck & Mr. Brabant called.* 13 Nov: *Drove my Father to call upon Mrs. Poore, & at Mr. Peck's at Rushall; found neither at home.*

1808: 4 Feb: *Called on Mr. Halliley's family, & on Mr. & Mrs. Peck.* 9 Apr: *Drove my Mother to Rushall to visit Mrs. Peck; found her & her husband & fine family at home. They are pleasant people.* 18 Apr: *Rode to Devizes, by Wick, that I might find the Hillier's House. Dined at Mr. Peck's, at Rushall, whither we went in a Post Chaise.*

PECKELSHEIM — Sofie Henriette Wilhelmine Peckelsheim at Weimar — *see also* Seckendorff[61]

Sofie Henriette Wilhelmine Peckelsheim (1764-1850) was the daughter of Friedrich Karl von Seckendorff, Freiherr [son of a baron] von Seckendorff-Aberdar (1736-1796) and Wilhelmine Johanna Charlotte (1742-1766). She married Dietrich Ernst Georg von Spiegel zu Peckelsheim, Freiherr von Spiegel zu Peckelsheim (1738-1789); they had at least 1 son:

1 Karl Emil von Spiegel zu Peckelsheim, Freiherr von Spiegel zu Peckelsheim (1782-1849); married, at Weimar, 18 April 1805, Emilie von Rotberg, Freiin [daughter of a baron] von Rotberg (1787-1870)

1800: 20 Apr: *In the Evening at Court, a beautiful Concert tho' the Jagemann did not sing a Clarinetist besides Baron & Baroness Zobel, Mad. de Pechelsheim her husband Privy Counsellor at Eisenach.*

PEDDER — William Newland Pedder[62]

William Newland Pedder (1796-1871), Church of England clergyman, was born at Andover, Hampshire, son of Revd William Pedder (1761-1831) and Sophia Newland (1766-1847). He was educated at Worcester College, Oxford (BA 1818; MA 1821), and was ordained deacon on 4 April 1819 and priest on 28 May 1820. His first clerical appointment was as curate of Upper Clatford, Hampshire, from 28 May 1820. He was then curate to his father at Andover with Foxcott from 9 May 1823 to 8 April 1830. He became vicar of Andover with Foxcott on 2 December 1830.

Pedder married Caroline Elizabeth Cotes (1799-1877), born at Bishop Burton, Yorkshire; they had 2 sons and 3 daughters:

1 William George (1832-1888), municipal commissioner, Bombay, Indian Civil Service; married, at Clevedon, Julia Frances Prescott (1848-1891)
1 Sophia Jane (1834-1921)
2 Elizabeth Georgina (1835-1898)
2 Digby Cotes (1837-1918), Lt-Col, Indian Army; married, 1889, Annie Lucy Gertrude Trevor (1867-1937)
3 Mary Florence (b. 1839)

1839: 29 Aug: *The prayers were read by the Vicar, the Revd. Mr. Pedder, and the Sermon preached by Archdeacon Brymer.*

PEEL — Jonathan Peel[63]

Jonathan Peel (1788-1841), brewer, was born at Accrington, Lancashire, the son of Jonathan Peel (1752-1834) and Esther Bolton (1762-1841). He was brother to Joseph and William Peel (*below*) and first cousin to Sir Robert Peel (*below*). He lived at Culham, near Newbury.

Jonathan Peel married, at St Michael's, Oxford, 5 January 1815, Elizabeth Tubb (1788-1868); they had 4 sons and 4 daughters:

1 William Accrington (1816-1881)
2 Edmund Yates (1816-1901)
3 Robert Bolton Wilde (1818-1869)
4 John Henry Westcar (1823-1891)
1 Emily Esther Anne (b. 1824)
2 Matilda Caroline (1827-1899)
3 Magdalene Susanna (1828-1903)
4 Ellen E. W. (b. 1830)

Peel was a partner in the brewery at Watlington. He contested Cheltenham unsuccessfully in the election of 24 July 1837. The result was as follows: Craven F. Berkeley (whig) 632; Jonathan Peel (tory) 298.

1837: 25 Jul: *At Cheltenham Craven Berkeley has succeeded against Peel, a Conservative.*

PEEL — Joseph Peel[64]

Joseph Peel (1799-1844), brewer, was born at Accrington, Lancashire, the fourth son of Jonathan Peel (1752-1834) and Esther Bolton (1762-1841). He was brother to Jonathan (*above*) and William Peel (*below*), and first cousin to Sir Robert Peel (*below*). He lived at Culham, near Newbury. He married, at Manchester Cathedral, 22 June 1834, Mary Greenwood (1809-1901); they had 2 sons and 2 daughters:

1 Hannah (b. 1835)
2 Mary (1837-1906)
1 Charles (1838-1885)
2 Joseph (b. 1841)

The votes in the Tewkesbury election of 25 July 1837 were as follows: W. Dowdeswell (tory) 219; John Martin (whig) 192; Joseph Peel (tory) 169.

1837: 16 Aug: *From F. Aston consulting me whether, without compromising his conservative principles, he can decline accepting the invitation of the Tewkesbury Conservatives to dine with them next week when it is intended to present to Mr. Peel, the unsuccessful Conservative candidate for that borough at the late election, a piece of plate.*

PEEL — Robert Peel[65]

Sir Robert Peel, 2nd baronet (1788-1850), prime minister, was born at Bury, Lancashire, the son of Sir Robert Peel, 1st baronet (1750-1830), MP and wealthy textile manufacturer, and Ellen Yates (1766-1803). He was educated at Hipperholme Grammar School, Harrow School, Christ Church, Oxford, and Lincoln's Inn. Peel was MP for Cashel, 1809-12; Chippenham, 1812-17; Oxford University, 1817-29; Westbury, 1829-30; and Tamworth, 1830-50.

He married, 1820, Julia (1795-1859), daughter of Sir John Floyd, 1st baronet; they had 5 sons and 2 daughters:

1 Julia (1821-1893)

1 Robert (1822-1895), Liberal Party politician and railway commissioner; succeeded as 3rd baronet; knighted 1869; married, at Westminster, 13 January 1856, Emily Hay (1836-1924)

2 Frederick (1823-1906); married, at St George's, Hanover Square, Westminster, 12 August 1857, Elizabeth Emily Shelley (1833-1865)

3 William Peel (1824-1858), naval officer; appointed KCB; awarded the VC for picking up a live shell with the fuse still burning and throwing it over the parapet just before it burst (18 October 1854, siege of Sevastopol); served in the Indian Mutiny; wounded at the relief of Lucknow; died of smallpox at Cawnpore, India

4 John Floyd (1827-1910), Capt., Scots Guards; married, 1851, Annie Jenney (1829-1904)

5 Arthur Wellesley (1829-1912), Liberal MP (1865-95) and speaker (1884-95); created 1st Viscount Peel; married, at Merevale, Warwickshire, 14 August 1862, Adelaide Dugdale (1839-1890)

2 Eliza (1833-1882)

At the age of 21 Peel became MP for Cashel, Tipperary, a rotten borough. His sponsor for the election was the chief secretary for Ireland, Sir Arthur Wellesley [later duke of Wellington]. His maiden speech in 1810 was described by the speaker, Charles Abbot, as 'the best first speech since that of William Pitt'. As chief secretary in Dublin in 1813, Peel proposed the setting up of a specialist police force, and in 1814 the Royal Irish Constabulary was founded.

Robert Peel was quickly marked out as one of the rising stars of the tory party. He first entered the cabinet in 1822 as home secretary, introducing a number of important reforms to British criminal law enforcement, most notably the establishment of the Metropolitan Police Force. He resigned as home secretary after Lord Liverpool became incapacitated and was replaced by George Canning. Canning favoured Catholic emancipation, while Peel had been one of its most outspoken opponents. After Canning's sudden death less than four months later and the brief premiership of Lord Goderich, Peel returned to the post of home secretary under the premiership of his long-time ally, the duke of Wellington. However, the pressure on the new ministry from advocates of Catholic emancipation was too great to resist, and an emancipation bill was passed the next year. As a result, Peel felt compelled to resign his seat as MP representing the graduates of Oxford University. He moved to the rotten borough, Westbury, retaining his cabinet position.

The tory government was replaced by a whig ministry in 1830 which lasted until 1834, when the tories returned to power. Robert Peel was selected as prime minister. He was in Italy at the time, and Wellington acted as caretaker for the three weeks he took to return. His ministry was a minority government and depended on whig goodwill for its continuation. The whigs formed a compact with Daniel O'Connell's Irish radical members to repeatedly defeat the government on various bills. Eventually Peel's ministry resigned and the whigs returned to power under Lord Melbourne.

In May 1839 Peel was offered another chance to form a government, this time by the new monarch, Queen Victoria. This would have been another minority government, and Peel felt he needed a further sign of confidence from his queen. Many of the higher posts in Victoria's household were held by the wives and female relatives of whigs; there was some feeling that Victoria had allowed herself to become too closely associated with the whig party. Peel therefore asked for some of this entourage to be dismissed and replaced by their Conservative counterparts. The request provoked a crisis; Victoria refused to change her household, and despite pleadings from the duke of Wellington, she relied on assurances of support from whig leaders. Peel refused to form a government, and the whigs returned to power.

Peel came to power a second time after a Conservative victory at the general election of 1841. The most notable act of his second ministry was the repeal the corn laws. This break with Conservative protectionism was triggered by the Irish Famine (1845-49). Tory agriculturalists were sceptical of the extent of the problem, and Peel reacted slowly to the famine. As realisation dawned, however, he hoped that ending the corn laws would free up more food for the Irish. His own party failed to support the bill, but it passed with whig and radical support on 15 May 1846. On 25 June 1846 the duke of Wellington persuaded the House of Lords to pass it. On that same night Peel's Irish Coercion Bill was defeated in the Commons by 292 to 219 by a combination of whigs, radicals, and tory protectionists. Following this, on 29 June 1846, Peel resigned as prime minister.

Sir Robert Peel was thrown from his horse while riding up Constitution Hill in London on 29 June 1850; the horse stumbled on top of him and he died three days later.

1824: 27 Sep.

1825: 2 Apr: *Tithes, absenteeship, the qualifications of Electors &c. came under the review of the several speakers, among whom Canning, Brougham, Peel, Burdett, Plunkett, North, Doherty, with some others, were very conspicuous.* 20 May, 17 Sep: *Just as we were leaving the village of Hartlebury I had a transient interview with my old acquaintance Villers, whose name I have twice mentioned in the course of this day's journeyings. He was riding with the lady, whom he has recently married, Miss Peel, daughter of a gentleman of that name, resident at Accrington in Lancashire, and engaged, I think, in the cotton trade, as most of that large clan are: she is also a cousin of the Secretary of State.*

1827: 8 Mar: *Mr. Dawson & Mr. Peel spoke at length on the misconceptions commonly hazarded about the treaty of Limerick.* 14 Apr: *The interval has afforded ample time for intrigue; the public voice seemed to point either to Canning or to Peel; the latter was loudly called for by the friends of Protestant ascendancy, and by those, who disapprove of the doctrines of the modern political economists: it was felt by them, that Peel could be depended on; that he was steady in principle, calm, judicious; that in sterling talent he was at least his rival's equal, & if inferior in brilliancy of eloquence that he yet possessed powers in that department of no ordinary nature.* 4 May: *Mr. Peel's speech was worthy of that great man, candid, open, logical, dignified, modest while he spoke of his own claims & services, animated and eloquent in descanting on those of others, who with himself had refused to take office under Mr. Canning.* 7 May: *In the House of Commons Mr. Canning utterly lost his temper, and exhibited an exacerbation quite unsuitable to his station; his opponents were the vehement Mr. Dawson, Mr. Peel, who was received with constant cheering.* 4 Jul: *The public sentiment in favour of his great rival, Mr. Peel, was strikingly evinced of late in the Theatre at Oxford, at the Commemoration, where that great man appeared, and not only at his entrance and exit was received by the most noisy & vehement applause, but at every interval in the business of the day, eager bursts of acclamation were unsparingly indulged in honour of him, while Canning's name, brought forward by a few, either to feel the pulse of the great concourse assembled, or by feigned respect to incite the audience to renewed applause of the real object of admiration and respect, regard was received with yells & hootings and other marks of disgust. An eye witness tells me, that a perfect canopy of caps waved over Peel as he left the Theatre, passing thro' the area: that the imperturbable calmness of his countenance & command of emotion were striking; but that he saw a tear trembling in his eye.*

1828: 23 Jan., 12 Feb., 24 Mar., 17 May, 28 May, 2 Jun.

1829: 7 Feb: *It was rather collected, that Peel was stedfast in his principles, and that the Premier, though readily expressing a wish, that the matter were settled, saw little prospect of such a termination.* 7 Feb: *Of Mr. Peel's apostasy few felt any apprehensions; he was considered as the leader & champion of the Protestant Interest, an honourable & steady leader in the forefront ... But his conversion, and the resolution adopted by the Duke of Wellington & himself, and assented to by the rest of the Cabinet, are to be dated, it now appears, from August last, although, as far as can be judged, the acquiescence of the Sovereign has been only lately, shall I say — extorted?* 13 Feb: *Mr. Peel has brought into the House of Commons his bill for suppressing the Roman Catholic Association in Ireland, which is to be a preliminary to the proposed legislative measure for the emancipation of the Papists.* 26 Feb., 1 Mar., 7 Mar: *On Thursday Mr. Peel brought forward his eventful proposition on behalf of the Roman Catholics, made a speech of four hours in length, was complimented by the friends of the measure, and cogently answered by its opponents, especially by Sir Robert Inglis.* 8 Apr., 26 Jun: *It is also positively anticipated, that Mr. Peel will erelong withdraw from the administration, or, at least, from what is called the management of the House of Commons.*

1830: 31 Jan., 22 Jun., 24 Jun: *Sir Robt. Peel has a measured, dignified tone in speaking; not natural, nor very pleasing; it is equable, flowing and generally fluent: he is extremely cautious, rather affects liberality of opinions, makes a semblance of concession to the judgment of others. Such was the impression left on my mind by his speech this night, in which, however, there were two or three able & eloquent passages; but I heard him to a disadvantage.*

1832: 27 Mar., 10 Apr., 17 May.

1833: 15 Feb., 13 Mar., 6 Nov: *Met Sir Robert Peel in an open carriage: he stopped for a moment to give some directions to our coachman, about a parcel. I did not at first recognize him, but mistook him for one of his brothers.*

1834: 9 Sep., 18 Nov: *I saw a newspaper by which it appeared that the Duke of Wellington has received his Majesty's commands to form a ministry, has actually accepted office, but that the final arrangements must be postponed until his Grace has communicated with Sir Robert Peel, who, unluckily, is at this moment in Italy, at Florence, with his family.* 2 Dec., 12 Dec: *Sir Robert Peel returned from the Continent on Tuesday last... The Duke of Wellington, awaiting his return, has carried on the routine business of the various state departments as interim Minister, almost single-handed; and now, with a noble generosity, resigns the helm of government into the hands of the younger statesman, who is appointed Premier, to hold the offices of First Lord of the Treasury and Chancellor of the Exchequer.*

1835: 20 Feb., 6 Apr., 9 Apr: *Breakfasted at the Bell Hotel, where the worthy conservatives learnt with pain what they must have anticipated, that Sir Robert Peel has resigned his post of Premier, and that his administration is dissolved. He will, doubtless, be succeeded by a rifaccimento of the Melbourne Administration.* 12 Jun.

1839: 10 May: *Recd. a letter from Round acquainting me that there was every prospect that a firm Conservative government would be formed: that at the suggestion of Lord Melbourne, the Queen had sent for the D. of Wellington, who had advised her to call on Sir Robt. Peel, to take measures for forming an administration: that the Queen had recd. Sir R.P. in a very satisfactory manner.* 11 May: *Found a letter from Round: the bright hopes of a vigorous, conservative government being formed are fast melting away.* 12 Aug.

1842: 17 Mar: *Frederick has a prospect of receiving a political appointment thro' Peel, who acknowledges a claim upon him, which he has not yet had an opportunity of discharging by placing him in a public office.*

1844: 28 Nov., 2 Dec.

1845: 25 Jan., 17-18 Feb., 16 Mar., 24 Mar., 2 Apr., 9 Apr., 11 Apr.

1847: 18 May.

1850: 2 Jul: *Much anxiety or curiosity as to the condition of Sir Robert Peel, who was violently thrown from his horse on Saturday last, and whose life is considered to be in great danger.* 3 Jul: *The late accident has proved fatal to Sir Robert Peel: thus a gifted and eminent man is departed from among us, and it is difficult to conjecture what will be the results of this striking and impressive event, as regards the future government of the country.*

PEEL — **Robert Peel** [66]

Robert Peel (1803-1869), Church of England clergyman and schoolmaster, was born at Richmond, Yorkshire, the son of Robert Peel. He was educated at Edenbridge, Kent, and Trinity College, Cambridge (BA 1828). He was ordained deacon on 15 June 1828 and priest on 28 June 1829. Peel was appointed stipendiary curate of Lower Lemington, Gloucestershire, on 15 June 1828, and from 1834 he kept a school at Edenbridge. He later served as headmaster of Hampton Grammar School, Middlesex, from 1839 to 1866, and curate of Hampton from 1846 his death in 1869.

Peel married Elizabeth (b. ±1804), born at Croydon, Surrey; they had 2 sons and 3 daughters:

1 Robert Raine (b. 1834)
1 Margaret (b. ±1837)
2 Mary (b. ±1838)
3 Ellen (b. 1840)
2 William Emery (±1844-1889)

1829: 17 Jun., 18 Jun: *Dr. Warneford's guests were Messrs. Scholefield, Ford, Hall, Jeaffreson, Prosser, Peel, Malcolm, Adams & myself.* 29 Oct: *... two names were inserted, those of Mr. Whitmore Jones, the new possessor of Chastleton, & Mr. Peel, the Curate of Bourton on the Hill.*

PEEL — **William Peel** [67]

William Peel (1793-1869), farmer and landed proprietor, was born at Accrington, Lancashire, the third son of Jonathan Peel (1752-1834) and Esther Bolton (1762-1841). He was brother to Jonathan and Joseph Peel (*above*) and a cousin to Sir Robert Peel (*above*). He married, first, at St Nicholas's, Liverpool, Lancashire, 15 April 1818, Anne Jane Steers (1798-1828); they had 3 sons and 2 daughters:

1 Spencer (1819-1860), army officer
2 Charles Steers (1819-1873), Church of England clergyman
3 Francis William (1823-1895), Church of England clergyman
1 Susannah Ellen (1824-1887)
2 Margaret Jane (1825-1904)

Peel married secondly, at St Mary's, Clitheroe, Lancashire, 1829, his cousin Sophia Ann Drake (±1792-1853), born at Rochdale, Lancashire, the daughter of Revd Thomas Drake (1745-1819) and Eleanore Yates (1760-1824). Peel farmed 286 acres and employed twelve men at Broadstone Hill House, Enstone, Oxfordshire.

1854: 16 Aug: *E. Clifford returned to dinner, having gone from Turkdean, where was a very hilarious party of dancers numerous, and ill arranged, as it would appear, to sleep at Salperton House, now rented by Mr. Peel, formerly of Broadstone, Oxon, and family. The late Mrs. Peel was sister of Mrs. Niblet of Haresfield, and, as such, the Peels known to the Cliffords, between whom and the Nibletts there is a close intimacy.*

PEGGE — Christopher Pegge — *see also* Morland[68]

Sir Christopher Pegge (1765-1822), physician, was born at Westminster, the only son of Samuel Pegge the younger (1733-1800), barrister, antiquary, poet, and musical composer, and his first wife, Martha (1732-1767), daughter of Henry Bourne, an eminent Derbyshire physician. He was educated at Oriel College (MA 1789; BMed 1789), where he was elected a fellow, and Christ Church, Oxford (DMed 1792). Pegge resigned his Oriel fellowship in 1790 to take up the post of Lee's reader in anatomy at Christ Church. His duties as reader involved the delivery of two courses of lectures per year. His lecturing style was described as both 'spirited' and 'easy and correct'. At first his lectures were extremely popular; it was 'not thought to be the thing to leave Oxford without attending one course'. Subsequently, however, Pegge came to be regarded as something of a bore. In 1790 he was also elected a physician to the Radcliffe Infirmary, a position he held until 1808, when he was forced to reduce his workload due to his asthma.

Pegge married, 29 March 1791, Amy, daughter of Kenton Couse of Whitehall, London; they had 1 daughter:

1 Mary (b. 1791); married Revd R. M. Boultbee of Merton College, Oxford

Pegge was elected a fellow of the Royal Society in 1795 and a fellow of the College of Physicians in 1796. In 1799, soon after the duke of York's inspection of the Oxford Loyal Volunteers, in which Pegge served as a major, Pegge was knighted by George III. In 1801 he was appointed regius professor of physic, in which capacity he gave occasional lectures on aspects of animal economy and held the mastership of a charitable foundation, the Ewelme Hospital. Otherwise he had few duties.

1804: 2 Mar: *At Sir C. Pegge's lecture on the Human Economy, the Bones & Muscles the subject of the day.* 3 Mar: *Sir C. Pegge's second lecture on the Human Economy which embraced the muscles, & nerves & introduced Galvanism.* 12 Nov: *Called with Round on Lady Pegge.* Supped at Sir Christopher's meeting Round.

1805: 19 Mar: *Called upon Round, Rashleigh & Lady Pegge. Called upon Round, Rashleigh & Lady Pegge.* 22 Mar: *Joined the Pegge & Morland Party. Walked back at ½ past 9 getting to College by 11.* 27 Mar: *Walked with Sir C. & Lady Pegge & Mrs. Cleaver.*

1806: 19 Mar: *conversed with Bright, Hall & Sir C. Pegge.* 21 Mar.

PEGLER — Humphrey Pegler[69]

Humphrey Pegler (1806-1875), farmer, was born at Maugersbury, Gloucestershire, the third son of John Pegler (1776-1850) and Mary Ann Hayward (1776-1847). He had numerous siblings in Maugersbury and Stow—5 brothers and 2 sisters, including:

1 John (1799-1875); *see below*
2 Theophilus Haddock (1803-1882)
3 Leonard Hayward (1808-1873)
4 Carleton (1810-1840)
1 Carolina (1813-1874)
2 Jane (b. 1815)
5 Charles (1817-1891)

Pegler married Lucy (1807-1864); they had at least 3 sons:

1 Humphrey Theophilus (1845-1896)
2 John Carlton (b. 1847)
3 Francis (b. 1848)

Pegler farmed at Bledington, about 4 miles from Maugersbury.

1838: 26 Apr: *Called at Mr. H. Pegler's, who was from home; but looked over his yards, to see the cattle, especially a fine bull, and some cows and stirks which were part of the recent importation from Cumberland, by which I profited.*

1839: 3 Apr: *A note from Mr. H. Pegler of Bledington, with additional particulars as to the pedigree of a cow, which he has procured for me, and which is one of a lot recently imported into this neighbourhood from Cumberland, being of a very superior stock, descended from the famous bull Comet.*

1844: 20 Aug.

1850: 17 Jun: *Received a letter from Mr. H. Pegler, Guardian of the parish of Bledington.* 18 Jun., 27 Jun: *Mr. H. Pegler exhibited a zeal without excess; it became necessary to enter into explanations of matters familiar to experienced guardians to clear up his doubts and suspicions: and he originated an enquiry, but not in a bad temper.* 5 Sep: *Mr. H. Pegler, Guardian of Bledington, a clever, but restless and meddling man, imagining that the system of our house needs reform, and failing in a first attempt to shew mismanagement, had taken up the Shoe question as a debateable manner, matter and argued it with warmth, & not without unhandsome imputations against the Clerk and Governor.*

1852: 2 Dec., 21 Dec: *Humphry Pegler, of Bledington, called to consult me on some private law business of his own.*

1853: 24 Mar: *The Brothers Pegler sought me, after the Magistrates meeting was closed, to get advice and information as to the regulations according to which contests for the Election of Guardians are carried on.* 15 Dec.,

1854: 18 Feb: *A long interview with H. Pegler of Bledington.* 10 Jun.

PEGLER — John Pegler[70]

John Pegler (b. ±1801), veterinary surgeon and farmer, was born at Maugersbury, Gloucestershire, the eldest son of John Pegler (1776-1850) and Mary Ann Hayward (1776-1847). He was elder brother to Humphrey (*above*).

Pegler married late in life, at Highworth, Wiltshire, 1861, Ann Watts (b. ±1821). He lived at Lower House, Maugersbury, and farmed 170 acres, employing four men.

1836: 18 Aug: *Rode to Stow, and attended a meeting of subscribers to the Police Association, which was attended by Messrs. Pole, Jeaffreson, W B Pole, Winter, Beman, Harris, Collett, Pegler, T. Collett & others.*

1838: 22 Feb: *The appellant brought forward two very experienced witnesses, Pegler & J. Clifford, of whom the former was one of the Committee appointed to value the hamlet for the Rate, & the latter a disinterested neighbour, and not a rate payer.* 9 Aug.

1839: 30 Jan: *A note from J Pegler, the Veterinary Surgeon, to tell me that an Asst. P.L.C. (probably Neave) is to dine to-day at Sir*

Geo. Phillipps at Weston Park after visiting C Norton Union, and means to visit the Stow Board of Guardians tomorrow.

1840: 16 Aug: *Wrote to Mr. J. Pegler, Veterinary Surgeon, that he need not look out longer for a steady harness horse, as the ladies (the Daniells) for whom I was enquiring, had suited themselves.*

1842: 27 Mar., 27 Nov: *A note from J. Pegler which I answered about a horse clipper.*

1843: 12 Feb: *Wrote to Mr. Pegler, Maugersbury, respecting a present of fruit and forest trees, which he has kindly made me.*

1844: 27 Jan: *A few lines from J. Pegler, Maugersbury, offering his team to bring a load of timber from thence, as he understood I had bought some at a late sale there.* 28 Jan.

1845: 4 Jun., 10 Jun: *Recd. a letter from J Pegler on Justice matters, in reply to one which I had addressed to him.* 21 Jun.

1846: 15 Nov: *One of my horses being ill, sent for J. Pegler, the Veterinary Surgeon, who pronounced the disease, inflammation of the lungs, and treated it accordingly.* 16 Nov: *J Pegler came to visit the sick horse, and with him I went in his gig to Stow: the poor horse very ill, but improved in his state as the day advanced.*

1850: 8 Feb.

1853: 21 Jan., 23 Mar. 24 Mar: *The Brothers Pegler sought me, after the Magistrates meeting was closed, to get advice and information as to the regulations according to which contests for the Election of Guardians are carried on.* 25 Mar., 6 Apr., 11 Apr., 16 Apr., 10 Jun., 15 Dec.

1854: 20 Apr., 8 Jun., 6 Jul.

PELHAM — Charles Anderson-Pelham [71]

Charles Anderson-Pelham, 2nd Lord Yarborough, 1st earl of Yarborough (1781-1846), MP, DL, landed proprietor, and yachtsman, was born at Brocklesby, Lincolnshire, the eldest son of Charles Anderson-Pelham, 1st Lord Yarborough (1749-1823), and Sophia (1752-1786), daughter and heir of George René Aufrère and Arabelle Bate.

Pelham was educated at Eton College and Trinity College, Cambridge. He was MP for Grimsby in 1803-07 and Lincolnshire in 1807-23; he succeeded as 2nd Lord Yarborough in 1823. He was recorder of Grimsby in 1823-32, and of Newport, Isle of Wight in 1825-32. In 1831 he was made DL for the Isle of Wight, and was promoted in the same year to lieutenant-colonel of the North Lincolnshire Regiment of Yeomanry and vice admiral of Hampshire and the Isle of Wight. For many years he was commodore of the Royal Yacht Squadron. He was created earl of Yarborough on 30 January 1837.

Pelham married, at Lambeth Palace, 11 August 1806, Henrietta Maria Charlotte (1788-113), second daughter of John Bridgeman-Simpson and only surviving child of Henrietta Frances, daughter and heiress of Sir Thomas Worsley, 6th baronet, of Apuldurcombe, Isle of Wight. Charles and Henrietta had 2 sons and 1 daughter:

1 Charles Anderson Worsley (1809-1862); styled Lord Worsley, 1837-46; succeeded as 2nd earl of Yarborough; married, at Brighton, 19 December 1831, Maria Adelaide (1814-1897), second daughter of Cornwallis Mause, 3rd Viscount Hawarden, and Jan Crauford, younger daughter of Patrick Crauford Bruce of Taplow Lodge, Buckinghamshire

2 Dudley Worsley (1812-1851), Capt., RN; married, 15 October 1839, Madalina Sinclair, sister and co-heir of Sir Robert Charles Sinclair, 9th baronet of Murkle, and second daughter of Adm. Sir John Gordon Sinclair, 8th baronet of Murkle, and Anne de Courcy, only daughter of Adm. Michael de Courcy

1 Charlotte (d. 1875); married, 19 November 1831, Sir Joseph William Copley, 4th baronet, of Sprotborough, Yorkshire

Pelham died on 5 September 1846 on board his yacht *The Kestrel*, off Vigo, Portugal.

1843: 8 Sep: *Several boats belonging to men of war, or yachts, were in attendance for officers or owners; Lord Yarborough, Commodore of the Yacht Club fleet, whom we had noticed, an elderly man; with gold laced cap, and blue jacket, rowed off in his own beautifully appointed four oared boat ...*

1846: 5 Jun., 8 Jun: *Next came St. Lawrance, where, almost wholly shut out by high hedges, lofty trees, or high walls, a large Elizabethan mansion, or villa, the property and frequent residence of the Earl of Yarborough, a nobleman with large estates in the Island, Lincolnshire & elsewhere, a great patron of Yachting, Commodore of the Yacht Club meeting at Cowes, and more commonly in favourable seasons to be heard of cruising in his favourite Kestrel than elsewhere;—his Lordship's second son, Capt. Pelham, R.N. has a cottage residence contiguous to that of his noble father at St. Lawrence.* 9 Jun: *This Sir R. Worsley's niece and heiress married Lord Yarborough, and so the property has passed into the Pelham family.*

PELHAM — George Pelham — *see* Rycroft [72]

George Pelham (1766-1827), bishop of Lincoln, was the third son of Thomas Pelham, 1st earl of Chichester (1728-1805), and Ann Frankland (1730-1815). He was also brother to Thomas (*below*). He was educated at Westminster School and Clare College, Cambridge (MA 1787), and was awarded a DCL from Lambeth in 1803.

Pelham was prebendary of Chichester, 1790-1803, and simultaneously vicar of Laughton, Sussex, 1790-1800. He was also appointed vicar of Bexhill in 1792 and of Hellingly in 1800, and held both these livings until his death in 1827. He was bishop of Bristol in 1803-07, and both bishop of Exeter and rector of Shobrooke, Devon, in 1807-20. He was appointed bishop of Lincoln in 1820 and held the see until his death. He was also clerk of the closet to the king.

Pelham married, 1792, Mary, third daughter of the Revd Sir Richard Nelson Rycroft, 1st baronet (d. 1786), 'notorious for his greed of lucrative office', and Penelope, daughter of Revd Richard Stonehewer. There were no children of the marriage.

1804: 19 Aug: *To the Cathedral Morn. Service performed by the Dean & Mr. Humphries, the Sermon, a good one by the Bishop.*

1806: 11 Mar: *Received from the Bish. of Bristol a polite negative to the request of private ordination without a title.* 14 Mar: *Replied in general terms to the Bishop of Bristol's letter.*

1823: 10 May.

1827: 11 Feb: *The reported decease of the Hon. & Revd. Dr. Pelham, Bishop of Lincoln, is now confirmed. He was brother of Lord Chichester, who also died not long ago, and successively held the Sees of Bristol, Exeter and Lincoln. His illness was occasioned by a cold caught, when attending the funeral of the Duke of York, and that duty, performed on a night intensely cold, has been well nigh fatal to others ...To return to Bishop Pelham; he was not distinguished by literary eminence, professional learning, or a strong mind; his rank was his chief recommendation to the bench, and while his conduct was not open to reproach, yet he was not regarded with that high respect, which most of his brethren command: he was esteemed a Courtier among the Bishops. There was a time, when from circumstances alluded to before (10 May 1823) I considered myself to have a slight claim to his patronage.*

PELHAM — Thomas Pelham [73]

Thomas Pelham, 2nd earl of Chichester (1756-1826), was the eldest son of Thomas Pelham, 1st earl of Chichester (1728-1805), and Ann Frankland (1730-1815). He was brother to George (*above*). He was educated at Westminster School and Clare Hall, Cambridge, and was MP for Sussex in 1780-1801. He succeeded to the Lords in his father's barony as Lord Pelham on 29 June 1801, and succeeded his father as 2nd earl of Chichester in 1805. He was secretary of state for home affairs, 1801-03, and chancellor of the duchy of Lancaster, 1803-04.

1801: 11 Sep: *Received a letter from Mr. Rycroft, & wrote to Lord Pelham.*

1823: 10 May: *Called on different acquaintances at Giggleswick & Settle, & dined at the former place with Mrs. Bolland, meeting the Pearts, Robinsons & Geldards, and Mr. Rycroft, eldest Son of a baronet of that name, who has estates in this neighbourhood, at Little Stainforth, Calton Hall, and Coniston, but resides on his estates in Kent near Farnham. Sir Nelson Rycroft's younger Brother, Sir Henry Rycroft, Knight Harbinger to the King married Mrs. Naper, the widow of the Hon. James Naper, brother to the late Lord Sherborne, & daughter of my Uncle Mr. F.J. Travell, Rector of Upper Slaughter. A sister of Mr. Rycroft's (for he was not then knighted) was married to Dr. Pelham, Bishop of Exeter, and now of Lincoln, and Brother to the Earl of Chichester. By this chain of connexion, I was in 1801 promised the appointment of private Secretary to Lord Chichester, then Lord Pelham, and recently appointed Secretary of State for the Home department; after some weeks expectation of an immediate introduction into that post, his Lordship caused to be intimated to me, that he should not require such services, because, I believe, his own appointment as Secretary for the Home department was only temporary, and I was disappointed of my promised place. Shortly after, I entered the University, and my views were decidedly turned to the Clerical profession.*

PELHAM-CLINTON — Henry Pelham-Clinton [74]

Henry Pelham-Clinton, 4th duke of Newcastle (1785-1851), landed proprietor, was born at Walton, Essex, the son and heir of Thomas Pelham-Clinton, 3rd duke of Newcastle (1752-1795), and Anna Maria (1760-1834), fifth and youngest daughter of William Stanhope, 2nd earl of Harrington. He was educated at Eton College. He was styled as Lord Clinton until 1794, and then as the earl of Lincoln until May 1795, when he succeeded his father as 4th duke of Newcastle.

Pelham-Clinton married, 18 July 1807, Georgiana Elizabeth (1789-1822), second daughter of Edward Miller Mundy of Shipley, Derbyshire. Georgiana died giving birth to their thirteenth child.

1828: 2 May.

1829: 7 Feb: *In the Upper house, Lord Eldon, the Duke of Newcastle, Lord Winchilsea, Lord Falmouth, Lord Redesdale &c. spoke with great energy.*

1832: 6 Jun: *Among the most unflinching opponents of the revolutionary measure we find the Duke of Newcastle, the Earl of Winchilsea, Lord Kenyon, the Earl of Carnarvon still in their places to declare their unqualified disapprobation.*

1838: 18 Dec.

PELLEW — Fleetwood Broughton Reynolds Pellew [75]

Fleetwood Broughton Reynolds Pellew (1789-1861), naval officer, was the second son of Edward Pellew, 1st Viscount Exmouth (1757-1833), and Susan Frowde (1756-1837). In March 1799 he began his naval career on board the *Impétueux*, then commanded by his father. He was later transferred with his father to the *Tonnant*, and in 1805, to the *Culloden* on the East India station. In September 1805 Pellew was promoted to lieutenant aboard the *Sceptre*, but he returned shortly afterwards to the *Culloden*. He was then appointed by his father to command the sloop *Rattlesnake*, and then, successively, the frigates *Terpsichore* and *Psyche*. In both frigates he repeatedly engaged Dutch vessels and Malay pirates. On 12 October 1807 Pellew was confirmed in the rank of commander, but was appointed by his father as acting captain of the 74-gun HMS *Powerful*. The following year he took command of the 50-gun *Cornwallis*, and then the 38-gun *Phaeton*. In October 1808, Pellew was involved in a damaging error of judgement when he demanded water from the Dutch colony at Nagasaki. He took two Dutchmen hostage, but his request was refused. The incident did not improve relations with the Japanese, who only allowed the Dutch to trade on their coast, and even then only through a limited factory at Nagasaki.

Pellew's commission as captain was confirmed on 14 October 1808. Continuing in the *Phaeton*, he took part in the capture of Mauritius in 1810 and of Java in 1811. In August 1812 the *Phaeton* returned to England with a large convoy of Indiamen. Pellew received the thanks of the East India Company and a present of 500 guineas.

Pellew next went out to the Mediterranean in the *Iphigenia* (36 guns), and in January 1813 he took command of the *Resistance* (46 guns). In October 1813 HMS *Resistance* was part of the squadron that silenced the batteries at Port d'Anzo and captured a convoy of twenty-nine vessels that had taken refuge there. In February 1814 the *Resistance* was ordered home and paid off, apparently because of a mutiny; several men were severely flogged as punishment and several were condemned to death. Their sentence, however, was quashed on account of a technical error in the proceedings; though there was no official reference, it was said that the men had been goaded to mutiny by Pellew's harshness.

In June 1814 Pellew was appointed CB, and in January 1836 the king made him a knight commander of Hanover (KCH). On 9 November 1846 he was promoted to rear admiral, and in December 1852 he was appointed commander-in-chief on the East Indies and China station. There was a strong expression of public opinion against his appointment to take command at the age of 63 in what was likely to be a troublesome war in Burma's pestilent climate.

In April 1853 Pellew hoisted his flag on board the *Winchester*, which returned to Hong Kong the following September. The men applied for leave at Hong Kong, but because of the heat in the town, the filthy conditions, and the poisonous spirits sold there, it was not considered a favourable location. Pellew decided, therefore, that the men should not have their leave until the weather at least became cooler. He neglected, however, to inform them of his reasons for denying their leave. This resulted in the circulation of mutinous expressions. When Pellew ordered the drum to beat to quarters, the men refused to obey, and the officers, with swords drawn, were sent to force them up. Some three or four were wounded, and the mutiny was quelled.

Upon the news reaching England, *The Times* pointed out that mutinies had occurred aboard both the *Winchester* and the *Resistance* shortly after Fleetwood Pellew had assumed command. The newspaper demanded his immediate recall. Notwithstanding this public pressure, the Admiralty had already decided that Pellew had demonstrated a lamentable want of judgement. He was summarily recalled.

Pellew had attained the rank of vice admiral on 22 April 1853. He became admiral on 13 February 1858, but had no further service. He died at Marseilles on 28 July 1861 and was buried in the protestant cemetery in Florence, where his first wife had been buried.

Pellew married, first, at St James's, Piccadilly, 5 June 1816, Harriet Frances (1794-1849), only daughter of Sir Godfrey Webster, 4th baronet; they had 1 son and 2 daughters:

1 Thomas Chaplin Fleetwood (1818-1819)

1 Harriet Bettina Frances (1821-1886)

2 Maude Mary (d. 1884)

Pellew married secondly, 22 February 1851, Cécile De Melfort (1831-1914), daughter of Edward Drummond, count of Melfort. They divorced in 1859.

Fleetwood Pellew's career was made by his father, who exploited death vacancies and the impracticability of communicating with the Admiralty to promote his son to the rank of captain at just 19 years old. This premature elevation seems to have warped Fleetwood's character. He was, like his father, a brave and resourceful seaman, but a harsh, overbearing, and insensitive disciplinarian. The two mutinies that defined his career were the result of his zeal and his failure to take his men into his confidence. His selection for the East Indies and China station command in 1852 reflected the scarcity of senior officers of suitable political persuasion; Pellew was always regarded as a doubtful choice, even by those who had backed him.

Pellew was a favourite of William IV, and the two men shared many values. He married for money, and possessed the independent means to survive his long years ashore in some style. This entry has been provided at length because Fleetwood Pellew was a close friend of George Witts, and their friendship adds to our knowledge of George's character. George was rebellious, forthright, and strong-headed; he and Pellew appear to have been kindred spirits.

1820: 4 Jul: *We derived much satisfaction to-day in the receipt of a letter from my Brother. It appears, that the news of his promotion to the rank of Captain in the Royal Artillery, which places him on half pay, was brought to him at Malta, by his friend the Hon. Captn. Pellew, a son of Lord Exmouth, commanding the Revolutionnaise. That officer was conveying to Constantinople, Mr. Frere, the Diplomatist; to hold the situation of Minister Plenipotentiary to the Porte, in the Interval between the departure of Sir R Liston the actual Ambassador, & the arrival of his successor, Lord Strangford. Captn. Pellew having warmly pressed George to accompany him & Mrs. Pellew, who sails with her husband on the Voyage, two short hours sufficed him to prepare for his departure, obtain the General's leave, & bid farewell for a time to the Island, where he has so long been on active service. A fortnight brought them to the end of their cruize, and the Palace of the British Embassy. Nothing can be more animated & interesting than my Brother's sketch of the voyage, country & society: nor are many better calculated to appreciate & describe such scenes.*

1823: 8 Jul: *I was afterwards so fortunate as to find a friend in Town my brother's intimate friends Captain & Mrs. Fleetwood Pellew. They were residing in Grafton Street with Mrs. T. Chaplin, aunt of Mrs. Pellew, who educated her. Capt. Pellew is one of the sons of the gallant Admiral Lord Exmouth, and himself in the Navy: of late years he has commanded a Frigate in the Mediterranean, the Revolutionnaire, where his intimacy with my brother commenced.*

PELLEW — George Pellew [76]

George Pellew (1793-1866), Church of England clergyman, was the third son of Edward Pellew, 1st Viscount Exmouth (1757-1833), and Susan Frowde (1756-1837). He was brother to Fleetwood Broughton Reynolds Pellew (*above*). George was educated at Eton College and Corpus Christi, Oxford (BA 1815; MA 1818; B&DD 1828). He was appointed vicar of Nazeing, Essex, in 1817, and vicar of Sutton on the Forest, Yorkshire, in 1820. He was subsequently seventh canon in Canterbury Cathedral, 1822-28; prebendary of Osbaldwick at York, 1824-28; rector of St George the Martyr, Canterbury, 1827-28; prebendary of Wistow at York, 1828-52; rector of St Dionis Backchurch, London, 1828-52; dean of Norwich, 1828-66; and rector of Great Chart, Kent, 1852-66. Pellew was one of the last Church of England clergymen to accumulate pluralities on such a scale. As dean of Norwich he had a seat in convocation, where he took a very active part in the debates, the recordings of which show him to have been a moderate churchman.

Pellew married, 1820, Frances (1780-1870), second daughter of Henry Addington, prime minister and first Viscount Sidmouth, and his first wife, Ursula Mary Hammond; they had 1 son and 5 daughters, including:

1 Frances Ursula (1821-1840)

2 Georgiana Susan (1822-1896)

1 Henry Edward (1828-1923); succeeded as 6th Viscount Exmouth; married, first, 5 October 1858, Eliza (d. 1869), daughter of William Jay, judge, of New York; at least 1 son:

1 Charles Ernest (1863-1945); succeeded as 7th Viscount Exmouth

3 Marian Hilaré Adelaide (1831-1901)

In 1847 Pellew published *The Life and Correspondence of Addington, First Viscount Sidmouth*. Although mentioned only fleetingly in the diaries, his life is of interest mostly because of his brother Fleetwood's close friendship with George Witts, the diarist's brother. Also, his wife Frances's first cousin was Charles Bathurst, one of Francis Witts's closest friends.

1847: 4 Feb: *C Bathurst, who purposes to send me a copy of the memoirs and correspondence of his uncle, Visct. Sidmouth, lately published by his son in law, the Dean of Norwich, Hon. & Revd. Dr. Pellew.* 21 Apr: *Began the perusal of the Life of Lord Sidmouth by the Hon. G. Pellew, Dean of Norwich—an interesting work.*

PELLEW — Samuel Humphrey Pellew [77]

Samuel Humphrey Pellew (1754-1843), surgeon in the Royal Marines, was the son of Capt. Samuel Pellew, RN (1712-1765) and Constance [Constantia] Langford (1725-1812). He married Jane Bawden [Ganden] (1754-1821). Pellew was the uncle of Fleetwood and George Pellew (*above*). He was assistant surgeon at HM dockyard in Plymouth and collector of HM customs in Falmouth for fifty years.

1823: 8 Jul., 13 Aug: *The information comes from Mr. Pellew, Collector of the Customs at Falmouth, agreeably to the arrangement, which I made in Town with his nephew, Captain F. Pellew, and from a Capt. Heathcote, of the Ionian Service, an old acquaintance of my poor brother's, who was a passenger with him on board the Packet, and had taken a particular charge of him.*

PEMBERTON — Edward Leigh Pemberton, solicitor, of Salisbury Square, Fleet Street [78]

Edward Leigh Pemberton (1795-1877), solicitor, was born in the parish of St Clement Danes, Westminster, the son of Robert Pemberton (1760-1804) and Margaret Leigh (1772-1841). He married, at St George the Martyr, Queen Square, Holborn, London, 23 December 1820, Charlotte Compton Cox (1798-1877); they had 6 sons and 1 daughter:

1 Emily Leigh (1821-1898)

1 Edward (1823-1910), DL and Conservative party politician; appointed KCB; married, 1849, Matilda Catherine Emma (d. 1906), daughter of Revd Francis James Noe
2 Robert Leigh (1826-1850)
3 Charles Leigh (1827-1921), Church of England clergyman
4 Loftus Leigh (1832-1907)
5 Wykeham Leigh (1833-1918), Maj.-Gen.
6 Henry (1835-1895)

Before the 1820s the firm appears to have been called Messrs Jones and Green, of Salisbury Square, Fleet Street. By 1818 it was located at 45 Salisbury Square and known as Green, Pemberton & Leigh. From January 1822 the firm became Green, Pemberton & Crawley, of the same address. By 1834 it had become Green, Pemberton, Crawley & Gardiner.

1835: 20 May: *Mr. Pemberton forwarded to me a Stamp Office legacy receipt for the legacy of £200 left to me by Lady Elcho.*

1836: 14 Aug: *A letter from Mr. Pemberton, acting Executor of Lady Elcho, apologizing for negligence in having till now omitted to inform me that her Ladyship had by her will bequeathed £200 to be invested in 3 pr. Cent Cons. in the names of Lord Wemyss and ... Mr. P. desires me to take the proper measures with my Bankers, Messrs. Hoare.* 15 Aug., 20 Sep: *Letters from E.F.W., Dr. Warneford, and Mr. Crawley, partner to Mr. Pemberton.* 21 Sep.

1839: 6 May: *Acting by the advice of his Solicitor, Mr. Pemberton, his Lordship had gone, accompanied by him, to take the oaths, which, in consequence of his infirmity, he had omitted doing during this queen's reign.*

1854: 21 Jul: *Busy in preparing a letter to Mr. Pemberton, Lord Wemyss's professional adviser in London, as to the Stanway Charities.* 24 Jul., 28 Jul., 2 Aug.

PENFOLD — George Saxby Penfold[79]

George Saxby Penfold (±1770-1846), Church of England clergyman, was born at Broadwater, Sussex, the son of Hugh Penfold (1727-1791), of Epsom, Surrey, and Susannah Saxby (b. 1731). He was educated at Merton College, Oxford (BA 1792; MA 1814; B&DD 1825). Penfold was appointed rector of Pulham, Dorset, in 1797, and of Christ Church, Marylebone, in 1828. He was finally appointed rector of Kingswinford, Staffordshire, in 1832.

Penfold married, at Westminster, Middlesex, 12 September 1792, Sarah Fleming (d. 1856). It is not known if there were any children.

1827: 3 Dec: *We came to Stanway on a visit to Lady Elcho for a few days, and found there a large party ... Next Dr. & Mrs. Penfold; she is a portly dame of high stature, and not far, I should think, below threescore: her husband, a little man, quick, polite, ready in conversation, a London preacher of celebrity: he is Rector of one of the new churches taken out of St. Mary le bone, Christ Church; he has twice edified my Stanway parishioners from the pulpit, and is much admired by Lady Elcho and her guests.* 6 Dec., 9 Dec: *Dr. Penfold read prayers at Stanway both at morning and evening service; he could not preach, having brought only two sermons, and those discourses he had delivered.*

1828: 6 Jan: *Dr. Penfold mentioned to me, that his academical degrees had been irregularly obtained: as an author he is unknown.*

PENNANT — ***see*** **Dawkins Pennant**

PENNINGTON — William Pennington[80]

William Pennington (1744-1829), master of ceremonies, was baptised on 26 March 1744 at Culmstock, Devon. One record states that he was born in 1738. He was employed as comptroller of the customs in Wilmington, New Hanover, North Carolina, from 1764 to 1776, and resided in Brunswick, North Carolina. By 1776 he was in Staten Island, New York. He was presumably a loyalist, as he appears to have returned to England at some point after 1776. Pennington married, 1792, Penelope Sophia (1752-1827), daughter of Edward Weston of Bath.

At some point after 1785, William Pennington was appointed as master of ceremonies at Bristol Hotwell. He wore a gold medallion strung on a blue ribbon to emphasise the dignity of his office. His published regulations were as follows:

> That a certain row of seats be set apart at the upper end of the room for ladies of precedence and foreigners of fashion. That every lady who has a right of precedence deliver her card to the Master of Ceremonies on her entering the room. That no gentleman appear with a sword or with spurs in these rooms, or on a ball night, in boots. That on ball nights when minuets are danced, ladies who intend dancing there will sit in a front row for the convenience of being taken out and returning to their places. That on all occasions ladies are admitted to these rooms in hats, not excepting the balls given to the Master of the Ceremonies. That the subscription balls will begin as soon as possible after 7 o'clock and concluded at 11, on account of the health of the company. It is earnestly requested that when a lady has gone down the dance she will be so polite as not to retire till it is concluded.

Bristol Hotwell became popular in the late seventeenth century, but by the late eighteenth century it was getting out of fashion—although the Irish and HEIC communities still favoured it. Hotwell was a summer resort and Bath a winter one, so that many traders moved their shops from Bath to catch the summer trade. The spa was also cheap—lodgings cost just 10 shillings a week and half price for servants.

As the resort increased in popularity, two assembly rooms, one boasting a 'man cook', were opened, in addition to the New Vauxhall pleasure gardens and Bristol's first theatre. So many visitors crowded into the pump rooms at the fashionable hours that there was little room for horses to be tethered. Terraces of houses were soon built with rooms to let, many of which still survive; Dowry Square and Albemarle Row are examples. As in Bath, a master of ceremonies was appointed to oversee the balls and dances.

The Prince Street assembly rooms further east were built in 1755. They were were designed by William Halfpenny; the façade was a compound of Palladian and Vanbrughian motifs, in limestone. The great room measured 84 feet in length and 34 feet in width and height, with outstanding acoustic qualities. The general scheme of decoration was designed on broad Palladian principles and a considerable use was made of Rococo interior ornamentation.

In the *Universal British Register*, the following was said of the Prince Street assembly rooms in Clifton:

> There are also two very large elegant public rooms; the one called the Old, or Upper Room; the other, which is opposite, is called the Lower or New Room. At these rooms are public breakfasts, during the season, every Monday and Thursday alternately, with cotillons and country dances, for which each person pays 1s. 6d. The balls are on Tuesdays; subscription for walking in the rooms and gardens, and reading the newspapers, is 5s. and for the balls one guinea; this at each room. Subscribers to the balls are allowed two tickets, which admit two ladies; not subscribers 5s. each ball.

It is unlikely that anything much had changed by the time the Witts family arrived in Clifton. In 1811 the venue became the Regency Theatre, to rival the Theatre Royal. It was later used by Great Western Railway, and then became a warehouse. It was finally demolished in 1956. A hotel now stands on the site.

1803: 31 Dec: *Made several visits with George: to the adorable Misses Price & Hughes; the sensible Jnr. Mc.Brides: the good assured Smiths; fulsome Mrs. Pennington: & the pleasant family of Mrs. Moncaster.*

1804: 31 Aug: *Walked in the Evening with Mr. Holmes & Ryan. At a dull card party at Mrs. Pennington's.* 14 Oct.

1805: 5 Feb: Called on the Townsend's & Pennington's. 29 Nov: *Accompanied my Mother & the Townsends to Ashe's Concert at Bristol, which was fully attended conversed chiefly with Mrs. Pennington & F. Daubeny.*

1806: 27 Feb: *In the Evening went early to Mrs. Pennington's much talked of assembly...... an immense crowd, heat intolerable & dancing very fatiguing; but every body resolved to be amused, four Rooms open; two for Cards; one for Dancing, another for retiring to: refreshments bad, served out some sandwiches & Porter after a considerable effort.* 1 Mar: *Walked to the Wells, called upon Mrs. Pennington.*

PENYSTON — Francis Penyston and the Penyston family of Cornwell, Oxfordshire [81]

Francis Penyston (1794-1828), JP and landed proprietor, was the son of Francis Penyston (1756-1827) and Rebecca (1756-1807), daughter of Ralph Assheton (1719-1759), of Downham and Cuerdale, and Rebecca (d. 1812), eldest daughter and co-heir of William Hulls, merchant, of London, Freelands, Kent, and Popes, Hertfordshire. Francis was educated at Eton College and Oriel College, Oxford (BA 1815). He became an Oxfordshire JP, and appears to have died childless.

Francis's parents, Francis and Rebecca Penyston, were friends of Edward and Agnes Witts. In her diary, Agnes mentioned some of the Penystons' children who did not survive. On 2 October 1788, she wrote, 'I went to pay a Lying in Visit to Mrs. Penyston all in grand form Miss Apleton with her, but it proved a very pleasant visit & a very nice little Girl....' And on 29 December 1788, 'Mr. Witts went to see Mr. Western, & found him much better much concern'd to hear of the death of Mr. Penystons little Girl'. A son was born the following year, and on 7 October 1789 Agnes wrote, 'I went to see Mrs. Penyston, who I found very pleasing & agreable, her little Boy was asleep so could not see him'. Francis and Rebecca Penyston had at least 6 daughters and 2 sons:

1 Mary (b. & d. 1788)
1 Thomas Fairmeadow (1789-1802)
2 Frances (1791-1873)
3 Harriot (1793-1840)
2 Francis (1794-1828); *see above*
4 Charlotte (1796-1822)
5 Jane (1798-1835)
6 Sophia (1802-1804)

It appears that none of the sisters married.

1823: 8 Jan: *Penyston 230108 Dined at Oddington with Lady Reade and Sir John. The usual showy display, & well lighted cheer. A large party as of old, Sir H. & Lady Dryden, Sir C. & Lady Imhoff, Mr. & Mrs. Lechmere, the Penystones &c.* 9 Dec: *We dined at Mr. & Mrs. Rice's, at Oddington Parsonage, meeting Mr. Penystone of Cornwell in Oxfordshire his son and daughter.*

1824: 27 Aug: *I attended a meeting at Halford Bridge Inn in Warwickshire of the proprietors of the Stratford & Moreton Rail road ...we met Mr. Langstone, of Sarsden, Oxon, M.P. for Woodstock, Mr. Penystone.* 9 Nov: *We dined at Mr. E. Leigh's at Broadwell, meeting Mr. Penyston of Cornwell, Oxon, his son & daughter.*

1825: 20 Sep., 4 Oct.

1826: 5 Jun: I dined at Mr. Twisleton's at Adlestrop ... the two Mr. Penystons. 18 Jul.

1827: 2 Oct.

1829: 4 Dec: *We dined at Mrs. Hastings's at Daylesford House, meeting a very pleasant party. There were five from Adlestrop .... two Miss Penystones.*

1833: 21 Jan: *Dined at Mrs. Hastings's, Daylesford House.... The Miss Penystons came to tea.*

1834: 23 Jul: *We met Sir John Reade, his Son and eldest daughter from Shipton Court. Mr. and Mrs. Arkwright, the Dean of Gloucester, the Misses Penystone, Mr. Winter, Miss Chapuset, and Mr. Vavasour were of the party.* 29 Jul: *To Daylesford, accompanied by Mr. Wellford, to dine at Mrs. Hastings's.... Miss Jane Penystone.... In the evening the party was joined by the Dean of Gloucester, his daughters Maria and Emma, and the other two Miss Penystones.*

1836: 27 Oct.

1837: 10 Oct.

1844: 1 May: *We met Sir C. and Lady Imhoff, Mr. and Mrs. Winter, Miss Penystone, Mr. Underwood, and Mr. and Mrs. Walters.* 4 Sep.,

1846: 11 Jul: *Drove with M.W. to call on the Winters at Daylesford, who were not at home. If afterwards appeared that Mrs. W. accompanied by Miss Penyston had drive to call on us, and we met them as we returned.*

1847: 6 Jul., 30 Sep.

1848: 11 Aug.

1850: 25 Jun.

1853: 10 Dec: *A note of invitation from Miss Penyston, to a dance on the 22d. Inst. at Cornwell.* 13 Dec:
With Mrs. W. Vavasour drove in the close carriage to Oddington, to dine with the Dean of Gloucester; where we met Miss Penyston.

PEPYS — Charles Christopher Pepys [82]

Charles Christopher Pepys, 1st earl of Cottenham, 1st Viscount Crowhurst (1781-1851), lord chancellor, was born in Wimpole Street, Cavendish Square, London, the second son of Sir William Weller Pepys, 1st baronet (1740-1825), master in chancery, and Elizabeth (1756-1830), eldest daughter of William Dowdeswell. His father, Sir William, was a distant relation, but not a descendant, of the diarist Samuel Pepys. Charles was educated at Harrow School and Trinity College, Cambridge, and called to the bar in 1804. He married, at St George the Martyr, Queen Square, Holborn, London, 30 June 1821, Caroline Elizabeth (1802-1868), daughter of William Wingfield (1772-1858) and Charlotte Mary Digby (1772-1807); they had fifteen children, including the following 4 sons and 7 daughters:

1 William John (1825-1881); succeeded as 3rd earl of Cottenham
1 Caroline (1827-1902)
2 Louisa (1828-1831)
2 Henry Leslie (1830-1891)
3 Lucy (b. 1834)
4 Adelaide (b. & d. 1834); died an infant
3 Frederick (1835-1874)

5 Elizabeth Theresa (1837-1897)
6 Evelyn (1839-1910)
4 Walter Courtenay (1840-1914)
7 Louisa (b. & d. 1843); died an infant

Pepys was appointed solicitor general in 1834, and in the same year became master of the rolls. Following Lord Melbourne's second administration in April 1835, Pepys was appointed lord chancellor in January 1836, and elevated to the peerage as Baron Cottenham, of Cottenham in the county of Cambridge. He held office until the ministry's defeat in 1841. In 1846 Pepys again became lord chancellor in Lord John Russell's administration. He succeeded his elder brother as 3rd baronet in 1845. In 1849 he also succeeded a cousin as 4th baronet of Juniper Hill. He resigned due to ill health in 1850. He was made earl of Cottenham and Viscount Crowhurst after his retirement.

1839: 6 May: *In the body of the House was the Lord Chancellor, with a few other Peers, and Sir John Campbell, the Attorney Genl. was addressing the House on what appeared to be a Scotch Appeal case, having reference to matters connected with the city of Glasgow.* 7 May.

1842: 15 Mar: *During this interval we recognized many persons of note—the Duke of Wellington, coming early as usual, sitting in a place which he always occupies, looking feeble, and evidently having lost his hearing on one side, occasionally conversing with other peers, very much with Lord Redesdale, but chiefly reading an act, or bill, or other document—Lords Brougham, Cottenham & Campbell, were present, making with Lord Lyndhurst a quartett of Chancellors past and present; we heard them all speak in presenting petitions, and Lord Cottenham delivered a written judgment.*

PERCEVAL — Dudley Perceval [83]

Dudley Montagu Perceval (1800-1856), deputy teller of the exchequer, was the sixth son of the assassinated prime minister Spencer Perceval (1762-1812) and Jane Wilson (1769-1844). He was educated at Harrow School and Christ Church, Oxford. Like his elder brother, Spencer, he was given free legal training at Lincoln's Inn, but was not called to the bar. He spent two years as an administrator at the Cape of Good Hope, where he married, at Cape Town, 24 July 1827, Mary Jane Bourke (1802-1888), daughter of the governor; they had 1 son and 1 daughter:

1 Charles Spencer (1829-1889), barrister-at-law
1 Isabelle Jane (1831-1921)

Perceval's duties were not onerous, nor was he much inconvenienced by his colonial exile, living, as he did, in the largely British-inhabited enclave of Wynberg, near the military camp. As he admitted to his brother, 'I go about & dine at two or three English homes, & play at whist or Billiards, & talk nonsense in politics, and take my ride in the afternoon & so forth, much as you would do at a small country town in England.'

Back in England Perceval obtained a Treasury post and defended his father's reputation after it was attacked in Napier's *History of the Peninsular War*. In 1853 he stood unsuccessfully against William Gladstone in the election for an MP to represent Oxford University.

1853: 5 Jan: *I also wrote to the Revd —T. Short, fellow of Trinity College, Oxford, Chairman of the Committee for conducting the election of Mr. Perceval, intimating my intentions of voting for that gentleman, as soon as my engagements would allow of my coming to Oxford.* 5-8 Jan., 18 Jan, 21 Jan., 23 Jan: The newspaper announces the success of Mr. Gladstone, who is in a majority of 124 above Perceval.

PERCY — Hugh Percy [84]

Hugh Percy (1784-1856), bishop of Carlisle, was the third son of Algernon, 1st earl of Beverley, and Isabella Susannah, second daughter of Peter Burrell of Beckenham, Kent. He was educated at Eton College and St John's, Cambridge (MA 1805; DD 1825), and entered the Church. Percy served as rector of Bishopsbourne, 1808-22; rector of Ivychurch, Kent, 1809-22; chancellor and prebendary of Exeter, 1810-16; chancellor of Salisbury Cathedral, 1812-56; prebendary of Canterbury, 1816-25; prebendary of St Paul's, 1816-56; archdeacon of Canterbury, 1822-25; dean of Canterbury, 1825-27; bishop of Rochester, 1827 (for a few months); and bishop of Carlisle, 1827-56.

Percy married, first, 1806, Mary, eldest daughter of Charles Manners Sutton, archbishop of Canterbury. He married secondly, 1840, Mary, daughter of Sir William Hope-Johnstone.

1827: 2 Jul: *After an unprecedented delay the vacant Bishopric of Rochester has at last been filled and by the same divine, whom the voice of common rumour has for many weeks assigned to the situation, the Hon. Dr. H. Percy, Dean of Canterbury, a brother, I believe, of Lord Louvaine.* 21 Sep: *The successor to the late Bishop of Carlisle is appointed in the person of the new Bishop of Rochester, Dr. Percy, who having held his see only two months, can have known little of it. He vacates only his Bishopric by his translation, for his deanery of Canterbury had been given to a brother of Lord Bagot.*

PERING — Benedict Pering [85]

Benedict Pering (±1783-1851), Church of England clergyman, was born at Exeter, son of Benedict Pering (±1750-1814), rector of St Mary Arches and St Olave, Exeter, and his wife, Sarah (1761-1837). He was educated at Wadham College, Oxford (BA 1805; MA 1810), where he was a fellow from 1812 to 1817. Pering appears to have obtained his first curacy at North Walsham, Norfolk, in June 1808. At the time of his death he was rector of Fersfield, Norfolk, having been appointed to the living in 1843, and rector of Dawlish, Devon. In the 1851 census he was registered as living at Newton Abbott, Devon, with his wife, Mary Carter (b. ±1787); they had married at Beccles in 1817. Apart from these few facts, little is known of Benedict Pering. It seems odd that after a warm friendship in the first year of college, his acquaintance with Francis Witts virtually ceased. It may have been that Pering was simply not in attendance at college, but it is more likely that they simply drifted into other friendships. Certainly there are no later diary entries that make reference to Pering.

1802: 10 Feb: *Dined with Mr. Mitchell, meeting there Messrs. Perrin & Williams Scholars of Wadham.*

11 Feb: *Breakfasted with Pering called upon Mrs. Wall employed in arranging my Rooms.... Perrin accompanied me to the Kitchen & introduced me to the Hall, where at the Commoners Table, I dined very comfortably at three o'clock. Spent the Evening at the King's Arms; sitting for an half an Hour with Pering before Prayers at nine.* 14 Feb: *At Pering's, meeting Evans, Powell of Exeter Coll., Edgell, Hastings, Rashley, Davis, & Williams.* 20 Feb., 26 Feb., 5 Mar: *Walked with Stevens. Pering spent the Evening with me.* 6 Mar: *Breakfasted with Pering & walked with him, gathering fossils to the furthest Extremity of Shotover Hill.* 12 Mar: *Walked with Pering.* 28 Mar: *Breakfasted with Pering &c.* 29 Mar: *Walked with Pering to Godstowe & Whiteham.* 1 May, 2 May, 4 May, 6 May, 7 May: *Breakfasted with Pering. Walked with Pering on the banks of the Canal. Sat with him after Supper.* 8 May: *Pering*

breakfasted with me. called on Hastings. Sat with Pering after dinner accompanied him to Mr. Kidd's Lecture on the fluoric acid & the Vegetable acids. Stevens & myself supped with Pering. 9-10 May, 14-15 May, 20-21 May, 5-7 Jun., 9 Jun., 12 Jun., 14-16 Jun., 19 Jun: *Had a few of my intimates with me Evans, Edgell, Pering &c.* 23 Jun., 4-5 Jul., 25 Jul.

1803: 22 Nov.

1804: 5 Feb., 19 Mar.

PERKINS — Duncombe Steele-Perkins — *see also* Charles Crawley[86]

Duncombe Steele-Perkins (1795-1882), Church of England clergyman, was born at Sutton Coldfield, Warwickshire, the son of Shirley Farmer Steele-Perkins (1768-1852) and Elizabeth (d. 1801), daughter of Joseph Duncombe of Sutton-Coldfield. He was educated at Trinity College, Oxford (BA 1820), and was appointed curate of Broadway, Worcestershire, and rector of Clifton, Leicestershire. The vicar at Broadway was Charles Crawley, another acquaintance of Francis Witts.

Perkins married Ann Gist (b. ±1794); they had at least 1 son and 1 daughter:

1 Ann Gist (1833-1833)
1 Duncombe (1838-1905), doctor of medicine

The couple lived later at Orton-on-the-Hill, Leicestershire.

1825: 14 Mar: *We found Mrs. Moncell from Cheltenham an inmate, and the circle at dinner was increased by the addition of Mr. Eddy, the Rector of Toddington & his daughter, Mr. Perkins, Curate of Broadway, & Mr. F. Aston.* 15 Mar: *Mr. Eddy and Mr. Perkins left Stanway, and Miss Hughes arrived from Cheltenham.*

1827: 4 Dec: *Mr. and Mrs. Perkins dined here; they reside at Farmcombe in the parish of Broadway, of which he is the Curate; she was Mr. Gist's eldest daughter, an amiable person: the current of their loves did not run smooth, but at length the Lady's friends consented to the union, which for all I can see, was suitable enough, though Mr. P. is neither well looking nor elegant.* 6 Dec: *We called at Wormington Grange. I accompanied Miss Kinloch, Mrs. Penfold and my wife in Lady Elcho's coach. We were received by Mrs. Perkins.*

1844: 21 Feb: *The members of the family attendg. as mourners were Mr. Gist, Lord Rossmore, and his brother, Col. Westenra, brothers of the deceased sister lady, Mr. Perkins and Mr. W. Young, who had married sisters of Mr. Gist, and Mr. W. Gist, the brother.*

PERKINS — Frederick David Perkins[87]

Frederick David Perkins (1792-1856), Church of England clergyman, was born in Devon, the son of Revd John David Perkins (1764-1845) and Bridget Maria Jane Northcote (1763-1835). He was educated at Brasenose College, Oxford (BA 1814; MA 1825), and entered the Church. He was appointed vicar of Stoke with Sowe, Warwickshire, in 1817, rector of Swayfield, Lincolnshire, in 1820, and rector of Down Hatherley, Gloucestershire, in 1827. Perkins was chaplain to King William IV and later to Queen Victoria between 1830 and 1856.

1837: 26 Jul: *Dined at the Pole's, at Wyck Hill; meeting Sir Charles & Lady Imhoff, with Miss Chapuset, and the Revd. F. D. Perkins, a Clergyman beneficed near Coventry, a King's Chaplain, and a Magistrate.* 28 Jul: *Rode after breakfast by appointment to Stow, to meet Mr. Perkins, the Clergyman whom I named as a guest at Wyck Hill on Wednesday. He is much interested in the administration of the Poor Law Amendment Act, as an Ex. off Guardian in the Union of Foleshill in North Warwickshire, and being an advocate at his Board for discontinuing the use of two ill adapted old Workhouses, hired by the Union, and for erecting one new Workhouse on the approved plan, was desirous of inspecting ours at Stow.*

PERKINS — John Perkins[88]

John Perkins (1776-1849), wine merchant and servant at Wadham College, Oxford, married, at Witney, 1798, Elizabeth (1774-1852), daughter of Edward and Mary Higgins; they had 2 sons and 6 daughters:

1 Elizabeth (1800-1867)
1 John (1803-1850); *see below*
2 Sarah (1804-1879); died unmarried
3 Mary Ann (1807-1808); died an infant
2 William Francis (1809-1889), bailiff at Oxford University; died unmarried
4 Harriet (1811-1818); died a young child
5 Mary Ann (1814-1833)
6 Maria (1817-1897); died unmarried

John Perkins was a college attendant at Wadham, and as such he looked after Francis Witts. The two men respected each other and maintained contact. Perkins' younger son, William, became one of Francis Witts's godsons.

1804: 2 Oct: *Heard from Perkins. Wrote to him & to Mr. Travell.*

1829: 26 Feb: *After tea & coffee I returned to my lodging between ten and eleven o clock, but not without looking in at John Perkins's in Broad Street, and asking after the health of his wife & family. This worthy man, once my attendant at College, by industry and good conduct has greatly risen in the world; though still a College servant, he carries on the trade of a Wine-merchant; his eldest Son, a Chorister of Magdalen first, then Servitor of Christ Church, is now a Clergyman, and resides in Scotland as domestic chaplain to the Earl of Galloway; his second Son, my godson, having served his time with a surgeon & apothecary at Abingdon, is going up to London to complete his medical studies.*

1833: 12 Sep: *A letter from John Perkins Senr. to announce that he had packed up and sent by waggon to Upper Slaughter my Son's books &c. from Magdalen Hall.*

1836: 14 Aug: *Before breakfast a visit from John Perkins Senr. who had driven his son, and two daughters to Stow yesterday.*

1839: 5 Jun: *Left home with Perkins, in my open carriage attended by my servant, for Oxford, before 7 o cl. A.M: took the road by Burford and Witney: breakfasted at the latter place; and reached Oxford soon after one o clock. Drove to Perkins Senr. in Broad Street, where I was very hospitably received, and found a sleeping room prepared for me as well as for John Perkins.* 6 Jun., 6 Jul., 7 Jul: *John Perkins Senr. attended at morning Service.* 9-10 Jul., 11 Jul: *The Perkins family had called, and partaken of luncheon at Upper Slaughter Rectory.* 9 Aug.

1840: 30 Aug: *John Perkins Senr., now visiting his son at L Swell, called with a parcel of German wool, which his daughter had procured for MW. from at Oxford.*

1842: 13 Jul: *John Perkins Senr. looked in on me in the evening respecting some transaction as to wine with my Son.*

1844: 8 Oct: *At Oxford, after a circuit to the Railroad station to deposit those who were travelling to London, we were set down at the Star Coach Office, from whence I proceeded, accompanied by Perkins and Vavasour, to Wadham College, where my old rooms of forty years since had been prepared for me,—a kind attention as to the choice of room which had been managed by J. Perkins, Senr.*

1845: 13-14 Feb., 23 Jun: *Returned home by Lower Swell and Eyford: called at the former place on the Perkins's, where we found their friends from Oxford on a visit—Mr. & Mrs. Perkins Senr.* 29 Jun: *The elder Perkins, now on a visit to his son at Lower Swell, came to church here, and called on us afterwards.*

1846: 14 Jul: *In the evening Miss S. Perkins called, and drank tea with us. She is at present visiting her brother at Lower Swell, whose wife and child are visiting their relations at Ryde.* 24 Aug: *Mr. and Mrs. Perkins, with his daughter, and sister Maria called upon us, and partook of refreshment here; they walked about our village &c. and I accompanied them on their way home.*

1847: 11 Jul: *After evening service John Perkins Senior called; and sat for an hour with us after dinner: he and his aged wife are now visiting their son at Upper Swell; the old man is much broken, slightly paralytic; his mind somewhat weakened, bursting into tears on accosting an old friend.*

1848: 29 Apr: *J. Perkins called, accompanied by his father and daughter. He has recovered greatly from his late attack The old man is very much broken, and feeble both in body and mind.* 3 May: *Visited him & his wife, his father and mother, and sister: J.P. Junr. continues in the same state of health as when we met lately: the old man is very declining.*

PERKINS — John Perkins — *see also* Green [89]

John Perkins (1803-1850), Church of England clergyman, was born at Oxford, the son of John Perkins (above). Through the good influence of his father he matriculated in 1820 as servitor at Christ Church, Oxford (BA 1824; MA 1827), receiving free accommodation, some free meals, and exemption from lecture fees. At Oxford, servitors were originally expected to act as servants to the fellows of their college, but by 1852 this requirement had fallen largely into disuse.

Having graduated from Oxford, Perkins was ordained deacon on 21 May 1826 and priest on 10 June 1827. He was appointed, 21 December 1832, by the dean and chapter of the Cathedral Church of Christ in Oxford, vicar of Lower Swell. He held the living until his death. As Francis Witts explains in his diary, he was previously a domestic chaplain to George Stewart, the earl of Galloway (1768-1834), a rear admiral in the Royal Navy.

Perkins married Eliza (b. 1807), daughter of William and Mary Green of Gosport, Hampshire; they had 1 daughter:

1 Eliza (1835-1895); married John Taylor (b. ±1834), bookseller; at least 1 son and 3 daughters:
    1 John Mancie (b. ±1862)
    1 Florence E. (b. ±1863)
    2 Alice Mary (b. ±1865)
    3 Ellen Rose (b. ±1866)

In the 1871 census Perkins' widow and daughter were both registered living in the same house in Blackheath, south London, with John Taylor, his daughter's husband, and four of their children. Also living there was Mary Green, aged 84, probably Eliza's mother. Eliza's elder sister was Martha Ellyett Green (b. 1795).

1829: 26 Feb: ... *his eldest Son, a Chorister of Magdalen first, then Servitor of Christ Church, is now a Clergyman, and resides in Scotland as domestic chaplain to the Earl of Galloway; his second Son, my godson, having served his time with a surgeon & apothecary at Abingdon, is going up to London to complete his medical studies.*

1833: 12 Jan: *The Revd. J. Perkins arrived from Oxford... I inducted him into the Vicarage of Lower Swell, to which he has recently been presented by the Dean and Chapter of Christ Church, the vacancy occurring by the demise of the late Vicar, The Revd. C. Sandby. Mr. J. P. was servitor or Bible Clerk of Ch. Ch. having received his previous education at Magdalen College School, where he was a Chorister.* 14 Jan: *Mr. Perkins had been engaged in the forenoon, looking over the Vicarial land at Lower Swell, and endeavouring to come to an arrangement with the old tenant, J. Merchant, as to its future occupation by him: but no definite agreement was made.*

1834: 30 Jul., 5 Aug.

1836: 20 Sep: *A call from John Perkins Junr. who had come from Oxford to Lower Swell, accompanied by Mr. Underwood, an Architect, to select on the Vicarage land a site for a Parsonage which he proposes to begin building with funds obtained from Queen Ann's bounty, the Pincot Charity, the Dean & Chapter of Christ Church &c.*

1837: 16 May, 8 Jul: *Recd. a letter from John Perkins Junr. to acquaint me that the Chapter of Christ Church had given him a further sum of £100 in aid of his intention of building a Vicarage House at Lower Swell, and that he is about to borrow £200 from the Governors of Queen Anne's Bounty, and requesting me with W. B. Pole to become Commissioners for making enquiries respecting dilapidations.* 9 Jul., 12 Jul: *Recd. a letter from J. Perkins requesting me to certify that the land on which he purposes to build the Vicarage house at Lower Swell is a part of the land appertaining to the Vicar, in right of the Benefice.* 13 Jul., 8 Aug.

1838: 25 Jan: *Before returning with my Son had an interview, at the Unicorn Inn, with John Perkins, who had come from Oxford this morning, accompanied by his Architect, Mr. Underwood, to make arrangements with Clifford, the Builder, who has contracted for the erection of his parsonage about to be built at Lower Swell.* 24 Jul: *A morning visit from J. Perkins Junr. who with his wife and Father came to Stow yesterday Even. to see the progress made in the Erection of his new Vicarage House at Lower Swell, which is in great forwardness, roofed, and will be ready for his residence early in next Spring.* 17 Aug., 21-22 Aug., 4-5 Oct.

1839: 26 Mar: *Rode to Stow; called by the way at L Swell, where saw Perkins, who arrived yesterday to take up his abode at his new Vicarage, bringing his furniture &c. from Oxford.* 27 Mar: *John Perkins, V. of Lower Swell, came to dine & spend the evening with us en famille.* 2 Apr., 4 Apr: *Rode to Stow: joined, at Lower Swell, Perkins, his sister, and little girl, with whom walked as far as to the Spa.* 20 Apr: *Drove MW. by Eyford to Lower Swell to call on Mrs. Perkins, whom we found at home with her husband's youngest sister: Perkins himself gone to Oxford, his duties as one of the chaplains of Carfax Church requiring his presence there to-morrow.* 30 Apr., 1 May, 11 May, 13 May, 15 May: *About twelve o cl. Perkins and his sister came from L Swell—and remained to luncheon—the former bringing his gun, and making some havoc in our rookery.* 23 May, 1 Jun: *Drove MW. to Lower Swell to call on the Perkins's. Arranged with JP. that we should travel together in my open carriage on Wednesday next, to Oxford, to vote at the election for a professor of Logic: returned by Eyford, bringing with us Maria Perkins and her niece, the Vicar's darling little girl.* 4 Jun., 5 Jun: *Left home with Perkins, in my open carriage attended by my servant, for Oxford, before 7 o cl. A.M: took the road by Burford and Witney: breakfasted at the latter place; and reached Oxford soon after one o clock. Drove to Perkins Senr. in Broad Street, where I was very hospitably received, and found a sleeping room prepared for me as well as for John Perkins.* 6 Jun., 16 Jun., 6-7 Jul., 9-11 Jul., 24 Jul., 2 Aug., 9 Aug., 21-22 Aug., 25 Aug.

1840: 4 Apr: *Mr. and Mrs. Perkins, accompanied by their little girl paid us a morning visit.* 18 Apr., 21 Apr: *Rode to Stow; on my*

way called on Perkins, and settled with him as to the service of my Church on Sunday next; he has undertaken to do my duty as well as his own and W B Pole's, without calling Winter to aid. 12 May, 14 May: *Home to dinner before six o clock; soon after which hour Mr. Perkins came for the sport of rook-shooting in our pleasure ground, and remained with us till after tea time, when I accompanied him homeward.* 25 May, 18 Jun., 25 Jun., 10 Jul., 13 Jul: *After an early dinner drove by Eyford to drink tea with the Perkins's at the Vicarage, Lower Swell; where we found besides Miss Perkins, Mrs. P's elder sister, Miss Green.* 16 Jul., 19 Jul., 23 Jul., 30 Jul., 18 Aug: *Walked to Lower Swell; called on John Perkins, who walked home with me, but did not come in.* 20 Aug., 25 Aug., 30 Aug., 10 Sep., 15 Oct., 24 Oct., 24 Nov:
E.F. W. sent his servant over with a parcel, and to Lower Swell for a little pig given him by Perkins. 28 Nov.

1841: 4 Mar.

1842: 9 Jan: *Recd. a note from Perkins, requesting me to fix the hour at which I would officiate for him on Sunday next at Lower Swell, agreeably to a promise I had made to him.* 15 Jan., 3 Feb., 10 Feb., 10 Feb., 25 Feb., 3-4 Mar., 5 Mar: *Walked to Lower Swell to visit the Church there, which is amply sufficient for the population, it was newly pewed, and enlarged in 1829: Perkins accompanied me, and I took luncheon at his house.* 24 Mar., 21 Apr., 27 Apr., 2 May, 12 May, 21 May, 23 May, 1 Jun: A dinner party. 15 Jun., 23 Jun., 7 Jul., 20 Jul: *With Wellford walked to Lower Swell and back; partook of luncheon with J Perkins, visited his church &c.* 21-23 Jul., 25 Jul., 27-29 Jul., 4 Aug., 11 Aug: *Rode to Stow Called at Perkins's, saw him and his Brother William: Perkins promised to perform one service for me on Sunday next at Slaughter.* 14 Aug., 25 Aug., 1 Sep: *I put my shoulder to the wheel, and the work being done, left Stow very late for home, John Perkins walking by the side of my horse as far as to his own premises.* 22 Sep., 3 Nov., 16 Nov., 20 Nov., 22 Nov., 19 Dec., 20 Dec: *I wrote to Perkins requesting his attendance at that hour, and his company afterwards at dinner.* 28 Dec.

1843: 9 Feb., 14 Aug., 16 Aug., 20 Aug., 17 Sep., 22 Sep: *Called on J Perkins; saw him and his wife; thanked him for his kind clerical assistance during my absence at Brighton.* 11 Nov., 16-17 Nov., 23 Nov.

1844: 8 Feb., 17 Apr: *Perkins is the President of the Club for the year.* 20 Apr., 2 May, 16 May, 25 Jul., 29 Jul., 1 Aug., 22 Aug., 29 Aug., 4-6 Sep., 18-19 Sep., 3 Oct., 8 Oct: *After a very early breakfast, set out for Oxford—to the foot of Stow hill in E.F.W.'s carriage—there met the "Wonder" Coach—to Oxford with Genl. E. Lygon, Mr. Pole, and J. Perkins inside—outside passengers, bound on the same errand as myself.* 11 Oct., 24 Oct., 31 Oct., 7 Nov., 14 Nov., 21 Nov., 5 Dec., 11-12 Dec., 16 Dec., 19 Dec., 26 Dec.

1845: 21 Jan., 23 Jan., 27 Jan., 30 Jan., 6 Feb., 13 Feb., 20 Feb., 13 Mar., 26 Mar., 31 Mar., 24 Apr., 1 May, 12 May, 26 May, 19 Jun., 25-26 Jun., 29 Jun.,

1846: 14 Jul: *In the evening Miss S. Perkins called, and drank tea with us. She is at present visiting her brother at Lower Swell, whose wife and child are visiting their relations at Ryde.* 24 Jul., 3-4 Aug., 18 Aug., 24 Aug: *Mr. and Mrs. Perkins, with his daughter, and sister Maria called upon us, and partook of refreshment here; they walked about our village &c. and I accompanied them on their way home.* 3 Sep., 17 Sep., 29 Oct., 5 Nov., 12-13 Nov., 19 Nov., 26 Nov., 3 Dec., 9-10 Dec.

1847: 25 Jan., 28 Jan., 12 Feb., 17 Feb., 25 Mar., 1 Apr., 8 Apr., 29 Apr., 20 May, 24 May: *Drove to Lower Swell: called on the Perkins's: much conversation with him as to Mr. Hunt, the Auditor ...* 27 May, 24 Jun., 30 Jun., 22 Jul., 30 Jul: *Wrote to J. Perkins, now at Oxford, requesting him to pay for me a bill I owe to Randal, Hatter.* 5-6 Aug., 19 Aug., 21 Aug., 25 Aug: *invited to meet his Lordship were .... Messrs. Perkins and Potter.* 31 Aug., 2 Sep., 7 Sep., 14 Oct.

1848: 20 Jan., 7 Mar., 25 Mar: *Wrote to Mrs. Perkins a note of enquiry as to the health of her husband, of whom I had been informed that he had experienced a paralytic stroke on Monday last.* 26 Mar: *Received a note from Mrs. J. Perkins: her husband is gradually and slowly recovering.* 4 Apr: *Walked to Lower Swell, and called on Perkins, whom I saw, as also his wife and daughter. Perkins is more recovered from his late attack than I had expected; his speech is articulate.* 14 Apr., 29 Apr: *J. Perkins called, accompanied by his father and daughter. He has recovered greatly from his late attack The old man is very much broken, and feeble both in body and mind.* 3 May: *Visited him & his wife, his father and mother, and sister: J.P. Junr. continues in the same state of health as when we met lately: the old man is very declining.* 29 May, 12 Jun:
E.F.W. accompanied me in a walk to Lower Swell, to call on J. Perkins. We found him languid and feeble. 19 Aug: *Called at Lower Swell, on John Perkins, whom I found much in the same state as when I saw him last, weak, and unequal to much exertion.* 5 Oct., 9 Nov.

1850: 29 Jan: *I should have mentioned on Sunday a kind visit received by me from W. Perkins and his niece ... I am happy to say they were able to give a comfortable report of the state of the worthy Vicar of Lower Swell, who has been for the past week in a very precarious state from an attack of Typhus fever; he is now pronounced out of danger.* 1 Mar: *I walked to the Vicarage at Lower Swell, to enquire after the health of John Perkins: saw Mrs. Perkins, and sat with her for a short time. P. is yet very weak; though convalescent, not able to do the duties of his church.* 18 Apr: *Death has again been busy in our vicinity—Poor John Perkins, V. of Lower Swell, paid the debt of nature yesterday: he had been of a delicate & feeble constitution for several years, crippled by paralysis for more than a twelvemonth, and failing ever since this year opened, so that Mr. Hayward had long anticipated a fatal issue, and it appeared doubtful, whether the fatal dart would be first hurled in the Vicarage at Lower Swell, or in the Rectory at Upper Slaughter. He was in many respects an estimable person, familiarized to me by an acquaintance begun in his boyhood. He leaves a widow, and one daughter not grown up not in ample circumstances.* 30 Apr., 2 May, 11 Jun: *Called on Mrs. Perkins, whom I saw, as also her daughter.* 5 Jul: *A letter from Mr. Oakely Hill, Bledington, bringing under my notice the case of poor Mrs. Perkins, who, it seems, is left with an income not exceeding £60 per ann. for the support of her daughter and herself, and requesting advice and assistance so as to procureing for her an allowance from the Clerical Charity of this diocese.* 6 Jul: *To Mr. O. Hill, expressing regret that Mrs. Perkins is so slenderly provided for; advising an application for the Clerical Charity through the Rural dean, and suggesting that, if it would suit her views, she is eligible to a house in Mrs. Edwards's College at South Cerney.* 12 Jul: *Mrs. Perkins and her sister called on me to take my advice as to several points — the proving of her late husband's will—application for relief from the County Clergy Charity fund of the diocese &c.* 17 Jul: *A note from Mrs. Perkins, announcing her intention of calling on me to-morrow at half past ten AM. to meet Mr. Morgan; I suppose, to prove her late husband's will. Replied that I should be ready to receive her.* 18 Jul., 19 Jul: *Mrs. Perkins and her sister, Miss Green, also came by appointment to meet Mr. Morgan, the Solicitor, of Stow, who brought with him a commission, in virtue of which I administered to her the customary oaths preliminary to probate of her late husband's will.* 24 Jul: *Wrote to E.F.W, sending my letter by the waggoner who came from Stanway with a load of coal: threw out an enquiry whether Sophy would wish me to purchase the cottage Piano-forte to be sold at Mrs. Perkins's sale next week.* 26 Jul: *A letter from Mrs. Perkins, who sends me £3. 12 in discharge of an account for newspapers supplied to her late husband which had been paid by Mr. Jennings.* 26 Jul: *Received a letter from Mrs. Perkins with further particulars as to her income, which will be increased beyond her expectations by family arrangements.*

PERKINS — William Francis Perkins [90]

William Francis Perkins (1809-1889), bailiff at the University of Oxford, was born at Oxford, the younger son of John Perkins (*above*). He was the godson of Francis Witts and named after him, but there was little intimacy between them. Contrary to the diary entry for 26 February 1829, Perkins does not seem to have completed his medical studies in London, or if he did he did not practise for long. He returned to Oxford, and by 1861 he had become a bailiff at the university. He lived at 62 Holywell Street with his unmarried sisters Sarah and Maria. He died unmarried.

1829: 26 Feb: *After tea & coffee I returned to my lodging between ten and eleven o clock, but not without looking in at John Perkins's in Broad Street, and asking after the health of his wife & family. This worthy man, once my attendant at College, by industry and good conduct has greatly risen in the world; though still a College servant, he carries on the trade of a Wine-merchant; his eldest Son, a Chorister of Magdalen first, then Servitor of Christ Church, is now a Clergyman, and resides in Scotland as domestic chaplain to the Earl of Galloway; his second Son, my godson, having served his time with a surgeon & apothecary at Abingdon, is going up to London to complete his medical studies.*

1842: 11 Aug: *Rode to Stow Called at Perkins's, saw him and his Brother William: Perkins promised to perform one service for me on Sunday next at Slaughter.*

1850: 29 Jan: *I should have mentioned on Sunday a kind visit received by me from W. Perkins and his niece ... I am happy to say they were able to give a comfortable report of the state of the worthy Vicar of Lower Swell, who has been for the past week in a very precarious state from an attack of Typhus fever; he is now pronounced out of danger.* 30 Apr: *Wrote to W. Perkins a letter of condolence on the death of his brother.* 2 May: *also a very proper and kind letter from W. F. Perkins in answer to that which I had written to him of Tuesday last.* 25 Sep: *To W. F. Perkins, Oxford, with a bill for newspapers supplied to the Perkins's of Lower Swell &c., which the Newspaper agent had presented to Mr. Jennings for payment.*

PERING — Allen Pering, agent to the Clothworkers Company [91]

Allen Pering (±1776-1866), solicitor, was the son of Thomas Pering of Dartmouth, Devon. He was also probably a close relation of Allen Pering (b. 1717) and another Allen Pering who had married, at Stoke Damerel, Devon, 8 December 1768, Sarah Patrick.

Pering was articled to attorney Richard Preston, of Dartmouth, on 16 December 1791, and later moved to London where he was admitted to the Freedom of the City of London on 2 September 1800. He practised as Pering & Co., solicitors, 5 Laurence Pountney Place, City of London, and Clothworkers Hall, 41 Mincing Lane, solicitor and clerk to the Cloth Workers Company. He lived at Norwood, Surrey.

1840: 29 Nov: *Received a letter from Mr. Jennings, inclosing copies of letters from Mr. Perring, Agent to the Clothworkers Company, to Messrs. Parker and Warter, and of the latter to Mr. Jennings; by which it appears that the Clothworkers offer £8100 for our premises in Fenchurch Street.*

1842: 15 Mar., 17 Mar: *Mr. A. Pering, as Solr. to the Clothworkers Company proved the agreement entered into by him with my Son and myself on the part of the Company and the approval of the contract by the Court of Exchequer on behalf of the Company.*

PERROTT — George Wigley Perrott [92]

George Wigley Perrott (1785-1831), JP and landed proprietor, was the son of George Perrott (d. 1806), of Pershore, Worcestershire, and Jane Wigley (1764-1835). He married, 1808, Charlotte Louisa Elizabeth, daughter of Joseph Yates (1764-1820), of Peel Hall, Lancaster, and Charlotte St John (1763-1803); they had at least 4 sons and 1 daughter:

1 Edmund Thomas Wigley (±1810-1851)
2 Robert (1812-1831); died at sea
3 William Stafford (1813-1865); educated at Queen's College, Oxford; went to Australia; returned and died at Fladbury
4 Henry (±1814-1882)
1 Anna Maria Louisa (1816-1868); married, at Leamington Spa, Warwickshire, 8 October 1844, Richard Rose (1821-1901)

1823: 14 Mar., 25 Apr: *Dr. Warneford and myself dined and slept at Cracomb four miles beyond Evesham, in the parish of Fladbury, on the upper road to Worcester, the seat of Mr. Perrot....—I should have mentioned Mrs. Perrot sooner: she appears to be a person of very considerable talent & extensive acquirements; she is now busy in preparing a work on the Ornithology of Worcestershire to be published in parts with an expensive series of portraits of the different birds illustrated by a scientific and interesting account of their habits &c. The drawings (we saw above 50 of them), are remarkably well executed. Mrs. Perrot is a proficient in Music, appears to have a great talent for conversation & activity of mind, devoting herself to the education of her family of four boys & a girl, & competent to superintend the classical studies of the former.* 26 Apr.

1826: 1 Aug: *To the right the view is bounded by a range of low hills, on the side of which is Cracombe, the seat of Mr. Perrot, whose hospitalities I once enjoyed, and beneath the high sloping ground are the villages of Fladbury & Cropthorne.*

1829: 24 Nov.

PERROTT — Thomas Perrott [93]

Thomas Perrott (±1770-1850), lieutenant-colonel of the Oxfordshire Militia, married, at Glympton Park, Oxfordshire, 26 February 1811, Anne Morgan Davies (1788-1872), only daughter of Rhys Davies (±1756-1809), solicitor, of Kythellyd, Glamorganshire. The Perrotts only stayed for a short period at Adlestrop; little has been discovered about them other than their marriage in 1811, which was widely reported. Perrott had long been involved in the Oxfordshire Militia; he was promoted to major in 1803, and in his will he proudly claimed to be a lieutenant-colonel. He and Anne were childless. They lived later at Rodney House, Clifton.

According to Francis Witts's diary entry for 10 February 1835, Miss Anne Davies had been brought up by Elizabeth Way (1765-1846), née Western, the widow of Sackville Lloyd (1762-1812), who assumed the additional surname Wheate on inheriting the Glympton Park estate. This would explain why Anne married Thomas Perrott at Glympton. There was presumably a Lloyd and Davies connection, but this has not yet been discovered. A confusing factor is that there is no such place as Kythellyd, Glamorganshire, where Anne's father Rhys Davies was registered as a solicitor. Apparently it should have been Cathylyd [Rhyndwyglydach Lower], but this does not clarify matters. The Berrington estate papers in the Glamorgan Archive Service probably hold more detail.

1829: 24 Nov: *Mr. Cartwright next proposed that the Aynho branch should be disunited, and was seconded by Col. Perrot, of Sandford Park, Lieut. Col. of the Oxford Militia, a very respectable gentleman & Magistrate resident on the line of road....*

1833: 29 Oct: *Proceeded to Adlestrop to call on Col. & Mrs. Perrott recently come to reside there: they formerly rented Sandford House in Oxfordshire, and are much esteemed. He is Lieut. Col. of the Oxfordshire Militia. They have a good fortune, but no family.*

1834: 31 Oct: *Mrs. Witts and myself dined with Mr. & Mrs. Perrot at Adlestrop. Edward did not accompany us, having been obliged to leave his portmanteau to follow him from Prinknash, which had not arrived.*

1835: 10 Feb: *Drove Mrs. Witts to Adlestrop to call on the Perrots: but were not admitted: Mr. Perrot being confined to his room by indisposition.* 21 Feb., 25 Feb: *With Mrs. Witts & my Son dined at Adlestrop at Mr. Perrots; a very agreeable party. We met the Revd. Mr. & Mrs. Way of Glympton Park, Oxon, Captain Leigh, and Mr. & Mrs. Whitmore Jones. Mrs. Way was widow of Mr. Lloyd, nephew and heir of Misses Wheate, singular old maiden ladies, proprietors of the Glympton Estate... Mrs. Perrot, whose maiden name was Davis, was brought up by Mrs. Way. The latter lady had been in former years intimate in the family of my Uncle, Ferdinand Travell: of course we had many topics of conversation.*

1836: 4 Oct:

PERRY — John George Perry[94]

John George Perry (1802-1870), inspector of prisons for the home department, was born in London or the London area. He received his education at St Bartholomew's Hospital and established himself in practice as a surgeon in Great James Street, Bedford Row, where he resided for several years. Sir Benjamin Brodie, his former tutor, being on intimate terms with the home secretary Sir James Graham, recommended Perry as a candidate to fill the vacancy of inspector of prisons. Perry was reportedly not a man of outstanding talent, but he was a thorough man of business, industrious, and methodical. He was a man 'well up' in practice, and of unassuming and urbane manners.

In the 1861 census Perry was listed as being married to Elizabeth (b. ±1811), and living at 12 Westbourne Street, just off Bayswater Road, London.

1844: 13 Jan: *The latter course was insisted upon by Mr. Barneby, in conformity with the opinion held by Sir James Graham, on the report of Mr. Perry, an inspector of Prisoners.*

1850: 7 Aug: *Dr. Evans, the leading physician of Gloucester, an eminent and talented man, made a very interesting report as to the sanitary state of the Gaol & its inmates, rebutting the assertions of the Prison Inspector, Mr. Perry, in a late report to the Secretary of State.*

PETERS — John William Peters[95]

John William Peters (1791-1861), JP and Church of England clergyman, was born in London, the eldest son of Revd Matthew William Peters (1741-1814) and Margaret Susannah Knowsley (b. 1757). His father was prebendary of Lincoln and rector of Knipton, Leicestershire, and Woolsthorpe, Lincolnshire. Peters was educated at Sidney College, Cambridge (BA 1814; MA 1817), and was ordained deacon on 25 September 1814 and priest on 9 July 1815. His first clerical appointment was as stipendiary curate of Coston, Leicestershire, from 25 September 1814. He was next appointed curate of Southrop, Gloucestershire, on 25 May 1819, and then rector of Quenington on 2 January 1823. He served at Quenington until 6 March 1834. He was also appointed to the curacies of Ampney St Mary and Ampney St Peter.

Peters married, first, Catherine (1801-1846), daughter of Sampson Colclough of Baconfield, Newark; they had at least 4 sons and 2 daughters:

1 Margaret Ann (1817-1896)
1 John (1819-1904)
2 Edmund Henry (1820-1904)
2 Mary Ann (1823-1872)
3 Christopher (b. 1824)
4 Samuel (1835-1911)

Peters married, secondly, Mary (1813-1856), daughter of Richard Bowly of Cirencester. Mary contributed several hymns to the Plymouth Brethren's *Psalms, Hymns and Spiritual Songs*. John Peters seceded from the Church of England in 1834.

1828: 14 Oct: *After breakfast I proceeded to Gloucester, being fortunate enough to meet with a conveyance in the little Phaeton of an acquaintance & magistrate, the Revd. Mr. Peters of Quenington, who was going also to the Sessions for the first time, I believe, since he qualified to act. Ill health had prevented him at an earlier period, he having suffered for two years past from derangement of the Stomach or other viscera. He is a mild, gentlemanlike, sensible person.*

PETERS — Thomas Peters[96]

Thomas Peters (1812-1890), Church of England clergyman, was born at Hindley, Lancashire, the son of Ralph Peters (1775-1838) and Frances Blackburne (1784-1845). He was educated at Rugby School and St Alban Hall, Oxford (BA 1835). Peters was rector and patron of Eastington, Gloucestershire. He married, 1840, Frances Curtis Hayward (±1812-1890); they had at least 1 son and 1 daughter:

1 Frances Elizabeth (1842-1905)
1 Ralph Entwistle (1843-1874)

1848: 27 Jun: *Several new magistrates qualified ——Mr. Peters, Incumbent of Eastington, who married a sister of Curtis Hayward.* 18 Oct: *We met Mr. Phelps of Chevenage and his sister (at dinner, Lysons Hempsted). — Mr. Peters, of Eastington, a Clergyman & Magistrate, but not in the habit of attending Quarter Sessions, with his lady.*

1851: 29 Apr.

PETTAT — Charles Richard Pettat[97]

Charles Richard Pettat (1813-1873), JP and Church of England clergyman, was born in Gloucestershire, the second son of Thomas Pettatt (*below*) and Ann Frances. He was educated at Rugby School and University College, Oxford (BA 1834), and was rector of Ashe and Deane, Hampshire, from 1845 to his death in 1873. Charles married, at Salperton, 12 September 1839, his cousin Anne Caroline Browne (1810-1895). In the 1841 census the young couple was registered as living with Anne's family at Great Witcombe. No children were recorded in either the 1851 or 1871 censuses. In the early years of their marriage, Charles and Anne appear to have alternated between the Browne homes at Great Witcombe and Salperton. They also appear to have been on friendly terms with Thomas Jones Howell, who would have been a near neighbour at Great Witcombe. Francis Witts's diary entry for 29 January 1845 is interesting; Col Beach would have been a close connection of Charles Pettat's grandmother.

1842: 12 Jan., 5 Mar: *A letter from Howell, chiefly to remind me to procure the insertion of C Pettatt's name on the Commission of the Peace for Gloucestershire.* 29 Apr: *Drove MW. to call at Salperton: saw Mrs. Browne, and Mr. and Mrs. C. Pettat.* 14 Dec: *Afterwards I drove MW. and Emmelyn to Witcomb to call on Lady Cromie, and on Mr. and Mrs. Charles Pettatt.*

1844: 10 Apr: *There came to dinner Mr. and Mrs. Charles Pettatt from Whitcomb.*

1845: 29 Jan: *Mrs. Charles Pettat and Miss Browne called from Salperton: Col. Beach has lately promised to present Charles Pettat to the living of Ashe in Hants, and not far from his residence, now vacant by the decease of the late incumbent.* 2 Apr., 4 Apr., 16 Jun.

1847: 23 Jul.

PETTAT — Thomas Pettat — *see also* Browne [98]

Thomas Pettat (1772-1839), Church of England clergyman, was born at Stonehouse, Gloucestershire, the son of John Pettat (1739-1811) and Martha (1752-1826), eldest daughter of Sir Howe Hicks, 6th baronet. During their residence at Bownham House, Rodborough (1790-93), Edward and Agnes Witts were on friendly terms with the Pettat family. Thomas Pettat's sister Martha Susannah (1767-1843) married, 1793, John Browne (1773-1850), of Salperton Park, an acquaintance of Francis Witts.

Thomas was educated at University College, Oxford (BA 1794; MA 1797). He was presented to the living of Hatherop in 1797 by William Ponsonby, and served as rector there until 1839. He was rector of Quenington for a short period, 1797-98, and vicar of Stonehouse from 1798 to 1803. In 1803 he was appointed by the king to the rectorship of Beverstone, although he lived at Southrop from 1809 to around 1835. The living at Beverstone came about through the Hicks connection.

1823: 17 Sep: *The Clerical Stewards were Dr. Timbrill, Rector of Beckford ... Mr. Selwyn, a Prebendary of Gloucester ... & the Revd. Wadham Huntley, Rector of Eastington & Aston Blank, also absent & represented by the Revd. T. Pettat of Southrop, brother to Mrs. Browne of Salperton.* 19 Sep: *I dined at the Ordinary at the King's Head Inn, Mr. Estcourt in the Chair, sitting between Mr. Hanford, a very agreeable Worcestershire Roman Catholic Squire, & Mr. T. Pettat.*

1824: 11 Oct.

1825: 25 Oct: *Lord Sherborne then took the chair: we had a pleasant party; Mr. Browne of Salperton, his brother in law, Mr. T. Pettat, who is incumbent of Hatherop and Beverstone.*

1826: 16 Jun., 5 Sep.

1829: 19 Feb: *I went alone to dine with the Brownes at Salperton: Mr. & Mrs. Lawrence of Sandywell Park, and T. Pettat, Mrs. Browne's nephew, a young dragoon officer.* 1 Apr., 22 Sep.

1835: 6 Apr.

1837: 18 Aug.

1838: 14 Aug.

PETTAT — Thomas John [99]

Thomas John Pettat (1808-1857), army officer, was the eldest son of Thomas and Anne Pettat, and brother to Charles Pettat (above). In 1829 he was a cornet. He then became a lieutenant by purchase in the 7th Regiment of Light Dragoons. He retired as a captain in the Queen's Own 7th Hussars.

1846: 4 Dec: *Went to dine with the Wallers at Bourton; meeting Harry Waller, two Misses Larkin, Captain Pettatt, Mr. Wollaston, Mr. and Mrs. Winter. A pleasant party Mr. Hastings Woodman was also a guest at the Wallers, brought by his relations, the Winters.*

PETTY — Henry Petty-Fitzmaurice [100]

Henry Petty-Fitzmaurice (1780-1863), chancellor of the exchequer, was the son of Prime Minister William Petty, 1st marquess of Lansdowne [better known as the earl of Shelburne], and his second wife, Lady Louisa, daughter of John FitzPatrick, 1st earl of Upper Ossory. He was educated at Westminster School and Edinburgh University, and married, 1808, Louisa Emma Fox Strangeways. He succeeded his half brother as 3rd marquess of Lansdowne in 1809.

Petty-Fitzmaurice was MP for Calne in 1802-06, and both MP for Cambridge University and chancellor of the exchequer in 1806-07. He was MP for Camelford in 1807-09. Later in his political career he was given the following appointments: minister without portfolio, May–July 1827; secretary of state for home affairs, July 1827–January 1828; lord president of council, November 1830–November 1834, April 1835–September 1841, and July 1846–February 1852; and minister without portfolio, December 1852–February 1858.

1826: 14 Sep: *Both these poets are near neighbours and favoured guests of that distinguished peer & politician: a great many years had elapsed, since I had seen him, then Lord Henry Petty, the pupil, at Edinburgh, of Dugald Stewart: there is an air of simplicity, certainly not of elegance, about the Marquis; but a look of strong sense mingled with kindliness of disposition.* 15 Sep.

1827: 25 Apr: *The newspapers speak confidently of a coalition between Mr. Canning and the Whig party: Lord Lansdown is said to be on the eve of taking office.* 30 Apr., 4 May, 19 May: *Mr. Canning has at length completed the formation of his cabinet. Whatever difficulties impeded the final arrangements, they have been removed, and Marquis Lansdowne takes a seat in the Cabinet without holding office.* 20 Jul: *Be that as it may, the locum tenens, Mr. Sturges Bourne, steps out of the Home Office to make room for the Marquis of Lansdowne.* 7 Sep.

1828: 13 Jun: *The Marquis of Lansdown pleaded the Romish cause.*

1832: 10 Apr: *Lord Lansdowne was moderate in his tone.*

1833: 10 Nov: *During my early residence in Edinburgh this eminent character [Dugald Stewart] received as pupils into his family some young Englishmen of distinguished families, the present Marquis of Lansdown.*

1835: 19 Apr: *The newspapers announce the near completion of a Whig Ministry under Lord Melbourne as Premier... comprising Lord Lansdowne.*

1839: 1 Sep.

1840: 26 Jul.

PHELPS — John Delafield Phelps [101]

John Delafield Phelps (1764-1842), bibliophile, was the son of John Delafield Phelps (1734-1771) and Esther Gully (1730-1789). He was educated at Oriel College, Oxford (BA 1785), and Lincoln's Inn (1789), and became an exchequer bill loan commissioner and a barrister.

John Phelps's wealth was derived from his family's clothier business in the Dursley and Cam area. He was lord of the manor in Dursley, but he lived most of the time at Chavenage, near Tetbury, where he was lessee of the manor house. Phelps was an ardent bibliophile and made a notable collection of Gloucestershire books, prints, and pamphlets, now housed in the Gloucestershire Collection in Gloucester City Library. He was among the eighteen founding members of the Roxburghe Club, formed at their first meeting for dinner at St Albans Tavern on 17 June 1812. The club is the oldest society of bibliophiles in the world. Its membership is limited to forty, all own of whom either own distinguished libraries or collections, or have a scholarly interest in books. It is, in the twenty-first century, the world's pre-eminent literary society. Among other precious books, Phelps owned a Shakespeare First Folio.

John's brother James Phelps (1766-1829) was educated at Oriel College, Oxford (BA 1787; MA 1790). He was rector of Brimspfield, Cranham, and Alderley from 1802 to 1829. He married Marianne [Mary Anne] Blagden Hale (1782-1847), daughter of John Blagden [who took the name Hale] and Anne Hale of Alderley.

John Delafield Phelps died childless and was buried at Dursley. His estate passed to his nephew, William John Phelps (1813-1891) (*below*), son of his brother James.

1801: 26 Sep: *Miss Guydickens, & Mrs. Tindal & Mrs. Phelps called in the morning.* 28 Sep: *Spent the Evening at Mr. Phelps's, where I was delighted with his pictures, chiefly brought from Spain. His Jupiter & Io by Corregio bears every mark of being an original & is undoubtedly one of the finest pieces I ever saw in his last manner. The pasto so peculiar to him is here an evidence of its authenticity, & the opinion of good judges confirms it. I saw also, but could not examine so particularly, a Rubens, a Titian & another Corregio.—We met Mrs. Tindal there.*

1822: 15 Oct: *Mr. Phelps, lately one of the Commissioners in the investigation of Ilchester gaol & the alledged improprieties practised there, Mr. Goldney, Mr. Ludlow Walker &c.*

1823: 15 Jul., 17 Sep., 14 Oct.

1824: 27 Apr., 13 Jul., 19 Oct.

1826: 10 Jan., 14 Sep.

1827: 10 Jul., 16 Oct.

1828: 15 Jul., 14 Oct.

1829: 14 Jul., 22 Sep., 20 Oct.

1830: 20 Apr.

1834: 15 Aug.

1836: 10-11 Aug., 12 Sep., 13 Sep: *Phelps betook himself to Chevenage, his residence near Tetbury.* 1 Oct.

1837: 4 Aug.

1838: 2 Jan., 16 Oct.

PHELPS — Thomas Phelps [102]

Thomas Phelps (±1782), Church of England clergyman, was born at Berwick St John, Wiltshire, the son of John Phelps (b. ±1760), farmer, and his wife, Anne (b. ±1764). He was educated at Jesus College, Oxford (BA 1806; MA 1809), and was ordained deacon on 20 September 1806 and priest on 20 September 1807. His first clerical appointment was as curate of Castlemartin, Pembrokeshire; this was followed by curacies at Llanddowror, Carmarthenshire, and Uzmaston, Pembrokeshire.

Phelps's father John owned the 420-acre Higher Bridmore Farm in the Berwick St John parish, near Shaftesbury. This was sold in 1802. Little has been discovered about the family.

1804: 20 Oct: *About two o clock left Cheltenham for Oxford in the Heavy Coach unusually heavily laden. Mr. Phelps of Jes. Coll. on the inside.*

PHELPS — William John Phelps [103]

William John Phelps (1813-1891), JP, landed proprietor, and barrister-at-law, was born at Minsterworth, the second son of James Phelps (1766-1829) and Marianne [Mary Anne] Blagden Hale (1782-1847). His uncle was John Delafield Phelps (1764-1842) (*above*). William was educated at Oriel College, Oxford (BA 1835; MA 1838), and Lincoln's Inn (1839). He was a Gloucestershire JP and high sheriff for the county in 1860. He lived at Chestal, Dursley, a large new house built above the Phelps's ancestral property in the valley below. The older house was demolished.

William Phelps married, at St Mary de Lode's, Gloucester, 3 February 1839, Patience Ravenhill (1814-1879); they had 3 sons and 4 daughters:

1 Maria Arlett (b. 1840)
1 William (b. 1842)
2 Jane (1845-1884)
2 Henry (b. 1847)
3 Esther/Hester (b. 1850)
4 Elizabeth R. (b. 1853)
3 John James (1858-1918); married, at Langham, Westminster, 20 March 1888, Clara Skerry

---

1848: 18 Oct: *We met Mr. Phelps of Chevenage and his sister.*

1850: 17 Oct: *At length we attained the eminence overlooking the town of Dursley in the valley beneath with W. Phelp's new Elizabethan mansion not far distant, with Uley and Stouts hill, and Uley Berry, and Owlpen in the distance.*

PHELPS — William Law Phelps [104]

William Law Phelps (1775-1834) was a solicitor from Puckrup, near Tewkesbury. He practised at Evesham between 1803 and 1834. He was married to Anne; they had at least 1 son:

1 Charles (1826-1904)

William Law Phelps was buried at Twyning, Gloucestershire.

1823: 14 Mar: *The business proposed was to examine the Attorneys Bills ... which on a first view appeared exorbitant. The three Solicitors had been desired to produce their bill; one of them, Mr. Hodson of Pershore, refused to sign the bill produced by the two others, Mr. Phelps of Evesham, and Mr. Griffiths of Broadway, stating, that he considered some of the charges unreasonable.*

PHILIPS — George Philips [105]

Sir George Philips, 1st baronet (1766-1847), industrialist and politician, was the second son of the eight children of Thomas Philips (1728-1811), a Manchester merchant, and Mary Jolley (d. 1806). His father was a partner in the pioneering firm J. and N. Philips, the largest tape manufacturer in Europe with mills in Staffordshire and Lancashire and warehouses in Manchester. He was also involved in a hatting business that served a growing American market in the late 1780s.

George Philips was one of the wealthiest and most successful entrepreneurs of the industrial revolution. First, his father's business, J. and N. Philips, continued to prosper under his management, producing huge rewards; he withdrew over £250,000 of generated profit between 1807 and 1831. Secondly, another of his businesses, the Salford twist mill, an offshoot of J. and N. Philips and managed by the extremely capable G. A. Lee (1761-1826), became one of

Manchester's largest and most technologically advanced cotton-spinning factories. It included one of Manchester's first iron-framed buildings and was the first mill to use gas lighting.

George was socially and politically ambitious. He entered parliament as MP for Wootton Bassett in 1820, thus representing, until 1830, one of the corrupt boroughs he aspired to abolish. He was later MP for South Warwickshire in 1832-34. He left parliament in 1834 to retire to his estate at Long Compton, Warwickshire.

George Philips married Sarah Anne (1769-1844); they had at least 1 son:

1 George Richard (1789-1883); *see below*

1838: 6 Feb: *Thence leaving the Oxford & Birmingham road into which we had entered at Long Compton, ascended a long and very steep hill to a lodge entering forming one of the entrances to Weston Park, the seat of Sir Geo. Phillips.* 7 Feb: *The report which he brought back, was on the whole favourable; he describes the farmers as a kind, friendly race of people, the facilities of obtaining the necessaries of life as much on a par with those attainable in most country villages; the land held with the curacy as productive; that Sir Geo. Phillips is a kind and hospitable neighbour, who with his lady are active in charity to the poor.* 13 Jun: *Sir G. P. has large property in the parishes of Long Compton and Whichford, and while Lady P. presides over the charities of the former, her daughter in Law takes in charge those of the latter place.* 31 Jul: *After luncheon M W. & myself accompanied by E.F. W. and Sophy made an excursion for two hours or more in our open carriage: our first point was to Weston Park, the seat of Sir Geo. Phillips; we entered his demesne at the top of the hill above Whichford, and descended through his plantations, and by his farm buildings and Steward's residence.* 5 Sep: *The late accident has prevented them from accepting invitations to dinner this week at Sir Geo. Philips's at Weston House, and at Mr. Dickens's at Cherrington.*

1839: 30 Oct: *A note from J Pegler, the Veterinary Surgeon, to tell me that an Asst. P.L.C. (probably Neave) is to dine to-day at Sir Geo. Phillipps at Weston Park after visiting C Norton Union, and means to visit the Stow Board of Guardians tomorrow.*

PHILIPS — George Richard Philips [106]

Sir George Richard Philips, 2nd baronet (1789-1883), was the only son of Sir George Philips, 1st baronet (*above*), and Sarah Ann, daughter of Nathaniel Phillips of Hollinghurst. He was educated at Eton College and Trinity College, Cambridge (BA 1812; MA 1816). The family's wealth came from extensive textile interests in Manchester, a family business which his father had inherited and greatly expanded. George (junior) followed in his father's political interest for the whig party. He was MP for Horsham in 1818-20, Steyning in 1820-24, Kidderminster in 1835-37, and for Poole in 1841-52. He was also a JP and DL for Warwickshire and Worcestershire, and high sheriff for Warwickshire in 1859. He succeeded as 2nd baronet in 1847.

Philips married, at Doveridge, Derbyshire, 18 November 1819, Sarah Georgiana Cavendish (1790-1874), daughter of the 2nd Lord Waterpark. They lived at Weston Park, Long Compton, Warwickshire, and had at least 3 daughters:

1 Juliana Cavendish (1821-1898); married, at St George's, Hanover Square, 23 March 1839, Adam Duncan-Haldane (1812-1867)
2 Emily Anne (1823-1899); died unmarried
3 Louisa Georgiana (1827-1870); married, at St George's, Hanover Square, 17 July 1847, James Sinclair (1821-1881)

1847: 14 Sep: *Of those who took the high table seats at the Dinner, the Marquis of W. Lord Redesdale, Mr. Phillips, of Weston Park.*

PHILIPS — Mark Philips [107]

Mark Philips (1800-1873), MP, educational reformer, and landed proprietor, was born at Philips Park, Whitefield, Lancashire, the son of Robert Philips (1760-1844), a prosperous merchant, and Anne Needham. He was educated at the Manchester Academy while it was in York, and then at the University of Glasgow. His younger brother, Robert Needham Philips, was MP for Bury.

Mark Philips, together with Charles Poulett Thomson, were the first MPs for Manchester in 1832 following the Reform Act. Philips represented the city in parliament until 1847, and was an active member of the anti-corn law league. A champion for universal education, in 1837 Philips chaired a meeting that led to the creation of the Lancashire Public Schools' Association, which was instrumental in establishing a system of publicly funded schooling. He also played an important role in establishing England's first free public library in 1852.

Philips was president of his old school Manchester Academy from 1842 to 1846, and from 1871 until his death. He was high sheriff for Warwickshire for 1851. He donated money to many causes, including £1,000 towards the fund for the provision of open spaces and parks for the City of Manchester. He died at his home, Welcombe House, Snitterfield, near Stratford-upon-Avon.

Francis Witts confused the two Philips families. It seems likely that George Philips and Mark Philips were related, but Mark Philips was not Sir George's son. Mark was the member for Manchester, but he did not live at Weston Park.

1838: 13 Jun: *His Son Mark Philips, residing at Weston Park, with his parents, is an adherent of the Whig administration, and one of the representatives of Manchester.*

PHILLIMORE — John Phillimore [108]

Sir John Phillimore (1781-1840), naval officer, was the third son of Joseph Phillimore (1750-1831), vicar of Orton on the Hill, Leicestershire, and Mary Machin (1754-1810). He was brother to Joseph Phillimore (1775-1855) (*below*).

Phillimore entered the Royal Navy and saw service during the French Revolutionary and Napoleonic Wars. He was involved in several notable actions during his career, including both battles of Copenhagen; he sent Sir Hyde Parker's famous signal to Nelson in the first, and fought off Danish gunboats in the second. On 25 February 1814, commanding HMS *Eurotas*, Phillimore came across the French frigate *Clorinde*. A long battle ensued, which eventually left *Eurotas* totally dismasted. Twenty of her men had been killed and forty wounded, with Phillimore among the latter. *Eurotas*'s first lieutenant took over while Phillimore was carried below to be seen by the surgeon. The *Clorinde*, meanwhile, had also been badly damaged during the engagement and had suffered even greater casualties—forty killed and eighty wounded. A jury-rig was erected aboard the *Eurotas* and the chase was resumed during the night; the *Eurotas* had nearly caught up to its foe when there came upon the scene two more British ships, HMS *Dryad* and HMS *Achates*. *Dryad* brought *Clorinde* to with a single shot. Knowing they could not escape, the Frenchmen surrendered.

Phillimore was appointed CB in 1815, but his wounds prevented him from returning to active service for some years. He was knighted in 1821. In 1823 he received command of the 46-gun frigate HMS *Thetis*.

Phillimore was at times a controversial figure. He caused a scandal when he thrashed the naval historian William James with a stick for apparently misrepresenting his conduct. On another occasion he invited rebuke from the Navy Board for his request for more paint for his ship. He nevertheless became an aide-de-camp to the young Queen Victoria, and took important steps to reform how the lower ranks and ordinary seamen were treated in the Navy.

Phillimore married, at St Mary's, Bathwick, Somerset, 17 February 1830, Catherine Harriett (1808-1841), daughter of Rear Adm. Raigersfeld; they had 2 sons and 3 daughters:

1 John Bouchier (1831-1865)
1 Catherine Rebecca (b. 1832)
2 Henry Bouchier (1833-1893), Rear Adm.; married, at Great Amwell, Hertfordshire, 5 January 1865, Anne Ellen Bourdillon (1845-1931); 3 sons and 6 daughters
2 Mary (b. 1835)
3 Rebecca Boucher (b. 1836)

1823: 8 Aug.
1827: 20 Jul.

PHILLIMORE — Joseph Phillimore[109]

Joseph Phillimore (1775-1855), MP and lawyer, was the eldest son of Joseph Phillimore (1750-1831), vicar of Orton on the Hill, Leicestershire, and Mary (1754-1810), daughter of John Machin of Kensington. He was brother to Sir John Phillimore (1781-1840) (*above*). Joseph Phillimore was educated at Westminster School and Christ Church, Oxford (BA 1797; BCL 1800; DCL 1804), and was regius professor of civil law at Oxford from 1809 to his death in 1855. He was MP for St Mawes in 1817-26, and Yarmouth, Isle of Wight, in 1826-30. In 1833 he was appointed as the principal commissioner for the final adjudication of the French claims under the treaties of 1815 and 1818. He was also judge of Gloucester consistory court, 1846-55.

Phillimore married, at Little Missenden, Buckinghamshire, 19 March 1807, Elizabeth (1780-1859), daughter of Revd Walter Bagot, vicar of Blithfield, Staffordshire; they had 7 sons and 1 daughter:

1 John George (1808-1865)
2 Walter William (1809-1815)
3 Robert Joseph (1810-1885)
1 Mary (1816-1886)
4 Charles Bagot (1817-1894)
5 Greville (1821-1884)
6 Augustus (1822-1897)
7 Richard (1823-1843)

Phillimore lived at Shiplake House, Oxfordshire.

1823: 8 Aug.
1827: 20 Jul.
1829: 27 Feb, 24 Nov.
1848: 24 Aug: *The Bishop was accompanied by his Chancellor, Dr. Phillimore.*
1851: 29 Apr: *The legal documents were read by the Chancellor, Dr. Phillimore.*

PHILLIMORE — Robert Phillimore[110]

Robert Phillimore (1783-1852), Church of England clergyman, was the fifth son of Joseph Phillimore (1750-1831), vicar of Orton on the Hill, Leicestershire, and Mary (1754-1810), daughter of John Machin of Kensington. He was brother to Sir John Phillimore (1781-1840) and Joseph Phillimore (1775-1855) (*above*). Robert was educated at Westminster School, Christ Church, Oxford (BA 1806; MA 1808), and Lincoln's Inn (1808). He was perpetual curate of Hawkhurst, 1812-14, and was appointed vicar of Shipton-under-Wychwood, Oxfordshire, in 1814, and vicar of Slapton, Buckinghamshire, in 1815. He died unmarried.

1823: 8 Aug: *We dined at Mr. Ford's, the Rector of Little Risington, meeting Mr. & Mrs. E. Leigh, Mr. & Mrs. R. Wynniatt, Dr. Warneford & Mr. R. Phillimore, Rector of Shipton, Oxon, brother to Dr. Phillimore, a civilian, Professor of Civil law at Oxford, and one of the Commissioners of the Board of Controul. He is also M.P. and was the original father of the late marriage act, which was so over-nursed in both houses, that it soon died a natural death. Another brother is Captain of a Frigate, a brave & skilful seaman, who distinguished himself in the late American struggle by the capture of a Frigate. He now commands the Thetis.*

1827: 20 Jul: *We dined at Mr. Ford's at Little Risington, and met Mr. Phillimore, Rector of Shipton under Wychwood, Mr. Phillimore is Brother of the Civilian, Dr. Phillimore, who is Professor of Civil Law at Oxford, one of the Commissioners of the Board of Control, M.P. for Yarmouth, Hants, & politically connected with the so-called Grenville Party: another brother, Sir John Phillimore, is a distinguished Naval Captain, whose prowess was conspicuous in a battle with an American Frigate, which he fought & captured in the last war with our Transatlantic neighbours.*

1844: 8 Oct.

1850: 12 Aug: *At Burford Mr. Phillimore, the Vicar of Shipton, got into the coach, and travelled with me to Oxford.*

PHILLIPPS — Robert Biddulph Phillipps[111]

Robert Biddulph Phillipps (1798-1864) was the son of Robert Phillipps (1742-1822), of Longworth, Lugwardine, Herefordshire, and Mary Anne Biddulph (d. 1839). James Phillipps (1751-1809), of Huntington, Homer, and Bryngwyn, Much Dewchurch, Herefordshire, was his uncle. His aunt, Frances Phillipps, daughter of Thomas Phillipps and Sarah Ravenhill, had married Reginald Wynniatt in 1774.

Robert Biddulph Phillipps married, at Marylebone, Westminster, 5 August 1834, Elizabeth (1793-1852), daughter of John Barneby (1757-1817) and Elizabeth Bulkeley (1770-1833); they had 2 daughters:

1 Elizabeth Bulkeley (1835-1909)
2 Mary Anne (1838-1858)

Catherine Phillipps (*see* diary entry, 24 May 1827) was a daughter of James Phillipps (1751-1809), and therefore Robert Biddulph Phillipps' cousin. Sir Thomas Phillipps was also a cousin.

1827: 24 May: *We met a party from Herefordshire, a Mr. & Mrs. Lockie, the Lady a relative of the Wynniatts, Mr. Wynniatt of Stanton, Miss C. Phillips, & Mr. Bowen; a pleasant visit, and I did not find myself much fatigued.*

1836: 6 Sep.

1840: 30 May: *Dined at Guiting Grange at the Wynniatts. Met Sir Thomas Phillips, of Middle Hill with his eldest daughter; Mr. and Mrs. Robert Phillips from Herefordshire, and Mr. Bowen.*

1844: 17 May: *Dined at Guiting Grange, meeting Mr. and Mrs. Robt. Phillips from Herefordshire, agreeable people with whom we were already acquainted.*

PHILLIPPS — Samuel March Phillipps[112]

Samuel March Phillipps (1780-1862), permanent under-secretary for home affairs, was born at Crakemarsh, Staffordshire, the second son of Thomas March, of More Crichel, Dorset, and Susan, fourteenth daughter of Edward Lisle of Crux-Easton, Hampshire. His father assumed the additional surname of Phillipps upon succeeding to the estate of Garendon Park, Leicestershire, in 1796, under the will of his cousin, Samuel Phillipps.

Samuel March Phillipps was educated at Charterhouse, Sidney-Sussex College, Cambridge (BA 1802; MA 1805), and the Inner Temple (1806). He devoted his leisure hours to researching the laws of evidence and the state trials. In 1827 he accepted the post of permanent under-secretary for home affairs, which he held until 1848, when he retired and was sworn of the privy council. He married, 1812, Charemelle (d. 1825), second daughter of Charles Grant and sister of Charles Grant, Lord Glenelg. He died at Great Malvern.

1835: 20 Mar: *Wrote to Mr. Pole an account of the unpleasant collision with Mr. Ackerley, and suggested to him the propriety of waiting on the Under-Secretary of the Home Department, Mr. March Phillips, and on Col. Rowan, Chief Commissioner of the Metropolitan Police in order to anticipate any application which might be made in those quarters by Mr. Ackerley.* 27 Apr: *Mr. Under Secretary Phillipp's reply to Mr. Ackerley's letter is printed along with it... The Under Secretary, in the dry, official style, acknowledges the receipt of Mr. Ackerley's letter, and by Lord John Russell's directions has to inform him that no persons employed in the Metropolitan Police are employed as constables at Stow.* 6 May.

1837: 12 Apr: *Received a letter from Pole communicating the purport of some conversation he had held with Mr. M. Phillips, the Under Sec. of the Home department.*

1845: 9 May: *From Mr. Under Secretary Phillips of the Home Office a very satisfactory letter respecting the Prisoner Woodlands whom I tried at the adjourned Sess. and sentenced to six months imprisonment.*

PHILLIPPS — Thomas Phillipps — *see also* **Fenwick** [113]

Sir Thomas Phillipps, 1st baronet (1792-1872), bibliophile, was illegitimate, the only child of Thomas Phillipps (1742-1818) and Hannah, daughter of James Walton, of Warley, and Mary Greenroyd. His paternal grandfather, William Phillipps, farmed at Broadway, Worcestershire, and his father was the prosperous senior partner of Phillipps, Lowe & Co., calico manufacturers and printers, of Manchester. On retiring from business, Thomas Phillipps (senior) moved to Broadway, and in 1794 he bought Middle Hill. Two years later he was joined there by his young son. The boy's mother Hannah Walton had no part in his upbringing, although she lived on until 1851.

Phillipps was educated at Rugby School and University College, Oxford, and developed strong antiquarian interests. He wrote to the veteran antiquary Sir Richard Colt Hoare offering to help with his history of Wiltshire. Hoare welcomed the offer and set the young Phillipps to work copying documents at Salisbury. The two men remained on consistently friendly terms until Hoare's death in 1838.

Phillipps was made 1st baronet in the coronation honours of 1821. From an early age he was an avid book and manuscript collector. His two most precious acquisitions were the famous manuscripts of the gospels of Matilda of Tuscany and the Gundulf Bible, which he bought for £172 and £189 respectively. Phillipps never stopped his manic collecting, and at the Wilks sale in 1847 he bought the Caxton *Recuyell of the Historyes of Troy* and the first folio of Shakespeare. He failed to secure the Gutenberg Bible, the price of which he ran up to £500 (more than double the previous record for this book), and he lost out to Lord Ashburnham when he tried to buy the duke of Buckingham's Stowe manuscripts, but between 1849 and 1862 he competed strongly for Guglielmo Libri's fabulous—if dubiously acquired—collections.

Phillipps married, first, 1819, Henrietta Elizabeth (1794-1832), third daughter of Maj.-Gen. Thomas Molyneux; they had 3 daughters:

1 Henrietta Elizabeth Molyneux (1819-1879); married, 1842, James Orchard Halliwell (1820-1889), who took the additional surname Phillipps in 1872 following the death of his father-in-law; 4 daughters
2 Maria Sophia Bampfylde (1821-1858); married, at St Mary's, Cheltenham, 1 August 1844, Revd John Walcot; 2 sons and 4 daughters
3 Katherine Somerset Wyttenbach (1823-1913); married, 1848, Revd John Edward Addison Fenwick (1825-1903); 5 sons and 2 daughters

Phillipps married secondly, 2 June 1842, Elizabeth Harriet Anna, eldest daughter of Revd W. J. Mansel and Harriet Charlotte Oliver. As the companion of his later years, Elizabeth showed great forbearance in the face of his increasing eccentricity, particularly in relation to a disruptive family matter with far-reaching consequences.

In 1839, as a Cambridge undergraduate, James Orchard Halliwell wrote to Sir Thomas Phillipps asking for historical information to assist him in his studies. He was only 18, and Phillipps was impressed by the young man; Halliwell agreed to examine Cambridge libraries for him, and in return, Phillipps printed the catalogue of scientific manuscripts that Halliwell had assembled. He also invited him to stay at Middle Hill. Halliwell visited Phillipps in February 1842, and promptly fell in love with his daughter, Henrietta. Sir Thomas was initially sympathetic to the match, but soon fell out with Halliwell over the question of a dowry. However, Henrietta was of age, and she and Halliwell eloped in August, soon after her father's second marriage. Sir Thomas's rage at this act of defiance was unbridled and lasting, especially after evidence emerged in 1845 that Halliwell had stolen manuscripts from Trinity College, Cambridge. Thereafter, Phillipps did his best to thwart and denigrate his son-in-law, and to make his daughter's life a misery. She tried her utmost to effect a reconciliation and remained on good terms with her sisters, both of whom married clergymen.

In his old age Phillips became preoccupied with the fate of his book and manuscript collection; he had negotiations with the Bodleian Library and the British Museum, but nothing came of them. Most of all he was determined that his son-in-law should not lay hands on it, even though Middle Hill itself was entailed on his wife. It was this, as well as a growing urgency for more space, that in 1863 led Phillips to take the lease of Thirlestaine House in Cheltenham, a large and uncomfortable mansion with additional art galleries. Thirlestaine had been left empty at the death of the 2nd Lord Northwick, and in 1867, having already lived there for around five years, Phillipps bought the house. It took two years for a wagon train to transport the library across the Cotswolds to its new home. Phillipps remained at Cheltenham until his death in 1872.

Sir Thomas Phillipps clearly irritated Francis Witts with his unbusinesslike attitudes, especially as Witts had lent him £6,000 on mortgage (*see* 20 June 1828); but Phillipps's services to scholarship and his saving of manuscripts for the nation were remarkable. Vellum manuscripts, then not held in great esteem, were used in great numbers by goldbeaters, tailors, and glue makers for their respective trades. Phillipps could not bear to see this waste and spent vast fortunes and a great deal of time in finding them, buying them, and saving them from destruction. In Gloucestershire, in particular, great thanks should be made for his publishing of the continuations to Ralph Bigland's *Gloucestershire*.

1824: 2 Nov: *Sir Thomas and Lady Phillipps, from Middle Hill, Mr. & Mrs. S. Gist, two Miss Gists, & Mr. W. Gist, & Mr. Wynniatt joined the dinner party (at Stanway). Sir T.P. was lately created a Baronet; he cannot boast of being an hereditary gentleman; his father, the first owner of Middle Hill of his name, raised himself from menial employments to considerable wealth by successful enterprize in the most money making times of the cotton manufactory.... He is an Antiquary, book collector; who has yet perhaps still more experience to buy than he has yet paid for, but report says, much trash has already been foisted upon him.... The Baronet, however, behaves as he ought to do, by abstaining from all reference to the matters litigated; not so his Lady, who was betrayed into some strong and ill timed comments to her husband's dismay and the amusement of the hearers.*

1825: 24 Jan: *The business, which took me to Broadway, was to look over some property in that and the adjoining parish of Willersey, recently purchased by Sir Thomas Phillipps of Middle Hill, who is desirous of borrowing £6000 on Mortgage of it in part payment of the purchase money. I rode over this land with Mr. Averill, his Solicitor.* 9 Jul: *It appeared, that Sir. T.P.'s attorney had been with ours this day & completed the business.*

1826: 30 Jun: *Lady Elcho had invited Sir Thomas Phillipps, Mr. Wynniatt, Mr. & Mrs. R. Wynniatt & Mr. Bowen, all of whom came to dinner.... he has just lost a contested Election, having been induced to offer himself for the borough of Grimsby, with little prospect of success. This was unlucky, for Sir T.P. can ill afford to throw away money; with a fine rental & large settled property, he is a very embarrassed man: even now borrowing money on mortgage of unsettled estates; and I am at this time in correspondence with his agent, Mr. Averill of Broadway, about a sum of £1000 advanced to him last year, under an engagement for repayment at this time, but for which he is about to find us farther security on an estate near Middle-hill. He will then owe us £6000 on Mortgage: that is, Mrs. Backhouse has, for her life, the income, the principal being included under our marriage settlement. Of course, I refrained from any conversation on these matters with Sir T. Phillipps.*

1828: 20 Jun: *I called on Mr. Averill, the Attorney, respecting a delay in the payment of the Interest on Mortgage due to Mrs. Backhouse by Sir T. Phillipps. I was vexed to find, that the Baronet had been at Middle hill to receive his rents, but had set out again for London, & eventually for the Continent, without making arrangements for the liquidation of this & other like claims upon him.*

1829: 11 Feb: *Two professional persons passed the greater part of the day here examining the title deeds of that part of Sir. T. Phillipps's property, which is in mortgage to my trustees. The arrears of the interest being not yet liquidated, and no satisfactory guarantee for their punctual discharge being offered, we have been under the necessity of recalling the principal under the penalty of further legal proceedings, if not repaid.* 2 Apr: *Mr. Averill appeared for Sir. T. Phillipps to pay off the remaining £1000 and the Interest due.* 22 Sep.

1840: 30 May: *Dined at Guiting Grange at the Wynniatts. Met Sir Thomas Phillips, of Middle Hill with his eldest daughter; Mr. and Mrs. Robert Phillips from Herefordshire, and Mr. Bowen: three of the Misses Wynniatt at table.* 1 Dec: *The property is chiefly in the hands of Sir Thos. Phillips, Bart. of Middle Hill in the parish of Broadway. Buckland is in Gloucestershire, and was anciently the property of the Thynnes, probably, a branch of the noble family of Bath.*

1847: 19 Jun: *Lady Phillips from Middle Hill called, accompanied by her unmarried daughter in law, and a Mr. Fenwick, an Oxonian to whom the young lady is engaged.*

1853: 7 Jan: *Betook myself to the Angel Hotel, where I was very comfortably accommodated, and spent the evening in the Coffee room where were many members of convocation — among them Sir Thomas Phillips of Middle Hill, near Broadway, the noted Antiquary; we did not recognize each other, many years having lapsed since we had met — each had forgotten the features of the other.*

PHILLIPPS — William Phillipps [114]

William Phillipps (±1802-1876), Church of England clergyman, was born at Broadway, and was almost certainly a cousin of Sir Thomas Phillipps (1792-1872) (*above*). Sir Thomas owned the advowson for Buckland, and his grandfather, William Phillipps, had been a farmer at Broadway.

Phillipps was educated at Corpus Christi, Cambridge (BA 1826), and was appointed curate of Charlton-Abbots, Gloucestershire, in 1828. He was curate of Buckland in 1841-47, and became rector there in 1848. He held the living until his death. In the 1851 census Phillipps was registered as a widower. By 1861 he had remarried and was living at the rectory at Broadway with his wife Mary (±1798-1869) and his unmarried son, John Higford Phillipps (±1836-1903). By 1871 Mary had died and John was still unmarried and living at the rectory. John Higford Phillipps died in Bedale, North Yorkshire.

1850: 16 Sep: *The following Clergymen were present—Mr. Head, from Aston Somerville, Mr. Covey, from Alderton; Mr. Harvey from Winchcombe; Mr. Whalley, from Toddington; Mr. Wedgewood, from Dumbleton, a new Incumbent; Mr. Goldsmith, from Hinton on the Green, with a Son; Mr. Phillips from Buckland.*

PHILLIPS — Mrs Phillips of Cheltenham

1825: 7 Jun: *We received an unexpected visit this morning from Mrs. Phillips of Cheltenham, widow of the late Capt. Phillips, to who the house, No. 2 Bellevue Place, occupied by my poor mother, belongs.* 16 Jun.

PHILLIPS — Phillips, labourer at Stanway

1825: 7 Jun: *Before he set out news was brought from Stanway, that a labourer of the name of Phillips there had that morning attempted his life by cutting his throat; he did not fully accomplish his object, but his life was considered by Mr. Bancks, the Apothecary from Winchcomb to be in imminent danger.*

PHILLIPS — Phillips of Bourton-on-the-Hill

1843: 3 Feb: *Recd. a letter from Sir C R Cockerell in answer to mine explaining to him why the conviction against—Phillips, of Bourton on the Hill was abandoned.*

PHILLIPS — Charles Phillips [115]

Charles Phillips (±1787-1859), judge, was born at Sligo and educated at Trinity College, Dublin (BA 1806). He entered the Middle Temple in London in 1807, and was called to the Irish bar in 1812. While in London he engaged in literature, which thenceforth occupied his leisure. He joined the Connaught circuit, and speedily became known for his florid oratory, which, though condemned by the bar, was effective with juries. He was employed in most of the 'crim. con.' cases of the period, and some of his extravagant speeches were published in separate form. He took a considerable part in the agitation for Roman Catholic emancipation. In 1821 Phillips was called to the English bar, where his fame as a pleader preceded him. In a comparatively short time he became leader of the Old Bailey bar.

By the beginning of the 1830s Phillips had formed a friendship with Henry Brougham, who soon became lord chancellor; the two men corresponded on legal and political questions until Phillips's death. In 1842 Phillips was appointed a commissioner of the bankruptcy court at Liverpool, but his time there was marred by clashes with his fellow judge and by the death of one of his sons. In 1846 he returned to London as a commissioner of the insolvent debtors' court. In 1857 he produced the widely read pamphlet *Vacation Thoughts on Capital Punishment*, which urged for the total abolition of the death penalty.

Charles Phillips's sensitive and imaginative nature inspired the romanticism of his writing and the eloquence and exaggerations of his advocacy. He was easily wounded by criticism and too eager to justify himself; under pressure, he was susceptible to lapses of judgement. He was not a great advocate, though significant for the success he achieved with his forensic style, which by English standards was unusually passionate and rhetorical. He was a tall man, with expressive features and a good speaking voice.

1826: 7 Aug: *They could not go to trial without him: Messrs. Curwood, Ludlow & C. Phillips without him, would be as chaff before the wind; able men as they are, before Mr. Scarlett, supported by Messrs. Campbell, Russel, Talfoard and Justice.*

1827: 11 Apr: *I passed three hours in the Nisi Prius Court. There was no cause of much interest, but I heard the conclusion of an address to the Jury by Mr. C. Phillips, the celebrated Irish Barrister, extremely fluent and ready; words seemed to flow at will, & epithets were lavished with redundancy. His countenance is expressive and handsome, his accent very Hibernian.*

PHILLIPS — Edward Francis Phillips [116]

Edward Francis Phillips (1798-1939), civil servant, was born at Westminster, son of John and Frances Phillips of Pall Mall. He served in the civil service at Malta. He died at at Brompton 12 May 1839. His sister, Mary Elizabeth (1795-1837), married, 4 June 1819, Revd James Gibson (1785-1850), rector of Worlington, Suffolk, which would explain his reason for being at Worlington, during a period of leave that he was taking in England in 1823.

1823: 6 Jul: *I received another letter relating to my poor brother's melancholy state from a gentleman signing himself E. F. Phillips, and dating from Worlington Parsonage near Mildenhall, Suffolk. This gentleman is recently arrived from Malta, where he saw George early in May in very indifferent health but in a sane state of mind.*

PHILLIPS — Henry Phillips [117]

Henry Phillips (1801-1876), singer, was born at Bristol, the son of Richard Phillips, an actor, and his wife, née Barnett, a singer and actress. He began his career at Covent Garden Theatre, but he was not initially successful. In 1824, however, he sang Caspar in a version of Weber's *Der Freischütz* at the English Opera House with great success, and thenceforth rose rapidly in public estimation. Phillips soon became prominent at the provincial musical festivals and was much engaged for theatre and concert work. In 1843 he turned from theatre work to giving lectures on music, which he continued at various intervals until the end of his career.

In 1845, having visited America, Phillips returned to Britain to sing in Vincent Wallace's *Maritana*. In 1846 and 1847 he sang in Mendelssohn's *Elijah* under the composer's direction. In 1846 Mendelssohn composed the Ossianic scena *On Lena's Gloomy Heath* specially for Phillips, but neither men were fully satisfied with the piece. In 1848-49 Phillips's voice declined drastically. He made various attempts in the 1850s to reestablish himself on a smaller scale, but frequently failed. These attempts included performances with his elder daughter, Florence, a singer. His younger daughter, Alice, was also a singer.

Henry Phillips was married to Francis (b. ±1814); they had at least 1 son and 4 daughters:

1 Blanche (b. ±1840)
2 Florence J. (b. ±1842)
3 Alice (b. ±1843)
4 Lucy (b. ±1846)
1 Herbert H. (b. ±1851)

In the 1861 census Phillips was listed as professor of music, Florence was listed a teacher of music, and Alice as a vocalist.

1826: 31 Mar., 12 Sep., 13 Sep: *Phillips was introduced to the audience in "When forced from dear Hebe to go", his fine mellow deep tones, and his chaste and correct style of singing, though somewhat lacking in spirit, were greatly admired, and the Stewards were complimented for bringing him forward in preference to Bellamy.* 14 Sep., 25 Sep.

1829: 22 Sep: *Of Vaughan, Phillips, & W. Knyvett, it must be acknowledged that though correct, chaste and tuneful, they are deficient in energy & vigour.... Phillips was very correct and effective in "Angel of Life" — the Music by Callcott; he wants the energy and the matchless judgment of poor Bartleman, but the quality of his voice is fine & mellow, and he sings with great taste.*

PHILLIPS — John Phillips [118]

John Phillips (±1794-1845) was chiefly a plumber, but also advertised himself as a painter, plumber, and glazier.

1845: 1 Mar: *Messrs. Beman, Shelton, T. Cook, Gillett, and Fletcher attended: also Mr. Phillips, of Stow, as working engineer, to whose advice we defer, and who will be entrusted with erecting the lift-pump, laying down pipes &c.*

PHILLIPS — William Spencer Phillips [119]

William Spencer Phillips (1795-1863), Church of England clergyman, was the son of William Spencer of Great Bardfield, Essex. He was educated at Trinity College, Oxford (BA 1815; MA 1817; BD 1827), where he was a fellow in 1822-29, dean in 1823, tutor in 1824, and philosophy lecturer in 1828. He was vicar of Devynock, Brecknockshire, in 1832-33, perpetual curate of St John's, Cheltenham, in 1829-63, and vicar of Newchurch with Ryde, Isle of Wight, in 1839-63.

1834: 15 Oct: *At the Palace a large party assembled to dinner.... Mr. & Mrs. Phillips; he resides at Gloucester, and is the Bishop's chaplain.*

1835: 9 Apr: *Called on Mr. Spencer Philipps, the Chaplain of our diocesan, to whom I wished to pay the late Mrs. Mary Hunt's subscription for 1835 to the Society for the Propagation of the Gospel.*

1837: 4 Jan.

1838: 3 Jan., 22 Aug: *He was accompanied by Mr. Phillips as his Chaplain, Archdeacon Thorpe, who usually attends in that capacity, being engaged in Bristol to-day, as Steward of a Clerical Charity there.*

1839: 2 Jan.

PHILLPOTTS — Henry Phillpotts[120]

Henry Phillpotts (1778-1869), bishop of Exeter, was a younger son of John Phillpotts (1743-1814), landlord of the Bell Hotel, Gloucester, and Sibella Glover (1752-1833). He was younger brother to John Phillpotts (*below*). Henry was educated at Magdalen College, Oxford (BA 1795; MA 1708; B&DD 1821), and entered the Church. He was appointed vicar of Kilmersdon, Somerset, in 1804, vicar of Bishop Middleham in 1805, and vicar of Stanton-le-Street, County Durham, in 1806. He then became rector of Stanhope in Weardale in 1820 and dean of Chester in 1828, and from 1831 to his death in 186 he served as bishop of Exeter.

Phillpotts married, at North Cerney, 22 September 1804, Deborah Maria Surtees (1782-1863); they had 8 sons and 6 daughters:

1 Elizabeth Stephenson (1806-1864); died unmarried
1 William John (1807-1888), archdeacon of Cornwall
2 Maria (b. 1808)
2 Henry (1809-1880)
3 Charlotte Cassandra (1810-1892)
3 Edward Copleston (1813-1866), Church of England clergyman
4 George (1814-1845)
5 Arthur Thomas (1815-1890)
4 Julia (b. 1816)
5 Sibella (1818-1889)
6 John Scott (1820-1872)
7 Octavius (1823-1869)
8 Charles Edward (1827-1909)
6 Constance (b. 1827)

1804: 5 Nov: *At a sermon by Philpott of Magdn. on the Establishment of King William.*

1827: 28 May: *Dr. Philpotts, a native of Gloucester, was Fellow of Magd. Coll. Oxford, when I was undergraduate, was then a young man, and esteemed one of the ablest and most promising scholars of his day.* 7 Sep: *I read this morning Dr. Philpott's second letter to Mr. Canning on the Roman Catholic question; a very powerful and able pamphlet, dated May 7. 1827.*

1828: 25 Mar: *The Deanery of Chester vacant by the elevation of Dr. Coplestone to the episcopal bench has very properly been given to Dr. Philpotts, the able Champion of Protestantism against the Roman Catholic pretensions.*

1829: 26 Feb: *It would surely have been wiser to declare himself (Tournay—Peel v Inglis) openly at once: perhaps, he was the more induced to give his suffrage at last, as he was exposing himself to odium and suspicion by entertaining as his guest at his lodgings the Dean of Chester, Dr. Philpotts, whose tergiversation has brought upon him general censure from the opponents of the Papists.*

1847: 15 Dec: *Of the thirteen Bishops, Dr. Philpot of Exeter addresses Lord J.R. in a long, laboured, able, argumentative, caustic, pungent, and polemical reply to the letter which the Minister sent as an answer to their Lordships.*

1848: 26 Apr: *The view taken by Bishop Philpotts has been warmly taken up by Clergy in that diocese and elsewhere, and petitions against the Proviso have been drawn up and signed; and are strongly advocated in the English Churchman, a journal which speaks the sentiments of the Tractarian or Ultra High Church party.*

PHILLPOTTS — John Phillpotts[121]

John Phillpotts (±1775-1849), MP, JP, and barrister-at-law, was the eldest son of John Phillpotts (1743-1814), landlord of the Bell Hotel, Gloucester, and Sibella Glover (1752-1833). He was elder brother to Henry Phillpotts (*above*). John was called to the bar at the Inner Temple in 1822, and went on the Oxford circuit and Gloucester sessions. He married, 1797, Sarah, daughter of Thomas Chandler of Ashcroft Hall, Gloucestershire; they had at least 1 son:

1 Thomas (1807-1890), Church of England clergyman; *see below*

Phillpotts was a JP for the counties of Gloucestershire and Cornwall, and sheriff for Gloucester in 1816. He was alderman in 1819, and MP for Gloucester in 1830-31, 1832-34, and 1837-47.

1826: 25 Jan., 16 Jun: *Mr. Philpotts will find an opponent at the starting post; Capt. Berkeley, brother to Col. Berkeley, having not unambiguously intimated, that in the event of Philpotts standing he will enter the lists against him; nor is the course new to him, as he has already been a candidate for Gloucester on former occasions.*

1828: 17 Apr.

1830: 22 Apr: *The Court, however, were unanimous against them; on the part of Stow Messrs. Justice & Greaves did themselves great credit; Messrs. Philpott & Alexander were engaged for the Respondents.*

1834: 13 Oct: *From information communicated to Howell by Hyett, who had it from Mr. Philpotts, it appears that the latter has been retained against us.*

1835: 4 Jan: *For Gloucester City four candidates start: Messrs. Hope and Cother on the Tory Interest, and Mr. Philpotts and Captain Berkeley on the Whig Interest.* 5-7 Jan.

1837: 25 Jul.

1838: 2 Jan.

PHILLPOTTS — Thomas Phillpotts[122]

Thomas Phillpotts (1807-1890), JP and Church of England clergyman, was born at Gloucester, the only son of John Phillpotts (±1775-1849), MP for Gloucester, of Porthgwydden, Cornwall, and Sarah, daughter of Thomas Chandler. He was educated at Eton College and King's College, Cambridge (BA 1830; MA 1833), where he was a fellow from 1828 to 1831. He was ordained deacon in 1830 and priest on 15 June 1833. Phillpotts was appointed curate of Newnham, Gloucestershire, and of St Austell, Cornwall, in 1830. He was then vicar of Gwennap in 1836-44, and of St Feock in 1844-74. Phillpotts was honorary canon of Truro from 1877 to his death in 1890, and chaplain to his uncle, the bishop of Exeter, from 1878 to 1883. He was also a JP for Cornwall.

Thomas Phillpotts married, first, at St Matthew's, Brixton, Surrey, 8 February 1831, Mary Emma Penelope (b. 1810), daughter of Ulysses Theophilus Hughes, RN; they had 1 son and 6 daughters:

1 Emily Sibella (b. 1834)
2 Helen (1836-1878)
3 Georgina Sophia (1837-1923)
4 Mary C. (b. 1839)
5 Emma Penelope (1842-1931)
6 Alice Maud (b. 1844)
1 John Hughes (1845-1871); died unmarried

Phillpotts married secondly, 1881, Mary Elizabeth, daughter of Revd Charles Paul and widow of Capt. F. Webber of the 45th Foot.

It seems surprising that Francis Witts would not have known that this young clergyman was a son of the Gloucester MP, but Phillpotts was a whig and Witts was a tory; he would probably not have regarded him or his family favourably. Furthermore he wrote that Phillpotts was curate of 'Newland' when it should have been 'Newnham' [on-Severn].

1840: 13 Apr., 24 Apr: *Mr. Philpot, Perpetual Curate of Newland, and Curate of Madresfield; with this gentleman I had no previous acquaintance.*

PHIPPS — Constantine Henry Phipps [123]

Constantine Henry Phipps, 1st marquess of Normanby (1797-1863), home secretary, was born at Mulgrave Castle, Whitby, Yorkshire, the eldest son of Henry Phipps, 1st earl of Mulgrave, and Martha Sophia, daughter of Christopher Thompson Maling. He was educated at Harrow School and Trinity College, Cambridge, and entered politics as a young man. He was MP for Scarborough in 1818-20, Higham Ferrers in 1822-26, and Malton in 1826-30. His postings included governor of Jamaica, 1832-34; lord privy seal, July–December 1834; lord lieutenant of Ireland, 1835-39; secretary of state for war, February–August 1839; and secretary of state for for home affairs, 1839-41.

Phipps married, 1818, Maria (1798-1882), daughter of Sir Thomas Henry Liddell, 6th baronet. He succeeded his father as 2nd earl of Mulgrave in 1831 and was created 1st marquess of Normanby in 1838.

1835: 19 Apr: *The newspapers announce the near completion of a Whig Ministry under Lord Melbourne as Premier... Lord Mulgrave to be Lord Lieutenant of Ireland, with Lord Morpeth as his Secretary.*

1839: 6 May: *Various political rumours were floating in the atmosphere of the House of Lords, and its purlieus; among others that Lord Melbourne and John Russel were about to retire from the administration, the former to be replaced in the post of Premier by the Marquis of Normanby, and the latter by Lord Morpeth at the Home Office.* 11 May: *It is understood that her Majesty objects to the removal of certain ladies holding office in her Court, more particularly the Marchioness of Normanby, and the Duchess of Sutherland, both nearly connected with political rivals of the intended Premier, as wife and sister.*

PHIPPS — Henry Norris Phipps [124]

Henry Norris Phipps (1808-1881), horse dealer, was born at Stow-on-the-Wold, the son of Thomas Phipps (1778-1844) and Jane Norris (1770-1846). He was descended from the Phipps family of Broadwell, and was probably a cousin of James and Thomas Phipps (*below*).

Henry was a horse-dealer living at Scotts Farm, Marsh Gibbon, Buckinghamshire. He married, 1834, Jane Trafford (1802-1869) of Horspath, Oxfordshire; they had 1 son and 3 daughters:

1 Sarah Louisa (1834-1862)
2 Jane (b. 1836)
1 Thomas Henry (1841-1904)
3 Martha (b. ±1846)

Phipps married secondly, 1870, Sarah Clapton (1830-1913) of Filkins, Oxfordshire.

1842: 21 May: *The case, one against H. Phipps, Horsedealer, for refusing to pay toll, and assaulting the Turnpike Gate Keeper at Stump's Cross, adjourned till June 24. in consequence of the illness of the prosecutrix.*

PHIPPS — James Phipps and Thomas Phipps of Broadwell [125]

James Phipps (±1785-1854), farmer and house proprietor, was born at Broadwell, the son of Richard Phipps. He was probably a cousin of Henry Norris Phipps (*above*) and a brother of Thomas Phipps (*below*). He was married to Mary (b. ±1783); they had at least 4 sons:

1 John (b. ±1827)
2 George (b. ±1830)
3 Joseph (b. ±1832)
4 Daniel (b. ±1834)

In 1851 James and his family were living at Cownham Farm.

Thomas Phipps (±1772-1854), farmer, was born and lived at Broadwell, Gloucestershire. He farmed 90 acres, employing four men. He was unmarried and lived with his widowed sister, Anne Cambray (b. ±1774). They were most likely siblings of James (*above*). It is unclear to which of the brothers the diary entry relates.

1836: 22 Dec: *It appeared pretty clear that the imputation, which originated with a farmer of Broadwell, Phipps, had its origin in an old grudge between him and Tidmarsh.* 29 Dec: *The enquiry into the alleged misconduct of Tidmarsh, the R.O. was resumed, and the oral testimony of Phipps and Hodgkins was taken.*

PHIPPS — William Phipps — *see also* Thomas Collett [126]

William Phipps (±1835-1844), young patient at Gloucester Infirmary, was the son of George Phipps (±1804-1877) and his wife, Elizabeth (±1804-1839). George Phipps was an agricultural labourer, born at Littleton, Dorset. The family presumably lived close to the Lower Slaughter and Upper Slaughter boundary, for they appear in the censuses for both villages; however, they attended the Upper Slaughter church. Apart from the death of poor young William, the family does not feature in the diaries. George and Elizabeth had at least 2 sons and 2 daughters:

1 Thomas (b. ±1831)
1 Sarah (b. ±1833)
2 William (±1835-1844)
2 Mary Anne (b. & d. 1839)

Elizabeth died in April 1839 just weeks after giving birth to Mary Anne, who followed her to the grave six weeks later. George Phipps married secondly, at Upper Slaughter, 28 August 1839, Anne Deborah (b. ±1816), born at Hampton, Worcestershire, the daughter of carpenter Thomas Collett. Her address in the marriage certificate was given as Upper Slaughter; neither George nor Anne could write, so they gave their marks. They had at least 3 sons and 2 daughters:

1 Joseph (b. 1840)
1 Eliza (b. ±1815)
2 William Henry (1849-1901)
3 Henry (b. ±1852)
2 Elizabeth (b. ±1857)

1844: 4 Jan: *visited the Infirmary ... and visited a lame young man from U. Slaughter, a patient; another from my parish, a sickly little boy with ophthalmia, had died of dropsy two or three days since.* 6 Jan: *Wrote to Mr. Hill, Secr. to the Gloucester Infirmary for information as to the appropriation of the clothes of little W. Phipps, lately deceased there.* 9 Jan: *Also from Mr. E. G. Hill in ansr. to mine of the same date respecting the clothes worn by the poor little boy Phipps, who lately died at the Infirmary.*

PIATTI — Carlo Alfredo Piatti [127]

Carlo Alfredo Piatti (1822-1901), cellist and teacher, was born in via Borgo Canale, Bergamo, Italy, son of the violinist Antonio Piatti. He began his studies on the violin before switching to the cello, which he studied under his grandfather, the great cellist Gaetario Zanetti. After two years, Piatti joined the theatre orchestra, where he played for three months. He made his concert debut aged 15 and started touring aged 16. Franz Liszt invited him to appear as a guest performer at one of his recitals; stunned by what the boy could do on a borrowed cello, Liszt presented him with a superb new instrument. Piatti went on to become one of the most celebrated cellists of his day, as popular for the pieces he wrote as for the robust and unsentimental way he performed them.

From 1838 Piatti travelled across Europe, playing with extraordinary success at the most important venues of the continent. In 1844 he appeared before the London public at a philharmonic concert, and during the autumn of 1850 he frequently played solos at the National Concerts, which were held at Her Majesty's Theatre, under the direction of Balfe. Piatti also appeared at the Sacred Harmonic Society's opening concert of the season on 5 December 1851, replacing Lindley on his retirement. Upon the establishment of the Popular Concerts in 1859, Piatti began a long association which only ended with his retirement in 1898.

1851: 21 May: *Quartetts of surpassing excellence were performed by him with Herr Schmid, and Mr. Mellon, on the Violin and Viola, and Signor Piatti, a capital Viollincellist.*

PICKERING — Richard Pickering[128]

Richard Pickering (1766-1822), Church of England clergyman, was the son of Thomas Pickering of Acworth, Yorkshire. He was educated at Lincoln College, Oxford (BA 1788; MA 1791; BD 1801), and was appointed rector of Winterbourne Abbas, Dorset, in 1811. He was then rector and patron of Wilcot from 1820 to 1822. This attribution is tentative, but it seems that Pickering owned property in this area of Wiltshire and is therefore the most likely candidate.

1806: 24 Oct: *We took the field with 10 or 11 brace of Greyhounds, more than 20 Gentlemen present, amongst whom were Mr. Pickering & his Lady, Mr. E. Poore, Mr. Dyke, Mr. Gibbs.*

PIDDOCKE — John Piddocke[129]

John Piddocke (1764-1841+), Church of England clergyman, was born at Ashby-de-la-Zouch, Leicestershire, the son of John Piddocke and Sarah Rochford, who had married on 9 July 1761. He was educated at Christ Church, Oxford (BA 1785; MA 1808), and was ordained deacon on 7 June 1789 and priest on 19 June 1791. His first clerical appointment was as curate of Whitwick and Worthington, Leicestershire, from 7 June 1789. He was later vicar of Clifton upon Dunsmore from 10 June 1795 to 8 August 1831, and a resident at Ashby-de-la-Zouch. His wife died young in 1798 at Ashby, and in 1841 he was registered as living in Market Place, Ashby.

1838: 26 Mar: *Then there was the Revd. Sir Nigel Gresley and his lady, Mr. Piddocke, an old Clergyman and Mag. resident at Ashby, his Son in law, Mr. Boyer, Mr. & Mrs. Merewether, and the Curate of Ashby, Mr. Fell.*

PIERPOINT — Mr Pierpoint, grocer, of Argyle Street, Bath

1808: 5 May: *In Queen Square most part of the morning, walking with Rowden &c. Afterwards with my Father & Mother called on the Reads, & on the Grocer Pierpoint in Argyle St.*

PIGGOTT — Anna Piggott and the Piggott and Smyth-Piggot families of Brockley[130]

By 1839 the estate at Brockley was owned by John Hugh Smyth-Piggott (1792-1853) of Ashton Court. The line of inheritance from the 1740s follows John Biggs (1713-1795), who changed his name to Piggott upon inheriting the Brockley estate from his maternal uncle, John Piggott. He married, 1740, Anna Coward (d. 1810) of Spargrove, Somerset; they had least 1 son and 1 daughter:

1 John (1741-1816); educated at Eton College and Christ Church, Oxford; died unmarried at Calais

1 Anna (d. 1813); married, 1762, William Provis; at least 1 daughter:

  1 Ann; married, 1815, John Hugh Smyth (1792-1853), of Aston Court, who assumed the name Smyth-Piggott

---

1804: 25 Aug: *Mr. Townsend called on us & accompanied Mrs. Bates, my Father & Mother & myself on a Jaunt to Brockley Combe, a picturesque, rocky woody valley in Somerset 8 miles distant: passed thro' a rich & beautiful valley, & the sweet villages of Ashton Bourton, Backwell & Farley: in view of Sir. H. Smith's at Ashton Court, Mr. Gore's at Barrow Court, Mr. Seymour's, late Mr. Turner's, at Belmont, Mrs. Piggott's of Brockley.*

1839: 4 Sep: *The approach to Weston is a steep descent, at the foot of which are is a spacious and enjoyable mansion house, belonging, I believe, to the Pigotts, embosomed in trees, recently erected in the Tudor style.* 5 Sep: *Mr. Pigott, the proprietor, has made an excellent turf road thro' his plantations over the western declivity, which gradually winding up the hill, passes almost close to the North Eastern extremity angle of the camp by which it is crowned, and commands a very fine view of Weston, and Sand bays, which are separated by the rocky islet of Birnbeck.*

PIGGOTT — Charles Piggott[131]

Sir Charles Piggott, 3rd baronet (1835-1911), army officer, was the son of Sir Thomas Piggott, 2nd baronet, and Georgiana Anne Brummell. He was severely wounded in the Crimea in 1855, serving as a lieutenant in the 90th Foot. He married, first, 30 October 1856, Mary Louisa (d. 1873), daughter of Capt. Charles Hallowell-Carew; they had 1 son and 1 daughter:

1 Florence Louisa (d. 1877)

1 Charles Berkeley (1859-1897)

He married secondly, 14 July 1880, Margaret Mary Pole, daughter of Sydney Cosby and Emily Ashworth. Piggott was a JP and DL for Buckinghamshire.

1851: 22 May: *Went to breakfast with my old friend Round at his apartments in St. James's Square ... His younger son, Edmund, a banker at Chelmsford, and married, who seems a very pleasant and intelligent young man, came in while we were at breakfast, accompanied by a fine, handsome young Baronet, Pigott.*

PIGOTT — Jane Pigott [Piggott][132]

Jane Pigott, née Dunnington (±1752-1841), was born at Manchester. She married, ±1773, Arthur Leary Pigott (1749-1819), MP and judge, eldest son of John Pig[g]ott (d. 1776) and his wife, Jane. Arthur Pigott had been born in Barbados and was attorney-general for Grenada in 1780. He then went to England, where he was a lawyer and politician. He was solicitor-general to the Prince of Wales in 1787, and attorney-general in the Grenville ministry between 1806 and 1807. He was knighted in 1806. Several sources state that Jane and Arthur Pigott were childless, but the *DNB* claims they had a daughter, although her identity is unknown.

1804: 10 Sep: *To Mr. Whalley's Mendip Lodge 14 Miles. Set out after an early breakfast, in two Sociables, & myself on horseback. Mrs. Honor & Miss Pigott, Mrs. Bates, my Father & Mother, Mrs. Parry Price, Miss Martin, Mr. C. & Mrs. C. & Mrs. Doyle.* 14 Sep: *With Mrs. Bates & Mrs. H. Pigott to the Synagogue, where we joined a party with Mrs. McMahon.* 30 Sep: *Mrs. Massey Miss Rawsons &c. Mr. Port, Mrs. H. Pigott, Mr. Townsend &c. called.*

PIGOT KAY — Mrs Pigot Kay

1836: 13 Sep: *At a late hour breakfast was ready, and then first I learnt the name of my nameless lady of yesterday, Mrs. Pigot Kay.*

PIGOTT — Gillery Pigott [133]

Sir Gillery Pigott (1813-1875), judge, was born at Oxford, the fourth son of Paynton Pigott (1770-1862), of Archer Lodge, Sherfield, Hampshire, and Banbury, Oxfordshire, and Lucy (d. 1860), third daughter of Richard Drope Gough. His father assumed the additional names of Stainsby-Conant in 1836. Pigott was educated at Revd William Carmalt's school in Putney before entering the Middle Temple in 1836. He married, at St George's, Hanover Square, Westminster, 26 June 1836, Frances (1814-1894), daughter of Thomas Drake (b. 1779), of Ashday Hall, near Halifax, and his wife, Sarah (b. 1774). Gillery and Frances had at least 5 sons and 5 daughters:

1 Francis Drake (1837-1901)
1 Rosalie Archer (1840-1924)
2 Gillery Paynton Francis Drake (1843-1847)
3 Frederic Thomas (1847-1847)
2 Alice Isabella (1848-1920)
4 Arthur Gough (1850-1878)
3 Mabel Lucy Sarah (1852-1894)
4 Edith Caroline (1853-1931)
5 Cecil Ernest (1855-1893)
5 Beatrice Barbara (1859-1947)

Pigott was called to the bar in 1839, and went on the Oxford circuit. He was MP for Reading in 1860-63, and on 3 October 1863 he was made a baron of the court of exchequer. He was knighted on 1 November 1863.

1851: 13 Feb: *At Sewell's office discussed the same subject with him, and looked at it the opinion given by Mr. Pigott as to the case submitted to him by Sewell on behalf of Capt. Leigh, respecting the Broadwell Stone quarries.* 1 Apr: *Mr. Skinner and Mr. Pigott were counsel for the prosecution (of Hathway); Sergeant Allen, and Mr. Huddleston for the defence: the number of witnesses for the prosecution was great.*

1853: 24 May: *I took the opportunity of conferring with Mr. Burrup, the Archdeacon's registrar as to the proceedings to be taken against John Hambidge at the Midsummer Sessions—principally as to employing Pigot as Counsel.*

PIGOTT — William Pigott [134]

William Pigott (±1810-1881), Church of England clergyman, was the fourth son of John Pigott of Dover. He was educated at New College, Oxford (BCL 1839), where he was a fellow from 1831 to 1851, bursar in 1839, dean of civil law in 1840, and sub-warden in 1844. He was vicar of Whaddon, Buckinghamshire, from 1850 to his death in 1881. Pigott died unmarried.

1846: 15 Aug: *We dined at Daylesford with the Winters: a large and pleasant party—the Dean of Gloucester, Mr. and Mrs. Wiggin, and John Talbot Rice, Mr. and Mrs. C. Pole, Miss Adams, Mrs. W. Vavasour, and Emma V. and a Mr. Pigot, a fellow of New College, a temporary Curate of Mr. Twisleton at Adlestrop.*

PILE — Robert Pile [135]

Robert Pile (±1775-1808) was a farmer and landed proprietor. He married, at Urchfont, Wiltshire, 14 September 1801, Sarah Hibberd (1776-1849); they had at least 1 son:

1 Simon (1804-1848)

There is a possibility that this was the Robert Pile who was said to be responsible for creating the white horse hill figure at Alton Barnes. He reportedly hired a journeyman painter by the name of John Thorne and paid him £20 to design the horse. Thorne then subcontracted the work to John Harvey. Pile's father may have been responsible for a similar white horse at nearby Pewsey.

1808: 30 Jan: *Compiling a funeral Sermon from Dr. Jones, to be preached at the funeral of Robt. Pile, Monday.* 1 Feb: *Assisted at the Funeral of R. Pile, attended by the members of the Club & an immense croud.*

PINCHIN — Thomas Pinchin — *see also* Embrow [136]

Thomas Pinchin (±1775-1857), agricultural labourer, lived at Eyford. He married, 19 November 1798, Ann Tufley (±1761-1848); they had at least 2 daughters:

1 Catherine; married, 13 June 1826, Samuel Price of Northleach
2 Eliza; had at least 1 illegitimate daughter:
  1 Ruth (1829-1849); married Thomas Ebrow, born at Hook Norton; no further records of the marriage or subsequent life have been discovered

Pinchin was listed in the census as an agricultural labourer pauper, born at Lower Swell.

1847: 7 Dec.

1848: 20 Sep: *Walked to Eyford, to visit the aged wife of Thomas Pinchin, who is dangerously ill.* 24 Sep: *Officiated at the funeral of the aged Anne Pinchin.*

1850: 7 Jun: *Visited Pinchin and Norris, aged inhabitants of Eyford.* 3 Aug.

1851: 22 Apr.

1852: 23 Jan., 2 Feb., 28 Apr., 14 May, 28 Dec.

1853: 27 May: *Walked to Eyford, where I administered the Holy Communion to aged and infirm persons.—Mrs. Ryan, Mary Ryan, Thos. Pinchin, and Widow Banting.* 9 Dec: *Walked to Eyford: visited T. Pinchin and his daughter Emborough aged & invalid.*

PIPON — Mrs Pipon at Mr Townsend's

Agnes Witts did not mention Mrs Pipon, although she did mention the dinner party and the venison. There are numerous families in Ireland bearing the name Pipon; this 'Mrs Pipin' may have been connected to the Clifton Irish set.

1804: 29 Jul: *with my Father & Mother & Mrs. Ryan: called on Mrs. Massey. A Haunch of Venison pleasant Dinner at Mr. Townsends, Mr. Baillie & Son, Mrs. Hankey & Daughter, Mrs. Pipon & ourselves.*

PITCHER — John Earle Pitcher [137]

John Earle Pitcher (±1803-1836), Church of England clergyman, was the fourth son of John Earle Pitcher (d. 1843), merchant, of St Pancras, London, son of Isaac Pitcher, plantation owner, of St Kitts. His father John Earle (senior) had been born on the island of St Kitts, West Indies. Pitcher was educated at Oriel College, Oxford (BA 1826; MA 1829), and was ordained deacon on 5 June 1831 and priest on 24 November 1832. His only clerical appointment appears to have been as assistant curate at Bourton-on-the-Water from 5 June 1831. He died young.

1832: 11 Mar: *Mr. Pitcher called on me at dinner time, and was kind enough to partake my meal and pass the evening with me. He is Curate of Bourton on the Water.* 19 Mar: *I dined with Mr. Pitcher, at Bourton, meeting Messrs. Croome, Ford, and Watson-Pole.* 25 Apr., 7 Jun: *In the course of the forenoon I called on the Davies's in Wellington Parade, on the Bishop's Secretary, Mr. Holt, with the Papers of my neighbour, Mr. Pitcher, who is about to be ordained Priest, early in the next month.*

PITT — Charles Pitt[138]

Charles Pitt (1803-1874), Church of England clergyman, was the son of Joseph Pitt (*below*) and his third wife, Anne Orlidge (1776-1819). He was educated at Christ Church, Oxford (BA 1822; MA 1825), and entered the Church. He was rector of Ashton Keynes in 1834-66, and vicar of Malmesbury in 1829-74. He married, at Brinkworth, Wiltshire, 1 February 1842, Theresa Elizabeth Brock (1814-1888); they had 4 sons and 4 daughters:

1 Charles Wightwick (1842-1914)
2 Walter Henry (b. 1844)
1 Theresa Elizabeth Maria (1845-1922)
2 Henrietta (1847-1937)
3 Anne (1848-1908)
3 George Lewis (1853-1901)
4 Frances Matilda (1856-1920)
4 William James (b. 1858)

1826: 6 Jan.

PITT — Cornelius Pitt[139]

Cornelius Pitt (1787-1840), Church of England clergyman, was the eldest son of Joseph Pitt (*below*), builder of Pittville, Cheltenham, and his first wife, Mary Robbins (1765-1788). He was educated at Oriel College, Oxford (BCL 1810) and Lincoln's Inn (1813), qualifying as a barrister-at-law. It is not clear why he gave up a career in law for the Church, although his lack of patronage may have been the reason. He was presented to the living of Hazleton by Lord Chancellor Eldon in 1824 and served as rector. He then became rector of Rendcomb in 1831.

Cornelius Pitt married, at St Mary de Crypt, Gloucester, 5 May 1818, Anne Eliza Robbins, née Horrocks (1786-1825), daughter of John Horrocks (1768-1804) of Edgeworth, Lancashire, and Penwortham Lodge, near Preston, Lancashire. She was a sister of Mrs Mary Whitehead. Her first husband, Robert Robbins, a barrister and presumably a cousin, died tragically when Anne was pregnant with their fifth child. Her children with Robert Robbins were named William, George, Percy, Caroline, and Elizabeth. It was supposed that Cornelius's father, Joseph Pitt, opposed the match and disowned the couple. Cornelius and Anne had 1 son and 1 daughter:

1 Joseph (±1819-1893), Church of England clergyman; educated at Oriel College, Oxford (BA 1841; MA 1844); appointed rector of Rendcomb, 1844; married, 1846, Mary Barbara Strong; retired to Torquay. Reginald Graham recorded the following description in his memoirs: 'I must not forget a quaint character who had a peculiar fascination for me and many others; this was the Rev. Joseph Pitt of Rendcomb Rectory, a fox-hunting parson of the old school. At the time I speak of he was about sixty years of age, with a grim, rugged face, shaggy eye-brows, and a twinkle in his eye which betokened the fund of comic humour concealed under that weather-beaten visage. Very clerical was his costume: always a tall hat somewhat ruffled, a profusion of white neckcloth, a long black greatcoat, and inevitable umbrella, which he carried in his hand, even when mounted for the chase. In deep sonorous tones he addressed everybody as "Sir," but most of his friends called him "Joe."'
1 Henrietta-Sarah (1820-1888); married, 1841, Thomas Miller of Preston, Lancashire

Francis Witts noted on 20 May 1825 that Anne Eliza was in dangerous health, and indeed she died a few weeks later, in July 1825. On 26 February 1840, Cornelius Pitt failed to return home at his usual time; his family, quite alarmed, twice sent out their groom and footman to search for him. On the second search, at 3 a.m., they found him—stiff and lifeless—lying on the ground within yards of where he had been spotted the night before, in perfect health. He had been at a petty sessions held at the house of correction on the main road in Northleach, and then at the town's workhouse to attend a meeting of the local poor law guardians. After that he had gone with another of the magistrates, the Revd William Price, as far as Fossebridge, but had turned down Mr Price's offer of dinner at his house, saying he had business to attend to at Chedworth. After leaving Chedworth in apparent good health Pitt set off home, but presumably suffered a stroke or heart attack. The inquest recorded death by natural causes. Witts probably wrote of Pitt's death, but his diary from 6 September 1839 to 18 March 1840 is missing.

1824: 9 Jul: *Dr Price's dinner party Mr. & Mrs. C. Pitt; (he is just instituted to the living of Hazleton, void by the death of M. Waller of Hall Barn & Farmington).*

1825: 20 May: *Mr. Pitt's eldest son, the Rector of Hazleton in this Diocese & Curate of Chedworth, a cotemporary of mine in Oxford, and a worthy man and good Magistrate, was so unfortunate as to forfeit his father's favour by marrying a widow Mrs. Robins, who had a family by her former husband, a connexion of Mr. Pitt's, & for whom Mr. Cornelius Pitt was in trust; as the Lady was of unexceptionable character, the elder Mr. Pitt has been generally blamed for making this union the ground of his rejection of an estimable son, who had previously to this connexion & rupture with his father been called to the bar. His prospects there, without powerful support or a liberal provision, being unpromising, he entered into orders, and owes to Lord Stowell, who has had opportunities of knowing him as curate of Chedworth, the living, he now holds, and to which he succeeded on the death of Mr. Waller: it is expected also, that his Father will in so far relax from his animosity, as to give him the living of Rendcomb, which is in his gift, when it shall be vacant. Mr. C. Pitt's wife is now in dangerous health.* 25 Oct.

1830: 10 May: *In the church the prayers were read by Mr. Vavasour, the Rector of Stow, & the sermon was preached by Mr. Cornelius Pitt, Rector of Hazelton, & Curate of Notgrove.*

1834: 15 Aug.

PITT — JOSEPH PITT[140]

Joseph Pitt (1759-1842), banker, merchant, MP, and landed proprietor, was the fourth son of Joseph Pitt, carpenter, of Badgeworth, near Cheltenham, and Ann Golding of Brokenborough, Wiltshire. He married, first, at Fairford Gloucestershire, 29 August 1786, Mary Robbins (1765-1788), daughter of Cornelius Robbins of Didmarton; they had 1 son:

1 Cornelius (1787-1840); *see above*

Pitt married secondly, at Stratton, Gloucestershire, Ann (1760-1792), daughter of Andrew Daubeny of Bristol; there were no children of the marriage. He married thirdly, at St James's, Bristol, 4 March 1794, Ann (1776-1819), daughter of Joseph Orlidge of Bristol; they had 4 sons and 2 daughters:

1 Joseph (1796-1869), solicitor; by 1841 he lived at Eastcourt with his widower father and two sisters; by 1861 he lived at Lichfield, Staffordshire, and worked for the Inland Revenue in the 'distributor of stamps department'; died unmarried

1 Anne (1797-1876); lived with her sister Henrietta at Ryde, Isle of Wight; died unmarried
2 William Gregson (1798-1846); *see below*
3 Charles (1800-1874); *see above*
2 Henrietta (1802-1867); lived with her sister Anne at Ryde, Isle of Wight; died unmarried
4 George Hicks (1803-1843), civil servant, HEIC; married, at Bombay, 3 March 1836, Wilhelmina Petrie Bell (1810-1855); 2 sons and 3 daughters

Joseph Pitt was a bailiff at Cirencester by 1790 and a steward by 1793. He was high steward at Cricklade in 1812-26, and capital burgess at Wootton Bassett in 1814-30. Finally, he was MP for Cricklade in 1812-31.

Joseph Pitt was one of the few first generation self-made men to enter parliament during the early nineteenth century. As a boy he 'used to hold gentlemen's horses for a penny', but he was bred to business by an attorney and established a successful practice in Cirencester. It was there that he became a partner in the bank of Pitt, Gardner, Croome, Bowley and Wood, which had branches in Tetbury and Cheltenham. With others, he set up a second bank in Cheltenham, with a branch at Burford, Oxfordshire; and in a third partnership, he set up a bank at Tetbury, Gloucestershire, with an agency at Dursley. He was also a partner in the London bank of Bosanquet, Beachcroft, Pitt and Anderson, and in the brewery Gardner, Pitt and Company.

Pitt invested speculatively in land, purchasing the manor of Minety, Gloucestershire, from Lord Rivers for £21,000 in 1791, and the neighbouring estate of Eastcourt, in Crudwell, Wiltshire, from the Earle family for £28,000 in 1807. He made Eastcourt his principal residence. In 1800 Pitt acquired from the earl of Essex a considerable area of agricultural land known as the Marsh, to the north of Eastcourt House. His first contribution to the architecture of Cheltenham was the Royal Crescent, built in 1812. In the early 1820s he began to develop his estate in Cheltenham as the new spa of Pittville.

In 1812 Pitt sold his legal practice to Joseph Bevir; although he used Bevir's services occasionally, he mostly relied on another Cirencester attorney, Joseph Randolph Mullings. Pitt had long been connected with the householder borough of Cirencester; as bailiff and returning officer—appointed by the patrons the Earls Bathurst—he evidently had some influence over elections there. It was, however, for the enlarged freeholder borough of Cricklade, where he had purchased the lordship of the manor from the 2nd earl of Carnarvon in 1811, that he was first returned to parliament at the general election of 1812. He was credited with the control of a seat on the ministerial interest, which he occupied himself until 1831.

In Gloucestershire Joseph Pitt is best remembered for his investment in Cheltenham, and specifically for 'Pittville', an estate and residential suburb, but it cost him dearly and was never a commercial success. At the gala opening ceremony for the Pittville Pump Room on 20 July 1830 Pitt stayed away, possibly because he was already disillusioned with the enterprise. He later claimed that it had cost him £40,000.

Pitt's financial affairs became more and more encumbered; crippling debts were only partially offset by the sale of some of his properties. It was estimated that he owed £150,000 at the time of his death and that the interest payments on his mortgages came to £6,000 a year, compared to the £4,000 he received in revenue from the properties. Nothing was left for his children, although most had received substantial gifts during their father's lifetime.

1820: 11 Apr.

1823: 14 Jan.

1825: 20 May: *This speculation will doubtless be lucrative to the first projector, Mr. Pitt M.P. for Cricklade, whose Estate will be parcelled out for the new erections, which on paper make an imposing appearance.... Mr. Pitt is one of those fortunate members of the legal profession, whom great sagacity, lucky opportunity, & the skill of seizing on favourable circumstances have elevated from a very humble to a very prosperous situation in life. His enterprizes as Attorney, banker, speculator in land and many other ways of gaining or losing fortunes, have been eminently successful. Cirencester was the scene, where his prosperity was first laid, and he has been extremely lucky in his Cheltenham dealings. At one period he possessed himself, by an exchange with Jesus College, Oxford, of the patronage of the Curacy of this place, & meditated the erection of a Chapel of ease; I was in communication with him for some time on this subject, and had I been disposed to embark a considerable sum, might, perhaps, at this time, have been the Incumbent of Cheltenham with one or more dependant Chapels, but the scheme was not particularly agreeable to myself or my dearest connexions, and the negociation ceased: as did also his project of building a chapel on a misunderstanding between him & those persons, who were disposed under certain conditions to become subscribers to it.*

1826: 10 Jan., 1 Apr: *The building project on the other side of the town on Mr. Pitt's estate is, however, I am told, in abeyance, the pecuniary embarrassments of the bankers probably account for this.*

1827: 6 Jul., 12 Oct.

1829: 13 Jan.

1830: 1 May: *The spirited proprietor & projector, Mr. Pitt, my old acquaintance, M.P. for Cricklade, one of those fabri fortunæ suæ, who in the course of a long life, are enabled by natural talent, lucky speculations, & great acuteness, boldness and perseverance, to rise from the lowest ranks in society to wealth and consequence, must, I fear, find this an unprofitable concern, less advantageous than if the money, which it has cost, had been invested in 3 per Cent. annuities.*

1834: 11 Aug.

1837: 18 Aug.

PITT — Mary Pitt — *see also* Goodrich [141]

Mary Pitt (±1759-1836) was the only child of John Pitt (1725-1805), attorney and MP for Gloucester (1789-1805), of Palace Yard, Gloucester, and Mary, daughter of Frances Roberts. She married, 1801, her cousin James Pitt (±1759-1806), born at Maisemore, Gloucestershire, the younger son of Revd James Pitt of Maisemore Court. James Pitt was educated at Worcester College (BA 1780) and Oriel College, Oxford (MA 1783; BD 1790). He was ordained deacon on 30 October 1785 and priest on 18 December 1785, and served as rector of Brimpsfield with Cranham from 16 January 1798 to his death. It appears that he acquired the advowson. There were no children of the marriage.

It appears that Mary resided in her late father's house. For some reason which is not clear, much of the Maisemore estate devolved to James rather than his elder brother William. Mrs Goodrich [Harriet, née Pitt] would have been anxious to remain on good terms with her very wealthy aunt.

1827: 3 Aug: *Mrs. Pitt of Gloucester, & Mrs. Goodrich, with her eldest son, came to tea in the evening.*

1834: 14 Aug: *Cranham has no resident gentleman or clergyman ... The living is in the gift of Mrs. Pitt of Gloucester; it is held with the adjoining benefice of Brimpsfield in the same patronage: a Mr. Moore is the present incumbent.*

PITT — William Pitt [142]

William Pitt (1759-1806), prime minister, was born at Hayes Place, Kent, the second son of William Pitt, later 1st earl of Chatham (1708-1778), prime minister, and Hester (1720-1803), daughter of Richard Grenville and Hester, Countess Temple. Pitt became the youngest prime minister when he came to office in 1783 at the age of 24. Following the union with Ireland in 1801, Pitt sought to inaugurate the new kingdom by granting concessions to Catholics. One way of doing this was to abolish the political restrictions under which they suffered. The king did not share the same view; he argued that to grant additional liberties would violate his coronation oath, in which he had promised to protect the established Church of England. Unable to change the king's strong views, Pitt resigned on 16 February 1801, but was prime minister again from 1804 until his death in 1806. He was also the chancellor of the exchequer throughout his premiership. Pitt was a strong and highly competent leader who steered Britain through the period of the French Revolution, the wars with France, and the early years of Napoleon. Francis Witts admired him greatly.

1806: 23 Jan: *Received with great sorrow the rumour of the great Mr. Pitt's decease.* 24 Jan: *Learnt the confirmation of the deplorable intelligence, which was anticipated yesterday.*

1844: 4 Jun.

PITT — William Gregson Pitt [143]

William Gregson Pitt (1798-1846) was the son of Joseph Pitt (*above*) and his third wife, Anne Orlidge (1776-1819). He became the manager of the County of Gloucester Bank at Cheltenham, into which his father's bank had been merged. Pitt married, at St Peter and St Paul, Aston, Warwickshire, 14 August 1832, Charlotte Spooner (1812-1887); they had 7 sons:

1 William Wilberforce (1833-1857)
2 Francis Arthur (b. & d. 1835)
3 Robert Hawkins (1835-1857)
4 George Lewis (1836-1837)
5 Henry Dowdeswell (1838-1899)
6 Francis Joseph (1840-1929)
7 Walter Lewes (1842-1914)

1835: 6 Jan: *Several Gentlemen took the oaths as Magistrates, some who had never before qualified, although they had been long on the Commission, others who had been recently appointed under a cold seal. Among them were Capt. Frederick Berkeley, the Hon. Grantley Berkeley, Messrs. Probyn, Surman, Agg, Clutterbuck, W. Pitt and Lt. Col. Pearce.*

PLANK — Samuel Plank of Wedhampton [144]

Samuel Plank (b. 1752), schoolmaster, was born at Urchfont, Wiltshire, the son of Francis and Elizabeth Plank. He married, at Urchfont, 16 January 1800, Ann (1767-1845), the daughter of John and Mary Wild. They do not appear to have had any children.

1807: 9 Mar: *Visiting Samuel Plank a devout man, a cripple, who had written to beg to see me.* 12 Mar: *Called in the Evening upon Samuel Plank.* 25 Mar., 27 Mar., 26 Dec.

1808: 15 Apr: *Administered the Sacrament to Saml. Plank.*

PLATT — Thomas Joshua Platt [145]

Sir Thomas Joshua Platt (1788-1862), judge, was the son of Thomas Platt (1760-1842), solicitor, of London, and his wife, Catherine (1777-1843). He was educated at Harrow School and St John's and Trinity College, Cambridge (BA 1810; MA 1814). Platt was admitted as a student to the Inner Temple in 1806, and was called to the bar in 1816. As an advocate on the home circuit he was praised both for his energy and for the clarity and simplicity of his language. Going by the size of his family his energy also extended to the bedroom. Francis Witts found him far too soft, prone to giving what he considered undue leniency.

Thomas Platt took silk in 1834, and in 1845 succeeded Baron Gurney as baron of the court of exchequer. He was knighted in the same year. He married, at St George's, Bloomsbury, Middlesex, 4 April 1814, Augusta Cuming (1795-1885). They had an extremely large family, including at least 5 sons and 8 daughters:

1 Catherine (b. 1814)
2 Susanna (b. 1816)
1 Charles (b. 1817); died young
3 Augusta (b. 1818)
4 Mary (1819-1900); married, at Old Saints, St Pancras, Middlesex, 16 September 1843, Paget Wotton Clarke (1812-1870); 1 daughter
2 Charles (b. 1820)
5 Georgiana (b. 1822)
6 Juliana Frances (b. 1825)
7 Emily Octavia (b. 1827)
3 Thomas Duodecimus (1829-1902)
4 Frederick William (b. 1830)
8 Angelica Helen (b. 1832)
5 Herbert Edwyn (b. 1834)

Thomas Duodecimus Platt's name indicates that he was the twelfth child, although among Platt's known offspring he comes in at number ten.

1845: 2-3 Apr., 29 Apr: *Woodlands was tried by me; his companion, who had escaped, was apprehended in the interval between the Adjd. Sess. and the Assizes, and was tried by Mr. Baron Platt, who adjudged him to only one month's imprisonment.* 9 May: ... *and from Mr. Under Secretary Phillips of the Home Office a very satisfactory letter respecting the Prisoner Woodlands whom I tried at the adjourned Sess. and sentenced to six months imprisonment, whereas Mr. Baron Platt, at the assizes, sentenced his partner in the offence to only one month's imprisonment.*

1847: 5 Apr: *Mr. Baron Platt being seriously ill was incapacitated from going the circuit, and Sergt. Gaselee officiated in his room.*

1852: 29 Mar: *Sat by the Presiding Judge, Mr. Baron Platt, all the time till the Court broke up. His Lordship gave rather an elaborate charge to the Grand Jury, adverting strongly and judiciously to the necessity of a sound education of the people, not merely an intellectual training, so as to cultivate the understanding and infuse secular Knowledge, but a training of the soul and infu an imparting of solid scriptural & evangelical truth. He also dwelt much, & much to the purpose, on the corrupting influence of beer houses.* 30 Mar: *Took my seat near Mr. Baron Platt throughout the day.... I noticed a strong tendency in the Judge to give great weight to every minute fact or suggestion which could be construed in favour of the accused.*

PLAYFAIR — John Playfair [146]

John Playfair (1748-1819), mathematician and geologist, was born at Benvie, near Dundee, the eldest son of James Playfair (1712-1772), minister of Liff and Benvie, and Margaret Young (1720-1805). Playfair attended the University of St Andrews to qualify for the Church. Having graduated in 1765, he completed his theological studies in 1770, when he was licensed as a minister.

In 1770 he moved to Edinburgh, where he became friends with William Robertson, Adam Smith, and Joseph Black. In 1785 he became joint professor of mathematics with Adam Ferguson at the University of Edinburgh, where each session he taught three courses, two of which focused on geometry and trigonometry.

1833: 10 Nov: *Standing in an area: at one corner of which a square edifice with columns, detached from the observatory, is the appropriate monument or cenotaph of the late distinguished Mathematician and Natural Philosopher, Professor Playfair, one of the most renowned of Scottish departed Savans, whose pupil I was.*

PLAYNE — George Playne [147]

George Playne (1802-1885), surgeon, was born at Gloucester, son of nonconformists William Playne and Margaret Gauntlett. His father was a saddler and harness-maker and had married his mother at Newnham-on-Severn on 21 April 1794. When he was 14 years old, George was apprenticed to Samuel Mutlow, the apothecary at the Gloucester Infirmary. He gained his licentiate in medicine from the Apothecaries Society, and went on to qualify MRCS. He was afterwards appointed to the Gloucester Infirmary as apothecary and house surgeon.

In 1839, after some twenty-two years at the hospital, Playne decided to emigrate to Australia. He was 37 years old. He arrived there on 15 November 1839 and soon formed a business partnership with Daniel Jennings. He purchased the occupancy rights and livestock to one of largest holdings in Victoria (around 200,000 acres, with 10,000 sheep) called Campaspe Plains Station. The Campaspe partnership between George Playne and Daniel Jennings was dissolved in 1844, and Playne set up in Melbourne to practise medicine again.

In the city, Playne became a prominent member of the colonial establishment; he was secretary at the Melbourne Club, 1844-48, and a magistrate from 1843 to 1854. He lobbied for improved tenure for squatters, and assisted with efforts to form a new colony separate from New South Wales, serving as secretary of the separation committee and joint treasurer to the delegate committee. He also helped to establish a medical association, for which he was president in 1851, and a hospital, and to form a new bank.

Playne was a friend and supporter of Lt-Gov. La Trobe, and had a strong influence on the development of a civilised society in Victoria. In 1850 he built one of the finest mansions in South Fitzroy. His dream of owning a large city house and a country property at Tanti on the Mornington Peninsula was realised, but keeping up a gentlemanly existence became impractical with the shortage of labour after 1851 and the rise in squalor and drunkenness when the gold rush started. In 1854 Playne left Melbourne on the *Golden Age*, bound for England. He never married and died in 1885. He was buried at Kingston-on-Thames, Surrey.

1827: 18 Oct: *After the ballot was over & the numbers had been declared, resolutions were proposed by Mr. Griffith and unanimously agreed to, that the present House Apothecary, Mr. Playne, should be appointed House Surgeon.*

1839: 9 Jul: *Received a letter from Mr. A. Wood, the Surgeon of the Gloucester the unsuccessful candidate last week for the office of Surgeon to the County Gaol. A new professional prize now offers itself to him. Mr. Playne, one of the Surgeons of Gloucester infirmary, has rather suddenly, but not quite unexpectedly, left this country for New South Wales; and A. Wood, who on a former occasion, lost the appointment only by one vote, applies to me for my vote and interest in his favour.* 10 Jul.

PLAYNE — William Playne [148]

William Playne (1772-1850), clothier, JP, and DL, was born at Woodchester, Gloucestershire, the son of Thomas Playne (1748-1788) and Martha Walkley (1747-1824). His parents married at Avening in February 1773, meaning that William and his elder sister Mary were illegitimate; 'son of Thomas Playne' was discreetly written on William's baptism register entry at Woodchester on 22 November 1772. After Thomas Playne's death, the family's clothier business was carried on under Martha's management. She retired in 1797 and the business was renamed William Playne and Co. and placed under the young man's management.

The Playne woollen mills were formerly in Woodchester, but in 1790 Edward Hoskins, the owner of Longfords Mill, Avening, conveyed his interest in the mill to Peter Playne, brother to Thomas, and Martha, Thomas Playne's widow, by lease and re-lease. In 1799 the mills were mortgaged for £1,000 to Thomas Lees. In 1808 William Playne and his wife and Peter Playne and his wife levied a fine on the property, which was then described as two clothing mills and a corn mill with workshops, a dyehouse, stable, and cow-house. The cloth made at Longfords consisted principally of superfine black and white, single buff cassimeres, livery cloth, and Spanish stripes.

In 1806 Longfords Lake was constructed by building a dam 150 yards long across the Avening stream. The area flooded forming a 15-acre lake. By 1813, Peter Playne and his nephew William had built a new mill called Lake Mill. Because they did not have complete confidence in the dam's ability to withstand such a great force of water, they built Lake Mill parallel to the valley, well away from the direct flow should the dam burst. Water was taken to the mill by way of a leat. In 1813 William and Peter Playne divided the mill property between themselves. William retained the original mills and workshops, which were supplied by the old pond, and his uncle Peter had Lake Mill (which contained three wheels), the dyehouses, and stove. Rack Hill was also divided. The corn mill was retained throughout the early nineteenth century. In 1829 William Playne mortgaged the two clothing mills, dyehouse, corn mill, and workshops to Wood, Pitt & Co. for £5,000. By this date, William Playne seems to have acquired control of the whole site; his uncle Peter had turned to manufacturing cloth at Dunkirk, Inchbrook, and Horsley Mills. During the 1820s, three steam engines were installed in Longfords Mills, and in March 1838, a power loom was installed in the mills in addition to the ninety hand looms, ten of which were out of use. At this time the rental value of the mills was £573 per annum, the highest in Minchinhampton.

In 1812 Philip Sheppard, of Minchinhampton, mortgaged his estates and sold Avening to William Playne. In 1814 he sold Gatcombe Park to David Ricardo. He moved to Dunkirk to escape his creditors and died there in 1838.

There is some confusion regarding Avening. The VCH states that a lower mill in Avening was sold in 1800 to John Blackwell, clothier, of Nailsworth, who re-converted it for fulling and conveyed it to William Overbury, wool-stapler, of Tetbury, in 1807. Overbury (d. ±1828) devised his estate to his widow for life and she sold the mill, which by then included a steam-engine, to the elder William Playne, of Longfords, in 1833. In 1838 the mill was used in the cloth industry by the partnership of William Playne, John Wise, and Peter Playne Smith. This information poses some questions and may refer to Spring Mill, slightly lower down the valley.

Longfords prospered and William Playne became a county magistrate. He built the house 'Longfords' on the hillside above the mill. Little is known of his early life, but it is likely that his first wife was Catherine; they appear to have had 1 son:

1 William (1804-1884); *see below*

Catherine died in 1804 and was buried at Minchinhampton shortly after William's birth. William Playne married, secondly, Mary Kimber (1776-1859) of Sapperton. Interestingly, there had been something akin to a marriage alliance between the yeoman Kimber family of Sapperton and the Playnes. William's brother George (1781-1847) had married Ann Kimber, and William Kimber, yeoman of Sapperton, married Hester Playne, William's sister, on 5 January 1805.

1836: 24 Nov: *Another letter arrived by the post, from Mr. Playne, of Longfords near Minchinhampton, a leading Clothier, and for a few years past a Mag. of the County: he is advanced in years, engaged in a very extensive trade, a good conservative, and a man of sound sense & business habits.* 25 Nov.

1837: 27-28 Jun.

1838: 16 Oct.

1839: 1-2 Jan., 8 Apr: *Mr. Playne joined us late in the evening.*

1844: 2 Jan., 7 Mar., 9 Apr., 21 Apr.

1845: 4 Mar., 15 Apr., 7 May, 1 Jul.

1847: 30 Jun.

PLAYNE — William Playne [149]

William Playne (1804-1884), clothier and JP, was born at Minchinhampton, the son of William Playne (1772-1850) and his wife, Catherine (d. 1804) (*above*). He married, at Minchinhampton, Gloucestershire, 8 October 1836, Mary Ann Ellis-Viner (1815-1868); they had 3 sons and 3 daughters:

- 1 Frederick Carl (b. 1837)
- 1 Catherine Ann (1838-1863); married, as his second wife, Thomas Marling (1803-1876); 1 son:
    - 1 William Playne (1863-1895); died unmarried
- 2 Henrietta Mary (b. 1841)
- 2 Arthur Twisden (1843-1923)
- 3 Edward (b. 1845)
- 3 Emily Frances (1845-1913)

On 1 March 1858 Playne was initiated into the freemasons' lodge at Sherborne, Stroud. He was high sheriff for Gloucestershire in 1871-72.

1852: 17 Mar.

PLEYEL — Marie Pleyel [150]

Marie-Félicité-Denise Pleyel, née Moke (1811-1875), singer, was born in Paris. She studied with Henri Herz, Friedrich Kalkbrenner, and Ignaz Moscheles, and by the age of 15 she was known in Belgium, Austria, Germany, and Russia as an accomplished virtuoso. She was engaged to Hector Berlioz in 1830, but after three months, while Berlioz was in Italy, she broke the engagement to marry Camille Pleyel (1788-1855), scion of the piano-manufacturing family. After their separation in 1835 (her many love affairs were notorious), Marie's concert career flourished. She received praise from Felix Mendelssohn, Franz Liszt, Frédéric Chopin, and François-Joseph Fétis. From 1848 to 1872 she was professor of piano at the Brussels Conservatory, where she established a school of piano playing in Belgium. Her few compositions for piano are of minor importance.

Marie-Félicité-Denise Pleyel blazed through France, Belgium, Austria, Russia, Germany, and England, leaving a trail of rave reviews and delirious fans. She came to England in 1846 and met with huge success.

1852: 9 Jun: *This great treat was succeeded by one of a very different character, but highly attractive — the performance of Madame Pleyel on the Pianoforte, a most brilliant piece of execution.*

PLUMER — Thomas Hall Plumer [151]

Thomas Hall Plumer (1795-1852), barrister-at-law, was the son of Thomas Plumer and Marianne (b. 1777), daughter of John Turton. His parents had married at Eccleshall, Staffordshire, in 1794. Plumer was educated at Eton College, Balliol College, Oxford (BA 1816; MA 1819), and Lincoln's Inn. He was examiner in the court of chancery in 1821 and a commissioner of bankrupts.

1805: 7 Nov: *Sat half an hour with my excellent friend Mrs. Carrick, & accompanied her, & Miss Turton, with her little nephew & niece Plummer & their Governess, a Miss Goodchild, to Bristol in a carriage.*

PLUMPTRE — John Plumptre [152]

John Plumptre (1754-1825), Church of England clergyman, was born at Mansfield, Nottinghamshire, the eldest son of Revd Septimus Plumptree and Catherine Young. He was educated at Eton College and King's College, Cambridge (BA 1777; MA 1780), where he was a fellow from 1776 to 1778. He was later awarded a DD from Lambeth in 1808. He was appointed vicar of Stone, Worcestershire, in 1778, and rector of Wichenford in 1790. He was also prebend of Worcester, 1787-1808, and dean of Gloucester, 1808-25. Plumptre married, 7 April 1781, his cousin Diana (d. 1825), daughter of Revd Robert Plumptre; they had at least 3 sons and 2 daughters:

- 1 John Francis (1782-1864); *see below*
- 1 Tryphena Mary (±1784-1873)
- 2 Annabella (b. ±1787)
- 2 Henry Scawen (1789-1862), Church of England clergyman
- 3 Robert Bathurst (1791-1883), Church of England clergyman; married, 7 April 1825, Susanna Nicholl (d. 1849)

1823: 31 Jan: *An Evening party at the Deanery. The venerable Dean, Dr. Plumptre, suffering under an attack of his inveterate malady, the Stone, could not meet his friends.* 22 Dec: *I dined and slept at Stanway Vicarage with Fred. Aston, meeting a very intelligent and well informed man, apparently of sound principles, the Revd. Mr. Plumptre, Senior Tutor and fellow of University College. He is a nephew of the Dean of Gloucester.*

1825: 15 Dec: *The vacancy arises by the recent death of Dr. Plumptre; the late Dean was a very respectable divine, formerly private tutor to Earl Bathurst.*

1840: 22 May: *We all took luncheon at Captn. Witts's, meeting Apphia; while we were there the Misses Plumtre, residents at Malvern, called to make a morning visit. These ladies are daughters of the late Dean of Gloucester, and were acquaintances of Mrs. Backhouse and Mrs. Witts.*

PLUMPTRE — John Francis Plumptre [153]

John Francis Plumptre (1783-1864), schoolmaster, was born at Stone, Gloucestershire, the eldest son of John and Diana Plumptre (*above*). He was educated at Eton College and King's College, Cambridge (BA 1804; MA 1807), where he was elected a fellow in 1803. He was assistant master at Eton in 1803-22, and a fellow of the college in 1822-64. He married Caroline Carter of Foxley, Wiltshire. Plumptre's sermons at Eton chapel were a perpetual source of amusement to his student congregation; so bigoted was his protestantism that he stigmatised Catholic emancipation as 'the wickedest thing since the crucifixion'.

1840: 13 Apr: *It was settled that the following Gentlemen should be ap invited to attend as Officiating Clergymen, at Medical Attendant, and Pall Bearers; the Revd. Dr. Card, and Revd. Mr. Simms, Vicar and Curate of the parish; Mrs. Addison; Revd. Messrs. B. Lechmere, Plumtre.* 24 Apr: *At the hour named they began to assemble:—the Revd. Dr. Card, the Vicar of Great Malvern, professed to be too unwell to meet the rest, and preferred remaining alone in a separate apartment. Mr. Plumtre, Fellow of Eton College, having no parochial duties, a very worthy but singular person, who resides a great deal at Malvern, was the first who arrived; I had met him formerly at Gloucester at the house of his Father, the late Dean.*

PLUMPTRE — Lydia Plumptre[154]

Lydia Plumptre (1762-1846) was the daughter of Robert Plumptre (d. 1788), master of Queen's College, Cambridge, and his wife, Ann. She had at least three brothers: Joseph, James, and Robert; and at least four sisters: Diana, Anne, Arabella, and Jemima. Lydia never married but it was common at that time for elderly spinsters to be accorded the title of 'Mrs'. She died at Upton-on-Severn in January 1846.

1826: 25 Jan: *We dined at our old friend's Mrs. M. Hunt's in Palace Yard: besides Miss Caroline & Miss Maria Hunt, Mr. & Mrs. Hone & their Son, Mr. F. Hone, & Mrs. Lydia Plumptre were of the party. Mrs. L. Plumptre is sister of the late Dean's wife, a very respectable maiden lady.*

1828: 18 Jan., 18 Mar., 19 Mar: *Mr. & Mrs. Whitcomb, & Mr. & Mrs. Seymour dined at Mrs. Hunts: Mrs. L. Plumptre came to tea.* 21 Mar.

1829: 24 Sep: *We had determined not to visit the Ordinary to-day, judging that it would be more agreeable to our hospitable old friend, that we should dine with her. Mrs. Lydia Plumtre, Sister to the wife of the late Dean Plumtre, a sensible old maiden lady resident at Gloucester, was added to our party.*

1832: 7 Jun.

1835: 6 Apr: *Waited also on Mrs. Lydia Plumptre, an old and valued friend of Mrs. M. Hunt, with whom, as having transacted some minor business for Mrs. M.H. during the time of her absence from Gloucester, I had some matters to settle.* 9 Apr.

1840: 13 Apr: *I accepted an invitation to dinner at Mrs. M. Hunt's, to meet her Shropshire friends; Mrs. Lydia Plumtree was of the party.*

PLUNKET — William Conygham Plunket[155]

William Conygham Plunket, Baron Plunkett (1764-1854), lord chancellor for Ireland, was the fourth, but second surviving, son of Revd Thomas Plunket (d. 1778), presbyterian minister, of Enniskillen, co. Fermanagh, and Mary, daughter of David Conyngham of Letterkenny, co. Donegal. He was educated at Trinity, Dublin (1779), King's Inns (1780), and Lincoln's Inn (1784). As well as being MP for Midhurst in 1807 and for Dublin University in 1812-27, Plunket was solicitor-general for Ireland in 1803-05, bencher, attorney-general for Ireland in 1805-07 and 1822-27, and lord chancellor for Ireland in 1830-34 and 1835-41.

1825: 7 Feb: *Mr. O'Connel, a Roman Catholic Barrister, of considerable talents, and powerful in oratory, is the Coryphæus of this dangerous assembly, and the unlucky Mr. Plunkett, the Irish Attorney General, has lately in vain arraigned him for an inflammatory tirade uttered in one of the sittings of this body; but the Jury would not find him guilty.* 2 Apr.,

1827: 8 Mar., 22 Apr: *That Mr. Plunkett is talented and eloquent, cannot be denied; but he is a zealous advocate of the Roman Catholic claims; he may be a sound lawyer, but he is a vacillating politician, vibrating between Whig & Tory.* 25 Apr., 30 Apr: *Mr. Plunkett goes to the Upper House with the rank of Baron Plunkett.*

PLUNKETT — Henrietta Maria Plunkett[156]

Henrietta Maria Plunkett, Lady Fingall (±1733-1808), was the only daughter and heir of William Wollascot of Woolhampton, Berkshire. She married, 19 March 1755, Arthur James Plunkett, 7th Baron Fingall (1731-1793); they had at least 4 sons and 1 daughter:

- 1 Arthur James Plunkett (1759-1836), leader of the Irish Roman Catholics; notwithstanding, headed a corps of yeomen in the suppression of the 1798 rebellion; succeeded as 8th Baron Fingall, 1793; married, 1785, Frances, daughter of John Donelan of Ballydonelan, co. Galwa; at least 1 son and 1 daughter:
  - 1 Arthur James Plunkett (1791-1869); styled Lord Killeen 1793-1836; succeeded as 9th Baron Fingall, 1836; married, at Corbalton, Ireland, 11 December 1817, Louisa-Emilia Corbally
  - 1 Harriet; married, 11 September 1817, John Jones (d. 1848) of Llanarth Court, Monmouthshire
- 2 Luke (d. 1794), Capt., Austrian service
- 1 Theresa (1763-1853); married, 1788, James Dease of Turbotston, co. Westmeath
- 3 Robert Plunkett (1765-1823); *see below*
- 4 William (1770-1806), Col, Austrian service

1804: 15 Jul: *With Miss Manners. With my Father & Mother & Mrs Massey to Lady Fingal's dull Evening Conversation.* 19 Aug: *To a dull half hour's conversation at Countess Fingall's.* 27 Sep: *In the evening with McMahon & finished by a pleasant party at Lady Fingals.* 30 Dec.

1805: 12 Mar., 10 Nov., 24 Nov.

1806: 19 Jan: *Passed great part of the Evening at the Dowager Countess Fingal's where a very numerous Circle was assembled. Introduced to the Earl & Countess Fingal, engaged in various Conversation with the Roberts's, O Callaghans, Dewe's, Dr. Carrick, Hon. R. Plunkett &c.* 21 Jan: *I contrived to reach a dance at Lady Teresa Dease's, before ten o clock, where I danced with a Miss Holford from Cheshire in obedience to Lady Teresa's Commands, with Miss Dease, & with my amiable friend Miss Gould. conversation with Lord Fingal, a man of great sense & moderation, the excellent Lady Ford, Mrs. Gould, Mr. Baggot, Mr. Probyn &c.* 22 Jan: *Late in the Evening joined a party at the Dow. Countess Fingal's; had a good deal of pleasant conversation with Lord Fingal, Dr. Carrick, Mr. Gould, a remarkably pleasant man, Mr. James Bagot, the Newnham's &c.* 2 Feb., 16 Feb., 16 Mar: *To the sombre Conversazione at the Dowr. Countess Fingal's, which was enlivened to me by the presence of many of my favourites, as the Goolds, Gillibrand's & Salters.* 22 Mar.

1825: 2 Apr: *A strong effort was made, that the Roman Catholic Associators might be heard by counsel at the Bar of the Houses of Parliament, and a deputation, headed by Lord Killeen, eldest Son of Lord Fingal, and Messrs. O Connel, Shiell, Brice &c. as advocates, repaired to London, but were not allowed to plead their cause.*

PLUNKETT — Robert Plunkett[157]

Robert Plunkett (1765-1823), landed proprietor, was the third son of Arthur James Plunkett, 7th earl of Fingall (1731-1793), and Henrietta Maria Wollascot (d. 1808) (*above*). He was one of the Irish Catholic set in Clifton. His sister, Theresa Dease, lived at Belle Vue House, Richmond Place [now Terrace], and this may have been where Robert had been staying.

1803: 23 Aug: *Mr. Plunkett called in the Morning on his way through Richmond to Town, to the former of which I accompanied him back.* 28 Dec: *Mr. Plunkett called.*

1805: 12 Feb: *Walked with Mr. Plunkett & Col. Brown.* 4 Mar., 9 Mar., 27 Nov.

1806: 17 Jan: *To the Library, conversed with Mr. Foster, Mr. Plunkett, Dr. Davis & Mr. Newnham.* 19 Jan: *Passed great part of the Evening at the Dowager Countess Fingal's where a very numerous Circle was assembled. Introduced to the Earl & Countess Fingal, engaged in various Conversation with the Roberts's, O Callaghans, Dewe's, Dr. Carrick, Hon. R. Plunkett &c.* 28 Jan., 31 Jan., 20 Feb., 25 Feb., 6 Mar., 11 Mar.

PLYMLEY — Panton Plymley — *later* Panton Corbett[158]

Panton Plymley (1785-1855), JP, MP, and landed proprietor, was the second, but first surviving, son of Revd Joseph Plymley, afterwards Corbett (1759-1838), of Longnor, Shropshire, and his first wife, Jane Josepha (1763-1787), daughter of Thomas Panton, merchant, of Leghorn. Panton Plymley, as he was first known, was born at Bank House on the 4,000-acre Longnor estate, which had been in the Corbett family since the reign of Henry VI. The estate came into his father's ownership on the death of his maternal uncle Robert Corbett [formerly Flint], in accordance with whose will the family assumed the name of Corbett by royal licence on 20 November 1804.

Panton Plymley was educated at Pembroke College, Oxford, and Lincoln's Inn (1801). He was called to the bar in 1806, and was MP for Shrewsbury in 1820-30. He married, 16 May 1814, Lucy Favoretta, daughter of Dr Trevor Jones of Lichfield, Staffordshire; they had 2 sons and 1 daughter:

1 Favoretta (1815-1887); married, at St George, Hanover, Jamaica, 7 April 1842, John James Edward Hamilton (1808-1847), son of Adm. Sir Edward Joseph Hamilton, 1st baronet
1 Richard (1816-1843)
2 Edward (1817-1895)

1804: 6 Mar: *Drank wine with Trevenen, Messrs. Ingram, Plymly, Crawley, Yeomans &c.*

POLE — Abraham Pole[159]

Abraham Pole (±1777-1844), banker, was the third son of Sir Charles Van Notten [later Pole], 1st baronet of Wolverton (1735-1813), and Millicent, daughter and co-heir of Charles Pole of Holcroft, Lancashire. His elder brothers were Peter (1770-1850) and Charles (1772-1864) (*below*). There was a younger brother, Henry (1781-1865), who features only fleetingly in the diaries, and a sister, Susannah, who married, 1802, Isaac Minet. All three siblings, Abraham, Revd Henry, and Susannah, were living together at Weymouth Street, Marylebone, London, at the time of the 1841 census.

1834: 7 Aug.
1836: 6 Sep., 24 Oct.
1838: 5 Feb., 12 May, 17 May.
1840: 24 Oct.

POLE — Charles Pole — *later* Van Notten-Pole[160]

Charles Pole (1772-1864), banker, was the second son of Sir Charles Van Notten [later Pole], 1st baronet of Wolverton (1735-1813), and Millicent, daughter and co-heir of Charles Pole of Holcroft, Lancashire. His elder brother was Peter (1770-1850) (*below*), and his younger brother was Abraham (±1777-1844) (*above*). There was another younger brother, Henry (1781-1865), who features only fleetingly in the diaries, and a sister, Susannah, who married, 1802, Isaac Minet.

Pole's father was of Dutch descent. He was senior partner in the prosperous London mercantile and banking firm Van Notten of Devonshire Square, Bishopsgate. He also invested in a Hampshire estate. Charles and his brother Peter entered the family business, signing the London merchants' loyal declaration in 1795. They subscribed £20,000 each to the loyalty loan for 1797.

Charles married, 2 November 1795, Felizarda Matilda (1776-1872), daughter of Richard Buller (1732-1824), a merchant of London and Portugal, and Felizarda Guerhelmina Burmester (b. 1733); they had at least 6 sons and 1 daughter:

1 Charles Richard (1797-1879); *see below*
2 William (1798-1900); *see below*
1 Millicent (1799-1880)
3 Watson Buller (1803-1900); *see below*
4 Mundy (1804-1900); *see below*
5 Arthur Cunliffe (1806-1873)
6 Lambert (1808-1906); *see below*

Charles Pole was a close associate of Francis Witts and features extensively in the diaries. The closeness of their 'friendship' is difficult to determine, but it was founded on mutual respect. Witts was also on friendly terms with three of Charles's sons.

1822: 1 Oct: *The annual meeting and dinner of the Stow Book Society was afterwards held, which I attended, and at which I was chosen Secretary, in the room of Sir Henry Dryden, who resigned. Mr. Pole, of Wick Hill, presided.* 17 Dec: *We dined at Mr. C. Pole's at Wick Hill.*

1823: 9 Jul: *I looked into Mr. Pole's counting house in Nicholas Lane. where I had five minutes chat with his son.* 30 Jul: *Mr. Pole, our able & indefatigable Treasurer, to whom the Institution is under the greatest obligations, was absent.* 21 Oct., 23 Oct: *We dined at Mr. Pole's at Wick Hill.* 25 Nov., 18 Dec.

1824: 28 Jul: *The Report was read by our indefatigable Treasurer, Mr. Pole.*

1825: 22 Sep., 25 Oct., 14 Dec: *The annual general meeting of the Stow Provident Bank was holden this day. Dr. Rice presided. In the absence of Mr. Pole ... Two of the most respectable banks in London have been compelled to stop payment, Sir P. Pole & Co. & Williams & Co. both of whom very largely connected with Country Bankers. The head of the former house is elder brother of our neighbour Mr. Pole of Wick Hill, the Bank director, who has been summoned to London, to give those counsels, which his great financial experience enables me him to bestow. I believe, that he is not at all connected with his brother in commercial or banking transactions. Mr. Pole's own concern is a Dutch agency house, long established, and to this he adds a connexion with the Sun fire Office, of which he is director & chairman of the board, as also an extensive business in the cotton line at Manchester.*

1826: 13 Dec.

1827: 7 Sep: *Our friend Miss Rollinson came from Farmington to pass two or three days with us. The Poles from Wick Hill came to meet here; at least Mrs. Pole & her son Mr. Watson Pole, Col. & Mrs. Clitherow. Col. Clitherow is in the 3d. Regiment of Guards; of course a very gentlemanly man of the world; he married Mr. Pole's eldest daughter, being divorced from his first wife.* 12 Sep., 12 Dec.

1828: 17 Oct., 17 Dec.

1829: 31 Jul., 10 Aug: *We dined to-day at Mr. Pole's at Wyck Hill. Mrs. C. R. Pole sings very pleasingly, and her three children seem nice, healthy little people. Mr. C. R. Pole was in Town. The Fords, with Watson Pole.* 12 Aug., 9 Dec.

1832: 17 May.

1833: 31 Oct.

1834: 14 Jul: *Mr. Pole called to confer with me respecting the misunderstanding with Mr. Ford as to the Police Association, Stow.* 15-18 Jul., 26 Jul., 31 Jul: *Dined at Wyck Hill: the party meant as a reconciliation dinner. It consisted of Ford, his wife, three daughters and two school-boy sons.* 12-13 Aug., 16 Aug., 19 Aug., 25 Aug., 28 Aug., 30 Aug., 15 Sep: *Drove Mrs. Witts to Wyck Hill; visited Mr. & Mrs. Pole, and Mrs. Clitherow.*, 20 Sep., 25-26 Sep., 30 Sep., 2 Oct., 23 Oct: *Messrs. Pole, Ford and the Dean of Gloucester met me; much business was transacted. Jeaffreson detained at home by indisposition; I had a letter from him on the subject of the Prosecution menaced by Croad, and on other matters.* 24-25 Oct., 27 Oct., 30 Oct., 3 Nov., 20 Nov., 21 Nov: *A dinner party. Mr. and Mrs. Pole, W. B. Pole and Capt. Pole—Capt. Leigh—Winter—Mr. & Mrs. and the two Misses Vavasour were our guests.* 27-28 Nov., 17-18 Dec., 22 Dec: *Mr. Pole came by appointment to discuss with me the measures necessary to be taken in consequence of the attack made upon us, as Managers of the Savings Bank, by Mr. Baillie on Wednesday.* 24 Dec., 26 Dec., 29-30 Dec.

1835: 1 Jan., 3-4 Jan., 10 Jan., 14-17 Jan., 19-22 Jan., 27-28 Jan., 31 Jan., 1-2 Feb., 4-5 Feb., 12 Feb., 26 Feb., 28 Feb., 4-5 Mar., 20 Mar., 22 Mar., 27 Mar., 2 Apr., 5 Apr., 9 Apr: *Wrote to Mr. Pole to inform him that the trial of Edmund Jeffrey was postponed till Monday.* 13 Apr., 18 Apr: *Mr. Pole called, with whom, I had a conference of four hours on various matters. We discussed the issue of the Stow Murder, the conduct of Mr. Ackerley, the controversy with Mr. Baillie &c. Mr. Pole has returned from London alone: Watson having experienced a relapse has gone down to Brighton with Mrs. Pole.* 21 Apr: *Mr. Pole, and Mr. Cameron dined with us to-day.* 23-24 Apr., 27 Apr: *it occurred to me as most expedient to put Mr. Pole, who, I knew, was returning to London to-morrow, in possession of the correspondence, that he might wait on Mr. Phillipps the Under Secretary, with whom he is personally acquainted.* 28 Apr., 6-8 May, 13 May: *Received a letter from Mr. Pole, who admits that the extract from the True Sun newspaper which I forwarded to him on the 8th. Inst. requires some notice... He mentions that Cobbett has cursorily noticed the Police Association at Stow in his register, and threatens in a future number to return to the subject.* 15-16 May, 20 May, 23 May: *After I returned, Mr. Pole called... Held a long conversation with Mr. Pole on the matters of the Police Association, Mr. Ackerley, and his eccentric proceedings.* 28 May, 30 May: *Drove with Mrs. Witts to Wyck-hill to call on the Poles: found Mr. and Mrs. Pole and Watson at home.*

1836: 25-26 Jul., 1 Aug: *A conference with Sophia Hunt on Wadenhoe affairs was interrupted by the arrival of Mr. Pole, who remained for an hour or more.* 9 Aug., 16 Aug: *With Mrs. W., Howell, and E.F.W. dined at the Poles, at Wyck Hill.* 18 Aug., 27 Aug., 29 Aug., 1 Sep., 15-16 Sep., 21 Sep., 27 Sep., 28 Sep: *Mr. Pole supplies me with iron pipes from the quantity which he has procured for the supply of Stow with water, and I am to replace them.* 4 Oct., 6 Oct., 25 Oct., 10 Nov: *The Dean of Gloucester, and Jeaffreson were my Colleagues: Pole absent, having an attack of gout.* 14 Nov., 16 Nov., 19 Nov., 22-23 Nov., 28 Nov., 1 Dec., 3 Dec., 5 Dec., 9 Dec., 11 Dec., 21-22 Dec., 29 Dec.

1837: 7 Jan: *Mr. Pole, who left Wyck Hill on Monday for Town for the winter, has written to me a sketch of his scheme and prices for supplying water to the Union Work house, in case the Guardians should prefer treating with him to sinking a well on the premises.* 12-13 Jan., 17-19 Jan., 21 Jan., 3 Feb., 11 Feb., 13 Feb., 19 Feb., 23 Feb., 26-27 Feb., 18 Mar., 21 Mar., 12 Apr., 21 Apr., 19 May: *Wrote a note to Mr. Pole, who is expected today at Wyck Hill, to request him to fix a time and place when & where we may confer on the business of the Stow Police Association.* 22 May: *Much engaged with Justice business—a long conference with Mr. Pole and his son Watson on various matters—the Police association, the supply of water to the Workhouse, the working of the Poor Law in this Union &c.* 29 May: *A letter from Mr. Pole, who returned to Town this morning on Police matters, with papers annexed.* 3 Jun., 12 Jun., 15 Jun., 3 Jul., 26 Jul: *Dined at the Pole's, at Wyck Hill.* 27 Jul: *Accompanied Mr. Pole, & W. B. Pole to the new Workhouse.* 16 Aug., 31 Aug: *Chesterman is busy in fixing the steam apparatus for cooking: directions were given as to water closets, the Bell and Turret, the supply of water from Mr. Pole's reservoir.* 4 Sep., 14-15 Sep, 17 Sep., 26 Sep., 29 Sep., 3 Oct: *Recd. a note from Mr. Pole requesting me to perform the duty on Sunday next at Lower Swell in his Son's absence.* 12 Oct., 8 Nov: *Drove MW. to Wyck Hill to call on various branches of the Pole family now collected there. Found assembled at the luncheon table Mr. and Mrs. Pole, Mr. & Mrs. C. R. Pole, Mrs. Clitherow, Mrs. Rudge, W. B. Pole, Mr. and Mrs. Winter.* 9 Nov., 23-24 Nov., 13 Dec., 28 Dec.

1838: 6 Jan: *Found several letters awaiting me: one from Mr. Pole written before he left Wyck Hill for town with his family for the winter.* 4 Apr., 15 May, 17 May, 23 May, 25 May, 7 Jul., 27 Jul., 31 Aug., 1 Sep: *Found Mr. and Mrs. Pole at home lately returned from a Tour.* 8 Sep., 21 Sep: *In Stow met Mrs. Pole, who spoke to me with the greatest feeling and tearful anxiety on the subject of my proposed retirement from the Justice Room.* 24 Sep: *Had a long conference with Mr. Pole, who kindly called to offer his mediation to reconcile the feud which exists in fact, though not in form, between me and my brother Mag. the Dean of Glouc. and Mr. Ford.* 25-27 Sep., 29 Sep: *We dined at Wyck Hill, meeting an old acquaintance, and very agreeable person, Mrs. Hicks Beach, who is on a visit to the Poles, also the Polsons and Billingsley.* 18 Oct., 20 Oct., 22 Oct., 25 Oct., 27 Oct: *Mr. Pole, and his daughter, Mrs. Rudge paid us a morning visit.* 1 Nov., 12 Nov., 15 Nov., 29-30 Nov., 12-13 Dec., 27 Dec., 29 Dec: *Had an interview with Mr. Pole at Pain's, on Police and other matters, in anticipation of his removal with his family from Wyck Hill to London for the Winter.*

1839: 6 Jan., 23 May, 20 Jun., 26-27 Jun., 3 Jul., 6 Jul., 17 Aug., 19 Aug.

1840: 5 May-8 May, 14 May, 15 May: *and to Mr. Pole, who is expected at Wyck Hill tonight, in answer to his letter received yesterday.* 5 Jun., 9 Jun., 11 Jun., 25 Jun., 8 Jul., 14 Jul., 16 Jul., 23 Jul., 30 Jul., 6 Aug., 13 Aug., 19-20 Aug., 27 Aug., 30-31 Aug., 3 Sep., 10 Sep., 12 Sep., 24 Sep., 29 Sep., 1-2 Oct., 7 Oct., 9 Oct: *Our good friend, Miss Rollinson, left us after luncheon, and went to Wyck Hill, on a visit to the Pole family.* 9 Oct., 29 Oct., 5 Nov., 10 Nov., 12 Nov: *A full bench of magistrates—the Dean of Gloucester, Messrs. Pole, Ford, R. Waller and myself, assisted by Messrs. C. R. Pole, E. Rudge, W B. Pole, Baillie, Winter, Lewes.* 19 Nov., 26 Nov.

1842: 7 Jan., 31 Mar., 26 May, 23 Jun., 20 Jul: *A dinner party; we were favoured with the company of Mr. and Mrs. Pole, Watson Pole.* 21 Jul., 11 Aug., 25-26 Aug., 1 Sep., 22 Sep., 28-29 Sep., 30 Sep: *Wrote a note to Mr. Pole, excusing myself from dining at*

Wyck Hill to-day, as I had been invited by him yesterday; having sent my phaeton to Stow to-day for a trifling repair, I had no means of conveyance. 7 Nov: *Drove MW. to Wyck Hill to call on the Poles and Rudges.* 10 Nov., 18 Nov., 19 Dec., 22 Dec., 28-30 Dec.

1843: 10 Aug., 17 Aug., 21 Sep., 26 Sep., 28 Sep., 30 Sep: *Drove with MW. to Wyck Hill to call on Genl. and Mrs. Clitherow lately arrived there; found them and Mrs. Pole at home.* 25-26 Oct., 9 Nov., 14 Nov., 23 Nov., 13-14 Dec., 21-22 Dec., 28 Dec.

1844: 25 Jan., 29 Feb., 25 Apr., 4 May, 11 May, 14 May, 17 May, 5 Aug: *With MW. drove to Wyck Hill; called on Mr. and Mrs. Pole, and Mr. and Mrs. Rudge; the latter not at home.* 9 Aug., 14 Aug: *We dined at Mr. Poles;—a sumptuous entertainment.* 8 Oct., 8 Nov., 12-14 Nov., 17 Nov., 8 Dec.

1845: 7 Jan., 27 Jan., 29 Jan., 2 Feb., 27 Feb., 8 Apr., 29 May: *To the Justice room, where Mr. Pole, who is come from Town to Wyck Hill for the season, and Mr. R. Waller, were my colleagues on the bench.* 2 Jun: *Drove with MW. to Wyck Hill, to call on the Poles, lately returned from Town into the Country: met with them at home.* 11 Jun: *Other guests were Mr. and Mrs. C Pole, Watson Pole, and the eldest Son of C R Pole, a fine youth educated for the army.* 12 Jun., 14 Jun., 25-26 Jun., 27 Jun: *We dined at Wyck Hill; —a large, and pleasant party, and handsome entertainment.*—the company consisted of Mr. and Mrs. C Pole, W. B. Pole ...

1846: 25 Jun., 4 Jul., 16-17 Jul: *Mr. Ford consulted me as to a letter which he had written but not dispatched, to Mr. Cooke, Cubbington, informing him that Mr. Pole, is grievously annoyed at the proposed placing of a stone communion table in the chancel of the Church at Wick Risington, and at the introduction of chanting into the service there; but chiefly at the former, which he considers objectionable, as being a badge of Ultra High Church or Tractarianism.* 23 Jul., 30 Jul., 22 Aug: *After we returned home, Mr. C. Pole called, being very full on the uneasiness he experiences by the tendency of Mr. Cooke and his family to introduce what he considers disturbing novelties into the Church and service, a stone altar-table, chanting &c.* 24 Sep., 5 Nov., 12-13 Nov., 26 Nov., 9-10 Dec., 17 Dec.

1847: 17-18 Feb., 20 Mar., 31 Mar., 27 Apr: *On the way met and had a long parley with Mr. Pole, who is come from Town to pass a few days at Wick Hill.* 29 Apr., 10 Jun: *Mr. Pole and his lady are returned to Wyck Hill from Town.* 12 Jun., 17 Jun., 23-24 Jun., 29 Jul., 19 Aug: *At the Provident Bank had a long conversation with Mr. Pole, who is much annoyed by his Rector G L Cooke making alterations in the Church Service at Wick Risington, chanting &c. which are distasteful to the Poles.* 26 Aug., 30 Aug., 16 Sep., 23 Sep., 28 Sep., 30 Sep., 14-15 Oct., 28 Oct., 11 Nov., 18 Nov., 25 Nov., 8 Dec.

1848: 13-14 Jan., 16 Jan., 19 Jun., 22 Jun., 6 Jul., 7 Aug., 10-11 Aug., 17 Aug: *Mr. and Mrs. C Pole entertain very handsomely; much good cheer, and a well appointed table.* 14 Sep., 26 Sep., 5 Oct., 26 Oct., 7 Nov: *Mr. Pole, of Wick Hill, has presented to the parishioners a very substantial plain oak communion table, with chairs of the same material, which he had intended for his church at Wick Risington, as a peace offering in consequence of the objection made by him to the placing of a stone communion table by the Rector, which created some time ago much uneasiness—but Mr. Cooke or his family held the proffered table & chairs very cheap, and spoke disparagingly of the taste and style displayed in them—whereupon the Squire took umbrage and transferred them to Upper Swell.* 9 Nov., 16 Nov.

1849: 27 Dec.

1850: 18 Jan., 25 Jan., 31 Jan., 7 Feb., 14 Feb., 21 Feb., 26 Feb., 28 Feb., 7 Mar., 14 Mar., 28 Mar., 10 May: *Mr. Pole also paid me a long visit.* 22 May, 30-31 May, 5-6 Jun., 13 Jun., 15 Jun., 27 Jun., 18 Jul., 22 Jul., 25 Jul: *Wrote a note to Mr. Pole, excusing myself on the score of illness, from fulfilling my engagement to dine at Wyck Hill to day.* 26 Jul: *Mr. Pole and his grandson rode thro' the village and enquired of my Servant as to my health.* 1 Aug., 29 Aug., 2 Sep., 12 Sep., 26 Sep., 1 Oct., 3 Oct., 31 Oct., 6 Nov., 21 Nov., 28 Nov., 9 Dec., 11-12 Dec., 26 Dec., 29 Dec.

1851: 16 Jan., 23 Jan., 30 Jan., 6 Feb., 13 Feb., 20 Feb., 13 Mar., 19 Mar., 22 Mar., 27 Mar., 3 Apr., 16 Apr., 17 Apr., 24 Apr., 6 May: *Wrote to Mrs. Dolphin that I would communicate with Mr. and Mrs. Pole as to her calling, when they returned to Wick Hill, explaining to her that both were laid up at Brighton, being great invalids.* 8 May: *To the Provident Bank, where I met Morrison, Winter, W. B. Pole &c. Mr. Pole is suffering at Wyck Hill from a severe attack of gout.*

1852: 22 Jan., 29 Jan., 5 Feb., 12 Feb., 26-27 Feb., 4 Mar., 11 Mar., 28 Oct., 4 Nov., 18 Nov., 25 Nov., 2 Dec., 9 Dec., 16 Dec., 22-23 Dec., 30 Dec.

1853: 13 Jan., 20 Jan., 28 Jan: *Mr. Pole called on me, bringing with him a note intimating his wish, if agreeable to the family to shew his respect to his old acquaintance by following his remains to the grave with his Carriage. I explained to him that W. Vavasour had determined on not availing himself of such kind offers, seeking greater privacy.* 3 Feb., 10 Feb., 17 Feb., 24 Feb., 3 Mar., 10 Mar., 12 Mar., 24 Mar., 31 Mar., 1 Apr: *The newspaper reports the death of my old acquaintance G.L. Cooke, Rector of Cubbington, Warw. and of Wick Risington ... Of late years from a High Churchman he had become what is called Puseyite, influenced, perhaps, by his children, holding opinions somewhat extreme; and so causing dissention and uneasiness at Wick where altruism in very distasteful to the Pole family.* 14-15 Apr., 21 Apr., 28 Apr., 5 May, 19 May, 2 Jun., 23 Jun., 8 Dec., 13 Dec., 14 Dec: *The party at Wyck Hill included Mr. and Mrs. Rudge, their son and daughter, staying with the Poles, Canon Ford and his daughters, Jemima and Dulcy, Captain Leigh, Mr. and Mrs. W B Pole and myself.* 15 Dec., 22 Dec., 28-29 Dec.

1854: 23 Feb., 9 Mar., 16 Mar., 23 Mar., 30 Mar., 13 Apr., 20 Apr., 4 May, 11 May, 18 May, 25 May, 8 Jun., 15 Jun., 21 Jun: *Wrote a note to Mrs. C V N Pole, accepting her invitation to dinner at Wyck Hill on the 30th. Inst. if my health continue as favourable as at present.* 29 Jun: *Dined at the Poles, Wyck Hill, accompanied by Edmund Clifford:a small party; the Watson Poles, Mr. and Mrs. Richmond, and two boys, and ourselves.* 13 Jul., 20 Jul., 27 Jul., 10 Aug., 17 Aug.

POLE — Charles Richard Pole — *later* Van Notten-Pole[161]

Charles Richard Pole (1797-1879), banker, was the eldest son of Charles Pole (1772-1864) and Felizarda Matilda Buller (d. 1872). He married, 22 September 1824, Anne Eliza, daughter of Edward Rudge and Anne Nouaille; they had 2 sons and 2 daughters:

1 Anna Matilda (1826-1916); died unmarried
2 Millicent Felizarda (1827-1894); died unmarried
1 Charles (1828-1909)
2 Edward Clitherow (1830-1922)

The family lived at Wyck Hill House, Wyck Rissington.

1829: 31 Jul: *Several of our neighbours dined with us to-day. Sir Edward and Mr. East, Mr. & Mrs. Pole, Mr. Charles Pole, & Watson Pole, Mr. & Mrs. Ford & their son, & Dr. Warneford formed the party. The Poles, now at Wyck Hill for the summer, were accompanied by the wife of their eldest son, a very pleasing, gentle person; Mr. C. R. Pole was in town; he is in Partnership with his father as a Dutch merchant and Banker: Mrs. C. R. Pole was daughter of Mr. Rudge, a gentleman of considerable fortune, residing at Abbey Manor house, near Evesham.* 10 Aug: *We dined to-day at Mr. Pole's at Wyck Hill. Mrs. C. R. Pole sings very pleasingly, and her three children seem nice, healthy little people. Mr. C. R. Pole was in Town. The Fords, with Watson Pole.* 18 Aug., 29 Oct: *We elected Mr. C. R. Pole (Son of Mr. Pole, of Wyck Hill,) a Trustee: he had been long a manager, and it was desirable, that he should be made a trustee, in order, that he might concur with his father, in whose mercantile house in town he is a partner, & generally resident.*

1833: 11 Sep: *Met C. R. Pole and his wife, from Abbey Manor, staying a few days at the Foley Arms Hotel.* 12-13 Sep.

1834: 28 Aug: *To Stow. Attended at the Provident Bank Office, and in the Justice Room. Messrs. Pole and Jeaffreson assisted me at both places. Messrs. Escott, W. B. Pole, and C. R. Pole also present.*

1836: 1 Dec.

1837: 2 Nov., 8 Nov: *Drove MW. to Wyck Hill to call on various branches of the Pole family now collected there. Found assembled at the luncheon table Mr. and Mrs. Pole, Mr. & Mrs. C. R. Pole, Mrs. Clitherow, Mrs. Rudge, W. B. Pole, Mr. and Mrs. Winter.*

1838: 27 Oct: *Mr. Pole, and his daughter, Mrs. Rudge paid us a morning visit.* 5 Nov., 12 Nov., 14-15 Nov., 29 Nov.

1840: 23 Jul., 29 Oct., 12 Nov: *A full bench of magistrates—the Dean of Gloucester, Messrs. Pole, Ford, R. Waller and myself, assisted by Messrs. C. R. Pole, E. Rudge, W B. Pole, Baillie, Winter, Lewes.* 14 Nov.

1842: 28 Jul., 20 Aug., 27 Sep.,

1843: 26 Sep.

1845: 11 Jun: *Other guests were Mr. and Mrs. C Pole, Watson Pole, and the eldest Son of C R Pole, a fine youth educated for the army.* 13 Jun.

1846: 15 Aug., 19 Aug., 1 Oct.

1848: 11 Aug., 17 Aug., 30 Aug., 15 Sep., 26 Sep: *Mr. Pole presided: he had brought with him his son, C R. Pole, and his grandson, a younger Charles, an officer in the Guards.* 5 Oct.

POLE — Henry Pole — *later* Van Notten-Pole [162]

Henry Pole (1781-1865), Church of England clergyman, was the youngest son of Sir Charles Van Notten [later Pole], 1st baronet of Wolverton (1735-1813), and Millicent, daughter and co-heir of Charles Pole of Holcroft, Lancashire. His elder brothers were Peter (*below*), Charles, and Abraham (*above*). Henry was educated at Christ Church, Oxford, and lived at Waltham Place, Berkshire. He married, 14 July 1814, Anne, daughter of John Blagrave (1785-1864) of Lambourn; they had 1 son and 3 daughters:

1 Frances (1815-1904)
2 Anne (1817-1904); married her cousin Lambert Pole; *see below*
1 Henry (1819-1906)
3 Agnes (b. 1820)

At the time of the 1841 census, Henry was with his brother Abraham and sister at Weymouth Street, Marylebone, London.

1840: 20 Jul: *Mrs. C. Pole made a morning visit, accompanied by her very pleasing daughter-in-law, the wife of her son, Lambert Pole; he married his first cousin, a daughter of the Revd. Henry Pole.* 30 Jul: *Messrs. Pole, Ford, and Waller sat with me as Magistrates, and several Gentlemen were assessors:– Winter, W. B. Pole, Lambert Pole, Revd. H. Pole (brother of Mr. Pole, and resident in Hants. Father in law of Mrs. Lambert Pole).* 29 Oct: *Met R. Waller, Mr. Pole, Watson Pole, C R. Pole, E. Rudge, a son of the Revd. H. Pole, Winter &c. at the Savings Bank, and at the Justice Room.*

1846: 22 Sep: *Mr. and Mrs. Rudge, accompanied by Mr. and Mrs. Henry Pole, called on us from Wyck Hill.*

POLE — Lambert Pole — *later* Van Notten-Pole [163]

Lambert Pole (1808-1906), general merchant and banker, was the sixth son of Charles Pole (1772-1864) and Felizarda Matilda Buller (d. 1872). He married, 8 May 1839, his cousin Anne (1817-1904), daughter of Revd Henry Pole and Anne Blagrave; they had 1 son and 5 daughters:

1 Anna Felizarda (1840-1903); married, at Croydon, Surrey, July 1868, Thomas W. Wedlake (1829-1917); 3 sons and 1 daughter
1 Lambert Henry (1842-1884)
2 Agnes Geraldine (1844-1909); died unmarried
3 Frances Harriet (1845-1932); died unmarried
4 Phillippa Eliza (1847-1873); died unmarried
5 Edith Matilda (1849-1941); married, 21 August 1877, Edward Shepherd

Despite a serious illness in 1844, Lambert lived to the ripe old age of 98.

1837: 16 Sep: *Accordingly Lambert Pole has set out for Londonderry, where he will find Watson Pole.* 25 Sep., 3 Oct.

1839: 22 Aug.

1840: 16 Jul., 30 Jul: *several Gentlemen were assessors:- Winter, W. B. Pole, Lambert Pole, Revd. H. Pole (brother of Mr. Pole, and resident in Hants. Father in law of Mrs. Lambert Pole).* 20 Jul: *Mrs. C. Pole made a morning visit, accompanied by her very pleasing daughter-in-law, the wife of her son, Lambert Pole; he married his first cousin, a daughter of the Revd. Henry Pole.* 21 Jul., 30 Jul., 20 Aug., 27 Aug., 12 Sep.

1842: 10-11 Aug., 19 Aug.

1844: 14 Sep: *Met W B Pole who gave a very bad account of his brother Lambert, still in a very precarious state.* 8 Oct: *Mr. Pole was travelling to London to the sick bed of his youngest son, who continues in a very precarious state: Mrs. Pole is at Wyck Hill, whither Mr. P. brought her from Town a few days since, in great distress on account of the alarming indisposition of her son Lambert—indeed, as the family is very united and attached, all feel the calamity heavily.* 8 Dec: *The long continued and great apprehension entertained that the life of Mr. Lambert Pole, who has been brought to death's door by internal abscesses, could not be saved, has at length yeilded to better prospects.*

1846: 28 Oct: *With MW. drove to call on the newly married couple at Upper Swell; Mr. & Mrs. W. B. Pole: before arriving there met Mr. Lambert, and learnt from him that there was great distress at Wyck Hill.*

POLE — Mundy Pole [164]

Mundy Pole (1804-1900), army officer, was the fourth son of Charles Pole (1772-1864) and Felizarda Matilda Buller (d. 1872). He was educated at Balliol College, Oxford (BA 1826), and was commissioned in the Army, rising to the rank of major in the 46th Regiment. He married, 13 July 1841, Anne Frances Salwey, née Manley, daughter of Adm. I. G. Manley and widow of Arthur Salwey. There were no children of the marriage. Despite his serious illness, Mundy lived to 96 years old. At probate he left £65,783 13*s* 3*d*.

1833: 1 Feb: *We dined at Mr. Leighs's at Broadwell, and met Sir Chas. and Lady Imhoff, Miss Chapuset, Mr. & Mrs. Vavasour of Stow, Messrs. W. B. and Mundy Pole.*

1834: 21 Nov., 26 Dec., 30 Dec.

1837: 14 Sep: *To the Savings Bank, where met Mr. Pole, who is under great anxiety respecting his son Capt. Mundy Pole, who has been for some time quartered at Londonderry, and of whom it has been intimated to the family by a letter from a brother officer, that he was seized on the point of embarkation for Portsmouth with so alarming an attack of obstruction in the bowels, that as his brother officers were forced to leave him, though in the hands of good medical attendants, it was very necessary that one of his family should immediately come to him.* 15 Sep: *Recd. a note from Mr. Pole, who has no tidings by this post of his son Mundy: this leaves the family in suspence and affliction, and we are deprived of the pleasure of seeing the party at dinner today.* 17 Sep., 20 Sep., 25 Sep: *Drove M W. to call at Wyck Hill, where we found Mrs. Pole and Mrs. Clitherow at home: the accounts from Londonderry of Mundy Pole continue to improve.* 3 Oct., 10 Oct: *Between my services at U. Slaughter, officiated at Lower Swell in the absence of Mr. W B Pole, who is still in attendance on his Brother, Mundy, in Ireland; who still continues very weak.* 11 Oct., 8 Nov: *Mundy Pole reached Wyck Hill from Ireland about the time that I went to Settle, and is now gone to Town in a convalescent state, meditating embarkation with his regiment for the W. Indies, if medical men consider him sufficiently recovered.*

1847: 15 Oct: *also Lt. Col. Pole and his lady. He is one of Mr. Pole's younger Sons, and has lately returned with his regiment from foreign service: having been stationed for many years in New South Wales and India. His marriage to the daughter of an Officer in the army took place in India: his regiment is now quartered at Chatham, whither he soon returns. Lt. Col. P. has enjoyed good health, & in an unfavourable climate has risen rapidly in his profession.*

1852: 25 Nov: *At the Provident Bank, met Mr. Pole, Lt. Col. Pole, Mr. Royce, E.F. W., Mr. Wiggin &c.*

POLE — Peter Pole — *later* Van Notten-Pole[165]

Sir Peter Pole, 2nd baronet (1770-1850), politician and banker, was the eldest son of Sir Charles Van Notten [later Pole], 1st baronet of Wolverton (1735-1813), and Millicent, daughter and co-heir of Charles Pole of Holcroft, Lancashire. His brothers were Charles, Abraham, and Henry (*above*), and his sister was Susannah, who married, 1802, Isaac Minet. (*See* Charles Pole (1772-1864) for more information on the family).

Peter Pole married, 24 December 1798, Anna Guerherlmina, daughter of Richard Buller (1732-1824), a merchant of London and Portugal, and Felizarda Guerhelmina Burmester (b. 1733). She was sister to Felizarda Matilda (1776-1872), who had married Peter's brother Charles on 2 November 1795. Peter and Anna had 4 sons and 5 daughters:

1 Anna (1799-1822); died unmarried
1 Peter (1801-1887); succeeded as 3rd baronet, 1850; *see below*
2 Richard Pole (1802-1893); *see below*
3 Samuel (1802-1863), Bt Maj.; died unmarried
2 Amelia (1804-1817); died a child
4 Edward (1805-1879), army officer; married, at Tiverton, Devon, 1839, Mary Tidball; 2 sons
3 Matilda (1807-1887); married, 11 August 1846, her cousin Watson Buller Van Notten-Pole (1803-1900)
4 Wilhelmina (b. 1808); married, 19 January 1832, Thomas Eaton Swettenham
5 Maria (1811-1904); married, at St Marylebone's, Westminster, 19 January 1832, Edward Thomas Turnour, 4th Earl Winterton (1810-1879); 3 sons and 6 daughters

Peter Pole succeeded his father as 2nd baronet in 1813. He was MP for Yarmouth, Isle of Wight, in 1819-26.

Pole's banking firm, Pole and Company, was one of the largest of its day in London. However, despite its reported yield of £40,000 per annum for the previous seven years, it was the first casualty of the banking panic of December 1825. The bank allegedly paid out £1,250,000 in a week, which dangerously weakened its reserves; it was forced to suspend payment on 12 December 1825 and subsequently dissolved. 'The shock given to public credit', observed the *Annual Register*, 'was tremendous as it was known that they kept accounts with forty-four country banks, several of whom, in all probability, would also stop payment'. According to one historian, 'the agitation of the City exceeded everything that had been witnessed for a century'. The same month Pole divested himself of his interests in two London mercantile firms, including the family concern of Peter and Charles Van Notten.

Pole retired at the 1826 dissolution of parliament. He had evidently managed to save much of his personal fortune. He sold Wolverton Park to the duke of Wellington in 1837 and inherited the Gloucestershire property of Todenham from his brother Abraham in 1844. At his death in August 1850 he left estates in Hampshire, Gloucestershire, Northamptonshire, and Kent. By his will these were divided between his sons.

1840: 1 Aug: *It appears that I was in error on Thursday last; the Gentleman, whom I mistook for Mr. Henry Pole, turns out to be the Revd. R. Pole, nephew of Sir C. Pole, and second son of Sir P. Pole, being beneficed in Hants: he married a Miss Elmhirst.* 26 Nov: *To the Savings Bank, where met Messrs. Pole, Watson Pole, Rudge, Capt. Pole (Son of Sir P. Pole, a dragoon officer).* 26 Nov: *To the Savings Bank, where met Messrs. Pole, Watson Pole, Rudge, Capt. Pole (Son of Sir P. Pole, a dragoon officer,) R. Waller, Ford, and Winter.*

1850: 2 Sep: *To W. B. Pole, a note of condolence and enquiry, having noticed in yesterday's paper the decease of Sir Peter Pole, uncle to Mr. W.B.P. and Father to Mrs. W B Pole: they had set out for London, where the Baronet died at the age of 79, after a long and slow decay.*

POLE — Peter Pole — *later* Van Notten-Pole[166]

Sir Peter Pole, 3rd baronet (1801-1887), JP and landed proprietor, was the eldest son of Sir Peter Pole, 2nd baronet (1770-1850). He was educated at Brasenose College, Oxford (MA 1821). He married, first, 28 July 1825, Louisa (d. 1852), daughter of Edmond Henry Pery, 1st earl of Limerick, and Mary Alice Ormsby; they had 1 son and 2 daughters:

1 Alice Louisa Chandos (1832-1901); married, at St Andrew's, Marylebone, Westminster, 21 October 1862, Charles Thomas Weatherley (1827-1894); 3 sons and 3 daughters
2 Margaret Caroline Chandos (1834-1914); married, 28 April 1864, Thomas Baker (1832-1910)
1 Cecil Charles (1829-1876); born at Florence, Italy; married Frances Anna (±1843-1921), daughter of Henry Rice (1813-1896) and Emma Lowndes-Stone; at least 3 sons and 4 daughters:
    1 Annie Louise (1862-1950)
    1 Cecil Pery (1863-1948); succeeded as 4th baronet
    2 Ethel Margaret (1865-1957)
    2 Gerald Charles (1866-1947)
    3 Florence Maud (1868-1960)
    3 Chandos Edward (1872-1947)
    4 Cicely (b. 1877)

Sir Peter Pole married secondly, 24 September 1863, Louisa, daughter of Samuel Lands.

1851: 17 Mar: *Sir Peter Pole, of Todenham, made his appearance, as newly placed on the commission, and to take the oaths to-morrow. As long and intimately acquainted with his Uncle of Wyck Hill, and his cousin and brother in law of Upper Swell, he soon formed a liaison with me, appearing very ready to put himself forward. The baronet will chiefly reside at Todenham; he seems to be about fifty years old; he married a daughter of Lord Limerick, and has a family—one son, at least, grown up, and who has been in the army, but has left the service. Sir P.P. also has been in the army.* 18 Mar: *Sir Peter Pole, and the Revd. L. Darell, new magistrates took the oaths.* 19 Mar: *Sir P. Pole had made himself rather prominent at the meeting yesterday, introducing himself to all whom considered leading Magistrates, and, among others, had intimated to Col. Browne, second in command of the Gloucestershire Regiment of Yeomanry Cavalry, his wish that his eldest son should hold a commission in that corps.* 22 Mar: *Received a letter from C. Pole, who, in reply to my letter respecting his great nephew, Sir P. Pole's son, writes very candidly, but in no very flattering terms—representing the young man, who soon got tired of the army, as idle, fond of pleasure, and a Mother's spoiled child.* 27 Mar., 31 Mar.

1852: 17 Mar: *A small but pleasant dinner party of Magistrates at the Bell in the Evening, Curtis Hayward presiding—Purnell, Francillon, Sir Peter Pole, Mullings, Baker ...* 29 Mar., 2 Dec.

POLE — Richard Pole [167]

Richard Pole (1802-1893), Church of England clergyman, was the second son of Sir Peter Pole, 2nd baronet (1770-1850), and Anna Guerherlmina Buller. He was educated at Balliol College, Oxford (BA 1823; MA 1826), and was rector of Wolverton, Hampshire, 1844-79. He married, 26 November 1836, Elizabeth Anna, daughter of Richard Elmhirst.

1840: 1 Aug: *It appears that I was in error on Thursday last; the Gentleman, whom I mistook for Mr. Henry Pole, turns out to be the Revd. R. Pole, nephew of Sir C. Pole, and second son of Sir P. Pole, being beneficed in Hants: he married a Miss Elmhirst.*

POLE — Watson Buller Pole — *later* Van Notten-Pole [168]

Watson Buller Pole (1803-1900), Church of England clergyman, was the third son of Charles Pole (1772-1864) and Felizarda Matilda Buller (1776-1872). He was educated at Rugby School and Balliol College, Oxford (BA 1825), and entered the Church. He was rector of Upper Swell, 1828-81, and Condicote, 1840-81. He married, 11 August 1846, his cousin Matilda (1807-1887), daughter of Sir Peter Pole, 2nd baronet (1770-1850), and Anna Guerherlmina Buller; there were no children.

Watson had a close relationship with Francis Witts—closer than that of his father—but there were differences in opinion that occasionally crept to the surface; for example, Watson Pole's dislike of the new poor laws in 1837. Nevertheless, as both men were closely involved in local administration they were in frequent contact, most often at the justice room and the Provident Bank.

1825: 12 Mar: *We dined at Mr. Ford's, at Little Risington,. Mr. Watson B. Pole was also of the party.*

1826: 28 Jul.

1827: 4 Jul: *We had a few of our bachelor clerical neighbours to dinner to-day: Mr. Hurd, Mr. Baillie, Mr. Jones, Mr. Hankins, Mr. Winter and Mr. W.B. Pole, one of the Sons of Mr. Pole of Wyck Hill, who has lately taken Deacon's orders, and is the Curate of Oddington.* 7 Sep., 12 Sep.

1828: 23 Apr., 2 Jul., 22 Jul., 27 Sep., 8 Oct: *My wife and I dined at Mrs. Hastings's, meeting a large party, William & Watson Pole.*

1829: 21 Jan: *We had a party of our friends to dinner. Mr. Ford, Mr. Winter, and Mr. W. B. Pole. Mr. Ford slept here.* 31 Jul., 10 Aug., 22 Sep: *Col. & Mrs. Clitherow & Revd. W. B. Pole (they were guests at the Palace, having come from Wyck Hill, M Col. Clitherow being cousin of the Bishop;)*

1832: 19 Mar.

1833: 14 Jan: *Mr. W. B. Pole joined our domestic circle at dinner.* 1 Feb: *We dined at Mr. Leighs's at Broadwell, and met Sir Chas. and Lady Imhoff, Miss Chapuset, Mr. & Mrs. Vavasour of Stow, Messrs. W. B. and Mundy Pole.*

1834: 9 Mar., 24 Jul., 26 Jul., 31 Jul., 7 Aug., 9 Aug., 13 Aug: *Met Mr. Pole and his son Watson, who had arrived last evening.* 20-21 Aug., 28 Aug., 4 Sep., 25 Oct., 30 Oct., 13 Nov., 21 Nov., 17 Dec., 24 Dec., 26 Dec.

1835: 4 Jan: *Notes passed to-day between Mr. Pole and myself, with reference to the business of the Prov. Bank, to the Stow Police Establishment, to the Northleach Police Establishment, and to the temporary appointment of a Clergyman to officiate at Upper and Lower Swell during the indisposition of Watson Pole. I took his duty this afternoon at Lower Swell. He has been more or less unwell for some months; his malady being general debility, probably arising from some derangement of the digestive organs; latterly, being alarmed by losing almost entirely the sight of his right eye, probably, from some sympathetic connection with the derangement of his viscera, he has gone for medical advice to Cheltenham, whence he proceeds to London for further medical aid, and to join his Father and Mother there, who leave Wyck Hill for the metropolis to-morrow.* 11 Jan., 18 Jan., 18 Apr: *Watson having experienced a relapse has gone down to Brighton with Mrs. Pole.* 30 May: *Drove with Mrs. Witts to Wyck-hill to call on the Poles: found Mr. and Mrs. Pole and Watson at home.*

1836: 16 Aug., 18 Aug., 21 Dec.

1837: 2 Mar., 23 Mar., 30 Mar., 4 Apr., 27 Apr., 3-4 May, 12 May, 16 May, 18 May, 22-23 May, 31 May, 1 Jun., 12 Jun, 29 Jun., 3 Jul: *Found Mr. & Mrs. P. and W B P. at home.* 8 Jul., 27 Jul: *Accompanied Mr. Pole, & W. B. Pole to the new Workhouse.* 13-14 Sep., 16 Sep., 25 Sep., 3 Oct: *Recd. a note from Mr. Pole requesting me to perform the duty on Sunday next at Lower Swell in his Son's absence.* 4 Oct., 8 Oct., 10-11 Oct., 14-15 Oct., 8 Nov: *Drove MW. to Wyck Hill to call on various branches of the Pole family now collected there. Found assembled at the luncheon table Mr. and Mrs. Pole, Mr. & Mrs. C. R. Pole, Mrs. Clitherow, Mrs. Rudge, W. B. Pole, Mr. and Mrs. Winter.* 13 Dec.

1838: 11 Jan., 16 Jan., 23 Jan., 1 Feb., 5 Feb., 7-8 Feb., 21-22 Feb., 1 Mar., 8 Mar., 12 Apr., 26 Apr., 30 Apr., 2 May, 15 May, 17 May, 31 May, 12 Jul., 3 Aug., 11 Aug., 19 Aug., 22 Aug., 31 Aug., 25 Sep., 27 Sep., 4 Oct., 12 Dec., 17 Dec., 27 Dec.

1839: 17 Jan., 14 Feb., 28 Feb., 6 Mar: *As I returned met at L Swell W B Pole, who walked some considerable distance conversing with me on various topics.* 7 Mar., 12 Mar: *At Geo. Pain's met with W B Pole, who engaged me in a long and on his part warm discussion on Poor Law Management; he is of the opposers of the new system, and has fixed on a case within our Union where a distressed family, the head being visited with mental derangement, are in circumstances of almost unavoidable distress calculated to create warm sympathy.* 14 Mar., 17-18 Mar., 21 Mar., 28 Mar., 23 May, 6 Jun., 27 Jun., 11 Jul., 22 Aug., 25 Aug.

1840: 19 Mar., 20 Mar: *Wrote to W B Pole my feelings at considerable detail with reference to the painful conversation I had yesterday with Winter in his presence.* 21 Mar: *Wrote to W B*

Pole a further letter of explanation on the subject which had been warmly discussed between Winter and myself on Thursday; also sent him Mrs. Pearce's letter received by me yesterday in elucidation of the case. 26 Mar., 4 Apr., 6 Apr: *at the Library met with W B Pole, who was fearful that a severe cold which made him dread exposure to the night air would prevent him from dining with us on Wednesday next.* 8 Apr: *A dinner party at home—Mr & Mrs. Waller from Farmington—Mr. & Mrs. Ford, with Dulcibella and Sophia Ford—Mr. Bowen, who slept here—and W B. Pole made up the party.* 9 Apr., 18 Apr., 21 Apr., 7 May: *and a note from W B Pole inviting me to dinner as to-day in Craig's Court, and again on Saturday, if I remained so long in Town.* 8 May: *Answered the note I had received yesterday from W B Pole, thanking him for the invitations to dinner at Craig's Court, which it was out of my power to accept, and apologizing for not having called upon his mother.* 25 May, 1 Jun: *Called on Mr. Pole: his son Watson with him. Much conversation on many points private and public; among the latter on constabulary, and poor Law matters.* 18 Jun., 25 Jun., 9 Jul., 16 Jul., 21 Jul., 23 Jul., 25 Jul., 30 Jul., 13 Aug., 20 Aug., 27 Aug., 10 Sep., 12 Sep., 24 Sep., 29 Sep., 2 Oct., 8 Oct., 24 Oct., 29 Oct., 5 Nov., 12 Nov: *A full bench of magistrates—the Dean of Gloucester, Messrs. Pole, Ford, R. Waller and myself, assisted by Messrs. C. R. Pole, E. Rudge, W B. Pole, Baillie, Winter, Lewes.* 22 Nov., 24 Nov., 26 Nov.

1841: 4 Mar.

1842: 12 Jan., 18 Jan., 20 Jan., 3 Feb., 10 Feb., 17 Feb., 24-25 Feb., 27 Feb., 11-12 Mar., 14 Mar., 22-24 Mar., 31 Mar., 19 May, 23 May, 26 My, 9 Jun., 16 Jun., 23 Jun., 4 Jul., 7-8 Jul., 14 Jul., 20 Jul: *A dinner party; we were favoured with the company of Mr. and Mrs. Pole, Watson Pole.* 21 Jul., 28 Jul., 25 Aug., 27-28 Jul., 4 Aug., 11 Aug., 18 Aug., 25 Aug., 29 Aug., 8 Sep., 15 Sep., 22 Sep., 27 Sep., 29 Sep., 13 Oct., 24 Oct., 3 Nov., 10 Nov., 22 Dec.

1843: 17 Jan., 19 Jan., 26 Jan., 9 Feb., 16 Feb., 11 Aug., 26 Sep., 12 Oct., 26 Oct., 7 Nov., 9 Nov., 16 Nov., 23 Nov., 30 Nov., 13-14 Dec., 21 Dec.

1844: 11 Jan., 8 Feb., 15 Feb., 22 Feb., 29 Feb., 14 Mar., 21 Mar., 4 Apr., 18-19 Apr., 26 Apr., 2 May, 6 May, 9 May, 10 May, 16 May, 14 Aug, 22 Aug., 29 Aug., 14 Sep., 19 Sep., 26 Sep., 11 Oct., 31 Oct., 7 Nov., 28 Nov., 5 Dec., 11-12 Dec., 19 Dec., 26 Dec.

1845: 7 Jan., 9 Jan., 16 Jan., 30 Jan., 6 Feb., 20 Feb., 27 Feb., 13 Mar., 15 Mar., 20 Mar., 10-11 Apr., 22 May, 26 May, 29 May, 5 Jun., 9 Jun., 11-12 Jun., 26-27 Jun., 5 Jul., 23 Jul., 24 Jul: *Wrote to Harry E Waller, M. H. Estcourt, and W B Pole invitations to dinner on the 29th. Inst.—W. B. Pole declines accepting the invitation, as he is leaving home preparatory to his marriage on the 11th. Aug. to his cousin the daughter of Sir Peter Pole: the attachment is of 15 or 16 years standing; objections were formerly made by the Parents on both sides as to consanguinity, but these scruples are at last surmounted, and the lovers now no longer young, are to be united at last, with ample pecuniary means on both sides.* 6 Aug., 28 Oct: *With MW. drove to call on the newly married couple at Upper Swell; Mr. & Mrs. W. B. Pole: before arriving there met Mr. Lambert.* 10 Nov., 12 Nov., 26 Nov., 24 Dec., 31 Dec.

1847: 9 Jan., 27 Jan., 4 Feb., 18 Mar., 25 Mar., 29 Mar., 1 Apr., 15 Apr., 24 May, 27 May, 29 May, 7-8 Jul., 15 Jul., 22 Jul., 5 Aug., 25 Aug., 16 Sep: *W B Pole was confined to his room owing to a hurt in the leg.* 21 Sep., 23 Sep., 25 Oct., 8 Nov., 18 Nov., 22 Nov., 8 Dec., 23 Dec., 30 Dec.

1848: 3 Feb., 10 Feb., 17 Feb., 2 Mar., 16 Mar., 6 Apr., 17 Apr., 27 Apr., 11 May, 16 May, 22 May, 29 May, 1 Jun., 8 Jun., 14 Jun., 6 Jul., 7-8 Aug., 11 Aug., 14 Sep., 24 Oct., 2 Nov., 7 Nov., 9 Nov.

1849: 12-13 Dec., 20 Dec., 27 Dec.

1850: 10 Jan., 24 Jan., 31 Jan., 7 Feb., 14 Feb., 21 Feb., 28 Feb., 1 Mar., 7 Mar., 14 Mar., 18 Mar., 21 Mar., 28 Mar., 19 Apr., 29 Apr., 15 May: *Mr. W. B. Pole kindly called on me.* 27 Jun., 8 Jul: *a sore correspondence between W B Pole and Hippisley on a question relating to the administration of baptism, in which the former, I am afraid, is wrong.* 10 Jul., 1 Aug., 29 Aug., 10 Sep., 12 Sep., 18 Sep., 26 Sep., 30 Sep: *Met and parleyed with W. B. Pole.* 1 Oct., 3 Oct., 24 Oct., 31 Oct., 6 Nov., 21 Nov., 28 Nov., 11-12 Dec., 19 Dec., 21 Dec., 26 Dec.

1851: 9 Jan., 16 Jan., 23 Jan., 30 Jan., 6 Feb., 13 Feb., 20 Feb., 27 Feb., 13 Mar., 27 Mar., 3 Apr., 10 Apr., 17 Apr., 24 Apr., 8 May, 15 May.

1852: 22 Jan., 29 Jan., 5 Feb., 12 Feb., 19 Feb., 4 Mar., 25 Mar., 27 Mar., 1 Apr., 12 Apr., 15-16 Apr., 19 Apr: *Received a note from Mrs. W. B. Pole, accepting my invitation to dinner on Thursday for herself and her husband.* 22 Apr: ... *other Guests were Sir Henry Vavasour, Mrs. W. Vavasour, Mrs. M. Vavasour, Mr. Stavely, Mr. and Mrs. W B Pole, Mr. and Mrs. Winter. All went off agreeably, Mrs. W. V. sang, and conversation did not flag.* 6 May, 12-13 May, 19-20 May, 27 May, 3 Jun., 7 Jun., 25 Oct., 28 Oct., 9 Dec., 16 Dec., 21-22 Dec., 30 Dec.

1853: 13 Jan., 20 Jan., 10 Feb., 17 Feb., 24 Feb., 3 Mar., 10 Mar., 22 Mar., 24 Mar., 31 Mar: *Having dressed at G. Pain's, and the Carriage having come from U.S. bringing Mr. Ball, who had been taken up at Lower Slaughter Turnpike Gate, I went to dine with Mr. and Mrs. W.B. Pole at Upper Swell.* 7 Apr., 14 Apr., 21-22 Apr., 28 Apr., 5 May, 13 May, 19 May, 24 May, 26 May: *I had Recd. this morning a kind note from Mr. W B Pole inviting me to dine there in a family way, after the business of the day at Stow, and take Mrs. W. V. home at night. To this I assented by a message conveyed to Mrs. W.B. Pole by Mrs. W. Vavasour.* 8 Jun., 8 Dec., 14-15 Dec., 22 Dec., 29-30 Dec.

1854: 2 Feb., 4 Feb: *Luncheon at W B Pole's; he accompanied me to the Cottage of an alleged pauper Lunatic, where we were met by Hayward as Medical Adviser.* 6 Feb., 9 Feb., 16 Feb., 23 Feb., 2 Mar., 8 Mar: *W B Pole, having heard of my spasmodic attack, kindly called on me.* 9 Mar., 16 Mar., 30 Mar., 6 Apr., 13 Apr., 20 Apr., 23 Apr., 25 Apr., 27-28 Apr., 25 May, 8-9 Jun., 15 Jun., 22 Jun., 24 Jun., 29 Jun., 6 Jul., 13 Jul., 20 Jul., 27 Jul., 3 Aug., 10 Aug., 14 Aug., 17 Aug.

POLE — William Pole — *later* Van Notten-Pole[169]

William Pole (1798-1900), barrister-at-law, was the second son of Charles Pole (1772-1864) and Felizarda Matilda Buller (d. 1872). He was educated at Eton College, Balliol College, Oxford (BA 1829; MA 1824), and the Middle Temple. He married, 17 November 1852, Harriet, daughter of Hieronimus Burmester. There were no children of the marriage. William effectively saw out the nineteenth century, dying on 30 December 1900, aged 102. At probate, he left £32,897 *6s 9d*. Two of his brothers, Mundy and Watson Buller, also died in 1900; a third, Lambert, lived until 1906. They were an extremely long-lived family.

1828: 8 Oct: *My wife and I dined at Mrs. Hastings's, meeting a large party, William & Watson Pole.* 19 Dec.

1829: 20 Mar.

1836: 25 Oct: *Mr. Pole assisted me in this very irksome duty: he was accompanied by his son William, the Barrister.*

1847: 7 Oct: *On my return home, met and held a parley with Mr. William Pole.*

POLHILL — William Polhill [170]

William Polhill (1795-1868), army officer, was the second son of Edward Polhill (1761-1837), tobacco merchant of York Place, Marylebone, and Sarah Ward, née Spooner (1768-1836), daughter of John Spooner of Barbados [*The Topographer and Genealogist* states her name as Jane Ward, née Spooner]. His parents married on 18 January 1787. He was baptised on 17 January 1796.

Polhill was commissioned as a cornet in the 16th Light Dragoons in July 1813, and was present at the battle of Waterloo. He was also present at the ball given by the duchess of Richmond. His tunic and vest, elaborately embroidered with gold and silver thread, together with the plume from his shako, are preserved in the Museum of the Royal United Service Institution, Whitehall.

Polhill was promoted to lieutenant in December 1815 and transferred to the Life Guards in October 1816. In January 1819 he moved to the 23rd Light Dragoons. On his retirement from the Army, Polhill went to live at Millbrook, Broadwell, where he held in his garden an annual celebration for the victory at Waterloo. In the 1861 census he was listed as farming 200 acres and employing eight men. He was known to be eccentric; one of his antagonists in the parish of Broadwell was the equally eccentric Adm. Jodrell Leigh (d. 1863), who lived at the manor house. Polhill died unmarried in 1867.

There is a question mark over the business of William Polhill's descendants. Beneath his name in a surviving family tree there is a short vertical line leading to the name Maria. She may have been his illegitimate daughter.

1826: 17 Apr: *We dined at Mr. Dolphin's at Eyford. We met there Mr. Talbot, Mr. & Mrs. R. Wynniatt, our old friend Mr. J. Dolphin, Mr. Bowen, & Mr. Polhill: the latter gentleman is almost entirely domiciliated at Eyford, at least during the winter & spring.*

1827: 16 Aug: *Besides these Mr. & Mrs. Stavely and the assiduous Captn. Polhill, long Mr. Dolphin's fidus Achates, and guest for months at a time, were staying in the house.*

1828: 5 Nov: *We dined at Eyford. The Dolphins have a large party in their house; Mrs. & three Miss Knights, Mrs. Payne, Miss Rollinson and her nephew, & Mr. Polhill.*

1829: 10 Jun: *We had a party of friends & neighbours to dinner. From Eyford Mrs. Payne & Mr. Polhill; Mr. & Mrs. Dolphin being now in Town, & having left her mother staying at their house, as also Polhill, who may almost be said to live there, assisting his friend in the management of his farm, and forgetting the habits and gaieties of a life-guardsman, contenting himself in a hospitable seclusion, which has been rendered the more acceptable by a curtailment of his resources incident to fashionable extravagance &, to say the least of it, indiscretion. Let us hope, however, that there is real good at bottom; Polhill's manners are gentlemanly & cheerful, & he is a very constant and attentive member of my congregation.*

1833: 13 Sep: *Polhill called between services.* 24 Oct.

1834: 10 Aug: *Polhill called after Evening Service.* 15 Aug., 6 Nov., 13 Nov.

1835: 14 Jan: *Mr. Polhill, who occupied the mansion house along with the farm which he rents from Mr. Dolphin, has lately retired to a new house, a farm house of a superior description, lately just erected about a quarter of a mile from the mansion house. It is said that Mrs. Dolphin, from resources of her own, over which her husband had no controul, but which she applied to this use, has paid for the erection of this farmhouse.* 17 Jan: *Walked to Eyford to call on Mr. Polhill at his new residence. He was not at home.* 25 Jan., 26 Jan: *Mr. Polhill called and gave an account that our friend, Mr. Browne, of Salperton, was suffering under severe illness.* 5 Feb., 22 Feb., 12 Apr., 17 Apr., 7 May, 20 May.

1836: 5 Aug., 5 Sep: *Polhill joined our dinner party.* 12 Sep., 22 Oct., 26 Oct., 1 Dec.

1837: 16 Jun., 27 Jul., 4 Nov: *Rode to Stow with Tarn and Polhill.* 3 Dec: *Attended while Hayward, who had been sent for by Polhill, the boy's Employer, placed the limb in the proper position, and assisted him in binding it up.* 5 Dec., 8 Dec.

1838: 21 Jun., 9 Aug., 1 Sep., 8 Nov.

1839: 14 Feb., 21 Feb., 11 May.

1842: 19 May.

1843: 21 Sep., 26 Oct., 14 Nov.

1844: 11 Jan., 22 Jan., 29 Feb., 28 Mar., 2 Oct: *Much engaged in Justice business at home;—particularly with Capt. Polhill, as to a trespass in pursuit of game on his land by a person not having a certificate: received a letter on this subject from Mr. Morgan.* 3 Oct.

1845: 6 Feb., 27 Mar., 10 Apr., 19 Jun.

1846: 27 Jun: *Wrote to Mr. Polhill, forwarding to him the letter I recd. from Mr. Pearce yesterday, containing an explanation as to the circumstances under which leave to go to Broadwell for a day or two had been allowed to a pauper inmate of the Workhouse from that parish.* 6 Jul., 9 Jul., 23 Jul., 13 Aug., 3 Sep., 17 Sep., 24 Sep., 8 Oct., 5 Nov., 31 Dec.

1847: 3 Jun: *After the business of the Union, I was engaged for nearly an hour, as a Magistrate, in hearing the complaints of Mr. Polhill and Mr. Potter as to an unwholesome nuisance at Broadwell.* 14 Sep., 14 Oct., 28 Oct., 11 Nov., 25 Nov., 9 Dec: *This charge, though supported by Mr. Polhill, will, I fully believe, prove to be without reasonable ground, and originates very much in personal antipathy against Mr. Beman.* 14 Dec., 16 Dec., 23 Dec.

1848: 11 Jun: *Wrote to Vernon Dolphin explaining to him that I did not receive his letter till 5 P.M. yesterday, and therefore could not meet him at Bourton at the hour he had named.——Enclosed my note under cover to Mr. Polhill, to whom I wrote a few lines, requesting him to forward my note to V.D. if he had left Broadwell .. Encountered Mrs. Hutchinson and Miss C Knight, with whom conversed as to the agitating affair of Vernon Dolphin's visit to Mr. Polhill at Broadwell. The latter had not invited, nor expected him, and, on finding him at his house, came to Eyford to announce to Mrs. Dolphin the arrival of her husband.* 15 Jun: *Learnt from Mr. Wilkins that Vernon Dolphin had quitted the neighbourhood, some arrangement having been made as between the husband and wife, in which Harry Waller and Mr. Polhill were the negociating parties.* 22 Jun: *Mr. Ford and myself held a Petty Sessions: Mr. Polhill, with whom I conversed on the affairs of Mr. and Mrs. Dolphin, was present with us.* 6 Jul., 7 Aug: *... making extensive repairs, additions and alterations to the mansion house at Eyford; as resolved to dismantle, and even pull down, the farm house at the Parks, erected only a few years ago for the residence of Mr. Polhill, and since occupied by W. Smith, Moore &c.*

1850: 1 Aug., 7 Nov., 28 Nov.

1851: 13 Feb: *Much interest was this day excited as to this case, most of the resident Owners and occupiers of land in Broadwell, with many others, being present, also, of gentlemen, W B Pole, Winter, Polhill, Potter, W. Vavasour, E.F. W.* 15 May.

1852: 22 Apr.

1853: 15 Dec.

1854: 24 Jun., 27 Jul.

POLLARD — Sophia Pollard of Dublin [171]

Sophia Pollard, née Bull (d. 1835), was the daughter of William Bull of Dublin. She married, 10 June 1782, William Pollard, of Castle Pollard, Westmeath, who died some time before 1824. They had at least 1 son and 3 daughters:

1 Sophia; married John Hill Foster
1 William Dutton Pollard (1789-1839)
2 Louisa Anne Pakenham (b. 1792)
3 Anna Maria; married, 1836, Matthias Kenny (±1788-1874); no children

Sophia Pollard was the younger sister of Anne Bull, who married William Vavasour, thus making Sophia (senior) Richard Vavasour's aunt.

1835: 5 May: *Mr. Vavasour had heard to-day of the sudden death of his Aunt, Mrs. Pollard.*

1845: 19 Feb: *A medical gentleman, Dr. Kenny, from Ireland, who had been many years back the professional attendant of the Vavasours, and of their connections, the Pollards, and who, some few years ago, married Miss Pollard, happened very opportunely to have lately arrived at Cheltenham after a sojourn abroad.*

POLLOCK — Jonathan Frederick Pollock[172]

Sir Jonathan Frederick Pollock, 1st baronet (1783-1870), attorney-general, was the third son of David Pollock (d. 1815), saddler, of Charing Cross, Westminster, and Sarah Homeria, daughter of Richard Parsons, receiver-general of customs. He was was educated at Trinity College, Cambridge (BA 1806; MA 1809), where he was elected a fellow in 1807, and Middle Temple (1802). He was called to the bar in 1807. Pollock was MP for Huntingdon, 1831-44; attorney-general, December 1834–April 1835 and September 1841–April 1844; and chief baron of the exchequer, 1844-66. He was knighted in 1834 and created a baronet in 1866.

Pollock married, first, 1813, Frances Rivers (d. 1827); and secondly, 1834, Sarah Anne Amowah. There were numerous children from both marriages.

1834: 17 Dec: *The following ministerial appointments are announced ... Mr. F. Pollock, Attorney General.*

1839: 6 May: *Mr. W. spoke of the prospects of his client with sanguine confidence, and mentioned that their leading counsel, Sir Fredk. Pollock, a man of high authority, considered their case as a strong one.* 7 May, 10 May: *Recd. a letter from Round acquainting me that there was every prospect that a firm Conservative government would be formed ... and Sir Fred. Pollock and Mr. Cresswell were to hold the posts of Attorney and Solr. Genl.*

1845: 2 Apr: *The Judges, the Lord Chief Baron, Sir Fred. Pollock, and Mr. Justice Platt, arrived from Monmouth in the usual course, being met by the High Sheriff at Over Bridge.* 3 Apr: *Charteris sat by the D. of Beaufort, who again was on the right hand of the Chief Baron, so that I was near enough to appreciate the lively and talented talk of Sir. F. Pollock, who appeared to great advantage as contrasted with his heavy brother, Platt.*

POLSON — Hugh Polson — *see also* Billingsley *and* Thackwell[173]

Hugh Polson (1807-1873), Church of England clergyman, was the son of John Hugh Pasley Polson (1781-1829), of Upton Helions, Devon, and Frances Sarah (1777-1821). He was educated at Exeter College, Oxford (BA 1829). He married, at Charlton-on-Otmoor, Oxfordshire, 12 December 1830, Georgina (1811-1873), daughter of Capt. George Crawley and Charlotte Yonge, both of the Crawley Boevey family. Hugh and Georgina had 2 sons and 3 daughters:

1 Arthur (b. ±1832)
2 George Henry (±1834-1889)
1 Catharina Rosalie (1836-1903)
2 Catharina (±1836)
3 Georgiana Alethe (b. 1838)

Hugh Polson was curate at Bourton-on-the-Water, and later at Woolstone, Berkshire. By 1861 the family was living at 92 Windsor Terrace, Plymouth, and Hugh was listed as a clergymen without cure of souls. There is a title deed dated 1868 showing Hugh and Georgina Polson to have bought property at Yolland, Devon, worth £29,000; they could not have been poor. Georgina died at Southernhay, Exeter, on 10 November 1873, followed two weeks later, at Monaco, by her widower.

Hugh Polson's sister Charlotte married, 1842, John Cam Thackwell, and his other sister, Elizabeth, married, 1838, John Richard Frederick Billingsley (1805-1878). Billingsley was born in Eynsham and matriculated in 1823 at Lincoln College, Oxford (BA 1829; MA 1830). He became curate of Bourton-on-the-Water in 1834 and later moved to Wormington as rector. At some point in the late 1840s his wife Elizabeth died, quite possibly after giving birth to their daughter Lydia Marcie. The disconsolate widower later entered into liaisons with servants which brought him into disgrace.

Hugh Polson also had a connection with the Daubeny family through his wife (*see* diary entry, 18 October 1842). It was probably through the Crawley/Daubeny/Waller connection that he came to Bourton in the first place, but this has not yet been investigated.

1836: 27 Jul: *Messrs. Polson and Geo. Daubeny called before dinner.* 2 Aug., 16 Aug: *With Mrs. W., Howell, and E.F. W. dined at the Poles, at Wyck Hill, where we met a large party from the Fords Mr. & Mrs. F. and their youngest Son, accompanied by Mrs. F.'s brother, Capt. Rooke, and his lady, a very agreeable woman: Mr. Mrs. and Miss Polson, Geo. Daubeny, W. B. Pole, and Winter made the party at the dinner table.* 22 Aug: *Looked in at the Polsons, and at Billingsley's.* 24 Aug., 3 Sep., 27 Sep., 12 Oct: *Entertained at dinner Mr. and Mrs. Polson, Mr. Billingsley and Geo. Daubeny.* 12 Nov., 30 Nov., 2 Dec., 9 Dec., 16 Dec., 20 Dec.

1837: 16 Jan., 20 Jan., 26 Jan., 12 Feb., 15 Feb., 17 Feb: *Entertained at dinner Mr. & Mrs. Cameron, Mr. & Miss S. Vavasour, Messrs. Ford, Billingsley, Polson, & Daubeny.* 2 Mar., 13 Apr., 17 Apr: *Polson has ceased to be Curate.* 19 Apr., 25 Apr: *I drove to Bourton on the Water to dine at the Polson, where I met Ford, Bowen, R. Waller, Billingsley & Geo. Daubeny.* 26 Apr: *Mr. and Mrs. Polson and Geo. Daubeny walked over to make a morning visit, and enquire after Mrs. Backhouse.* 28 Apr., 9 May, 13 May, 16 May, 23 May, 31 May, 14 Jun., 16 Jun., 20 Jun., 3 Jul., 19 Jul: *My son dined with Mr. Daubeny at Bourton: who is now residing at Polson's house; the latter being on an excursion with his family in the Isle of Wight.* 28 Aug., 31 Aug., 6 Sep: *After our return recd. a morning visit from Mr. and Mrs. Polson, who brought with them Mrs. R. Waller and Sir Thomas Crawley, Uncle to Mrs. Polson, who is passing a few days with his niece.* 6 Sep: *After our return recd. a morning visit from Mr. and Mrs. Polson, who brought with them Mrs. R. Waller and Sir Thomas Crawley, Uncle to Mrs. Polson, who is passing a few days with his niece.* 20 Sep., 26 Sep., 7 Oct., 10 Oct., 17 Nov., 5 Dec., 8 Dec., 15 Dec., 19 Dec.

1838: 2 Feb., 5 Mar: *Called at Mr. Polson's door to make enquiries after Mrs. P. who was lately confined of a daughter.* 8 Mar., 20 Apr., 25 Apr., 30 Apr., 7 May, 9 May, 22 May: *Mrs. Polson with her eldest boy, conducted by Geo. Daubeny, came soon after: (Mr. Polson is absent in Devonshire;) they all drank tea here.* 1 Jun: *Mr. & Mrs. Polson imparted to me in confidence that a marriage was contemplated between Polson's sister, Bessy, a very nice, pleasing girl, who is just returned into Devon, after a visit of a twelvemonth at Bourton, and our good friend Billingsley, which seems likely to contribute to the happiness of all parties.* 13 Jun., 16 Jun: *Mr. & Mrs Polson made a morning visit to us.* 25 Jun., 14 Jul., 28 Jul., 8

Aug., 20 Aug., 24 Aug., 7 Sep., 20 Sep: *Mr. and Mrs. Polson called in the course of the day.* 25 Sep., 29 Sep., 2 Oct: *Met Polson, when I called at his house, but did not go in, as his lady had gone to Oxford.* 5 Oct., 22 Oct: *Returning home I met Mr. & Mrs. Polson, accompanied by a relation (Mr. C. Crawley) who had been making a morning visit at our house.* 6 Dec: *At the desire of the latter I signed Polson's Testimonial in order to his being licenced to the Curacy of Bourton on the W., and promised to take his duty at L. Slaughter on Sunday the 16th. when he will be absent in Devonshire, whither he goes to be present at his sister's marriage.* 4 Dec: *When I reached home, I found Billingsley come to make a parting visit previously to leaving Bourton on the W. for Exeter to-morrow, where his Union with Miss. E. Polson is fixed for the 13th. Inst.* 16 Dec., 28 Dec.

1839: 18 Jan., 29 Jan., 27 Feb., 1 Mar., 4 Mar., 14 Apr., 27 Apr., 1 May, 17 May, 24 May, 1 Jun., 7 Jun., 19 Jun: *Billingsley and his Lady from Wormington, accompanied by Miss Polson, who is staying with her sister, made a morning call.* 26 Jun., 9 Jul., 1 Aug.

1840: 25 May, 2 Jun: *My son's horse having been brought from the Naunton Inn, with an intimation that he was fishing in Aston Brook, and would be here to dinner, I walked across our farm in the expectation of meeting him. I first fell in with Waller and Polson, piscatores, and confabulated for a season with them, and shortly afterwards overtook E.F.W.* 5 Jun., 17 Jun., 15 Jul., 18 Jul., 25 Jul: *Mr. and Mrs. Polson called, but so late and so near our dinner hour that they would not dismount, but held a parley with me at the door.* 5 Aug., 31 Aug., 10 Sep., 15 Sep., 19 Sep., 7 Oct: *Received a party at dinner—Miss Rollinson, who arrived to stay two days with us from Farmington Lodge, Mr. & Mrs. R. Waller, Mr. & Mrs. Cameron, Mr. and Mrs. Polson, and Capt. Leigh.—All went off pleasantly.* 7 Nov., 25 Nov: *I rode to Bourton on the Water to make enquiries after Mr. Polson, of whom I had heard yesterday that he was seriously indisposed. Saw Mrs. P. for a moment, who is uneasy about her husband: his malady seems to be a derangement of the liver; Pitt, the Surgeon of Burford, who had been called in yesterday, had not yet attended.*

1841: 5 Mar: *R. Waller told me yesterday that Polson had finally determined on giving up his curacy.*

1842: 1 Feb: *A letter to MW & myself jointly from Mrs. Polson from Florence, with an animated account of the travels of herself, husband and children, very amusing and a little enthusiastic, but full of kind and grateful feelings towards us.* 18 May: *Drove E.F.W. and Sophy with MW. to call at Wormington Rectory on the Billingsleys: where spent from half an hour to an hour: the first visit since the birth of their little girl: and since the marriage of Miss Poulson to Mr. Thackwell, a gentleman residing at or near Newent.* 18 Oct: *I had pleasure also in meeting Geo. Daubeny, now on a visit to his brother in law, Martin Crawley, whom he had accompanied to the meeting in the Grand Jury room. He has for the present retired from the Curacy of Guildford to the duties of which he has found his health unequal — has been abroad—partly with the Polsons — who are just returned to England, and now fixed for a time at Prestbury.* 30 Nov: *Mr. Polson called on us: I had met him, and strolled with him about the Town; with his wife and children, since their return from their foreign tour, they have he has been residing without any professional engagement at Prestbury.* 2 Dec., 3 Dec: *On our way back through Prestbury we called on the Polsons, sitting some time with them.* 8-9 Dec.

1843: 25 Jan: *At Bourton met Mr. and Mrs. Polson, who are on a visit to the Wallers.* 13 Aug: *Wrote a note to Mr. Polson in the forlorn hope of being able to obtain from him assistance for the service of my church, so as to enable us to make an excursion to the coast.* 14 Aug., 19-20 Aug.

1845: 10 May: *Mr. Aitkens not having distinctly explained whether my services would be required to-morrow at Lower Slaughter Church, I wrote a note to R Waller, and found that they were unnecessary, as if A. had not otherwise provided for the church, Polson was at Bourton on the Water, and would officiate there.*

1847: 12 Jun: *Mr. and Mrs. Polson called on us, and passed an hour with us on their way homewards (Woolston, Berks) from the Billingsleys at Wormington, whence they had brought their younger boy, as also a little girl, a daughter of the Billingsleys; it was pleasant to see the kindly warmth with which the Polsons revisited old neighbours.* 6 Oct: *A letter from Mr. G. F. Newmarch, who writes to enquire whether Mr. Polson is still looking out for a living to purchase.* 7 Oct., 21 Oct: *Found a letter from Mr. Polson in answer to that which I had lately addressed to him: he has given up all thought of purchasing a living.*

1850: 25 Sep: *EFW sends me a letter he had received from Mrs. Polson, whom I imagine he had met in travelling, who writes most kindly of me and of my dear departed wife, expressing a wish that I would visit Polson and herself at Woolston. She also adverts to misconduct on the part of Billingsley, which, I fear, is not a false charge.* 8 Oct.

PONSONBY — **Charles Frederick Ashley Cooper Ponsonby**[174]

Charles Frederick Ashley Cooper Ponsonby, 2nd Baron de Mauley (1815-1896), MP and landed proprietor, was the eldest son of William Francis Spencer Ponsonby (1787-1855) and Henrietta Frances Spencer (d. 1844). He was educated at Eton College and was MP for Poole, 1837-47, and Dungarvan, 1851-52. He married, 9 August 1838, his first cousin, Maria Jane Elizabeth Ponsonby (d. 1897); they had 4 sons and 2 daughters:

1 Helen Geraldine (d. 1949)
2 Emily Priscilla Maria (d. 1926)
1 William Ashley Webb (1843-1918); succeeded as 3rd Baron de Mauley of Canford
2 Maurice John George (1846-1945); succeeded as 4th Baron de Mauley of Canford
3 Frederick John William (1847-1933)
4 Edwin Charles William (1851-1939)

Ponsonby succeeded his father as 2nd Baron de Mauley of Canford in 1855. The family estate was Langford House, near Lechlade.

1853: 4 Apr: *Grand Jury, which included among its members, Nigel Kingscote MP., Sir W Codrington, Hon.—— Ponsonby, Son of Lord De Mauley, Sir J.F. Davis, Sir M. Crawley Boevey, Purnell, Curtis Hayward, Hale, &c.* 5 Apr: *Eighteen sat down to table, including myself and Mr. T. Purnell, Clerical Magistrates, and the High Sheriff. Of the party were Sir. M. Boevey, the Hon—Ponsonby, Purnell, Hale, C. Hayward, &c.*

POOLE — **Isaac Poole**[175]

Isaac Poole (±1809-1881), farmer, was born at Swerford, Oxfordshire, by coincidence the same parish where Francis Witts spent his early childhood years. He married, first, Hannah (1802-1875); they had at least 1 son:

1 Sydney (b. 1839); farmed at Little Hinton, Wiltshire; married, at Little Rissington, Gloucestershire, 16 October 1865, Elizabeth, daughter of John Fox, farmer, of Rissington

He married, secondly, Frances (b. ±1816). Isaac Poole farmed about 40 acres at Bourton-on-the-Water.

1852: 26 Mar: *Isaac Poole called to pay a half year's rent of the land he rents of me at Bourton.*

1853: 25 May: *Met Isaac Poole at or near the fields which he rents of me at Bourton; walked over the land with him. It is improved since it has been in his occupation; I agreed to his proposal as to assisting him in repairing a mound.*

POORE — Edward Poore and the Poore family of Wedhampton, Wiltshire [176]

Edward Poore (1773-1814), attorney and landed proprietor, was the son of Edward Mullins Poore (1742-1795) and Anna-Maria (1747-1812), second daughter of James Montagu, of Lackham, Wiltshire, descended from the earls of Manchester. Edward—Ned—had been articled as a clerk to an attorney and was destined for the law, but it is unclear what he was doing during the time that Francis Witts was at Urchfont. The Mrs Poore referred to in the diaries is presumably his mother, Anna-Maria.

Poore married, first, at St Martin-in-the-Fields, Westminster, 11 December 1794, Martha Ann (1769-1801), second daughter of George Wolff, Danish consul in England; they had 1 son and 1 daughter:

1 Edward (1795-1838); succeeded his great-uncle Sir John Methuen Poore, 1st baronet (1745-1820), as 2nd baronet of Rushall, Wiltshire; married, at Edinburgh, 5 January 1818, Agnes Marjoribanks (1795-1868); 1 son and 5 daughters
1 Matty Wolff (1796-1828)

He married secondly, 3 July 1802, Elizabeth, second daughter of Revd Edward Gilman; they had 2 sons and 2 daughters:

1 J. Phillip Heathcote (b. 1799)
2 Richard Francis Gibson (1804-1852)
1 Eleanora Charlotte Montagu (d. 1900); married, 1839, William Long
2 Annette Gibson (1803-1866); married, 1822, Revd Joseph Haythorne of Hill House, Gloucester

The Poore family, originally of Rushall, were well-to-do; it is clear why Agnes Witts should have wished to associate herself with them.

1806: 21 Sep: *Mrs. Poore of Wedhampton, & her Sister, Mrs. Smith, Mrs. Legge, & Miss Frusler called upon my Mother at Stert.* 25 Sep., 9 Oct., 24 Oct., 5 Nov., 13 Nov., 22 Dec., 27 Dec.

1807: 6 Feb., 11 Feb: *Dined at Wedhampton not unpleasantly with Mrs. Poore & Mrs. Smith.* 16 Feb., 25 Mar., 14 Apr., 16 May, 22 May, 25 May, 2 Jun., 4 Jun., 23 Jun., 28 Jun., 5 Jul., 19 Jul., 23 Jul., 28 Jul., 30 Jul., 9 Aug., 11 Aug., 20 Aug., 23 Aug., 26 Aug., 3 Sep.

1808: 21 Jan., 21 Feb: *Proceeded in the double bodied White Lion Coach, an uneasy vehicle: roads worse & worse, as we advanced: my companions were Mr. Headley of Calne, Ned Poore, &c.* 29 Mar: *Called on Mrs. Poore, admitted to her Bedside for an instant her operation over about a week.* 30 Aug.

POPE — George Uglow Pope [177]

George Uglow Pope (1820-1908), Tamil and Sanskrit scholar, teacher, and missionary, was born at Prince Edward Island, Canada, son of devout Methodists John Pope (1791-1863) and Catherine Uglow. He and his family migrated to England when he was an infant. He left for South India in 1839 and arrived at Sawyerpuram near Tuticorin.

Pope became a scholar of Tamil, Sanskrit, and Telugu. He set up several schools and taught Latin, English, Hebrew, mathematics, and philosophy. He was created DD at Lambeth in 1864 and became a fellow of the University of Madras in 1859. He was created MA at Oxford in 1886. Pope married, first, at Cuddlalore, Madras, India, 1 January 1842, Mary Anderson Carver (1824-1845); they had 2 daughters:

1 Catherine Anderson (1843-1872)
2 Mary Carver (1845-1896)

Pope married secondly, at Madras, Tamil Nadu, India, 29 June 1848, Henrietta Page Van Someron (1830-1911); they had 2 sons and 1 daughter:

1 Henrietta (d. 1911)
1 John van Someren (1850-1930)
2 Arthur (1858-1927)

1850: 1 Feb: *A special meeting S.P.G. at Stow to-day. Drove thither; called at the Rectory, where met Ford, who had come to preside at the meeting, as Rural Dean; we were joined by Messrs. Vernon, one of the Secretaries of the Parent Society, and Mr. Pope, Missionary in the district of Tinivelly in the Diocese of Madras.... Mr. Pope's address was long and exceedingly interesting, detailing his experience for ten years as a Missionary in Southern India; he is by descent of Wesleyan origin; calm, composed, measured in tone, rather too low in voice, but very fluent, very impressive, very clear in his explanations.*

PORT — John Port — *see also* D'Ewes, Granville, *and* Ram [178]

John Port (1730-1807), landed proprietor, was born John Sparrow, the son of Burslem Sparrow (1702-1769), ironmaster, and Frances Newell (b. 1706). His father was from a Staffordshire family that had originally come from Wales. John took the surname Port on succeeding to Ilam on the death of his uncle George Port, formerly Newell. He married, at Upton-cum-Chalvey, Buckinghamshire, 4 December 1770, Mary Pauline (1745-1814), daughter of John D'Ewes (1693-1780), of Wellesbourne, Warwickshire, and Anne Granville (1707-1761) of Buckland, Gloucestershire; they had 4 sons and 4 daughters:

1 Georgina Mary Anne (1771-1850); married, 1789, Benjamin Waddington; at least 2 daughters:
    1 Frances (1791-1876); married, 1 July 1817, Christopher Charles [Christian Karl Josias von] Bunsen (1792-1860); 5 sons and 5 daughters
    2 Augusta (1802-1896); married, 1823, Benjamin Hall (1802-1867), commissioner of works, 1855 ('Big Ben' is said to have been named after him), and MP for Monmouth. Hall was created a baronet in 1838 and entered the House of Lords in 1859 as Baron Llanover under Prime Minister Palmerston
1 John (1773-1837); married, at St George's, East Stonehouse, Devon, 5 November 1795, Mary Parke (1777-1837); 2 sons and 3 daughters:
    1 Louisa Hannah (1797-1858)
    1 John Desbrowe (1799-1802)
    2 George Richard (1800-1882)
    2 Georgina Mary Anne (b. 1802)
    3 Harriet (1804-1877)
2 George Rowe (1774-1794); served in the Royal Navy
3 Bernard (1776-1854), rector of Ilam
2 Louisa (1778-1817); married Revd Brownlow Villiers Layard (1779-1861); 10 sons and 3 daughters
4 Bevil (1780-1804)
3 Harriet (1781-1824)
4 Frances [Fanny] Anne (1783-1860); married, 11 August 1803, Abel John Ram (1776-1823), son of Abel Ram (1753-1836) and Elizabeth Stopford (b. 1758) of Clonatin, co. Wexford; 1 son and 2 daughters:
    1 Abel John Ram (1804-1883), Church of England clergyman; married, 11 April 1833, a cousin, Jane Stopford (1806-1873); 3 sons and 2 daughters
    1 Frances Mary Anne (1808-1889); died unmarried at Bournemouth
    2 Unknown

Mrs Mary A. Delany, née Granville (1700-1788), the great favourite of King George III and Queen Charlotte, took over the education of her great-niece Georgiana Mary Ann Port in 1778 when Georgiana was 7 years old. The girl came to live with her in London. The Port family lived at Ilam Hall, a Tudor mansion in Staffordshire; they sold it in 1809 to David Pike Watts, who completely remodelled it.

The Port family were great favourites of Revd John [D'Ewes] Granville of Calwich; Mary was his favourite sister. The Port children were frequently at Calwich Abbey, or staying with the Granvilles on their frequent visits to Cheltenham, Clifton, and other places. Francis Witts developed an infatuation for Fanny Port in 1801, but it was not to be; his means and prospects would not have been deemed good enough.

1801: 30 Jan: *Doubtful weather, but fine enough for walking. Mr. Granville, Mrs. G. Miss Port, Miss Rook &c.* 15 Jun: *After dinner sat for a quarter of an hour with Mr. Port and his Daughter.* 28 Oct: *I danced three dances with Fanny Port, a charming girl.* 31 Oct: *Fanny Port breakfasted with us, I saw much of the Granvilles & her during the course of the day.* 2 Nov: *The dinner & Evening were most pleasant Fanny Port in particular a sweet young woman.* 3 Nov., 4 Nov: *We met there the Granvilles &c. Fanny Port pleasing as ever.* 5 Nov., 6 Nov: *Also early in the morning to the Well, & to the Turnpike with Fanny.* 7 Nov: *Walked to Sandford & Charlton, & afterwards with my Mother, Mrs. Granville, & the amiable Fanny Port.* 8 Nov: *In the Evening came Mrs. & Miss Wyndham forming a party, which would have been dull, had not the Granvilles & my friend Fanny stept in to enliven conversation.* 9 Nov: *Dined & spent the Evening with the Granvilles meeting Mr. & Mrs. Hunt. As usual there most agreeable. Fanny & I alone did not play at Cards.* 10 Nov: *Adjourned to a party at Mr. Newell's, the great Cheltenham Apothecary, where I was against my desire forced to play at Cards, & could not enjoy the Conversation of Fanny or of any of the friends, whom I met there.* 11 Nov., 14 Nov: *Miss Sophia & Miss Louisa Jones dined with us, the former, repairing with us to tea & Cards at Mr. Rooke's, where her powers of attraction fell before the unassuming preeminence of the amiable Fanny, who with the Granvilles, Mrs. Newell, & Miss Markham were also there.* 16 Nov., 17 Nov: *Fanny as usual worth all the rest... Walked with the Granville party, conversing mostly with Fanny, who becomes every day more interesting.* 19 Nov., 20 Nov: *Dined at Mr. Granville's, meeting Mr. & Mrs. Newell, & Mr. & Miss Hughes. Of course most agreeable; the Evening we spent there also, Fanny playing us, & dressed in blue ribbands looking charmingly.* 22 Nov., 23 Nov: *Walked with the Granvilles &c. Fanny it may be supposed the centre of attraction. Took leave of them with bitterness of heart previous to their Departure for Bath tomorrow.*

1802: 2 Jan: *With them we repaired to Alfred St. to dinner; there, as some former pages shew, that I have not been insensible to her merit, the lovely Fanny occupied much of my thoughts & observations: she was amiable & obliging, soft & beautiful as before, & not the worse now for a severe attack of an Influenza. To her Brother the Revd. Bernard Port very lately of Brazenose College I was introduced, & found in him a very pleasant Companion. In the Evening the party separated. Bernard Port & I went to the Theatre.* 3-5 Jan., 11 Sep: *Found at that Charming place (Calwich) Mr. & Mrs. Granville, Mr. Delabere Fanny & Bernard Port.* 12-13 Sep., 16 Sep., 17 Sep: *Rode with Mrs. Granville & Fanny to the summit of Wever.* 18 Sep., 20 Sep: *Attended Mrs. Granville & my Mother in the Gig. Riding tête à tête with the Dear Fanny.* 27 Sep., 28 Sep., 30 Sep., 10 Oct.

1803: 27-28 Dec., 30-31 Dec.

1804: 3 Jan., 4 Jan: *Called on the Ports, sitting some time with Miss Leyard, Harriet, & her Father. Poor Leyard afterwards was taken terribly ill.* 7 Jan., 9-10 Jan., 16 Jul., 27 Jul., 4-5 Aug., 11 Aug., 17-18 Aug., 3-4 Sep., 11 Sep., 19 Sep., 24-25 Sep., 30 Sep., 6 Oct., 8 Oct.

1805: 12 Feb: *Dined en famille at Mr. Port's, to meet Mr. DelaBere.* 15 Feb., 22 Feb: *Called at Mr. Port's: felt considerable emotion in seeing Mrs. J. Ram the first time since her Marriage—a look of Death was on her.*

1806: 16-17 Jan., 24 Jan., 28 Jan., 30 Jan., 5 Feb., 7 Feb: *Walked a little way afterwards with Mrs. Salter & Capt. Port.* 9 Feb., 11 Feb: *Called upon poor Mr. Port, whom I found better, tho' very low.* 27 Feb., 1 Mar., 6 Mar., 9 Mar., 15 Mar.

1812: 5 Aug: *We found Mr. & Mrs. Dewes of Wellesbourne with their Son, Mr. Granville's guests: he is Mr. G's elder Brother. Miss Louisa Port, Mr. G's great niece, resides with them.* 6 Aug: *The Revd. B. Port, Rector of Irlam, Mr. Granville's nephew, & an old acquaintance of mine, called on us.* 12 Aug: *We dined at Wooton Hall. This pleasant and retired place, the property of Mr. Davenport of Cheshire is now rented by my old acquaintance A. J. Ram, Son of Col. Ram, Member for Wexford, who married Miss F. Port, Mr. Granville's niece. He has a lovely young family. We found there, inmates of the House, Mrs. Port & her unmarried Daughter, Mrs. Ram's mother & Sister, with whom I had long ago been intimate ...*

1823: 16 Feb: *A mock heroic entitled the Whippiad, arising out of an academical feud between Mr. Halliwell, a tutor of Brazen-nose and my old acquaintance, Bernard Port, now Incumbent of Ilam in Derbyshire, and circulated in M.S., was much admired by his contemporaries, and was really a witty and sarcastic jeu d'esprit.*

1825: 31 Mar: *The other, Louisa Port, a niece of Mrs. Ram, who enjoyed the benefit of Mrs. Granville's maternal care in her education, is married to a Mr. Webster. But I must not proceed with the history of all the Calwich connections, which whom I have so long known, & always felt an interest in.*

1828: 3 Apr: *Mrs. Delany was Aunt to my excellent old friend, now no more, Mr. Granville; consequently to Mr. Dewes of Wellesbourne, & Mrs. Port, and Mrs. Waddington.*

POTOCKI — Stanisław Kostka Potocki [179]

Stanisław Kostka Potocki, Count Potocki (1755-1821), was a Polish noble, politician, writer, publicist, collector, and patron of art. He visited Rome in 1780, where he was painted by Jacques-Louis David. He was great podstoli of the crown in 1781-84, and in 1792 he became an artillery general. He fought in the War in Defence of the Constitution.

Potocki was a deputy of Lublin and one of the leaders of the patriotic party on the Four-Year Sejm, a parliament of the Polish–Lithuanian commonwealth held in Warsaw. From 1792 to 1797 he lived abroad. From 1807 he was a member of the governing commission, Komisja Rządząca, and chairman of the education chamber, Izba Edukacyjna. In 1809 he became chairman of the council of state and the council of ministers, and from 1810 he was director of the commission of national education, Komisja Edukacji Narodowej. In 1818-20 he was chairman of the senate.

Potocki collected art, mainly paintings, graphics, and antique ceramics. His collection was exhibited in Wilanów in 1805, and led to the establishment of one of the first museums in Poland.

1800: 22 Mar: *Dined with my Father & Dukinfield at Court: among other people of Rank Count Potocki formerly ambassador of Poland at the Sublime Porte, and brother of the famous Ignatius*

Potocki: tho' of different principles from that unfortunate nobleman, whose son is at present one of the gentlemen at the Belvedere.

POTTER — Robert Potter [180]

Robert Potter (±1816-1896), Church of England clergyman and schoolmaster, was born at Clitheroe, Lancashire, the son of Richard Potter (1770-1853), corn dealer, and Elizabeth Noton (1778-1854). He was educated at Shrewsbury and Manchester Grammar School, and then at Peterhouse, Cambridge (BA 1840; MA 1843). He was appointed mathematical master at Bristol College in 1840, and was later curate at Broadwell, 1846-56, vicar of Bulkington, Warwickshire, 1856-77, and vicar of Corley, 1877-96.

Potter married, at Exeter, 20 October 1842, his cousin, Mary Frances (1821-1903), second daughter of the late James Potter (b. ±1820, Jamaica planter, of Heavitree, Devon; they had 7 sons and 6 daughters:

1 Robert (1843-1865)
1 Elizabeth Rebecca (1846-1929)
2 William (1847-1899)
2 Emily Mary (1848-1910)
3 James Richard (1849-1849)
3 Anne Edith (1849-1871)
4 Emily Mary (b. 1849)
4 Henry Samuel (1852-1929)
5 Mary Frances (1854-1915)
5 John Fredrick (1855-1874)
6 Edward Christopher (b. 1857)
7 Michael Cressy (1858-1948)
6 Gertrude Augusta (1861-1951)

In 1851 Potter had a pupil, William Pocock (b. ±1834), living with him and his family. Pocock was born in Paris, the son of Lt William Innes Pocock, RN, and Anne, daughter of Thomas Wilson of Ive's Place, Maidenhead. By coincidence, Thomas Wilson was a close acquaintance of Broome Witts of Cookham

---

1846: 26 Aug: *Drove to Broadwell: left our cards at the Rectory for Mr. and Mrs. Potter: he has lately fixed there, as Curate, in the room of Mr. Underwood; apparently from the North Country, and a sensible man, of whom the Bp. of Hereford, in whose diocese he has been curate, speaks in favourable terms.* 21 Sep., 24 Dec.

1847: 7 Apr., 11 May: *Wrote a note to invite Mr. Potter to dine with us on Friday: he accepted the invitation.* 14 May: *We had a dinner party—of gentlemen; Mr. Vavasour, Mr. R Waller, Mr. Turner, Mr. Potter, and Mr. Barrow were our guests.* 3 Jun., 10 Jun., 25 Aug., 3 Sep., 6 Sep., 8 Sep., 21 Sep., 25 Nov., 8-10 Dec., 15 Dec: *Received a letter from Mr. Potter, who persists in his charges against Mr. Hayward.* 16 Dec., 20 Dec., 28 Dec: *A letter from Mr. Potter, who finds fault with the minutes and resolutions of the Board.* 29 Dec., 30 Dec: *Mr. Hayward was in attendance to meet any charge which might be preferred against him by Mr. Potter: but that gentleman did not come, sending a letter to me, and pleading illness as preventing him.* 31 Dec.

1848: 7-8 Jan., 11 Jan., 13 Jan: *Mr. Potter addressed me in a public letter, in which he maintained his charge against Mr. Hayward, and desired to be heard on other charges against him.* 8 Feb: *A large & agreeable party: the Bp. of Madras, the Rural dean, Ford, with his daughters Jemima and Dulcibella, Mr. and Mrs. Winter, Mr. and Mrs. Potter...* 26 Apr., 11 May, 29 May, 7 Jun., 23 Aug., 29 Sep.

1850: 6 Feb: *Mr. Potter called, with whom I conversed on his proposed application to the Magistrates of Warwickshire, for the vacant Chaplaincy of their County Gaol; and promised him a testimonial of character and fitness for the office.* 9 Feb., 13 Feb: *A letter from Mr. Potter, gratefully acknowledging the favourable terms in which I had couched.* 28 Feb., 12 Jun., 15 Jul: *Received a letter from Mr. Potter, Curate of Broadwell, to whom I had mentioned that the Chaplaincy of our County Gaol is vacant, he having been a candidate for a like post at Warwick some months ago. He, however, on consideration, declines offering himself—the probability of success being very doubtful.* 18 Sep., 24 Sep., 29 Nov.

1851: 10 Feb: *I wrote to invite Mr. and Mrs. Potter, of Broadwell, to join the party, which they engaged to do.* 12 Feb: *Mr. and Mrs. Royce, with Miss Laurent, Mrs. Royce's half-sister, Mr. and Mrs. R. Waller, and Mr. and Mrs. Potter, dined with me.* 13 Feb., 23 Apr., 8 May, 14 May.

1852: 1 Apr., 14 Apr., 17 May, 20 May.

1853: 26 Feb., 1 Mar., 2 Mar: *I should have mentioned that Potter had borne a useful part in the oratory of the day. We had much lively, informing and agreeable conversation throughout the evening.* 3 Mar., 30 Mar., 21 Apr., 5 May, 24 May, 13 Dec.

1854: 23 Mar., 10 Apr., 3 May, 13 Jun., 19 Jul.

POUNCE — George Pounce, Lady Elcho's butler — *see also* Eddy [181]

George Pounce (1806-1878), butler, was the son of James Pounce and Catherine Reeves. He was baptised in 1806 at Hammersmith and married, 8 May 1837, Catherine Eddy (1796-1882). By 1861 the couple had moved to Jersey, where they lived the rest of their lives. They initially lived at Bifrons Cottage, St Lawrence, where George farmed 4 acres. By 1881 Sarah was a widow living 'from funds' in Rue du Bas, St Helier.

1835: 7 Mar:—*to her Butler, Pounce, £40—besides a year's wages.*

1838: 18 Dec: *while the Daughter has disgraced herself by a clandestine marriage with one Pounce, formerly a handsome footman to Lady Elcho, in which capacity he served, when Miss C. Eddy first saw him, and he wore the D. of Newcastle's livery, when she married him.*

1840: 12 Jun: *Mrs. Pounce, so greatly altered that I did not at first recognize her, and who was naturally much embarrassed in what way to meet my wife and me for the first time since her ill-conditioned union with a quondam footman of Lady Elcho: of course we took only such distant notice as was necessary to avoid incivility.*

POWELL — Alexander Powell [182]

Alexander Powell (1782-1847), MP and landed proprietor, was the son of Francis Powell, of Salisbury, and Anna Maria, daughter and heir of Sydenham Burrough of Salisbury. He was educated at Exeter College, Oxford (BA 1804), and lived at Hurdcott House, near Wilton, Wiltshire. He was MP for Downton, 1826-30.

Powell married, at Willingham, Cambridgeshire, 7 July 1807, Joanna (1787-1848), daughter of Revd George Henry Law, rector of Willingham, Cambridgeshire; they had 5 sons and 4 daughters:

1 Anna Maria (1808-1845); married, at St Mary's, Bryanston Square, Marylebone, Westminster, 1 June 1830, Richard Strachey (1781-1847)
1 Alexander Pitts Eliott (1809-1882); married, at Westbury, Wiltshire, 14 March 1839, Mary Elizabeth Vere Booth Tyndale (1812-1891)
2 Charles (b. & d. 1810)
2 Joanna (1812-1889); married, at St Editha's, Baverstock, Wiltshire, 17 June 1839, Thomas Garrett (1808-1885)
3 Jane (1813-1896); married, at Banwell, Somerset, 29 September 1836, Reginald Pole (1801-1888)

3 Edward (b. & d. 1816)
4 Catherine Augusta (1818-1883); married, at Baverstock, Wiltshire, October 1843, Charles Raikes Davy (1818-1885)
4 George Francis Sydenham (1820-1888); married, at Christian Malford, Wiltshire, 4 August 1852, a cousin, Mary Dorthea Everilda Law (1830-1921)
5 Henry Lionel (1824-1837); died young

1802: 14 Feb: *At Pering's, meeting Evans, Powell of Exeter Coll., Edgell, Hastings, Rashley, Davis, & Williams.* 20 Feb., 24 Jun: *Edgell & Powell dined & supped with me.*

POWELL — James Cotton Powell [183]

James Cotton Powell (1809-1851), Church of England clergyman, was born in the parish of St Thomas's, Hackney, Middlesex, the son of James Powell (b. 1774) and Catherine Cotton (1774-1840). His father was the proprietor of a family business, James Powell and Sons—also known as Whitefriars Glass—glassmakers, leadlighters, and stained glass window manufacturers. The company had existed since the seventeenth century, but rose in fame in the nineteenth century due to the Gothic Revival, which created a greater demand for stained glass windows.

James Powell was educated at Trinity College, Cambridge (BA 1831; MA 1834). He was a student at Lincoln's Inn, but changed course and entered the Church, becoming curate of St James, Clapton, Middlesex. He married, 3 March 1840, Louisa Lloyd.

1836: 27 Sep: *Wrote to the Revd. J. C. Powell, Ass. Sec. S.P.G. to acknowledge the receipt of the packet of reports of the Society's proceedings in the West Indies, which had been forwarded to me some days ago.*

POWELL — William Frederick Powell [184]

William Frederick Powell (1804-1890), Church of England clergyman, was the son of Richard Powell, physician, and his wife, Mary. He was educated at Peterhouse, Cambridge (BA 1827; MA 1830), and entered the Church. He was curate of Great Malvern, 1830-33; perpetual curate of Stroud, 1833-39; vicar of Cirencester, 1839-68; honorary canon of Gloucester, 1854-81; and canon of Hereford, 1878-90. He died unmarried.

1834: 15 Oct: *At the Palace a large party assembled to dinner ... Mr. Powell, the excellent incumbent of Stroud, formerly Curate of Great Malvern.*

1837: 4 Jan.

1838: 3 Jan.

1839: 2 Jan.

1840: 15 Apr: *Wrote to Mr. Powell, the Incumbent of Cirencester, formerly Curate of Malvern, to announce to him the decease of my Aunt.*

1848: 2 Feb: *These vehement men are Mr. Powell, the Incumbent of Cirencester, Mr. Huntley, of Boxwell, both in this diocese, and both very estimable, but over strenuous Clergymen, with whom I have been long acquainted, and Mr. Jebb, an incumbent of the Diocese of Hereford.* 24 Aug: *Mr. A. and Sophy had gone to Cirencester yesterday to be the guests of Mr. Powell.*

1851: 29 Apr.

POWER — Alfred Power [185]

Sir Alfred Power (1805-1888), poor law commissioner, was the sixth son of John Power of Market Bosworth, Leicestershire, and later of Lichfield, Staffordshire. He was educated at Clare College, Cambridge, and the Middle Temple. He was called to the bar in 1830 and served on the Midland circuit. Power was assistant poor law commissioner for England, 1834-43; chief poor law commissioner for Ireland, 1849-73; and vice-president of the local government board, Ireland, 1872-79. He was appointed KCB in 1873. He married, at Cambridge, 30 September 1836, Lucy Anne (b. 1814), daughter of Thomas Starkie; they had at least 3 sons:

1 Thomas Starkie (1837-1878); died at Edinburgh
2 William Addison (1839-1888); died at Dublin
3 Charles (b. 1841)

Like Edwin Chadwick, Alfred Power was an ideologue, a disciple of the new political economy, with dogmatic views on the question of poor relief. Perhaps because of his friendship with Chadwick he was appointed as an investigator for the 1833 factory commission. He was accused at mass demonstrations of siding with the factory owners; on one occasion his effigy was burnt in a town's market place. Power was said to be rigid and arrogant as a young man, lacking both a sense of humour and a sense of proportion. He was one of the original nine assistant commissioners to the poor law commission.

At the time of the 1841 census, the Power family lived at Abberley House, Great Malvern, Worcestershire. No census record for 1851 has been discovered, but it is known that the family was in Ireland at that time.

1842: 12 Jul., 14 Jul: *By half past twelve o'clock Mr. Power, the Asst. P. L. C. arrived from Cheltenham, agreeably to promise; this union is now within his district; he was employed in superintending the West Riding and Lancashire Unions.* 18 Aug., 25 Aug: *Recd. a letter from Mr. Power, Asst. P. L. C. with a form of card used in the Dollgelly Union as a check on Out-relief given.* 1 Sep.

POWER — Edward Power [186]

Edward Power (±1801-1860), printer and stationer, was born at St Briavels in the Forest of Dean. He kept a small business as a printer and stationer near the Cross at Gloucester. In 1849 his premises were at 6 Westgate Street, Gloucester, and by 1851 they were at 4 Westgate Street, slightly nearer to the Cross. He was married to Harriet; they had at least 6 sons and 3 daughters:

1 Edward (b. ±1825)
2 Henry (b. ±1828)
1 Harriet (b. ±1828)
3 William (b. ±1835)
4 Daniel (b. ±1836)
2 Jane Priscilla (b. 1838)
5 Albert (1839-1878)
3 Caroline (b. 1842)
6 Joseph (b. 1843)

1844: 18 Apr: *Also a letter from Power, Printer, Gloucester, accompanying a copy of the new Rules for the government of the Bridewells in the County, just out of the Press.*

POWERSCOURT — *see* Wingfield *and* Twisleton

POWYS — Thomas Atherton Powys [187]

Thomas Atherton Powys, 3rd Baron Lilford (1801-1861), landed proprietor, was the son of Thomas Powys, 2nd Baron Lilford (1775-1825), and Anna Maria Atherton (d. 1820). He was educated at Eton College and Christ Church, Oxford. He married, 1830, Mary Elizabeth, daughter of Henry Richard Fox, Baron Holland, and Elizabeth Vassall. Powys succeeded as 3rd Baron Lilford in 1825.

1823: 17 Sep: *The Ordinary for Gentlemen is held alternately at the two principal Inns; this day it was at the King's Head. I dined there; Mr. C. Leigh in the chair. I may here as well enumerate some of the principal persons and families, who attended the music meeting on this and the following days ... Lord Lilford.*

1835: 25 Mar: *The ground slopes from the Mansion House towards the river, and commands distant views of Lilford House, Park and Woods, the seat of Lord Lilford.* 27 Mar.

1847: 11 Aug.

POYNDER — George Poynder [188]

George Poynder (1791-1877), physician, was born at Kennington, Lambeth, Surrey, the son of John Poynder (1751-1800) and Sarah Wix (1756-1802). He was educated at Eton College and began his career at the Bethlehem Hospital. In 1824 he was appointed as the Gloucester lunatic asylum's first superintendent, with a salary of £200 per year. He left in 1828 to become the first superintendent at the Kent County Asylum, later Oakwood Hospital. He married Margeretta [Marguerette] Russell (1804-1871); they had 3 sons and 2 daughters:

1 Robert (1834-1929)
1 Emma (1837-1870)
2 Clement (b. 1835)
2 Agnes (1838-1904)
3 Alfred (1839-1906)

By 1871 George was retired and living with his wife Margeretta at Worthing, Sussex.

1824: 30 Apr: *I visited the Lunatic asylum, going over every part of the institution with the resident Medical man, Mr. Poyner, & attended thro' the female ward by the matron, Mrs. Chambers. Both these persons seem to be remarkably well suited to their station, intelligent, active, tranquil, cheerful.*

1828: 15 Jun: *I went to the Lunatic Asylum a Mr. Hitch, from Tewkesbury, in the place of an excellent officer, who recently resigned—Mr. Poynder—whom the Managers of the Institution much regret, but it was believed by him, that the confinement incident to his situation was injurious to his health.*

POYNER — Robert Poyner [189]

Robert Poyner (1791-1870), manservant, was born at Taynton, Gloucestershire, the son of Edward Poyner (1751-1825) and Mary Child (b. 1755). It is unclear when he entered the service of Francis Witts, but it may have been a number of years before he was first mentioned in Witts's diaries. He married, at St Mary's, Cheltenham, 5 December 1833, Elizabeth Holton (b. 1811). She was twenty years his junior. They had 2 sons and 2 daughters:

1 Elizabeth Ann (b. 1838)
2 Ellen (1841-1842); died an infant
1 George Robert (b. 1845)
2 William Edward (1847-1927), coal miner; married, at Cardiff, Matilda (1850-1941), born at Newport; 4 sons and 6 daughters

There is a gap in Francis Witts's diaries between 15 November 1833 and 3 March 1834 in which he may have mentioned Poyner's marriage. By 1838 Poyner had left Witts's service—presumably on cordial terms—and entered that of Margaret Jones in Palace Yard, Gloucester. She was well-known to Francis Witts. Margaret Jones offered Poyner a house for his family, something Witts had not been able to provide. In the 1851 census Poyner was not listed at Palace Yard, but his wife Elizabeth was, as a housekeeper living at number 25. Their sons George and William were also registered there.

By 1861 Robert Poyner had returned to his native village of Taynton. He was listed in the census as a widower and agricultural labourer. With him in his household was his unmarried daughter Elizabeth, his son George, and a grandson, Edwin (b. 1859). It has not been discovered when Poyner's wife Elizabeth died, but it must have been between 1851 and 1861. Edwin, his grandson, is a mystery. He may have been the illegitimate son of his daughter Elizabeth. Robert Poyner died at Newent Union Workhouse in 1870, and was buried at Taynton.

Poyner's youngest son, William, stayed at Cardiff for a while after his marriage and then returned to Old Church House, Taynton, with his young family. He worked as an agricultural labourer. He later returned to south Wales and became a coal miner.

1826: 30 Sep: *Poor Robert, who is an useful & honest fellow, has been complaining for some months, and it now appears, a fistula is formed; he is about to place himself under the charge of the eminent surgeon, Mr. Fletcher, and, perhaps, eventually, will avail himself of my recommendation, and get into the infirmary; should he recover, he will resume his place in our family.* 19 Oct: *At the infirmary weekly board, where my servant, Robert Poyner, was admitted on my recommendation; Mr. Fletcher has performed the operation for fistula successfully.*

1827: 20 Jan: *Our old servant, R. Poyner, returned with us; he having been since the middle of October in the infirmary, and though now convalescent, still looks very ill.*

1829: 4 Apr: *I sent my servant off by an early coach to meet my phaeton and horse, which the gardener was to bring to Andoversford, and with which Robert was to wait for me at Cheltenham.* 14 Jul., 22 Sep.

1833: 5 Nov: *Wrote to Mr. J. Smith, Taynton, near Newent, on business of my Servant, Robert Poyner.*

1835: 20 Jun: *Robt. Poyner on Prov. Bank business.*

1838: 24 Aug: *Wrote to Robt. Poyner, a former Servt. residing at Gloucester, in reply to a note which he had sent to me desiring me to remit to him a part of his capital as a depositor in the Stow Prov. Bank.*

PRAED — Bulkley John Mackworth Praed [190]

Bulkley John Mackworth Praed (1799-1876), banker, was the second son of William Mackworth (1756-1835), serjeant-at-law, of Devon, and Elizabeth (1765-1810), daughter of Benjamin Winthrop, governor of the Bank of England. He was educated at Harrow School and St John's College, Cambridge. Praed changed his surname by royal licence to Mackworth Praed. He married, first, 22 December 1828, Emma (1806-1836), daughter of Mungo Dick of Pitkerrow, co. Forfar; they had 3 sons and 1 daughter:

1 John Bulkley (1830-1831); died an infant
2 Bulkley John (1831-1860)
3 Winthrop (1831-1890)
1 Georgina Susan (1833-1910)

Praed married secondly, at Chichester, Sussex, 14 July 1840, Elizabeth (1819-1852), daughter of Patrick Persse Fitzpatrick; they had 6 sons and 3 daughters:

1 Herbert Bulkley (1841-1920)
2 William (1844-1848); died a child
3 Fitzpatrick William (1845-1914)
4 Arthur Campbell Bulkley (1846-1901)
1 Margaret Hannah Colthurst Bulkley (1847-1856)
5 William (1849-1911)
2 Alice Elizabeth (1850-1918)
3 Louisa Kathleen Georgina (1851-1869)
6 Ernest Bulkley (1852-1853); died an infant

Praed married thirdly, at St Marylebone, Westminster, 26 April 1859, Emily Maria (1821-1905), daughter of William Fane; they had 2 sons and 1 daughter:

1 Julian Fane (1860-1876)
2 Algernon Henry (1861-1952)
1 Hester Fane (d. 1923)

William Mackworth Praed, the second son of Praed's second marriage and one of the 'fine young family', died aged 4, the year after Francis Witts's visit.

1847: 11 Aug: *We partook of luncheon, by appointment, with Mrs. Praed, the lady of the tenant of Wadenhoe House, her husband being absent in town, on his business as a banker, being a partner in the firm of Praeds & Co. We found Mrs. P. an elegant and polite hostess, surrounded with a fine young family, partly her own children, partly Mr. P's by a former wife.*

PRAED — William Praed [191]

William Praed (1747-1833), banker and MP, was the eldest son of Humphrey Mackworth Praed, of Trevethoe, and Mary, daughter of William Forester of Dothill Park, Shropshire. His mother was the widow of Sir Brian Broughton Delwes, 4th baronet, of Broughton, Staffordshire, uncle to Bulkley John Mackworth Praed (*above*). William Praed was educated at Eton College and Magdalen College, Oxford. He married, 19 June 1778, Elizabeth Tyringham, daughter of Barnaby Backwell, banker; they had 7 sons and 3 daughters, including:

1 James Backwell (1779-1837); married, 1813, Sophia (d. 1854), daughter of Charles Chaplin, MP
2 William Tyringham (1780-1846)
1 Elizabeth Tyringham Praed (b. 1781), twin to Humphry
3 Humphry Mackworth (b. & d. 1781), twin to Elizabeth
4 Humphry (b. 1782)

Praed was MP for St Ives in 1774-75 and 1780-1806, and Banbury in 1806-08. He became a partner in his father's Truro bank in 1779, and founded, in around 1801, the London bank of Praed Co., 189 Fleet Street. He was instrumental in having the bill for the Grand Junction Canal passed by parliament in 1790.

1832: 27 Mar: *Great talent has been shewn on both sides of the house, but the preponderance of weight eloquence and judgment and acuteness appears to me to have been on the side of the Anti-reformers—Sir Robert Peel, Mr. Croker, Sir R. Inglis, Sir E. Sugden, Sir C. Wetherell, Mr. Praed, Lord Mahon, Lord Porchester and many others spoke with great force and convincingness.*

PRATT — George Charles Pratt [192]

George Charles Pratt, 3rd baron, 2nd marquess, and 3rd earl of Camden (1799-1866), MP and landed proprietor, was born in Arlington Street, Middlesex, the son of John Jeffreys Pratt, 2nd baron, 1st marquess, and 2nd earl of Camden (1759-1840), and Frances (±1766-1829), daughter of William Molesworth and Anne Smith. Pratt was educated at Eton College and Trinity College, Cambridge, and was styled Lord Brecknock in his early years. He succeeded as 3rd baron in 1835, and 2nd marquess and 3rd earl in 1840. Pratt was MP for Ludgershall, 1821-26, Bath 1826-30, and Dunwich, 1831-32. He married, 27 August 1835, Harriet, daughter of Revd George Murray, bishop of Rochester; they had 3 sons and 8 daughters, including:

1 John Charles (1840-1872); married, at St James's, Westminster, 12 July 1866, Clementina Augusta (1848-1886), youngest daughter of George Spencer Churchill, duke of Marlborough, and Charlotte Augusta, daughter of Henry Jeffery Flower, Viscount Ashbrook

---

1834: 12 Sep: *The Bishop and his family left Lady L. after an early dinner of which we partook. Just as they were setting out Lord Brecknock, Son of Earl Camden, called on the Bishop, who had been formerly his Tutor.*

PRATT — John Tidd Pratt [193]

John Tidd Pratt (1797-1870), barrister and civil servant, was born in London, the second son of John Christian Frederick Pratt (1768-1840), surgeon, of Kensington, and Susanna Thomas. He was educated at the Inner Temple (1819) and called to the bar in 1824. He married, 20 May 1821, Anne (1803-1875), daughter of Maj. Thomas Campbell; they had 2 sons and 4 daughters:

1 William (1822-1867)
1 Elizabeth Anne (b. 1824)
2 Maria M. A. (b. 1828)
2 Charles Pallmer (1829-1886); married, at Dover, Kent, 16 September 1874, Moncrieffe Mesham; 3 sons and 2 daughters
3 Mary (b. 1834)
4 Jane (b. 1836)

In 1828 Pratt was appointed as consulting barrister to the national debt commissioners. An act of that year assigned him the duty of certifying the rules of savings banks, which up to that point had simply been submitted to quarter sessions. The following year he was given the additional duty of certifying the rules of friendly societies, as well as receiving their returns of sickness and mortality every five years. In subsequent years the certification of the rules of loan societies (1835), building societies (1836), and societies for the pursuit of literature, science, and the fine arts was added to the consulting barrister's list of responsibilities.

John Tidd Pratt was the author of numerous legal manuals and published on the law relating to savings banks (1828), friendly societies (1829), the poor (1833), and highways (1835). He was one of the founders of the Reform Club, a trustee of the Soane Museum, and a fellow of both the Royal Society of Literature and the Society of Antiquaries.

1828: 14 Oct: *The new Savings Bank act having a clause, that the Rules of these institutions should be enrolled after being sanctioned by a barrister (Mr. Tidd Pratt) appointed by the Commissioners for the Reduction of the National debt.* 17 Oct.

1837: 10 Jun: *Not finding them at their Office left a few lines with Tidd Pratt's last circular pamphlet on Friendly Societies, containing a set of resolutions, rules, tables &c.* 16 Jun., 11 Aug.

PREVOST — George Prevost [194]

Sir George Prevost, 2nd baronet (1804-1893), Church of England clergyman, was born at Roseau on the island of Dominica, the only son of Sir George James Marc Prevost, 1st baronet (1767-1816), governor-in-chief of British North America, and Catherine Anne (1766-1821), daughter of Maj.-Gen. John Phipps. He succeeded as 2nd baronet in 1816 and was educated at Oriel College, Oxford (BA 1825; MA 1827).

Prevost was a pupil and disciple of John Keble, whom he frequently visited at Southrop. He married, at St George's, Bloomsbury, Middlesex, 18 March 1828, Jane Williams (1807-1853); they had 2 sons and 2 daughters:

1 Harriet (1829-1868)
1 George Phipps (1830-1885), Col
2 Charles (1831-1902); succeeded as 3rd baronet; married, at Bisley, Gloucestershire, 22 January 1856, Sarah Margaret (1832-1919), daughter of Revd Thomas Keble
2 Charlotte Mary (b. 1834)

Prevost was curate to John Keble's brother Thomas at Bisley, Gloucestershire, from 1828 to 1834, when he was instituted to the perpetual curacy of Stinchcombe in the same county. He was later rural dean of Dursley, 1852-66; proctor of the diocese of Gloucester and Bristol, 1858-65; archdeacon of Gloucester, 1865-81; and honorary canon of Gloucester, 1859-93. From its inception, Prevost was an ardent supporter of the Tractarian movement; he contributed to *Tracts for the Times* and translated the *Homilies of St. John Chrysostom on the Gospel of St. Matthew* (1843) for the Library of the Fathers.

1837: 4 Jan: *The Establishment of the Society was moved by the D. of Beaufort, and seconded by the Revd. Sir Geo. Prevost, son of the late General of that name, Incumbent of the small vicarage or curacy of Stinchcombe, who has given £400 to the funds of the Society.*

1838: 3 Jan.

1839: 2 Jan.

1847: 31 Aug.

1850: 8 Nov: ... *and others, men of note in various ways, with whom I am slightly acquainted, or whom I only know by sight — such as Sir Geo. Prevost, Alex. Watson & others of the Tractarian Party.*

1851: 29 Apr., 23 Oct: *A circular from Sir George Prevost, on behalf of a society formed for obtaining signatures to petitions to the Upper and Lower houses of convocation, praying that measures be taken to obtain the sanction of the government to a revival of the active working of Convocation — a matter much urged at present by the Tractarian party in the Church, but which appears to me very likely to do harm.*

PRICE & Co. — merchants of Gloucester [195]

Price & Company was founded in Gloucester in 1740. In the 1820s and early 1830s the firm existed as a partnership between William Price (d. 1838) and William Tupsley Washbourne (d. 1842); it was known as Price & Washbourne and traded from the north warehouse at Gloucester Docks. Price & Washbourne were primarily timber merchants, although they also imported corn.

William Price was a founder and director of the Gloucestershire Banking Company. He was sheriff for Gloucester in 1819, mayor in 1822, and a JP for the city and the county. He bought the manor and estate of Tibberton in 1837. His son William Philip Price (*below*) inherited the property the following year.

Price & Washbourne appears to have ceased trading from Gloucester Docks by 1846, but Price & Co. continued in the timber trade from High Orchard, Gloucester.

1851: 27 Jan: *To Messrs. Price and Co. Gloucester for the terms of Passage to New York by their ship advertised to sail on the 27th March.* 1 Feb: *Recd. a packet from Messrs. Price and Co. Gloucester, with printed particulars of the terms of passage by their ships about to sail to New York and Quebec.*

PRICE — Benjamin Price Withers — *see also* Dupuis, Waller, *and* Wells [196]

The Price Withers family was complicated. Benjamin Price Withers (d. 1771) inherited the manor of Westbury, Buckinghamshire, from his cousin Cambell Price. His only son Benjamin Price Withers (1768-1805), born at Westbury, married, at Tewkesbury, 24 March 1790, Susannah Buckle of the Mythe, Tewkesbury. They had 1 son:

1 James (b. ±1792-1806)

The Price Withers properties at Mixbury in Oxfordshire, Westbury in Buckinghamshire, and Brackley in Northamptonshire devolved to Price Withers' godson, Benjamin Gurden (b. 1788), who assumed the name Price in 1808. He married, at Wendlebury, Oxfordshire, 1816, Eliza Anne (1797-1878), eldest daughter of Revd George Dupuis (1757-1839) and Caroline Elizabeth Stevens (1771-1843); they had at least 3 daughters:

1 Unknown
2 Georgiana Lucy; married, 1842, Nathaniel Armstrong Wells, eldest son of Nathaniel Wells of Piercefield, Monmouthshire
3 Julia Rachel-Stevens; married, at Paris, Thomas Bullock Webster, 15th Bombay Native Infantry, fourth son of E. W. B. Webster of Hendon

---

1837: 8 Dec: *Though still heavily oppressed with cold, and otherwise indisposed and out of spirits, made an effort to go out with my wife and Son to dine at Mr. R. Waller's, where we met Mr. and Mrs. Chamberlayne, Mr. and Mrs. and Miss D. Ford, Miss Polson, Mr. Billingsley, and two relatives of Mrs. R. Waller, Miss Dupuis, her sister, and Miss Price, her niece.* 15 Dec: *Rejoined my wife at the Rectory, where found all the party at home: Mr. & Mrs. R. Waller, Miss Dupuis, and Miss Price.*

1839: 23 Jan: *Saw Mr. & Mrs. R.W. and Miss Price, niece of Mrs. R.W.* 20 Apr: *Returning home, we met Mrs. Dolphin, near her own house, accompanied by Robt. Waller & his wife, with her Sister, Mrs. Price, and her niece Miss Price.*

1845: 17 Feb: *Met with him, Mrs. Waller, her niece, Miss Price, Messrs. Stenson and Aitkens—walked with them towards Little Risington.*

PRICE — Charles Price [197]

Charles Price (1777-1853), physician, was born in Somerset and educated at Wadham College, Oxford (BA 1797; MA 1801; BMed 1802; DMed 1804), where he was a fellow until 1821. He was elected a fellow of the College of Physicians in 1805, and served as physician in the Middlesex Hospital from 1807 to 1815. He was appointed physician extraordinary to William IV in 1832.

1806: 18 Mar: *Breakfasted with my excellent but indolent friend Dowell, where I was met by Dr. Price, & Round; Trevenen also called in.* 19 Mar: *Breakfasted at Dr. Price's, meeting Dowell.* 20 Mar., 21 Mar: *Breakfasted with Dr. Price, meeting Dowell.* 22 Mar.

1829: 26 Feb: *I subsequently met my old friend Dr. Price, fellow of my college, and in great practice as a Physician at Brighton.*

PRICE — Elizabeth Price and the Price family at Clifton — *see also* Hughes [198]

Elizabeth Hughes, née Price (1784-1813), was from a moderately affluent family of good standing in Clifton. According to the diaries of Agnes Witts, Mr and Mrs Price lived at 'The Cottage' at Prestbury; 'Miss Price' was their niece. Agnes Witts also referred to Miss Price's school, which appears to have been in Clifton.

Elizabeth Price became a close friend, or perhaps a companion, to Elizabeth Hughes (1768-1850), only daughter of the wealthy attorney Thomas Hughes (1732-1794), of Cheltenham, who had married, 1763, Elizabeth Bridges (1728-1786), a wealthy heiress, of Keynsham Abbey, Somerset. It seems that Elizabeth Hughes took some accommodation at Richmond Place, Clifton; Elizabeth Price may have lived there with her, perhaps as a companion. Whatever the case, the two women were frequently together. Elizabeth Price married Hughes's younger brother, Robert (1771-1827), and had 1 son:

1 Charles Robert (1809-1810); died an infant

Elizabeth Hughes, née Price, died of consumption [tuberculosis] in 1813. Her friend and sister-in-law Elizabeth Hughes died unmarried in 1850.

1803: 27 Dec: *Went in the Evening to a card party at a Miss Price's with her & our friend a Miss Hughes in Richmond place, which the presence of three lively Miss Marriotts rendered agreeable to my Brother & myself.* 30 Dec., 31Dec: *Made several visits with George: to the adorable Misses Price & Hughes.*

PRICE — George Price[199]

George Price (1780-1861), Church of England clergyman, was the son of Ralph Price of Lyminge, Kent. He was educated at Wadham College, Oxford (BA 1802; MA 1808), and was vicar of Eastwood, Essex, 1826-57, and rector of Fryerning, 1826-61.

1803: 1 Nov: *Walked with Edgell & Rashleigh & with Newbigging, & sat in the Evening with Dowell meeting at his Rooms, Thomas & George Price.* 4 Nov.

1806: 22 Mar: *Dined in the Common Room; Rogers, Price, Dr. Cooper, Stevens & Hall.*

PRICE — James Scarlett Price[200]

James Scarlett Price (±1800-1876), solicitor, was born at Bushley in Worcestershire. He married, 1837, Anne Capel (b. ±1800) of Painswick; they had at least 1 daughter:

1 Sarah (b. ±1843)

Price began his career as a partner of George Newmarch of Cirencester. He and his family lived in Sheep Street in a gabled house, the freehold of which he bought in 1860. This house now forms half of what has become the Bay Tree Hotel.

1825: 9 Jul: *In passing through Burford, I called at the office of Messrs. Newmarch & Price.*

1839: 22 Mar.

1842: 26 Jan: *A letter from F. Newmarch, stating that, in consequence of Mr. Price of Burford having commenced a canvass on his behalf in the neighbourhood of Witney and Burford for the Clerkship of the Crickley Hill district of Turnpike Roads, he had determined to sally forth as to day to solicit votes for himself, and proposed to dine and sleep here.*

1843: 21 Aug: *Mr. Price, Solr., of Burford, and Mr. Wells of Bourton on the Water, also travelled with us to the Farringdon road station, and to London.*

1844: 10 Oct.

1850: 3 Mar., 30 Dec.

1852: 8 Dec: *Mr. Price, Solicitor, Burford, called upon me for the copy of the Registry of the death of the late Mrs. Payne, Mrs. Dolphin's Mother.* 9 Dec.

1853: 1 Feb., 3 Feb.

PRICE — Joseph Price[201]

Joseph Price (±1785-1860), farmer, was born at Bourton-on-the-Water and lived at Upper Slaughter. He married, 1810, Sarah Boulton (d. 1826); they had 2 sons and 2 daughters:

1 Anne (b. 1812); married, at Upper Slaughter, 1 March 1836, Henry Hartwell of Bourton-on-the-Water

1 William (1814-1886), agricultural labourer and shepherd; married Jane and lived at Elmley Castle, Worcestershire

2 Hannah (b. & d. 1817)

2 Thomas (1818-1891)

Price married secondly, at Upper Slaughter, 20 April 1829, Hannah Pew (1781-1843) of Upper Slaughter. At the time of the 1841 census he was living with Hannah and his son Thomas. He was a farmer, but presumably not on a large scale.

1826: 13 Jan: *While we were at dinner John Smith unexpectedly arrived from Upper Slaughter with the horses, being sent by my leading parishioners to consult me on the propriety of holding an inquest on the body of Sarah Price, wife of a small farmer in my parish, who poor soul was found dead in bed on Tuesday morning last. She had been in indifferent health for some time past, but of late had recovered strength, and was much better. She died without a struggle by the side of her husband, who was ignorant of the fatal event, till he awoke at the usual hour, and found her a corpse. She was a very respectable woman of her class, an industrious, prudent, careful wife & mother: may GOD protect her poor children, the eldest of whom cannot be above sixteen!* 16 Jan.

1829: 2 Nov: *At a meeting of the Trustees of the Upper Slaughter Church & Charity Estate, holden this day, a tender was presented by Mr. Robert Comely, of Lower Slaughter, for the farm now tenanted by Mr. Jos. Price, but which will be vacant at Lady day next.*

1840: 1 Apr.

1842: 25 Nov: *Administered the holy Sacrament privately to Hannah Price, who is in a very declining state of health.*

1843: 18 Jan: *Funeral of Hannah Price.*

1847: 9 Mar.

1851: 24 Mar: *Attended a vestry meeting — E Lea, J B Collett, S. Collett, W Dix, & Jos. Price were present.*

PRICE — Thomas Price[202]

Thomas Price (b. ±1783) was the son of John Price of Kew Stoke, Somerset. He matriculated at Wadham College, Oxford, on 22 January 1802, but nothing else is known of him.

1802: 30 Apr: *The party in the inside of the coach beside myself were ... On the outside were Price & Simmons, freshmen of our College, Williams of Jesus, Owens of Oriel.*

PRICE — William Price[203]

William Price (1784-1860), Church of England clergyman, was born at Charlton House, between Steventon and Wantage, Berkshire, the son of William Henry Price (1753-1826), of Charlton House, and grandson of William Price (1720-1792), master of the Ironmongers' Company (1772), of London.

Price was educated at Pembroke College, Oxford (BA 1803; MA 1806), where he was elected a fellow. He was ordained deacon on 21 February 1807 and priest on 28 February 1808. He was appointed rector of Coln St Dennis, Gloucestershire, on 27 January 1810, and chaplain of Coln Rogers on 12 June 1813. His father spent his final years with him at his rectory at Coln St Dennis, and died there. Price was domestic chaplain to Anne Keppel, née Miller, countess of Albermarle, until her death in 1824. He was also appointed rector of Farnborough, Berkshire, in 1815; his only sister, Mary (1785-1840), died at the rectory there.

In addition to his clerical responsibilities, Price was a tax commissioner and a JP. He was also Francis Witts's equivalent at Northleach, where he was chairman of the board of guardians of the workhouse; the two men were long-standing friends. He married, first, 21 November 1810, Mary (1788-1828), daughter of James Davis of Uppins, Buckinghamshire; they had 2 sons and 3 daughters:

1 Anne (1812-1875); married John Benjamin Andrews (1815-1881), only son of Benjamin Andrews of Stowting, Kent; apparently no children
1 William Henry (1813-1889); educated at Pembroke College, Oxford (BA 1835; MA, 1838); fellow, 1840-59; bursar, 1855; served as rector of Farnborough, 1836-61; rector of Fawley, Berkshire, 1838-55; rector of Somerton, Oxfordshire, 1861-74; and rector of Coln St Dennis, 1874; married, 29 March 1859, Lucy Maria (1826-1886), daughter of Daniel Taunton of Walton House, Oxfordshire; no children
2 Mary (1814-1895); married, 26 June 1845, Revd Thomas William Goodlake (d. 1875), rector of Swindon (nr Cheltenham) Gloucestershire; 3 sons and 3 daughters:
    1 Thomas Surman (1847-1915); died at Swindon, Gloucestershire
    2 William Henry Gerrard (1848-1878), Lt, RN; served aboard HMS *Shannon*; married, at St John's, 16 May 1876, Cheltenham, Catherine Maud, only daughter of Samuel Julian of co. Kerry; 1 son:
        1 Thomas Julian (1877-1951)
    1 Mary Elizabeth (b. 1846); listed, 1881, as an unmarried annuitant, living at 14 Westbourne Street, Knightsbridge, Westminster
    2 Henrietta Gertrude (1852-1929)
    3 Grace Emily (1853-1937); married, 6 June 1871, Charles Crocker of Wargrave, Berkshire; 1 son:
        1 Charles Edward Goodlake (1874-1936)
    3 John Price (1854-1877)
3 Henrietta [Harriet] (b. ±1816); listed, 1881, as living with her half-sister Charlotte at 232 St Mary's Street, Wallingford; died unmarried
2 Bartholomew (1818-1898); educated at Pembroke College, Oxford (BA 1840; MA 1843); fellow and junior dean, 1844; tutor and mathematics lecturer, 1845; public examiner 1847-48 and 1853-55; bursar, 1851; moderator, 1852; Sedleian professor of natural philosophy, 1853; proctor, 1858; vicegerent 1864; hon. fellow of Queen's College, 1868; elected FRS and FRAstrS; visitor of Greenwich Observatory; married, 20 August 1857, Amy Elizabeth, daughter of William Cole Cole, JP, of Highfield, Exmouth; 2 sons and 5 daughters:
    1 William Arthur (1860-1954); married, at St Giles's, Oxford, 28 December 1910, Mabel Frances Vernon Harcourt (1874-1965)
    2 Bartholomew George (1870-1947); officer, Royal Fusiliers; married, at the British Embassy church, Paris, 23 June 1919, Joan Colvin (1878-1969); 1 son:
        1 Bartholomew Colin C. (1922-1993)
    1 Amy Maud (1858-1949); died unmarried
    2 Mary Eliza Mabel (1862-1939); died unmarried
    3 Alice Margaret (b. 1864)
    4 Rose Emelyn (1866-1894); died unmarried
    5 Elenor Rokeby (1868-1956); died unmarried

Price married secondly, 15 July 1829, a widow, Harriet (d. 1865), daughter of James Davis, of Uppins, and sister of Price's first wife; they had 2 sons and 2 daughters:

1 Charlotte (b. ±1832); listed, 1881, as living with her half-sister Harriet at 232 St Mary's Street, Wallingford; died unmarried
1 George. (b. 1834); died unmarried
2 James (b. 1836)
2 Adelaide (b. ±1839); married, 3 November 1869, Bernard John McNulty (±1833-1878), civil engineer, born at Limerick, Ireland; lived at Chelsea, 1871; she apparently died soon after, but no record has been found; no children

---

1820: 11 Apr.

1823: 10 Jan: *Attended the quarterly Petty Sessions at Northleach Bridewell, after which I went to dine and sleep at Mr. Price's, the Rector of Coln St. Dennis.*

1823: 15 Jul., 21 Oct.

1824: 9 Jul: *We dined at Mr. Price's, the Rector of Coln St. Dennis.* 13 Jul., 7 Sep: *We had a dinner party ... Mr. & Mrs. Price & Mr. C. Goold from Coln St. Dennis.* 11 Oct.

1825: 30 Apr: *Our young friend Charles Gould, who still remains under the tuition of Mr. Price, came over from Coln St. Dennis, and dined with us, returning in the Evening.* 18 Jul: *We dined at Mrs. Price's at Coln St. Dennis.*

1826: 13 Apr., 22 May, 26 Jul.

1827: 6 Jul., 10 Jul., 12 Oct., 16 Oct.

1828: 15 Jul.

1829: 13 Jan., 14 Jul., 29 Sep.

1834: 15 Aug., 4 Oct: *Drove to Northleach, accompanied by Otway, to assist Mr. Price in the examination of witnesses against a man named John Laight, of Winson, charged on suspicion of stealing five sheep on the 16th Sept.* 10 Oct., 28 Nov: *Mr. Price, of Coln St. Dennis, called to consult with me as to the steps necessary to be taken in respect of a case of infanticide which has recently occurred at Northleach.* 1 Dec.

1835: 2 Jan., 20 Jan., 13 Mar., 2 Apr., 10 Apr.

1837: 17 Mar., 18 Aug.

1838: 14 Aug.

1839: 22 Mar., 6 Apr., 9 Apr.

1840: 27 Aug: *Mr. Price of Coln St. Dennis, Chairman of the Northleach Union attended as well as Howell, to observe the course of our proceedings.*

1842: 8 Feb., 23 Mar., 12 Apr., 22 Apr., 27 Apr., 20 May: *Mr. Price of Coln St. Dennis called, and took luncheon with us: he had accompanied a fellow of Pembroke College, Oxford, a Mr. Cox, Senr. Bursar, to Aston Farm, which is the property of that Society, and Price had left him fishing in Aston Brook.* 8 Oct., 16 Oct., 18 Oct.

1843: 3 Jan., 16-17 Oct.

1844: 19 Mar., 9 Apr., 1 May, 1 Oct: *After luncheon with F. A. walked to visit the House of Correction, met Mr. Price just returned from U. Slaughter, whither he had ridden to confer with me on matters pertaining to the Gaol Bridewell and other Justice business.* 8-9 Oct.

1845: 17 Jan., 12 Mar., 4 Apr., 7 May, 7 Jul.

1846: 23 May, 17 Jul.

1847: 23 Mar., 18 May, 29 May, 24 Jun., 28 Jun.

1848: 19 Jun: *Mr. Price of Coln St. Dennis, and his youngest daughter by the first wife, called on us.* 25 Jun., 27 Jun., 24 Aug., 11 Oct.

1850: 31 Jul.

1852: 24 Feb., 3 Mar., 25 Mar.

PRICE — William Philip Price — *see also* Price & Company[204]

William Philip Price (1817-1891), JP, DL, MP, timber merchant, and businessman, was the eldest son of William Price (1788-1838), merchant, and Frances George (1791-1860). His father was sheriff for Gloucester in 1819, mayor in 1822, and JP for the city and county. William Price (junior) was extensively engaged as a timber merchant at Gloucester and Grimsby, and as head of the firm Price & Son, established in 1740. He became JP for Gloucestershire in 1842, high sheriff in 1849, and DL in 1852, in which year he entered parliament as MP for Gloucester. He held the seat until 1859, and then again from 1865 to 1873. Price was chairman of Gloucestershire Banking Company, 1860-85. He was a member of the committee of management of the Gloucester and Berkeley Canal Co., 1840-70, and the first chairman of the directors, 1870 to April 1873. He was deputy chairman of the Midland Railway, 1864-70, and chairman, 1870-1873. He was also chairman of the Gloucester and Dean Forest Railway until 1873.

William Price married Frances Anne (1818-1890), daughter of John Chadborn (1784-1839) and Eliza Anne King (1776-1839); they had 1 son and 3 daughters:

1 William Edwin (1841-1886); married Margaret (1849-1911); 3 sons:
   1 Morgan Phillips (1885-1973), geologist; lived at Tibberton, Gloucestershire
   2 William Robert (1886-1975)
   3 William M. (b. 1887)

1 Gertrude (1846-1905); married, at Rudford, Gloucestershire, 31 March 1869, Charles George Brooke-Hunt (1845-1912), naval officer, of Bowden Hall; 2 daughters:
   1 Violet Edith Gwenllyan (1870-1910)
   2 Lilian Frances (1873-1929)

2 Edith (1848-1934); died unmarried

3 Alice Gwenthan (±1858-1923); married, at Newent, Gloucestershire, July 1886, Charles Lee-Williams (1853-1935); at least 1 son:
   1 Owen L. Lee (1887-1973)

1845: 15 Apr., 7 May.

1847: 11 Jul: *Here I foregathered with Mr. Price, of Tibberton Court near Gloucester, a merchant of that port, a very clever and intelligent young man, for some time very favourably known to me as a brother magistrate, and who, having married a lady, whose fortune was mainly derived from the coffers of the wellknown Gloucester Banker and Miser Jemmy Wood, has not been afraid to accept an invitation to offer himself as representative of the city with which he is connected by birth, and by business.*

1848: 3 Jan., 22 Nov.

1850: 28 Jan: *travelled to Cheltenham, as I had from thence in the morning to Gloucester, with W. P. Price.*

1851: 29 Apr.

1853: 4 Jan., 5 Jan: *W P. Price and his supporters threw all their influence into the Admiral's scale and the Blues, who had not anticipated so signal a defeat, doubtless, were highly mortified.*

PRICHARD — Thomas Octavius Prichard[205]

Thomas Octavius Prichard (1808-1847), physician, served as superintendent for two years at Glasgow Royal Lunatic Asylum. In 1838 he was appointed founding superintendent of the Northamptonshire County General Lunatic Asylum, which was funded by public subscription for private and pauper lunatics. By 1844 Prichard had built the number of patients up from 70 to 260. He claimed never to have put patients under physical restraint, but he resigned in 1845 following allegations of professional misconduct. He later opened a private asylum at Abington Manor, near Northampton.

Thomas Prichard married Elizabeth (b. ±1812); they had at least 1 son and 3 daughters:

1 Elizabeth (b. 1839)
2 Fanny Louisa (b. 1840)
3 Ellen Octavia (b. 1841); married Charles H. Terry
1 Lewis Lloyd (b. ±1849)

At Abington Manor, Prichard was assisted by two cousins, Thomas and William. Thomas (±1812-1878) married Prichard's widow, Elizabeth, and continued the management of the asylum.

1835: 10 May: *Received a letter from Sophia Hunt with a very unfavourable account of the state of her sister, Caroline's mind and health. Dr. Prichard, an eminent Physician, whose studies have been directed to the subject of mental alienation, and who has published an approved work on diseases of the mind, has been called in.*

PRIEST — at Oxford

There is no record of anyone at Oxford at this period with the name of Priest.

1806: 19 Mar: *Conversed with Sir. J. Riddell, Priest, More, Trevenen, Micklem, Jenkins.* 20 Mar: *Conversed with Stacie, the More's, Darke, Burney, Marsh, Priest, Cabbell &c.*

PRINCE — John Prince[206]

John Prince (1753-1833), Church of England clergyman, was born in London, the son of John Prince. He was of modest origins, and quaintly categorised in the *Oxford Alumni* as 'pleb'. Prince was educated at Oriel College, Oxford (BA 1775). He was appointed vicar of Enford, Wiltshire, a living in the gift of mayor and commonalty and citizens of the City of London, governors of Christs Hospital.

1807: 7 Aug: *Visitation at Lavington found Archb. Danberry with many Clergymen, Messrs. Key, Spencer, Smith, Prince, Jones, Basset, Richards, Dr. Skinner, Williams, Rogers &c. &c.*

PRINN — George Bragge Prowse Prinn — *see also* Dodington Hunt *and* William Hunt Prinn[207]

George Bragge Prowse Prinn (1767-1839), JP and landed proprietor, was born at Yeovil, the son of George Prowse, of an ancient Somerset family, and Elizabeth (d. 1800), daughter of William Bragge (1708-1778) and Elizabeth Hunt (1711-1741), of Hatfield Peverel, Essex. Prowse was educated at University College, Oxford (MA 1787). He inherited Charlton Park estate from his cousin William Hunt Prinn (±1772-1821) (*below*), and thereby added Prinn to his name.

George Prowse Prinn was appointed high sheriff for Gloucestershire in 1839 and rose to become colonel of the Somerset Militia. No obvious record has come to light indicating a marriage or any children. He died at the Somerset Hotel, Strand, in January 1839.

After Prowse Prinn's death, the Charlton estate passed to Jane Eliza Russell, daughter of Maj.-Gen. James Dodington Sherwood. She was the second wife of Sir William Russell, 1st baronet (1773-1839), a Scottish physician who was created a baronet on 18 February 1832 for his services in the field of medicine. He died at Charlton Park on 26 September 1839. The estate was conveyed to Jane Eliza's son, Lt-Gen. Sir William Russell, 2nd baronet (1822-1892), who served in the Crimean War and in the Indian Mutiny of 1857.

1827: 9 Apr: *The High Sheriff this year is Col. Prinn, late Prowse, the inheritor of the landed property of my old acquaintance, Mr. Prinn of Charlton Park, near Cheltenham.*

PRINN — William Hunt Prinn — *see also* Dodington Hunt[208]

William Hunt Prinn (±1772-1821), landed proprietor, was educated at Corpus Christi College, Oxford. He married, 1802, Hester (d. 1822), youngest daughter of John Salmon of Eastcot House, Wookey, near Wells, Somerset. Prinn inherited the Charlton estate from Dodington Hunt (d. 1803). He was succeeded by his cousin George Bragge Prowse (*above*), who assumed the name Prinn on entering into the family estates.

1805: 26 Jul: *At the Rehearsal with Mr. Prinn &c.*

PRIOR — George Sayle Prior[209]

George Sayle Prior (1799-1884), Church of England clergyman, was born at Tewkesbury, the eldest son of George Prior and Dinah Boyes, who had married at Eastleach Turville, Gloucestershire, 28 February 1791. He was educated at Queen's College, Oxford (BA 1823), and was ordained deacon on 25 May 1823 and priest on 21 December 1823. His first clerical appointment was as curate of Coldridge, Devon, from 10 July 1823. This was followed by curacies at Bondleigh, from 20 September 1826, and Eggesford, from 21 December 1833, both in Devon. In 1840 he was appointed chaplain at Lisbon and remained there until 1861. On returning to England he served as rector of St Breock, Cornwall, 1861-73. The curacy of Toddington is not listed on the Church of England database nor in *Oxford Alumni*, but neither source is totally comprehensive.

Prior was married to Mary (1820-1894); they had 2 sons and 3 daughters:

1 Diana Matson (1842-1929)
2 Frances Josling (1844-1933); married, at St Breocke, Cornwall, 21 September 1864, Ernest Augustus Prideaux-Brune (1839-1868); 1 son and 1 daughter
1 George Sayle (1847-1920); married, at St James's, Emsworth, Hampshire, 22 June 1870, Philadelphia Simmons Matson (1848-1920); 1 son and 3 daughters
2 Frederick Henry (1848-1933); educated at Magdalen Hall, Oxford; married Euphemia Erskine Dawson (1861-1933); 2 sons
3 Horace Matson (1850-1877)

1839: 7 May: *Mr. Prior, the Curate of Toddington, was there, bringing with him the parish registers of Toddington and Didbrook.*

PRIVETT — John Privett[210]

John Privett (±1780-1846), butcher (listed in the census as a farmer), lived at Market Place, Stow-on-the-Wold.

1838: 5 Apr: *Of the new Guardians who presented themselves with credentials from their respective parishes, were Mr. Chamberlayne, for Maugersbury, Privett, for Stow.* 19 May, 8 Aug., 2 Nov., 16 Nov.

1845: 9 Jan: *To the Workhouse, where I conferred with Mr. Pearce on the subject of a letter which I had recd. from him this morning, wherein he wished for advice as to the course to be taken by Privett, the late Butcher, whom he considers to have been falsely charged with indecencies and immoralities, of which he has been, in his old age, and very recently, not for the first time, publickly reminded by insulting popular demonstrations.*

1846: 30 Dec: *A candidate for the place of schoolmistress at the Union Workhouse called upon me—widow of John Privett, our late butcher.*

PROBERT — John Probert, police constable at Northleach[211]

John Probert (b ±1823), labourer and police constable, was born at Berkeley, Gloucestershire, the son of James Probert (1790-1855) and Sarah Ann Browning (1790-1847). He was 5 feet 11½ inches in height. He was dismissed on 24 January 1850 for unknown reasons.

1846: 10 Sep: *An affray occurred on Sunday evening last, in the public house at Barrington Wharf, it being the night of Barrington feast, which ended in the death of a man present, and the serious wounding of another, both injuries being caused by rash or unlucky blows inflicted by a Police Constable, Probert, stationed at Northleach.*

PROBYN — Mr Probyn of the North Gloucestershire Militia

This person is not known, but he was probably of the Probyn family of Newland, Gloucestershire.

1806: 21 Jan., 9 Feb: *walked a little with Mr. Probyn of the North Gloc. Mil., whom also I pressed into Mrs. Salter's service.* 12 Feb.

PROBYN — John Probyn — *see also* Dighton[212]

John Probyn (1761-1843), Church of England clergyman, was the son of Edmund Probyn of Newland. He was educated at Christ Church, Oxford, and served as dean and archdeacon of Llandaff, 1796-1843. He married, at Newland, Gloucestershire, 28 November 1785, Anne Jones (1763-1846); they had at least 3 sons and 1 daughter:

1 John (1785-1863); *see below*
2 Edmund (1788-1837), vicar of Longhope and Abenhall
1 Maria (1797-1875); married Charles Mein Dighton (1797-1826); 3 sons
3 Thomas (1798-1871), Lt, 17th Bombay Native Infantry; resigned his commission, 1834; married Margaret; at least 2 sons and 5 daughters

---

1823: 14 Jan.
1830: 12 Jan.

PROBYN — John Probyn[213]

John Probyn (1785-1863), JP and landed proprietor, was born at Newland, the eldest son of John Probyn (*above*). He lived at the manor house in Longhope. He was married to Anna (b. ±1795); they had at least 1 daughter:

1 Blanche (b. ±1833)

1835: 6 Jan: *Several Gentlemen took the oaths as Magistrates ... Probyn.*
1844: 8 Apr.

PRODGERS — Edwin Prodgers[214]

Edwin Prodgers (1786-1861), Church of England clergyman, was the son of Edward Prodgers of Worcester. He was educated at Trinity College, Oxford (BA 1807; MA 1810; BD 1827), and was rector of Ayott St Peter, Hertfordshire, 1842-61.

1840: 5 Oct: *Recd. a few obliging lines from Lord Rossmore, covering a letter which he had received from the Revd. Edwin Prodgers, Minister, I believe, of Brixton, Surrey, speaking in terms of approbation of the sermon which I preached at Stanway on occasion of the death of Lady Rossmore.* 6 Oct.

PROSSER — John Prosser [215]

John Prosser (b. ±1804), Church of England clergyman, was born at Hereford, the second son of John Prosser. He matriculated at Magdalen Hall in 1823, but does not appear to have completed his degree. He was appointed stipendiary curate of Bourton-on-the-Hill and Moreton-in-Marsh chapel on 4 March 1824; he may have remained there until at least 1845. His wife was Elizabeth Boughton (±1795-1841).

The diary entries are unclear. It is possible that some of the entries attributed to Joseph below refer to John. John and Joseph Prosser do not appear to have been related, although they may have been cousins.

1840: 27 Oct: *Several Clergy of my acquaintance were there, Billingsley accompanied by his wife, Mr. Malcolm of Toddington, and his son, who is curate of Wellesbourne in Warwickshire, Mr. Marshall of Evesham, Mr. John Eddy, Mr. Prosser of Moreton, Mr. Coyle of Blockley &c.*

PROSSER — Joseph Camplin Prosser [216]

Joseph Camplin Prosser (1805-1870), Church of England clergyman, was the third son of William Prosser of Tewkesbury. He appears to have become a curate for Dr Warneford at Bourton-on-the-Hill before he went to Oxford; he matriculated at Magdalen Hall on 21 October 1829. The diary entry for 8 September 1826 mentions two Mr Prossers; the latter appears to be W. M. Prosser, presumably an elder brother, but it may be that John Prosser (*above*), curate at Bourton-on-the-Hill, was a cousin. Joseph Prosser became rector of Itton in 1832 and rector of Newchurch, Monmouthshire, in 1829.

1826: 19 Apr., 8 Sep: *Lord Redesdale presided, I dined and slept at Dr. Warneford's. Mr. Ford, Mr. Malcolm, two Messrs. Prosser, Mr. Collier, Mr. Jeaffreson &c. were of the party.*

1828: 23 Apr.

1829: 18 Sep., 22 Sep.

1830: 14 Apr.

PROSSER — William Prosser — *see also* John Forbes [217]

William Prosser (±1804-1863), stone mason, was born at Monmouth. In 1851 he was registered as living at 4 Tivoli Street, Cheltenham; ten years later he was living with his wife, Sarah (b. ±1802), at Queen's Retreat, Cheltenham. At some point he was in partnership with Robert Todd, and they employed John Forbes as an architect. In 1834 Forbes was holding a bond to order on behalf of William Prosser; he forged Prosser's signature to pay a butcher's bill of £4 and to take the difference, which the butcher paid in cash. The case came up before Mr Justice Coleridge, and Forbes was sentenced to transportation to Australia. In the end the sentence was commuted to a short prison term, which he served at Gloucester.

1835: 13 Apr.

PROSSER — Richard Prosser and the Prosser family of Lower Slaughter [218]

Richard Prosser (±1778-1861), farmer and maltster, lived at Lower Slaughter. He was married to Elizabeth (b. ±1775); they had at least 1 son and 2 daughters:

1 William C. (±1817-1911), farmer; married Mary Anne; farmed 82 acres employing three men and a boy

1 Mary (±1820-1854)

2 Charlotte (b. ±1821)

By 1861, at the age of 83, Prosser was still working as a maltster. He lived at the Farm House, Lower Slaughter. He died very shortly after the census was taken.

1837: 1 May: *At Prosser's house endeavoured to find some clue to her offence committed there yesterday: it now transpired that a cheese had been stolen.*

1840: 23 Sep: *R Prosser, who came to inform me that he & others had been robbed on Wednesday in last week of linen hung out to dry, and had a clue, as he supposed, to the plunderer.*

1842: 10 Sep: *Walked with E.F.W. and Sophy to L. Slaughter to speak with R. Prosser as to some accommodation which he, in his capacity of Trustee to the House of the Baptist Minister at Bourton, can give in respect of Edward's cottages there.*

1846: 27 Jul: *R Prosser having pressed upon me that it would be to my advantage to purchase for £900 eleven acres of excellent grass land in the parish of Lower Slaughter, late Smith's ... I went to look at the fields.* 28 Jul., 29 Jul: *Called on R. Prosser, and declined purchasing the land at Lower Slaughter, which he had offered to me.*

1847: 4 Jun: *Drove with MW. to Bourton on the Water, callg. on the way at Prosser's, Lower Slaughter, on Prov. Bank business.* 13 Nov.

1849: 19 Dec: *Business with R. Prosser as to Income Tax assessed on him in regard of his profits in trade.*

1854: 22 May: *Paying a bill to W C Prosser, learnt some edifying particulars as to the close of the life of his amiable sister, Mary, lately deceased after a lingering decline.* 26 May, 3 Jun: *Walked with Edm. Clifford to Lower Slaughter. Called on Mrs. Prosser, to condole with her on the loss of her good daughter, Mary.* 24 Jun.

PROTHEROE — Edward Protheroe [219]

Edward Protheroe (1774-1856), MP and merchant, was the eldest son of Philip Protheroe (d. 1803) (*below*) and Mary Brain. He was educated at Harrow School and Christ's College, Cambridge. He married, 1796, Anne, daughter of John Waterhouse of Halifax, Yorkshire; they had 1 son:

1 Edward Davis (1798-1852); *see below*

Protheroe was sheriff for Bristol in 1797-98, mayor in 1804-05, and MP in 1812-20. He held extensive properties in Gloucestershire and Bristol, but his main residence was at Newnham, Gloucestershire. By 1811 he was living in London at 39 Harley Street.

Protheroe subscribed in 1809 to the bill from which emerged the Severn and Wye Railway and Canal Company. In 1812 he bought collieries from his uncle John Protheroe in the Forest of Dean at a cost of 20,000 guineas. It was in coal mining, as well as iron mining and smelting, that he later developed an extensive industrial empire.

1833: 18 Apr: *The house adjoins a more elaborate and somewhat grotesque castellated Villa, still, I believe, the property of one of the opulent mercantile family of the Protheroes.*

1836: 14 Jul: *Higher up the hill we visited the mouth of one of the deepest and largest mines of the district, where the coal is raised from a pit nearly 200 yards below the surface. The works belong to Mr. Protheroe, who has an extensive concern in this district.*

PROTHEROE — Edward Davis Protheroe [220]

Edward Davis Protheroe (1798-1852), MP and landed proprietor, was the son Edward Protheroe (1774-1856) (above), MP for Bristol (1812-20), and Ann Waterhouse. The family seat was at Newnham, Gloucestershire. Protheroe was educated at Christ Church, Oxford, and was MP for Evesham, 1826-30, Bristol, 1831-32, and Halifax, 1837-47. He was also a commissioner of public records. He took the additional surname of Davis in 1845 and died unmarried.

1840: 20 Oct: *A very large attendance of Magistrates; among them, and among those with whom I was especially in intercourse, were Prothero, MP. for Halifax ...*

PROTHEROE — Philip Protheroe[221]

Philip Protheroe (1747-1803), West India merchant, banker, and shipowner, was in partnership with Robert Claxton. In 1794 he became a founding partner of the Bristol City Bank (Ireland, Protheroe & Co.). By the time of his death on 30 August 1803, he had acquired landed property in Gloucestershire and in his ancestral counties of Carmarthenshire and Pembrokeshire. In his will he made cash bequests in excess of £112,000.

Philip Protheroe married Mary Brain (1744-1819); they had at least 4 sons and 1 daughter:

1 Edward (1774-1856); *see above*
1 Sarah (±1779-1860); married, at St Augustine the Less, Bristol, 1 January 1799, James Vaughan (1773-1857); 4 sons and 2 daughters
2 Philip (1781-1846)
3 Lewis (1782-1827)
4 Henry (17[?]-1840); died at Rouen, France

1804: 20 Sep: ... *in view of Knoll a place belonging to Mr. Worrall, & another beneath it, the property of Mr. Protheroe a Bristol lawyer, & merchant, enjoying singular advantages of situation & prospect.*

PROWER — John Mervyn Prower[222]

John Mervyn Prower (1784-1869), Church of England clergyman, was born at Purton, Wiltshire, the son of Revd John Prower (1747-1827) and Anne Lipyeatt (1747-1811). He was educated at Wadham College, Oxford (BA 1806; MA 1835), and was appointed honorary canon of Bristol and vicar of Purton, Wiltshire.

Prower married, 1809, Susannah Coles (b. 1786), born at Codoxton House, Neath, Glamorgan; they had at least 1 son:

1 John Elton (1812-1882), officer, 67th Regt

Prower was widowed before 1851. The marriage settlement between him and Susannah Coles is held at Gloucestershire Archives. It has not been studied in detail, but it mentions the following other parties: Sarah Coles, spinster, of Purton, Wiltshire; Charles Brandon Trye, surgeon, of Gloucester; William Montague of Gloucester; John Elton of Hucclecote; and John Merrott Stephens of Maisemore.

1802: 23 Jun: *Bathed. Walked with Pering & Prower.* 8 Aug: *Walked with Dove & Brown & Prower.*

1803: 29 Dec: *A good & merry supper. A good deal of conversation with the hosts, hostesses etc, Caroline Hillhouse, Lieut. Prower Schol. of Wadham.*

1804: 2 Jan: *took a second very late breakfast with Prower & Mr. Johnston. The former & myself afterwards joined two of the Miss Smiths & with them made the complete circle of the Hill & back with them to their house; chatty & agreeable.* 3 Jan., 8 Jan., 11 Jan: *Dined very pleasantly with Prower at the Wilts Mess. Having dressed at his lodgings where I proposed to sleep after a ball where we were invited.* 13-16 Jan., 18 Jan., 26 Jan.

1805: 18 Mar: *Drank wine with Dowell, meeting Prower.* 19 Mar., 21 Mar.

1806: 18 Mar: *Walked round the Parks with Prower.* 20 Mar: *Lounged a little with Prower.*

1839: 5 Jun: *In virtue of seniority I occupied a post of honour by the side of the Warden, Dr. Symonds, who laid himself out to be very agreeable and conversible; opposite to me was my old contemporary & acquaintance, Prower, a North Wiltshire Clergyman.*

1844: 8 Oct: *Found a crowd of members of convocation gathering for the fray; among whom recognized a few acquaintance, but very few of my own standing; one cotemporary only, I think, the Revd. J. M. Power, Rector of Purton, Wilts.*

1848: 24 Aug: *Canon Prower, from Purton, my ancient college acquaintance and contemporary, now a Wiltshire Rural Dean and as such raised by Bp Monk to the profitless dignity of honorary canon of Bristol Cathedral.*

PROWSE — *see* Prinn

PROWSE JONES — *see* Jones

PRUEN — Septimus Alexander Conant Pruen[223]

Septimus Alexander Conant Pruen (±1817-1865), attorney and coroner, was born in the East Indies, possibly Calcutta, the son of John Pruen (1776-1839) and Susannah Langford (1779-1856). He married, 1845, Louise Griffiths (b. 1820); they had at least 2 sons:

1 Frederick Langford (b. ±1846)
2 George Griffiths (b. 1851)

1848: 2 Aug., 28 Aug.

1850: 15 Jul: ... *his competitors are Mr. Septimus Pruen, Attorney, Cheltenham, Mr. Holt, Junr. Attorney, Gloucester, and a Mr. Smith, formerly a medical Practitioner, of Winchcomb.* 16 Jul., 1 Aug: *Mr. W. H. Leigh, of Adlestrop, called on the fruitless errand of canvassing me in favour of Mr. Pruen, the candidate for the vacant Coronership. He is supported by the Whig, Radical, and Berkeley interest.* 3 Aug: *It is stated that the majority of votes at the close of the poll in the three polling places yesterday was in favour of Mr. Pruen, so that Lovegrove has been defeated.* 11 Oct., 14 Oct: ... *in the same carriage with whom I travelled to Gloucester, Mr. Barnett, the Coroner, and Mr. S. Pruen, the new Coroner, being also in our carriage.* 28 Oct., 31 Oct.

PRUEN — William Ashmead Pruen[224]

William Ashmead Pruen (1782-1840), Church of England clergyman, was the son of Thomas Pruen (b. 1736), of Gloucester, and Catherine James (b. 1739) of Eastington, near Stonehouse, Gloucestershire. He was elder brother to John Pruen, and therefore uncle to Septimus Alexander Conant Pruen (*above*).

William Pruen was educated at Worcester College, Oxford (BA 1805; MA 1808; BD 1819). He was perpetual curate of Fladbury, Worcestershire, 1809-38, and vicar of Snitterfield, Warwickshire, 1838-40. He married, at Cropthorne, Worcestershire, 29 May 1806, Margaret Hudson Boyce (1783-1848); they had 2 sons and 4 daughters:

1 Mary (1808-1863)
2 Margaret (1808-1881)
3 Anne (1809-1865)
4 Elizabeth (b. 1811)
1 William Stafford Smith (1817-1831)
2 Hudson Boyce (1823-1895), Church of England clergyman

1823: 25 Apr: *Mr. W. Pruen, Curate to Mr. Stafford Smith, has long had an academy at Fladbury, in some repute: he is originally from Cheltenham and brother to the Revd. T. Pruen, Curate of Dursley, who had not the advantage of an University Education, & entered the church after trying more than one line in life.*

PUGET — John David Puget[225]

John David Puget (1760-1805), banker, was born in the parish of St Botolph, Bishopsgate, London, the eldest son of John Philip Puget (1729-1767) and Esther Dunn (d. 1814). He was the elder brother of Rear Adm. Peter Puget (1765-1822), who charted Puget's Sound on the north-western Pacific coast of North America, now Washington State. Puget's ancestors had fled France for England during Louis XIV's persecution of the Huguenots. By the mid-eighteenth century they had varied their religious allegiance and become dissenters.

John Puget was a director of the Bank of England from 1790 to his death in 1805. He lived at Poynter's [Pointer's] Grove, Totteridge, Hertfordshire, and married, 1796, Catherine (1772-1842), daughter of James Hawkins (d. 1807), bishop of Raphoe, and Catherine, daughter of Gilbert Keene. John and Catherine had at least 1 son and 3 daughters:

1 Catherine Esther (b. 1797); baptised in the parish of St Andrew, Holborn, London

2 Elizabeth (b. 1798); born in John Street; baptised in the parish of St Andrew, Holborn, London; married, as his second wife, James Browne (1793-1854) of Claremont House, co. Mayo; at least 1 son and 1 daughter:

  1 Catherine (b. ±1826)

  1 James (b. ±1827)

3 Esther Catherine (1800-1874); born in John Street; baptised in the parish of St Andrew, Holborn, London; married, 7 August 1823, Vice Adm. Granville George Waldegrave, 2nd Baron Radstock (1786-1857), son of William Waldegrave, 1st Baron Radstock (1753-1825), and Cornelia Jacoba Van Lennep (d. 1839); at least 1 son and 2 daughters:

  1 Granville Augustus William Waldegrave (1833-1913); succeeded as 3rd Baron Radstock

  1 Elizabeth Cornelia (1824-1903); died unmarried

  2 Catherine Esther (1826-1898); died unmarried at Le Havre, Normandy

1 John Hey (1803-1867); educated at Glasgow University (1816-20), New College, Oxford (matriculated only), and Trinity College, Cambridge (BA 1825; MA 1828); married, at Cheriton, near Dover, his cousin Isabella, eldest daughter of Francis Hawkins, senior judge of Barelly, East India; at least 2 sons and 3 daughters:

  1 John Hey (1827-1894), Col, 8th King's Royal Irish Hussars; married, 1863, Florence Annie de Arroyave (1840-1897)

  1 Isabella Mary (b. 1828); married, at Totteridge, 27 September 1849, Francis Shoe

  2 Frances (b. 1829)

  2 Granville William (1830-1888); died at Kensington, Middlesex

  3 Emma Hey (b. 1839); married, at Totteridge, 31 July 1860, John Davison

The family seem also to have maintained a town house in John Street, Spitalfields, where most of the children were born. In the 1841 census, Puget's widow Catherine was still a resident at Totteridge. She lived there with her daughter Elizabeth Browne and grandchildren Catharine and James. She died the following year.

John David Puget was referred to as 'of Dublin and Totteridge'. There was a Dublin connection to the family which has not yet been fully explored. It seems likely that Puget set up a wing of his banking activities there, and he presumably met Catherine in Dublin. Alternatively, he may have been working alongside his brother-in-law, William George Digges Latouche (1747-1803), who had married Puget's elder sister Grace (1759-1843) at the church of St George the Martyr, Queen Square, London, on 14 November 1787. Latouche appears to have headed up, or been a partner in, the Dublin bank La Touche.

La Touche Bank had been founded by another Huguenot, William George Digges La Touche (1746-1803), whose father, David Digues La Touche (1671-1745), born near Blois in France, had fled to an uncle in Amsterdam upon the revocation of the Edict of Nantes. There he had entered Caillemotte's Huguenot regiment. He came to England with the Prince of Orange and fought at the battle of the Boyne. After his regiment was disbanded he chose to remain in Dublin, first as a maker of poplins and later as a banker.

After his first meeting with John David Puget in June 1801, Francis Witts wrote his name as 'Peyett'. In the same month, Agnes Witts met the Puget family twice; in her diary she spelt their name 'Pigout'. Accordingly, it appears that the family had long since given up maintaining the soft 't', as in the original French version of 'Pugét'.

1801: 1 Jun: *Mr. & Mrs. Manning, Mr. Bosanquet & Mr. Peyett, called afterwards. Mr. Garrow & Mr. Ellill spent the Evening with us.* 6 Jun: *I also walked over Mr. Peyett's Grounds, which are very compact & pretty.*

1802: 18 Jan: *With Jno. Fiott called upon Mr. Pugett; & upon Mr. Ellill.* 20 Jan: *Walked down to Highgate & thence drove myself conveniently hither in a Taxed Cart. Met here at dinner Mr. Lee, Mr. & Mrs. Pugett, Mrs Garrow & Mr. Marsham. Played at Commerce.*

1803: 9 Oct: *Mr. & Mrs. Puget called at the Park: Walked all the Party to Highwood & called on the Bowzer's.*

PUGH — Alexander Pugh[226]

Alexander Pugh (1788-1855), agricultural labour, was born at Upper Slaughter. He married, at Lower Slaughter, 1815, Mary Webley (1786-1857), born at Little Rissington; they had at least 1 son and 1 daughter:

1 William (1817-1892); *see below*

1 Charlotte (b. ±1822); listed, 1841, as living with her brother William at 'Sabrina Cottages, Island', presumably Alney Island, Gloucester

---

1840: 21 Apr: *In the Evening wrote a recommendation of a patient, Charlotte Pugh, to the Governors of the Gloucester Infirmary; also a note on her behalf to Mr. Hill, the Secretary of the Infirmary.*

1853: 18 Feb: *Parish business in the evening, advising Alex Pugh under a difficulty.*

1854: 15 Apr: *Visited sick and aged parishioners—Widows Wilcox and Lanchbury, and A Pugh's wife.* 11 Jul.

PUGH — Jacob Pugh[227]

Jacob Pugh (±1795-1868), carpenter, was born at Upper Slaughter. He was probably a brother to Alexander (*above*). He was married to Hannah (b. ±1796), born at Colesbourne; they had at least 1 son:

1 Emmanuel (b. ±1840)

The family lived at 6 Corpus Street, Cheltenham.

1838: 28 Jan: *Wrote to Mr. Gabb, Perp. Cur. of Charlton Kings, in answer to his letter of the 28th. Ult inclosing 10/- to be given by him to my parishioner, Jacob Pugh, living at Charlton as a donation to him out of the charity resources of this Parish.*

PUGH — William Pugh[228]

William Pugh (1817-1892), agricultural labourer, was born at Upper Slaughter, the son of Alexander Pugh (1788-1855) and Mary Webley (1786-1857). He married, 1847, Elizabeth Paynter (1821-1904), the Witts family cook. Elizabeth was born at Ashton Keynes, the daughter of Joseph Paynter (1793-1876) and Mary Cary (b. ±1797). In the 1851 census William was listed as an agricultural labourer. He and Elizabeth emigrated to Canada, reportedly in 1853. In 1861 they were living at Owen Sound, Grey, Ontario. By 1880 they had moved to Michigan. William died at Calumet, Houghton County, Michigan, and Elizabeth died at Osceola Township in the same county.

The date given for William and Elizabeth Pugh's emigration to Canada, 1853, does not tie up with the diary entries for 1854. It is likely that this is an error and the emigration occurred later.

1847: 14 Dec: *Our cook, Elizabeth Painter, married this morning by me to William Pugh, of this village.*

1852: 7 Dec: *Wrote to the authorities of the Great Western Railway a testimonial in favour of William Pugh of this parish, but resident in London, who seeks the office of Porter in that establishment.*

1854: 17 May: *A begging letter from Wm. Pugh, late a parishioner here, but who was assisted by our parochial charity in removing himself and family to London, where he represents himself and them as lately suffering from severe illness and in much distress: he hopes for relief from the parish of his Settlement.* 19 May: *To my Churchwarden's (E. Lea) to advise with him as to sending help to W. Pugh, from whom I received a pressing application on Wednesday. Conferred thereon with Mrs. Lea.* 20 May: *Mrs. Lea called, bringing her husband's consent to my suggestion of sending £2. 0. 0. to assist W. Pugh in his present distress, provided he forward from the Clergyman of his parish or the Medical man who has attended his family in sickness, a certificate of such sickness and distress.... Wrote a letter to that effect to W. Pugh.* 24 May: *Received a certificate from a Surgeon at Lambeth, who had attended W. Pugh and his wife in their late attack of Small Pox, and spoke favourably of their conduct and character. Wrote to W. Pugh a note to accompany a Post office order to-morrow for £2. 0. 0 — on the U S. Charity Estate account.*

PULLER — Selina Puller and the Puller family of Painswick[229]

Selina Puller, née Wall (1750-1831), was the daughter of Charles Wall (1757-1815) and Harriet Baring (1768-1838). She married, at All Hallows, London Wall, 29 May 1771, Richard Puller (1747-1826), merchant, of London and Painswick Court, Gloucestershire; they had 5 sons and 3 daughters:

1 Christopher (1774-1824); educated at Eton College and Christ Church, Oxford; called to the bar at the Inner Temple, 1800; knighted, 1823, on succeeding Sir R. H. Blossett as chief justice of Bengal, but died in Calcutta, five weeks after arriving in India; married, at St Michael's, St Albans, Hertfordshire, 9 August 1804, Louisa (±1772-1857), daughter of Joseph King, of Taplow, and niece of Daniel Giles, of Youngsbury, Hertfordshire, to which estate she succeeded in 1840; at least 1 son and 2 daughters, including:
    1 Christopher William Giles (1807-1864), MP for Hertford; married, 2 July 1831, Emily, daughter of William Blake; 5 sons and 4 daughters
    1 Mary Louisa Puller (1811-1815)
2 Henry (1782-1813)
1 Selena Eliza (1785-1872)
3 Edward (1786-1800)
2 Charlotte Louisa (1788-1828)
4 Richard (1789-1831)
3 Harriet (1790-1870)
5 George (1792-1844); educated at Merton College, Oxford (BA 1814)

1829: 19 Oct: *We set out about eleven o'clock, and went by Cheltenham, where both they and myself had some errands. I accompanied them to call on a Mrs. Puller, an old & infirm lady, who with two unmarried daughters resides in a handsome house at Pitt-ville. They did formerly live at Painswick; Mrs. Puller's son, Sir Christ. Puller, was an eminent barrister on the Oxford circuit, and afterwards Chief Justice at Calcutta, where the Climate carried him off, within a few weeks after his arrival.*

PULSFORD — Charles Pulsford[230]

Charles Pulsford (±1782-1841), Church of England clergyman, was the son of Luke Pulsford and Jane Gould of Wells. He matriculated at Merton College, Oxford, in 1799, but migrated in 1806 to Jesus College, Cambridge (BA 1807; MA 1827). Pulsford was vicar of Barton St David, Somerset, 1810-30; prebendary of Wells, 1815; rector of Kingweston, 1819-26; canon-residentiary of Wells, 1826-41; and vicar of Burnham, 1827-41. He married, 1841, Laetitia Sarah, daughter of Edward Berkeley Napier of East Pennard.

1807: 17 Aug: *to the village of Usley & Deptford Inn where I had the pleasure to meet & dine with an acquaintance the Revd. Mr. Pulsford of Wells.*

PURNELL — John Bransby Purnell[231]

John Bransby Purnell (1820-1869), eldest son of Purnell Bransby Purnell, of Stancombe Park, was educated at Corpus Christi, Oxford. Little is known of him. He does not appear to have married and most records show that he continued to live at Stancombe Park. He was a JP and commissioner of assessed taxes. His father died in 1866 and his elder brother William Paston Purnell, an army officer, died in May 1869. John died unmarried in August 1869, at just 49 years old.

1845: 15 Apr.

1848: 6 Jan., 21-22 Mar.

1851: 31 Mar., 20-21 May, 22 May: *Accompanied John Purnell, and his two namesakes, of Kings Hill and Staverton, to the Crystal Palace, where I remained from 1 PM. till 5 P.M.* 23 May: *Accompanied Mr. Purnell of Kings Hill, his son, and John Purnell, on a visit to Northumberland House.*

1852 17 Mar.

1853: 5 Jan., 15 Mar., 4 Apr.

1854: 31 Mar: *He kindly came to acquaint me that he had received a letter from John Purnell, to the effect that he had named my curacy to his cousin Edmund Clifford, son of my old acquaintance & brother Justice, Clifford of Frampton, who is at present an unemployed Clergyman.* 22 Jul: *Wrote to J B Purnell, inviting him to pass a week here, from Aug 3. to Aug 10.* 25 Jul: *Received a letter from J. B. Purnell, who accepts my invitation to visit me from Aug 3. to the 10th.* 3 Aug: *Returned home by 5 P.M. and found John Purnell arrived from Stancombe Park.* 4 Aug., 6-7 Aug., 8 Aug: *Soon after 2 P.M. E.F.W. Sophy and J Purnell went to Stow in my son's open carriage to be present at the meeting of the Cotswold Archers.* 10 Aug: *J B. Purnell left us in the course of the forenoon, for Cheltenham, on his way to Stancombe Park; apparently he had much enjoyed his visit.*

PURNELL — Purnell Bransby Purnell and the Purnell family — *see also* Cooper [232]

Purnell Bransby Purnell (1791-1866), JP, DL, and landed proprietor, was the eldest son of Robert Bransby Cooper (1762-1845), MP for Gloucester (1818-30), and Anne Purnell (1763-1804). His parents had married at Dursley, Gloucestershire, on 6 May 1784. Robert Bransby Cooper came from an old Norfolk family. He was the son of Revd Samuel Cooper and Maria Bransby, daughter of James Bransby and Anna Maria Paston. The Paston family, famous for their fifteenth-century letters, was prominent in Norfolk. Sir Astley Paston Cooper was Robert's youngest brother and therefore Purnell's uncle. He became the most eminent surgeon of his day and was created a baronet in 1821. He was appointed surgeon to the king in 1828. Anne Purnell, Purnell's mother, was the daughter and heir of William Purnell (1737-1805) and Jane Compeer (1729-1792) of Ferney Hill House [also called New House], Dursley. Purnell's younger brother was Robert Jermyn Cooper (1795-1873).

Purnell Bransby Cooper changed his name to Purnell by royal licence on 22 February 1805 in pursuance of the will of his maternal grandfather, whose estates he inherited upon his majority in 1811. He was educated at Eton College and Christ Church, Oxford, and married, at Frampton-on-Seven, 13 July 1813, Charlotte Anne (1791-1862), daughter of Nathaniel Clifford and Mary Packer of Frampton Court; they had at least 2 sons and 4 daughters:

1 Charlotte Anne (1815-1816); died an infant
2 Frances Mary (1817-1897); died unmarried
1 John Bransby (1820-1869); *see below*
2 William Paston (1821-1869), Col, 90th Foot; lived at Formosa Cottage, Cookham, on the banks of the River Thames; married, at Cookham, 27 July 1865, Elizabeth Susan Young (1837-1925); died at Cookham, Berkshire, and was buried at Stinchcombe, Gloucestershire; 3 daughters
3 Helen (1825-1889); died unmarried at Stancombe Park, Stinchcombe
4 Rose (1830-1834); died an infant

Purnell was chairman of the local board of guardians (Dursley Union) from 1836 to 1848. He was prominent in organising the building of the union workhouse, and was active in working for those unfortunate individuals wrongfully put in lunatic asylums. He was also chairman of the quarter sessions from 1842 to 1863, and a member of the Oxford and Cambridge Club, and of the Queen's Hotel, Cork Street, London. His family home was at Stancombe Park, Stinchcombe.

1801: 19 Dec: *Rode with my Uncle over to Mr. Cooper's at Dursley. Walked with that Gentleman & his two Boys to Mr. Baker's at Stout's Hill near Uley, & scaited there for some hours.*

1823: 8 Apr., 15 Jul.

1824: 13 Jan.

1826: 10 Jan.

1827: 24 Apr., 10 Jul., 16 Oct.

1828: 15 Apr., 14 Oct.

1829: 13 Jan., 14 Jul., 22 Sep.

1830: 12 Jan., 20 Apr.

1832: 29 Mar.

1834: 4 Nov: *A letter from Mr. Bathurst, inclosing one from P. B. Purnell, a Magistrate residing near Dursley, on the subject of the scale of fees payable to Petty Sessions Clerks.* 5 Nov., 22 Dec.

1835: 1 Jan: *Also a printed scale of Petty Sessns. Clerks fees, proposed to be moved as an amendment at the Quarter Sessions on the scale proposed by the Committee of Accounts. This emanates from Mr. Purnell, being forwarded to me with his Compts.* 4 Jan., 6 Jan.

1836: 11 Aug., 20 Oct.

1837: 2 Jan., 5-6 Jan., 3-4 Feb., 6-8 Mar., 10-11 Apr., 26-28 Jun., 4 Aug., 16-18 Oct.

1838: 1 Jan: *Found Bathurst at the Shire Hall, where we were joined by Purnell, and were deeply engaged all the day and till past midnight in auditing the County accounts.* 2-3 Jan., 9-11 Apr., 2-3 Jul., 5 Jul: *As usual, in intimate intercourse on the business of the Sessions, and otherwise, with Bathurst, Purnell, Baker &c.* 15-16 Oct., 31 Dec.

1839: 1 Jan., 3 Jan: *After breakfast at the Bell, accompanied Bathurst to the opening of his court, and remained there or in Purnell's Court the greater part of the forenoon.* 8-10 Apr., 1-2 Jul.

1840: 29-30 Jun., 1 Jul., 19-21 Oct.

1841: 27 Feb: *A letter from C Bathurst, acknowledging the receipt of mine of the 24th. respecting the Committee of Accounts, written in no very friendly feeling towards Purnell. A letter from Purnell, with more details as to the revival of the Sessions dinner fund, stimulating me to exertion in the cause, and pointing out many, whom he judged I could influence, of whom several dead, and several left the country.* 2 Mar: *A letter from C Bathurst, in reply to mine of the 27th. Inst. written with a less sore feeling towards P. B. Purnell, so that I hope the cloud may disperse.*

1842: 5-6 Jan., 18 Jan: *It is thrown out, whether Sergt. Ludlow would not be a fit Chairman, if he cease to go on the Oxford Circuit, and in default of a more eligible person Codrington leans to Purnell, taking care, however, that he shall not be put forward as the Whig Candidate.* 19 Jan: *it appeared to me that the best policy for our party at the present juncture would be to come forward as proposers of Purnell.* 11-13 Apr., 14 Apr: *Purnell, Bathurst, and I went down to the Shire Hall for a few last words on County business, and the two former remained to close the minutes of the Sessions.* 16 Apr., 21 Apr., 28 Apr., 6 May, 16 May, 31 May, 27-30 Jun., 21-22 Sep., 5 Oct., 7 Oct., 10 Oct., 18-19 Oct., 1 Nov: *Received a letter from Mr. Bathurst on Purnell's conduct in the Chair at the Quarter Sessions with reference to the disagreeable questions as to Prison discipline and dietary, especially as to the attack made on the management of the Northleach Bridewell.* 4 Nov., 7-8 Nov., 13 Nov., 17 Nov., 24-26 Nov., 1 Dec., 5 Dec.

1843: 2 Jan., 3 Jan: *Mr. Purnell admitted that the investigation had been conducted with great impartiality, ability, and courteousness; but regretted that it had not been of a more public nature; and, especially, with reference to the charges against Northleach Bridewell.* 4 Jan., 6-7 Jan., 8 Jan: *and from Bathurst a third communication on Purnell's resignation of the second chair at Q.S.* 14 Jan., 19 Jan., 22 Jan., 7 Feb., 11 Feb., 14 Feb., 9 Oct: *Purnell prevented from attending by the remains of serious illness, spasmodic asthma, from a severe attack of which he is slowly recovering.* 16 Oct: *To the Shire Hall where engaged with Messrs. C. Hayward and Lysons in auditing County Accounts till past six in the Evening: Mr. Purnell not joining us in consequence of his serious illness, but he arrived at Glouc. in the evening, looking wretchedly, and miserably weak, yet preparing for the business of to-morrow, when he will preside.* 17-18 Oct., 1 Dec: *To the Shire Hall, where was subsequently joined by P B Purnell, his Father, J C Hayward, Mr. Crawley Boevey, Mr. Sayers, members of the Prison rules and Gaol Committee; also Mr. Fuljames, the County Surveyor, Mr. Riddiford from the office of the Clerk of the Peace, Mr. Mason, the Governor; and Mr. R Cooper, the Chaplain of the Gaol.*

1844: 1 Jan., 2 Jan: *Accompanied the County Chairman, Purnell, to open the Court, which, slenderly attended at first, was very much crowded after midday.* 3 Jan., 29 Feb: *Received a letter from P. B. Purnell, pressing me to take the chair in one of the Courts for the trial of prisoners at the Adjourned Sessions at Gloucester next week.* 1-2 Mar., 12 Mar., 16 Mar., 8-10 Apr., 14 Apr., 20 Apr., 25 Apr., 1 May, 3 May, 28 May, 15 Aug., 29 Sep: *A letter from P B Purnell, printed as a circular, and sent to each Magistrate in the County, on the time and plan of contracting for provisions and other supplies for the Gaol and Houses of Correction—much ado about nothing—my friend writes too much.* 1 Oct., 15 Oct., 29 Oct., 3 Nov: *A letter from C. Bathurst, who is very uneasy as to the unnatural controversy between the brothers Purnell and Cooper, which is now become a paper war, the elder having thought it necessary to reply to the younger in yesterday's county papers: and so the ball may be bandied backwards and forwards weekly for an indefinite time: but who can or will venture, unasked, to interfere?* 10-11 Nov., 15 Nov., 7 Dec., 11 Dec., 13-14 Dec., 17 Dec: *Recd. a letter from Purnell, at least signed and dictated by him, informing me that he had fractured his thigh by a fall on the ice, while skating; that he, of course, would not be able to preside on the County day at the Epiphany Sessions, and had written to request Archd. Timbrill to take the chair for him.* 18 Dec., 25 Dec: *Recd. a letter from C Bathurst, who sent me a letter he had received from Mr. Clifford of Frampton Court, brother in law of Purnell, to whom he had written for information, giving a description of Purnell's accident, which seems to have been very serious, and he has suffered greatly, both from the fracture and from general illness occasioned by or consequent on it.* 27 Dec., 28 Dec: *Recd. a letter dictated by, and signed by, Purnell, who is suffering greatly, though he speaks of a slight improvement.* 30-31 Dec.

1845: 7 Jan., 20 Jan., 21 Jan: *Recd. a letter from C Bathurst, who forwards to me one written to him by Purnell, very long and curious with most minute details, and graphic picturing of all his sufferings from the fracture of his thigh bone, and consequent serious illness: he enters into minutiæ as to the contrivances for his accommodation in respect of movement for the offices of nature, describing all with the accuracy of a minute philosopher.* 22-25 Jan., 27 Jan: *A letter from Purnell, still a pitiable Sufferer, on the feud between himself and his Brother, the Chaplain of the County Gaol.* 28-29 Jan., 4 Feb., 8 Feb: *A letter from Purnell acknowledging the receipt of my last letter to him: he has still no use in his fractured limb.* 31 Mar., 2-3 Apr., 14 Apr: *To the Bell Hotel, where I found Purnell, and had a long conference with him on County matters.* 15 Apr., 20 Apr., 15 Apr., 20 Apr: *Recd. a letter from R J Cooper, the Chaplain of Gloucester Gaol: he is very angry with me for supporting his brother, the Chairman, in his attack upon him, particularly, because at the Q.S. I seconded Purnell's motion that the matters alleged by him against the Chaplain should be referred to the Board of Vis. Justices of the Gaol.* 6-7 May, 30 Jun., 1 Jul.

1846: 21 May, 29-30 Jun.., 1-2 Jul., 14-15 Jul., 21 Jul., 11 Aug., 25 Aug., 19-22 Oct., 11-12 Nov., 18 Nov: *We were kindly received by the pleasing Mrs. Hayward ... We passed a pleasant evening, with music, and looking at portfolios, especially those brought by Lysons containing a valuable collection of engravings of antiquities, especially of tesselated pavements, both from Italy, Spain, & France, & from England. These had been acquired by his Uncle and Father, the celebrated Antiquarians, and were now produced in consequence of Purnell's having lately discovered the remains of a Roman Villa on his property at Stancombe.* 19 Nov: *Early breakfast at Quedgley; after which Purnell and I took leave of our friendly host and hostess, proceeding in his open carriage to the Gloucester Railway Station.*

1847 4-5 Jan., 16 Mar., 22-23 Mar., 31 Mar., 5 Apr., 16 May, 18 May, 29 May, 28-30 Jun., 17 Aug: *A letter from P. B. Purnell, inviting me to his house on the 24th. Inst. to meet Mr. and Mrs. Curtis Hayward, and Mr. and Mrs. Lysons, at dinner and to sleep, and on the following day to view the site of the Roman Villa which he has been disinterring on his grounds at Stancombe Park.* 19 Aug: *Wrote to P. B. Purnell, forwarding to him for his perusal R. J. Cooper's letter to Howell, that he might know, if he had not otherwise been informed, that his brother, the Chaplain, was seeking office as Prison Inspector.* 22 Aug., 10 Sep., 18-20 Oct., 3 Dec., 7 Dec.

1848: 3-5 Jan., 18 Jan., 22 Jan., 20-22 Mar., 26-28 Jun., 23 Sep., 3 Oct., 6 Oct., 16-17 Oct., 22 Nov.

1849: 10 Dec: *A letter from Purnell: he was taken ill soon after I left the Committee at Gloucester on Wednesday last.* 11 Dec., 22 Dec., 31 Dec.

1850: 1 Jan: *A very well deserved vote of thanks was moved by Lord Fitzhardinge, and seconded by the Duke of Beaufort, recognizing the great services rendered by Purnell to the County, and to the community at large, in his unwearied and persevering labours, in respect of the conditions of the Private Lunatic Asylums in this County.* 2 Jan., 12 Jan., 20 Jan: *From Purnell I received a basket of wild fowl, a kind remembrance at this season.* 21 Jan., 28 Jan., 6 Feb., 4-5 Mar., 9 Mar: *A kind & feeling letter from Purnell with reference to my present great anxiety.* 12 Mar., 25 Apr: *Recd. letters in reference to my grievous loss from P. B. Purnell ...* 27 Apr: *Wrote to Purnell to acknowledge his obliging letter of condolence.* 1-2 Jul., 7 Aug., 20 Sep: *A letter from Purnell, alluding to County business, but chiefly written to notify that he was about to send me a neck of venison.* 22 Sep: *Purnell's promised neck of venison having arrived this morning, wrote notes of invitation to dinner on Wednesday next ...* 25 Sep: *To Purnell, to thank him for the neck of venison he had sent.* 2 Oct: *Received a letter from Purnell, who invites me to spend the latter days of the Quarter Sessions week at Stancomb Park.* 3 Oct: *Wrote to Purnell, accepting his invitation to Stancomb Park, if my health with allow.* 14-15 Oct., 16 Oct: *it was past eleven o clock, when we arrived at the Berkeley Road station, where Purnell's Clarence met us, and conveyed us to Stancombe Park by 12 o clock. Mrs. P. and her daughters had sat up to receive us, not without alarm at the delay, and the tea furnished by the fair hands of Miss P. was very refreshing, before we retired to bed.* 17 Oct: *Purnell had planned a very enjoyable excursion which occupied four hours from mid-day to 4 P.M.* 18 Oct: *An excursion to Berkeley Castle, in two carriages.* 19 Oct: *After breakfast, at 11 AM. I took leave of John Purnell and his amiable sisters, and proceeded in Purnell's carriage, which he drove, and which conveyed also Mrs. P. with Mrs. and Miss Niblett, to the Berkeley Road Station.* 14 Dec., 30 Dec., 31 Dec: *The Lord Lieutenant, the Marquis of Worcester, Lord Ellenborough, Sir W. Codrington, Sir M. Crawley Boevey, with a host of other leading Magistrates were present.... The tribute selected was from the manufactory of an eminent London House, Messrs. Handcock, and consisted of a circular drawing room table with a pillar & claw leg, the materials being of rosewood and ebony, richly inlaid with silver in a very beautiful, antique, Etruscan pattern.... The Lord Lieutenant in very well chosen and well considered terms of subdued compliment dilated on the valuable services of the County Chairman, to which the latter responded in fitting language and set phrase.*

1851: 31 Jan., 5 Feb., 11 Feb., 1 Mar., 6 Mar., 17 Mar., 31 Mar., 19 May: *When I returned to my hotel I found John Purnell in the coffee-room, who is living with his father in the house, having arrived to-day; The County Chairman has been staying here for a fortnight, much interested in the Great Exhibition, but suffering from lameness, and varicose veins.* 20 May: *I sat up for some time in conversation with the Purnells, father and son. I was struck with the visible marks of exhaustion and indisposition which the countenance of the elder displayed: he admitted that he was suffering from the excitement, and unequal to the exertions consequent on a visit to London at this season, enduring much pain from his lameness, and inconvenience from his legs, inflamed with varicose veins.* 21 May: *My friends set me down at my hotel, where I found John Purnell, in considerable agitation, alone in the coffee-room, waiting for intelligence from his Father's apartment, with whom the eminent surgeon, Bransby Cooper, was, watching the symptoms of his complaint. It seems that his cousin, Bransby, had been called in during the day, who had also summoned Dr. Bright to a consultation.* 21 May: *Purnell of Stancombe Park is confined to his room with indisposition.* 23 May.

1852: 7-11 Mar., 13 Mar., 15-18 Mar., 8 Jun: *My friend, the County Chairman, is staying at the Queen's — we met at breakfast.* 9 Jun., 10 Jun: *To the Queen's Hotel, to call on P.B. Purnell, now in town, whom I accompanied on a visit to the Government Exhibition at Gore House, Kensington.*

1853: 3-5 Jan., 14-15 Mar., 4-5 Apr., 10 Jun., 27 Jun.

1854: 28-29 Jan., 31 Jan., 4 Feb: *from Purnell on the almost exhausted subject of his retirement from the County Chair, and resumption of it, which he seems to regard as impracticable.* 7 Feb., 11 Feb., 14 Feb., 23 Feb., 12 Mar., 14 Mar., 19 Mar., 22-23 Mar., 16 Apr: *A letter from Purnell, very kind in its expression, in answer to mine of the 14th. Inst.* 2 Jun., 7 Jun: *A letter from P. B. Purnell in reply to mine to him of the 3d. Inst., in which I intimated my intention, in consequence of ill-health, to retire from the public business of the County as far as regards attendance at Quarter Sessions & Assizes. The tone of the letter is most friendly, & even affectionate.* 1 Jul: *Purnell appears to have adverted to my past public services in terms of warm encomium, no doubt borne away by personal regard, and over rating both my talents and my Services—but he seems to have met with a cordial response from the other members of the Court.*

PURNELL — Robert John Purnell [233]

Robert John Purnell (1789-1862), landed proprietor, was born at Bradford-on-Avon, Wiltshire, the son of Robert Hooper (1752-1824) and Mary Baily (1752-1837). He married, 1811, Mary Anne (d. 1842), daughter of Revd Lewis Hughes and Anne Purnell; they had 1 son and 3 daughters:

1 Mary Anne (±1813-1893); married, at Dursley, 1848, Henry Miniken-Horsley (1811-1882); 2 sons and 1 daughter
2 Hester (±1813-1842)
1 Thomas (1814-1892), Church of England clergyman; *see below*
3 Emily Hughes (1821-1844)

Purnell's wife Mary was the niece of Lt-Col Thomas Purnell (d. 1802) of Kingshill, Dursley; it was via her that the Purnell name perpetuated. This Thomas was variously named 'Thomas Purnell Purnell' and 'Purnell Thomas Purnell'. He was a man of influence. He appears to have studied at Lincoln's Inn in 1769, but it is unknown if he ever practised law. In 1784 he was appointed sheriff for Gloucestershire for the lords of the council. In 1760 was a partner in Fromebridge Mill with William and John Purnell, presumably his brothers. William was probably William Purnell of Ferney Hill, who died in 1805. They were clothiers, or more likely financiers of clothiers.

The mystery regarding the background to Robert John Purnell's inheritance is unlocked by an entry in *The London Gazette*:

> *Whitehall, August 21, 1826.*
> The King has been pleased to give and grant unto Robert John Hooper, of Lyme Regis, in the county of Dorset, Esq. and unto Mary Anne his wife, only child of the Reverend Lewis Hughes, late of Llanfechelh. in the county of Anglesey, Clerk, deceased, by Anne his wife, who was the sister of Thomas Purnell Purnell, late of Kingshill, in the parish of Dursley, in the county of Gloucester, Esq. deceased, His royal licence and authority, that they may, in compliance with a clause contained in the last will and testament of the said Thomas Purnell Purnell take and henceforth use the surname of Purnell, and also bear the arms of Purnell ...

Robert Hooper duly took the surname of Purnell in 1826 following the death of Lt-Col Purnell's 'beloved wife' Anne Purnell, née Phillimore (1743-1826), sister to John Phillimore of Symonshall, Uley. This was in compliance with the lieutenant-colonel's extremely lengthy and detailed will.

Mary, Robert John Purnell's wife, was presumably a cousin of some degree to Anne Purnell (1763-1804), of Ferney, who married Robert Bransby Cooper. Kingshill House does not appear to have been the main family residence—Robert John Purnell died at Bradford, Wiltshire, where he was born—but it is noteworthy that Mary Anne, the eldest daughter, was married at Dursley, showing that Kingshill House was also used.

1851: 21 May: *Returned to my hotel, where I met Mr. Purnell of Kings-hill near Dursley, and his Son, the Rector of Staverton. The elder P. is used to live at the Queen's Hotel; but, having been disappointed in procuring an apartment, is, with his son, in lodgings, but resorting hither to meet the County Chairman and his son, and others with whom he is acquainted.* 22 May: *Accompanied John Purnell, and his two namesakes, of Kings Hill and Staverton, to the Crystal Palace, where I remained from 1 PM. till 5 P.M.* 23 May: *Accompanied Mr. Purnell of Kings Hill, his son, and John Purnell, on a visit to Northumberland House.*

PURNELL — Thomas Purnell [234]

Thomas Purnell (1814-1892), Church of England clergyman, was the son of Robert John [Hooper] Purnell and Mary Anne Hughes (*above*). He was educated at Brasenose College and New Inn Hall, Oxford, and was vicar of Staverton, Gloucestershire, from 1841 to his death in 1892. He married, at Cheltenham, 1844, Ann Wilkinson (1826-1874); they had 3 sons and 5 daughters:

1 Annie St Clair (1845-1923)
1 Robert Hughes Wilkinson (1848-1920)
2 Otto Fenwick (1852-1914)
3 Lewis Johnson (1856-1934)
2 Emily Nora (1858-1911)
3 Ellen Mabel Margaret (b. 1860)
4 Jessie Mary Maud (b. 1862)
5 Hester Adelaide (1867-1949)

1851: 21-23 May.
1853: 5 Apr.
1854: 17 May, 15 Jul.

PURVIS — Charles Purvis and the Purvis family at Clifton [235]

Charles Purvis (1743-1810), JP and landed proprietor, was born at Darsham, Suffolk, the son of Rear Adm. Charles Wager Purvis (1715-1777). He married, 27 January 1774, Elizabeth (1753-1816), daughter of Edward Holden Cruttenden; they had 2 sons and 2 daughters:

1 Elizabeth (b. 1775); married, 8 July 1817, Revd Edward Ravenshaw, rector of West Kington, Wiltshire
1 Charles (1777-1859)
2 Sarah Anne (1781-1817); died at Bath
2 Edward Purvis (1786-1873)

Elizabeth Purvis died at Bath but was buried at Darsham, Suffolk.

1804: 8 Jan: *Partook of a hearty luncheon at Mr. Marriotts: & afterwards walked with the Mesdemoiselles of that party, Misses Horton & Purvis, Captn. Horton & Prower on the Downs.* 21 Dec: *Went late to a smaller not very animated party at Mrs. Purvis's in Glo'ster Row.*

PUSEY — Edward Bouverie Pusey [236]

Edward Bouverie Pusey (1800-1882), Church of England clergyman and theologian, was the second child of Philip Pusey (1746-1828), landowner, and Lady Lucy Sherard (1770-1858), daughter of the earl of Harborough and widow of Sir Thomas Cave. Edward's father was the youngest son of Jacob Bouverie, 1st Viscount Folkestone, who took the name Pusey when he inherited extensive property at Pusey, a small village in Berkshire. Edward was educated at Eton College and Christ Church, Oxford, and was elected in 1824 to a fellowship at Oriel College. Between 1825 and 1827, he studied oriental languages and German theology at the University of Göttingen.

In 1828 Pusey married Maria Catherina Raymond Barker (1801-1839), youngest daughter of John Raymond Barker, of Fairford Park, by his second marriage. Edward and Maria had at least 1 son and 2 daughters:

1 Lucy N. (b. 1830)
1 Phillip Edward (1831-1880)
2 Mary Amelia; married, at Oxford, 1854, Revd James Graham Brine; thirteen children

In 1828 the duke of Wellington, then prime minister, appointed Pusey to the regius professorship of Hebrew with the attached canonry of Christ Church. Pusey became a student of the Church Fathers and the Caroline Divines, who revived pre-Reformation traditions. One of his sermons, preached before the university in May 1843, caused such concern among the university authorities that they suspended him from preaching for two years. The immediate effect of this suspension was the sale of 18,000 copies of the condemned sermon, *The Holy Eucharist, a Comfort to the Penitent.* Through this publicity, Pusey became one of the most influential people in the Anglican Church. He played no direct part in establishing the Oxford movement, but it nonetheless came to be popularly known as Puseyism, and its adherents Puseyites. Pusey was a highly influential member of the High Church party, of which he was a leader.

In private, Pusey led a simple existence. He had few personal friends, and rarely mingled in general society; though bitter to opponents, he was gentle to those who knew him, and his munificent charitable works secured him a warm place in the hearts of many to whom he was personally unknown. In his domestic life he faced severe trials; his wife died young in 1839, and his only son Phillip, a like-minded scholar who shared many of his literary labours (and who edited an excellent edition of St Cyril's commentary on the minor prophets), died in 1880 after many years of suffering. From that time Pusey was seen by only a few people. His strength gradually declined, and he died on 16 September 1882 after a short illness.

1837: 4 Dec: *Far different was another publication which I concluded this evening, a Sermon by the learned and pious Dr. Pusey, Heb. Prof. at Oxford, preached before the Univ. on Nov. 5.*

1838: 5 Jan., 19 Feb: *There was much general conversation, on politics, all being conservatives, and besides touching on topics of a local nature, the state of parties in and the interests of the Church were discussed, as well generally, as more privately between myself and Mr. Kennaway, who is apparently a very amiable, pious man bred up among the Evangelical Clergy, but moderate, and now disposed, I should say, to keep a middle course between that party and the High Church section owning Pusey and Newman as their leaders, and at present exercising no small influence, probably, to good, in the Church.*

1839: 11 Mar., 5 May.

1840: 22 Sep: *I also called on Mr. and Mrs. Riddell, at their lodgings near the new Church at Leckhampton, by whom I was obligingly received, but had not time to stay long: his manner continues to be hurried and abrupt, and he is still vehement in any view he takes of opinions and persons; especially bitter, at present, in his censure of those who adhere to the opinions of Dr. Pusey and Mr. Newman, whom, by a vulgar error, unworthy of a scholar, he designates as Papists.*

1842: 21 Jan., 21 Aug.

1843: 16 Aug: *The subject of Dr. Pusey's sermon on the Lord's supper, lately published, and for expressions in which held to be dissonant from the doctrine of the Church of England he has been suspended from preaching before the University of Oxford, was introduced by Mr. Cooke.*

1844: 26 Sep., 8 Oct: *The greater number of the non placets were young men; Dr. Pusey did not appear, Newman & J. Keble were present.*

1845: 13 Feb.

PUZZI — Giovanni Puzzi [237]

Giovanni Puzzi (1792-1876), musician, was born at Parma, Italy. He was something of a child prodigy, having made a name for himself as a soloist while still very young. He performed widely in Europe during his youth. By 1809 he had become a member of Emperor Napoleon Bonaparte's private band, and soon afterwards, in 1815, he became principal horn with the Paris Opera. By the 1820s Puzzi had emigrated to England, where he became the first professor of horn at the Royal Academy of Music. He played in the Italian Opera Orchestra at the King's Theatre, the Philharmonia Society, and the Concert of Ancient Music. Later Puzzi became a leading organiser of chamber music concerts for the London aristocracy. Much of the source material for his lucrative chamber and solo repertoire was based on Italian opera.

1834: 15 Aug: *Mrs. Howell, Emmeline and William set out before breakfast to pass the day at Cheltenham with some friends, and attend a concert by some distinguished vocalists, Grisi, Tamburini and Ivanhoff, with Puzzi on the horn.*

PYE — Henry Anthony Pye [238]

Henry Anthony Pye (1766-1839), JP and Church of England clergyman, was born at Faringdon, Berkshire [now Oxfordshire], the only son of Henry James Pye (1745-1813), MP for Berkshire (1784-90), and Mary (1705-1796), daughter of Col William Hook and Martha, daughter of W. Corbet. He was educated at Merton College, Oxford (BA 1786; MA 1789), where he was elected a fellow. Pye was ordained deacon on 25 April 1789 and priest on 19 December 1790. He served as perpetual curate of Wolvercott, Oxfordshire, 19 December 1790 to 4 June 1802; vicar of Great Wolford, Warwickshire, 7 September 1793 to 2 December 1821; and rector of Lapworth, Warwickshire, 15

November 1793 to 8 May 1810. Pye was a pluralist, and in addition to the above appointments, he was made perpetual curate of Cirencester, 28 December 1806; prebendary of Worcester Cathedral and canon of the 4th prebend, 24 January 1818; rector of Harvington, Worcestershire, 16 July 1818; and rector of Gamlingay, Cambridgeshire, 26 August 1835. He was also a Gloucestershire JP.

Henry Pye married Frances Ursula (1767-1850), daughter of Thomas Wilkinson (b. 1738), of Amsterdam, and Sarah Mainwaring (b. 1742); they had at least 2 sons and 5 daughters:

1 Anna Maria (1796-1890); died unmarried at Bath
2 Harriet Frances (1797-1817); died unmarried at Cirencester
3 Sarah Elizabeth (1798-1818); died unmarried at Cirencester
1 Henry Anthony (1799-before 1839); educated at Magdalen College, Oxford (BA 1820; MA 1823)
4 Jemima (1802-1881); married, at Worcester, 16 November 1826, Charles John Dimsdale, 5th Baron Dimsdale of the Russian Empire (1801-1872); at least 1 son:
  1 Robert Dimsdale (1828-1898); succeeded as 6th Baron Dimsdale of the Russian Empire
2 William (1805-1891); *see below*
5 Emma (1807-1901)

1820: 11 Apr.

1823: 14 Jan.

1824: 27 Apr., 13 Jul.

1828: 15 Jan., 17 Jul: *I dined to-day with the Bishop of Gloucester; the party consisted of his Lordship and Miss Bethell, the Archdeacon of Gloucester, Messrs. Baker, of Stouts Hill, Pye, Prebendary of Worcester, & Incumbent of Cirencester.* 18 Jul: *the Sermon was preached by my old acquaintance the Revd. H. A. Pye, Prebendary of Worcester, Rural Dean of the Deanery of Cirencester, & Incumbent of that place. It was a very excellent discourse, well delivered, & suitable to the occasion.*

1836: 23 Jul: *A letter from Mr. Pye, Incumbent of Cirencester and Preb. of Worcester.* 10 Aug.

1837: 4 Aug.

1838: 16 Oct.

PYE — William Pye[239]

William Pye (1805-1891), Church of England clergyman, was the second son of Henry Anthony Pye (*above*). He was educated at Christ Church, Oxford (BA 1827; MA 1830), and married, 1831, Margaret Cripps (1803-1890); they had at least 1 son and 3 daughters:

1 Frances (b. ±1832)
2 Harriet (b. ±1836); died unmarried
1 William Henry (±1837-1886); educated at Marlborough College
3 Catherine S. (b. ±1844)

Pye was rector of Sapperton in 1833-83, and held the rectory alongside that of Stratton. In 1878 he resigned the Stratton living after some disagreement with certain members of his congregation, in particular the Playne family. The living was sequestered for six years following Pye's resignation. He died at Clevedon, Somerset.

1845: 2 Apr: *Mr. Pye, the Rector of Sapperton, officiates as Sheriff's Chaplain, and Mr. Burrup acts as Under Sheriff.*

1846: 11 Aug: *Called with Col. Browne and the Rev Mr. Pye, on the High Sheriff at the Kings Head.*

1848: 16 Aug: *Received a letter from Mr. Raymond Cripps, the Treasurer of our Union, who intimates that, as it is necessary, in consequence of the decease of his brother William, who was one of his sureties for the due discharge of his office as Treasurer, that another be substituted in his name, he would propose either his brother Frederick, or his brother in law W. Pye, Rector of Sapperton.* 24 Aug: *Mr. Pye, Rector of Sapperton, who brought with him his lady and daughter.*

PYNDAR — John Pyndar of Madresfield Court, Worcestershire — *see also* Lygon[240]

John Reginald Pyndar, 3rd Earl Beauchamp (1783-1853), landed proprietor, was the second son of William Lygon, 1st Earl Beauchamp (1747-1816). His family name was Lygon, but he took the name Pyndar (the family's patronymic) by royal licence in 1813.

John Pyndar [Lygon] was educated at Christ Church, Oxford (BA 1806; MA 1808). He married, first, 1814, Charlotte (1787-1846), daughter of John Henry Scott, 1st earl of Clonmell; and secondly, 1850, Catherine (d. 1875), widow of Henry Murray and third daughter and co-heir of Sarah, Baroness Braye. He succeeded his elder brother William Lygon (1782-1823) as 3rd Earl Beauchamp.

1825: 10 May, 16 May.

1827: 2 Aug: *Earl B. is married to a sister of Earl Clonmel's; before his accession to the title, he bore the name of Pindar, which he had taken with an estate left to the second son of the family by an uncle.... His brother Edward is of the same rank in the army, & commands the other regiment of Life guards; Edward is unmarried, his elder brother is united to a daughter of Earl St. Germains; these brothers, with a sister, Lady Louisa Lygon, live in great harmony, but, I apprehend, are not on the pleasantest terms with the present Earl Beauchamp.*

1846: 12 Aug.

PYNE — Thomas Pyne[241]

Thomas Pyne (±1802-1873), Church of England clergyman, was born in London, the son of Thomas Pyne (1773-1851) and Sarah Gainesford (d. 1808). He was educated at St John's College, Cambridge (BA 1824; MA 1832), and was appointed, in 1840, tutor and travelling companion to the Princes William Anantamissa and John Ansale of Ashanti. William and John had been brought to England as hostages for a term of six years in accordance with a treaty signed in 1831.

Pyne was perpetual curate of Hook, Surrey, in 1843-73. He was a member of council of the Chronological Institute of London, 1851-52, and was elected a fellow of the Royal Astronomical Society in 1868. He married, first, at Wonston, Hampshire, 8 October 1850, Rosanne Mary (1821-1853), daughter of Cdr Richard Davison Perkins Pritchard (1788-1849) and Mary Ann Davis (1791-1842). He married secondly, at Hook, Surrey, 15 May 1860, Elizabeth (1831-1911), daughter of Maj. Thomas Waters, Royal Marines, of Surbiton, Surrey. Thomas and Elizabeth had 2 sons and 3 daughters:

1 Elizabeth Rosanne (1861-1954)
2 Agnes Bonville (1862-1956)
1 Percy Thomas (1863-1946)
3 Julia Carolyn (1865-1950)
2 Reginald Gaynesford (1867-1934)

Thomas Pyne was author of the following works: *The Sabbath*; *Peace on Earth*; *Vital Magnetism*; *The Law of Kindness*; *Memoir of the Rev. Robert Francis Walker*; *Pagan Rome* (from the French); *Abolition of Capital Punishment*; and *Glance at the Heavens*.

1846: 17 Jul: *To B. L. Witts to make enquiry respecting a Revd. Mr. Pyne, residing in the neighbourhood of Kingston on Thames, who professes to cure epilepsy by vital magnetism. A pauper from Lower Swell has been under his care, and wishes to return to make a further trial of the system.* 24 Jul: *Wrote to Perkins forwarding part of a letter which I received to-day from B. L. Witts in answer to my letter of enquiry as to the Revd. Mr. Pyne, living near Kingston on Thames, who treats epileptic patients by vital magnetism — in other words, I suppose by mesmerism.*

PYNSENT — Thomas Pynsent [242]

Thomas Pynsent (±1808-1881), JP and landed proprietor, was born at Highweek, Devon, the son of Charles Pynsent (b. 1788). He was initiated as a freemason on 26 February 1838 at the Lodge of Union, Chudleigh, Devon. He married, at St Mary's, Marylebone, Westminster, 13 July 1843, Jane (1809-1891), daughter of James Goodeve Sparrow (1770-1838) and Anne Clowe (b. 1770). Jane had previously married, 1826, her distant cousin Fiske Goodeve Harrison (1793-1872), son of John Hayes Harrison and Sarah Thomas Fiske.

Fiske Goodeve Harrison was born at Copford Hall, Essex, and educated at Charterhouse (1806-10) and St John's College, Cambridge. He served in the East Essex Regular Militia and rose to the rank of major. Upon inheriting his mother's estates after her death, he changed his surname to Fiske-Harrison. He became lord of the manor of Copford upon his father's death in 1839. He served as JP and high sheriff for Essex in 1827.

In 1840 Jane took legal action for her marriage to be nullified on the basis of her husband's impotence and her continued virginity. Fiske refused to come forward to be examined but Jane was examined and declared to be a virgin; she eventually obtained the necessary nullification.

Thomas Pynsent and Jane had 3 daughters:

1 Margaret Jane (1845-1920)
2 Florence Lombe (1847-1943); born at Florence, Italy
3 Jane Augusta (1850-1902)

1844: 30 Apr: *Accompanied MW. to call at Eyford on Mrs. Payn, now left there alone, Mrs. Dolphin being gone to Paris to attend the accouchement of Mrs. Pynsent.* 13 Oct: *Mr. & Mrs. Pynsent (ci-devant Mrs. Fiske Harrison) called are now visitors at Eyford, and were at Church.* 22 Oct., 28 Oct., 4 Nov: *I called at Eyford; saw Mrs. Dolphin, and Mr. and Mrs. Pynsent.* 8-9 Nov., 12 Nov., 15 Nov., 1 Dec., 8 Dec., 10 Dec.,

PYRKE — Duncombe Pyrke [243]

Duncombe Pyrke (1809-1893), JP, DL, barrister-at-law, and landed proprietor, was born at Littledean, Gloucestershire, the son of Joseph Pyrke (1774-1851) (*below*) and Elizabeth Apperley (1785-1858). He was educated at St Alban Hall, Oxford, and Lincoln's Inn (1864), and became a barrister-at-law.

Pyrke married, at Salisbury Cathedral, 16 December 1833, Harriet Jemima (1811-1893), daughter of Revd William Marris (1780-1811); they had 1 son and 1 daughter:

1 Augusta Harriet (1835-1891); married Octavius Cobb Rooke (1827-1888)
1 Duncombe (1836-1905); married, at Gloucester, 3 February 1857, Susan Evans (1833-1912), possibly a cousin; 3 sons and 1 daughter:
  1 Reginald Duncombe (1858-1943)
  2 George Apperley (1859-1877)
  1 Constance (1861-1901)
  3 Valentine Evans (1864-1939)

1847: 5 Apr.

1850: 1 Jul: *At the Great Western station joined by Lefroy, Mr. Halliwell, and a sister of Mr. Duncombe Pyrke.*

1853: 18 Apr: *The infection was caught by Miss F. visiting at Gloucester the wife of Captain Octavius Rooke, Adjutant of the South Gloucester Militia, who has lately married a daughter of Mr. Pyrke, and who was supposed to have so far recovered from the complaint that all danger of communicating the malady was passed.*

1854: 11 May: *from Mr. Duncombe Pyrke, a Brother Magistrate, requesting my vote in favour of one W. Beard, a candidate for the office of Wardsman at Northleach Bridewell, formerly holding the same post at Little Dean Bridewell, now closed.*

PYRKE — Joseph Pyrke [244]

Joseph Pyrke (1774-1851), verderer of the Forest of Dean and landed proprietor, was born at Littledean, the son of Joseph Watts Pyrke (1741-1805) and Charlotte Evans (1747-1835). He was educated at Oriel College, Oxford, and lived at Deane Hall. He married, at St Mary de Lode's, Gloucester, 2 January 1805, Elizabeth (1785-1858), daughter of Thomas Apperley (d. 1818) and Ann Wynn (1731-1818) of Wotton, Gloucester; they had 1 son and 4 daughters:

1 Charlotte Eliza (1806-1871); died unmarried
2 Julia (b. & d. 1807)
1 Duncombe (1809-1893); *see above*
3 Louisa Mary (1811-1865); married, at Littledean, Gloucestershire, 17 October 1833, Revd Thomas Leech Tovey (1804-1842); 1 son and 2 daughters
4 Emilia (1814-1875)

1826: 16 Jun.
1827: 24 Apr., 10 Jul.
1835; 10 Jan.
1840: 1 Jul.
1845: 2-3 Apr.

PYTT — Robert Henry Pytt, surgeon, of Burford [245]

Robert Henry Pyt (1779-1850), surgeon, was born at Gloucester, the son of John Pytt (1743-1822) and his wife, Hannah (d. 1830). He married, at St John the Baptist's, Burford, Oxfordshire, 14 April 1807, Mary Elizabeth Macey (1788-1824); they had 5 sons and 7 daughters:

1 Erasmus Henry (1808-1832)
2 Robert Henry (1809-1833)
1 Mary Ann (1810-1821)
2 Elizabeth Mary (1812-1867)
3 Jane Letitia (1813-1826)
4 Frances Hannah (1814-1833)
5 Ann (b. 1816)
6 Margaret Catherine (1818-1904)
3 John William (1819-1845)
4 William (1821-1852)
5 Roland H. (1822-1847)
7 Hannah (1822-1856)

1828: 7 Oct: *Pitt, of Burford, an able practitioner, was sent for, towards the last, but when all hope was over. And so has the flower drooped & died: alas! poor Bessy Rice.*

1840: 25 Nov: *I rode to Bourton on the Water to make enquiries after Mr. Polson, of whom I had heard yesterday that he was seriously indisposed. Saw Mrs. P. for a moment, who is uneasy about her husband: his malady seems to be a derangement of the liver; Pitt, the Surgeon of Burford, who had been called in yesterday, had not yet attended.*

Q

QUEEN VICTORIA — *see* Saxe-Coburg-Gotha

QUICKE — Andrew Quicke and the Quicke family of Newton St Cyres [1]

Andrew Quicke (1825-1891) was born at Newton St Cyres, the fifth son of John Quicke (1783-1859) and Frances Catherine Cumming (1790-1862). By 1851 he was a fundholder, married to Julia (b. ±1835), living at 6 Walton Villas, Chelsea. He died at Boulogne-sur-Mer, France; whether he had moved there for pleasure or to escape creditors is unknown.

1840: 13 Sep: *After evening service I drove to Wormington, where I was very kindly and hospitably received by Mr. & Mrs. Billingsley: and passed the evening very pleasantly. He has under his tuition a youth of 15, a son of Mr. Quicke, of Newton St. Cyres, near Crediton....*

R

RAIKES — Miss Raikes at Malvern

This Miss Raikes is likely to have been one of the Raikes family of Gloucester, but there is insufficient information to identify her.

1802: 29 Jul: *Walked on the Malvern Hills. Conversed with Mr. Dillon, Miss Tonkins, May &c. A Dance in the Evening where I danced with Misses Burt, May, Raikes & the divine Charlotte.*

RAIKES — Henry Raikes[1]

Henry Raikes (1782-1854), Church of England clergyman, was born in Broad Street, City of London, the second son of Thomas Raikes (1741-1813), merchant and governor of the Bank of England (1797), and Charlotte (d. 1810), daughter of Henry Finch. He was a nephew of Robert Raikes, the founder of the Sunday school movement, and his grandfather, also Robert Raikes, was the founder of the *Gloucester Journal*. Henry was educated alongside Francis Witts at Elmore, and then at Eton College (1793-1800) and St John's College, Cambridge (BA 1804; MA 1807). He spent most of 1805 travelling abroad. After visiting Austria and Hungary he sailed to Greece, where he met George Hamilton Gordon, 4th earl of Aberdeen, a contemporary of his at Cambridge. Together they spent the winter exploring the interior of the Peloponnese and the sites of the temples and cities of Boeotia. The following year, as the guest of Lord Collingwood, Raikes accompanied the Mediterranean squadron on its cruise off the coasts of Sicily and Africa.

Henry Raikes became curate of Betchworth in Surrey, and was later curate of Shillingstone in Dorset, Burnham in Buckinghamshire, and Bognor in Sussex. He married, 16 March 1809, Augusta, eldest daughter of Jacob John Whittington of Yoxford, Suffolk; they had 3 sons and 2 daughters, including:

1 Henry Raikes (1811-1863), barrister, of Llwynegrin Hall, Mold, Flintshire; married Lucy Charlotte (d. 1889), daughter of Archdeacon Francis Wrangham
1 Emily August (b. & d. 1820)
2 Cecilia (±1821-1913); married, 8 August 1854, Revd David Dale Stewart (1819-1900)

In 1828 Raikes became examining chaplain to his old friend John Bird Sumner, bishop of Chester. In 1830 he was appointed chancellor of the diocese of Chester. His influence grew rapidly, and he became well known in the city and diocese as a preacher, a public speaker on religious occasions, and an active philanthropist. A leading evangelical, Henry Raikes was prominent in the activities of the Church Missionary Society.

1826: 28 Aug: *A distant view of Elmore court, the place, where I first went to school, on an eminence not far from the Severn. It is a deserted mansion of Sir W. Guise's: in 1793, when I was an inmate within its walls, & left it on my parents removal to Scotland, incident on my Father's reverse of fortune ... some of my old schoolfellows are among my intimate acquaintance in the County, & sitting on the same bench with me as Magistrates, Genl. Guise, Mr. Edwd. Jones, Col. Webb, M.P. for Gloucester, Charles Crawley &c.: Others, as the Raikes's, are now removed from the County.*

RAIKES — Richard Raikes and the Raikes family of Gloucester[2]

Richard Raikes (1743-1823), Church of England clergyman, was the fourth son of Robert Raikes, printer, of Gloucester. His family hailed from Treberfydd, Brecknockshire. He was an uncle to Henry Raikes (1782-1854) (*above*). Richard was educated at Eton College and St John's College, Cambridge (BA 1767; MA 1770). He was appointed perpetual curate of Maisemore, Gloucestershire, in 1793, treasurer and prebendary of St David's Cathedral in 1797, and prebendary of Hereford in 1809. He held all four posts until his death in 1823. He married, 1774, Ann, daughter of Samuel Mee of Gloucester.

1829: 2 Apr: *Since I was last in the Cathedral a monument has been erected in the outer choir to the memory of a pious and amiable old Pastor, long an inhabitant of Gloucester, who died two or three years or more past: the Revd. R. Raikes, brother to the Founder of the system of Sunday Schools.*
1839: 2 Jan.

RAIKES — Robert Raikes — *see also* Robert William Hippisley[3]

Robert Raikes (1818-1901), Church of England clergyman, was the son of Thomas Raikes and Elizabeth Armstrong of Treberfydd, Brecknockshire. The Raikes of Brecknockshire were related to the Raikes of Gloucester. He was educated at Exeter College, Oxford (BA 1841; MA 1846), and was high sheriff for Brecknockshire in 1851. He married, at Eynsham, Oxfordshire, 1841, Frances Taunton.

Robert Raikes held High Church views similar to those of his brother-in-law Robert William Hippisley, husband to Raikes's sister Grace Louisa (1814-1892). With Henry Hippisley, Robert William's brother, Raikes established a Tractarian church at Treberfydd.

1847: 25 Aug: ... *invited to meet his Lordship were Mr. Ford with his daughters Dulcy and Sophia, my son and his wife, Mr. and Mrs. Hippisley, who were accompanied by their Visitors, Miss Digby, and Mr. Raikes, a young brother of Mrs. Hippisley.*

RAINE — William Raine[4]

William Raine (±1774-1858), Church of England clergyman, was the son of Joseph Raine of Batsford. He was educated at Queen's College, Oxford (BA 1795; MA 1798), and became rector of Widford, Gloucestershire, in 1812, and perpetual curate of Swinbrook, Oxfordshire, in 1838.

1824: 27 Aug.
1825: 19 Jul.
1826: 19 Apr., 3 Oct., 9 Nov.
1842: 23 May.
1852: 3 Mar: *A letter from the Revd. W. Raine of Swinbrook, an Oxfordshire Magistrate, and old acquaintance, requesting information and advice as to Emigration to Australia, on behalf of one of his poor parishioners.* 19 Mar.

RALFE — Henry Ralfe[5]

Henry Ralfe (1791-1869), artillery officer (HEIC), was born at Petersfield, Hampshire, the son of Revd William Ralfe (1743-1825), rector of Maulden, Bedfordshire, and his wife, Annabella (d. 1830). He had three brothers: William, James, and Charles. James was indentured in November 1792 to attorney-at-law Robert Serle of Winchester, Hampshire.

Henry Ralfe was a captain in the Bengal Artillery, HEIC. In 1819 he returned from Calcutta to England on board *La Belle Alliance*.

He married, at Greenock, Renfrewshire, 27 August 1828, Margaret Clubley, née Carnegy (1799-1859), widow of W. A. Clubley. The couple lived at Coburg House, the Parade, Chudleigh, and do not appear to have had any children. Ralfe's sister, Annabella (1795-1856), was the second wife of Thomas John Lloyd Baker.

1836: 12 Sep: *Mr. and Mrs. Baker, Mr. & Mrs. Rolfe (Mr. R. being a brother of Mrs. Baker) Mr. Phelps, Mr. Clifford and his Son.* 13 Sep: *Mr. Rolfe is a retired East India Officer in the Artillery Service, and resides near Chudleigh: thither they were travelling.*

RAM — Abel John Ram and the Ram family — *see also* Port[6]

Abel John Ram (1776-1823), landed proprietor, was born in London, the son of Col Abel Ram (1753-1830), of Clonatin, co. Wexford, and Elizabeth Stopford. His father was MP for Wexford in 1801-06 and 1807-12. Abel (junior) was educated at Corpus Christi, Oxford, and married, 1805, Frances Port (1784-1860); they had 1 son and 2 daughters, including:

1 Abel John Ram (1804-1883)

The Ram family were well known in the Cheltenham area. They seem to have lived at Sandford, where they were acquainted with the Hughes and Delabere families. Agnes Witts referred to them numerous times in her diaries.

It was at Cheltenham that Abel John Ram first met Fanny Port. During 1801 Francis Witts was smitten with her, and it was with a heavy heart some four years later that he received the news of her marriage. While the Ram family were at Cheltenham and Clifton, Francis Witts was also acquainted with Abel's three sisters. The family had an estate at Highfield Grove, Hampshire, as well as Clonatin in Wexford.

1802: 27-28 Aug., 31 Aug., 1 Sep: *Afterwards at the Rooms conversing chiefly with Miss Bush & Miss Ram.* 3 Sep: *walked with Miss Bush & Mrs. Neville & Abel John Ram.* 6-9 Sep., 21 Sep., 22 Sep: *Breakfasted with Baker in the Public Room. Afterwards walked with A.J. Ram, his three sisters & Baker thro' the delightful woods opposite the Inn.* 23 Sep.

1805: 22 Feb: *Felt considerable emotion in seeing Mrs. J. Ram the first time since her Marriage – a look of Death was on her.* 26 Feb: 26 Feb: *At a very crowded Ball at York House in the Evening, where I danced with Miss Whyte; Mrs. John Ram alone could dispel the ennui, I felt.* 27 Feb: *Called on the Rams & found poor Fanny very poorly.* 2 Mar., 15 Mar.

1806: *At an early hour my Father & Mother left me upon a visit to Mr. Ram's in Berks.*

1812: 6 Aug: *We dined at Wooton Hall. This pleasant and retired place, the property of Mr. Davenport of Cheshire is now rented by my old acquaintance A. J. Ram, Son of Col. Ram, Member for Wexford, who married Miss F. Port, Mr. Granville's niece. He has a lovely young family.*

1825: 31 Mar: *Mrs. Granville has since educated two of her husbands nieces of the name of Port; the elder, a very lovely & most estimable person, is now the Widow of Mr. A. J. Ram, Son of Col. Ram, formerly MP. for Wexford, by whom she has one son and two daughters: the Widow & children, in the wreck of the Ram's once large property, and since the husband's decease, who was a very worthy person, though inconsiderate, have found a city of refuge at Calwich.*

RAMSDEN — Thomas Lugden Ramsden[7]

Thomas Lugden Ramsden (1805-1875), Church of England clergyman, was educated at St John's College, Oxford (BA 1826; MA 1829). He was appointed stipendiary curate of St Clement Eastcheap with St Martin Orgar in 1828, and of Mitcham in 1831. He later became vicar of Forest Gate, Essex, in 1852.

1832: 17 May: *Mr. Browne, from Salperton, with his daughter Caroline, Mr. H. Waller, the two Miss Wallers, with Mr. Ramsden, the present resident Curate of Farmington, with ourselves, formed the circle at the dinner table.*

RANDALL — Thomas Randall[8]

Thomas Randall (1805-1887), hatter and hosier, traded from 22 High Street, Oxford, between 1839 and 1864. He lived at Grandpont House and was a prominent figure in Oxford, serving as JP and alderman, and mayor in 1859-60. He married, first, his cousin Elizabeth Figgins, née Randall (1803-1829), eldest daughter of Josiah Randall of Cornmarket; and secondly, at St Mary Magdalen, Oxford, 31 July 1830, Elizabeth Frances (1809-1895), daughter of George Cecil, solicitor, of Beaumont Street. Thomas and Elizabeth Francis had 1 son and 1 daughter:

1 Eliza Cecil (b. 1837)

1 Thomas (b. 1840)

1840: 8 Jun: *A letter from Randall, Hatter, Oxford, who has lost the measure of my hat, and wishes me to send it, that he may forward to me another.* 9 Jun.

1847: 6 Mar: *To Randall, hatter, Oxford, ordering a new hat.* 30 Jul.

1848: 7 Mar.

RANDOLPH — John Randolph[9]

John Randolph (1749-1813), bishop of London, was born at Oxford, the third son of Thomas Randolph (1701-1783), president of Corpus Christi College, Oxford, and Thomazine Honywood (1707/8-1783). He was educated at Westminster School and Christ Church, Oxford (BA 1771; MA 1774; BD 1782; DD 1783). From 1779 to 1783 he was a tutor and censor at Christ Church, where he helped the dean, Lewis Bagot, to enforce discipline. He was a tutor to William Wyndham, later Baron Grenville, and Richard Polwhele, the latter of whom complained that his 'manner was frigid, and his words were few'. He was appointed professor of poetry in 1776, proctor in 1781, regius professor of Greek in 1782, and regius professor of divinity in 1783. He married, 13 September 1785, Jane (d. 1836). John Randolph was bishop of Oxford in 1799-1807, Bangor in 1807-09, and London in 1809-11.

1802: 3 Jan: *Laura Chapel was well attended; it is a fine oval building, & most warm & commodious. Dr. Randolph read Prayers & preached. He is celebrated & abating, his Vehement Gesticulation & voice his Sermon equaled the expectations which knowing his reputed Eminence I had formed.* 10 Jan: *Skaited with George & Fiott; Mr. Bowzer's family & Miss Nicholson's as Spectators. Read a Sermon in the Evening of Dr. Randolph; J. Fiott reading the Service.*

1803: 27 Nov: *Evans & Dowell passed the Evening with me; we went to a dull Lecture of the Bishop of Oxford's.*

1804: 5 Feb., 21 Oct: *Called on Round & Baillie & on the Bishop of Oxford.* 4 Nov., 11 Nov., 14 Nov., 16 Nov.

RANSFORD — Edwin Ransford[10]

Edwin Ransford (1805-1876), singer and composer, was born at Bourton-on-the-Water, the son Joseph Ransford (1773-1851), grocer, of Bourton, and Mary (1770-1860), daughter of James and Ann Beale. He first appeared on the stage as an extra in the chorus at the King's Theatre, Haymarket, and was afterwards employed in the same capacity at Covent Garden. He married, March 1825, Hannah (±1805-1876); they had at least 1 son and 1 daughter:

1 William Edwin (1826-1890)
1 Mary Elizabeth (b. 1827)

During Charles Kemble's management of Covent Garden, Ransford sang the baritone role of Don Caesar in Samuel James Arnold's *The Castle of Andalusia*, and was engaged soon afterwards by Arnold for the English Opera House. During the autumn seasons of 1829 and 1830 he was at Covent Garden, and in 1831 he played leading characters under R. W. Elliston at the Surrey Theatre, where he won great acclaim. Later that same year he appeared at Sadler's Wells as Captain Cannonade in John Barnett's opera *The Convent*, or, *The Pet of the Petticoats*. On 3 November he played Giacomo in the first English production of Auber's *Fra Diavolo* at Drury Lane. In 1832 he was with Joe Grimaldi at Sadler's Wells, playing Tom Tuck in Andrew V. Campbell's nautical drama *The Battle of Trafalgar*; Ransford made a great hit in the play with S. C. Neukomm's song 'The Sea'. He afterwards fulfilled important engagements at Drury Lane, the Lyceum, and Covent Garden. At Covent Garden he played the Doge of Venice in *Othello* on 25 March 1833, when Edmund Kean made his last appearance on the stage; he was also in the cast, as Sir Harry, when Charles Kemble made his final appearance, as Charles Surface in *The School for Scandal*. Ransford's own final theatrical engagement was with W. C. Macready at Covent Garden in 1837-38.

After his retirement from the stage, Edwin Ransford sang for a time at concerts, and then, from 1845 onwards, produced a series of popular musical entertainments in which he took the leading roles. For some years he was in business as a music-seller and publisher, and during the 1840s and 1850s he issued many popular songs. His business started in Charles Street, Soho Square, and moved to 461 Oxford Street in 1850. He later went into partnership with his son William Edwin, a talented singer, in 1869. Ransford was considered a genial and popular man. He was buried at Bourton-on-the-Water.

1837: 24 Jun: *At half past seven rode to Bourton on the Water, in compliance with a summons Recd. from Mr. Ford, whom with Messrs. Billingsley, Wilkins, Kendall, Ransford Senr. & Junr.*

1845: 6 Jun.

1847: 14 Sep: *There were present three professional singers, Messrs. Ransford and two others associated with him, now on a professional tour in the neighbourhood: they performed in a very spirited and pleasing manner.*

1848: 2 Jun: *... were present, of honorary members, Messrs. W. and Jos. Bryan, Wilkins, Stenson, J. Bennett, Palmer, Ransfords, Senr. and Junr ——&c ——The younger Ransford, the London Singer, on a visit to his family, and on a professional tour with his musical son and daughter, giving concerts in country towns, like a Scottish Wilson, indulged us with many songs well sung with a fine voice.*

RANSFORD — Joseph Ransford [11]

Joseph Ransford (1773-1851), grocer, of Bourton, was born at Cheltenham, the son of John Ransford [Rainsford] (1735-1818) and Mary Taylor (1740-1820). He married, at Bourton-on-the-Water, 4 July 1796, Mary (1770-1860), daughter of James and Ann Beale; they had 5 sons and 5 daughters:

1 John (1797-1866); married, at Kingham, Oxfordshire, 26 September 1826[?], Elizabeth Fowler (b. 1801); 3 sons and 2 daughters
2 James (1799-1868); married, at Edgefield County, South Carolina, USA, a cousin, Hester Rainsford (b. 1815), born at Edgefield
1 Anne (1801-1847); died at Coventry
2 Mary (1803-1888); married Thomas Collett (1805-1869); at least 3 sons and 3 daughters
3 Edwin (1805-1876); *see above*
3 Harriett (1807-1885); married, at Bourton-on-the-Water, 10 November 1830, John Hanks (1806-1842)
4 Elizabeth (1809-1852); married John Charles Guest (1819-1896)
4 Thomas (1811-1873); *see below*
5 Hannah Dunscombe (b. 1813); married, at Bourton-on-the-Water, 14 March 1851, Edwin Thompson (b. 1829)
5 Alfred (1816-1900); married, at Leamington Priors, Warwickshire, 24 October 1850, Mary Ann Wadams (1810-1888)

1837: 24 Jun: *At half past seven rode to Bourton on the Water, in compliance with a summons Recd. from Mr. Ford, whom with Messrs. Billingsley, Wilkins, Kendall, Ransford Senr. & Junr.*

1838: 1 Jun.

1840: 5 Jun.

1845: 6 Jun.

RANSFORD — Thomas Ransford [12]

Thomas Ransford (1811-1873), grocer, was born at Bourton-on-the-Water, the son of Joseph Ransford (1773-1851) and Mary Beale (1770-1860) (*above*). He married, at Little Rissington, Gloucestershire, 19 March 1839, Eliza Ruth Hanks (1820-1861); they had 3 sons and 5 daughters:

1 James Beale (1840-1920)
1 Emily Ann (1842-1922); married, at Coventry, October 1868, Charles Stibbert Slater (1844-1899)
2 Mary Sophia (1843-1870)
3 Elizabeth Margaret (1852-1935); died unmarried at Cheltenham
4 Sarah Eliza (b. 1853); listed, 1911, as living unmarried at Cheltenham with her sister Elizabeth Margaret
5 Florence (1858-1941); died unmarried at Cheltenham
2 Alfred (1860-1936); died at Docking, Norfolk
3 Oliver (b. 1861)

1837: 11 Aug: *Mr. Kendall is appointed Treasurer, Dr. Stenson, Consulting Physician, Mr. Wells, Surgeon and Apothecary, Mr. Ransford Junr. Secretary.*

1838: 4 May: *Met R Waller, Messrs. Wilkins, Kendall, Kimber, Wells, and T. Ransford.* 1 Jun.

1839: 7 Jun: *Went from thence to the so-called Assembly rooms, where Messrs. Waller, Polson, and myself with several other honorary members of the Society, met the ordinary members, and went through the routine business of the day, the re-election of Trustees, Directors, Treasurer, appointment of Secretary in lieu of Mr. T. Ransford, who has removed to Coventry, &c.*

RASHLEIGH — George Rashleigh [13]

George Rashleigh (1784-1874), Church of England clergyman, was born at Boughton, Kent, the son of Peter Rashleigh (1746-1836) and Frances Burvill (1757-1823). His paternal grandparents were Jonathan Rashleigh (1693-1764) and Mary Clayton (1708-1770). Rashleigh was educated at Oriel College, Oxford (BA 1805; MA 1807), and was ordained deacon on 27 September 1807 and priest on 25 September 1808. His first clerical appointment was as curate of Meopham, Kent, from 27 September 1807. He was later appointed curate of Harrietsham on 7 February 1814, vicar of Horton Kirby, Kent, on 13 April 1818, and rector of Lower Hardres, Kent, on 24 March 1827. He married, at Gatcombe, Hampshire, 2 November 1813, Maria Worsley (1791-1853); they had 3 sons and 2 daughters:

1 Mary Frances (1817-1894); married, at Horton Kirby, Kent, 23 August 1848, Andrew William Burnside (1791-1863); 1 son and 1 daughter
2 Louisa Maria (1819-1910); died unmarried at Dartford, Kent
1 Henry Burvill (1820-1916); married, at Longfield, Kent, 14 September 1847, Sarah Maria King (1828-1923); 2 sons and 2 daughters
2 Charles Edward (1825-1904); married, at St Austell, Cornwall, 1849, his cousin Charlotte Hinxman (1823-1917), daughter of William Rashleigh (1777-1855) and Caroline Hinxman (1782-1842); 1 daughter
3 William Boys (1827-1890); married, at Dartford, Kent, 2 July 1863, Frances Portia (1836-1906), daughter of Revd James King (1801-1864) and Maria Carleton (1806-1841); 2 sons and 5 daughters

---

1803: 20 Nov: *Called on G. Rashleigh & Mr. Williams.* 25 Nov: *Edgell, Evans, the two Rashleighs & Carless with me in the Evening.*
1804: 29 Jan: *Looked in on Rashleigh where George also was.* 9 Mar: *Spent the Evening not very lively with G. Rashleigh, Stackhouse & Edgell.* 4 Nov.
1806: 28 Jun: *Bath: made an unsuccessful call upon Mrs. Bates, but meeting George Rashleigh walked over the Town with him.* 1 Jul: *Called upon George Rashleigh at the New Inn.*

RASHLEIGH — Jonathan Stackhouse Rashleigh [14]

Jonathan Stackhouse Rashleigh (1782-1863), Church of England clergyman, was born at Wickham, Hampshire, the son of Revd Jonathan Rashleigh (1740-1806) and Catherine (1745-1788), daughter of Revd William Stackhouse (1710-1771) and Catherine Williams (1718-1771). His paternal grandparents were Jonathan Rashleigh (1693-1764) and Mary Clayton (1708-1770); he was therefore first cousin to George Rashleigh (*above*). He was educated at Wadham College, Oxford (BA 1805; MA 1811), and was ordained deacon on 22 December 1805 and priest on 20 December 1806. He succeeded his father as rector of Wickham, Hampshire.

Rashleigh married, at Whitchurch, Hampshire, 7 July 1807, Caroline (1785-1866), daughter of Adm. John Stanhope (1744-1800) and Caroline Dent (1763-1830); they had 4 sons and 6 daughters:

1 Caroline (1808-1831); died unmarried at Wickham
2 Mary (1809-1873); married John Edward Buller (1802-1881); 2 sons and 8 daughters
3 Louisa (1812-1860); died unmarried at Wickham
1 Charles Stackhouse (1813-1867); died unmarried at Westbrook House Asylum, Alton, Hampshire
2 William Henry (b. & d. 1816)
4 Jane (1819-1882); died unmarried at Southampton
5 Henrietta (1820-1875); died unmarried at Fareham
3 Philip George (1821-1882); married, at St George's, Birmingham, 14 June 1847, Eliza Mappin Mapping (1830-1896); 5 sons and 4 daughters
6 Emily (1827-1889); died unmarried at Fareham
4 Stanhope (1829-1908); married, at St Paul's, Edmonton, 18 June 1857, Lydia Louisa Walker (1831-1909); 3 sons and 2 daughters

---

1802: 14 Feb: *At Pering's, meeting Evans, Powell of Exeter Coll., Edgell, Hastings, Rashley, Davis, & Williams.* 28 Feb: *to St. Mary's with Rashleigh & Williams, hearing from Mr. Gray of St. Mary Hall a rational Sermon.* 16 Mar: *Walked with Rashleigh.* 20 Mar: *Walked round the Parks with Williams & Rashleigh.* 23 Mar., 4 May: *Pering, Williams, Rushleigh, & Gamlin breakfasted with me.* 6-7 May, 9-10 May, 15 May, 22 May, 24 May, 3 Jun: *rowed with Edgell & Rashleigh.* 6 Jun., 8 Jun., 20 Jun., 4 Jul., 6-9 Jul.
1803: 1 Nov: Walked with Edgell & Rashleigh. 22 Nov., 25 Nov: *Edgell, Evans, the two Rashleighs & Carless with me in the Evening.* 10 Dec.
1804: 29 Jan: *Looked in on Rashleigh where George also was.* 9 Mar: *Spent the Evening not very lively with G. Rashleigh, Stackhouse & Edgell.*
1805: 19 Mar.

RATHBORNE — Wilson Rathborne [15]

Wilson Rathborne (1748-1831), naval officer, was born at Balnakil, near Loughrea, co. Galway, the son of Richard Rathborne, a protestant clergyman. In September 1763 he was entered as an able seaman in the *Niger*, commanded by Sir Thomas Adams, on the Newfoundland station. After six years' service, Rathborne followed Adams to the *Boston*, and ten months later to the *Romney*, in which he returned to England in 1770. In 1773 he joined the sloop *Hunter* as an able seaman. He became midshipman around a year later, but seeing no prospect of further promotion, he accepted a warrant as master of the *Hunter*. It was not until 1780 that Rathborne was allowed to return to England.

Rathborne's career began to accelerate when he joined the *Bedford* as lieutenant under Cdre Edmund Affleck. He was present in the actions off the Chesapeake on 16 March and 5 September 1781, and at St Kitts in January 1782. He also saw action under Adm. George Rodney's overall command under the lee of Dominica on 9 and 12 April 1782. In the summer of 1783 the *Bedford* returned to England and was paid off. At the time of the armament of 1787, Rathborne was in the *Atlas*, carrying Sir Edmund Affleck's flag; afterwards he was appointed to the *Colossus*, one of the Channel fleet, in which he remained until 1791. In December 1792 he was appointed to the *Captain*, in which he went to the Mediterranean in 1793, and took part in the occupation of Toulon, the reduction of Corsica, and the action of 14 March 1795, in which he was severely wounded in the right arm and lost his right eye. He was invalided back to England, and on 9 November 1795 he was promoted to the rank of commander.

In 1797 Rathborne was given command of the *Good Design*, convoying the trade from Leith to the Elbe, or to Elsinore. In December 1799 he was appointed to the brig *Racoon*, which he commanded in the Channel, the Mediterranean, and the West Indies. On 18 November 1802 he was promoted to captain and posted to the frigate *Santa Margarita*; he returned to England the following year when the *Santa Margarita* was ordered to join the Channel fleet. On 4 November 1805, in company with the *Phoenix*, commanded by Sir Richard John Strachan, Rathborne fell in with the French ships that had escaped from Trafalgar under Dumanoir. Harassed by the *Santa Margarita* and the *Phoenix*, the French vessels were brought to action and were all taken. Very soon after this success, Rathborne was appointed to the *Foudroyant*; he objected to the move and the Admiralty permitted him to remain in the *Santa Margarita* until December 1807, when the ship, being quite worn out, was paid off. For the next two years Rathborne commanded the sea fencibles off the Essex coast, and from 1810 to 1813 he had charge of the impress service in the Tyne. In 1822 he was appointed superintendent of the ordinary at Chatham, a post which he held until 1825.

Rathborne married, in 1805, Cecilia Mary, daughter of John French of Loughrea, co. Galway; they had 3 sons.

1798: 5 Aug: *Our Commodore Captn. Rathborne of the Good Design Armed Vessel of 14 Guns weighed anchor about twelve o'clock, when our Convoy consisting of six Merchantmen to the Elbe, and two to the Weser, bore down for the mouth of the Firth.* 7 Aug., 9 Aug., 12 Aug.

RAWDON-HASTINGS — George Augustus Rawdon-Hastings — *see also* Yelverton [16]

George Augustus Rawdon-Hastings, 2nd marquess of Hastings (1808-1844), landed proprietor, was the second, but only surviving, son of Francis Rawdon-Hastings, 1st marquess of Hastings (1754-1826), and Flora, *suo jure* countess of Loudon (1780-1840), daughter of John Macleod. He was a godson of the Prince of Wales. Rawdon-Hastings was styled earl of Rawdon from 1817 to 1826. He was a lord of the bedchamber in 1830-31, and bearer of the golden spurs at the coronation of William IV. He married, 1831, Barbara Yelverton (1810-1858), who was in her own right Baroness Grey de Ruthyn. Rawdon-Hastings died at Southampton at the age of 36, and Barbara married, secondly, Reginald Henry, who, by royal licence took the name of Yelverton in lieu of Henry. Barbara Yelverton died of a stroke in Rome and was buried in the English cemetery there.

1838: 24-25 Mar., 26 Mar: *His Lady is Baroness Grey de Ruthyn in her own right; they are both young, and she widely different in habits and temperament from her Lord.... Soon after breakfast accompanied M.V. and his brother in a walk to Cole Orton house the seat of Sir George Beaumont, distant about two miles from Ashby, where the Marquis of Hastings's fox hounds were to meet, Sir G.B. giving a public breakfast to the sportsmen.*

RAWLINSON — Abram Lindow Rawlinson — *see also* Lindow [17]

Abram Lindow Rawlinson (1805-1875), solicitor, was born at Charlbury, Oxfordshire, the son of Abram Tyzack Rawlinson (1777-1845) and Eliza Eudocia Albinia (1781-1863), daughter of Henry Martin Creswicke (1757-1781) and Eugenia Collins (1759-1831). He practised as a solicitor at Chipping Norton, Oxfordshire.

Rawlinson married, at Marriage Winterbourne, Gloucestershire, 9 July 1831, Sarah Smith (1794-1869); they had 2 sons and 1 daughter:

1 Anna Eudocia (1834-1920); died unmarried
1 Abram Henry (1836-1837); died an infant
2 Abram Creswicke (1838-1910); married, at Holy Trinity, Chelsea, 6 August 1867, Laura Elizabeth Anne Farwell (1840-1886); 1 son and 5 daughters

Abram Lindow Rawlinson was a first cousin of Henry Lindow, who had changed his name from Rawlinson to Lindow.

1829: 24 Nov: ... *to elect a Clerk or Clerks to the Chipping Norton, Stow, Burford & Banbury Turnpike Trust in the room of Mr. Churchill ... The candidates were Mr. Rawlinson, Son of Mr. R. of Chadlington, an influential and talented Oxfordshire Magistrate & Commissioner, and nephew to my neighbour, Mr. Lindow, of Lower Slaughter, a young man, said to be of some promise, just become an Attorney, and about to settle at Chipping Norton.*

1834: 7 Nov., 28 Nov., 17 Dec.
1836: 30 Aug., 10 Sep., 27 Sep., 27 Oct., 31 Dec.
1837: 4 Sep.
1838: 16 Feb., 21 Feb., 12 May.
1842: 22 Apr., 27 Apr., 1 Nov., 3 Nov.
1843: 26 Sep.
1844: 20 Aug., 24 Sep., 1 Oct., 14 Dec., 19 Dec.
1846: 5 Sep.
1847: 28 Sep.
1850: 25 Jun., 26 Nov: *My Son rode to Chipping Norton and back to consult Mr. Rawlinson as to arrangements connected with the Stow Cricket Club.*
1852: 2 Dec.

RAWLINSON — Abram Tyzack Rawlinson and the Rawlinson family of Grassyard Hall [18]

Abram Tyzack Rawlinson (1777-1849), JP and landed proprietor, was the son of Henry Rawlinson (1743-1786) and Martha Tyzack (1743-1808) of Grassyard Hall, Caton-with-Littledale, Lancashire. Abram had a twin brother, Henry, who was some twenty minutes his junior; Abram therefore inherited the Grassyard Hall estate, although he later moved to Charlbury, near Chipping Norton, Oxfordshire. Henry inherited the wealth of his uncle, William Lindow (d. 1786), a prosperous West India merchant who had resided in Lancaster with his wife Abigail (1740-1790). The Rawlinson family hailed originally from Chadlington, Oxfordshire, and had changed their name from Rollinson to Rawlinson (*see below*, Rollinson).

Abram married, at St George's, Hanover Square, Middlesex, 18 August 1800, Eliza Eudocia Albinia (1781-1863), daughter of Henry Martin Creswicke (1757-1781) and Eugenia Collins (1759-1831); they had 6 sons and 5 daughters:

1 Anna Maria (b. 1801)
2 Eudocia Martha (1802-1825); died unmarried
3 Maria (1804-1897); married, at Chadlington, Oxfordshire, 7 April 1832, Brooke Smith (1804-1881); 2 daughters
1 Abram Lindow (1805-1875); *see above*
4 Georgiana (1806-1885); married, at St George's, Hanover Square, Middlesex, 1849, Lewis Wilson Heath (1811-1881)
5 Caroline (1808-1820); died a child
2 Henry Creswicke (1810-1895), Assyriologist and diplomat; created 1st baronet; married, at St George's, Hanover Square, Middlesex, 2 September 1862, Louisa Caroline Hancourt Seymour (1830-1889); 2 sons
3 Edward (1811-1812); died an infant
4 George (1812-1902), professor and Church of England clergyman; married, at Oxford, 7 July 1846, Louisa Wildman Chermside (1826-1915); 4 sons and 8 daughters
5 Richard Smith (1814-1850); died unmarried in India
6 Edward Augustus (1815-1859); married, at Westbury-on-Trym, Gloucestershire, 1841, Susan Jane Sharpe (b. 1817); 1 son

The *DNB* states that Abram Tyzack Rawlinson was a notable breeder of racehorses.

1801: 11 Nov: *Mr. Rawlinson dined with us & repaired with us in the Evening to Mrs. Hughes, where I enjoyed a most pleasant evening supping there.* 12 Nov: *Mr. Delabere, Miss Hughes, & Mrs. Brown called in the morning, as also Captn. Rawlinson.*

1805: 11 Jul: *Accompanied my Mother, Mrs. Bates, a Miss Rawlinson & a Mr. Cookson to the Play.* 16 Jul: *A large party in two Carriages visited Prestbury gardens very pleasantly. The Ellistons, Mrs. Bates, Mr. Cookson, Miss Rawlinson & ourselves.*

1836: 30 Aug., 27 Oct.

RAWSON — Thomas Jekyll Rawson and the Rawson family at Clifton [19]

Thomas Jekyll Rawson (1764-1843), JP and landed proprietor, was born at Nottingham, the son of Thomas Rawson (±1737-1801), hosier and member of Nottingham junior council, and Prisca (1734-1764), daughter of William Lee, framework knitter, and Ann Marsh. The Jekyll name came from his paternal grandfather, William Rawson (1710-1780), who had married, at Thirkleby by Thirsk, Yorkshire, 25 March 1733, Elizabeth, daughter of Thomas Jekyll (1679-1758). Thomas's parents, Thomas and Prisca, had married at St Mary's, Nottingham, on 5 August 1762. His mother, Prisca, died at his birth.

Thomas Jekyll Rawson married, at St Oswald's, Ashbourne, Derbyshire, 14 September 1794, Sarah, youngest daughter of Richard Hayne, JP, of Ashbourne Green Hall, Ashbourne, Derbyshire, and Mary, eldest daughter of Revd William Newton of Ashbourne; they had 3 daughters:

1 Frances (1795-1828); married, at St George's, Hanover Square, Middlesex, 21 July 1825, Sir Thomas Le Breton, attorney-general and bailiff of Jersey (1848-57), son of Sir Thomas Le Breton and Anne Hue
2 Harriett (1797-1859); married, at St Oswald's, Ashbourne, 9 April 1818, Daniel (d. 1859), son of Daniel Smith, of Mayfield, Staffordshire, and Sarah Bingley
3 Selina (1798-1838); married, at St Oswald's, Ashbourne, 18 August 1821, George James (1795-1850), only son of Charles Pennington, of Nottingham, and Ann Robinson

In her diaries, Agnes Witts mentioned the family being at Clifton and Cheltenham, as well as Ashbourne, where they were acquainted with the Granvilles.

1804: 1 Aug: *to Ashton for Raspberries & Cream ending in a supper at Mrs. Massey's, consisting of Mrs. Massey, the Rawsons, Miss Monck, Miss Fortescue, Adm. & Col. Jones, Hankey & myself.* 27 Sep: *Conversed much with the Rawsons Mrs. Carrick &c.* 30 Sep: *Mrs. Massey Miss Rawson. Mr. Port, Mrs. H. Pigott, Mr. Townsend &c. called.*

RAYER — Richard Rayer[20]

Richard Rayer (1775-1844), farmer, was born at Upper Slaughter, the son of William Rayer and Anne Clarke. He was one of Lady Elcho's two principal tenants at Stanway, farming in the parish of Cutsdean. Rayer later became a tenant of Lady Elcho's son, Francis Charteris, 8th earl of Wemyss and 4th earl of March (1772-1853). It is not known how Francis Witts's debt of £300 came about. Given Rayer's Upper Slaughter provenance, it might have been for some expenditure he had incurred in that parish, or maybe at Stanway when he received the gift of the living there from his mother's first cousin, Lady Hereford. Richard Rayer married, at Little Rissington, Gloucestershire, 25 September 1799, Mary Bennett (1777-1865); they had 6 sons and 5 daughters:

1 Jane (1800-1810)
2 Ann (1802-1878)
1 John (1803-1863)
3 Mary (1806-1875)
2 Richard (1806-1875)
3 George (1807-1812)
4 William (1809-1812)
5 Edward (1810-1858)
4 Eleanor (b. 1813)
5 Sarah (1814-1876)
6 George (1817-1889)

'Cleeve' was stated as Rayer's residence at the time of his death. It appears that by 1841 he had retired from farming and settled at Bishop's Cleeve. He was buried at Cutsdean.

1835: 15 May: *Wrote to Messrs. Hoare directing them to pay on my account to the town correspondents of Messrs. Lechmere & Co. Bankers, Tewkesbury, the sum of £300. This arrangement is with the view of discharging a debt on bond to that amount which I incurred many years ago to Mr. Richard Rayer, and which had been transferred by him to Mr. George Cook of Stanway.*

RAYMOND BARKER — John Raymond Barker[21]

John Raymond Barker (1743-1827), landed proprietor, was the son of John Raymond of Tower Hill, London. He took the additional name Barker by royal licence in 1789 when he succeeded Esther Lambe, née Barker, granddaughter of Andrew Barker who had settled at Fairford in 1650. John Raymond Barker married, first, Martha (d. 1796), daughter of Daniel Booth, governor of the Bank of England (1779-81), of Hutton Hall, Essex; they had 7 sons and 5 daughters:

1 Daniel (1770-1827); married, 1797, Sophia Anne, youngest daughter of John Ives of Norfolk; at least 3 sons and 2 daughters:
  1 John Raymond (1801-1888); *see below*
  2 George Ives (±1803-1887), Capt., Gloucestershire Regt of Yeomanry Cavalry
  3 Henry Charles (±1805-1889), rector of Daglingworth
  1 Sophia Anne (1805-1876); married, at St Mary's, Marylebone, 9 January 1827, as his second wife, Bernard Brocas (1801-1839) of Beaurepaire, Hampshire; 3 sons and 4 daughters:
    1 Bernard (1827-1861)
    2 Lionel Raymond (1829-1862)
    1 Sophia Anne (1830-1900)
    3 Reginald (1832-1883)
    2 Emily (1833-1886)
    3 Isabel (b. 1836)
    4 Henrietta Maria (1838-1913)
  2 Harriet Ives (1811-1854); married Revd Francis William Rice (1804-1878), vicar of Fairford (1827-78), son of Revd Edward Rice and Charlotte Lascelles; 1 son and 1 daughter:
    1 Ellen (1832-1924)
    1 Arthur de Cardonnel (1836-1911); succeeded as 6th Baron Dynevor
2 James (1771-1832), banker; died in the parish of St John, Hackney, Middlesex
1 Esther (1772-1797); married, April 1794, John March of the parish of St George's, Hanover Square, Middlesex; at least 1 daughter:
    1 Esther (b. 1797)
2 Elizabeth (b. 1773)
3 Henry (b. 1774)
3 Martha (b. 1776)
4 Thomas (1778-1866); married, 13 December 1824, Eliza Jane, daughter of Thomas Somers Cocks (b. 1737)
5 Charles (1779-1838); married, first, at St George's, Bloomsbury, Middlesex, June 1811, Elizabeth Barnardiston; secondly, at St George's, Hanover Square, London, 1827, Mary Caroline Hammersley (1777-1843); at least 3 sons and 2 daughters from his first marriage, including:
  1 Charles (1812-1875)
  2 Frederick Mills (1815-1890), Church of England clergyman; married, at St Michael's, Littlemore, Oxfordshire, 16 July 1853, Elizabeth Mason (1829-1916), eldest daughter of William Hackett of Aylestone Hall, Leicestershire; legally separated, 1872; at least 1 son:

1 Edward Pusey (1857-1929); married, 9 January 1883, Rose Mary Crawford (1861-1924)
1 Katherine (±1815-1892); died unmarried
2 Elizabeth (b. 1817)
3 Henry Barnardiston (1821-1894), barrister-at-law and first-class cricketer for Cambridge University CC and Marylebone CC (1840s); married, at St Mary's, Bryanston Square, 22 July 1852, Caroline Maria (1832-1911), born in Bengal, daughter of James Lawrell; at least 4 sons and 2 daughters:
1 Henry Wykeham (1854-1920), stockbroker
2 Cecil Stuart (1857-1931), solicitor
3 Aubrey Barnardiston (1858-1945); died at Melbourne, Victoria, Australia
4 Edmond Campbell (b. 1859)
1 Ethel Caroline (1862-1947); died unmarried
2 Evelyn Lawrell (1865-1942); died unmarried
4 Mary (b. 1780)
6 Frederick (1786-1819), Church of England clergyman; ordained priest, 2 December 1810; curate of Marston Meysey, appointed 12 June 1813; curate of Great Barrington, appointed 1814; vicar of Taynton, 21 February 1814 to 1819; vicar of Little Barrington, 17 April 1815 to 1819
7 George (b. 1787)
5 Fanny (d. 1838)

Of the twelve children of John Raymond Barker and Martha Booth the only missing birth record is for Fanny. All fourteen of Raymond Barker's children were baptised at the presbyterian chapel in Carter's Lane, London, which has made it easier to confirm the births. In Raymond Barker's will it appears that apart from his two daughters from his second marriage, his surviving sons were Daniel, Thomas, Charles, and James, and his daughters were Martha and Fanny. Their mother, Martha Booth, died when her hairpiece caught fire after dinner one night in 1796.

John Raymond Barker married, secondly, Margaret (±1766-1851), daughter of Thomas Boddington of Hackney; they had at least 2 daughters:
1 Georgiana Maria (1800-1878); died unmarried
2 Maria Catherina (1801-1839); married, 1828, Revd Edward Bouverie Pusey (1800-1882), theologian; at least 1 daughter:
1 Mary Amelia; married, at Oxford, 1854, Revd James Graham Brine; thirteen children

John Raymond Barker was responsible for developing the landscaped gardens at Fairford Park. He died in January 1827. His eldest son, Daniel Raymond Barker (1770-1827), husband to Sophia Anne Ives, died seven months later. Their son John Raymond Raymond Barker (1801-1888) succeeded to the Fairford estate.

Thomas Raymond Barker (1778-1866), fourth son of John Raymond Barker, was caught up in a scandalous divorce. In 1805 he became involved with Anne Loveden of Buscot Park. Her husband, the MP Edward Loveden, was often away on county business; Anne felt neglected, and young Thomas, 'who had the reputation of flirting with every woman he came near', became a frequent visitor. Fairford Park was a short distance from Buscot, and Thomas's father was a close friend of Edward Loveden. He was himself a constant visitor to Buscot; Loveden had supported him at college and had even lent him an expensive horse. In 1805, friends and servants noticed a growing attachment between Anne and Thomas, and it was brought to the attention of her husband. The divorce case was notorious; it put a serious strain between John Raymond Barker and his son, but not sufficient for him to exclude him from his will.

1804: 11 Dec: *The Entrance to the Village of Fairford is very pretty, & the neatness of several comfortable little residences, as well as of the Houses & Cottages in general, bear witness to the good management of the place, under the care of Mr. Raymond Barker, & his Brother in Law, Mr. Morgan. The object of our Curiosity here was the Church, which we examined with due attention.*

RAYMOND BARKER — John Raymond Raymond Barker [22]

John Raymond Raymond Barker (1801-1888), JP, DL, and landed proprietor, was the grandson of John Raymond Barker (*above*). He married, first, 6 May 1823, Harriot Ives (1798-1830), daughter of William Bosanquet of London; they had 2 daughters:
1 Augusta Raymond (1827-1895); married, 1 January 1856, Sir Lumley Graham, 4th baronet (1828-1890)
2 Leonora Raymond (1829-1906); died unmarried

Raymond Barker married secondly, 14 December 1841, Katherine Reynolds-Moreton (1815-1892), youngest daughter of Thomas, 1st earl of Ducie; they had 1 son:
1 Percy Fitzhardinge (1843-1895); married, 25 June 1874, Morna Georgina Hawley (1848-1919)

1828: 15 Jul: [At the Quarter Sessions].

1829: 22 Sep: [At the Music Festival]. *Mr. & Mrs. Raymond Barker & party.*

1830: 12 Jan., 14 Apr: [Harriet] *How far the females of the family have succeeded with the eldest son, the Incumbent of Fairford, I know not; probably, he will yeild soon, if he have not already succumbed; as his wife, a sister of his parishioner, Mr. Raymond Barker, whom he has recently married, is strongly biassed in the same way; moreover his Curate, a youth recommended from Wadham College, is reported to hold similar opinions.*

1834: 10 Oct: *I rode to Northleach to attend at the Petty Sessions … Met Messrs. Barker …*

1835: 29 Jan: *We met Sir Charles Imhoff, Messrs. Twisleton, Cameron, and Barker. The latter gentleman is a younger brother of Mr. Barker of Fairford, and Curate of Churchill: a very pleasing young man.*

1836: 29 Aug: *Mr. Weare the Clergyman of Chipping Norton, and Barker, the Curate of Churchill, both pleasant and worthy young men, came to dinner.* 30 Aug: *Mr. Lockwood and Mr. Barker joined the home circle at dinner.* 9 Jun., 27 Sep: [of Churchill].

1837: 17 Mar: *The Turnpike meeting was attended by Lord Sherborne, Waller, Barker …*

1839: 24 Apr: *Wrote letters to Mr. Raymond Barker, to the Hon. James Dutton …*

1840: 30 Jun: *The Magistrates with whom … I was most in communication were …*

1842: 8 Feb: *…Tractarian love of novelties in Church services twice everyday, baptism by immersion &c coined by Mr. Barker, the new Incumbent of Bledington; the Bp. had suggested that Ford & I should quietly recommend him to discontinue practices likely to breed controversy and give offence in his parish and among his neighbours.* 23 May, 16-17 Aug., 27 Sep.

1844: 22 Mar: *A letter from J R Barker Esqr. requesting my advice …* 30 Mar., 2 Apr., 9 Apr.

1847: 22 Mar., 31 Aug.

1848: 26 Jun., 24 Aug: [H. Raymond Barker] … *Mr. Barker, Rector of Daglinworth.*

1850: 1 Jan: [G. R. Barker], 30 Dec: [G. R. Barker].

1851: 29 Apr., 19 May: … *repairing to the Metropolis — Raymond Barker.*

1852: 15 Mar: *A meeting of the County rate Committee (Purnell, Curtis Hayward, Raymond Barker & myself) was held.*

1853: 4 Apr: *Raymond Barker, High Sheriff, and Francis Rice, his brother in law, and Rector of Fairford, acted as his Chaplain.*

1854: 14 Feb: *The members of the Police Committee present were ... Barker.*

READ — Paul Read[23]

Paul Read (1799-1856), schoolmaster, was born at Gillingham, Dorset, the son of Andrew Read (1757-1827) and Unity Thick (1757-1838). He married, at Mitcheldean, Gloucestershire, 20 July 1822, Mary (b. ±1799), born at Frome, Somerset, daughter of John Newport and his wife, Amelia. They had at least 2 sons and 1 daughter:

1 Henry Newport (1824-1887), Church of England clergyman
1 Sarah Emily (b. 1825)
2 Robert Arthur (b. 1830)

Paul Read ran a small school in George Street, Stroud.

1837: 5 Feb: *Wrote to a Mr. Read of Stroud, to request him to permit his servant H. Bateman to come home to see her Mother, one of my parishioners, now dangerously ill of a pleurisy: visited her & others suffering under the prevalent epidemic.* 14 Feb: *A letter from the Mr. Read to whom I wrote on the 5th. Inst. complaining that his servant H. Bateman whom he had allowed to come home to see her Mother during her illness, had used him ill by writing to give up her service without returning at all, by which his family was put to great inconvenience, & requesting me to use my influence to procure her return.* 15 Feb: *Wrote a few lines to Mr. Read to beg him not to be severe in marking the fault of his servant H. Bateman, whom we have induced to return to her situation in his family, her mother being out of danger, and slowly recovering.*

READE — Jane Reade[24]

Lady Jane Reade, née Hoskyns (±1757-1846), was the second daughter of Sir Chandos Hoskyns, 5th baronet (1720-1782), and Rebecca May. She had married, 13 January 1784, Sir John Reade, 6th baronet (1762-1789), son of Sir John Reade, 5th baronet (1721-1773), and Harriet Barker, daughter and heir of William Barker of Sonning, Berkshire. Her husband had succeeded as the 6th Baronet Reade, of Bardon Court, Beedon, Denford, Northamptonshire, and Shipton Court, Oxfordshire, in 1773. They moved to Oddington in 1787, and John died two years later, aged only 27. They had 2 sons and 1 daughter:

1 John Chandos Reade (1785-1868); *see below*
2 George Compton Reade (1788-1866), officer, Grenadier Guards; married, at St Mary's, Marylebone, Middlesex, 6 March 1809, a cousin, Maria Jane (1787-1837), daughter of Sir Hungerford Hoskyns, 6th baronet (1753-1802), and Catherine Stanhope (1755-1790); at least 3 sons and 2 daughters:
  1 John Stanhope (1811-1883); married, in the United States, 1836, Louisa Walton (1815-1899); 2 sons and 2 daughters:
    1 Catherine L. (1843-1907)
    1 George Compton Reade (1845-1909); succeeded as 9th baronet, 1890
    2 Walter Charles (1853-1895)
    2 Maria Louisa (1855-1931)
  2 George (1812-1863), Lt, Madras Army, HEIC; married Jane Anne, daughter of J. Norton; at least 1 son:
    1 Chandos Stanhope (1851-1890); joined HEIC civil service, Madras; succeeded as 8th baronet, 1868; married, at St George's, Hanover Square, Middlesex, 11 March 1880, Maria Emma Elizabeth Conway; no children; died at St Leonards-on-Sea
  3 Chandos (1817-1833)
  1 Caroline Jane (1822-1864)
  2 Maria Louise (1831-1886); married her cousin John Edmund (1799-1870) (*see below*, Thomas Reade)
1 Julia Jane (1789-1837)

1801: 20 May, 22 May: *About 9 o'clock we repaired to a brillant Assembly at Lady Read's Curzon Street, May Fair, where was a very fine shew of Ladies, more so, than of Gentlemen.*

1823: 8 Jan: *Dined at Oddington with Lady Reade and Sir John. The usual showy display, & well lighted cheer.*

1824: 6 Apr: *We had a dinner party; Lady & Miss Reade, Mr. & Mrs. Egerton Leigh, Mr. R. Wynniatt ...* 9 Nov.

1826: 2 Nov: *We dined, Miss Witts accompanying us, at Oddington, at Lady Reade's. It was a large, formal party with much display; the spacious suite of rooms open.*

1827: 25 Jul: *We had a party to dinner. Lady Reade came accompanied by her daughter & her younger son, Mr. George Reade, now in a visit with his family at Oddington, his son, a tall lad of sixteen, accompanied them.*

1828: 19 Dec: *We dined at Oddington, at Lady Reade's, and met a large party.*

1829: 20 Mar: *We dined at Lady Reade's at Oddington, meeting, as usual, a large party.* 25 Jun.

1832: 10 Apr: *We all went to dine with our worthy old friend Lady Reade, at Oddington—a handsome entertainment and numerous party. Besides Miss Reade and her brother Sir John, who was on a visit to his Mother with his three daughters attended by their respectable governess, Miss Granger ...*

1833: 18 Jan: *We dined at Lady Reade's at Oddington: a party of seventeen. Sir John Reade's birth-day: who was present.*

1834: 23 Jul., 3 Oct., 10 Oct.

1835: 26 Jan: *Drove Mrs. Witts to Oddington, where we called on Lady Reade. Miss Reade is a great invalid.*

1837: 12 Apr: *Lady Reade will, I fear, be greatly overpowered by the loss of her only daughter and attached companion: I should not wonder if it accelerated her death; with a delicate constitution and at a great age such a shock may prove fatal.* 26 Apr: *Called at the door of Oddington house, and, as Lady Reade had not yet received any visitors, left our cards with enquiries after her.* 29 May: *Drove MW. to call on Lady Reade at Oddington: she seemed in tolerable health and spirits: but is, as we were informed by the friend staying with her, her granddaughter, Miss Reade, Miss Impey, and Miss Grainger, much agitated when her daughter's death is adverted to.* 27 Sep.

1838: 6 Jun: *Thence to call on Lady Reade, whom we did not see, as she was confined to her bed in consequence of an accident which befel her last Saturday, by falling in her entrance hall, and bruising her face and arms seriously: she is going on very favourably.* 14 Aug: *Lady Reade with a Mrs. Williams, and Mr. Hoskyns made a morning visit.* 16 Aug., 28 Sep: *Called at Oddington on Lady Reade, whom we found at home, in good health and spirits.* 13 Oct.

1839 2 Feb., 5-6 Feb., 25 Feb., 12 Jun: *We called at Lady Reades, as we returned, where we were received by the good old lady, whose younger Son is staying with her.*

1840: 30 Mar: *Drove MW to call on Lady Reade at Oddington; her Ladyship confined to her chamber, and too much indisposed to see us. Took luncheon with her two granddaughters, Emily and*

Clara, daughters of Sir John Reade, and with Miss Emily Reade of Bath, who has been passing the winter at Oddington. 28 Jul: *Called at Lady Reade's; admitted to the good old Lady, whom we thought a good deal altered in appearance.* 4 Aug: *We passed on to Oddington to dine with a family party at Lady Reade's—where we met Mrs. Roberts, Mrs. Williamson, Sir John Reade, his son and daughters, and two nieces, daughters of Mr. George Reade.* 11 Aug: *Compton Reade with his sister Clara rode over from Oddington to make a morning visit.* 30 Aug: *Also from Lady Reade, who continues anxious that I should endeavour to procure the insertion in the St. James's Chronicle of the extract from Bp. Heber's writings against drunkenness, which I transmitted ineffectually to the Editor of the paper to appear in its columns some months ago, that it might fall under the Eye of her Son who perseveres, I am afraid, in his bad habits of indulgence in wine to excess.* 2 Sep: *Wrote to Lady Reade, in answer to the letter I had received from her on the 30th. Ult.* 21 Sep., 26-28 Sep.

18 Nov: *We had a rough drive to and from the Rectory at Daylesford, whither we went to dine with the Winters; meeting Sir Charles and Lady Imhoff, the Dean of Gloucester, Emma and John Talbot Rice, Compton & Clara Reade, and Mr. Lewes. A pleasant party.*

1842: 12 Jan., 18 Jan., 2 May: *Called on Lady Reade, who looked very feeble, and broken since I saw her last.* 17 Aug., 24 Aug.

1844: 15 Apr: *Mr. Reade (Compton) and J. T. Rice made a morning visit.* 6 May: *Returning we called at Oddington at Lady Reade's door to make enquiries, and leave cards: we heard that her Ladyship has of late rallied wonderfully, and left her bed room; two of her granddaughters (Mr. G. Reade's daughters) are staying with her, but were from home.* 14 Sep., 1 Dec.

1845: 9 Jan: *There were also present Messrs. Winter, W. B Pole ... Compton Reade.*

1846: 11 Jul., 2 Sep., 17 Dec: *Recd. information of the decease of our old friend and neighbour, Lady Reade, at Oddington, which happened yesterday. Her ladyship had passed her 90th year: had long been a frail being, subject to frequent inflammatory attacks, but retained her faculties wonderfully till nearly the last. She was a charitable, amiable, pious woman and her loss will be great to her family and to the poor of Oddington.*

READE — John Chandos Reade[25]

Sir John Chandos Reade, 7th baronet (1785-1868), landed proprietor, was the son of Sir John Reade, 6th baronet (1762-1789), and Jane (±1757-1846), second daughter of Sir Chandos Hoskyns, 5th baronet (1720-1782), and Rebecca May. He was educated at Harrow School and Christ Church, Oxford. He succeeded as 7th baronet in 1789, aged 4. Reade married, at St James's, Piccadilly, 6 January 1814, Louisa (±1785-1821), youngest daughter of David Murray, of South Warnborough, and Elizabeth Harley. Alexander Murray, 7th Lord Elibank, was her uncle. John and Louisa had 2 sons and 3 daughters:

1 Compton (1814-1851); died unmarried
2 John Chandos (b. 1816); died young
1 Louisa Jane (1817-1837); died unmarried
2 Emily (1819-1897); classified an imbecile; died unmarried
3 Clara Louisa (1821-1853); married, at Oddington, Gloucestershire, 13 October 1846, John Talbot Rice (1820-1899); no children

Sir John Chandos Reade left all of his real and personal estate to a servant, Joseph Wakefield, whom he directed to take the name Reade.

1823: 8 Jan: *Dined at Oddington with Lady Reade and Sir John. The usual showy display, & well lighted cheer.*

1825: 17 May: ... *Mrs. Lechmere having been sister to the late admirable Lady Reade, whose death a few years since was so just a cause of affliction to Sir John Reade of Shipton, whom she left with a family of young children.*

1826: 2 Nov.

1829: 29 Nov.

1833: 21 Jan.

1834: 23 Jul: *We met Sir John Reade, his Son and eldest daughter from Shipton Court.*

1837: 10 Oct.

1838: 3 Aug., 8 Aug., 7-8 Sep., 25 Sep: *The annual meeting of the distr. Comm. of the Xtian Knowl. Soc... . Compton Reade, Escott, & others and passed off satisfactorily.*

1839: 2 Feb: *Mr. Chamberlayne called, accompanied by his friend Mr. Doyne; with the former confidential conversation as to Sir J. Reade and family, Lady Reade, and serious grounds for uneasiness arising out of the habits of Sir John.* 5 Feb: *When I left home it was my intention to go to Oddington to see Lady Reade on the delicate busines which Mr. Chamberlayne opened out to me on the 2d. Inst: but I recd. from him a note covering a letter which he had recd. from lady R. expressive of great anxiety on the subject, the obligation she felt to him and me for wishing to aid her in her uneasiness, but intimating an unwillingness to see me at Oddington, or till she should have had another interview with Mr. Chamberlayne.* 6 Feb., 31 May.

1840: 30 Aug: *Also from Lady Reade, who continues anxious that I should endeavour to procure the insertion in the St. James's Chronicle of the extract from Bp. Heber's writings against drunkenness, which I transmitted ineffectually to the Editor of the paper to appear in its columns some months ago, that it might fall under the Eye of her Son who perseveres, I am afraid, in his bad habits of indulgence in wine to excess.*

1844: 29 Feb: *Mr. Reade, eldest son of Sir John ... were present.* 25 Jul.

1846: 2 Sep: *It is announced that her sister Clara is ere long to be married to John Talbot Rice, the Dean of Gloucester's youngest Son, not in any profession; not having passed an examination for a degree at Oxford, where he was of Exeter College: One feels vexed that so pleasing a young person as Clara Reade should have engaged herself to a young man, with so little mental power; in moral character he is very respectable. Her health is delicate: it is said they are to reside at the Rectory, Great Risington, and he, whose present occupation is farming, will, probably, manage the Rectory farm.* 8 Oct: *While I was at Stow, Sir John C. Reade called with his daughter Clara.* 15 Oct: *John Talbot Rice and Clara Reade were married on Tuesday last.*

1847: 20 Oct.

1850: 31 Jan., 16 Jul: ... *thence to Great Risington, where called upon Mr. and Mrs. J. T. Rice, whom we found at home, as also Emily Reade, sister to Mrs. J.T.R.*

1852: 27 Oct: ... *So also did Mrs. J. Talbot Rice, accompanied by her sister, Emily Reade.*

READE — Thomas Reade — *see also* Irvine[26]

Thomas Reade (1762-1837), landed proprietor, was the second son of Sir John Reade, 5th baronet (1721-1773), and Harriet Barker, daughter and heir of William Barker of Sonning, Berkshire. He married Catherine (d. 1830), daughter of Sir John Hill; they had at least 1 son and 3 daughters, including:

1 Lucy (b. 1798)

1 John Edmund (1799-1870), poet and novelist; born at Broadwell, Gloucestershire; married, 1 October 1847, his cousin Maria Louise (1831-1886), daughter of George Compton Reade; 1 daughter:
    1 Agnes Coralie (b. ±1858); married, 1881, Arnold Highton, who then assumed the additional surname of Reade
2 Maria (b. 1801)

Thomas was apparently the younger twin to Sir John Reade, 6th baronet (1762-1789). According to local gossip in the Shipton area, Oxfordshire, the legitimacy of the twins was in question.

1801: 19 Nov: *Sat for half an hour with Miss Hughes, & in the Evening at Mrs. Boswells, where we met a large but an uninteresting party; conversed much with Miss Hughes & Miss Read.*

1802: 21-22 Aug., 22 Aug: *Walked in the Evening with my Father & Mother & Mrs. & Miss Reade.* 23 Aug., 24 Aug: *Drank Tea with my Father & Mother at Mr. & Mrs. Reade's.* 7-8 Sep.

1824: 27 Oct: *I accepted the office of Trustee to a Settlement made by Mr. Reade of Bath in favour of his children with his eldest son & a Mr. Batchellor of Bath. Though not highly valuing the father, by whom the request was made, yet I was anxious to serve his wife & family, who have suffered in many respects from the want of sense and prudence, which is but too notorious in him. Besides I am already in trust for his eldest daughter Mrs. Irvine, who married a relation of the Chamberlaynes of Maugersbury, a Commander in the Royal Navy. Mr. Reade is the surviving brother of the late Sir John Reade, & uncle of the present Baronet.*

1825: 14 Jun.

1829: 25 Jun: *We dined at Lady Reade's.... Mrs. Reade & her two daughters from Bath are staying at Oddington; the health of the former has declined greatly, especially since the decease of her daughter Lucy, some time since; the lot of this respectable lady has been painful; a husband fond of low company, and deficient in sense; a Son talented and a small poet, but without useful practical abilities; a daughter married to Captain Irving, in bad health, and not in flourishing circumstances, another bornée in understanding— these are not elements of peace or tranquillity of mind, particularly, where strength of mind is wanting. Mrs. Reade had been a very kind friend to my son, when he was at Lyde House School.*

1837: 9 Feb: *A letter from Mr. Reade, son of the late Mr. Reade of Bath, announcing to me his Father's decease some days since, which, indeed, I had seen noticed in the public papers.* 11 Feb., 14 Feb., 19 Feb., 14 Mar., 18 Mar., 1 Apr.

1838: 6 Jun., 16 Aug: *Called at the Unicorn Inn, on the Misses Irvine, who had expressed a wish to see me and to introduce to me their nephew, the only son of Capt. Irvine. R.N. by his wife, late Miss Reade, daughter of Mr. Reade of Bath, now deceased.*

1839: 14 May: *We had not met for many years; not to communicate with each other since his ill-starred marriage to Miss Reade, cousin of Sir J. Reade, in 1821.*

1840: 19 Mar., 30 Mar: *... and with Miss Emily Reade of Bath, who has been passing the winter at Oddington.* 26 May: *Miss Emily Jane Reade, and her unmarried sister as represented by Mr. Batchellor.*

1842: 18-19 Mar., 2 May.

1844: 2 Dec.

1846: 2 Sep: *We were received by Mrs. Matthews, late Miss Emily Reade of Bath, now the wife of a gentleman resident on his property in Somersetshire, without any profession, not far from Wincanton.*

1852: 8 May: *Mr. & Mrs. John Talbot Rice, & Miss Reade, called while I was out.*

1854: 8 Mar.

READING — Sergeant Reading at Moreton

1852: 4 Apr: *... to take the place of Sergt. Reading, the late officer in charge of the Station at Moreton in Marsh, who has left the force to take the place of Relieving Officer of the Shipston Union.*

RECAMIER — Jeanne-Françoise Julie Adélaïde Récamier [27]

Jeanne-Françoise Julie Adélaïde Récamier (1777-1849), better known as Juliette, was married in 1793, at the age of 15, to Jacques-Rose Récamier (1751-1830), a rich banker nearly thirty years her senior. Beautiful, accomplished, and with a love for literature, Mme Récamier became a leader of Parisian society. The habitués of her house included many former royalists and others, such as Gen. Bernadotte and Gen. Moreau, who had more or less defected to the government. This, her friendship for Germaine de Staël, and her refusal to act as lady-in-waiting to Napoleon's wife, Empress Joséphine de Beauharnais, brought her under suspicion. Mme Récamier was eventually exiled from Paris on Napoleon's orders. After a short stay at her native Lyon, she moved to Naples.

1802: 22 May: *Walked with him & Stephens in Ch. Ch. Meadow & saw the famous Mad. Ricamier.*

REDESDALE — *see* Mitford

REDMAYNE — Thomas Joseph Redmayne [28]

Thomas Joseph Redmayne (1795-1862), landed proprietor, was born at Stainforth and was married to Jane (1809-1862). They lived at Taitlands, also called Stainforth House, built between 1831 and 1847 in the Greek revival style.

1837: 5 Apr: *The Stackhouses, Brownes, Redmaynes, Fosters &c., resident at or near Great Stainforth have given the munificent sums of £300, £200, £100 each and in all between £1300 and £1400 have been pledged by a few proprietors.*

1847: 29 Mar: *Wrote to Mr. Birkbeck to obtain the votes and interest of two ladies of his family, and of Mr. Redmayne, Stainforth.*

REEVES — officer at Gloucester County Gaol

There were two officers of the name Reeves at Gloucester Gaol. They were probably related, and one may have assisted the other in getting appointed. This officer is unknown, but the other, Christopher, is listed below.

1847: 20 Apr: *A letter from Reeves, an officer of the County Gaol, a candidate for the vacant office of Keeper of Littledean Bridewell.* 29 May: *Insisting on our principle declared on the 18th. that it is indispensably necessary to have a deputy Governor experienced in prison management on the Separate System, we determined to exercise that Veto, and, on the Governor nominating Mr. Jeens, we refused to sanction his appointment, and directed that pro tempore the duties of Deputy Governor should be performed, when necessary, by Reeves and Cooper; two officers of tried good standing in the Gaol.*

REEVES — Christopher Reeves [29]

Christopher Reeves (1799-1866), keeper at Northleach House of Correction, was born at Warminster, Wiltshire. He served as an officer at Gloucester Gaol before becoming keeper at Northleach. He was married to Elizabeth Russell (b. 1800), and lived at Chedworth.

1844: 11 May: *Recd. a letter from C Reeves, one of the Subordinate Officers at Gloucester Gaol, bespeaking my vote and interest in his favour, as a candidate for the office of Keeper of the H. of Correction at Northleach.* 1 Oct: *He accompanied us to the House of Correction, where we conversed together, looking over the Bridewell books, and making enquiries of Reeves, the new Keeper, who appears to do his work well.*

1845: 22 Feb: *A letter from Reeves, Keeper of Northleach Bridewell, that a prisoner whom I had committed thither had paid the penalty imposed upon him.* 24 Feb.

1848: 30 Mar: *Received a letter from M W. — who forwards a letter addressed to me by Reeves, the Keeper of the House of Correction at Northleach, who doubts as to the accuracy of a recent game commitment of mine.* 3 Apr.

1850: 31 Jul.

1853: 17 Mar.

REEVES — John Reeves [30]

John Reeves, hotelier, kept Reeves Hotel, College Green, Bristol, before moving to Weston-super-Mare in 1824. There he took the lease on a hotel which had been built in 1808 as a speculation financed by Richard Parsley, William Cox, J. P. Capell, and Richard Fry. It was built on the site of a farmhouse that had been destroyed by fire in the late eighteenth century.

The hotel opened in July 1810 and was leased to James Needham, a Bristol hotelier. At the time it was described as having 'every convenience,' including 'A select Boarding Table—Neat Post Chaises—Good Stabling and lock-up Coach Houses.' It also had facilities for making its own beer and a bathing machine. The hotel was not an immediate success, and had to close after eleven months due to a lack of custom. In 1814 it reopened, and benefitted from a higher number of visitors to Weston due to the arrival of the first coach services from Bristol around this time. It was called Fry's Hotel in 1822 and Reeves Hotel by 1829, following its purchase by John Reeves. By 1839 it was run by William Reeves, presumably John's son, and by 1842 the hotel was listed as 'Reeves' Hotel', but the proprietor was a Thomas Rogers. The hotel still exists today as the Royal Hotel.

———

1839: *The approach to Weston is a steep descent ... detached from the beach by two small inclosures of green land, is the principal Hotel, kept by Reeves, formerly landlord of the hotel near College Green, Bristol, which is now amplified into an hospitium of higher pretensions, and greater shew as the Royal Western.*

REEVES — John Sims Reeves [31]

John Sims Reeves (1818-1900), singer, was born at Woolwich, London, the son of John Reeves, a Royal Artillery bandsman, and his wife, Rosina. He was christened John Reeves and added 'Sims' later to his name. Reeves's first professional appearance was as a baritone in H. R. Bishop's *Guy Mannering* at Newcastle in December 1838. Later he performed at the Grecian Saloon, London, under the name Johnson. His voice settled in the tenor range, and in 1842 and 1843 he was engaged by W. C. Macready at Drury Lane, where the repertory included works by Handel and Purcell. During the summer of 1843 he took some lessons with Giulio Bordogni in Paris, and until late 1845 he sang in provincial theatres.

Reeves married, 1850, Charlotte Emma Lucombe (±1823-1895), a soprano, with whom he sang in opera performances and concerts. They had five children, of whom Herbert Sims Reeves and Constance Sims Reeves became professional singers. In March 1851 Reeves appeared at the Théâtre Italien, Paris, and from that point onwards, and for more than twenty years, he was at the forefront of his profession. He sang privately for Queen Victoria and Prince Albert, and Macfarren, Costa, and Sullivan were among the composers who wrote tenor parts specifically for him.

———

1852: 7 Jun: *The immense audience were witnesses to the excellences of the performance, and the sublimity of the music. The chorus parts were magnificently given—The principal vocalists were Messrs. Sims Reeves—Herr Staudig —Mr. Lawler, in the absence of Herr Formes,—suffering from hoarseness, Madame Clara Novello, Miss Dolby and Miss Byers.—S. Reeves & Staudigl sang to perfection.*

REICHARDT — Alexander Reichardt [32]

Alexander Reichardt (1825-1885) was a Hungarian-born tenor and composer. He regularly appeared at performances in Britain from 1851 until a few years before his death.

In 1852 Madame Spontini was invited by Berlioz to accompany him to London for the playing of the finale of *La Vestale* at the New Philharmonic Society's concert. She went to the concert with her brother, Gaspar Spontini, the composer of the opera. Alexander Reichardt sang the tenor part of Licinius, and Pierre Josef Staudigl, a distinguished bass, sang the high priest's part. While in London, Reichardt and Staudigl also performed in concerts with Clara Novello. After his retirement Reichardt settled in Boulogne. He died there in 1885.

———

1852: 9 Jun: *Clara Novello, and Miss Williams sang delightfully as Soprano and Contralto, the two Germans, Reichardt and Staudigl, were the Tenor and Baritone.*

REID — John Reid and the Reid family of Cheltenham [33]

John Reid (1756-1813), plantation owner, was born at Wakefield, Trelawney, Jamaica, the second son of John Reid (1710-1777) and Mary Haughton (1715-1780). He married, at Hanover, Jamaica, January 1778, his cousin Mary Haughton James (1759-1847), daughter of Col Montague James and Mary Haughton. Mary's parents had also married at Hanover, twenty-four years earlier, on 2 April 1754. John and Mary lived in Cheltenham at St Julia's Cottage, which appears to have been in what is now Oxford Passage. 'Mrs Reid at St Julia's Cottage' features regularly in the diaries of Agnes Witts.

The New Monthly Magazine of 1814 stated that John Reid 'was interred in Tewkesbury church [presumably the Abbey] next to his relation Lady Clerck'. This was Lady Anne Clarke (d. 1800), aunt to John Reid's wife, Mary Haughton James. Lady Anne Clarke was the widow of Sir Simon Clarke, 7th baronet (1727-1777), and youngest daughter and co-heir of Philip Haughton, a wealthy Jamaica plantation owner, and Catherine, youngest daughter of Joseph Tharpe of Bachelor's Hall, Jamaica. When she married Simon Clarke, Anne brought with her £100,000 and an estate called 'Retirement' in St James, Jamaica, as well as other lands in Hanover, Jamaica. John Reid's mother-in-law, Mary Haughton, was Lady Anne Clarke's elder sister. When her father died in 1765, she inherited Green Island in Hanover, Jamaica, which was presumably of similar value to the estate inherited by Anne. Reid's wife Mary would have been very wealthy, but Reid was himself a wealthy man in his own right. He owned the Wakefield estate at Trelawney, Jamaica, manufacturing sugar and rum with the use of slave-labour.

John and Mary Reid were childless. The 'Miss Reid' in the diaries of Agnes Witts was Elizabeth Reid Quarrell (1784-1880), described in Reid's will as his 'adopted daughter'. She was the daughter of William Dawes Quarrell and his wife Alice of Trelawny, Jamaica. They had both died before 1813. When Elizabeth Reid Quarrell died unmarried at 4 Cornwall Road, Bayswater, her will, proved on 1 November 1880, showed her effects to be worth under £2,000.

1802: 31 Aug: *Drank Tea at Mrs. Reid's meeting Miss Hughes.* 1 Sep., 5 Sep.

1804: 16 Oct: *Called on Mrs. Reid, Mr. & Mrs. Baillie, Mr. & Mrs. Worsley.* 17 Oct.

1805: 24 Jul.

REINAGLE — Joseph Reinagle [34]

Joseph Reinagle (1762-1825), cellist and composer, was the son of Joseph Reinagle, a Hungarian, and Annie Laurie. As a bandsman with the Empress Maria Theresa's army, Joseph Reinagle (senior) landed in Scotland in 1745 with the Young Pretender, Prince Charles Edward Stuart. After the prince's defeat, Reinagle lodged with the Laurie family in Scotland, and married their daughter Annie. Joseph and Annie's son Joseph grew up to become a cellist and composer.

1802: 3 Jun: *At the Music Room with Stevens & Brown. Reinagle's benefit.*

REITZENSTEIN — the Reitzenstein family at Weimar [35]

Christiane Henriette von Reitzenstein (1784-1837) and Caroline Friederike Freiin von Reitzenstein (1785-1845) were the daughters of Georg Christoph Freiherr von Reitzenstein (1753-1840) and his wife, Eleonore Luise (1748-1810). Caroline married, 1802, Friedrich August Leopold, Graf von Beust (b. 1776). Other members of the family have not been investigated.

1799: 13 Dec: ... *where helping three young Ladies who had just begun to learn to scate: namely Mademoiselle de Fumel, & the two Fraülein Reitzenstein.*

1800: 15 Mar: *Mad. Flavie, & the two Reitzensteins very pleasant.*

RENNELL — Thomas Rennell [36]

Thomas Rennell (1786-1824), Church of England clergyman, was born at Winchester, the only son of Thomas Rennell (1754-1840), dean of Winchester, and Sarah Blackstone. He was educated at Eton College and King's College, Cambridge (BA 1810; MA 1813; BD 1822). After his ordination as priest on 27 October 1811 he was at once appointed assistant preacher at the Temple by his father, who was the master. Father and son were regarded as equally effective and popular preachers there.

Thomas Rennell (junior) became editor of, and a frequent contributor to, the *British Critic,* the organ of the Hackney Phalanx, a group of high church tory defenders of Anglican orthodoxy. He had already shown himself to be a champion of orthodox Anglican divinity in his critique of Unitarianism, entitled *Animadversions on the Unitarian Translation or Improved Version of the New Testament*, which he published anonymously in 1811.

In 1816 Rennell was appointed vicar of Kensington, where he proved himself to be an active and conscientious parish priest. In the same year he was elected Christian advocate at Cambridge. He was for several years examining chaplain to John Fisher, bishop of Salisbury, who in 1823 gave him the mastership of St Nicholas's Hospital and the prebend of South Grantham in Salisbury Cathedral. He was elected a fellow of the Royal Society on 25 April 1822, in spite of opposition from those who resented his *Remarks on Scepticism*. In the same year Rennell produced a reply to the *Apocryphal New Testament* by the radical bookseller William Hone, and in 1823 he was one of the most distinguished churchmen to publish a defence of the Established Church and its clergy in the wake of Henry Brougham's attacks on their wealth and political partisanship.

Thomas Rennell married, 14 October 1823, Frances Henrietta, eldest daughter of John Delafield of Kensington. A few weeks later he was stricken down with a fever and died at Winchester on 30 June 1824. He was buried in Winchester Cathedral.

1824: 7 Jul: *I notice in the papers with great regret the death of Mr. Rennel, the Vicar of Kensington, and Son of the able Dean of Winchester. The loss of Mr. R. is very serious to the church.*

1827: 27 Feb.

RENNIE — Captain Rennie at Clifton [37]

Capt. Rennie's identity is unknown, but he may have been a relation of John Rennie (*below*), on a visit to Clifton. He was in Clifton with a Miss Rennie.

1804: 29 Dec: *Walked to Bristol & with Capt. Rennie.*

RENNIE — John Rennie [38]

John Rennie (1761-1821), engineer, was born at Phantassie, Haddingtonshire [now East Lothian], the fourth son and youngest of the nine children of James Rennie (1715-1766), farmer and brewery owner, and Jean Rennie (1720-1783). He had a precocious interest in machinery, which was nurtured by the well-known millwright Andrew Meikle (1719-1811), inventor of the threshing machine and modifier of the windmill. Fortunately for Rennie, Meikle lived on his father's estate.

In 1783 Rennie took a study tour around England, making notes on canals, bridges, and machinery along his route. His destination was Birmingham, where a letter from Robison procured him an introduction to James Watt. As luck would have it, Watt was in need of a millwright to extend the mechanical scope of his steam engine. He was greatly taken with Rennie, and the next year he and Boulton offered the young man the management of their London business, which entailed the responsibility of erecting the engines they supplied.

Rennie's career developed quickly. He took on a multitude of river navigation and harbour improvements, fen drainage schemes, and waterworks schemes. In London, he was a key figure in the expansion of the commercial docks during the French wars. He acted as engineer of the London docks (1800-05) and, with Ralph Walker, the East India docks (1803-6). He also built extensions and some remarkable sheds at the West India docks (1809-17), and commissioned by the Admiralty, made wartime improvements to the Thames naval dockyards, including a superb steam-powered smithy at Woolwich. His detailed scheme of 1807 for a wholly new dockyard at Northfleet, however, was not carried out.

Rennie's grandest work under a government contract was the mile-long protective breakwater at Plymouth Sound, which was started in 1811 and completed in 1848. To Rennie's gratification, its scale was admired by Napoleon when he arrived as a prisoner at Plymouth in 1815. His crowning achievement, however, was the trio of metropolitan bridges spanning the Thames: Waterloo Bridge, Southwark Bridge, and London Bridge. All three were constructed by Edward Banks (1770-1835), of the early contracting firm, Jolliffe and Banks, which had also built many of Rennie's canals. Waterloo Bridge (1811-17) was his masterpiece; though privately promoted, it was the most prestigious bridge project Britain had yet seen.

Rennie and Telford were the greatest civil engineers of their day, and Francis Witts was fortunate in being able to join John Rennie on numerous relaxed occasions at dinner and in conversation. Rennie would have been in Bristol on these occasions to supervise the construction of the floating docks.

John Rennie married, at Christchurch, Surrey, 6 November 1790, Martha Ann Mackintosh (1771-1806); they had nine children, including the following 5 sons and 2 daughters:

1 George (1791-1866), engineer; carried on his father's work
2 John (1794-1874), engineer; carried on his father's work; knighted, 1831; married, at St Marylebone, 15 September 1835, Selina Harriet Garth Collerton (1811-1897)
3 William (1796-1818)
1 Jane (1800-1869)
2 Anna Maria (1802-1872); married, at St James's, Westminster, 4 June 1828, Charles Robert Cockerell (1788-1863), architect
4 Matthew Boulton (1804-1881)
5 James (1806-1883)

1804: 7 Aug: *Dined at Dr. Carrick's, meeting Mr. & Mrs. Goldney, Mr. & Mrs. Drummond, &c. Mr. Rennie; very pleasant.* 10 Aug: *Called on Mrs. Riddell, Mr. Rennie, Mrs. Massey.* 21 Dec: *Accompanied my mother on visits to the M. Rennie's and their sisters.*

1805: 4 Jan: *Called upon the agreeable Mr. Rennie, & Mr. & Mrs. Newnham.* 28 Jan., 15 Feb., 5 Mar.

1806: 15 Jan.

RENS — Francis James Rens [39]

Francis James Rens (1775-1834), teacher of French, otherwise known as Jacobus Franciscus Wap, was the son of Joannes Wap (1739-1813) and Agatha Rens (1737-1809). He appears to have been connected to the Van Notten Pole family, and given his skill in accountancy, he may have worked for them in some capacity prior to leaving the Netherlands. Wap [Rens] married, at Rotterdam, August 1802, Gertrudis van Heukelom (1762-1842), a widow thirteen years his senior. She had previously been married to Jacobus Godefridus Midderigh. Jacobus Franciscus Wap and Gertrudis had 1 son and 1 daughter:

1 Joanna Agatha (b. & d. 1803); died an infant
1 Johanes Jacobus Franciscus (1806-1880); became a noted Dutch author

The 1820s and early 1830s was a turbulent period in the Netherlands with the nation splitting into two separate countries, predominantly along the religious boundary. Finally, in 1830, Belgium seceded from the kingdom, a step that was recognised by the Netherlands only in 1839. Notwithstanding the turmoil, it seems that marital issues comprised the true reason for Wap's arrival in England. Quite why he took the name of Rens instead of Wap is unclear, but it may have been to hide his identity from his elderly wife. Most of what we know is contained in the diary entries below.

1828: 17 Dec: *I have been in frequent correspondence with Mr. Pole respecting the appointment of a gentleman, whom in many respects he considered well suited for our purpose. The circumstance of his being a foreigner, and speaking English imperfectly was in his disfavour; but then he would have the less opportunities of disclosing the accounts of depositors, to whom he would be a perfect stranger; ... To Mr. Pole he was well known, as a merchant in distress, who had been in affluent circumstances in the Netherlands, of which country he was a native, & from whence he had come to England to obtain a scanty subsistence by teaching French, which he thoroughly understands & speaks as a native. ... he was thoroughly master of the mysteries of book-keeping and wrote an excellent mercantile hand; he wrote English with great facility; though he spoke our language like a foreigner, he fully understood it in conversation; he was not unwilling to exchange his uncertain prospects as a teacher in London for the certainty of a permanent situation in our establishment, where he might, by tuition in French, eke out the slender stipend, one Guinea per week, which it was in our power to offer him.* 27 Dec: *The gentleman, who has been appointed accountant of the Provident Bank is arrived, & entered upon his duties yesterday. This day he gave Edward a first lesson in French. Mr. Rens appears a very quiet, polite, well informed, respectable.*

1829: 7 Jan: *We had two or three guests to dinner F. Aston, Mr. Baillie, & Mr. Rens We are confirmed in our favourable opinion of him, and I am glad to find, that he is a Protestant.* 11 Apr: *Mr. Rens arrived to dinner, whom I had invited to stay over to-morrow. He is a truly respectable, gentlemanly, unobstrusive, well-informed person.* 13 Apr.. 12 Jun., 7 Aug., 17 Oct., 13 Nov.

1830: 28 Jan: *The snow has prevented Mr. Rens from attending as often as he otherwise would have done, as French Master, but he gave several lessons, by which Edward has profited.* 29 Apr., 30 Apr: *The morning was passed in making calls, and walking about, to the great gratification of my friend Rens, who, though he had formed a very favourable idea of Cheltenham from the descriptions, which he had heard, found the reality to exceed his anticipations.* 1-2 May.

1834: 13 Mar: *After our return Mrs. Witts & I called on the Easts, from whom we learnt with great grief the melancholy news of the murder of our worthy friend Rens, Actuary of the Stow Provident Bank.* 14 Mar: *The melancholy tidings of the murder of poor Rens was confirmed by an article in the Cheltenham paper, which I procured at Bettison's Library.* 18 Jul: *Rode to Stow through very heavy thunder rain to meet Messrs. Ford, Jeaffreson and Pole, and examine evidence in the matter of the pros. against Clifford and Cox for the robbery and murder of F. J. Rens... The evidence of George Keen, as corrected by that of J. D. Charles, goes far to prove the existence of a jealous feeling on the part of Cox.* 21 Jul: *With Mr. Jeaffreson at Mr. Brooke's pursuing the investigation into the murder of poor Rens.* 24 Jul., 26 Jul., 7-9 Aug., 13 Sep: *On the 9th Inst. after our departure for Peach Field Lodge, the Clerk of Mr. Croad, the Attorney of Gloucester, who was employed for the defence of Clifford and Cox, the prisoners committed by myself and other Magistrates on suspicion of the murder of the late F. J. Rens, called to deliver a notice of action against Messrs. Ford, Jeaffreson and myself for false imprisonment.* 22 Sep., 26 Sep., 30 Sep: *It appears that Mr. Ford, actuated by curiosity, and, perhaps, wishing to extract something from the Prisoner, had gone yesterday to the Bridewell & sent for him. In the presence of the Keeper he asked him whether he had any communication to make, to which at first he made no reply, but on Ford's repeating the question, guarding him at the same time against saying anything to prejudice himself, and telling him that he could not hold out any promise of favour or benefit to him, the prisoner trembled exceedingly, and before Ford could procure writing materials to take down his words burst forth—"Please, Sir, I murdered the poor Gentleman".* 27 Oct., 7 Nov.

1835: 13 Feb., 18 Feb., 20 Mar., 13 Apr: *And now came on the trial of Edmund Jeffrey ... perpetrator of the murder of poor Rens.* 14 Apr: *Repaired before breakfast to the Gaol to confer with the Chaplain on the importance of ascertaining from Edmund Jeffrey, whether he really had any accomplice in the murder of poor Rens.* 15 Apr: *It has been mentioned that Edmund Jeffrey was intimate with a worthless young man, Thornton, who was transported last year, subsequently to the murder of Mr. Rens, for poultry stealing. Is it improbable, that he was Jeffrey's guilty* *associate?*23 Apr: *The bookseller at Stow has published a little pamphlet containing a narrative of the murder of poor Rens, of the consequent investigations, and of the trial and execution of E. Jeffrey.*

1836: 29 Jul., 2 Sep.

REVELL — James Revell[40]

James Revell (1815-1891), bookbinder, was born at Cambridge. He married, at St Mary's, Cheltenham, 20 November 1838, Eliza (±1816-1885), born at Bourton-on-the-Water, the daughter of William Tye (1786-1851) and Elizabeth Busson (b. 1791); they had at least 5 sons and 2 daughters:

1 Fanny (b. ±1841)
1 Henry (±1843-1891)
2 Elizabeth (b. ±1845)
2 James (b. ±1848)
3 Frank (±1851-1870)
4 Charles (b. ±1853)
5 William (b. ±1856)

The three elder children were born at Leamington Spa, Warwickshire, indicating that James and Eliza had only recently settled at 68 High Street, Cheltenham, when Francis Witts first found James Revell. By 1861 the family had moved to 4 Portland Terrace. After Eliza's death, James moved to Coventry, where he died in 1891.

1851: 19 May: *Looking out a Bookbinder; my former tradesman having betaken himself to Australia — Left some books to be bound with one Revell.*

1852: 21 Apr: *A note from Revell, Bookbinder, Cheltenham, with his bill for work done, and soliciting payment on the score of poverty, and illness in his family.* 22 Apr., 24 Apr.

1853: 9 Mar: *Revell, Bookbinder, Cheltenham, sends me his bill, begging payment.* 10 Mar., 12 Mar.

REYNELL — Henry Reynell and the Reynell family in London[41]

Henry Reynell (1744-1811), stationer, was awarded the Freedom of the City of London in 1767. He married, May 1773, Rebecca (±1748-1805), presumably a cousin, the sister of Carew Reynell (b. ±1749); they had at least 3 sons and 3 daughters:

1 Carew Henry (b. 1777)
2 Henry Willock (b. 1779)
1 Elizabeth (b. 1783)
3 George (1784-1859), stationer; born at St James's, Westminster; awarded the Freedom of the City of London, 1829
2 Caroline (b. 1786)
3 Harriet Elizabeth (b. 1790)

It seems probable that the 'Mr. Reynell Junr' was George. The family had Bristol and Irish connections; one Carew Reynell (±1739-1781) was bishop of Derry.

1801: 3 Jul: *Accompanied Lady Lyttelton & Miss Eycott afterwards to Mrs. Adams's, in Harley Street, where we met a select party; Mrs. Goodenough, Mr. Reynell, & a very well informed & well judging Gentleman Mr. Wilkins.* 4 Jul: *... party at Lady Lyttelton's ... Mr. Reynell Junr. a well informed young man, anxious to obtain information, le Vicomte de Bruges, Mr. Wood, Mrs. Doig, Miss Olies, le Vicomtesse de Bruges, Mrs. & Miss Reynell.*

REYNOLDS — Joseph Reynolds[42]

Joseph Reynolds (1816-1884), farmer, was born at Lower Slaughter, the son of John Reynolds (1776-1853) and Anne Dalby (1778-1824). He married, December 1842, Maria (1813-1876), daughter of Crescens Smith (1787-1838) and Maria Malpas (1788-1848) of Blockley; they had 1 son and 4 daughters:

1 Maria Elizabeth (1843-1922)
2 Anne (1845-1933)
3 Miriam (1847-1920)
4 Ellen (1850-1935)
1 Joseph Crescens (1851-1906)

The family lived at Slaughter Hill Farm, Lower Slaughter. Joseph was a tenant farmer with 256 acres, employing seven labourers.

1836: 20 Nov: *After evening service Reynolds came from L. Slaughter with a youngster of very bad character in the custody of the Bourton policeman: Mr. R's house was broken open this morning, while the family were at meeting at Bourton, all the inmates being absent, and while the congregation were at Church at L. Slaughter.* 24 Nov: *Heard the evidence against T. Betteridge on suspicion of stealing from Reynolds's house once more recapitulated, but dismissed the charge as not sufficiently proved to warrant a commitment, although there is little doubt on my mind that he is the guilty person.*

1837: 29 Apr: *Engaged during great part of the morning in consulting with Reynolds of Lower Slaughter and others respecting a corpse of an infant which had been found floating in the mill-pound at L.S.* 30 Apr: *There seems no great chance of detecting the offender; he, doubtless, is an inhabitant of the village, and the same who lately broke open, Mr. Reynolds's house, under similar circumstances.* 8 Jun: *It soon appeared that three of these had no chance, and the competition rested between Kearsey, Milbourn, and J. P. Reynolds.*

1838: 5 Apr., 1 Nov., 6 Nov.

1847: 9 Mar.

1850: 28 Nov: *He is a native of Lower Slaughter, and had been employed by Mr. Reynolds, farmer, whom he plundered on both occasions. The man was apprehended by the Police at Stratford, offering for sale silver spoons, stolen from Mr. R. —*

1851: 6 Mar: *Conferred with Jos. Reynolds as to the emigration of Benj. Carey.*

1853: 13 Mar: *Afternoon service, prayers: W Vavasour attended Church; called on me to consult me as to his annoyances in the matter of the manor of L Slaughter, which he holds by lease under Sir Geo. Whitmore, but the tenants (Reynolds) obstruct him.*

1854: 4 May: *The principal business was the conviction of two labourers of Upper and Lower Slaughter for taking fish from the water meadow carrier in Reynolds's farm in Lower Slaughter ... Jos. Reynolds intimated that he was surprised and dissatisfied at the amount of the fine; shewing great displeasure.* 14 Jun., 6 Jul: *Mr. Pearce, most injudiciously, maintained that, however others might be actuated by proper motives, one Guardian at least was his enemy (J. Pegler) who had owned to another (Jos. Reynolds) that he should not be satisfied till he had got rid of all the Pearces from the establishment. This Pegler vehemently denied; but, no doubt, something of the sort was said, and Reynolds very likely to report it in the most offensive manner.*

REYNOLDS-MORETON — *see* Moreton

RICARDO — the Ricardo family of Gatcombe Park[43]

David Ricardo (1772-1823), stockbroker and economist, was the son of Abraham Israel Ricardo (1734-1812), a devout Jew and prominent member of the Spanish and Portuguese Jewish community in London, and Abigail del Valle (1752-1801). His father held strong views, particularly in matters of religion, politics, and education, and insisted on strict, unquestioning compliance from his children. David, an independently minded youth, reacted strongly against his rigid upbringing. He fell in love with Priscilla Ann (1768-1849), daughter of Edward Wilkinson (1728-1809), a Quaker surgeon, and married her at Lambeth, Surrey, on 20 December 1793. He and Priscilla had 3 sons and 5 daughters:

1 Osman (1795-1881)
1 Henrietta (1796-1838)
2 Priscilla (1797-1839)
3 Fanny (1800-1820)
2 David (1803-1864)
4 Mary (1805-1839)
3 Mortimer (1807-1876)
5 Birtha (1810-1856)

David and Priscilla had married despite the objections of both their families. Estranged from his father, David could not expect to receive any support from that quarter, and so embarked upon what was to become a hugely successful financial career. As a jobber on the stock exchange and a loan contractor for government stock, he soon amassed a sizeable fortune, allowing him to begin a gradual retirement from business in 1815.

From 1812 the family's London home was at 56 Upper Brook Street. To this was added in 1814 a country seat, Gatcombe Park. At Gatcombe the Ricardos entertained lavishly, often hosting large, sumptuous dinner parties that extended well into the small hours. Ricardo, a slim man of below average height with a high-pitched voice, was himself temperate in habits; but he was also sociable, humorous, and addicted to intelligent debate and conversation. His friend Maria Edgeworth described him as 'altogether one of the most agreeable persons, as well as the best informed and most clever, that I ever knew'.

Ricardo's interest in political economy was aroused in 1799 on a visit to Bath when he chanced upon a copy of Adam Smith's *The Wealth of Nations* in a travelling library. He later wrote a famous work, *Principles of Political Economy and Taxation* (1817). He was appointed high sheriff for Gloucestershire in 1818, and in 1819 he became MP for Portarlington, an Irish rotten borough. He held the seat until his death in 1823.

David and Priscilla had eight children between 1795 and 1810. Of the three sons, two—Osman and David—were to become MPs, and the third—Mortimer—became a captain in the Life Guards and a DL of Oxfordshire. Osman Ricardo (1795-1881), JP, DL, and MP for Worcester (1847-65), was educated at Trinity College, Cambridge (BA 1816). He inherited the estate of Bromsberrow, near Ledbury, Herefordshire, in 1823. He married, 1817, Harriet Mallory (±1799-1875), but did not have any children. His younger brother, David Ricardo (1803-1864), MP for Stroud (1832-33), married, at Sunbury-on-Thames, Surrey, 1 June 1824, Catherine St Quinton (1802-1871); they had at least 2 sons and 1 daughter:

1 George Robert (1826-1831)
1 Catherine (1829-1905)
2 Henry David (1833-1873)

1826: 15 Sep: *And this seems the proper place for inserting a list of some of the leading families & individuals, whose presence on this occasion served so many good purposes; benefiting the charity ... the Ricardos, two families.*

1828: 15 Apr., 14 Oct.

1829: 13 Jan., 22 Sep: ... *the two Brothers, Osman & David Ricardo Esqrs.—with their respective ladies.* 20 Oct.

1830: 12 Jan., 20 Apr: *The High Sheriff is David Ricardo Esqr. a magistrate, with whom I am well acquainted, of Gatcomb Park, near Minchin Hampton, second son of the wealthy political economist of that name, now deceased, whose theories of finance have so blindly, as some think, been followed, in the adjustment of the currency, to the great injury, as is alledged, of the country, much of the existing distress being traced by many to the system constructed on his principles.*

1835: *Howell confirms what has been already hinted in the newspapers, that Lord John Russell will at length be seated in the House of Commons for the District borough of ... Mr. Ricardo, however, a Whig of the old school, and first member for the borough under the Reform Act, is indignant; he, like Hyett, had, probably, retired from the representation of the Borough in disgust.*

1837: 5 Jul.

1840: 16 Sep., 20 Sep: *Recd. a letter from Mr. Ricardo, who regrets that a previous pledge will prevent him from voting for the admission of E. Kendrick into the London Orphan Asylum.*

1843: 19 Oct: *Long conversation with Mr. Ricardo on prison alterations, future proceedings of the County as to the course to be pursued.*

1844: 2-3 Jan., 8 Apr.

1845: 30 Jun: ... *other magistrates who attended the Prison Committee were Archd. Timbrill, Messrs. Viner, Ricardo and Hyett.*

1846: 12 Aug: *In the immediate vicinity are properties belonging to the Earl of Beauchamp, Dr. Beale Cooper, and Mr. Ricardo, whose seat at Bromeberrow is not far distant.*

1850: 21 Jan., 24 Feb: *David Ricardo has drawn up, and caused to be printed, and circulated among the Magistrates of Gloucestershire, certain tables illustrating the Receipt and Expenditure of the County at decennial periods from 1800 to 1840.* 31 Dec.

1852: 16 Mar: *Mr. D. Ricardo exhibited his usual disposition to oppose even the smallest and most reasonable claims on the county rates.*

1853: 4 Jan: *There was a numerous assemblage of the magistracy;—the Lord Lieutenant, the Marquis of Worcester, MP. Nigel Kingscote, MP., R J Mullings MP., O Ricardo MP.—Sir M. H. Beach, Hon. Gustavus Talbot &c.*

RICE — Edward Rice — *see also* Cameron, Escott, Reade, *and* Wiggin [44]

Edward Rice (1776-1862), Church of England clergyman and dean of Gloucester, was the son of George Rice (d. 1779), MP, of Newton, Carmarthenshire, and Cecil Talbot (1735-1793). Cecil's father, William Talbot (d. 1782), was created Earl Talbot in 1761, but having no male issue, he was created, in 1780, Baron Dynevor of Dynevor for life, with a special remainder in favour of his daughter Cecil, who was by that time a widow. She succeeded, 1782, as *suo jure* Baroness Dynevor. On her death she was succeeded by her eldest son, George Talbot Rice (1765-1852) (*below*). He was succeeded in turn by his son, George Rice Trevor (1795-1869), and on his death he was succeeded by his cousin, Francis William Rice (1804-1878), the eldest surviving son of Edward Rice (1776-1862).

Edward Rice was educated at Christ Church (BA 1798) and All Souls, Oxford (MA 1802; B&DD 1820). He was appointed precentor and prebendary of York in 1802, vicar of Sutton-in-the-Forest, York, in 1804, and rector of Great Barrington and Great Rissington, Gloucestershire, in 1810. He then served as prebendary of Worcester in 1815-25, and was appointed rector of Oddington in 1820 and dean of Gloucester in 1825. He married, 1800, Charlotte (d. 1832), illegitimate daughter of Gen. Francis Lascelles and Anne Catley (1745-1832), a celebrated singer. Her parents' relationship was no fleeting affair; including Charlotte, they had 6 sons and 4 daughters:

1 Francis (b. 1768); married, at Dumfries, 1793, Margaret, daughter of William Bushby of Tinwald, Dumfrieshire
2 Edward Paoli (b. 1770)
3 Hugh (b. 1772)
1 Frances (b. 1774); married Robert Jenner
4 Rowley (b. 1775)
2 Jane; married Revd Montagu John Wynyard, chaplain to the queen
3 Charlotte (d. 1832); married Revd Edward Rice
5 George Robert (d. 1824)
4 Elizabeth (1784-1828); married, 1803, Herbert Jenner Fust
6 Edward Robert (b. 1787); married, 1808, Anne Taylor

Gen. Lascelles and Anne were reported to have married in 1780, but no records exist to confirm this. Edward and Charlotte Rice had 5 sons and 6 daughters:

1 Francis William (1804-1878); *see below*
1 Charlotte (1805-1882); married, 1835, Alexander Cameron (1806-1873)
2 Cecil (1808-1852); married, 1837, Charles Augustus Arney (1809-1879)
2 Maria (1810-1886); married, 1839, Edward Bankes (1795-1867)
3 Elizabeth (1810-1828)
4 Lucy Horatia (1811-1895); married, 1832, William Sweet-Escott (1806-1884)
3 George (1811); listed at Oddington, 1841
4 Henry (1813-1896); married, 1837, Emma Lowndes-Stone (1818-1907); 2 sons and 7 daughters:
    1 Frances Anna (±1843-1921); married Cecil Charles Van Notten Pole (1829-1876)
    2 Katherine Emily (d. 1882)
    3 Cecil Louisa (d. 1901)
    4 Florence Maria Caroline (d. 1908)
    5 Georgiana Clara (d. 1938)
    6 Amy Augusta Mary (d. 1929)
    7 Beatrice Helen (d. 1921)
    1 Edward William (1855-1924)
    2 Henry Charles Talbot (1862-1931)
5 Frances Emma (1814-1860); married, 1842, William Wiggin (1820-1901)
5 John Talbot (1819-1899); *see below*
6 Mary [Louisa] (1821-1845)

1820: 11 Apr., 25 Apr: *The first meeting for this Season of the Stow Clerical Society was held this day. Nineteen Clergy dined together as usual, and I presided instead of Dr. Rice, now keeping Residence on his Prebend at Worcester.*

1822: 3 Oct: *We dined at Dr. & Mrs. Rice's at Oddington. I had, as usual, on Thursdays, passed the forenoon in transacting business at the Justice Room & Provident bank at Stow.*

1823: 23 Apr: *First meeting of the Stow Clerical Society for this year: Hon & Revd. E. Rice, Prebendary of Worcester & Rector of Oddington & Great Risington (Brother to Lord Dynevor).* 15 Jul., 30 Jul., 7 Oct., 8 Oct: *I dined and slept at Batsford Park, the seat of Lord Redesdale. The party consisted of the Hon. & Revd. E. Rice, D. D. Rector of Great Risington and Oddington, at the latter of which places he resides. He is also Prebendary of Worcester & Precenter of York. He is a most estimable man, with whom I have long been on terms of intimacy, acting as his colleague in the various public business of the neighbourhood, as magistrate and otherwise. His wife, formerly Miss Lascelles, daughter of the late Genl. Lascelles, of the Harewood family; her mother was Miss Catley, formerly a celebrated singer and public performer: with them were their two eldest daughters.* 21 Oct: *We dined at Mr. & Mrs. Rice's, at Oddington Parsonage.*

1824: 7 Sep: *We had a dinner party: the Hon. Mr. & Mrs. Rice, and two daughters, from Oddington, Mrs. Rice, from Bourton on the Water.* 16 Sep: *Mr. Baillie, Curate to Mr. Rice at Great Risington, & private Tutor, to one of his younger sons, Henry, with his pupil, dined with us to-day.* 5 Oct., 19 Oct: ... *But for a mistake in the wording of a will, which made its operation different from the design of the testator, this Bedfordshire property would have devolved to my friend & neighbour at Oddington, Lord Dynevor's brother.*

1825: 19 Jul., 4 Oct., 14 Dec., 15 Dec: *Dr. Rice, announced to us to-day his being nominated Dean of Gloucester, & received our congratulations... Dr. Rice will vacate his Prebend of Worcester.*

1826: 30 Mar., 31 Mar: *I dined at the Deanery; Mrs. Rice & her many daughters were flourishing, & my old friend, the Dean, hospitable & in good spirits.* 18 Jul., 26 Jul: *We had a dinner party: the Dean of Gloucester, with his two elder daughters & his eldest son.* 22 Aug: *We dined at the Dean of Gloucester's at his parsonage at Oddington.* 5 Sep., 7 Sep., 14 Sep., 2 Nov., 21 Dec.

1827: 15 Apr., 24 Apr.

1828: 22 Jul: *We received some of our neighbours to dinner; Mrs. Rice & two of her daughters from Oddington.* 12 Aug., 23 Aug., 2 Sep: *I dined and slept at Mr. Baillie's at Great Risington, meeting the Dean of Gloucester & his eldest son; his two next Sons, George & Henry, came to tea in the Evening.* 1 Oct., 7 Oct: *During the interval between the meeting of the Christian Knowledge Society, and the annual Book Society dinner the gentlemen present were much grieved to learn the tidings of the death of the fourth daughter of our friend & neighbour, the Dean of Gloucester, which occurred about three o clock this afternoon. Miss Elizabeth Rice, a very lovely and unaffected young woman of eighteen, esteemed by most the flower of the flock, had not been many days ill.*

1829: 13 Jan., 15 Jan: *He is at present in residence, with part only of his family at the Deanery; Mrs. Rice is at Oddington with her eldest Son and most of her children; Miss Cecil and Miss Lucy Rice, with George & Henry are at Gloucester.* 4 Feb., 20 Mar., 15 May: *We dined with the Egerton Leighs at Broadwell, meeting the Dean of Gloucester, his son Francis, & his daughters Cecil and Maria ... These young ladies are handsome & elegant, surpassing in beauty their cousin Miss Leigh, who yet is a well looking girl.* 20 May, 25 Jun., 22-23 Sep., 11 Nov.

1830: 14 Apr: *This young man is imbued with what are called Evangelical principles not in a less degree, I believe, than his compeer, Baillie, the Dean's Vicegerent at Great Risington; & as such both are in high favour with the influential Lady, Mrs. Dean, who with one, if not more, of her daughters, has of late adopted puritanical views with great zeal; labouring to convert the good Dr. Rice, who has not yet embraced the new doctrines to the full extent, though, apparently, somewhat warped towards them.* 10 May.

1831: 11 Dec.

1832: 7 Jun: ... *and at the Deanery, where I saw Misses Cecil & Emma Rice, the Dean being gone to his Son's at Fairford, to be present at the wedding of his fourth daughter, Lucy, who is married to-day to the Revd. Mr. Escott, late Curate of Churchill and Cornwell.*

1833: 18 Oct.

1834: 15 Jul: *Dined at the Dean of Gloucester's, Oddington.... The Misses Maria and Emma Rice, in the light ballad style, sweetly [sang].* 23 Jul., 26 Jul., 29 Jul: *In the evening the party was joined by the Dean of Gloucester, his daughters Maria and Emma.* 31

Jul., 8 Aug., 29 Sep: *I wrote to the Dean to apprize him what had been done as to Edwin Jeffrey.* 3 Oct: ... *at the Parsonage we saw Miss Maria Rice and her brother Henry.* 9 Oct., 23 Oct., 30 Oct., 13 Nov., 17 Dec., 24 Dec.

1835: 7 Jan., 13 Jan., 14 Feb: *Mr. Cameron called, and we persuaded him to remain and dine with us. He announced to us that he was about to be married to Miss Rice, the eldest daughter of the Dean of Gloucester.*

27 Feb: *Mr. Cameron called to consult me on some painful differences which had arisen between the Dean of Gloucester and himself in relation to the treaty for marriage between Miss Rice and Cameron. The disagreement arose out of the refusal of the Dean to make such pecuniary arrangements as were adequate to Cameron's views of a sufficient income.* 28 Feb., 8 Apr., 21 Apr., 7 May, 21 May, 28 May, 4 Jun., 17 Jun., 28 Jul., 3 Aug: *We entertained the Dean of Gloucester, with his Son, Henry, & his daughters Cecil and Lucy: Louisa the former is engaged to be married to a Mr. Harnay, an officer.*

1836: 28 Jul., 3 Aug., 10 Aug., 24 Aug., 30 Aug., 6 Sep., 27 Oct., 10 Nov., 17 Nov., 19 Nov., 22-24 Nov., 26 Nov: *Going to Stow, I met a bride and bridegroom descending the hill in a chariot: Cecil Rice, the Dean of Gloucester's eldest unmarried daughter having this morning been united to an officer in the army, I believe, a subaltern, by name Arney, who has been recruiting for two years past at Gloucester — not a very bright match.* 30 Nov: *I had heard that that day was fixed for the wedding, and supposed the invisible person occupying the other place in the carriage to be the happy man: whereas it was the Dean, and on his way, accompanied by his daughter, to Gloucester, to attend the chapter audit.* 8 Dec., 15 Dec., 21 Dec., 29-30 Dec.

1837: 7 Jan: *He brought a good report of his Mother and Grandmother, and was very full of a long day which he passed on Wednesday with the Rice family at Oddington, having been invited to be present at the Wedding of the Dean's eldest unmarried daughter, Cecil, to Mr. Arney, to which a large party, in all nearly 40, had been asked.* 30 Jan., 12 Apr., 11 May, 18 May, 25 May, 1 Jun., 24 Jun., 6 Jul., 20 Jul., 2 Aug., 10 Aug., 17 Aug., 7 Sep., 14 Sep., 21 Sep., 26-28 Sep., 5 Oct., 10 Oct., 12 Oct., 2-4 Nov., 8-9 Nov., 11 Nov., 15-16 Nov., 23 Nov., 12-15 Dec., 20 Dec., 28 Dec.

1838: 3 Jan., 5 Feb., 8 Mar., 15 Mar., 24 May, 31 May, 14 Jun., 28 Jun., 12 Jul., 2 Aug., 8 Aug., 16 Aug., 22-23 Aug., 30 Aug., 31 Aug: *Adverted to the unkind comments and insinuations made on my conduct by the Dean of Gloucester.* 1 Sep: *Arthur Morgan, Mr. Tarn's Clerk, having taken the Complainant Hilling, the owner of the drill for which exemption from toll was claimed, to his principal, with a view to them proceeding to an appeal, Trenfield the Attorney of Winchcombe, who was assisting his Father & Brother in law Brookes as Mag. Clerks, intimated to the Dean of Glouc. and Mr. Ford what was going on, at the same time giving his opinion, as a professional man, that my views of the case, and the course I had adopted were just and correct.* 6 Sep: *With regard to the matter in dispute he believes me to have been right throughout—I mean as to the mode of conducting the case of exemption from tolls—blames the Dean for his harsh comments and insinuations, but believes that Ford did not use the words "secret design" at which I took offence.* 21 Sep: *Recd. a very handsome letter from the Lord Lieut. of the County, Lord Segrave, to inform me that he had recd. a joint letter from the Dean of Gloucester and Mr. Ford, acquainting him that it was my intention to withdraw my services as a Magistrate for this County.* 22 Sep: *Answered Lord Segrave's letter to the effect as stated by me yesterday, premising a very summary statement of the circumstances which had induced me to declare an intention of withdrawing from the Justice room at Stow, and of what had passed in correspondence between Mr. Ford, the Dean of Gloucester, and me.* 24 Sep: *Had a long conference with Mr. Pole, who kindly called to offer his mediation to reconcile the feud which exists in fact, though not in form, between me and my brother Mag. the Dean of Glouc. and Mr. Ford.* 25-26 Sep., 27 Sep: *At half past three joined Mr. Pole and the Dean of Gloucester in the Justice room.* 4 Oct., 11 Oct., 16 Oct., 18 Oct., 8 Nov., 15 Nov., 6 Dec., 12 Dec., 20 Dec.

1839: 4 Jan: *We did not go beyond the limits of the Park, strolling in the plantations, on the terrace &c. but chiefly conversing in Howell's study on all manner of topics—my altercation with Ford and the Dean of Gloucester, my correspondence with Lord Segrave, and return to the Stow bench.* 9 Apr., 16 May, 23 May, 30 May, 13 Jun., 25 Jul., 15 Aug., 22 Aug.

1840: 10-11 Jun., 16 Jul., 23 Jul., 28 Jul: *Drove MW. to Oddington. Called at the Rectory. The Dean of Gloucester was from home. Received by Miss Rice, who appeared in delicate health; her sister Louisa is much recovered from her late serious illness, which, it was feared, would end in decline; but it is still in a precarious state.* 5 Aug: *Received a note from the Dean of Gloucester, with an apology for his not attending the meeting to-day: his lukewarmness is much to be regretted; last December the weather was too cold, now too hot: the truth is that the Dean is listless, careless, and self-indulgent, without public spirit: however, he transmitted £1. as a donation.* 13 Aug., 27 Aug., 31 Aug: *In Barrington Lane met and parleyed with the Dean of Gloucester.* 3 Sep., 10 Sep., 17 Sep., 21 Sep: *Miss Louisa Rice, the Dean of Gloucester's youngest daughter, who has been suffering from an indisposition of many months standing, believed to be a decline, but who has of late rallied greatly, though still very delicate, was also calling on the Vavasours.* 24 Sep., 29 Sep., 8 Oct., 15 Oct., 5 Nov., 12 Nov., 18-19 Nov.

1842: 20 Jan., 27 Jan., 3 Mar., 5 Mar., 18 Apr: *Met at Stow Mr. and Mrs. Wiggin, lately married; the lady being Emma Rice, the Dean's Daughter, the Gentleman a young Oxonian, not yet in orders, and some years his wife's Junior, a Gentlemanly, accomplished young man, as we have heard, and son of a London merchant.* 19 May, 21 May, 23-24 May, 26 May, 2 Jun: ... *the Dean of Gloucester, with whom F. had been in communication, hoped, I suppose, rather than expected, that a remonstrance addressed by him & me to Stokes would prevent such a scandal and exposure, and had suggested that I should prepare such a letter as we might jointly sign, and dispatch, with a view of averting so serious a mischief, as related both to Ford & Stokes, and the harmony of the neighbourhood.* 3-4 Jun., 9 Jun., 16 Jun., 7-8 Jul., 14 Jul., 21 Jul., 4 Aug., 8 Aug., 10 Aug., 16 Aug., 18 Aug., 25 Aug., 22 Sep., 11 Oct., 3 Nov., 19 Dec., 30 Dec.

1843: 17 Jan., 19 Jan., 16 Aug., 29 Sep., 12 Oct., 14 Oct., 26 Oct., 2 Nov., 16 Nov., 13-14 Dec.

1844: 11 Jan: *The Dean of Gloucester, Ford, W B Pole, Polhill, Debary, were also present, and the Dean with Ford, sat with R Waller and me as Mag.* 25 Jan., 26 Jan: *Wrote to the Dean of Gloucester with the address of a biscuit baker at Bath — by whom we are supplied with that article.* 27 Feb., 29 Feb., 2 Mar., 9 Apr., 10 Apr., 27 Apr., 6 May, 25 Jul., 29 Jul: ... *wrote to the Dean of Gloucester, inviting him and others of his party to dinner on Wednesday next.* 1 Aug., 7-8 Aug., 26 Aug., 29 Aug., 5 Sep., 18-19 Sep., 24 Sep., 26 Sep., 10-11 Oct., 31 Oct., 21 Nov., 5 Dec., 11-12 Dec., 19 Dec., 26 Dec.

1845: 16 Jan., 6 Feb., 24 Feb: *Heard of the decease of the youngest daughter of the Dean of Gloucester at Oddington, on*

Friday last: she has long been in a very declining state; she was the only unmarried daughter. 26 May: ... *those who remained to partake of an early dinner were the Dean of Gloucester, Messrs. Ford, Hippisley, Hurd, Twisleton, Waller, Aitkens, Wiggin...* 19 Jun.

1846: 25 Jun., 23 Jul., 29 Jul: *A dinner party: the Dean of Gloucester, Mr. and Mrs. Wiggin, J. T. Rice, Mr. and Mrs. W. Vavasour, Miss Vavasour, and Henry Lindow made up our party.* 6 Aug., 13 Aug., 15 Aug., 26 Aug., 3 Sep., 10 Sep., 17 Sep., 24 Sep., 29 Sep., 1 Oct., 8 Oct., 15 Oct., 12 Nov., 3-4 Dec., 9 Dec., 31 Dec.

1847: 27 Jan: *Recd. a letter from the Dean of Gloucester, now in residence there, drawing my attention to ill-conduced beer-houses in the parish of Oddington, & other matters of justice business in which the Dean is interested.* 5-6 Feb., 17 Apr., 10 Jun., 6 Jul., 13 Jul., 31 Jul., 19 Aug., 2 Sep., 11 Sep., 14 Sep., 28 Sep., 30 Sep., 5 Oct., 28 Oct., 25 Nov., 8 Dec., 23 Dec.

1848: 11 May, 16 May, 1 Jun: ... *letter from the Dean of Gloucester on a nuisance of which he complains.* 8 Jun., 16 Jun., 6 Jul., 14 Sep., 26 Sep., 29 Sep., 12 Oct., 2 Nov., 9 Nov.

1849: 12 Dec.

1850: 10 Jan., 30 Apr: *From the Dean of Gloucester a very kind letter of condolence on my late heavy bereavement.* 2 May, 27 May: *The Dean of Gloucester made me a very friendly call.* 31 May, 6 Jun., 13 Jun., 20 Jun., 1 Aug., 29 Aug., 26 Sep., 1 Oct., 31 Oct., 6 Nov., 9 Dec., 11 Dec., 19 Dec.

1851: 18 Jan: ... *from the Dean of Gloucester, now in residence at the Deanery, with suggestions as to matters which he wishes to have discussed at the annual meeting of the Trustees of the United Stow and Moreton Turnpike trust on Thursday next.* 23 Jan., 27 Jan., 30 Jan., 31 Mar., 13 Apr., 19 Apr., 22 Apr., 24 Apr., 15 May.

1852: 23 Jan., 27 Apr: *Wrote to the Dean of Gloucester, asking him for a subscription towards reimbursing Mr. Brookes the money he is out of pocket for fees paid to counsel in the prosecution of Hambidge.* 29 Apr: *Received a letter from the Dean of Gloucester, who declines subscribing towards the reimbursement of the money R Brookes is out of pocket by extra fees in the prosecution of John Hambidge, thinking that the work was ill done.* 19 May: *Wrote notes of invitation to a dinner party on Wednesday next, to Mrs. J. Talbot Rice, Mrs. Dolphin. Wiggin, the Dean of Gloucester, and Mrs. Hippisley.* 20 May: ... *but the Dean of Gloucester declines it.*

1853: 24 May, 6 Jun., 8 Dec: *From the Dean of Gloucester, an invitation to dinner at Oddington on Tuesday next.* 13 Dec: *With Mrs. W. Vavasour drove in the close carriage to Oddington, to dine with the Dean of Gloucester.*

1854: 19 Jul.

RICE — Frances Rice[45]

Frances Rice, née Ingram (±1760-1834), of Coln St Aldwyn, Gloucestershire, was the daughter of Thomas Ingram (d. 1806), lord of the manor of Bourton. She married, at Coln St Aldwyn, 30 November 1778, by licence, John Rice (d. 1802) of Quenington. Frances died a widow in 1834 having settled the estate on a distant cousin named in her uncle's will, Bowyer Vaux, a Birmingham surgeon. It is unclear how she came to be the patron of Archibald Morrison.

1824: 3 Aug: *We dined at Mrs. Rice's, Bourton on the Water, who spends some summer months at her house there every year; at other times she resides with her protegé Mr. Morrison and his wife, also a former protegée, at Stoneleigh, in Warwickshire, where he is Curate, & takes pupils. The Morrisons are now with Mrs. Rice.* 7 Sep: *We had a dinner party: the Hon. Mr. & Mrs. Rice, and two daughters, from Oddington, Mrs. Rice, from Bourton on the Water.*

1825: 9 Aug: *Croome party: Mrs. Rice. brought a large party to Mr. Croome's table... . Mr. Morrison is of Wadham College, and Curate of Stoneleigh in Warwickshire; he takes pupils; two of these are with him now; inmates of Mrs. Rice's roomy mansion.* 17 Aug: *Dined at Mrs. Rice's at Bourton on the water. There was a large party.* 26 Aug: *We had Mrs. Rice and her friends to dinner: Viz. Mr. & Mrs. Morrison, & Mr. Wilson.*

1828: 14 Aug: *...to dine with our old acquaintance, Mrs. Rice, at Bourton on the Water.* 27 Aug.

1834: 17 Jul: *Wrote to Morrison, now staying at Mrs. Rice's at Bourton to request him to bury a corpse for me to-morrow.* 29 Jul. 2 Aug: *At the former place called on Mrs. Rice with Mrs. W. and Wellford.* 6 Dec: *Our neighbour and old acquaintance, Mrs. Rice, of Bourton on the Water, died this morning, advanced in years, after a gradual decline for several weeks past.* 19 Dec: *Drove Mrs. Witts to Bourton on the Water to call on Mr. & Mrs. Morrison, who leave that place to-morrow; Mr. M. & his wife having been there since a day or two before the decease of Mrs. Rice, by whom they had been both educated, and who regarded them as her adopted children.*

1835: 13 Jan.

RICE — Francis William Rice[46]

Francis William Rice (1804-1878), Church of England clergyman, was the eldest son of Edward Rice (1776-1862) and Charlotte Lascelles (d. 1832)(*above*). He was educated at Westminster School and Christ Church, Oxford (BA 1826; MA 1847), and served as vicar of Fairford from 1827 to his death in 1878. He married, first, 1830, Harriet Ives, daughter of Daniel Raymond Barker (1811-1854); they had 1 son and 1 daughter:

1 Ellen (1832-1924)
1 Arthur de Cardonnel Rice (1836-1911); succeeded as 6th Baron Dynevor

Rice married secondly, 1856, Eliza Amelia (1826-1896), eldest daughter of Revd Henry Carnegie Knox, rector of Lechlade; they had 3 sons and 2 daughters:

1 Francis (b. 1859)
2 Cecil Mina (1860-1924)
3 William Talbot (1861-1945)
1 Alice Sophia (1862-1939)
2 Mary Charlotte (1863-1923)

1827: 5 Oct: *I dined at the worthy curate's of Great Risington ... and Mr. Rice, the Dean of Gloucester's son, who had left his Father & Mother with the rest of the family at Brighton, and returned into Gloucestershire for a few days pheasant shooting.*

1828: 2 Sep: *I dined and slept at Mr. Baillie's at Great Risington, meeting the Dean of Gloucester & his eldest son; his two next Sons, George & Henry, came to tea in the Evening.*

1829: 4 Feb: *Messrs. Ford & F. Rice formed the party; the latter recently admitted to Priest's orders, & presented by his father, the Dean of Gloucester, to the Vicarage of Fairford, vacant by the decease of Dr. Michell, late Prebendary of Gloucester.* 15 May: *We dined with the Egerton Leighs at Broadwell, meeting the Dean of Gloucester, his son Francis.* 20 May.

1834: 30 Sep: *This busy day concluded with the annual meeting and dinner of the Stow Book Society. Mr. F. W. Rice and Mr. Cameron were elected members.*

1835: 1 Feb: *Mr. F. Rice wrote me a few lines, expressing a wish that certain books should be ordered into the Book Society at Stow, of which he is a member.*

1837: 8 Feb., 6 Oct: *Of those leaning or embraced in the principles of the Evangelical school, I observed the Incumbent of Campden, Mr. Kennaway, with two friends, Hall Junr., F. Rice, Elridge, Bennet Hoskins.*

1838: 15 Oct: *At the Coffee room met with Mr. F. Rice, Rector of Fairford, and eldest son of the Dean of Gloucester, who was on his road to Dynevor Castle in Wales, to visit his Uncle, Lord Dynevor.*

1844: 5-6 Dec.

1853: 4 Apr: *Raymond Barker, High Sheriff, and Francis Rice, his brother in law, and Rector of Fairford, acted as his Chaplain.* 6 Apr: *Mr. Hale, the High Sheriff, and his niece, Miss Rice, daughter of Francis Rice, a very sensible, but somewhat singular young person, were those with whom I was most in communication.*

RICE — George Talbot Rice [47]

George Talbot Rice, 3rd Baron Dynevor (1765-1852), MP and landed proprietor, was the eldest son of George Rice (d. 1779), of Newton, Carmarthenshire, and Cecil Talbot, *suo jure* Baroness Dynevor (1735-1793), daughter and heir of William Talbot, Baron Dynevor. He was educated at Christ Church, Oxford, and succeeded as 3rd Baron Dynevor in 1793. He was MP for Carmarthen, 1790-93, and lord lieutenant of Carmarthenshire, 1804-52. He married, 20 October 1794, Frances, third daughter of Thomas Townsend, 1st Viscount Sydney, and Elizabeth Powys; they had 1 son and 6 daughters:

1 George (1795-1869), MP for Carmarthen (1820-31 and 1832-52); educated at Christ Church, Oxford; married, 27 November 1824, Frances Anne, eldest daughter of Gen. Lord Charles Fitzroy; succeeded as 4th Baron Dynevor of Dynevor, 1852; 4 daughters:
  1 Frances Emily (±1827-1863)
  2 Caroline Elizabeth Anne (±1829-1887)
  3 Selina (1836-1918)
  4 Elianore Mary (1839-1897)
1 Frances (±1796-1884); died unmarried
2 Cecil (±1797-1883); died unmarried
3 Harriet Lucy (±1799-1879); died unmarried
4 Carolina (±1804-1878); died unmarried
5 Catherine Sarah (±1806-1887); died unmarried
6 Maria Elizabeth (±1814-1883); died unmarried

1824: 19 Oct: *Among the Magistrates present were, Lords Dynevor, Ducie, Sherborne & Apsley: the Hon. H. Morton, Sir W. Guise, Mr. R B Cooper, Mr. Goodrich, Mr. Byles, Dr. Timbrill, Mr. Keysall, Mr. Ford, Mr. Goldney, Mr. Phelps, Mr. Newman, Archd Sandiford, &c ... Lord Dynevor & his son, the Hon. G. Rice Rice, MP. for Carmarthenshire, qualified as Magistrates, and are likely to act in the same division as myself, their occasional residence being at Barrington Park, in which & the adjoining parishes of Great Risington and Taynton in Oxfordshire his Lordship has considerable property. Lord Dynevor is a very pleasant and affable man, and well versed in public business. His principal Seat is at Dynevor Park in Wales; he has only one son and several daughters. Mr. Rice is on the eve of marriage with a daughter of Lord H. Fitzroy. He is also about to assume the name of Trevor; having recently succeeded by the death of Visct. Hampden to a very considerable estate in Bedfordshire, subject to a large jointure to Lady Hampden, formerly Miss Brown, eldest daughter of Mr. Commissioner Brown (of the Excise) resident in Edinburgh, where, in my boyhood, I was very intimate in the Brown family. The Lord Hampden in question was succeeded in his title by his brother, the Honble. Mr. Trevor, who died after enjoying the title about three weeks, & he also left Mr. Rice a large property in money The Rice's were connected with Lord Hampden's family by intermarriages. But for a mistake in the wording of a will, which made its operation different from the design of the testator, this Bedfordshire property would have devolved to my friend & neighbour at Oddington, Lord Dynevor's brother.*

1837: 1 Jun: *Two or three nights ago, Ackerley collected at a public house in Stow a crowd of curious people, chiefly of the lower classes, to whom he descanted on the water-works now being constructed, on the Weights and measures, and all his old exciting points, reviling in most unmeasured terms Lord Dynevor, Pole, Ford and myself.*

1838: 5 Feb., 15 Oct: *At the Coffee room met with Mr. F. Rice, Rector of Fairford, and eldest son of the Dean of Gloucester, who was on his road to Dynevor Castle in Wales, to visit his Uncle, Lord Dynevor.*

1842: 25 May.

1844: 29 Feb: *Satisfactory letters of acquiescence and support were read from Lord Dynevor, Genl. Lygon, Sir J. Cathcart, the Dean of Gloucester, Mr. Pole, Mr. Chamberlayne &c.*

1847: 5 Oct.

1851: 23 Jan.

1852: 12 Apr: *Mr. Moore, Surgeon, called in the evening, to ask for information whether any recent Act. of Parlt. had passed forbidding the interment of deceased persons within the walls of Churches. I am not aware of any such prohibition ... The doubt had arisen as to the burial of Lord Dynevor who died rather suddenly at Barrington Park on Good Friday of an attack of gout at the heart, aged 86 years. His Lordship had long been in a feeble state, both of body and mind.*

RICE — John Talbot Rice — *see also* Reade [48]

John Talbot Rice (1819-1899) was the fourth son of Edward Rice (1776-1862) and Charlotte Lascelles (d. 1832) (*above*). He matriculated at Exeter College, Oxford, but never took a degree. He married, first, 1846, Clara Louisa Reade (1820-1853); there were no children of the marriage. He married secondly, 1855, Elizabeth Lucy Boyd (1827-1914).

1838: 6 Jan: *Very unpleasant travelling & the roads very indifferent, as far as Andoversford, where I baited, and passed half an hour or more with the Dean of Gloucester's youngest Son, John Talbot, lately entered of Exeter Coll., rather a promising youth.*

1839: 25 Jul.

1840: 18 Nov.

1842: 24 May: *We met also the Dean of Gloucester, John Talbot Rice, and Mrs. Wiggin; Mr. W. gone to Oxford for the day.* 20 Jul: *A dinner party; we were favoured with the company of Mr. and Mrs. Pole, Watson Pole, Mr. Wynniatt with his daughter Harriet, and son in law, W. Lowndes, Mr. and Mrs. Winter, and J. T. Rice; the evening passed off pleasantly.* 6 Oct.

1843: 7 Dec.

1844: 15 Apr: *Mr. Reade (Compton) and J. T. Rice made a morning visit.* 31 Jul: *Mr. and Mrs. Wiggin and John Talbot Rice came from Oddington.*

1846: 25 Jun., 29 Jul., 15 Aug., 2 Sep: *It is announced that her sister Clara is ere long to be married to John Talbot Rice, the Dean of Gloucester's youngest Son, not in any profession; not having passed an examination for a degree at Oxford, where he was of Exeter College: One feels vexed that so pleasing a young person as Clara Reade should have engaged herself to a young man, with so little mental power; in moral character he is very respectable. Her health is delicate: it is said they are to reside at the Rectory, Great Risington, and he, whose present occupation is farming, will, probably, manage the Rectory farm.* 8 Oct., 15 Oct., 25 Nov., 8 Dec.

1847: 26 Jan., 13 Mar., 20 May, 31 Jul: *Drove with M.W. to call on Mr. & Mrs. J. T. Rice at Great Risington, whom we found at home, and with them the Dean of Gloucester.* 25 Nov.

1848: 14 Jun: *A dinner party. Our company consisted of Mr. and Mrs. Wiggin, Mr. and Mrs. W. B. Pole, Mr. and Mrs. J. T. Rice, Mr. and Mrs. W. Vavasour, and Emma Vavasour.* 15 Aug: *My wife and daughter with my two elder grandchildren drove to call on Mrs. J. T. Rice at Great Risington.* 17 Aug., 12 Oct.

1849: 13 Dec.

1850: 14 Feb., 16 Feb., 31 May, 19 Jun: *We called on Mrs. J. T. Rice at Great Risington; her husband was in Town, and we found with her a daughter of Mr. Francis Rice.* 16 Jul., 19 Sep., 7 Nov., 20 Nov., 27 Nov: *A dinner party. Mr. & Mrs. J. T. Rice, Mr. Wiggin, Mr. & Mrs. and Miss Morrison, Mrs. R. A. Scott, and Mr. Ogle were our guests, added to our home party.*

1851: 13 Mar.

1852: 15 Feb., 8 May, 19 May: *Wrote notes of invitation to a dinner party on Wednesday next, to Mrs. J. Talbot Rice, Mrs. Dolphin. Wiggin, the Dean of Gloucester, and Mrs. Hippisley.* 22 May: *A note from Mrs. J. Talbot Rice, who, with her husband, accepts my invitation to dinner on Wednesday next.* 26 May: ... *a dinner party: in addition to our home party, the guests were Mr. and Mrs. J. T. Rice, Mr. & Mrs. Wiggin, Mr. and Mrs. Hippisley, Mrs. Dolphin, and Miss Kirby.* 27 Oct., 29 Dec.

1853: 24 Feb., 7 Apr., 13 Dec., 15 Dec.

1854: 9 Feb., 28 Mar., 21 Jun: *At the Station met and chatted with J. T. Rice on his way to Town.*

RICE — Richard Rice[49]

Richard Rice (1824-1902), Church of England clergyman, was born at Hayton, Cumberland, the eldest son of Revd Richard Rice (1792-1868) and Mary Goodenough (1802-1869), who had married at Broughton Poggs, Oxfordshire, on 24 April 1821. Rice (senior) was probably curate at Broughton Poggs at the time of his marriage, for he appears to have come from Buscot in Berkshire. He was a cousin of some degree to Edward Rice, dean of Gloucester.

Richard Rice (junior) was educated at Queen's College, Oxford (BA 1846; MA 1851), and was second master at Northleach Grammar School from 1849 to 1868. He was also curate of Hampnett and vicar of Little Barrington, Oxfordshire, 1866-1902. He married, at Hampnett and Stowell, Gloucestershire, 5 October 1856, Maria Wells (1826-1907); they had 3 sons and 2 daughters:

1 Richard (1858-1947)
2 Ernest (b. 1860)
1 Lilian (1863-1889)
3 Hugh Goodenough (1865-1947)
2 Cecily Wells (1867-1931)

1850: 30 Jul: *Sauntering in the garden (Northleach) with my friends, who were visited during the forenoon by Mrs. Rice, the wife of a clergyman beneficed and resident near Farringdon, and mother of the under-master of the Northleach grammar school, who is also curate of Hampnett.—A younger brother of this gentleman, also an assistant in a school, called.* 18 Sep.

RICHARDS — George Richards[50]

George Richards (1767-1837), poet and Church of England clergyman, was born at Halesworth, Suffolk, the son of James Richards, later vicar of Rainham, Kent. He was educated at Blundell's School, Tiverton, Christ's Hospital, London, and Trinity College, Oxford. Charles Lamb knew him at school, and called him 'a pale, studious Grecian'. He matriculated as a scholar at Trinity in 1786 and gained two chancellor's prizes: in 1787 for Latin verse, on the subject 'Rex, a violenta regicidae manu ereptus, cum regina Oxoniam invisens', and in 1789 for an English essay entitled 'On the Characteristic Differences between Ancient and Modern Poetry'. In 1791 George Simon, Earl Harcourt, gave anonymously a prize for an English poem, 'The Aboriginal Britons', which Richards won. Simon and Richards later became lifelong friends.

Richards graduated BA 1788, MA 1791, and BD and DD 1820. In 1790, when he was ordained, he was elected to a fellowship at Oriel College; he remained a fellow until 1796. He was appointed Bampton lecturer in 1800, and select preacher in 1804 and 1811. In 1795 he became rector of Lillingstone Lovel, Oxfordshire, and from 1796 he was vicar of Bampton. Richards also published the following: *Songs of the Aboriginal Bards of Britain* (1792); *Modern France: a Poem* (1793); *Matilda, or, The Dying Penitent* (1795); *The Divine Origin of Prophecy Illustrated and Defended* (Bampton lectures, 1800); *Odin*, a drama (1804); and *Miscellaneous Poems* (2 vols, 1804).

Richards married, at Oxford, 6 October 1796, Anna Maria Parker. They do not seem to have had any children.

1829: 22 Sep: *Lord W. Somerset is brother of the Duke of Beaufort, Prebendary of Bristol, and Rector of Tormarton ... I rather think, he still holds a family living also in Brecknockshire, near Crickhowell, Llangattock, a good piece of preferment, but requiring a knowledge of the antient British tongue. He became an adult pupil of Mr. Richards at Bampton, & quietly passed within the wicket.*

1830: 22 Jun: *The Revd. Dr. Richards, formerly one of the portionaries of Bampton, Oxfordshire, is the Vicar, a very highly esteemed divine; he took pupils in earlier years: I have heard, that when it was intimated to him by authority, that it was necessary, in order to complete the improvements in this quarter, that his Parsonage house should be taken down, he not only assented to the measure, but declined the proposal of the Commissioners of Woods & Forests to rebuild it entirely at the public expence, and gave them the sum of £3000 towards the costs about to be incurred.*

RICHARDS — Henry Richards — *see also* Croome *and* Daubeney[51]

Henry Richards (1799-1871), Church of England clergyman, was born at Farlington, Hampshire, the son of Griffith Richards (1755-1825) and Anne Longcroft (1762-1838). He was educated at Exeter College, Oxford (BA 1822; MA 1825; BD 1833), and entered the Church. Richards was appointed stipendiary curate of Stapleton, Gloucestershire, on 13 March 1824, and stipendiary curate of nearby Horfield on 17 March 1828. He married, at St Paul's, Bristol, 23 October 1823, Caroline (1799-1885), daughter of Revd James Daubeny (1748-1817) and Helene Drewett (1755-1843), daughter of Andrew Daubeny (1724-1807) and Mary Drewett (b. 1734). Henry and Caroline had 2 sons and 2 daughters:

1 Helena Caroline (1826-1852)
1 Edward Griffith (1827-1863)
2 Charles Henry (1831-1885)
2 Mary Elizabeth (1834-1865)

1833: 13 Apr: *The incumbent of this parish is the Revd. H. Richards, whom I formerly knew, when he was Curate to Mr. Croome at Bourton on the Water, where, however, he did not remain long. He married a Miss Daubeny, sister of the late Mrs. Croome, and of the Revd. Edward Daubeny of Ampney near Cirencester.* 20 Apr.

RICHARDS — William Richards [52]

William Richards (1760-1823), Church of England clergyman, was born at Burton Bradstock, Dorset, the son of Richard Richards (1718-1774) and Elizabeth Davis (1718-1774). He was educated at Trinity College, Oxford, but does not appear to have taken his degree. He was appointed rector of Little Cheverell, Wiltshire, on 24 May 1796, and stipendiary curate of nearby Tilshead on 7 October 1815.

Richards married, at Bridport, Dorset, 30 August 1788, Hannah Ewens (1768-1835); they had 5 sons and 8 daughters:

1 William (b. 1790), naval officer; served in the *Medusa* frigate; promoted to lieutenant in the *Queen*, 1813; married (wife unknown); 3 sons:
  1 William Thomas Cook (1820-1869)
  2 Edward (b. 1825)
  3 John (b. 1830)
1 Martha Anna (1793-1847); married, 1812, J. F. A. Wiltens of Cliff Hall
2 Eliza (b. ±1794)
3 Harriett (b. 1796)
2 Charles (b. 1798)
3 John (1799-1878)
4 Sophia (1800-1867)
5 Charlotte (b. & d. 1802)
6 Jane (1804-1878)
7 Caroline (1806-1878)
4 George (1807-1874), Church of England clergyman; became vicar of Chitterne, 1862; married, at Heytesbury, Wiltshire, 1 July 1863, Anne Elizabeth Knight (1825-1907); at least 1 daughter:
  1 Sophia Anne (1867-1938)
8 Marianne (1810-1877)
5 Edward (1811-1886); married, at Prestbury, Gloucestershire, 18 April 1850, Henrietta Humphries (1823-1881)

1807: 18 Feb: *Dined at Mr. Tinker's at Littleton & passed the Evening very pleasantly, going in the Lavington Chaise, met Mr. & Mrs. Richards, Mr. Bafret, Mr. Bernard, Mr. Eldridge &c.* 11 May, 7 Aug: *Visitation at Lavington found Archb. Danberry with many Clergymen, Messrs. Key, Spencer, Smith, Prince, Jones, Basset, Richards, Dr. Skinner, Williams, Rogers &c. &c.* 25 Aug: *Called with Mr. Royce on Mrs. Richards.*

1808: 17 Mar: *Rode to Little Cheverel & called on Mrs. Richards respecting the Clergy Funds.* 28 Apr.

RICHARDSON — Miss Richardson at Totteridge — *see also* Fiott [53]

Miss Richardson was presumably the daughter of Nicholas Richardson and Elizabeth, daughter of Revd Thomas Fiott (b. ±1699), rector of St Martin, Guernsey. Her father was the only son of Clement Richardson, of Guernsey, and was presumably a cousin to some degree of John Fiott (1749-1797), merchant, of London, who had known Channel Islands connections. Her parents married in 1752.

1803: 7 Oct: *Miss Richardson & Miss Fiott left Totteridge for Layton.*

RICHARDSON — Miss Richardson of Yorkshire [54]

Miss Richardson was a connection or friend of the Backhouse family. She accompanied Margaret Backhouse to Gloucestershire in 1808. She may be the Ann Richardson, 'Gentlewoman', who was still living at Giggleswick in 1822.

1808: 1 Feb., 1 May: *to Gloucester. Arrived at that place by nine, where I had the happiness to meet my friends, Mrs. Backhouse, Miss Richardson & my beloved Margaret.*

RICHARDSON — tenant of Francis Witts at Bucklersbury, London

1838: 9 Sep: *Recd. a letter from Mr. Jennings acquainting me that our tenant Clarke wishes to transfer the remaining 6½ years of his lease in the house at in Bucklesbury to a Mr. Richardson, who is willing to pay the present rent £100 per ann. for the remainder of the lease, provided he can get a further lease of 21 or 23½ years from the expiration of the present term at £90 per ann.* 28-29 Sep., 8 Oct.

1839: 5 Jan., 12 Jan., 5 Jul: *Recd. a letter from Mr. Jennings with information and advice how to act in respect of Mr. Richardson, one of our tenants in Bucklersbury, who has fallen into embarrassments by over-speculation, and fails in making good the payment of three quarters rent now due.* 6 Jul., 14 Aug., 17 Aug.

1840: 23 Oct: *A letter awaited me from Mr. Jennings, to apprize me that one of our London Tenants, Richardson, who is somewhat in arrear of rent, had proposed to his creditors a composition at 5/ in the pound, and requesting to know whether I would come into those terms.* 26 Oct.

1842: 15 Feb.

RICHARDSON — William Richardson [55]

William Richardson (1808-1851) was born at Kirkby Lonsdale, Westmorland, the son of John and Elizabeth Richardson. There is no record for him either at Oxford or Cambridge. He was vicar of the new church at Stainforth until 1865. In the 1851 census he was listed as unmarried, living at Stainworth with Isabel Holgate, his widowed housekeeper, and her two children. In the 1861 census he was listed as staying at Leek in Staffordshire at the home of Charles Heaton, a physician. It may be surmised that he was undergoing some form of treatment. Nothing more has been discovered. The inscription on his tomb states that he was born in 1811, but this is a mistake. He was born 1808, but not baptised until 1813.

1844: 9 Oct: *Letters from the Revd. Richardson, Incumbent of Stainforth, soliciting, a subscription or donation to the Ripon Church-building Society, and addressing me as the organ of a District Committee, established at Settle, and acting for a sub-committee at Stainforth.* 13 Oct: *Wrote to the Revd.—Richardson, incumbent of Stainforth, with a remittance of £5.* 24 Oct.

RICHMOND — Henry Sylvester Richmond [56]

Henry Sylvester Octavius Richmond (1808-1872), Church of England clergyman, was born at Turvey, Bedfordshire, the son and presumably the eighth child of Legh Richmond (1772-1827) and Mary Chambers (b. 1778) of Bath. He was educated at Queen's College, Cambridge (BA 1831; MA 1834), and entered the Church. Richmond was vicar of Breedon-on-the-Hill and Ratby, Leicestershire, 1833-41; curate of Denton, Kent, 1841-43; curate of Framfield, Sussex, 1843-44; curate of Barlborough, Derbyshire, 1844-47; chaplain to the workhouse at Bath, 1847-50; curate of Stoke Golding, Leicestershire, 1852; and rector of Wyck Rissington, Gloucestershire, 1853-72. He married, 1836, Caroline Eliza Close (1808-1892); they had 3 sons and 3 daughters:

1 Legh Atherton (1838-1895); died unmarried
2 Douglas Close (b. 1839)
1 Mary Isabella (b. 1841)
3 Henry Sylvester (1843-1908)
2 Frances Maria (1844-1930); died unmarried
3 Catherine (1848)

1853: 7 Apr: *Mr. Ford named that the Benefice of Wick Risington had been already presented to a Mr. Octavius Richmond, son of the formerly well-known Legh Richmond, an Evangelical Clergyman of high estimation, known as by other writings, so particularly by his piece of Biography—"the Dairyman's daughter". Mr. O.R. is represented as a married man in middle life, with a family, and pupils, now holding a curacy near Newport Pagnell.* 22 Dec.

1854: 2 Feb., 15 Mar: *Wrote notes of invitation to dinner on the 23d. to Ford, Morrison, Royce, Hippisley, and Richmond.* 18 Mar., 23 Mar: ... *were soon followed by Mr. Hippisley, Mr. Royce, Mr. Ball, Mr. Richmond. These were my guests at dinner.* 3 May, 17 May: *Mr. Richmond called on me and E Clifford, and advised with me as to the School house &c. built on the glebe at Wick Risington.* 25 May, 30 Jun: *Dined at the Poles, Wyck Hill, accompanied by Edmund Clifford:a small party; the Watson Poles, Mr. and Mrs. Richmond, and two boys, and ourselves.* 19 Jul., 22 Jul: *I drove to call on Mr. and Mrs. Richmond at Wick Risington, whom I found at home.* 3 Aug.

RICKETTS — Robert Tristram Ricketts [57]

Sir Robert Tristram Ricketts, 1st baronet of The Elms and Beaumont Leys (1772-1842), naval officer, was born at Basingstoke, Hampshire, the son of John Ricketts (b. 1737) and Harriot Grace Roberts (b. ±1742). He was promoted to lieutenant in 1793 and retired as rear admiral of the blue. He was made baronet of The Elms, Gloucester, and Beaumont Leys, Leicester, on 15 February 1828, while ranked vice admiral.

Ricketts married Rebecca Eliza (1780-1859), daughter of Richard Gumbleton and N. N. Hamilton O'Hara; they had 4 sons and 2 daughters:

- 1 Cornwallis (1803-1885), Adm.; succeeded as 2nd baronet; married, first, 31 May 1834, Henrietta Plumb (1812-1838), daughter of John Plumbe Tempest and Sarah Plumbe; 2 sons:
  - 1 Robert Tempest Tempest (1836-1901); born at Rome; succeeded as 3rd baronet
  - 2 Robert (b. & d. 1838); given the same name as his elder brother; born and died an infant at Florence, Italy; there is a note in the 1839 parish register stating that his body was removed to the family vault

  Henrietta died at Florence giving birth to her second son; she was buried at Swindon, near Cheltenham. Cornwallis married secondly, 29 January 1852, Caroline Augusta, daughter of Henry Pelham Pelham-Clinton, 4th duke of Newcastle-under-Lyne, and Georgina Elizabeth Mundy; 1 son and 5 daughters:
  - 1 Augusta Henrietta Mary (±1852-1910); married, 24 April 1876, James Young Stephen; 2 sons and 1 daughter
  - 2 Evelyn Emily Anna Maria (1854-1901); died unmarried at Knaresborough, Yorkshire
  - 3 Constance Charlotte Rose (1856-1932); married, at St George's, Hanover Square, Middlesex, Charles Edward Stuart Ratcliffe (1854-1928); 1 son and 3 daughters
  - 1 Frederick William Rodney (1857-1925); succeeded as 5th baronet; married, 29 May 1879, Alice Eve Grace (d. 1931), daughter of Charles Fox Webster and Louisa Alice Frances Calder; 3 sons and 1 daughter
  - 4 Gertrude Charlotte Eleanor (±1859-1939); died unmarried
  - 5 Mildred May (±1862-1922); died unmarried at Weymouth
- 1 Harriet Dorothea (1809-±1889); married, first, at Cheltenham, 12 December 1844, Revd John Charnock; secondly, St James's, Westminster, 20 February 1868, Edmund Haworth (1797-1879)
- 2 William Hamilton (1810-1830); died in India
- 2 Lavinia Ann (1812-1874); died unmarried at Cheltenham
- 3 Simpson Hicks (1816-1858), Cdr; married, 14 June 1855, Emma Gertrude, daughter of William George Pigou and Jane Mildred Smith; 2 sons
- 4 St Vincent William (1820-1866); married, 6 April 1842, Georgiana Mary (1821-1867), daughter of Mary Dashwood-King (1788-1873) and Augustus FitzHardinge Berkeley (1789-1872), illegitimate son of Frederick Augustus Berkeley, 5th earl of Berkeley, and Mary Cole; 3 sons and 1 daughter

---

1835: 7 Jan: *The Bishop and Mrs. Monk had apologized for not asking us to join their dinner party to-day, their table being full, but insisted on our spending the Evening with them... We found there Sir Robert Ricketts, an admiral, who resides at Cheltenham.*

RIDDELL — James Riddell and the Riddell clan of Ardnamurchan and Sunart, co. Argyll [58]

Sir James Riddell, 1st baronet (1726-1797), was the third son of George Riddell, of Kingloss, co. Linlithgow, and Christiana, daughter of Andrew Paterson of Kirkton. Sir James Riddell and his second wife, Sarah (*below*), were close friends of Edward and Agnes Witts in Edinburgh. Riddell was a cultured man. He graduated LLD and became a fellow of the Society of Antiquaries and superintendent-general to the British Fisheries Society.

Riddell married first, 7 February 1754, Mary (1735-1762), daughter and heir of Thomas Milles (1695-1765) and Helen Ferrier (1703-1742) of Billockby Hall, Norfolk; they had 4 sons and 1 daughter:

- 1 James (1757-1763); died an infant
- 2 Thomas Milles (1759-1796), 'lord of the manor of Billockby in Norfolk'; lived at Larbert, Stirling; married, 1784, Margaret, daughter of Dugald Campbell of Locknell, Argyll; 2 sons and 5 daughters:
  - 1 James (1787-1861); *see below*
  - 1 Catherine Drummond (b. 1788); married, at Colombo, Ceylon [Sri Lanka], 3 April 1830, Caroline Stuart Rodney (1810-1898); 2 sons and 2 daughters:
    - 1 Thomas Milles Stratford (1832-1854)
    - 2 Rodney Stuart (1838-1907); succeeded as 4th baronet
    - 1 Louisa M. (b. 1842)
    - 2 Frances Elizabeth (b. 1852)
  - 2 Mary Milles Geva (b. 1789)
  - 3 Sarah Burden (b. 1791)
  - 4 Eleanor Frazer (b. 1793)
  - 5 Margaret (b. 1794)
  - 2 Campbell Drummond (b. 1796)
- 3 George James (1759-1783), army officer; lived at Loddon Stubbs, Norfolk; killed in a duel with David Cuninghame, Mary Milles's nephew
- 4 Andrew Paterson (1760-1761); died an infant
- 1 Mary Christian Paterson (1761-1762); died an infant

Riddell married secondly, 1775, Sarah Swinburne (1731-1817) (*below*), daughter and heir of Henry Foster, of Yorkshire, and widow of John Swinburne.

Agnes Witts mentioned various members of the Riddell family in her diaries—most commonly Col Riddell and Mr M. Riddell—but often did not clarify the identity of individuals. When the Witts family arrived back in Edinburgh in April 1801 they became re-acquainted with the Riddells; they later also renewed their acquaintance in other fashionable areas of England. Lady Riddell lived her later years in Bath.

1801: 7 Apr: *The little Riddells came in the evening.* 8 Apr: *Mrs. Riddell called early in the morning.* 18 Apr: *We afterwards repaired to Miss McFarlan's, where we met M. Riddel, Mr. & Mrs. Dewar.* 9 Aug: *Went to Portman Chapel with Lady Lyttelton & Miss Eycott, met Mr. Riddell.* 14 Aug: *Mr. Riddell called & sat long with us.* 13 Oct: *My Mother as well as myself were in Mrs. Doig's box, very agreeably: the remaining Company consisted of Mrs. Scott & Mrs. Eycott, & two most agreeable persons, the former of whom I had long wished to know, & the latter I had formerly seen much of at Edinburgh. Mr. Matthias, & Mrs. W. Riddell. I conversed chiefly with them, who had a real taste for what was passing.* 14 Oct: *Called on Mrs. Daniell & upon Mrs. W. Riddell without success.* 17 Oct: *Called afterwards upon Mrs. Riddell No. 4 Sackville Street with my Mother.*

1804: 15 Jul: *Mr. Riddell & Mr. Stewart called.* 8 Aug: *Called upon Mr. Riddell, Mrs. Parris, Col. Bowen, Mrs. Massey.* 10 Aug: *Called on Mrs. Riddell, Mr. Rennie, Mrs. Massey.* 30 Aug.

1805: 9 Jul: *Called with my Father on Col. Riddell & with my Mother on Mrs. Auriol & Mrs. Campbell.*

RIDDELL — James Riddell[59]

Sir James Riddell, 2nd baronet (1787-1861), was the son of Thomas Milles Riddell (1759-1796), of Labart, Stirling, and Margaretta, daughter of Donald Campbell of Lochnell, co. Argyll. He was educated at Christ Church, Oxford (BA 1807), and succeeded his grandfather as 2nd baronet in 1796. He married, 1822, Mary, youngest daughter of Sir Richard Brooke, 5th baronet; they had 1 son:

1 Thomas Milles (1822-1883), officer, 7th Dragoon Guards; served in the Kaffir War; succeeded as 3rd baronet, 28 September 1861; married, 16 July 1851, Mary, daughter of John Hodgson of St Petersburg. At his death the baronetage devolved to his cousin, Rodney Stuart Riddell

---

1806: 19 Mar: *Conversed with Sir. J. Riddell, Priest, More.* 20 Mar: *conversed with Sir James Riddell.*

RIDDELL — Sarah Ridell[60]

Sarah Riddell, née Burdon (1731-1817), was the widow of Sir James Riddell, 1st baronet (1728-1796). She had previously been married to John Swinburne. She lived her later years in Bath.

1802: 2 Jan: *Nor did we omit to call upon Lady Riddell in the Lower Crescent, which with the Circus, Millsom Street, Gay Street, & the Upper Rooms present an excellent Specimen of modern stile in architecture. Lady Riddell is in good health enjoying a most charming House.* 3 Jan: *We dined at Lady Riddell's, meeting Countess D'Alton daughter of Lord Trimlestown, lively, French, & agreable. To our Circle was added in the Evening a Mr. Barratt, in some points an Enigma, a Continental pedestrian, & a linguist, still an amusing Character. Not less so the Honbl. Mr. Barnewall Countess D'Alton's Brother instructive & inquisitive. Col. Riddell & a Miss Cavan led up the rear.* 6 Jan., 8 Jan.

1808: 6 May: *Called on Mr. Worthington in the Upper Crescent, & on Lady Riddell.*

RIDDIFORD — George Riddiford[61]

George Riddiford (±1810-1877), local government officer, was born at Wotton-under-Edge and began his career as a solicitor's clerk, rising to become chief clerk in the Clerk of the Peace Office for Gloucestershire. In the 1851 census he was listed as a visitor in the house of Gilbert Babbage, mercer, in Southgate Street. Riddiford's family featured in the 1861 census. He married, at Dursley, Gloucestershire, 19 October 1840, Emily Foxwell (1819-1876), born at Woodchester; they had at least 3 daughters and 4 sons:

1 George L. (b. ±1841)
1 Kate (b. ±1846)
2 James (b. ±1848)
2 Mary (b. ±1850)
3 Percy (b. ±1853)
3 Helen (b. ±1855)
4 Charles (b. ±1857)

1842: 11 Apr: *To the Grand Jury Room at the Shire Hall, where I was afterwards joined by C Bathurst and Purnell, my colleagues on the Committee of accounts, and transacted the usual business with them, Mr. Burrup (for Mr. E. Bloxsome) Mr. Riddiford, Mr. Lefroy, Mr. Keiley, Mr. Whitehead &c.* 27 Jun.

1843: 2 Jan., 9 Oct., 16 Oct., 1 Dec: Mr. Riddiford from the office of the Clerk of the Peace.

1844: 1 Jan., 20 Jan., 8 Apr., 10 Apr., 1 May, 17 Aug., 14 Oct., 26 Oct., 29 Oct., 12-13 Nov., 17 Dec., 24 Dec., 30 Dec.

1845: 2 Jan., 12 Mar: *The County Chairman has sent Mr. Riddiford to investigate the matter at the Bridewell.* 31 Mar., 14-15 Apr., 17 Apr., 7 May, 24 May, 10 Jun., 30 Jun., 3 Jul.

1846: 29 Jun., 19 Oct.

1847: 7 Jan., 22 Mar., 28 Jun., 18 Oct.

1848: 3 Jan., 7 Jan., 20 Mar., 20 Jun., 26 Jun., 16 Oct., 22 Nov.

1849: 31 Dec.

1850: 15 Jan., 18 Jan., 20 Jan., 2 Feb., 7-8 Feb., 12 Feb., 20 Feb., 22 Feb., 2 Mar., 11 Mar., 14 May, 26 Jun., 1-2 Jul., 31 Aug., 14 Sep., 14-15 Oct., 2 Nov., 16 Nov., 19 Nov., 28 Dec., 30 Dec.

1851: 17 Mar.

1853: 3 Jan., 14 Mar., 27 Jun.

RIDDLE — Joseph Esmond Riddle[62]

Joseph Esmond Riddle (1804-1859), classical scholar and Church of England clergyman, was born at Bristol, the son of Joseph Riddle. He was educated at St Edmund Hall, Oxford (BA 1828; MA 1831), and was appointed Bampton lecturer in 1852. He was incumbent of St Philip and St James, Leckhampton, Cheltenham, from 1840 to 1859. From 1828 to 1830 Joseph Riddle lived at Ramsgate, where he took pupils and began a translation of Immanuel Scheller's folio Latin dictionary, *Lexicon totius Latinitatis*, which was published at the Clarendon Press, Oxford, in 1835. Several abridgements followed, and in 1838 a *Complete English–Latin Dictionary* was published, followed, in 1849, by *A Copious and Critical Latin–English Lexicon, Founded on the Dictionaries of Dr W. Freund*. He married Margaret Sharwood (1816-1901); they had 1 son and 1 daughter:

1 Margaret Alice (1851-1917)
1 Arthur Esmond (1853-1927)

Francis Witts hired Joseph Riddle as a tutor for his son Edward. He was also a curate for Witts at Upper Slaughter, the only curate Witts took until 1854 when, in severe ill health, he appointed Edmund Clifford. Riddle was a painstaking and laborious scholar, a vigorous defender of evangelical principles against the Tractarian movement, and an earnest but unimpassioned preacher.

1833: 12 Jan: *Mr. Riddle went this afternoon to Cheltenham, to preach the Sermon for the National Society...* 14 Jan., 20 Jan: *Mr. Riddle preached the same discourse, which he delivered last week at Charlton.* 26 Jan., 28 Jan., 12 Mar: *I joined my kind friend and judicious adviser at his rooms, whence he sallied to take counsel with the excellent Mr. Ogilvie, fellow of Balliol, but was disappointed, as that gentleman, it appeared, was absent from Oxford. Mr. Riddle, on his return from Balliol, called on Mr. Hill, the respectable Vice Principal of St. Edmund Hall, to impart to him the circumstances of the case, and to take his opinion; with whom he had a long conversation respecting those halls and colleges, at which it was most likely, that such a youth might be admitted.* 13 Mar., 1 Apr: *Our friend, Mr. Riddle, left us this morning for Bristol, being summoned thither by his Father under very distressing circumstances.* 8 Apr., 9 Apr: *After breakfast, Mr. Riddle came to us from Bristol, and having heard our arrangements returned home to pack up and transport his clothes and books to our new abode, into which we removed, when we had settled our bill at the Hotel. Leaving Mrs. W. to unpack & arrange her matters, Edward and myself took a walk to Bristol by Brandon Hill.* 10 Apr., 12-13 Apr., 18-19 Apr., 20 Apr: *We walked to Bristol, to call on Mr. Riddle's family in Old Market Street.* 21-22 Apr., 23 Apr: *After luncheon Mr. Riddle left us to go to Bristol to pass the day preparatory to his travelling to morrow by coach to Cheltenham, where my open carriage is to meet and convey him to Upper Slaughter, from whence he is to proceed to Oxford on Thursday to meet my Son and myself who propose to travel direct from Bristol to the former place.* 1 Sep: *It was left in my care as a parting present from Mr. Riddle to my Son.* 12 Sep.

1834: 18 Nov., 2 Dec., 16 Dec.

1835: 11 Jun., 13 Jun., 17 Jun.

1836: 21 Oct: *Found a letter from Mr. Riddle, dated from Malvern, whither he and his bride went on their marriage, which took place a short time since.* 22 Oct: *Wrote to Riddle to press him and his bride to pass a night here next week on their way to Town, proposing to them to come on Wednesday.* 25 Oct., 26 Oct: *Between 3 & 4 o clock Mr. and Mrs. Riddle arrived from Malvern to pass the day, and sleep here.* 27-28 Oct., 1 Nov.

1837: 21 Dec: *Also from Mr. Riddle, from whom I had not heard for a long time, and who writes to congratulate us on my son having passed his University examination with honours.*

1838: 22 Jan., 1 Mar., 11 Jun.

1839: 5 Jun: *Mr. Riddle also came to seek me: he has been settled since Lady day at Oxford, with his lady, and is likely to remain here some time: when I last heard from him, he was Curate of Harrow, but he is unstable, and seldom remains long in one residence: the life of a student, and the habits of a town suit him better than the avocations of the parish priest: hence frequent removals, and experiments; for some months, and during last winter, he resided on a Curacy near Tetbury, with which he seems to have been heartily sickened.*

1840: 22 Apr: *In the course of our rambles stumbled on Mr. Riddle, who is about to settle at Cheltenham, as the Minister of the newly completed church in the parish of Leckhampton, and suburbs of Cheltenham.* 29 Apr: *Trye did not consider Riddle as very deeply imbued with what are called Evangelical opinions.... I also called on Mr. and Mrs. Riddell, at their lodgings near the new Church at Leckhampton, by whom I was obligingly received, but had not time to stay long: his manner continues to be hurried and abrupt, and he is still vehement in any view he takes of opinions and persons; especially bitter, at present, in his censure of those who adhere to the opinions of Dr. Pusey and Mr. Newman, whom, by a vulgar error, unworthy of a scholar, he designates as Papists.*

1842: 2 Dec., 5 Dec: *Called on Mr. Riddle, at his residence at Cotswold Villas, near St. Philip's Church, Leckhampton, not far from the Park, but did not meet with him at home.* 8 Dec., 9 Dec: *Drove MW. to call on Mr. and Mrs. Riddle, whom we found at home: his residence is not far from his church, which though strictly speaking, not a district Church, or Chapel of Ease to the parish Church at Leckhampton, since it partakes in some measure of the character of a Proprietary Chapel, is virtually a District Church, to which by arrangement with Mr. Trye, the Rector of Leckhampton, a district, which may be called the Town district, is assigned, to Mr. Riddle, while Mr. Trye superintends the rural part of his parish.*

1844: 30 Dec: *Met and travelled in the same coach with Mr. Edwards, the Incumbent of Prestbury, who, with me, lamented the line taken by Riddle, now Incumbent of the new church at Leckhampton, and whose very dissenter-like, ultra-low-church views and opinions, particularly as expressed at a late meeting of the Religious Tract Society at Cheltenham, have obtained much notoriety.*

1850: 8 Nov.

RIDEOUT — Charles Rideout[63]

Charles Rideout (1796-1866), district surveyor of the Post Office, was born at St Albans, Hertfordshire, the son of Revd Richard Rideout (1759-1841) and Sarah Nicoll (1758-1809). He married, at St Mary de Lode's, Gloucester, 4 August 1826, Charlotte Washbourn (1797-1861), daughter of Thomas Washbourn (1770-1824), alderman, and Elizabeth Kendall (1776-1803); they had 2 sons and 1 daughter:

1 Nicoll Searancke Charles (1827-1870)
2 Caranchi (b. 1828)
1 Sarah Anne Nicoll (1832-1881)

In 1861 Charles and Charlotte were registered as living at Wotton Hill, Gloucester.

1839: 5 Feb: *I recd. a note from the District Surveyor of the Post Office, Mr. Rideout, apprizing me that a new Postmaster is appointed at Moreton in Msh. in the room of J Lardner, decd. and that it will be an accommodation in the management of the concerns of the Post Office there, if my bag with those of other gentlemen be made up in future at the Stow Post Office and not at Moreton, as hitherto.*

1842: 2 Jun., 10 Jun: *Wrote to Mr. Rideout, director of Postoffice arrangements in this district, suggesting to him a hint respecting the conveyance of the post from Moreton to Stow and back by the "Little Wonder" Coach, which had occurred to different persons who had canvassed the matter yesterday.* 17 Jun.

1843: 2 Nov.

1850: 12 Oct., 22-23 Oct., 25 Nov., 28-29 Nov.

1854: 20 Apr.

RIDLEY — Henry Ridley[64]

Henry Ridley (1753-1825), Church of England clergyman, was born at Heaton, Northumberland, the son of Matthew Ridley (1711-1778) and Elizabeth White (1722-1764). He was educated at University College, Oxford (BA 1774; MA 1776; B&DD 1802). He was made a prebendary at Gloucester in 1804, and was then appointed rector of Kirkby Underdale, Yorkshire, in 1805. He became rector of St Andrew-cum-St Mary, Hertford, in 1817. Ridley married, at Whickham, Durham, 3 June 1775, Elizabeth Willis (1755-1780); they had a large family.

1825: 15 Dec: *At Gloucester too Dr. Ridley has lately paid the debt of nature, whereby his brother in law, the Lord Chancellor, has been enabled to provide for the Revd. H. Wetherell.*

RIVINGTON — booksellers, printers, and publishers — *see also* John Ellill[65]

The famous firm of Rivington was founded by John Rivington (1720-1792) and his younger brother James Rivington (1724-1802). Their respective families were large and many of their sons worked for the firm. Margaret Ellill (1754-1828), sister to John Ellill, of Totteridge, married, 26 April 1777, Francis Rivington (1745-1822), eldest son of John Rivington (1720-1792); they had fourteen children. Some of their daughters were at John Ellill's house at Totteridge in January 1802 when Francis Witts dined there. John Ellill was a lead merchant and the Rivingtons would have needed lead to make up their type for printing; before his sister had married into the Rivington family he was probably acquainted with them via his business.

1801: 21 May: ... *we alighted at the foot of Ludgate Hill; & repairing to Mr. Rivington's the Bookseller found Edwd. Witts & my Brother awaiting our arrival.*

1802: 11 Jan., 13 Jan: *Mr. Ganvio, Mr. Ellill & Miss Rivingtons dined here. Fiott & myself walked to Barnet. Mr. Hopegood made a morning visit.*

ROBERTS — the Roberts families of Dowry Square, Hotwells, and the Mall, Clifton[66]

The Roberts families feature extensively in the diaries of Agnes Witts, but nothing tangible has been discovered about them. Agnes often referred to a 'Mrs Roberts' in the same sentence as a 'Mrs E. Roberts', but only one forename is certain: Charles Roberts, presumably a son of one of these families. It is likely that these families, so well known to Agnes, were seasonal visitors to Bristol and not permanent residents. Mrs Roberts and Mrs E. Roberts later relocated to Cheltenham.

1806: 14 Jan: *Danced also with the pleasing Miss Roberts; conversed much with Capt. Webb.* 16 Jan., 19-21 Jan., 24 Jan: *Walked with C. Roberts.* 27 Jan., 9 Feb., 12 Feb., 16 Feb., 23 Feb., 25 Feb., 27-28 Feb., 1-3 Mar., 16 Mar.

ROBERTS — Henry Roberts[67]

Henry Roberts (1816-1884), Church of England clergyman, was born at Saintbury, Gloucestershire, the son of Revd James Frederick Roberts (b. 1774) and his wife Sarah (b. 1793). His parents had married at Saintbury on 5 September 1813. He was educated at Radley College and Jesus College, Cambridge (BA 1841; MA 1844), and married Lucretia Marshall (1818-1881); they had 1 son and 2 daughters:

1 Lucy Russell (1846-1869)
2 Mary Lucretia (1851-1881)
1 James Alfred (1858-1923)

When Roberts was a curate without a parish the family lived with Lucretia's parents, Charles and Letitia Marshall. Charles was a farmer on a substantial scale, with 747 acres, employing thirty-five men.

1854: 17 Mar: Roberts 540317 *Received a letter from E.F.W.... Report of a call he had made on Mr. Roberts, a Clergyman unemployed, at Snowshill, who, if needful, might have been temporarily engaged by me; but it is likely that he may soon take permanent duty.* 20 Mar., 24 Mar., 26 Mar: *Mr. Roberts came on horseback from Snowshill, in time for the morning service: a quiet, civil, unpresuming man of about thirty years of age. Monotonous and somewhat provincial in performance of the duty in the desk—preached a good plain sermon. He performed the afternoon duty: dined with me, and rode back to Snowshill:—this will, probably, be the arrangement while he assists me.* 2 Apr., 9 Apr., 16 Apr: *Mr. Roberts came punctually to undertake the services of my church, probably for the last time Presented him with the quiddam honorarium of £2. 2. 0 for each of four Sundays.*

ROBERTS — Robert Roberts[68]

Robert Roberts (1807-1891), Church of England clergyman, was born at Wartling, Sussex, the son of Revd Robert Roberts, rector of Wadenhoe, and his wife, Hannah. He was educated at Corpus Christi, Cambridge (BA 1830), and took over his father's rectorship at Wadenhoe, Northamptonshire, in 1831. He became rector of All Saints', Aldwincle, in 1838, and held both livings until his death in 1891. He married Anne (b. ±1812), born at Langford, Somerset; they do not appear to have had any children.

1835: 25 Mar., 29 Mar.

1838: 30 Aug: *Mr. Roberts, the Incumbent of Wadenhoe, whose father purchased the advowson or next presentation, will present himself to Aldwinkle, but as he means to continue to reside at Wadenhoe is looking out for an Orthodox Clergyman, with some private fortune, to take the Curacy.*

1847: 13 Aug., 3 Nov., 10 Nov.

ROBERTS — William Roberts[69]

William Roberts (b. 1798), solicitor, was born at Churchdown, Gloucestershire, the son of William M. B. Roberts (1768-1808) and Margaret Jones (1769-1843). He married, at Longhope, Newland, Gloucestershire, 9 November 1820, Mary Ann Probyn (b. 1799); they had at least 2 sons:

1 Charles (b. 1828)
2 Thomas L. (b. 1833)

By 1881 Roberts was a widower living at 25 High Street, Coleford, with his son Charles, an auctioneer and also a widower.

1842: 14 May: *A letter from an Attorney, Roberts of Coleford, canvassing for my vote in his favour, when the Magistrates of Gloucestershire make an appointment of Clerk to a new Court of Requests about to be established by Act of Parliament in lieu of the ancient Jurisdiction of St. Briavel's, about to be annulled.* 16 May, 16 May, 29 May, 18 Sep.

ROBERTSON — Miss Robertson of Edinburgh

1801: *Miss Robertsons &c called in the morning.*

ROBERTSON — Colonel and Mrs Robertson of 70 Grosvenor Street, London

1801: 17 May, 23 May: *sat near half an hour at Mrs. Robertson's No. 70 Grosvenor Street.*

ROBINS — the Robins family at Clifton

1806: 16 Feb: *walked to Bristol with DeMauny, returned with him & Robins... With Robins in Bristol & to Clifton.* 23 Feb: *To the Post Office, Bristol, walked a little with Robins.* 25 Feb., 26 Feb: *Walked with Robins, the Ch. de Mauny, Mr. Kelly, Mr. Sheridan, all of whom I ought to avoid.* 15 Mar: *I walked a little with Robins; to Bristol with Cox.* 16 Mar.

ROBINSON — Mr Robinson of Edinburgh

1801: 13 Apr: *spent my time pleasantly with Mr. R. Newbigging. Among others, the Company consisted of two Mr. Cockburns, Mr. Rolland, Major Robinson &c.*

ROBINSON — Mr Robinson of Charterhouse Square, London

1806: 26 Feb: *Wrote letters upon business to Mr. Horne & a Mr. Robinson, an Attorney in Charter House Square.*

ROBINSON — Disney Robinson [70]

Disney Robinson (1804-1869), Church of England clergyman, was born at Harborne, Staffordshire, the son of Revd Richard George Robinson (1736-1825), vicar of Harborne, and Mary Woolhouse Thorp (1771-1839). He was educated at St John's College, Cambridge (BA 1828; MA 1831), and was ordained priest in 1830. He served as perpetual curate of Woolley, Yorkshire, from 1833 to 1868.

Robinson married, 1833, Fanny, daughter of Robert Hodgson of Haigh Hall, near Wakefield. He lived the latter years of his life at Henbury, near Bristol, and died at Torquay. He was the author of at least three books: *The Law and Gospel*; *The Christian's Privilege*; and *The Shield of Truth*.

1846: 11 Aug: *The Lord Lieutenant was not present, though expected at Gloucester this evening to be in readiness in case of his being called under a subpoena to give evidence on a trial expected to come on to-morrow, for a libel consisting in the superscription of an envelope sent by post at Cheltenham to Mrs. Barker, with whom it is notorious that Earl Fitzhardinge lives in a criminal manner, such envelope having been traced to a Revd. Disney Robinson, a Clergyman residing at Cheltenham, who, in intemperate zeal, addressed the envelope to Mrs. B. "adulteress and Sabbath breaker.*

ROBINSON — Frederick John Robinson [71]

Frederick John Robinson, 1st Viscount Goderich (1782-1859), prime minister, was the second of the three children of Thomas Robinson, 2nd Baron Grantham (1738-1786), diplomat and MP, and Lady Mary Jemima Grey Yorke (1756-1830). He was educated at Harrow School, St John's College, Cambridge, and Lincoln's Inn. He became MP for Carlow in 1806, and a year later he was elected MP for Ripon; he retained that seat until 1827.

In 1807 Robinson acted as secretary to a special mission to Vienna, and in May 1809 he became a protégé of Lord Castlereagh, one of the four contestants for Pitt's mantle. It was Castlereagh who appointed him his under-secretary in the war office and who subsequently became his patron. Robinson resigned with Castlereagh in the autumn of 1809 and, in deference to him, declined an office in Perceval's newly formed government. Under Lord Liverpool, Robinson rose from the ranks of the junior Pittites to become a senior tory. His promotion to chancellor of the exchequer in January 1823 was said to have been due partly to the support of his predecessor Vansittart, one of Castlereagh's confidants, and partly to the appeal of his 'amiable and gentlemanlike' manner among the powerful independent country gentlemen in the Commons. Budget surpluses enabled Robinson to reduce assessed taxes and to abolish or reduce duties. They also gave him the opportunity to make grants to house the Royal Library in the British Museum and to purchase the Angerstein collection for the National Gallery. These achievements, together with his support for Catholic relief and the abolition of slavery, led to Robinson being regarded as one of the most liberal members of the government; he was given the nicknames 'Prosperity Robinson' and 'Goody'. The final year of his chancellorship was by far the least successful. A run on the banks in the last months of 1825 led to a commercial crisis. The government responded the following year with a bill to restrict the issue of paper money below the value of £5, but in face of strong opposition in the Commons, Robinson consented to weakening its terms.

Liverpool's resignation through ill health in February 1827 and Canning's appointment as his successor in April shattered the tory–whig divide that had dominated parliamentary politics since 1812. Among the tories, Canning's liberalism, particularly on the Catholic question, led the anti-Catholic ministers to refuse to serve under him. The tories therefore separated into four main groups. The proliferation of parties was such that the king was obliged to play a significant role in the negotiations leading to the formation of Canning's government; to some this raised the spectre of the resurgence of another party—that of the crown. It was against this background that Robinson eventually became prime minister. In the tortuous negotiations leading to Canning's appointment to the post in April, Robinson had been considered, but was rejected; however, although he was not one of Canning's intimate friends, his liberalism and experience made him an essential member of the new government. Robinson accepted the post of colonial secretary, and agreed to take the lead in the Lords as the newly created Viscount Goderich.

On 8 August 1827 Canning died, and the king immediately turned to Goderich to be the next head of government; this was subject to the reorganised cabinet agreeing to the same terms as its predecessor—namely that it should continue to be a coalition of moderate tories and whigs and that measures for parliamentary reform and Catholic relief were off the table. The king was anxious for the post of chancellor of the exchequer to be given to one of Canning's oldest friends, William Sturges Bourne, but Bourne declined it. Goderich then offered it to Huskisson and the coalition whig George Tierney, but they also refused. He therefore turned to J. C. Herries, the financial secretary of the Treasury under Liverpool but an anti-Catholic politician. Goderich knew that the offer would be approved by the king but he was unprepared for the level of hostility it created within the government. It led to the collapse of Goderich's administration after only five months.

Goderich continued his public career as colonial secretary and president of the Board of Trade and of the India board. He gave his last speech in the Lords in 1847. He died at Grantham House in Putney in 1859.

1827: 2 May, 4 May, 7 May: *In the Lords poor Visc. Goderich is baited in much the same manner by Lord Londonderry, Lord Winchilsea, Lord Ellenborough &c.* 15 Jun: *Lord Redesdale especially brought forwards certain resolutions declaratory of just principles on this branch of political economy, as appeared to him, but contrary to the modern doctrines, which were canvassed at some length, answered by Lord Goderich, & though not carried, recorded on the Journals...* 12 Aug: *It seems to be settled, that the members of Mr. Canning's Ministry shall endeavour to govern the Country, though their leader is no more. His Majesty has sent for Lord Goderich, who will take the Post of Premier, and he must, doubtless, have recourse to a larger infusion of Whig principles into the Cabinet, in order to keep up the requisite number of public officers of State.* 7 Sep: *There seems no doubt, that there has been much discussion and struggle for mastery among the members of the Cabinet, so much so as to threaten a dissolution of their ill omened & recent combination. Lord Goderich has a very arduous task in hand; it may be doubted, whether he has talent and influence enough to rule his* fellows.

1828: 6 Jan., 11 Jan: *The political bubble has burst, and the unnatural coalition between apostate Tories & inconsistent Whigs is at an end; in a word, the ministry is broken up. For some time past it has been whispered, that considerable dissention prevailed in the Cabinet; it was known, that Ministers were in a minority as regarded the house of Lords, and the Parliament was to assemble on the 22d. Inst. Lord Goderich some two or three weeks since was stated to have sent in his resignation; & the premiership was actually offered to & refused by Lord Harrowby: then it was said, that Lord Goderich had consented to hold the reins of the State Coach some time longer, & it was added, that the King had yeilded an unwilling assent to the future admission of Lord Holland into the cabinet.* 30 May.

ROBINSON — Oswin Robinson [72]

Oswin Robinson (1825-1873), Church of England clergyman, was the fifth son of William Robinson (1792-1854) and Catherine Oswin (1791-1862) of Coventry. He was educated at New Inn Hall, Oxford (BA 1849; MA 1854), and married, at Stow-on-the-Wold, 26 October 1850, a widow, Susanna Bevis, née Taylor (1813-1891). Oswin and Susanna had at least 2 sons and 1 daughter:

1 Ann (1851-1852); died an infant
1 Oswin Nicholas (1854-1878)
2 Augustus Theodore (1856-1928)

Robinson and his wife arrived in New York on 21 May 1851 with Susanna's three children from her previous marriage:

1 James (b. ±1844)
1 Sarah (b. ±1846)
2 Jane (b. ±1848)

America clearly did not suit them. By 1861 they were back in England living at Gloucester Street, Malmesbury, Wiltshire, where Robinson remained an unemployed clergyman.

1850: 12 Jun: *Hippisley performed the afternoon service, his curate Mr. Robinson, reading the lessons with a very good voice, and well. This young man, late a pupil of Mr. Dean of Wick, and ordained on Trinity Sunday, holds, now doubt, the extreme opinions advocated and acted upon by his Rector and his former tutor.* 27 Jun: *A great want of temper and judgment was shewn by Mr. Robinson, the curate of Stow, who, unlike other Clergymen who occasionally attend to advocate the cause of a pauper, presented himself to denounce one of the parishioners, as imposing on the liberality of the Board, being lazy, and abusive to himself in the course of a pastoral visit.* 18 Sep., 24 Oct: *Met R W Hippisley, who is greatly annoyed by the conduct of his curate, Robinson ... Lodging at an obscure tradesman's at Stow, it seems that he has connected himself with a widow daughter of the house, some years his Senior, and encumbered with three children by her deceased husband. The result has been that the woman is or professes to be with child by him, and marriage at a very short notice indispensable.*

1851: 18 Apr., 28 Apr: *Learnt, with regret, that great excitement prevails at Stow in consequence of R W Hippisley having made such disclosures to the Bishop of Jamaica respecting the character of Mr. Robinson, that his appointment as temporary Chaplain at Belize has been cancelled.* 1 May, 5 May, 8 May: *Mr. Robinson left Stow to-day with his wife and her children, for Liverpool——thence to betake themselves by the first packet to the United States.*

ROBINSON — Robert Ansley Robinson [73]

Robert Ansley Robinson (1806-1880), JP, was born in Sussex and lived at 10 Berkeley Place, Cheltenham. He was a Gloucestershire JP. In 1855 he was cited by Ornwell Lloyd Evans for adultery in a divorce case. By 1871 he was living at Marylebone. Robinson married late in life, 1872, Mary Ann Broadbent (1823-1905). He died in London.

1852: 15 Mar: *... arrived at the Great Western Station soon after ten o'clock, meeting there Mr. Ansley Robinson, and Mr. Lefroy ... The former, a Chelt. Magistrate, much in the confidence of Lord Fitzhardinge, presented me with a lithograph sketch of a magnificent piece of plate about to be presented to his Lordship by a large body of subscribers as a testimony of the respect and regard of the many who have during a long series of years enjoyed the sports of the field with his Lordship's foxhounds.* 29 Mar., 9 Jun: *Made a long visit to the Exhibition of the Royal Academy. Met there Mr. Ansley Robinson.*

ROBINSON — William Robinson and the Robinson family of Settle [74]

William Robinson (1789-1872), banker, was born at Chatburn, Lancashire, the son of Josias Robinson (1749-1827) and Susannah Dixon (1758-1824). He married, at Giggleswick, Yorkshire, 8 October 1819, his cousin Jane Peart (1786-1843); they had at least 2 sons:

1 William (1823-1881)
2 John (1825-1886)

In 1835 William Robinson succeeded his father-in-law John Peart as a partner in the Craven Bank.

1823: 10 May: *Called on different acquaintances at Giggleswick & Settle, & dined at the former place with Mrs. Bolland, meeting the Pearts, Robinsons & Geldards.* 12 May.

1825: 13 Sep: *I took an early dinner at Giggleswick with Mrs. Bolland, where I met Mrs. A. Currer, Miss A. Ingleby, of Austwick, Mrs. Willis, & Mr. Robinson, a very respectable young Solicitor, settled at Settle, and married to Miss Peart, Mrs. Bolland's niece, my dear wife's old schoolfellow at Preston in Lancashire.*

1827: 3 Mar.

1837: 24 Oct., 28-29 Oct.

1838: 15 Sep., 17 Sep.

1840: 12 Jun., 1 Aug.

1843: 8 Nov: *MW. recd. a letter from Mrs. Hartley communicating the very recent decease of Mrs. Robinson of Settle — a worthy woman, my wife's schoolfellow and contemporary,—and long friend, who had been for some time in a low and depressed state both of body and spirits, but was hastily carried off at last by a rapidly increasing disease of the liver.*

1853: 29 Mar: *A letter from Mr. Robinson, Skipton, informs me that Jane Lonsdale has endorsed to her nieces, the Misses Cooper, the note of hand she holds of mine for £600.* 7-8 Apr., 13 Apr.

ROBINSON — William Scott Robinson [75]

William Scott Robinson (1803-1875), Church of England clergyman, was born in the parish of St Marylebone, Middlesex, the son of George Abercrombie Robinson (1758-1832) and Margaret Southwell (d. 1824). He was educated at Exeter College, Oxford (BA 1826; MA 1829), and was appointed rector of Dyrham, Gloucestershire, in 1828, and Farleigh Hungerford, Wiltshire, in 1832. He married, at the church of St Botolph, Bishopsgate, London, 12 February 1828, Matilda Maxwell (1803-1878), daughter of John Innes (1767-1838) and his wife, Sarah: they had 2 sons and 6 daughters:

1 Matilda Scott (1829-1869)
1 William Le Fleming (1830-1895)
2 John Innes (1833-1891)
2 Fanny Gordon (1837-1902)
3 Anna Smith (b. 1839)
4 Clara Frances (1842-1904)
5 Eliza Scott (1844-1924)
6 Sophia Jane Hemyss (1846-1927)

1829: 1 Apr: *The High Sheriff is Mr. Blathwayt of Dyrom Park, between Petty France & Bath, a young man of good fortune, who now & then attends the Sessions as a magistrate; his chaplain, the Revd. Mr. Robinson, is clergyman of his parish, and appears a pleasing young man.* 2 Apr: *A very good and pertinent sermon ... a clergyman, at least one not preaching in his own village church, should wait till he has been some years in the profession, before he uses such sentences as begin with, "I earnestly exhort," "I anxiously beseech you". "I solemnly call on you by that sacred authority, with which I am invested" &c.*

ROBISON — Dr Robison at Oxford

1804: 30 Jan: ... *called on Mr. Michele & on Odell, & D. Robison.* 31 Jan: *At Dr. Robison's first mathematical lecture.*

ROCKE — *see also* Evans

It seems likely that Jem Evans's mother, Sarah (d. 1803) was born Sarah Rocke. In which case, Miss Rocke may be a sister, or a niece.

1802: 24 Jun: *All called at Mr. Evans's, who with his Lady & Miss H. Rocke had come the Evening before.* 4 Jul: *Mr. & Mrs. Evans Miss Rocke, J. Evans, Edgell, Stevens, Pering, & Rashleigh breakfasted with me.*

RODICK — Maria Amelia Rodick[76]

Maria Amelia Rodick, née Witts (1769-1830), was the daughter of Broome Witts (1738-1769) and Elizabeth London (1738-1837). She was baptised at the presbyterian chapel in Carter Lane, Blackfriars, London. Her brothers were Broome Phillips (1767-1848) and Edward London (1768-1841), and she was a second cousin to Francis Witts, her grandfather Edward being elder brother to Francis's grandfather, Broome.

Maria married, at St Mildred's, Bread Street, London, 22 January 1795, Archibald Rodick (1772-1859), second son of Archibald Rodick of Wellingbrough, Northamptonshire; they had 7 sons:

1 Edward (b. & d. 1795)
2 Edward London (1797-1864); married, at St Mark's, Kennington, Surrey, 31 January 1838, his cousin Jane Morton (1818-1915); at least 5 sons and 10 daughters:
  1 Maria (b. 1841)
  2 Jane (b. 1844)
  3 Anne (1845-1934); died unmarried at West Ashford, Kent
  4 Sophia Jessy (1848-1931)
  1 John R. J. (b. ±1846)
  5 Amelia Maria Augustine (1847-1859); died a child
  6 Sophia Jane (1848-1931); died unmarried at West Ashford, Kent
  2 Julius C. F. Augustine (b. ±1849)
  7 Ellen (b. 1850-1917); died unmarried at West Ashford, Kent
  8 Agnes (1852-1915)
  3 Archibald Edward (1853-1934)
  4 Edward (b. 1855)
  9 Laura (1857-1888); died unmarried
  10 Emily (1860-1881); died unmarried at Thanet, Kent
  5 Frank (1863-1948)
3 Henry (1798-1872); born deaf; died unmarried
4 James (1801-1838); died at Halstead, Essex
5 George (b. & d. 1802)
6 George (1804-1852); died at Lambeth; buried at Norwood cemetery, Norwood Road, Lambeth
7 Septimus (1809-1886)

Archibald Rodick appears to have commenced his career with the East India Company as a clerk. Later he was a banker in Wellingborough, Northamptonshire, in partnership with Archibald Morton, Charles Morton, and his own son, Edward London Rodick. The bank went through a difficult time in 1822 and finally went under during the banking crisis of 1825, when all the partners went bankrupt. The two sons of the family, Edward and Henry, were taken into their uncle Broome Phillips Witts's silk business. Maria died in 1830 and Archibald eventually lodged with his son Henry at the Silk Mill, Pebworth, Essex. Henry appears to have remained unmarried. Edward London married, 1838, Jane Morton (1818-1915), showing that the connections between the Rodick and Morton families remained close. Jane was more than twenty years Edward's junior. They had a large family of at least fifteen children.

Jane, at the time of 1911 census, was living at 100 Newlands Park, Sydneham, as a widow on independent means. Living with her there were four of her children: Anne, Sophia, Ellen, and Frank — all unmarried.

1801: 21 Jul: *Came in a coach with my Father & Mother, to spend some time with Mrs. Witts at Champion Hill near Camberwell Surry. We found there Edward & her Daughter Mrs. Rodick with one Boy.*

1802: 3 Feb.

1827: 17 Nov: *After dinner, the will was produced and read over by Mr. B.P. Witts ... £1000 thereof to Mr. Witts of Brunswick Square; the same to Mr. E L Witts; the same to Mrs. Rodick, their Sister, for life, and to her children after her decease. Mr. Rodick, the Husband, is precluded from any interest in this bequest, he being a bankrupt, and his affairs in the hands of assignees. He was a banker at Wellingborough, and failed during the panic for a very large amount: not chargeable, I believe, with any dishonest proceedings, but having been guilty of great indiscretion, in placing unlimited confidence in a connexion, to whom he entrusted for speculation very large funds, principally, of course, arising from the deposits made by his customers; Mr. & Mrs. Rodick have a large family, Sons, and now grown up; two of them, I think, are in partnership with Mr. B.P. Witts, and are very respectable young men.*

1830: 28 Feb: *A letter from my cousin Miss Witts, now staying with her sister in London, announces to me by the desire of Mr. Witts of Brunswick Square, the awfully sudden & unexpected death of his sister, Mrs. Rodick.... Some weeks ago, she had experienced a spasmodic attack in the chest, which was called Asthmatic; she consequently confined herself to the house, being somewhat indisposed, but was considered quite convalescent, when she came with Mr. Rodick to Town, who was summoned on his own bankruptcy business. It is now ascertained, that the poor woman laboured under an incurable disease of the heart, which was likely to terminate thus instantaneously in death. She has left five sons, young men of estimable characters, whose conduct has been such as never to cause their parents any distress, but who have acted in the most becoming and dutiful manner during their afflictions of their parents.* 23 Jun: *Pursuing the line of Fleet Street, Ludgate Hill & St. Paul's Church Yard, we stopped in Cheapside at the corner of Friday Street, that I might call at the Counting House of my relative Mr. Witts, who, I found, had left London this very day for Cheltenham on a short excursion to recruit his health, & for a little recreation: there I met one of his nephews & partners in his silk-trade, Mr. Rodick, whom I have always heard mentioned as an estimable person; he is unfortunately so deaf as to require the aid of a trumpet.* 25 Jun: *To dinner at Mrs. Witts's, Brunswick*

Square—a party Messrs. Bailey, Hibbert, Bassevi, Jones, Misses Witts and Whitehouse (then afterwards a Capt. Orange, Messrs. Rodicks × 3).

1832: 14 Jun.

1835: 24 Mar., 11 Jun.

RODWELL — John Rodwell[77]

John Rodwell (±1780-1852), bookseller, was born at Great Thornham, Suffolk, the son of Thomas and Bridget Rodwell. He was in partnership with John Martin and traded as Rodwell & Martin, booksellers and publishers, of 46 New Bond Street and 40 Argyll Street, London. Upham and Beet took over the bookselling business. John Rodwell lived above the shop at New Bond Street with his wife, Henrietta (b. ±1780), and two daughters, Frances and Henrietta, both born in around 1815.

1832: 28 Sep: *Wrote to Mr. Rodwell for a supply of books for the Stow Book Society.*

1833: 28 Oct., 4 Nov.

1834: 24 Jul., 21 Sep., 1 Oct., 11 Oct., 24 Oct., 26 Nov., 2 Dec., 22 Dec.

1835: 2 Jan., 23 Jan., 6 Feb., 1 May.

1836: 29 Jul., 28 Sep., 4 Nov., 14 Nov., 9 Dec. 19 Dec.

1837: 10 Jan., 13 Feb., 3 Mar., 10 Mar., 15 Apr., 8 May, 19 May, 17 Jun., 21 Jul., 27 Sep., 11 Oct., 24 Nov., 18 Dec., 29 Dec.

1838: 26 Jan., 2 Feb., 17 Feb., 6 Apr., 18 Apr., 8 May, 12 May, 18 May, 16 Jun., 17 Aug., 26 Sep., 5 Oct., 5 Nov., 9 Nov., 16 Nov., 16 Nov., 24 Nov., 1 Dec., 10 Dec., 24 Dec., 28 Dec.

1839: 1 Feb., 12 Feb., 22 Mar., 20 May, 28 Jun., 6 Jul., 12 Jul.

1840: 20 Mar., 27 Mar., 27 Jun., 22 Jul., 24 Jul., 29 Sep., 13 Nov., 28 Nov.

1842: 15 Jan., 21 Jan., 28 Jan., 11 Feb., 1 Apr., 8 Apr., 22 Apr., 3 May, 6 May, 27 Jul., 28 Sep., 14 Oct., 25 Oct., 3 Nov., 23 Dec.

1843: 20 Jan., 3 Feb., 10 Feb., 17 Feb., 13 Oct., 30 Oct., 10 Nov., 24 Nov., 8 Dec.

1844: 22 Jan., 2 Feb., 9 Feb., 15 Mar., 22 Mar., 20 Apr., 4 May, 24 Jul., 2 Aug., 6 Aug., 27 Sep., 5 Oct., 8 Nov., 15 Nov., 26 Nov., 13 Dec.

1845: 10 Jan., 17 Jan., 28 Jan., 31 Jan., 21 Feb.

1846: 27 Jun., 30 Sep., 9 Oct., 26 Oct., 6 Nov., 26 Dec.

1847: 22 Jan., 5 Feb., 12 Feb., 8 Mar., 19 Mar., 26 Mar., 30 May, 26 Jun., 10 Jul., 16 Jul., 23 Aug., 4 Oct., 26 Oct., 19 Nov., 10 Dec.

1848: 14 Jan., 27 Jan., 25 Feb., 7 Mar., 26 Mar., 4 May, 21 Aug., 1 Sep., 27-28 Sep., 13 Oct., 3 Nov.

1850: 30 Jan., 12 Mar., 21 Mar., 28 Mar., 3 May, 20 Jul., 25 Jul., 24 Aug., 28 Aug., 2 Oct., 12 Oct., 9 Nov., 18 Nov., 22 Nov., 3 Dec.

1851: 3 Jan., 10 Jan., 21 Jan., 7 Feb., 11 Apr., 25 Apr., 14 May.

1852: 17 Jan., 13 Feb., 15 Feb., 14 Mar., 22 Apr., 22 Oct: *A circular from Messrs. Upham and Beet. Booksellers, Bond Street, Successors to Mr. Rodwell, deceased, intimating that they have entered on his business, and asking to be continued in the supplying of books for the Stow Book Society.*

ROFF — Moses Roff[78]

Moses Roff (1817-1860), tailor, was the son of Thomas Roff (±1784-1868) and Mary Brindle. His parents were Baptists of Bourton-on-the-Water. Moses married Sarah Green (1819-1895), and they had at least 1 son:

1 William Barnard (1846-1907)

Moses was admitted to the county asylum on 10 January 1848.

1846: 14 Jul: *... from the R.O. Gloucester Union, acknowledging my remittance of £5.10.6 in payment of the bill for the maintenance of Mr. Roff at the Lunatic Asylum.* 31 Aug: *Wrote to Dr. Hitch for a report of the state of Moses Roff, a patient in the Gloucester Lunatic Asylum.* 3 Sep., 27 Oct: *Walked to Bourton on the Water, to hand to Roff the account due for his son's maintenance &c. in the Gloucester Lunatic Asylum; saw his wife and daughter.* 5 Nov.

1847: 16 Jan., 10 Apr., 13 Apr: *... from Mr. Illes, Fairford Lunatic Asylum, that they would receive M. Roff at 12/- per week;—from Dr. Williams, Superintendent Gloucester Lunatic Asylum, that my letter to him respecting M.R. would be laid before the Committee of Visitors yesterday; and that I should hear further on the subject.* 14 Apr: *Walked to Bourton on Water; conferred with Mr. Wilkins, Mr. Wells, and Thomas Roff, as to the conveyance of Moses Roff to the private house at Fairford for the reception of insane persons, to which it seems most convenient that he should be taken.* 20 Aug., 27-28 Aug., 22 Sep.

1848: 8 Jan., 14 Feb., 16 Feb., 20 Sep: *... the principal case being an order of removal from Bourton on the Water to Long Compton of the wife and child of Moses Roff. A former order regarding the same parties had been quashed by consent in consequence of some technical errors, or informalities in its wording. An order of maintenance in the Lunatic Asylum at Gloucester, saddling the parish of Long Compton with the charges, was made yesterday.*

ROFF — Robert Roff[79]

Robert Roff (1800-1862), smallholder farmer, was born at Stow-on-the-Wold, the son of Robert Roffe (1768-1848) and Elizabeth Mullis (1770-1805). Roff farmed 9 acres at Lower Swell. He married, at Barcheston, Warwickshire, 27 March 1820, Anna Penson (1799-1862); they had 5 sons and 4 daughters:

1 Lucy Penson (1822-1866)
1 Samuel Drury (1824-1894)
2 Thomas (1825-1907)
3 Henry (b. 1828)
4 Josiah (1831-1916)
2 Mary (b. 1833)
3 Sarah Anna (1835-1891)
4 Martha (1838-1919)
5 Charles Gersham (1840-1917)

1852: 24 May: *A long interview with Mr. Cridland, the Surveyor of taxes for this district, as to charges of immoral and dissolute conduct, amounting in fact to assaulting with intent to commit a rape a daughter of one Roff of Lower Swell & Stow, a tradesman at the latter place, and chief, as preacher of a sect of Antinomian Dissenters.*

ROFF — Thomas Roff[80]

Thomas Roff (±1784-1868), annuitant, but probably a tailor before retirement, was born at Clapton-on-the-Hill. He married, at Bourton-on-the-Water, 26 July 1810, Mary Brindle (b. ±1782); they had at least 4 sons and 1 daughter:

1 Moses (1817-1860); *see above*
1 Sarah (1819-1853)
2 Henry (b. 1822)
3 William (b. & d. 1823)
4 Stephen (b. & d. 1828)

By 1851 Thomas was a widower living with his unmarried daughter, Sarah.

1834: 30 Sep.

1839: 2 May.

1846: 7 Jul: *Transacted parish business there with Mr. Wilkins: also with Roff, and J. Lardner.* 27 Oct.

1847: 20 Aug: *Wrote to Mr. Illes, Lunatic Retreat, Fairford on behalf of Roff, of Bourton, who called on me for advice as to his son, a patient in confinement there, and the future arrangements necessary in the event of the fund being exhausted which is now applied to the poor man's maintenance.* 27 Aug., 28 Aug: *T. Roff from Bourton came, with whom conferred as to the state of his lunatic son, the demand of support made on the father by the son's wife, the necessity that the parties should have recourse to parochial relief, and the manner in which their claim to relief ought to be substantiated.*

1854: 4 Aug.

ROGERS — Captain Rogers at Cheltenham

1802: 27 Aug: *Drank tea at Mr. Nevilles, meeting Miss Markham, Dr. Sanders, Mr. Cruickshanks, Captn. Rogers.*

ROGERS — Mrs Rogers, widow, of Upper Slaughter

Mrs Rogers does not appear on census records for either Eyford or Upper Slaughter.

1849: 14 Dec: *Visited other sick parishioners——Mrs. Rogers.* 18 Dec., 24 Dec., 28 Dec.

1850: 14 Jan: *Visited and prayed with Mrs. Rogers, who seems to continue in the same state.* 22 Jan., 25 Jan., 5 Feb., 13 Feb., 2 Mar., 22 Mar: *Visited Mrs. Rogers, who still lingers, and is bed-ridden; prayed by her.* 29 Apr., 3 Jun., 18 Jun., 13 Jul: *Visited Mrs. Rogers, still lingering in grievous infirmity of body, and prayed with her.* 22 Jul., 5 Aug., 7 Sep., 21 Oct., 5 Nov., 25 Nov., 25 Nov., 2 Dec., 23 Dec: *Visited Mrs. Rogers, whose state of health seems to be improved.*

1851: 11 Feb., 14 Feb., 21 Mar., 9 Apr., 19 Apr.

1852: 6 Mar.

ROGERS — George Rogers [81]

George Rogers (1771-1836), Church of England clergyman, was born at Leek, Staffordshire, the son of John Rogers and his wife, Hannah. He was educated at Christ Church, Oxford (BA 1793; MA 1796), and was appointed vicar of Market Lavington, Wiltshire, in 1805. He married, 1806, Harriet Bourdieu, fourth daughter of James Bourdieu of Combe, near Croydon, Surrey; they had at least 1 son and 1 daughter:

1 Harriet Bourdieu (1808-1838); died unmarried
1 George Bourdieu (1810-1872)

1807: 7 Aug: *Visitation at Lavington found Archb. Danberry with many Clergymen, Messrs. Key, Spencer, Smith, Prince, Jones, Basset, Richards, Dr. Skinner, Williams, Rogers &c. &c.* 14 Aug: *Called & left my card for the Revd. Mr. Rogers at Lavington.* 18 Aug: *Mr. Rogers the Vicar of Lavington made a long morning visit.* 25 Aug., 12 Dec.

1808: 14 Jan., 17 Mar., 15 Apr.

ROGERS — George Henvill Rogers [82]

George Henvill Rogers (1770-1847), Church of England clergyman, was born at Iwerne Courtney, Dorset, the son of Revd Richard Colmer Rogers and Elizabeth Henville. He was educated at Wadham College, Oxford (BA 1791; MA 1796), where he was a fellow until 1813 and chaplain from 1813 to his death in 1847. He was also vicar of Southrop, 1812-47, and appears to have died unmarried.

1802: 16 Feb: *At Mr. Rogers Lecture in Xenophon's Anabasis.* 18 Feb.

1829: 26 Feb: *I sat by the sub-warden, ... opposite to me was Mr. Rogers, now Chaplain of the College, and in my day, the Junior Tutor; he succeeded to a College living, Sotherop in Gloucestershire, but pleads his Chaplaincy as an excuse for non-residence. In fact the responsibility of parochial duty would be overpowering to a mind like his, and to live out of college, excepting in the long vacation rambles, would be a misery to him.*

1832: 15 Mar.

ROGERS — John Rogers — *see also* Joseph Jennings [83]

John Rogers (1768-1840), of Upper Footing, Surrey, was the son of John Rogers (1729-1796), of Sun Court, Cornhill, and Mary Neal. He married, 1798, Elizabeth Wellford (d 1845); they had at least 1 son:

1 John (1807-1872); married, at Holy Trinity, Clapham, Surrey, 31 January 1833, Harriet Thornton (1812-1891); 5 sons and 5 daughters:
  1 John Thornton (1834-1900)
  2 Reginald Wellford (1835-1910), vicar of Cookham, Berkshire; married, 1871, Emelia Sophia Thornton
  1 Gertrude Elizabeth (1837-1917)
  3 Henry Middleton (1840-1915); joined the Bengal Civil Service; married, 1880, Rose Janet Fell
  2 Mary Selina (1841-1911)
  4 Arthur Parry (1843-1907), officer, 68th Foot; became a JP of Devon; married, 1868, Florence Maria Unwin
  3 Margaret Alice (1844-1924)
  5 Walter Francis (1846-1895); married Louisa Curteis
  4 Clara Louisa (1848-1849)
  5 Harriet June (1854-1935)

John Rogers (junior) was a Berkshire JP and was elected a fellow of the Royal Society. He married, 1833, Harriet Thornton. His father, John Rogers (senior), was the elder brother of Rebecca Rogers (1777-1860), who married London draper David Jennings (1753-1819), father of the architect Joseph Jennings (1806-1889), who acted as an agent for Francis Witts. The connection between John Rogers and Broome Witts is not known, but it was probably a business connection which turned into a close friendship.

1801: 21 Sep: *Mrs. Pages, Mr. Rogers, all very agreeable & a Mr. Lindsay dined with Mrs. Witts.* 22 Sep: *Came up to town in Mrs. Witts's carriage, with my cousins & Mr. Rogers.*

1805: 2 Aug: *Uncle Witts's beautiful little place the Retreat: upon the Banks of the Thames; facing the Cliefden Woods: found Mr. & Mrs. Rogers upon a visit to my Uncle & Aunt; the Lady very agreeable.*

1825: 3 Jul: *Besides this, there is an unfortunate coolness between the Vicar of the latter parish and my Uncle; Mr. Whately has been always on terms of civility with him till a short time ago, when he took an unreasonable offence, in consequence of my uncle's friend, Mr. Rogers, purchasing an estate in the parish with the Advowson.*

1827: 14 Nov: *He mentions that his brother Mr. Witts, of Brunswick Square, an eminent silk manufacturer, & Mr. Rogers, of Streatham, an opulent man, who is retired, I believe, from trade as an underwriter, and who married a sister of George Wellford, are the Executors.* 17 Nov.

1832: 13 Jun: *We had much sensible and agreeable conversation after dinner, and in the evening our party was increased by the arrival from Town of Mr. Rogers, Wellford's excellent brother-in-law, in readiness to attend the funeral of my deceased Aunt.* 14 Jun.

1837: 2 May: *Wrote to Mr. Rogers to apologise for not having before sent to him and Mrs. R. a copy of the lithograph of Lady L. and to request their acceptance of one which I propose forwarding to Mr. Jennings to be conveyed by him to his Uncle.* 3 May, 26 May.

1840: 25 Mar: *A letter from the Secretary of the Union Life Assurance Office ... Mr. Rogers being Chairman of the Directors, and B. P. Witts, one of the Board, accounts for this private application being made to me.*

ROGERS — Samuel Rogers [84]

Samuel Rogers (±1781-1852), Church of England clergyman, was born in London, the son of Samuel and Dorothy Rogers. He was baptised at St George the Martyr, Queen Square, Camden, Middlesex, and was educated at Wadham College, Oxford (BA & MA 1804), and Lincoln's Inn (1802). He was rector of Orton Longeville, Huntingdonshire.

1804: 3 Feb.

1806: 19 Mar., 22 Mar.

ROGERS — William Rogers and the Rogers family of Stow-on-the-Wold [85]

William Rogers (1770-1860), tailor, was born at Little Rissington, Gloucestershire, the son of Bennett Rogers (b. 1745) and Martha Wilks (b. 1748). He lived at 53 Market Place, Stow-on-the-Wold, with his wife Jane (±1767-1848); they had at least 1 son and 3 daughters:

- 1 Henry (1794-1856), tailor; traded from 74 Market Place, Stow; married Elizabeth Smith (1804-1878), born at Burford, Oxfordshire; at least 2 sons and 2 daughters:
  - 1 Henry (1823-1900); married Caroline (b. ±1823), born at Stow; he was a widower by 1891
  - 2 Frederick (±1826-1870)
  - 1 Selina (±1826-1905); married, 1878, John Hatch (1814-1889)
  - 2 Louisa A. (1844-1921); married, 1864, Thomas Wood (1839-1913)
- 1 Elizabeth (b. 1809)
- 2 Amelia (b. ±1810)
- 3 Martha (±1810-1842)

1834: 18 Jul: *A close and anxious enquiry as to the statements made by W. Rogers to John Hide on May 29. Rogers suppressed the truth, equivocated and shewed callous indifference... evidence of his daughter, Martha, who detailed some facts of a very suspicious description, implicating her Father, and proving that the conversation held by him with Hide was deeply impressed on his mind, though he swore to us that it had entirely passed off his memory. Committed Rogers on suspicion of being accessory to the murder for re-examination on Monday next, when we shall resume the enquiry, and continue the examination of other witnesses ...* 21 Jul., 23 Jul: *Took the evidence of Elizabeth Rogers and her mother, who came to make further disclosures and explanations as to the murder of poor Rens.* 24 Jul: *... took the farther deposition of Martha Rogers in pursuance of the enquiry as to the murderers of Mr. Rens.*

1835: 13 Apr: *And now came on the trial of Edmund Jeffrey... M. Rogers, who saw him go out on his last walk.*

ROLLIN — Alexandre Auguste Ledru-Rollin [86]

Alexandre Auguste Ledru-Rollin (1807-1874), lawyer and politician, entered politics when he was elected deputy for Le Mans in 1841. The violence of his electoral speeches led to his trial at Angers and sentencing to four months' imprisonment. He was also fined but appealed successfully on a technical point. His speeches at working-men's banquets in Lille, Dijon, and Chalons heralded the revolution of 1848. In 1849 Rollin escaped to London where he joined the executive of the revolutionary committee of Europe, with Lajos Kossuth and Giuseppe Mazzini among his colleagues. In 1857 he was accused of complicity in an obscure attempt against the life of Napoleon III of France, and condemned in his absence to deportation. Under Louis Philippe he made large contributions to French jurisprudence, editing the *Journal du palais*, 1791-1837.

1848: 19 May: *France has just passed through, or is passing through, the horrors of the second revolution within the short space of three months ... the same parties as before, with a few exceptions, and especially Lamartine and Ledra Rollin, have been nominated to carry on the public service.* 29 Jun.

ROLLINSON — Mary Rollinson of Chadlington — *see also* Dolphin, Hippisley, *and* Rawlinson [87]

Lock Rollinson (±1745-1788), landed proprietor, of East End, Chadlington, Oxfordshire, was a close friend of Edward Witts, Francis's father. Back in the 1770s, when they were both single and young, Lock and Edward travelled together, touring Ireland in 1770-71 and France in 1774. After that date there are no further references to Lock Rollinson in the Witts family papers. Lock's sister, Martha (d. 1780), married Ferdinand Tracy Travell and was the mother of Martha Travell/Buxton/Whalley and Jane Travell/Naper/Rycroft.

Lock married Mary Jones (d. 1795), of East Farleigh, Kent; they had 1 son and 3 daughters:

- 1 Mary (1779-1858); died unmarried; *see below*
- 1 James Lock (1780-1802)
- 2 Martha (1782-1864); married John Dolphin of Lower Slaughter (*see* Dolphin)
- 3 Ann (1783-1855); married Henry Hippisley of Lambourn (*see* Hippisley)

Mary Rollinson (1779-1858), the eldest child, features frequently in the diaries. She lived at 18 Bennett Street, Bath, and was a regular visitor to her family and connections in Gloucestershire. Her sister, Martha Dolphin, was with her at Bath at the time of the 1851 census, and it seems quite possible that Martha stayed there on regular occasions. Following their brother James Lock Rollinson's early death in 1802, the three sisters inherited the Chadlington Manor estate, making them relatively wealthy. When Mary died unmarried in 1858 she left just under £35,000—a considerable sum.

Mary frequently visited the Wallers, of Farmington, but it is not clear why this friendship or attachment should have been so strong. Robert Waller was the son of Maria Dolphin, sister to Mary Rollinson's brother-in-law John Dolphin, but this seems a somewhat distant link. There may well have been other ties to the Waller family which are not immediately apparent. There was also a connection with the Pole family, but the details are unclear.

The Mr Rawlinson mentioned by Francis Witts in November 1801 was probably Abram Tyzack Rawlinson (*see above*). Rawlinson's father changed his name from Rollinson to Rawlinson, and appears to have inherited the Charlbury/Chadlington estate. Abram was therefore a cousin to Mary. The connection between the Rawlinson and Rollinson families was mentioned in a deed of 10 June 1806, by which the three sisters acquired the assets from the Chadlington estate.

1801: 10 Nov: *Mr. Fowkes & Mr. Rollinson from Gloucester Captain of the Oxford Militia dined with us.* 11 Nov: *Mr. Rawlinson dined with us & repaired with us in the Evening to Mrs. Hughes, where I enjoyed a most pleasant evening supping there.* 12 Nov: *Called upon the Granvilles. Mr. Delabere, Miss Hughes, & Mrs. Brown called in |46 the morning, as also Captn. Rawlinson.* 16 Nov: *At Gloucester we stopt at the King's Head, where we met Captn. Rollinson & Miss Rooke, the latter of whom conducted my Mother to visit Miss Delabere.*

1827: 28 Aug: *We drove to Farmington, and called at the elder Mr. Waller's, where we had the pleasure of seeing our old and good friend, Miss Rollinson, looking very well. She accompanied her brother in law, Mr. J. Dolphin into Gloucestershire, he being come to visit his two nephews at Farmington and Eyford.* 29 Aug. 7 Sep: *Our friend Miss Rollinson came from Farmington to pass two or three days with us. The Poles from Wick Hill came to meet here; at least Mrs. Pole & her son Mr. Watson Pole.* 10 Sep: *Miss Rollinson left us to pass a day or two with the Dolphins at Eyford. She is an upright, cheerful, friendly, sensible woman; warmly attached to her sisters and their numerous children, and with ample means to benefit them; but more especially devoted to the Dolphins of Copford, with whom she resides.*

1828: 2 Nov: *John Dolphin, who with his aunt, Miss Rollinson, arrived at Eyford yesterday from Moccas.* 2 Nov: *In the Evening my wife and myself dined at Farmington Lodge, at the Wallers. We met the Fords, Mrs. Boudier, Sir Frederick Johnstone, a pleasing young man, who on attaining his majority will come into possession of a very large property, Mr. Dutton, Mrs. Waller & her two daughters, Miss Rollinson & Mr. J. Dolphin Junr. We were very glad to meet Miss R. and her nephew.* 5 Nov: *We dined at Eyford. The Dolphins have a large party in their house; Mrs. & three Miss Knights, Mrs. Payne, Miss Rollinson and her nephew.*

1832: 17 May: *We dined to-day with Mrs. Waller at Farmington to meet Mr. & Mrs. John Shirley. This most pleasing and amiable bride, lovely and simply engaging, is the elder of the two daughters of my deceased friend and neighbour, the Revd. John Dolphin... The Revd. Mr. Shirley's sister married Lord Suffield... This connection of the two parties by relationship and friendship with Lord Suffield has led to the intermarriage of Mr. Shirley and Catherine Dolphin, who are now making a tour of visits to their friends, ... with the Hippisleys, at Bath with Miss Rollinson.*

1834: 16 Aug., 18 Aug., 20 Sep.

1835: 1 Apr: *A letter awaited me from Miss Rollinson to announce the decease of my amiable cousin, Miss Buxton.*

1837: 17 Nov: *Our old friend Miss Rollinson came from Farmington Lodge, but returned at night.*

1838: 18 Oct., 20 Oct.

1839: 16 Apr: *Called on Miss Rollinson, 18 Bennet Street, and passed half an hour agreeably: meeting her nephew, Mr. H. Hippisley, on a visit to her with his bride, a pleasing young person, daughter of a Berkshire clergyman, by name Nelson.* 18 Apr., 24 Jun.

1840: 2 Oct., 7 Oct: *Received a party at dinner—Miss Rollinson, who arrived to stay two days with us from Farmington Lodge.* 8-9 Oct.

1842: 8 Jul., 12 Jul: *Drove MW. to Stow; called at the Rectory on the Hippisleys and Miss Rollinson, now on a short visit to them, whom we saw.*

1847: 11 Jun., 30 Aug: *MW. received a letter from our friend Miss Rollinson.* 16 Sep: *Miss Rollinson was on a visit to the Poles, having arrived on Tuesday last from Farmington Lodge; she promises to come to us on a visit on Monday next.* 20-24 Sep., 25 Sep: *After luncheon our good friend, Miss Rollinson left us to visit R W Hippisley at the Rectory Stow: I believe we had mutually enjoyed each others Society; Miss R. is a little prejudiced; but well principled, sensible, & well informed.* 26 Sep., 28 Sep.

ROLLS — Henry Rolls [88]

Henry Rolls (1782-1838), Church of England clergyman, was the third son of Henry Rolls of Southam, Warwickshire. He was educated at Christ's College, Cambridge (BA 1816), and Balliol College, Oxford (MA 1819). He was curate of Boxworth, Cambridgeshire, 1813-16; rector of Barnwell St Andrew, Northamptonshire, 1818-29; rector of Barnwell All Saints', 1819-20; and rector of Aldwincle All Saints', 1820-38. Rolls married secondly, 1838, Sarah Anne. He died in Paris.

1835: 25 Mar: *Besides George Hunt, Thomas Hunt, and myself, who attended as Mourners, four gentlemen of the neighbourhood had been invited. Mr. Yorke of Thrapstone...Mr. Isham from Polebrooke... also the Revd. Mr. Rolls, an agreeable and kind hearted Clergyman, the incumbent of the adjoining parish of Aldwinkle.* 29 Mar: *Returned to Wadenhoe to attend the afternoon Service at the Church there, accompanying the three Misses Hunt. The service was well performed and a good sermon preached by Mr. Rolls, who with his daughter called at Wadenhoe house afterwards.*

1838: 30 Aug: *It is that of Aldwinkle the adjoining parish to Wadenhoe, the late incumbent of which, Mr. Rolls, died lately abroad.*

ROOKE — Miss Rooke at Cheltenham

1801: 30 Oct., 31 Oct: *Mrs. Shakerly Miss Rooke, & Miss Tucker drank tea with my Aunts.* 14 Nov., 20 Nov., 26 Nov.

ROOKE — Charles Rooke — *see also* Dawson [89]

Charles Rooke (1746-1827), army officer, was born at West Drayton, Middlesex, the son of Capt. Brudenell Rice Rooke (1692-1776) and Anne Millington (1703-1771). His brother, Sir Henry Willoughby Rooke (1782-1869), was present at the battle of Waterloo, and later became a general. Charles was a lieutenant-colonel in the 3rd Regiment of Guards at the end of the American Revolutionary War, and might have retired from service had it not been for the breaking out of hostilities with France in 1794. Thirty regiments of fencible light dragoons were raised; Rooke was selected to command the Windsor Foresters, levied in the neighbourhood of Windsor. He received his commission as full colonel on 1 May 1794, the same day that his friend, Sir Nathaniel Dukinfield, of Stanlake Lodge, Berkshire, received his as lieutenant-colonel. Both men had been recommended by the earl of Radnor, lord lieutenant of Berkshire, and their commissions had been signed by the king.

The Royal Windsor Foresters, a regiment of fencible cavalry, consisted of six troops. It was posted to Scotland during the invasion scare of 1797 and was disbanded in 1799/1800. While in Scotland Charles Rooke and his family became close friends with Edward and Agnes Witts; there are many references to the family in the diaries of Agnes Witts. Another mutual friendship was with Sir Nathaniel Dukinfield. It appears that Charles was also on good terms with King George III; this friendship may have attributed to the formation and name of the Royal Windsor Foresters. Charles was later allowed to reside in the 'Stone Tower' at Windsor Castle, where he died 1827.

Charles Rooke married, at Giggleswick, Yorkshire, 17 October 1776, Elizabeth, daughter of Ambrose Dawson; they had 2 sons and 3 daughters:

1 Elizabeth Dinah (b. 1777)
2 Jane Elizabeth (b. & d. 1779)
1 John Charles (1781-1813), Lt-Col; served in Egypt and Portugal; died of wounds at San Jean de Luz
2 Henry Willoughby (1782-1869), Maj.-Gen.; appointed CB and KCH; married, at St John's, Camden, Hampstead, Middlesex, 12 May 1803, his cousin Selina Mary (1772-1859), daughter of Maj. Henry Rooke (1742-1821); 3 sons and 2 daughters:
  1 George Charles (1805-1840)
  1 Jane (1807-1836)
  2 Willoughby John Edward (1810-1902)
  3 William Frederick (1813-1845)
  2 Caroline Elizabeth (1818-1881)
3 Mary Hannah (1786-1870)

1801: 6 Jul: *At Standlake we found Mr. & Mrs. & two Miss Rookes visitors; Mr. White formerly surgeon in the Windsor Foresters had dined there. Standlake is an old brick house, apparently very commodious.* 7 Jul: *walked with Col. Rooke, my Father & Lloyd Dukinfield until overtaken by the rain.* 8 Jul., 10 Jul: *Mr. and Mrs. Rooke &c. left us this morning for Oxford.*

1833: 9 Nov: *Dunbar, though it was so dark, that I could only distinguish its long street, brought to my mind vivid recollections of my boyhood. We passed several weeks here one summer during the vacation. My Father and Mother were attracted to the place, partly by the convenience it afforded for sea bathing, but more by the circumstance, that three or four English regiments of Fencible Cavalry were encamped in its vicinity, and among them the Windsor Foresters, with the Colonel & Lieutenant Colonel of which Corps, Col. Rooke and Sir Nathaniel Dukinfield, and their ladies, my parents were intimately acquainted.*

ROOKE — Frederick William Rooke and the Rooke family of Bath and Lackham — *see also* Ford [90]

Frederick William Rooke (1782-1855), naval officer, was born at Stanhoe, Norfolk, the son of George Rooke (1756-1807) and Mary Marriot (1760-1821). He entered the Royal Naval Academy in 1796, and embarked, on 1 March 1797, as midshipman on board the 74-gun *Cumberland*, lying at Portsmouth. In the following July Rooke removed to the *Sirius* (36 guns), stationed in the North Sea, and from February 1798 to March 1799 he was in the *Ramillion* (74 guns). He then returned to the *Sirius* for two years, and was present at the capture of the frigate *Dédaigneuse*. A fourteen-month posting in the *Boaddicea* (38 guns) was then followed by a posting to the *Clyde* (38 guns) in July 1803. In the *Clyde* he served in the Baltic and the North Sea until December, when he became acting lieutenant of the *Ariadne* (24 guns), off Havre de Grace. In January 1805 he was nominated sub-lieutenant of the *Attentive* gun-brig in the West Indies, and was confirmed a lieutenant in November 1805. On 12 December he was appointed to the *Achille* (74 guns), attached to the Channel fleet. On 10 October 1805 Rooke received charge of the signal-station at Swanage, and held the posting for six months. In July 1807 he was again appointed to the *Achille*, employed first in the Channel, then off the coast of Spain, and then at the siege of Flushing, where he served on shore. Having contracted Walcheren fever, he convalesced for 10 months until 3 August 1810, when he was appointed to the *San Juan* (74 guns), bearing the broad pendant of Cdre C. V. Penrose at Gibraltar. While officially attached to the *San Juan*, Rooke served in the flotilla and was in frequent action with the enemy during the siege of Cadiz. He also commanded a division of gun-boats in the defence of Tarifa. For these services he was advanced to the rank of commander on 21 March 1812. After this, Rooke was given no further postings, but he accepted the rank of retired captain on 25 March 1845.

Frederick Rooke married, first, at Walcot, Bath, Somerset, 4 May 1813, Anne (1793-1829), daughter of Robert Wallace and Elizabeth Scott; they had 9 sons and 3 daughters:
1 William Wallace (b. & d. 1814)
1 Emily Anne (1814-1893); married, at Rampisham, Dorset, 9 May 1843, Revd John Paley (b. 1816)
2 William Wallace (1816-1864); married, at Lacock, Wiltshire, 15 September 1842, Julia Rooke Humphreys (1811-1896)
3 Frederick John (1817-1894), Church of England clergyman; married, at Walcot St Swithin, Bath, Somerset, 21 February 1843, Jane Elizabeth Marcon (1819-1857)
2 Eliza Sophia (1818-1874); married, at Lacock, Wiltshire, 12 September 1844, Thomas Abdy Fellowes (1821-1895)
3 Maria Georginia (1820-1892); became a nun; died unmarried
4 Alexander Beaumont (1821-1914); married, at Hardenhuish, Wiltshire, 3 September 1844, a cousin, Ellen Clutterbuck Rooke (1820-1892)
5 Francis (1823-1852)
6 Seton Paterson (1824-1901); became a Roman Catholic priest
7 Alfred (b. & d. 1826)
8 Octavius Cobb (1827-1881) Capt.; married August Harriet Pyrke (1835-1891)
9 Frederick William (1829-1866)

Anne died in 1829 following the birth of Frederick. Rooke married, secondly, 1833, Harriett Hyde.

1827: 5 Oct: *I dined at the worthy curate's of Great Risington, where the accustomed hospitality prevailed. The party consisted of Mr. Ford, and his brother-in-law, Capt. Rooke, of the Navy.*

1828: 9 Aug: *We went to dine at Little Risington at Mr. Ford's, meeting a large family party: Mr. & Mrs. Boudier from Farmington, accompanied by Mrs. E. Rooke, a smart old lady from Bath, Mrs. Ford's Aunt, two maiden sisters of Mrs. Ford's, Miss Rookes, and in the evening, Mrs. Ford's infirm & aged uncle Rooke, who resides with the Fords, a rich old bachelor, & martyr to the gout.*

1836: 16 Aug: ... *Capt. Rooke, and his lady, a very agreeable woman.*

1837: 14 Aug., 14 Aug.

1838: 10 Aug., 13 Aug.

1839: 4 Sep: *Two of these have been erected by one of the Misses Rooke, sisters of our neighbour Mrs. Ford, and with whom we are acquainted.*

1840: 8 Jul: *From thence to call on the Fords, where we were received by Mr. & Mrs. F. two daughters, Sophia & Dulcibella, and niece, Emily Rooke.*

1843: 14 Oct: *Mrs. P. we had known as Miss Rooke, daughter of Captn. Rooke of Lackham; she has lately married a Clergyman of small fortune, beneficed in the East riding of York.*

1853: 18 Apr: *The infection was caught by Miss F. visiting at Gloucester the wife of Captain Octavius Rooke, Adjutant of the South Gloucester Militia, who has lately married a daughter of Mr. Pyrke.*

ROPER — Mary Roper [91]

Mary Roper, Lady Dacre, née Fludyer (1755-1808), was born at Lee Green, Kent, the daughter of Sir Thomas Fludyer (1711-1769) and Mary Champion (1737-1761). She married, at Lambeth Palace chapel, Lambeth, Surrey, 2 March 1773, Trevor Charles Roper, 18th

Lord Dacre (1745-1794). On 1 February 1802 Gillray published *A Bouquet of the Last Century*, a wicked caricature of Lady Dacre.

1801: 25 May: *Dined with Dow. Lady Dacre Bruton Street.*

ROSE — Joseph Rose[92]

Joseph Rose (±1796-1876), farmer, was born at Wormington, Gloucestershire, the son of James and Jane Rose. He was an unmarried farmer at Broadwell.

1838: 5 Apr: *Of the new Guardians who presented themselves with credentials from their respective parishes, were ... Rose, for Broadwell.*

1843: 16 Nov.

1851: 3 Feb: *Capt. Leigh called to apply for a summons to Mr. Rose of Broadwell to shew cause why he should not be fined for wilful trespass and damage done to a public stone quarry in the parish of Broadwell, which is set out in the award for getting stone for the repair of the Highways—he having dug and carted away stone from thence for his own private purposes.*

ROSENHAGEN — Anthony Rosenhagen[93]

Anthony Rosenhagen (±1776-1853), superintendent comptroller of army accounts, was a British subject born in France. In 1798 he was earning £40 a year as a junior clerk of the bills, and by 1812 he was private secretary to the chancellor of the exchequer. He later became comptroller of army accounts. In his early life he lived in Wimpole Street, London. He married, first, 26 October 1819, Louisa Craven Barnard, but she died just seven weeks later. His second wife has not been identified, but he married, thirdly, Frances (b. ±1788). By 1851 Rosenhagen was living at 32 Promenade, Cheltenham, and was listed as a widower and blind.

1823: 11 Sep: *Our evening circle was increased by the addition of Mr. & Mrs. Rosenhagen, & their guest M. Costantini. Mr. R. a very agreeable and respectable gentleman, labouring under a sad defect of vision, is just relinquishing his post as Comptroller of Army Accounts... Mrs. Rosenhagen is of the Packhurst family of Ripple, in Worcestershire, a branch of that settled at Catesby in Northampton-shire, of which stock was the learned author of the valuable Hebrew & Greek Lexicons adapted to the old & new testaments.*

1824: 23 Apr: *We dined at Mr. & Mrs. Rosenhagen's.*

1826: 8 Feb.

1837: 4 Jan.

ROSS — the Ross family of Edinburgh

1801: 15 Apr: *The chief persons there (Gregory's for dinner) were Mr. and Mrs. & Miss G. Brown, Miss Ross, Miss McKenzie &c.* 27 Apr: *... went to supper at Lady H. Blair's, where our reception was as usual hearty & obliging, Dr. & Mrs. Gregory & Miss Ross met us there.*

ROSS — Captain Ross at Clifton

1804: 23 Aug: *Walked with my Father & Mother, Mr. Ryan, Mr. Holmes, Capt. Ross &c.*

ROSS —John Lockhart Ross[94]

John Lockhart Ross (1811-1891), Church of England clergyman, was born at Edinburgh, the son of George Ross. He was educated at Oriel College, Oxford (BA 1833; MA 1836). He was vicar of Fifield and Idbury, Oxfordshire, 1840; vicar of Avebury, Wiltshire, 1852-63; rector of St George in the East, 1863-73; and rector of St Dunstand in the East, 1873. He married Isabella Seton-Steuart (1816-1893); they had 3 sons and 1 daughter:

1 George Henry William (b. 1853)
2 Reginald R. H. (b. 1855)
3 Henry Stuart Lockhart (b. 1857)
1 Lillias Elizabeth Grace (b. 1859)

By 1881 John and Isabella were living at Portobello House, Mortlake, Surrey.

1842: 27 Apr: *This meeting being closed, there followed the first dinner for the season of the Stow Clerical Society before which several new members were elected: viz Messrs. Ross (incumbent of Fifield;) ...*

ROUND — Charles Gray Round[95]

Charles Gray Round (1797-1867), MP, JP, DL, and barrister-at-law, was born at Colchester, Essex, the son of Charles Round (1770-1834) and Charlotte Green (1773-1831). He was a cousin of John Round (*below*). Charles was educated at Balliol College, Oxford (BA 1818; MA 1821), and became a barrister at Lincoln's Inn in 1822. He also served as recorder of Colchester, JP and DL for Essex, chairman of the quarter sessions, and MP for North Essex, 1837-47. He married, at Colchester, Essex, 4 July 1838, Emma Sarah Brock (1819-1892). There do not appear to have been any children.

1845: 30 May.

1847: 18 May, 20-21 May, 25 Jul: *A circular from Mr. C. G. Round's Committee at Oxford announcing that the election for the University is fixed for Thursday next... . I fear that C. G. Round has low church tendencies; he is not a man of commanding talent, though a scholar, and a man of business; he comes also recommended to one by his relationship to my old friend; yet still I withhold my vote from him, though he numbers among his supporters most of the Heads of Houses, but he is too openly upheld by the low Church party and the Protectionists.*

ROUND — John Round[96]

John Round (1783-1860), MP and high steward of Colchester, was born at Danbury Park, Essex, the eldest surviving son of John Round (1734-1813), barrister, of Colchester, and Catherine (d. 1802), daughter of Edward Green, of Lawford Hall, Essex, and widow of Revd Richard Daniel. He was born on 8 March 1783, making him just two weeks younger than his close friend Francis Witts. He was educated at Balliol College, Oxford (BA 1805; MA 1808), and was created DCL in 1814. He was a JP and DL for Essex, and was appointed high sheriff in 1834. He was also MP for Ipswich, 1812-18, and Maldon, 1837-47. He married, at St George's, Hanover Square, Westminster, Middlesex, Susan Constantia (1789-1845), daughter of George Caswall (d. 1825), of Sacombe Park, Hertfordshire, and Ann Newman (1760-1829); they had 3 sons and 5 daughters, including:

1 John (1816-1887); educated at Balliol College, Oxford (BA 1838; MA 1841), and the Inner Temple (1838); lived at West Bergholt Hall, Essex; married Laura (±1827-1864) (*see below*), youngest daughter and co-heir of the poet Horatio Smith; 1 son and 2 daughters:
    1 John Horace (1854-1928), historian and genealogist; appointed hon. historical adviser to the crown in peerage cases; president, Essex Archæological Society, 1916-21; vice-president, English Place-Name Society; died unmarried

1 Laura Constantia (1855-1864); died in France or possibly in Lucerne, Switzerland, with her mother

2 Violet Grace (1856-1934); married, at St Michael's, Chester Square, London, 5 January 1889, Frederick David Charles Shaw Kennedy (1858-1942)

2 Frederick Peel (1818-1884)

3 Edmund (1820-1891), barrister-at law and banker; educated at Balliol College, Oxford (MA 1844), and the Inner Temple (registered as a student there in 1842); called to the bar, 31 January 1845; member of the south-eastern circuit; became a JP for Essex; married, 10 October, 1846, Louisa Caroline, daughter of Charles George Parker of Springfield Place, Essex

1 Constantia Catherine Anne (1823-1892); married, at Hove, Sussex, 9 May 1848, as his second wife, Rear Adm. Henry Alexander Story (1813-1879), who died at Avranches, Normandy

2 Eliza-Mary (1827-1837); died a child

John Round's wife Constantia died in a fire in London on 27 May 1845. The *Gentleman's Magazine* described the tragedy in some detail:

> A fire very suddenly occurred at Raggett's Hotel, in Dover-street, Piccadilly, at one o'clock in the morning, and, though few persons in the house had retired to rest, five of them lost their lives, namely, Mrs. John Round, wife of the member for Maldon; Mr. Raggett, the proprietor of the hotel; Miss Raggett, his daughter (who, missing her footing on the escape, fell to the ground with great violence, and died soon after); Mrs. Jones, a servant of Lord Huntingdon's; and another female servant.

Constantia and her daughter, also named Constantia, had just returned from the theatre and were still waiting for their supper when the fire rapidly engulfed the building. Only the younger Constantia escaped. Three years later she married Henry Alexander Story (1813-1879). After the tragic death of his wife, John Round retired from public life; at the time of the 1851 census he was living with his daughter Constantia and son-in-law in Torquay with Henry's 5-year old daughter, Amelia, from his previous marriage. Henry and Constantia appear to have lived for some time in France, where Henry died in 1879. John Round's three sons survived, but of his five daughters, only Constantia grew to adulthood.

John Round was the only university friend Francis Witts remained in contact with throughout his life. Being of different colleges, the two men did not meet until 25 February 1803, in their second year at Oxford. After that they do not appear to have met again until February 1804. Thereafter they became close friends.

Round's eldest son, John Round, was a barrister. He married Laura Smith, a lively woman and well-connected in literary circles; W. M. Thackeray reputedly named Laura in *Pendennis* after her. She died at Lucerne, Switzerland, on Saturday 27 August 1864, and was buried at Danbury. John and Laura's eldest daughter, Laura Constantia, died in the same year. The fact that they were in Switzerland indicates that mother and daughter were probably receiving treatment for tuberculosis.

Round's second son, Frederick Peel, is something of a mystery. On 18 July 1842 he was appointed usher to the Order of the Thistle, and later he was appointed usher of the Green Rod, but beyond these appointments he scarcely features in any records. In *Visitation of England and Wales*, Howard and Crisp reported Frederick Round to be living at 15 Brunswick Terrace, Brighton, the home of his elder brother; and in the *The Court Journal and Fashionable Gazette* (1859) Frederick Round's presence was recorded at Her Majesty's levée of March 1859. All other records are silent. He may have spent some time abroad; indeed Francis Witts mentioned in his diary entry for 15 July 1847 that he was at that time at the German baths. He died unmarried. The third son, Edmund, had a distinguished legal career, and married, but died childless. The male Round line came to an end with the death of John Horace Round in 1928.

1803: 25 Feb: *A Rubber party & Oysters in the Evening at Round's. Dowell Belfield & myself.*

1804: 4 Feb: *Sat in the morning with Dowell & Round. At the Billiard Table with Evans & Williams. Passed the evening with Dowell, meeting Round & Mr. Belfield of Oriel. Played five rubbers.* 9 Feb: *Walked with Dowell & called with him on Round.* 13-14 Feb., 17 Feb: *Dined at Dickenson's with Round meeting the adjutant of the OLV.* 22 Feb., 5 Mar., 8 Mar: *Breakfasted with Round, Dowell & F. Dunne.* 21 Oct., 25 Oct., 9 Nov., 12 Nov: *Walked with Dowell & Round. Called with Round on Lady Pegge.* 18 Dec: *Heard from Round.*

1805: 9 Jan: *Wrote to Mr. B.P. Witts & J. Round.* 7 Feb., 10 Feb., 21-22 Feb., 17 Mar: *Breakfasted with Dowell meeting Round.* 19 Mar., 21 Mar: *At an Examination at the Schools, where Round & Moore of Exeter very much distinguished themselves.* 26 Mar: *Drank wine at Rounds.* 28 Mar., 12 Sep., 24 Sep.

1806: 20 Jan: *Began a letter to Round.* 21 Jan: *... & a letter upon general subjects to my friend Round.* 3 Mar: *... a letter to Round respecting my intended visit to Oxford, in answer to one, which I received from him.* 10 Mar: *Received a letter from Round, upon my coming to Oxford, & respecting two Curacies.* 18 Mar: *Breakfasted with my excellent but indolent friend Dowell, where I was met by Dr. Price, & Round; Trevenen also called in.* 19 Mar: *Called upon Round ... Dined in the Balliol Hall with Round, adjourning afterwards to the Junr. Common Room.* 20-22 Mar.

1807: 20 Jan: *Heard from my friend Round.* 21 Jan., 12 Mar., 27 Apr., 29 Jul., 15 Dec.

1808: 18 Feb., 10 Mar., 20 Mar., 19 Apr.

1823: 9 Jul: *I breakfasted with my old friend, Mr. Round, late Member for Ipswich, at his house in Albemarle Street: Mrs. Round with her four children were in Hertfordshire at her Father's, Mr. Caswall's, of Sacombe Park.* 9 Jul: *...then proceeded with Round to the Bank of England, where he was going to receive Dividends, in the New 4. per cent. Office. The celerity, self possession & punctuality, with which this is effected by the Clerks amid the hum and buzz of claimants is truly astonishing.*

1824: 11 Aug: *We had the pleasure of a visit for some hours from our friends Mr. & Mrs. J. Round, who are on their way with three of their children to Tenby and other parts of Wales. They came to us from Mr. Barter's at Sarsden, where they had been passing a day, and after an early dinner proceeded in the evening to Cheltenham.*

1829: 26 Feb: *On our way thither I stumbled on my excellent friend Round, crossing from Balliol College to his lodgings... We now rarely see each other, but keep up a correspondence by letter.*

1830: 22 Jun: *Our first visit was to my worthy friend, Mr. Round, in Albemarle Street, whom we found at home, in good health & spirits, though inconvenienced by a trifling local complaint in one of his legs; he received us with that kindness, which is congenial to his nature, & in accordance with those friendly feelings, which have always subsisted between us, since we formed an intimacy, when we were Under-graduates at the University... We talked confidentially of the accession of fortune, which he has gained by the decease of a maiden aunt of Mrs. Round, an ancient & eccentric Miss Caswall, recently deceased, & whom I once met many years since at his house in Town.* 24 Jun: ... *our kind friends, Mr. & Mrs. J. Round, called in their open carriage by appointment, to take us to the Regent's Park, & Zoological gardens ... At half past six we repaired to Albemarle Street, and were introduced to our friends two youngest children, lively and interesting little girls.*

1834: 25 Nov: *A letter from my friend Round, who is in good health, as is all his family.*

1835: 14 May, 20 May: *A letter from Round informing me that he and Mrs. Round will be in Town next week, when he hopes that my engagement to Miss Jane Witts will bring me thither, and afford an opportunity for our meeting.* 25 May.

1837: 21 Jan: *Also a very long and friendly letter from my old & worthy friend John Round.* 27 Jan., 4 Mar., 30 Mar., 28 Jul: *The Conservative Press of the day claim for that cause the preponderance on the elections which have already taken place: among other Conservatives who have displaced Whig members I observe my old friend Round, who has beaten Lennard at Maldon.* 15 Aug: *Wrote to John Round, congratulating him on his return for Maldon.* 29 Aug., 7 Sep., 20 Sep., 16 Nov: *Recd. a letter from my excellent friend Round, communicating to me the death of his youngest daughter, aged 11 years, which has plunged his amiable and united family in great grief.* 17 Nov., 2 Dec: *A very kind letter from Round congratulating me on my Son having passed his examination with credit.* 9 Dec., 13 Dec., 30 Dec.

1838: 9 Jan., 7 Mar., 30 Mar: *Recd. a letter from J Round, whose seat for Maldon is in jeopardy.* 5 Apr: *Recd. a short letter from Round, written from the Comm. Room in the H. of C. where his tenure of his seat for Maldon will be decided.* 7 Apr: *Recd. a letter from J Round, imparting the welcome intelligence that the Comm. of the H. of C. appointed to decide as to the validity of his return for Maldon had come to a determination in his favour.* 8 Apr., 10 Nov., 19 Nov.

1839: 22 Jan., 10-11 Feb., 26 Feb., 3 Apr., 24 Apr., 5 May: *From the Temple I made my way to Davies Street, Berkeley Square, to call on my good friend, John Round.* 6 May: *Thence to Davies Street, where most cordially received by Round, and introduced by him to his two elder Sons, John and Frederick, fine young men, both of them members of Balliol College, and the younger having just passed his examination for his AB. degree... Mrs. Round with her two sons, Round and myself formed an easy, friendly family party; Miss R. came in to the Drawing room, when we taking coffee, not yet introduced, not handsome, but elegant and accomplished.* 8 May, 10-11 May, 25 May, 28 May.

1840: 24 Mar., 5-6 May, 7 May: *Breakfasted with Round at his house in Davies Street—his second son Frederick, a pleasing youth, formed a trio with his Father and myself: his eldest son was not at home, and Mrs. Round and her daughter did not make their appearance.* 16 Sep.

1841: 26 Feb.

1842: 16 Jan., 12 Feb., 15 Mar., 17 Mar: *My son and I breakfasted in Davies Street, Berkeley Square, with my worthy old friend, J Round, MP. for Maldon, and his two elder sons, John and Frederick... Frederick, the second Son, is a more studious and, probably, more talented young man; like his brother having passed through the University of Oxford, at Balliol, their Father's College, with credit, where the third son Edmund now is.* 7 May.

1844: 16 Feb: *Recd. a letter from my old friend, J Round, M.P. after a long silence.* 20 Feb.

1845: 10 May: *Received a letter from my old friend Round, MP. for Maldon, announcing to me that he has contracted with the Ecclesiastical Commrs. for the sale to them of his Mansion at Danbury Park, to be appropriated as a residence for the Bishop of Rochester, under the new Ecclesiastical arrangement, which assigns to that Prelate that part of the diocese of London, which is included in the County of Essex, to be held with the small ancient diocese of Rochester.* 30 May: *There we learnt to our deep regret that the Mrs. Round, who was the victim of the dreadful conflagration at Ragget's hotel, in Albemarle Street, London, some days since, was really our old friend.* 31 May: *Wrote to poor J. Round a letter of condolence on his late melancholy loss.* 6 Jun: *I received a very melancholy but interesting letter from poor Round in reply to mine written to condole with him on the dreadful catastrophe, which had befallen his wife, giving me particulars of her funeral &c.* 18 Jun., 5 Jul: *A letter from poor Round.*

1846: 5 Sep., 10 Oct.

1847: 21 May: *Received a letter from my old friend, John Round, MP. for Maldon, bespeaking my support of his relation and friend C G Round who is to be proposed as a representative for the University in the room of Estcourt.* 25 May, 28 May, 10 Jun., 23 Jun., 25-26 Jun., 5 Jul., 8-9 Jul., 15 Jul: *A letter from J. Round, now attending the Assizes at Chelmsford: he proposes being with us by dinner time on Monday next, and remaining till Thursday.* 19 Jul: *Our old friend Round arrived by 5 PM from Hereford, and seemed please to revisit us. He appears to enjoy good health, and is a hale man for his years, but very deaf. His eldest son and daughter are travelling in Germany, but soon rejoin him at Brighton, where he will henceforth generally reside. His second son, the Usher of the Green Rod, is likewise abroad, at the German Baths. His youngest Son, who is married is the junior partner in a provincial Bank at Chelmsford. My old friend retires finally from parliament at the approaching dissolution, relinquishing his seat for Maldon. His spirits are good, and he abounds in anecdote.* 20 Jul: *With Round took a drive in the phaeton: to Maugersbury, where we met E.F.W. and Sophy, with Emma Vavasour on their way to Stow.* 21 Jul: *Breakfasted at an early hour with Round, my son rising to take leave of our friend.* 28 Aug.

1848: 6 Feb: *Received a letter from my old friend J Round, now residing at his house at Brighton.* 7 Feb., 9 Feb: *Wrote to Mr. Sadler, Sutton under Brailes, as residing in the neighbourhood of Shipston; to make enquiry as to Capt. Story, agreeably to the request made to me by Mr. Round.* 16 Feb: *A letter from J Round in reply to my letter stating what I had learnt as to Capt. Story: the good father has given his consent to his daughter's marriage to that officer.* 9 Mar: *From Barter I heard such an account of the Story family, of their levity of character, and habits, that I much fear that Constantia Round has small hopes of happiness in wedded life, and that my poor old friend will have much anxiety in his latter years arising out of the injudicious attachment formed by his darling daughter.* 27 Apr: *letter from J. Round announces that his daughter is to be married to Capt. Story on the 9th. Inst. May.* 2 May: *Wrote to Round, congratulating him, as far as might be, on his daughter's approaching marriage: but there is reason to fear that she is not about to make a very eligible connection.* 20 Dec: *A kind and long letter, chiefly on his family concerns, from my old friend John Round, dated from Torquay, where he has been residing for sometime past with his daughter, Mrs. Story, and her husband, the former having been recommended by her medical adviser to resort to a mild climate for the correction of a disposition to pulmonary complaint; she has derived much benefit from so doing.*

1850: 17 Apr., 28 Apr., 2 May, 9 Aug., 4 Dec.

1851: 7 Mar., 30 Apr., 19 May: *I found notes awaiting my arrival in Town: one from my old friend John Round, with an invitation to breakfast with him on any day most convenient to myself.* 20 May, 22 May: *Went to breakfast with my old friend*

Round at his apartments in St. James's Square—they are on the upper floor, and the ascent of the long Staircase was very trying to my breath, but they are cheerful & comfortable, commanding the airy enclosure of the square. Round wears well, and except that he is extremely deaf, enjoys life, and the society of his children. In the winter he assembles them round him at his house in Brighton, the Spring he passes in London, in Summer he travels chiefly with his eldest Son, a gentleman artist of great skill in landscape drawing, in picturesque parts of England, Wales and Scotland, and in the autumn is domiciliated with his daughter and her husband, Capt. Storey of the preventive Service, who are settled at Torquay. His younger son, Edmund, a banker at Chelmsford, and married, who seems a very pleasant and intelligent young man, came in while we were at breakfast, accompanied by a fine, handsome young Baronet, Pigott.

1853: 13 Mar: *A friendly letter from Round, now 70 years of age:—his eldest son about to marry a daughter of Horace Smith, the man of letters, one of the authors of the Rejected addresses.* 1 May, 3 May.

1854: 12 Jul: *Also a very kind letter from Round, now on a tour of the Lakes, dated Windermere, enquiring after my health, having read in a provincial paper of my retirement from the Chair of the Finance Committee of the County, and asking my opinion as to the character of the College at Cheltenham as a place of education for an orphan boy in whom he takes an interest.* 12 Jul.

ROUNDELL — Dorothea Roundell — *see also* William Palmer [97]

Dorothea Palmer, née Roundell (1792-1867), was the third and youngest daughter of the six sons and three daughters born to Revd William Roundell (1746-1821), of Gledstone and Screven, and Mary (1752-1818), youngest daughter of Revd Henry Richardson (1711-1778), rector of Thornton. Her parents had married in 1775. Dorothea married, 10 September 1810, Revd William Jocelyn Palmer (1777-1853), rector of Mixbury, Oxfordshire; they had 6 sons and 5 daughters (*see* William Palmer). Francis Witts would have been aware of the Roundell family of Gledstone through his wife Margaret's Yorkshire connections.

1838: 17 Sep: *I must have passed at no great distance from Gledstone House, the seat of the Roundells.* 24 Nov: *Mr. Palmer is in other respects a very estimable man; and of considerable ability; being one of a large and talented family of brothers: he married the youngest Miss Roundell, of Gledstone house in Craven.*

ROVEDINO — Carlo Rovedino [98]

Carlo Rovedino (1751-1822), singer, first performed in London in 1777 with Rauzzini Sacchini. Back in Italy Rovedino performed in comic opera in Venice, 1780-81, and Naples, 1784-85, singing Salieri and Cimarosa arias. Between 1789 and 1792 he was part of the Italian company that enchanted Paris with various comic operas. He later moved back to London. He was reported performing at numerous cities, but most notably London and Dublin.

1801: 2 Jun: ... *principal actors in the Opera Rezira, were Sign. Viganoni, Sign. Rovedino & his wife & Madl Banti. The former, particularly Rovedino are very fine, but totally outdone by the harmonious Banti, whose voice & singing surpassed all my expectations.*

1824: 26 Aug: *We dined at Mrs. Dolphin's at Eyford, meeting ... as also a professional performer from town, a Mr. Rovedino, son of a celebrated singer of that name—and himself a beautiful singer, exhibiting on the stage of the Opera house, but with a voice better suited to a drawing room. Of course we had a good deal of beautiful music.*

ROWAN — Captain Rowan

1836: 10 Aug: ... *the five candidates who had experience in prison management were Capt. Rowan, Tregenza, Hoare, Mance, and Saunders: all these, with the exception of Rowan were present... His correspondence with Bathurst and Bloxsome indicated him as a man of good sense and gentlemanly feelings.* 27 Aug: *On my road to Stow found a letter from Bathurst respecting the appointment of a Gaoler. It appears that Capt. Rowan is disposed to withdraw from the contest on the plea that he is unwilling to stand in the way of a gentleman connected with the County who has a family, and to whom the income of the place is a matter of much importance.* 6 Sep., 13 Sep.

ROWAN — Charles Rowan [99]

Charles Rowan (±1782-1852), army officer and police officer, was born in co. Antrim, the fifth son of Robert Rowan (1754-1832), of Garry, co. Antrim, and North Lodge, Carrickfergus, and Mary, daughter of Hill Wilson of Purdysburn, co. Down. He was commissioned in 1797 an ensign in the 52nd Regiment of Foot, and saw active service during the Napoleonic Wars, in Sicily, 1806-08, Sweden, 1808, and in the Peninsular War. Rowan also fought at the battle of Waterloo. He returned to England with his regiment in 1818, and was stationed in the Midlands until 1821, when, as commanding officer, he took the 52nd Foot to Dublin. He retired from the Army by sale of his commission in 1822.

In 1829, Charles Rowan was selected by Sir Robert Peel as founding senior commissioner of the Metropolitan Police. Peel was probably acting on advice from the duke of Wellington and Sir George Murray, Wellington's quartermaster-general during the Peninsular campaign and secretary of state for war and the colonies in his government. Murray had been particularly impressed by Rowan's conduct at Waterloo. Rowan was to provide the military discipline and organisation needed by the new police force, and the junior commissioner, barrister Richard Mayne, was to provide the legal expertise. Over the next twenty years, these two men provided a solid foundation on which the Metropolitan Police could build.

1835: 20 Mar: *Wrote to Mr. Pole an account of the unpleasant collision with Mr. Ackerley, and suggested to him the propriety of waiting on the Under-Secretary of the Home Department, Mr. March Phillips, and on Col. Rowan, Chief Commissioner of the Metropolitan Police.*

1836: 14 Nov., 11 Dec.

ROWDEN — Edward Rowden [100]

Edward Rowden (1780-1869), Church of England clergyman, was born at Cuxham, Oxfordshire, the son of Revd Francis Rowden (1724-1822) and Sophia Goodenough (1739-1813). He was educated at New College, Oxford (BA 1802; MA 1806), where he was a fellow until 1812. He was appointed vicar of Highworth, Wiltshire, in 1804. Rowden married, at Cowley, Oxfordshire, 13 August 1811, Elizabeth (1782-1825), daughter of Revd Nathan Wetherell (1726-1807), dean of Hereford, and Richarda Croke (1743-1812); they had 4 sons and 4 daughters:

1 Sophia Elizabeth (1812-1890)
2 Frances (1813-1857)
1 Edward Wetherell (1814-1870); *see below*
3 Maria (1815-1888)
2 Francis Marmaduke (1815-1903), Church of England clergyman
3 George Croke (1820-1863), Church of England clergyman
4 Jane Margaret (1821-1909)
4 Charles Wetherell (1825-1868)

It is not clear why Francis Witts referred to Edward as John unless it was a second name which he used by preference.

1808: 3 May: *Walking at times with the party, which was Shopping, with Rowden, Smith, Wilkins, &c.* 5 May: *In Queen Square most part of the morning, walking with Rowden &c.*

1823: 22 Sep.

1836: 23 Nov: *Received a very satisfactory letter from E.F.W, who has decided on returning home for the Xmas vacation on Tuesday next, when he will bring with him for a day or two his friend Edward Rowden of Wadham, son of my old College acquaintance John Rowden, Incumbent of Highworth, Wilts, that he may accompany my son to Stow Ball, which is fixed for that day.*

1837: 2 Mar.

ROWDEN — Edward Wetherell Rowden [101]

Edward Wetherell Rowden (1814-1870) was the eldest son of Edward Rowden (1780-1869) and Elizabeth Wetherell (1782-1825) (*above*). He was educated at New College, Oxford (BA 1838; MA 1842), where he was appointed bursar in 1847, dean of arts in 1848, sub-warden in 1849, and registrar in 1853. He was created DCL in 1856. Rowden married, at St Matthew's, Brixton, Surrey, 21 January 1851, Mary Ann (1828-1901), born at Langwm, Pembrokeshire, daughter of John Condliffe Cooper and Mary Brown (b. ±1787), who was born at Burton, Pembrokeshire. Mary Ann's parents had married at Burton in 1817. Edward and Mary Ann had 3 sons and 3 daughters:

1 Edward (1853-1893)
2 Harry Wetherell (1853-1921), army officer
1 Mary Harriet (1854-1939)
3 John (1856-1857)
2 Jessie Theresa (1857-1937)
3 Clara (1859-1923)

1836: 23 Nov., 29 Nov: *A few lines from E.F.W. announcing that in consequence of his friend Rowden being obliged to attend a lecture they could not leave Oxford till a late hour and should travel in a gig.* 30 Nov.

1837: 2 Mar: *There was a very comfortable letter from my Son, giving an account of an excursion last week to Highworth, where he had been the guest of the Rowdens, and from thence accompanied their party to a large and agreeable assembly at Swindon.* 21 Mar., 7 Aug: *It seems that on Saturday, he had a letter from F. Rowden, dated from Dublin, whither he and poor Ryland Chater had gone on an excursion, stating that the latter had been seized with fever, which had proved to by be typhus, and that he way was in a very precarious state.* 17 Sep., 21 Sep., 22 Sep: *The Misses Vavasour with Rowden and my son accompanied me to the Workhouse.* 23 Sep., 25 Sep: *E. Rowden left us after breakfast, to return to Highworth: he is a gentlemanly pleasing young man, with good principles, and amiable; but not talented, and having a good deal of useful and general information, and clearness of views yet to gain.* 11 Oct: *Also to Rowden to inform him that I proposed proceeding on my Journey into Yorkshire from Gloucester, on Thursday the 19th. after attending the quarter Sessns. and pressing him to accompany me on my Excursion.* 16 Oct: *A letter from F. Rowden, accepting my invitation to accompany me into Yorkshire, and promising to be with me on Wednesday, that we may leave Gloucester together on Thursday.* 18 Oct., 19 Oct: *Rose at 6 AM. and in half an hour met F. Rowden at the Bell, where had a comfortable breakfast, before leaving Gloucester at seven by the Victoria, a pair horse coach, which reached Worcester by ten, and Birmingham by one o clock.* 20 Oct: *I had taken an inside place, and Rowden one outside, but as the evening closed, he betook himself to a warm corner within.* 22 Oct., 24-27 Oct., 30 Oct: *After an early dinner Rowden and myself left our excellent and hospitable friends in a chaise for Clithero, where we arrived about half past six in the evening, and retired after tea to our beds to be ready for starting by the coach for Manchester at 5 to-morrow morning.* 31 Oct: *Rowden preferred an outside berth.* 10 Nov: *Recd. a letter from E. Rowden, giving an account of his journey homewards after he had parted from me at Birmingham.*

1839: 5 Jun: *I omitted to name that in the convocation house I shook hands with many old acquaintances—Billingsley, Rowden, Lysons &c.*

1853: 4 Apr: *Mr. W.H. Cooke and Mr. Rowley Lloyd, Barristers, canvassed me for my vote in Convocation in favour of Mr. E. Rowdens fellow of New College, one of the candidates for the vacant office of Registrar of the University.* 16 Apr: *Received a letter from Mr. Rowden, pressing one to go to Oxford to vote for him on the 27th.* 29 Apr: *It appears by the newspapers that W.E. Rowden has been the successful candidate for the office of Registrar of the Univ. of Oxford: beating his two Competitors, Mr. Cornish, of Corpus, and Mr. Rawlinson of Exeter, by a large majority.*

ROWE — Mrs Rowe at Clifton

1806: 18 Jun: *In the Evening at a very pleasant party at Mrs. Goold's ... The Auriols, Mrs. Rowe, Garden, Adair &c. of the Party.*

ROWE — Mrs Rowe, aunt of Mary Anne Dolphin — *see also* Payne [102]

Little has been uncovered regarding Mrs Rowe. Her maiden name was Tanfield and she was a sister of Mary Payne, who had four known sisters: Katherine (b. 1757); Martha (b. 1762); Dorothy (1767-1840); and Ann (1769-1847). Dorothy married, 22 June 1793, as his second wife, Revd Basil Bury Beridge (1737-1808). Ann died unmarried. This Mrs Rowe is therefore likely to be Katherine or Martha.

1835: 23 May: *Called on Mrs. Dolphin, to pay my respects to her Mother, Mrs. Payne, whom, being indisposed, I did not see. Saw Mrs. Dolphin, her aunt, Mrs. Rowe ...*

1837: 4 Jul: *In the evening, Mrs. Payne and her sister, Mrs. Rowe, called from Eyford.* 11 Jul: *Mrs. Rowe and Mrs. Harrison left Eyford this morning, for Essex.*

ROWLEY — George Rowley, superintendent of pensioners, Bombay [103]

George Rowley (d. 1848), superintendent of pensioners, Bombay, first appeared in the HEIC records as an ensign in 1797. He became a career officer and was promoted to major in 1846. He died in 1848.

1848: 15 Feb: *At the desire of Sophia Hunt, to whom the measure has been suggested by a Col. Ottey, of the E.I. Company's service, I wrote, as Exor of M C Hunt, to Major Rowley, Superintendent of Pensioners, Bombay, as to Edward Hunt.* 30 May: *Recd. a letter from Mr. Boye, Paymaster of the Bombay Pensioners, with a full account of the present circumstances of Mr. Edward Hunt. This letter is a reply to one written by me on Feb. 15. last to Major Rowley Superintendent of Pensioners, Bombay establishment.*

ROYCE — David Royce [104]

David Royce (1817-1902), Church of England clergyman, was born at Oakham, Rutland, the third son of Baptists Matthew and

Charlotte Royce. He was educated at Christ Church, Oxford (BA 1840; MA 1845), where he was chaplain from 1844 to 1851. Royce was perpetual curate of Cowley, Oxford, in 1840-50, and was presented by his college to the living of Lower Swell as vicar in 1850. He married, 1850, Elizabeth Anne (1819-1903), daughter of John and Mary Ann Mould of Oundle, Northamptonshire. No children were listed in either the 1861 or 1871 censuses. David Royce was a founding member of the Bristol and Gloucestershire Archaeological Society; on his death his widow donated many of his books to the society, laying the foundation for the society's library.

1850: 27 Aug: *Recd. a letter from the Revd. David Royce, recently instituted to the Vicarage of Lower Swell, requesting me to induct him into his Church on Thursday or Friday next.* 29 Aug: *A note from Mr. Royce, who accepts my proferred hospitality, and who accordingly arrived here to tea in the evening in my carriage, which I sent to meet the coach at the foot of Stow Hill—He appears gentlemanly, well informed, and well intentioned—much conversation with him as to his present and future position as Vicar of Lower Swell, and on general topics.* 30 Aug: *Drove Mr. Royce to Lower Swell, and formally inducted him to the Benefice—Called with him on Merchant, the Churchwarden, and assisted at a conference as to the temporalities of the Vicarage, particularly, with reference to the numerous allotment tenants now in occupation of the greater part of the glebe.* 5 Sep., 11 Oct., 12 Oct., 26 Oct., 31 Oct: *Mr. Royce joined our party at dinner.* 18 Nov., 23 Nov: *Walked to Lower Swell, and called on Mr. and Mrs. Royce, the Vicar having since we last met, married the Step-daughter of a Lincolnshire Clergyman, a Miss Mould, daughter of a gentleman formerly resident at Oundle——She appeared an agreeable young woman, of easy manners, and well looking.* 6 Dec.

1851: 25 Oct: *Mr. Royce called and consulted me on different points relating to his Vicarage & parish.* 30 Oct., 30 Jan., 2 Feb., 6 Feb., 12 Feb: *Mr. and Mrs. Royce, with Miss Laurent, Mrs. Royce's half-sister, Mr. and Mrs. R. Waller, and Mr. and Mrs. Potter, dined with me.* 21 Feb., 25 Feb., 28 Feb., 7 Mar: *Wrote to G. Pain to mention that Mr. Royce is a candidate for admission into the Stow book Society.* 14 Mar., 12 Apr., 23 Apr., 25 Apr., 28 Apr., 15 May: *Mr. Royce sought me out there, and laid before me a rough plan of the enlargement of the Church at Lower Swell, which he contemplates, and which, indeed, is very necessary, as the population of the village is much increased and the accommodation for divine worship is very inadequate. It is proposed to append to the present edifice a North Aisle, and Mr. Buckler of Oxford is the Architect to whom the work will be entrusted.*

1852: 22 Jan., 30 Jan., 1 Mar., 9 Mar: *In the forenoon Mr. Royce, and Miss Laurent called upon me; Mrs. R. is gone to visit an aged and perhaps, dying relative at Oakham. Mr. R. was desirous of bearing testimony to the generally good character of a young man of his parish, now in confinement at Northleach Bridewell under my warrant of remand, on a charge of setting fire with another to a plantation at Swell Wold.* 12 Mar., 24-25 Mar., 3 Apr., 14 Apr., 24 Apr., 17-18 May, 20 May: *Dressed at the Unicorn for dinner at Mr. Royce's, where found Mr. Laurent (not Lawrence,) Mrs. Royce's step-father...* 4 Nov., 25 Nov., 21 Dec., 29-30 Dec.

1853: 14 Jan., 18 Jan., 25 Jan., 23 Feb: *Wrote to invite Mr. Royce to dinner on the same occasion, who accepted the invitation.* 2 Mar., 30-31 Mar., 9 Apr., 15 Apr., 24 May, 22 Jun., 15 Dec., 29 Dec.

1854: 13 Feb., 9 Mar., 15 Mar., 23 Mar., 30-31 Mar., 3 May, 5 Jun., 29 Jun., 19 Jul.

RUCK — Edmund Naunton Ruck[105]

Edmund Naunton Ruck (1816-1893), farmer, was born at Down Ampney, the son of Edmund and Ann Ruck. He farmed 700 acres, employing fifty-six men. He married, at Cricklade, Wiltshire, January 1839, Jane Bathe (1814-1858); they had 1 son and 2 daughters:

1 Mary (1839-1916)
2 Hannah (1841-1921)
1 Edmund Bathe (1851-1858)

1844: 2 Feb: *Wrote to Mr. Edmund Ruck of Down Ampney, Secretary to the Committee of Tenant farmers who have summoned a meeting at Cirencester on Monday next, to establish an agricultural protection society, expressing my apprehension that it will not be in my power to attend the meeting, my approval of it, and my readiness to co-operate in any temperate and well considered measures which may be adopted at it.* 29 Feb: *This measure was favoured by Mr. E. Ruck, Secretary to the Society formed at Cirencester for agricultural protection, and upheld by Messrs. Winter and W B Pole, who held aloof because it did not form part of the scheme.*

RUDDLE — Amelia and George Ruddle[106]

Amelia Ruddle, née Whitehouse (1805-1862), was born in Liverpool, and married, 1828, George Ruddle (b. 1804). In the 1861 census George was listed as a retired officer, DL, and JP. Amelia's mother, Mary Whitehouse, was registered in the same census as living with her and her husband at The House, Ashchurch, Tewkesbury.

1836: 21 Jul: *Found there B. L. Witts, who had arrived during our absence from Walton House, near Tewkesbury, the residence of Mr. Ruddall, a connection of his Mother's by marriage.*

1840: 29 Jul: *Recd. a letter from B. L. Witts ... He proposes visiting us on the 3d. Aug. and leaving us on the evening of the following day for his relation's, Mr. Ruddle's, at Walton House, near Tewkesbury.*

1844: 12 Sep., 25 Sep.

1847: 11 Oct: *A letter from Mrs. Woodroffe, who with her husband, after a tour during the honeymoon in North Devon &c. is now on a visit to her relations, Mr. and Mrs. Ruddle, at Walton House near Tewkesbury.*

1853: 21 Jun: *Received a visit from Mr. & Mrs. Ruddle, Mr. Hastings Wodman, and Miss Townsend. They remained with me to luncheon, and set out in heavy rain to Mr. Ruddle's house near Tewkesbury, whence they came yesterday, and, after calling on Miss Penyston at Cornwell, and visiting Daylesford, had slept at Stow. Miss Townsend, daughter of a deceased Solicitor of Rugby, and niece of the Vicar of Aston Blank, is also niece of Mrs. Ruddle, who was a Miss Whitehouse, and a niece of Mrs. Witts of Brighton, her mother having been one of the many daughters of the Lake family. Another Miss W. married Mr. Townsend of Rugby, and a third is the second wife of Mr. J Williams Martin, of Shoborough House, Twyning, an old acquaintance and brother Magistrate of mine: Mr. Ruddle also has latterly been placed in the commission for Gloucestershire, is Deputy Lieutenant for the County, a Captain in the Worcestershire Militia, a Magistrate for the Borough of Tewkesbury, & Chairman of the Tewkesbury Union —— a sensible man with good manners & habits of business.*

1854: 14 Feb: *The members of the Police Committee present were Purnell, Holland, Curtis Hayward, G Parry, Winterbotham, Ruddle, C. Trye, Brickdale, Barker, Talbot and myself.*

RUDGE — Edward Rudge [107]

Edward Rudge (1763-1846), botanist and antiquary, was born at Evesham, Worcestershire, the son of Edward Rudge (1717-1790) and Elizabeth Long (1729-1820). His father was a merchant and alderman of Salisbury, and possessed a large portion of the abbey estate at Evesham. Edward was educated at Queen's College, Oxford, but took no degree. He married, 1791, Anne Nouaile (1761-1836); they had 2 sons and 1 daughter:

1 Edward John (1792-1861); married Felizarda Pole; *see below*
1 Anne Eliza (1797-1879); married Charles Pole
2 Samuel Nouaille (1801-1865)

At a young age Edward's attention was turned to botany by his uncle, Samuel Rudge (d. 1817), a retired barrister and amateur botanist. Samuel formed a herbarium, which he passed to his nephew in his will, and encouraged him in his interest. Edward purchased a fine series of plants from the Guianas, collected by M. Martin, and subsequently studied the flora of that region in detail. He published, between 1805 and 1807, *Plantarum Guianæ rariorum icones et descriptiones hactenus ineditæ*. Between 1811 and 1834 Edward conducted a series of excavations in the portions of the estate of Evesham Abbey under his control. He communicated his discoveries of relics and ruins to the Society of Antiquaries in London, and the society published them in volume 5 of their *Vetusta Monumenta*, alongside a detailed account written by Rudge's son, Edward (*below*), of the masonry discovered during the excavation.

1829: 10 Aug: *We dined to-day at Mr. Pole's at Wyck Hill. We met there Mr. & Mrs. Rudge, the father and mother of Mrs. C. R. Pole, as also of Mr. E. Rudge, who married Miss Felizarda Pole. The elder Mr. Rudge is a great amateur in horticulture; by his property near Evesham he has much influence in the elections for that borough. Mrs. Rudge seemed a very sensible, well informed woman. She joined her daughter & Mrs. Pole at the piano forte; it is strange to see two grandmothers, the one accompanying with the instrument, the other with the voice the mother of their grandchildren.*

1844: 14 Aug.

1846: 22 Aug: *Drove with M W. to Wyck Hill to call on the Poles, and on Mrs. and Mrs. E. Rudge, now on a visit there. Were not received; tidings having just arrived of the dangerous condition of Mr. Rudge Senr. of Abbey Manor near Evesham, and his son had just set out to visit his father, as anticipated on his death-bed. The elder Mr. Rudge is 83 years of age, and has been in a precarious state for some time past.* 28 Oct.

RUDGE — Edward Rudge [108]

Edward Rudge (1792-1861), barrister-at-law, was the eldest son of Edward Rudge (1763-1846) and Anne Nouaile (1761-1836) (*above*). He was educated at Caius College, Cambridge (BA 1815; MA 1818), and Lincoln's Inn (1815). He was called to the bar in 1819, and elected a fellow of both the Society of Antiquaries (1834) and the Royal Society (1847). He was also a JP and DL for Worcestershire. Rudge married, 1825, Felizarda (1802-1880), second daughter of Charles Pole [later Van Notten-Pole] (1773-1864) and Felizarda Matilda Buller (1776-1872) of Wick Hill House, Gloucestershire; they had 3 sons and 2 daughters:

1 Edward Charles (1828-1909)
1 Millicent (b. & d. 1831)
2 Augusta Felizarda (1838-1898)
2 William John (1839-1910)
3 Walter Reginald (1842-1906)

Edward followed his father in his interests, notably as an antiquary. He wrote *Some Account of the History and Antiquities of Evesham*.

1829: 10 Aug.

1837: 8 Nov.

1838: 20 Oct., 27 Oct.

1840: 12 Sep., 28-29 Oct., 12 Nov., 14 Nov., 26 Nov.

1843: 2 Nov: *Met and parleyed with Sir C. & Lady Imhoff, Mr. and Mrs. Winter, Mr. and Mrs. Rudge.* 7 Nov., 14 Nov.

1844: 5 Aug., 9 Aug., 14 Aug., 29 Aug: *Mr. & Mrs. Rudge with W B Pole brought their eldest son to be confirmed.*

1846: 22 Aug., 22 Sep., 28 Oct: ... *met Mr. Lambert, and learnt from him that there was great distress at Wyck Hill, poor Mr. Rudge being dangerously ill, and great fears entertained. It is a melancholy dispensation; just after the death of his father in extreme old age, and so just come to the enjoyment of a large fortune; himself in middle life, as people are want to say, of those not much beyond fifty years of age, with a numerous young family: a man of blameless character, quiet, sensible, well informed, gentlemanly.* 5 Nov.

1847: 28 Sep.

1853: 28 Jun: *New Magistrates who qualified were Mr. Rudge of Abbey Manor near Evesham, and his son, and Mr. Potter, partner in the timber trade with W. P. Price.* 14 Dec.

RUDGE — Thomas Rudge [109]

Thomas Rudge (±1753-1825), Church of England clergyman, was born in the parish of St Mary de Lode, Gloucester, the son of Thomas Rudge (1726-1809) and Anne Baret (1720-1759). He was educated at Merton College and Worcester College, Oxford (BA 1780; MA 1783; BD 1784). He was appointed rector of St Michael's and St Mary-de-Grace, Gloucester, and vicar of Haresfield in 1784, and chancellor of the diocese of Hereford in 1817. He was also archdeacon of Gloucester, 1814-25. Rudge was the author of *The History of the County of Gloucester* (1803). He married Sarah King (1755-1821), born at Iron Acton, Gloucestershire; they had at least 7 sons and 3 daughters:

1 Hannah Maria (1779-1814)
1 Charles King (1781-1839)
2 Thomas King (1783-1783)
3 William King (1784-1785)
4 Samuel King (1785-1789)
5 James (1786-1815)
6 Frederick (1787-1867), Church of England clergyman
2 Emily (b. 1791)
3 Caroline (b. 1795)
7 Henry (b. 1798)

1820: 17 May: *At the archdeacon's visitation at Stow, the Sermon was preached by Mr. Archdeacon Rudge.* 3 Jun: *Mr. Rudge, the Archdeacon of Gloucester, held his Visitation at Stow, where a small proportion of the clergy of the Deanery attended. The Archdeacon preached, but was from indisposition ill able to discharge the duties of the day. He is much broken. He is Chancellor of the Diocese of Hereford, Rector of St. Michael's Church, Gloucester, & of Haresfield, near that city.*

1824: 5 May.

1825: 9 Mar: *The Gloucester Journal mentions the decease of the Revd. Thomas Rudge, Archdeacon of this Diocese, in advanced life. He was also Chancellor of Hereford: he was indebted for both these dignities to the regard of Bishop Huntingford, now prelate of the latter diocese & predecessor of Bish. Ryder in this. Mr. Rudge was also Rector of St. Michael's in the City of Gloucester, & of Haresfield near Gloucester, where he resided. He was besides Incumbent of Dursley, which is, I believe, an appendage of the Archdeaconry. At his Visitations he was not accustomed to deliver charges, but preached a Sermon once in three years on those occasions.*

RUMSEY — Henry Wyldbore Rumsey [110]

Henry Wyldbore Rumsey (1809-1876), surgeon, was born at Chesham, Buckinghamshire, the son of Henry Nathaniel Rumsey (1766-1843), and Frances Elizabeth Catherine Murray (1782-1846). He lived 80 Barton Street, Gloucester, and later at Priory House, London Road, Cheltenham. He married, at St Mary's, Cheltenham, 28 May 1835, Fanny Sophia Langston (1810-1887); they had 2 sons and 2 daughters:

1 Frances Elizabeth (b. 1837)
1 Henry Langston (1838-1924)
2 Margaret Blanche (1841-1920)
2 Robert Frederick (1843-1920)

1839: 11 Jul: *Recd. a circular letter from a Mr. Ramsey, a Surgeon at Gloucester, a candidate for the vacancy at the Infirmary: he is supported by Mr. Lysons, who addressed a few lines to me in his favour.* 12 Jul.

1850: 27 Nov: *Received a letter from Dr. Ramsay, assistant Superintendent of the Lunatic Asylum.*

RUSHOUT — John Rushout [111]

John Rushout, 2nd Baron Northwick (1770-1859), landed proprietor, was born at Northwick, Worcestershire, the son of John Rushout, 1st Baron Northwick (1738-1800), and Rebecca (1740-1818), daughter of Humphrey Bowles (1700-1784) and Hannah Hurst (b. 1715). He was educated at Harrow School, where he was governor between 1801 and 1859. He was elected a fellow of the Society of Antiquaries in 1800, the same year he succeeded his father as 2nd Baron Northwick. He died unmarried at the age of 89.

1820: 3 Mar.

1823: 25 Nov: *I dined and slept at Dr. Warneford's, meeting Lords Redesdale and Northwick, Mr. Pole, Mr. Jeaffreson, Mr. Ford, Mr. Saumarez and Mr. Eyre. Lord Northwick's residence is at Northwick Park, Worcestershire, in the parish of Blockley; he is advancing in years, still unmarried, a man of very polite manners, rather of the old school; has travelled a great deal, and converses very agreeably on many topics of history & research, which have at different times engaged his attention. He is a connoisseur in coins.*

1825: 21 Jun., 22 Sep: *I rode to Batsford to dine and sleep at Lord Redesdales. There I met Lord Northwick, Mr. & Mrs. Pole of Wick Hill, three Miss Selwyns, elderly young ladies.*

1826: 18 Dec: *I dined and slept at Lord Redesdale's. The old Peer is, as usual, full of talk and information, very communicative, confidential & kind.*

1828: 23 Aug.

1829: 22 Sep.

1832: 10 Apr.

1836: 17 Aug.

1837: 12 Feb., 24-26 Feb.

1838: 14 Feb., 19 Feb: *It was nearly six o cl. when we reached Northwick Park, and when we had changed our dress, were introduced to a large party.* 20 Feb: *The Peer met his three Clerical guests at an early breakfast in the library at nine o clock; having first conducted us into his picture gallery and given us a cursory view of his treasures.*

1840: 27 Oct.

1842: 29 Nov.

1843: 27 Aug.

1845: 9 May: *Accompanied M.W. to Thirlestane House, the residence of Lord Northwick, to see his large collection of pictures.*

1850: 10 Jan.

1851: 14 May.

1854: 9 Aug: *We reached Northwick Park some time before 2 P.M. and learnt that Lord Northwick was at home, having arrived from his house at Cheltenham on yesterday evening. On sending in my card we were immediately admitted, and ushered into the picture gallery, where we were soon after joined by his Lordship, who most obligingly performed the part of our Cicerone—an office, in which he especially delights, when his acquaintance visit his cherished treasures. He is, in fact, one of the rarest curiosities of his collection—fourscore and five years old, somewhat bowed, his hands and feet distorted by gout, with silvery locks, and somewhat dim eyes, yet gracious and courteous, after the manner of the vieille cour, fluent and copious.*

RUSSELL — the Russell family at Clifton — *see also* Auriol [112]

Charlotte Eliza Russell (1727-1808) was the daughter of John Russell (±1697-1752) and Anne [Sarah[?]] Rixon (b. 1698). She married, at the British factory chaplaincy, Lisbon, Portugal, 20 February 1751, James Peter Auriol (1713[?] or 1724[?]-1779), East India merchant.

Charlotte's father, John Russell, was an interesting person. He came from obscure origins but was very well-connected; Thomas Pelham-Holles, 1st duke of Newcastle (1693-1768), brother to Henry Pelham (1694-1754), prime minister (1743-54), affectionately called him 'Bumbo'. Russell was a quasi-official agent at Gibraltar and the Barbary states when the latter were run by tyrannical emperors. He was first married to Catherine Moore, who presumably died young. He married secondly, at St James, Westminster, ±1719, Anne Rixon; they had 2 sons and 3 daughters:

1 John (1721-1798), naval officer; wife and children unknown
1 Elizabeth (b. 1723)
2 Charlotte Eliza (1727-1808); married James Peter Auriol
3 Steuart (1731-1769); named after her father's friend Adm. James Steuart (d. 1757); married, at the British factory chaplaincy, Lisbon, Portugal, 15 June 1751, Samuel Eyre (1704-1794); 2 daughters:
  1 Susannah Harriet (1755-1833)
  2 Charlotte Louisa (b. 1757)
2 Wager (b. 1732); named after his father's friend Adm. Sir Charles Wager (1666-1743); married Jane; 1 daughter:
  1 Charlotte (b. 1761)

John Russell ended his career as British consul at Lisbon, a reward for his previous hard work in challenging environments. He died in 1752. Wager tried to follow his brother John into the navy but was unsuccessful. In January 1760, he was appointed a captain in Seabright's Foot in room of Henry Reddish. In the Seven Years' War, he served as a captain in the 83rd Regiment; the Portuguese made complaints against him and the 'devilish English'. He may at one time have entered Portuguese service as Tenente Col Wager Russell. Nothing is known of Wager's wife Jane, including the date of their marriage. As well as his daughter Charlotte, Wager may have had a son, João Wager Russell, but the evidence is nebulous. There was also a John Russell who married another Jane, but as João is John in Portuguese this was probably the same person. John and Jane had at least 1 son:

1 Francis Wager (1788-1845)

There are still families bearing the surname Wager Russell in Portugal to this day.

As to the Mr and Mrs Russell and Miss Russell at Clifton, we are little the wiser. They may have been children or grandchildren of John Russell, RN, or of Wager Russell, but equally, they may have been connected to the Russell family from Staffordshire, whom Agnes Witts had been acquainted with at Calwich Abbey when staying with the Granvilles. The only definite Auriol/Russell connection appears in Agnes Witts's diary entry of 10 December 1804: 'Mrs Auriols niece Miss Russell call'd before I ventured out ...' This was most likely Charlotte, Wager Russell's daughter.

1804: 17 Sep: *A pleasant party in the evening at the Townsend's. The Manners's, Russell's, Van der Horsts &c.* 24 Dec: *... called upon Mrs. Russell, a very obliging woman, & Mr. Newnham.*

1805: 30 Jan: *Received an unexpected invitation in the morning to Mrs. Salter's Dance this Evening, &, waving the ceremony of Introduction, made my appearance there; we staid till nearly three o'clock, had a good supper, & a pleasant party on the whole. Danced with Cecilia Wolseley, Miss Anson, Miss Salter the younger, Miss Russell & Maria Wolseley.* 2 Feb., 8 Mar: *Walked with Mrs. & Miss Russel.*

1806: 3 Feb: *Danced with Miss Smith, Miss Russel, Miss Monck, & Miss Wolseley.*

RUSSELL — wine merchant at Bath

1808: 30 Mar: *Rode to Clifton. returned the upper road to Bath, to the Elephant & Castle, where I slept after supping with Mr. Russel, the Wine Merchant.*

RUSSELL — of Wick Rissington, patient at Gloucester Infirmary

1844: 6 Dec: *Wrote to Mr. Hill, Secretary to Gloucester Infirmary, desiring him on the part of our Union to provide a pair of shoes for the patient Russel of Wick Risington.*

RUSSELL — Hannah Russell[113]

Hannah Russell (b. ±1795) was born at Buscot, Berkshire [now Oxfordshire]. She was sentenced to 6 months' imprisonment for larceny at the Gloucester Epiphany quarter session on 1 January 1839. In the 1841 census she was listed as living at Maugersbury, Stow-on-the-Wold, with her husband, John (±1787-1847). They had at least 3 sons and 2 daughters:

1 William (±1818-1879); died at Stow

1 Elizabeth (b. ±1830); married, at Stow, 1859, William Thomas Smith (b. 1831); at least 1 son and 1 daughter:

  1 John (1860-1930)

  1 Norah (b. 1865)

2 Mary (b. ±1832)

2 George (b. ±1834)

3 Charles (1840-1843)

By 1851 Hannah was a widow living at Little Rissington with her daughters Elizabeth and Mary. These two girls had been born in Wyck Rissington and their brother George had been born in Holyport, in the far east of Berkshire. It seems quite likely that the patient from Wyck Rissington in the entry above was of this same family. Nothing further has been found.

1838: 13 Oct: *The latter announces that the Police has not yet apprehended Hannah Russell, who, with her husband, has run away, they have also contrived to get their children away to accompany them.* 22 Oct: *Rode to Stow, to meet Mr. Pole, and examine witnesses with a view to the Committal of Hannah Russell, the woman charged with stealing clothing and articles of furniture from the Workhouse.* 18 Oct: *The theft committed by H. Russel was reported: it seems that she has gone out of the neighbourhood, and, eluding the vigilance of the police, is removed with her husband and three children.*

1839: 3 Jan: *In Purnell's Court two trials took place of prisoners whom I had committed ... and H. Russell, for stealing a quantity of linen, blankets, sheets, and wearing apparel from the Stow Union Workhouse, pleaded guilty, and was sentenced to six months imprisonment.*

RUSSELL — John Russell[114]

John Russell, 1st Earl Russell (1792-1878), prime minister, was the third son of John Russell, 6th duke of Bedford (d. 1839), and his first wife, Georgiana Elizabeth Byng, daughter of George, 4th Viscount Torrington. He was brother to both Francis Russell, marquis of Tavistock, and Lord George William Russell. John was educated by Dr Moore at Sunbury, Middlesex, at Westminster School (1803-04), and privately by Dr Edmund Cartwright (1804-05) and by Revd John Smith at Woodnesborough, Kent (1805-08). He matriculated at Edinburgh University in 1809 and graduated in 1812. Russell married, first, 1835, Adelaide (d. 1838), daughter of Thomas Lister of Armitage Park, Staffordshire; and secondly, 1841, Frances Anna Maria Elliot Murray Kynynmound, daughter of Gilbert Elliot Murray Kynynmound, 2nd earl of Minto. He was created Earl Russell in 1861, KG in 1862, and GCMG in 1869.

Russell entered parliament as MP for Tavistock in 1813, and held the seat until 1817. He was then MP for the following constituencies: Tavistock, 1818-20; Huntingdonshire, 1820-26; Bandon Bridge, 1826-30; Tavistock, 1830-31; Devon, 1831-32; Devon South, 1832-35; Stroud, 1835-41; and London, 1841-61. He became a privy councillor in 1830 and afterwards served in the following posts: paymaster-general, December 1830–December 1834 (in cabinet from June 1831); commissioner on civil administration of the Army, 1833-34 and 1835-37; secretary of state for home affairs, April 1835–September 1839; ecclesiastical commissioner, 1835-37; secretary of state for war and colonies, September 1839–September 1841; prime minister, 6 July 1846–27 February 1852 and 3 November 1865–6 July 1866; commissioner on new bishoprics, 1847; secretary of state for foreign affairs, December 1852–February 1853 and June 1859–November 1865; cabinet member without office, February 1853–June 1854; lord president of council, June 1854–February 1855; fourth charity commissioner, 1854-56; member of the special mission to Vienna, February–April 1855; and secretary of state for colonies, May–July 1855.

1828: 24 Mar: *In the beginning of the month the subject of the Corporation and Test Acts was brought before the House of Commons by Lord John Russel, a son of the Duke of Bedford, a whig, and esteemed a man of talent.*

1833: 18 Apr.

1835: 20 Feb: *This is an ominous and dispiriting defeat for Sir Robt. Peel's administration... the desire of opening the Session with a triumph against the ministry, have influenced the Whig and Radical party, united under the guidance of Lord John Russel, to propose in opposition to Sir C. M. Sutton their staunch liberal partizan, Mr. Abercromby.* 4 Apr: *The aspect of political affairs is very alarming: and there is every reason to apprehend that Sir Robert Peel and the Conservative administration must retire from the helm of the State. The leader of the Opposition, Lord John Russel, has been trying the strength of the relative parties by a motion as to the appropriation of the possible surplus revenue of the Church of Ireland.* 19 Apr: *The newspapers announce the near completion of a Whig Ministry under Lord Melbourne as Premier... Lord John Russell to be Secretary of State for the Home Department, and Leader of the House of Commons.* 27 Apr., 6 May, 13 May: *Howell confirms what has been already hinted in the newspapers, that Lord John Russell will at length be seated in the House of Commons for the District borough of Stroud.* 16 May: *Received a letter from my Son from Prinknash Park... On the evening of Edward's arrival at Prinknash, Lord John Russell and Col. Fox called at Howell's... My son represents [Russell] as a very mean looking, bilious person. He has recently married the widow of the late Lord Ribblesdale.* 12 Jun.

1839: 6 May: *Various political rumours were floating in the atmosphere of the House of Lords, and its purlieus; among others that Lord Melbourne and John Russel were about to retire from the administration.* 2 Sep.

1847: 21 Apr., 23-24 Apr., 27 Apr., 15 Dec., 22 Dec.

1852: 22 Feb: *The Whig Ministry have resigned. Lord John Russell goes out.*

RUSSELL — **Thomas Russell**[115]

Thomas Russell (b. ±1813), superintendent of police, was born in Ireland. He married Catherine (b. ±1815), who hailed from Cheltenham. He was one of the superintendents Thomas Lefroy had handpicked to bring with him when he was appointed chief constable at Cheltenham in 1839. Russell was later a commission agent and seems to have moved around from job to job, never again achieving a senior position.

1844: 30 Dec: *A complaint against the High Constable is expected to-morrow in consequence of his having dismissed Russel, the acting, thief-taking, and clever Superintendent at Cheltenham.* 31 Dec: *The expected attack on the Chief Constable on account of his dismissal of Mr. Russell from the post of Superintendent at Cheltenham was not made: Capt. Sinclair, the Mag. who had taken the matter up, having, by reference to the Constabulary Act, discovered that Lefroy had acted conformably to law: nor did he even make any comment on the transaction, as to be regretted, or unwise &c. which he had also threatened.*

1845: 15 Apr: *Sergeant Organ of the County Constabulary was appointed Governor of the Bridewell at Lawford's gate in the room of the deceased governor: there were many candidates, and, among them, Russel, late Superintendent of Police at Cheltenham, whom the Chief Constable had removed from his office for misconduct, but who was warmly supported by Cheltenham Magistrates; but Mr. Mirehouse, as connected with Lawford's Gate House of Correction, took care to expose the previous misconduct of Russel in a charge substantiated against him of an indecent assault upon a Policeman's wife, sometime since, which the Chief Constable had visited with a certain degree of punishment, short of dismissal, on the suggestion of the Magistrates before whom the case was heard.*

RUSSELL — **William Oldnall Russell**[116]

Sir William Oldnall Russell (±1784-1833), legal writer and judge in India, was the eldest son of Samuel Oldnall, rector of St Nicholas, Worcester, and North Piddle, and Mary, daughter of William Russell of Powick. In 1816, in accordance with the will of his maternal grandfather, William took the surname Russell, retaining Oldnall as a forename. He was educated at Christ Church, Oxford (BA 1804; MA 1807), and was admitted as a member of Lincoln's Inn in 1805. He was called to the bar in 1809 and became a serjeant-at-law in 1827. In 1819 he published a *Treatise on Crimes and Misdemeanours* (2 vols), which was by far the most significant output of his professional life.

In 1832 Charles Grant, president of the India board, appointed Russell chief justice of Bengal, whereupon Russell was knighted. Russell arrived at Calcutta in July 1832, but he became sick soon afterwards. He died on 22 January 1833 aboard the steamer *Enterprize* off the coast of Prince of Wales Island (Penang), where he had gone to recover his health. He was buried on the island the same day.

1826: 7 Aug: *Serjeant Wilde had been retained, & was expected every moment from the Western circuit ... They could not go to trial without him: Messrs. Curwood, Ludlow & C. Phillips without him, would be as chaff before the wind; able men as they are, before Mr. Scarlett, supported by Messrs. Campbell, Russel, Talfoard and Justice.*

1827: 15 Apr: *The judges ... They came attended by the Sheriff and his chaplain, also their Marshall, Mr. Blick: the company invited to meet them were Mr. Taunton & Mr. Russel, Barristers; .... Mr. Russel is rising into eminence in his profession. He is author of a valuable work on Crimes & misdemeanours, which is a manual of forensic jurisprudence, extremely valuable to the profession, and to those, who preside in Courts: even the Judges frequently refer to it, and to Chairmen in Quarter Sessions it is very useful.*

RUSSELL PAKINGTON — *see* Pakington

RUTHVEN — **James Ruthven**[117]

James Ruthven, 7th [5th] Lord Ruthven of Freeland (1777-1853), landed proprietor, was the son of James Ruthven, 6th [4th] Lord Ruthven of Freeland (1733-1789), and Mary Elizabeth (1767-1820), daughter of David Leslie-Melville, 6th earl of Leven, and Wilhelmina, countess of Leven. Clearly something is wrong here; Mary Elizabeth could not have given birth at the age of 10. It may be presumed that her correct date of birth was some ten years or so earlier. *The Complete Peerage* states that the peerage became extinct on the death of the unmarried 2nd earl in 1701, but that the heir to entail of the estates assumed the peerage. On this basis James was 7th Lord Ruthven of Freeland. He held the rank of major in the 90th Foot and succeeded as 7th Lord in 1789. According to *The Complete Peerage* he died unmarried, but in the Edinburgh parish archives there is a clear marriage registration, dated 18 December 1813, between James Ruthven and Mary Hamilton Campbell (1789-1885), daughter of Walter Campbell, 9th of Skipness and 3rd of Shawfield, and Mary Campbell. There were no children, and James was succeeded in the barony by his sister Mary Elizabeth Thornton Ruthven (1784-1864), who married, 1806, William Hore of Harperstown.

The Hon. D. Ruthven was James's brother, David (1787-1808), who was placed in the Bengal civil establishment in 1805, and died at Madras in 1808. In *The Ruthven Family Papers*, Samuel Cowan gives different numberings to the Lords Ruthven.

1806: 27 Jan: *... to a Rout & dance given by Mrs. M. Causland, which would have been more pleasant, if I had known more of her guests & there had been fewer children. We were accompanied by Mrs. C. Roberts. I danced with Miss M. Morse, Mrs. J. Auriol, Mrs. Parris & Miss Binden. Conversed with C. Roberts, Ryan, the Hon. D. Ruthven &c.* 2 Mar: *Passed the Evening most pleasantly & supped at the Goolds; besides the family party & myself, no one but Lord Ruthvan, a great deal of pleasant Conversation & music.* 11 Mar: *Dined in a large, dashing party at Gillibrand's the Adair family, Lords Kilwarden & Ruthven; Major Cochrane & P.J. Miles, formed the party.*

RYAN — Edward Ryan [118]

Sir Edward Ryan (1793-1875), judge in India and civil service commissioner, was the eldest son of John Burke Ryan of Grosvenor Place, London. He was educated at Trinity College, Cambridge (BA 1814; MA 1817), and married, at Teignmouth, Devon, 13 December 1814, Louisa (1789-1866), sixth daughter of William Whitmore of Dudmaston Hall, Bridgnorth, Shropshire. They had at least 9 sons and 3 daughters:

1 Edmund Burke (1816-1850)
1 Frances Hanway (1817-1838)
2 Louisa (1819-1906)
2 John Cavendish (1820-1822)
3 Wolryche Whitmore (1821-1867)
3 Mary Anna (b. 1823)
4 Edward Moody (1824-1879)
5 Robert Henry (b. 1825)
6 Fredrick York (1827-1829)
7 Charles Lister (1832-1920)
8 William Cavendish Bentick (1833-1889)
9 Edward Henry (1837-1929)

In 1817 Ryan was called to the bar at Lincoln's Inn and began practising on the Oxford circuit. In 1825 he published, with William Oldnall Russell, *Crown Cases Reserved for Consideration and Decided by the Twelve Judges of England from the Year 1799*. In November 1826 he was appointed a puisne judge of the supreme court at Calcutta and knighted (27 November). He arrived at Calcutta in 1827 and narrowly escaped death from fever several times during his chief justiceship. By 1842 Ryan had resigned the post and returned to England.

1842: 24 May: *We dined at Maugersbury with the Franks's, a pleasant party; meeting Lady Ryan and her younger son: she is an agreeable person, half sister to Mrs. Franks, Whitmore Jones &c. and wife of Sir E. Ryan, a Judge, who has recently returned from the Bench at Calcutta with a pension, not now staying with the Franks's, being gone to Town.*

RYAN — John Ryan — *see also* Manning [119]

John Ryan (±1740-1808), polymath, physician, planter, slave-owner, freemason, merchant, and naturalist, was arguably one of the most interesting people that Francis Witts ever met. He was probably born on the island of Montserrat in the West Indies, or possibly 200 miles to the north-west on the island of St John in the Danish West Indies. Information is patchy; he is likely have been the son of William Ryan (d. 1753) and had brothers named Henry and William. He was also probably a cousin of William Manning of Totteridge. The Ryan family were residents of long standing in Montserrat, having settled there in the late seventeenth century during the reign of Charles II. They remained Catholic, and in the 1750s and '60s, like many West Indian Catholic sons, John Ryan was sent, with his brothers Henry and William, to the Jesuit College at St Omer, Normandy.

The Ryan family, along with the Bakers, their protestant relations by marriage, were British and Irish merchant-planters who, by the early eighteenth century, had migrated to the Danish West Indies from the British Leeward Islands. Although they became neutral subjects of the Danish crown, they also maintained personal and commercial ties with the British Empire. In this way, they successfully established a number of sugar plantations and took advantage of the brisk entrepôt trade that developed on St Croix in the Danish West Indies during this period. The Ryan family (or possibly John Ryan alone) owned a passenger and cargo vessel that constantly plied between the Leeward Islands and St Croix. The family shipped a good deal of sugar to Denmark, and also supplied the besieged French colony of Saint Domingue with British and Irish goods, together with African slaves. In return, Saint Domingue was given an international market for its plantation produce.

John Ryan eventually settled at St Croix. In addition to his his native English and school-learnt French, he adopted Dutch and Danish by necessity. The Dutch were the first owners of the islands that later became Danish, and Dutch (Nederlandsch) was the main language spoken there. John was the owner of estates in the King's, Queen's, and East End quarters of St Croix, and his brothers Henry and William became successful planters in their own right; Henry owned an estate, Plessens, in the Prince's quarter of St John.

In 1777, at St Croix, Ryan was installed as the provincial grand master of the freemasons' grand lodge of England. He was also a member of a freemasons' lodge in Copenhagen; when in Denmark he lived at Frederiksberg, at that time a separate town to Copenhagen. He was a noted naturalist, herbalist, collector, and patron; the following was the proposal for his election as a fellow of the Royal Society:

> John Ryan Esqr of Great Marlborough Street, a Gentleman well versed in various branches of Philosophy and particularly in Natural History, being desirous of the honour of becoming a Fellow of the Royal Society, we whose names are undersigned do from our personal knowledge recommend him as deserving of that honour, and as likely to be a most useful Member. Proposers A. B. Lambert; George Pearson; Thos Martyn; Joseph Correa de Serra; George Shaw; Maxwell Garthsore; Tho Bowdler; Chas Hatchett.

From this we learn that in addition to his homes at St Croix and Frederiksberg, Ryan maintained a London house, although it may have been the address of a fellow learned colleague merely used for convenience. Ryan was also a fellow of the Linnean Society of London. In 1802 he gave his address as Copenhagen, but by 1808, the year of his death, he gave it as St Croix, so he appears to have retired there.

John Ryan was first mentioned by Agnes Witts in her diary entry of 5 August 1798. He was a fellow passenger on the vessel *George and Mary*, which the Witts family took from Leith to Hamburg. What he was doing in Scotland is not clear, but he was remarkably well-travelled. Three weeks later, on 26 August 1798, Agnes wrote that John Ryan was on the move again: 'Mr. Ryan call'd on us before he set off for Amsterdam'. By October 1800 Ryan had discovered that the Witts family were living in Copenhagen; we know from Agnes Witts's diary that their acquaintance picked up again. After the Witts family was evacuated from Copenhagen, Ryan caught up with them again in London, and Agnes recorded that she saw him again at Clifton three years later, on 20 July 1804; it is most likely that he was in Bristol to board a ship for the West Indies. It is known that Ryan returned to Bristol in 1806, but as for personal details such as his family, information is scarce. It is not known whether he was married.

1798: 13 Aug: *After dining with the Captain on Board, we left the Vessel in a Shore Boat, and landed on a Place called the Foresaddle Back; Mr. Ryan and our Party went to the Hotel Copenhagen.* 15 Aug: *The Company besides ourselves consisted of two Gentlemen Mr. Ryan and Mr. White. We had a most excellent and worthy man in our fellow Passenger, Mr. Ryan: whose kindness to part of our Family who were afflicted with that almost unavoidable concurrence the Sea Sickness, will ever deserve our highest Gratitude, and the Information which as a Man of Learning well acquainted with the world, he was calculated to give, was to the younger part of our Party most extensively useful.*

1801: 2 Jun: *Called after breakfast upon Mr. Ryan Steevens's Coffee house New Bond Street. He was more angry than ever with the measures of the British Government towards Denmark.* 6 Jun., 8 Jun: *Mr. Ryan called in the Morning.*

1804: 23 Jul: *Walked in the Evening with my Father & Mother, Mr. Ryan, the Manners's &c.* 29-30 Jul., 4 Aug., 21 Aug., 23 Aug., 26 Aug., 30-31 Aug., 1-2 Sep., 5 Sep., 7 Sep., 9 Sep., 25 Sep., 27 Sep., 4 Oct.

1805: 10 Jan: *Bristol, &c. met Ryan, Miss Fortescue, Wolseleys &c.*

1806: 17 Jan: *Went down in a postchaise with my Mother & Mr. Ryan; joined Mrs. Salter &c.* 18 Jan: *Accompanied Ryan in the Morning to Queen Square.* 27 Jan., 11 Feb., 25 Feb., 27 Feb., 6-7 Mar., 13-14 Mar.

RYAN — Patrick Ryan and the Ryan family of Eyford [120]

Patrick Ryan (±1795-1865), gardener, was born in Ireland and lived at the Gardener's Lodge, Eyford, with his wife Lucy (±1790-1854) and daughter Mary Anne (b. ±1825), also born in Ireland.

1834: 28 Oct: *Wrote to the Revd. James Griffith, Rathkeale, Co. Limerick, at the request of Mrs. Ryan, the wife of the gardener at Eyford, to make enquiries about a sum of money to which her daughter is entitled, and which is stated to be under the control of Mr. Griffith and another, as Executors of the will of the child's maternal grandfather.*

1835: 3 Mar: *Received a letter from the Revd. James Griffiths, Rathkeale, Ireland, in answer to one addressed by me to that gentleman in October last. He replies that the money bequeathed to Mary Anne Ryan, daughter of the Eyford Gardener, by her deceased Grandfather, has been invested in Mr. G.'s name as Trustee for the infant, in the Limerick Savings Bank.*

1844: 9 Apr., 12 Apr., 30 Apr., 10 May, 2 Oct., 4 Oct., 9 Oct: *Letters from ... M. A. Ryan, respecting a deposit which she proposes to make in the Provident Bank at Stow.* 11 Oct., 5 Nov., 15 Nov., 20 Nov.

1847: 26 Jan., 11 Jun., 24 Jul: *Visited the Ryan family at the Mansion House; the daughter an invalid.* 21 Aug: *Capt. Frobisher, accompanied by Ryan, Mrs. Dolphin's gardener, and his daughter, called.*

1848: 28 Jan., 18 Mar., 2 Apr, 7 Aug: *Mary Ryan called on us; full of uneasiness as to proceedings at Eyford.*

1849: 18 Dec.

1850: 14 Jan: *It seems that Mrs. D. in correspondence, or by her amanuensis, Mary Anne Ryan, has exaggerated ...* 19 Feb., 3 Aug.

1851: 15 Feb.

1852: 23 Jan: *Walked to Eyford; visited Mrs. Ryan, who is confined to her bed by a bad humour in her leg.* 30 Jan., 2 Feb., 14 Feb., 12 Mar., 20 Apr., 22 May, 8 Dec: *Called on Mrs. Ryan, the Gardner's wife.*

1853: 20 Apr., 24 May: *Received a note from M. Ryan, Eyford, desiring to know when I will administer Holy Communion privately to her sick mother.* 27 May.

1854: 13 Mar: *Mrs. Ryan, confined by a complication of maladies to her couch.* 13 Jun: *Walked to Eyford, to call on poor Mrs. Ryan, suffering grievously from a cancerous tumour over the eyes, and from internal disease in the urinary passages.* 28 Jun.

RYCROFT — Henry Rycroft [121]

Sir Henry Rycroft (1766-1846), knight harbinger to King George III, was the second husband of Francis Witts's cousin Jane (1765-1797), younger daughter of Ferdinand Tracy Travell. He was the second son of Sir Richard Rycroft, 1st baronet (1736-1786), and Penelope Stonehewer, and younger brother to Sir Nelson Rycroft, 2nd baronet (1761-1827), of Farnham, Surrey. Henry was appointed knight harbinger to King George III in 1797. This office, created in 1660, was a department within the transportation establishment of the court. The knight harbinger and his subordinates below stairs were responsible for finding accommodation for the court while on the move. The knight harbinger was appointed by the lord chamberlain's warrant. Originally the office was held for life, but after 1695, it was only held 'during good behaviour'. Rycroft's two predecessors had each held the office for about thirty years, and he held it himself until at least 1837. The remuneration originally consisted of 10*s* a day and 40 marks a year, totalling £193 16*s* 8*d* a year, plus riding wages and fees of honour which yielded around £60 per year. Henry Rycroft was knighted for his services in 1816.

Jane and Henry Rycroft did not have any children, and there are very few other references to them in the diaries. In the early 1790s there was frequent correspondence between Agnes Witts and Jane Rycroft, but this petered out and Jane died in 1797.

1801: 18 Aug: *Received a most gratifying Letter from Mr. Rycroft, in which he offers to me the situation of Secretary to Lord Pelham, Secretary of State for the Home Department, which I immediately accepted in an answer, which I instantly wrote to him.* 19 Aug., 2 Sep., 4 Sep., 11-12 Sep., 28 Sep.

RYCROFT — Jane Rycroft — *see* Naper

RYCROFT — Richard Henry Charles Rycroft [122]

Sir Richard Henry Charles Rycroft, 3rd baronet (1793-1864), landed proprietor, was the eldest son of Sir Nelson Rycroft, 2nd baronet (1761-1827), and Charlotte (1771-1803), daughter of Henry and Frances Read. He was the nephew of Sir Henry Rycroft (*above*). Richard succeeded as 3rd baronet in 1827. He married, 18 May 1830, Charlotte Ann Josephine (1805-1874), eldest daughter of William Tennant, of Little Aston Hall, Staffordshire, and Maria Charlotte, daughter of Charles Pelham, 1st Baron Yarborough. They had at least 2 sons:

1 Nelson (1831-1894); succeeded as 4th baronet
2 Charles Alfred William (b. 1839)

1823: 10 May: *Called on different acquaintances at Giggleswick & Settle, & dined at the former place with Mrs. Bolland, meeting the Pearts, Robinsons & Geldards, and Mr. Rycroft, eldest Son of a baronet of that name, who has estates in this neighbourhood, at Little Stainforth, Calton Hall, and Coniston, but resides on his estates in Kent near Farnham. Sir Nelson Rycroft's younger Brother, Sir Henry Rycroft, Knight Harbinger to the King married Mrs. Naper, the widow of the Hon. James Naper, brother to the late Lord Sherborne, & daughter of my Uncle Mr. F.J. Travell, Rector of Upper Slaughter. A sister of Mr. Rycroft's (for he was not then knighted) was married to Dr. Pelham, Bishop of Exeter, and now of Lincoln, and Brother to the Earl of Chichester. By this chain of connexion, I was in 1801 promised the appointment of private Secretary to Lord Chichester, then Lord Pelham, and recently appointed Secretary of State for the Home department; after some weeks expectation of an immediate introduction into that post, his Lordship caused to be intimated to me, that he should not require such services, because, I believe, his own appointment as Secretary for the Home department was only temporary, and I was disappointed of my promised place. Shortly after, I entered the University, and my views were decidedly turned to the Clerical profession.*

1830: 24 Jun: *The only other guests, besides ourselves, were Sir Richard & Lady Rycroft, a bride & bridegroom. I had met with him several years ago at Settle in very different society, & did not find him altered or improved. By his Father's decease he is now the baronet. His Lady was a Miss Tennant, whose parents reside at Brighton, of good family, but neither attractive in person nor in countenance, nor bringing much fortune. We thought, there was not much in mind or manners to recommend her; but brides are apt to take airs, and in a few months Lady Rycroft may be seen to more advantage. It was in May 1823, that I first made Sir H. Rycroft's acquaintance.*

1837: 5 Apr: *The proposition of Mr. Dawson has been most generously met by wealthy proprietors in the township of Great & Little Stainforth; as to the latter Mr. Clapham gives £100 and our Tenants, the Armisteads, £30 though they have no landed property in the Township: it does not appear that Sir Richard Rycroft has been applied to as yet.*

RYDER — Dudley Ryder [123]

Dudley Ryder, 1st earl of Harrowby (1762-1847), politician, was born in the parish of St George, Hanover Square, London, the eldest of the three sons of Nathaniel Ryder, 1st Baron Harrowby (1735-1803), and Elizabeth, daughter of Richard Terrick, bishop of London. He was the brother of Henry (*below*). Ryder was educated at Harrow School and St John's College, Cambridge (MA 1782; Hon. LLD 1833). He was also awarded a DCL in 1814 from the University of Oxford.

Ryder entered parliament in 1784 as MP for Tiverton and retained the seat until 1803. His notable appointments were as follows: under-secretary of state for foreign affairs, 1789-90; paymaster-general, 1790; privy councillor, 1790; comptroller of the household, 1790-91; member of the India Board of Control, 1790-91; vice-president of the Board of Trade, 1791-1801; chairman of the finance committee, 1791; treasurer of the Navy, 1799-1801; chairman of the corn committee, 1800; foreign secretary, 1804; chancellor of the duchy of Lancaster with a seat in the cabinet, 1805-06; ambassador extraordinary and minister plenipotentiary to Berlin, Vienna, and St Petersburg, 1805; president of the Board of Control for India Affairs, 1809; member of the cabinet, without office, 1809-12; lord president of the council, 1812-27. Ryder went on special mission to Brussels in 1815 to confer with Wellington. He retired from office on Canning's death in 1827 and was offered the prime ministership, but refused it.

Ryder succeeded his father as 2nd Baron Harrowby in 1803, and was created earl of Harrowby and Viscount Sandon in 1809. He married, 30 July 1795, Susan Leveson-Gower (1772-1838), third daughter of Granville Leveson-Gower, 1st marquess of Stafford; they had 4 sons and 5 daughters, including:

1 Dudley (1798-1882); succeeded as 2nd earl of Harrowby; married, 15 September 1823, Frances (1801-1859), fourth daughter of John Stuart, 1st marquess of Bute
2 Granville Dudley (1799-1879); married, 30 May 1825, his cousin Lady Georgiana Augusta (1800-1865), third daughter of Henry Charles Somerset, 6th duke of Beaufort, and Charlotte Sophia Leveson-Gower, second daughter of Granville Leveson-Gower, 1st marquess of Stafford, by his third wife
3 Frederick Dudley (1806-1882); married, 14 August 1839, Marian Charlotte Emily (d. 1873), only child of Thomas Cockayne of Ickleford House, Bedfordshire
1 Susan (1796-1827); married, 4 July 1817, Hugh Fortescue, 2nd Earl Fortescue
2 Mary (d. 1900); married, 15 July 1828, Adm. Edward Saurin (d. 1878)
3 Georgiana Elizabeth (1804-1844); married, 12 December 1825 John Stuart-Wortley, 2nd Baron Wharncliffe
4 Harriet Charlotte Sophia (d. 1899); married, 15 August 1839, Revd Lord Charles Hervey
5 Louisa (d. 1899); married, 19 February 1833, Capt. George Matthew Fortescue (1791-1877)

1825: 19 Jul: *The others were the late Col. Barry, Lord Harrowby, Lord Ashtown, Lord Montague, and Mr. Barclay, also an eminent quaker banker: others occasionally joined our circle round the pump room fire for an hour before breakfast.*

1827: 14 Apr: *It is stated also, that several of the high officers of State have sent in their resignation. Now as to the ministers remaining in office, they are all advocates of the Roman Catholic claims; the Earl of Harrowby, Mr. F. Robinson, Mr. Wynne, and Mr. Huskisson.* 28 Aug: *Lord Harrowby retires from the Government, and his post of Lord President of the Council is conferred on the Duke of Portland, who, though a member of the cabinet, had of late been without office.* 11 Jan: *The premiership was actually offered to & refused by Lord Harrowby.*

1832: 10 Apr: *The leading peers who have seceded from the ranks of the Anti-reformers, and have given in a qualified adhesion to the measure, are Lord Harrowby and Lord Wharncliffe.* 10 May: *Nothing decisive has transpired as to the new ministry: it appears, that the King has put himself into communication with the Duke of Wellington, Lord Lyndhurst and Lord Harrowby.* 6 Jun.

1835: 6 Feb: *On this Commission are appointed the Archb. of Canterbury and York, the Bishops of Lincoln & Gloucester, the Bishop of London, the principal Ministers of State, Lord Harrowby, and certain eminent Civilians.*

1836: 4 Nov.

1844: 8 Oct., 28 Nov., 16 Dec.

1848: 28 Mar.

RYDER — Henry Ryder [124]

Henry Ryder (1777-1836), bishop of Gloucester, was the fifth son of Nathaniel Ryder, 1st Baron Harrowby, and Elizabeth, daughter of Richard Terrick, bishop of London. He was the younger brother of Dudley (*above*). Ryder was educated at St John's College, Cambridge (MA 1798; DD 1813), and entered the Church. He was curate of Sandon, Staffordshire, 1801; rector of Lutterworth, Leicestershire, 1801-14; vicar of Claybrooke, 1805-15; canon of Windsor, 1808; dean of Wells, 1812-31; bishop of Gloucester, 1815-24; bishop of Lichfield and Coventry, 1824-36; and prebendary of Westminster, 1831-36. There was some opposition to Ryder's appointment as bishop of Gloucester in 1815 owing to his strong evangelical views. He married, 1802, Sophia (1780-1862), daughter of Thomas March Phillipps of Garendon Park, Leicestershire; they had at least 10 sons and 3 daughters:

1 Henry Dudley (1803-1877), canon residentiary of Lichfield
1 Anna Sophia (1805-1893)
2 Charles Dudley (1806-1825)
2 Harriet Amelia (1808-1885)
3 George Dudley (1810-1880)
4 Arthur Dudley (1811-1880)
5 William Dudley (1813-1894)
6 Thomas Dudley (1815-1886)
3 Sophia (1817-1901)
7 Edward Lisle (1818-1846)
8 Alfred Phillips (1820-1888), Adm.; knighted
9 Richard Calthorpe Whitmore (1822-1897)
10 Spencer Charles Dudley (1825-1873)

1824: 4 Feb: *Attended the consecration of Bathwick new Church by the name of St. Mary's; the duties of the Bishop of Bath and Wells being performed by Bishop Ryder, of Gloucester.* 29 Mar., 24 May: *It is generally understood, that Bp Ryder had set his heart on the Diocese of Bath & Wells, but accepted Lichfield and Coventry on finding, that Dr. Law had received the promise of the former, on Dr. Beadon's decease.* 27 Jun., 19 Oct.

1832: 10 Apr: *Several of the Bishops also have declared themselves in favour of the second reading.* 9 May, 17 May: *On Sunday last, a charity Sermon was advertised to be preached at St. Bride's Church by the Bishop of Lichfield and Coventry: placards were issued to collect a mob with a view of interrupting and insulting the Prelate in the discharge of his duty. He had voted for the Second reading of the bill, but against ministers in the division on Lord Lyndhurst's motion. Though a meek, and fair far from stout, man, Dr. Ryder did not flinch from his duty.*

S

SABINE — Joseph Sabine and the Sabine family — *see also* Baring-Gould *and* Hunt[1]

Joseph Sabine (1744-1814), army officer, was born at Tewin House, Hertfordshire, the son of John Sabine (1712-1776) and Susannah Osborne (1726-1759). He was the grandson of Gen. Joseph Sabine (1661-1739), a man with a distinguished military career. After fighting in 1695 at the siege of Namur during the Nine Years' War, Sabine served in Flanders throughout the War of the Spanish Succession, commanding his regiment at the battle of Blenheim in 1704 and the battle of Oudenarde and the siege of Lille in 1708. He was an MP in the government interest for Berwick, where he was also governor until 1730. In March 1727 he was made lieutenant-general, and in July 1730 he was promoted to general. In 1730 he was sent as governor to Gibraltar, where he died in 1739.

Joseph Sabine married, at Condover, Shropshire, 13 August 1769, Sarah (1758-1788), daughter of Thomas Hunt, of Boreatton, Shropshire (1704-1777), and Sarah (1715-1766), daughter of Edward Witts of Witney, Oxfordshire. Sarah Hunt, née Witts, was the sister of Francis Witts's grandfather, Broome Witts (1713-1768), and therefore great aunt to Francis. The children of the Sabine family were first cousins once removed to Francis Witts.

Sarah Sabine, née Hunt, appears to have been close to Apphia, Lady Lyttelton, and to Francis's father, Edward Witts. It was the missing likeness of Mrs Sabine that formed the basis of some correspondence between brother and sister back in 1793. The Sabine family does not feature much in Francis Witts's diaries, although there are numerous references in the diaries of his mother Agnes. Along with Ferdinand Travell, Joseph Sabine was a trustee of the marriage settlement between Edward and Agnes Witts.

Although originally from Ireland, the Sabines had lived in Hertfordshire since 1715. Joseph Sabine found the estate so encumbered when he inherited it that he was eventually forced to sell Tewin House, but he and Sarah continued to live in the county. They had 4 sons and 3 daughters:

- 1 Joseph (1770-1837); died unmarried
- 1 Caroline Susanna (1771-1842); married, at St Marylebone, Westminster, 21 June 1797, Henry Browne (1754-1830) of North Mymms Place; 1 son and 5 daughters:
  - 1 Caroline (1798-1855); married, at Langham, 11 August 1831, James Power
  - 2 Amelia (1799-1878); died unmarried
  - 3 Anna Maria (1801-1876); died unmarried
  - 4 Harriet (b. 1803)
  - 5 Juliana (1806-1874); died unmarried
  - 1 Henry Sabine (1808-1843); married, at Plymouth, 26 February 1840, Isabel Harriet Anne Bremer (1815-1866)
- 2 John (1773-1805), Maj.; married, 1800, Maria Magdalen (1775-1839), daughter of Adm. Sir Thomas Pasley, 1st baronet; at least 1 son:
  - 1 Thomas (1804-1884), Adm.; changed his name to Pasley by royal licence, 1809; succeeded as 2nd baronet; appointed KCB
- 2 Diana Amelia (1774-1858); married, 1801, William Baring-Gould (1770-1846) of Lew Trenchard, Devon; 5 sons and 3 daughters:
  - 1 Harriet (1801-1857)
  - 2 Margaret (1803-1853)
  - 1 Edward (1804-1872); married, 1832, Sophia Charlotte (d. 1863), daughter of Adm. Francis Godolphin Bond
  - 2 William (1805-1839)
  - 3 Charles (1807-1881)
  - 4 Henry Sabine (1810-1811)
  - 3 Emily Sabine (1812-1893)
  - 5 Alexander (1814-1899)
- 3 Henry (1779-1781); died an infant
- 3 Sarah (1783-1834); appears to have died unmarried
- 4 Edward (1788-1883), Gen.; appointed KCB; married, at St Olave's, Chichester, Sussex, 14 December 1826, Elizabeth Julianna (1807-1879), daughter of William Leeves of Tortington, Sussex; at least 1 son and 1 daughter:
  - 1 Alphonse Gillman (b. 1845)
  - 1 Elizabeth (dates unknown)

Sarah died a month after the birth of Edward in 1788. Caroline, then aged 17, kept house for her father and 'mothered' the younger children until her marriage to Henry Browne in 1797. She and Henry had a family of six children. Henry was a very wealthy man, being chief of the HEIC's settlement at Canton [Guangzhou], China. He was keenly interested in new farming methods and in the experiments of 'Turnip' Townshend of Bakewell. He was elected a fellow of both the Society of Antiquaries and the Royal Society. He bought North Mymms Place from the duke of Leeds around the time of his marriage. Caroline's father got on well with his son-in-law and made North Mymms his home until his death in 1814.

Joseph Sabine's eldest son Joseph (1770-1837) was essentially a country man. He had an absorbing interest in horticulture and rare plants and ornithology, especially in British birds. He practised law until 1808, when he was appointed inspector-general of taxes. He held this position until 1835. He was an original member of the Linnean Society, founded in 1788, and as the honorary secretary of the Royal Horticultural Society, he straightened its accounts and methods. For these services the society presented him with a gold medal. He was a fellow of the Royal Society from his 60th birthday until his death, and at 67 he was actively interested in the Zoological Society. These 'facts' seem at complete odds with Francis Witts's diary entry for 24 June 1830.

Diana Amelia Sabine (1774-1858) married William Baring (1770-1846), son of Charles Baring (1742-1829) and Margaret Drake (1742-1803), heir of William Drake Gould of Lew Trenchard. Charles Baring accordingly changed his name to Baring-Gould in 1795. Diana's son, Edward Baring (1804-1872), also changed his name to Baring-Gould in accordance with a provision in his grandmother Margaret's will. He married Sophia Charlotte Bond. Their son, Sabine Baring-Gould (1834-1924), was the famous writer perhaps best known for the hymn 'Onward Christian Soldiers'. Sabine Baring-Gould met and fell in love with a Yorkshire mill girl, Grace Taylor (1850-1916), daughter of Joseph Taylor of Horbury. Grace could not read or write, so Baring-Gould sent her away to be educated for two years. He then married her at the church of St Peter and St Leonard, Horbury, Yorkshire, on 24 May 1868. George Bernard Shaw is said to have based his play *Pygmalion* on the story of Sabine and Grace.

Edward Sabine (1788-1883) had his education supervised by his brother Joseph, eighteen years his senior, and his brother-in-law, Henry Browne. He became an officer in the Royal Artillery, but the duke of Wellington granted him general leave of absence on the understanding 'that he was usefully employed in scientific pursuits'. On 9 May 1813 the packet *Manchester* sailed out of Falmouth bound for Canada with a 'Mr. Sabine', surgeon, on board, accompanied by his cousin Edward in the official capacity of astronomer. This 'Mr. Sabine' may have been Edward's cousin John Lewis Sabine, but no details have been discovered about him. Eight days out from Falmouth the *Manchester* was attacked by the *Yorktown*, an American privateer; in the ensuing battle, which lasted twenty hours, Edward Sabine and his young soldier attendant were said to have handled a gun 'to good effect'. The *Manchester* was, however, 'compelled to strike her colours'. Two months later she was recaptured by a British frigate, and, after a short spell of service at Quebec, Edward returned to England. Two expeditions followed in search of the Northwest Passage: in 1818 in the *Isabella* under Cdr Ross, and in May of the following year under Sir Edward Parry. Edward became a recognised authority on Arctic bird life and a general in the Army. He was elected a fellow of the Royal Society in 1818, and was treasurer in 1850-61 and president in 1861-71. He was also president of the British Association for the Advancement of Science. He was appointed KCB in 1860, and died in 1883 at the ripe old age of 95. He was married with at least two children.

1801: 22 May, 26 May.

1823: 9 Apr: *Mrs. Baring Goold, who with her daughter was on a visit to Mrs. Hunt, & about to leave Gloucester to-day on a visit of a short duration to my Aunt Lady Lyttelton at Pickham Grove. Mrs. B. Goold is daughter of the late Mr. & Mrs. Sabine. Mrs. S. was Sister to Mrs. Hunt, of Boreatton in Shropshire & consequently cousin to my Father; the late Mr. Hunt's Mother having been a Witts, Sister to my Grandfather. The Baring Goold's reside at Teignmouth in Devon. Her brother Jos: Sabine was employed in the Tax Department, perhaps, is now; & is in many respects a scientific character. He is Secretary to the horticultural Society, and a distinguished Ornithologist. Another brother, Edward, is Captn. in the Royal Artillery, & a person of eminent attainments in the philosophical Sciences. He accompanied the Navigators, Captn. Ross & Captn. Parry, on their Expeditions to the North Pole, or, more correctly, in search of a Northwest passage, as Astronomer to the expedition; but did not sail with the adventurous & able Captn. Parry in his third Voyage .... To return to Captn. Sabine; he has been again, &, I believe, still is engaged in taking, under the sanction & direction of the government, astronomical observations, which have for their object the elucidation of many highly important points of Geography, Geometry, & Navigation. These researches have carried him on the coast of Africa, &, I believe, will require a voyage to the extremity of Northern Europe, & another visit to the regions of the icy Sea.*

1827: 23 Apr: *We passed the evening at Mrs. Hunt's, who has now staying with her Miss Sabine, with two friends of hers, Miss Irtons. I never have had the pleasure of meeting my cousin, Miss Sabine, before. She is sister of Mr. Sabine, Capt. Edward Sabine, of scientific fame, Mrs. Browne, Mrs. Baring Gould &c. and resides at Bath. She appears a woman of cultivated mind & understanding and much accomplished. A specimen of her drawings, which we saw, bespeaks her a superior artist in a peculiar style. With water colours, she pourtrays a minute miniature panorama of extensive & interesting scenery, with groupes of figures, buildings, shipping &c. Thus she expands before you the environs of Teignmouth, Devon; the glorious scenery round Keswick, embracing in one panorama Derwent Water, Borrowdale, Bassenthwaite Lake &c.* 14 Jul: *The former lady, with her two relatives Misses Caroline & Maria Hunt, I found on the point of setting out for Malvern, on an excursion of a few days. I found with them Mr. E. Baring Gould, son of Mr. B. Gould, who married my relative, Miss Sabine, & elder brother of the youth, who was pupil of Mr. Price and is now a student at Cambridge.*

1830: 24 Jun: *My distant relation, Mr. Sabine, is or was nominal Treasurer of the Zoological Society; in reality, he did not discharge the duty, nor had any controul over the funds, although his name was on the list of the Officers; and his unfortunate mismanagement of the affairs of the Sister Society, the Horticultural, which has been lately developed, induced the members of the Zoological to wish, that he had not even a nominal place in the management of their concerns. Not that any want of integrity has been proved against M. Sabine in the discharge of his duties as Secretary of the Horticulturists, but he suffered the affairs of that institution to fall into great embarrassment, carelessly incurred very exorbitant & unnecessary expence, was jealous of any interference, & inattentive to the requests of the members of the Society. The result has been the necessity of retiring from the concern altogether, not without disgrace & loud censure; & a system of economy has been adopted by the directors of the Institution strongly contrasted with that lavish disbursement, which Mr. Sabine sanctioned, & which so nearly led to the bankruptcy & dissolution of the society.*

1840: 6 May: *Left my card at No. 2 Portland Place with Mrs. Browne, at the same time giving in charge to her servant a watch, late my Aunt Lyttelton's, which had been several years since promised by her to Mrs. Power, Mrs. Browne's daughter: the watch presented an enamelled Miniature of Mrs. Sabine, formerly Miss Hunt of Boreatton, Mrs. Browne's mother.*

SADLER — Michael Thomas Sadler[2]

Michael Thomas Sadler (1780-1835), MP for Newark (1829-34), was a partner in an Irish linen importing company in Leeds and travelled frequently in Ireland on business. He was active in public life as a social reformer. His reputation was such that when the Brontës played their game of 'Islanders' in 1827, Charlotte reported that Anne chose Sadler as one of her three great men of England. He spoke and voted against Catholic emancipation, but was a prime mover in promoting the Factories Act.

1829: 25 Mar: *Mr. Sadler is a Merchant of Leeds, whose affairs have taken him a good deal into Ireland, and who has paid great attention to the state of society, & the political relations of that unhappy island.*

SADLER — Samuel Farmer Sadler[3]

Samuel Farmer Sadler (±1760-1816), Church of England clergyman, was educated at Pembroke College, Oxford (BA 178; MA 1788), and was vicar of Sandhurst, near Gloucester. He married Catharine Ann Parsons (b. 1760); they had 2 sons:

1 Samuel Farmer (1795-1862), Church of England clergyman; *see below*
2 James Hayes (1795-1845), Church of England clergyman; lived in Portman Square, London, and Keynsham Bury, Cheltenham

SADLER — Samuel Farmer Sadler[4]

Samuel Farmer Sadler (1795-1862), Church of England clergyman, was born at Sandhurst, Gloucestershire, the son of Samuel Farmer Sadler and Catharine Ann Parsons (*above*). He was educated at Balliol College, Oxford, and became rector of

Sutton-under-Brailes, Gloucestershire. He married, at Moreton-in-Marsh, Gloucestershire, 21 April 1840, Ann Beatrix (1804-1866), daughter of Henry Hulton (1765-1831) and Louisa Caroline Campbell (d. 1863); they had at least 1 son:

1 Samuel Campbell Hulton (1842-1904), solicitor; joined his uncle's firm in Manchester which survives to this day

---

1826: 19 Apr.

1827: 16 May: *The Sermon was preached by Mr. Sadler, Incumbent of Sutton under Brailes, a remote nook of Gloucestershire, not far from Shipston on Stour... . Mr. Sadler is Son of a clergyman, who had the living of Sandhurst, near Gloucester, where he has an Uncle still living, and cousins, with whom we are acquainted: Lieut. Sadler, of the royal Navy, his cousin, is a fine young man & officer, an intelligent and well informed person.* 2 Oct.

1828: 7 Oct.

1829: 20 May, 6 Oct.

1830: 10 May.

1834: 20 Aug., 20 Nov.

1835: 17 Jun.

1837: 16 Jan., 12 May, 16 Aug., 26 Sep.

1838: 25 Apr., 30 Jul., 22 Aug., 25 Sep., 24 Oct., 7 Dec.

1839: 1 May, 17 May.

1840: 25 May.

1842: 10 Feb: *The Bishop has issued a Commission to R W Ford, as Rural dean, with Waller, Sadler, and myself to survey and report upon the amount of Church accommodation in the deanery.* 11 Feb., 22 Feb., 24-25 Feb., 26 Mar., 23 May, 16 Aug.

1844: 17 Sep: *A letter from Mr. Sadler, Sutton under Brailes, apologizing for his inability to attend the meeting of the Stow Distr. Comm. S.P.G. to-morrow.* 11 Oct.

1845: 25-26 Jun.

1846: 20-21 Jun., 24 Jun., 26 Aug: *A letter from S. F. Sadler, explaining that an engagement which he could not put off prevents him from attending the meetings at Stow to-day.*

1847: 6-7 Jul., 20-21 Jul., 4 Sep., 21 Sep.

1848: 7 Feb: *Wrote to Mr. Sadler, Sutton under Brailes, as residing in the neighbourhood of Shipston; to make enquiry as to Capt. Story, agreeably to the request made to me by Mr. Round.* 8 Feb., 15 Feb., 26 Apr., 16 May, 16 Aug., 23 Aug., 12 Oct.

1850: 3 Jan: *Mr. Sadler writes to know whether I should like to possess a lithograph portrait of my old friend Mr. Malcolm.* 8 Jan: *Wrote to Mr. Sader, Sadler expressing the satisfaction it would give me to be allowed to possess myself of a copy of the lithograph portrait of the excellent Mr. Malcolm.* 2 May: *Received from Mr. Sadler a very kind letter of condolence on my late heavy loss.* 7 May, 25 May, 1 Jun., 12 Jun., 18 Sep., 24 Sep., 24 Oct., 26 Oct., 1 Nov: *A letter from Sadler made it doubtful whether he would fulfil his engagement to dine, and sleep here today, his little boy being indisposed:——however, he did arrive before dinner-time, the alarm as to his Son's illness being abated.* 2 Nov: *Conversation with Howell and Sadler, the latter of whom left us between 11 & 12 o clock to return home.* 12 Nov.

1851: 23 Apr.

1852: 22 Oct., 29 Oct.

1853: 18 Feb., 22 Feb.

SAINSBURY — John Sainsbury of Urchfont[5]

John Sainsbury (1733-1816) was born at Market Lavington, Wiltshire, the son of James Sainsbury. He was buried at Urchfont.

1806: 12 Sep.

1807: 14 Jan., 17 Dec: *Called upon Mrs. Butcher, Mrs. Legg, John Sainsbury, a wretched object.* 21 Dec: *Visited poor John Sainsbury.* 24 Dec., 29 Dec.

1808: 4 Jan., 8 Jan: *Administered the Sacrament privately at John Sainsbury's.* 20 Jan., 26 Jan., 20 Feb.

ST ALBYN — Langley St Albyn — *see* Gravenor

ST AUBYN — James Piers St Aubyn — *see also* Marmaduke Vavasour[6]

James Piers St Aubyn (1815-1895), architect, was born at Powick, Worcestershire, the second son of Revd Robert Thomas St Aubyn (1786-1875) and Frances Fleming St John (1792-1863), daughter of John Francis Seymour St John (1761-1822), prebendary of Worcester, and Frances Fleming. He was known to his family and friends by his middle name, Piers. He was educated at Penzance Grammar School before beginning his studies in architecture. He married, at Stoke Damerel, Devon, April 1852, Eliza Phillpott. There do not appear to have been any children of the marriage.

Piers St Aubyn was articled to Thomas Fulljames in Gloucester and acted as clerk of works for the building of Edward's College, South Cerney, in 1838-39. He was elected to the Royal Institute of British Architects in 1837 on the nomination of George Basevi, Edward Blore, and William Railton, and became a fellow of the institute in 1856, having been proposed by Benjamin Ferrey, Giles Gilbert Scott, and F. C. Penrose. St Aubyn was primarily a church architect; he built a considerable number of new churches and undertook even more restorations. He practised on his own account in London and Devonport, taking his former pupil and assistant Henry John Wadling into partnership. His church work was firmly in the Gothic revival mainstream of his time, and rarely departed from the forms of the Decorated period; it therefore lacks originality or flair. St Aubyn's greatest professional disappointment was his failure to secure the commission to build Truro Cathedral; he lost by one vote to John Loughborough Pearson. His most notable achievement was the restoration of St Michael's Mount, described as among the greatest achievements of nineteenth-century architecture.

James Piers St Aubyn was a nephew of Mary Anne Vavasour (1795-1881), who was a slightly younger sister of his mother.

1843: 20 Dec: *A letter from Marmaduke Vavasour, written under the impression that I am a Worcestershire Magistrate, and bespeaking my good offices in favour of a nephew of Mrs. M. V., a Mr. St. Aubin, an Architect, who is soliciting the post of County Surveyor in Worcestershire.*

1848: 24 Aug: *Nothing can be more suitable, unpretending & simple than this little Church. The Architect, Mr. St. Aubyn, of a good Devonshire, or Cornish family, and nephew of Mrs. Marmaduke Vavasour, was present ... he was a pupil of our County Surveyor, Mr. T. Fulljames, of Gloucester, he was engaged for a long time, as Clerk of the Works, in superintending the building of Edward's College, South Cerney.*

ST CLAIR — David Latimer St Clair[7]

David Latimer St Clair (1784-1861), naval officer and JP, was born at Chichester, Sussex, the son of William St Clair and Augusta Tinling, who had married at St Philip's, Menorca, on 25 June 1773. St Clair commenced his career in the Royal Navy as a midshipman aboard HMS *Royal Sovereign*. He was promoted to lieutenant in 1802, and commander in 1812. He bought Staverton Court in Gloucestershire, and married, at St Marylebone's, Westminster, Middlesex, 13 April 1819, Elizabeth Isabella (1806-1857), daughter of John Farhill of Chichester; there were no children of the marriage.

1835: 9 Apr.

1839: 1 Jan., 11 Apr., 2 Jul: *The prominent topic of the day was a debate on education within the Gaol, the subject being urged in a strange, rambling, injudicious manner by Capt. St. Clair, one of the Magistrates of the Cheltenham district.*

1844: 31 Dec: *The expected attack on the Chief Constable on account of his dismissal of Mr. Russell from the post of Superintendent at Cheltenham was not made: Capt. Sinclair, the Mag. who had taken the matter up, having, by reference to the Constabulary Act, discovered that Lefroy had acted conformably to law: nor did he even make any comment on the transaction, as to be regretted, or unwise &c. which he had also threatened.*

1845: 15 Apr., 7 May.

1847: 5 Jan: *When the Chairman moved the Court to build a new Chapel at the County Gaol, making at the same time, and under the same expenditure, other necessary alterations for better accommodation in various ways, he was vehemently resisted by Craven, Berkeley, Capt Sinclair, Col. Jenner, Sir John Guise &c.* 5 May, 18 May: *The only Magistrate who spoke on the side of the victor besides the Lord Lieut. was Capt. Sinclair.* 29 Jun.

ST CLAIR-ERSKINE — James St Clair-Erskine [8]

James St Clair-Erskine, 6th baronet and 2nd earl of Rosslyn (1762-1837), army officer, landed proprietor, and politician, was born at Rosslyn, Midlothian, the son of Lt-Gen. Sir Henry Erskine, 5th baronet (1710-1765), and Janet Wedderburn St Clair (1735-1797), daughter of Sir Peter Wedderburn and Sarah St Clair (b. 1720). He succeeded his father as 6th baronet and, in 1805, he succeeded his maternal uncle Alexander Wedderburn as 2nd Earl Rosslyn. He married, 1790, Harriet Elizabeth Bouverie (1771-1810); they had 3 sons and 2 daughters:

- 1 Charlotte Henrietta (b. 1791)
- 1 Henry Alexander (b. & d. 1792)
- 2 James Alexander St Clair (1802-1866); succeeded as 3rd earl of Rosslyn; married, at Dysart, Fife, 10 October 1826, Frances (1794-1858), daughter of William Wemyss (1760-1822), of Wemyss, and Frances Erskine (1754-1798); 2 sons and 2 daughters:
  - 1 Fanny Elizabeth (b. 1827)
  - 1 James Alexander George (1830-1851)
  - 2 Harriett Elizabeth (b. 1831)
  - 2 Francis Robert (1833-1890); succeeded as 4th earl of Rosslyn; married, at Hanover Square, London, 8 November 1866, Blanche Adeliza Fitzroy (1839-1933); 2 sons and 3 daughters
- 3 Henry Francis (1804-1829), Capt., Guards; died unmarried
- 2 Janet (1805-1880); married, 10 November 1829, Bethell Walrond of Dulford House, Devon

James St Clair-Erskine had a distinguished military career and was MP for Castle Rising, Morpeth, and Kirkcaldy Burghs. He was lord privy seal, 1829-39, a of the lord of the Treasury, 1834, and lord president of the council, December 1834–April 1835.

1829: 36 Jun: *Another proof of the Duke of Wellington's readiness to amalgamate with the Old Whigs is to be found in the appointment of the Earl of Rosslyn to the office of Lord Privy Seal, which had been long kept open, its duties being performed by Lord Ellenborough. His Lordship is a Lieutenant General.*

1830: 20 Apr.

1834: 17 Dec.

ST JOHN — Henry St John [9]

Henry St John, 4th Viscount Bolingbroke and 5th Viscount St John (1786-1851), landed proprietor, was born at Lydiard Tregoze, Wiltshire, the second, but first surviving, son of George Richard St John, 3rd Viscount Bolingbroke and 4th Viscount St John (1761-1824), and Charlotte (1757-1803), daughter of Thomas Collins, George Richard's former tutor. Henry was educated at Christ Church, Oxford, and succeeded as 4th Viscount in 1824. He married, at St George's, Hanover Square, Westminster, 3 June 1812, Maria Mildmay (1790-1836); they had 2 sons and 5 daughters:

- 1 Anne Jane Charlotte (1814-1881)
- 2 Isabella Letitia (1816-1893)
- 3 Emily Arabella Jane (1817-1855)
- 4 Maria Jane Louisa (1820-1861)
- 5 Isabella (b. ±1820)
- 1 Henry Mildmay 1820-1899); succeeded as 5th Viscount Bolingbroke; *see below*
- 2 Spencer Mildmay (1822-1849); died at Kanpur, Uttar Pradesh, India

The St John family was involved in a double scandal. After the births of Henry St John and his siblings, their father George Richard St John, 3rd Viscount Bolingbroke, embarked on a sexual relationship with his younger half-sister Mary Beauclerk. She had been born in 1766 to George Richard's mother and Topham Beauclerk, her second husband, although they married in 1768, two years after Mary's birth. The half-siblings, George and Mary, had a child in Paris, but for a time it was passed off as George and Charlotte's. Charlotte was anxious to save her marriage and hoped by this ruse to preserve the family name from infamy. However, Mary became pregnant by George for the second time in 1788 and delivered their second child, again in France.

In 1789 George Richard St John abandoned Charlotte and his legitimate children. He and Mary left Britain with their two small children to live together on the Continent. They travelled under the name 'Barton' and left instructions to their families not to try to find them. The story quickly spread and was eventually reported in *The Times* on 7 July 1789. Mary went on to bear George another two sons. All their children lived to adulthood, and one of them, Robert St John, known as Bob St John, was much loved by the politician Charles James Fox and his mistress, later wife, Elizabeth Armistead.

By May 1794 George had abandoned Mary Beauclerk and the four boys for a Belgian noblewoman, Isabella Charlotte Antoinette Sophia Hompesch, Baroness von Hompesch. He persuaded her to marry him bigamously and to live with him in obscurity, first on the Continent, then in Britain, and finally in the United States. In 1797 Mary Beauclerk married Count Franz Jenison von Walworth, an Anglo-Bavarian, by whom she had legitimate children, and after Charlotte's death in 1803, George Richard St John was freed to lawfully marry Isabella Hompesch, which he did on 1 August 1804. Their eldest children were illegitimate, but George and Isabella went on to have a further two daughters and two sons while married. George Richard St John died, aged 63, at Pisa in Italy. He was succeeded in his titles by his eldest surviving son, Henry St John, 4th Viscount Bolingbroke.

Henry's eldest son, Henry Mildmay, involved the family in a second scandal. After succeeding as 5th Viscount Bolingbroke, Henry Mildmay did not return to the family seat at Lydiard Park, Wiltshire, but stayed in London. In 1852 he met Ellen Medex, the half-Jewish daughter of Charles and Miriam Medex. Although Henry and Ellen never married, they masqueraded as Mr and Mrs Morgan for over thirty years, living at various addresses in London and Brighton. During these years Ellen gave birth to four children, only one of whom, Ellen Rose (b. 1863), survived. She was baptised Ellen Rose St John Morgan. Despite there being no evidence of a marriage, Ellen Medex was buried at Highgate cemetery as 'Ellen, Viscountess Bolingbroke'.

After Ellen Medex's death, Henry moved back to Lydiard Park. He met Mary Elizabeth Emily Howard, a young servant girl, and installed her as his housekeeper. When away from Lydiard, Henry and Mary lived in Bath as a couple, calling themselves Mr and Mrs Wilson. Mary gave birth to two boys, one in 1882 and the other in 1885; they were kept at Bath under the eye of a governess. In 1893, when Mary became pregnant a third time, she prevailed on Henry to marry her, which he did in secret that year at Bath registry office. The child was stillborn, but three years later she gave birth to a boy, who was christened Vernon Henry St John, the only legitimate heir to the title.

Henry became engaged in a long-running feud with the peerage publications, including *Debrett's*, *Dod's*, and *Burke's Peerage*. In order to 'legitimise' his children so that the eldest son could inherit the title, he tried to pass them off as the offspring of his non-existent marriage to Ellen Medex. Although the peerage books had previously accepted that he was married, they began to unravel the lies and removed all reference of his marriage and heirs apparent, instead installing one of Henry's cousins, Canon Maurice St John, as heir presumptive to the title. Henry Mildmay St John died in November 1899. After the funeral the existence of his wife Mary and heir Vernon Henry was revealed; the scandal was reported in all the British newspapers. Mary continued to live at Lydiard Park and died in February 1940.

1805: 19 Mar: *Drank wine with Prower meeting St. John & Adams.*

SAINTON-DOLBY — *see* **Dolby**

SAINTSBURY — George Saintsbury [10]

George Saintsbury (1796-1860), under-treasurer to the Society for the Propagation of the Gospel in Foreign Parts, was born in the parish of St Ann, Blackfriars, London, the son of John Saintsbury (1765-1824) and Ann Davis (1768-1854). He resigned as under-treasurer in April 1840, and in the 1851 census he was listed as residing at 42 Pembridge Villas, Kensington, and living off private means, being a stockholder in various railway and dock companies. He married, at St Peter's, Cheesehill, Winchester, Hampshire, 20 December 1826, Elizabeth Wright (±1807-1877); they had 2 sons and 4 daughters:

1 Georgina (1829-1921); died unmarried at Hambledon, Surrey
1 Francis Saintsbury (±1832-1865), army officer; died at Bengal, India
2 Elizabeth Sophia (1835-1916); married, 1863, Henry George Green (1828-1910); 4 sons and 1 daughter
3 Josephine Frances Mary (1838-1925); died unmarried at Southampton
4 Emily Anne (1841-1862)
2 George Edward Bateman (1845-1933); married Emily Fenn (1844-1924); 2 sons:
    1 Lewis (1871-1922)
    2 Christopher (1876-1959)

At the time of his death George Saintsbury was secretary and superintendent of Southampton docks.

1837: 28 Jan: *Wrote to Mr. Saintsbury, Under Treas. and Receiver of the Society for the Propagation of the Gospel, with a remittance of subscriptions which I had received from the members of the Stow Distr. Comm.* 3 Feb., 26 May, 28 May.
1838: 24 Jul.
1839: 23 Feb., 1 Jun., 13 Aug.

SALMON — Eliza Salmon [11]

Eliza Salmon, née Munday (1787-1849), singer, was born at Oxford, the daughter of a Mr Munday (first name unknown) and a soprano singer of the Mahon family of musicians. This performing family consisted, most likely, of a father and mother and the following children: singers James, Sarah [later Mrs John Second], and three more girls [later Mrs Munday, Mrs John Warton, and Mrs Ambrose]; and two instrumentalists, John and William. In *The Oldest Music Room in Europe* John H. Mee wrote that a Miss Mahon 'was allowed nine or ten [benefit] concerts [at Oxford in] 1776 and 1787,' although this may refer to any of the four Misses Mahon.

Eliza made her first appearance at Covent Garden in the Lenten oratorios on 4 March 1803, and enjoyed immediate success. She sang in the first performance of the Messiah at Covent Garden in 1805. She was gifted with a charming manner, a voice of beautiful tone, and a face 'of dazzling fairness', but her tendency to embellish her solos was criticised.

On 11 February 1806 Eliza married James Salmon (1780-1827), organist of St Peter's, Liverpool. In 1813, suffering financial difficulties, he joined the Army and was posted with his regiment to the West Indies, where he died. Mrs Salmon performed regularly at the Three Choirs Festival, and at oratorios and concerts in London. She travelled extensively to fulfil her engagements, and in 1823 was said to have earned £5000. Her voice collapsed suddenly during one of the Concerts of Ancient Music in May 1825, and her career ended. It was said to be the result of a breakdown of her nervous system due to 'intemperance'. She attempted, without success, to attract pupils. She married, secondly, Revd Hinde, but he died in about 1840, leaving her destitute. She died in poverty in 1849.

1823: 17 Sep: *The exquisite Vaughan, the powerful & scientific notes of Mrs. Salmon, the liquid & thrilling tones of Miss Stephens, the spirit and execution of Caradori, Mr. Sapio's fine tenor, the taste & simplicity of Miss Travis, the deep rolling tones of Bellamy, tho' far inferior to the exquisite judgment science & refinement of Bartleman, afforded a rich treat.* 18 Sep.
1826: 12 Sep.

SALMON — William Salmon [12]

William Salmon (1748-1826), attorney, was born at Devizes, Wiltshire, the son of William Salmon (1729-1781). William Salmon (senior) had started out as a young attorney in Devizes in around 1750, and was the first of three generations of attorneys with the same name serving as town clerk and solicitor to the borough of Devizes. His firm was passed to his son, William Salmon (1748-1826), who in 1793 became the principal owner of Devizes Castle. William Salmon (junior) also became a partner in the town's first bank, later known as Salmon, Tylee & Co., situated in St John's Street. He became known locally as 'King' Salmon and was described as 'running the Corporation'. He was joined in the family legal firm by his son William Wroughton Salmon (d. 1855), who also succeeded to ownership of the castle in 1809.

William Salmon (1748-1826) married, 24 June 1773, Sarah Mortimer; they had at least 1 son and 1 daughter:

1 Sarah (b. 1775)
1 William Wroughton (±1776-1855), attorney; married Eliza (b. ±1779), born at Bradford-on-Avon

---

1806: 15 Aug: *Supped with the same party (Tylee's etc) & Mr. W. Salmon.* 21 Aug: *Called upon the Messrs. Salmons.* 4 Nov: *In pursuance of an invitation dined with the Mayor & Corporation of Devizes upon occasion of the Election of Members for the Town; Mr. Smith & Mr. Estcourt being re-elected. Met a very large & select party & dined at ½ past four in the Town Hall. Conversed chiefly with the Mr. Salmons, F. Merewether, Mr. Estcourt, Mr. C. Lucas, Compton, Jaques &c.* 7 Nov: *Met & conversed with Mr. & Mrs. J. Tylee, C. Tylee, Miss Tylee, Mr. & Mrs. M.W. Salmon, Ch. Mayo, Mrs. & Miss Spalding &c.*

1807: 9 Jan, 30 Jan., 5 Feb., 13 Apr: *Wrote to Mr. W. W. Salmons.* 30 Apr: *Drove my Mother to Devizes, where my Father meeting us, we passed a fire at Mr. Salmon's Office.* 6 May, 27 May.

1808: 14 Jan: *Accompanied my Father & Mother in a Chaise to Devizes Assembly. Conversed with the Tylee family, the Salmons.* 1 Apr., 8 Apr.

SALTER — Christopher Salter and the Salter family at Clifton, Bath, and Stoke Poges [13]

Christopher Salter (1789-1839), JP, DL, and landed proprietor, was born at Bath, the son of Elliot Salter (±1735-1790), naval officer, and Elizabeth Johnston [?] (1761-1822). He was grandson of Elliot Salter (1700-1739) of Stoke Court, Buckinghamshire. Christopher's father Elliot Salter was made a lieutenant in the Royal Navy on 3 July 1765. In 1776, during the American Revolutionary War, he was posted to the Newfoundland station as captain of HMS *Renown*, flagship of Vice Adm. John Montagu. There is a record of an Elliott Salter who married, in New York State, 30 April 1783, Elizabeth Johnston (1761-1822); it seems possible that Salter had previously courted a woman of a loyalist family, and at the end of the war in February 1783, had returned to marry her. This is conjecture, but the parts all fit. It seems that Salter had also been married before, for on 16 February 1792, a Miss Salter, daughter of the late Capt. Elliot Salter, RN, married, at Bath, Edward Gibbons, younger son of the late Sir John Gibbons, baronet and KCB.

The Salter family owned Stoke Court—also known as West End House—at Stoke Poges, Buckinghamshire, from 1660 to 1828. During the early to mid-eighteenth century the Salter family had let this property to the Rogers/Grey family, and it was here that Thomas Grey (1716-1771) composed his *Elegy Written in a Country Churchyard* (1750). In 1758, after the death of his mother and aunts, Thomas Grey gave up the lease of Stoke Court. By that stage ownership of the property had passed to Capt. Elliot Salter, who later resided there. Little is known about Capt. Salter; his wife Elizabeth died at Brighton, but the date and location are tentative. Apart from the sizeable Stoke property, Capt. Salter inherited property in Buckinghamshire and elsewhere from his childless cousin George Wingfield (1737-1785) of Leopard Court, Worcestershire.

Christopher Salter also appears to have lived at Stoke Court. Like his father, little is known about him. He became high sheriff for Buckinghamshire in 1812, and married, at Paris, 1 September 1818, Maria Watson. They had at least 1 daughter:

1 Elizabeth Isabella Caroline (1819-1900); married, at Ilfracombe, Devon, 1851, as his third wife, Sir Charles Henry Darling (1809-1870), KCB and governor of Newfoundland and Labrador (1855-57); 4 sons:
    1 Charles Henry (1852-1931), army officer
    2 William James (b. 1856)
    3 James Bruce (1857-1935)
    4 Ralph Sydney (1859-1913)

Christopher had at least three sisters: Maria (1777-1864), Isabella (1784-1842), and Caroline (dates unknown). Isabella Helena married, at Brighton, 28 April 1829, a widower, John Wilmer Field (1775-1837) of Heaton Hall and Helmsley Lodge, Yorkshire. She died and was buried at Boulogne, Nord Pas de Calais, France. Nothing has yet been discovered about Caroline other than she and Isabella were living together at Caen, Normandy, with their brother Christopher in 1826. Maria married, 1797, Rear Adm. William Pierrepont (1767-1813), and had five children, all born at Pierrepont's estate of Farley Hill [later Unsted Park], Bramley, near Godalming, Surrey. Of these five, only the eldest, Anne Sumner, baptised 1802, and the youngest, Henry Bennett, born 1810, reached adulthood. Anne, the eldest, married, at St Swithin's, Walcot, Bath, June 1823, John Uniacke, mayor of Chester (1839 and 1840). She died at Clifton, Bristol, in 1862. The second eldest, William, was born on 5 May 1803 and died in 1819 at Queen's Square, Bath, aged 15. Charles was born in 1806 and Maria, the second daughter, in 1809; they died on 27 April and 29 June 1814 respectively, at Farley Hill, where their father had died in August the previous year. They were buried with him at St Peter's and St Paul's, Godalming, and their names were added to his monument in the church.

1805: 30 Jan: *Received an unexpected invitation in the morning to Mrs. Salter's Dance this Evening, &, waving the ceremony of Introduction, made my appearance there; we staid till nearly three o'clock, had a good supper, & a pleasant party on the whole.* 5 Mar., 12 Mar: *In the Evening a very good Ball at York House; danced with Miss Ford & Miss C. Salter.*

1806: 16-20 Jan., 22 Jan: *Walked with Mrs. & the Miss Salters till dinner.* 23 Jan: Called upon Mrs. Salter & her Daughters. 25 Jan., 29-30 Jan., 1 Feb., 2 Feb: *Returned to Clifton with Mrs. Salter & Mrs. Becher... ... after a very pleasant visit (to Mrs Carrick) joined the Salter party, but left them rudely & abruptly, fancying I spied a disinclination to my making one of their Cortege on the Mall, where the Middlesex Band was playing. Blamed myself afterwards for venturing to interpret a look & gesture, & for allowing my temper to be ruffled and suspicion raised; but the circumstances impressed upon my mind doubts of the propriety of my assiduities in that Quarter, which still possess me. I must be more guarded, & less susceptible.* 5-7 Feb., 9-10 Feb., 11 Feb: *Accompanied them to the York House Ball; danced with Isabella Salter, & Cecilia Wolseley, our Tea party consisted of Mrs. Salter, her young Ladies, Ryan, Mrs. Chollet & my Mother; conversed much with Mrs. S. Auriol, Mrs. Gillibrand.* 12-13 Feb. 16 Feb., 19-20 Feb., 22-28 Feb., 2-4 Mar., 8-11 Mar., 15-16 Mar., 19-22 Mar., 27 Jun.

SAMPSON — Edward Sampson — *see also* Daubeney [14]

Edward Sampson (1773-1848), JP, was born at Henbury, Gloucestershire, the younger son of Edward Sampson, merchant, and Mary, daughter of Thomas Brown of Salperton, Gloucestershire. His parents married in 1768 and had four children: Mary (1769-1821), John (1771-1830), Edward (1773-1848), and Catherine (1774-1813). Edward married, 1807, Joanna (±1772-1846), daughter of George Daubeney (1742-1806), of Redland, and Martha Baker; they had at least 1 son:

1 Edward (1810-1897); married, at Long Ashton, Somerset, 12 November 1838, Belinda (1813-1881), daughter of Benjamin Way, of Denham Place, Buckinghamshire, and niece of Sir John Smyth of Ashton Court

---

1829: 10 Oct: *dined and slept yesterday with our friends, the Browne's, at Salperton; We met a large party; Col. & Mrs. W. Beach, Mr. & Mrs. Trye, and Mr. Sampson, the young man, whom we lately met at Bourton on the Water, and who is a connection of our host's.*

1832: 15 Mar: *Breakfasted with Dr. Daubeny, Professor of Chemistry, at his house in the Ashmolean Museum. The party consisted of his brother in law, Mr. Croome, the Rector of Bourton on the Water, his son Charles, Messrs. Daubeny, a grandson of the late Archdeacon of Wilts., Mr. Samson, son of a rich Alderman of Bristol, Edward and myself.*

1833: 18 Apr.

1835: 6 Apr., 15 May: *Took advantage of an interval between the showers to drive Mrs. Witts to Bourton on the Water, where we called at Mr. Daubeny's, to pay our respects to Mrs. Sampson, his Aunt.* 22 May.

1837: 4 Aug.

1842: 13 Apr.

1843: 17 Oct: *Breakfasted at the Bell with Mr. Samson.*

1844: 2 Jan., 16 Aug., 8 Oct., 14-15 Oct., 14 Dec: *He has applied to Mr. Sampson, a Magistrate of the Bristol district, resident at Henbury, advanced in years, but hale, whose early experience as a legal practitioner will give him advantages in some respects as to the audit of Solicitors' bills &c.* 28 Dec: *Mr. Sampson declines becoming a member of the Committee of Accts.*

1845: 2 Apr., 15 Apr., 1 Jul.

1846: 10 Aug., 12 Aug: *Breakfasted at 8AM. with Savage, Sampson Junr. and Dr. Greaves.*

SANDBY — Charles Sandby [15]

Charles Sandby (1761-1833), Church of England clergyman, was born in the parish of St Dunstan in the West, London, the son of William Sandby (b. 1737) and Ann Bowes (b. 1737). He was educated at Christ Church, Oxford (BA 1783; MA 1786), and was ordained deacon on 6 June 1784 and priest on 11 June 1786. His first clerical appointment was as curate of Great and Little Hampton, Worcestershire, from 27 January 1791 to 10 February 1791. He was then vicar of Lower Swell, Gloucestershire, 1795-1833; rector of Great Comberton, Worcestershire, 1799-1808, vicar of Belton, Leicestershire, 1807; and rector of Honeychurch, Devon, 1816.

1827: 14 Jan: *I have had an interview with the Bishop, & resigned the Curacy of Lower Swell.... Mr. Sandby has never been in Gloucestershire since I have held the curacy, to which Bp. Huntingford appointed me in 1813, the living being then sequestered.... I have had no correspondence with my Vicar, nor even known his abode. In fact, I believe, he was sometimes in durance, often in concealment, and serving churches in obscurity and remote quarters of the Country ... In early life, he was a man of expence & dissipated character; in latter life he assumed the tone of the serious party in the Church.*

1833: 12 Jan.

SANDERS — John Sanders [16]

John Sanders was schoolmaster at Millbank Penitentiary, but little apart from his correct name has been discovered.

1836: 2 Aug: *By the way received a circular from Mr. Saunders, now Schoolmaster at the Millbank Penitentiary, and one of the Candidates for the vacant place of governor of our county gaol.* 10 Aug: *Saunders is School-Master at Millbank Penitentiary, a post he has held for 11 years, and had in that capacity great advantages for acquiring a knowledge of prison discipline.*

SANDFORD — Daniel Sandford [17]

Daniel Sandford (1766-1830), Scottish episcopal bishop of Edinburgh, was the second son of the Revd Dr Daniel Sandford (d. 1770), of Sandford Hall, Shropshire, and Sarah, daughter of Revd John Chapone. He was born at Delville, near Dublin, in the house of Dean Delaney, and was educated privately and at Christ Church, Oxford (BA 1787; MA 1791). He married, at St Swithin's, Walcot, Bath, 11 October 1790, Helen Frances Catherine (1769-1837), eldest daughter of Erskine Douglas, a staunch Jacobite. Sandford had met Helen in Bath, where his mother had gone to live after his father's death. Daniel and Helen had 3 sons and 4 daughters:

1 Eleanor Sarah (1791-1815)
1 Erskine Douglas (1793-1861)
2 Frances Catherine (1795-1875)
2 Wilhelmina Jemima (1797-1883)
3 Daniel Keyte (1798-1838)
3 Sarah (1800-1864)
4 John (1801-1873)

In 1792 Sandford resigned as curate of Hanworth, near Sunbury, Middlesex, to take up an invitation from English Anglicans in Edinburgh to open an episcopal chapel. Edward and Agnes Witts first heard Sandford preach on Sunday 19 January 1794 at St George's chapel. They struck up a friendship which lasted until the Witts family left for Germany. Sandford's congregation first worshipped in West Register Street, then Rose Street, and from 1818, at St John's, a prominent church at the west end of Princes Street. In January 1806 he was elected bishop of Edinburgh, the first Englishman to become a Scottish episcopalian bishop. His administration saw a growth in the number of congregations in southern Scotland, largely owing to a migration from the north of the country, England, and Ireland, into the central industrial belt. He died in Edinburgh on 14 January 1830.

Interestingly, in his diary entry for 23 January 1833, Francis Witts assumed that Daniel Sanford's wife had been a Campbell. This probably stemmed from the belief that she was related to Margaret Charteris, née Campbell, wife of Francis Charteris, earl of Wemyss; they had all met together at the Whitehouse, near Edinburgh. In all likelihood, the connection with Francis Charteris was probably through the Douglas family. Charteris later inherited considerable estates in Peeblesshire, including the castle and the barony of Neidpath, as the male heir of the body of his great-great-grandmother, Anne, first wife of David, 4th earl of Wemyss, and only daughter of William Douglas, 1st duke of Queensberry.

1801: 2 Apr: *I waited upon the Browns, upon Mr. Sandford, upon Capt. Stephens &c.* 12 Apr: *Mr. Sandford was kind enough to accomodate me with Caesar's Commentaries.* 23 Apr: *My father & Mother were in the Evening at Mr. Sandford's & Mr. Brown's.* 25-26 Apr: *At Church in the afternoon, when Mr. Sandford preached a very good Sermon.* 4 May: *Called at Whitehouse, upon Mr. Sandford, Lady Catherine Charteris, &c.* 28 Sep: *Received a letter from Mr. Sandford, wrote to Mr. Rycroft.*

1802: 20 Mar: *At the coffee house met with my worthy friend Mr. Sandford.* 21 Mar: *Breakfasted with Mr. Sandford at the Star.*

1830: 23 Jan: *The public journals announce the decease of the venerable Dr. Sandford, Bp. of Edinburgh. This distinguished person claims peculiar mention from me, and I was greatly indebted to him in early life, when my Parents lived in the Scottish Metropolis from 1793 to 1798. He was on very friendly terms with them, and as there was no opportunity of my obtaining confirmation in Scotland, & it was my parent's desire, that I should partake of the holy Sacrament before we went abroad, Mr. Sandford was so kind as to take me under his own tuition gratuitously, to superintend my reading of a religious sort, to examine me as to my faith & progress in Christian Knowledge, and to impress on my mind sound principles of religion and morality. On my return from Denmark, I had an opportunity of renewing my intimacy with this amiable divine, & once since during my residence at the University, whither he came to take the degree of D.D —Dr. Sandford was by birth an Englishman, & in early days was, I believe, a Student of Christ Church; when a young man, not having been long in orders, he married a Scotch lady of good family, a Miss Campbell, I think, and moved with her to Edinburgh, where he received pupils into his family, chiefly young Englishmen & others from Scotland, on high terms.*

1833: 10 Nov: *In York Place are two Episcopal Chapels, the smaller one dedicated to St. George was a recent building when I firstknew knew Edinburgh, and was then frequented by the best families, a Clergyman of the name of Cleeve being the Minister; he was Incumbent of Wooler in Northumberland, a fine reader; but he did not maintain respect by his private character, & the far superior talents and piety of Mr. Sandford.*

SANDHAM — Major Sandham

1847: 4 Apr: *Received a distressing letter from poor Howell, stating that on his arrival yesterday in Town, he had met with a letter from his friend, Major Sandham, communicating to him that a strong rumour prevailed that three Officers had been killed in an affray with the Kaffirs in South America, Africa of whom one was Frederick Howell, Surgeon in the Rifles, lately arrived in the Colony of the Cape of Good Hope.*

SANDHAM — Grace Sandham — *see* Backhouse

SANDIFORD — Charles Sandiford [18]

Charles Sandiford (1752-1826), Church of England clergyman and JP, was born in London, the son of Revd Rowland Sandiford, vicar of Christ Church, Newgate Street, London. He was educated at St Paul's and Sidney College, Cambridge (BA 1773; MA 1776), and was ordained deacon on 29 May 1774 and priest on 8 April 1776. His first clerical appointment was as curate of Awre and Blakeney chapel from 8 February 1780, but by 18 November 1780 he had become vicar. He was also vicar of Tirley, Gloucestershire, 1788-1826, and appointed chancellor of Bath and Wells in 1813 and archdeacon of Wells in 1815. Sandiford was a JP for Gloucestershire.

1823: 14 Jan.

1824: 13 Jul., 19 Oct.

1825: 12 Apr., 14 Jul: *I dined at the Palace with the Bishop of Gloucester. The party consisted of Archdeacons Sandiford and Timbrill, Mr. Ford, Mr. Douglass, Vicar of Newland, & Mr. Evans, Master of the College School.*

1826: 13 Apr: *It appears that Mr. Sandiford, Archdeacon of Wells, & Vicar of Awre and Tirley in this County is deceased. This worthy septuagenarian had for many years been very infirm from paralytic attacks, and died at Bath. He was a very intelligent man, and for many years an excellent magistrate of this County, being a complete man of business.... My first acquaintance with him was in the capacity of Chaplain to Bp. Beadon, when I was ordained Deacon in 1806. The ample orb of Mr. Sandiford's wig was at first rather awful to me, who was to be subjected to his Examination; but nothing could be more superficial or summary than the process was. An allusion to the new & stricter line of examination then lately adopted in the University of Oxford was alledged as a reason, why the enquiry on occasion of ordination needed not to be followed up closely; & in fact all parties, the Bp. & his wife, the Chaplain & the neophyte, were in a hurry to get breakfast over in order to proceed to Westminster Abbey, to be present at the first day's impeachment of the late Lord Melville.*

SANDON — Lord Sandon — *see* Ryder

SATCHELL — Stevens, Wilkinson and Satchell

Stevens, Wilkinson and Satchell, of Queen Street, Cheapside, was a firm of solicitors.

1839: 6-7 May.

SAUMAREZ — Mr Saumarez at Dr Warneford's

1823: 25 Nov: *I dined and slept at Dr. Warneford's, meeting Lords Redesdale and Northwick, Mr. Pole, Mr. Jeaffreson, Mr. Ford, Mr. Saumarez and Mr. Eyre.*

SAUMAREZ — James Saumarez [19]

Sir James Saumarez, 1st Baron de Saumarez (1757-1836), naval officer, was born at St Peter Port, Guernsey, the third son of Matthew Saumarez (1718-1778), physician, of Guernsey, and his second wife, Carteret, daughter of James le Marchant. In command of the frigate HMS *Crescent*, Saumarez was involved in one of the first major single-ship actions of the French Revolutionary Wars when he captured the French frigate *La Reunion* on 20 October 1793. As a reward, Saumarez was knighted by King George III. Saumarez was Nelson's second in command at the battle of the Nile where he distinguished himself once more, forcing the surrender of the *Peuple Souverain* and the 80-gun *Franklin*. Between 6 and 12 July 1801, after a repulse at Algeciras, he routed a far superior combined force of French and Spanish ships at the battle of the Gut of Gibraltar. For his services, Saumarez received the Order of the Bath and the Freedom of the City of London.

Saumarez and Nelson had served together in 1797 and 1798 but their relationship was often strained. They first clashed after the battle of Cape St Vincent. Saumarez had forced the surrender of the *Santissima Trinidad* but was unable to capture her because Jervis was forced to break off the engagement. Nelson attempted to console Saumarez by telling him that the Spanish had confirmed the *Trinidad* had indeed surrendered, to which Saumarez tersely replied, 'Whoever doubted it sir? I hope there is no need for such evidence to establish the truth of a report of a British officer'. In May 1798, when Saumarez was appointed to Nelson's squadron in the Mediterranean, Nelson preferred to confer with Troubridge, even though, as the senior captain, Saumarez was technically second in command. And on the quarterdeck of HMS *Vanguard* after the battle of the Nile, when Saumarez suggested to Nelson that the tactic of doubling the French line had been a dangerous one as it had meant exposing British ships to 'friendly fire', Nelson cut him short and angrily went below without giving him a chance to explain. Nelson decided that Saumarez should escort the prizes home and they never served together again.

After the Treaty of Amiens, Saumarez went home to his family in Guernsey. When war broke out again, he was given command of the naval forces defending the Channel Islands. He therefore was not present at the battle of Trafalgar.

James Saumarez married, at Guernsey, 27 October 1788, his cousin Martha (1768-1849), daughter of Thomas Le Marchant (1731-1791) and Mary Dobrée (1731-1791); they had 3 sons and 5 daughters:

1 James (1789-1863); succeeded as 2nd Baron de Saumarez
1 Emilia (b. 1791)
2 Mary Dobrée (1792-1812)
3 Martha Harriet (1794-1848)
4 Carterette (1796-1814)
5 Amelia (1800-1838)
2 Thomas Le Marchant (1803-1834); *see below*
3 John St Vincent (1806-1891); succeeded as 3rd Baron de Saumarez

---

1820: 7 Jan: *I had my first interview with Adm. Sir James Saumarez, Father of my pupil, who is now with his family at Bath lately arrived from their residence in Guernsey. I found him a man of polite manners, of a fine erect person, and intelligent countenance. One likes to rest upon the features of a hero: and the exploits of Sir James Saumarez at Aboukir, and elsewhere, in the late long war, entitled him to rank very high in the list of British naval Commanders.* 24 Mar: *Sir James & Lady Saumarez with their two Daughters called here on their journey from Bath into Northamptonshire, where their eldest Son resides.*

1821: 19 Jan: *We dined at Sir James Saumarez's. We met there among others his Brother, Mr. R. Saumarez, late an eminent Surgeon at Newington, but now retired from professional practice. This Gentleman is author of a Treatise on Physical Science.*

SAUMAREZ — Richard Saumarez[20]

Richard Saumarez (1764-1835), surgeon, was born at St Peter Port, Guernsey, the fifth son of Matthew Saumarez (1718-1778), physician, of Guernsey, and his second wife, Carteret, daughter of James le Marchant. He was younger brother to James (*above*). Richard enrolled as a medical student at the London Hospital in about 1781, and was apprenticed to William Blizard, who had recently been appointed surgeon. Saumarez was admitted as a member of the Company of Surgeons on 7 April 1785; he received a modified licence which forbade him to practise in London or within 7 miles of the City, but this restriction was abolished the following year. From 1786 he lived at Newington Butts in Southwark, just south of the Thames.

Saumarez married, at St Peter Port, 6 January 1786, Marthe (1762-1802), daughter of Jean le Mesurier (1717-1793), lawyer and governor of Alderney, and Martha Dobrée (1727-1764); they had 6 sons and 2 daughters:

1 Carteret (1789-1867)
1 Richard (b. & d. 1790)
2 Richard (1791-1864), Adm.
3 Frederick Walshman (1794-1885), naval officer; became mentally ill
4 Thomas (1796-1823)
2 Martha (1797-1864)
5 Paul (1798-1876), Church of England clergyman; became mentally ill
6 John (1799-1813)

In 1788 Saumarez was appointed surgeon to the Magdalen Hospital, Streatham. He resigned on 1 March 1805, and became an honorary governor of the hospital in recognition of his services. He gradually developed a large and lucrative practice in London until 1818, when he retired to Bath. He was elected a fellow of the Royal Society of Edinburgh in 1822, and of the Royal Society in 1834.

On 13 November 1801 Saumarez's wife Marthe died of consumption, and he subsequently married Elizabeth Enderby, a rich widow and the great-aunt of Gen. Gordon of Khartoum. It was by her desire that they retired to Bath. Saumarez's children Frederick and Paul became mentally ill before their father's death and were placed under the care of the court of chancery. The third son, Richard (1791-1866), became an admiral, and spent twenty years campaigning on behalf of the mentally ill and against the vast expense of chancery proceedings.

1821: 19 Jan: *We dined at Sir James Saumarez's. We met there among others his Brother, Mr. R. Saumarez, late an eminent Surgeon at Newington, but now retired from professional practice. This Gentleman is author of a Treatise on Physical Science.*

SAUMAREZ — Thomas Saumarez[21]

Thomas Le Marchant Saumarez (1803-1834), naval officer, was the second son of Adm. James Saumarez (*above*). He married, at Milford, Wiltshire, 1829, Catherine Spencer A. Beresford (1807-1877), daughter of Lt-Col Spencer Vassall. He was killed in action on 4 July 1834, aged 30, at Montevideo, Uruguay. Catherine married secondly, 1841, Eardley Wilmot Michell (1813-1885).

1820: 7 Jan: *My pupil, Mr. T. Saumarez, returned from Bath to resume his studies.* 24 Mar: *Sir James & Lady Saumarez with their two Daughters called here on their journey from Bath into Northamptonshire, where their eldest Son resides.* 22 Jul: *My pupil, Thomas Saumarez, finally left me this day, and relieved me from a burdensome responsibility and duty. Without any direct moral defect in character, he was a most unpleasant inmate; not only slow of apprehension, treacherous in memory, without application and observation, but sullen, unsocial, awkward.*

SAUNDERS — Arthur Cardinal Saunders[22]

Arthur Cardinal Saunders (1823-1905) was born at Steynton, Pembrokeshire, the fifth son of David Hugh Saunders of Steynton, Pembrokeshire. He was educated at Pembroke College, Oxford (BA 1846; MA 1848), and entered the Church. He was curate of Great Barrington, Oxfordshire, vicar of Magor with Redwick, Monmouthshire, 1860-81, and later rector of Lydiard Millicent, Wiltshire. He married, at Chepstow, Monmouthshire, 29 September 1857, Jane (1836-1919), daughter of Newdigate Poyntz (1785-1853) and Alice Brinn (1805-1875); they had 3 sons and 3 daughters:

1 Caroline Alice (1861-1921)
1 Arthur Newdigate (b. 1863)
2 Katherine Lucy (1865-1947)
3 Mary Elizabeth Poyntz (1868-1940)
2 Frederick Stephen P. (b. 1872)
3 Nathaniel Argent (1873-1946)

1850: 18 Sep.
1852: 2 Dec.

SAUNDERS-DUNDAS — *see* **Dundas**

SAVAGE — Henry Savage[23]

Henry Savage (1737-1823), naval officer, first appeared in Royal Navy records on 20 July 1758. In 1782 he was commanding the frigate HMS *Boreas* in the West Indies, but on 12 April of that year, during the battle between Sir George B. Rodney and the Count de Grasse, he was captain of the 74-gun HMS *Hercules*. In the heat of the action, when alongside a ship of far superior force, Savage jumped on an arm-chest on the quarterdeck and, to encourage his men, sang a few lines of 'O! what a charming thing's a battle!' The *Hercules* had seven men killed and nineteen wounded in the action.

During the Spanish and Russian armaments in 1790 and 1791, Capt. Savage commanded HMS *Pomona*, a small frigate. In 1795 he took command of HMS *Albion*, a 74-gun ship without a poop, employed in the North Sea; on 27 April 1796 he had the misfortune of being wrecked in the *Albion* on the Middle-Sand in the Swin.

Savage was promoted to rear admiral of the red in 1800, rear admiral of the white in 1804, vice admiral of the white in 1805, vice admiral of the red in 1809, admiral of the blue in 1810, and admiral of the white in 1814. He was married but his wife's name is unknown. She died in 1810, aged 75 years. In his will Savage asked that his remains be laid, with as little expense as possible, in the vault of St James's chapel, Tottenham Court Road, next to his great friend Capt. Somerset, RN.

1801: 28 May: *Dined very pleasantly at Mrs. Daniell's: met there Lady Lyttelton, Admiral Savage, Sir N. Rule &c. Walked home with Lady Lyttelton.*

SAVAGE — John Savage — *see also* Wiltshire[24]

John Savage (1785-1870), sugar refiner, mayor of Bristol, and JP, was born at Tetbury, the son of Revd John Savage (1745-1803), of Tetbury, and Charlotta (1756-1846), daughter of Walter and Charity Wiltshire. His parents were well-acquainted with Edward and Agnes Witts. In 1850, after the death of his mother, John Savage sold the old house of Tetbury Close to Joseph Woods, a banker of Tetbury. Savage, however, retained much of the lands. He married, 21 October 1811, Elizabeth (±1790-1870), daughter of Robert Claxton (d. 1812), alderman, and Rachel Mardenborough; they had 4 sons and 1 daughter:

1 William (1811-±1900), Church of England clergyman; appointed vicar of Burcombe, Wiltshire, 1869
2 Francis (±1813-1882)
3 John Claxton (±1813-1836); educated at Oriel College, Oxford (BA 1834)
4 Henry (b. 1816)
1 Maria (±1823-1842)

The sugar-refining Savage and Claxton families were in partnership with Philip Protheroe with interests in St Kitts and Nevis. Their claims following emancipation were unsuccessful. The Claxton family came from St Kitts and Nevis; it appears that Robert Claxton had been born in the West Indies. This goes some way to explaining the family's 'sugar' interests, which were almost certainly the source of the wealth. In Robert Claxton's will he left £3,000 to each of his younger sons, Christopher, Robert, William (1798-1873), and Philip Protheroe Claxton, who was 21, and £4,000 each to his daughters Elizabeth and Margaret.

John Savage was an alderman and mayor of Bristol for two years running, from 1829 to 1831. In the 1841 census he was listed as a magistrate living at Henleaze with his wife Rachel [Elizabeth], née Claxton (b. ±1790), his son Francis (b. ±1813), who was listed as a sugar refiner, and his daughter Maria (b. ±1823). John Savage was buried in Bathford churchyard, the burial place of his mother's family, the Wiltshires of Shockerwick.

1833: 21 Apr: *The Mayor, Mr. Stanton, was present, also Aldermen Daniel, & Savage, and others unknown to me; they came without state and as private individuals.*

1835: 6 Apr.

1839: 1 Jan.

1845: 3-4 Apr.

1846: 10 Aug., 12 Aug: *Breakfasted at 8AM. with Savage, Sampson Junr. and Dr. Greaves.*

SAWBRIDGE — Miss Sawbridge — *see also* Whalley

Mary Dulcibella Sawbridge (1820-1881) married William Whalley in 1846.

1846: 20 Jul: *Mr. and Mrs. William Whalley called, while we were at the Vicarage. He took to himself a wife, a Miss Sawbridge, while we were in the Isle of Wight: the lady is lady-like, of a suitable age, a Clergyman's daughter; we had made her acquaintance before, when she was a visitor of Mr. Francis, both at Upper Slaughter and Stanway.*

SAWYER — Charles Sawyer[25]

Charles Sawyer (1787-1876), landed proprietor and JP, was born at White Waltham, Berkshire, the son of John Sawyer (1766-1845) and Sarah Dickins. He married, 10 October 1812, Henrietta (1788-1864), daughter of Adm. Sir George Bowyer, 1st baronet of Radley (1739-1799), and Henrietta Brett (1753-1845); they had 5 sons and 2 daughters:

1 Edmond (b. 1815)
1 Henrietta (b. 1819)
2 Henry John (1820-1852)
3 Charles (b. 1821)
2 Charlotte (b. 1825)
4 Robert (b. 1826)
5 William George (b. 1830), Church of England clergyman

Sawyer lived at White Waltham with a large family. He was a local JP. One of his sons was also a JP and the others were barristers.

1832: 13 Jun: *To dinner with my friend Wellford came Mr. Charles Sawyer, a Magistrate residing near Maidenhead, a very worthy, serious, and intelligent person of good fortune, much respected in this district.*

SAXE-COBURG AND GOTHA — Albert and Victoria[26]

Prince Albert Francis Charles Augustus Emmanuel of Saxe-Coburg and Gotha (1819-1861) was born at Schloss Rosenau, near Coburg, Bavaria, the second son of Ernest III, duke of Saxe-Coburg-Saalfeld, and his first wife, Louise of Saxe-Gotha-Altenburg. When he was 7, his father divorced his mother on the grounds of adultery; she was sent to live in Switzerland and forbidden to see her children. Albert was educated at Bonn University. He married, 1840, his first cousin, Queen Victoria, and they had nine children. Albert died on 14 December 1861 at the early age of 42. The contemporary diagnosis was typhoid fever, but recent opinion points out that he had been ill for at least two years before his death, which may indicate that he suffered from a chronic disease such as Crohn's disease, renal failure, or cancer.

Queen Alexandrine Victoria (1819-1901) was the daughter of Prince Edward, duke of Kent and Strathearn (1767-1820), the fourth son of King George III and Victoria of Saxe-Coburg-Saalfeld (1786-1861). Both the duke of Kent and King George III died in 1820. Victoria was raised under close supervision by her mother Princess Victoria, the sister of Leopold (*below*). She inherited the throne at the age of 18 since her father's three elder brothers had all died leaving no legitimate surviving children.

1830: 31 Jan: *In these tirades Mr. Alexander was supported & assisted by another red-hot Anti-catholic divine from Ireland, a protégé of Sir Harcourt Lees, by name Crosby, a chaplain of the Duke of Cumberland, Incumbent of Lewisham, a living, which he contrived to obtain, by what interest I know not; this man wrote a most violent letter in the Morning Journal to the*

Duke of Wellington, charging him with all the sins, to which a politician is liable, & with traitorous views on the crown itself, by plotting a union between his son & the Princess Victoria, the presumptive heiress of the crown. 26 May, 23 Jun: *The Portrait of the Princess Victoria, by R. Westall, R.A. is a very pleasing picture, of a very intelligent, fair-haired child; much is said of the promising talents, disposition &c. of this, probably, eventual occupant of the British throne.*

1833: 13 Sep.

1837: 29 May: *In the meantime the presumptive heiress of the throne, the Princess Victoria of Kent, attained her eighteenth birthday and on Wednesday last, and as having entered on her 19th. year is capable of ascending the throne without a regency, as Queen in her own right, should there be a demise of the crown.* 19 Jul: *The newspapers convey the tidings of the prorogation of Parliament on Monday last by the interesting young Queen in person, which was an affecting as well as striking and splendid affair.* 9 Nov: *A foggy, moist day, true November weather, very unpropitious for the splendid procession and banquet appointed in the metropolis, the Queen having accepted an invitation to dine in state at Guildhall with the Corporation, it being Lord Mayor's day.*

1838: 28 Jun: *Auspicious weather for the Queen's Coronation, which was celebrated generally with great spirit and zeal.* 2 Sep: *Read a Sermon preached before the Queen by Dr. Hook, as her Chaplain, which has been supposed to have given great offence at Court and to Ministers.* 9 Dec.

1839: 16 Apr., 7 May, 10 May: *Recd. a letter from Round acquainting me that there was every prospect that a firm Conservative government would be formed: that at the suggestion of Lord Melbourne, the Queen had sent for the D. of Wellington, who had advised her to call on Sir Robt. Peel, to take measures for forming an administration: that the Queen had recd. Sir R.P. in a very satisfactory manner, that everything was likely to be arranged smoothly.* 11 May: *Found a letter from Round: the bright hopes of a vigorous, conservative government being formed are fast melting away: it is generally rumoured in Town, and believed, that the Queen has revoked the carte blanche which she at first gave to Sir Robt. Peel, and refuses to consent to such changes in the household as he considers absolutely essential to the stability of his government.*

1840: 21 Jun., 1 Jul., 12 Jul: *Edward Oxford, the youth who fired two loaded pistols at the Queen & Prince Albert has been acquitted of treason on the ground of insanity; ample evidence was adduced of his own insanity derived from his father and grandfather.* 22 Nov: *By the newspaper received this day, it appears, that the Queen was safely delivered of a Princess at Buckingham palace yesterday afternoon. Her accouchement has taken place rather sooner than was expected.*

1842: 30 Jan., 7 Feb., 1 Jun: *The newspapers announce another attack on the life of the Queen by a young miscreant of the lower Classes, firing a pistol at her as she was returning with Prince Albert in an open carriage from an airing, on Constitution Hill.* 19 Jun.

1843: 27 Aug., 4-8 Sep., 9 Sep: *The Queen and the Duchess of Kent, who had arrived on a visit to her daughter yesterday, first drove past us in a coach and pair, with plain liveries, the carriage dark coloured, and with nothing to indicate rank; another carriage presen followed with the suite; Prince Albert, and another gentleman had preceded in a light open two-wheeled carriage, unnoticed, to the pier.* 10 Sep: *I cannot say that I caught the features either of the Queen or Duchess of Kent, who, with the little Princess Royal, occupied the open carriage, drawn by four horses with outriders, and footmen in royal livery: the postillions in a plain livery: an equerry riding by the side: but the cortége was suitable to the rank and place.* 11 Sep: *It is stated that her Majesty embarks tomorrow for Ostend on a visit to the King and Queen of the Belgians at Brussels.* 12 Sep: *Before breakfast, walking on the Esplanade, Eastward, watched from a distance the embarkation of the Queen and Prince with their suite for Ostend: a beautiful sight; no ships of war in view, but a fleet of six or seven steamers besides; the beautiful royal steam-yacht, which manoeuvred between and round them, while the whole were turning their hands heads up the channel, in a very skilful manner.* 15 Sep.

1844: 28 May: *I explored the beach between the Railway terminus, and the foot of Shakespeare's Cliff, inspecting the piling and other substructions of the railway buildings, and the timber viaduct, which are interesting works of engineering — while there a salute from the Heights announced the landing of the King of Saxony,* who arrived in the roads, as was expected, in the Princess Alice, Post office steamer, which had been sent to Ostend for his conveyance on a visit to the Queen, and, as it is said, on a tour in England.* 4 Jun: *There are numerous bed rooms and dressing rooms, of odd irregular shapes, owing to the form of the building so appropriated, converted from fort to a mansion, capable of accommodating a large circle, and the great Duke often entertains numerous parties here; we visited nearly all the apartments, rendered interesting as the abode of the aged Statesman and ablest general of the age, and as, some time since, the temporary residence and retreat of the Queen and her consort with her two elder children.* 8 Oct: *It is stated on good authority that the Duke of Wellington expressed great indignation at the resistance to his nomination, looking on it as an act of insubordination, and himself having discovered that suffrage was not contemplated in the statute: his Grace expressed not only a readiness, but an anxiety, to come and preside, and appoint, in person, though it would be very inconvenient, as he was required to meet the King of the French on his landing at Portsmouth to-day, on a visit to the Queen.*

1848: 19 Mar: *The Queen of England has given birth to another princess.* 18 Jul.

SAXE-COBURG AND GOTHA — Leopold Georg Christian Friedrich Saxe-Coburg Gotha[27]

King Leopold Georg Christian Friedrich Saxe-Coburg Gotha (1790-1865) was the youngest son of Franz Frederick Anton, duke of Saxe-Coburg-Saalfeld and Countess Augusta Reuss-Ebersdorf. He later became a prince of Saxe-Coburg and Gotha after the territorial swap by his father of Ehrenburg Palace in the Bavarian town of Coburg. As a child Leopold was appointed colonel of the Izmaylovsky Guards Regiment in Russia. Seven years later, he became a major-general. When Napoleonic troops occupied the duchy of Saxe-Coburg in 1806, Leopold went to Paris. Napoleon offered him the position of adjutant, but he refused. Instead, he took up a military career in the Imperial Russian cavalry. He campaigned against Napoleon and in 1815 reached the rank of lieutenant-general in the Imperial Russian Army.

In 1816, Leopold married Princess Charlotte of Wales, daughter of the prince regent; he was created a British field-marshal and knight of the garter. On 5 November 1817, Princess Charlotte delivered a stillborn son and died the following day. In 1840, Leopold arranged the marriage of his niece, Queen Victoria, the daughter of his sister, Princess Victoria of Saxe-Coburg-Saalfeld, to his nephew, Prince Albert of Saxe-Coburg and Gotha, the son of his brother, Ernst I, duke of Saxe-Coburg and Gotha.

Leopold turned down the throne of Greece. After Belgium asserted its independence from the Netherlands in 1830, the Belgian

National Congress considered several candidates and eventually asked Leopold to become king of the newly formed country.

1830: 6 Feb: *A very general belief prevails, & it has been very confidently asserted both in the Continental & British Journals, that Prince Leopold of Saxe Cobourg is fixed upon by the Courts of Paris & London, with the consent of that of St. Petersburg, as the future Sovereign of Greece; not, indeed, with the title of King, but with the royal power.* 26 May: *The other important political event, which has been announced to Parliament, is the resignation of the throne of Greece by Prince Leopold of Saxe Cobourg.*

1833: 13 Sep: *We drove to the Northern extremity of the hills in the direction of Cradley ... chiefly tenanted by the poor, for whose benefit a school has been built at the joint expence of the Duchess of Kent, who contributed £60, the King of the Belgians who gave £50, and my Aunt Lyttelton, who added £40 to increase the size of the school house.—The Duchess of Kent with her daughter, the Princess Victoria, passed a summer here three years since, and her brother, Prince Leopold, staid some weeks with his royal relatives.*

SAXE-COBURG-SAALFELD — Princess Victoria of Saxe-Coburg-Saalfeld[28]

Victoria of Saxe-Coburg-Saalfeld (1786-1861), mother of Queen Victoria, was the fourth daughter of Franz Friedrich Anton, duke of Saxe-Coburg-Saalfeld (b. 1750), and his wife, Augusta Caroline Sophia, the daughter of Count Reuss-Ebersdorf. She married, 1803, Emich Charles, prince of Leiningen (d. 1814), with whom she had a son, Charles, and a daughter, Feodore. She was then persuaded by her brother Prince Leopold, the widower of Princess Charlotte, George IV's heir, to secure the English succession by marrying Edward, duke of Kent (1767-1820), the fourth son of George III and Queen Charlotte. They married at Coburg in 1818 and Princess Alexandrine Victoria was born in 1819. The duke died of pneumonia the following year.

Lord Melbourne considered the duchess of Kent foolish and weak-minded, but she was pious. Once queen, Victoria threw off the domination of her mother and a difficult three years followed. After her coronation, Queen Victoria kissed her aunt Queen Adelaide, but only shook her mother's hand. In 1840, following Victoria's marriage to the duchess's nephew, Prince Albert, there was a family reconciliation and the duchess spent twenty harmonious years at court and with her grandchildren.

1833: 13 Sep: *We drove to the Northern extremity of the hills in the direction of Cradley, where the woods are said to be fine: in this quarter of the parish are many scattered cottages, chiefly tenanted by the poor, for whose benefit a school has been built at the joint expence of the Duchess of Kent, who contributed £60, the King of the Belgians who gave £50, and my Aunt Lyttelton, who added £40 to increase the size of the school house.—The Duchess of Kent with her daughter, the Princess Victoria, passed a summer here three years since.*

1830: 26 May, 23 Jun: *Great care is taken with her education, & her mother, the Duchess of Kent, is generally spoken of as an amiable, sensible, well principled & well-conducted person.*

1843: 9 Sep: *The Queen and the Duchess of Kent, who had arrived on a visit to her daughter yesterday, first drove past us in a coach and pair.* 10 Sep: *I cannot say that I caught the features either of the Queen or Duchess of Kent, who, with the little Princess Royal, occupied the open carriage.* 15 Sep.

1848: 18 Jul.

SAXE-GOTHA — the ducal family of Saxe-Gotha-Altenburg[29]

Ernest II, duke of Saxe-Gotha-Altenburg (1745-1804), was the third, but second surviving, son of Frederick III, duke of Saxe-Gotha-Altenburg and Luise Dorothea of Saxe-Meiningen. During 1768-69 Ernest took an educational journey to the Netherlands, England, and France, and met important people in politics, science, and the arts. In 1772 his father died and Ernest became duke of Saxe-Gotha-Altenburg. As an enlightened ruler he promoted an educational system and supported the theatre, art collections, and libraries, as well as the natural sciences in his duchy. He was interested particularly in astronomy and physics. With the astronomer Franz Xaver von Zach, Ernest established the Observatory of Gotha, one of the foremost observatories in Europe and a renowned centre for the study of astronomy. He married Marie Charlotte Amalie Ernestine Wilhelmine Philippine, prinzessin von Sachsen-Meiningen (1751-1827); they had two sons, Emil Leopold August (1772-1822) and Frederick (1774-1825).

Emil succeeded his father in 1804. Two years later, during the Napoleonic Wars, he joined the Rhine Confederation. He had an aversion for the hunt and riding, and a preference for dancing, wearing silk socks and feminine clothes. Among his friends he called himself 'Emilie'. Goethe called him 'angenehm und widerwärtig zugleich'—'agreeable and disgusting at the same time'. He married, 1797, Louise Charlotte of Mecklenburg-Schwerin. They had only one daughter, Luise Dorothea Pauline Charlotte Fredericka Auguste (1800-1831); therefore Emil became the maternal grandfather of Albert, prince consort of Queen Victoria.

On Emil's death in 1822, his brother Frederick succeeded as duke of Saxe-Gotha-Altenburg. He died unmarried and the line of Saxe-Gotha-Altenburg ended. After his death, Frederick's lands were repartitioned among his Wettin relations. Ernest I of Saxe-Coburg-Saalfeld (1784-1844) received Gotha and changed his title to duke of Saxe-Coburg and Gotha.

1800: 28 Jun: *Having received during our Residence at Weimar great Civilities from some of the Princes of the House at Gotha who had frequently expressed a wish of seeing us at their Court, we gladly went somewhat out of our direct Road to see that neat little Town ... Our acquaintance with both Princes Sons of the Reigning Duke at the Court of Weimar prepared the Path for the Civilities shewed to us by the whole Family for which we shall ever remain grateful. Not merely the Individuals of the Ducal Family but even the private persons of the Noblesse strove to make our stay of four days perfectly agreable.—For the male part of our Family a Dinner was every day appointed at Court, where the Duke & his eldest Son & his Wife together with Prince Frederic always appeared tho' the Duchess herself in Summer never joins in the public Society... The Duchess Reigning, Sister of the Reigning Duke of Meiningen, is in the Opinion of those Persons who know her best not so amiable a Character as the Duke, her Consort: altho' in her friendly Behaviour towards our Party who except perhaps from the Representation of her Sons were entirely unknown to her, the greatest politeness and Condescension towards Strangers was manifest.... . Prince Frederic, an amiable young Man of 25 Years, is well looking, and resembles part of the Royal Family of England. His disposition is friendly and obliging, without striking Abilities he is extremely polite and amiable, beloved by all, without Haughtiness or Pretensions... . The Character of the Prince Hereditary is by no means that of an amiable man, & so open does he lay himself to the Observation of all with whom he is in Company that there is but one general Opinion about him. At the age of 27 Years, this Prince neither beloved nor even popular is capricious, haughty, whimsical... . The Reigning Duke Ernest II. aged 55 Years came to government of the Duchies of Gotha and Altenbourg in the Year 1772... . His Highness is of a middling Stature, & fair, his features are correct and in early years he must have been handsome: in his manners condescending, affable, nay at times jovial: fond of solitude & retirement he is most contented when alone in his English Garden, easy in his manners, and endowed with an engaging politeness, he is nevertheless and with reason averse from relaxing in the formal Etiquette of his Court. His literary Abilities are above the Common rate, his Application and Desire of gaining further Enquiries are great, and his knowledge is Superior to that of most Persons of his rank: Of his Connection with the Illuminati so often imputed to him, I shall not venture to mention: particularly as I had no Opportunity of knowing the Opinion of his Highness in Philosophical or Political Concerns.*

SAXE-MEININGEN — Princess Adelaide of Saxe-Meiningen [30]

Princess Adelaide of Saxe-Meiningen (1792-1849) was born at Meiningen, Thuringia, Germany, the eldest child of George I, duke of Saxe-Meiningen, and Luise Eleonore, daughter of Christian Albrecht, prince of Hohenlohe-Langenburg. She was titled Princess Adelaide of Saxe-Meiningen, duchess in Saxony, and styled serene highness from her birth until the Congress of Vienna (1814-15), when the entire House of Wettin was raised to the style of highness.

Following the death of Princess Charlotte in 1817, a crisis relating to the succession demanded action by the unmarried sons of George III. William, duke of Clarence, already had ten illegitimate children by the popular actress Dorothea Jordan, but they were obviously debarred from the succession. A double wedding was held at Kew Palace in Surrey, England, on 11 July 1818: Adelaide married William, duke of Clarence, and William's brother, Prince Edward, duke of Kent, married Victoria, dowager princess of Leiningen. William and Adelaide settled amicably in Hanover, and by her influence William drank less, swore less, became more tactful, and generally improved his behaviour. There were two live births—daughters named Charlotte and Elizabeth—who survived a short while, and other miscarriages and still births. William and Adelaide became king and queen in 1830. In general Adelaide was considered a good and popular queen, but her interference during the passage of the 1832 Reform Bill (she was thought to have manipulated William) brought about many problems. Following William IV's death in 1837, Adelaide spent most of the remaining twelve years of her life at Witley Court in Worcestershire.

1844: 3 Jun: *It being announced that the Queen Dowager would embark here to day for the Continent, whither she is going on a visit to some of her relations, we wended our way with the many to catch a glimpse of the good Adelaide.*

1845: 8 Jul: *And the good Queen Dowager, whose health requires a country residence in a warm genial situation, with pure air, and who has tried several places of the nobility, in different counties, which she has taken on lease, but never retained any of them long, has occupied Witley Court now for a longer sojourn than has been her wont: holding her court there, dispensing thence her charities far and near; and surrounded by the many estimable persons whom she has attached to her establishment.*

SAXE-WEIMAR — Prince William Augustus Edward of Saxe-Weimar-Eisenach [31]

Prince William Augustus Edward of Saxe-Weimar-Eisenach (1823-1902) was the son of Prince Charles Bernard of Saxe-Weimar-Eisenach (1792-1862) and Princess Ida of Saxe-Meiningen, whose sister Adelaide was wife to King William IV. His military career began in 1841 when he joined the 67th (South Hampshire) Regiment of Foot as an ensign. He married, 1851, Lady Augusta Katherine Gordon-Lennox, daughter of Charles Lennox, 5th duke of Richmond; she was created countess of Dornburg by the grand duke of Saxe-Weimar the day before the wedding.

Prince William's royal connections ensured that he proceeded quickly through the ranks. He was promoted to major in the Grenadier Guards on 20 June 1854 and served in the Crimean War, in which he fought at the battle of Alma, the siege of Sevastopol, the battle of Balaclava, and the battle of Inkerman.

1844: 3 Jun: *another hired carriage conveyed her Majesty's nephew, Prince Edward of Saxe Weimar, a very fine young man, the Marquis of Ormond, and two other gentlemen of the Suite, the spectators cheering; but the limited space did not admit of a large concourse.*

SAXE-WEIMAR-EISENACH — Karl August, grand duke of Saxe-Weimar-Eisenach, and the ducal family [32]

Karl August, grand duke of Saxe-Weimar-Eisenach (1757-1828), was the eldest son of Ernst August II Konstantin, duke of Saxe-Weimar-Eisenach (1737-1758), and Anna Amalia (1739-1807), daughter of Duke Karl I of Braunschweig-Lüneburg-Wolfenbüttel. His governor was Count Johann Eustach von Görtz, a German nobleman of the old strait-laced school, but in 1771 his mother ousted Görtz and appointed as his tutor Christoph Martin Wieland. In 1774 the poet Karl Ludwig von Knebel came to Weimar as tutor to Karl August's brother, the young Prince Frederick Ferdinand Constantin, and in the same year the two princes set out, with Count Görtz and Knebel, for Paris. At Frankfurt Knebel introduced Karl August to the young Johann Wolfgang Goethe, marking the beginning of a momentous friendship.

In 1775, after Karl August had returned to Weimar, he assumed the government of his duchy and married Princess Luise of Hesse-Darmstadt (1757-1830), daughter of Ludwig IX of Hesse-Darmstadt (1719-1790), landgrave of Hesse-Darmstadt (1768-90). One of the young grand duke's first acts was to summon Goethe to Weimar. In 1776 Goethe was made a member of the privy council. The duke was a heavy drinker and a good sportsman, but he also had more serious tastes; following in the footsteps of his renowned mother, he took an active interest in literature, art, and science. He funded Goethe's foundation of the Fürstliche freie Zeichenschule Weimar, and encouraged the expansion of Weimar classicism.

In 1788 Karl August served in the Prussian Army as major-general in active command of a regiment. As such he was present, with Goethe, at the battle of Valmy in 1792, and the siege of Mainz and the battle of Pirmasenz in 1794. The disastrous campaign of Jena followed in 1806, and it was probably only thanks to the famous encounter between Napoleon and Karl August's wife, Luise, that his duchy was not confiscated. Karl August and Luise had 4 sons and 3 daughters:

- 1 Luise Auguste Amalie (1779-1784)
- 2 Unnamed princess (b. & d. 1781)
- 1 Karl Friedrich (1783-1853); succeeded as grand duke; married Maria Pavlovna (1786-1859), third daughter of Tsar Paul I of Russia (1754-1801); 2 sons and 2 daughters:
    - 1 Marie Luise Alexandrina (1808-1877); married Friedrich Carl Alexander (1801-1883), son of Friedrich Wilhelm III, king of Prussia and elector of Brandenburg (1770-1840)

2 Augusta Maria Luise Katharina (1811-1890); married Wilhelm Friedrich Ludwig, king of Prussia and emperor of Germany (1797-1888); numerous children, including:
1 Frederick (1831-1888); became Frederick III, emperor of Germany and king of Prussia for ninety-nine days in 1888, the year of the three emperors; married Victoria Adelaide Mary Louisa (1840-1901), daughter of Queen Victoria; numerous children, including:
1 Wilhelm II (1859-1941); succeeded as last king of Prussia and emperor of Germany
1 Karl Alexander August Johann (1818-1901); succeeded as grand duke; married Wilhelmina Marie Luise (1824-1897)
2 Paul Alexander (1805-1806); died an infant
2 Unnamed prince (b. & d. 1785)
3 Karoline Luise (1786-1816); married Frederick Ludwig, hereditary grand duke of Mecklenburg-Schwerin; 2 sons and 1 daughter:
1 Albrecht (1812-1834)
1 Helene (1814-1858); married Ferdinand, duc d'Orleans, eldest son of King Louis Philippe of France
2 Magnus (1815-1816); died an infant
3 Unnamed prince (b. & d. 1789)
4 Karl Bernhard (1792-1862); became colonel of a regiment in the service of the king of the Netherlands after the Congress of Vienna; married, Ida (1794-1852), daughter of Georg Friedrich Karl, duke of Saxe-Meiningen Hildburghausen; 4 sons and 3 daughters:
1 Luise (1817-1832); died at Windsor Castle
1 Wilhelm Karl (1819-1839)
2 Wilhelm August Eduard (1823-1901); married Augusta Catherine (1827-1904), daughter of Charles Gordon-Lennox, 5th duke of Richmond, and Caroline Paget
3 Hermann Bernhard (1825-1901)
4 Friedrich (1827-1892)
2 Anna (1828-1864)
3 Amalia Maria da Gloria Augusta (1830-1872)

Karl August had numerous mistresses and numerous illegitimate children. (*See* Knebel.)

Karl August's mother was Anna Amalia Saxe-Weimar-Eisenach (1739-1807), daughter of Duke Karl I of Brunswick and a niece of Frederick the Great. In 1756, at the age of 16, she married the 18-year-old duke, Ernst August II, but he died in 1758, leaving Anna Amalia as regent for their infant son. She remained as regent until 1775 when her son, Karl August, reached 18 years of age. Despite her heavy official responsibilities, Anna Amalia cultivated intellectual interests, especially in music. She was the friend and patroness of Goethe, Herder, Schiller, and Wieland, and turned Weimar into the most important cultural centre in Germany during the Age of Enlightenment. The Weimar Theatre was destroyed by fire in 1774, but Anna Amalia continued the tradition of the singspiel in later years with performances, in the amateur theatre, of her own compositions to texts by Goethe.

Anna Amalia was responsible for bringing together some of the most important characters in the enlightenment movement. Her and her son's court shone brightly, and their influence far exceeded the otherwise modest status of the duchy. Edward and Agnes Witts took Francis and George to Weimar in autumn 1798 and they stayed almost two years. They were at court on many occasions and Agnes frequently played cards at the same table as Anna Amalia. When Edward and Agnes told the dowager duchess they were leaving Weimar they were even offered a private dinner by the ducal family. Agnes's diary entries are of greatest interest (*The Diary of a Cotswold Lady — volume 2*), but Francis also recorded events from his perspective as a 16 and 17 year old in 1798, 1799, and 1800.

1798: 2 Sep: *The Reigning Duchess, Louise Princess of Saxe Darmstadt, is aged 45 Years, Her figure is rather majestic, than handsome, her face pleasing, tho' the features are not regular, she is affable, yet not free in her Conversation, she always maintains the Dignity of her rank, without stiffness or Affectation, & suits her conversation admirably to the person with whom she speaks. Adapted much to reading, particularly to History & Politics, an adherent of Lavaters System, & always more ready to obtain Knowledge than to display her own talents, and acquirements.*

The Reigning Duke, a man of 43 Years old, is a small figure, & rather a forbidding Countenance, fond of Music, & of reading, attached to particular people, & fond of the fair Sex. Ambitions that his Court & Town should be visited by Strangers, yet fond of ease & social joviality. This genius is martial, & violent, fond of exercise, & passionately attached to the Chase which he pursues with great ardor. If anything, inclined to expence, and fond of travelling to foreign Courts &c. Without much taste, he is fond of improving his Park, in which however he is chiefly assisted by Privy Counsellor Göethe, & Baron Wohlzagen.... among the many learned who were attracted to this Town During Minority of the present Duke by the Duchess Mother Amalia Princess of Brunswick now above 60 Years of Age, a Woman who without great Part, or extensive Science &c. endowed with some weakness gave a fine Example in her Regency, by extending the splendor of the Character of the Dominions of her Son.... The Hereditary Prince, a youth of 17 Years, is tall & well made, rather of a dark complexion, his Natural Abilities are good, he is good tempered, & inclined to be friendly, his Manners are more constrained than could be wished, arising from the flattery which has been bestowed on hım, & the particular partiality of his amiable Mother. His habit of body is at present weak, & he is in general Averse to all bodily Exercise.... The little Prince Bernard is only 8 Years old, his Character of Course not yet decided, tho' he appears to partake much of that of his father. Several other Children, the fruit of this marriage both older & younger than the Prince Hereditary have died & these three are alone alive... The Princess, between 14 & 15 years of age, small in stature is a Brunette, lively, & clever extremely fortunate in her Governess, a Mademoiselle de Knebel.

1799: 20 Jan: *in the Evening to Concert & Supper at Court very full. The Duchess Mother for the first time.* 23 Aug: *It being a fine but rather dark Day we played late in the Evening with the Prince &c at Prison Bases.* 28 Aug: *To Mr. Schmids. To the Park to play at Prison Bases with the Prince.* 22 Oct: *A very pleasant Day; in the Evening to a Ball at the Duchess Mothers very pleasant.* 24 Oct: *The talkative Frau Wenheit was if anything overrated by the Berkin on the whole except Becker & Götz the play was represented in a superior Manner being Duchess Amalia's Birth Day.* 11 Dec: *to the Duchess Mother's to Dinner with Dukinfield & my Mother. very agreeable.* 13 Dec: *my Mother at a large Card Party at the Duchess Mother's.* 22 Dec: *to a Tea party given by the Duchess: where we grown up Folks amused ourselves by playing all sorts of foolish Childrens Games, very tiresome indeed.*

1800: 30 Jan: *Fine Weather indeed, sun &c. &c. to illuminate our worthy Duchesses Birthday.* 31 Jan: *Massquerade where all the world almost were, as also our whole party, being the Day held in celebration of the Duchesses Birthday, it was select in company of the Noblesse.* 2 Feb: *in the Evening to Court which being the Duchesses Birthday was very splendid. Mademoiselle Jagemann sung finely, & the Concert was very pretty.* 5 Feb: *Dukinfield & myself dined very comfortably at the Duchess Mothers: a large party: I sat very agreeably by Monsr. d'Einsiedel.* 18 Feb: *my Father and Mother dined at the Duchess Mothers.* 24 Feb: *my Parents at a Party at Cards at the Duchess Mothers.* 28 Feb: *nevertheless joined in a Court Sledging Party, more than 20 Sledges and numerous Outriders round the Town and Webicht, afterwards till 10 o'clock to a lively Ball at the Princes, in the small Salle at Court.* 2 Apr: *my Father dined at the Duchess Mothers.* 13 Apr: *Three young Englishmen Beloulerant introduced rather embarassing as neither could speak French; & the Duchess was circumstances left nearly ten minutes almost alone with them and could make neither of them understand her. Their Names besides Duncan Forbes of Culloden, Mr. Bouverie, & a Mr. Edkins from Berkshire.*

1828: 28 Jun: *The public papers announce the death of the Grand Duke of Saxe Weimar. This respected Prince died suddenly at Torgau as he was returning from Berlin to his own states; he was, I believe, above seventy years of age, and his attack, which carried him off suddenly, was of an apoplectic nature ... The now reigning Duke was a youth of my own age, but far inferior in talent to either of his Parents; borné, shy and awkward; the Duke wished him to associate with the English youths in order to shake off some of his mauvaise honte & acquire ease of manner; but I apprehend, he still continues an ordinary personage; yet highly connected, for he married a Russian Princess, a Sister of the present & late Emperor, a woman of spirit and talent, as I have heard... . The Duke had one other son, a Prince Bernhard; he was a fine manly boy, when I knew him, and a good soldier, I heard, afterwards; but he became enamoured of French Bonapartean politics, and, therefore, ill esteemed in Germany; in what station he now ranks I am ignorant.*

1830: 26 Feb: *The foreign journals announce the death of the Dowager Duchess of Saxe Weimar, a princess of high attainments & virtues, and eminently distinguished in her sphere.*

SAXONY — Frederick Augustus [33]

King Frederick Augustus Joseph Maria Anton Johann Nepomuk Aloys Xavier (1750-1827), of the House of Wettin, was king of Saxony from 1805 to 1827. He was also Elector Frederick Augustus III of Saxony, 1763-1806, and Duke Frederick Augustus I of Warsaw, 1807-13.

1827: 14 May: *The public papers mention the death of the King of Saxony, Frederick Augustus 4, on the 5th. Inst. at Dresden. This prince was in his 77th. year; the Roman Catholic monarch of a Protestant people. Before being raised by Napoleon Buonaparte to the regal rank, when he was Elector of Saxony, I was introduced at his court, during our stay of about three months at Dresden in 1800.*

SAYER — John Sayer — *see also* Crawley [34]

John Sayer (1787-1836), Church of England clergyman, was born at Doddington, Kent, the son of John and Charlotte Sayer. He was educated at Merton College, Oxford (BA 1811; MA 1829), and was ordained deacon on 17 November 1811 and priest on 19 September 1813. His first clerical appointment was as curate of Lezant, Cornwall, from 17 November 1811. He was then vicar of Arlingham, Gloucestershire, from 1814 to 1836. He married Elizabeth Thomas (b. ±1800); they had at least 1 son and 2 daughters:

1 Mary Elizabeth (b. 1818)
2 Charlotte Anne (b. 1819)
1 John (1823-1886), chancery barrister; listed living at Arlingham, 1851, with his 91-year-old grandmother, Mary Thomas; married, at Flaxley, Gloucestershire, 13 September 1849, Charlotte Sybella Crawley (1824-1900), born at Ravensthorpe, Northamptonshire, daughter of William Crawley-Boevey (1790-1858) and his cousin Charlotte Crawley (1799-1878); 4 sons and 2 daughters:
  1 Mary (1853-1908)
  1 George (1853-1920)
  2 William (1854-1912)
  3 John (1856-1917)
  4 Arthur (b. 1856)
  2 Sibella Fanny (1863-1940)

1823: 15 Jul.
1824: 27 Apr.
1825: 12 Apr., 18 Oct.
1826: 10 Jan.
1827: 24 Apr., 10 Jul.
1828: 15 Jan., 15 Apr., 15 Jul., 18 Jul.

1829: 13 Jan., 16 Jul: *I passed an hour with a party of my brother Magistrates at the King's Head; ... Sayer &c. The last named gentleman amused us by performing some very tuneful strains on a clever little instrument newly imported, and called the German Æolian harp. It appeared to be a small frame work of brass, capable of being held in the mouth between the lips, and furnished with a scale of steel springs pitched according to the gamut; this had five notes, and the player by emitting or drawing in his breath causes such a vibration of the strings as to produce very sweet & harmonious warblings, now louder, now softer, now rapid, now slow. A person with an ear for music, or a knowledge of the science, might even play simple airs upon this diminutive toy, the effect being extremely pleasing.* 17 Jul: *The Revd. J. Sayer, Rural Dean of the Deanery of Gloucester, and Vicar of Arlingham, preached the sermon.* 20 Oct.

1830: 12 Jan., 20 Apr.
1836: 20 Oct.

SAYERS — Andrew Sayers [35]

Andrew Sayers (1799-1874), Church of England clergyman, was born in Dublin, the son of Richard Sayers (d. 1826) and Thomasina Knight (1783-1833). He was educated at St Mary Hall, Oxford (BA 1831; MA 1849), and was ordained deacon on 10 June 1827 and priest on 1 June 1828. His first clerical appointment was as curate of Thenford, Northamptonshire, from 10 June 1827. He was later appointed stipendiary curate of Down Hatherley, Gloucestershire, on 6 January 1831, curate of St John the Baptist, Gloucester, on 16 May 1832, and curate of nearby St Aldate, Gloucester, on 22 October 1832. These posts were supplemented by the curacies of Pauntley, from 24 December 1834, and Upleadon, from 26 February 1835. He was later rector of St Mary de Crypt, Gloucester, 1841-70, and vicar of Upleadon. Gloucestershire, 1834-74. Sayers married, at Old Church, St Pancras, London, 16 February 1824, Louisa Sarah (1795-1866), daughter of William Charles Yelverton, 2nd Viscount Avonmore (1762-1814), and Mary Reade (1769-1834). There do not appear to have been any children.

1834: 15 Oct: *At the Palace a large party assembled to dinner ... Mr. Sayers, a Clergyman, and, I believe, private tutor to the Bishop's little boy.* 17 Oct.

1839: 2 Jan., 9 Apr.
1842: 29 Jun.

1843: 3 Jan: *I had also found that Mr. Sayers, one of the Visiting Magistrates of the Gaol, and a Clergyman, viewed the matter in the same light as we did.* 16 Sep: *Received a letter from the Revd. A Sayers, Incumbent of St. Mary de Crypt Church at Gloucester, a circular dated Aug. 12. and accompanied by a very attractive lithograph of the chancel of that church, as it will appear, if the projected restorations and enlargement shall take place.* 18 Sep: *Wrote to Mr. Sayers—expressing surprize that it was thought that my name on a committee for promoting the restoration and enlargement of the church of St. Mary de Crypt could be of any service to the cause, since I have no connection with the parish.* 9 Oct., 17 Oct., 1 Dec.

1844: 3 Jan., 6 Mar., 10 Apr., 14 Oct., 30 Dec.

1845: 4-7 Mar., 6 May, 1 Jul., 2 Jul: *Breakfasted at the Bell—and afterwards with A Sayers, Robt. Hale, and E.F.W. visited the Church of St. Mary de Crypt, examining its many excellencies of architecture, and its antiquities, together with the extensive alterations and restorations now in progress.* 3-4 Jul.

1846: 29 Jun., 11 Aug., 25 Aug., 18 Nov.

1847: 5 Apr., 29 May.

1848: 3 Jan., 20 Mar., 16 Oct.

1850: 7 Aug., 14 Oct., 8 Nov.

1851: 29 Apr.

1853: 21 May.

SCARLETT — James Scarlett [36]

James Scarlett, Baron Abinger (1769-1844), lord chief baron of the exchequer, was born at Duckett's Spring, St James's parish, Jamaica, the second son of Robert Scarlett, of Duckett's Spring, and Elizabeth Wright, a widow, the daughter of Col Philip Anglin of Paradise estate, Jamaica. He was educated at Trinity College, Cambridge (BA 1790; MA 1791; LLD 1835), and was a barrister at the Inner Temple in 1791. He was king's counsel in 1816 and MP for the following constituencies: Peterborough, 1819-30; Malton, 1830-31; Cockermouth, 1831-32; and Norwich, 1832-34. He was knighted in 1827 and was attorney-general for a short time in the same year, and again in 1829. In 1834 he was made lord chief baron of the exchequer. In 1835 he was created Baron Abinger of Abinger, Surrey.

1826: 7 Aug: *Mr. Scarlett, retained by Mr. Lawrence, the Defendant, had arrived from the Northern Circuit, sanguine of success.*

1827: 26 Apr: *The news of the day is, that Mr. Scarlett has accepted the vacant office of Attorney General, Sir Ch. Wetherell being among the number of those, who have resigned. Mr. Scarlett is one of the ablest pleaders of the day, and a decided Whig.* 2 May: *Mr. Scarlett (now knighted).*

1828: 12 Feb: *Sir Charles Wetherell is appointed Attorney General in the room of Sir James Scarlett.*

1830: 31 Jan: *At last the Government was incensed, the Whig Attorney General, Sir. J. Scarlett, was instructed to proceed against Alexander & Isaacson & others ...* 24 Jun: *Sir James Scarlett, the Attorney General, rose to reply to Brougham, and his speech appeared to me very unworthy of the high character, which he bears as an acute & judicious advocate. It was dull, unimpressive, prosing.*

1834: 15 Aug: *Looked in to the Nisi Prius Court, where we rejoined Howell, and heard part of a speech by Sir James Scarlett, who had been retained on an important Special Jury Cause, Blakemore v. the Glamorganshire canal company.* 12 Dec: *... and Sir James Scarlett to be Lord Chief Baron of the Exchequer, in the room of Lord Lyndhurst.*

1837: 4 Aug: *Lord Abinger, the Lord Chief Baron, and Sir. J. T. Coleridge from the Queen's Bench were the Circuit Judges, two of the most eminent lawyers of the day.*

SCARSBROOK — Richard Scarsbrook [37]

Richard Scarsbrook (1782-1852), innkeeper and landlord of the Unicorn, Stow-on-the-Wold, was born at Hook Norton, Oxfordshire, the son of Thomas Scarsbrook (b. 1752) and Mary Hancock (b. 1742). He was married to Jane (±1791-1851); they had at least 2 daughters:

1 Jane (1825-1853); married, at Stow-on-the-Wold, 23 June 1846, William Marchant Gale; at least 1 son:
  1 Richard (b. 1846)
2 Elizabeth (b. ±1831)

1842: 27 Sep: *There was an excellent dinner provided at the Unicorn by Mr. Scarsbrook.*

1843: 29 Sep., 11 Sep: *Wrote to Mrs. Scarsbrick, to secure places for Saturday next in the Wonder Coach.*

1844: 17 Aug: *Wrote notes to the coachman of the "Wonder" to secure places for the Backhouses on Tuesday next, and to Mrs. Scarbrook to send a fly to meet them when the coach arrives at the foot of Stow hill.*

1845: 11 Feb., 6 Jul.

1851: 22 Feb: *Wrote to Mrs. Scarsbrook, Unicorn Inn, Stow, to order post horses to take my chariot to Stanway on Monday next to bring my son's family hither on a visit.* 30 Mar., 10 Apr: *The recent death of poor Mrs. Scarsbrook, the respected landlady of the Unicorn Inn, has thrown a damp on the Spirits of all who knew her. She was unwell on Friday last: constipation and inflammation of the bowels hurried her to the grave. She was an excellent wife and mother; a cheerful, active, clever, managing woman, particularly qualified for her position; acceptable to persons of every class, from the peer to the peasant—and withal a truly benevolent and extensively charitable creature, befriending all within her reach.*

1852: 22 Jan: *Thither I repaired by 12 o clock, it being held at the Unicorn Inn, now deprived by Death, after a lingering illness, of its aged landlord, Scarsbrook, whose bustling, active, and benevolent wife had preceded him to the grave, some months ago. The establishment is about to pass into the hands of one Heather, Butler for several years to Mr. Chamberlayne.*

1853: 19 Mar., 24 Mar.

SCHALL — Karl Leopold Anton Schall [38]

Karl Leopold Anton Schall (1780-1833), actor, was born at Breslau, the son of a wealthy merchant. He educated himself in the fine arts and intended to be a writer, but he migrated to the stage. He was a minor actor who carried out some directorial tasks, which according to George Brandt, suggests the limitations of the Weimar company. He later also became a playwright. According to Francis Witts he was an Englishman, but this was an error. In his youth Schall was a fine dancer, but in later years his corpulence suited him more to the role of Shakespeare's Sir John Falstaff. Together with Max Habicht and Friedrich Heinrich von der Hagen, he translated the French edition of the *The Arabian Nights* into German. In later years he also became a journalist in his native Breslau.

1798: 2 Sep: *An Englishman of the Name Schall, is a poor actor except in the Character of sneaking Villain, his fort is the Chamberlain in Emilia Galotti &c.*

1799: 12 Nov: *... best Actors Vohsin, Malkolmi, Graff, Schall, Haide, Vohs & Becker.* 20 Nov., 4 Dec., 14 Dec., 16 Dec.

1800: 20 Jan., 3 Feb: *Cordemann Vohsin, Schlanzovsky, Schall & Graff played very well.* 18 Feb.

SCHERER — Alexander Nicholas Scherer [39]

Alexander Nicholas Scherer (1771-1824), Russian-German physicist, chemist, and pharmacist, was born at St Petersburg in Russia. In 1794 he graduated from the University of Jena and later served as a lecturer at the gymnasium in Weimar. In 1800 he was appointed a professor of physics at the University of Halle, and shortly afterwards worked as a manager at a stoneware factory in Potsdam. In 1803 he relocated to the University of Dorpat as a professor of chemistry, and the following year returned to St Petersburg as a professor of chemistry and pharmacy at the medico-surgical academy. In 1815 he became a full member of the St Petersburg Academy of Sciences. His most famous work was *Codex medicamentarius Europaeus* (1811).

1799: 17 Aug: *To Mr. Scherer's Lecture on Chemistry; the subject of which was the spacing of wood.*

SCHILLER — Johann Christoph Friedrich von Schiller — *see also* Schwabe [40]

Johann Christoph Friedrich von Schiller (1759-1805), playwright and author, was born at Marbach, Württemberg, the only son of military doctor Johann Kaspar Schiller (1733-1796) and Elisabeth Dorothea Kodweiss (1732-1802). Because his parents wanted him to become a pastor, they had the pastor of the village instruct him in Latin and Greek. Pastor Moser was a good teacher, and later Schiller named the cleric in his first play *Die Räuber* after him. As a boy, Schiller was excited by the idea of becoming a cleric and often put on black robes and pretended to preach. In 1766, his father took an assignment to the garrison in Ludwigsburg, and there young Schiller came to the attention of Karl Eugen, duke of Württemberg. Schiller entered the Karlsschule Stuttgart in 1773, where he eventually studied medicine. During most of his short life, he suffered from illnesses that he tried to cure himself.

While at the Karlsschule, Schiller read Rousseau and Goethe, discussed classical ideals with his classmates, and wrote his first play, Die Räuber (The Robbers). The play dramatises the conflict between two aristocratic brothers: the elder, Karl Moor, leads a group of rebellious students into the Bohemian forest where they become Robin Hood-like bandits, while Franz Moor, the younger brother, schemes to inherit his father's considerable estate. The play's critique on social corruption and its affirmation of proto-revolutionary republican ideals astounded its original audience. Schiller became an overnight sensation; because of this play he was later made an honorary member of the French Republic. In 1780, Schiller obtained a post as a regimental doctor in Stuttgart, but he disliked the job. In order to attend the first performance of Die Räuber in Mannheim, he left his regiment without permission; for this he was arrested and sentenced to fourteen days' imprisonment. Karl Eugen forbade him from publishing any further works. Schiller fled Stuttgart in 1782, going via Frankfurt, Mannheim, Leipzig, and Dresden to Weimar, where he settled in 1787. In 1789, he was appointed professor of history and philosophy in Jena, where he wrote only historical works. In 1790 he married Charlotte von Lengefeld (1766-1826); they had at least 2 sons and 2 daughters:

1 Karl Friedrich Ludwig (1793-1857)
2 Ernst Friedrich Wilhelm (1796-1841); married Maria Magdalena Josefa Walburgis Antoinette Klementine Pfingsten (1781-1853)
1 Karoline Luise Henriette (1799-1850); married Franz Karl Emanuel Junot (1786-1846)
2 Luise Henriette Emilie (1804-1872); married Adalbert Heinrich von Gleichen-Russwurm (1803-1883)

From Jena, Schiller returned with his family to Weimar in 1799, and Goethe convinced him to return to playwriting. These two literary greats founded the Weimar Theatre under the auspices of the duke, and it became the leading theatre in Germany. Their collaboration helped lead to a renaissance of drama in Germany. For his achievements, Schiller was ennobled in 1802 by the duke of Weimar, adding the nobiliary particle 'von' to his name. He remained in Weimar until his death from tuberculosis in 1805.

Neither Goethe nor Schiller are mentioned specifically in the diaries of Francis Witts. However, it is hard to believe that the Witts family did not encounter them during two years' residence in Weimar with frequent visits to court. It is entirely possible that Francis did not merely write to Goethe regarding his membership of the Weimar library, but applied to him in person. There are gaps in the diaries indicating lost volumes where references may have been made. Furthermore, the somewhat offhand way in which Francis referred to the dowager duchess and the prince hereditary could indicate a similar indifference towards Schiller and Goethe; it is possible that he neglected to mention meeting them. But in such a small place as Weimar, he must at least have seen Schiller on numerous occasions. This is all but confirmed in the diary entry for 17 April 1838, in which Witts recalled, 'In early life at Weimar, I was present at the first representation of Schiller's magnificent dramas "Die Piccolomini" and "Wallenstein's Tod".' It is almost inconceivable that Schiller would not have been at the theatre in person on such occasions.

1798-1807: *The Journal of the Tour in Germany*, noted in personal journals and rough books, 1798-1800; written up by Witts between 23 January and 4 February 1807: *The whole Edifice is light & airy, the Ornaments, Classical, & Elegant, the Colours, good & the Guilding Chaste.—If any thing it were to be wished that the Number of Theatrical Masks some of them most hideous & disgusting were not so great. The Stage itself is small & it were to be wished that under the direction of Göthe the Decorations were more adapted & elegant.—However such little Reproaches are counterpoised by the Company at present on this Theatre which under the administration of the great Göthe who so well understands the management of the Theatre, is become one of the chief Dramatis Personae in Germany, & are capable of leading the path in representing with success for the first time the best pieces of a Kotzebue, a Schiller, a Göthe and an Iffland. During my Residence here they represented Kotzebues, Graf Burgund, several of his Comedies besides, his Gustav Vasa, his Sonnenjungfrau, & his Bayard, Schillers three Pieces Wallenstein, Piccolomini, Wallensteins Lager, his Robbers, his translation of Macbeth his Maria Stuart, Goethes Mahomet from Voltaire &c.*

1799: 19 Aug: *The "Musen Almanach von Schiller. 1798" occupied me. In such a Magazin must naturally be inserted some bad as well as the good: in the Almanach for 1798 the best appears to me to have been written by Goethe, Schiller, Matthison, & Mademoiselle d'Imhoff under the Initials A & F. To the Taylors Apprentice &c.* 20 Aug: *Received from Mr. Schmid the first volume of "Geschichte des Abfalls der vereinigten Niederlande von der spanischen Regierung. von Friedrich Schiller. Leipzig. 1788".* 24 Aug: *To Mr. Boettiger, from whom I brought "Élémens de l'Histoire de France, depuis Clovis jusque'à Louis XV... . carried there "Schillers Geschichte des dreyssigjährigen Krieges."* 25 Aug., 19 Nov.

1801: 21 Apr: *I read Schiller's Robbers & Fiesco in the original.* 24 Apr., 29 Apr.

1828: 12 Feb., 28 Jun: *I must not allow my pen to run on with these gossiping fragments of my boyish days, when scarcely eighteen, drest in the Smart Uniform of the Windsor Foresters, I occupied my Station at the Ducal table, or concert, or ball; walked or lounged the live long summer evening in the Duke's beautiful English Garden or Park, waltzed with pretty German Fraülein, attended the Theatre, to hear the noble dramas of Schiller for the first time performed.*

1833: 22 Apr.

1838: 17 Apr: *In early life at Weimar, I was present at the first representation of Schiller's magnificent dramas "Die Piccolomini" and "Wallenstein's Tod"—these celebrated poems have been frequently reperused by me, and I have now accompanied the perusal of Lt. Col. Mitchell's work with a constant reference to Schiller.*

SCHLAGENTEUFEL — the Swedish family Schlagenteufel at Weimar

1799: 1 Sep: ... *dined drank Tea & supped at Court—where many strangers particularly a Dutch Family Pabst. Father, son & daughters & Swedish Family Schlagenteufel.*

SCHLANZOVSKY — Madame Schlanzovsky [41]

Little has been discovered regarding Madame Schlanzovsky. She was known as a dancer and her first recorded stage appearance was in 1782. She performed at Hamburg in September 1797 in the role of Ophelia, and was well received. She performed at Weimar from 1797 for two or three seasons.

1799: 4 Dec: ... *best actors Graff, Malkolmi, Schlanzovsky, Vohs, Becker, Genast, Haide, Weyrauch.* 16 Dec.

1800: 15 Jan., 3 Feb: *Schlanzovsky played very well.*

SCHLUTZ — the Schlutz [Schulz] family from Gotha

The name Schlutz seems unusual. It is probably a transliteration for Schulz, but even so, no person has yet been identified. Schulz is a common Jewish-Ashkenazi family name in northern Germany. The German word Schulz originates from the local official known as Schultheiß or Dorf-Schulz(e), a local law enforcement officer equivalent to a police officer, magistrate, bailiff, or mayor. This person does not appear in the diaries of Agnes Witts, who merely reported, 'We all 4 went to a very large Tea party at Mr. Gores, principaly to hear some noted Musicians from Gotha, one a Woman on the Violin another a Girl of 12 Years old on the Piano Forte while the father was capital on the VioConcelo'.

1800: 7 Mar: *Tea party & Concert at Mr. Gores about 60 people. Three Musicians from Gotha Father, Mother, & Child a girl of 12 years old, all excellent in their Way. Mr. Schlutz on the Violoncello, his Wife, on the violin, and his Daughter on the Harpsichord.*

SCHMID — Ernst Augustus Schmid [42]

Ernst August[us] Schmid (1746-1809) was a writer, linguist, translator, and connoisseur of literature. He served as tax collector (1782) and secretary (1794), and was a counsellor to Duchess Anna Amalia during her regency. He was also one of the tutors to her two sons. He had wanted to create a literary society in Weimar, but failed due to lack of interest, possibly due to the high price of books, magazines, and newspapers. He worked in the duke's library (now known as the Duchess Anna Amalia Library), and became senior librarian from 1803 until his death in 1809. In a letter dated 8 December 1789, Friedrich Schiller (1759-1805) recommended to his future wife Lotte [Charlotte von Lengefeld] and his sister Caroline the Weimar library, 'where a bored man, Schmid, who teaches English and Italian, can provide you with good books'. Schmid wrote the first extensive dictionary of German and Spanish—the first part (Spanish–German) appeared in 1795 and the second (German–Spanish) in 1805—but he is best known as the translator of Lord James Burnett Monboddo's six-volume work, *Of the Origin and Progress of Language*, published in English between 1773 and 1792.

1798: 2 Sep: *This Collection is better filled with ancient than modern books, but however several new Publications are to be met with always. It is taken Care of by three Librarians, the Head of whom Schmid is a very agreable man, without great Abilities his Talent for learning Languages, has lead him to read so many Books in all Languages, that he has gathered many Anecdotes & Facts which render him an agreable Instructor for he is well enabled to give Lessons in his own, in the ancient, in the Italian & Spanish Tongues. As an Author, his merits lie in translating, his best work is Lord Monboddy translated—& a Spanish & German dictionary, He is a would be Poet, but his verses are tedious & often incorrect totally without fire or genius.*

1799: 14 Aug., 16 Aug., 19-21 Aug., 23 Aug: *To Mr. Schmids who gave me a Poem of his own Composition & Translation.* 26 Aug., 28 Aug., 30 Aug., 23 Aug: ... *to Mr. Schmid who also drank Tea with us.* 28 Oct., 30 Oct: *walked with our whole party in the Morning to Mr. Schmids.* 2 Nov: *went to Mr. Schmids My Mother & Mr. Dukinfield to a Concert by a Demoiselle Kirschgessner: on the Musical Glasses. The accompaniment spoilt the whole Effect of her good Play.* 5 Nov., 7 Nov., 9 Nov., 11 Nov., 14-15 Nov., 18 Nov.

1800: 4 Jan: ... *called on Mr. Schmid. received a copy of Wielands Alcestes from him in Loan.*

1805: 29 Nov: *Wrote letters recommending Mr. V. Jones Junr. to Messrs. Schmidt & Böttiger.*

SCHMID — Herr Schmid, violinist

1851: The *concert was of that character now called "Chamber music" — one of a series given by a celebrated German violinist, Herr Moligne, at the Beethoven rooms in Queen Anne Street West... . Herr Moligne played exquisitely in duets with his daughter, who accompanied him on the Piano-forte and quartetts of surpassing excellence were performed by him with Herr Schmid, and Mr. Mellon, on the Violin and Viola.*

SCHOLEFIELD — Jeremiah Scholefield [43]

Jeremiah Scholefield (1765-1846), Church of England clergyman, was the son of Jeremiah Scholefield of Abberford, Yorkshire. He was educated at Trinity College, Oxford (BA 1787; MA 1790; BD 1799), and was ordained deacon on 20 December 1789 and priest on 21 December 1794. His first clerical appointment was as curate of Shipton-on-Cherwell, Oxfordshire, from 21 December 1789. He was later rector of Barton-on-the-Heath, Warwickshire, from 1808 to 1846. He married, at St John's, Eltham, Kent, 26 September 1809, Margaret Holmes (1780-1861); they had 4 sons and 5 daughters:

1 Catherine Margaret (b. 1810)
2 Sophia Maria (b. 1812)
3 Julia Susanna (1813-1888)
4 Elizabeth Charlotte (b. 1815)
1 William Brooke (b. 1816)
2 Michael Henry (b. 1818)
3 Charles Keeling (1820-1862)

5 Ellen Gertrude (b. 1822)

4 Arthur Frederick Heber (1825-1894)

1826: 18 Jul: *Lord Redesdale in the chair, & afterwards dined with a party at Dr. Warneford's among whom were Mr. Penyston, the Dean of Gloucester, Mr. Hall, Mr. Malcolm, Mr. Scholefield.* 22 Aug: *We dined at the Dean of Gloucester's at his parsonage at Oddington, meeting the Scholefield's of Barton on the heath, the Vavasours &c.*

1828: 19 Dec.

1829: 27 Feb., 27 Jun., 18 Sep.

1834: 15 Jul: *Dined at the Dean of Gloucester's, Oddington. Met the Poles and the Scholefields ... Miss Julia Scholefield surprised me; a very fine, powerful voice, good taste, and well taught: with attention will still improve and approach the skill and power of a professional performer.*

1836: 27 Oct.

1837: 10 Oct: *Then there were three Misses Rice, Mr. and Mrs. Ford, and two daughters; Mr. & Mrs. Scholefield, and two daughters; they were accompanied by a young Spaniard, M. Zamora.*

1838: 30 Jul: *The mansion, the residence of the amiable & estimable Colvilles: the rectory of the less approved Scholefields; both enjoyable places.*

SCHÖNDORF — Herr Schöndorf at Mr Gore's

1799: 6 Nov: *... to Mr. Gore's where met Messrs. Foster, Mounier, Schöndorf, de Manion, de Vaux &c.*

SCHRADER — Mrs Schrader at Lady Lyttelton's

1801: 30 Aug: *Drank tea & spent the Evening at Lady Lytteltons, where we met Miss Stone & Mrs. Schrader.*

SCHRÖDER — Friedrich Ludwig Schröder[44]

Friedrich Ludwig Schröder (1744-1816), actor, theatrical manager, and playwright, was the most celebrated German actor of his day. His parents were legendary figures of the German stage: his stepfather, Konrad Ernst Ackermann, was a brilliant and much-beloved comic actor, and his mother was the renowned actress Sophie Schröder. Friedrich's true inspiration, however, came from Konrad Ekhof, who joined Ackermann's company in 1764.

Schröder was on the stage from the age of 3. He lived for a time in a deserted theatre, learning acrobatics from travelling companies that occasionally worked there. Greatly influenced by the acting of Konrad Eckhof, Schröder further developed the realistic school and raised the standard of taste in Germany with his excellent ensemble productions, initiating reforms in costume, scenery, and acting. He introduced Shakespeare to Germany and produced his own translations of eleven of Shakespeare's plays (1776-80). He also produced his own plays and those of the new *Sturm und Drang* movement. The play referred to by Francis Witts was *Der Ring Ein Lustspiel in fünf Akten*, a comedy in five acts. The second part was called (in English) 'The Unfortunate Marriage'.

1798-1807: *The Journal of the Tour in Germany*, noted in personal journals and rough books, 1798-1800; written up by Witts between 23 January and 4 February 1807.

The German Theatre and Opera House is under the Direction of the famous Actor and the no less celebrated Author of Plays (many of which from le dire en passant he has translated from the English) Schroeder: his Company led by himself is after that at Berlin superior to any in Germany, and his Orchestra remarkably fine: indeed in Hamburgh where some of the greatest of Muscicians in Europe reside, the art is carried to a very high degree of Perfection. The French Theatre and Opera House here is also extremely well supported partly by noble Emigrants. At a Play represented there at which I was present, the Actors were remarkably good the Scenery and dress well managed and the Effect highly preserved.

1799: 24 Oct: *The Weather not being very propitious did not walk out but after fencing &c. went to the Play quite new, by Kotzebue himself there, being called die beyde Klingsberge and founded on the two Pieces der Ring and des Ringes zweiter Theil by Schröder.*

SCHRÖDER-DEVRIENT — Wilhelmine Schröder-Devrient[45]

Wilhelmine Schröder-Devrient (1804-1860), singer, was born in Hamburg, the daughter of a celebrated baritone and a renowned actress. She received early training in movement and diction from her parents and, as a child, appeared in the theatre in both ballet and children's roles. She made her operatic debut in Vienna in 1821 as Pamina in Wolfgang Amadeus Mozart's *Die Zauberflöte*. In the following year Carl Maria von Weber chose her to play the role of Agathe in his *Der Freischütz*, and she also appeared as Leonore in a noted revival of Ludwig van Beethoven's *Fidelio* in Vienna. Both roles brought her tremendous acclaim. Indeed, she was often credited with securing success for *Fidelio*, which had been revived after a poor reception in its premiere. Richard Wagner felt that Schröder-Devrient had awakened in him his vocation as a composer. She later created the roles of Adriano in Wagner's *Rienzi*, Senta in *Der fliegende Holländer*, and Venus in *Tannhäuser*. From 1822 to 1847 she sang primarily in Dresden, Saxony, but also appeared in Berlin, Weimar (Saxe-Weimar-Eisenach), Paris, and London, achieving her greatest successes in highly dramatic roles such as Donna Anna in Mozart's *Don Giovanni*, Leonore in Beethoven's *Fidelio*, and in Weber's *Euryanthe* and Vincenzo Bellini's *Norma*.

1837: 10 Jun: *About half past six my son arrived from Oxford, rather tired with a week of bustle, during which he had mingled with his studies much of gaiety in the society of different parties of acquaintance congregated during the Commemoration week; Mad. Schroeder Devrient and Clara Novello as Vocalists had attracted him at a Concert.*

SCHWABE — Traugott Lebrecht Schwabe[46]

Traugott Lebrecht Schwabe (1737-1812) was court advocate, mayor of Weimar (1775-76), and later a secret government councillor. In addition, in 1776 he was involved in the appointment of Johann Gottfried Herder to the senior pastor. He married Sophia Dorothea Weber.

Schwabe was the father of another mayor of Weimar, Carl Leberecht Schwabe, with whom the riddle of the skull of Friedrich Schiller began. Three days after his death on 9 May 1805, Schiller was hastily buried in the Kassengewölbe, a mausoleum in Weimar's Jacobs cemetery for distinguished citizens whose families did not have a family vault. The burial was quick and unceremonious. Schiller's widow Charlotte von Lengefeld had planned to move her husband's coffin to an individual grave later on, but the cheaply made coffin burst and his remains ended up mixed with those of other people in a mass grave. In 1826, the Weimar mayor, Karl Lebrecht Schwabe, an enthusiast of Schiller's writings, decided to dig up the poet's remains. He hired three day labourers and the cemetery's gravedigger to help. By that time Schiller's body was decomposed beyond recognition. Schwabe reported that the stench of decay was so strong that only smoking prevented him and his men from getting sick. He described the Kassengewölbe as a 'chaos of decay and rot'. Illegally, he unearthed a total of 23 or 27 skulls. Schwabe took them home, placed them all on a table and decided that the largest must be Schiller's. Johann Wolfgang von Goethe later secretly took the skull home, where he kept it on a blue velvet cushion underneath a bell jar. He even wrote a poem about it entitled 'Lines on Seeing Schiller's Skull' ('Bei Betrachtung von Schillers Schädel'), in which he described the skull as a 'mysterious vessel'. The skull, along with the body believed to correspond to it, was moved to the Weimarer Fürstengruft, Weimar's ducal vault, in 1827, to be joined by Goethe's remains in 1832, creating a shrine to German classicism.

1798-1807: *The Journal of the Tour in Germany*, noted in personal journals and rough books, 1798-1800; written up by Witts between 23 January and 4 February 1807. It is not really clear if Francis Witts is referring to the father or the son, but it was just a fleeting reference, and probably to the father.

SCOTT — John Scott[47]

John Scott, 1st earl of Eldon (1751-1838), lord high chancellor, was born in Love Lane, Newcastle-upon-Tyne, the third son and eighth of the thirteen children of William Scott (1696/7-1776), a 'hoastman' or coal factor, and his second wife Jane (±1709-1800), daughter of Henry Atkinson of Newcastle-upon-Tyne. He was educated at Newcastle Grammar School and University College, Oxford (BA 1770; MA 1773; DCL 1801). He was a barrister of the Middle Temple and was appointed king's counsel in 1783. He was MP for Weobley in 1783-96 and Boroughbridge in 1796-99, chancellor of Durham in 1787-99, solicitor-general in 1788-93, and attorney-general in 1799. He was knighted 1788 and in 1799 he was created 1st Baron Eldon. In 1801 he was made lord high chancellor, in which office he remained (apart from a short break 1806-07) until 1827. John Scott (1805-1854) succeeded his grandfather as 2nd earl of Eldon.

1824: 27 Jun: *There appeared a strong inclination on the part of some members of the administration to grant this boon; even a Bishop, Dr. Ryder, professed, that he saw no harm in granting the petition, but other opinions happily prevailed, and the unshaken firmness of the admirable Lord Chancellor Eldon, with the able arguments of Bishops Law & Burgess, carried a large majority with them against the motion in the House of Lords.*

1826: 4 Feb: *Parliament met on Thursday last; the Session was opened by Commission: a slight indisposition prevented the King's attendance. Lord Gifford ... sat on the Woolsack, during Lord Eldon's absence from indisposition. The veteran lawyer & politician is confined to his chamber by a violent attack of gout.*

1827: 4 May: *In the House of Peers, the venerable Lord Eldon vindicated his retirement on the same principle as Mr. Peel, adding, that having long deliberated on the propriety of resigning his high office, on the score of advanced age, and on other grounds, it was to be looked for, that he should embrace the present opportunity.*

1828: 2 May, 13 Jun.

1829: 7 Feb.

1830: 10 May: *In the mean time, as Curate of Chedworth, he had an opportunity of cultivating Lord Stowell's good-will, who, considering with others of his acquaintance, that he had been unfairly used by his father, procured for him from his brother, the Lord Chancellor, Eldon, the living of Hazelton, when it was vacant by the death of the late Mr. Waller of Farmington.*

1833: 11 Mar: *The Duke of Wellington & Lord Eldon expressed their resolution to support the Ministers, Lords Longford, Wicklow, Roden, well disposed Irish peers, assented to the necessity and pledged themselves to support the Measure.*

1844: 8 Oct: *The space appropriated to the Heads of houses, and Doctors, was very much crowded; the Bishops of Llandaff and Chichester being the only prelates present:—many peers attended—Lords Eldon, Sandon, Ashley and others.*

SCOTT — Richard Ashley Scott and the Scott family of Banks Fee — *see also* Morrison[48]

Richard Ashley Scott [Moss] (1796-1860), land tax commissioner for Gloucestershire, was born at Stow-on-the-Wold, Gloucestershire, the only child of Richard Moss and his wife, Mary (±1773-1854). Little is known of this family.

John Scott (1707-1795) bought the Banks Fee estate in about 1753 and built a substantial property there. In his extremely lengthy will he mentioned his late wife Jane and left an annuity to a maiden sister, Hannah, who lived at Dartmouth Street, Westminster. He also made provision for his mentally-ill daughter, Catherine. The main estate devolved to his daughter Charlotte. John Scott also stated that he had manors, messuages, and copyhold estates in the counties of Gloucester, Middlesex, and Hertford. There was also a bequest for his illegitimate daughter, Elizabeth Phillips, who was living with him at Banks Fee at the time of his death. Scott had three other illegitimate children from the same mother; they were John Samuel Philips, who was then serving in the Royal Navy, and Mary and George, who were both at boarding school.

It is not known what happened to Charlotte. No will, probate, or record of any death has so far been uncovered. However, the spinster Elizabeth Scott (1746-1838) was registered as the owner of Banks Fee, and it seems probable that she had been born Charlotte Elizabeth, but preferred to use Elizabeth as her main name.

In her will Elizabeth left everything to Mary Moss and her son Richard Ashley Moss, then living at Drummond Street, Somers Town, London. Accordingly, mother and son changed their surname to Scott. Richard Ashley Scott married, at Longborough, Gloucestershire, 18 August 1847, Caroline Frances (1822-1909), daughter of Archibald Charles Henry Morrison (1793-1866) and Frances Mary Wilton (1801-1879). There were no children of the marriage. After Richard Scott died, Caroline remained a widow and went to live at Cheltenham with her two maiden sisters, Julia and Mary. The Banks Fee estate was sold in 1859.

1837: 23 Dec.

1844: 19 Oct: *Visiting sick parishioners and others in distress, especially the Fortys—the father being more and more pressed by his Creditor, Mrs. Scott of Banksfee, who, under the influence of her son, seems resolved to prosecute him to the utmost extremity of the law.* 22-23 Oct.

1846: 19 Sep: *My tenant Forty, who has evaded the Bailiffs for two years past, was arrested this morning, and conveyed to Gloucester Gaol at the suit of Mrs. Scott, of Banks fee, for the costs in the action which she brought against him.* 29 Dec: *Recd. letters from Morrison ... announces the engagement and approaching marriage of his eldest daughter to Mr. Scott, of Banksfee, with which he and Mrs. M. are greatly pleased: she is a fine, well looking, well educated young woman; her intended must be a good deal her Senior, and is a strange looking, unprepossessing man, almost unknown in the neighbourhood, but, I daresay, sensible, and well informed, hitherto chiefly residing in town: M. speaks very favourably of him from personal observation, and the report of others: at all events, it will be what is called a good match, the Lady's fortune being I suppose, nil, and the Gentleman son & heir of an old lady of good property and Estate.*

1847: 30 Apr., 7 Jun: *The marriage between the eldest daughter and Mr. Scott is still contemplated; has been postponed in consequence of the gentleman's ill health.* 19 Aug: *Informed of the marriage of Mr. Scott of Banksfee to Miss Morrison, eldest daughter of the Vicar of Longborough.*

1848: 19 Jan., 15 Apr: *While I was thus employed, my ladies paid visits to Mrs. John Scott at Banksfee.* 16 May: *Met and conversed with Mr. and Mrs. W B Pole, Mr. and Mrs. and Miss Morrison, and Mrs. R A Scott.* 20 Jun., 23 Aug., 30 Aug: *Entertained several of our neighbours at dinner: and Mr. and Mrs. Scott.* 11 Sep., 10 Nov.

1850: 25 Feb: *Mrs. R. W. Scott and Miss Morrison very kindly drove from Longborough to make enquiries after my wife.* 9 Mar., 10 Jun., 15 Jul: *to Banksfee, to call on Mr. and Mrs. Richard Scott, whom also we did not find at home. It is a very pretty, but rather inaccessible place, which I had never visited before.* 20 Jul., 25 Jul., 29 Jul., 19 Sep., 24 Sep., 8 Nov., 19 Nov., 23 Nov: *A letter from Mr. R. Scott, dated from London, apologizing for not dining here on Wednesday, when, however, Mrs. Scott purposes to be of my party.* 27 Nov: *A dinner party. Mr. & Mrs. J. T. Rice, Mr. Wiggin, Mr. & Mrs. and Miss Morrison, Mrs. R. A. Scott, and Mr. Ogle were our guests, added to our home party.* 6 Dec: *Mrs. R. Scott, and her sister, Miss Morrison, kindly called upon me, but near the village the pretty poney drawing their little carriage strained some joint, and suddenly became dead lame; so that they were obliged to leave both carriage & poney, and returned home in my carriage.*

1851: 2 Jan: *... from Mr. R. Scott of Banksfee, with kind wishes at the commencement of the new year, and thanks for the attention I had shown to Mrs. Scott and her sister, when their pony fell lame some time ago at Upper Slaughter.*

1852: 17 May, 9 Nov: *Mrs. R. A. Scott & Miss Morrison were guests, passing the morning with Mrs. W. Vavasour and her sister. Mrs. W. Dod appeared in high spirits as a bride, and looked well.*

1853: 19 May, 24 May.

1854: 25 Apr: *To Morrison a note of condolence on the death of the aged Mrs. Scott, of Banksfee, who departed this life suddenly two or three days ago. Mr. and Mrs. R. Scott (nee Morrison) will now become possessed of the Bankfee property and Mansion.* 10 Jun: *Drove with E. Clifford to call at Banksfee on Mr. and Mrs. Scott, now possessed of that residence and property by the recent decease of Mr. S's mother. Found them at home, with a large family party of Morrisons collected in the grounds at Banksfee to welcome W. Morrison, who had availed himself of the facility afforded by the Railway to come from Oxford for the day to see his friends.* 20 Jun.

SCOTT — Claude Scott[49]

Sir Claude Scott, 1st baronet (1742-1830), banker and MP, was born at Bromley, Kent, the son of Claude and Mary Scott. He was a self-made entrepreneur in the corn trade, making most of his money during the 1790s with government grain contracts. He married, 8 September 1767, Martha, daughter and heir of John Eyre of Stepney; they had 4 sons and 1 daughter:

1 Claude (b. 1769); presumably died young
2 Thomas (b. 1770); presumably died young
1 Martha (b. 1771)
3 Samuel Claude (1772-1849); succeeded as 2nd baronet; married, at St Georges, Bloomsbury, Middlesex, 4 February 1796, Ann Ommanney (1776-1849); at least 1 son:
    1 Claude Edward (1804-1874)
4 Thomas (b. 1779)

Scott was MP for Malmesbury in 1802-06 and Dungannon in 1809-12. Through his corn trade he made a large fortune which he invested in East India Company stock; he lived 'splendidly' near Bromley, on an estate he purchased in 1797. By 1810 Scott had retired from business and purchased the Lytchet Minster estate in Dorset from John Jeffery. He moved there from Kent for the sake of his wife's health. In the election of 1812 he was an unsuccessful candidate for Bridport. It seems to have been his last attempt to return to Westminster. By 1818 he was described as 'immensely rich and does a good deal of good by employing the people to improve the roads etc.... he is a man of very strong clear sense, and never pretends to knowledge that he has not. By this plain conduct he has acquired the esteem of the gentlemen in his neighbourhood, who are a very aristocratic body.' Scott was created 1st baronet in 1821. In about 1824 he became principal in the London bank of Scott, Dent & Co. He died on 27 March 1830, one of seven London bankers who died within two months of one another.

1833: 10 Sep: *After breakfast left Upper Slaughter with Mrs. Witts and Mrs. Backhouse in our close carriage to visit my Aunt Lady Lyttelton at Peachfield Lodge ... Miss Parrott her guest—an elderly maiden lady—sister of Mr. P., a partner in Sir C. Scott's banking house, London.*

1838: 16 Jul: *They prospered in life, and the late Mr. Parrot, brother of Mrs. E.L.W., who died not long since, was acting partner in the banking house of Sir Claude Scott and Co., a person of great respectability.*

1840: 28 Apr., 5 May, 7 May, 13 May, 23 Jun., 7 Jul: *Wrote to Messrs. Hoare desiring them to place £150 to the a/c of M E.F. W. with Sir C. Scott and Co. to be ready for his travelling expences: also to Sir C. Scott & Co to advise them that such a sum will be paid in by Hoare to my Son's credit, with a view to his being furnished by them with Circular notes to that amount on their Continental Correspondents, agreeably to the system now usually arran adopted. There are certain London Bankers, of whom Sir C. S. & Co. are one firm, by whom these notes are issued.* 9 Jul., 18 Jul.

1842: 19 Feb., 15 Mar., 17 Mar.

SCOTT — Walter Scott[50]

Sir Walter Scott, 1st baronet (1771-1832), poet and novelist, was born in College Wynd in the Old Town of Edinburgh, the tenth child of Walter Scott (1729-1799) and Anne Rutherford (1739[?]-1819). He was the first English-language author to have had truly international appeal during his lifetime, with many contemporary readers in Europe, Australia, and North America. Many of his works remain classics of both English-language literature and Scottish literature. Famous titles include *Ivanhoe*, *Rob Roy*, *The Lady of the Lake*, *Waverley*, *The Heart of Midlothian*, and *The Bride of Lammermoor.* Although primarily remembered for his extensive literary works and his political engagement, Scott was an advocate, judge, and legal administrator by profession; throughout his career he combined his writing and editing work with his daily occupation as clerk of session and sheriff-depute of Selkirkshire. A prominent member of the tory establishment in Edinburgh, Scott was an active member of the Highland Society and served a lengthy term as president of the Royal Society of Edinburgh (1820-32).

Between the ages of 4 and 26, Walter Scott lived at 25 George Square, Edinburgh. The Witts family lived in an apartment at No. 2 George Square for a year from July 1793, so it seems highly likely that Francis Witts would have known Scott as a young man, or at the very least have seen him on occasion. Walter Scott wrote anonymously, but he became known as an author in 1826, when his name was finally revealed.

1824: 10 May: *St Ronan's well. By the author of Waverley, Quintin Durward &c. 3 Vols. 1824. 12mo" A man, who is always talking, cannot always talk well; and a writer, who is perpetually before the public, will sometimes write carelessly, languidly, and irrationally.* 28 Sep: *Redgauntlet. By the author of Waverley &c. 1824. 3 Vols." This is a very spirited, interesting book. The first volume, unlike any of the former productions of the great known unknown, is cast in the epistolary form, the latter volumes in the narrative & journal style.*

1825: 1 Mar: *"The Inheritance. 3 Vols. 12mo 1824" An excellent novel by an anonymous author, a former production of whose pen received the encomium of that excellent admirable critic and judge of literary merit, the author of Waverley.* 3 Sep.

1827: 1 Dec: *"Chronicles of the Canongate. By the author of Waverley. 2 Vols. Edin. 1827. 12mo." The mystery, which has been thrown over the manufacture of those unrivalled works, which had long been universally ascribed by the public to Sir Walter Scott, has at length been removed, by the avowal of the admirable baronet himself, made at a public dinner at Edinburgh some months since, when he was rather precipitately induced to admit himself to be the sole author, and to receive the homage justly paid to him in that character.*

1828: 15 Jun., 29 Sep.

1833: 15 Oct., 9-10 Nov.

SCOVELL — John Scovell [51]

John Scovell (1812-1877), farm bailiff, was born at Northchapel, Sussex, the son of Peter Scovell (1774-1838) and Ann Futcher (1779-1845). In 1841 he was living at Haslemere in Surrey. In 1842 he became the land agent to Harriet, Lady Cockerell. He married, at Bourton-on-the-Hill, Gloucestershire, 24 November 1853, Elizabeth Broad (1828-1914), daughter of Thomas Stayt; they had 1 son and 2 daughters:

1 John (1855-1918)
1 Elizabeth Ann (1857-1889)
2 Frances Mary (b. 1860)

1847: 16 Apr: *Wrote to Asst. P.L.C. Graves with a paper on the cultivation and disease of the Potatoe, which I received yesterday from Mr. Scovell, Bailiff to Lady Cockerell.*

1850: 5 Apr: *Justice business at home—one application induced me to write a note to Mr. Scovell, Lady Cockerell's Bailiff.* 7 Apr.

SCROPE — Anne Scrope — *see also* Lee Warner *and* Wynniatt [52]

Anne Scrope (1755-1829), of Walcot, Somerset, was formerly Ann Brydges, widow of Francis William Thomas Brydges of Tyberton Court, Herefordshire. She was the mother of Catherine Wynniatt, née Brydges, and Anne Lee Warner, née Brydges. She married secondly, 1798, Joshia Scrope of Long Sutton, Lincolnshire (d. 1820). She died at Walcot, Bath, and was buried at Tyberton, Herefordshire.

1824: 2 Jul: *We dined at Mr. R Wynniatt's at Guiting Grange, meeting Mrs. Wynniatt (Mr. R. W's mother,) Mrs. Scrope (Mrs. R. W's mother,) Mr. & Mrs. Woodyatt, Mr. Bowen & Mrs. Wynniatt of Staunton.*

SEATON — William Seaton [53]

William Seaton (1802-1868), Church of England clergyman, was born at Bristol, the son of William Seaton (1786-1852) and his wife, Hannah (1791-1862). He appears to have been an indecisive person. He was admitted at Queen's College, Cambridge, on 9 April 1825, but does not appear to have stayed there. He then matriculated at Peterhouse, Cambridge, on 10 December 1830, but changed his mind once more and matriculated at Magdalen Hall, Oxford, on 24 November 1831. There is no record of him taking any degrees. He became curate of St Thomas's, Bristol, some time shortly before 1844, and was perpetual curate of Christ Church, Pennington, Lancashire, 1854-62. He was then perpetual curate of St Thomas's, Lambeth, Surrey, 1862-68. Writing anonymously as 'the Churchgoer', Joseph Leech, editor of the *Bristol Times*, wrote somewhat tongue-in-cheek of a service he attended on 13 January 1844 officiated by Seaton: 'The service was performed and the sermon preached by the Curate, the Rev. W. Seaton. His style is earnest and energetic, and I have no doubt calculated to be eminently useful ... The sermon was from Revelations, and was a very useful and judicious discourse.' Leech's style was gentle sarcasm.

Seaton married, first, 4 August 1823, Mary Ann (1801-1850), daughter of James Winns (1764-1841); they had at least 4 sons and 1 daughter:

1 William (b. 1826)
1 Sarah Caroline (1835-1908)
2 Samuel Alfred (±1836-1898)
3 Charles Abdiel (b. 1839), Church of England clergyman; married, at St George's, Bloomsbury, Middlesex, 21 September 1893, Susanna Rowe
4 Hugh (1840-1905)

By 1851 Seaton was listed as a widower and 'clergyman without cure of souls', visiting Revd Frederick Hose, vicar of Dunstable. He married secondly, at St Mary's, Islington, Middlesex, 9 October 1851, Henrietta (1815-1894), daughter of Richard Hasell (1779-1864) and Mary Bartlett (1791-1869); they had at least 3 sons:

1 Ernest Prince Pennington (1853-1912); married, at Lewisham, Kent, 17 April 1879, Mary Jane Betts Avery (1856-1942)
2 Arthur William (1854-1921)
3 Octavius Herbert (±1856-1933), Church of England clergyman

1833: 21 Apr: *the Sermon was preached by a Mr. Seaton, who is esteemed by many an eloquent divine... He has recently been engaged as assistant in the extensive parish of St. Philip and Jacob, where he wished to obtain a permanent appointment, as the Minister of a large new Church recently erected in that parish... he aimed at confining his duties to the public service on Sundays, and refused to take part in the laborious weekly offices of the ministry in that very populous suburb, the respectable incumbent of St. Philip and Jacob, Mr. Day, declined giving him the appointment which he solicited.*

SECKENDORF — Franz Karl Leopold Freiherr von Seckendorf-Aberdar [54]

Franz Karl Leopold Freiherr von Seckendorf-Aberdar (1775-1809), poet and Weimar government official (Regierungsrat), was born at Wonfurt in the district of Hassberge. He studied at Jena, and in 1798 came as a government assessor to Weimar, where he became acquainted with Goethe, Schiller, and Wieland. In 1802 he moved to a government post in Stuttgart, but was alleged to have behaved in a treasonable manner and was imprisoned in Schloss Hohenasperg. Released in 1805, he went to Vienna. At the outbreak of the war in 1809 he resigned as a captain in the Vienna Militia, and fought with Gen. Johann Baron von Hiller's VI Armee Korps, covering the left wing of the main Austrian Army. On 3 May 1809, retreating towards Linz, the Austrian Army fought a savage action against Marshal André Masséna's corps at the battle of Ebelsberg. Franz Seckendorf was discovered dying in a burning barn at Ebelsberg, Linz, on 6 May 1809.

1798-1807: *The Journal of the Tour in Germany*, noted in personal journals and rough books, 1798-1800; written up by Witts between 23 January and 4 February 1807.

There is also a Club of Savans, the admittance into which is very easy, these meet every Thursday to dinner & Supper in the Hofjägers at the Saxon Post, & is a Society by which a young Man can profit much, having there an Opportunity of becoming acquainted with some of the most famous men in the Town & Neighbourhood. The Secretary, M. de Seckendorff is a very well informed young Man, singular in his manners, reserved to the world, & open to particular people.

1799: 18 Nov: Disagreeable cold, damp weather walked in the Gardens with Gulliver Maj Seckendorff & Martin.

1800: 10 Apr: *Rather a cloudy morning and wind in the Afternoon: nevertheless walked both morning and afternoon met Seckendorff, going in full Parade on his Cream coloured Nag to Leipzig: attending thither August von Kotzebue & his Family, who were going to Livonia.*

SECKER — Charles Hubert Secker[55]

Charles Hubert Secker (1812-1900), farmer, was born at Widford, Oxfordshire, and lived at the manor house. He married Elizabeth (b. ±1827), daughter of John Lovett (1798-1888) and Rachel Bateman (b. 1802); they had at least 6 sons and 4 daughters:

1 Kate (b. ±1857)
1 Charles Allan (1859-1890)
2 John Percival (1860-1902); married, in Worcestershire, July 1886, Alice Field (b. 1865)
2 Alice Mary (b. 1861)
3 Hubert Henry (±1862-1952)
3 Florence Rachel (1865-1959)
4 Sidney Bateman Lovett (±1866-1923)
5 Frank Hatton (±1867-1937)
6 Arthur Monro (1869-1964)
4 Elizabeth Hilda (1872-1952)

1839: 21 Jun: *Mr. R. Waller called to join me in hearing evidence sufficient to justify our committal of the remaining housebreaker at Widford, who was apprehended yesterday near Abingdon, and brought hither by Otway, accompanied by Mr. Secker.* 23 Aug: *Wrote to Mr. Lewes requesting him to put down my name as a subscriber of five shillings to a piece of plate about to be given to Mr. Secker, as a compliment for his spirited conduct in the late house-breaking case at Widford.* 9 Aug.

SEEBECK — Thomas Johann Seebeck[56]

Thomas Johann Seebeck (1770-1831), physicist, was born at Reval [now Tallinn], Estonia, to a wealthy Baltic German merchant family. He received a medical degree in 1802 from the University of Göttingen, but preferred to study physics. In 1808 he became the first physicist to produce and describe the amalgam of potassium. In 1810 he observed the magnetic properties of nickel and cobalt, and in the same year, at Jena, Seebeck described the action of the spectrum of light on the chloride of silver. He observed that the exposed chemical would sometimes take on a pale version of the colour of light that exposed it, and recorded the action of light for a considerable distance beyond the violet end of the spectrum. Seebeck also worked on the *Theory of Colours* with Goethe. In 1818 he discovered the optical activity of the solutions of sugar.

In 1821 Seebeck discovered the thermoelectric effect, in which a junction of dissimilar metals produces an electric current when exposed to a temperature gradient. He found that a circuit made from two dissimilar metals with junctions at different temperatures would deflect a compass magnet. He initially believed this was due to magnetism induced by the temperature difference, but it was soon realised that it was an electrical current that was induced, which by Ampere's law deflects the magnet. More specifically, the temperature difference produces an electric potential (voltage) which can drive an electric current in a closed circuit. Today, this effect is known as the Peltier–Seebeck effect. It is the basis of thermocouples and thermopiles.

1798-1807: *The Journal of the Tour in Germany*, noted in personal journals and rough books, 1798-1800; written up by Witts between 23 January and 4 February 1807.

Of strangers there are many. The chief are Count Marschall, the Egloffstein, Seebach, Helldorf, Luc, Lasberg, Wolfskiel, Gormar, Oldorthausen, Families &c. all of whom almost have some Office either in the Civil, Military or Immediate Court Service.

SELFE — Henry Selfe[57]

Henry Selfe (1810-1870), barrister-at-law, was born at Rose Hill, near Worcester. His original surname was Page, but he changed it to Selfe on succeeding to his maternal grandmother's property at Trowbridge, Wiltshire. He was educated at Glasgow University and was called to the bar in 1834. Selfe practised on the Oxford circuit and at the parliamentary bar until 1856, when he was appointed magistrate at the Thames Police Court in London. In 1863 he exchanged this position for the Westminster Court, where he remained until his death. In 1858 he was associated with Col Ffrench and Mr Aspinall Turner on the Weedon Commission, which inquired into the state of the Army Clothing Department and the defalcations in war stores sent to the Crimea. Selfe married, 1840, Anna Maria (1812-1899), eldest daughter of William Spooner, archdeacon of Coventry and rector of Elmdon, near Rugby; they had 4 sons and 3 daughters:

1 James Alfred (1841-1913)
2 Edward Henry (1844-1880)
3 William Lucius (1845-1924), judge; knighted in the 1897 diamond jubilee honours; married, at Holy Trinity, Clapham, Middlesex, 10 August 1876, Ellen Bicknell (1844-1929)
4 Sydney Gerard Frederick (1847-1910), Lt-Col
1 Edith Annie (b. 1849)
2 Florence Mary (1851-1948)
3 Rose Emily (1852-1929); died unmarried

Selfe was an active member of the Canterbury Association of New Zealand and became honorary London agent for the provincial government.

1845: 10 May: *Received a letter from Mr. Greaves, the Barrister, strongly recommending Mr. Selfe, a Barrister on the Oxford circuit, of some standing, and with a fair share of business, and a steady sensible man and fair lawyer, who, this late in the day, is a candidate for the office of Auditor of the Oxfordshire and Warwickshire Poor Law District.* 11 May, 13 May, 22 May: *Received a letter from Mr. Selfe as to the Auditorship of our district of Poor Low Unions.*

SELWYN — John Selwyn[58]

John Selwyn (1753-1823), Church of England clergyman, was born at Blockley, the son of Charles Jasper Selwyn (1725-1794) and Elizabeth Coxeter (1730-1776). He was educated at Pembroke College, Oxford (BCL 1783). He was appointed rector of Ludgershall, Wiltshire, 1777; master of Wigston's Hospital, Leicester, 1793; succentor of Salisbury Catherdal; and rector of Coulstone, Wiltshire, 1798. Selwyn married Bridget (1753-1823), daughter of William Dyer (1722-1805) and Bridget Charleton (1726-1792); they had 4 sons and 2 daughters:

1 George Brydges (1778-1803)
1 Albinia (1780-1860)
2 John (1782-1810)
2 Bridget (1783-1867)
3 Charles William (1786-1820)
4 Henry Thomas (1788-1831)

1823: 17 Sep: *The Clerical Stewards were Dr. Timbrill, Rector of Beckford, a strong headed, intelligent, active man; a leading magistrate of this county & of Worcestershire, & Treasurer of the Clergy Charity: Mr. Selwyn, a Prebendary of Gloucester, but precluded, as I understand, by mental infirmity from attending.*

1825: 22 Sep: *I rode to Batsford to dine and sleep at Lord Redesdales. There I met Lord Northwick, Mr. & Mrs. Pole of Wick Hill, three Miss Selwyns, elderly young ladies, daughters of a former Incumbent of Blockley, who have for many years resided in the village of Batsford.*

SETON-KARR — John Seton-Karr [59]

John Seton-Karr (1812-1884), Church of England clergyman, was the eldest son of Andrew Seton, of Kippilaw, co. Roxburgh, and Alicia Rawlinson of Ancoats Hall, Lancashire. His father was a member of the Bengal Civil Service and assumed the additional name and arms of Karr by royal licence on 16 May 1815. John Seton-Karr was educated at St Mary Hall, Oxford (BA 1838), and entered the Church. He was vicar of Berkeley, Gloucestershire, from 1839 to his death in 1884, and also served as domestic chaplain to the duke of Roxburghe. Seton-Karr succeeded his father at Kippilaw in 1832, and married, 1855, Anna Campbell, daughter of Archibald Douglas of Glenfinart, co. Argyll. She was the widow of Richard Campbell of Auchinbreck, Argyll.

1850: 18 Oct: *Mr. Seton Karr is Vicar of Berkeley, a young man, whose mother was discreditably known many years since as being on intimate terms with Lord Fitzhardinge at Cheltenham, yet then living with her husband, whose Son the Vicar is believed to be; but it would appear that he resembles his patron and his mother in laxity of morals, and, having before his ordination been more than suspected of improper familiarity with a married lady, is now under prosecution in the ecclesiastical courts for alleged immoral conduct. The Bishop has required him to abstain from clerical duty until the decision of the courts has been pronounced; and the services of the parish are confided to a curate.*

SEWELL — Messrs Sewell, solicitors, of Newport, Isle of Wight

1846: 5 Jun: *Wrote to Messrs. Sewell, Solrs., Newport I.W., requesting a ticket of admission to be sent to enable us to inspect Lord Yarborough's mansion house at Appledurcomb, not far from Ventnor.* 7 Jun.

SEWELL & NEWMARCH — solicitors of Cirencester — *see* Joseph Sewell

Until the 1840s George Newmarch (1791-1857) handled all of Francis Witts's important legal matters. By the 1840s Joseph Sewell (*below*) had entered the partnership. He eventually took a senior position and the firm was renamed Sewell & Newmarch. For the purposes of the index general references to the firm are listed under Joseph Sewell.

SEWELL — Joseph Sewell — *see also* Newmarch [60]

Joseph Sewell (1814-1890), solicitor, was born at Peckham, Surrey, the son of Benjamin Sewell (1774-1849) and Mary Ann Neck (1781-1850). He married, at Freebridge Lynn, Norfolk, 16 June 1842, Anne Elizabeth (1821-1882), daughter of John Hudson (1794-1869) and Anne Rebecca Moore (1797-1880); they had 9 sons and 4 daughters:

1 Anne Mary (b. 1843)
1 John Joseph (1844-1920); married Annie Christine Sophia Otto (1841-1883)
2 Emma Sophia (1845-1921)
2 Thomas Moore (1846-1917)
3 Harriet Maria (b. & d. 1847)
3 Henry Frederick (1848-1929)
4 Harriet Maria (b. & d. 1850)
4 Edward Clare (1851-1942)
5 Francis Demainbray (1852-1855); born at Cirencester; buried at Lower Swell
6 Charles (1855-1893); married, at Christ Church, Lancaster Gate, Westminster, 27 February 1889, Mary Helen Meikle Welden (1867-1889)
7 Arthur Demainbray (1857-1902); married, at St Mary's, Sunbury-on-Thames, Surrey, 12 October 1898, Edith Mary Blake (1871-1904); died at 'Grena', Goulburn, New South Wales, Australia
8 Francis Warneford (1859-1946); married Isabel Russel Couper (1865-1948)
9 Benjamin Ernest (b. & d. 1860); born at Cirencester; buried at Lower Swell

Joseph Sewell was in partnership with George Newmarch (1791-1857) and eventually took the senior position in the firm. These entries need to be read in conjunction with entries for Sewell & Newmarch (*above*). Francis Witts liked Joseph Sewell and did much to encourage the expansion of his legal firm, particularly when Sewell took over Jackson Clark's legal practice. Witts was also instrumental in ensuring Sewell's appointment as clerk to the commissioners of taxes—which created further friction between Francis Witts and Richard Ford.

1842: 12 Jan., 3 Mar., 18 Mar., 25 Oct., 30-31 Oct.

1843: 2 Feb., 18-19 Aug., 25 Sep., 25 Nov., 16 Dec.

1844: 28 Jan., 8 Mar., 25-26 Mar., 29 Mar., 1 Apr., 4 Apr., 29 Jul., 31 Jul.

1844: 22-23 Apr.

1845: 18 Jan., 21 Jan., 22 Apr: *Recd. a letter from Mr. Sewell about putting down a beer house at Lower Swell: the Atkins Wright property there has been purchased by his Father in law, Mr. Hudson, an eminent Agriculturist in Norfolk, and the Beer house is one of the houses on the Estate.* 23 Apr.

1846: 11 Jun: *Received a letter from Sewell and Newmarch respecting the £1000 to be advanced on mortgage to Mr. Lockhart.* 12 Jun., 17 Jun., 22 Jun., 9-10 Jul., 14 Jul., 18 Jul. *Mr. Sewell called by appointment after breakfast, bringing with him the deed securing repayment of the additional £1000 lent by us to Mr. Lockhart on mortgage of his estates in Bucks.* 29 Jul., 3 Aug., 6-7 Aug., 11 Jul., 12 Jul: *At 9 AM left Gloucester in a fly with Mr. Sewell, who had come from Cirencester, true to his appointment, for Redmarly, to look over a farm there which may suit us as an investment for the money arising out the sale of our houses in Fenchurch Street.* 15 Aug: *Mr. Sewell came to breakfast from Lower Swell, where he had left Mrs. Sewell on a visit to her brother, now residing at the Bowle farm—Mr. Hudson,*

Mrs. Sewell's father, has recently purchased the considerable estate, late belonging to the Atkyns Wright family, in Lower Swell, and is occupying that position of it, which was leased for many years by Jos. Clifford, placing one of his sons there to manage it. 20 Aug., 26 Aug., 4-5 Oct., 11-12 Oct., 16 Oct., 18 Oct., 23 Oct., 29 Oct., 2 Nov., 4 Nov., 24-25 Nov., 1 Dec.

1847: 8 Jan., 19 Feb., 24 Jun., 27 Aug., 31 Aug., 1 Sep., 6-8 Sep., 15 Sep., 18 Sep., 21 Sep., 25 Sep., 28-29 Sep., 2-3 Oct., 5 Oct., 9 Oct., 20 Oct., 23-24 Oct., 25 Oct: *Mr. Sewell dined and spent the evening with us. In conference between him, E.F.W., and myself as to the state of the negociation respecting the living of Stanton.* 28 Oct., 1 Nov., 5-6 Nov., 9 Nov., 16-17 Nov.

1848: 31 Mar: *Messrs. Sewell and Newmarch notify that Mr. Marling has will repayid with interest the temporary loan made by me of £200: on Apr. 16. S & N offer me an investment on Mortgage for £1000.* 1 Apr., 15 Apr., 19-20 Apr., 22 Apr., 8-9 Aug.

1849: 18 Dec.

1850: 10-11 Jan., 17 May, 15 Jul., 17 Jul: *In the morning, at breakfast time, we had been visited by Mr. Sewell, who, being in the neighbourhood, called to enquire after my health.* 21 Aug., 24 Aug: *Received a letter from Jackson Clark as to the scheme of Sewell opening an office at Stow, to fill the vacancy occasioned by Mr. Morgan's decease — Afterwards received a visit from Sewell, who, having had a letter from Jackson Clark as to the scheme of Sewell opening an office at Stow, to fill the vacancy occasioned by Mr. Morgan's decease. —Afterwards received a visit from Sewell, who, having had a letter from Jackson Clark, had travelled from London, where he was, to discuss the proposition with his friends in this neighbourhood.* 27 Aug: *Received a letter from Mr. Jackson Clark, informing me that Mr. Sewell had made arrangements with Mrs. Morgan for the purchase of the good-will of her late husband's professional business, and so established himself as a practitioner at Stow in Morgan's offices.* 29 Aug., 1-2 Sep., 5 Sep., 12 Sep., 17 Sep., 26 Sep., 28 Sep., 3 Oct., 24-26 Oct., 31 Oct., 6 Nov., 9 Nov., 14 Nov., 21 Nov., 1 Dec., 3 Dec., 5 Dec.

1851: 16 Jan., 22 Jan., 4-7 Feb., 13 Feb., 20 Feb., 25 Feb., 27 Feb., 10 Apr., 17 Apr: *To Mr. Sewell's office, where I conferred with him on his appointment to the office of Clerk to the Commrs. of Taxes.* 24 Apr., 30 Apr., 1-2 May, 8 May, 11 May, 14-15 May.

1852: 11 Mar., 25 Mar., 30 Mar., 1 Apr., 1 Jun., 3 Jun., 9 Jun., 25 Oct., 28 Oct., 4 Nov., 11 Nov., 14 Nov., 18 Nov., 1-2 Dec.

1853: 8 Jan., 13 Jan., 20 Jan., 27 Jan., 10 Feb., 17 Feb., 23-24 Feb., 3 Mar., 11 Mar., 24 Mar., 31 Mar., 5 Apr., 7 Apr., 14 Apr., 20-21 Apr., 29 Apr., 19 May, 2 Jun., 8 Dec., 10 Dec., 15 Dec., 20 Dec., 25 Dec., 28-29 Dec.

1854: 30 Jan., 2 Feb., 11 Feb., 23 Feb., 2 Mar., 5 Mar., 23 Mar., 6 Apr., 13 Apr., 20-21 Apr., 11 May, 18 May, 25 May, 10 Jun: *A letter from Mr. Sewell to announce that he & Newmarch are about to take into partnership a Mr. Francis, from Norfolk, to be resident at Stow, and conduct the business of the firm in this part of the country — Sewell still superintending it personally, as at present, by weekly attendance. He intimates that Mr. F. will be ready, if elected, to take the office of Clerk to our Union, if elected. All this promises well; and so I observed in my reply to Sewell, who is now at Cirencester, and will receive my letter to-morrow by his messenger, who goes thither, taking my letter with him.* 14 Jun: *Sewell came to dine with me tête á tête, as it turned out.* 21-22 Jun., 6 Jul., 13 Jul., 3 Aug., 10 Aug.

SEYER — Samuel Seyer [61]

Samuel Seyer (1757-1831), Church of England clergyman, was born at Bristol, the son of Samuel Seyer (1719-1776) and Ann Ebsworthy (1724-1787). He was educated at Corpus Christi College, Oxford (BA 1776; MA 1780). He was appointed perpetual curate of Horfield in 1813, and was rector of Filton, Gloucestershire, from 1824 to his death in 1831. Seyer was the author of *Memoirs Historical and Topographical of Bristol and its Neighbourhood; from the earliest period down to the present time* (1821).

Seyer married, at All Saints', Wraxall, Somerset, 18 April 1781, Elizabeth Turner (1757-1819); they had 4 daughters:

1 Sibylla (1782-1847)
2 Mary (1786-1834)
3 Frances (b. & d. 1788)
4 Elizabeth (b. 1793)

1804: 31 Dec.

SEYMOUR — Edward Seymour [62]

Edward Seymour (±1768-1820), Church of England clergyman, was born at Market Lavington, Wiltshire, the son of Lord William Seymour (1724-1800) and Hester Matravers (1738-1812), and grandson of Edward Seymour, 8th duke of Somerset (1695-1757). He was educated at Oriel College, Oxford (BA 1792; MA 1795), and was appointed vicar of Fisherton-de-la-Mere, Wiltshire, in 1793.

1808: 27 Apr: *Attended the Clergy meeting, as Steward of the Pottern Deanry. Paid my arrears. The party at Dinner consisted of Dr. Welles, Mr. Francis, Mr. Mayo, Mr. Ledyard, Mr. Dodwell, Mr. Williams, Herbert Hawes, Mr. Seymour, & Mr. Goddard. A very good dinner, & wine tolerable. Some quarreling ensued & much folly was uttered.*

SEYMOUR — George Penrose Seymour [63]

George Penrose Seymour (1766-1827), JP, DL, and landed proprietor, was born at Belmont, near Bristol, the son of Thomas Seymour (b. 1721) and Ann Penrose. He married, at Yatton, Somerset, 7 July 1790, Louisa Cam (1766-1853); they had 2 sons and 2 daughters:

1 George Turner (1793-1880), Church of England clergyman
1 Louisa Cam (1795-1861)
2 Henry Cam (1803-1847)
2 Harriot Ann (1808-1886)

Seymour bought the Belmont estate and in 1813 bought the neighbouring estate of Tyntesfield for his clerical son, George Turner Seymour.

1804: 25 Aug: *Mr. Townsend called on us & accompanied Mrs. Bates, my Father & Mother & myself on a Jaunt to Brockley Combe, a picturesque, rocky woody valley in Somerset 8 miles distant: passed thro' a rich & beautiful valley, & the sweet villages of Ashton Bourton, Backwell & Farley: in view of Sir. H. Smith's at Ashton Court, Mr. Gore's at Barrow Court, Mr. Seymour's, late Mr. Turner's, at Belmont.*

SEYMOUR — Henry John Hyde Seymour [64]

Henry John Hyde Seymour (1795-1860), naval officer and landed proprietor, was born at Easterton, Wiltshire, the son of Col Francis Compton Seymour (1755-1822) and Leonora Perkins (1760-1795). He married, at Melksham, Wiltshire, 20 November 1821, Charlotte (1800-1869), daughter of Sir Samuel Whitcombe (1751-1816) and Mary Aubrey (1764-1843); they had at least 2 sons and 4 daughters:

1 Julia Mary (1824-1841); died unmarried at Malmesbury, Wiltshire
1 Henry (1825-1911), Church of England clergyman; married, at Morden, Surrey, 4 November 1851, Susannah Biscoe Tritton (1826-1889)

2 Charlotte Payne (1825-1892); married, 7 August 1845, Charles James Willoughby (1822-1875)
2 Edward Adolphus (1829-1893)
3 Mary Alice (±1830-1918); married, at Dorking, Surrey, 20 July 1854, Constantine Estlin Pritchard (1820-1869)
4 Frances (±1830-1902); married, at Chelsea, London, 3 June 1856, George Francis Coke (1830-1885)

1828: 18 Mar: *We dined at Wotton, at Mrs. Hopkinson's.... We met Mr. Whitcombe, a Solicitor of Gloucester, & Chapter Clerk, a man of good abilities & information, his brother, whose adventures in Greece I have formerly mentioned and a Mr. Seymour, brother in law to Mr. Whitcomb, who has been a naval officer, but now resides in Wales.* 19 Mar.

SEYMOUR — John Hobart Culme Seymour [65]

Sir John Hobart Culme Seymour, 2nd baronet (1800-1880), Church of England clergyman, was born at Plymouth, the son of Adm. Sir Michael Seymour, 1st baronet (1768-1834), and Jane Hawker (1775-1852). He was educated at Exeter College, Oxford (BA 1821; MA 1824), and was ordained deacon on 25 May 1823 and priest on 11 April 1824. Seymour's first clerical appointment was as curate of Westhampnett, Sussex, from 26 May 1823. He was then appointed as follows: vicar of Horley and Hornton, Oxfordshire, 1 October 1824; prebend of Lincoln and chaplain-in-ordinary to the queen, 1827; canon of Gloucester, 1829; and rector of Northchurch, Hertfordshire, 1830. Seymour married, first, at St George's, Hanover Square, Westminster, 12 April 1833, Elizabeth Culme (1808-1841); they had 1 son:

1 Michael (1836-1920), Adm.; succeeded as 3rd baronet

Seymour married secondly, at All Souls, Marylebone, Westminster, 10 February 1844, Maria Louisa (1814-1887), daughter of Charles Smith (1756-1814) and his wife, Augusta (1772-1845); they had 1 son and 4 daughters:

1 Laura Maria (1845-1893)
1 Henry Hobart (1847-1920)
2 Jane Eliza (±1847-1905)
3 Caroline Mary (1848-1857)
4 Charlotte Augusta (1856-1940)

1829: 4 Feb: ... *It is now given to the Revd. J. H. Seymour, Chaplain to the Bishop of Chichester, and, I suspect, the same clergyman, who has of late officiated in the King's private chapel at the Cottage in Windsor park.* 16 Jul: *At half past five I went to the Palace to dine with the Bishop, other guests were the Revd. Messrs. Seymour, Lysons, Douglas, Sayer, Shirley & Ford. Mr. Seymour is the new prebendary of Gloucester and private Chaplain to the King at his Cottage in Windsor Park; he is also examining Chaplain to the Bishop of Chichester; a most pleasing and agreeable young man; very handsome, and of polished manners. He is son of the late Sir Michael Seymour, a distinguished officer in the Navy, and having been early left an Orphan with a sister, was a protegé of the King: he is about thirty years old, and was educated at Winchester College, whence he removed to Exeter College, Oxford. I believe, he has a living in Oxfordshire.* 17 Jul., 24 Sep.

1832: 29 Mar: *Of the Stewards Mr. Holford, Son of George Holford Esqr. of Weston Birt, an old and valiant valued acquaintance of mine, attended: also Mr. Prebendary Seymour, with whom I had a slight previous acquaintance made at the table of the late Bishop of Gloucester.*

SEYMOUR — Webb John Seymour [66]

Webb John Seymour (1777-1819), amateur geologist, was the fourth son of Webb Seymour, 10th duke of Somerset. He was educated at Christ Church, Oxford (MA 1797), where he developed an interest in anatomy and chemistry; he even set up a chemical laboratory in his rooms. After graduation, Seymour went to Edinburgh and became friends with Francis Horner, the philosopher Thomas Brown, and John Playfair. He took several trips with Playfair across Scotland, and a few to England, studying the geology. Seymour also learned mathematics from Playfair and studied political economy as well as Bacon's *De Augmentis Scientiarum and Novum Organum*. He was elected a fellow of the Royal Society of Edinburgh in 1799, and of the Royal Society of London in 1802. He died unmarried.

1801: 12 Apr: *An evening party at Mr. Browns called us out about eight o'clock; if nothing else, at least we enjoyed a good supper, we met there Lord Webb Seymour, Mr. McPherson, Mr. Duff &c.*

1833: 10 Nov: *During my early residence in Edinburgh this eminent character received as pupils into his family some young Englishmen of distinguished families, the present Marquis of Lansdown, the late Lord Ashburton, the Earl of Warwick, the late Lord Webb Seymour, brother of the Duke of Somerset.*

SHACKLEFORD — William Shackleford [67]

William Shackleford (1805-1857), coach maker, was born at Oxford, the son of William Shackleford (1785-1847) and Sarah Wright (1783-1863). He lived at 6 Grosvenor Place. He married, first, Rebecca Alden (1799-1846); they had 2 sons and 3 daughters:

1 William Copley (1836-1916)
2 Alfred Seymour (b. 1838)
1 Sarah Rebecca (b. 1841)
2 Rebecca Alden (b. 1843)
3 Miriam (1845-1915)

Shackleford married, secondly, Ann Lewis (1822-1879); they had 2 sons and 2 daughters:

1 Annie Lewis (b. 1848)
2 Agnes Catherine (1850-1925)
1 Arthur Lewis (1853-1916)
2 Lewis John (1856-1917)

1854: 1 Feb: *my chief errand being to give orders for the repair of my open carriage, at Shackleford's Coachmaker; the business, late Garratt's, being discontinued, since his decease, I was obliged to go to another builder. Meant to have brought home an open carriage on loan, while my own is under repair, but not being able to procure one at all commodious, determined on using my chariot, while the phaeton is in the Coachmaker's hands.* 5 Feb., 25 Mar: *Wrote to Shackleford, the Coachmaker at Cheltenham, urging him to complete without delay the repairs of my Phaeton.* 29 Mar., 19 Apr.

SHARD — Sarah Shard [68]

Sarah Shard (1775-1858) was the daughter of Edward Stone (1743-1811) and Sarah Witts (1745-1834). She married, in London, 16 June 1807, Charles Shard, a widower, of Lovell's Hill, Berkshire, and Peckham, Surrey, the son of James Shard (b. 1738). There were no children of the marriage. Charles Shard had originally married, at Bradenham, Buckinghamshire, 8 February 1787, Sarah Lillie (1763-1804); they had 1 son and 1 daughter:

1 Charles (1791-1847); owned Hedgerley Park, Buckinghamshire; married, at St George's, Hanover Square,

Westminster, 28 November 1811, Harriot Sarah Dawson (1789-1879); 1 daughter:

1 Harriett Frances (b. 1815)

1 Sarah (1793-1867)

Interestingly the incumbent who married Charles Shard and Sarah Lillie in 1787 was Edward Stone, Charles's future father-in-law. Sarah Stone would therefore have known the Shard family. She was first cousin to Francis Witts, her mother Sarah being elder sister to Francis's father, Edward Witts.

1827: 24 May: *We were agreeably surprized by a visit from Captain Witts, which was not, indeed, wholly unexpected, as we had reason to think, he would call on us on his return from Berkshire, where he had been to see my Uncle. He came, indeed, directly from Lacey Green, in Bucks, the seat of my cousin, Mrs. Shard.* 16 Nov: *I did not see my poor Aunt this evening, but found assembled my Cousin Mrs. Shard, and Messrs. Witts of Brunswick Square & E L Witts of Champion Hill… . Many years have passed since Mrs. Shard & myself have met.*

1829: 24 Aug: *Mrs. Shard took her mother to Town, when Lady Lyttelton was there; they all occupied one house.*

1830: 21 Jun.

1834: 9 Mar: *Returning from church, found a letter from Anne Witts, apprising us of the decease of our Aunt Stone, some days since at Lacey Green. At her advanced age, loaded as she was with infirmities, a burden to her affectionate daughter, Mrs. Shard, and impaired in faculties both mental and bodily, this cannot but be considered a happy release.*

1836: 15 Aug: *The colony of Witts's at Malvern, with Mrs. Shard, approve of the proposition I made respecting a lithograph print of my Aunt, and the picture has been placed in Mr. Lane's hands with the expectation that in a month the work will be executed.* 28 Oct.

1837: 23 Feb: *A letter from my cousin Mrs. Shard, now recovered from a serious indisposition, requesting me to look out for a curacy with a title for orders for her protegé, Charles Gray.* 25 Feb., 19 Mar., 28-29 Sep., 13 Nov.

1838: 13 Jan., 30 May, 2 Jun., 14 Jun., 17 Jul.

1840: 18 Mar., 13 Apr., 22 Apr., 25 Apr., 2 May, 5 May, 9 May, 27-28 Jun., 5 Jul., 25 Jul., 15 Aug: *Recd. a letter from Sophy Daniell. The sisters are on the point of leaving Mrs. Shard's, and taking possession of the cottage which they have engaged at Penn in Bucks.* 16 Oct., 18 Oct., 26 Oct.

1841: 1 Mar: *Wrote to Sophy Daniell, requesting her to desire Mrs. Shard to burn any letters of my Father's, Mothers, Brother's, or mine, which might be found among Lady Lyttelton's papers.*

1842: 17-18 Nov., 24 Nov.

1843: 16 Jan., 26 Jan., 23 Nov., 28 Nov., 27 Dec: *Wrote to Mrs. Shard in answer to a letter recd. from her a month or more ago, and at E.F. W's desire, requesting her to stand as Godmother to the baby.*

1844: 4 Jan: *Recd. a letter from Mrs. Shard in answer to mine of the 27th. Inst. purporting that she will act as Sponsor to the dear infant at Stanway; to whom she sends a silver pap-boat of venerable antiquity, having been presented to Richd. Parish Witts, probably a century ago.* 6 Jan., 31 Jan., 5 Feb: *Wrote to Mrs. Shard with an account of the christening &c.*

1845: 26 Apr: *Wrote to Mrs. Shard with an enquiry after her health, having heard from Eliza Daniell that she had been much indisposed.* 5 May.

1848: 31 Jan: *Recd. a letter from my cousin Mrs. Shard.* 16 Feb.

1850: 19 Apr., 18 Jun: *Recd. a kind letter from my cousin Mrs. Shard with an invitation to visit her at Lacy Green.* 8 Jul: *Wrote to Mrs. Shard in answer to her letter received some time ago, proposing to visit her.* 17 Jul., 5 Aug: *Wrote to Mrs. Shard, proposing to visit her from the 12th. to the 17th. Inst.* 9 Aug., 12 Aug: *Mr. Gray, being invited to dinner at Mrs. Shard's, accompanied me thither in my carriage … entered the premises of Mrs. Shard, where I received a most cordial welcome from my aged almost octogenarian cousin. Her faculties are nearly unimpaired: there is a little deafness, and slight defect of memory as to recent events, but a vigorous mind as to the past, much interest in past and passing events, much right mindedness mingled with a few strong prejudices, the remains of much elegance and gracefulness of manner, with cordiality & a conciliatory address. Infirmity confines her to her drawing room & bedroom, and prevents her from partaking of the family meals, yet it is rather disinclination than an inability to move which confines her to the house and to these apartments.* 14 Aug., 20 Aug., 28 Aug., 21 Sep., 25 Sep., 1 Oct., 13 Oct., 4 Dec., 14 Dec., 17-18 Dec.

1851: 18 Jan: *A friendly letter from Mrs. Shard.* 22 Mar., 7 May.

1852: 21 Jan: *Recd. a letter from Mrs. Shard, who, though very infirm, writes a wonderfully correct and lively account of herself and inmates, with comments on passing events, allusions to books, kind expressions of attachment to absent connections, and in a patient, contented, and religious tone and spirit.* 26 Apr., 3 Nov.

1854: 11 Feb., 17 Feb: *Letter from Mrs. Shard in answer to mine lately written: she desires my acceptance of her oil painting of St. Peter, executed by herself, and formerly in the possession of my Aunt Lyttelton, to be mine for my life, and afterwards to be her Godsons, Freddy's.* 22 Feb., 4 Mar: *Received by Railway the package containing Mrs. Shard's picture of St. Peter; a very good production as by an amateur.* 9 Mar., 22 Mar., 31 Mar., 19 Apr., 9 May, 16 Aug: *A letter from Mrs. Shard with kind enquiries after my health, and details of her own weak state, and the illness of some of those nearly connected with her.*

SHARP — Mr A. Sharp at Edinburgh

1801: 19 Apr: *Drank tea & supped with Mr. & Mrs. Brown, Mr. A. Sharp being also there.*

SHARP — Mr Sharp of Lancaster

1840: 1 Aug.

1847: 3 Apr., 8 Apr: *A letter from Mr. Sharp of Lancaster, Secretary to the North Western Railway, in answer to mine of the 3d. Inst.* 10 Apr.

SHARP — Granville Sharp and the Sharp family — *see also* Baker[69]

Granville Sharp (1735-1813), author and slavery abolitionist, was the ninth and youngest son of Thomas Sharp (1693-1758), archdeacon of Northumberland, and Judith Wheler (d. 1757). His grandfather was John Sharp, archbishop of York, and two of his brothers became Anglican clergymen.

1829: 27 Oct: *"Memoirs of Granville Sharp Esqr. composed from his own Manuscripts and other authentic documents in the possession of his family, and of the African Institution. By Prince Hoare. With observations on M^r. Sharp's biblical criticisms by the Right Rev^d. Lord Bishop of S^t. Davids (Burgess) Lond. 1820 4to."* *M^r. Granville Sharp was an eminent person in his day; eminently persevering, eminently upright, eminently pious, charitable, and affectionate to his relations and friends.*

1836: 12 Sep: *The library and dining room contain some good family portraits: an excellent resemblance of my old acquaintance, now deceased, the Revd. Mr. Baker, of Stout's-hill, Father of my host: a good portrait of himself in a shooting dress: good likenesses in Crayons of the present Mrs. B; and of the son and daughters of Baker by his former wife, Miss Sharp, daughter of an eminent London Surgeon, and niece of the excellent Granville Sharp, whose portrait is also here.*

SHAW-HELLIER — *see* Hellier

SHAYLER — **Thomas Shayler** [70]

Thomas Shayler (±1804-1854), schoolmaster, was born at Arrow, near Alcester, Warwickshire. His wife Elizabeth (b. ±1799) was also born at Arrow, and together they were schoolmaster and schoolmistress in the village. At the time of the 1851 census they lived at Priory Street, Alcester, with their daughter Sarah (1835-1854). Thomas was buried in his home parish of Arrow.

1854: 27 Jul: *To the Workhouse, where I presided at a special meeting of Guardians to receive and read the testimonials of candidates for the office of Clerk. Three candidates, Mr. Francis, Mr. Wright, and Mr. Shayler, a Schoolmaster of Buckland near Broadway, with good character as to his position as Schoolmaster, but having no experience in Poor Law matters; it was soon settled that his testimonials should be returned to him, and his pretensions passed over.*

SHEEPSHANKS — Miss Mary Sheepshanks — *see* William Carey

SHEEPSHANKS — Miss Susanna Sheepshanks — *see* Walter Levett

SHEKELL — **William Bonner Shekell** [71]

William Bonner Shekell (1815-1857), farmer, was the son of Thomas Shekell (1780-1852), JP and farmer, and Hannah Hilton (±1788-1863). Thomas farmed 250 acres employing seven labourers and four women. In the 1851 census William was said to farm 131 acres and employ four men. Legend has it that William fell out with the incumbent at Pebworth, where he lived, and was buried in a spinney on the outskirts of the village. However, this is unlikely as the burial was recorded in Pebworth's parish register by the vicar, James Fowle.

1844: 29 Feb.

SHELDON — **Ralph Sheldon** [72]

Ralph Sheldon (1741-1822), MP and landed proprietor, was born at Norfolk House, Westminster, the son of William Sheldon (1715-1780), of Weston, Warwickshire, and Margaret Frances Disney Rooke (1721-1776), daughter of James Rooke of Bigsweir House, Monmouthshire. He came from an old recusant Catholic family and was educated at St Gregory's, Douai, in 1755. Sheldon married, first, at Maestricht, Holland, April 1780, Jane Holbourne (1740-1812), second daughter of Adm. Francis Holburne of Menstrie, Clackmannan, and Lymington, Hampshire; they had 1 son and 3 daughters:

1 Catherine (1781-1818)
1 Edward Ralph Charles (1782-1836)
2 Jane Louisa (1783-1871)
3 Frances Anne (1785-1832)

Sheldon married secondly, 1818, Sarah Broom, of Great Titchfield Street, London, but they did not have children. He was MP for Wilton in 1804-22 and mayor in 1808-09. He was also appointed colonel of the Oxford Loyal Volunteers in 1803 and lieutenant-colonel of the Warwickshire Militia 1808. Ralph Sheldon was an old acquaintance of the Witts family, and Agnes Witts referred to him numerous times in her diaries, the first instance being on 13 April 1789. He was a cousin of Col Charles Rooke, another friend of Edward and Agnes Witts.

1802: 10 Feb: *We called without success upon Dr. & Mrs. Wall & Mr. Sheldon in St. Giles's opposite to St. John's Coll. & thence by St. Mary Hall, towards Merton & Pembroke; thro' Peckwater into Christ Church.* 27 Feb: *Mr. Sheldon was so polite as to call on me; after sitting a quarter of an hour he accompanied me to his own house & introduced me to the Ladies.* 7 Mar: *At Mr. Sheldons in the Evening ... The Sheldons most agreeable, meeting there Maurice of Oriel, & Dr. & Miss S. Wall. Playing on the Harp & Piano & singing. Supped there.*

1803: 2 Nov.

1804: 19 Oct: *In the forenoon called on Nevilles, Sheldons &c.*

1838: 13 Jun: *Weston Park and house were the ancient demesne of a Roman Catholic family of the name of Sheldon, with the last representative of which I was formerly acquainted.*

SHELTON — **Samuel Shelton** [73]

Samuel Shelton (±1780-1867), farmer, was born at Bisham, Berkshire, the son of William Shelton (1732-1823) and Elizabeth Horwood (1744-1832). He rented Luckley Farm, measuring 522 acres, from James Henry Leigh of Adlestrop. It was a substantial farm and Shelton employed eighteen labourers. He married, first, at Bisham, Berkshire, 5 February 1801, Sarah Hall (1780-1806); and secondly, at Longborough, Gloucestershire, 1807, Mary Alcock (1791-1875). Samuel and Mary had at least 2 sons:

1 Thomas Hathaway (1814-1868)
2 Charles (1817-1856)

1836: 27 Aug: *At Stow I met Messrs. Vavasour, Tarn, Beman, Shelton, Freeman on the premises proposed for a temporary W.H.*

1837: 20 Jul.

1838: 11 Jan., 1 Feb., 8 Feb., 15 Feb: *the other Guardians who spoke were Shelton and Wilkins: the former said that my character stood so high that he thought I might treat such insinuations as had been made with the same contempt as if they had been anonymous attacks; and the latter asserted his persuasion that I retained the confidence of the Guardians and of the country generally as entirely as I possessed it when some months ago a public testimonial of respect had been presented to me.* 8 Mar., 5 Apr., 20 Apr: *Messrs. Beman, Comely, Shelton, W. Bryan have accepted the invitation.* 26-27 Apr., 9 Aug., 1-2 Nov., 6 Nov.

1840: 14 May, 17 Sep., 15 Oct.

1842: 3 May, 5 May.

1843: 27-28 Jan.

1844: 22 Feb: *Arrived at home I found that Messrs. Wells, of Hampnett, Bryan, and Shelton Junr. had been seeking me, whence I concluded that a meeting was in contemplation at Stow for the preliminary steps necessary towards the establishment of an Agricultural Protection Society, and I, therefore, determined, contrary to my first intention, to go forward to Stow, when the horses had been baited.* 24 Feb., 29 Feb., 5 Mar., 11 Mar., 19 Aug: *Mr. Shelton called to ask me to visit Mr. Jeaffreson before he leaves Longborough for town.* 30 Aug.

1845: 1 Mar.

1847: 8 Apr: *The retirement of Mr. Shelton, the guardian for Longborough, is to be regretted.* 14 Sep.

1850: 30 Aug: *Mr. Shelton of Luckley farm, who called on me in the evening for advice as to Tax business.* 31 Oct.

1853: 29 Jan: *Wrote to S. Shelton, Luckley Farm, as to one of my parishioners sons, who has fallen into bad health, while in his service.* 3 Feb., 15 Dec.

SHEPHERD — Miss Shepherd at Clifton

1804: 14 Aug: *Called on Mrs. Bates, Miss Shepherd, the Townsends &c.* 6 Sep: *Drank Tea with Miss Shepherd.*

SHEPPARD — Edward Sheppard — *see also* Wallington [74]

Edward Sheppard (1764-1849), clothier, JP, and DL, was the second son of William Sheppard (1734-1814) and Ann (1737-1820), daughter of William Hulbert and Elizabeth Wyatt of Frome, Somerset. The Sheppards of Gatcombe, Minchinhampton, were among his relations. He was on good terms with the diarist's parents, Agnes and Edward Witts, when he was a young, single man living in Uley. He first dined with them at Bownham House on Thursday, 9 June 1791, and the following Monday, 13 June, Edward and Agnes returned his visit, dining at his house in Uley.

Sheppard married, at Bredon, Worcestershire, 9 January 1797, Mary (1775-1845), daughter of John Darke (1735-1805) and his wife, Anne (1733-1798); they had 8 sons and 7 daughters:

- 1 Mary Rebecca (1798-1886); died unmarried
- 1 John Darke (1799-1813); died young
- 2 Anne (1800-1879); married, at Wotton-under-Edge, Gloucestershire, 21 September 1820, John Wallington (1797-1888); 1 son and 1 daughter:
  - 1 John Williams (1822-1910); married, 1852, Henrietta Maria, youngest daughter of Col William Beach of Oakley Hall, Hampshire
  - 1 Anne Elizabeth (±1825-1907); married, 1856, William Twogood of Uplands, Somerset
- 2 Edward (1801-1848); died at Leapcastle, King's County, Ireland
- 3 Hulbert Henry (1803-1804); died an infant
- 3 Frances Elizabeth (1804-1877); died unmarried
- 4 Robert William (1806-1830); died unmarried at the Isle of Wight
- 5 Richard Calvert (1807-1863)
- 4 Eleanor Martha (1808-1883); died unmarried
- 5 Caroline (1810-1866); married, at Wotton-under-Edge, Gloucestershire, 13 May 1835, Kenelm Henry Digby (1811-1891); 6 sons and 3 daughters
- 6 Berkeley (b. & d. 1810)
- 6 Emily (1812-1896); died unmarried
- 7 Arthur Francis (1813-1905), Church of England clergyman; married, at St Julian's, Shrewsbury, 13 June 1855, Catharine Gilbanks (b. 1819)
- 8 Thomas Henry (1814-1888), Church of England clergyman
- 7 Harriet Jane (1816-1889); married, at Quatford, Shropshire, 28 April 1846, as his second wife, Revd Thomas Fremeaux Boddington (1804-1871); 3 sons and 4 daughters

Edward Sheppard was high sheriff for Gloucestershire in 1819, and a JP and DL of the county. He was a successful clothier and owned a large mill in Uley. In about 1815 he commissioned George Stanley Repton to build him a mansion, which he named The Ridge. It was situated on the crest of the hill between Wotton-under-Edge and Uley, with splendid views across Stinchcombe Hill towards the Severn and the Forest of Dean.

In 1837 during a down-turn in the clothing trade, Edward's business failed and he became bankrupt. Sheppard's Mill appears to have employed more than 800 people and the collapse of the business had a dramatic effect on the area. Sheppard retired to Fir Grove, Quatford, Bridgnorth, Shropshire, where his daughter Harriet and son-in-law Revd Thomas Fremeaux Boddington lived. He died there in 1849.

1826: 16 Jun., 15 Sep.

1835: 7 Feb: *Mr. Baker, in his own peculiar, dry manner, reported to Bathurst, with a desire that it might be communicated to me, a conversation which had incidentally passed between himself, Col. Kingscote & Mr. Sheppard. The latter gentlemen, ever prone to find fault, prejudiced men, & sour Whigs, seized an opportunity of cavilling at the proceedings of the Quarter Sessions, the attempted reforms of the Committee of accounts* ... 13 Mar: *Wrote to T. J. Ll. Baker, forwarding to him his memorable letter, reporting the conversation between himself, Col. Kingscote, and Mr. Sheppard.*

1850: 18 Oct: *Mr. and Mrs. John Wallington, from Dursley, joined the party at Stancombe Park at dinner, accompanied by a daughter, an accomplished performer on the Piano. J W. is a magistrate, and pleasant person with whom I have long been well acquainted; his lady also I have known for some years, the daughter of a former magistrate and clothier, some years since deceased, Edward Sheppard, of the Ridge.*

SHEPPARD — Thomas Cotton Sheppard [75]

Sir Thomas Cotton Sheppard, 2nd baronet (1785-1848), landed proprietor, was the second son of Sir Thomas Sheppard (1746-1821), of Thornton Hall, Buckinghamshire, and Elizabeth (d. 1800), daughter of Dr William Cotton of Crakemarsh Hall, Staffordshire. On 3 April 1806, after the death of his elder brother William (1778-1803) and in accordance with the will of his maternal grandfather, he took by royal sign manual the name and arms of Cotton before that of Sheppard. Thomas had two sisters:

- 1 Maria (1776-1798); married, 14 December 1795, William Lowndes of Whaddon Hall, Buckinghamshire; probably died at childbirth giving birth to 1 daughter:
  - 1 Maria Selby (1798-1856); born at Whaddon, Buckinghamshire; died unmarried
- 2 Elizabeth (b. 1777); married, 22 July 1813, Thomas Hart of Uttoxeter

Elizabeth was an acquaintance of Agnes Witts w hen the latter stayed at Calwich Abbey.

Thomas Cotton Sheppard lived at Crakemarsh Hall, Staffordshire. He married, 10 December 1822, Mary Ann (d. 1845), only daughter of Revd George Turner of Wragby, Lincolnshire. There do not appear to have been any children of the marriage. The diary entries for 1802 are interesting, for they make Thomas Sheppard appear an adult, and not merely a youth of 17.

1802: 8 Oct: *Rode with my Father to Mr. Wheeler's at Craiekmarsh where we dined meeting Mr. Cotton.* 12 Oct: *Mr. & Miss Hughes came Mr. Wheler & Mr. Cotton dined at Calwich.*

1812: 5 Aug: *Two daughters of Mr. Wheler of Crakemarsh were also on a visit at Calwich. Mr. Cotton Shepherd & Mr. Wheler, both well known to me of old, were added to our dinner party. Miss Shepherd accompanied the former, as also the Revd. Lownds... Within one mile of Uttoxeter a road to the left leads to Cheadle; we pursued the right hand road towards Ashborn. A mile farther is Crakemarsh situate in rich meadows among lofty trees. A mansion house and ornamented Cottage here both belong to Cotton Shepherd Esqr., the former is at present tenanted by Trevor Wheler Esqr. eldest Son of Sir Charles Wheler of Warwickshire, as Mr. Shepherd is eldest Son of Sir Thomas Shepherd of Bucks. Both these Gentlemen are remarkably pleasant hospitable men.*

SHERBORNE — *see* Dutton

SHERIDAN — Charles Francis Sheridan [76]

Charles Francis Sheridan (1750-1806), author and politician, was born at 12 Dorset Street, Dublin, the second child of Thomas Sheridan (±1719-1788), actor and lecturer on elocution, and Frances Sheridan, née Chamberlaine (1724-1766), novelist and playwright. He was elder brother to Richard Brinsley Sheridan (*below*). Apart from a short period at Mr Whyte's school in Dublin, Charles was educated by his father, who was anxious for him to become an orator.

In 1772 Charles Sheridan was appointed secretary to the British ambassador to Sweden. He later wrote *A History of the Late Revolution in Sweden* (1778), which established his literary reputation. Back in England he entered Lincoln's Inn on 11 May 1775 and was called to the Irish bar in 1780. At the Irish general election of 1776, MP for co. Cork Sir Robert Tilson Deane, who wished to obtain a peerage, purchased for Sheridan one of the seats for the borough of Belturbet from Lord Lanesborough. Despite assistance such as this, Sheridan kept a low profile for the fourteen years he was in parliament. At the general election of 1783 he was returned for the borough of Rathcormack via government influence with Richard Tonson, who also wished for a peerage and duly became Lord Riversdale.

In spring 1783 Sheridan married Letitia Christiana (±1760-1813), daughter of Theophilus Bolton; they had at least 2 sons and 3 daughters:

1 Thomas Henry (d. ±1813); died at Shiraz, Persia
2 Charles
1 Frances Nannette; married Charles Satterthwaite of Liverpool
2 Letitia Elizabeth
3 Caroline Alicia (±1790-1850); married, 2 December 1810, Col Michael Riddell (1783-1844), Madras Cavalry (HEIC); 1 son and 2 daughters:
  1 Letitia (b. 1811); born at Cheltenham; married, at Edinburgh, 22 December 1840, Thomas Wyllie Webster (1808-1877); 1 son and 2 daughters
  1 Michael Chaplin (1822-1853)
  2 Carolina (d. 1833)

Sheridan's political career ended in 1790. He published two pamphlets: the first, *An Essay on the True Principles of Civil Liberty and Free Government* (1793), upheld the view of Ireland as an independent kingdom, while the second, *Some observations on a late address to the citizens of Dublin with thoughts on the present crisis* (1797), attributed the troubled state of the country to the example of France. On the whole, however, Sheridan spent his retirement in various unsuccessful experiments; for instance, in trying to design a perpetual motion machine. He was a member of the Royal Dublin Society and the Royal Irish Academy. He did not enjoy good health and died at Tunbridge Wells on 24 June 1806, aged 56. *The Gentleman's Magazine* declared him to be 'a gentleman of most distinguished talents as an author, both in history and political controversy, and no man was more universally beloved and respected in private life'. It appears that the Sheridans sometimes lived at Clifton, probably as a seasonal visitors, as Charles and Letitia were acquaintances of Edward and Agnes Witts.

1805: 27 Nov: *At a party at a Mrs. Sheridan's called a very good one to me very dull & uncomfortable. Conversed with Miss Elfords.*

1806: 8 Feb., 26 Feb: *Walked with Robins, the Ch. de Mauny, Mr. Kelly, Mr. Sheridan, all of whom I ought to avoid.* 28 Feb: *returned from Bristol with Mr. Sheridan.*

SHERIDAN — Richard Brinsley Sheridan [77]

Richard Brinsley Sheridan (1751-1816), playwright, was the third child of Thomas Sheridan (±1719-1788), actor and lecturer on elocution, and Frances Sheridan, née Chamberlaine (1724-1766), novelist and playwright. The family moved to London in 1754 and in 1762 Richard was sent to Harrow School, where he remained until 1767 or '68. In London, a former physician Lewis Ker tutored Sheridan in Latin and mathematics, while Domenick Angelo taught him fencing and horsemanship. Angelo's son became Sheridan's friend, and both boys were also educated by Richard's father, Thomas. Thomas moved the family to Bath in 1770, teaching elocution there and giving his Attic entertainments.

In 1773 Richard married Elizabeth Ann [Eliza] Linley (1754-1792), who had sung superbly in oratorios at Oxford. Strikingly beautiful with a magnificent soprano voice, she was painted at least four times by Gainsborough, while Reynolds described one of his two paintings of her as St Cecilia as the best he had ever painted. She was the daughter of Thomas Linley, a musician Thomas Sheridan had first met in 1764 and hired to take part in his Attic entertainments. Eliza died in 1792 and Richard subsequently married, 1795, Esther Jane (1776-1817), daughter of Revd Newton Ogle and Susanna Thomas. Richard and Esther had 1 son:

1 Charles Brinsley Sheridan (1796-1843)

Thomas Sheridan had intended a legal career for his son, but Richard gave up his studies at the Middle Temple and decided on writing as a career. His first play, *The Rivals*, was withdrawn after the first night on 17 January 1775, but Sheridan rewrote it in ten days and its popularity has lasted ever since. In 1778 Sheridan wrote *The Camp*, which commented on the ongoing threat of a French invasion of Britain, and in 1779 his most famous play, *The School for Scandal*, was first performed. It is considered to this day to be one of the greatest comedies of manners in English. An ongoing rivalry existed between Sheridan and his fellow playwright Richard Cumberland, a friend of the Witts family; he included a parody of Cumberland in his play *The Critic*.

In 1776, having quickly made his name and fortune, Sheridan, his father-in-law, and one other partner, bought a half interest in the Drury Lane theatre; two years later, they bought out the other half. Sheridan was the manager of the theatre for many years and later became sole owner with no managerial role. His later plays were all produced there.

In 1780, Sheridan entered parliament as the ally of Charles James Fox on the side of the American colonials in the political debate of that year. In 1787 he demanded the impeachment of Warren Hastings, the first governor-general of India. His speech in the House of Commons was described by Edmund Burke, Charles James Fox, and William Pitt as the greatest ever delivered in ancient or modern times. In 1793, during the debates on the Aliens Act, which was designed to prevent French Revolutionary spies and saboteurs from flooding into the country, Edmund Burke made a speech in which he claimed there were thousands of French agents in Britain ready to use weapons against the authorities. To dramatically emphasise his point he threw down a knife onto the floor of the House of Commons. Sheridan is said to have shouted out 'Where's the fork?' which led to much of the House collapsing in laughter.

When Sheridan failed to be re-elected to parliament after thirty-two years in 1812, his creditors closed in; his final years were harassed by debt and disappointment. On hearing of his debts, the American Congress offered him £20,000 in recognition of his efforts to prevent the American War of Independence. This he declined. In December 1815 Sheridan became ill, and was largely confined to bed. He died in poverty, and was buried in the Poets' Corner of Westminster Abbey. In 1825 the Irish writer Thomas Moore published a sympathetic two-volume biography *Memoirs of the Life of Richard Brinsley Sheridan*. It became a major influence on subsequent perceptions of the playwright.

1826: 20 May: *"Memoirs of the life of the Right Honourable R.B. Sheridan. By Thomas Moore. London 1825. 2 Vols 8vo." This is a work, which has excited much attention ... He became for many years the chosen friend & ally of C. Fox, though a coolness existed between them before the death of the latter; fought in the foremost ranks, with Burke in the famous trial of Governor Hastings; on this occasion Sheridan's celebrated speeches were considered at the time among the finest specimens of modern oratory; he opposed Pitt systematically, leagued with the opposition of the day; obtained a great influence at Carlton House, and though never holding a high Ministerial office, when his party was in power, was in many respects a most influential person.* 14 Sep: *After a hasty & scrambling dinner, I retired to Wellington Parade to dress for the Concert: it was after I left the room, that the poet Moore's health was given, which he acknowledged in a light jocose manner, but which was not cordially received by some rigid professors in morals & politics: some, it was said, refused to fill their glass to the toast; & truly the laxity of the poet's morality, his bitter party spirit, his acrimonious and insidious political publications, and, above all, his atrocious attack on the king, aggravated by gross and wilful misrepresentation, in the life of Sheridan, are enough to excite a prejudice against him ...*

SHIELDS — Mrs Shields of Devizes

1806: 9 Aug: *Passed the Evening at Mrs. Gents. Tea, walking & supper, very pleasant, the Tylee Family, Mrs. Sutton, Mrs. Shields & daughter formed the party.*

1807: 24 Jun.

SHILLUM — William Shillum [78]

William Shillum (b. ±1818), horse keeper, was born at Longborough. He was listed in the 1851 census as a horse keeper, living at Moreton-in-Marsh and married to Elizabeth Breakspear (b. ±1813), a washerwoman.

1834: 15 Nov: *Walked with E.F.W. to Bourton to Messrs. Wilkins & Kendal's office, where I met Mr. Ford, and held a bed of justice. Committed to Gloucester Gaol the horse-stealer, Simpson, whom I had sent to Northleach Bridewell for re-examination on the 1st. Inst. Shillum, the partner in Simpson's guilt, is still at large.* 26 Nov: *I called on Mr. Wilkins to press upon him the propriety of proceeding against Shillum for the offence of horse-stealing.*

SHIPLEY — Samuel Shipley [79]

Samuel Shipley (1762-1850), Church of England clergyman, was born at Ashbourne, Derbyshire, the son of Daniel Shipley (1723-1802). He was educated at Oriel College, Oxford (BA 1786; MA 1788), and was ordained deacon on 26 June 1785 and priest on 18 December 1785. He was appointed vicar of Ashbourne with Mapleton, Derbyshire, on 30 October 1806, and held the living for his life. He was married, but his wife is not known. In his will everything devolved to nephews and nieces.

1802: 28 Sep., 6 Oct: *Mr. Furnival, Mr. Shipley, Mr. Harland, Mr. & Mrs. Bingham & Miss Edwards dined with us.*

SHIPTON — Percival Maurice Shipton [80]

Percival Maurice Shipton (1826-1906), Church of England clergyman, was the eldest son of James Maurice Shipton (1789-1886) and Eliza Atkins (1796-1884) of Walmer Hall, near Cheltenham. He was educated at Eton College, Exeter College, Oxford, and Magdalene College, Cambridge. Shipton was curate of Dudley, Worcestershire, in 1852-53, and of Toddington, Gloucestershire, in 1853-55. He was then rector of Clapton-in-Gordano, Somerset, in 1855-60, and finally rector of Halsham, Yorkshire, in 1860-1905. He married, first, 1858, Matilda Agnes (±1838-1863), eldest daughter of Edward Stanley Curwen of Workington Hall, Cumberland. She died at Dieppe, Normandy, in August 1863. He married, secondly, Adeline Bates (1840-1928); they had 1 son:

1 John Perceval (1871-1945)

1854: 17 May: *Towards luncheon time my son and daughter arrived on horseback from Stanway, bringing with them Mr. Ball, and Mr. Shipton, the Curate of Toddington, altogether a stranger to me, and a person with little to recommend him except a gentlemanlike manner.* 26 May: *The latter (E.C.) rode on to call on Mr. Shipton at Toddington; eventually the three out together, and had luncheon at Stanway; returning from thence, Mr. Shipton being on his way to dine at Mr. Ball's at Lower Guiting, E.C. foolishly allowed Mr. S. to mount his mare, and leap her over several walls. One of these she refused, threw her rider over her head: he fell, having sustained but little harm; but the mare cut and disfigured one knee sadly.* 31 May: *E. Clifford had been calling on, and spending the time of our absence with, Mr. Shipton at Toddington, who returned to dine here.* 4 Jul., 7 Aug: *Mr. Shipton Curate of Toddington, an old schoolfellow of E. Clifford and J Purnell, came to visit us: we accommodated him with a bed, by coupling Georgie with Elizth.* 9 Aug., 13 Aug: *Recd. a note from Mr. Shipton, returning thanks for my hospitable reception of him last week.*

SHIRER & SONS [81]

Shirer & Sons, Imperial Circus, Promenade, were linen and woollen drapers and carpet suppliers.

1846: 23 Sep: *Wrote to Shirer and Co. Cheltenham with a remittance for goods supplied.*

SHIRLEY — James Shirley [82]

James Shirley (1802-1870), landed proprietor, was the sixth son of Evelyn Shirley (1756-1810), of Ettington Park, Stratford-on-Avon, Warwickshire, and Lough Fea Castle, co. Monaghan, and Phyllis Byam (1763-1836), daughter of Charlton Wollaston (1733-1764) and Phillis Byam (1736-1829). He married, in London, 1831, Catherine Louisa (1808-1867), daughter of John Dolphin (±1775-1831) and Martha Rollinson (1782-1864); they had 3 sons and 4 daughters:

1 Horatio Henry (1834-1900); died unmarried at Cheltenham
1 Katharine Frances (1836-1916); died unmarried in Dorset
2 Georgiana Louisa (1837-1898); died unmarried in Dorset
2 Evelyn William (1840-1911), Cdr; died unmarried at Thanet, Kent
3 Mary (1842-1911+); presumably died unmarried
3 James Charlton (1843-1905); died unmarried at 24 Montpelier Street, Brampton Square, Middlesex
4 Selina Caroline (1850-1915); died unmarried at Southbridge House, Dorchester, Dorset

Francis Witts was incorrect in his attribution of James's forename as 'John'. It is singular that all seven children died unmarried.

1832: 17 May: *We dined to-day with Mrs. Waller at Farmington to meet Mr. & Mrs. John Shirley. This most pleasing and amiable bride, lovely and simply engaging, is the elder of the two daughters of my deceased friend and neighbour, the Revd. John Dolphin... The Revd. Mr. Shirley's sister married Lord Suffield... This connection of the two parties by relationship and friendship with Lord Suffield has led to the intermarriage of Mr. Shirley and Catherine Dolphin, who are now making a tour of visits to their friends, ... with the Hippisleys, at Bath with Miss Rollinson.*

SHIRLEY — Walter Augustus Shirley [83]

Walter Augustus Shirley (1797-1847), Church of England clergyman, bishop of Sodor and Man, was educated at New College, Oxford (BA 1819; MA 1823; DD 1846). He was appointed vicar of Shirley, Derbyshire, in 1828, and served as rector of Whiston, Yorkshire, in 1838-39. He was then rector and patron of Brailsford, Derbyshire, in 1839, prebend of Lichfield and archdeacon of Derby in 1841-46, and bishop of Sodor and Man in 1847.

1829: 16 Jul: *I At half past five I went to the Palace to dine with the Bishop, other guests were the Revd. Messrs. Seymour, Lysons, Douglas, Sayer, Shirley ... Mr. Shirley is a friend of Mr. Seymour's, and on a visit to him; he is, I believe, brother of Mr. Shirley, of Eatington, Warwickshire, the Member for the County of Monaghan.*

SHORT — Thomas Short [84]

Thomas Short (1789-1879), schoolmaster, was educated at Trinity College, Oxford (BA 1812; MA 1814). He was a fellow at Trinity, 1816-79, a tutor, 1816-59, and bursar, 1838. He was also assistant master of Rugby College, 1810-16.

1853: 5 Jan: *I also wrote to the Revd. —T. Short, fellow of Trinity College, Oxford, Chairman of the Committee for conducting the election of Mr. Perceval, intimating my intentions of voting for that gentleman, as soon as my engagements would allow of my coming to Oxford.* 7 Jan.

SHRAPNELL — Henry Jones Shrapnell [85]

Henry Jones Shrapnell (1792-1837), surgeon, was born at Dursley, Gloucestershire, the son of William Fisher Shrapnell (1765-1817) and Mary, daughter of Henry Jones, of the South Gloucestershire Militia. He began his career working with his father, a surgeon to the South Gloucestershire Militia. He was also a friend, like his father, of Edward Jenner. He spent many of his formative years as Jenner's assistant, becoming a member of the Royal College of Surgeons in 1814. It was noted that 'young Henry Shrapnell, when not busy with his patients spent much of his time in his [Jenner's] study, sorting and labelling specimens, trying to reduce to order what remained obstinately and interestingly disordered'. In 1823 Shrapnell had a paper published in the *London Medical Gazette* describing his own research into the anatomy of the human ear, part of which is known to this day as the 'Shrapnell Membrane'. He was elected a fellow of the Geological Society of London in 1826. In 1829 he had financial problems and had to spend time in the King's Bench Prison as an insolvent debtor.

In his youth Shrapnell ran away to Gretna Green to marry his first cousin, Maria (b. 1803), daughter of John Marklove and Elizabeth Jones of Berkeley. Years later, at Berkeley, Gloucestershire, 17 September 1822, he married her formally. They had 2 sons and 2 daughters:

1 William Henry (b. 1823)
1 Mary Anne Elizabeth (1826-1842)
2 Emily Maria (b. 1828); lived in Berkeley, 1841, aged 13, with her aunt Ann King, née Jones, widow of attorney-at-law George King of Slimbridge; married, at St Leonard's, Shoreditch, London, 10 August 1865, John McWilliam; appears to have had a previous liaison with her cousin John Gale Marklove (b. 1827), resulting in the illegitimate birth of 1 son:
  1 Francis Worthington [Shrapnell] (1850-1874)
2 Francis Robert Maurice (1832-1833)

1824: 31 Mar: *This painful duty was undertaken by Webb, attended by Dr. Baron, the Physician attending Mr. Hicks's family, & Mr. Shrapnell, the Surgeon, who first saw the deceased, and a melancholy task it was.*

1827: 18 Oct: *Mr. Shrapnell would have spoken in reply to the comments made on his letters and statements in the Gloucester Journal, but was not permitted as not being a governor, though claiming the privilege as president of a lodge of Free-masons subscribing to the institution.*

SHUTE — Hardwicke Shute [86]

Hardwicke Shute (±1785-1845), surgeon, appears to have been born at Bristol. He married, first, at Ashton, near Bristol, June 1809, Marianne (1776-1814), daughter of Arthur Wolfe, 1st Viscount Kilwarden (1739-1803), and Anne Ruxton (1745-1804).

Viscount Kilwarden was an Irish peer, politician, and judge, who held office as lord chief justice of Ireland. Upon receiving news of Robert Emmet's uprising on 23 July 1803, Kilwarden left his residence in Clondalkin on the western outskirts and set out for Dublin Castle; accounts differ as to whether he went to the castle for protection or because he had been officially summoned. He was with his daughter Marianne and grandnephew, Revd Richard Straubenzie Wolfe. Near his intended destination Kilwarden's coach was waylaid. He and his grandnephew were bundled out onto the street by a group of Emmet's followers and hacked to death with pikes. Marianne alone escaped.

Hardwicke Shute and Marianne Wolfe had at least 2 sons:

1 Arthur William (1811-1855); born and baptised at Bath; buried at Hempstead, Gloucester
2 Hardwicke (1812-1884), Church of England clergyman; born and baptised at Bath; vicar of Little Milton and later Great Milton, Oxfordshire; married Sarah Frances; appears not to have had children, but Edith (b. ±1847), his niece, probably a daughter of Arthur, lived with them; died at Kingston, Surrey

Hardwicke Shute married secondly, at St John the Baptist, Gloucester, 19 December 1816, Mary Elizabeth, born at Chiswick, Middlesex, the only daughter of George and Harriet Gregory; they had at least 3 sons:

1 George Byng Hardwicke (1818-1892), medical practitioner; born at Gloucester; died at Alderbury, Wiltshire
2 Edward Parker (1822-1895), farmer; farmed 382 acres in Corfe Mullen, Dorset; died unmarried at Kingston, Surrey
3 Harry Fitzgerald (1826-1914); married, at Eastington, Gloucestershire, 9 May 1853, Annie Sarah Cother (1830-1892), daughter of Samuel Commeline (1791-1870) and Sarah Wilton (1783-1861); 4 sons and 3 daughters:
  1 Gerald Edward (1854-1930)
  1 Gertrude Laura (1856-1934)
  2 Arthur Blagdon (1858-1936)
  2 Agnes Howard (1860-1934)

3 Charles Commeline (1862-1944), Church of England clergyman
3 Marion Alice (1864-1902)
4 Theodore Gayer (1866-1931)

1825: 12 Jul.

1827: 1 Jan: *Under this advice, we were not long in deciding to go to Gloucester, where under Mrs. Backhouse's roof, I can avail myself of the counsel of Dr. Shute, of whose science & judgment & attention we entertain a good opinion.* 3 Jan: *Dr. Shute came to me in the evening, and passed an hour or two with us. Though he evidently partakes of the apprehensions of Mr. Hayward, yet like him he hopes the unfavourable symptoms may arise from extensive disorder of the digestive organs; and to that he means to direct his attention, as the most curable view of the case.* 5 Jan: *The suspicions, which I entertained as to an incipient hernia, and which Dr. Shute & Mr. Hayward both considered well founded, have been confirmed by Mr. Cother, the eminent surgeon here, whom I have consulted, & by whose advice I have this day put on a truss.* 10 Jan: *Dr. Shute wishes me to walk out, but the exercise on first going out always brings on a spasm, and I can only move at a very gentle pace.* 14 Jan., 16 Jan: *I have a daily visit from Dr. Shute, who is a very attentive physician, & being extremely well informed and sensible, I enjoy his visits, which often are prolonged for half an hour or more.* 20 Jan., 22 Jan., 27 Mar., 27 Apr: *Had a last interview with Dr. Shute previous to our return home to-morrow.* 10 Jul., 18 Oct.

1828: 18 Jan: *We dined at Mrs. Mary Hunt's, meeting Dr. Shute.* 18 Mar., 21 Mar., 15-16 Jun., 16 Jul: *Before breakfast I had called on Dr. Shute, and taken his advice about some lingering dyspeptic symptoms still hanging about me and distressing me.*

1837: 4 Aug.

1839: 11 Feb.

1842: 10 Mar: *Letters from Dr. Hitch of the Lunatic Asylum, Gloucester, to solicit my vote for his appointment as a Physician of the Gloucester Infirmary, in the room of Dr. Shute, who retires, as an individual subscriber, and as one of the Trustees of a Charity in this parish subscribing to the Infirmary.* 18 Mar., 15 Apr.

1843: 18 Oct.

1845: 2 Apr: *Dr. Shute, who is in very declining health, is to retain his situation as Visiting Physician, but his salary is to be reduced from £100 to £50 per ann.*

1846: 22 Oct: *Quarterly meeting: numerously attended Mr. Gambier Parry in the Chair: present, among many more, Messrs. Purnell, Hyett, Baker, Whitcomb, Hall, Avery, Cols. Cother and Hawkins, Messrs. Helps, Clarke, Worthington, Walters &c. — Some favourable to the new system of rules, others opposed to them.—Messrs. Murray Browne and Shute so hostile as to withdraw by letter their subscriptions.*

SHUTE BARRINGTON — *see* **Barrington**

SIBSON — Anne Sibson [87]

Anne Sibson, née Alcock (1801-1873), schoolmistress, was born at Upper Slaughter, the daughter of Thomas and Rhoda Alcock. She married Henry Sibson (1795-1877), born in the parish of St James, Westminster, the son of Thomas and Charlotte Sibson. Anne and Henry had at least 2 sons and 1 daughter:

1 Maria (b. 1830)
1 Alfred (1834-1909)
2 Edward (b. 1838)

Henry Sibson was an artist and sculptor working in the 1820s at the cathedral of Notre Dame, Paris. He wrote memoirs which were acquired, unpublished, by the Tate Archive in 1999. They reveal a fascinating insight into the possible inspiration behind the protagonist in Victor Hugo's novel *The Hunchback of Notre Dame*:

> The [French] government had given orders for the repairing of the Cathedral of Notre Dame, and it was now in progress ... I applied at the Government studios, where they were executing the large figures [for Notre Dame] and here I met with a Mons. Trajan, a most worthy, fatherly and amiable man as ever existed—he was the carver under the Government sculptor whose name I forget as I had no intercourse with him, all that I know is that he was humpbacked and he did not like to mix with carvers.

In a later entry in his memoirs, Sibson wrote about working with the same group of sculptors on another project outside Paris, and again mentioned the reclusive government sculptor, this time recalling his name as 'Mon. Le Bossu' (le bossu is French for 'the hunchback'):

> Mon Le Bossu (the Hunchback) a nickname given to him and I scarcely ever heard any other ... the Chief of the gang for there were a number of us, M. Le Bossu was pleased to tell Mon Trajan that he must be sure to take the little Englishman.

Hugo began writing *The Hunchback of Notre Dame* in 1828 and the book was published in 1831. He had a strong interest in the restoration of the cathedral, and its architecture features as a major theme in the book.

1837: 10 Feb: *A letter came also from Mrs. Sibson, wife to an artist in London, and daughter of my old parishioners Thos. & Rhoda Alcock, empowering me, if her Father and Mother are in distress, to let them have necessaries of fuel and mutton at her expence to the amount of a sovereign, which she will repay me.* 11 Feb., 16 Feb: *Also from Mrs. Sibson, in answer to mine of the 11th. in which I adverted to the probability of her Father's death, which has now taken place, & the daughter empowers me to give directions as to his funeral at her expence.* 13 Mar., 24 Mar., 11 May: *A grateful letter from Mrs. Sibson, who has repaid the money I advanced on her acct. to the assist her Parents and meet the charge of the funeral of her Father.* 29 Apr: *Wrote to Mrs. Sibson, wife of a modeller in Town, daughter to the late Rhoda Alcott, stating what I had paid for her on account of her mother's funeral, and how the amount might be repaid.* 30 Oct: *Anne Sibson, of London, writes me word that she has to paid to Mr. Jennings on my account the £1. 18. 0. which I advanced for the funeral expences of her mother, Rhoda Alcock.*

SIERS — George Siers [88]

George Siers (b. ±1806), manservant, was born at Longdon, Worcestershire. He married, 15 March 1837, Martha Davis (d. 1850); they had at least 5 sons and 2 daughters:

1 Mary Ann (b. 1837); born at Lower Slaughter
2 Elizabeth (b. 1838); born at Upper Slaughter
1 George Henry (1842-1908); born at Upper Slaughter; married, at St Martin's ,Worcester, 25 October 1868, Mary Ann Done (1848-1929); 2 sons and 4 daughters:
  1 George Henry (b. 1869)
  2 William Robert (1872-1900)
  1 Elizabeth (b. 1874)
  2 Agnes M. (b. 1877)
  3 Louisa (b. 1884)

4 Emily (b. 1887)
2 David (b. 1843); born at Upper Slaughter
3 Joseph (b. ±1845); born at Upton-on-Severn
4 William (b. ±1847); born at Upton-on-Severn
5 Job (b. ±1849); born at Earls Croome

After his dismissal from service in the Witts family, George returned to Upton-on-Severn, but later gained a position as coachman at Earls Croome, Worcestershire. Martha died there in 1850, possibly not long after giving birth to Job.

1837: 23 Feb: *After breakfast appeared George Siers from Upton on Severn, the man of whom Abraham Gibbs had given me information, and whose character I had received from Mr. Kent.* 24 Feb: *Wrote on behalf of my new servant to Martha Davis, the woman to whom he is engaged, to explain the course to be adopted as to the publication of banns between herself and Geo. Siers at Upton on Severn and Slaughter.* 3 Mar: *Wrote to the Revd. Abel Smith of Hanley Castle, Actuary of the Upton on Severn Savings Bank on business of my servant, George Siers.*

1842: 9 Jan: *My son's servant rode over from Stanway to be present as Godfather to our Servant's (G. Sier's) infant son baptized this afternoon, and brought a letter from E.F.W.* 12 Dec.

1844: 16 Dec: *Came at length to the conclusion that I must part from Geo. Siers, our house-servant, who has now lived with us several years.* 17 Dec: *Willm. Dix called to vindicate himself in respect of the imputation charged on him for improper intimacy with Geo. Siers's wife, which he vehemently denied, though he could not but own his frequent visits, which he declared to be perfectly innocent, and intreated me not to persist in my resolution of dismissing the husband.* 27 Dec: *A letter from J. Bateman, about to leave Mr. Aplin's service; and desirous of knowing when he may wait on me to offer his services in the room of G. Siers.*

1845: 3 Jan: *John Bateman having come from his service with Mr. Aplin, near Banbury, to see his poor mother in her declining state, and to offer his services to me in the room of George Siers, I engaged him, subject to the character he may receive from his present master, to whom I wrote.* 29 Jan: *Mary Bateman died during last night: nevertheless John Bateman came to wait upon us, Geo. Siers being gone for a day or two into Worcestershire to prepare a place for himself and family, when he finally leaves my service.* 1 Feb: *Geo. Siers returned from Worcestershire, and resumed for a short season his place in our family.* 11 Feb: *My old servant George Siers left me, and was succeeded by John Bateman.* 15 Feb., 21 Mar: *A letter from G. Siers, requesting me to recommend him to Mr. Berwick Lechmere as a fit person to fill the office of Hall Keeper, now vacant at the County Courts, Worcester.* 22 Mar: *Wrote to Mr. Berwick Lechmere, speaking favourable by G. Siers, but explaining that his wife's levity and misconduct had caused me to dismiss him from my service. — To George Siers, that I had so written to Mr. B.L.* 25 Mar., 4 Apr: *Found letters awaiting me from Leopold Dryden, from Geo. Siers, from J C Geldard.*

SIEVIER — Robert William Sievier [89]

Robert William Sievier (1794-1865), engraver, sculptor, and scientist, was born in London. He decided to become an engraver after gaining a silver medal from the Society of Arts in 1812 for a pen-and-ink drawing. To improve his knowledge of the human form, Sievier learned to model in clay and studied anatomy under Joshua Brookes. Subsequently, in around 1823, he gave up engraving in favour of sculpture. His portrait busts included those of Lord Chancellor Eldon, Sir Thomas Lawrence, and Prince Albert, the prince consort. He also executed several memorial statues, including one of the physician Edward Jenner. In the latter part of his life, Sievier abandoned sculpture and devoted himself to science; he was involved in rubber production and in the early development of electric telegraphy.

1824: 11 Jul: *The lingering affair of the monument to Sir G. O. Paul was again brought forward. It is now proposed to employ a rising young artist, by name Sevier, who is to execute the monument in memory of Dr. Jenner, now in progress, and also to be erected by subscription.* 13 Jul: *the Revd. G. Crawley, having great skill in drawing likenesses, has furnished from memory a sketch of the departed Baronet, which in the principal features is a great resemblance, and which he has given to Mr. Sevier as an aid for the modelling his bust.* 19 Oct.

1825: 9 Nov: *I dined with Mr. Montague, meeting, besides his own family, Mrs. Church, the wife of his partner in the extensive Ironworks, Mr. Sievier, and the Revd. J. Bishop. Mr. Sievier is the Sculptor employed to design and execute the two monuments now erecting in the Cathedral to Sir G. Paul & Dr. Jenner. He was, I am told, bred up an engraver, & has only of late turned his talents to the art of sculpture.*

SILVER — Thomas Silver [90]

Thomas Silver (1776-1853), historian and Church of England clergyman, was born at Winchester, Hampshire, the son of John Nicholas Silver (1748-1837) and Frances Humphreys (d. 1824). He was educated at St John's College, Oxford (BCL 1807; DCL 1812). Silver was Rawlinson professor of Anglo-Saxon in 1817-22, and then moved to the Church. His first clerical appointment was as curate of Ickford, Buckinghamshire, from 21 February 1818. He was then vicar of Great Staughton, Huntingdonshire, from 4 July 1822 to 16 July 1823, and of Charlbury, Oxfordshire, from 12 July 1828 to his death in 1853. He died unmarried.

1834: 28 Nov: *Also to Mr. A. L. Rawlinson in answer to a note which I had received from him yesterday to propose the Revd. Dr. Silver, Vicar of Charlbury, as a member of the Stow Book Society.* 17 Dec., 19 Dec: *Wrote to Dr. Silver, of Charlbury, to apprize him that he had been elected a member of the Book Society on Wednesday last.*

SIMMONS — George Simmons [91]

George Simmons (1804-1866), road surveyor, was born at Stanway, Gloucestershire, the son of Isaac Simmons (1774-1841) and Elizabeth Lawrence (1781-1864). He married, at Turkdean, Gloucestershire, 28 October 1834, his cousin Mary Ann Lawrence (1811-1871), born at Turkdean; they had at least 2 sons and 2 daughters:

1 George (1837-1898)
1 Eliza (b. 1839)
2 Isaac L. (b. 1847)
2 Mary A. (b. 1852)

1837: 4 Jun: *Today I recd. a letter from F. Aston to inform me that Geo. Simmons of Stanway intends to offer himself as a candidate for the vacant post of Rel. Off. of our Union.* 8 Jun: *I supported him as a tried and experienced person with high character, after an failing in obtaining support for another candidate, Simmons of Stanway, a very respectable and competent person, but not prepossessing in appearance, and generally unknown to the Guardians.*

SIMMONS — Elizabeth Simmons of Church Stanway[92]

Elizabeth Simmons (1822-1898), daughter of Isaac and Elizabeth Simmons (below), was lady's maid to Margaret Witts. After Margaret's death she returned home to Church Stanway where she occupied herself as a dressmaker. By 1861 she was back at the rectory at Upper Slaughter, this time as lady's maid to Sophia Witts. By 1871 Elizabeth was married to Thomas Hartwell (1837-1919), a photographer born at Bourton-on-the-Water, who was some fifteen years or so her junior. The couple lived at Banbury, Oxfordshire. By 1891 they were living at Broadway, Worcestershire, and with them was Elizabeth's sister, Charlotte. Elizabeth died in July 1898 at the age of 76.

1848: 10 Jul: *Arrived at the Plough Hotel, Cheltenham at 11 o cl. where we were joined by Elizabeth Simmons, a young person from Stanway, who comes into our service as Lady's maid instead of Amy Hollins, who leaves us.*

1850: 12 Apr: *Poor creature! She* [Margaret] *is sadly oppressed, and very patient, though constantly dwelling on her sufferings, and her helplessness: no one can have more attentive nurses than the three female servants, and especially Elizabeth Simmons, her own personal maid, a kind, affectionate, intelligent young woman.* 20 Apr: *Making arrangements of a domestic nature as to my future establishment of servants. Elizabeth Simmons, my poor wife's affectionate personal attendant, to remain till July, when her second year of service has expired; then, if not before, to suit her own convenience, we are to part.* 14 Jun: *E Simmons received a note from Sophy as to work in which she is employed.* 9 Jul: *Busy in domestic matters, settling bills, and paying wages to good Elizabeth Simmons, my poor wife's faithful and kind attendant, who leaves my service with a silver watch which I have given her in testimony of my gratitude and regard.* 21 Aug: *The fever continues to prevail at Stanway; no death has occurred for a month past. Poor Elizabeth Simmons is now suffering under it, and delirious.* 5 Sep: *Called at Elizabeth Simmons's as I left the village: she is declared by the medical attendant to be out of danger, having experienced a bad attack of the prevalent fever.*

1852: 7 Apr: *Walked with my darling Georgie to call on poor Elizabeth Simmons, who has been suffering for three months from a bad liver complaint, and is still very feeble and ill.* 1 Nov: *Walked with my dear son and daughter to Church Stanway, & visited the widow Simmons and her daughters,—ever mindful of the useful & affectionate services of Elizabeth S. in my poor wife's declining state, and at the close of her life.* 12 Nov: *called at the Simmons's—Elizabeth S. now quite recovered from the attack of fever, but suffering from derangement of liver.*

1854: 23 Apr: *Wrote to Mrs. W. B. Pole to recommend Elizth. Simmons as a servant, having been informed that the Lady's maid is going to leave the service, and WBP. & his wife to set out for Town to-morrow.* 27 Apr: *A note from Eliz. Simmons, purporting that her health will prevent her taking any place of service at present.*

SIMMONS — Isaac Simmons and the Simmons family of Church Stanway[93]

Isaac Simmons (1774-1841), smallholder farmer, was born at Church Stanway, the son of Robert Simmons and Mary Sharp. He married, at Turkdean, Gloucestershire, 14 December 1802, Elizabeth (1781-1864), daughter of George Lawrence (b. 1745) and Hannah Taylor; they had at least 3 sons and 2 daughters:

1 George (1804-1866); *see above*
2 Isaac (1807-1859), innkeeper at Woodmancote; married Harriett (±1814-1885); at least 2 daughters:
  1 Charlotte (1838-1913)
  2 Rosa (1840-1913)
3 Robert (b. 1809)
1 Charlotte (1811-1897)
2 Elizabeth (1822-1898); *see above*

Isaac Simmons was a smallholder farmer working just 8 acres. William Mason (b. ±1821), male servant, was listed as living with the family in 1841. In the 1851 census he was referred to as a farm labourer.

1848: 20 Jun: *Walked to Church Stanway, to Chidley's, Simmons's &c.*

1850: 26 Apr: *Walked to Church Stanway; called on Mrs. Simmons, and bore testimony to the faithful and affectionate services done to my poor wife in her long illness by her daughter Elizabeth.*

SIMMS — Edward Simms[94]

Edward Simms (1803-1897), Church of England clergyman, was the only son of Samuel Simms of Bath. He was educated at Wadham College, Oxford (BA 1827; MA 1830), and entered the Church. He was curate at Malvern in 1840 or slightly before, and went on to become vicar of Dudley, followed by Wilton, Wiltshire. In 1856 he moved to Plaitford, Wiltshire, where he remained until 1860. It is not clear where he was for the period 1860-70, although Sussex is a possibility; his son's entry in *Alumni Oxoniensis* describes him as being of 'Lindfield, Sussex, cler.' In 1870 Simms became vicar of Escot in Devon, a post which he retained until 1877. He retired to Bushey Park, Salterton, Devon, where he lived until his death in July 1897.

1840: 13 Apr: *It was settled that the following Gentlemen should be invited to attend as Officiating Clergymen, at Medical Attendant, and Pall Bearers; the Revd. Dr. Card, and Revd. Mr. Simms, Vicar and Curate of the parish.*
24 Apr: *At the hour named they began to assemble:—the Revd. Dr. Card, the Vicar of Great Malvern .... lastly Mr. Simms, the Curate of Great Malvern.* 26 Apr: *The service was performed by Dr. Card, and Mr. Simms: the latter reads monotonously.*

SIMPSON — Anne Simpson — *see also* John Dean Paul[95]

Anne Simpson (1747-1821) was the daughter of Thomas Lyon, 8th [6th] earl of Strathmore (1704-1753), and Jean [Joan] Nicholson (1713-1778). She married, 1768, John Simpson (1740-1802) of Bradley Hall, Durham; they had at least 2 daughters:

1 Maria Susannah (1773-1845); married, at Upper Harley Street, Westminster, 26 March 1796, Thomas Liddell, 2nd Baron Ravensworth (1775-1855), son of Sir Henry Liddell, 5th baronet, and elder brother of Revd Henry George Liddell (1787-1872)
2 Frances Eleanor (1776-1833); married, 1799, Sir John Dean Paul, 1st baronet of Rodborough, Gloucestershire (1775-1852); 3 sons and 4 daughters

The fact that one of Lady Anne's daughters, Frances Eleanor, married John Dean Paul would largely explain why she was with Anne Snow on 3 August 1803. In his memoirs Augustus Hare provides an interesting insight into Lady Anne:

> The vicissitudes of her eventful life, and her own charm and cleverness, combined to make Lady Anne Simpson one of the most interesting women of her age, and her society was eagerly sought and appreciated. Both her daughters had married young,

> and in her solitude, she took the eldest daughter of Lady Paul to live with her and brought her up as her own child. In her house, Anne Paul saw all the most remarkable Englishmen of the time. She was provided with the best masters, and in her home life she had generally the companionship of the daughters of her mother's sister Lady Liddell, afterwards Lady Ravensworth, infinitely preferring their companionship to that of her own brothers and sisters. Lady Anne Simpson resided chiefly at a house belonging to Colonel Jolliffe at Merstham in Surrey, where the persons she wished to see could frequently come down to her from London. The royal dukes, sons of George III, constantly visited her in this way, and delighted in the society of the pretty old lady, who had so much to tell, and who always told it in the most interesting way.

In 1803 Lady Anne was living at Heatham House, Whitton Road, Twickenham; Agnes Witts made a point of seeking out the house, but did not call. On 6 July 1803, Agnes wrote, 'in the Morning walk'd before Tea to several parts of Twickenham principaly to take a view of Ldy. Anne Simpsons house.' Lady Anne died in March 1821 at Merstham House, Surrey.

1805: 3 Aug: *At Sunbury, finding our poor friend Mrs. A Snow, with whom we found Lady A. Simpson & Mrs. Park.*

SIMPSON — John Simpson[96]

John Simpson (b. 1816), horse thief, was sentenced at the Gloucester assizes, 4 April 1835, to life imprisonment for horse stealing. He was presumably transported to Australia, but he did not arrive there. Two of his accomplices, Henry Stiles and William Smith, were convicted at the same time for the same term and arrived in New South Wales on 7 September 1835 on the vessel *John Barry*. It is not known what happened to John Simpson; he may have died *en route*.

1834: 15 Nov: *Walked with E.F.W. to Bourton to Messrs. Wilkins & Kendal's office, where I met Mr. Ford, and held a bed of justice. Committed to Gloucester Gaol the horse-stealer, Simpson, whom I had sent to Northleach Bridewell for re-examination on the 1st. Inst. Shillum, the partner in Simpson's guilt, is still at large.*

SIMPSON — William Simpson[97]

William Simpson (1744-1831), minister at the kirk of Tron, was born at Wilton, Roxburghshire, the second son of James Simpson, minister of Wilton, and Ann Cranston. Simpson was presented to the kirk at Tron by the town council on 25 February 1789. He was made DD in 1810. He married, first, 1775, Jean Douglas Balderston (d. 1786); they had at least 2 sons and 2 daughters:

- 1 Euphemia (b. 1776)
- 2 Ann (b. 1778)
- 1 James (1780-1853), advocate and author; wrote *A Visit to Flanders after the Battle of Waterloo*
- 2 George (1782-1807)

Simpson married secondly, 1794, Isabella (1742-1825), daughter of James Ker of Bughtrig.

William Simpson was a friend of the Witts family in Edinburgh and was frequently mentioned by Agnes Witts in her diaries. In his diary entry for 17 April 1801, Francis Witts referred to William's son, James Simpson, his friend during the Edinburgh years. James Simpson was called to the bar in 1801. In early life he was acquainted with Sir Walter Scott, and was among those to whom the author submitted *Waverley* for criticism before publication.

1801: 14 Apr: *Mr. Simpson, Mr. Jones, Miss Robertsons &c called in the morning.* 15 Apr: *Made various visits to Mr. Simpson, Miss Campbell of Shirvan, Lady Sinclair, & Mrs. Sands.* 17 Apr: *Mr. J. Simpson called in the morning, and I walked a little with him.* 29-30 Apr., 2 May.

SINCLAIR — Captain Sinclair at Lord Elcho's

Capt. Sinclair is likely to have been a younger brother of Sir John Sinclair, 1st baronet of Ulbster (1754-1835), of Thurso Castle, Caithness (*see below*, Diana Sinclair). It seems probable that Capt. Sinclair was a captain of the Rothesay and Caithness Fencibles.

1801: 9 Apr: *In the evening Captn. Sinclair joined our party, which was at least very merry.*

SINCLAIR — Diana Sinclair[98]

Diana Jane Elizabeth Macdonald (1769-1845), daughter of Alexander, 1st Baron Macdonald, married, 1788, Sir John Sinclair, 1st baronet of Ulbster (1754-1835), of Thurso Castle, Caithness, as his second wife. They had at least 1 son and 1 daughter:

- 1 George (1790-1868); succeeded as 2nd baronet; married, 1 May 1816, Catherine Camilla Tollemache (d. 1863); at least 1 son and 1 daughter:
  - 1 Tollemache (1825-1912), MP; succeeded as 3rd baronet
  - 1 Adelaide Mary Wentworth (±1830-1873)
- 1 Julia (d. 1868)

Sir John Sinclair was MP for Caithness and president of the Board of Agriculture in 1793-98 and 1806-14. He was a privy councillor in 1810 and cashier of excise (Scotland) in 1811-30. He was colonel of the Rothesay and Caithness Fencibles in 1794, and lieutenant-colonel and commandant of the Caithness Volunteers in 1803. He was promoted to colonel of the volunteers in the same year. Sinclair was also an influential author on both finance and agriculture; his 21-volume pioneering work *Statistical Account of Scotland* was published between 1791 and 1799.

1801: 15 Apr: *Made various visits to Mr. Simpson, Miss Campbell of Shirvan, Lady Sinclair, & Mrs. Sands.*

SITWELL — Francis Sitwell[99]

Francis Sitwell (1770-1813), MP and landed proprietor, was the second son of Francis Hurt [later Sitwell] (1746-1793), of Renishaw Hall, Eckington, Derbyshire, and Mary (1750-1792), daughter of Revd Richard Warneford of York. His brother was Sitwell Sitwell. He married, at Lowick, Northumberland, 21 September 1795, Ann, daughter of Ilay Campbell of Succoth, Argyll; they had 3 sons and 3 daughters:

- 1 Susan Anne Hurt (b. 1796)
- 1 Francis (1797-1884); married Johannah Tallack (1794-1856); at least 1 son:
  - 1 Francis (1826-1898)
- 2 Mary Amelia (1798-1844); married, at Edinburgh, 30 April 1824, John Tait, advocate
- 2 Alexander (1799-1807)
- 3 Ann Jane (1801-1869); married, 12 July 1824, John Campbell (1798-1830), son of Sir Archibald Campbell, 2nd baronet of Succoth (1769-1846), and Elizabeth Balfour; at least 2 sons:
  - 1 Archibald Islay (1825-1866); succeeded as 3rd baronet
  - 2 George (1829-1874); succeeded as 4th baronet
- 3 William Hurt (1802-1865); married, 29 January 1828, Sarah Honoria (1811-1892), daughter of Jonathan Simon Cooper (1777-1850) and Anna Maria Kirchhoffer (1777-1832); 4 sons and 3 daughters:

1 William Henry (1829-1850)
2 Albert Hurt (1834-1894), Church of England clergyman
1 Anna Mary Elizabeth (b. 1836)
3 Honorius Sisson (1839-1891)
2 Isla Ashley (1841-1880)
3 Sara Honoria Rosa (1849-1880)
4 Harold Cooper (d. 1884)

Sitwell succeeded his father at Barmoor Castle, Northumberland, in 1793. On 29 August 1796 Agnes Witts wrote, 'between Dinner & Tea walk'd to Stevenson, late Lady Sinclairs, now just taken by Mr. Sitwell who we found there, & very politely shew'd us the place.' Quite why Sitwell was there is not clear, but there was a connection with Lord Elcho. Francis Sitwell was MP for Berwick-upon-Tweed in 1803-06, but made no reported speech and did not contest Berwick in 1806. As a Pittite he offered instead for Haddington Burghs on the strength of Lord Elcho's interest at Lauder, but did not go to the poll.

Francis Sitwell's father, Francis Hurt, inherited the immense wealth of his kinsmen the Sitwells in 1776. In 1793 Francis (junior) was set up as a Northumbrian country gentleman under the terms of the will of his father's cousin, Samuel Phipps (d. 1791). In 1806 he was described as having 'lately addicted himself to agricultural pursuits', and in that year established a cattle show.

1801: 6 May: *With my Lord round all the young plantations, I rode in with Miss Kate to Haddington on my Lords (he must) & then bored away stupid as an owl in a well stuffed coach to dine with the Sitwell's at Stevenston.* 7 May: *Returned round –?–field & Stevenston (thank Heaven) without meeting Sitwell.*

1805: 9 Jan: *At supper a scramble of good things & good company, but highly amusing. Much with F. Sitwell, a hearty racketing fellow, with whom I renewed an old acquaintance.*

SIVORI — Ernesto Camillo Sivori [100]

Ernesto Camillo Sivori (1817-1894), violinist, was born at Genoa. He was taught by Restano, Paganini, Costa, and Dellepiane, who found him to possess an extraordinarily precocious talent. From 1827 Sivori began his career as a travelling virtuoso, which lasted almost without interruption until 1864. In 1839 he commenced his series of tours playing all over Europe and the United States. He played Mendelssohn's concerto for the first time in England in 1846, and was in England again in the seasons 1851 and 1864. Sivori lived for many years in Paris, and died at Genoa on 18 February 1894.

1852: 9 Jun: *The first part was Beethoven's grand Choral Symphony, a magnificent piece of music. Hector Berlioz, an eminent composer was Conductor, the leader Sivori, a celebrated Violinist.*

SKETCHLEY — Sarah Sketchley and the Sketchley family of Liverpool — *see also* Chater [101]

Sarah Penelope Sketchley (1808-1887) was born at New York, the daughter of William Sketchley (±1775-1839) and Sarah McCully (±1786-1866). She was baptised some nine years later at Stoke-on-Trent, Staffordshire. William Sketchley was a merchantman captain. He commanded the Magdalen, a transatlantic vessel of some importance as it carried diplomatic papers between the British and United States governments during the months leading up to the War of 1812. As commander of the packet ship Manchester, Sketchley was the first to arrive in the United States in 1820 with the news of the death of King George IV. He also commanded the Martha (1821) and the Minerva (1822).

Capt. Sketchley's sister-in-law was Anne Deborah McCully (d. 1861), the second wife of James Chater, a Baptist minister in Ceylon, whose first wife Anne Thomas had died at St Helena in 1820 during a homeward voyage having given birth to twin girls. This left a family of seven, the two eldest boys having already died in 1815 with the loss of the East Indiaman *Arniston* off the coast of Africa. One of the eldest surviving children was John Ryland Chater (1813-1837). (The Ryland in his name had either been given in honour of the Manchester philanthropist John Ryland or because of a family connection with him.) John Ryland Chater was educated at Magdalen College, Oxford (BA 1837), where he was a contemporary of Edward Witts. The latter met Chater's cousin Miss Sarah Sketchley (their mothers had been sisters) and formed an affection for her. This went down badly with Edward's father, Francis Witts, and successful efforts were made to forestall an engagement and marriage. The final chapter closed with John Ryland Chater's premature death in Dublin in 1837.

Sarah had been born at New York so presumably her mother, Sarah McCully, travelled occasionally with her husband. Alternatively, Sarah McCully may have been an American citizen, but this seems unlikely as her sister Ann Deborah McCully married a Baptist minister in England and was presumably from England or Ireland. The two Sarahs, mother and daughter, travelled together at least a further two times to New York. The first time they arrived on the *William Thompson* on 27 May 1824, and the second time they arrived on the *Cambridge* on 23 March 1840. On this second occasion they were charged with the melancholy duty of tidying up the affairs of their husband and father, Capt. William Sketchley, who had died at New York on 14 November 1839 and been buried in New Jersey.

By the time of the 1841 census, mother and daughter were living at 32 Percy Street in Liverpool's Georgian district; they appear to have enjoyed some affluence. They later moved to Kensington, London, where Sarah (senior) died in 1866. By 1881, Sarah (junior) was living at 32 Hereford Street, Kensington, an annuitant, with her 79-year-old Liverpudlian friend Miss C. F. B. Henderson. Sarah Penelope Sketchley died unmarried.

1837: 15 Apr: *Much serious conversation with E.F.W. as to his line of study at Oxford, with a view to his passing through his examination with honours, as to the taking of his BA degree, and entering into Orders, not without reference to a partiality which he has conceived for Miss Sketchley, a lady to whom he was introduced last summer at Oxford.* 18 Apr: *A letter from E.F.W. announcing his safe arrival at Oxford yesterday, and inclosing a letter from Miss Sketchley to which he had referred in his conversations with his Mother and myself on Saturday and Sunday last.* 1 May: *His object being to consult with us on the affair of his attachment to Miss Sketchley, and on the course to be pursued in consequence of the communication from Mr. Duncan, which I had forwarded to him on the 28th. Ult. Much conversation with M.W. and myself on this interesting point.* 19 Apr: *Wrote to Mrs. Currie Duncan, requesting her and Mr. D. to ascertain such particulars as they can collect at Liverpool, respecting the condition, character, connections and the like of the Sketchleys.* 26 Apr: *A friendly letter from Mr. Currie Duncan in reply to the one I wrote to his wife on the 19th., the account he sends of the Sketchley family is very satisfactory on almost all points, he promises to gain quietly further information.* 2 May: *Wrote to Mr. Duncan to thank him for his letter of the 24th. Ult. and to request him to communicate any further information he may collect as to the Sketchleys, mentioning that E.F.W. does not at the present moment propose to take any decisive step in the affair.* 14 May: *A letter from Mr. Duncan with further details as to the Sketchley family, on the whole rather satisfactory than otherwise.* 24 May: *A letter to Mrs. Backhouse from Liverpool contained such representations or misrepresentations of the Sketchley family as caused us much musing.* 25 May: *Wrote to my Son; sent him an extract from Miss Gardner's letter to Mrs. Backhouse, as far as it related to the Sketchleys, and acquainted him that his Mother would write by this post to her cousin to desire her to endeavour to procure on good authority a confirmation or a refutation of the facts and opinions she had communicated about them in her letter received yesterday.* 3 Jun: *M.W. recd. a letter from M. Gardner in reply to that which she had written on the 25th. Ult. requesting her to procure a confirmation or refutation of the unfavourable representations which her letter to Mrs. Backhouse had conveyed as to the Sketchleys.* 13 Jun: *A conversation with my son, renewed from Sunday morning, on the information as to Miss Sketchley's connections, received through Miss Gardner, as showing that the lady, however amiable, talented and accomplished she may be, has little to recommend her, in respect of connection.* 30 Jun: *Conversing seriously with my son on the subject of the Sketchleys; he has finally relinquished all thoughts of forming a connection with Miss S. and in this has been strengthened by ascertaining from W. Vavasour that they are considered by persons moving in good society at Liverpool as of a dubious condition, intimacy with whom would exclude from the best circles.* 14 Jun: *MW. recd. a packet of letters from the Gardner family written before the letter relative to the Sketchleys which my wife recd. from M. Gardner on the 3d. Inst.—and not containing any further information as to those ladies.* 30 Jun: *Conversing seriously with my son on the subject of the Sketchleys; he has finally relinquished all thoughts of forming a connection with Miss S. and in this has been strengthened by ascertaining from W. Vavasour that they are considered by persons moving in good society at Liverpool as of a dubious condition, intimacy with whom would exclude from the best circles.* 15 Jul: *All is tending towards what I anticipated when the connection with Miss Sketchley was abandoned by him: his partiality for Sophy Vavasour is maturing into a steady attachment; except in respect of the lady's prospects as to fortune being scanty, we do not see any reason to oppose my Son's wishes: she is not handsome, but she is sensible, amiable, well and prudently brought up, and the family connections very respectable.* 28 Aug: *Conversation with E.F.W. about a letter which he recd. to-day from S.P.S. Liverpool.* 29 Aug: 29 Aug: *Wrote to Round, requesting him to frank a letter which I inclosed to him, and which E.F.W. had written to Miss Sketchley in reply to the one he had recd. from that lady yesterday.*

SKILLERN — Richard Solloway Skillern [102]

Richard Solloway Skillern (1773-1836), schoolmaster and Church of England clergyman, was the son of Joseph Skillern of Gloucester. He was educated at All Souls, Oxford (BA 1796; MA 1800), and was twenty years the master of the Crypt School in Gloucester. He was also vicar of Chipping Norton from 1808 to 1835.

1826: 7 Oct: *I rode to Chipping Norton to prepare for a design, which I had long contemplated, the erection of a tablet, recording the deaths of my revered Parents & lamented brother, in the Church of that place, where the remains of the former are interred. Before I reached the Town, I met the Incumbent, Mr. Skillern, with whom I had some acquaintance, who very obligingly returned with me to assist me in selecting a proper place for the proposed tablet. Mr. S., now far advanced in years, was Master of the Crypt School in Gloucester, & is an intelligent old man: his benefice is in the gift of the Dean & Chapter of Gloucester.*

SKILLICORNE — William Nash Skillicorne [103]

William Nash Skillicorne (1807-1887), JP, DL, and landed proprietor, was born at Swindon, near Cheltenham, Gloucestershire, the son of Richard Skillicorne Skillicorne (1779-1834) and Anna Maria Ballinger (1781-1856). He was educated at Worcester College, Oxford (BA 1830; MA 1833), and was a JP and DL for Gloucestershire. He married, at Eynsham, Oxfordshire, 28 October 1856, Mary Ann Greenwood (1823-1914); they had 1 son and 3 daughters:

1 Anna Maria Nash (1859-1938)
1 William Nash (1861-1915)
2 Edith Mary (1862-1918)
3 Elizabeth Nash (1865-1934)

1828: 20 Aug.
1852: 4 Nov.
1853: 27 Jun.
1854: 4 Feb: ... *from Mr. Skillicorne, as Chairman of a Committee at Cheltenham for carrying out a scheme of exhibition of horticulture with kindred arts, to be brought out next summer there, within a miniature Chrystal palace.*

SKINNER — Allan Maclean Skinner [104]

Allan Maclean Skinner (1809-1885), barrister and judge, was born at Chelsea, Middlesex, the son of Brig.-Gen. John Skinner (1752-1827) and Ann Maclean (1773-1864) of Chelsea. He was educated at Eton College and Balliol College, Oxford (BA 1832), and was a barrister-at-law at Lincoln's Inn (1834) and the Inner Temple (1837). He joined the Oxford circuit and was appointed revising barrister in 1837, and both recorder of Windsor and deputy recorder of Gloucester in June 1852. He resigned the office of revising barrister in 1857 upon his appointment as one of Her Majesty's Council. In the same year he was invited by the Society of Lincoln's Inn to be a master of the bench, and was appointed judge of county courts in South Staffordshire in 1859. He married, at Bridgend, Glamorgan, October 1837, Caroline Emily Harding (1812-1901); they had 3 sons and 6 daughters:

1 Clifton Newman (b. 1834)
2 John Edwin Hilary (1839-1894)
1 Caroline Rachel (b. 1840)
2 Anna Cordelia (b. 1840)
3 Florence Marion (1842-1918)
4 Katherine Louisa (b. 1844)
5 Maud Elizabeth (1844-1904)
3 Allan Maclean (1846-1901)
6 Euphemia Effie Isabella (1847-1939)

In 1861 the family lived at Brocton Villa in Brocton, Staffordshire.

1846: 11 Aug: ... *the case which I heard was not one of interest; a controversy as to the ownership of a small house near Bristol, in which were engaged Sergeant Talfourd, Greaves, Keating & Skinner.*
1852: 30 Mar: *Agreeably to what had been arranged between myself and Mr. Brookes, who was Attorney for the prosecution (of Hambidge), Mr. Keating, Q.C., had been retained as Senior, and Mr. Skinner as Junior Counsel.*

SKINNER — John S. Skinner [105]

John S. Skinner (1749-1823), schoolmaster and Church of England clergyman, was born at Poole, Dorset, the son of John and Anne Skinner. He was educated at Trinity College, Oxford (BA 1772; MA 1792; B&DD 1792), and was ordained deacon on 14 June 1772 and priest on 25 September 1774. His first clerical appointment was as vicar choral at Salisbury Cathedral from 22 September 1779 to 31 December 1822. He was master of Salisbury Close Free Grammar School from 1 May 1780 to 15 July 1801. He was also appointed vicar of Shrewton on 15 March 1782 and rector of Poulshot on 30 September 1801. John Skinner was married and had at least 1 son:

1 John Thomas (1781-1826)

1806: 12 Aug: *Rode to Polshot to call upon Jem Evans, on a visit there at Dr. Skinner's.* 22 Aug., 24 Sep: *Rode to the Clergy meeting at Devizes for the purpose of raising a fund for the orphans & widows of the Clergy of the County of Wilts, to which I subscribed my quota. Conversed chiefly with Ward of Bradford Dr. Skinner, Ledyard, C. Mayo, &c. met Mrs. Hillier &c.*

1807: 7 Aug., 14 Aug: *Called upon Dr. Skinner & his son, received subscriptions to the Clergy Fund.*

SKINNER — Thomas Skinner [106]

Thomas Skinner (1807-1879), upholsterer, was born at Witney, the son of Quakers Thomas and Mary Skinner. He married, at Thornbury, Gloucestershire, 1839, Margaret Elizabeth Long (1816-1869), born at Berkeley, Gloucestershire; they had 4 sons and 4 daughters:

1 Henry G. (1840-1874)
2 Thomas John (1842-1915)
3 James Edward (1844-1886)
4 Robert Alfred (1845-1892)
1 Lydia (1848-1918)
2 Maria Formosa (1852-1920)
3 Sarah Octavia (1854-1940)
4 Margaret Elizabeth (1856-1953)

All of the children except Henry, the eldest, were born in Australia. The family must have left England in about 1842, but by 1851 they had returned and were living at Stone, near Thornbury. They did not settle for long, and left again for Australia in 1852 in the *Formosa*. Presumably Maria was born on board, or at least conceived on board. Thomas died at Hobart, Tasmania, in 1879.

1838: 19 Mar: *The tradesman to whom we had been recommended by Mr. Lyne, the Auctioneer, of Kingham, is named Skinner, and does a great deal of business in this way.* 2 Jun: *Also to Skinner the Upholsterer at Witney, by whom the principal part of E.F.W's furniture has been provided, to arrange with him as to the Bank into which the amount of his bill shall be paid to his acct.* 5-8 Jun., 10 Jun: *Omitted to mention yesterday the receipt of a letter from Skinner, announcing that £200 had been paid in by Hoare on my a/c to his Bankers at Witney & placed to his a/c in part discharge of his bill against E.F.W. for furniture &c.* 21 Jul., 25 Jul.

SKIPPER — John Benson Skipper [107]

John Benson Skipper (1807-1891), Church of England clergyman, was born in the parish of St Aldate, London, the son of John Skipper (b. 1770) and Elizabeth King (b. 1775). He was educated at Emmanuel College, Cambridge (BA 1830; MA 1836), and was ordained deacon on 6 June 1830 and priest on 5 June 1831. His first clerical appointment was as curate of Broadway, Worcestershire. In December 1841 he was licensed to the perpetual curacy of Ashchurch, Gloucestershire. He later served as vicar of Marden, Wiltshire, from 1844 to 1874.

Skipper married, at Burwell, Newmarket, Cambridgeshire, 18 August 1830, Charlotte (1805-1881), daughter of the Salisbury Dunn (1753-1823) and Ann Riste (±1763-1832); they had 6 sons and 2 daughters:

1 Louisa Vaughter (1832-1885)
1 John Benson (1834-1834)
2 Archibald John (1835-1893)
3 Charles Philip (1838-1901)
4 Herbert (1840-1919)
5 Alfred Theophilus (1842-1919)
2 Charlotte Elizabeth (1846-1921)
6 William (b. 1846)

After 1874 Skipper retired to Tonbridge. He died at Dover in 1891.

1840: 27 Oct: *The advowson or next presentation* [Broadway] *has been purchased by the Revd. Skipper, who resides in the mean parsonage, and is the stipendiary curate, and the church lately built is partly on the site of a former chapel of Ease, in a street or road leading from the main street of the village towards the parish Church.*

1842: 1 Nov: *After luncheon I left home in my phaeton to dine and sleep at the Vicarage, Stanway, where, when I arrived, I found that my son and daughter had gone with Mr. & Mrs. Dryden to Ashchurch, to be present at the opening of a National School room lately erected in that parish; the incumbent, Mr. Skipper, entertained his friends and neighbours, giving a collation before the commencement of divine service performed on the occasion, after which Mr. Close preached a suitable and able sermon.*

SKRIMSHIRE — Fenwick Skrimshire [108]

Fenwick Skrimshire (1775-1855), physician, was born at Wisbech, Cambridgeshire, the son of William Skrimshire (1739-1814) and Elizabeth Fenwick (b. 1740). He was married to Charlotte (1785-1866), daughter of James Cobb; they had 5 sons and 2 daughters:

1 Susan (b. 1808)
1 Charles Brown (b. 1809)
2 Henry Fenwick (1810-1861), Church of England clergyman; educated at St Catherine's College, Cambridge; married, at Hertford, 19 July 1842, Ann Louisa Catherine Collings (d. 1847)
3 Arthur James (1814-1906); married, at St George's, Bloomsbury, Westminster, 20 June 1843, Emily Penelope Stedman (1813-1891)
2 Charlotte Emma (b. 1815)
4 Frederick Cobb (1816-1891); married, at Braddan, Isle of Man, 7 August 1855, Frances Elizabeth Handcock
5 Edward Augustus (1820-1896)

Fenwick Skrimshire was a physician and naturalist living in Peterborough. He published a number of works on popular science and medicine.

1835: 30 Mar: *Wrote a note to Mr. Westcott, the Apothecary at Oundle respecting the fees due to Dr. Skrimshire.*

SKRINE — Henry Skrine [109]

Henry Skrine (1755-1803), barrister, traveller, and topographer, was the eldest of the three children of Richard Dickson Skrine (1719-1791), landowner and JP, of Warleigh Manor, Bathford, Somerset, and Elizabeth (1726-1800), daughter and heir of John Tryon of Collyweston, Northamptonshire. He was educated at Winchester College and Christ Church, Oxford (BCL 1781). He became a barrister of Stone Buildings, Lincoln's Inn, and was called to the bar in 1782, but whether he ever actually practised law is uncertain.

Skrine's inherited wealth enabled him to spend his time chiefly in travelling and writing. In 1792 he published *Three successive Tours in the North of England, and great part of Scotland*, and this was followed by *Two successive Tours through the whole of Wales, with several of the adjacent English Counties* (1798) and *A general Account of all the Rivers of note in Great Britain, &c. concluding with a minute description of the Thames* (1801). A manuscript journal of his two journeys to France in 1788-89, containing an interesting account of revolutionary Versailles, is in the Skrine family papers kept at Warleigh Manor.

Skrine married, first, at St Giles-in-the-Fields, Middlesex, 1787, Marianne (1767-1788), eldest daughter of John Chalié, a wealthy wine merchant of Wimbledon, Surrey; they had 1 son:

1 Henry (1788-1853); married, at Westbury on Trym, Gloucestershire, 21 January 1812, Caroline Anne Spry (1794-1867)

Marianne died after giving birth to Henry, and Skrine married secondly, at St George's, Hanover Square, Westminster, 1790, Letitia Sarah Maria (1762-1813), daughter and heir of John Harcourt of Dan-y-parc, Crickhowell, Brecknockshire. Henry and Letitia had 2 sons and 5 daughters:

1 John Harcourt (1791-1847)
2 Thomas Henry (1792-1815)
1 Isabella (b. 1793)
2 Letitia (1794-1796)
3 Anne (b. 1795)
4 Henrietta (1797-1832)
5 Catherine (1799-1814)

Skrine was high sheriff for Brecknockshire in 1795, when he apparently lived at Dan-y-parc, which his wife had inherited. He subsequently moved to the family home of Pyports House, Cobham, Surrey, and then again to Walton-on-Thames in 1796 or '97.

1801: 27 Oct: ... *Lady Harries & Miss Hughes; at the house of the latter we dined meeting her brother a pleasant Lawyer in Lincolns Inn, & Mr. and Mrs. Skrine, great English Travellers, almost to a mania, he a very singular, & she a very agreeable person. He has written two Tours, besides a long description of British Rivers.*

1805: 3 Aug: ... *we agreed to repair to Walton, where we expected to find very good accommodations. In this we were frustrated finding only moderate beds & a moderate & tardy dinner. Mrs. Skrine called & sat with us in the Evening.* 4 Aug: *Mrs. Skrine's hospitality made our day pass very pleasantly.* 5-6 Aug.

1853: 17 Jun: *Near to it* [Hersham church] *is a mural monument in memory of a gentleman at whose house near the Village I visited some fifty years ago —a Mr. Skrine, of Warley near Bath, with whom my father and mother were acquainted.*

SKYNNER — the families of Arnold, Anthony, Skynner, Hunt, and Witts

These threads have not yet been unravelled. Unfortunately the pedigree copied by Francis Witts is no longer in the Witts family papers.

1824: 20 Oct: *I called on Mrs. M. Hunt. She had kindly copied for me a pedigree in her possession illustrative of the connection of the families of Arnold, Anthony, Skynner, Hunt, Witts &c. which throws considerable light on the family descent, of which before as relates to my Grandmother Witts & her connexions, I had but vague ideas.*

SLANEY — Robert Aglionby Slaney [110]

Robert Aglionby Slaney (1791-1862), barrister-at-law, was born at Shifnal, Shropshire, the eldest son of Robert Slaney (1764-1834), of Hatton Grange, Shropshire, and Mary (1770-1836), daughter of Thomas Mason of Shrewsbury. He was educated at Trinity College, Cambridge (1809), and the Inner Temple (1810). He was called to the bar in 1817. Slaney married, first, at Hatton Grange, Shrewsbury, Shropshire, 7 February 1812, Elizabeth (1784-1847), daughter of Dr William Hawkins Muckleston (1755-1787) and Frances Presland (1761-1837); they had 3 daughters:

1 Elizabeth Francis (1813-1870); married, May 1835, Thomas Campbell Eyton (1809-1880)
2 Mary (1817-1866); married, at Ellesmere, Shropshire, 8 May 1839, William Watkin Edward Wynne (1801-1880)
3 Frances Catherine (1823-1896); married, in Shropshire, October 1845, William Kenyon (1815-1884)

Slaney married secondly, at London, April 1854, a widow, Catherine Anne Archer, née Buckston (1801-1883), daughter of Revd George Buckston of Bradborn Hall. Slaney succeeded to Hatton Grange in 1834. He was MP for Shrewsbury in 1826-34, 1837-41, 1847-52, and 1857-62.

1835: 24 Feb: *He* [Rowland Hunt of Boreatton] *has left three or four children by his widow, who was a Miss Lloyd, who, with Mr. Slaney, lately representative for Shrewsbury, and Miss Hunt, is left guardian of the infant family... While my son was a pupil of Archdeacon Butler at Shrewsbury School, he was not unfrequently a guest at Boreatton.*

1839: 4 Jan.

SLAPP — Thomas Peyton Slapp [111]

Thomas Peyton Slapp (1777-1849), Church of England clergyman, was born at Botesdale, Suffolk, the son of Thomas Slapp (1743-1805), attorney, of Botesdale, and Ann Katherina Kendall (1739-1812). He was educated at Bury St Edmunds, Merchant Taylors' School, and Christ's College, Cambridge (BA 1798; MA 1801), and was ordained deacon on 22 September 1799 and priest on 18 December 1808. His first clerical appointment was as curate of Nettlestead, Suffolk, and Riddlesworth, Norfolk. He was then rector of Little Brandon, Norfolk, 1811-18; rector of Bracon Ash, 1811-49; perpetual curate of Old Buckenham, 1815-49; and rector of Rickenhall Inferior, Suffolk, 1827-49. He married, at St Peter's, Dublin, 22 December 1807, Olivia Beatty (1792-1823); there do not appear to have been any children.

Thomas Peyton Slapp was a very wealthy man. In his will of 24 May 1849 he appointed his nephew, Richard Reeve, of Old Buckenham, sole executor. He gave generous legacies to family members, his staff, and to various hospitals and charities.

This attribution is tentative, but Thomas Peyton Slapp is the only person who fits the information given in the diaries. It may be presumed that he formed a friendship with Richard Charles Head Graves at Cambridge, but what they were doing at Cote remains unknown at present.

1804: 5 Jan: *Walked to Cote, where I found a pleasant party at Dowells; his Mother, himself, Mr. Slap, & Graves of Pem. Coll.* 24 Jan: *Dined & slept at the former's House at Cote, where I experienced a friendly reception, & was extremely pleased. Besides the family & Slap, the party consisted of Mr. & Mrs. Foster, the Lamottes, Capt. Holosworth, Col. Coke, Mr. & Mrs. John Alleyne.* 25 Jan: *Accompanied Mrs. Dowell, Slap & Willm. On their walk thro' Westbury.*

SLATTER — Thomas Slatter [112]

Thomas Slatter (1785-1831), Church of England clergyman, was born at Oxford, the son of Thomas and Mary Slatter. He was educated at Christ Church, Oxford (BA 1805; MA 1808), and was ordained deacon on 24 December 1809 and priest on 17 June 1810. His first clerical appointment was as chaplain at Christ Church, Oxford. He was then rector of Shipton-on-Cherwell, Oxfordshire, from 1813 to his death in 1831. Slatter was married to Elizabeth (±1784-1870), born at Great Wolford, Warwickshire; they had at least 1 son and 1 daughter:

1 Harriet (b. 1815); married, at St Mary the Virgin, Oxford, 4 September 1845, Henry Kilbee (b. 1814), son of Henry Kilbee and Frances Taylor; at least 2 sons:
  1 Percival Thomas (1847-1923)
  2 Thomas Slatter (1849-1939)
1 Thomas Baker (b. 1817); married, at All Saints', Paddington, 24 August 1849, Jemima Elizabeth (b. 1831), daughter of Richard Powell Benneworth (b. 1806) and Jemima (b. 1807); at least 1 son:
  1 Thomas Richard (1850-1874); born at Tendring, Essex

Slatter died rather young. His son did not rise to follow his profession; in 1861 Thomas Baker Slatter was the gate keeper to the Victoria Docks, London.

1802: 8 Mar: *To the Music Room in the Evening, with Stevens, Evans &c. Mad. Mara, Welsh & Hill, Vicary & Slatter. Judas Maccabeus. Mad. Mara sung charmingly "Pious orgies Pious Airs". Father of Heaven &c.*

SLINGER — Matthew Proctor Slinger [113]

Matthew Proctor Slinger (1790-1875), farmer and landed proprietor, was born at Clapham, Yorkshire, the son of Simon Slinger (b. 1736) and Agnes Noddle (d. 1798). He married, at Warton, Lancashire, 29 May 1819, Ellen (1797-1881), daughter of William Lawson (1757-1829) and Elizabeth Peacock (b. 1760); they had at least 3 sons and 1 daughter:

1 Francis Procter (1820-1857)
1 Elizabeth (1822-1903); died unmarried
2 William (b. ±1824)
3 Robert (1826-1907)

In his 1823 diary, Francis Witts referred to a certain 'Slingsby'. It appears reasonably safe to assume that this was an error for Slinger. In 1841 Slinger was farming numerous portions of land in Long Preston belonging to Mary Ann Tennant.

In both the 1861 and 1871 censuses Slinger was listed as a landed proprietor, retired, living with his wife Ellen and unmarried daughter Elizabeth (b. 1822) at Newfield House, Austwick, next door to his son Robert's farm, at Far End, Austwick, just 3 miles or so from Giggleswick. The graves 50 and 78 at St Oswald's, Horton-in-Ribblesdale, contain many of the family, but there are various other Slinger names that were probably not children. The Proctor and Slinger families intermarried and there were numerous strands of these names.

1823: 12 May: *Very much engaged in business, with Messrs. Hartley, Geldard, Moorhouse, Slingsby & others till twelve o clock, then rode to Stainforth Hall, and accompanied by our tenant & his Father to the higher parts of our Estate there.*

1825: 9 Sep: *We found the tenant M P Slinger in very bad spirits; he seems to want energy and judgment & to be of a very penurious disposition. There is little chance of his continuing the farm.* 13 Sep: *The whole morning was consumed in consultations with Mr. Hartley and Mr. Geldard on the steps to be taken, when I was gone, respecting the letting of the farms... we, therefore, were at liberty to come to a settlement with Slinger as to the Sherwood House farm, which he took for seven years at £90 per ann.* 13 Oct: *I received a letter to-day from Mr. Hartley announcing to me, that he had agreed to let the Stainforth Hall farm to a respectable tenant of the name of Buck, for the sum of £330 per ann. This is a heavy reduction in our income; but, I am persuaded, is as good a rent as we could obtain. Slinger by his murmurs has certainly decried the farm...*

SLOANE STANLEY — William Sloane Stanley [114]

William Sloane Stanley (1780-1860), MP and landed proprietor, was the first and only surviving son of Hans Sloane (1739-1837), of South Stoneham, Hampshire, and Sarah (1748-1783), daughter and co-heir of Stephen Fuller, merchant and Jamaica agent, of Clement's Lane, Lombard Street, London. His parents were cousins. He was educated at Eton College (1791), St Andrews University (1798-99), and the Belvedere, Weimar (1799-1800). He married, at St George's, Hanover Square, Westminster, 23 June 1806, Gertrude (1783-1870), daughter of Frederick Howard, 5th earl of Carlisle (1748-1825), and Margaret Caroline Leveson-Gower-Howard (1753-1824); they had 3 sons and 4 daughters:

1 Gertrude (1807-1894); died unmarried; lived in 1881 at Upperton Road, Eastbourne, with her sister Frederica
1 William Hans (1810-1896); married, at St George's, Hanover Square, Westminster, 22 May 1834, Honoria Elizabeth (1808-1887), born at Kinsale Ireland, the daughter of Gen. Joseph Gubbins of Stoneham, Hampshire; 1 son and 1 daughter:
  1 Elizabeth (b. 1836)
  1 Hans (1840-1888); married, 7 June 1866, Emilie Josephine Edwards
2 George (1811-1896), Church of England clergyman; married, at Compton-Bassett, Wiltshire, 11 April 1835, Laura Maria (1812-1904), daughter of William Webber (1766-1818) and Harriet Nicholson (1779-1858), and sister of Matilda, who married Thomas Assheton Smith; 5 sons and 5 daughters:
  1 Florence Laura (1838-1913)
  1 Cecil George (1840-1891)
  2 Frederick (1840-1917)
  3 Francis (1841-1904); succeeded to the Tedworth estate on the death of his aunt Matlida Assheton Smith, 1859; married, 15 August 1866, Charlotte Rose; 2 sons
  2 Blanche (1842-1879)
  3 Grace (1847-1929)
  4 Rose Laura (1849-1891)
  4 William Felix (1851-1923)
  5 Evelyn (1853-1938)
  5 Henry Charles (1856-1933)
2 Frederica (1811-1887); died unmarried; lived in 1881 at Upperton Road, Eastbourne, with her sister Gertrude
3 Caroline (1814-1880); married, 1 July 1833, John Thomas Mott (1809-1884); 1 son and 4 daughters:
  1 John Stanley (1838-1927)
  1 Gertrude Sophia (1842-1932)
  2 Harriet Elizabeth (1843-1928)
  3 Frederica Lucy (1846-1926)
  4 Laura Caroline Josephine (1848-1852)
4 Augusta (b. 1815)
3 Henry (b. 1817)

William Sloane Stanley succeeded his father in 1824, having taken the additional name of Stanley on 28 December 1821 upon inheriting the Paulton estate from his cousin Hans Stanley, chargé d'affaires in Paris, who had died unmarried in 1780. Sloane Stanley was MP for Orford in 1807-12 and Stockbridge in 1830-31. He was sheriff for Hampshire in 1828-29. Sloane Stanley's relationship with his father went from bad to worse during his early adulthood. There were hints of trouble to come during his education in Scotland and Germany, when he ran up debts and was accused of gambling. Money was at the bottom of their squabbles. A full and interesting biography can be found in the *History of Parliament*. The 1801 diary entry may not be the same Sloane, but it fits a previous pattern.

1799: 16 Aug: *To the "Erb Prinz" where we visited Messrs. Hammersley & W. Sloane, just arrived the younger Mr. Hammersley & Mr. S. to go to the Belvedere.*

1801: 30 Oct: *Met Mr. Legge & poor Mr. Sloane in a dreadful yellow jaundice.*

SLY — *see* George James

SMALLRIDGE — Charles Smallridge [115]

Charles Smallridge (±1800-1868), solicitor and proctor, was born in the parish of St Marylebone, Westminster, Middlesex, the son of William and Anne Smallridge. He married, at Gloucester, 1840, Mary Thomas (1809-1877); they had 3 sons and 8 daughters:

1 Mary M. (b. 1828)
2 Dorothy Anne (1830-1895); married Henry M. Sheldon of Staverton, Gloucestershire; died at Boulogne; at least 1 daughter:
  1 Mary Louise (b. 1864); married, at Boulogne-sur-Mer, 11 August 1887, Capt. T. W. Sandes
3 Frances Elizabeth (b. 1831); married, at All Souls, Hampstead, 29 July 1869, Revd Alfred Bond of Ogbourne St George, Wiltshire
1 Charles Vere (1835-1836)
4 Helen Isabella (b. 1836), married, at Gloucester, 1856, Alfred William Wheeler (1821-1893); 4 sons and 2 daughters:
  1 Beatrice Helen (1859-1906)
  1 Percy Augustus Vere (1861-1923)
  2 Blayney Alfred (1863-1946)
  3 Gerald Alfred (b. 1865)
  4 Ernest Alfred (b. 1866)
  2 Frances Winifred (1867-1956)
5 Catherine Therese (1837-1923); died unmarried
6 Penelope Vere (1838-1847); died young
7 Winifred Octavia (1840-1868); died unmarried
8 Flora Alice (1842-1877); died unmarried
2 Charles Edgar Blayney (1843-1921); died at Wandsworth, London
3 Henry Augustus Hale (1845-1900); married, at St George, Queensland, Australia, 18 August 1877, Johannah Foley (b. 1848); 5 daughters:
  1 Florence Alice Henrietta (1879-1958)
  2 Mable May (1881-1949)
  3 Margaret Mary Frances (1884-1904)
  4 Penelope Rose (1887-1967)
  5 Johanna (dates unknown)

1852: 30 Mar: *Mr. Smallridge of Gloucester was the Attorney for the defence* [of Hambidge], *and Messrs. Huddlestone & Powell were his counsel.*

1853: 21 Apr: *At Mr. Sewell's office learnt that Mr. Herschell, the Chaplain of the County Prison, Mr. Wilkins, Solr. to the Trustees of the late Hambidge of Icomb, Mr. Smallridge, Solr. of Gloucester, who had acted as Attorney for the prisoner, when J. Hambidge was tried for the alleged murder of his father, and has been otherwise mixed up with his concerns, especially as to a settlement of the property bequeathed by the Father, were to meet at Stow to-day.*

SMART — William Smart [116]

William Smart (±1805-1845), poacher, died at Cheltenham Union Workhouse. Suspicions were entertained that he had been badly treated at Northleach House of Correction.

1845: 4 Mar: *We consulted together on an intimation conveyed by letter to Bloxsome from Mr. Barnett, one of the County Coroners, that he was engaged in holding an inquest on one William Smart at Cheltenham, who had died in the Workhouse there, and of whom it was insinuated that his death was accelerated by harsh treatment and injudicious medical attendance, during his confinement for poaching in Northleach House of Correction.* 7 Mar: *Met and conversed with Lefroy on Police matters, and with Mr. Talbot on the proceedings before the Coroner on the inquest of W. Smart.* 12 Mar: *I took the opportunity of making some enquiries, and inspecting the Journals of the Med. Officer, Keeper, and Visiting Magistrates, as to the treatment of W. Smart, a prisoner, on whose body an inquest is now pending at Cheltenham.* 14 Apr., 15 Apr: *As to the imputations against the discipline and management of Northleach Bridewell, and the inquest still sitting on the body of W. Smart, the Chairman adopted my advice, and recommended the court not to enter upon any investigation until the inquest should be closed.* 29 Apr., 7 May: *Howell accompanied me in my carriage to attend the Adjourned Quarter Sessions, fixed for this day, for an enquiry as to the proceedings of the Officers of the Bridewell at Northleach in respect of the treatment of W. Smart deceased.*

SMITH — the Smith family of Clifton [117]

The Smith family, unlike other affluent members of the Clifton set, were neither of Irish nor HEIC stock; they were prominent Bristol merchants, originally linen drapers. In the early eighteenth century Robert Smith owned tracts of land in Clifton, including Clifton Wood House with 8 acres adjoining. He built houses on this land to be let out to visitors to the Hotwells. For several seasons they were let to Selina, countess of Huntingdon, but in the early 1750s, being short of money, Robert Smith sold Clifton Wood House to Thomas Goldney III for £2,000. There are references in the Goldney papers to the late Robert Smith dating from 1753. Robert Smith appears to have been succeeded by Thomas and Samuel Smith, linen drapers, presumably his sons.

Morgan Smith, a sugar refiner and another member of the family, also had dealings with Thomas Goldney. In 1752 he set up a bank with Goldney and others named Goldney, Smith & Co. This bank later amalgamated with other enterprises, becoming Miles' Bank, and through further amalgamations in the nineteenth and twentieth centuries it became the National Westminster Bank, which survives to this day.

Joseph Smith (1745-1815) was another wealthy member of the Smith family; he still held property at Clifton Wood in the early nineteenth century. How and where he fits into the Smith lineage has not yet been ascertained, but presumably he was a son of either Thomas or Samuel, and a grandson of Robert. Joseph was a merchant of considerable standing. He served as high sheriff for Bristol in 1789 and mayor in 1794. He married Sarah Pope (b. 1760); they had 3 sons and 2 daughters:

1 Orton (1777-1856)
2 Brooke (b. 1778)

3 Joseph Pope (1780-1839)
1 Sarah (1782-1830)
2 Marianne (1788-1880)

At the time of the 1851 census Marianne was unmarried and staying with her brother Orton in St Michael's Square, Southampton. They were acting as executors for a relation.

The Smith family was first mentioned by Agnes Witts in her diary on 28 April 1802: 'A very fine Day, a remarkable clear air, walk'd to Bristol to some Shops, & visited Miss Brice, before we came home visited Miss Smiths at Clifton Wood who had been very civil about Ball Tickets.' The family requires further research, but there are certain strands already uncovered which may or may not tie together. One common link may be the Sweeting family. Jonathan Sweeting (1788-1868) married, first, 1809, Martha Marriott (1791-1822), and secondly, at Stokesley, Yorkshire, 1824, Hannah. In 1832, with Hannah and two children, Jonathan and Thomas, Sweeting sailed from Stokesley to Upper Canada. Then there was Henry Sweeting Smith (1773-1841), son William Smith (d. 1824) of Bristol. He married Sarah Smith. Could there have been a link? Francis Witts was friendly with a Henry Smith, and yet Henry was not one of Joseph Smith's sons; there may, therefore, have been cousins in the Clifton set. It seems quite likely; all were from monied families. It is unknown as yet where the name Sweeting came from and whether there were connections between the Marriott, Sweeting, and Smith families that antedated the marriage of Jonathan Sweeting to Martha Marriott in 1809. There seem to be links between these families, but they may be misleading.

1802: 28 Apr: *With my Parents to Bristol. Called upon Miss Brice: & on our return upon the Miss Smiths.* 29 Aug: *Walked in the Evening to Tea with my Father & Mother at Mrs. Smith's.*

1803: 29 Dec: *George & myself to Dowry Square to Mrs. Adams's. Merry & pleasant Ball—with two of the pleasant unaffected Miss Marriott's, Miss Adams simple & naive, Miss Becket, who wd. be but for an unhappy cast of the eye, one of the most beautiful & finest women in England, as well as the most lively, & with my old friend Miss Smith. A good & merry supper. A good deal of conversation with the hosts, hostesses etc, Caroline Hillhouse, Lieut. Prower Schol. of Wadham, & Capt. Becket of the Coldstream & his Brother a Barrister, who accompanied their sister & Lady Smith.* 31 Dec: *Made several visits with George: to the adorable Misses Price & Hughes; the sensible Jnr. Mc.Brides: the good assured Smiths; fulsome Mrs. Pennington: & the pleasant family of Mrs. Moncaster.*

1804: 2 Jan: *The former & myself afterwards joined two of the Miss Smiths & with them made the complete circle of the Hill & back with them to their house; chatty & agreeable.* 7 Jan: *Captns. Smith & Horton, Mr. Port, Harriet & Miss Leyard, Miss Duce's etc. there.* 17 Jan: *Some pleasant men there Horton, Dawkins, Smith, Lear etc. etc.* 18 Jan: *I accompanied Horton & Lear to the Queen's Ball at Bristol; full, gay, amusing: the Marriotts, Moncasters etc. there; great fun with Dowell, Horton, Smith, Lear, Susan Gibbons, The Marriott's, Smiths, Prower, Eagles etc. etc. etc.* 21 Jan: *Conversed chiefly with John Dawkins, Smith & Hook, Hart Davis, Harriett, etc.* 28 Jan: *A most amusing Evening, during which I had much conversation with Dawkins, Smith, Hooke, Johnson, the Leyards, Hillhouses, Smiths etc. The latter formed a side table at almost Jovial Supper with Smith, Hook, Johnson & myself.* 11 Feb: *Walked & lounged with Dowell & Smith of the Bedford.* 20 Jul: *Walked in the Evening with my Father & Mother & with the Smiths of Clifton Woods.* 25 Aug: *Heard from Henry Smith.* 12 Sep: *Wrote to Smith.* 30 Dec: *... with my Father & Mother upon Mrs. Smith, Mrs. Auriol, & Mrs. Gould.*

1805: 6 Feb: *Danced with the pleasing Mrs. Brown, Miss Ford, Marianne Smith, & Miss Adair.* 21 Mar: *Breakfasted with Adams, meeting Prower, Vashon, Smith & Strong.* 10 Nov: *Walked with the Miss Smiths & Mrs. Carrick.*

1806: 3 Feb: *Danced with Miss Smith, Miss Russel, Miss Monck, & Miss Wolseley.* 10 Feb: *Walked a little with Mrs. Newnham & S. Townsend with Miss Smiths.* 16 Feb: *... for a short time with the Salters, also with the Smiths.* 22 Feb: *Conversed chiefly with Cecilia Wolseley & Miss Smith.*

SMITH — curate of Naunton

Despite many attempts the identity of this curate has not been discovered. The incumbent at Naunton was John Hurd, an invalid. He appears to have appointed this curate in 1844.

1844: 29 Aug: *Many of the clergy of the neighbouring parishes attended — Dean of Gloucester, Messrs. Wiggin, Ford, Hurd, Smith, Spring, Dolphin, Hippisley, Perkins, Twisleton, Oakley Hill, Underwood, Bowen, Pantin, and others.* 12 Sep: *... also from Mr. Smith, Curate of Naunton, on the same subject.*

1846: 26 Aug., 21 Sep.

SMITH — Albert Richard Smith [118]

Albert Richard Smith (1816-1860), author, public lecturer, and mountaineer, was born at Chertsey, Surrey, the son of Richard Smith (d. 1857), surgeon, and his wife, Maria. He was educated at Merchant Taylors' School, London (1826-31), and Middlesex Hospital (1835-38). In 1838 he qualified as a surgeon and apothecary and attended at the Hôtel Dieu hospital in Paris. He later joined his father's medical practice at Chertsey. In 1849 Smith went on a tour to Constantinople and the Near East. On his return he published *A Month at Constantinople*. Shortly afterwards he appeared at Willis's Rooms in a public entertainment about his travels called 'The Overland Mail', which proved a hit. In August 1851 Smith ascended Mont Blanc, and the following year he published *The Story of Mont Blanc*. He also produced an entertainment at the Egyptian Hall called 'Mont Blanc', describing the ascent of the mountain and the Englishman abroad; it became the most popular exhibition of its kind ever known. In May 1854 he gave his performance at Osborne House before Queen Victoria and Prince Albert. Smith's 'Mont Blanc' show ran for 2,000 performances over six years and helped to popularise mountain climbing in mid-Victorian Britain.

1852: 8 Jun: *In the course of the evening repaired to the Egyptian Hall, Piccadilly, to be present at a very popular entertainment, the Ascent of Mont Blanc. It was impossible to procure admission to the reserved seats, which had all been preengaged: so I contented myself with a place in the Area, which was crowded to excess—there was besides a gallery brimful. Albert Smith is a very clever literary character, redundant in wit and humour, author of much popular light reading, an energetic traveller.*

SMITH — Charles Smith [119]

Charles Smith (1807-1882), farmer, JP, and landed proprietor, was born at Bridlington, Yorkshire, the son of Charles Smith (1763-1811) and Judith Berkin (1772-1817). He was a JP and substantial farmer living at Southrop House. He married, at Le Havre, Normandy, 4 January 1837, Mathilde Adelaide Cathinka (1815-1888), daughter of Antoine Marie Labouchère (1775-1829) and Catharina Meinche Knudtzon (1781-1860); they had 7 sons and 5 daughters:

1 Cathinca Judith (1842-1866)
1 George (1844-1915)
2 Norna Frances Clementine (1845-1929)
2 Gerald Henry Labourchère (1845-1884)
3 Charles Broder Knudtzon (1847-1871)
3 Mathilde Emma Harriet (1848-1928)
4 Thorwald Clewelyn (1850-1932)
5 Harald Anthony (1851-1922)
6 Ronald Augustus Royds (1852-1883)
4 Hilda Mary Charlotte (1854-1932)
5 Brenda Katherine Louisa (1856-1940)
7 Eric Alexander Lisle (1858-1928)

Charles Smith farmed 1,300 acres and employed sixty-two labourers. By 1871 the family had moved to nearby Filkins.

1845: 2 Apr: *The Gentlemen of the County, and personal friends of the High Sheriff, soon began to congregate — Mr. Daubeny (Ampney) Lyon (Miserden) Kaye (late of Sandywell Park, now of Ampney) Smith (Southrop) Col. Fendall (Sevenhampton) Henry, Frederick, and Raymond Cripps, C Pettatt, and several others.* 15 Apr.

1847: 29 Jun: *Sir Michael H. Beach, and his friend Mr. Smith of Southerop, a very agreeable travelled man, and a distant relation of the Vavasours of Rochdale, i.e. of Marmaduke V., Mrs. V. of "the Cottage" &c.*

SMITH — David Smith [120]

David Smith (1800-1869), maltster, was born at Cold Aston. He married Elizabeth (b. 1802); they had at least 2 sons and 1 daughter:

1 Matthew (b. ±1823)
2 Moses (b. 1825); born at Lower Guiting
1 Caroline Emily Payn (b. 1829); born at Lower Guiting

The family were Baptists and the children were baptised at Bourton-on-the-Water by Revd Thomas Coles. In 1829 Smith was farming at Lower Guiting and by 1841 at Clapton-on-the-Hill. By 1851 he had changed profession.

1842: 3 Jun.

1847: 14 Sep: *... shewing me the best specimens: Messrs. Beman, Shelton, D. Smith, Bryan &c.*

SMITH — Edward Smith, later Dodsworth — *see also* pedigree below, under George Smith [121]

Sir Edward Smith, 2nd baronet (1768-1845), landed proprietor, was the eldest son of Sir John Silvester Smith, 1st baronet of Newland Park, Yorkshire (1734-1789), and Henrietta Maria (1736-1795), daughter of John Dodsworth of Thornton Watlass, Yorkshire. Smith succeeded to the baronetcy in 1789, and married, 22 September 1804, Susanna (d. 1830), youngest daughter of Col Henry Dawkyns of Standlynch Park, Wiltshire; they had at least 1 daughter:

1 Catherine (dates unknown)

Smith succeeded to the estate of Thornton Watlass on the death of his maternal uncle, Revd Frederick Dodsworth (1783-1822), canon of Windsor (*below*), and changed his name by royal licence to Dodsworth. He was succeeded by his younger brother, Charles (1775-1857), who became 3rd baronet. (*See below,* George Smith.)

1807: 24 Jul: *Wrote to Mrs. Heard & Sir Edward Smith.* 10 Aug: *Heard from Sir Edwd. Smith.*

SMITH — Elizabeth Anne Smith [122]

Elizabeth Anne Smith, née Marriott (±1769-1844), was born the second daughter and co-heir of Revd James Marriott of Horsemonden, Kent. She married, 13 May 1797, Sir John Wyldbore Smith, 2nd baronet (1770-1852); they had 7 sons and 2 daughters:

1 John James (1800-1862); succeeded as 3rd baronet
2 William Marriott (1801-1864), Church of England clergyman; succeeded as 4th baronet
1 Anne Eliza (1803-1859)
3 George Roxburgh (1804-1805); died an infant
4 Henry Curtis (1806-1834), Church of England clergyman
2 Lydia Bosworth (1808-1876); *see below*
5 Reginald Southwell (1809-1895), Church of England clergyman
6 Francis (1810-1851), Church of England clergyman
7 Edward Heathcote (1813-1870), army officer

1835: 23 May: *Saw Mrs. Dolphin, her aunt, Mrs. Rowe, and Mrs. Harrison: also Lady Smith, wife of a Dorsetshire Baronet, and her invalid daughter, who, with a pretty little girl of the name of Bragge.*

1852: 8 May: *Miss Smith, daughter of the late Sir J. Wildbore Smith of Dorsetshire is a very gifted person, very accomplished, a poetess, a composer, and a fine musician, both singing & playing with great taste & gracefulness — She favoured us with many of her choice productions, some very beautiful.*

SMITH — Elizabeth Smith [123]

Elizabeth Smith (1776-1806), scholar and translator, was born at Burn Hall, near Durham, the eldest daughter of George Smith (1751-1822), banker, of Tent Lodge, Coniston, and Julia (1754-1836), daughter and sole heir of Richard Mott of Carlton, Suffolk. Sir Charles Felix Smith was her brother. Elizabeth's extensive learning was acquired in spite of many disruptions in her life. In June 1785 the family moved to Piercefield Park, near Chepstow, Monmouthshire. After the declaration of war with France, her father's business collapsed and his valuable library was broken up. In 1794 he took a commission in the Army, serving for some years in Ireland. For a few months in 1796 Elizabeth and her mother joined him in Sligo, where Elizabeth studied the Irish language. In summer 1799 they moved to Ballitor, co. Kildare, where she once again had access to a good library. Until they moved to Coniston in 1801 she did not have a settled home, and spent much of her time visiting friends in London, Shirley, and Bath.

Aside from a governess who taught her French and a little Italian when she was very young, Elizabeth was largely self-taught. In 1789 she became governess to her siblings and began an influential friendship with Henrietta Maria Bowdler. In 1794 she began learning Arabic and Persian from her brother's oriental dictionary, and in 1796 she studied Hebrew from a Bible belonging to Henrietta Bowdler's mother. Between 1795 and 1799 she learned Spanish, German, Arabic, Persian, Greek, Latin, Hebrew, some Syriac, and Erse, as well as music, mathematics, and astronomy. She died unmarried on 7 August 1806 in Coniston.

1817: 8 Sep: *The first of these, the property of Mr. North, and on sale, is, however, not so enviable a spot, as the second, belonging to Col. Smith, whose lot it has been to reside in places remarkable for picturesque beauty, as Piercefield on the banks of the Wye was once his abode. His present residence is charming, & I have since been told, that the views from his grounds, to which strangers are admitted without interruption, are peculiarly grand and striking.*

I cannot omit to mention, that this Gentleman was Father, and this place the dwelling, of the late lamented Miss Smith, so well known by her amiable character, her accomplishments, and her learning. 9 Sep: *We surveyed the valley & expanse of water as far down as Coniston Hall on the one side & below Fent Lodge, Col. Smith's seat, on the other.*

SMITH — F. Smith, surveyor of roads

1835: 13 Mar: *The former working Surveyor, F. Smith, being found unequal to the duties intrusted to him... the management of the road from Barrington to Frogmill, being the great Cheltenham road, was transferred to Mr. Stokes...*

SMITH — George Smith [124]

George Smith (1772-1811), Church of England clergyman, was fortunately the subject of a short obituary notice in the March 1811 edition of the *Salisbury and Winchester Journal*. A different George Smith was incorrectly attributed to the Urchfont appointment in the *Cambridge Alumni*. Contrary to what was said there, the vicar of Urchfont was George Smith, second surviving son of Sir John Silvester Smith, 1st baronet of Newland Park, Yorkshire (1734-1789). He was educated at Christ's College, Cambridge (BA 1795). His elder brother, Sir Edward Smith (1768-1845) (*above*), succeeded as 2nd baronet on 1789, and when one sees that the diarist wrote to him on 24 July 1804 and received a reply on 10 August 1807, it all falls into place. Francis Witts wrote in the misguided hope that Sir Edward might influence his younger brother.

The basic pedigree is as follows: Sir John Silvester Smith, 1st baronet (1734-1789), son of John Smith (b. 1686) and Ann Hodgson (b. 1699), married, at Thornton Watlass, Yorkshire, 20 July 1761, Henrietta Maria (1736-1795), daughter of Revd John Dodsworth (b. 1736). They had 5 sons and 4 daughters:

1 John Silvester (b. 1763)
2 John Christopher (b. 1764)
1 Anna Maria (b. 1766)
2 Henrietta (b. 1767)
3 Edward (1768-1845); succeeded as 2nd baronet; married, 22 September 1804, Susanna Dawkyns
3 Charlotte (1770-1788); died a teenager
4 George (1772-1811)
4 Elizabeth (1774-1851)
5 Charles (1775-1857); succeeded as 3rd baronet; married, 8 June 1808, Elizabeth (b. 1789), daughter of John Armstrong and Sophia Blayney; 7 sons and 7 daughters, all of whom adopted by royal licence the surname Dodsworth, or later Smith-Dodsworth:
  1 John (1809-1852)
  1 Sophia (1810-1879); died unmarried
  2 Edward Frederick (1811-1833); died a young man, unmarried
  3 Charles (1812-1832); died a young man, unmarried
  2 Henrietta Maria (1814-1882); married, at St Mary's, Marylebone, Westminster, 1 December 1858, Revd Robert Whytehead (1808-1871); at least 1 daughter:
    1 Margaret (b. ±1836)
  4 Matthew (1819-1858); succeeded as 4th baronet; married, in Lancashire, 23 September 1852, Anne Julia Crowder (1828-1890); 3 sons and 1 daughter:
    1 Charles Edward (1853-1891); succeeded as 5th baronet
    1 Henrietta (1854-1926); died unmarried
    2 Matthew Blayney (1856-1931)
    3 Frederick Cadwallader (1858-1900), army officer, 11th Foot
  5 George (b. ±1820)
  6 Frederick (1822-1885); died at Monte Carlo
  3 Elizabeth (1825-1867); married Joseph D. Tetley
  4 Frances (1825-1857); married, 4 September 1857, Revd James Le Maistre
  5 Hannah (b. ±1826)
  6 Catherine (b. ±1826); married John Dalton (1784-1864)
  7 Cadwaller James [or James Cadwallader as he was baptised] (1826-1850), ensign by purchase, 14th Foot; died unmarried
  7 Charlotte Salisbury (1833-1912); died unmarried; lived, 1861, at Ventnor, Isle of Wight, with her sister Sophia

George Smith was appointed rector of Manningford Abbots, near Pewsey, in 1797, and vicar of Urchfont, near Devizes, in 1802. He died at Hotwells in March 1811.

1806: 8 Mar: ... *with a direction to a Revd. Smith No. 6 Westgate Buildings, to whom I wrote respecting a Curacy advertised in the Bath Chronicle.* 12 Mar: *After an early breakfast, rode over to Bath, where I passed the forenoon. Called upon the Revd. G. Smith respecting an advertised Curacy.* 20 Mar., 23 Mar: *Made a fruitless call upon Smith at Glocester House... ... Walked upon the Mount with Smith discussing particulars relating to his House.* 19 Jun: *Received an unpleasant letter from Smith which afterwards gave me considerable uneasiness.* 24 Jun: *Great uneasiness respecting our Treaty with Smith. Walked with my Father to call upon him at Glocester House in vain ... Had a long conversation with him on the Downs afterwards.* 25 Jun: *Wrote a note to Smith.* 26 Jun: *Called upon Smith in the forenoon.* 27 Jun: *Called upon Smith soon after breakfast.* 1 Jul: *Called upon George Rashleigh at the New Inn, & upon Smith... With my Father & Mother in the Evening, which was worn by considerable uneasiness respecting Smith's affair &c.* 2 Jul: *Uneasy all day; this affair with Smith disturbing me.* 3 Jul: *Called upon Smith after breakfast. Much contentious conference & uneasiness respecting his business.* 4 Jul: *Visited Smith for an hour or two after breakfast.* 5 Jul: *Rode to Bath after breakfast. After baiting there, harnessed my Grey in a Taxed Cart, & drove him to Erchfont; passed the Evening unpleasantly with Smith.* 6 Jul: *After a late breakfast & coming to a conclusion with Smith, walked to Stert.* 17 Jul: *Arranging matters with Smith.* 19-20 Jul., 22 Jul: *Rode to Erchfont in hopes of arranging matters with Smith but a sudden dispute made one quickly return, & occasioned two letters to & from him to me & one to & from Jaques.* 23 Jul: *Rode over to Smith to make future arrangements; an odious occupation.* 24 Jul: *Passed the greater part of the day with Smith at Erchfont.* 26 Jul: *Rode over to Erchfont to settle matters with Smith, from whom I parted without regret.* 22 Aug., 12 Sep., 13 Oct., 30 Oct., 1 Nov., 15 Dec.

1807: 14 Jan., 30 Jan., 12 Feb., 10 Mar., 24 Mar., 4 Jun., 6-8 Jun., 10 Jul., 1 Aug., 7 Aug., 24 Aug.

1808: 30 Jan: *Wrote to the Bishop of Sarum respecting my engagements with Smith.* 5 Feb: 6 Feb: *Received a letter from Smith, my Vicar, from Chippenham, whither he seems to become with a view of dislodging me; painful enough.* 8 Feb: *At Devizes conversed with Mr. Gibbs &c. Repaired to the White Hart; whence to Smith's lodgings. Dined with him, & held a long conversation upon business, leading, I presume, to my finally leaving Erchfont at the expiration of my term.* 9 Feb: *Walked over parts of the town of Chippenham before breakfast. Visited & conferred with Smith.* 7 Mar: *Heard from Smith in Town; an embarrassing letter, which required a letter to the Bishop of Salisbury.* 14 Mar: *Wrote to the Revd. G. Smith.*

1824: 25 Apr.

SMITH — George Smith — *see also* James Smith[125]

George Smith (1823-1882), carter, was born at Upper Slaughter, the second son of John Smith (1784-1840) and Matilda Elmer (1789-1849). He lived at Bourton-on-the-Water with his wife, Jane (1826-1899), born at Chasleton, Oxfordshire; they had at least 4 daughters and 2 sons:

1 Emma Maria (±1848-1931); married, at Bourton-on-the-Water, 26 December 1869, Joseph Mosen (1847-1922); 10 sons and 6 daughters; died at Raetihi, New Zealand
2 Elizabeth (±1851-1933)
1 John (b. ±1854)
3 Mary J. (b. ±1858)
4 Ellen (b. ±1863)
2 Walter John (1867-1912)

There are no records for George and his family on the assisted sailings to Australia; furthermore, even if they had gone, it is unlikely they would have been able to afford the passage money to return to England. It may be assumed, therefore, that they got cold feet and remained in England; George presumably never met his brother James again. (*See below*, Matilda Smith.)

1852: 26 May: *Wrote to Canon Ford, who had prepared an application paper on behalf of George Smith and his wife and two children, inhabitants of Bourton, but settled parishioners here, who are eager to emigrate to South Australia, in company with others from Little Risington, about to be dispatched thither, and there to join James Smith the brother of George.*

SMITH — Hugh Smith[126]

Hugh Smith (b. 1778), Church of England clergyman, was born in London, the second son of Hugh Smith, barrister-at-law of Lincoln's Inn. He was educated at Charterhouse and Trinity College, Cambridge (BA 1815; MA 1818), and was admitted at Lincoln's Inn in 1797. However, he changed his mind in favour of the Church. He was ordained deacon on 25 March 1815 and the same year was appointed rector of Weston-sub-Edge, Gloucestershire, on 2 December 1815. He remained there until 1846, when he was appointed rector of Stoke d'Abernon, Surrey. He held that living until 1862. He married Eleanor Ann (b. 1781), daughter of Sir Francis Blake, 2nd baronet (1737-1818), and Elizabeth Douglas (d. 1823); they had at least 5 sons:

1 Hugh Wallis (1811-1901); married, 1855, Julia Funck, a widow and daughter of William Fitzgibbon
2 Henry (b. 1819)
3 Robert William (b. 1820)
4 George Frederick (1824-1914); married Caroline, fourth daughter of Revd Francis Ellis-Jervoise
5 Charles Francis (b. 1827)

In 1861 Hugh and Eleanor Smith were living with servants in Marlborough Square, Kensington.

The above attribution regarding Eleanor's parentage supposes that, in the case argued and determined in the ecclesiastical courts at Doctors' Commons in 1828, the executor named Revd Hugh Smith and the daughter named Eleanor were the same Hugh Smith and Eleanor who married. There is a possibility that this is not correct.

1825: 21 Jun: *The Sermon was preached by the Revd. Hugh Smith, Incumbent of Weston sub edge, with a good though rather studied delivery.*

SMITH — James Clutterbuck Smith[127]

James Clutterbuck Smith (b. ±1768), Church of England clergyman, was the son of Matthew Smith of Greenwich. He was educated at Oriel College, Oxford, and was appointed curate of Woolwich on 22 June 1802. This attribution is tentative.

1805: 18 Aug: *At church in the morning a moderately good sermon on sobriety by the Curate, Mr. Smith.*

SMITH — James Smith[128]

James Smith (1819-1894), agricultural labourer, was born at Upper Slaughter, the eldest son of John Smith (1784-1840) and Matilda Elmer (1789-1849). He lived at Bourton-on-the-Water, and married, at Aston Somerville, Worcestershire (about 14 miles north-west of Bourton), 5 February 1848, Sarah Anne (1829-1906), daughter of William Matthews (b. 1790) and his wife Martha (1798-1837) of Snowshill. James and Sarah had 4 sons and 7 daughters:

1 William (b. 1848); born at Aston Somerville
1 Sarah Ann (1854-1895)
2 Emma Sophia (1856-1884)
2 John (1858-1875)
3 Charlotte (b. 1859)
3 James H. (1861-1941)
4 Mary (b. 1863)
5 Jessie (1864-1927)
4 Henry (b. 1867)
6 Eleanor Nell (1869-1965)
7 Louisa (1872-1935)

In 1851 James and Sarah sailed from Plymouth to Australia on board the *Sea* with their eldest son William. They arrived at Hobsons Bay, Victoria, on 20 August 1851, and settled in Tasmania, where they had a further ten children. Francis Witts made an error in his diary entry for 24 February 1851, writing 'John' instead of 'James'. (*See below,* Matilda Smith.)

1851: 24 Feb: *Both these being Trustees of our Church and Charity land, consulted them on the advisability of assisting John Smith, a settled parishioner of this parish, resident at Bourton on the Water, having a wife and child, to emigrate to Port Philip in Australia, where he has a sister married, and doing well. I proposed that, out of the surplus funds of our Trust.* 25 Feb: *Wrote to S. Walcot Esqr. Secretary to the Government Emigration Board, requesting to be furnished with the necessary papers for the emigration of James Smith and his family to Port Philip.* 3 Mar: *Conferred with the wife of James Smith and with Benj. Carey as to emigration to Australia.* 10 Mar: *Wrote to Mr. Walcott, Secretary to the Colonial Emigration Board, with papers for the Emigration of James Smith & family properly filled up.* 19 Mar: *Received a packet from the Government Colonial and Emigration Office, containing the papers relative to the Emigration of James Smith to Australia.* 24 Mar: *The business of the parish trust being entered on with a view to furthering the proposed emigration of James Smith and family out of the surplus funds of the Estate, J B Collett retracted the consent he had given … and it was notified to J. Smith that the intention of assisting him to emigrate was abandoned. J.B.C's conduct was disapproved by all the Rate payers present.* 28 Mar: *E Lea and J B Collett called by appointment after breakfast, the latter being desirous of retracting his opposition to the emigration of James Smith and family at the expence of the Parish Trust … Conferred with James Smith and his wife on the matter.* 29 Mar: *Despatched to the Colonial and Emigration Office, by Post office orders, £6 — for the passage money to Port Philip of James Smith, his wife and their child.* 8 Apr., 11 Apr: *Recd. from the Emigration Board, a letter containing the embarkation order for James Smith, wife and child to Port Philip — they are to be at the agent's office at Plymouth on May 12.* 12 Apr: *Drove to Bourton on the Water; gave further directions to Palmer at the shop as to the outfit of James Smith, his wife and child; desired him to communicate to them at what time they are to repair to Plymouth to meet the vessel which is to convey them to Australia... . Called at Mr. Wilkins's office to speak to him on the same subject; Mrs. W. is very kind in clothing the child, and giving comforts to the woman.* 21 Apr., 30 Apr., 3 May: *Conferred with Palmer as to the outfit for the emigrants, James Smith, his wife and child.* 10 May: *Transacted business with Edward Lea, as Co-Trustee of the Church and Charity Estate of this parish; arranging for the departure of James Smith his wife and child for Plymouth on Monday next, on his route to Port Philip, Australia; the journey to Plymouth to be taken under the charge of one Trotman, of Bourton on the W., — an Ex Policeman of the Gloucestershire Constabulary, who will conduct the party with their luggage by railway, and deposit them in the Government barracks at Plymouth assigned for Emigrants.*

SMITH — John Smith [129]

John Smith (b. 1777), maltster, was born at Great Rissington, Gloucestershire, the son of William and Anne Smith. In 1841 he was apparently unmarried, living with his father, William (b. ±1755), also a maltster.

1843: 18 Aug: *After an early breakfast walked to Bourton on the Water; at the office of Messrs. Wilkins and Kendal met Messrs. Ford and R Waller, with whom long engaged in taking depositions as to a charge preferred against one John Smith, late a farmer and Maltster at Great Risington, of having set fire to a rick of hay the property of Mr. W. Hyatt: a strong body of circumstantial evidence, leading to the conclusion that the act was committed under impulses of malice by the party charged.* 2 Dec., 4 Dec: *Walked to Bourton on the Water by appointment to meet Messrs. Ford and Waller at the offices of Messrs. Wilkins and Kendall, to deliberate on fresh matter, which has transpired with reference to the charge of Arson against John Smith of Great Risington.* 12 Dec: *A note from Mr. Ford summoned me to Messrs. Wilkins and Kendall's office at Bourton on the Water to further deliberations as to the coming trial of John Smith of Great Risington on a charge of arson, and to transact other Magisterial business.* 14 Dec: *Mr. Ford informed me that the Grand Jury had ignored the bill against John Smith of Great Risington; I never expected that he would be found guilty. — but I had anticipated that the charge would have gone before the petty Jury.*

SMITH — John Smith

John Smith appears to have been a servant and gardener of the Witts family. Nothing has been discovered and his children were not baptised at Upper Slaughter.

1826: 13 Jan: *While we were at dinner John Smith unexpectedly arrived from Upper Slaughter with the horses, being sent by my leading parishioners to consult me on the propriety of holding an inquest on the body of Sarah Price.*

1839: 19 Mar: *Considerable annoyance in consequence of the absence of our Gardener, J Smith, who has left the Village, and his work, as is believed, in consequence of his being over head and ears in debt, leaving behind him his wife and family, who are, doubtless, cognizant of his movements.* 26 Mar.

SMITH — John Smith of Combe Hay, Somerset — *see* **Leigh** *and* **John Smith Leigh**

SMITH — John Carrington Smith [130]

John Carrington Smith (1766-1843), lieutenant-colonel in the Army, married, 1799, Charlotte Juliana Butler (1769-1830), daughter of Viscount Mountgarret and sister to the earl of Kilkenny. John and Charlotte had at least 1 son:

1 Edmund Carrington (1801-1857)

Smith served in India. In his will he mentioned having property worth approximately £11,000 to £12,000. He left everything to his son Edmund.

1836: 14 Sep: *The Mag. present were, R. B. Cooper, in the chair, Lord Ellenborough, Mr. Seale Evans, Fulwar Craven, Col. Carrington Smith, and Edmund Hopkinson, who like myself came to watch the proceedings against the swindling horse dealer and stealer.*

SMITH — Joseph Grace Smith [131]

Joseph Grace Smith (±1787-1859+), judge, was born in the parish of St Mary, Islington, Middlesex, the son of Joseph Smith (1757-1839) and Maria Grace (1760-1847). He was baptised in the Baptist chapel in James Street, Stepney, Middlesex. He married, at St John's, Devizes, Wiltshire, 3 March 1818, Hannah (1791-1863), youngest daughter of Benjamin Webb Anstie (1747-1824) and Hannah Overbury (1758-1808); they had at least 1 son and 1 daughter:

1 Anna Maria (b. 1821)

1 Philip Anstie (1824-1879)

Smith lived at Winkfield House in Wiltshire and was a county court judge.

1848: 17 Oct: *The pamphlet published in the name of Dr. C. Bompas, but probably the production of his Uncle, Mr. Grace Smith, a Barrister, and recently appointed Judge of a county court district in Wilts and Somerset.* 22 Nov: *Mr. Grace Smith, formerly a provincial barrister of Bristol, a man of great experience, knowledge in his profession and acuteness, and now Judge of a County Court, his district being in Somersetshire and Wilts.*

SMITH — Joshua Smith [132]

Joshua Smith (±1732-1819), MP and landed proprietor, of Erlestoke Park, near Devizes, was born in London, the eldest son of John Smith, merchant, of Lambeth, and Mary, daughter of Griffin Ransome of Lambeth. He married, at St Andrew's, Gatton, Surrey, 17 August 1766, Sarah (b. 1747), daughter of Nathaniel Gilbert, judge and member of the legislative council of Antigua. They had 4 daughters:

1 Augusta (1772-1845); married by special licence, 29 March 1798, Charles Smith (1756-1814) (possibly a cousin), son of Charles Smith and Judith Lefevre; 3 sons and 6 daughters:
  1 Augusta (1799-1836)
  1 Charles Joshua (1800-1831)
  2 Spencer (b. 1806)
  2 Charlotte Judith (b. 1809)
  3 Maria Louisa (dates unknown)
  3 Drummond (d. 1832)
  4 Sarah Eliza (dates unknown)
  5 Frances (dates unknown)
  6 Emma (dates unknown)

2 Emma (b. 1774)

3 Elizabeth [Eliza] (dates unknown); married William John Chute (1757-1824)

4 Maria (d. 1843); married, 18 August 1787, Charles Compton (1760-1828); 1 son and 2 daughters:
 1 Spencer Joshua Alwyne (1790-1851); became marquess of Northampton
 1 Frances Elizabeth (b. 1791)
 2 Elizabeth (unknown)

Smith was a director of the HEIC (1771-73), a shipowner, and timber merchant. He was also MP for Devizes, 1788-1818.

Because the name Smith is so common, it is very easy to misattribute, but it seems likely that the young Mrs Smith referred to in the diaries was Augusta Smith, who was on friendly terms with one of the Tylee family, both families being of the upper strata of Devizes society. Equally confusing is the 'Compton' reference. In this circumstance it seems probable that this was Charles Compton, husband to Maria Smith, and not related to the Compton families of Urchfont and Eastcott.

1806: 4 Nov: *In pursuance of an invitation dined with the Mayor & Corporation of Devizes upon occasion of the Election of Members for the Town; Mr. Smith & Mr. Estcourt being re-elected.* 5 Jul: *Met & conversed with Messrs. Compton & Smith.*

1807: 24 Jan: *Recovering the fox was found impossible, & I left the party with Butcher, returned thro' the beautiful village of Stoke & by Mr. Smith's elegant Mansion ...*
6 May: *Mr. Jones called in a post chaise to convey me to the Election Dinner at Devizes Mr. Smith & Mr. Estcourt being re-elected.* 22 Jul: *Called upon the Tylees, & pleasantly received Mrs. Smith a very attractive young woman.* 3 Aug: *Mrs. Smith & Miss Tylee called, my Mother returned with them to Devizes in the Chaise.*

SMITH — Lydia Bosworth Smith [Lees] [133]

Lydia Bosworth Smith (1808-1876), doctor of medicine and poet, was the second daughter of Sir John Wyldbore Smith, 2nd baronet (1770-1852), and Elizabeth Anne Marriott (±1769-1844). The name Bosworth came from Lydia's maternal grandfather. She married, at Edinburgh, 4 April 1855, as his second wife, Henry Lees (1813-1872). Although she formally retained the surname 'Smith', Lydia used her husband's name also. One source states that she graduated MD. At the time of the 1851 census Henry Lees was visiting the Smith family, who also lived at Blandford in Dorset. He was listed as 'married'. Presumably his first wife had died or he had obtained a divorce; the details are sadly lacking.

1852: 11 May: *Miss Lydia Smith sat at the head of her table, the other guests, besides the Vavasours and myself, were James Wynniatt, Miss Kirby, and Mr. Paxton, Mrs. Dolphin's Steward. Miss L.S., who leaves Mrs. Dolphin tomorrow, sang and played a great deal, chiefly her own compositions; those on sacred themes, Hagar, Ruth, David & Jonathan, are very beautiful & touching—she has wonderful powers of execution both as to finger & voice, with great tenderness and grace; and the improvised, elaborate compositions, with variations on a theme given—I selected "Suoni la tromba", are truly beautiful.* 27 Oct: *Mrs. Dolphin and Miss Lydia Smith, her guest since Monday, called on me.* 28 Oct., 29 Oct: *A large party to luncheon, with music—Mrs. Dolphin, Miss L Smith, Miss Walmesley, two Misses Wynniatt, Tom and Jem Wynniatt, Mrs. W. Vavasour, Sophy and myself formed the party.* 27 Dec: *Heard at "the Cottage" that Miss Lydia Smith has taken the fatal plunge which rumour had represented her as having already perpetrated: she is said, on Miss Walmsley's authority, to have gone off last week with Dr. Lees—a physician of Blanford,—a married man with eight or nine children. This is stated to have been a heavy blow to Mrs. Dolphin.*

SMITH — Matilda Smith [134]

Matilda Smith, née Elmer (1789-1849), was born at Deddington, Oxfordshire, the daughter of Henry Elmer (b. 1750) and Ann Butcher (1752-1831), who died at Upper Slaughter. She was baptised at Deddington on 21 August 1789. Matilda married John Smith (1784-1840); they had at least 3 sons and 6 daughters:
 1 Jane (b. 1812); born at Deddington, Oxfordshire
 1 George (1813-1814); died an infant at 5 months
 2 Mary Anne (b. 1816)
 3 Elizabeth (1816-1908); married, at Upper Slaughter [or Northleach], 6 February 1837, Isaac Williams (1812-1859), of Little Rissington, son of Samuel Williams (1788-1861) and Hannah Read (1788-1859); 4 sons and 2 daughters:
  1 Harriett (1838-1900)
  1 Dennis (b. & d. 1843)
  2 George (1845-1911)
  2 Matilda Jane (1857-1916)
  3 John (dates unknown)
  4 Isaac John (d. 1908)
 2 James (1819-1894); *see above*
 4 Harriet (b. 1821)
 3 George (1823-1882); *see above*
 5 Emma (b. 1826)
 6 Louisa (1828-1909); married John Webley (1827-1916); at least 1 daughter:
  1 Ann (1855-1930)

Elizabeth, Matilda's third daughter, and her husband Issac Williams departed with their children from Plymouth on board the *Severn* and arrived at Victoria, Australia, on 9 December 1856. They emigrated freely, but three of Isaac's brothers had been sent to Australia as convicts: Job (1820-1878); Emanuel (1822-1872); and George (1824-1846). According to a family pedigree, Elizabeth died at Caulfield, Victoria, Australia.

1836: 3 Sep: *Wrote to the Secretary of the Gloucester infirmary to ascertain whether Matilda Smith could be admitted as a patient on the parish subscription next week.* 6 Sep: *Received a letter from the Infirmary at Gloucester in answer to my enquiry, stating that Matilda Smith might be admitted as an out-patient on Thursday next.*

1843: 8 Nov: *Wrote to Dr. Twisleton to put him on his guard against the arts and misrepresentations of my parishioners, Matilda and Louisa Smith, who, from information given me by the latter, in her folly, were likely, as I judged, to try to impose on his good nature.*

SMITH — Nathaniel Smith [135]

Nathaniel Smith (1781-1869), surgeon and fellow of the Royal College of Surgeons, was born in London. In 1861 he lived at 14 Lansdown Place, Clifton, as a widower with 2 unmarried daughters:
 1 Henrietta Maria (b. 1815)
 2 Sarah Anne (b. 1817)

1848: 22 Nov: *There appeared also Mr. N. Smith, an eminent surgeon of Bristol, uncle to Dr. Bompas, and brother of Mr. Grace Smith.*

1850: 1 Jan: *As to the Fishponds Asylum the Bompas family has retired with Mr. Nathl. Smith from the management.*

SMITH — Peter Smith [136]

Sir Peter Smith (b. ±1781), chief clerk in the colonial office, was born in Scotland. He entered the service as an extra clerk on 20 August 1810 and stayed in the post until 5 April 1816. His other appointments were as follows: translator, 5 January 1814; clerk, 5 July 1819; supernumerary assistant clerk, 28 March 1822; senior clerk, 5 January 1824; and chief clerk, 1 July 1843. He retired on 1 January 1860. Smith handled military matters and questions relating to the conferment of colonial honours. Upon his retirement in 1860 he was awarded the Order of St Michael and St George. He lived at 3 New Finchley Road, Hampstead, and was unmarried.

1842: 12 Dec: *Our party was increased before dinner by the arrival from Town of Mr. Smith, an old and intimate acquaintance of Howell, a Senior Clerk in the Colonial Office, a valetudinarian, and rather peculiar and old bachelorlike in his habits, but of great experience in his line, a very useful and valuable public servant.* 13 Dec: *After breakfast accompanied Howell and Mr. Smith on a long and very enjoyable walk to the Rough Park, and through the Beech woods, even to the summit of Cooper's* hill. 14 Dec. *After breakfast I drove Miss Dowell to call on the Wintles at Saintsbridge, while I took Mr. Smith to Gloucester; and visited with him the principal public buildings there; the Shire Hall, Gaol, Cathedral, Port & Spa.* 15-17 Dec.

SMITH — Robert Smith [137]

Robert Smith (1793-1872), farmer, was the son of William Smith (1743-1815) and Hannah Rimell (1751-1827). In 1851 he lived with his wife Ann (1788-1867); they had at least 1 son:

1 John William Tysoe (b. 1829-1875)

The family lived at Hinchwick Farm, Condicote. It measured 680 acres and employed twenty-nine labourers.

1850: 11 Nov: *Mr. Beman called to consult me on a matter which he wishes to refer to my arbitration as between himself and Mr. Smith of Hinchwick.* 15 Nov: *Wrote to Mr. Smith, Hinchwick in reference to his dispute with Mr. Beman about Poor Rates.* 5 Dec: 5 Dec: *To the Unicorn, accompanied by Winter, where I adjudicated, as Arbitrator, a matter which has been long in dispute between Mr. Beman, as outgoing tenant of Hinchwick farm, and Mr. Smith, the incoming tenant ... Mr. Hancock, Attorney of Shipston, appeared for Mr. Smith.*

SMITH — Samuel Smith [138]

Samuel Smith (1814-1866) was the son of Thomas Smith (1778-1847) and Alley Pearce (1776-1847). He emigrated to Australia to work for a relation, Thomas Arkell. In late 1823 or early 1824 Thomas Arkell entered into what turned out to be a lifelong relationship with Sophia Millage, née Langley (1802-1887). After a marriage of only 20 months she had left her husband Richard Millage to live with Arkell, bringing her baby Elizabeth with her. Arkell brought Elizabeth up as if she was his own daughter. Samuel Smith married Elizabeth Millage (1822-1900) and they had eleven children:

1 Thomas Arkell (1840-1911)
2 Henry (1842-1887)
1 Lucy Ann Arkell (1844-1912)
3 George Sydney (1845-1909)
2 Emma Sophia (1848-1877)
3 Susannah Elizabeth (1850-1927)
4 Hannah Rebecca (b. 1851)
4 Edwin Australia (1853-1883)
5 Frederick Darling (1855-1934)
5 Ada Maretta (b. & d. 1859)
6 Florence Maretta Gertrude (1861-1882)

Samuel died in 1866 at Trunkey Creek, Australia.

1832: 7 Jun: *I also called on Samuel Smith, son to my neighbour, Mr. Dolphin's tenant at Eyford, a fine looking youth of eighteen, who has been seized lately with a scrophulous affection in the hip, calculated to excite great apprehension, and has been removed hither to be under the care of the eminent Surgeon, Fletcher.*

1836: 20 Nov: *Young Samuel Smith of Eyford called for a certificate of his baptism.*

1838: 26 Feb: *Wrote to the Secretary of State for the Colonies on behalf of the Smith family of Eyford, to enquire about emigration to New South Wales, who is the recognized Emigration Agent to that Colony, what part of the passage money is defrayed by Government in the case of Agricultural labourers emigrating with families, when a ship will sail &c.? The enquiry was suggested in a letter from Sam. Smith, who emigrated about a year ago, accepting an invitation from a Colonist, from the neighbourhood of Cheltenham, named Arkell, now advanced in life, who has acquired a valuable property in land, stock &c. and wished for a young Gloucestershire farmer to come out to assist him in cultivating his property in the interior, in Bathurst County.* 2 Mar: *Received a letter from the Australian Emigration Agent attached to the Colonial Office, with a number of printed documents respecting emigration to New South Wales & Van Dieman's land, which were sent in reply to my letter to the Colonial Secretary on the 26th. Ult. and which I communicated to my neighbour E. Lea, that they might be available to the Smith family.*

SMITH — Sarah Smith [later Bartley] [139]

Sarah Smith (±1783-1850), actress, was probably born in Liverpool in 1783, but accounts of her parentage are conflicting. She adopted the surname Smith on her mother's second marriage, which apparently took place in 1793. By this time she had already appeared on stage in Salisbury as Edward in Mrs Inchbald's comedy *Every One has his Fault*.

At the age of 16 Sarah Smith played Joanna in Thomas Holcroft's *The Deserted Daughter*. She then spent three years under Stephen Kemble at the Edinburgh Theatre Royal. Disillusioned by her experience there, she retired from the stage, but was soon driven back to it by her need to earn a living. She obtained work on Tate Wilkinson's York circuit, and remained there until his death in 1803. She then moved on to Birmingham and thence to Bath, where she enjoyed popular success; she was hailed as the 'Siddons of Bath', although the compliment may not have pleased her. At Bath she was noticed by Thomas Harris, who engaged her for Covent Garden, where she first appeared on 2 October 1805 as Lady Townly in Vanbrugh's *The Provoked Husband*.

Smith was reluctant to take part in comedy, and Sarah Siddons enjoyed the monopoly on characters that she wished to perform. She refused to play secondary parts to Mrs Siddons but also refused to be bought out of her contract. Harris thought her 'unaccommodatingly fastidious'. On the expiration of her contract in 1808, Smith departed for Dublin, where she was warmly received. She then returned to London, where her reception was more cordial than it had been formerly. In 1811 she migrated to Drury Lane, and in January 1813 she created the character of Teresa in S. T. Coleridge's tragedy *Remorse*.

On 23 August 1814 she married the widowed actor George Bartley (±1782-1858); their happy union produced two children. Sarah Siddons' retirement in 1812 had left Sarah Bartley as the reigning queen of tragedy on the London stage, but her position was soon usurped by Eliza O'Neill. In 1818 the Bartleys went to America, where Sarah secured her reputation and made a fortune. They returned to England in 1820 and undertook a provincial tour. Sarah appeared at Covent Garden in November 1823 as Mrs Beverley in Edward Moore's *The Gamester*, but thereafter she performed infrequently. The death of her son in 1843 and that of her daughter shortly afterwards greatly affected her, and she died from heart disease at her Bloomsbury home on 14 January 1850.

1808: 24 Feb: *Visited Covent Garden Theatre to see the new Comedy: Begone dull care; not a very interesting—piece: Fawcett's acting extremely good, the whole well supported; Miss Smith highly prepossessing.* 25 Feb: *In the Evening to Covent Garden Theatre, where I was much amused by a very interesting Drama a Swedish Fable, entitled the Wanderer, or the Rights of Hospitality. Miss Smith very great, Charles Kemble excellent as the Hero.*

SMITH — Sydney Smith [140]

Sydney Smith (1771-1845), Church of England clergyman, author, and wit, was born at Woodford, Essex, the son of Robert Smith (1740-1827), merchant, and Maria (±1750-1801), daughter of Isaac Olier, a Huguenot. He was educated at Winchester College and New College, Oxford, and entered the Church in 1794 as curate at Netheravon on Salisbury Plain. After a return to Oxford, where he learnt thoroughly both French and German, Smith became private tutor to Michael Hicks-Beach, son of Smith's squire at Netheravon. A Continental tour had been planned, but the invasion of Switzerland by France in February 1798 forced a rethink; Weimar was discarded as a destination in favour of Edinburgh. Smith set off north with his pupil on 1 June 1798. He did not enjoy his tutorial duties—Hicks-Beach was a lazy young man of mediocre intellectual ability, whose main interest was socialising—but he loved Edinburgh and quickly built up a network of friends which included Henry Brougham, a friend to Francis Witts.

One evening shortly before the Christmas of 1801, during a meal with friends, Smith suggested, half in jest, that they should start a literary review. The idea was taken up enthusiastically and gained financial support from Archibald Constable, a leading Edinburgh bookseller. The first issue of the *Edinburgh Review* came out on 10 October 1802, and Smith did much to establish its literary reputation. Of the 101 articles in the first four issues, he was responsible for nineteen; only Brougham, credited with twenty-one, wrote more. Smith ranged widely, writing on matters as diverse as philosophy, travel, drama, and theology. He was the best communicator among the reviewers, and also possessed the most scabrous wit. Smith was a canon of Bristol, and frequently in the Bristol and Bath vicinity; it was during this period in his life that he was seen in Bath by Francis Witts.

On Smith's return to London, Lord and Lady Holland became his chief patrons. In October 1806 they persuaded Lord Chancellor Thomas Erskine to make him rector of the affluent living of Foston-le-Clay, 12 miles north-east of York. During these London years Smith also became a popular preacher. He had the use of three pulpits: Berkeley chapel in John Street, Mayfair; Fitzroy chapel a little further north in the parish of St Pancras; and the Foundling Hospital. Smith's doctrinal views were conventional—he was an uncritical follower of the theology of William Paley—and his sermons were firmly moral in their tone. What made him famous was his fiery delivery. Smith's *Sermons* were published in two volumes in 1809.

Sydney Smith married Catharine Amelia Pybus (1768-1852); they had 3 sons and 2 daughters:

1 Saba (1802-1866); married, at St George's, Hanover Square, Westminster, 13 March 1834, Sir Henry Holland, 1st baronet Holland of Sandlebridge (1788-1873); 3 daughters
1 Noel Percy (b. & d. 1803); died an infant
2 Douglas (1805-1829); died unmarried
2 Emily (1807-1874); married, at York, 26 December 1827, Nathaniel Hibbert (1794-1865); 1 son and 2 daughters
3 Wyndham (1813-1871); died unmarried

Sydney Smith was hugely influential and successful. He was an innovative and unconventional rector, putting into practice what would later be called the social gospel. He planted a number of small gardens with fruit trees, allowing the villagers to gather the produce, and also set aside part of his glebe for allotments at nominal rents. He excelled as a makeshift doctor, keeping copious notes on all his patients and ordering drugs for them from London. In January 1814 he was made a magistrate, and subsequently dispensed his own brand of humane justice in preference to the rigours of statute law. He was especially lenient towards poachers. He enjoyed a distinguished career in the Church with a substantial income, but is best remembered for his wit and satire; '[Lutterell's] idea of heaven is eating pâté de foie to the sound of trumpets,' was one of his best-known mots.

Smith was not only an important contributor to the growth of libertarian thought in England, he was also, as G. K. Chesterton later pointed out, the inventor of nonsense, a very English style of humour. He suffered a heart attack and died in Green Street on 22 February 1845. He was buried next to his beloved son, Douglas, in Kensal Green cemetery. It seems that Francis Witts was an admirer of Sydney Smith, but he improperly 'knighted' him in 1802.

1802: 4 Jan: *Sir Sydney Smith was one of the first figures: his sight as also that of Lord Nelson's Father, a venerable old Gent. was very gratifying to me.*

1838: 22 Aug: *Here he particularly alluded to certain personal and unjustifiable attacks which had been made against himself, principally by Sydney Smith, and also by others of less note, by whom he had been exposed to much obloquy and undeserved reproach.*

1845: 8 May: *After returning to Prinknash I read aloud to the family circle, a very clever, witty, posthumous pamphlet by the Revd. Sidney Smith, on the subject of endowing the Romish Clergy in Ireland, which he greatly recommends.*

SMITH — Thomas Assheton Smith [141]

Thomas Assheton Smith (1776-1858), MP, landed proprietor, quarry owner, and cricketer, was born in Cavendish Square, London, the second of the nine children of Thomas Assheton Smith (1752-1828), landowner and MP, and Elizabeth (d. 1814), daughter of Watkin Wynne of Foelas, Denbighshire. His paternal grandfather was Thomas Assheton of Ashley, Cheshire; his father added 'Smith' to his surname when he inherited estates at Tidworth in Hampshire and Vaynol in Caernarvonshire from his uncle, William Smith.

Smith (junior) was educated at Eton College and Christ Church, Oxford. He married Matilda, second daughter of William Webber, of Binfield Lodge, Berkshire, but had no children. On the death of his father in 1828, Smith inherited the Tidworth and Vaynol estates. As part of the latter, he took over the complex of slate quarries known as Dinorwig, which was situated on Elidir mountain, near Llanberis.

Smith was Conservative MP for Andover in 1821-31, and Caernarvonshire in 1832-41. He was master of the Quorn hounds in 1806-16, and of a Hampshire pack at Penton in 1826, and afterwards at Tidworth. In his youth he was a great cricketer and later he became an enthusiastic yacht owner. He introduced several novelties in yacht construction.

1848: 24 Jul: *this range of quarries, very extensive, but far less so than those we had visited in the morning, are the property of Mr. Asheton Smith, who has great estates here.* 25 Jul: *Again proceeding inland, and losing the sea, we passed Vaenol, a seat of Mr. Asheton Smith.*

SMITH — Thomas Smith and the Smith family of Eyford [142]

Thomas Smith (1778-1847), farmer at Eyford, married, at Honeybourne, Worcestershire, 11 March 1801, Alley Pearce (1776-1854), born at Weston-sub-Edge. Thomas and Alley had ten children, including the 3 known sons and 6 known daughters:

1 Elizabeth (1802-1879); married, 8 June 1820, Edward Lea (1795-1858)
2 Anne (±1804-1836); married, at Upper Slaughter, 14 November 1833, John Tysoe of Lower Swell
1 William Smith (b. 1805)
3 Harriett (1808-1855); married, at Upper Slaughter, 4 June 1835, Edward Tysoe (1805-1853) of Lower Swell
4 Sophia (1810-1884); married, 4 November 1830, Henry Arkell (1803-1878) of Boddington
5 Lucy (1811-1837); died unmarried
2 Samuel (1814-1866); emigrated to Australia; *see above*
6 Hannah (b. & d. 1816); died an infant
3 George Edwin (1819-1883); emigrated to Australia; *see above*

1834: 6 Aug: *Drove Mrs. Backhouse and Mrs. Witts to Eyford. Edward walked to meet us there.*

1835: 19 Mar., 27 May: *Called on the Smiths.*

1836: 10 Oct: *Walked to Eyford, to visit Lucy Smith, who has again fallen into a very feeble & precarious state of health.* 16 Oct: *Walked to Eyford with M.W. to enquire after Lucy Smith, who is getting weaker, almost confined to bed, & supposed to be going off in a dropsy.* 28 Oct., 6 Dec: ... *called on poor Lucy Smith, now confined to her bed, suffering under all the worst symptoms of decay by dropsy: her Brother went yesterday to Liverpool to be ready to sail to New South Wales.*

1837: 9 Jan: *Went to Eyford and administered the sacrament privately to Lucy Smith, who is more and more declining to the grave.* 14 Jan: *Walked with MW. to Eyford to enquire as to state of Mr. Smith, who had been seized with inflammation on the lungs on his return from a journey on Thursday Even.* 15 Jan: *He is no better, Hayward in almost constant attendance, and Dr. Baron sent for. Lucy Smith, whom I saw, appeared sinking fast.* 17 Jan: *The Father still lies in a very precarious state: the daughter at the point of death, surrounded by their numerous and attached relations and connections* 18 Jan: *Lucy Smith died last night, she was a patient, pious, amiable sufferer.* 21 Jan: *Poor Lucy Smith was buried.* 22 Jan: *Rather a more unfavourable report of Mr. Smith; his son in law E. Lea seriously ill with the prevailing epidemic.* 23 Jan: *In my ride called to enquire after Mr. Smith, who is better, as also E. Lea, who is, however, much indisposed.* 27 Jan: *Walked to Eyford, and visited Smith, now considered out of danger, and slowly recovering.* 13 Feb.

1838: 1 Feb: *The appointment was ... opposed by Comely in a speech, by Colletts (three) Smith, Wests, Gillett &c.* 8 Feb: *Those insinuations originate in the bad feeling of my neighbour & parishioner Smith, the Guardian for Eyford, a man of plausible exterior, but of an unforgiving temper, prone to think and free to speak ill of others.* 15 Feb: *I took occasion to advert to the personalities which had been circulated in so improper a manner as to my motives and conduct in this controversy, stating my determination to give a public denial to the insinuation that I was manoeuvring to obtain the Chaplaincy for my son, and that I had caused him to preach a Sermon of my writing pointed at Smith the Guardian of Eyford... and that in Smith's presence, who appeared very angry and very strongly to feel the force of what I said, not so much from a sense that he had done me wrong, as smarting under the chastisement he received.* 25 Feb: *Well pleased to see my neighbour Smith of Eyford again at Church; a proof, I trust, that he has repented of his uncharitable surmises and censures which made it necessary that I should publickly deny the false insinuations in circulation against me, as to my motives in respect of the question of appointing a chaplain to the Workhouse.* 8 Mar., 22 Mar: *I lean to this chiefly in consequence of the uneasiness I have experienced from the personal imputations laid to my charge by Smith, the Eyford Guardian.* 5 Apr: *I felt so deeply wounded by the unwarrantable imputations which had been thrown upon me by Smith that I was strongly tempted to cease from further connection with the Guardians.* 27 Dec.

1839: 1 Jun.

1842: 29 Jan: *Visited Mrs. Smith, Eyford, who is dangerously ill.* 31 Jan: *Visited Mrs. Smith, who continues in a precarious state. Privately administered to her the holy Communion, also to her three daughters Mrs. Lea, Mrs. E. Tysoe, and Mrs. Arkell.* 4 Feb., 9 Feb., 14 Feb.

1843: 29 Sep.

1844: 10 Feb., 22 Mar: *Walked with MW. to Eyford: called on the Smiths, who are about to leave the farm.*

1847: 6 Mar: *Recd. a note from J. Bryan, Stow, Undertaker, announcing the death of Mr. Smith, farmer of Bledington, and that it is proposed that he be interred at Upper Slaughter on Tuesday next: he was for very many years a tenant resident at Eyford, and some of his children are buried here.* 9 Mar: *Mr. Smith from Bledington was buried here to-day.*

SMITH — William Smith [143]

William Smith (1805-1879), farmer, was born at Weston-sub-Edge, the eldest son of Thomas Smith (1778-1847) and Alley Pearce (1776-1854) of Eyford (*above*). After Mrs Dolphin had given him notice at Eyford, William took a position at Chadshunt in Warwickshire, and by 1851 he was at New House Farm, Bibury, on a farm of 733 acres, employing twenty-nine agricultural labourers. He married Ann G. (b. 1815), born at Longborough, Gloucestershire; they had at least 5 daughters:

1 Ann Gibbs (b. ±1840)
2 Susan (b. ±1841)
3 Kate (b. ±1843)
4 Sophia (b. ±1844)
5 Fanny (b. 1846)

1837: 4 Apr: *The winner of last year, Standard, then the property of W. Bryan of Lower Slaughter now of V. Dolphin, and on both occasions rode by W. Smith of Eyford, came in fifth.* 11 Aug.

1839: 7 Jun: ... *besides a considerable party of ordinary members and musicians about fifteen dined on very good and well cooked viands at the high table, being Trustees & Honorary members—Waller, Polson, Wilkins, Kimber, W. Smith, E. Lea, J. Bennett, Ransford, T. Collett, W. & Jos. Bryan, C. Barton &c.*

1840: 5 Jun: *At half past one sat down to dinner, R Waller taking the Chair, about sixty dined, and of these eighteen or twenty were honorary Members,—Ford, Polson, Wilkins, Kendall, Welles, two Bryans, W. Smith, Palmer, T. Collett, Ransford, J Bennett, Hanks, Kimber &c.* 10 Jun: *A vestry meeting had been called, and some of the farmers attended & met me, but the absence of W. Smith prevented our going to business, which was to regulate the amount to be assessed on him.* 11 Sep: *Walked with MW. to the Parks Farm, Eyford, to shew civility to by calling on the*

Tenant and his wife (Mr. W. Smith) who have lately taken up their residence there, and whom we saw. 25 Oct: *Recd. a letter from a Mr. Cooper of Henley in Arden, who is steward to a gentleman of the name of Knight, owner of a considerable farm in Warwickshire, which William Smith, who has received notice to quit the Parks farm at Eyford, from Mrs. Dolphin, is desirous to take. W.S. had referred the parties to me for a character as to skill in husbandry, responsibility &c.—W.S. came to me on my sending for him in the evening, to put me in possession of facts which might enable me to speak with sufficient confidence as to his responsibility.* 26 Oct: *Wrote to Mr. Cooper, of Henley in Arden, in reply to his letter received yesterday, with a favourable report as to W Smith.*

SMITH — William Smith [144]

William Smith (1811-1881), solicitor and farmer, lived at Fen Farm, Winchcombe. He farmed 160 acres, employing twenty men and women and three boys. Late in life he married Elizabeth (b. 1839); they had 3 sons and 1 daughter:

1 Agnes (b. ±1859)
1 William (b. ±1861)
2 Edmund (b. ±1864)
3 Edwin (b. 1866)

1844: 11 Jan: *The parties charged were defended by Mr. Smith, Attorney, Winchcomb.* 29 Aug.

1848: 2 Aug: *Mr. Pruen, a Solicitor, of Cheltenham, a Mr. Russel, of the same place, and a Mr. Smith of Winchcombe.* 28 Aug.

SMITH-STANLEY — Edward George Geoffrey Smith-Stanley

Edward George Geoffrey Smith-Stanley, 14th earl of Derby (1799-1869), was prime minister on three separate occasions: February–December 1852; February 1858–June 1859; and June 1866–February 1868. He was known before 1834 as Edward Stanley, and from 1834 to 1851 as Lord Stanley. He is one of only four British prime ministers to have had three or more separate periods in office; his ministries, however, all lasted less than two years, and he held the post for a total of just over four years.

1852: 27 Feb: *The Conservative party now in the ascendant; Lord Derby Prime Minister, Disraeli Chancellor of the Exchequer, Messrs. Walpole, Lord Malmesbury, and Sir John Pakington, Secretaries of State for the Home, Foreign & Colonial Departments—Duke of Northumberland, First Lord of the Admiralty, Mr. Henley at the Board of Trade, Sir E. Sugden, Lord Chancellor &c.—Good men and true, but can they maintain their ground against active, experienced, and unscrupulous opponents?*

SMYTH — Hervey Smyth [145]

Sir Hervey Smyth, 3rd baronet (1734-1811), army officer, was born at Ampton, Suffolk, the son of Sir Robert Smyth, 2nd baronet, and Louisa Carolina Isabelle, daughter of John Hervey, 1st earl of Bristol. He was a page of honour to George II before entering the Royal Horse Guards as a cornet at the age of 19. On 8 November 1756, at the beginning of the Seven Years' War, Smyth became a captain in the 15th Foot. In 1758 he participated in the expedition against Louisbourg, Île Royale [Cape Breton Island], where he was slightly wounded. He won the admiration of Brig.-Gen. James Wolfe, who wrote to Lt-Gen. Lord George Sackville on 30 July that 'Little Smith ... is a most indefatigable, active, and spirited man and has a just claim to your favour and friendship'. On 4 May 1759 Wolfe appointed Smyth one of his aides-de-camp for the campaign against Quebec. The British force arrived at Île d'Orléans on 27 June and the siege of the city began. On 22 July Wolfe sent Smyth to Quebec under a flag of truce, escorting a large number of women captured the previous day by Lt-Col Guy Carleton during an attack on Pointe-aux-Trembles [Neuville]. On the evening following their capture, in a gesture of gallantry, Wolfe had entertained at table those of the women from distinguished families; he was angered, therefore, when his aide-de-camp was rudely received by Quebec's besieged inhabitants and protested this treatment to Lt-Gen. Louis-Joseph de Montcalm. Nine days later Smyth participated in the disastrous attack at Montmorency Falls, and on 13 September he was severely wounded in the battle of the Plains of Abraham, where Wolfe himself was killed. In his will Wolfe left him and several other officers 100 guineas each 'to buy swords & rings in remembrance of their Friend'. Hervey Smyth succeeded as 3rd baronet in 1783.

1801: 29 Sep: *Sir Hervey Smith drank Tea, & spent the Evening with us.*

SMYTH — Jane Smyth — *see also* Upton *and* Way [146]

Jane Smyth, née Whitchurch (1739-1818), was the daughter of Joseph Whitchurch of Heath House, Stapleton. She married Thomas Smyth (d. 1800) of Stapleton; they had at least 2 sons and 2 daughters:

1 Florence (1769-1852); married John Upton (±1766-1832) of Ingmire Hall, Westmorland; *see below*
1 Hugh (1772-1824); succeeded as 3rd baronet of Long Ashton; married, 20 May 1797, Margaret (1756-1819), fifth daughter of Christopher Wilson (1714-1792), bishop of Bristol, sixteen years his senior; no children of the marriage, although he already had an illegitimate son by Elizabeth Howell, whom he purportedly married in 1822
2 John (1776-1849); succeeded as 4th baronet; *see below*
2 Mary (1778-1850); married Benjamin Way (1770-1834) of Denham Place, Buckinghamshire; their second daughter Eliza married her first cousin, Thomas Upton (1800-1843), son of Florence

Jane and Thomas's eldest son Hugh succeeded his uncle Sir John Hugh Smyth (±1735-1802) as 3rd baronet of Long Ashton, but died without a legitimate heir. He was succeeded as 4th baronet by his younger brother John, who died childless. The baronetcy became extinct, but the property devolved to Florence, Hugh and John's sister, who had married John Upton (±1766-1832) of Ingmire Hall, Westmorland. Florence lived at Ashton Court and changed her name back to Smyth. Following her death in 1852, the estate devolved upon her grandson, John Henry Greville Upton (1836-1901), the son of cousins Thomas Upton (Florence's son) and Eliza Way. John Henry Greville also changed his name to Smyth and was later created 1st baronet Smyth of Ashton Court.

There was an unsuccessful claim to the estate in 1853. One Thomas Provis purported to be Sir Richard Smyth, a long-lost son of Sir Hugh (1772-1824). The claim was heard at Gloucester crown court in August 1853 and dismissed as an imposture.

1853: 22 Apr: *Received a letter from a Solicitor, Mr. Cattlin, Ely Place, desiring me to search my registers for a marriage entry, and entries of a birth and death from 1795 to 1800, all with reference to a presumed marriage of a Mr. Smyth, and with a view to help to establish a claim set up to the large estates of the Baronet Smyth family at Ashton, Somerset, Stapleton, Gloucestershire, and elsewhere.*

SMYTH — John Smyth [147]

John Smyth (1776-1849), landed proprietor, was the second son of Thomas Smyth (d. 1800), of Stapleton, and Jane Whitchurch (1739-1818). He was the younger brother of Sir Hugh Smyth, 3rd baronet. John succeeded as 4th baronet in 1824. He died unmarried in 1849, and the baronetcy became extinct.

1833: *The late Archdeacon Trevelyan, brother to Sir John Trevelyan, a much esteemed Clergyman, was incumbent of Henbury; his successor, the Revd. Mr. Way is a young man, a connection of Sir John Smith, of Ashton Court, in Somersetshire.*

1839: 27 Aug: *Long Ashton is an extensive village, with many enjoyable residences, besides the Court, the seat of Sir John Smyth, which presents an extensive front, and is pleasantly situated on a gently Eminence, in the centre of a luxuriantly wooded park... In days long since gone by, when an Undergraduate at the University, and occasionally resident with my parents at Clifton, I sometimes visited the Lady Smith of that generation with her relations the Marriotts, and more than 33 years ago, very soon after going into Orders, I officiated on one occasion in the ancient parish church of Long Ashton.*

SMYTH — Margaret Smyth, Lady Smyth — *see also* Beckett, Marriott, *and* Upton [148]

Margaret Smyth, née Wilson (1756-1819), was the fifth daughter of Christopher Wilson (1714-1792), bishop of Bristol. She was sister to Elizabeth Marriott, Dorothy Upton (d. ±1796), wife of John Upton, and Mary, Lady Beckett. Margaret married, 1797, Sir Hugh Smyth, 3rd baronet of Ashton Court (1772-1824). Sir High does not himself feature in the diaries.

Sir Hugh was sixteen years younger than Margaret, and apparently independent, extravagant, and an avid huntsman. Why a spirited young man should have chosen to marry an old spinster-daughter of a bishop remains a mystery. The only logical explanation is that he was hard-pressed for money, but this has not been investigated. The marriage was childless, but Hugh had an illegitimate son with his lover Elizabeth Howell, whom he purportedly married in 1822.

1804: 4 Jan: *Accompanied Harriet & Betsy Marriott to Lady Smith's at Ashton Court: Miss Beckett & her aunt were both at home & Lord Stourton & his two sons called while we were there. The house is beautifully situated on the declivity of a hill: of a most romantic castellan stile of building; the oldest date is in the reign of Henry 4th. near 400 years ago. Repton has proposed several plans to Sir Hugh, some of which will be adopted.* 3 Jan: *Drank Tea with Lady Smith's party, & passed the Evening very pleasantly.* 25 Aug: *Mr. Townsend called on us & accompanied Mrs. Bates, my Father & Mother & myself on a Jaunt to Brockley Combe, a picturesque, rocky woody valley in Somerset 8 miles distant: passed thro' a rich & beautiful valley, & the sweet villages of Ashton Bourton, Backwell & Farley: in view of Sir. H. Smith's at Ashton Court.*

1805: 31 Jul: *A party in the Evening & supper at Miss Hughes's: less unpleasant then usual: the Markhams, Lady Smith & Miss Sparrow &c.*

SMYTH — Charlotte Smyth — *see also* Poore[149]

Charlotte Smyth, née Montagu (1757-1811), was the fourth daughter of James Montagu (1713-1790), of Lackham, Wiltshire, descended from the earls of Manchester, and Eleanor Hedges (b. 1727). She married Revd Richard Smyth (1756-1837), who was born at Stapleford Tawney, Essex, the third son of Revd Sir William Smyth, 6th baronet (±1719-1777), and Abigail (1716-1787), daughter of Andrew Wood of Shrewsbury. He was educated at St John's College, Cambridge, and was rector of Stapleford Tawney and Theydon Mount, Essex, from 1780 to his death in 1837. He was also rector of Little Warley, Essex, from 1800 to his death. It is not known if the couple had any children. One reference refers to a son Richard, but it does not seem reliable and nothing firm has been discovered.

Charlotte Smyth's obituary in the *Gentleman's Magazine* was overflowing with praise:

> [She was] perhaps the most celebrated person of her time, for exquisite beauty and symmetry of form which happily received additional lustre from high mental accomplishments ... Her death, it is supposed, was accelerated by the death of her nephew, Capt Frederick Montagu, who so gallantly distinguished himself at the late battle of Albuera, and gloriously fell in the arms of Victory.

1806: 25 Sep: *Walked with my Father & Mother to pay a morning visit to Mrs. Poore of Wedhampton, and her Sister, Mrs. Smith, the former my parishioner ...*

1807: 6 Feb: *Called upon Mrs. Poore & her sister Mrs. Smith at Wedhampton.* 11 Feb: *Dined at Wedhampton not unpleasantly with Mrs. Poore & Mrs. Smith.* 16 May: *... fine enough to drive my Mother to call upon Mrs. Poore at Wedhampton, with whom we met Mrs. Smith.* 22 May: *Mr. Butcher Senr., Mr. & Mrs. W. Butcher, Miss Carter, Mrs. Poore, Mrs. Smith & Miss Legg drank tea & supped with us.* 2 Jun: *Walked to Wedhampton called on Mrs. Poore & Mrs. Smith.* 4 Jun: *Drove my Mother to tea at Wedhampton with Mrs. Poore, Mrs. Smith still there.* 23 Jun: *Drove my Mother upon the Andover Road in the Evening & called upon Mrs. Warrener with whom we found Mrs. Poore & Mrs. Smith.*

SMYTH-PIGGOTT — *see* Piggott

SNEYD — the Sneyd family of Ashcombe Park, Leek — *see also* Newdigate [150]

Radulphus Sneyd (1723-1793), landed proprietor, of Ashcombe Park, Leek, Staffordshire, was married to Barbara Bagot (1725-1797); they had at least 7 sons and 8 daughters:

1 Frances (1750-1809); married Francis Newdigate (±1752-1835)
1 Walter (±1752-1829)
2 Ralph (1753-1808); married, at Westminster, 14 December 1780, Penelope Moore
3 Edward (1754-1776)
2 Charlotte (1756-1829)
3 Sarah (b. 1756)
4 Barbara (1757-1829)
5 Anne (1758-1826)
6 Elizabeth (1759-1827)
7 Mary (1760-1823); died unmarried
4 William (1761-1823)
5 John (1763-1836)
8 Henrietta (1765-1854)
6 Henry (1767-1800)
7 George (1768-1815)

1802: 13 Sep: *Rode with Mr. Granville & Fanny. Walked. Miss Sneads dined at Calwich.* 1 Oct: *Miss Sneyd, Mr. Newdigate & Mrs Palmer dined at Calwich.*

SNOOK — Henry Snook

1807: 17 Dec: *Called upon John Dunford, Harry Snook, Mrs. Cook, Matthew North &c.*

1808: 18 Mar: *Mr. Harry Snook called. Read with attention Dr. Gillies's new History of old times.*

SNOW — Mr Snow of Naunton

1820: 28 Feb: *The Anabaptist meeting House at Naunton was erected by Subscription for the use of the Church (as they term it) assembling there. Since the demise of its regular Minister some years since there has been no appointment of a permanent successor (ordained according to their tenets:) the worship has been uncertainly performed, & the Sacraments not administered. The adherents of the party now holding Antinomian doctrines & recently seceders from our church, who consider Mr. Snow as their leader & pastor, gained entrance some time ago into this meeting, and a majority of the Subscribers profess the new opinions.*

SNOW — Anne Snow, Valentina Snow, and the Snow family — *see also* Paul *and* Clitherow[151]

The diaries refer to Ann[e] Snow (1752-1810) and Valentina Snow (1747-1826). The Snow and Paul families were from the London banking fraternity, connected by several intermarriages. Robert Snow (1720-1772), of Mill Hill, Middlesex, married, at St Mary's, Hendon, Middlesex, 4 April 1742, Valentina (1723-1756), daughter of George Paul (1680-1755) and Susannah Malin (1695-1757); they had 3 sons and 3 daughters:

- 1 Thomas (b. & d. 1743)
- 2 George (1745-1822); married, 24 July 1766, Elizabeth (1745-1772), daughter of Sir Onesiphorus Paul, 1st baronet (1706-1774), and Catherine Paul of Hill House, Rodborough, Gloucestershire; the Paul family also had property in Langton, Dorset; 1 son and 2 daughters:
  - 1 Robert Snow Paul (1768-1849); married, at Langton, Long Blandford, Dorset, 1795, Charlotte Ellis (±1760-1838); inherited the Rodborough and Woodchester estate following the death of his uncle, Sir George Onesiphorus Paul, 2nd baronet (1746-1820); changed his name to Paul
  - 1 Jane (1770-1847); married, at Langton, Dorset, 12 January 1795, James Clitherow (1766-1841); no children
  - 2 Valentina Elizabeth (b. & d. 1772); died at five months, shortly after the death of her mother

  George married, secondly, Elizabeth Woodcock; 3 sons:
  - 1 George Snow (1782-1815); died at Ostend, West-Vlaanderen, Belgium
  - 2 Edward (1783-1790); lived at Langton, Long Blandford, Dorset
  - 3 Thomas (1785-1867), Church of England clergyman; married, at Micheldever, Hampshire, 19 December 1815, Maynard Eliza D'Oyly (1785-1866); 3 sons and 3 daughters:
    - 1 George D'Oyly (1818-1885), Church of England clergyman
    - 1 Harriett Maynard (1820-1899)
    - 2 Thomas Rochfort (1821-1904)
    - 2 Eliza D'Oyly (1822-1857)
    - 3 Charles Hastings (1824-1900); married, 1850, Helen Clara Piers (±1826-1913)
    - 3 Isabella Maud (1826-1850)
- 1 Valentina (1747-1826); died unmarried
- 2 Ann[e] (1752-1810); died unmarried
- 3 Robert (1754-1835); married, at Waterford, Ireland, 1777, Margaret Strahan; at least 1 son:
  - 1 Robert (b. 1778); married Margaret Strahan, presumably a cousin; 3 sons and 1 daughter:
    - 1 William (1807-1886); took the name Strahan; married, 9 February 1837, Elizabeth Anne Dorothea Fisher
    - 2 Robert (b. 1805)
    - 1 Margaret (b. 1810)
    - 3 Henry (1811-1874), Church of England clergyman; *see below*
- 4 Francis (1755-1794); married, at Salisbury, January 1775, John Paul; at least 1 son:
  - 1 Robert Paul (1778-1805); died at sea off Trinidad

From the diary of Agnes Witts it may be surmised that George Snow's second wife, Elizabeth Woodcock, probably died in or just before 1788. Agnes's diary entry for 2 June 1788 reads as follows: '... left Salisbury before 9: a pleasant open drive of 22 miles to Blandford, where we went without stopping, the Crown a good Inn & the Town chearfull while Dinner was getting, walket up to Mr. Snows at Langton more than a mile to see his three Boys, fine children in a melancholly situation poor things ...'

In the diaries of both Agnes and Francis Witts, 'Miss Snow' refers to Valentina, whereas Ann is always referred to as 'Miss Ann[e] Snow' in full. The Snow family tree lists Ann without a final 'e', as does Francis Witts, but Agnes always added the 'e' at the end. The family tree also shows that Valentina died in 1800, but this is an error; she died at Sunbury in November 1826. Regarding the entry for 26 February 1808, it is unclear who Mr V. Snow is. It is not clear how and where Agnes came to know the Snow family, but both Valentina and Anne were probably her most frequent correspondents.

1801: 17 May: *Miss Snow called upon us early after breakfast, and much pleased us by their warm friendship.* 19-20 May, 22 May, 26-27 May, 29 May, 31 May: *Accompanied Mr. R. Snow & the two Sempstresses, to Church at the Trinity Chapel.* 2 Jun., 4 Jun., 7 Jun., 10 Jun., 2 Jul: *Dinner at the Snows where we met with a hearty reception; & in the evening were joined by Mrs. Beavert, Miss Hickes, Mr. & Miss Webb, & Mr. T. Snow.* 5-6 Jul., 8 Sep., 15 Sep., 17-19 Sep., 23 Sep., 6 Oct., 12-13 Oct., 15 Oct., 17 Oct., 19 Oct., 21-22 Oct., 24-25 Oct.

1803: 2 Sep: *Found Miss Ann Snow laid up with a bad leg.* 3 Sep: *Househunting for Miss Snows.* 26 Sep.

1805: 2 Aug: *Very bad account from Sunbury of Mrs. A. Snow's health.* 3-5 Aug.

1808 26 Feb: *Paid Mr. V. Snow a visit immediately after breakfast. The good lad is occupying Lady Middletons House in Portman Square... Sat an hour with the Mrs. Snow's: Mrs. Anne deplorably altered & her maladies hopeless; met there Mr. & Miss Webb, & Mrs. Clitherow.*

1810: 6 Oct: *The Evening we spent as usual most agreeably at Mr. Snow's. Mr. Snow, Mr. D. Paul, Miss Webb, Col. & Mrs. Clithero &c.*

1827: 7 Sep.

SNOW — Henry Snow[152]

Henry Snow (1811-1874), Church of England clergyman, was born in the parish of St James, Westminster, Middlesex, the son of Robert Snow (b. 1778) (*above*) and Margaret Strahan. He married, at Cirencester, Gloucestershire, 30 July 1846, Jane Mary Louisa Howman (1826-1892); they had 1 son and 6 daughters:

- 1 Jane (1848-1888)

2 Edith (b. 1850)
1 Henry Arthur (1852-1876)
3 Mary M. (b. 1855)
4 Jessie Louisa (1857-1933)
5 Katharine Annie (b. 1860)
6 Grace Susan (b. 1861)

By 1843 Henry Snow had become the vicar of Bibury in Gloucestershire. He was still there in 1871, living at the vicarage in Bibury with his wife, Jane, and daughters, Edith, Mary, Jessie, Katharine, and Grace. There is no evidence of him being at Oxford or Cambridge. Francis Witts probably did not realise that he was the great-nephew of his mother's favourite friends Anne and Valentina.

1842: 3 Mar: *To the Justice room, but not till 4 o clock, where Ford & R Waller were my colleagues: present also Winter, Vavasour, Bowen, Snow of Windrush (a Clergyman not long since appointed to that living with Sherborne), Lewes &c.* 27 Apr., 8 Jul.

1843: 16 Aug: *Mr. Snow, the newly instituted incumbent of Bibury, presided at the meeting, and Mr. Perkins was chosen to fill the chair during next year.* 7 Dec.

1844: 19 Mar.

SODEN — *see* Von Soden

SOLE — Mr Sole, solicitor [153]

Messrs Sole, Turner, and Turner were solicitors operating from No. 68, Aldermanbury.

1842: 12 Dec: *... also a letter from a Mr. Sole, Solicitor to the Assignees of Mr. Gilson, Tenant of Nos. 5 & 6 Bucklersbury, making certain propositions with reference to G's bankruptcy.*

SOLLY— Isaac Solly [154]

Isaac Solly (1769-1853), Baltic merchant, was born in Jefferys Square in the parish of St Mary Axe, London, the son of Isaac Solly (1724-1802) and Elizabeth Neal (1741-1819). He was a merchant in the Baltic trade. During the Napoleonic Wars, Isaac Solly and Sons were principal contractors supplying hemp and timber to government dockyards. Between 1817 and 1827 the business traded from 15 St Mary Axe. In addition to this business, Solly was a director of the Million Bank in 1791 and commissioner of the Lieutenancy of the City of London in 1811. He served as chairman of the London Dock Company, founding chairman of the London and Birmingham Railway, chairman of the British and American Steam Navigation Company, and governor of the Royal Exchange Assurance Corporation, having been appointed director in 1817. He was also among the original proprietors of the London University. He was declared bankrupt in 1837 during the banking crisis of that year. He lived at 2 Jeffreys Square, St Mary Axe, in a house that now lies under the site of the Gherkin.

Solly married, at St Martin Orgar and St Clement Eastcheap, London, 23 July 1795, Mary Harrison (1771-1854); they had 6 sons and 4 daughters:

1 Elizabeth (1796-1818)
2 Mary (1797-1880)
1 Isaac (1799-1870)
2 John (1801-1823)
3 Charlotte (1803-1871)
3 Samuel (1805-1871), surgeon
4 William M. (b. 1807)
5 Edward (1809-1810)
4 Lavinia (b. 1812)
6 Henry (1813-1903), social reformer and founder of working men's clubs

---

1804: 1 Jan: *Our comfort sadly interrupted by a letter from Mr. Solly to George recalling the latter immediately.*

SOMERSET — Captain Somerset, staff officer of the district

1846: 15 Jul: *Wrote to Capt. Somerset, Staff Officer of the District, who is expected tomorrow at Stow to pay the Pensioners, on behalf of the widow of B. Carey, that she may receive his quarter's pension.* 16 Jul: *When at Stow I had an interview with Capt. Somerset, the staff officer of the district as to the pension of the late B. Carey.* 28-29 Jul.

SOMERSET — Charles Henry Somerset [155]

Charles Henry Somerset (1767-1831), army officer, MP, colonial governor, and landed proprietor, was born at Badminton, Gloucestershire, the second son of Henry Somerset, 5th duke of Beaufort (1744-1803), and Elizabeth (1747-1828), second and youngest daughter of Adm. Edward Boscawen. Charles Henry was the brother of Arthur John Henry Somerset, Robert Edward Henry Somerset, Fitzroy James Henry Somerset, and Henry Charles Somerset, marquis of Worcester. Charles was educated at Westminster School and Trinity College, Oxford. He married, first, at St John the Baptist, Hillingdon, Middlesex, 17 June 1788, Elizabeth (1766-1815), daughter of William, 2nd Viscount Courtenay; they had 3 sons and 3 daughters, including:

1 Elizabeth (1790-1872); married, at St George's, Hanover Square, Westminster, 18 July 1812, Henry Wyndham (1790-1860)
2 Mary Georgiana (1793-1856); married, at Westminster, 25 June 1833, Stirling Freeman Glover (1796-1866)
1 Henry (1794-1862), Lt-Gen.; appointed KCB; married, at Gretna Green, Dumfriesshire, 20 March 1817, Frances Sarah Heathcote (1800-1886); 5 sons and 5 daughters
3 Charlotte Augusta (1799-1864)
2 Villiers Henry Plantagenet (1803-1855), Church of England clergyman

Elizabeth died at Cape Town, South Africa, and Charles married secondly, 1821, Mary (1788-1860), daughter of John, 4th Earl Poulett; they had 1 son and 2 daughters:

1 Poulett George Henry (1822-1875); married, at St George's, Hanover Square, Westminster, 15 April 1847, Barbara Augusta Nona Mytton (1822-1870)
1 Mary Sophia (1823-1869); died unmarried
2 Augusta Anne (1824-1881); married, at St George's, Hanover Square, Westminster, 1 August 1863, Sir Henry Winston Barron, 1st baronet (1795-1872)

Charles Somerset had a political career as well as a military one. He was MP for Scarborough in 1796-1802 and Monmouth in 1802-13. His principal appointments were as follows: lord of the bedchamber to the prince of Wales, 1791-97; comptroller of the household, 1797-1804; privy councillor, 1797; joint paymaster-general, 1804-06 and 1807-13; and governor of the Cape of Good Hope, 1813-27. At Pitt's death Lord Charles lost his place as joint paymaster-general and was considerably embarrassed by the advent to power of his former Whig friends, who were not, however, unmindful of him. At first Fox, with an eye on garnering support from the duke of Beaufort, considered him for the constableship of the Tower; and in April 1806, Lord Grenville wondered whether he was 'of sufficient calibre for the Cape'. Lord Charles went to the Cape in 1813 with a salary of £10,000 p.a. He remained there, an energetic if somewhat autocratic governor, until 1826.

1831: 3 Sep.

SOMERSET — **Granville Charles Henry Somerset**[156]

Lord Granville Charles Henry Somerset (1792-1848), politician, was the second of the ten children of Henry Charles Somerset, 6th duke of Beaufort (1766-1835), and his wife, Charlotte Sophia (1771-1854), daughter of Granville Leveson-Gower, 1st marquess of Stafford (1721-1803), and his third wife, Susannah. He was the younger brother of Henry Somerset, 7th duke of Beaufort. Granville was educated at Christ Church, Oxford, and married, 27 July 1822, Emily (1797-1869), daughter of Robert Smith, 1st Baron Carrington; they had 3 sons and 2 daughters:

1 Granville Robert Henry (1824-1881); married, at Westminster, 18 August 1857, Emma Philadelphia Dashwood (1827-1906)
1 Emily Catherine Anne (1826-1908); married, at Westminster, 10 May 1859, Henry Ayshford Sanford (1822-1905)
2 Constance Henrietta Sophia Louisa (1827-1893); married, at Hertford, 20 August 1857, Rowland Smith (1826-1901)
2 Leveson Eliot Henry (1829-1900); married, at St Asaph, Denbighshire, 18 January 1872, Evah Penelope Rowley (1845-1904)
3 Raglan George Henry (1831-1924); died unmarried

Somerset succeeded his late uncle Lord Arthur to the family seat for Monmouthshire unopposed in 1816 and held it until his death. His elder brother Henry already had a seat for Monmouth Boroughs. Lord Granville, a member of Grillion's Club since 1815, was a ministerialist like the rest of his family; all his known votes before 1820 were in favour of the Liverpool administration. He voted against Catholic relief on 9 May 1817. On 26 February 1819, in his first known speech, he opposed any alteration in the coal duties. He was subsequently a Conservative politician, having accepted junior office under Lord Liverpool in March 1819, when his elder brother resigned his place. He was lord of the Treasury 1819-27 and 1828-30; privy councillor, 1834; commissioner of woods, forests and land revenues, 1834-35; and chancellor of duchy of Lancaster, 1841-46.

1827: 9 Apr., 14 Apr.

1828: 1 Feb: *Both houses of parliament met on Tuesday, and the King's speech ... my old acquaintance, Lord Granville Somerset takes his former seat at the board of the Treasury.*

1829: 13-14 Jan., 18 Feb.

1832: 17 May: *I now come to the actual state of things, as regards the executive power, and this will be best explained by two letters from Lord Granville Somerset, which I have received, one yesterday, the other to-day.*

1834: 21 Dec: *Further intelligence is communicated in the newspapers as to the Ministerial appointments. The Earl of Aberdeen holds the Office of Colonial Secretary, while Earl De Grey is to preside at the Admiralty; Earl Maryborough is to be Post-master General; Lord Lowther, Treasurer of the Navy and Vice President of the Board of Trade; Lord Granville Somerset, Chief Commissioner of Woods and Forests.*

1836: 10 Aug.

1839: 12 Aug., 14 Aug.

1842: 18 Jan.

SOMERSET — **Henry Charles Somerset**[157]

Henry Charles Somerset, 6th duke of Beaufort (1766-1835), politician and landed proprietor, was the eldest son of Henry, 5th duke of Beaufort (1744-1803) and Elizabeth (1747-1828), second and youngest daughter of Adm. Edward Boscawen. He was educated at Westminster School and Trinity College, Oxford. He married, at Lambeth, Surrey, 16 May 1791, Charlotte Sophia (1771-1854), daughter of Granville Leveson-Gower, 1st marquess of Stafford (1721-1803), and his third wife, Susannah. Henry and Charlotte had 4 sons and 8 daughters:

1 Henry Charles (1792-1853); succeeded as 7th duke of Beaufort; *see below*
2 Granville Charles Henry (1792-1848); *see above.*
3 William George Henry (1793-1794); died an infant
1 Charlotte Sophia (1795-1865); married, 12 August 1823, Frederick Gough-Calthorpe (1790-1868)
2 Elizabeth Susan (1798-1876); married, first, 16 April 1822, Edward O'Bryen (d. 1824); secondly, at Stoke Gifford, Gloucestershire, 11 November 1829, James Orde (1777-1850)
3 Georgiana Augusta (1800-1865); married, at Westminster, 30 May 1825, Granville Dudley Ryder (1799-1879)
4 Edward Henry (b. & d. 1802)
4 Susan Carolina (1804-1886); married, at Westminster, 11 May 1830, George Horatio Cholmondeley (1792-1870)
5 Louisa Elizabeth (1806-1892); married, at Great Badminton, Gloucestershire, 22 October 1832, George Finch (1794-1870)
6 Isabella Frances Anne (1808-1831); married, 8 April 1828, Thomas Henry Kingscote (1799-1861)
7 Harriet Blanche (1811-1885); married, 9 August 1833, Randolph Stewart (1800-1873)
8 Mary Octavia (1814-1906); married, 28 November 1837, Walter Rockcliffe Farquhar (1810-1900)

Henry Charles Somerset was styled marquess of Worcester until 1803 when he succeeded as 6th duke of Beaufort. He was nominated and invested as a knight of the garter on 17 January 1805, and was installed on 23 April the same year. Since no knight had been installed since 1801, there were seven vacancies at the time. He bore the queen's crown for the coronation of William IV and Adelaide of Saxe-Meiningen on 8 September 1831.

Somerset was MP for Monmouth in 1788-90, Bristol in 1790-96, and Gloucestershire in 1796-1803, at which point he succeeded to his father's seat in the House of Lords. He was lord lieutenant of Monmouthshire and Brecknockshire from 1803, and of Gloucestershire from 1810; he became constable of St Briavel's Castle and warden of the Forest of Dean in 1812, and high steward of Bristol in 1834; he held all these posts for the rest of his life.

1822: 15 Oct.

1823: 17 Sep., 14 Oct.

1824: 13 Jan., 1 Apr.

1826: 30 Mar., 14-15 Sep.

1827: 14 Apr., 18 Oct.

1829: 13 Jan., 22-23 Sep.

1830: 10 May.

1832: 29 Mar., 17 May.

1833: 8 Apr.

1835: 21 May.

SOMERSET — **Henry Charles Somerset**[158]

Henry Charles Somerset, 7th duke of Beaufort (1792-1853), army officer and landed proprietor, was the first son of Henry Charles Somerset (*above*). He was educated first by Revd Walter Fletcher at Dalston, Cumberland, before attending Westminster School, where he stayed until 1805. Edward Vernon, bishop of York, then took over his education, and he finally matriculated at Christ Church, Oxford. Somerset married, first, at Westminster, 25 July 1814, Georgiana Frederica (1792-1821), daughter of Henry Fitzroy (1765-1794) and

Anne Wellesley (1768-1844). Her grandfather was Charles Fitzroy, 1st Baron Southampton. Henry and Georgiana had 2 daughters.

1 Charlotte Augusta Frederica (1816-1850); married, 5 December 1844, Philipp Roger Franz von Neumann (1781-1851)

2 Georgiana Charlotte Anne (1817-1884); married, at Great Badminton, Gloucestershire, 29 December 1836, Christopher William Bethell-Codrington (1805-1864)

Somerset married secondly, 1822, Emily Frances (1800-1889), half-sister of his first wife and daughter of Charles Culling Smith; they had 1 son and 6 daughters:

1 Henry Charles Fitzroy (1824-1899); succeeded as 8th duke of Beaufort; married, at Hampton, Middlesex, 3 July 1845, Georgiana Charlotte Curzon (1825-1906); 5 sons and 1 daughter; *see below*

1 Emily Blanche Charlotte (1828-1895); married, 20 July 1848, George Hay (1827-1897)

2 Rose Caroline Mary (1829-1885); married, at Highworth, Wiltshire, 4 October 1846, Francis Frederic Lovell (1821-1906)

3 Henrietta Louisa Priscilla (1831-1863); married, 26 June 1855, John Morant (1825-1899)

4 Geraldine Harriet Anne (1832-1915); died unmarried

5 Katherine Emily Mary (1834-1914); married, 20 July 1858, Arthur Walsh (1827-1920)

6 Edith Frances Wilhelmina (1838-1915); married, 10 September 1863, William Henry Forester Denison (1834-1900)

Henry Charles Somerset was MP for Monmouth in 1813-31 and 1831-32, and Gloucestershire West in 1835. He was styled marquess of Worcester until 1835 when he succeeded his father as 7th duke of Beaufort. In 1810, as marquess of Worcester, he joined his uncles Edward and Fitzroy in the Peninsular campaign, and became aide-de-camp to the duke of Wellington, whose niece he subsequently married. While on home leave, after the writ had been delayed so that he could be present, he was returned for Monmouth on his father's interest. He was not opposed there until 1820. A ministerialist, he paired with the government for the continuation of the property tax on 18 March 1816, despite the protests of his constituents. Soon afterwards he accepted a seat at the Admiralty Board, and was lord of the Admiralty from 1815 to 1819. He was primarily a sportsman and socialite and had no inclination for business; he acquired notoriety for his high-spirited pranks and scrapes, not least his liaison with the courtesan Harriette Wilson. He voted against Catholic relief on 21 May 1816, 9 May 1817, and 3 May 1819, though his belated vote was on the latter occasion disallowed.

1835: 1 Jan: *It is suspected that Augustus Morton will offer himself as the Whig Candidate for the Eastern division to sit as colleague of Codrington, and so to leave the field open in the Western division to the Marquis of Worcester, the Tory Candidate.* 4-5 Jan.

1836: 30 Aug., 13 Sep.

1837: 2 Jan., 4 Jan.

1840: 20 Sep.

1842: 22 Feb: *E.F.W. went after breakfast to meet the Duke of Beaufort's fox-hounds at Farmington Grove: his Grace having promised to attend to gratify his sporting friends in this neighbourhood.*

1843: 3 Jan: *He* [Lord Edward] *was not buried, as he had wished, at Badminton, where his wife's remains repose, some obstacle being interposed, it is said, by his nephew, the Duke of Beaufort.*

1845: 3 Apr.

1847: 14 Sep: *Very unpleasant rumours in circulation as to the finances of the Duke of Beaufort.*

1850: 1 Jan.

1851: 23 Jan: *The Duke of Beaufort, though rather restored from a very dangerous illness under which he has been lately labouring, cannot be regarded as otherwise than in a precarious state of health.* 18 Apr.

SOMERSET — Henry Charles Fitzroy Somerset[159]

Henry Charles Fitzroy Somerset, 8th duke of Beaufort (1824-1899), army officer, politician, and landed proprietor, was born in Paris, the eldest son of Henry Somerset, 7th duke of Beaufort, and Emily Frances, daughter of Charles Culling Smith. He was educated at Eton College. Somerset was made a lieutenant in the 1st Life Guards in 1843, and following in the family tradition he was aide-de-camp to the duke of Wellington in 1842, and to Viscount Hardinge in 1842-46. He was made a captain in the 7th Dragoons in 1847, and a lieutenant-colonel in 1858. He retired from the Army in 1861. Somerset was MP for East Gloucestershire, 1846-53; high steward of Bristol, 1854-99; master of the horse, 1858-59 and 1866-68; and lord lieutenant of Monmouthshire, 1867-99. He was also appointed privy councillor on 26 February 1858 and a knight of the garter on 19 March 1867. He married, at Hampton, Middlesex, 3 July 1845, Georgiana Charlotte (1825-1906), daughter of Richard William Penn Curzon-Howe, 2nd earl of Howe (1796-1870), and Harriet Georgiana (1799-1836), daughter of Robert Brudenell, 6th earl of Cardigan, and Penelope Anne Cooke; they had 5 sons and 1 daughter:

1 Henry Adelbert Wellington Fitzroy (1847-1924); succeeded as 9th duke of Beaufort; married, at Trinity church, Sloane Street, Westminster, 9 October 1895, Louise Emily (1864-1945), widow of Carlo, Baron de Tuyll, and second and youngest daughter of William Henry Halford, of Oldown, Gloucestershire, and of the Old Bank, Bristol, and Ellen, daughter of Revd William Tower of How Hatch, Essex

2 Henry Richard Charles (1849-1932); married, 6 February 1872, Isabella Caroline Somers-Cocks (1851-1921)

3 Henry Arthur George (1851-1926); implicated in the notorious Cleveland Street scandal of boy prostitutes in 1889 involving Prince Albert Victor of Wales (1864-1892); fled to France where he lived in exile for the remainder of his life; died unmarried at Hyeres, Provence-Alpes-Côte d'Azur, France

4 Henry Edward Brudenell (1853-1897); married, 17 August 1880, Fanny Julia Dixie (1859-1939)

5 Henry Fitzroy Francis (1855-1881); died unmarried

1 Blanche Elizabeth Adelaide (1856-1897); married, at Great Badminton, Gloucestershire, 21 July 1874, John Henry de la Poer Beresford (1844-1895)

1845: 3 Apr: *The Marquis of Worcester made his first appearance as foreman of the Grand Jury, and was said to have acquitted himself well.*

1846: 10 Aug: *Marquis of Worcester, foreman of the Grand Jury. I took a seat in the Crown Court, and watched the proceedings there* ... 11 Aug: *The Marquis of Worcester with Sir W. Codrington, Robt. Hale, Brownes, & others attended, but only for a very short time, to express their good will, and intention to support the institution.* ... 26 Aug: *A note generally circulated, but without signature, intimates that the Marquis of Worcester having sent venison as a compliment to the yeomanry of the neighbourhood of Stow, has intimated his intention of meeting them at dinner on Friday next, on which occasion my attendance is requested.*

1847: 5 Jan., 6 Apr., 29 Jun., 7-8 Jul., 6 Aug: *The Marquis of Worcester and Sir C W Codrington were quietly elected representatives for the Western division of this County on Wednesday last.* 26 Aug., 14 Sep: *The Marquis of Worcester arrived to preside at the entertainment, coming from Gopsall Hall, the seat of his Father in law, Lord Howe, in Leicestershire ...*

1850: 31 Dec.

1851: 4 Jan., 23 Jan: *The Duke of Beaufort, though rather restored from a very dangerous illness under which he has been lately labouring, cannot be regarded as otherwise than in a precarious state of health. By his decease the Marquis of Worcester would be raised to the House of Peers, and the Division would lose one of its conservative representatives.* 31 Mar., 1 Apr., 4-5 Apr., 18 Apr.

SOMERSET — John Thomas Henry Somerset[160]

Lord John Thomas Henry Somerset (1787-1846), army officer, was the eighth son of Henry, 5th duke of Beaufort, and Elizabeth, second and youngest daughter of Adm. Edward Boscawen. He was educated at Westminster School and Trinity College, Oxford. He married, at Brussels, 4 October 1814, Catherine (1790-1865), daughter of Arthur Annesley, 1st earl of Mountnorris (1744-1816), and his second wife, Sarah (1763-1849), third daughter of Sir Henry Cavendish, 2nd baronet, and Sarah, *suo jure* Baroness Waterpark. John and Catherine had at least 1 son and 1 daughter:

1 Frances Georgina Elizabeth (1816-1862); married, as his second wife, James Whatman Bosanquet (1804-1877)

1 Alfred Plantagenet Frederick Charles (1829-1915); married, 24 September 1857, Adelaide Harriet Brooke-Pechell (1833-1920)

1826: 31 Aug: *... Lord John Somerset, youngest brother of the Duke of Beaufort, occupies the larger seat.* [Hempstead] *He is in the army, & married to a daughter of the late Earl of Mount-norris.*

1827: 15 Apr.

1829: 22 Sep.

1834: 12 Aug: *We were at the Bell in conversation with Lord John Somerset, Dr. Cooke, Archd. Onslow and other anxious blues.* 15 Aug: *Many were the county gentlemen, nobles and clergy, yeomen &c. with whom I mingled in conversation—among them Lords Ellenborough, Edward & John Somerset, the handsome hero of the day, of whom it were to be wished that his talent and habits of business equalled the enthusiasm of his adherents ...*

1836: 22 Dec: *A letter or rather note from Lady John Somerset, acknowledging the receipt of the print of my Aunt Lyttelton which I had presented to Lord John and herself...*

1842: 30 Jun.

SOMERSET — Robert Edward Henry Somerset[161]

Lord Robert Edward Henry Somerset (1776-1842), army officer, politician, and landed proprietor, was the fourth son of Henry, 5th duke of Beaufort, and Elizabeth, second and youngest daughter of Adm. Edward Boscawen. He was brother to Lord Arthur John Henry Somerset, Charles Henry Somerset, Fitzroy James Henry Somerset, and Henry Charles Somerset, marquis of Worcester. He was educated at Westminster School and married, at Powderham, Devon, 17 October 1805, Louisa Augusta (1781-1823), daughter of William, 2nd Viscount Courtenay, and Frances Clack (d. 1782); they had 2 sons and 5 daughters, including:

1 Louisa Isabella (1808-1888); died unmarried

2 Frances Caroline (1809-1890); married, 23 April 1840, Theophilus Clive (1808-1875)

3 Matilda Elizabeth (1815-1905); married, 9 August 1842, Horace Marryat (1818-1887)

1 Edward Arthur (1817-1886); married, at Bedminster, Gloucestershire, 13 September 1849, Agatha Miles (1828-1912)

4 Georgiana Emily (1819-1910); married, 10 November 1852, Robert Neville Lawley (1819-1891)

Lord Edward Somerset, as he was usually known, had a distinguished army career during the Napoleonic Wars. In 1799, while on active service in Holland, he came in on the family interest for Monmouth Boroughs. His father was a friend of Pitt's government, and Edward, when he attended, followed the same line. In 1802 he made way for his elder brother Charles. On his father's death in October 1803, Edward replaced his eldest brother Henry as county member for Gloucestershire and retained the seat until he was defeated for the western division in 1832. He voted with Fox and Pitt against Addington's ministry on defence on 23 and 25 April 1804, and was listed a friend of Pitt's on the latter's return to power, voting against the censure motion on Melville on 8 April 1805. He was joint deputy paymaster-general in 1807-13, lieutenant-general of ordnance in 1829-30, and surveyor-general in 1834-35. He was finally MP for Cirencester in 1834-37. He retired from the Army as a general in 1841.

1824: 1 Apr.

1826: 16 Jun: *... joining the procession of Lord Edward Somerset & his friends to the Shire Hall ... Lord Edward addressed the freeholders in a plain manly style; but his Lordship is more famed for fighting than for talking; his campaigns in Spain, his brave exploits on the field of Waterloo, his affability and attention to the real business of the house of Commons are better claims to the attachment of his constituents than finely rounded periods.* 15 Sep., 7 Oct: *At the lower end of the farthest Northern Aisle is an iron door communicating with a Mausoleum of the Dawkins family, which has a considerable estate & mansion house at Over Norton in this parish, now occupied by Lord Edward Somerset, and at Salford, a village in the vicinity.*

1827: 9 Apr.

1828: 15 Jan.

1829: 13-14 Jan., 2 Apr: *We were much crowded at table, but had a good dinner and pleasant party. I sat near the head of the table between my friends Dr. Cooke & T. J. L. Baker, near me were Sir W. Guise, Webb, Lord E. Somerset.* 26 Jun: *Lord Edward Somerset, our County Member, has also been recently appointed to an important post, that of Lieutenant General of the Ordnance, from which Sir W. Clinton has been removed.* 22 Sep.

1830: 10 May.

1833: 8 Apr.

1834: 31 Jul: *Lord Edward Somerset is to be returned for Cirencester in the room of Lord Apsley, who takes his seat in the House of Lords.* 12 Aug., 15 Aug.

1835: 4 Jan., 6 Jan.

1836: 6 Sep., 13 Sep.

1837: 10 Jul.

1843: 3 Jan., 2-3 Feb., 6 Feb., 10-11 Feb., 14 Feb.

1844: 8 Mar.

1848: 12 Mar., 12 Apr.

SOMERSET — William George Henry Somerset[162]

Lord William George Henry Somerset (1784-1861), Church of England clergyman, was the sixth son of Henry, 5th duke of Beaufort, and Elizabeth, second and youngest daughter of Adm.

Edward Boscawen. He was educated at Westminster School and Jesus College, Cambridge. He married, first, 29 May 1813, Elizabeth (1790-1843), eldest daughter of Lt-Gen. Sir Thomas Molyneux, 5th baronet (1767-1841), and Elizabeth Perring; they had 5 sons and 1 daughter:

1 Henry Charles Capel (1816-1905); married, 10 September 1840, Elizabeth Alicia O'Connell (1818-1892)
1 Emily Georgiana Elizabeth (1818-1894); married, at Dorchester, Dorset, 31 December 1839, Charles George Newcomb (1817-1862)
2 William (1822-1902); married, at Bath, Somerset, 2 August 1842, Helen Donald (d. 1849)
3 FitzRoy Molyneux Henry (1823-1901); married, at Edinburgh, 1 March 1849, Jemima Drummond Nairne (1831-1874)
4 John Plantagenet Edward Henry (1826-1838); died young
5 Boscawen Thomas George Henry (1833-1893); married, at Tiverton, Devon, 24 September 1863, Florence Smallwood Clarke (1832-1874)

Somerset married secondly, 1844, Frances Westby, widow of Cornelius O'Callaghan and daughter of Henry Brady of Raheen Manor, co. Clare.

After a military career early in his life, Somerset entered the Church. His clerical appointments were as follows: vicar of Stoke Gifford, Gloucestershire, 1814-34; rector of Llangattock with Llanelly, Brecon, 1814-51; rector of Magor with Redwick, Monmouthshire, 1821-26; prebend of Bristol, 1822-51; rector (sinecure) of Llanfihangel Cwm Du, with Crickhowell, Brecon, 1823-51; and rector of Tormarton with Acton Turville, Gloucestershire, 1826-51.

1829: 22 Sep: *Lord W. Somerset is brother of the Duke of Beaufort, Prebendary of Bristol, and Rector of Tormarton near Petty France. I rather think, he still holds a family living also in Brecknockshire, near Crickhowell, Llangattock, a good piece of preferment, but requiring a knowledge of the antient British tongue. This was not one of his Lordship's early acquirements, but a powerful stimulus being offered, in the shape of a good income, he applied himself diligently, & in a few months mastered the difficulties of Celtic pronunciation sufficiently to read the liturgy & preach intelligibly to his Welsh congregation.*

SOMMERS — Mrs and Miss Sommers

1801: 5 May: *Mrs. General Forbes, Mrs. Buchan-Hepburn, Miss Bryars, Mrs. & Miss Sommers came to dinner,* [at Lord Elcho's] *also a Mr. Gowdy a parson, a little deaf withal.*

SOMMERS — John Sommers Cocks[163]

John Sommers [Somers] Cocks, 1st Earl Sommers (1760-1841), MP and landed proprietor, of Castleditch, Herefordshire, was born at Droitwich, Worcestershire, the eldest son of Charles Cocks, 1st Lord Somers, baron of Evesham (1725-1806), and Elizabeth (1739-1771), daughter of Richard Eliot, MP. (The spelling of the surname was used interchangeably.) He was educated at Harrow School, Westminster School, and St Alban Hall, Oxford. He married, first, at Claines, Worcestershire, 19 March 1785, Margaret (1760-1831), daughter of Revd Treadway Russell Nash, historian of Worcestershire; they had 3 sons and 1 daughter:

1 Edward Charles (1786-1812), Maj.; died at the battle of Burgos, Peninsular War
2 John (1788-1852); succeeded as 2nd Earl Somers; married, at St James's, Westminster, 4 March 1815, Caroline Harriet Yorke; 1 son and 5 daughters:
  1 Caroline Margaret (1817-1894)
  2 Isabella Jemima (1818-1838)
  1 Charles (1819-1883); succeeded as 3rd Earl Somers
  3 Harriet Catherine (1823-1893)
  4 Emily Maria (1830-1879)
  5 Caroline Margaret (dates unknown)
3 James (1790-1856), Church of England clergyman
1 Margaret Maria (1791-1852)

Sommers Cocks married secondly, 1834, his cousin Jane (1775-1868), daughter of James Cocks, banker of London, and widow of Revd George Waddington. He was MP for West Looe, 1782-84; Grampound, 1784-90; and Reigate, 1790-1806. He succeeded as 2nd Lord Sommers on 30 January 1806, and was created Earl Sommers on 17 July 1821. He was lord lieutenant for Herefordshire from 1817 until his death.

1825: 17 May.

1828: 17 Jun: *Tuesday being the day, on which Eastnor Castle, the seat of Earl Somers, is permitted to be seen, we drove thither in Captain Witts's phaeton, my servant attending us on horseback.*

1832: 10 Apr: *Among other seceders from the Antireform majority of last Autumn we find Lords Somers, Northwick, Coventry &c.*

1836: 22 Jul.

1837: 1 Mar.

SOTHEBY — Miss Sotheby

1804: 26 Aug: *To Dowry Chapel, Miss Sotheby walking with us. Mr. Hawes officiated.*

1805: 17 Nov: *with Car. Townsend, the Ansons etc. Called with my Mother upon Miss Sotheby.*

SOUTH — Mrs South of Urchfont

1806: 30 Oct: *Found Mrs. T. & her whole family of seven daughters at home: the eldest a sweet girl. A Mrs. South with them.* 9 Nov: ... *Evening at Erchfont, to which Mrs. Tinker's family came, calling upon us, namely Mr. & Mrs. Tinker, Mrs. South, & the two elder Miss Tinkers.*

SOUTHEY — Robert Southey[164]

Robert Southey (1774-1843), poet laureate, was born in Wine Street, Bristol, the son of Robert Southey and Margaret Hill. He was educated at Westminster School, London, where he was expelled for writing an article condemning flogging in *The Flagellant*, a school magazine, and at Balliol College, Oxford. He later said of Oxford, 'All I learnt was a little swimming ... and a little boating.' Although his fame has been eclipsed by his contemporaries and friends William Wordsworth and Samuel Taylor Coleridge, Southey's works still enjoy some popularity. In this biographical index, entries are usually reserved for people the diarist knew, met, or corresponded with, but given Francis Witts's enthusiasm for Southey's work it seems right to include him.

1824: 22 Nov: *"The Book of the Church. By Robert Southey Esqr. LDD, &c. 2 Vols. Lond. 1824." Mr. Southey, to whose excellent writings, both in prose and verse, the State, the Church, and sound in principles in general, are as much indebted as the cause of literature itself, has here performed a very great service to the public.*

1826: 17 Nov: *"Vindiciæ Ecclesiæ Anglicanæ. Letters to Charles Butler Esqr. comprising Essays on the Romish Religion, and vindicating the Book of the Church. By Robt. Southey Esqr. Lond. 1826. 8vo." This is a valuable work ...*

1827: 21 May: *"History of the Peninsular war. By Robt. Southey Esqr. L.L.D. &c. In three Volumes. Vol. 2. Lond. 1827.*

4to." The Poet Laureate publishes this work in detached Volumes at distant periods; an inconvenient mode for the reader; but suitable to a voluminous history, for which the Author is gradually collecting & concocting the materials.

1835: 25 May.

1842: 15 Mar: *Mr. John Warter, eldest son of Mr. Warter of Meole, a clergyman in Sussex, married to a daughter of the poet Southey, who has been recently appointed one of the Trustees of my late Uncle Broome in room of Mr. Rogers, deceased.*

SOUTHWELL — Edward Southwell[165]

Edward Southwell, 21st Lord Clifford (1767-1832), landed proprietor, was the son of Edward Southwell, 20th Lord Clifford (1738-1777), and Sophia Campbell (±1743-1828). He married, 1789, Mary Elizabeth, second daughter of Joseph Deane [Bourke], 3rd earl of Mayo, archbishop of Tuam. The couple were childless.

1833: 18 Apr: *His Lordship was a man of retired habits, particularly, towards the close of life: he seldom mixed in publick business, or emerged from the circle of his immediate friends & connexions.*

SPALDING — Dr Samuel Spalding of Devizes[166]

Samuel Spalding (1751-1811), physician, was the second son of Alexander Spalding, of Holm, Kirkcudbright, and Jean Gordon, daughter of Alexander Gordon, cadet of Lochinvar, of Shirmers. His younger brother, the fourth son, was John Spalding (1763-1815), Kirkcudbright MP for Wigtown Burghs (1796-1803), of Holme and Shirmers. Samuel married Sarah (1746-1833), daughter of Joseph Watkins (1702-1790) and Magdalene Gibbs (d. 1794); they had at least 1 daughter:

1 Frances Emma Valentina (±1790-1847); married, 4 April 1809, Maj. George Evans of the brigade of the Portsmouth district of Gosport, Hampshire; 2 sons and 1 daughter (adopted the surname Evans-Gordon):
  1 Emma Georgina Mary Anne (1810-1885)
  1 Charles Samuel Spalding (1813-1901), Capt., 76th Foot
  2 Henry Andrew Grant Evans (1818-1865), army officer, 22nd Regt

There are a handful of fleeting references to the Spalding family in the diaries, but to echo Francis Witts's comments they do come across as ridiculous or pretentious. One snippet has come down to us. In a note to Mrs Stephen Hillman, Mrs Spalding esteemed it a pleasure 'to join Mrs Hillman's party if she intends going to the Play tonight ... Dr and Mrs Spalding mean to shew themselves at the Theatre, if only for an hour'.

1806: 18 Jul., 20 Jul: *A late dinner at Dr. Spalding's: he a plain man of sense, his Lady very eccentric, his Daughter insignificant.* 22 Jul: *To a rout at Dr. Spaldings: a large party, the Hostess more garrulous than ever; I principally conversed with Mr. Mayo & Miss H. Hillier, a very interesting creature.* 29 Jul., 11 Aug: *Dined at Dr. Spalding's, Mr. Spalding his Brother an elegant & agreeable man. The Dr. & his wife highly ridiculous... returned by nine after some sad singing by Miss Spalding.* 18 Aug., 26 Sep: *walked with Mrs. & Miss Spalding, with whom I had an explanation respecting an alteration in the Lady's verses falsely attributed to me.* 17 Oct, 27 Oct., 29 Oct: *Dr. & Mrs. & Miss Spalding called upon us & we proceeded together to dine at Mr. C. Mayo's at Stoke, where we made a very agreeable visit.* 7 Nov.

1807: 2 Jan., 6 May.

1808: 14 Jan.

SPANGLER — Johann Samuel Spangler[167]

Johann Samuel Spangler (b. 1770), schauspieler (actor), was born at Dresden, the son of Johann Spangler. He was married to Johanna Karoline Dorothea (b. 1776), who was a 'schauspielerin' from Stralsund on the Baltic coast. Spangler was elected to the freemasons' lodge of Große Loge Preßen gennant Royal York zur Freundschaft in 1805, and appears to have been active in Weimar up to 1807.

1798: 2 Sep.

1800: 17 Mar: *... well acted by Vohs, Malkolmi, Vohsin, Weyrauch, Spangler, Genast, Haide, & Becker.* 31 Mar.

SPARROW — Miss Sparrow at Cheltenham

1805: 31 Jul: *A party in the Evening & supper at Miss Hughes's: less unpleasant then usual: the Markhams, Lady Smith & Miss Sparrow &c.*

SPARROW — Miss Sparrow at Eyford

1842: 6 Sep: *Walked with Miss Daniell to Eyford: called on Mrs. Payne, Mrs. Dolphin being from home: saw her with her guests, Mrs. Ware and Miss Sparrow.* 10 Sep., 14 Sep.

SPEIRS — the Speirs family of Elderslie, Dunmore Park, and Edinburgh[168]

Mary Speirs, née Buchanan (±1735-1818), was the daughter of Peter Buchanan of Silverbank and Auchentorlie. She was the second wife of Alexander Speirs (1714-1782), of Elderslie, and a widow for thirty-six years. Her eldest son Archibald (1758-1832) inherited the Elderslie estate, and her second son Peter (1761-1829) was an eminent Glasgow merchant in tobacco and other merchandise; he built the large cotton spinning mill that brought Fintry into the industrial world. Mary's Edinburgh town house was at 59 George Street. She appears to have also had a country home near Dunmore Park, between Falkirk and Stirling. According to Agnes Witts, it was very close to the banks of the River Forth; the Witts family visited on 23 September 1794. The Speirs seem to have been associated with or related to the Mure family. There were at least four daughters; from the diaries we know that two of them were named Helen and Grace.

1801: 6 Apr: *Mrs. Mure looking younger, if possible & the Spiers's all arrayed in black.* 9 Apr: *Mrs. & Miss Spiers's called upon us in the forenoon.*

SPENCE — Miss Spence, governess to the daughters of Canon Ford

1829: 3 Jul: *... not prevent our dining to-day with the Fords, the Evening after sundry laudable exertions of finger & voice by the young musical aspirants of the house, my friend's four little daughters, we had a brief but great treat in three songs admirably sung by Miss Spence, the young ladies governess, who seems to be a perfect proficient in music.*

SPENCER — Charles Christopher Spencer — *see also* Backhouse

Charles Christopher Spencer (1827-1880) was the eldest son of Revd Charles Spencer, vicar of Bishop's Stortford. He was educated at Queen's College, Oxford (BA 1842; MA 1847), and was rector of Benefield, Northamptonshire, 1851-77. He married, 1851, Jane, third daughter of John Backhouse, under-secretary of state for foreign affairs.

1850: 31 Oct: *Recd. a letter from Fanny Backhouse.... her sister Jane is engaged to marry a clergyman in the Isle of Wight, by name*

Spencer, who, I believe, was one of the Curates of the Tractarian Mr. Bennet of St. Paul's, Chelsea, to whom, his family, and ministry, the Miss Backhouse are much attached. 9 Nov.

1851: 30 Mar: *The marriage between Jane Backhouse and the Revd. Mr. Spencer will take place soon after the Brother's wedding, which may be solemnized in Easter week.* 7 May: *Received cards announcing the marriage of the Revd. C. C. Spencer to Jane Backhouse.*

SPENCER — George John Trevor Spencer [169]

George John Trevor Spencer (1799-1866), bishop of Madras, was the son of William Spencer (1769-1834). His grandfather was Lord Charles Spencer and his great-grandfather was Charles Spencer, 3rd duke of Marlborough. He was educated at University College, Oxford. He served as perpetual curate of Buxton until his appointment as bishop of Madras in 1837. He attained the post through the influence of his brother-in-law John Hobhouse, 1st Baron Broughton. After resigning the see in 1849, Spencer was appointed minister of the English protestant Marbœuf chapel in Paris. He was later chancellor of St Paul's Cathedral, and finally rector of Walton on the Wolds, Leicestershire.

1842: 12 Jul.

1848: 3 Feb., 7 Feb., 8 Feb: *A large & agreeable party: the Bp. of Madras, the Rural dean, Ford, with his daughters Jemima and Dulcibella ...*

SPENCER — Edwin Spencer, tailor at Stow-on-the-Wold [170]

Edwin Spencer (1813-1870), tailor, was born at Stow-on-the-Wold, the son of William Spencer (1781-1845), agricultural labourer, and Mary Farmer (1781-1850). He married, at Coventry, 6 August 1833, Ann (1807-1870), born at Wappenbury, Warwickshire, the daughter of John and Hannah Hall. They lived at 19 Sheep Street and do not appear to have had children. Edwin had several siblings in Stow, including the following 3 brothers and 4 sisters:

1 Selina (b. 1802)
2 Caroline (1804-1865)
3 Naomi (1806-1874)
4 Matilda (1808-1857)
1 Frederick (1810-1887)
2 Nimrod (1816-1861)
3 Arthur (b. 1818)

By 1861 Edwin and Ann had moved to Coventry, where they both died.

1845: 29 May: *Met Mr. Spencer, a Tailor at Stow, with Messrs. Lea and Davis, as Trustee of the Upper Slaughter Church and Charity Estate, and Church warden of U.S., and finally agreed with Spencer to take as an apprentice Robert Clack, a young parishioner of Upper Slaughter, who has lost a leg by amputation at Gloucester Infirmary.* 12 Jun: *Robt. Clack of Upper Slaughter, the poor fellow whose leg has been lately amputated, was apprenticed to Spencer, tailor, Stow—the apprentice fee being paid by the Trustees of the Upper Slaughter Church and Charity Estate.*

SPENCER — John Charles Spencer [171]

John Charles Spencer, 3rd Earl Spencer (1782-1845), politician and landed proprietor, was the eldest son of George John Spencer, 2nd Earl Spencer. He was educated at Harrow School and Trinity College, Cambridge, and began a lengthy career in politics. He was MP for Okehampton, 1804-06; Northamptonshire, 1806-12; and Northamptonshire South, 1832-34. He was chancellor of the exchequer and leader of the House of Commons in 1830-34. He was styled Viscount Althorpe from 1783 to 1834, when he succeeded his father as 3rd Earl Spencer.

1833: 29 Feb., 11 Mar: *I have noticed the supposed healing measure introduced by Lord Althorp in the H. of Commons.* 13 Mar: *The Irish Disturbances bill, having passed through the House of Lord's, has been introduced into the commons by Lord Althorp, where its first reading has been fiercely but ineffectually contested by a desperate minority of radicals and repealers for several successive nights.*

1834: 16 Nov: *The newspapers announce the dissolution of Lord Melbourne's administration, an event not generally expected. The decease of Earl Spencer and his Son Lord Althorp's elevation to the Peerage have led to this issue. It is stated that the King told Lord Melbourne that, as Lord Spencer could no longer hold the office of Chancellor of the Exchequer, it must be considered that the Ministry was defunct.*

SPENCER-CHURCHILL — George Spencer-Churchill [172]

George Spencer-Churchill, 6th duke of Marlborough (1793-1857), politician and landed proprietor, was born at Bill Hill, Wokingham, Berkshire, the eldest son of George Spencer [later Spencer-Churchill], 5th duke of Marlborough (1766-1840), and Susan (1767-1841), daughter of John Stewart, 7th earl of Galloway. He was educated at Eton College and Christ Church, Oxford, and entered politics. He was MP for Chippenham in 1818-20, and for Woodstock in 1826-31, 1832-35, and 1838-40. He was styled the marquess of Blandford from 1817 to 1740, and was lord lieutenant of Oxfordshire in 1842-57.

Spencer-Churchill married, first, at St George's, Hanover Square, Westminster, 13 January 1819, his first cousin, Jane (1798-1844), daughter of George Stewart, 8th earl of Galloway; they had 3 sons and 1 daughter:

1 Louisa (±1820-1882); married Robert Spencer, son of Francis Spencer, 1st Baron Churchill
1 John Winston (1822-1883); succeeded as 7th duke of Marlborough
2 Alfred (1824-1893); married Harriet, daughter of Frederick Gough-Calthorpe, 4th Baron Calthorpe
3 Alan (1825-1873); married Rosalind Dowker

He married secondly, 10 June 1846, Charlotte Augusta (1818-1850), daughter of Henry Flower, 4th Viscount Ashbrook; they had 1 son and 1 daughter:

1 Almeric Athelstan (1847-1856); died young
1 Clementina Augusta (1848-1886); married John Pratt, 3rd Marquess Camden

Spencer-Churchill married thirdly, 18 October 1851, his first cousin, Jane Francis Clinton (1818-1897), daughter of Edward Richard Stewart and granddaughter of John Stewart, 7th earl of Galloway; they had 1 son:

1 Edward (1853-1911); married Augusta, daughter of Maj. George Drought Warburton

---

1840: 26 Mar: *W B Pole informed me that he had learnt from his Father that there was another change in Otway's views: that he had resigned the office of Superintendent of in the Essex Constabulary to accept that of Porter at the principal lodge at Blenheim Park, to which he had been recommended by the Metropolitan Commissr. of Police, who had been requested by the new Duke of Marlborough to send him a proper person.*

1844: 18 May: *A packet from Otway with a document circulated by the D. of Marlborough, being the copy of a letter written to him by Mr. Bowles, the Incumbent of Woodstock, illustrating the secret history of the opposition recently got up to the return of the M. of Blandford for Woodstock.*

SPITZEDER — Johann Baptist Spitzeder[173]

Johann Baptist Franz Peregrinus Spitzeder (1764-1842), actor and noted bass singer, was born in Salzburg, Austria, the son of Franz Anton Spitzeder (1732-1796). His father had complained to Archbishop Colloredo when Mozart was appointed in his place as keyboard tutor at the Kappelhaus. From 1786 to 1788 Spitzeder (junior) was in Gustav Friedrich Grossmann and Christian Wilhelm Klos's company; he was engaged in Cologne, Düsseldorf, Bonn, and Aachen. From there he moved to the theatre in Bonn, which opened on 3 January 1789, when the 19-year-old Ludwig von Beethoven played viola in the orchestra. From November 1796 Spitzeder was in Karl Haßloch's company in Kassel; his debut in Weimar was on 27 September 1799 as Osmin in Mozart's singspiel *Die Entführung aus dem Serail* (*The Abduction from the Seraglio*). In 1804, having gone through a period of severe financial hardship, Spitzeder was briefly employed at the theatre in Vienna. Later in life he was music director at various theatres.

1798: 2 Sep: *The Opera is not now* (summer 1800) *in so flourishing a Condition as when first I came, Stermins as bass, was much superior to Spitzeder, & Weyrauch acted excellently in the Opera buffa, but as for the rest, they have no tolerable Tenor, & besides Mad.selle Jagemann not one good Actress.*

1799: 26 Oct: *Two Songs by her inimitable Graf Almavira by Haltenhof who shewed much more Spirit & sung better than usual. Figaro by Weyrauch as usual most amusing & Doctor Bartholo by Spitzer very well indeed.* 4 Dec: ... *best actors Vohs, Becker, Genast, Haide, Weyrauch, Spitzeder, & Schall.,* 7 Dec: *The best performers were Jagemann, Matiegzeck, Weyrauch, & Spitzeder.*

1800: 26 Feb., 3 Mar., 8 Mar: ... *well done by Jagemann, Vohsin, Spitzeder & Weyrauch.*, 5 Apr.

SPRING — George Thomas Spring[174]

George Thomas Spring (1819-1855), Church of England clergyman, was the second son of Revd Frederick Spring, Madras chaplain, of Tillicherry, India, and his wife, Jane. He was educated at St Edmund Hall, Oxford (BA 1840; MA 1843), and married, at St Peter in the East, Oxford, 31 December 1844, Emma, daughter of Revd John Hill; they had at least 1 son and 2 daughters:

1 Emma S. (b. ±1845)
2 Fanny J. (b. ±1848)
1 George H. (b. ±1849)

In the 1851 census the family was registered at Aylesbury, Buckinghamshire; Spring was listed as chaplain to the Buckinghamshire Infirmary. He was perpetual curate of Hampton Gay, Oxfordshire, from 1851 to his death in 1855, and appears also to have been a local curate in Gloucestershire.

1844: 29 Aug: *Many of the clergy of the neighbouring parishes attended—Dean of Gloucester, Messrs. Wiggin, Ford, Hurd, Smith, Spring, Dolphin, Hippisley, Perkins, Twisleton, Oakley Hill, Underwood, Bowen, Pantin, and others...*

SPRY — John Hume Spry[175]

John Hume Spry (1778-1854), Church of England clergyman, was born at Bristol, the son of Revd Dr Benjamin Spry (1741-1806) and Harriet Bromfield (1760-1784). He was educated at Oriel College, Oxford (BA 1799; MA 1802; B&DD 1824), and was Bampton lecturer in 1815. He was rector of St Marylebone in 1824-54 and appointed prebend of Canterbury in 1828. Spry married, relatively late in life, at St Marylebone, Westminster, Anne Elizabeth Spence (1796-1846). He married secondly, at the Old Church, St Pancras, London, 17 August 1848, Emily Anne Chapman (1799-1864), widow of Revd R. H. Chapman and daughter of Maj. James Allen and his wife, Louisa.

1828: 25 Mar: *A Prebend of Canterbury void by the decease of Dr. Marlow, has been given to a very excellent man, Rector of Mary-le-bone, Dr. Spry: he was formerly Fellow of Oriel, preached the Bampton Lectures, was Minister of the Free Church at Birmingham, and within these few years placed at the head of the vast parish of St. Mary le bone, now divided into five districts.*

1832: 15 Mar.

1845: 30 Jan.

SPURRIER — Miss Spurrier, visitor at Eyford

1835: 19 Apr: *Mrs. Dolphin and her visitor, Miss Spurrier, passed with us the interval between morning and afternoon services.* 26 Apr., 28 Apr: *Mrs. Dolphin takes Miss Spurrier to her friends in town to-morrow.*

SQUIRES — Mrs Squires at Urchfont

1807: 3 May.

STABLES — Louisa Stables and the Stables family of Betchworth, Surrey[176]

Louisa Stables (1779-1834), visitor at Clifton, was born at Croydon, Surrey, the daughter of John Stables (1750-1835), an HEIC man, and Dorothy (b. 1750), daughter of Sarah Lawrence (b. 1727) and George Paplay of Kingston, Jamaica, Betchworth, Surrey, and Red Lion Square, London. Her parents, John and Dorothy, had married on 16 January 1773. We know of Louisa's name from the diaries of Agnes Witts, and from the same source, that her aunt was a Sarah Hay, née Paplay (b. 1758), although *The Gentleman's Magazine* spells it 'Hey'. Unfortunately searching for Hay and Stables usually produces results relating to horses, so investigation was not simple. A brass plate in Betchworth church, however, has provided some basic information on this family.

Sarah Paplay married, on 5 April 1783, William Hey (±1733-1797), a British lawyer and customs commissioner who became chief justice of Quebec in 1766. He helped to formulate the legal system for the province and sat in the House of Commons from 1774 to 1776. Sarah's sister Dorothy and her husband John Stables had at least 3 sons and 4 daughters:

1 Harriet (1774-1827)
2 Maria (1775-1821)
3 Frances Dorothy (1777-1832)
4 Louisa (1779-1834)
1 Edward (1782-1815), army officer; died on the field of Waterloo, 18 June 1815
2 Frederick (1789-1815), army officer; fought at Waterloo and died of his wounds, 11 July 1815
3 Henry (1788-1830), Col; fought at Waterloo and survived, but suffered from his wounds for the remaining fifteen years of his life

It is uncertain which of the Miss Stables suffered from a deformity, as mentioned by Francis Witts, and quite how many of the Stables sisters were at Clifton. George Romney painted Dorothy Stables with her daughters Harriet and Maria in 1777 and 1778.

Louisa Stables' maternal grandfather George Paplay was a slave-owner and probably a merchant, given that he acted as prize agent in Jamaica in 1763-64. At probate, he was was stated to have owned 335 male slaves and 281 female. None were listed as boys, girls, or children. The estate at probate was valued at £135,539.15 in Jamaican currency, of which £29,983.13 was the stated value of the enslaved people. In his will, proved 5 March 1770, George Paplay made numerous bequests of annuities totalling several hundred pounds per annum. There were also monetary legacies, including £2,000 to Sarah Livingston, wife of Philip Livingston; £7,000 to his daughter Dorothy Stables; £6,000 to his daughter Sarah Hey; and £5,000 to his daughter Catherine. His mother-in-law (possibly from a second wife) Sarah Baxter and sister-in-law Miss Anna Baxter were also left small legacies. Paplay left the rest of his real and personal estate to his son Edward Manning Paplay, except for a house and land at Sunninghill, Berkshire, which he left to his daughter Dorothy. Dorothy's husband John Stables left the Sunninghill estate to his daughter Harriet in his will of 1795.

1806: 25 Feb: *To a York House Ball at the usual late hour. Had the mortification of dancing two dances with a very deformed Lady, Miss Stables, at Mr. & Mrs. Roberts's particular desire.* 4 Mar: *Idled my time away in the Evening shamefully. My Father & Mother visiting the Miss Stables's.* 15 Mar: ... *in a small party at Lady Ford's; Mrs. & Miss O Callaghan, Mrs. Salter & Isabella, Honble. Mr. Yorke, Cox, & the Miss Stables. Miss Ford upon the Piano, Miss M. Stables upon the Harp in a very superior style, & Miss O Callaghan very moderately singing.*

STACKHOUSE — *see* WYNNE PENDARVES

STACPOOLE — Joseph Stacpoole [177]

Joseph Stacpoole was the son of James Stacpoole and Elinor Ronayne. He married a Miss Evans (forename unknown). He was presumably the Joseph Stacpoole, lawyer of the Middle Temple, who was the subject of a case brought before the assizes in Maidstone on 20 March 1777. Stacpoole was under the belief that he was being embezzled by a person named John Parker, and an incident took place in which a pistol Stacpoole had in his possession discharged, injuring Parker. The case was brought before the Maidstone assizes at the above date, but Stacpoole and two others were found not guilty of wilfully and maliciously shooting at John Parker.

1806: 4 Feb: *Supped at Mrs. J. Auriol's; besides ourselves, the notorious Mr. Stackpole & his wife.* 12 Feb: *When all were assembled, the Room presented a goodly shew, & had not Lord Kilwarden taken a liberty by bringing Mr. Stacpoole, uninvited, Mrs. Salter would have nothing to regret.*

STACY — Daniel George Stacy [178]

Daniel George Stacy (1785-1863), Church of England clergyman, was the son of Henry Stacy of Oxford. He was educated at Pembroke College, Oxford (BCL 1813), and was a fellow of New College from 1809 to 1832. He was appointed bursar at New College in 1825 and dean of canon law in 1826. He was vicar of Hornchurch, Essex, from 1831 to his death in 1863.

1805: 1 Aug: *Met Stacey & Trevenen & walked down the High Street with them.*

1806: 20 Mar: *Conversed with Stacie, the More's, Darke, Burney, Marsh, Priest, Cabbell &c.*

STAFFORD — Miss Stafford at Clifton

Nothing has been found regarding this woman, and it is unclear if her family name was Stafford or Stafford-Jones. It may be that Mrs Lindsay was a relation.

1802: 5 Sep: *Drank tea at Lady Jervis's meeting Mrs. Lindsay & Miss Stafford.* 8 Sep: *Walked with Mrs. Lindsay & Miss Stafford Jones &c.*

1806: 27 Feb: *Accompanied my Father & Mother, Mrs. Cary & Miss Stafford.*

STANHOPE — Edwin Francis Stanhope [179]

Edwin Francis Stanhope (1727-1807), landed proprietor, was born at Stanwell House, Middlesex, the son of Charles Stanhope (1700-1759) and Cecelia Stede (1704-1773). He married, at St George's, Hanover Square, Westminster, 9 August 1753, Catherine (1725-1807), daughter of John Brydges, marquess of Carnarvon, Viscount Wilton (1702-1727), and Catherine Tollemache (1684-1754); they had 1 son and 1 daughter:

1 Henry Edwyn (1754-1814), Adm. of the Blue; created 1st baronet, 1807; married, at Newport, Rhode Island, USA, 23 August 1783, Margaret [Peggy] Malbone (1761-1809); 1 son and 4 daughters:
  1 Peggy (1785-1812)
  2 Catharine (1786-1790)
  3 Anna Eliza (1789-1819)
  4 Caroline (1791-1800)
  1 Edwyn Francis Scudamore (1793-1874); succeeded as earl of Chesterfield; *see below*
1 Catherine (1755-1790)

1801: 27 May: *In the Evening to a party at Lady Lyttelton's, which was musical; The Harp, Grand Piano Forte & voice; the chief performers were, Miss Hadsley, Miss Bowles, Miss Canning, Miss Kearney, the Misses Halifax, Miss Stanhope, le Compte de Montmorency &c.* 3 Jun: *Repaired in the Evening to Lady Lytteltons, where was rather a squeeze & music., Miss Guydickens's, Lady E. Lee, Mr. E. Stanhope, & a French Count & Countess &c.* 10 Jun:
Lady Lytteltons, accidental Music began, Miss Halifaxes sung, & Miss Morley; it was quite a squeeze: a Mr. Wood a nephew of Mr. Sheridan also sung in a very singular style. We met there the Hanbury's, Guydickens, Mrs. Scott & Miss Morley, Sir N. Dukinfield, Sir H. & Major Vavasour, Mr. Doig, Mr. Edwin Stanhope, Comte de Bruges, Miss Nevilles, Mr. & Mrs. Chambers, Miss Hungerford, &c.

STANHOPE — Edwyn Francis Stanhope [180]

Edwyn Francis Stanhope, 2nd baronet, earl of Chesterfield (1793-1874), landed proprietor, was the only son of Adm. Sir Henry Edwin Stanhope (1753-1814), 1st baronet. Stanhope inherited Holme Lacy on the death of the duchess of Norfolk, Frances, née Fitzroy-Scudamore, in 1820, and changed his name to Scudamore-Stanhope. He married, at St George's, Hanover Square, Westminster, 20 January 1820, Mary (1799-1859), born at Calcutta, the daughter of Thomas Dowell; they had 3 sons:

1 Henry Edwyn Chandos (1821-1887)
2 Berkeley Lionel (1824-1919)
3 William Pitt (1827-1891)

1826: 8 Mar: *The property of the Duchess of Norfolk, who lived separate from her husband in a state of derangement at the*

Mansion of Hom Lacy, and survived him some years, having died without issue, came eventually to be divided, between her three nearest of kin, Sir Edwyn Stanhope, son of an Admiral and himself a captain in the royal navy & a baronet, General Burr, and Mr. Parsons...

1829: 22-23 Sep.

STANHOPE — Philip Henry Stanhope [181]

Philip Henry Stanhope, 5th Earl Stanhope (1805-1875), MP and landed proprietor, was born at Walmer, Kent, the eldest son of Philip Henry, 4th Earl Stanhope (1781-1855), and Catherine Lucy (1785-1843), fourth daughter of Robert Smith, 1st Baron Carrington, of Upton, and Anne, daughter of Lwyns Boldero-Barnard of Cave Castle, Yorkshire. He married, at Westminster, 10 July 1834, Emily Harriet (1816-1874), daughter of Maj.-Gen. Sir Edward Kerrison (1776-1853) and Mary Martha Ellice (1793-1860); they had 4 sons and 2 daughters:

1 Arthur Philip (1838-1905); succeeded as 6th Earl Stanhope
2 Edward (1840-1893)
1 Mary Catherine (1844-1876)
3 Henry Augustus (1846-1933)
4 Philip (1848-1923); created 1st Baron Weardale
2 Adeline Aguilar (b. 1850)

Stanhope was MP for Wootton Bassett in 1830-32, and for Hertford in 1832-33 and 1835-52. He was styled Viscount Mahon from 1816 to 1855, when he succeeded as 5th Earl Stanhope.

1832: 27 Mar: *Great talent has been shewn on both sides of the house, but the preponderance of weight eloquence and judgment and acuteness appears to me to have been on the side of the Anti-reformers—Sir Robert Peel, Mr. Croker, Sir R. Inglis, Sir E. Sugden, Sir C. Wetherell, Mr. Praed, Lord Mahon, Lord Porchester and many others spoke with great force and convincingness.*

STANLEY — Thomas Stanley [182]

Thomas Stanley (1776-1857), cabinet maker, upholsterer, and undertaker, was born at Snowshill, Gloucestershire, the son of Richard Stanley (1729-1804) and Ann Hyatt (1735-1818). He married, at Tewkesbury, 7 July 1810, Mary (1789-1864), daughter of Richard Williams (1740-1824) and Mary Coslett (1753-1823); they had 1 daughter:

1 Eliza (1831-1847)

The family lived at 14 Northgate Street, where Thomas was in business.

1828: 14 Apr: *My accommodations for sleeping &c. at Mr. Stanley's, our Upholsterer in Northgate Street, were very comfortable. I have made an arrangement to have a bed there, when I visit the County town, and shall doubtless find it more convenient than taking up my abode at the Hotel.* 16 Jul: *I had taken up my lodgings at Stanley's, the Upholsterer's in Northgate Street, as I did at the last Sessions, and was very comfortably accommodated.* 14 Oct.

1829: 12 Jan., 14 Jul., 20 Oct: *I deposited my carpet bag at my customary lodgings at Stanley's, in the Northgate Street.*

1830: 12 Jan., 2 Mar., 20 Apr.

1834: 11 Oct: *Wrote to Stanley, to bespeak an apartment at his house during the next week, when I attend the Quarter Sessions at Gloucester.*

1835: 7 Apr.

1836: 15 Oct., 17 Oct., 31 Dec.

1837: 2 Jan., 6 Mar., 10 Apr., 4 Aug., 16 Oct.

1838: 1 Jan., 9 Apr., 2 Jul., 15 Oct.

1840: 11 Apr., 12 Apr., 27 Jun., 6 Aug: *Also from Stanley, the Upholsterer and Undertaker of Gloucester, who had been employed in the funeral of Lady Rossmore.* 11 Aug., 17 Oct., 19 Oct.

1842: 8 Apr., 11 Apr: *Reached Gloucester before mid-day, and took up my abode at Stanley's—he is now relieved from apprehension as to the health of his only child, who, when I was here at the Michs. Sessns. was in a very alarmingly precarious state, and remained ill for more than three months.* 14 Apr., 22 Apr., 5 Jun., 25 Jun., 27 Jun., 14 Oct., 18-19 Oct., 30 Dec.

1843 2 Jan., 22 Jan., 1-2 Feb., 16 Oct., 28 Oct., 31 Oct., 1 Nov., 20 Nov., 25 Nov., 30 Nov., 1 Dec.

1844: 1 Jan., 16 Feb, 18 Feb: *A letter from Stanley announces that I am invited to be present at the funeral of Mrs. Gist, my Son also.* 5 Apr., 8 Apr., 12 Aug., 15 Aug.

STANLEY — Thomas Stanley [183]

Thomas Stanley (1814-1881), druggist, was born at Snowshill, Gloucestershire, the son of Abraham Stanley (1770-1838) and Mary Abbits (1778-1814), who had married at Ebrington, Gloucestershire, on 11 December 1806. Thomas married, at St Mary's, Warwick, 19 October 1837, Ann Richardson Lucas (1812-1887); they had 4 sons and 3 daughters:

1 Charles Lucas (1838-1911)
2 Abraham (1840-1911)
1 Alice Mary (b. & d. 1845)
2 Lucy (b. & d. 1846)
3 Ann Richardson (b. & d. 1848)
3 Job Richardson (1849-1929)
4 Frederick Abbits (b. & d. 1856)

1843: 24 Jan: *In the Evening Thomas Stanley, nephew of my good host at Gloucester, once a druggist at Broadway, where he was unsuccessful in business, called to bespeak my interest with the County Member, Codrington, that he might obtain the appointment of Tidewaiter at the Port of Gloucester, to assist him in obtaining which I wrote in his favour to Mr. Codrington.*

STANTON — Daniel Stanton [184]

Daniel Stanton (1778-1832), JP, merchant, and sugar refiner, lived at Clift House, Ashton. He was a Bristol councillor in 1826-34 and mayor in 1832-33, as well as a Gloucestershire JP.

1833: 21 Apr: *The Mayor, Mr. Stanton, was present, also Aldermen Daniel, & Savage, and others unknown to me; they came without state and as private individuals.*

STANTON — William Henry Stanton [185]

William Henry Stanton (1790-1870), JP and MP, was born at Thrupp House, Thrupp, Gloucestershire, the son of William Stanton (1758-1841) and Anne Caruthers (1768-1842). He married, 1823, Jane (1795-1869), eldest daughter of Roger Smith of Manor House, Walworth; they had 5 sons and 1 daughter:

1 William Henry (b. 1824)
2 William Henry (1826-1910)
3 Alfred John (1827-1906)
1 Emily Jane (1829-1895)
4 James Thomas (1831-1906)
5 Frederick Smith (1833-1892)

Stanton was Liberal MP for Stroud, 1841-52, and a Gloucestershire JP.

1845: 1 Jan: *Reached Prinknash with Howell by 5 P.M. and saw all the young people, at and after dinner, till it was time for them to set out for the party at a Mr. Stanton's to which they were invited.*
1846: 11 Aug.

STAUDIGL — Josef Staudigl [186]

Josef Staudigl (1807-1861), bass singer, was born at Wöllersdorf in Lower Austria. He had already been singing in London when he appeared, in 1842, at Covent Garden in the first English performance of *Les Huguenots*. He played the role of Marcel, and the following year he appeared in the English première of Bellini's *Norma* as Oroveso. Through foreign engagements, especially in London, he became one of the most famous bass singers of his age. He was greatly admired on the operatic stage, but even more so as an interpreter of Lieder and an Oratorio singer.

1852: 7 Jun: *The chorus parts were magnificently given ... The principal vocalists were Messrs. Sims Reeves ... Herr Staudigl ... S. Reeves & Staudigl sang to perfection.* 9 Jun.

STAVELEY — Thomas Kitchingman Hutchinson Staveley — *see also* Dolphin, Knight, *and* Hutchinson [187]

Thomas Kitchingman Staveley (1791-1860), army officer, MP, and landed proprietor, was the eldest son of Michael Hutchinson, doctor of physic, and Mary Tanfield. He was the great-grandson of Susanna Staveley, wife of Mr Tanfield, of Carthorp, and daughter of Gen. Miles Staveley (d. 1722) of Stainley. Mary Ann Dolphin was his half-sister.

Thomas inherited Gen. Staveley's estate and adopted the surname Staveley in lieu of Hutchinson by royal licence on 29 December 1815. He was a captain in the Royal Engineers and MP for Ripon in 1832-35. He married, first, 1820, Mary Claridge (d. 1851); there were no children. He married secondly, 1852, Anne Elizabeth (1819-1881), daughter of Michael Andrew Burmester (1781-1851), army staff surgeon, and Mary Barlow (1786-1823); they had at least 1 son and 2 daughters:

1 Miles (1853-1867); died of diphtheria aged 14
1 Roseberry Mary (1856-1931)
2 Martha Charlotte (1859-1935)

1827: 16 Aug: *Besides these Mr. & Mrs. Stavely and the assiduous Captn. Polhill, long Mr. Dolphin's fidus Achates, and guest for months at a time, were staying in the house. Mr. Stavely is half brother to Mrs. Dolphin, being Mr. Payne's eldest Son by her first husband, a medical man, by name Hutchinson; this son was, I have understood, in the Engineers, and having been adopted by an old Genl. Stavely, inherited from him a fortune & took his name. He resides chiefly on his property in Yorkshire, near Rippon.*
1844: 15 Nov.
1850: 4 Jan: *... and very full of a visit she had received during this week from her brother, Mr. Stavely, and his lady.*
1852: 9 Mar: A long letter from Mrs. Dolphin, written from the residence of her brother Mr. Staveley, near Ripon. 14 Mar., 17 Apr. *Mr. Stavely is expected this evening at Eyford, on a visit to his sister, as also a Miss Burmester, a young lady to whom the widower Stavely, now, I believe, hard upon sixty years of age, is shortly to be married. The lady, about thirty years old, was, I believe, a relation of the late Mrs. Staveley.* 19 Apr: *To Mrs. Dolphin, to invite Mr. Staveley to dinner on Thursday next, if it be agreeable to him to leave her and Miss Burmester. Mr. S. and Miss B. attended divine service at my church yesterday. In the evening a note came from Mrs. D. with an acceptance of my invitation on the part of Mr. S.* 21 Apr., 22 Apr: *... other Guests were Sir Henry Vavasour, Mrs. W. Vavasour, Mrs. M. Vavasour, Mr. Stavely, Mr. and Mrs. W B Pole, Mr. and Mrs. Winter. All went off agreeably, Mrs. W.V. sang, and conversation did not flag.* 25 Apr., 1 Jun., 2 Jun: *Mr. S. to be married at Bath to Miss Burmester on Saturday.* 5 Jun: *Mrs. Dolphin gone to be present at her brother Stavely's wedding to-day.*

STAYT — Edward Stayt [188]

Edward Stayt (1807-1864), farmer, was born at Sezincote, the son of William Stayt (1769-1843) and Mary Hambridge (1772-1843). He farmed 100 acres employing six labourers at Swell Hill, Lower Swell. He married, at Westcote, Gloucestershire, 9 March 1842, Ellen Potter (b. 1820), born at Sarsden, Oxfordshire; they had 2 sons and 3 daughters:

1 Mary Ellen (1844-1907)
2 Clara Anne (1846-1931)
1 Henry Edward (1847-1924)
2 William Robert (1848-1918)
3 Nancy (b. 1850)

1844: 22 Feb., 24 Feb.
1845: 18 Jun: *Wrote to Mr. Stait (farmer) as to a dispute between him and a servant.*
1852: 2 Dec.

STEELE — John Maxwell Steele — *see also* Graves [189]

Sir John Maxwell Steele, 4th baronet (1812-1872), barrister-at-law and landed proprietor, was born at Hampstead, Dublin, the eldest son of Sir Richard Steele, 3rd baronet. He was educated at Brasenose College, Oxford (BA 1833), and Lincoln's Inn (1831). He succeeded as 4th baronet in 1850, and assumed the additional surname of Graves by royal licence in 1861. He was high sheriff for Gloucestershire in 1866.

John married Elizabeth Graves (1817-1877), born at Mickleton Manor, Gloucestershire, the daughter and heir of Richard Morgan Graves (±1752-1835) and his wife, Elizabeth Shermor; they had 1 daughter:

1 Frances Elizabeth (1845-1874)

Elizabeth was a cousin of the poor law commissioner John Thomas Graves (1806-1870).

1844: 3 Jan.
1851: 31 Mar.
1852: 18 Mar: *At half past six Lefroy's small dining room contained a large party — Lady Steele, wife of an Irish Baronet, a magistrate, to whom Cheltenham is more pleasant as a residence than the manor house at Mickleton, which fell to his lot with the heiress Miss Graves; who, perhaps, would prefer the country to the town abode.——Sir Maxwell was not of our party.* 29 Mar: *Sir Maxwell Steele presided over his fellows, as it turned out, very creditably.*

STEELE-PERKINS — *see* Perkins

STEERE — Lee Steere Steere — *see also* Witts *and* Richard [190]

Lee Steere Steere [Witts] (1774-1832), landed proprietor, was born in Portman Square, Westminster, the son of Richard Witts (1747-1813) and Martha Steere (1755-1815). After the death of his maternal grandfather, Lee Steere, in 1785, his father Richard Witts appears to have acted as his trustee, managing a wealthy estate with less than careful attention. Lee Steere Witts matriculated at Worcester College, Oxford, in June 1794, and two years later took the name Lee Steere Steere in accordance with his grandfather's will—a condition of his inheritance. In 1797 Lee proposed marriage to a Miss Daniel, a neighbour in Harley Street, but nothing came of it.

A detailed account of the problems between Richard Witts and his son is given in the introduction in volume 1, pages 124-129. Because of his father's mismanagement of his inheritance, Lee became estranged from his father, and seemingly from the remainder of the family. Although Lee Steere Steere was Francis Witts's first cousin there was virtually no connection between them beyond childhood. Equally, there are few references in Agnes Witts's diaries. Agnes met Lee's grandmother, Martha Steere's mother, on 23 May 1785 and 2 June 1785, but the young man is not mentioned. On 23 May 1785, she wrote, 'A universal bright fine Day M^r. & M^rs. R. Witts breakfasted with us, several others friends call'd on us, & we went with my Bro^r. & Sis^r. & M^rs. Steer to three exhibitions.' Edward Witts, Francis's father, feared the young man was prone to idleness, and on 16 February 1796 wrote as much to his sister Apphia, Lady Lyttelton:

> I agree with you in the goodness of Heart of the young Heir—but from the unfortunate mode of Education, he has hitherto gone thro', I hardly think he has Strength of Understanding sufficient to impell him, for the ensuing three year's to finish, what the Variety of Masters, & the Severity of the Trustees have left undone—and a Sage Mentor, on entering into the World, would be, a very valuable acquisition, whether he travells in his own Country or out of it. He has shown no propensity to Vice of any kind—& therefore might more easily be led into the best Course of Manly Studies & Employments, independant of Litterature, but I fear he has a natural Idleness, as well as but little Inclination to Exercise, which is absolutely necessary to form great part of the Enjoyments of Life.

Eighteen months later, on 17 November 1797, Edward wrote again to his sister:

> My Dear Lady Lyttelton, I have lately met with some Gentlemen who were witness to a very very serious offer of Marriage from Mr. Lee Steere at Harrowgate to a Miss Daniel, the Daughter of a rich east Indian, who with his Wife & Son & two daughters Mr. Steere followed from York Races where he recived as he said the first Shot thro' his Heart—from Miss Daniel—The Mother a very vulgar odd Woman was very sanguine for the Match—but the Father gave his Daughter her Choice, & he was refused—& in consequence left Harrowgate, but with a determination to visit the family again in Harley Street, where they live as well as himself. Mr. Taite a Man very eminent in the Law here & Membr. of Parlt. told me he consulted him on the bussiness, & that he gave him very cautious advice, to know the family a little longer before he made his proposals—but his ardor was too great—& in an short absence Mr. Tait was on a visit he made his proposals & was refused, Mr. Tait said his Conduct was in no degree improper, except a little dashing about his Curricle & Horses—& that he opened to him his fortune & view in Life, confessing he knew very little of the world & wished for a private life—he asked him if he knew his Uncle & Aunt in Endinburg & spoke frequently of them—but to his great surprise never mentioned having either Father Mother, Brother or Sister to any one of the Party at Harrogate.—I have written an Acct. of this transaction to his Father, as I thought it right he showd know it: but it a sad proof of his stubborn Rebellion against his father in not asking his Consent on so material a point. The young Lady was a prodigeous fine Singer in the Italian Stile, nor very pretty but a genteel & Elegant figure. I belive they have a place in Yorkshire, as well as their House in Harley Street.

The Mr Tait referred to was William Tait (d. 1800), an Edinburgh lawyer and MP for Stirling Burghs (1797-1800). Interestingly, although Lee Steere was spurned by Miss Daniell, her brother married Lee's sister, Eliza.

Following his estrangement from his father, Lee Steere Steere married, at St Marylebone, Westminster, 21 June 1798, Sarah Harrison (b. 1778); they had 4 sons and 2 daughters:

- 1 Elizabeth (1802-1886); married, first, at St Marylebone, Westminster, 26 June 1823, Revd Henry John Ridley (1790-1834); secondly, at Ockley, Surrey, 28 September 1843, James Scarlett, 1st Baron Abinger (1769-1844); apparently no children
- 1 Lee (1803-1890), JP, DL, and MP for West Surrey (1870-80); married, at Hessle Mount, Yorkshire, 30 January 1826, Anne Watson (b. 1806), born in Hull; 6 sons:
  - 1 Lee (1826-1912), army officer, 88th Regt; married, at Hessle Mount, Yorkshire, 1851, his cousin Margaret (±1828-1898), born in Hull, the daughter of Keiro Watson; lived at Haisthorpe Hall, Bridlington, Yorkshire, and was listed as retired by 1861; lived at 4 Belle Vue, Bridlington, by 1881; moved back to Jayes after his father's death in 1890 and was succeeded there by his nephew Henry; 8 daughters:
    - 1 Sarah Fiducia Lee (b. ±1858)
    - 2 Fideene (b. ±1859)
    - 3 Emily (b. ±1860)
    - 4 Janet (b. ±1861)
    - 5 Harriett (b. ±1865)
    - 6 Margaret (b. 1869)
    - 7 Eva (b. 1871)
    - 8 Grace Muriel Lee (b. 1875)
  - 2 Henry (1828-1899); married, at St James's, Westminster, 4 August 1857, Elizabeth Mary Fitzroy (1827-1899); 1 son:
    - 1 Henry Charles (±1859-1933); 1 son:
      - 1 John H. G. (1895-1914); died in action at Ypres
  - 3 James George (1830-1903); became a midshipman in the merchant service; at sea for fifteen years, finally as commander of the *Devonshire*, a well-known East Indiaman; emigrated to Western Australia in early 1860 and leased 100,000 acres of land in the southern part of the colony; one of the first elected members of the Western Australian legislative council, 1867; won his seat again in 1870 and was chosen to lead the elected members; represented Western Australia at the federal conventions of 1891 and 1897 and was a member of the constitutional committee at both; knighted, 1888; appointed KCMG, 1900; married, at St John's, Hampstead, Middlesex, 16 June 1859, Catherine Anne, daughter of Sir Luke Leake; 5 sons and 8 daughters:
    - 1 Edith Anne (b. & d. 1860)
    - 1 Edward John (1863-1957)
    - 2 Unnamed girl (b. & d. 1866)
    - 3 Marian Rose (b. 1867)
    - 2 Charles James (1868-1940)
    - 4 Mabel Constance (1870-1930)
    - 3 Hubert Arthur (b. 1872)
    - 5 Bertha Mary (1873-1961)
    - 6 Amy Florence (1874-1960)
    - 7 Nina (b. & d. 1876)
    - 8 Alice Maude (b. 1877)
    - 4 Wilfred (1878-1934)
    - 5 Lancelot Henry (b. & d. 1882)

4 John Robert (1832-1881)
5 Charles William (±1838-1900)
6 Augustus Frederick Lee (1841-1903); emigrated to Haisthorpe, York, Western Australia; suffered financial problems (according to an advertisement in the *Perth Gazette and W. A. Times* of 1869) and was forced to make an arrangement with his creditors; seems to have named his estate after his eldest brother's home; married, at Perth, Western Australia, 16 February 1859, Ellen Elizabeth Roe (1840-1887); 3 sons and 4 daughters:
   1 Matilda Annie (b. & d. 1860)
   1 Herbert John (1862-1942)
   2 Ethel Elizabeth (b. 1864)
   2 Ernest Augustus (1866-1957); knighted
   3 Beatrice Maude (1868-1940)
   4 Eva Matilda (1872-1943)
   3 Algernon George (1875-1899)
2 Sarah (b. 1804)
2 Robert Harrison (b. 1807)
3 John Lee (b. 1809)
4 George (b. 1810)

Francis Witts said nothing more of his cousin Lee Steere Steere in his diaries that survive. However, his diary for the period June to December 1832 is missing, and as Lee Steere Steere died on 4 September 1832, it may be that Witts mentioned him then.

1827: 17 Nov: *The remaining £500, 3 per Cent Red. Ann. are left under the same restrictions as the £1000 to Mrs. Rodick, to Mrs. Daniel, daughter of my late uncle, Mr. Richd. Witts, and wife of a Solicitor, who having been guilty in his profession of gross acts of dishonesty, has been compelled to expatriate himself, and lives, I think, somewhere in France. Poor Mrs. D., who is, I am inclined to believe, an estimable person, with bad health, resides at Lyme in Dorsetshire, on slender means, with two daughters, her only surviving children; a son, who had obtained a commission in the East India Company's military service, having fallen an early victim to the climate of the East. Mrs. Daniel is the only one of my Uncle Richard's family, whom my Uncle has named in his will: Mr. Lee Steere, the eldest Son, took with the fortune, which was very ample, the name of his maternal grandfather, & has been from the period of his coming of age alienated from his father's family: having been at variance with his Father, who was an incautious man, and having, more through carelessness than any improper motive, failed to keep regular accounts of expenditure on his Son's account during his minority subsequently to his grandfather's decease, was unable to render such a statement as was satisfactory to the interested advisers of the young man, who had yielded himself to their guidance, & who succeeded in detaching him from both his parents & indeed his whole family.*

1840: 5 Jul: *Mr. D. was a Solicitor in London in earlier life, moving in a very respectable sphere, and partner in a very good house; but many years ago he was guilty of evil practices, amounting, I apprehended, to forgery, to the great injury of the property of his wife's brother, Lee Steer, and on that account was forced to expatriate himself ...*

STENSON — Nathaniel Stenson [191]

Nathaniel Stenson (1775-1862), physician, was the son of Matthew and Elizabeth Stenson of Kensington, Westminster. He married, at Bourton-on-the-Water, 23 September 1802, Elizabeth Snook. By the time of the 1841 census he was a widower, living with his son William (*below*).

1828: 14 Aug: ... *we met rather a motley party: Dr. Stenson, the Physician of the Village, a good practitioner, but not a favourite of the higher classes out of his own Village; he is a Baptist, & what is termed very serious; a well intentioned man, but who has not lived in good Society, having been settled in earlier life at Brentford as an Apothecary.*

1837: 16 Jun., 11 Aug: *We met Messrs. Ford, Waller, Daubeny, Dr. Stenson, Stenson Junr., Coles, Kimber, Palmer, Ransford, W. Smith, Jos. Bryan, Kendall, Wells &c.*

STENSON — William Snooke Stenson — *see also* Waller *and* Mason Cox [192]

William Snooke Stenson (1817-1888) was born at Bourton-on-the-Water, the son of Nathaniel Stenson (1775-1862) and Elizabeth Snooke. He was listed as a gentleman, living on his own means. He married late in life, at Bourton, 15 November 1876, Mary Elizabeth Louisa Waller (1849-1929); they had 1 son and 1 daughter:
1 William Waller (1877-1925)
1 Mary Gladys Waller (1880-1955)

1837: 11 Aug.

1838: 1 Jun.

1839: 27 Apr., 17 May: *Messrs. Ford, R. Waller, Wilkins, Kendal, Polson, W Stenson, Kimber &c. were present.*

1842: 8 Jul: *Among the players were Messrs. Colville, Harry Waller, R Waller, T. Wynniatt, Guise, Stenson, H. Lindow, W. Vavasour, Aitkins, W Bryan, Winter, W. B. Pole, E. F. W.*

1843: 3 Jun., 11 Aug: *About eighteen members of the Club were present; among them Mr. Colville & his brother Col. Colville, Messrs. R. Waller, Stenson, Aitkens, W. Vavasour, E. F. Witts, W. B. Pole, Dickens, Underwood, Barrow, Brookes, H. Ford, T. Wynniatt, Westmacott, &c. Mr. and Mrs. Franks were also spectators.*

1844: 20 Aug: *Visited the cricket field, where met my son who reported well of his wife and children, Messrs. Colville, R Waller, Stenson, Rawlinson &c.* 4 Oct.

1845: 17 Feb., 6 Jun.

1847: 4 Jun: *Between four & five the high table broke up to repair to the Rectory where Mrs. Waller regaled with tea & coffee the Revd. Messrs. Ford, Hunt, Turner & myself—also Mr. Stenson—the Waller children delighted in the band, and flags.* 21 Jul: *My son left us about three o clock for Leamington, Sophy and myself walking with him to the Turnpike gate at Lower Slaughter, where he was joined by R. Waller, and W. Stenson in a fly.* 2 Oct: *R. Waller, with Mr. Aitkens and Mr. Stenson, were gone to Westwell to shoot.* 5 Oct.

1848: 2 Jun., 16 Aug: E.F.W. *rode to Bourton to call on Mr. W. Stenson.* 18 Aug: *E.F.W, Sophy, and Broome went to call on the Wallers and Mr. W Stenson at Bourton on the Water.*

1853: 3 Jun: *At five P.M. the high table broke up, and we of the Rectory party, finding that the ladies had gone to visit Mr. Stenson's greenhouse, followed them thither, where we also found Mr. Arthur Neale. I had never before seen the treasures on a small scale fostered by Mr. Stenson, and was much pleased with his beautiful show of seedling geraniums, cinerarias, and, above all, calceolarias.*

STEPHENS — Catherine Stephens [193]

Catherine Stephens (1794-1882), singer and actress, was the daughter of Edward Stephens, a carver and gilder in Park Street, Grosvenor Square. Having shown, like her elder sisters, some musical ability, she was placed under Gesualdo Lanza, with whom she remained for five years. Under his care she sang at Bath, Bristol,

Southampton, Ramsgate, Margate, and other places. She appeared early in 1812 in subordinate parts at the Pantheon as a member of an Italian opera company, headed by Madame Bertinotti Radicati. She was compared to Angelica Catalani and Elizabeth Billington and had considerable success in opera and concert halls.

In 1838 she married George Capel-Coningsby, 5th earl of Essex, an octogenarian widower who died in 1839. Lady Essex survived him forty-three years, and took an interest in theatrical matters.

1823: 17 Sep: *The exquisite Vaughan, the powerful & scientific notes of Mrs. Salmon, the liquid & thrilling tones of Miss Stephens, the spirit and execution of Caradori, Mr. Sapio's fine tenor, the taste & simplicity of Miss Travis, the deep rolling tones of Bellamy, tho' far inferior to the exquisite judgment science & refinement of Bartleman, afforded a rich treat.* 18 Sep: ... *performers distinguished themselves greatly. Mrs. Salmon, Miss Stephens, Miss Travis, Messrs. Vaughan, Bellamy & Hawes.*

1826: 12 Sep., 13 Sep. *Miss Stephens, the sweetest ballad singer of her age, and deservedly high in her reputation, enchanted the audience in "I've been roaming"; and her duet with Madame Caradosi, "Su' l'aria", from Mozart, was deservedly encored. It was, indeed, beautiful, and not less so Caradosi's solo, sung with admirable delicacy and grace.* 14-15 Sep., 25 Sep.

STEPHENS — George Hopewell Stephens [194]

George Hopewell Stephens (1759-1819), naval officer, was born in the parish of St Botolph without Aldgate, Middlesex, the son of Griffith-Niccoll Stephens. He was commissioned lieutenant in the Royal Navy on 7 April 1778, and was appointed first lieutenant aboard the 44-gun *Janus*, commanded by Capt. Bonovier Glover. The *Janus* was part of Capt. William Cornwallis's squadron which fought a superior French force in the Windward Passage on 20-22 March 1780. When Capt. Glover died of natural causes during the action, Stephens was obliged to assume command; he was able to cause significant damage to the 74-gun French flagship *Annibal* by manoeuvring off her quarters, although in so doing the *Janus* suffered badly aloft. Glover's reputation had recently been tarnished by his officers bringing him to a court-martial, and after the action Stephens was somewhat unfairly castigated by Cornwallis for allowing Capt. Glover to die below in his cabin rather than on deck.

Stephens was commanding officer on HMS *Goelan* in 1793, and was later promoted to commander. As captain he was given command of *Oiseau* and *Tremendous*, flagship in Adm. Pringle's squadron, in 1797. He became caught up in the mutinies of that year and was threatened by his crew on board HMS *Tremendous* with a court-martial on charges of cruelty and mistreatment. The mutinous spirit was temporarily quashed with a general pardon, and Stephens requested a regular court-martial to clear his name. This was held on board HMS *Sceptre* and Stephens was honourably acquitted and returned to duty. Shortly afterwards the crew of HMS *Tremendous* broke out into an open mutiny that spread to other ships in the harbour at Cape Town. Adm. Pringle, who was onshore at the time, ordered the batteries around the harbour to be manned and aimed at *Tremendous*, the source of the mutiny. With over 100 guns pointed at his flagship he demanded the crews return to obedience and give up the ringleaders within two hours, or he would order the *Tremendous* destroyed. Realising that Pringle was sincere in his intent, the mutineers surrendered ten minutes before the deadline.

For a short period from November 1799 to December 1800, Stephens commanded the 98-gun *Barfleur* in the Channel with the flag of Rear Adm. Cuthbert Collingwood. On 13 January 1801 he was replaced by Capt. William Bligh (1754-1817), of 'mutiny of the *Bounty*' fame, aboard the 56-gun ex-Indiaman *Glatton*, which Stephens had only joined a few weeks previously; he was thus deprived of the opportunity of fighting at the battle of Copenhagen on 2 April. Stephens was appointed to the 74-gun *Brunswick*, serving in the North Sea and the Channel and as flagship to the second-in-command at Portsmouth, Rear Adm. John Holloway. Stephens next went out to Jamaica with Cdre William Essington's squadron of five sail of the line in October 1801, and then joined Rear Adm. Sir John Thomas Duckworth's fleet of twenty-eight sail of the line in the West Indies from January to September 1802. In 1813 Stephens was promoted to rear admiral of the blue, and in 1814 to rear admiral of the white.

It seems that Stephens was sent back to Britain to take up his new command on the same ship as the Witts family. He married, at Ealing, 29 November 1800, Anna Maria (1774-1823), daughter of John Bligh (1735-1794) and Elizabeth Titcher (1739-1822). John Bligh was elder brother to Adm. Sir Richard Rodney Bligh and third cousin to William Bligh (1754-1817). George and Anna had at least 1 son:

1 William Stephens (b. 1813); married, at All Saints', Southampton, Hampshire, 16 April 1846, Catherine Saunders Smith (1821-1895); 7 sons and 1 daughter

---

1801: 1 Apr., 2 Apr: *I waited upon the Browns, upon Mr. Sandford, upon Capt. Stephens &c.*

STEPHENS — Maurice FitzGerald Townshend Stephens [195]

Maurice FitzGerald Townshend Stephens (1792-1872), DL, JP, and Church of England clergyman, was the third son of Richard Boyle Townsend, MP, and Henrietta Newenham. He was educated at Christ Church, Oxford (BA 1812; MA 1815), and became vicar of Thornbury in 1823. He held the living until his death in 1872. Townsend married, 1826, Alice Elizabeth (d. 1831), only daughter of Henry Richmond Shute (d. 1855) of Iron Acton, Gloucestershire; they had 1 son and 2 daughters:

1 Henry John Townsend (b. 1827)
1 Geraldine Henrietta (b. 1829)
2 Alice Gertrude (b. 1830)

Alice was the niece and heir of Henry Stephens of Chavenage House, near Tetbury, Gloucestershire, who died intestate in 1822. Following his death the estate passed to his sister's children; first to Richmond Shute who died in 1823, and then to Alice, only daughter of Henry Richmond Shute of Iron Acton. A provision in the will of another Henry Stephens (d. 1795), the last of the elder line of this family, stipulated that an heir through the female line was to drop his or her own name and adopt by royal licence the arms and name of the Stephens family. Maurice Townsend did this on 27 January 1827.

1828: 15 Apr., 15 Jul., 14 Oct.
1829: 22 Sep., 24 Sep., 20 Oct.
1830: 12 Jan., 20 Apr.
1832: 29 Mar.
1833: 13 Apr: *Thornbury is a living in the gift of Christ Church, Oxford: the present incumbent is the Revd. Maurice Townsend Stephens, a gentleman of Irish extraction, with whom I am well acquainted as a brother magistrate on the bench at Gloucester.*
1834: 15 Aug.
1835: 5 Jan.

STEPHENSON — George Stephenson [196]

George Stephenson (1781-1848), colliery and railway engineer, was born at Wylam, Northumberland, the second son of Robert Stephenson, foreman at the Wylam colliery pumping engine, and Mabel, daughter of Richard Carr, dyer, of Ovingham. Stephenson had various coalpit-related experiences in his youth which built the empirical knowledge fundamental to his later success. He advanced, in several essential details, the design and construction of the locomotive.

By the time experiments were being made on the Middleton wagonway, Stephenson was working for the grand allies at Killingworth colliery. He was familiar with the work of engineers Chapman and Hedley, and it seems likely that he had observed at close quarters the Blenkinsop rack-rail locomotive at work on the Coxlodge and Fawdon wagonway. Indeed, Stephenson's own engine, the *Blucher*, constructed at the West Moor colliery workshop during the first half of 1814, followed Blenkinsop's design in detail. However, since the Killingworth wagonway was laid with wooden edge-rails with a metal strip surface, the *Blucher* had two critical operational weaknesses. First, its single straight-flue boiler offered limited steam-raising power when compared with the Trevithick-type return-flue installed in the Wylam engines. In the absence of the rack-rail transmission its tractive effort was relatively poor. Secondly, it proved too heavy for the wooden track, although this can hardly have been a fatal flaw considering that a second locomotive was constructed early in 1815. To these shortcomings Stephenson applied his remarkable engineering talents and dogged persistence, transforming the Killingworth wagonway into the focal point of railway experiment and design after 1815.

The problem of poor tractive effort was soon alleviated, but by no means solved, by the simple expedient of increasing the diameter of the boiler flue and applying the power directly to the wheels by connecting rods, thus reducing the need for crudely manufactured gearing. Further developments were directed towards increasing the longevity of the track; one approach was reducing the damage inflicted by the engine itself. To this end Stephenson collaborated with William Losh, the senior partner in the Newcastle iron-making firm Losh, Wilson, and Bell. Together they produced the so-called 'steam spring', an arrangement of pistons on each axle bearing the weight of the boiler and its attachments. Far more effective were Stephenson's patent improvements to the track, which involved a new method of jointing and more sophisticated rail chairs. These were also produced in association with Losh, and by the end of 1818 the Killingworth wagonway had been relaid with cast-iron edge-rails bearing the Losh–Stephenson patent.

Of the early locomotive builders, Stephenson alone proved capable of viewing railway development as an entity. In perceiving the vital link between locomotive and track he succeeded in demonstrating the economic and practical advantages of mechanical traction. The smooth edge-rail was superior in an engineering and technical sense to both the tram plate and Blenkinsop's rack-rail. In addition, the Stephenson–Losh design improvements reconfirmed the principle first established by Trevithick that the weight of a locomotive was sufficient to provide the necessary adhesion on the rails. The *Blucher* may have been far less sophisticated in its boiler design to the Trevithick and Hedley engines, but in its mode of operation it ranks as the first 'modern' locomotive, reliant upon the force of adhesion via flanged wheels. When it was put to work on the Killingworth wagonway the number of horses was reduced from fifty to thirty. By 1820, when the cast-iron track was relaid with wrought-iron edge-rails, haulage by horses had all but disappeared.

Stephenson was recruited to the Stockton and Darlington Railway project, inaugurated by act of parliament in 1821 to link the collieries of south-west Durham with the mouth of the River Tees. Appointed as engineer to the line with a salary of £300 per annum, Stephenson strongly urged the advantages of steam locomotives over horse traction. He re-surveyed the whole of the proposed line, and early in 1823 a new parliamentary act was obtained with alterations to the original route conducive to locomotive haulage. On 23 May 1823 the first rail was laid. Stephenson advocated the use of malleable iron rails rather than 'inferior' cast iron; he succeeded in persuading the railway company's management committee to form the line with two-thirds of the former.

Stephenson went on to build the first public inter-city railway line in the world to use steam locomotives: the Liverpool and Manchester Railway, which opened in 1830. He is renowned as the 'Father of Railways'; his rail gauge of 4 feet 8½ inches remains the standard gauge for most of the world's railways.

1838: 24 Mar: *Travelled inside with a person of considerable eminence in the department of science as applied in modern improvements, Mr. Stevenson, the Civil Engineer, who may be considered paramount authority on all points connected with Steam, Steam-Engines, particularly, as applied to railroads, rail-roads, coal mines, gas-works & the like.*

STERNBERG — Anthony Augustus de Sternberg [197]

Anthony Augustus de Sternberg (1794-1858) was a minor Prussian nobleman. His parentage is unknown, and the information available relates more to his wife Catherine. Sternberg married, at St Nicholas's, Brighton, Sussex, 30 May 1836, Catherine Augusta (1791-1859), daughter of John Harrison, surgeon and apothecary, and Jane Mary Parkinson of Coopersale, Essex. She was goddaughter to Joseph Steele, of Acrewalls, Frizington. He was surgeon at the London Hospital and a good friend of her father's. When her father died in 1815, Catherine agreed to live with Dr Steele at 9 Trinity Square, London, as his housekeeper and companion. Following his death in 1835 she inherited the estates of Birks and Crosslacon and Frizington Parks.

After their marriage, Antony and Catherine lived at 15 Royal Crescent, Bath. However, by February 1840 they had signed a formal separation agreement and parted ways. The house in Bath was sold in June 1840 and Catherine continued to live at Trinity Square in London; meantime, her mineral rights in Cumberland brought her a significant income. In 1844 she purchased 1 Waterloo Crescent, Dover, and land at Belsfield, Bowness-on-Windermere, where she commissioned the Kendal architect George Webster to design her a residence. She made donations to Arlecdon church and the national school in Cleator Moor, but her greatest charitable interest was reserved for the Whitehaven Infirmary in Howgill Street, Whitehaven. There she donated money for a new fever wing, which opened in 1857. She was unable to attend the opening ceremony, but dedicated the wards to the memory of her father John Harrison and godfather Joseph Steele. Her estranged husband, Baron de Sternberg, died on 7 November 1858 in Westminster. Catharine died on 21 June 1859 in London.

1851: 19 May: *Mr. Hare, who, with Mrs. Hare, is on a visit to the Baron de Sternberg at his residence in George Street Portman Square, and who invites me in the Baron's name to breakfast, as affording an opportunity for us to meet and discuss matters of business.* 21 May: *Proceeded in a Cab to George Street, Portman Square, to the lodgings of Baron de Sternberg; by whom, and by his guests & visitors, Mr. & Mrs. Hare, I was kindly received. The Baron is said to be a Livonian; a portly, square, German figure and countenance betoken a vigorous constitution in advancing years; his manners are courteous and mild ... Several years since the Baron married a wealthy English heiress of mature years, and the couple lived in the fashionable world of Bath, and elsewhere in opulence and in general society. But a separation took place in course of time, occasioned, I believe, by ill-founded jealousy on the part of the lady. Children there were none; and a partition of income was agreed upon, the Baron living in Town, as a bachelor, the Baroness chiefly residing at Dover.*

STEVENS — Frederick Stevens, solicitor [198]

Frederick Stevens, solicitor, was a partner in the firm Stevens, Wilkinson and Satchell, of 6 Queen's Street, Cheapside.

1839: 6 May: *I betook myself thither in an omnibus, and found myself in due time in Queen Street, Cheapside at the business house of Messrs. Satchell Stevens, Wilkinson and Satchell, where I learnt that my labour was in vain, that Mr. Wilkinson was already gone to the H. of Lords, and that thither I must follow him, where I should find him by applying at the office of Mr. Thompson, Parliamentary Agent.* 7 May: *Remained till nearly 12 o cl. in the Coffee Room at Ibbotson's awaiting the arrival of a clerk from Messrs. Stevens, Wilkinson and Satchell, who had been promised to be with me by eleven o cl. to point out to me the places in the Stanway Register Books, which I shall be called upon to produce and read at the bar of the H. of Lords, and to mark them for ready reference.*

STEVENS — Robert Stephen Stevens [199]

Robert Stephen Stevens (1780-1856), Church of England clergyman, was born at Rotherhithe, Southwark, Surrey, the son of Robert and Elizabeth Stevens of Ansford, Somerset. He was educated at Wadham College, Oxford (BA 1800; MA 1806), where he was proctor in 1811, sub-warden in 1822, and a fellow until 1824. He became perpetual curate of Denham, Suffolk, in 1813, and was vicar of South Petherwin from 1824 to his death in 1856. He was married to Katherine (b. ±1785), who was born at Bristol. Robert was buried at Portishead, Somerset.

1802: 24 Feb: *Breakfasted with Paget, meeting Hastings, Edgell, Alford & Stevens.* 25 Feb, 27-28 Feb., 2 Mar., 5 Mar., 7-8 Mar., 16-18 Mar., 21-22 Mar., 27 Mar: *With Stevens in the Bodleian & spent the Evening with him.* 28 Mar., 6 May, 8-9 May, 15-16 May, 22 May, 12 Jun., 16 Jun., 18 Jun., 4 Jul., 6 Jul.

1806: 18 Mar: *Dined at Dr. Price's, meeting Stevens, Round, & a Mr. Latham of B.N.C.* 21-22 Mar.

1824: 19 Feb: *I had the gratification to-day of receiving a letter from my old acquaintance, Mr. Stevens, Fellow and Tutor of Wadham College, announcing the termination in his favour of the contest, which has been proceeding for some time for the Vicarage of South Petherwyn, near Launceston, in the gift of the University of Oxford, and vacant by the death of Dr. Shaw of Magdalen College. ... I have known him intimately from my first entrance into the University.* 15 Apr: *My worthy old friend, Mr. Stevens, the new Rector of South Petherwyn, arrived from Oxford to pass a day with us; in cheerful spirits from the late success, which attended his election, & most grateful to those, who contributed to the attainment of his object.* 17 Apr.

STEVENS — Thomas Stevens [200]

Thomas Stevens (1809-1888), Church of England clergyman and assistant poor law commissioner, was born at Bradfield, Berkshire, the son of Revd Henry Stevens (1766-1842), rector of Bradfield, and Maria Tinney (1769-1843). He was educated at Oriel College, Oxford (BA 1832; MA 1836), and served as assistant poor law commissioner, 1836-39. He succeeded his father as rector of Bradfield and was a JP for Berkshire and Oxfordshire. It appears that Thomas Stevens was an acquaintance or friend to Edward Witts during Edward's time at Balliol College, Oxford.

Stevens married, first, at Newcastle-under-Lyme, Staffordshire, 1839, Caroline Octavia Tollet (1810-1840); and secondly, at Cotesbach, Leicestershire, 5 April 1843, Susannah Marriott (1823-1866). He and Susannah had 5 sons and 8 daughters:

1 Mary Anne (1844-1927)
2 Caroline (1846-1877)
1 Henry (1847-1907)
3 Susannah (1849-1924)
2 Thomas (1851-1910)
3 Robert (1853-1923)
4 Elizabeth (1855-1869)
5 Margaret (1856-1938)
4 John (b. & d. 1858)
6 Frances (1859-1943)
5 William Henry (1862-1935)
7 Anne Marriott (1863-1931)
8 Catherine Octavia (1865-1959)

1836: 15 Jul: *Before nine I rejoined my family: all pretty well. I had expected to find Stevens with them, he having written to E.F.W. that he would arrive as today; but no Stevens made his appearance.* 16 Jul: *A letter to E.F.W. from Stevens, explaining the engagements at many P. L. Unions which prevented his fulfilling his promise of being with us this week.* 26-28 Jul., 6 Aug., 14 Aug., 19 Aug., 23-24 Aug., 25 Aug: *After breakfast, Mr. Stevens accompanied me in my open carriage to Stow, to attend the weekly meeting of the Board of Guardians.* 26 Aug., 7 Oct., 11 Oct: *Received a letter from Stevens, who proposes to pass Friday next with us, and will, perhaps, come on Thursday Even. from Witney.* 13 Oct: *E.F.W., who had ridden to Stow, returned with me about 6 P.M. when we found Stevens arrived from Witney to stay a day or two with us.* 14-15 Oct., 21 Oct., 1 Nov: *Received a letter from Stevens, announcing that the Poor Law Commrs. have removed him from his present district to complete the formation of Unions in Leicestershire, Rutlandshire, Derbyshire, and North Staffordshire, and that his place is to be supplied in Berks, Oxon, and Gloucestershire by Mr. Hall, an Asst. Commr. of longer standing than himself, and retiring on account of indifferent health from the more laborious duties which Stevens is about to undertake.* 4 Nov., 10 Nov., 14 Dec., 29 Dec: *I received a very friendly letter from Stevens, now spending his Xmas with his family at Bradfield, who expresses himself well satisfied with his new district, and to have succeeded beyond his expectation in dissolving Gilbert's Act Incorporations.*

1837: 11 Jan., 20 Feb., 31 Mar., 18 Apr., 5 May, 25 May, 1 Jun., 3 Jun., 20 Jun: *A letter from Stevens, the Asst. P.L.C. vindicating himself, as against the resolution of our Board of Guardians, from blame in respect of the removal of our late rel. off. Day: and giving a hasty account of his operations in his district.* 15 Jul.

1838: 26 Mar: *Of these one was my good friend, Stevens, the Asst. P.L.C. who superintends the working of the Poor Law in this district, & who came from Lichfield purposely to meet me.* 27 Mar.

1839: 5 Jan: *He informed me that our old friend Stevens, the Asst. P.L.C., is about to retire from the Commission at Lady-day, and to enter into Orders; also to marry a lady from the neighbourhood of Lichfield.*

1841: 3 Dec: *A letter from Stevens, formerly Asst. P.L.C. and in charge of this district, and, as such, much domesticated here, a worthy, religious, rightminded person. Of late years we have had no intercourse by letter or otherwise. He has taken orders, and married; held some small preferment in Staffordshire, which he has resigned, and now resides with or near his father, the Rector of Bradfield, near Reading, as I believe, assisting him in his duty, and watching over his almost worn out state of helplessness: will be also successor to his living and property at Bradfield, when he dies.* 6 Dec:... *to Stevens a long letter in reply to his recd. on the 3d. Inst.* 28 Dec: *Found a long and very interesting letter from Stevens in answer to mine of Dec. 6. giving an affecting account of the afflictions he has gone through, in the loss of his wife eleven months after their marriage, and of other near and dear connections.*

1842: 10 Jan: ... *answered the very melancholy and affecting letter which I had received from Stevens on Dec. 28.*

STEVENS — Timothy Stevens [201]

Timothy Stevens (1791-1839), attorney and town clerk, was born at Cirencester, the son of Timothy Stevens (d. 1817), bookseller and stationer, of Cirencester, and Eliza Hanley. In November 1807 he was indentured as an apprentice for five years to William Stevens, of Cirencester, an attorney of the king's bench and common pleas at Westminster and presumably an uncle. On the completion of his apprenticeship Timothy appears to have returned to Cirencester where he lived in Park Street and practised as an attorney. He was also town clerk for Cirencester.

1834: 26 Jul.

1835: 15 Jan: *Received a letter from Mr. T. Stevens, Attorney at Cirencester, and Clerk to the Petty Sessions there, respecting a trial on a charge of felony which had taken place at the last Sessions.* 16 Jan.

STEWART — the Stewart family at Clifton

1802: 29 Apr: *Called upon Mrs. Barnewall, Mr. McBride, Mrs. Stewart, Mrs. Bates.*

1804: 30 Jul: *In the Evening walked with Mr. & Miss Stewart. At a party at Lady Jervis's: conversed chiefly with Miss Monck & Miss Fortescue: played at Commerce.* 31 Jul: *Called upon Mrs. Stewart & Mrs Carrick.*

STEWART — former gardener to Edward and Agnes Witts at Rodborough

1805: 19 Aug: *With my Father through Charlton to Mr. Angerstein's Villa where our old gardener Stewart, now his loaded us with delicious fruit and flowers, as well as with honest heartfelt acknowledgement for past favours.* 23 Aug: *Walked with my Father & mother to Woodlands, Mr. Angerstein's, where Stewart our old gardener received us most handsomly tho' lamed poor fellow by an accident. We saw his pretty wife, delighted in his Conservatory, & feasted on fruit.*

STEWART — Archibald Douglas Stewart, later Drummond-Stewart [202]

Sir Archibald Douglas Stewart of Grandtully, 8th baronet (1807-1890), landed proprietor, was the son of Sir George Stewart, 5th baronet (1750-1827), and Catherine, daughter of John Drummond, of Logiealmond, and sister of Sir William Drummond of Logiealmond. His parents married in 1792, and he succeeded as 8th baronet in 1871 on the death of his brother, Sir William George Drummond-Stewart, 7th baronet (1795-1871). Archibald married, at St Mary's, Bryanston Square, Westminster, 4 May 1875, Mary, eldest daughter of John Fraser of Bunchrew, Inverness-shire.

1823: 3 Oct: *I went to dine and sleep at Lady Elcho's at Stanway ... Lady Rossmore, my mother, & Miss Church are still at Stanway, as also Mr. R. Stuart, a very fine lad, son of a Gentleman of fortune in East Lothian, and pupil of the Revd. Mr. Bland at Kenilworth. This young man is nephew of Sir W. Drummond.*

STEWART — Edward Richard Stewart — *see also* Charteris [203]

Edward Richard Stewart (1782-1851), landed proprietor, was the son of John Stewart, 7th earl of Galloway (1736-1806), and his second wife, Anne (±1742-1830), daughter of Sir James Dashwood, 2nd baronet, and Elizabeth Spencer. He married, 10 November 1805, Katherine (±1781-1863), daughter of Francis Wemyss Charteris, Lord Elcho, and Susan Tracy-Keck. Katherine was a second cousin to Francis Witts. She and Edward had 3 sons and 3 daughters:

1 Edward (1808-1875), Church of England clergyman; married, 27 February 1838, Louisa Anne (d. 1892), daughter of Charles John Herbert and Louisa Middleton; 2 sons and 5 daughters:
  1 Winifred (d. 1919)
  2 Katharine Elizabeth (d. 1912)
  3 Louisa Winifred (d. 1929)
  4 Augusta Francis Harriet
  5 Jane (d. 1908)
  1 Herbert (1843-1885), Maj.-Gen.; appointed KCB; died at the battle of Metammeh, Egypt, 16 February 1885
  2 William Anthony (1847-1883), Church of England clergyman
1 Susan Katherine (1809-1874)
2 Algernon (1811-1875); married, October 1833, Charlotte Clement (d. 1861), daughter of Col J. Albeck Clement; 2 sons:
  1 Charles Edward (1836-1904), Col
  2 Algernon Augustus (1839-1905), Maj.-Gen.
2 Katherine (b. 1812)
3 Arthur (1813-1879); married, 29 July 1840, Mary, daughter of Revd Dr Spencer Madan; 2 sons and 3 daughters:
  1 Sophia Louisa (d. 1929)
  2 Jessie Charteris (d. 1903)
  3 Mary (d. 1942)
  1 Walter (1841-1896), Rear Adm.
  2 Alan (1844-1924)
3 Jane Frances Clinton (1817-1897); married, at Blenheim Palace, Woodstock, Oxfordshire, 18 October 1851, as his third wife, George Spencer-Churchill, 6th duke of Marlborough (1793-1857), son of George Spencer-Churchill, 5th duke of Marlborough; 1 son:
  1 Edward (1853-1911)

1824: 17 Dec: *Lady Elcho has also other inmates, Lady Catherine Stewart, two sons and a daughter. Her Ladyship is Lady Elcho's second surviving daughter & wife of the Hon. Edw. Stewart, Chairman of the Commissioners for auditing the public accounts. Mr. Stewart has held several official Stations of a similar nature, & is a brother of the Earl of Galloway Of his two sons here, the eldest is an Etonian, the youngest is a schoolboy rather younger than Edward. Lady Catherine in early life was a very pretty woman, & having always lived in the first circles her manner & address are peculiarly elegant.* 24 Dec: *Mr. Stewart and his second son, Algernon, reached Stanway from Town to breakfast. I regretted,that they had not arrived on an earlier day, Mr. S. being a very well informed and conversible man.* 29 Dec.

1830: 23 Jun: *Mr. Edward Stewart, indeed, looked in before dinner, but he was engaged to dine out; Lady Catherine Stewart with her daughters are now in Paris; Mr. Edward Stewart, Junr. the eldest son, having finished his Oxford career, at Oriel, where he was placed in the catalogue of those, who distinguished themselves at the examinations, but not high in the list, is keeping terms at one of the Inns of Court, whether he is an assiduous student of the law, I should doubt; particularly, as with many high & fashionable connections, he is quick & clever, & fond of gay society, in which he moves in the most fashionable circles... His next brother, Algernon, has a civil appointment at Ceylon, the third Arthur is in the Dragoons.*

1835: 27 Feb: *Received a letter from the Hon. Edward Stewart, Chairman of the Board of Customs, and Son in law of Lady Elcho, to announce to me the decease of our venerable and excellent friend, in her 92d. year.* 28 Feb.

STILES — Henry Stiles [204]

Henry Stiles (1809-1879), attorney and superintendent registrar at Northleach, was born at Cheltenham. He married, at Sandford St Martin, Oxfordshire, 17 January 1835, Anne (1808-1874), daughter of Nathaniel Castle (1775-1830) and Ann Merry (b. 1781); at least 4 sons and 4 daughters:

1 Helen (b. 1836)
1 George Sydney (1838-1839); died an infant
2 Anne (1841-1913)
3 Charlotte Elizabeth (1843-1914)
2 Henry Aubrey Alfred (1844-1845); died an infant
3 Charles (b. 1845)
4 Helen (1845-1927)
4 Henry Warner (1847-1857)

1853: 1 Nov: *Justice business at home: on one case received a letter from Mr. Styles, Magistrates' Clerk at Northleach.*

STILES — Robert Stiles [205]

Robert Stiles (1795-1848), postman at High Street, Moreton-in-Marsh. He was married to Jane (±1800-1856); they had at least 3 sons and 4 daughters:

1 Edward (b. ±1826)
2 Charles (b. ±1827)
1 Jane Elizabeth (b. ±1832)
2 Anna Maria (b. ±1834)
3 Martha (b. ±1836)
3 William (b. ±1837)
4 Louisa (±1839-1917)

1840: 24 Jun: *A note from Mr. Jackson Clark with reference to a subscription in aid of Robt. Styles the Postman, deprived of his situation under the Post office for a small (if any) fault.*

STOCKHAUSEN — Margarethe Stockhausen [206]

Margarethe Stockhausen (1803-1877), soprano, was born Margarethe Schmuck in Guebwiller, Alsace, the daughter of a notary. She married Franz Stockhausen (1789-1868). From 1827 to 1840 she appeared frequently in London and the provinces with great success. Her repertory included oratorios and operatic excerpts.

1830: 21 Jun: *Madame Stockhausen and other Artistes come down for two concerts to be held at the Music room on tomorrow and Wednesday Evenings; the Speeches &c. to be recited in the Theatre on Wednesday.*

STOKES — John Allen Stokes [207]

John Allen Stokes (1786-1858), surveyor and civil engineer, was born at Shrewsbury and trained as a civil engineer. He lived at Little Hampton Lodge in the parish of Great Hampton and Little Hampton, Evesham, Worcestershire. He married Hester, and in 1851 they had three young nieces and a governess living with them. Stokes had a long career as a surveyor of turnpikes in the area and was well respected.

1822: 19 Oct. *Was the only Commissioner of the Evesham second district of roads, who adhered to an engagement to meet Mr. Stokes, the Surveyor, at Broadway hill, to view a proposed new line of road, which would materially diminish the steepness of the ascent.*

1823: 14 Mar: *Broadway Hill is wonderfully improved under the scientific management of our Surveyor, Mr. Stokes; and the whole line in excellent order.* 25 Apr: *Nothing can exceed the solidity and level surface of this road formed of large gravel blended with a blue limestone; the greatest skill is shewn by Stokes in taking his line; he trusts nothing to the eye, but measures all his work by a level, in this & other points of his practice he follows ...*

1825: 24 Jan., 19 Jul.

1835: 30 Jan., 13 Mar.

1838: 22 Mar., 14 Aug., 23 Aug., 30 Aug.

1839: 11 Mar., 22 Mar., 6 Apr: *... poor Mr. Stokes, the Surveyor, who certainly has broken down here for the first time in the management of the road, and how or why it would be hard to say, received from the Commrs. his dismissal from the post of surveyor, without a comforting or mollifying word—such was the prevailing temper of the Commissioners—and the meeting broke up.*

1840: 8 Oct.

1842: 13 Jan., 20-25 Jan., 27 Feb., 5 Mar., 23 Mar., 30 Mar., 25 May, 2-4 Jun., 9 Jun., 11 Jun., 16 Jun., 3-4 Nov.

1843: 27 Jan.

1844: 25 Jan., 27 Jan., 21 Mar., 31 Oct., 1 Nov., 5-6 Nov.

1845: 4 Jan., 7 Jan., 20 Feb., 24 Feb., 28 Feb., 16 Mar., 26 Mar., 7 May, 1 Jul.

1846: 29 Jul., 21 Sep., 6 Oct.

1847: 27 Jan., 27 Apr., 3 May, 30 Jun.

1850: 7 Mar.

1851: 14 May.

1852: 22 Jan: *... directions were given to the Surveyor (Stokes) to reduce the rate of wages paid to the common labourers on the road.* 25 Mar., 28 Mar., 1 May, 3 May, 3 Dec., 7 Dec.

1853: 25 Jan: *Having been informed that W. Edgeworth and his wife, toll-takers at Lower Slaughter Turnpike gate, have received from Jackson, the renter, notice to quit on an early day, I wrote to Mr. Stokes, recommending W.E. to him as a fit person to be employed by the trustees as Toll-taker at any gate which may be kept in hand.*

STOKEY — Frederick Stokey [208]

Frederick Stokey (1820-1905), innkeeper, was born in Marylebone, Westminster, the son of Frederick Joseph Jones Stokey (1801-1852), probably the same Frederick Stokey who at the time of the 1841 census was a manservant to Samuel Wix, vicar and hospitaller of the hospital of St Bartholomew the Less, Middlesex, and his wife, Charlotte (1801-1870). Frederick Stokey (junior) married, at All Souls', Marylebone, 22 March 1847, Phoebe Austin (±1819-1894), born at Sibford, Oxfordshire, the daughter (presumably illegitimate) of William Smith; they had at least 4 sons and 3 daughters:

1 Catherine Charlotte (1848-1932)
1 Frederick William (1849-1939)

2 Henry Reece (1851-1904)
3 Thomas Charles (1852-1908)
2 Elizabeth Phoebe (±1853-1891)
4 Alexander Austin (1855-1911)
3 Mary Levina (b. 1860)

Stokey was the proprietor of the Wellington public house in Sherborne Street, Bourton-on-the-Water, now known as the Duke of Wellington and still in business.

1853: 9 Mar: *Wrote to Stokey, Innkeeper, Bourton on the Water to bespeak his Clarence to convey R Waller, & myself ...*

STOLLARD — Joseph Stollard, turnpike keeper

There were two Joseph Stollards, both born at Ashton-under-Hill, Gloucestershire [now Worcestershire], which lies about 15 miles north-west of Lower Slaughter. There is insufficient information to make a precise identification.

1836: 11 Jan: *Recd. from Jos. Stollard, a sort of memorial addressed to me and Ford, claiming certain allowances on his leaving L. Slaughter Turnpike gate.*

1837: 15 Jun: *At first A. asserted that he could not find sureties, but two came forward subsequently, creatures of his own and ignorant men, Jos. Stollard of Bourton, and Richd Gardner of Stow, who with him entered into the required Recognizances.*

STONARD — attorney in Virginia

1845: 29 April: *Considerable sums have already been recovered at distant intervals on this account: and much through the agency of the Stonards; so that it seems advisable to leave the matter in their hands.*

1850: 3 May: *A letter from Miss Backhouse, Wavertree, kindly expressed as to my poor wife—and desiring my opinion as to a letter from Mr. Stonard, the Virginian lawyer, who has been employed to collect debts due to the Backhouse family from America, which she has forwarded to Mr. Wilson for his judgment as to its contents, with a request that he will send it on to me.* 6 May: *Mr. Wilson having forwarded to me without any comment the letter written by Mr. Stonard, the agent in Virginia for recovering debts due to the Backhouse family, which purports that further endeavours to obtain payment are hopeless.*

STONE — Mr Stone of Cheltenham

1839: 24 Jul: *Mr. Pearce called, accompanied by his connection, Mr. Stone, a retired Cheltenham tradesman.*

1844: 7 Oct: *Had recd. a letter from Mr. Stone of Cheltenham, uncle of Mrs. Pearce, to whom I wrote some days since, but who from absence had only lately recd. my letter, and will visit his niece shortly.* 10 Oct.

STONE — Henry Stone [209]

Henry Stone (b. ±1803), librarian and shopman, was born at Fillongley, Warwickshire, and boarded with George and Mary Pain as late as 1871. In the 1871 census he was listed as 'librarian'; presumably he had taken over the Stow Book Society librarianship from George Pain, his former employer. He was unmarried and after 1871 he disappears from record.

1834: 26 Sep: *I employed myself in preparing the draft of a letter ... While so engaged, Henry Stone, Shopman to Mr. Pain, Watchmaker, Stow, came with notes from Mr. Pole and Mr. Winter, to inform me, that yesterday one Thornton of Stow, Tailor, and repairer of watches, had brought to Pain's shop a part of the gold repeater of the late unfortunate Mr. Rens.* 30 Sep: *Pain could recognize it by bringing to him a part of the works, & finding that Henry Stone knew the watch, resolved on putting the whole watch into his Master's hands, to save himself from anticipated trouble, careless what the effect might be as to Jeffrey.*

1847: 8 Aug:... *also to Mr. Pain, desiring him to come or send Henry Stone to rectify a time piece which is out of order.*

STONE — Sarah Stone, née Witts — *see also* Shard *and* Richard Meade [210]

Sarah Stone, née Witts (1745-1834), was Francis Witts's aunt, being the sister of his father, Edward. She married, at Chipping Norton, Oxfordshire, 27 June 1769, Edward Stone (1743-1811), son of Edward 'Edmund' Stone (1702-1768) and Elizabeth Grubb (1705-1751). Her father-in-law was famous for his discovery of aspirin. He received his BA from Wadham College, Oxford, in 1724, and was rector of Horsenden, Buckinghamshire, from 1737 until his death in 1768. He moved to Chipping Norton in 1758, and there he discovered that willow bark cured pain. He wrote to the Royal Society in 1763 to inform them of this, and later the active ingredient in the bark was identified as aspirin.

Like his father, Edward Stone (junior) went to Wadham, Oxford (BA 1762), and then entered the Church. He succeeded his father as rector of Horsenden, and held the living from 1769 until his death in 1811. He was also perpetual curate of Princes Risborough. Edward and Sarah had at least 1 daughter:

1 Sarah (1770-1858); married, at St Marylebone, Westminster, 16 June 1807, widower Charles Shard (1764-1814) of Lovell's Hill, Berkshire, and Peckham, Surrey; no children

They may have also had a son, another Edward, but if he existed he died without issue. Edward Stone died on 15 February 1811 and was buried at Winkfield in Berkshire.

The connection between the Stones and the Meades was via Richard Meade's grandparents, Thomas Meade (1703-1770) and Elizabeth Stone (1709-1772), half-sister to Edward 'Edmund' Stone (1702-1768) and daughter of Edward Stone (1672-1741) and his second wife, Elizabeth Grubb (1670-1753), who had married on 23 April 1707. There are several conflicting pedigrees where the dates vary, so extra careful research is needed here.

1801: 1 Jun: *In the morning called upon & had much interesting conversation with Mrs. Stone.* 30 Aug., 4 Sep., 13 Sep., 16-17 Sep.

1802: 5 Aug., 9 Oct.

1827: 14 Nov: *Of my Father's brothers and sisters, only Lady Lyttelton & Mrs. Stone survive, the former nearly 84 the latter 82 years of age, I believe.—On reference to my pedigree I find, I am right in the ages of my Uncle & Aunts.* 16 Nov: *Many years have passed since Mrs. Shard & myself have met. She arrived here from her residence at Lacey Green in Buckinghamshire, beyond High Wycomb, on hearing of my Uncle's decease, & her society and support will be very consoling to my aunt during the trying scenes of this week.*

1828: 24 Sep.

1829: 24 Aug: *The accounts of my Aunt Stone are very good.* 25 Aug.

1830: 21 Jun: *Mrs. Stone hardly every moves & her daughter scarcely quits her.*

1834: 9 Mar: *Returning from church, found a letter from Anne Witts, apprising us of the decease of our Aunt Stone, some days since at Lacey Green.*

1838: 14 Jun: *It turns out to consist of two handsome old fashioned silver pint cups, having been a portion of the personalties which fell to the share of my Aunt Stone, a few years since, when she, together with Lady Lyttelton, as next of Kin, succeeded to the personalty of an old and almost forgotten collateral relation, Richard Parish Witts.*

1840: 6 May.

1850: 12 Aug.

STORMONTH — James Stormonth[211]

James Stormonth (1753-1809), lawyer and agent, was born at Kingoldrum, Angus, the son of Alexander Stormonth (d. 1763) and Giles Ogilvie (b. 1727). He married, at Airlie, Angus, 2 June 1786, Isabella Wedderburn; they had 1 son and 5 daughters:

1 Isobel (1787-1867)
2 Elizabeth Betsy (1788-1874)
1 Alexander (1790-1838)
3 Katherine (1791-1863)
4 Jean (1792-1795)
5 Margaret (1795-1874)

James Stormonth was listed in the Edinburgh directory as a writer, presumably meaning that he practised law or insurance in some manner. He acted as agent to Lord Elcho and lived at 9 St James Square, Edinburgh.

1801: 3 Apr: *Went in the forenoon to the Cowgate Chapel, having before called upon Mr. Stormonth.* 4 Apr: *Our dinner at Lord Elcho's was very late, but very cordial: no one was there, but Mr. Stormonth.* 10 Apr., 13 Apr., 16 Apr., 1 May.

1806: 15 Feb: *Wrote letters on business in my Father's name to Mr. Stormonth & to Mr. Elrige.*

STORY — Henry Alexander Story — *see also* Round[212]

Henry Alexander Story (1813-1879), naval officer, was the son of Revd Philip Laycock Story (1782-1843) and Lydia (1786-1854), daughter of Sir Francis Baring, baronet (1740-1810), and Harriet Herring (1750-1804). He was a lieutenant in the Royal Navy in 1838, commander in 1846, captain in 1855, rear admiral in 1873, and a retired vice admiral in 1878. He married, first, at St George's, Hanover Square, Westminster, 27 October 1845, Amelia Caroline Spence (1824-1847), daughter of Edwin Sandys Dashwood (1794-1846) and Amelia Hare (1795-1857); they had at least 1 daughter:

1 Caroline Amelia (1846-1904)

Henry married secondly, 9 May 1848, Constantia Catherine Anne (1823-1892), daughter of John Round, JP and DL, of Danbury Park, Essex. He died in 1879 at Avranches, Basse-Normandy. Constantia died in 1892 at Aveyron, France.

1848: 6 Feb: *... he begs me to make some enquiry as to the conduct and character of Commander Story R. N. whom his only daughter has met at Baden, and who has proposed for her hand. The lady has attached herself to her admirer, but the good Father hesitates, as it is not many months since the gentleman lost a second wife, and to be so early a suitor appears strange. Capt. Story is well connected, but my old friend wishes for information as to the circumstances attending the decease of his last wife, who left one infant child. It appears she died at Shipston, and R. thinks I can procure intelligence.* 7 Feb., 8 Feb., 15 Feb., 16 Feb: *A letter from J Round in reply to my letter stating what I had learnt as to Capt. Story: the good father has given his consent to his daughter's marriage to that officer.* 9 Mar: From Barter *I heard such an account of the Story family, of their levity of character, and habits, that I much fear that Constantia Round has small hopes of happiness in wedded life, and that my poor old friend will have much anxiety in his latter years arising out of the injudicious attachment formed by his darling daughter.* 27 Apr: *... letter from J. Round announces that his daughter is to be married to Capt. Story on the 9th. Inst. May.*

1849: 20 Dec: *A kind and long letter, chiefly on his family concerns, from my old friend John Round, dated from Torquay, where he has been residing for sometime past with his daughter, Mrs. Story, and her husband, the former having been recommended by her medical adviser to resort to a mild climate for the correction of a disposition to pulmonary complaint; she has derived much benefit from so doing.*

STOTT — George Stott[213]

George Stott (1814-1911), Church of England clergyman, was born at Coventry, the son of George Stott and his wife, Susanna. He was educated at Worcester College, Oxford (BA 1837; MA 1840), where he was elected a fellow in 1839. Stott was appointed curate of Didbrook and Hales. He did not marry, and by 1881 he was in High Barnet, where he eventually died at 96—a good age for someone always worried about his health.

1844: 31 Jan: *When we returned to the Vicarage, a cheerful party assembled at luncheon; to whom was added Mr. W. Gist, who happened to call: a neighbouring Clergyman, Mr. Stott, Fellow of Worcester, and Curate of Didbrook, lately come into the neighbourhood, had called before our meal, but could not be persuaded to join the party.* 21 Feb: *Proceeding thither after divine service in my carriage my son and I overtook Mr. Stott, the Curate of Didbrook, walking, and conveyed him to his destination.* 18 Nov.

1848: 26 Aug.

1850: 24-25 May, 29 May: *Mr. Stott, by appointment, rode over from Didbrook to meet the party: he remained to dine with us, riding home in the cool of the evening.* 22 Jun., 2 Sep.

1851: 4 Feb: *Mr. Stott joined our party at dinner (Stanway). He is in indifferent health, and there is some reason to fear that he will resign the curacy of Didbrook, thinking the place damp and unhealthy. He goes to-morrow to recruit his health at Brighton, whither his sister preceded him yester this morning.* 15 Apr., 23 Apr., 9 May.

1854: 23 Jun: *Mr. Stott made a long morning call, from Blockley, where he is on a visit. His health is somewhat improved, but he has no clerical engagement, and is perhaps unequal from throat complaint to undertake regular duty. He has been living with his excellent Sister, Miss Stott, as invalids in search of health, at Tunbridge Wells and Ventnor &c.; her lungs being seriously affected.*

STRAFORD — Joseph Cooper Straford[214]

Joseph Cooper Straford (1794-1859), solicitor, was born at Tewkesbury, the son of Joseph Straford and Diana Long. He practised as a solicitor at Cheltenham with offices at Bath Street.

1836: 12 Sep: *Conferred with Mr. Straford, the Clerk, on a case, in which two of my parishioners are interested, as prosecutors, and which will be heard on Wednesday before the Cheltenham Magistrates.*

1840: 23 Oct: *My parishioner, Mrs. Collett, claimed my advice and presence at the office of Mr. Straford, the Solicitor, where she had some business to transact respecting which he wished to confer with her in my presence.*

STRATFORD — *see* WINGFIELD-STRATFORD

STRATTON — Anthony Stratton — *see also* Cook[215]

Anthony Stratton (1812-1900), farmer, was born at Stow-on-the-Wold, the son of Robert Mansell Stratton (1782-1869) and Jane Cook (1781-1849). He married, 1845, Elizabeth Davis (1820-1905); they had 2 sons and 3 daughters:

1 Charlotte (1846-1922)
1 William Cook (1848-1861)
2 Jane Elizabeth (1850-1944)
3 Sarah Cook (1852-1928)
2 Valentine (1856-1916)

In the 1861 census the family was living at Rectory Farm, Upper Slaughter, which measured 387 acres and employed ten men and nine boys. Living at home were Charlotte and Valentine.

1851: 10 May: *Mr. Thomas Cook, of Fox Farm, called on me with reference to my Rectory Farm, in which, on Mr. Davis's retirement he wishes to place his nephew, Mr. Anthony Stratton, whom he adopted when a boy, and has brought up to the farming business. A.S. is a steady, respectable, and not very young man, married to his cousin Davis, daughter of Mrs. D., one of the Cook family, & sister to Mrs. John Davis, her husband having also been brother to John D.* 13 May, 18 May, 20 May.

1852: 22 Jan., 11 Feb: *Engaged with A Stratton in considering on the farm and at the Hill Barn alterations.* 24 Mar., 4 May, 14 May, 28 May, 10 Nov., 17 Nov.

1853: 27 Jan., 7 Feb., 14 Feb., 23 Mar., 22 Apr., 2 May, 14 May, 18 May, 28 May, 30 May, 4 Jun., 19 Dec. 23 Dec., 31 Dec.

1854: 11 Feb., 17 Feb., 7 Apr., 17 Apr., 28 Apr., 29 May, 28 Jul., 16 Aug.

STRATTON — George Frederick Stratton — *see also* D'Ewes *and* Leigh[216]

George Frederick Stratton (1779-1833) was born in the parish of St Mary and St Marylebone, Middlesex, the eldest son of George Stratton (1734-1800) and Hester Eleanor Light. His father had been appointed a writer in the East India Company's service on 31 October 1750, and had proceeded to Fort St George, Madras, in 1751, where he had had an uneventful but prosperous career. In 1768 he became a member of the governor's council, but never rose to the highest station. He married, 1768, Hester Eleanora; they had 3 sons and 2 daughters:

1 Aurora Georgina (1782-1783); died an infant
2 Wilhelmina Sarah (1785-1849); married, 1809, Egerton Leigh (1779-1865); 1 son and 6 daughters
1 George (1779-1833); *see below*
2 William (b. 1781), twin to John; died shortly after birth
3 John (1781-1819), twin to William; married, 20 June 1809, Frances Maria (1782-1850), daughter of John and Frances Bower Jodrell; 1 son and 4 daughters:
    1 Georgina Maria (1812-1892); married, 18 March 1831, William Curtis (1804-1870)
    2 Harriet Vittoria (1814-1900); married, 14 August 1832, Sir Michael Hicks Hicks-Beach (1809-1854), MP
    3 Elizabeth Julia (1815-1885); married, first, Col Wedderburn (died before 1843); and secondly, 8 August 1843, Thomas Drake, who changed his name to Thomas Tyrwhitt-Drake (1818-1888)
    4 Emily Ann (1816-1883); married, 18 September 1838, Henry Barnett, MP, JP and DL, of Glympton Park
    1 John Locke (1818-1903); married, first, at Turweston, Mary Scott Horrocks (d. 1851); and secondly, 2 October 1855, Mary Willes (1837-1914)

In 1780 and 1793 Great Tew estate was bought in two separate parts by George Stratton (senior), using the fortune he had amassed in India. The manor house had evidently fallen into disrepair as he and his family lived in a smaller Georgian dower house slightly to the south of it. He died in March 1800 and was succeeded by his son George Frederick Stratton, who had the manor house demolished in about 1803.

George Frederick Stratton (1779-1833) was educated at St John's College, Cambridge (BA 1801; MA 1804) and Lincoln's Inn (1807). He was also awarded a DCL from Oxford in 1806. He was high sheriff for Oxfordshire in 1806-07, and was elected a fellow of the Royal Society in 1807. In 1808 he engaged the Scots botanist and garden designer John Loudon, who laid out north and south drives in Great Tew Park and planted ornamental trees in and around the village, which today enhance its picturesque appearance. Stratton married, at Wellesbourne, Warwickshire, 1 January 1805, Anne (1778-1861), only daughter of Bernard D'Ewes (1743-1822) and Anne Delabere (1750-1780) of Wellesbourne.

In 1815-16 Matthew Robinson Boulton, son of the manufacturer Matthew Boulton, of Soho, Birmingham, bought Great Tew estate. It is unclear what George Frederick Stratton did next. He appears to have died at New Orleans, Louisiana, in 1833, but what took him there is unknown. The diary entry for 16 June 1826 has been given in detail as it supplies some fascinating information. George Stratton was certainly unfortunate in his business dealings, and Francis Witts was probably being unfair in his appraisal; it is interesting that Loudon went on to achieve a high reputation. What Anne Stratton did after the sale of Great Tew is also unclear; she may have accompanied George to America, but this is unlikely. In her later life she lived at Barnards Green, Malvern.

1805: 23 Mar: *Thro' Kidlington, & leaving Wotton on the left took bread & cheese at a small public House Kilganon Castle: thence by a green lane of about four miles, leaving Glympton on the left, to a cluster of houses called Cuckold's Holt: by a Bridle Road to Gt. Tew, Mr. Stratton's, a noble Park & situation for a House; the old mansion of the Kecks pulled down: Stratton lives in a small Stewards House in the Village, which is very neat: between Cuckold's Holt & Gt. Tew.*

1825: 31 Mar: *Mrs. Granville's fortune, which was not inconsiderable, descends to her niece, Mrs. Stratton, wife of George Stratton Esqr. formerly of Great Tew in Oxon, and brother to our acquaintance Mrs. Egerton Leigh.*

1826: 16 Jun: *Mr. Stratton, formerly possessor of Great Tew in Oxfordshire, to come forward as their candidate. The requisitionists make up in number what they want in weight: hardly a country gentleman or clergyman is to be found in the list, but hosts of attorneys, innkeepers, little farmers, shopkeepers, dissenters &c. To call Stratton the farmer's friend is exceedingly absurd: blessed with a noble fortune, he dissipated it many years since in idle speculations; one was the inviting to farm his fine estate a Scotch adventurer of the name of Loudon with strange wild notions of improvement which consisted only in indiscriminately overturning all established principles and practices of the country... Great Tew was sold & resold, till at last it has fallen into the hands of Mr. Bolton a man of sense and high character, the representative of the gentleman, who formed the great mechanical establishment at Soho near Birmingham, whom wise speculations enabled to acquire that estate, which Stratton was forced to sell, because with activity of imagination proportionate to his lack of judgment he ran into every wild speculation which crossed his path, whether of*

Scotch farmers, or quacks boasting the discovery of an infallible remedy for the yellow fever. Nor has Mr. Stratton better claims to the farmer's support by his conduct as Vice President and Secretary of the Oxfordshire agricultural Society, or by his own practical performances, when he professed to follow the plough: he was turned out of the former posts, ne respublica quid detrementi caperet, & his Scotch or Irish bailiffs always plundered him & humbugged him. He has, however, other sources of popularity, one is, that he has for many years commanded a body of Yeomanry in the Northern division of the County; & he has for many late years been a most indefatigable supporter and advocate of Evangelical principles and of the Bible Society, in which latter well organised body he holds, indeed, in Warwickshire, Oxfordshire & parts of Gloucestershire the rank of itinerant chairman; i.e. is ready to preside, wherever no gentleman of the neighbourhood, in which the meeting is held, is disposed to patronize Ultra exaggeration in religious matters. Nor is Stratton well plumed for contest; his noble has for many years been reduced to a ninepence; & tho' by the death of his father in law, his resources have been materially enlarged, yet by no means to such an extent as to justify his embarking in a struggle for the representation of a county. In fine it is easy to foresee, that he will be worsted in his conflict; for all the gentry of the County are determined with influence & purse to support Ashurst, and keep out a man, whom they regard as an intruder; who possesses, indeed, great fluency of speaking, but is lamentably devoid of judgment. All the attorneys, and dissenters, & supporters of the bible society will fail in their object; & Stratton after a flash in the pan, will return to his rented place between Alcester & Evesham with a shrunken purse, and irritated spirit. Mr. Stratton is brother to Mrs. Egerton Leigh, and married Miss Dewes, daughter of Mr. Dewes of Wellsbourne & niece of my old and afflicted friend Mr. Granville... Mr. Stratton is brother to Mrs. Egerton Leigh, and married Miss Dewes, & niece of my old and afflicted friend Mr. Granville. 2 Sep.

1829: 15 May: *We dined with the Egerton Leighs at Broadwell, meeting the Dean of Gloucester, his son Francis, & his daughters Cecil and Maria, Mr. & Mrs. Twisleton, Mr. Vavasour, and two Miss Strattons, nieces of Mrs. E. Leigh, on a visit at Broadwell. They are daughters of her younger brother, John Stratton, a Captain in the Oxfordshire Militia, now deceased. I was well acquainted with him; his widow survives him, she was a Miss Joddrel of Cheshire, and a connection of Egerton Leigh.* 25 Jun., 24 Nov.

1833: 26 Oct: *The Misses Leigh from Broadwell rode over to request me to come to their Mother, who was anxious to advise with me on a matter of importance. Accompanied them to Broadwell, where I found Mrs. Leigh in distress arising out of the increasing feebleness of her aged mother, Mrs. Stratton, resident with them under very distress lamentable circumstances, springing out of the very culpable conduct of G. F. Stratton, her eldest Son, whose want of principle has led him to ruin, and forced him into voluntary exile.*

1836: 30 Aug: *We had hardly entered it, when we were greeted by the strains of a band of musicians; it proved to be the day of meeting of the Wychwood Forest Cricket Club, who with their tents pitched, were playing on a beautiful lawn skirted by the fine forest trees near the Ranger's Lodge, a mansion now unoccupied, but which has at various times been the abode of G. F. Stratton, the Duke of Beaufort, Sir H. Lambert, Mr. Goodlake and others.*

1840: 24 Apr: *Mrs. Stratton (widow of Geo. Fred. Stratton, now residing at Barnards Green).*

1850: 4 Sep: *Park Hall was formerly rented by G. F. Stratton— The distance from Stanway is about seventeen miles.*

STRAUBENZEE — Catherine van Straubenzee[217]

Catherine van Straubenzee (1787-1870) was the daughter of Charles Spencer van Straubenzee (b. 1750) and Anne Theophilia Davison, and granddaughter of Phillip William Casimir van Straubenzee (1723-1765) and Jane Turner (d. 1772). She married, 4 May 1809, Capt. Francis Farrington Gardner, RN (1773-1821), son of Adm. Alan Gardner, 1st Baron Gardner of Uttoxeter, and Susannah Hyde Gale. Catherine and Francis had 3 sons and 2 daughters:

1 Francis Charles (1810-1836)
2 Stewart William (1812-1882); married, at Agra, India, 28 August 1834, Jane Gardner (1817-1869)
3 Alan Hyde (1814-1858)
1 Catherine Georgiana (b. 1815)
2 Susanna Amelia (b. 1820)

Francis Farrington Gardner rose to become a rear admiral. He died at Le Havre, France, in 1821.

The van Straubenzee name came to the United Kingdom with Phillip William Casimir van Straubenzee, a Belgian captain in the Dutch Blue Guards, who had joined Bonnie Prince Charlie in support of the Jacobite rising of 1745. As the Jacobite army headed south into England, van Straubenzee met Jane Turner, of Kirkleatham, daughter of Cholmley Turner, MP for Yorkshire (1727-41). Sir William Turner, lord mayor of London (1669), of Kirkleatham, had bequeathed in his will a substantial amount of money to Cholmley, his great nephew. Cholmley Turner refused to give his consent to his daughter's marriage and so Phillip and Jane eloped. Phillip transferred his allegiance to Hanover and became an officer in the British Army. He was naturalised as a British citizen by act of parliament in 1759 at the request of George II.

1806: 7 Mar: ... *amused myself as well as I could for the rest of the Evening; some of the most notable personages were little Miss Straubenzee, Mrs. J. Auriol etc.*

STRICKLAND — Thomas Alfred Strickland[218]

Thomas Alfred Strickland (1802-1852), Church of England clergyman, was born at Ripon, Yorkshire, the third son of Sir George Strickland (1729-1808) and Elizabeth Laetitia (1734-1813), fifth daughter of Sir Rowland Winn, 4th baronet, and Susanna Henshaw. He was educated at Merton College, Oxford (BA 1824; MA 1831), and became rector of Bredon, Worcestershire, in 1837. He held the living until his death in 1852. Late in life he married Ann Katherine Fitzgerald (b. ±1823), born in Ireland; they had 2 sons and 1 daughter:

1 George (b. 1841), Church of England clergyman; married, at Cheltenham, 28 June 1870, Emily (b. ±1842), born in Ireland, the daughter of Gerland Dillon; at least 1 son:
    1 Thomas Alfred G. (b. 1871); born at Penrith, Cumberland
1 Alice Geraldine (b. ±1843); died unmarried
2 Thomas Hoy Forestor (1849-1875); died unmarried at Cawnpore, India

It seems impossible that Strickland's mother could have been 68 years old at the time of his birth; the accuracy of Cokayne, *Complete Baronetage*, in this particular instance is therefore open to question.

1838: 2 Dec: *A budget of letters ... lastly a long and very proper letter from Aston, announcing to me that he has accepted the living of Northleach, that he shall probably remove thither towards the end of Jany, that he fully expects that E.F.W. will be his successor, &c. desiring to hear soon from us what our views and wishes are, and, in particular, whether he shall write a second letter to Mr. Strickland, the Rector of Bredon, to whom he has announced his removal from the Curacy of Cutsdean, to request that Gentleman, if he have no friend whom he has a desire to place there to reserve it for a short time open, until it be ascertained, whether his successor at Stanway would wish to hold Cutsdean with it, as has been customary for a long series of years.* 5 Dec: *From Aston I recd. a letter in reply to mine of the 2d. and written to inform me that Mr. Strickland, the Rector of Bredon, had desired him to beg for the Curacy of Stanway for a brother in law of his, highly recommended.*

1840: 20 Jul: *While I was with him a Mr. Fowle, an old College intimate, called on him, coming from Bredon, where he is fixed as Mr. Strickland's Curate.*

1847: 1 Dec.

STRONG — Charles Strong[219]

Charles Strong (±1783-1864), Church of England clergyman, was born at Tiverton, Devon, the son of Richard Henry Strong. He was educated at Wadham College, Oxford (BA 1805; MA 1810), and was ordained deacon on 11 October 1807 and priest on 21 April 1811. He was appointed rector of Broughton Gifford, Wiltshire, on 22 May 1811, and remained so until 1844. He was also appointed stipendiary curate of Cannington, Wiltshire, on 5 February 1816, and curate at Locking, Somerset, in around 1815. Locking was where the diarist's close friend William Dowell served as vicar between 1812 and 1824. It seems likely that Dowell and Strong remained close friends since their years together at Oxford.

Charles Strong married Anne Margrete; they had at least 1 son:

1 Charles Edward (1814-1899), Church of England clergyman; born at Locking, Somerset; baptised, 8 July 1815, by Revd William Dowell; educated at Wadham College, Oxford; curate at St Lawrence Lydeard, Somerset, 1841

By 1851 Charles Edward was living with his father at Gravesend, Kent; he was listed as a widower clergyman without cure of souls. Ten years later they were both at Clifton, and Charles Edward was simply listed as unmarried. By 1871, several years after his father's death, Charles Edward had married, secondly, Anne (b. ±1803), who was born at St Lawrence Lydeard; they had presumably met when Charles Edward was a curate there. She was twelve years his senior. They lived at Withycombe Raleigh, Devon. By 1891 Charles Edward was a widower once more; he died eight years later.

1805: 21 Mar: *Breakfasted with Adams, meeting Prower, Vashon, Smith & Strong.*

STRONG — William Strong[220]

William Strong (1819-1866), carpenter, was born at Bourton-on-the-Water, the son of Robert Strong (1789-1862) and Mary Hookham (1790-1831). He married, at Stow-on-the-Wold, 19 October 1846, Jane Blizard (1821-1902), also born at Bourton; they had at least 4 sons and 3 daughters:

1 Sarah Anne (1848-1922)
1 Robert William (1848-1929); married, at Brentford, Middlesex, 1912, Olive Nicholson Jesty (1883-1960)
2 Richard Blizard (1850-1903); married, at Stow-on-the-Wold, 1 March 1875, Emily Ann Collett (1855-1909), born at Lower Guiting; 3 sons and 1 daughter:
  1 Annie Elizabeth (1875-1947)
  1 Otto John (1882-1959)
  2 Arnold Tom (1889-1957)
  3 Edgar Victor (1893-1953)
2 Mary Hannah (1851-1913)
3 Thomas (1853-1904); married, 8 January 1881, Caroline Ann Shipton; 5 sons and 1 daughter:
  1 Frank (b. 1882)
  1 Ida Annie (b. 1883)
  2 William E. (b. 1884)
  3 Richard W. (b. 1886)
  4 Guy (b. 1887)
  5 Harry (b. 1890)
4 Henry John (b. 1856), draper's traveller and draper at Woburn, Bedfordshire, by 1881; married Clara (b. ±1847)
3 Harriet Elizabeth (1861-1920)

The family lived at 84 Market Place, Stow-on-the-Wold, where William was a carpenter employing three men.

1838: 1 Jun.

1844: 18 Feb., 18 Mar.

STUART-WORTLEY-MACKENZIE — John Stuart-Wortley-Mackenzie[221]

John Stuart-Wortley-Mackenzie, 2nd Baron Wharncliffe (1801-1855), was a Conservative politician. He served briefly as under-secretary of state for war and the colonies between December 1834 and January 1835.

1835: 11 May: *He is opposed by the Conservative party, by whom Mr. Stuart Wortley, a Son of Lord Wharncliffe is brought forward.*

1837: 27 Jul., 28 Jul., 10 Aug.

STUCKÉ — Henry John Stucké[222]

Henry John Stucké (1830-1866), tailor, was born in the parish of St Marylebone, Westminster, the son of Heinrich Sucké (1796-1882) and his wife Phoebe (1793-1885) of Norwood Green. He was a master tailor at 7 Clarence Street, employing fourteen men. He married, at Reading, Berkshire, July 1862, Emma Lansley (b. ±1841); they had 1 son and 2 daughters:

1 Gertrude (b. 1864)
1 William Henry (1865-1931)
2 Mary Emma (b. 1867)

1854: 27 Apr: *A note from Stucké, the Cheltenham tailor, apologizing that the clothes I had ordered were not finished when the carrier called for them on Tuesday.*

STURGES BOURNE — William Sturges Bourne[223]

William Sturges Bourne (1769-1845), politician and poor law reformer, was born as William Sturges, the only son of the Revd John Sturges (1736/7-1807), prebendary of Winchester, and Judith, daughter of Richard Bourne of Acton Hall, Worcester. He was educated at Winchester College and Christ Church, Oxford (BA 1790; MA 1793), and practised as a barrister. In 1803 he inherited £2000 p.a. from his uncle Francis Bourne and happily took the name Bourne in accordance to his uncle's stipulation, whereupon his friend George Canning promptly dubbed him 'Scroggs', by which nickname he became generally known in Canningite circles.

Sturges had been an MP for some years and in various seats before becoming MP for Ashburton in 1827. He was given the following appointments: secretary to the Treasury, 1804-06; lord of the Treasury, 1807-09; privy councillor, 1814; commissioner of the Board of Control, 1814-16 and 1818-22; secretary of state for home affairs, July 1827; commissioner of woods, forests and land revenues, July 1827–February 1828; poor law commissioner, 1832-33; and ecclesiastical commissioner, 1832-35. He married,

2 February 1808, Anne, daughter of Oldfield Bowles of North Aston, Oxfordshire; they had 1 daughter:

1 Ann (b. 1809)

1827: 30 Apr: *Mr. Sturges Bourne is to have the Home Department, but, it is added, pro tempore.* 20 Jul: *Be that as it may, the locum tenens, Mr. Sturges Bourne, steps out of the Home Office to make room for the Marquis of Lansdowne; Mr. Sturges Bourne retires to the cool shades of the New Forest, of which he is appointed Keeper in the room of the lamented Duke of York.* 7 Sep.

SUCKLING — Robert William Suckling [224]

Robert William Suckling (1809-1881), naval officer, was born at Burnham, Suffolk, the second son of Horace Suckling (1770-1828) and Catharine Jackson (1773-1861). He entered the Royal Navy in 1823 and was promoted to lieutenant in 1838. He commanded HMS *Rattlesnake* in 1847. He married, at St Marylebone, Westminster, 17 July 1851, Charlotte Caroline (1819-1867), daughter of Henry Frederick Amedroz (1795-1850) and Emma Milbourne (1786-1883); they had 1 daughter:

1 Mary (b. 1825)

1851: 19 May: *Capt. Suckling was employed on the Surveying service with the late Capt. Stanley, in the Rattlesnake in Torres Straits &c. on board which ship Willoughby Howell served as midshipman.*

SUDELEY — *see* Charles Hanbury Tracy

SUGDEN — Edward Burtenshaw Sugden [225]

Sir Edward Burtenshaw Sugden, 1st baronet (1781-1875), lord chancellor, was the son of Richard Sugden, hairdresser, of Duke Street, Westminster, and Charlotte Burtenshaw of St George's, Hanover Square, Westminster. Despite his father's modest profession, Edward's family were of sufficient means for him to be educated privately. He entered Lincoln's Inn in 1802, and was called to the bar in 1807. Edward Sugden was knighted in 1829 and created a baronet in 1852. He was MP for Weymouth and Melcombe Regis in 1828-31, St Mawes in 1831-32, and Ripon in 1837-41. In addition he was solicitor-general in 1829-30, privy councillor in 1835, lord chancellor of Ireland in 1834-35 and 1841-46, and lord chancellor in 1852. He married, 23 December 1808, Winnifred (1781-1861), daughter of John Knapp; they had 7 sons and 7 daughters, including:

1 Henry (b. 1811)
1 Juliet (b. 1812)
2 Charlotte (b. 1815)
3 Caroline (b. 1816)
2 Frank (b. 1817)
3 Arthur (b. 1822)
4 Sophia (b. 1825)
5 Harriet (b. 1826)
6 Augusta (1827-1903)

1829: 7 Feb: *Mr. O'Connel was preparing to make his appearance at the door of the House of Commons, and claim that admittance, as the representative of the County of Clare, which great authorities, Lord Colchester and Mr. Sugden, the eminent barrister, assert, he cannot gain under the present state of the law.* 26 Jun: *Sir E. B. Sugden, a very able Chancery lawyer, son of a celebrated London Hair-dresser, and grandson of a Skipton Barber, being made Solicitor General.*

1830: 31 Jan.

1832: 27 Mar: *Sir Robert Peel, Mr. Croker, Sir R. Inglis, Sir E. Sugden, Sir C. Wetherell, Mr. Praed, Lord Mahon, Lord Porchester and many others spoke with great force and convincingness.*

1834: 17 Dec: *The following ministerial appointments are announced, in addition to those which I have already noticed ... Sir Edward Sugden; Lord Chancellor of Ireland.*

1852: 27 Feb: *The Conservative party now in the ascendant ... Sir E. Sugden, Lord Chancellor &c.*

SULIVAN — George James Sulivan — *see also* Thomas Beale Browne [226]

George James Sulivan (±1791-1866), army officer, businessman, JP, DL, and landed proprietor, was born at Madras, India, the son of Sir Benjamin Sulivan (1747-1809), barrister-at-law, and Elizabeth (1771-1824), daughter of Rear Adm. Sir Digby Dent (1739-1817). His father had been born at Cork, Ireland, the son of Benjamin Sullivan Mór (1720-1767) and Bridget Limric (1720-1802), and his maternal grandfather, Rear Adm. Sir Digby Dent, had been born at Portsmouth, the son of Capt. Cotton Dent, RN (d. 1761), captain of Greenwich Hospital, and Catherine Bowerbank (b. 1717).

Sir Digby married three times, and George's grandmother, Elizabeth Greentree Challoner (1746-1786), of St Helena, was his second wife. They married before 1769 and had 3 sons and 6 daughters; she died in childbirth on 7 November 1786 at their home in Fareham.

George's father, Benjamin Sulivan, went to India with the intention of practising at the Calcutta bar, but he halted first at Fort St George, where he was consulted by a Mr Whitehall on the legal aspects of the verdict of the coroner's jury regarding the death of Lord Pigot. Following this, Benjamin decided to stay in Madras. In 1778 he offered his services as standing counsel, arguing that the government required professional assistance in trials at quarter sessions and appeals from decisions of the mayor's court. As the only person on the spot to have been 'educated regularly as a barrister', Sulivan won his appointment as standing counsel (later called government advocate) a few months later, with a salary of 250 pagodas per month.

Sir Benjamin Sulivan and Elizabeth Dent married in India on 17 May 1790. Sir Benjamin died in India, and his widow returned to England and died at Clifton in 1824. Their son George James Sulivan spent his early life in India before sailing to England. He married, at Abbots Langley, Hertfordshire, 4 April 1816, Mary Plomley (1795-1866), daughter of Revd Stiverd Jenkins (1766-1842) and Elizabeth Portal (b. 1766); they had at least 3 sons and 5 daughters:

1 Ellen (1817-1871); baptised at St Mary's, Cheltenham
1 George Frederick Augustus Filmer (1819-1896), Col, Royal Scots Greys; married, 12 May 1842, Emily Anne, only daughter of Richard Prime of Walberton, Sussex
2 Mary Eliza (±1821-1906); married, at Alverstoke, Hampshire, 12 August 1840, Thomas Beale Browne (1810-1888); 3 sons and 1 daughter
3 Margaret (±1822-1823); died an infant
4 Emily Esther (±1828-1858)
2 Robert Desmond (±1829-1872)
5 Eliza Charlotte Albinia (±1831-1917)
3 John Filmer (1834-1924), Church of England clergyman

The children tended to be baptised late, making the true birth dates difficult to calculate. For instance, Mary Eliza was baptised at St Mary's, Cheltenham, in 1827, and yet she married in 1840, and certainly would have been older than 13. The 1881 census states she was 80, so a birth date of 1821 is probably about right. Margaret died before baptism, so her date is merely a guess. Ellen and George Frederick were baptised together in 1825.

The family lived at Arlington Street, Westminster, and at Ditchamgrove, Petersfield, Hampshire, and then, by 1851, Kington House, Piddletown, Dorset. A little earlier Sulivan had bought a grand country home, Wilbury Park in Amesbury, Wiltshire. Wilbury House was begun in 1710 by William Benson, and the name appears to have been composed of the Wil of Wilton and the bury of Amesbury, both being neighbouring houses and both believed to have been designed by Inigo Jones. Sullivan bought this house, presumably using the profits from his business; he was a director of the European Life Insurance and Annuity Company of 10 Chatham Place, Blackfriars. He was also a JP and DL for Bedfordshire, and high sheriff in 1840. In addition, he was a captain in the Royal Horse Guards Brigade and a major-general in the Portuguese service in 1851.

1840: 17 Jul: *Drove MW. to call on the Brownes at Salperton; saw Mrs. B. and Mr. T. Browne; the latter is in much better health than formerly, and less absorbed in Ultra-Protestantism; indeed, his rage is now farming, and his condition would have been changed from single blessedness to married felicity some weeks ago, but for the indisposition of the lady, a daughter of Capt. Sullivan, a Gentleman of large fortune resident at Wilbury Park in Wilts.* 18 Aug: *To Mr. Browne, Salperton, to congratulate him and Mrs. Browne on the marriage of their Son to Miss Sullivan, which took place a few days since.* 20 Nov: *Rode to Salperton to call on the Browne family. Received by Mrs. Browne, by whom I was introduced to her daughter in law, Mrs. Beale Browne, a very pleasing, elegant, well looking and agreeable young person. Tom has, apparently, been fortunate in the connection he has made: the lady had a pretty fortune, and is well connected, being a daughter of a Gentleman of the name of Sullivan, resident at Wilbury in Wilts. Her Mother was a Miss Jenkins, daughter of the Revd. Stiverd Jenkins of Locking, Somerset, and was at one time greatly admired by my poor deceased friend Dowell, then Vicar of Locking.*

SUMMERSBY — Jenny Summersby

Jenny Summersby or Summersbee was probably from Stow-on-the-Wold as there were families of that name at Stow and Chipping Norton.

1834: 21 Jul: *The deposition of Jenny Summersby, the nurse who attended on the corpse of Mr. Rens from his death till his burial, was also important. Other witnesses were also examined.*

SUMNER — Charles Richard Sumner[227]

Charles Richard Sumner (1790-1874), bishop of Winchester, was born at Kenilworth, the third son of Revd Robert Sumner (1748-1802), vicar of Kenilworth and Stoneleigh, and Hannah (1756/7-1846), daughter of John Bird, alderman of London. He was younger brother to John Bird Sumner, archbishop of Canterbury. Their mother was the niece of William Wilberforce, and Charles and John were therefore second cousins to Samuel Wilberforce, whom Charles consecrated to the episcopacy.

Charles Sumner was educated at Eton College and Trinity College, Cambridge (BA 1814; MA 1817). He was ordained deacon on 5 June 1814 and priest on 2 March 1817. He married, at the English chapel of Geneva, 24 January 1816, Jennie Fanny Barnabine (1794-1849); they had 4 sons and 3 daughters.

At Brighton in 1820, Sumner was introduced by the Conynghams to George IV; he dined with the king and talked with him afterwards for three hours. He made a favourable impression. In April of the following year, without waiting for the approval of Prime Minister Lord Liverpool, King George announced to Sumner that he intended to promote him to a vacant canonry at Windsor. Liverpool refused to sanction the appointment, and an angry correspondence took place between the two, which ended in a compromise. The canonry was given to Dr James Stanier Clarke, and Sumner succeeded to all of Clarke's appointments, which included the posts of historiographer to the crown, chaplain to the household at Carlton House, and librarian to the king. George IV also made Sumner his private chaplain at Windsor, with a salary of £300 a year.

On 21 May 1826 Sumner was consecrated at Lambeth as bishop of Llandaff, an office which he held with the deanery of St Paul's (from 25 April 1826) and the prebendal stall of Portpoole (from 27 April 1826). Within a year he made his first visitation of the diocese. When the rich bishopric of Winchester became vacant by the death of George Pretyman Tomline in 1827, George IV hastened to bestow it upon Sumner, remarking that this time he had determined that the see should be filled by a gentleman. Sumner was confirmed in the possession of the bishopric on 12 December 1827, and the next day was sworn in as prelate of the Order of the Garter. He was just 37 years old when he became the head of this enormous diocese (which then included the archdeaconry of Surrey, and hence much of the metropolis south of the Thames), with its vast revenues and a castle for the bishop's use. He was the first bishop of Winchester to be enthroned.

1826: 28 Apr: *The new Bishop of Llandaff is fixed upon; Dr. C.R. Sumner being raised to the bench, and with that See is to hold, as his predecessor Bp. Vanmildert did, the lucrative Deanery of St. Paul's. Dr. Sumner owes his promotion to Court favour, being private Chaplain and librarian to his Majesty.*

1827: 19 Feb., 25 Mar., 30 Oct., 30 Nov: *The Bishop of Llandaff, Dr. Sumner, is raised to the vacant see of Winchester, a strange leap from the bottom to the top of the ladder from the poorest to almost the richest See in the kingdom… and it is considered a proof of the continued influence of the Marchioness of Conyngham over the royal mind*

1828: 6 Oct., 29 Aug.

1836: 15 Nov.

SURMAN — John Surman Surman — *see also* Goodlake[228]

John Surman Surman (1809-1880), JP and landed proprietor, was the son of John Hughes Goodlake (1788-1821), of Letcombe Regis, Berkshire, and Elizabeth (1807-1843), daughter of William Surman and niece and heir of John Surman of Swindon Hall, near Cheltenham. John Surman Surman was born as John Surman Goodlake, but took the surname Surman in 1831 by act of parliament in accordance with a provision in the will of John Surman. He lived at Swindon Hall with his unmarried sister, Mary Doorman Goodlake (1817-1860).

1835: 6 Jan: *Several Gentlemen took the oaths as Magistrates, some who had never before qualified, although they had been long on the Commission, others who had been recently appointed under a cold seal. Among them were Capt. Frederick Berkeley, the Hon. Grantley Berkeley, Messrs. Probyn, Surman, Agg, Clutterbuck, W. Pitt and Lt. Col. Pearce.*

1839: 1 Aug.

1845: 4-7 Mar.

1847: 4 Jan., 5 Apr., 29 May, 28 Jun., 18 Oct.

1848: 20 Mar.

1850: 7 Aug., 14 Oct.

1852: 18 Mar: *The village of Swindon ... Of these the wealthiest is Mr. Surman, one of the legatees of the miser banker of Gloucester, Jemmy Wood; S's name was Goodlake, and he is unmarried, a sister living with him, a pleasing person.*

1853: 6 Oct: *At dinner there was a pleasant reunion of residents of the village; Mr. and Mrs. Sherlock Willis, and her sister, Miss Waile; and Mr. Surman with his sister, Miss Goodlake. J. Surman and sister left us to join a Cheltenham evening party.* 7 Oct: *After breakfast, accompanied Lefroy to call on Mr. Surman, his neighbour, whom we found at home, receiving us in his handsome house, and splendidly furnished suite of apartments. Much therein reminds one of the riche parvenu, but there is something intrinsically good, kind, and liberal in the man, especially towards his near connections, tho' mingled with vulgarity, and a want of general information.*

1854: 1 Jul.

SUTCLIFFE — William Sutcliffe[229]

William Sutcliffe (1759-1840), physician, was apprenticed in 1778 to his father Abraham Sutcliff[e] (1721-1798), who had been born at York. As a boy, Abraham had been a weaver by trade, but finding this hard, he went at the age of 16 to be an errand-boy to a Mr Ecroyd, a surgeon in Kendal. He gradually taught himself Latin from the prescriptions written by his master, and by borrowing various books he gained knowledge of medical matters in general. He saved enough money to be able to walk to Edinburgh over two or three winters to attend classes there. Edinburgh was then the best place to study medicine in the English speaking world, but being a Quaker, Sutcliffe was not allowed to be awarded a university degree. In time, however, he became an accomplished classical scholar and proficient in medical science. He moved to Settle, perhaps because it was a well-known centre for Quakers, and started a practice as an apothecary, presumably in about 1740 He built the premises on the Cheapside/Duke Street corner of the Market Place, possibly in around 1753. In 1786 he retired to Sheffield, where he died in 1798.

William, an active Quaker, occupied the family premises after his father's retirement. He qualified as a doctor and was surgeon to the First Craven Legion of Yeomanry for a short time. His apprentice surgeons were Lawrence Fearenside (1794), John Holdsworth (1792), and Thomas Williams Simmonds (1796). Simmonds went on to study in London and Edinburgh and became very knowledgeable in natural history. It is not known if Sutcliffe married or had children.

1825: 11 Sep: *The party consisted of Mrs. Ingram, two daughters and a son, Mrs. A. Currer, Mr. W. Hartley, Mr. Sutcliffe & myself... Mr. Sutcliffe is the medical authority of the parish & district; shrewd, clever, eccentric, full of paradox, experienced.* 12 Sep: ... *returning to dinner at Mr. Hartley's, who had invited Mr. Oliver Farrer, of Clapham Lodge, and his brother William, Mr. W. Clayton, and Mr. Sutcliffe.*

1837: 28 Oct.

SUTTIE — George Grant Suttie[230]

Sir George Grant Suttie, 5th baronet (1797-1878), army officer and landed proprietor, was the son of Sir James Suttie, 4th baronet (1759-1836), and Katherine Isabella Hamilton. He was an officer in the Scots Fusilier Guards. He married, at Gosford, Haddingtonshire, 3 September 1829, Harriet (1805-1858), seventh daughter of Francis Charteris, 9th [7th] earl of Wemyss (1795-1883), and Louisa (1798-1882), fourth daughter of Richard Bingham, 2nd earl of Lucan (1764-1839), and Elizabeth (1770-1819), daughter and co-heir of Henry Belasyse, 2nd earl of Fauconberg, of Newborough. George and Harriet had at least 4 sons:

1 James (1830-1878); succeeded as 6th baronet in June 1878, but died 4 months later; married, at St Andrew's episocpal chapel, Kelso, 6 August 1857, Susan Harriet, eldest daughter of James Henry Robert Innes Ker, 6th duke of Roxburghe, and Susanna Stephanie, daughter of Lt-Gen. Sir James Charles Dalbiac, KCH; 1 son and 4 daughters:
  1 Susan Harriet (1859-1946)
  2 Victoria Alberta (1868-1900)
  1 George (1870-1947); succeeded as 7th baronet
  3 Susan Harriet (d. 1841)
  4 Harriet (d. 1941)
2 Francis (1832-1884)
3 George (1835-1875)
4 Robert (1841-1933)

1829: 30 Jun: *Illness also is likely to cause some disappointment to Lady Elcho as to the expected arrival of Lord & Lady Wemyss from London with their unmarried daughters; the two youngest of whom are seized with the scarlet fever, & will not be able to visit their grandmother; but the rest of the family are likely to arrive in a few days. Lady Harriet Charteris is about to marry Mr. Suttie, eldest son of Sir James Suttie, an East Lothian Baronet, of very large fortune; the future bridegroom is represented to be a very handsome and estimable man; I remember his mother a beautiful woman.*

1839: 17 Jul: *Lady Wemyss was sitting with her daughter Lady Harriet Suttie, and the ladies Jane and Caroline Charteris. Lord Wemyss had gone out on horseback, attended by his Son in law. Sir Geo. Suttie.*

SUTTON — Eleanor Sutton[231]

Eleanor Sutton, née Addington (1749-1839), was the daughter of Anthony Addington (1713-1790) and Mary (±1722-1778), daughter and heir of Revd Haviland John Hiley (1689-1753), physician to William Pitt, of Reading, Berkshire, and Eleanor Terrell (d. 1768). Eleanor was the sister of Henry Addington, 1st Viscount Addington (1757-1844), prime minister, 1801-04. She married, 1 August 1771, James Sutton (±1733-1801), of Roundway House, New Park, the son of Prince Sutton, clothier, of Devizes, and Mary Willey. This connection between the Sutton and Addington families brought Henry Addington to Devizes, where he became MP. James and Eleanor had at least 2 sons and 3 daughters:

1 George William (dates unknown); died an infant
1 Mary (±1777-1791)
2 Eleanor (1779-1829); married Thomas Grimston Estcourt (1775-1853); 6 sons and 4 daughters
2 James (b. 1783); died an infant
3 Sarah Charlotte (1788-1841); married Robert J. Matthews

The Gentleman's Magazine states that on 18 May 1840, Mary, third daughter of James Sutton, of Devizes, died at Bath, aged 83, widow of Crispianus Load (1744-1813). This suggests a birth year of approximately 1757, which does not compute unless James Sutton had had a previous, unknown wife. Crispianus and Mary had actually married in 1798, and Mary was his second wife. It may be that there was another James Sutton in Devizes, possibly a brother or cousin to Prince Sutton.

James Sutton's mother, Mary Hiley, inherited the New Park estate on the death of her unmarried brother George Willey in 1770, and James inherited it from his elder brother Willey Sutton in

1775. The estate had been crown land until the mid-seventeenth-century when an unknown purchaser bought it. The Willey [or Willy] family—probably George Willy the elder, of Devizes, or his father—built the first house there in the early eighteenth century. James Sutton had profitable business interests in Devizes and London, and in 1777 he embarked on what is modestly termed in a surviving account book as 'alterations at New Park'. They were finished in 1783. James Wyatt was selected as architect and the resulting house was a splendid mansion. Roundway House was finally demolished in 1955.

1806: 22 Jul: ... *to Mrs. Sutton of New Park, Sister to Lord Sidmouth, a very lady like person, who with her Daughter & Miss Estcourts were the most pleasing persons in appearance in the circle.* 25 Jul., 7 Aug: *Walked in Mrs. Sutton's beautiful woods, passed the Evening very pleasantly.* 9 Aug: *Passed the Evening at Mrs. Gents. Tea, walking & supper, very pleasant, the Tylee Family, Mrs. Sutton, Mrs. Shields & daughter formed the party.*

1807: 8 Jan: *Mrs. Sutton called but I did not see her.* 24 Jun: *Drove my Mother to call upon Mrs. Sutton at New Park. Very handsomely received by Mrs. S. & Mrs. Estcourt, found there Mrs. Sutton of Devizes, Mrs. Shield, & Miss Haraland.* 27 Jul: ... *to dine at New Park, where we found a most pleasant reception from Mrs. Sutton & Mr. & Mrs. J. Estcourt Norhangers; only Mr. Estcourt Senr. & his Lady & two Daughters & a Miss Matthews. Music by Mrs. J. Estcourt & Miss C. E.—a very agreeable visit.*

1808: 27 Jan: *Mrs. Sutton & Mrs. Estcourt called.*

1826: 4 Feb.

1826: 26 Jan: *We passed the evening in a friendly way with Lady George Sutton & her sisters, the Mrs. Pearts, who reside near Mrs. Backhouse, being also old acquaintances of my poor Mother's.*

SWALE — Hoggarth John Swale and the Swale family of Langcliffe Hall [232]

Hogarth John Swale (1810-1893), Church of England clergyman, was born at Kendal, Cumberland, the son of John Swale (1770-1812) and Ann Hoggarth (1773-1859) of Langcliffe Hall. He appears to have dropped one of the 'gs' from his mother's name. He was educated at Queen's College, Oxford, where he was awarded a scholarship (BA 1832; MA 1836). Swale was the first vicar of Settle in 1838, and at some point he was the chaplain at the British Embassy in Paris. It is interesting that his daughter was married in Paris; indeed, the family appears to have been abroad at the time of the 1861 census.

Hogarth Swale married, first, at Giggleswick, 22 April 1841, Mary (1818-1844), daughter of George Thackrah Lambert (b. 1786) and Ellen Peart (1794-1825); they had 1 son and 1 daughter:

1 Ellen Eliza (1842-1913); married, in Paris, 11 June 1864, Ralph Assheton Nowell (1831-1912)
1 John Lambert (1844-1876)

Mary presumably died giving birth to John, or soon after. Hogarth married secondly, at St Mary's, West Brompton, Middlesex, 12 May 1851, Emily Charlotte, daughter of William Henry Gater; they had 5 sons and 1 daughter:

1 Harold (1853-1919)
2 Hugh (1857-1890)
1 Edith (b. 1861)
3 Gerald (b. 1863)
4 Cecil (1865-1938)
5 Francis Hewit (1871-1895)

Swale had three sisters; they must have been the young ladies that Francis Witts met:

1 Mary (b. 1802)
2 Ann (b. 1804)
3 Barbara (b. 1805)

1837: 22 Oct., 23 Oct: *Returned to Hartley's sometime before dinner, to meet two of the Misses Swale.* 27 Oct.

1838: 14 Sep., 15 Sep: *Mr. & Mrs. Robinson—Miss Lambert,—John and Mary Swale.*

SWEET — John Sweet [233]

John Sweet (d. 1822) was co-founder of the nurserymen firm Sweet & Miller of Durdham Down. He co-founded the business in 1786 with John Miller.

1804: 4 Sep: *On the Downs, at the Brigade & Miller's & Sweet's with my Father & Mother.*

SWEET — Stephen Sweet [234]

Stephen Sweet (±1770-±1841), bookseller, married, at St James's, Westminster, ±1803, Jane Nicoll; they had 2 sons and 1 daughter:

1 Louisa Emma (1805-1890)
1 Henry (1808-1885)
2 George (1816-1879)

The law bookselling firm was founded as Stephen Sweet in 1799. There appears to have been some form of merger with Alexander Maxwell's firm, founded in 1800. By 1802 the two traded as Sweet & Maxwell.

1844: 29 Nov: *Wrote to Mr. Sweet, law-bookseller, for particulars as to price, discount &c. of a new Edition of Burn's Justice about to be published.* 1-2 Dec., 9 Dec., 11 Dec.

SWEET-ESCOTT — *see* Escott

SYMONS — Benjamin Parsons Symons [235]

Benjamin Parsons Symons (1785-1878), vice-chancellor of Oxford University, was born at Cheddar, Somerset, the son of John Symons. He was educated at Wadham College, Oxford (BA 1805; MA 1810; BD 1819; DD 1831), where he was a fellow in 1812, bursar in 1814-23, and sub-warden. On 16 June 1831 he was elected warden of the college. He was vice-chancellor of Oxford University from 1844 to 1848. He resigned the wardenship on 18 October 1871, but continued to reside in Oxford until his death in 1878.

1802: 15 May: *A sad riot in College Simmonds & Steward.* 30 Apr: *The party in the inside of the coach beside myself were ... On the outside were Price & Simmons, freshmen of our College.*

1806: 21 Mar: *of the party were Stevens & his Wife, Matthias of B.N.C., Budd of C.C.C., Marsh, Marshall of Ball. Dr. Price, Michel, Simmons, Round, Dr. Cooper, Mr. Jebb, Mr. Davis.*

1829: 26 Feb: *I called also on the Sub-warden, Mr. Symons; he was out, but I met him returning to the College, and accepted his invitation to a dinner given in the Hall.*

1831: 20 Jun: *In the course of the past week an event not unworthy of being mentioned by me has occurred at Oxford, having reference to my own college, namely, the resignation of the Wardenship of Wadham by Dr. Tournay, in favour of Mr. Symons, fellow and Tutor. The abdication of the former and the election of the latter have taken place, and were accompanied by an expression of esteem and respect to these two most valuable persons, conformable to the taste of the times, and far better earned by them, than by many, on whom such tokens of regard have been conferred. To Dr. Tournay a handsome candelabrum was presented by a deputation, consisting of the two senior fellows, and to Mr. Symons an Epergne & Plateau after dinner in the hall.*

1832: 15 Mar: *I dined in the Hall of Wadham College, with my learned and worthy acquaintance and contemporary, Dr. Symons, Warden of that Society.*

1836: 11 Nov., 21 Nov., 25 Nov., 23 Dec.

1838: 10-11 Jul.

1839: 5 Jun: *In virtue of seniority I occupied a post of honour by the side of the Warden.*

1842: 1 Mar: *A letter from the Warden of Wadham Coll.* 2 Mar., 4 Mar., 19 Nov., 22 Nov.

1844: 26 Sep., 3 Oct., 8-9 Oct., 31 Oct.

1845: 9 Jan., 13 Jan., 24 Jan., 26 Jan., 11 Feb: *To Dr. Symons, accepting his obliging invitation to his house during the necessary time of my remaining at Oxford on the 13th. and 14th.* 13-14 Feb., 28 Jun.

1847: 26-27 Apr.

SYMONS — Jelinger Cookson Symons — *see also* Kendall[236]

Jelinger Cookson Symons (1809-1860), barrister-at-law and assistant commissioner to the royal commission on the handloom weavers, was the son of Revd Jelinger Symons (1778-1851), vicar of Radnage, Buckinghamshire, and Maria, eldest daughter of John Airey of Northumberland. He was educated at Trinity Hall, Cambridge (BA 1832), and was called to the bar at the Middle Temple in 1843. He practised on the Oxford circuit. He married, at St James's, Paddington, 16 June 1845, Angelina (±1824-1913), third daughter of Edward Kendall of Austrey, Warwickshire, and Cheltenham, Gloucestershire; they had at least 2 sons:

1 Jelinger Edward (1846-1934)
2 Edward Warwick Jelinger (1849-1915), Church of England clergyman

Symons was appointed by the home office one of the nine assistant commissioners to the royal commission on the handloom weavers. In 1840 he was appointed one of the six sub-commissioners of the children's employment commission. He visited the Yorkshire coalfield, where he was appalled by the sexual immorality resulting from the mixing of male and female labour underground. He also served as a tithe commissioner.

1845: 7 Mar: *Left Gloucester by Railway for Cheltenham before 3 PM. travelling in the same carriage with Mr. Baker of Lypiatt Park, and Mr. Jelinger Symons, the Barrister.*

1847: 21 Apr: *Received a packet of documents from the Committee of Privy Council on Education with a letter from Mr. Jelinger Symons, the Barrister.*

1848: 21 Mar., 15 Apr.

1850: 6 Nov: *fixed for an examination of the boys of the Union School, Mr. Jelinger Symons, the Government Inspector having reported unfavourably of the qualifications of the Schoolmaster, Hornsby.* 22 Nov.

1851: 7 Jan: *Received a letter from Mr. Jelinger Symonds, Inspector of Workhouse schools, addressed to me as Chairman of the Stow on the Wold Union.* 8 Mar: *After breakfast I accompanied my son in his carriage to Winchcombe, to meet Mr. Jelinger Symons, the inspector of Workhouse schools under the Comm. of privy council on Education.*

1852: 18 Mar: *Another daughter of Mr. Kendal is married to Mr. Jelinger Symons, the Barrister.*

1853: 16 Apr: *Drove to Stow: to be the Workhouse, where I met Mr. Jelinger Symons, Inspector of Workhouse.*

1854: 24 May: *Mr. Pearce having written to inform me that Mr. Jelinger Symons purposes to visit the Workhouse school to-morrow,*

T

TAGART — John Davies Tagart[1]

John Davies Tagart (1814-1885), chemist, was born at Bath, the son of William Tagart (1774-1817) and Amy Lathy (1776-1840). He was married to Jane (b. ±1815), who was born at Cheltenham. At the time of the 1851 census they had a nephew, Charles Edward Woodroffe (b. ±1842), born in London, living with them at 389 High Street, Cheltenham. By 1871 John Tagart had married, secondly, Kate Sale (b. ±1831), born at Oxted, Surrey. He and Kate had 1 son and 1 daughter:

1 John Edward Robinow (1864-1927); born in Edinburgh; died at Hastings, Sussex

1h Lucy (b. ±1866); born in Edinburgh

Little is known of John Davies Tagart other than an injunction that was brought against him on 3 March 1842 to stop him selling a medicine he advertised as 'Sir James Murray's Fluid Magnesia'. He died at Lewes, Sussex, and was buried at Cheltenham.

The bulbs of the squill plant were used to make medicine. It was taken to treat mild heart failure, irregular heartbeat, 'nervous' heart complaints, and certain vascular problems. It was also taken as a 'heart tonic'. White squill was made from the bulb of *Drimia maritima*. Francis Witts suffered from a heart condition, and he died from a heart attack in August 1854.

1844: 10 Sep: *Wrote to Tagard Chemist, Cheltenham, for a box of pills.*

1845: 9 Feb: *Wrote a note to Tagart, Chemist, Cheltenham, for a supply of pills.* 22 Jun.

1847: 10 Sep: *Wrote to Tagart, Chemist, Cheltenham for a box of Squill pills.*

1848: 23 Oct.

1850: 7 Feb., 22 Mar.

1851: 6 Mar.

TALBOT — George Talbot[2]

George Talbot (1763-1836), JP and landed proprietor, was the son of Revd George Talbot (d. 1782) and Anne Bouverie, daughter of Jacob des Bouverie, 1st Viscount Folkestone. He was educated at Exeter College, Oxford (BA 1783; BCL 1786), and married, 1789, Charlotte Elizabeth, daughter of Revd Thomas Drake. They had 2 daughters:

1 Mary Anne (1789-1851); married, at St Marylebone, Westminster, 18 May 1815, Francis Lawley (1782-1851) of Spoonhill

2 Charlotte (1792-1879); married, at St George's, Hanover Square, Westminster, 26 June 1818, William Mount (1787-1869); 2 sons and 3 daughters:

  1 Mary Anne Jane (1819-1892)

  2 Charlotte Elizabeth (1822-1853)

  1 William George (1824-1906)

  2 Thomes Edward (1828-1841)

  3 Francis John (1831-1903), archdeacon of Chichester

The family lived at Temple Guiting.

1823: 15 Jul., 14 Oct.

1824: 13 Jan.

1826: 30 Mar., 17 Apr: *We dined at Mr. Dolphin's at Eyford. We met there Mr. Talbot, Mr. & Mrs. R. Wynniatt.* 22 Apr., 15 Sep., 3 Oct: *The meeting of the Stow Book Society ... Mr. Talbot presided in the room of Mr. East, who is absent from Adlestrop.*

1827: 30 Jun: *On our return in the afternoon we called for half an hour at Mr. Bowen's parsonage at Temple Guiting, who welcomed us very hospitably shewed us his handsome church, new to Edward, and took us a little circuit in Mr. Talbot's grounds, which neither Margaret nor Edward had ever visited, & which are very pleasantly and tastefully laid out ... The family is in Town: so it is, that fashionable people desert their country seats, their rich parks, & lovely gardens in the finest season.* 2 Oct., 16 Oct.

1828: 12 Feb., 17 Dec.

1829: 13 Jan., 28 Apr., 22 Sep., 24 Nov.

1830: 20 Apr.

1833: 6 Nov: *We had previously passed a seat of Lord Middleton's, which is now and has long been occupied by Mr. F. Lawley, late MP. for Warwickshire and Son in Law of our neighbour Mr. Talbot.*

1834: 30 Sep., 17 Dec.

1835: 1 Jan., 5 Jan., 10 Jan., 14-15 Jan., 17 Jan., 21 Jan.

1836: 30 Aug: *Engaged before breakfast in writing letters: to T. J. Ll. Baker, reminding him of the great agricultural sale of the Stock &c. of the late Mr. Talbot, to take place on the 6th. Sept.* 1 Sep., 6-7 Sep., 10 Oct.

1837: 1 Jun.

1842: 7 Apr.

1846: 27 Oct.

TALBOT — George Gustavus Chetwynd-Talbot[3]

George Gustavus Chetwynd-Talbot (1810-1896), Church of England clergyman and JP, was born at Ingestre, Staffordshire, the son of Charles Chetwynd Chetwynd-Talbot, 2nd Earl Talbot (1777-1849), and Frances Thomasine Lambart (1782-1819). He was educated at Christ Church, Oxford (BA 1828; MA 1831), and was ordained deacon on 7 July 1833 and priest on 20 December 1834. His first clerical appointment was as curate of Ingestre from 7 July 1833. He was then appointed rector of Withington on 23 December 1834. He married, at Withington, Gloucestershire, 25 June 1842, Emily Sarah (1815-1876), daughter of Henry Elwes (1787-1850), of Colesbourne House, and Susan (1784-1832), daughter of Anthony Hamond, of Westacre, Norfolk, and Sarah Case. George and Emily had 2 sons and 4 daughters:

1 Emily Margaret (1843-1886); married, at Northleach, Gloucestershire, 15 December 1864, John Habington Barneby Lutley (1840-1906); 1 son and 4 daughters:

  1 Gwendolen Emily Frances (1866-1932)

  2 Ethel Susan (1868-1945)

  3 Geraldine Violet (1869-1897)

  4 Gertrude Emily (1872-1937)

  1 John Talbot (1873-1946), Col

1 George Canning (1845-1891); educated at Rugby School; married, at Winchcombe, Gloucestershire, July 1875, Edith Mary Brocklehurst (1850-1932); at least 1 son:

  1 John Arthur William (1876-1918)

2 Caroline Sarah (1848-1850); died an infant

2 Gustavus Arthur (1848-1920); married, at Freebridge Lynn, Norfolk, January 1880, a cousin, Susan Frances Elwes (1853-1934); 3 sons and 2 daughters:

1 Reginald George (1881-1939)
1 Cecil Emily (1884-1949)
2 Constance Evelyn Mary (1887-1949)
2 Gilbert Gustavus (b. 1888)
3 Humphrey Richard (1889-1914)
3 Emma Frances (1853-1875)
4 Adela Henrietta (1856-1892)

1837: 15 Aug: *Dined at the Wallers, Farmington Lodge, meeting the Bride and Bridegroom from Bourton on the W. (R. Waller and his wife) Mr. Talbot, a son of Lord Talbot's, Rector of Withington, a Magistrate for the County, and a very pleasing young man...* 18 Aug.
1838: 3 Jan., 14 Aug.
1839: 22 Mar., 6 Apr., 9 Apr.
1840: 30 Jun., 16 Oct.
1842: 23 Mar., 12 Apr., 16 Oct., 18 Oct.
1843: 3 Jan., 2-3 Feb.
1844: 31 Dec.
1845: 7 Mar., 12 Mar., 3 Apr., 15 Apr., 7 May.
1847: 12 May, 18 May.
1850: 1 Jan., 25 Apr.
1853: 4 Jan., 28 Jun.
1854: 14 Feb., 23 Mar.

TALBOT — James Talbot [4]

James Talbot, 3rd Baron Malahide (1767-1850), diplomat, was born at Malahide Castle, Dublin, the son of Col Richard Wogan Talbot Demalahide (1736-1788) and Margaret O'Reilly, *suo jure* Baroness Talbot of Malahide (1740-1834). He was educated at Trinity College, Dublin, and Gray's Inn. He married, 26 December 1804, Ann Sarah (1785-1857), daughter of Samuel Rodbard of Evercreech House, Somerset; they had 7 sons and 6 daughters:
1 James (1805-1883); succeeded as 4th Baron Malahide
1 Margaret Nugent (1807-1887)
2 Samuel Rodbard John Neil (1808-1863)
3 Richard Gilbert (1810-1879)
2 Anne (1811-1832)
4 John Mervin (1813-1830)
3 Harriett Mary Everard (1814-1881)
5 George (1816-1886)
6 Edward Plantagenet Airey (1817-1904)
4 Mary Ann [Marianne] Flora Etruria (1819-1878)
5 Charlotte Etruria (1822-1855)
7 William Leopold Porsenna (1824-1881)
6 Susan Anne (1827-1919)

James Talbot succeeded his brother Richard as 3rd Baron Malahide in 1849. He served in the diplomatic service from 1796 to 1801 in the Swiss cantons and Sweden, although he was forced by unknown circumstances to leave Stockholm. He met the Witts family in Copenhagen, during which period he featured in Agnes Witts's diaries. He returned to Edinburgh with the Wittses aboard HMS *Kite*.

1801: 3 Apr: *Lord Kellie & Mr. Talbot rendered their morning's visit instructive & agreeable.* 4 Apr: *Our dinner at Lord Elcho's was very late, but very cordial: no one was there, but Mr. Stormonth, & in the Evening Mr. Talbot & Dr. Beake, who proposed to follow Mr.Drummond on the ensuing day.* 1 May, 16-17 May, 4 Jun., 9 Jun.

TALBOT — John Chetwynd-Talbot [5]

John Chetwynd-Talbot (1806-1852), barrister-at-law, was born at Ingestre, Staffordshire, the son of Charles Chetwynd Chetwynd-Talbot, 2nd Earl Talbot (1777-1849), and Frances Thomasine Lambart (1782-1819). He was elder brother to George Chetwynd-Talbot (*above*). He was educated at Christ Church, Oxford (BA 1827; MA 1829), and Lincoln's Inn (1829). He was admitted to the Middle Temple in 1836 and became queen's counsel and a bencher in 1843. He married, at York, 26 August 1830, Caroline Jane (1810-1876), daughter of James Archibald Stuart-Wortley-Mackenzie, 1st Baron Wharncliffe (1776-1845), and Lady Caroline Elizabeth Mary Crichton (1779-1856); they had at least 2 sons:
1 John Gilbert (1835-1910)
2 Edward Stuart (1844-1934)

1829: 15 May: *We dined with the Egerton Leighs at Broadwell, John Talbot came to tea.*

TALFOURD — Thomas Noon Talfourd [6]

Thomas Noon Talfourd (1795-1854), MP and judge, was born at Reading, Berkshire, the son of Edward Talfourd (1769-1833), brewer, and Anne Noon (1773-1858). He received his education at Hendon and Reading Grammar School, and at the age of 18 he was sent to London to study law under Joseph Chitty, the special pleader. Early in 1821 Talfourd joined the Oxford circuit, having been called to the bar earlier in the year. Fourteen years later, he was created a serjeant-at-law, and in 1849 he succeeded Thomas Coltman as judge of the court of common pleas. In 1835 he was elected MP for the borough of Reading, and was re-elected in 1837. He chose not to run in the general election of 1841, but stood again in the general election of 1847 and was elected. In the House of Commons Talfourd introduced a copyright bill in 1837, but the dissolution of parliament in the same year following the death of William IV meant that it had to be reintroduced in the new parliament in 1838, when it met with strong opposition. Talfourd re-introduced it again in 1839, 1840, and 1841. It finally became law in 1842, albeit in modified form and at a time when Talfourd was not in parliament. Charles Dickens dedicated *The Pickwick Papers* to Talfourd.

Thomas Noon Talfourd married, at St John's, Hackney, Middlesex, 31 August 1822, Rachael (1792-1875), daughter of John Towill Rutt; they had at least 4 sons and 2 daughters:
1 Francis (1827-1862), barrister and dramatist
1 Mary (1829-1901)
2 Charles Lamb (1830-1836)
3 William Wordsworth (1831-1900)
2 Catherine (1833-1915)
4 Thomas Noon (1836-1885)

1826: 7 Aug.
1834: 30 Sep.
1846: 11 Aug.
1851: 31 Mar: *Mr. Justice Talfourd was the presiding Judge. Mr. Justice Patteson presided at Nisi Prius ... I arrived in Court just after Talfourd had finished his charge to the Grand Jury, which he very gracefully, eloquently, and properly closed with a well considered and pertinent tribute of admiration and esteem to the memory of Sergeant Ludlow, for many years his rival and Competitor on this Circuit.*
1853: 4 Apr.

TALMAGE — John Mayow Talmage[7]

John Mayow Talmage (1813-1883), Church of England clergyman, was born at Headington, Oxfordshire, the son of Charles Talmage (1771-1845) and Ann Mayow. He was educated at Christ Church, Oxford (BA 1834; MA 1838), where he was chaplain from 1836 to 1845. He was appointed rector of Fifield with Idbury, Oxfordshire, in 1843. Talmage married, first, at Charlbury, Oxfordshire, 23 January 1845, Louisa (1816-1863), eldest daughter of Francis South of St David's Hill, Devon. He married secondly, at St Stephen's, Shepherd's Bush, Westminster, 4 September 1866, Susan (1842-1915), eldest daughter of William Jones Penkivil, barrister-at-law; they had at least 2 sons:

1 John Mayow Lionel (1868-1909)
2 Algernon Mayow (1871-1939)

1844: 5 Dec: *At a subordinate meeting of the Book Society the Revd. Talmage, of Fifield, was elected a member.*

1845: 26 Mar: *Of Clergymen of adjoining deaneries or dioceses, Messrs. Hutchinson, Talmage, Lockwood, Winter, and Crawley...*

1846: 21 Sep.

1850: 18 Sep.

1852: 14 Apr., 22 Apr.

1853: 30 Mar.

1854: 3 May.

TAMBURINI — Antonio Tamburini[8]

Antonio Tamburini (1800-1876), baritone singer, was born in Faenza, then part of the Papal States in Italy. As a youth he studied the horn with his bandmaster father and voice with Aldobrando Rossi and Bonifazio Asioli. He made his operatic debut at 18 years old in Cento in Pietro Generali's *La contessa di colle erbose*. He sang in Piacenza, Naples, Livorno, and Turin, before appearing in 1822 at La Scala, Milan, in Rossini's *Matilde di Shabran*, Saverio Mercadante's *Adele e Emerico*, and the first performance of Donizetti's *Chiara e Serafin*. He often worked with the tenor Giovanni Battista Rubini and the soprano Giulia Grisi, and was renowned for his good looks and impressive stage presence. He was most famous, however, for his association with Bellini's operas, such as *I Puritani*. Alongside Grisi, Rubini, and the bass Luigi Lablache, Tamburini was one of the so-called 'Puritani Quartet' of leading international singers. In 1843 the quartet was reunited on stage, albeit with Giovanni Mario replacing Rubini, at the premiere of Donizetti's *Don Pasquale*.

Tamburini was a particular favourite with London and Paris audiences. He was married to the contralto Marietta Gioia-Tamburini, and they often sang together. Tamburini returned to Italy for a brief time, and then in 1844 he moved to St Petersburg, Russia, where he stayed until his retirement a decade later. He was known for his musicianship and versatility; during a performance in Palermo he was said to have taken the costume and role of a young soprano too frightened to sing.

1834: 15 Aug: *Mrs. Howell, Emmeline and William set out before breakfast to pass the day at Cheltenham with some friends, and attend a concert by some distinguished vocalists, Grisi, Tamburini and Ivanhoff, with Puzzi on the horn.*

TANCRED — Thomas Tancred — *see also* Ibbetson *and* Mills[9]

Sir Thomas Tancred, 6th baronet (1780-1844), landed proprietor, was born at Aldborough Manor, Aldborough, Yorkshire, the son of Sir Thomas Tancred, 5th baronet (1749-1784), and Penelope (1745-1837), daughter of Thomas Assheton-Smith of Bowdon, Cheshire. He succeeded as 6th baronet in 1784. He married, in Staffordshire, 25 April 1805, a cousin, Harriet Lucy (1781-1864), daughter of Revd Offley Crewe (1765-1836) and Harriet Assheton-Smith (1765-1865); they had at least 4 sons and 1 daughter:

1 Thomas (1808-1880); succeeded as 7th baronet, 1844; married, 16 April, 1839, Jane (1818-1901), third daughter of Prideaux John Selby of Twizell House, Northumberland; 6 sons and 4 daughters:
  1 Thomas Selby (1840-1910); succeeded as 8th baronet
  1 Lucy Sybille (1842-1933)
  2 Henry Assheton (b. 1844)
  2 Gertrude Annie (b. 1848)
  3 Edith Jane (b. 1849)
  3 Prideaux Francis (b. 1850)
  4 Clement William (1852-1888)
  5 Seymer Mitford (1856-1929)
  6 Harry George (b. 1857)
  4 Bertha Eveline (1860-1952)
1 Harriet Anne (1812-1847)
2 Henry John (1816-1884); educated at Rugby School; served in a hussar regiment of the Austrian Army; bought land in New Zealand and settled there in 1850; married, 30 July 1857, Georgeanna Janet Grace Richmond; no children
3 Robert William (1818-1846)
4 William (1818-1864)
2 Susan (1821-1910)

The Witts family knew Thomas Tancred in Weimar where he was presumably studying at the Belvedere under M. Mounier. He was only fleetingly mentioned by Francis Witts, but he appeared in the diaries of Agnes Witts on 15 December 1798: 'Sr. Thos. Tancred, Mr. Mills, Mr. Walker & Mr. Ibbetson here before they went to the Opera'.

Tancred's two sons Thomas and Henry John both emigrated to New Zealand, and Thomas himself died there. He was buried at Old Napier cemetery, Hawkes Bay.

1846: 18 Jun: *About a mile from Cowes Castle, along the beach, westward, close to the water's edge, is West cliff or Egypt, a castellated villa, the property of Sir T. Tancred, but usually occupied by some distinguished member of the Yacht club.*

TAPLIN — George Taplin, Mr Brookes's clerk[10]

This attribution to George Taplin (1831-1879), missionary and teacher, is highly speculative. No one of the name Taplin was recorded in the censuses for 1841 or 1851, and Francis Witts only mentioned him in his diaries during a period of two years. George Taplin was born on 24 August 1831 at Kingston-upon-Thames, Surrey. At 12 years old he went to live with his maternal grandfather in Andover, Hampshire, and was educated there in a private school. His father died when he was 14 and in 1842 he became a solicitor's clerk at Andover. The question is whether or not there was a connection that led George to leave Andover for South Australia. His employer died in March 1849 and this may have been what precipitated his emigration. If this attribution is correct, it is also surprising that the diarist should have given a mere 16-year-old boy the dignity of the term 'Mr'. However, putting these doubts and questions to one side, the following is George Taplin's story.

A committed Congregationalist, from the age of 15 George Taplin had desired to become an overseas missionary. He arrived in Adelaide in the *Anna Maria* on 12 October 1849 and worked initially as a labourer and a lawyer's clerk. In June 1851 Taplin was recruited for the ministry by Revd T. Q. Stow. He lived with Stow, studying and working in the garden for his board and lodging. On 28 February 1853, at Payneham, Taplin married Stow's servant Martha Burnell, who also aspired to missionary work. In October 1853 they went to Currency Creek and later to Port Elliot, where in February the next year Taplin opened a school. The Central Board of Education took it over but he remained as teacher until 1859. That year the Aborigines Friends Association appointed Taplin as their first missionary-teacher with a salary of £200 to work in the lower Murray districts. The site he chose for a settlement on the shores of Lake Alexandrina was a traditional camping ground called Raukkan (The Ancient Way), known to Europeans as Point McLeay.

Taplin was ordained by the Congregational Church in 1868 so that he could administer sacraments and solemnise marriages. The next year the chapel was completed and opened. He was keenly interested in Ngarrindjeri culture and society and learned their language; he used it in his preaching, and translated and published Bible tracts. Taplin also published invaluable anthropological studies which were far superior to contemporary works on South Australian aboriginals. He died of heart disease in 1879, and was survived by his wife and six children.

1846: 26 Jun: *to Mr. Taplin, Mr. Brookes's Clerk, as to a prosecution against a prisoner charged with felony, and to be tried at the Quarter Sessions next week.* 9 Dec: *To Mr. Brookes's office, where conferred with Mr. Taplin on Justice business.*

1847: 27 Jan., 30 Dec.

1848: 28 Apr., 20 Sep., 5 Oct.

TARN — Miles Brookes Tarn [11]

Miles Brookes Tarn (±1781-1870), solicitor, was born at Shipton, Oxfordshire, but appears to have come from an old Cumbrian family. He married, 1815, Lucy Ann Renfield (±1798-1853), who was born at Arundel, Sussex. He was listed in 1830 as an attorney, but later referred to himself as a solicitor, but this was common in his profession. From Stow-on-the-Wold he moved first to Leamington Priors, and later, after the death of his wife, to Newton Abbott, Devon, where he lived with his sister Mary Tarn. He died at Newton Abbot in 1870.

1834: 14 Jul: *Mr. Tarn called relative to the pros. of persons detected at Banksfee shooting wild-fowl on Sunday June 29.* 17 Jul: *Mr. Tarn prosecuted to conviction six men from Longborough detected by the Police in the act of shooting wild fowl under circumstances which we considered to bring them within the scope of the Game Act.* 5 Aug., 7 Nov: *Wrote to Mr. Tarn, Stow, in the name of the Magistrates, tendering to his acceptance a check for Ten Guineas, as a small renumeration for his assistance in the enquiry as to the perpetrators of the cruel murder of poor Rens.* 8 Nov.

1835: 13 Feb., 18 Feb., 23 Feb., 2 Apr., 4 Apr., 13 Apr: *In the course of the Evening, Mr. Tarn called on me to state that subsequently to the trial of Edmund Jeffrey, Mr. Bonner, the Attorney employed for the defence had communicated to him, that the Prisoner in his private communications with him, had admitted that he had an accomplice in the murder.*

1836: 25 Aug., 27 Aug., 29 Aug., 10 Dec.

1837: 6 Feb., 13 Jul., 20 Jul., 7-8 Sep., 26 Sep.,12 Oct., 4 Nov., 11 Nov.

1838: 11 Jan., 5 Feb., 8 Mar., 5 Apr., 20 Apr., 23 Apr: *I found a note from Mr. Tarn excusing himself from accepting my invitation to dinner on Friday next on the plea of ill health.* 27 Apr., 9 Aug., 1 Sep.

1839: 23 Jul.

1843: 25 Sep: *The latter explained the circumstances under which the property had been bought by him, and the conveyance not signed by the person in question; adding that Mr. Tarn, the late Solr. of Stow, who acted for Forty, had assured him that the signature of the individual alluded to was of no importance.* 2-3 Nov.

TAUNTON — William Elias Taunton [12]

Sir William Elias Taunton (1773-1835), judge, was born at Oxford, the eldest son of Sir William Elias Taunton, town clerk of Oxford and clerk of the peace for the county, and Frances, daughter of Stephen Grosvenor, sub-treasurer of Christ Church, Oxford. He was educated at Westminster School and Christ Church, Oxford (BA 1793; MA 1796), where in 1793 he gained the chancellor's prize for the English essay. He was admitted a student of Lincoln's Inn in 1794, and was called to the bar in Easter term 1799. He joined the Oxford circuit. In 1801 he became a commissioner of bankrupts, and in 1806 he succeeded Charles Abbot as recorder of Oxford. Taunton married, 1814, Maria, youngest daughter of Henry William Atkinson, provost of the Company of Moneyers. He was created king's counsel in 1821 and elected a bencher of his inn in 1822. On 12 November 1830 he was appointed a justice of the king's bench and was knighted five days later.

1827: 11 Apr: *...Taunton, whose learning and tact are of the first order, answered him ably: Mr. Serjt. Bosanquet sums up well, and appears thoroughly conversant with the judicial duties.* 15 Apr: *Mr. Taunton is King's Counsel, and may be considered as leader of the circuit: he is a very able lawyer, and experienced pleader; his voice & appearance are disagreeable, but his manner cool, collected, deliberate and impressive. He is the eldest Son of the late Town Clerk of Oxford, Sir Elias Taunton, who lived in my undergraduate days in a suburban staring brick house on the Isis, which he had called Grand Pont, and which the capped & gowned wits easily transmuted into Grand Punt.*

1828: 17 Apr: *Mr. Taunton, Kings Counsel, a lawyer of great experience & ability, was brought down from town to lead, at an expence of fully a hundred Guineas, including travelling expences &c.*

1829: 3 Apr: *Mr. Taunton, clear, distinct, logical, singularly happy in making himself understood by persons not of that profession, the learning of which he possesses in no ordinary degree.*

1830: 22 Apr.

1832: 3 Jan., 29 Mar.

1842: 13 Apr.

TAWNEY — Bradnam Tawney [13]

Bradnam Tawney (1745-±1810), Church of England clergyman, was educated at Magdalen College, Oxford (BA 1766; MA 1769; BD 1788). He was a minor canon of Winchester Cathedral, chaplain of Winchester College, vicar of Preston Candover, Hampshire, and rector of St Thomas and St Clement's, Winchester, 1788-1810. He married, March 1770, the eldest daughter of Jabez Jugger, a well-known grocer and distiller in Oxford. She died in 1811.

1803: 31 Oct: *My acquaintance Mr. Tawney on the Roof where I travelled part of the way attracted by him & a sensible agreeable Clergyman.*

TAYLOR — Mr Taylor, cousin of James Currie Duncan

1835: 9 Jun: *Mr. Taylor, a cousin of Mr. Currie Duncan, not a very young man, but an undergraduate of Cambridge, and preparing himself for the Church, apparently a well informed and worthy person, who had come to Town to attend his relation as bridegroom's man.* 10-11 Jun.

TAYLOR — James Taylor [14]

James Taylor (1771-1847), Church of England clergyman, was the son of Revd John Taylor (d. 1793) of Clifton. His father was rector of St Ewen's, Bristol, and perpetual curate of Clifton from 20 May 1762 to 26 April 1793. James was educated at St John's College, Oxford, and was ordained deacon on 31 May 1795 and priest on 20 December 1795. He was appointed perpetual curate of Clifton on 25 December 1795, and served the parish until his death in 1847. He was married to Eliza (b. ±1840), who was born in Ireland. They lived at Mall Buildings, Clifton.

1833: 11 Apr: *The minister, is Mr. Hensman, a very popular clergyman, was at one time the officiating & responsible Pastor of the Congregation at Clifton Church, during the absence of the incumbent, Mr. Taylor, a man of very indifferent character.*

TAYLOR — John Duncombe Taylor — *see also* Vanderhorst [15]

John Duncombe Taylor (1774-1835), merchant and slave owner, was from a wealthy slave-owning family with sugar plantations in Antigua. For many years he was a resident of Clifton, but he returned to his native Sion Hill, Antigua, where he died on 28 February 1835. It is unclear what happened to the property; it appears that John Duncombe Taylor unsuccessfully claimed the estates of Little Sion and Sion Hill as owner-in-fee, but the reasons are not clear.

Duncombe Taylor married, at Clifton, 1798, Mary Cooper Vanderhorst (1767-1823), daughter of Elias Honorius Vanderhorst (1738-1816) and Mary Raven Cooper [or Cowper] (1742-1797) of Charleston, South Carolina; they had 1 daughter:

- 1 Cordelia (1807-1875); married Alexander Moffat (1801-1848), who changed his name to Duncombe; 4 sons and 2 daughters:
  - 1 Henry Duncombe (1833-1862)
  - 2 William Duncombe Vanderhorst (1833-1925)
  - 1 Jessica Mary Duncombe (1835-1885)
  - 3 Ernest Cooper (1837-1880)
  - 2 Blanche Cordelia (1840-1918)
  - 4 Charles Byam Duer (±1845-1897); born in Antigua

The Vanderhorst family was established in South Carolina towards the end of the seventeenth century by Elias Vanderhorst's grandfather, a subaltern from Rotterdam who had followed William of Orange to England in 1688. From there he had emigrated to Charleston, where his son was born. Elias's mother Mary was also born in South Carolina; her family had left Paris to join Charleston's Huguenot community. Elias inherited a considerable fortune when his father died during his infancy. In 1759 and 1760 he served in the wars against the Cherokees and afterwards became a merchant. He married Mary Raven Cooper [Cowper] in 1763; they had ten children, but only 2 sons and 5 daughters survived infancy:

- 1 Elizabeth Cooper (1753-1820); died unmarried
- 1 Elias (1763-1874); married, in South Carolina, 30 March 1784, unknown
- 2 Mary Cooper (b. 1767); married John Duncombe Taylor of Antigua
- 3 Harriet Cooper (1769-1837); married Henry Thomas Shewen of Swansea
- 2 Thomas Cooper (1773-1849); born at Charleston, South Carolina; married, at St Stephen's, Bristol, 1799, Mary Hannah Beale (1770-1806)
- 4 Anne Catherine (1780-1864); married John Rees of Carmarthen
- 5 Carolina Mary (1784-1802); died unmarried

An unfortunate business venture made Elias dependent on his mother-in-law's income. Health and financial problems probably prompted his emigration in 1774 with his family and mother-in-law to Bristol, where once again he established himself as a merchant. On 3 October 1787 Elias Vanderhorst became a burgess of Bristol, but he does not appear to have exercised his right to vote.

1804: 21 Jul: *At a party at Ashton in the Evening, the Taylors, Miss Vanderhorst, Manners's, Weir, Horton &c.* 12 Sep: *Walked with Miss Van Der Horst & Miss Taylor to Bristol.* 23 Dec: *to visit the Vander Horsts: found Mr. Taylor, Miss V & Miss T. at home.*

1805: 2 February: *Walked to Bristol, with Miss Russel & with Mr. & Mrs. Taylor.* 10 Nov.

1806: 20 Jul: *met by a Miss A. Taylor, other Company to Tea, particularly, Mrs. Hillier & her interesting Daughter nearly blind, Mrs. Carrick's cousin whom I conversed with for a long time.*

TAYLOR — Richard Taylor and the Taylor family of Totteridge [16]

Richard Taylor (d. 1804) appears to have been a neighbour of the Arrowsmith family at Totteridge. It seems likely that he was of the same Taylor family that lodged at Charlton while visiting Cheltenham in August 1802. There are numerous references to this family in the diaries of Agnes Witts, but it is confusing that in his will of 1804 Richard Taylor made no mention of a wife.

1802: 22 Aug: *Called upon Mr. & Mrs. Taylor, & Sir. W. Altham.*

1803: 7 Oct: *Miss Richardson & Miss Fiott left Totteridge for Layton.The rest of the party except Mr. Arrowsmith called on Mr. & Mrs. Taylor & the Marshams.* 16 Oct., 19 Oct: *Mr. Bowzer's & Mr. Taylor's Family came to the Park to Tea & Supper.*

TEAL — John Teal [17]

John Teal (1800-1874), agricultural labourer, was born at Broadwell, the son of Thomas and Mary Teal. He was married to Susannah (±1810-1887) and they lived 'behind Noon' at Stow-on-the-Wold with 1 son and 5 daughters:

- 1 Sophia (b. ±1824)
- 2 Mary Ann (b. ±1827)
- 3 Elizabeth (b. ±1830)
- 4 Emma (b. ±1834)
- 5 Fanny (b. ±1837)
- 1 George (b. 1840)

Both John and Susannah were agricultural labourers. In 1838 John Teale was imprisoned again for a sentence of four months for the crime of larceny. By 1871 John and Susanna lived in Sheep Street with their grandson William Tuffley (±1864-1911). By 1881 Susanna was a widow and still living with her grandson William.

1834: 9 Aug: *Delayed by other magisterial business, among the rest, by an atrocious assault committed by one Teale, who on being served with a notice of recognizance by Otway the Senior Off. of Police, threw himself into a most towering rage, and in a struggle bit the top of Otway's right thumb clean through, nail and all.* 16 Oct: *Nothing very interesting, except, as far as I was concerned, the trial of Teal, of Stow, for an assault on Otway, by savagely biting his thumb, when in the discharge of his duty as a constable. Teal found guilty, and sentenced to four months imprisonment, to hard labour.*

1835: 7 May: ... *the list of names consists of the very refuse of society in the ... men, such as Clifford, Cox & Teale, who have been brought into trouble and under the suspicion of the Magistrates.*

TEAST — Sydenham Teast[18]

Sydenham Teast (1789-1868), shipbuilder, JP, and DL, was born at Bristol, the son of Sydenham Teast (1754-1813) and Eleanor Buckle (1764-1841). His father was a Bristol-based Quaker merchant in the African ivory and timber trade, and a whaler, fur-trader, shipbuilder, and shipowner. He was also involved in the slave trade, and refitted the slaver *Hector* in 1776. He constructed Redcliffe Parade in Bristol in the 1770s, and built two dry docks at Wapping on the Avon in 1755, and a further two at Canon's Marsh on the mouth of the River Frome in 1790. On 9 September 1782, Teast's company launched the *Hermione*, a fifth-rate 32-gun frigate, the only warship built by the yard. In 1861, Sydenham Teast (junior) was listed in the census as an unmarried man living at Durdham Down.

1845: 15 Apr.

1847: 23 Mar: *At the Gloucester Station had a parley with Col. Browne, Mr. Clutterbuck, and Mr. Teast, and with the latter walked from the Cheltenham Railway Station to the Plough.*

TEBBUTT — John Chew Tebbutt[19]

John Chew Tebbutt (±1805-1873) was born at Sudborough, Northamptonshire, the son of Sanders Tebbutt (1778-1832) and Ann Chew (1782-1806). He was an ale and porter brewer, and a farmer of 700 acres, employing twenty-six men and six boys. He married, at Godmanchester, Huntingdonshire, Mary Ann Aldwincle (1812-1890); they had 7 sons and 3 daughters:

1 Sophia Anne (1834-1938)
1 Frederick John (1836-1909)
2 Charles Augustus (b. & d. 1837)
3 Charles Edward (1838-1898)
4 Sanders (1839-1899)
2 Marianne [Marion] (1842-1928)
5 George Henry (1846-1883)
6 Joseph Alfred (1849-1886)
3 Anne (b. 1851)
7 Alfred (b. 1855)

1835: 24 Mar: *The navigation of the river is, however, still very incomplete. Thrapstone appeared to be a thriving Market town. Here I left the coach to pursue its route through Huntingdon to Cambridge, and was met at the Inn by Mr. J. C. Tebbutt, the Steward of the Wadenhoe estate.* 25 Mar: *Much engaged all the forenoon in conferences with Miss Hunts, with Mr. Tebbutt, the Steward, and the Undertaker from Oundle.* 27 Mar: *Accompanied Mr. George Hunt and Mr. Tebbutt in a walk over parts of the Wadenhoe property.* 28 Mar., 30 Mar: *Engaged the whole day in business with the Ladies and Mr. Tebbutt.* 31 Mar., 25 May, 5 Jun.

1836: 15 Jul., 16 Oct., 1 Nov.

1837: 21 Apr., 6 May, 11 Nov.

1847: 11 Aug., 14 Aug., 2-3 Nov.

TELFORD — Thomas Telford[20]

Thomas Telford (1757-1834), civil engineer, was born at Eskdale, Dumfriesshire, the son of John Telford, shepherd. His father died soon after he was born, and at the age of 14 he was apprenticed to a stonemason. He worked for a time in Edinburgh before moving to London in 1782. There he met architects Robert Adam and Sir William Chambers, and was involved in building extensions to Somerset House. Two years later Telford found work at Portsmouth dockyard. Although largely self-taught, he was becoming knowledgeable in the specification, design, and management of building projects.

In 1787, through the patronage of William Pulteney, Telford was appointed surveyor of public works in Shropshire. In 1790, as Shropshire county surveyor, Telford designed a bridge to carry the London–Holyhead road over the River Severn at Montford; it was the first of some forty bridges he was to build in Shropshire, including major crossings over the Severn at Buildwas and Bridgnorth. The bridge at Buildwas was Telford's first iron bridge.

After establishing himself as an engineer of road and canal projects in Shropshire, Telford designed numerous infrastructure projects in his native Scotland, including harbours and tunnels. Such was his reputation as a prolific designer of highways and bridges, he was dubbed 'The Colossus of Roads', and was elected as the first president of the Institution of Civil Engineers. He retained the post for fourteen years until his death. He never married.

1826: 10 Jan: *Mr. Telford was requested to survey the river, select a proper site and give in correspondent plans.* 31 Aug: *Mr. Telford is, I understand, the presiding genius here; this able engineer is a native of Eskdale on the Scottish borders, and was a mason in the same parish, which gave birth to Sir John & Sir Pulteney Malcolm .... My excellent friend, Malcolm, Rector of Toddenham ... has told me, that Telford first came up as a mason to London about 1782 to work at the Adelphi, then building. His talent & scientific turn of mind, with the patronage of powerful & discerning men, among whom was Sir James Pulteney, who employed him largely on his estates and collieries, canals &c. in Shropshire, have gradually advanced him to the very summit of his profession; so that at the present time the execution of all public works, docks, canals, bridges, roads &c. of great importance, is submitted to his judgment, both by government & other public bodies.*

1827: 2 Apr: *We walked to Over bridge to view the site of the new bridge over the Severn, building, under the direction of Mr. Telford, by the County.*

1828: 15 Jun: *I can only express my admiration of the elegance & the boldness, the delicacy and the symmetry of the design & the effect. Mr. Telford, whose design it is, speaks of the bridge...*

1829: 28 Apr: *I am persuaded, it will remain for centuries a testimony of the profound science of Mr. Telford, who speaks in the most favourable manner of the workmanship, which has been contracted for by a person of the name of Cargill. The approaches are in great forwardness: and the old crazy bridge may soon be abandoned.* 14 Jul.

1830: 30 Mar., 20 Apr: *A rumour was whispered, that the new bridge, which had been built at the expence of the County at Over, had given way, & was in danger of falling, & Mr. Telford was called upon to report on the security of the structure.*

TELLER — Marie Luise Teller[21]

Marie Luise Teller (1755-1810), actress, was originally from Regensburg, Bavaria. She joined the Weimar company in early 1799 and remained there until her death. After a rather uneven start (she lost her role in Schiller's *Die Piccolomini* having been told she was 'unteachable'), she nonetheless became a regular in secondary roles. She was particularly known for her diction, but little is known about her life. There was a young actress, Sophie Teller, at Weimar, who played a gypsy boy in Goethe's *Gotz von Berlichingen*, and it is tempting to think she may have been Marie Luise's daughter.

1798: 2 Sep: *Mad. Teller is at an advanced age with a disgusting face one of the best actresses I know, her Fortis the Gräfin Orsina in Lessings Emilia Galotti, her Gräfin Terzky, & her Lady Macbeth are almost inimitable.*

1799: 24 Oct: *Teller as Gräfin Derburg was very great considering that it is only a secondary Character.* 30 Sep., 14 Dec., 23 Dec.

1800: 3 Mar: *Extremely well acted by Haide, Vohs, Cordemann, Caspar, Graff, Spitzeder, and Teller.* 12 Mar.

TEMPLE — Henry John Temple, Viscount Palmerston [22]

Henry John Temple, 3rd Viscount Palmerston (1784-1865), prime minister, was born at 4 Park Street [later 20 Queen Anne's Gate], Westminster, the eldest of the five children of Henry Temple, 2nd Viscount Palmerston (1739-1802), and his second wife, Mary (1754-1805), daughter of Benjamin Mee, a London merchant and Bath resident. He was educated at Harrow School (1795-1800) and the University of Edinburgh (1800-03). He succeeded his father to the title of Viscount Palmerston on 17 April 1802, before he had turned 18. He then went to St John's College, Cambridge (1803-06). When war was declared against France in 1803, Henry joined the volunteers mustered to oppose a French invasion; he was one of the three officers in the unit for St John's College. He was also appointed lieutenant-colonel commander of the Romsey Volunteers.

Henry Temple, Viscount Palmerston, was in government almost continuously from 1807 until his death in 1865. He began his parliamentary career as a Tory and concluded it as a Liberal. He was MP for Newport, Isle of Wight, 1807-11; Cambridge University, 1811-31; Bletchingly, 1831-32; Hampshire South, 1832-34; and Tiverton, 1835-65. His most important government postings were foreign secretary, 1830-41; home secretary, 1852-55; and prime minister, 1855-58 and 1859-65.

For two decades, Palmerston was at the centre of foreign affairs, not only in Europe, but also in Turkey, Afghanistan, the Middle East, and Asia. He bankrolled the two wars with China in 1842 and 1860, but managed to escape culpability for the disasters of the Crimean War, having been home minister under the earl of Aberdeen at the time. Indeed, it was Palmerston who would pick up the pieces and gain much of the credit for the war's successful conclusion. Palmerston demonstrated both decisiveness and subtlety in his handling of the Indian Mutiny; troops were despatched and the situation normalised, but he was strong enough to resist most of the calls for harsh retribution. He supported more lenient measures and dissolved the East India Company, bringing India under the direct rule of the British government.

Palmerston was out of office for a year and a half, and during that time he helped form the Liberal Party, which came together in June 1859 on the back of support for Italian Resorgimento. He returned to government as prime minister in the same month. In his second administration he managed to retain Britain's neutrality during the American Civil War, despite provocation and lobbying from both sides. He allowed British shipyards to build Confederate ships, but only on a commercial, not political, basis. He supported Denmark over ownership of Schleswig-Holstein, but to avoid the possibility of engaging in a continental war, he did not intervene when Prussia invaded in February 1864. In 1865, following a vote of censure, Palmerston called a general election which he won with a convincing majority, but he did not see the new parliament convened. He died of a fever on 18 October 1865 after catching a chill while riding in his carriage.

1826: 16 Jun: *Another contest, which has attracted much attention is that for the University of Cambridge; the Candidates being Lord Palmerston & Mr. Bankes, the Attorney General (Sir Singleton Copley) & Mr. Goulburn, the Chief Secretary of Ireland.*

1827: 2 May.

1828: 23 Jan., 1 Feb., 28 May: *I own, I cannot feel much regret at the resignations of Huskisson and Lord Palmerston; the former I have long been led, to consider as a politic & able but dangerous statesman, the latter of an inferior order, both as to talent & principle.*

1835: 19 Apr: *The newspapers announce the near completion of a Whig Ministry under Lord Melbourne as Premier ... comprising ... Lord Palmerston.*

1852: 22 Feb: *The Whig Ministry have resigned. Lord John Russell goes out, being defeated in the House of Commons on a motion by Lord Palmerston that the old militia be organised, and not a local militia.*

TEMPLE-NUGENT-BRYDGES-CHANDOS-GRENVILLE — Richard Temple-Nugent-Brydges-Chandos-Grenville [23]

Richard Temple-Nugent-Brydges-Chandos-Grenville, 1st duke of Buckingham and Chandos (1776-1839), landed proprietor, was born in London, the son of George Nugent-Temple-Grenville, 1st marquess of Buckingham (1753-1813), and Mary Elizabeth (1758-1812), eldest daughter and co-heir of Robert, Earl Nugent, and his third wife, Elizabeth, dowager countess of Berkeley, daughter of Henry Drax of Ellerton Abbey, Yorkshire. Richard was educated at Brasenose, Oxford, and was MP for Buckinghamshire from 1797 to 1813. He succeeded as 2nd marquess of Buckingham in 1813, and was created duke of Buckingham and Chandos in 1822.

Richard married, at Westmorland chapel, Marylebone, Westminster, 16 April 1796, Anna Elizabeth, *de jure* Baroness Kinloss (1779-1836), second but only surviving daughter and heir of James Brydges, duke of Chandos, and his second wife, Anne Elizabeth, daughter of Richard Gamon. Richard and Anna had at least 1 son:

1 Richard (1797-1861); succeeded as 2nd duke of Buckingham and Chandos

---

1823: 17 Sep: *I may here as well enumerate some of the principal persons and families, who attended the music meeting on this and the following days. The Duke & Duchess of Beaufort and the Ladies Somerset, the Duke of Buckingham on one morning from Cheltenham.*

1824: 10 Jul: *My Aunt Lady Lyttelton arrived from Cookham to stay a day or two here... Among other places, she had formed one of the many guests at Stowe, the Seat of the Duke of Buckingham, on occasion of the Christening of the Marquis of Chandos's eldest Son, the heir of the Dukedom, which was celebrated with great and expensive festivities. The ancient alliance between the Grenvilles & Lytteltons entitled my Aunt to appear, as on a former occasion, among the family friends of the Temples & Chandos's.*

1827: 14 Apr: *... and connected with the Duke of Buckingham; but his Grace is in himself a cypher, his bodily infirmities increase, & though with most of his connections he be a strenuous supporter of the Roman Catholic interests, yet he has been unable to instill his opinions on that head into his son, the Marquis of Chandos, who firmly and strongly resists all concessions to the Papists.* 4 May.

1830: 6 Feb., 23 Jun.

1832: 10 Apr.

1836: 4 Nov.

1853: 5 Jan: *to-day I received from Mr. Short of Trinity, Chairman of a Committee sitting at Magdalene Hall, an application in favour of the Marquis of Chandos, who, as it is stated, has consented to offer himself to oppose Gladstone. But hardly had I received this appeal forwarded to me from home, than I ascertained from another Member of Convocation attending the Sessions that Lord Chandos declines standing...*

TENCH — John Tench[24]

John Tench (1764-1848), Church of England clergyman, was the son of Revd John Tench of Davenham, Cheshire. He was educated at Brasenose College, Oxford (BA 1787; MA 1789; BD 1808), where he was proctor in 1800 and a fellow until 1813. He was appointed rector of Great Rollright, Oxfordshire, in 1811, and held the living up to his death.

1802: 14 Mar: *Heard a moderate Sermon at St. Mary's in the morning from Mr. Tench of Brazenose.*

1829: 7 Feb., 24 Nov.

TERROT — Charles Hughes Terrot[25]

Charles Hughes Terrot (1790-1872), Scottish episcopal bishop of Edinburgh, was born at Cuddalore, India, the son of Capt. Elias Terrot, HEIC, of Huguenot descent, who was killed at the siege of Bangalore within weeks of his son's birth. His mother, Mary Terrot, née Fonteneau, returned to England and settled with her son at Berwick-upon-Tweed. From the age of 9 Charles was educated at the home of Revd John Fawcett, of Carlisle, and later attended Carlisle Grammar School. In 1808 he entered Trinity College, Cambridge, and graduated BA in 1812. He became a fellow of Trinity in 1813 and served as a deacon in Bristol the same year, before moving to Chester as a priest. He returned to Scotland in 1814 to serve as an incumbent in Haddington. In 1833 he served in St Paul's in Edinburgh, and became dean in 1837 and bishop in 1841. During this time he lived at 19 Northumberland Street in Edinburgh's Second New Town. He was elected a fellow of the Royal Society of Edinburgh in 1840, and served as the society's vice-president from 1844 to 1860. He was also a member of the Architectural Society of Scotland.

Terrot married Sarah Ingram Wood (d. 1855); they had 2 sons and 7 daughters:

1 Elias Charles (b. 1816)
1 Sarah Anne (1820-1901)
2 Elizabeth Louisa (1828-1908)
3 Charlotte
4 Catherine
2 Charles William
5 Anna Jemina
6 Mary Anne Elizabeth
7 Helen Harriet (d. 1904)

1833: 23 Oct: *Received a letter from Mrs. Howell, from Prinknash, written in her husband's absence in Town, inclosing a letter to him from Mr. Blair, recommending the Revd. Mr. Terrott of Edinburgh as a fit person with whom to place my son. This is the same gentleman whose name had been very favourably mentioned by Mr. Ellis.* 25 Oct: *Wrote to Mr. Terrott at Edinburgh, expressing my intention of bringing my Son to Edinburgh for the winter.* 30 Oct: *A letter from Mr. Malcolm communicating to me the information he had obtained through a friend at Edinburgh as to gentlemen there taking private pupils; of whom two only are named, a Preacher of the Scotch Church, on very moderate terms, and Mr. Terrot ... Wrote to Howell, explaining what I had done in writing to Mr. Terrot, and that I should, probably, go to Edinburgh with Edward next week, but was desirous first to hear from him.* 2 Nov: *Received an answer from Mr. Terrot, from Edinburgh; but though he states that he has room for my Son, his terms being £150 for the period of the College Session, it is doubtful whether the situation will answer our views.* 4 Nov: *Replied to Mr. Malcolm's letter received on the 30th Ult. apprizing him of my intention of taking Edward to Edinburgh, and of placing him, if possible, under the care of Mr. Terrot.* 10 Nov: *Returning to our hotel I dispatched a note to the Revd. Mr. Terrot, requesting an interview for the following morning, to which I received a verbal answer in the affirmative.*

1835: 23 Feb: *Read Common Sense, a poem published in 1819 by Mr. Terrot, with whom my son resided last winter in Edinburgh.*

TERRY — Michael Terry[26]

Michael Terry (1818-1903), Church of England clergyman, was born at Botley, Hampshire, the son of Edward and Jane Terry. He was educated at Lincoln College, Oxford (BA 1841; MA 1844), and held various curacies in Gloucestershire in his early life. In the 1851 census he was registered as curate of St Luke's, Finsbury, and in 1861 he was at Great Stanmore. He married, at Kensington, Westminster, 1863, Charlotte Sarah (1831-1888), daughter of John Hunter (1794-1869) and Caroline Wilkinson (1790-1862); they had 4 sons and 1 daughter:

1 Arthur Michael (b. 1864)
2 Hubert Lanphier (1865-1925)
1 Ellen [Ella] Charlotte (1866-1942); died unmarried
3 Francis John (1867-1935)
4 Cyril Edward (1870-1947), Lt-Col

Terry was (temporary) vicar of Kelstern, Lincolnshire, in 1864-66, and was appointed perpetual curate of Awsworth, Nottinghamshire, in 1869. By 1891 he was a widower and retired, living at Chichester as a lodger. His daughter Ellen was visiting him at the time of the census. By 1901 Michael Terry was living at 9 Allison Grove, Camberwell, and Ellen, unmarried, was living with him.

1847: 22 Oct: *Walked to Wick Risington to make my first call on Mr. Terry, a new curate lately arrived there, to replace Mr. Barrow. He is, I believe, a fellow of Lincoln College, and has been Curate of Norton near Gloucester.* 23 Oct: *Mr. Terry, the Curate of Wick Risington, returned my call; he appears an intelligent, not very polished person, not reserved, and somewhat deaf.* 26 Oct: *Mr. Terry, the new curate of Wick Risington joined our circle: — a plain looking and not very polished man, but well informed.* 27-28 Oct., 16 Dec.

1848: 19 Jan., 1-2 Mar., 26 Apr., 28 Apr., 29 May, 7 Jun., 19 Jun., 6 Jul., 23 Aug., 2 Sep., 13 Sep., 29 Sep., 22 Oct: *To Mr. Terry, inviting him to dine with us on that day.* 25 Oct: *A dinner party — Mr. and two Misses Ford, Dulcibella and Sophia, —— E.F.W. and Sophy coming from "the Cottage", with Mr. Vavasour, and Mr. Terry, were our guests.*

1851: 20 May: *Accosted by Mr. Terry, the former curate of Wick Risington, who now holds a curacy in a London Church.*

TEUL — John Teul[27]

John Teul (b. ±1826), Baptist minister, was born at Shipton-under-Wychwood, Oxfordshire. He was married to Mary Thorn (b. ±1829), who was born at South Molton, Devon. At the time of the 1851 census they had one daughter, Mary Burgess (b. ±1846), who was also born at South Molton. This seems to indicate that John had lived for some time in Devon and then moved to Gloucestershire with his family. They lived at Waterloo House, Naunton. Apart from the 1851 census entry for Naunton, there are no records relating to the family.

1853: 14 Jan: *Also received a visit from a Soi-disant Revd. Teull a Baptist Minister of Naunton, who sought my advice as to the course he should take in respect of a slanderous report in circulation charging him with improper familiarity with the wife of a labourer of that place.*

TEUSCHER — Anna Catherina Teuscher [28]

Anna Catherina Teuscher (1786-1852) was born in the canton of Thurgau, Switzerland, about 35 km north-west of Zürich. Francis Witts made a reference to Marienfield [Marienfeld in German], 'her native town', but no such town has been located. Anna's sister lived at Frauenfeld im Thurgau, the capital of the canton.

1852: 20 Apr: *In the Evening received a note from Mrs. Dolphin, who consults me as to her faithful servant, Mrs. Teuscher, making a will, disposing of her savings in service and of a house and garden in her native town, Marienfield, in the Thurgau. T. is ill, & in a very precarious state.* 23 May, 28-29 May, 31 May ... *she wished to leave as to her personal property, Railway shares & money in a Savings Bank, to a small amount, she was firm in her resolution to bequeath it to her dear mistress, with whom she has lived nearly 20 years. — I expressed that Mrs. D. would much prefer her leaving all to her relations, but she appeared positive; at the same time saying she would make provision according to her final judgment after the arrival of a sister, who is expected to visit her to-morrow.* 5 Jun: *Prayed with her. Advised with her and her sister as to her making a will.* 17 Nov: *A very long letter from Mademoiselle Teucher from Frauenfeld, in the Thurgau, requesting me to forward a certificate of her sister Catherine's burial. She enters at length into the history of herself and sister, dwells on the misunderstanding between Mrs. Dolphin and herself, and requests information as to the property left by her Sister, whether she made a will &c.* 19 Nov., 10 Dec: *Furnished Mr. Harris Undertaker, Stow, with a certificate of the burial of A. M. Teuscher, which he had requested me yesterday to provide, being desired so to do by Mr. Paxton.* 30-31 Dec.

1853: 2 Mar.

THACKWELL — John Cam Thackwell [29]

John Cam Thackwell (1807-1892), landed proprietor, was born at Wilton Place, Dymock, Gloucestershire, the son of John Thackwell (b. 1765), JP and DL, and Winifred Seabright. He married, at Exeter, 13 April 1842, Charlotte Eleanor (±1811-1880), daughter of John Hugh Pasley Polson (1781-1829), of Upton Helions, Devon, and Frances Sarah (1777-1821); they had 3 sons and 4 daughters:

1 Charlotte Ellen (1842-±1844); died an infant
1 John (1844-1914); married Alice Annie (b. ±1857); at least 1 daughter:
  1 Alice Maude Mary (b. ±1878)
2 William Polson (1846-1922), married, 1884, Katherine Maude (1858-1943); at least 2 daughters:
  1 Olive Winifred (1888-1952)
  2 Katherine Joan (b. 1896)
2 Katherine Emily (1848-1871)
3 Arthur Joseph (b. 1852); married Emma (b. ±1859); at least 1 son:
  1 Charles Frederick (b. 1884)
3 Isabel Charlotte Mary (1854-1892); died unmarried (suicide)
4 Helen Elizabeth (1856-1945); died unmarried

1842: 18 May: *Drove E.F.W. and Sophy with MW. to call at Wormington Rectory on the Billingsleys: where spent from half an hour to an hour: the first visit since the birth of their little girl: and since the marriage of Miss Poulson to Mr. Thackwell, a gentleman residing at or near Newent.*

THOMAS — Alfred and John Thomas of Urchfont

1806: 15 Aug: *Dined with the J. Tylee's a very pleasant party Mr. C. Mayo & his Sister, Mrs Newman Mr. Neat, Mrs. C. Tylee, Mr. & Mrs. Gent & Mrs. Hillier, & Mr. Thomas.* 24 Aug: *Dined with John Gale an excellent man, though suffering from a wrist disorder. John Thomas called in.*

1807: 8 Mar: ... *dined at John Gale's, their own family & Miss Gabrielle, Mr. Dimond, & John Thomas in the Evening; pleasant enough.*

1808: 3 Jan: *Dined with the Gales, meeting Mrs. Jaques, John & Alfred Thomas ... .*

THOMAS — John Godfrey Thomas [30]

Sir John Godfrey Thomas, 6th baronet of Wenvoe Castle (1784-1841), Church of England clergyman, was the son of Sir John Thomas, 5th baronet of Wenvoe Castle (1749-1828), and Mary (1758-1845), daughter of John Parker, of Hasfield Court, Gloucestershire, and his wife, Mary. Thomas matriculated at St Mary Hall in 1800, but then dropped out of the scene for three years before re-entering at Wadham College (BA 1803; MA 1806). He became vicar of Bodiam, Sussex, in 1809, and vicar of Wartling, Sussex, in 1811. He succeeded his father as 6th baronet of Wenvoe Castle, Glamorgan, in 1828.

Thomas married, first, 1 April 1808, Frances (1770-1816), daughter of Stephen Ram of Ramsfort, co. Wexford, Ireland; they had 1 son:

1 Edmond Stephen (1810-1852); succeeded as 7th baronet

He married secondly, at Holt, Wiltshire, 10 March 1817, Elizabeth Ann Grey (1785-1854), eldest daughter of Revd John Vignobles, of Cornahir, co. Westmeath, Ireland, and widow of Lt-Col Grey, of the 30th Foot, who was killed at Badajoz in April 1812. John and Elizabeth had 3 sons and 5 daughters:

1 Eliza Julia (1818-1908)
2 Julia (1820-1895)
3 Caroline Margaret (1822-1896)
4 Paulina (1823-1914)
1 Godfrey John (1824-1861)
2 John (1826-1861)
3 Charles (1828-1871)
5 Fanny

1803: 31 Oct: *Thomas & Brown (the Revd.) sat with me in the Even.* 1 Nov: *Breakfasted with Thomas.* 2-4 Nov.

1804: 14 Feb., 18 Feb., 21-23 Feb.

THOMAS — Josiah Thomas [31]

Josiah Thomas (1760-1820), Church of England clergyman, was the son of Walter and Mary Thomas. He was educated at Charterhouse and St John's College, Cambridge (BA 1782; MA 1789), and his clerical appointments were as follows: vicar of St Merryn, Cornwall, 1785-91; rector of Street with Walton, Somerset, appointed 1791; rector of Backwell, appointed 1796; prebendary of Wells, appointed 1798; vicar of Kingston-Deverill, Wiltshire, appointed 1813; and archdeacon of Bath and vicar of Christ Church, Walcot, Bath, 1817-20. He married, at Walcot Street, Bath, 22 February 1794, Susanna Isabella (1762-1835), only daughter of Dr Henry Harington of Bath; they had 4 sons and 4 daughters:

1 Elizabeth Ann (1794-1882)
1 Henry Harington (1795-1874)
2 Mary Ann (1796-1872)
2 Charles Thynne (1797-1874), Lt-Col
3 Jane Ann (1798-1893)
3 Edmund (b. 1799)
4 George Hudleston (1801-1839), Capt.
4 Frances Anne (1802-1804)

1820: 3 Jun: *Read in the newspaper the account of the death of Mr. Archdeacon Thomas. This learned & sound divine will be a great loss to the Church of England.*

THOMASON — Henry Botfield Thomason [32]

Henry Botfield Thomason (1802-1843), landed proprietor, was the son of Sir Edward Thomason (1769-1849) and Phillis Brown (1771-1851), daughter of Samuel Glover (1742-1808) and Phillis Bown (1747-1819). His father was a manufacturer and inventor in Birmingham, and was knighted by King William IV. His grandfather was Edward Thomason (1740-1793), a manufacturer of buckles.

Henry Thomason married, first, 1824, Elizabeth (1798-1879), daughter of Richard Yardley (1765-1823) and Mary Stringer (b. 1774); they had 2 sons and 3 daughters:

1 Elizabeth Yeoville Yardley (1824-1856)
1 Henry Richard Yeoville Yardley (1826-1901), architect; married, at St Barnabas's, Erdington, Warwickshire, 12 March 1863, Harriett Rollason (1839-1899); 2 sons and 2 daughters:
  1 Edward Henry (b. 1864)
  1 Florence Mary (1865-1929)
  2 Edith Harriett (1867-1930)
  2 Philip Rollason (1869-1958)
2 George Buchorest Yeoville (1828-1896)
2 Adelaide Yeoville Yardley (1830-1891)
3 Mary Anne Yeoville Phillis Yardley (1835-1900); married, 2 June 1858, Richard Austin Herbert

Strangely, Thomason seems to have taken a second wife while his first wife Elizabeth was still alive; in fact, Elizabeth outlived him by some 36 years. No record of any divorce has been discovered, yet the records clearly state that Henry Botfield Thomason married secondly, at Ludlow, Shropshire, 28 August 1838, Jane Price, daughter of Sir John Pinhorn (1744-1831) of Ringwood Park, Isle of Wight. Henry Botfield Thomason bought Peachfield Lodge in 1840, but did not live long to enjoy it.

Following Henry's death in 1843, Jane married secondly, 21 April 1847, Sir Robert Gyll, of Wyrardisbury House, Buckinghamshire. In the 1861 census, Elizabeth lived with her son, the noted architect Henry Richard Yeoville Yardley Thomason. She died at Edgbaston, Warwickshire, in 1879.

1840: 23 Jun: *Very many persons had inspected the premises, but there was, in fact, no competition; nor any company in the Auction room except our own Solicitor and his brother, who was instructed to buy in the property if it did not reach the price at which my son was willing to let it go—£1000—and two inhabitants of Malvern, who, with Abraham Gibbs, were requested to bid on our part, as shadows, if I may so term it, and Mr. H. B. Thomason, a gentleman resident at Mathon Lodge ... Mr. Thomason is a son of Sir Edward Thomason, a celebrated Manufacturer of plated, plated goods &c. at Birmingham, whose shew-rooms have for many years been well known and universally visited.* 25 Jun: *Wrote to Messrs. Hoare remitting to them a cheque for £100 on the Birmingham Banking Company, drawn in my favour ye the day before yesterday by Mr. Thomason, as his deposit on the purchase of Peach Field Lodge.* 27 Jun: *... from Hoares who send back the cheque on the Birmingham Bankg. Company drawn by Mr. Thomason, which I forwarded to them on the 25th. Inst. because it is made payable at Birmingham only, and they have no correspondent there.* 3 Jul., 4 Jul: *Received a letter from Messrs. Hoare announcing that there had been paid in to my account with them by Messrs. Cripps £100—this is the produce of the cheque drawn in my favour on the Birmingham Company by Mr. H. B. Thomason, which Hoares sent back to me because not payable in London, and which Cripps's have got cashed at Birmingham, remitting the account to me at Hoares.* 7 Jul., 8 Jul: *Wrote to Mr. Thomason in reply to his letter received on the 3d. Inst. and to Mr. Gibbs on the same subject, the disposal of the pheasants &c. at Peach Field Lodge.* 11-12 Jul., 18 Jul., 20 Jul., 28 Jul: *Received a letter from Mr. Thomason on various points relative to the title to Peach Field Lodge.* 29 Jul., 6-8 Aug., 12 Aug., 19 Sep: *Recd. a letter from Mr. Thomason; he is not ready with the remainder of the purchase money for Peach Field Lodge, and desires that an arrangement may be made for two or three months, that the deeds having been signed may remain in our hands, and that he may be allowed to defer payment, on an engagement to pay the amount with interest at a season more convenient to himself.* 20 Sep, 22 Sep, 23 Sep: *Wrote to Mr. Thomason in answer to his letter recd. on the 19th.; declined affording the accommodation sought.* 24-25 Sep., 30 Sep., 1 Oct., 7 Oct., 9 Oct., 14 Oct: *My son having executed in London the conveyance of Peach Field Lodge to Mr. Thomason, I executed it this morning, and forwarded it by post with a few lines to Mr. Thrupp.* 2-4 Nov.

THOMPSON — Mr Thompson, a lawyer in London

This person has not been identified. He was the legal adviser to Mrs Timbrell, who, with her sisters, were the heirs to the Tracy estate. They also owned the advowson of the living of Upper Slaughter. These ladies were highly significant to the life of Francis Witts. In the summer of 1805, Edward and Agnes Witts made contact with Mrs Timbrell and her sisters, and by careful nurturing and negotiation they paved the way for Francis to succeed eventually to the rectory of the parish. This took place following the death of Francis's uncle Ferdinando Tracy Travell in 1809.

1823: 24 Dec: *... nor do I think the Timbrells had any surviving relatives; there was not even old intimacy or regard; on the contrary at times the Morris's & Lawrence's were objects of bitter sarcasm and vituperation. But in a lucky moment Mr. W. Morris contrived to lend the old ladies a large sum of money to enable them to pay off the bill of their then legal adviser, a Mr. Thompson of London, & so connected himself with them as that they were unable afterwards to disengage themselves. Mr. Thompson had at one period the good fortune of being the intended heir; but on some offence given the will made in his favour was rescinded.*

1826: 7 Aug: *... when Mrs. Lightbourne died in the close of 1823, mentioned the disposition, which she made of her property in favour of Mr. Walter Lawrence, superseding a former will made in favour of her former legal adviser, Mr. Thompson of London. By that older will, besides the bequest to Mr. Thompson, a tenement in Whittington & £10000 were bequeathed to a man named Freeman, a Cheltenham Apothecary ...*

THOMPSON — the Misses Thompson at Camberwell, Surrey — *see also* Benjamin Tomkins

In July 1801, the Witts family left London for a few days to stay with Mrs Witts at Champion Hill, Camberwell, where they were visited by Mr and Mrs Tomkins, who came with their nieces, the two Misses Thompson.

1801: 28 Jul: *Mr. and Mrs. Tomkins & two Miss Thompsons drank tea in the afternoon with Mrs. Witts.*

THOMPSON — Henry Thompson and the Mmes Thompson at Cheltenham [33]

Henry Thompson (1749-1820) was the son of Richard Thompson (1721-1773) and Ann Pearson (1725-1811), who had married at

Bridekirk, Cumberland, on 20 October 1745. In order to better understand the Cheltenham circle, it is appropriate first to list Richard and Ann's children; they had 5 sons and 4 daughters:

- 1 Richard (1746-1776), Church of England clergyman; educated at Queen's College, Oxford (BA 1768; MA 1771); ordained deacon, 2 June 1776; died soon after; probably unmarried
- 2 John (1748-1824); appears to have died unmarried
- 3 Henry (1749-1820); married, at Enfield, Middlesex, 18 June 1792, Judith (1771-1850), daughter of Thomas Teshmaker (1736-1771) and Sara Coster (1750-1832); 3 sons and 3 daughters:
  - 1 Henry Teshmaker (1793-1855)
  - 2 Pearson (1794-1872); *see below*
  - 1 Sarah Ann (1796-1868)
  - 2 Esther (1797-1833)
  - 3 Richard Thomas (1798-1799); died an infant
  - 3 Elizabeth (1800-1878); married Edward Armitage (1796-1878); 1 son and 5 daughters:
    - 1 Edward Henry (1821-1877)
    - 1 Jane (1822-1874)
    - 2 Susanna Thompson (b. 1826)
    - 3 Ann (b. 1826)
    - 4 Sarah A. (b. 1827)
    - 5 Louise (b. 1828)
- 4 Isaac (1751-1757); died a child
- 1 Elizabeth (1753-1807); appears to have died unmarried, probably before 1807
- 2 Mary (1755-1794)
- 3 Isabella (b. 1757); married, at Bridekirk, Cumberland, 7 February 1784, Thomas Benson
- 4 Sarah (1759-1761); died an infant
- 5 Allan (b. 1761)

Henry Thompson (1749-1820) moved to Cheltenham in around 1801 and immediately set about establishing himself as a landowner and property developer. He bought up to 400 acres of Revd John de la Bere's estate, and a further 30 acres in 1804; he continued to purchase land as it came on the market. Thompson built the Montpellier Spa in 1809, and rebuilt it in 1817; the dome was added by his son Pearson in 1825-26. Henry died at his home, Vittoria House [Hygeia House pre-1813], on 2 November 1820, aged 72.

There were three Mmes Thompson: Mrs Thompson; Mrs H. Thompson; and Mrs P. Thompson (for Mrs Pearson Thompson). We know that Mrs H. Thompson was Judith Thompson, née Teshmaker (1771-1850), because on Thursday 2 April 1818 Agnes Witts wrote the following: 'Miss Hallifax call'd on me to visit Miss Grosvenors & introduce her to them, she afterwards walk'd with me to make a useless call on Mrs. H. Thompson & her Daughter Mrs. Amatage ...'

Because there are vast gaps in the early diaries (Francis Witts only started writing his diary seriously in 1820, the year Henry Thompson died), Francis Witts made no specific mention of Henry Thompson. However, given the family's importance to the Wittses and the many relevant entries in the diaries of Agnes Witts, this pedigree is of interest. (*See below*, Pearson Thompson.)

THOMPSON — Mr and Mrs A. Thompson at Clifton

1804: 1 Sep: *At an entertaining Party at Mrs Waddington's, Mr. & Mrs. A. Thompson Mr. & Mrs. Ball, Mrs. & Miss Buikstocks, Napier's &c. much literary conversation.*

THOMPSON — Henry Thompson[34]

Sir Henry Thompson, 3rd baronet (1796-1868), Church of England clergyman, was the son of vice admiral of the blue [later red] Sir Charles Thompson, 1st baronet (1740-1799), and Jane (1766-1833), daughter of Robert Selby and Elizabeth Miln. He was educated at Harrow School and Oriel College, Oxford (BA 1819; MA 1821). He was curate in charge at Holy Trinity, Bembridge, Isle of Wight, and rector of Holy Trinity, Fareham, Hampshire (he and his mother Lady Jane Thompson had funded the building of the church at Fareham), and in 1845 he was given the living of Frant, Sussex, by the earl of Abergavenny. He succeeded his elder brother Norborne in 1826 to become 3rd baronet.

Thompson married, first, at St Mary's, Portsea, Hampshire, 26 February 1828, Hannah Jean (1803-1829), fourth daughter of Sir George Grey, 1st baronet; they had 1 daughter:

- 1 Hannah Jane (1829-1899)

Hannah presumably died during childbirth, or soon after. Thompson married secondly, at Brighton, Sussex, October 1835, Emily Frances Anne (1807-1883), youngest daughter of Ralph Leeke and Honora Frances Harvey Thursby (1771-1843) of Longford Hall, Shropshire; they had 2 sons and 2 daughters:

- 1 Frances Anne (±1838-1862)
- 1 Henry Charles (1843-1863)
- 2 Ralph Hervey (b. & d. 1846)
- 2 Caroline Eleanor (1848-1900)

1832: 9 Mar: *The gallery seats are let to persons of a higher description. Sir H. Thompson Bart., a young divine of the so-called Evangelical party, has undertaken the ministry of this Church, which, as well as Trinity Church, is subordinate to the old church of St. Mary's.*

THOMPSON — Henry Thompson[35]

Henry Thompson (1797-1878), Church of England clergyman, was born at Southwark, Surrey, the son of Thomas and Margery Thompson. He was educated at St John's College, Cambridge (BA 1822; MA 1825), where he was awarded a scholarship in 1818 and the Browne medal in 1820. He was curate of St George's, Camberwell, Surrey, 1824-27; curate of Salehurst, Sussex, 1827-28; curate of Wrington, Somerset, 1828-53; and vicar of Chard, 1853-78. Henry married, 1823, Anne Harrison (1805-1872), daughter of Revd James Bell, vicar of Lympne, Kent, and Ann Stiven (1781-1839); they had 1 son and 2 daughters:

- 1 Anna Bell (b. 1826)
- 1 Henry Bell (1827-1887)
- 2 Mary Bell (b. 1830)

Henry Thompson was the author of *The Life of Hannah More With Notices of Her Sisters* (1838).

1833: 13 Oct: *My Son in the Evening read aloud a Funeral Sermon on the excellent Hannah More, preached at Wrington, Somerset, where she was lately interred by the Revd. H. Thomson, Curate of that place.*

1839: 29 Aug: *Mr. Thompson is a lively, active, talented man. Curate of Wrington: I believe he has published a Memoir of Mrs. Hannah More in one Volume, and, if I mistake not, a work entitled Pastoralia, of considerable esteem, also some single sermons, and others printed occasionally in the Christian Remembrancer.*

THOMPSON — Pearson Thompson[36]

Pearson Thompson (1794-1872), solicitor, JP, and landed proprietor, was the son of Henry Thompson and Judith Teshmaker (*above*). He inherited part of his father's estate in 1820 and bought his brother Henry's share for £2,800 in 1825; Henry lived in Cumberland and had never shown much interest in the Cheltenham inheritance. In his early life, Pearson practised as a solicitor in London. He married, at Enfield, Middlesex, 10 October 1817, Dorothy, daughter of William Scott of Austin Friars; they had 1 son and 4 daughters:

1 Pearson Scott (1823-1878)
1 Elizabeth
2 Catherine
3 Marianna
4 Helen Dorothy (b. & d. 1837)

After inheriting his portion of father's property, Pearson Thompson moved to Cheltenham to develop the estate. He had a house built in Vittoria Walk in 1825, but the date he and his family began living at Hatherley Court has not been confirmed. It is also uncertain when Hatherley Court was built. One daughter, Helen Dorothy, was born there in August 1837, and died there six weeks later.

Pearson Thompson employed J. B. Papworth as his architect from 1824 onwards to design both the layout of the Montpellier estate and the Montpellier Pump Room Rotunda. Papworth also designed a number of large houses in Cheltenham's wealthy Lansdown district, which was owned by Thompson. Richard Roy, a fellow developer, lived in one of them. He and Thompson were members of a committee formed to provide fashionable public entertainments such as musical promenades and summer balls. In 1836, while considering the various proposals for railway lines to Cheltenham, they founded a local joint-stock bank.

Pearson Thompson and Richard Roy developed an estate in Brighton, and in 1841 and '42 they lent money to John Duncan, who was developing the Ladbroke estate. When Duncan went bankrupt the creditors put Thompson and Roy in charge of carrying out the development; aspects of its layout and general character owe much to the Montpellier estate at Cheltenham. Thompson's principal role during the Ladbroke development was to provide the capital, and he remained at home at Hatherley Court in Cheltenham most of the time, where he served as a Gloucestershire JP. His investment in the Ladbroke estate, however, had 'so involved his affairs as to compromise the whole of his property', but whether or not he was on the verge of bankruptcy is not clear. In 1849 Pearson Thompson emigrated to Australia, and this rather suggests that he had conceded financial defeat. He practised at the bar in Sydney for a while, and then went to Castlemaine, Victoria, the epicentre of a large goldmining district. He was successful in his enterprises and became a magistrate.

1826: 8 Feb: *Before setting out, walked up the Sherborne Well walk, and as far as Thompson's Montpellier Pump room. The proprietor, Mr. Pearson Thompson, is building there on a very large scale. He is greatly extending the pump room and its contiguous buildings, & will doubtless, make it by the next summer a very sumptuous edifice. Reading, billiard & promenade rooms, are, I understand, to be under the same roof, and the whole will be surmounted by a very handsome dome covered with copper, in the elevation of which many workmen are now busily employed.* 30 Sep: *We stopped at Cheltenham for half an hour or more, and walked to the Montpellier Spa, to view a very magnificent room, which Mr. Pearson Thomson, the proprietor of that Spa and its attached walks & drives, has erected. We found it, as it had been represented, a very fine edifice.*

THORNHILL — *see also* **Goodrich**

Nothing has been discovered regarding Miss Thornhill, but there may have been some connection with the Thornhill family of Hopton, Suffolk, although this suggestion is purely conjectural. Miss Thornhill's fiancé (according to the diaries), William John Pitt Goodrich (1809-1838), was educated at Oriel College, Oxford, and went on to the Inner Temple where he was called to the bar. He died on 17 August 1838, and whether they actually got married is not known, but as no record has been found relating to a marriage they presumably did not.

1836: 13 Sep: *Mrs. Goodrich and two daughters were absent in Devonshire for sea bathing: four Misses Goodrich, pleasing, accomplished, elegant, and well informed: Miss Thornhill, a young lady engaged to William Goodrich: W. Goodrich himself made our party.*

THORNTON — George Thornton [37]

George Thornton (b. ±1785) was married to Elizabeth (b. ±1785). They were both born at Stow-on-the-Wold, and in the 1851 census, George was listed as an inmate of Wotton Lunatic Asylum in Gloucester.

1834: 26 Sep: *Henry Stone, Shopman to Mr. Pain, Watchmaker, Stow, came with notes from Mr. Pole and Mr. Winter, to inform me, that yesterday one Thornton of Stow, Tailor, and repairer of watches, had brought to Pain's shop a part of the gold repeater of the late unfortunate Mr. Rens.* 30 Sep: *Thornton, probably, if he had possessed the facility of getting rid of it without detection, would have so disposed of it; for he is not a very reputable character…*

1835: 13 Apr: *Thornton the tailor, who dabbles in watches … was half-drunk, vulgar, and impudent; braving the suspicions which he must have been aware his concern in the transaction with Jeffrey about the watch must excite. He had the assurance to claim the reward offered for the discovery of the murderer, and was duly rebuked by the Judge.*

THORNTON — John Thornton [38]

John Thornton (1814-1844), labourer, was born at Stow-on-the-Wold, the son of George and Fanny [Frances] Thornton. In 1830 Francis Witts sent him for trial at the Lent assizes, charged with stealing 1 shilling and 3 pence from the premises of Thomas Bown on 1 March 1830. In addition, he was charged with the theft of some oranges and sugar. The court records described him thus: '16 years of age, height 4 feet 10¾ inches; dark hair, dark eybrows, dark eyes, face rather flat and broad, rather short nose, brown complexion, mole on the left cheek, a mark on his chin, scar on his right elbow, scar on joint of the first finger right hand, scar second joint first finger left hand, two moles on the back of his neck, not read.' He was found not guilty, and was discharged on 17 April 1830. This would have angered Witts.

Some years later, Thornton was sentenced to seven years' transportation for larceny at the midsummer sessions of 1 July 1834. He was received on board the prison hulk *Justicia* at Woolwich on 16 July 1834, removed on 27 June 1835, and sailed on board the *Mary Ann* to New South Wales on 6 July 1835. He arrived there on 31 October 1835. He was imprisoned at Newcastle, where he arrived on 11 November 1835. Under 'remarks' he was described as pock-pitted. He became a farm labourer and died on 16 January 1844.

1834: 16 Jul: *Received a packet from Mr. Brookes covering a letter to him from Mr. Wooler respecting the pros. of Cox and Clifford, and a paper containing the substance of information communicated to Messrs. Brookes and Otway at Glouc. Gaol on Saturday last by Sandalls and Thornton sentenced at the last Quarter Sessions to seven years transportation.*

1835: 15 Apr: *It has been mentioned that Edmund Jeffrey was intimate with a worthless young man, Thornton, who was transported last year, subsequently to the murder of Mr. Rens, for poultry stealing. Is it improbable, that he was Jeffrey's guilty associate?*

THORNTON — Watson Joseph Thornton [39]

Watson Joseph Thornton (1802-1855), Church of England clergyman, was the second son of Henry Thornton (1760-1815) and Mary Ann Sykes (1765-1815) of Chobham, Surrey. He was educated at Trinity College, Cambridge (BA 1824; MA 1827), and entered the Church. He served as both rector of Llanwarne, Herefordshire, and prebendary of Hereford from 1833 to his death in 1855, and was appointed canon of Hereford in 1842. Watson married, at Donnington, Herefordshire, 12 April 1842, Frances Anne (1817-1855), daughter of Richard Webb of Donnington Hall, Herefordshire; they had 2 sons and 1 daughter:

1 Frances Marianne (1843-1912)
1 Henry Sykes (1848-1916)
2 Charles Inglis (1850-1929)

Together with Francis Witts and Richard Hare, Thornton was one of the executors of Thomas Welch Hunt (1797-1824), who with his bride Caroline was murdered by brigands during their honeymoon in Italy.

1836: 16 Jul.

1842: 9, Jul., 15 Jul: *Recd. a letter from Mr. Hare with a Power of Attorney inclosed for the sale of as much 3 pr. Ct. Cons. standg in the name of myself, Mr.H. and Mr. Thornton, as Trustees of the personal Estate of the late T. W. Hunt, as should be sufficient to pay certain law expences on the foreclosure of a mortgage, and arrears of interest due therefrom to Miss. C Hunt.*

1844: 27 Jan: *Wrote to the Revd. W. J. Thornton, Llanwarne Rectory, Ross, my co-trustee as to the estate of the late T. W. Hunt, on the subject of the disputed turnpike securities of the Hunt family.* 31 Jan., 27 Feb., 8 Mar., 11 Mar., 25 Mar., 28 Mar., 30 Mar., 1-2 Apr., 4 Apr., 6-7 Apr., 12 Apr., 14-21 Apr., 24-30 Apr., 1-4 May, 8 May, 28-31 May, 1 -3 Jun., 26-27 Jul., 4 Aug., 5 Nov., 8 Nov., 18 Nov., 21-22 Nov., 28 Nov., 30 Nov., 4 Dec., 10 Dec., 18 Dec., 24 Dec., 26 Dec.

1845: 2 Jan., 6 Jan., 11 Jan., 25 Jan., 29 Jan., 31 Jan., 5 Feb., 14 Feb., 18 Feb., 21Feb.

1846: 22 May, 28-29 May, 7 Jun., 16 Jun., 4 Jul., 8 Jul: *Received a letter from Mr. Thornton, who approves of my suggestion that the business of Whitby's mortgage be left in the hands of Messrs. Cox and Williams, but that as to other concerns relating to the Wadenhoe Trust, some other Solicitor be employed to be named by Mr. Cox and Mr. Braikenridge: the former being the confidential adviser of Mr. Hare, and the latter of Mr. Geo. Hunt.* 26-28 Jul., 31 Jul., 1 Aug., 5-7 Aug., 9 Aug., 6 Oct., 9 Oct., 12-13 Oct., 17 Oct., 23 Oct., 7 Nov., 12 Nov., 21 Nov., 24 Nov., 10-11 Dec.

1847: 5 Mar., 9-10 Mar., 20-21 Mar, 25-26 Mar., 4 Apr., 16-19 Apr., 21 Apr., 23 Apr., 6-7 Jun., 11-19 Jun., 7 Jul., 10 Jul., 13-14 Jul., 21 Jul., 23 Jul., 2 Aug., 10 Aug., 13 Aug., 7 Sep., 20 Sep., 23 Sep., 9 Oct., 12 Oct., 18 Oct., 23-24 Oct., 29-30 Oct., 1 Nov., 6 Nov., 9 Nov., 15-16 Nov., 30 Nov., 27-28 Dec., 30-31 Dec.

1848: 1 Jan, 7 Jan., 15 Jan., 19 Jan., 1 Mar., 3 Mar., 10 Mar., 15 Mar., 28 Mar., 3 Apr., 7-9 Apr., 12-14 Apr., 17 Apr., 20-21 Apr., 24-25 Apr., 28 Apr., 1 May, 3-6 May, 9-11 May, 14-21 May, 25 May, 27 May, 29 May, 1 Jun., 3 Jun., 8-9 Jun., 13 Jun., 18-20 Jun., 23 Jun., 3 Jul., 5 Jul., 29 Jul., 31 Jul., 8 Aug., 10 Aug., 12 Aug., 14-15 Aug., 21 Aug., 15 Sep., 23 Sep., 25 Sep., 27-30 Sep., 3 Oct., 5 Oct., 7 Oct., 10 Oct., 12-13 Oct., 15 Oct., 21 Oct., 30-31 Oct., 2 Nov., 6 Nov., 8 Nov., 10 Nov., 14 Nov., 16-17 Nov.

1849: 11 Dec., 14 Dec., 22 Dec., 25 Dec., 28 Dec.

1850: 4 Jan., 9 Jan., 11-12 Jan., 17-18 Jan., 23 Jan., 25-27 Jan., 5 Feb., 8-9 Feb., 16 Feb., 9 Mar., 18-19 Mar., 25 Mar., 28-29 Mar., 30 Mar., 1 Apr., 9-11 Apr., 13 Apr., 19 Apr., 23 Apr., 30 Apr., 2 May, 8 May, 12-14 May, 18-19 May, 22-23 May, 4 Jun., 11 Jun., 16 Jun., 20-21 Jun., 3 Jul., 6 Jul., 23 Jul., 31 Jul., 6 Sep., 19 Oct., 28 Oct.

1851: 6 Jan., 10 Jan., 13 Jan., 15 Jan., 18 Jan., 20 Jan., 26 Jan., 28 Jan., 2 Feb., 8 Feb., 11 Feb., 17 Feb., 19-20 Feb., 23-24 Feb., 1 Mar., 3 Mar., 9-10 Mar., 2 Apr., 8 Apr., 2 May, 5-6 May, 10 May, 17-18 May, 22-24 May, 29 May.

1852: 7 Feb., 11 Feb., 28 Mar., 3 Apr.

1853: 11-12 Mar., 15 May, 24 May.

THORP — Charles Thorp [40]

Charles Thorp (1803-1861), Church of England clergyman, was born at Hook Norton, Oxfordshire, the second son of William Thorp (1762-1835) and Elizabeth Watts (1765-1847). He was educated at Magdalen Hall, Oxford (BA 1834; MA 1839). Thorp was ordained deacon on 14 June 1835, and appointed on that same day as curate of Sandford St Martin, Oxfordshire. He was chaplain to Northleach House of Correction, 1847-56, and rector of Nympsfield, Gloucestershire, where he died in 1861.

Thorp married Jane Ellerton Hubbuck (1804-1864), born at Caversham, Oxfordshire; they had at least 2 sons:

1 Charles Ellerton (1850-1891)
2 Edward Ellerton (1851-1923)

1847: *The Revd — Thorpe was elected Chaplain of Northleach House of Correction in the room of Mr. Ireland, deceased.*

1848: 11 Oct: *Inspected the Bridewell, met Mr. Thorpe, the Chaplain, and advised as to the enlargement of the Chapel.*

1849: 10 Dec: *Mr. Thorp, Chaplain of the Bridewell at Northleach, called, partly to ascertain from me what deductions were likely to be made from his stipend in consequence of the deliberations of the County Finance Committee; partly, to obtain from me a testimonial of his good conduct as the Chaplain of one of the Gloucestershire Houses of Correction, which he might transmit, with the testimonials of other magistrates, to the authorities in the County of Norfolk, he proposing to offer himself as Candidate for the vacant Chaplaincy of the Bridewell at Swaffham, the income of which is double of that now received by him.*

1850: 15 Feb: *... accompanied by the Chaplain, Mr. Thorpe, we called at the Vicarage, and paid a short visit to the Astons, all of whom, with the exception of the younger Frederick, who was gone to Cheltenham, we saw.* 31 Jul.

1852: 15 Nov.

THORP — Thomas Thorp [41]

Thomas Thorp (1797-1877), Church of England clergyman, was born at Pontefract, Yorkshire, the eldest son of Robert William Disney Thorp (1766-1849), of Leeds, and Ann Catherine Grant (d. 1827). He was educated at Pontefract School, Richmond, Yorkshire, and Trinity College, Cambridge (BA 1819; MA 1822; BD 1842). He was archdeacon and chancellor of Bristol, 1836-73, and rector of Kemerton, 1839-77. He died unmarried.

1835: 12 Jun: *I proceeded to the cool cloisters behind Westminster Abbey, and waited on the Bishop of Gloucester at his Prebendal residence. His Lordship received me, though at this time engaged in preparing for an Ordination on Sunday next. The candidates were at that moment passing their Examination before his Lordship's Chaplain, Mr. Thorp.*

1837: 4 Aug., 17 Sep: *My Son received a kind letter from Archd. Thorp in his capacity of Examining Chaplain of Bp. Monk, in reply to a letter which Edwd. wrote to him some time since, soliciting direction and advice as to the line of reading preparatory to his Examination for Deacon's orders.* 24 Dec.

1838: 22 Aug.

1839: 2 Jan.

1844: 22 Mar.

1848: 26 Apr.

1851: 29 Apr.

THRING — William Davison Thring [42]

William Davison Thring (1783-1854), Church of England clergyman, was born at Sutton Veny, Wiltshire, the son of Brouncker Thring (1752-1812) and Mary Bayley, née Watts (1762-1825). He was educated at Wadham College, Oxford (BA 1804; MA 1825; B&DD 1830), and was ordained deacon on 2 March 1806 and priest on 21 February 1807. His first clerical appointment was as curate to his father. He became rector of Sutton Veney and Fisherton Delamere, Wiltshire, in 1829, and held the living until his death in 1854.

Thring married, at St James's, Piccadilly, Westminster, 28 July 1814, Jane Dugdale (1791-1869); they had 3 sons and 5 daughters:

1 Jane (1815-1878)
1 William Dugdale (1816-1872)
2 Richard Southby Otto (1817-1875)
2 Arabelle (1820-1889)
3 Mary (b. 1822)
4 Fanny (b. 1823)
3 John Everett (1826-1895)
5 Margaret Lucy (1829-1873)

The living at Fisherton Delamere was in the gift of Thring's old college friend at Wadham, John Davis of Fisherton Delamere House. After Thring's death, one of the Davis family—Thomas John Davis—followed him as rector.

1802: 3 Jun: *At Thring's meeting Evans, Alford, &c.*

1804: 21 Oct: *Breakfasted with Evans & Thring.* 22-23 Oct., 24 Oct: *Passed the evening with Evans & Thring.* 25 Oct.

1806: 31 Dec. *Called upon Mr. J. Tylee; met & walked with Thring.*

1807: 9 Apr: *Received a letter from Thring.* 29 May: *Rode off early on a visit to W. Thring, at Great Sutton, two miles beyond Heytesbury, about twelve miles from Erchfont over the plain; found my way very well by observing the various landmarks. Heytesbury a lively village & the country pretty. Sir W. Acourt's a pleasant place—Great Sutton Parsonage an old Abbey, I presume retired, & well wooded: The village large & clean. Dined & slept. Dr. & Mrs. Thring very civil.*

1832: 14 Mar: *In the course of the forenoon I called on an old College acquaintance and contemporary, who happened to be in Oxford, Dr. Thring, Rector of Sutton Veny, near Warminster, who recently took his degree to enable him to hold a second piece of preferment in the same county.*

THRUPP — Edward Thrupp [43]

Edward Thrupp (1809-1877), Church of England clergyman, was born at Paddington, Westminster, the third son of Joseph Thrupp (1748-1821) and his second wife, Mary Pillow (1769-1845). For the complex history of this family see the detailed entry below regarding Edward's elder brother, Joseph. Edward Thrupp was educated at Wadham College, Oxford (BA 1830; MA 1834), and entered the Church. He was appointed curate at Great Malvern and Coddington, Herefordshire, and later served as vicar of Feltham, Middlesex, from 1848 to his death in 1877.

Thrupp married, at St Mary de Lode, Gloucester, 3 July 1838, Katherine [Catherine] Stewart (±1815-1860), born in Ireland; they had at least 2 sons and 3 daughters:

1 Edward Kirkpatrick (1839-1872)
2 Morton Frederic (1840-1917)
1 Catherine Mary Amelia Helen (1842-1911)
2 Helen (1843-1851)
3 Edith Mavesyn Ann Hill (1852-1872)

It seems almost certain that Edward Thrupp's appointment as curate at Great Malvern was through the influence of Lady Lyttelton, who was friendly with/associated to the Thrupp family. It is almost too great a coincidence for it to have occurred without her 'input'.

1834: 9 Sep: *Besides the inmates of the house we had Dr. Card, the Vicar of Great Malvern, Mr. Thrupp, the Curate ...* 10 Sep.

1836: 19 Jul., 21 Jul: *Left my card for Mr. Thrupp who was from home ... Mr. Thrupp, shewing less judgment in his conversation than one could have desired.*

1840: 13 Apr., 24 Apr., 23 Jun: *Soon afterwards were waited on by Mr. Edward Thrupp, who came from his residence at Coddington to meet his brother, who had passed Sunday there, and had been in engaged yesterday on business at Worcester, whence he arrived between eleven and twelve o clock ...*

THRUPP — Joseph William Thrupp — *see also* Burgoyne *and* Parrott [44]

Joseph William Thrupp (1799-1873), solicitor, was born in the parish of St George, Westminster, the son of Joseph Thrupp (1743-1821) and his second wife, Mary Pillow (1769-1845). The Thrupp family were long associated with a coach building firm established in Worcester in the early eighteenth century. The founder was probably John Thrupp (1690-1755), husband to Dorothy Bishop (b. 1693). Their son Joseph (1743-1821), born at Hallow, Worcestershire, went to London in about 1765 and ran a coach making business in George Street [Balderton Street since 1886], Grosvenor Square. His best known coach building descendant was George Athelstane Thrupp (1822-1905), although there were also a number of other notable descendants who were not coach, carriage, or harness makers.

The Thrupp family business later consolidated in Oxford Street, and despite the rebuilding of the street as late as 1884-86, the firm retained their showrooms and works at the Grosvenor estate, Nos 421-429, Oxford Street. The scatter of trades in this part of the street was similar in 1890 to what it had been fifty years before, and the only speciality discernible besides coaches was leather goods. In an 1890 directory, two makers of leather breeches, four boot makers, and one saddler were recorded. Joseph's London business was continued by his nephew Henry East Thrupp (1774-1852), father of coach builder Robert Thrupp (1813-1871), together with Joseph's much younger fourth son Charles Joseph Thrupp (1791-1872), who left his nine surviving children £30,000. Of those nine children was George Athelstane Thrupp (1822-1905) and Ellen Thrupp (1829-1914). In 1869 Ellen married George's business partner George Henry Maberly (1836-1901). The firm existed up to 1967 as part of the Rootes Group.

Joseph Thrupp (1743-1821) married, first, at St George's, Hanover Square, Westminster, Mary (1757-1795), daughter of John Burgan and Dorothy Foulstone; they had 5 sons and 3 daughters:

1 Dorothea Ann (1779-1847)
1 Joseph (1781-1783)
2 Maria Ann (1782-1860)
2 John Augustus (1785-1844)
3 Josepha Augusta (1787-1788)
3 Josiah Augustus (1789-1816)
4 Charles Joseph (1791-1872)
5 Henry Joseph (1793-1862)

He married secondly, at the same church, 5 May 1797, Mary Pillow (1769-1845); they had 6 sons and 3 daughters:

1 Mary (1798-1877)
1 Joseph William (1799-1873); *see below*
2 James (1801-1871)
3 Robert (1803-1808)
2 Ann Elizabeth (1804-1863)
3 Jane Caroline (1807-1882)
4 Edward 1809-1877), Church of England clergyman; *see above*
5 Frederick (1812-1895)
6 Horace (1814-1904)

Joseph William Thrupp (1799-1873), solicitor, was a partner in the firm Burgoynes, Thrupp, and Clark of 160 Oxford Street. He married, at St Marylebone, Westminster, 24 August 1826, Ruth Louisa (1804-1886), daughter of Thomas John Burgoyne (1775-1847) and Ruth (1779-1837), daughter of Richard and Charlotte Parrott of Quebec Street, London. They had 1 son and 1 daughter:

1 Francis Joseph (1827-1867), Church of England clergyman famous for his writings on hymns; educated at Winchester College and Trinity College, Cambridge; ordained, 1852; given the college living of Barrington, Cambridgeshire; elected a member of the board of theological studies at Cambridge; select preacher, 1865; wrote *Ancient Jerusalem* (1855), *Introduction to the Psalms* (2 vols, 1860), and *A Translation of the Song of Songs* (1862); contributed to the *Speaker's Commentary* and to William Smith's *Dictionary of the Bible*; married, at St George's, Hanover Square, 12 April 1853, Elizabeth Bligh Glennie (1831-1909)
1 Adelaide (1830-1908)

The connection between the Witts and Thrupp families was derived from the Burgoyne/Parrott side. When Apphia Witts [later Lady Lyttelton] went to India in 1769, she was accompanied by a young lady's maid, Ruth Fuller (b. 1755), who had been born at Salford, Oxfordshire, a village close to Chipping Norton. Ruth married, at Salford, 20 June 1776, Richard Parrott (1755-1807), banker, of Quebec Street, London. Their daughter, Anne (1783-1865), married, 1838, Edward London Witts, cousin of the diarist. Lady Lyttelton maintained a life-long link with the Parrott family, and when Ruth Burgoyne married Joseph William Thrupp, that link widened. Apphia had a great fondness for maintaining links, often distant and tenuous, with far flung cousins and connections. This tenuous link of family with friends is demonstrated in a diary entry by Agnes Witts of 12 November 1789:

> Mr. Witts & I went to London, for me to appear in the Court of Chancery call'd upon Mrs. Guydickens, who kindly went with me there, the bussiness was soon over, & she went with me shopping till near Dinner time when we dined very comfortably in Bayswater Street, Miss Hanburys came to Drink Tea & staid the evening, & after Supper we went to Sleep at Mr. Parrots in Quebec Street very comfortably.

Agnes had presumably been in correspondence with Lady Lyttelton as to where she and Edward might stay during their visit, and Lady Lyttelton had no doubt arranged for their temporary lodging with the Parrott family in Quebec Street.

1834: *12 Sep: The Thrupps, Mr. and Miss Burgoyne called at Peach Field Lodge. 13 Sep: Lady L. had a large party to dinner: sixteen sat down to table, and the aged hostess did the honours with great spirit, and courteous attention to her guests: enjoying herself extremely. There were a Mrs. and Miss Norris, residents in London, and, it proved, relatives of our neighbour, Mrs. H. Waller, of Farmington Lodge—Mr. & Mrs. Thrupp.*

1840: 14 Apr: *To Mr. Thrupp, a Solicitor, in Oxford Street, in whom Lady Lyttelton had placed confidence.* 17-18 Apr., 21 Apr., 24 Apr., 30 Apr., 2 May, 5 May: *After breakfast called on Mr. Thrupp at his office in Oxford Street, No. 160, where he received me with much attention, and I went through my business relating to my Aunt's will and other matters connected with it very satisfactorily... Dined pleasantly at 55 Upper Brook Street, with Mr. and Mrs. Thrupp, en famille: he is a well informed, agreeable & sensible person; they have two very nice children.* 6-8 May, 14 May, 16 May, 19-22 May, 8 Jun., 11 Jun: *Recd. a letter from Mr. Thrupp in answer to mine of May 22. and June 8. He still considers the legacies to the School of Ancient Industry, and the Infant School bequeathed by my Aunt to have failed in consequence of those schools having been discontinued: he proposes to meet my Son and me at Malvern at the time of the sale of the premises—on the 23d. Inst.* 12 Jun., 14-15 Jun., 23 Jun., 27 Jun., 3 Jul., 5 Jul: *Called on Mr. Thrupp by appointment, who introduced me to his partner, Mr. Burgoyne, an elderly gentleman, who married a Sister of the late Mr. Parrot, a partner in Sir Claude Scotts' house, and son of a very worthy person, who originally went out to India with my Aunt Lyttelton, as her servant. Miss Parrot, who has married my cousin E L Witts was her daughter. Mr. Burgoyne is Father to Mrs. Jos. Thrupp.* 7 Jul., 12 Jul., 12 Jul., 20 Jul., 29 Jul., 7 Aug., 12 Aug., 12 Sep., 20 Sep., 22 Sep., 25 Sep., 30 Sep., 1 Oct., 14 Oct., 2-7 Nov.

1842: 22 Jan., 5 Feb., 18 Feb., 15 Mar: *After breakfast proceeded with Edward to Mr. Thrupp's offices, with whom I transacted business, relating to the winding up of the affairs of my late Aunt Lyttelton.* 17 Mar: *We proceeded towards our hotel, shopping by the way, and reached it before six o clock in time to dress for dinner with Mr. and Mrs. Thrupp at their private residence in Upper Brook Street, where we met Mrs. E. L. Witts, and were joined in the evening by her nephew and Mrs. Thrupp's cousin, Mr. Geo. Parrot, a young man connected, either as a Junior partner or Clerk, with Sir Claude Scott's bank, of which his late Father was the resident and managing partner.* 16 Mar: *To our Hotel to dress for dinner at B P Witts's in Brunswick Square, whither we went in a cab, and whence we returned in a hired coach with Mrs. E. L. Witts, the Widow of Champion Hill, who is staying in Town with her niece Mrs. Thrupp.* 30 Jun., 1 Jul.

1852: 8 Nov., 24 Nov: *Recd. a letter from Mr. Burgoyne, head of the firm in which Mr. Thrupp is a partner, in reply to mine of the 8th. Inst. The dividend payable to Lady Lyttelton's estate out of Boldero's bankrupt Estate is inconsiderable ...*

1854: 7 Mar: *Recd. a letter from Mr. Jennings, who is a candidate for the office of Surveyor to the Merchant Tailor's Company; now vacant, and is anxious that I should use in his favour any influence I may have with Mr. Thrupp, the London Solicitor, who is a member of the Court of that company, and so is one of the parties entitled to vote for the candidates.* 17 Mar, 25 Mar.

THURLES — Miss Thurles of Urchfont

1807: 16 Jul: *Mrs. Legg & Miss Thurles called late.* 19 Jul.

THYNNE — *see* Chester-Master

TIBBS — Somerset Tibbs[45]

Somerset Tibbs (1808-1868), dentist, was born at Aldbury, Hertford, the son of Samuel and Ann Tibbs. He married, 3 January 1831, Hannah Culverhouse; they had 1 daughter:

1 Ann (b. 1831); baptised on 25 January 1831 (a remarkably short pregnancy)

It seems likely that Hannah died during childbirth or shortly after, for in July 1832 Tibbs married, secondly, Clarissa Michelin; they had 3 sons and 4 daughters:

1 Clarissa Anne (b. 1837); appears to have died soon after birth
1 Percival William (b. 1838)
2 Clarissa (b. 1840)
2 Somerset (b. & d. 1842)
3 Jessica Frances (b. 1844)
4 Somersine Hannah (b. 1851)
3 John Arthur Somerset (b. 1853)

In 1841 Somerset Tibbs was living at Regent Street; he was still at 58 Regent Street in 1858.

1847: 5 May: *My wife visited Mr. Tibbs, the Dentist, to have her mouth renovated; the operation went off successfully, to all appearance.*

1848: 7 Nov: *Engaged with Mr. Tibbs, the dentist.*

TICEHURST — Rowland James Ticehurst[46]

Rowland James Ticehurst (1817-1888), solicitor, was born at Battle, Sussex, the son of William Ticehurst (1768-1852), schoolmaster, and Ann Clark (1779-1858). William Ticehurst had first been married to Sophia (d. 1801), but she died young, possibly after giving birth to a son named Rowland, who died in infancy in 1802. Rowland Ticehurst married secondly, at Devizes, Wiltshire, 1843, Anna Clark (b. ±1815); they had at least 3 sons and 2 daughters:

1 Rowland (1844-1924)
2 Augustus Rowland (b. 1846)
1 Frances (1847-1923)
3 Frederic (b. ±1848-1916)
2 Hildred Carlyle St. Clair (b. ±1850)

Rowland James Ticehurst was in partnership with Edmund Lambert Newman and William Henry Gwinnett (1809-1891) of Cheltenham. In 1861 he and Anna lived at 15 Royal Crescent, Cheltenham.

1845: 8 Feb: Mr. *Ticehurst, a Partner in the house of Gevinnett, Newman, and Ticehurst, Solrs. Cheltenham, arrived from Stow, where he had been on a similar errand to Mr. Vavasour, with the will of the late Lady Burdett.*

TICKELL — the Tickell family at Tunbridge Wells

1805: 1 Oct: *A party at Mrs. Moore's of about twenty very pleasant, Miss Windham, the Bucknalls, O'Callaghan, Tickells etc.*

TIDD PRATT — *see* Pratt

TIDMARSH — Samuel Tidmarsh[47]

Samuel Tidmarsh (±1793-1855), union workhouse relieving officer, was born at Broadwell, Gloucestershire. He was married to Jane (±1795-1870). In the early 1840s he and Jane ran a small shop and beer house at Evenlode. In 1851 they were farming 60 acres in Evenlode, employing two labourers.

1836: 11 Dec: *A letter from Hall, the Assist. P.L.C. in answer to mine written to him on Friday last: he considers the charge made against the Rel. Off. Tidmarsh very serious, advises the course proper to be taken, and will, if he can, be at Stow, on the 22d. when the case is to be investigated, but this is uncertain.* 12 Dec: *Wrote to Beman on the subject of the charge brought against the Rel. Off. Tidmarsh, pointing out the penalties to which he has rendered himself liable...* 22 *It appeared pretty clear that the imputation, which originated with a farmer of Broadwell, Phipps, had its origin in an old grudge between him and Tidmarsh ... The latter [Tidmarsh] had made himself obnoxious to the censures of persons unfavourably inclined towards him by persisting, in keeping a Beerhouse at Evenlode, although, when he was appointed Rel. Off., he had pledged himself to discontinue the occupation.* 23-24 Dec., 29 Dec.

1838: 26 Nov: *Transacting business with Tidmarsh the Rel. Officer of the Union.* 29 Nov.

1839: 2 May: *The board after a little discussion confirmed and adopted all the proceedings of the Board of last year; and the Rel. Off. were asked whether they would now accept the united offices of R.O. and Coll. of rates on the terms which they had declined: viz £60 per ann. as the maximum for both—Tidmarsh appeared to refuse the offer with firmness.*

1842: 13 Mar., 6 Jun: *S. Tidmarsh was convicted of misapplication of the funds of the Stow Union, and fined thrice the amount of the money misapplied (15/9) and a nominal fine of five shillings.* 4 Jul: *To the Workhouse, where met Mr. Beman by appointment, also Mr. Pearce; and conferred with them on the alleged misconduct of the Relieving Off. Tidmarsh, and the course to be pursued in the case.* 12 Jul., 14 Jul., 25 Jul., 27 Jul: *The P. L. C. have issued an order for the dismissal of S. Tidmarsh.* 28 Jul: *The dismissal of Tidmarsh, the R. O, was formally carried out.* 15 Sep., 29 Sep: ... *and an investigation into an alleged misapplication of the funds of the Union by the late Rel. Off. Tidmarsh took up much time, both at the Board and afterwards before the Magistrates.*

TIERNEY — George Tierney[48]

George Tierney (1761-1830), politician, was born at Gibraltar, the third son of Thomas Tierney, a native of Limerick, and his wife, Sabina (d. 1806). His father was a London merchant, prize agent at Gibraltar, and a man of some affluence. He spent his later years in Paris, but his wife lived in England where their children were educated. George was educated at Boteler's School, Warrington, Eton College, and Peterhouse College, Cambridge. He entered Lincoln's Inn in 1780 and was called to the bar in 1784, but did not practise. He entered parliament as MP for Colchester in 1789-90. He was then MP for Southwark, 1796-1806; Athlone, 1806-07; Bandon Bridge, 1807-12; Appleby, 1812-18; and Knaresborough, 1818-30. He was appointed privy councillor on 1 June 1803. In addition, he was treasurer of the Navy, June 1803–May 1804; president of the Board of Control, October 1806–April 1807; and master of the Mint, May 1827–February 1828.

George Tierney married, 9 July 1789, Anna Maria (1768-1844), daughter of Michael Miller of Bristol; they had 1 son and 3 daughters:

1 Louisa Mary (b. 1793)
2 Anna Maria Tierney (1796-1864)
3 Madeline (1796-1854)
1 George (1800-1882)

1827: 4 May: *In the House of Commons, Messrs. Brougham, Tierney &c. Sir F. Burdett, Sir R. Wilson &c. took their seats on the*

Treasury benches & spoke in favour of Canning's ministry. 19 May: Mr. Tierney is made master of the mint with a seat in the cabinet. 7 Sep: *The great bone of contention has been the Chancellorship of the Exchequer ... Mr. Huskisson was talked of, but his health is not sufficient for the fatigues of the post: Mr. Tierney, but his age incapacitated him.*

TILLEARD — John Tilleard [49]

John Tilleard (1793-1870), solicitor, was born at Lambeth, Surrey, the son of James Tilleard (b. 1758), solicitor, and Mary Brayne (b. 1756). He married, at St Mary's, Mortlake, Surrey, 8 September 1814, Elizabeth (1789-1859), daughter of Joseph Oliver Allman (1761-1807), solicitor, and Dorothy Mawman (1766-1811); they had at least 2 sons and 2 daughters:

1 John Adams (1815-1875)
1 Eleanor Mary Ann (1817-1882)
2 Thomas Allman Bower (1818-1882)
2 Katharine Dorothy (1821-1916)

In 1831 their 15- or 16-year-old son, John Adams Tilleard was awarded his articles of clerkship, articled to his father. The partnership was named Tilleard and Miller, of Old Jewry, in 1829. By 1843 it had become John Tilleard and Son of 34 Old Jewry. In the 1861 census John Tilleard was living in Streatham with his son John Adams Tilleard and his daughter-in-law Eleanor (b. ±1820).

1846: 21 Dec: ... *to Mr. Thornton, in answer to his last letter, desiring him to communicate to Mr. Hare and Mr. Cox that we had fixed on Mr. Tilleard as our Solicitor to be consulted on Hunt affairs, when necessary.*

1848: 16 May, 19 May, 5 Aug., 10 Aug., 29 Aug., 31 Aug., 1 Sep., 3 Sep., 11 Sep., 14-15 Sep., 19 Sep.

TILSLEY — Edwin Tilsley [50]

Edwin Fawler Tilsley (±1810-1889), solicitor, was born at Chipping Norton, the son of Thomas Tilsley. In 1829 he was articled to George Fawler Tilsley, of Chipping Norton, presumably an uncle. He married, 1845, Frances [Fanny] Elizabeth Boughton Prosser (1826-1899); they had at least 1 son and 2 daughters:

1 Frances Eliza Henrietta Louisa (b. 1850)
2 Louisa (b. 1852)
1 Albert Edwin George Fawler (b. 1862), clerk to his father

Edwin Tilsley was a solicitor at Moreton-in-Marsh, and held the office of clerk of the union.

1835: 19 Mar: *Mr. Ackerley now, thoroughly warmed, shifted his ground, and preferred a direct charge against the Police Officers; he stated that they were generally obnoxious; Messrs. Jeaffreson, Winter, Brookes, and Tilsley, rebutted this in most decided terms, alledging that the men had won the good opinion of all respectable people, and were only obnoxious to the obnoxious.*

1854: 18 Jul: *A printed letter from a person in the name of Wright, from Moreton in Marsh, signifying that he is a candidate for the Clerkship of our Union. He says he has been employed as Assistant Clerk of the Shipston Union — probably as Clerk to Mr. Tilsley of Moreton, the Solicitor, who holds the office of Clerk of the Union.*

TIMBRELL — John Timbrell [51]

John Timbrell (1773-1865), archdeacon of Gloucester and JP, was born at Bretforton, Worcestershire, son of Thomas Timbrill of Pershore. At birth his name was Timbrill, but the family chose to alter it to Timbrell. He was educated at Worcester College, Oxford (BA 1793; MA 1796; BD 1803; DD 1816), and entered the Church. He was appointed vicar of Beckford with Ashton-under-Hill in 1797, and of Breforton, Worcestershire, in 1816. He was archdeacon of Gloucester 1814-1865 and vicar of Dursley from 1825 to his death. He married Elizabeth Edwards 1796-1848); they had at least 3 sons and 3 daughters:

1 Elizabeth (1826-1827)
1 John Carwardine (1829-1848)
2 Jane (1831-1894)
2 Robert (1831-1832)
3 Robert (1833-1877)
3 Catherine (1835-1864)

1820: 11 Apr.

1822: 15 Oct.

1823: 14 Jan, 8 Apr., 15 Jul., 17 Sep., 14 Oct.

1824: 13 Jan., 10 Mar., 24 Apr., 13 Jul., 19 Oct.

1825: 12 Apr., 16 May: *By a letter from Mrs. Backhouse received to-day, it appears, that the Bishop of Gloucester has made a selection, from among the Incumbents of his Diocese, of an Archdeacon. His choice has fallen on Dr. Timbrill, Rector of Beckford, and of Bretforton in the adjoining County of Worcester. Dr. Timbrill is also Treasurer of the Clerical Charity for the diocese of Gloucester, and an active magistrate: in fact, a very useful man of business* 14-15 Jul., 18 Oct.

1826: 10 Jan., 30-31 Mar., 10 May, 11 Jul.

1827: 16 May, 16 Oct.

1828: 15 Jan., 15 Apr., 16 Jun., 15 Jul., 17 Jul., 14 Oct.

1829: 13 Jan., 1-2 Apr., 28 Apr., 20 May: *The Visitation of the Archdeacon of Gloucester, Dr. Timbrill, was held this day at Stow, which I attended, as usual. The Archdeacon himself preached an excellent discourse ...* 14 Jul., 22-23 Sep., 20 Oct.

1830: 21 Jan., 20 Apr., 10 May.

1834: 16 Oct.

1836: 10-11 Aug.

1837: 5 Feb., 13 Feb., 7 Mar., 23 May, 27 Jun., 4 Aug.

1838: 3 Jan., 10 Apr., 3 Jul., 24 Aug: *It seems that Gist has given this preferment to a Son of Archd. Timbrill, a boy of ten years of age; consequently, it is to be held for 14 years. There is a comfortable parsonage house, and the main drawback is the irregularity of conduct for which the Patron, who resides within a mile of the Village, is notorious: his habits of intoxication, and licentious conversation being such that it is almost impossible for a decent clergyman to associate with him.* 29 Aug: ... *but Lord Rossmore arrived at the Grange on Saturday, and exerted his influence with his son in law to retract the authority he had given to Archd. Timbrill to select a clergyman to hold the living for a time, he (Lord R.) having some Irish Clergyman whom he wishes to patronize, and place in the vacant situation.* 16 Oct.

1839: 1 Jan., 9 Apr., 24 Apr., 12 May, 17 May: *We dined, a tolerably large party, at the Unicorn, at three o clock, where was good fare, and not anything to be complained of but the fulsome and tiresome habit which the Archdeacon has, in common with his Diocesan of giving toasts, the healths of dignitaries, officials, and other individuals present or absent, with a wearisome and somewhat disgusting tone of flattery.* 2 Jul.

1840: 25 May, 30 Jun., 20 Oct.

1841: 4 Mar.

1842: 5-6 Jan., 31 Jan., 4 Feb., 12 Apr., 23 May, 28-29 Jun., 18 Oct.

1843: 3-4 Jan., 17 Aug., 6 Oct., 17 Oct: *Dr. Timbrill, as Senior Magistrate was called to the Chair, and presided at the dinner, the party consisting of 22 Magistrates; the Archdeacon, after his fashion, being rather over zealous in compliments and toasts, the ball of giving and returning thanks was kept up vigorously, till several of the party, myself among the number, withdrew to an exhibition at the Theatre.*

1844: 22 Feb., 29 Feb., 1-2 Mar., 6 Mar., 8 Apr., 10 Apr., 9 Aug., 13 Aug., 8 Oct., 14 Oct., 18 Oct., 16-17 Dec., 30-31 Dec.

1845: 2 Jan., 24 Jan: *Replied to Purnell's letter recd. yesterday as far as it related to the controversy between him and his brother, and Dr. Timbrell's management of that business at the late Sessions.* 27 Jan., 19 Feb: *My son has met Dr. Timbrill who professes to have caught a bad cold from his attendance at Oxford last week, and to be unequal to undertake the duties of second Chairman at the Adjourned Sessions at Gloucester on Mar. 4; so that those duties are likely to devolve on me.* 21 Feb., 26 Feb., 1 Mar., 15 Apr., 1 May, 26-27 May, 30 Jun., 1 Jul.

1846: 30 Jun., 20-21 Oct., 18 Nov.

1847: 16 Mar., 23 Mar., 18 May, 29 May, 28-30 Jun., 10 Sep., 18 Oct., 1 Nov.

1848: 3 Jan., 13 Jan., 16 May.

1850: 8 Nov.

1851: 4 Feb: *With my dear daughter in law, and Broome, drove to Beckford to call on Archdeacon Timbrill and his daughters.* 17 May: *Dr. Timbrill in full vigour, not withstanding his great age. He has been 27 years Archdeacon, and was instituted to his living of Beckford as long ago as in 1797.*

1853: 18 Jan., 22 Jan., 24 May.

TIMBRELL — the Timbrell sisters, Patience, Judith, and Rebecca [52]

Patience (1740-1814), Judith (1745-1812), and Rebecca (1749-1823) were the daughters of William Timbrell (1705-1774) and Patience Gleadow (b. 1711). They inherited the Tracy estates at Sandywell, Upper Slaughter, Lower Swell, and elsewhere from Thomas Tracy (±1716-1770), MP, of Sandywell Hall. Thomas was the seventh son (probably) of John Tracy (1681-1735), of Stanway, Gloucestershire, and Anne, daughter of Sir Robert Atkyns, MP and chief baron of the exchequer, of Lower Swell and Sapperton, Gloucestershire. John and Anne had married on 7 August 1699. Their family supposedly numbered fifteen, but not all of their children are known as the parish registers for Lower Swell and Stanway are incomplete and damaged by mice and damp.

Thomas Tracy's paternal grandparents were Ferdinando Tracy (1659-1682) and Katherine (1660-1722), daughter of Anthony Keck (1630-1695) and Mary Thorne (1640-1702). Ferdinando and Katherine married on 22 July 1680. Thomas's paternal great-grandparents were John Tracy, 3rd Viscount Tracy of Rathcoole (1617-1687), and Elizabeth, third, but first surviving, daughter of Thomas Leigh, 1st Baron Leigh, and Mary (d. 1688), daughter and co-heir of Sir Thomas Egerton. They were married in around 1655.

As Ferdinando Tracy was a younger son of the viscount, his grandson Thomas was of a junior line. Thomas's great-uncle, William Tracy (1657-1712), succeeded as 4th Viscount Tracy of Rathcoole in 1687. The peerage eventually became extinct on the death of the 8th Viscount in 1797. One source states that Thomas's father John Tracy (1681-1735) was a godson of his grandfather John, 3rd Viscount Tracy. This seems probable as John's father Ferdinando died in 1682, a year after John's birth, while his grandfather lived until 1687.

Thomas Tracy joined the Army as an ensign in the 9th Foot in 1737, but retired sometime between 1740 and 1752. In 1751 he was considered as a candidate for Gloucester on the corporation interest, and in 1752 James West believed that he would be willing to stand at Tewkesbury. Nothing is known of any further attempts by Tracy to enter parliament until 1763, when he was returned unopposed for Gloucestershire on the Berkeley interest. He served as MP for Gloucestershire from 27 April 1763 to his death on 24 June 1770. Tracy voted with the opposition over Wilkes and general warrants, and was a member of the Wildman's Club. He was classed variously during his career: as a 'sure friend' by Newcastle on 10 May 1764 ; as a 'pro' by Rockingham in July 1765 and as a 'whig' in November 1766; as a 'country gentleman' by Townshend in January 1767; and as a 'friend' by Newcastle again in March 1767. In his last recorded vote on 27 February 1767, Tracy voted against the Chatham administration on the land tax. He was returned unopposed in 1768. There are no surviving speeches attributed to him.

Thomas Tracy married, 15 April 1746 (with 'a great fortune', according to a letter from James West to Henry Pelham dated 25 July 1752), Mary, daughter and heir of Sir William Dodwell (d. 1727) of Sevenhampton, Gloucestershire. With this marriage Thomas acquired Sandywell Park, Whittington, and lands in Whittington and nearby Sevenhampton. The *History of Parliament* states that there was one daughter of the marriage, but this is incorrect. There was a son, Dodwell (1746-1768), born on 19 March 1746 and baptised at Sevenhampton on 22 March that year. He died at Paris on 11 January 1768; what he was doing there is unclear, but he was probably on the Grand Tour. He was buried at Stanway on 18 February 1768. His memorial reads as follows:

> ... a youth (from his amiable disposition and distinguished parts) of the most promising hopes, but these alas were blasted, when in the flower of his age he was snatched from the arms of his afflicted parents and friends, January 11th, 1768, at Paris, on his return from his travels in the 21st year of his age.

Following Thomas's death two years later, Mary remained as a widow at Sandywell Park until her own death in 1799. She was buried at Stanway. With Mary lived two other 'Mrs. Tracys'. One of these we know to have been her unmarried sister-in-law, Elizabeth Tracy (1718-1793). Elizabeth died at Sandywell Park and was buried at Stanway on 6 November 1793. Agnes Witts was in Edinburgh at the time and recorded the event in her diary:

> *Monday 11 November 1793*
> Quite a perfect dry day, having been a frost in the night, & a sharp North wind, a little sun but a great tendency to fog & very cold, I never went out, having much to do & to think on, my spirits very low & much agitated, by the confirmation of Mrs. Eliza Tracys death, & receiving all the particulars of it in a Letter from Betty Guydickens.
>
> *Wednesday 13 November 1793*
> A very miserable day of wind & rain, little better than Sunday last of course an intire Stay at home day, not ill suited to my numerous employs went into Mourning for my much valued Friend & Aunt Mrs. Elizabeth Tracy, of whose Death, Funeral & Wile I had a very particular account in a long informing Letter from my Sister Travell.

The death of Elizabeth Tracy was a great blow to Agnes; her Aunt Betty had been one of her most frequent correspondents. Afterwards she corresponded frequently with Mary Tracy; she may have been trying to build upon the family connection in view of her and her husband's financial difficulties.

The other Mrs Tracy resident at Sandywell was presumably Agnes's other aunt, Martha (1712-1802). She died on 29 September 1802 and was buried at Stanway on 8 October 1802. Agnes was visiting her Granville friends at Calwich Abbey when she made a note of her aunt's death in her diary:

> *Saturday 2 October 1802*
> Another very similiar day, but still more wonderfuly warm, such an evening seldom if ever known at the season, Mrs. Granville & I in the Gig Mr. Witts Father & Son on horseback, went to Mrs. Fernihoughs Grove Cottage a mile or two from Ashborne where we found a large party of Ladies one of the prettiest places of the kind I ever saw, all but Mr. Delabere & I walk'd till after dark wrote to E. Guydickens on our Aunt Marthas death & rec'd a charming letter from Lady Elcho.

Martha's passing did not cause Agnes the sorrow she had felt at the loss of her Aunt Betty, and she did not go into mourning. Francis Witts did not record the event at all.

Somewhat surprisingly, Mary Tracy died intestate. Litigation over her estate lasted until 1807. The three sisters, Patience Timbrell (1740-1814), Judith Timbrell (±1745-1812), and Rebecca Lightbourne, née Timbrell (1749-1823), distant relations and heirs at law, were then declared heirs to the bulk of the estate. In 1809 they received a conveyance from Mary's surviving trustees, Charles Hanbury Tracy and his wife Henrietta. Other claimants were compensated with land at Upper Slaughter or with cash; Rebecca's estranged husband, Thomas Lightbourne, surrendered his rights in return for an annuity. Judith died in 1812 and Patience in 1814, both devising their shares to Rebecca, who died in 1823, leaving her estate to Walter Lawrence Lawrence. To discharge her debt and legacy to the Cheltenham solicitor Theodore Gwinnett, Lawrence surrendered part of the Brockhampton estate, including its principal house, to Gwinnett in 1825.

Agnes Witts wisely advised her son Francis to use the family connection with the Tracy lineage to cultivate the goodwill of the three sisters; they owned the advowson to the living at Upper Slaughter, then held by Francis's uncle, Ferdinando Tracy Travell (1740-1809). This advice was well given; following Ferdinando's death, the sisters presented the living to Francis Witts. Witts eventually bought the advowson from Walter Lawrence Lawrence in December 1831 for £1,016. It was a bargain, probably agreed for the benefit of Francis Witts and his descendants.

1805: 1 Aug: ... *calling upon my patroness, the Miss Timbrels &c. Mrs. Travell called.*

1806: 3 Jan: ... *a letter of Congratulation to Mrs. Timbrells, who have gained their Cause.*

1824: 24 Dec: *The three sisters were pleased with the attention paid to them by a branch of the Tracy family, none of whom had before in any way recognised them, and on a subsequent interview, when I was introduced to them, gave me the promise of the living of Upper Slaughter, when it should be vacant, if my character and conduct in the interval should be such as to merit their patronage. They said, they should have satisfaction in doing what Mrs. Tracy had left undone, and as I was her godson, they considered my claim to patronage from her as strong. Mrs. Tracy was the heiress of a Sir William Dodwell ...*

TINDAL — Mr Tindal, a distant relation to Francis Witts

1801: 22 May: *I was introduced to a distant Relation, Mr. Tindal, who again presented me to the Turkish Chargé d'affaires.* 26 Sep: *Miss Guydickens, & Mrs. Tindal & Mrs. Phelps called in the morning.* 28 Sep.

TINDAL — Nicholas Conyngham Tindal [53]

Sir Nicholas Conyngham Tindal (1776-1846), solicitor-general, was born at Coval Hall, the son of Robert Tindal, solicitor, of Chelmsford, and Sarah Pocock. He was educated at Chelmsford Grammar School and Trinity College, Cambridge (BA 1799; MA 1802). In 1802 he entered as a student at Lincoln's Inn, and in 1834 he was awarded an honorary DCL degree from the University of Oxford.

Tindal was with Brougham as counsel for Queen Caroline in her trial in 1820. He entered parliament as MP for the Wigtown burghs and became solicitor-general on 20 September 1826; it was a time of change caused by Copley's appointment as master of the rolls. Tindal was knighted in the same year, and returned to parliament for Harwich. In 1827, when Copley became lord chancellor, a vacancy was created at the University of Cambridge; Tindal was elected against William John Bankes by 479 votes to 378. On 9 June 1829 he succeeded William Draper Best, 1st Baron Wynford, as chief justice of the common pleas, and held the post until his death.

Tindal married, 2 September 1809, Merelina (1788-1818), daughter of Capt. Thomas Symonds (1731-1793) and Elizabeth Malet; they had 4 sons and 3 daughters:

1 Nicholas (1810-1842)
2 Louis Symonds (1811-1876), Adm.
3 Robert John (1813-1814); died an infant
1 Merelina (b. 1813); died an infant
2 Merelina (1815-1852)
4 Charles John (±1816-1853), barrister; died unmarried
3 Isabella Juliana (b. & d. 1818); died an infant

1826: 18 Sep: ... *and Mr. Tindal is raised to the post of Solicitor General.*

1827: 2 May: *Law Appointments Solicitor General—Sir N.C. Tindal.*

1829: 25 Mar: ... *so it was referred to the more pliant and liberal Solicitor General, Sir Nicholas Tindal.* 26 Jun.

1844: 15 Aug.

TINKER — Leonard Tinker [54]

Leonard Tinker (1775-1807), draper, of Eastcott, Wiltshire, was apprenticed in December 1791 to William Cunnington of Heytesbury. He married, at Great Cheverell, April 1796, Jane Sainsbury (d. 1799); they had 1 daughter:

1 Maria (b. 1797)

Leonard Tinker married, secondly, Elizabeth Lye.

1807: 6 Jan: *Walked to Easticott to call upon Leonard Tinker, who could not see me.* 14 Jan: *Engaged from 11 to 4 in attending the funeral of the late Mr. L. Tinker from Eastcott to West Lavington, which was handsome & expensive, but the weather was extremely unfavourable. Among the Gentlemen present were Messrs. D. & B. Compton, Williams, William Tinker, Smith, Garent, Sainsbury &c.* 23 Jan: *Rode to Eastcott, & called upon the Widow Tinker, & to Littleton upon Mrs. Tinker, her Daughters &c. where I made a pleasant visit.* 5 Feb: *[Rode] to Devizes, where I had several errands: particularly as commissioner to the Administration of Leonard Tinker's Effects, which took me to Mr. W. Salmon's.*

TINKER — William Tinker and the Tinker family of Littleton — *see also* Giddings [55]

William Tinker (1766-1831), landed proprietor, was born at Imber, Wiltshire, the son of Philip Tinker (1729-1791) and Ann Sainsbury. He lived at Littleton Panell, West Lavongton, and married, at West Lavington, Wiltshire, 20 February 1787, Sarah Amor (1764-1829). They had 4 sons and 8 daughters:

1 Sarah Ann (1788-1832)
2 Harriot (b. & d. 1789)
3 Mary (b. 1790)
1 William (b. 1791)
4 Louisa (1793-1845)
2 Robert Amor (b. & d. 1794)
5 Caroline (1795-1873)
6 Sophia Amor (b. 1797)
3 Robert Amor (b. & d. 1798)
7 Amelia (b. 1801)
8 Ellen (1804-1844)
4 Robert Amor (1805-1862)

The picture is made more complicated as there was also a Tinker Hawkins family at Urchfont; presumably they were closely related.

1806: 30 Oct: *Drove my Mother to Littleton to call upon Mrs. Tinker, the road through Lavington being very bad drove round by Devizes & Pottern, the latter part very beautiful. Found Mrs. T. & her whole family of seven daughters at home: the eldest a sweet girl.* 9 Nov.

1807: 3 Jan: *Accompanied my Father upon a walk to call upon Mrs. Tinker's family.* 23 Jan: *Rode to Eastcott, & called upon the Widow Tinker, & to Littleton upon Mrs. Tinker, her Daughters &c. where I made a pleasant visit.* 7 Feb: *Mr. Tinker called early to tempt me hunting; but without success.* 15 Feb., 18 Feb: *Dined at Mr. Tinker's at Littleton & passed the Evening very pleasantly, going in the Lavington Chaise, met Mr. & Mrs. Richards, Mr. Bafret, Mr. Bernard, Mr. Eldridge &c.* 22 Mar., 8 Aor., 20 Apr., 20 May, 21 May, 24 May, 7 Jul., 22 Aug., 12 Dec.

1808: 14 Jan., 19 Feb., 15 Apr.

TIPPING — Thomas Tipping [56]

Thomas Tipping (1823-1884), postmaster, was born at Tetbury, Gloucestershire. He was the postmaster at Stow-on-the-Wold, and his wife, Maria (b. ±1827), born at Lower Slaughter, was the postmistress. They had at least 1 daughter:

1 Marianne

In 1851 the Tipping family lived at 85 Market Place, which was presumably also the address of the post office. Maria must have died some time after 1861 as Thomas subsequently appears to have married Anne (1823-1891), born at Maisey Hampton, Wiltshire. Thomas Tipping acted as a clerk to Arthur Charles Llewyllin Morgan (±1815-1850), and later for Joseph Sewell (±1814-1890). In the 1871 census, Thomas and Anne were living at Park House, Lower Swell, and Thomas was listed as a 'solicitor's managing clerk'. By 1881 he was listed as a 'retired solicitor's clerk'.

1850: 29 Jun: *Wrote to Mr. Tipping, postmaster at Stow, with directions to forward my letters and newspapers to me at Gloucester next week.* 6 Aug., 10 Aug., 21 Aug: *From T. Tipping, Clerk to Mr. Morgan, I received a note soliciting the appointment held by Mr. M of Clerk to the Commissioners of taxes for this district.* 27 Aug: *A letter to the same effect from Mr. Sewell, who mentions the terms of his arrangement with Mrs. Morgan, and that he has retained the services of Tipping, Morgan's late clerk.... This was brought by Tipping, from whom I received further information on the same points.* 10 Oct: *to Mr. Tipping, Postmaster, to forward my letters to Lidney Park.* 9 Dec.

1851: 22 Jan: *Received a note from Mr. Tipping on Tax business.* 20 Apr: *Wrote to Tipping, the Postmaster at Stow, requesting him to find out Lapper, and to send him to meet Mr. F. at Northleach.*

1852: 22 Oct.

1853: *27 Jan., 31 Jan., 13 Mar., 31 Mar., 26 Apr., 16 May, 25 May: Much engaged during the forenoon in business — with Tipping, on Tax and Registration of voters.* 10 Jun., 22 Dec., 28 Dec.

1854: 1 Jan., 25 May: *To Mr. Sewell's office, where procured from Tipping a Post Office order for £2. 0. 0 for W. Pugh, and consulted him as to Tax returns.* 27 Jul., 3 Aug., 7 Aug.

TOBIN — Henry Wilhelm Tobin [57]

Henry Wilhelm Tobin (±1809-1903), army officer, was the son of Joseph Tobin (b. ±1775), a retired general in the Royal Artillery, and his wife, Harriet (b. ±1779). He married late in life, 1861, Anna Maria Dunscombe (b. ±1838); they had at least 2 daughters:

1 Ordine (b. ±1858)
2 Jessy (b. ±1859)

Henry Tobin commenced his military career as an ensign in Malta. Besides serving in the North Gloucester Militia, he was in the 77th Foot and the 48th Foot. He transferred to the latter regiment as lieutenant without purchase in 1839. He died at Liskeard, Cornwall.

1853: 12 Mar: *After breakfast I went to Stow in the Bourton Clarence, picking up R. Waller by the way. Mr. Pole joined us to perform the duties of Deputy Lieutenant in the enrolment of only six volunteers to serve in the North Gloucester Militia. Capt. Tobin and Mr. Cripps attended as Adjutant and Surgeon.* 15 Apr: *... to attend a Militia meeting. Deputy Lieutenants Pole and R. Waller gave me the meeting, and Capt. Tobin, Adjutant of the North Gloucester Reg.*

TOCKER — John Alexander Tocker [58]

John Alexander Tocker (1812-1899), Church of England clergyman, was born at Jaulnah, India, the son of Maj. John Tocker, of the HEIC, and Sarah Boardman. He was educated at Trinity College, Cambridge (BA 1834; MA 1837), and was appointed curate of Little Barrington in 1838. He served there, and as curate of Highworth, Wiltshire, until 1842.

Tocker married, at Ryde, Isle of Wight, 21 January 1856, Loetitia Adeline (1827-1882), daughter of Robert Booth (1793-1858) and Antonetta Edwards (1791-1878). In 1861 he was living at Camden Place, Camberwell, while his wife was with her mother at Bathford, Bath. He disappears from the *Clergy List* in 1868, but in 1881 he was listed as a retired clergyman living at Ilfracombe with his wife Loetitia. He died at Bath.

1838: 25 Apr: *My son was elected a member; also Mr. Dandridge, the new Incumbent of Little Barrington Sherborne, and Windrush, and his curate, a Mr. Tocker.* 13 Jun., 8 Aug., 22 Aug: *On arriving at Ford's we found besides his own family, the Bishop and his Chaplain, Mr. & Mrs. Escott, Mr. G. L. Cooke, Mr. Cameron, and Mr. Tocker, the Curate of Windrush.*

1839: 1 May, 21 Aug.

1840: 25 May, 17 Jun., 5 Aug.

1842: 21 Aug: *Recd. a letter from Mr. Tocker, late Curate of Little Barrington, now of Highworth, recommending a person of Barrington, a candidate for the place of R. O. in our Union.* 1 Sep., 3 Sep.

TODD — Edward James Todd [59]

Edward James Todd (1802-1869), Church of England clergyman, was born at St Constantine, Cornwall, the fourth son of Lovell Todd (1767-1846) and Rebecca Mitchell (b. 1769). He was educated at

Worcester College, Oxford (BA 1825), and was ordained deacon on 30 October 1825 and priest on 29 October 1826. His first clerical appointment was as assistant curate of Seaton and Beer, Devon, from 30 October 1825; he was then appointed curate of Axminster on 20 September 1826. He was vicar of Sherborne from 1843 to his death in 1869. He married Mary Ann (b. 1802) and together they had at least 1 son:

1 Edward Hallett (1836-1914)

Edward Todd was the co-owner, with Francis Witts, of the manor of Upper Slaughter. He was also the landlord of the farmer Edward Lea, who lived at the manor house. How this came about is unclear, but as he must have had connections with Lord Sherborne; he may have bought the property as an investment. Francis Witts had bought the two acres of 'pleasure ground' in front of the rectory in 1832, so presumably Lord Sherborne was not averse to divesting himself of property. It appears that Todd bought the manor house in around 1852-53.

1845: 26 Mar.

1850: 8 Jul: *The sermon, a very long, but a good one, on John 16. 33. was preached by Mr. Todd, the Incumbent of Windrush.*, 20 Jul., 26 Jul.

1852: 24 Oct., 29-30 Oct., 15 Nov: *Met Mr. Todd in the village, who had come to Mr. Lea's on arrangements as to his farm. He obligingly brought me a present of a basket of Portugal onions.* 4 Dec., 16 Dec.

1853: 26 Jan., *Mr. Todd, having come to Upper Slaughter to give directions as to alterations at the farm occupied to E Lea, and particularly as to laying on water to supply the yards and farm-buildings, requested me to assist him with advice ...* 22 Mar: *Received a visit from Mr. Todd, who is now busy in repairs on his newly acquired farm premises, late Lord Sherborne's.* 24 May.

1854: 3 Feb., 9 Jun., 21 Jun.

TODD — William Todd [60]

William Todd (d. ±1823), slave-owner and London timber merchant, was in partnership with Frederick William Curthorpe. He bought the Cranham estate, but for some unknown cause went bankrupt in 1822, just two years after 'Todd's Cottages' were completed. He died the following year.

William Todd and Frederick William Curthorpe's business premises were at Langbourn Chambers, which appear to have been located at 16 and 17 Fenchurch Street, London. By 1832 another member of the Todd family, Fleming Thomas Todd, was still in business at Langbourn Chambers. Down the road at 110 Fenchurch Street, Thomas Todd (1763-1836), merchant, and the Todd Brothers, a firm of West India merchants, were in business by 1842. Thomas was married to Eliza Rochfort Utten (1770-1847), and was later in partnership with his son Richard James Surry Todd. They owned slaves and sugar plantations in Jamaica in the Trelawney and St Anne parishes. These Todds of 110 Fenchurch Street were probably of the same family as their neighbours at Langbourn Chambers, but no clues as to a connection are given in William Todd's will; he left what remained of his estate to his brother John and sister Elizabeth.

Another Todd with involvement in the wider family business was Benjamin Richard Todd (±1764-1830), who was buried at St John, Barbados. He married, at St James, Barbados, 22 May 1798, Margaret Rudder Wood. William Todd (d. ±1823) left a minor bequest to two members of the Wood family, and the UCL reference states that Benjamin was William's executor, although in his will William stipulated that his executor should be one Charles Jenkins.

There is considerable mystery concerning William Todd, and it may be that this is a misattribution. In January 1826 Francis Witts wrote as if Todd was still in residence at Cranham, and in *The Stranger's Guide through Cheltenham* (1834), Henry Davies wrote, 'Mr Todd has long since abandoned this faëry of his own creation and it is now the property of —— Read Esq.' It is difficult to know what Davies meant by 'long since'. Todd's bankruptcy—which would have been a disgrace and possibly kept quiet—and subsequent death a year later may not have been known in the area.

Whatever the truth is, a William Todd bought much of Cranham beech woods at Ladlecombe, east of Cranham. He created a summer retreat there in a glade by the Birdlip road, comprised of several thatched buildings with verandas, sometimes described as Swiss cottages or villas. One contained the principal rooms, and another the service accommodation and kitchens. Sporting facilities, including a billiard room, were housed in the other buildings. There were also fish ponds at the site. Some of the buildings date from the eighteenth century, although the retreat was first specifically recorded in 1821; most of the buildings were probably built between 1815 and 1820. The architect was reputed to have been John Buonarotti Papworth (1775-1847).

Todd's Cottages had gone out of use by 1861, and the whole site was bought in 1878 by William Frederick Hicks-Beach. In 1898, Hicks-Beach leased the site to Dr Pruen, who founded the Cotswold Sanatorium there. He built new thatched cottages with verandahs as wards for the patients. Dr Pruen lived in Cranham Lodge, and his colleague Dr Etlinger took up residence at Ladlecombe cottage until 1913; thereafter a succession of doctors and their families lived in the cottage. It was at Ladlecombe, while a patient at the sanatorium, that George Orwell corrected the proofs of *Nineteen Eighty-Four*.

1826: 28 Jan:... *some years had elapsed since I had travelled it, & in that time a very picturesque groupe of cottages has been erected in one of the glades, close by the road ... They are called Cranham Cottages, and consist of several very tasteful thatched buildings with verandas, painted casements, flower beds &c; looking exactly one of those scenes, which the theatre exhibits, of rural elegance, or a description in a novel, or a plan and view in Repton or some other artist's elegant work on building cottages and laying out grounds. A Mr. Todd has built them, and resides there, not altogether as the elegant hermit of the Beech woods, for he has a large interest and speculation in the beech timber growing around him, and on one occasion, when he mingled in the Society of Gloucester at a ball, wine had so drawn forth his vulgarity, that he insulted the company, was turned with some companions out of the room, and forced to make a humble apology, in the newspaper. But that is past: the man is not tolerated; but his cottages are not unworthy of a visit.*

TODD — William D'Arcy Todd [61]

Sir William D'Arcy Todd (1770-1848), army officer, was born at Kendal, Westmorland, the son of William Todd and grandson of Fryer Todd of West Auckland, co. Durham. He was a captain in the Army and paymaster of the 53rd Regiment. Little has been discovered about him. He was knighted at some point and died in 1848. He also may have served in the King's German Legion. He married, at Richmond, 28 or 29 September 1802, Charlotte, daughter of William Tonkin of Lisbon (who had died before 1802); they had at least 2 daughters:

1 Charlotte (b. 1805)
2 Mary Tonkin (b. 1806)

We learn from the diaries that Todd's wife Charlotte had a sister called Sophy, but beyond that little is known. Francis Witts was clearly besotted with Charlotte, and in the entry for 18 September 1803 one can sense a touch of jealousy in the words 'met him'. William Todd served in the Peninsular War, 1807-09.

1802: 28 Jul: *At Malvern dined. Was introduced to the May's &c. &c. but particularly to the lovely Charlotte Tonkins. Mr. Dillon & Miss Tonkin, sung Italian.* 29 Jul: *Walked on the Malvern Hills. Conversed with Mr. Dillon, Miss Tonkins, May &c. A Dance in the Evening where I danced with Misses Burt, May, Raikes & the divine Charlotte who sung after supper Italian finer than I had ever heard off the Stage with Dillon.*

1803: 5 Sep: *Mrs. D'Arcy Todd, the loveliest woman on the face of the Earth, & her sister Miss Sophy Tonkins called in the forenoon.* 6 Sep: *Drank Tea at Mrs. Tonkyn's. Singing from the lovely Charlotte & a great deal of conversation with her.* 12 Sep: *Rowed my Father & Mother to Richmond & back, calling on the charming Mrs. Todd, & Mr. & Mrs. May.* 17 Sep: *Rowed in the forenoon; & walking to Richmond called & sat with the lovely Charlotte & her Sister Sophy.* 18 Sep: *Called at the Todds, all of us. Met him, Charlotte & her Sister Sophy: as charming as ever. Walked together on the River side in the Evening.* 22 Sep., 4 Oct., 20 Oct.

TOMBS — William Tombs[62]

William Tombs (1810-1890) was a veterinary surgeon. He and his wife Elizabeth (1813-1886) were born at Great Barrington. They married late in life and do not appear to have had any children.

1836: 3 Nov: *Adjourned, after the ordinary business, with Messrs. Tombs and Harris, to the Workhouse, where inspected the house, and gave directions.*

1838: 11 Jan., 5 Apr.

1840: 25 Jun.

TOMKINS — Benjamin and Mary Tomkins at Champion Hill[63]

Benjamin Tomkins (1762-1817), of Upper Thames Street, London, married, at St James's, Clerkenwell, Middlesex, 21 April 1782, Mary [Sarah?] Ivey (b. 1762); they had at least 4 sons and 4 daughters:

1 Benjamin (b. 1782); married, 9 June 1830, at St Olave's, Hart Street, Mary, third daughter of T. Davy of Golden Square
2 James (b. 1784)
3 John (b. 1787)
1 Mary Ann (b. 1788)
2 Elizabeth (b. 1792)
4 Charles (b. 1794)
3 Martha (1800-1865)
4 Hannah (dates unknown); married, 2 June 1818, John Shepherd of Frome, Somerset

It appears that the Tomkins family were nonconformists, or possibly Quakers; they attended the same chapel as Elizabeth Witts, née London (1738-1837), of Champion Hill. They would also have been known to Broome Phillips Witts in City business circles.

In his will Tomkins asked to be buried, with just one carriage and the least expense possible, in the vault at the meeting house of the independents, at the bottom of Old Gravel Lane, St George in the East, Stepney. He also referred in his will to his dear wife Sarah, which throws up a discrepancy.

1801: 28 Jul: *Mr. and Mrs. Tomkins & two Miss Thompsons drank tea in the afternoon with Mrs. Witts.*

TONKIN — Charlotte Tonkin — *see* Todd *and* D'Arcy Todd

TORDIFFE — John Tordiffe[64]

John Tordiffe (1805-1846), Church of England clergyman, was born at Plumbland, Cumberland, the son of William and Elizabeth Tordiffe. He was educated at Queen's College, Oxford (BA 1829). Records are scarce, but he seems to have been married to Mary Anne (d. 1860); they had at least 4 daughters:

1 Harriet (b. 1836)
2 Isabella (b. 1839)
3 Ellen (1842-1843)
4 Mary Anne (b. 1844)

John Tordiffe was curate of Hampnett and chaplain to the workhouse.

1823: 10 Jan: *As to the School at Northleach it is endowed with a portion of the Tithes of the living at Chedworth & the appointment of the masters is in Queen's College Oxford. The candidate for the Exhibition must be nominally at least a pupil of the School. The Vicar of Northleach, the Head Master & the Bailiff of the Town nominate. At present the School is in utter decay: there is no head Master: the Revd. Mr. Tordiffe, chaplain to the Bridewell, is under Master, & teaches a few children the rudiments of Grammar, having an allowance to officiate as head Master should any pupils be found.*

1828: 14 Oct: *Mr. Tordiffe, the chaplain of this bridewell having removed from Northleach to a small living; which he holds in Somersetshire (Chilcompton, I believe) his situation was vacant.*

1838: 3 Feb: *Bathurst requests me to comment upon it, and to give my opinion as to a communication he had received from Mr. Tordiffe, Chaplain of Northleach Bridewell, who writes to say that the hours named in the prison rules for the commencement of the Services on Sunday are highly inconvenient, and interfere with the hours fixed for duty at the churches which he serves.* 5 Feb: *Mr. Tordiffe having called at U. Slaughter, followed me to Stow; he has changed his mind; and determined to retain his Curacy at Hampnett, in the confidence that he will not be called on to relinquish the chaplaincy of Northleach Bridewell even though unable to perform the duties on Sundays at the hours prescribed in the prison regulations.*

1842: 8 Oct: *Examined Mr. Tordiffe, the Chaplain, Mr. Bedwell, the Surgeon, the Keeper, two Turnkeys, and Miller.* 16 Oct.

1843: 12 Oct.

1844: 6 Jan., 27 Apr., 1 May, 5 Aug.

1846: 14 Jul: ... *from F. Aston, announcing the sudden death of Mr. Tordiffe, the Chaplain of Northleach Bridewell, on Saturday last, under the impression that I should like to communicate on the subject with Purnell.* 15 Jul., 17 Jul: *F. Aston and I walked to the funeral of Mr. Tordiffe at Hampnett ... Poor Mr. Tordiffe, at all times, a nervous and excitable person, of irreproachable conduct, correct in the discharge of public and private duties, had, perhaps, never quite recovered from the painful shock his feelings had sustained, when an enquiry was instituted by the government some years since into the management of the Bridewell at Northleach, Poor Tordiffe's age was 41.* 24 Jul: *Received a letter from C Bathurst, who generously offers to give £30 to Mrs. Tordiffe, if the circumstances in which T. left his family justify call in my opinion for such an act of charity.* 30 Jul., 6 Aug., 8 Aug: *Ford called on me to communicate what passed at the ann. meetg. of the Subscribers to the Clerical Charity of the Diocese held on Thursday at Gloucester, at which he was present. A very liberal annuity was voted from the funds of the Charity to poor*

Mrs. Tordiffe, who is also to be accommodated with a house in Edward's College, South Cerney.

1847: 29 Mar: *MW. recd. a note from Mrs. Aston in which I am requested to apply to Mr. Cockey, Mr. Birkbeck &c. to obtain votes for the admission of one of the children of the late Mr. Tordiffe of Hampnett, into the Wanstead orphan asylum.* 29 Mar: *Wrote to Mr. Birkbeck to obtain the votes and interest of two ladies of his family, and of Mr. Redmayne, Stainforth, in favour of M A Tordiffe's admission into the Wanstead Infant Orphan Asylum, either at the approaching or the November election: in the same strain wrote to Mr. Cockey: also to F. Aston that I had so done.* 2 Apr.

TORRENS — Henry Whitelock Torrens [65]

Henry Whitelock Torrens (1806-1852), secretary to the Board of Customs, Calcutta, was born at Canterbury, Kent, the eldest son of Maj.-Gen. Sir Henry Torrens KCB (1779-1828), adjutant general of the forces and military secretary to the duke of York, and Sarah (1781-1863), daughter of Col Robert Patton (1743-1812), governor of St Helena, and Constantia Adriana Sally Mapletoft (1756-1811), who had married at St Helena on 9 March 1803.

Torrens was educated at Charterhouse and Christ Church, Oxford, where he was rusticated along with the duke of Wellington's sons for painting the doors of the college red. In 1828, having first tried the law and a foreign office clerkship, Torrens accepted a writership in the East India Company's service. He was a famous linguist and many of the princes and dignitaries in India asked specifically for him to act as their interpreter. In 1838 he published what would become known as his most substantial work, the first volume of a translation of the *Arabian Nights*.

Torrens married, first, at Hajjepore, Patna, India, 21 November 1832, Elizabeth Mary Roberts (1803-1834); they had 2 sons:

1 Henry D'Oyly (1833-1889), Lt-Gen., governor and commander-in-chief, Malta; appointed KCT and KCMG
2 George (b. & d. 1834)

Elizabeth appears to have died giving birth to George, who also died. Torrens married secondly, at Calcutta, Bengal, India, 20 November 1835, Louisa Ann Rebecca Law (b. 1817); they had 3 sons and 5 daughters:

1 Henrietta Frances (1836-1909)
2 Constance Adriana (1838-1928)
3 Mary Jane (b. 1840)
1 Arthur Fleming Emile (1845-1906)
4 Minnie Emily Frederica (1848-1849); died an infant
5 Louisa (b. & d. 1850); died an infant
2 Charles Patton (1851-1932), assistant surveyor of India
3 Gerard Philip (1852-1905)

Henry Whitelock Torrens died at Calcutta on 16 August 1852.

1825: 9 Aug: *Mr. Morrison is of Wadham College, and Curate of Stoneleigh in Warwickshire; he takes pupils; two of these are with him now; inmates of Mrs. Rice's roomy mansion: the elder, Mr. Torrens, a very elegant & accomplished young man, of considerable scholastic attainments: He too as well as his fellow pupil dined with us. Mr. T. is of Christ Church; but under a cloud; having incurred the penalty of rustication by some riotous behaviour in a moment of intoxication. The two sons of the Duke of Wellington were in the same scrape, & were sentenced to the same penalty: but the great captain was displeased & removed his sons to Cambridge. Sir H. Torrens judged more wisely, & has placed his son under Mr. Morrison's care till the period of his banishment is passed.* 17 Aug.

TOUCHET — Mary Touchet — *see* Elton *and* Henry

TOURNAY — William Tournay [66]

William Tournay (1762-1833), Church of England clergyman, was born at Dover, Kent, the son of Thomas Tournay (1728-1795) and Muriel Elizabeth Worger (1735-1798). He was educated at Wadham College (BA 1784; MA 1790; BD 1802; DD 1806), where he was a fellow from 1789 to 1799, and warden from 1806 to 1831. His clerical appointments were as follows: perpetual curate of Whitfield near Dover; rector of St James, Dover; vicar of Hougham, 1796; prebendary of Peterborough, 1817; and prebendary of St Paul's, 1818.

1829: 26 Feb: *I paid my respects to Dr. Tournay, the Warden, by calling at his door, but was not admitted. He was, in fact, placed in an awkward situation. Being a leading man in the University, & generally respected for his sound judgment & principles, he had taken a line not indicative of those qualities, which were commonly imputed to him, by expressing an intention of being neutral on the present occasion.*

1831: 20 Jun: *In the course of the past week an event not unworthy of being mentioned by me has occurred at Oxford, having reference to my own college, namely, the resignation of the Wardenship of Wadham by Dr. Tournay, in favour of Mr. Symons, fellow and Tutor... As Prebendary of Westminster and Peterborough, with other preferment, he is a well endowed Clergyman, but it is a rare instance of self-denial in those, who enjoy the prizes of the clerical profession, to relinquish part of their emoluments voluntarily, and in resigning the Wardenship he gives up a handsome income.*

TOWNSEND — James and Mary Townsend and the Townsend family of Upper Slaughter [67]

James Townsend (1762-1852), agricultural labourer, was born at Coln St Aldwyn. In the 1851 census he lived with his widowed daughter-in-law Mary (1789-1852), born at Bourton-on-the-Hill. James married Alice (±1766-1840); they had at least 4 sons and 2 daughters:

1 John (b. 1798); married, at Upper Slaughter, 18 November 1822, Hannah Kilby of Naunton; 1 daughter:
    1 Anne (b. 1823)
2 Thomas (1799-1849)
3 James (d. 1807)
1 Mary (b. 1808)
2 Alice (b. 1811); at least 1 illegitimate son and 1 illegitimate daughter:
    1 John (b. 1828)
    1 Anne (b. 1832)
4 William Townsend (1814-1894), agricultural labourer; born at Upper Slaughter; married Ruth (1809-1855), born at Wolford; at least 1 son and 1 daughter:
    1 James (b. 1842)
    1 Mary (b. 1845); born at Eyford

1840: 13 Jul: *Also conferred with Mrs. Collett who has for the present, at least, recovered her influence over her daughter, who has disclosed to her the particulars of her clandestine intercourse with W. Townsend, has been brought to see her error, and to relinquish the connection; she is to be removed from the village to Cheltenham, where her sister has employment as a dress maker.*

1847: 12 Apr., 16 Apr: *Visiting Townsend, an aged and sick parishioner.*

1848: 21 Jan., 22 Jan., 24 Jan.

1849: 10 Dec., 14 Dec., 26 Dec.

1850: 5 Jan., 7 Jan., 16 Jan., 4 Feb., 4 Mar., 19 Mar, 20 Mar: *Read prayers with James Townsend.* 23 Mar., 8 Apr., 29 Apr., 3 Jun., 24 Jun., 22 Jul., 2 Aug., 5 Aug: *Visited sick parishioners, administered the Holy Communion to Widow Townsend, her aged father in law, and sister in law, and prayed with Mrs. Rogers.* 7 Sep., 25 Sep., 21 Oct., 5 Nov., 25 Nov., 3 Dec.

1851: 4 Jan., 13 Jan., 31 Jan., 10 Feb., 11 Feb: *Visited sick parishioners——Mrs. Rogers, and Ruth Townsend's child.* 14 Feb., 21 Feb., 28 Feb., 4 Mar., 22 Mar., 5 Apr., 15 Apr., 2 May, 6 May, 16 May.

1852: 16 Jan., 28 Jan., 10 Feb: *Visited and prayed with Shepherd Townsend and the Widow T.* 21 Feb., 6 Mar., 12 Mar., 23 Mar., 26 Mar: *Visited my old parishioner, Shepherd Townsend, now confined to his bed, approaching his ninetieth birthday.* 2 Apr: *Administered the holy communion privately to old Shepherd Townsend, now confined to his bed, and very feeble, his daughter in law the Widow Townsend.* 5 Apr., 12 Apr., 17 Apr., 21 Apr., 27 Apr: *Visited the Townsends — an afflicted house: the old Shepherd bedridden with a cancerous sore on his back; — the widowed daughter in law recently tapped a second time for the dropsy, & lying in a very feeble state.* 1 May. 7 May, 11 May, 15 May, 19 May, 29 May, 5 Jun: *Visited and prayed with old Townsend, & his widow daughter-in-law. The old man seems approaching his end. Both are very helpless and feeble.*

TOWNSEND — Joseph Townsend [68]

Joseph Townsend (1739-1816), Church of England clergyman, was born in the parish of St Christopher le Stocks, London, the fourth son of Chauncy Townsend (1708-1770), London merchant, and Bridgett (d. 1762), daughter of James Phipps, governor of Cape Coast Castle. He was educated at Clare College, Cambridge (BA 1762; MA 1765), and later studied physic at Edinburgh. He was a popular preacher among the Calvinistic Methodists, and occasionally officiated at Lady Huntingdon's chapel at Bath. He was rector of Pewsey, Wiltshire, from 1763 to his death in 1816. He married, first, at St Agnes, Cornwall, 27 September 1773, Joyce Nankivell (1743-1785); they had 5 sons and 3 daughters:

1 Charlotte (1774-1837)
1 Thomas (1776-1822)
2 Sophia (1777-1798)
2 Charles (1780-1865)
3 Henry (1782-1812)
4 James (1785-1864)
3 Joyce (dates uknown)
5 Joseph (dates unknown)

Townsend married secondly, 1790, a widow, Lydia Hammond, née Clerke. In 1786 he published *A Dissertation on the Poor Laws*. He also wrote *A Journey through Spain*.

1806: 29 Oct: *Dr. & Mrs. & Miss Spalding called upon us & we proceeded together to dine at Mr. C. Mayo's at Stoke, where we made a very agreeable visit, ... Met Mr. Townsend, R. of Pewsey, & author of a Journey in Spain ... Conversed a great deal, & mostly upon literary & political subjects with Mr. Townsend & Mr. Mayo.*

TOWNSEND — Maurice Fitzgerald Townsend — *see* Stephens

TOWNSEND — Richard Townsend [69]

Richard Townsend (b. ±1785), keeper of the house of correction at Northleach, was married to Ann (b. ±1780), matron at the same house of correction. Richard and Ann were both born in Gloucestershire, but it is unclear where. Being a prison officer, Richard is likely to have had a military background.

1834: 1 Nov: *Then came Townsend, the Keeper of the House of Correction at Northleach, who is under a cloud, in consequence of an adventure which befel him at Gloucester, when he was intoxicated and fell into the company of loose women.* 10 Nov., 21 Nov., 15 Dec: *Townsend, the Keeper of Northleach Bridewell, came to submit to me a letter which he had received from Mr. R. B. Cooper, in which that Magistrate finds fault with him for a supposed irregularity in the management of the Bridewell.*

1835: 13 Apr: *And now came on the trial of Edmund Jeffrey ... Townsend was first called, and hesitated a good deal, when it was pressed upon him in cross examination that he had held out inducements to the prisoner to confess.* 24 Apr.

1840: 17 Oct.

1842: 16 Oct.

1844: 11 May: *Recd. a letter from C Reeves, one of the Subordinate Officers at Gloucester Gaol, bespeaking my vote and interest in his favour, as a candidate for the office of Keeper of the H. of Correction at Northleach, which Townsend is about to resign.*

TOWNSEND — Thomas Townsend and family — *see also* Munro *and* Newnham [70]

Thomas Townsend (d. 1824), slave and sugar plantation owner, of Grenada, was probably the son of Thomas Townsend (1724-1792) and his wife Martha (1714-1789), both of Godmanchester, Huntingdonshire. In his grant of arms, 1797, Townsend referred to himself as 'of Poyle Park, Surrey and Godmanchester, Huntingdonshire'. However, another source gives his mother's name as Susan, née Warburton (d. 1799), so his parentage remains uncertain.

It is not clear when Townsend first went to Grenada, but it was probably shortly after 1762. Grenada was captured by the British on 4 March 1762 during the Seven Years' War, and was formally ceded to Britain by the Treaty of Paris on 10 February 1763. In 1766 the island was rocked by a severe earthquake, and the following year there was a slave uprising, which was suppressed. During the American Revolutionary War France recaptured Grenada on 4 July 1779 when Comte d'Estaing stormed Hospital Hill; a British relief force was then defeated in the naval battle of Grenada on 6 July. The island was restored to Britain four years later with the signing of the Treaty of Versailles on 3 September 1783.

While the slave population on Grenada exceeded 20,000, the white population numbered only about 1,000, and there was constant fear of a slave uprising. Furthermore, there was dissent among the white population, which was comprised of English, Irish, Scots, and French, the majority of whom were Catholic. The protestant minority was always trying to exert its authority, which created on-going tension. Townsend appears to have been a controversial figure on the island. He published a paper on 23 July 1772, entitled *A Plain Narrative of Sundry Facts and Consequences Which Have happened in the Island of Grenada Since its Submission to the British Arms in 1762, in Order to Shew What Were the Real Causes Which First Produced and Have Since Supported.* Townsend fell out with the governor, William L. Leyborne, who suspended him as a councillor on 24 July 1772 on account of his conduct at the council meeting of 23 July; the suspension was no doubt connected to Townsend's publication of his paper. However, a reconciliation seems to have occurred, as in 1774 the governor appointed Townsend treasurer.

It is not known when or why Townsend and his family returned to England; it may have been before or after the French occupation. Once in England he used some of his fortune to buy Poyle Park, near Farnham, Surrey. Later he bought 3 and 4 Rodney Place, Clifton, and he appears to have purchased property in Wiltshire. When his daughter Elizabeth made her will in 1817 (she died in 1819), she appointed her father, Thomas, of Pickwick House, Wiltshire (this must have been the grade II listed Pickwick House at Corsham), as executor along with her son Matthew. Townsend finally sold the Belmont estate in Grenada in 1817 to James Bain [Baillie?], who was financed by the company Leitch & Smith.

Townsend did not mention his wife's name in his will, but going by his daughter Caroline's baptismal record, it appears that she was called Elizabeth. She was clearly still alive when Townsend died in 1824. Thomas and Elizabeth had at least 7 daughters:

- 1 Elizabeth (±1774-1819); born at Belmont estate, Grenada; married, probably in Grenada, probably 1793 or 1794, Matthew Munro (1761-1797); 1 son and 2 daughters:
  - 1 Matthew (1795-1866); married, at Edmondsham, Dorset, 16 February 1822, Philadelphia Jane Caroline Monro (1800-1867); 1 daughter:
    - 1 Caroline Harriet (1823-1897)
  - 1 Elizabeth Barbara (b. 1796[?]); married, at Southampton, 14 December 1821, Robert Aitchison
  - 2 Charlotte Isabella (b. 1797); born at Poyle Park, Surrey, 31 March 1797; probably died young
- 2 Susanna (1775-1853); married, 22 November 1804, William Moore Newnham (1755-1832); 1 son and 1 daughter:
  - 1 Sophia Elizabeth
  - 1 George William (1806-1893)
- 3 Sophia (1777-1853); born at Belmont estate; died unmarried
- 4 Charlotte (dates unknown); died unmarried
- 5 Jane (dates unknown); died unmarried
- 6 Caroline (1783-1858); died unmarried
- 7 Louisa (b. 1785); born at Westminster, 5 July 1785; baptised, 7 August 1785; died unmarried

Most of the family information is derived from Thomas Townsend's will, proved on 13 May 1824. In it he referred to himself as 'Thomas Townsend formerly of Grenada but now residing at Clifton, Gloucestershire'. He had, in contemplation of his marriage, secured jointure of £300 p.a. for his wife on certain plantations in Grenada, but was unsure whether his wife had released such property. He left the Grenada estates in trust to James Bain, or Baillie, of Bedford Square, John Ross of Grenada, and his grandson Matthew Munro. They were instructed to sell the estates and thereby provide his wife with a total of £1,000 p.a. (including the jointure), and his five daughters, Sophia, Charlotte, Jane, Caroline, and Louisa, with the residual estate. In a codicil dated 23 March 1820, Townsend stated that he had purchased 3 and 4 Rodney Place, Clifton, and added these properties to the total property under his trust. In a further codicil dated 1 July 1823, he redirected this property to his wife for life, and then to his 'four unmarried daughters'; at the same time he added Andrew Loughnan, of Bedford Square, as an additional trustee.

Ideas of 'integration' with one of the Townsend girls may have been floating in the minds of Francis Witts and his mother Agnes. The younger of the sisters would have been of Francis's age or only fractionally older, and there was sugar wealth in the family. The summer and early autumn of 1804 was a period of extensive socialising with the family. See especially diary references to Caroline Townsend on 16 and 22 January 1805.

1804: 16 Jul., 22 Jul: *In the Evening walked with my Father & Mother, the Townsends & Capt. & H. Manners &c.* 23 Jul., 26-27 Jul., 8 Aug., 14 Aug., 17 Aug., 20-21 Aug., 23 Aug: *Mr. Townsend called.* 24-25 Aug., 27-28 Aug., 31 Aug., 9-18 Sep., 20 Sep: ... *the whole party at Mr. Townsend's, I accompanied Mrs. Hopkinson & Miss Lang, Mr. Townsend & his six daughters (Mrs. Munro, Susan, Charl., Carol, Jane & Sophia) in Mrs. H's coach & a Sociable to the New Passage 10 miles.* 22-25 Sep: *Afterwards to a large party at Mrs. McMahon's where the Lady of the mansion & two Miss Mosses sung tolerably: thence to the Ball then, but not unpleasant: danced with Miss White & Caroline Townsend.* 26 Sep., 28-30 Sep., 1-5 Oct., 6-11 Oct., 13-14 Oct., 22-23 Dec., 25 Dec: *Called on good Mr. Townsend.* 28 Dec: ... *party at Mr. Townsends & music; conversed much with my agreeable friend Mrs. Newnham.*

1805: 1 Jan., 5 Jan., 11-12 Jan., 14 Jan: *Walked to Bristol, & with Mr. Townsend & Newnham, & Deace.* 16 Jan., 19 Jan., 22 Jan: *A violent head-ach rendered me very unequal to exertion all the Evening, during which, however, I was not a little amused by a would be love sick letter from a soi-disant Caroline Townsend.* 24 Jan., 1 Feb., 5-6 Feb., 26-27 Feb., 8-9 Mar., 11 Mar., 14-15 Mar., 13 Sep., 9 Nov: *Called on Mrs. Townsend etc. & Mrs. Monro etc.* 17 Nov., 25-26 Nov., 29 Nov.

1806: 15 Jan., 22 Jan., 5 Feb., 11 Feb., 24 Feb.

TOWNSEND — Thomas Townsend — *see also* Whitehouse[71]

Thomas Townsend (1804-1888), Church of England clergyman, was born at Rugby, Warwickshire, the son of Thomas Townsend. He was educated at Worcester College, Oxford, and married, 1850, Elizabeth (1813-1906), born at Sutton-under-Brailes, Gloucestershire [now Warwickshire], the daughter of Thomas Garrett (1776-1837) and Alice Watkins (b. 1785). They had 2 daughters:

1. Barbara Helen Rosa (1851-1847); died unmarried
2. Emily Alice (1853-1925); died unmarried

H. W. Townsend, of Rugby, presumably a cousin of Thomas, married, at Bebington, Cheshire, 8 August 1833, Elizabeth Anne, eldest daughter of William Whitehouse. At the same time, James Thomas Lake Whitehouse married Esther Louise, youngest daughter of the late Revd Richard Lowndes Salmon, vicar of Sandbach.

1845: *8 Jan: I walked to L. Slaughter Turnpike gate for my letters met Mr. Aitkens who joined me; from him learnt that a Mr. Townsend from Northamptonshire, I believe, is to be the new Incumbent of Aston Blank—through what interest I am not aware.* 12 Mar: *The latter privately communicated with me as to Mr. Townsend, the new Vicar of Aston Blank, that his character had been represented to him (Aston) by a friend in Warwickshire, where he had held different curacies, in an unfavourable light.* 26 Mar., 1 Apr: *Recd. from F. Aston a long rambling letter respecting Mr. Townsend, the Vicar of Aston Blank: as to whom he persists that his character is so damaged that he ought to be avoided, but says that he is precluded from entering into details, or mentioning his informant.* 25 Jun.

1847: 6 Apr: *From the Cheltenham Station into the Town I walked with Mr. Townsend, the Vicar of Cold Aston, who was returning from Gloucester.* 7 Apr.

1850: 18 Sep: *Confirmation L Ris. Revd. Mr. Boudier, and Mrs. B. and Miss Wise: —— Revd. T. Townsend, and his Bride; — Revd. Mr. Harene.*

1853: 21 Jun: *Received a visit from Mr. & Mrs. Ruddle, Mr. Hastings Wodman, and Miss Townsend... Miss Townsend, daughter of a deceased Solicitor of Rugby, and niece of the Vicar of Aston*

Blank, is also niece of Mrs. Ruddle, who was a Miss Whitehouse, and a niece of Mrs. Witts of Brighton, her mother having been one of the many daughters of the Lake family. Another Miss W. married Mr. Townsend of Rugby, and a third is the second wife of Mr. J Williams Martin, of Shoborough House, Twyning, an old acquaintance and brother Magistrate of mine... H. Woodman is entitled to a share in the Daylesford property, now about to be sold by auction, and having come to England to attend the funeral of the late Sir C. Imhoff, when on a visit to old friends of his late mother near Tewkesbury, saw and fell in love with Annie Townsend, then visiting her Aunts, Mrs. Ruddle and Mrs. Martin. H.W. is 38 years of age, the young lady hardly 18, with little or no fortune, but pretty, and very pleasing. The wedding is not likely to be long deferred, and the fiancés, after their Union, are likely to repair to Germany ...

1854: 17 Jul: *Mr. Townsend, of Aston Blank, was present at our sitting, and afterwards at the New Inn, whither we adjourned to hear another case, from Stow, a disgusting exposure of the low state of morals among the labouring classes.*

TOWNSON — Robert Townson — *see also* John Witts [72]

Robert Townson (1762-1827), natural historian and traveller, was born at Spring Grove, Marshgate, Richmond, Surrey, the youngest child of John Townson (1721-1773), London merchant and insurer, and Sarah (1731-1805), daughter of James Shewell (1708-1786) and Sarah Smith (d. 1748). The Shewells were partners in the brewery trade with Samuel Whitbread and the publishing business with Thomas Longman. Sarah Shewell was in fact the wife of Charles Aldcroft (d. 1774), a London haberdasher, with whom she had one child, James Aldcroft (1752-1796), who later took the name Townson. Before they married in 1766, John Townson and Sarah Shewell had carried on a concealed 'criminal conversation' since about 1753, which yielded four children—Mary (1754-1822), Ann (1756-1811), John (1760-1835), and Robert (1762-1827). John Townson died in 1773 at Hackney. A neighbour there, John Witts (1750-1816), who married Robert's sister Ann in 1774, was inducted vicar of Cardington, Shropshire, in 1777. The Townson family took up residence beneath the Lawley, a famous hill in Shropshire, in an area in beautiful countryside which was greatly to influence Robert's later career.

From about 1777 to 1783 Townson was apprenticed in Manchester. He found, however, that business did not interest him; he set off to travel, largely on foot, through France and Italy to Sicily. In 1787, he paused on his return journey to study chemistry and assaying under Balthasar Georges Sage (1740-1824) at the École des Mines in Paris. In 1788 he enrolled as a student of medicine and chemistry, and later of botany, at Edinburgh University. He had intended on a career in surgery, but soon discovered that his greatest interest lay in the study of natural history. In 1790 he was duly elected president of the student Edinburgh Natural History Society, and in 1791, having been proposed by the geologist James Hutton, he became a fellow of the Royal Society of Edinburgh.

In 1791 Townson enrolled as a student of natural history at the University of Göttingen, and travelled there via Uppsala and Copenhagen. While in Göttingen he took a year off to travel to Vienna and throughout Austrian Habsburg lands. He returned to Göttingen and published his first works, on reptilian physiology, in 1794 and 1795. He returned home in 1795 and the following year was awarded the degree of LLD by Edinburgh University. He settled again in Shropshire, where he wrote *Travels in Hungary* (1797), which contained pioneering botanical, entomological, and petrographic observations, as well as spirited descriptions of exploits in the Tatra Mountains and the caves of Slovakia.

Townson became certain of the importance of conducting mineralogical surveys. In 1797 he applied to the Sierra Leone Company to fund a survey, but was rejected on the grounds that the findings might distract attention from agriculture. He then applied to the East India Company to undertake mineralogical surveys in India, but was also unsuccessful. In Shropshire, Townson wrote *Philosophy of Mineralogy* (1798), *A Poor Man's Moralist* (five editions, 1798-1804), and *Tracts and Observations in Natural History* (1799). This last work was his most important; it completed his account of his pioneering experiments in reptilian physiology and offered a remarkable account of the geology of Shropshire.

Disillusioned by his failures to obtain patronage abroad, Townson returned to travelling in England and Europe. Between 1802 and 1805 he spent much of his time compiling a *History of Yorkshire*, which he eventually abandoned through a lack of subscribers. In May 1805, after the death of his mother, Townson decided to follow his brother, an officer in the Royal Marines, to Australia. Having gathered his collections at his house in Shropshire and burnt his manuscripts, he set off in December 1806. He had been promised land by the British government and assured that he was the type of settler most needed, but on his arrival in Australia he found that the governor, William Bligh (1754-1817), was of a completely different opinion. In protest, Townson became one of the 'rum rebels' who helped depose Bligh in 1808. In 1811 he was finally granted land and settled at Varro Ville, near Sydney; but his scientific aspirations to explore Australia had been thwarted by Bligh and the primitive state of democracy in the colony. His attempts to investigate the natural history of this new country were equally frustrated.

At Varro Ville Townson became a successful farmer and wine producer, using the scientific methods which had proved so uninteresting to his contemporaries. By 1820 he wanted to return to Britain, but he was unable to dispose of his estates; he remained at Varro Ville, somewhat embittered, until his death there on 27 June 1827. He was buried in St John's churchyard, Parramatta, on 3 July. He left goods worth under £10,000.

The above information, taken primarily from the *Dictionary of National Biography*, does not wholly tie up with what is said in the diaries. The identity of the 'Dr Townsend' met by Francis Witts in May 1801 at Lady Lyttelton's house cannot be known for certain, but Townson seems a likely candidate. The connection with John Witts would fit, but there was no-one of the name Townsend or anything similar appointed governor of Botany Bay. Furthermore, in 1828 Francis Witts mentioned that Townson left a fortune of £20,000, which is at variance with what is stated in *DNB*.

1801: 30 May: *To Lady Lyttelton's, where we met Dr. Townsend late Governor of Botany Bay ...*

1828: 25 Jan: *I received information to day from my Cousin, Miss Witts, from Peach Field Lodge, which gave us great pleasure; that a maternal Uncle, Dr. Townson, who has recently died in New South Wales, has left the two Sisters and their brother three fourths of his fortune, estimated at £20000... The surviving uncle, Capt. Townson, is settled in Van Diemen's land.* 16 Jun.

1838: 17 Jul: *The cousins Anne and Apphia are in good health, but wonderfully increased in size, particularly, the former. The sisters, with their brother, are drawing to a close their Australian long protracted affairs; and it appears that they will divide between them as much as £18000, the proceeds of the property accumulated in New South Wales by their maternal uncles, Capt. & Dr. Townson, old Settlers in the Colony, but chiefly by the former.*

TOWSE — John David Towse [73]

John David Towse (1760-1842), attorney-at-law and clerk to the Fishmongers' Company, was born in Crooked Lane, London, the son of John Towse (1735-1803), deputy clerk to the Fishmongers' Company, and Margaret Allen (1724-1798). He married, first, at St Michael's, Crooked Lane, London, 17 October 1792, Anna Jennings (1774-1806); they had 1 son and 3 daughters:

1 Anna Margaret (1801-1804)
2 Caroline (1804-1807)
1 [unnamed] (b. & d. 1806)
3 Anna (1806-1807)

He married secondly, 11 August 1808, Anna Beckwith (1788-1858); they had 3 sons and 4 daughters:

1 John Beckwith (1809-1889)
2 William Beckwith (1810-1889)
1 Caroline Beckwith (1816-1902)
3 Robert Beckwith (1818-1868)
2 Elizabeth Beckwith (1821-1912)
3 Louisa Beckwith (1823-1922)
4 Laura Beckwith (1826-1920)

Towse was clerk to the Fishmongers' Company from 1809 to 1839. He was also clerk to the Cooks' Company.

1832: 14 Jun: *As we passed through Maidenhead we called at the Sun Inn on a deputation of the Court of the Fishmonger's company, consisting of the Prime Warden, Mr. Mills, Mr. Hewson, a friend of Wellford's, a very worthy and amiable man, & the fat, bustling, important Clerk of this wealthy Company, Mr. Towze.*

TRAILL — William Traill — *see also* Charteris [74]

William Traill (1746-1831), professor of mathematics, was the son of Revd William Trail (1712-1756), minister of St Monance in Fife, and Mary (1731-1756), daughter of Revd Robert Trail, minister of Panbride. Both his parents died in 1756 of a malignant fever.

Traill, who added a second 'l' to his name, studied at Marischal College, Aberdeen. In 1766 he was appointed to the chair of mathematics competing against Playfair and Robert Hamilton. He was a founder member of the Royal Society of Edinburgh in 1783. He married, first, Mary Watt; they had at least 1 son:

1 Alexander (1780-1859)

He married secondly, at Edinburgh, 10 April 1799, Frances (1753-1848), daughter of Francis Wemyss, 7th (5th) earl of Wemyss (1723-1808), who later took the name Charteris, and Catherine Gordon (1725-1786). Frances was a sister to Francis Charteris, Lord Elcho (1749-1808), and a first cousin to Agnes Witts. William Traill died at Bath in 1831. His widow, Frances, died at Bath in 1848, aged 95.

1801: 18 Apr: *In the evening came (to Lord Elcho's) Dr. & Lady F. Traill, Mr. & Mrs. Howard, Mr. & Mrs. Greathead, Lady Hamilton Dalrymple.*

TRAVELL — the Travell family of Swerford, Oxfordshire

John Travell (1699-1762), of Swerford, married, at Stanway, Gloucestershire, 12 May 1725, Anne Tracy (1701-1763). They had 5 sons and 8 daughters:

1 John (b. 1726); baptised at Stanway, 9 April 1726
1 Frances Mary (±1727-1768); died unmarried
  1 Francis (1763-1790)
  2 George (1767-1808)
2 Ann (1730-1735); born at Adlestrop; baptised, 7 July 1730; buried at Swerford, 21 July 1735
3 Frances (d. 1735); buried at Swerford
3 William (b. 1731); baptised at Swerford, 20 December 1731
4 Anne (±1737-1826); died unmarried aged 88 at Cheltenham; buried, 8 February 1826
4 Ferdinando Tracy (1740-1808); married, at Chadlington, Oxfordshire, 5 September 1763, Martha Rollinson (1739-1780); 2 daughters:
  1 Martha (1764-1839)
  2 Jane (1765-1797); buried at Cuckfield, Sussex
5 Letitia (b. & d. 1741); baptised 29 June 1741; buried at Swerford, 11 September 1741
6 Catherine (1742-1804); died unmarried
5 Robert (1743-1744); baptised at Swerford, 21 February 1743; buried, 23 April 1744
7 Jane (b. & d. 1745); baptised at Swerford, 3 July 1745; buried, September 1745
8 Agnes (1748-1825); baptised at Swerford, 15 December 1748; married, at Upper Slaughter, 12 June 1775, Edward Witts (1746-1816); buried at Chipping Norton, 18 January 1825; 3 sons:
  1 Francis (1783-1854)
  2 George (1785-1823)
  3 Edward (1786-1794)

John Travell's wife, Anne Tracy (1701-1763), was the great-granddaughter of John Tracy, 3rd Viscount Tracy of Rathcoole (1617-1687), from whom the Tracy lineage can be traced. John Tracy married, about 1655, Elizabeth, third, but first surviving, daughter of Thomas Leigh, 1st Baron Leigh, and Mary (d. 1688), daughter and co-heir of Sir Thomas Egerton. John and Elizabeth possibly had several children, but at least the following 2 sons:

1 William (1657-1712); succeeded as 4th Viscount Tracy of Rathcoole; married, first, 12 July 1679, Frances, daughter of Leicester Devereux, 6th Viscount Hereford; 1 daughter:
  1 Elizabeth (1679-1747)

  William married secondly, 30 August 1688, Jane (d. 1708), third and youngest daughter of his maternal uncle, Sir Thomas Leigh, of Hamstall Ridware, Staffordshire, and Jane, daughter of Patrick Fitzmaurice, 18th baron of Kerry and Lixnaw; at least 1 son:

  1 Thomas Charles (1690-1756); succeeded as 5th Viscount Tracy of Rathcoole; married, first, 27 December 1712, Elizabeth (d. 1719), eldest daughter of William Keyt of Ebrington, Gloucestershire; at least 2 sons:
    1 William (1715-1752)
    2 Thomas Charles (1719-1792); succeeded as 6th Viscount Tracy of Rathcoole; married, 10 February 1755, Harriet (d. 1795), daughter of Peter Bathurst, of Clarendon Park, Wiltshire, and Selina, daughter of Robert Shirley, 1st Earl Ferrers; appears to have died childless and intestate

    Thomas married, secondly, Frances (d. 1751), eldest daughter of Sir John Pakington, 4th baronet, of Aylesbury, and Frances, daughter of Sir Henry Parker, 2nd baronet, of Honington; at least 2 sons:

    1 John (1722-1793); succeeded as 7th Viscount Tracy of Rathcoole; died unmarried
    2 Henry Leigh (1733-1797); succeeded as 8th Viscount Tracy of Rathcoole; married, 12 December 1767, Susannah (d. 1783), daughter of Anthony Weaver of Morvill, Shropshire; died without an heir and the peerage became extinct
2 Ferdinando (1659-1682); married, 22 July 1680, Katherine (1660-1722), daughter of Anthony Keck (1630-1695) and Mary Thorne (1640-1702); at least 1 son:

1 John (1681-1735); married, 7 August 1699, Anne (±1683-1761), daughter of Sir Robert Atkyns, MP and chief baron of the exchequer; fifteen children, including the following 8 sons and 4 daughters:

- 1 John (b. 1703); born at Lower Swell; presumably died an infant
- 1 Anne (1701-1763); born at Lower Swell; married, at Stanway, 12 May 1725, John Travell (1699-1762) of Swerford, Oxfordshire; *see above*, the Travell family
- 2=Robert (1706-1767), MP for Tewkesbury (1734-41) and Worcester (1748-54); born at Lower Swell, elder twin of John; married, 7 August 1735, Anna Maria, daughter of Sir Roger Hudson, director of the South Sea Co.; buried at Stanway, 5 September 1767
- 2=John (1706-1773); born at Lower Swell, twin of Robert; married Catherine Lindsay; no children
- 4 Anthony (1708-1769); took his grandmother's maiden name Keck in 1729 in accordance to the will of his great-uncle Francis Keck, enabling him to inherit the manor of Great Tew, Oxfordshire; married, 3 August 1736, Susan, daughter of James Hamilton, 4th duke of Hamilton; 2 daughters:
  - 1 Henrietta Charlotte (1742-1817); married, 1774, Edward Devereux, 12th Viscount Hereford (1741-1783); no children
  - 2 Susan (1746-1835); married, 1771, Francis Charteris, Lord Elcho; *see* Charteris
- 5 Edward (1709-1723); born at Lower Swell; buried at Stanway, 4 June 1723
- 2 Martha (1712-1802); died 29 September 1802 aged 90; buried at Stanway
- 6 Thomas (±1716-1770), MP for Gloucestershire (1763-70); married, 15 April 1746, Mary (1724-1799), daughter and heir of Sir William Dodwell (d. 1727) of Sevenhampton, Gloucestershire; see Timbrell sisters; 1 son:
  - 1 Dodwell (1746-1768); died 11 January 1768 at Paris, aged 21
- 3 Eliza (1718-1793); born at Stanway; died unmarried at Sandywell Park
- 7 William (1721-1729); buried at Stanway, 17 May 1729
- 8 Charles Richard (1724-1725); buried at Stanway, 22 March 1725
- 4 Frances (1729-1808); married Gustavus Guydickens (1732-1802)

TRAVELL — Anne Travell

Anne Travell (1738-1826) was the diarist's aunt. She was sister to Agnes Witts, Catherine Travell (1742-1804), and Ferdinando Tracy Travell (1740-1809). She was unmarried and lived at Cheltenham. See the introduction in volume 1 for more family information.

1801: 17 Nov: *At my Aunt's party in the Evening, were two Card Tables, all the Granvilles, Miss A Snell, the Miss Jones.*

1804: 5 Oct., 16 Oct., 17 Oct: *Walked with my aunt, Mrs. Worsley & Mrs. Reid.* 18-19 Oct.

1805: 23 Mar: *Walked with Mrs. Travell & Martha Buxton to my Father's very pretty old place of his own creation Swerford Park, the most romantic Dell, I have seen in Oxfordshire; now occupied by a Mr. & Mrs. Chinner, people unworthy of so nice a place. Our dinner party besides my Uncle & Aunt consisted of Mrs. Whalley & Martha & Jane Buxton.* 24-26 Mar., 5 Jul: *Reached my Aunt's house by one of the London Coaches from Oxford at ½ past six in the morning. Had great pleasure in meeting my Father & mother. Was introduced to Jane Napier, with whom I was greatly pleased.* 6-7 Jul., 13 Jul: *A sad constrained dinner at Mrs. Travells, the family party broken by Miss Hughes & in the Evening by Mrs. Bates & her Party—Walked with the young Ladies: never less at my Ease.* 14 Jul: *Between Churches Mrs. Travell & Jane Napier called & Miss Markham.* 17 Jul: *Tea & a Party at my Aunts dull & tiresome.* 21 Jul., 28 Jul., 30 Jul: *Dined at my Aunts' meeting Miss Hughes & Miss Herries & Sir R. Herries.* 1 Aug., 8 Aug.

1822: 18 Oct: *I returned home: met my horses at Cheltenham, where I called on my Aunt Mrs. Travell, whom I had not seen for a long time; she appeared to me much broken. The Miss Guydickens' were her guests.* 20 Dec: *We called this morning on my Aunt, Mrs. Travell, whom we found in good health, considering her very advanced age.*

1823: 7 Apr: ... *in very heavy rain for Cheltenham, where I passed the remainder of the day & slept at my Mother's. My Aunt Travell, & her inmate Miss Louisa Whalley, came to tea.* 14 Jul: ... *Cheltenham, where I called on my aunt Mrs. Travell. I found with her my cousin Mrs. Whalley, Mr. Whalley's unmarried sister, and Miss Louise Whalley, daughter of the late Mr. C. Whalley.* 16 Aug: *My wife and Mother went to Cheltenham, to my Aunt Travell's in order to procure mourning.* 10 Sep: *We left home on a visit of a few days to my Aunt Mrs. Travell at Cheltenham, where we found staying with her Mrs. Whalley & Miss Marianne Whalley, a daughter of the late Mr. C. Whalley.* 27 Sep: *I returned to Upper Slaughter, leaving Margaret with her Mother. I passed an hour or two on my way with Mrs. Travell, at Cheltenham.* 18 Oct: *We returned home, calling for an hour or two at my Aunt Travell's at Cheltenham, where we found the Miss Guydickens's on a visit as also Mrs. Whalley & Miss M. Whalley still inmates.* 13 Dec.

1824: 7 Jan: ... *Information, which we had received that my Aunt Travell had been taken ill, and was in danger, induced me to go over to Cheltenham this day. I found my mother still very weak & confined to her chamber, and my aunt relieved from the alarming attack, which had endangered her life. Her disorder was an obstruction of the bowels; but though she has obtained present ease, I cannot help anticipating a decay at no distant time. The constitution cannot stand many shocks at 85 years of age, and the digestive organs seem to perform their office very insufficiently. I found the poor old lady grateful for my attention, devout, and placid.* 12 Jan: *In passing thro' Cheltenham I had made hasty enquiries and found that both my mother and aunt were going on tolerably well.* 16 Jan, 11 Mar., 30 Mar: *I also found my Aunt Travell much recovered; Miss Buxton is on a visit to her.* 2 Apr., 21 Apr: *We dined at my Aunt Travell's.* 24 Jul., 18 Oct., 22 Oct.

1825: 7 Jan: *I dined with my Aunt Travell, meeting Mrs. Whalley and her son William.* 8-9 Jan., 10 Jan: *I drank tea at Mrs. Travell's. Much of my time was taken up in writing letters to absent relations, connections & friends.* 25 Jan., 31 Jan., 11 Apr: *I found my aged relative confined to her sofa by a wound on the leg, which has afflicted her now for a month, and at her very advanced age, 86, there is certainly reason for apprehension. Her spirits appear good, but she is thinner & more feeble.* 15 May, 19 May, 21 May, 8-10 Jun., 15 Jun., 11 Jul., 15 Jul., 5 Aug: 17

Nov: ... *at Cheltenham called on my Aunt Travell, whom I found fully as well as when I saw her last. Maria & Fanny Whalley were still her guests.*

1826: 9 Jan., 17-18 Jan., 2 Feb: *On my arrival, I found, that the last struggle was past, & that my aunt, my mother's surviving sister, had breathed her last about one o clock this morning. ... Had my Aunt lived till May she would have been 88 years of age. ... Cheltenham had been her place of abode for many years; she was the eldest of four daughters of John Travell Esqr. of Swerford, and on his demise, they removed to Cheltenham as an eligible residence for single gentlewomen, near their relatives at Stanway & Sandywell Park; a little country town, not then a public place; my Mother was the youngest. The two intermediate sisters died; one Miss Frances Travell, a great while ago: my Aunt Catherine in 1804. For many years, the unmarried sisters inhabited a house in the George Inn Yard, now an appendage, I think, to that inn, but in former days one of the best houses in the place.* 7 Feb: *After dinner, by the last coach to Cheltenham I went thither to be in readiness to attend Mrs. Travell's funeral to-morrow morning. I passed the evening with the Whalley family: besides Miss Buxton and her mother, there was Mr. William Whalley from Swerford, and Miss Louisa Whalley. I slept at Sheldon's Hotel.* 8 Feb: *The funeral took place between 9 & 10 o clock A.M.*

TRAVELL — Catherine Travell

Catherine Travell (1742-1804) was the diarist's aunt. She was sister to Anne Travell (1738-1826), Agnes Witts, and Ferdinando Tracy Travell. Catherine was unmarried and lived at Cheltenham. See the introduction in volume 1 for more family information.

1801: 30 Oct: *At Harwards's &c. where I met Mr. Myers &c. In & out at the Repository Lottery walked with My Aunt Catherine, Mr. Delabere.* 4 Nov: *My Aunt Travell very unwell.*

1804: 15 Oct:... *found Mrs. C. Travell extremely broken & ill.* 25 Oct: *Learnt by a letter from Mr. Travell the decease on Monday of my good Aunt Catherine.*

TRAVELL — Ferdinando Tracy Travell — *see also* Buxton, Naper, Rycroft, *and* Witts[75]

Ferdinando Tracy Travell (1740-1808), Church of England clergyman, was born at Swerford, Oxfordshire, the son of John Travell (1699-1762) and Anne Tracy (±1705-1763). As with other members of the Travell and Witts families, information on Ferdinando is covered extensively in the introduction of volume 1. He married, at Chadlington, Oxfordshire, 5 September 1763, Martha Rollinson (1741-1780); they had 2 daughters:

1 Martha (1764-1839); married, first, John Buxton (1756-1790); secondly, 1796, William Morgan Whalley (1772-1846); *see* Buxton *and* Whalley for detail

2 Jane (1765-1797); married, first, William Naper (1749-1791); secondly, Sir Henry Rycroft (1766-1846); *see* Naper *and* Rycroft for detail

Ferdinando was the elder brother of Agnes Witts and the uncle of the diarist. He was possibly named after his great-grandfather, Ferdinando Tracy (1659-1682), but it is not known why. This Ferdinando died at an early age of an unknown cause. In 1680 he married Katherine Keck and they had 1 son:

1 John (1681-1735); married Anne, daughter of Sir Robert Atkyns of Sapperton; 9 sons and 1 daughter:
  1 John (d. 1740)
  2 Robert (d. 1767)
  3 John (d. 1773)
  4 Ferdinando (d. 1729)
  5 Anthony Keck (1712-1769)
  6 Thomas (1716-1770)
  7 William (1722-1729)
  8 Edward (d. 1724)
  9 Charles Richard (1724-1726)
  1 Ann (1701-1763); married John Travell (1699-1762); probably 5 sons and 7 daughters:
    1 Frances (1725-1735); died a child
    2 Ann (d. 1735); died an infant
    1 John (1725-1745)
    2 Francis (1728-1801); died unmarried but had illegitimate children
    3 William (b. 1731)
    3 Anne (1738-1826); died unmarried
    4 Ferdinando Tracy (1740-1808); *see above*
    4 Letitia (b. 1741)
    5 Catherine (1742-1804); died unmarried
    5 Robert (b. 1743)
    6 Jane (b. & d. 1745)
    7 Agnes (1748-1825); married Edward Witts

The parish register for Swerford is a messy and jumbled book, but some entries are very clear. It becomes obvious that John Travell and his wife Anne had many children but few survived beyond childhood.

In later life Ferdinando was much in the company of Frances Eeles (1747-1823), living at 14 Great Cumberland Street, London. It is also possible that he and Frances were responsible for much of the bringing up of Ferdinando's orphaned grandson, James Lennox William Naper (1791-1868), son of Ferdinando's late daughter, Jane. James's younger sister, Jane (1792-1853), seems to have been brought up by, or at least spent much time with, her aunt, Martha Whalley.

Ferdinando provided a large proportion of the funding necessary for Francis Witts to be educated at Oxford. This explains much of the correspondence between Francis and his uncle. Some of the exchanges relating to money were strained; the detailed exchanges between January and March 1805 were probably a combination of discussions relating to money and Francis's upcoming career. The discussion in Cheltenham in July 1805 was also not 'joyous'. It is clear from the diaries that Ferdinando retained family property at Swerford in Oxfordshire.

1801: 1 May, 14 May: *I sallied along Oxford Street, which, if regular, would be the finest range of buildings in the world, to No. 14 Great Cumberland Street, where I had the satisfaction of being kindly received by my Uncle Ferdinand ...* 15 May, 19 May, 25 May, 28 May, 2 Jun., 19 Aug: *Wrote to Mr. Rycroft, Mr. Travell & Lord Elcho.* 7 Nov: *Mr. Travell of Slaughter arrived to dinner.* 10 Nov: *Walked with my Uncle & with Mr. Delabere.* 13 Nov: *Mr. Travell left Cheltenham.*

1802: 30 Jan: *Fog & rain. George came down, from London. Wrote to Mr. Travell.* 2 Feb., 6 Feb., 27 Mar., 13 Jul., 16 Jul: *Heard from Mr. Travell & wrote to him.* 25 Jul.

1803: 17 Oct., 5 Nov., 30 Dec.

1804: 22 Feb: *Passed part of the morning with Mr. Travell at the Kings Arms.* 11 Mar., 16 Mar., 24 Sep., 2 Oct., 4 Oct., 8 Oct., 25 Oct: *Learnt by a letter from Mr. Travell the decease on Monday of my good Aunt Catherine. Learnt by a letter from Mr. Travell the decease on Monday of my good Aunt Catherine.* 6 Nov., 10 Nov., 16 Nov: *Dined with Mr. Travell at the King's Arms.* 22-24 Dec., 29 Dec., 31 Dec.

1805: 1 Jan., 12 Jan., 14 Jan., 28 Jan., 31 Jan., 2 Feb., 13 Feb., 16 Feb., 27 Feb., 8 Mar., 12 Mar., 14 Mar., 21 Mar., 23 Mar: *A fine clear day, hard frost in the morning after a cold meat & ale breakfast, took my knapsack & steered my Course towards my Uncle's at Swerford at ½ past six o clock reached his house before one: about 19 miles.* 20 Jul: *A family party in the Evening, with Mr. Travell, at my Aunts', Miss Hughes to make a break:—far from joyous.* 21 Jul: *Between Churches a long conversation upon business with Mr. Travell.* 24 Jul: *A business conversation with Mr. Travell.— Unpleasant letters & domestic disquiet embittered the day.* 3 Aug: *Received letters waiting for us, one for me from Mr. Travell.* 12 Aug: *Called at Mr. B. P. Witts's who was absent on a Tour in Derbyshire; found at his House a letter from Mr. Travell.* 15 Aug: *Wrote to Mr. Witts of the Retreat, Mr. Travell, & Tom Dodd.* 21 Aug., 15 Sep., 28 Sep., 18 Nov., 22 Nov., 24 Nov., 27 Nov.

1806: 19 Jan: *Recd. a letter upon business from Mr. Travell.* 20 Jan: *Received another letter upon business from Mr. Travell, and wrote one upon the same subject to Mr. Dawkins.* 30 Jan., 25 Feb: *Wrote to Mr. Travell upon business. Received a letter from the Revd. Mr. Cumberland, which reduces to a shadow my expectations of the Curacy of Ampney; perhaps Providence does not esteem me as yet worthy to labour in the vineyard.* 2 Mar., 13 Mar: *... and another requesting a remittance to meet me at Oxford to Mr. Travell.* 19 Mar., 17 Jul., 29 Jul., 30 Jul., 8 Aug., 5 Sep., 13 Sep., 19 Sep., 26 Sep., 4 Oct., 6 Oct., 27 Oct., 30 Oct., 1 Nov., 13 Nov., 15 Dec., 25 Dec.

1807: 1-2 Jan., 21 Jan., 29-30 Jan., 2 Feb., 10 Feb., 12 Feb., 18 Feb., 10 Mar., 11 May, 19-20 May, 25 May: *Called with my Father on Mr. Travell.* 7 Jul., 12 Jul., 15 Jul., 25 Jul., 3 Aug., 22 Aug., 29-30 Aug., 3 Sep., 9 Dec., 18 Dec.

1808: 13 Jan., 4-5 Feb., 18 Feb., 26 Feb., 1 Apr., 8 Apr., 27 Apr., 6 May: *Shopping with the Backhouses &c. Mr. Travell, Dr. Baker, & Mrs. F. Baker, called on us.*

1822: 20 Dec: *Sacred to the Memory of The Revd. F. T. Travell M A. Who died on the 27th day of September 1808 In the 69th. Year of his age Having been 45 Years Rector of this parish.*

1825: 16 May: *Dr. Jenkinson has from early youth suffered from a nervous debility of the muscles of the neck, causing a painful involuntary motion of the head, probably arising from premature growth, which in my Uncle F.T. Travell had produced a similar infirmity.*

1833: 9 Apr: *My Predecessor & Uncle, Mr. Travell, had procured this painting, probably, the remains of a still larger picture, at the time, when he fitted up the chancel with a handsome, but not very appropriate, mahogany altar-piece.*

1835: 25 Feb: *Mrs. Perrot, whose maiden name was Davis, was brought up by Mrs. Way. The latter lady had been in former years intimate in the family of my Uncle, Ferdinand Travell: of course we had many topics of conversation.*

Travell 350324 speaking of Northampton I met h might have mentioned a divine of the 167th. Century, Dr. John

1842: 21 Nov: *The remains were interred in a single bricked vault, at the East end of the Chancel, in the churchyard, beside the Grave of our little infant girl, and near the graves of my late Uncle and predecessor, the Revd. F. T. Travell, and his wife.*

TRAVELL — Jane Tracy Travell — *see* Naper

TRAVIS — Deborah Travis — *see also* Knyvett [76]

Deborah Travis (1797-1876), singer, was born at Shaw, Lancashire, the daughter of John Travis and his wife, Mary. She was one of the Lancashire chorus singers at the Concerts of Ancient Music from 1813 to 1815, and appeared as a principal from 1815. She was much in demand, especially as an oratorio singer, until her retirement in 1843. She married, at St Mary's, Prestwich, 15 November 1826, as his second wife, William Knyvett (1779-1856), the third and youngest son of Charles Knyvett (1752-1822).

1823: 17 Sep: *The Dettingen Te Deum, the Overture to Esther, Dr. Boyce's Anthem (Charity) and W. Knyvett's new Coronation Anthem were the Musical treats for the morning. Of the vocalists, Miss Travis, Messrs. Vaughan, Bellamy ... the taste & simplicity of Miss Travis...* 18 Sep.

1826: 12 Sep: *... to the remaining singers, who appeared at the rehearsal; suffice it to mention Vaughan, William Knyvett and Miss Travis, all remarkable for chaste execution & a faultless accuracy, combined with taste & sweetness, indicative of the genuine English school to which they belong ...* 13 Sep: *Miss Travis sung in a most correct & tasteful manner "Lo! here the gentle lark" and was accompanied by Nichols on the flute ...* 14 Sep: *Miss Travis sang delightfully, "what though I trace".* 25 Sep.

TRENFIELD — Dennis Trenfield [77]

Dennis Trenfield (1804-1868), solicitor, was born at Tewkesbury, Gloucestershire, the son of John Trenfield (1784-1848) and Elizabeth Dukes (1784-1860). He was a solicitor at Winchcombe and clerk to the Winchcombe Union. His brother John (b. ±1812) was presumably in practice with him as a solicitor. He married, at Stow-on-the-Wold, Eliza (b. ±1809), daughter of R. Brookes of Stow; they had at least 1 son:

1 John Dennis Brookes (1838-1903)

Trenfield disgraced himself by forging a promissory note for £200, and was convicted at the March 1858 assizes to ten years' penal servitude. Prior to his trial he attempted suicide by discharging a pistol in his face; he broke his jaw-bone and lodged two bullets, one of which remained in the back of his neck. He died in 1868.

1836: 31 Jul: *A letter from Mr. Trenfield on the subject of a fraud perpetrated at Winchcomb Fair on Thursday on two parishioners of mine, G. Collett and R. Humphries, by giving a £10 note of a Gloucester Bank which stopped payment many years ago in payment for a poney.*

1837: 28 Feb: *Drove with F. Aston in his phaeton to Winchcombe, where called on Trenfield, Clerk to the Winchcombe Union, by whom we were accompanied to the new Workhouse recently finished and now occupied.* 24 Mar.

1838: 28 Mar., 1 Sep.

1839: 19 Aug.

1842: 11 Mar., 24 Apr., 27 Apr., 8 Jul.

1843: 27 Dec.

1844: 21 Feb., 9 Aug., 5 Oct., 9 Oct.

TREVALYAN — Walter Calverley Trevelyan [78]

Sir Walter Calverley Trevelyan, 6th baronet (1797-1879), landed proprietor, was born at Cambo, Hallington, Northumberland, the son of Sir John Trevelyan, 5th baronet (1761-1846), and Maria (1772-1852), daughter of Sir Thomas Spencer Wilson, 6th baronet of Charlton (1726-1798), and Jane Weller (1749-1818). He was educated at University College, Oxford (BA 1820; MA 1822), and succeeded as 6th baronet in 1846. Walter married, first, 1835, Pauline Jermyn (1816-1866); they had 1 son:

1 Alfred Wilson Trevelyan (1831-1891); succeeded as 7th baronet of Nettlecombe

---

1822: 20 Nov: *My young Friend, and Curate at Stanway, Frederick Aston, accompanied by his college friend, Mr. Walter Calverley Trevelyan, left us after passing two days with us.*

TREVENEN — Edward Trevenen [79]

Edward Trevenen (1785-1846), Church of England clergyman, was born at Helston, Cornwall, the son of John Trevenen (1755-1825) and Lydia Johns (1753-1786) of Cury, Cornwall. He was educated at Pembroke College, Oxford (BA 1808), and was ordained deacon on 28 August 1808 and priest on 24 September 1809. His first clerical appointment was as curate of St Mawgan with St Martin in Meneage from 29 August 1808. He was then rector of Drewsteignton, Devon, from 1810 to his death in 1846. He married, at St John's, Hackney, Middlesex, 27 August 1818, Marianne (1792-1829), daughter of James Cazenove (1744-1827) and Marianne Sophia Duboulay (1762-1849); they had 5 daughters:

1 Lydia Johns (1819-1820)
2 Marianne (1821-1896)
3 Elizabeth (1822-1896)
4 Harriet (1825-1909)
5 Louisa (1826-1838)

1803: 13 Nov: *Evans breakfasted with me. Sacrament Sunday. Walked with Evans. Odell called upon & dined with Dowell, meeting Evans & a Mr. Trevannon.* 19-20 Nov., 22-23 Nov.

1804: 1 Feb., 19 Feb., 25-26 Feb., 6 Mar., 10-11 Mar., 26 Jul., 16 Aug., 5 Sep., 24 Sep: *Wrote to Trevenan & Mr. Travell.* 25 Oct: *Trevenen called.* 3 Nov: *Passed the evening with Dowell, meeting Davis & Trevenen.* 9 Nov., 10 Nov: ... *a pleasant party where I met James, Trevenen, Mr. Scott B. &c. &c.*

1805: 24 Jan., 18 Mar., 22 Mar: *Dowell & Trevenen took an early dinner with me, after which we walked to Abingdon, where, in the Market House, the Bohemian Silver Miners performed a Concert.* 1-2 Aug.

1806: 15 Jan., 18 Mar: *Breakfasted with my excellent but indolent friend Dowell, where I was met by Dr. Price, & Round; Trevenen also called in.* 20 Mar.

TRIMMER — Charles Trimmer [80]

Charles Trimmer (1825-1907), Church of England clergyman, was the son of Edward Trimmer of Gloucester. He was educated at Corpus Christi, Oxford (BA 1847; MA 1850), where he was elected a fellow in 1851. Trimmer was a friend of Henry Elwes, of Marcham, Berkshire, with whom he was staying at the time of the 1851 census. By 1861 he was living at 66 St George's Place, Cheltenham, as a clergyman without cure of souls. Presumably he was a local curate during 1850, but it is not clear where. He remained unmarried, and in 1891 he was a lodger in Cavendish Street, Marylebone, and in 1901 a visitor in Sussex. He died at Tonbridge, Kent.

1850: 12 Jun., 24 Sep., 24 Oct.

1851: 23 Apr.

TRINGHAM — Miss Tringham [Tringhams] at the Fords' ball, Clifton

1804: 11 Jan: *Dancing enough & pleasant & good glees were sung nor did we cease till near 5 o clock. The principal belles were Miss Tringhams, Miss Castle, Miss Holder's, Miss S. Gibbons &c. &c. I danced with most of these & on the whole was thoroughly amused.*

TRISTRAM — Jane Tristram at Stoutshill, Uley [81]

Jane Tristram [later Piers] (±1788-1871) was born at Belbroughton, Worcestershire, the only daughter of Revd Thomas Tristram (±1756-1796) and Louisa (1766-1838), daughter of Maj.-Gen. John Barrington (1723-1764) and Elizabeth Vassal (1734-1764). Louisa was well connected; she was a niece of William Wilbram Viscount Barrington, the bishop of Salisbury Revd Shute Barrington, and Vice Adm. of the White Samuel Barrington. She married Revd Thomas Tristram at St Michael's, Bedwardine, Worcester, on 16 April 1787. The precise relationship has not been investigated, but Revd William Lloyd Baker, of Stoutshill, and Revd George Barrington, of Grantham, Lincolnshire, were trustees named in the settlement made before the marriage.

Jane married, at Gloucester, 21 December 1813, Octavius Piers (1789-1848), son of Sir Pigott William Piers (1742-1798) and Elizabeth Smyth; they had 4 sons and 1 daughter:

1 Eliza Jane (1817-1893)
1 Henry (1818-1901)
2 William Dewe (1821-1882)
3 Edward William (b. 1822)
4 Claudius Buchanan (1831-1905)

1801: 19 Dec: *The Tea was very good. Mrs. Cooper her daughter & her Governess with whom we walked back to Dursley, joined the party on the tea. As also Mrs. H. Baker, Miss Gregory & Miss Tristram.*

TROTMAN — Fiennes Trotman [82]

Fiennes Trotman (1785-1835), landed proprietor and JP, was born at Siston Court, Pucklechurch, Gloucestershire, the son of Fiennes Trotman (1752-1824) and Hester Miller (1752-1833). He married, about 1815, Harriet Henrietta (1792-1823), daughter of Francis Litchfield (1769-1812) and Anne Miller; they had 1 daughter:

1 Harriette Elisabeth (1820-1875)

1830: 12 Jan.

TROTMAN — Robert Trotman [83]

Robert Trotman (1819-1861), police officer and carrier, was born at Bagpath, near Kingscote, Gloucestershire, the son of Thomas Trotman (1794-1877) and Edith Taylor (1789-1871). He was registered as a 6-foot-tall agricultural labourer when he enlisted in the Gloucestershire Constabulary on 5 September 1842 with warrant number 516. He married, at Bourton-on-the-Water, Gloucestershire, 1 September 1847, Ann (1826-1867), daughter of William and Hannah Lock; they had at least 1 son:

1 John Austen Bryan (1857-1946)

1851: 10 May: ... *under the charge of one Trotman, of Bourton on the W.,—an Ex Policeman of the Gloucestershire Constabulary, who will conduct the party with their luggage by railway, and deposit them in the Government barracks at Plymouth assigned for Emigrants.* 17 May: *Settled with Trotman, Bourton on the Water, the expences incurred in the conveyance of the Emigrant Smiths to Plymouth.*

TRYE — Charles Brandon Trye [84]

Charles Brandon Trye (1806-1884), Church of England clergyman and JP, was the second son of Gloucester surgeon Charles Brandon Trye (1757-1811) and Mary (1766-1848), daughter of Samuel Lysons of Rodmarton. His elder brother was Henry

Norwood Trye (*below*). He was educated at Brasenose College, Oxford (BA 1829; MA 1832), and was rector of Leckhampton, 1830-84. He married, 22 May 1832, Jane Riland (1810-1889), daughter of Edward Pickard (d. 1859); they had 4 sons and 2 daughters:

1 Sarah Mary (1834-1912)
1 Henry Norwood (1835-1902)
2 Charles Brandon (1839-1840)
3 Reginald Edward (1843-1928)
4 Riland John (b. & d. 1844)
2 Jane Eleanor (1847-1911)

1839: 11 Apr.

1840: 29 Apr: *Met and conversed with Mr. Lewes, Mr. & Mrs. Billingsley, and Mr. Trye, the Rector of Leckhampton. The latter explained to me the circumstances under which the new Church in his parish has changed its character, and become a proprietary Church; the contributions assigned to it from the Diocesan Church-building Society were relinquished, when it appeared that a deficiency of resources to such an extent prevailed, that there could be no probability of the Church being completed otherwise than by accepting large advances from the Trye family ... Trye did not consider Riddle as very deeply imbued with what are called Evangelical opinions.*

1842: 9 Dec: *Drove M.W. to call on Mr. and Mrs. Riddle ... it partakes in some measure of the character of a Proprietary Chapel, is virtually a District Church, to which by arrangement with Mr. Trye, the Rector of Leckhampton, a district, which may be called the Town district, is assigned, to Mr. Riddle, while Mr. Trye superintends the rural part of his parish.*

1845: 6 May.
1846: 20-21 Nov.
1847: 5 May, 7 May, 29 May.
1850: 7 Aug.
1854: 14 Feb.

TRYE —Henry Norwood Trye [85]

Henry Norwood Trye (1798-1854), landed proprietor and JP, was baptised at Rodmarton in 1798 and again at Leckhampton in 1800. He was the eldest son of surgeon Charles Brandon Trye (1757-1811) and Mary (1766-1848), daughter of Samuel Lysons of Rodmarton. He was educated at Oriel College, Oxford, and inherited Leckhampton Court on the death of his father in 1811. Henry was a Gloucestershire JP and high sheriff for Gloucestershire in 1837. As a freemason he was initiated into the Faith and Friendship Lodge, Berkeley, on 20 December 1819. He married, at St Peter's, Leckhampton, Gloucestershire, either 3 or 4 June 1824, Alicia Harriet Longworth (±1800-1866); they had 1 son:

1 Henry Norwood (1835-1902)

1823: 24 Dec.

1826: 16 Jun., 31 Aug: ... *we passed Hardwick Court, the mansion of my friend T.J. Lloyd Baker, a magistrate, & lately High Sheriff, of the County: the estate was purchased of Lord Hardwick, who derives his tithe from hence; before it passed by purchase into that noble family, it was for nearly three centuries the property of the Trye's, a family of Norman extraction. The present representative of this house has a seat at Leckhampton near Cheltenham, and is a magistrate for the County; his father was a very eminent surgeon at Gloucester.*

1829: 10 Oct: *Dined and slept yesterday with our friends, the Browne's, at Salperton; We met a large party; Col. & Mrs. W. Beach, Mr. & Mrs. Trye (the Squire of Leckhampton, now resident at Cheltenham, a justice also).* 20 Oct.

1836: 10 Aug.

1837: 26 Jun: *Another topic which occupied us was perusing and considering the evidence lately taken by the Sheriff, Trye, as to a charge made against the Executioner employed on occasion of the fulfilling the last sentence of the Law on the murderer Bartlett, sentenced at the last Assizes.* 4 Aug: *Had a gentleman presided at the Infirmary dinner the party would have been very agreeable: there were present the High Sheriff (Trye), Grantley Berkeley, Bathurst ...*

1838: 3 Jan.
1839: 2 Jan., 11 Apr.
1850: 8 Nov.

TRYE — Isabella Trye [86]

Isabella Trye (1800-1847) was born and baptised at Leckhampton, Gloucestershire, the third daughter and fourth child of surgeon Charles Brandon Trye (1757-1811) and Mary Lysons (1766-1848). She was sister to Charles and Henry (*above*). She married, at Walcot, Bath, 25 July 1826, Revd Emilien Daniel Benoit Frossard (1802-1881), a protestant minister at Nismes; they had 2 sons and 2 daughters:

1 Charles Louis (1827-1901)
2 Émilien Sigismond (1829-1898)
1 Mary Isabella (1830-1903)
2 Jeanne Amelia (1835-1921)

1845: 30 Jun: *Howell looked in for a short time ... and that he has settled to send his son Edward to be pupil to a French Protestant Clergyman, married to an English lady, a Miss Trye, at Nismes, until he be required to join the regiment.*

TUCKER — Miss Tucker at Cheltenham [87]

Miss Tucker was a friend of Miss Rooke and Miss Rachel Delabere (1755-1802), who lived and died in Gloucester. Other than this nothing is known, although there may have been a connection with Josiah Tucker (1713-1799), who was dean of Gloucester and apparently looked after some of his eight sisters.

1801: 31: Oct: *At Harwards also as usual. Mrs. Shakerly Miss Rooke, & Miss Tucker drank tea with my Aunts.*

1802: 3 Jan: *Half an Hour after Church I sat tête à tête with the Dear Fanny, till interrupted by Miss Tucker bringing a bad account of Miss Delabere.*

TUCKER — Francis Tucker [88]

Francis Tucker (1772-1849), tallow chandler, was the founder of Francis Tucker & Company. Before the age of gas and electricity, wax candles were in vast demand. The tallow industry on Kensington High Street was run by several Catholic families led by James Wheble (1729-1801), who was from a prominent recusant family in Winchester. By 1766 Wheble had based himself in Kensington, and within a few years his business occupied miscellaneous properties in the High Street and on the west side of Young Street, where a warehouse was rated in his name from 1772 onwards. So successful was Wheble's enterprise that when he died in 1801 he was said to be worth upwards of £200,000—a figure roughly confirmed by his will. Francis Tucker (1772-1849), another Catholic, was already established as a tallow chandler in South Molton Street, off Oxford Street, when he took over Wheble's business. The firm finally disappeared in 1974.

1852: 17 Nov: *Letter, circular from Cotteril, Kensington, Wax & tallow chandler, that he has retired from the business, and solicits a continuance of my orders for his successors, Messrs. Tucker.*

1853: 30 Dec: *To Messrs. Tucker & Co. wax chandlers &c. Kensington, with a cheque on Hoare for £6. 12. 0 in payment of a bill for candles supplied.*

1854: 9 Jul: *Received a note from Messrs. Tucker, Chandlers, Kensington, who claim payment for a candle box which, I believe, was returned.* 10 Jul., 29 Jul.

TUDER — William and Harriot Tuder of Cheltenham and Malvern Wells[89]

William Tuder (1783-1849), army officer and JP, was born at Romsey, Hampshire, the son of Revd William Tuder (1755-1820) and Elizabeth Camilla Walker (1759-1840), of Putney, Middlesex, who had married at St George's, Hanover Square, Westminster, on 6 February 1779. William Tuder is not to be confused with William Tudor (1769-1845), army surgeon.

William Tuder features in the 1830 *Pigot's Directory* for Tenby as husband to 'Elizabeth'. She must have died before 1844 as she is not listed in the 1844 directory. By this time Tuder was as a major in the Army. He did not mention Elizabeth in his will, but devolved his estate to two surviving sisters, Elizabeth Camilla Edwards (1781-1840) and Frances Tuder (b. 1790), the latter of whom died unmarried. He was mentioned in the will of Stephen Cole, brother to his first wife, Harriot Cole, who left him a substantial bequest. William had a brother, Lt John Kelly Tuder, RN (±1787-1845), and two other sisters, Sophia (1792-1839) and Lucy (1788-1847).

William Tuder married, first, Harriot (1768-1822), daughter of Maj. Thomas Rea Cole (1739-1807), of Twickenham, and Isabella (1742-1806), eldest daughter of Sir Henry Ibbetson. Thomas Rea Cole, an officer of the 98th Regiment, was the second son of Stephen Cole of Heatham Place, Middlesex. He married Isabella Ibbetson at York on 21 June 1764; they had at least 2 sons and 1 daughter:

- 1 Stephen Thomas (1765-1835); married, 15 January 1795, Lady Elizabeth Henrietta (1778-1857), daughter of Edward Stanley, 12th earl of Derby (1752-1797); 5 sons and 2 daughters
- 1 Harriot (1768-1822); baptised at Leeds, Yorkshire; married Capt. William Tuder
- 2 Henry (1770-1815); married, at Dublin, 26 July 1806, Jane Eliza Owen (1780); 1 son and 2 daughters

The Cole family had substantial brewing interests at Twickenham, and in 1822 William Tuder became a partner in the firm with Harriot's surviving brother, Stephen. William and Harriot do not appear to have had any children. In 1818 they appear to have been living at the Cole family residence of Folly House, Twickenham.

1825: 14 May: *In the secluded churchyard we discovered a flat stone monument in memory of a very hospitable and worthy old acquaintance of ours, who died at Malvern Wells towards the close of 1822. She was the wife of Captn. Tudor, a very respectable Welch Gentleman: Mrs. Tudor's indifferent health caused them to reside chiefly at Malvern Wells, Tenby and Cheltenham. It was at the latter place, that we enjoyed their society and hospitality.*

TUDOR — William Tudor[90]

William Tudor (±1756-1838), clerk to the Gloucestershire sessions, was born at Barnwood, Gloucestershire, the son of William Cole (1735-1783) and Susannah Thatcher (1736-1816), also known by the name of Glossop. He was the brother of Mary Cole (1767-1844), who purportedly married, 1785, Frederick, Lord Berkeley, the 5th earl (1766-1810). William changed his name to Tudor and was appointed clerk of the peace by his patron, the 5th earl of Berkley, in 1800. In the Berkeley peerage claim of 1811, in which the earl attempted unsuccessfully to prove his eldest son's legitimacy, Tudor was the principal witness to testify to his lordship's purported first marriage to Mary Cole.

1839: 1 Jul: *It appears that the real Clerk of the Peace for the County, Mr. Tudor, has lately died. He was brother of the Countess Berkeley, and had holden the office, which had been conferred on him by the late Earl of Berkeley, when Lord Lieutenant, for many years, during which he never officiated in his own person, and Mr. Bloxsome has constantly acted as his efficient deputy.*

TUFNELL — Edward Carleton Tufnell[91]

Edward Carleton Tufnell (1806-1886), civil servant and educationist, was a younger son of William Tufnell (1769-1809), barrister, and Mary (1776-1829), daughter of Thomas Carleton. His father was a developer of Barnsbury, London, where he was lord of the manor; Tufnell Park was named after him. He was also whig MP for Colchester, 1806-07. Edward was educated at Eton College, privately by Christopher Jeaffreson (1769-1846), at Balliol College, Oxford, and at Lincoln's Inn.

Edward Tufnell was appointed an assistant commissioner by the royal commission on the poor laws in July 1832. He was to conduct local investigations into the working of the poor law. He was a supporter of Edwin Chadwick, and gave evidence to his constabulary commission in 1838. From the establishment of the poor law board in 1847 to his retirement in June 1874, Tufnell was an inspector of the administration of government grants to workhouse schools in the London area. He married, 1846, Mary (1824-1877), only daughter of Col William Macadam; they had 3 sons and 1 daughter:

- 1 Carleton (1847-1893), Cdr
- 2 Edward (1848-1909), Conservative MP for South-East Essex (1900-06)
- 1 Mary (1850-1928)
- 3 Frederick (1860-1920), Church of England clergyman

1823: 21 Mar: *We dined at Mr. Jeaffreson's at Longborough, meeting Sir C. & Lady Cockerell, Mr. & Mrs. E. Leigh, their brother & sister, Mr. & Mrs. Dumbleton, Mr. & Mrs. Hall, of Batsford, with his pupil, Mr. Tuffnell.*

TUFNELL — Edward Wyndham Tufnell[92]

Edward Wyndham Tufnell (1814-1896), first bishop of Brisbane, was born at Bath, the son of Lt-Col John Charles Tufnell (d. 1841), banker and army officer, and Uliana Ivaniona Margaret (d. 1848), daughter of Revd John Fowell of Bishopsbourne, Kent. He was educated at Eton College and Wadham College, Oxford (BA 1837; MA 1842; Hon. DD 1859). Tufnell was curate of Broadwindsor, Dorset, in 1837-40, and Broadhinton, Wiltshire, in 1840-46. He was then rector of Beechingstoke, Wiltshire, in 1846-57, and of St Peter and St Paul, Marlborough, in 1857-59. In 1850-59 he was also a prebendary of Salisbury Cathedral. Tufnell was consecrated first bishop of Brisbane in Westminster Abbey by J. B. Sumner, archbishop of Canterbury, on 14 June 1859. He sailed in the *Vimiera* on 5 May 1860 with five priests, two deacons, four laymen, and £7,000 in donations and the promise of further annual contributions. He reached Brisbane in September. The new diocese included all of Queensland south of the twenty-first parallel; its five parishes had a scattered population of 25,000 and were served by three clergymen, including Benjamin Glennie.

In 1865-67 Tufnell sought further funds in England, but illness and other factors prolonged his visit. The delay reduced his already slender popularity in Queensland. Though dignified, devout, and high principled, and a good administrator with sound policies, Tufnell had not related well to his flock; he seemed unable to identify with the crudity of colonial life, and his moderate High Churchmanship widened the gap. His stipend was modest and he used private means generously for diocesan purposes, but he was criticised for devoting money to the see endowment and to Bishopsbourne, his gracious episcopal residence. But despite his weaknesses, Tufnell's pioneering achievements were significant, although at the time they went largely unrecognised. His resignation, submitted after his return to England in February 1874, was received in Brisbane without surprise or regret. Tufnell went on to serve as curate of Charing, Kent, in 1877-79, vicar and rural dean of Croydon, Surrey, in 1879-82, and vicar of Felpham and residentiary canon of Chichester Cathedral in 1882-96. He was married to Laura Louisa (1840-1930); they had 1 son and 1 daughter:

1 Ida Mary Uliana (b. 1870)
1 Arthur Wyndham (1872-1920)

1842: 14 Aug: *A letter from Mr. Dalton ... but will send in his place the Revd. Tuffnell, Curate of Broad Hinton, Wilts, and Fellow of Wadham College, who may be expected by the Little Wonder coach to-morrow evening.* 16 Aug: *Mr. Ford brought with him the Revd. E. W. Tuffnell, as a deputation from the Parent Society, who had reached Little Risington last evening.* 11 Sep: *A letter from Mr. Tuffnell, who returned the report which I had prepared for the annual meeting of the Distr. Comm. S. P. G., which he had taken with him from Stow.* 12 Sep.

TULLY — James Dillon Tully[93]

James Dillon Tully (1785-1827), army surgeon, was born at Loughrea, Galway, Ireland. He joined the Army, and in 1801, at the age of 16, he became hospital mate. On 17 September 1802 Tully was appointed assistant surgeon to the 58th (Rutlandshire) Regiment of Foot, and in 1807 he was appointed surgeon to the 35th (Sussex) Regiment of Foot. In 1815 he was appointed staff surgeon and took on the local rank of deputy inspector of hospitals, Ionian Islands. Plague broke out in the Ionian Islands at the end of 1815, spreading throughout Corfu and reaching Cephalonia in May 1816. Tully produced a detailed record of the epidemic entitled *The history of the plague as it has lately appeared in the islands of Malta, Gozo, Corfu and Cephalonia* (London, 1821). In 1818 he arrived in Malta.

Tully married, at Malta, 2 September 1818, Indiana Elizabeth Maria (b. ±1801), daughter of John Reinaud, collector of HM revenue and magistrate at Vittoriosa, Malta, and Sarah Maria Willimot (1779-1837); they had 1 daughter:

1 Adelaide Elizabeth Miles (1822-1852)

In 1820 Tully was transferred to take over the management of the ordnance hospital in Valletta, and in 1824 he was appointed deputy inspector of hospitals. He died of yellow fever at Jamaica in 1827.

1823: 22 Aug: *I received this day a letter from Mr. H. Lye, Surgeon of the Camden Packet, giving a long & minute report of my poor brother's case. The opinion formed by Dr. Tully, Staff Surgeon at the Military Hospital, at Malta.*

TURBERVILLE — George Turberville[94]

George Turberville (1758-1839), Church of England clergyman, was born at Tewkesbury, the son of George Turberville (1725-1774) and his wife, Elizabeth (d. 1774). He was educated at Trinity College, Oxford (BA and MA 1787), and entered the Church. He was vicar of Hanley Castle, Worcestershire, and was appointed rector of Bromsberrow, Gloucestershire, in 1812. He was then rector of Whichford, Warwickshire, from 1823 to his death in 1839. He married, at St Augustine the Less, Bristol, 16 November 1780, Elizabeth Osborne (b. 1757); they had 1 son and 2 daughters:

1 Ann Margaretta (1782-1857)
2 Eleanor (1788)
1 Edmund (1789-1858)

1827: 3 Aug: *My aunt had invited two or three persons to dinner, to which we sat down before five o clock. Besides the family quintetto from the two houses, there were Mr. Turberville, Mr. Hays & Miss Wemyss. Mr. Turberville is an old acquaintance of mine, & brother Magistrate, as he acts for Gloucestershire, as well as for Worcestershire, & frequently attends at our Assizes and Sessions; he is Rector of Hanley, an extensive and rambling parish, stretching from near Upton to the top of the Malvern Hills above the Wells, its breadth being not so considerable as its length. His parsonage house is about two miles on the Malvern side of Upton, close by the road. He is also incumbent of Whichford in Warwickshire, a living, to which he was presented of late years by Lord Beauchamp.*

1834: 10 Sep: *Again a large dinner party: 17 sat down to table. Besides the inmates of Peach Field Lodge, and my cousin John, there were Mr. Turbervile, Rector of Hanley ...*

1836: 22 Jul: *... Formerly Mr. Turbervile, as Incumbent of Hanley Castle, officiated on Sundays at the Wells House; other opportunities of public worship were denied to the inhabitants.* 29 Jul.

1837: 30 Jan: *Received a letter from Mr. Turberville, Rector of Hanley Castle, Worcestershire, and Whichford, Warwickshire, in consequence of an application he has had from Mr. Cameron for the curacy of Whichford, vacant by the present curate's retirement, who having unexpectedly lost his wife wishes to withdraw from it.* 31 Dec:
In consequence of hearing that Mr. Cameron is likely to leave the Curacy of Whichford in Warwickshire, wrote to my acquaintance, Mr. Turberville, the Rector, resident at Hanley Castle on his other preferment, soliciting him not to decide finally as to a successor to Cameron, without giving my Son an opportunity of offering his services, provided on further consideration it should appear desirable that Edward should apply to Bp. Monk for permission to retire from his Curacy to another on which there is a clerical residence at which he should settle as a family man.

1838: 6 Jan: *One from Mr. Turberville, in reply to mine of the 31st. Ult. promising, in the event of Cameron leaving the Curacy of Whichford, to give my son the refusal of that cure, and entering into some details as to the emoluments, size of the house, land attached &c. which may render it somewhat questionable whether the Curacy would suit my Son's views.* 3-4 Feb., 7 Feb., 12 Feb: *Wrote to Mr. Turberville to say, that, having visited Whichford, it seemed likely to answer my Son's purpose, and to beg him to keep the Curacy open for a few days till the Bp. of Gloucester shall have consented or refused to permit my son to resign the curacy of Upper Slaughter.* 16 Feb., 20 Feb., 26 Feb., 12 Mar., 20 Mar., 28 Mar., 31 Mar., 23 Apr: *He had passed two or three days very satisfactorily amid our friends at Malvern, and had called on Turberville at Hanley who recd. his future curate very cordially.* 17 Jul., 19 Oct., 11 Nov: *E.F.W. rode over from Whichford to consult me on a letter recd. by him this day from Mr. Turberville on the subject of the amount of stipend payable to my son (See Oct. 19.)* 22 Nov., 27 Nov., 3 Dec., 9 Dec., 12 Dec., 14 Dec., 21 Dec., 31 Dec.

1839: 15 Feb., 12-13 Apr., 23 Apr., 20 Jun., 5 Jul: *Mr. Turberville, in correspondence with Mr. Clifton, the Bp. of Worcester's Ch Secretary, still demurs about paying my Son the full amount of stipend due to him as Curate of Whichford ...* 9-10 Jul., 2 Sep: *... she lent me the Gloucester Journal of Saturday last, from which I observed that on the 27th. died George Turberville, the aged Rector of Hanley Castle and Whichford, probably after a short illness. It appears that he was 83 years of age. We had just cause to be dissatisfied with his conduct in the relation which he bore to my Son, urging with pertinacity an unjust and untenable claim...*

1840: 24 Apr., 18 Oct., 27 Oct.

TURNER — Miss Turner, a guest of the Snow family

1801: 1 May: *Evening with the Snows, Mr. T. Snow, Miss Turner & Miss Bennet a very pretty woman met us there.* 22 May, 4 Jun: *In the Evening we repaired to Miss Snows, where we met Col. & Mrs. Clitherow, Mr. & Mrs. Webb, a very handsome woman. Miss Webb, Miss Turner, Mr. & Mrs. Walker, &c.*

TURNEY — Samuel Turney [95]

Samuel Blandford Turney (1829-1915), chemist, was born at Paddington, Westminster, the son of Samuel and Jane Turney. He was married to Mary (b. ±1826), born at Chilton, Somerset; they had at least 4 sons and 2 daughters:

1 Jane Pierrepoint (b. ±1855); born at Cambridge; died unmarried
2 Lucy Marian (b. ±1857); born at Cambridge; died unmarried
1 John Davey (b. 1860)
2 Edward George (b. ±1862); died unmarried
3 Herbert B. (b. ±1866)
4 Frederick E. (b. ±1869)

The family lived at 183 Union Street, Plymouth.

1852: 5 Nov: *A letter from a person of the name of Turney, Islington, stating himself to be the nephew of Mr. John Blandford, and that his uncle, who is deceased, has left him heir to his land &c. at Upper Slaughter, as to which he requests information ... Who this Turney is, and how his nephew, remains to be explained.* 6 Nov., 11 Nov: *Received a letter from Mr. Turney, the heir of Mr. John Blandford, from which it appears that he is likely soon to visit this village, to look after his property here.* 25 Nov: *In the evening received a call from Mr. Turney, Great Nephew of the late Mr. John Blandford, a young Chemist about to settle in business at Cambridge, who had travelled from Town to Bourton on the Water to-day, whence he came in a gig. He produced to me the probate of J Blandford's will, shewing that he is the inheritor of his small property here, and Executor of his will. It appears that JB. died in Ireland in January last.*

TURNER — Anne Turner [96]

Anne Turner (b. ±1820) was born in Gloucestershire.

1846: 21 Aug: *Wrote to Anne Turner, our former cook, now in service at Cheltenham, desiring her to meet me at Cheltenham on Tuesday next to receive from me the amount of her deposits in the Stow Prov. Bank, which, under an authority she had given me, I had received yesterday.*

TURNER — Charles Beresford Turner [97]

Charles Beresford Turner (1816-1891), Church of England clergyman, was born at Hagley, Worcestershire, the son of Revd John Turner (1775-1847). He was educated at Balliol College, Oxford (BA 1838), and entered the Church. He was appointed curate of Lower Slaughter and Clapton, and resided at Bourton-on-the-Water from April 1847 to February 1848. At the time of the 1851 census Turner was curate at Shelsley Beauchamp, Worcestershire, and by 1861 he was curate of Pitton and Farley, Wiltshire. He was then vicar of North Eling, Hamphire, from 1863 to 1884.

Turner married, 1852, Mary Matilda Davies (1827-1890); they had 2 sons and 2 daughters:

1 Mary Katherine (b. 1857)
2 Agnes Caroline (1861-1906)
1 Arthur Beresford (1862-1910)
2 Helen P. (b. ±1864)

1847: 1 Apr: *Messrs. W B Pole, Clarke, and Turner were present: the latter is the gentleman about to undertake the Curacy of Lower Slaughter and Clapton, residing at Bourton on the Water: he appears a sensible, intelligent man, and is a Son of a recently deceased incumbent of Hagley.* 4 May: *At Bourton left my card at the lodgings of Mr. Turner, the new curate, who was from home.* 8 May: *Mr. Hunt declined, Mr. Turner accepted our invitation.* 10 May, 14 May: *We had a dinner party — of gentlemen; Mr. Vavasour, Mr. R Waller, Mr. Turner, Mr. Potter, and Mr. Barrow were our guests.* 27 May, 31 May, 4 Jun., 6-7 Jul., 10 Jul., 30 Jul: *... to Mr. Turner, informing him what are the real facts of the relief given to Widow Cross and her family.* 20 Aug: *Wrote to Mr. Turner, — an invitation to meet the Bishop of Gloucester, and others here on Wednesday evening next.* 23 Aug: *Mr. Turner called on us at breakfast time, desiring to be present at the hearing of a case of larceny charged against a boy, Son of one of his parishioners of Lower Slaughter.* 2 Sep., 4 Sep., 8 Sep., 5 Oct: *R Waller, who was driving Messrs. Turner and Stenson to Stow to join the Cricket party, conveyed me as far as to Lower Slaughter Turnpike gate on my way home.* 14 Oct., 20 Nov: *Mr. Turner, the Curate, is about to leave Bourton for a better curacy in Worcestershire.* 29 Dec: *Mr. Turner, who had called at Upper Slaughter after we left home, followed me to Stow, where I signed his testimonial to satisfy the Bishop of Worcester of his orthodoxy and good moral character. He is going from Bourton on the Water on Saturday next, leaving that curacy to take the charge of the parish of Shelsley Beauchamp, in Worcestershire.*

1848: 3 Feb., 7 Mar.

TURNER — George Turner and the Turner families of Westcote [98]

George Turner (1793-1872), farmer, was born at Little Rissington, Gloucestershire, the son of Robert Turner and Eleanor Bennett (b. ±1772). He farmed 92 acres at Westcote, employing three men. He married, at Westcote, 30 March 1835, Elizabeth Ann Williams (1801-1882); they had at least 3 sons:

1 Thomas (1831-1879)
2 Charles (b. 1838)
3 George (b. 1842)

Thomas Bennett Turner (1796-1860), farmer, was born at Little Rissington, Gloucestershire, the younger brother of George. He farmed 20 acres at Westcote. He was unmarried and lived with his maiden sister, Elizabeth (b. ±1805), and unmarried brother, William (b. ±1811). Also at Westcote was another younger brother, Francis Turner (1804-1866), a cattle dealer, who married, at Cheltenham, 14 November 1843, Elizabeth Bricknell (1817-1901). Francis and Elizabeth had 1 son and 2 daughters:

1 Mary (b. ±1844)
2 Susannah (b. ±1847)
1 Francis (b. 1850)

It seems most likely that George would have been the guardian for Westcote, but the three were all brothers.

1838: 5 Apr: *Of the new Guardians who presented themselves with credentials from their respective parishes, were Mr. Chamberlayne, for Maugersbury, Privett, for Stow, E. Tysoe, for L Swell, J. Cooke for U Swell, Akerman for W. Rissington, Hambidge for Icomb (Glouc) Roberts for Great Risington, Edginton for Great Barrington, Reynolds for L Slaughter Rose, for Broadwell, Stow for Adlestrop, Turner for Westcote...*

TURNER — George Turner[99]

George Turner (1832-1873), agricultural labourer and soldier, was born at Naunton, Gloucestershire, the son of William Turner (1803-1855), later a resident of Lower Slaughter, and Sara (b. ±1809), who was born at at Guiting. George was committed to prison on 16 June 1850 with a six-month sentence for stealing a watch. Afterwards he enlisted in the Army, but that life did not suit him and by early 1857 he was back at Lower Slaughter. He was committed to prison again on 28 May 1857 for forging a cheque for £20. From his committal reference we know that he was 5 feet 7 inches in height, with dark hair and hazel eyes. His visage was described as long and his complexion fresh. By 1871 he was married to Eliza (b. ±1829); they had 1 daughter:

1 Barbara (b. 1863)

By 1871 the family was living at Sheep Street, Stow-on-the-Wold, and in the census George was listed as having consumption. He died in 1873.

1850: 26 Jul: *A note from Sergt. Gallop, Glouc. Constabulary, as to the property found on the person of the Prisoner, George Turner, when charged with stealing Mrs. Griffin's watch &c.*

1852: 31 Dec: *Wrote to the Secretary of War, for information from that office as to George Turner, a young man of Lower Slaughter, who enlisted into the 63d Inf. in Aug. last, and has not been heard of since.*

1853: 30 Dec: *To the Commanding Officer of the 1st. Comp. 63d. Inf. stationed at Dublin, on behalf of Private Turner, now at Lower Slaughter, on furlough, who asks for an advance of pay to take him back to his Regiment.*

TURNER — Henry Turner[100]

Henry Turner was a fishmonger of 8 Coventry Street, Haymarket. His shop was very famous and had been in business for many years when Francis Witts first mentioned it in his diaries in 1834. Before Henry Turner, Mr Robertson had been the proprietor, and in the eighteenth century Sir Joshua Reynolds, Dr Johnson, Burke, Gibbon, and Boswell were among the clientele. In February 1847 Turner was declared insolvent. He went bankrupt in December 1847, but he somehow weathered the storm and was soon back in business. It appears that the business finally closed in 1859.

1834: 19 Nov: *Wrote to Messrs. Turner and Co. Fishmongers for a dish of fish for a dinner party on Friday.*

1836: 30 Jul: *Wrote to Turner & Co., Fishmongers for a dish of fish for Wednesday next.*

1837: 15 Feb: *Wrote to Messrs. Turner, Fishmongers, Coventry Street, Piccadilly, to order a dish of fish for Friday.*

1838: 9 Aug: *Omitted to mention a letter which I wrote yesterday to Messrs. Turner, Fishmongers, London, for fish for a party on Friday.*

1840: 5 Jan: *Wrote to Turner & Co. Fishmongers, London, to order a dish of fish for a party on Wednesday.* 10 Apr: *Wrote to Messrs. Turner & Co.—Fishmongers, with a remittance for their bill for fish supplied.* 16 Apr.

1842: 30 May: *Wrote to Turner & Co. Fishmongers, London, for a dish of fish for a dinner party on Wednesday next.*

1843: 13 Feb: *Wrote to Turners, Fishmongers, London, for a dish of fish for a party on Wednesday next.*

1844: 29 Jul: *Wrote to Messrs. Turner, Fishmongers, for a dish of fish for dinner on Wednesday.* 1 Aug: *Wrote to Messrs. Turner, Fishmongers, with a remittance.* 21 Aug: *Wrote to Messrs. Turner, fishmongers, London, for a supply of fish for a party on Friday.*

1845: 9 Jun: *Wrote to ... Turner, the London fishmonger, for a dish of fish on Wednesday.*

1847: 12 May: *Wrote to Turner, fishmonger, London, to order a dish of fish for a party to-morrow.* 30 Jul: *Wrote to Turner, fishmonger, London, with a cheque for £4. 18. 6 for fish supplied.* 1 Aug., 19 Sep: *Wrote to Turner, Fishmonger, London, to order a dish of fish for a dinner party.*

1848: 23 Jan: *A letter from the official assignee of Turner, our London Fishmonger, who is a bankrupt, and to whom we owe a small bill for fish supplied.* 24 Jan: *To Mr. Jennings, requesting him to pay the little bill due to Turner, the Fishmonger.* 11 Jun: *Wrote to Turner, fishmonger, London, for a dish of fish for a party to dinner on Wednesday.* 26 Aug: *Wrote to Turner, fishmonger, London, ordering a dish of fish for a dinner party on Wednesday next.* 22 Oct: *Wrote to Turner, fishmonger, London, to send fish for a dinner party on Wednesday next.*

1850: 22 Jan: *Wrote to Turner, Fishmonger, London, for a barrel of Oysters.* 28 Oct: *Wrote to Turner, fishmonger, London, with an order for fish for dinner parties on Wednesday and Friday.* 25 Nov: *Wrote to Turner, fishmonger, London, with an order for fish for dinner party on Wednesday.*

1851: 9 Feb: *Wrote to Turner, fishmonger, London, for a dish of fish for company on Wednesday next.*

1852: 19 Apr: *To Turner, fishmonger, London, for a dish of fish for my dinner party on Thursday.* 9 Nov: *Also to Turner, Fishmonger, London, to order a dish of fish for a dinner party on Friday.*

1854: 31 Jul: *Wrote to Turner, fishmonger, to order fish for a party on Friday next.* 7 Aug: *Wrote to Turner, Fishmonger, with a cheque for £3. 2. 0. the amount of his bill for fish supplied to me.*

TURNER — John Matthias Turner[101]

John Matthias Turner (1786-1831), bishop of Calcutta, was born at Oxford, the son of Thomas Turner. He was educated at Christ Church, Oxford (BA 1804; MA 1807; DD 1829), and entered the Church. He was vicar of St Helen's, Abingdon, Oxfordshire, in 1823, rector of Wilmslow, Cheshire, in 1824-29, and bishop of Calcutta in 1829-31. He married, at Edinburgh, 4 July 1814, Louisa Lewis Robertson (1782-1828).

1829: 21 Feb: *The newspapers announce that the Revd. J. M. Turner, Rector of Wilmslow, Cheshire is raised to the see of Calcutta, vacant by the resignation of Bp. James... Of the new prelate it is stated, that he was of Christ church, Oxford; (I think, that I remember him there a Servitor or Bible Clerk;) ...*

1832: 15 Mar., 25 Apr.

TURNER — Thomas Turner[102]

Thomas Turner (1782-1859), banker, was born at Gloucester, the son of John Turner (1752-1832), of Down Hatherley, and Hester (1759-1814), daughter of Thomas Smyth (b. 1720) and Mary Broughton. He was in partnership at the Gloucester Bank with his father and Robert Morris of Cheltenham. The Gloucester Bank failed during the national banking crisis of 1825-26, but it was generally felt that Thomas Turner was unfortunate rather than imprudent.

Turner married, first, at Barnwood, Gloucestershire, 22 November 1814, Louise Woodbridge (1789-1821), daughter of David Walters (±1756-1833) and Harriott Woodbridge; they had 2 sons:

1 Thomas (1816-1833)

2 James Woodbridge (1819-1820)

He married secondly, at Foy, Herefordshire, 1824, Sarah (1789-1864), daughter of John Jones.

In 1820 Turner built Hillfield House, set in fairly extensive grounds on what is now known as Denmark Road. He became treasurer to the Gloucester Infirmary and to the Three Choirs Festival, and despite the bank's failure, he retained his collection of old masters. He died in 1859 at Spa Villas. He published privately *A Narrative of a Journey Associated with a Fly from Gloucester to Aberystwyth* (1849).

1823: 24 Sep: *Called at Mr. Turner's house at Wotton half a mile from Gloucester to look at his collection of paintings. This gentleman, who is a banker at Gloucester, has several very interesting paintings, but as he was not at home nor was there a catalogue, the pleasure to be derived from inspecting them was much diminished.*

1825: 17 Dec: ... *we heard this day, that Messrs. Turner & Morris of Gloucester & Cheltenham have stopped payment.*

1826: 17 Jan: *The Messrs. Turner are about to embark in a new concern at Gloucester; they have entirely separated themselves from their partner Mr. Morris, whose indiscretions, it is alledged, have principally contributed to the suspension ...* 22 Feb: *The proposed union of Messrs. Turner with Messrs. Gladstone, Montague & Nicholls will not take effect.* 27 Feb: *Messrs. Turners have issued another manifesto to the public, which is rather unsatisfactory, in as far as, while it continues to assert the adequacy of their means to the full discharge of their engagements, it proposes a slow and gradual liquidation of their debts.*

1829: 30 May: *She is come back in pretty good health & excellent spirits; accompanied by Miss Charlotte Jones, daughter of Mrs. Jones, with whom Mrs. B. has been staying. Her father was a Clergyman & Rector of Foy in Herefordshire, of which parish her Brother is now the incumbent. There is a large family; three sisters are married; one of them to Mr. T. Turner, late Banker at Gloucester, in partnership with his Father & Mr. R. Morris, whose affairs proved so disastrous at the time of the late panic. Mr. T. Turner is generally esteemed & pitied.*

1841: 5 Mar: *Wrote to Mr. Turner of Gloucester, to thank him in the name of Mrs. Backhouse, as well as of M.W. and myself for his kind attention in sending to us a copy of a work he has lately printed for private distribution, being a pleasing account of a tour made in South and North Wales by himself and Mrs. Turner, in the summer of 1837. The narrative is drawn up in a pleasant good natured, serious, tasteful spirit, interspersed with numerous quotations from poets, and illustrated by several good engravings.*

1842: 25 Nov: *Also to Mr. Turner, Banker, Gloucester, for information as to the present value of Berkeley and Gloucester Canal shares, of which Mrs. Backhouse held three of the nominal amount of £100 each, which she took in part liquidation of a balance due to her on a banking account, when Messrs. Turner and Morris failed.* 3 Dec: *Also a letter from Mr. Turner, informing me that the £100 Gloucester and Berkeley Canal shares cannot be considered worth more than £10 each—"a noble reduced to a nine pence".*

1846: 2 Jul: ... *among those present were Purnell, Hale, B. Baker, Whitcombe, and Robinson (the latter a gentleman resident at Painswick,) who may be viewed as upholding the propositions of the Committee; Governors opposed to the rules now submitted by the Committee, were chiefly Mr. Avery, a Solicitor of Gloucester, a voluble speaker, one of the leaders of the old House Committee, Col. Cother, and Mr. Turner, the Treasurer —neutral, but rather leaning to the new system...* 11 Aug.

1848: 10 Jan., 14 Jan.

1850: 16 Jan: *Also to Mr. Turner, Treasurer to the Gloucester Infirmary, with a cheque for £16. 16. 0.* 24 Jan.

1851: 22 Jan: *Wrote to Mr. T. Turner, Treasurer to the Gloucester Infirmary, with a cheque on Messrs. Hoare for £14. 14. 0. being the amount of the annual Subscriptions of the Stow on the Wold Union, the Upper Slaughter Charity Trustees, the Stanway Charity Trustees and myself.* 26 Jan.

1852: 27 Jan., 31 Jan.

1853: 15 Jan., 18 Jan.

1854: 28 Jan., 1 Feb.

TURTON — Maria Turton [103]

Maria Turton (1786-1841) was the daughter of John Turton (±1745-1824) and Mary Meysey (1754-1838) of Sugnall, near Eccleshall, Staffordshire. Her parents married at Claines, Worcestershire, on 17 March 1774, and had at least 2 sons and 2 daughters:

1 Mary Ann [Marianne] (1775-1857); married, at Eccleshall, Staffordshire, 1794, Sir Thomas Plumer (1753-1824); 5 sons and 2 daughters:
  - 1 Thomas Hall (1795-1852)
  - 1 Marianne (1798-1884)
  - 2 Charles John (1800-1887)
  - 2 Eliza Frances (1802-1838)
  - 3 Henry Richard Hugh (1803-1879)
  - 4 Spencer Percival (1810-1876)
  - 5 John Julius (1813-1875)

1 William (1783-1853)

2 Henry (1785-1861)

2 Maria (1786-1841); died unmarried

The Miss Turton was probably Maria, and her little nephew and niece would have been two of the above Plumer children. The nephew was probably Thomas Hall Plumer (1795-1852), barrister-at-law. He was educated at Eton College, Balliol College, Oxford (BA 1816; MA 1819), and Lincoln's Inn. He was examiner in the court of chancery in 1821, and a commissioner of bankrupts.

1805: 7 Nov: *Sat half an hour with my excellent friend Mrs. Carrick, & accompanied her, & Miss Turton, with her little nephew & niece Plummer & their Governess, a Miss Goodchild, to Bristol in a carriage.*

TUSTIN — Thomas Tustin [104]

Thomas Tustin (1799-1866), plasterer and bricklayer, was born at or near Evesham, Worcestershire, the son of Joseph Tustin (b. 1775). He was in business with William Tustin at Bath Terrace, Cheltenham, as a plasterer and bricklayer. He married, first, before 1828, an unknown wife, probably Susan (±1797-1835); they had 2 sons:

1 Frederick Henry (1828-1912)

2 Edward Thomas (1830-1896)

Tustin married secondly, 14 October 1841, Elizabeth (1804-1881), daughter of William Doleman, basket weaver. In 1841 he lived at Casino Cottage, named after the casino which no longer exists. The street is now named St James' Place; early in the nineteenth century it only had one dwelling in it—Casino Cottage, facing a timber yard and adjacent to Great Norwood Street.

1840: 3 Apr: *Wrote to T. Tustin, Cheltenham, the Bricklayer, whom I employed late last year in rectifying and curing my dining room chimney, which was used to smoke, putting in a new grate &c.—to desire him, if he is willing to undertake the work, to fix a time for inspecting the Stow workhouse as regards its chimneys & flues ...* 5 Apr., 8 Apr., 9 Apr: *I presided at the weekly meeting of the Guardians of the Union ... Tustin was appointed to do the necessary work for heating the wards and other apartments in the Workhouse which require alteration in that respect ...* 18 Apr: *At the Workhouse inspected the repairs going on under Tustin in making new chimneys and fire places in the two wings.* 3 May, 14 May: *To the Workhouse, where I met Tustin, the Cheltenham Bricklayer, and inspected with him the work he has been doing there.*

TUTHILL — George Leman Tuthill [105]

Sir George Leman Tuthill (1772-1835), physician, was born at Halesworth, Suffolk, the only son of John Tuthill, an attorney at Halesworth, and Sarah, only daughter of James Jermyn. He was educated at Caius College, Cambridge (BA 1794; MA 1809; MD 1816), and married, in around 1795, Maria, daughter of Richard Smith of Halesworth. He and Maria had at least 1 daughter:

1 Laura Maria (1800-1863); married Thomas Bowett, solicitor

It appears that after their return to England from Weimar, via a Mediterranean sojourn, the Tuthills went once more to Paris, where George Tuthill became one of the numerous British subjects detained there by the revolution. After several years' captivity, Mrs Tuthill successfully petitioned Napoleon for her husband's release. This was probably in about January 1806; in a letter to Thomas Manning dated 10 January 1806 from St Germain-en-Lay, Tuthill alluded to his hopes.

George Tuthill was physician to Westminster Hospital and to the Bridewell and Bethlehem hospitals. He was knighted in 1820.

1799: 15 Aug: *Mrs. Tuthill who called on my mother was by the bad Weather obliged to stay till pretty late.* 19-20 Aug., 22-23 Aug.

1801: 17 May: *... he had returned from the Mediterranean six months, and had a daughter.*

TWISLETON — Frederick Benjamin Twisleton [106]

Frederick Benjamin Twisleton, 10th Baron Saye and Sele (1799-1887), Church of England clergyman, was born at Gaydon, Northamptonshire, the son of Thomas James Twisleton (1770-1824) and Anne Ashe (1771-1847). He was educated at Winchester College and New College, Oxford (BCL 1825; DCL 1832), and entered the Church. He was appointed prebendary of Hereford and rector of Broadwell and Adlestrop in 1825, and held the livings until 1852. He was later archdeacon of Hereford from 1863 to 1867. He married, first, at Cheriton, Kent, 4 June 1827, Emily (1798-1837), second daughter of Richard Wingfield, 4th Viscount Powerscourt (1762-1809), and his second wife, Isabella Brownlow (d. 1848). Frederick and Emily had 5 sons and 2 daughters:

1 Emily Wingfield (±1827-1917); married, first, 7 August 1849, Thomas Guy, son of Thomas Gisborne and Elizabeth Fyche Palmer; and secondly, 2 April 1872, John Haward Griffiths
1 John (1830-1907); succeeded as 11th Baron Saye and Sele; married, 24 April 1856, Augusta Sophia, daughter of Thomas Robert Hay-Drummond, 11th earl of Kinnoull, and Louisa Burton Rowley; 4 sons and 6 daughters:
  1 Beatrice Emmeline Augusta (1857-1929)
  1 Geoffrey Cecil (1858-1937); succeeded as 12th Baron Saye and Sele
  2 Edwyna Susan Elizabeth (1860-1931)
  3 Edith Ellen Louisa (1861-1929)
  4 Alexandra Caroline Frances (1862-1938)
  2 Eustace Edward (1864-1943)
  5 Maud Mary (1866-1937)
  6 Gertrude Emily (1869-1948)
  3 Ivo Henry John (1872-1947)
  4 William Cecil (1879-1906)
2 Cecil Brownlow (1831-1870); married, at Paris, 17 December 1861, Maria Louisa, daughter of John Hardy; 2 sons and 1 daughter:
  1 Emily Cecilia (1862-1934)
  1 Henry Edward (1866-1932)
  2 Cecil John (1867-1899)
3 Ivo de Vesci Edward (1833-1875); married, 26 July 1864, Isabella Emily, daughter of Charles Francis Gregg; 2 sons and 2 daughters:
  1 Bertram Ralph Ivo (1865-1886)
  1 Dorothy Margaret Isobel (1868-1961)
  2 Eva Caroline (1873-1963)
  2 Nathaniel Ivo Edward (1876-1963)
4 Wingfield Stratford (1834-1923); married, at St John's, Paddington, Westminster, 6 October 1863, Alice Susan Yorke (1836-1922); 4 sons and 1 daughter:
  1 Winifred Emily Cecil (d. 1945)
  1 Gerard Yorke (1864-1926)
  2 Alberic Arthur (1865-1919)
  3 Caryl Wentworth (1869-1948)
  4 John Temple (1877-1970)
5 Frederick Nathaniel Fiennes (1836-1896); married, 16 August 1887, Isabella Margaret, daughter of Thomas Martinson Richardson
1 Isabella Elizabeth Catherine (1837-1915); married, 11 June 1857, Richard Frederick, son of Richard Webb and Frances Hannington; 1 son:
  1 Algernon Edward (1865-1952)

Frederick Benjamin Twisleton married secondly, 1857, Caroline, third daughter of Chandos Leigh, 1st Baron Leigh of Stoneleigh. On 14 February 1849 he changed his name by royal licence to Frederick Benjamin Twisleton-Wykeham-Fiennes. Although politically a Liberal, Frederick Twisleton was a good friend of Francis Witts.

1823: 9 Dec: *Mr. T. is nephew of Mrs. Leigh Senr. and of Lord Say & Sele; Son of the Hon. & Revd. Mr. Twisleton, Archdeacon of Ceylon, who, by a singular latitude consented to by the Bp. of Gloucester, is Incumbent of the united parishes of Adlestrop and Broadwell, though living in another hemisphere at the time of his institution & induction by proxy. Mr. B. Twisleton is a Fellow of New College, and chaplain to the Bp. of Hereford.*

1824: 9 Nov.

1825: 6 Jun: *Accompanied by F. Aston, I dined at Mr. Twisleton's at Adlestrop. This polite and agreeable young man has recently become Rector of that and the united parish of Broadwell, having before been Curate of Adlestrop. The living is in the gift of Mr. Leigh of Stoneleigh Abbey, whose first cousin Mr. Twisleton is, being nephew to Mrs. Leigh (Dowager). His Father the Hon. & Revd. Dr. Twisleton was brother of a late Lord Say & Sele: a man of talent, but gay & expensive in early days, and in latter life reclaimed, he had long lived in high estimation and respect in the island of Ceylon as principal chaplain & latterly as Archdeacon under the new see of Calcutta.* 2 Aug., 20 Sep.

1826: 3 Mar., 15 Mar: *Lady Elcho & Miss Church came from Stanway to stay a day or two with us. — Mr. & Mrs. R. Wynniatt, Mr. Ford, Mr. Twisleton & Mr. Bowen dined with us.* 5 Jun: *I dined at Mr. Twisleton's at Adlestrop, & there met the amiable old Bishop of Hereford, Dr. Huntingford, returning from Hereford to Winchester.* 5 Jul., 18 Jul., 28 Jul., 15 Sep: *The names of the Stewards for 1829 were then announced and received with much applause. Mr. Thos. Kingscote, nominated by Mr. Moreton, Mr. Estcourt Junr. by Mr. Dutton, Mr. Waller of Farmington by Mr. Dolphin. The Clerical Stewards are the Bishop of Gloucester, Lord William Somerset (brother to the Duke of Beaufort, Prebendary of Bristol, & Rector of Tormarton) and Mr. Twisleton, respectively nominated by Mr. Bankes, Mr. Bowles & myself.* 9 Nov., 21 Dec.

1827: 21 Feb., 3 Jul: *We took a drive to Adlestrop to pay the compliment of a wedding visit to Mr. & Mrs. Twisleton, the young Rector having lately married the Hon. Emily Wingfield, Sister of the late aunt of the present Lord Powerscourt. The Lady possesses more blood than beauty, but is represented to be amiable, & accomplished: these good qualities make up for a small fortune.* 12 Sep., 25 Sep.

1828: 12 Feb., 23 Apr., 28 May: *We had a party of our neighbours to dinner to-day: Mr. & Mrs. Twisleton ...* 25 Jun., 2 Jul., 20 Aug., 23 Aug., 27 Sep., 7 Oct., 19 Dec.

1829: 20 Mar., 15 May, 17 Jun., 27 Jun., 3 Jul., 12 Aug., 22-23 Sep., 16 Oct: *a dinner party in the evening; Mr. & Mrs. E. Leigh & Miss Leigh, Mr. & Miss Croome, Mr. & Mrs. Twisleton.*

1830: 14 Apr., 10 May.

1832: 25 Apr.

1833: 29 Oct.

1834: 13 Mar: *To the left we passed the little village and church of Ashow, the incumbent of which is Mr. Charles Twisleton, the younger brother of our friend, the Rector of Adlestrop.* 24 Jul., 30 Sep., 31 Oct.

1835: 1 Jan., 29 Jan., 17 Jun.

1836: 4 Oct., 3 Nov.

1837: 16 Jan., 30 Jan., 21 Apr., 7 Jun: *A note from Mr. Twisleton accompanying a pamphlet, which when I have perused he requests me to forward to some of my clerical neighbours.* 14 Jun., 20 Jun: *Recd. the melancholy information of the death of Mrs. Twisleton, the amiable and pious wife of our neighbour and acquaintance, the Rector of Adlestrop... . Mrs. T. was a daughter of Lord Powerscourt, Aunt of the present peer of that name, who is a minor; a mild, charitable, religious, domestic, sensible, but shy and retiring person.* 21 Jul.

1838: 17 Jan., 6 Feb., 20 Mar., 8 Aug., 16 Aug: *Thence to the Rectory, where I met Twisleton with all his fine family of motherless children, and their maternal Aunt, Mrs. Newcome, the widow of an Irish Clergyman, and sister of the late Lord Powerscourt.* 7 Sep., 25 Sep.

1839: 12 Apr., 21 Aug.

1840: 25 May, 14 Jun., 16-17 Jun., 4 Aug., 29 Sep., 24 Nov.

1842: 15 Apr., 27 Apr., 23-24 May, 6 Jun., 9 Jul., 21 Jul., 12 Aug., 19 Aug., 1 Nov.

1843: 8 Nov., 14 Nov.

1844: 13 Jan., 1 Feb., 17 Apr., 24 Apr: *We entertained at dinner Vavasour, Dryden, Twisleton and Bowen — Dryden having returned to-day from Leamington to rejoin his wife at Stow—a cheerful party.* 29-30 Aug., 7 Nov., 4 Dec., 7 Dec., 11 Dec.

1845: 7 Jan., 19 Jan., 21 Jan., 26 Jan., 6 Feb., 14 Feb., 20-21 Feb., 22 Mar: *Dr. Twisleton, as a Connection of Mr. Dryden, came shortly after my son to attend the funeral, and was soon followed by Lord Leigh, who, out of respect and regard for his connection Mr. Dryden, had made a point of being present, leaving Stoneleigh park Abbey this morning, and proposing to return this evening.* 26 Mar., 26 May, 25 Jun.

1846: 15 Aug., 13 Nov., 17 Dec. 31 Dec.

1847: 7 Apr: *The subject proposed for a paper to be read by the Rector of Adlestrop, but which was not forthcoming, was "the Divinity and eternal generation of our blessed Saviour"—the disappointment arose from the unexpected decease, a few days since, of Lord Saye and Sele, whose barony and considerable estate descends to my old friend and neighbour, Fredk. Twisleton.* 23-24 Apr., 16 Jul., 28 Sep., 23 Dec.

1848: 3 Feb: *A note from Lord Saye and Sele, inviting M.W. and me to dinner on Tuesday next.* 8 Feb: *In the evening went with M.W. to Adlestrop, to dine with Lord Saye & Sele—A very bad, dark, stormy, and rainy night, both as we went and returned. Our first visit to the Peer since he has succeeded to the title... His appointments suitable to his present rank and fortune, both in respect of table, wine, and attendance.* 14 Feb., 22 Feb: *His father, Dr. Twisleton, Archd. of Ceylon, and a younger Brother of the Lord S. and S. of that day, was a very gay and dissipated young man. Even when a pupil at Westminster School he devoted himself to private theatricals, and at a very early age became entangled with a Miss Wattell a Stage heroine, as young and giddy as himself. Her he married, and poverty, dissention, and separation were the result of the ill conditioned union. She bare him no live child, and on their being parted, she went on the stage as a means of support, he prosecuting his studies at Oxford. At Edinburgh, as an actress, she became the mistress of one Stein, a merchant, who kept her until she had borne him a Son, and eventually separated from her. This connection enabled Mr. Twisleton to obtain a divorce; after which he married a Miss Ashe, the mother of the present Lord and his two brothers.—Till Lord S & S. succeeded to the title and estates, which were left to him by his deceased cousin —— who had never married, but had lived a dissipated & eccentric life, always of late years recognizing his cousin, the Rector of Adlestrop, as his heir and successor, these not very creditable family histories had been lulled to sleep, and were hardly remembered, except as recorded in one to two memoirs of persons long since deceased, particularly in those of one Reynolds, an Actor & wit, and companion of the early life of the Archdeacon.——Now it became necessary to revive them; and chiefly to prove that the Son of Mrs. Twisleton, born after her separation from her husband, and before their divorce, could not be his Son by reason of non-access. Extraordinary success has attended the researches made by Lord S. & S's Solicitors.* 29 Feb., 28 Dec.

1849: 18 Feb: *Recd. a letter from Lord Saye and Sele, who accepts our invitation to dinner on Tuesday next.*

1850: 16 Mar.

TWISS — Horace Twiss [107]

Horace Twiss (1787-1849), lawyer and politician, was born in the parish of St Giles-in-the-Fields, London, the eldest son of Francis Twiss (1760-1827), of Bath, and Frances (1759-1822), daughter of Roger Kemble, actor and theatrical manager. He was educated at the Temple and called to the bar in 1811. He married, first, 2 August 1817, Ann Lawrence Serle (1790-1827); they had 1 daughter:

1 Fanny Horatia Serle (1818-1874); married, first, Francis Bacon (d. 1840); secondly, John Thadeus Delane, editor of *The Times*

Twiss married secondly, at St George's, Hanover Square, Westminster, 3 April 1830, Ann Louisa Greenwood, daughter of

Revd Alexander Sterky, a Swiss minister and reader to the Princess Charlotte. Ann was the widow of Charles Greenwood, a Russia merchant. Horace and Ann had 1 son:

1 Quintin William Francis (1835-1900), Treasury clerk

Horace Twiss was MP for Wotton Bassett in 1820-30, Newport, Isle of Wight, in 1830-31, and Bridport in 1835-37. He held the following appointments: commissioner of bankrupts, 1819-27; counsel to the Admiralty and judge advocate of the fleet, 1824-28; king's counsel, 1827; bencher, 1827, reader 1837, and treasurer, 1838, of the Inner Temple; under-secretary of state for war and colonies, 1828-30; and vice-chancellor of the duchy of Lancaster, 1844-49.

1826: 13 Jan.

1827: 19 Apr: *The counsel on both sides, Messrs. Ludlow & Twiss, conducted the business with great talent & judgment and Mr. Baron Vaughan charged the Jury with much impartiality and distinctness; perhaps, went over the ground rather too often, incurring the risk of confounding the Jury in the desire of leaving nothing unsaid.*

1828: 17 Jun: *Among the subordinate appointments are Mr. Horace Twiss, to be Under Secretary in the Colonial Office; & Mr. Geo. Bankes to be Secretary to the Board of Controul... With Mr. Twiss I have been long acquainted from the circumstance of his having been a leading counsel at our quarter Sessions; he is a very talented man, nephew to John Kemble & Mrs. Siddons, fluent in speech, with a considerable fund of humour, a good lawyer, rather irritable, and incautious as a pleader; an ambitious man...*

TYLEE — John Tylee and the Tylee family of Devizes — *see also* Gent[108]

John Tylee (1737-1812), brewer, was born into a Quaker family. He was a nephew of Charles Rose, and together they were innholders in 1766 and in partnership as brewers by 1768. By 1783, Rose was dead, and the firm had been transformed into Tylee and Gent. Under the subsequent names of Gent and Tylee, J. & T. Tylee, and Tylee & Co. it is traceable to 1844. By 1822-23 the brewery was located at the Maltings, Northgate Street. At the time that Francis Witts was at Urchfont, John Tylee's partner was James Gent (d. 1829). It appears that through various transformations the brewery eventually became Wadworths, which exists today. John had at least 3 sons and 1 daughter:

1 John (b. 1775); married, about 1800, Gracion Hunt (1780-1837); at least 2 two sons:
  1 Charles (1801-1871)
  2 Edward (b. ±1805)
2 Thomas (b. 1777)
3 Charles (b. 1778)
1 Hannah (b. 1780)

The family was very influential in Devizes. By the time of the 1861 census John Tylee (junior) had given up all pretence of his brewing heritage and listed himself as 'banker'.

1806: 22 Jul: *Was introduced to a Miss Tylee...* 29 Jul: *Called with my Mother upon Mrs. J. Tylee, a very pleasant little woman.* 4 Aug: *Passed a very pleasant Even. at Mrs. J. Tylee's: Mrs. Gent, Mrs. Hillier ...* 7 Aug., 9 Aug., 15 Aug: *Dined with the J. Tylee's a very pleasant party Mr. C. Mayo & his Sister, Mrs Newman Mr. Neat, Mrs. C. Tylee, Mr. & Mrs. Gent ...* 22 Aug: *Called at Mrs. J. Tylee's meeting Mr. J. Tylee & Charles Mr. Barrie, Mrs. Hillier & Harriet, Miss Tylee &c.* 23 Aug: *Drank Tea & supped at Mr. J. Tylee's, walking in the Interval. Miss Tylee, C. Tylee, Alfred Wyatt, Mrs. Hillier & Harriet, Mr. Maurice & Miss M. Gibbs. Very agreeable.* 25 Aug: *Walked about the Town with me & with Alfred Wyatt & C. Tylee. Dined at the Elder Mr. Tylee's, very pleasantly meeting Mereweather Mrs. Tom Tylee, her Husband, Alfred Wyatt &c.* 27 Aug., 6-8 Oct., 13 Oct., 27 Oct., 31 Oct., 1 Nov., 7 Nov: *Met & conversed with Mr. & Mrs. J. Tylee, C. Tylee, Miss Tylee, Mr. & Mrs. M.W. Salmon, Ch. Mayo, Mrs. & Miss Spalding &c.* 31 Dec.

1807: 2 Jan., 26 Jan: ... *called upon Miss Tylee, with whom I found Mrs. J. Tylee & Mrs. Gent.* 30-31 Jan., 5 Feb: *Also met & conversed there with Mr. Estcourt, Salmon Junr., Eldrige, Tom Tylee.* 10 Mar: *Mr. C. Tylee, & Miss Tylee called; the latter bringing me a letter from my dear friend Mrs. Carrick ...* 16 Mar., 20 Mar., 6 Apr., 20 Apr., 24 Apr., 29 Apr., 11 May, 3 Jun., 9 Jun., 24 Jun., 29 Jun: *In the Evening drove my Mother to drink tea at Mrs. C. Mayo's at Beeching Stoke; met Mrs. J. Gent, Miss H. Tylee, Mr. & Mrs. Lancaster.* 8 Jul., 15 Jul: *Drove my Mother thro' Lavington, Worton, & Seend to Devizes to dine at Mrs. John Tylee's. My Father walked & met us. Miss Tylee completed the party.* 22 Jul., 3 Aug., 10 Aug., 24 Aug., 25 Aug: *Mr. & Mrs. J. Tylee & Charles, drank tea & passed the Evening with us.* 31 Aug., 7 Dec: *Called upon the Tylees of both houses. Saw & conversed with Mr. C. Tylee, his Brothers & Sisters.* 10 Dec., 16 Dec: *Called upon the Hilliers, met Ch. Tylee & Michael Wyatt, called on John Tylee, whose infant is deplorably ill, called upon Mr. Tylee & his daughter.*

1808: 11 Jan., 13-14 Jan., 15 Jan: *Breakfasted most pleasantly at Mr. John Tylee's:... called upon Mrs. Hill, & the other Tylee Family: conversed with the Miss Tylees, Charles Hill, &c.* 25 Jan., 5 Feb., 7 Feb., 14 Mar., 23 Mar., 11 Apr., 20 Apr., 29 Apr.

TYLER — John Tyler of Redland[109]

John Tyler (1735-1810), landed proprietor, married, 1776, Martha (1748-1816), daughter of John Chatfield (1704-1765) and Frances Sturt (1712-1781); they had at least 1 son and 2 daughters:

1 Lucy (1782-1854); married, at Redlands, Gloucestershire, 13 August 1807, Isaac Spooner (1774-1849); 3 sons and 4 daughters:
  1 Lucy (1808-1884)
  2 Barbara (1809-1825)
  1 Isaac (1810-1879)
  2 John (1811-1823)
  3 Charlotte (1812-1887)
  4 Frances (1813-1897)
  3 Charles Herbert (dates unknown)
2 Charlotte Mary Amey (1784-±1823); died unmarried
1 John Chatfield (1787-1851); born at Westbury-on-Trym, Gloucestershire; married, at St George's, Hanover Square, Westminster, 28 March 1826, Amelia Henley (1801-1887), daughter of Charles Fitzroy (1762-1831) and Princess Amelia of Hanover (1783-1810), sixth daughter of King George III and Charlotte of Mecklenburg-Strelitz; 6 sons and 4 daughters:
  1 Henry Whatley (1827-1908)
  1 Josephine (1828-1868)
  2 Charlotte (1830-1896)
  2 John (1831-1901)
  3 Lucy (1833-1907)
  3 Charles (b. 1834)
  4 Edward (1838-1875)
  5 Frederick J. (b. 1841)
  4 Mary (b. 1848)
  6 James (b. 1851)

1805: 9 Mar: *Called on the Tylers at Redlands.*

1806: 25 Feb: *Conversed with the Salters, Ryan, Tyler, Gould & Gillibrand party, Robin, Miss Holford, the Poetess, the Roberts's &c.*

TYLER — Peter Tyler — *see also* Barrett-Lennard[110]

Peter Tyler (1715-1763), army officer, married Anna Maria (1719-1782), daughter of Henry Roper, 8th Lord Teynham (±1676-1723). Her father committed suicide by shooting himself. Her half-brother was Thomas Barrett-Lennard, 17th Baron Dacre (1717-1786), late husband to Anna Maria Barrett-Lennard, née Wilson (d. 1806), dowager Lady Dacre. Peter and Anna Maria Tyler had 3 sons and 2 daughters:

- 1 Charles (1760-1835), Adm.; knighted; commanded HMS *Tonnant* at Trafalgar; originally second in line from Collingwood's flagship HMS *Royal Sovereign*, but due to *Tonnant*'s speed, swapped to third in line and became quickly and intensely engaged; first forced the Spanish *Monarca* to surrender (although she later attempted to escape) before colliding with the *Algésiras*, which soon became hopelessly entangled in *Tonnant*'s rigging. Charles married, first, Anne (d. 1784), only daughter of Charles Rice, RN; and secondly, 25 November 1788, Margaret (d. 1835), daughter of Abraham Leach of Pembrokeshire; died at Beaufort Buildings, the Spa, Gloucester, on 28 September 1835; three children from each marriage, including the following son from his first marriage:
  - 1 Charles (d. 1846), naval officer; died a captain on the retired list
- 2 Francis Henry (dates unknown)
- 1 Mary (dates unknown)
- 3 George Peter (dates unknown)
- 2 Frances Anne (dates unknown)

Peter Tyler was a captain in the 52nd Regiment. The Mr Tyler who met the Witts family on 25 May 1801 would have been one of the above three brothers, sons of Peter and Anna Maria.

1801: 25 May: *Dined with Dow. Lady Dacre Bruton Street, where we enjoyed a very handsome reception; we met there Mr. & Mrs. Leonard, Mr. Tyler, & another Gentleman.*

TYNDALL — Thomas Tyndall[111]

Thomas Tyndall (1764-1804), banker, was the son of Thomas Tyndall (±1723-1794) and Alicia Smith (1733-1764), and the grandson of Onesiphorus Tyndall (1689-1757), banker and merchant, of Bristol, and Elizabeth Cowles (1696-1730). After Elizabeth's death in 1730, Onesiphorus Tyndall remained a widower, living for many years in the parish of Christchurch in Bristol. In 1743 he inherited from his brother John a house in the Royal Fort, then on the northern fringes of the city, which consolidated the family's close connection with the area. Thomas (senior) was Onesiphorus's youngest son, and succeeded him as a partner in the Old Bank. Between 1753 and 1767 he purchased a number of fields in the area and turned them into an ornamental park. He built a stately house on the crest of the hill on the site of a Civil War fortification, and named it Fort Royal (now known as Royal Fort House). Its design, by James Bridges, was a compromise between the separate designs of architects Thomas Paty, John Wallis, and Bridges himself. This led to different classical styles—Baroque, Palladian, and Rococo—for three of the house's façades. The house was built between 1758 and 1761 by Thomas Paty, with plasterwork by Thomas Stocking.

Tyndall employed Humphry Repton from 1799 to landscape the gardens which form a small part of Tyndall's Park, which extended to Whiteladies Road in the west, Park Row in the south, and Cotham Hill to the north. Over the years, due to family financial pressures, large parts of the park were sold for housing development. The Bristol Grammar School was also built on land purchased in 1877. Only a small part of the original area remains, known as Royal Fort Gardens. The locations of drives in the Royal Fort Park are reflected in street plans today. The Royal Fort was occupied by members of the Tyndall family until 1916, when Henry Herbert Wills bought it and gave it to the university.

Thomas Tyndall (1764-1804) married, at Sydmonton, Hampshire, 28 October 1786, Marianne (±1761-1805), daughter of Lambert Schimmelpennick, of Berkeley Square, Bristol, a member of a branch of a noble Dutch family in the shipping trade at Bristol, and Jane Thompson; they had 6 sons and 4 daughters:

- 1 Thomas (1787-1841); married, at Westbury-on-Trym, Gloucestershire, 7 April 1812, Mary Sybella Hill (1791-1822); at least 1 son and 2 daughters:
  - 1 Thomas Onesiphorus (1814-1869); married, 25 April 1844, Caroline Lucy (1810-1882), daughter of Sir Charles Abraham Elton, 6th baronet (1778-1853); at least seven children
  - 1 Maria Gertrude (1819-1864); married, 1859, her sister's widowed husband, James Cookson (1816-1888) of Neasham Hall, Durham; 1 daughter:
    - 1 Florence (1862-1927)
  - 2 Sybella Frances (1821-1853); married, 1847, James Cookson (1816-1888) of Neasham Hall, Durham; 2 sons and 1 daughter:
    - 1 Joseph Tyndall (b. 1848)
    - 2 Francis (b. 1853)
    - 1 Emmeline Maria (b. 1850)
- 1 Alicia (1789-1793); died a child
- 2 Onesiphorus (1790-1855); married, 1829, Margaret Stuart, daughter of Col Bruce of Fife; changed his name to Tyndall Bruce
- 2 Marianne (1792-1864); married, 1815, Marcus McCausland (1787-1862), eldest son of Connolly McCausland (1754-1827), of Fruit Hill, Drenagh, co. Derry, and Theodosia Mahon (±1746-1822); 1 son and 9 daughters:
  - 1 Theodosia Sydney (1818-1903)
  - 2 Henrietta Caroline (1821-1897)
  - 3 Marianne (1822-1863)
  - 4 Katherine Geraldine (1822-1859)
  - 5 Julia (1825-1826)
  - 6 Georgina (1826-1836)
  - 1 Conolly Thomas (1828-1902)
  - 7 Elinor Georgiana (1830-1852)
  - 8 Adelaide (1831-1917)
  - 9 Ellin M. Causland (dates unknown)
- 3 William (1793-1863); married, at Worcester, 3 October 1814, Magdalene Caroline (1793-1852), daughter of John Impett (1758-1809) and Maria Raitt (1764-1824); 3 sons and 3 daughters:
  - 1 William Henry (b. & d. 1816)
  - 1 Caroline Georgina (1817-1890)
  - 2 Mary Adelaide (1818-1898)
  - 2 William Charles (1821-1827)
  - 3 Marianne Luise (1826-1851)
  - 3 Graham (1828-1867)
- 3 Henrietta (1794-1869)
- 4 Caroline (1796-1843); married, 1821, Robert Bright (1795-1869), of Abbots Leigh, the first physician to classify common symptoms of kidney disease (1827); Bright's disease is named after him; 7 sons and 3 daughters:

1 Richard (1822-1878)
2 Robert Onesiphorus Bright (1823-1896)
3 Tyndall (1824-1902)
4 George (1826-1919)
1 Caroline Margaret Ann (1828-1917)
5 Charles Edward (1829-1915)
6 Arthur (1831-1857)
7 Reginald (1833-1920)
2 Isabel Marianne (1835-1920)
3 Constance (1838-1924)

4 Charles (1797-1832); married, at Clifton, 29 May 1823, Theodosia McCausland (d. 1825); 1 son and 1 daughter:
1 Charles Mahon (1826-1881)
1 Theodosia (1828-1893)

5 George (1798-1848)

6 Edward (1800-1849), Lt, RN; married, at Stoke Damerel, Devon, 15 February 1830, Louisa, youngest daughter of Lt-Col Du Vernet, RA; 3 daughters:
1 Louisa Miriam Sophia (1831-1864)
2 Julia Caroline Maria (1833-1901)
3 Alice Martha Anna (b. 1836)

1804: 18 Aug: *In Mr. Tindal's Grounds in the Evening.*

1833: 8 Apr: *Leaving St. Michael's hill to our left, we passed what I used to known as Tindal's Park, the margin of which is now fringed with little Villas, of recent erection, and pretty rows of houses; since my acquaintance with Clifton, which I have not visited, I think, since 1806.*

TYNDALE — **Thomas George Tyndale** [112]

Thomas George Tyndale (1777-1865), Church of England clergyman, was born at Bathford, Somerset, the son of George Booth Tyndale (1743-1779) and Elizabeth Annesley (1745-1816). He was educated at Trinity College, Oxford (BA 1799; MA 1802), and was vicar of Wooburn, Buckinghamshire, and rector of Holton, Oxfordshire, 1819-56. Tyndale married, at Swallowfield, Berkshire, 22 February 1809, Mary Anne (1774-1826); they had 3 sons and 2 daughters:

1 Anne Biscoe (1810-1877)
2 Elizabeth Vere (1811-1902)
1 William Earle (1813-1895)
2 Henry Annesley (1816-1891)
3 George Thomas (1818-1916)

1825: 3 Jul: *The incumbent of Wooburn is the Revd.——Tindal, who has another living, Holton in Oxfordshire, where he resides, keeping a Curate at Wooburn. Mr. Tindal formerly resided here, where I have called upon him with my Uncle; he is a Clergyman attached to the puritanical party: & such have most of his curates been.*

TYSOE — **Edward Tysoe** [113]

Edward Tysoe (1805-1853), farmer, was born at Lower Swell, Gloucestershire, the son of John Tysoe (1759-1839) and Mary Stayt (1776-1828). He married, at Upper Slaughter, 4 June 1835, Harriet (1808-1855), daughter of Thomas Smith (1778-1847), of Eyford, and Alley Pearce (1776-1847) of Weston-sub-Edge; they had at least 1 son:

1 John (b. 1837)

Edward's brother John married, at Upper Slaughter, 14 November 1833, Anne Smith, sister to Harriet. Anne and Harriet had at least two further sisters: Sophia Arkell and Elizabeth Le. At the time of the 1851 census Edward Tysoe was farming 290 acres at Bledington, employing nine labourers. His widowed mother-in-law Alley was living with him and his family.

1838: 5 Apr: *Of the new Guardians who presented themselves with credentials from their respective parishes, were Mr. Chamberlayne, for Maugersbury, Privett, for Stow, E. Tysoe, for L Swell ...*

1839: 2 May, 30 May.

1842: 31 Jan.

1843: 21 Aug: *Before leaving home received a note from Mrs. E. Tysoe, Lower Swell, with contributions to a small amount, collected by her for the Society for the Propagation of the gospel in foreign parts.* 22 Aug.

1844: 22 Feb: *A numerous party of tenant farmers were soon collected (Messrs. Shelton, Cook, Staite, Bennet, Gibbs, Tysoe, Merchant, Green, Gillett, Williams, R. Davis, Bolser, & others).* 24 Feb.

1847: 22 Dec: *Visited poor Emily Lea, far gone in consumption, and whose days are numbered: prayed with her,—an interesting and lovely girl of eighteen: her parents and her Aunt Tysoe were present.*

U

UNDERWOOD — Henry Jones Underwood[1]

Henry Jones Underwood (1804-1852), architect, was born at Bristol, the son of William Robert Underwood (1772-1854) and Sarah Jones (1777-1842). He was the brother of architects Charles Underwood (*c.* 1791-1883) and George Allen Underwood. Henry trained in London as a pupil of H. H. Seward before joining the office of Sir Robert Smirke. In 1830 he moved to Oxford where much of his work involved designing churches or schools. He built St Paul's parish church, Walton Street, and the library of the Oxford Botanic Garden in the Greek Revival style, but he is best known for his Gothic Revival architecture. His church at Littlemore for Newman became a model for other churches.

Underwood married, at Ryde, Hampshire, 11 August 1841, Mary Worthington. There do not appear to have been any children. In 1852 he committed suicide at the White Hart Hotel, Bath.

1836: 20 Sep: *A call from John Perkins Junr. who had come from Oxford to Lower Swell, accompanied by Mr. Underwood, an Architect, to select on the Vicarage land a site for a Parsonage which he proposes to begin building with funds obtained from Queen Ann's bounty, the Pincot Charity, the Dean & Chapter of Christ Church &c.*

1838: 25 Jan: *Before returning with my Son had an interview, at the Unicorn Inn, with John Perkins, who had come from Oxford this morning, accompanied by his Architect, Mr. Underwood, to make arrangements with Clifford, the Builder, who has contracted for the erection of his parsonage about to be built at Lower Swell.*

UNDERWOOD — Richard Underwood[2]

Richard Underwood (1815-1877), Church of England clergyman, was the son of Richard and Harriett Underwood of Hereford. He was educated at St John's College, Oxford (BA 1841; MA 1843), and entered the Church. He was curate of Broadwell from at least 1842 to 1845, and vicar of All Saints', Hereford, from 1859 to 1877. In the 1851 census Underwood was listed as a clergyman without the cure of souls, a visitor at the home of James and Ann Herring at Horsham, Sussex. He never married and in 1861 and 1871 he was living at Hereford with his widowed mother, Harriett (b. ±1781).

1842: 20 Jan., 27-28 Apr., 26 May: *Wrote notes of invitation to Messrs. Martin, Debary, Underwood &c.* 29 May, 1 Jun: A dinner party: our Guests being Mr. & Mrs. Perkins, Mr. Underwood (Curate of Broadwell,) ... 2 Jun., 16 Aug., 31 Aug., 20 Sep., 27 Sep., 28 Dec.

1843: 11 Aug., 16 Aug., 26 Sep., 9 Nov., 13 Dec.

1844: 17 Apr., 20 Apr., 26 Apr., 1 May, 10 May, 21 Aug., 29 Aug., 4 Sep., 7 Sep: *With M.W. drove to Longborough to make a first visit to Mr. and Mrs. Underwood, and their daughter, parents and sister of the respectable Curate of the parish, now, and for some time past, resident with him... Mr. U. Senr. is a Herefordshire man, and was brother to a Canon of Hereford, and Vicar of Ross: — was a Solicitor, and secretary to Bp. Huntingford, when he held that the See of Hereford.* 18 Sep., 24 Sep., 7 Oct., 11 Oct., 4 Dec: *All the Underwoods from Broadwell called upon us: the Curate with his father, mother and sister.*

1845: 7 Jan., 21 Jan., 30 Jan., 13-14 Feb., 20 Feb., 22 Mar: *Mr. Underwood performed the service.* 26 Mar., 31 Mar., 3 May: *Mr. Underwood called.* 25 Jun., 27 Jun.

1846: 5 Sep: Drove to Broadwell: left our cards at the Rectory for Mr. and Mrs. Potter: he has lately fixed there, as Curate, in the room of Mr. Underwood ...

UPHAM — John Upham of Upham's Library[3]

John Upham was a bookseller in Lower Walks, Bath.

1808: 4 May: *To Barlow's the Wine Merchant's, Upham's library &c. Walked with my beloved Margaret in Sidney Gardens &c.*

UPHAM & BEET — booksellers of Bond Street[4]

Upham and Beet bought the business previously run by John Rodwell and John Martin, which had traded as Rodwell & Martin, booksellers and publishers, of 46 New Bond Street and 40 Argyll Street, London. They supplied books to the Stow Book Society, which Francis Witts frequently referred to as the Stow Library. Their final premises were at 46 Bond Street, London.

1852: 22 Oct., 2 Nov., 6 Nov., 14 Nov., 27 Nov., 16 Dec., 24 Dec.

1853: 21 Jan., 7 Feb., 8 Mar., 11 Mar., 11 Mar., 22 Apr., 27 Apr., 20 May, 8 Jun., 24 Jun.

1854: 10 Feb., 18 Feb., 23 Feb., 7 Apr.

UPTON — John Upton and the Upton family at Clifton — *see also* Marriott *and* Smyth[5]

John Upton (±1766-1832), landed proprietor, was the son of John Upton, of Westmorland, and Mary, daughter of George Noble of Weston, co. Durham. He married, first, Dorothy (d. 1796), daughter of Christopher Wilson, bishop of Bristol; they had 1 son:

1 John (1796-1867); inherited the family estate of Ingmire Hall, Westmorland; died unmarried

Dorothy died either in childbirth or soon after. Upton married secondly, 1799, Florence (1769-1852), daughter of Thomas Smyth, of Stapleton, and sister of Sir Hugh Smyth, 3rd baronet, of Ashton Court. John and Florence had 1 son:

1 Thomas (1800-1843); succeeded to Ingmire Hall, Westmorland, on the death of his half-brother John; married, 1829, Eliza Way (1800-1870), daughter of Benjamin Way of Denham Place, Buckinghamshire; 2 sons:
    1 Unnamed; died in infancy
    2 John Henry Greville [later Smyth] (1836-1901); inherited the Ashton Court estate through his grandmother, Florence, and changed his name to John Henry Greville Smyth; created 1st baronet Smyth of Ashton Court

John Upton had three sisters: Mary (1764-1839), who married John Morland (1765-1819) of Capplethwaite; Margaret (±1780-1871), who remained unmarried and lived at Clifton (presumably the 'Miss Upton' in the diaries); and Jane (dates unknown), presumably the 'Jenny' referred to by Francis Witts on 17 August 1804. Upton also had two sisters-in-law living in the Bristol and Clifton area: Elizabeth Marriott and Margaret, Lady Smyth. Both were the daughters of Christopher Wilson. Margaret, Lady Smyth, was the sister of John Upton's first wife, Dorothy, and was married to the brother of his second wife, Florence. She was therefore John Upton's sister-in-law twice over.

1804: 1 Jan: *Called on Mr. Marshall, walked with Miss Upton, & with my mother & George visited Lady Francis Flood & the Leyards.* 3 Jan: *Compelled much against my will to accompany Miss Upton on a walk across the downs.* 28 Jan: *Accompanied in the Evening my Father & Mother Miss Upton & Mrs. Barton to the meeting of the Harmonic Society at Gloster House...* 21 Jul: *Walked Miss Upton & Hen. Manners.* 26 Jul: *Walked alone with Hankey & Miss Upton in the Evening.* 31 Jul., 2 Aug., 6 Aug., 17 Aug: *A grand Rout & Supper at Mr. J. Jervis's: Count Bonnelarhi of the party: pleasant on the whole long & interesting conversation with Eliz. & the Ports, Brandrams, Monck's, Adairs, Jenny Upton &c. &c.* 21 Aug., 29 Aug., 1 Sep., 6 Sep., 11 Sep., 23 Sep., 21 Dec: *... & the customary Badinage with Miss Upton...* 22 Dec: *Called upon the Townsend's & Uptons...*

1805: 31 Jan: *In the Evening at Mrs. Uptons Rout which the Wolseley party rendered agreeable to me.* 9-10 Nov., 14 Nov.

1806: 13 Feb., 15 Mar.

USHER — Henry Usher[6]

Henry Usher (±1816-1896), Church of England clergyman, was born at Lincoln, the son of Richard and Mellicent Usher. It is not known where he was educated, but it does not appear to have been at either Oxford or Cambridge. He was married to Alvira (±1819-1890), born at Holbeach, Lincolnshire; they had at least 1 son and 1 daughter:

1 Alexander (b. ±1843)

1 Selena Louisa (b. 1851)

In 1851 Usher was curate of Oddington, Oxfordshire, and by 1861 he was listed as curate of Broadwell, Gloucestershire. By the time of the 1871 and 1881 censuses, he was rector of Saltfleet, Lincolnshire.

1850: 19 Sep.

1851: 11 Apr: *Preparing for the discussion likely to take place at the approaching Ruri-decanal meeting on the question proposed by Mr. Usher, Curate of Oddington.* 23 Apr.

1852: 22 Jan: *... also with Mr. Usher, from whom I received a letter yesterday, pleading the cause of Mr. Wiggin, who is liable to indemnify a farmer of Oddington who had been charged a heavy sum for toll for over-weight in respect of a load of sand required for the building of the new church at Oddington.* 23 Jan., 27 Jan., 14 Apr.

1853: 30 Mar., 13 Dec.

1854: 16 Mar., 15 Apr., 19 Jul.

V

VALLÉ — Barto Vallé [1]

Barto Vallé's Italian Warehouse, Haymarket, was founded at Haymarket in 1761 by Bartolommeo Vallé. Another Italian food shop was established in the eighteenth century and already known as the 'Old Italian Warehouse' in 1753. Vallé's business was also known as Bartolommeo Vallé and Brother, Bartho Vallé & Brother, and Vallé, Bartholommeo. The original address was the Old Italian Warehouse, at the Orange Tree and Two Oil Jars, No. 175, St James's, Haymarket, London. By 1763 Vallé was offering produce from Cyprus, Corfu, Russia, North Africa, the East Indies, France, Spain, Holland, and Hungary. In the 1817 directory, the business was listed as 'B. Valle' at 21 Haymarket, and in the 1827 directory as 'Fred Valle' at the same address. The eastern side of Haymarket was at the time described as 'a pleasant promenade' with 'many eminent tradesmen's houses'. There were many foreigners settled in the neighbourhood and during the earlier eighteenth century the chapel in Oxenden Street had held services in Italian. The business was taken over in 1911 by Robert Jackson & Co., of Piccadilly, and was still selling 'Barto Vallé's Cream Virgin Olive Oil' in the 1920s.

1835: 26 Jun.

1842: 7 Apr.

1844: 6 Aug: *To Mr. F. Vallé, Haymarket, with an order for three dozen of Moselle.* 10 Aug., 16 Aug., 5 Sep: *Recd. a letter from Mr. Vallé, Wine merchant, in the Haymarket, in answer to mine of the 6th. Inst.* 7 Sep.

1848: 15 Apr: *From Barto Valle, Wine merchant, London, with a bill for Claret which he has lately supplied to me.* 17 Apr., 19 Apr.

VANDELEUR — Alice Vandeleur [2]

Alice Vandeleur, née Burton (b. ±1722), was the daughter of Thomas Burton and Dorothy Forster. She married, 28 March 1765, Crofton Vandeleur (1726-1795), son of John Vandeleur and Francis Ormsby. Alice and Crofton had 6 sons and 4 daughters:

- 1 Frances (1766-1832); died in Paris
- 2 Dorothy (1767-1850)
- 1 Thomas Burton (1767-1835), Irish barrister and judge
- 2 Crofton (d. 1806), Maj.-Gen.; commanded HM troops on Antigua; married Elisabeth Croasdaile (1782-1860); died of fever, 31 October 1806, and was buried in the churchyard at Falmouth, Antigua; 1 son:
  - 1 Crofton Thomas Croasdaile (±1806-1876)
- 3 Alice (b. 1771)
- 3 Richard (b. 1773)
- 4 Emily (b. 1774)
- 4 Frederick (1776-1813); died at the battle of Vittoria, Portugal
- 5 John Ormsby (1777-1828); married, 1805, Frances Moore (1777-1833); 2 sons, including:
  - 1 Crofton Moore (1808-1881)
- 6 William (1780-1843)

The above dates are conflicting in various records and should be carefully checked before quoting. The Irish branch of the Vandeleur family was descended from Maximillian Vandeleur, a Dutch merchant from the town of Middelburg in the province of Zeeland, who had settled in Kilrush, Ireland, in the seventeenth century.

1806: 4 Feb: *Supped at Mrs. J. Auriol's; besides ourselves, the Lady & her Husband, Gillibrand, the notorious Mr. Stackpole & his wife & a Mr. Jenner formed the party. Mr. & Mrs. Frampton & Mrs. & Miss Vandeleur had gone before supper.*

VANDERHORST — Elias Vanderhorst and the Vanderhorst family of Clifton — *see also* Taylor [3]

Elias Vanderhorst (1738-1816), merchant, was born at Charleston, South Carolina, the son of John Vanderhorst (1718-1740) and Mary Elizabeth Foissin (1715-1768). The Vanderhorst family was established in South Carolina towards the end of the seventeenth century by Elias's grandfather, a subaltern from Rotterdam who had followed William of Orange to England in 1688. From there he had emigrated to Charleston, where his son was born. Elias's mother Mary was also born in South Carolina; her family had left Paris to join Charleston's Huguenot community. Elias had at least two brothers, Arnoldus, whose son became governor of South Carolina, and William, and a sister, Elizabeth, whose grandson was the artist Washington Allston.

Elias inherited a considerable fortune when his father died during his infancy. In 1759 and 1760 he served in the wars against the Cherokees and afterwards became a merchant. He married, 1763, Mary [Elizabeth] Raven Cooper [or Cowper] (1742-1797); they had ten children, but only 2 sons and 5 daughters survived infancy:

- 1 Elizabeth Cooper (1753-1820); died unmarried
- 1 Elias (1763-1874); married, in South Carolina, 30 March 1784, unknown
- 2 Mary Cooper (b. 1767); married John Duncombe Taylor of Antigua
- 3 Harriet Cooper (1769-1837); married Henry Thomas Shewen of Swansea
- 2 Thomas Cooper (1773-1849), born at Charleston, South Carolina; married, at St Stephen's, Bristol, 1799, Mary Hannah Beale (1770-1806)
- 4 Anne Catherine (1780-1864); married John Rees of Carmarthen
- 5 Carolina Mary (1784-1802); died unmarried

An unfortunate business venture made Elias dependent on his mother-in-law's income. Health and financial problems probably prompted his emigration in 1774 with his family and mother-in-law to Bristol, where once again he established himself as a merchant. On 3 October 1787 he became a burgess of Bristol. On 4 May 1792 George Washington, as president, and Thomas Jefferson, as secretary of state, signed the appointment of Elias Vanderhorst as US consul for the port of Bristol and its environs. Elias declined his reappointment as consul in early 1816 and died shortly afterwards.

Many of the Vanderhorst family papers went to Eliza Vanderhorst who died unmarried in 1814. She left most of her possessions to her niece, Cordelia Duncombe Taylor. Cordelia married Alexander Moffat, of Antigua, who then took the name Duncombe. Thomas Cooper Vanderhorst also died without children and some of his papers passed to Cordelia.

1804: 21 Jul: *At a party at Ashton in the Evening, the Taylors, Miss Vanderhorst, Manners's, Weir, Horton &c.* 27 Aug: *a dull Party at the Manners's; met the Townsends & Miss Van Der Horst.* 30 Aug., 12 Sep., 13 Sep: *In the Evening accompanied two of the Miss*

Townsends & the Miss Manners's to Mrs. Van Der Horsts in the Garrison Parade in Queen Square. 17 Sep., 19 Sep., 23 Dec: *to visit the Vander Horsts: found Mr. Taylor, Miss V & Miss T. at home.*
1805: 5 Jan.

VANE — Eleanor Vane at Clifton — *see also* Straubenzee [4]

Eleanor Vane (1736-1818) was the youngest daughter of Sir George Vane (1685-1750), of Long Newton, Durham, and Ann Machon (1687-1769), who had married at the cathedral church, Durham, on 27 September 1722. She never married and was referred to by Agnes Witts as 'Old Mrs Vane' (Friday 14 March 1806), the term 'Mrs' being commonly used for elderly spinsters. Eleanor was then accompanied by her great-niece, Catherine van Straubenzee (1787-1870), daughter of Charles Spencer van Straubenzee (b. 1750) and Anne Theophilia Davison, and granddaughter of Phillip William Casimir van Straubenzee (1723-1765) and Jane Turner (d. 1772). On her mother's side, Catherine was also great-granddaughter of Sir George Vane.

Some sources state that Eleanor died in 1794, but this appears to be an error. She lived in New Bond Street, Bath, and was buried at St Michael's, Bath, on 21 February 1818, aged 81.

1806: 14 Mar: *Adjourned from there to a party at Mrs. Vane's, numerous & hot; played speculation with the young people.*

VANE — Charles William Vane [5]

Charles William Vane [formerly Stewart], 3rd Marquess Londonderry (1778-1854), army officer and politician, was born in Mary Street, Dublin, the son of Robert Stewart, 1st Marquess Londonderry (1739-1821), and his second wife, Frances (1750-1833), eldest daughter of Charles Pratt, 1st Earl Camden. He was half-brother to Lord Castlereagh. He was educated at Eton College, 1790-94, and entered the Army as a lieutenant at the age of 16, in Macnamara's Foot. Stewart (as he was then called) served in Flanders in 1794 and was ADC to the king in 1803. He distinguished himself under Sir John Moore in the Peninsular War, and was severely wounded at the battle of Kulm in 1813. He was promoted to major-general in 1810, lieutenant-general in 1814, and general in 1837.

Stewart was MP for Thomastown in 1800 and for co. Derry in 1800 and 1801-14. He was under-secretary for war and the colonies in 1807-09, and in 1813-14 he was envoy extraordinary and minister plenipotentiary to Berlin, and military commissioner with the allied armies. He married, first, at St George's, Hanover Square, Westminster, 8 August 1804, Catherine (1774-1812), fourth and youngest daughter of John Bligh, 3rd earl of Darnley; they had at least 1 son:

1 Frederick William Robert (1805-1871); succeeded as 4th Marquess Londonderry

He married secondly, at St George's, Hanover Square, Westminster, 3 April 1819, Frances Anne Emily (1800-1865), daughter of Sir Henry Vane-Tempest, 2nd baronet of Long Newton, Durham. Frances was therefore related to Eleanor Vane (*above*). As a result of his marriage Charles took by royal licence the name Vane in lieu of that of Stewart. He succeeded as 3rd Marquess Londonderry in 1822.

1827: 4 May: *The Marquis of Londonderry boldly, bluntly and uncomprisingly denounced Mr. Canning's policy altogether, and gave that as his ground for relinquishing his situation as Lord of the Bedchamber, professing to believe, that the Duke of Wellington had been very ill used.* 7 May: *In the Lords poor Visc. Goderich is baited in much the same manner by Lord Londonderry, Lord Winchelsea, Lord Ellenborough &c.*

VAN HAREN — Duco van Haren [6]

Duco van Haren (1747-1801), a Friesian nobleman, was the eldest son of the Dutch poet Onno Zwier van Haren (1713-1779). The van Harens were a distinguished Dutch family of German origin and, at this time, Hanoverian sympathies. Duco van Haren retired to Weimar in 1797 and died there in 1801. His son Pieter Willem (1774-1850) entered the Hanoverian service in the second half of 1790s, transferring later to England, where he appears to have served as an officer in the Royal Marines.

1798: 28 Aug., 2 Sep: *There is also a Club of Savans, the admittance into which is very easy, these meet every Thursday to dinner & Supper in the Hofjägers at the Saxon Post, & is a Society by which a young Man can profit much, having there an Opportunity of becoming acquainted with some of the most famous men in the Town & Neighbourhood. The Secretary, M. de Seckendorff is a very well informed young Man, singular in his manners, reserved to the world, & open to particular people. This Club is visited also by the Prince Hereditary:—attended by his Tutor a Dutchman, by name de Haren, a man of real worth, but haughty, & sometimes rather Frivolous.*
1799: 1 Sep: *dined drank Tea & supped at Court ... The Prince at Rudolstadt, in his way to which place, his Coach was overturned, M. de Haren much hurt by Baron de Schardt falling on him.*

VAN NOTTEN POLE — *see* Pole

VANSITTART — Nicholas Vansittart [7]

Nicholas Vansittart, Baron Bexley (1766-1851), chancellor of the duchy of Lancaster, was born in Old Burlington Street, Westminster, the son of Henry Vansittart (1732-1770), former governor of Bengal, and Emilia [Amelia] (1738-1819), daughter of Nicholas Morse, governor of Madras. He was educated at Christ Church, Oxford (1784), the Inner Temple (1786), and Lincoln's Inn (1788). He was called to the bar in 1791 and elected a bencher of Lincoln's Inn in 1812. In 1793, and in successive years, Vansittart published a number of pamphlets in support of Pitt's government; in 1796 he entered parliament as member for Hastings. In 1801 he went on a diplomatic mission to Denmark, and on his return he was made joint secretary of the Treasury, an appointment he again received in Grenville's administration. For a short time in 1805 he was secretary for Ireland.

In 1809 Perceval offered Vansittart the chancellorship of the exchequer, which he declined. However, on Perceval's assassination in 1812, Vansittart accepted the post, which he held until 1823. During his chancellorship he had the distinction of living at 10 Downing Street. In carrying out his duties, he showed only mediocre ability and contrived to make himself exceedingly unpopular. In 1823 he was created Baron Bexley and chancellor of the duchy of Lancaster, with a seat in the cabinet. He held this position until 1828. During the remainder of his life, which lasted until 1851, he took an active part in aid of religious and charitable societies.

Vansittart married, at All Saints', Fulham, 22 July 1806, Catharine Isabella (1778-1810), daughter of Sir William Eden, 1st Baronet Auckland. He is of particular interest in the diaries as he was rescued from Denmark by the Royal Navy alongside with the Witts family, and with them arrived at Leith on board HMS *Kite*.

1801: 1 Apr: *Captn. S. Digby, brought us safe into Leith Roads, where we moored about Midday ... Mr. Drummond, Mr. Talbot, Mr. Vansittart, Dr. Beeke, Mr. Chapman, & family, Mr. Fenwick, & family, Mr. Avison, Captn. Stephens, Lieut. Falconer, my Father's family, &c: Our baggage passed through the Customhouse without difficulty, & we dined a large party at the Leith Coffeehouse.*

1805: 17 May: *Mr Vansittart's chambers are No. 5, Stone Buildings.* 31 Jul: *Mr. Vansittart & Lord Leven called & sat some time with me.*

1823: 25 Jan: *The newspapers announce, that Mr. Vansittart retires from the Post of Chancellor of the Exchequer—He has been considered an able financier, but his health is said not to be equal to the fatigues of a Parliamentary campaign. In early life I met him at Copenhagen, when in the Winter of 1801-2 I was Secretary to Mr. Drummond (now Sir W. Drummond) Chargé des Affaires at that Court. Immediately before the rupture with the Northern powers and the first attack by a British fleet on Copenhagen, Mr. Vansittart was dispatched under Lord Sidmouth's administration, then just appointed, to co-operate with Mr. Drummond in the important negociations of the time. He was accompanied by Dr. Beeke, now Dean of Bristol. On the failure of the negociations and advance of the fleet we all returned to Britain on board of a sloop of war detached for that purpose. Since that time I have not had any personal acquaintance with Mr. Vansittart. He has the character of being a very pious man: he never shone as a debater in parliament.* 12 Feb: *It is announced that Mr. Vansittart is appointed Chancellor of the Duchy of Lancaster, in the room of C. B. Bathurst Esq. of Lidney Park in this County, formerly a Chairman of our Quarter Sessions.* 18 Feb: *Mr. Vansittart is raised to the peerage by the title of Baron Bexley.*

VAN STRAUBENZEE — *see* **Straubenzee**

VASHON — James Volant Vashon [8]

James Volant Vashon (1783-1845), Church of England clergyman, was born at Ludlow, Shropshire, the son of James Volant Vashon (1742-1827) and Jane Bethell (1743-1785). He was educated at Wadham College, Oxford (BA 1806; MA 1810), and was rector of Salwarpe, Worcestershire, 1818-45. He married, in Kent, 14 November 1821, Mary Ann (1796-1862), daughter of Christopher Mayhew (1756-1803) and Sarah Garrett (1756-1811); they had 1 son and 1 daughter:

1 James Garrett (1822-1831)
1 Marianna (1834-1887)

1805: 21 Mar: *Breakfasted with Adams, meeting Prower, Vashon, Smith & Strong.* 26 Mar: *Drank wine at Rounds. Met Messrs. Fort, J. Dunne, Gravenell, Barton, Vashon, Wilson, Moore & Leech: a pleasant party enough.*

VASSALL-FOX — Henry Richard Fox, later Vassall-Fox [9]

Henry Richard Fox [later Vassall-Fox], 3rd Baron Holland of Holland and 3rd Baron Holland of Foxley (1773-1840), politician, was the only son of Stephen Fox, 2nd Baron Holland (1745-1774), and Lady Mary Fitzpatrick (1747-1778). He succeeded as 3rd Baron Holland in 1774. He was educated at Oxford, and afterwards travelled on the Continent, meeting, in Naples, Elizabeth Vassall (1770-1845), wife of Sir Godfrey Webster. Lord Holland spent 1795 with Elizabeth Vassall at Florence and Lucca. They returned to London in May 1796, and their eldest son, Charles Richard Fox, was born on 6 November 1796. Sir Godfrey divorced his wife in 1797, and she and Lord Holland were then married, at Rickmansworth, Hertfordshire, on 6 July 1797. They had 4 sons and 3 daughters:

1 Charles Richard (1796-1873)
2 Stephen (1799-1800)
3 Henry Edward (1802-1859); succeeded as 4th Baron Holland
1 Mary Elizabeth (1806-1891)
2 Mary Elizabeth Pryer (1807-1888); married, 24 May 1830, Thomas Atherton Powys (1801-1861)
3 Georgiana Anne (1809-1819)
4 Charles Richard (1826-1873)

In 1800 Holland assumed the name of Vassall to safeguard his children's rights to his wife's West Indian fortune.

Lord Holland took his seat in the Lords in 1796. In 1806, his uncle, Charles James Fox, became foreign secretary and Holland was sworn a privy councillor later that year. Holland led the opposition to the Regency Bill in 1811, and attacked the orders in council and other strong measures of the government taken to counteract Napoleon's Berlin decrees. He denounced the treaty of 1813 with Sweden which bound Britain to consent to the forcible union of Norway, and he resisted the bill of 1816 for confining Napoleon in St Helena. He was chancellor of the duchy of Lancaster in 1830-34 and 1835-40 in the cabinets of Lord Grey and Lord Melbourne, and was still in office when he died in October 1840.

1827: 25 Apr: *The newspapers speak confidently of a coalition between Mr. Canning and the Whig party: Lord Lansdown is said to be on the eve of taking office; but not Lord Holland, nor Mr. Brougham.* 30 Apr: *There is little doubt, that Canning has affected a coalition with the Whigs, but the Marquis of Lansdown, Lord Holland and Mr. Brougham are not to take office as yet.* 4 May, 7 Sep.

1828: 11 Jan., 1 Feb.

1834: 28 Dec.

1835: 19 Apr.

VAUGHAN — John Vaughan [10]

Sir John Vaughan (1769-1839), barrister-at-law and attorney-general, was born at Leicester, the third son of James Vaughan (1740-1813) and Hester Smalley (1740-1791). He was educated at Rugby School and Queen's College, Oxford. Having left Oxford without a degree, he was admitted to Lincoln's Inn in 1786, and called to the bar in 1791. Vaughan joined the midland circuit, where his style of advocacy brought him popularity with juries. He was elected recorder of Leicester on 14 February 1798, and was created serjeant-at-law on 12 February 1799. A strong supporter of Pitt, Vaughan threw himself into the movement for raising funds for the war with France by public subscription.

Vaughan married, first, 20 December 1803, Augusta (1782-1813), second daughter of Henry Beauchamp, 13th Baron St John of Bletso; they had six children, including the following 2 sons and 3 daughters:

1 Augusta (1805-1880)
2 Barbara (1806-1869)
3 Hester (1807-1847)
1 John James Vaughan (1809-1881), Church of England clergyman
2 Henry Halford (1811-1885), judge

He married secondly, at St Marylebone, Westminster, 4 August 1823, Louisa (1785-1860), eldest daughter of Sir Charles William Rouse-Boughton and widow of St Andrew, 14th Baron St John of Bletso; they had 2 sons and 1 daughter:

1 Emily (1824-1898)
1 Charles Lyndhurst (1828-1895), Church of England clergyman
2 Edward St John (b. 1830)

Vaughan was appointed solicitor-general to Queen Charlotte on 1 May 1814, and was promoted to attorney-general in the Trinity vacation of 1816. In the Easter term of the same year he was appointed king's serjeant, and conducted the crown's case in March 1820 against Sir Francis Burdett for seditious libel following

Burdett's comments upon the 'Peterloo massacre' of 1819. In August 1821 Vaughan led for the crown in the prosecution for seditious conspiracy of George Edmonds and others, who had resolved to elect a 'legislatorial attorney' to represent Birmingham in parliament. He was raised to the exchequer bench following the resignation of Sir Robert Graham and was knighted on 24 November 1828.

1827: 9 Apr: *The judges of Assize opened their commission here this evening, The circuit had been allotted to Mr. Baron Garrow, and Mr. Baron Vaughan; but the former was seized with gout...* 10 Apr: *After divine service the business of the Assizes commenced, Mr. Baron Vaughan presiding in the Crown Court, whither I repaired. He appears an acute man, of very gentlemanlike manners, fluent in his address to the Jury, but not pretending to eloquence.* 19 Apr: *The counsel on both sides, Messrs. Ludlow & Twiss, conducted the business with great talent & judgment and Mr. Baron Vaughan charged the Jury with much impartiality and distinctness; perhaps, went over the ground rather too often, incurring the risk of confounding the Jury in the desire of leaving nothing unsaid.*

VAUGHAN — Thomas Vaughan [11]

Thomas Vaughan (1782-1843), singer, was born at Norwich, where he was a chorister at the cathedral under John Christmas Beckwith. His father died while he was still very young and he entered the musical profession under the patronage of Canon Charles Smith. In June 1799 he was elected lay clerk of St George's chapel, Windsor, where he attracted the notice of George III. On 28 May 1803 he was admitted a gentleman of the Chapel Royal, and about the same time he became vicar-choral of St Paul's Cathedral and lay vicar of Westminster Abbey. In 1806 he married Elizabeth Tennant, a soprano singer well known from 1797 in oratorio performances; they had 4 sons and 2 daughters:

1 Thomas Charles (b. 1806)
1 Elizabeth Sarah (b. 1809)
2 Anne (b. 1809)
2 Edward William (b. 1810)
3 John Stephen (b. 1812)
4 James Ford (b. 1816)

After ten or eleven years of married life Thomas and Elizabeth separated, and Elizabeth Vaughan was heard as Mrs Tennant at Drury Lane Theatre.

In 1811 Vaughan joined Charles Knyvett in establishing vocal subscription concerts in opposition to the Vocal Concerts, but on the death of Samuel Harrison in 1812 the two enterprises were merged, and from 1813 Vaughan became principal tenor soloist at all the prominent concerts and festivals. He sang at the Three Choirs Festivals from 1805 to 1836, and took part in the performance of Beethoven's ninth symphony in 1825. For twenty-five years he was the leading singer of oratorio in England. He died in 1843 and was buried in the west cloister of Westminster Abbey.

1823: 17 Sep: *The exquisite Vaughan, the powerful & scientific notes of Mrs. Salmon, the liquid & thrilling tones of Miss Stephens, the spirit and execution of Caradori, Mr. Sapio's fine tenor, the taste & simplicity of Miss Travis, the deep rolling tones of Bellamy, tho' far inferior to the exquisite judgment science & refinement of Bartleman, afforded a rich treat.* 18 Sep: *The performers distinguished themselves greatly. Mrs. Salmon, Miss Stephens, Miss Travis, Messrs. Vaughan, Bellamy & Hawes.*

1826: 12 Sep: ... *suffice it to mention Vaughan, William Knyvett and Miss Travis, all remarkable for chaste execution & a faultless accuracy, combined with taste & sweetness, indicative of the genuine English school to which they belong, and which has been graced by the names & talents of Bartleman, Harrison & Greatorex.* 13 Sep: *Vaughan was correct & sweetly harmonious; and Webbe's glee "When Winds breathe soft" by him & the other English Singers was a most winning, soothing melody, and well merited the encore, which it received.* 15 Sep: *Vaughan was delicate and graceful in "Softly rise"; and Phillips deservedly encored in a beautiful ballad, which he sang with a mellow strain and tasteful simplicity.* 25 Sep.

1829: 22 Sep: *Vaughan was chaste, elegant and correct in that beautiful cantata, "See, from the silent grove Alexis flies", which he delights to sing, and amateurs of good taste and feeling equally delight to hear; the music is by Pepusch, and he was admirably accompanied on the Violoncello by Lindley. But amidst the brilliancy of the modern school Vaughan's style is getting out of date, wanting force and point, and, perhaps, the quality of his voice is rather impaired: strange it is, that these singers last so long, and maintain their powers and station so successfully; Vaughan and Braham & Knyvett have kept their ground these thirty years or nearly.* 23 Sep: *Madame Malibran and Mr. Vaughan performed a delightful duet by Marcello—"Qual anelante cervo."* ... *Vaughan's first air was from Judas Maccabaeus, in which he was accompanied on the Violoncello by Lindley with unrivalled skill.*

VAUGHAN WILLIAMS — Edward Vaughan Williams — *see* Williams

VAVASOUR — Caroline Vavasour — *see also* William Vavasour [12]

Caroline Susan Vavasour (1816-1878) was the second daughter of Lt-Gen. Sir Henry Maghull Mervin Vavasour (*below*) and Anne (d. 1837), eldest daughter of William Vavasour of Dublin. She married, 1842, her first cousin William Vavasour (1819-1863) (*below*). After William's death, Caroline married secondly, 1868, William Wiggin (1820-1901). For entries regarding Caroline Vavasour after 24 September 1842 *see* William Vavasour.

1840: 11 Aug., 12 Sep: *Mrs. V. informed me in confidence that her son had formed an engagement with his cousin Caroline Vavasour, daughter to Lady Vavasour, with whom and her unmarried daughters he is now travelling.*

1841: 10 Aug: *E.F.W. and Sophy brought with them W. Vavasour to dine with us: he is looking forward to a marriage with his cousin, Sir H. Vavasour's sister, about the 24th. it will take place in London, whither Lady V. and her daughters are lately arrived from abroad. E.F.W. is to perform the ceremony.*

1842: 3 Feb., 5 Feb: *Called at "the Cottage"; where found Mr. & Mrs. V. and Mrs. W. Vavasour; the W. V's returned last Thursday night from Dublin.* 31 Mar., 12 May, 28 May,

VAVASOUR — Emily Vavasour — *see also* Dryden [13]

Emily Vavasour (1813-1845) was the eldest daughter of Richard and Julia Vavasour. See the entry for Richard Frederick Vavasour for full family details. Emily was born at Rochdale, Lancashire. She married, 1839, Leopold Erasmus Dryden (1792-1846). They lived at East Woodhay in Hampshire and had 1 daughter:

1 Helen (1840-1885); married William Macfarlane

For entries after 12 June 1839 *see* Dryden.

1837: 12 Jan., 23 Aug: *Rode with my son to Stow: he joined E. & S. Vavasour in a ramble while I transacted business* ... 12 Sep., 21 Nov., 23 Dec.

1838: 23 Jan., 11 Apr: ... *Also that Leopold Dryden had proposed to, and been accepted by Emily Vavasour.* 14 Apr., 17 Apr., 8 May, 12 May, 16 May: *E.F.W. conducted Emily Vavasour, as Bride maid ...* 17 May, 21 May, 23 May, 4 Jun., 9 Jun: *In the Evening a cheerful and kind note from E.F.W. brought by Mr. Vavasour's servant from Whichford, whither he had taken Emily to pass a day or two with her sister.* 12-13 Jun., 23 Jul., 25 Jul., 30 Jul., 2 Aug: *Called at the Rectory, and sat for half an hour with the Rector, his lady, and Emily Vavasour, Leopold Dryden, who is there on a visit to the lady of his choice, consulted with me on matters of a legal nature connected with his preferment at Leek Wotton.* 8-9 Aug., 11 Aug., 13 Aug., 16 Aug., 20 Aug., 29 Aug., 6 Oct., 23-24 Oct.

1839: 22 Jan: *Emily gone to-day to Whichford to be with her sister while E.F.W. is absent at Worcester at the Ordination.* 3 Feb., 5 Feb., 15 Feb., 16 Mar., 18 Mar., 21 Mar., 26 Mar., 28 Mar., 3 Apr., 12 Apr: *Rode to Stow: called at the Rectory, where saw Mr. and Mrs. V. and Emily, to whom I presented in my wife's name a little bridal remembrance: she is recovering from her late indisposition, and, I presume, will become Mrs. L. Dryden in the month of May.* 22 Apr., 25 Apr., 1 May, 3 May, 18 May, 25 May, 10 Jun, 12 Jun: *Mrs. Witts and I went in our open carriage to breakfast at the Rectory, Stow, on occasion of the wedding of Leopold Dryden and Emily Vavasour.*

VAVASOUR — Emma Vavasour — *see also* Dod [14]

Emma Matilda Vavasour (1818-1907) was the third daughter of Lt-Gen. Sir Henry Maghull Mervin Vavasour (*below*) and Anne (d. 1837), eldest daughter of William Vavasour of Dublin. Emma was the niece of Julia Vavasour and the sister of Caroline, who married William Vavasour. She was therefore also a cousin to Sophy Witts, née Vavasour, which explains the closeness between them. She married, 1852, John Whitehall Dod (1823-1878). For entries regarding Emma after 24 August 1852 *see* Dod.

1840: 11 Aug.

1842: 9 Jan., 17 Jan: *The whole party, except Leo. Dryden, who was unwell, and with the addition of Miss Vavasour, daughter of Lady V. who with her mother is now staying at Leamington, went to the Warwickshire Hunt Ball, at Stratford on Wednesday, a very brilliant assembly.*

1844: 21 Jan: *Mr. Vavasour, with his nephew, Sir Henry Vavasour... He has been educated much abroad, travelled much with his parents on the Continent, and lately returned from Naples, and its environs, where Lady V. has been sojourning with her youngest daughter, who has engaged herself to marry a Swiss officer in the Neapolitan service.* 16 Apr: *Mrs. W. Vavasour has recd. from abroad intelligence that a projected and settled union between her sister and a Swiss Officer in the Neapolitan Service, Amadée de Moralt, has been broken off, the gentleman probably finding the lady's fortune less than he expected, and pleading a prior engagement with better prospects revived... Emma Vavasour grieves, and wears the willow, kindly pitying, and romantically exonerating from blame her late swain; Lady V. may chew the bitter cud for miscalculation, in preferring the continent and foreign lovers to England and a home connection; and others of the family will consider that the young lady has had a narrow escape...* 16 Jun.

1846: 15 Aug., 21 Aug., 31 Aug., 31 Oct., 2 Dec., 9 Dec., 31 Dec.

1847: 11 Feb., 8 Mar: *Called at "the Cottage": Mrs. Vavasour gone to see the family at Maugersbury—Emma Vavasour ill with measles.* 15 Apr., 20 Apr., 13 Jul: *To Maugersbury House, where found the W. Vavasours at home, with Emma, who is lately returned from visits to Lady Styles at Chester, and Mrs. Donnington Jefferson in Yorkshire.* 20 Jul., 2 Aug., 23 Aug., 8 Sep., 16 Sep., 18 Sep., 30 Sep., 14 Oct: *... as we arrived met Emma Vavasour on horseback, on the way to call at the Vicarage, Stanway.* 26 Oct., 7 Nov., 22 Nov., 2 Dec., 10 Dec.

1848: 16 Feb: *... return home found Mrs. W. Vavasour and her sister Emma, who had walked from Maugersbury.* 4 Mar., 17 Mar., 15 Apr., 11 May, 12 Jun., 14 Jun., 19 Jun.

1850: 3 May, 25 May, 29-30 May, 4 Jun., 6 Jun., 20 Jun., 27 Jun.

1851: 20 May: *Drove to Sussex Square, situate in the fine modern appendage to the West end in the Bayswater region, to call on Emma Vavasour, who is visiting at the residence of Admiral Cator, with whose family she is a frequent guest for months at a time.* 22 May, 26 May.

1852: 7 Jun: *He announced to me what had not before been disclosed to my son and his wife, that an engagement had been formed in Yorkshire some months ago between Emma Vavasour, his sister, and a Mr. Whitehall Dod, only son and child of one of the representatives for North Shropshire, a young man connected with the Cayley family. He is somewhat younger than Emma: the connection is represented to be very eligible in point of station and fortune. He is now in Asia Minor, at Smyrna, with his Yacht, but is expected soon to return to England.*

VAVASOUR — Henry Maghull Vavasour and the Vavasour family of Spaldington, Yorkshire [15]

Sir Henry Maghull Mervyn Vavasour, 2nd baronet (1767-1838), army officer and landed proprietor, was the son of Lt-Col Henry Nooth [later Vavasour](1741-1813) and Anne Assheton-Yates (1738-1818), of Spaldington, daughter of Maghull Yates (d. 1757) and Elizabeth Trafford (d. 1728). Henry's paternal grandparents were Bridget Mervyn (d. 1769) and Henry Nooth (d. 1784), son of James Nooth, vicar-choral of Wells Cathedral, of Huguenot ancestry, and a Miss Winchcombe.

Through her mother, Elizabeth, Anne Assheton-Yates was the heir of Thomas Vavasour of Spaldington. Henry (the elder) took the name and arms of Vavasour on 26 March 1791, as directed by the will of Thomas Vavasour. He was created a baronet on 20 March 1801. With the union of Great Britain and Ireland in 1801, all new baronetcies were styled 'of the United Kingdom', and all holders of baronetcies created after that event have borne the title of baronets of the United Kingdom. Vavasour of Spaldington, having been created first, became the premier baronetcy as Vavasour of Spaldington and Melbourne, co. York.

The family of Vavasour came to England with William the Conqueror. They took their name, says Camden, from their office, being the king's vavasours, a little inferior to the dignity of a baron. Anciently they had had the article Le affixed to their name. Thomas Vavasour, 19th in descent from Manger le Vavasour, first of his family to settle in England, married Dorothy, daughter of Sir Ferdinando Leghe (d. 1679) of Middleton. Thomas settled his estate on his sole daughter, Mary Vavasour, and her descendants, on condition of their assuming the name and arms of Vavasour. Mary married, 1680, Sir Ralph Assheton, baronet, and had two sons, who died young, and three daughters. Anne, the eldest daughter, inherited her mother's estate at Spaldington, and married, 1701, Humphrey Trafford, of Trafford. They had five children—Humphrey, Cecil, Sigismund, Anne, and Elizabeth—but only Elizabeth (d. 1788) had children. She married Maile Yates, of Maghull, and had 3 daughters:

1 Anne-Assheton; married Sir Henry Vavasour, 1st baronet
2 Mary (d. 1794); married, first, John Aspinall, sergeant-at-law; secondly, Henry Aspinall, of Lincoln's Inn
3 Catherine Eleanora; married Robert Campbell of Asknish, Argyllshire

Maj.-Gen. Sir Henry Maghull Mervyn succeeded his father as 2nd baronet on 15 March 1813. He married, 28 November 1807, Ann (d. 1845), eldest daughter of William Vavasour of Dublin; they had 1 son and 3 daughters:

1 Anna Mervynia (1812-1898); married, 1839, Joseph Dunnington-Jefferson (1807-1880)

1 Henry Mervyn (1814-1912); succeeded as 3rd baronet; married, 27 August 1891, Alice Emily Georgiana Olivia Codrington (1848-1920)
2 Caroline Susan Vavasour (1816-1878); married, first, her cousin William Vavasour (1819-1863); secondly, at Bathwick, Somerset, 28 January 1868, William Wiggin (1820-1901)
3 Emma Matilda (1818-1907); married, 1852, John Whitehall Dod (1823-1878)

For Caroline up to September 1842, *see* Caroline Vavasour; after that date, *see* John Whitehall Dod. For Emma up to August 1842, *see* Emma Vavasour; after that date, *see* William Vavasour.

1801: 6 Jun: ... *to Mrs. Doig's, where we found neither a very numerous, nor a very pleasant party. Mr. Mosley &c. Sir D. Carnegie, Mrs. Scott, Major Vavasour &c.* 10 Jun: *Lady Lytteltons, accidental Music began, Miss Halifaxes sung, & Miss Morley; it was quite a squeeze: a Mr. Wood a nephew of Mr. Sheridan also sung in a very singular style. We met there the Hanbury's, Guydickens, Mrs. Scott & Miss Morley, Sir N. Dukinfield, Sir H. & Major Vavasour* ...

1827: 25 Sep: *Then we had Mr. & Mrs. Vavasour, and they brought with them Sir Henry & Lady Vavasour: Lady Vavasour is sister to the Rector of Stow; her spouse, the head of the Vavasours, a Major General, mean in appearance, and singularly plain; but well informed, and conversible, and has been much abroad. His conversation would be more agreeable & intelligible, but that a Sabre which in some skirmish cleft his nose, has given him a snuffling tone & inarticulate pronunciation, which makes the purport of his observations hard to be caught: he is deaf withal, and therefore, perhaps, his voice is raised to a discordant pitch; he is blind too of an eye, and the sightless but not motionless ball is barely shrouded under a pair of spectacles; but these are trifling deductions from the estimable qualities, for which I am well disposed to give him credit. His family seat is near York, but they are abandoning it for a long sejour on the Continent: having their children's education in view; why will English gentry take their treasures to France & Italy? losing the benefits of attachment to their native land but formed in tender years, risking their religious principles, and gaining superficial elegances at the expence most commonly of substantial and really useful acquirements.*

1838: 8 Jan: *He married a sister of the Rector of Stow, who survives him; he is succeeded by his only son Henry, a pleasing young man of three & twenty, there are two or three daughters.*

1842: 9 Jan., 17 Jan., 17 Aug.

1844: 21 Jan: *He has been educated much abroad, travelled much with his parents on the Continent, and lately returned from Naples, and its environs, where Lady V. has been sojourning with her youngest daughter, who has engaged herself to marry a Swiss officer in the Neapolitan service.* 16 Apr: *Lady V. may chew the bitter cud for miscalculation, in preferring the continent and foreign lovers to England and a home connection...* 24 Sep.

1845: 24 Apr: *Mrs. W. Vavasour is also a great invalid: and Lady Vavasour, in an alarming state of health, in great debility, has removed from Melbourn Park to the immediate neighbourhood of Exeter, for medical advice, and change of climate.* 2 Jun: *She brought a very indifferent account of the health of Lady Vavasour, now at Heavitree near Exeter, and supposed to be very near her end.* 8 Jun: *A note from Vavasour announced the death of Lady Vavasour near Exeter; to this I replied.* 17 Jun.

VAVASOUR — Henry Mervyn Vavasour [16]

Sir Henry Mervyn Vavasour, 3rd baronet (1814-1912), was born at Melbourne Hall, Melbourne, near Pocklington, Yorkshire, the only son of Sir Henry Maghull Mervyn Vavasour (1767-1838) and Ann Vavasour (d. 1845). Henry succeeded as 3rd baronet in 1838 and married, at St James's, Westminster, 30 June 1853, Louisa Anne (1823-1889), daughter of Richard Griffin, 3rd Baron Braybrooke (1783-1858) (known as Richard Neville until 1797 and Richard Griffin between 1797 and 1825), and Jane (1799-1857), daughter of Charles Cornwallis, 2nd Marquess Cornwallis. They had 2 daughters:

1 Unnamed infant (b. & d. 1854)
2 Constance (1856-1927); married, 1902, Alfred Bertie Hobart Hampden

---

1837: 4 Sep: *E.F.W. dined at the Vavasours to meet Mr. Vavasour, only son of Sir Henry V., and nephew of the Rector of Stow, who accompanied his Uncle from Bath, whither he had come to attend the funeral of his Aunt Miss F. Vavasour.* 5 Sep.

1838: 8 Jan: *E.F.W. had ridden to Stow, whence he brought back intelligence of the decease of Sir Henry Vavasour, of Milbourn Hall in the East Riding of Yorkshire, after a short illness.* 30 Apr: *Wrote to Newmarch on the same subject; also on my son's concerns, that since it appeared necessary that there should be additional Trustees to his marriage Settlt. it was probable that on the lady's side Sir H. Vavasour would be appointed, and that Edwd. would take it as a favour, if Frederick Newmarch would consent to act in that capacity.*

1844: 21 Jan: *Mr. Vavasour, with his nephew, Sir Henry Vavasour; formed part of my congregation, and remained till nearly the time of evening service, taking luncheon with us: they walked. I had not met Sir H. V. since he was a schoolboy; his countenance is plain, but his manners good and quiet, and I should judge him to be sensible and well informed. With a nominally good estate, and considerable expectations, his mother being liberally jointured, this young man has but a scanty income at present, so as to render a residence at his seat in Yorkshire inexpedient. He has been educated much abroad, travelled much with his parents on the Continent, and lately returned from Naples, and its environs, where Lady V. has been sojourning with her youngest daughter, who has engaged herself to marry a Swiss officer in the Neapolitan service.* 30 Jan.

1850: 4 Jun., 20 Jun: *Mr. Vavasour joined me after I had been conferring on Poor Law administration with Mr. Winter and Mr. Beman, and I accompanied him to "the Cottage", where I had been invited to dinner, Mr. Ogle being the only other guest. Mr. and Mrs. W. Vavasour and Emma, Mr. & Mrs. V., Ogle & myself formed the party.* 27 Jun: *Mr. Vavasour drove with me some distance on my way homeward; the departure of his son, Caroline, & Emma for London on their parliamentary business is deferred.*

1851: 6 Mar: *E.F.W. called on me to consult me as to his Correspondence with Sir H. M. Vavasour in respect of their Co-Trust — and the idle scruples of the latter about accepting an investment by mortgage of the sum of £3000, recently paid over by Sir H.V. to W. Vavasour in right of his wife.* 20 May.

1852: 17-18 Apr., 20 Apr: *On my way home met Sir H. Vavasour and his sister, who had been calling upon me, and were riding further for exercise.* 22 Apr: ... *other Guests were Sir Henry Vavasour, Mrs. W. Vavasour, Mrs. M. Vavasour, Mr. Stavely, Mr. and Mrs. W B Pole, Mr. and Mrs. Winter. All went off agreeably, Mrs. W.V. sang, and conversation did not flag.* 24 Apr., 26 Apr., 29-30 Apr., 1 May, 6 May, 11-13 May, 7 Jun: *I betook myself to the Queen's Hotel, Cork Street, and had hardly settled myself there, when Sir H. Vavasour called upon me, for whom I had brought a small parcel from his sister. He announced to me what had not before been disclosed to my son and his wife, that an engagement had been formed in Yorkshire some months ago between Emma Vavasour, his sister, and a Mr. Whitehall Dod, only son and child of one of the representatives for North Shropshire, a young man connected with the Cayley family. He is somewhat younger than Emma: the connection is represented to be very eligible in point of station and fortune. He is now in Asia Minor, at Smyrna, with his Yacht, but is expected soon to return to England.* 10 Nov., 13 Nov.

1853: 28 Jan: *The funeral is fixed for Wednesday next at Broadwell; Sir H.M. Vavasour, Marmaduke Vavasour, and myself are invited to attend: the former are probably to be my guests.* 1-3 Feb., 19 Mar: ... *who informed me of the recent death of Mrs. Campbell of Bath, an old lady a connection of the Baronet Vavasour's family* ... 20 Mar:

She has heard from her Brother, Sir Henry Vavasour, that, as to her share of the old Vavasour estate at Spaldington, Mrs. Campbell has left to him one moiety, and the other equally divided between his three sisters, Mrs. Jefferson, Mrs. W. Vavasour, &c. Mrs. Whitehall Dod. 15 Apr: *She communicated to me, but not before I had received the intelligence from another quarter, that her brother Sir. Henry is engaged to marry the Hon. Louisa Neville, a younger daughter of Lord Braybrooke: reported to be pleasing, 31 years of age, and with a fortune of £10,000: he is 38 years old, and the connection is altogether suitable: the recent windfall by Mrs. Campbell's decease places him in easy, though not in affluent circumstances.* 26 Jun: ... *to join his wife, who has been visiting Mr. and Mrs. Whitehall Dod, at their residence near Conway, and who accompanies them to-morrow to the metropolis, that all may attend the wedding of Sir H M Vavasour, which is fixed for Thursday next; the ceremony to be performed at St. James's Church, Piccadilly, in which parish Lord Braybrook's Town house in Burlington Street is situate.*

1854: 8 Jun: ... *chatted for a few minutes with Mrs. W. Vavasour. Her Brother, Sir Henry, is made happy by the birth of a daughter.* 19 Jul: *The newspaper announces the death of the infant daughter of Sir H. and Lady Vavasour, five weeks old.—Wrote to Mrs. W. Vavasour a note of condolence on the occasion.*

VAVASOUR — John Vavasour of Rochdale, Lancashire [17]

John Vavasour (b. 1791), merchant, was born at Rochdale, Lancashire, the third son of merchant Thomas Hippon Vavasour (1750-1819), of the Butts, Rochdale, Lancashire, and Penelope (1757-1826), daughter of Edmund Smith and Penelope Bill. For details of John's siblings *see* Julia Vavasour under the entry for Richard Frederick Vavasour (*below*).

1834: 18 Nov: *While we were absent, Mr. John Vavasour called & left his cards.*

1838: 24 Mar: *Before dinner time arrived Mr. John Vavasour, Marmaduke's Brother, from Rochdale, where he had been visiting the family connections.* 25-27 Mar.

1848: 13 Nov: *Received a letter from Mr. Vavasour, informing me of the decease of a brother of Mrs. V., a half pay officer, at Jersey: he has long been in a deplorable state of health. Marmaduke Vavasour, when resident at Broadwell, whence once brought this gentleman to dinner at Upper Slaughter.*

VAVASOUR — Marmaduke Vavasour and the Vavasour family of Ashby-de-la-Zouch [18]

Marmaduke Vavasour (1797-1879), Church of England clergyman, was the youngest son of merchant Thomas Hippon Vavasour (1750-1819), of the Butts, Rochdale, Lancashire, and Penelope (1757-1826), daughter of Edmund Smith and Penelope Bill. He was brother to Julia, the wife of Richard Frederick Vavasour (*below*), rector of Stow-on-the-Wold. For more details of Marmaduke's siblings *see* Julia Vavasour under the entry for Richard Frederick Vavasour.

Marmaduke Vavasour was educated at Brasenose College, Oxford (BA 1822; MA 1822), and was ordained deacon on 22 December 1822 and priest on 21 December 1823. His first clerical appointment was as stipendiary curate to his brother-in-law, Richard Vavasour, at Stow-on-the-Wold, from 22 December 1822. He was then appointed stipendiary curate of Lower Swell on 22 May 1827, and of Broadwell with Adlestrop on 9 December 1828. He was vicar of Ashby-de-la-Zouch, Leicestershire, from 1833 to 1875, and honorary canon of Peterborough from 1851 to his death in 1879.

Vavasour married, at Severn Stoke, Worcestershire, 19 October 1826, Mary Anne (1795-1881), daughter of John Francis Seymour St John (1761-1832), prebendary of Worcester, and Frances Fleming (1764-1853); they had at least 3 sons and 5 daughters:

- 1 Penelope (1827-1858); married, at Ashby-de-la-Zouch, Leicestershire, 23 January 1849, John Morewood Gresley (1816-1866); 5 sons:
  - 1 Nigel Walsingham (1850-1909), Church of England clergyman
  - 2 Geoffrey Ferrers (1851-1935), Church of England clergyman
  - 3 William Stuckley (1852-1923)
  - 4 Roger St John (1854-1935), Church of England clergyman
  - 5 Laurence Stafford (1855-1941)
- 1 John St John (b. & d. 1829); born and died at Broadwell, Gloucestershire
- 2 Frances Barbara (1830-1871); married, at Ashby-de-la-Zouch, Leicestershire, 11 January 1853, Montagu Webster (1820-1904), Church of England clergyman; 3 sons and 3 daughters:
  - 1 Edward Montagu (1854-1936)
  - 1 Louisa Janet (1856-1929)
  - 2 Reginald Henry (b. 1858)
  - 2 Mary Anne Penelope (1860-1938)
  - 3 Arthur Vavasour (1868-1933)
  - 3 Ethel Barbara (1871-1944)
- 3 Mary Anne Elizabeth (1831-1905); married, at Ashby-de-la-Zouch, Leicestershire, June 1853, John Denton (1830-1903), Church of England clergyman; 3 sons and 3 daughters:
  - 1 Charles St John (1858-1933)
  - 1 Mary Cecil Penelope (1859-1927)
  - 2 Alice Louise (1861-1927)
  - 2 Henry St Aubyn (b. 1862)
  - 3 Florence Edith (b. 1864)
  - 3 John Fleming St Andrew (1872-1949)
- 4 Louisa Jane (1832-1901); married, at Ashby-de-la-Zouch, Leicestershire, July 1867, Joseph Taylor (b. 1830), solicitor; 2 sons and 1 daughter:
  - 1 Arthur Vavasour (1868-1942)
  - 1 Edith Louisa Josephine (b. 1868)
  - 2 Robert Joseph (b. 1869)
- 2 Marmaduke Walter (1833-1877); married, at Kingsclere, Hampshire, April 1860, Sybil Catherine Holdsworth (1842-1926); 1 son and 1 daughter:
  - 1 Marmaduke Vavasour (1861-1902)
  - 1 Caroline Sybil Frances (1862-1906); died unmarried
- 5 Augusta Sophia (1836-1922); married, at Ashby-de-la-Zouch, Leicestershire, June 1864, Edward William Cradock Middleton (1839-1887)
- 3 John Francis Stukeley St John (1837-1900), Church of England clergyman; married, at North Church, Hertford, 21 April 1868, Eleanor Elizabeth Brooke (1838-1924); 5 sons and 1 daughter:

1 Richard St John (1869-1937)
2 Walter Hippon (1870-18810)
3 Nigel Marmaduke (1871-1952)
4 Edmund Brooke (1873-1899)
1 Eleanor Maude (1874-1938)
5 Thomas Francis Stukeley (1876-1914)

Marmaduke Vavasour's youngest son, John Francis Stukeley Vavasour, was rector of Farmington, Gloucestershire, in 1872-73, and then of Snelland, Lincolnshire, from 1872 to 1900. Francis Witts was his godfather.

1823: 22 Mar., 3 Apr: *I dined at Mr. Vavasour's, the Rector's of Stow, meeting his brother in law, Mr. M. Vavasour.*

1827: 21 Feb: *It happened, that Mr. Marmaduke Vavasour, brother-in-law to the Rector of Stow, and who has been a good deal in this neighbourhood, having been ordained to the Curacy of Stow, and assisted the Dean of Gloucester two or three years ago at Oddington, was looking out for a professional engagement; having on his marriage last summer relinquished a Curacy, which he held in Worcestershire...* 25 Jun: *We made calls ... & Mr. & Mrs. M. Vavasour, who are come to reside in the house late occupied by Mr. Lee Compere; Mr. Vavasour being curate of Lower Swell in my room; he has but just entered on his charge.*

1826: 27 Sep: *I dined and slept at Mr. M. Vavasour's at Broadwell, meeting Messrs. Jeaffreson, Bowen, Winter & Jones. Mrs. M. Vavasour did not make her appearance; she is daily expecting her accouchement. Mr. M. Vavasour succeeds Mr. Jones as Curate of Broadwell, & Mr. W. B. Pole, follows Mr. M. Vavasour as Curate of Lower Swell.*

1829: 17 Jun., 27 Jun., 3 Jul., 11 Aug.

1830: 14 Apr., 10 May, 26 May.

1832: 27 Apr: *We had a party of our neighbouring friends to dinner—Mr. & Mrs. East, Mr. & Mrs. M. Vavasour, Mr. & Mrs. Ford, Miss Ford & Mr. W. Ford, and Mr. F. Aston, who slept here.*

1833: 12 Mar., 14 Oct., 6 Nov: *Ashby we regarded with interest as the future residence of our friend M. Vavasour.*

1836: 24 Aug: *Mr. Marmaduke Vavasour, in addition to the subscriptions of larger amount raised in the parish and neighbourhood, has resorted to the measure of soliciting half crown subscriptions in the places where he is known, in order to increase the resources for this greatly needed addition to the Church accommodation in his parish.*

1837: 13 Mar.

1838: 6 Jan: *A letter from Marmaduke Vavasour, congratulating us on Edward's having passed his University Examination with so much credit, and on his having taken Deacon's Orders; expressing much satisfaction at the engagement between my son and his niece Sophy Vavasour, of whom he speaks in very favourable and, I am convinced, just terms of approbation; and finishing by soliciting me on the score of old friendship, and the approaching connection between the families, to be Godfather to his seventh child, a boy, with whom Mrs. M. Vavasour has lately presented him.* 9 Jan., 9 Mar: *A letter from Marmaduke Vavasour, pressing me to fix a time for visiting him & his lady at Ashby de la Zouch, there to stand as Godfather to his infant son.* 10 Mar., 15 Mar., 23 Mar., 24 Mar: *Very cordially received by my friends the M. Vavasours; much conversation as to the prospects of my son and his fiançee.* 25 Mar: *Marmaduke Vavasour's duties are very heavy; he is assisted in them by a Curate...* 26-27 Mar., 1 May, 16 May: *Marmaduke Vavasour, who with his wife had arrived on the preceding evening from Ashby de la Zouch, preceded us to be ready to perform the sacred rite.* 17 May, 23 May.

1839: 12 Jun: *Mr. Marmaduke Vavasour came from Ashby de la Zouch to perform the marriage ceremony: Edward and his wife were of course of the party, also Mr. Charles Dryden, brother of the Bridegroom, a London Solicitor. Thus it was entirely a family party, not even Bridesmaids. Mr. & Mrs. Vavasour & their Son of course attended.* 13 Jun.

1838: 18 Mar: *The Sponsors were Capt. Witts, Marmaduke Vavasour, and Apphia Witts.* 25-26 Mar., 1 May.

1841: 5 Mar.

1842: 14 May: *After midday left the agreeable circle at the Vicarage, Stanway, Marmaduke Vavasour, Mrs. DeBurgh, and her child were also on the wing to pass a few days with the Vavasours at Stow.* 12 May: *Met by my son and Marmaduke Vavasour, who has been passing a day or two at Stanway.* 13-14 May, 8-9 Jun.

1843: 20 Dec., 23 Dec.

1847: 29 Jun., 19 Aug: *I dressed for dinner at the Unicorn Inn, where M W. called for me in the Chariot. We proceeded to dine at Mr. Winter's at Daylesford; where we met Marmaduke Vavasour and his daughter Penelope on a visit there... M Vavasour looks well, and his daughter appears to be a very pleasing girl.* 26 Aug.

1851: 20 May: *Met a large party of the Vavasour connection; Marmaduke, with his married daughter, Mrs. Gresley, and her husband, an unmarried daughter, and a niece, Mrs. De Burgh.*

1852: 7 Apr: *E.F. W. drove to Ashchurch to meet Mrs. M. Vavasour, who had been staying with her nonagenarian Mother, Mrs. St. John, at Worcester, and is to pass the time at the Vicarage till Monday next, when she goes to visit the W. Vavasours at Lower Slaughter.* 17-18 Apr., 23 Oct., 4 Nov., 6 Nov., 8-15 Nov., 18 Nov.

1853: 28 Jan., 1 Feb: *He had travelled by Worcester and Evesham; and thence by a fly to "the Cottage" at Stow, expecting a cordial reception from his sister; but the morbid feeling in which she and her son indulge operated to prevent a meeting between the brother and sister, greatly to the surprise and distress of the former.* 2-4 Feb., 5 Feb: *My worthy, amiable, well informed and well principled friend, M. Vavasour, left me after breakfast, going to Cheltenham, where, and at Worcester, he purposes staying a day to two with friends before his return to Ashby de la Zouch.* 13 Feb., 20 Jun.

VAVASOUR — Richard Vavasour and the Vavasour family of Broadwell — *see also* **Arbuthnot, Burdett, Walmesley,** *and* **Witts** [19]

Richard Frederick Vavasour (±1784-1853), Church of England clergyman, was born in Dublin, the son of William Vavasour (1744-1819), a lawyer of Kildare Street, Dublin, and Anne (1747-1823), daughter of William Bull and Anne Brooke-de Capell Brooke. The Vavasour family was complicated and there is frustratingly little information. The picture is further obscured by the Vavasours' amazing tendency of marrying within the family. It is a triumph of familial identity that during that time of less than easy communications there should have been such a degree of contact and intermarriage. Richard Frederick Vavasour married a Rochdale Vavasour, and his sister married a Spaldington Vavasour; Richard's son, William, also married a Spaldington Vavasour, who through his aunt also happened to be a first cousin. There were four groupings of the family: the Hazlewood, Yorkshire, Vavasours (the most senior branch); the Melbourne and Spaldington, Yorkshire, Vavasours (the second branch); the Rochdale, Lancashire, Vavasours; and the Dublin Vavasours (the junior branch). They were all related and clearly they all kept in touch.

Kildare Street was in the fashionable area of Dublin and the Vavasours that had made it their home were well-to-do. In the churchyard of St Matthew's, Irishtown, near Kildare Street, are the tombs of members of the Vavasour family dating from 1762. Among them is that of William Vavasour (1744-1819), father to Richard Frederick Vavasour. William was the son of Peter Vavasour (1722-1782), a younger son of the Vavasour house of Spaldington and an officer in the dragoons. When quartered in Ireland, Peter had married Mary Hayes, an heir in ward to the earl of Bessborough. She was the daughter of Capt. William Hayes (d. 1720), of Dublin, and Jane Des Mynieres—a widow when she married William Hayes—the third daughter of Henry Ponsonby, uncle of William Ponsonby, 1st Baron Bessborough (1659-1724). The earl of Bessborough, Brabazon Ponsonby (1679-1758), son of William, who succeeded as 2nd baron and was created 1st Earl Bessborough in 1739, was a second cousin to Mary Hayes. He was also her guardian. Peter Vavasour, Mary's husband, was buried at St Matthew's, Irishtown, and presumably Mary was buried there too.

In 1792 William Vavasour (1744-1819) took a lease of 60 acres of marshland between Beggar's Bush and Ringsend, and reclaimed it by embanking the River Dodder; he named it Vavasour Square. He also held substantial property at Williamstown to the north-west of Dublin. What is now The Avenue, Williamstown, was previously known as Vavasour Avenue. William had at least one known sister, Frances (1741-1816), who married Thomas McAuliffe (1754-1818).

Anne Bull (1747-1823), wife of William Vavasour, had a younger sister, Sophia, who married William Pollard, and a niece, Sophia Forster Pollard, who married John-Hill Forster (son of Forster-Hill Forster) who ended up the in the Marshalsea prison, Dublin—a debtor's prison. Sophia moved to Cheltenham and features in the diaries—adding some colour.

Besides Richard Frederick, William Vavasour and Ann Bull had three children: Henry William (±1783-1851), a captain in the Royal Engineers; Anne (d. 1845), who married Sir Henry Maghull Mervyn Vavasour, 2nd baronet (1767-1838), of Melbourne Hall, near Pocklington, and of Spaldington, Yorkshire; and Frances (d. 1837), who remained unmarried and died at Bath. Henry had a distinguished military career; as the Vavasour family was so pertinent to the later Witts family it is worth relating his career at length.

Henry involved himself with Louisa, daughter of Sir George Dunbar (±1750-1811) and Jane Rowe (d. 1830). Whether they were ever married is unclear, but presumably not, as his daughters born at Quebec were listed as the daughters of Henry William Vavasour and Louisa Rudall. Louisa had previously married, at St Pancras, 3 September 1806, George Rudall (1781-1871), lieutenant in the South Devon Militia, of Crediton, Devon. They had at least 1 daughter, Louisa Maria (1811-1831). George Rudall lived for the remainder of his life with his nephew, Francis, in Warren Street in the parish of St Pancras, where he worked as an instrument maker.

Notwithstanding the social ostracism their association may have aroused, Henry and Louisa presumably cohabited for the reminder of their lives; being stationed overseas would have been of benefit in this circumstance. Henry and Louisa appear to have had at least five children, including:

1 Henry J. (b. 1819); born in Canada; became an ensign by purchase in the 18th Foot, 7 December 1838
2 Mervin (±1821-1866); born at Montreal; married, at Manchester, 23 October 1860, Frances Elizabeth Hartwell Dickson; at least 2 daughters
1 Florence (b. 1823); born at Quebec
2 Georgiana (b. 1825); born at Quebec

Henry William Vavasour received a commission as second lieutenant in the Royal Engineers in 1804, and was one of the first of this corps to study surveying at the Trigonometrical Survey. Promoted to lieutenant on 1 March 1805, he served in the Cape Colony from 7 January 1806 to 11 February 1809, when he became a second captain and was posted to Ireland. On 9 April 1811 he was sent to Gibraltar; while based there he took part in the Peninsular War and the defence of Tarifa, Spain, receiving a promotion to captain on 21 July 1813. After a brief tour of duty at Chatham, England, he was sent to British North America. He arrived at Quebec on 1 October 1815, and was initially stationed there.

Vavasour served as senior engineer at Fort George, Upper Canada, where he was responsible for surveying military reserves and roads, and building and maintaining forts on the Niagara frontier. His duties at Fort George brought him into closer contact with the civilian population than most regular army personnel. As a result, he was aware of the post-war unrest in the area, and in 1818 recommended the establishment of a board of inquiry to investigate the claims of civilians who had suffered losses or had not been paid for services rendered during the war of 1812 with the United States.

Vavasour had applied for land near Niagara in the previous year but was rejected under the terms of an order in council of 1797 that denied grants to soldiers on full pay. Lord Dalhousie visited the Niagara frontier in July 1819, and although he first commented that Vavasour was 'particularly intelligent & entertaining', he later noted in his journal that he found the officer to be 'a Bombastic & discontented soldier, constantly speaking without any regard to truth.' Vavasour returned to Quebec in September 1823 and served there until his departure for England on 27 June 1825.

Henry Vavasour was next stationed in Scotland from 1826 to 1829. In October of the following year he was promoted to lieutenant-colonel and became commanding engineer in Ceylon, a post he occupied for almost six years. He held the same post at Chatham from 1837 to 1839, and at Harwich from 1841 to 1845. He was promoted to colonel on 22 April 1845, and served in Dublin as senior engineer from 1847 to 1849. On 7 July he was again posted to British North America, this time as commanding engineer for the Province of Canada with headquarters in Montreal. In this capacity he was responsible for all military surveying, fortifications, and works, including the maintenance of the canals on the Ottawa and Rideau rivers. He was one of the few British officers to have served as a junior officer on the Canadian frontier and later to hold a commanding position in Canada. Referred to in an obituary as a 'gallant and much respected officer,' Henry Vavasour died in office and was interred in the military burial ground at Montreal.

Henry's brother, Richard Frederick Vavasour (±1784-1853), married, 1 July 1812, at St Chad's, Rochdale, Julia (1789-1865), daughter of Thomas Hippon Vavasour (1750-1819) and Penelope (1757-1826), daughter of Edmund Smith and Penelope Bill. Thomas Hippon Vavasour was born at Rothwell, near Oulton, Yorkshire, the son of John Vavasour, a tanner, of the Butts, Rochdale. He and his wife Penelope had at least 4 sons and 6 daughters:

1 John (b. 1779); died young [?]
2 Walter (b. 1780)
1 Mary (b. 1781)
2 Elizabeth (b. 1783)
3 Ann (b. 1784)
4 Penelope (b. 1786)
5 Jane (b. 1787)
6 Julia (b. 1789)
3 John (b. 1791)
4 Marmaduke (1797-1879); *see above*

In the baptismal records there are clearly two Johns born to Thomas and Penelope, so it appears that the first John died young. Thomas Hippon was also presumably the brother of Marmaduke

Vavasour (1747-1798), who held property in Rothwell. The Vavasour family in Rothwell dates back to at least 1283, from which date there existed a family seal. This branch of the Vavasours was descended from the Vavasours of Hazlewood.

The Smith side of the family is also quite detailed. Thomas Hippon Vavasour, of the Butts House, Rochdale, Lancashire, married, 1777, Penelope (1757-1826), daughter of Edmund Smith and Penelope (1735-1761), born at Alton, Staffordshire, daughter of Robert Bill (1684-1751) and Lydia Hurst (1694-1769). Penelope Smith died in 1761, shortly after giving birth to a second daughter, Lydia. (For members of Julia Vavasour's extended family featured in the diaries, *see also* Arbuthnot, Burdett, *and* Walmesley.) Edmund Smith married, secondly, Mary Raynor. They had numerous children, including the following son and 3 daughters:

1 Mary
2 Jane
1 Isaac
3 Ann; married John Walmsley of Castlemere

Edmund Smith's brother, Thomas Smith (d. 1806), of Castleton Hall, married, 23 February 1774, Penelope Firth (1750-1823); they had several sons who died young and 4 named daughters:

1 Esther; married Sir William Burdett
2 Ellen; married John Entwisle of Foxholes, Rochdale
3 Harriet; married Sir Robert Arbuthnot
4 Mary; married Col Hugh Baillie of the Dragoon Guards

The Rochdale Vavasours were originally woollen merchants and had been living at Rochdale since at least the beginning of the eighteenth century. Later the family business interests appear to have widened. Thomas Hippon Vavasour, who had been born at Rothwell, Yorkshire, moved to Rochdale, where there were existing Vavasour connections.

Richard Frederick Vavasour (±1784-1853) and Julia Vavasour (1789-1865) had 1 son and 2 daughters:

1 Emily (1813-1845); married, 1839, Leopold Erasmus Dryden (1792-1846); lived at East Woodhay, Hampshire; 1 daughter:
    1 Helen (1840-1885); married, at St Mary's, Putney, Surrey, 30 August 1872, Walter Henry MacFarlane (1821-1897); 1 son and 3 daughters:
        1 Emmeline Vavasour (1873-1951)
        2 Mabel Gerard (1878-1962)
        3 Ethel Dorothy Dryden (1880-1959)
        1 Walter De Burgh (1881-1942)
2 Sophia (1815-1871); married, at Stow-on-the-Wold, 16 May 1838, Edward Francis Witts (1813-1886); 3 sons:
    1 Francis Edward Broome (1840-1913); *see below* under Witts
    2 Frederick Richard Vavasour (1843-1900); *see below* under Witts
    3 George Backhouse (1846-1912); *see below* under Witts
1 William Thomas (1819-1863); *see below*

Richard Vavasour was educated at Trinity College, Dublin (BA). He was collated in November 1812 and in 1816 he was made a prebendary of Kilmacduagh. In 1822 he resigned, and accepted preferment in England. He and Julia appear to have lived for some time at Rochdale; their eldest daughter Emily was born there in 1813, and baptised at St Chad's on 8 December 1813. Richard was inducted as stipendiary curate at Stow-on-the-Wold on 5 June 1822, and just over two months later, on 15 August 1822, he became rector, a position he was to hold for thirty-one years until his death in 1853. The advowson belonged to Henry Hippisley, so presumably some arrangement was struck. It is not known how the friendship between Henry Hippisley and Richard Vavasour began, but they presumably met at Oxford, where Richard was admitted *ad eundem* in 1834; he may also have been at Oxford after taking his degree at Trinity College, Dublin. What is clear is that the Hippisley family retained a friendly interest at Stow. Richard Vavasour was succeeded by a younger member of the family, Robert William Hippisley (1818-1901).

1823: 22 Mar., 3 Apr: *I dined at Mr. Vavasour's, the Rector's of Stow, meeting his brother in law, Mr. M. Vavasour.* 23 Apr.

1824: 17 Feb., 26 May. 7 Sep: *We had a dinner party: the Hon. Mr. & Mrs. Rice, and two daughters, from Oddington, Mrs. Rice, from Bourton on the Water, Mr. & Mrs. Price & Mr. C. Goold from Coln St. Dennis, & Mr. Vavasour formed the circle.* 16 Dec.

1825: 22 Jun., 15 Dec.

1826: 3 Mar., 28 Mar., 28 Jul., 22 Aug., 21 Dec.

1827: 21 Feb., 25 Jun., 21 Sep., 25 Sep., 2 Oct.

1828: 12 Feb., 23 Apr., 25 Jun., 2 Jul., 20 Aug.

1829: 27 Feb., 20 Mar., 15 May 20 May, 25 Jun., 12 Aug., 6 Oct., 24 Nov., 9 Dec.

1830: 14 Apr., 10 May.

1831: 11 Dec.

1832: 25 Apr.

1833: 1 Feb., 18 Oct., 25 Oct., 31 Oct.

1834: 23-24 Jul., 26 Jul., 7-9 Aug., 28 Aug., 18 Sep: *Edward drove his Mother to Stow to call on Miss Hippisley at the Vavasours.* 26 Sep., 30 Sep., 9 Oct., 19 Oct., 20 Oct., 23-25 Oct., 30 Oct., 7 Nov., 8 Nov., 19 Nov., 21 Nov., 27 Nov., 4 Dec., 17-18 Dec., 24 Dec.

1835: 1-2 Jan., 13 Jan., 15 Jan., 22 Jan., 29 Jan., 4-5 Feb., 12 Feb., 19 Feb., 26 Feb., 5 Mar., 2 Apr., 23 Apr., 27 Apr., 5 May: *Mr. Vavasour had heard to-day of the sudden death of his Aunt, Mrs. Pollard.* 27-28 May, 3-4 Jun., 17-18 Jun.

1836: 28 Jul., 4 Aug., 24 Aug., 27 Aug., 29 Aug., 8 Sep., 15 Sep., 22 Sep., 27 Sep., 29 Sep., 4 Oct., 6 Oct., 13 Oct., 22 Oct., 25 Oct., 27 Oct., 3 Nov., 10 Nov., 17 Nov., 24 Nov., 6 Dec., 8 Dec., 15 Dec., 21-22 Dec., 27 Dec., 29-30 Dec.

1837: 12 Jan., 9 Feb., 9 Mar., 13 Mar., 23 Mar., 30 Mar., 4-5 Apr., 13 Apr., 19 Apr., 4 May, 16 May, 23 May, 25-26 May: *Mr. Vavasour and his two daughters called upon us.* 1-2 Jun., 10 Jun., 14 Jun., 21-24 Jun, 29-30 Jun., 4 Jul: *Mr. & Mrs. Vavasour and their eldest daughter had called during our absence.* 11-13 Jul., 15 Jul., 21 Jul., 25 Jul., 2 Aug., 6 Aug: *In a walk with my son in the evening, he communicated to me what I was not at all surprized at hearing, that he had declared himself definitively not only to Sophy Vavasour, but to her parents, and had been accepted as the future husband.* 8 Aug., 9 Aug: *Rode to Stow, and had a long and satisfactory conversation with Mr. & Mrs. Vavasour on the engagement between my son and their daughter.* 9 Aug: *Rode to Stow, and had a long and satisfactory conversation with Mr. & Mrs. Vavasour on the engagement between my son and their daughter.* 10 Aug., 14 Aug: *We were to have passed the evening at the Vavasours, and to have met the Imhoffs and the Chamberlaynes &c. but tidings of the alarming state of Mr. Vavasour's sister at Bath hurried him off thither this morning, and the party was postponed.* 19 Aug., 20 Aug., 24 Aug., 27 Aug., 31 Aug: *Mr. Vavasour is not yet returned from Bath, but his sister has paid the debt of nature, and is to be buried tomorrow.* 4 Sep., 12 Sep: *These ladies, with a Mrs. Baillie, and a Mrs. Entwerle were coheiresses of the name of Smith, daughters of a wealthy manufacturer, I believe, at Rochdale, and Cousins of Mrs. Vavasour.* 14-15 Sep., 19 Sep., 22-23 Sep., 25-26 Sep., 29 Sep., 4 Oct., 6 Oct., 10 Oct., 12 Oct., 14 Oct., 2 Nov., 4 Nov., 9-10 Nov., 16 Nov., 21 Nov., 30 Nov., 1

Dec: *My son drove his mother to call on the Vavasours at Stow, and he remained to dine there.* 2-4 Dec., 7 Dec., 12-14 Dec., 16 Dec: *Mr. C. gives the painting; the expence of framing and fixing it and making the necessary alterations in the Chancel will be defrayed by Mr. Hippisley as Patron and Vavasour as Rector.* 21 Dec., 23 Dec., 28 Dec., 30 Dec.

1838: 9 Jan., 11 Jan., 13 Jan., 17-18 Jan., 21 Jan: *My son dined at the Rectory, & brought home a kind note from Vavasour, congratulating me on the manner in which he had performed the duty, the composition of the sermon &c.* 23 Jan., 28-29 Jan., 1-2 Feb., 5-6 Feb., 8 Feb., 14., 15 Feb: *Thence to the Vavasours, where my Son had been passing the forenoon, and where there was great and well-founded anxiety in consequence of a letter received this morning by Mr. V. announcing that his son had been for a fortnight seriously ill at Woodside near Liverpool with a pulmonary inflammation.* 17-18 Feb., 20-21 Feb., 24 Feb: *E.F.W. rode to Stow, and returned to dinner with the news that Vavasour reached home yesterday Even. accompanied by his Son, who has recovered very rapidly from his late serious indisposition.* 25-26 Feb., 8 Mar., 12 Mar: *E.F.W. rode before breakfast to Stow, whence he accompanied Mr. Vavasour and Sophy in their open carriage to Whichford, which neither the lady nor her father had yet seen.* 15 Feb., 17 Feb: *Conferred with Vavasour in a tête-à-tête at his Cottage on the settlements to be made on his daughter in contemplation of her marriage with my Son.* 22 Mar: *Called at the Rectory, where Vavasour conferred with me on the settlement proposed in contemplation of Edward's marriage, exhibiting to me some documents as to his property at Broadwell, and on which he proposes to give a security for £2000, the fortune of his daughter, to which she will be entitled on the decease of her parents; also as to a sum of £4000 belonging to Mrs. Vavasour, in her own disposal, and with which the Broadwell property was purchased, her Trustees having a mortgage on that property for the amount.* 28-29 Mar., 31 Mar., 4-6 Apr., 7 Apr: *Held a family conference with him as to the tenor of the settlements to be made on the marriage of my son, previously to the arrival of Mr. Vavasour, who came about two o clock to meet Mr. N.* 14 Apr., 21 Apr., 25 Apr., 28 Apr., 30 Apr: *After luncheon drove Sophy V. back to Stow: called at the Rectory, saw all the family party, conferred with Mr. V. as to the Settlements on the approaching marriage.* 2-3 May, 8 May, 10 May, 12 May, 15 May: *Mr. and Mrs. Vavasour, E.F.W., Sophy and myself were parties to these deeds, which were duly signed and witnessed after explanations made by Mr. N. at the Rectory.* 16 May: *Mr. Vavasour leading his daughter, the bride. Sophy was much agitated, and looked very pale, but very interesting, simply and elegantly dressed.* 17 May: *Mr. V. and Emily, with her fiancé Leopold Dryden, Mr. and Mrs. M. Vavasour, Capt. Leigh & Billingsley were our guests.* 23-24 May, 4 Jun., 9 Jun., 13 Jun., 16 Jun: *Our dear children left us about midday for Stow, whither they went in our open carriage, to proceed thence to Whichford in Mr. Vavasour's phaeton.* 19 Jun., 10 Jul., 12 Jul., 16 Jul., 25 Jul., 30 Jul., 2 Aug., 8-11 Aug., 13 Aug., 16 Aug., 20 Aug., 23 Aug., 29 Aug: *Vavasour gone to Dublin.* 5 Sep., 21 Sep., 25 Sep., 27 Sep., 4 Oct., 11 Oct., 18 Oct: *I was not released till half past four o clock, when I accompanied Vavasour to the Rectory, to borrow a cloak and shawl as a shelter on my way home: saw the ladies for a few moments.* 24 Oct: *Called at the Vavasours, saw Mr. V. and Emily, who returned from Whichford yesterday.* 25 Oct., 15 Nov., 22 Nov., 27 Nov., 30 Nov., 3 Dec: *Passing through Stow called at the Rectory, and saw Mr. Vavasour, who is anxious that Edward should resign Whichford, and go to Stanway, but though he did not say so in express terms, I gathered that from communications they had recd. from Whichford it was likely that I should find my son and his wife very reluctant to come into our views.* 4 Dec: *However, as I pondered the matter, it occurred to me on calmer reflection that I might lay myself open to the charge of precipitation, and that Mr. and Mrs. Vavasour were entitled to express an opinion on the subject, when they should have heard what had passed at Whichford yesterday.* 5-6 Dec., 7 Dec: *But was induced to take a middle course, and once more urge Vavasour to visit Stanway, and then, when he had seen it, say whether he wont would recommend their accepting the Curacy.* 8 Dec: *Vavasour walked from Stow to breakfast, with a sanguine feeling that all will yet turn out satisfactorily as to the question of our childrens' removal to Stanway, which he thinks a measure recommended by every consideration of prudence.* 9 Dec., 11-13 Dec., 20 Dec: *Found at the Inn a note from my son to intimate that he and his wife were at the Rectory, where I called for a few minutes, and saw them and the Vavasours.* 21 Dec: *About noon E.F.W. and Sophy accompanied by Vavasour came from Stow in a chaise, took luncheon with us, and remained for two hours or more.*

1839: 22 Jan., 28 Jan., 31 Jan., 5 Feb., 7 Feb., 15 Feb., 24-25 Feb., 28 Feb., 2 Mar., 7 Mar., 16 Mar., 18 Mar: *Called at the Rectory: saw Mr. Vavasour: Mrs. V. and Emily still a good deal indisposed.* 21 Mar., 27 Mar: *Mrs. B; as also her husband is an invalid, and Cheltenham is supposed not to agree with her; they have some idea of renting Vavasour's newly built cottage in Broadwell.* 26-28 Mar., 3-4 Apr., 12 Apr., 22 Apr., 1 May, 3 May, 13 May, 16 May, 17 May, 25 May, 30 May, 10 Jun., 12 Jun: *Mr. Marmaduke Vavasour came from Ashby de la Zouch to perform the marriage ceremony: Edward and his wife were of course of the party, also Mr. Charles Dryden, brother of the Bridegroom, a London Solicitor. Thus it was entirely a family party, not even Bridesmaids.* 15 Jun., 25-27 Jun., 11 Jul., 22 Jul., 25 Jul., 2 Aug., 15 Aug., 21 Aug.

1840: 18 Mar: *Mr. Vavasour arrived from Stow yesterday. Mrs. Vavasour and William did not reach Stanway till past three o clock, from Leke Wotton, in their open carriage; Mrs. V. had been passing ten days with Mrs. Dryden, superintending her accouchement and nursery: she reports favourably of both Mother and infant.* 25 Mar., 2 Apr., 9 Apr., 11 Apr., 18 Apr., 21 Apr., 30 Apr., 2 May, 12 May: *Called at the Rectory, where found Mr. and Mrs. Vavasour, and Mr. and Mrs. Dryden, with their infant: the Drydens have been staying at Stow for some days; Emily looks delicate, her baby is a very nice looking child.* 14 May, 19-21 May, 25 May: *Mr. Vavasour officiated in the reading desk, and when the services in the church were concluded, set off for Cheltenham to be at hand to afford his services as a friend and clergyman, at the last hours of Sir W. Burdett, an Irish Baronet, with whom and his lady there has long been an intimacy as regards the Vavasour family.* 10-12 Jun., 15-16 Jun., 27 Jun., 18 Jul., 20-21 Jul., 25 Jul., 30 Jul., 1 Aug., 3 Aug., 5-6 Aug., 12-13 Aug., 20 Aug: *Called on the Vavasours at the Cottage, who communicated to me an approaching change in their position. Mr. W. Hippisley, youngest Son of the late H. Hippisley, and at whose option it was under family arrangements to call on Mr. V. to resign the Rectory of Stow, when he was should be in Priest's orders, but as to whom there was reason to expect that it would not be his interest to avail himself of that power, has intimated to Mr. V. that he has entered into such arrangements with his brothers, besides an engagement for an early marriage, that it is his design to take the Rectory of Stow, about next Midsummer twelvemonth. In the meantime he has arranged to become Curate to Mr. Vavasour, for a year from next Midsummer, about which time he expects to be ordained Deacon, and is to inhabit the Rectory house, putting it into repair; with a view to these arrangements the Vavasours purpose to withdraw from the Rectory at Michaelmas next to their Cottage.* 25 Aug., 10 Sep., 12 Sep., 15 Sep: *On my return met Mr. and Mrs. Vavasour in their carriage with Miss Hippisley: they had been at our door, but MW. was out in the Village, and had since met them.* 20-21 Sep., 29 Sep., 1 Oct., 3 Oct., 10 Oct., 12 Oct., 2 Nov., 5 Nov., 12 Nov., 14-15 Nov., 17 Nov., 24 Nov: *Called on the Vavasours at Foss Cottage, who were not at home, but we met and held a parley with them afterwards in the Market place, and at the Library.*

1841: 4 Mar.

1842: 18 Jan., 20-21 Jan., 25 Jan., 27 Jan., 5 Feb., 7 Feb., 10 Feb: *Conferred with E.F.W. and Sophy on a new aggravation of the matters at issue between Vavasour and R W Hippisley, now brought to a sort of crisis.* 11 Feb: *Wrote a long and elaborate letter to Ford on the dispute between R W Hippisley and Vavasour, pointing out a course by which it is not improbable that matters can be set straight for the advantage of both parties, and while I decline undertaking the office of Mediator, suggesting to Ford what it seems to me he might do in the matter.* 12-18 Feb., 22 Feb., 3-5 Mar., 7 Mar., 10 Mar., 31 Mar., 7-8 Apr., 21 Apr., 27 Apr., 12 May, 17-18 May, 23 May, 28 May, 31 May, 8-9 Jun., 24 Jun., 7-8 Jul., 23 Jul., 26 Jul., 28 Jul., 4 Aug., 11-12 Aug., 16 Aug., 22 Aug., 25 Aug., 29 Aug., 19 Sep., 27 Sep., 29 Sep., 12 Oct., 19 Oct., 10 Nov., 16-17 Nov., 20-21 Nov., 23 Nov., 25 Nov., 2 Dec., 22 Dec., 27-28 Dec.

1843: 7 Jan., 26 Jan., 11 Aug., 14 Aug., 19 Sep., 27 Sep., 19 Oct., 25 Oct., 9 Nov: *Mr. Vavasour informed me that R W Hippisley has at last signified his intention to assume the Rectory of Stow, calling on Mr. V. to resign, which he will do on an early day.* 16 Nov., 29 Nov., 7 Dec., 15 Dec., 19 Dec., 22 Dec., 26 Dec., 29 Dec.

1844: 6 Jan., 9 Jan., 21 Jan., 31 Jan., 6 Feb., 16-17 Feb., 19 Feb., 27 Feb., 20-21 Mar., 26 Mar: *Mr. Vavasour had dined and slept at the Vicarage yesterday, on his way to Ashchurch to take the rail for Liverpool, and thence to Dublin, on business.* 16-17 Apr., 22 Apr: *Mr. Vavasour returned from Ireland on Thursday last.* 24 Apr., 13 May, 18 May, 23 Jul., 7 Aug., 14 Aug., 23 Aug., 27 Aug., 3-5 Sep., 7 Sep., 19 Sep., 24 Sep., 8 Oct., 12 Oct., 25 Oct., 25 Nov.

1845: 6 Jan: *Mr. and Mrs. V. are at Leamington, visiting the Drydens, and in great distress in consequence of a very unfavourable medical opinion havg. been given as to Emily Dryden's state of health, which, uttered unguardedly, has overpowered herself, her husband, and parents.* 9 Jan., 16 Jan: *Vavasour also looked in, and walked with me to the foot of Stow Hill, as I went to meet my carriage; very full of the hopes and fears as to the state of poor Mrs. Dryden, and as to the will of the late Lady Burdett: dilating also with much satisfaction on the many good qualities of heart and head which he ascribes to his son in law EFW.* 21 Jan., 8 Feb., 19 Feb: *A removal to Cheltenham appeared to be expedient; intimation of the danger was conveyed to Mr. and Mrs. Vavasour.* 24 Feb., 3-4 Mar., 7 Mar., 12 Mar: *In the evening we received a letter from E.F.W.—no hope remains that Emily Dryden can long survive: she herself is prepared to depart—Sophy is resigned to the approaching loss of her sister—Mr. Vavasour overwhelmed.* 13 Mar., 15 Mar., 18 Mar: *A letter from Mr. Vavasour, announcing the death of poor Emily Dryden, which happened yesterday.* 19 Mar., 20 Mar: *There had been much hesitation as to the place of sepulcture ... at length Broadwell was chosen, for the like reason, and because Mr. D. had held the curacy of that parish, in which also Mr. Vavasour's residence is situate.* 22 Mar: *Nearly half an hour elapsed, before the procession to Broadwell was ready to start — Mr. V. joined his afflicted Son in law and Son in the Coach, and the fourth place was occupied by E.F.W.* 26-27 Mar., 29 Mar., 31 Mar., 8 Apr., 24 Apr: *Mr. & Mrs. Vavasour continue in a state of great depression of spirits, utterly overcome by the loss of their daughter.* 3 May, 14 May, 21 May, 27-28 May, 30 May, 2 Jun., 4 Jun., 8 Jun., 23 Jun., 28 Jun., 5 Jul.

1846: 24 Jun., 11 Jul., 21 Jul., 24 Jul., 17 Aug., 14 Sep., 17 Sep., 12 Oct., 29-30., 9-10 Nov., 21 Nov., 26 Nov., 31 Dec.

1847: 23 Feb., 28 Feb., 27-28 Feb., 27-28 Apr., 3 May, 5-6 May, 10-14 May, 19 May, 26 Jun., 3 Jul., 6 Jul., 22 Jul., 19 Aug., 2 Sep., 25 Oct., 22 Nov.

1848: 4 Mar., 14 Mar., 16 Mar., 12 May, 23 May, 12 Jun., 6 Jul., 5 Aug., 7 Aug., 30 Aug., 7 Sep., 18 Sep., 20 Oct., 22 Oct., 24-25 Oct., 13 Nov: *Received a letter from Mr. Vavasour, informing me of the decease of a brother of Mrs. V., a half pay officer, at Jersey: he has long been in a deplorable state of health. Marmaduke Vavasour, when resident at Broadwell, whence once brought this gentleman to dinner at Upper Slaughter.* 16 Nov.

1849: 20 Dec.

1850: 23 Jan., 21 Feb., 28 Feb., 4 Mar., 7 Mar., 14: *Recd. a note from Mr. Vavasour, announcing the decease of Mrs. Walter Vavasour, second wife & widow of a deceased Brother of Mrs. Vavasour of the Cottage.* 15 Mar., 20-21 Mar., 25 Mar., 28 Mar., 3 Apr., 11 Apr: *Mr. Vavasour came to meet me and make enquiries as to my poor wife.* 14 Apr., 16 Apr., 19 Apr: *Mr. Hayward preceded the corpse; Canon Ford, Mr. Vavasour ...* 21 Apr., 30 Apr., 4 May, 8 May, 10 May, 16 May, 18-19 May, 28 May, 30-31 May, 4 Jun., 6 Jun., 20 Jun., 27 Jun, 23 Jul., 16 Aug., 24-25 Aug., 29 Aug., 12 Sep., 18 Sep., 22 Sep., 24-25 Sep., 1 Oct., 3 Oct., 25 Oct., 28 Oct., 1 Nov., 6-9 Nov., 14 Nov., 29 Nov., 5 Dec., 12 Dec.

1851: 16 Jan., 20 Jan., 23 Jan., 27 Oct., 20 Feb., 27 Feb., 13 Mar., 4 Apr., 8 Apr., 14 Apr., 17 Apr., 23-24 Apr., 8 May, 12-13 May.

1852: 18 Jan., 26 Jan., 29 Jan., 3 Feb., 12 Feb., 19 Feb., 11 Mar: *Called for her at "the Cottage", where saw Mr. and Mrs. V. — the former rather indisposed.* 19 Mar: *Bad account of Mr. Vavasour, who having been poorly for some little time, had some serious attack on Monday night last, which might arise from some derangement of the liver, or malady of the heart, and required prompt medical attendance.* 21 Mar., 22 Mar: *Conferred with Mr. Hayward as to Mr. Vavasour's state, which he considers precarious, believing that there is organic disease of the heart; that he ought to be very cautious as to diet, exercise, excitement &c.:—that sudden death may be the consequence of a sudden spasm...* 24 Mar., 1 Apr., 8 Apr., 13-14 Apr., 18 Apr., 26 Apr: *Mr. V. looking ill, and thinking he ails nothing, and should be quite well, if the wind should cease to blow from the East.* 29 Apr., 1 May,
6 May, 10 May, 12-13 May, 20 May, 25 May, 27-28 May, 25 Oct., 4 Nov., 10-14 Nov., 15 Nov: *The early tidings from Stow were that there was no discernible change in Mr. Vavasour's state.* 16-18 Nov., 20 Nov., 22-24 Nov., 26 Nov., 1 Dec., 5-6 Dec., 9 Dec., 14 Dec., 16 Dec: *A change for the worse in poor Vavasour's state; I saw him for a few moments; he appeared to suffer greatly from difficulty of breathing, restlessness, and bodily distress; but drove out accompanied by Sophy ...* 22 Dec., 27 Dec., 30 Dec.

1853: 5 Jan: *He grows daily weaker, and is in a very languishing state.* 11 Jan., 20 Jan., 24 Jan., 27 Jan: *The last sad scene is over. Mr. Vavasour breathed his last between 3 & 4 AM.* 2 Feb: *After breakfast we left home for Stow, to attend the funeral of our friend Vavasour, Marmaduke & Sir H. Vavasour going with me in my chariot, and Broome outside...* 9 Mar., 11 Mar.

1854: 29 Jan., 10 Feb., 17 Mar., 29-30 Mar., 1 Apr., 25 Apr., 12 May, 3 Jun., 6 Jun., 29 Jun., 5 Jul., 31 Jul.

VAVASOUR — Sophia Vavasour — *see* Sophia Witts

VAVASOUR — Thomas Vavasour of Rochdale[20]

Thomas Vavasour (b. 1777), merchant, was the eldest son of Thomas Hippon Vavasour (1750-1819), of the Butts, Rochdale, Lancashire, and Penelope (b. 1757), daughter of Edmund Smith and Penelope Bill. He was christened on 25 July 1777 and the church record is very clear: 'Thomas son of Thos. Vavasour Chapman [trader] & Penelope of Butts'. Thomas and Penelope had only married on 3 April 1777; the wedding was likely a hastily planned affair. Thomas was the eldest brother of Julia and Marmaduke.

1829: 17 Jun: *We dined at Mrs. Hastings's, and met a large party Mr. & Mrs. Twisleton, Mr. & Mrs. M. Vavasour, Mr. T. Vavasour & Mrs. Winter.* 3 Jul: *A deluge of rain, reducing the hay still unricked to the dismal appearance of dung, did not prevent our dining to-day with the Fords, where we met Mr. & Mrs. Twisleton, Mr. & Mrs. M. Vavasour, & Mr. T. Vavasour.*

VAVASOUR — William Thomas Vavasour[21]

William Thomas Vavasour (1819-1863), landed proprietor, was the only son of Richard and Julia Vavasour (*above*). He seems to have had a delicate constitution, and for the sake of his health he lived the life of a country squire without the burdens of a serious profession or public office. He married, September 1842, his first cousin, Caroline Susan (1816-1878), daughter of Lt-Gen. Sir Henry Maghull Mervyn Vavasour, 2nd baronet.

In the diaries, William Vavasour comes across as a spoilt and indulged young man. Although his health was poor, he managed to go fox hunting, fishing, and shooting. He enjoyed a long continental holiday in 1840 and, other than a short stint as a clerk in Liverpool between 1837 and 1839 he does not seem to have worked much in his life. There were no children of the marriage and he died in 1863. Caroline married secondly, 1868, William Wiggin (1820-1901).

1835: 5 Jun: *William Vavasour came in the forenoon to fish with Edward, & staid dinner with us.*

1836: 24 Nov., 26 Dec: *William Vavasour called, having forced his way on his poney through opposing snow drifts to see Edward and his friend Chater, who had, however, sallied forth on foot, and made a circuit over the hill to speculate on the depth of the snow, and the extent of the obstruction caused by the drifts.* 28 Dec: *Will. Vavasour came in the forenoon to drive his sisters home.*

1837: 24 Jun: *The Proclamation over, took luncheon at the Rectory, where welcomed the return of Will. Vavasour to his family to pass a few days, this being the first time he has visited them since he left them to enter into a great mercantile Counting house at Liverpool as Clerk: the lad has, I understand, conducted himself remarkably well during the few months of his engagement.* 28-30 Jun., 1 Jul., 10 Nov., 17 Nov., 4-5 Dec., 7 Dec.

1838: 15 Feb: *Thence to the Vavasours, where my Son had been passing the forenoon, and where there was great and well founded anxiety in consequence of a letter received this morning by Mr. V. announcing that his son had been for a fortnight seriously ill at Woodside near Liverpool with a pulmonary inflammation.* 20 Feb., 24 Feb: *E.F.W. rode to Stow, and returned to dinner with the news that Vavasour reached home yesterday Even. accompanied by his Son, who has recovered very rapidly from his late serious indisposition.* 8 Mar., 25-26 Sep., 11 Oct., 23-24 Oct.

1839: 16 Mar: *W.V. returned from Liverpool in indifferent health.* 26-28 Mar., 3 Apr., 11 Apr., 3 May, 16 May, 18 May, 25 May, 12 Jun., 15 Jun., 20 Jun., 11 Jul., 22 Jul., 4 Aug: *We learned from Hayward that W. Vavasour returned yesterday evening from Stanway, having accompanied Edward & Sophy to Malvern &c., suffering under a grievous attack of the malady. Spasmodic Asthma, to which he is subject.* 5 Aug., 9 Aug., 21 Aug.

1840: 18 Mar., 26 Mar., 7 Apr., 9 Apr., 11 Aug: *Received a very interesting and satisfactory letter from E.F.W. dated Wildbad, Aug. 2. Our dear travellers all quite well, and continue to be delighted with their tour. They have deviated somewhat from their proposed route to visit Wildbad, where they had been staying from July 30 to Aug. 2. They were induced to follow this route by W. Vavasour, who came to meet them at Baden Baden; and whom they accompanied to Wildbad, where they joined Lady Vavasour and her daughters, with whom W.V. is travelling.* 12 Sep: *Called at the Rectory: received by Mrs. Vavasour; Miss Hippisley is on a visit there, whom I was glad to meet. Mrs. V. informed me in confidence that her son had formed an engagement with his cousin Caroline Vavasour, daughter to Lady Vavasour, with whom and her unmarried daughters he is now travelling.*

1842: 17 Jan., 3 Feb., 31 Mar., 8 Apr., 12 May, 28 May, 31 May, 6 Jun., 24 Jun., 8 Jul., 6 Aug., 13 Aug., 25 Aug., 29 Aug., 8 Sep., 20 Sep., 29 Sep., 6 Oct., 11 Oct., 1 Nov., 16 Nov., 20 Nov., 27-29 Dec.

1843: 9 Feb., 16 Feb., 10-11 Aug., 19 Aug., 19 Sep., 21 Sep., 27 Sep., 14 Dec.

1844: 22 Jan., 30-31 Jan., 6 Feb., 8 Feb., 15 Feb., 22 Feb., 19 Mar., 2 Apr., 4 Apr., 16 Apr., 19 Apr., 22 Apr., 24-25 Apr., 2 May, 10 May, 13 May, 15 May, 30 Jul: *We dined at the Vavasours, meeting Mr. and Mrs. W. Vavasour, lately returned from a visit in Hants, Mr. and Mrs. Dryden, and our dear children.* 2 Aug., 24 Sep: *W. Vavasour and his wife are on a visit to Lady Vavasour at Melbourn.* 30 Jul., 14 Nov: *W. Vavasour our Assessor there; he is lately returned with his lady from Melbourne Park, where they have been paying a long visit.* 21 Nov., 25 Nov., 27-28 Nov., 26 Dec.

1845: 6 Jan., 23 Jan., 8 Feb., 12 Feb., 24 Feb., 27 Feb: *W. Vavasour and his wife I also saw; the former suffers less from the abscess in his hand.* 3 Mar., 13 Mar., 22 Mar., 8 Apr., 24 Apr: *Mrs. W. Vavasour is also a great invalid: and Lady Vavasour, in an alarming state of health, in great debility, has removed from Melbourn Park to the immediate neighbourhood of Exeter, for medical advice, and change of climate.* 4 May, 17 Jun.

1846: 24 Jun., 6 Jul., 29 Jul., 15 Aug., 21 Aug., 31 Aug., 30-31 12 Sep., 24 Sep., 5 Oct., 30-31 Oct., 5 Nov., 12 Nov., 28 Nov., 30 Nov., 2 Dec., 9 Dec., 11 Dec., 31 Dec.

1847: 11 Feb., 20 Feb., 8 Mar., 11 Mar., 15 Apr., 19-20 Apr., 27 Apr., 7 May, 11-13 May, 17-18 May, 8 Jul., 12-13 Jul., 2 Aug: *Received a letter from E.F.W. with a good account of all at the Vicarage, Stanway. Emma Vavasour is now their guest, W.V. and his wife having gone to the Isle of Wight.* 19 Aug: *We proceeded to dine at Mr. Winter's at Daylesford; where we met Marmaduke Vavasour and his daughter Penelope on a visit there, Mrs. Vavasour and her husband with Emma V., Mr. and Mrs. Pole, Mr. and Mrs. Colville.* 26 Aug., 8 Sep., 14 Sep., 16 Sep., 23 Sep., 30 Sep., 14 Oct., 26 Oct., 7 Nov., 11 Nov., 22 Nov., 25 Nov., 2 Dec., 9-10 Dec., 23 Dec.

1848: 3 Feb., 16 Feb: ... *return home found Mrs. W. Vavasour and her sister Emma, who had walked from Maugersbury.* 19 Feb., 22 Feb., 2 Mar., 4 Mar., 7 Mar., 16-17 Mar., 15 Apr., 11-12 May, 14 May, 16 May, 8 Jun., 12 Jun., 14 Jun., 19 Jun., 6-7 Jul., 15 Jul., 11 Aug., 16-17 Aug., 31 Aug., 14 Sep., 26 Sep., 28 Sep., 7 Oct., 30 Oct.

1850: 18 Jan., 7 Feb., 13 Feb., 20-22 Feb., 28 Feb., 28 Mar., 4 Apr., 19 Apr., 21 Apr., 3-4 May, 25 May, 29-30 May, 4 Jun., 5-6 Jun., 17 Jun., 20 Jun., 27 Jun: *Mr. Vavasour drove with me some distance on my way homeward; the departure of his son, Caroline, & Emma for London on their parliamentary business is deferred; W.V. continues much of an invalid.* 23 Jul., 11 Aug., 16 Aug., 23 Aug., 29 Aug., 5 Sep., 24 Sep., 1 Oct., 28 Oct., 1 Nov., 5 Nov., 14 Nov., 21 Nov., 28 Nov., 29 Nov: ... *Mrs. W.V. likes to sing, but does not sing agreeably.* 12 Dec.

1851: 7 Jan: *Wrote to invite Mr. and Mrs. W. Vavasour to dine with us to-morrow en famille. E.F.W. took this note with him to Stow, whither he rode, and brought a reply from Mrs. W.V. who accepts my invitation to dinner and to sleep here: W.V. excuses himself on the score of indifferent health which leads him to decline invitations to dine from home. Yet he persists with intense ardour in his devotedness to fox hunting.* 8-9 Jan., 23 Jan., 30 Jan., 13 Feb., 20 Feb., 27 Feb., 6 Mar., 13 Mar., 3 Apr., 8 Apr., 23 Apr., 8 May, 12-13 May.

1852: 26 Jan., 3 Feb: *Called on the Vavasours, where saw Mr. & Mrs. V. and Mrs. W.V; the latter returned home yesterday from her visit to her friends in Yorkshire. There seems to be now little doubt that Mr. and Mrs. W.V. will become the Tenants of the mansion house at Lower Slaughter.* 8 Feb., 19 Feb., 1 Mar: ... *chatted with the Royce party, and Mrs. W. Vavasour, on her way to take up her abode at Lower Slaughter.* 3 Mar., 7 Mar: *Mrs. W. Vavasour attended the morning service, and I walked back with her to Lower Slaughter.* 10-11 Mar., 14 Mar., 16 Mar., 19 Mar: ... *having brought Mrs. W. Vavasour, to spend two or three hours with her relation, Mrs. Foster.* 21-22 Mar., 24-25 Mar., 28-29 Mar., 3 Apr., 4 Apr: *W. Vavasour & Mrs. W.V. attended the morning service, and called on me afterwards——W. Vavasour said to be still suffering at night—not able at times to lie down, and curtailed of sleep.* 6 Apr., 8 Apr: *Received a note from Mrs. W. Vavasour, who accepts my invitation to dinner on Tuesday next for herself and Mrs. M.V. — Willm. V. declines on the plea of apprehension of risk from the night air: the truth being that he loves his own ease, and dislikes the restraints of society.* 9 Apr., 12-14 Apr., 16 Apr., 18-20 Apr., 22 Apr., 26 Apr., 29 Apr., 1-2 May, 5-6 May, 9-13 May, 16 May, 19 May, 23 May, 25 May, 28-30 May, 4 Jun., 6 Jun., 23 Oct., 29 Oct., 4 Nov., 6 Nov., 9 Nov., 11 Nov., 13-14 Nov., 20 Nov., 25 Nov., 27 Nov., 6 Dec., 9 Dec., 11 Dec., 16 Dec., 22 Dec: *Mrs. W.V. has been staying at the Cottage for a night or two, and declined my offer to take her back to Lower Slaughter.* 30 Dec.

1853: 11 Jan: *W. Vav. Is exceedingly attentive to his Father; but the confinement to the house, and the incompatibility of the air as unsuited to his Asthmatic constitution make it necessary, as the medical attendant declares, that he should continue his habitual horse exercise, and go home to sleep in the valley at his own house..* 18-20 Jan., 27 Jan: *Willm. Vavasour, much indisposed, had gone home to sleep at Lower Slaughter, was sent for, and only arrived when his father had been gone nearly an hour—His grief exceeded due bounds, so as to incapacitate him from for the pious cares which the moment required; he could neither give necessary orders, nor afford his disconsolate mother the consolation she so greatly needed.* 28 Jan., 2 Feb., 9 Feb., 16 Feb., 20 Feb., 25 Feb., 28 Feb., 6 Mar., 11 Mar: *Mrs. W. Vavasour, who has been on horseback, visiting the Watson Poles, called as she returned from U. Swell; and, having dismissed her groom & the horses, sat a little while with me, & subsequently walked with me to Lower Slaughter...* 13 Mar., 19-20 Mar., 24-25 Mar., 19 Mar., 5 Apr., 15 Apr., 17 Apr., 25 Apr., 28 Apr., 1 May, 8 May, 11-13 May, 17 May, 20-21 May, 29 May, 1 Jun., 26 Jun: *W.V. to join his wife, who has been visiting Mr. and Mrs. Whitehall Dod, at their residence near Conway, and who accompanies them to-morrow to the metropolis, that all may attend the wedding of Sir H M Vavasour, which is fixed for Thursday next; the ceremony to be performed at St. James's Church, Piccadilly, in which parish Lord Braybrook's Town house in Burlington Street is situate.* 8 Dec., 11 Dec., 13 Dec., 15 Dec., 19 Dec., 24 Dec., 28-29 Dec.

1854: 2 Jan., 11 Jan., 29 Jan., 6 Mar., 16-17 Mar., 26 Mar., 29-30 Mar., 1-2 Apr., 9 Apr., 12-13 Apr., 16-18 Apr., 21-23 Apr., 25-27 Apr., 30 Apr., 2 May, 4 May, 12 May, 14 May, 16 May, 17 May: *From the account given I suspect that W.V. drives an ill trained team in a random, Wild Irish, style, yet knows the Coachman's work.* 18 May, 21-24 May, 26 May, 28 May, 3 Jun., 6 Jun., 8 Jun., 14-15 Jun., 18 Jun., 21-22 Jun., 24-25 Jun., 29 Jun., 2 Jul., 5-7 Jul., 9 Jul., 13 Jul., 16 Jul., 19-20 Jul., 23 Jul., 27-29 Jul., 31 Jul., 4 Aug., 6 Aug., 10-11 Aug., 13 Aug.

VENABLES — George Venables and the Venables family of Cookham [22]

George Venables (1793-1860), landed proprietor and paper manufacturer, was born at Cookham Mills, Cookham, Berkshire, a younger son of William Venables (1761-1819), a paper manufacturer at Cookham, and Mary Green (1762-1819). George's eldest brother William (1785-1840) went to London in about 1806 and entered business as a wholesale stationer (presumably supplied by his father) with two partners in Brewer Street, Golden Square. After the death of one partner he dissolved his connection with the other and operated alone, before moving, in about 1816, to 17 Queenhithe, at which premises he kept his business for the remainder of his life. By 1826 William was in partnership with one Mr Wilson, possibly Thomas Wilson of Ive's Place, Maidenhead. They were joined in about 1831 by William Tyler. William Venables (junior) rose to become lord mayor of London in 1825-26 and MP for London in 1831-32.

In his will, William Venables (senior) left equal shares in the residue of his estate to his children. Charles, of Hampton Grey House, Woodstock, Oxfordshire, and George, of Cookham, were both paper manufacturers with mills at Wooburn and Taplow, Buckinghamshire, south-east of Wycombe, near the Berkshire border. George Venables married, at St Mary Magdalen, Oxford, 13 September 1832, Mary Davenport (1812-1883); they had 4 sons and 1 daughter:

1 Mary Davenport (1833-1914)
1 George Davenport (1835-1876)
2 William Henry (1836-1904)
3 Charles Francis (1839-1893)
4 Samuel (1840-1902)

1842: 17 Mar: *Mr. Venables, still, I believe, a paper-maker at Cookham, proved, as attesting witness, the Execution of my Uncle's will, Mr. Wilson, that he & my Aunt died without issue....*

VENOUR — John Venour and the Venour family of Wellesbourne, Warwickshire [23]

John Venour (1734-1787), landed proprietor, was born at Wellesbourne, Warwickshire, the son of Thomas Venour (1701-1752) and Ann Banbury (1710-1755). He married, first, at Strelley, Nottinghamshire, 31 October 1758, Mary Edge (1727-1765); and secondly, at Rugeley, Staffordshire, 15 May 1766, Catherine (1745-1825), daughter of Robert Landor (1708-1781) and Mary Noble (1706-1798). John and Catherine had 5 sons and 5 daughters:

1 Thomas (1767-1790)
2 John (1768-1839), Church of England clergyman; educated at Rugby School and Worcester College, Oxford (BA 1789; MA 1792); appointed stipendiary curate at Cubley with Marston Montgomery, Derbyshire, 12 May 1793; became acquainted with the Witts family while they were staying at Calwich

Abbey, Derbyshire, 10 June 1793; later appointed rector of Bourton-upon-Dunsmore, Warwickshire, 1818. He married, at Sherborne, Dorset, 1 March 1808, Maria (1781-1857), daughter of Stephen Briggs and Magdalen Pasley; 5 sons and 3 daughters:

1 John Askell (1809-1815)
2 William Briggs (1809-1829)
3 Thomas Henry Blackburn (1812-1878)
4 Stephen Charles (1813-1859)
1 Magdalene (1815-1857)
2 Elizabeth Catherine (b. & d. 1817)
3 Maria (1820-1855)
5 John Malcolm (1822-1823); died an infant

1 Sophia (1769-1848)
2 Mary Anne (1770-1847)
3 Robert (b. & d. 1772)
4 William (1773-1803)
3 Eliza (1774-1802)
4 Caroline (1776-1837)
5 Harriet Isabella (1778-1826)
5 Walter Askell (1781-1850)

1806: 2 Jul: ... *in the Evening a little with Mr. Deacon, Mrs. & Miss Venour, & the Goolds.*

VEREKER — Charles Vereker [24]

Charles Vereker, 2nd Viscount Gort and Baron Kiltarton of Gort (1768-1842), army officer and MP for Limerick (1794-1800 and 1802-17), distinguished himself on 5 September 1798 when he was severely wounded opposing a French invasion at Coloony, co. Sligo. He succeeded as 2nd Viscount Gort and Baron Kiltarton of Gort in 1817.

1834: 13 Sep: *Walked with the Astons to Stanway house and gardens in the chance of meeting with Lord and Lady Gort, who had proposed coming from Cheltenham to visit Stanway and Toddington under the conduct of F. Aston, to whom Lord Ellenborough had written to request these attentions at his hand.*

VERNON — Miss Vernons at Clifton

1803: 31 Dec: ... *the rest of the party being gone before to Mrs. McCausland's Rout of 90 persons great & small; a wondrous collection of Masters & Misses; some of the latter among the order of beauties; Miss Vernons in particular conversed much with Mrs. Adams, her Son Frank etc. etc.*

VERNON — Caroline Vernon at Stanway [25]

Caroline Vernon (1751-1837) was the daughter of Henry Vernon (1718-65), of Hilton Park, Staffordshire, and Henrietta (1719-1786), daughter of Thomas Wentworth, 3rd earl of Strafford. She was maid of honour to Queen Charlotte from 1768 to 1818. Caroline had three brothers and four sisters, the most famous of whom was her elder sister Henrietta (1745-1828).

In 1764, just a month after their initial meeting, Henrietta married Richard Grosvenor, 1st Baron Grosvenor (1731-1802), despite him being fourteen years her senior. Richard was a notorious gambler and womaniser and the marriage turned out to be a mistake. Henrietta's attention fell on the king's brother, Henry, duke of Cumberland, who happened to be the same age as her. The couple met in secret in inns around the country. One time, while they were out at a friend's house in Cavendish Square, Henrietta asked for a private meeting with the duke to talk about her brother. They were excused, but after a half hour their host decided they had talked for long enough and went to interrupt. She found Henry on top of Lady Grosvenor, 'with her petticoats up' on her couch. The subsequent adultery trial was soon the talk of the town; Henrietta and Henry's 'letters' to each other were enough to secure Richard Grosvenor damages of £10,000. After seven years of marriage, Henrietta and Richard were separated in 1771. Richard died in 1802, and Henrietta married Lt-Gen. George de Hochepied, 6th Baron de Hochepied. She retired to a quiet life with him until her death in 1828.

It is unclear how the friendship between Susan, Lady Elcho and Caroline Vernon arose, but the connection may have been via Susan's sister, Charlotte, who from 1761 to 1774 was a maid of honour like Caroline.

1823: 6 Sep: *Miss Vernon, more than a septuagenarian, was another guest: formerly a maid of honour to Queen Charlotte & sister to the notorious Lady Grosvenor; a corrected character, it is said, ladylike in manner, but a bitter foe of old Cork & O: animosity not unfrequently exploding between them.*

1826: 11 Apr. *Miss Vernon arrived on a visit to Lady Elcho from London.*

VERNON — Frances Vernon — *see also* **John Borlase Warren** [26]

Frances Maria Vernon (1784-1837) was the daughter of Adm. John Borlase Warren (1753-1822) and Caroline Clavering (d. 1839). She married George Venables-Vernon, 4th Baron Vernon, and had at least 1 son:

1 George John Warren (1803-1866), MP; succeeded as 5th Baron Vernon, 1835

1837: 2 Oct: *A letter from F. Aston accompanying a present of grouse, in which he mentions that the wealthy Lady Vernon, lately deceased, has left to Miss Church an annuity of £100 per ann.*

VERNON — Henry John Vernon [27]

Henry John Vernon (1816-1895), Church of England clergyman, was born at Bilton, near Rugby, Warwickshire, the son of Edward Vernon (b. 1780) and Theodosia Frances Morrice (1785-1875). He was educated at Magdalen Hall, Oxford, and was ordained deacon in 1839. Having held the curacy of Newchurch on the Isle of Wight for seven years, Vernon was appointed assistant travelling secretary of the Society for the Propagation of the Gospel in 1846. He held this post for twenty years, after which he served as vicar of Eckington, Worcestershire, until 1877. He married, at St Nicholas, Brighton, 26 April 1849, Caroline Ann (1820-1883), only daughter of Revd Spencer Rodney Drummond; they had 1 daughter:

1 Laura Louisa Lilia (1851-1929); married, 1884, David Archer Vaughan Colt-Williams

---

1848: 7 Feb: *This deputation is to consist of the Bishops of Madras and Antigua, Mr. Thomson, a former Missionary of the Society in the diocese of Madras, and Mr. Vernon, one of the Secretaries of the Parent Society.* 22 Feb: *Mr. V. is an elegant young man, lately appointed Under Secretary of the S.P.G.—a very elegant and agreable person, who has been Curate of Mr. Spencer Phillips at Northew Church in the Isle of Wight.*

1850: 15 Jan., 1 Feb., 10 Sep.

1852: 9 Jun.

1854: 23-24 Mar.

VESEY —Thomas Vesey [28]

Thomas Vesey, 3rd viscount de Vesci (1803-1875), MP and landed proprietor, was born in Dublin, the son of John Vesey, 2nd viscount de Vesci (1771-1855), and Frances Letitia (1770-1840), daughter of

William Brownlow. De Vesci sat as MP for Queen's County in 1835-37 and 1841-52. In 1857 he was elected an Irish representative peer and entered the House of Lords. He married, at St Mary's, Wilton, Wiltshire, 19 September 1839, Emma (1819-1884), daughter of Gen. George Augustus Herbert, 11th earl of Pembroke and 8th earl of Montgomery (1759-1827), and Countess Catherine Semyonovna Vorontsova (1784-1856). Thomas and Emma had 2 sons and 2 daughters:

1 Frances Isabella (1840-1915); became marchioness of Bath
1 John Robert William (1844-1903); succeeded as 4th viscount de Vesci of Abbey Leix
2 Beatrice Charlotte Elizabeth (1845-1876)
2 Eustace Vesey (1851-1886), army officer

1828: 28 May: *We had a party of our neighbours to dinner to-day: Mr. & Mrs. Twisleton, & the Hon. Mr. Vesey, Son of an Irish peer, Viscount De Vesci, a cousin of Mrs. Twisleton.*

VESEY-FITZGERALD — William Vesey-FitzGerald[29]

William Vesey-FitzGerald, 2nd Baron FitzGerald and Vesey (1783-1843), MP and landed proprietor, was the elder son of James Fitzgerald (1742-1835) and Catherine Vesey (1759-1832), who was created Baroness Fitzgerald and Vesey in the peerage of Ireland in 1826. He was educated at Christ Church, Oxford, and became an MP. He held the seat for Ennis in 1808-12 and 1813-18, for Clare in 1820-28, Newport in 1829, Lostwithiel in 1830, and for Ennis again in 1831-35.

Vesey-FitzGerald was involved in the famous scandal surrounding the relationship between the duke of York and Mary Ann Clarke; he rendered services to the government and the court in bringing facts to light, and thereby secured his appointment as a lord of the Irish Treasury in 1809 and a privy councillor in Ireland in February 1810. His motives were impugned by Mrs Clarke in letter which she published in 1813, but despite her assertions being founded on the truth, there was not enough evidence to damage Vesey-Fitzgerald's reputation and she was condemned to nine months' imprisonment for libel.

In 1812 Vesey-FitzGerald was made a privy councillor and lord of the Treasury in England. He was also chancellor of the Irish exchequer and first lord of the Irish Treasury; he held these offices until they were merged with the English Treasury in 1816. Between 1826 and 1828 he served as paymaster of the forces under, successively, Lord Liverpool, George Canning, and Lord Goderich. In 1828 the duke of Wellington appointed him president of the Board of Trade and treasurer of the Navy. He was thus required to contest the Clare constituency once again, but in this he was defeated. The contest was noteworthy because Vesey-FitzGerald's opponent, Daniel O'Connell, went on to spearhead Catholic emancipation in Ireland. Vesey-FitzGerald managed to get elected for Newport in 1829, and served as president of the Board of Trade and treasurer of the Navy until February 1830, when he resigned. He briefly represented Lostwithiel in 1830 and then Ennis from 1831 until 1835.

Vesey-FitzGerald succeeded his mother as 2nd Baron FitzGerald and Vesey in 1832. As this was an Irish peerage it did not entitle him to a seat in the House of Lords, but in 1835 he was created Baron FitzGerald of Desmond and of Clan Gibbon in the county of Cork, in the peerage of the United Kingdom, and was able to take a seat. He again held office as president of the Board of Control under Sir Robert Peel between 1841 and 1843.

1828: 17 Jun: *The Duke of Wellington has now, it is to be presumed, completed his administration by the appointment of the Right Hon. W. Vesey Fitzgerald, a man of ability, and long conversant with official habits, to the Presidency of the Board of Trade.* 28 Jun., 9 Jul.

VICTORIA — *see* **Saxe-Coburg-Gotha**

VIGANONI — Giuseppe Viganoni[30]

Giuseppe Viganoni (1753-1822), singer, was born at Bergamo, Italy, and made his London debut at the King's Theatre on 11 December 1781. Fanny Burney referred to him as a 'feeble singer, not much in favour with the public that season'. Viganoni returned to London at the King's Theatre in 1795 and received £1,000 and a benefit. He reappeared on 15 March 1796 singing a principal role in *I due gobbi*, and later on 7 April as Oreste in *Ifigenia in Tauride*. The *Morning Chronicle* of 16 March 1796 reported that Viganoni had a 'small but a very pleasing voice' and sang with passion and sentiment; his 'science is perfect; and he manages his powers with very polished skill'. The *Monthly Mirror* of February 1796 was also very positive:

> Viganoni, the new singer, has great taste and uncommon flexibility; as an actor he stands first on the Italian stage; and on the English there are not many before him. He is one of the very few public performers in the kingdom, that can look and walk like a gentleman.

He was a tenor and particularly known for his renditions of operas by Giovanni Paisielli. He sang mainly on the Continent, and died at Venice in 1822.

1801: 2 Jun: ... *principal actors in the Opera Rezira, were Sign. Viganoni, Sign. Rovedino & his wife & Madl Banti. The former, particularly Rovedino are very fine, but totally outdone by the harmonious Banti, whose voice & singing surpassed all my expectations. The Music of the Opera was by Bianchi. As in Alzira Mad. Banti ran away with all my admiration...*

VILLERS — William Villers[31]

William Villers (±1791-1861), Church of England clergyman, was born at Wolverhampton, Staffordshire, the son of Simon Villers and Elizabeth Salt (b. 1759). He was educated at Balliol College, Oxford (BA 1813), and was ordained deacon on 8 January 1815 and priest on 29 June 1817. His first clerical appointment was as curate of Upper Swell, Gloucestershire, from 31 January 1815. He was then appointed curate of Broadwell with Adlestrop on 13 February 1815, and later curate of Kidderminster on 17 February 1835. He was vicar of Bromsgrove from 1846 to his death in 1861.

Villers married, at Altham, Lancashire, 14 July 1825, Susannah (1799-1865), daughter of Jonathan Peel (1752-1834) and Hester Bolton (1762-1841); they had 3 sons and 1 daughter:

1 Elizabeth Jane (1827-1899)
1 William Richard (1828-1908), Church of England clergyman
2 Edward Wildman Batavi (1830-1915)
3 Robert John (1832-1896), Church of England clergyman

1825: 12 Mar: *We dined at Mr. Ford's, at Little Risington, meeting Sir Robert and Lady & Miss Chester. Sir Robert holds the Office of Master of the Ceremonies at Court, his Lady is a sister of Mr. Ford's: their eldest Son, who held the situation of Assistant Master of Ceremonies for a short time, died some time since of a decline; he was a very elegant youth, & had been a pupil of Mr. Villers, when he resided as Curate of Upper Swell.* 17 Sep: *The living belongs to my old friend Revd. W. Villers, and is in the gift of Sir John Sebright, whose son was pupil to Mr. Villers, both when he resided as Curate of Upper Swell and Broadwell, and when he removed for a time to Edinburgh, to superintend the education of this and other pupils.... Mr. Villers, whom I lately mentioned, is Minister of the new church at Kidderminster, Mr. Onslow having placed him in that situation, for which he is peculiarly fitted, being a very excellent preacher, and having, since he left Gloucestershire, familiarized himself with large congregations in populous places, for he filled the situation of curate in St. Philip's church, Birmingham, to the great satisfaction of the people for a considerable length of time. Mr. Villers acquired the patronage of the Archdeacon of Worcester by superintending his son's education ....*

1829: *We dined at Mr. Jeaffreson's at Longborough ... Villers was, as he had been on the preceding day at Stow, the Lion of the day. He looks well, is cordial, cheerful, sensible, well-informed, and sure to conciliate esteem and good-will, as he ever was. He strongly pressed me to visit him in Worcestershire, & I feel much tempted to do so, if the matter can be arranged next summer. He resides at Waresley Green, near Kidderminster, where he is Minister of a new and large church: and in the immediate vicinity of his own house.*

1833: 2 Nov: *Wrote to Howell, acquainting him with the proposed arrangements as to the journey to Edinburgh, and inclosed a letter to Mr. Villers, the Minister of the New Church at Kidderminster, to serve as an introduction to Howell, when he visits that part of his Factory district.*

1834: 29 Sep: *The plan is to remain at Prinknash till Friday morning, and then to start for Kidderminster in the first instance, there probably to remain a day or two on a visit to my old acquaintance, the Revd. W. Villers, minister of the new Church in that Town.* 8 Oct.

1842: 15 Nov: *Mr. R W Hippisley wrote to invite us to partake of luncheon at his house on the 23d. Inst. which is fixed for the performance of two services on occasion of the opening of the new Organ recently erected by subscription in the Church at Stow, on which occasions sermons are to be preached by the Revd. W. Villers, formerly Curate of Stow, and still borne in most favourable recollection by the parishioners.*

1843: 9 Nov: *To the Justice room, where transacted magisterial business with Mr. Pole; present, Vavasour, Villiers, W. B. Pole — Mr. Villiers, Rector of Shenstone, near Lichfield, heretofore Curate of Lower Swell, Broadwell and Stow, a talented and popular man, had this week visited Stow, as he did last year about the same season, to preach a sermon in aid of the funds for erecting an Organ a considerable debt yet remaining due.* 10 Nov.

VILLIERS — Eleanor Villiers — *see* Lechmere

VINER ELLIS — *see* Ellis

VIZARD — William Vizard and the Vizard family of Dursley [32]

Henry Vizard (1775-1866), banker and solicitor, came from a family of bankers and solicitors in Dursley, Gloucestershire, established by John Vizard in 1758. William Vizard (1808-1875) was born at Dursley, the son of John Vizard (1772-1814) and Anna Maria Weight (1783-1830), and nephew of Henry (*above*). He married, about 1839, Maria Budden Jeffries (1811-1892); they had at least nine children (based on their forenames), including the following son and 7 daughters:

1 Marian (b. 1840)
2 Constance Anne (1841-1916)
3 Gertrude Mary (b. 1844)
4 Ella (1846-1931)
5 Bertha Septima (1848-1923)
1 Herbert (1850-1932)
6 Nora Octavia (1851-1932)
7 Ada Nona (1853-1924)

Members of the Vizard family practised in London, where a different William Vizard—presumably a relation—acted for Queen Caroline when King George IV tried to divorce her in 1820. The partnership of William Vizard and James Leman of 51 Lincoln's Inn Fields as attorneys, solicitors, conveyancers, money scriveners, auditors and receivers, dissolved on 31 December 1852. In 1851 William and his wife Maria lived at Montagu Grove, Hampstead, Middlesex.

1844: 5 Dec: *Received politely by Mr. Huntley; Mr. Vizard, I believe, A Solicitor from Dursley, was in attendance...*

1847: 23 Jan: *A letter from the Office of Messrs. Vizard & Leman Solrs.—London, addressed to me by error: should have been addressed to E.F.W; as one of the Exors. of the late Lady Burdett ...*

VOHS — Johann Heinrich Andreas and Friederike Margarethe Vohs [33]

Johann Heinrich Andreas Vohs (±1762-1804), actor, was born at Kleve, a city on the lower Rhine at the German–Dutch border. Little is known about his early years. In 1789 he was a member of the national theatre in Bonn, and shortly afterwards he made his debut in Weimar in the role of Eduard Ruhberg in *Verbrechen aus Ehrfurcht*. He married, 1793, Friederike Margarethe Porth (1777-1860), who had recently become an actress in Weimar. Both gained Goethe's respect as actors.

Vohs contributed to the reorganisation of the Weimar company in 1793, and Goethe appointed him director of the theatre, albeit with powers restricted to narrowly defined artistic areas. In 1794 Vohs assumed various other responsibilities within the company, including the management of the theatre library, sets, and costumes. He was relieved of his post in 1796 due to personnel problems.

After his directorship, Vohs concentrated on his own roles, reciting the prologue in the costume of Max Piccolomini and then playing the role of a cuirassier in the premiere of Schiller's *Wallenstein's Lager* on 12 October 1798. In the role of Max Piccolomini in the two other parts of the trilogy, Vohs was criticised for speaking some parts with excessive sentimentality or for not engaging enough youthful verve. His performance in the title role of Schiller's adaptation of *Macbeth* on 14 May 1800 received better reviews; despite Vohs having forgotten some of his lines, Schiller embraced him after the performance. In the premiere of *Maria Stuart*, Vohs played Mortimer and his wife played the role of Maria Stuart.

Financial difficulties prompted Vohs to accept the position of director at the newly organised theatre in Stuttgart in September 1802, though he did perform that summer during the company's guest appearances in Lauchstädt and Rudolstadt. Ill health kept him from having much success in Stuttgart, and he died two years later. His wife, Friederike Margarethe, remained for a time in Stuttgart and then moved to Frankfurt. In 1818 she married Friedrich August Werdy, and continued acting.

1798: 2 Sep: *During my Residence here they represented Kotzebues, Graf Burgund, several of his Comedies besides, his Gustav Vasa, his Sonnenjungfrau, & his Bayard, Schillers three Pieces Wallenstein, Piccolomini, Wallensteins Lager, his Robbers, his translation of Macbeth his Maria Stuart, Goethes Mahomet from Voltaire &c. &c. Vohs is one of the best Actors of lovers, heros &c. in Germany, his Max Piccolomini is masterly, his Charles*

Moor excellent, and so in most Characters which he attempts his voice is powerful & his action very fine. Some Scenes by him in the Sonnenjungfrau as Rolla are excellent -His wife is a tolerable actress, naïve with sensibility, she acts with success Margaretha Löwenhaupt, Thekla, &c... The Theatre does not remain at Weimar, during Summer, it then goes to Lauchstädt, Rudolstadt, & Nuremburg—Actors are here tolerably well paid, Vohs & his wife 1500 Dollars, & Madselle Jagemann at 600 Pr. Ann.

1799: 24 Oct: *Vohs as Graf Klingsberg exhibited all his prowess to the very best advantage it would be impossible to act the Characters better... The Character of Madame Frieburg acted by Vohsin, was kept up in the most masterly stile The beauty of her Face, the softness of her voice the interesting manner which she has of acting all rendering the Feelings of the Author in that Character in the most favourable Light.* 30 Oct: *Vohs acted well as also Teller indeed none of the rest had in the piece an opportunity of shewing themselves off.* 7 Nov., 12 Nov: ... *best Actors Vohsin, Malkolmi, Graff, Schall, Haide, Vohs & Becker.* 20 Nov: *The best Actors were General von Horstwall by Graff, his Son by Vohs. Graf Wernau by Malkolmi, his daughter Linora by Vohsin. Baron Rahming by Schall, his wife by Beck.* 20 Nov., 4 Dec: ... *best actors Graff, Malkolmi, Schlanzovsky, Vohs, Becker, Genast, Haide, Weyrauch, Spitzeder ...* 14 Dec: ... *to a new play by Ziegler Der Lorberkranz, rather interesting than other wise & from it being acted well very pleasing however there is no originality its being almost a scene of Imitation The best acted Characters were Graf von Grauenstein Oberster, Graff, der Erbprinz Rittmeister, Vohs* ... 16 Dec., 23 Dec.

1800: 15 Jan., 20 Jan., 30 Jan., 3 Feb., 12 Feb., 18 Feb., 3 Mar: *Extremely well acted by Haide, Vohs, Cordemann, Caspar, Graff, Spitzeder, and Teller.* 8 Mar., 12 Mar: ... *well acted by Vohs, Teller, Beckin, Metzner, Becker ...* 17 Mar., 5 Apr.

VON SODEN — August Warren Hastings, Baron von Soden — *see also* Hastings, Winter, *and* Woodman [34]

August Warren Hastings, Baron von Soden (1818-1859), landed proprietor, was born at Stuttgart, Württemberg, the son of Rudolph Philipp August von Soden (1785-1849) and Rosalie Chapuset de St Valentin (1793-1818), daughter of Baron Chapuset of Stuttgart. His parents had married at Daylesford, Gloucestershire, on 26 July 1817. His mother Rosalie was a niece to Mrs Hastings and sister to both Louisa Chapuset, who married Thomas Bartholomew Woodman, and Marie Chapuset, who married Thomas Winter. August married Caroline Luise Eugenie Friedrike Freiin von Holzschuher, and together they had at least 1 daughter:

1 Marie Caroline Friedrike Eleonore

After Rosalie's death, Rudolph von Soden married twice more: Eleonore Harsdorf was his second wife, and Helene Drechsel von Deuffstetten (b. 1805) was his third.

1837: 10 Oct: *The company consisted of Lord Redesdale and Miss Mitford, Sir C. & Lady Imhoff, a Baron Soden, who accompanied them, and who is a great nephew of the late Mrs. Hastings, an unhealthy-looking young man, speaking only German, my little remaining skill in that language being brought into play to converse with him... It is understood that Governor H. left every thing in his widow's power: she has left Daylesford estate, with the mansion, furniture, &c. to her son Sir C. Imhoff, for his life, but without any provision for his lady in the event of her surviving him: her money in the funds is understood to be divided between Mrs. Woodman and Mrs. Winter chiefly, perhaps, also some part to Baroness Soden.*

VON WEBER — *see* Weber

VON WERTHER — *see* Werther

VORES — Thomas Vores [35]

Thomas Vores (1804-1875), Church of England clergyman, was baptised in the parish of St Marylebone, Westminster, the son of Thomas Vores (1760-1820) and Elizabeth Chamley (1771-1853). He was educated at Wadham College, Oxford (BA 1826; MA 1828), where he was a tutor from 1828 to 1834, and dean in 1831. He later served as vicar of St Mary in the Castle, Hastings, from 1841 to his death in 1875. Vores married, at Banwell, Somerset, 12 January 1835, Elizabeth Plomley Jenkins (1804-1871); they had 1 son and 1 daughter:

1 Anna (1832-1894)
1 Thomas Stiverd Plomley (1835-1918)

1844: 8 Oct: *The Vice Chancellor's health was given in an eloquent speech by the Revd. Mr. Vores, formerly fellow and tutor of Wadham, now a clergyman at Hastings, and feelingly responded to by Dr. Symons.*

1845: 13 Feb: *Mr. Vores, a former fellow and Tutor of Wadh. Coll., now a Clergyman beneficed at Hastings, a popular preacher, of low Church views, a polished and insinuating person, with great fluency of expression, was, like myself, an inmate with the Vice Chancellor.* 14 Feb.

VULLIAMY — Sarah Vulliamy — *see also* Rice [36]

Sarah Vulliamy, née de Gingins (1758-1841), was the daughter of Jean Rodolphe Dit L'Indien de Gingins-la Sarraz (1712-1778). She married, at St James's, Westminster, 17 April 1779, Benjamin Vulliamy (1747-1811) of clock-making fame. They had 7 sons and 4 daughters:

1 Benjamin Lewis (1780 1854)
1 Mary (1781-1868)
2 Sarah (1783-1841)
2 Francis (1785-1846)
3 Justin Theodore (1787-1870)
3 Frances Lucy (1789-1846)
4 Lewis (1791-1871)
5 Henry (1793-1800)
4 Lucy (1795-1804)
6 Henry (1797-1800)
7 Arthur Frederick (1803-1892)

Sarah's father was a Swiss officer formerly of the East India Company's service. She had been born his natural daughter and heir to his English property, which placed the Vulliamys firmly within the more prosperous ranks of this expatriate community. It is unclear what created the bond of friendship between Mrs Rice and Mrs Vulliamy other than the fact that both had been born illegitimate.

Benjamin Vulliamy was the son of Justin Vulliamy, a clockmaker of Swiss origin, who had moved to London in around 1730. Benjamin earned a reputation as a builder of mantel clocks, decorative timepieces that adorned the halls of high society, and his talent earned him a royal appointment in 1773. Through this he came to receive an endowment of £150 a year and the title of 'king's clockmaker' for George III. In around 1780, Vulliamy was commissioned to build the regulator clock, the main timekeeper of the King's Observatory, Kew, which served as an unofficial prime meridian and was responsible for the official London time until 1884, when the Greenwich Royal Observatory assumed both responsibilities.

W

WADDILOVE — Richard Waddilove [1]

Richard Waddilove (1790-1850), landed proprietor, was born at Rylstone, Burnsall, north of Skipton, Yorkshire, the son of Richard Waddilove (b. 1745) and Mary Sowerby (1758-1808). He appears to have died without family. In his will he bequeathed his estate to two friends, Thomas Mason Johnson and Henry Blake.

1844: 4 Oct: *Mr. Waddilove, of Rilston sent us a box of moor game, which arrived this evening, a compliment paid to us in return for our civility, when in Craven, in allowing him the liberty of shooting over our Scale House property.* 5 Oct.

1850: 29 Mar: *The late Mr. Waddilove of Rilston, who died a short time since, has left by will £1000 to meet other subscriptions, and £200 towards the building of a schoolhouse there.* 5 Jul.

WADDINGHAM — John Waddingham [2]

John Waddingham (1799-1890), railway entrepreneur, was born at South Ferriby, Lincolnshire, the son of Thomas Waddingham (1769-1845) and Ann Husband (1773-1852). Along with George Hudson, he made his fortune with the Midland Railway Company. In 1849 Waddingham purchased the Guiting Grange estate from Revd Reginald Wynniatt (the younger). Wynniatt had inherited a fourth share in the estate in 1819 from his father, who had been passed it in the will of Mary Snell, widow of Powell Snell (d. 1813). He purchased the remaining shares in 1826. At this date the estate comprised the following: Guiting Grange Manor [also known as Guiting Power Manor], together with the mansion house, deer park, and lands in Guiting Power; a small allotment of land in Temple Guiting; a moiety of the manor of Naunton along with the manor house and around 203 acres of land and various cottages in Naunton; and the manor of Westcote, Westcote Farm, and other lands and cottages within the manor, including Gawcombe Farm. The estate was augmented further by John Waddingham, notably by the purchase of Aylworth Manor in 1854, and Roundhill Farm, Naunton, in 1880.

Waddingham married, at Leeds, 1837, Margaret (d. 1880), daughter of James Wilkinson of Bradford, Yorkshire; they had 2 sons and 1 daughter:

1 John (1838-1908)
2 Thomas James (1840-1938)
1 Margaret Anne (1843-1918); succeeded to the Guiting estate on the death of her eldest brother in 1908; married, 1876, Frederick Richard Vavasour Witts (1843-1900), second grandson of the diarist; 3 daughters:
    1 Sophia Margaret Vavasour (1877-1959); married, as his second wife, 20 January 1920, Samuel Gray Richardson (1851-1934); died at Penzance
    2 Mabel Elizabeth Vavasour (1878-1961); married Jack Cheetham
    3 Ethel Frances Vavasour (1881-1950); married Capt. John Kennard; 2 sons and 2 daughters

---

1852: 30 Mar: *At the railway station we met Mr. Waddenham, of Guiting Grange, which residence, however, he does not occupy, though he has greatly enlarged & improved it, but lives in the outskirts of Cheltenham. He is one of those lucky speculators in Railways who has amassed and secured a large fortune, was closely mixed up at one time with the noted Hudson, and participated in some of the odium cast on the transactions of that Railway King - In Gloucestershire, whether as Gentleman, Magistrate or Grand Juror, he is not popular—a novus homo, making money in a doubtful way, and sprung from an obscure origin, is not likely to be very acceptable to the old County Squires, whose lands, though often hampered with mortgage, have descended through several generations.*

1853: 2 Mar: *Mr. Waddingham has made a liberal offer for the purchase of all Dolphin's Estates, but Mrs. D. treats it as greatly below the value.*

WADDINGTON — Benjamin Waddington — *see also* Port [3]

Benjamin Waddington (1749-1828), landed proprietor, was born at Walkeringham, Nottinghamshire, the son of Joshua Waddington (1710-1780) and Anne Ferrand (1716-1806). He married, at St Swithin's, Walcot, Bath, 25 February 1789, Georgina Mary Ann (1771-1850), daughter of John Port and Mary D'Ewes of Ilam, Derbyshire. Georgina was a famous protégé of Mrs Mary Delany, née Granville (1700-1788), whose friends included Horace Walpole, Queen Charlotte, and George III, and who was known to combine science and craft in her many creative endeavours. Benjamin and Georgina had a least 6 daughters:

1 Harriet (b. & d. 1790)
2 Frances (1791-1876); *see below*
3 Mary Anne (1792-1793)
4 Emilia (1794-1819)
5 Matilda (b. & d. 1797)
6 Augusta (1802-1896); became baroness of Abercarn and of Llanover; *see below*

Benjamin Waddington bought the Llanover estate from the Cecil family, of The Dyffryn, Glamorgan, in about 1792. With the agreement of all his daughters, he settled the estate on his youngest daughter, Augusta (1802-1896). In 1823 she married Benjamin Hall (1802-1867), of Abercarn, and the neighbouring estates of Llanover and Abercarn were united. Benjamin Hall was created Baron Llanover in 1859, and Augusta is best remembered as Lady Llanover, 'Gwenynen Gwent'.

Frances (1791-1876), Benjamin and Georgina's eldest surviving daughter, married Christian Charles Bunsen (1791-1860), and one of their ten children, Karl de Bunsen (1821-1887), married his second cousin Mary Isabell Waddington, thus uniting the two branches of the Waddington family.

1804: 11 Aug: *At a party at Miss Ports: Mr. & Mrs. & Miss Waddington with two young ladies, the Murrays, Blunts, Mrs. Massey & ourselves. Very dull. Mrs. Waddington beautiful, elegant & well informed.* 13-14 Aug., 22 Aug., 1 Sep: *At an entertaining Party at Mrs Waddington's, Mr. & Mrs. A. Thompson Mr. & Mrs. Ball, Mrs. & Miss Buikstocks, Napier's &c. much literary conversation.* 4 Sep: *Dined stupidly enough at Mr. Port's to meet the Waddington Party.*

1828: 3 Apr: *Mrs. Delany was Aunt to my excellent old friend, now no more, Mr. Granville; consequently to Mr. Dewes of Wellesbourne, & Mrs. Port, and Mrs. Waddington, the eldest Miss Port, herself now advanced in years, once a beautiful, always a talented woman, in whose society I have often been, was brought up by Mrs. D. Mrs. Waddington married an opulent gentleman, who having made a fortune in trade, purchased a good estate in Monmouthshire, Lanover near Abergavenny, which has been the place of their residence.*

WAKELAM — William Walter Wakelam [4]

William Walter Wakelam (b. 1827) was the son of William John Wakelam and his wife, Sarah, of Bourton-on-the-Water. William was baptised by Thomas Cole, a protestant dissenting minister.

1853: 14 Dec: *The Rel. Off. called upon me as to the removal of the Lunatic Wakelam from Bourton, which was is likely to take place... To Mr. Waller's at Bourton, and there, having obtained the opinion of Mr. Moore as to the insanity of W. Wakelam, whom we personally examined at the Police Station, made an order for his conveyance to-morrow by the Rel. Officer, to the licenced house for reception of Lunatics at Hook Norton, kept by Mr. Mallam.*

1854: 3 Feb: ... *to Mr. Wilkins, Bourton on the Water, for some further information as to the antecedents in W. Wakelam's history, to enable me to state a case fully for an opinion by the P.L.C. as to the making an order for his maintenance as a Lunatic on the parish of his Settlement, or on the County if that course can be taken legally, supposing him to be an American Citizen.* 6 Feb., 8 Feb., 6 Apr: *Called on Mrs. Gregory to enquire as to a letter from the lunatic Wakelam written to Martha Lea, and forwarded through Mr. Pearce for my judgment & perusal. It refers to his confinement in the Lunatic private asylum at Hook Norton.* 25 May, 3 Jun.

WAKEMAN — Mary Wakeman of Little Malvern [5]

Mary Wakeman, née Williams (*c.* 1760-1840), was the daughter of Thomas Williams, of Trellynia, co. Flint, and his wife, Elizabeth. In the mid-eighteenth century the manor of Little Malvern was owned by Mary's mother Elizabeth, who conveyed it in 1766-67 to Edmund Lechmere, evidently for the purposes of some settlement. In 1771, as a widow, she still appears to have held the manor with her daughter Mary, possibly as a tenant. Mary still eventually inherited the property.

Mary married, 1796, Walter Wakeman (d. 1801), of the Mythe, Tewkesbury, who also owned property at Beckford, Gloucestershire. He had been honoured in 1788 with a morning call by King George III on his visit to Tewkesbury and the Mythe Tute. Mary was Walter's second wife; his first was Anne, widow of a Mr Chinn. After their marriage, Mary and Walter lived at Little Malvern, and died without issue. Mary left Little Malvern Court to her kinsman William Berington, of Hereford, son of her second cousin Charles. When he died in 1847 the manor passed to his son Charles Michael, who enjoyed it until his death in 1897, when it passed to his son Capt. William Berington.

In most records Mary Wakeman is referred to as Mrs Wakeham. Chamber's *A General History of Malvern* offers some information to confirm Mary's maiden name as Williams, and further information is provided in the correspondence of Mary Barrett Browning:

> Great is our surprise to hear that Mrs Wakeman has let Malvern for a year to a Mr Burns a Catholic, because she is too poor to keep up both houses: he comes in May, & she goes to Sarnsfield—poor Miss Harper is to occupy a room at Mr Jenkin's opposite—she is much the same, never likely to be well—it is sad to think that the good old lady must be so imposed upon by her steward & people about her, as to be so straigthened [*sic*]—I send you poor Miss Price's kind note.

The Wakeman family at Beckford remained Catholic following the Reformation. Benedict Wakeman died in 1765 at Beckford, and it seems likely that Walter was his son or grandson. (*See below*, William Wakeman.)

1825: 14 May: *The farthest extent of our drive was to Little Malvern, a lovely rural village on the slope of the hill, embosomed in trees, & boasting a singularly romantic ancient church, half in ruins, festooned with ivy and other wild plants. Close to it is the old manor house, chiefly of lath and plaster, retaining one diminutive turret, rising in old fashioned gable ends exhibiting modern windows, but grouping well in the picture, as it lies in the lap of a luxuriant foliage, commanding a fine distant view over the vale of the Severn, while the foreground and home accompaniments are rich and picturesque. It is the residence of Mrs. Wakeman, an opulent Roman Catholic lady, advanced in years, and connected with a Gentleman of the same name and faith, who enjoys a good estate at Beckford in Gloucestershire.* 1827: 1 Aug.

WAKEMAN — William Wakeman [6]

William Wakeman (1739-1836), landed proprietor, was the son of Henry Wakeman (1709-1787) and Mary Bracy (1710-1766). He succeeded to the Beckford estate on the death of his father, and lived there, unmarried, throughout his extremely long life. It seems quite likely that he was a brother of Walter Wakeman of the Mythe. He had three maiden sisters: Teresa (1747-1833), Ann (1751-1833), and Appolonia (1755-1830).

1843: 6 Oct: *The late Mr. Wakeman, the Roman Catholic Squire of Beckford, explained to Dr. Timbrill that this door was that through which the excommunicated were expelled, and afterwards on penitence re-admitted.*

WALCOT — Mr Walcot, wine merchant of London

1845: 24 May: *A letter from a Mr. Walcot in London, of whom Howell had ordered for me six dozen of Claret of different sorts; the wine arrived in cases.* 28 May, 30 May, 13 Jun, 18-19 Jun., 21 Jun.

WALCOTT — Stephen Walcott [7]

Sir Stephen Walcott (1806-1887), secretary to the Colonial Land and Emigration Commission, was born at Barbados, the son of Robert John Walcott, a slave owner. After moving to England he entered at Lincoln's Inn and was called to the bar in 1829. In 1832 he was appointed an assistant commissioner for inquiring into the working of the poor laws in England. Three years later he went to Canada with the governor-general as chief secretary to the government. He returned to England in 1838, and his next appointment was as secretary to Her Majesty's Colonial Land and Emigration Commission and to the South Australian Colonisation Commission. The latter had been established by a commission from Queen Victoria on 14 January 1840.

In July 1860 Walcott became second colonial land and emigration commissioner, and in January 1877 he succeeded to the position of sole commissioner. He received the companionship of the Order of St Michael and St George in 1872, and was made a knight commander of the order in 1877. By the end of 1877 the Treasury lords refused to approve a budget for the commissioners for the coming year. Walcott informed the colonial office that he would be resigning on 31 March 1878, and on this date the Colonial Land and Emigration Commission was abolished.

Walcott married, at Quebec, 30 January 1838, Frances Isabella Davidson (1816-1849); they had 3 daughters:

1 Elizabeth Isabel (1839-1867)
2 Jessie (1842-1917)
3 Fanny Constance (1845-1922)

1851: 21 Feb: *Two labouring men came to consult me about Emigration to Australia. Wrote on their behalf to Mr. Walcot, Secretary to the Government Emigration Board, for information on the subject.* 25 Feb., 10 Mar., 12 Apr.

WALDRON — a protégé of Thomas Lloyd Baker of Hardwicke Court

1836: 5 Sep: *Mr. Baker, accompanied by his elève, young Waldron, arrived to dinner, and to pass some days with us.* 6 Sep: *After breakfast Baker and young Waldron set out in their gig for Upper Guiting, to attend the sale of the celebrated South-down flock of the late Mr. Talbot, and I followed them on horseback an hour afterwards.* 7-8 Sep., 12 Sep.

WALE — Augusta Caroline Wale and the Wale family of Shelford, Cambridgeshire[8]

Augusta Caroline Wale (1825-1925) was the third daughter of Gen. Sir Charles Wale, KCB (1763-1845) and his third wife, Henrietta Brent (1788-1853). She married, at Chesterton, Cambridgeshire, 3 July 1856, Richard Dill (1822-1912); they had 4 sons and 2 daughters:

1 John Frederick Gordon (1859-1925)
2 Richard Marcus Gordon (1860-1917)
3 Robert Charles Gordon (1862-1918)
1 Augusta Helena Cecily Gordon (1864-1946)
4 George Francis Gordon (1865-1907)
2 Mildred Henrietta Gordon (1867-1932)

Augusta's father, Gen. Sir Charles Wale, had a daughter, Isabella Martha, by his second wife, Isabella Johnson. She married Sherlock Willis, and they had 7 sons and 1 daughter. Wale had a further 6 sons and 4 daughters by his third wife, Henrietta Brent. These daughters were named Henrietta, Louisa, Augusta, and Cecil-Marianne. By 1853 the only one remaining unmarried was Augusta, so it is probable that she was the 'Miss Waile' mentioned by Francis Witts.

1853: 6 Jan: *At dinner there was a pleasant reunion of residents of the village; Mr. and Mrs. Sherlock Willis, and her sister, Miss Waile; and Mr. Surman with his sister, Miss Goodlake.*

WALE — Job Wale[9]

Job Wale (b. 1802), stone mason, was born at Temple Guiting, Gloucestershire, the son of William and Jane Wale. From his prison record we know that he was 6 feet 1¾ inches in height, with brown hair, grey eyes, a fresh complexion, and an oval visage. He was committed on 23 April 1839 by Francis Witts for stealing a ewe teg (a female sheep between one and two years of age). He was convicted at Gloucester assizes on 3 August 1839 with a sentence of transportation for life. He was one of 230 convicts transported on the *Woodbridge* on 10 October 1839, which arrived in New South Wales on 26 February 1840. In 1844 he was shipped from Norfolk Island to Tasmania on the *Maitland*, and appears to have received a 'ticket of leave' in 1849. Tickets of leave were a form of passport given to prisoners who were released before the end of their sentence, meaning that they were free to pursue a new life in the new colony.

1839: 9 Aug: *Job Wale, the Sheep stealer, from Kineton, was sentenced to transportation for life: he was tried by Mr. Justice Alderson, who took occasion to pass a high compliment on Otway, for the manner in which, on this occasion, he had discharged his duty as Constable, and ordered him from the County rates a remuneration of £5.*

WALKER — Adam Walker[10]

Adam Walker (±1731-1821), philosopher and inventor, was born at Patterdale, Westmoreland, the son of a woollen manufacturer. His reputation as a student at the age of 15 procured him the post of usher at Ledsham School in the West Riding of Yorkshire. Three years later he was appointed writing-master and accountant at the free school at Macclesfield, where he studied mathematics. He made some ventures in trade which were unsuccessful, and lectured on astronomy at Manchester. After four years at Macclesfield, the success of his lectures encouraged him to set up a seminary at Manchester on his own account. He gave this up a little later, however, to become a travelling lecturer in natural philosophy. After visiting most of the great towns in Great Britain and Ireland, he met Joseph Priestley, who induced him to lecture in the Haymarket in 1778. Meeting with success, he took a house in George Street, Hanover Square, and read lectures every winter to numerous audiences. He was engaged as lecturer by the provost of Eton College, Edward Barnard, whose example was followed by the heads of Westminster, Winchester, and other public schools. In his leisure, Walker amused himself by perfecting various mechanical inventions. Among them were engines for raising water, carriages powered by wind and steam, a road mill, a machine for watering land, and a dibbling plough.

Adam Walker was married to Eleanor; they had 3 sons and 1 daughter:

1 William (±1766-1816)
2 Adam John (±1769-1839)
3 Deane Franklin (1778-1865)
1 Eliza (d. 1856); married Benjamin Gibson of Gosport, Hampshire

---

1801: 3 Jul: *We dined with her Ladyship afterwards, meeting Mr. Walker a well known lecturer in Philosophy possessed of much general knowledge.*

WALKER — Anne Walker — *see also* Barr[11]

Anne Walker, née Barr (1785-1848), was the daughter of Martin Barr of Henwick Hall, Hallow, Worcestershire. She married, 1804, Jonathan Walker (1781-1842). She bought Peckham Grove, where Lady Lyttelton lived before she moved to Peachfield Lodge. By the time of the 1841 census she was living with her brothers Martin and George and sister Maria back at Henwick Hall. Mr Walker is not mentioned in the diaries, so Anne may have been estranged, although an enigmatic entry of 27 April 1840 may indicate his ongoing presence.

1827: 2 Aug: *Our family party were assembled at dinner at my Aunt's but adjourned for tea to Captain Witts's; a Mrs. Walker, residing at Pickham Grove, my Aunt's late abode, a near neighbour on the common, joined our circle.*

1829: 26 Aug: *Mrs. Walker, a very estimable woman, but a great invalid, who resides at Pickham Grove, my Aunt's former abode, came to tea, and passed the evening.* 27-28 Aug.

1830: 19 Apr: *I was not long before I went to Montpellier Parade, in search of my cousins Captain & Mrs. Witts, who had been paying a visit for a few days to their friend & neighbour at Malvern, Mrs. Walker, who has been residing during this Winter at Cheltenham.*

1833: 10 Sep., 12 Sep: *Called on Mrs. Walker at Pickham—her Mother, Mrs. Barr—and an unmarried sister were her guests.*

1834: 10 Sep., 12 Sep.

1836: 18 Jul., 19-20 Jul., 22 Jul.

1838: 23 Apr: *He experienced kind attentions from all, including our poor friend, Mrs. Walker, at Pickham, who is sinking under a dropsy.* 20 Jul: *After breakfast called on poor Mrs. Walker at Pickham Grove, who, tho' in a wretched state of health from dropsy and other ailments, wished to see me.*

1840: 24-25 Apr., 27 Apr: *Wrote a few lines to Mr. Cole, Portrait Painter, Worcester, this Artist some years ago painted an excellent picture of my late Aunt, which it is my son's wish should be hung up with other family portraits in Upper Slaughter: Mr. C. had intimated through Mr. Walker a wish to varnish it...* 23 Jun.

1842: 9 Apr., 16 Apr., 22 Apr.

1845: 8 Jul.

1846: 13 Jul.

1847: 29 Sep, 8 Oct., 7 Nov.

1848: 1 May: *Mrs. Barr and her children left us for Mrs. Walker's at Henwick, near Worcester ... Mrs. Walker's health is very precarious: with her reside her unmarried sister, and an unmarried brother, to both of whom Mrs. C.B. is attached, as they are to her & her children.* 26 Jul: *M.W. received a letter from Eliza Daniell, announcing the death of Mr. George Barr, at Henwick; where he resided with his sister, Mrs. Walker, and Miss Barr.* 27 Aug: *The newspapers announce the death of Mrs. Walker at Henwick Hall.*

WALKER — Charles Ludlow Walker [12]

Charles Ludlow Walker (1787-1856), merchant, shipowner, and JP, was born at Harborne, Worcestershire, the son of Thomas Walker (1756-1805) and Harriet Ludlow (b. 1763). He married, at Areley Kings, 16 November 1816, Mary Anne (1794-1869), daughter of Reginald Pyndar (1755-1831) and his wife, Mary (1762-1849); they had 2 sons and 2 daughters:

1 Charles Pyndar Beauchamp (1817-1894)
1 Mary Anne (1821-1857)
2 Charles (b. 1831)
2 Elizabeth (1838-1907)

Charles Ludlow Walker lived at Redland, Bristol, and was a Gloucestershire JP. He was influential in Bristol affairs: he was one of the witnesses for the bill for the Great Western Railway and was a partner in the Harfords and Bristol Brass and Copper Company.

1820: 15 Oct.

1827: 16 Oct.

1830: 12 Jan.

1846: 5 Apr.

WALKER — David Walker [13]

David Walker (1761-1831), printer, was based in Hereford, where he bought the *Hereford Journal* in 1791. He bought the *Gloucester Journal* and presumably also the printing interests from the Raikes family in 1802. The *Gloucester Journal* was established in 1722 by Robert Raikes and William Dicey, who were already partners in a Northampton newspaper. Raikes, who carried on the paper alone from 1725, was succeeded at his death in 1757 by his son Robert. Robert Raikes (junior), a practical and successful businessman, used the paper to further his philanthropic aims.

David Walker was married to Elizabeth (1767-1845); they had 2 sons and 2 daughters:

1 Alexander (1788-1838)
1 Elizabeth (1791-1880)
2 Ann (b. 1793)
2 David Mowbray (±1791-1871); *see below*

1826: 25 Sep: *The miscellaneous expences of the meeting are extremely heavy: Messrs. Walker's Bill for printing, advertising &c. exceeded £130.*

WALKER — David Mowbray Walker — *see also* Meyler [14]

David Mowbray Walker (±1791-1871), printer and publisher, was the son of David and Elizabeth Walker (*above*). He was the proprietor of the *Gloucester Journal* and a Gloucestershire JP. He married, first, an unknown woman; they had 1 daughter:

1 Ellen Eliza (1828-1898)

He married secondly, at St Mary's, Lambeth, Surrey, 17 June 1836, Elizabeth Long (1809-1889); they had at least 1 son:

1 George F. (b. 1836)

1846: 25 Aug: *Walked to the Lunatic Asylum, where I found Curtis Hayward presiding at the meeting of Visitors; the other members present were H. C. Clifford, C. Crawley, A Sayers, T B Ll Baker, and D M Walker.*

WALKER — James Walker [15]

James Walker (±1771-1841), primus of the Scottish Episcopal Church, was the son of Alexander Walker of Fraserburgh, Aberdeenshire. He was educated at Marischal College, Aberdeen, and St John's College, Cambridge (BA 1789 & 1793; MA 1796; DD 1826). He was tutor to Sir John Hope, 11th baronet of Craighall (1781-1853), and travelled with him and his brother Hugh for two or three years, which included a period of tuition at the Belvedere, Weimar, where he appears to have taken on additional duties. Agnes Witts mentioned James Walker in her diaries several times between September 1798 and June 1800, therefore it may be surmised that the Hopes and Revd Walker were at Weimar for at least a year and nine months.

On his return to Scotland Walker was appointed minister at St Peter's chapel, Edinburgh, where he remained until 1829. He became dean of Edinburgh in 1808, and served as bishop of Edinburgh from 1830 to his death in 1841. He was appointed pantonian professor at the Episcopal Theological College, Edinburgh, in 1830, and primus of the Scottish Episcopal Church in 1837. He held both these posts until his death. He was the first protestant clergyman to establish a regular service in Rome in 1819, and he was sub-editor of the *Encyclopaedia Britannica*.

1798: 2 Sep: *Mr. Walker, a Clergyman of the Church of England, keeps up the youths of that Country in the Practice of their Religion, & gives to foreigners ample Instruction in the English Language.*

1799: 19 Aug: *To Belvedere in the hopes of playing at cricket in which I was disappointed: spoke to Mr. Walker.*

1800: 27 Jan: *In the Evening. Mr. Walker & the two Mr Hops & Mademoiselle d'Outel. Played at Pope Joan.* 27 Feb: *Mr. Walker drank Tea with us.* 3 Apr: *On our return in the Evening, we took leave of the Fenwicks & of Miss Walker.*

WALKER — James Walker — *see also* Billingsley [16]

James Walker (1794-1854), Church of England clergyman, was the son of Robert and Elizabeth Walker. He was educated at New College, Oxford (BA 1816; MA 1819), where he was chaplain from 1815 to 1823. Walker was ordained deacon on 27 September 1818 and priest on 19 December 1819. His first clerical appointment was as curate of Withington, Gloucestershire, from 21 September 1826;

this was followed by the rectorship of Raddington, Chipstable, Somerset, from 4 January 1833. He married, at Eynsham, 1824, Fanny [Frances] Billingsley. They lived for a while at Charlton Kings while James was curate at nearby Withington. The family emigrated to Australia on board the *Arabian* and arrived at Launceston, Van Diemen's Land, on 27 August 1841. They moved to New South Wales in 1843. Walker was initially a missionary, but later became headmaster at The King's School, Parramatta.

1835: 19 Jun: *With E.F.W. dined at Billingsley's, met Escott, Walker & a boy son of the latter.*

1837: 16 May: *E.F.W. and myself dined with Billingsley, meeting Messrs. Lewes, W B Pole, Walker, Waller, Polson, Bowen and Vavasour.*

1838: 22 May: *In the evening Billingsley walked over with two fine boys, his nephews, sons of Mrs. Walker of Charlton Kings, to shoot some rooks.*

1840: 13 Sep: *After evening service I drove to Wormington, where I was very kindly and hospitably received by Mr. & Mrs. Billingsley ... He has under his tuition a youth of 15, a son of Mr. Quicke, of Newton St. Cyres, near Crediton; also Mr. Gist's eldest son, a puny boy; and a fine lad, son of Mr. Walker of Charlton Kings.*

1842: 26 Apr: *Saw only Sophia Ford, and learnt the satisfactory particulars received of Fred. Ford's safety. Having gone out to settle in one of the Australian colonies, and reached Launceston in Van Dieman's Land in safety, where he parted from Mr. Walker, who, with his family, is settled at George Town as a Missionary, he proceeded in a schooner to Port Philip with all his property.*

WALKER — James Walker [17]

James Walker (1809-1883), corn merchant, was born at Compton Abdale, Gloucestershire, the son of Thomas Walker (1752-1814) and Mary Dyer (1771-1857). He married, at Eastington, Northleach, Gloucestershire, 19 March 1842, Ann (1821-1899), daughter of Charles Powell (1783-1834) and Martha Weatherstone (1788-1855); they had 3 sons and 5 daughters:

1 Mary (1842-1916)
1 Joseph (1844-1879)
2 Thomas (1848-1911)
2 Annie (1850-1927)
3 James (b. 1852)
3 Rebecca E. (1853-1940)
4 Martha (b. 1856)
5 Mabel (b. 1867)

The family lived at Coal Yard Farm, Northleach.

1838: 25 Aug: *Wrote to Walker, Corndealer at N Leach, to order a supply of oats and beans.*

1840: 27 Jun: ... *to Mr. James Walker, Stow Northleach, with a remittance for Oats supplied to me, and an order for more.* 16 Oct: *After which, and paying for a quantity of Oats which had been supplied to me by the Corn dealer, Walker, I rejoined M W. at the Vicarage.*

1842: 15 Feb.

1843: 6 Feb: *Wrote to Walker, Corn dealer, Northleach, with a remittance for oats supplied.*

1846: 24 Nov: *Omitted to mention a letter which I wrote to Walker of Northleach, Corn merchant, for a supply of oats.* 29 Nov.

1847: 19 Jan., 22 Jan: ... *from Jas. Walker, Northleach, acknowledging my late remittance of his of £7. 0. 0 for oats.* 4 Apr: *Wrote to Mr. Walker, Corn-dealer, Northleach, desiring him to furnish me with five quarters of oats.*

1849: 26 Dec: *To Mr. James Walker, Northleach, with a cheque for oats supplied, and with an order for more.*

1850: 5 Apr., 15 Jul., 19 Jul., 8 Oct., 28 Oct., 1 Nov.

1851: 22 Mar.

1852: 5 Jun., 9 Jun.

WALL — Elizabeth Wall [18]

Elizabeth Wall, née Whitmore (1783-1843), was born at Bridgnorth, Shropshire, the daughter of William Whitmore (1745-1816) and Frances Barbara Lister (1750-1792). She married, at Quatt Malvern, Shropshire, 3 August 1802, Revd John Wall (1775-1817), rector of Quatt, near Bridgnorth; they had at least 2 sons and 1 daughter:

1 John Whitmore (1803-1833)
1 Elizabeth (1808-1828)
2 Henry Edward (1809-1837); *see below*

1832: 10 Apr: *We all went to dine with our worthy old friend Lady Reade, at Oddington ... we met Mr. & Mrs. Ford & Miss Ford, Mr. & Mrs. Whitmore Jones, accompanied by a Sister of Mr. W. Jones's (a widow, Mrs. Wall) and her son, a fellow of New College.*

WALL — Henry Edward Wall [19]

Henry Edward Wall (1809-1837) was the second son of Revd John Wall, of Stockton, Shropshire, and Elizabeth Whitmore (*above*). He was educated at New College, Oxford.

1832: 10 Apr: *We all went to dine with our worthy old friend Lady Reade, at Oddington ... we met Mr. & Mrs. Ford & Miss Ford, Mr. & Mrs. Whitmore Jones, accompanied by a Sister of Mr. W. Jones's (a widow, Mrs. Wall) and her son, a fellow of New College.*

WALL — Martin Wall [20]

Martin Wall (1747-1824), physician, was the son of John Wall (1708-1776), of Worcester, and Catherine Sandys (1709-1796). He was educated at Winchester College, New College, Oxford (BA 1767; MA 1771), St Bartholomew's Hospital, London, and Edinburgh University (BMed 1773; DMed 1777). He was a fellow of New College, Oxford, from 1763 to 1778, and clinical professor there from 1785 to his death in 1824.

Wall began practising medicine at Oxford in 1774, and on 2 November 1775 he was elected physician to the Radcliffe Infirmary. His work on the use of opium for low fevers during the typhus epidemic at Oxford was published in 1786. He was elected a fellow of the College of Physicians in 1787, and Harveian orator and a fellow of the Royal Society in 1788. He drank tea with Dr Samuel Johnson at Oxford in June 1784; Boswell called him 'this learned, ingenious, and pleasing gentleman'.

Martin Wall married Mary (1754-1841), daughter of John and Ann Hawkins; they had at least 1 son and 3 daughters:

1 Mary Hawkins (b. 1779)
2 Sophia Elizabeth (b. 1781); married, at Oxford, 3 January 1805, Revd Gilbert Heathcote (1765-1829)
3 Catherine Emily (b. 1783)
1 Martin Sandys (1785-1871), chaplain-in-ordinary to the prince regent and to the British Embassy at Vienna

Dr Wall was an old friend of Edward and Agnes Witts.

1801: 20 May.

1802: 10 Feb: *We called without success upon Dr. & Mrs. Wall.* 11 Feb: *Breakfasted with Pering called upon Mrs. Wall employed in arranging my Rooms.* 7 Mar: *The Sheldons most*

agreeable, meeting there Maurice of Oriel, & Dr. & Miss S. Wall. 4 Jun: *Wrote to George, Mr. Matthews, & Mr. Granville, at the Walls in the Evening a pleasant party.* 24 Jun: *To the play with the Walls.* 26 Jul: *Called on the Walls, &c: the Warden, Brown.*
1803: 19 Nov: *At a large & pleasant party at Dr. Wall's.*

WALLBANK — Thomas Wallbank [21]

Thomas Wallbank (±1805-1881), farmer, was born at Clapham, Yorkshire. He married, first, at Giggleswick, Yorkshire, 6 December 1828, Agnes Bleazard (1806-1841); they had 1 son and 2 daughters:

1 Isabella (b. 1832)
1 Robert (b. 1835)
2 Agnes (b. 1838)

Wallbank married secondly, at Settle, Yorkshire, April 1842, Ellen Metcalfe (1817-1891); they had at least 4 sons and 4 daughters:

1 Thomas (1845-1922)
2 James (1845-1922)
1 Esther Mary (b. 1847)
3 William (b. 1847)
2 Ellen (b. 1850)
3 Nancy (1852-1919)
4 Mary Jane (b. 1855)
4 Adam (1859-1936)

1838: 13 Sep: *Wrote a note to Mr. Hartley by Christ. Geldard, when he went after breakfast to Settle, requesting him to send a messenger to Ingleborough Lodge, to ascertain from the Messrs. Farrer the character of T. Wallbank, the highest bidder for the Stainforth Hall farm; who had referred to them ...* 17 Sep: *... but Wallbank declined fulfilling his bargain, on the plea that his brother had peremptorily refused to enter on the farm in partnership with him, objecting on the ground that the rent offered was excessive.*

WALLER — the Waller family

The Waller family was descended from Aldred de Waller (d. 1183) of Newark, Nottinghamshire. The family's most prominent member was David de Waller, who for thirty years served as master of the rolls to King Edward III. More recent generations of the family lived at Hall Barn, Beaconsfield, Buckinghamshire. Edmund Waller (1725-1788) married Martha, daughter of Rowland Philipps of Haverford. They had two sons: Edmund (1757-1810) and Henry (1760-1824). Henry (*below*) succeeded his brother Edmund to the family estates in 1810.

WALLER — Harry Waller — *see also* Dolphin [21]

Henry [Harry] Waller (1760-1824), Church of England clergyman and landed proprietor, was born at Farmington, Gloucestershire, the son of Edmund Waller (1725-1788) and Martha Phillips (1732-1788). He was educated at Christ Church, Oxford (BCL 1787), and ordained deacon on 6 December 1783 and priest on 18 December 1784. His first clerical appointment was as rector of Farmington from 27 December 1786. He was also vicar of Winslow in 1789, and of Hazleton, Gloucestershire, from 1793 to his death in 1824. He married, at St George's, Hanover Square, Westminster, 15 May 1797, Maria (1768-1838), daughter of John Dolphin, of Eyford, Gloucestershire, and Margaretta Eeles (1740-1793); they had 3 sons and 2 daughters:

1 Eliza (1800-1869)
1 Harry Edmund (1804-1869); *see below*
2 Maria (b. 1809)
2 Robert Blackwell (1810-1871), Church of England clergyman; *see below*
3 Stephen Richard (1813-1875), Church of England clergyman; *see below*

The family resided at Farmington Lodge. Waller removed himself to Boulogne in 1821 to escape his creditors, and died there in 1824.

1802: 1 Jan: *After dinner we repaired to Mrs. Whalley's, meeting a Mrs. & Miss Waller & Miss Beaufort Irish people. The Evening did not pass disagreeably; & a cold Chicken for supper concluded the events of the day.*
1829: 10 Oct: *... dined and slept yesterday with our friends, the Browne's, at Salperton; We met a large party ... Mrs. Waller, her two daughters, and her son Robert (now of Brazennose)...*
1832: 17 May: *We dined to-day with Mrs. Waller at Farmington to meet Mr. & Mrs. John Shirley.*
1834: 18 Aug: *Rode to Farmington, to call on Miss Rollinson at Mrs. Waller's; found the ladies at home. Met John Browne, Harry and Robert Waller.*
1835: 25 Apr: *Mrs. Waller and her younger daughter called.*
1837: 20 May: *Miss Waller was at Bath: Maria being unwell, did not appear.* 31 Jul: *Called also on Mrs. Waller, whom we found better in health than usual.* 7 Aug.
1838: 25 Jun: *Drove to Farmington with M.W. to call on Mrs. Waller.*

WALLER — Harry Edmund Waller — *see also* Boudier *and* Elwes [22]

Harry Edmund Waller (1804-1869), JP, DL, and landed proprietor, of Hall Barn and later of Farmington Grove, was born at Farmington, Gloucestershire, the eldest son of Henry Waller and Maria Dolphin (*above*). He was educated at Eton College and Brasenose College, Oxford. He married, 15 June 1826, Caroline Elizabeth (1806-1840), daughter of John Larking of Clare House, East Malling, Kent; they had 3 sons and 5 daughters:

1 Edmund (1828-1898); educated at Mr James Chorncok's School, Ripon, and Brasenose College, Oxford; called to the bar, 1853; married, at St Mary's, Bryanston Square, Westminster, 7 July 1859, Lucy (1831-1878), daughter of Henry Elwes (1787-1850) and Susan (1784-1832), daughter of Anthony Hamond, of Westacre, Norfolk, and Sarah Case; at least 1 son and 2 daughters:
    1 Edmund (b. & d. 1860)
    1 Caroline Lucy (1861-1863)
    2 Rachel Elizabeth Frances (1868-1954); married, at St Peter's, Farmington, 3 September 1889, Cecil Fane de Salis (1857-1948); 9 sons and 4 daughters
1 Adela Dorothea (1830-1890); died unmarried at Worcester
2 William Noel (1831-1909); died unmarried at Farmington Lodge
2 Georgina Mary (1833-1894); married, at Northleach, 1855, Edward John Beckett Marriott (1818-1882), born at Bangalore, Karnataka, India, second son of Gen. Thomas Marriott (1773-1847) of the Bank, Worcester; no known children
3 Emily Maria (1834-1919); married, at Farmington, 15 May 1862, Lt-Gen. Edward William Boudier (1819-1890), son of Revd John Boudier (1787-1874) and Marianne Rooke (1790-1887). Boudier commenced his military career in the Madras Army in January 1836, and served in the Crimean War (in which his brother was an army chaplain) and the Indian Mutiny, after which he continued as an officer in the Indian Army, still based in Madras, and retired to Torquay in 1881. He and Emily Maria had 1 son and 3 daughters:
    1 Georgiana Mary (b. 1863)
    2 Caroline Elizabeth (1867-1954); married, at Newton Abbot, Devon, January 1888, Revd Edward Mapleton Dew (b. 1859)

1 Harry Edmund (1871-1955); bought a farm in California upon his father's death; died at Napa County, California, USA

3 Emily Dorothea (1874-1941); died unmarried at Stone, Staffordshire

4 Caroline Matilda (1836-1871); died unmarried

3 Harry (1837-1857); died unmarried

5 Elizabeth (1840-1892); died unmarried at Farmington

Harry Waller was a JP and DL, and high sheriff for Gloucestershire in 1834-35. He sold Hall Barn, Beaconsfield, in 1832, and inherited from Miss Sophia Elizabeth Lawrence, his second cousin once removed, 2,800 acres at Kirkby Fleetham, North Yorkshire, and Clint, south of Ripon. Harry was keen on horse racing, and his horse won the Ascot Gold Cup in 1852.

1825: 25 Oct: *I attended the Annual Meeting of the Commissioners of the Crickley Hill district of Turnpike roads ... & Mr. H. Waller. The latter gentleman qualified: he is lately come of age, and is about to fix his residence on his Gloucestershire property at Farmington, which he recently endeavoured to dispose of: his Buckinghamshire seat, Hall-barn, near Beaconsfield, is let for a term of years. He seems a well disposed youth, but not particularly prepossessing: his purpose of paying his father's debts to the amount of £20,000 is much to his credit.*

1826: 15 Sep: *And this seems the proper place for inserting a list of some of the leading families & individuals, whose presence on this occasion served so many good purposes; benefiting the charity ... Mr. & Mrs. H. Waller, Mrs. & the Misses Waller ... The names of the Stewards for 1829 were then announced ... Mr. Waller of Farmington by Mr. Dolphin.*

1827: 6 Jul: *Afterwards I dined at Mr. Waller's at Farmington, meeting Mr. & Mrs. Ford, Mr. & Mrs. Boudier, Mrs. Waller & her two daughters. A pleasant visit. Mr. Waller seems a very promising young man. I have known him from boyhood, though we never exchanged visits at Farmington during his father's life time, who was a singular character, and far from estimable; yet as having married Mr. J. Dolphin's sister, a very respectable woman, we were frequently thrown together. Mrs. Waller has gone through many trials; she has had to endure her husband's misconduct, as regarded his duties to herself, the embarrasment of affairs, to which mismanagement had led and extravagance had aided, her husband's exhausted constitution and his latter years weighed down with the burdens of a decaying mind and body, in that retreat at Boulogne, which so many impoverished English gentry resort to. But when her husband died, the scene brightened. Her son was much attached to her, and had been educated at Brazennose; he honourably resolved to pay his deceased Father's debts, as far as they were not usuriously contracted, and that intention he has fulfilled, though under no legal obligation: the Estates were entailed on him, both those in Bucks, at Beaconsfield and near Aylesbury, and those in Gloucestershire; so that he came into an ample income; but failing in the sale of his Gloucestershire property to Lord Sherborne or others, which was in contemplation, he prudently resolved for the present at least to make Farmington his residence, as a less expensive place than Hall Barn, his seat in Buckinghamshire, which he has let. Farmington also is more suitable for field sports, and now, that it is put in good repair, & well fitted up, it is a very comfortable residence. He has married a young Lady, whom he met at Boulogne, well connected, accomplished, pleasing, elegant & handsome, but with little fortune; her name, Larkins, and an elder sister is now on a visit to them. Mrs. W. Senr. with her two unmarried daughters, & her younger Sons, two schoolboys, occupies Mr. Willan's mansion house in the Village, & the two families seem on the pleasantest footing.... Mr. Waller himself, under an unpromising exterior, seems to possess good sense & good principles, with the desire of making himself useful as a Country Gentleman; for the duties of the Magistracy he appears to have a turn, & most desirable is it, that the younger Squires should engage in the country business of the neighbourhood, & not leave all to the clergy, as is too often the case, while their attention is absorbed in fox hunting, racing, London amusements, or the gay frivolities of Cheltenham, Brighton &c. The Country Gentlemen are but too often averse to those duties, which become them most, and are most advantageous to their neighbourhood.* 16 Aug., 28-29 Aug., 12 Oct.

1828: 15 Jan., 28 May: *We had a party of our neighbours to dinner to-day: Mr. & Mrs. Dolphin; Mr. & Mrs. Waller, Miss Maria Waller & Mr. Winter ...* 14 Oct., 20 Oct.

1829: 19 Feb: *I went alone to dine with the Brownes at Salperton: I met Harry Waller & his wife ...* 2 Apr., 22 Sep., 23 Sep.

1830: 12 Jan.

1833: 18 Oct.

1834: 12 Aug., 15-16 Aug., 18 Aug., 6 Nov., 1 Dec: *The High Sheriff, Harry Waller, was present, assisting us: though, as Sheriff, precluded from acting as Magistrate.*

1835: 10 Jan: *The High Sheriff, H. Waller, opened the business of the day in a brief speech well delivered ...* 14 Jan., 17 Jan., 20 Jan., 19 Mar., 10 Apr.

1836: 6 Sep., 11 Oct: *Waller wrote to invite me to dine and sleep at Farmington on Friday after the Petty Sess. at Northleach Bridewell.* 25 Nov: *The post brought a letter from Cockey, acknowledging the receipt of the parcel I had sent with the particulars of the living of Bourton, and giving the result of the deliberations of the Warden & fellows of Wadh. which are that Waller shall fix a price, which, if the marketable price, & not a fancy price, will, probably, be accepted.*

1837: 17 Mar., 7 Apr: *Having met Waller, who is Chairman of the Union, and his brother Robert, they accompanied me to the Workhouse, which is very eligibly situate at the entrance of the Town coming from Oxford, near the road, with a handsome front.* 19 Apr., 13 May, 16 May, 23 May, 10 Jun., 12 Jun., 14 Jun., 16 Jun., 27-28 Jun., 5 Jul., 7 Aug., 15 Aug: *Dined (M.W., E.F.W. and myself) at the Wallers, Farmington Lodge, meeting the Bride and Bridegroom from Bourton on the W. (R. Waller and his wife) ...* 10 Oct., 30 Dec.

1838: 25 Jun: *Met H. Waller going out on horseback, who chatted with us in the village near his house, as we declined going in, Mrs. W. being absent in Town.* 3 Oct.

1839: 20 May: *We returned home by Farmington, calling at the Lodge; but Mr. Waller was from home, and Mrs. W. gone out airing.* 11 Jun: *Very delightful weather. Rode to Salperton; called on the Brownes; saw all the family except Caroline, who is in Town. Mrs. Browne has been seriously ill, but is recovered. Met there Mr. and Mrs. Waller, from Farmington, she is convalescent: there were two Waller boys, and two sweet girls daughters of Col. Beach.* 24 Jun: *Mr. & Mrs. Waller at home: met also Mrs. Aliers, a sister of Mrs. Waller, with a son and daughter; Robt. Waller, and Miss Caroline Browne.*

1840: 8 Apr: *A dinner party at home - Mr & Mrs. Waller from Farmington ...* 10 Apr., 11 May, 1 Jul., 28 Jul: *H. W. was absent at Goodwood races.* 31 Jul: 2 Oct: *Dined at the Wallers at Farmington Lodge, a very agreeable party - meeting our good old friend, Miss Rollinson, who is staying there.* 16 Oct., 20 Oct., 7 Nov., 27 Nov: *To H. Waller, to congratulate him on Mrs. H.W's safe delivery & the birth of a daughter on Tuesday last: sending a servant over to enquire after her and the infant ...*

1842: 2 Jul., 5 Jul: *The second son of H E Waller, a fine boy, rode from Farmington with a note from his Father, inviting M W. and me to dinner on Friday next, to wh. I sent an affirmative answer.* 8 Jul: *It was the first time we had visited Farmington Grove since the lamented decease of Mrs. H. W. - her sister, Miss Aiken, sits at the head of her Brother in law's table, and appears domiciliated there; all the Children, eight motherless orphans, the eldest under fourteen, the youngest under two years of age, are at home.* 8 Jul: *... when the storm abated I rode home, to dress for dinner at Farmington Grove, whither M W. and I went in the Chariot through a violent storm of rain, and where we passed a very pleasant evening ...* 16 Oct., 18 Oct: *To the Bridewell, where met the two Visiting Justices (the Wallers) and Price.* 29 Oct: *Met the two Wallers and Mr. Akers, who married one of the late Mrs. Waller's sisters.* 16 Nov: *Wrote to Mr. Aitkens requesting him to take my evening service on Sunday next, which he will endeavour to do, but it will be inconvenient, since his Rector is incapacitated from duty on that day, in consequence of the decease of his wife's sister, Miss Dupuis, a very pleasing and amiable person whose loss will be deeply felt by Mrs. Waller.*

1844: 23 Feb., 27 Feb., 1 May, 16 May: *Wrote to Mr. Waller of Farmington, with particulars as to the Character and qualifications of ...* 27 Jul.

1845: 12 Mar., 8 Jul.

1846: 24 Jul., 27 Jul., 3 Nov., 4 Dec.

1847: 21 Jun: *Harry Waller called and partook of luncheon here: he explained the low condition to which Vernon Dolphin has sunk, a state almost approaching to want.* 4 Aug: *Harry Waller and his cousin, John Dolphin, called: the latter is now on a visit at Farmington, the father of seven children, and an amiable, respectable Norfolk Clergyman.* 30 Aug.

1848: 1 Apr., 23 May: *Harry Waller has lately built a school room for the children of the parish.* 15 Jun: *Learnt from Mr. Wilkins that Vernon Dolphin had quitted the neighbourhood, some arrangement having been made as between the husband and wife, in which Harry Waller and Mr. Polhill were the negociating parties.* 5 Jul: *M W. & I set out with the intention of calling on Mrs. Dolphin at Eyford, but being overtaken on our way thither by Harry Waller, who was also going thither ...*

1851: 23 Jan., 21 May.

1850: 2 Aug: *Mr. Waller of Farmington, accompanied by Mr. Boudier, paid me a visit.*

1853: 3 Jun: *The party at the Rectory was increased by the arrival from Farmington, of four Misses Waller, and their Governess.*

WALLER — Robert Blackwell Waller — *see also* Dupuis [23]

Robert Blackwell Waller (1810-1871), Church of England clergyman, was the second son of Henry Waller and Maria Dolphin (*above*). He was educated at Brasenose College, Oxford (BA 1832; MA 1835), and was ordained deacon on 21 December 1833 and priest on 20 December 1834. Waller's first clerical appointment was as stipendiary curate of Farmington from 22 December 1833. He became rector of Bourton-on-the Water in 1836 and held the living until his death in 1871. The living appears to have been in the gift of his brother, Harry, as the diary entry of 25 November 1836 implies that the warden of Wadham College was interested in buying it.

Robert Waller married, at Wendlebury, Oxfordshire, 18 July 1837, Louisa (1806-1874), daughter of Revd George Dupuis (1757-1839) and Caroline Elizabeth Stevens (1771-1843); they had 6 sons and 1 daughter:

1 Robert (1838-1914); died unmarried at Farmington
2 John Hampden (1839-1934); married, at St Margaret's, Westminster, 6 June 1871, Elizabeth Jamieson (1844-1915); at least 1 son and 2 daughters:
  1 Ida Elizabeth (1872-1951)
  2 Violet Louise (1875-1894)
  1 Alured Jamieson (1880-1934)
3 Hugh Sydney (1840-1924); married, at St Peter's, Pimlico, Middlesex, 14 December 1876, Alice Emma Pegler (1854-1928); 3 sons and 2 daughters:
  1 Katherine Alice (1877-1943)
  1 Robert Lawrence (1878-1938)
  2 Arthur Sydney (1882-1952)
  3 Harold Edward (b. 1883)
  2 Maria Dorothea Sydney (1887-1967)
4 Walter Richard (1843-1912); died unmarried at Bourton-on-the-Water
5 Lawrence (1844-1877); joined the freemasons' Prince of Wales lodge, Stow-on-the-Wold, 17 February 1873; appears to have died unmarried at Bourton-on-the-Water
6 Raymond Edward (1846-1892); appears to have died unmarried at Darrawella, Ceylon, 13 February 1892, from injuries sustained from a fall from his horse
1 Mary Elizabeth Louisa (1849-1929); married, at Bourton-on-the-Water, 15 November 1876, William Snooke Stenson (1817-1888); 1 son and 1 daughter:
  1 William Waller (1877-1925)
  1 Mary Gladys Waller (1880-1955)

1828: 30 Jul: *We had a little party of our young neighbours to dinner: Messrs. Robert & Stephen Waller from Farmington ... Robert Waller is with a private tutor at Cottingham, near Rockingham, Northamptonshire ...*

1829: 22 Sep., 10 Oct.

1834: 12 Aug., 18 Aug., 4 Dec., 24 Dec.

1835: 15 Jan., 20 Jan., 29 Jan., 5 Feb., 12 Feb: *A letter from Robert Waller, accepting an invitation which I had sent him to dine and sleep here to morrow.* 13 Feb: *Robert Waller came to dine and sleep here. We had a gentleman's dinner party.* 14 Feb., 13 Mar: *Drove my son to Northleach to attend a meeting of the Commissioners of the Crickley Hill Turnpike Trust ... Mr. R. Waller with a friend, the Hon—Rous were also present at the meeting.*

1836: 24 Aug., 5 Nov., 10-11 Nov., 21 Nov., 23-24 Nov.

1837: 7 Apr., 17 Apr., 25 Apr., 1 May, 4 May, 12 May, 15 May, 12-13 Jun., 20 Jun., 5 Jul., 8 Jul., *E.F.W. took an early dinner with Waller and Billingsley at Bourton.* 31 Jul: *Saw Miss W. Robert Waller was married to Miss Dupuis, youngest daughter of the incumbent of Wendlebury, Oxon, on the 18th. they had been long engaged to each other.* 7 Aug., 11 Aug., 12 Aug: *Mrs. R. Waller appears a pleasing, unaffected young woman, not pretty, but with a very intelligent countenance, and natural, lady like manner.* 15-16 Aug., 18 Aug., 22 Aug., 24 Aug., 31 Aug., 6 Sep., 13 Sep., 15-16 Sep., 22 Sep., 26 Sep., 10 Oct., 17 Oct., 2 Nov., 6-7 Nov. 9 Nov., 29-30 Nov., 4 Dec., 8 Dec: *Though still heavily oppressed with cold, and otherwise indisposed and out of spirits, made an effort to go out with my wife and Son to dine at Mr. R. Waller's, where we met Mr. and Mrs. Chamberlayne, Mr. and Mrs. and Miss D. Ford, Miss Polson, Mr. Billingsley, and two relatives of Mrs. R. Waller, Miss Dupuis, her sister, and Miss Price, her niece.* 15 Dec.

1838: 7 Jan: *E.F.W. performed duty in the afternoon at Lower Slaughter to assist R. Waller, who is visiting with his lady at her father's at Wendlebury ...* 1 Feb., 6 Feb: *I omitted to mention yesterday the receipt of a few lines from R. Waller announcing to me that his mother had died at Farmington on Sunday evening.* 7-8 Feb., 10 Mar., 15 Mar., 22 Mar., 12 Apr., 19-20 Apr., 26 Apr., 4 May, 7 May: *Mrs. R. Waller was confined this morning - a son and heir.* 10 May, 17 May, 31 May, 1-2 Jun., 13-14 Jun., 21 Jun., 12-13 Jul., 2-3 Aug., 8 Aug., 10 Aug., 14 Aug., 22 Aug., 7 Sep., 22 Sep., 25 Sep., 2 Oct., 16 Oct., 22 Oct., 24-25 Oct., 30 Oct., 1 Nov., 6 Dec., 11-13 Dec., 20 Dec., 27 Dec.

1839: 1-2 Jan., 17 Jan., 23-24 Jan., 31 Jan., 7 Feb., 14 Feb., 21 Feb., 28 Feb., 4 Mar: *Mrs. R. Waller gone to Wendlebury to see her aged father, the Revd. Dupuis, who is believed to be very near his latter end: not expected to survive many days.* 7 Mar: *Mr. Ford gone from home, and Mr. Waller prevented from attendance by the state of his Father in law, who is understood to be at the last extremity.* 14 Mar., 21-22 Mar., 25 Mar: *Drove MW. to Bourton on the Water, where called at the Rectory, and admitted by Mrs. R. Waller, who seemed greatly affected on first seeing us, this being the first time we have met since her Father's recent decease.* 28 Mar., 6 Apr., 9 Apr., 11 Apr., 20 Apr., 25 Apr., 1-2 May, 11 May, 13 May, 15-17 May, 22 May, 30 May, 13 Jun., 20-21 Jun., 24 Jun., 26-27 Jun., 11 Jul., 25 Jul., 10-11 Aug., 15 Aug.

1840: 19 Mar., 26 Mar., 28 Mar., 31 Mar., 1-2 Apr., 9-10 Apr., 30 Apr., 12 May, 14-15 May, 25 May, 27-28 May, 30 May, 2 Jun., 4-5 Jun., 8 Jun., 11 Jun., 25 Jun., 30 Jun., 9 Jul., 13 Jul., 16 Jul., 23-24 Jul: *Drove MW. to Bourton on the Water: we called at the Rectory, and paid a cheerful morning visit to Mrs. R. Waller, with whom we found her infirm Mother, Mrs. Dupuis, whose powers both of mind and body seem to be much decayed, and her sister, Miss M. Dupuis.* 30 Jul., 5-6 Aug., 13 Aug., 20 Aug., 27 Aug., 3 Sep., 10 Sep., 17 Sep., 24 Sep., 29 Sep., 1 Oct., 7-8 Oct., 15 Oct., 20 Oct., 24 Oct., 29 Oct., 4-6 Nov., 12 Nov., 19 Nov., 26 Nov.

1841: 4-5 Mar.

1842: 20-21 Jan., 27 Jan., 10 Feb., 11 Feb., 17 Feb., 22 Feb., 24-26 Feb., 3 Mar., 10 Mar., 24 Mar., 26 Mar., 31 Mar., 7-8 Apr., 12-13 Apr., 21 Apr., 27 Apr., 12 May, 20 May, 22-23 May: *R Waller did not join the dinner party, in consequence of the recent death of his Brother Stephen's wife, who sank after child birth, leaving him a young widower with three very young children; a lamentable event!* 3 Jun., 9 Jun., 28-30 Jun., 8 Jul., 21 Jul., 28 Jul., 2 Aug., 11 Aug., 16 Aug., 16 Aug., 25 Aug., 31 Aug., 15 Sep., 29 Sep., 6 Oct., 8 Oct: *To the Bridewell, where met the two Visiting Justices (the Wallers) and Price.* 10 Oct., 14 Oct., 16 Oct., 18 Oct., 24 Oct., 29 Oct., 3-4 Nov., 21 Dec., 30 Dec.

1843: 3 Jan., 17 Jan., 26 Jan., 9 Feb., 16 Feb., 8 Aug., 11 Aug., 16 Aug., 18 Aug., 20 Aug., 2 Sep., 17 Sep., 20-21 Sep., 28-29 Sep., 18 Oct., 24 Oct., 26-27 Oct., 2 Nov., 16 Nov., 23 Nov., 4 Dec., 7 Dec., 19 Dec., 21 Dec., 28 Dec.

1844: 3 Jan., 11 Jan., 18 Jan., 1 Feb., 8 Feb., 29 Feb: *Mr. R. Waller kept apart, though present at the meeting for some reason undeclared.* 14 Mar., 21 Mar., 29 Mar: *Mrs. Robt. Waller with her two eldest boys called on us; I escorted them back to near Bourton Robt. Waller attending the Assizes.* 2 Apr., 4 Apr., 15 Apr., 17-19 Apr., 2 May, 10 May, 29 Jul., 12 Aug., 20 Aug., 29 Aug., 16 Sep: *Called on the Wallers; received by Mrs. R.W. and Miss Dupuis, her sister.* 18 Sep., 24 Sep., 26 Sep., 4 Oct., 7 Oct., 10-11 Oct., 28 Oct: *Answered a note which I had recd. from R Waller, who pleaded that his lady was in labour as an excuse for not meeting me at Stow to-day on Justice business.* 29 Oct., 31 Oct., 21 Nov., 19-20 Dec., 27 Dec.

1845: 2 Jan., 16-17 Jan., 23 Jan., 6 Feb., 17 Feb: *Met with him, Mrs. Waller, her niece, Miss Price, Messrs. Stenson and Aitkens - walked with them towards Little Risington;—home to dinner.* 24 Feb., 28 Feb., 8 Mar., 11-12 Mar., 19-20 Mar., 26 Mar., 31 Mar., 1 Apr., 4 Apr., 10 Apr., 15 Apr., 28 Apr., 30 Apr: *After our return Mrs. R Waller, her niece Mrs. Wells, and two of the Waller boys, walked from Bourton to call on Sophy; we walked back with them to some distance beyond Lower Slaughter.* 1 May, 7 May, 10 May, 15 May, 26 May, 29-30 May, 3 Jun., 6 Jun: *Mr. Wells, who married Mrs. R Waller's niece, they being now on a visit at the Rectory, accompanied us: he is son of Mr. Wells of Piercefield, and a man of colour; unfortunately without profession or occupation; it was an imprudent match, for the gentleman, disobliging his own family, is without resources, and the lady, a very pleasing young women, attached herself to him contrary to the wishes of her friends, whose means also are also very confined—Mr. W. is now almost hopelessly seeking employment.* 25 Jun., 2-4 Jul.

1846: 20 Jun., 24 Jun., 3 Jul: *Mr. Aitkens called to remind me of the duty to be done by me at Lower Slaughter on Sunday next. Mrs. Aitkens was confined last night; Mrs. Waller on Sunday night last.* 7 Jul: *Called at R. Waller's, who is recovering from an indisposition which has hung upon him for some time past. He gave a favourable account of his lady and her infant.* 15-16 Jul., 23 Jul., 27 Jul., 28 Jul., 6 Aug., 8 Aug., 26 Aug., 24 Sep., 8 Oct., 29 Oct., 31 Oct., 5 Nov., 16 Nov., 19 Nov., 21 Nov., 25-26 Nov., 4 Dec: *... went to dine with the Wallers at Bourton; meeting Harry Waller, two Misses Larkin, Captain Pettatt, Mr. Wollaston, Mr. and Mrs. Winter. A pleasant party ...* 10 Dec., 17 Dec.

1847: 4 Feb., 22 Feb., 14 Mar., 17-18 Mar., 30 Mar., 1 Apr., 7 Apr., 15 Apr., 17 Apr., 4 May, 10 May, 13-14 May, 25 May, 27 May, 31 May, 4 Jun: *Between four & five the high table broke up to repair to the Rectory where Mrs. Waller regaled with tea & coffee the Revd. Messrs. Ford, Hunt, Turner & myself - also Mr. Stenson - the Waller children delighted in the band, and flags.* 10 Jun., 14 Jun., 22 Jun., 24 Jun., 29-30 Jun., 20-21 Jul., 23 Jul., 2 Aug., 5 Aug., 8 Sep., 16 Sep., 29-30 Sep., 2 Oct., 5 Oct., 14 Oct., 28 Oct., 1 Nov., 11 Nov., 20 Nov., 25 Nov., 9 Dec., 14 Dec., 23 Dec.

1848: 19-20 Jan., 1 Feb., 3 Feb., 7 Feb., 16-17 Feb., 22 Feb., 29 Feb., 7 Mar., 14 Mar., 16 Mar., 1 Apr: *... land-tax due to me, although I have not yet been paid by Robt. Waller, who is generally tardy in this matter.* 13 Apr., 15 Apr., 18 Apr., 25 Apr., 11 May, 16 May, 25 May, 1-2 Jun., 8 Jun., 13 Jun., 15 Jun., 6 Jul., 9 Jul., 8 Aug., 12 Aug., 18 Aug., 23-24 Aug., 31 Aug., 14 Sep., 16 Sep., 27 Sep., 24 Oct., 26 Oct., 8 Nov.

1849: 20 Dec.

1850: 2 Jan., 11 Jan., 14 Feb., 28 Feb., 5 Mar., 7 Mar., 14 Mar., 28 Mar., 11 Apr., 16 Apr., 19 Apr., 4 May, 22-23 May, 28 May, 4 Jun., 14-15 Jun., 20 Jun., 4-5 Jul., 8 Jul., 15 Jul: *Wrote to R. Waller, reminding him that he has failed to pay me the annual amount of Land Tax upon his benefice relieved redeemed but not exonerated, and which is mine by purchase from the Croome family, since 1846.* 1-2 Aug., 27 Aug., 29 Aug., 6-7 Sep., 12 Sep., 18 Sep., 22 Sep: *Purnell's promised neck of venison having arrived this morning, wrote notes of invitation to dinner on Wednesday next to Mr. Ford, R Waller, Vavasour, Chamberlayne, and Ogle.* 24-26 Sep., 2 Oct., 6 Nov., 29 Nov., 9 Dec., 19 Dec., 29 Dec.

1851: 16 Jan., 1 Feb., 7 Feb., 12 Feb., 27 Feb., 13 Mar., 10 Apr., 13-14 Apr., 17 Apr., 24 Apr., 2-3 May.

1852: 21-22 Jan., 29 Jan., 2 Feb., 12-13 Feb., 26 Feb., 27 Feb: *Wrote to R Waller, as to the state of our accounts, what I owe him for hay supplied to me, what balance is due to me for Land tax payments in arrear.* 11 Mar., 25 Mar., 8 Apr., 20 Apr., 22 Apr., 6 May, 10 May, 17 May, 20 May, 3 Jun., 16 Nov., 2 Dec., 16 Dec., 30 Dec.

1853: 13 Jan., 15 Jan., 29 Jan., 14 Feb., 16 Feb., 19 Feb., 24 Feb., 2 Mar., 8-10 Mar., 12 Mar., 17 Mar., 31 Mar., 15 Apr., 19

Apr., 21 Apr., 11 May, 24-25 May, 3 Jun., 23 Jun., 13-14 Dec., 25-6 Dec., 28 Dec.

1854: 2 Feb., 23 Feb., 10 Mar: *Robert Waller, the younger, kindly sent by his parents to enquire how I am, called upon me.* 1 Apr., 6 Apr., 15 Apr., 20 Apr., 24 Apr., 4 May, 19 May, 6 Jun: *A kind note of enquiry from Mrs. R. Waller, accompanying a present of a brace of fine trout.* 7 Jun., 13-15 Jun., 29 Jun., 17-18 Jul., 27 Jul., 29 Jul.

WALLER — Stephen Richard Waller[24]

Stephen Richard Waller (1813-1875), Church of England clergyman, was the third son of Henry Waller and Maria Dolphin (*above*). He was educated at Shrewsbury School and Brasenose College, Oxford (BA 1834; MA 1837). He was curate of Lower Mitton, near Stourport, in 1849, and rector of St Cuthbert's, Bedford, from 1868 to his death in 1875. He married, first, at Donnington Wood, Shropshire, 20 September 1838, Lucy (1808-1842), daughter of Revd Charles Richard Cameron (b. 1780) and Lucy Lyttleton Butt (±1782-1858), a noted writer of children's books on religious themes. They had 2 sons:

1 Stephen Bethel (1838-1843)
2 Charles Henry (1841-1911)

Lucy died soon after Charles's birth, and Stephen married secondly, 1845, Harriet Eliza Lea (1819-1858). Stephen and Harriet had at least 6 sons and 2 daughters:

1 Alfred Lawrence (1846-1866)
2 Walter Augustus Ewen (1849-1921)
1 Agnes Eliza (1850-1939)
3 Percy (1852-1922)
4 George Herbert (1854-1873)
5 Edward Cecil (1855-1930)
2 Emily Marion (1857-1939)
6 Theodore Harry (1859-1950)

1827: 28 Dec: *William Ford, an Etonian, about a year older than Edward, and Stephen Waller, a younger son of Mr. Waller, two or three months younger than my boy, dined & slept here. Stephen Waller is about to be placed at Shrewsbury School, the arrangement with Archdeacon Butler having been made by me. We invited him in order to make the future schoolfellows well acquainted with each other.*

1828: 30 Jul: *We had a little party of our young neighbours to dinner: Messrs. Robert & Stephen Waller from Farmington, and John & Charles Croome from Bourton. Of these Stephen Waller is a schoolfellow of Edward's at Shrewsbury ...* 8 Aug: *This afternoon we lost our dear boy, who returns to morrow to Shrewsbury School. We sent him in the phaeton with the servant this evening to sleep at Cheltenham, where he would meet his schoolfellow, Stephen Waller, & proceed by coach to-morrow.*

1837: 20 May: *Her sons Robert and Stephen were with her: the latter on a visit of a fortnight from the neighbourhood of Wolverhampton, where he has charge of a new Church and large congregation in the coal district.*

1842: 23 May: *R Waller did not join the dinner party, in consequence of the recent death of his Brother Stephen's wife, who sank after child birth, leaving him a young widower with three very young children; a lamentable event!*

WALLINGTON — John Wallington — *see also* Sheppard[25]

John Wallington (1797-1882), JP, clothier, and landed proprietor, was the second son of Edward Wallington, of Dursley, and his wife and cousin, Arabella, daughter of John Wallington of Chelsea. John married, at Wotton-under-Edge, Gloucestershire, 21 September 1820, Anne (±1800-1879), daughter of Edward Sheppard (1764-1849) and Mary Darke (1775-1845) of the Ridge, Wotton-under-Edge; they had 1 son and 1 daughter:

1 John Williams (1822-1910), Col; appointed KCB; married, 1852, Henrietta Maria, youngest daughter of Col William Beach of Oakley Hall, Hampshire; 4 sons and 3 daughters:
  1 John Arthur Beach (1853-1901)
  2 Edward William (1854-1933)
  3 Charles Digby (1856-1934)
  1 Henrietta M. (b. ±1859)
  2 Augusta Frances (b. ±1860)
  3 Alice Julia (b. ±1862)
  4 Frank Maxwell (1870-1946)
1 Anne Elizabeth (±1825-1907); married, 1856, William Twogood of Uplands, Somerset

---

1828: 18 Jul: *Among the persons present (SPCK) were Mr. R. B. Cooper, M.P., who always stands forward to support the cause of the Church and the orthodox party, Messrs. Ford, Jeaffreson, Douglas, Sayer, Hardwicke, Wallington, Drs. Michell, Kempthorne, Bishop, Evans, and several other Clergymen ...*

1837: 4 Jan., 11 Apr.

1843: 2 Sep: *Amid the throng recognized Mr. and Mrs. John Wallington from Gloucestershire.* 5 Sep: *Chatted with Mr. and Mrs. John Wallington.*

1844: 8 Apr.

1847: 5 Apr.

1850: 18 Oct: *Mr. and Mrs. John Wallington, from Dursley, joined the party at Stancombe Park at dinner, accompanied by a daughter, an accomplished performer on the Piano. J.W. is a magistrate, and pleasant person with whom I have long been well acquainted; his lady also I have known for some years, the daughter of a former magistrate and clothier, some years since deceased, Edward Sheppard, of the Ridge.*

1851: 29 Apr.

WALLIS — Thomas Wallis[26]

Thomas Wallis (1787-1843) was a landed proprietor and a Gloucester JP and DL. He bought Tibberton Court, Gloucestershire, in 1822, and lived there until 1837. He later lived at Oakford House, Devon. Little has been discovered about him. His place of birth, parents, and the source of his wealth are unclear, but the diary entry of 4 April 1829 indicates that he had held a civil position in India, had been secretary to an admiral, and had had the opportunity, presumably through trade, of making a fortune.

Wallis married first, at St Marylebone, Westminster, 30 March 1816, Charlotte Augusta Amelia (1799-1875), youngest daughter of Sir George Bolton (d. 1806), of Tutshill House, Tidenham, Gloucestershire, and Catherine Bannatyne, née Lawley, a widow and the daughter and heir of John Lawley. Charlotte's parents had married at St Marylebone on 2 October 1794.

Sir George Bolton, tutor and inventor of gun-locks, was schooled in military tactics and mathematics preparatory to an army career, but was instead appointed instructor to the royal princesses, daughters of George III, in writing, geography, and arithmetic. Being of independent means, Bolton indulged his interest in firearms by seeking to improve the musket gun-lock; in both military and sporting firearms it was so defective that accidents were frequently caused by guns going off at half-cock in the heat of battle or when forging through dense vegetation. His design of a self-acting and detached bolting lock was constructed by mathematical instrument makers. The Board of Ordnance had several examples made for trial at Woolwich, but although the performance was deemed admirable, cost ruled out a general adoption. Bolton designed a simpler version and described both models in his *Remarks on the present defective state of fire-arms, with an explanation of a newly invented patented gun-lock* (1795). The locks were obtainable from the gunsmith Fisher of High Holborn, and Bolton was knighted 1799. Through his wife he inherited the Upper Diamond estate in St Vincent, a plantation worked by slave labour.

In 1828 Wallis's wife Charlotte eloped with Charles James Nelson Birkett (1800-1842), who up to 1828 was in partnership with Abraham Townsend and John Strangwayes as dry salters of Old Swan Stairs, London. By 1830, in consequence of the elopement, Thomas Wallis had obtained a divorce. Charlotte did not settle with Birkett but married one Frank Howard on 19 December 1833.

Thomas Wallis remarried, at Brixton, 11 September 1833, Mary Anne, third daughter of Evan Roberts of Grove House, Brixton, Surrey. He died at Boulogne on 14 November 1843. There do not appear to have been any children from either marriage.

Another source in the Gloucestershire Archives states that the Price family was associated with the Tibberton Court estate from 1837, but according to Wallis's will, proved in 1844, he was still the owner at the time of his death. It may be assumed that the Price family were tenants who went on to buy the estate.

1829: 4 Apr: *After breakfast I went to the Shire hall in the hope of hearing the action for criminal conversation between Mr. Wallis, a magistrate of the County, & his former friend, Mr. Burkitt, who seduced the lady from a kind, indulgent & worthy man, after a sojourn of some weeks under their roof last October. Wallis had been formerly in a civil situation, Secretary to an Admiral, in the Navy, where he had the opportunity of making a good fortune, with which he returned in middle life, a well looking man, from India, & married a lady many years younger than himself, by whom he has had no family. He had purchased Tibberton Court near Gloucester, where he had settled, & from general opinion and the opportunities I have had of seeing him at the Sessions, I should say, he was a sensible, upright man, and a man of business. I tried in vain to obtain admittance into the Court ...*

1836: 21 Oct: *Left Gloucester by a Bristol coach at 12 o cl. travelled with Mr. Wallace, a Mag. who formerly lived near Gloucester, but who has now quitted that residence.*

WALMESLEY — Elizabeth Walmesley — *see also* Arbuthnott, Burdett, Kirby, Lydia Smith, *and* Vavasour [27]

Elizabeth Walmesley (1802-1881+) was the daughter of John Walmesley (1769-1822) and Ann Smith (b. 1777). John Walmesley, of Castlemere, Rochdale, was high sheriff of Lancashire in 1819 and a person of some substance. Elizabeth remained unmarried, but she had two married sisters: Mary Ann (b. ±1800), who married Henry Brown (b. ±1792), JP, of Devon, who lived at Stratfield Turgis in Hampshire; and Hannah (1803-1863), who married Rear Adm. D. H. O'Brian (1784-1867) of New House, Hoddesdon, Hertfordshire. Elizabeth Walmesley was a cousin to Julia Vavasour; their mothers were half-sisters. The precise relationship can be traced as follows: Edmund Smith (1729-1777) married, 23 September 1755, at Alton, Staffordshire, Penelope (1735-1761), daughter of Robert Bill (1684-1751) and Lydia Hurst 1694-1769). Edmund and Penelope had two daughters: Penelope (1757-1826) and Lydia (b. & d. 1761). Penelope (senior) died shortly after giving birth to Lydia, presumably from complications at her birth. Penelope (junior) married, 1777, Thomas Hippon Vavasour of the Butts House, Rochdale, Lancashire. Edmund married, secondly, Mary Raynor, and had several further children, including Mary, Jane, Isaac, and Ann. Ann Smith married John Walmsley of Castlemere.

Edmund Smith's brother, Thomas Smith (d. 1806), of Castleton Hall, married, 23 February 1774, Penelope Firth (1750-1823). They had several sons who died young and four daughters: Esther, Ellen, Harriet, and May. Esther married Sir William Burdett; Ellen married John Entwisle of Foxholes, Rochdale; Harriet married Sir Robert Arbuthnot; and Mary married Hugh Baillie, a colonel in the Dragoon Guards.

It is not clear how Elizabeth Walmesley came to be a close friend to Marianne Dolphin.

1846: 11 Dec: *Had a few moments interview at Eyford with Miss Walmsley and W. Vavasour. The latter had walked over to call on Miss W. who is visiting Mrs. D. and the lady was returning part of the way homeward with the Gentleman.* 22 Dec., 31 Dec.

1848: 9 Apr., 11 Apr., 19 Apr., 29 Apr., 5 May, 24 Sep., 3 Oct., 8 Nov., 12 Nov., 15-16 Nov.

1850: 2 May, 11 May, 22 May, 24 Jun., 29-30 Jun., 9-10 Jul., 12 Jul: *Miss Walmesley, as also Mr. Winter and his daughter, came by appointment to take luncheon with us, remaining till five P.M. - we walked to Eyford &c.* 14 Jul., 4 Aug., 6 Aug., 11 Aug., 16 Aug., 18 Aug., 20 Aug., 22-25 Aug., 28 Aug., 1 Sep., 17-18 Sep., 30 Sep., 4 Oct., 6 Oct., 13 Oct: *Miss Walmsley called between the services, giving a sad account of poor Mrs. Dolphin's health, who returned home on Monday last.* 14 Oct., 20 Oct., 22 Oct., 26-27 Oct., 3 Dec., 7 Dec.

1852: 24 Oct: *Miss Walmesley now on a visit at Eyford, called on me after each of the services. Much conversation with her as to Mrs. D's position.* 25 Oct., 27 Oct., 6 Nov., 2 Dec: *Much conversation with Miss Walmsley as to Mrs. Dolphin's position, the management of her concerns, her disjointed and disorganized establishment at Eyford, her pecuniary embarrassments, and critical situation arising from her relation to Mr. Dolphin, her dissentions with members of her own family, her reckless and impetuous, and indiscreet mode of conducting herself, under circumstances of no common difficulty.* 5-6 Dec., 8 Dec., 13 Dec: *Miss Walmsley called on me, & sat a long time complaining much of Mrs. Dolphin, and opening out many points and matters any thing but creditable to her. Something must be laid to the account of vexation at seeing others preferred to herself, and her advice disregarded: but still there is much to blame in Mrs. D's proceedings.* 14 Dec: *A note from Miss Walmsley, who sends me a copy of the letter she has written to Mrs. Dolphin intimating her departure from Eyford tomorrow .... Miss Walmsley called to consult me as to the course she should take in consequence of a letter recd. this morning from Mrs. Dolphin, couched in unfriendly terms, censuring her for interfering in her domestic concerns, as to certain late quarrels among the Eyford servants, & generally reproaching her with unkindly opposing her views, not assenting to her; thus unmistakeably shewing that she would gladly be rid of her presence at Eyford ...* 22 Dec., 24 Dec: *Recd. a letter from Miss Walmsley, in answer to mine of Thursday she describes Mrs. Dolphin as suffering under a bad attack of fever; yet not believed to be in danger. Miss W. had not been long enough with Mrs. D. to form any very accurate notion as to the position of her affairs, whether she is likely to return to Eyford or not.* 26 Dec.

1853: 19 Dec: *Called at the Vavasours, where, besides the ladies of that name, I met Miss Walmsley, just arrived on a visit.* 22 Dec., 24 Dec., 31 Dec.

1854: 27 Apr: *After my return home, and before I could dine, most unexpectedly called upon by Mrs. Dolphin & Miss Walmsley just come to Eyford, but for what length of time, or under what views as to the future, did not appear; for, finding that I was going to dinner, and noticing that I was much tired, they only remained long enough to give me a friendly greeting ...* 30 Apr., 5 May: *Miss Walmsley paid me a long visit after breakfast; she leaves Eyford to-morrow ...I trust Miss W. will entirely abandon her from this time.* 6 May, 3-4 Jun., 6 Jun., 10-11 Jun., 13 Jun: *Met Miss Walmsley in the Eyford garden, detained at Eyford by the vehement solicitations of Mrs. Dolphin, whose impetuous impulses mar her own schemes & projects, while they are a perpetual source of uneasiness to all connected with her.—Miss W. leaves Eyford tomorrow.* 14 Jun: *W.V. invited E. Clifford to accompany him in his four in hand carriage to Adlestrop Station, whither he was going to convey Miss Walmsley on her way to her home by rail.*

WALSH — Francis Clarke Walsh [28]

Francis Clarke Walsh (1822-1900), Church of England clergyman and teacher, was born at Netherbury, Dorset, the son of Benjamin Walsh (1778-1856) and Mary Bidwell Clarke (1782-1832). He was educated at St Paul's School and University College, Oxford (BA 1845; MA 1867). He married, at Hallow, Worcestershire, 26 December 1848, Mary Pickernell (b. 1822). There do not appear to have been any children.

This attribution is tentative as there is no firm identification, but Walsh did have Gloucestershire connections and he may have been a curate at Winchcombe for a few years. Whether or not he was the same Revd Walsh who had been curate at Cutsdean is also not at all clear. He may have gone to Malta for the winter and then returned to Gloucestershire in 1847.

In 1871 Walsh was a teacher at Leamington Priors, Warwickshire. By 1881 he was with his father-in-law at Up Hatherley, Gloucestershire, and listed as a clergyman without cure of souls. By 1891 he was at Painswick, and he died at Stroud in 1900.

1846: 3 Oct: *Called on Mr. Bowen at Temp Temple Guiting, whom I found in better health than he has of late been; but still a greater sufferer from his chronic complaint. With whom was Mr. Walsh, the Curate of Cutsdean, making a visit: this gentleman has resigned his curacy on account of delicate health, and is going abroad, to Malta, as he suffers from a pulmonary affection.*

1847: 16 May: *Morning Service E.F.W. officiated, reading prayers: he not returning to his duty at Stanway, which Mr. Walsh had undertaken.* 21 May, 7 Sep., 8 Sep: *Revds. R. W. Ford, C. B. Turner, E. F. Witts, Walsh, Clarke, Crompton, Potter, Pantin, Hippisley, Winter, Morrison, Waller, Wiggin, Hunt and Williams.*

1850: 19 Mar: *Mr. Walsh also, from Winchcombe, very kindly drove to call here, and make personal enquiries.* 21 Aug: *E.F.W. and Mr. Walsh paid a visit to me, and partook of luncheon here ...* 22 May, 26-28 May.

1852: 22 May: *As Mr. Walsh is now for a few days at his house at Winchcomb, my son wishes me to invite him to dinner on Wednesday next. I wrote accordingly.*

1854: 6 Mar: *He was followed by Mr. Walsh, who having dined and slept at my Son's last evening & night, had heard this morning ...* 17 Mar., 17 Jun., 21-22 Jun.

WALTERS — James Woodbridge Walters — *see also* Hyett [29]

James Woodbridge Walters (1793-1852), JP and landed proprietor, was baptised in the church of St Mary Magdalen, Richmond, Surrey, the son of David Walters (±1756-1833) and Harriott Woodbridge (1764-1809). He was a younger brother of Louise Woodbridge Walters (1789-1821), who married, at Barnwood, Gloucestershire, 22 November 1814, Thomas Turner (1782-1859), banker, of Gloucester.

In the early nineteenth century the Walters family built up a large estate centred on Barnwood House. In 1813 David Walters bought the house and 32 acres of former copyhold land owned by Sir Charles Hotham, 10th baronet (1766-1811). He added to the estate, which passed at his death to his son James.

Walters married, first, at St Mary de Lode, Gloucester, 2 March 1819, Sarah (1800-1824), daughter of Revd Henry Cay Adams (1762-1808) and Frances Marston (d. 1828); they had at least 3 sons:

1 David (1820-1836)
2 James (b. & d. 1822)
3 Henry (1824-1872), army officer; married, 7 July 1853, his cousin Caroline Woodbridge; no children

Sarah died at Henry's birth or shortly after. James married secondly, 29 April 1828, Stephana (1800-1890), daughter of Joseph Seymour Biscoe and his wife, Stephana, who later lived at Cheltenham. Stephana (junior) was born on 7 May 1800 and baptised on 19 September 1801 at St Mary's, Bletchingley, Surrey. She and James had at least 2 sons:

1 Frederick James (1830-1832)
2 William (1832-1912); married, 1866, his cousin Louisa Mary Woodbridge (1840-1929); 4 sons and 3 daughters:
   1 Henry Beauchamp (1867-1944)
   2 George Francis James (1868-1874)
   1 Nina Grace (1870-1940)
   3 Vincent Edward (1873-1939)
   4 David Francis (1875-1897)
   2 Mary Stephana (1879-1953)
   3 Lucy Kathleen (1883-1974)

Frances Adams, née Marston, mother of James Woodbridge Walters' first wife Sarah, inherited Buenos Ayres, later known as Painswick House, and its rococo landscape garden from Benjamin Hyett (1741-1810), her cousin's husband. Hyett's wife was Sarah Adams (1746-1804), a friend and correspondent of Samuel Johnson. The Hyetts were on friendly terms with the diarist's mother and father, Agnes and Edward Witts. Frances Adams inherited Buenos Ayres for life with reversion to her son William Henry Adams (1795-1877), who assumed the surname Hyett in 1813. William Henry was an MP and agricultural scientist, and much enlarged the estate in the early and mid-nineteenth century. In 1847 he acquired the freehold of his properties.

James Woodbridge Walters was a JP and a sheriff for Gloucester. At the time of the 1851 census he was living with his wife Stephana and their son Henry at 2 Hesketh Crescent, Torquay. Walters died the following year leaving large debts, and the house was by bought by a consortium and converted into an asylum.

1826: 11 Jul: *The Quarter Sessions were attended by a numerous bench of Magistrates. Dr. Cooke & Mr. Cripps M.P. presided in the respective courts; among the gentlemen present, were ... Walters ...*

1835: 6 Jan: *On returning to the Spa Hotel I found that Mrs. Monk had kindly sent her carriage to take my Son with her party to Barnwood, where a juvenile dance was given by Mr. Walters to the children of several of the families in Gloucester and its neighbourhood.* 10 Jan.

1842: 18 Oct.

1844: 1 May.

1845: 2 Apr.

1846: 22 Oct., 18 Nov.

WALTERS — Ralph Walters — *see also* Moorhouse[30]

Ralph Walters (1801-1865), solicitor and landed proprietor, was born at Newcastle-upon-Tyne, the son of attorney Robert Walters (1763-1837) and Isabella (1765-1842), daughter of Ralph Clayton, serjeant-at-law, of Newcastle-upon-Tyne. His parents had married at St Andrew's, Newcastle, on 20 December 1788. Isabella's sister, Anne (d. 1834), married, at the same church, 13 February 1790, Henry Moorhouse (1759-1794), maternal uncle to Margaret Witts. Henry and Anne had two children, William Henry and Margaret, both of whom died in infancy. Having inherited from his parents and his aunt, it appears that Ralph Walters wished to scoop up the remainder of the property—that of Ravenflatt and Cracoe.

Walters commenced his legal career in partnership with his father and Peregrine George Ellison, but it was dissolved in 1828. He was also secretary for the committee of twelve gentleman overseeing the Newcastle Asylum for Female Penitents.

Walters married, at Bovey Tracey, Devon, 28 September 1824, Elizabeth (1798-1840), daughter of Robert Hole (1742-1822) and Anne Pitts (d. 1809); they had 5 sons and 3 daughters:

1 Robert Hole (1825-1854)
2 Henry (b. & d. 1826)
3 William Henry (1827-1857)
4 Charles (1829-1830); died an infant
1 Anne Eliza (1830-1886)
2 Mary Moorhouse (1834-1865)
3 Lydia (1836-1865)
5 Charles Croker (1838-1840)

1834: 20 Jul: *Wrote to Mr. Ralph Walters, Newcastle, Executor to the late Mrs. Moorhouse, acknowledging his letter of the 9th, intimating an intention of early paying the £500 charged on the Ravenflat property, acquainting him with Mrs. Witts's readiness to accommodate him in respect of the plate bequeathed to her in her late Uncle's will.* 31 Jul., 1 Aug., 6 Aug., 9 Oct: *A letter from Mr. Newmarch respecting the property at Cracoe, covering copy of a letter from Mr. Walters Senr.: a difficulty has been stated, which I do not distinctly understand, arising out of the leasehold tenure of part of the Cracoe estate.* 11 Oct: *Mr. Newmarch arrived before dinner, intending to stay with us till Monday morning. Conferred with him on the difficulty raised by Mr. Walters as to the Cracoe property. It is not very distinctly stated, but we infer that Mr. W. considers a part, if not the whole to be leasehold, in which case Dr. H. Moorhouse could not legally entail it ...* 18 Oct., 20 Oct., 11 Nov: *A letter from Mr. Newmarch, from Newcastle, by which it appears that Mr. Walters does, indeed, claim the greater part, if not the whole of the Ravenflat and Cracoe property, on the ground that, being leasehold, it could not legally be made subject to entail ...* 12 Nov: *Wrote to Mr. Geldard to explain to him the impediments raised by Mr. Walters to our succession to the property at Ravenflat and Cracoe ...* 17 Nov: *Mr. Newmarch arrived ... His report of his interview with the Messrs. Walters at Newcastle was rather less discouraging than I expected it.* 21 Nov., 26 Nov., 12 Dec.

1835: 20 Jan: *Conferred with Mr. Newmarch respecting the Ravenflat and Cracoe property. Directed him to write to Mr. R. Walters to urge him to furnish us with the Abstract of title and other documents promised ...* 11 Feb., 14 Feb., 21 Feb: Mr. Newmarch arrived to dinner with a Mass of Papers, abstracts of title &c ... 7 Apr: *From Mr. Newmarch also I received a letter and parcel containing Mr. Wilbraham's opinion on the case ... Mr. Wilbraham is of opinion that our claim to the freehold is unquestionable, that as to the leasehold we have a claim to as much thereof as shall be a full equivalent for the value of the ... but that owing to the great difficulty... he would recommend a compromise between ourselves and Mr. Walters.* 18 Apr., 26 Apr., 29 Apr., 23 May.

1836: 29 Jul: *Mr. Newmarch had reached Northleach from Cheltenham before us. He laid before us two opinions which he had taken from Knight and Parry, Chancery Barristers, on our claim to the Rilston, Cracoe and Ravenflat estates ...* 4 Aug., 6 Aug., 13 Aug., 15 Aug., 23 Aug., 26 Aug., 30 Aug., 7 Sep: *Found a letter from Newmarch ... Mr. Parry of the Chancery Bar, who was visiting near Cirencester, and who retains the same view of our case as against Mr. Walters, which he did before & will draw the Bill accordingly.* 14 Nov., 16 Dec., 30 Dec.

1837: 10 Jan., 29 Jan., 5 Mar., 12 Mar., 2 May, 11 May, 13 May, 20-21 May, 24 May, 31 May, 2 Jun: *Newmarch came before breakfast from Cirencester, with whom we had a long conference respecting our chancery suit, and the conditions on which it would be right to compromise with Walters.* 10 Jun., 30 Jun., 7 Jul., 10 Jul: *Arrived there at ½ past 10 o cl. and had an hour's conference with Newmarch at his office on our Ravenflat affair, when we agreed to accept the terms of compromise last proposed by Mr. Walters ...* 9 Aug., 18 Aug: *Our negociation with Mr. Walters is also drawing to a close, he having approved the draft of the compromise to be made between us ... Recd. a letter from Newmarch, who communicates that the settlement of the affair with Walters is going on well, and progressing towards an early termination, but that it has been necessary to relinquish our claim on the plate, as at the advanced age, and in the infirm state of Walters Senr. delay is dangerous.* 1 Sep., 13 Sep., 15 Sep., 19 Sep., 29 Sep: *Also to Newmarch consulting him whether, as there does not seem a probability that Messrs. Walters will be able to complete the conveyance to us of the Ravenflat farm during the ensuing month, and as the legal ownership still rests with Mr. Walters Senr. as Trustee, it would not be desirable to request of him to furnish me with a notice to quit to be served on the Tenants before the 26th. Oct.* 15 Oct., 18 Oct., 21 Oct., 10 Nov., 21 Nov.

1838: 16 Feb: *On a cursory survey it appears that the sum of nearly £1000 will have been expended by us in this litigation* ... 28 Sep.

WANSEY — John Wansey of Grove Lane, Camberwell[31]

John Wansey (1748-1820), clothier, of Grove Lane, Camberwell, and Hackney, was the son of George Wansey (1713-1762) and Hester [Esther] Green (1713-1794). He married, 31 March 1772, Sarah Raymond (1750-1803); they had 4 sons and 4 daughters:

1 George (1774-1778)
1 Sarah (1775-1837)
2 Elizabeth (±1782-1869); married, 1800, her first cousin, Henry Wansey (1774-1855) of Sambourne House, Warminster, Wiltshire
2 George (1782-1784)
3 Mary (b. 1784)
3 John (±1785-1832)
4 Mary Ann (b. 1786)
4 George (1790-1875)

The Wanseys, like the Camberwell Wittses, were nonconformists involved in the cloth industry, creating an extra social bond. The Miss Wansey mentioned by Francis Witts was probably Sarah.

1801: 31 Jul: *Mr. and Mrs. Wansey & Miss Wansey drank tea with Mrs. Witts also.*

WARD — Edward Ward, clerk of works at the Stow and Chepstow workhouses

1837: 7 Nov: *Also to Mr. Ward, late Clerk of the Works to the Union at Stow, but now removed to Chepstow to superintend in the same capacity the erection of a Workhouse there.* 1 Dec: *Also a letter from E. Ward, late Clerk of the Works to the Stow Union, acknowledging the receipt of a cheque for £7. 8. ...*

WARD — George Henry Ward[32]

George Henry Ward (1785-1849), landed proprietor, was born at Islington, Middlesex, the son of George Ward (1751-1829) and Mary Woodfall (1753-1813). He was the elder brother of William (*below*). He married, at St Andrew's, Enfield, Middlesex, 12 September 1817, Mary Saunders. There were no known children.

George Ward (senior), a successful merchant in the City of London, bought the Bellevue estate in Cowes, Isle of Wight, in 1793. The estate consisted of a house, garden, yard, and seven fields amounting to just over 17 acres in all. In around 1799 Ward rebuilt Bellevue mansion, renaming it Northwood House, and the estate became known as Northwood Park. After his death the estate was inherited by his son, George Henry, who was locally nicknamed 'King Ward' because of his extensive property holdings in the Cowes area. In around 1837 Northwood House was rebuilt and remodelled. Papers from Northwood House held at the British Library include architectural drawings from Nash's office as well as others bearing the name of G. J. J. Mair. George Henry Ward died in 1849 and the estate was inherited by his nephew, William George Ward.

1846: 18 Jun: *Northwood park, the seat of Mr. Ward, overhangs with its groves the town of West Cowes, into which we descended ...* 19 Jun.

WARD — John Ward[33]

John Ward (±1782-1842), Church of England clergyman, was born at Bristol, the son of John Ward. He was educated at Wadham College, Oxford (BA 1806; MA 1809), and was ordained deacon on 27 April 1806 and priest some three months later on 2 August. It appears that his first clerical appointment was as curate of Bradford-on-Avon, but this is not shown on the Church of England database. He was appointed rector of Littleton-on-Severn, Gloucestershire, on 25 April 1807, and served the parish until 9 September 1829. He was appointed rector of nearby Compton Greenfield, Gloucestershire, on 28 November 1810, and held the living until his death at Kingsdown, Bristol, in 1842. As a contemporary of Francis Witts at Wadham, it is surprising that he does not feature more prominently in the diaries.

1806: 24 Sep: *Rode to the Clergy meeting at Devizes ... Conversed chiefly with Ward of Bradford ...*

WARD — John William Ward[34]

John William Ward, 4th Viscount Dudley and Ward (1781-1833), politician, was the only child of William Ward, later 3rd Viscount Dudley and Ward (1750-1823), and Julia (1754-1833), daughter of Godfrey Bosvile of Gunthwaite, Yorkshire. He was educated by private tutors and at the University of Edinburgh, Oriel College, Oxford, and Corpus Christi, Oxford (BA 1802; MA 1813). Ward was MP for Downton, 1802-03; Worcestershire, 1803-06; Petersfield, 1806-07; Wareham, 1807-12; Ilchester, 1812-18; and Bossiney, 1819-23. He was appointed privy councillor in 1827, and served as secretary for foreign affairs from April 1827 to May 1828. He succeeded as 4th Viscount Dudley and Ward in 1823, and died unmarried.

1827: 26 Apr: *It is now said, that Lord Dudley and Ward is to hold the seals of the Foreign Office ... I remember him, & was somewhat acquainted with him, when he was at Edinburgh in very early life; I think, he was a pupil of Dugald Stewart at the same time as the Marquis of Lansdown, Lord Ashburton &c.: he was then very potent in Greek, and a little scornful as to the deficiency of that commodity in the College of Edinburgh.*

1828: 23 Jan., 28 May: *Disunion reigns in the cabinet; for it is announced, that Mr. Huskisson and Lord Palmerston have resigned their offices, & it is surmised, that the rest of the liberal party in the administration, Mr. C. Grant, Mr. Lamb, Lord Dudley &c. will also retire.* 30 May, 2 Jun.

1833: 10 Nov: *During my early residence in Edinburgh this eminent character received as pupils into his family some young Englishmen of distinguished families ... The late Earl of Dudley was also pursuing his studies at the same period in Edinburgh.*

1834: 9 Sep: *Besides the inmates of the house we had Dr. Card, the Vicar of Great Malvern, Mr. Thrupp, the Curate, Col. and Mrs. Parker, from Cheshire, people of fortune and highly connected, well bred and agreeable, and a Mr. Sims, private Tutor to the eldest son of the present Lord Ward, a clergyman who has succeeded to the title of Ward, with the entailed estates of the late Earl Dudley and Ward, the former title being extinct, his Lordship having died without heirs.*

WARD — Sophia Ward[35]

Sophia Ward (1786-1861) was probably a former servant of the Witts family in Chipping Norton, although the connection is not clear. She lived at Tight End [or Tite End], near the church.

1843: 28 Nov: *Wrote to Mr. Eldridge, Vicar of Chipping Norton, inclosing half a sovereign, which I requested him to give to Sophia Ward, a person on whose behalf Mrs. Shard had solicited me in her late letter.* 30 Nov.

1850: 25 Sep: *To Mrs. Shard, assuring her of my sincere sympathy on occasion of Anne Gray's severe illness, and sent her a cheque on Hoare for £5.—promising a like remittance at Michs.—1851, if Sophia Ward, of Chipping Norton, for whose benefit the contribution is made, should be alive and need it.* 13 Oct.

WARD — William Ward[36]

William Ward (1761-1838), bishop of Sodor and Man, was born in Saintfield, near Belfast. He was ordained into the Anglican ministry as a deacon in 1788 and a priest in 1789. He was appointed bishop of Sodor and Man in 1828 and held the see until his death in 1838. He married, 1805, Anne Hammersley (d. 1841); they had 2 sons and 5 daughters, including:

1 Charlotte Anne Dorothea (1807-1828)
1 William Harry Perceval (±1812-1875), Church of England clergyman
2 Anne Louisa (1813-1875)
2 Thomas William (1816-1829)
3 Caroline (b. 1817)
4 Mary (d. ±1844)

1828): 6 Jan: *The Gazette, a better authority than the newspapers, now determines, who is to be the new prelate of the insular (Sodor and Man) diocese, the same, whom general report has recently pointed out; a Dr. W. Ward, of whom till very lately I never heard, but who is understood to have been Tutor, or otherwise connected with Lord Goderich & his elder brother, Lord Grantham.* 29 Aug.

1834: 23 Aug: *Among persons of note who were pointed out to us were the Marquis & Marchioness Thomond, Dr. Ward, Bishop of Sodor and Mann, &c.*

WARD — William Ward [37]

William Ward (1787-1849), MP, director of the Bank of England, and first-class cricketer, was born at Highbury Place, Islington, the second son of George Ward (1751-1829), of Northwood Park, Cowes, and Mary Woodfall (1753-1813). He was younger brother to George Henry (*above*). William Ward was educated at Winchester College and spent some time at Antwerp gaining experience in a banking-house. On his return in 1810, his father, a London merchant and large landowner in the Isle of Wight and Hampshire, took him into partnership. Ward became known as an expert on foreign exchanges, and was elected a director of the Bank of England in 1817. In 1819 he gave evidence before the parliamentary committees on the restrictions on payments in cash by the Bank of England.

Besides his career in finance, Ward was MP for the City of London, 1826-31, and a prominent right-handed batsman and occasional slow lob bowler. His first-class career in cricket began in the 1810 season, but was interrupted by the Napoleonic War until 1816. Ward played until 1845. His score of 278 for the MCC *v.* Norfolk at Lord's in 1820 was the highest individual innings in first-class cricket until W. G. Grace scored first-class cricket's first triple-century in August 1876.

Ward married, at St Giles-in-the-Fields, 26 April 1811, Emily (1792-1848), fifth daughter of Harvey Christian Combe, alderman, prosperous brewer, and radical London politician; they had 5 sons and 4 daughters:

1 William George (1812-1882); *see below*
1 Emily Mary (1813-1839)
2 Harvey Herman (1815-1816)
3 Henry (b. 1816)
4 Matthew (1818-1843)
2 Alicia Frances (1819-1869)
3 Caroline Elizabeth (b. 1821)
4 Georgiana Mary (b. 1825)
5 Arthur Robert (1829-1884)

1826: 14 Sep: ... *the well known and obtrusive Matthew Wood, ... of his friend Mr. Ward, Bank Director & M.P. for the city of London, whose party and family had joined Mrs. Wood's, and on the strength of all these dignities pressed for precedence.*

WARD — William George Ward [38]

William George Ward (1812-1882), theologian and philosopher, was born in London, the eldest son of William Ward and Emily Combe (*above*). He was educated at Christ Church and Lincoln College, Oxford (BA 1834; MA 1837), and was a fellow of Balliol College, 1834-45. He was also mathematical and logic lecturer at Balliol, junior bursar in 1841, and senior bursar in 1842. Ward was prominent in the Oxford movement. He wrote *Ideal of a Christian Church* in 1844, which was condemned in convocation the following year; for this publication he was deprived of his MA degree. Ward seceded to Rome shortly afterwards, and was for many years editor of the *Dublin Review.* Pius IX conferred on him the degree of DD.

1845: 9 Jan: *Recd. a letter from Dr. Symons on the subject of the coming conflict at Oxford on the matter at issue as to Mr. Ward, Fellow of Ball. Coll. and a leader among the Tractarians, which now so grievously agitates the University and the Church.* 13 Jan., 21 Jan., 26 Jan., 7 Feb., 8 Feb: *Much conversation with E.F.W. as to the coming struggle at Oxford as to the censure and degradation of Mr. Ward; his mind is not yet quite made up whether he shall go up to vote against him in Convocation.* 9 Feb., 12-13 Feb., 16 Feb., 23 Feb.

WARD — William Ward [39]

William Ward, Viscount Ednam, of Ednam, co. Roxburgh, and 2nd Earl Dudley of Dudley Castle (1817-1885), landed proprietor, was born at Bury St Edmunds, Suffolk, the son of William Humble Ward, 10th Baron Ward of Birmingham (1781-1835), and Susanna Beecroft. He was educated at Eton College and Christ Church, Oxford, followed by Trinity College, Oxford. He inherited the estate of his second cousin, John William Ward (*above*), who had died unmarried. Ward married, first, at St George's, Hanover Square, Westminster, 24 April 1851, Selina Constance de Burgh (1829-1851), who died later in the year in Germany, where she had gone for treatment for a lung complaint. He married secondly, 1865, Georgina Elizabeth (1846-1929), daughter of Sir Thomas Moncreiffe, 7th baronet (1822-1879), and Louisa (1825-1898), daughter of Robert Hay, 10th earl of Kinnoull. William and Georgina had 6 sons and 1 daughter:

1 William Humble (1867-1932); succeeded as 3rd Viscount Ednam of Ednam
2 John Hubert (1870-1938)
3 Robert Arthur (1871-1942)
1 Edith Amelia (1872-1956)
4 Reginald (1874-1904)
5 Cyril Augustus (1876-1930)
6 Gerald Ernest Francis (1877-1914)

1836: 27 Oct: *Lord Ward, an Oxonian, a very handsome youth, heir to the vast property of the late Earl Dudley and Ward.*

1845: 8 Jul: *He is as yet under Guardians, the period of his majority having been delayed by the will of Earl Dudley, as I suppose, beyond the usual term.*

WARD HUNT — George Ward Hunt — *see also* Hunt [40]

George Ward Hunt (1825-1877), MP and landed proprietor, was born at Buckhurst, Berkshire, the only surviving son of Revd George Hunt (1786-1853) and Emma Gardiner (1796-1862). He was educated at Eton College, Christ Church, Oxford, and the Inner Temple, and was a prominent Conservative politician and statesman, serving as chancellor of the exchequer and first lord of the Admiralty in the first and second ministries of Benjamin Disraeli.

Hunt entered the House of Commons in 1857 as MP for Northamptonshire North, having made several unsuccessful previous attempts. He was a secretary to the Treasury from 1866 to 1868, in the ministry of the 14th earl of Derby. He was then appointed to the exchequer when Disraeli took office. The story goes that when he stood up to present his one and only budget speech to parliament, he discovered that he had left the ministerial 'red box' containing it at home. This is said to have been the origin of the tradition whereby a chancellor shows the assembled crowd the box by holding it aloft when he leaves for the House of Commons on budget day.

George Ward Hunt married, at St Marylebone, Westminster, 5 December 1857, Alice Eden (1833-1894); they had 5 sons and 5 daughters:

1 George Eden (1859-1892)
1 Mary Caroline (b. 1860)

2 Emma (1862-1915)
2 Walter Robert (1864-1940)
3 Allen Thomas (1866-1943)
3 Alice Margaret (1867-1926)
4 Gertrude Sophia (1870-1952)
5 Constance (1871-1938)
4 John Frederick (b. 1873)
5 Edward (b. 1875)

The Hunt family is covered extensively in the introduction in volume 1. This entry should more sensibly be listed under 'Hunt', but as George Ward Hunt was most frequently referred to as 'Ward Hunt', he is listed here. In volume 1 he is referred to as H32.

1850: 9 Jan: *Received a letter from Mr. Ward Hunt, son of Mr. Geo. Hunt ...*

1853: 12 Mar: *I wrote letters to Mr. Ward Hunt and Mr. Thornton, adverting to the decease of Mr. George Hunt: a letter of condolence to the former ...* 16 Mar., 4 Apr: *Among the host of barristers present was Ward Hunt, who reported favourably of the health of his mother and the rest of the family ...*

WARDE — George Warde [41]

George Warde (1725-1803), army officer, was the second son of Col John Warde of Squerryes Court, Westerham. He was a close childhood friend of James Wolfe, 'the Conqueror of Quebec'. In 1778 he became a colonel in the Royal Horse Guards, and in 1791 he was appointed commander-in-chief, Ireland, a post which earned him the rank of general in 1796. Warde was instrumental in repulsing two French invasions of Ireland in 1796 and 1798. He married, late in life, at St Mary's, Lambeth, Surrey, 31 January 1781, Charlotte (1729-1813), daughter of Spencer Madan and Charlotte Cornwallis (d. 1794); they had at least 1 son:

1 Charles Warde (1787-1869) Capt., RN; born at Oxford; died unmarried

---

1801: 14 May: *After breakfast I sallied out in quest of Sir N. Dukinfield, whom I with some difficulty found in No. 22 Princes Street Cavendish Square with Gen. Warde.* 12 Jul: *Our party consisted of Sir. N., my Father, Lloyd, Henry, & myself. Read before dinner. Mr. G. Warde came in the Evening, a well informed and civil Gentleman.* 19 Jul: *Mr. and Mrs. G. Warde came in the Evening, pleasant persons.*

WARDLAW — the Wardlaw family

Edward and Agnes Witts were on friendly terms with a Wardlaw family in Edinburgh, and it seems likely that the Wardlaws mentioned by Francis Witts were of the same family, on a trip to the fashionable watering places of Bath and Cheltenham.

1802: 4 Jan: *As it was, Miss Wardlaw, who with her Mother & Brother was now is at Bath danced with me down two Sets.* 8-9 Aug.

WARE — Mrs Ware — *see also* Boothby *and* Tanfield

Mrs Ware has not been identified, but it is known she was the daughter of John Tanfield and the sister of Mary Payne. It seems likely that she was either Catherine (b. 1757) or Martha (b. 1762).

1838: 15 Jan: *Her sister, Mrs. Ware, has been sometime a visitor at Eyford.*

1839: 7 Jul: *After morning service had a long and painful visit from Mrs. Dolphin. She is just returned from Town with her Mother and Aunt Ware ...* 10 Jul: *Walked with MW to Eyford to call on the ladies there; received by the four widows or widows bewitched, Mrs. Ware, Mrs. Payn, Mrs. Harrison, and Mrs. Dolphin ...* 28 Jul., 19 Aug., 25 Aug.

1842: 6 Sep., 4 Oct: *Mrs. Payn and Mrs. Ware had also called during our absence.* 9 Oct: *Recd. a note from Mrs. Dolphin, intimating a wish that her connection Mr. Boothby, now visiting at Eyford, might preach here to-day, to which I wrote an affirmative answer.... Between the services we were visited by the party from Eyford,—Mr. & Mrs. Boothby and a daughter, Mrs. Payne, Mrs. Ware, and Mrs. Dolphin.* 12 Oct: *I dined at Eyford House; the party consisted of Mrs. Dolphin. Payne, Mrs. Ware, Mr. Wynniatt, Miss Anne W., Mr. & Mrs, and Miss Boothby.* 12 Oct., 26 Oct.

WARING — Jane Waring [42]

Jane Waring (1808-1876), pauper, was born at Bledington, and from the diary entries it appears that she was of feeble mind. In the 1841 census she was resident in the workhouse with 3 young sons:

1 Thomas (b. ±1833)
2 John (b. ±1835)
3 Richard (b. ±1839)

On 11 September 1845 she was sentenced by Richard Ford and Robert Waller to one month's imprisonment in Northleach House of Correction for misbehaviour at Stroud Union Workhouse. Her son John, born in Bledington, went on to lead a respectable life. In 1891 he was married and working as a plate layer on the railway.

At the time of the 1851 and 1861 censuses, Jane was still lodged in the Union Workhouse at Stow. In 1851 Thomas and Richard were still there, but John had left.

1838: 10 Aug: *Mr. Pearce called to report to me the escape from the Workhouse of a pauper, A. Waring, who has repeatedly evaded the observation of the officers, and got off.* 11 August: *Jane Waring has not come back; she had been traced by a devious course for some distance, when nothing further could be ascertained as to the route she had taken: probably, the poor creature is rambling somewhere, and one cannot but feel anxious least she should come to some harm.* 15-16 Aug., 18 Aug: *In the Evening, Mr. Pearce called to inform me that Jane Waring had found her way back to Stow, after wandering over the Country by Cheltenham, Gloucester, N. Leach &c. and was lodged in the W. House.*

WARNEFORD — Samuel Wilson Warneford [43]

Samuel Wilson Warneford (1763-1855), Church of England clergyman and philanthropist, was born at Uckfield, Sussex, the younger son of Revd Francis Warneford (1732-1784), of Warneford Place, Sevenhampton, and Catherine (d. 1757), daughter of Samuel Calverley, a wealthy drug merchant of Southwark, and his wife, Catherine. The Calverleys resided in Ewell, Surrey, and their wealth greatly enriched the Warnefords.

Samuel Wilson Warneford was educated at University College, Oxford (BA 1783; MA 1786; BCL 1790; DCL 1810). He was ordained in 1787 and became curate of Norton Broyne [later Brize Norton], Oxfordshire. He married, 1796, Margaret (1775-1840), previously a ward of court, eldest daughter of Edward Loveden Loveden [later Edward Pryse Pryse, MP], of Buscot, Berkshire, and his wife, Margaret. Warneford's wife was sickly but rich, and in face of strong hostility from Edward Loveden, a marriage settlement was reached linking the two families' fortunes. Deaths in both families subsequently further augmented Warneford's capital; his wife, for example, was left £34,000 by her grandfather.

Warneford was vicar of Bures St Mary, Essex, in 1795-98, and became rector of Lydiard Millicent, Wiltshire, in 1809, where he purchased the advowson. He held the rectorship until his death, but sold the advowson to Pembroke College, Oxford, in 1828. In 1810 Warneford also bought the advowson of both the vicarage of Bourton-on-the-Hill and the rectory of Moreton-in-Marsh, Gloucestershire, having received a dispensation to hold the second living. He was an honorary canon of Gloucester from 1844 to his death, but he is best remembered for his philanthropy.

Warneford became one of the governors of the Radcliffe Infirmary, Oxford, to which he donated approximately £70,000 from 1812 onwards; the infirmary was renamed the Warneford Lunatic Asylum in 1843. The churches of Bourton-on-the-Hill and Moreton-in-Marsh were refitted and improved by Warneford at a cost of £1,000 each. His gifts and support were numerous, but this is not the place to list them all. His sister Philadelphia (1767-1834), a wealthy woman in her own right, contributed to many of the charities he supported.

1822: 27 Sep: *I dined at Dr. Warneford's, Bourton on the Hill, after a fatiguing turnpike meeting there, at which Lord Redesdale presided. Slept at Bourton on the Hill & returned the following morning.*

1823: 13 Mar: *I dined and slept at Dr. Warneford's at Bourton on the Hill: a large party.* 14 Mar., 24 Apr: *After the ordinary business of the day at Stow, I proceeded to Bourton on the Hill, where I dined & slept at Dr. Warneford's ...* 25 Apr., 8 Aug., 25 Nov: *I dined and slept at Dr. Warneford's, meeting Lords Redesdale and Northwick, Mr. Pole, Mr. Jeaffreson, Mr. Ford, Mr. Saumarez and Mr. Eyre ...*

1824: 6 Aug.

1825: 5 Apr: *We had a dinner party.... Dr. Warneford ...* 19 Jul., 20 Sep.

1826: 17 Jun: *Dr. Warneford having been thought of, a Doctor of mature years & a shovel hat being doubtless a most suitable candidate, he was nominated by Mr. Ford, while I seconded my old acquaintance ...* 5 Jul., 18 Jul., 8 Sep.

1828: 18 Apr: *Mr. Chr. Jeaffreson was at one time curate of Moreton, & relinquished that situation in consequence of his evangelical bias, strongly contrasted with the opinions of his Rector, Dr. Warneford ...*

1829: 31 Jul: *Several of our neighbours dined with us to-day. & Dr. Warneford formed the party.* 12 Aug., 18 Sep: *... Dr. Warneford is Patron as well as Incumbent, a rich man as well as an earnest friend to the Church; having no family of his own, and living at no great expence, though keeping a handsome establishment, he can afford to be generous out of his ample income, & will yet leave a very considerable fortune to his nieces, the daughters of the elder brother of the House, Col. Warneford of Warneford Place in Wilts....* 19 Sep: *Miss Warneford appeared at breakfast: I had not seen her for nine years: she is much aged & very feeble, but when sitting in her chair less of a cripple, than I had expected. When she attempts to walk, the ravages of paralysis are painfully visible; the use of one side being almost wholly gone. But she is patient and cheerful ...* 24 Nov.

1834: 5 Mar., 7 Mar., 19 Sep: *... drove to dine and sleep at Dr. Warneford's at Bourton on the Hill.* 20 Sep., 17 Nov.

1835: 31 Mar: *After dinner sat for an hour or two with Dr. Warneford ... at the Stoneleigh Hotel.*

1836: 16 Sep., 20-21 Sep., 1 Oct., 4 Oct., 22 Oct., 25 Oct., 16 Dec.

1837: 18 Mar., 21-22 Mar., 30 Mar., 2 Jun., 16 Aug., 16 Nov.

1838: 5 Feb., 14 Feb., 13-14 Mar., 2 Apr., 30 Oct., 30 Dec.

1839: 2 Jan., 17 Jan.

1840: 24 Mar., 22 Apr., 6 Jun.

1842: 27 Apr., 20 Dec.

1843: 27 Jan: *Before commencing business we called on the venerable Dr. Warneford, whom we found in comfortable health and spirits; confined, as is his wont, in the winter season, to his fire side, but enjoying a green old age, in full possession of his faculties ...* 14 Nov.

1844: 27 Jan: *Called on Dr. Warneford, and found him in full vigour of mind ... but not free from gout, attended by some degree of Erysipelas.* 30 Nov.

1846: 8 Aug., 12 Aug.

1847: 27 Jan: *Called on Dr. Warneford, whom we found in firm health, considering his age and chronic infirmity: his faculties of mind unimpaired, sight and hearing good. He still takes the same lively interest in what regards the Church and the State; is still acute, and diligent in the management of his private affairs ...* 3 Feb., 24 Jun.

1850: 3 Jan., 8 Jan.

1853: 16 Mar., 16 Mar.

1854: 12 May.

WARNER — *see* Lee Warner *and* Daniel Lee Warner

WARRE — John Tyndale Warre and the Warre family of Hestercombe — *see also* Greg[44]

John Tyndale Warre (1756-1819), landed proprietor, was born at Bristol, the son of George Tyndale (1704-1771) and Margaretta Bampfylde (b. 1722). He was heir to the Warres of Hestercome, an ancient Somerset family, and the nephew of Coplestone Warre Bampfylde (d. 1791). In accordance to the terms of his uncle's will, he changed his name to Warre. He was high sheriff for Somerset in 1796.

Warre married, at Bristol, 10 January 1789, Elizabeth, only daughter and heir of John Farell of Bristol; they had 1 daughter:

1 Elizabeth Maria Tyndale Warre (1791-1872); inherited the Hestercombe estate upon her father's death; died unmarried

There was another Warre family headed by James Warre (1756-1833) of London and Oporto. The two families were almost certainly related. James married Eleanor (±1759-1847), daughter of Thomas and Elizabeth Greg of Belfast. The 'Miss Gregg' mentioned by Francis Witts in his diary entries of 2 and 5 October 1804 was probably Eleanor Warre's niece.

1804: 23 Aug: *A Promenade & Ball very fully attended & hot at York House for the Benefit of the little Polish Count Bosuwlaski. Great deal of Conversation with many people. Danced with Miss Warre & Miss Augusta Manners.*

WARREN — Charles Warren[45]

Charles Warren (1798-1866), army officer, was born at Bangor, Caernarvonshire, the third son of John Warren (1767-1838), dean of Bangor, and Elizabeth Crooke (1771-1825). He entered the Royal Military Academy at Woolwich, but was soon offered a commission in the infantry by the duke of York. He was gazetted an ensign in the 80th Foot on 24 November 1814, and joined the depot at Colchester on 24 January 1815. Warren commanded a detachment from Ostend in the duke of Wellington's march on Paris after Waterloo, and entered the city with the allied army.

Warren had a distinguished army career which included service in India, South Africa, and China. On 25 November 1845 he was promoted to regimental lieutenant-colonel commanding the 55th Regiment, with which he served in Ireland during the disturbances of 1846-47. He also fought in the Crimean War. He was promoted in 1858 to major-general.

Warren married, in Paris, 17 April 1830, Mary Ann (1808-1846), daughter of William Hughes (b. 1778) and his wife, Margaret; they had 3 sons and 3 daughters:

1 John (1831-1854)
1 Margaret (1832-1912)
2 Mary (1835-1838)
3 Charlotte (1837-1846)
2 Charles (1840-1927)
3 William (1841-1907)

1848: 11 Nov: *Justice business at home as to extending the furlough of a soldier in declining health, which occasioned me to write to Lt. Col. Warren, C.B. commanding the 18th. Inf. Reg. quartered at Dublin.*

WARREN — John Borlase Warren [46]

Sir John Borlase Warren, 1st baronet (±1754-1822), MP and naval officer, was the son and heir of John Borlase Warren (d. 1763) of Stapleford and Little Marlow. He entered Emmanuel College, Cambridge, in 1769, but did not take a degree. In 1775 he was created a baronet—the baronetcy held by his ancestors, the Borlases, had become extinct in 1689. He married, 1780, Caroline (1766-1839), daughter of Sir John Clavering (1722-1777) and Diana West (1731-1766); they had at least 2 sons and 2 daughters:

1 George John (1783-1801); died at the battle of Abu Qir, Alexandria, Egypt
1 Frances Maria (1784-1837); married George Charles Venables-Vernon, 4th Baron Vernon (1779-1835); at least 1 son:
  1 George John (1803-1866); succeeded as 5th Baron Vernon
2 William Henry (b. 1788)
2 Diana Martha Clavering (b. 1790)

Warren was MP for Great Marlow in 1774-84, during which period his career in the Royal Navy began in earnest. In April 1794 he was commodore of the frigate squadron assisting in the blockade of Brest off the north-west coast of France, during which his squadron captured a number of French frigates. In 1795 Warren commanded one of the two squadrons carrying troops for the Quiberon expedition, and the following year his frigate squadron off Brest was said to have captured or destroyed 220 vessels. In October 1798, when a French fleet carrying 5,000 men sailed from Brest intending to invade Ireland, their plan was frustrated in no small part by Warren's squadron during the action of 12 October 1798.

In 1802, Warren was sworn of the privy council and sent to St Petersburg as ambassador extraordinary. In 1806 he captured a large French warship, the *Marengo*, at the action of 13 March 1806. He was commander-in-chief on the North American station in 1807-10 and 1813-14, and was promoted to admiral in 1810.

It seems that Francis Witts approached Warren in October 1802 asking for an appointment as his secretary, similar to his former position in Copenhagen with William Drummond.

1802: 11 Oct: *Wrote to Lord Elcho & Sir J. Borlase Warren.*

1837: 2 Oct: *Lady V., doubtless, appreciated justly her attentions to Lady Warren, Lady V.'s mother, with whom Miss C. now resides as Dame de Compagnie, in a similar capacity as for so many years with Lady Elcho.*

WARRENDER — George Warrender [47]

Sir George Warrender, 4th baronet (1782-1849), politician and banker, was the eldest son of Sir Patrick Warrender, 3rd baronet of Lochend (1731-1799), and Helen, daughter of James Blair of Dunbar. He was educated at Edinburgh, Christ Church, Oxford, and Trinity College, Cambridge. He succeeded his father as 4th baronet on 14 June 1799, and was made lieutenant-colonel of the Berwick, Haddington, Linlithgow, and Peebles Militia in 1805. He married, at St James's, Westminster, 3 October 1810, Anne (1791-1871), second daughter of George Evelyn Boscawen, 3rd Viscount Falmouth. There do not appear to have been any children.

Warrender was MP for Haddington Burghs in 1807-12, Truro in 1812-18, Sandwich in 1818-26, and Westbury in 1826-30. He was lord of the Admiralty from October 1812 to February 1822, commissioner of the Board of Control from February 1822 to February 1828, and appointed privy councillor on 4 February 1822. He was director (extraordinary) of the Bank of Scotland from 1822 to 1828. Warrender purchased the picturesque estate of Clifden in Buckinghamshire.

1825: 29 Jun: *We ascended to Clifden, and were not denied admittance to the grounds ... it has recently been purchased by Sir George Warrender, a Scotch Baronet, formerly a Lord of the Admiralty, and now one of the Commissioners for the Affairs of India. His seat in Scotland is near Dunbar: we were contemporaries and acquainted, when we studied together in the Junior classes of the College at Edinburgh, previously to 1798.* 8 Jul.

1837: 22 Jul: *Very kindly recd. by his Lordship and family: a late dinner, as they were expecting Lord and Lady Belhaven from Town, who did not arrive till eleven o cl., having been long on the road from Sir Geo. Warrender's seat at Clifden, which they had made their first halting place.*

WARRINER — Ann Warriner [48]

Ann Warriner, née Long (±1740-1815), married, 1759, Gifford Warriner (1745-1820), born at Beechingstoke, Wiltshire, the son of Gifford Warriner and his wife, Elizabeth. Ann and Gifford had at least one son:

1 Gifford; married, 1787, Betty Hutfield; at least 1 son:
  1 Gifford (1788-1880); declared a lunatic in 1821; later lived at Conock Cottage from at least 1838 to his death

Gifford and Ann Warriner lived at Conock Manor, an imposing eighteenth-century Georgian manor house. It is not clear which of the Mrs Warriners Francis Witts was referring to in his diaries, but it was probably the elder. The family was of some standing; Gifford Warriner was high sheriff for Wiltshire in 1791.

1806: 9 Oct: *... whence I returned to Wedhampton with Mrs. Poore & Mrs. Warrener.* 27 Dec.

1807: 14 Apr: *Drove my Mother to call upon Mr. Jones vwvw& Mrs. Warrener at Conock.* 1 May, 4 May: *In the Evening Mrs. Warrener & Mrs. L. Mayo, Mr. Mayo & Mrs. Jones visited us to tea.* 23 Jun., 6 Jul., 28 Jul., 11 Aug., 26 Aug., 30 Dec: *... then thro' Wedhampton to Conock; & called upon Jones & his Aunt Warriner.*

1808: 7 Mar: *... called upon Mr. Jones & Mrs. Warriner; rode with Jones & Hill to Devizes.*

WARTER — Edward Warter [49]

Edward Warter (1811-1878), JP and Church of England clergyman, was born at Pontesbury, Shropshire, the younger son of Henry Degory Warter (1770-1853) and Emma Sarah Moore Wood (1786-1863) (below). He was educated at Shrewsbury

School and Magdalene College, Cambridge (BA 1834; MA 1837), where he was elected a fellow in 1835. He was later a tutor and president at Magdalene. Warter was rector of Great Hanwood, Shropshire, in 1849-58, and of Aldrington, Sussex, in 1852-78. He was a JP for Shropshire. He married, first, at Bedford, April 1852, Charlotte Gertrude Harries (1814-1854); and secondly, at Hendon, Middlesex, Rosamund (1826-1893), only daughter of Revd Frederick Holmes, professor at Bishop's College, Calcutta. Edward and Rosamund had at least 1 son:

1 Hugo Francis Witts (1857-1865); presumably named after the diarist

---

1845: 10 Jul: *Our party at dinner was increased by the arrival of Mr. Edward Warter, who had, indeed, accompanied John Witts from Meole this morning.* 11 Jul: *By the roadside is the small, singular-looking modern brick church, the benefice being in the patronage of Mr. Warter of Cruck Meole, the present Incumbent living in the Parsonage, far advanced, I believe, in years; but Edward Warter, though the youngest son of the family, will succeed, I believe, to his father's property in Hanwood and to the advowson, under some peculiar custom of the manor, I presume, analogous to, or identical with, Borough English.* 12 Jul: *Mr. E. Warter called at my cousins between breakfast and luncheon time—John Witts accompanied MW. and me to call on Mr. and Mrs. Warter; they inhabit a very comfortable moderate sized Mansion house, situate very near, perhaps a little too near, the Meole Brook in a pleasure ground: we were admitted into a comfortable dining room, and into a bed room occupied by Mrs. Warter, who is still too much an invalid to join the family below.*

WARTER — Henry Degory Warter — Parker & Warter, solicitors [50]

Henry Degory [Diggory] Warter (1770-1853), solicitor, was born at Cruck Meole, Shropshire. He was a solicitor in partnership with William Parker at 1 Carey Street, Chancery Lane, London. He married, 19 March 1805, Emma Sarah Moore Wood (1783-1863), born at Calcutta, Bengal, the daughter of William Wood (1745-1813), of Marsh Hall and Hanwood, Shropshire, and his wife, Esther (d. 1804). Henry and Emma had at least 4 sons:

1 John Wood (1806-1878); married, 1834, Edith May, daughter of the poet Robert Southey; *see below*
2 Henry Degory (1807-1884)
3 William (1808-1809)
4 Edward (1811-1878); *see above*

Francis Witts used Henry Warter on an increasing basis as his London solicitor, and their families were connected. In his diary entry for 2 August 1826, he said, 'Mrs. Warter is sister to Mrs. John Witts', and on 17 July 1838 he said, 'Capt. Witts is in better health than usual, but his wife is very ailing; they are soon going to town, to meet her favourite nephew, Mr. John Warter, and his lady.' Capt. John Witts had married Maria Wood (±1770-±1855), elder sister to Emma Sarah Moore Wood (*above*).

1826: 2 Aug: *For the same reason we were unable to introduce ourselves to Mr. & Mrs. Warter of Cruck Meole, about four miles from Shrewsbury, who had been so good as to express a wish of shewing kindness to our dear boy. Mrs. Warter is sister to Mrs. John Witts, and her husband is a Shropshire gentleman with a pretty good estate ...* 21 Oct: ... *At the latter place they had seen our dear Edward, who has been very kindly treated by Mr. & Mrs. Warter, who give him a general invitation to their house ...*

1830: 25 Jun: *To dinner at Mrs. Witts's, Brunswick Square ... & Mr. H. Warter.*

1836: 24 Dec: *Wrote to Mr. Jennings ... also to consult with Mr. H. Warter, whether I could give or withhold my assent, or declare myself neutral, without reference to the Trustees under the will of my Uncle, or to the parties contingently interested in the property, Capt. Witts and B. P. Witts.* 29 Dec.

1837: 14 Feb., 17 Feb.

1838: 17 Jul: *Capt. Witts is in better health than usual, but his wife is very ailing; they are soon going to town, to meet her favourite nephew, Mr. John Warter, and his lady.*

1839: 5 Jan., 12 Jan., 14 Jan., 14 Aug., 17-18 Aug.

1840: 31 Mar: ... *Mr. Jennings considers the arrangement very satisfactory; and has consulted in the business, as far as concerns the legal effect of the transaction, Mr. Henry Warter, as our London Solicitor.* 4 Apr., 24 Jun., 27 Jun., 3-4 Jul., 17 Aug., 20 Aug., 25 Aug., 29 Aug., 31 Aug., 9 Sep., 24 Nov., 29 Nov.

1841: 1 Mar., 3 Mar.

1842: 8-10 Feb., 15 Feb., 17 Feb., 19 Feb., 21 Feb., 23 Feb., 25 Feb, 27 Feb., 2 Mar., 4 Mar., 15 Mar: *Mr. John Warter, eldest son of Mr. Warter of Meole, a clergyman in Sussex, married to a daughter of the poet Southey, who has been recently appointed one of the Trustees of my late Uncle Broome in room of Mr. Rogers, deceased.* 17 Mar., 20 Mar., 23 Mar., 5-7 Apr., 9 Apr., 13 Apr., 19 Apr., 22 Apr., 27 Apr., 29 Apr., 3 May, 14 May, 30 May, 1 Jun., 4 Jun., 7 Jun., 11 Jun., 16-17 Jun., 19 Jun., 25 Jun., 29 Jun., 23-25 Jul., 28 Jul., 3-4 Aug., 7 Aug., 25 Aug., 27 Aug., 4 Sep., 7 Sep., 10 Sep., 12 Sep., 15 Sep., 25-26 Sep., 30 Sep., 3-4 Oct., 7 Oct., 25 Oct., 30-31 Oct. 3 Nov., 12 Nov., 14 Nov., 16 Nov., 23 Nov., 12 Dec., 18 Dec., 21 Dec., 25 Dec.

1843: 11 Jan., 13 Jan., 15 Jan., 17 Jan., 10 Feb: *Received a letter from Mr. H. D. Warter: the Transaction with the Clothworkers Company is closed, and the sum paid, agreeably to the contract with us is £9512. 10. that being the value of £10000 3 per Ct. Cons. at 95? pr Ct.—the highest point to which they have of late attained, and so an income of £300 per ann. is secured to us at the present price of stock.* 11 Feb., 16 Feb., 18 Feb., 18 Aug., 20 Aug., 23 Aug., 19-20 Nov., 22 Nov., 24 Nov., 28 Nov., 30 Nov. 2 Dec.

1844: 21-22 Jan., 24 May: *He gives a good account of my cousin John Witts, and a very bad one of Mrs. Warter Senr. whose decease is, probably, near at hand.* 30 May: *MW. recd. a letter from Apphia Witts; Mrs. Warter still lingers; John Witts is pretty well in health.* 2 Sep., 6 Sep., 3-4 Nov.

1845: 29 Mar., 2 Apr., 9 Jul., 10-12 Jul.

1846: 29 May, 11-15 Jun., 17 Jun., 22 Jun., 28 Jun., 14 Jul., 21 Jul., 24-25 Jul., 29 Jul., 12 Aug., 15 Aug., 27 Aug., 5 Oct., 17 Oct., 23 Oct., 2 Nov., 5 Nov., 21 Dec., 23 Dec.

1847: 4 Feb: *Received letters from H. D. Warter, with particulars of a property in ground rents in the Wandsworth road offered to us for purchase for my consideration; one of the same of which Jennings referred in his letter received yesterday ...* 5 Feb., 9-10 Feb., 23 Feb., 27 Feb., 5-6 Mar., 11-13 Apr., 15 Apr., 20 Apr., 16-17 May, 19 May, 23 May, 1 Jul., 10 Aug., 14 Aug., 31 Aug., 1-2 Sep., 11-12 Sep., 21-22 Sep., 29-30 Sep., 1 Oct., 4-5 Oct., 9 Oct., 7-8 Dec., 10 Dec., 16 Dec., 19 Dec., 21 Dec., 23-24 Dec., 29 Dec., 31 Dec.

1848: 2 Jan., 26 Jan., 29 Jan., 24 Mar., 27 Mar., 29 Mar: *Having made our survey, Mr. Jennings & I got into a Cab cab, and betook ourselves to Mr. H. Warter's office in Carey Street, where we conferred with him as to the St. George's Ground rents, and Mr. Jennings took with him from thence a number of deeds relating to it the property which he will want as a guide in receiving the Ground rents. Here I parted from Mr. Jennings, and remained for some little time with Mr. Warter, conversing with him on business, as to the payment of the balance due to him on his account for business done &c., and as to our mutual friends and connections in Shropshire.* 15 Apr.

1850: 19 Jul.

1853: 9 Apr: *Having noticed in the newspaper the death of Mr. Warter, of Cruck Meole, at 82 years of age, I wrote to Apphia Witts, requesting her to assure her brother and Mrs. J. Witts, and through them Mrs. Warter and other members of that family, of my condolence: thus also seeking information as to the health & welfare of my Shropshire relations, and keeping alive an intercourse which their secluded habits render rare and occasional.*

WARTER — John Wood Warter [51]

John Wood Warter (1806-1878), Church of England clergyman and antiquary, was the eldest son of Henry Warter and Emma Wood (*above*). He was educated at Shrewsbury School and Christ Church, Oxford (BA 1828; MA 1834; BD 1841). He served as chaplain to the embassy at Copenhagen in 1829-33, and was vicar of Heene with West Tarring and Durrington, Sussex, from 1834 to his death in 1878. Warter was an intimate friend of the poet Robert Southey, whose eldest daughter, Edith May (1804-1871), he married at Keswick, Cumberland, on 15 January 1834. John and Edith had 2 sons and 3 daughters:

1 Edith Frances (1836-1863)
1 Henry Degory (1837-1889)
2 Ellen Isabella (b. & d. 1837)
3 Ellen Caroline (1839-1929)
2 John S. (1840-1866)

Warter was an old-fashioned churchman of the 'high and dry' school. He published many tracts and sermons reflecting his orthodox divinity, and was frequently in dispute with the ecclesiastical commissioners. Although most of his works concerned religious and antiquarian topics, his greatest service to scholarship was his collection of material relating to Robert Southey, published as *Life and Correspondence of Robert Southey*. Warter edited volumes 6 and 7 of Southey's *Doctor*, and a one-volume edition of the whole work (1848). He also edited Southey's *Commonplace Book* in four volumes (1849-51), and four volumes of *Selections from Southey's Letters* (1856).

1838: 17 Jul: *Capt. Witts is in better health than usual, but his wife is very ailing; they are soon going to town, to meet her favourite nephew, Mr. John Warter, and his lady.*

1842: 15 Mar., 17 Mar.

1843: 4 Sep: *There also we heard that the Church of West Tarring, the benefice of Mr. John Warter, is little more than a mile distant from Worthing, but is now undergoing repair; he and his family being absent from home on a visit to their friends.*

WATERFALL — James Waterfall [52]

James Waterfall (1786-1840), Quaker grocer and retailer, was born at Coventry, the son of John Waterfall (1745-1829) and Sarah Farr (1750-1815). He was a confectioner, pastry cook-cum-grocer, and druggist at 377 High Street, Cheltenham. He married, at Tewkesbury, 23 November 1810, Elizabeth Booth (1792-1867); they had 6 sons and 3 daughters:

1 Charles (1811-1881)
2 John Seymour (1812-1873)
3 Edward (b. 1814)
4 William (1818-1902)
1 Elizabeth (b. 1823)
2 Annie (b. 1825)
5 Arthur (b. 1828)
3 Helen (1833-1834)
6 James (1834-1915)

In 1851, Waterfall's widow Elizabeth lived at 11 Portland Street, Cheltenham, as a lodging house keeper.

1837: 19 Feb: *A letter from Waterfall of Cheltenham, naming a servant likely to suit me, which I answered ...*
21 Feb: *To Waterfall, desiring him to continue to look out for a servant, particularly, as regarded the man whom he named to me by a letter received on Saturday, but who had not made his appearance on Monday, as I had expected.*

1846: 12 Sep: *Wrote to E.F. W.—also to Mr. Waterfall about a bill due by us to late Walls and Fisk ...*

WATHEN — Obadiah Paul Wathen [53]

Obadiah Paul Wathen (1783-1868), clothier and landed proprietor, was born at Woodchester, Gloucestershire, the fifth son of Sir Samuel Wathen (1748-1835), of Woodchester, and Margaret (1748-1826), daughter of Benjamin Peach (1719-1778) and Elizabeth Gaisford (1726-1787). He married, at the church of St Mary, St Denys and St George, Manchester, 7 October 1806, Margaret (1781-1854), daughter of James Bateman (1748-1824), of Tolson Hall, Westmorland, and Margaret Nicholson (1750-1819); they had 4 sons and 4 daughters:

1 Margaret Peach (1807-1850); married Thomas Plummer Dunn (1802-1867), whose pyramid-shaped tomb at the Woodchester parish graveyard is distinctive
2 Elizabeth Bateman (1810-1907)
1 James Bateman (1811-1886)
2 Samuel Paul (1812-1813)
3 Agnes Paul (1818-1886)
4 Augusta Maria (1819-1853)
3 John Bateman (1821-1906), Church of England clergyman
4 Herbert Lloyd Basset (1822-1844)

Wathen's wife Margaret died in 1854 in Prestbury, near Cheltenham, and he died at Lynch House in Somerset some fourteen years later. Agnes and Edward Witts were on friendly terms with various members of the Wathen family when they lived in Rodborough between 1789 and 1793. The Wathens were wealthy clothiers in the Stroud valleys.

1825: 20 May: *These reports relate to a laxity of principle and improper heat of temper as regards Mr. Hale, indiscretion on his part in keeping under his roof an unfortunately vicious youth, his own son, and other minor charges alledged by Mr. O.P. Wathen of Woodchester, who yet does not chuse his name to be brought forward.*
14 Jun: ... *it appears from Mr. Hale's representations, that Mr. Wathen's son was the last person to cast the first stone; being a spoiled child his complaints were too hastily listened to by his parents, who were, doubtless, ignorant, that charges might have been brought against him of indelicate language & the utterance of coarse sentiments.*

WATKINS — Charles Severne Watkins [54]

Charles Severne Watkins (1782-1813), army officer, was born at Rock, Worcestershire, the only son of Revd Richard Watkins (1744-1805) and Ann Malpas (1744-1796). He was educated at Eton College and Wadham College, Oxford. Watkins was a lieutenant in the 3rd (Prince of Wales) Regiment of Dragoon Guards, and married, at Clifton Campville, Staffordshire, 12 July 1810, Sarah Biokerton. They do not appear to have had any children.

1802: 15 May: *Afterwards with Williams Rashleigh & Pering in the High St. where we met Watkins & Hastings terribly drunk. Brought them home at last with difficulty. At night they made a bonfire of their furniture.*

WATKINS — George Nowell Watkins [55]

George Nowell Watkins (1771-1844), Church of England clergyman, was born at Froyle, Hampshire, the son of George Watkins and his wife, Ann. He was educated at St Mary Hall, Oxford (BA 1792; MA 1795), and was perpetual curate of Long Sutton, Hampshire, from 1806 to his death in 1844. He married, at St George's, Bloomsbury, Westminster, July 1810, Mary Boswell (1790-1869), youngest daughter of Thomas Aston and Susanna[h] Prosser, of Bedford Place, and elder sister of Frederick Aston. George and Mary had least 1 son (not listed here) and 1 daughter:

1 Mary Baldwin (1811-1885); married, 1830, Henry Burningham (b. 1799), barrister-at-law; at least 1 son:
  1 Henry George Charles (b. 1831), Capt., 58th Foot

1820: 5 Jan: *We spent the Evening at Mrs. Aston's: my old pupil Frederic A. had been with us much in the morning. We had delicious music. Mr. Aston's daughter, Mrs. Watkins, is a most superior private singer: and indulged us with several delightful songs ...* 19 May: *My young friend Frederick Aston arrived from his Brother-in-law's, Mr. Watkins's, Berkley near Frome ...*

1823: 15 Feb: *I went yesterday to dine & sleep at Stanway Vicarage. Mrs. Watkins, Frederick Aston's youngest Sister, was his guest: her husband is the Revd. Nowell Watkins; as usual, her exquisite singing enchanted me; though certainly her voice is not what it once was: but her taste & expression remain the same.*

1826: 23 Jun: *They are set out on visits to his brother in law, Watkins, Curate of Blagdon, Somerset, and Blizard of Donnington near Ledbury.*

1827: 10 Jan: *... Mr. Watkins, with his wife and daughter being come to spend several weeks with him and Mrs. F. Aston; Mr. Watkins can serve Stanway & Cutsdean, while Frederick does my duty. I therefore did not hesitate to accept his services for the 21st.*

1828: 12 Aug: *... since Mrs. Aston's decease, his daughter Mrs. Watkins, with her husband, has resided with him; but this arrangement is now terminated by Mr. W. taking a Curacy in Leicestershire.*

1833: 31 Oct.

1840: 21 Aug.

1844: 6 Aug: *Mr. and Mrs. Aston and Mrs. Watkins paid us a visit, and took luncheon with us: we had not seen Mrs. W. for many years; lately become a widow, having lost her husband, who was many years her senior, and had long been a great invalid, she is about to take up her residence in another house in the same parish—Froyle, Hants—in which she has long lived, with Mr. W. who had a small Chapelry in the neighbourhood: her only child, Mrs. Burningham, the wife of a barrister, resides, and has long resided, near her in the same parish.* 1 Oct.

1848: 11 Oct., 4 Nov: *Recd. a letter from F. Aston, written from Froyle in Hants, the residence of his sister, Mrs. Watkins.*

WATLING — Charles Henry Watling [56]

Charles Henry Watling (1794-1871), Church of England clergyman, was born at Leominster, Herefordshire, the son of Robert Watling (1739-1814) and Mary Brewer. He was educated at Merton College and Jesus College, Oxford (BA 1817; MA 1820; BD 1827), and was appointed perpetual curate of Charlton Kings in 1830 and vicar of Tredington, Worcestershire, in 1839. He married, at Childwall, Lancashire, 27 August 1833, Emily (1813-1880), third daughter of Thomas Colley Pitter of Aigburth Hall, near Liverpool; they had 3 sons and 1 daughter:

1 Charles Wyatt (1835-1902)
1 Mary Elizabeth (1838-1916)
2 John Thomas (1841-1895)
3 Henry Fairchild (1843-1872), Church of England clergyman

1833: 26 Jan: *Mr. Riddle went to Cheltenham preparatory to officiating at Charlton Kings to-morrow in the room of Mr. Watling, who is still absent from his cure.*

1840: 29 Apr. *Three Clergymen were appointed Trustees of the Church, Messrs. Trye, Edwards, and Watling, the latter of whom being an old, tried, and kind friend of Riddle, had been mainly instrumental to his appointment.*

WATSON — Alexander Watson [57]

Alexander Watson (1815-1865), Church of England clergyman, was born in Southwark, Surrey, the son of Joseph Watson (1765-1829), headmaster of an asylum on Old Kent Road for the deaf and dumb. He was educated at Shrewsbury School and Trinity College and Corpus Christi, Cambridge (BA 1837; MA 1840), and afterwards at Durham University. He was ordained deacon in 1839 and priest in 1840.

Watson was curate of St Andrew's, Manchester, 1839-40; assistant minister at St John's, Cheltenham, 1841-50; vicar of St Marychurch with Coffinswell, Devon, 1851-55; rector of Bridestowe with Sourton, 1856-58; vicar of Bedford chapel, Bloomsbury, London, 1859-61; and curate of St Mary's, Soho, 1863-64. He was involved in a chancery suit concerning Bedford chapel, and became insolvent as a result.

Watson was married to Hannah (b. ±1819), born at Eccles, Lancashire; they had at least 2 sons and 4 daughters:

1 Alexander Hook (1841-1908)
1 Hannah G. (b. ±1843)
2 Annie R. (b. ±1844)
2 Herbert Edward (b. 1846)
3 Charlett J. (b. ±1847)
4 Harrietta B. (b. 1850)

1850: 23 Apr: *Wrote to Mr. Watson, the Incumbent of St. John's, Cheltenham ...* 25 Apr., 8 Nov.

1851: 10 May.

WATSON — William Henry Watson [58]

Sir William Henry Watson (1796-1860), MP, army officer, and barrister-at-law, was born at Nottingham [another source states Bamburgh, Northumberland], the son of Capt. John Watson, of the 76th Foot, and Elizabeth, daughter of Henry Grey of Bamburgh, Northumberland. He was educated at the Royal Military College, Marlow, and was commissioned as a cornet in the 1st (Royal) Dragoons by the duke of York on 14 November 1811. He was promoted to lieutenant on 7 May 1812 while serving in the Peninsular War. The 1st Dragoons were reduced in 1814, and in April 1815 Watson exchanged into the 6th (Inniskilling) Dragoons. He served with this regiment in Belgium and France, sharing in the Waterloo prize money in the process. He was also present at the allied armies' entry into Paris.

Watson was placed on half pay on 25 March 1816, and entered Lincoln's Inn as a student on 19 June 1817. He worked diligently and was soon able to practise as a special pleader; he continued as a special pleader until 1832, when he was called to the bar by

Lincoln's Inn. Watson joined the northern circuit, where he found work and became popular, taking silk and becoming a bencher of his inn in 1843. He was MP for Kinsale, 1841-47, and Hull, 1854-56, and was knighted in 1856.

Watson married, first, at Newcastle-upon-Tyne, Northumberland, 17 August 1826, Anne (1802-1828), daughter of William Armstrong (1778-1857) and Anne Potter (1780-1848); they had 1 son:

1 John William (1827-1909)

He married secondly, at Midhurst, Sussex, 5 August 1831, Mary Capron (1806-1878); they had 1 son:

1 William Henry (1834-1899)

In his diary, Witts referred to Watson as an Irishman, and therefore this attribution must be considered tentative. However, no other barrister of this name has been discovered.

1828: 17 Oct: *The dull monotony, which had prevailed during the Sessions, was this morning unexpectedly interrupted by a fracas between one of the Magistrates on the Bench, & one of the Barristers. Mr. Goodrich, an experienced man, but warm in temper, yet not quarrelsome, interposed some remark by no means uncalled for or likely to give offence, while Mr. Watson, an Irishman, and a quick impetuous gentleman, was addressing the Court. The latter, who has been accustomed of late to take undue liberties in Mr. Cripps's Court, where he chiefly practises, and where disorder & irregularity are but too prevalent, from the informal manner, familiarity & easy temper of the presiding magistrate, took this interruption of Mr. Goodrich very ill ...*

WATTS — Anne Watts and the Watts family of Eyford [59]

Anne Watts (±1756-1842) was the widow of Richard Watts (±1755-1819). She and Richard had at least 4 sons and 1 daughter:

1 Samuel (b. 1788); married Hannah; at least 1 daughter:
    1 Mary Anne (b. 1823)
2 Thomas (b. 1790)
3 Robert (b. 1793)
1 Hannah (b. 1796); married, at Upper Slaughter, 28 September 1828, John Farmer of Bourton-on-the-Water
4 John (1799-1872); born at Upper Slaughter; married, at Lower Swell, Gloucestershire, 15 January 1825, Ann Elizabeth Hensley (1801-1830); 4 sons:
    1 George (1826-1854)
    2 Henry (b. 1827)
    3 Charles (1828-1837)
    4 Frederick (b. & d. 1829)
    Ann was buried by Francis Witts on 12 September 1830. John married, secondly, Elizabeth (b. ±1810); 2 sons and 1 daughter:
    1 Alfred (b. 1832)
    2 Edwin (1835-1838)
    1 Emma (b. 1837)

In the 1841 census Anne Watts was listed as being independent, living with her daughter-in-law Elizabeth Watts (b. ±1810), her grandsons Henry (b. 1827) and Alfred (b. 1832), and her granddaughter Emma (b. 1837). John Watts was listed in the baptismal records as a servant, and he may have been in service with Marianne Dolphin at Eyford Park. He died in 1872 at Stow-on-the-Wold.

1838: 9 Jan: *Walked to Eyford, administered the Sacrament to A. Watts, an estimable old parishioner, now become very feeble, and perhaps, approaching her end.* 12 Jan., 15 Jan., 17 Jan: *Walked to Eyford, visited A. Watts, who seems to be rallying: visited several aged and infirm parishioners.* 26 Jun: *Visited an aged parishioner at Eyford, A. Watts, for whom I had prepared a will which she executed.* 20 Oct.

1842: 20 Nov: *Mr. Vavasour performed the evening duty, and preached: he also buried the remains of good old Anne Watts, late of Eyford, and who died at her son's at Lower Slaughter, whither she had latterly removed, on the day after Mrs. Backhouse; I had paid her a ministerial visit on the very day of my Mother in law's decease, and noticed that she was rapidly sinking under a dropsy, which had not long betrayed itself.*

1851: 22 Apr.

1852: 23 Jan., 7-8 May, 11 May, 15 May, 29 May.

WATTS — Sarah Watts of Eyford [60]

Sarah Watts (±1772-1848) was the wife of Robert Watts (1775-1864). They were not native to Eyford and had four married daughters, but little more is known. In the Upper Slaughter parish register, 2 sons and 6 daughters are recorded:

1 Anne (b. & d. 1797)
2 Sarah (b. 1798)
3 Elizabeth (b. 1800)
1 Robert (b. 1805); *see below*
4 Anna (b. 1806)
2 Samuel (b. 1808)
5 Priscilla (b. 1811)
6 Sabina (1813-1893); married, at Stow-on-Wold, 27 December 1833, James Ivins; died at Nuneaton, Warwickshire; at least 1 son:
    1 George (b. 1848); born at Broadway, Worcestershire

It seems likely that Robert (junior) (b. 1805) married a Sarah, and had at least 1 daughter: Hannah (b. 1828). On 4 March 1832 Emily was born to Sarah. In the parish register Francis Witts wrote the following:

> This child is admitted to be illegitimate, the woman's husband, if living, being in Canada where he has been residing nearly two years. The person charged by Sarah Watts as Father of the child, has paid a sum of money to the overseer of Eyford, to indemnify that place against any charges incident on the breeding up of the child.

If Robert (junior) had indeed gone to Canada, it is not known whether he returned.

1847: *Visited—Watts, a poor woman at Eyford, who is in a dangerous state from cancer in the bladder.* 7 Dec., 11 Dec., 24 Dec: *I called on J Davis; and at Eyford on Sarah Watts who still lingers in a very distressed state.*

1848: 11 Jan: *Visited Sarah Watts of Eyford, still lingering in a very suffering state.* 28 Jan., 8 Feb: *Officiated at the funeral of Sarah Watts of Eyford.*

WATTS-RUSSELL — Michael Watts-Russell [61]

Michael Watts-Russell (1816-1875), Roman Catholic lay preacher, was born at Ilam, Staffordshire, the son of Jesse Watts-Russell (1786-1875) and Mary Watts (1792-1840). He was educated at Eton College and Christ Church, Oxford (BA 1838). He took orders and became rector of Benefield in Northamptonshire. He married, at Norton parish church, Faversham, Kent, 29 April 1841, Augusta Baker (1813-1852); they had 3 sons and 3 daughters:

1 Augusta Gertrude Mary (1842-1918)
2 Catherine Ellen (1843-1917)
3 Etheldreda Stephanie (1845-1847)

1 Wilfrid Mary Michael (1846-1879)
2 Michael John Charles (1848-1912)
3 Julian (1850-1867)

The family lived at Biggin Hall, Northamptonshire. F. W. Faber was a neighbour at Elton, and Watts-Russell came to share his advanced Tractarian views. After consulting Newman, he became Faber's spiritual director. In November 1845 Watts-Russell, with his wife and children, joined Faber at Oscott where they were all received into the Catholic Church. On Faber's encouragement, Watts-Russell took a house in Birmingham, but he soon moved with his family to Italy. After his wife's death he became a secular priest. He died at Pershore, Worcestershire.

1847: 10 Aug: *All this part of the building was completed under the incumbency of the late Michl. W. Russel, prior to his Secession from the Church, and betrays the strong leaning which resulted in his renouncing the faith of his fathers.... Biggin Hall, the seat of Mr. Watts Russel, a wealthy proprietor in this County and in Derbyshire, is on high ground, surrounded by old timber and modern plantations to the right about two miles from O: ... Here we were introduced to the Incumbent & his lady Mr. & Mrs. Day, pleasing persons. Mr. Day was tutor to some part of Mr. Watts Russel's family, and is a Cambridge man. Mr. W.R. presented him to the living, when it was vacated, about a year and half ago, by the secession to Rome, of his son, Mr. Michl. W.R., who with his wife went over to the popish Church, about the same time that Mr. Faber, Incumbent of Elton, Huntingdonshire, professed himself a Roman Catholic.* 17 Aug.

WAY — Henry Hugh Way — *see also* the Smyth family of Ashton Court *and* the Upton family [62]

Henry Hugh Way (1807-1890), Church of England clergyman, was the second son of Benjamin Way of Clifton and Denham Place, Buckinghamshire. He was educated at Merton College, Oxford (BA 1829), and was vicar of Henbury from 1830 to 1860.

1826: 15 Sep: *And this seems the proper place for inserting a list of some of the leading families & individuals, whose presence on this occasion served so many good purposes; benefiting the charity ... Revd. Mr. & Mrs. Way.*

1833: 18 Apr: *The late Archdeacon Trevelyan, brother to Sir John Trevelyan, a much esteemed Clergyman, was incumbent of Henbury; his successor, the Revd. Mr. Way is a young man, a connection of Sir John Smith, of Ashton Court, in Somersetshire.*

WAY — William Way [63]

William Way (1773-1845), Church of England clergyman, was the son of Benjamin Way (1740-1808), of Denham Place, Buckinghamshire, and Elizabeth Ann Cooke (1746-1825). He was also uncle of Henry (*above*). He was educated at Christ Church, Oxford (BA 1795; MA 1798), and lived at Glympton Park, Oxfordshire. He was rector of Denham and vicar of Hedgerly, Buckinghamshire, from 1798 to his death in 1845. He married, 2 February 1816, Elizabeth Wheate, née Western (1765-1846), daughter of Maximilian Western (1739-1801) and Elizabeth Ffolkes (1748-1804), and widow of Francis Sackville Lloyd Wheate (d. 1812), whom she had married at St Marylebone, Westminster, on 1 June 1799.

The manor of Glympton descended through the Wheate family until the early nineteenth century. It was owned successively by William Wheate (d. 1659), his son Thomas (d. 1668), his grandson son Sir Thomas (d. 1721) (created baronet in 1696), and his great-grandson Sir Thomas (d. 1746). The latter Sir Thomas Wheate had no sons, and on the death of his widow Mary in 1765, the manor was bought, presumably from his nephew Sir Jacob Wheate, for his daughters Sarah (d. 1805), Anne (d. 1807), and Mary Lloyd (d. 1803), who held it jointly. They were succeeded by Mary's son Francis Sackville Lloyd (1762-1812), who assumed the additional surname Wheate. After his death, Francis's widow Elizabeth, née Western (1765-1846), and her second husband William Way held Glympton until Elizabeth's death in 1846.

1835: 25 Feb: *With Mrs. Witts & my Son dined at Adlestrop at Mr. Perrots; a very agreeable party. We met the Revd. Mr. & Mrs. Way of Glympton Park, Oxon, Captain Leigh, and Mr. & Mrs. Whitmore Jones. Mrs. Way was widow of Mr. Lloyd, nephew and heir of Misses Wheate, singular old maiden ladies, proprietors of the Glympton Estate.*

WEALE — Robert Weale [64]

Robert Weale (1799-1883), assistant commissioner of the new poor laws, was born at Godalming, Surrey, the son of James Weale (1763-1836) and Barbara Bull (1766-1822). Weale married, at Eastbourne, Sussex, 2 December 1823, Kate (1802-1864), daughter of John Morey (b. 1776) and Catherine Turner (b. 1776); they had 3 sons and 2 daughters:

1 Robert Morey (1825-1910)
1 Marian Bayley (b. 1828)
2 Charles James (b. 1830)
2 Barbara Rose (1833-1931)
3 George Henry Harding (1836-1876)

1839: 5 Jan: *Remained for two hours at Cheltenham to allow the horse time to rest and bait; during which I shopped, and conversed a good deal with Mr. Weale, Asst. P.L.C. whom I met in the Plough Coffee room, and who was in his way from Stroud to Worcester, having yesterday been the guest of the Guardians of the Stroud Union, by whom he had been entertained at dinner, as a compliment on his leaving the district hitherto under his charge, comprehending the greater part of Gloucestershire, Worcestershire & Somersetshire.* 9 Jan.

WEARE — Thomas William Weare [65]

Thomas William Weare (1814-1871), Church of England clergyman and schoolmaster, was born in the parish of All Saints', Hereford, the eldest son of Lt-Col Thomas Weare. He was educated at Westminster School and Christ Church, Oxford (BA 1836; MA 1838), and remained a member of the college until 1853 when he married. In March 1838 Weare joined the Oxford lodge of the freemasons. He was vicar of Chipping Norton for a short time, and then of Cowley, Oxford. By 1841 he had taken up the post of second master at Westminster School, a position he held for twenty years. By 1867 he had been appointed rector of Isfield, Sussex.

Weare married, at Hertingfordbury, Hertfordshire, 23 August 1853, Louisa Emma Mary (1818-1865), daughter of Henry Fynes-Clinton (1781-1852) and Katharine Octavia Majendie (1797-1871); they had 1 son and 3 daughters:

1 Henrietta Anna Louisa (1856-1916)
2 Esther Katherine Clinton (1858-1927)
1 Edwin Thomas Clinton (1859-1921)
3 Lucy Isabella (1860-1948)

1836: 29 Aug: *Mr. Weare the Clergyman of Chipping Norton, and Barker, the Curate of Churchill, both pleasant and worthy young men, came to dinner.* 27 Oct.

1837: 4 Sep: *Mr. Weare, the Vicar of Chipping Norton is Chaplain with a salary of £30 per ann.* 6 Oct.

WEBB — Mr Webb, land surveyor, of Worcester

Francis Witts may have been referring to either Messrs Webb and Buck, land surveyors, of Worcester, or to Mr F. P. Webb, land surveyor, of Evesham. It was probably the former.

1848: 14 Nov: *Wrote to Mr. Bloxsome for information, whether a land Surveyor of Worcester, by name Webb, had ever been employed so as to be recognised by the County rate Committee. Lord Redesdale is desirous ...*

WEBB — Edward Webb and his sister Frances Webb[66]

Edward Webb (1779-1839), MP and landed proprietor, was the second son of John Webb (±1730-1795) and Arabella Bushell of Sevinbroke, Oxfordshire. He was educated at Elmore School and by William Shaw at Fortyhill, Enfield, until 1794. Edward's elder brother John went to Bengal as a writer in the East India Company's service in 1790, and returned home on the death of his father in 1795. Edward was left £4,000 in his father's will to be invested at 4 per cent until he came of age, plus a sum of £1,000 to be paid to him on the death of his mother. Both bequests were additional to his entitlement under his parents' marriage settlement. Soon after his father's death, Edward obtained the East India Company writership for which he had applied in 1794; he arrived in India in September 1795. His brother John Webb died on 21 March 1797 of an illness contracted in the East, having bequeathed Edward £2,000 to be invested in stocks until he attained his majority. Under the provisions of their father's will, any surplus from the proceeds of the sale of property in Gloucestershire and London beyond what had been allocated to provide for their mother was also to be made over to Edward in his own right.

Edward was still in Bengal when his mother made her will on 24 February 1801, directing that her property at Dauntley should be sold to provide £5,000 for her daughter Frances, with any balance going to Edward. She died on 11 June 1801 and Edward came home to settle in Gloucestershire, where he became active in the militia. By 1811 he had acquired Gloucestershire estates at Stoke Bishop and Norton Court, plus land in Monmouthshire containing lead mines, and leasehold property in Worcestershire and Berkshire. He married, 1807, Jane Mary Catherine (1781-1814), daughter of Sir John Guise, 1st baronet of Highnam Court, Gloucestershire, and Elizabeth Wright; they had 1 daughter:

1 Elizabeth Frances (b. 1809)

Edward Webb was created DCL at Oxford in 1823. He was president of the Anchor Society in 1818, and MP for Gloucester in 1816-32; he was defeated in May 1838. He was one of the Gloucester common council in 1819, and made captain of the Royal North Gloucester Militia on 22 March 1803, and lieutenant-colonel of the 1st Eastern Battalion of the Gloucestershire Militia on 14 April 1809. His sister Frances Webb (d. 1846), of Stoke Bishop, was a friend of Elizabeth Newell, who had married James Jones of Stadhampton. Elizabeth outlived her husband, and on her death in 1818, she bequeathed all her property to her friend Frances. Elizabeth had left instructions in her will (dated 1806) that Miss Webb should leave the whole property to one person who should take the name of Newell. Frances Webb accordingly left Adwell and Radnage to a relation, John W. Birch, clerk assistant to the House of Lords, and he took the name Newell Birch. It was at this home, Adwell House, Tetsworth, near Thame, Oxfordshire, that Edward retired to live with his sister.

On his return from India in 1801 or 1802, Edward had lived at the family property, Sneyd Park in Stoke Bishop, near Bristol; as Francis Witts had known him as a schoolfellow at Elmore, it was only natural that he should have re-kindled his friendship when he and his family were at Clifton. Edward had three sisters, one of whom is referred to in the diary; this must have been Frances, for whom provision had been made in her mother's will.

In 1839 Edward Webb took a voyage to the United States with his daughter Elizabeth Frances. He was greatly weakened by sea sickness on his voyage to America, and was taken ill at Niagara Falls. He died at New York on 18 September 1839 and was buried at Elmore.

1805: 1 Jan., 21 Jan: *Dined with the Dowells & slept at Cote, my Father accompanied me part of the way thither. Llewellyn, Slade Baker, Edw. Webb & his sister, & F. Daubeny dined with us.* 19 Nov: *In the evening to the Clifton Ball ... Conversed with Webb, Daubeny, Mr. Dowell etc.*

1806: 14 Jan: *Danced also with the pleasing Miss Roberts; conversed much with Capt. Webb.* 17 Jan., 21 Jan: *Mounted a hackney between four & five to repair to Capt. Webb's at Stoke, where a large & pleasant party were assembled, & most hospitably & handsomely entertained.* 3 Feb., 3 Mar.

1808: 29 Mar: *At Cote. Found my friend, very ill; Mr. & Mrs. Dowell, Mr. Hetling, Miss Webb & Mr. Jos. Hutchinson made the Evening's party, played Whist in the Evening.*

1824: 31 Mar: *On the rumour reaching the King's head, that a Gentleman unknown, who had dined with the Sheriff, was lying a corpse at the Infirmary, Col. Webb, the Member for Gloucester, Genl. Guise & myself hastened thither to recognize the person, & arrange how best to communicate the calamity to the sufferer's family.*

1825: 18 Oct: *The Michaelmas Quarter Sessions commenced.*

1826: 30 Mar., 16 Jun., 11 Jul., 6 Aug., 31 Aug: *... distant view of Elmore court, the place, where I first went to school ...some of my old schoolfellows are among my intimate acquaintance in the County, & sitting on the same bench with me as Magistrates, Genl. Guise, Mr. Edwd. Jones, Col. Webb, M.P. for Gloucester ...* 15 Sep.

1829: 1-2 Apr., 14 Jul., 16 Jul., 22 Sep.

1830: 21 Jun: *A little way before the ascent of the hill began, we passed, on the right, a modern Elizabethan Porter's lodge, this is the way to Adwell, the residence of my old Schoolfellow and acquaintance Mr. Webb, the M.P. for Gloucester. I believe the property really to belong to his maiden sister, to whom it was left by a relative; Webb is a widower with one daughter; his wife, who died many years since, was sister of Sir B. W. Guise. Miss Webb and her brother live together.*

1832: 29 Mar.

1833: 18 Apr: *... to our right were Sneyd Park ... formerly the property of my old school-fellow & acquaintance, Edward Webb Esqr., for many years representative of the City of Gloucester, whose hospitality in by-gone years I had here enjoyed.*

1838: 3 Jul: *The Whig Radicals then put forward the old, but for some years retired representative of their political opinions Col. Webb, and the result was the reelection of Hope by a large majority.*

WEBB — John Webb[67]

John Webb (1776-1869), Church of England clergyman, was the son of William Webb of Aldgate, London. He was educated at St Paul's School and Wadham College, Oxford (BA 1798; MA 1802). As well as being a minor canon of Gloucester, he was appointed rector of Tretire with Michaelwood, Herefordshire, in 1812, and vicar of St Mary, Cardiff, in 1821. Webb married, 1820, Sarah Ann Reynolds (1776-1849); they had 1 son and 1 daughter:

1 Thomas William (1807-1885), Church of England clergyman
1 Frances (b. 1847)

1823: 17 Sep: *The service was read by Mr. Webb, one of the Minor Canons.*

1826: 13 Sep: *Mr. Webb, a Minor Canon, read the lessons with the Voice of a Stentor.*

1827: 1 Apr: *Mr. Webb, the Minor Canon, assisted at the Sacrament.*

WEBB — Richard Webb and Richard Holden Webb, visitors of the Snow family[68]

Richard Webb (±1740-1818), landed proprietor, is rather a mystery. In his son Richard Holden Webb's entry in *Oxford Alumni* he was referred to as 'Richard Webb of Anscomb, Berkshire', but there is no such place. He did, however, inherit an estate through his wife at Bray, Berkshire. He obviously had a London home as well as this estate. In his will, proved 23 December 1818, he referred to himself as Richard Webb of Ham Common, Surrey, and mentioned estates at Kingswood, near Wotton-under-Edge, Gloucestershire, and Bray, Berkshire.

Richard Webb married Elizabeth (b. 1743), born at Tooks Court in the parish of St Andrew, Holborn, London, the daughter of Robert Holden and Elizabeth Winch; they had at least 1 son and 1 daughter:

1 Elizabeth Mary (b. 1770); married, 1822, Capt. Booth of the 15th Hussars
1 Richard Holden (1776-1851), army officer and landed proprietor; educated at Eton College and Christ Church, Oxford; married, at Essendon, Hertfordshire, 2 October 1797, Frances (1772-1848), daughter of Capt. Robert Orme (1732-1790) and Audrey Townsend (1732-1781); 5 sons and 2 daughters:
  1 Audrey Georginia Ann (1799-1858); married, at St Marylebone, Westminster, 1831, Hugh Hill
  2 Jane Charlotte (1801-1893); married, first, H. P. Hadow; secondly, J. Walker
  1 Richard Townshend (b. 1802); married, at Bombay, India, 26 October 1824, Caroline Payne
  2 William Morse (1803-1842); married Janet Gray
  3 John Sterry (1804-1827)
  4 Robert Holden (1806-1880), Church of England clergyman; married, at Westbury-on-Trym, Gloucestershire, 21 September 1841, Anne Ford
  5 Stephen Francis (1814-1892); married Mary Ann Jones

We know from the diaries of Agnes Witts that the above family is the correct attribution. On 7 September 1806 she wrote the following:

> A most beautiful bright day & as fine an evening, at one o'clock went in the Punt on the water, as far as Hampton Court bridge, very pleasant going, but so tedious returning against the stream that Mrs. Snow & myself were both sick spent the evening at Mr. Webbs, Mrs. Holden Webb there.

1801: 1 Jun., 4 Jun: *In the Evening we repaired to Miss Snows, where we met Col. & Mrs. Clitherow, Mr. & Mrs. Webb, a very handsome woman. Miss Webb, Miss Turner, Mr. & Mrs. Walker, &c.* 2 Jul., 5 Jul.

1808: 26 Feb: *Sat an hour with the Mrs. Snow's ... met there Mr. & Miss Webb, & Mrs. Clitherow.*

WEBB — Richard Webb[69]

Richard Webb (b. 1811), schoolmaster, was born at Hatherop. He married, at Stow-on-the-Wold, Elizabeth (b. ±1819). They lived in Coxwell Street, Cirencester, and had five children. By the time of the 1881 census Richard and Elizabeth were retired and living in Ramsgate, Kent, with two unmarried daughters.

1847: 26 Apr: *A letter from one Webb of Cirencester, formerly a School master at Stow, asking testimonials and advice from me with a view to his offering himself as a candidate for the vacant post of Clerk & deputy Governor, Gloucester Gaol.* 27 Apr: *Wrote to Mr. R Webb, Cirencester, declining to give a testimonial to him on the ground that I had never much opportunity to judge of his competency to discharge difficult official duties ...*

WEBB — William Webb[70]

William Webb (±1744-1806), Church of England clergyman, was the son of James Webb of Eccleshall. He was educated at Trinity College, Oxford (BA 1768), and served as vicar of Ashbourne and rector of Mapleton.

1802: 12 Sep: *To Ellaston Church where a Mr. Webb performed.* 15 Sep: *Mr. Webbe dined with us.* 19 Sep: *At Ellaston Church in the morning. Mr. Webb officiated in reading ...* 26 Sep., 28 Sep.

WEBER — Miss Weber[71]

Miss Weber was presumably one of the surviving two daughters of theatre producer/presenter Franz Anton von Weber (1734-1812), uncle of Constanze, Wolfgang Amadeus Mozart's wife. It seems that out of eight children born, two boys and two girls survived. Von Weber worked in Weimar in collaboration with Goethe. He married secondly, 1785, Genevieve Burner (1764-1798); the composer Carl Maria von Weber (1786-1826) was their son.

1799: 25 Dec: *Mademoiselle de Löwenstein presented a Mademoiselle Weber played very well on the Harp: but the Room was too large and the Harp but a bad Instrument.*

WEBSTER — George Mountjoy Webster[72]

George Mountjoy Webster (1774-1861), Church of England clergyman, was the son of William Theophilus Mountjoy Webster of Reading. He was educated at St John's College, Oxford (BA 1798; MA 1802; BD 1808; DD 1845), where he was a fellow until 1817. He was rector of Codford St Mary, Wiltshire, from 1816 to his death in 1861.

1808: 12 Apr: *Mr. Webster the Curate of Bromham there.*

WEDDERBURN — John Wedderburn of Ballindean[73]

Sir John Wedderburn, 6th baronet of Ballindean (1729-1803), landed proprietor, was born into a family of impoverished Perthshire gentry. At 17 years old he fought alongside his father in Ogilvy's regiment at Culloden. He escaped capture and, after a short period in France, sailed to Jamaica where he lived for many years and eventually became the island's largest landowner. His father was not so lucky; he was executed by hanging on Kennington Common on 28 November 1746.

The baronetcy was forfeited, but despite the attainder, Wedderburn assumed its legitimacy and became *de facto* 4th baronet in 1746. In 1769 he returned to Scotland with a slave, one Joseph Knight, who, inspired by Somerset's case in England in which the English courts had held that slavery did not exist under English law, brought suit against Wedderburn for his freedom. Knight won his claim, establishing the principle that Scots law would not uphold the institution of slavery.

Wedderburn married, first, 1769, Margaret (d. 1775), daughter of David Ogilvy, who, but for attainder, would have been earl of Ainslie. They had 1 son and 2 daughters:

1 Margaret (1772-1807)
2 Jean (1773-1861)
1 David (1775-1858); succeeded as 7th baronet of Ballindean; created a baronet of the United Kingdom on 10 August 1803, with a remainder to the heirs male of his great-grandfather, the 4th baronet; from this date, the assumption of the attainted baronetcy ceased

Wedderburn married secondly, 1780, Alicia, second daughter of James Dundas of Dundas; they had 2 daughters:

1 Anne (d. 1867)
2 Louisa Dorothea (d. 1836)

Wedderburn ended his days as a wealthy country gentleman, having restored his family fortune and recovered the title baronet of Blackness and Ballindean.

1801: 9 Apr: ... *called at Mr. Fletcher's, Mr. Brown's, & Sir J. Wedderburn we met & recognized.* 28 Apr: ... *supped with the Browns, where we met Mr. Wedderburn & Miss M. Graham.*

WEDGWOOD — John Wedgwood[74]

John Wedgwood (1766-1844), potter, landed proprietor, and founder of the Royal Horticultural Society, was born at Burslem, Staffordshire, the eldest son of Josiah Wedgwood (1730-1795) and his wife, Sarah (1734-1815). He was a partner in the Wedgwood pottery firm in 1790-93 and again in 1800-12. He was educated at Warrington Academy and Edinburgh University, and had an interest in botany and horticulture, particularly in the cultivation of tropical fruit and other exotic plants. Wedgwood founded the Royal Horticultural Society after suggesting the idea to William Forsyth, head gardener to King George III, in a letter dated 29 June 1801. He chaired the first meeting of the society on 7 March 1804. He lived in Abergavenny, Wales, Cote, near Bristol, and at Kingscote, Gloucestershire.

Wedgwood married, 1794, Louisa Jane (1771-1836), daughter of John Bartlett Allen (1729-1803) and Elizabeth Hensleigh (1738-1790); they had 4 sons and 3 daughters:

1 Sarah Elizabeth (1795-1857); died unmarried
1 John Allen (1797-1882), Church of England clergyman
2 Thomas Josiah (1797-1860), Col; married, 1836, Anne Maria Tyler (1790-1855)
2 Caroline Louisa Jane Wedgwood (1799-1825)
3 Charles (1800-1823); died unmarried at Birhampoor, India
3 Jessie (1804-1872); married, 26 October 1830, a cousin, Henry Allan Wedgwood (1799-1885); 3 sons and 3 daughters
4 Robert (1806-1881), Church of England clergyman; *see below*

1805: 22 Jan: *After breakfasting with my agreeable friends at Cote, & admiring two beautiful water colour Views of Rome in Mr. Wedgewood's House, I left the Dowells, William walking with me part of the way to Bristol.*

WEDGWOOD — Robert Wedgwood[75]

Robert Wedgwood (1806-1881), Church of England clergyman, was the son of John Wedgwood (*above*) and Louisa Jane Bartlett Allen of Cresselly, Pembrokeshire. He was the grandson of Josiah Wedgwood, founder of the family's pottery business. He was educated at Charterhouse and Emmanuel and Trinity College, Cambridge (BA 1828; MA 1831). He was curate of Preston Candover with Nutley, Hampshire, in 1841-45, and of Woking, Surrey, in 1847-50. He was then rector of Dumbleton, Gloucestershire, from 1850 to his death in 1881.

Wedgwood married, at Guildford, Surrey, September 1847, Mary Halsey (b. 1827); they had 5 daughters:

1 Elleanor Mary (b. 1851)
2 Henrietta (b. 1853)
3 Edith Louisa (b. 1854)
4 Anne Sophia (b. 1856)
5 Eliza Millicent (b. 1860)

1850: 16 Sep: *The following Clergymen were present ... Mr. Wedgewood, from Dumbleton ...* 8 Nov: *At half past two left by train for Cheltenham with Vavasour, Riddle, E.F.W, Mr. Wedgwood, Mr. Boyd &c.*

1852: 7 Apr: *Mr. Wedgwood, the Rector of Dumbleton, called on me.*

WEICHSEL — Charles Weichsel — ***see also*** **Billington**[76]

Charles Weichsel (1767-1850), violinist, was born at Soho, Westminster, the son of Carl Friedrich Weichsel (1728-1811) and Fredericka Weirman (d. 1786). His father, a native of Freiburg, Saxony, was principal oboist at the King's Theatre and Vauxhall Gardens. Charles studied the violin with Wilhelm Cramer and made his début in 1774 with his sister Elizabeth. He played standing on a stool and was sketched by the artist Rowlandson. He led the King's Theatre band and Philharmonic Society during the early nineteenth century. His sister, Elizabeth Billington, née Weichsel (1765-1818), was one of the most famous singers of her day.

Weichsel married, first, at St Martin-in-the-Fields, Westminster, 18 August 1804, opera soprano Stefana Rovedino (d. 1806). He married secondly, at St Luke's, Middlesex, 27 November 1838, Jane Sumner, a widow.

1801: 13 Oct: ... *her (Mrs Billington's) Brother led the band with a masterly violin.*

WEIGALL — Henry Weigall[77]

Henry Weigall (1829-1925), artist, was the son of Henry Weigall (1798-1882), sculptor, and Selina Smith (±1801-1883). He was part of a very talented family. His father was a sculptor, gem engraver, die-sinker, and modeller. Henry, sometimes called 'Henry Weigall Jr', exhibited at the Royal Academy from 1846 to 1914. He worked as a miniature painter during the early part of his career, before turning to portrait painting in oils and subject painting. He painted numerous portraits of well-known people, including Prime Minister Benjamin Disraeli, and created sculptures. His miniature of the duke of Wellington is in the Royal Collection.

Weigall married, at Westminster Abbey, 15 August 1866, Rose Sophia Mary (1834-1921), daughter of Priscilla Fane, countess of Westmorland, the duke of Wellington's favourite niece. Henry and Rose had 6 sons and 1 daughter:

1 Fitzroy Henry Francis (1867-1961)
2 Julian William Wellesley (1869-1945)
3 Gerald John Villiers (1870-1944)
4 Louis Arthur Frederick (1874-1957)
5 William Ernest George Archibald (1874-1952)
6 Evelyn Henry Villiers (1876-1946)
1 Caroline Rachel Selina Priscilla (1879-1967)

1853: 7 Jun: *Called on a young miniature painter H. Weigall, visited his studio: some beautiful paintings in progress; a finished miniature portrait of the Duke of Wellington, portraits in oil &c. a rising young artist, and talented man.*

WEIPPERT — John Erhardt Weippert [78]

John Erhardt Weippert (1766-1823), instrumentalist and composer, was from Schweinfurt in Franconia. He was father, grandfather, and uncle to numerous English musicians; the family was numerous and it is not precisely clear which members made up what became known as John Weippert's Band. He married, first, at St George's, Hanover Square, Westminster, 28 December 1791, Mary Spence (1770-1810); they had 1 son and 1 daughter:

1 Julia Caroline (1792-1812); married the actor William Lovegrove
1 John Thomas Lewis (1798-1843); married, 1821, Isabella Stevenson (1799-1831); 1 son and 1 daughter:
 1 John Charles (1822-1867)
 1 Sybell Julia (1824-1908)

He married secondly, at St Pancras, Middlesex, 29 April 1812, Lydia Wigforth (1790-1868); they had 1 son and 1 daughter:

1 Julia Ann (1812-1902)
1 Erhard William (1815-1885)

1829: 22 Sep: *There was sufficient space to perform the necessary evolutions with spirit and ease this evening; & the Stewards had engaged a celebrated & fashionable band (Weippert's) from Town for the occasion.*

WEIR — Henry Weir, Royal Navy officer on HMS *Kite* [79]

Sir Henry Weir (±1775-1841), naval officer, was promoted to lieutenant in 1794. He successively commanded the *Phoenix*, a hired lugger, the brigs *Monkey* and *Ferreter*, and the cutter *Alban*. On 31 March 1807 the *Ferreter* was captured in the River Ems by seven Dutch gun-boats after a severe night action in which many of Weir's crew were killed. Weir was next appointed to the *Alban* the following November, and continued in her until promoted to command the *Calypso*, an 18-gun brig, on 28 June 1810. On 14 June 1811 he captured a Danish privateer of 10 guns, and destroyed another of the same description on the coast of Jutland. On 6 July 1812, in conjunction with Capt. T. P. Stewart of the *Dictator*, Weir attacked a Danish force in the Sleeve, consisting of the frigate *Nayaden*, the 20-gun *Laaland*, and the 18-gun *Samsoe* and *Kiel*. The Danish vessels were defeated and partly captured, but at length left for wrecks due to navigational difficulties. For this gallant action Weir was advanced to post rank on 22 July 1812. On 12 January 1814 he was appointed to the 20-gun *Thais*, and served in her for some time on the East India station.

Sir Henry Weir was married to Phillis Wickerman and died at Loches, France. He and Phillis had 2 daughters:

1 Clarissa Ann Percival (1800-1880)
2 Helen (1801-1859)

This attribution is highly probable, but cannot be confirmed. There was no officer of the name of 'Wear' in the Royal Navy in 1801, when Francis Witts mentioned the name in his diary. As a point of interest, HMS *Kite* returned to the fleet off Denmark, and Adm. Horatio Nelson transferred his flag to the ship from 19 June to 1 July 1801.

1801: 2 Apr: *At dinner we met a large party. All our Ship's Crew, two of the Officers, Mr. Dewar, & Mr. Wear, & Mr. Fletcher the Advocate ...*

WEIR — Elizabeth Weir [80]

Elizabeth Weir (b. 1831) was probably the daughter of Robert Webb (±1795-1851), a forester at Stanway, and Jane Blair (b. ±1795), a schoolmistress at Stanway. Robert and Jane had married in 1817. Francis Witts rendered Elizabeth's name as Weare, but she was probably of very little interest to him and presumably left his service under less than satisfactory terms.

1854: 3 Jun: *From Mrs. Humpheys, Cheltenham, asking for the character of Elizabeth Weare, a former kitchen maid.—Replied that, as she had left my service before Michs. last, and lived in two families since, I declined giving any character.*

WELDEREN — Jan Walraaf Van Welderen, Count Welderen [Walderen/Wilderen] [81]

Count Jan Walraaf Van Welderen (1725-1807), diplomat, married, 1759, Anne (1721-1796), daughter of William and Anne Whitwell of Oundle, Northamptonshire. She was the sister of John Griffin Griffin, 4th Baron Howard de Walden (1719-1797), born John Whitwell. Van Welderen and Anne had at least 1 daughter:

1 Louis Anne Graaf Van Welderen (b. 1760)

Van Welderen arrived in England in 1762 as an ambassador of the states general of the Netherlands (Wilderen is now part of modern-day Belgium). He may have been appointed as he spoke English and had English connections. He was in England until 1780, when he was forced to return to the Netherlands prior to the onset of the fourth Anglo-Dutch War of 1781-84. During the war he appears to have served as a captain on the Dutch vessel *Ajax*. Lady Howard would have been his sister-in-law; Catherine Griffin, née Clayton (±1747-1807), was the second wife of John Griffin Griffin, 4th Baron Howard de Walden (1719-1797).

1801: 19 Jul: ... *called upon Lady Howard, to whom I was introduced, as also to Count Wilderen, formerly the Dutch Minister.*

WELLES — Francis Welles — *see also* Gwinnett *and* Newmarch [82]

Francis Welles (1755-1816), attorney, was born at Prestbury, the son of Thomas and Susanna Welles. His grandfather Francis Welles (1699-1756) was the vicar of Prestbury, as was his elder brother Thomas in 1795. Thomas was also appointed rector of Badgworth with Shurdington in 1806. Francis (junior) studied the law and became an attorney in Cheltenham. In 1808 the first stone of a new market house in Cheltenham, paid for by the lord of the manor of Cheltenham, was laid by 'Francis Welles and Theodore Gwinnett, his Stewards'. In 1811 the partnership between Theodore Gwinnett, Charles Newmarch, and Francis Welles, attorneys and solicitors, of Cheltenham, was dissolved. In the meantime, in 1806, under the Enclosure Act of that year, Francis Welles was awarded the largest portion of land at Pittville. He built Marle Hill House between 1806 and 1810. He died at Cheltenham and was buried at Prestbury on 2 February 1816.

Surprisingly little is known of Welles's family life. He had more than one daughter. His youngest daughter, Martha, married, at Southampton, 1825, Revd George Parry Hollis (b. ±1797).

1823: 24 Dec: *The Attorneys, Welles, Gwynnett & Newmarch, who succeeded to the office in Cheltenham of Mrs. Tracy's Steward, Mr. Markham, took up and prosecuted at their own expence and hazard the cause of these sisters, and after much research, many difficulties, and great anxiety, established their claim in such a manner, as to leave little doubt of their ultimate success. At this juncture, in 1805, it occurred to my Father and Mother to make themselves known to the three sisters, and to solicit their patronage for me on the decease of my uncle Ferdinand Travell, the Rector of Upper Slaughter ...*

WELLESLEY — Arthur Wellesley [83]

Arthur Wellesley, 1st duke of Wellington (1769-1852), army officer, politician, and prime minister, was the third of the five surviving sons to Garret Wesley, Viscount Wellesley and 1st earl of Mornington (1735-1781), and Anne, eldest daughter of the 1st Viscount Dungannon. Wellesley was commissioned as an ensign in the Army in 1787 and served in Ireland as aide-de-camp to two successive lords lieutenant of Ireland. A colonel by 1796, Wellesley saw action in the Netherlands and India, where he fought in the Fourth Anglo-Mysore War at the battle of Seringapatam. He was appointed governor of Seringapatam and Mysore in 1799, and as a newly appointed major-general, he won a decisive victory over the Maratha Confederacy at the battle of Assaye in 1803. Wellesley rose to prominence as a general during the Peninsular campaign of the Napoleonic Wars, and was promoted to the rank of field marshal after leading the allied forces to victory against the French at the battle of Vitoria in 1813. Following Napoleon's exile in 1814, Wellesley served as ambassador to France and was granted a dukedom. During the Hundred Days in 1815, he commanded the allied army which, together with a Prussian army under Blücher, defeated Napoleon at Waterloo. Wellesley's battle record is exemplary; he ultimately participated in some sixty battles during the course of his military career.

Wellesley devoted himself to politics after retiring from an active military career. He was twice British prime minister as part of the Tory party: from 1828 to 1830, and for a little less than a month in 1834. He oversaw the passage of the Catholic Relief Act in 1829, but opposed the Reform Act in 1832. Wellesley continued as one of the leading figures in the House of Lords until his retirement, and remained commander-in-chief of the Army until his death.

1824: 20 Apr: *The Duke of Wellington is now here* [Cheltenham] *for the benefit of his health. I saw him to-day for the first time. He was walking with my acquaintance, Lord Apsley, eldest son of the Earl of Bathurst. The great Captain of the age is much attached to this agreeably young nobleman. The Duke's countenance is very striking, but carries with it the appearance of a great wear and tear of constitution.*

1826: 18 Jan.

1827: 26 Jan: *The Duke of Wellington succeeds the Duke of York, as Commander in chief of the Forces. His Grace retains his seat in the Cabinet and the Master Generalship of the Ordnance, but does not take the Income of the latter office any longer.* 14 Apr., 4 May, 15 Jun., 28 Aug.

1828: 11 Jan., 23 Jan., 1 Feb., 2 May, 28 May: *A few days will unravel what is at present obscure, and with all sound Tories & Anticatholics, I am bound to wish success to the Duke of Wellington & Mr. Peel.* 2 Jun., 13 Jun., 17 Jun., 17 Jun., 23 Aug.

1829: 7 Feb., 7 Mar., 25 Mar., 8 Apr., 26 Jun.

1830: 31 Jan., 6 Feb., 19 Apr., 22 Jun.

1832: 10 Apr., 9-10 May, 17 May, 6 Jun.

1833: 8 Feb., 29 Feb., 11 Mar.

1834: 18 Nov., 2 Dec., 12 Dec.

1835: 12 Jun.

1839: 6 May, 10 May.

1842: 15 Mar., 12 Apr.

1843: 3 Jan.

1844: 31 May, 4 Jun., 8 Oct.

1845: 16 Jun: *Began reading a compilation entitled Maxims and opinions of the Duke of Wellington, with a prefatory memoir of his life.* 18-19 Jun., 23-24 Jun., 28 Jun.

1852: 18 Nov: *The improvement in the weather to-day very opportune, this being the appointed day for the public obsequies of the great Duke of Wellington in St. Paul's cathedral where his remains will rest beside those of our great naval hero, Nelson, at the national cost.*

WELLFORD — George Wellford — *see also* Rogers [84]

George Wellford (1785-1861), Church of England clergyman, was the son of John Wellford of Tower Dock, London. He was educated at Exeter College, Oxford (BA 1813; MA 1815), and ordained deacon on 1 May 1814. His first clerical appointment was as curate of Bourton-on-the-Hill, Gloucestershire, from 10 February 1815. He was appointed stipendiary curate of Bray, Berkshire, on 20 April 1818, and chaplain of Jesus Hospital in Bray.

The Wellford, Rogers, and Thornton families were connected by marriage. John Rogers (1768-1840), of Upper Footing, Surrey, married, 1798, Elizabeth Wellford, presumably George Wellford's sister. Their son, John (1807-1867), a JP and fellow of the Royal Society, of River Hill, married, 1833, Harriet Thornton. The diary extract of 10 September 1824 provides much of the background, while Agnes Witts's diary entries for 1814 show that George Wellford acted as curate for Francis Witts in September 1814. Wellford does not appear to have married.

1805: 15 Jul: *Tea & a Party at my Aunts dull & tiresome. The Berringtons, Louisa Jones, Mr. Welford & Mr. Jeffries, Fowlkes &c.* 19 Jul.

1824: 10 Sep: *Our old friend Mr. Wellford came on a visit to us. I must retrace a little his history. He is son of some very old and intimate friends of my Uncle Broome Witts, & as such was introduced to my by him in 1814, when Mr. Wellford, at a more advanced age than is usual, was about to enter into the Church His views had in earlier life been directed to trade, which he had quitted from a desire to enter into the Church, although his family were dissenters. He had consequently gone to Exeter College. I was able to forward his wishes, & oblige my Uncle, by giving him a title for orders on this living, and he resided here in the Rectory house, as Curate, during a visit of three months, which we made in Yorkshire. His next Curacy was Moreton in Marsh, Dr. Warneford having engaged him, as soon as he left us: and a most painstaking and conscientious Paster he proved himself ... Shortly after Mr. Wellford became Curate of Bray, near Maidenhead, where his sentiments & opinions were all congenial.* 13 Sep: *Mr. Wellford left us to pass a day in & near Moreton in Marsh, that he might visit his old parishioners & neighbours.* 14 Sep., 18 Sep: *Our friend Mr. Wellford left us for Bray.*

1825: 29 Jun: *Our friend Mr. George Wellford, Curate of Bray, rode over in the evening to tea, and to welcome us to Berks.* 1 Jul: *Mr. Wellford is chaplain to some Almshouses, not far from the church, from which he derives an emolument of £20 per ann. besides very comfortable apartments in the gateway leading to the antique brick quadrangle ...* 4 Jul: *The Vicarage of Bray is in the gift of this very respectable prelate, who on the decease of a late worthy vicar, the Revd. Mr. Townsend, gave the living to the Revd. Mr. Levett, Incumbent of Carlton near Skipton, Yorkshire, & late Tutor of Christ Church, to hold till his nephew should be in priest's orders. Mr. Townsend, who died, when we were at Cookham Grove three years since, was of the Evangelical party in the church, and much attached to his Curate, George Wellford ... although Mr.*

Legge & Mr. Wellford have not been brought up in exactly the same school of divinity, yet such has been the right feeling, such the good sense, and just appreciation of merit as belonging to each, that on the approaching institution of Mr. L. to the vicarage, the connexion, as between Vicar and Curate, is not to cease. 6 Jul: *Mr. Wellford dined with us to-day; he was accompanied by his brother, Mr. Francis Wellford, whom a bad state of health has compelled to withdraw from the pursuits of trade.* 13 Aug.

1827: 12 Jun: *Mr. G. Wellford drove over from Bray to tea and spent an hour with us. He looked ill, and has been indisposed. He retains the Curacy of that parish under the new Vicar Mr. Levett, who succeeded about a twelvemonth since to the living, on the decease of the late amiable young Incumbent, Mr. Legge, whom I met two years since at my friend Wellfords' lodgings in the Hospital at Bray.* 13 Jun., 22 Aug., 26 Aug., 28-29 Aug., 2-3 Sep., 14 Nov., 17 Nov: *Mr. Rogers & Mr. Wellford did not make their appearance till two o clock, coming, from Bray, and they returned thither after the funeral, Mr. R. not judging, that it was necessary for him to be present, when the will was opened, as one of the Executors was in the house.*

1828: 18 Apr.

1829: 11 Feb., 13 Mar.

1832: 20 Mar., 25 Mar., 25 Apr., 8 Jun., 12 Jun., 14 Jun.

1834: 22-23 Jul., 28 Jul: *In the evening our friend Wellford arrived to tea in his gig from Oxford which he had sent forward on Saturday by his servant, leaving Bray himself this morning by a Cheltenham coach.* 29 Jul., 31 Jul., 1-5 Aug., 23 Aug., 12 Sep., 28 Nov: *Received a letter from my friend Wellford, written in terms of warm and exalted piety and Christian hope, recounting an attack of apoplexy with which he was visited on the 1st. Inst. and from which he was restored by prompt and energetic medical aid steadily administered.* 12 Dec.

1835: 4 Mar., 10 Jun.

1837: 2 May, 24 Jul.

1838: 30 Jan., 3 Aug., 5 Aug., 27 Nov.

1842: 13-14 Feb., 26 Feb., 15 Mar: *Jos. Wilson, a very rich old gentleman, a connection of the Bishop of Calcutta, who had married a sister of Geo. Wellford, and had been intimate with my late Uncle and Aunt, thus was enabled to prove that there never was any issue of that marriage ...* 4 May, 11 May, 9 Jun., 29-30 Jun., 1-2 Jul., 4 Jul., 7 Jul., 12 Jul: *I drove out after early tea in the phaeton to the foot of Stow hill to meet my old friend Wellford coming from Bray on a visit to us, and travelling by the Great Western railway to Farringdon Station, and thence by the "Little Wonder" coach.* 13-21 Jul., 4 Aug., 23 Aug., 6 Oct., 9 Oct., 29 Oct.

1843: 5 Jan., 16 Jan., 15 Sep., 30 Sep.

1844: 20 Jan., 27 Nov.

1845: 9 Jan., 12 Jan., 16 Jun.

1846: 3 Sep.

1847: 13 Feb., 9 Apr., 17 Apr., 6 Sep.

1848: 20 Jul., 14 Oct: *From Geo. Wellford I received a long letter, in his usual strain—conveying the intelligence of the death of his sister. Mrs. Hayley, some weeks ago.*

1850: 12 Feb., 17 Apr., 25 Apr.

1851: 4 Jan.

1852: 3 Mar: *A letter from Geo. Wellford, after a long interval during which our correspondence has been interrupted; very friendly; a new Vicar of Bray having been appointed, in lieu of Mr. Levett, resigned, he is about to quit the curacy, and to confine himself to the duties he has so long performed, and to the chaplaincy of the hospital at Bray, which he has so long held.* 7 Mar., 9 Mar.

1853: 9 Apr., 12 Apr.

WELLINGTON — *see* Wellesley

WELLS — Nathaniel Wells — *see also* Price *and* Withers [85]

Nathaniel Wells (1779-1852), JP and landed proprietor, was born at St Kitts, the son of Welsh merchant William Wells (1730-1794) and a black slave, Joardine [Juggy] Wells (d. 1811). After inheriting his father's plantations, Wells became a wealthy landowner and magistrate, and the second black person, after Capt. John Perkins, to hold a commission in the armed forces of the crown. He was also Britain's first black high sheriff.

Wells married, at St George's Hanover Square, Westminster, 9 June 1801, Harriet (1780-1820), daughter of Revd Charles Este (1752-1828) and Cordelia Croft (1748-1828); they had 5 sons and 5 daughters:

1 William Meyrick (1803-1823); died unmarried at Piercefield House

1 Harriet Claxton (1804-1888); married, 5 March 1831, Revd Frederick Cuthbert Beresford Earle (1803-1864); 1 son and 2 daughters:

- 1 Josephine Harriet (1838-1863)
- 2 Cordelia Adelaide Emily (1842-1844)
- 1 Beresford Nathaniel (1844-1910)

2 Nathaniel Armstrong (1806-1846); married, at the British Embassy, Paris, 26 February 1844, Georgina Lucy (1819-1901), born at St Germain de Loisé, Perche, Normandy, the daughter of Benjamin Price (1786-1871) and Eliza Anne Dupuis (1797-1878); 1 son:

- 1 Nathaniel Armstrong (1847-1900), Church of England clergyman; born at Caen, Normandy; married, at St Pancras, Middlesex, 7 October 1880, Mary Grace Andrews (1859-1948); apparently no children

3 Charles Rush (1807-1848); married, at Chatteris, Isle of Ely, Cambridgeshire, 12 May 1831, Vincentia Money Chatfield (1807-1881)

4 John Tighe (1808-1869), Church of England clergyman; married, at St Luke's, Chelsea, Middlesex, 4 July 1833, Ellen Margaret Bayford (1813-1898); 3 sons and 9 daughters:

- 1 Ellen Harriet (1834-1890)
- 2 Harriet Este (1836-1890)
- 1 John Nathaniel (1837-1856)
- 3 Frances Delia (1839-1911)
- 4 Julia Maria (1840-1845)
- 5 Margarate Vincentia (1843-1899)
- 6 Caroline Sophia (1844-1911)
- 2 Charles Augustus Este (1846-1923)
- 7 Mary (b. 1849)
- 8 Emily Blanche (1850-1932)
- 9 Georgina (b. 1852)
- 3 William Henry Bayford (1854-1931)

2 Delia Frances (1809-1845); died unmarried at Bath

5 Henry Llewellyn (1810-1822); died a child at Piercefield House

3 Henrietta Maria (1813-1872); married, at Chepstow, Monmouthshire, 26 July 1843, James Barnard Bryan (b. 1816)

4 Grace Emily Georgiana (1814-1841); married, at Chepstow, Monmouthshire, 26 November 1836, George Watkins (1807-1890); 3 daughters:

- 1 Grace Emily (1837-1928)
- 2 Harriet Sarah (1838-1894)
- 3 Marian Cordelia (1840-1929)

5 Caroline Angeline (1816-1852); died unmarried at Bath

The son referred to in the diary entry for 30 April 1845 was Nathaniel Armstrong Wells. He was the author of *The Picturesque Antiquities of Spain; Described in a Series of Letters*, published in 1846, the year of his death. His posthumous son became vicar of Holy Trinity, Frome, Somerset.

1804: 21 Sep: *Persfield Grounds ... the property, now, of West Indian Mr. Walls, in whose hands it will not probably remain longer than in those of his predecessors. The grounds & estate are terribly neglected & running to waste, & the House a prey to Dry Rot.*

1845: 30 Apr: *After our return Mrs. R Waller, her niece Mrs. Wells, and two of the Waller boys, walked from Bourton to call on Sophy; we walked back with them to some distance beyond Lower Slaughter.* 6 Jun: *Mr. Wells, who married Mrs. R Waller's niece, they being now on a visit at the Rectory, accompanied us: he is son of Mr. Wells of Piercefield, and a man of colour; unfortunately without profession or occupation; it was an imprudent match, for the gentleman, disobliging his own family, is without resources, and the lady, a very pleasing young women, attached herself to him contrary to the wishes of her friends, whose means also are also very confined—Mr. W. is now almost hopelessly seeking employment.*

WELLS — Thomas Wells [86]

Thomas Wells (1790-1861), farmer, was born at Ascott-under-Wychwood, Oxfordshire, the son of Thomas and Ann Wells. He was married to Sarah (1795-1840); they had 1 son and 6 daughters:

1 Eliza (b. 1821)
2 Mary Ann (b. 1821)
1 John (b. 1826)
3 Maria (1827-1907)
4 Ellen (b. 1828)
5 Emily (1831-1867)
6 Emma (1833-1905)

Wells had been a farmer at Hampnett, with 1,150 acres and sixty-five male employees.

1846: 19 May: ... also from Mr. Wells, Vice Chairman of the Northleach Union ... 17 Jul., 29 Jul., 8 Oct.

WELLS — William Wells [87]

William Wells (1799-1859), surgeon and registrar, was born at Bourton-on-the-Water, the son of William Wells, surgeon, and his wife, Sarah. There was another surgeon in Bourton in 1821 by the name of Silas Wells, possibly an uncle. Wells was married to Ann Courtenay (b. ±1803), who was from Okehampton, Devon; they had 2 sons and 2 daughters:

1 Jane Maria (b. 1836)
2 Georgiana Clara (b. 1840), twin to Courtenay
1 Courtenay (b. 1840), twin to Georgiana
2 George John Campbell (b. 1841)

There is an anecdote concerning Dr Wells and his mare:

> Mr Wells, the elderly, kindly surgeon of Bourton-on-the-Water in the early nineteenth century, would forgive his apprentice almost anything except over-riding his favourite mare who knew the practice so well that when the apprentice got lost in the hills and valleys of the Cotswolds he dropped the reins and the mare took him safely home.

1836: 14 Nov.

1837: 19 Jan., 16 Mar: *Presided at the Board of Guardians: contracts made with the Med. Off. Hayward & Wells, on the same terms as last year.* 29 Apr: *Engaged during great part of the morning in consulting with Reynolds of Lower Slaughter and others respecting a corpse of an infant which had been found floating in the mill-pound at L.S., writing to the Coroner to hold an inquest, to Mr. Wells, the Med. Off. of this district of the Union to attend at the inquest ...* 11 Aug., 9 Sep.

1838: 4 May, 1 Jun.

1840: 17 Sep: *Conferred with the two Medical Officers of the Union, Messrs. Hayward and Wells ...*

1842: 16 Feb: *Mr. Wells called to open himself to me with reference to unpleasant feuds existing between him and a former Assistant of his, who has now set himself up as Apothecary in opposition to him at Bourton.* 31 Dec.

1843: 18 Aug., 21 Aug.

1844: 7 Apr., 23 Aug., 25 Aug., 11 Nov.

1845: 23 Feb., 2-3 May, 22 May.

1846: 30 Aug.

1847: 6 Apr., 9 Apr: *Mr. Wells called on me last evening, and stated that he had no doubt that the young woman had experienced an attack of that disease ...* 10 Apr., 14 Apr., 3 Jun., 12 Sep., 14 Nov., 18 Nov.

1848: 21 Jan., 24 Oct., 8 Nov.

1850: 6 Oct.

1852: 27 Apr: *... present at the Vaccination by Mr. Wells of many of the children of this village and Eyford ...*

1854: 17 Apr.

WELSH — Thomas Welsh [88]

Thomas Welsh (1781-1848), singer, was born at Wells, Somerset, the son of John Welsh and his wife, the daughter of the elder Thomas Linley (1733-1795). At the age of 6 he became a chorister at Wells Cathedral, where his singing soon attracted an eager audience. Sheridan heard of him and persuaded Linley to engage him for the 1792 Bath concerts. Welsh's first opera appearance was in 1792 in Thomas Attwood's *The Prisoner*, written especially for him, and he performed at Drury Lane Theatre in 1795 in Attwood's *The Adopted Child* and Storace's version of *Lodoiska*. John Kemble promoted him as an actor and coached him in the part of Prince Arthur in Shakespeare's *King John*. In the meantime Welsh continued his musical education under Karl Friedrich Horn, Johann Baptist Cramer, and Karl Friedrich Baumgarten. In 1802 he was admitted as a gentleman of the Chapel Royal.

Welsh produced two farces at the Lyceum Theatre, an opera, *Kamskatka*, at Covent Garden, and music for several plays. He sang as a bass and became most renowned as a singing teacher. His first wife is unknown, but he married secondly, 9 June 1827, Mary Ann Wilson (1802-1867); they had 1 daughter:

1 Mary Ann Lucy (1828-1901); married, at Woodchester, Gloucestershire, Carlo Alfredo Piatti (1822-1901), Italian cellist, teacher, and composer

Mary Ann Wilson had created a great sensation when she made her début as Mandane in Arne's *Artaxerxes* at Drury Lane in January 1821. Her career was lucrative but short, as her exertions led to a breakdown in her health and the ruin of her voice.

1802: 8 Mar: *To the Music Room in the Evening, with Stevens, Evans &c. Mad. Mara, Welsh & Hill, Vicary ...* 9 Mar: *... adjourned to the miscellaneous Concert. Mad. Mara & Welsh delightful. The former particularly in "Farewell ye limped Streams" "So che dovrei" &c.*

WEMYSS — *see* **Charteris**

WERE — Ellis Bowden Were [89]

Ellis Bowden Were (1810-1891), Church of England clergyman, was born at Wellington, Somerset, the son of Thomas Waltham Were (1784-1862) and Elizabeth Saunders Bowden (1786-1863). He was educated at Queen's College, Oxford (BA 1832; MA 1836), and by 1838 he was vicar of Chipping Norton. By 1843 he had moved to become vicar of Stamford Baron in Lincolnshire. His movements and marital arrangements after this point are uncertain, but he probably remained unmarried. He was admitted to a lunatic asylum on 21 November 1846, and again on 8 June 1891; it therefore seems that he suffered spans of mental instability. His death at Beckenham, Kent, was recorded at Lewisham.

1838: 12 Jun: *Col. and Mrs. Dawkins from Over-Norton, accompanied by Mr. Were, the Clergyman of C Norton.*

1839: 23 Jul: *Wrote to Mr. Were, the Incumbent of Chipping Norton, inclosing a cheque on Messrs. Hoare for £5., as my contribution towards the fund now being raised for repairs and repewing of the Church at that place.* 25 Jul.

1840: 18 Oct: *Wrote to Mr. Were, the Clergyman of Chipping Norton, for information as to the report transmitted in the letter which I received from Mrs. Shard on the 16th.., that our family vault had been filled up during the alterations and repairs in Chipping Norton Church.* 25 Oct: Recd. a letter from Mr. Were in reply to mine of the 18th.... 26 Oct.

WERTHER — Jacob Friedemann, Count von Werther [90]

Jacob Friedemann, Count von Werther (1739-1806), landed proprietor, was of the Beichlinger line of the Thuringian noble family of Werther. He was the youngest child of Count Georg von Werthern (1700-1768) and Jacobine Henriette, Countess von Flemming (1709-1784). He married, 1773, Nassau an der Lahn Johanna Luise vom und zum Stein, an older sister of the Prussian minister and reformer Baron Karl vom und zum Stein; they had at least 1 daughter:

1 Henriette Caroline Luise (1774-1836); married, 1801, Friedrich Christian Ludwig von Senft and Pilsach (1774-1853)

In 1774 Count von Werther was sent to the Spanish court in Saxony's diplomatic service. On his return, he and his family settled in Weimar where they had connections to the Weimar court.

1798: 2 Sep: *Still, some few people do receive Society in the Evening, the Helldorffs, Werthern, Fouquet, Fumel, Rictgenstein &c.*

WEST — Hannah West — *see also* Bateman [91]

Hannah West, née Bateman (1817-1887), was the daughter of Robert Bateman (1780-1823) and Mary West (±1785-1844). In her earlier life she had been in service with the Read family in Stroud, but had returned home to nurse her mother, Mary, the village schoolmistress at Upper Slaughter—to the annoyance of the Read family. She later went into service with Eliza Daniell, only for the same thing to happen, although this time her mother was dying.

Hannah married Edward Dobbins West (1806-1883), a gamekeeper and farmer of 60 acres in Cutsdean, and presumably a cousin; they had at least 1 son and 1 daughter:

1 Mercy (1850-1872)

1 Frederick Edward (b. ±1852)

By 1871 the family had been joined by Hannah's brother, Joseph Bateman, who was listed in the census as an indoor servant. By 1881 Joseph was still there, in addition to Hannah's niece, Phoebe (1852-1914).

1846: 15 Jul: *Wrote to E.F.W. the letter conveyed by J Bateman, who went today to Cutsdean to see his sister, Hannah West, who is dangerously ill.* 15 Aug: *Visited Hannah West, who is still very ill: she is staying with her relations, the Bryans at Lower Slaughter.* 29 Aug: *Visited sick neighbours; J. Davis and Hannah West; both great sufferers.*

WEST — Thomas West [92]

Thomas West (1799-1867), farmer, was born at Lower Slaughter and baptised at Bourton-on-the-Water, the son of Thomas West and his wife, Elizabeth. He farmed 188 acres at Icomb, employing seven labourers. He was married to Mary (1795-1869); in the 1851 census at least 1 son and 1 daughter were listed at home:

1 Mary (b. ±1828)

1 Thomas (b. ±1830)

1838: 1 Feb.

1840: 25 Jun: *The business of the Board went forward in the ordinary manner until three o clock, when I vacated the chair, which was taken by Mr. West, to carry on the remaining business ...*

1844: 13 Nov: *Wrote to Mr. West, Guardn. of Icomb ...*

1852: 18 Nov: *To the Workhouse, where conferred with Mr. Pearce & Mr. West, the Guardian of Icomb ...* 2 Dec.

1854: 20 Apr., 8 Jun., 22 Jun., 6 Jul.

WESTCOTT — Peter Westcott [93]

Peter Westcott (b. ±1801), surgeon, was in partnership with John Mould at Oundle in 1824 as a surgeon and apothecary. He moved to Leamington Spa where his son William, an only child, was born on 17 December 1848. William, it was said, was 'effectively born to medicine'. In 1875 he applied for admission to an un-named 'Mystic Order' (possibly the Societas Rosicruciana in Anglia), and was asked to state 'all you care to reveal of your past life'; he wrote, 'I hardly know anything of interest to reveal. Both parents died before I was ten years old & I was left to the care of my half uncle, an elderly Bachelor Surgeon.' The half-uncle, Richard Westcott Martyn (1792-1879), was in practice at Martock in Somerset, where his nephew joined him after obtaining his MB degree in November 1871. At Martock William soon became a prominent citizen.

1835: 25 Mar: *At eleven o clock the preparations for the funeral of our deceased friend were nearly completed ... Mr. Westcott was present ...* 30 Mar: *Wrote a note to Mr. Westcott, the Apothecary at Oundle respecting the fees due to Dr. Skrimshire.*

WESTENRA — Warner William Westenra — *see also* Charteris *and* Gist [94]

Warner William Westenra, 2nd Baron Rossmore (1765-1842), MP and landed proprietor, was born at Rathleague, Queen's County, Ireland, the eldest son of of Henry Westenra and Harriet, daughter and co-heir of Col John Murray, MP (Ireland), of co. Monaghan, and sister of the dowager Baroness Rossmore of Monaghan. Warner was educated at Oswestry and Trinity College, Dublin (1783). He was MP for co. Monaghan from August to December 1800, and in the UK parliament from 1800 to 1801. He married, first, 1791, Mary Anne [Marianne] (d. 1807), second daughter of Charles Walsh of Walsh Park, co. Tipperary; they had 4 sons and 1 daughter:

1 Henry Robert (1792-1860), MP (whig) for co. Monaghan (1818-30, 1831-32, May-July 1834, and 1835-42) and lord lieutenant for the same (1843-52); educated at Westminster School and Trinity College, Dublin (admitted, 4 July 1810); married, first, at Edinburgh, 25 January 1820, Anne

(±1794-1844), illegitimate daughter of Douglas Hamilton, 8th duke of Hamilton; secondly, at Camla, co. Monaghan, 19 May 1846, his cousin, Josephine Julia Helen (1832-1912), second daughter of Henry Lloyd, of Farrinrory, co. Tipperary, and Harriet Amelia, daughter of Sir John Craven Carden, 1st baronet of Templemore, co. Tipperary, and Frances Maria, sister of Warner William Westenra, 2nd Baron Rossmore; no surviving children from his first marriage, but from his second, 4 sons and 2 daughters:

1 Frances Kathleen (1849-1925)
2 Norah Josephine Harcourt (1850-1934)
1 Henry Cairns (1851-1874); succeeded as 4th Baron (Ireland) and 3rd Baron (UK)
2 Derrick Warner William (1853-1921); succeeded as 5th Baron (Ireland) and 4th Baron (UK)
3 Richard Hamilton (1854-1880)
4 Peter Craven (1855-1932)

2 Richard (1794-1838); died at co. Monaghan
3 John Craven (1798-1874); married, first, 31 March 1834, Eleanor Mary Jolliffe (1770-1839); secondly, at Broadwater, near Worthing, Sussex, 23 July 1842, Anne Daubuz (1808-1882); 1 daughter:

1 Mary Anne Wilmot (1847-1894)

4 Charles (b. 1800)
1 Marianne (1801-1844); married, 17 July 1824, Samuel Gist (1795-1845); 3 sons and 7 daughters:

1 Marianne Westenra (1825-1895); married Edward Du Pré (1821-1895); 3 daughters
2 Margaret Elizabeth (1828-1829)
3 Mary (b. 1829)
4 Elizabeth Perkins (b. 1831)
1 Samuel (1832-1904)
5 Ann (b. 1834)
6 Eleanor Mary Augusta (b. 1835)
7 Elizabeth (1836-1896); died unmarried
2 William Westenra (1837-1878)
3 Henry Westenra (1838-1907); married, first, 20 September 1859, Eleanor Maria, youngest daughter of Revd Thomas Du Pré, rector of Willoughby; widower by 1861 and married secondly, 1875, Charlotte Caroline Eudall

Warner William Westenra married, secondly, 3 June 1819, Augusta Charteris Wemyss (1781-1840), fourth and youngest daughter of Francis Charteris, styled Lord Elcho (1749-1808), and Susan Tracy-Keck (1745-1835); there were no children of this second marriage. Westenra succeeded to the Irish peerage in 1801. In March 1838 he was created Baron Rossmore of Monaghan in one of the coronation peerages of Queen Victoria. Augusta died suddenly at Wilton House, Cheltenham, on 28 July 1840, and Warner died on 10 August 1842 at Rossmore Park, Ireland.

1823: 6 Sep: *Lastly on the preceeding evening had arrived my fair & fat cousin Lady Rossmore, Lady Elcho's youngest daughter, from Ireland, where she had left her Lord.* 17 Sep., 23 Oct.

1824: 2 Nov: *The Mr. Gist, who dined at Stanway to-day, and is eldest son of the riche parvenu residing at Wormington Grange in this vicinity, has recently been married to Mary Anne Westenra, daughter of Lord Rossmore, an amiable young person, but possessed neither of talent nor beauty.*

1826: 17 Jun: *I found poor Lady Rossmore under considerable agitation and uneasiness, owing to letters received from Ireland, intimating, that her step-son, Mr. Westenra, who has, contrary to my surmises, succeeded in securing his return for the County of Monaghan, on the popular, that is, the Roman Catholic interest, turning out his old colleague, Colonel Leslie, has been wounded in a duel, arising out of the contest ...* 26 Jun: *We left home to pass a few days with Lady Elcho at Stanway, with whom we found her daughter Lady Rossmore, who had arrived three weeks since from Ireland. My fair cousin has not grown thin since I saw her, in 1823, but looks in good health.*

1829: 30 Jun., 11 Jul: *Lord & Lady Rossmore are at present on a visit to Lady Elcho. I had not seen her Ladyship since the summer of 1826, and I thought her looking well, though complaining of indifferent health. My fair cousin & her Lord were recently arrived from Ireland; his Lordship I had only once before met, and I was not led to admire him more on a second interview than I had at the first. He appears to me a bad specimen of his rank & country; advanced in years, he has a good stout figure, & is tall, but his features, regular, though not indicative of talent or of an amiable disposition, are horribly disfigured by thick and amorphous whiskers.*

1830: 23 Jun.

1835: 12 Jun.

1838: 29 Aug., 20 Sep.

1840: 2 Aug: *Much shocked by finding in the newspapers a notice of the demise of my relation, Lady Rossmore. It seems she arrived from Ireland on Monday or Tuesday last at Cheltenham, and died very suddenly at that place on Tuesday.* 5-6 Aug., 11 Aug., 2 Sep: *Received a letter from F. Aston, with a communication from Lord Rossmore, whom he had found very much debilitated and depressed at Cheltenham.* 3-4 Sep., 6 Sep., 9 Sep., 11 Sep: *Recd. a letter from Lord Wemyss in answer to mine of the 4th. Inst. approving of the course I had taken with reference to a funeral sermon on the occasion of the death of Lady Rossmore.* 13 Sep: *After an early breakfast set out in my open carriage in with my servant to Stanway, to perform the duties there, and preach the promised sermon on the death of Lady Rossmore.* 15 Sep., 22 Sep: *My chief business was to wait on Lord Rossmore. I found the old peer in a calmer state, and more resigned than I had been led to expect.* 24 Sep., 5-6 Oct: *Recd. a few obliging lines from Lord Rossmore, covering a letter which he had received from the Revd. Edwin Prodgers, Minister, I believe, of Brixton, Surrey, speaking in terms of approbation of the sermon which I preached at Stanway on occasion of the death of Lady Rossmore, and which his Lordship had forwarded to Mr. P. for his perusal.*

1841: 28 Feb: *Received a letter from Lord Wemyss in answer to mine of the 22d. He thinks that the Monument to Lady Rossmore should be placed in the body of Stanway Church.* 1 Mar.

1842: 3 Dec: *We afterwards visited the Shop of Geo. Lewis, the Sculptor, who executed the monument erected at Stanway in memory of Lady Rossmore.*

1844: 16 Feb., 21 Feb: *The members of the family attendg. as mourners were Mr. Gist, Lord Rossmore, and his brother, Col. Westenra, brothers of the deceased sister lady, Mr. Perkins and Mr. W. Young, who had married sisters of Mr. Gist, and Mr. W. Gist, the brother.*

WESTERN — Charles Western[95]

Charles Western (1760-1835), Church of England clergyman, was born at Great Abington, Cambridgeshire, the son of Thomas Western (1735-1781) and Jane Calvert (1736-1819). He was educated at Hertford College, Oxford, and was appointed rector of Kingham in 1785, a position he held for fifty years. He married, at St James's Palace, Westminster, 7 July 1784, Mary Peniston Goostrey (1762-1849); they had 4 sons and 1 daughter:

1 Thomas (1785-1790)
2 Charles William (1786-1786)
1 Hannah Maria (1787-1851)
3 Maximillian (b. & d. 1789)
4 Charles Maximilian Thomas (1790-1824), army officer; born at Tiverton, Devon; joined the Portuguese service having gained a commission in the Army as lieutenant-colonel; married Harriet Clarke and had five children, four of whom were born in Portugal

---

1823: 23 Apr: ... *first meeting of the Stow Clerical Society for this year: Mr. Western, Rector of Kingham, Oxfordshire ...*
1826 19 Apr.
1828: 23 Apr., 2 Jul., 20 Aug.
1829: 17 Jun., 12 Aug., 24 Nov.
1830: 14 Apr.
1832: 25 Apr.
1833: 21 Jan.
1834: 20 Aug., 31 Oct.

WESTMACOTT — Horatio Westmacott [96]

Horatio Westmacott (1806-1862), Church of England clergyman, was born at Westminster, the third son of Sir Richard Westmacott (1775-1856), professor of sculpture at the University of Oxford, and Dorothy Margaret Wilkinson (1778-1834). His elder brother, Richard Westmacott (1799-1872), succeeded their father as professor of sculpture at Oxford. Horatio was educated at Corpus Christi, Cambridge (BA 1827; MA 1835), and was ordained deacon on 15 October 1831 and priest on 8 December 1832. His first clerical appointment was as stipendiary curate of Brent Knoll, Somerset, from 17 October 1831. Having purchasing the advowson, he appointed himself rector of Chastleton, Oxfordshire, in 1838. He held the living for the rest of his life.

Westmacott married, at Westminster, 2 June 1838, Penelope Spencer Ruscombe (1815-1894), daughter of Joseph Ruscombe Poole (1775-1843) and Elizabeth Spencer Stone (1785-1822); they had 6 sons and 2 daughters:

1 Edward Vesey (1840-1911)
2 Richard (1841-1925), Maj.-Gen.; knighted
3 Herbert (1842-1926), Church of England clergyman
4 Edmund Dickinson (1844-1928)
1 Bertha (1846-1895)
2 Isabel (1847-1900)
5 Ruscombe Field (1849-1925), Lt-Col
6 Walter (1853-1939), Church of England clergyman

1838: 20 Mar: *Mr. Adams is removing to a college living in Northants. and resigns the living of Chastleton, which since his Father's death he has held with a fellowship of St. John's, Oxf. but the advowson and next presentation of which he has sold to a Clergyman of the name of Westmacott.* 5 Sep., 25 Sep., 26 Sep: *Also to Whitmore Jones, from whom I had recd. a note yesterday to nominate the Revd. H. Westmacott a member of the Book Society, requesting him to inform that gentleman that he had been elected a member.*

1842: 6 Oct: *Wrote to Mr. Westmacott respecting his wish that the Edinburgh Review may be ordered into the Stow Library.* 9 Oct.

1843: 11 Aug., 26 Sep.
1844: 27 Jan., 1 Aug., 29 Aug., 3 Oct.
1847: 18 Mar., 19 Mar., 23 Mar., 13 May, 9-10 Oct., 14-15 Sep.
1848: 8 Feb.

WESTON — Moses Weston [97]

Moses Weston (1818-1899), agricultural labourer, was born at Longborough, Gloucestershire, the son of Henry Weston (1767-1847) and his wife, Hannah (1772-1858). He married, at Kidderminster, Worcestershire, October 1852, Elizabeth (1828-1888), daughter of Thomas Cooper (b. 1808); they had at least 4 sons and 2 daughters:

1 Henry (1850-1917); married, at Lichfield, Staffordshire, October 1876, Sarah Ann Hulme (1852-1927); 1 son and 3 daughters:
  1 Albert Henry (b. 1878)
  1 Violet Priscilla (1879-1934)
  2 Ada A. (1889-1975)
  3 Ellie M. (b. 1895)
1 Elizabeth (b. 1854)
2 Moses (1856-1927); married, at Birmingham, October 1876, Sarah Ann Young (1853-1927); 4 sons and 3 daughters:
  1 Alfred (1877-1955)
  1 Florence (1878-1976)
  2 William Henry (1881-1951)
  2 Edith Emily (1882-1944)
  3 Albert Victor (1884-1903)
  4 Leonard (1885-1965)
  3 Gertrude (1888-1946)
3 Thomas (1858-1904)
2 Emily (b. 1861)
4 Frederick (b. 1865); married, at Worcester, January 1896, Ellen Maria Lewis (1865-1943); 1 son and 1 daughter:
  1 Sidney F. (b. 1890)
  1 Eveyln A. (b. 1903)

Shortly after their marriage at Kidderminster, Moses and Elizabeth moved to nearby Chaddesley Corbett, Worcestershire, where all of their children were born.

1834: 18 Dec: *The most important matter was an enquiry respecting a fire which had broken out about 6 o clock this morning in a rick yard at Longborough, the fourth fire within the last four years in that parish: and, no doubt, the deed of an incendiary... Under all the circumstances we concurred with Jeaffreson in the propriety of committing the lad for a few days to Northleach Bridewell, for reexamination, in order that time might be afforded for further investigation. The lad's name is Moses Weston.* 24 Dec: *After a long investigation and examination of witnesses, we discharged the boy detained under suspicion of being concerned in the incendiarism at Longborough, the proof being insufficient to go before a Grand Jury ...*

WETHERELL — Charles Wetherell [98]

Sir Charles Wetherell (1770-1846), politician and lawyer, was born at Oxford, the third son of Nathan Wetherell (d. 1807), dean of Hereford and master of University College, Oxford, and Ricarda (1743-1812), daughter of Alexander Croke of Studley Priory, Oxfordshire. He was educated St Paul's School and University College, Oxford, followed by the Inner Temple, where he was admitted in 1790. He was called to the bar in 1794 and admitted at Lincoln's Inn in 1806. He married, first, 1826, his cousin Jane Sarah Elizabeth (d. 1831), daughter of Sir Alexander Croke; they had 1 daughter:

1 Meredith Maria (1804-1841)

He married secondly, 1838, Harriet Elizabeth Warneford.

Wetherell was MP for Rye in 1812-13, Shaftesbury in 1813-18, Oxford in 1820-26, Hastings in 1826, and Plympton in 1826-30. He was solicitor-general from January 1824 to September 1826, and attorney-general from September 1826 to April 1827 and February 1828 to March 1829. He was knighted in 1824. Wetherell died on 17 August 1846 at Preston Hall, Kent, after being injured in a carriage accident on 10 August.

1825: 15 Dec.

1826: 29 Jan: *The only candidate now named is the Solicitor General, Sir C. Wetherell, of Magd. Coll. and Son of the old Dean of Hereford, who was also Master of University Coll. He is a man of talent, and a strenuous opponent of the Catholic claims: but some may not consider an ambitious Barrister a proper representative.* 18 Feb., 18 Sep.

1827: 26 Apr.

1828: 12 Feb., 15 May.

1829: 25 Mar: *The Attorney General, Sir C. Wetherell, made also a most strong impression; his long and energetic oration was a true Phillipic; scornful, sarcastic, full of defiance, manly, personal, while his reasoning was potent and the close combatting of a practised advocate.* 26 Jun.

1830: 24 Jun.

1832: 27 Mar.

1833: 12 Mar.

1845: 9 Feb.

WETHERELL — Henry Wetherell[99]

Henry Wetherell (1775-1857), Church of England clergyman, was born at Oxford, a younger son of Revd Nathan Wetherell (d. 1807), master of University College, Oxford, and dean of Hereford, and Ricarda Croke (1743-1812). He was a younger brother of Charles (*above*). Henry was educated at Magdalen College, Oxford (BA 1795; MA 1798), and was a fellow of University College in 1802. He was chaplain to the duke of Kent, prebendary of Gloucester in 1825, and archdeacon of Hereford from 1825 to 1852. He was also appointed rector of Thruxton, Herefordshire, in 1799, and of Kentchirch in 1818.

1825: 15 Dec: *At Gloucester too Dr. Ridley has lately paid the debt of nature, whereby his brother in law, the Lord Chancellor, has been enabled to provide for the Revd. H. Wetherell, one of the Sons of Dean Wetherall, of Hereford, & Head at one time of University College: brother also to the present Solicitor General. Mr. Prebendary Wetherell has also been selected by Bp. Huntingford to be Archdeacon of Hereford, in which diocese he holds the living of Thruxton.*

1826: 16 Jun., 14 Sep.

1827: 1 Apr., 22 Apr., 24 Apr.

1829: 2 Apr., 22 Sep.

1832: 29 Mar.

1847: 6 Apr.

1848: 11 May.

1851: 31 Mar.

WETHERELL — James Wetherell[100]

James Wetherell (1786-1857), Church of England clergyman, was born at Cowley, Oxfordshire, a younger son of Revd Nathan Wetherell (d. 1807), master of University College, Oxford, and dean of Hereford, and Ricarda Croke (1743-1812). He was a younger brother of Charles and Henry (*above*). He was educated New College, Oxford (BCL 1813), and appointed perpetual curate of Upton St Leonards in 1815, and vicar of Lyonshall, Herefordshire, in 1816. He was prebendary of Hereford from 1821 until his death.

1825: 15 Jul: *A distinct secretary to be appointed for the Diocesan Meeting; and the Revd. Wetherell, Perpetual Curate of Upton St. Leonard's, a resident in Gloucester, was named.*

1826: 17 Jun. *The Sermon was preached by Archdeacon Wetherell, the Prebendary now in residence. It was good doctrine, but delivered in a dull, halting manner.*

1827: 15 Apr, 22 Apr.

1838: 4 Jan: *Mr. P. is Rural Dean of Gloucester Deanery, and Incumbent of Upon St. Leonard, to which he was presented by Bp. Monk on the resignation of Mr. J. Wetherell, who at all times a weak person, is now, I believe, in confinement.*

WETHERELL — Richard Wetherell[101]

Richard Wetherell (1773-1858), Church of England clergyman, was born at Oxford, the third son of Revd Nathan Wetherell (d. 1807), master of University College, Oxford, and dean of Hereford, and Ricarda Croke (1743-1812). He was the younger brother of Charles (*above*) and elder brother of Henry and James (*above*). He was educated at University College, Oxford (BA 1795; MA 1798), and entered the Church. He was appointed rector of Westbury-on-Severn in 1798, of Wyck Rissington in 1809, and of Notgrove in 1810.

Wetherell married, at Ticehurst, Sussex, 23 November 1796, Caroline Duff, née May (1778-1833), only surviving child of Thomas May, of Pashley, Sussex, and Sarah, daughter of J. Gray. She was the widow of Capt. Duff. Caroline and Richard had 7 sons and 6 daughters:

1 Mary (b. 1797)
1 Richard (1800-1893)
2 Elizabeth (b. 1802)
3 Caroline (b. 1805)
2 Thomas May (1807-1873); *see below*
3 Nathan (1808-1887)
4 Charles (1810-1845), Church of England clergyman
5 Henry (b. 1812)
4 Frances Richarda (b. 1813)
6 William (1815-1864), Church of England clergyman
5 Eleanor (b. 1816)
6 Charlotte (1818-1834)
7 Edward (1823-1894)

Richard and Caroline were beneficiaries of compensation for the enslaved people on Virgin Valley in St James, Jamaica.

1845: 7 Apr: *I proceeded to Bourton Bridge, where I took up Mr. Ford, and drove with him through Aston Blank to Notgrove—roads bad—village has an air of desertion—the Rector, Wetherell, non resident—all the farmers, even his tenant, dissenters,—the Curate, Mr. Hill, an estimable man, but with a slender income, and married to a farmer's widow, living in a treeless, gardenless, comfortless cottage, yet friendly and hospitable and giving us a good plain luncheon.*

WETHERELL — Thomas May Wetherell[102]

Thomas May Wetherell (1807-1873), Church of England clergyman, was born at Westbury-upon-Severn, Gloucestershire, the second son of Richard Wetherell and Caroline May (*above*). He was educated at Trinity College, Dublin (BA 1830), and Magdalen College, Oxford (MA 1837). In 1835, between his degrees, he was appointed chaplain to the mayor of Winchester. He later served as vicar of Flaxley, Gloucestershire, from 1852 to his death in 1873. He married, at St Martin-in-the-Fields, Westminster, 1833, Anne, youngest daughter of Henry Winchester, alderman of the City of

London, of Oakfield Lodge, Hawkhurst, Kent. This attribution is speculative, but as the living at Wyck Rissington was held by Thomas's father, Richard, it seems likely that Thomas was the curate mentioned by Francis Witts.

1840: 14 Aug: ... *He was accompanied by his son Frederick, and a Mr. Wetherall, a young man who, it is intended, shall become a candidate for Deacon's orders with the Curacy of Wick Risington as his title.*
22 Aug: *Rode to call on Mr. Ford ... but met him and Mr. G. L. Cooke, by the way at Wick Risington, where we held a long parley together on various points. G.L.C. is come to officiate at his own Church at Wick R. to-morrow, and to give orders for repairs to the parsonage house, with a view to its being hereafter the residence of a Curate; at present the cure is vacant, and some difficulty will be found in procuring a supply till Christmas, when the gentleman selected, Mr. Wetherall, is to be ordained Deacon.*

WEYRAUCH — Vincent Weyrauch [103]

Vincent Weyrauch (1765-1802) was an actor and singer. He was engaged to perform under Michael Schlager in Freiberg, Saxony, for the winter of 1784-85, and at the Weimar Theatre in 1785. He was then engaged under Gustav Friedrich Wilhelm Großmann in Frankfurt, Köln, Aachen, Düsseldorf, and Hannover from 1786 to 1788, and with Böhm's company in Pyrmont and Kassel in 1788. In 1788-89 he was engaged under Johann Friedrich Toscani and Peter Carl Santorini in Kassel, Marburg, and Hofgeismar. In all of the above he performed in comic roles in comedies and musical comedies. In the winter season of 1789-90 he was part of Franz Anton von Weber's theatre company in Meiningen.

Weyrauch married, at Meiningen, 8 November 1788, Jeanette von Weber (1768-1834), aunt of the composer Carl Maria von Weber; they had 1 son and 2 daughters:

1 Victoria Elisabeth (1790-1850)
2 Wilhelmina Sophia Friederike (b. 1795)
1 August Heinrich (1799-1835)

In the season of 1790-91, Weyrauch was engaged in Hanover, Pyrmont, and Kassel. He re-appeared at the court theatre in Weimar for the 1793-94 season, and after a year in Frankfurt he returned to Weimar and remained there until 1800. He was apparently close to Goethe. He performed in Danzig and Königsberg in 1800-01, before moving to St Petersburg where he died in 1802.

1798: 2 Sep: *The Opera is not now (Summer 1800) in so flourishing a Condition as when first I came, Stermins as bass, was much superior to Spitzeder, & Weyrauch acted excellently in the Opera buffa, but as for the rest, they have no tolerable Tenor, & besides Mad.selle Jagemann not one good Actress.*

1799: 26 Oct: *Figaro by Weyrauch as usual most amusing & Doctor Bartholo by Spitzer very well indeed.* 3 Nov: ... *as also Weyrauch & Becker as the Jeweller.* 7 Nov: *To the Play Die Versöhnung by Kotzebue a pretty interesting piece a Comedy where Becker, Madame Beck, Malkolmi, Vohsin & Weyrauch played very well.* 4 Dec: ... *best actors Graff, Malkolmi, Schlanzovsky, Vohs, Becker, Genast, Haide, Weyrauch.* 7 Dec: *The best performers were Jagemann, Matiegzeck, Weyrauch, & Spitzeder.*

1800: 26 Feb., 8 Mar: ... *well done by Jagemann, Vohsin, Spitzeder & Weyrauch.* 17 Mar: ... *well acted by Vohs, Malkolmi, Vohsin, Weyrauch, Spangler, Genast, Haide, & Becker.* 21 Mar: ... *particularly by Jagemann and Weyrauch, without whom indeed few Operas here are tolerable. Weimar will lose much when the latter goes to St. Petersburg.* 29 Mar: *Mad. Weyrauch ...* 2 Apr: ... *the Characters of Weyrauch and Malkolmi extremely well done the former, poor man, most excessively agitated on being applauded extremely when going out the Play for the next night, it being the last time of his acting here.*

WHALLEY — the Whalley family of Ecton, Northamptonshire [104]

The Whalley family is first mentioned in the diaries of Agnes Witts. On Wednesday 25 November 1789, during a visit in Northamptonshire, she wrote, 'Mr. Whalley call'd here in the Morning, play'd at Whist & Cribbage & at Ving'tun ...' Five days later, on Saturday, 28 November 1789, she wrote, 'we went in the two Chaises to Drink Tea at Mr. Whalleys at Ecton'. She was presumably referring to Palmer Whalley (1738-1803), rector of Ecton, the son of Eyre Whalley (1703-1762), also rector of Ecton, and Barbara (1704-1770), daughter of Thomas Palmer, rector of Ecton from 1720 to 1732. Eyre Whalley was a friend of Benjamin Franklin, one of the founding fathers of the United States. He married Barbara Palmer at St Paul's Cathedral, London, on 23 March 1737, and they had 2 sons and 3 daughters:

1 Palmer (1738-1802); *see below*
1 Barbara (1740-1810)
2 Anne (1742-1783)
2 John (1743-1745); died an infant
3 Sarah (1747-1818)

Palmer Whalley was appointed rector of Ecton in 1763 and rector of Wilby in 1782. He held both livings until his death in 1803. During his forty-year ministry he was confined to his room for long periods due to illness; during one of these bouts he composed and circulated among his parishioners the poem 'The Sick Minster's Short But Affectionate Address to His People'.

It is not clear how the friendship between the Whalley and Travell families came about, but Ferdinando Travell was at Oxford (Wadham) at the same time as Palmer Whalley (Lincoln), and they were of the same age, so it may be assumed that this was the foundation.

Palmer Whalley married, at St Mary Le Wigford, Lincoln, 1766, Mary Gardner (1738-1804); they had at least 2 sons and 2 daughters:

1 John Palmer (b. 1767)
1 Mary (1771-1776)
2 Thomas (1775-1830)
2 Elizabeth (b. 1782)

Following the Northamptonshire visit, the Ecton Whalleys do not appear again in the Witts family papers. The family belongs more to the index of the diaries of Agnes Witts, *The Complete Diary of a Cotswold Lady*, but has been included here for the sake of completeness.

WHALLEY — the Whalley family of Kington, Herefordshire [105]

It is not known if there was a connection between the Whalley families of Ecton and Kington, but probably not as the Kington branch hailed from Lancashire. However, hints of a connection are to be found here and there.

William Whalley (±1737-1795), Church of England clergyman, was the son of Giles Whalley, gauger, of Ashton-in-Mackerfield, Lancashire. He was educated at Manchester School and Brasenose College, Oxford (BA 1739; MA 1762). He was appointed headmaster of Kington Grammar School, Herefordshire, in 1766, and held the office until 1792, when he was presented by the earl of Oxford to the rectory of Presteign in the same county. Whalley died there in 1795. He married Katherine, and had at least 3 sons and 1 daughter:

1 William Morgan (1772-1846); *see below*
2 Charles (1774-1812); *see below*
1 Catherine (b. ±1777)
3 Frederick (1780-1864); *see below*

There is a letter held at the Gloucestershire Archives, dated 1774, from William Whalley, of Kington, to his 'best friend' Revd Ferdinando Tracy Travell of Upper Slaughter. It contains, among general gossip, a reference to subscriptions for a county infirmary. It is very likely that this friendship was what brought Charles Whalley to Stow-on-the-Wold and William Morgan Whalley to his curacy at Swerford, which then led to intimacy with Ferdinando's widowed daughter Martha.

The dates of William Morgan Whalley's ordination as deacon and priest are not given in the Church of England database, and it is not known when Ferdinando Travell appointed him as his curate at Swerford, although it was probably after Whalley's graduation in 1795. A rare surviving letter from Edward Witts to his sister, Apphia, Lady Lyttelton, dated 16 February 1796, provides a little further information:

> ... perhaps you have already heard from Mrs. A. Travell of the intended match (or perhaps it is by this time completed)—of Mrs. Buxton ... to the eldest Son of Mr. Whalley an old fellow Collegian of Mr. Stone's at Wadham.—she had certainly known him many years, even from Childhood—& at midsummer last or Michaelmas, he was ordained, and made Curate to Mr. Travell at Slaughter—we hear he is amiable & Sensible—which is all she has to depend upon—, as he can have but little knowledge of the world, and certainly no fortune—as his father had but few years enjoyment of a good Living, given him by Lord Oxford: & a large family & wife to provide for—he is probably ten years younger—they are still to live on with her Father who makes no objection to this Match—which compleats the fourth in his family—all equally surprising to their friends and Relations.

More information follows under the entry for William Morgan Whalley.

WHALLEY — Charles Whalley — *see also* Horne [106]

Charles Whalley (1774-1812), solicitor at Stow-on-the-Wold, was the second son of William Whalley (±1737-1795), of Kington, Herefordshire, and his wife, Katherine (*above*). He was brother to William Morgan and Frederick (*below*). He married Sarah Lewis, and had at least 3 sons and 3 daughters:

1 Unknown daughter
1 Henry (b. 1801)
2 Arthur Charles (b. 1802); educated at Pembroke College, Oxford (BA 1824); married, at Bath, 10 September 1842, Anne Georgina, second daughter of the late Maj. Audain of the 16th Regt
2 Louisa Marianne (1803-±1847); married, 1834, James Thomas Horne of Cumberland Street, Portman Square, Westminster (*see below*); at least 4 sons:
    1 Edward Lewis (±1838-1870), Church of England clergyman; educated at Exeter College, Oxford; appointed curate of Great Marlow, Buckinghamshire; died at Great Marlow
    2 Charles James (1839-1910), Lt-Col, Bedfordshire Regt (1892); married, at Rostrevor, co. Down, Ireland, 18 April 1882, Elizabeth Douglas Stewart (1841-1918); died at Elidor, Weymouth, Dorset; children unknown
    3 Frederick Elidor (±1842-1867), Church of England clergyman; educated at Rugby School and Exeter College, Oxford; appointed curate of Hambledon, Buckinghamshire; died at Brighton
    4 Henry Edward St John (1846-1871); educated at Rugby School and Exeter College, Oxford; died at Lewes, Sussex
3 Sarah Marianne (1804-1893); married, at Old Radnor, Radnorshire, 25 January 1830, Frederick William Whinyates (1793-1881); 5 sons and 3 daughters:
    1 Harriet (d. 1830)
    1 Frederick Thomas (1833-1915)
    2 Edward Henry (b. 1835)
    3 Albert William Orme (1841-1878)
    2 Amy Octavia (1843)
    4 Charles Elidor (1846-1872)
    3 Emily Marianne (dates unknown)
    5 Francis Arthur (dates unknown)
3 Frederick Elidor (1811-1830), Cornet, 6th Regt of Light Cavalry, Bengal; died at Bengal

Ferdinando Travell's friendship with William Whalley was instrumental in bringing Charles Whalley to Stow-on-the-Wold, but there was also a connection with the Horne family. William Horne, along with Revd John Dolphin, John West, and Anne Travell, is listed in a deed of 1813 as one of the remaining trustees of a marriage settlement going back some time. This William Horne was probably the distinguished barrister and politician Sir William Horne (1773-1860), born at Hereford, the second son of Revd Thomas Horne (d. 1824) and Frances Ann Price of Weobley, Herefordshire. His father kept a private school called Manor House, in Chiswick, where Lord Lyndhurst was educated; after attending this school, William was admitted at Lincoln's Inn on 3 June 1793 and called to the bar on 23 June 1798. Horne practised at the chancery bar, and was a commissioner of bankrupts from 1807 to 1818. In 1812 he was elected MP for Helston, Cornwall, and in 1818, having lost his seat in the Commons, he became a king's counsel. This was followed by his appointment on 6 November 1818 as a bencher of his inn. When Brougham became lord chancellor, Horne was appointed law officer to assist him in the court of chancery. He became solicitor-general on 26 November 1830, and was knighted in the same year.

Horne married, 12 August 1799, Ann (d. 1823), daughter of James Hesse, of Bedfordshire; they had at least 4 sons and 3 daughters. After Ann's death he married secondly, at Marylebone, 17 May 1825, Ann Davison (d. 1849), widow of Henry Davison of Ponfield, Hertfordshire. They had 1 son and 1 daughter. As can be seen above, Charles Whalley's daughter Louisa Marianne married James Thomas Horne, son of Edward Horne and nephew of Sir William.

In another, more remote, connection, Frances Eeles, Ferdinando Travell's great female companion (their actual relationship may only be guessed at), lived at 14 Great Cumberland Street, the same street in which Edward Horne resided.

While still a young man, Charles Whalley left Stow-on-the-Wold and took a position with the HEIC in India. He was sheriff of Calcutta in 1809-10, and died at Calcutta in June 1812.

1803: 7 Aug: *Heard from Ch. Whalley & answered him.* 3 Dec.

1804: 13 Feb: *Heard from my parents & wrote to C. Whalley.*

1805: 8 Aug: *Wrote to Mrs. Travell Mr. B.P. Witts & Mr. C. Whalley.* 12 Aug: *Had great difficulty in learning tidings of Mr. C. Whalley.* 3 Aug: ... *another fruitless search after C. Whalley with my Father.* 22 Aug: *Wrote to C. Whalley.* 30 Aug: *Wrote to C. Whalley.*

1807: 10 Mar: *Heard from Ch. Whalley.*

1823: 7 Apr: ... *I passed the remainder of the day & slept at my Mother's. My Aunt Travell, & her inmate Miss Louisa Whalley, came to tea.*

1823: 9 Jul: *Called at the Comptrollers of Army Account's Office in Whitehall, to see my relation Miss Buxton, who resides in the Official residence of her brother-in-law, Mr. Fred. Whalley, Secretary of that department. Found both Mr. F. W. & Miss Buxton at home ... I dined at Whitehall with Miss Buxton and Mr. Fred. Whalley ... A Henry Whalley was also of the party: he is son of the late Mr. C. Whalley, a solicitor, formerly of Stow, and afterwards in India, where he died, who was brother to Mr. W. Whalley, Fred. Whalley etc. This young man is a Clerk in the Comptroller's Office, & acts as secretary to his uncle Frankland Lewis M.P. who is a member of a Commission for the investigation of certain departments of government in Scotland & Ireland.* 14 Jul: ... *I called on my aunt Mrs. Travell. I found with her my cousin Mrs. Whalley, Mr. Whalley's unmarried sister, and Miss Louisa Whalley, daughter of the late Mr. C. Whalley.* 10 Sep: *We left home on a visit of a few days to my Aunt Mrs. Travell at Cheltenham, where we found staying with her Mrs. Whalley & Miss Marianne Whalley, a daughter of the late Mr. C. Whalley.* 2 Oct: ... *where we found the Miss Guydickens's on a visit as also Mrs. Whalley & Miss M. Whalley still inmates.*

1825: 15 Jan: *We dined at Mrs. Travell's, meeting her inmate Mrs. Whalley, and one of the late Charles Whalley's sons, a schoolboy.*

1826: 7 Feb.

WHALLEY — Ferdinand William Whalley [107]

Ferdinand William Whalley (1799-1875), landed proprietor, was the eldest son of William Morgan Whalley (1772-1846) and Martha Buxton, née Travell (1764-1839). He was educated at St Mary Hall, Oxford. He was said to have had a 'weak mind', but what this meant is unknown. He married, at St Mary the Virgin, Oxford, 25 June 1840, Harriet (±1800-1848), of Littlemore, Oxford, the fourth daughter of Betsey Thorpe, widow, of Littlemore. In the 1851 census Whalley was listed as a landed proprietor, fund holder, and widower, living in the Dyer Ward, presumably Dyer Street, Cirencester.

1839: 24 Jun: *Took luncheon at the Wallers. From Miss Rollinson heard many particulars as to the last illness of our Cousin, Mrs. Whalley, and respecting her family ... Ferdinand Whalley, the unfortunate eldest of the family, unfortunate both in mind and body, has signified his intention of ceasing to reside with his family, and by so doing, and selecting not an unsuitable house, has released his brother and sisters from much unpleasant responsibility. He has made his election to take up his abode at Sandford, in Oxfordshire, with the widow and daughter of a Clergyman, named Thorpe, formerly Curate of Hook-norton, and afterwards Incumbent of Sandford, decent people, in humble circumstances.*

1850: 20 Nov: *Recd. a letter from Ferdinand W. Whalley, now a resident at Cirencester, who is about to invest money in the purchase of a government annuity, and therefore requires an extract of my parish register, to show the date of his baptism according to a form prescribed in the Government Annuity office.*

WHALLEY — Frederick Whalley [108]

Frederick Whalley (1780-1864), secretary at the comptroller's office, Whitehall, was born at Kington, Herefordshire, the third son of William Whalley (±1737-1795) and his wife, Katherine. He was brother to Charles (*above*) and William Morgan (*below*). In 1811 Whalley was assistant secretary at the comptroller's office, Whitehall, but by 1822 he had been promoted to secretary in the department for general business. He married, March 1809, Martha Buxton (1787-1819), and lived at Park Street, Grosvenor Square, Westminster. Frederick and Martha had 2 sons:

1 Frederick William Charles Buxton (1811-1881); *see below*

2 James Park (1817-1911), Church of England clergyman; educated at Rugby School and University College, Oxford (BA 1839); appointed rector of East and West Wretham, Norfolk, and diocesan inspector of schools; married, 12 September 1850, Agnes Ellen Birch (1824-1910); 4 sons and 2 daughters:

  1 Frederick James (b. 1851), army officer; educated at Sandhurst; entered service in the 8th Regt of Foot, 1872; served in Afghanistan, 1877-80; married, at St Peter's, Cranley Gardens, Kensington, 21 July 1881, Isabella Sarah Burnett (b. 1860)

  2 Robert Seymour (1852-1903); married, at Oakhill, Somerset, 10 July 1884, Constance Margaret Strachey (1863-1935); at least 1 son:

    1 Frederick Seymour (1885-1958)

  1 Margaret Agnes Katharine (1853-1873)

  3 Laurence Travell (1854-1907), barrister-at-law of Lincoln's Inn and later estate agent at Capel, Dorking, Surrey; married Isabel Henrietta Napier (1863-1945); at least 1 son and 1 daughter:

    1 James (1898-1907)

    1 Flora (b. 1899)

  2 Beatrice Jane (1856-1944)

  4 Pryor Buxton (1858-1943), Church of England clergyman; seems to have died unmarried

Frederick Whalley married secondly, at Cheltenham, 19 August 1835, Anne (1790-1857), daughter of the late John Foote of Lee, Kent. In the 1851 census, Whalley was recorded as living at Moorfield, Clevedon, Somerset, with his maiden sister, Catherine, his wife, Anne, and his unmarried sister-in-law, Mary Foote (b. ±1791). In 1861 he lived with his sister Catherine and eldest son Frederick William Charles Buxton, barrister-at-law, who was not practising at the time.

1801: 29 May: *I had the pleasure of meeting Mr. Mills & Lieut. Falconer; Mr. & Mrs. Browne &c & Mr. F. Whalley were also there.*

1822: 20 Dec: *We called this morning on my Aunt, Mrs. Travell ... With her is a nephew of hers, a sweet child, youngest Son of her late sister Mrs. F. Whalley. Miss Buxton together with her Brother-in-law, Mr. F. Whalley, who is Secretary to the Comptroller's Office ...*

1823: 9 Jul: *Called at the Comptrollers of Army Account's Office in Whitehall, to see my relation Miss Buxton, who resides in the Official residence of her brother-in-law, Mr. Fred. Whalley, Secretary of that department. Found both Mr. F. W. & Miss Buxton at home ... I dined at Whitehall with Miss Buxton and Mr. Fred. Whalley ... meeting M. W. Whalley, a young man, who has been educated at Westminster School & Christ Church and is intended for the church. He is second son of my cousin, Mrs. Whalley, the Mother of Miss Buxton, by her second husband, the Revd. W. M. Whalley, incumbent of Waltham Abbey, but resident on his wife's estate, at Swerford, Oxfordshire, the old family property of the Travells, which she inherited on the decease of my Uncle & predecessor in the living of Upper Slaughter, F. T. Travell, my Mother's brother. A Henry Whalley was also of the party: he is son of the late Mr. C. Whalley, a solicitor, formerly of Stow, and afterwards in India, where he died, who was brother to Mr. W. Whalley, Fred. Whalley etc. This young man is a Clerk in the Comptroller's Office, & acts as secretary to his uncle Frankland Lewis M. P. who is a member of a Commission for the investigation of certain departments of government in Scotland & Ireland.*

1825: 25 Jan: ... *besides Mrs. Whalley we met Mrs. Charles Whalley and her two agreeable daughters; also her eldest Son, Mr. Henry Whalley, who is a clerk in the Comptroller's Office, Whitehall, of which his Uncle Frederick is the Secretary, & also acts as private Secretary to another Uncle, Mr. Frankland Lewis, who is at the head of an important commission ...*

1826: 9 Jan: *We sat for an hour or two at Mrs. Travell's, who is very tolerably well. Mrs. Whalley, Miss Buxton & her little nephew & charge, James Whalley, are her present guests.* 7-8 Feb.

WHALLEY — Frederick William Charles Buxton Whalley [109]

Frederick William Charles Buxton Whalley (1811-1881), barrister-at-law, was the eldest son of Frederick Whalley (1781-1864) and Martha Buxton (1787-1819) (*above*). He was educated at Westminster School, Christ Church, Oxford (BA 1833), and Lincoln's Inn (1842). At the latter he was registered as William Buxton Whalley. He married, at Cheltenham, 27 June 1845, Frances Augusta Caroline (1816-1898), only child of of Maj. William Medows Hammerton of Hammerton, Tipperary. Little is known of Frederick William's life. At the time of the 1861 census he was staying with his father at Clevedon, Somerset, a barrister but not in practice. He later lived at Clifton, and then at 5 Grosvenor Place, Bath, and finally at 46 Queen's Gate Terrace, South Kensington, where he died. Probate was granted to his brother James Park Whalley and to his barrister nephew, Laurence Travell Whalley. At his death he left £11,834 19*s* 3*d*.

1826: 8 Feb: *The funeral took place between 9 & 10 o clock A.M. At an early hour, by the Mail from London, Mr. Frederick Whalley, & his eldest Son, a fine Westminster Schoolboy of 15, arrived ...*

WHALLEY — Martha Whalley [110]

Martha Whalley, née Travell (1764-1839), was the eldest of the two daughters of Ferdinando Tracy Travell (1740-1808) and Martha Rollinson (1741-1780). She married, first, John Buxton (1756-1790); they had 1 son and 3 daughters:

1 Harriett (b. & d. 1785)
1 George (b. & d. 1786)
2 Martha (1787-1819); married, March 1809, Frederick Whalley (1780-1864) (*above*), her step-father's younger brother
3 Jane (1789-1835); died unmarried

Martha married secondly, 1795, William Morgan Whalley (1772-1846) (*below*); 2 sons and 3 daughters:

1 Harriet (1797-1872); died unmarried; *see below*
1 Ferdinand (1799-1875); *see below*
2 William (1801-1871); *see below*
2 Maria (1802-1873); *see below*
3 Frances (1804-1866); died unmarried; *see below*

William and Martha later became estranged, and he acquired the incumbency of Waltham Abbey. Only basic details are known regarding their three daughters. Harriet (1797-1872), the eldest, remained unmarried. In the 1841 census she was at Swerford, and in 1851 she was recorded visiting her cousin Jane Naper at Moccas, Herefordshire. She was still resident at Moccas in 1861, eight years after Jane's death. Harriet died at Cirencester, where she had been living at 4 Chesterton Terrace, just four doors away from her brother William, rector of Toddington, and also near to her brother Ferdinand. Maria (1802-1873) married, 1841, Edward Bowly (1808-1882), brewer, of Siddington, the son of Samuel and Sarah Bowly. Edward was a widower; he had married first, at the Quaker meeting house in Nailsworth, 1832, Susannah Wilkins (±1802-1840). Frances Anne (1804-1866) remained unmarried. In both the 1851 and 1861 censuses she was registered as living with her sister and brother-in-law at Siddington.

The events of 8 February 1826 poisoned the relationship between Francis Witts and his cousin Martha Whalley. Francis had not only been outmanoeuvred on the very substantial sum left by his aunt, but to his chagrin he also discovered that the relatively modest sum (in the circumstances) of £400 [about £39,000 in 2019 values], in the form of a bond borrowed for his mother's use, still stood against him and was not going to be written off. The result was a family schism that never fully healed. It was not until 1846—twenty years after the break—that some semblance of normality returned, with civil exchanges between Martha's unfortunate son, William, and Francis and Edward Witts.

It is not known what lay behind Martha's behaviour, but it may be assumed that there was resentment in the Whalley household that Francis's mother, Agnes, had previously outmanoeuvred them in regard to the living of Upper Slaughter, and that this was a form of pay-back.

1802: 1 Jan: *Breakfasted with Mrs. Whalley at the Centre House in Albermarle Row, having first walked by Hopesquare & Granby Row, to Princes Buildings, which is reckoned the best situation in Bristol Hotwells, & from the back Rooms of which a beautiful view of St. Vincents Rock & the Country beyond Bristol is commanded ... At Mrs. W. Whalley's was her Mother, & the two Miss Buxtons, the elder of whom is in better Health.*

1803: 2 Aug: *Wrote to Mrs. Whalley.*

1805: 23 Mar: *Walked with Mrs. Travell & Martha Buxton to my Father's very pretty old place of his own creation Swerford Park, the most romantic Dell, I have seen in Oxfordshire; now occupied by a Mr. & Mrs. Chinner, people unworthy of so nice a place. Our dinner party besides my Uncle & Aunt consisted of Mrs. Whalley & Martha & Jane Buxton.* 26 Mar., 5-6 Jul.

1823: 10 Sep., 2 Oct., 23 Dec: *I called on Mrs. Travell & Mrs. Whalley ...*

1824: 24 Jul: *My two cousins Maria & Fanny Whalley, the younger daughters of Mrs. Whalley, two very pleasing and amiable young women of twenty and twenty two years of age, came on a visit to us ...* 29 Jul.

1825: 7 Jan: *I dined with my Aunt Travell, meeting Mrs. Whalley and her son William.* 15 Jan., 25 Jan., 31 Jan., 11 Apr., 19 May: *We found with her the two younger ladies of the Whalley family, Maria & Fanny, most pleasing, well informed, and interesting persons.* 21 May, 8 Jun: ... *Maria & Fanny Whalley are still her guests.* 11 Jul., 15 Jul., 5 Aug: *Mrs. Whalley is now her only guest. Her daughters returned to Swerford on Tuesday: the elder, Maria, after a decided attack of smallpox ...* 17 Oct: *Maria Whalley was her inmate.* 17 Nov.

1826: 9 Jan., 2 Feb: *Soon after breakfast I received a letter begun by Mrs. Whalley and concluded by Miss Buxton containing an alarming account of my Aunt Travell's state ... To her niece, my cousin, Mrs. Whalley, my Aunt had a very warm attachment, as also to all her family ...* 7 Feb., 8 Feb: ... *nearly everything is left to Mrs. Whalley and her children by her second husband. The amount of the property I cannot exactly say; perhaps, £8000 or £9000.... The excuse alledged is the very impoverished state of Mrs. Whalley and her family, which is much worse than I ever supposed, and this, doubtless, was placed in so strong a light, that my aunt fancied, it was a duty to reinstate them as far as she could: forgetting, that their own imprudence had thus reduced their ample means ... I had borrowed of her £400 some years ago, which I shall now have to repay to her Executors, Mrs. Whalley's two children, Miss Buxton & Mr. W. Whalley. But this is not all; when my poor father and mother furnished the house, which my Mother occupied during her latter years, she advanced them a like sum, for which I gave my security, my aunt saying, it did not matter to her; provided the interest was paid during her life, as she should not want the principal afterwards; and yet the bond, I then gave, stands in force against me ...* 11 Feb: *We stopped at Cheltenham long enough to call on the Whalley family. We judged, that Christian charity required this visit at our hands. Mrs. Whalley did not appear; she either was too ill to come down, or said, she was ... The bond for £400—borrowed for my Mother's use, should have been cancelled by them, after the explanation, which I gave them on Wednesday. But they have chosen their part.*

1835: 1 Apr: *A letter awaited me from Miss Rollinson to announce the decease of my amiable cousin, Miss Buxton... To her Mother, Mrs. Whalley, her loss will be irreparable.*

1838: 8 Oct: *We did not meet any of the Whalley family, but thought we saw two of the ladies in the grounds.*

1839: 14 Jun: *Recd. a letter from my cousin Wm. Whalley, announcing the decease of his Mother at her house in Bath on the 13th. Inst. Few particulars are told, save that the case was hopeless from the commencement of the attack a fortnight before ... She was a clever, selfish, woman—at variance with a strange, weak, worthless, second husband, whom, much younger than herself, and without fortune, she married to please herself, and from whom though the father of five children, she at last found it absolutely necessary to separate ... always in feeble health, but like a cracked pitcher lasting longer than many a utensil without a flaw ...* 24 Jun: *Took luncheon at the Wallers. From Miss Rollinson heard many particulars as to the last illness of our Cousin, Mrs. Whalley, and respecting her family. She was about 70 years of age, and all her children attended her death bed, with the exception, I believe, of her eldest son, Ferdinand. Her husband was not present, nor had they, I presume, met for many years. Yet Mrs. Whalley, by her will, showed that she entertained no unforgiving temper towards him, as she has left him for his life about £100 per ann., as much as she had at her disposal.*

1843: 4 Oct: *Met Mr. W. Whalley and his sister Harriet with two ladies going to see the mansion-house at Stanway, the ruins of Hayles Abbey &c.*

1848: 24 Aug: ... *near the village of Siddington, and passed along it in the direction for Cricklade, having on our right the residence of Mr. Bowly, a gentleman who married, to his second wife, my cousin Maria Whalley ...*

WHALLEY — Thomas Sedgwick Whalley[111]

Thomas Sedgwick Whalley (1746-1828), Church of England clergyman, poet, and traveller, was born at Cambridge, the third son of John Whalley, master of Peterhouse College, and his wife, the only child of Francis Squire, canon and chancellor of Wells Cathedral. His mother died at Winscombe Court, Somerset, in 1803, aged 96. Whalley was educated at St John's College, Cambridge (BA 1767; MA 1774), and was appointed rector of Hagworthingham, Lincolnshire, in 1772. For over fifty years the duties were discharged by a curate. Whalley was canon of Wells from 1777 to 1826.

Thomas Whalley married, 1774, Elizabeth (d. 1801), only child of Edward Jones, of Langford Court, Somerset, and widow of John Withers Sherwood. The marriage brought Whalley a great fortune and the estate at Langford Court. In about 1776 Whalley purchased the centre house in the Crescent at Bath (20 Royal Crescent), but he still spent his summers at Langford Court. Frances Burney described him in her diary as 'immensely tall, thin and handsome, but affected, delicate, and sentimentally pathetic'.

In the summer of 1783, for financial reasons, Whalley and his wife broke up their establishments in England and went abroad. Langford Court was let for many years and eventually sold in 1804. When he arrived in Paris Marie-Antoinette called him 'Le bel Anglais'. Whalley spent his springs and winters in southern France, Italy, Switzerland, and Belgium for a long period. He often spent the summer at Mendip Lodge [Langford Cottage], on the Mendip hills, built by Dr Whalley between 1787 and 1793, where the grounds had grottoes and terrace walks. Sarah Siddons visited him there.

Whalley was created DD of Edinburgh University on 10 July 1808. The next winter he bought a house in Baker Street, London, and for some years lived there in great style. After the peace of 1814 he went abroad again. On his return in 1818 he purchased the centre house in Portland Place, Bath, and in 1825 he bought the lease of a house at Clifton. He left England in 1828 for the last time. Whalley died of old age on 3 September 1828, a few weeks after his arrival at La Flèche in France.

1804: 10 Sep: ... *to Mr. Whalley's Mendip Lodge 14 Miles. Set out after an early breakfast, in two Sociables, & myself on horseback.*

WHALLEY — William Morgan Whalley — *see also* **Buxton** *and* **Travell**[112]

William Morgan Whalley (1772-1846), Church of England clergyman, was born on 30 December 1772, at Kington, Herefordshire, the eldest son of William Whalley (±1737-1795) and his wife, Katherine. He was educated at Queen's College, Oxford (BA 1795), and married, at Upper Slaughter, 1796, Martha Buxton, née Travell (1764-1839). They had 2 sons and 3 daughters. (*See above*, Martha Whalley.)

Whalley was the main legatee of his father-in-law, Ferdinando Tracy Travell, and inherited the property at Swerford, some of which he sold in 1817; he was still resident at Swerford in 1823. William became estranged from Martha, and at the same time he became the incumbent of Waltham Abbey, a living which for some reason, as yet undiscovered, was in the gift of Mrs Guydickens. It may have been how the family provided for a separation between the pair.

1804: 16 Mar: *Wrote to Mr. Whalley & Mr. Travell.* 19 Mar: *Wrote to Mr. Whalley.*

1805: 25 Mar: *Our dinner party was increased by the visiting & Mr. Whalley, who had returned from his Duty at Slaughter, a very fine handsome man.* 26 Mar., 5-6 Jul.

1839: 24 Jun: *Took luncheon at the Wallers. From Miss Rollinson heard many particulars as to the last illness of our Cousin, Mrs. Whalley ... Yet Mrs. Whalley, by her will, showed that she entertained no unforgiving temper towards him, as she has left him for his life about £100 per ann., as much as she had at her disposal. It appears, which I did not know before, that he has for some time been residing with his maiden sister at Hereford.*

1844: 8 Dec: *A letter from Mr. Aplin, Solicitor, Banbury, requesting extracts from my parish register as to the births, marriages and deaths of the Travell and Whalley families, so that a pedigree may be deduced to complete a title for the sale of a part of the Swerford Estate.* 10 Dec., 17 Dec.

1845: 17 Jan.

1846: 24 Jun: *Received a letter from Mrs. Guydickens containing an offer to my son of the Perpetual Curacy of Waltham Abbey, Essex, vacant by the death of W. M. Whalley.*

WHALLEY — William Whalley [113]

William Whalley (1801-1871), Church of England clergyman, was the second son of William Morgan Whalley (1772-1846) and Martha Buxton, née Travell (1764-1839). He was educated at Westminster School and Christ Church, Oxford (BA 1823; MA 1830). He was appointed curate of Swerford, Oxfordshire, in 1824, and served as vicar of Toddington and Didbrook, Gloucestershire, from 1843 to his death in 1871. William married, at Walcot, Bath, 9 June 1846, Mary Frances (1812-1850), daughter of Revd John Sikes Sawbridge (1765-1836), rector of Welford, Berkshire, and Frances Jane Framingham Thruston (1778-1837); they had 2 daughters:

1 Mary Frances (1849-1903); lived at Watermoor Road, Cirencester; died unmarried
2 Laura Helen (b. & d. 1850)

In the 1871 census William was listed as living at Cotswold Lodge, Cirencester, with his unmarried daughter, Mary.

1823: 9 Jul: *Called at the Comptrollers of Army Account's Office in Whitehall, to see my relation Miss Buxton, who resides in the Official residence of her brother-in-law, Mr. Fred. Whalley, Secretary of that department. Found both Mr. F. W. & Miss Buxton at home ... I dined at Whitehall with Miss Buxton and Mr. Fred. Whalley ... meeting M. W. Whalley, a young man, who has been educated at Westminster School & Christ Church and is intended for the church. He is second son of my cousin, Mrs. Whalley, the Mother of Miss Buxton, by her second husband, the Revd. W. M. Whalley, incumbent of Waltham Abbey, but resident on his wife's estate, at Swerford, Oxfordshire, the old family property of the Travells, which she inherited on the decease of my Uncle & predecessor in the living of Upper Slaughter, F. T. Travell, my Mother's brother.*

1825: 7 Jan: *I dined with my Aunt Travell, meeting Mrs. Whalley and her son William.* 18 Jan: *William Whalley, arrived from Swerford to breakfast at nine o clock, but it was half past 10 AM. before we could reach the Church.*

1826: 7-8 Feb., 11 Feb: *W. Whalley was in the act of setting out for Swerford, and our arrival did not detain him even for a few minutes.*

1839: 14 Jun: *Recd. a letter from my cousin Wm. Whalley, announcing the decease of his Mother at her house in Bath on the 13th. Inst.* 16 Jun., 24 Jun: *Took luncheon at the Wallers. From Miss Rollinson heard many particulars as to the last illness of our Cousin, Mrs. Whalley, and respecting her family ... I was also in the dark as to the residence of William Whalley, the Son, who, it seems, is Curate of Siddington, near Cirencester. He took the Curacy under the understanding that his engagement would not exceed a twelvemonth, at the expiration of which term the Rector, the Hon. & Revd. C Bathurst, brother of Earl Bathurst, was expected to return, his absence being occasioned by ill-health; but as the indisposition is protracted, so the Curacy may, probably, be held longer by W. Whalley.*

1843: 10 Jan: *Lord Sudeley has presented the benefice with its appendages, Didbrook, Hayles, Stanley Pontlarge, to my cousin, William Whalley ...* 4 Oct: *Met Mr. W. Whalley and his sister Harriet with two ladies going to see the mansion-house at Stanway, the ruins of Hayles Abbey &c.*

1844: 21 Feb., 16 Nov: *I walked to and from Didbrook, and inspected the new parsonage almost completed there at the expence of Mr. W. Whalley, the Vicar of Toddington and Didbrook.*

1846: 24 Jun: *I recommended E.F.W. to make enquiry of his neighbour, William Whalley, who is likely to know the facts as to a piece of preferment so long held by his father.* 20 Jul: *Mr. and Mrs. William Whalley called, while we were at the Vicarage. He took to himself a wife, a Miss Sawbridge, while we were in the Isle of Wight: the lady is lady-like, of a suitable age, a Clergyman's daughter; we had made her acquaintance before, when she was a visitor of Mr. Francis, both at Upper Slaughter and Stanway.* 30 Oct: *... the loving and cheerful party were increased by the accession of Mr. and Mrs. W. Whalley from Toddington.*

1847: 2 Mar: *Took a walk with our dear children to Didbrook, where met and parlayed with Mr. & Mrs. Wm. Whalley.*

1850: 26 Mar: *... but the melancholy news announced of the death of Mrs. Whalley, at Toddington, on Saturday last after a premature confinement, the Infant having also died. W. Whalley better in health and spirits than he has lately been, but much overpowered: the case very pitiable; a marriage of a very few years standing; one little girl survives; the husband nervous and of uncertain health; death coming hastily, soon after the husband and wife had removed into a handsome new house provided for the Vicar by his patron, Lord Sudeley ...* 16 Sep. *... His brother, Wm. Whalley, having returned for a short time to Toddington, where he has placed a Curate, has again left that place, in a very shattered state of spirits, and, I am told, being quite unequal to exertion, is also temporarily resident with the Bowly's at Siddington.*

1851: 4 Feb: *The report of Mr. Whalley's state is unfavourable: he is depressed in spirits, nervous, and hypochondriac, residing at the new house assigned to him by Lord Sudeley, as Vicar of Toddington, with a Curate, who has been engaged for a limited term.*

1852: 2 Nov: *With E.F.W. and Sophy drove to call on Mr. Whalley at Toddington. He was gone on a visit to his sister, Mrs. Bowly, at Siddington—The house occupied by him is not the parsonage, but a new and handsome brick building in antique style, lately erected by Lord Sudeley, himself a very skilful architect. It is adjacent to the village, to the mansion house, and to the Church, but dark and damp, as embosomed in lofty elms, and not far from a sluggish brook. The house is exceedingly commodious, well arranged, & finished in the best manner; may, perhaps, hereafter become the residence of some member of Lord Sudeley's family; Whalley is about to leave it as too large for his solitary state, returning to the old parsonage—W. is a shaken infirm, prematurely old man, fond of reading, but inactive, not disposed to make himself useful, or to adorn his profession; disappointed, dejected and helpless, having lost his wife, and being without energy.*

WHATELY — Thomas Whately [114]

Thomas Whately (1773-1864), Church of England clergyman, was born at Ware, Hertfordshire, the son of Joseph Whately (1730-1797) and Jane Plumer (1740-1821). He was educated at Christ's College, Cambridge (BA 1795; MA 1800), and was appointed vicar of Cookham, Berkshire, on 1 May 1797. He served the Cookham parish until 1837, when he became rector of Chetwynd, Shropshire. He held the Chetwynd living until his death in 1864. Whately married, 12 January 1813, Isabella Sophia, second daughter of Sir William Weller Pepys, 1st baronet (1741-1825), and Elizabeth Dowdeswell (1756-1830); they had 6 sons and 2 daughters:

1 William Walter (1814-1817)
2 Charles (1815-1895)
1 Sophia Jane (1817-1899)

3 William Joseph (1818-1909)
2 Elizabeth Rachel (1820-1879)
4 Henry Thomas (1822-1879), Church of England clergyman
5 George Hamilton (1824-1864)
6 Arthur Pepys (1829-1909)

1825: 3 Jul: ... *there is an unfortunate coolness between the Vicar of the latter parish and my Uncle* ...

1827: 17 Nov: *Whately, the Vicar of Cookham, met us at the entrance of the Church Yard, and performed the service without much earnestness or devotion; yet the fault was, I believe, in the manner only, and indicated a nervousness habitual to the man, probably, constitutional.* 18 Nov.

1832: 14 Jun.

WHEATON — Anne Wheaton of Swerford

1805: 25 Mar: *Our party early interrupted by the arrival of Miss Anne Wheaton & her dear Champion, Mr. John Newton, in an Equipage fifty years old at least, in every part a great entertainment to us young people, who were more inclined to laugh at than to admire the Spinster & her favourite.*

WHEELER — George Domvile Wheeler [115]

George Domvile Wheeler (1816-1890), Church of England clergyman, was born at Walcot, Bath, the son of Revd George Wheeler (1777-1838), curate of Shipton Moyne, and Margaret Domvile. He was educated at Redlands School, Bristol, and matriculated at Oriel College, Oxford, in 1832. He migrated to Wadham College (BA 1836; MA 1841), where he was a fellow from 1841 to 1843. Wheeler was ordained deacon in 1839, and his first clerical appointment was as curate of Blockley, Gloucestershire. He was later appointed vicar of Great Wolford, Worcestershire, in 1843, and rector of Barcheston in 1846. He was a JP for Gloucestershire and Worcestershire, and appointed honorary canon of Worcester Cathedral in 1875 and rural dean of South Kineton in 1888. Wheeler married, 1843, Charlotte Emily (d. 1851), third daughter of Adm. Bateman; they had 1 surviving daughter:

1 Margaret Lucy Jane (1846-1920); died unmarried at Bourton-on-the-Water

He married secondly, 1857, Sarah Ann (1826-1909), daughter of Capt. Chetwynd; they had at least 3 sons and 2 daughters:

1 Emilie Annie (1862-1918); died unmarried at Bourton-on-the-Water
1 George Domvile Chetwynd (1858-1947), Church of England clergyman, lepidopterist, and author of *The Butterflies of Switzerland and the Alps of Central Europe*
2 William Charles Edmund (b. 1859)
3 Walter Compton (1861-1920), Church of England clergyman
2 Agnes Eva (1864-1865); died an infant

Wheeler was a prominent and well-loved personage at Great Wolford for almost fifty years. On his death in April 1890, the *Evesham Journal* reported as follows:

> When it became known that the Vicar was no more, there were universal expressions of sorrow amongst the parishioners, and in all parts of the village signs of mourning were to be observed. Not only was this so at Great Wolford, but in the parishes where the late canon was almost as well known and as much respected as he was at home.

1845: 13 Feb: *My fellow travellers were Messrs. Perkins, Debary, Wheeler (Wadh. Coll) Rector of Gt. Wolford.*

WHEELER — William Wheeler [116]

William Wheeler (b. 1808), Church of England clergyman and later convert to Rome, was the eldest son of William Wheeler of Hurley, Berkshire. He was educated at Magdalen College, Oxford (BA 1827; MA 1830; BD 1838), where he was a fellow from 1836 to 1843. He was rector of Old and New Shoreham from 1843 until he became a Roman Catholic in 1855.

1843: 28 Aug: *The living is in the gift of Magdalen College, Oxford; was lately held by Mr. Biddulph, now by Mr. Wheeler: and, I believe, Old Shoreham church forms a part of the benefice: New Shoreham affording a very small proportion of the income* ...

WHELDALE — West Wheldale [117]

West Wheldale (1766-1828), Church of England clergyman, was born at Boston, Lincolnshire, the son of West Wheldale (d. 1788) and his wife, Ann (d. 1819). He was educated at Manchester School, Brasenose College, and Magdalen College, Oxford (BA 1790; MA 1792), and elected a fellow of Brasenose in 1791. Wheldale was ordained deacon on 19 September 1790 and priest on 25 March 1791. His first clerical appointment was as curate of Frampton, Lincolnshire, where he eventually became vicar in 1804. He was also appointed rector of Christ Church, Spitalfields, in 1804.

1804: 4 Mar: ... *to St. Peter's in the afternoon where Mr. Wheldale of Braznose preached.*

WHELER — Trevor Wheler [118]

Sir Trevor Wheler, 8th baronet (1763-1830), landed proprietor, was the son of Sir Charles Wheler, 7th baronet (1730-1821), and Lucy (1731-1800), daughter of Sir John Strange (1696-1754), master of the rolls, and Susanna Strong (1701-1747). He married, at Ashbourne, Derbyshire, 20 March 1792, Harriet (1771-1806), daughter of Richard Beresford (1731-1790) and Alice Garle (1739-1815); they had 2 sons and 5 daughters:

1 Trevor (1792-1869); succeeded as 9th baronet
1 Harriet (1794-1846)
2 Lucy (1796-1855)
3 Anna Marie (1797-1880)
4 Charlotte Theresa (1800-1867)
2 Francis J. Wheler (1801-1878), Maj.-Gen.; succeeded as 10th baronet
5 Agnes (1805-1879)

The family lived at Crakemarsh Hall, Uttoxeter.

1802: 20 Sep: ... *to Craiemarsh on the Uttoxeter road; an extremely beautiful country of six miles. Found Mr. & Mrs. Wheeler at home.* 8 Oct: *Rode with my Father to Mr. Wheeler's at Craiekmarsh where we dined meeting Mr. Cotton* ... 12-13 Oct.

1812: 5 Aug: *A mile farther is Crakemarsh situate in rich meadows among lofty trees. A mansion house and ornamented Cottage here both belong to Cotton Shepherd Esqr., the former is at present tenanted by Trevor Wheler Esqr. eldest Son of Sir Charles Wheler of Warwickshire, as Mr. Shepherd is eldest Son of Sir Thomas Shepherd of Bucks. Both these Gentlemen are remarkably pleasant hospitable men.... Two daughters of Mr. Wheler of Crakemarsh were also on a visit at Calwich. Mr. Cotton Shepherd & Mr. Wheler, both well known to me of old, were added to our dinner party.*

WHELON — William Whelon [119]

William Whelon (1822-1865), secretary to the North Western Railway Company, was born at Lancaster, the illegitimate son of

Jane Whelon. He married, at St Mary's, Lancaster, 23 January 1844, Ellen Holden (1819-1907); they had 3 sons and 3 daughters:

1 Elizabeth (b. 1845)
2 Lucy (b. 1846)
1 Charles Edmond (1850-1918)
2 William (1851-1891)
3 Alfred Westfield (1854-1935)
3 Mary Ellen (b. 1860)

Whelon held an important position in the North Western Railway, but some financial problem overwhelmed him and he committed suicide in May 1865.

> SHOCKING SUICIDE. The whole of of North Lancashire has been startled by the announcement of the suicide of Mr. William Whelon, a gentleman of high position, and carrying on business at Lancaster and Preston, through pecuniary difficulties and the fear of exposure. Mr. Whelon rose from a poor office boy to be the secretary of the Little North-Western Railway then he became a merchant and ...

1854: 10 Jul: *Received a letter from Mr. Whelon, Secretary to the North Western Railway, containing a draft in my favour from the Craven Bank for £18. 16. 8. being the half year's Interest due to me (less Income tax) on my loan to the Company of £800.*

WHIPPY — Benjamin John Whippy [120]

Benjamin John Whippy (1796-1868), landed proprietor, was born in London, the eldest son of Benjamin Whippy, of Peachley, Worcestershire, and Mary Fenner, née Godfrey, daughter of Thomas Godfrey and widow of Capt. Fenner. Benjamin was grandson of Thomas Whippy, of Bellbroughton, Worcestershire, and Esther Tristram. He married, 4 December 1828, Jane Susannah, born at Charlbury, the second daughter of Benjamin Holloway, of Lee Place, Oxfordshire, and Georgiana, daughter of Gen. Thomas Roberts. They lived at Lee Place, Charlbury, and do not appear to have had any children. Whippy was involved in the Lord Churchill's Club, a charitable society, as the manager of the Finstock branch and later as manager of the Charlbury branch.

1836: 27 Oct: ... *Mr. & Mrs. Whippy from Lea Place, Charlbury; Mr. & Mrs. James of Evenlode: Mr. and Mrs. Clarke of Compton; Mr. Hall of Batsford & his Son, Robert: Mr. Marriott, an Oxonian, Son of Genl. Marriott; there were others whose names have escaped me, or whom I did not know.*

WHISH — Martin Richard Whish [121]

Martin Richard Whish (1781-1852), Church of England clergyman, was born at Northwold, Norfolk, the son of Revd Richard Whish (1750-1810), rector of West Walton, Norfolk, and Philippa Sandys (1758-1851). He was educated at King's Lynn and Caius College, Cambridge (BA 1804; MA 1807), and entered the Church. Whish served as vicar of Bedminster, Bristol; prebendary of Salisbury, 1806-52; rector of St Mary Redcliffe, Bristol; perpetual curate of St Thomas, Bristol; and vicar of Abbott's Leigh, 1806-52. He married, at Alderley, Gloucestershire, 30 October 1810, Elizabeth (1784-1826), daughter of John Blagden [who took the name Hale] (1740-1808), and Anne Hale (1751-1814) of the ancient family of Hale of Alderley. Martin and Elizabeth had at least 1 son:

1 John Matthew Hale (1822-1891)

1826: 30 Mar: ... *and Mr. Whish, the Sheriff's Chaplain & Brother in law.... Mr. Whish, who married Miss Hale, is a man of considerable ability, as I am told, and resides at Barnwood near Gloucester: he is one of the Evangelical party and a Chaplain of Bishop Ryder.* 15 Jun.

1833: 17 Apr.

WHITBY — Thomas John Whitby [122]

Thomas John Whitby (1775-1844), coal merchant of Red Lion Wharf, Upper Thames Street, was the son of Thomas Whitby (1742-1813) and Ann Margaret Hasse (1753-1815). He lived at 68 Queen Street in the parish of St Martin Vintry, London. He was initially in business with his father, Thomas Whitby, in the firm Thomas Whitby and Co., before going into partnership with Luke Whitby (1784-1821). Their firm was called Thomas and Luke Whitby of 66 Queen Street, Cheapside. Luke had 4 sons, one of whom was Luke Falkener Whitby (1810-1885); it is unclear which Luke was in partnership, but it was probably the senior, born in 1784. It seems probable that after the death of Luke (senior) in 1821, the business began sliding away from under Thomas Whitby. He had, however, been a merchant on a considerable scale; on 30 May 1799 he was awarded the Freedom of the City of London.

1839: 12 Jul: ... *also from Mr. Hare, dated Lyme Regis, on matters connected with the Wadenhoe Trust, particularly as to Thos. Whitby's Mortgage: the man is become a Bankrupt, & it is questionable whether the property mortgaged, a wharf &c. on the Thames, in London, will, by its sale, realise the principal money lent, with the arrears of interest.* 19 Jul.

1846: 8 Jul: *Received a letter from Mr. Thornton, who approves of my suggestion that the business of Whitby's mortgage be left in the hands of Messrs. Cox and Williams ...*

1847: 15 Jun: *Recd. two letters from Mr. Hare on the interminable dispute as to Whitby's wharf ...*

WHITCOMBE — John Aubrey Whitcombe and Whitcombe & Helps, solicitors [123]

John Aubrey Whitcombe (1793-1872), solicitor, was the eldest son of Sir Samuel Whitcombe (1752-1816), of Hempsted Court, and Mary (1764-1843)(*below*), illegitimate daughter of Sir John Aubrey, 6th baronet. He married, at Barnwood, 1 November 1825, Julia (1802-1885), third daughter of David Walters of Barnwood House; they had 8 sons and 6 daughters:

1 John (b. 1826)
1 Louisa (1827-1895); married, at St Mark's, Gloucester, 20 December 1864, Theophilus Taylor (1823-1884)
2 John Henry (1829-1863); died at Greymouth, Grey, New Zealand
3 David Aubrey (1830-1832); died an infant
4 Thomas (1831-1841); died a child
2 Emily (1833-1834); died an infant
5 George (1834-1921); married, at Stroud, June 1859, Jessie Leckie Wilton (1836-1864)
6 William (1835-1850); died a child
3 Harriet Walters (1837-1848); died a child
4 Mary (1838-1852); died a child
5 Emma (1839-1927); died unmarried
6 Charlotte (1842-1868); died unmarried at Gloucester
7 Charles Edward (1845-1921); married, at Wentworth, Ontario, Canada, 22 May 1907, Gertrude Elizabeth Wilson (b. 1877)
8 Frederick (1846-1847); died an infant

John Whitcombe was a solicitor in his father's practice and took his articles in 1809. He later became the senior partner in

Whitcombe & Helps. In the 1851 and 1861 censuses the family was registered as living at Hillfield House, Kingsholm, Gloucester.

1828: 18 Mar: *We dined at Wotton, at Mrs. Hopkinson's.... We met Mr. Whitcombe, a Solicitor of Gloucester, & Chapter Clerk, a man of good abilities & information, his brother, whose adventures in Greece I have formerly mentioned ...* 19 Mar: *Mr. & Mrs. Whitcomb, & Mr. & Mrs. Seymour dined at Mrs. Hunts ...*

1829: 25 Sep.

1832: 28 Feb: *Engaged with Mr. Whitcombe, Solicitor, of Gloucester, and with Miss Hunts on business relating to the Executorship.* 30 Mar.

1835: 28 Mar., 1 Apr., 6-7 Apr., 14 Apr., 30 Apr., 3 May, 7 May, 5 Jun., 14 Jun., 16 Jun., 20 Jun.

1836: 6 Sep., 8 Sep., 14 Sep., 31 Dec.

1837: 2 Jan., 5-6 Jan., 4 Feb., 6 Feb., 6 Mar., 8 Mar., 11 Apr., 6 May, 28 Jun., 14 Jul., 20 Jul.

1839: 17-18 Mar.

1840: 3 Jun.

1843: 18 Oct.

1844: 27 Jan.

1845: 28-29 Jan., 2 Feb., 4-5 Feb., 4 Jun., 8-9 Jun.

1846: 2 Jul., 11 Aug., 22 Oct., 18 Nov.

1847: 12 Jun., 17-18 Jun., 13 Jul., 3 Nov., 8 Nov., 10 Nov., 24 Nov., 11 Dec., 17 Dec.

1848: 4 Jan., 18 May, 23 May, 27-29 Jun., 4 Nov., 6 Nov., 8 Nov., 12 Nov., 14 Nov.

1850: 27 Jan., 24 Jun., 26 Jun.

1851: 29 Apr.

WHITCOMBE — Mary Whitcombe [124]

Mary Whitcombe, née Aubrey (1764-1843), was born at Amberg-Sulzbach, Bayern, Germany, the illegitimate daughter of first cousins Sir John Aubrey, 6th baronet, and Martha Catherine Carter (d. 1815). Her mother was the daughter and co-heir of George Richard Carter of Chilton. Her father's first wife, Mary, died on 14 June 1781, and he married, secondly, Martha Catherine Carter on 26 May 1783.

Mary married, at St John the Baptist, Dorton, Buckinghamshire, 7 May 1792, Sir Samuel Whitcombe (1752-1816); they had 7 sons and 3 daughters:

- 1 John Aubrey (1793-1872); *see above*
- 2 Samuel Richard (1794-1850); married Eliza Pike; 2 sons and 3 daughters:
  - 1 Aubrey (1834-1855)
  - 1 Eliza M. A. (1836-1916)
  - 2 Charlotte Aubrey (1838-1916)
  - 3 Honore (b. 1840)
  - 2 Francis Henry Aubrey (1849-1935)
- 1 Mary Martha Emma (1796-1834); married, first, 2 May 1816, Capt. Hugh Ross, RN (d. 1828); secondly, Thomas Phillips; several children, one of whom was named William
- 3 Charles (1797-1884), Church of England clergyman; appointed vicar of Great Sherston [Sherston Magna], Wiltshire
- 2 Margaretta Theresa (1798-1807); died a child
- 3 Charlotte (1800-1869); married, at Wells, Somerset, 21 November 1821, Henry Seymour (1795-1860); 2 sons and 6 daughters:
  - 1 Jane Seymour Treherne (1816-1903)
  - 2 Charlotte Payne (1822-1892)
  - 3 Julia M. (1824-1841)
  - 1 Henry (1825-1911)
  - 4 Jane (d. 1903)
  - 2 Edward Adolphus (1829-1893)
  - 5 Frances (1830-1902)
  - 6 Mary Alice (1830-1918)
- 4 Henry Somerset (1802-1891); died unmarried
- 5 Thomas Douglas (1804-1882); *see below*
- 6 William Guise (1806-1832), army officer; died unmarried at Great Sherston; *see below* under Thomas Douglas Whitcombe
- 7 Edward (b. & d. 1808)

1829: 25 Sep: *Mrs. Hunt's house had its ample share of callers, some of whom we saw; Lady Crawley and family, Mrs. Colchester & daughters, Lady Whitcombe & her son, Mrs. James Commeline & her daughters &c.*

WHITCOMBE — Thomas Douglas Whitcombe [125]

Thomas Douglas Whitcombe (1804-1882), naval officer, was the fifth son of Sir Samuel Whitcombe (1752-1816), of Hempsted Court, and Mary Aubrey (1764-1843). He married, at St Clement Danes, Westminster, 14 July 1834, Elizabeth Kirkaldie (1814-1880); they had 6 sons and 4 daughters:

- 1 Charles Douglas (1836-1904); died in New Zealand
- 1 Julia (1837-1921)
- 2 Henry Aubrey (b. 1839)
- 2 Caroline Elizabeth (1841-1920)
- 3 Mary Sophia (1842-1930)
- 4 Selina Katherine (1844-1930)
- 3 William Eustace (1848-1930)
- 4 Edward John (1850-1926)
- 5 Seymour Frederick (1852-1935)
- 6 George Hawkes (1854-1917)

The diary entry is interesting, but the true story of Thomas's brother William is even more fascinating. Being adventurous—and presumably something of a romantic—William presumably accepted overtures from representatives of the movement for Greek independence. His career there is not known, but Thomas found him and brought him home. On his return, William wrote a book, *Sketches of Modern Greece*; in the introduction he expressed his wish to go back to Greece, but he never did. On 25 June 1830 he was granted through purchase a commission as ensign in the 2nd West Indian Regiment of Foot, commanded by Gen. Francis Fuller. This was not a regiment to attract gentlemen of worth, and was known more as a refuge for 'black sheep'. After inspecting the regiment on 7 January 1832, Maj.-Gen. Sir James Carmichael Smyth reported on some of its problems:

> three out of five of the captains have been obliged to go home from debility and that total loss of energy brought on by drinking brandy and water.... The excitement caused by a change of scene and a change of quarters seems absolutely necessary to keep the greater numbers of officers in the tropical climate from this most ungentlemanlike and disgraceful indulgence.

William served actively with this regiment until the end of 1831, but early in 1832 he was put on the sick list. On 17 April, General Smyth awarded him a year's leave 'on account of ill health'. He had until 30 April 1833, and he returned to England, where on 13 July he was promoted to lieutenant. His nephew gave a brief account of what followed:

> After a short stay with his mother he went to pay a visit to my Uncle Charles (fourth child of Samuel and Mary Whitcombe,

> Vicar of Magna Sherston from 1830 to 1884, the year of his death) at Sherston, and while there fell desperately in love with some girl at Corsham, a village a few miles from Sherston. He had a desperate quarrel with her, and went to Corsham, staying at the Inn there, while trying to make it up. He was seemingly unsuccessful, for after an interview, the people at the Inn heard him parading his room the greater part of the night; stamping, exclaiming, and seemingly tearing up papers. There was then a heavy fall, and rushing up he was found lying dead on the floor surrounded by torn up papers.

William was buried in the aisle of his brother's church in Sherston. A tablet to his memory can still be read: 'erected as a tribute of affection by his surviving brothers'.

1828: 18 Jan: *Mr. T. Whitcomb came to tea. This young man is brother to a Solicitor in Gloucester, where his father was a Knight and of the same profession; he himself has been in the East Indies, whither he went, I believe, in the naval line. But he is chiefly interesting at present in consequence of a residence in Greece, from which he has recently returned ... Mr. T. Whitcomb was induced to visit Greece in company with a brother, to seek after another member of the family, the youngest son, who had volunteered into the Greek service, and there had fallen into bad connexions ...*

WHITE — passenger on the brig *George and Mary* to Hamburgh

1798: 5 Aug: *The Company besides ourselves consisted of two Gentlemen Mr. Ryan and Mr. White.*

WHITE — surgeon to the Royal Windsor Foresters

1801: 6 Jul: *At Standlake we found Mr. & Mrs. & two Miss Rookes visitors; Mr. White formerly surgeon in the Windsor Foresters had dined there.*

WHITE — Miss White at Clifton — *see also* Jervis

Miss White was probably a niece of John Jervis-White-Jervis (1766-1830), barrister. John Jervis-White-Jervis was born at Bally Ellis, co. Wexford, the son of John Jervis Jervis-White and Elizabeth Whitthorn. He was a barrister in Dublin and took, by royal licence in 1793, the name of Jervis after his own surname of White.

1804: 5 Sep: *To the fair at Bristol, with Lady Jervis & Miss White, Mrs. McMahon, Ryan ...* 25 Sep: *to a large party at Mrs. McMahon's where the Lady of the mansion & two Miss Mosses sung tolerably: thence to the Ball then, but not unpleasant: danced with Miss White & Caroline Townsend.* 12 Oct: *Walked with the Manners's Sir J. J. W. Jervis, Miss White &c.*

1805: 29 Jan: *A good Ball in the Evening at York House; danced with Miss White & Miss Anson agreeably.*

WHITE — Miss White, a friend of Marianne Dolphin

1843: 7 Oct: *On my return home I found Mrs. Dolphin with her friend Miss White calling on M.W. ...*

WHITE — Mr White, a barrister at Barnard's Inn

1846: 15 Jun: *... to Mr. White of Barnard's Inn, that I am unable to give any information as to the affairs of Dodsworth, formerly tenant at Scale House ...* 10 Jul: *... a letter from an Attorney of Barnard's Inn, by name White, with an enquiry as to the Exors. of Dr. Moorhouse's will ...* 11 Jul: *Wrote to Mr. White, Barnard's Inn, in answer to the letter received from him yesterday, stating that Dr. Moorhouse had made no will ...*

WHITE — Andrew Douglas White, officer in the Royal Engineers, Ordnance Survey [126]

Andrew Douglas White (1793-1837), army officer, was born at Sydney Cove, New South Wales, Australia, the illegitimate son of naval surgeon John White (±1756-1832) and convict Rachel Turner (b. ±1760). His father had joined the Royal Navy on 26 June 1778 as 3rd surgeon's mate aboard HMS *Wasp*. In October 1786 he was appointed chief surgeon of the expedition to establish a convict settlement at Botany Bay. The so-called First Fleet of 1788 contained 778 convicts aboard eleven ships. In December 1792, about the same time that John White applied for leave to England, control of the colony passed to Maj. Francis Grose, who took over from the departed Capt. Arthur Philips. Grose was notorious for doling out land grants to fellow officers and other favourites, and White received 100 acres at present-day Petersham, which he named Hamond Hill Farm.

John White formed a liaison with convict Rachel Turner in Sydney. She was convicted at Middlesex Gaol and sentenced to seven years' transportation from the Old Bailey on 12 December 1787. She sailed aboard the *Lady Juliana* in June 1789 and arrived in Sydney Cove on the Second Fleet in June 1790. She served as John White's housekeeper in 1792; their son, Andrew Douglas, was born on 23 September 1793, and baptised at Sydney on 3 November that year.

John White's application for leave was eventually granted, and on 17 December 1794 he sailed on HMS *Daedalus*, taking with him his 15-month-old son. He reached London in July 1795, and once there, became reluctant to return to New South Wales. He chose to resign his appointment in August 1796. White served aboard various merchant ships for three years, before becoming surgeon at Sheerness Navy Yard. He remained there until 1803, and afterwards became surgeon at Chatham Yard. He was superannuated in 1820 at the age of 63. He married in about 1800, and had 1 son and 2 daughters:

1 Richard Hamond White; Lt, RN
1 Clara Christiana; married, as his second wife, Ralph Bernal, MP
2 Augusta Catherine Anne; married Lt Henry Sandham, RE, who rose to become a lieutenant-general

John White spent his last years at Brighton, and died at Worthing on 20 February 1832, aged 75, leaving an estate valued at £12,000. His illegitimate son Andrew Douglas was brought up in England by a sister of his friend, Lt Henry Waterhouse. After his education Andrew joined the Royal Engineers as a second lieutenant on 1 July 1812. He was promoted to first lieutenant on 21 July 1813 and seems to have gone to Flanders in late 1813 as part of the British force under Lt-Gen. Thomas Graham.

Andrew White remained on the Continent in 1814, and served as the junior officer on the Royal Engineer staff at Waterloo, a surprisingly young group for a branch of service with a reputation for slow promotion. The commanding officer was Lt-Col James Carmichael Smyth, a 35-year-old Londoner with experience in the Peninsular War and at the Cape of Good Hope. His two subordinates were 29-year-old East Anglian Capt. Sir George Hoste, and a 26-year-old Sussex man serving as brigade-major, Capt. John Oldfield. The second captains were Frank Stanney and Alexander Thompson, the former a 25-year-old Londoner and the latter a Scot of the same age. The first lieutenants were John William Pringle, a 24-year-old Scot who had served in the Peninsular campaign; Marcus Anton Waters, a 24-year-old Dubliner; Francis Bond Head, a 22-year-old from Kent; Francis Yarde Gilbert, a 21-year-old Cornishman; John Sperling, adjutant, a 21-year-old from Surrey who had been at Bergen-Op-Zoom; and finally White, 21 and from New South Wales.

In early 1815 Wellington ordered Carmichael Smyth to prepare a map of the area south of Brussels. It was partly drawn by Lt Sperling, but it was incomplete when Wellington called for it in June 1815. The original sketches were rushed from Brussels by Lt Waters, and Wellington marked on the map where he wished his troops to be deployed. He passed it to Sir William Howe de Lancey, his quartermaster-general, who was wounded on the battlefield while carrying it. Capt. Oldfield saved the map and wrote its history on it.

White survived the battle unscathed and returned to England to receive his Waterloo medal in 1816. In the years following he was stationed at Chatham, where he joined the freemasons' Royal Kent Lodge of Antiquity on 20 January 1819.

White returned to Sydney late in 1822, and there was reunited with his mother after nearly thirty years. She had married Thomas Moore, a wealthy farmer and philanthropist, in Sydney in January 1797, but had not had any more children. White returned to England in July 1824 and was promoted to second captain in the Royal Engineers on 6 December 1826. He was placed on half-pay on 6 October 1831 and returned to Australia in 1833. He married, at St John's, Parramatta, June 1835, Mary Anne MacKenzie, niece of Lt-Col John Piper CB, of the 4th Foot. White died on 24 November 1837 of unknown causes. There were no children of the marriage.

No local newspaper lamented the passing of Australia's only Waterloo veteran. Nonetheless, Andrew Douglas White is generally recognised as Australia's first decorated soldier and first returned serviceman. His mother treasured her son's Waterloo medal until her own death a year after his.

1825: 12 Mar: *We dined at Mr. Ford's, at Little Risington, There were also of the party two officers of the Engineers, Messrs. White & Lancey: these gentlemen with a third, of the name of Gosset, have been stationed for some time at Stow to survey this district for the grand trigonometrical map, which is in a course of publication under the direction of the board of Ordnance.*

WHITE — Anne White[127]

Anne White (b. ±1815) was listed in the 1841 census as a female servant in the Stanway household of Edward Witts. She was presumably personal attendant to Edward's wife Sophy. Nothing is known of her after she had left Francis Witts's employment. She was not recorded in the 1851 census for Upper Slaughter.

1845: 19 Jan: *Wrote to E.F.W. a letter to be dispatched to Stanway by our groom to-morrow as to the sending A. M. Andrews to be a temporary housemaid, as to Anne White accompanying Sophy to Stapleton ...* 20 Jan: *In consequence of the alarm of fever in our family, Anne White is not to go to Stapleton as Sophy's attendant.* 29 Jan:
Dr. Wing called—two servants ill—the Cook not worse: Anne White indisposed, but not believed to have caught the fever ... 23 Feb., 26 Feb., 27 Feb: *Dr. Wing called, and considered Ann White better.* 1 Mar: Anne White continues ill; but Dr. Wing, who visited her to-day, does not consider her complaint dangerous ... 7 Mar: *I reached home before 7 P.M. and had the comfort of finding all pretty well—Anne White is on the recovery ...* 11 Mar., 14 Mar: *Dr. Wing called: his patient, Anne White, is recovering.* 18 Mar: *Dr. Wing called;—his patient, A White, is convalescent.*

1846: 6 Jul: *Jealousies, bickerings &c. love quarrels between John Bateman and Anne White begin to be very troublesome, and seem likely to end in their both leaving our Service.* 7 Aug: *As I expected, the misunderstanding between Bateman and Anne White has ended in our accepting from the latter a warning to quit our service, and giving a warning to the same effect to the former. AW. accuses JB. of neglecting her, after an engagement to marry her, of which we were cognizant, and of attaching himself to Farmer Dix's daughter ...* 12 Aug., 29 Aug: *Anne White left our service.*

WHITE — Joseph Blanco White[128]

Joseph Blanco White (1775-1841), clergyman and author of Irish-Spanish descent, was born in Seville into a Catholic family and christened José Maria. He was at first destined for the family mercantile business, but through the influence of his Spanish mother he was channelled towards the Church. After six years of study he developed doubts about Christianity, and when the French invaded Spain he fled to Cadiz, and escaped to England in 1810. In London he was helped by Lord Holland and Lord John Russell who had both travelled in Spain and knew the country well. Through the influence of Richard Wellesley he was employed by Juigné, a French refugee priest and printer in London, to produce a monthly periodical called *Español.*

In England White turned once more to Christianity, preferring Anglicanism to Catholicism. After finishing with his magazine work, he signed the 39 articles on 10 August 1814 to qualify himself as an English clergyman. In 1825 he published his *Evidences Against Catholicism*, and in 1826 the University of Oxford conferred on him a masters degree in recognition of his services to the Church of England.

White settled in Oxford as a member of Oriel College, and was on friendly terms with Newman, Pusey, and others, who later became part of the Oxford movement. In 1829 he voted for Peel, which isolated him to some extent at Oxford. This, and the offence he took at being treated as a 'foreigner', caused him to leave the University in 1831. He moved to Dublin, where he joined his friend Whately, who had recently become archbishop there. In 1835, after several years of oscillating in his views, White turned to unitarianism and moved to Liverpool. From there he contributed to the *London and Westminster Review*. He died after a long illness in 1841.

1827: 10 Feb: *"Practical and internal evidence against Catholicism; with occasional strictures on Mr. Butler's book of the Roman Catholic Church. In six letters addressed to the impartial among the Roman Catholics of Great Britain & Ireland. By the Revd. Jos. Blanco White &c. London 1825 8vo." This valuable work deserves to be ranked with the ablest productions of the modern champions of Protestantism ...*

1829: 26 Feb: *The other individual, to whom I allude, was the celebrated Blanco White; can he vote for Peel, who is the most popular of all the writers ...*

WHITE — Sampson White[129]

Sampson White (1765-1826), Church of England clergyman, was born at Fyfield, Hampshire, the son of Revd Henry White (1733-1788) and Elizabeth Cooper (1734-1815). He was educated at Oriel College, Oxford (BA 1786; MA 1789), and entered the Church. He was appointed vicar of Uphaven, Wiltshire, in 1789, and served as rector of Maidford, Northamptonshire, from 1798 to his death in 1826. He married, at St Mary's, Selborne, Hampshire, 21 August 1798, Hannah White (1770-1858), possibly his cousin, and probably great-niece of the naturalist Gilbert White (1720-1793). Sampson and Hannah had 1 son and 4 daughters:

1 Emma (1799-1821)
2 Harriet (1800-1823)

1 Samson Henry (1802-1871), Church of England clergyman
3 Maria (1804-1839)
4 Elizabeth (b. 1810)

1807: 2 Sep: *Called at Mrs. Giffard's for the Revd. Mr. White's Subscription to the Clergy in vain.*

WHITE — William White[130]

William White (1765-1823), Church of England clergyman, was born at Milton Lilbourne, Wiltshire, the son of William and Ann White. He was educated at Merton College, Oxford (BA 1788; MA 1790), and served as rector of Teffont Evias, Wiltshire, from 26 April 1799 to his death on 11 October 1823.

1807: 21 May: *Mr. & Mrs. Compton, Mr. & Mrs. Tinker with their two daughters, & the Revd. Mr. White of Teffont came to us to tea & supper, & staid till near twelve.*

WHITEFOOT — William Whitefoot[131]

William Whitefoot (±1749-1813[?]), nonconformist clergyman, was born at Dorrington, Shropshire, the son of nonconformists Thomas and Mary Whitefoot. He became a member of the countess of Huntingdon's circle, and appears to have studied at Trevecca College, which was founded by the countess in 1768. Whitefoot then moved across the country to Woodford congregational church in Essex, which was founded in about 1790. It was registered by Whitefoot in 1795 as Providence chapel for independents.

1801: 27 Dec: *To Wotton Meeting in the Afternoon with my Mother & Uncle hearing a most methodistical ranting Sermon from a Mr. Whitefoot a preacher in Mr. Rowland Hill's Tabernacle at Wotton.*

WHITEHALL DOD — ***see*** **Dod**

WHITEHEAD — Miss Whitehead at Bourton-on-the-Water — ***see also*** **William George** ***and*** **Cornelius Pitt**[132]

Miss Whitehead was probably a daughter of John Whitehead and Mary Horrocks, who had married in 1796 at Bolton le Moors, Lancashire. If this attribution is correct, she was an elder sister to John Horrocks Whitehead (*below*).

1824: 3 Aug: *We dined at Mrs. Rice's, Bourton on the Water ... Mr. & Mrs. George of Bourton on the Water, with her sister, Miss Whitehead ...*

WHITEHEAD — William Whitehead[133]

William Whitehead (1786-1871), registrar of births and deaths, was born at Gloucester. He married Esther (±1790-1850), and they had at least 3 sons and 2 daughters:

1 Alfred (1810-1859); married, at Gloucester, ±1836, Elizabeth Whittard (1808-1842); at least 3 sons and 2 daughters:
  1 Caroline Emma L. (b. 1837)
  2 Mary Eliza (b. 1838)
  1 Alfred (b. 1839)
  2 Henry Ambrose (b. 1841)
  3 Richard William (b. 1842)
1 Maria (b. 1826)
2 Frederick (1827-1902); married, at Gloucester, 1857, Susannah Elizabeth Kilminster (b. 1839); 1 son and 5 daughters:
  1 Annie Pauline (b. 1858)
  2 Agnes Ophelia (1861-1923)
  3 Kate Augusta (1864-1923)
  4 Gertrude Adeline (b. 1865)
  5 Henrietta Clara (b. 1866)
  1 Henry Ambrose (1868-1944)
3 Bernard (b. 1827)
2 Mary (b. 1831)

In the 1861 census Whitehead was listed as a widower and registrar of births and deaths, living at 50 College Court with his son Frederick, unmarried granddaughter Mary, and his grandson Alfred. Whitehead's eldest son, Alfred, was a bookseller, stationer, musical instrument seller, professor, and teacher of the pianoforte.

1842: 11 Apr: *To the Grand Jury Room at the Shire Hall, where I was afterwards joined by C Bathurst and Purnell, my colleagues on the Committee of accounts, and transacted the usual business with them, Mr. Burrup (for Mr. E. Bloxsome) Mr. Riddiford, Mr. Lefroy, Mr. Keiley, Mr. Whitehead &c ...*

1843: 16 Oct: *Much engaged with the different County officers, Messrs. Bloxsome Senr. and Junr., Wilton, Lefroy, Riddiford, Keiley, Mason, Whitehead &c.*

1844: 1 Jan: *We were attended by the usual County Functionaries, Mr. Bloxsome, Mr. E. Bloxsome, Mr. Riddiford, Mr. Lefroy, Mr. Keiley, Mr. Mason, Mr. Fulljames, Mr. Whitehead &c.* 14 Oct., 30 Dec.

1845: 14 Apr., 30 Jun.
1846: 29 Jun., 19 Oct.
1847: 22 Mar., 28 Jun., 18 Oct.
1848: 3 Jan., 20 Mar., 16 Oct.
1849: 31 Dec.
1850: 1 Jul., 14 Oct.
1851: 17 Mar.
1853: 3 Jan., 14 Mar., 27 Jun., 19 Dec.

WHITEHEAD — John Horrocks Whitehead — ***see also*** **William George** ***and*** **Cornelius Pitt**[134]

John Horrocks Whitehead (1808-1846), merchant and HEIC naval officer, was born at Preston, Lancashire, the son of John Whitehead and Mary Horrocks, who had married at Bolton in 1796. In 1801 John Whitehead was brought into the business Horrockses, Miller & Co. by his father-in-law, John Horrocks (1768-1804), baron of the Lancashire cotton industry and MP for Preston (1802-04), of Penwortham Lodge, near Preston, Lancashire. Mrs Cornelius Pitt, née Anne Eliza Horrocks, was Mary's sister and aunt to John Horrocks Whitehead.

After serving in the HEIC, John Horrocks Whitehead became a partner in the trading firm Shaw, Whitehead & Co. He died at Singapore in 1846, and was buried at the old cemetery at Fort Canning. He was mentioned in the Singapore newspaper regarding his involvement with St Andrew's church, near Raffles Hotel, Singapore.

1824: 9 Jul: *Miss Horrocks, daughter of the Member for Preston, & niece to Mrs. C. Pitt, Mr. Whitehead of the East Indian Company's naval Service, nephew to Mrs. C. Pitt, Mr. E. Hughes, a fellow of Jesus Coll. Oxford, Mrs. Price, Senr. & Miss Davis, Mrs. W. Price's Sister.*

WHITEHOUSE — William Whitehouse at Mrs Witts's, Brunswick Square[135]

William Whitehouse (1770-1844), merchant, of New Ferry, Cheshire, married, at St Anne's, Liverpool, 12 November 1798, Mary (1779-1865), eldest daughter of William Charles Lake

(1753-1836), merchant and landed proprietor, and Ann Orange (1758-1810); they had 6 sons and 5 daughters:

1 William (1800-1878); died unmarried

2 Thomas Lake (1801-1878); married, at Bebington, Cheshire, 8 August 1833, Esther Louisa (1812-1846), youngest daughter of the late Revd Richard Lowndes Salmon, vicar of Sandbach; at least 1 daughter:

 1 Henrietta Sophia (1836-1909); died unmarried

3 Richard (b. 1802)

1 Elizabeth Anne (b. 1804); married, at Bebington, Cheshire, 8 August 1833, Henry William Townsend (1790-1840), born at Rugby, Warwickshire, the son of Thomas Townsend (b. 1770); 2 sons and 1 daughter:

 1 George William (1834-1919)

 1 Louisa Henrietta (1839-1841)

 2 Thomas Lake Whitehouse (1840-1848)

2 Amelia (1805-1862); married, at Liverpool, 5 August 1828, George Ruddle (b. 1804), a retired officer (1861 census), DL, and JP, living at Walton House, Ashchurch, Gloucestershire

3 Clarissa Barbara (1807-1864); lived with her sister Amelia at Ashchurch, Gloucestershire; died unmarried

4 Charlotte Mary (1808-1881); married, at St Andrew's, Bebington, Cheshire, 5 November 1836, Robert Ellison Gorst (1813-1868); at least 2 sons:

 1 William Arthur (1837-1920)

 2 Peter Freeland (1838-1918), Church of England clergyman; appointed rector of Saxby

5 Sophia Bashford (1809-1887); married, first, at Ashchurch, Gloucestershire, 17 July 1841, John Williams Martin (1795-1859); secondly, in Paris, 5 October 1864, William Forster Cormack (1812-1891); at least 1 son from her first marriage:

 1 Charles Stanhope (1845-1886)

4 Charles Augustus (b. 1811)

5 William Frederick (1812-1860); married, at St Mary's, Tewkesbury, Gloucestershire, 21 August 1845, Mary Ann Isis Hepworth (1823-1863)

6 Edward Orange Wildman (1816-1890); married, first, at All Saints', Southampton, 16 December 1847, Emma Parry (1828-1862); 1 daughter:

 1 Adele Emma Wildman (1849-1930)

 Married, secondly, Hannah Statham (1838-1869); 1 son and 1 daughter:

 1 Arthur Statham Wildman (b. 1865)

 1 Hilda Mary Wildman (1868-1902)

The Whitehouse family married extensively into the Lake and Townsend families.

1830: 25 Jun: *To dinner at Mrs. Witts's, Brunswick Square—a party Messrs. Bailey, Hibbert, Bassevi, Jones, Misses Witts and Whitehouse ...*

1835: 11 Jun: *The bridal party on their return to Brunswick Square were joined by other friends ... a Mr. Fleming and a Mr. Whitehouse.*

1842: 13 May: *Marmaduke Vavasour had driven to Twyning to visit his old acquaintance, Mr. John Williams Martin, and be introduced to his young wife, a niece of Mrs. Witts of Brunswick Square, late a Miss Whitehouse: this the second wife, many years his Junior, the former had been as much older than himself, and, I believe, his Godmother.*

1844: 12 Sep: *With Mr. Duncan drove to Stow; he made enquiries there as to the coach to Cheltenham ...*
and thence to visit the Ruddles, connections of the Lakes, Whitehouses, Duncans, Martins &c., at Walton House near Tewkesbury ...

1853: 21 Jun: *Received a visit from Mr. & Mrs. Ruddle, Mr. Hastings Wodman, and Miss Townsend... Miss Townsend, daughter of a deceased Solicitor of Rugby, and niece of the Vicar of Aston Blank, is also niece of Mrs. Ruddle, who was a Miss Whitehouse, and a niece of Mrs. Witts of Brighton, her mother having been one of the many daughters of the Lake family. Another Miss W. married Mr. Townsend of Rugby, and a third is the second wife of Mr. J Williams Martin, of Shoborough House, Twyning, an old acquaintance and brother Magistrate of mine.*

WHITFORD — Thomas Whitford [136]

Thomas Whitford (1836-1903), butler, was the son of Thomas Whitford (1806-1848) and Ann Packer (1805-1886), of Stanway. His father was a farming bailiff, and may have been employed as such by the earl of Wemyss. Tom Whitford began his career as a gentleman's servant to Edward Witts. He then became a footman to James Henry Legge Dutton, 3rd Baron Sherborne. He married, 1869, at St George's, Hanover Square, Elizabeth Jane Howell (1836-1908) and became a lodging house keeper at 9 Royal Parade, Cheltenham. Thomas and Elizabeth had 5 sons and 1 daughter:

1 Arthur Thomas (1871

2 Frank (b. 1871)

3 Frederick George (1873-1955)

1 Elizabeth Jane (b. ±1876)

4 Bertie Edward (b. ±1876)

5 Edward John (b. 1879)

In 1881 Whitford was butler to Baron Sherborne at Sherborne, with Elizabeth living nearby at Northleach, raising their children. After the death of the 3rd Baron, Thomas became butler to James St Vincent, 4th Lord de Saumarez (of Guernsey) in Grosvenor Place, Knightsbridge. He died at Plymouth in 1903.

1848: 7 Sep: *Broome, attended by his squire, Tom Whitford, rode on his poney to join the party at "the Cottage" ...* 9 Sep: *Broome with his attendant, Tom, and on his poney, remained till after luncheon.*

WHITMORE — Charles Shapland Whitmore [137]

Charles Shapland Whitmore (1805-1877), judge, was born at Lower Slaughter, Gloucestershire, the third son of Gen. Sir George Whitmore (1775-1862) (*below*) and Cordelia Ainslie (1780-1857). He was educated at Rugby School and Trinity College, Cambridge, and was admitted at the Inner Temple in 1827. In 1830 he was called to the bar and joined the Oxford circuit. He was made queen's counsel in 1855, a bencher in 1856, reader in 1868, and treasurer in 1869. He was recorder of Lichfield in 1848-52 and of Gloucester in 1852-77, and judge of Southwark county court in 1857-77. Whitmore resided at Rutland Gate, Hyde Park, and later at Lower Slaughter. He married, at St George's, Hanover Square, Westminster, 2 December 1845, Elizabeth Katherine (1818-1883), daughter of Lt-Col Robert James Brownrigg (1790-1822) and Mary Elizabeth Emma Nesbitt (1797-1867); they had at least 3 sons:

1 Charles Algernon (1851-1908)

2 William Walter (1853-1925)

3 Edward Henry (1858-1905)

1837: 22 Sep: *Messrs. Peake and Whitmore are the Barristers selected for this duty in the Eastern Division.*

1853: 13 Mar: *W Vavasour ... called on me to consult me as to his annoyances in the matter of the manor of L Slaughter, which he holds by lease under Sir Geo. Whitmore, but the tenants (Reynolds) obstruct him in the enjoyment, claiming a right to destroy rabbits; in correspondence on the subject with Sir G. W's son, the Recorder of Gloucester, with whom I advise him to have a conference ...* 5 Apr.

WHITMORE — George Whitmore[138]

Sir George Whitmore (1775-1862), army officer and landed proprietor, was the son of George Whitmore (1739-94) and Mary Walls (b. 1744). He was grandson of Lt-Gen. William Whitmore (1714-1771), MP for Bridgnorth. George was presumably born at Lower Slaughter Manor as he was baptised at Bourton-on-the-Water. He inherited the Lower Slaughter estate in 1794, but like many before and after him, he did not reside there and the property was let out for long periods.

As colonel commandant, Sir George Whitmore headed the Royal Engineers detachment on Malta between 1811 and 1829. There he became a great friend of the governor, Sir Thomas Maitland, and designed the military hospital at the Villa Bighi in conjunction with Vice Adm. Sir Pulteney Malcolm. When Sir Thomas Maitland was high commissioner of the Ionian Islands, Whitmore designed the Palace of St Michael and St George in Corfu. He was promoted to major-general and made a knight of the Royal Guelphic Order (KCH), a Hanoverian order of chivalry instituted in 1815 by the prince regent (later George IV). Knights under this order were not usually supposed to adopt the title 'Sir' unless they were also conferred with the honour of KB (knight bachelor), which for Whitmore does not seem to have been the case. Notwithstanding this, Whitmore took to using the title and was well known as 'Sir George'. He married, 1798, Cordelia Ainslie (1780-1857); they had at least 7 sons and 3 daughters:

1 George St Vincent (1798-1851); married, 22 February 1827, Isabella Maxwell, daughter of Sir John Stoddart and Isabella Wellwood-Moncreiff; 5 sons and 4 daughters:
  1 Cordelia Nugent (b. 1828)
  1 George Stoddart (1829-1903)
  2 Montagu Stopford (1831-1880)
  2 Mary Moncreiff (b. 1833)
  3 Annette Dashwood (1834-1835); died an infant
  3 Henry Ainslie (1837-1857)
  4 Charles William (1838-1839); died an infant
  4 Emily Atkinson (1840-1924)
  5 John (1845-1904)
2 Ainslie Henry (1800-1843)
1 Mary (b. 1802); married, 3 February 1827, Nicolas Orlando Walter Tyrell Leroux Nugent
2 Cordelia Winifreda (1804-1851); married, 25 August 1827, Vice Adm. Montagu Stopford, son of James George Stopford, 3rd earl of Courtown, and Mary Scott; 1 son and 3 daughters:
  1 Annette Jane (d. 1921)
  2 Mary Cordelia (d. 1912)
  3 Emily Winifreda (d. 1891)
  1 George Montagu (1828-1860), Maj.
3 Charles Shapland (1805-1877); *see above*
4 William Lechmere (1807-1866); married, 17 October 1837, Sara Patience Mee; 2 sons and 2 daughters:
  1 George Ainslie Lechmere Aston (1841-1878)
  1 Marian Serena (1844-1926)
  2 Mortimer Durant (1848-1892)
  2 Grace Emily (b. 1854)
5 Mortimer Robert (1809-1884); married, 22 November 1836, Cecilia Hall, daughter of Adm. Henry Byng; 1 daughter:
  1 Ada Byng (b. 1838)
3 Emily Harriet Octavia (1812-1870); died unmarried
6 Francis Locker (1814-1894), Lt-Gen.; served in the Crimea and Canada; married, 18 January 1848, Eliza, daughter of John Ledsam; 2 daughters:
  1 Winifred Mary (1851-1934)
  2 Maud Mildred (1862-1944)
7 Edmund Augustus (1819-1890), Gen.; appointed KCB; served in the Crimea; died unmarried

In the 1851 census Sir George Whitmore was registered as living at 113 Blackheath Road, Greenwich, with his wife Cordelia, his widowed daughter Mary Nugent (b. ±1802), and his unmarried daughter Emily Harriet Octavia (1812-1870). The Lower Slaughter estate appears to have descended to Sir George's third son, Charles Shapland, but it is not immediately clear why as Charles's elder brother, George St Vincent, had at least one son, George Stoddart Whitmore (1829-1903).

1835: 20 May: *Attended Sir Geo. Whitmore's Court Leet and Court Baron at Lower Slaughter.*
1838: 18 May, 31 Oct.
1853: 13 Mar., 5 Apr., 4 May.

WHITMORE — William Wolryche Whitmore[139]

William Wolryche Whitmore (1787-1858), MP and landed proprietor, was the eldest son of William Whitmore, of Dudmaston Hall, Quatt, Shropshire, and his first wife, Frances Barbara, daughter of John Lyster of White Whitmore. He was a half brother to John Henry Whitmore-Jones (*below*). William was educated at Shrewsbury School and married, 1810, Lucy Elizabeth Georgiana (d. 1840), daughter of Orlando Bridgman, 1st earl of Bradford. He succeeded his father to the Dudmaston estate in 1816, and was MP for Bridgnorth, 1820-32, and Wolverhampton, 1832-1834, and high sheriff for Shropshire, 1838-39.

1825: 17 Sep: *The present representatives of the borough are Mr. Whitmore, of Dudmaston Hall in this vicinity, a gentleman of talent, who frequently addresses the house, principally on points of finance & political economy, and a namesake, Mr. Whitmore of Apley Park, a place also in the immediate neighbourhood ...*
1829: 11 Aug.

WHITMORE-JONES — John Henry Whitmore-Jones[140]

John Henry Whitmore-Jones (1796-1853), army officer, JP, DL, and landed proprietor, was born at Dudmaston Hall, Shropshire, the sixth son of William Whitmore and his second wife, Mary Louisa Thomas. He was half-brother to William Whitmore (*above*). In 1814, a distant ancestor, Arthur Jones, made his will, leaving Chastleton to 'My Kinsman, John Henry Whitmore, of Dudmaston, Salop.' Whitmore was educated at Christ Church, Oxford, and then entered the Army, but retired on his marriage to Dorothy, daughter of Col Clutton, of Pensax Court, Worcestershire, on 1 January 1821. John and Dorothy had 4 sons and 6 daughters:

1 John Arthur (b. ±1822)
1 Mary Elizabeth (b. ±1825)
2 William (b. ±1826)
2 Jenetta (1827-1904); born at Bigsweir; married, at Chasleton, 18 December 1862, as his second wife, John Harris (1816-1897); at least 1 son:
  1 Thomas Whitmore (1864-1917); married his cousin Irene Dickins
3 Frances Barbara (b. ±1828); born at Swerford, Oxfordshire; married Charles Dickins; at least 1 daughter:

1 Irene (d. 1955); married her cousin Thomas Whitmore Harris, who took the name Whitmore-Jones
4 Joanna Dorothea (b. 1829); born at Chastleton; married Revd Thomas Harris (1811-1895), rector of Swerford, Oxfordshire; no known children
3 Walter Thomas (±1831-1872); born at Chastleton
5 Louisa Georgiana (1833-1915); born at Chastleton; married, July 1864, Revd Charles John Elliot Walkey (1833-1895), son of Revd Charles Collyns Walkey (1804-1887) and Milborough Anne Huyshe (1802-1883); 3 sons and 1 daughter:
1 Charles Elliot John (1867-1954)
2 Rowland Huyshe (b. 1869), artist; married, 13 November 1896, Marian Isabella Marshall
3 Walter Whitmore (b. & d. 1873)
1 Julia (dates unknown)
6 Ellinor Marian (1834-1881); born at Chastleton; married John Franks of Ballyscaddane Castle, co. Limerick, eldest son of cousins Sir John Franks, judge of the supreme court, Bengal, and Catherine Franks of Carrig, co. Cork
4 Wolryche Harry (±1838-1874); born at Chastleton

John duly inherited the Chastleton estate in 1828, and took the additional surname of Jones. He was captain of Queen Adelaide's Own Oxfordshire Yeomanry, and died in 1853, leaving ten children. The sons all died unmarried, and the eldest daughter, Mary Elizabeth Whitmore-Jones, held the property, by consent of her sisters (all of whom were married), from the death of their youngest brother in 1874 until 1900, when she resigned it to her nephew, Thomas Whitmore Harris. The estate still remains in the Whitmore family but the house was sold to the National Trust in 1992.

1829: 11 Aug: *My wife & myself dined at the Easts at Adlestrop. The guests were Mr. & Mrs. Whitmore Jones ... Mr. Jones was an aged country squire; I believe, an old Bachelor, and died last spring; Mr. Whitmore was remotely related to him, being a younger brother of Mr. Whitmore of Dudmaston, in Shropshire, M.P. for Bridgnorth ... The gentleman, who has succeeded to Mr. Jones's property, & takes his name, is now residing at the Rectory house at Swerford, till some alterations are completed at Chastleton; he was in the dragoons, is an ardent Nimrod, has a ready & voluble tongue, & great flow of spirits. His lady accompanies well on the Piano forte ...* 29 Oct.

1832: 10 Apr: *We all went to dine with our worthy old friend Lady Reade ... Mr. & Mrs. Whitmore Jones, accompanied by a Sister of Mr. W. Jones's (a widow, Mrs. Wall) and her son ...*

1834: 26 Jul: *Mr. Whitmore Jones sat as Worcestershire Magistrate ...* 25 Sep., 25 Oct.

1835: 25 Feb.

1836: 10 Sep., 27 Sep., 4 Oct., 24 Oct., 27 Oct: *Whitmore Jones is a cadet of the family of Whitmore of Dudmaston near Bridgnorth, and was is the heir of the late Arthur Jones, of Chastleton, an old fashioned Bachelor Squire, who selected this young man, as one of his nearest of kin, to take his name and estates ... Mrs. W. Jones is a very accomplished Musician, and was instructed by Miss Novello's mother.* 31 Dec.

1837: 1 Mar: *I was not quite a stranger to some of them, having met Mrs. Holland and her sister, Miss Isaacs, at Chastleton; they are nearly connected with the Whitmore Jones's.* 12 May, 22 Sep., 26 Sep., 9 Nov., 16 Nov.

1838: 19 Feb., 12 May, 24 May, 27 Jul: *Edward, who first heard of the attack of lumbago which has seized me, last evening, at Mr. & Mrs. Whitmore Jones's party ...* 23 Jul., 27 Jul: *I hurried home to a hasty dinner, and dressed to accompany Mrs. W. in our Chariot to an Evening party and concert at the Whitmore Jones's at Chastleton.* 26 Sep.

1839: 21 Feb., 13 May.

1840: 26 Mar., 16 Apr., 9 Jul: *The rest of the party were Whitmore Jones, rattling and dashing at every subject with his usual volubility and good humour ...* 24 Oct.

1841: 27 Feb., 4 Mar.

1842: 12 Jan., 18 Jan., 10 Mar., 24 May, 14 Jun., 16 Jun., 21 Jul., 27 Sep., 29 Dec.

1843: 27 Jan., 21 Sep., 14 Dec.

1844: 22 Feb., 29 Feb.

1846: 3 Dec.

1847: 8 Jul.

1850: 28 Mar., 1 Apr., 25 Jun: *Thence to Chastleton by the Daylesford grounds, & across Adlestrop Hill; called in on Mr. & Mrs. Whitmore Jones, whom we found at home, with two of their daughters ... I had only once before visited Chastleton House, many years ago, when its hospitable owners, now rather confined in their means, from large outgoings, and a numerous family, unable too to relieve themselves by family arrangements contemplated on the eldest Son's coming of age, gave a large party and concert, Clara Novello, the accomplished public singer, being the principal performer. Poor young Whitmore Jones, a very promising lad then, and afterwards an Oxonian, has fallen into a hopeless state of epilepsy and fatuity, but is not likely to bring a miserable life to an early termination.* 27 Jun., 1 Aug., 12 Sep., 1 Oct., 24 Oct., 31 Oct., 21 Nov., 11 Dec., 26 Dec.

1851: 27 Feb., 3 Apr., 24 Apr., 19 May.

1852: 22 Jan., 5 Feb., 13 May, 2 Dec.

1853: 20 Jan., 17 Feb., 23 Feb: *My groom brought from Stow the intelligence of the sudden death, on Tuesday night, of Whitmore Jones: I saw him in apparently good health on Thursday last: and he attended on Monday the funeral of Sir Chs. Imhoff.* 24 Feb: *The report of Mr. Whitmore Jones's decease is not confirmed: the rumour had been very prevalent at Stow.* 3 Mar: *... There heard with much regret that poor Mr. Whitmore Jones is lying in a dangerous condition at Bengeworth. A fortnight ago it was currently rumoured that he had died suddenly; but there was no foundation for the report ... he was found, as it is alleged, on the floor of his bedroom, having been struck, I imagine with apoplexy: great apprehensions as to the event of the seizure were entertained: and it appears that to day Mrs. W.J. with many of her children have left Chastleton for Bengeworth on the receipt of very alarming tidings.* 6 Mar: *Mrs. W. Vavasour called on me after the afternoon service.—She reported the death of poor Whitmore Jones on Friday.*

WHITTELL — Miss Whittell at the Lefroys [141]

Joshua Francis Whittell (1805-1867), landed proprietor, of Helmsley, Yorkshire, married, 3 February 1831, Phoebe (1813-1883), daughter of Anthony Lefroy (1777-1857) and Elizabeth Wilkin (1780-1852); they had at least 1 son and 4 daughters:

1 Eugene Thomas Curzon (b. 1833-1863)
1 Henrietta Phoebe (b. 1836)
2 Anna Maria (b. 1837)
3 Julia (b. 1849)
4 Blanche Lefroy (1852-1940)

1853: 6 Jan: *... I had a very kind reception from Mrs. L. and was introduced to Miss Whittle, a niece of Lefroy's, now on a visit to him, and whose residence is with her parents at Helmsley in Yorkshire.*

WHYTE — Mark Anthony Whyte and Miss Whyte at Clifton [142]

Mark Antony Whyte (±1764-1838), JP, barrister-at-law, and landed proprietor, was born into a slave-owning and slave-trading Quaker family at Liverpool, the son of Antony Whyte, merchant, and Elizabeth, daughter of Robert Slater and Jane Gill. He was educated at Warrington Academy, Jesus College, Cambridge, and Lincoln's Inn, and called to the bar on 16 June 1792. Whyte married, by licence, 1798, Maria Louisa (1773-1855), born at Launde Abbey, Leicestershire, the daughter of John Simpson and Jane Finch. After his marriage Whyte apparently ceased practising. The couple lived at Barrow Hill, near Rocester, Staffordshire.

Mark Whyte's great-grandfather was Andrew Gill, of Chesterfield, and his uncle was Gill Slater, a Quaker who invested in the slave trade. Whyte inherited a portion of the slave-worked sugar plantations at Queensbury, on the island of St Vincent, from another uncle, Thomas Slater.

Whyte was on friendly terms with another Rocester Quaker, a bibliophile called Thomas Bainbrigge. The two men were instrumental in establishing the Friendly Society of Rocester in 1832, and donated most of the money needed to found the Quaker meeting hall there.

Maria Louisa Whyte was a bibliophile and art connoisseur. Her collection included the famous painting *An Elderly Couple* by Jan Gossaert [Jean Gossart], now in the National Gallery (reference NG1689), which she had bought at Christie's on 13 May 1847. It appears that on Bainbrigge's death she also acquired some of his collection.

Mark and Maria Whyte do not appear to have had any children. Mark died in 1838 and Maria in 1855. By her will of 12 January that year she bequeathed Barrow Hill and her painting and book collection there to her niece, Louisa Jane Finch Simpson (d. 1865), widow of Henry Dawson (d. 1849). On Mrs Dawson's death in 1865, her son, Capt. Arthur Finch Dawson (1836-1928), inherited the house and its valuable contents.

This then takes us to the identity of Miss Whyte. Only one daughter of Antony and Elizabeth Whyte has been discovered; this was Jane (b. 1767), younger sister to Mark Antony. On 26 February 1805, Francis Witts's 22nd birthday, Agnes Witts wrote, 'Again very windy but rather more mild Mr. & Mrs. Ram & Miss Port here before I went out when I made many visits, & calls ...' This is relevant to us for it shows that the Ram family were then resident at Clifton. Mark and Maria Whyte were close friends with Abel John Ram (1776-1823), who had married, 1805, Frances Port (1784-1860). The families were often in each other's company. If Mark and Maria had not bothered accompanying the Rams to Clifton, it seems that Jane had.

1805: 26 Feb: *At a very crowded Ball at York House in the Evening, where I danced with Miss Whyte ...* 27 Feb., 4 Mar.

1812: 5 Aug: *Immediately on crossing this Stream we are in the village of Rocester, which is in no respect remarkable; Cotton mills & weaving employ the population of this place. Soon after we ascended Barrow Hill, near the summit of which Mr. Whyte's house & grounds command a fine view down the fertile valley of the Dove.* 6 Aug.

WIGGIN — William Wiggin [143]

William Wiggin (1820-1901), Church of England clergyman, was born at Ardwick, Lancashire, the second son of Timothy Wiggin (1773-1856) and Catherine Holme (1782-1845). He was educated at Exeter College, Oxford (BA 1841, MA 1847), and was appointed rector of Oddington in 1844. He held the living until 1871, when he became rector of Hampnett. Wiggin married, first, at St Mary de Lode, Gloucester, 29 March 1842, Frances Emma (1814-1860), fifth daughter of Edward Rice (1776-1862), dean of Gloucester, and Charlotte Lascelles (1775-1832); they had 8 sons and 2 daughters:

1 Edward Hugo Rice (1843-1879); married, at Chester, 1873, Henrietta Baxter (1845-1933); at least 1 daughter:
  1 Cecil Frances Sarah Rice (1874-1970)
2 Henry William Rice (1844-1910); born at Offington; died, presumably unmarried, at Meddacombra estate, Ceylon
3 Augustus Holme (1846-1893); moved to Toronto, 1871, then to the USA; married Hannah L. Hansen; died at Albert Lea, Freeborn, Minnesota; 1 son and 1 daughter:
  1 Eva Stena (1886-1893)
  1 Thomas Henry (1889-1893)
1 Emmeline Maria Louisa (1847-1919); married, at Northleach, Gloucestershire, 4 September 1873, George William Goodeve (1849-1919); 3 sons and 3 daughters:
  1 George William (1874-1956)
  2 Edwin Henry (1875-1928)
  1 Emmeline Frances (1878-1881)
  2 Gladys Emma M. (1879-1896)
  3 Lionel (1881-1915)
  3 Violet Eva (1883-1950)
4 Edwin Rice (1849-1913), coffee and tea planter; died in Ceylon, presumably unmarried
5 Arthur Robert (1850-1903); married, 1872, at Holywell, Flintshire, Mabel Grace (1857-1919), daughter of John Scott Bankes; went to Ceylon to join his brother Edwin and co-manage a plantation; died at Lindula, Ceylon; at least 1 daughter:
  1 Dorothy Wynne (1881-1957)
6 Frederick John Rice (1852-1882); married Elizabeth Anne Griffith (b. 1855); died at South Pueblo, Colorado, USA; at least 1 daughter:
  1 Marguerite Eleanor Wiggin (b. 1876)
7 Herbert Rice (1853-1882), coffee planter; born at Oddington; moved to Ceylon
2 Caroline Eva (1855-1942); died unmarried at Cheltenham
8 Francis Holme (1859-1905); married, at Edmonton, Middlesex, 19 December 1889, Margaret Carey (1868-1906); 3 sons and 4 daughters:
  1 Noel Holme (1890-1917), Lt, 36th Brigade Royal Field Artillery; died at Kut-el-Amara, Iraq
  2 Arthur Francis Holme (1892-1935)
  1 Eva Margaret Holme (b. 1893)
  2 Mary Holme (b. 1894)
  3 Douglas Holme (1895-1914)
  3 Hilda Frances Holme (1901-1982)
  4 Frances Holme (1905-1990)

The Wiggin tribe demonstrated ample fecundity and overseas adventurism. Emmeline's husband, George William Goodeve, appears to have been the founder of the family's tradition in managing coffee and tea plantations in Ceylon [now Sri Lanka]. At least four of the sons died in Ceylon and two died in the United States.

Frances Emma Wiggin died soon after giving birth to Francis Holme. William married secondly, 1868, Caroline Susan Vavasour, née Vavasour (1816-1878), the widow of her cousin William Vavasour (1819-1863). By the time of the 1881 census the household also included William's son-in-law, George Goodeve, who had married his daughter Emmeline, and their 6-year-old son George, who had been born in Ceylon. George Goodeve (senior), although only 31, was listed in the census as a retired coffee planter.

William Wiggin was distantly related to Margaret Witts (*see* diary entry, 21 August 1844).

1842: 18 Apr: *Met at Stow Mr. and Mrs. Wiggin, lately married; the lady being Emma Rice, the Dean's Daughter, the Gentleman a young Oxonian, not yet in orders, and some years his wife's Junior, a Gentlemanly, accomplished young man, as we have heard, and son of a London merchant.* 2 May: *Left our cards at the Parsonage for Mr. and Mrs. Wiggin, who are gone within this day or two on visits for some weeks.* 24 May.

1844: 9-10 Apr., 6 May, 31 Jul., 21 Aug: *While we were out, Mr. Wiggin called; he is a relation of Mrs. Backhouse.* 24 Aug., 26 Aug., 29 Aug., 11 Sep., 18-19 Sep., 21 Sep., 26 Sep., 30 Sep., 11 Oct., 27 Oct., 28 Oct., 31 Oct.

1845: 7 Jan., 23 Jan., 6 Feb., 26 Mar., 25 Jun.

1846: 24 Jun., 21 Jul., 23-24 Jul., 27 Jul., 29 Jul: *A dinner party: the Dean of Gloucester, Mr. and Mrs. Wiggin, J. T. Rice, Mr. and Mrs. W. Vavasour, Miss Vavasour, and Henry Lindow made up our party.* 15 Aug., 26 Aug., 21 Sep., 19 Nov., 25 Nov.

1847: 28-29 Mar., 5-7 Apr., 5-7 Jul., 17 Jul., 8 Sep., 11 Sep., 21 Sep., 28 Sep., 30 Sep., 1 Nov., 19 Nov.

1848: 29 Feb., 11 May, 29 May, 7 Jun., 14-16 Jun., 7 Aug., 18 Aug., 23-24 Aug., 20 Sep., 26 Sep., 29 Sep., 6 Oct., 23 Oct., 1 Nov., 9 Nov., 12-13 Dec., 20 Dec., 27 Dec.

1850: 10 Jan., 31 Jan., 9 Feb., 18 May: *Mr. Wiggin showed me the plans of the new church which he proposes to build at Oddington, and hopes to commence next year. The designs are very good, and the Architect, Mr. Dankes, is creditably known by other works of a like character ...* 31 May, 12 Jun., 20 Jun., 25 Jun., 27 Jun., 18-19 Sep., 24 Sep., 1 Oct., 22-23 Oct., 25 Oct., 31 Oct., 7 Nov., 21 Nov., 27-28 Nov., 5 Dec., 19 Dec., 26 Dec.

1851: 31 Mar., 23-24 Apr., 30 Apr., 1 May, 8 May, 26 May.

1852: 22-23 Jan., 17 Mar., 19 Mar., 14 Apr., 22 Apr., 6 May, 17 May, 19-20 May, 26 May: ... *dinner party: in addition to our home party, the guests were Mr. and Mrs. J. T. Rice, Mr. & Mrs. Wiggin, Mr. and Mrs. Hippisley, Mrs. Dolphin, and Miss Kirby.* 11 Nov., 18 Nov., 25 Nov., 22 Dec., 30 Dec.

1853: 18 Feb., 21 Feb., 27 Feb., 15 Mar., 30 Mar., 1 Apr., 21 Apr., 28 Apr., 24 May, 26 May, 2 Jun., 22 Jun., 10 Dec., 13 Dec., 15 Dec., 22 Dec., 29 Dec.

1854: 22 Jun., 24 Jun., 6 Jul., 19-20 Jul.

WIGHTMAN — William Wightman[144]

Sir William Wightman (1784-1863), barrister-at-law and judge, was born in the parish of St Clement Danes, Westminster, the son of William Wightman, of an old Dumfriesshire family, and his wife, Elizabeth. He was educated at University College and Queen's College, Oxford (BA 1805; MA 1809), and was an honorary fellow of the latter from 1859 to his death in 1863. He was admitted at Lincoln's Inn in 1804 and called to the bar in 1821. In 1830 Wightman transferred himself to the Inner Temple and joined the northern circuit. He was engaged in many celebrated cases, particularly the prosecutions arising out of the Bristol riots, and was knighted in 1841. He married, 1819, a daughter of James Baird of Lasswade, near Edinburgh. Wightman died of a stroke in the judges' lodgings at York on 10 December 1863.

1852: 29 Mar: ... *dined with the Judges, Wightman & Platt ...*

WILBERFORCE — Samuel Wilberforce[145]

Samuel Wilberforce (1805-1873), bishop of Winchester, was born at Clapham, Surrey, the third son of William Wilberforce (1759-1833) (*below*) and Barbara Anne Spooner (1771-1847). He was educated at Oriel College, Oxford (BA 1826; MA 1829; B&DD 1845), and was elected an honorary fellow of All Souls' College. He was on the council of Keble College from 1871 to his death in 1873. Wilberforce's career in the Church ran as follows: curate of Checkendon, Oxfordshire, 1828-29; rector of Brighstone, Isle of Wight, 1830; rector of Alverstoke, Hampshire, 1840; prebendary of Winchester, 1840-44; archdeacon of Surrey, 1841-44; dean of Westminster 1844-45; bishop of Oxford 1845-69; and bishop of Winchester, 1869-73. He was also appointed lord high almoner and prelate of the Order of the Garter.

Wilberforce married, at Woolavington, Sussex, 11 June 1828, Emily (1807-1841), daughter of Revd John Sargent (1780-1833), evangelical rector of Lavington, Sussex, and Mary (1778-1861), daughter of the banker Abel Smith. Samuel and Emily had at least 4 sons and 2 daughters:

1 Emily Charlotte (1830-1917)
1 Herbert William (1833-1856)
2 Agnes (b. & d. 1837)
2 Reginald Garton (1838-1914)
3 Ernest Roland (1840-1907)
4 Albert Basil Orme (1841-1916)

Despite his long career—both distinguished and controversial—Wilberforce features poorly in the diaries, but this may have been because Witts did not live long enough to see him emerge as a defender of orthodoxy in the early 1860s. He moderated the hostility of evangelical critics; the Anglo-Catholics, starved of episcopal representation, increasingly forgot their reservations and adopted him as their champion. By the time of Gladstone's appointment as prime minister, Wilberforce was no longer viewed as a controversial figure, but one whose stature in the Church was unquestionably assured. For a long and detailed life, see the *DNB* entry.

1842: 18 Dec.

1845: 13 Feb.

1847: 26 Jun., 6 Jul.

1848: 13 Jan.

WILBERFORCE — William Wilberforce[146]

William Wilberforce (1759-1833), MP, philanthropist, and slavery abolitionist, was born at Hull, the only son of Robert Wilberforce (1728-1768), merchant, and Elizabeth (d. 1798), daughter of Thomas Bird of Barton, Oxfordshire. He began his political career in 1780, eventually becoming the independent MP for Yorkshire, 1784-1812. In 1785 he became an evangelical christian, which precipitated major changes to his lifestyle and a lifelong concern for reform. In 1787, Wilberforce came into contact with Thomas Clarkson and a group of anti-slave-trade activists, including Granville Sharp, Hannah More, and Charles Middleton. They persuaded him to take on the cause for abolition, and he soon became one of the leading English abolitionists.

Wilberforce headed the parliamentary campaign against the British slave trade for twenty years until the passage of the Slave Trade Act of 1807. In later years, he supported the campaign for the complete abolition of slavery; he resigned from parliament in 1826 because of his failing health, but continued his involvement after this date. The campaign led to the Slavery Abolition Act of 1833, which abolished slavery in most of the British Empire.

Wilberforce married, at St Swithin's, Walcot, Bath, 30 May 1797, Barbara Anne (1771-1847), daughter of Abraham Spooner (b. 1751); they had 4 sons and 2 daughters:

1 William (1798-1879); married, 19 June 1820, Mary Frances Owen (1800-1880); 3 sons:
    1 William (1821-1900)
    2 Robert (1824-1825); died an infant
    3 Edward (b. 1834)
1 Barbara (1799-1821)
2 Elizabeth (1801-1832)
2 Robert Isaac (1802-1857); married, at Bridlington, Yorkshire, 16 June 1832, Agnes Everilda Frances Wrangham (1800-1834); 2 sons:
    1 William Francis (1833-1905)
    2 Edward (1834-1914)
3 Samuel (1805-1873); *see above*
4 Henry William (1807-1873); married, 24 July 1834, Mary Sargent (1811-1878); 6 sons and 4 daughters:
    1 John William (1835-1847)
    2 Arthur Henry Bertrand (1839-1904)
    1 Mary Florence (1840-1841); died an infant
    3 Ambrose Newman (1841-1842); died an infant
    2 Caroline M. (1844-1915)
    3 Agnes Everilda Mary (1845-1890)
    4 Henry Edward (1847-1938)
    5 John (b. 1850)
    6 Wilfred Ignatius (1850-1910)
    4 Mary Philippa (b. & d. 1853)

1824: 5 Feb: *The well meant, but injudicious and rather fanatical urgency of Messrs. Wilberforce, Buxton & others, forming a strong party in & out of the House of Commons ...* 27 Jun.

1826: 26 Apr: *At the pump room we saw the celebrated Mr. Wilberforce. I had never before seen him, except in the House of Commons some years ago, when Sir F. Burdett made a scornful reply to a quiet speech of his in defence of loyal principles & in reprobation of seditious practices. He was then a plain, upright, grave, elderly man: now he is withered, shrunk, bowed even to deformity, a wreck: but there is something still expressive in his eye, a seriousness over his features, which indicates the repose of a good man on the verge of life.*

WILBRAHAM — Edward Wilbraham [147]

Edward Wilbraham (1785-1859), barrister-at-law, was born at Horsley [Nailsworth], Gloucestershire, the son of Edward Wilbraham, of the Cheshire Wilbrahams, and Mary, daughter of William Matthews. He was a bencher at Lincoln's Inn in 1842 and a QC. In 1845 he became a director of Equity & Law Life Assurance. For such an eminent person, Edward Wilbraham has left a very small biographical footprint. He lived in Torrington Square, Bloomsbury, and appears to have been unmarried. Among other bequests at his death, he left £300 to the village school in his native Horsley, where he was both born and buried.

1824: 27 Apr.

1835: 21 Feb: *... Conferred on their content and determined upon submitting a case to Mr. Wilbraham of the Chancery Bar for his opinion.* 5 Mar., 7-8 Apr., 11 Apr., 15 May.

WILCOX — Charles Wilcox of Upper Slaughter [148]

Charles Wilcox (1809-1877), agricultural labourer, was the son of Edward and Susan Wilcox (*below*). He married, first, Mary (±1809-1869), born at Icomb, Worcestershire; they had 1 son and 3 daughters:

1 Anne (b. & d. 1845)
1 George (b. ±1846); married Sarah Elizabeth Gibbs (b. 1850), born at Stretton-on-Fosse, Warwickshire; they appear to have lived in Essex
2 Anne (1850-1851)
3 Mary (b. 1851)

Mary died in 1869 and Charles married secondly, at Upper Slaughter, 5 March 1872, Jane Bridgman, née Gardner (b. ±1829), daughter of Thomas Gardner and widow of William Bridgman (1828-1869), son of Michael and Elizabeth Bridgman. William and Jane had married at Lower Slaughter on 12 October 1850. Jane appears to have had a life full of grief and sadness; out of nine children only two survived her.

1845: 15 Feb: *We settled that ... also that C Wilcox should be appointed by me Parish Clerk.*

1854: 17 Jun: *Visiting C Wilcox, the parish Clerk, who is suffering from a bad cold &c.* 23 Jun.

WILCOX — Edward and Susan Wilcox of Upper Slaughter [149]

Edward Wilcox (1783-1865), agricultural labourer, was born at Upper Slaughter, the son of Thomas Wilcox (1762-1845) and Mary Combs (±1761-1828). He married Susan (1781-1855), from Aston Blank; they had at least 3 sons and 5 daughters:

1 Diana (1805-1818); buried under the registered name 'Dinah'
1 William (b. 1807)
2 Charles (1809-1877)
2 Jane (b. 1813)
3 George (b. 1817)
3 Mary (1819-1839)
4 Sarah (b. 1823)
5 Hannah (b. 1827)

1850: 5 Feb: *... prayed with the widow Rogers; visited Mrs. Collett, Widows Gardner, E. Wilcox's wife, and Mrs. Dix ...*

1851: 4 Mar.

1852: 10 Feb., 21 Feb., 19 May: *Visited the Townsends—read prayers to them and Susan Wilcox.* 5 Jun: *... Both are very helpless and feeble.—So also Susan Wilcox, whom I also visited.*

1853: 6 May, 9 May: *Administered the Holy Communion privately to Sus. Wilcox, her daughter in law, wife of C.W. and Mary Collett.* 14 May, 18 May.

WILCOX — Elizabeth Wilcox of Upper Slaughter [150]

Elizabeth Wilcox, née Norris (±1790-1855), was born at Eyford. She married, at Upper Slaughter, 28 May 1827, Wiliam Wilcox of Eyford. When Francis Witts visited her in 1851 she was living as a lodger at Upper Slaughter in the home of Matthew David (b. ±1794), an agricultural labourer, born in Little Rissington. His 14-year-old daughter, Ruth, was there too. Elizabeth may have been acting as some sort of housekeeper.

1846: 26 Dec.

1848: 12 Feb.

1850: 9 Sep: *Visited aged and sick parishioners ... the Gregorys ... Widow Wilcox ...* 21 Oct., 25 Nov., 13 Dec.

1851: 4 Jan., 31 Jan., 4 Mar., 5 Apr., 15 Apr., 2 May, 17 May: *Visited Widow Wilcox, who is suffering from Erysipelas.*

1852: 28 Jan., 6 Mar., 23 Mar., 2 Apr: *Administered the holy communion privately ... and the Widow Wilcox—three feeble creatures,—as one of them said weak in body, but it was to be hoped strong in faith.* 7 May, 10 Dec.

1853: 6 May, 17 Dec.

1854: 28 Jan., 8 Feb., 25 Feb., 22 Mar., 15 Apr., 19 May, 23 Jun., 11 Jul., 29 Jul., 16 Aug.

WILCOX — Joseph Wilcox of Upper Slaughter[151]

Joseph Wilcox (1799-1846), agricultural labourer, of Quenington, was born at Upper Slaughter, the son of Thomas Wilcox (1762-1845) and Mary Combs (±1761-1828). He was a younger brother of Edward (*above*).

1846: 28 Jun: *Afternoon service, prayers, after which the funeral of Jos. Wilcox, a native of this parish, brought from Quenington, where and at Bibury he has long resided—a labourer.*

WILDE — the Wilde family at Cheltenham

1801: 5 Nov: *Mrs. Wilde called ...* 23 Nov: ... *Conversed most with Mrs. Gray, & Miss Wilde & young D'Alton.* 24 Nov: *In the Evening a Rout at Mrs. Coutt's ... chiefly conversing with my friend Mrs. Gray & Miss M. Wilde.* 25 Nov: *Walked with Miss M. Wilde.*

WILDE — Thomas Wilde[152]

Sir Thomas Wilde (1782-1855), lord chancellor, was born in Warwick Square, Newgate Street, London, the second son of Thomas Wilde, attorney, of London and Saffron Walden, Essex, and Mary Ann Knight. He was educated at St Paul's School and was admitted an attorney in 1805. He was the younger brother of Sir John Wilde, and James Wilde, 1st Baron Penzance, was his nephew. Thomas entered the Inner Temple and was called to the bar in 1817. He was retained in 1820 for the defence of Queen Caroline, and distinguished himself in cross-examination. Having thereby gained some celebrity early on, the way was opened to an extensive common-law practice. Queen Caroline, meantime, expressed her gratitude by making him one of her executors alongside Stephen Lushington.

In 1824 Wilde was made serjeant-at-law, and in 1827 he was made king's serjeant. He was MP for Newark in 1831-32 and 1835-41, and for Worcester in 1841-46. He was appointed solicitor-general in 1839, knighted in 1840, and succeeded Sir John Campbell as attorney-general in 1841. In 1846 Wilde was appointed chief justice of the court of common pleas. He held the office until 1850, when he became lord chancellor. He was then created Baron Truro of Bowes in the county of Middlesex. Wilde remained lord chancellor until the fall of the Russell ministry in 1852.

1826: 7 Aug: *Serjeant Wilde had been retained, & was expected every moment from the Western circuit; he had been paid his three hundred guineas ...* 28 Aug: *Messrs. Lawrence & Newmarch have inserted in the Gloucester Journal an explanation of the absence of Mr. Serjeant Wilde, whereby the Sandywell cause was withdrawn.*

1846: 10 Aug: *The business of the Assizes was begun ... Wilde, sat at Nisi Prius.*

WILDMAN — John Wildman and the Wildman family[153]

John Wildman (1793-1877), army officer, was born in London, the third son of Thomas Wildman (1740-1795), of Bedford Square, London, and Bacton Hall, Suffolk, and the second son of Sarah (1750-1830), Wildman's second wife and daughter of Henry Hardinge of Durham. Thomas Wildman was lawyer and consigliere to the Beckfords of Fonthill Magna, Wiltshire. John was also a nephew of the political reformer John Horne Tooke.

John Wildman matriculated at Christ Church, Oxford, but appears to have changed his mind about gaining a degree. He became a colonel in the Army, presumably by purchase, and married, 1824, Margaret (1800-1825), daughter of Francis Charteris, 8th earl of Wemyss, and Margaret Campbell. Margaret died at Devonshire Cottage, Richmond, on 22 October 1825, shortly after their marriage. John did not remarry, and stayed close to the Charteris family for the remainder of his life. In the 1851 census he was listed as a visitor at 39 Brook Street, Hanover Square, and in the 1871 census as a visitor at Hanover Chambers, 23 Hanover Square.

John's elder brother, Thomas Wildman (1787-1859), was also a colonel in the Army. He had fought at the battles of Corunna and Waterloo. The Wildman family—known for being unscrupulous lawyers—had obtained Quebec estate, a large sugar plantation in Jamaica, from William Beckford when he was experiencing financial problems. The wealth generated from this plantation provided Thomas Wildman with the means to purchase Newstead Abbey in 1818 for £95,000 from a Mr Clawton, who had bought it from Lord Byron for £14,000. Like Beckford, Byron had been suffering from financial difficulties; he had been trying to sell the abbey since 1812. Thomas Wildman had gone to Harrow with Lord Byron and the two were old friends; Byron's half-sister Augusta said Wildman had 'soul enough to value the dear Abbey', and he was considered to be the man who saved Byron's home. Wildman spent £100,000 restoring it, hiring the architect John Shaw to make improvements. He also amassed a large collection of Byron memorabilia there, and hosted many visitors including Franz Liszt. Thomas Wildman served as high sheriff for Nottinghamshire in 1821-22.

1825: 28 Oct: *I received an intimation from Lady Elcho of the decease of Lady Margaret Wildman, one of the many daughters of Lord Wemyss. This poor young lady has fallen victim to consumption at the age of 26, exactly a year after her union with Captain Wildman, a cavalry officer, who is left in great affliction.*

1829: 11 Jul: *Our object in our drive to-day was to pay our respects to Lord & Lady Wemyss, who arrived at Lady Elcho's two or three days ago, accompanied by the Ladies Louisa and Harriet Charteris and Col. Wildman, his Lordship's widowed son-in-law.*

1836: 26 Jul: *Lady Wemyss's party to Cheltenham consisted of herself, her two daughters, Lady Grey of Groby, and Lady Jane Charteris, Col. Wildman ... 27 Jul.*

1839: 17 Jul: ... *The family will not prolong their stay beyond ten days. Lord and Lady Belhaven, Col. Wildman, and young Charteris, Lord Elcho's eldest son, an Oxonian, are expected.*

1840: 18 Jul: *Lady Jane & Lady Caroline Charteris, and Major Wildman are staying at Stanway, and were very friendly and pleasant.* 19 Jul: *The Ladies Charteris, Major Wildman and myself took a long evening walk as far as the Cottages at Toddington.* 20 Jul.

1842: 16 Jul: ... *at 7 o clock we sat down ... the party consisting of Lord and Lady W.—Ladies Jane & Caroline Charteris, Colonel Wildman, Mr. Marshall and myself.* 17 Jul., 31 Jul.

1844: 26 Jul: *Mr. Wildman, and Mr. Campbell made up the party ...*

1847: 26 Jul.

1849: 28 Dec: *Another letter was sent in the packet, received from Gosford House, written by Col. Wildman, giving a melancholy report of Lord and Lady Wemyss, both of whom are confined to their beds, he very feeble and declining ...*

1851: 24 May: *I met ... the ladies Jane and Caroline Charteris escorted, as usual, by Col. Wildman.*

WILKINS — Charles Wilkins[154]

Sir Charles Wilkins (1749-1836), orientalist, was born at Frome, Somerset, the son of Hugh Wilkins and Mary Wray. His mother was niece of the engraver Robert Bateman Wray and the banker Charles Wray, a partner in Hoare's Bank in London. Charles Wray procured a writership in the East India Company's Bengal establishment for his great-nephew, Charles Wilkins.

In 1770 Wilkins became superintendent of the company's factories at Malda, Bengal. Encouraged by Warren Hastings, he took up the study of Sanskrit and became the first Englishman to master the language. Wilkins returned to England in 1786, most likely due to the departure of his friend and patron Warren Hastings and the state of his health. The following year he married Elizabeth Keble in London. The couple resided at Bath for a time, and then returned to London; they were living there in 1788 when Wilkins was elected to the Royal Society in recognition of his pioneering studies of Sanskrit and his typographical achievements. His first wife died around that time, and late in 1789 Wilkins married Lucy Shingler at Hawkhurst, Kent. He was knighted in 1833.

Although Wilkins never completed his dictionary of Sanskrit, he produced three lexicographical publications, the first of which seems to have been a fragment of that project. His second publication was a glossary of words in Indian languages connected with land revenue, and the third was his revision of John Richardson's *A Dictionary: Persian, Arabic, and English* (1806). Persian was the *lingua franca* of Indian diplomacy, and it was via this language that western scholars first began to explore Sanskrit literature.

Wilkins was precisely the type of cultivated person that Lady Lyttelton chose to associate with. She may well have known him in the English community in Calcutta.

1801: 4 Jul: ... *party at Lady Lyttelton's consisting of Dr. Garnett, whose conversation did not gratify me much more than his pamphlet, Mr. Moore, Mr. Wilkins, who, I am told, assisted in translating the Sanscrit ...* 9 Oct: *Evening at Mrs. Doig's where met Lady Lytt, Mr. and Miss Morley, Mr. & Miss Wilkins.*

WILKINS — John North Wilkins[155]

John North Wilkins (1788-1854), solicitor, was born at Bourton-on-the Water, the son of Baptist minister Revd William Wilkins (1753-1812) and Elizabeth North (1753-1798). He was baptised in the Baptist church at Bourton in October 1788. He married, 1820, Anna Eliza Cobb (1799-1877) of Banbury; they had at least 5 sons and 3 daughters:

- 1 William (b. 1821); probably died young
- 1 Elizabeth (1822-1909); died unmarried at Hastings
- 2 William Henry (1824-1880), solicitor and parliamentary agent; lived at Barnes, Surrey, 1861, and Kingston, Surrey, 1871; married Mary (b. ±1827), born at Wandsworth, Surrey; 2 sons and 1 daughter:
  - 1 William Howell (b. ±1852)
  - 1 Ada (b. ±1858)
  - 2 Edward (b. ±1866)
- 3 John Edward (1826-1889), barrister; arrived at New York, 1853, and renounced his allegiance to the king of Hanover when asked to state his intention to become a US citizen; married, at Cook, Illinois, USA, 7 April 1856, Margery W. Steele (b. 1834), born at Montreal, Canada; returned to England and by 1881 was living at 10 Wyndham Place, Marylebone, Westminster, and practising as a barrister; died at Chicago, Cook County, Illinois, USA; no known children
- 4 Albert (b. 1828), architect; lived, unmarried, at Kingston-on-Thames, 1881; not heard of after
- 2 Emily Anne (1830-1833); died an infant
- 5 Francis (b. 1833), banker's clerk; lived at Gloucester, 1851; not heard of after
- 3 Letitia Augusta (1835-1892); lived with her sister Elizabeth at Hastings, 1891; died unmarried

Wilkins was a solicitor in partnership with William Kendall at Bourton-on-the-Water. Kendall married, at Bourton, April 1825, Wilkins' half-sister, Letitia, daughter of Revd William Wilkins and his second wife, Letitia, daughter of John Field and Anne Cromwell. Although John Wilkins was one of the leading dissenters of Bourton, he rubbed along well with Francis Witts. For personal matters, however, Witts used the services of Newmarch of Cirencester. John Wilkins was involved in the Friendly Society of Bourton and was also a guardian of the Stow Union Workhouse.

1828: 20 Oct: *I went by appointment to the Office of Messrs. Wilkins & Kendal, Solicitors, Bourton on the Water, to complete a purchase, which we had recently made of Mr. Dolphin ...*

1829: 24 Nov: *Messrs. Aplin of Chipping Norton, and Wilkins of Bourton on the Water, Attorneys, who had coalesced on this occasion, and presented themselves to the Commissioners to share in the emoluments and duties of the office.*

1830: 20 Apr: ... *He is not again to return to fill the post of Judge Advocate at Gibraltar ... are to be transferred for the most part to the Civil Judge, there, a Mr. Baron Field, who has held a judicial post at New South Wales (& is a connexion of Mr. Wilkins, the Attorney at Bourton on the Water) ...* 22 Apr.

1833: 18 Oct.

1834: 16-17 Jul., 4 Sep., 22 Sep., 15 Nov., 26 Nov.

1835: 6 Jan., 5 Feb., 16 Feb., 18-21 Mar., 3 Apr., 24 Apr., 27 Apr., 16 May, 21 May, 28 May, 1 Jun., 16 Jun, 16 Jul: *In the Evening a long conference with Mr. Wilkins on the purchase of land for the erection of a workhouse.*

1836: 23 Jul., 25 Jul., 2 Aug., 22 Aug., 25 Aug., 24 Sep., 10 Oct. Mainly dealing through 1836 with the Ackerley affair.

1837: 25 Jan., 6 Feb., 12-13 Feb., 4 Apr., 8 Apr., 11 Apr., 14 Apr., 29 May, 31 May, 1 Jun., 7 Jun., 10 Jun., 12 Jun., 16 Jun., 19-20 Jun., 24 Jun., 5 Jul., 7 Jul., 11 Jul., 13-15 Jul., 19-20 Jul, 24 Jul., 11 Aug., 6 Sep., 11 Sep., 30 Sep., 11 Oct., 18 Nov., 12-15 Dec: The action brought by D'Oyley.

1838: 11 Jan., 2 Feb., 8-9 Feb., 14-15 Feb., 5-7 March., 29 Mar., 31 Mar., 5 Apr., 20 Apr: *Messrs. Beman, Comely, Shelton, W. Bryan have accepted the invitation, Mr. Wilkins has declined it on the plea of reluctance to dine any where from home ...* 27 Apr: *Messrs. Beman, Bryan, Comely and Shelton had accepted the invitation; Messrs. Wilkins & Tarn had excused themselves on the score of ill-health ...* 4 May, 7 May, 9 May, 18 May: *Attended at Lower Slaughter a court Leet & Baron of Sir G. Whitmore, over which Mr. Wilkins presided: he solicited my presence, it being necessary that two Copyholders should attend, and absence or death prevented more than one besides me from coming.* 22 May, 30 Jun., 9 Jul., 7-8 Oct., 29 Oct., 31 Oct., 1 Nov.

1839: 17 May, 22 May, 7 Jun: *besides a considerable party of ordinary members and musicians about fifteen dined on very good and well cooked viands at the high table, being Trustees & Honorary members—Waller, Polson, Wilkins, Kimber, W. Smith, E. Lea, J. Bennett, Ransford, T. Collett, W. & Jos. Bryan, C. Barton &c.—There was much of good humour, hilarity, and good feeling, assisted by libations of punch, toasts, speeches, returning of thanks and music ...*

1840: 15 May, 30 May, 5 Jun: *At half past one sat down to dinner, R Waller taking the Chair, about sixty dined, and of these eighteen or twenty were honorary Members ... Wilkins, Kendall ... three hours of loyal and complimentary toasts, punch often brewed & replenished, the Wick Band enlivening the company with its really well performed music, much cheerfulness and good humour ...* 8 Jun., 13 Jun., 19 Jun., 25 Jun., 5-6 Aug., 10 Sep., 17 Sep., 15 Oct., 7 Nov.

1842: 11 Feb., 25-26 Feb., 19 Mar., 3 May, 28 May, 9 Jun., 16-17 Jun., 21 Jul: *I was overtaken as I walked from Lower Slaughter Turnpike Gate to Stow, by Mr. Wilkins, who gave me a seat in his gig, with whom I conferred on magisterial business in which he was professionally concerned.* 9 Aug., 15 Aug., 18 Aug., 5 Sep., 3 Oct., 8 Nov.

1843: 8 Feb., 18 Aug., 30 Sep., 7 Oct., 10 Oct., 18 Oct., 27 Oct., 2 Nov., 27 Nov., 2 Dec., 4 Dec., 7 Dec., 12 Dec., 19 Dec.

1844: 1 Feb., 23 Mar., 27 Mar., 30 Mar., 2 Apr., 6 Apr., 10 Aug., 12 Aug., 4 Oct., 10 Oct., 29 Oct., 17 Dec., 28 Dec.

1845: 8 Feb., 28 Feb: *T. Fulljames called agreeably to his appointment,—with whom I walked to Bourton Bridge, where we met Messrs. Ford and R Waller, with Mr. Stokes, also Mr. Wilkins, and surveyed the site, consulting on the best plan of widening the bridge ...* 16 May, 6 Jun., 7 Jul.

1846: 7 Jul., 29 Oct., 12 Nov.

1847: 10 Apr., 14 Apr., 4 May, 10 Jun., 19 Aug., 21 Aug., 28 Oct., 22 Sep., 30 Sep., 14 Oct., 21 Dec.

1848: 8 Jan., 14 Feb., 16 Feb., 2 Mar., 16 Mar., 2 May, 2 Jun., 10 Jun., 15 Jun: *Learnt from Mr. Wilkins that Vernon Dolphin had quitted the neighbourhood, some arrangement having been made as between the husband and wife, in which Harry Waller and Mr. Polhill were the negociating parties ...* 17 Aug., 12 Sep., 20 Sep., 21 Oct., 24 Oct., 10 Nov., 23-24 Nov., 1 Dec., 5 Dec., 7 Dec., 14 Dec.

1850: 20-22 Feb., 28 Feb., 14 Mar., 22 May, 3 Dec., 21 Dec.

1851: 27 Jan., 7 Feb., 13 Feb., 26-27 Feb., 28 Feb: *Wrote a note to Mr. Royce, to accompany an architectural drawing by Mr. Wilkin's son, settled as an architect at Cirencester, formerly a pupil of Mr. Fulljames, for a schoolroom. Mr. W. Junr. offers it to Mr. R's notice not in the expectation of its being adopted, or of any emolument, but as an opportunity of making known his acquirements in his profession.* 13 Mar., 19 Mar., 29 Mar: *Mr. Wilkins followed me thither; conferred with him about these people, as to whom Mrs. W. and her daughter are very charitably disposed, and willing to assist by clothing the child, and otherwise.* 12 Apr.

1852: 1 Apr., 8 Apr., 3 Jun., 5-6 Nov., 18 Nov., 2 Dec., 16 Dec., 22 Dec.

1853: 21 Jan: *Having learnt in a conversation with H. W. Lindow yesterday, that certain impressions of an unfavourable nature had been made on his mind as to the management of our Union concerns, and particularly, as to the employment of Mr. Wilkins in a late parish settlement & lunatic case, and to the Union of the offices of Clerk and Guardian in one person, Mr. Pearce, Exparte views on this subject having been conveyed by John Pegler, who is a busy critic of Union management, ill disposed towards Wilkins, & desirous of change, especially if it should result in a discomfiture of Dissenters, wrote to HWL. At considerable length, pointing out to him the real facts of the matters complained of, and shewing that there is another side of the affairs, different from that which has been presented to him.* 19 Mar., 21 Mar., 23-24 Mar., 30 Mar., 7 Apr., 13 Apr., 16 Apr., 3-4 May, 6 May: *A note from Mr. Wilkins accompanied an obliging present of a dish of trout.* 7 May, 9 May, 23 Jun., 10 Dec.

1854: 3 Feb., 6 Feb., 7 Apr., 15 Apr., 11 May, 3 Jun., 8 Jun., 24 Jun., 17 Jul: *Mr. Wilkins has had an attack of apoplexy; but prompt medical treatment has relieved him.* 22 Jul: *Heard to-day of the decease yesterday morning of Mr. Wilkins, the Attorney of Bourton on the Water—- On Sunday he had an attack of Apoplexy—on Friday he is called to his account—a younger man than I am ...* 23 Jul: *In the Evening I received a note from Mr. W. Wilkins Son of the late Mr. W., asking me to allow my Servant John Beale to be one of the bearers to the grave of his poor Father's remains on Thursday next: JB., being a Bourton man, may have been in some manner employed heretofore in the Wilkins family.* 24 Jul: *Wrote to Mr. W. Wilkins that I should readily spare John Beale to attend at the funeral of his Father, adding a few words of sympathy and condolence ...*

WILKINS — Thomas Wilkins [156]

Thomas Wilkins (b. 1804), a labourer at Stow-on-the-Wold, was charged on 19 July 1854 for having 'carnally known a female ass' at Naunton on 24 June that year. Nothing more has been discovered about Wilkins and it is not known what his sentence was. He was not included in the Stow 1851 census. Although he was recorded as a labourer in the prison record, Francis Witts stated that he was a postman.

1854 18 Jul: *Mr. R Waller called by appointment to be present at the examination of Thos. Wilkins of Winchcomb, postman from Naunton to Winchcomb, charged with bestiality—a disgusting case, clearly established by the evidence.*

WILKINSON — Miss Wilkinson and Miss Amelia Wilkinson at Clifton and Cheltenham [157]

Little has been discovered relating to the Wilkinson family at Clifton. There appears to have been two Misses Wilkinson, one of whom, presumably the younger, was named Amelia. In the diaries of Agnes Witts they both feature at Clifton between 1803 and 1807. Agnes made her first reference to them on 3 September 1803:

> ... up so early as to be on Richmond Terrace between 7 & 8 to be present at the melancholly procession of the Funeral of Captain Mosshead of the S. Devon Militia the whole Regt. drawn up & the Band playing appropriate pieces very Solemn & affecting the greater part of the time in Miss Wilkinsons Lodgings ...

From this it may be surmised that the sisters had taken lodgings at Richmond Terrace. Over the next three to four years Agnes mentioned them more than forty times in her diary, the last reference being on 4 September 1807. Eight years later the two sisters arrived at Cheltenham, and a further ten or so references followed between 6 December 1815 and 24 November 1817, after which period Agnes did not mention them again. There seems to have been a connection between the Misses Wilkinson and the Auriol family, but this has not yet been unravelled.

1804: 14 Jan: *Accompanied the Marriots & my Father & Mother who had previously been at Sir Ed. William's to Miss Wilson's small party the Horton's Wilkinson's etc. etc. Passed the Evening pleasantly in conversation.* 30 Dec:
Walked with Mrs. Cooper, Miss Willins, & Miss A Wilkinson ...

1805: 26 Jan: *Passed the Evening alone, my Father & Mother being at the Miss Wilkinsons.* 7 Mar: *Walked to Bristol with Miss A. Wilkinson.*

1806: 14 Jan: *... to Barry's Library in Bristol & returned with the conversible Miss A Wilkinson.*

WILKINSON — George Wilkinson [158]

George Wilkinson (1814-1890), architect, was born at Witney, Oxfordshire, the eldest son of William Anthony Wilkinson (1783-1838) and Mary Hunter (1784-1864). He was the elder brother of William Wilkinson (1819-1901), presumably also an architect, who practised in Oxford. George won a competition in 1835 to design a workhouse for the Thame Poor Law Union and went on to design a total of two dozen workhouses in England; these included those at Northleach (1835), Stow-on-the-Wold (1836), and Woodstock (1836-37), each with wings laid out in an H-plan. Wilkinson built Tenbury Workhouse (1837) on a double courtyard plan, and for two others, Witney (1835-36) and Chipping Norton (1836), he used the unusual design of a saltire with four wings radiating from an octagonal central block. For Wolverhampton he adapted this layout to incorporate six wings. In 1839 Wilkinson was invited to Ireland as the architect of the Poor Law Commission. He was made a fellow of the Royal Institute of British Architects in 1878.

Wilkinson married, at St Mary's, Witney, Oxfordshire, 18 December 1850, Mary (1816-1864), daughter of John Williams Clinch (1788-1871), the Witney brewer, banker, and landowner; they had at least 4 daughters:

1. Annie Elizabeth (1857-1904)
2. Edith (dates unknown)
3. Florence (dates unknown)
4. Alice (dates unknown)

1836: 28 Jul: *We regarded the agreement made last week with Clifford as final, subject to the opinion which the Architect might give as to the land being suitable for the erection of the proposed building; and Mr. Wilkinson was to be requested to meet the Building Comm. on Monday next to view the site.* 30 Jul., 22 Nov., 22 Dec: *Mr. Wilkinson, the Architect, attended the board with the plans of the workhouse, suggesting the propriety of certain alterations, and that measures should be taken for the supply of water on the premises by sinking a well, or otherwise.*

1837: 16 Mar., 3 Aug., 31 Aug: *Visited both the Workhouses and at the New Workhouse had an interview with Wilkinson, the Architect, who was inspecting the building.* 5 Sep., 20 Nov., 23 Nov: *As I was on the point of setting out for Stow, detained by a call from Mr. Wilkinson, the Architect of our Union, to explain that he had been prevented from fulfilling his engagement at the Workhouse on Monday last ...* 21 Dec.

1838: 24-25 Jan., 9 Jul.

WILKINSON — John Wilkinson, solicitor of Messrs Lake, Wilkinson, and Lake [159]

John Wilkinson was a solicitor in partnership with Messrs Lake at 10 Newsquare, Lincoln's Inn.

1842: 3 Apr: *recd. a letter from Messrs. Lake, Wilkinson, and Lake, Solrs. Lincoln's Inn, desiring me to forward an extract from my Parish Register of the baptism of Frances, daughter of a Visc. Courtenay in 1763, at which time the Peer seems to have resided at Eyford.*

WILKINSON — Josiah Wilkinson, solicitor of Messrs Satchell Stevens, Wilkinson, and Satchell [160]

Josiah Wilkinson was a solicitor in partnership with William Stevens and John Satchell at Queen Street, Cheapside. The partnership was dissolved by mutual assent in 1845.

1839: 6 May: ... *and found myself in due time in Queen Street, Cheapside at the business house of Messrs. Satchell Stevens, Wilkinson and Satchell, where I learnt that my labour was in vain, that Mr. Wilkinson was already gone to the H. of Lords, and that thither I must follow him, where I should find him by applying at the office of Mr. Thompson, Parliamentary Agent.* 7 May.

WILLAN — Mr Willan at the Dolphins' dinner party

1824: 19 Feb: *Dolphin's dinner party—Miss Browne of Salperton, Mr. G. Hutchinson, half brother to Mrs. Dolphin, a well informed conversible travelled man, Mr. Willan & the Revd. Mr. Bragge, Cousin to Mr. Dolphin (the two latter of the sporting genus).*

WILLARD — John Harry Willard [161]

John Harry Willard (1770-1845), landed proprietor, was born at Eastbourne, Sussex, the son of Thomas George Willard (1729-1794) and Harriet Davis (1740-1807). He married, at Cheam, Surrey, 18 July 1815, a widow, Charlotte Antrobus, née Vardon (1778-1865), daughter of Samuel Vardon (b. 1755) and Charlotte Ling (1755-1813). Willard was lieutenant-colonel in Brighton's Royal Sussex Militia. He was also a correspondent of the duke of Richmond.

1833: 18 Jan: *We dined at Lady Reade's at Oddington: a party of seventeen. Sir John Reade's birth-day: who was present. Sir Charles & Lady Imhoff, Miss Chapuset, a Col. & Mrs. Willard, on a visit to Lady R. agreeable people of the world ...* 21 Jan: *Dined at Mrs. Hastings's, Daylesford House. Met nearly the same party as we did on Friday at Oddington; Sir John & Miss Reade, Col. & Mrs. Willard ...*

WILLCOX — T. Willcox & Son [162]

The firm was probably T. Willcox & Son of St Michael's Hill, Bristol.

1844: 10 Apr: *Magistrates met in the Grand Jury room ... to receive some explanation as to certain tenders delivered in yesterday for the buildings at the gaol ... in the course of the morng. and the answer led to the acceptance of Messrs. Wilcox of Bristol, as contractors for the work, being men of capital and great experience in large works ...*

WILLIAM IV — *see* Brunswick-Lüneburg

WILLIAMS — Revd Williams at Oddington

This young clergyman has not been identified. He followed Revd Mr Houghton to the curacy in 1847, but had departed some time before 1851.

1847: 28 Mar: *A letter from Mr. Wiggin, dated Deanery, Gloucester, who is in trouble, in consequence of a servant of his late strange curate of Oddington, Mr. Houghton, persisting in holding a cottage of which Mr. H. had the occupation as Curate, to the great inconvenience of Mr. Williams, the present Curate, and annoyance of the Dean and Wiggin—Mr. Williams is directed to call on me, and this letter is to prepare me for his visit, and to request me to take some steps as a Magistrate to eject the woman.* 7 Apr., 29 Apr., 6-7 Jul., 8 Sep., 21 Sep.

1848: 8 Fe 1848: 8 Feb., 22 Feb., 26 Apr.

WILLIAMS — Mrs Williams of Victoria park, Manchester

1851: 30 Apr: *Received a letter from Mrs. Williams, a lady residing at or near Manchester, and a connection of the Skipton Lonsdales, Chamberlains, and Coopers, requesting information as to the pedigree of the Banks's of Bank Newton, in Craven, as far as I can afford it from document in the title deeds of our Beck House property.* 3 May, 6 May.

WILLIAMS — Cox and Williams, solicitors — *see also* Cox of Meyrick *and* Cox, solicitors

Cox and Williams were solicitors of Lincoln's Inn Fields.

1842: 6 Nov: *Wrote to Mr. Hare in reply to his letter recd. yesterday, and to Messrs. Cox and Williams ...*

1846: 8 Jul.

1847: 16 Apr., 22 Apr., 25-26 May, 10 Jun.

1850: 9 Jan: *From Mr. Williams I also received a letter with inclosures containing copies of three letters which had passed between him and Mr. Braikenridge ...* 5 Feb.

WILLIAMS — Alice Williams [163]

Alice Williams, née Witts (1742-1800), was the eldest of the nine children of Broome Witts (1713-1768) and Apphia Anthony (1713-1760), and therefore the eldest aunt of Francis Witts. There is only a single entry in Agnes Witts's diary referring to Alice, dated 13 May 1789:

> ... went soon after Breakfast taking Lady Lyttelton with us to see Mrs. Williams in her retreat at Rotherhithe, a small hut shell in a Garden, her appearance & the visit alltogether very singular.

Alice married Thomas Williams, but nothing has been discovered about him. It is possible that he accompanied his mother in May 1789, in which case he would have met her once.

1840: 8 May: ... *and from a Mr. Good of Ilchester, written in consequence of my letter to the Editor of the Sherborne Journal of Apr. 25, which, by a copy of that paper forwarded by Miss Daniell, has, I see, been inserted in its columns. Mr. Good is the person whom Capt. Witts suspected of having furnished the false statement as to my Aunt's history: having been in early life, clerk to Mr. Williams, the discreditable Attorney who cajoled my Aunt Alice Witts into a disastrous marriage with him; (she died nearly 40 years ago) ...*

WILLIAMS — Charles Frederick Williams [164]

Sir Charles Frederick Williams (1774-1845), barrister-at-law, judge, and commissioner for the court of bankruptcy, was born at Dursley, Gloucestershire, the third son of Richard and Alice Williams. He was educated at Lincoln's Inn and called to the bar on 26 April 1804. He went on the western circuit and for many years practised at the Somerset and Bristol sessions. He married late in life, 22 April 1822, Elizabeth, fourth daughter of Ralph Brown Wylde Browne, of Glazeley, Shropshire, and Mary Anne, sister of Thomas Whitmore of Apley Park, Shropshire.

Williams was known by the soubriquet 'Minimus' on account of his stature, being a mere 4 feet 11½ inches tall. He was an excellent horse rider, and before entering the legal profession was a member of the militia. He was once wounded in a duel, and his account of it could often be heard after dinner. He was an excellent mimic and especially happy in his imitation of countrymen. It was said that he would have made a capital actor, having great command and self-assurance.

Williams had an estate at Gooseham, Cornwall, and a house in Hyde Park Square. A portrait by William Grove of Sir Charles, posing with his hands together, lounging comfortably on an upholstered chair with papers and inkstand on a table to his right, is on view at Sherborne Park, Gloucestershire.

1826: 5 Sep: *Lord Sherborne was in the chair, & had sent a very fine haunch of venison. Mr. Browne, Mr. Pettatt, Mr. Ford, Mr. Price, Mr. Croome, Mr. Lewis, the Dean of Gloucester, Mr. Lawrence & Mr. Newmarch were of the party. Lord Sherborne brought with him his friend Mr. Fredk. Williams, a man of diminutive stature, but redundant in wit, and withal an able counsellor on the Western Circuit, who played first fiddle at our Symposiacs with humour & good humour: some of his acted stories would rival the Mimic Matthews.*

WILLIAMS — David Williams [165]

David Williams (1784-1823), schoolmaster, was the son of John Williams of Ystradmeric [Ystrad Meurig], Cardiganshire. He was educated at Wadham College, Oxford (BA 1805; MA 1810), where he was a fellow in 1812-13. Williams was headmaster of Ystradmeric Grammar School.

1802: 10 Feb: *Dined with Mr. Mitchell, meeting there Messrs. Perrin & Williams Scholars of Wadham.* 14 Feb: *At Pering's, meeting Evans, Powell of Exeter Coll., Edgell, Hastings, Rashley, Davis, & Williams.* 15 Feb: *Walked up Headington Hill with Williams.* 16 Feb: *At Mr. Rogers Lecture in Xenophon's Anabasis. Walked with Williams.* 17 Feb: *Walked with Williams. At Mr. Mitchell's Lecture in Grotius.* 18 Feb: *Walked with Williams. At Mr. Roger's Lecture in Xenophon.* 20 Feb: *With Williams in the afternoon, who spent the Evening & supt with me.* 21 Feb: *Walked with Williams.* 22 Feb: Fine weather. *Rowed down the river & back with Evans, Alford, Paget & Williams.* 23 Feb: *Walked with Williams. Spent the Evening in his Rooms with himself & Alford.* 24 Feb: *With Williams.* 25 Feb: ... *with Evans in the Morning. Walked with him & Williams.* 26 Feb: *Walked with Williams, who spent the Evening with me.* 27 Feb: *Walked with Williams. Strolled with Stevens.* 28 Feb: ... *to St. Mary's with Rashleigh & Williams ...* 29 Feb: *Breakfasted with Evans. Walked with Williams.* 3 Mar: *Breakfasted with W. Alford, walked with Williams, & spent the Evening with him.* 4 Mar: *Fine weather. Breakfasted with Williams, & walked with him.* 7 Mar: 7 Mar: ... *with Williams, to hear Crowe the University Orator ...* 10-12 Mar., 17 Mar., 19-20 Mar., 26 Mar., 2 May, 4 May, 6 May, 9-10 May, 12-13 May, 15 May, 17-20 May, 22-23 May, 24 May: *With David Williams on the Water.* 14-16 May, 4 Jul., 6 Jul., 14 Jul: *Dined in the Common Room with Williams.*

1803: 7 Nov., 14 Nov: *Spent the Evening with Evans, meeting Burge & Williams.* 23 Nov: *At a party at Williams's, extremely unpleasant.* 11 Dec: *Evans breakfasted with me. He & Williams passed the Evening with me.*

1804: 4 Feb., 7-8 Feb., 13 Feb., 22-23 Feb.

WILLIAMS — Edward Williams [166]

Sir Edward Williams, 5th baronet (1728-1804), landed proprietor, was the brother of Sir Henry Williams, 4th baronet of Gwernevet. Sir Henry died without an heir in 1741, and Edward succeeded as 5th baronet. He married, first, 1749, Mary, daughter and co-heir of Isaac Leheup of Gunthorpe, Norfolk. Mary died at Llangoed Castle in 1763, aged 34, and Edward married, secondly, Mary, daughter and co-heir of John Riley of Epsom, Surrey.

Sir Edward was MP for Breconshire in 1788-89, and one of the principal promoters of the Brecknock Agricultural Society. He died at Clifton in 1804 without a surviving son, and the baronetcy became extinct. Mary, his daughter and heir, married Thomas Wood, of Littleton Park. Sir Edward's grandson, Thomas Wood (1777-1860), was MP for Breconshire (1806-47) and a brother-in-law to Lord Castlereagh.

1803: 28 Dec: *Accompanied my Brother in the Evening to Sir Ed. Williams's Club for half an hour ...*

1804: 14 Jan: *Accompanied the Marriots & my Father & Mother who had previously been at Sir Ed. William's to Miss Wilson's small party the Horton's Wilkinson's ...* 25 Jul: *At the Cathedral Service & Sir E. Williams's Burial. Foster & Humphries performing.*

WILLIAMS — Edward Vaughan Williams [167]

Sir Edward Vaughan Williams (1797-1875), judge, was the eldest surviving son of John Williams (1757-1810), serjeant-at-law, and Mary, daughter of Charles Clarke of Foribridge, near Stafford. He was educated at Winchester College, Westminster School, and Trinity College, Cambridge (BA 1820; MA 1823), and entered Lincoln's Inn in 1818. He was called to the bar in 1823 and initially joined the Oxford circuit where he soon found work. He later joined the south Wales circuit when it became independent, and travelled also on the Chester circuit.

Williams was created serjeant-at-law in 1846 and on the same day was appointed a justice of the court of common pleas. He was knighted in 1847. Sitting *in banco* at Westminster, he was acknowledged to be one of the most powerful constituents of the court; because of his deep learning and common sense, he probably gave rise to fewer new trials on the grounds of misdirection than any of his fellow judges. His judgments were cautious, concise, and extremely accurate, although at times he was perhaps too cautious; in his books in particular he allowed doubtful points to remain unresolved which his authority might otherwise have settled. Williams was compelled by increasing deafness to retire from the bench in February 1865. On his retirement he was sworn of the privy council and gave valuable assistance between 1865 and 1868. He married, 1826, Jane Margaret Bagot; they had 6 sons, the fifth of whom, Sir Roland Vaughan Williams, became a lord justice of appeal in 1897.

1834: 12 Aug: ... *Thence to the Bell Hotel, where we found Bathurst, who detailed to me some extraordinary comments made by the Judge presiding at the Crown Side, Baron Williams, respecting the prosecution against Clifford and Cox...* 13 Aug: *There was a small majority against the finding the bills, actuated, no doubt, by an unwillingness to come to a conclusion at variance with the very broad hints thrown out by Baron Williams in his charge ...* 13 Sep.

1839: 9 Aug: *They were tried by Mr. Justice Williams, who directed £15 out of the County rate ...*

1850: 7 Aug: *The two Judges of Assize, Lord Campbell, Lord Chief Justice of the Queen's Bench, and Sir Edwd. Vaughan Williams, one of the Justices of the Common Pleas, arrived in the afternoon, escorted by the High Sheriff, as usual, and immediately repaired to the Cathedral, where they attended divine service.* 8 Aug: *Sir E. V. Williams, presiding in the Crown Court, is, no doubt, an accomplished and sound lawyer, but prosaic and prolix, with a hesitating, nervous, and embarrassed delivery. He is an old Westminster, contemporary with Howell, & on friendly terms with him now.*

1853: 4 Apr: *Repaired to the Crown Court, in which Talfourd presided, and where the roll of Magistrates had been called, and the charge given to the Grand Jury. Vaughan Williams was the presiding judge at Nisi Prius.*

WILLIAMS — Henry Bold Williams [168]

Henry Bold Williams (1809-1873), military officer and lawyer, was born at Exeter, the youngest son of Joshua and Everilda Williams of Perridge House. He was educated at the Middle Temple and called to the bar in 1842. He married, at Cheltenham, 16 August 1832, Annie Hodson, whose late father had been a major in the HEIC. In the 1851 census Henry was listed as a barrister, not practising, living with his wife at Littlehempston, Devon. By 1861 Henry was a widower, living at 2 Berkeley Villas, Cheltenham; he was listed as a retired major, HM's service, but his service details are lacking. Records show that he was a shareholder in railway stock.

1847: 29 May: *At Cheltenham, met and parleyed with Lefroy and Mr. Bold Williams; and setting out with little delay in my carriage, I reached home by half past six P.M.*

1854: 1 Feb.

WILLIAMS — James Williams of Oddington

1839: 29 May: *Wrote to C Bathurst for information as to a James Williams lately killed on a tram-road near Lydney by accident, under an impression that the man may be an Oddington person, who has deserted his wife and family and left them chargeable to the Stow Union.*

WILLIAMS — Jane Williams of Upper Slaughter

Jane Williams, née Collett (±1804-1844), was born at Upper Slaughter, but no baptism record has been found. She married, at Upper Slaughter, 31 May 1825, William Williams.

1843: 15 Aug: *Received a letter from Dr. Hitch, announcing that Jane Williams has recovered her sanity at the Asylum sufficiently to return to her family, provided she be not exposed to much labour and anxiety ...* 18 Aug: *Wrote to Dr. Hitch in answer to the letter which I recd. from him yesterday on Tuesday, stating the arrangements I had made as to Jane Williams ...*

1844: 25 Aug., 26 Aug: *Poor Jane Williams died—a happy release—I privately baptized her infant—and wrote to Dr. Hitch to name her decease.* 28 Aug: *Funeral of Jane Williams.*

WILLIAMS — John Williams [169]

John Williams was the curate of Market Lavington from 1783 to 1823, but nothing further has been discovered as there are too many clergyman of that name and period.

1807: 14 Jan: *Engaged from 11 to 4 in attending the funeral of the late Mr. L. Tinker from Eastcott to West Lavington, which was handsome & expensive ... Among the Gentlemen present were Messrs. D. & B. Compton, Williams, William Tinker, Smith, Garent, Sainsbury &c.* 8 Jun: *Attending poor Joseph Legg's funeral M. Lavington ... Mr. Williams met us at the Church yard wicket.* 7 Aug., 22 Aug: *Rode to Lavington & W. Lavington called upon Mr. Williams at the latter place with whom I agreed to do my Erchfont Duty during my approaching absence.* 12 Dec.

1808: 27 Apr.

WILLIAMS — John Williams [170]

John Williams (1779-1857), Church of England clergyman, was born at Sidmouth, Devon, the son of John Williams. He was educated at St Edmund Hall, Oxford (BA 1805; MA 1808; BD 1815; DD 1818), and entered the Church. He was curate of Woodchester, Gloucestershire, from 1805 to 1833, and rector from 1833 to his death in 1857, thus demonstrating over half a century's commitment to his parish. He married Elizabeth (1783-1870); they had 4 sons and 6 daughters:

1 Eliza (1808-1842)

2 Mary Anne (1810-1819)
1 John (1812-1815); died an infant
3 Hester Kezia (1814-1838)
2 John (1815-1838)
4 Christiana (1819-1856)
5 Emily (1821-1822); died an infant
3 Herbert (1823-1843)
4 Alfred (1825-1845)
6 Fanny (1831-1834); died an infant

Tragically all but one of John's children predeceased him, and they all predeceased his wife Elizabeth.

1850: 8 Nov: *Dr. Williams of Woodchester, a very low Churchman, complained of the term "deep & indignant sorrow" as used in the proposed address to the Bishop, wishing that "holy indignation" should be substituted for it; but he was not seconded ... as the fear of discord seemed generally to pervade the meeting, the address was speedily carried with only one dissentient, Dr. Williams.——*

WILLIAMS — John Williams [171]

John Williams (b. ±1820), of Islip, Oxfordshire, formerly of Stow-on-the-Wold, was sentenced on 5 January 1847 at the county sessions, Gloucester, to six months' imprisonment for larceny. He was recorded as 27 years old and 5 feet 10 inches in height, with curly light brown hair, grey eyes, a round face, and a fair complexion. Williams was charged on the oath of Thomas Gleed, of Moreton-in-Marsh, for stealing a trunk, a box, and other articles.

1846: 26 Nov: *To the Justice room: much business; principally, the completion of the matter postponed last Thursday, the prisoner, John Williams, committed for trial at the Epiphany Q.S. ...*

WILLIAMS — Joseph Williams [172]

Joseph Williams (1795-1875), clarinetist, was born at Hereford. Little is known of his personal life, but there are countless references to him as 'Mr Williams' on theatre and concert bills and programmes; by 1821 he was making a name for himself as an accomplished clarinetist. At the 1826 Three Choirs at Gloucester, he was paid a fee of 15 guineas. In February 1841, John Fane, 11th earl of Westmorland (1784-1859), styled Lord Burghersh at that time, a founder of the Royal Academy of Music, offered Joseph Williams 'the first clarionet' at the Ancient Concerts. Francis Witts's reference to 'Willman' in 1823 was almost certainly a slip of the pen.

1823: 17 Sep: *... such masters in execution as Cramer, Lindley, Marshall, Nicholson on the Flute, Willman on the Clarionet, Bochsa on the harp, it was impossible not to be delighted ...*

1826: 25 Sep: *I shall set down the terms, on which the principal performers were engaged ...*

1829: 23 Sep: *... she was accompanied by Williams, the celebrated performer on the Clarionet, who does wonders with an instrument seldom made capable of soft and pleasing strains ...*

WILLIAMS — Robert Williams [173]

Robert Williams (b. 1779), Church of England clergyman, was born at Baeumaris, Anglesey, the son of William Williams. He was educated at Jesus College, Oxford (BA 1801; MA 1818), and was curate at Charlton Kings by at least 1823. By 1830 Charles Henry Watling was the newly inducted curate, and Williams had either died or moved on.

1824: 22 Apr: *Walked to the Village of Charlton Kings ... The Curate, the Revd. Williams, of Jesus College, is very justly liked & respected; being a well informed, sensible and accomplished man.*

1827: 10 Apr: *Attended the Service at the Cathedral .... The Sermon was preached by my old acquaintance, the Revd. Mr. Williams, Minister of Charlton Kings, and Fellow of Jesus Coll. Oxford (and Chaplain to the Sheriff).*

WILLIAMS — Thomas Williams of Bourton-on-the-Water [174]

Thomas Williams (±1809-1850), agricultural labourer, was married to Hannah (b. ±1815); they had at least 1 son and 3 daughters:

1 Elizabeth (b. ±1836)
1 John (b. 1838)
2 Anne (b. ±1843)
3 Elizabeth (b. ±1849)

1848: 13 Nov: *Williams, my son's tenant at Bourton on the Water, against whom he has been obliged to take proceedings in the County Court, as being in arrear of rent, called to endeavour to make an arrangement with ... Wrote to my Son, explaining the position in which he is placed in respect of his Bourton tenant, Thos. Williams ...* 17 Nov.

WILLIAMS — William Gunter Williams [175]

William Gunter Williams (b. 1822), Church of England clergyman, was born at Kintbury, Berkshire, the eldest son of William and Ann Williams. He was educated at Queen's College, Oxford, and ordained deacon on 21 September 1845. He was listed as curate at Great Rissington in the census of 1851, but little else has been discovered about him.

1850: 12 Jun: *Those assembled were Messrs. Biscoe, Sadler, Wiggin, Hippisley, Trimmer, Usher Dean, Robinson, Boggis, Potter, Morrison, Williams & myself ... Mr. Williams, Curate of Great Risington, then read a calm, judicious paper, on the question how far the literal obedience of the rubrics was binding on the Minister ...* 18 Sep., 24 Sep.

1854: 19 Jul.

WILLIAMS — William White Williams [176]

William White Williams (1815-1880), physician, was born at Dursley, Gloucestershire, the son of Mileo and Catherine Williams. He was probably a nephew of Sir Charles Frederick Williams (*above*). He married Eleanor (b. ±1815), born at Berkeley; they had at least 1 son and 1 daughter:

1 Charles Frederick (1841-1927)
1 Helen Pearce (1843-1933); died unmarried at Cheltenham

In the 1851 census Eleanor was listed as a matron. In 1861 William was listed as a 45-year-old widower living at the asylum with his daughter Helen Pearce, who was born at Hayes, Middlesex, and son Charles Frederick, born at South Newington, Oxfordshire. William was qualified as MD, FLS, and MRCP, and was consulting physician at the Gloucester county asylum. Later in life he lived at Whithorne House, Charlton Kings, Cheltenham.

1846: 8 Sep: *A letter from a Dr. Williams, Hayes, Middlesex, accompanying some very satisfactory testimonials as to his professional skill, talents, and general character. Dr. W. is a candidate for the vacant situation of resident superintendent of the Gloucester Lunatic Asylum.*

1847: 10 Apr: *Wrote to Dr. Williams, Superintendent, Gloucester Lunatic Asylum, and Mr. Illes of the Fairford Lunatic*

Asylum, to ascertain whether Moses Roff of Bourton could be admitted into either of these asylums, he having relapsed into a state of insanity. 13 Apr., 25 Jun., 28 Jun., 30 Jun., 24 Aug: *from Dr. Williams, Superintendent of the Lunatic Asylum, Gloucester ...*

1848: 19 Jun., 22 Jun.

1850: 23 Nov: *Wrote to Dr. Williams, Superintendent of the Lunatic Asylum, Gloucester ...*

1852: 28 Mar., 30 Mar.

1853: 20 Feb: *Wrote to Dr. Williams, Superintendent of the Gloucestershire Lunatic Asylum ...* 23 Feb., 1 Mar., 5 Mar., 10 Mar., 16-18 Mar.

1854: 29 Apr., 4 May.

WILLIAMS-WYNN — Watkyns Williams-Wynn [177]

Sir Watkyns Williams-Wynn, 5th baronet of Wynne-stay (1772-1840), MP and landed proprietor, was the son of Sir Watkin Williams-Wynn, 4th baronet, and his second wife, Charlotte, daughter of George Grenville, a former prime minister. His aunt Hester, Charlotte's sister, had married William Pitt, 1st earl of Chatham, therefore Watkyns was cousin to Pitt the Younger. Due to his great influence in the area, he was often referred to as the 'Prince of Wales'! He was at one point an aide-de-camp to William IV.

1825: 17 Sep: *The ruins of a Monastery are very extensive and picturesque, affording a rich treat to the Antiquary; but I could only obtain a distant glimpse of them as I left the town.... The ruins, with almost the whole town, are the property of Sir Watkin Williams Wynne.*

WILLIAMSON — Mrs Williamson at Lady Reade's

1840: 28 Jul: *Called at Lady Reade's; admitted to the good old Lady, whom we thought a good deal altered in appearance: Mrs. Roberts and Mrs. Williamson are on a visit to her.* 4 Aug. *We passed on to Oddington to dine with a family party at Lady Reade's—where we met Mrs. Roberts, Mrs. Williamson, Sir John Reade, his son and daughters, and two nieces, daughters of Mr. George Reade.*

1846: 11 Jul: *Called on Lady Reade, with whom we found her old friend Mrs. Williamson ...*

WILLIS — John Willis of Redhorn, Wedhampton, Wiltshire

1807: 23 Jun: *Visiting John Willis at Redhorne struck with a Palsy.* 25 Jun., 27 Jun., 19 Jul.

WILLIS-FLEMING — the Willis Fleming family of Binstead [178]

Christopheria Willis-Fleming, née Buchanan (1799-1860), was the widow of John Fleming Barton Willis-Fleming (1781-1844), who died at Athens. They had 2 sons and 1 daughter:

1 John Browne (1815-1872)
2 Thomas James (1819-1890)
1 Charlotte (1821-1874)

1846: 26 May: *The Church at Binstead, almost wholly rebuilt, is a sweet, rural, secluded place of worship, in excellent taste, of the Early English style; beyond it a spacious, thick oakwood or coppice, sloping to the beach, thro' a glade in which I found my way to the shore, expecting to be able to return on sand or shingle, but found myself entangled in a tenacious white mud, hardly practicable for walking, though intermingled with stones. Floundered along to a jetty, and a cottage on the shore, whence I obtained the guidance of the woman inhabiting it to prevent the intrusion of strangers on the private grounds of Mrs. Fleming, widow of a late MP. for Hants, who resides here.* 28 May: *A light yacht, of, perhaps, thirty tons burthen, which had been built, in a shed, near our house, on the Strand, was launched at half past one to-day. It belongs to a Mr. Fleming, a son of the lady residing near Binstead, into whose lovely grounds I obtained admission on Tuesday: he is Commodore of the Ryde Yacht club: the hull was safely launched to be g towed to Cowes there to be rigged and fitted out. Crowds on the beach greeted with loud hurrahs its descent into the water; we watched it as it came down the frame from a row boat, which we had engaged.*

Willis Percival & Co. — Willis Percival & Co., bankers [179]

Willis Percival & Co., founded in 1700, was one of London's oldest private banking partnerships. At the time of its failure it had three partners—Henry Willis, Samuel Tomkins, and Samuel Leith Tomkins. The firm's origins go back to Thomas Williams' goldsmith business, which in 1677 traded at the sign of The Crown in Lombard Street. By 1698 Benjamin Tudman, a 'goldsmith and bancker [sic] in Linnen' was at the address. In about 1708 he was joined by Stephen Child, formerly of the bankers Child & Co., and the business was renamed Tudman & Child. Frequent name changes followed as new partners joined and departed until the bank finally became Willis, Percival & Co. in around 1814. The bank financed international trade, in particular cargoes of sugar from the West Indies in the 1780s. In 1878 the collapse of a large customer, a Greek firm of importers called Gerussi Brothers & Co., of Finsbury Circus, caused the bank to suspend payment with liabilities of about £500,000. It was acquired by Capital & Counties Bank (est. 1877) in 1878.

1835: 28 Mar: *In the evening wrote to Mr. Whitcombe, Gloucester, to Messrs. Willis, Percival & Co., Bankers, London.* 1 Apr., 15 Apr., 27 Apr., 29 Apr., 3-4 May, 7 May, 9 May, 23 May, 30 May, 2 Jun., 10 Jun.

1836: 12 Jul., 11 Oct.

1837: 24-25 May, 28-29 May, 7 Jun., 3 Sep.

WILLIS — Sherlock Willis [180]

Sherlock Willis (1796-1873), homeopathic medical practitioner, was born at Pickwick, Wiltshire, the son of John Law Willis (1765-1841) and Louisa Maria Duberley (1768-1831). He married, first, at Bodiam, Sussex, 17 November 1820, Margaret Vignoles (1797-1830); and secondly, at Brussels, 19 May 1834, Isabella Martha (1810-1893), daughter of Gen. Sir Charles Wale (1765-1845) and Henrietta Brent (1788-1853). Sherlock and Isabella had 7 sons and 2 daughters:

1 Sherlock Vignoles (1836-1913); born at Rome
2 Charles Woodley (1837-1866)
3 John Armine (1839-1866)
4 Horace George (1841-1922); born at Rome
5 Cecil Sherlock (1843-1898)
1 Louisa (b. 1845)
2 Isabella Margaret (1847-1935); born at Paris
6 Reginald Charles Bruce (1848-1935)
7 Robert Henry (1853-1928)

1852: 18 Mar: *The village of Swindon with its Manor House, occupied by Mr. Sherlock Willis, its ancient Church restored, its parsonage now tenanted by a new Incumbent, the Revd. Lewis Griffiths ...*

1853: 6 Jan: *At dinner there was a pleasant reunion of residents of the village; Mr. and Mrs. Sherlock Willis, and her sister, Miss Waile; and Mr. Surman with his sister, Miss Goodlake.—Mr. S.W.*

is a well educated, well informed, travelled man, living in Swindon Manor House, and his ladies agreeable persons. A brother of his has lived near Gloucester, with whom I have been acquainted for some years. Mr. S. W. takes an interest in Union matters, and is the Elected Guardian for Swindon.

WILLOUGHBY — Sarah Willoughby of Adlestrop

1847: 28 Jun: *A letter from Dr. Williams, the Superintendent of the Lunatic Asylum, in answer to mine requesting a report of the state of Sarah Willoughby.* 30 Jun: *Wrote a few lines to J. Perkins; begging him to communicate to his parishioner, Betterton, the mother of S. Willoughby, the account I had received from Dr. Williams as to the state of that lunatic.* 24 Aug: ... *to inform me that poor Mrs. Willoughby, of Adlestrop, a patient in that institution, sent thither by me, and who, when taken out for exercise with others, beyond the boundaries of the asylum, had escaped.*

1848: 4 Sep: *Received a letter from Winter as to the insane woman, Willoughby, of Adlestrop ...*

WILLSON — unknown correspondent

It is rare to find someone who cannot be tied down in one form or another, but this Mr Willson is a mystery—and an especially intriguing one regarding Witts's reference to 'matters of taste'.

1805: 25 Nov: *Wrote to Willson.*

1806: 28 Feb: *Wrote a letter, chiefly upon matters of taste to Willson.* 26 Jul: *Received a letter from Willson.* 29 Jul: *Wrote to Margaret, to Mr. Travell, & to Willson ...* 24 Sep: *Heard from Willson.*

WILMOT — Mr Wilmot at Cheltenham

1804: 17 Oct: *Mr. Delabere, Mr. & Mrs. Worsley & Mr. Wilmot called. Dined alone. In the evening Mr. Wilmot & Lady Herries. Aunt C. worse.* 18 Oct: *Called on Mrs. Wilmot. Mrs. Worsley called.* 20 Oct: *Called on Mr. Delebere & Mr. Wilmot & Mrs Baillie ...*

WILMOT-HORTON — Robert John Wilmot-Horton [181]

Sir Robert John Wilmot-Horton, 3rd baronet (1784-1841), politician, pamphleteer, and colonial administrator, was the only son of Sir Robert Wilmot, 2nd baronet (1752-1834), of Osmaston, near Derby, and his first wife, Juliana Elizabeth Byron (1754-1788). He was educated at Eton College and Christ Church, Oxford. Wilmot-Horton was under-secretary of state for war and the colonies between 1821 and 1828, and governor of Ceylon between 1831 and 1837. He was a member of the Canningite faction and MP for Newcastle-under-Lyme, 1818-30.

Wilmot-Horton reorganised the colonial office, dividing the empire into administrative regions, each with a senior clerk responsible for its administration. He is best remembered, however, for advocating that poor British and Irish families should be allowed to emigrate to the colonies and be granted land there; he was chiefly responsible for securing two parliamentary grants in 1823 and 1825 to fund an experiment to settle poor Irish families in Canada. He married, at Croxall, Derbyshire, 6 September 1806, Anne Beatrix (1787-1871), daughter and co-heir of Eusebius Horton of the Catton Hall estate in Derbyshire; they had 6 sons and 3 daughters:

1 Eusebius (b. 1807)
2 Robert Edward (1808-1880); succeeded as 4th baronet
3 Christopher (1809-1864)
1 Anne Augusta (1811-1843)
4 John (1814-1882)
2 Harriet (1818-1897)
5 Frederick (1819-1855)
3 Emily Julia (1821-1866)
6 George Lewis (1825-1887); succeeded as 5th baronet

Until 1823 Robert lived at his family's estate of Osmaston Hall. He inherited the Catton Hall estate on the death of his father-in-law in 1823, and pursuant to the latter's will, added Horton as a second surname.

1829: 7 Mar: *It had been proposed by Mr. Wilmot Horton, as a security, in a recent publication on the subject, that Roman Catholics should be precluded from speaking or voting, or at least from voting in either house of parliament on any topic relating to the Church ...*

1833: 6 Nov: *Approaching nearer to Derby, we noticed on the right Osmaston Hall, the seat of Sir R. Wilmot- Horton ...*

1838: 4 Apr: *Mrs. B. was daughter of Sir Eardley Wilmot.*

1839: 5 Jan: *Also a letter from Newmarch offering to us a mortgage for £10000 on some property of Sir. R. Wilmot Horton in Cheshire of nearly the value of £30000: N. considers the Security so eligible that, though it exceeds by £4000 the sum about to be repaid to us by the Exors. of Mr. Blackwell, it would be desirable for us to take the mortgage, if by sale of Trust monies in the funds, or funded property of our own or Mrs. B., we can make up the required sum.* 8 Jan: 12 Jan., 14 Jan., 16 Jan: *Sir R. & Lady W. Horton have a life Interest in this estate, and by their Marriage Settlt. Lady Horton has a power to charge it with £10,000.* 22 Jan., 2 Feb., 4 Feb: *It appears probable that the mortgage to Sir R. W. Horton may be finally arranged, the deed executed, and the money paid by the 12th. Inst. when Newmarch proposes being in Town for that purpose.* 8 Feb., 19 Feb., 21 Feb., 26 Feb., 26 Feb., 3 Aug., 8 Aug.

1842: 28 Feb., 1 Sep: *A letter from Newmarch respecting the deductions from Int. payable by Horton's Exors. to us on account of Income Tax ...* 18 Dec.

1843: 25 Jan: *Recd. a letter from Messrs. Hoare intimating that Lady Horton's agents had paid to my account with them £194. 3. 4.* 3-4 Mar., 9 Aug., 13 Aug., 18-19 Aug., 26 Aug., 26 Sep., 29 Sep., 25 Oct., 21 Dec.

1844: 22 Jan., 24 Jan., 24 Jul.
1845: 24 Jan.
1847: 24 Jan., 24 Jul.
1848: 26 Jan., 27 Jul.
1850: 24 Jan., 24 Jul.
1851: 24 Jan.
1852: 24 Jan.
1853: 25 Jan.
1854: 26 Jul.

WILSON — Mr Wilson, a pupil of Mr Morrison

1825: 9 Aug: ... *Mr. Torrens, and Mr. Wilson, the other Stoneleigh pupil, were the performers. Mr. Torrens sang Italian Buffa songs with taste & spirit.* 17 Aug: ... *dined at Mrs. Rice's at Bourton on the water. There was a large party. Mr. Torrens, & Mr. Wilson, Mr. Morrison's pupils.* 26 Aug: *We had Mrs. Rice and her friends to dinner: Viz. Mr. & Mrs. Morrison, & Mr. Wilson.*

WILSON — Daniel Wilson [182]

Daniel Wilson (1778-1858), bishop of Calcutta, was born at Church Street, Spitalfields, the son of Stephen Wilson (d. 1813), a wealthy London silk manufacturer, and Ann Collett (d. 1829), daughter of Daniel West, one of George Whitefield's trustees. He was educated at St Edmund Hall, Oxford (BA 1802; MA 1804; DD 1832), where he was later tutor or vice-principal. As curate to Richard Cecil at Cobham and Bisley, Surrey, Wilson became a strong evangelical preacher. He was minister of Worton, Oxfordshire, 1807-12; assistant curate at St John's chapel, Bedford Row, Bloomsbury, 1808-12; sole minister at St John's chapel, 1812-24; and vicar of St Mary's, Islington, 1824-32. In 1832 he was consecrated bishop of Calcutta and first metropolitan bishop of India and Ceylon. He founded an English church at Rangoon, Ceylon, in 1855, and St Paul's Cathedral, Calcutta (consecrated 1847). Wilson was succeeded as vicar of St Mary's, Islington, by his son, Daniel (1805-1886), who held the living for fifty-four years.

1829: 26 Feb: *The vote given by two individuals excited much surprize; that Daniel Wilson, the Evangelical Rector of Islington, the eloquent preacher ...* 29 Nov.

1832: 25 Apr: *The Bishopric of Calcutta has been at last accepted by the well known Daniel Wilson...*

1833: 12 Mar.

1839: 5 May.

1842: 15 Mar: *Mr. Jos. Wilson, a very rich old gentleman, a connection of the Bishop of Calcutta, who had married a sister of Geo. Wellford, and had been intimate with my late Uncle and Aunt ...*

1844: 8 Oct. 9 Oct: *Rose early, and betook myself before 8 AM. to breakfast at the Star Hotel—there in the coffee room met and conversed with the Revd.—Wilson, Rector of Islington, and Price, of Coln St. Dennis.*

1845: 26 Mar.

WILSON — Frances Wilson at Clifton [183]

Frances Wilson (±1753-1821) appears frequently in the diaries of Agnes Witts. She was the fourth out of six daughters of Christopher Wilson (1715-1792), bishop of Bristol (1783-92). Her eldest sister was Anne (d. 1785), who married Revd Samuel Disney; then came Elizabeth (1747-1821), who married Randolph Marriott; the third, Mary (1749-1823), married Sir John Beckett; Margaret (1756-1819), the fifth, married Sir Hugh Smythe; and finally, the sixth and youngest, Dorothy (±1758-1796), married John Upton of Ingmire Hall.

1804: *Accompanied the Marriots & my Father & Mother who had previously been at Sir Ed. William's to Miss Wilson's small party the Horton's Wilkinson's etc. etc.*

1805: *Alone in the evening, my Father & Mother being at a party at Miss Wilson's.*

1806: *Visited Miss Wilson's route, which was numerous & not unpleasant.*

WILSON — John Wilson [184]

John Wilson (1784-1854), lawyer and professor of moral philosophy, Edinburgh, was the son of John Wilson of Paisley, Renfrewshire. He was educated at Magdalen College, Oxford (BA 1807; MA 1810), and Lincoln's Inn, where he became a student in 1806. He became an advocate of the Scottish bar in 1815. Wilson was a poet, critic, and prose writer, the 'Christopher North' of *Blackwood's Magazine* and its chief editor from 1817. He was also the author of *Noctes Ambrosianæ*. He was professor of moral philosophy at Edinburgh from 1820 to 1851.

1804: 17 Feb: *Dined at Dickenson's with Round meeting the adjutant of the OLV., Wilson of Magd. the Dunns, Dowell, Moons &c.*

1805: 26 Mar: *Drank wine at Rounds. Met Messrs. Fort, J. Dunne, Gravenell, Barton, Vashon, Wilson, Moore & Leech: a pleasant party enough ...* 12 Aug: *Called without success upon Dove & Wilson, found the Broughams at home.* 7 Nov.

1806: 19 Mar: *Dined in the Balliol Hall with Round, adjourning afterwards to the Junr. Common Room, where Gamlin, Wilson & a Merton man, Mr. Burney...*

1833: 15 Oct: *In the Evening Edward & I alternately read aloud a spirited paper from an old number of Blackwood's Magazine, probably written by Professor Wilson, and descriptive of the fine scenery of Wastdale in Cumberland ...*

1844: 22 Nov: *Began Wilson's Voyage round Scotland: he is Brother of Professor Wilson, a clever, spirited and agreeable writer ...* 17 Dec: *Finished reading Wilson's Voyage round Scotland, an informing, amusing, well written book.*

WILSON — John Wilson [185]

John Wilson (1789-1873), Church of England clergyman, was the son of Mary and William Wilson (*below*). He was educated at St Paul's School and Trinity College, Oxford (BA 1810; MA 1814; BD 1826; DD 1852), where he was a scholar, 1812-16, fellow, 1816-50, tutor, 1816-19, senior bursar, 1822, and president, 1850-66. He was rector of Garsington, Oxfordshire, from 1850 to 1866, and a fellow of the Society of Antiquaries, London, and of the Royal Society of Northern Antiquaries, Copenhagen.

1842: 15 Jul: *... recd. a letter from J Backhouse on the subject of the American claims of the Backhouse family, and on the course he proposes to adopt for the recovery of monies still due from that source; with a correspondence on the business with his relative, the Revd. J. Wilson, and an American house at Liverpool, for the consideration of MW. and myself.*

1844: 1 May: *Wrote to J Backhouse in answer to his letter recd. yesterday, expressing our readiness to concur in any reasonable expence and proper measures approved by him, and Mr. Wilson, who is one of the parties entitled to a share in any money recovered from America on account of the Backhouse claims ...*

1845: 29 Apr: *Recd. a letter from the Revd. J. Wilson, my wife's cousin, fellow of Trin Coll. Oxford, and resident at Wood or Water Eaton in Oxfordshire, accompanying a packet of papers, with reference to the claims of the Backhouse family on parties in the United States of America, indebted at the time of the American war to the mercantile house of Backhouse at Liverpool.*

1850: 3 May, 6 May: *Mr. Wilson having forwarded to me without any comment the letter written by Mr. Stonard, the agent in Virginia for recovering debts due to the Backhouse family, which purports that further endeavours to obtain payment are hopeless, I wrote to Miss Backhouse, returning to her this letter, and intimating an opinion that it is vain to prosecute the claims any further.*

WILSON — John Wilson [186]

John Wilson (1800-1849), singer, was born in Edinburgh, the son of John Wilson, a coach driver, and Mary Edwards. He was a member of the choir of Duddingston parish church during the ministry of the painter John Thomson (1778-1840). For some time he was precentor of Roxburgh Place relief church, where his fine tenor voice drew great crowds. From 1825 to 1830 he was precentor of St Mary's church, Edinburgh, and while there he published *A Selection of Psalm Tunes* (1825). After this he devoted himself entirely to teaching music and giving concerts.

Wilson studied singing in Edinburgh with Finlay Dun and then in London with Gesualdo Lanza and Domenico Crivelli, and took harmony and counterpoint lessons from George Aspull. He made his operatic début in March 1830 in Edinburgh, when he appeared as Harry Bertram in *Guy Mannering*. He performed at Covent Garden in roles such as Don Carlos in Linley's *The Duenna*, and from 1835 to 1838 at Drury Lane in operas such as Balfe's *The Siege of Rochelle*. He made his American début in 1838 at the National Theatre, New York, and went on to undertake a 20-month tour of American cities with Jane Shirreff. This tour helped cultivate a taste for opera in the United States.

After his return from America Wilson decided to leave the stage to become an exponent of Scottish song. He started to give lecture recitals with titles such as 'Nights with Burns', 'Jacobite Songs', and 'Mary Queen of Scots', which were extremely successful both in England and America. He sang for Queen Victoria at Taymouth Castle in 1842. His musical entertainments led to the publication of his edition of *The Songs of Scotland* (1842), which included such previously unknown songs as 'Hail to the Chief'. In 1849 Wilson embarked on another North American tour, but he died of cholera in Quebec city on 8 July 1849.

1844: 13 Apr: *The performer was Mr. Wilson, for these two years or more advantageously known, as a tasteful singer of old Scotch songs, possessing a good voice, much command of it, pathos or humour, as the topic requires, and a gentlemanlike manner.*

1845: 6 Jun: ... *Ransford, both having excellent voices, and one, a Stationer in London, being also a Professional Singer, both in the Metropolis, and in the Provinces, and now on a musical tour, giving in various Towns an entertainment, after the manner Wilson the Scottish vocalist* ...

WILSON — Mary Wilson [187]

Mary Backhouse (1758-1822) married, at Glasgow, 1781, Revd William Wilson (1738-1818), son of John Wilson and Margaret Douglass. William Wilson was educated at Brasenose College, Oxford (BA 1760; MA 1762), and served as rector of West Shefford, Berkshire, from 1776 to his death in 1818. William and Mary were the parents of Revd John Wilson (1789-1873), rector of Garsington, Oxfordshire (*above*).

1822: 30 Dec: *Yesterday we received the news of the death of an Aunt of my wife, Mrs. Wilson, formerly Miss Backhouse, relict of the Revd. Mr. Wilson, a Berkshire Clergyman. Of late years she had resided at Headington, near Oxford, to be near her son, the Revd. John Wilson, Fellow of Trinity College. No intercourse was kept up between the Wilsons and the Backhouse family, consequently we had no acquaintance with her: family feuds of old date brought about this estrangement.*

WILSON — Thomas Wilson [188]

Thomas Wilson (1734-1829), landed proprietor, of Ive's Place, Maidenhead, and of Eshton Hall, Gargrave, Yorkshire, married Mary Gale. One of their daughters, Anne, married Lt William Innes Pocock, RN, who apparently inherited the Maidenhead property. It seems likely that Thomas Wilson was the Mr Wilson who witnessed Broome Witts's will. He may also have been in business with the Venables family of Cookham.

1842: 17 Mar: *Mr. Venables, still, I believe, a paper-maker at Cookham, proved, as attesting witness, the Execution of my Uncle's will, Mr. Wilson, that he & my Aunt died without issue...*

WILSON — Thomas Patten, later Wilson-Patten [189]

Thomas Wilson-Patten (1770-1827), landed proprietor, was the son of Thomas Patten, of Bank Hall, Warrington, and Dorothea, daughter of Peter Bold, MP, and Anna Maria Wentworth. He married Elizabeth, daughter of Nathan Hyde of Ardwick. Thomas and Elizabeth were tenants at the beautiful Jacobean Wootton Lodge, close to Calwich Abbey. Thomas changed his name to Wilson in accordance with the will of his cousin, Revd Thomas Wilson. When his son came of age in 1823, Thomas was able to resume using the name Patten.

1812: 6 Aug: *We made a morning visit to Mr. & Mrs. Wilson at Wooton Lodge, about two miles beyond Ellaston. This singular place is beautifully situated on an abrupt rock overhanging a fine deep glen issuing as it were, from the bosom of Wever, & richly finely clothed with wood.*

WILTON — Charles Pleydell Neale Wilton [190]

Charles Pleydell Neale Wilton (1795-1859), Church of England clergyman, was born at Upper Swell, Gloucestershire, the son of William Wilton (1771-1809) and Charlotte Jelf. He was the grandson of Henry Wilton and Sarah Pleydell, of Gloucester, and a nephew to John Pleydell Wilton (*below*). Charles was educated at St John's College, Cambridge (BA 1817; MA 1827), and was appointed curate of Awre, Gloucestershire, and later curate of Stowting, Kent, in 1826. He married, 1823, Elizabeth Plaistowe (1797-1839).

Wilton was appointed chaplain for New South Wales in October 1826, and arrived at Sydney with his wife in April 1827 aboard the *Elizabeth*. He had a distinguished clerical career in Australia and was well respected. Elizabeth died at Newcastle, New South Wales, in 1836, having been predeceased by two children. On 14 October 1839 Charles married Charlotte Albinia, eldest daughter of Benjamin Sullivan, police magistrate at Raymond Terrace. Wilton was, to the end, a conscientious churchman and active in encouraging science. He died on 5 June 1859 at Newcastle, and was survived by his widow, a son and a daughter.

1825: 9 Aug: *Mrs. Rice. brought a large party to Mr. Croome's table: among them were the Revd Mr. Wilton and his wife; he is Curate of Blakeney and Awre, and son of a former Incumbent of Upper Swell, who died in 1804/1809, leaving a large and distressed family... A sister of his, Now Mrs. Morrison, was a protegée of Mrs. Rice, and with her husband, who also owes his education to the same benevolent lady, was a guest at Mr. Croome's feast.*

WILTON — Henry Hooper Wilton [190]

Henry Hooper Wilton (1795-1881), lawyer, was the son of Henry Wilton (1765-1822) and Peggy Hooper, née Fryer (1763-1845). He received his articles of clerkship under his uncle Robert Wilton in 1819, and succeeded him as town clerk in 1827. He married Harriet Jones (1804-1881); they had at least 3 sons and 6 daughters:

1 Harriet Margaret (1828-1914); married, 1862, Alfred John Stanton (1825-1906)
1 Henry (1829-1845)
2 Frederick (b. 1830); died an infant
3 Charles Turner (1832-1923); married, 1860, Millicent Mary Mirehouse (1837-1925)
2 Elizabeth (1833-1913); married, 1853, Robert Snaith Hichens (1828-1868)
3 Julia Anne (1834-1916); married, first, 1856, Henry Matthew John Bowles (1826-1884); secondly, 1886, Henry D'Obrain (1840-1896)

4 Charlotte Jane Griffith (1835-1925); married, 1874, Arthur Ellis (1818-1891)
5 Frances Mary Caroline (1839-1914); married, 1867, Charles Jerdein (1835-1908)
6 Cristina/Christina (1841-1908); married, 1893, John Henry Lace (±1840-1899)

In the 1861 census the family was registered as living at Whitminster House. The household included Henry's unmarried sister Harriet Wilton (1800-1880).

1834: 22 Jul: *Wrote to H. H. Wilton, the Treas....*
1837: 16 Oct.
1842: 22 Sep., 24 Sep., 27 Sep.
1843: 2 Jan., 9 Oct., 16 Oct.
1844: 16 Aug., 3 Sep., 6 Sep., 14 Sep., 14 Oct., 30 Dec.
1845: 14 Apr.
1846: 8 Sep: *A letter from Mr. Wilton, Treasurer of the County of Gloucester, accompanying the yearly balance sheet of the receipts and expenditure of the County ...* 11 Sep., 15 Sep., 19 Oct.
1847: 22 Mar., 5 Apr., 10 Sep., 18 Oct.
1848: 3 Jan., 20 Mar., 28 Aug., 3 Sep., 16 Oct.
1849: 31 Dec.
1850: 13 Feb: *A letter from Mr. Hooper Wilton, who is very sore about the late curtailment of his salary as County Treasurer ...* 14 Feb., 24 Feb: *Letter from H. H. Wilton; influenced, perhaps, by my late letter to him, he withdraws the letter ...* 10 Oct., 14 Oct., 29 Oct. 1 Dec., 5 Dec., 30 Dec.
1853: 27 Jun.

WILTON — John Pleydell Wilton and the Wilton family of Gloucester[191]

John Pleydell Wilton (1774-1839), surgeon, was the son of Henry Wilton (1738-1804) and Sarah Pleydell (1732-1807) of Westbury-on Severn. His parents had married at St Mary de Crypt, Gloucester, on 24 August 1759, and had at least 6 sons and 2 daughters:

1 Charles Henry (1761-1832); married, first, 1776, Sarah Baden (±1760-1793); secondly, 1795, Eunice Wise (b. ±1767)
2 Henry (1765-1822); married, 1787, Peggy Hooper, née Fryer (1763-1845); *see above*
3 Robert (1766-1827), Gloucester town clerk (1813-27); married, 1792, Sarah Fryer (1761-1839), sister of Peggy (*above*)
1 Mary Maria (1767-1834); married, 1788, William Mutlow (±1761-1832), cathedral organist
4 James (1769-1836); lived in France for some of his adult life; died unmarried
2 Elizabeth (b. 1769); probably died an infant
5 William H. (1771-1809); married, 1793, Charlotte Jelf (1772-1810)
6 John Pleydell (1774-1839); married, at St Mary de Crypt, Gloucester, 8 February 1796, Mary Lightfoot (1774-1861), born at Selsley, Gloucestershire; at least 5 sons and 5 daughters:
    1 John William (1796-1867); married, 1823, Mary Anne Cholmondeley Mason (1798-1890)
    2 Robert (1798-1877); married, 1824, Charlotte Maria Hallett (1804-1866); *see below*
    3 William (1799-1880), surgeon; married his cousin Sarah Wilton (1801-1888); went to Australia and both died in New South Wales
    1 Mary (1801-1840); married, 1833, Percy Galindo (1796-1860)
    2 Caroline (1804-1872); married, 1828, Capt. Thomas Gregory, RN (1792-1871)
    4 Unnamed son (b. & d. 1806)
    5 George Pleydell (1808-1874)
    3 Kate Ann (1810-1845); married, 1833, William Russell Skey (1805-1844)
    4 Emma Vittoria (1813-1855); married, 1837, Henry Milnes (1796-1864) of Leominster
    5 Elizabeth Marsh (1816-1915); married, 1841, Stephen Hack (1816-1894); lived much of their lives in Australia but returned and died in Gloucestershire

John Pleydell Wilton was a house pupil at Middlesex Hospital from 1790 to 1799. By 1807 he was a surgeon at the Gloucester gaol on a salary of £47.

1825: 12 Jul: *... very minute & detailed comments were presented to the Sessions by the Surgeon, Mr. Wilton, as to the propriety of an improved dietary; & his recommendations were in great measure confirmed by Dr. Shute.*
1826: 11 Feb: *We left Gloucester for Upper Slaughter; Mrs. Backhouse accompanied us. A neighbour of Mrs. Backhouse, and Mr. J. Wilton, the medical man, promised to watch & report proceedings from Wellington Parade.*
1839: 21 Jun: *Recd. a circular from Mr. Hickes, a Surgeon at Gloucester, announcing the recent decease of Mr. Wilton, the excellent Surgeon of the County Gaol ...*

WILTON — John William Wilton[192]

John William Wilton (1796-1867), surgeon, was the son of John Pleydell Wilton (above), surgeon, of Gloucester, and Mary Lightfoot. He was a cousin of Henry Hooper Wilton (above). He married, at Awre, Gloucestershire, 17 November 1823, Mary Anne Cholmondeley (1799-1880), daughter of Lt-Col Mason, of Spa Road, Gloucester, and Susannah, daughter of Roynan Jones of Nass House. They had at least 6 sons and 8 daughters:

1 George Henry (1824-1848); married Susannah Fletcher; had a son (b. 1848) who was partially educated in Germany
1 Elizabeth Cholmondeley (b. & d. 1826)
2 Harriet (1827-1828); died an infant
2 John Pleydell (1829-1913); married, 1861, Marion Milnes (1834-1913)
3 Francis (1830-1888)
4 Edward (1832-1892); married, 1868, Mary Huxtable (1842-1883)
5 William Spencer (1883-1885); died an infant
3 Mary (1835-1873); married, 1863, Samuel Powning Coldridge (1827-1905)
6 Charles William (1838-1882); married, 1870, Kezia Slaughter (1842-1917)
4 Charlotte (1839-1899); married, 1877, Herbert Milnes (1831-1909)
5 Elizabeth Kate (±1840-1911)
6 Annie (b. 1842)
7 Lucy (1842-1921); married, 1860, Horace Bartleet (1832-1901)
8 Harriet Susannah (1844-1925); married, 1882, William de Pipe Belcher

John Wilton studied at St Bartholomew's Hospital and practised at 11 King Street, Gloucester, where he was surgeon to the Gloucester Infirmary. He was created MRCS on 6 December 1816 and FRCS on 11 December 1843, being one of the original 300 fellows. He died at Gloucester on 23 May 1867. His son John

(1829-1913) followed his father and grandfather in a medical career, and was appointed surgeon of the Gloucester Militia in 1873.

1827: *There were, no doubt, several younger practitioners anxious for the appointment, as a step in their profession, as an opportunity of gaining greater experience, and as qualifying them to take pupils with considerable premiums; Messrs. J. Wilton, Shrapnell, Meyler, Heane &, I believe, one or two more, were candidates ...*

1845: 7 May: *Mr. Wilton, as an eminent Medical practitioner, had been sent from Gloucester ...*

1846: 11 Aug.

WILTON — Robert Pleydell Wilton [193]

Robert Pleydell Wilton (1798-1877), solicitor, was the son of John Pleydell Wilton (1774-1839) and Mary Lightfoot (1774-1861) (*above*). He married, 24 August 1824, Charlotte Maria L. Hallett (1804-1866); they had at least 2 sons and 7 daughters:

1 Frances Maria (1826-1911); died unmarried
2 Henrietta Caroline (1827-1894); married, 1845, John George Maclean
1 Robert Pleydell (1929-1866); married, 1851, Mary Emily Taylor
3 Agnes Kate (1830-1903); married, 1839, John Poole Haines
4 Emma Jane (1832-1919); married, 1851, Revd Richard Parkinson
5 Charlotte Helen (1835-1908); died unmarried
6 Jessica Leckie (1836-1864); married, 1859, George Whitcombe
2 Frederick (1837-1878); married, 1866, Marion Milnes
7 Florence (1839-1897); married, 1863, William Henry Davies

1846: 18 Nov: *Messrs. Hayward, Purnell, Dr. Timbrill and myself remained in consultation with Mr. R. Wilton, the solicitor to the Asylum, when it appeared that the whole matter was surrounded with legal difficulties ...*

1847: 16 Mar., 19 Aug: *Recd. from Mr. R. Wilton, Gloucester, a packet containing the deed of dissolution ...* 31 Oct.

WILTSHIRE — John Wiltshire [194]

John Wiltshire (1788-1867), landed proprietor and DL, was born at Shockerwick House, Bathford, Somerset, the son of John Wiltshire (1762-1842) and his wife, Charlotte. He was the grandson of Walter Wiltshire (1719-1799) and his wife, Charity. He was educated at New College, Oxford, and lived at Shockerwick, where he appears to have owned the advowson. He married Frances (1801-1860), daughter of Revd Richard Burdett Ness (1758-1829) and Jane Liddiard (b. 1760) of Gloucester; they had at least 2 sons and 3 daughters:

1 John Walter (1821-1889)
1 Louisa Jane (1823-1891); married, at Bathford, 1 December 1847, Lt Fitzjames Stuart MacGregor (1816-1886), son of Lt-Gen. J. A. Paul MacGregor; 1 son and 6 daughters:
    1 Louisa Jane Georgina (1847-1914)
    2 Charlotte Maria Fredericka (1851-1885)
    3 Frances Emily (1852-1874)
    4 Laura Wilhelmina (b. 1854)
    5 Harriet Isabella (1856-1891)
    6 Linda Eliza Catherina (1858-1921)
    1 James Richard Burdett Stewart (1862-1906)
2 Helen Mary (1826-1911); married, at Bathford, 5 February 1846, John Hampden (1819-1891), eldest son of Revd John Hampden, rector of Hinton Martell, Dorset; 1 son and 3 daughters:
    1 Constance Louisa Sophie (1833-1914)
    2 Helena Margaretta (1846-1936)
    3 Eleanor (b. 1847)
    1 Hobart (b. 1850)
2 William (b. 1827)
3 Laura Ann (1830-1871)

In his will of 1842, John Wiltshire (senior) bequeathed the estate to John, but also mentioned his nephew John Savage. John Savage (1785-1870), sugar refiner, JP, and mayor of Bristol, was born at Tetbury, the son of Revd John Savage (1745-1803), of Tetbury, and Charlotta (1756-1846), daughter of Walter and Charity Wiltshire. Francis Witts's parents, Edward and Agnes, had been good friends of the Wiltshire family of Bathford, and with the Savages of Tetbury.

Shockerwick House is an impressive Grade 1 building set in 19 acres of parkland. It was built in around 1750, although some additions were made in the 1790s, possibly by John Palmer. The Shockerwick estate was acquired by the Wiltshire family in about 1745 from the executors of Anthony Carew, whose family had owned the previous house.

Walter Wiltshire (d. 1765) seems to have been the first of his family to have bought property in the parish. He owned Wiltshire's Rooms, one of Bath's two lucrative gaming establishments. Beau Nash had an interest in Wiltshire's establishment, but this was kept a secret. When his income from Wiltshire's Rooms began to decline, Nash became convinced that he was being defrauded of his rightful interest and unwisely took Wiltshire to court. The court ruled that the profits of gaming were immoral, and Nash not only lost his case but also his good reputation. Wiltshire lost too, but in a different way; noting the evidence given in court, the vestry of St Peter and St Paul fined him £500 for keeping a gaming house within the abbey's parish. Despite their public quarrel, when Nash died in 1762 Wiltshire was one of the chief mourners at his funeral at the abbey. Walter himself died just three years later.

John, the elder of Walter Wiltshire's sons, was the founder of a successful carrier's business in which his younger brother, also Walter (1719-1799), was a partner. John died comparatively young and Walter (junior) inherited the estate at Shockerwick and the lease of Wiltshire's Rooms. He was a prominent citizen of Bath, serving as common councilman, alderman, and three times mayor of the city. The painter Thomas Gainsborough, who lived at Bath between 1760 and 1774, was one of his friends. Wiltshire conveyed Gainsborough's paintings to their destinations safely and without charge, and in return, Gainsborough made Wiltshire gifts of some of his paintings. These were dispersed about a century later at a sale at Shockerwick; one, 'Orpin, the Parish Clerk', now hangs in the Tate Gallery. Walter Wiltshire (junior) died in 1799 at the age of 81, and Shockerwick passed to his son, John (d. 1842).

In December 1805, having come to Bath to take the waters, Prime Minister William Pitt the Younger visited Shockerwick to view the paintings there by Gainsborough and other distinguished artists. During his visit he was informed in a despatch arrived by courier of the defeat at Austerlitz. According to John Wiltshire's son John (1788-1866), then aged 17, Pitt exclaimed, 'Heavy news indeed, do get me some brandy'. Pitt was so agitated that the young John Wiltshire feared he might collapse. The prime minister had been in failing health for several years, and this news was indeed a fatal blow; he died in London a few weeks later.

Princess Victoria, later Queen Victoria, visited Shockerwick with her mother when, in 1830, she came to Bath to open the Royal Victoria Park. John Walter Wiltshire (d. 1889), son of John Wiltshire (junior), was the last member of the family to own Shockerwick.

1826: 14 Sep: ... *at the hospitable board of Mr. & Lady Frances Bankes, who allowed me to introduce any of my acquaintances, and, besides Margaret & her Mother, Mr. Ford & his sister, Mr. & Miss Wiltshire &c. availed themselves of my introduction.*
1829: 22 Sep.

WINCHESTER — William Winchester [195]

William Winchester (1815-1888), Church of England clergyman and later privy chamberlain to Pope Leo XIII, was the son of Henry Winchester (1777-1838) and Elizabeth, daughter and heir of John Ayerst of Hawkhurst. His father was MP for Maidstone in 1830-31, sheriff of London in 1826-27, alderman in 1826-38, and lord mayor in 1834-35; he married William's mother, Elizabeth Ayerst, on 24 November 1803. Henry Winchester was said to have been an irascible and cantankerous man who carried the seeds of discontent into all his spheres of endeavour. A scurrilous magazine of the period, *Figaro in London*, lampooned him as follows:

> Alderman Winchester has been labouring under a very severe malady. He has positively had a violent attack of *wit*. We are happy to say that there are not the smallest fears of a *relapse*. Wit with Winchester is like the measles with a child;—he has it *once*, and then there is an end of it.

Henry Winchester became president of St Thomas's Hospital on 11 February 1835, and was also a vice-president of the Society for the Promotion of Arts, Manufactures and Commerce, and treasurer of the Printers' Pension Society. His personal affairs, which were known to be unhappy, were worsened by the deaths of his children, including that of his youngest son at the Mansion House on 17 June 1835. Winchester's business dealings had been encumbered for some time, and he was officially ordered to surrender as a bankrupt on 1 March 1838. He died a week later '... at a lunatic asylum, to which he had been removed, having unhappily brooded with such intense melancholy on his domestic calamities as to have been bereft of his senses.' No will or grant of administration has been found. He was succeeded by his second and only surviving son William (1815-1888). (*See* the diary entry for 3 January 1839.)

William Winchester was educated at Christ Church, Oxford (BA 1838; MA 1840). He was appointed an assistant chaplain in the Bengal Ecclesiastical Establishment in August 1840, and proceeded to India in the *Zenobia* on 12 October 1840. He was on furlough in 1851, but returned to India and was shortly afterwards posted in 1853 to Dacca, where he remained until he retired. During the Mutiny of 1857-58, Winchester 'fearlessly exposed himself in assisting the wounded' at Dacca. It is recorded that he was present at an engagement with two companies of mutinous sepoys of the 73rd Native Infantry and a detachment of native artillery at Lal Bagh, Dacca, on 22 November 1857, for which he received the India Medal without clasp.

William Winchester retired from the Bengal Ecclesiastical Establishment in 1859. He married, 1861, Elizabeth Maria, eldest daughter of Maj.-Gen. Edward Gwatkin, of the 31st Bengal Native Infantry, and widow of Maj. Robert Barlow Palmer Byng. Shortly after their marriage, the couple moved to Rome where the Winchester became privy chamberlain to Pope Leo XIII. He died at Rome in 1888 and was buried together with his wife, who had died there in 1868.

William Winchester was a knight commander of the Holy Sepulchre in Jerusalem, and in his will he bequeathed the cross of this order, together with his chamberlain's chain of office and his 'India Medal'. The medal eventually ended up in the collection of John Tamplin and was sold at auction on 19 September 2003.

1839: 2 Jan: *Of the Clergy there were present ... Winchester ...* 3 Jan: *An assistant Curate to Mr. Parsons at Upton St. Leonards, dined and slept at Prinknash, by name Winchester, recently ordained, a Xt. Ch. man, said to have distinguished himself at the Univ: he resides with his widowed Mother at Glouc. and appears amiable, but shy and reserved: and no wonder, for I understand that his Father, the late Alderman Winchester, of London, having fallen into embarrassment, terminated his days by suicide.*

WINDHAM — William Windham [196]

William Windham (1750-1810), politician, was the only son of Col William Windham, of Felbrigg, Norfolk, and Sarah Hicks of Tanfield, Essex. He was educated at Eton College, Glasgow University, and University College, Oxford. He married, 1798, Cecilia Forrest. He was MP for Norwich in 1784-1802, St Mawes in 1802-06, New Romney in 1806, and Higham Ferrers in 1807-10. He was secretary at war with a seat in the cabinet from July 1794 to February 1801, and was appointed a privy councillor on 16 July 1794. He was secretary of state for war and colonies from February 1806 to March 1807.

1801: 8 Jun: *On the Ministerial side Mr. Wilberforce seemed to me the best orator: Mr. Abbot, Mr. Addington, Mr. Baker, Mr. Yorke, Mr. Windham, Mr. O'Hare & Lord Hawkesbury chiefly arrested my attention ...*

WINDSOR — Mrs Windsor, actress at Bristol and Bath [197]

It is not known who Mrs Windsor, née Daniel, married or precisely when, but it was presumably early in 1804. She was a solo singer at Vauxhall Gardens in 1800, and performed there again as Miss Daniel in 1803. On 1 October 1804 Francis Witts saw her in Elizabeth Inchbald's play *The Child of Nature*. Five days later, at Bath, she performed as Laura in *Lock and Key*, a musical farce in two acts, written by Prince Hoare.

1804: 1 Oct: *To the play at Bristol in the Evening with my Mother, Lady Hunloke, Sue & Caroline Townsend & Col. Hill. The Child of Nature, the Farm House & my Grandmother. The Actors very indifferent. Egerton, a Miss Jameson, her first appearance, Mrs. Windsor, & Mr. Mallinson, the best.*
1805: 11 Mar: ... *Incledon excelling in Don Carlos in the Duenna, & Patrick in the Poor Soldier, & unrivalled in the storm. Mallinson, Lovegrove, Blisset, Webber & Mrs. Windsor above mediocrity.*

WING — Charles Wing, medical practitioner at the Stow-on-the-Wold Union Workhouse [198]

Charles Wing (1792-1869), surgeon, was born at Stamford, Lincolnshire, the son of William and Elizabeth Wing. He qualified MRCS on 3 July 1814 as a general practitioner, and lived at St John's Wood, Westminster, until 1846. Before moving to Bourton-on-the-Water, Wing was surgeon to the Metropolitan Hospital for Children and Blue Coat School, Westminster. He was a member of the Royal Institution, the Westminster Medical Society, and the Harveian Society. Wing wrote the *Evils of the Factory System* and contributed to *The Lancet* with articles on the subject of 'Spinal Deformity' in 1839 and 1840.

In the 1851 census Wing was registered as living at 94 North End Road, Fulham, and in the 1861 census at 3 Down Place, Hammersmith, Middlesex. On both occasions he was listed as a practising surgeon. He married Harriet (b. ±1797), who was born at Maidenwell, Lincolnshire.

1843: 18 Aug: *Another disagreeable duty was performed by us in sending, on a certificate of Messrs. Wells and Wing, as medical practitioners, to the Lunatic Asylum at Gloucester, Richd. Fox of Bourton on the Water ...*

1844: 5 Dec.

1845: 15 Jan: *Our cook taken ill, is attended by Dr. Wing.* 16 Jan., 18 Jan., 20 Jan, 22 Jan., 24 Jan., 27 Jan., 29-30 Jan., 1 Feb., 3 Feb., 7 Feb: *Wrote to Mr. Aitkens on the subject of his nominating Dr. Wing as a candidate for admission into the Stow Book Society, a very ill-judged proposition, as professional persons, not clergymen, have been hitherto, generally, been considered ineligible, and an attempt to open the door to other than the gentry and clergy of the neighbourhood is likely to give offence, and be resisted.* 12 Feb., 14 Feb., 26-27 Feb, 1 Mar., 13-14 Mar., 18 Mar., 5 Jul: *... a letter from Pearce ... also that Dr. Wing was censured for neglecting his duty as Medical officer, in not properly visiting a pauper patient ...*

1846: 7 Jul: *We had previously visited the premises of his neighbour, Dr. Wing, who was busily engaged in arranging in the grounds surrounding his house, booths, orchestra, tents &c. for a rural fete to be given tomorrow on occasion of the annual meeting of the Bourton on the Water lodge of Odd Fellows, a society in which the little doctor takes singular interest.*

WINGFIELD — **Charles Wingfield**[199]

Charles Wingfield (1787-1846), surgeon, was the son of the Revd John Wingfield of St Chad, Shrewsbury. He was trained as a house surgeon at St Bartholomew's Hospital and served as assistant surgeon at the General Hospital in Calcutta, but took a furlough in 1813 and never returned. He then worked as a surgeon in Liverpool and was eventually struck off the roll in Calcutta in 1818. He married, at Liverpool, 22 September 1819, Hannah Brancker (1788-1870); they had at least 1 daughter:

1 Mary (1821-1825)

In 1817 the post of surgeon to the Radcliffe Infirmary in Oxford became vacant; there was a contested election which Charles Wingfield won narrowly by 71 votes to 70. Wingfield became one of the leading surgeons in Oxford and took an active part in the early days of the Providential and Medical and Surgical Association. He remained surgeon to the Radcliffe Infirmary for the rest of his life. He was elected a fellow of the Royal College of Surgeons in January 1844.

1827: 18 Oct: *The first question to be decided, was whether these gentlemen were equal to the performance of the duties required of them, now the structure was enlarged; and on this point the most positive assurance, that they were, was given by their own explanations, & by those of Dr. Baron & Dr. Shute, the Physicians of the establishment, and Dr. Wingfield, aSurgeon of eminence at Oxford, Surgeon of the Radcliffe Infirmary, and once who had received his education at Gloucester Infirmary.*

1832: 14 Mar: *I hastened for an explanation to Edward, who explained to me, that, when riding with two companions a spirited hack, his horse had run away with him, and in leaping a five-barred gate, had caught his heels in the upper bars, & thrown his rider, who sustained a very serious injury on the left elbow. Yet he was able to ride at a slow pace to Oxford, whither one of his companions, having hurried forward, had secured the attendance of Mr. Wingfield, an eminent Surgeon. Under his skilful management the injury was in a fair way to be entirely remedied ...* 5 Apr: *We had the comfort of receiving this evening our dear son, who returned to us from Oxford for the Easter Vacation. He is not in such good health as we could wish, and continues still under Mr. Wingfield's care.*

WINGFIELD — **Emily Wingfield** — *see* **Twisleton**

WINGFIELD — **Isabella Wingfield**[200]

Isabella Wingfield, née Brownlow (d. 1848), was the daughter of William Brownlow, of Lurgan, co. Armagh, and Catherine Hall. She married, 1796, Richard Wingfield, 4th Viscount Powerscourt (1762-1809).

1827: 25 Sep: *Mrs. Hastings invited us this day to make up for the disappointment on Thursday last ... Mr. & Mrs. Twisleton from Adlestrop were accompanied by Mrs. T's mother, the Lady Powerscourt.*

WINGFIELD-STRATFORD — **John Wingfield-Stratford**[201]

John Wingfield-Stratford (1810-1881), landed proprietor, was born at 12 Stratford Place, Westminster, the son of Lt-Gen. John Wingfield (1772-1850) and Frances Bartholomew (d. 1827). He married, at Rendcomb, Gloucestershire, 10 December 1844, Jane Elizabeth (1825-1897), daughter of Gen. Sir John Wright Guise, 3rd baronet, and Charlotte Diana Vernon; they had 7 sons and 6 daughters:

1 Isabella Margaret (1846-1933); married, 14 January 1868, Revd James Newton Heale
2 Frances Charlotte (1847-1926); married, 24 November 1875, Sir Henry Michael Hawley (1848-1909); 3 sons and 3 daughters:
  1 Henry Cusack Wingfield (1876-1923); succeeded as 6th baronet
  2 Cyril Francis (1878-1914)
  3 Michael Charles (1879-1934)
  1 Winifred Mary (1880-1891)
  2 Gladys Florence (1885-1922)
  3 Olive Victoria (1887-1981)
1 Edward John (1849-1903), Lt, Scots Guards; died unmarried
2 Henry Verner (1851-1923), Capt., Rifle Brigade; served in the Wadri expedition, 1881; died unmarried
3 Cecil Vernon (1853-1939), Lt-Col, RE; married, 12 October 1881, Rosalind Isabel, daughter of Revd Edward Vesey Bligh and Lady Isabel Mary Frances Nevill; at least 2 sons and 1 daughter:
  1 Esmé Cecil (1882-1971), army officer and English historian
  2 Geoffrey Edward (b. 1887), Col
  1 Rosalind Frances Cecily (1893-1975)
3 Emily Rose (1855-1904); married, 9 September 1875, Lt-Col Henry Waugh Renny-Tailyour; 1 daughter:
  1 Eileen Mary (d. 1969)
4 Leonard Guise (1856-1941); married, 13 December 1880, Alethe Sylvia, daughter of Capt. Alexander Nixon Montgomery; 1 son and 4 daughters:
  1 Maud Frances Jane (1882-1947); married, 20 June 1912, Bernard Bowles Colbeck
  1 Mervyn Edward John (1883-1922), Capt.
  2 Murielle Alethe Victoria (1887-1931); married, 1912, Richard Osbaldeston Spencer-Smith (b. 1875); died at Clinique de Collonge, Territet, Switzerland
  3 Agnes Mary (dates unknown)
  4 Hermione (1890-1966); married Gilbert John Victor Shepherd (1887-1969)
4 Florence Mary (1858-1947); married, 10 April 1883, Henry Laurence Daly, son of Gen. Sir Henry Dermot Daly and Susan Elizabeth Ellen Kirkpatrick; 1 son:
  1 Jocelyn Dermot (d. 1925)

5 Howard W. (1859-1940); married, 22 October 1902, Christian Margaret, daughter of David Scott Duncan
6 Richard Nevill (1861-1942); married, 16 December 1891, Grace Dorothea, daughter of Capt. Alexander Nixon Montgomery; 1 son and 1 daughter:
  1 Esmé John Richard (1897-1918), Sub-Lt, RN; killed in action
  1 Georgina Grace Ida (1899-1980)
7 Francis Mervyn (1865-1932); married, 16 January 1906, Nora, daughter of George Matthey; 1 son and 1 daughter:
  1 Mervyn Verner (1907-1982)
  1 Georgina Frances (1910-1924)
5 Georgiana Maud (1868-1945); married, 2 June 1891, Maj. Howard Guise, son of Revd Vernon George Guise and Mary Harriet Lane; 1 daughter:
  1 Jane (1893-1966)
6 Violet Alice Ethel (1869-1916); married, 25 January 1893, Cdr Bertie Angelo Cator; 1 daughter:
  1 Elizabeth (b. 1899); married, at West Malling, Kent, 20 April 1922, Revd Edward Eustace Hill (1876-1958)

1845: 14 Mar: *There was also Mr. Stratford son of Colonel Stratford, of Kent, who married Miss Guise, eldest daughter of Sir John, a very pretty and pleasing young person—she was one of the party, and I much admired her unaffected manners: her husband sensible, quiet and gentlemanlike.*

WINTER — Revd Winter at Champion Hill

There was no Church of England minister by the name of Winter in the vicinity of Champion Hill at the time of Francis Witts's mention. The Wittses of Champion Hill were a mixture of Quakers and nonconformists, so this may have been a Baptist minister, or one of some other denomination.

1801: 27 Jul: *Mrs. Favell, Mr. Martin an American, the Revd. Mr. Winter with his wife & Daughter & the two gentlemen dined with us.*

WINTER — Mr Winter, a pupil of John Fowell Jones

1827: 5 Jun: *There were also at the Symposium of our host & hostess, the Egerton Leighs and his brother, the Revd. Peter Leigh, Mr. Jones & his dandy pupil, Mr. Winter ...*

WINTER — Thomas Winter [202]

Thomas Winter (1797-1872), Church of England clergyman, was born at Chipping Norton, Oxfordshire, the son of Thomas and Anne Winter. He was educated at Lincoln College, Oxford (BA 1819; MA 1821), and was ordained deacon on 28 May 1820. On the same day he was appointed to his first clerical position as curate of Daylesford, Gloucestershire. He was later appointed stipendiary curate of Condicote on 17 August 1823. He served as rector of Daylesford from 1825 to his death in 1872.

Winter married, 1837, Maria Chapuset (1804-1889), born in Stuttgart in the German kingdom of Württemberg. She was the niece of Marian Hastings, née Chapuset (1747-1837). Marian had been born Anna Maria Apollonia Chapuset and was known as Baroness Imhoff until her divorce. She had also been known as Anna Maria Appolonia von Chapuset-von Imhoff. Thomas and Marie had at least 1 daughter:

1 Marian (1838-1919); died unmarried; buried at St James's, Nether Worton, Oxfordshire

Thomas Winter was an important person to Francis Witts and the relevant diary extracts are substantial. Sadly, he left a very modest footprint and not much is known of him. After Charles Imhoff's death in 1853, Winter became the custodian of the Hastings' papers.

1823: 23 Apr., 9 Dec: *The only other guest besides ourselves was Miss Chabuzet, a German relative of Mrs. Hastings, widow of the late distinguished Governor General of India, who continues in advanced life to reside at Dalesford. Mrs. Hastings's German extraction & early history is well known.*

1824: 19 Feb: *Sir Charles & Lady Imhoff, and Miss Chabuzet, with ourselves, formed the party. Sir C. Imhoff, a Major Genl. in our Service, is of German Origin, being son of Mrs. Hastings, the wife of the Governor General of India, by her first husband Baron d'Imhoff, whose second wife & family by the Second Couche I knew intimately in my early days at Weimar.* 6 Apr: *We had a dinner party; Mr. & Mrs. Egerton Leigh, Mr. R. Wynniatt, Mr. Bowen, & Mr. Winter ...* 9 Nov.

1825: 29 Jul: ... *Mr. Winter, lately instituted to the Rectory of Daylesford, Worcestershire, of which he was before curate, the presentation being in Mrs. Hastings, widow of the late celebrated Governor Hastings ...* 3 Nov.

1826: 3 Mar: *We met a pleasant party: Mr. & Mrs. East, Miss Chabuzet, Mr. Twisleton, Mr. Jones, Mr. & Mrs. Vavasour.* 19 Apr., 23 May: *Mr. Hurd and Mr. Winter joined our party at dinner.* 14 Jun: *afterwards I drank tea at Mr. Winter's lodgings.* 6 Aug., 2 Nov.

1827: 14 Jan., 4 Jul., 25 Jul., 16 Aug., 3 Sep: *We drove to make our first call on Mrs. Hastings at Daylesford. It has pleased this ancient Lady, after we have been 18 years settled here, to find us out & visit us.* 12 Sep., 25 Sep: *Mrs. Hastings most politely invited us this day to make up for the disappointment on Thursday last ...There was a large party: Mr. Winter officiated as chaplain & carved the haunch of venison.* 2 Oct.

1828: 12 Feb., 23 Apr., 28 May, 2 Jul., 22 Jul., 27 Sep., 7-8 Oct., 19 Dec.

1829: 21 Jan: *We had a party of our friends to dinner. Sir C. Imhoff and Miss Chapuset.* 25 Feb: *I prepared for a journey to Alma mater, in which I was to be accompanied by my friend and neighbour, Mr. Winter, who was to meet me at Gawcomb Turnpike gate on the road to Witney, where we had agreed to dine & sleep.* 27 Feb., 1 Mar., 20 Mar., 20 May, 17 Jun, 25 Jun., 27 Jun., 11-12 Aug., 29 Sep., 16 Oct., 13 Nov., 4 Dec.

1830: 14 Apr., 26-27 May.

1832: 25 Apr.

1833: 18 Jan., 21 Jan., 1 Feb., 17 Oct., 25 Oct., 30 Oct.

1834: 23-24 Jul., 26 Jul., 29 Jul., 31 Jul., 7-9 Aug., 19-20 Aug., 28 Aug., 30 Sep., 23 Oct., 25 Oct., 31 Oct., 21 Nov., 17 Dec.

1835: 1 Jan., 10-13 Jan., 15-17 Jan., 21-22 Jan., 29 Jan., 5 Feb., 12-13 Feb., 19 Feb., 26 Feb., 19 Mar., 2 Apr., 5 Apr., 9 Apr., 7 May, 12 May, 28 May, 4 Jun.,

1836: 28 Jul., 4 Aug., 16 Aug., 18 Aug., 22 Aug: *Soon after our return my son and I went in our open carriage to dine with Winter at Daylesford.* 24-25 Aug., 29 Aug., 31 Aug., 8 Sep., 27 Sep., 29 Sep., 6 Oct., 13 Oct., 27 Oct., 3 Nov., 10 Nov., 17 Nov., 24 Nov., 1 Dec., 21-22 Dec., 29 Dec.

1837: 12 Jan., 19 Jan., 23 Feb., 9 Mar., 23 Mar., 30 Mar: *She retained her faculties to the last, her death bed was attended by her nearest relations, Sir Chas. and Lady Imhoff and Miss Chapuset.* 13 Apr., 19 Apr., 26 Apr: *Sir Charles I. and Winter are gone to Town, as Executors, to prove Mrs. Hasting's will.* 6 May: *Called on Winter at Daylesford, whom we found at home, and Miss Chapuset with him.* 11 May, 18 May, 22 May, 22 Jun., 24 Jun., 29 Jun., 6 Jul., 14 Jul: *Entertained a party of our neighbours at dinner ... Sir C. and Lady Imhoff, Mr. Winter and Miss Chapuset, from Daylesford*

... 20 Jul., 26-27 Jul., 10 Aug., 17 Aug., 24 Aug., 31 Aug., 7 Sep., 14 Sep., 21 Sep., 26-27 Sep., 10 Oct: *The Imhoffs were also accompanied by Hastings Woodman, Great nephew of the deceased Governor, and standing in the same relation to Mrs. Hastings, being son of Mr. Woodman, formerly Rector or Brackley & Daylesford by Mademoiselle Chapuset, elder sister of our friend Marie, both being Germans, and nieces of Mr. Hastings. Of the latter I should have sometime since recorded that on the 3d. Inst. she became the wife of our friend, Winter, Rector of Daylesford. It has been a long engagement, and both being highly esteemed by a numerous circle of friends and acquaintance, many good wishes are put up for their happiness.* 12 Oct., 2 Nov., 6 Nov: *Drove M W. to Daylesford to call on our old friends Winter and Marie Chapuset in their new character of man and wife, united after a long engagement, and, I trust, having much happiness in prospect.* 8-9 Nov., 16-17 Nov., 23 Nov., 29 Nov., 14 Dec., 21 Dec., 28 Dec.

1838: 11 Jan., 18 Jan., 25 Jan., 1 Feb., 8 Feb., 15 Feb., 22 Feb., 1 Mar., 5-6 Mar., 8 Mar., 15 Mar., 22 Mar., 5 Apr., 12 Apr., 19-20 Apr., 25-27 Apr., 10 May, 17 May, 24 May, 31 May, 6 Jun., 13-14 Jun., 21 Jun., 28 Jun., 12 Jul., 2 Aug: *Mrs. Winter was safely delivered of a daughter on Monday last; it is doubtful whether the infant will live, but the Mother is going on well.* 9 Aug., 16 Aug., 23 Aug., 30 Aug., 31 Aug: *From Churchill we proceeded by Cornwell to Daylesford House, to call on Mrs. Hastings: she was indisposed, and confined to her dressing room; but we passed a pleasant half hour or more, taking luncheon with Miss Chapuset, Mrs. Winter, and Miss Adams, who is staying with Mrs. H.* 6-7 Sep., 25 Sep., 27-28 Sep., 3-4 Oct., 11 Oct., 18 Oct., 24 Oct., 1 Nov., 6 Nov: 8 Nov., 29 Nov., 12 Dec., 20 Dec., 24 Dec., 27 Dec.

1839: 17 Jan., 24 Jan., 28 Feb., 7 Mar., 14 Mar., 21 Mar., 4 Apr., 1-2 May, 11 May, 13 May, 16-17 May, 23 May, 29-30 May, 6 Jun., 13 Jun., 20 Jun., 26-27 Jun., 11 Jul., 22 Jul., 15 Aug., 19 Aug., 22 Aug.

1840: 19 Mar: *A long and very unpleasant argument, amounting almost to an altercation, with Winter on Poor Law matters, which he urged very pertinaciously, and with an eagerness bordering on personality.* 20 Mar: *Wrote to W B Pole my feelings at considerable detail with reference to the painful conversation I had yesterday with Winter in his presence.* 21 Mar: *Wrote to W B Pole a further letter of explanation on the subject which had been warmly discussed between Winter and myself on Thursday; also sent him Mrs. Pearce's letter received by me yesterday in elucidation of the case ...* 26 Mar: *When the sitting was over joined Messrs. Ford and Waller as Magistrates in the Justice room; Messrs. Winter and W B Pole were present. I met the former with the usual shake of the hand, and no reference was made to the unpleasant argument last week.* 2 Apr., 9 Apr., 16 Apr., 18 Apr., 21 Apr., 30 Apr., 25 May, 28 May, 4-5 Jun., 10 Jun., 11 Jun: *The Daylesford question was brought before Mr. Ford, by Pearce, as Clerk to the Union, and supported by me, who argued for the legality and reasonableness of the Order issued by the Board of Guardians; Winter took up the parable on the part of the absent Parish Officers of Daylesford ...* 17-18 Jun., 25 Jun: *He expressed an opinion that the Guardians of our Union were quite in order as to the point in dispute between them and Mr. Winter on the part of Daylesford; that our proceedings had been all correct ...* 26 Jun: *Thence drove through the grounds to Daylesford Village, called at the Winters, but were not admitted, as they were dressing to go out to dinner ...* 16 Jul., 21 Jul., 23 Jul., 30 Jul., 5-6 Aug., 13 Aug., 20 Aug., 27 Aug., 10 Sep., 17 Sep., 24 Sep., 29 Spe., 8 Oct., 15 Oct., 24 Oct., 29 Oct., 5 Nov., 12 Nov., 18 Nov: *We had a rough drive to and from the Rectory at Daylesford, whither we went to dine with the Winters; meeting Sir Charles and Lady Imhoff ... A pleasant party.* 19 Nov., 26 Nov.

1841: 4 Mar.

1842: 20 Jan., 27 Jan., 3 Feb., 10 Feb., 17 Feb., 24 Feb., 1 Mar., 3 Mar., 10 Mar., 10 Mar., 23-24 Mar., 31 Mar., 7 Apr., 21 Apr., 27 Apr., 12 May, 19 May, 26 May, 6 Jun., 9 Jun., 14 Jun., 16 Jun., 23 Jun., 7-8 Jul., 20 Jul: *A dinner party; we were favoured with the company of Mr. and Mrs. Pole, Watson Pole, Mr. Wynniatt with his daughter Harriet, and son in law, W. Lowndes, Mr. and Mrs. Winter, and J. T. Rice; the evening passed off pleasantly.* 21 Jul., 28 Jul., 4 Aug., 15 Aug., 18 Aug., 25 Aug., 31 Aug., 8 Sep., 15 Sep., 22 Sep., 27 Sep., 1 Oct., 6 Oct., 13 Oct., 3 Nov., 13 Nov., 22 Dec: *A very serious charge by Mr. Winter against Edginton, Contractor for the supply of bread to the 1st. distr. of the Union, was entered into ...* 27 Dec.

1843: 19 Jan., 26 Jan., 15-16 Feb., 21 Sep., 26 Sep., 12 Oct., 14 Oct: *Met and held parley with Mr. and Mrs. Winter, and their little girl in the grounds near Daylesford, as we were going to call on them.* 2 Nov., 9 Nov., 16 Nov., 30 Nov., 28 Dec.

1844: 25 Jan., 15 Feb., 22 Feb., 29 Feb., 21 Mar., 4 Apr., 17-18 Apr., 25 Apr., 1-2 May, 6 May, 25 Jul., 5 Aug: *A letter from Mr. Winter, written on the eve of his departure with Mrs. W. for a tour on the Rhine, to Stutgard &c.* 14 Sep: *Drove to Daylesford; called at the parsonage, and received a favourable account of Winter, who, with Mrs. W. and their little girl, are expected back from their foreign tour, to Stuttgard, Baden-Baden &c. in a few days.* 30 Sep., 3 Oct., 7 Oct., 10 Oct., 31 Oct., 21 Nov., 5 Dec., 11-12 Dec., 26-27 Dec.

1845: 9 Jan., 16 Jan., 30 Jan., 6 Feb., 25 Feb., 27 Feb., 13 Mar., 20 Mar., 26-27 Mar., 10 Apr., 17 Apr., 24 Apr., 1 May, 22 May, 29 May, 10 Jun: *By the way we called at Daylesford on the Winters; Mr. W. was out; we were received by Mrs. W.—much lamentation as to the injury they would experience by the line of the Oxford, Worcester & Wolverhampton railway passing so near their house; however they have secured from the Directors of the Company a large compensation.* 12 Jun., 14 Jun., 24 Jun., 26 Jun., 9 Jul., 11 Jul., 16 Jul., 6 Aug., 13 Aug., 15 Aug., 26 Aug., 3 Sep., 10 Sep., 17 Sep., 24 Sep., 29 Sep., 1 Oct., 8 Oct., 15 Oct., 24 Oct., 5 Nov., 12 Nov., 19 Nov., 26 Nov., 4 Dec., 10 Dec., 31 Dec.

1847: 16 Jan: *Mr. & Mrs. Winter called upon us.* 4 Feb., 11 Mar., 7-8 Apr., 15 Apr., 20 Apr: *Winter confined to his bed with an attack of Influenza.* 12 May, 27 May, 3 Jun., 10 Jun., 24 Jun., 8 Jul., 15 Jul., 20 Jul: *We proceeded to Daylesford: called on the Winters: W. kindly accompanied Round and myself in a drive thro' the grounds attached to Adlestrop House ...* 22 Jul., 19 Aug., 26 Aug., 28 Aug., 1 Sep., 8 Sep., 14 Sep., 28 Sep., 30 Sep., 14 Oct., 16-17 Oct., 25-26 Oct., 3 Nov., 11 Nov., 18 Nov., 25 Nov., 15 Dec., 20 Dec., 23 Dec. 30 Dec.

1848: 15 Jan., 27 Jan., 3 Feb., 8 Feb., 10 Feb., 17 Feb., 24 Feb., 2 Mar., 16 Mar., 6 Apr., 27 Apr., 11-12 May, 18 May, 1 Jun., 8 Jun., 23 Jun: *Mr. Winter called, and partook of luncheon with us: ... He also tendered his services for three of four Sundays, to enable me to make an excursion to the sea ...* 26 Feb., 4 Jul., 6 Jul., 8 Jul., 27 Jul., 29 Jul., 5 Aug., 7 Aug., 17 Aug., 20 Aug., 30-31 Aug., 2 Sep., 4 Sep., 12 Oct., 24 Oct., 9 Nov.

1849: 12 Dec.

1850: 10-11 Jan., 24 Jan., 7 Feb., 21 Feb., 2 Mar., 7 Mar., 9 Mar., 14 Mar., 21 Mar., 28 Mar., 11 Apr., 19 Apr., 8 May, 17 May, 30 May, 30-31 May, 13 Jun., 17 Jun: 24-25 Jun: *After luncheon sallied forth in the Winter's family four-wheel, with its sturdy and safe poney—first to Daylesford House, now only occupied by servants, Sir Charles Imhoff being now resident at his house in town ...* 11-12 Jul., 18 Jul., 1 Aug., 29 Aug., 5 Sep., 26 Sep., 1 Oct., 3 Oct., 23 Oct., 25 Oct., 27 Oct., 6-7 Nov., 14 Nov., 21 Nov., 28 Nov., 5 Dec., 12 Dec., 19 Dec.

1851: 9 Jan., 16 Jan., 23 Jan., 30 Jan., 6 Feb., 13 Feb., 27 Feb., 13 Mar., 27 Mar., 3 Apr., 10 Apr., 17 Apr., 23-24 Apr., 1 May, 8 May, 11 May, 15 May, 22 May: *During part of the time I joined Mr. and Mrs. Winter, who arrived in Town with Sir Charles Imhoff yesterday or the day before, and are staying with him in Portugal Street ...*

1852: 22 Jan., 29 Jan., 5 Feb., 12 Feb., 19 Feb., 4 Mar., 11 Mar., 25 Mar., 27 Mar., 1 Apr., 3 Apr: *Called on the W. Vavasours at Lower Slaughter, where I also met Mr. and Mrs. Winter, and their daughter ...* 8 Apr., 15 Apr., 19 Apr., 22 Apr., 29 Apr., 6 May, 12 May, 12-13 May, 27 May, 3 Jun., 7 Jun., 25 Oct., 28 Oct., 2 Dec., 16 Dec., 23 Dec., 30 Dec.

1853: 13 Jan., 3-4 Feb., 10 Feb., 18 Feb., 20 Feb., 24 Feb., 10 Mar., 7 Apr., 28 Apr., 5 May, 11 May, 13 May, 19 May, 26 May, 2 Jun., 8 Dec., 15 Dec., 22 Dec., 19 Dec.

1854: 2 Feb., 9 Feb., 16 Feb., 23 Feb., 9 Mar., 16 Mar., 23 Mar., 30 Mar., 6 Apr., 13 Apr., 20 Apr., 27 Apr., 4 May, 11 May, 18 May, 25 May, 8 Jun., 18 Jun., 22 Apr., 24 Jun., 6 Jul., 13 Jul., 19-20 Jul., 27 Jul., 10 Aug., 17 Aug.

WINTERBOTHAM — Lindsey Winterbotham [203]

Lindsey Winterbotham (1799-1870), solicitor and banker, was the son of Revd William Winterbotham (1763-1829), a Baptist minister at Plymouth who had been fined £200 and imprisoned for four years at Newgate Gaol. He was charged in 1793 at Exeter assizes for preaching a sermon 'advocating an extension of civil and religious liberty'. Revd Winterbotham later became the Baptist minister at Shortwood Tabernacle, near Nailsworth, between 1804 and 1829.

Lindsey Winterbotham subscribed to the same religious views as his father, and acted as a deacon of the Bedford Street congregational chapel in Stroud. He married Sarah Anne Selfe Page (b. ±1809); they had at least 4 sons and 1 daughter:

1 Henry Selfe Page (1837-1873)
2 Arthur Brend (1838-1892)
1 Sarah Anne (b. ±1840)
3 Edward W. (b. ±1842)
4 William H. (b. ±1843)

The family lived at Bank House, High Street, Stroud. Lindsay was the general manager and inspector of branches for the Gloucestershire Banking Company, and had previously been a solicitor at Tewkesbury and mayor of that town. Two of Lindsey and Sarah's children, Henry Selfe and Arthur Brend, became MPs. In 1885 Arthur joined Thomas Hunt to establish the firm Hunt & Winterbotham, woollen cloth manufacturers, of Cam.

1837: 22 Sep: *A host of attorneys were present: the leading agents for the Conservative party being Mr. Cox of Cheltenham, and Mr. Barnett of Tetbury, for the Whigs. Mr. Winterbotham and Mr. Gyde, both of Cheltenham.*

1848: 27 Jun: *Several new magistrates qualified ... Mr. Winterbotham of Stroud, a dissenter, and ci-devant Attorney, a man of talent, and a liberal, as, I suppose, are most of the rest ...* 17 Oct.

1850: 15 Jan., 28 Jan., 1 Jul., 7 Aug., 14 Oct., 8 Dec., 10 Dec., 14 Dec: *sent to Mr. Winterbotham by the return of the post a few lines to accompany Mr. M's letter to me ...* 30 Dec.

1851: 7 Feb: *... one of these from Mr. Winterbotham, the manager of the Cirencester and Stow branches of the Gloucestershire Banking Company, announces the miserable condition, both bodily and mental, of Raymond Cripps, formerly manager of the Stow & Cirencester branches of the Gloucestershire Banking Company ...* 17 Mar.

1852: 9 Mar., 15 Mar.

1853: 3 Jan., 14 Mar., 7 Apr: *Mr. Winterbotham, the manager of the Stroud, Cirencester, and Stow Branches of the Gloucestershire Banking Company, sought an interview with me as to the change likely to occur in the establishment here, in consequence of Mr. Kimber's resignation of his office as Clerk ...* 27 Jun.

1854: 14 Feb.

WINTLE — James Wintle — *see also* Crawley *and* Fulljames [204]

James Wintle (1770-1860), solicitor, JP, DL, and landed proprietor, was born at Gloucester, the son of James and Sarah Wintle. The Wintles hailed from Westbury-on-Severn and Newnham-on-Severn, where they had been landed proprietors since the fifteenth century. James married, 1813, Harriet Fulljames (1777-1845), aunt of the county surveyor Thomas Fulljames. They had at least 1 son and 1 daughter:

1 Harriet (1816-1889); married, 1845, Charles Yonge Crawley (1813-1876)
1 James (1818-1899), solicitor and farmer, of Newnham-on-Severn; married, at All Saints', Bishop's Wood, Herefordshire, 29 August 1850, Eliza Ives (1824-1863), daughter of Edward Partridge and Eliza Ives; at least 4 sons and 4 daughters:
  1 Marion Ives (1851-1914)
  1 Douglas James (1853-1947); married, at Conwy, Caernarvonshire, 1893, Elizabeth Wheeldon
  2 Robert Amyatt (1854-1923)
  2 Agnes Eliza (b. 1856); married, at Westbury-on-Severn, Gloucestershire, 1878, Cecil Frederick Hall (b. 1846)
  3 Gladys Josephine (1858-1933); died unmarried
  3 Thomas Gilbert (b. 1860); married, at Paddington, Middlesex, 1891, Margaret Constance Jackson (b. 1861)
  4 Clara Harriet (1861-1941); died unmarried at Poole, Dorset
  4 Edward Ives (1863-1878)

The family lived in Upton St Leonards at Saintbridge House, which James Wintle largely rebuilt in 1835. At the time of the 1841 census they were staying at Minsterworth. Harriet died in 1845, and by the time of the 1851 census, James was staying at Greyfriars, Gloucester, with his daughter Harriet and son-in-law Charles Crawley.

1826: 27 Jan: *I left my family in Wellington Parade this afternoon, being engaged to dine at my friend Mr. Howell's at Prinknash Park, whither I went in a post chaise. Mr. and Mrs. Wintle & a lady with them: Mr. W. is a very worthy, good sort of man, residing at Saint Bridge near Gloucester, and enjoying a handsome independence.* 16 Jun., 6 Aug: *I rode out to dinner at Prinknash Park, where I met Mr. Wintle, Mr. Macleod ...*

1829: 14 Jul.

1830: 12 Jan., 20 Apr.

1834: 15 Aug., 17 Oct.

1836: 12 Aug: *We returned only in time to dress for dinner, & to our home party were added Mr. Wintle of Saintbridge, and his nephew T. Fulljames, the Architect and County Surveyor.*

1838: 16 Oct: *We returned only in time to dress for dinner, & to our home party were added Mr. Wintle of Saintbridge, and his nephew T. Fulljames, the Architect and County Surveyor.*

1842: 13 Apr., 14 Apr: *Dressed at Prinknash, and having detained the Fly, accompanied Howell, William and Emmelyn, to dinner at Saintsbridge at Mr. Wintle's, where a large party was assembled—Mr. and Mrs. W. with their son, a young Solicitor, just establishing himself at Gloucester, their daughter, Mr. & Mrs. Viner Ellis, Dr. and Mrs. Maddy, with the party from Prinknash, made up the circle at dinner.* 18 Oct.

1844: 2 Jan., 15 Aug.

1845: 1 Apr., 13 Apr.

1851: 29 Apr: *Wintle, my good brother Magistrate, tho' somewhat feeble through age, retains all his amiability of character and good sense.*

WINTLE — Thomas Wintle[205]

Thomas Wintle (±1774-1855), Church of England clergyman, was the son of Thomas Wintle, rector of Wallingford, Berkshire, and grandson of James Wintle of Gloucester. He was a cousin in some degree to the two James Wintles (*above*). Thomas was educated at St John's College, Oxford (BA 1795; MA 1799; BD 1804), and was appointed rector of Tidmarsh, Yorkshire, in 1814, and rector of Leckford, Hampshire, in 1840.

1829: 18 Feb: *Two Committees were promptly formed in Oxford ... They meet under the presidency of Mr. Wintle of St. John's, an active man of business.*

WINTLE & ARKLE — Wintle & Arkle, wine merchants[206]

Wintle & Arkle were wine merchants of 40 Eastgate Street, Gloucester.

1837: 24 May: *Wrote to Messrs. Wintle, Wine Merchants, Gloucester, who had sent me yesterday a case of Sherry, which I had not ordered; and which I shall return; it is charged a higher price than I am used to give.* 26-27 May.

WITHERS — *see* Price Withers

WITTS — the Witts family

The diary references to the family are very numerous. Instead of being listed in alphabetical sequence by forename, the entries are best listed by category. The sequence adopted is as follows:

Parents—Edward (1746-1816); Agnes, née Travell (1748-1825)
Brothers—George (1785-1823); Edward (1786-1794)
Wife—Margaret, née Backhouse (1785-1850)
Son—Edward Francis (1813-1886)
Daughter-in-law—Sophia, née Vavasour (1815-1871)
Grandsons—Francis Edward Broome (1840-1913); Frederick Richard Vavasour (1843-1900); George Backhouse (1846-1912)
Uncles and aunts—Broome (1744-1827); Amelia, née London (1742-1832); Richard (1747-1815); John (1751-1816)
First cousins—Richard (1775-1834); John (1777-1857); Ann (1775-1839); Apphia (1781-1859)
First cousins once removed—Broome Phillips Witts (1767-1845); Edward London Witts (1768-1841)
Second cousins
More distant relations

Other cousins who were born as Witts such as Lee Steere Witts and Eliza Witts have been listed under their adopted names: Lee Steere Steere and Eliza Daniell. Detailed biographical information is generally given in the introduction of volume 1, and therefore only additional information has been included in these entries.

WITTS — Edward Witts — *father*

Edward Witts (1746-1816).

1798: 27 Aug: *My Father first procured a Passport in the Name of his Family from Sir James Cranfurd valuable for an Year: this as was indeed foreseen was unnecessary but at any Rate it is worth While to carry such a Convenience.*

1799: 28 Oct: *Walked in the Evening to the Play Der Friede am Pruth went my Father & Mr. Dukinfield.* 5 Nov., 10 Nov., 14 Nov., 19 Nov., 24-30 Nov., 1-3 Dec., 18 Dec.

1800: 8 Jan., 11 Jan., 14 Jan., 20 Jan., 23 Jan., 25-26 Jan., 1 Feb., 8-9 Feb., 16 Feb., 18 Feb., 22-25 Feb., 1-2 Mar., 10 Mar., 15-16 Mar., 22 Mar., 26 Mar., 30 Mar., 1-2 Apr., 6-7 Apr., 9 Par., 13-15 Apr., 19 Apr.

1801: 2 Apr., 6 Apr., 8-11 Apr., 22-23 Apr., 26-27 Apr., 3 May, 12 May: *Upon landing at the Glocester Coffeehouse Piccadilly, we did not find my Father & Brother in their apartment; they were dining at Lady Lytteltons, but kindly returned soon to welcome us to Town.* 17 May. 19-20 May, 29 May, 2 Jun., 6 Jun., 7-8 Jul., 10 Jul., 12-13 Jul., 22 Jul: *Walked with my Father thro' Camberwell.* 24-25 Jul., 27 Jul: *Walked with my Father thro' Peckham & Camberwell.* 30 Jul: *Walked with my Father to Hayly Hill commanding a fine view of the Metropolis & of Surry.* 31 Jul: *Walked with my Father to London, & returned to tea at Champion Hill. Dined with Lady Lyttelton.* 2-4 Aug., 8-12 Aug., 15 Aug., 18-19 Aug., 24-26 Aug., 28-29 Aug., 31 Aug., 2 Sep., 8-12 Sep., 26-27 Sep., 29 Sep., 2 Oct: *My Father dined in the city.* 6 Oct., 9-10 Oct., 12 Oct., 19 Oct: *... visited with my Father & Mother a boarding house No. 11 Stafford Place Buckingham Gate ...* 21 Oct., 24-25 Oct., 2 Nov., 5 Nov: *Received & wrote a Letter to my father.* 7-8 Nov., 16 Nov., 18 Nov., 24-25 Nov., 6 Dec: *The Day chequered by the wished for arrival of my Father from London.—Did not go out.* 8 Dec., 11-12 Dec., 16-17 Dec., 22 Dec., 25 Dec.

1802: 1 Jan: *I walked with my Father over the Hotwells & Clifton. The situation which I should most like is Sion Row, or the Rows of houses near Durham Downs.* 26-28 Jan., 1-4 Feb., 12 Feb: *My Father & Mother breakfasted with me in my Rooms.* 28-29 Feb., 11 Mar., 16 Mar., 18 Mar., 29 Mar., 28-29 Apr., 2 May, 10 May, 19 May, 3 Jun., 5 Jun., 10 Jun., 18 Jun., 23 Jun., 5 Jul., 9-10 Jul., 12 Jul., 17 Jul., 22 Jul., 25-26 Jul., 30-31 Jul., 6-12 Aug., 22 Aug., 24-25 Aug., 27 Aug: *Walked with my Father to the Royal Spa, where we met Mr. Cruickshanks.* 27-30 Aug., 2 Sep., 4-5 Sep., 7 Sep., 27 Sep., 30 Sep., 2 Oct., 8 Oct.

1803: 9-13 Aug., 15-18 Aug., 20 Aug., 22-24 Aug., 26-29 Aug., 2 Sep., 4 Sep., 7-8 Sep., 10-16 Sep., 21 Sep., 23-24 Sep., 26-30 Sep., 1 Oct., 5-6 Oct., 10 Oct., 20 Oct., 6 Nov., 16 Nov., 20 Nov., 26 Dec.

1804: 11 Jan: *My Father & Mother played cards & supped at Mr. Parris's.* 13-14 Jan., 16 Jan., 19 Jan: *Enlivened by the rather unexpected fortunate return of my dear Father.* 22 Jan., 24-25 Jan., 28 Jan., 30 Jan., 5 Feb., 13 Feb., 15 Feb., 14 Mar., 17-18 Jul., 20 Jul., 22-26 Jul., 29 Jul., 6 Aug., 9 Aug., 14 Aug., 16 Aug., 18-26 Aug., 1 Sep: *Walked with my Father & Mother & C. Massey & Miss Upton before dinner.* 3-4 Sep., 6 Sep: *... to the fair with my Father & Mother, the Balls ...* 9-10 Sep., 16 Sep., 10 Sep., 16 Sep., 23 Sep., 30 Sep., 3 Oct., 5 Oct., 12 Oct., 13-14 Nov., 17 Nov., 27 Dec., 29-30 Dec.

1805: 5-6 Jan., 18 Jan., 21 Jan., 3 Feb., 13 Feb., 17 Feb., 1 Mar., 3 Mar., 5-9 Jul., 11-12 Jul., 14 Jul., 16-17 Jul., 20 Jul., 25-26 Jul., 30 Jul., 1 Aug: *After a cold dinner set off in a Post Chaise for Oxford with my Father & mother ...* 5-6 Aug., 10 Aug., 12-14 Aug., 17 Aug., 19 Aug: *With my Father through Charlton to Mr. Angerstein's Villa where our old gardener Stewart, now his loaded us with delicious fruit and flowers, as well as with honest heartfelt acknowledgement for past favours ...* 21-23 Aug., 25-26 Aug., 29 Aug., 2 Sep., 11-12 Sep., 14 Sep., 16 Sep., 20 Sep., 24 Sep., 29 Sep., 18 Nov., 20 Nov., 22-26 Nov., 28 Nov.

1806: 15 Jan., 24 Jan., 28 Jan., 30 Jan., 2 Feb., 4-5 Feb., 7-8 Feb., 12 Feb., 16 Feb., 21 Feb., 26-27 Feb.. 4 Mar., 6 Mar., 12 Mar: *Unable to join the Party at Lady Wolseleys in the Evening.*

My Father & Mother not having an engagement, we were all at home. 13 Mar., 17 Mar., 22 Mar., 24 Jun., 28-30 Jun., 3 Jul., 7 Jul: 17 Jul: *Rode to Erchfont;. After dinner took a walk with my Father & Mother ...* 22 Jul., 25-28 Jul., 31 Jul., 3 Aug: *Drove my Father as far as Stert upon the road to Erchfont ...* 5 Aug., 10 Sep., 10 Sep., 12-13 Sep., 17 Sep., 21 Sep: *My Father too indisposed to go to Church.* 25 Sep., 28 Sep., 7-9 Oct., 11-12 Oct., 18 Oct., 22-23 Oct., 7 Nov., 13 Nov.

1807: 1 Jan., 3 Jan., 13 Jan., 18 Mar., 23 Mar., 26 Mar., 6 Apr., 8 Apr., 22 Apr., 30 Apr., 3 Jun., 7 Jun., 26 Jun., 29 Jun., 5-6 Jul., 9 Jul., 14-15 Jul., 23 Jul., 30 Jul: *Drove my Father to Devizes on various Errands.* 1-2 Aug., 5-6 Aug., 22 Aug., 31 Aug.

1808: 12-15 Jan., 26 Jan., 23-24 Feb., 29 Apr: *My Father & Mother set out for Bath, about half past nine in a Chaise. Accompanied them to Devizes.* 2 May: *My Father & Mother's charming lodgings in Alfred Street received me first; thence I escorted my Ladies to No.1 Queen Square.* 3 May, 5 May.

1812: *On Monday the 3d. of Aug. 1812, my wife and myself began a Northern Tour, leaving my Father & Mother at Upper Slaughter, who wished to remain some time longer there, and keep house in our absence.*

1825: 16 Sep: *The living of St. Chad's formerly belonged to Dr. Adams, a former Master of Pembroke College, Oxford, and an intimate fried of Dr. Johnson. My father & Mother, who enjoyed his familiar acquaintance, always spoke of him with much regard, and used to visit him both at Shrewsbury and Oxford.*

1833: 8 Apr: *The principal adventurer in the affair was an old acquaintance of my Father's, an East Indian gentleman, by name Auriol, who, on his return from abroad, settled at Clifton ...* 9 Apr: *Before breakfast, I sallied out in quest of lodgings, & first took a survey of the Mall, where at No. 17 I find found a very suitable set of apartments, not many doors distant from where I had lodged with my Parents in the early days of my Undergraduateship.* 9 Nov. ... *Dunbar, though it was so dark, that I could only distinguish its long street, brought to my mind vivid recollections of my boyhood. We passed several weeks here one summer during the vacation. My Father and Mother were attracted to the place, partly by the convenience it afforded for sea bathing, but more by the circumstance, that three or four English regiments of Fencible Cavalry were encamped in its vicinity, and among them the Windsor Foresters, with the Colonel & Lieutenant Colonel of which Corps, Col. Rooke and Sir Nathaniel Dukinfield, and their ladies, my parents were intimately acquainted.* 10 Nov: *... at the corner house on the Southern side of the Square, at its Eastern extremity: there it was that my Parents had to nurse their three sons when suffering from hooping cough and measles, and to mourn over the loss of the youngest, Edward, whose delicate constitution sunk under the attack of these combined diseases ...*

1834: 9 Mar: *Returning from church, found a letter from Anne Witts, apprising us of the decease of our Aunt Stone ... Thus of all my Father's brothers and sisters Lady Lyttelton only remains.*

WITTS — Agnes Witts — *mother*

Agnes Witts, née Travell (1748-1825).

1799: 2 Nov: ... *went to Mr. Schmids My Mother & Mr. Dukinfield to a Concert by a Demoiselle Kirschgessner: on the Musical Glasses.* 10 Nov: ... *my Father Mother & Brother were at the Opera of Figaros Hochzeit where they were rather tired.* 19 Nov., 23 Nov., 27 Nov., 2-3 Dec., 11 Dec., 13-14 Dec., 18 Dec.

1800: 1 Jan: ... *to the Opera Cosa Rara, my Mother & Dukinfield.* 6 Jan., 11 Jan., 14 Jan., 22 Jan., 5 Feb., 8-10 Feb., 16 Feb., 18 Feb., 24 Feb., 2 Mar., 5 Mar: ... *My Mother and Dukinfield in the Evening to Das Räuschchen a tiresome Play.* 10 Mar., 12 Mar., 26 Mar., 30-31 Mar., 1-2 Apr., 5-7 Apr., 14-15 Apr., 19 Apr.

1801: 8 Apr., 11 Apr., 22-23 Apr., 26-27 Apr., 3 May, 5 May: *I had the pleasure of walking with my Mother & Miss Charteris thro' his Lordship's own plantations to the River Tyne, which flows thro' Haddington.* 13 May: *After having taken a tolerably good lodging No. 3. Conduit Street I proceeded with my Mother into Cavendish Square ...* 20 May, 22 May, 27 May, 29 May, 1-2 Jun., 4 Jun., 6-7 Jun., 14 Jul., 25 Jul., 2 Aug., 4 Aug., 10 Aug., 12 Aug., 15 Aug., 18-19 Aug., 24-29 Aug., 31 Aug., 2 Sep., 8-12 Sep., 26 Sep., 6 Oct., 9-10 Oct., 12 Oct. 13 Oct: *My Mother as well as myself were in Mrs. Doig's box, very agreeably ...* 17 Oct., 19 Oct., 5-6 Nov., 8-9 Nov., 17 Nov., 26 Nov: *Left Cheltenham, after an early breakfast, for my Uncle's Mr. Witts's at Nibley, in a Hack Chaise with my Mother.* 29 Nov., 6 Dec., 25 Dec., 27 Dec.

1802: 1 Feb., 4 Feb., 12 Feb., 16 Feb., 22 Feb., 28-29 Feb., 11 Mar., 16 Mar., 18 Mar., 29 Mar., 28-29 Apr., 2 May, 10 May, 3 Jun., 5 Jun., 10 Jun., 18 Jun., 23 Jun., 5 Jul., 9-10 Jul., 12 Jul., 25 Jul., 30 Jul., 5-12 Aug. 18 Aug: *Walked in the Evening with my Mother to the Rooms; dreadfully dull.* 22 Aug., 24-25 Aug., 27 Aug., 29-30 Aug., 1-2 Sep., 4-5 Sep., 7 Sep., 20 Sep: *Attended Mrs. Granville & my Mother in the Gig. Riding tête à tête with the Dear Fanny ...* 28 Sep., 2 Oct., 7-8 Oct.

1803: 9-10 Aug., 12-13 Aug., 15-18 Aug., 20 Aug., 22-24 Aug., 26-29 Aug., 2 Sep., 4 Sep., 7-8 Sep., 10-16 Sep., 21 Sep., 23-24 Sep., 26 Sep., 28-30 Sep., 1 Oct., 5-6 Oct., 10 Oct., 14 Oct: *With Mrs. Arrowsmith & my Mother in the Chaise to Nichs. School at Southgate & back with Mr. A in the Phaeton.* 20 Oct., 31 Oct., 3 Nov., 9 Nov., 22 Nov., 29-30 Nov., 7 Dec., 26 Dec., 28 Dec.

1804: 11 Jan., 13-14 Jan., 18-19 Jan., 22 Jan., 25 Jan., 27-28 Jan., 30 Jan., 5 Feb., 13 Feb., 15 Feb., 14 Mar., 17-18 Jul., 20 Jul., 22-24 Jul., 26 Jul., 29 Jul.,31 Jul., 6 Aug., 9 Aug., 14 Aug., 17-26 Aug., 28 29 Aug., 1 Sep., 3 4 Sep., 6 Sep., 8 10 Sep: ... *to Mr. Whalley's Mendip Lodge 14 Miles. Set out after an early breakfast, in two Sociables, & myself on horseback. Mrs. Honor & Miss Pigott, Mrs. Bates, my Father & Mother, Mrs. Parry Price, Miss Martin, Mr. C. & Mrs. C. & Mrs. Doyle ...* 15-16 Sep., 18-19 Sep., 23 Sep., 26 Sep., 30 Sep., 3 Oct., 5-6 Oct., 12 Oct., 13-14 Nov., 17 Nov: *Wrote home ...* 21 Dec., 24 Dec., 27 Dec., 29-30 Dec.

1805: 3 Feb., 13 Feb., 17 Feb., 23 Feb., 26 Feb., 1 Mar., 3 Mar., 12 Mar., 21 Mar., 26 Mar., 5 Jul: *Reached my Aunt's house by one of the London Coaches from Oxford at ½ past six in the morning. Had great pleasure in meeting my Father & mother. Was introduced to Jane Napier, with whom I was greatly pleased.* 6 Jul., 8-9 Jul., 11-14 Jul., 25-26 Jul., 30 Jul., 1 Aug., 5-6 Aug., 10 Aug., 12-14 Aug., 17 Aug., 21-23 Aug., 26 Aug., 29 Aug., 10-12 Sep., 14 Sep., 16 Sep., 20 Sep., 24 Sep., 29 Sep., 16 Nov., 18 Nov., 20 Nov., 22-26 Nov., 28-29 Nov.

1806: 15 Jan., 17 Jan., 23-24 Jan., 28 Jan., 30-31 Jan., 2 Feb., 4 Feb., 6-8 Feb., 11-12 Feb., 16 Feb., 25-27 Feb., 4 Mar., 6 Mar., 8 Mar: *Accompanied my Mother upon a long walk to visit Mrs. Dowell, at Cote, who was not at home; I did the honours of the House & Garden.* 12-13 Mar., 22-23 Mar., 24-25 Jun., 28-29 Jun., 3-4 Jul., 7 Jul., 17 Jul., 19 Jul: *In the Evening drove my Mother upon the London Road as far as Bishop's Cannings.* 22 Jul., 25-26 Jul., 28-29 Jul., 31 Jul., 1-2 Aug., 5 Aug., 7 Aug., 11-12 Aug., 15 Aug., 17 Aug: *Returned to dinner at Devizes. Wrote to my Mother.* 22-23 Aug., 26-27 Aug., 1 Sep., 4 Sep., 6 Sep., 9 Sep., 12 Sep., 15 Sep: *Brought my Mother to Erchfont to make arrangements & conveyed her back.* 17 Sep: *Drove to Devizes to reconduct my Mother to Erchfont. My Father walked & they took up their abode in the Vicarage for the first time.* 19 Sep., 22-23 Sep., 25-26 Sep., 28 Sep., 1 Oct., 6-9 Oct., 12 Oct., 17-18 Oct., 22-23 Oct., 27 Oct., 30 Oct., 5 Nov., 10 Nov., 15 Nov., 26-27 Dec.

1807: 1-2 Jan., 5 Jan., 31 Jan., 13 Feb., 16 Feb., 20 Mar., 26 Mar., 14 Apr., 18 Apr., 23 Apr: *Drove my Mother to visit Mrs. L. Mayo, whom with her brother we found at home.* 27 Apr., 30 Apr., 1 May, 16 May, 18 May, 23 May, 25 May, 27 May, 2 Jun., 4 Jun., 9 Jun., 23-24 Jun., 6-9 Jul.,15 Jul., 22-24 Jul., 1-3 Aug., 6 Aug., 10 Aug., 13 Aug., 15 Aug., 22 Aug., 24 Aug., 26 Aug., 31 Aug.

1808: 12 Jan., 14-15 Jan., 23-24 Jan., 9 Apr., 11-12 Apr., 15 Apr., 29 Apr., 2-3 May, 5 May.

1812: 3 Aug: *On Monday the 3d. of Aug. 1812, my wife and myself began a Northern Tour, leaving my Father & Mother at Upper Slaughter, who wished to remain some time longer there, and keep house in our absence.*

1820: 15 Feb: *Returned from Cheltenham, whither I went yesterday to visit my poor Mother now again suffering by a very severe fit of the gout.* 10 Apr., 13 Jun: *My Mother arrived to-day on her customary summer visit, last from Cheltenham, where she had been spending a few days with my Aunt Mrs. Travell: as she had been before for a month with Lady Lyttelton near Malvern.* 15 Aug: *My Mother left us to join her friend Lady Elcho lately arrived at Stanway.* 9 Sep: *The Stanway party came to dine with us, consisting of Lady Elcho, my Mother, my cousins the Miss Guydickens's, & the companion of Lady Elcho, Miss Church.*

1822: 30 Sep: *I dined and slept at Lady Elcho's at Stanway, meeting, besides Miss Church and my Mother, the Gist family.* 4 Oct: *My Mother arrived from Stanway on a visit ...* 3 Dec: *My Mother left us for her residence at Cheltenham.* 20 Dec: *We dined and slept at my Mother's in Belle Vue Place.*

1823: 13 Jan: *We staid an hour or two at Cheltenham to call on my Mother, who has been suffering severely by an inflammatory attack on the chest, which has left her very low both in strength & spirits ...* 17 Feb: *I went to Cheltenham to pass a day or two with my Mother, who, I rejoice to say, is very much recovered ...* 7 Apr., 11 Apr., 13 Jun: *My Mother arrived from Cheltenham on a visit in good health and spirits.* 14 Jul: *My mother left us on a visit to Lady Elcho at Stanway.* 22 Jul., 13 Aug: *Soon after the receipt of this mournful information, I mounted my horse for Stanway to impart it to my poor Mother, to tell her, I was her only surviving child.* 14 Aug: *I returned home to breakfast, & my Mother followed me some hours afterwards, preferring to pass the first days of grief in the society of Margaret and myself.* 16 Aug., 20 Aug., 23 Aug: *my Mother returned this day to Stanway in as good spirits as we can expect.* 6 Sep., 3 Oct., 30 Oct: *My mother arrived from Stanway.* 25 Nov: *My Mother left us for Cheltenham. Her birthday was on the 23d. she was then 75 years old. Since she has been with us this time, she has never breathed the outward air, and so has avoided the cough often so troublesome to her ... These symptoms of decline cause us much anxiety.* 23 Dec: *On arriving at my mother's, I had the grief to find her extremely ill; she had been attacked with one of those violent inflammations on the chest, to which she is so subject, and had been in considerable danger on the preceding day.* 24 Dec., 30 Dec: *I again repaired to Cheltenham to visit my poor mother, whom I found still in a very precarious state.*

1824: 1 Jan: *I returned from Cheltenham, leaving my mother very weak and ill ...* 12 Jan., 26 Jan., 11 Mar: *... spending the morning with my mother at Cheltenham, who is quite well.* 30 Mar., 2 Apr., 19 Apr., 22 Apr., 26 Apr., 1 May, 22 May, 8 Jun: *My Mother came to us from Cheltenham for her usual summer visit, and, thank GOD, considering her age and infirmities, she now enjoys good health.* 21 Sep: *My Mother left us for Stanway, where she is going to pass some time with Lady Elcho.* 27 Sep., 1 Nov: *I went to Stanway by Lady Elcho's invitation to meet some of her neighbours at dinner ... my Mother & Miss Church The addition to the dinner party ...* 17 Dec., 22 Dec: *My Mother still continuing very unwell, labouring under great oppression of breath, accompanied with much drowsiness, was with difficulty persuaded this day to see Mr. Bancks, the Apothecary of Winchcomb, who took from her several ounces of blood by which operation she seemed in some degree relieved.* 24 Dec: *It was with much anxiety and fear that I left my mother in such an uncomfortable state of health, unwilling to leave Stanway for her own house and medical friend at Cheltenham ...* 29 Dec: *Continued bad accounts of my poor Mother's health, coming from Stanway, carried me there to-day.*

1825: 1 Jan: *I rode over to Stanway to breakfast in consequence of a letter from Miss Church, giving me an account of Mr. Wood's opinion of my poor Mother.* 4 Jan: *I received a letter from Miss Church acquainting me with my Mother's arrival at Cheltenham on Monday, whither she accompanied her, and that she was not the worse for the little journey, but on the whole as Miss Church thought, rather better.* 6 Jan: *A great change for the words had taken place & I found, that little or no hopes of my Mother's restoration were entertained. There was evidently a great tendency to dropsy, the face swelling, with a running from the eyes and mouth.* 7 Jan: *There was no change for the better, but the difficulty of rousing my Mother seemed increased ... On my return I found my poor Mother more roused, than at any previous time since I had arrived. She spoke of her approaching end, of which she seemed thoroughly aware from the first interview with Dr. Christie ... She desired to be buried as my poor father had been, and by his side in the Vault at Chipping Norton Church.* 8 Jan: *It was very evident, that my dear Mother was rapidly approaching her end ... Dr. Christie told me, death was so fast approaching, that I must remain at my post.* 09 Jan: *Death rapidly advanced during the night and morning, and at mid-day my beloved Mother breathed her last. She went off gently, & the last fearful struggle past, her features resumed the usual placidity, and lost the distortion, which for some days had disfigured them. Thus am I at length bereft of Father, Mother & Brother! GOD's will be done! GOD be thanked for the blessings still left to me, an excellent wife & promising child. Great reason have I to speak well of my departed Parent. She was a most affectionate wife & mother, a well principled Christian, warm in her friendship, strong in point of judgment, well informed, had an extensive knowledge of life, and in her best days, even to a late period, shone in society & conversation. She was 76 years of age, having been born in 1748.*

WITTS — George Witts — *brother*

George Witts (1785-1823).

1799: 10 Nov., 23 Nov., 25 Nov: *To the Play der Amerikaner went my Brother & Dukinfield ...* 28 Nov., 2 Dec., 9 Dec., 11 Dec: *To the Play in the Evening went George & Dukinfield ...*

1800: 18 Jan: *George & Dukinfield at the Zauberflöte.* 21 Jan: *I went accompanied by Dukinfield & George to drink tea with Mr. Martin a'Court ...* 26 Jan., 5 Feb., 8 Feb., 21-22 Feb., 5 Mar., 21 Mar: *... with my Brother to Tarare an Opera which I had before seen & which was tolerably acted.* 9 Apr., 15-16 Apr., 20 Apr.

1801: 4 Apr., 8 Apr., 23 Apr: *My Father & George walked to Leith ...* 1 May, 3 May: *... my Father & Brother took leave of us, as they proceeded to London in a Berwick Smack.* 12 May, 17 May, 20 May, 24 May, 27 May, 30 May, 4 Jun., 10 Jun: *My Brother* *entered his 17th. Year.* 16 Jul: *Received & answered a letter from George* ... 20 Jul: *In the Evening we walked all round St. James's Park, & coming home to supper met with my Brother.* 23-24 Jul., 28 Jul: *Dined with Edward: Broome & George dined there* ... 2 Aug., 5 Aug: *George came up to us in the Evening.* 19 Aug., 23 Aug: *George spent the day with us.* 25 Aug: *Called in the forenoon upon Mr. B. P. Witts & Mr. E. Witts & My Bro. at Messrs. Pryce and Darlot in the City.* 26 Aug., 30 Aug: ... *walked with Harriet in the Evening & with George to Paddington, where was a great concourse of people at the Canal.* 6 Sep: *George spent the day with us* ... 13 Sep., 17 Sep., 20 Sep: *George also at Champion Hill.* 27 Sep., 30 Sep: *Went into the city visited both the Mr. Witts's. & George's lodgings* ... 4 Oct., 17 Oct., 20-21 Oct., 25 Oct., 29 Oct: *Wrote to George.* 29 Dec.

1802: 8 Jan., 9 Jan: ... *skaited with Fiott on the long Pond: George joined the Party in the Evening.* 10 Jan: *Skaited with George & Fiott* ... 11 Jan: *A Ball in the Evening at Mr. Ellill's; Geo. also there: very animated & agreable...* 30 Jan., 4 Feb., 7 Feb: *Our dear George with us dined at Lady Lyttelton's.* 9 Mar., 16 Mar., 11 May, 4 Jun., 25 Jul., 22 Aug., 26 Aug., 7 Sep.

1803: 25 Feb., 17-18 Aug., 22 Aug., 28 Aug: *By breakfast George came down from Town* ... 29 Aug: *Walked with George, who walked his Horse, as far as East Sheen on his road to London, before breakfast.* 2 Sep: ... *Met George there. Walked with him thro' the Strand to Temple Bar* ... 4 Sep., 10-11 Sep, 17 Sep., 26 Sep: *Called & sat great part of the Morning with George & his friend Galiffe.* 27 Sep., 17 Oct., 31 Oct., 6-7 Nov., 9 Nov., 15 Nov., 28 Nov., 1 Dec., 26-28 Dec., 29 Dec: *George & myself to Dowry Square to Mrs. Adams's. Merry & pleasant Ball* ... 30-31 Dec.

1804: 1 Jan: *Our comfort sadly interrupted by a letter from Mr. Solly to George recalling the latter immediately* ... 2 Jan: *Forced to part from George whom I accompanied to Bristol & saw him safe in Fromont's Coach.* 6 Jan., 10 Jan., 13 Jan: *Wrote to George a long letter.* 25 Jan. ... *passed the Evening alone writing to George.* 29 Jan., 1 Feb., 17 Feb., 19 Feb., 23 Feb: ... *wrote to Galiffe & George.* 6-7 Mar., 14 Mar., 18 Mar., 25 Oct., 4 Nov: *From Friday the 26th October till Saturday Nov. 3d. Engaged in London on George's account in painful business, the progress of which I decline inserting.* 12 Nov.

1805: 27 Mar., 31 Mar., 26 Jul., 6 Aug: *Welcomed by my brother at the Ship Tavern at Woolwich* ... 7 Aug: *George called in the forenoon after having passed his Examination in Mathematics with Dr. Hutton* ... 8 Aug: *Accompanied George to the fencing school, where he shewed himself an apt scholar.* 9 Aug: *George with us a few minutes in the morning. A short walk in the Evening.* 11 Aug: *Considerably depressed by domestic uneasiness. In the Evening George was with us.* 14 Aug: *George called & sat some time late with us. He had been in London having passed his Examinations & gained his Commission in the Artillery* ... 15 Aug., 16 Aug: *Accompanied George to the field day of the Artillery, with which I was well pleased.* 17-18 Aug., 19 Aug: *George put his Uniform on & joined his Regiment.* 21-22 Aug., 24 Aug: *Breakfasted at the Barracks with George & Collyer.* 26 Aug: *George came late to take leave of us.* 1 Sep., 30 Nov: *A domestic Evening; not unembittered by chagrin respecting my Brother, whose intended departure for the Continent was announced to us from an indifferent person.*

1806: 4 Feb: *We had the satisfaction of hearing from my Brother from Bremen; he is oppressed by Rheumatism in consequence of his busy movements in Germany, but in hope of soon returning.* 5 Feb., 11 Feb: *Had the satisfaction of knowing, by a letter from my Brother, that he is safely arrived from the Continent in Yarmouth roads.* 23 Feb: *Wrote letters upon business to George & Mr. Horne.* 25 Jun., 31 Jul., 15 Aug: ... *wrote to a Creditor of George's* ... 26 Sep: *Wrote to Mr. Travell, and a letter upon George's business.* 17 Oct., 28 Oct.

1807: 5 Feb., 24 May, 23 Jul., 31 Jul., 9 Dec.

1808: 30 Apr.

1820: 4 Jul: *We derived much satisfaction to-day in the receipt of a letter from my Brother. It appears, that the news of his promotion to the rank of Captain in the Royal Artillery, which places him on half pay, was brought to him at Malta, by his friend the Hon. Captn. Pellew, a son of Lord Exmouth, commanding the Revolutionnaise. That officer was conveying to Constantinople, Mr. Frere, the Diplomatist; to hold the situation of Minister Plenipotentiary to the Porte, in the Interval between the departure of Sir R Liston the actual Ambassador, & the arrival of his successor, Lord Strangford. Captn. Pellew having warmly pressed George to accompany him & Mrs. Pellew, who sails with her husband on the Voyage, two short hours sufficed him to prepare for his departure, obtain the General's leave, & bid farewell for a time to the Island, where he has so long been on active service. A fortnight brought them to the end of their cruize, and the Palace of the British Embassy. Nothing can be more animated & interesting than my Brother's sketch of the voyage, country & society: nor are many better calculated to appreciate & describe such scenes.*

1822: 1 Dec: *We were gratified by receiving a letter from my Brother Captn. Witts, of the Royal Artillery, from Malta; his last communication received towards the end of August, represented him to be in very indifferent health, and that he intended, if he could meet with an agreeable opportunity by sea, before winter set in, to return to England to recruit his health, which is impaired by many years residence in the Mediterranean. Now, indeed, being on half pay, he is his own master, but partiality to the countries, in which he has so long resided, res angustel, the love of travelling, and seeing the world, have kept him in the Mediterranean: but not always at Malta; he has resided much at or visited Naples, the Ionion Isles, Corfu &c. the Greek Archipelago, Smyrna, the Troad, Constantinople, the Coasts of Syria & Egypt. He now talks of coming to England next Spring. We had been very uneasy at the unusually long time, which had elapsed since he last wrote, and dreaded worse accounts of his health, which, it seems, is recruited.*

1823: 4 Jul: *We were afflicted with receiving most painful accounts of my brother from Malta, whose arrival from the Mediterranean we had been anxiously expecting for some time. In his last letters he had spoken of his shaken nerves & impaired health, but anticipated with satisfaction a return to England and removal from a hot climate, which he expected would recruit his strength* .... 6 Jul: *I received another letter relating to my poor brother's melancholy state from a gentleman signing himself E. F. Phillips* ... *This gentleman is recently arrived from Malta, where he saw George early in May in very indifferent health but in a sane state of mind* .... 7 Jul: *In pursuance of my intention to endeavour to make somearrangements in consequence of the melancholy account of my poor brother's state I left home this morning for London* ... 8 Jul: *I first directed my steps to the office of Messrs. Greenwood & Cox, the Army Agents, in Craig's Court, Charing Cross, as being my brother's agents* ... *I was afterwards so fortunate as to find a friend in Town my brother's intimate friends Captain & Mrs. Fleetwood Pellew* ... *From Captain Pellew I learnt, that the Gentlemen, who had written to me respecting George, were both employed in the civil department in Malta* ... *Captain Pellew kindly promised to write to his Uncle Saml. Pellew Esqr., Comptroller of the Customs at Falmouth, to ascertain in what state of body & mind my brother might be on his arrival by the Mediterranean Packet ...* 13 Aug: *The suspence, in which we have been plunged for so long a time respecting my unhappy brother, is now closed in a most painful manner by the receipt of letters from Falmouth, giving intelligence of his decease on the 8th. inst. GOD rest his soul! The information comes from Mr. Pellew, Collector of the Customs at Falmouth, agreeably to the arrangement, which I made in Town with his nephew, Captain F. Pellew, and from a Capt. Heathcote, of the Ionian Service, an old acquaintance of my poor brother's, who was a passenger with him on board the Packet ...* 21 Aug: *Received a letter from Captn. Heathcote containing some particulars of my poor brother, parts of which I shall transcribe ...* 20 Oct: *A melancholy occupation awaited me this evening in looking over some boxes, forwarded from Falmouth, containing my poor brother's effects, papers &c...*

1824: 30 Mar: *... at my Mother's met Mr. F. Newell, who acted as Commissioner to administer to my Mother an oath, as to the amount of my late poor brother's effects, it being necessary, that she, as nearest of kin, should administer. With the arrears of pay remaining in his agents hands the whole is under £100 and will only suffice to pay his debts and expences of administration.*

WITTS — Margaret Witts — ***wife***

Margaret Witts, née Backhouse (1786-1850).

1805: 16 Jul: *Wrote to Margaret.* 27 Jul: *Heard from Margaret ...* 29 Jul., 11 Aug., 16 Aug., 3 Sep., 11 Sep., 26 Sep., 4 Oct., 19-20 Nov.

1806: 24 Jan: *Found upon my return to Clifton a delightful letter from my beloved Margaret ...* 29 Jan: *Wrote a long letter to my beloved Margaret.* 14 Feb., 20 Feb., 6 Mar., 13 Mar., 29 Jul., 22 Aug., 9 Sep., 15 Sep., 30 Sep., 4 Oct., 17 Oct., 30 Oct., 3 Nov., 13-14 Nov., 16-17 Dec., 27 Dec., 29 Dec.

1807: 12 Jan., 27 Jan., 30 Jan., 10 Feb., 17 Feb., 9 Mar., 23 Mar., 31 Mar., 16 Apr., 20 Apr., 5 May, 10 May, 25 May, 1 Jun., 6 Jul., 18 Jul., 22 Jul., 4 Aug., 8 Aug., 20 Aug., 24 Aug., 6 Dec., 10 Dec., 16-17 Dec., 21 Dec., 26 Dec., 28 Dec., 28 Dec.

1808: 2 Jan: *Heard from my dearest Margaret.,* 4 Jan., 7 Jan., 11 Jan., 15 Jan., 18 Jan., 23 Jan., 25 Jan., 27 Jan., 8-9 Mar., 15 Mar., 17 Mar., 21-22 Mar., 26-27 Mar., 1 Apr., 3 Apr., 7 Apr., 12 Apr., 19 Apr., 23 Apr., 27 Apr., 1 May: *Engaged in parish business & preparing for my departure to meet my beloved Margaret at Glo'ster. --- to Gloucester. Arrived at that place by nine, where I had the happiness to meet my friends, Mrs. Backhouse, Miss Richardson & my beloved Margaret.* 2 May: *My Father & Mother's charming lodgings in Alfred Street received me first; thence I escorted my Ladies to No.1 Queen Square. Where my Father & Mother came to welcome them.* 3 May, 4 May: *Walked with my beloved Margaret in Sidney Gardens &c.* 5-6 May.

1817: 30 Aug: *At the Sun Inn, after a comfortable breakfast, I had the happiness of again embracing my wife & child, who came in Mrs. Backhouse's Carriage to convey me to their lodgings at Bardsea, three miles distant.*

1820: 5 Jan: *My wife put herself again under the medical charge of our old and skilful friend Col. Cooper ...* 5 Feb: *I trust, the medical advice my wife has received during our stay at Bath, & the use of the waters, will essentially strengthen her constitution.*

1823: 1 Feb: *I left my dear wife & boy at Mrs Backhouse's ...* 19 Feb: *I rejoined my wife at Mrs. Backhouse's at Gloucester.* 17 May: *I arrived about 12 o clock, rejoicing to find myself again in my domestic retreat, and having much to relate to my dear wife & her mother of the business, which I had transacted while absent ...* 14 Aug: *I returned home to breakfast, & my Mother followed me some hours afterwards, preferring to pass the first days of grief in the society of Margaret and myself.* 24 Aug: *My dear wife's birth-day. She was born in 1786. GOD be thanked, that of late her delicate health seems rather re-established. I can never be sufficiently grateful for her constant affection, warm participation in my pleasures and griefs, anxiety to make me comfortable. She is a pattern to wives in her judicious care of her family, kind heartedness to her poor neighbours, and prudence in her own expences. I have to thank GOD for an union with a woman of virtuous & religious principles, good sense, and amiable temper.* 18 Sep., 27 Sep: *I returned to Upper Slaughter, leaving Margaret with her Mother.* 16 Dec.

1824: 24 Jan: *My dear wife has been suffering during this & the past cold weeks from bilious spasms.* 11 Mar: *Found my dear wife suffering severely, as she has done for many weeks, from bilious spasms.* 2 Apr., 24 Apr., 26-27 Apr., 1 May: *Leaving my wife with her Mother, in the hope that with change of air, and more genial weather, her health will be recruited ...* 17 May: *I rejoined my dear wife at Gloucester, and had the comfort to find her health considerably amended ...* 22 May, 24 Aug: *My dearest wife's birth-day: she is this day 38 years old. May GOD long preserve her to be a blessing to her son and myself! may her very delicate health be improved!*

1825: 10 Jan: *My dear wife and child arrived from Upper Slaughter.... Margaret's health and strength are little equal to severe trials, and in her mother's society she would find comfort.* 12 Jan., 19 Jan., 24 Jan., 5 Feb., 14 Feb., 15 Feb: *I was sorry to find my dear wife suffering from a sick head-ache. The late bright sunshine and Easterly winds have not agreed with her, & she has suffered more within this month from spasm and palpitation, than during the colder months of winter.* 15 Jun., 15 Jul., 17 Sep., 22 Oct., 7 Nov.

1826: 1 Apr., 24 Apr: *We set out from home this morning to pass a few days at Bath: our principal cause for going to that place being, that Margaret might have an opportunity of availing herself of the skill of a dentist ...* 25 Apr: *My dear wife began to take the waters ...* 29 Apr: *My dear wife much indisposed. The operation by the dentist, and the cold wind together have caused a bad swelled face: added to this is a bilious attack ...* 2 May, 1 Aug., 5 Aug., 11 Sep., 14 Sep., 16 Sep., 25-26 Sep.

1827: 16 Apr., 23 Apr., 8 May, 4 Jun., 16 Jun., 12 Jul., 31 Jul., 4 Aug.

1828: 14 Jan., 3 Mar., 10 Mar., 17 Mar., 18 Apr., 20 Jun., 18 Jul., 14 Aug., 13 Oct., 17 Oct.

1829: 12 Jan., 19 Feb., 27 Feb., 30 Mar., 2-4 Apr., 27 Apr: *Margaret was suffering in some degree from a cold ...* 2 May, 30 May: *Twenty one years ago this day I was married to my dear wife ...* 17 Jul., 7 Aug., 24 Aug., 28-29 Aug., 22 Sep., 23 Sep: *Margaret and myself retired from the Cathedral, and partook of luncheon at the Deanery ...*

1830: 28 Jan: *It has also been very trying to my dear wife, who has had a recurrence for some time past of those trying painful spasms, which in former winters have been so wearing to her strength.* 19 Apr., 23 Apr., 30 Apr., 1 May, 3 May, 27 May: *Our intention is to repair at first for a week to the Metropolis, where I have not been for seven years, and my dear wife and son were never in London.* 21-23 Jun., 24 Jun: *... Edward and myself accompanied Mrs. F. Witts on foot on a long stroll through various streets in the West end of the Metropolis ...* 25 Jun: *The morning's walk and sights had so fatigued our dear companion as to render it necessary, that she should repose before we went to our dinner engagement ...* 2 Aug.

1832: 27 Feb., 5 Mar: *Accompanied Mrs. Backhouse and my wife to Cheltenham. Took up our abode in comfortable lodgings No. 396 High Street.* 10 Mar., 26 Mar., 29-30 Mar., 6 Jun., 8 Jun., 13 Jun.

1833: 18 Jan: *We dined at Lady Reade's at Oddington ...* 13 Mar., 9-10 Apr., 11 Apr: *After breakfast took a walk with my wife by the Zig-zag path to the Hotwells, Dowry Square &c ...* 13 Apr., 15 Apr., 17-18 Apr., 21 Apr: *Mrs. Witts and myself walked after breakfast to Bristol, to attend divine Service at the Mayor's chapel in College Green ...* 22 Apr., 10 Sep: *After breakfast left Upper Slaughter with Mrs. Witts and Mrs. Backhouse in our close carriage to visit my Aunt Lady Lyttelton at Peachfield Lodge ...* 11-13 Sep., 15 Oct., 22 Oct., 25 Oct., 28-29 Oct., 8 Nov., 10 Nov.

1834: 3 Mar: *Left home for Leamington with Mrs. Witts and Mrs. Backhouse, to stay some days there.* 6 Mar., 8 Mar., 10 Mar., 12-13 Mar., 19-21 Jul., 25 Jul., 2 Aug., 5-6 Aug., 13-14 Aug., 16 Aug., 18 Aug: *Mrs. Witts and her mother, left home for Cheltenham to pass a few days there, that the former may have an opportunity of consulting a dentist ...* 21-26 Aug., 30 Aug., 10 Sep., 15-16 Sep., 18 Sep., 23 Sep., 26 Sep., 1 Oct., 3 Oct., 7 Oct., 14-15 Oct., 18 Oct., 20-22 Oct., 31 Oct., 3 Nov., 11-12 Nov., 17-18 Nov., 23 Nov., 26 Nov., 7 Dec., 12 Dec., 19 Dec.

1835: 5 Jan: *After an early breakfast, at eight o'clock, we set off in the Chariot for Gloucester: Mrs. Backhouse, E.F.W., my wife and myself ...* 7-9 Jan., 14 Jan., 17 Jan., 22 Jan., 26-27 Jan., 2-3 Feb., 8 Feb., 10 Feb., 19 Feb., 24-25 Feb., 2 Mar., 13 Mar., 21 Mar., 27 Mar., 29 Mar., 1 Apr., 4 Apr., 6-7 Apr., 14 Apr., 20 Par., 27 Apr., 5 May, 9 May, 13 May, 15 May, 21 May: *Mrs. Witts accompanied me in the phaeton to Stow, and returned, driven by the servant ...* 23 May, 25 May, 30 May, 3-4 Jun., 7 Jun., 9 Jun., 11 Jun: *Received a joint letter from my Wife and my Son ...* 12 Jun., 16 Jun.

1836: 14-15 Jul., 20-21 Jul., 23 Jul., 30 Jul., 1-2 Aug., 6 Aug., 11 Aug., 13 Aug., 15-17 Aug., 23 Aug., 29 Aug., 31 Aug., 3 Sep., 17 Sep., 21 Sep., 24 Sep., 27 Sep., 16 Oct., 20 21 Oct., 27 Oct., 2 Nov., 5 Nov., 16 Nov., 25 Nov., 29 Nov., 6 Dec., 11 Dec., 20 Dec., 25 Dec.

1837: 4-5 Jan., 7 Jan., 14 Jan., 20 Jan., 3 Feb., 1-2 Mar., 4 Mar., 13 Mar., 16 Mar., 19 Mar., 3-4 Apr., 8 Apr., 10 Apr., 12 Apr., 18 Apr., 20-21 Apr., 25-26 Apr., 28 Apr., 1-2 May, 6-7 May, 9 May, 12 May, 16 May, 20 May, 23 May, 25-26 May, 29 May: *Drove MW. to call on Lady Reade at Oddington ...* 3 Jun., 5 Jun., 10 Jun., 13-15 Jun., 17 Jun., 20 Jun., 26 Jun., 28 Jun., 30 Jun., 2-3 Jul., 5 Jul., 11 Jul., 17 Jul., 19 Jul., 24 Jul., 31 Jul., 8 Aug., 9 Aug: *Mrs. W. opened to her Mother the state of matters between E.F.W. and Sophy Vavasour.* 12 Aug., 15 Aug., 21 Aug., 24 Aug: *My dear wife's birthday who enters into her 52d. year.* 28 Aug., 1 Sep., 3 Sep., 6 Sep., 12 Sep., 20-21 Sep., 25-28 Sep., 10-11 Oct., 13 Oct., 18 Oct., 21 Oct., 25-26 Oct., 1 Nov., 5-6 Nov., 8 Nov., 10 Nov., 12 Nov., 21 Nov., 25 Nov., 27-28 Nov., 8 Dec., 13 Dec., 15 Dec.

1838: 3-4 Jan., 6 Jan., 8 Jan., 26 Jan., 31 Jan: *Hayward called, considered Mrs. Backhouse as going on well: he prescribed for MW. who is suffering from indigestion.* 7 Feb., 13 Feb., 15 Feb: *MW. had received a letter from A. Currer, dated from Blythe, in the Back Settlements of Upper Canada ...* 19 Feb., 9 Mar., 14 Mar: *... Much conversation with him, in which my Son took part with his Mother and myself ...* 22-23 Mar., 28 Mar., 7 Apr., 11 Apr., 14 Apr., 21 Apr., 23 Apr: *Much engaged during the day in various shopping, which wholly occupied MW.* 7-8 May, 11 May, 16 Mat, 18 May, 22-23 May, 26 May, 2 Jun., 4 Jun., 6 Jun., 8-9 Jun., 13-14 Jun., 23 Jun., 25 Jun., 28 Jun., 30 Jun., 1-2 Jul., 4 Jul., 6-7 Jul., 19-21 Jul., 23 Jul., 27 Jul., 30-31 Jul., 3 Aug., 8 Aug., 13 Aug., 15-16 Aug., 20 Aug., 22 Aug., 27 Aug., 31 Aug., 9 Sep., 12 Sep., 14-15 Sep., 20-21 Sep., 28 Sep., 1 Oct., 5 Oct., 7 Oct., 9-10 Oct., 17 Oct., 20 Oct., 23 Oct., 30 Oct., 1 Nov., 5 Nov., 10-12 Nov., 14 Nov., 20 Nov., 30 Nov., 5-7 Dec., 9-11 Dec., 15 Dec., 19 Dec., 30 Dec.

1839: 2 Jan., 5 Jan., 17 Jan., 22 Jan., 29 Jan., 3 Feb., 23 Feb., 4 Mar., 8 Mar., 18-19 Mar., 25 Mar., 27 Mar., 30 Mar., 8 Apr., 11-12 Apr., 16 Apr., 18 Apr., 20 Apr., 23-24 Apr., 1 May, 6-9 May, 14-15 May, 20 May, 24 May, 28 May, 30 May, 1 Jun., 12 Jun., 17 Jun., 2 Jul., 6 Jul: *M.W. recd. a letter from Wavertree from her Uncle Backhouse, containing a remittance of £26. 13. 4 being our share of a sum forwarded from Virginia in liquidation of the claims of the Backhouse family on the descendants of their debtors in that country.* 10 Jul., 12 Jul., 14-17 Jul., 22 Jul., 24 Jul., 28 Jul., 10 Aug., 12 Aug., 23 Aug., 26-27 Aug., 29-31 Aug., 2 Sep., 5 Sep.

1840: 18 Mar: *M.W. and I went in the close carriage after breakfast to Stanway, to the christening of our grandchild.* 20 Mar., 25 Mar., 30 Mar., 3 Apr., 8 Apr., 13 Apr: *My wife had an engagement at Cheltenham to hire a cook, and for shopping &c. ...* 14-16 Apr., 22-24 Apr., 27 Apr., 29 Apr., 5-9 May, 11 May, 14 May, 16 May, 20 May, 22 May, 27 May, 29 May, 8 Jun., 11-12 Jun., 16 Jun., 23-25 Jun., 28 Jun., 30 Jun., 1 Jul., 3 Jul., 8-9 Jul., 14-15 Jul., 17 Jul., 19 Jul., 21 Jul., 24-25 Jul., 28 Jul., 1 Aug., 4-5 Aug., 24 Aug., 30 Aug., 11 Sep., 15-16 Sep., 19 Sep., 22 Sep., 1 Oct., 9 Oct., 12-14 Oct., 16 Oct., 21-23 Oct., 29 Oct: *MW, much indisposed with a bad head ache and bilious attack, could not join us at dinner, or in the evening.* 31 Oct., 4 Nov., 10 Nov., 14 Nov., 20 Nov., 24-25 Nov., 30 Nov., 1 Dec.

1841: 26-28 Feb., 1 Mar: *Mr. Hayward called. MW. going on satisfactorily.* 2 Mar., 5 Mar.

1842: 5 Jan., 7 Jan., 1 Feb., 8 Feb., 15 Feb., 25 Feb., 28 Feb., 4 Mar., 12 Mar., 15 Mar., 17-18 Mar., 29 Mar., 9 Apr., 12-13 Apr., 15-16 Apr., 18-20 Apr., 23 Apr., 26 Apr., 29 Apr., 2 May, 4 May, 10 May, 12-13 May, 17-19 May, 24-25 May, 27 May, 1 Jun., 3 Jun., 10 Jun., 15-17 Jun., 20 Jun., 27-30 Jun., 2 Jul., 5 Jul., 8 Jul., 12 Jul., 15-17 Jul., 22 Jul., 29 Jul., 2 Aug., 7 Aug: *MW. also begins to find the anxiety and fatigue prejudicial to her health.* 8 Aug: *I regret to say, he finds his Mother in delicate health, owing to the fatigue and anxiety consequent on Mrs. Backhouse's precarious state, in whom no great change was observed by us or Mr. Hayward to-day ...* 11 Aug: *MW. I hope, better in health than a few days since, but very delicate, and liable to suffer from attendance on her mother.* 13 Aug., 19 Aug., 21-23 Aug., 24 Aug: *May dear wife's 56th. birthday: may GOD preserve her to be a blessing to her family, strengthen her bodily health, and support her under the trials reserved for her!* 26 Aug., 30 Aug., 9 Sep: *All this is very trying to my wife, who is poorly and overcome with anxiety.* 23 Sep., 25 Sep: *MW. in a delicate state of health, but her complaints chiefly proceeding from anxiety and watching over her mother: she takes medicine to counteract debility ...* 27 Sep: *Mrs. W. much as she has been of late; worn with anxiety and close attention to her mother.* 29 Sep., 3-5 Oct., 7 Oct., 11 Oct., 15 Oct., 18-19 Oct., 22 Oct., 27 Oct., 4 Nov., 7 Nov., 13 Nov: *... he would be with us without fail in the evening, and sleep here, that he might shew a right respect to his departing grand-mother, and afford comfort and support under the expected shock to his dear Mother.* 14 Nov., 15 Nov: *Mr. Hayward called to visit MW. whose health does not appear to have been materially affected by the trial of yesterday: yet she is very nervous, and somewhat excited ...* 17 Nov., 18 Nov: *My dear wife is more calm and comfortable, less nervous, and excitable, now that the principal arrangements for the funeral are over.* 20 Nov: *My poor wife agitated, anxious, excitable, and very weak in body, but took a few turns in the garden ...* 21 Nov., 22 Nov: *My poor wife, whose spirits had been upheld by an effort yesterday, experienced a re-action, and was to-day much* *debilitated, depressed, and excitable ...* 24 Nov: *MW. and I were in better health and spirits than for some days past.* 25-26 Nov., 27 Nov: *My dear wife went to Church: the service was very long: the singers, meaning well and respectfully, were somewhat tedious and harrassing with funeral Psalms and Anthems.* 28-30 Nov., 1-4 Dec., 5 Dec: *Called on Dr. Baron to request him to visit MW. which, it was arranged, he should do to-morrow ...* 8 Dec., 9 Dec: *Dr. Baron visited MW. changed her medicine, and expected that she would find so much benefit from it that it would not be necessary for him to visit her again.* 12 Dec., 15 Dec., 19 Dec., 21 Dec., 23 Dec., 25 Dec., 27 Dec.

1843: 2 Jan: *MW. purposed to go to Stanway to-day on a visit to our children, and a fly had been ordered to convey her.* 3-5 Jan., 9 Jan., 11 Jan., 23 Jan., 25 Jan., 28 Jan., 30 Jan., 1 Feb., 13 Feb., 10-11 Aug., 14-16 Aug., 18-19 Aug., 24 Aug: *My dear wife entered on her 58th year: may it please GOD to preserve her as long as life may be a blessing and comfort to herself!* 27 Aug., 29 Aug., 2 Sep., 3 Sep: *To afternoon prayers at Hove Church in a fly with MW; walking home.* 7 Sep: *I hastened to our lodgings in a fly, to bring MW. into what struck me as the best manner of enjoying the sight without fatigue or pressure.* 8 Sep: *With MW. took a drive for an hour, by the beach, the Steynes, a little way along the Lewes road, then back under the fine Viaduct ...* 10 Sep., 13 Sep: *With MW. paid, probably, a last visit to the very enjoyable and refreshing chain pier, the sea tame; now that the court is gone the large vessels have departed ...* 15-16 Sep., 19-20 Sep., 25 Sep., 27 Sep., 29-30 Sep., 3 Oct: *After luncheon left home in our phaeton with M.W. on a visit to our dear children at Stanway ...* 4 Oct., 7 Oct., 9 Ocr., 13-14 Oct., 17-19 Oct., 27 Oct., 3 Nov., 7-8 Nov., 9 Nov: *My wife and I kept aloof on principle: the whole cast of the affair was too theatrical, too much a display of artistical skill, too manifest a seeking of the praise of men, too open a design on the purse of the public.* 11 Nov., 13 Nov., 16 Nov., 18 Nov., 20 Nov., 24 Nov., 27 Nov., 29 Nov., 1 Dec: *Breakfasted early, and left home with MW. early in our open carriage for Cheltenham ...* 6 Dec., 9 Dec., 11-12 Dec., 14 Dec., 15 Dec: *MW. has experienced two attacks, one yesterday, and one this morning, of bleeding at the nose ...* 16 Dec: *Mr. Hayward called, and gave medical advice to MW. who has had no recurrence of hæmorrhage since yesterday ...* 19 Dec., 26-30 Dec.

1844: 2 Jan., 4-7 Jan., 11 Jan., 13 Jan., 15 Jan., 17-18 Jan., 20 Jan., 22 Jan., 25 Jan., 29 Jan., 31 Jan., 15-17 Feb., 19-20 Feb., 22 Feb., 27 Feb., 29 Feb., 2 Mar., 8 Mar., 10-11 Mar., 13 Mar: *MW. less severely affected than myself, but still under the influence of a catarrh.* 14-17 Mar., 19 Mar., 21-23 Mar., 26-28 Mar., 30 Mar., 2-3 Apr., 8-11 Apr., 13-14 Apr., 16 Apr., 18 Apr: *Both MW. and myself are suffering from Influenza.* 19-20 Apr., 24-26 Apr., 30 Apr., 1 May, 3-4 May, 6-7 May, 11 May, 15 May, 19 May, 24 May, 30 May, 1 Jun: *MW. and I made an excursion to-day to Folkstone and Sandgate.* 2 Jun., 23 Jul., 26 Jul., 5 Aug., 7 Aug., 9-10 Aug., 13 Aug., 15-16 May, 24 Aug: *Left home about 11 A.M. with my wife and the Backhouses in our two carriages for my Son's residence at Stanway.* 31 Aug., 1-2 Sep., 4 Sep., 7 Sep., 17 Sep., 24-25 Sep., 27 Sep., 30 Sep., 1-2 Oct., 7 Oct., 9-10 Oct., 14 Oct., 16 Oct., 18-19 Oct., 21-22 Oct., 29 Oct., 7 Nov., 15-17 Nov., 19 Nov., 21-22 Nov., 24-25 Nov., 30 Nov., 3-4 Dec., 10 Dec., 16 Dec., 20 Dec., 31 Dec.

1845: 1-2 Jan., 6 Jan., 8 Jan., 13 Jan., 17 Jan., 21 Jan., 26 Jan., 31 Jan., 1 Feb., 5-8 Feb., 11 Feb., 24 Feb., 27 Feb., 3-6 Mar., 11 Mar., 18 Mar., 24 Mar., 26 Mar., 28-29 Mar., 4 Apr., 7-9 Apr., 17 Apr., 23 Apr., 26-27 Apr., 29-30 Apr., 1 May, 5 May, 9 May, 15 May, 17 May, 21-22 May, 24 May, 27 May, 30-31 May, 2-4 Jun., 8 Jun., 10 Jun., 14 Jun., 16-17 Jun., 19-20 Jun., 23-25 Jun., 29-30 Jun., 1-2 Jul., 4 Jul., 11-12 Jul.

1846: 21 May: *MW. Sophy, Broome and I enjoyed a long saunter or sitting on the Pier, watching steamers arrive and depart.* 30 May: *With MW. and dear Broome enjoyed a pleasant row, for two hours, Westward, along the sweetly wooded coast, as far as the entrance to Wootton Creek and back.* 31 May, 1 Jun., 8-9 Jun., 11 Jun: *With MW. took a long walk: achieved the steep ascent of St. Boniface Down to its summit near the road crossing the heights towards Appuldurcomb ...* 13-15 Jun., 18 Jun., 19 Jun: *In the forenoon MW. and I sat for a long time in great enjoyment in a shady spot below the Castle, where an old man lets out chairs at a penny an hour.* 20 Jun., 24 Jun., 27 Jun., 4 Jul., 6 Jul., 11 Jul., 15 Jul., 17-18 Jul., 21 Jul., 25 Jul., 30 Jul., 3-6 Aug., 12 Aug., 17 Aug., 20 Aug., 22 Aug., 24 Aug: *My dear wife's sixtieth birthday. May GOD protect and preserve her! She is an affectionate wife and mother, a kind hearted friend and neighbour, a sensible woman, diligently endeavouring to do her duty in the station in which GOD has placed her.* 26 Aug., 31 Aug., 2 Sep., 8 Sep., 10 Sep., 12 Sep., 14 Sep., 17 Sep., 21 Sep., 24-25 Sep., 29 Sep., 30 Sep: *Mr. Hayward visited and prescribed for MW: whose cough continues obstinate, the biliary system being deranged.* 1-3 Oct., 7 Oct., 12 Oct., 21 Oct., 28 Oct., 30 Oct: *After breakfast, with MW. and Miss Vavasour, went in our close carriage to Stanway, to attend the Christening of my third grandson ...* 2 Nov., 5 Nov., 9 Nov., 12 Nov., 24 Nov., 10 Dec., 22 Dec., 25 Dec., 31 Dec.

1847: 5-7 Jan., 20 Jan., 29 Jan., 1 Mar., 8 Mar., 12-13 Mar.,18-19 Mar., 22-23 Mar., 25 Mar., 29-31 Mar., 6 Apr., 14-15 Apr., 17 Apr., 20 Apr., 22 Apr., 27 Apr., 29 Apr., 4-5 Apr., 7 May, 10 May, 13 May, 15 May, 20 May, 23-24 May, 26-27 May, 31 May, 1 Jun., 3-4 Jun., 7 Jun., 9-12 Jun., 16-17 Jun., 19 Jun., 22 Jun., 24 Jun., 27-28 Jun., 30 Jun., 1 Jul., 3 Jul., 8 Jul., 13 Jul., 15-16 Jul., 22-24 Jul., 26 Jul., 29 Jul., 31 Jul., 4 Aug., 7 Aug., 9-11 Aug., 13 Aug., 17 Aug., 29-20 Aug., 23 Aug., 28 Aug., 30-31 Aug., 2 Sep., 4 Sep., 8 Sep., 11 Sep., 14-15 Sep., 18 Sep., 22-26 Sep., 28 Sep., 30 Sep., 2 Oct., 8 Oct., 10 Oct., 15 Oct., 18 Oct., 21-22 Oct., 25-26 Oct., 28 Oct., 30 Oct., 3-4 Nov., 6 Nov., 11 Nov., 15 Nov., 18 Nov., 20 Nov., 22 Nov., 2 Dec., 17 Dec., 24 Dec., 29 Dec.

1848: 4 Jan., 7 Jan., 14 Jan: *With my wife visited Emily Lea; put up prayers with her and others of her family ...* 17 Jan., 3 Feb., 10 Feb., 16-17 Feb., 22 Feb., 2-4 Mar., 6-7 Mar., 15 Mar., 22-24 Mar., 30-31 Mar., 3 Apr., 9 Apr., 11 Apr., 15 Apr., 25 Apr., 28-29 Apr., 2 May, 4-6 May, 8 May, 11-12 May, 16 May, 18 May, 22-23 May, 25 May, 29 May, 1 Jun., 3-4 Jun., 9-10 Jun., 12 Jun., 16 Jun., 20 Jun., 22-23 Jun., 27-29 Jun., 6-7 Jul., 10 Jul., 15 Jul., 17 Jul., 4 Aug., 7-8 Aug., 10 Aug., 13 Aug., 15 Aug., 19 Aug., 24 Aug: *MW's birthday: entering on her 63d. year. May GOD protect and preserve ...* 27 Aug., 30 Aug., 1-2 Sep., 6 Sep., 8 Sep., 11 Sep., 14-15 Sep., 18-20 Sep., 2-3 Oct., 5-6 Oct., 11-12 Oct., 18 Oct., 29 Oct., 2 Nov., 7 Nov., 16 Nov.

1849: 14 Dec., 24 Dec: *M.W. has been of late so much indisposed, and appeared to suffer particularly to-day from the cold, and has such shortness of breath, with debility, and restless nights, that I wrote to desire Mr. Hayward to visit her ...* 25 Dec: *Mr. Hayward visited MW. at breakfast time, and found her much out of order ...* 27 Dec: *Mr. Hayward called at breakfast time, and visited MW. whose pulse he found too quick ...* 28 Dec: *M.W. appears languid, probably, from the aperients administered to her ...* 29 Dec: *Mr. Hayward called to visit MW., whom he found rather improved since he last saw her; but the pulse, though reduced, is still too high; and the tongue foul: she has experienced languor to day ...* 30 Dec: *MW. seems still to improve in health; more freedom in breathing; sleeps better; but did not venture to Church ...* 31 Dec: *Left MW. after a tolerably comfortable night with good hope that she is gradually recovering a better state of health.* 1850: 2 Jan: *Received a letter from M W. who believes herself to be rather better than when I left her ...* 3-4 Jan., 6 Jan: *Mr. Hayward called to visit M W. and made some change in her medicine: the pulse lower ...* 7 Jan: *Mr. Hayward again called on us; did not find Mrs. Witts worse; indeed the pulse improved; but privately intimated a wish that if it could be conveniently arranged, we should before long call in a Physician, he being desirous to have his view of her case confirmed or corrected ...* 8 Jan: *Having without much difficulty prevailed on her to admit of a visit from Dr. Baron, I finished my letter to E.F. W. with the intelligence that he was likely to be here to-day ...* 9-10 Jan., 11 Jan: *My wife did not seem the worse for receiving these visitors, but remains much the same as for some days past ...* 12 Jan., 14 Jan., 17 Jan: *After breakfast wrote a note to Mr. Hayward, begging his early attendance on M W.* 18 Jan., 19 Jan: *M W. did not leave her bed till 3 P.M. or her chamber at all during the day.* 20-21 Jan., 23-24 Jan., 27-31 Jan., 2 Feb: *Mr. Hayward visited M W. and thought her going on comfortably. The bowels are still constipated ...* 4-9 Feb., 10 Feb: *Mr. Hayward called on M W. He admitted her case to be complicated, that she was better in one respect, and worse in another— the worse being the effusion in the lower extremities ...* 12-14 Feb., 15 Feb: *All seems much the same with our patient as of late; drowsiness, quick pulse, dry mouth, restless nights; the digestive organs, and the kidneys, appear in a better order, but the dropsical symptoms are not materially abated ...* 16-18 Feb., 20-21 Feb., 22 Feb: *M W. remains nearly in the same state; the breath was very painfully obstructed in going upstairs to bed ...* 23-24 Feb., 26 Feb: *Mrs. Lea visited my wife in her sitting room for a short time, and was shocked to find her so feeble and suffering ...* 28 Feb., 1-3 Mar., 5 Mar., 6 Mar: *M W. continues in the same state; she admitted to her dressing room to day Anne Yearps, a respectable old servant of ours, married to a tradesman of Lower Slaughter, who was anxious to see her. Much conversation, and very satisfactory, with my dear wife, as to arrangements which she wishes me to make in the event of her death ...* 8 Mar: *Engaged in preparing for M W's signature a document expressive of her wishes in the event of her decease ...* 9 Mar., 10 Mar: *Mr. Hayward called, and thought M W. weaker and more sinking ...* 12-13 Feb., 14 Feb: *Hayward visited M W: found her languid and the dropsical symptoms unabated.* 15-18 Mar., 19 Mar: *M W. suffered much to day from languor, & faintness, increased distension and shortness of breath: yet moved from her bed room to her little sitting room, & thence in the evening to the dining room, as had been accustomed: very feeble and lethargic in the evening.* 20 Mar: *Hayward visited M W. whom he found exceedingly languid and exhausted, in part because she had taken a very active aperient, Elaterium, which he had administered with a view to drawing off water from the System by the alvine excretions. In this he succeeded, and the system rallied, so that the great exhaustion went off, and in the evening the drowsiness was not so overpowering as usual ...* 21 Mar., 22 Mar: *An early visit from Mr. Hayward, who found his poor patient in a state of great exhaustion, owing to the violence of a medicine, Elaterium, taken on going to bed last night. It had, however, answered the purpose in draining the cavities of the body of a large accumulation of water: the sufferer revived in the afternoon, but the appetite was bad, and the tense condition of the frame from effusion under the skin unabated. Sleep in a recumbent posture for a continuance is impossible to be had without a sense of suffocation, so that the night as well as the day is mostly passed in an arm chair ...* 23-24 Mar., 25 Mar: *M W. did not suffer so much by the dose of Elaterium which she had taken, as before: the evacuation very copious ...* 26 Mar., 27 Mar: *Hayward called, and found his patient improved in some respects; the Elaterium treatment seems to have drawn off much water from the cavities & upper part of the body, but the dropsy in the lower extremities appears unabated ...* 28-29 Mar., 30-31 Mar., 1 Apr: *She now does not leave her dressing room for the dining room in the evening, nor her bed chamber till afternoon. Great debility, and pain in the body and lower extremities with palpitation of the heart ...* 3 Apr., 7 Apr., 9 Apr: *Mr. Hayward visited us. M W. was in the forenoon and early afternoon in a state of great prostration ...* 10-11 Apr., 12 Apr: *Poor creature! She is sadly oppressed, and very patient, though constantly dwelling on her sufferings, and her helplessness: no one can have more attentive nurses than the three female servants, and especially Elizabeth Simmons, her own personal maid, a kind, affectionate, intelligent young woman.* 14 Apr: *The tidings brought to my bedside when I was called purported that there had been no material change in my dear wife's state during the night: but, on visiting her, when dressed, I found her exceedingly weak, but perfectly sensible, and recognizing all around her, though the voice was hardly audible, and inarticulate ... She passed off almost as an infant does to sleep, not a convulsion, however slight, hardly one sterterous rattle, and the soul was severed from the body, to speed, I firmly believe, as I earnestly trust, to bliss; for she was a virtuous, loving wife, a tender mother, a good daughter, a kind mistress, a friendly neighbour; unaffectedly and simply pious, patient and charitable; excellent in the management of her family, attentive to her poor neighbours, prudent, amiable & sensible—"at veniet felicius ævum quando iterum tecum, scin modo dignus, ero"—Immediately on the close of the awful scene, I dispatched my groom with a few lines to my Son, informing him of our loss, and before three o clock he came to me ...* 17 Apr: *The last remains of the beloved one were this day consigned to the coffin: visited the chamber of death, once more, to see the now closed casket, which contains all that is mortal of her who has been a blessing to me for nearly 42 years.*

WITTS — Edward Francis Witts — *son*
Edward Francis Witts (1813-1886).

1817: 30 Aug: *At the Sun Inn, after a comfortable breakfast, I had the happiness of again embracing my wife & child, who came in Mrs. Backhouse's Carriage to convey me to their lodgings at Bardsea, three miles distant.* 9 Sep: *We were soon ourselves to become passengers across the lake, as the arrangements, which we had made for our tour included the return of our little boy and female attendant from this place to Beck House by Kendal. Four years and a little more do not give the disposition of mind suited for the contemplation of nature's charms, and the charge of a child is rather troublesome on such excursions, as that, which we were now making, however cherished on ordinary occasions. Yet parental solicitude led us not to quit our treasure till we had landed him safe on the point opposite to the Ferry House, from whence he continued his route to Kendal in his Grandmother's Carriage, which returned to meet us in the Evening at Ambleside.*

1820: 2 Mar: *My dear Son Edward's seventh birthday. May the Almighty give strength to the powers both of his mind & body, & may his Parents train him up in the ways of religion & in useful learning!*

1822: 20 Dec: *I went yesterday to Cheltenham to meet our dear Edward on his return from School for the Christmas holidays. He arrived in a Bath Coach in perfect health and spirits, the same affectionate engaging child as ever.*

1823: 1 Feb: *I left my dear wife & boy at Mrs Backhouse's. The latter goes in a day or two to School. GOD bless him! he is a delight to his Parents. Endowed with very good natural talents, and competently advanced in school learning, I cannot be too grateful to Providence for bestowing on us a child so rich in every affectionate & amiable quality of the heart ...* 2 Mar: *Our dear Edward's 10th. birthday. GOD grant that he may continue in health, and increase in religious and useful learning!* 20 Jun: *Our dear Edward returned home for the Midsummer holidays. GOD be blessed, that he is in good health. Mr. Hale writes to me in the most satisfactory manner of his conduct at school, as well as of his improvement.* 5 Jul: *We parted from our beloved Edward, who returned to School by Gloucester, where he would arrive at Mrs. Backhouse's in the Evening, & proceed to Lyde House to-morrow.* 16 Aug., 20 Aug., 16 Dec: *The arrival of our dear Edward from school for the Holidays was a source of unfeigned delight to us. His grandmother Backhouse accompanied him from Gloucester, to spend the Christmas with us. Our joy was not a little heightened by the excellent report, which Mr. Hale gives us of general good conduct, and proficiency in learning.*

1824: 3 Feb: *Mrs. Backhouse left us for Gloucester; carrying our dear boy with her; who will pursue his journey to Lyde House school to-morrow.* 2 Mar: *My dear Edward's birthday. He is eleven years old.* 17 Jun: *Our dear Edward came home for the midsummer holidays; he seems in excellent health & spirits, and Mr. Hale writes a most satisfactory account of his progress in his learning and good behaviour.* 6 Aug: *Our beloved boy left us this day to return to school, in good health. May the Almighty watch over him! His warm affection, simplicity of heart, and quickness of apprehension endear him to all, who know him.* 15 Dec: *A real holiday in the return of our dear boy from school. Thank GOD, he appears in very good health Mr. Hale makes a very satisfactory report of his progress in his studies and general good behaviour.*

1825: 10 Jan., 15 Jan: *I returned to my melancholy duties at Cheltenham early this morning, accompanied by my dear boy.* 17 Jan: *The mournful and last duty of attending the remains of my Mother to the grave devolved upon me. My dear boy was my companion ...* 19 Jan., 24 Jan., 5 Feb: *I parted from my dear Son, who returns to School on Monday next.* 2 Mar: *My dear Son is this day twelve years old....* 15 May: *In the evening we took our schoolboy to the Wells ...* 14 Jun: *I had the happiness of finding my dear boy in admirable health and spirits, and of receiving an excellent account of his conduct, abilities and application ...* 15 Jun: *At Wellington Parade I had the pleasure of being greeted by my dear son in excellent health and spirits ...* 15 Jul., 5 Aug: *Our beloved boy's holidays terminated this day ... I took him after an early breakfast to Cheltenham, whence he was to proceed by the Birmingham coach to Bath. Mr. Croome lent me his gig and horse, and I took with me his second son, who is also a pupil of Mr. Hale's.* 16 Sep., 16 Dec: *We had the happiness of saluting our dear Edward on his return to us this day for the Christmas ...*

1826: 17 Jan., 23 Jan., 8 Feb: *On arriving at Gloucester I missed the bounding step and cheerful greeting of our dear boy; he had set off this morning to resume his studies at Bath in good health and tolerable spirits ...* 2 Mar., 24 Apr: *Immediately after our arrival, I walked to Dr. Hale's on Sion Hill, to see our dear boy ...* 26 Apr: *Our dear boy passed the afternoon and evening with us.* 29 Apr: *It being a half holiday, our dear boy passed the afternoon and evening with us ...* 30 Apr., 1 May, 5 May, 16-17 Jun., 24 Jul., 28 Jul., 1 Aug: *The time was now come for our dear Edward's journey to Shrewsbury ...* 14 Sep., 21 Oct., 15 Dec: *Our dear Edward returned from School: he seems well in health, grown, cheerful and contented with his new world at Shrewsbury, & as far as I can as yet judge, has made considerable progress. Dr. Butler has placed him higher than I expected; in the middle fifth ...*

1827: 2 Feb: *Our dear boy left us this afternoon on his way to Shrewsbury.* 2 Mar., 16 Jun: *I had the happiness of finding my dear boy with his Mother, & both well; he arrived yesterday evening from Shrewsbury for the holidays, in good health, excepting a little cold & cough, and bringing from Dr. Butler the assurance, that his conduct during the last half year has been good.* 12 Jul., 31 Jul: *The time is drawing near for our dear Edward's return to School ...* 1 Aug., 3 Aug., 4 Aug: *My dear boy's holidays were verging to a close, and by eight o'clock he was seated in Captain Witts's phaeton; who was so kind as to take him to Worcester, and see him off by the Shrewsbury coach, his place being already engaged.* 14 Dec: *The glad time was returned for our dear Edward's holidays ... and Archdeacon Butler's report of his conduct is couched in the emphatic word, satisfactory.*

1828: 14 Jan., 1 Feb: *This afternoon our dear boy left us for Shrewsbury to resume his Studies under Archdeacon Butler.* 2 Mar: *Our dear Edward's birthday, who is fifteen years of age....* 16 Jun., 19 Jun: *We reached the Crown Inn about two o clock, & stopped or strolled about till three, when I was at my post, awaiting the arrival of my son; the heavy rumbling Shrewsbury Hibernia Coach was pretty true to its time, & came freighted with school boys on the deck, & school girls in the hold. Edward soon discovered me ...* 20 Jun: *Our comfort in the arrival of our dear boy was in some degree abated by the circumstance, that Archdeacon Butler's report of him was rather less favourable than usual. He intimated, that he had been idle & trifling, at the same time acknowledging his good abilities and seemed to wish, that I should excite him on these points. This produced some earnest & painful conversation ...* 18 Jul., 8 Aug: *This afternoon we lost our dear boy, who returns to morrow to Shrewsbury School. We sent him in the phaeton with the servant this evening to sleep at Cheltenham, where he would meet his schoolfellow, Stephen Waller, & proceed by coach to-morrow.* 9 Aug., 10 Dec., 27 Dec.

1829: 12 Jan: *We left home after breakfast for Cheltenham in the close carriage, the weather being very cold & frosty. My dear wife & Son proposed to convey me so far on the way to Gloucester ...* 22 Jan., 30 Jan., 2 Mar., 18 Jun: *... which brought back our dear Edward, who left Shrewsbury by the coach this morning for the Midsummer ...* 24 Jun: *We dined at Mr. Croome's at Bourton on the water; Edward accompanied us; although almost too young to mix in society, yet we deemed it better not to leave him behind us alone, when we go out, and occasionally joining in the parties of the neighbourhood during the holidays will accustom him to good company, and give him a distaste for low company.* 25 Jun., 17 Jul., 7 Aug., 11 Dec: *We experienced the great delight of welcoming our dear Son to-day; he arrived last evening by the coach from Shrewsbury at Cheltenham, where he was met by our man-servant with the open carriage. He had fine weather for his journey, is much grown and seems in good health. He brought with him a character from his school, which could not but make us rejoice.*

1830: 28 Jan: *The day, however, was arrived for the departure of our dear Edward, & we grieved to lose him.* 2 Mar: *The seventeenth birthday of my dear son.* 27 May, 17 Jun., 23-24 Jun.

1831: 11 Dec., 18 Dec.

1832: 2 Mar: *My dear Son this day enters his twentieth year. GOD preserve and protect him! strengthen his bodily health, and give him grace to resist temptation, to pursue his studies diligently, and to walk humbly, faithfully, piously and prudently!* 13 Mar: *Left home after a very early breakfast for Oxford, on a visit to my son, and to exercise my suffrage as a Member of Convocation,*

on the approaching occasion of a contest for the new Sanscrit Professorship. 14 Mar., 16 Mar: ... *I consequently breakfasted in Edward's rooms ...* 27 Mar: *If it please GOD to preserve the life of my son, he will, probably, take holy orders, and then, at my death, or cession, may quietly take my place in the ministry of his native parish. The value of the advowson will in the mean time be increasing, if eventually to be sold, as my years increase. The liberality of my excellent Mother in law, so remarkable in matters of importance, has enabled me to make these purchases, and my Son has given them his full concurrence ...* 5 Apr: *We had the comfort of receiving this evening our dear son, who returned to us from Oxford for the Easter Vacation. He is not in such good health as we could wish, and continues still under Mr. Wingfield's care.* 29 Apr., 4 May:
Our dear son returned to Balliol to resume his studies ... 6 Jun.

1833: 12 Mar: *Our object in visiting Oxford was to fix on a college or hall on the books of which we might place my son's name; with a view to his resuming his academical career in Easter Term ... We afterwards passed some time in the shop of a bookseller, Graham, and when Mr. R. went by appointment to wait on Dr. Cardwell, I remained alone in his rooms at Edmund Hall. On his return I found, that the Principal of St. Alban Hall on mature consideration declined admitting my Son ...* 24 Mar: *"Advice to a young man upon first going to Oxford, in ten letters from an uncle to his nephew. By the Revd. Edward Berens, M.A. Late Fellow of Oriel College. Lond. 1832 12mo." An admirable little manual by the Archdeacon of Berks, which I procured, when in Oxford, and have presented it to my son, in the hope and anxious desire, that on resuming his studies at the University, he may model his conduct upon the platform here laid down ...* 1 Apr: ... *after the departure of Edward & Mr. Riddle for Oxford ...* 9 Apr: *After breakfast, Mr. Riddle came to us from Bristol, and having heard our arrangements returned home to pack up and transport his clothes and books to our new abode, into which we removed, when we had settled our bill at the Hotel. Leaving Mrs. W. to unpack & arrange her matters, Edward and myself took a walk to Bristol by Brandon Hill.* 10-12 Apr., 13 Apr: *Agreeably to the arrangements which I had made, I travelled homeward to-day to be in readiness to perform my clerical duties to-morrow: leaving Mrs. Witts, Edward & Mr. Riddle at Clifton.* 15 Apr., 17 Apr., 19 Apr: *I accompanied Mr. Riddle & Edward in a walk across Durdham Downs to the immediate vicinity of Sneyd Park, through delightful fields traversed by a footpath. The views, the verdure, and the bursting foliage were most agreeable.* 21-22 Apr. 11 Sep: *"Abbott's young Christian, or a familiar illustration of the principles of Christian duty. By Jacob Abbott, Principal of the Mount Vernon School, Boston, America. Abridged. Printed by the religious tract society 18mo." It was left in my care as a parting present from Mr. Riddle to my Son ...* 12 Sep: *A letter from John Perkins Senr. to announce that he had packed up and sent by waggon to Upper Slaughter my Son's books &c. from Magdalen Hall.* 13 Sep—to 13 Oct: *My Son in the Evening read aloud a Funeral Sermon on the excellent Hannah More ...* 14 Oct: *Howell inclosed a letter from his friend, Mr. Blair, an Advocate of consideration in Edinburgh, written in reply to enquiries made by Howell as to a proper situation there, in which my Son may be placed during the Winter.* 15 Oct., 16 Oct: *Walked with Edward, before breakfast, by the old and almost deserted Spa, to the Montpellier Walks & Spa ...* 19 Oct., 22 Oct., 24 Oct., 25 Oct: *Wrote to Mr. Terrott at Edinburgh, expressing my intention of bringing my Son to Edinburgh for the winter ...* 28 Oct., 30 Oct., 1 Nov: *Received an answer from Mr. Terrot, from Edinburgh; but though he states that he has room for my Son, his terms being £150 for the period of the College Session, it is doubtful whether the situation will answer our views ...* 4 Nov: *Replied to Mr. Malcolm's letter received on the 30th Ult. apprizing him of my intention of taking Edward to Edinburgh, and of placing him, if possible, under the care of Mr. Terrot ...* 5 Nov: *Soon after 11 o'clock started on our Northern Journey with my son ...*

1834: 18 Jul., 22 Jul: *Edward absent at Stow; it being the day of meeting of the Cricket Club ...* 24 Jul., 26 Jul., 29 Jul., 2 Aug., 4-6 Aug., 8 Aug., 11-13 Aug., 14 Aug: *But Edward accompanied us part of the way to Cranham; but left us to pursue his favourite study of botany in the woods.* 15-16 Aug., 18 Aug., 23 Aug., 25-28 Aug., 8-9 Sep., 12 Sep., 13 Sep: *Botanized successfully with my Son ...* 1-15 Sep., 16 Sep: *E.F.W. went to Stow to join the Cricketers, and dined there.* 18 Sep., 22-23 Sep., 25-26 Sep., 29 Sep., 3 Oct: *Wrote to E. F. Witts, directing to him at Kidderminster, where we presume him and Howell now to be. Gave an account to him of the proceedings against Edwin Jeffrey ...* 8 Oct., 13-15 Oct.,17-18 Oct., 28 Oct: *A letter from my Son, dated from Frome, and giving an account of the peregrinations of Mr. Howell and himself since we parted ...* 30-31 Oct., 6-8 Nov., 15 Nov., 18-19 Nov., 20 Nov., 27 Nov., 4 Dec., 7 Dec., 12 Dec., 15-17 Dec., 23-24 Dec., 30 Dec.

1835: 1-2 Jan., 5-8 Jan., 9 Jan: *Edward had ridden to Prinknash in the forenoon to call on the Howells, and had afterwards gone to dine en famille at the Palace, from whence he accompanied Mrs. Monk and the ladies of her party to the Ball given this Evening at the Bell Hotel ...* 13 Jan., 15 Jan., 17 Jan., 22 Jan., 27 Jan., 29 Jan., 5-6 Feb., 11-12 Feb., 14 Feb., 16 Feb., 19-20 Feb., 23-27 Feb., 3 Feb: *My Son rode to Prinknash Park to pass a day or two with the Howells.* 7 Mar., 10 Mar: *My Son walked to Bourton on the Water & staid to dine with his friend, Mr. Billingsley.* 13-14 Mar., 16-17 Mar., 19 Mar., 23 Mar: *Left home, accompanied by my son, on my route into Northamptonshire ...* 29 Mar., 2-3 Apr., 5-6 Apr., 9 Apr., 13 Apr., 15 Apr: ... *the rest of the day and slept under the roof of our valuable friends the Howells, in their domestic circle. Besides my Son I found there, Mr. Donald Hume Macleod, a brother of Mrs. Howell ...* 16 Apr: *Edward and I left our kind Prinknash friends about one o'clock by the Bath Coach for Cheltenham ...* 24 Apr., 7 May: *My Son having received some days since a letter from his friend, Augustus Foster, of Trin. Coll. Cambridge ... My Son had become intimate with him at Edinburgh, where they were both inmates with Mr. Terrot, who had represented Mr. Foster to me as a very estimable youth ...* 8 May: *Wrote to Howell to accept his invitation to my son, as far as concerned his circuit in England and Wales, but declining it as to Ireland, whither Edward had no wish to go ...* 10 May, 13 May: *A letter from Howell on the subject of the contemplated tour in Germany. He chiefly objects to it on the ground of the uneasiness which his Mother and myself are likely to experience during our Son's absence ...* 14 May, 16-17 May, 21 May: *A letter from my son, dated at Kidderminster, whence he and Howell were about to proceed to Ludlow and Salop ...* 22 May, 26 May, 30 May: *My Son returned late in the Evening from his excursion in North Wales ...* 4-5 Jun., 11 Jun., 13 Jun., 18-19 Jun.

1836: 11 Jul., 13-16 Jul., 18 Jul: *After breakfast, accompanied by E.F.W., set out for Peach Field Lodge on a visit to my Aunt, Lady Lyttelton, in my open carriage ...* 19 Jul., 21-25 Jul., 26 Jul: *With E.F.W., between two & three o'clock, left home in our open carriage for Stanway, where we were very kindly received by Lord Wemyss.* 27-29 Jul., 2 Aug., 5-9 Aug., 11 Aug: ... *arrived by 5 o cl. at the house of my excellent friends, the Howells... The young man from U. Slaughter had reached Prinknash Park on horseback half an hour before me, and brought a good account of his Mother and*

Grandmother. 13 Aug., 15-18 Aug., 19 Aug: *Howell and E.F. W. left us before breakfast for Witney to visit the Mills there.* 20 Aug., 22-24 Aug., 26 Aug: *At a very early hour in the morning E.F. W. set out on his projected tour through Somerset and Devon.* 28 Aug: *In consequence of my having hinted in my letter that E.F. W. was on the eve of an excursion into Devon, Caroline H. sends a very kind invitation to him to spend a little time with them at Ilfracomb, taking a bed at their house, and making excursions with them to objects of curiosity and interest in that part of N. Devon.* 30 Aug., 2-3 Sep., 6 Sep: *A letter from E.F. W., dated Torquay on Saturday Even, gave a farther and animated account of his tour in S. Devon: he had been successful in finding nearly forty plants new to him; was in good health and spirits, and enjoyed his pedestrian exercise* ... 7 Sep., 11 Sep., 15 Sep., 20 Sep., 22 Sep., 27-30 Sep., 4 Oct: *E.F. W. dined with Billingsley.* 6-7 Oct., 11 Sep., 12 Oct: *Engaged in settling accounts with my son previously to his return to Oxford on Saturday* ... 13 Oct., 15 Oct., 21 Oct: *She brought a letter from E.F. W. which she had received yesterday, giving an account of his arrival at Magd. Hall, his journey thither with Stevens, and his present occupations: all satisfactory.* 23 Oct., 27 Oct., 31 Oct: *Received a long and satisfactory letter from Edward, giving an account of his studies, and, particularly, the outline of the scheme of reading, which, with the advice of Messrs. Jacobson and Cockey, he has formed with a view to obtaining the honours of a Class at his second examination before taking his Bachelor's degree.* 2-5 Nov., 10-11 Nov., 15-16 Nov., 23 Nov: ... *he will bring with him for a day or two his friend Edward Rowden of Wadham, son of my old College acquaintance John Rowden, Incumbent of Highworth, Wilts, that he may accompany my son to Stow Ball, which is fixed for that day.* 25 Nov., 29 Nov., 1 Dec., 3 Dec., 7-9 Dec., 14-16 Dec., 20-23 Dec., 26 Dec: *William Vavasour called, having forced his way on his poney through opposing snow drifts to see Edward and his friend Chater, who had, however, sallied forth on foot, and made a circuit over the hill to speculate on the depth of the snow, and the extent of the obstruction caused by the drifts.* 29-30 Dec.

1837: 5 Jan., 7 Jan: *My son had driven down to meet me, and to order some clothes &c. for himself.* 9 Jan., 11-15 Jan., 20 Jan., 23 Jan: *E.F. W. left us early in the morning, to keep term at Oxford.* 26 Jan: *Recd. a letter from E.F. W. very satisfactory, who is comfortably settled to his studies* ... 30 Jan., 6 Feb., 12 Feb., 15 Feb., 21 Feb., 1-2 Mar., 4 Mar., 8 Mar: *In half an hour after I reached home, my Son came from Oxford, a phaeton from Stow having been sent to meet him at Barrington Inn.* 9 Mar., 11 Mar., 13 Mar., 16 Mar., 17 Mar: *Immediately after I arrived there, my son and Billingsley came by the Mazippa coach from Cheltenham, having had but little rest and no sleep, as the Bachelor's Ball, a very brilliant affair, had not terminated till 7 o'clock in the morning.* 18 Mar., 21 Mar., 25 Mar., 30 Mar., 1 Apr: *My Son and myself with our men servants, and many labourers and others of the village were soon on the spot, and by a copious supply of water brought from the brook in buckets* ... 4 Apr: *My son had ridden to Sudely to be present at the annual Cheltenham Steeple Chace, and returned to dinner.* 5-6 Apr., 13 Apr., 15 Apr: *Much serious conversation with E.F. W. as to his line of study at Oxford, with a view to his passing through his examination with honours, as to the taking of his B.A. degree, and entering into Orders, not without reference to a partiality which he has conceived for Miss Sketchley, a lady to whom he was introduced last summer at Oxford.* 17 Apr: *E.F. W. left us for Magd. Hall to keep Easter term.* 18 Apr: *A letter from E.F. W. announcing his safe arrival at Oxford yesterday, and inclosing a letter from Miss Sketchley to which he had referred in his conversations with his Mother and myself on Saturday and Sunday last.* 21-22 Apr., 28 Apr: *Wrote to E.F. W. sending him a copy of Mr. Duncan's letter received on the 26th.* 1 May: *Agreeably surprised by the arrival of my son to breakfast from Oxford, he having ridden over, with an intention of returning in the Evening but he was induced to stay all night.* 2 May: *E.F. W. left us long before breakfast on his return to Oxford.* 7 May, 10 May, 13 May: *A letter from my son, to acquaint us that he meant to be with us this evening, and to remain till Wednesday next.* 14 May: *Much conversation with E.F. W. on his views of settling in life.* 16 May, 17 May: *My son started for Oxford soon after six o'cl. A.M.* 20 May, 24 May, 25 May: *Wrote to my Son; sent him an extract from Miss Gardner's letter to Mrs. Backhouse, as far as it related to the Sketchleys, and acquainted him that his Mother would write by this post to her cousin to desire her to endeavour to procure on good authority a confirmation or a refutation of the facts and opinions she had communicated about them in her letter received yesterday.* 28 May: *A very satisfactory reply from my son to the letter I wrote to him on the 25th.* 3 Jun: *Recd. a letter from my son, who proposes returning to Slaughter on Friday next: a satisfactory account of his studies engagements &c.* 5 Jun: *Wrote to my Son, lightly touching on the letter received from Miss Gardner on the 3d. Inst. also sent him a remittance.* 9-10 Jun., 12 Jun., 13 Jun: *A conversation with my son, renewed from Sunday morning, on the information as to Miss Sketchley's connections, received through Miss Gardner, as showing that the lady, however amiable, talented and accomplished she may be, has little to recommend her, in respect of connection.* 14 Jun., 15 Jun: *My son started on horseback at an early hour for Cirencester, whither he went in the expectation of finding a rare plant in Lord Bathurst's woods, park which he explored in vain under the guidance of the Misses Croome; he dined with Mr. Robert Croome, and rode home by moonlight.* 16-17 Jun., 20-21 Jun., 24 Jun: *My son rode with me to Stow about mid-day to attend at the ceremony of proclaiming Queen Victoria: the Under Sheriff having deputed the Clerk to the Mag. to make proclamation in his stead.* 28 Jun: ... *E.F. W. had gone to Stow to accompany Will. and Sophy Vavasour on a ride to Sudely Castle &c.* 29 Jun., 30 Jun: *Conversing seriously with my son on the subject of the Sketchleys; he has finally relinquished all thoughts of forming a connection with Miss S. and in this has been strengthened by ascertaining from W. Vavasour that they are considered by persons moving in good society at Liverpool as of a dubious condition, intimacy with whom would exclude from the best circles.* 3-6 Jul., 8-13 Jul., 15 Jul: *Rode with E.F. W. to Stow: much conversation with him as to his future prospects, his going into the Church, and settlement in life* ... *All is tending towards what I anticipated when the connection with Miss Sketchley was abandoned by him: his partiality for Sophy Vavasour is maturing into a steady attachment; except in respect of the lady's prospects as to fortune being scanty, we do not see any reason to oppose my Son's wishes: she is not handsome, but she is sensible, amiable, well and prudently brought up, and the family connections very respectable.* 17 Jul., 19 Jul., 21-23 Jul., 25 Jul: *My son passed the evening with the Vavasours.* 2 Aug: *E.F. W. having taken a ride during the cessation of the rain was overtaken by a violent storm at Stow, and remained to dine and pass the evening at the Vavasours.* 4 Aug: *My object in seeking a conference with his Lordship was to obtain his promise to receive my son as a Candidate for ordination at the Xmas ordination, when he will have passed his examination for his Bachelor's degree, and nothing will remain to be done towards the degree, but the merely putting on the gown, early in Lent Term.* 6 Aug: *In a walk with my son in the evening, he communicated to me what I was not at all surprized at hearing, that he had declared himself definitively not only to Sophy Vavasour, but to her parents, and had been accepted as the future husband.* 7 Aug: *Edward recd. a letter which gave him great distress.* 8 Aug: *E.F.W.—dined at the Vavasours.* 9 Aug: *Rode to Stow, and had a long and satisfactory conversation with Mr. & Mrs. Vavasour on the engagement between my son and their daughter.* 10-12 Aug., 14-15 Aug., 17-21 Aug., 23-24 Aug., 27-29 Aug., 31 Aug., 4-5 Sep., 7 Sep., 11-12 Sep., 14-15 Sep., 17-19 Sep., 21-23 Sep., 25 Sep., 28-29 Sep., 3 Oct., 5-6 Oct., 10-11 Oct., 15 Oct: *A letter from E.F.W. announcing his safe arrival at Oxford ...* 18 Oct., 21 Oct., 23 Oct., 2 Nov., 7 Nov., 13-14 Nov., 16-17 Nov., 19 Nov., 27-28 Nov., 30 Nov: *My dear Son arrived to breakfast, having ridden from Oxford to Stow after four o cl. yesterday on an Oxford hack, and passed the evening and slept at the Vavasours under the impression that we were dining at the Robert Waller's.* 1 Dec., 2 Dec: *A very kind letter from Round congratulating me on my Son having passed his examination with credit.* 4 Dec: *Settled accounts with my Son previous to his going to Oxford to-morrow to pack up his books &c.* 5-8 Dec., 12 Dec: *This being the day fixed for the Annual Stow Ball, E.F.W. went to dine and sleep at the Rectory, Stow, meaning to accompany the Vavasours to the Ball.* 13 Dec., 20 Dec: *My Son left us about 3 P.M. in the phaeton for Andoversford, whence he intended to proceed to Gloucester by Coach to offer himself for Examination to morrow as a Candidate for Deacon's Orders.* 22 Dec., 24 Dec., 25 Dec: *My Son read the morning prayers and preached, and assisted me in the administration of the Sacrament.* 27-28 Dec., 30-31 Dec.

1838: 3 Jan., 6-9 Jan., 10 Jan: *Settling accounts with my Son, and auditing his Oxford Bills.* 13-14 Jan., 17-19 Jan., 21 Jan., 22 Jan: *My Son left us for Oxford to take his B.A. degree on Wednesday ...* 24-25 Jan., 28-29 Jan., 1-3 Feb., 4 Feb: *Recd. a letter from Mr. Turberville, offering my son the vacant curacy of Whichford.* 6 Feb: *After an early breakfast left home with E.F.W. in the phaeton for Whichford to look out at the Parsonage &c., with a view to the forming a judgment whether it would be a suitable residence and curacy for my son.* 7-9 Feb., 11 Feb., 12 Feb: *Wrote to Mr. Turberville to say, that, having visited Whichford, it seemed likely to answer my Son's purpose, and to beg him to keep the Curacy open for a few days ...* 14-16 Feb., 18-26 Feb., 28 Feb., 1-4 Mar., 6 Mar., 8 Mar., 10-11 Mar., 12 Mar: *E.F.W. rode before breakfast to Stow, whence he accompanied Mr. Vavasour and Sophy in their open carriage to Whichford, which neither the lady nor her father had yet seen.* 14 Mar: *Much conversation with him, in which my Son took part with his Mother and myself, about our affairs, as to the proper provisions for a settlement on his approaching marriage.* 15 Mar., 17-20 Mar., 22-24 Mar., 28-31 Mar., 1 Apr., 3-5 Apr., 7-8 Apr., 11 Apr., 13-18 Apr., 20-25 Apr., 27-30 Apr., 1-5 May, 7-8 May, 9 May: *A letter from E.F.W. who seems satisfied with his proceedings at Whichford, and is very busy in settling himself there.* 10-11 May, 13-15 May, 16 May: *To us all a day of deep interest; may GOD Bless the union of my Son with his bride; may they be happy in each other ...* 17-18 May, 21-23 May, 25 May, 27-28 May, 30 May, 2 Jun., 4 Jun., 9-12 Jun., 13 Jun: *Edward and Sophy accompanied us, they having previously arranged to return and spend the remainder of the week at the two parental rectories of Stow and U. Slaughter.* 14-16 Jun., 19 Jun., 21 Jun., 28 Jun., 30 Jun., 10 Jul., 12-13 Jul., 21 Jul., 23 Jul., 25 Jul., 27 Jul., 30-31 Jul., 2-3 Aug., 6-8 Aug., 10-16 Aug., 18-20 Aug., 22-24 Aug., 26 Aug., 29-30 Aug., 4-5 Sep., 8-9 Sep., 20 Sep., 23 Sep., 25-27 Sep., 2-3 Oct., 6-9 Oct., 11-12 Oct., 19 Oct., 23-24 Oct., 29 Oct. 31 Oct., 6-9 Nov., 13 Nov., 17 Nov., 20 Nov., 22 Nov., 26-27 Nov., 1 Dec: *Stated my own earnest wish that Edward should take the Curacy of Stanway, that I had already written to urge him to accept it, and proposed to go to Whichford further to press the point on Monday, that I would take the earliest opportunity of intimating to the Bp. the result and should my son decline removing to Stanway, then I should be happy to nominate such successor as His Lordship might recommend.* 3 Dec: *Passing through Stow called at the Rectory, and saw Mr. Vavasour, who is anxious that Edward should resign Whichford, and go to Stanway, but though he did not say so in express terms, I gathered that from communications they had recd. from Whichford it was likely that I should find my son and his wife very reluctant to come into our views.* 4 Dec: *My son came down as I was on the eve of setting out homeward, in considerable agitation of spirits, and ready, I believe, to have ratified the acquiescence in my views which they had been expressed before we parted last night.* 5-8 Dec., 9 Dec: *Wrote to E.F.W. to apprize him that Vavasour and I had visited Stanway yesterday—that V. proposed going to morrow to Whichford to advise him about the removal to Stanway, but that unless they came cordially and with full preparation of the heart to be pleased they had better not come at all.* 11 Dec., 12 Dec: *Wrote to the Bp. of Glouc. & Bristol to acquaint him that my son had accepted the Curacy of Stanway ...* 14-15 Dec., 18 Dec., 20-21 Dec., 24 Dec., 30 Dec.

1839: 2 Jan., 4-5 Jan., 7 Jan: *Also to E.F.W. proposing to him to come over from Whichford either on Wednesday, Friday, or Saturday to execute the lease of the house in Bucklersbury.* 12 Jan., 14 Jan., 17 Jan., 22 Jan., 25 Jan., 27 Jan., 30 Jan., 2-4 Feb., 10 Feb., 15 Feb., 22-24 Feb., 1 Mar: *Wrote to E.F.W. with reference to the domestic vexations under which, we understood him & his wife to be suffering, offering any assistance or accommodation in our power.* 2-4 Mar., 8 Mar., 10 Mar., 12-14 Mar., 16-17 Mar., 22 Mar., 25-28 Mar., 29 Mar: *After we had dined my son came from Stanway, on his way to rejoin his wife at Stow.* 30 Mar., 7 Apr: *Recd. a letter from my son, expressing satisfaction with his change of residence, a wish that we should visit him at the Vicarage, and giving details as to domestic and other arrangements.* 11-13 Apr., 20 Apr., 23-24 Sep., 30 Apr., 1 May, 3 May, 9-10 May, 12-14 May, 17 May, 30-31 May, 12 Jun., 14 Jun., 19 Jun: *I drove to Stanway, and reached the Vicarage by half past one o clock, where very affectionately welcomed by my children ...* 28 Jun., 5 Jul., 9-10 Jul., 16-17 Jul., 19 Jul., 25 Jul., 27 Jul., 30 Jul., 2 Aug., 4-5 Aug., 11 Aug., 14 Aug., 20-22 Aug., 29 Aug., 2-4 Sep.

1840: 18 Mar: *M.W. and I went in the close carriage after breakfast to Stanway, to the christening of our grandchild.* 25 Mar., 28-31 Mar., 6-7 Apr., 9-13 Apr., 16 Apr., 18 Apr., 20 Apr., 22-24 Apr., 26-27 Apr., 29-30 Apr., 1 May, 3 May, 5 May, 7-10 May, 12 May, 14 May, 18-22 May, 28-30 May, 8 Jun., 11-12 Jun., 15 Jun., 17 Jun., 20 Jun., 23-24 Jun., 27 Jun. 28 Jun: *Received a letter from my Son acquainting me with a measure on which he has decided, and which he intends to put in force on the 13th. July. He proposes to pass about two months with his wife and infant in an excursion up the Rhine, and into Switzerland.* 1-3 Jul., 6-7 Jul., 12 Jul: *Wrote to E.F.W. on various points with reference to the property at Malvern and otherwise previously to his departure from England ...* 13-14 Jul., 18-19 Jul., 23-25 Jul., 2 Aug: *Recd. a most gratifying letter from E.F.W. dated at Frankfort on the Main on Sunday 26th. Ult.* 3 Aug., 5-7 Aug., 11 Aug., 13 Aug., 18-19 Aug., 25-26 Aug., 31 Aug., 4 Sep., 7 Sep: *Recd. a very delightful letter from my Son, dated Domo d'Ossola on the 28th. Inst. Ult.* 9 Sep., 12 Sep., 19-21 Sep., 25 Sep., 29 Sep: *Heard from our dear children. E.F.W. writes from Innsbrück on the 19th. (Saturday) and is compelled to postpone his return to England for a week, owing to disappointment in his progress through the Tyrol, in which he has been delayed longer than he expected.* 30 Sep., 1 Oct., 7 Oct., 9-10 Oct., 12 Oct: *Our dear children rode over to Slaughter from Stanway to see us, looking extremely well, and being in excellent spirits.* 13-14 Oct., 18 Oct., 26-30 Oct., 1-5 Nov., 6 Nov: *Our dear children left us in the afternoon for Stanway ... We had all enjoyed each other's society much ...* 12 Nov., 15 Nov., 17-18 Nov., 22-24 Nov., 28 Nov., 30 Nov., 1 Dec.

1841: 26 Feb., 2 Mar: *My dear Son's birthday: he is twenty eight years of age this day. Much affectionate thought of him and his, and earnest prayer for his and their temporal and eternal welfare.* 3 Mar., 5 Mar.

1842: 9 Jan., 12 Jan., 17-19 Jan., 21-26 Jan., 29 Jan., 31 Jan., 3 Feb., 5 Feb., 10-11 Feb., 15-17 Feb., 19-27 Feb., 2 Mar: *My son's birthday: he this day entered on his 30th. year: may GOD bless, protect, guide and restrain him and his so that he and they may thro' Christ's merits come at last to his everlasting glory!* 4-5 Mar., 7-9 Mar., 11-12 Mar., 14-17 Mar., 19-23 Mar., 30-31 Mar., 5 Apr., 7-8 Apr., 16 Apr., 22-23 Apr., 29 Apr., 3 May, 5 May, 12-13 May, 16-18 May, 20 May, 24 May, 30-31 May, 1-4 Jun., 6 Jun., 8 Jun., 16 Jun., 19-20 Jun., 22 Jun., 24 Jun: *Met my son at the Cricket ground, where there was a small muster of players.* 29 Jun., 1 Jul: *... also to E.F.W. on the topic which we had anxiously discussed at Gloucester on Wednesday.* 3-4 Jul., 6 Jul., 8-9 Jul., 13 Jul: *John Perkins Senr. looked in on me in the evening respecting some transaction as to wine with my Son.* 15-16 Jul., 17 Jul: *A late breakfast—after which divine service. I read the prayers, and my son preached a very good sermon.* 22-23 Jul., 26 Jul., 27 Jul: *... to Perkins, Oxford, at my son's request, with a cheque on Hoare for £20, on account of wine supplied to him by Perkins.* 30 Jul: *Recd. a very agreeable and satisfactory letter from E. F. W, dated Barmouth, giving a full account of the prosperous and enjoyable journey ...* 31 Jul., 1 Aug., 3 Aug., 8-9 Aug., 11-13 Aug., 15 Aug., 18 Aug., 22-23 Aug., 25 Aug., 27 Aug: *Our dear children and grandchild took luncheon, and passed two or three hours with us on their way from Stow to Stanway.* 29 Aug., 1 Sep., 4 Sep., 6 Sep., 8-10 Sep., 12 Sep., 15 Sep., 20 Sep., 23-24 Sep., 27 Sep: *Our dear children came from Stanway soon after mid-day to pass a couple of days with us, bringing the dear Broome.* 28-30 Sep., 3 Oct., 7-8 Oct., 10 Oct., 14 Oct., 18-20 Oct., 22 Oct., 24 Oct., 27 Oct., 29 Oct., 1 Nov., 10 Nov., 13 Nov: *I wrote to my Son, explaining to him the actual state of things, and requesting him to come with his dear wife and child as early as possible to-morrow, that he might, if it should so please GOD, see his Grand mother once more alive.* 14-21 Nov., 24 Nov: *Our dear children and grand-child left us to-day for Stanway; their society during these triste and anxious duties which have come upon us has been a great comfort ...* 28 Nov., 1 Dec: *Most agreeably surprized by the unexpected arrival of our dear children and grandchild from Stanway.* 2-3 Dec., 7 Dec., 12 Dec., 14 Dec., 17 Dec., 19 Dec., 22 Dec., 26 Dec., 28 Dec.

1843: 1-2 Jan., 4-6 Jan., 9-13 Jan., 24 Jan: *... Also to E.F.W. who soon after came with Sophy, having ridden from Stanway, and spent two hours with us—a great treat.* 26 Jan., 31 Jan., 1-2 Feb., 8 Feb., 10 Feb., 10-12 Aug., 16 Aug., 18 Aug., 28-30 Aug., 2 Sep., 4 Sep., 6 Sep., 18 Sep: *Our dear children came from Stanway to welcome us home ...* 23-25 Sep., 27 Sep., 30 Sep: *A letter from E.F.W. from Prinknash Park: they had performed well and enjoyed much their little excursion through the clothing vallies to Berkeley Castle and back; they will return to Stanway to-day, and invite us to visit them there next week.* 2-6 Oct., 7 Oct: *After breakfast we left our dear children, having passed with them some very pleasant days.* 11-12 Oct., 15 Oct., 19-20 Oct., 23-28 Oct., 6 Nov., 20 Nov., 22 Nov., 27 Nov: *After breakfast M.W. and I went in our phaeton to pass two or three hours with our dear children at Stanway ...* 5 Dec., 9 Dec., 15 Dec., 18 Dec., 19 Dec: *Recd. from Stanway in a short note from E.F.W. brought by his servant the very comfortable intelligence that our dear Sophy was brought to bed about 3 o cl. this morning of a fine boy; the labour easy, and all doing well.* 20 Dec: *In the evening a note from my son, brought to Eyford by the Guiting Postman, giving a delightful account of the dear mother and babe at the Vicarage, Stanway.* 24 Dec: *A note from my dear Son with an excellent account of his dear wife and infant: himself also and Broome quite well.* 27 Dec., 29 Dec.

1844: 6 Jan., 11-12 Jan., 15 Jan, 24 Jan., 29-31 Jan., 3 Feb., 6 Feb., 16 Feb., 18-22 Feb., 24 Feb., 26-27 Feb., 29 Feb., 2 Mar., 7 Mar., 9 Mar., 15-16 Mar., 21-22 Mar., 29 Mar., 2-4 Apr., 9 Apr., 15-19 Apr., 21 Apr., 23-24 Apr., 25 Apr: *My son rode to Shipton Downs, Idbury &c.—to make geological observations, returning to Stow, where his servant met him to ride back his horse to U Slaughter, E.F.W. returning with me in the phaeton.* 27 Apr., 1 May, 3 May, 6-7 May, 10 May, 13 May, 15 May, 18-19 May, 27039 May, 23-26 Jul., 30-31 Jul., 1 Aug., 3 Aug., 6 Aug., 14 Aug., 17 Aug., 20-21 Aug., 24 Aug., 31 Aug., 3-4 Aug., 7 Sep., 9 Aug., 18 Sep., 20 Sep., 24 Sep., 2-4 Oct., 6-10 Oct., 12 Oct., 18 Oct., 21 Oct., 28 Oct., 31 Oct., 7 Nov., 11 Nov., 14-17 Nov., 18 Nov: *... my son has discovered a Roman camp, perhaps not hitherto noticed ... which may have communicated with a gate by which egress was had for water and forage, the former being at hand in a spring under Bigbury, near which is a hump of earth of considerable size, evidently not natural, which, probably, indicates the site of ancient buildings.* 20-22 Nov., 25 Nov., 28 Nov., 8-9 Dec., 15-17 Dec., 26 Dec., 30 Dec.

1845: 1 Jan., 6 Jan., 9 Jan., 11 Jan., 13-20 Jan., 26 Jan., 28-29 Jan., 4 Feb., 6 Feb., 8 Feb., 12-13 Feb., 17 Feb., 19-20 Feb., 24 Feb., 27 Feb., 4 Mar., 8 Mar., 12-15 Mar., 19 Mar., 20 Mar: *Received a letter from E.F.W. with a comfortable account, under the circumstances, of dear Sophy, who bears the loss of her sister with grief, but with resignation ...* 22 Mar., 25-26 Mar., 29 Mar., 31 Mar., 9 Apr., 13 Apr., 15-17 Apr., 21-30 Apr., 1-4 May, 7-8 May, 16 May, 18-20 May, 24 May, 26-27 May, 2-3 Jun., 5-7 Jun., 11-13 Jun., 15 Jun., 17-19 Jun., 21-22 Jun., 27 Jun., 1-3 Jul., 5-6 Jul., 12 Jul.

1846: 15 May: *E.F.W. left us after luncheon to pursue his geological researches at Atherfield, and in its neighbourhood, going by a Newport and Cowes coach to Atherf Blackgang Chine Hotel, where he purposes to sleep, and to return to-morrow.* 21 May, 23 May, 29 May, 31 May, 1 Jun., 4-5 Jun., 8 Jun., 10 Jun: *E.F.W. went on a geological excursion to Blackgang Chine, Atherfield Rocks &c., setting out before breakfast ...* 14 Jun., 18-19 Jun., 24 Jun; 27 Jun: *Recd. a letter from E.F.W., who is disposed to decline accepting the living of Waltham Abbey ...* 28 Jun: *My Son had thrown out a suggestion, grounded on a former conversation with me, that, as an increase of income with his increasing family is now becoming very requisite, it might be desirable, if convenient to me, to endeavour to purchase the advowson or next presentation of the living of Stanton, which is likely soon to be vacated ...* 3 Jul., 7 Jul., 15 Jul., 17 Jul., 20 Jul., 25 Jul., 4 Aug., 8 Aug: *Recd. a letter from E.F.W. all well at Stanway: Sophy expects to be confined on an early day, and, therefore, Edwd. declines meeting me and Mr. Sewell on Wednesday next, to look over the estate at Redmarley ...* 11 Aug., 15 Aug., 18 Aug: *A letter from E.F.W. all well at Stanway Vicarage, and our dear Sophy expecting her confinement on any day.* 19 Aug., 24 Aug: *Recd. a letter from E.F.W. acknowledging my late remittance to him of £50. He gives a very good account of dear Sophy, and the children: the former seems to have made a sad miscalculation ...* 12 Sep., 18 Sep: *A letter from E.F. W. with a very good report of all at Stanway; save that the suspence as to Sophy's confinement still subsists.* 21 Sep., 25 Sep: *An early messenger from Stanway brought a letter from E.F. W. with the glad tidings that our dear Sophy had been safely delivered of a Son last evening; she had a good and a short time, and both the Mother and the infant are going on quite well. GOD be praised for this great mercy!* 28 Sep: *Received a letter from E.F. W. with a very excellent account of his dear wife and her baby.* 29 Sep., 3 Oct: *Found all at the Vicarage as I could wish: my dear daughter so wonderfully recovered as to be dressed, sitting in the drawing room, in excellent spirits, looking as if nothing had happened to her. The dear infant not so large a child as its elder brothers had been, at the same age, but a very lovely baby, perfectly healthy. It is to be name George Backhouse, the former name being given in memory of my deceased brother, the latter out of respect to the family family and maiden name of my dear wife. Broome and Frederick were bright, blooming boys ...* 5 Oct., 12 Oct., 16 Oct., 19-21 Oct., 2 Nov., 7 Nov., 9 Nov., 14 Nov., 9 Nov., 14 Nov., 22 Nov., 24 Nov., 26-28 Nov., 30 Nov., 2 Dec: *Our dear children & the infant returned from Maugersbury to the delight of the elder boys ...* 4-5 Dec., 11 Dec., 25 Dec., 28-30 Dec.

1847: 5-6 Jan., 14 Jan., 25 Jan., 29-30 Jan., 4-5 Feb., 8 Feb., 10-11 Feb., 15 Feb., 17 Feb., 19 Feb., 21-22 Feb., 24 Feb., 27 Feb., 1-2 Mar., 4 Mar., 8 Mar., 23 Mar., 29-30 Mar., 1 Apr., 5-6 Apr., 10 Apr., 12-14 Apr., 15 Apr: *When I returned from Stow, found my son's servant with a note, intimating that he had been sent to desire Anne Bateman to go to Stanway to supply the place of Sophy's cook, who is leaving them in a hurried, unhandsome manner; so that annoyance in respect of servants visits them as well as us.* 17 Apr., 20-21 Apr., 23 Apr., 25-26 Apr., 28 Apr., 30 Apr., 3 May, 5-7 May, 10-13 May, 16-20 May, 21 May: *Lost our dear children and grandchildren, who returned to-day to Stanway: their departure left a great blank ...* 29 May, 31 May, 1 Jun., 8 Jun., 10 Jun., 14 Jun., 16 Jun., 19 Jun., 22 Jun., 24-27 Jun., 29-30 Jun., 1 Jul., 3 Jul., 7-9 Jul., 12-13 Jul., 16 Jul., 19-21 Jul., 23 Jul., 26 Jul., 2 Aug., 13-14 Aug., 20 Aug., 25-26 Aug., 31 Aug., 2 Sep., 5 Sep., 7-8 Sep., 14-15 Sep., 19 Sep., 22 Sep., 28 Sep., 5 Oct., 11 Oct., 13 Oct., 19-20 Oct., 25-28 Oct., 1 Nov., 5 Nov., 9 Oct., 10 Oct: *Wrote to E.F. W. a very full account of all I had learnt from Mr. Sewell as to the living of Stanton, the cancelling of the contract for the purchase of the next presentation, and the Bishop's determination to accept W. H. Bloxsome's resignation ...* 17 Nov: *He and Sophy are greatly disappointed, but exonerate me from all blame ...* 25 Nov., 27 Nov., 2 Dec., 9 Dec., 11 Dec., 15 Dec., 24 Dec., 28 Dec.

1848: 10 Jan., 13 Jan., 20-21 Jan., 27 Jan., 31 Jan., 1 Feb., 7 Feb., 11 Feb., 15 Feb., 17 Feb., 22 Feb., 1 Mar., 3 Mar., 7 Mar., 12 Mar: *Our dear children and grandchildren arrived from Stanway ...* 14-18 Mar., 21 Mar., 31 Mar., 1 Apr: *Wrote to E.F. W., consenting to the building of the stable at Stanway Vicarage ...* 4 Apr: *A letter from a Stranger, a Mr. Prentice, dated from Cheltenham, a botanist, who asks for a direction to the true habitat of Thlaspi perfoliatum, a rare plant, known as indigenous by Bobart, afterwards lost, as was supposed, but re-discovered some years ago by my son and Mr. Billingsley ...* 10-11 Apr., 17-20 Apr., 25-26 Apr., 2 May, 4 May, 8 May: *Inspected the alterations, particularly the new stable and laundry, which are nearly completed, and very commodious.* 11-12 May, 20 May, 30 May, 4-6 Jun., 8-11 Jun., 13 Jun., 14 Jun: *Walked with dearest Sophy to Eyford slate quarries, whither E.F. W. had preceded us to collect any fossils which the Quarrymen might have put aside for him, and whom we found in the Slate Quarries.* 16-17 Jun., 30 Jun., 4-5 Jul., 7 Jul., 10 Jul., 13 Jul., 15 Jul., 18 Jul., 21-22 Jul., 26 Jul., 1 Aug., 7-8 Jul., 13-18 Aug., 26028 Aug., 6-7 Sep., 9 Sep., 12 Sep., 16 Sep., 26-27 Sep., 4-5 Oct., 14 Oct., 17-19 Oct., 24-25 Oct., 4 Nov., 8 Nov., 11-12 Nov., 17 Nov., 21 Nov.

1849: 13 Dec., 26 Dec., 29 Dec.

1850: 4 Jan., 7 Jan., 9 Jan., 12 Jan., 17 Jan., 21-22 Jan., 24-25 Jan., 29 Jan., 2 Feb., 6 Feb., 15-16 Feb., 18 Feb: *M.W. much in the same state; had the comfort of a visit from our dear children, who rode over to see us ...* 22 Feb., 27 Feb., 1 Mar., 5 Mar., 8 Mar., 11-12 Feb., 13-15 Feb., 18 Feb: *Wrote a note to E.F. W. with a report of his Mother's state ...* 19 Mar: *... she enjoyed seeing her children; dear Edward and Sophy riding from Stanway ...* 21-22 Mar.,25 Mar., 29-30 Mar., 2 Apr., 4 Apr., 6 Apr: *Wrote to E.F. W. with a report of his poor Mother's health.* 8 Apr., 10 Apr: *She was able to receive and in a degree to enjoy a visit from our dear children, who came on horseback from Stanway, and remained with us for three hours ...* 12 Apr: *He recommended me to send for my son early to-morrow, that he might come and visit his mother; I therefore late in the evening wrote to E.F. W. a statement of the present condition of things, begging to see him; this letter will be conveyed by my groom ...* 14 Apr: *She passed off almost as an infant does to sleep ...* 15 Apr: *... my dear Son relieved me from much that would have been very irksome ...* 16 Apr: *My Son wrote letters to the Editors of the two Gloucestershire, and one Oxfordshire papers ...* 18-19 Apr., 21-22 Apr., 26 Apr., 4 May, 8 May, 13 May: *... my dear children arrived from Stanway, with the kind intention of dining with me and riding home late in the Evening.* 21 May, 23 May, 27-28 May, 30 May, 5 Jun., 16 Jun., 22 Jun., 1-3 Jul., 10-11 Jul., 15-16 Jul., 18-20 Jul., 23-25 Jul., 29 Jul., 1 Aug., 16 Aug., 21 Aug., 24 Aug., 29 Aug: *Received a letter from E.F. W.—he urges my visiting him and dear Sophy on Tuesday next; and opens out to me a plan which is to be carried into effect immediately after the Confirmation at Stanway: viz. that he & Sophy with the younger children shall go to Brighton or Worthing, or elsewhere for a month, for sea bathing ...* 3-4 Aug., 9 Sep: *At breakfast time my son unexpectedly rode from Stanway, and partook of my meal—He came to announce that A. M. Andrews, his housemaid, daughter of my gardener, had fallen ill of fever, and was about to be removed in a fly to her father's house, where she accordingly arrived, and was attended by Mr. Collins ...* 11 Sep: *Received a note from E.F. W. He and Sophy have made up their minds to remain at Stanway, maugre the endemic there till Tuesday next, on which day they purpose setting off for the sea coast.* 14 Sep., 16 Sep., 18 Sep., 21-22 Sep., 27 Sep., 4 Oct., 9 Oct., 13 Oct., 15 Oct., 23 Oct., 26 Oct., 30-31 Oct., 1 Nov., 8-9 Nov., 12 Nov., 18 Nov., 22 Nov., 25-29 Nov., 7 Dec., 13 Dec., 21 Dec., 23 Dec., 28 Dec.

1851: 1 Jan., 6 Jan., 9 Jan., 15 Jan., 21 Jan., 25 Jan., 29-30 Jan., 1 Feb., 5-6 Feb., 12-13 Feb., 18 Feb., 20 Feb., 24-25 Feb., 27 Feb., 1 Mar., 6 Mar., 11 Mar., 16 Mar., 19 Mar., 24 Mar., 27 Mar., 30-31 Mar., 1 Apr: *I received a letter from E.F. W. who proposes, with his belongings, to arrive at Upper Slaughter by dinner time to-morrow.* 3-5 Apr., 13 Apr., 21-26 Apr., 6 May, 26 May, 28 May.

1852: 21-22 Jan., 25-26 Jan., 30-31 Jan., 6 Feb., 12-13 Feb., 17-19 Feb., 28 Feb., 8 Mar., 16-17 Mar., 23 Mar., 25-26 Mar., 29 Mar., 6 Apr., 8 Apr., 12-13 Apr., 15-17 Apr., 22 Apr., 27 Apr., 3 May, 8-9 May, 12 May, 16 May, 21 May, 24 May, 26-29 May, 4 Jun., 8-9 Jun., 25 Oct., 27-29 Oct., 31 Oct., 1-2 Nov., 5 Nov., 7 Nov., 11-17 Nov., 19-25 Nov., 9 Dec., 11 Dec., 18 Dec., 20-22 Dec., 27 Dec., 31 Dec.

1853: 4-6 Jan., 10-11 Jan., 13 Jan., 19 Jan., 24-25 Jan., 27 Jan: *The last sad scene is over. Mr. Vavasour breathed his last between*

3 & 4 AM.—My son had found him no worse than he had left him when he returned to "the Cottage" last night. He & Sophy retired to bed at half past 11 P.M.—were called at half past 3 AM. and were present when the awful moment came which recalled the spirit to its maker. 28 Jan., 20 Feb: *Letter from E.F.W. giving an improved account of dear Sophy's health and spirits.* 23 Feb., 2-3 Mar., 7 Mar., 9 Mar., 11-12 Mar., 21 Mar., 25-26 Mar., 28-29 Mar., 4 Apr., 13 Apr., 1 May, 3 May, 7 May, 9-14 May, 20 May, 23 May: *In the evening received a letter from my son, left at Lower Slaughter Turnpike gate, probably by some gentleman who had met with him at the Batsford cricket ground ... he likewise suggests change of scene & sea air, so that they contemplate going to the Coast, probably of South Wales, near Swansea or to Tenby, as soon as the boys come from school ...* 28 May, 6 Jun., 8-9 Jun., 16 Jun., 23 Jun: *Received a letter from E.F.W. dated "the Mumbles, near Swansea" ...* 9 Dec: *An agreeable surprize from the arrival of my son and daughter, on horseback, accompanied by Capt. Bell and Mr. Ball, who came about 5 P.M., dined with me, and set off on their return from for Stanway about 8 P.M.* 10 Dec., 14 Dec., 17 Dec., 20 Dec., 24 Dec., 26 Dec.

1854: 28 Jan., 3 Feb., 13 Feb., 21-22 Feb., 5 Mar: *Wrote to E.F.W—to inform him of the serious spasmodic attack under which I am suffering.* 6 Mar: *He was soon after followed by my dear children, accompanied by dear Georgie, who, on hearing of my illness, kindly resolved to come to pass the day and night here ...* 7 Mar., 11 Mar., 143 Mar: *My son rode over to see me, and remained with me for nearly two hours. He has been somewhat out of order in his digestive organs.* 17 Mar., 20 May, 23 Mar., 25 Mar., 29 Mar., 31 Mar., 7 Apr., 14 Apr., 21 Apr., 27 Apr: *It appears that E.F.W. and Sophy are meditating a trip to be absent one Sunday to the neighbourhood of Bridgend, Glamorganshire, to locate themselves at Southern down, a place visited by my Son last Summer, that Sophy may inhale the sea breeze, and her husband enjoy some fishing in the Ewenny.* 2 May: *To E.F.W. with a narrative of all my troubles and annoyances; naming that I have given up the intention of visiting the Howells ...* 5 May: *Letters from E.F.W. dated Southerndown—where they were sojourning in an Inn ...* 8 May: *Received a letter from E.F.W: tired of the monotony of Southerndown, he and his propose proceeding as to-day by railway to Merthyr Tydvil, & thence to Brecon, with the intention of returning home on Saturday.* 9 May, 12 May, 16 May, 17 May: *Had my children been aware how seriously I am indisposed, they would probably have come alone.* 22-23 May, 25-26 May, 27 May: *... my son remained here till after luncheon, waiting in the expectation of seeing Mr. Hayward, but, as he did not come, left us about 3 P.M. Hayward called about 5 P.M. and examined my lower extremities ...* 31 May: *But I could not enjoy the society of my children and their friend. Waiting too long for my dinner, a fit of indigestion came on, with great pain in the stomach, and sickness, which drove me to my bed. Edward and Sophy waited on me in turn with great solicitude, nor were the nursing attentions of the faithful Elizabeth Minors wanting ...* 1 Jun., 5 Jun: *Wrote to E.F.W. with a report of my health, and of what had passed since we parted.* 7 Jun: *A letter from E.F.W. suggesting that, as Lord Wemyss is expected at Stanway next week, the proposed visit to me by himself, Sophy & Georgie should be postponed till the week following, when Freddy can be of the party.* 9 Jun: *Wrote to E.F.W, in answer to his letter received on Wednesday, pressing him and his to come on a visit on the 19th.* 14 Jun: *Last week they spent 47 hours in Town, that Sophy might consult Sir Henry Holland, who considered that, as regards the neuralgic affection to which she is subject, there is no change for the worse, and that the same palliatives and course of treatment already observed ought to be persevered in ...* 18 Jun: *Before my note was dispatched, received one from my Son, acquainting me that, as Sophy was suffering sadly from toothache and face ache, their coming hither must be postponed till Tuesday.* 20 Jun: *Disappointed in my expectation of welcoming the Stanway party, E.F.W having sent a messenger to inform me (by note) that poor Sophy is still so great a sufferer from tooth and face ache as to be unable to travel to-day ...* 21 Jun: *Mr. Walsh rode from Winchcomb to meet E.F.W. and we had a pleasant trio at and after dinner ...* 22 Jun., 29 Jun., 4 Jul: *And towards 6 P.M. came my son and daughter in their carriage, Sophy having recovered from one of her periodical head-aches, which had visited her early in the day.* 7 Jul., 7-8 Aug., 12 Jul., 14 Jul: *E.F.W. accompanied me by invitation to luncheon with Lord and Lady Wemyss at the great house.* 15 Jul., 25 Jul., 2 Aug: *The party from Stanway arrived by detachments—first, on horseback, Broome and Edmund Clifford——then, in their own carriage E.F.W, Sophy and Bro Freddy:— lastly, in my close carriage, which I sent for them, Georgie with the Servants.* 4-5 Aug., 7 Aug: *My son and daughter, with Freddy, arrived from Stanway to dinner and to conclude their visit to me———A noisy party of laughing and frolicking old schoolmates—with music—singing by Sophy.* 8 Aug: *Much singing by Sophy between breakfast and luncheon time——E.F.W. went to Lower Slaughter, to make arrangements with the Vavasours as to the Archery meeting at Stow to-day.* 12 Aug: *E.F.W. and Sophy in their phaeton—Broome on his poney, Freddy with his papa and mamma, Georgie and the servants in my chariot.*

WITTS — Sophia Witts — *daughter-in-law*

Sophia Witts, née Vavasour (1815-1871), was born in Ireland, the eldest daughter of Richard Frederick Vavasour (±1784-1853) and Julia, née Vavasour (1789-1865).

1836: 27 Dec: *The Misses Vavasour slept here: their brother returned home on his poney.*

1837: 12 Jan: *My son sent home the Phaeton and horse by a man from Cheltenham, with a note intimating that he had accepted an invitation to dine to day with a family of the name of Bell, to meet Mrs. & the Misses Vavasour, and that he should return to-morrow by the Northampton Coach.* 17 Feb: *Entertained at dinner Mr. & Mrs. Cameron, Mr. & Miss S. Vavasour, Messrs. Ford, Billingsley, Polson, & Daubeny.* 25 Feb: *Sophy Vavasour called here.* 17 Jun: *... my son took a ramble with the Misses Vavasour, and walked home to dinner.* 28 Jun., 15 Jul: *All is tending towards what I anticipated when the connection with Miss Sketchley was abandoned by him: his partiality for Sophy Vavasour is maturing into a steady attachment; except in respect of the lady's prospects as to fortune being scanty, we do not see any reason to oppose my Son's wishes: she is not handsome, but she is sensible, amiable, well and prudently brought up, and the family connections very respectable.* 6 Aug: *In a walk with my son in the evening, he communicated to me what I was not at all surprized at hearing, that he had declared himself definitively not only to Sophy Vavasour, but to her parents, and had been accepted as the future husband.* 9 Aug., 21 Aug: *Drove M.W. to Stow to call on the Vavasours, the first visit she has paid since E.F.W's engagement with Sophy has been sanctioned by the Parents on both sides.* 23 Aug., 28 Aug., 12 Sep., 22 Sep., 4 Oct., 11 Oct., 14 Nov., 16 Nov., 23-24 Dec., 27 Dec.

1838: 6 Jan., 23 Jan., 4 Feb., 7 Feb: *But none of these things move my Son, who with Sophy V. professes a wish for seclusion, no desire for society, and a persuasion that they shall be all in all to each other.* 9 Feb., 8 Mar., 12 Mar., 17 Mar., 22 Mar., 24 Mar., 31 Mar., 11 Apr., 17 Apr., 28 Apr., 30 Apr., 2 May, 8 May, 10-12 May, 15 May, 16 May: *To us all a day of deep interest; may GOD Bless the union of my Son with his bride; may they be happy in each other ...* 21 May, 30 May, 4 Jun., 9 Jun., 12 Jun: *This day having been fixed for our visiting E.F.W. and his wife, we sent for post horses, being afraid of venturing, as we had intended, in our open carriage ...* 13 Jun., 15-16 Jun., 21 Jun., 28 Jun., 10 Jul., 12-13 Jul., 23 Jul., 27 Jul., 30-31 Jul., 2-3 Aug., 6-7 Aug., 8 Aug: *Sophy indisposed, having caught cold, which brought on an Asthmatic oppression in breathing to which she is occasionally subject.* 9-12 Aug., 13 Aug: *E.F.W. came from Stow about mid-day with a very satisfactory report of Sophy's amended health, she having passed a good night, and having passed had no return of Asthmatic affection.* 14-16 Aug., 17 Aug: *Sophy oppressed with a cold in the morning, but very well in the evening.* 18 Aug., 20 Aug., 22-23 Aug., 24 Aug: *To our very great regret learnt in the morning that poor Sophy was labouring under a recurrence of her former seizure of shortness of breathing, under which she had been suffering during the night, and which was, doubtless, occasioned by exposure to damp when riding or in the open carriage yesterday or on Wednesday ...* 25 Aug., 29 Aug., 3 Sep., 5 Sep., 25-27 Sep., 6 Oct., 8-9 Oct., 11-12 Oct., 23-24 Oct., 29 Oct: *A very pleasant letter from my son, giving an account of the visit he and his wife had paid to Dryden at Leek Wotton of their rides thither and home, and excursions to Warwick, Leamington, Stoneleigh, Coventry, Guy's Cliff &c.* 6-9 Nov., 20 Nov., 30 Nov., 3-9 Dec., 11 Dec., 20-21 Dec., 30 Dec.

1839: 2 Jan: *Recd. a letter from M.W. brought by Otway, it named that E.F.W. had been at U.S. yesterday from Stow, where he and Sophy arrived on Monday; but she is confined to her room by a bad cold and oppression on her breath.* 5 Jan., 12 Jan., 22 Jan., 10 Feb., 15 Feb., 1-2 Mar., 10 Mar., 12-13 Mar., 16 Mar., 26 Mar., 28-30 Mar., 11 Apr., 20 Apr., 23-24 Apr., 30 Apr., 1 May, 3 May, 9-10 May, 12-15 May, 17 May, 12 Jun., 19 Jun., 28 Jun., 5 Jul., 9-10 Jul., 15 Jul: *Sophy is now declared to be certainly enceinte, and her accouchement is expected in January next ...* 16 Jul., 25 Jul., 27 Jul., 30 Jul., 2 Aug., 4-5 Aug., 11 Aug., 20-23 Aug., 2-3 Sep.

1840: 25 Mar: *He brought a very good account of Sophy and the infant ...* 31 Mar: *E.F.W. rode over from Stanway to breakfast, and brought a very good account of Sophy and the infant ...* 6 Apr., 9-11 Apr., 16 Apr., 23 Apr., 26-27 Apr., 29 Apr., 8-9 May, 12 May, 14 May, 18-22 May, 2 Jun., 8 Jun., 11-12 Jun., 17 Jun., 20 Jun., 22 Jun., 24 Jun., 2 Jul., 6-7 Jul., 13 Aug., 18 Aug., 25 Aug., 7 Sep., 9-10 Oct., 12-13 Oct., 18 Oct., 26-28 Oct., 31 Oct., 1 Nov., 4-5-7 Nov., 12 Nov., 15 Nov., 24 Nov., 30 Nov., 1 Dec.

1841: 3 Mar.

1842: 9 Jan., 17-19 Jan., 29 Jan., 31 Jan., 3 Feb., 10 Feb., 15 Feb., 19 Feb., 21-22 Feb., 24-26 Feb., 4 Mar., 8 Mar., 12 Mar., 17 Mar., 22 Mar., 7 Apr., 16 Apr., 22-23 Apr., 29 Apr., 5 May, 12-13 May, 16 May: *This the anniversary of Edward's & Sophy's marriage; and their mutual attachment continues warm and unabated.* 17-18 May, 30-31 May, 1-4 Jun., 6 Jun., 8 Jun., 16 Jun., 20 Jun., 24 Jun., 29 Jun., 1 Jul., 6 Jul., 8 Jul., 15-17 Jul., 22-23 Jul., 26 Jul., 30 Jul., 8 Aug., 13 Aug., 22-23 Aug., 25 Aug., 27 Aug., 6-7 Sep., 10 Sep., 12 Sep., 15 Sep., 20 Sep., 24 Sep., 27-30 Sep., 6-7 Oct., 10 Oct., 18 Oct., 20 Oct., 22 Oct., 1 Nov., 13-18 Nov., 21-22 Nov., 24 Nov., 1-3 Dec., 26 Dec.

1843: 2 Jan., 4-5 Jan., 9 Jan., 11 Jan., 24 Jan., 26 Jan., 31 Jan., 10-12 Aug., 16 Aug., 18 Aug., 28 Aug., 2 Sep., 18 Sep., 24 Sep: *... and my daughter though in the family way, was not at all exhausted by the fatigue and hurry.* 27 Sep., 3-4 Oct., 5 Oct: *... Sophy is expected to be confined late in November, or very early in December.* 7 Oct., 19 Oct., 23 Oct., 25 Oct., 27-28 Oct., 20 Nov., 22 Nov., 27 Nov., 5 Dec: *Received a very satisfactory letter from my Son: all remains at the Vicarage, Stanway, as on yesterday week, when we were there, except that the Monthly Nurse is arrived, and dear Sophy still able to go to church, and drive out in the open carriage, walk short distances &c.* 15 Dec., 19 Dec: *Recd. from Stanway in a short note from E.F.W. brought by his servant the very comfortable intelligence that our dear Sophy was brought to bed about 3 o cl. this morning of a fine boy; the labour easy, and all doing well.* 20 Dec., 24 Dec., 26 Dec., 29 Dec.

1844: 6 Jan., 11 Jan., 24 Jan., 29 Jan., 31 Jan., 6 Feb., 15 Feb., 19-20 Feb., 22 Feb., 26 Feb., 29 Feb., 2 Mar., 21 Mar., 26 Mar., 2 Apr., 9 Apr., 15-16 Apr., 18-19 Apr., 23-26 Apr., 3 May, 10 May, 13 May, 15 May, 23-24 Jul., 26 Jul., 30-31 Jul., 1 Aug., 14 Aug., 17 Aug., 20-21 Aug., 31 Aug., 3 Sep., 7 Sep., 9 Sep., 18 Sep., 20 Sep., 24 Sep., 2 Oct., 4 Oct., 7 Oct., 9-10 Oct., 12 Oct., 18 Oct., 28 Oct., 31 Oct., 7 Nov., 11 Nov., 14-16 Nov., 18 Nov., 20-21 Nov., 28 Nov., 16 Dec.

1845: 6 Jan., 9 Jan., 13-15 Jan., 17-20 Jan., 26 Jan., 29 Jan., 4 Feb., 8 Feb., 12-13 Feb., 19 Feb., 24 Feb., 27 Feb., 4 Mar., 12 Mar: *... no hope remains that Emily Dryden can long survive: she herself is prepared to depart—Sophy is resigned to the approaching loss of her sister ...* 14-15 Mar., 20 Mar: *Received a letter from E.F.W. with a comfortable account, under the circumstances, of dear Sophy, who bears the loss of her sister with grief, but with resignation ...* 22 Mar., 25-26 Mar., 29 Mar., 31 Mar., 13 Apr., 17 Apr., 21-30 Apr., 1-3 May, 16 May, 19-20 May, 24 May, 2-5 Jun., 7 Jun., 17 Jun., 29 Jun., 5 Jul.

1846: 21 May, 1 Jun., 8 Jun., 14 Jun., 18-19 Jun., 24 Jun., 20 Jul., 25 Jul., 24 Aug., 31 Aug: *He gave a good account of his dear wife's condition: she has strangely miscalculated, but well ...* 17 Sep: *Mrs. V. had received a letter from dear Sophy, who describes herself as quite well, but hourly expecting her confinement.* 3 Oct: *Found all at the Vicarage as I could wish: my dear daughter so wonderfully recovered as to be dressed, sitting in the drawing room, in excellent spirits, looking as if nothing had happened to her. The dear infant not so large a child as its elder brothers had been, at the same age, but a very lovely baby ...* 12 Oct., 30 Oct., 16 Nov., 20 Nov., 22 Nov., 24 Nov., 26 Nov., 28 Nov., 30 Nov., 2 Dec., 4-5 Dec., 25 Dec.

1847: 14 Jan., 5 Feb., 15 Feb., 17 Feb., 24 Feb., 1-2 Mar., 10 Apr., 14-15 Apr., 26 Apr., 28 Apr., 5-7 May, 10-11 May, 13 May, 15 May, 17-21 May, 8 Jun., 13 Jun., 16 Jun., 19 Jun., 24 Jun., 26 Jun., 29 Jun., 3 Jul., 9 Jul., 12-13 Jul., 19-23 Jul., 27 Jul., 25-26 Aug., 7 Sep., 11-13 Oct., 25-28 Oct., 9 Nov., 17 Nov., 2 Dec., 15 Dec.

1848: 13 Jan., 31 Jan., 1 Feb., 22 Feb., 6 Mar., 12 Mar., 14-17 Mar., 18-19 Apr., 25 Apr: *My son rode from Stanway to see us: poor Sophy was unable to accompany him, as she is suffering from tooth-ache, and a swelled face.* 8 May, 11-12 May, 27 May, 3-16 Jun., 29-30 Jun., 4 Jul: *... when we received the very sad intelligence brought by a servant from Stanway in a note from my Son, that his beloved wife was thrown from her horse yesterday, had fallen violently on her head, and suffered a concussion of the brain.* 5 Jul: *Wrote to E.F.W.—sent our groom with my letter, who brought back a very satisfactory report of our dearest Sophy's state; she has rallied wonderfully ...* 7 Jul: *Drove with M.W. to Stanway and back; remaining at the Vicarage for two or three hours, chiefly in the company of my son, and his dear children; but our beloved Sophy was well enough to pass an hour with us.* 13 Jul., 18 Jul., 21 Jul., 26 Jul., 1 Aug., 10 Aug., 13 Aug., 16-18 Aug., 26 Aug., 6-7 Sep., 9 Sep., 24 Oct., 20-21 Nov.

1850: 4 Jan., 17 Jan., 24-25 Jan., 6 Feb., 18 Feb., 27 Feb., 1 Mar., 13 Mar., 19 Mar., 21 Mar., 26 Mar., 2 Apr: *Poor Sophy had been suffering from one of her periodical headaches, but in the Evening had thrown it off.* 4 Apr., 13 Apr., 16-17 Apr., 19 Apr., 21 Apr., 24-26 Apr., 8 May, 13 May, 21 May, 23 May, 27-28 May, 30-31 May, 5 Jun., 22 Jun., 11 Jul., 16 Jul: *... A pleasant party; music and singing in the drawing room; our dear Sophy being the most skilful performer.* 18-20 Jul., 24 Jul: *Wrote to E.F.W. ... threw out an enquiry whether Sophy would wish me to purchase the cottage Piano-forte to be sold at Mrs. Perkins's sale next week.* 25 Jul., 1 Aug., 16 Aug., 21 Aug: *My dear daughter could not accompany her husband, as she was suffering from a bad headache.* 3-4 Sep., 9 Sep., 14 Sep., 16 Sep., 21 Sep., 1 Oct., 9 Oct: *... letter from E.F.W. with the pleasant information that the Sea-air or bathing, or both, seem to have abated, if not removed, our dear Sophy's headache.* 22-23 Oct., 30 Oct., 1 Nov., 12 Nov., 25 Nov., 27-29 Nov., 7 Dec: *Sophy also has been incommoded by decaying teeth ...* 28 Dec.

1851: 6 Jan: *Dear Sophy continues to have a recurrence of headache, which we had hoped the Sea air and sea-bathing had entirely removed.—She is taking the advice of Mr. Copeland, a surgeon at Cheltenham.* 7-9 Jan., 4 Feb., 12-13 Feb., 20 Feb: *Received a letter from E.F.W. ... though he has been suffering from cold, and Sophy from head-ache.* 24-28 Feb., 1 Mar., 31 Mar., 2 Apr., 4 Apr: *Poor Sophy had been suffering in the morning by one of her sad periodical headaches, but had rallied by mid-day ...* 5 Apr., 22-24 Apr., 9 May, 13 May.

1852: 17 Jan., 20 Jan: *Poor Sophy suffered till luncheon time by an attack of her periodical and somewhat inexplicable bad headaches ...* 22 Jan., 27 Jan., 30 Jan., 6 Feb., 9 Feb: *Dear Sophy looks pale & fatigued with watching & nursing, and loss of customary air and exercise.* 17 Feb., 19 Feb., 8 Mar., 17 Mar., 25 Mar., 30 Mar., 12-13 Apr., 15-17 Apr., 24 May, 27-29 May, 1 Jun., 4 Jun., 27 Oct: *My dear children came from Stanway to stay till Friday, and to accompany me to dine at Eyford.... Sophy sang solos and duets with James Wynniatt ...* 28-29 Oct., 31 Oct., 1-2 Nov., 10-14 Nov., 16-17 Nov., 19-20 Nov., 22-23 Nov., 24 Nov: *Sophy had a slight attack of her periodical head-ache ...* 1 Dec., 16 Dec., 22 Dec., 24 Dec., 27 Dec: *My dear daughter in law has been suffering very much of late from Ear ache ending in abscesses; the pain has been very great, and rest much disturbed; & another abscess seems to be ripening to maturity. This is very sad; duty calling her to the sick room, and exposure to external air in travelling to and fro from Stanway being very prejudicial—Mr. Vavasour's state appears very serious ...*

1853: 1 Jan: *My messenger from Stanway brought me a letter from my Son, who gives but a sad report of poor Sophy's sufferings from Ear-ache, by which she is still harassed, and greatly distressed at her inability to visit her parents.* 10-14 Jan., 19 Jan., 25 Jan., 27 Jan: *The last sad scene is over. Mr. Vavasour breathed his last between 3 & 4 AM ... He & Sophy retired to bed at half past 11 P.M.—were called at half past 3 AM. and were present when the awful moment came which recalled the spirit to its maker.* 2 Feb: *... Sophy, not visible, & under the influence of head ache ...* 8 Feb: *She has been suffering from head-ache, restless and unrefreshing sleep, and depression of spirits caused not only be grief for the loss of her Father, but for the approaching separation from her dear boy, Freddy, just about to go to school for the first time.* 16 Feb., 7 Mar., 9-12 Mar., 28 Mar., 15 Apr., 9-10 May, 13 May, 19 May: *Letter from E.F.W., on the whole satisfactory: written after a long interview with Sir H. Holland, who entered fully into Sophy's case, and pronounced that there is no organic mischief, no injury of the brain, the headaches arising from something wrong with a superficial nerve: in fact, neuralgia is the complaint, and likely in time to wear off.* 9 Dec.

1854: 28 Jan., 22 Feb., 1 Mar: *I grieve to say poor Sophy was attacked with a very bad headache last Friday ...* 6 Mar., 20 Mar., 23 Mar., 25 Mar., 5 May, 22-23 May, 24 May: *Poor Sophy suffered from one of the bad headaches to which she is subject, but rallied, and recovered by 4 P.M.* 27 May, 29 May, 31 May, 1 Jun., 14 Jun: *Last week they spent 47 hours in Town, that Sophy might consult Sir Henry Holland, who considered that, as regards the neuralgic affection to which she is subject, there is no change for the worse, and that the same palliatives and course of treatment already observed ought to be persevered in ...* 18 Jun: *Before my note was dispatched, received one from my Son, acquainting me that, as Sophy was suffering sadly from toothache and face ache, their coming hither must be postponed till Tuesday.* 20 Jun., 29 Jun: *Poor Sophy has been very much reduced in strength by her late attack of swelled face and tooth-ache ...* 4 Jul: *And towards 6 P.M. came my son and daughter in their carriage, Sophy having recovered from one of her periodical head-aches, which had visited her early in the day.* 6 Jul., 8 Jul., 14 Jul., 15 Jul: *... Poor Sophy very much indisposed, with an inflamed sore throat, diarrhoea, and bad cold. Confined to her bed, and visited by the Medical man from Winchcomb, who, I trust, may soon restore her to her usual health.* 2 Aug., 4-5 Aug., 7-9 Aug., 11 Aug: *Poor Sophy unwell in the morning—She has not recovered all her strength since a bad attack of pain in the face sometime ago, accompanied with diarrhoea, and has lost flesh and appetite. I fear she and Edward exert themselves too much in riding, strong exercise, and the engagements of society: they need more repose.* 12 Aug., 14 Aug: *Sophy looks thin, but says she is quite well, and is in good spirits.*

WITTS — Francis Edward Broome Witts — *grandson — see also* Woodroffe [206]

Francis Edward Broome Witts (1840-1913), Church of England clergyman, was the eldest son of Edward Francis Broome Witts (1813-1886) and Sophia Vavasour (1815-1871). He was educated at Rugby School and Trinity College, Oxford (BA 1861, MA 1865), and entered the Church. He was vicar of Temple Guiting, Gloucestershire, 1866-80; vicar of Norton, 1880-86; patron, rector, and lord of the manor of Upper Slaughter, 1886-1913; rural dean of Stow-on-the-Wold, 1891-1913; and canon of Gloucester Cathedral. He married, 1875, at Weston-sub-Edge, Margaret Hole, née Bourne (1848-1921), daughter of George Bourne (1821-1901) and Jane Hole (1825-1854); they had 5 sons and 3 daughters:

1 Margaret Apphia Broome (1876-1969); married, 19 April 1899, George Frederick Woodroffe (1855-1938), *see* Woodroffe

2 Edith Jane Bourne (1877-1963); travelled to South Africa, 1920, to visit her brother Edward, farmer and resident there; returned to England with Edward on board SS *Ingria*, travelling first class, arriving at Southampton in December 1920; by 1939 lived at Hillesley House, Hillesley, near Wotton-under-Edge, Gloucestershire, with her unmarried brother George, recently widowed sister Margaret, and cousin Louisa M. Bourne; died unmarried

1 Edward Francis Broome (1879-1956), army officer and farmer in South Africa and later Upper Slaughter; educated at Eton College and Merton College, Oxford; sailed to England from South Africa in 1915 aboard SS *Briton*, risking German submarines; served as a lieutenant in the 2nd Volunteer Battalion, Gloucestershire Regt; returned to South Africa after the war but came back to England with his sister Edith

in 1920 (whether this was a short break or a permanent return is not clear but electoral registers show that Edward had returned permanently to England by at least 1929); lived at Upper Slaughter Manor with his unmarried sister Agnes by 1939; died unmarried

3 Agnes Edna Broome (1880-1968); served during the First World War in the Voluntary Aid Detachment; awarded the British War Medal and Victory Medal; lived at Upper Slaughter Manor with her brother Edward; died unmarried

2 George Bourne (1883-1958), Capt.; educated at Marlborough College; served as ARP warden from 1939; lived at Hillesley House, Hillesley, with his sister Edith, widowed sister Margaret, and cousin Louisa M. Bourne; died unmarried

3 John [Jack] Travell (1885-1954), Maj.; educated at Rugby School; married, at Rome, 1918, Gulielma Ewart Richardson (1891-1976); lived at 198a Warrington Terrace, Maida Vale, Westminster, in 1922, and at Sandford Mill House in the parish of Woodley and Sandford, Berkshire, by 1925

4 Frank (1887-1941), Brig.; educated at Radley College and Trinity College, Oxford (1906); received a temporary commission in the Irish Guards in August 1914, made permanent in 1916; served in France with distinction throughout the First World War: mentioned in dispatches three times, wounded three times, awarded the MC (1 November 1917) and DSO (2 June 1919). Given the following appointments between the wars: staff officer, Portsmouth and London, 1919-26; deputy assistant adjutant and quartermaster-general, London district, 1926-29; chief instructor at the Royal Military College, Sandhurst, 1930-33; commanding officer, 1st Battalion, King's Own Royal (Lancaster) Regt, 1933-35; assistant quartermaster-general, HQ Aldershot Command, 1935-37; aide-de-camp to George VI from 1939. Commanded the 8th Infantry Brigade, 1937-40, during operations in the battle of France, and served as area commander, Glasgow, from 1940. Married, at Satterthwaite, Cumberland, 17 August 1919, Ruth Leonide (1892-1971), daughter of Harold Brocklebank of Grizedale Hall, Cumberland, and of Twyford, Hampshire; died aged 54 of heart failure; buried at Buchanan churchyard, Stirlingshire

5 Frederick Vavasour Broome (1889-1969), Maj.-Gen.; educated at Radley College; passed into RMA Woolwich aged 16 and commissioned into the Royal Engineers, 1907. Joined 4 Co. Bengal Sappers and Miners and served with distinction during the First World War in France and Mesopotamia; commanded No. 2 Mobile Bridging Train during the bridging of the Tigris at the Shumran Bend on 23 February 1917, a major turning-point in the campaign; awarded the MC, DSO, and croix de guerre, and mentioned three times in despatches; between the wars saw active service in Kurdistan, Iraq, Shanghai, and Palestine, and during the second was deputy chief of the general staff of the BEF and later GOC, Southern Army, India. After retirement served as lieutenant-governor of the Royal Hospital, Chelsea, 1948-57. Married, 1929, Alice, eldest daughter of the late Arthur Wrigley, JP, of Wyck Hill, Gloucestershire; 1 son and 3 daughters; buried at Upper Slaughter

1 Alice Margaret (b. 1931)

2 Elizabeth Mary Broome (b. 1933)

3 Diana Katherine (1936-2006)

1 Francis Edward Broome (b. 1941)

Francis Edward Broome Witts died on 18 August 1913, at Unterschächen, Switzerland, and was buried at Upper Slaughter.

1840: 18 Mar: *M.W. and I went in the close carriage after breakfast to Stanway, to the christening of our grandchild.* 19 Mar., 25 Mar., 31 Mar., 16 Apr: *Arrived at Stanway by mid-day, where most kindly received by my dear children, whom with their delightful babe I found quite well ...* 23 Apr., 26-27 Apr., 29 Apr., 8-9 May, 14 May, 18 May, 20 May, 22 May, 30 May, 2 Jun., 12 Jun., 20 Jun., 22 Jun., 24 Jun., 28 Jun., 6-7 Jul., 18 Aug., 25 Aug., 7 Sep., 9 Oct., 12-13 Oct., 18 Oct., 26-28 Oct., 2 Nov., 6 Nov., 15 Nov., 30 Nov.

1841: 26 Feb: ... *Broome is still suffering slightly from a cough and cold.* 3 Mar.

1842: 9 Jan., 17 Jan., 19 Jan., 29 Jan., 31 Jan., 3 Feb., 10 Feb., 15 Feb., 19 Feb., 21 Feb., 24-26 Feb., 4 Mar., 8 Mar., 12 Mar., 17-18 Mar., 22 Mar., 7 Apr., 29 Apr., 5 May, 13 May, 17 May: *Dear Broome in high health and spirits.* 30-31 May, 1-2 Jun., 4 Jun., 8 Jun., 16 Jun., 20 Jun., 24 Jun., 6 Jul., 16-17 Jul., 22 Jul., 30 Jul., 8 Aug., 13 Aug., 22-27 Aug., 6-15 Sep., 20 Sep., 24-30 Sep., 6 Oct., 10 Oct., 1 Nov., 13-17 Nov., 24 Nov., 1-3 Dec., 26 Dec.

1843: 4-5 Jan., 9 Jan., 26 Jan., 31 Jan., 12 Aug., 16-18 Aug., 28 Aug., 18 Sep., 24 Sep., 27 Sep., 3-4 Oct., 7 Oct., 19 Oct., 23 Oct., 25 Oct., 27-28 Oct., 20 Nov., 27 Nov., 24 Dec., 26 Dec: *Our darling Broome delights in his new brother, and is in fine health and spirits.* 29 Dec.

1844: 6 Jan., 11 Jan., 24 Jan., 29 Jan., 31 Jan., 6 Feb., 19-21 Feb., 22 Feb: ... *the children both coughing; Broome severely affected: doubtless with the hooping cough.* 26 Feb., 29 Feb., 4 Mar., 7 Mar., 15 Mar., 20-21 Mar., 26 Mar., 2 Apr., 9 Apr., 15-16 Apr., 18 Apr., 23 Apr., 27 Apr., 3 May, 10 May, 13-15 May, 23-24 Jul., 26 Jul., 30-31 Jul., 1 Aug., 14 Aug., 17 Aug., 20-21 Aug., 31 Aug., 3 Sep., 9 Sep., 18 Sep., 20 Sep., 24 Sep., 2 Oct., 9-12 Oct., 18 Oct., 28 Oct., 31 Oct., 7 Nov., 15 Nov., 18-21 Nov., 28 Nov., 16 Dec., 26 Dec.

1845: 14-19 Jan., 31 Jan: *The birth-day of my darling grandson Broome—GOD bless him!* 4 Feb., 8 Feb: *In the village met our darling grandson Broome waiting for us, the picture of health, and beaming with glee on seeing us.* 4 Mar., 12 Mar., 15 Mar., 22 Mar., 12-13 Apr., 17 Apr., 21-25 Apr., 1 May, 3 May, 16 May, 20 May, 24 May, 2-3 Jun., 6-7 Jun.

1846: 21 May, 27 May: *Broome enjoyed his own special treat before we set out in a complete exhibition of Punch & Judy seen from the pretty garden of the hotel.* 30 May, 1 Jun., 13-14 Jun., 18 Jun., 24 Jun., 20 Jul., 3 Oct., 12 Oct., 30 Oct., 2 Nov., 16 Nov., 21-24 Nov., 30 Nov., 1-2 Dec., 4-5 Dec.

1847: 29 Jan: *Wrote to E.F.W:—also to my dear Broome to be received by him on his birthday—the 31st. Inst.* 1 Mar., 10 Apr., 15 Apr., 26-28 Apr., 3-7 May, 10 May, 13 May, 17 May, 19 May, 21 May, 8 Jun., 19 Jun., 24-26 Jun., 29 Jun., 3 Jul., 9 Jul., 12 Jul., 18 Jul., 22-23 Jul., 12-13 Oct., 25-26 Oct.

1848: 31 Jan: *The birth day of my beloved Grandson, Broome; he is this day eight years old: a very fine, healthy promising boy: may he be well brought up, and prove a blessing to all connected with him!* 1 Feb., 12 Mar., 15 Mar., 23 Mar., 18 Apr., 8 May, 11-12 May, 4-5 Jun., 9-16 Jun., 16 Aug., 18 Aug., 7-9 Sep., 24 Oct.

1849: 28 Dec: *The Stanway Packet also contained a very delightful letter to E.F.W. from Mr. Garratt, speaking in very affectionate and gratifying terms of our dear Broome, his excellent conduct in school, and his attention to his lessons.*

1850: 4 Jan., 17 Jan., 24-25 Jan., 1 Feb: *I omitted yesterday to mention the birth-day of our dear grandson, Broome, now ten years old: a very promising boy ...* 1 Mar., 22 Mar: *Received a letter from our dear Broome, with kind enquiry as to his poor Grandmother ...* 2-4 Apr., 9 Apr: *Wrote to dear Broome, to acknowledge the letter lately received from him by his poor Grandmother.* 17 Apr., 24 Apr., 3 May: *Procured for my dear grandson, Broome, a handsome Bible and prayer book, with index, Bagster's edition, handsomely bound in one volume ...* 7 May, 11 May, 22 Jun: *Great delight in seeing Broome who has brought an excellent character home from his school, together with a prize ...* 11 Jul., 19 Jul., 10 Aug., 21 Aug: *Darling Broome was taken back to school yesterday by his Papa, who liked much the new abode of Mr. Garrard at Park Hall, near Alcester.* 24 Aug., 26 Aug., 29 Aug., 31 Aug., 4 Sep: *Soon after 11 AM. set out on an excursion to Park Hall, to visit my dear Grandson, Broome. A Broadway fly with a pair of horses took dear Sophy, Freddy, and myself—E.F.W. rode thither and back.* 17-18 Sep., 28 Sep: *Drove in my open carriage to Broadway, to meet my darling Broome, coming to me for the Michaelmas holidays. The dear boy had arrived there before me, his father's servant having driven early from Stanway to Park Hall to bring him. He looked all health, and glee, and affection.* 29-30 Sep., 1-5 Oct., 9 Oct., 19 Oct., 21 Oct., 23 Oct., 30 Oct., 8 Nov., 16 Nov., 23 Dec., 26 Dec., 28 Dec.

1851: 6 Jan., 9 Jan., 15 Jan., 21 Jan., 4 Feb., 14 Feb., 18 Feb., 4 Mar., 11 Mar., 15 Mar., 19 Mar: *Received a letter from E.F.W. who was prevented from coming to attend at the Sessions yesterday, by intelligence received from Park Hall that our dear Broome had caught the measles.* 23-24 Mar., 27 Mar., 22 Apr., 24-25 Apr., 7 May, 10-11 May, 21-22 May.

1852: 16 Jan., 21-22 May, 2 Feb: *Visited by my dear grandson, Broome, who remained with me from 10 AM. till 3 P.M.* 17 Feb., 23 Feb., 20 Mar., 3 Apr., 7-8 Apr., 12 Apr: *Broome arrived on his poney, having gone to meet the foxhounds at Guiting.* 15 Apr., 17 Apr., 28 Apr., 4 May, 1 Nov., 3 Nov., 28 Nov., 16 Dec., 24 Dec: *The hounds met at Eyford, which brought dear Broome from Stanway to the meet, who after following them on his poney for two or three hours, found his way hither, and staid with me from 2 to 4 P.M.*

1853: 5-6 Jan., 10 Jan., 12-13 Jan., 25 Jan., 31 Jan., 2 Feb., 16 Feb., 18 Feb., 23 Feb., 2 Mar., 18 Mar., 28 Mar., 27 Apr., 13 May, 1 Jun., 26 Dec.

1854: 28 Jan., 13 Feb., 15-16 Feb., 30 Mar., 4 Apr., 14 Apr., 12 May, 31 May, 29 Jun: *My dear Broome also came home from Rugby, two days before he was expected, with a bad cough, which has hung on him for a fortnight or more, caused by putting on his clothes when damp after bathing in a shower of rain: but he is said to be now going on well. He has brought home with him two prizes, one for good conduct, the other for good Latin composition.* 4 Jul: *My dear Grandson, Broome, preceded the rest of his family by riding from Stanway, and arrived in time for luncheon——He appears in very good health, but with the remains of a cough. The report of his conduct and progress in his studies from Rugby is, on the whole, very satisfactory.* 5 Jul: *My eldest Grandson very much absorbed with his newly acquired treasure, a fowling piece—with which he did much execution among the Small birds, and made one unlucky shot which demolished several panes of glass in my staircase window to his great discomfiture.* 6-7 Jul., 8 Jul: *The dear boy was in very high spirits, having enjoyed shooting with his Uncle's leave near the Lower Slaughter coppices, and killed three or four couple of rabbits.* 11-12 Jul., 15 Jul: *Broome very much pleased with his success in gunnery, having killed this forenoon a hawk and a jay.* 26 Jul: *Agreeably surprized by a visit from my dear Grandson Broome, who kindly came to pass the day and sleep here, bringing messages from his Parents as to their visit next week &c. The dear boy enjoyed himself much in holiday games and sports with E Clifford——who enjoyed the companion as much as if they were of the same age. Broome is very loving, intelligent and well mannered: much improved by being at a public school, I think I may say.———My spirits not very good, my health declining.—Yet I enjoyed much the visit of my Grandson.* 27 Jul., 29 Jul., 31 Jul., 1-2 Aug., 5 Aug: *After breakfast my son and Broome left us for Moreton in Marsh to be present at a Cricket Match between the Moreton & Broadway Cricket Clubs ... Broome returned to us about 9 P.M. full of glee, the Moreton players having beaten the Broadway eleven.* 6 Aug., 9 Aug., 11-12 Aug.

WITTS — Frederick Richard Vavasour Witts — *grandson*

Frederick Richard Vavasour Witts (1843-1900) was the second son of Edward Francis Broome Witts (1813-1886) and Sophia Vavasour (1815-1871). He was educated at Rugby School and entered upon a military career. He became a major and an honorary lieutenant-colonel of the 2nd Volunteer Battalion of the Gloucestershire Regiment. He married, at Lower Guiting, 18 October 1876, Margaret Anne (1843-1918), only daughter of John Waddingham of Guiting Grange, Gloucestershire. Frederick and Margaret had 3 daughters:

1 Sophia Margaret Vavasour Waddingham (1877-1959); married, 1920, as his second wife, Samuel Gray Richardson (1851-1934)

2 Mabel Elizabeth Vavasour (1878-1961); married, at Winchcombe, Gloucestershire, July 1910, John [Jack] Cheetham (1873-1959), son of Joshua Milne Cheetham (1835-1902) and Sarah Crompton (1833-1905)

3 Ethel Frances Vavasour (1881-1950); married, at Guiting Power, Gloucestershire, 9 August 1910, Capt. Howard John Kennard (1882-1967), son of Robert William Kennard (1858-1929) and Rose Nicholl Byass (1859-1948);); they had 2 sons and 2 daughters:

- 1 Robert William (1912-1979)
- 2 John Nicholl (1913-1957), Capt.
- 1 Susan Margaret Rose (1915-1982)
- 2 Maurice Nancy (1917-2002)

1843: 26 Dec: *Our darling Broome delights in his new brother, and is in fine health and spirits: the infant a remarkably healthy and fine child: to be named Frederick Richard Vavasour, after his maternal Grandfather.* 29 Dec.

1844: 6 Jan., 11 Jan., 24 Jan., 29 Jan., 31 Jan: *As soon as might be afterwards the whole family party went to Stanway to the christening of the dear infant.* 6 Feb., 20 Feb., 22 Feb., 26 Feb., 29 Feb., 4 Mar., 7 Mar., 15 Mar., 20-21 Mar., 26 Mar: *Glad should we have been had we found matters quite satisfactory there, but the dear infant, through straining incident to the hooping cough, had a rupture yesterday evening, and the alarm had a prejudicial effect on its dear mother's health.* 2 Apr: *Recd. two notes from E.F.W. one to inform us that, being dissatisfied as to the attendance of the Apothecaries at Winchcomb, he & Sophy had determined on going for a day to Cheltenham with the infant for the advice of Mr. Copeland, a Surgeon there, as to the rupture, truss &c....* 9 Apr., 15 Apr., 19 Apr: *Mr. Hayward called by appointment, and vaccinated the baby.* 23 Feb., 26 Apr: *Hayward came to visit the dear infant—from some cause or other the vaccination has not succeeded.* 27 Apr., 3 May, 10 May, 13 May, 15 May 27 May, 23-26 Jul., 30-31 Jul., 1 Aug., 14 Aug., 20-21 Aug., 31 Aug., 3 Sep., 9 Sep., 18 Sep., 20 Sep., 24 Sep., 2 Oct., 9-12 Oct., 18 Oct., 28 Oct., 31 Oct., 7 Nov., 15 Nov., 19 Nov: *Mr. Hayward rode from Stow, and reported favourably of our dear little Frederick, whom he vaccinated last week, and the infection has taken, promising well.* 20-21 Nov., 28 Nov., 16 Dec., 26 Dec: *They had visited*

Cheltenham with their children, chiefly that Mr. Copeland, a surgeon of repute there, whom they had consulted as to a rupture in the dear infant caused by great straining when suffering by the Hooping Cough should examine into that matter; who reported that as there was still a perceptible tendency to protrusion at the Navel, he should recommend a continuance of pressure on the part—by a bandage, as heretofore used.

1845: 14-15 Jan., 17 Jan., 19 Jan., 4 Feb., 8 Feb., 4 Mar., 12 Mar., 15 Mar., 22 Mar., 13 Apr., 17 Apr., 21 Apr., 25 Apr., 3 May, 20 May, 24 May: ... *Mr. Copeland, the Surgeon of Cheltenham, to whom they had taken little Frederick for an opinion whether they might safely disuse a truss on the navel, pronounced that it had better be continued for the present, as there was still a slight tendency to rupture.* 2 Jun., 7 Jun.

1846: 20 Jun., 24 Jun., 20 Jul: ... *but poor Freddy looks very ill, much reduced in flesh, and delicate, having suffered from an attack of influenza, as it would appear, or bad cold, attended with much inward fever.* 25 Jul., 3 Oct., 12 Oct., 16 Nov., 5 Dec., 19 Dec: *Dear Freddy's birthday— 3 years old.*

1847: 1 Mar., 23 Mar., 29 Mar., 10 Apr., 15 Apr., 26 Apr., 28 Apr., 3 May, 5-7 May, 10 May, 13 May, 17 May, 19 May, 21 May, 8 Jun., 19 Jun., 24 Jun., 26 Jun., 29 Jun., 3 Jul., 9 Jul., 12 Jul., 18 Jul., 22 Jul., 25 Oct., 28 Oct: *Mr. Hayward visited our dear grandchild Freddy professionally: poor little fellow, his bowels and liver are a little out of order, and he looks pale, suffers also from toothache.* 5 Nov.

1848: 12 Mar., 18 Apr., 8 May, 12 May, 10 Jun., 12 Jun., 15-16 Jun., 7 Sep.

1849: 19 Dec: *My dear Grandson, Frederick, this day six years old ...*

1850: 21 Jan., 27 Feb., 16 Apr., 19 Apr., 24-26 Apr., 23 May, 22 Jun., 11 Jul., 4 Sep., 12 Sep., 16 Sep., 12 Nov., 25 Nov.

1851: 21 Jan., 24-27 Jan., 8 Mar., 31 Mar., 22 Apr., 25 Apr., 10 May, 11 May: *The younger children of E.F.W and Sophy are by their marriage Settlement entitled to £3000 payable out of the settled Estates in the parish of Giggleswick, and to £2000 the amount of their Mother's fortune; while Sophy's jointure is fixed at £300 per ann. payable out of the Giggleswick property. I propose to settle on the younger children of the marriage £5000, payable on their father's decease, and £100 per ann. as an additional jointure to Sophy, should she survive her husband, and continue a widow... This scheme will ensure to the younger children of the marriage £10000.*

1852: 17 Jan., 21 Jan., 22 Jan: *Freddy had been feverish and had not slept well, and, though less heavy, shewd symptoms of the measles, which, no doubt, are coming to maturity in him ...* 25 Jan., 27 Jan: *A letter from dear Sophy, written very cheerfully, with a bulletin of dear Freddy's state; he is going on well, but the measles have attacked him more severely than his younger brother ...* 31 Jan., 9 Feb., 17 Feb., 1 Apr., 7 Apr., 17 Apr., 24 May, 22 Nov., 24 Nov: *My grandsons very happy, running for some hours after the fox hounds ...* 25 Nov.

1853: 10 Jan., 13 Jan., 25 Jan., 8 Feb: *She has been suffering from head-ache, restless and unrefreshing sleep, and depression of spirits caused not only be grief for the loss of her Father, but for the approaching separation from her dear boy, Freddy, just about to go to school for the first time.* 16 Feb., 2 Mar., 18 Mar., 28 Mar., 27 Apr: ... *and the boys were ailing of the Mumps: their parents about to visit them at Park Hall &c.* 13 May, 27 May, 23 Jun.

1854: 28 Jan., 13 Feb: *Freddy went to School on Saturday: Broome to go to Rugby on Friday next ...* 20 Apr., 21 Jun., 4 Jul., 7-8 Jul., 2 Aug., 7 Aug: *My son and daughter, with Freddy, arrived from Stanway to dinner and to conclude their visit to me ...* 12 Aug.

WITTS — George Backhouse Witts — *grandson*[208]

George Backhouse Witts (1846-1912), civil engineer, archaeologist and JP, was the youngest son of Edward Francis Broome Witts (1813-1886) and Sophia Vavasour (1815-1871). He was educated at Rugby School and became a distinguished archaeologist. He was the author of the *Archaeological Handbook of the County of Gloucester* (1883). He married, 8 June 1878, Sybil Catherine (1842-1926), born at Cowes, Isle of Wight, the only child of Richard Holdsworth of The Elms, East Woodhay, Hampshire. She had recently been divorced (May 1877) from George's cousin, Marmaduke Walter Vavasour (1833-1877), following a suit brought at Marmaduke's petition. Just five months after the divorce, Marmaduke committed suicide, although it appears that the jury at the inquest returned an open verdict.

In the 1891 census the Witts household at Hill House, Leckhampton, included Sybil's two children from her first marriage, Caroline Sybil Frances Vavasour (1863-1906) and Marmaduke Vavasour (1861-1902), an invalid. They both predeceased their mother, which must have been a devastating blow to her after such a troubled life. In their wills she was left £1,613, 8*s* 10*d* by her son and £6,469 16*s* 7*d* by her daughter. George and Sybil had 1 daughter:

1 Sybil Holdsworth (1880-1958), trained as a nurse at the General Hospital, Cheltenham, between 1914 and 1917. By 1927 she was single and living at Hillesley House, near Wotton-under-Edge, but shortly afterwards she married someone of the surname Smith and moved to 25 Warrender Park Terrace, Edinburgh. In 1934, having passed her examination in 1921, she registered in Edinburgh as a qualified nurse. The last nursing record that has been discovered relating to her is dated 1943. She died at the Cottage, Gifford, near Haddington, East Lothian. There were no children of the marriage.

1846: 25 Sep: *An early messenger from Stanway brought a letter from E.F.W. with the glad tidings that our dear Sophy had been safely delivered of a Son last evening; she had a good and a short time, and both the Mother and the infant are going on quite well.* 3 Oct: *The dear infant not so large a child as its elder brothers had been, at the same age, but a very lovely baby, perfectly healthy. It is to be name George Backhouse, the former name being given in memory of my deceased brother, the latter out of respect to the family family and maiden name of my dear wife.* 12 Oct., 30 Oct: *The party present were Mrs. W. Vavasour, Emma Vavasour, & Mr. Lefroy: my son performed the rite, his excellent wife and the promising children, Broome & Frederick, with my wife and myself, and the attendant nurses, were the rest of the congregation. I stood as proxy for Mr. Charles Barr, as one of the Godfathers, the other, the Revd. Mr. Ashworth, an uncle of my dear Sophy's, being the husband of her mother's sister, was represented by Mr. Lefroy.* 16 Nov., 2 Dec., 5 Dec.

1847: 1 Mar., 10 Apr: *E.F.W. rode over from Stanway to dine with us, remaining more than two hours: we had expected him and Sophy yesterday or to-day to pass the morning with us: he came to explain that they had been prevented by the serious illness of the Baby, who had been suffering from a violent cold and congestion of the lungs* ... 12-15 Apr., 26 Apr., 5-7 May, 10 May, 19 May, 21 May, 8 Jun., 19 Jun., 24 Jun., 26 Jun., 29 Jun., 3 Jul., 9 Jul., 12 Jul., 19 Jul., 25 Oct.

1848: 12 Mar., 18 Apr., 8 May, 12 May, 10 Jun., 24 Sep: *To day is the birthday of my youngest grandson; he is a noble and promising boy, now entered on his third ...*

1850: 27 Feb., 16 Apr., 19 Apr., 26 Apr., 23 May, 31 May, 22 Jun., 11 Jul. 12 Sep., 16 Sep., 25 Nov., 24 Dec., 27 Dec: ... *leaving dear Georgy as my companion, who returned to Upper Slaughter in my phaeton with his Grandpapa, and Grandmamma Vavasour ...*

1851: 28 Feb., 8 Mar., 31 Mar., 22 Apr., 25 Apr., 10 May, 11 May: *The younger children of E.F.W and Sophy are by their marriage Settlement entitled to £3000 payable out of the settled Estates in the parish of Giggleswick, and to £2000 the amount of their Mother's fortune; while Sophy's jointure is fixed at £300 per ann. payable out of the Giggleswick property. I propose to settle on the younger children of the marriage £5000, payable on their father's decease, and £100 per ann. as an additional jointure to Sophy, should she survive her husband, and continue a widow... This scheme will ensure to the younger children of the marriage £10000.*

1852: 16-20 Jan., 22 Jan., 31 Jan: *Recd. a letter from E.F.W. brought from Stanway by the carter with a load of coal; both Freddy and Georgy are confined to the house by the delicacy consequent on the measles ...* 2 Feb., 6 Feb: *I hope the dear little George is in a way to recover; but he has had a severe attack of fever with enlargement of the submaxillary glands, and is very much reduced in strength.* 9 Feb., 12 Feb: *A letter from E.F.W. with a satisfactory account of dear George: the tumour under the Jaw has so far matured, as to admit of its being lanced, and discharge matter; and the dear boy seems greatly relieved.* 17 Feb., 1 Apr., 7 Apr., 17 Apr., 24 May, 22 Nov., 24-25 Dec.

1853: 10 Jan., 25 Jan., 7 Mar., 9-12 Mar., 28 Mar., 9 May, 13 May, 26 Dec.

1854: 28 Jan., 6 Mar., 20 Mar., 23 Mar., 20 Apr., 22 May, 27 May, 1 Jun., 4 Jul., 7-8 Jul., 2 Aug., 9 Aug., 12 Aug.

WITTS — Broome and Amelia Witts — *uncle and aunt*[209]

Broome Witts (1744-1827), landed proprietor, was born at Chipping Norton, Oxfordshire, the eldest son of Broome Witts (1713-1768) and Apphia (±1719-1760), born at Hackney, Middlesex, daughter of Edward Anthony (b. 1700). His parents had married at All Saints', Edmonton, Middlesex, on 25 June 1741. Broome married, at St Michael's, Queenhithe, London, 20 March 1772, Amelia (1743-1832), daughter of Edward London (b. 1710) and Elizabeth Phillips (b. 1710), both of the parish of St Michael Queenhithe, a Christopher Wren church in the City of London [now Upper Thames Street] that was demolished in 1876. At the time of his marriage, Broome was living in London in the parish of St Margaret Moses, a church which stood on the east side of Friday Street but was never rebuilt after it was destroyed by fire in 1666. He was therefore clearly with the Wittses of Friday Street and was presumably at that time in business with the family. His later activities, however, are something of a mystery. We discover from the diaries of Agnes Witts that by January 1791 he had taken possession, under a tenancy, of Nibley House, a Georgian mansion in North Nibley, Gloucestershire, with an accompanying farm.

In a letter written by Edward Witts to his sister Apphia, Lady Lyttelton, in March 1793, Edward said the following of their brother:

> My Brother Broome, came yesterday to me, by my desire: but his Visit turned out the very reverse, of what I expected. & whatever feeling you discoverd in his mind on the occasions, that arose when you was at Nibley—it was all evaporated before he came under my Roof: as instead of Sympathy or compassion—, he seemed to regret that our settled income was so secured, as to prevent him the effect of Bankruptcy. in truth that is all we have left; & tho' I asked him to be a Trustee to my Affairs, he said very calmly, he was so little of a Man of bussiness that he hardly ever choze to put pen to paper.—His contempt of the World, from having restored a once broken fortune, ought not to have appeard in a House of distress ...

Quite what fortune was broken is enigmatic, but Broome and Amelia, although childless, lived in a state of considerable comfort. On 23 December 1801, Edward, Agnes, and their eldest son, Francis (the diarist), were staying with Broome and Amelia at Nibley. In another rare surviving letter addressed to his sister Apphia, Edward reveals some interesting snippets of information:

> Nothing can be more gratifying to my Wife & myself than the Conversation of Mrs. Witts—whose strong good Sence, equal Spirits, & open & Candid Heart is a treat not often met with. for want of Society—good & honest as my Brother is, he is got very saturnine—and I am sorry to find dislikes the Country & his Neighbourhood—& laments his having taken it.—his Farm is the only occupation, & very usefull & successfull it proves—but his Hospitality and good Cheer, will fatten us all—you will not wonder when he tells me, his Butchers Bill only—is 150£ a year. they are both wonderfully surprised and attached to Frank, & are incessant in their kindness to him on all occasions—He has had many Rides & explored the Country—& one Skaiting day on the Saturday—in this Neighbourhood.

What benefit Broome may have achieved if Edward had gone bankrupt is unclear, but as Edward did at last succumb to bankruptcy three years later, we can only assume that Broome was the gainer—but in what manner remains tantalisingly obscure. The fact that Broome later paid for some of his nephew Frank's university education may be part of the answer. See pages 106-110 of volume 1 for more detail. In 1802 Broome Witts was able to exit from the tenancy at North Nibley, and he moved to Cookham in Berkshire.

1801: 26 Nov: *Left Cheltenham, after an early breakfast, for my Uncle's Mr. Witts's at Nibley, in a Hack Chaise with my Mother.* 29 Nov: *I did not go in the Evening to Wooton where Mr. & Mrs. Witts & my Mother went to Mr. R. Hill's Tabernacle.* 2 Dec: *Rode out with Mr. Witts, thro' a valley in Nibley Parish, the Hills enclosing which are very beautifully interspersed & clothed.* 3 Dec: *Rode with my uncle in the vale; first to Berkley. This town lies low; it is, however, rendered observable by being the scene of feudal grandeur demonstrated in Lord Berkley's venerable Gothic Castle ...* 6-8 Dec., 12 Dec: *Walked with my Uncle & Father to the Top of Nibley Nole, which commands a fine view over the adjacent Country: back thro' Lord Berkley's Beech woods.* 16 Dec., 18-19 Dec., 24 Dec: *Rode with my Uncle to Wotton.* 25 Dec., 27-28 Dec., 31 Dec.

1802: 13 Feb., *Wrote to Mrs. Witts of Nibley ...* 24 Feb., 9 Jul: *Heard from my Parents. Wrote to Mr. Witts of Nibley.* 14 Jul., *Heard from Nibley & wrote an answer.*

1805: 27 Mar: *Heard from Mr. B. Witts & replied to him ...* 2 Aug: *... posted through Benson Henley & Maidenhead: to my Uncle Witts's beautiful little place the Retreat: upon the Banks of the Thames; facing the Cliefden Woods ...* 3 Aug: *After breakfast & another animated conversation with my Uncle left his pretty little retreat with little regret, though with feelings rather embittered ...* 15 Aug: *Wrote to Mr. Witts of the Retreat ...* 3 Oct: *Wrote to my Uncle Broome ...*

1806: 21 Jul: *Wrote to my Uncle Witts.* 30 Jul: *Heard from Mr. Witts of Cookham ... Wrote to Mr. Witts.*

1825: 27 Jun: *This was the day fixed for commencing our visit to my uncle Witts; it is nearly three years since we were at Cookham Grove ... Both Mr. & Mrs. Witts are broken in appearance since we saw them; the former more than the latter; both having passed the limit of fourscore ... On the Berkshire side are some very elegant ornamented cottages with gardens; besides a handsome villa, the*

Retreat, which my Uncle formerly occupied before he made the purchase of Cookham Grove, where he has now resided for nineteen years. 29 Jun: *crossing by Cookham ferry, which is a lively feature in the view from my Uncle's house, & being his own property, managed under his own eye by servants, is no source of annoyance, though the windows of the sitting rooms closely border on the banks of the river ... and endowed with several estates in the parish; the founder placed the whole under the superintendance of the Fishmonger's company in London. My Uncle has for several years acted as representative of the Company, affording his gratuitous services in the payment of the stipends of the pensioners, letting the farms, receiving the rents &c.* 3 Jul: *My Aunt resorted to her usual place of worship at Maidenhead, a meeting of Presbyterian Dissenters, to which sect she belongs; whither my uncle usually accompanies her, except on the first Sunday in each month, when he receives the Sacrament in our Church.* 9 Jul: *We took leave of our kind host & hostess on our return home ...*

1827: 28 Apr: *On reaching home we found a letter from my Aunt Mrs. Witts, from Cookham Grove, communicating the very precarious state of my Uncle: it seems, that he has been seized with a spasmodic asthma, accompanied with some disease of the bladder, his legs swelling &c.* 11 Jun: *I left home on a visit to my Uncle at Cookham Grove ... My aunt seems better than she was two years ago: calm, though very anxious, viewing things as they are, and resigned through a long rooted and firm faith in the divine promises.* 16 Jun., 22 Aug., 14 Nov: *We were on the point of setting out for Stanway on a visit to Lady Elcho, when we received the melancholy information of the death of my Uncle.* 17 Nov: *After breakfast my Aunt received me in her dressing room, supported wonderfully, collected and calm beyond expectation: but she is under a strong excitement ...* 18-19 Nov.

1829: 11 Feb: *In a letter, which I received this day from Mr. Wellford, a very indifferent account is given of my Aunt, Mrs. Witts....* 13 Mar., 24 Aug.

1830: 28 Feb: *Mrs. Rodick, before she died, had just written to Mrs. Witts, to say, that she would come on a given day to Cookham grove, to visit her for a fortnight, or during the necessary stay of her husband in town: my Aunt will feel the shock severely, but she will bear it with calm & Christian fortitude.*

1832: 11 Feb: 20 Mar: *I received from my friend Wellford a letter, apprizing me of the very serious indisposition of my Aunt, Mrs. Witts, of Cookham Grove. She has been unwell for a fortnight, and the symptoms are such as to create very alarming apprehensions. At her very advanced age, nearly ninety, if I am not mistaken, her life cannot be very long protracted ...* 25 Mar., 8 Jun: *Letters had arrived this morning from Cookham Grove and Bray, written by Mr. B. P. Witts and George Wellford, announcing the death of my Aunt Mrs. Witts at Cookham on the evening of Tuesday the 6th....* 12-13 Jun.

1838: 14 Aug: *I had a few minutes conversation with Newmarch as to my private concerns, viz. the Endorsement proposed to be made on our Marriage Settlt. to remedy an omission in the deed of appointment of new Trustees, in consequence of the decease of my Uncle B. Witts ...* 2 Nov.

1840: 26 Oct: *Wrote to Mr. Jennings in answer to the letter from him which arrived during my absence ... though not disposed to deviate from the letter of my Uncle's will, unless the advantage were very decided.*

1841: 1 Mar.

1842: 13 Feb: *... because it has been notified to him that his presence will be required before the Judges and Comm. of Lords on our private Bill, to testify that there are no direct descendants of my Uncle & Aunt Broome Witts.* 2 Mar., 15 Mar., 17 Mar., 4 Jun.

1843: 15 Sep: *Many years had elapsed, more than thirty, since M.W. and I had visited them with my Uncle Broome Witts, from Cookham ...*

WITTS — Richard Witts — *uncle* — *see also* Lee Steere Steere

Richard Witts (1747-1815) was the third son of Broome Witts (1713-1768) and Apphia Anthony (±1719-1760). Richard does not feature in the family business and his activities are something of a mystery. Family information is given on pages 124-130 of volume 1. Richard married Martha Steere (1755-1815), and they had 2 sons and 1 daughter:

1 Lee Steere (1774-1832); *see* entry for Lee Steere Steere
2 Richard (1775-1834)
1 Eliza (1777-1829); *see* entry for Daniel

Richard died a few days before 14 January 1815, the date Agnes Witts made the following sorrowful entry:

> More or less constant small rain or mist the whole of the day, which made it gloomy enough & was but too consonant with our feelings on receiving the melancholy tidings of the sudden Death of our Brother Mr. Richard Witts in London ...

Francis Witts gives more detailed family information in his diary entry for 17 November 1827.

1801: 1 Aug: *In the afternoon my uncle Richard came down, as did all the young men later.* 2 Aug: *Repaired with my Father, Mother, & Brother to the Chapel of Ease at Camberwell: the Service was moderately performed but the Organ gratified me much. My uncle Richard set out towards Hale.* 28 Aug: *My Uncle Richard breakfasted with us.*

1827: 17 Nov: ... *The remaining £500, 3 per Cent Red. Ann. are left under the same restrictions as the £1000 to Mrs. Rodick, to Mrs. Daniel, daughter of my late uncle, Mr. Richd. Witts, and wife of a Solicitor, who having been guilty in his profession of gross acts of dishonesty, has been compelled to expatriate himself, and lives, I think, somewhere in France. Poor Mrs. D., who is, I am inclined to believe, an estimable person, with bad health, resides at Lyme in Dorsetshire, on slender means, with two daughters, her only surviving children; a son, who had obtained a commission in the East India Company's military service, having fallen an early victim to the climate of the East. Mrs. Daniel is the only one of my Uncle Richard's family, whom my Uncle has named in his will: Mr. Lee Steere, the eldest Son, took with the fortune, which was very ample, the name of his maternal grandfather, & has been from the period of his coming of age alienated from his father's family: having been at variance with his Father, who was an incautious man, and having, more through carelessness than any improper motive, failed to keep regular accounts of expenditure on his Son's account during his minority subsequently to his grandfather's decease, was unable to render such a statement as was satisfactory to the interested advisers of the young man, who had yielded himself to their guidance, & who succeeded in detaching him from both his parents & indeed his whole family. Mr. Richard Witts, the second Son, had a very comfortable provision, but, with weak intellect, has been led step by step into low habits and mean connexions; and having contracted two marriages very disgracefully, now lives with reduced means, without respectability, and unnoticed by his connexions, at St. Albans.*

WITTS — John Witts — *first cousin — see also* Robert Townson

John Witts (1777-1857), officer in the Royal Marines, was born at Hemington, Surrey, the only son of John Witts (1751-1816) and Ann Townson (1756-1811). He served in the Royal Marines and ended his career with the rank of captain. John was a substantial beneficiary in 1828 from the estate of his uncle Robert Townson. In 1835 there was a further bequest of £5,000 to John and his sisters from John Townson (1759-1835), Robert's elder brother (*Australian Dictionary of Biography*).

John Witts married Maria Wood (±1780-±1855), born at Calcutta, Bengal, the elder daughter of William Wood (1745-1813), of Marsh Hall and Hanwood, Shropshire, and his wife, Esther (d. 1804). There were no children of the marriage. No record of Maria's death has been discovered, and she did not leave a will. The last mention of her by Francis Witts was in his diary entry of 21 April 1854:

> Received a letter from Apphia Witts, who seems pleased at my enquiry after the health of herself and her brother and his wife. It appears that John & Mrs. Witts I169 are in comfortable health, so much so as to be expected by Apphia to visit her at Shrewsbury. But she [Maria Witts] describes herself as a great invalid, confined to her drawing room and adjoining bed room: little likely to go to see her brother at Cruck Meole, very unequal to regular attendance at Church, but can hear and see.

John died in July 1857, by which time Maria was already dead, so she probably died in around 1855.

1812: 4 Aug: *We were disappointed of meeting here my Cousin John Witts, Capt. in the Marines, who commands a recruiting party at Lichfield, but he was with his friends at Lydleys Hays, when we passed through.*

1825: 29 Mar: *My cousin, Captain Witts, arrived to pass a day or two with us. He is brother of the Miss Witts's, being the only Son of my late Uncle, the Revd. John Witts, Vicar of Cardington in Shropshire. Captain Witts is on the half-pay of the Marines, having seen a great deal of hard service in early life. He was at the battle of Aboukir, & for many years in different ships on the Mediterranean Station, serving on land in Egypt, at Ischia &c.—he has experienced shipwreck, hard work, bad climates & the wear & tear of the profession to such extent, that he has the appearance of age and is, indeed, in delicate health. He is married, but has no family: his wife, a Miss Wood, of Shropshire, is also subject to wretched attacks of ill-health. They have lately been residing at Pickham Grove, in Great Malvern ...* 31 Mar: *Captain Witts left us again for Malvern.* 9 May: *My cousin John Witts, and his estimable, sickly wife, and his two sisters are like ourselves guests of our worthy aunt ...* 15 May, 17 May: *I took a very pleasant walk with John Witts across the Malvern Hills into Herefordshire ...*

1826: 31 Oct: *Our family party was increased by the addition of my Cousin Captain Witts and his wife. They had been spending the summer abroad, chiefly on the banks of the Rhine, at Bonn, Godesberg &c. and proposed remaining longer, when they were induced to return by the increasing infirmities and dangerous state of Mrs. J. Witts's brother, Mr. Wood, a Shropshire Gentleman, to whose residence they repaired, and have been staying some time there & at Mr. Warter's at Cruck Meole, near Shrewsbury.* 1 Nov: *Captain & Mrs. Witts left us to-day and returned to Malvern.*

1827: 24 May: *We were agreeably surprized by a visit from Captain Witts, which was not, indeed, wholly unexpected, as we had reason to think, he would call on us on his return from Berkshire, where he had been to see my Uncle.* 26 May: *John Witts left us for Malvern, having been absent from thence a month.* 11 Jul., 31 Jul: *My aunt received us with the utmost affection and warmth of feeling, and Captain & Mrs. Witts, still her immediate neighbours, soon joined us.* 1 Aug: *We passed the forenoon and till an early four o clock dinner in a delightful drive. Captain & Mrs. Witts, with Edward, accompanied me in the Phaeton ...* 2-4 Aug., 16 Oct., 17 Oct: *After going with my cousin Capt. Witts into the Gaol &c., we took our places in Court, but he was soon oppressed with the heat and crowd, and left me.* 18-19 Oct., 17 Nov: *Captain Witts arrived, while I was with my Aunt, from Malvern ...*

1828: 16 Jun: *Captain Witts, has been a great sufferer of late, but is now convalescent: at one time he was reduced very low, & put himself under the care of Mr. Carden, an eminent Surgeon, at Worcester, whose advice he is now following & gradually gaining ground ...* 17-19 Jun., 23 Jul: *Our friends, Captain and Mrs. Witts arrived from Malvern to pay us a short visit ...* 28 Jul: *... anxious to-day by a violent spasm in the abdominal viscera, which attacked John Witts ...* 29 Jul., 1 Aug: *Our friends Captain & Mrs. Witts left us after an early dinner, and intended to sleep at Witney ...* 24 Sep.

1829: 24 Aug: *We were joined at tea by my four cousins from the next door, Captain & Mrs. Witts and the Miss Witts's ...* 27-29 Aug.

1830: 19 Apr: *I was not long before I went to Montpellier Parade, in search of my cousins Captain & Mrs. Witts, who had been paying a visit for a few days to their friend & neighbour at Malvern ...* 20 Apr., 23 Apr.

1832: 14 Jun: *Wellford and myself proceeded in a fly to Cookham Grove to attend at the funeral of our departed friend. We there found the two Messrs. Witts, Broome & Edward, and my cousin John, who with his wife had arrived from Malvern, travelling in their open carriage ...*

1833: 10 Sep: *Captain Witts dined, accompanied by Jane & Emma Witts ...* 11-12 Sep.

1834: 28 Jul., 18 Aug., 23-24 Aug., 8 Sep: *Captain and Mrs. Witts, and my two Cousins, the Miss Witts's from their respective cottages, joined the party at dinner, after the return of the Bishop and his lady and children from Great Malvern ...* 9-12 Sep., 22 Oct: *My wife received a letter from Miss Witts, giving a very indifferent account of the health of Mrs. John Witts ...*

1835: 7 Jan., 1 Apr: *Mrs. Witts had received a letter from Miss Witts, who with her sister is now in Town, where the sisters are domiciliated with Capt. and Mrs. J. Witts. Of the latter a very indifferent account is given, her eye sight is nearly gone, and she is in a very debilitated and exhausted state of health ...* 22 Apr: *Received a letter from Miss Witts from Town, giving a very indifferent account of the general health of Mrs. John Witts, and, particularly, of her defect of sight ...* 19 May.

1836: 18 Jul: *The report from Hayes Bank of Mrs. J. Witts's state very unfavourable... suffering under an inflammatory attack, which had been a few hours before accompanied by convulsive spasms in the face ...* 19 Jul:
Went to Capt. Witts's and sat half an hour or more in Mrs. W.'s sick room with my four cousins. The invalid better than yesterday, the inflammatory symptoms having disappeared, but miserably reduced and exhausted ... 20-22 Jul., 23 Jul: *... whither it shall please GOD that I may see again my aged Aunt, or my cousin John's feeble wife, may well be doubted; the life of both seems to hang on a thread.* 31 Jul: *... Lady L. is languid, but that Mrs. J. Witts has recovered her ordinary state of health ...* 15 Aug., 28 Sep., 21 Oct., 28 Oct., 18 Nov., 24-25 Dec.

1837: 11 Jan., 21 Jan., 31 Jan., 1-3 Feb., 26 Apr., 8 Aug: *Capt. and Mrs. J. Witts came in their open carriage unexpectedly, about mid-day, on a journey from London to Malvern, having slept last night at Enstone.* 28 Nov., 1 Dec., 28 Dec.

1838: 23 Apr: *Capt. Witts in better health than usual ...* 17-19 Jul., 10-11 Aug., 14 Aug., 19 Sep., 2 Nov.

1839: 27 Jan., 20-21 Mar., 28 Jun: *To Mr. Jeaffreson, to request to be informed of the address of his son, the Oculist, that I might communicate it to Capt. Witts; poor Mrs. W., almost dark, still hoping against hope, and, though, from general ill health, almost unequal to be moved, clinging to the delusion that relief may still be had by consulting some new practitioner, of whom men speak favourably.* 29 Aug., 5 Sep: *We had just breakfasted when Capt. Witts made his appearance, having stumbled on our Servant, he learnt that we were here. It seems that John & his wife, with the Sisters Anne & Apphia have been occupying lodgings here since they left Clevedon. Mrs. W. till within these two or three days has greatly revived ...* 16 Jul., 5 Aug.

1840: 18 Mar., 1 Apr., 4 Apr., 12-15 Apr., 22-29 Apr., 8-10 May, 12 May, 18-22 May, 15 Jun., 22-24 Jun., 29-30 Jul., 5 Aug., 7 Aug., 11 Aug., 14 Aug., 20 Aug: *Recd. a letter from John Witts, communicating that his own and his wife's health is so indifferent at present, and that they are so much less well than when the arrangement was made, that they must reluctantly relinquish the intention of visiting us to morrow.* 21 Aug., 24 Aug: *Recd. a letter from John Witts, who now proposes with his wife to visit us this week, coming either on Wednesday, Thursday, or Friday evenings. Wrote by return of post to say we shall be happy to see them.* 26-28 Aug., 31 Aug: *Capt. Witts's phaeton returned from Stow repaired and refitted ...* 1 Sep: *Capt. and Mrs. Witts left us after breakfast to return to Malvern: they seemed to have enjoyed their visit, and the change appeared to have benefitted his health.* 4 Sep., 9 Sep., 11 Sep., 18 Sep., 29 Sep., 2 Oct., 24 Nov.

1841: 3 Mar.

1842: 15 Feb., 15-17 Mar., 14 May, 4 Jun., 13 Jun., 19 Jun., 22 Aug: ... *they met John Witts there, who looked very aged and shaken; Mrs. J. W. said to be quite blind: they are fixed for the present at Meole.* 29 Aug., 28 Sep., 14 Nov., 16 Nov.

1843: 12 Dec.

1844: 24 May, 30 May, 16 Sep., 25 Sep.

1845: 29 Jan., 9 Jul: ... *He did not live in the village, the Parsonage being then not a suitable residence, but rented a house at some little distance, Lydleys Hayes—where he brought up his family, of which my cousins John and Apphia were are the survivors—his wife was a Townson, Sister to a medical Gentleman of considerable scientific acquirements, much devoted to Geology, Botany, and Antiquarian pursuits: who, with a brother, settled in Australia soon after the Colony of Botany bay was founded; and, dying there, had acquired considerable property, which devolved upon my Cousins.* 10 Jul: ... *He partook of luncheon with us; and so also did John Witts, who had driven in from Cruck Meole to pass the day with us.* 11-12 Jul., 15 Jul.

1847: 11 Apr., 20 Apr., 1 Jul., 30 Aug., 6 Sep., 4 Oct., 22 Oct., 24 Dec.

1848: 3 Mar: *MW. recd. from Apphia Witts a tolerable report of her self, her Brother John, and Mrs. John Witts.*

1850: 2 Feb., 20 Apr.

1853: 9 Apr., 21 Apr: *It appears that John & Mrs. Witts are in comfortable health ...*

WITTS — Ann Witts and Apphia Witts — *first cousins*

Ann Witts (1775-1839) and Apphia Witts (1781-1859) were unmarried daughters of John Witts (1751-1816) and Ann Townson (1756-1811). They were sisters to Capt. John Witts. Ann died in October 1839 during a gap in Francis Witts's diaries, but Margaret Witts recorded the event in her small pocket book diary on Wednesday 16 October 1839: 'Heard of Miss Witts's death'.

1822: 5 Sep: *My cousins Ann & Apphia Witts came on a visit to us. They had left Cookham Grove, where they had been spending some time with their Uncle & Aunt Witts.* 8 Oct: *Miss Witts's left us for Gloucester, where they propose passing a little time in lodgings till Lady Lyttelton can receive them at Pickham Grove.* 17 Oct: *During my stay at Gloucester I frequently saw my cousins Anne & Apphia Witts, who were in comfortable lodgings.*

1823: 23 Aug.

1824: 1 Apr., 20 May, 20 Jun., 13-14 Jul., 19 Oct: *After dining with my brother Magistrates, I spent the evening with my worthy Cousins the Miss Witts's.*

1825: 28 Jan: ... *my cousins, the Miss Witts's came to tea: they have recently returned to Gloucester, having passed a few weeks at Bristol.* 9 May, 16 May, 17 Oct: *Our cousins, Miss Witts's, who have been spending the summer at the village of Hempstead near Gloucester, but are now fixing themselves in lodgings at the Spa, called in the evening.*

1826: 11 Jul., 5 Aug., 8 Aug., 31 Aug: *Walked with my cousins, Miss Witts's to their pretty village of Hempstead. They occupy for the summer apartments in a cottage, close to the grounds of the Mansion house ...* 11 Sep: *The Miss Witts's had removed from Hempstead into the lodgings engaged for Lady Lyttelton, which they will occupy with her, while she remains at Gloucester.* 12 Sep., 14 Sep., 27 Sep.,10 Oct: *Our cousins, the Miss Witts's arrived from Gloucester, to pass some time with us.* 2 Nov., 21 Nov: *Our good cousins, the Miss Witts's left us for Gloucester: after staying a day or two with Mrs. Backhouse they will go to their old lodgings at Hempstead till near Christmas ...*

1827: 7 Jan: *My cousins, the Miss Witts's, now lodging in Worcester Street, drank tea with us this evening ...*
14 Jan., 18 Jan., 2 Apr: *Our good cousins, Miss Witts's, now lodging very near to Wellington Parade ...* 9 Apr., 11 Jul., 15 Oct: *Miss Witts's came in after tea, having arrived from Hempstead, where they have been lodging during the summer, this afternoon, and taken apartments in Gloucester for a few weeks, Malvern, that is, Peachfield Lodge, being their winter destination.*

1828: 16 Jun., 19 Jun., 7 Oct., 13 Oct.

1829: 24 Aug., 27-28 Aug.

1830: 28 Feb: *A letter from my cousin Miss Witts, now staying with her sister in London, announces to me by the desire of Mr. Witts of Brunswick Square, the awfully sudden & unexpected death of his sister, Mrs. Rodick.*

1833: 10-12 Sep.

1834: 9 Mar: *Returning from church, found a letter from Anne Witts, apprising us of the decease of our Aunt Stone, some days since at Lacey Green.* 10 Mar., 12 Sep: *Walked with Apphia Witts to Great Malvern and back.* 22 Oct.

1835: 5 Jan: *The Misses Witts have been in lodgings here some days, on their way from Malvern to London.* 7 Jan., 9 Jan., 22-23 Apr., 19 May, 8-13 Jun.

1836: 18-20 Jul., 15 Aug., 28 Sep., 21 Oct., 28 Oct., 25 Dec.

1837: 31 Jan., 19 Mar., 20 Apr., 12 May, 10 Jun., 2 Jul., 3 Sep., 5 Nov., 28 Nov., 1 Dec., 4 Dec., 29 Dec.

1838: 19 Feb., 7 Apr., 23 Apr., 15 May, 6 Jul., 10 Jul., 16-19 Jul., 9 Sep., 19 Sep., 20 Oct., 9 Dec., 24 Dec., 28 Dec.

1839: 27 Jan., 1 May, 19 Jun: *I drove to Stanway ... and cordially greeted by my cousins Anne and Apphia Witts, who take up a great deal of room in the small apartments of the Vicarage, and seem highly delighted by the reception they have experienced from Edward ...* 24 Jun: ... *At home I found the Misses Witts arrived from Stanway, on a visit of a few days, having brought a good account of our children.* 25 Jun., 1 Jul., 5 Jul., 14 Jul., 29 Aug., 5 Sep: *It seems that John & his wife, with the Sisters Anne & Apphia have been occupying lodgings here since they left Clevedon ....*

1840: 8 Apr., 13 Apr: *The property at Peachfield Lodge with all the buildings, garden, orchards &c. is devised to me to hold, together with the furniture and moveables on and about the premises, till my son attains his 27th. year (which he has done) and then to be assigned to him absolutely, but as I conceive without any entail, yet subject to a limited interest as to Pear Grove Cottage, in favour of Ann & Apphia Witts, as long as they live unmarried. That interest is now vested in Apphia who may reside there, if she chooses, free of rent and widow window tax, or, if she do not wish to reside there, has a power of letting it, for not more than two years at a time ...* 15 Apr., 18 Apr: *Apphia Witts is now on a visit to Mrs. Shard.* 23 Apr: *Conferring on many points with reference to the funeral and to the affairs of my deceased Aunt, with Capt. Witts, Apphia, the Misses Daniell, A. & S. Gibbs &c* ... 24-29 Apr., 9 May, 18-22 May, 22 Jun: ... *dined at Hayes Bank Cottage with Capt. and Mrs. J Witts, meeting Apphia, and had much conversation with them on many points relating to the property, furniture &c. of our deceased Aunt.* 23-24 Jun., 29 Jul., 5 Aug., 4 Sep: *My cousin, Miss Witts, arrived from Malvern on a visit to us this evening.* 9 Sep: *My cousin Apphia left us this day after luncheon on her way to London, to settle herself in lodgings.* 11 Sep., 16 Sep: *M.W. recd. a letter from Apphia Witts, who had a good journey to Town, and has settled herself in lodgings at 31 Keppel Street, Russel Square.* 30 Sep., 5 Nov: ... *Mr. Thrupp had paid over, as had been agreed, to Apphia Witts, £130, in consideration of her interest in Pear Grove Cottage ...* 24 Nov.

1841: 3 Mar.

1842: 17 Jan., 24-25 Jan., 4 Feb., 15 Feb., 4 Mar., 7 Mar: *Apphia Witts arrived from Stanway about 3 ocl—having been on a visit to my son since Thursday ...* 10 Mar: *Apphia Witts left us after luncheon for Oxford, on her way to Town in a fly.* 15 Mar., 19 Mar: *Our first point was to Ormond Street, to visit Capt. and Mrs. Witts, and Apphia.* 14 May: *Capt. and Mrs. Witts returned to Salop, from Town, and Apphia Witts follows them soon.* 22 Aug., 28 Sep.

1843: 12 Dec: *A letter to M.W. from A. Witts gives the usual report of herself, brother, and sister in law, at Shrewsbury and Meole, all in an ailing state, but Apphia the stoutest of the three.*

1844: 30 May, 25 Sep.

1845: 29 Jan., 4 Apr., 4 Jun., 17 Jun., 8 Jul: ... *we had determined on travelling to Shrewsbury by Worcester, Ludlow &c., because we did not wish to arrive at Apphia Witts's till to-morrow afternoon ...* 9-11 Jul.

1846: 15 Jun: ... *to Mr. Mainwaring, informing him of the death of my cousin, Anne Witts, and giving him the address of Captn. Witts, and his sister Apphia.* 15 Jul.

1847: 20 Apr., 23 Apr., 1 Jul., 22 Oct., 7 Nov., 9 Nov., 24 Dec.

1848: 3 Mar., 23 Jun.

1850: 2 Feb., 11 Feb., 24 Feb., 19 Apr.

1853: 9 Apr., 21 Apr.

WITTS — Richard Parish Witts — *first cousin once removed*

Very little is known of Richard Parish Witts (1748-1828), but the diarist's entry for 25 August 1828 explains all that is relevant. Francis Witts's comments about 'a low, worthless person' do not do him credit; it appears he was piqued at fortunes passing to hands other than his own.

1828: 25 Aug: *I received tidings through Miss Witts of the decease of a distant relative, of whom I knew little during his life, and had seldom heard his name, though he was my first cousin fir once removed. Mr. Richard Parish Witts died on the 12th Inst. at Malling in Kent, aged 80 years, and he was, I understand, of late years at least, of unsound mind. He was son of an early elder brother of my Grandfather, a Richard, who married a Jane Parish; & he had freehold property, I believe, at Witney; it does not clearly appear, to whom this descends; from looking at the pedigree, I should say, his legal heir is Broome Witts, of Brunswick Square, as descendant of Edward, the elder brother of Richard: unless there are descendants of Edward by his eldest Son, Edward, entitled to inherit; but the account sent to me points out a person of the name of Wright, as heir at law. Mr. Richd. Parish Witts died unmarried, & by a will made in 1777, it seems, that he made his "next of kin" heirs of his personalty; this is construed to mean his next of kin at the time of his decease, in which case, my Aunts, Lady Lyttelton & Mrs. Stone, his only surviving first cousins, are entitled to his personalty, and as such were written to by some maternal relations of the deceased, representatives of the Executors named in that will, both of whom are no longer living. What the amount of the personalty may be, whether considerable or small, does not yet transpire. Mr. Broome Witts has tendered his services to my two Aunts to administer to the will & transact the business for them. In the meantime the poor deceased, agreeably to his desire expressed shortly before he died, and which coincided with the directions left in his will, was buried in the Meeting house yard at Witney by the side of his Father & Mother... Lady Lyttelton has not received any distinct account of the personal property left by her deceased cousin, Mr. R. P. Witts, & which Mrs. Stone and herself inherit. It now appears, that the deceased did not leave his personalty in his will to his nearest of kin; but that all or almost all of the numerous legacies, which he left, having lapsed, his personalty descends to my two Aunts, as nearest of kin, while his freehold estate falls to his Uncle Edward Witts's great grandson, being Son of his Cousin Edward (not my father) by a second marriage. The descendants of his Uncle Edward by his first wife, a Helen Wyld of Nottingham, are females, daughters of a daughter married to a Walford, consequently cannot inherit: but he had a Son by his second wife, a person of low condition & the Son by that marriage again having male issue the estate devolves on him. I fear, from what has transpired, that he is a low, worthless person.*

1829: 25 Aug: ... *and into that of Mrs. Stone, a sum of £2000 each, being the proceeds of the personal estate of their cousin Mr. R. P. Witts ...*

1838: 14 Jun: *It turns out to consist of two handsome old fashioned silver pint cups, having been a portion of the personalties which fell to the share of my Aunt Stone, a few years since, when she, together with Lady Lyttelton, as next of Kin, succeeded to the personalty of an old and almost forgotten collateral relation, Richard Parish Witts, who had lived and died among the descendants of his maternal relations in Kent.*

1840: 6 May.

1844: 4 Jan.

WITTS — Edward Witts — *first cousin once removed* [210]

Edward Witts (b. 1736) and his family make a complete line that was little known to the diarist and which has been previously ignored. The diarist's great-uncle, Edward Witts (1701-1754), had three other children in addition to Broome Witts (1738-1769), father of Broome Phillips Witts. They were as follows: Sarah (b. 1734); Edward (b. 1736); and Richard (b. 1740). Out of these three, our interest is with Edward, the eldest male Witts of the eldest line. He married, at Nottingham, 14 June 1757, Helen Wylde (b. 1737). She appears to have died quite young, but no record has been found.

Richard Parish Witts (1787-1833), baptised as an Anglican at St Mary's, Witney, 1 January 1788, is recorded as being the son of Edward and Mary Witts; this seems to be a second marriage, and the evidence is borne out by the diary entry for 28 August 1828. Mary therefore logically appears to have been the 'Widow Witts', of Friday Street in the City, referred to by the diarist.

Richard Parish Witts was born in the parish of St Mildred, with the parish church adjacent to Friday Street. It seems likely from this that the family was closely involved in the business followed by the Wittses of Witney. In 1802, at the age of 14 or 15, Richard was apprenticed in the silk industry to his first cousin Broome Phillips Witts. It seems quite logical that much of the business devolved from the elder Edward Witts (b. 1701) to his son Edward (b. 1736), who presumably worked with his nephew Broome Phillips Witts, and that on the demise of this second Edward, Broome Phillips Witts took over as the senior partner. At this time, if it had not happened already, he moved the business towards silk manufacture. If, however, the diarist is right, and the family had fallen low, this does not accord with Widow Witts being the property owner. It seems more likely that the inheritance had followed the normal course, but that the diarist and his parents disapproved of the marriage match between Edward Witts and Helen Wylde and cast aspersions. It is obvious from the events that occurred that neither Richard Parish Witts (senior) (1748-1828) nor Broome Phillips Witts distanced themselves from this branch of the family, and this is further proven by the list dinner guests of 16 March 1842.

Richard Parish Witts (1787-1833) married, at Sudbury, Suffolk, 28 May 1809, Frances (1788-1879), daughter of Thomas Goldsmith; they had seven children, including the following 2 sons and 4 daughters:

1 Richard Goldsmith (1809-1842); *see below*
1 Frances [Fanny] Horner (1812-1853); married, 1834, William Bernard Taylor (1812-1853); emigrated to Australia and died at Melbourne; at least 5 sons and 3 daughters:
    1 William Henry (1836-1853)
    2 Edwin Witts (1837-1878)
    1 Fanny (1838-1923)
    3 Charles Everett (1840-1923)
    2 Ellen Elizabeth (1840-1904)
    3 Emily (b. 1841)
    4 Frederick Richard (1843-1910)
    5 Septimus (1844-1907)
2 Emma Lydia (1816-1905); married, 1843, Thomas James Hanbury
2 Charles Augustus (1818-1910); *see below*
3 Ellen Mary (1819-1901); married, 1862, her cousin William Frederick (1818-1894)
4 Anne Elizabeth (b. 1822)

There is an interesting document that reads as follows: 'Fishmongers, at a Court, 1st August 1820, The within named apprentice Richard Parish Witts was made free by the Service to Broome Phillips Witts ...' It is difficult to know what to read into this. Richard had been apprenticed to B. P. Witts back in 1802, and a usual apprenticeship would have lasted five to nine years—for Richard, ending when he was 21 years old. It may have been that Richard's apprenticeship was being formally closed long after the actual termination date, or perhaps that he was joining his first cousin as a member of the Fishmongers' Company. Whatever the case, it seems that Richard had moved by this time to his wife's home town of Sudbury in Suffolk and taken up trade there.

Richard was presumably a godson of his uncle Richard Parish Witts (1748-1828), and this would explain his baptismal name. In the will of Richard (junior), proved in October 1833, the preamble states: 'Silk Manufacturer and wine and spirit merchant of Sudbury, Suffolk (on the oath of my Cousin Richard Parish Witts of Town Malling in Kent and late of Witney, Oxfordshire)...' Richard left a considerable sum in his will, so the family were not as 'low' as the diarist made out in his entry for 25 August 1828. After Richard's death, his widow Frances eventually moved to No. 1 Camden Grove, Camberwell, where she lived with her son Charles Augustus, who was listed in the 1851 census as an unmarried banker's clerk. Frances was listed as an annuitant. She led a long life and died at the age of 91.

Richard and Frances's eldest son, Richard Goldsmith Witts (1809-1842), entered the merchant marine and was a mate on the sailing vessel *Kite* which was shipwrecked off the coast of China. The crew was captured by the Chinese and put on public display in bamboo-caned cages measuring hardly more than 3 feet cubed. Richard and other surviving crew members were rescued by British military forces. After a spell at Macao, Richard was put on the vessel *Ann*, bound for England, but died on board due to his ill-treatment at the hands of the Chinese.

The dinner guests at Brunswick Square on 16 March 1842 were presumably Charles Augustus Witts and either Ellen Mary Witts or Anne Elizabeth Witts.

1828: 25 Aug: *I received tidings through Miss Witts of the decease of a distant relative, of whom I knew little during his life, and had seldom heard his name, though he was my first cousin once removed. Mr. Richard Parish Witts died on the 12th Inst. at Malling in Kent, aged 80 years, and he was, I understand, of late years at least, of unsound mind. He was son of an early elder brother of my Grandfather, a Richard, who married a Jane Parish; & he had freehold property, I believe, at Witney; it does not clearly appear, to whom this descends; from looking at the pedigree, I should say, his legal heir is Broome Witts, of Brunswick Square, as descendant of Edward, the elder brother of Richard: unless there are descendants of Edward by his eldest Son, Edward, entitled to inherit; but the account sent to me points out a person of the name of Wright ... while his freehold estate falls to his Uncle Edward Witts's great grandson, being Son of his Cousin Edward (not my father) by a second marriage. The descendants of his Uncle Edward by his first wife, a Helen Wyld of Nottingham, are females, daughters of a daughter married to a Walford, consequently cannot inherit: but he had a Son by his second wife, a person of low condition & the Son by that marriage again having male issue the estate devolves on him. I fear, from what has transpired, that he is a low, worthless person.*

1842: 16 Mar: *Two or three were added in the evening, particularly, a Mr. & Miss Witts, descendants of the oldest branch of the family as formerly settled in Witney, and who had fallen, pretty much thro' the misconduct and intemperance of this young man's father and grandfather, into a low situation.* 8 Apr: *The newspaper to-day mentions the death of Mr. Witts, a remote connection of ours, and brother to a gentleman & lady whom I met in Brunswick Square on Mar. 16. when I named also the circumstance of the brother having been shipwrecked and a prisoner to the Chinese: he is stated to have died at Macao in consequence of the hardships he underwent in captivity.*

WITTS — Elizabeth Witts — *widow of first cousin once removed*

Elizabeth Witts, née London (1738-1837), was the daughter of Edward and Elizabeth London. She married, at St Mildred, Bread Street, 22 March 1764, Broome Witts (1738-1769), son of Edward Witts (1701-1754) and Mary Trigg (1701-1746), who had married at Nottingham in 1732. Broome and Elizabeth's marriage was witnessed by Broome's uncle and aunt, Broome Witts (1713-1768) and Apphia Witts, née Anthony, Elizabeth's father, Edward London, and sister, Amelia London, and Broome's cousins Alice and Apphia Witts, later Lady Lyttelton. During her amazingly long life, Elizabeth spent many years at Champion Hill, and then retired to Brighton. She had three children: Broome Phillips Witts, Edward London Witts, and Maria Amelia Rodick.

1801: 21 Jul: *Came in a coach with my Father & Mother, to spend some time with Mrs. Witts at Champion Hill near Camberwell Surry. We found there Edward & her Daughter Mrs. Rodick with one Boy.* 20 Sep., 22 Sep., 24 Sep., 21 Oct: *Miss Snow, & Mrs. Witts called on us, as also Dukinfield, who drank tea with us.*

1802: 20 Jan.

1830: 28 Feb: ... *Her aged mother, elder sister of my aunt at Cookham, a most vigorous and extraordinary woman, at 92, residing at Champion Hill, insisted on coming to town, to take a last farewell of her deceased and only daughter in death.*

1832: 14 Jun: *Mr. Edward Witts & his brother gave us a very indifferent report of their aged Mother, Mrs. W. of Champion Hill, the elder sister of my deceased Aunt, who had lately been very much shaken by a fall out of a low open carriage ...*

WITTS — Broome Phillips Witts — *second cousin*

Broome Phillips Witts (1767-1845) was the eldest son of Broome Witts (1738-1769), a draper of Chipping Norton, Oxfordshire, and Elizabeth London, daughter of Edward London, of Kingston-upon-Thames, and Elizabeth Phillips. His father was the eldest son of Edward Witts (1701-1754), a fustian weaver, and Mary Trigg (1701-1746). Broome Phillips Witts was baptised on 11 March 1767 at the English Presbyterian Carter Lane meeting house, St Paul's, in what the Anti-Jacobin referred to as '... the most respectable meeting-house the dissenters have in the metropolis'. Two years and one day earlier, an elder brother, Broome London Witts, had been baptised in the same building, but this elder Broome appears to have died shortly afterwards. Broome Phillips Witts maintained his dissenting heritage as did his mother Elizabeth and his aunt Amelia, who had married her brother-in-law's cousin, also Broome Witts, uncle to the diarist. Two cousins, therefore, both named Broome Witts, married two 'London' sisters.

It is not fully clear how the family rose in prominence and wealth. Indeed, the branches that remained in Aldbourne, Wiltshire, never achieved either, but as the diarist makes clear in 1842, Broome Phillips Witts maintained contact with his cousins—relations which the diarist and his parents never took an interest in.

Broome Phillips Witts's grandfather, Edward, married Mary Trigg at Nottingham in 1732. It seems they remained there for a few years as Broome's elder siblings, Sarah (b. 1734) and Edward (b. 1736), appear to have been born there. Following his marriage and the birth of his eldest two children, Edward (senior) moved from Nottingham onto the Witney and London stage with premises in Friday Street. Although seemingly a humble fustian weaver, Edward continued the family business in Witney and London adopted by his father, also Edward, following his father's marriage to Sarah Broome of Witney. It seems probable that the business, based on wool stapling, for which Witney was an acknowledged centre, was actually commenced by the Broomes. Since medieval times wool had come from vast flocks of Cotswold sheep, the famous 'Cotswold Lions'. In the fifteenth century the wool had been bought by staplers and taken first to London and then exported, largely to the Low Countries where weaving and clothmaking was at an advanced stage. As the years passed by, water mills in the escarpment communities such as the Stroud valleys and similar valleys in Wiltshire and Somerset, powered by plentiful streams from the hills, developed from grist to fulling; by the seventeenth century weavers and other artisans with names such as Webb and Witts began to migrate from the Low Countries to the west of England where their skills were at a premium. Economic incentives for this migration were often coupled with the need to escape religious persecution.

London marts controlled by powerful guilds monopolised the market. Exporting from the west of England was not possible without going via London, and the staplers evolved from buying and selling the raw wool to doing the same with the finished, or partially finished woollen cloth. It was logical for serious merchants such as the Broomes of Witney to have a London base, and at some point in the evolution of the family's fortunes they achieved guild membership status. Astute marriage alliances were probably the cause of this; it was a trend followed by the diarist's father Edward, who married into the Travell family, which also had guild members in the wool stapling trade. Broome Parish Witts was a liveryman of the Fishmongers Company, freed by redemption in 1792, and prime warden in 1840-42.

At the death of Edward Witts, Broome Phillips Witts's grandfather, in 1754, the family business was carried on by his son Broome, but following Broome's death in 1769 there is a period of some fifteen to twenty years for which we have little knowledge. This period ended when Broome Phillips Witts became old enough to get involved. At some point in the 1780s or early 1790s the business evolved from wool to silk, which was centred on Spitalfields. The silk industry had been established there by Huguenot refugees who had migrated after the revocation of the Edict of Nantes in 1685, bringing little with them apart from their skills. By settling in Spitalfields, outside the bounds of the City of London, they hoped to avoid the restrictive legislation of the City guilds. By 1687 more than 13,000 French refugees were settled in London, primarily around Spitalfields, but also in the nearby communities, and through them the silk industry flourished. There is more information on Broome Phillips Witts's business on pages 102 and 103 of volume 1, including his connection with George Courtauld and his business interests in Pebmarsh.

At some point in the late eighteenth century, Broome Phillips Witts, his mother Elizabeth, brother Edward London Witts, and sister Maria Amelia moved together to Champion Hill, Camberwell. Broome married, at Liverpool, 2 March 1809, Jane Lake (1787-1853), daughter of William Charles Lake (1753-1836) and Ann Orange (1758-1810). William was born in Berkeley County, South Carolina, and presumably returned to England as a loyalist. He was a successful Liverpool merchant and lived at Birkenhead Priory; this was before the town of Birkenhead had been built, when the Benedictine priory was merely surrounded by a few houses. William married, 1777, Ann Orange (1758-1810), who had been born in Virginia. She died at Birkenhead Priory. Some time shortly after 1819, William moved to Castle Godwyn, Painswick, Gloucestershire. Much of the family wealth had been built from trading in the Irish Shipping Packet Company and later in slaving, which William pursued in partnership with his brother Thomas.

Broome and Jane had at least 2 sons and 3 daughters:

1 Jane (1810-1855); married, 1835, James Currie Duncan
2 Emma (1812-1899); married, 1850, Revd Richard John Allen of Swilland, Suffolk; *see below*
1 Broome Lake (1816-1861); married, 1848, Maria Dickson; *see below*
2 William Frederick (1818-1894); married, 1862, his cousin Ellen Mary Witts (1821-1901)
3 Maria (1822-1904); married, 1847, John Edward Woodroffe (1822-1913); *see below* under Maria Witts

At some point early in the nineteenth century Broome Phillips Witts moved to Brunswick Square. He also had a country property at Kingston-upon-Thames where he died in January 1845. He was buried in the churchyard at All Saints', Kingston, Surrey. His widow lived on in Brighton, and died in 1853.

1801: 15 May, 30 May, 24 Jul., 28 Jul., 25 Aug: *Called in the forenoon upon Mr. B. P. Witts & Mr. E. Witts & My Bro. at Messrs. Pryce and Darlot in the City.* 20 Sep: *In the afternoon with B. P. Witts to Peckham meeting, where we heard a masterly extempore Sermon ...* 24 Sep: *Dined with Lady Lyttelton, meeting there Mrs. Witts of Champion Hill, whose sons came up in the Evening, B.P. Witts slept with me.* 3 Oct., 20 Oct.

1802: 8 Jan., 19 Jan., 3 Feb., 8 Feb.

1803: 24 Aug: *Mrs. B. P. Witts called ...* 28-29 Sep.

1804: 23 Aug., *Wrote to Mr. B.P. Witts.* 17 Sep., 5 Oct., 7 Oct., 4 Nov., 12 Nov., 28 Dec.

1805: 9 Jan., 8 Aug., 12 Aug: *Called at Mr. B. P. Witts's who was absent on a Tour in Derbyshire ...* 21 Nov.

1808: 22 Feb: *... walked with B.P. Witts, met various individuals of my acquaintance.*

1825: 13 Jun: *At Castle Godwin, a small place perched among the beech woods adorning the upland valley contiguous to Painswick resides a Mr. Lake, formerly of Liverpool, & father to the wife of Mr. B.P. Witts, of Brunswick Square, my second cousin, an opulent merchant largely engaged in the silk trade.*

1827: 14 Nov: *... He mentions that his brother Mr. Witts, of Brunswick Square, an eminent silk manufacturer, & Mr. Rogers, of Streatham, an opulent man, who is retired, I believe, from trade as an underwriter, and who married a sister of George Wellford, are the Executors ...* 17 Nov: *When the funeral procession was on the point of setting out ... followed by John Witts & myself, B P Witts & his brother, as mourners of the family ...*

1828: 25 Aug: *The family of the Witts's was originally a dissenting family: B. P. Witts's branch is still ...*

1830: 28 Feb: *A letter from my cousin Miss Witts ... announces to me by the desire of Mr. Witts of Brunswick Square, the awfully sudden & unexpected death of his sister, Mrs. Rodick.* 23 Jun: *From Broad Street we retraced our way through the heart of the city towards Brunswick Square, to call on Mrs. Witts, the lady of my cousin B.P. Witts.* 25 Jun: *To dinner at Mrs. Witts's, Brunswick Square.*

1832: 12 Jun: *Wellford drove me to Cookham Grove, where we passed an hour with Jane Witts, a very estimable and pleasing young woman, daughter of my cousin, Broome P. Witts, who was in Town, but expected back this evening.* 13-14 Jun.

1835: 8 Jun., 10 Jun: *After dinner we were joined by Mr. Blackford, a nephew of Mrs. B. P. Witts, an intelligent young man engaged in mercantile business ...* 14 Jun., 19 Jun.

1836: 3 Dec., 9 Dec., 14 Dec.

1837: 15 Feb: *Also a letter from B. P. Witts announcing the decease of his mother ...* 17 Feb.

1838: 14 Jun.

1839: 5 May: *I next bent my steps towards Brunswick Square, and called on the Witts's, where I found Mr. and Mrs. W. and their daughter Emma: the younger unmarried daughter being on a visit at Champion Hill to be out of reach of infection ...*

1840: 25 Mar., 13 Apr., 6 May, 7 May: *At five o clock the whole family from Brunswick Square arrived to dinner; Broome P. Witts & his lady, their daughter Mrs. Duncan, whom I had not seen since I united them together her to her husband some years since in St. Pancras Church, Emma Witts and her sister Maria, now grown a very fine young woman, and B. L. Witts, the Son and Brother of the above. We formed a friendly groupe of connexions, and the evening passed pleasantly.* 27 Jun., 30 Jun.

1842: 14 Mar: *Found a note from B P Witts inviting us to dinner at Brunswick Square to meet the whole clan of congregated Witts's on Wednesday ...* 15 Mar., 16 Mar: *To our Hotel to dress for dinner at B P Witts's in Brunswick Square, whither we went in a cab, and whence we returned in a hired coach with Mrs. E. L. Witts, the Widow of Champion Hill, who is staying in Town with her niece Mrs. Thrupp.* 17 Mar., 25-26 Nov.

1843: 31 Aug.

1845: 8 Jan:. *A letter from B. L. Witts, announcing the death of his Father, which took place on Monday evening at his house in Brunswick Square, London, whither the family had lately removed from their country residence at Surbiton near Kingston on Thames: he had been apparently only slightly indisposed with a cold, for a week: no danger was anticipated till within 48 hours of his decease, when inflammation of the bowels hastily carried him off: but his sufferings were little, his faculties retained till the last—and his family, with the exception of Mrs. Duncan, assembled round his bed: his age 78 years.* 7 Jun: *Recd. a letter from Maria Witts with an account of the sayings and doings of Laura and Constance Howell while guests in Brunswick Square ...*

1847: 25 Dec: *Received a letter from Broome Lake Witts, who announces to me his approaching marriage to a lady of the name of Dickson, daughter of a late Major Dickson: the young people are to be united in next month.*

1851: 23 May: *Mrs. Witts, I found at home, returned from a visit to Mrs. Allen, late Emma Witts, at her home near Ipswich, whence they came back yesterday. Mrs. Witts is but little altered during the years which had passed since we met: she has fixed her residence as a Widow at Brighton.* 28 May: *Having observed in the newspaper yesterday notice of the death of a Mrs. Dickson at Brighton, whom I believe to have been the mother of Mrs. B.L Witts, wrote to B.L.W. expressing my apprehension that his wife has experienced this loss.*

1853: 17 Jun: *The account received to-day by B.L.W. from Brighton of his mother's declining health was very unfavourable.*

WITTS — Edward London Witts — *second cousin*

Edward London Witts (1768-1841) did not take part in the family company but ran his own businesses. He also operated from Friday Street, at number 44, advertising himself as a stationer and paper hanger (1792-94). From 1794 he was at 34 St Paul's Churchyard in partnership with William Jennings, but this was dissolved in 1797. Other partnerships followed: Witts & Baldwin from 1800 to 1803, and Witts & Palmer from 1804 to 1805. Thereafter he appears to have traded alone. Edward remained a bachelor until late in life, living with his mother at Champion Hill. In 1838, at the age of 70, he took the plunge and married Ann Parrott (b. ±1784).

The 'vexatious letter' of 1805 mentioned by Francis Witts was probably in relation to Francis's wayward brother, George.

1801: 1 May, 20 May, 25 May, 4 Jul., 21 Jul: *Came in a coach with my Father & Mother, to spend some time with Mrs. Witts at Champion Hill near Camberwell Surry. We found there Edward & her Daughter Mrs. Rodick with one Boy.* 22-24 Jul., 28 Jul: *Dined with Edward: Broome & George dined there: as also Mr. Baldwin & two Clerks. returned to tea at Champion Hill.* 3 Aug., 25 Aug., 6 Sep., 20 Sep., 22 Sep., 24 Sep., 30 Sep., 7 Oct: *Called on Ed. Witts. Rowed from Hungerford Stairs to St. Paul's Stairs ...* 15 Oct.

1802: 19 May, 19 Jan., 4 Feb., 7 Feb: *To St. Paul's Churchyard calling on Mr. Witts, & also saw Mrs. Witts.*

1804: 26 Aug., 25 Sep.

1805: 6 Sep: *Wrote to Mr. Edwd. Witts.* 8 Sep: *A vexatious letter from Edward Witts.* 9 Sep., 11 Sep., 14 Sep.

1827: 14 Nov: *We were on the point of setting out for Stanway on a visit to Lady Elcho, when we received the melancholy information of the death of my Uncle. It was conveyed to me in a letter from Mr. Edward Witts of Champion Hill, nephew to my Aunt, and our distant cousin ...* 17 Nov.

1829: 11 Feb.

1830: 23 Jun: *Pursuing the line of Fleet Street, Ludgate Hill & St. Paul's Church Yard, we stopped in Cheapside at the corner of Friday Street, that I might call at the Counting House of my relative Mr. Witts, who, I found, had left London this very day for Cheltenham on a short excursion to recruit his health, & for a little recreation ...*

1832: 14 Jun: *Wellford and myself proceeded in a fly to Cookham Grove to attend at the funeral of our departed friend. We there found the two Messrs. Witts, Broome & Edward, and my cousin John, who with his wife had arrived from Malvern ...*

1835: 11 Jun: *Her worthy Uncle, the old bachelor, from Champion Hill, was the first to make his appearance of those friends & relations who were invited to attend the couple to church ...*

1838: 14 Jun: *... descended to the representatives of the elder branch of that portion of the family of which B.P.W. and his brother Edward with their numerous connexion are only known to me.*

1840: 13 Apr., 27 Apr., 5 May: *... and a note from Mr. Edwd. Witts of Champion Hill inviting me to that place to meet our Brunswick Square connexions on Thursday next ...* 16 Jul: *I wrote to Mr. E. L. Witts, Champion Hill, congratulating him on his marriage with Miss Parrott which took place on the 12th. Inst. an event of the early accomplishment of which we had been apprized by Miss Witts.* 7 May: *Called on Mr. Thrupp by appointment, who introduced me to his partner, Mr. Burgoyne, an elderly gentleman, who married a Sister of the late Mr. Parrot, a partner in Sir Claude Scotts' house, and son of a very worthy person, who originally went out to India with my Aunt Lyttelton, as her servant. Miss Parrot, who has married my cousin E L Witts was her daughter. Mr. Burgoyne is Father to Mrs. Jos. Thrupp.*

1842: 16 Mar: *To our Hotel to dress for dinner at B P Witts's in Brunswick Square, whither we went in a cab, and whence we returned in a hired coach with Mrs. E. L. Witts, the Widow of Champion Hill, who is staying in Town with her niece Mrs. Thrupp.* 17 Mar.

WITTS — Emma Witts — *second cousin once removed — see also* Richard John Allen

Emma Witts (1812-1899) was the second daughter of Broome Phillips Witts and Jane Lake. She married, 1850, Richard John Allen (1810-1867). There were no children of the marriage.

1839: 5 May: *I next bent my steps towards Brunswick Square, and called on the Witts's, where I found Mr. and Mrs. W. and their daughter Emma ...*

1840: 7 May: *At five o clock the whole family from Brunswick Square arrived to dinner ...*

1842: 16 Mar: *Mrs. Witts looked and moved like a lady in her usual calm manner: her daughter Emma as I had last seen her, always pleasing and amiable ...*

1844: 7 Aug., 4 Sep., 10 Sep., 11 Sep: *Our friends Emma and Maria Witts, accompanied by their brother in law, Mr. Currie Duncan, arrived, as we expected, to dinner, having come by rail-road and coach, and in our open carriage from the foot of Stow hill.* 25 Sep: *After luncheon our agreeable cousins, Emma and Maria Witts, left us, having, I hope, been mutually pleased with their visit, as we had been with seeing them, and becoming better acquainted with them.* 30 Sep.

1845: 5 Feb: *M.W. recd. a pleasant letter from Emma Witts with accounts of that family.*

1847: 26 Sep: *M.W. received a letter from Emma Witts: there is reason that we should expect a visit from Mr. and Mrs. J. E. Woodroffe about Oct. 22: the bride and bridegroom are now on a tour in North Devon.*

1848: 28 Mar.

1850: 29 Oct: *Wrote to Emma Witts, to congratulate her on her approaching marriage to a Suffolk Clergyman, by name Allen, resident in the neighbourhood of Ipswich.* 5 Nov., 14 Nov: *Received an envelope, with wedding cards of Mr. and Mrs. Allen, which proves that Emma Witts became the wife of the Vicar of Swilland yesterday.*

WITTS — Broome Lake Witts — *second cousin once removed*

Broome Lake Witts (1816-1861), Church of England clergyman, was the eldest son of Broome Phillips Witts and Jane Lake. He was educated at Eton College and Corpus Christi, Cambridge (BA 1839; MA 1842), and admitted at Lincoln's Inn on 10 April 1838. He was ordained deacon in 1840 and priest the following year. He was perpetual curate and then vicar of Hersham, Surrey, 1842-61. Broome married, 1848, Maria Sophia (b. ±1816), daughter of Maj. R. Lothian Dickson.

It appears that Broome had initially intended on a career in the law, but he changed his mind and entered the Church. Interestingly, despite his father's loyalty to the family's dissenting roots, Broome Lake Witts had moved towards the Established Church. Broome and Maria had four children:

1 Julia Mary (b. 1848)
2 Jane Lake (1850-1922)
1 Broome Lake (1853-1916); educated at Uppingham School and Trinity College, Cambridge; admitted at Lincoln's Inn, 12 November 1874; called to the bar, 13 June 1877; practised before the supreme court of Ceylon and in Queensland; died in Australia, 1916
3 Charlotte Sheffield (1857-1929)

Broome Lake (senior) was frequently in poor health. He died at Boulogne on 18 June 1861. Following his death, his widow and young family moved to Homefield Road, Wimbledon, Surrey.

1836: 21-22 Jul., 23 Jul: *Several letters awaited my arrival: one from B L Witts, from Castle Godwin, kindly acknowledging our civilities to him.*

1839: 8 May: *The younger Broome was convalescent, I paid him a visit in his airy sitting room at the top of the house.*

1840: 19 Mar., 23 Mar: *Wrote to B. L. Witts in reply to his letter received on the 19th. Inst.* 7 May, 29 Jul: *Recd. a letter from B. L. Witts, who was ordained Deacon very lately by the Bp. of Chester, as Curate of the Church at Everton near Liverpool; he is now with his family at Kingston upon Thames; but enters on the duties of his profession on the 9th. Aug.* 30 Jul., 3 Aug: *In the evening walked to Lower Slaughter Turnpike gate to meet B. L. Witts, who arrived from Town by the "Little Wonder" Coach, having left Paddington by the Great Western Railway at midday ... Our young friend looks delicate, and hardly equal to much clerical duty.* 4 Aug: *B. L. Witts, being obliged to pursue his journey towards Liverpool this evening, and having taken an early dinner, accompanied MW. and myself in the Chariot to Stow, where at six P.M. he took a place on the Novelty Coach for Cheltenham, meaning to proceed from thence to Gloucester, where his maternal Aunts, the Misses Lake, reside.* 19 Aug.

1842: 15-17 Mar.

1844: 24 Feb: *A note from B. L. Witts, accompanying two little pamphlets illustrating his doings as Curate of a district Church in the parish of Walton on Thames—at Hersham ...* 5 Mar.

1845: 8 Jan: *A letter from B. L. Witts, announcing the death of his Father ...* 9 Jan.

1846: 17 Jul., 24 Jul.

1847: 25 Dec: *Received a letter from Broome Lake Witts, who announces to me his approaching marriage to a lady of the name of Dickson, daughter of a late Major Dickson: the young people are to be united in next month; it would seem that the lady is well connected, but, I fear, has very little fortune; and his income is not large.* 28 Dec.

1848: 14 Jan: *Cards forwarded by the post in the usual nuptial fashion announced the marriage of B. L. Witts and Miss Dickson on the 12th. Inst.*

1850: 25-26 Apr., 11 Sep: *Wrote to Broome L. Witts, congratulating him on the birth of another child. I had noticed the announcement in the newspaper ...*

1851: 16 Apr., 10 May, 14 May, 20 May: ... *He writes that he has lately consulted a medical friend, and has been advised to retire for a time from the active duties of his profession, for the recovery of his health. Apprehensions of induration of the heart are entertained, and he is advised to travel and relax from all cares.* 24 May: ... *we moved onward to the Walton Station, where we arrived half an hour later than we should have done. There I found Broome L. Witts waiting for me, and his servant-boy to take my bag. A walk of half a mile through pleasant fields brought us to the village of Hersham ...* 25 May, 28 May.

1852: 12 Mar: *A letter from B. L. Witts, who with his wife & children is now in resident at Cromer, where he has been for some time taking temporary duty, in two small adjacent villages; but contemplates returning in summer to Hersham.* 27 Apr., 10 Dec.

1853: 7 May, 20 May, 28 May, 30 May, 3 Jun., 10 Jun., 15 Jun: *Walked to Hersham in little more than a quarter of an hour, & found my cousin and his family very comfortably settled in their new parsonage, an excellent house as regards the ground floor, with enjoyable dining & drawing room, & study, opening on a spacious garden and adjoining field ... Mrs. B.L.W. cordial & agreeable, and far advanced in pregnancy: her two little girls, very nice children, but the younger a little Pickle, or Tomboy.* 16-18 Jun.

1854: 31 Jan., 5 Aug.

WITTS — William Frederick Witts — *second cousin once removed*

William Frederick Witts (1818-1884), Church of England clergyman, was the second son of Broome Phillips Witts and Jane Lake. He was educated at Eton College and King's College, Cambridge (BA 1842; MA 1845), where he was Crosse scholar in 1842 and Tyrwhitt Hebrew scholar in 1844. He was a fellow at King's from 1840 to 1863. William was ordained deacon in 1844 and priest in 1851. He was curate of St Giles with St Peter's, Cambridge, 1844-61; chaplain and assistant master at Uppingham School, 1861-73; curate-in-charge of St John-the-Evangelist, North Woolwich, 1874-78; and rector of Ringwood with Harbridge, Hampshire, 1878-84. He married, 1862, his cousin Ellen Mary (1821-1901), daughter of Richard Parish Witts (1787-1833). There were no children of the marriage.

1839: 5 May: ... *his brother Frederick, at Cambridge, now a fellow of Kings College.*

1842: 16 Mar: ... *the two brothers, Broome and Frederick; the latter just arrived from Cambridge is a fellow of Kings, and a close student—will, probably, enter the Church, and has all the appearance of a talented young man, with a mind always, and, perhaps, too intensely at work.*

WITTS — Jane Witts — *second cousin once removed — see also* James Currie Duncan

Jane Witts (1810-1855) was the eldest daughter of Broome Phillips Witts and Jane Lake. She married, 12 June 1835, James Currie Duncan (1799-1854), son of George Duncan (1771-1831) and Christian Currie (1765-1818). There do not appear to have been any children of the marriage.

1835: 25 May: *Wrote to Round, who is now in Town, expressing my regret at being disappointed in meeting him there, in consequence of Miss Jane Witts having deferred the day of her marriage.* 27 May: *Wrote to Miss Witts, to fix the day of my arrival in town for the 8th. of June ...* 11 Jun: *Jane Witts appears likely to enjoy as much comfort in the connection formed this day as generally falls to the human lot ...*

WITTS — Maria Witts — *second cousin once removed — see also* John Edward Woodroffe

Maria Witts (1822-1904) was the youngest daughter of Broome Phillips Witts and Jane Lake. She married, 1847, John Edward Woodroffe (1822-1913). For detailed family information *see below*, Woodroffe.

1840: 7 May ... *and her sister Maria, now grown a very fine young woman ...*

1844: 7 Aug: *Letters crossing between MW. and Emma Witts make it pretty sure that the latter, with her sister Maria, will visit us after the Backhouses have left us.* 10 Sep: *Recd. a letter from Mr. Currie Duncan, who proposes to accompany Emma and Maria Witts hither to-morrow, and to proceed from hence by Cheltenham to Liverpool on the following day.* 11 Sep: *Our friends Emma and Maria Witts, accompanied by their brother in law, Mr. Currie Duncan, arrived, as we expected, to dinner, having come by rail-road and coach, and in our open carriage from the foot of Stow hill.* 14 Sep., 16 Sep: *Maria Witts received a letter from Capt. Witts with a good account of our Shropshire friends ...* 21 Sep., 25 Sep: *After luncheon our agreeable cousins, Emma and Maria Witts, left us, having, I hope, been mutually pleased with their visit, as we had been with seeing them, and becoming better acquainted with them.* 30 Sep., 16 Nov., 17 Dec.

1845: 12 Feb., 7 Jun: *Recd. a letter from Maria Witts with an account of the sayings and doings of Laura and Constance Howell while guests in Brunswick Square ...* 24 Jun.

1846: 4 Jun.

1847: 13 Aug: ... *from Maria Witts, announcing her approaching marriage to a Mr. Woodroffe, a Barrister of Lincoln's Inn, of Irish extraction, and asking me to give her away, standing in the place of her deceased Father: the ceremony to be performed at Kingston upon Thames by her eldest brother, in about a fortnight ...* 14 Aug: *Wrote to Maria Witts, congratulating her on her approaching marriage, and promising, if it were possible, to be present at the Wedding, and to give her away.* 18 Aug: *A letter from Maria Witts; her wedding had been fixed for the 26th.; was postponed till the 28th. to suit my engagements; but has been further put off, and no day fixed, owing to the Settlements being not yet ready.* 24 Aug: *... from Maria Witts who announces her wedding as fixed for the 9th. Sept.* 25 Aug: *Wrote to Maria Witts, explaining that my engagements on Sept 8. would preclude my being able to be present at her wedding on the day following.* 14 Sep: *The marriage of Maria Witts to Mr. Woodroffe was announced to us today ...* 4 Sep: *M.W. received a letter from Maria Witts to whom she had written ... to visit us towards the close of October, as they return from Devonshire, whither they propose are going to pass the honeymoon.*

WOLF — Maria Caroline Wolf[211]

Maria Caroline Wolf, née Benda (1742-1820), singer, pianist, and composer, was born at Potsdam, the daughter of Franz Benda, first violinist and composer at the court of Frederick II. Maria's aunt was Anna Franziska Hattasch, a chamber singer, and her uncle was the conductor Georg Benda; both had appointments at the court of the duke of Gotha. At some point around 1761, having received piano and singing lessons from her father, Maria left Potsdam and moved to Weimar, where she was employed at the court theatre. In 1770 she married Ernst Wilhelm Wolf, and from 1775 she took part in theatre productions directed by Goethe.

Francis Witts's two mentions of 'Benda' in his diaries may indicate that Maria used her maiden name as her professional name, or that one of her nephews was working at court as an aspiring actor/singer; the former is more likely, even though she would not have been in the first flush of youth. Ernst Wolf died in 1792 and Maria continued to live in Weimar until her death on 2 August 1820.

1799: 16 Nov: *The Costume of Mad. Jagemann bad, her singing very good. On the whole the Stage is too small to produce the desired effect. the best Performers were Benda Matiegzeck & Genast.*

1800: 26 Feb: *to the Theatre with my mother in the Evening, a new opera music by Salieri. Tarare or Axur the music beautiful, but rather unequal the Characters best acted were by Jagemann, Spitzeder, Weyrauch, Becker, Benda &c.*

WOLFE — John Wolfe[212]

John Wolfe (1769-1830), MP and landed proprietor, was educated at Trinity College, Dublin. He was MP for Ardee in 1790-97, and succeeded as Baron Kilwarden of Kilteel on the death of his mother. He was one of the Irish set at Clifton and remained unmarried.

1806: 4 Feb: *Called at Sir W. Wolseley's; all the good trio at home & Lord Kilwarden with them uttering anything but the words of wisdom.* 12 Feb: *When all were assembled, the Room presented a goodly shew, & had not Lord Kilwarden taken a liberty by bringing Mr. Stacpoole, uninvited, Mrs. Salter would have nothing to regret.* 11 Mar: *Dined in a large, dashing party at Gillibrand's the Adair family, Lords Kilwarden & Ruthven; Major Cochrane & P.J. Miles, formed the party.*

WOLLASTON — Henry John Wollaston[213]

Henry John Wollaston (1805-1869), Church of England clergyman, was the second son of Revd Henry John Wollaston (1770-1833), rector of Scotter, Lincolnshire, and Louisa Symons (1783-1833). He was educated at Sidney College, Cambridge (BA 1829), and was curate of Byfield, Northamptonshire, and then curate of Farmington, Gloucestershire, 1838-46. He died unmarried.

1838: 7 Sep: *Mr. Twisleton was of the party—Mr. Wollaston, the Curate of Farmington ...* 25 Sep.

1839: 6 Apr: *With Mr. Ford ... rode homewards as far as Bourton with Mr. F. by Farmington, to call on the Curate, Mr. Wollaston, to whom I am ashamed to say I had not previously paid this compliment: nor did I to-day, for we met him on his way to towards Northleach.* 22 May.

1840: 5 Aug., 2 Oct: *Dined at the Wallers at Farmington Lodge ... and Mr. Wollaston. Two agreeable unmarried sisters of Mrs. W.,—Misses Larkin, are on a visit at Farmington. Music in the Evening.*

1842: 27 Apr., 8 Jul., 31 Aug.

1844: 18 Feb., 19 Mar., 17 Apr.

1845: 12 Mar.

1846: 17 Jul., 4 Dec.

WOLLEN — Joseph Wollen[214]

Joseph Wollen (1803-1880), JP and surgeon, was born at East Harptree, Somerset, the son of William Wollen (1779-1809) and Sarah Wookey (1782-1863). He practised at Painswick, and married, at Wedmore, Somerset, 15 March 1836, Elizabeth Duckett (1804-1848). In 1841 Joseph and Elizabeth lived at New Street, Painswick. They had at least 1 son and 2 daughters:

1 Elizabeth (1836-1875); married, at Wedmore, Somerset, 20 September 1870, Richard Purnell Tyley (1834-1912)
2 Sarah (b. ±1838)
1 Joseph (1841-1882)

By 1851 Joseph was a widower and living back at Wedmore. He was listed as a county magistrate.

1842: 16 Oct: *It seems that Mrs. H. was in a precarious state from haemorrhage two months ago; rallied, and had been peculiarly well in strength and spirits since: this improvement had prevented all apprehension on the part of her poor husband and children, but the Medical attendant, Mr. Wollen, of Painswick, had entertained serious fears as to the issue ... Mr. Cother offered his congratulations on the successful result, and was about to take his leave, when Mr. Wollen, observing a recurrence of unfavourable symptoms, recalled him, and in a very short time my poor afflicted friend was a Widower—ten children motherless.* 20 Oct., 22 Oct.

WOLSELEY — William Wolseley and the Wolseley family at Clifton[215]

Sir William Wolseley, 6th baronet (1740-1817), landed proprietor, was the son of Sir William Wolseley, 5th baronet (±1692-1779), and Ann Fieldhouse. He succeeded as 6th baronet in 1779, and married, 1765, Charlotte Barbara, daughter of Zachary Chambers of Wimbledon, Surrey. They had 4 sons and 4 daughters:

1 William Edward (b. 1766)
1 Charlotte (1767-1861); married Gen. Sir Thomas Browne, KCB
2 Charles (1769-1846); succeeded as 7th baronet; married, 2 July 1812, Anne Wright
3 Robert (1770-1815), Church of England clergyman; married Mary Anne (b. 1783), only daughter of Revd George Watson Hand, archdeacon, and Ann Martha
4 Henry (1771-1836); married, 1793, Charlotte, daughter of John D. Halliday
2 Maria (b. 1772); married Revd John Ryland of Yoxall, Staffordshire

3 Caroline (d. 1833); married Robert Haig
4 Cecilia (d. 1857); married, at Calwich, Staffordshire, 30 June 1812, Revd Charles Prowett, rector of Stapleford, Hertfordshire

---

1805: 9 Jan: *Danced with my old friend Cecilia Wolseley ...* 10 Jan., 30 Jan: *Received an unexpected invitation in the morning to Mrs. Salter's Dance this Evening ... Danced with Cecilia Wolseley, Miss Anson, Miss Salter the younger, Miss Russell & Maria Wolseley.* 31 Jan: *In the Evening at Mrs. Uptons Rout which the Wolseley party rendered agreeable to me.* 21 Feb: *Passed the Evening alone, my Father & Mother being at Mr. Macbride's & Lady Wolseley's ...*

1806: 22 Jan: *Upon my return to Clifton called upon the admirable Lady Wolseley and her amiable Daughter Cecilia ...* 3 Feb., 4 Feb: *Called at Sir W. Wolseley's; all the good trio at home ...* 10 Feb: *To a small dull party at Lady Wolseley's, where I conversed chiefly with Cecilia ...* 11-12 Feb., 16 Feb., 22 Feb., 26-27 Feb., 2 Mar., 4 Mar., 6 Mar: *Repaired in the Evening to a party at Lady Wolseleys, numerous & warm, but visiting so congenial a family must always be pleasant. Conversed a great deal with the amiable Cecilia ...* 7 Mar., 12 Mar., 14 Mar: *... sitting by & chatting with Cecilia Wolseley all the Evening, who told me many a secret of my own, which I had no notion were in her keeping.*

1812: 5 Aug: *A large brick House at the entrance of the Town is inhabited by Mr. Wolseley, a Son of Sir W. Wolseley: the seat of the latter is at Wolseley Bridge, not far distant.*

WOOD — Dr Wood of Newcastle[216]

Dr Wood (d. 1822) was for many years head of an asylum at Newcastle which opened in 1767. After his death in 1822 he was succeeded by Dr Glenton. No more details have yet been uncovered.

1801: 8 May: *Our party to Dunbar 8 miles in the Union Coach consisted of a man & wife & two squalling children, a very well informed man Dr. Wood, head of a madhouse at Newcastle & a Miss Morton of the same place extremely well educated & well read.*

WOOD — Mr Wood at one of Lady Lyttelton's soirées

The diarist mentioned that this Mr Wood was a nephew of Sheridan—presumably Richard Brinsley Sheridan—but no connection has been discovered. Lady Lyttelton enjoyed having intellectuals, literati, and musicians around her, so a connection such as this would have been normal.

1801: 27 May, 10 Jun: *... a Mr. Wood a nephew of Mr. Sheridan also sung in a very singular style.* 4 Jul., 23 Oct.

WOOD — Alfred Joshua Wood[217]

Alfred Joshua Wood (1808-1888), surgeon, was born at Manchester and studied at St Bartholomew's Hospital. He began practising at Barton Street, Gloucester, where he was surgeon to the infirmary and the Magdalen Asylum. Next he was resident medical superintendent at Barnwood House Hospital for the Insane, and later he practised for some time at Ilfracombe. He retired to 3 Denmark Road, Gloucester, and died there on 18 March 1888. He was made MRCS on 22 January 1830, and a fellow of the Royal College of Surgeons on 11 December 1843, one of the original 300 fellows. He became a licentiate of the Society of Apothecaries in 1830 and gained his MD from St Andrews in 1858. In 1871 he was living with his wife, Frances (b. ±1812), who was matron of the lunatic asylum. They had 1 son and 2 daughters at home:

1 Elizabeth (b. ±1845)
1 William Bryan (b. ±1846), medical student (1871)
2 Bertha (b. ±1852)

1839: 23 Jun: *M W. recd. a letter from Miss Davies, to acquaint us that Mr. Alfred Wood, Surgeon, Gloucester, is a Candidate for the vacant office of Surgeon to the County Gaol, and to bespeak my vote.* 25 Jun: *Recd. a letter from Mr. A. Wood, soliciting my vote ...* 28 Jun: *To Mr. Alfred Wood, to promise him my support ...* 2 Jul: *Attended the Chairman to the opening of the Court, and assisted in the Grand Jury room, as usual, in the transaction of the County business. There was a large muster of magistrates, the more on account of the appointment to the vacant office of Surgeon of the County Gaol to be this day filled up. There were three candidates, Messrs. Hickes, A Wood, and Fletcher ...* 9 Jul: *Received a letter from Mr. A. Wood, the Surgeon of the Gloucester the unsuccessful candidate last week for the office of Surgeon to the County Gaol. A new professional prize now offers itself to him ...* 10 Jul., 12 Jul., 14-15 Jul., 25 Aug.

1846: 2 Jul., 11 Aug.

1848: 22 Nov: *There were present also two medical men conversant with lunacy, Dr. Conolly, and Dr. Wood ...*

WOOD — James [Jemmy] Wood[218]

James [Jemmy] Wood (1756-1836), banker, miser, and eccentric, was born in 1756, the third child and only son of Richard and Elizabeth Wood. He attended either Sir Thomas Rich's School or The King's School. Wood inherited the Gloucester Old Bank from his grandfather who had founded it in 1716. The bank was said to have been one of the oldest private banks in Britain, having survived the financial consequences of the Napoleonic Wars when many other banks went out of business. It operated from Wood's drapery shop in Westgate Street, Gloucester, and offered no interest on deposits of less than one year. The bank was believed to have employed only James Wood and two clerks. On the counter were nailed counterfeit coins as a warning to customers not to try and pass them off on the bank. Gloucester Old Bank was taken over by the County of Gloucestershire Banking Company in 1838, which eventually became part of Lloyds Bank in 1897.

There are numerous stories of Wood's miserliness, but it is unclear how many are true. Supposedly he visited Gloucester Docks to fill his pockets with small pieces of coal that fell off the boats being unloaded there, and wore the same old clothes for years on end. It is said that on a journey to London, when a fellow traveller made fun of Wood's ragged clothing, Wood bet him £5 that he could withdraw £100,000 from the bank on his arrival in the city. The fellow passenger took the bet and lost his money. Wood was renowned for walking everywhere rather than paying the cost of a carriage. One story records that once he travelled back to Gloucester from Tewkesbury in the back of a passing hearse, laid out in the space usually reserved for the deceased.

Wood's miserliness and wealth brought him national fame; he had Toby Jugs and a Staffordshire figure based on him. His distinctive profile of a protruding chin and nose and a sloping forehead made him prime fodder for caricaturists. The accusations of miserliness may have had a basis in fact but from his journals it is evident that Wood was not a recluse; he took part an active part in the activities of the city. He became nationally known as 'The Gloucester Miser'.

Wood was worth around £900,000, which reportedly made him 'the richest commoner in His Majesty's dominions'. Charles Dickens may have been inspired by the stories of the Gloucester Miser when he created the character of Ebenezer Scrooge in *A Christmas Carol*. A character by the name of Dismal Jemmy appears in *The*

Pickwick Papers, and Jemmy Wood, of Gloucester, is mentioned in *Our Mutual Friend*. It has also been speculated that the court case of Jarndyce *v.* Jarndyce in *Bleak House* may have been based on the case that arose following irregularities in Wood's will, which soaked up much of the estate's funds. It should also be noted that the court system of the time was so slow and expensive that there are a number of other possible cases on which Jarndyce could easily have been based.

Wood never married and had no children. He left around £900,000 to be shared equally between Sir Matthew Wood (*below*), the solicitor John Chadborn, and Wood's two other executors Jacob Osborne and John S. Surman. A damaged codicil was found leaving money to the City of Gloucester and to other beneficiaries; it was wrangling over the authenticity of this codicil that caused the settlement of the estate to be delayed. Chadborn hanged himself in 1839, and the obituary notice in *The Gentleman's Magazine* stated that since Wood's death he had '... been almost wholly engrossed with the proceedings consequent upon the disputed validity of the will.'

1836: 27 Aug: *This course called forth replies in explanation from Bathurst, Estcourt, and Goodrich; after which Alderman Wood made a rambling and absurd address to the Court in favour of Mason and against poor Rowan; committing himself by ill advised remarks on his own experience in prison management, on the City Prisons, and Gaolers, and on other irrelevant topics.*

1839: 1 Aug., 27 Aug: *If I have not been misinformed, this valuable institution benefitted largely, it was said to the amount of £13000, by the will of the maiden sister of the late Alderman Wood of Gloucester, of miserly reputation, and enormous wealth, which is now the subject matter of litigation ...*

WOOD — Mark Wood[219]

Sir Mark Wood, 1st baronet (1750-1829), MP, army officer (HEIC), and engineer, was the eldest son of Col Alexander Wood (1712-1778), of Burncroft, and Jane Mercer. He became a cadet of the HEIC Army in 1770, and went to India with his brother George. He married, at Calcutta, 1786, Rachel (d. 1802), daughter of Robert Dashwood; they had 2 sons:

1 Alexander (d. 1805)

2 Mark (1794-1837); succeeded as 2nd baronet; elected MP for Gatton; married, 1833, Elizabeth Rachel, daughter of William Newton; on his death the title became extinct

Wood was MP for Milborne Port, Gatton, and Newark, and received his baronetcy on 3 October 1808.

1823: 22 Sep: *In the afternoon I rode to Northleach to meet the Regulator coach ... In the coach I met with a conversible old Baronet, Sir Mark Wood, who gave me his address in town No. 66 Pall Mall, with a cordial invitation. I believe him to have been formerly in Service in India. He has estates in Surrey, Monmouthshire & Glamorganshire.*

WOOD — Matthew Wood[220]

Sir Matthew Wood, 1st baronet (1768-1843), MP and alderman, was the son of William Wood (d. 1809), serge maker, of Exeter and Tiverton, Devon, and Catherine Cluse (d. 1798). He was a member of the Worshipful Company of Fishmongers, a member of the court of aldermen of the City of London, sheriff of the City of London for 1809, and lord mayor of London from 1815 to 1817. He was elected unopposed as MP for the City of London at a by-election in June 1817, and held the seat until his death in 1843.

Wood was a prominent partisan and adviser of Queen Caroline on her return to England in 1820. He was left property by the feeble-minded sister of the banker James 'Jemmy' Wood, known as 'the Gloucester Miser' and one of the richest men in the country. She appears to have been a fan of Queen Caroline and had taken a shine to the alderman. Despite their shared surname, Matthew Wood was no relation.

Matthew Wood moved into his newly acquired property in Gloucester and, it appears, soon realised the vulnerability of the old banker and his fortune. In 1833 Jemmy gave the him rent-free use of Hatherley House, which his bank had acquired through a bankruptcy. In return Matthew Wood allowed Jemmy to send all his mail under parliamentary franked cover. Soon Matthew Wood had his sights on a baronetcy not only for himself, but also for the Gloucester Miser.

Jemmy Wood died in 1836. He left his entire estate, valued at over £900,000, to Mathew Wood and three other executors, but a court case ensued against them. Eventually, on 20 February 1839, in an extremely long and detailed verdict, Judge Jenner decided that the terms of the will were made by conspiracy and fraud, and ordered that the whole of the estate should be divided between two relations. However, within two years this verdict was overturned on appeal, and what was left of the estate after the immense legal costs was distributed equally among the beneficiaries.

1826: 14 Sep: *... the well known and obtrusive Matthew Wood, Alderman of London & M.P. who since the death of his name sake, the sister of the eccentric & wealthy Jemmy Wood, Alderman & Banker of Gloucester, has been a summer resident at the latter place, where the old lady left him a good house, in consideration of his championship of the late Queen Caroline, & where, peradventure, Alderman Matthew thinks it a good speculation to worm himself into the good graces, &, if possible, into the last will & testament ...*

1838: 16 Oct: *No Lord Lieut; nor Peers, nor MP's, save Sir M. Wood.*

1839: 1 Aug.

WOOD — Richard Wood[221]

Richard Wood (1805-1871), schoolmaster, appears to have been born in Fairford. He was married to Elizabeth (b. ±1805) and they had 4 sons:

1 Charles (b. ±1835)

2= Richard (b. ±1837)

2= Edward (b. ±1837)

4 Samuel (b. ±1840)

In the 1841 census Wood was listed as a schoolmaster at what was advertised as 'Gent's Boarding Academy'. His pupils were aged between 8 and 15.

1846: 17 Jul: *Those present were ... and Mr. Wood, a Schoolmaster at Northleach also attended.*

WOOD — William Wood of Devizes

William Wood has not been identified although he appears to have been prominent among the farmers and gentry of Devizes and its environs.

1806: 7 Aug: *Upon my return at Miss Tylee's with their family party Mr. & Mrs. Gent, Mr. W. Wood &c.* 22 Oct.

1807: 2 Jan: *Conversed with Mr. Brabant, Mr. Wood &c.* 20 Apr., 13 Aug., 14 Aug: *... returned thro' Devizes. Met & conversed with Mr. Wood.* 20 Aug: *Rode to Devize conversed with Mr. Jones,*

Mr. & Mrs. Jaques, Willm. Woods. 29 Aug.

1808: 14 Jan., 29 Apr., 1 May: *Rode off before twelve with Will. Wood as far as Rowde ...*

WOOD — William Wood[222]

William Wood was an apothecary in Cheltenham who in later years upgraded his description of himself to 'surgeon'. He practised at 11 Cambray Place, and was an acquaintance and colleague of Dr Edward Jenner and a member of the 'Vaccine Association'. Under a scheme for a dispensary in Cheltenham, members of the association offered their services gratuitously under the presidency of Edward Jenner. Members included Dr Boisragon, Dr Christie, Dr C. Parry, Mr Newell, Messrs Wood and Lucas, and Mr Seager, all physicians and surgeons of Cheltenham.

1823: 23 Dec: *Wood, the Apothecary, who has long attended her, was on the alert, and by copious bleeding and a blister ...*

1824: 29 Dec: *Continued bad accounts of my poor Mother's health, coming from Stanway, carried me there to-day. I returned, however, to dinner, having with much difficulty prevailed on my Mother to see Mr. Wood, her medical friend from Cheltenham, to whom I wrote accordingly ...*

1825: 1 Jan: *I rode over to Stanway to breakfast in consequence of a letter from Miss Church, giving me an account of Mr. Wood's opinion of my poor Mother.* 6 Jan: *While I was attending my usual duties as a Magistrate at Stow, I received a distressing communication from Dr. Christie, whom, it appears, Mr. Wood called to his aid yesterday evening.*

WOODCOCK — Miss Woodcock at Bredon[223]

Miss Woodcock was presumably a sister or niece of [Anna] Eleonora Woodcock, who married, at Heston, Middlesex, 28 August 1782, Revd John Keysall (1760-1836). Keysall was born at Holborn, London, the son of John Keysall (1735-1813) and Mary Browne (1736-1769). Anne [or Anna] appears to have died young. John Keysall married, secondly, Elizabeth Colton (1776-1864).

1826: 28 Jun: *Mr. Eddy and his son dined at Stanway. In the evening the party was increased by Mrs. Keysall and Miss Woodcock ... Miss Woodcock is a relation of the first Mrs. Keysall.* 29 Jun.

WOODHOUSE — John Chappell Woodhouse[224]

John Chappell Woodhouse (1750-1833), Church of England clergyman, was the son of Dr William Woodhouse of Lichfield. He was educated at Christ Church, Oxford (BA 1770; MA 1773; B&DD 1807), and entered the Church. He was rector of Donnington, Shropshire, 1773-1833; prebendary of Rochester, 1797-98; canon of Lichfield, 1798; archdeacon of Shropshire, 1798; dean of Lichfield, 1807-33; and rector of Stoke-on-Trent, Staffordshire, 1814-33.

1829: 27 Aug: *Lady Lyttelton received company to-day Dr. Woodhouse, the ancient Dean of Lichfield ...*

WOODLANDS — Richard Woodlands[225]

Richard Woodlands (1794-1868), agricultural labourer, was born at Kingscote, Gloucestershire, the son of John and Mary Woodlands. He lived at Ragnall, Wotton-under-Edge, Gloucestershire, and was married to Sarah Hazell (1797-1873), born at Lasborough, Gloucestershire; they had at least 2 sons and 4 daughters:

1 Harriet (b. 1818); born at Kingscote, Gloucestershire
2 Hannah (1820-1904); born at Kingscote, Gloucestershire; 1 illegitimate daughter:
  1 Emma Davis (b. 1843); born at Wotton-under-Edge, Gloucestershire
  Hannah married, at St Philip's, Bristol, 3 August 1851, Samuel Worlock (1816-1874), born at Bitton, Gloucestershire; 1 son and 4 daughters:
  1 Fanny (1846-1891)
  1 Samuel (1849-1926)
  2 Harriet (1853-1918)
  3 Zipporah (1857-1914)
  4 Sarah (1861-1928)
1 George (b. 1826); born at Kingscote, Gloucestershire; presumably died an infant
2 George (1828-1910), agricultural labourer; born at Ozleworth, Gloucestershire; married, at Wotton-under-Edge, 29 May 1859, Harriet Chapple (1836-1930), born at Leighterton, Gloucestershire; at least 3 sons and 5 daughters:
  1 Thomas (b. 1860)
  2 George (b. 1862)
  1 Sarah Jane (1865-1945)
  2 Eliza Ann (b. 1869)
  3 Emily (b. 1871)
  3 Frederick (b. 1874)
  4 Clara (b. 1878)
  5 Ada (b. 1888)
3 Charlotte (b. ±1832); born at Ozleworth, Gloucestershire; married, at St Philip's, Bristol, 4 December 1852, John Davis
4 Mary (b. 1834), wool spinner; born at Ozleworth, Gloucestershire

In the 1861 census there were also two grandchildren in the household, Samuel Worlock, ploughboy, born at Oldland, Gloucestershire, and Ann Rogers (b. ±1852), scholar, born at Bristol. It has not been discovered how Ann fits into the family.

Richard Woodlands, who could not read nor write, was sentenced by Francis Witts at the adjourned sessions at Gloucester on 4 March 1845 to six months' imprisonment for larceny. This is typical example of Witts's severity.

1845: 29 Apr: *The documents which he transmits are from the Home Office, requiring explanation as to a sentence passed at the Adjourned Sessions on a prisoner, named Woodlands, whom I tried and sentenced to six months hard labour in the Penitentiary.* 30 Apr., 9 May: *... from Mr. Under Secretary Phillips of the Home Office a very satisfactory letter respecting the Prisoner Woodlands whom I tried at the adjourned Sess. and sentenced to six months imprisonment, whereas Mr. Baron Platt, at the assizes, sentenced his partner in the offence to only one month's imprisonment.*

WOODMAN-HASTINGS — Warren Hastings Woodman-Hastings — *see also* Hastings, Townsend, *and* Whitehouse[226]

Warren Hastings Woodman-Hastings (1815-1897), landed proprietor and captain of the Royal Württemberg Cavalry, was the son of Revd Thomas Bartholomew Woodman (1760-1825) and Louisa von Chapuset. His father, Thomas, was the only son of John Woodman (1724-1816), of Cleveland Row, St James's, London, and Ann (b. 1731), daughter of Revd Penyston Hastings of Churchill, Oxfordshire. Ann was the only sister of Warren Hastings.

John Woodman was steward to the duke of Bridgwater. He was described as a 'cautious lawyer' and became one of Warren Hastings' attorneys in England. His son Thomas was educated at Westminster School and Trinity College, Cambridge (BA 1781;

MA 1784), and was admitted at Lincoln's Inn in 1779, but chose to enter the Church. He was vicar of Ivinghoe, Buckinghamshire, 1797-1803; vicar of Brackley, Northamptonshire, 1803-25; vicar of Wingrave, Buckinghamshire, 1803-04; prebendary of York, 1807; and finally rector of Daylesford, Worcestershire, 1814-15, and chaplain to the duke of Clarence. Thomas married, 22 July 1811, Louisa (d. 1825), second daughter of Baron von Chapuset of Stuttgart, Germany; following her mother's divorce and subsequent re-marriage, Louisa became a niece of Warren Hastings.

Warren Hastings Woodman-Hastings married, 1853, Annette (1836-1912), only daughter of Henry Townsend of Rugby. Little information about the couple has become apparent. They changed their surname from Woodman to Woodman-Hastings, possibly due to a stipulation in a will. They had 2 sons and 3 daughters:

- 1 Marian Charlotte Amelia (1854-1904); born at Baden Baden, Württemberg; married, at St Mary's, Great Malvern, Worcestershire, 10 July 1877, William Sanday (1843-1920)
- 1 Warren (b. & d. 1861); born at Baden Baden, Württemberg, 4 April 1861; died at the age of 4 weeks
- 2 Georgiana Hastings (1866-1955); born at Canon Frome, Herefordshire; married, at Tewkesbury, Gloucestershire, April 1891, Joseph Rushton Shortt (1860-1919); 1 daughter:
  - 1 Muriel Georgina Elizabeth Hastings (1892-1976)
- 2 Milo Warren (b. & d. 1869); died an infant; buried at Daylesford
- 3 Annette Maud Avondale (1872-1954); born at Maugersbury, Gloucestershire; died unmarried

Charlotte Julia Woodman-Hastings (1814-1886) was apparently an elder sister to Warren. It is interesting that she had also been induced to take the additional name of Hastings when she had been born 'Woodman'. Records are poor and there is little more information available for this family.

1837: 10 Oct: *The Imhoffs were also accompanied by Hastings Woodman, Great nephew of the deceased Governor, and standing in the same relation to Mrs. Hastings, being son of Mr. Woodman, formerly Rector or Brackley & Daylesford by Mademoiselle Chapuset, elder sister of our friend Marie, both being Germans, and nieces of Mr. Hastings ...*

1842: 27 Sep: *The party consisted of Mr. Franks, Sir C. Imhoff, who was accompanied by Mr. Impey, and Mr. Hastings Woodman ...*

1846: 24 Oct: *Met there Winter, and his wife's nephew, Hastings Woodman, an officer in the King of Bavaria's service.* 4 Dec: *A pleasant party Mr. Hastings Woodman was also a guest at the Wallers, brought by his relations, the Winters.* 10 Dec: *Dressed at the Unicorn for dinner at the Rectory, Stow, MW. calling for me in the carriage. A pleasant party: Mr. and Mrs. R. Waller, Mr. and Mrs. Winter, Mr. Hastings Woodman.*

1850: 25 Jun: *From Chastelton we returned to Adlestrop Hill, deviated by Adlestrop House and Village, and returned to Daylesford Parsonage in time to receive a visit from Mr. Hastings Woodman, and his sister, Miss W., great nephew & niece of Warren Hastings & his lady, nephew and niece of Mrs. Winter, and now on a visit to a Miss Penystone at Cornwell.*

1853: 5 Apr: *Among many other visitors of the Court with whom I was acquainted, was Hastings Woodman, the descendant, so to speak, of Governor and Mrs. Hastings, and now, I apprehend on the decease of Sir Charles Imhoff, entitled to a third share in the Daylesford property, which is upon sale.* 21 Jun: *Received a visit from Mr. & Mrs. Ruddle, Mr. Hastings Wodman, and Miss Townsend. They remained with me to luncheon, and set out in heavy rain to Mr. Ruddle's house near Tewkesbury, whence they came yesterday, and, after calling on Miss Penyston at Cornwell, and visiting Daylesford, had slept at Stow. Miss Townsend, daughter of a deceased Solicitor of Rugby, and niece of the Vicar of Aston Blank, is also niece of Mrs. Ruddle, who was a Miss Whitehouse, and a niece of Mrs. Witts of Brighton, her mother having been one of the many daughters of the Lake family. Another Miss W. married Mr. Townsend of Rugby, and a third is the second wife of Mr. J Williams Martin, of Shoborough House, Twyning, an old acquaintance and brother Magistrate of mine ... Hastings Woodman, in the service of the King of Wirtemburg, I believe a Cavalry officer, is great nephew both to the late Governor Hastings and the late Mrs. Hastings; being son of Mr. H's nephew, the late Revd. Woodman, Incumbent of Brackley, by his wife, a Miss Chapuzet, niece of Mrs. Hastings, and elder sister of Mrs. Winter... HW. is 38 years of age, the young lady hardly 18, with little or no fortune, but pretty, and very pleasing. The wedding is not likely to be long deferred, and the fiancés, after their Union, are likely to repair to Germany, the gentleman wishing to remain in service for a limited time at least. His sister, Miss Woodman, lives much with Miss Penyston, and, therefore, it was natural that H.W. wished to introduce to that lady his future wife. Hence the visit of the party to "the Hills," and their calling on me ...* 13 Dec: *With Mrs. W. Vavasour drove in the close carriage to Oddington, to dine with the Dean of Gloucester; where we met Miss Penyston, and Miss Woodman ...*

WOODROFFE — John Edward Woodroffe — *see also* Maria Witts[227]

John Edward Woodroffe (1822-1913), barrister-at-law, was born at Cork, Ireland. He married, September 1847, Maria (1822-1904), youngest daughter of Broome Phillips Witts and Jane Lake; they had 5 sons and 3 daughters:

- 1 Charles Henry Witts (1848-1888), JP for Hampshire; educated at Trinity College, Cambridge, and Lincoln's Inn; called to the bar, 1875; lived at Stydd House, New Forest, Hampshire; married, 18 August 1875, Catherine Mary (1848-1891), only child of John Goodale of Normanton, Derbyshire; divorced, 1886; Catherine died at Florence, Tuscany, Italy. It was Charles who brought forward the petition on the basis of 'malfunction of the parts of generation of the said Catherine Mary Woodroffe, otherwise Goodale and the said Charles Henry Woodroffe'. To this effect, he invited experts to inspect his 'parts and organs of generation ... to see whether his impotency cannot be relieved or removed by art or skill'. It is therefore rather puzzling that they had a son, but the whole business and the divorce seem to lead to the conclusion that in desperation Catherine had a liaison elsewhere. Nevertheless, as far as the records go, Charles and Catherine had 1 son:
  - 1 William Harold Goodale (1878-1953); educated at Emmanuel College, Cambridge; appears to have been a ward of his maternal uncle or great-uncle, W. R. Goodale of Oatlands, Moorland Park, Paignton, Devon; married, 1910, Alice Vivian Teague (1885-1966); died in Devon; at least two children, including 1 daughter:
    - 1 Alice (1913-1993)
- 2 William Tidd (1850-1859); died young
- 3 John Witts Allen (1851-1940); married Beatrice Fox-Young; 1 son and 2 daughters:
  - 1 Vera (1886-1969)
  - 2 Aileen Beatrice (1890-1985)
  - 1 Neville Leslie (1893-1914), 2nd Lt, Irish Guards; killed in action at the 1st Battle of Ypres
- 4 Duncan (1853-1917), vicar of Banstead, Surrey
- 5 George Frederick (1855-1938), clerk at the Bank of England (after 1877); educated at Winchester College; married, at

Upper Slaughter, 1899, Margaret Apphia Broome (1876-1969), eldest daughter of Francis Edward Broome Witts (1840-1913) and Margaret Hole, née Bourne (1848-1921); 4 sons and 2 daughters:

1 Frederick Witts (b. & d. 1900)
2 Geoffrey Broome Witts (1901-1982), stockbroker; educated at Winchester College; made lieutenant-colonel in the Territorials during the Second World War; married, at Madras Cathedral, 1929, Winifred Anne Wathen; twin daughters:
1= Susan (b. 1931); married, at Southwark Cathedral, 1960, Revd Crewdson Howard Lloyd (1931-1999); 3 sons:
1 Stephen Howard (b. 1961)
2 Andrew Woodroffe (b. 1963)
3 John Crewdson (b. 1965)
1=Jane (1931-2016); married, at Lower Kingswood, Surrey, 1957, Francis Oswald James Otway (1926-2009)
1 Margaret Joan (1902-1987); married, at St Mary's, Wimbledon, 19 June 1926, Percy Bantock Nevill (1887-1975)
2 Norah Apphia (1906-1988); married, December 1943, Eric Seale Haslam (1886-1967)
3 John Edward (1912-1998), solicitor; educated at Trinity College, Oxford; lived unmarried at 36 Lancaster Road, Wimbledon, 1939; married, 1972, Marilyn Northcote Toller (b. 1947); 3 daughters:
1 Kate Toller (b. 1974)
2 Apphia Witts (1977-1978)
3 Tabitha Witts (b. 1979)
4 Maurice George (1916-1932); died at Hertford, while at school

1 Ada Bickersteth (1857-1948); married, at Kensington, 12 November 1889, Lt-Col Charles Edward Lang (1849-1923), born at Corfu; 2 sons:
1 Conyers Frederick Woodroffe (1891-1969)
2 Norman Cyril (1894-1971)
2 Alice Jane (1860-1927); died unmarried at Bath
3 Ethel Mary (1866-1940); married, at St Stephen's, Kensington, 27 December 1888, Revd Francis Johnson Tuck (1856-1921); 4 sons and 1 daughter:
1 Gerald Louis Johnson (1889-1965)
2 Noel Johnson (1892-1964)
3 Duncan Johnson (1893-1916)
4 Percival Hubert Johnson (1900-1970)
1 Delia Mary Johnson (1908-1989)

Something rather odd must have happened in the early years, for when Capt. John Witts died in 1857 he bequeathed £1,000 to Maria Woodroffe, wife of John Edward Woodroffe, on the strict condition that it went to her personally and was not used for the payment of any debts that her husband may have accrued.

1847: 13 Aug: *... from Maria Witts, announcing her approaching marriage to a Mr. Woodroffe, a Barrister of Lincoln's Inn, of Irish extraction, and asking me to give her away, standing in the place of her deceased Father: the ceremony to be performed at Kingston upon Thames by her eldest brother ...* 14 Sep: *The marriage of Maria Witts to Mr. Woodroffe was announced to us today ...* 11 Oct., 17 Oct., 20 Oct: *... found Edward and myself in Court, having come over for the morning ... Maria Woodroffe, as usual, pleasing and agreeable in look and manner.* 11 Oct: *Shortly before dinner time Maria Woodroffe and her husband arrived from Cheltenham, on a visit to us. We found them very pleasing and agreeable. He is about 25 Years of age: a very talented and well educated man; having passed through Dublin College with credit. His Father, Dr. Woodroffe, now resident at Dublin, and infirm in health, retired from his profession, was for many years an eminent Surgeon at Cork, and has many children—three sons in the legal profession: one an Irish Barrister, another at the English bar, our guest, a third a Solicitor.*

1847: 25 Oct: *Called with Mr. Woodroffe at "the Cottage," where we saw Mr. and Mrs. Vavasour, with whom we partook of luncheon.* 26-27 Oct., 28 Oct: *An early breakfast to allow of Mr. and Mrs. Woodroffe being in time to proceed by Oxford to reach Town in the Evening. A fly took them to meet the Wonder coach ...* 24 Dec: *... she also heard form Dublin from Mr. Woodroffe, now arrived there on a visit to his family with his wife ...*

1848: 28 Mar: *Went to Brunswick Square, where I called on the Witts's and Woodroffe's, who live together ...* 19 Aug: *MW. received a letter from Mr. Woodroffe announcing that his wife had given birth to a son, and is doing well.*

1850: 25 Apr., 7 May.

1851: 23 May: *I drove in a cab to the far West, to visit Mrs. Woodroffe, in Inverness Road, terra incognita to me, being at the furthest part of Bayswater, opposite to Kensington Gardens, near Porchester Terrace, and at no great distance from the Great Western Railway terminus. Here are to be had fresher air, and glimpses of verdure ...* 24 May, 28 May: *Dined at the Woodroffe's in Inverness road ...*

1853: 16 Jun: *We halted for a few minutes near a house which has just been engaged for a country residence at Teddington by Mr. and Mrs. Woodroffe: they intend to give up their house in Inverness Road, Bayswater, and make Teddington their home, as beneficial to their young family, and sufficiently within reach of Town to admit of Mr. W. going to his chambers in Lincoln's Inn daily ...* 17-18 Jun.

WOODYATT — Thomas Woodyatt — *see also* **Keysall**[228]

Thomas Woodyatt (1771-1841), naval officer, was born at Malvern, Worcestershire. He was a lieutenant in the Royal Navy and served between 1799 and 1815. He married, 1818, Harriett (1775-1863), born at Claines, Worcestershire, the daughter of Michael and Penelope Biddulph of Ledbury, Herefordshire, and Copton Hall, Worcestershire. Thomas and Harriett lived at Holly Mount, Malvern. Princess Victoria stayed at Holly Mount when she visited Malvern in 1830, and the Woodyatt mansion was used by some of the royal entourage. There were no children of the marriage.

1824: 2 Jul: *We dined at Mr. R Wynniatt's at Guiting Grange, meeting Mrs. Wynniatt (Mr. R. W's mother,) Mrs. Scoope (Mrs. R. W's mother,) Mr. & Mrs. Woodyatt ... Mr. Woodyatt is brother of the late Mrs. C. Keysall, is in the navy, and resides at Malvern.*

1825: 17 Sep: *To the left, as we drew near Worcester, amid a cluster of trees was the church and village of Claines; the parish extends as far as the Foregate Street, Worcester: at Claines reside the Miss Woodyates, daughters of the eminent Physician, who recently died at Worcester, and sisters of my friend Charles Keysall's deceased wife.*

1830: 23 Jun: *She is about to visit Malvern this summer with the Princess, her daughter, & her usual suite; the Mansion of Mr. Woodyatt, with others adjoining, is engaged for their reception.*

WOOLER — Thomas Jonathan Wooler[229]

Thomas Jonathan Wooler (±1786-1853), journalist, radical, and police advocate, was born in Yorkshire. He started his life as a printer, but moved to London, and by 1808 he ran his own debating club, the Socratic Union, which met at the Mermaid tavern, Hackney. Wooler became closely associated with *The Reasoner* (1813-14), a literary magazine that published reports of debates held at the Globe and Mermaid taverns. In 1817 he published the first edition of *Black Dwarf* (1817-24), one of the most influential radical journals to follow the Napoleonic Wars. The journal's tone was satiric and its politics were those of radical constitutionalism.

Wooler was a gifted writer known for his ability to directly typeset his articles without first committing them to paper. Among his contributions to *Black Dwarf* were regular letters from the character named the Black Dwarf to various fictional correspondents. He was arrested in early May 1817 and faced two trials for seditious libel for two articles published in the third and tenth numbers of the *Dwarf*. The first article was entitled 'The right of petition' and the other, 'The past—the present—and the future'. Wooler was tried at Guildhall before Justice Charles Abbott and two special juries on 5 June 1817. The attorney-general, Samuel Shepherd, led the prosecution. Wooler defended himself brilliantly, with advice from Charles Pearson, the young City radical. He was acquitted in the second trial and, although found guilty in the first, serious procedural errors regarding the status and delivery of the jury's verdict led to a decision on appeal for a new trial. However, the government chose not to bring Wooler to trial on this occasion.

In late 1825 Wooler again appeared before the court of king's bench, where he failed to win a rule to show cause in his petition against the benchers of Lincoln's Inn for having denied his application to enter chambers to study to become a barrister. He exposed the exclusive practices of the inns of court in his *Case between Lincoln's Inn, the Court of King's Bench and Mr. T. J. Wooler* (1826). Wooler gradually drifted out of radical politics, commenting after the passing of the 1832 Reform Bill that 'these damned Whigs have taken all the sedition out of my hands'. Subsequently he worked as a legal advocate in the police courts. In 1845 Wooler published a legal handbook entitled *Every Man his Own Attorney*, intended to enable readers to avoid the expenses of a lawyer. He was married to Elizabeth, daughter of John Pratt of Kingsland; they had at least 1 son:

1 John Pratt Wooler (1824-1868)

It is most surprising that Witts should have used Wooler's services, but he was probably not aware of the character of the man he was working with. In his mistaken zeal to get Cox and Clifford convicted, he may have asked around and had Wooler suggested to him as a successful police advocate. It was most reassuring that the grand jury used 'minute sifting of the evidence' to bring no bill, for a little later the true murderer came to light proving that Cox and Clifford were innocent.

Wooler's son became a barrister, but drifted away from the legal profession to become a successful playwright. His greatest success was a farce in one act entitled *Allow Me to Apologize*.

1834: 16 Jul: *Received a packet from Mr. Brookes covering a letter to him from Mr. Wooler respecting the pros. of Cox and Clifford ...* 8 Aug: *... we were assisted by Mr. Wooler from London, who arrived yesterday evening ...* 12 Aug., 13 Aug: *but Wooler confidently asserted that the conduct of the Grand Jury was most extraordinary, that this minute sifting of the evidence was in fact the assuming to themselves a right to try the case, and that in all his experience he had never met with a similar proceeding ...*

WORDSWORTH — Charles Favell Forth Wordsworth [230]

Charles Favell Forth Wordsworth (1803-1874), barrister-at-law, was born at Harwich, the son of Robinson Wordsworth, a relative of the poet laureate. He was educated at the grammar school in Harwich and was called to the bar in January 1833. He specialised in railway law and became QC in June 1857. Wordsworth wrote numerous books, his most important being *The Law of Railway, Banking, Mining and Other Joint Stock Companies* (1845).

1850: 22 Jan: *Recd. a letter from a Mr. Charles Wordsworth, Paper Buildings, Temple, saying it had been reported that I meant to sell the Scale House property, and wishing, if it were so, to know the price.*

WORKMAN — Benjamin and Henry Workman, solicitors [231]

Benjamin and Henry were both born at Pershore, Worcestershire, the sons of Joseph Workman (1766-1825) and Sarah Turner (1773-1859). Benjamin Workman (1797-1877), solicitor, JP, landed proprietor, and farmer, married, but was a widower by 1861. In the 1861 and 1871 censuses he was listed as a JP, landowner, and farmer of 447 acres, living at Great Hampton, Worcestershire. His brother, Henry Workman (1801-1888), solicitor, DL, and farmer, was a widower by 1851 and, in that census, was listed as a solicitor and alderman of the borough of Evesham, and resident at Great Hampton. By 1861 he was also a DL and landowner of 342 acres. Both Benjamin and Henry were solicitors of Evesham; it is clear that Francis Witts held them in low regard.

1853: 15 Mar: *New Magistrates who qualified were ... Two Messrs. Workman, ci devant Solr. from Evesham or its neighbourhood.*

WORNUM — John and Frances Wornum [232]

John Wornum (1791-1857), army officer (HEIC), married, at Cheltenham, 1839, Frances Elizabeth (1802-1886), daughter of F. J. Jones of Seapoint, Dublin. Wornum retired from the HEIC Army as a major, and the couple lived at Leamington Priors. After she was widowed, Frances moved to Cheltenham.

1848: 2 Sep: ... *expected the arrival of Eliza Daniell to-day, but she never came. She has been visiting, at Gloucester, a Major and Mrs. Wornum, whose acquaintance she had formed at Leamington.*

WORRALL — George Worrall [233]

George Worrall (1768-1840), banker, JP, and landed proprietor, lived at Frenchay Park, near Bristol. Worrall was a partner in the Exchange Bank, Bristol, and in 1823 he acquired all of the upper portion of the common at Frenchay, and added two wings to the house. He was very active in the affairs of the parish, and was largely responsible for the building of the Frenchay church. He was a Gloucestershire JP and was appointed, 1834, captain of the Stapleton and Winterbourne Troop of the Gloucestershire Yeomanry Cavalry.

Worrall married Hannah (1778-1864), daughter and co-heir of Dr Thomas Rigge, of Clifton, whose other daughter married James Rooke. On James Rooke's death his two children, George and Elizabeth Rooke, were adopted by the Worralls. George and Elizabeth predeceased their adoptive parents, leaving them their property on condition that they took the name Rooke. Hannah, then a widow, did this in August 1840 by royal licence.

1804: 20 Sep: ... *in view of Knoll a place belonging to Mr. Worrall, & another beneath it, the property of Mr. Protheroe a*

Bristol lawyer, & merchant, enjoying singular advantages of situation & prospect ...

1826: 16 Jun.

1830: 20 Apr.

1837: 17 Oct: *Mr. Worrall seconded the amendment.*

WORSLEY — Charles Worsley[234]

Charles Worsley (1783-1854), Church of England clergyman, was the son of Henry Worsley of Gatcombe, Isle of Wight. He was educated at St Mary Hall and Wadham College, Oxford (BA 1804; MA 1807). He was appointed rector of Lesnewth, Cornwall, in 1813, and later served as incumbent at St Thomas's, Newport, Isle of Wight.

1805: 17 Mar: *Called on Worsley.* 30 Mar: *Walked with Dowell, Worsley & Drank wine & passed the Evening with Dowell.* 1 Apr: *Walked before breakfast with Dowell & Worsley.*

1806: 19 Mar: *Walked a little with Michell & with Worsley.* 20 Mar: *Dined in the Hall, conversing with Worsley.* 21 Mar: ... *walked with Adams & with Worsley round Ch. Ch. Meadow.*

WORSLEY — Ralph Worsley[235]

Ralph Worsley (1765-1848), Church of England clergyman, was the second son of Revd James Worsley, rector of Stonegrave, Yorkshire, and Dorothy, daughter of Sir Ralph Pennyman. He was educated at Westminster School and Trinity College, Cambridge (BA 1788; MA 1792). He was perpetual curate of St Olave's, York, 1790-1848; rector of Little Ponton, Lincolnshire, 1791-1829; and rector of Finchley, Middlesex, 1794-1848. He was also appointed canon of Ripon in 1792, and sub-dean of Ripon in 1801. He married, 1795, Elizabeth, second daughter of Thomas Gildart of Finchley, Middlesex.

1802: 28 Jan: *Walked out alone, & with the Ladies, Mr. Bowzer & the Revd. Mr. Worsley of Finchley joining us.*

1804: 16 Oct: *Called on Mrs. Reid, Mr. & Mrs. Baillie, Mr. & Mrs. Worsley.* 17-20 Oct.

WORTHINGTON — Charles Worthington[236]

Charles Worthington (±1762-1819), barrister-at-law, was born at Preston, Lancashire, the son of James and Anna Worthington. He was a barrister of Lincoln's Inn and of 11 Lansdown Crescent, Bath. He married, 1791, Elizabeth Maude; they had 1 daughter:

1 Charlotte Mary (b. ±1800); married, at Middlesex, 2 November 1821, Charles Crook, rector of Bath

The Worthingtons were northern folk, and from the diaries of Agnes Witts it becomes clear that Charles Worthington was a friend of the Backhouses; he took the part of Margaret's late father by giving her away on her marriage to Francis Edward Witts on 30 May 1808.

1808: 5 May, 6 May: *Called on Mr. Worthington in the Upper Crescent, & on Lady Riddell.*

WORTHINGTON — George Henry Worthington[237]

George Henry Worthington (1788-1864), army officer, was born in Lancashire. He married, at St Marylebone's, Westminster, 10 March 1830, Ann (1813-1854), daughter of George Worral Counsell (1758-1843) and Ann Trimnell (1775-1845); they had at least 1 daughter:

1 Anne Georgina Juliet Counsel (1832-1907)

The family lived in Blackfriar's Square, Gloucester. Worthington was a governor of the Gloucester Infirmary.

1846: 2 Jul., 22 Oct: *Quarterly meeting: numerously attended Mr. Gambier Parry in the Chair: present, among many more, Messrs. Purnell, Hyett, Baker, Whitcomb, Hall, Avery, Cols. Cother and Hawkins, Messrs. Helps, Clarke, Worthington, Walters &c.*

WRIGHT — Mr Wright at Bristol[238]

There is a possibility (but nothing more than that) that this was Thomas (b. 1775), the son of Joseph Wright (1734-1797), of Derby, and his wife, Hannah. Agnes Witts had had her portrait painted by Thomas Wright at Bath, and she and her family met him socially at Calwich Abbey, the home of their friends the Granvilles.

Thomas's mother Hannah was of lowly status, the daughter of a lead miner. On 21 May 1775, Thomas Wright was baptised at Wormhill, Derbyshire, a lead mining community. His father Joseph was in Italy at the time, and did not reach England until September. Joseph and Hannah also had a daughter, Anna Romana, born near Rome in August 1774; knowing that she was pregnant again, Hannah may have decided to return home much sooner than her husband.

Agnes mentioned Mr Wright somewhat enigmatically on 12 July 1799, while the Witts family were at Weimar:

> ... while Dinner is preparing we walk'd on the Bridge over the River Sallee, surveying the romantic scenery & imediately after went into the Castle to survey the Cabinet of natural curiosities which are well kept & arranged here we were join'd by our English friend Mr. Wright who is doing pennance by remaining at Jena to learn the German language, he return'd to the Inn with us drank Coffee & staid an hour or two till we set out for home ...

No other Wright of any note is mentioned in Agnes's diaries. Knowing her methods of maintaining a vast collection of friends and acquaintances, such a continuing connection with the family is feasible.

1806: 21 Feb: *Accompanied my Father to Bristol: left my card there with Mr. Wright ...* 22 Jun: To Bristol; *walked with Mr. Wright to the ruins of the Iron Bridge over part of the Canal, which fell as it was erecting two days ago & wounded severely several Workmen ...*

WRIGHT — Mr Wright, a relation by marriage to Broome Lake Witts

1853: 18 Jun: *After breakfast Mr. Wright, a gentleman who has married a lady descended from one of the Branches of the Witney Witts's, and so is not distantly related to Broome L. Witts, and who has a temporary residence at Esher, called ...*

WRIGHT — Charles Wright[239]

Charles Wright (b. 1820), solicitor's clerk, was born at Laughton, Lincolnshire; his family had moved to Gloucestershire in 1849 or 1850. Francis Witts was being partisan and unfair in being so dismissive of Charles Wright, who was only committed and persistent. He was the managing clerk of Edwin Tilsley, solicitor at Moreton-in-Marsh. Charles was married to Elizabeth (b. ±1819); they had 4 sons and 4 daughters:

1 Sarah Ann (b. ±1843)
1 John Burris (b. ±1846)
2 Alice (b. ±1847)
2 George William (b. 1850)
3 Charles H. (b. ±1852)
3 Elizabeth (b. ±1856)
4 Frank (b. ±1858)
4 Clara (b. ±1861)

By 1861 the family had moved to Lincoln, and by 1871 to Hulme, Manchester, where Charles became a law stationer.

1854: 17 Jul: *A printed letter from a person in the name of Wright, from Moreton in Marsh, signifying that he is a candidate for the Clerkship of our Union. He says he has been employed as Assistant Clerk of the Shipston Union—probably as Clerk to Mr. Tilsley of Moreton, the Solicitor, who holds the office of Clerk of the Union ...* 27 Jul., 29 Jul., 1 Aug., 3 Aug.

WRIGHT — Edward Wright[240]

Edward Wright (b. 1818), naturalist, was the eldest son of Thomas Wright of Otton, Essex. He was educated at Eton College and Christ Church, Oxford (BA 1839). He died in New Zealand.

1838: 8 May: *During my absence a young Oxonian, Mr. Wright of Xt. Ch. called with a friend, to us both being strangers, having driven over from Oxford to see the Thlaspi perfoliatum.*

WRIGHT — Frederick Wright, a friend of Thomas Howell[241]

Frederick Wright (d. 1873), lieutenant-colonel in the Royal Artillery, was born at Upton Pyne, Devon, the son of John Thomas Wright (1762-1838) and Catherine Jane Northcote (1764-1844). He joined the Royal Artillery as an ensign on 13 September 1805, and was promoted to lieutenant on 1 June 1806, captain on 22 April 1822, and major on 10 January 1837. He retired on half pay on 22 December 1846. He married, ±1816, Mary Elizabeth Hall (1801-1851); they had 1 son and 4 daughters:

1 Jaquetta (1817-1899)
2 Georgina Lucinda (1818-1901); married, at Canterbury, 8 August 1844, William Augustus Guy
3 Gertrude (1821-1880)
4 Katherine Fanny (1826-1889); died unmarried
1 Barrington Stafford (1832-1928), Church of England clergyman

Although retired, Frederick Wright was promoted to lieutenant-colonel in 1855. He died at 7 Westbourne Villas, Paddington, Middlesex. His executors were his daughter Katherine Fanny and his son-in-law William Augustus Guy.

1847: 14 May: *Also a letter from Howell ... forwards for my perusal a letter he received some time ago from his friend, Major Wright, dated Algiers, and giving an amusing and interesting account of Valencia, Algiers &c.*

1851: 27 May: *I found a note from Laura Howell, with an appointment to meet her and Miss Macdonnel with Major Wright at the Exhibition of the Royal academy.—Major W. is on half pay, an intimate of the Howells, a very agreeable, friendly, and travelled man: I had often been interested and amused by letters he had written from foreign countries in his frequent excursions, now at Madeira, now in Switzerland, and anon, perhaps in Russia. After a little search I found the trio, and will now name some other paintings ...*

WRIGHT — John Wright

John Wright, writer to the signet.

1854: 23 Jul: *Mrs. Dolphin sent two letters for my perusal—one from Mr. Wright—a Scotch Writer to the Signet, congratulating her on having obtained her deliverance from her ill-assorted Union; he addresses her as Mrs. Payne, using her maiden name; he writes in very proper terms hoping that the rest of her life may be passed in peaceful blessedness, and devotion to GOD according to his gospel: and that if they never meet again in this world, they may meet hereafter, where the recollection of this life's sorrows will only add to the joys of the redeemed—Little does this good man know the inward mind of her whom he thus piously addresses!*

WYATT — Alfred Wyatt — *see also* Hillier[242]

Alfred Wyatt (b. 1788), Oxonian, was the son of Thomas Wyatt and his wife, Mary, of Bromham, Wiltshire, which is located 3.5 miles north-east of Devizes. He was baptised at Rowde and was educated at Christ Church, Oxford (BA 1811; MA 1814).

There seems to have been a family connection between Alfred Wyatt and Michael Wyatt, who first met Francis Witts at Oxford in 1802, but nothing obvious has been uncovered. There was a connection to the architect Wyatts. Among several generations of Wiltshire Wyatts there were many prominent architects who designed a number of the country's well-known buildings. Thomas Henry Wyatt (1807-1880) designed Wilton church and the assize courts in Devizes; Benjamin Dean Wyatt (1775-1850) designed the Market Cross; and James Wyatt (1746-1813) designed Bowden House, near Lacock, and Fonthill Abbey. Matthew Wyatt II (1773-1831) married Anne, daughter of Brig.-Gen. George Hillier, of Devizes, and settled at Rowdeford House in 1818. Their son Matthew Digby Wyatt, another renowned architect and designer, was born at Rowde in 1820 and attended school in Devizes.

1806: 22 Aug: *The Venison remarkably well flavoured & drest. Conversed chiefly with Gaisford, C. Tylee, Tom Tylee, Alfred Wyatt &c.* 25 Aug: *Walked about the Town with me & with Alfred Wyatt & C. Tylee. Dined at the Elder Mr. Tylee's, very pleasantly meeting Mereweather Mrs. Tom Tylee, her Husband, Alfred Wyatt &c.* 27 Aug: *Called upon my friends the Hilliers. Met there Miss H. Tylee. Met & Conversed with Miss Tylee, Mrs. Lediard, Alfred Wyatt, Charles Tylee, W. Butcher &c.*

1807: 31 Aug: *Called at the Post at Devizes without success. Saw Alfred Wyatt & C. Tylee.* 7 Dec., 10 Dec: *Called upon Miss Hillier, where I met Miss C. Wyatt, Miss S. Hughes, & Miss H. Tylee.*

WYATT — Henry Herbert Wyatt[243]

Henry Herbert Wyatt (1822-1902), Church of England clergyman, was the only son of Thomas Wyatt (d. 1834), army officer (HEIC), of Calcutta. He was educated at Queen's College, Oxford (BA 1844; MA 1847), and entered the Church. He was perpetual curate of Holy Trinity chapel, Brighton, 1856-66; principal of Brighton Training College, 1863-86; vicar of Bolney, Sussex, 1872-86; and vicar of Conington, Northamptonshire, 1886. He married, 1849, Elizabeth; they had at least 2 sons and 1 daughter:

1 Edgar Herbert (1853-1933); died at Devonport, New Zealand
1 Grace Elizabeth (1855-1940)
2 Harold Frazer (1858-1925)

It is clear from the comments made by Francis Witts that Henry Wyatt was of the same family as Alfred and Michael Wyatt.

1853: 2 Feb., 1 Mar: *At last, at 10 P.M., came the Revd. H.H. Wyatt, Asst. Secretary, alone ... Mr. W. an agreeable & gentlemanlike person.* 2 Mar: *Mr. Wyatt and myself separately engaged in preparing for the special meeting S.P.G. to be held at Stow... Drove to Stow, accompanied by Mr. Wyatt.* 4 Mar: *I am pleased to have made Mr. W's acquaintance, and shall be glad of an opportunity of meeting him again. He is talented, right-minded, well informed, and agreeable. He is of that family of Wyatts of whom I knew something in early life, connected with the Estcourts &c. At one time he was Curate of Tetbury, at another of Loughborough.*

WYATT — Michael Wyatt [244]

Michael Wyatt (1780-1830), Church of England clergyman, was the son of Thomas Wyatt of Tamworth, Staffordshire. He was educated at Oriel College, Oxford (BA 1803), and St John's College, Cambridge (MA 1809). He was curate of Polesworth, Warwickshire, 1806; rector of Widford, Hertfordshire, 1808-12; rector of Ashley, Wiltshire, 1809; and rector of North Wraxall, Wiltshire, 1814-30. He also served as domestic chaplain to Charles Cornwallis 2nd Marquess Cornwallis Viscount Brome (1774-1823). Why he was spending time in Wiltshire is unknown, but there was presumably a family connection at Bromham, Wiltshire.

1802: 14 Mar: *Spent the Evening at Pagett's meeting Mr. Allworthy & a Mr. Wyatt of Oriel Coll.*

1807: 2 Jan: *... found Mrs. J. Tylee at home, with the Revd. Michael Wyatt & Miss Anstie.* 6 May: *Very pleasant & agreeably conversed with Mr. Long M.P. Estcourt, Revd. M. Wyatt, Tinker, Dr. Hill, Dr. Spalding &c.* 16 Dec: *Called upon the Hilliers, met Ch. Tylee & Michael Wyatt ...*

1808: 22 Feb: *... The other best performers were my friend Storau, Mrs. Mountain, Bannister &c. The Mayor of Garratt, followed part of which most amusing caricature I outstaid. Sat with Michael Wyatt.*

WYNCH — Paul Marriot Wynch and the Wynch family of Ashen [245]

Paul Marriott Wynch (1763-1841), senior merchant in the HEIC's Bengal Civil Service, married late in life, 1820, Sophia Martha Maling (b. 1810). The Wynch family came from Ashen, Suffolk. Paul and Sophia had at least two children; 1 son and 1 daughter:

1 Sophia Adeline Lydia (b. 1828); married William John Deane (1823-1895)
1 Charles George (1833-1876)

1851: 25 Mar: *Received a visit from Mr. Deane, the Curate of Wick Risington, who was accompanied by his Mother in law, Mrs. Wynch, a very lady-like and pleasing person....* 26 Mar: *Visited by Mr. and Mrs. Deane, Mrs. Wynch, and her son, a Rugbean, pupil to his brother in law.* 4-5 Apr.

1852: 18 Feb., 20 Feb., 24 Feb.

WYNDHAM — Henry Penruddocke Wyndham [246]

Henry Penruddocke Wyndham (1736-1819), JP and MP, was the eldest surviving son of Henry Wyndham, of St Edmund's College, Salisbury, and Arundel, daughter of Thomas Penruddocke of Compton Chamberlayne. He was educated at Eton College and Wadham College, Oxford. He was elected a fellow of the Society of Antiquaries on 6 February 1777 and a fellow of the Royal Society on 9 January 1783. He was a JP and an MP for Wiltshire, 1795-1812, but he rarely attended parliament.

1807: 11 May: *Drove Mr. Jones to the nomination of his cousin Rich Long, & H. P. Windham Esq., for the County at Devizes.*

WYNDHAM — Sophia Anne Wyndham at Cheltenham and Tunbridge Wells [247]

Sophia Anne Wyndham (1761-1830) was the second daughter of John Wyndham (1733-1765) and Elizabeth Dalton (1727-1785). She died unmarried at Hampton Court, Surrey. Her younger niece (whom she called her beloved niece in her will) was Harriet Sophia Shakespear, née Dyot-Bucknall (1799-1877), daughter of Thomas Skip Bucknall, MP, and Charlotte Elizabeth Wyndham. She married, at St George's, Hanover Square, Westminster, 19 October 1818, Arthur Shakespear. However, the Miss Bucknall present at Tunbridge Wells was most probably the elder niece (another beloved niece), Arabella Charlotte Hanmer, née Dyot-Bucknall (1788-1862), who married, at St Marylebone, Westminster, 14 July 1808, Thomas Hanmer. Arabella also died at Hampton Court.

1801: 8 Oct: *In the Evening came Mrs. & Miss Wyndham forming a party, which would have been dull, had not the Granvilles & my friend Fanny stept in to enliven conversation.* 10-11 Nov., 14 Nov.

1805: 10 Sep: *Called with my Mother upon Miss Windham.* 25 Sep: *at a party at Miss Windhams, which turned out a lively pleasant dance of six couple ....* 28 Sep., 30: *In the evening with Miss Windham & the Miss Bucknall, & drank tea & passed the evening with them en famille very pleasantly.* 1 Oct., 4 Oct: *Called on Miss Wyndham.*

WYNNE PENDARVES — Edward William Wynne Pendarves [248]

Edward William Wynne Pendarves (1775-1853), MP and landed proprietor, was the second, but only surviving, son of John Stackhouse, of Pendarves, and Susanna, daughter and heir of Edward Acton of Acton Scott, Shropshire. He was educated Harrow School and Trinity College, Oxford (1793), and was elected a fellow of All Souls in 1796. He married, 1804, Tryphena, daughter and heir of Revd Browse Twist of Bowden, Devon. He succeeded to the estates of his cousin Revd Luttrell Wynne in 1814, and those of his father in 1819. He took the additional name of Wynne by royal sign manual on 4 January 1815, and Pendarves in lieu of Stackhouse on 28 February 1815. He lived at Pendarves, near Camborne, Cornwall, and 36 Eaton Place, Belgrave Square. Wynne Pendarves was MP for Cornwall, 1826-32, and Cornwall West, 1832-53.

1803: 26 Dec: *Mr. Stackhouse of All Souls was a very pleasant fellow traveller; my friend Alford was also of the party as far as Bath.*

1804: 9 Mar: *Spent the Evening not very lively with G. Rashleigh, Stackhouse & Edgell.*

WYNNE — Richard Aubrey Wynne [249]

Richard Aubrey Wynne (1785-1805), Oxonian, was the son of Gabriel Wynne of Taunton Castle, Somerset. He was educated at University College, Oxford. He died of tuberculosis at Exmouth in 1805.

1803: 5 Nov: *Dined famously with Newbigging at St. John's Gandy, Messrs. Glead, Frith, Brodwen, Wynne & Mardenburgh made up the party; barring a short dispute, the Evening passed pleasantly enough.*

WYNNIATT — James Wynniatt [250]

James John Wynniatt (1832-1897), army officer, was born at Guiting Grange, a younger son of Reginald Wynniatt (1785-1860) and Catherine Brydges (1790-1865). He married, 1858, at Marylebone, Marie Götz [Goetz], born at Frankfurt; they had at least six children:

1 John Wenman (1858-1934)
1 Maude (b. 1860)
2 Brydges (b. ±1862)
2 Marie Wilhelmina (1865-1935)
3 Eustace Alexander Gordon (1867-1908)
4 Cecil (b. ±1871)

James was an officer of the 52nd Oxfordshire Light Infantry and 10th Hussars.

1852: 30 Mar: *Other guests came to dinner ... from Stanton Tom Wynniatt, his brother Jem, and his sisters Anne and Sophy ... his Brother, an enthusiast in music, has a powerful voice, which he exerts vigorously, shouting amain, and excuses himself on the plea that such was the style of the German Music Master, who taught him at Dresden, where he passed some months last year, in training for the military profession, but which he has not yet entered.* 7 Apr., 8 May: *Drove to dinner at Mrs. Dolphin's: the party consisted of Mrs. D., Miss Smith, Miss Kirby, James Wynniatt, and his sisters Susan and Harriet, now staying at Eyford.* 11 May, 14 Oct: *Wrote also to James Wynniatt to offer him a bed for Wednesday and Thursday night, on which days he is to dine at Eyford: this I do at Mrs. Dolphin's request, but readily.* 27 Oct., 28 Oct: *After breakfast James Wynniatt betook himself to Eyford ...* 29 Oct: *A large party to luncheon, with music—Mrs. Dolphin, Miss L Smith, Miss Walmesley, two Misses Wynniatt, Tom and Jem Wynniatt ...*

WYNNIATT — Reginald Wynniatt — ***see also*** **Daniel Lee Warner, Anne Scrope,** ***and*** **William Charles Lowndes-Stone** [251]

Reginald Wynniatt (1785-1860), landed proprietor, was the younger son of Reginald Wynniatt (1737-1819), of Stanton, Gloucestershire, and Frances Phillips (1752-1831) of Eaton Bishop, Herefordshire. Reginald inherited a quarter share in the estate of Guiting Grange from his father in 1819, which his father had held under the will of Mary Snell, widow of Powell Snell (d. 1813). Reginald purchased the remaining shares in 1826. At this date the estate comprised the following: Guiting Grange Manor [also known as Guiting Power Manor], together with the mansion house, deer park, and lands in Guiting Power; a small allotment of land in Temple Guiting; a moiety of the manor of Naunton along with the manor house and around 203 acres of land and various cottages in Naunton; and the manor of Westcote, Westcote Farm, and other lands and cottages within the manor, including Gawcombe Farm.

Reginald married, 1812, his cousin Catherine Brydges (1790-1865), daughter of Francis William Thomas (1751-1793) and Ann Brydges (1755-1829) of Tyberton Court, Herefordshire. Reginald and Catherine had at least fourteen children, an equal balance of 7 sons and 7 daughters:

1 Reginald (1813-1881); *see below*
1 Frances Ann (1814-1845); died unmarried
2 Wenman (1815-1841); drowned at London, Canada
2 Catherine (1817-1850); married, 1840, William Charles Lowndes-Stone; 1 son who died in infancy and 2 daughters:
  1 Catherine Charlotte (1841-1882); married, 1862, Capt. Robert Thomas Norton [later Lowndes-Stone-Norton] (d. 1895)
  2 Margaret Susan (1845-1932); married, 1871, Henry John Elwes (1846-1922)
3 Susan (1818-1895); died unmarried at Gloucester
3 Thomas William (1820-1881), JP; *see below*
4 Anne Mary (b. 1822); died unmarried at Elmore, Gloucestershire
5 Harriet (1824-1867); married, 1859, Revd J. E. Alcock, rector of Hawling; 2 daughters:
  1 Sophia Lucy
  2 Marian
6 Sophia (b. 1825); died unmarried at Cheltenham
4 Robert (b. 1827); presumably died an infant
7 Marianne (b. 1828); died unmarried at Prestbury, Gloucestershire
5 Robert James (1830-1860), naval officer; knighted, 1854; died unmarried; *see below*
6 James John (1832-1897); *see above*
7 Francis Brydges (1834-1849); died unmarried, a teenager

The diary entry for 2 March 1853 is very revealing. At some point after this date the Guiting estate was sold to John Waddingham and the Wynniatts retired to Stanton Court. In the 1851 census Reginald and his wife Catherine were registered at Stanton Court with seven of their unmarried children: Reginald, Thomas William, Susan, Anne, Harriett, Sophia, and Mary Ann. Shortly after this date Reginald (junior) moved to the Old Grange, Dymock. He married late in life. By 1861 only three unmarried children were at Stanton—Thomas William, Susan, and Anne—and by 1891, Susan and Anne were living at 4 Montpellier Grove, Cheltenham.

One Wynniatt son who receives virtually no coverage in the diaries was Robert James Wynniatt, an officer in the Royal Navy. In 1850, at the age of 21, he was made a member of the McClure Arctic Expedition, one of numerous British search efforts to determine the fate of the Franklin's lost expedition. The McClure expedition was distinguished as the voyage during which Robert McClure became the first person to confirm and transit the Northwest Passage by a combination of sea travel and sledging. McClure and his crew spent three years locked in the pack ice aboard HMS *Investigator* before abandoning it and making their escape across the ice. They were rescued by HMS *Resolute*, which was itself later lost to the ice. McClure returned to England in 1854, where he was knighted and rewarded for completing the passage. In 1860, Robert Wynniatt, by then ranked commander, was on board HMS *Nimrod* at Shanghai, during the Second Opium War. He died around that time, unmarried.

1823: 23 Jul: *The dinner party consisted, in addition to the family in the house, of Mr. Wynniatt, of Staunton, and the younger branches of the Gist family.* 8 Aug., 22 Dec: *I also met Mr. Wynniatt of Stanton.*

1824: 6 Apr: *We had a dinner party; Lady & Miss Reade, Mr. & Mrs. Egerton Leigh, Mr. R. Wynniatt ...* 7 May, 28 Jun: *I dined at Mr. Hurd's, the Rector of Naunton, meeting Mr. Wynniatt, Mr. R. Wynniatt ...* 2 Jul: *We dined at Mr. R Wynniatt's at Guiting Grange, meeting Mrs. Wynniatt (Mr. R. W's mother,) Mrs. Scrope (Mrs. R. W's mother,) Mr. & Mrs. Woodyatt, Mr. Bowen & Mrs. Wynniatt of Staunton.* 26 Aug., 17 Sep., 1 Nov: *I went to Stanway by Lady Elcho's invitation to meet some of her neighbours at dinner ... Mrs. R. Wynniatt and her eldest daughter & Mr. T. Wynniatt.*

1826: 17 Apr: *We dined at Mr. Dolphin's at Eyford. We met there Mr. Talbot, Mr. & Mrs. R. Wynniatt ...* 22 Apr., 15 May, 30 Jun: *Lady Elcho had invited Sir Thomas Phillipps, Mr. Wynniatt, Mr. & Mrs. R. Wynniatt & Mr. Bowen, all of whom came to dinner.* 25 Aug.

1827: 8 May: *We went on without alarm till very near Mr. Wynniatt's park wall, when I gave him a slight touch with the whip ... We took the horse to Mr. Wynniatt's stables, who allowed his men to assist in taking the broken carriage to Guiting Grange also, where it will remain till I send it to Gloucester to be repaired. I remaindered an hour with Wynniatt, and then walked home ...* 7 Aug: *We dined and slept with our friends, the Browne's at Salperton. Mr. & Mrs. R. Wynniatt, with their eldest son, made up the party: it was, as usual, pleasant and sociable.* 16 Aug.

1828: 5 Nov: *We dined at Eyford. The Dolphins have a large party ... Reginald Wynniatt came to dinner*

1829: 27 Feb., 22 Sep.

1833: 18 Jan: *We dined at Lady Reade's at Oddington ... Mr. Wynniatt, his eldest son & daughter, Mr. Chamberlayne with ourselves made up the party.* 24 Oct.

1834: 26 Jul., 28 Jul: *Henry Tracy called with young Reginald Wynniatt on his canvass for his brother ...* 11 Aug: *I noticed Messrs. Wynniatt, Greenaway, Lindow &c.* 5 Sep: *A dinner party ... Mr. Wynniatt and two daughters dined with us.* 24 Oct., 1 Nov.

1835: 14 Jan.

1836: 3 Aug: *We entertained the Dean of Gloucester ... also Mrs. Wynniatt with her eldest son, and two elder daughters ...* 30 Aug., 18 Nov: *Reginald Wynniatt the Elder called, having heard that I was indisposed.*

1837: 15 Aug: *Dined (M.W., E.F.W. and myself) at the Wallers, Farmington Lodge ... Reg. Wynniatt, Junr. with his Sisters Kitty and Fanny ...* 22 Aug: *We also met Mrs. & Miss Wynniatt ...* 25 Nov.

1838: 25 May, 15 Aug., 22 Dec.

1839: 16 May.

1840: 20 Mar., 27 May: *Drove MW. to Guiting Grange to call on the Wynniatt family on occasion of the recent marriage of Miss. C.W. to Mr. Lowndes, eldest Son of Mr. Lowndes Stone, an Oxfordshire Gentleman, whose estate and place at Brightwell adjoin Watlington.* 30 May: *Drove MW. to Guiting Grange to call on the Wynniatt family on occasion of the recent marriage of Miss. C.W. to Mr. Lowndes, eldest Son of Mr. Lowndes Stone, an Oxfordshire Gentleman, whose estate and place at Brightwell adjoin Watlington.* 17 Jul: *On our return home called at Guiting Grange to pay our respects to Mr. and Mrs. W. Lowndes, now visiting the Wyniatts, for the first time after their Union. Saw Mrs. Wynniatt, her son Tom, and eldest daughter, also the Bride and Bridegroom ...* 8 Oct.

1842: 22 Mar: *Reginald Wynniatt the younger, sent over in the evening the Lower Guiting Constables ...* 23-24 Mar., 26 Mar., 17 May, 8 Jul., 20 Jul: *A dinner party; we were favoured with the company of... Mr. Wynniatt with his daughter Harriet, and son in law, W. Lowndes ...* 8 Aug., 12 Oct.

1843: 19 Jan: *I set out to ride homeward with Bowen, R. Wynniatt, & his boys, but my horse was so restless that I was obliged to dismount and lead him home.* 11 Aug., 26 Nov: *Reginald Wynniatt Junr. called, and accompanied us to Evening church; the church at Lower Guiting being in a state not to be used for divine service ... this alteration has been disapproved by the elder Wynniatt, and has been a source of strife and heart-burning.*

1844: 17 Feb., 15 May: *MW. and I drove to Stanway: as we passed by Guiting Grange, we met and parleyed with Mr. Wynniatt and Mr. & Mrs. W Lowndes Stone; accepted an invitation to dine at the Grange on Friday next.* 17 May: *Poor Mrs. Wynniatt lamentably lame with paralysis.* 23 Aug: *A dinner party; entertained Mr. and Mrs. Chamberlayne, Mr. Wynniatt, Regd. Wynniatt, and two Misses W...* 29 Aug., 3 Sep: *Mrs. and Miss Susan Wynniatt called upon us.* 13 Sep., 16 Dec.

1845: 12 Mar: *Mr. Wynniatt, accompanied by Mr. Guise, eldest son of the Baronet, had called, and left a note inviting me to dinner at Guiting Grange on Friday ...* 13-14 Mar., 24 Mar., 26 Apr: *Wrote to R Wynniatt to condole with him and his family on the severe affliction which has befallen him. His second daughter, married to Mr. Lowndes Stone, of Oxfordshire, has lately been confined in London of a daughter, having already two children, a son and daughter.—Mr. W.L.S. left her in town for his Father's seat in Oxfordshire, intending to return to accompany her thither in a few days: he took with him his little boy: somewhere he caught a contagious disease, and in two days, I believe, was a corpse; the poor little boy died on the day following;—of course the widow & both families, at Guiting Grange and Brightwell, plunged in the deepest grief: the widow barely recovering after her accouchement.* 16 May: *Wrote a note of enquiry and condolence to R Wynniatt, as we had heard a very bad account of the state of Miss W's health, and that Mrs. Lowndes Stone had left Guiting Grange suddenly in great alarm as to the health of one of her surviving children ...*20 May: *Miss W. is fast sinking into the grave: the alarm as to Mrs. Lowndes Stone's child has been removed by its recovery from what proved to be a temporary indisposition ...* 23 May: *Called at Eyford ... heard there that poor Miss Wynniatt died last night.* 14 Jun.

1846: 5 Oct: *Mrs. and Miss Wynniatt called: the former so lame and helpless as to be unable to get out of her carriage, into which MW. entered, & there received her visit.* 9 Nov., 25 Nov: *A dinner party ... Mr. T Wynniatt with his sisters, Susan and Anne ...* 7-8 Dec.

1847: 12 Mar., 9 Jun., 2-3 Jul., 6 Jul., 13 Aug., 7-8 Sep., 16 Sep: *Mr. Wynniatt with his son Tom, and his daughters, Susan and Harriet ...* 12 Oct: *The Rectory House is spacious & very commodious; very well built, somewhat in the Tudor style, under the incumbency of Mr. Wynniatt, and shortly before he sold the advowson to Mr. W.H.B[loxsome] ...*

1850: 20 Jan: ... *Miss Susan Wynniatt, who with her sister, Sophy, is passing a day or two at Eyford, with Mrs. Dolphin who returned a few days since, in very sad health ...* 8 Nov.

1852: 30 Mar: *Other guests came to dinner ... from Stanton Tom Wynniatt, his brother Jem, and his sisters Anne and Sophy ...* 8 May: *Drove to dinner at Mrs. Dolphin's: the party consisted of Mrs. D., Miss Smith, Miss Kirby, James Wynniatt, and his sisters Susan and Harriet, now staying at Eyford.* 27 Oct., 29 Oct: *A large party to luncheon, with music—Mrs. Dolphin, Miss L Smith, Miss Walmesley, two Misses Wynniatt, Tom and Jem Wynniatt ...* 31 Oct.

1853: 2 Mar: *The effects of folly and expensive and thoughtless habits are developed at last in the Wynniatt family. Roginald Sonr. obliged to keep out of the way of his adverse creditors, and the establishment to be broken up at Stanton. Poor Mrs. W. and her silly daughters:—What will become of them?* 6 Jun: *Met the elder Wynniatt, on his way to Town, and we were fellow travellers throughout the journey.*

1854: 10 Jun: *Miss Walmsley paid me a visit: much confidential communication as related to the Wynniatt family, and Mrs. Dolphin.*

WYNNIATT — Reginald Wynniatt[252]

Reginald Wynniatt (1813-1881), JP and landed proprietor, was born at Dymock, Gloucestershire, the eldest son of Reginald Wynniatt (1785-1860) and Catherine Brydges (1790-1865). He lived at Old Grange, Dymock, Gloucestershire, and in the 1861 census he was listed as unmarried and living with his mother and sisters Sophia and Maria. Reginald married, at Kensington, 21 November 1869, Caroline Betha (1848-1919), daughter of William Vansittart (1813-1878) and Harriette Humphrys (1811-1852); they had 1 daughter:

- 1 Harriett (1870-1944); married, at Bradfield, Berkshire, 23 April 1896, Henry Mildmay Husey (1857-1916); 2 sons and 1 daughter:
  - 1 Ernest Wynniatt (1897-1958), Capt. RMA; awarded the Croix de Guerre (Belgium)
  - 1 Mary Wilder Wynniatt (1899-1963)
  - 2 Reginald Wynniatt (1902-1970)

In the 1881 census Reginald was listed as a magistrate, married, and living back at Stanton Court. He died a few weeks later at Steyning, Sussex. Following his death, Caroline married secondly,

13 September 1882, Horace Drummond Dean (1854-1930). She also died at Steyning.

1833: 18 Jan: *We dined at Lady Reade's at Oddington ... Mr. Wynniatt, his eldest son & daughter.*

1834: 28 Jul: *Henry Tracy called with young Reginald Wynniatt on his canvass for his brother ...* 11 Aug: *I noticed Messrs. Wynniatt, Greenaway, Lindow &c.*

1836: 3 Aug: *We entertained the Dean of Gloucester ... also Mrs. Wynniatt with her eldest son, and two elder daughters ...* 30 Aug.

1837: 15 Aug: *Dined (M.W., E.F.W. and myself) at the Wallers, Farmington Lodge ... Reg. Wynniatt, Junr. with his Sisters Kitty and Fanny ...*

1842: 22 Mar: *Reginald Wynniatt the younger, sent over in the evening the Lower Guiting Constables ...* 23-24 Mar., 26 Mar.

1843: 19 Jan: *I set out to ride homeward with Bowen, R. Wynniatt, & his boys ...*

WYNNIATT — Thomas Wynniatt[253]

Thomas Wynniatt (1779-1830), landed proprietor, was an elder son of Reginald Wynniatt (1737-1819), of Stanton, Gloucestershire, and Frances Phillips (1752-1831) of Eaton Bishop, Herefordshire. He was educated at Christ Church, Oxford (BA 1801; MA 1804).

1824: 1 Nov: *I went to Stanway by Lady Elcho's invitation to meet some of her neighbours at dinner ... Mrs. R. Wynniatt and her eldest daughter & Mr. T. Wynniatt.* 2 Nov.

1826: 30 Jun: *Lady Elcho had invited Sir Thomas Phillipps, Mr. Wynniatt, Mr. & Mrs. R. Wynniatt & Mr. Bowen, all of whom came to dinner.*

1827: 24 May: *We met a party from Herefordshire, a Mr. & Mrs. Lockie, the Lady a relative of the Wynniatts, Mr. Wynniatt of Stanton ...* 26 Aug.

1829: 27 Feb., 22 Sep.

WYNNIATT — Thomas William Wynniatt[254]

Thomas William Wynniatt (1820-1881), JP and landed proprietor, was the second son of Reginald Wynniatt (1785-1860) and Catherine Brydges (1790-1865). He was educated at St Mary Hall, Oxford. Following the family's financial disaster he moved to Stanton. In the 1861 census he was registered as living with his sisters Susan and Anne; all three were unmarried. Thomas remained at Stanton Court right up to his death. He died unmarried.

1840: 20 Mar., 27 May: *Saw Mrs. Wynniatt, her son Tom, and eldest daughter, also the Bride and Bridegroom ...*

1843: 19 Jan: *I set out to ride homeward with Bowen, R. Wynniatt, & his boys ...*

1846: 5 Oct: *Mrs. and Miss Wynniatt called: the former so lame and helpless as to be unable to get out of her carriage, into which MW. entered, & there received her visit.* 9 Nov., 25 Nov: *A dinner party ... Mr. T Wynniatt with his sisters, Susan and Anne ...*

1847: 16 Sep: *Mr. Wynniatt with his son Tom, and his daughters, Susan and Harriet ...* 30 Sep: *... dinner at the W. Vavasours at Maugersbury House ... T. Wynniatt, with his sisters Susan and Anne ...*

1850: 1 Jan: *My son came with T. Wynniatt about midday, and returned with him after the principal business ...*

1851: 31 Mar: *My Son returned with T. Wynniatt by train to Cheltenham, & home in T.W's open carriage ...* 2 Apr.

1852: 30 Mar: *Other guests came to dinner ... from Stanton Tom Wynniatt, his brother Jem, and his sisters Anne and Sophy ... T. Wyniatt sings in a gentlemanly style with a weak voice, but good taste ...* 7 Apr., 27 Oct., 29 Oct: *A large party to luncheon, with music—Mrs. Dolphin, Miss L Smith, Miss Walmesley, two Misses Wynniatt, Tom and Jem Wynniatt ...*

1853: 8 Jan: *... They also propose to me to advance £3000 on mortgage of some property of Mr. T. Wynniatt, at Stanton; further explanations on these points are to be given to me vivâ voce, on Thursday next.* 13 Jan: *To Mr. Sewell's office ... and the proposed loan on Mortgage of T. Wynniatt's Stanton property, respecting which I agreed to the arrangements proposed ... and lend the like sum on mortgage of the Wynniatt property and TW's share of a Settlement on younger children made on the marriage of his Parents ...* 27 Jan., 10 Feb.

WYNTER — Philip Wynter[255]

Philip Wynter (1792-1871), Church of England clergyman, was the son of Philip Wynter of Aldborough, Suffolk. He was educated at St John's College, Oxford (BA 1815; MA 1819; BD 1824; DD 1828), where he was a scholar from 1811 to 1814 and a fellow from 1814 to 1828. He was also dean of arts and tutor at St John's, 1822-28; catechetical lecturer, 1827; select preacher 1828 and 1833; president 1823-71; and vice-chancellor 1840-44. He was appointed canon residentiary at Worcester in 1868, and master of St Oswald's, Worcester, in 1869.

1829: 18 Feb: *Two Committees were promptly formed in Oxford, one of men, who considered Peel unworthy of being re-elected ... Among the opponents of the Minister we find Dr. Wynter ...*

1844: 26 Sep: *the Vice Chancellor, Dr. Wynter, President of St. John's, retires at the beginning of Michs. term from his office ...* 8 Oct: *Therefore, when the retiring Vice Chancellor, Dr. Wynter, made his speech, as usual, in Latin ...*

WYNTER — John St Thomas Wynter[256]

John St Thomas Wynter (1808-1891), surgeon, was the son of Maj. George Jacob Wynter (1782-1873), of Bedfordshire, and Hephzibah Wagstaff (1781-1850) of Onley, Buckinghamshire. He was a surgeon at Winslow, Buckinghamshire. He married, 1843, Frances (1808-1843), daughter of Philip Wynter (1753-1827) and Anne Elizabeth Hamilton (1769-1843). Frances was presumably a cousin of some degree. John married secondly, 1847, Emmeline Jane Howell (1822-1865); and thirdly, 1870, Maria Stuart Kirkland (1845-1912). There do not appear to have been children from any of the marriages.

1847: 18 May: *I received a letter from Howell, announcing the very unexpected intelligence that Emmeline had, at her place of seclusion, Mursley, in Buckinghamshire, where she is residing with a Clergyman named Horne,* whose wife is sister to Mrs. Parsons, late of Upton St. Leonards, formed a connection with a medical Gentleman, named Wynter, practising at Winslow a widower of 40 years of age, of respectable character, well spoken of by Mrs. Parsons and her Sister ...* 19 Jun: *Emmeline is to be married to Mr. Wynter, Medical practitioner at Winslow, on the 29th. Inst*

XIMENES — Morris [Moses] Ximenes[1]

Sir Morris [Moses] Ximenes (1762-1830), captain of the volunteers, was a member of the London Exchange, where he made a large fortune. In 1802 he was elected a warden of the Bevis Marks Synagogue, but declined to accept; when he was fined he resigned from the community and converted to Christianity. Ximenes appears to have adopted a military career, and was known as Captain Ximenes. He was knighted, and became high sheriff for Kent.

1801: 20 Jul: *Left Stanlake soon after Breakfast in a Post chaise. The Road we had passed before. It was rendered very lively upon occasion of a Review of Capt. Ximenes troop of Volunteers, when they were to receive their colours.*

Y

YELVERTON — *see also* Rawdon Hastings [1]

Barbara Yelverton, Baroness Grey of Ruthin (1810-1858), married, 1831, George Augustus Rawdon Hastings (1808-1844), a godson to the Prince of Wales. He was styled earl of Rawdon, 1817-26, and was a lord of the bedchamber, 1830-31, and bearer of the golden spurs at the coronation of William IV. Following Hastings' death, Barbara married, secondly, Reginald Henry, who took the name of Yelverton in lieu of Henry by royal licence. Barbara Yelverton died of a stroke in Rome and was buried in the English cemetery there.

1838: 26 Mar: *His Lady is Baroness Grey de Ruthyn in her own right; they are both young, and she widely different in habits and temperament from her Lord.*

YARBOROUGH — earl of Yarborough — *see* Pelham

YEARP — Richard Yearp [2]

Richard Yearp (1789-1867), Upper Slaughter parishioner, was born at Upper Slaughter, the son of Daniel (1759-1832) and Anne Yearp (1764-1831). They appear to have had 2 sons and 3 daughters:

- 1 Richard (1789-1867)
- 1 Elizabeth (1792)
- 2 Anna (1797-1862); married, at Upper Slaughter, 4 July 1822, William Dix (1795-1862); 1 son and 2 daughters:
  - 1 Catharine (1825-1873); married, 1851, Thomas Edgington (b. 1831)
  - 1 Alfred (1829-1920); married, at Witney, December 1866, Elizabeth Hemming (b. 1834)
  - 2 Mary Ann (b. 1832)
- 2 William (1799-1858), shoemaker; died unmarried
- 3 Rebecca (b. 1804); married, at Upper Slaughter, 15 August 1831, George Collett (1807-1879), blacksmith; 3 sons and 1 daughter:
  - 1 Charles (1832-1906)
  - 2 Edward (b. 1834)
  - 3 Frederick (1835-1874); died unmarried
  - 1 Martha (b. 1837)

Rebecca presumably died sometime after 1841, but no record has been found. In the 1851 census William Yearp (b. 1799) was listed as a shoemaker, living in the household of his brother-in-law, William Dix, farmer. George Yearp (±1803-1863) was a land surveyor and widower, born at Upper Slaughter but living in West Street, Chadlington, Oxfordshire. No baptism record has been found for him, but he was probably related.

1847: 20 Aug: *Conferred with W. Dix, whose brother in law, R. Yearp, is more or less deranged, and had disturbed us during the night, by knocking at our doors on a vain pretence ...* 14 Sep: *... and the family of Wm. Dix, with reference to Richd. Yearp, who is not in his right mind.* 27 Oct: *Visited a sick parishioner, R. Yearp, of whom it is hard to say, whether he is more diseased mentally or bodily.* 29 Oct., 9 Nov: *Mr. Collins, Surgeon, Bourton on the Water, called as to visiting R. Yearp, to ascertain the State of his mind, whether a lunatic, and fit to be removed to the Lunatic Asylum.* 11 Nov., 13 Nov., 16 Nov., 26 Nov.

YEARP — Thomas Yearp and the Yearp family of Lower Slaughter [3]

Thomas Yearp (±1812-1888), shoemaker, was born at Lower Slaughter, the son of Thomas Yearp, cordwainer, and his wife, Betty. He married Ann (±1810-1892), born at Ashton-under-Hill, Worcestershire, the daughter of Thomas Jackson (1780-1851) and Ann Gibbs (1781-1858); they had at least 3 sons:

- 1 Thomas (1845-1914); married Sarah Anne (b. ±1845)
- 2 William (1848-1920); married Selina (b. ±1848), born at Duntisbourne Leer, Gloucestershire; at least 1 son and 2 daughters:
  - 1 Beatrice (b. ±1849)
  - 2 Elsie (b. ±1855)
  - 1 Charles L. (b. ±1859)
- 3 Benjamin Berwick (1849-1882), wine and spirits merchant at Stow-on-the-Wold; traded from 'Wine Vaults', between Market Square and the White Hart; married Mary, who was from Cheltenham

---

1850: 6 Mar: *M.W. continues in the same state; she admitted to her dressing room to day Anne Yearps, a respectable old servant of ours, married to a tradesman of Lower Slaughter, who was anxious to see her.* 19 Aug: *... she is on a visit to her former fellow servant, Mrs. Yearp, wife of the shoemaker at L Slaughter.*

1851: 21 Jan: *Called on Thos. Yearp's wife, Lower Slaughter with her eldest boy's Provident Bank Cheque Book; he having made a deposit.*

1852: 1 Jun: *Called at Mrs. T. Yearp's to speak with her as to Emily Peard ...*

1853: 15 Jan: *Walked to Lower Slaughter to make enquiries of Mrs. T. Yearp as to Emily Peard, stated to be in a very impaired health, and straitened circumstances, at Cheltenham left with Mrs. Y. a Sovereign to be remitted by her to E.P., as a distressed and deserving old Servant.*

YEOMANS — Henry Yeomans [4]

Henry Yeomans (1784-1813), Church of England clergyman, was the son of William Yeomans of Worcester. He was educated at Pembroke College and University College, Oxford (BA 1807; MA 1810), and was rector of Little Wigborough, Essex, 1812-13.

1804: 6 Mar: *Drank wine with Trevenen, Messrs. Ingram, Plymly, Crawley, Yeomans &c.*

YONGE — Charlotte Theresa Yonge — *see* Dowell

YORK — the duke of York — *see* Brunswick-Lüneburg

YORKE — Charles Frederick Yorke and Daniel Yorke, bankers of Oundle [5]

Charles Frederick Yorke (1787-1857), banker, was baptised at Oundle, the son of James and Catherine Yorke. In the 1851 census he was listed as a banker and merchant living at 12 Narrow Bridge Street, Peterborough. He had at least 1 son and 2 daughters:

- 1 Ann (b. ±1810)
- 2 Elizabeth (b. ±1827)
- 1 Frederick William (b. ±1815), banker

Daniel Yorke (1794-1861), banker, was baptised at the village of

Southwick, near Oundle, Northamptonshire, the son of Adam and Sarah Yorke. It seems probable that Charles and Daniel were cousins to some degree. They traded under the names of the Peterborough Bank and the Oundle Bank. In August 1844 they had £12,545 of bank notes in circulation.

1835: 28 Mar: *In the evening wrote to ... Messrs. Yorke, Bankers, Oundle ...* 23 May, 25 May, 29 May.

1837: 4 Jun: *I failed to mention yesterday a letter received from Messrs. Yorke, Bankers, Oundle with a statement of my acct. with them as Exor. of Mrs. M. Hunt.* 7 Jun.

1838: 11 Jul., 20 Jul., 10 Dec., 22 Dec.

1847: 16 Aug., 12 Nov., 20 Nov.

1850: 5 Jan: *Wrote to Messrs. Yorke, Bankers, Oundle ...* 10 Jan., 12 Jan.

YORKE — Charles Philip Yorke [6]

Charles Philip Yorke (1764-1834), politician, was the second son of Charles Yorke of Tittenhanger. He was educated at Harrow School and St John's College, Cambridge. He was admitted at Lincoln's Inn in 1780, and called to the Middle Temple in 1787. He went on an Italian tour in 1788-89, and married, 1790, Harriott, daughter of Charles Manningham of Thorpe, Surrey.

Yorke was MP for Cambridgeshire, 1790-1810; St Germans, 1810-12; and Liskeard, 1812-18. His appointments included the following: secretary at war, February 1801–August 1803; privy councillor, 20 February 1801; secretary of state for home affairs, August 1803–May 1804; teller of the exchequer, February 1810; first lord of the Admiralty, May 1810–March 1812; and charity commissioner, 1818-21. Yorke was a captain of the Cambridgeshire Militia in 1792, a major in 1794, lieutenant-colonel in 1799, and colonel in 1806-11.

1801: 8 Jun: *... on the Ministerial side Mr. Wilberforce seemed to me the best orator: Mr. Abbot, Mr. Addington, Mr. Baker, Mr. Yorke, Mr. Windham, Mr. O'Hare & Lord Hawkesbury chiefly arrested my attention.*

1806: 8 Mar: *... at Mrs. Salters, meeting the Hon. Mrs. Yorke & Miss Bradby, Lady Ford & Miss Ford, Mrs. Otway, & Mr. Cox ...* 15 Mar: *... in a small party at Lady Ford's; Mrs. & Miss O Callaghan, Mrs. Salter & Isabella, Honble. Mr. Yorke ...*

YORKE — John Yorke [7]

John Yorke (1788-1862), JP, DL, and banker, was the only surviving son of William and Margaret Yorke of Thrapston, Northamptonshire. He lived at Thrapston House, Huntingdon Road, with his wife Juliana Frances Ann Yorke (1789-1875), who appears to have been a cousin. They had at least 1 son:

1 William (b. ±1827), solicitor and banker

At some point soon after the death of Stephen Eaton in 1834, John Yorke became a partner with George Eland and the Thrapston bank became known as the Thrapston and Kettering Bank. The Charter Act of 1844 limited the notes issued by banks. However, authority was given for John Yorke and George Eland of the Thrapston and Kettering Bank to issue notes amounting to the value of £11,559. John's son William Yorke later became involved, and after his death the business was carried on by the Eland family. In 1888 financial difficulties led to an offer by the Stamford, Spalding and Boston Bank to pay creditors 15 shillings in the pound (75 per cent) and take over the business. The Thrapston and Kettering Bank eventually became part of Barclays.

The Yorke family of Thrapston had connections with the Hunt family going back for more than a century; they had acted over the generations as advisors and stewards to the Hunts. Presumably there was also a connection to the Yorkes of Oundle and Peterborough.

Following the death of her husband, Juliana moved to 19 South Street, Mayfair, London, to be with her bachelor brother Charles Yorke (1790-1880), a retired general.

1835: 25 Mar: *At eleven o clock the preparations for the funeral of our deceased friend were nearly completed. Mrs. M. Hunt had desired to be buried in an unostentatious manner...Besides George Hunt, Thomas Hunt, and myself, who attended as Mourners, four gentlemen of the neighbourhood had been invited. Mr. Yorke of Thrapstone ...*

1847: 14 Aug: *Transacted business at the Thrapstone Bank relating to the Hunt property... Rejoined the Hunts at the parsonage, being introduced to the incumbent, Mr. Bagshaw, and his family.—Then called on Mrs. Yorke the lady of the Banker and principal inhabitant of the place in the outskirts of the Town.*

YORKE — Joseph Yorke [8]

Joseph Yorke (1807-1889), MP and landed proprietor, was the eldest son of Joseph Yorke, of Forthampton Court, and Catherine, daughter of James Cocks, banker, of London. He was educated at Eton College and St John's College, Cambridge. He married, 1834, Frances Antonia, daughter of Reginald Pole Carew, and succeeded his father in 1830. Joseph was MP for Reigate, 1831-32, and high sheriff for Gloucestershire, 1844-45. He was a cousin to Charles Philip Yorke.

1844: 15 Aug: *Mr. Yorke of Forthampton Court, High Sheriff—Mr. Erskine of Forthampton his chaplain ...*

YOUNG — Samuel Young — *see also* Call [9]

Sir Samuel Young, 1st baronet (1766-1826), landed proprietor, was the son of Adm. Sir George Young (1732-1810) and Anne Battie. He was created 1st baronet of Cookham in 1813. He married, 28 April 1796, Emily (1775-1847), daughter of Charles Baring (1742-1829), of Exmouth, and Margaret Gould (1743-1803), daughter of William Drake Gould and Margaret Belfield. Samuel and Emily had 5 sons and 2 daughters:

1 Lucia (d. 1890)
2 Louisa Caroline
1 George Young (1797-1848); succeeded as 2nd baronet; *see below*
2 Charles Baring (1801-1882)
3 Henry (1803-1881)
4 Horatio Beauman (1806-1879), Adm.
5 William Jackson (1809-1848)

1825: 8 Jul: *Formosa, the elegant Villa of Sir Samuel Young, in the parish of Cookham, is a sweet spot to look at, in summer must be a cool and refreshing retreat; but occupying, as it does, an islet ...*

YOUNG — George Young [10]

Sir George Young, 2nd baronet (1797-1848), naval officer, was the eldest son of Samuel Young and Emily Baring (*above*). He was a captain in the Royal Navy. He married, 23 June 1835, Susan (1804-1895), only daughter of William-Mackworth Praed (1756-1835), serjeant-at-law and revising barrister for Bath. Susan's mother belonged to the English branch of the Winthrops, a New England family. George and Susan had 5 sons and 1 daughter:

1 Elizabeth Susan (d. 1925)
1 George Young (1837-1930); succeeded as 3rd baronet

2 Edward Mallet (1839-1900), Church of England clergyman
3 William Mackworth (1840-1924), member of the Indian Civil Service; served as lieutenant-governor of Punjab, 1897-1902; knighted KCSI
4 Albert Stewart Winthrop Young (1842-1918)
5 Bulkley Samuel Young (1843-1866)

1853: 24 Jun: *A letter from Lady Young. the widow of a Baronet having property on the Thames, near Maidenhead, in the parish of Cookham, known as Formosa, adjacent to the property of my late Uncle at Cookham Grove.*

YOUNG — William Francis Young [11]

William Francis Young (1804-1881) married, 1836, Elizabeth Gist.

1844: 21 Feb: *The members of the family attendg. as mourners were Mr. Gist, Lord Rossmore, and his brother, Col. Westenra, brothers of the deceased sister lady, Mr. Perkins and Mr. W. Young, who had married sisters of Mr. Gist, and Mr. W. Gist, the brother.*

Z

ZOBEL — Johann Philipp von Zobel zu Giebelstadt-Darstadt[1]

Johann Philipp von Zobel zu Giebelstadt-Darstadt (1768-1850), Austrian secretary at Weimar, married Anna (1769-1863), daughter of Lt-Col Thomas Evans Durell of the Horse Guards. Durell was an equerry to King George III. The couple had eight children and many of their descendants migrated to England.

1800: 15 Apr: ... *my Father and Dukinfield at Bayard where they met & introduced themselves to Herr von Zobel and his wife formerly Miss Durell, Daughter of Col. Durell ...* 16 Apr: ... *called at Herr von Zobel at Secretary Autriches, with my Father ...* 17 Apr., 20 Apr.

Endnotes

The source references for each person are generally within alphabetical sequence of the source, or where alphabetically it seems appropriate to place it, therefore Ancestry.co.uk [Anc] and births, marriages and deaths [BMD] will usually come as early entries for any endnote. Authors are represented surname first in small capitals.

Main Specialist Websites

Ancestry.co.uk

For Ancestry.co.uk these pedigree records were accessed between 2012 and 2019, and unfortunately changes occur beyond the control of the editor. The formula used is 'Anc:' followed the by pedigree name, followed by a colon, and then the profile name (i.e. the profile code of the person who initiated the record on Ancestry). Very worrying for the editor is the frequency with which pedigrees appear and disappear, so that a pedigree sourced in 2014, may well have disappeared by 2017 to be replaced by other keen amateurs anxious to research their family. The reason for this has not been investigated, but it may simply be because the initiator failed to keep up his or her annual subscription. This haphazard researching is less than desirable, and all Ancestry pedigrees need to be used with great caution. Some are excellent, others full of errors. The editor has tried to test pedigrees and has discarded any which show errors, but even so no guarantee can be given and every researcher seeing the use of a pedigree should test it very carefully and cross-check with quality BMD records or other sources.

Births, marriages and deaths

These cover all BMD source material on Ancestry.co.uk including parish records and post-1834 formal registrations. Parish records often show baptism dates without actual birth dates, and therefore many birth date attributions pre-1834 need to be tested with personal research.

Census records

The 1841 census, the first ever detailed census, was an important source for research, but a poor record for accuracy due to many of the assessors rounding up or down birth dates to the nearest five years. The 1851 census is a much better record and thereafter every census improves slightly. The 1851 census was taken on 30 March 1851, so anyone said to be aged '51' was therefore 75 per cent likely to have been born in 1799 and not in 1800. The editor has used the symbol '±' when using census records to show that the date is approximate.

General websites

For general websites the formula use has been the website name, person name, or approximate description followed by the date viewed and the URL.

Darryl Lundy's thepeerage.com has been helpful and many major websites have been quoted without URL links. From this source, the formula used has been 'thepeerage.com:' followed by 'person', and then the hash character (#) and the person code. To a lesser degree Cracroft's Peerage has also been accessed and no URL links are given for this source.

UCL's website: Legacies of British Slave-ownership has been invaluable, especially for the diary entries between 1802 and 1806 in Clifton, but also surprisingly for many entries throughout the diaries.

Typographic representation of URLs is always a problem. Following the style guide from other publications, breaks in URLs are before a period and before or after any other punctuation or symbol (e.g., /, //, _, @). We have not broken a URL after a hyphen to avoid ambiguity.

Abbreviations

AGB	*Allgemeine Deutsche Biographie*, replaced 2019 by Neue Deutsche Biographie: <https://www.biographie-portal.eu/search>
ADB	*Australian Dictionary of Biography*: <http://adb.anu.edu.au/>
Anc	Ancestry.co.uk
BDA	Highfill, Philip H., Burnim, Kalman A., & Langhans, Edward A.: *A Biographical Dictionary of Actors, Actresses, Musicians, Dancers, Managers, and Other Stage Personnel in London, 1660–1800*, 16 vols, 1973–1995
BHO	British History Online (see also *VCH*, below): <https://www.british-history.ac.uk/>
BLG	*Burke's Landed Gentry*, centenary edition, 1937, edited by H. Pirie-Gordon DSC, FSA
BM	The British Museum
BMD	Births marriages and deaths, from various sources, Ancestry.co.uk, or parish records, all listed under this single three-letter acronym
BMJ	*The British Medical Journal*
B-1832-1	Burke, John, *A General and Heraldic Dictionary of the Peerage and Baronetage of the British Empire*, 1832, vol. 1
B-1832-2	Burke, John, *A General and Heraldic Dictionary of the Peerage and Baronetage of the British Empire*, 1832, vol. 2
B-1833	Burke, John, *A Genealogical and Heraldic History of the Commoners of Great Britain and Ireland*, 1833
B-1834	Burke, John, *A Genealogical and Heraldic History of the Commoners of Great Britain and Ireland*, 1834
B-1835-1	Burke, John, *A Genealogical and Heraldic History of the Commoners of Great Britain and Ireland, Enjoying Territorial Possessions or High Official Rank: But Uninvested with Heritable Honours*, 1835, vol. 1
B-1835-2	Burke, John, *A Genealogical and Heraldic History of the Commoners of Great Britain and Ireland, Enjoying Territorial Possessions or High Official Rank: But Uninvested with Heritable Honours*, 1835, vol. 2
B-1836	Burke, John, *A Genealogical and Heraldic History of the Commoners of Great Britain and Ireland Enjoying Territorial Possessions Or High Official Rank, But Uninvested with Heritable Honours*, 1836
B-1837-1	Burke, John, *A Genealogical and Heraldic History of the Landed Gentry*, 1837, vol. 1.
B-1837-2	Burke, John, *A Genealogical and Heraldic History of the Landed Gentry*, 1837, vol. 2.
B-1838-1	Burke, John, *A Genealogical and Heraldic History of the Commoners of Great Britain and Ireland, Enjoying Territorial Possessions or High Official Rank: But Uninvested with Heritable Honours*, vol. 1, 1838

B-1838-2	Burke, John, *A Genealogical and Heraldic History of the Commoners of Great Britain and Ireland, Enjoying Territorial Possessions or High Official Rank: But Uninvested with Heritable Honours*, vol. 2, 1838
B-1838-3	Burke, John, *A Genealogical and Heraldic History of the Commoners of Great Britain and Ireland, Enjoying Territorial Possessions or High Official Rank: But Uninvested with Heritable Honours*, vol. 3, 1838
B-1838-4	Burke, John, *A Genealogical and Heraldic History of the Commoners of Great Britain and Ireland, Enjoying Territorial Possessions or High Official Rank: But Uninvested with Heritable Honours*, vol. 4, 1838
B-1841	Burke, John; Burke, Sir Bernard; and Burke, Bernard, *A Genealogical and Heraldic History of the Extinct and Dormant Baronetcies of England, Ireland and Scotland*
B-1844	Burke, John; and Burke, Sir Bernard, *A Genealogical and Heraldic History of the Extinct and Dormant Baronetcies of England, Ireland and Scotland*, 1844
B-1844-Enc	Burke, John Bernard, *Encyclopædia of Heraldry, or General Armory of England, Scotland and Ireland: Comprising a Registry of all Armorial Bearings from the Earliest to the Present Time, including the Late Grants by the College of Arms*
B-1845	Burke, Bernard, *A Genealogical and Heraldic Dictionary of the Peerage and Baronetage of the British Empire*, 1845
B-1846-1	Burke, John, *A Genealogical and Heraldic Dictionary of the Landed Gentry of Great Britain & Ireland: A to L, 1846*
B-1846-2	Burke, John, *A Genealogical and Heraldic Dictionary of the Landed Gentry of Great Britain & Ireland: M to Z, 1846*
B-1847-1	Burke, John, *A Genealogical and Heraldic History of the Landed Gentry*, vol. 1
B-1847-2	Burke, John, *A Genealogical and Heraldic History of the Landed Gentry*, vol. 2
B-1848	Burke, John, and Burke, John Bernard, *Dictionary of the Peerage and Baronetage of the British Empire*, tenth edition, 1848
B-1850	Burke, John Bernard, *The Heraldic Register*, 1850
B-1852-1	Burke, John Bernard, *A Genealogical and Heraldic Dictionary of the Landed Gentry of Great Britain & Ireland*, vol. 1
B-1852-2	Burke, John Bernard, *A Genealogical and Heraldic Dictionary of the Landed Gentry of Great Britain & Ireland*, vol. 2
B-1854	Burke, John Bernard, *A Genealogical and Heraldic Dictionary of the Peerage and Baronetage of the British Empire*
B-1855	Burke, John Bernard, *A Genealogical and Heraldic Dictionary of the Landed Gentry of Great Britain & Ireland*, 2 vols
B-1860	Burke, John Bernard, *A Genealogical and Heraldic Dictionary of the Peerage and Baronetage of the British Empire*
B-1863-1	Burke, Sir Bernard, *A Genealogical and Heraldic Dictionary of the Landed Gentry of Great Britain and Ireland*, vol. 1, 1863
B-1863-2	Burke, Sir Bernard, *A Genealogical and Heraldic Dictionary of the Landed Gentry of Great Britain and Ireland*, vol. 2, 1863
B-1864	Burke, Sir Bernard, *The General Armory of England, Scotland, Ireland, and Wales: Comprising a Registry of Armorial Bearings from the Earliest to the Present Time*

B-1865-1	BURKE, Sir Bernard, *A Genealogical and Heraldic Dictionary of the Landed Gentry of Great Britain & Ireland*, vol. 1
B-1865-2	BURKE, Sir Bernard, *A Genealogical and Heraldic Dictionary of the Landed Gentry of Great Britain & Ireland*, vol. 2
B-1871-1	BURKE, Sir Bernard, *A Genealogical and Heraldic History of the Landed Gentry of Great Britain & Ireland*, vol. 1
B-1871-2	BURKE, Sir Bernard, *A Genealogical and Heraldic History of the Landed Gentry of Great Britain & Ireland*, vol. 2
B-1879-1	BURKE, Sir Bernard, *A Genealogical and Heraldic Dictionary of the Landed Gentry of Great Britain and Ireland*, vol. 1, 1879
B-1879-2	BURKE, Sir Bernard, *A Genealogical and Heraldic Dictionary of the Landed Gentry of Great Britain and Ireland*, vol. 2, 1879
B-1875-1	BURKE's *Genealogical and Heraldic History of the Landed Gentry*, vol. 1
B-1882-1	BURKE's *A Genealogical and Heraldic History of the Landed Gentry of Great Britain & Ireland*, vol. 1
B-1882-2	BURKE's *A Genealogical and Heraldic History of the Landed Gentry of Great Britain & Ireland*, vol. 2
B-1885	BURKE's *Genealogical and Heraldic History of the Peerage, Baronetage and Knightage*
B-1886-1	BURKE's *A Genealogical and Heraldic History of the Landed Gentry of Great Britain & Ireland*, vol. 1
B-1886-2	BURKE's *A Genealogical and Heraldic History of the Landed Gentry of Great Britain & Ireland*, vol. 2
B-1898	BURKE's *Genealogical and Heraldic History of Peerage, Baronetage and Knightage*, vol. 60, 1898
B-1898-1	BURKE, Bernard, *A Genealogical and Heraldic History of the Landed Gentry of Great Britain & Ireland*, vol. 1
B-1898-2	BURKE, Bernard, *A Genealogical and Heraldic History of the Landed Gentry of Great Britain & Ireland*, vol. 2
B-1899	BURKE's *Landed Gentry of Ireland,* 1899
B-1906	BURKE's *A Genealogical and Heraldic History of the Landed Gentry of Great Britain & Ireland*
B-1912	BURKE, Bernard: *Genealogical and Heraldic History of the Landed Gentry of Ireland*, 1912
B-1914	BURKE's *Genealogical and Heraldic Dictionary of the Peerage and Baronetage of the British Empire*
c-	Census or censuses, 1841–1911, followed by census year or years
CA	*Cambridge Alumni*, via Ancestry.co.uk
CB	*The Complete Baronetage*, in 5 vols, 1900, COKAYNE, George Edward
Carthusians	PARISH, W. D., *List of Carthusians, 1800–1879*, 1879
CCEd	The Clergy of the Church of England Database 1540–1835 <http://theclergydatabase.org.uk/>
CL	*The Clergy List*, 1841
CP	*The Complete Peerage*, in 13 vols, 1910–1959, COKAYNE, George Edward, *et al.*
Crockford	*Crockford's Clerical Directory*, followed by year number
DCB	*Dictionary of Canadian Biography*: <http://www.biographi.ca/en/index.php>

Debrett 1815	Debrett, John, *The Baronetage of England: Containing Their Descent and Present State, Their Collateral Branches, Births, Marriages, and Issue, from the Institution of the Order in 1611...*
Debrett 1822-I	Debrett, John, *The Peerage of the United Kingdom of Great Britain and Ireland*, vol. I, England
Debrett 1822-II	Debrett, John, *The Peerage of the United Kingdom of Great Britain and Ireland*, vol. II, Scotland and Ireland
Debrett 1824-I	Debrett, John, *Debrett's Baronetage of England*, vol. I
Debrett 1824-II	Debrett, John; *Debrett's Baronetage of England*, vol. II
Debrett 1827-I	Debrett, John, *Debrett's Baronetage of England*, vol. I
Debrett 1827-II	Debrett, John; *Debrett's Baronetage of England*, vol. II
Debrett 1832	Debrett, John, *The Baronetage of England*, 1832,
Debrett 1835	Debrett, John, *The Baronetage of England,* 1835
Debrett 1839	Courthope, William, *Debrett's Complete Peerage of the United Kingdom of Great Britain and Ireland*
Debrett 1840	Debrett, John, *The Baronetage of England,* revised, corrected and continued by Collen, G. W., 1840
EB	*Encyclopaedia Britannica*
E&W Wills	England & Wales, Prerogative Court of Canterbury Wills, 1384–1858
Eton	Stapylton, H. E. C. *Eton School Lists from 1791 to 1877*, 1884
DNB	*Oxford Dictionary of National Biography*: <https://www.oxforddnb.com/>
Foster-1881	Foster, Joseph, *The Peerage, Baronetage and Knightage for 1881*
Foster-1882	Foster, Joseph, *The Peerage, Baronetage and Knightage for 1882*
GA	Gloucestershire Archives, as specific from The National Archives
G&B	Gell, R., Bradshaw, T., *The Gloucestershire Directory*, 1820
GM	*The Gentleman's Magazine*, followed by volume number, year and page number
GPA	Gloucestershire Police Archives: <https://gloucestershirepolicearchives.org.uk/>
Grove	*The New Grove Dictionary of Music and Musicians*, 20 vols, 1995 edition
HP	*History of Parliament*: <https://www.historyofparliamentonline.org/>
Hunt	Hunt & Co. *Directory*, 1849, Gloucester, Bristol, etc.
LM	*The Lady's Magazine*, followed by year and page number
LG	*The London Gazette*, followed by year and page number
Lodge-1832	Lodge, Edmund, *The Peerage of the British Empire as at Present Existing: To which is added the Baronetage*
Lodge-1833	Lodge, Edmund, *The Peerage of the British Empire as at Present Existing: Arranged and Printed from the Personal Communications of the Nobility*
Lodge-1843	Lodge, Edmund, *The Peerage of the British Empire as at Present Existing: Arranged and Printed from the Personal Communications of the Nobility*
Lodge-1845	Lodge, Edmund, *The Peerage of the British Empire as at Present Existing: Arranged and Printed from the Personal Communications of the Nobility*
Lodge-1859	Lodge, Edmund, *The Genealogy of the Existing British Peerage and Baronetage: Containing the Family Histories of the Nobility*
MATB	Foster, Joseph, *Men at the Bar*, 1885
MI	Monumental Inscriptions
MM	*The Monthly Magazine* (and its successor *The New Monthly Magazine*)
NA	The National Archives

NBD	O'Byrne, William Richard, *A Naval Biographical Dictionary*, 1849
NPC	England & Wales, National Probate Calendar (Index of Wills and Administrations), 1858–1995
NPG	National Portrait Gallery
PI	Personal information supplied by descendants and other relations
Pigot	*Pigot's Directories*, various years for various locations—followed by place and year
OA	Foster, Joseph, *Alumni Oxoniensis* (1715–1886), 1888, via Ancestry.co.uk
Trans. BGAS	*Transactions of the Bristol and Gloucestershire Archaeological Society*
UCL–Slaves	UCL Department of History: Legacies of British Slave-ownership; online history
VCH	Victoria County Histories (BHO) British History Online, followed by county and parish
WFP	Witts Family Papers; WFP 173 to 235; the diaries of Agnes Witts (1748–1825)
Walford-1860	Walford, Edward, *The County Families of the United Kingdom, or, Royal Manual of the Titled and Untitled Aristocracy of England, Wales, Scotland, and Ireland*, published annually from 1860
Walford-1864	As above, enlarged
Walford-1869	As above, enlarged
Walford-1871	As above, enlarged
Walford-1882	As above, enlarged
Walford-1893	As above, enlarged
Walford-1919	As above, enlarged
WRC	Dalton, Charles, *The Waterloo Roll Call*, 1904
Williams	Williams, W. R. *The Parliamentary History of the County of Gloucester, including the Cities of Bristol and Gloucester, and the boroughs of Cheltenham, Cirencester, Stroud, and Tewkesbury, from the earliest times to the present day, 1213–1898*, 1898.

Letter A

1 Anc: Johnson/Harris Family Tree: jessicaina47; *CB*; *CP*; *DNB*; *HP*; PI: e-mail information—Polly & James à Court; MI: St Mary's, Cheltenham.
2 Webb, E. A., *The records of St. Bartholomew's priory [and] St. Bartholomew the Great, West Smithfield*: vol. 2, 1921, pp. 373-404.
3 *CP*; *HP*.
4 *CP*.
5 Wikipedia.
6 *DNB*; *HP*.
7 BMD; Boase, Frederic, *Modern English Biography*, 1892; United Grand Lodge of England Freemason Membership Registers, 1751–1921; NBD.
8 Kingsley, Nicholas, viewed 21 January 2019: <http://landedfamilies.blogspot.com/>.
9 BMD; *HP*; thepeerage.com: person M, #28500.
10 BMD; c-1841; Guiting Chapel History.
11 Great Western Railway Guide; *LG*.
12 *CB*.
13 BMD; *CA*; Kingsley, Nicholas, viewed 21 January 2019: <http://landedfamilies.blogspot.com/>; *WRC*.
14 *DNB*; WFP F185, 25 July 1793.
15 BMD; *B-1838-1*; *LM*, vol. 38, 1807.
16 Adams of Clifton, viewed 23 February 2019: <https://coadb.com/surnames/adams-arms.html>; Anc: Adams Family Tree: JacquieZV; *B-1838-4*, p. 434; *B-1871-2*, p. 1581 [Supplement]; *OA*
17 Anc; *OA*.
18 GA: Hyett and Adams Families; *VCH*, Gloucestershire, Painswick.
19 Anc: Hartley Family Tree: clawrenc707; c-1851.
20 *DNB*; *HP*.
21 BMD; census; *Proceedings of the Royal Society of London*, vol. 10; Wikipedia.
22 Anc: Family of Roderick James Craig: Rod Craig; BMD; *Burke 1838-4*, p. 26; *The European Magazine, and London Review*, vol. 40, 1801, p. 398; Gloucestershire, England, Church of England Baptisms, Marriages and Burials, 1538–1813, 1786; *HP*; *MM*, vol. 21, 1806, p. 373; E&W Wills; Phillimore, William Phillimore Watts, and Madge, Sidney Joseph, *Gloucestershire Notes and Queries*, vol. 2, issues 13-24, 1882, p. 620; UK, Poll Books and Electoral Registers, 1538–1893, for the years 1774 and 1776; Tann, Jennifer; *Gloucestershire Woollen Mills*, 1967.
23 Anc: Kirk-Traill Family Tree: antonygould; BMD; c-1841–1871; Pigot; *The Railway Times*, 22 August 1846; *VCH*, Gloucestershire, Cheltenham; *Walford-1893*, p. 7.
24 BMD; c-1841–1851; *DNB*.
25 Aris's *Birmingham Gazette*, 17 August 1840; BMD; c-1841; *OA*.
26 BMD; c-1841–1871; Wyck Risington Marriages, viewed 8 April 2017: <https://parishmouse.co.uk/3229/wyck-risington-marriages-1775-to-1812/>.
27 *B-1847-4*, p. 1498.
28 Anc: The Family Tree: swendeperle82; website, Harry Hurlbutt Albino, viewed 23 February 2019: <http://folkopedia.efdss.org/wiki/Harry_Hurlbutt_Albino>.
29 BMD.
30 BMD, c-1841; *Harper's Cheltenham Directory & Guide*, 1844.
31 *Ibid.*
32 *CA*.
33 *GM*, vol. 147, February 1830; *A Political Pilot*, 26 March 1831.
34 *The Aberystwyth Observer*, 19 February 1859; BMD; c-1841; *Medico-Chirurgical Transactions*, 1839.
35 *CA*.
36 Anc: Cook Family Tree: rillwater; *MM*; MI: church of St Editha, Tamworth; Alford Family Notes.
37 *Bridgwater and Somerset Herald*; *GM*, vol. 165, 1839; *OA*.
38 Wikipedia.
39 Anc: SCOONES: Fenella_L; CCEd; *OA*; *VCH*, Gloucestershire, Bledington, vol. 6, 1965.
40 *CA*; PI, kindly supplied by Brian Williams, Churchwarden, Swilland.
41 BMD; *CA*; c-1841; *GM*, vol. 186, 1849.
42 Anc: Tammy Woods family tree; Anc: Smith Family Tree: mdrms; BMD; *OA*.
43 Anc: RobertJones 1892 family tree; BMD; *OA*.
44 BMD; c-1851–1871; Gloucestershire, Gaol Registers, 1815–1879; Gloucester Epiphany Sessions, 4 January 1853; Gloucestershire, England, Prison Records, 1728–1914 for William Allington.
45 *LG*, part 1, 1837. (8 June 1837); *The Tradesman*, vol. 6, 1811.
46 Kingsley, Nicholas, viewed 21 January 2019: <http://landedfamilies.blogspot.com/>.
47 BMD; c-1841–1891.
48 BMD; Anc: tonysmith1066 family tree; Kingsley, Nicholas, viewed 21 January 2019: <http://landedfamilies.blogspot.com/>.
49 BMD; c-1841–1851.
50 *DNB*.
51 BMD; c-1841–1851.
52 BMD; c-1851; *OA*; *Crockford* 1865; *CL*; *Carthusians*.
53 *CA*.

54 BMD.
55 BMD; c-1851.
56 Anc: Hedley, Webb, May, Shaw, Chatwin, Gorey, Hammond, Jenkins, Mepham, Harkett, Harper Family Tree: Rosie Harper; Anc: Will & Erika's Family Tree: catharinesayer; *CP*; *HP*.
57 BMD; c-1841–1871; *Crockford*, 1865; *OA*; PI—the Parsons family.
58 Anc: susanhoneyman family tree. BMD; c-1841–1851; *OA*.
59 This attribution is tentative: *DNB*; *CA*; *LG*, part 2, 1835; *Pigot*, 1830; WFP F201.
60 WFP F207.
61 Anc: Hulse Family Tree; BMD; c-1841.
62 Anc: Hulse Family Tree; Articles of Clerkship, 1756–1874; BMD; c-1851–1871; *Oxford Chronicle and Reading Gazette*, 16 June 1866.
63 Anc: Potts Family Tree; BMD; c-1841–1861.
64 James Royds' account of the family (1826), viewed 10 April 2017: <http://www.fitzwalter.com/afh/Royds/roydshist3.html>; BMD.
65 BMD; c-1841–1861; thepeerage.com: person M, #627830.
66 *DNB*.
67 BMD; c-1841–1861; *Hunt*.
68 BMD; c-1841–1881; Anc: Doreen Muller Family Tree.
69 Boddington MI.
70 *The Sydney Gazette and New South Wales Advertiser*, 29 July 1820, 26 February 1824, 8 April 1833; Thomas Arkell, viewed 10 April 2017: <www.airgale.com.au>, Langley: <www.australianroyalty.net.au>.
71 Anc: Hoskyns Family Tree: JanetHoskyns; *BLG*; Kingsley, Nicholas, viewed 21 January 2019: <http://landedfamilies.blogspot.com/>.
72 Anc: Roots, Branches and Twigs: Chris Thomas; BMD.
73 BMD; c-1841; *CL*; *OA*; James Armistead, viewed 15 April 2017: <http://armistead.one-name.net/>.
74 *Ibid.*
75 Anc: PAF V5: Pullarm; Anc: shepherd Family Tree: shepherd790; BMD; Crawford, Lt-Col. D. G., *Roll of the Indian Medical Service 1615–1930*, vol. 2, 2012, p. 420; *GM*, vol. 89, part 2; vol. 126, 1819, p. 281; *List of Officers of the Royal Regiment of Artillery from 1716 to the Present Date*, 1869, p. 28; E&W Wills—will of Juliet Armstrong; WFP F194 and F201.
76 BMD; c-1841–1871.
77 *DNB*.
78 BMD; Anc: Larry Tyrell Family Tree; Dodsley, J., *The Annual Register, or, A View of the History, Politics, and Literature for the Year 1827*, vol. 69, 1828; BHO: *The Environs of London*: vol. 4; Hertfordshire Archives.
79 *HP*.
80 *DNB*.
81 BMD; c-1841–1861.
82 BMD; c-1851–1861; *The Aristocracy of London*: part I: Kensington, 1863; *GM*, vol. 91, 1821; Cumbria Records Office; Fishwick, Henry, *The History of the Parish of Rochdale in the County of Lancaster*, 1889; thepeerage.com: person M, #138294.
83 BMD; c-1841–1851; Anc: Joseph Askew Family Tree.
84 Anc: Wilding Family Tree: annewilding197; c-1841–1881; *Liverpool Mercury*; Rochdale Library Service; CCEd; *OA*; *ADB*, vol. 3.
85 *HP*.
86 BMD; c-1841–1881; CCEd; *Birmingham Journal*, 1 July 1826; *OA*; There are many entries relating to Frederick Aston in the diaries of Agnes Witts, commencing 11 June 1811 and lasting until her death in 1825. WFP, F216–F235.
87 BMD; c-1841–1851; Anc/Stimpson Family Tree.
88 BMD; c-1841–1871; *OA*.
89 *HP*; Kingsley, Nicholas: Atkyns, viewed 9 February 2019: <http://landedfamilies.blogspot.com/2016/12/242-atkyns-of-sapperton-swell-bowl.html>.
90 BMD; c-1841–1871; *OA*.
91 Anc: AlbertBulteelFisher: jonathanturner_1; *Journals of the House of Lords*, vol. 40, 1794, p. 379; John Lewis Auriol, viewed 15 April 2017: <https://www.myheritage.com/names/john_auriol>; *Pigot*, 1831; The Holburne Museum, viewed 15 April 2017: <https://www.holburne.org/zoffany/>; Clifton Hotwell Spa, viewed 15 April 2019: <http://osborne.house/profilego.asp?ref=28423139>; WFP F206.
92 BMD; c-1841–1881.
93 BMD; c-1841–1861; Lewis, S., *Worcestershire General and Commercial Directory for 1820*; Avery, Clara A., The Averell–Averill–Avery family: a record of the descendants of William and Abigail Averell of Ipswich, Mass.; 1850; Pittville, viewed 15 April 2017: <http://pittvillehistory.org.uk/index.php>.
94 BMD; c-1841–1881; *Hunt*.
95 *CB*; Wikipedia—Matthew Whitworth-Aylmer, 5th Baron Aylmer.
96 BMD; c-1841; Anc: Byrnes Family Tree.
97 BMD; c-1841–1851.

Letter B

1 Anc: Sheppard; BMD; Martínez-Fernández, Luis, *Fighting Slavery in the Caribbean: The Life and Times of a British Family in Nineteenth-Century Havana*, 1998; *Gore Directory for Liverpool*, 1766; Institute of Historic Building Conservation, viewed 4 May 2017: <http://www.ihbc.org.uk/context_archive/108/slavery>.

2 BMD; Duke University Library: Special Collection Holdings: Caribbean Islands, Backhouse, John, 1784–1845, Papers, 1740–1956, Merchant and British Under Secretary of State for Foreign Affairs, Business and personal correspondence of the Backhouse family, principally of John Backhouse; *MM*, vol. 29, 1810; *B-1846-1*.
3 BMD; *Grove*.
4 *DNB*.
5 BMD; c-1851.
6 BMD; *DNB*.
7 D'Alton, John, *King James's Irish Army List*, 1855.
8 *DNB*.
9 BMD; *OA*.
10 GA; Somerset Archaeological and Natural History Society *Newsletter* 70, summer 2004.
11 BMD; c-1841–1901; *Hunt*; Anc: Audrey's definitive tree: Audrey_Earl.
12 BMD; *HP*; *OA*; UCL–Slaves.
13 Robertson, George, *A Genealogical Account of the Principal Families in Ayrshire, More Particularly in Kyle and Cunninghame*, vol. 1, 1823.
14 BMD; *HP*.
15 BMD; *OA*; UCL–Slaves.
16 BMD; *HP*.
17 BMD; c-1841–1861; *OA*; *The Law Journal Reports*, vol. 21, 1843, p. 154; UCL-Slaves.
18 *HP*.
19 *ADB*; BMD; c-1841–1861; University of Reading: Archive of Baillière, Tindall & Cox.
20 *CB*; WFP F199.
21 BMD; *OA*.
22 BMD; *OA*; NA, E&W Wills—will of Reverend John Baker, Doctor of Law of Freshford, Somerset.
23 Anc: Glass/Simpson Family Tree: Patsi Brown; *DNB*; UCL–Slaves.
24 CCEd; *OA*.
25 c-1851.
26 *CA*; *GM*, vol. 103, part 1, 1833, p. 186.
27 Ball, Edward, *Slaves in the Family*, 1998. Chaplin, Joyce E., *An Anxious Pursuit: Agricultural Innovation and Modernity in the Lower South, 1730–1815*, 2012; Phillips, R., *Bristol Gaol Delivery Fiats, 1741–1799*, Bristol Record Society, 1989; *MM*, vol. 55, 1823.
28 Birmingham City Archives.
29 BMD; c-1841–1871.
30 NPC; *Crockfords Clerical Directory*, 1868; West Glamorgan Archive Service; Boddington MI.
31 *DNB*; E&W Wills—will of Catharina Ballard.
32 *CB*; *HP*.
33 BMD; *Slater's Directory*, 1851.
34 BMD; c-1841–1851; E&W Wills—will of Adam Bancks, Surgeon of Winchcomb; *Pigot's Directory*, 1830.
35 Anc: Ganly Family Tree; BMD; *CA*; *HP*.
36 *GM*, vol. 136, 1824; *OA*; *VCH*, A History of the County of Middlesex: vol. 7, Acton, Chiswick, Ealing and Brentford, West Twyford, Willesden, 1982; London Metropolitan Archives; *Illustrated London News*, 21 September 1850.
37 Wikipedia.
38 Anc: Holliday-Benkert Family Tree; BMD; c-1841–1901.
39 *GA*.
40 Anc: Baring Sealy Family Tree: Bobbie1959; *HP*; *The Nautical Magazine* for 1832, p. 168; Shrady, George Frederick, and Stedman, Thomas Lathrop, *Medical Record*, vol. 33, 1888, p. 123.
41 *HP*.
42 Wikipedia— Baring family properties; *HP*.
43 Anc: Anjels Web: Genakin; *DNB*.
44 Anc: Kerr Montgomery etc. Family Tree; BMD; *CA*; c-1851–1861; GA.
45 BMD; *CA*.
46 RBS Heritage Hub, viewed 13 July 2019: <https://www.rbs.com/heritage/companies/dimsdale-fowler-barnard-and-dimsdales.html>.
47 *B-1846-1*.
48 *CB*; *HP*.
49 *B-1838-4*; Richards of Wexford, viewed 13 July 2019: <https://sites.rootsweb.com/~cmricha/>.
50 c-1841.
51 *CL*; *OA*; The School Gateway, viewed 13 July 2019: <schoolgateway.westminster.org.uk>.
52 Adams, William James, *Bradshaw's Railway Gazette*, vol. 2, 1846; c-1851; *Cheltenham Chronicle*, 10 July 1855; *The Economist*, vol. 3, part 2, 1845; *Gloucestershire Chronicle*, 24 October 1846; *Gloucester Journal*, 7 June 1856; *Herapath's Railway Journal*, 1845.
53 Australian Convict Transportation Registers–Other Fleets & Ships, 1791–1868; Gloucestershire, England, Prison Records, 1728–1914.
54 *CP*; *Debrett 1840*; John Thomas Barnewall, viewed 13 July 2019: <https://www.geni.com/people/John-Barnewall-15th-Baron-Trimlestown/6000000022334939365>.
55 *DNB*.
56 Anc: Barr Family Tree: CharlesJDawson; *Berrow's News* 27 October 1831, obituary of Samuel; BMD; *GM*, 1848; *MM*, vol. 23, 1807; England & Wales, Non-Conformist and Non-Parochial Registers, 1567–1970 for Charles Barr; *The Spectator*, 24 July 1841; Charles Barr, viewed 13 July 2019: <museumofroyalworcester.org>.

57 *CP*.
58 *HP*; Andrew Roberts: Middlesex University.
59 *OA*.
60 Barbados Church Records, 1637–1887; BMD; c-1841–1901.
61 *GM*, vols 156-157, 1834; BMD; c-1841–1871; *OA*.
62 Les cahiers de la Société Augustin Barruel; Wikipedia.
63 Evans, John, *The History of Bristol, Civil and Ecclesiastical*, vol. 2, 1816.
64 *DNB*.
65 Anc: Barrie/Kumnick Family Tree: Di_Barrie; BMD; c-1841–1851.
66 BMD; c-1851–1861; *OA*; Sarsden House, viewed 4 May 2017: <https://www.parksandgardens.org/places/sarsden-house>.
67 *DNB*.
68 BMD; c-1841–1881.
69 BMD; c-1861; *OA*; *The Spectator*, 30 April 1842.
70 BMD; c-1841–1861.
71 *GM*, vol. 83, (113) part 1, 1813; GA: Register of deputations to gamekeepers, 1801.
72 Anc: Dave Bashford-Lucy Ward: DaveBashford; BMD; c-1841–1891; NA: Trafalgar ancestors; *Walford-1871*; UCL–Slaves; website: Fryer family, viewed 5 May 2017: <http://www.westmoorsmiscellany.co.uk/fryergullivercastleman/>.
73 BMD; *MM*, vol. 15, 1825; *Windsor and Eton Express*, 1 January 1825.
74 *HP*.
75 Anc: Dyer/Batchelor Family Tree: eeyore539; *OA*; Bath Abbey Cemetery–MI.
76 Anc: Tanner/Welsh Family Tree; BMD; c-1841–1901.
77 Anc: Ords of Durham–Northumberland Family Tree; *B-1834-1*; WFP F231.
78 *DNB*; *OA*.
79 *HP*.
80 c-1841–1861; *HP*; *OA*.
81 *CP*; *HP*.
82 *LG*, January 1850; The Dundas Family, viewed 4 May 2017: <http://dundasfamily.co.uk/>.
83 BMD; c-1841–1901.
84 *Ibid.*
85 *Ibid.*
86 Anc: Rudkin Family Tree; BMD; c-1841–1901.
87 *Galignani's Messenger: The Spirit of the English Journals*, Paris, 1819; *VCH*, Gloucestershire XIII, draft text by John Ju⊠i*CA*; LG, part 1, 1809.
88 England & Wales, Criminal Registers, 1791–1892; *The Spectator*, 22 October 1842; *Examiner: A Weekly Paper on Politics, Literature, Music and the Fine Arts*. 1842. p. 681.
89 BMD; c-1841–1851.
90 *DNB*; Wikipedia.
91 *CB*; thepeerage.com: person M, #120504.
92 BMD; National Library of Wales: Chirk Castle Estate Records; *The Names and Descriptions of the Proprietors of Unclaimed Dividends on Bank Stock, and on the Public Funds, Transferable at the Bank of England: Which Became Due on and Before the 5th January, 1812, and Remained Unpaid the 31st December*, 1814; Griffiths, George Edward & Ralph, *The Monthly Review*, 1800; People in Books, Diaries, Historical Documents, etc., viewed 13 July 2017: <https://www.opcdorset.org/fordingtondorset/Files2/DorchesterPeople2.html>.
93 *AGB*.
94 *EB*.
95 BMD; *HP*; Wikipedia.
96 *DNB*.
97 BMD; Pope, Charles, *The Merchant, Ship-Owner, and Ship-Master's Custom and Excise Guide*, eighth edition, 1831; WFP F199.
98 BMD; *CA*; WFP 213.
99 BMD; c-1841–1881; MI: St Peter and St Paul, Northleach, footstone details.
100 *DNB*.
101 Anc: Burmester/Belcher/Cogswell/McMaster/Davey Trees: John Davey; *OA*.
102 BMD; CCEd; c-1851; Devon Archives and Local Studies Service (South West Heritage Trust); *OA*.
103 BMD; Edward William Derrington Bell, viewed 5 May 2017: <https://www.findagrave.com/memorial/11268433/edward-william_derrington-bell>; <http://www.vconline.org.uk/edward-w-d-bell-vc/4585969261>.
104 BMD; c-1871; *GM*, August 1831; Henry Bell, viewed 5 May 2017 <http://freepages.rootsweb.com/~cbye/genealogy/brandling/brandling/charles/index.htm>.
105 Anc: Sue Rintoul Family Tree: Sue Rintoul; c-1851–1871; *OA*; Henry Walford Bellairs, viewed 5 May 2017: <https://www.geni.com/people/Rev-Henry-Bellairs/6000000027927089402>.
106 *DNB*; *Grove*.
107 Anc: The Murphy Bellamy Family Tree: wfbellamy; Elwick, George, *The Bankrupt Directory: Being a Complete Register of All the Bankrupts, with Their Residences, Trades, and Dates when They Appeared in the London Gazette, from December 1820 to April 1843*; *LG*, part 1, 1828; certificate of the burial at Tidmington, co. Worcs., of John Byrkin Bellamy: Shakespeare Birthplace Trust; Warwickshire, Parish Registers, 1535–1984.
108 E&W Wills—will of John Henry Belli Bivar; John Henry Belli-Bivar, viewed 5 May 2017: <http://genealogy.links.org: Belli Bivar>.
109 Anc: Beman family tree: Jean Harding; BMD; c-1841–1891.

110 BMD; c-1841–1891.

111 BMD; c-1841–1901.; Register: Bristol, Lewin's Mead Chapel (Presbyterian), 1759–1786; *GM*, vol. 140, 1826; *The European Magazine: And London Review*, vol. 45, Philological Society of London, 1804; PAGET, J. W., *The Law Journal*, vol. 5, 1827; SEYER, Samuel, *Memoirs Historical and Topographical of Bristol and Its Neighbourhood: From the Earliest Period Down to the Present Time*, vol. 2, 1823.

112 BMD; c-1841–1881; Little Rissington MI.

113 c-1841.

114 *DNB*.

115 CCEd; GREGORY, Jeremy, *The Speculum of Archbishop Thomas Secker*, 1995.

116 *Essex Archaeology and History News*, Winter 2007.

117 *Accounts and Papers of the House of Commons*, vol. 38, 1846; *LG*, vol. 2, 1820; E&W Wills—will of George Bentley, Auctioneer of Worcester; *Pigot and Co.'s National Commercial Directory*, Worcestershire, 1835.

118 CART, T. J., *A Dictionary of Literary Pseudonyms in the English Language* 2015; c-1841–1851; *OA*; National Library of Scotland: Scott, Walter, acquisition of first edition of *The vision of Don Roderick*; a poem, 1811.

119 DACK, Catherine Nora, 'Urbanization and the Middling Sorts in Derbyshire Market Towns: Ashbourne and Wirksworth 1660–1830', Ph.D thesis, University of Leicester, 2010; FAREY, John, *General View of the Agriculture and Minerals of Derbyshire: With Observations on the Means of Their Improvement*, 1813; GLOVER, Stephen, *The History of the County of Derby*, vol. 2, 1829; MOGG, Edward, *Paterson's Roads, Being An Accurate Description of All The Cross Roads in England and Wales, with Parts of the Roads of Scotland*, 1831; *Remains, Historical and Literary, Connected with the Palatine Counties of Lancaster and Chester*, 1843; viewed 6 May 2017: <http://www.ourashbourne.co.uk/person/francis-beresford>: <http://genealogy.links.org/ francis-beresford>.

120 Parliamentary Archives: Manuscript Collection; viewed, 6 May 2017: <https://www.geni.com/people/Georgiana-Mary-Berkeley-Seymour/6000000002188383914>.

121 BMD.

122 *CP*; *DNB*; *HP*; LEECH, Joseph, *The Rural Rides of the Bristol Churchgoer*, 1982, reprinted 2004.

123 *DNB*; *MM*, vol. 13, 1820; UCL-Slaves.

124 UCL-Slaves; Joseph Berwick.

125 Anc: Best/Wood Tree: wallhayes; *CP*; *HP*.

126 *The Athenaeum: A Magazine of Literary and Miscellaneous Information*, vol. 4, 1808; WFP F208.

127 *DNB*.

128 c-1861.

129 BMD; c-1841.

130 *The Royal Calendar, and Court and City Register for England, Scotland, Ireland and the Colonies*, vol. 7, 1845.

131 c-1841–1851.

132 *Hereford Journal*, 3 November 1824; *LG*, part 1, 1827.

133 Anc: Parlour Family Tree: Richard Parlour; BMD; c-1851–1861; *OA*; Sussex Archives; *The Law Journal Reports*, vol. 8, 1839, p. 267, E&W Wills—will of Mary Beverley.

134 BMD; *Grove*; BURDEN, Michael, New College, Oxford University: 'Mrs Billington's embonpoint; scandal, hysteria, and Mozart'; given at the British Society for 18th-century Studies Annual Conference, St Hugh's College, Oxford, 4 January 2008; Wikipedia.

135 BMD; c-1841–1871; NA: WO Records.

136 BMD; c-1841; GLOVER, Stephen, *The History of the County of Derby*, vol. 2, 1829, p. 597.

137 *DNB*.

138 BMD; c-1841–1871, *OA*; thepeerage.com: person M, #587743.

139 *CA*.

140 BMD; c-1841–1851.

141 ARMSTRONG, Mostyn John, *History and Antiquities of the County of Norfolk*, 1781, p. 28; *GM*, 1838; KEARSLEY, George, *Kearsley's Complete peerage, of England, Scotland and Ireland*, vol. 1, 1802, p. 239; *OA*; E&W Wills—will of George Graham Blackwell of Ampney Park , Gloucestershire; Eardley John Blackwell, viewed 6 May 2017: <https://www.myheritage.com/names/eardley_blackwell>; *The Annual Register: or a View of the History, Politics and Literature*, for the Year 1822, vol. 41, p. 233.

142 *CB*; *Debrett 1840*, p. 733.

143 BMD; c-1851–1861; *B-1852-1*; George William Blathwayt, viewed 6 May 2017, <https://www.nationaltrust.org.uk/dyrham-park>.

144 BMD; CCEd; c-1841; *Gloucester Journal*, Saturday 6 November 1875; *LG*, 1858, p. 3585.

145 Anc: Descendants of Thomas Insall including Smiths Wells & Woods Families; BMD; c-1881.

146 BMD; c-1851–1861.

147 BMD; *DNB*; *The Royal Society*, 1829, p. 4.

148 Anc: Thos Dunn of Glaven: Raywdunn; *DNB*.

149 Anc: Whitney-Schoenfeldt Family Tree: cschoenfeldt; BMD; CCEd; c-1841–1901; *OA*.

150 Anc: SANFORD Family Tree: susanlking2705; BMD; c-1841–1871; GA: Articles of co-partnership in business of banking (The Dursley and Uley Bank): Messrs George Watts of Bath, gent, Edward Bloxsome of Dursley, gent, Thomas Watts of Uley, cheese factor and James Player of Dursley, gent (1807); *Hunt*; National Library of Australia, viewed 6 May 2017: <https://catalogue.nla.gov.au/Record/3543613>.

151 East India Company at Home, 1757–1857; viewed 13 July 2019: <https://blogs.ucl.ac.uk/eicah/sezincote-gloucestershire/sezincote-case-study-the-cockerell-family/>; Louisa Dent, viewed 13 July 2019: <https://www.geni.com/people/Louisa-Dent/6000000031961963627>.

152 *ADB*, vol. 3.

153 Theobald Boehm, viewed 13 July 2019: <http://www.flutehistory.com/Players/Theobald_Boehm/index.php3>.

154 Anc: More/Taylor: suemore68; BMD; 1911; *CA*; c-1861–1901; *White's Directory of Essex*, 1848—list of inhabitants of Earls Colne.

155 Bruce, Wallace, A., *Gloucestershire History* No. 2 (1988).
156 BMD; c-1851–1871.
157 Bigelow, Harry Augustus, *Introduction to the law of real property*, part 2, 1919, p. 694; BMD; *Collectanea topographica et genealogica*, 1838 p. 261; Hilton Price, F. G., *A Handbook of London Bankers*, 1876; NA: Ref: B 3/300, *In the matter of Charles Boldero, Edward Gale Boldero, Sir Henry Lushington and Henry Boldero, bankers, bankrupts*, vol. 4, 2 January 1812; Vesey, Francis, *Reports of Cases Argued and Determined in the High Court of Chancery, from the Year MDCCLXXXIX to MDCCCXVII: With a Digested Index*, vol. 19, 1845, p. 692.
158 Anc: Old Settle: KenAndSarahLister; Bolland Family Papers, Yorkshire Archaeological and Historical Society; Bolland, viewed, 13 July 2019: <ncbpt.org.uk/folly/exhibitions ... /bolland_family>.
159 *CA*; Henry John Bolland, viewed 13 July 2019: <wyndhammarsh.co.uk/genealogy/familygroup: Bolland>.
160 *The Annual Register, Or, A View of the History, Politics, and Literature for the Year*, vol. 74, 1833; BMD; Bolton, Henry Carrington, *The family of Bolton in England and America, 1100–1894 a study in genealogy. Embodying the Genealogical and biographical account of the family of Bolton*, published in 1862 by Robert Bolton, rewritten and extended to date, 1895, p. 11; E&W Wills—will of Sir Robert Bolton, General in the Army and Colonel of the 7th Regiment of Dragoon Guards of Swerford Park, Oxfordshire.
161 BMD; c-1841–1881; *The Lancet*, vol. 2, 1840, p. 736. *LG*, vol. 2, p. 3782; Provincial Medical and Surgical Association, *The Transactions of the Provincial Medical and Surgical Association*, 1845, p. 378.
162 *Reports of Cases Argued and Determined in the Ecclesiastical Courts at Doctors' Commons, and in the High Court of Delegates ...: Containing Cases from Michaelmas Term 1827, to [Easter Term 1833] ... and Some Cases of an Earlier Date in the Supplement[s, 1700–1827]*, vol. 3, pp. 24-56; *OA*; MI: Evesham, viewed 13 July 2019: <http://www.eveshamparish.com/uploads/7/6/7/2/7672331/inscriptions.pdf>.
163 Anc: Berube/Adamson 2015: sonette68; *CA*; CCEd; E&W Wills—will of George Bonner.
164 BMD; c-1861.
165 Anc: Charles Boothby—Family tree; BMD; Boothby, C., *Under England's flag from 1804 to 1809: the memoirs, diary and correspondence of Charles Boothby, captain of Royal Engineers*, 1900; Boothby, C., *The prisoner of France: memoirs, and correspondence of diary Capt. Charles Boothby, R.E. During his last campaign*, 1898; *OA*.
166 *DNB*.
167 *DNB*.
168 Parker, James Gordon, 'The Directors of the East India Company, 1754–1790', 1977, PhD thesis, MSS 480523, University of Edinburgh, History and Classics PhD Thesis Collection.
169 *DNB*; Sir John Bernard Bosanquet, viewed 13 July 2019: <http://www.historyhome.co.uk/people/bosanquet.htm, The Silk Road to Leytonstone, viewed 13 July 2019: <http://www.leytonpast.info/page211.html>.
170 *DNB*.
171 BMD; Berkeley, George Monck, and Berkeley, Eliza, *Poems*, 1797, p. ccciv; Lodge, John, *The Peerage of Ireland: Or, a Genealogical History of the Present Nobility of that Kingdom. Revised, Enlarged and Continued to the Present Time*; by Mervyn Archdall, 1789.
172 *Grove*; Giovanni Bottesini, viewed 13 July 2019: <https://www.allmusic.com/artist/giovanni-bottesini-mn0001416775/biography>.
173 Garland, Henry and Mary (editors) *The Oxford Companion to German Literature*, 1997; Wikipedia.
174 BMD; *CA*; c-1841–1901; Payne, James Bertrand, *Armorial of Jersey*, 1859.
175 *VCH*, Oxfordshire; Handsworth; Great Tew Church MI; Matthew Robinson Boulton, viewed 13 July 2019: <https://www.gracesguide.co.uk/Matthew_Robinson_Boulton>.
176 Anc: Hull Wilkinson Pennicott Bozen Batt Ware Duggan Family tree; thepeerage.com: person M, #52400.
177 BMD; Bourne of Hackinsall by Nigel Watts; c-1841–1901; *OA*; WFP F86–F129.
178 Anc: Gumpper, Monroe, Brown, and Simon Family Tree: Karl Gumpper; *CP*; *HP*.
179 *The East India Register and Directory*, 1804, p. 186; *GM*, vol. 84, part 1, 1814, p. 571; *GM*, vol. 173, 1842, p. 109.
180 BMD; CCEd; c-1841; *The Christian Observer*, vol. 9, 1811, p. 816; E&W Wills—will of Thomas Bowen.
181 Henry Carrington Bowles, viewed 21 July 2019: <https://sites.rootsweb.com/~bowlesfamily/the_bowles_of_london_and_middlesex.htm>.
182 Anc: Phillips Family Tree: royphillips43; BMD; c-1841–1861.
183 *OA*.
184 *DNB*; *OA*.
185 BMD; c-; 1851–1881; Peaty, I. 'The Cotswold Brewery, Cirencester', *Journal of the Brewery History*, 1994.
186 BMD; New Inn and Tavern, viewed 13 July 2019: <http://www.bristolslostpubs.co.uk/>.
187 BMD; The Fry Family Tree: Frenchay Village Museum, March 2016; *The Gazette*, April 1788, p. 208; *GM*, vol. 93, 1803, p. 83; Hassell, John, *Picturesque Rides and Walks*, vol. 1, 1817; *VCH*, *A History of the County of Middlesex*, vol. 5, 1976; Jones, Arthur, *Hertfordshire 1731–1800 as Recorded in the Gentleman's Magazine*, 1993; *Kent's Directory for the Year 1794. Cities of London and Westminster, & Borough of Southwark*; Sugar Refiners & Sugarbakers Database, viewed 13 July 2019: <http://www.mawer.clara.net/sugarssac.html>; Wilson, Harry Bristow, *The History of Merchant-Taylors School, from its foundation to the present time*, vol. 2, 1814, p. 1215.
188 *The Asiatic Journal and Monthly Miscellany*, vol. 5, 1831; *Asiatic Journal and Monthly Miscellany*, 1835, p.45; *The Asiatic Journal*, 1842; BMD; *The Court Journal: Court Circular & Fashionable Gazette*, vol. 5, 1833 p. 702; *GM*, vol. 103, part 1, 1833, p. 371; *The Indian Mail*, issue 1, 1843, p. 633; *The United Service Journal*, 1833, p. 522.
189 *CP*; *HP*.
190 Anc: Brabant Family Tree; BMD; c-1851; NA: Marriage settlement between Robert Brabant and Elizabeth Hughes 1808; *Coventry Telegraph*; *VCH*, Wiltshire.
191 *HP*; Reay FSA FRHistS, Justin, 'The Naval Bradbys of the Hamble'.
192 BM; Fell, Alfred, *The Early Iron Industry of Furness and Districts: An Historical and Descriptive Account from Earliest Times to the End of the Eighteenth Century with an Account of the Furness Ironmasters in Scotland 1726–1800*, 2013; NPG.

193 Anc: Keen Family Tree; Anc: Benjamin Morgan and John Callaghan Merged 31 December 2008 Family Tree; BMD; c-1851–1861; *The Ecclesiastical gazette, or, Monthly register of the affairs of the Church of England*, vols. 7-8, 1845, p. 249; *OA*.

194 *The Asiatic Journal and Monthly Register for British and Foreign India, China, and Australia*, vol. 6, 1831, p. 154; *The Asiatic Journal and Monthly Register for British and Foreign India, China, and Australia*, 1834, p. 178; BMD; E&W Wills—will of Paris Bradshaw, Lieutenant Colonel in the Service of the East India Company of Patna, East Indies; St Andrew's Parish Register, Clifton; Paris William Augustus Bradshaw, viewed 13 July 2019: <https://www.geni.com/people/Paris-William-A-Bradshaw/6000000042816578817>; Kent, England, Tyler Index to Parish Registers, 1538–1874 for Mary Ann Carr.

195 *The collected works of Jeremy Bentham*, vol. 1, 1989, p. 260; BMD; *CA*; c-1861; Dorset History Centre: Correspondence of Hayne family, including letters from Lucy Bragge (daughter of Lovelace Hayne) at Sadborrow; *HP*; E&W Wills—will of Thomas Vernon Dolphin; *OA*; Thorncombe Village Trust, viewed 13 July 2019: <http://www.thorncombe-village-trust.co.uk/>.

196 *DNB*.

197 Bristol City Council Archives; c-1841–1881; *OA*.

198 Bristol City Council Archives; BMD; c-1841–1851; *OA*; *Telephone Directory* 1907.

199 BMD; c-1841–1851.

200 Bigg-Wither, Reginald Fitz Hugh, *A History of the Wither Family*, 1907, p. 87, BMD; *B-1906*, p. 314; *CB*; Hill, Constance, *Jane Austen: Her Homes and Her Friends*, 1902, p. 73; Tucker, George Holbert, *Jane Austen the Woman: Some Biographical* Insights, 1995, p. 34; *VCH*, Hampshire.

201 BMD; Christies, Portrait of Mrs John Allnutt, née Eleanor Brandram, half-length; Jeremiah, Melwyn, MI in the Church of St Stephen, Walbrook in the City of London, 2008; E&W Wills—will of Samuel Brandram, Colourman of Lee, Kent, 25 November 1808; NPG; Who Were the Brandrams? viewed 14 July 2019: <http://www.thamesdiscovery.org/frog-blog/who-were-the-brandrams>.

202 BMD; CCEd; *Taunton Courier*.

203 Anc: Wendy Ross Family Tree: Wendy Ross; BMD; *DNB*; Faye Brereton-Goodwin, Brereton Families of Ireland, viewed 14 July 2019: <http://breretonhistory.ca/Feb%202015%20Brereton%20of%20Ireland%20Vol%202.pdf>.

204 BMD; Bristol Industrial Archaeological Society (BIAS): Stiles, Robin, *The Old Market Sugar Refinery 1684–1908*; Sugar Refiners & Sugarbakers Database, viewed 13 July 2019: <http://www.mawer.clara.net/sugarssac.html>.

205 BMD; c-1851; Centre of South Asian Studies, Cambridge.

206 Anc: clement Family Tree: mmel19; BMD; c-1841–1861; *OA*; Oxford History, viewed 14 July 2019: <http://www.oxfordhistory.org.uk/mayors/>.

207 *CB*; *OA*.

208 Hatchard and Company, *Christian Observer*, 1835, pp. 130-131; *OA*.

209 *OA*.

210 BMD; c-1841–1891.

211 BMD; c-1841–1891; *DNB*.

212 BMD; *DNB*; *MM*, vol. 28, 1809, p 109.

213 BMD: c-1841–1851; *OA*; Broadhurst Family Tree, viewed 14 July 2019: <http://www.broadhurst-family.co.uk/FamilyTree/>.

214 *CA*; CCEd; c-1841; E&W Wills—will of John Brocklebank.

215 CCEd; *OA*; Slave Registers of former British Colonial Dependencies, 1813–1834; British Women's Emancipation since the Renaissance, viewed 14 July 2019: <http://www.historyofwomen.org/>.

216 BMD; c-1851–1881; *CA*; Peter Bellinger Brodie, viewed 14 July 2019: <http://www.bellsite.id.au/gdbtree/HTMLFiles/HTMLFiles_85/P28269.html>.

217 Anc: Stratton_2012-11-20: palmajack; BMD; c-1841; *Oxford Journal*, 30 January 1893.

218 *DNB*; *HP*; University College, London, Brougham Papers; WFP F214.

219 *GM*, 1806, p. 291; *GM*, 1810, p. 495; Kay, John, *A Series of Original Portraits and Caricature Etchings: With Biographical Sketches and Anecdotes*, 1842, vol. 2, p. 75; *The Scots Magazine and Edinburgh Literary Miscellany*, vol. 67, 1805; Ellis, William Smith, *Notices of the Ellises of England, Scotland, and Ireland, from the Conquest to the Present Time, 1857-1866*, p. 141; Cracroft's Peerage—Viscount Hampden; Wedderburn, Alexander, *The Wedderburn Book 1296–1896*, vol. 1, 1898; Robert Brown of Firth, viewed 14 July 2019: <https://www.geni.com/people/Robert-Brown-of-Firth/6000000019419301838>.

220 BMD; CCEd, Longe, John, *The Diary of John Longe (1765–1834), Vicar of Coddenham*, 2008, p. 263; *OA*; *The British Critic and Quarterly Theological Review*, 1826, p. 258.

221 *Slater's Directory of Gloucestershire*, 1850.

222 Anc: Patrice: TXGALS; BMD; Burke's *Family Records*; c-1841–1851; GA: Marriage Settlement Brown/Lloyd Baker 1832; *Selected Papers on Social and Economic Questions*, 1918; Benjamin Chapman Browne, viewed 14 July 2019: <https://www.gracesguide.co.uk/Benjamin_Chapman_Browne>.

223 BMD; Colville, Dorothy, North Mymms—Parish and People; Foster, Joseph, *The baronetage and knightage; Gentleman's Magazine, or Monthly Intelligencer*, vol., 147, 1830, p. 571; vol. 48, 1840, p. 427; *The Hertfordshire Naturalist*; E&W Wills—will of Caroline Susanna Browne; Survey of Astronomical History, viewed 14 July 2019: <https://shasurvey.wordpress.com/>; *VCH*, Hertfordshire.

224 BMD; *B-1906*, p. 207; c-1881; *OA*; Parish Register, Salperton.

225 Anc: John Sharp Family Tree: howard_nicholson1; *CA*; c-1861; *Ecclesiastical Gazette*, 1839; GA.

226 BMD; *OA*.

227 c-1851–1861.

228 BMD; c-1851.

229 *CA*.

230 CCEd.

231 c-1841; *OA*; Geological Society of London, viewed 6 May 2017: <https://www.geolsoc.org.uk/Groups-and-Networks/Specialist-Groups/History-of-Geology-Group/Online-Resources>.

232 BMD; c-1861–1871; *DNB*.

233 BMD; *CA*; Buller surnames, viewed 6 May 2017: <https://www.genealogy.com/forum/surnames/topics/buller/>.
234 *DNB* and Wikipedia.
235 *DNB*.
236 *B-1845*; Information provided by multiple sites. See also the families of Arbuthnott and Vavasour.
237 BMD; c-1841–1851; *Pigot's Directory*, 1839.
238 BMD; c-1841–1851; *NBD*.
239 *OA*.
240 *DNB*; *OA*.
241 *OA*.
242 BMD; c-1841.
243 Staveley Genealogy, viewed 14 July 2019: <https://www.staveley-genealogy.com/old_sleningford.htm>.
244 Ibbetson, Julius Caesar, *A Picturesque Guide to Bath, Bristol Hot-wells, the River Avon, and the Adjacent Country*, 1793.
245 *OA*.
246 BMD; *VCH*, Gloucestershire, Alvington, volume 5, Bledisloe Hundred, St Briavels Hundred, the Forest of Dean, 1996.
247 BMD; *OA*.
248 *DNB*.
249 BMD; c-1871–1881; Foster, Joseph, *Oxford Men and Their Colleges, 1880–1892*, 1893, p. 273 & p. 533; *Register of Wadham College*; Wikipedia: Montagu Burrows.
250 BMD; c-1851–1861; Morris & Co. *Commercial Directory & Gazetteer of Newnham 1876*; *OA*; Hyett, Francis Adams, Bazeley, William, Austin, Roland, 1874, *Supplement to the Bibliographer's Manual of Gloucestershire Literature*, 1915, p. 612.
251 BMD; *CA*; WFP F180.
252 *HP*.
253 BMD; Bishop Bickersteth's Visitation Returns; CCEd; c-1841–1861; *OA*.
254 BMD; c-1851–1861.
255 BMD; c-1861; *Pigot's Directory*, 1830.
256 Anc: Bush, Henry Statton artist: Alex Panayotti; Anc: Dyer/Batchelor Family Tree: eeyore539; *LM*, vol. 24, 1793, p. 616; E&W Wills—will of Robert Bush of Clifton, PROB 11/1754, 1829; WFP F201.
257 BMD; c-1851; *The Christian Remembrancer*, vol. 1, 1841, p. 468; UCL–Slaves.
258 BMD; c-1851–1881; *OA*.
259 BMD; Hunt, Henry, *Memoirs of Henry Hunt, Esq*, vol. 1, 1820, p. 251; *LG*, part 1, 1824, p. 413.
260 *CP*.
261 *DNB*; *CA*.
262 *Hunt*.
263 BMD; c-1861; *Dictionary of Ulster Biography*; *Home Rule: An Irish History 1800–2000*; *New York Times*, 1879.
264 BMD; WFP, *et passim*.
265 Anc: Jamiaquino; Cambridgeshire County Record Office.

Letter C

1 Anc: Ager Family Tree: Geoffrey Ager BMD; *DNB*; *OA*.
2 Anc: Reformers, Abolitionists, Suffragists and More: DawnMO83; BMD; *HP*.
3 *CB*; *HP*; WFP F186-219.
4 *DNB*.
5 BMD; c-1841.
6 *DNB*; *OA*; Twickenham Museum, viewed 14 July 2019: <http://www.twickenham-museum.org.uk/detail.php?aid=32&ctid=1&cid=15>; Whitminster MI.
7 BMD; c-1841–1871; Alexander Abercromby Cameron, viewed 14 July 2019: <https://www.noblecircles.com/genealogy/index.php>.
8 BMD; Richards, J. *The Legal Observer, Or, Journal of Jurisprudence*, vol. 31, 1846, p. 300.
9 *CP*.
10 *DNB*; National Galleries of Scotland, viewed 14 July 2019: <https://www.nationalgalleries.org/art-and-artists/42122/john-francis-campbell-islay-iain-%C3%B2g-%C3%ACle-1822-1884>.
11 Anc: Campion family tree: BettyHolden70; BMD; c-1841–1901; England & Wales, Criminal Registers, 1791–1892.
12 BMD; Drummond, Pippa, *The Provincial Music Festival in England, 1784–1914*, 2016, p. 38; *GM*, vol. 29, 1830, p. 283.
13 *DNB*.
14 BMD; Geoghegan, Patrick, *Irish Lives; The Irish Times*; *GM, and Historical Chronicle*, vol. 58, part 1, 1788, p. 189; Jerdan, William: *Men I Have Known*, 1866, p. 106.
15 *BLG*; Hartpury Parish Historic Notes.
16 Anc: Holbrow Stanton Gosling Waterfield Family Tree: chrisrooney46; BMD; *B-1846-1*, p. 186; c-1841–1881; Haine, Colleen, *The Cloth Trade along the Painswick Street*, 1985.
17 Hamilton, A., *The Town and Country Magazine, or, Universal Repository of Knowledge, Instruction, and Entertainment*, vol. 6, 1774, p. 716; *Kent, Directory*, 1740; *The Sentimental Magazine: Or, General Assemblage of Science, Taste, and Entertainment. Calculated to Amuse the Mind, to Improve the Understanding, and to Amend the Heart*, vol. 3, 1775, p. 47.
18 Anc: Wilkinson/Chesson Family Tree: BLekias; *B-1879*-1, vol. 1. p. 266; MI: Christchurch, Cheltenham; Scatcherd & Letterman, *London and Its Environs; or the General Ambulator, and Pocket Companion for the Tour of the Metropolis and its Vicinity*, 1820, p. 42.

19 Anc: Percival-Smith Family Tree: chrisps131; BMD; c-1891; Southwick Hall, viewed 14 July 2019: <http://www.southwickhall.co.uk/home.htm>; *VCH*, Northamptonshire, Little Addington, vol. 3, 1930.
20 *Grove*.
21 Anc: Dawe, Claude-Hounsell, Fox-Strangeways: janweeks1; BMD; *OA*.
22 c-1851–1871; *OA*.
23 *DNB*; *OA*.
24 *DNB*.
25 BMD; c-1841, Upper Slaughter Parish Register.
26 BMD; *DNB*; *OA*.
27 Birmingham: Archives, Heritage and Photography Service, ref. MS 3375/410873; BMD; CCEd, *GM*, part 2, 1805, p. 773; *OA*; *Registers of Wadham College, Oxford*.
28 BMD; Burke's *Family Records*, 1897, pp 138-9; *CA*; Cornwall Record Office: Carlyon of Tregrehan; WFP F208.
29 *CB*; *HP*.
30 BMD; *DNB*.
31 BMD; Mayo, Charles Herbert, *A Genealogical Account of the Mayo and Elton Families*, 1908.
32 BMD; *OA*; *Registers of Wadham College, Oxford*; website: Frederick Hamilton Carrington, viewed 14 July 2019: <https://www.wikitree.com/wiki/Carrington-770>.
33 BMD; *CA*; CCEd; CL; Dodsley, J., *The Annual Register, or, a View of the History, Politics, and Literature for the Year*, 1806, p. 490; *OA*; *Walford-1860*, p. 174.
34 Anc: A Prior to Now Combe Down family tree: Richard Hill; BMD; *DNB*; *HP*.
35 BMD; c-1841; *VCH*, Gloucestershire, vol. 11, Bisley and Longtree Hundreds, 1976.
36 Anc: James Michael White Family Tree: James Michael White; BMD; *Burke-1875*, vol. 1, p. 215; *MM*, vol. 40, 1815, p. 564; website: Swanzy, Henry Biddall, The families of French of Belturbet and Nixon of Fermanagh, and their descendants, 1908; *Walford-1882*, p. 109.
37 Göler, Leopold, *Die Schauspielerinnen Manon und Fanny Caspers und ihre Beziehungen zu Goethe und Thorwaldsen. In: Mannheimer Geschictsblätter*, 1932, pp. 223-238; Sämtliche Werke, Johann Wolfgang von Goethe, vol. 19, 1808; Franziska Caspers, viewed 14 July 2019: <https://gw.geneanet.org/pierfit?lang=de&n=caspers&oc=0&p=Franziska>.
38 CCEd, *DNB*.
39 BMD; *CB*; c-1861.
40 BMD; c-1841–1861; *DNB*.
41 Anc: Forster Family Tree: Paul Bowman; BMD; c-1851–1861; *Hunt*.
42 Anc: South African Cave Tree: SheilaCave36; BMD; c-1841–1901; *OA*; RBS Banking History.
43 *HP*.
44 *HP*.
45 *DNB*.
46 GA: Price family of Tibberton Court; *Pigot Directory*, 1830; *VCH*, Gloucestershire, vol. 4, the City of Gloucester, 1988; Winchcombe parish register 1785.
47 BMD; *DNB*.
48 *DNB*.
49 BMD; c-1851–1871.
50 BMD; Museum of Royal Worcester, viewed 14 July 2019: <https://www.museumofroyalworcester.org/>.
51 BMD; B-1846-1, p. 203; CCEd; *OA*; *VCH*, Essex, vol. 6, 1973; *VCH*, Gloucestershire, vol. 6, 1965. 52 BMD; B-1846-1, p. 203; *The Statutes of the United Kingdom of Great Britain and Ireland*, vols 30-33, 1832, p. xxv.
53 Smith, Leonard, *Cure, Comfort and Safe Custody: Public Lunatic Asylums in Early Nineteenth-Century England*, 1999, p. 62.
54 BMD; *OA*.
55 *The Annual Register of World Events*, vol. 85, 1844, p. 312; Barton, Henry D., *The Law Journal Reports*, vol. 7, 1838, pp. 34-40; BMD; *B-1836*, p. 642; *LG*, part 2. 1833, p. 1463; *OA*; *The Spectator*, 17 August 1833, p.11; Whitbourne Court History, viewed 14 July 2019: <http://herefordshirepast.co.uk/buildings/whitbourne-court/>.
56 BMD; *B-1906*, p. 295; *GM*, 1834, p. 442; Wallace, Frank, *Spiritual Songsters*, 2015.
57 *OA*.
58 *DNB*; *Grove*.
59 Anc: INGRAM: ANNE BRYANT; BMD; Anc: Barnes 100: Kerry Challoner Anderson; c-1841–1871; GA.
60 BMD; c-1841–1871; GA: Charleton family papers.
61 Anc: Family Tree: assemblyorder; *CP*; *GM*, vol. 147, 1830, p. 174; Lodge, Edmund, *The Peerage of the British Empire as at present existing*, 1840, p. 522; WFP.
62 Anc: Chater Family Tree: kchater1; *The Asiatic Journal and Monthly Register for British and Foreign India, China, and Australia*, vol. 28, 1829, p. 624; Chater, James, viewed 10 November 2018: <http://pigott-gorrie.blogspot.com/2008/06/a-missionary-in-ceylon-henry-robert.html>; *GM*, vol. 162, 1837, p. 438; *The Monthly Repository of Theology and General Literature*, vol. 15, p. 733; *OA*; Skeen, William, *Mountain Life and Coffee Cultivation in Ceylon: A Poem on the Knuckles Range, with Other Poems*, 1870, p. 174, note 45; Whelan, Timothy D., *Baptist Autographs in the John Rylands University Library of Manchester, 1741–1845*, 2009, p. 366; *Arniston*—Wikipedia.
63 Anc: Garway-Heath family tree: garway1; BMD; c-1841–1861; *Gardner's Directory of Oxfordshire*, 1852. *MM*, vol. 58, 1824, p. 379.
64 BMD; *DNB*.
65 Anc: Applegates-McChesney-Jarosz-Dziedzic: Terrence K Applegate; *DNB*.
66 BMD; *B-1912*, p.178; 1912 c-1841–1881; *Nottinghamshire Guardian*, 14 October 1852; *Slaters Commercial Directory*, 1858–1859.

67 BMD; *B-1847-1*, p. 212; Darwin, Charles, *The Correspondence of Charles Darwin: 1821–1836*, vol. 1, 1985, pp. 618-9; *DNB*; MI at St Mary's church, Watford—'In memory of ... Lt Col Charles Chester ... of the XXIII Regt Bengal Native Infantry who fell in the Mutiny and Rebellion in India AD MDCCCLVIII. Erected by their brother officers'; thepeerage.com: person F, #405572.

68 GA: Chester-Master Family; Saunders and Otley, *The Annual Peerage of the British Empire*, vol. 1, 1829, p. 232; *Williams*.

69 BMD; c-1841–1861, Iowa c-1856, Book 1 of Naturalization Declarations, 1832–1856, Dubuque County, Iowa. Des Moines: Iowa Genealogical Society, 1982; Oldt, Franklin T., *History of Dubuque County, Iowa; being a general survey of Dubuque County history, including a history of the city of Dubuque and special account of districts throughout the county, from the earliest settlement to the present time*, vol 2, p. 14; *Repertory of patent inventions and other discoveries and improvements in arts, manufactures and agriculture*, vol. 14, 1840, p. 4.

70 BMD; *CA*; *GM*, 1838, p. 108; List of the Royal Society, for the Year 1794, vol. 13, p. 5, Johnston, William, *Medical Observations and Inquiries*, vol. 6, 1784, pp. 31-47; *VCH*, Gloucestershire, vol. 4, 1988, pp. 382-410.

71 BMD; *CP*; thepeerage.com: person M, #28804; Theal, George McCall, *History of South Africa Since September 1795*, 2010, p. 35.

72 BMD; Fox-Davies, Arthur Charles, *Armorial Families: A Directory of Gentlemen of coat-armour*, vol. 1, 1899, p. 362.

73 Anc: Dunn family tree; Anc: Ingram Family_2017; BMD; c-1851–1881; MI—Newent, Gloucestershire, St Mary's Churchyard & Watery Lane Cemetery.

74 BMD; *Oxford Journal*, 21 September 1805; *The Universal Magazine of Knowledge and Pleasure*, 1805, p. 593; Anne Tanner, viewed 14 July 2019: <https://www.genealogy.com/forum/surnames/topics/tanner/2197/>; Marbury Hall, viewed 14 July 2019: <http://www.feathersmediums.co.uk/a-house-with-spirit.html >; John Smith-Barry, viewed 14 July 2019: <https://williamgray101.wordpress.com/2016/09/07/john-smith-barry-1793-1837/>.

75 *Lloyds Weekly Newspaper*, 13 May 1849; Roll, Eric, *An Early Experiment in Industrial Organization: History of the Firm of Boulton and Watt 1775–1805*, 2013, p.117 UCL–Slaves: Bourdieu, Chollet & Bourdieu; Van Ruymbeke, Bertrand and Sparks, Randy J., *Memory and Identity: The Huguenots in France and the Atlantic Diaspora*, 2003; WFP F208, 17 January 1806.

76 BMD; c-1841–1901; *CP*; *OA*.

77 Anc: Campbell-Wyber Family Tree-JAB-January2017; BMD; c-1841–1851, *CL*; *OA*.

78 Anc: Stockie/O'Brien Family Tree: James Stockie; *Pigot's Directory*, 1830.

79 Anc: Heath Family Tree: RebeccaHeath75; BMD; c-1851; *Slater's Directory of Gloucestershire*, 1850.

80 BMD; c-1841–1851; *Hunt*; *VCH*, Gloucestershire, vol. 4, the City of Gloucester, 1988; Gloucestershire Transport History, viewed 21 July 2019: <http://glostransporthistory.visit-gloucestershire.co.uk>.

81 BMD; *CP*; *HP*.

82 BMD; c-1861; Tibbetts, G. R., Churchill Family of Deddington, viewed 21 July 2019: <http://www.deddingtonhistory.uk/__data/assets/pdf_file/0004/12685/ChurchillsFin3.pdf>.

83 c-1851; *Slaters Commercial Directory*, 1858/9.

84 Beavan, Charles, *Reports of Cases in Chancery: Argued and Determined in the Rolls Court During the Time of Lord Langdale, Master of the Rolls*, vol. 6, 1845, pp. 314-323 Greenwood *v.* Churchill; BMD; Tibbetts, G. R., Churchill Family of Deddington,viewed 21 July 2019: <http://www.deddingtonhistory.uk/__data/assets/pdf_file/0004/12685/ChurchillsFin3.pdf>.

85 BMD; c-1841–1861, *Pigot's Directory*, 1830, *Slaters Commercial Directory*, 1858/9.

86 Anc: COOPER/DETLEFSEN FAMILY TREE: helengrace88; *DNB*; *OA*.

87 BMD; c-1851–1871; Gloucestershire, England, Gaol Registers, 1815–1879; England & Wales, Criminal Registers, 1791–1892; *Parliamentary Papers*, vol. 29, part 1, *Appendix to the Second Annual Report of the Commissioners under the Poor Law Amendment Act*, 1836, p. 268.

88 Anc: Clackl Family Tree, Mary Goodfellow; BMD; c-1841–1861; *OA*.

89 *CA*.

90 Anc: Barratt Clayton Dowler tree: WmHouston2; BMD; c-1841–1901.

91 Anc: Annable family tree: 1Branch; Australia, Convict Index, 1788–1868; BMD; c-1861–1881; England & Wales, Criminal Registers, 1791–1892.

92 Anc: Duggan Family Tree: stephanieottawa; c-1841–1851; *The Ecclesiastical gazette, or, Monthly register of the affairs of the Church of England*, vols 7–8, 1845, p. 230; Leech, Joseph, *Rural Rides of the Bristol Churchgoer*; Yatton Church, viewed 21 July 2019: <http://www.yattonchurches.org/>.

93 c-1841–1851; GA.

94 *DNB*; *OA*; Pickering, William, *Oxford University Statutes*, vol. 1, 1845 p. 39.

95 BMD; *Pigot and Co.'s National Commercial Directory* ... Worcestershire, 1835, p. 652; Richards, J., *The Legal Guide*, vol. 1, 1839, p. 76.

96 Evans, Robert, and Humphreys, Maggie, *Dictionary of Composers for the Church in Great Britain and Ireland*, 1997, p. 65; E&W Wills—will of Charles Erlin Jackson Clarke; The succession of organists at Durham Cathedral, viewed 21 July 2019: <http://www.duresme.org.uk/>.

97 Wilbour, Benjamin Franklin, *Little Compton Families*, 2003, p. 191.

98 Anc: Taylor Family Tree: junejesney; BMD; Moulton-Barrett, viewed 18 February 2019: <https://www.browningscorrespondence.com/biographical-sketches/?id=1849>; UCL–Slaves.

99 *DNB*.

100 BMD; c-1841—1891; *Kelly's Directory*, 1856; *OA*; UCL–Slaves.

101 BMD; Burke, J. and J. B., *Heraldic illustrations*, vol. 1, 1844, plate xxxviii; c-1841; *CL*; *GM*, 1837, p. 548; E&W Wills—will of Benjamin Claxson, d. 1777; *OA*; *VCH*, Gloucestershire, vol. 4, the City of Gloucester, 1988.

102 Anc: Janes + Thickett Families: Bob Janes; Baines, E., *History, Directory & Gazeteer, of the County of York*, 1822, p. 219; BMD; c-1851; *The Scots Magazine, or, General Repository of Literature, History, and Politics*, vol. 77, 1815, p. 556.

103 BMD; *DNB*.

104. BMD; c-1841–1881; Gloucestershire Society for Industrial Archaeology; Skempton, A. W., *A Biographical Dictionary of Civil Engineers in Great Britain and Ireland: 1500–1830*, 2002, pp. 140-1.

105 BMD; Burke's *Family Records*, 1897, pp 162-3; c-1841–1861; *OA*.
106 BMD; *CB*; CCEd; c-1851; *OA*.
107 BMD; c-1851–1881; *CA*.
108 BMD; *B-1846-2*, p. 1498; *A Genealogical and Heraldic Dictionary of the Landed Gentry of Great Britain & Ireland: Supplement, corrigenda and general index*, 1849, p. 309; *CA*; MI: Frampton-on-Severn, viewed 21 July 2019: <http://www.framptoncourtestate.co.uk/>.
109 BMD; *B-1865-1*, p. 1109; c-1841–1881; *Debrett 1840*, p. 363; National Library of Wales: Morgan-Clifford Manuscripts; Wikipedia: Henry Morgan Clifford.
110 BMD; c-1841–1851.
111 BMD; c-1841–1851. *Pigot Directory* 1830.
112 Anc: King/Edkins Family 240514: nicola stevens; BMD; c-1841–1861.
113 Anc: Gallatin Family Tree: lauriemiller98; BMD; c-1841–1851.
114 BMD; c-1841–1881.
115 BMD; *The British Magazine and Monthly Register of Religious and Ecclesiastical Information, Parochial History, and Documents Respecting the State of the Poor, Progress of Education*, vol. 19, 1841, p. 475; c-1841; *Pigot and Co.'s National Commercial Directory ...* Worcestershire, 1835 p. 677.
116 *The Bankers' Magazine, and Journal of the Money Market*, vol. 4, 1846, p. 436; Barclays Group Archives, viewed 21 July 2019: <https://www.archive.barclays.com/>.
117 BMD; c-1841; James Clitherow, viewed, 21 July 2019: <http://www.bhsproject.co.uk/families_clitherow.shtml>.
118 Anc: Waring Family Tree: FredWaring51; *DNB*.
119 BMD; *B-1846-1*, pp. 236-7; *The Plantagenet Roll of the Blood Royal*: The Mortimer-Percy vol., p. 324; Ricardo, David, *The Works and Correspondence of David Ricardo*: vol. 8, Letters 1819–June 1821, 1952, p. 243; Witchell, M. E. N., Hudleston, C. R., *The Family of Clutterbuck*, 1924, pp. 52-7.
120 BMD; c-1851–1871.
121 BMD; c-1851–1881.
122 *DNB*.
123 BMD; *OA*;
124 BMD; *DNB*; *HP*.
125 BMD; *CB*; *DNB*; *HP*; Webster, Anthony, *The Richest East India Merchant: The Life and Business of John Palmer of Calcutta, 1767–1836*, 2007, pp. 53-4.
126 Anc: Michael Howery Family Tree: HoweryM; BMD; c-1851–1871; *OA*; Frome Museum, viewed 21 July 2019: <https://fromemuseum.wordpress.com/collection/metalworking/cockey/>.
127 Bodleian Library: Papers of the Codrington Family; *CB*; *HP*; *Williams*.
128 BMD; *CB*; *CP*; *HP*; *OA*.
129 BMD; *DNB*; UCL–Slaves.
130 *East India Kalendar or Asiatic Register 1797–1799*, p. 116; *The East India Register and Directory*, 1815, p. xxiii; *The Genealogist*, vol. 23, 1907, p. 60; *Morning Chronicle*, 28 December 1803, p. 3; Records of Holy Trinity, Westbury-on-Trym.
131 Baker, George, *The History and Antiquities of the County of Northampton*, vol. 2, 1841, p. 266; BMD; Charlotte Coker, viewed 18 February 2019: <https://www.myheritage.com/names/charlotte_coker>; Cracroft's Peerage; *Notes and Queries*, 1883, p. 308; E&W Wills—will of John Coker; WFP F203, F220-6.
132 BMD; Wright, E. G., *Collections Towards the History and Antiquities of the County of Hereford*: pt. 1, 1812; *The Universal Magazine of Knowledge and Pleasure*: vol. 75, 1784, p. 110.
133 c-1841–1881; Worcester Porcelain Museum.
134 BMD; *The British Critic, and Quarterly Theological Review*, 1827, p. 538; c-1841–1871; MI: Ventnor: St Catherine's Church.
135 BMD; c-1851–1911.
136 BMD; c-1841, Shakespeare Birthplace Trust: Reference: ER 3/4794.
137 *DNB*.
138 *DNB*.
139 *DNB*.
140 c-1851, criminal records: Gloucester Assizes 31 March 1838.
141 BMD; c-1851; Fosbroke, Thomas Dudley, *Abstracts of records and manuscripts respecting the County of Gloucester; Formed into a History*, 1807, p. 276.
142 BMD.
143 c-1841.
144 BMD, specifically baptisms at Upper Slaughter recorded at Bourton; c-1841–1851.
145 Anc: Gates family tree: Ariesgates11; BMD, specifically baptisms at the Baptist Chapel, Bourton-on-the-Water.
146 Anc: kennett: awalters196; BMD, specifically baptism at Upper Slaughter.
147 BMD.
148 BMD, specifically baptisms at Upper Slaughter recorded at Bourton; c-1841–1851.
149 BMD, specifically baptism at Upper Slaughter.
150 BMD, specifically baptisms at Upper Slaughter, c-1841–1851.
151 Anc: Burt Family Tree: hamletcat; BMD, specifically baptisms at Upper Slaughter recorded at Bourton; c-1841–1891.
152 BMD.
153 BMD; c-1841–1851.
154 BMD, specifically baptisms at Upper Slaughter recorded at Bourton; c-1841–1891; Brian Collett Family History Research, viewed 21 July 2019: <http://www.collettfamilyhistory.net/>.

155 Anc: Burt Family tree; BMD; c-1841–1901.
156 BMD; c-1841–1851.
157 BMD; c-1841–1861.
158 BMD; c-1841–1851.
159 Anc: Clemson and Hiscock Family Tree: Carole_Hiscock; BMD.
160 BMD; c-1851–1861; Witney Blanket Story, viewed 21 July 2019: <http://www.witneyblanketstory.org.uk/wbp.asp>.
161 BMD; c-1851–1861; *The Navy List*, 1845, p. 58; White FRGS, James, *Place-names in the Thousand Islands, St Lawrence River*, 1910.
162 Anc: Hamrick/McGuire/Hansen/Devine/ Ratterree Family Tree; BMD; *DNB*; *Kellys Gloucestershire Directory* 1856; Cohen, Rachel. *The New Yorker*, 6 October 2003, 'The Very Bad Review—Two Victorian men of letters, One review from hell'.
163 BMD; *CA*; *GM*, 1799, p. 992, 1836, p. 677.
164 *Cardiff and Merthyr Guardian, Glamorgan, Monmouth, and Brecon Gazette* 23 September 1848; *GM*, 1833, p. 63.
165 BMD; c-1841–1851; E&W Wills—will of George Twisleton Colvile.
166 BMD; c-1851, *OA*.
167 BMD; c-1851; WikiTree, viewed 21 July 2019: <https://www.wikitree.com/wiki/Colvile-18>.
168 Anc: Day Family Tree: jamesfday888; Anc: White Family Tree; Hayter Family Tree; BMD; c-1851–1881.
169 BMD; *CA*; CCEd; c-1841–1881; GA: Commeline family of Gloucester; MI: St Lawrence's Churchyard, Sandhurst, Gloucestershire; *Wiltshire Notes & Queries*, vol. VIII 1914–16, 1917.
170 *CA*; CCEd; *OA*.
171 *CA*; *GM*, 1853, I., p. 328.
172 CCEd; *OA*.
173 Anc: Janes + Thickett Families: Bob Janes; BMD; GA: Commeline family of Gloucester.
174 BMD; c-1841–1881; GA: Commeline family of Gloucester.
175 MI: Urchfont Church.
176 *DNB*.
177 *CP*.
178 BMD; c-1841–1851; *DNB*; MI: Stanway, Gloucestershire, St Peter's Churchyard. Interestingly, the *DNB* entry on Richard Cook by L. A. Fagan, revised by Annette Peach is wrong. The beginning part of the entry reads: 'Cook, Richard (1784–1857), history painter, was born in London and was baptized on 17 October 1784 at St Giles Cripplegate, London, the son of Richard Cook (*fl.* 1785–1804), painter, and Jane, née Tuck whom he married at St Leonard, Shoreditch, on 22 July 1784. Farington recorded in his Diary for 18 November 1816 that, according to the sculptor John Rossi, 'Cooke [*sic*] the new Associate, is a native of Gloucestershire. His father, who was a farmer, has retired from business, having sufficient to live upon' would appear to be inaccurate (*Farington, Diary*)'. In fact Farington was right! There is a Stanway birth parish record for Richard, baptised 30 December 1784; Farington, viewed 21 July 2019: <https://www.paul-mellon-centre.ac.uk/media/_file/articles/facsimile-transcription-1.pdf>.
179 BMD.
180 BMD; c-1841; GA: D1395—Deeds and Manorial Records: Testamentary and Trusts.
181 BMD; c-1841.
182 BMD.
183 BMD; c-1851–1861.
184 BMD; c-1851–1861.
185 BMD.
186 BMD; *The British Magazine and Monthly Register of Religious and Ecclesiastical Information, Parochial History, and Documents Respecting the State of the Poor, Progress of Education, etc.*, vol. 12, 1837, p. 585; *GM*, vol. 14, 1840, p. 670; GA; *MM*, vol. 35, 1813, p. 564; *OA*.
187 BMD; c-1841–1851; *DNB*; *OA*.
188 Anc: Durrant Family Tree; BMD; c-1841–1911; *Pigot's Directory of Gloucester*, 1830.
189 Anc: Reynolds Family Tree; BMD; *Pigot's Directory of Gloucester*, 1830.
190 *DNB*; Church of St Andrew, Donhead St Andrew, viewed 26 July 2019: <https://www.wiltshire-opc.org.uk/genealogy/index.php/parish-directory/item/267-donhead-st-andrew?jjj=1564155261101>; The Diaries of Charlotte Grove, viewed 26 July 2019: <http://www.claretjug.info/>.
191 BMD; c-1841–1851, 1861; *MATB*, p. 98; Sufton Court, viewed 26 July 2019: <https://www.historichouses.org/houses/house-listing/sufton-court.html>.
192 BMD; *Debrett's Baronetage of England: Containing an Account of All Existing English Baronets, with Alphabetical Lists of Such as Have Been Advanced to the Peerage, Or Whose Titles Have Become Extinct, etc.*, 1832, p. 741.
193 Anc: Tilbury Family Tree; BMD; c-1851.
194 c-1851; website: gloucestershirepolicearchives.org.uk.
195 Anc: Cooper Family Tree: MaryCooper43.
196 BMD; c-1871, 1881; *Chelmsford Chronicle*, 24 April 1868; *OA*.
197 BMD; British History Online: *Survey of London*, vol. 40; *HP*; Lincolnshire Archives. National Archives: Meniconi Family.
198 BMD; *Debrett 1832*, 1832, p. 741; *DNB*; *HP*.
199 BMD; c-1841–1871; *OA*.
200 BMD; c-1841; *GM*, vol. 179, 1846, p. 441.
201 *American Vital Records from the Gentleman's Magazine, 1731–1868*, 1987, p. 65; Anc: The Gages et al of S. Africa; Anc: Lloyd Family Tree–10 Oct 2018: warrenlloyd56; BMD; c-1841–1871; *GM*, vol. 179, 1846, p. 307.
202 Anc: Gentle Castle Family Tree: Lucy Castle; BMD; *DNB*; Churchill, John, *The London Medical Directory*, 1846, p. 36.
203 BMD; *DNB*.

204 Anc: Copley family tree: SIMONCOPLEY; *CA*; *DNB*.
205 BMD; *B-1886*-1, p. 410; c-1851; NPC, probate–Catherine Louisa Jane Corbett Holland Craddock (1906); *LG*, part 1, 1839, p. 951; *GM*, vol. 11, 1839, p. 554; Wickhamford Manor House, viewed 26 July 2019: <https://www.badseysociety.uk/places/wickhamford-manor-house>.
206 Patterson, Michael, *The First German Theatre: Schiller, Goethe, Kleist and Büchner in Performance*, 1990; von Seckendorf, Leo, *Korrespondenzen der Goethezeit: Edition und Kommentar*, 2014, p. 743.
207 BMD; c-1851–1861.
208 Anc: Janes + Thickett Families: Bob Janes; BMD; *CB*; Savile, Cecil George and Reade, Compton, *The House of Cornewall*, 1908; Sir Velters Cornewall, viewed 26 July 2019: <https://armorial.library.utoronto.ca/stamp-owners/COR004>.
209 BMD; *CA*; CCEd; *CL;* c-1851–1861; Philip Durell Monamy Cornwall, viewed 26 July 2019: <https://www.cichw1.net/pmbg3aa.html>.
210 *Grove*; Wikipedia.
211 Brand, C. F. and C. P., *Italy and the English Romantics*, 1957, appendix B; *The Literary Gazette*, vol. 11, 1827, p. 672.
212 BMD; c-1841; *DNB*.
213 BMD; c-1851; *Journal of the Society for Army Historical Research*, winter 1968, vol. XLVI no. 188.
214 BMD; c-1841–1861.
215 Anc: Dupe Family Tree: ChristopherDupe; BMD; *The General Chronicle and Literary Magazine,* vol. 4, 1812, p. 446; *GM*, 1850, p. 89; MI: St Lawrence's Churchyard, Sandhurst, Gloucestershire; E&W Wills—will of William Cother; Sparkes, Alan, 'The Reform of Gloucester's Municipal Corporation 1835', viewed 20 February 2019: <http://www.bgas.org.uk/tbgas_bg/v125/bg125311.pdf>; *Williams*.
216 BMD; c-1841–1861.
217 BMD; *The Post Office London Directory*, Kelly's Directories Limited, 1843, p. 142; Apprenticeship indenture of Thomas Finch, viewed 26 July 2019: <https://www.exploringsurreyspast.org.uk/collections/getrecord/SHCOL_3073_8_1_1_2>; *The Spectator*, 20 July 1844, *The British Banner*, 12 November 1851, p. 13.
218 *CA*.
219 BMD; c-1841–1861.
220 *DNB*.
221 *CP*.
222 *CP*; *HP*.
223 BMD; *CA*; c-1851; *The European Magazine, and London Review*, vol. 84, Philological Society of London, 1823. p. 281; *Foster-1881*, p. 218.
224 c-1841.
225 BMD; c-1851–1901; James Cox, Mitchell Families on line, viewed 26 July 2019: <http://mfo.me.uk/getperson.php?personID=I19095&tree=E1>.
226 *OA*.
227 Blacker, Beaver H., *Gloucestershire Notes & Queries*, vol. 7, 1896, p. 76; BMD; c-1841–1861; *OA*; Holden, Robert Mackenzie, *Historical Record of the Third and Fourth Battalions of the Worcestershire Regiment*, 1887, p. 310.
228 BMD; c-1841–1901.
229 BMD; *Bath Chronicle and Weekly Gazette*, 16 July 1795; Phillimore, W. P. W., & Blagg, Thomas M., (eds.) *Gloucestershire Parish Registers, Marriages*, vol. XVII; Temple Phillips, H., *Bristol Medico-Chirurgical Journal*, vol. 85, pp. 41-44; University of Bristol Library Special Collections, DM2337/D/1, Diary of Joseph Mason, 1763.
230 BMD, Stow-on-the-Wold burials.
231 BMD; c-1841–1881.
232 BMD; *CA*; c-1841–1891; *VCH*, Gloucestershire.
233 BMD; CCEd; c-1851; *GM*, vol. 52, 1842, p. 673; *MM*, vol. 42, 1816, p. 187; Southey, Rosemary, PhD thesis, 'Commercial Music Making in Eighteenth-Century North East England: A Pale Reflection of London?' vol. II, p. 10.
234 Anc: Struthers (JaniceStruthers): JaniceStruthers; Anc: Taylor Family Tree: Angela Taylor; BDA, vol. 3, Corye to Dynion, pp. 24-29; BMD; c-1841–1851; *DNB*; England & Wales, Criminal Registers, 1791–1892 for Frederick Cramer; *Grove*; Proceedings of the Old Bailey, viewed 12 May 2019: https://www.oldbaileyonline.org/browse.jsp?div=t18440819-195; Workhouse Admission and Discharge Records, 1764–1930.
235 BMD; *CB*; *Foster-1881*, p. 150.
236 BMD.
237 BMD: *CP*; Robert Walter Craven, viewed 26 July 2019: <https://www.findagrave.com/memorial/68372385/robert-walter-craven>.
238 *LG*, part 1, 1836, p. 792; William Crawford MP, viewed 26 July 2019: <https://www.geni.com/people/William-Crawford-MP/6000000012028350623>; Robert Wigram Crawford, viewed 26 July 2019: <https://www.gracesguide.co.uk/Robert_Wigram_Crawford>.
239 *DNB*.
240 *The Globe*, p. 1, 30 January 1834; *LG*, part 2, 1816, p. 1373, part 4, 1846, p. 3932.
241 BMD; c-1861.
242 BMD; CCEd; *OA*; Crawley Boevey, Sir Thomas, viewed 26 July 2019: <https://www.combedown.org/tng/getperson.php?personID=I627&tree=bryan-daubeney-fortt>.
243 BMD; CCEd; c-1841–1861; *OA*; Crawley Boevey, Sir Thomas, viewed 26 July 2019: <https://www.combedown.org/tng/getperson.php?personID=I627&tree=bryan-daubeney-fortt>. thepeerage.com: person M, #32103; Frederick Duke Yonge, viewed 26 July 2019, https://www.geni.com/people/Frederick-Yonge/6000000029266526821.
244 Anc: Janes + Thickett FamiliesTree: Bob Janes; BMD; c-1851, thepeerage.com: person M, #297529.
245 BMD; CCEd; c-1861; *GM*, vol. 157, 1835, p. 321; Griffiths, J. E. *Pedigrees of Anglesey and Caernarvon families*; Crawley-Vincent Manuscripts, viewed 26 July 2019: <https://archiveshub.jisc.ac.uk/search/archives/e634749d-906a-3352-aef9-efe0f958979d>.

246 BMD; *CB*; Crawley Boevey, Sir Thomas, viewed 26 July 2019: <https://www.combedown.org/tng/getperson.php?personID=I627&tree=bryan-daubeney-fortt>.

247 BMD; *CB*; Crawley Boevey, Sir Thomas, viewed 26 July 2019: <https://www.combedown.org/tng/getperson.php?personID=I627&tree=bryan-daubeney-fortt>.

248 BMD; Foster, Joseph, *The Peerage, Baronetage and Knightage of the British Empire*, p. 152; website: thepeerage.com: person M, #32113, *OA*; Crawley Boevey, Sir Thomas, viewed 26 July 2019: <https://www.combedown.org/tng/getperson.php?personID=I627&tree=bryan-daubeney-fortt>.

249 Austen, Jane, *Jane Austen's Letters*, 2011, p. 513; BMD; *The European Magazine, and London Review*, vol. 64, 1813, p. 368; *Foster-1881*, p. 506; *LG*, part 2, 1831, p. 90.

250 BMD; c-1851, 1881–1901; *OA*; *Melksham Directory*, 1855, p. 84, viewed 26 July 2019: <http://www.twhc.org.uk/directory/Melksham1855.pdf>.

251 BMD.

252 BMD; c-1851–1881.

253 BMD; c-1851–1881; Newton, Lucy, Centre for International Business History, University of Reading: thesis: 'Change and continuity: the development of joint stock banking in the early nineteenth century', viewed 26 July 2019: <http://www.reading.ac.uk/web/files/business/empd040-07.pdf>.

254 BMD; *B-1906*, p. 390; c-1851–1881; *OA*.

255 BMD; *HP*.

256 BMD; c-1851.

257 BMD; c-1841; *Williams*.

258 Lloyds Banking Group Archives (London): Reference GB 386 A/53/17.

259 Bedfordshire Archives & Records Service: Abstract of Title of William Bodger to freehold property at Clifton; BMD; Charlton Kings MI; *Gloucestershire History* No. 16 (2002) pages 9-22, Moore-Scott, Terry, 'The Manorial Estates of Leckhampton; *The Law Journal*, vol. 8, 1830, p. 144.

260 Anc: Hillyar/Harvey Family Tree: paulinemarsh52; BMD; c-1841–1851; Birmingham City Archives; *Edinburgh Gazette,* 12 October 1827; *The Genealogical Magazine*, vol. 6, 1903, p. 308; Gloucestershire, England, Prison Records, 1728–1914; *LG*, part 1, 1836, p. 29; *MM*, vol. 44, 1817, p. 380; *Pigot's Directory*: Cheltenham, 1830.

261 Anc: Warren Lloyd Family Tree; BMD; *Debrett, 1835*, p. 421; *DNB*; *LG*, part 1, 1839, p. 1139.

262 BMD; *CA*; CCEd; *GM*, vol. 94, part 1, 1824, p. 475; *The Poll for a Knight of the Shire to Represent the County of Leicester*, vol. 6, 1775, p. 82.

263 BMD; *Burke-1844*, p. 604; *CB*.

264 BMD; *CA*; John Lake Crompton, viewed 26 July 2019: <https://www.geni.com/people/John-Crompton-Rev/6000000015529523073>; Notes on the life of Harriet Crompton, viewed 26 July 2019: <https://www.anotherurl.com/photos/family/forrest/harriet_crompton.htm>; John Lake Crompton, viewed 26 July 2019: <https://www.wikitree.com/genealogy/PENTIN>.

265 BMD.

266 *The Annual Register*; vol. 41, 1822, p. 215; BMD; CCEd; *GM*, vol. 9; vol. 163, 1838, p. 214; *OA*.

267 *The Athenaeum*, vol. 3, 1808, p. 591; BMD; *Burke-1846-1*, p. 204; Cheshire Archives and Local Studies: Certified copy of marriage dated 26 July 1832 of John Crooke Freeman of Leyland; *GM*, vol. 163, 1838, p. 331; *GM*, vol. 178, 1845, p. 73; *GM*, vol. 72, 1861, p. 215; *MM*, vol. 25, 1808, p. 461; *Norfolk Chronicle*, 17 November 1860; The Family of Cameron Bryant, viewed 26 July 2019: <https://worldconnect.rootsweb.ancestry.com/cgi-bin/igm.cgi?op=GET&db=cbryant6&id=I088722>.

268 *NBD*: Crole, Charles.

269 BMD; *Bath Chronicle and Weekly Gazette*, 4 April 1895; Bourton-on-the-Water cemetery MI; CCEd; c-1851–1891; *OA*.

270 BMD; *GM*, vol. 110, 1811, p. 294; Rudder, Samuel, *The History and Antiquities of Cirencester*, 1800, p. 183.

271 c-1841.

272 BMD; c-1851; *Pigot's Directory* 1830.

273 c-1851–1861.

274 BMD; *B-1838-1*, p. 246; Lennox Russell, Constance Charlotte Elis, *Swallowfield and its Owners*, 1901, pedigree facing p. 229; *Lodge-1859*, p. 652; thepeerage.com: person F, #376215; WFP F204.

275 *DNB; Grove*.

276 BMD; CCEd; *OA*.

277 BMD; CCEd, *DNB; OA*.

278 Davies, H., *A View of Cheltenham, in its Past and Present State*, 1843, p. 202; *DNB;* Jameson, Thomas, *A Treatise on Cheltenham Waters and Biliary Diseases*, 1814.

279 BMD; CCEd; *CL*; Halford Church MI; E&W Wills—will of Richard Crump; *OA*; Charles Collins Crump, viewed 26 July 2019: <http://gramstedt.com/getperson.php?personID=I13226&tree=all>.

280 BMD; *CA*; c-1841–1881.

281 BMD; *DNB*; Richard Shuttleworth Cruttwell, viewed 26 July 2019: <https://www.combedown.org/tng/getperson.php?personID=I40&tree=crutwell>.

282 *DNB*.

283 BMD; c-1841; *DNB*.

284 BMD; Dudley, Thomas Briscoe, *A Complete History of Royal Leamington Spa*, 1901, p. 120; John Cullis, viewed 26 July 2019: <http://leamingtonhistory.co.uk/ranelagh-gardens/>.

285 *DNB; HP*. Le Faye, Deirdre, *Jane Austen's Letters*; WFP F173–F195.

286 Anc: Holcombe Family Tree; BMD; *CA*; CCEd; *GM*, vol. 95, part 1; vol. 137, 1825, p. 378; *VCH*, Gloucestershire, Elrington, Christopher, *Gloucestershire,* vol. 10, Westbury and Whitstone Hundreds; MI: Leonard Stanley, St Swithun's Churchyard.

287 *DNB*.

288 BMD; *CB*; thepeerage.com F, #237812.

289 *Alphabetical List of the Officers of the Indian Army: With the Dates of Their Respective Promotion, Retirement, Resignation, Or Death, Whether in India Or in Europe, from the Year 1760 to the Year 1834 Inclusive, Corrected to September 30, 1837*, 1838, pp. 62-63; Anc: Oxborough /Griffore/Miller/Greeley Tree; *The Asiatic annual register*, vol. 8, 1809, p. 165; *The Asiatic Journal and Monthly Miscellany*, vol. 33, 1840, p. 171; BMD; *GM*, vol. 41 (195), 1854, p. 445; *The Scottish Jurist: Containing Reports of Cases Decided in the House of Lords, Courts of Session, Teinds, and Exchequer, and the Jury and Justiciary Courts*, 1858, p. 723; Sutherland and Knox, *Noblemen and Gentlemen's Seats, Villages*, 1857, p. 117, p. 173; *The United Service Magazine*, 1844, p. 320 and vol. 74, 1854, p. 630.

290 Anc: Wildberger/Sears Family Tree; MI: Gloucester Cathedral.

291 *The Athenæum: A Journal of Literature, Science, the Fine Arts, Music, and the Drama*, 1834, p. 811; *Bath Chronicle*, 28 January 1798; Penley, Belville S., *A History of Dramatic Representations in Bath*, 1892, p. 87 and p. 99; Johnston, Roy, *The Musical Life of Nineteenth-Century Belfast*, 2017; Temperley, Nicholas, *Musicians of Bath and Beyond: Edward Loder (1809–1865) and His Family*, 2016, p. 78; *Monthly Mirror*, August 1802; Slater, Isaac, *Slater's National Commercial Directory of Ireland*, 1846, p. 382; Greene, John C., *Theatre in Dublin, 1745–1820: A Calendar of Performances*, 2011.

292 BMD; Archives of Ontario; Henry Speight: Upper Wharfedale, 1900.

293 *DNB*.

294 *Parliamentary Papers*, vol. 43, 1843, p. 4; *Reports from Commissioners*, 1845, vol. III, p. 184.

295 BMD; c-1841–1911; *Cheltenham Chronicle*, 8 December 1923; *OA*; thepeerage.com: person F, #223181.

296 BMD; c-1841–1901; *OA*.

Letter D

1 *Debrett 1839*, p. 1144; *Debrett 1840*, p. 733; Richard D'Alton, viewed 30 July 2019: <http://www.feniangraves.net>; Landed Estates in Connacht and Munster, viewed 30 July 2019: <http://landedestates.nuigalway.ie/>.

2 Henderson, Thomas Finlayson, article published 1885: 'Augustus Frederick, Duke of Sussex (1773–1843)'.

3 Bridgwater, Patrick, *The German Gothic Novel in Anglo-German Perspective*, 2013, p. 292; Heckmann, Ruth, *Tonsetzerinnen: Zur Rezeption von Komponistinnen in Deutschland um 1800*, 2016, p. 322; Stark, Susanne, *Roman in Englisch-deutscher Perspektiven : Kulturelle Berührungspunkte Zwischen Englisch- und Deutschsprachigen Ländern*, 2000, p. 85; website: Caroline Schelling, viewed 30 July 2019: <https://www.carolineschelling.com/dramatis-personae/>.

4 *The Jurist*, vol. 2, 1839, p. 263; *The Legal Observer, Or, Journal of Jurisprudence*, vol. 31, 1846, p. 32; *The New Zealand Journal*, vol. 4, 1843, p. 177; Nichols, John Gough, *The Topographer Genealogist*, vol. II, 1853; Nigel D'Oyly, viewed 30 July 2019: <https://www.sjpl.org/caroombrowse?page=429&order=title&sort=asc>.

5 Grace's Guide, viewed 15 May 2019: <https://www.gracesguide.co.uk/Thomas_Daft_and_Son>; *Osborne's London & Birmingham railway guide*, 1840, p. 228.

6 *DNB*.

7 Anc: Todd Family Tree: grandcru52; BMD; *B-1837-2*, p. 103; c-1851; *MM*, vol. 37, 1814, p. 273; *MM*, 1816, p. 465; *Stamford Mercury*, 25 October 1816; *Walford-1882*, p. 591; genuki.org.uk: Bishops Hull Marriages 1562–1812; Dales of Newcastle Upon Tyne, viewed 30 July 2019: <http://www.rootschat.com/forum/index.php?topic=729018.9>.

8 Anc: Dallas-Smith Family Tree: Rod Dallas; BMD; CCEd; c-1841–1851; *DNB; OA*.

9 BMD; c-1841–1891; *OA*.

10 The University of Edinburgh, viewed 30 July 2019: <http://ourhistory.is.ed.ac.uk/index.php/Andrew_Dalzel_(1742-1806)>.

11 Anc: Humphrey, Probyn, Raikes, Cary, Wilson, Dyble: Jeremy Dyble; *B-1846-1*, p. 95; E&W Wills—wills of John, Mary and Anna Maria Dandridge; Southall, Mary, *A Description of Malvern*, 1822, p. 48; Anna Maria Dandridge, viewed 30 July 2019: <https://www.geni.com/people/Anna-Bassett/6000000003095810310>.

12 BMD; *B-1837-2*, p. 18; c-1851; *CL*; Owen, W., *Miscellaneous Correspondence*, vol. 3, 1764, p. 557; *OA*.

13 *DNB;* UCL–Slaves.

14 Anc: Walkinshaw Family Tree: Ian Stewart; BMD; British Library: Asian and African Studies, IOR/L/AG/23/10/1 no. 1922, DANIELL, George Noble 1804–1823; Howard, Joseph Jackson, and Crisp, Frederick Arthur, *Visitation of England and Wales* notes: vol. 3, 1898: arms of George Daniell; Merivale, J. H. *Reports of Cases Argued and Determined in the High Court of Chancery—1815 to 1817* (1817) vol. III Toulmin v. Steere, pp. 210-225; NPC for Eliza Frances Daniell; UCL–Slaves.

15 Anc: Armstrong Cooper Douglas Family Tree; BMD; *CA*; c-1841–1881; *Literary and Biographical Magazine, and British Review*, vol. 11, 1793, p. 318; *OA*.

16 Anc: Janes + Thickett Families, family tree: Bob Janes; BMD; *OA*; wikitree, Osbaldeston-50; Riches to Rags, viewed 30 July 2019: <http://www.ewyaslacy.org.uk/-/Riches-to-Rags-The-Bankruptcy-of-Thomas-Daniell-of-Michaelchurch-Court-Lord-of-the-Manor-of-Ewyas-Lacy-By-Bob-Steele/1835-1851/rs_ewy_0137>.

17 CCEd; *DNB*.

18 BMD; *CB*; thepeerage.com: person F, #300965.

19 Anc: thomas-moriah-darke: 138016719; BMD; *OA*.

20 BMD; c-1841–1891; Cricinfo; *OA*.

21 Anc: Darnell Family Tree: annedith; BMD; *DNB*.

22 *HP*; Wikipedia— Sir John Dashwood-King, 4th Baronet.

23 BMD.

24 BMD; CCEd; c-1851–1891; *OA*.

25 Anc: Daubeny/Thompson Family Tree II: riklinda_1; CCEd; *DNB*.

26 Anc: Symonds Family Tree: geologicalkandrew; *DNB*.

27 Anc: Symonds Family Tree: geologicalkandrew; Symonds Family Tree: geologicalkandrew; BMD; CCEd; *OA*.

28 BMD; *B-1838-4*, p. 740; *MM*, vol. 21, 1806, p. 235.

29 BMD; *HP*; *Williams*.

30 BMD; B-1865-1, p. 107; B-1869-1, p. 112; c-1911; Fox-Davies, Arthur Charles, *Armorial families: A Directory of Gentlemen of Coat-Armour*, p. 94.

31 *A List of the Officers of the Army and of the Corps of Royal Marines*, 1821, p. 238; MI: tablet: Christ Church, Bath.

32 BMD; *GM*, vol. 174, 1843, p. 443; GA: D182/IV/12: Marriage Settlement between the Rev. James Daubeny of Stratton, clerk and Helena Daubeny of Bristol; *OA*.

33 BMD; *GM*, vol. 48, 1840, p. 202; Joseph Walters Daubeny, viewed 30 July 2019: <https://www.findagrave.com/memorial/175122937/joseph-walters-daubeny>.

34 BMD; Samuel Whitfield Daukes, viewed 30 July 2019: <http://www.peek-of-hazelwood.org.uk/search.php?mylastname=Daukes+&myfirstname=&mybool=AND&offset=0&search=Search>; Wikipedia: Samuel Daukes.

35 *The Athenaeum*, vol. 3, 1808, p. 379; *The Monthly Repertory of English Literature*, 1810, p. 333; Sophia Longley, viewed 30 July 2019: <https://www.werelate.org/wiki/Person:Sophia_Longley_(1)>.

36 Anc: caroline-barbara-gooch; BMD; CCEd; *OA*; Walter-Davenport-Bromley, viewed 30 July 2019: <https://www.geni.com/people/Walter-Davenport-Bromley/6000000038949948913>.

37 Faulkner, Thomas, *History and Antiquities of Kensington*, 1820, p. 407; *Survey of London*: vol. 37, Northern Kensington, 1973.

38 BMD; *OA*.

39 England & Wales, Criminal Registers, 1791–1892.

40 Anc: Dightons of Clifford Chambers: John Cooper; BMD; CCEd; *OA*, c-1881.

41 c-1841–1851.

42 Anc: Dightons of Clifford Chambers: John Cooper; BMD; CCEd; *OA*.

43 *HP*; cracroftspeerage.co.uk.

44 Anc: Underwood/Kain family: Peter Underwood; CCEd; *CL*; *OA*.

45 Anc: Williams Family Tree: ColinWilliams42; *American Vital Records from the Gentleman's Magazine, 1731–1868*, 1987, p. 150; Brown, Lena Boyd, and Oliver, Vere Langford, *More Tombstones of the British West Indies*, 2007, p. 69; St Kitts National Archives.

46 BMD; CCEd; *GM*, vol. 77, part 1, 1807, p. 385; *OA*.

47 BMD.

48 BMD; *OA*; *VCH*, Wiltshire, vol. 8, Warminster, Westbury and Whorwellsdown Hundreds; Wadham Register.

49 *DNB;* Ofir Friedman, viewed 3 March 2019: <https://www.geni.com/people/Sir-John-Francis-Davis-1st-Baronet/6000000021599814881?through=6000000021604893668>.

50 Anc: Kelly family tree: Corrina Deeth; BMD; c-1851; Foster, Joseph, *Grantees of Arms*, vol. 1, 1915, p. 99; *Monthly Paper: The National Society for Promoting the Education of the Poor*, December, 1854; Southey, Robert, and Southey, Charles Cuthbert, *The Life of the Rev. Andrew Bell: ... Prebendary of Westminster, and Master of Sherburn Hospital, Durham. Comprising the History of the Rise and Progress of the System of Mutual Tuition*, vol. 2, 1844, p. 304; St George-in-the-East Church, viewed 30 July 2019: <http://www.stgitehistory.org.uk/history.html>.

51 BMD.

52 BMD; c-1841–1851.

53 BMD; c-1851; *Hunt*.

54 BMD; CCEd; *OA*.

55 Rutter, Owen, *A Brief History of the Firm of Messrs. Davison, Newman & Company*, 1938; Wikipedia.

56 BMD; c-1841–1851.

57 Anc: Morway-Kelliher family tree: Valentina Espinola; *HP*.

58 thepeerage.com: person M, #124641; *HP*.

59 Anc: Mark Heal EXTENDED tree 28-2-19: MarkElliotAnstrutherHeal; *HP*.

60 Anc: PEEL FAMILY TREE: SHARONCMAUD; *HP*.

61 BMD; c-1851; North Yorkshire County Record Office: Dawson of Langcliffe.

62 Anc: Victorians family tree: MarchHare2; BMD; c-1841–1851; *CA*; *GM*, vol. 179, 1846, p. 86.

63 Anc: Lisa Allen Family Tree: tooligan; BMD; c-1851.

64 c-1851.

65 BMD.

66 BMD; c-1851, 1881–1891.

67 BMD; c-1851; *Parliamentary Papers*, vol. 9, part 2, 1846, p. 575.

68 Anc: deacon Family Tree: timddeacon; Bedford family, viewed, 3 March 2019: <https://lists.rootsweb.com/hyperkitty/list/bedford-surname@rootsweb.com/thread/24606358/>; BMD; *B-1847-1*, p. 318; *OA*; WFP F208.

69 *The Archaeological Journal*, vol. 1, 1846, p. 251; *Bentley's History and Directory of the borough of Evesham*, 1840; c-1841; The Newsletter of the Trust for the Victoria County History of Herefordshire; Series 2, No. 17; spring 2014, p. 9.

70 Anc: glase.robinson.hill-public family tree: BMD; c-1851–1891; Warren Patrick Glase; *GM*; *OA*.

71 BMD; John Dearman, viewed 25 August 2019: <https://www.red1st.com/axholme/getperson.php?personID=I1750043982&tree=Axholme>.

72 Anc: Carson Family Tree: LIZUPATREE; BMD; *B-1898-2*, p. 107; Catholic Parish Registers, The National Library of Ireland; Dublin, Ireland; Microfilm Number: Microfilm 09148/03; c-1851; *CP*; *Debrett's Peerage*; Farrar, *Henry*, *Irish Marriages: Being an Index to the Marriages in Walker's Hibernian Magazine, 1771 to 1812*, 1897.

73 *Gazette de Brunswig*, 1756, p. 71; *Le grand dictionnaire historique, ou le melange curieux de l'histoire sacree et profane*, vol. 2, 1759, p. 18.

74 Anc: Saunders: Bernadette Giblin; BMD; c-, 1851–1871; *OA*.

75 *Grove*.

76 *Memoirs of Frederica Sophia Wilhelmina, Princess Royal of Prussia*, vol 1. p. 208, 1828.
77 BMD; *DNB*.
78 *Biographie universelle, ancienne et moderne*, vol. 59, p. 341.
79 BMD; *British Magazine and Monthly Register of Religious and Ecclesiastical Information, Parochial History, and Documents Respecting the State of the Poor, Progress of Education, Etc.*, vol. 6. p. 465, 1834; CCEd; c-1851, 1871–1881.
80 *DNB*.
81 Jean Gabriel René François de FOUCQUET, viewed 30 July 2019: <https://gw.geneanet.org/pierfit?lang=fr&n=de+foucquet&oc=0&p=jean+gabriel+rene+francois>.
82 HÄRTL, Heinz and DE GRUYTER, Walter, *Briefwechsel I (1788–1801)*, p. 577, 2013; Philibert de Fumel, viewed 30 July 2019: <https://gw.geneanet.org/mbelliard?lang=en&n=de+fumel&oc=0&p=philibert>.
83 Anc pedigree, hugoblomfield; *CA*.
84 Anc: ConleyTAT family tree; *GM*, vol. 3, p.101, 1857; *Baily's Magazine of Sports & Pastimes*, vol. 22, p. 373.
85 *DNB*.
86 François-Marie Joseph Poulain de Mauny, viewed 30 July 2019: <https://gw.geneanet.org/alecomte22?n=poulain+de+mauny&oc=&p=francois+marie+joseph>.
87 DE BARRAU, Hippolyte, *Documens historiques et généalogiques sur les familles et les hommes remarquables du Rouergue dans les temps anciens et modernes*, 1854, p. 452; *Journal des débats politiques et littéraires*, p. 2, 1814; MANSEL, Philip, *The French Emigres in Europe and the Struggle against Revolution, 1789–1814*, p. 117, 1999.
88 ISRAEL, Jonathan, *Democratic Enlightenment: Philosophy, Revolution, and Human Rights 1750–1790*, 2013, p. 831; Ernst Carl Constantin von Schardt, viewed 30 July 2019: <http://geneagraphie.com/getperson.php?personID=I627408&tree=1>.
89 *DNB*; *OA*.
90 *DNB*.
91 BATEMAN, John, *The Great Landowners of Great Britain and Ireland*, 1878, p. 112; BMD; c-1851; *LG*, part 3, 1843, p. 2304; *OA*.
92 BMD; c-1841–1851; The History of Dents, viewed 30 July 2019: <https://www.dentsgloves.com/en/history/>.
93 *AGB*.
94 BMD; c-1861–1871; Devonshers of co. Cork, viewed 30 July 2019: <https://www.genealogy.com/forum/surnames/topics/devonshire/4/>; DEVONSHER (KILSHANNIG), viewed 30 July 2019: <http://landedestates.nuigalway.ie/LandedEstates/jsp/estate-show.jsp?id=2764>.
95 BMD; *CA*; GRANVILLE, Roger, *The History of the Granville Family: Traced back to Rollo, first Duke of Normandy with Pedigrees, etc.*, 1895.
96 BMD; BURNETT, D. Graham, *Trying Leviathan: The Nineteenth-Century New York Court Case That Put the Whale on Trial and Challenged the Order of Nature*, 2010, p. 101; c-1841–1851; *The Lancet London: A Journal of British and Foreign Medicine, Surgery, Obstetrics, Physiology, Chemistry, Pharmacology, Public Health and News*, vol. 2, 1835, pp. 200-201; William Dewhurst, viewed 30 July 2019: <https://www.ucl.ac.uk/bloomsbury-project/institutions/theatre_anatomy.htm>.
97 *DNB*.
98 BMD; c-; 1841–1881; Indian Mutiny 1857-9, viewed 30 July 2019: <http://glosters.tripod.com/IM8.htm>.
99 BMD, *Oxford Chronicle and Reading Gazette*, 1 January 1848; Biographies of Oxford pub landlords, viewed 30 July 2019, http://www.stsepulchres.org.uk/burials/index_pubs.html; 1846 Pubs of Oxford–Oxford History, viewed 30 July 2019: <http://www.oxfordhistory.org.uk/people_lists/oxford_pubs/pubs_1846.html>.
100 *EB*.
101 BMD; *Chelsea Royal Naval Exhibition: Official Catalogue & Guide*, 1891; E&W Wills—will of Stephen Thomas Digby; Royal Navy Captain List, 1805.
102 Anc: A ORIGINAL TREE DAINTON/MCCLURE/ MCCA BE: painterann; BMD; c-1851–1871; thepeerage.com: person F, #259664.
103 BMD; CCEd; *OA*.
104 *DNB*.
105 *Grove*.
106 Anc: Andrew Bateup: Andrew Bateup; Anc: Maude Family Tree: juliembracken; BMD.
107 Anc: Dix Edgington Family Tree; Anc: German-Geach Family Tree; BMD; c-1841–1851.
108 BMD; NICHOLLS, H. G., *The Forest of Dean*, 1858; *OA*.
109 KAIN, Roger J. P., and PRINCE, Hugh C., *The Tithe Surveys of England and Wales*, 2006, p. 36; c-1841.
110 *Kent's Original London Directory*, 1823, p. 100; Lloyd's Register, The archaeological excavation, viewed 25 August 2019: <https://www.lr.org/en-gb/who-we-are/lr-in-london/site-uncovered/>.
111 Anc: Mytton-Mills of Lindridge Worcestershire; Anc: Mosse-Robinson Family Tree; BMD; c-1851–1871; *The Strabane Morning Post*, 17 June 1823; *Slater's Cheltenham Directory*, 1859.
112 *The Annual Register, or, A View of the History and Politics of the Year 1842*, vol. 83, p. 151; BMD; c-1851–1861; *B-1833*, p. 298; *B-1850*, p. 93; The seize quartiers of the family of Bryan Cooke, and of Frances his wife, 1857.
113 BMD: Upper Slaughter parish register.
114 *DNB*; Exeter Working Papers in British Book Trade.
115 *DNB*; *HP*; *OA*.
116 BMD; *CA*; Frederick Dodsworth, viewed 31 July 2019: <https://genealogy.links.org/links-cgi/readged?/home/ben/camilla-genealogy/current+c-dodsworth6183+2-2-0-1-0>; British History Online: vch/wilts/vol3; thepeerage.com: person M, #57967.
117 Anc: Dodsworth Family Tree: Trevor_Nancarrow; William Dodsworth, viewed 31 July 2019: <https://genealogy.links.org/links-cgi/readged?/home/ben/camilla-genealogy/current+c-dodsworth35077+2-2-0-1-0>; thepeerage.com: person M, #57967.
118 CCEd; *OA*.
119 *DNB*.
120 *Grove*.
121 BMD; *CA*.

122 BMD; CCEd; c-1841–1851, 1861; *Kelly's Gloucestershire Directory*, 1856; *Lewis Worcestershire Directory* 1820; *OA*.

123 Anc: Helka Family tree: darjenmc; Anc: Janes + Thickett Families: Bob Janes; BMD; *CA*; CCEd; c-1851; *OA*; Staffordshire Records Office, deeds; *The Times*, 14 November 1797; *VCH*, Gloucestershire; *VCH*, Staffordshire.

124 BMD; Burke, J., ed., *The Annual Register*, edited by; *Cassey Shropshire Directory* 1871; c-1861; *VCH*, Gloucestershire; E&W Wills—will of Revd Thomas Bowen.

125 BMD; c-1851–1861; *HP*; Stroud MI; *The Treble Almanack for the Year 1804*, p. 67.

126 BMD; *CA*; CCEd.

127 *DNB*.

128 BMD; *The Athenaeum*, vol. 1, 1807, p. 321; *Sporting Magazine*, vol. 29, 1807, p. 185; *The Legal Observer, or, Journal of Jurisprudence*, vol. 26, 1843; The Dove Family, viewed 31 July 2019: <http://www.prattens.co.uk/FAMILIES/DOVE/start.html>.

129 Anc: post: 28 Oct 2012: pennywythes1; *OA*.

130 *HP*; *OA*.

131 *Williams*.

132 Anc: NWQ All ancestors: cambrensis12; BMD; CCEd; c-1851, *OA*.

133 CCEd; *OA*; Wadham College Registers.

134 Anc: The Dowells of Holme Lacy: JimandMargaret455; BMD; *CA*; CCEd; *OA*; Wadham College Registers; WFP F213 & F214; William Loney, viewed 31 July 2019: <https://www.pdavis.nl/Background.htm>; thepeerage.com: person F, #685498.

135 Anc: Towells Family Tree: Eizabeth Stinchcombe; Anc: Christiaan Engelbrecht Family Tree: Christiaan Engelbrecht; BMD; c-1851; *DNB*; *Pigot*; *VCH*, Gloucester.

136 Anc: Hull Wilkinson Pennicott Bozen Batt Ware Duggan Tasmania 1 November 2016: Olmorijo Olmorijo; *DNB*; *OA*.

137 BMD; *B-1841*, p. 34; c-1841–1851; *GM*, vol. 142, 1827, p. 283; *The Spectator*, 27 September 1828, Page 14.

138 BMD; c-1881; Warwickshire County Record Office.

139 BMD; *CA*; *HP*; *The Medical and Physical Journal*, 1802, p. 154, evidence on Dr Jenner's petition; MI: Bath Abbey Cemetery.

140 Andrew Robert Drummond, viewed 31 July 2019: <https://www.clanmacfarlanegenealogy.info/genealogy/TNGWebsite/getperson.php?personID=I27316&tree=CC>; Cadland House, viewed 31 July 2019: <https://historicengland.org.uk/listing/the-list/list-entry/1000280>; Frederica Manners, viewed 31 July 2019: <https://gw.geneanet.org/olivierdrieux?lang=en&n=manners&oc=0&p=elizabeth+Frederica>.

141 BMD; c-1841–1861; *CP*; Journal of Ensign John Drummond, viewed 31 July 2019: <http://www.garethglovercollection.com/journal-of-ensign-john-drummond/>.

142 BMD; *DNB*; *HP*; Logiealmond, viewed 9 March 2019: <http://www.clanmacfarlanegenealogy.info/genealogy/TNGWebsite/getperson.php?personID=I27101&tree=CC>.

143 Anc: Torstsenson Family Tree: keith burns; BMD; *CA*; c-1841–1881; *CB*; CCEd; *OA*; thepeerage.com: person M, #372284, M, #372285, M, #372287, M, #372286; Julius Hutchinson, viewed 31 July 2019: <https://www.werelate.org/wiki/Person:Julius_Hutchinson_(1)>.

144 Anc: MacFarlane Family Tree: johnmurray3131; BMD; *CA*; CCEd; *Foster-1882*, p. 191; Walter Henry MacFarlane, viewed 31 July 2019: <http://www.barbsweb.co.uk/history/oldham2.htm>; NPC: Ethel Dorothy Dryden Macfarlane.

145 Anc: Old Settle: KenAndSarahLister; c-1841–1851.

146 Anc: Lady Gee and Me: anni3030; BMD; c-1881; *GM*, vol. 169, 1840, p. 670; Dukinfield family, viewed 31 July 2019: <https://www.stirnet.com/genie/data/british/dd/dukinfield1.php>.

147 Bromley, David & Janet, *Wellington's Men Remembered: A Register of Memorials to Soldiers who Fought in the Peninsular War and at Waterloo*, vol. 1, 2012; WFP F213.

148 Anc: Taylor: kekelu*CA*; BMD; *B-1838-2*, p. 533; *B-1834*, p. 75; c-1841–1851; E&W Wills—will of Thomas Dumbleton; Glanville-Richards, William Urmston Searle, *The Registers of Windlesham, Surrey, 1677–1793*, 1881, p. 57; Elizabeth (Jodrell) Leigh, viewed 31 July 2019: <https://www.wikitree.com/wiki/Jodrell-24>.

149 *CB*; *MM*, vol. 26, 1808, p. 191.

150 BMD.

151 Anc: Lord Forbes Family Tree: jacobs849; *HP*; MI: St Mary's Church, Helmsley.

152 *HP*; *DNB*; Thomas Slingsby Duncombe, viewed 31 July 2019: <http://www.chartistancestors.co.uk/thomas-slingsby-duncombe-1796-1861/>.

153 *B-1845*, p. 370.

154 NA: Bond on marriage of Hart Davis and Charlotte Dundas, daughter of Lady Eleanor Dundas of Canon Hall, Scotland; Scott, Walter, *The Edinburgh Annual Register*, vol. 9, 1820, cccccxiii; Eleanora Elizabeth Home, viewed 31 July 2019: <https://www.clanmacfarlanegenealogy.info/genealogy/TNGWebsite/getperson.php?personID=I61283&tree=CC>; Eleanora Elizabeth Dundas, viewed 31 July 2019: <https://wellcomelibrary.org/item/b1903149x#?c=0&m=0&s=0&cv=0&z=-0.5582%2C-0.0665%2C2.1164%2C1.3294> Lady Elenora Home, viewed 31 July 2019: <https://tunearch.org/wiki/Lady_Elenora_Home_(1)>.

155 Anc: Gumpper, Monroe, Brown, and Simon Family Tree: Karl Gumpper; *HP*; *CP*.

156 *Ibid*.

157 *CB*; *CP*.

158 BMD, Urchfont Parish Registers 1746–1801.

159 Anc: Tracey Family Tree: kossuth2; Anc: Nelson Dunford Family Tree: nataliemm24; BMD; c-1841–1861.

160 Anc: Kelly-Dunlop-Ross (Draft, Research): buzzkelly; *HP*; Robertson, George, *A Genealogical Account of the Principal Families in Ayrshire, More Particularly in Kyle and Cunninghame*, vol. 1, 1823; WFP F186–F196.

161 Anc: J D Mahoney 2018—Direct Line & Others: whiteswan138; CCEd; c-1851; E&W Wills—will of James Dunne; *OA*.

162 Anc: seckold Family Tree: Seckolddi; Archives of Ontario; BMD; CCEd; *OA*; PI from Trevena Whitbread, great-great-granddaughter; *VCH*, Gloucestershire; Wadham College Records.

163 CCEd; BMD; *CA*; c-1871–1891; *GM*, 1859, p. 418; *The Law Times Reports of Cases Decided in the House of Lords, the Privy Council, the Court of Appeal ...* [new Series], vol. 94, 1906, pp. 90-92; *The Literary Gazette and Journal of the Belles Lettres, Arts, Sciences*, &c, 1843, p. 212.

164 Anc: Devine, Langsford, Hughes-Hallett, Lush Family Tree: Anne Varker; BMD; *CA*; CCEd; c-1841–1851; *MM*, vol. 5, 1816, p. 84; *VCH*, Oxfordshire.
165 Betham, Revd William, *The Baronetage of England, or, The History of the English Baronets, and such Baronets of Scotland, as are of English Families*, 1803, p. 191; BMD; c-1841; *Debrett 1815*, p. 1412; *LG*, December 1799; website: Holy Trinity Memorials, viewed 31 July 2019: <http://pittvillehistory.org.uk/bios/Trinity%20memorials/Holy%20Trinity%20intro.html>.
166 BMD; CCEd; *OA*.
167 Anc: Wrightson Family Tree: Angela Wrightson; BMD; *CA*.
168 BMD; E&W Wills—will of Hannah Felicia Dutton; Historic Canterbury, viewed 9 March 2019: <http://www.machadoink.com/Tyre%20&%20Dutton%20Family.htm>; *List of the Governors and Officers of the Asylum for the Support and Education of the Deaf and Dumb Children of the Poor*, 1817, p. 64; *The Second Report of the British and Foreign Bible Society*, vol. 6, 1806, p. 214; MI: St Paul's Cemetery, Longport, Canterbury; Twickenham Museum: John Serle, viewed, 10 March 2019: <http://www.twickenham-museum.org.uk/detail.php?aid=161&ctid=1&cid=10>.
169 Anc: Mills Roberts: Appledore5; BMD; *CP*.
170 *CA*; *DNB*.
171 *CA*; CCEd.
172 BMD; England & Wales, Criminal Registers, 1791–1892; Gloucestershire, England, Gaol Registers, 1815–1879.
173 *VCH*, Wiltshire, vol. 10, 1975, the parish of Woodborough.
174 BMD; c-1851–1871; *OA*.

Letter E

1 BMD; *CA*; CCEd; *DNB*; Williams, William, ed. Breverton, Terry: *The First American Novel—the Journal of Penrose*, 2007.
2 Anc: Ellis Family Tree: PeterEllis25; BMD; *HP*.
3 BMD; CCEd; *OA*.
4 BMD; *CA*; Carthusians.
5 Witney, viewed 31 July 2019: <http://www.witneyblanketstory.org.uk/wbp.asp>.
6 *Debrett 1835*, p. 421; *DNB*; *HP*.
7 BMD; *DNB*; *HP*; *OA*.
8 BMD; c-1841–1891.
9 BMD; CCEd; *OA*.
10 Anc: Jenkins Family Tree: Richard Henry Nicholas Jenkins; BMD; CCEd; *GM*, vol. 161, 1837, p. 650; *OA*.
11 Anc: family tree: Victoriana: John Eddy; BMD; CCEd; c-1841–1861; *CL*; *OA*.
12 BMD; CCEd; c-1841–1861; Justin Courtier Le Grice (Edgell), viewed 31 July 2019: <https://legrice.net/webtrees/individual.php?pid=I2&ged=legrice.ged>; Wadham College Register.
13 Anc: ronjames18, Edgeworth Family tree; Anc: Kerr/Orrow Family tree; BMD; c-1841–1871.
14 *MM*, vol. 27, 1809, p. 523.
15 *Pigot's Directory*, 1830.
16 Anc: Samantha Martin Family Tree: Samantha Martin; BMD; c-1851; Gloucestershire, England, Land Tax Records, 1713–1833, 1825.
17 Anc: Samantha Martin Family Tree: Samantha Martin; BMD; c-1841–1871.
18 BMD; *OA*.
19 BMD; c-1851–1871; GPA.
20 BMD; *OA*.
21 BMD; c-1851.
22 Birmingham City Archives.
23 *DNB*; *Eton*; Oliver, Vere Langford, *Caribbeana, being Miscellaneous Papaers relating to the History, Genealogy, Topography, and Antiquities of the British West Indies*, 1914; UCL–Slaves.
24 *The Gardeners' Chronicle and Agricultural Gazette*, 1846, p. 623; *Perry's Bankrupt Gazette*, 23 June 1849.
25 *DNB*.
26 BMD; *GM*, vol. 90, part 2; vol. 128, 1820, p. 84; NA: Attested Copy Lease and Release, Centre for Buckinghamshire Studies: D-CH/A/3-4, 1787.
27 An Act for Vesting the Settled Estates, Late of John Dolphin, Esquire, Deceased, in the County of Stafford, in Trustees, to be Sold for Payment of the Portions of the Younger Children, 1795; Anc: Sercombe-Baijer-Giffard Family Tree: sercombe1859; BMD; Collections of the Nova Scotia Historical Society, vol. xvi, 1912, p. 171; NA: Attested Copy Lease and Release, Centre for Buckinghamshire Studies: D-CH/A/3-4, 1787; *The Royal Kalendar, and Court and City Register for England, Scotland, Ireland, and the Colonies*, 1822, p. 170; NA: West Sussex Record Office, WISTON–The Wiston Archives, lease to Isaac Eeles; Eeles, viewed 31 July 2019: <https://amershammuseum.org/history/>.
28 *Ibid.*; MI; E&W Wills—will of William Eeles; MI: Charlton near Woolwich.
29 Egloffstein, viewed 15 March 2019: <https://www.stammreihen.de/showalbum.php?albumID=60...50>.
30 *AGB*: Friedrich Hildebrand Freiherr von Einsiedel.
31 BMD; *CA*; *OA*.
32 BMD; c-1841–1851.
33 Anc: Barbados Families: ajparker42; c-1851; *DNB*; *OA*.
34 BMD; CCEd; c-1851–1861; *OA*; Robert G. Eldridge, Toronto, NSW, Australia.
35 Burke, Edmund, *Annual Register*, vol. 49, 1809, p. 561; E&W Wills—will of William Eldridge; *GM*, vol. 77, part 1, 1807, p. 385; *MM*, vol. 31, 1811, p. 598; *VCH*, Wiltshire, vol. 10, 1975, Devizes.

36 BMD; *CB*; c-1851; *HP*.
37 Anc: The Beer Ellis Family Tree: arthurcmurray; BMD; c-1841–1871.
38 *OA*; Richard Ellerton, viewed 31 July 2019: <http://e-rootz.net/Trees/Richard1678.htm>.
39 BMD; Buck, J. W., *Cases in Bankruptcy ... Containing reports of cases decided by Lord Chancellor Eldon, and by Vice Chancellors Sir Thomas Plumer and Sir John Leach, from Michaelmas Term 1816 to Michaelmas Term 1820, etc.*, vol. 1, 1820, p. 568, *DNB*; *The Law Journal*, vol. 6, 1828, p. 209; *LG*, part 1, 1812, p. 818; Montefiore, Joshua, *A Commercial Dictionary: Containing the Present State of Mercantile Law, Practice, and Custom Intended for the Use of the Cabinet, the Counting-house, and the Library*, 1803, p. xxxiii; *A Report of the Case of the King Against Bebb and Others, Assignees of Castell and Powell, Bankrupts, on an Extent: With Explanatory Notes, and an Appendix of Some Cases and Records in Extents which Have Not Been Before*, 1811, p. 220; *Wakefield's Merchant and Tradesman's General Directory for London: Westminster, Borough of Southwark and Twenty-two Miles Circular from St. Paul's, for the Year, 1794. Containing an Accurate List of the Names and Places of Abode of the Merchants, Manufacturers, and Principal Tradesmen*; Letter–Martin Morrison to John Ellill, viewed 31 July 2019: <https://www.dukesfield.org.uk/transcription/letter-martin-morrison-to-john-ellill-12-mar-1808/>.
40 Anc: Fletchers: John Rainer; BMD; c-1851; thepeerage.com: person F, #692613; Pedigree of the Elliot Family of Amroth, viewed 31 July 2019: <http://ukgo7.com/carmarthenshirefhs/elliotsofamroth.pdf>; thepeerage.com: person M, #692612.
41 BMD; c-1841–1871.
42 *Army List*, 1805; BMD; c-1841–1851, *DNB*; *European Magazine, and London Review*; *GM*, vol. 93, part 1, 1823, p. 189; MI: St Mary's, Berkeley.
43 BMD; c-1841–1881; Eaton, Thomas, *A Concise History and Description of the City and Cathedral of Worcester*, 1829; E&W Wills—will of William Viner; GA.
44 Anc: Ords of Durham–Northumberland Family Tree; *B-1834*; WFP F231; Henry Ellison, viewed 31 July 2019: <http://www.douglashistory.co.uk/famgen/getperson.php?personID=I168609&tree=tree1>; Colonel Robert Ellison, viewed 31 July 2019: <https://www.geni.com/people/Colonel-Robert-Ellison-Grenadier-Guards/6000000034600032974>; Henrietta Isaacson, viewed 31 July 2019: <https://www.geni.com/people/Henrietta-Isaacson/6000000005438494616>.
45 Anc: Swanson Ainsworth FTM2017: tracycpg; *DNB*; *The Bankrupt Directory; Being a Complete Register of All the Bankrupts from Dec. 1820 to Apr. 1843*, p. 132; Robert William Elliston, viewed 12 March 2019: <https://www.wikitree.com/wiki/Elliston-15>.
46 Family of John Eldridge and Anne Potter, viewed 15 March 2019: <www.home-manley.net/fam96.html>.
47 *MM*, 1812, p. 181; *LG*, vol. 2, 1820, p. 2161; Mayo, Charles Herbert, *A Genealogical Account of the Mayo & Elton Familes*, 1908, pp. 55-56.
48 Anc: Campbell Family Tree: Lucy Elton; BMD; Burke, Edmund, *Annual Register*, vol. 81, 1840, p. 293; *Debrett 1840*, p. 192; *DNB*; *GM*, vol. 56, 1844, p. 646; Frederick Bayard Elton, viewed 31 July 2019: <https://www.gravestonephotos.com/public/gravedetails.php?grave=405896&scrwidth=1600>.
49 BMD; *Debrett 1840*, p. 192; *NBD*; thepeerage.com: person M, #398804.
50 *DNB*.
51 BMD; CCEd; c-1851; *OA*.
52 Anc: JB & AB Families: John Elwes; *BLG*; BMD; c-1841–1851; *DNB*; *Eton* 1805; Gilmartin, Kevin, *Sociable Places: Locating Culture in Romantic-Period Britain*, 2017, p. 173; Miller, Norman, article: *The Daily telegraph*, 20 September 2016; *OA*; Sarah Elwes, viewed 15 March 2019: <edpopehistory.co.uk/entries/elwes-sarah/1799-05-03-000000>.
53 BMD; c-1851.
54 Anc: Emra Family Tree: Caryl Virginia Emra; BMD; CCEd, John Emra, viewed 12 March 2019: <https://www.myheritage.com/names/john_emra>; *OA*; Oliver, Vere Langford, *Caribbeana: being miscellaneous papers relating to the history, genealogy, topography, and antiquities of the British West Indies*, 1910, p. 290, UCL-Slaves.
55 *AGB*: Hubert Engels.
56 BMD; *GM*, vol. 161, 1837, p. 655; *GM*, vols 174-175, 1843, p. 87; Rochdale Church MI.
57 *DNB*; *OA*; Scott, Webster and Geary, *The Assembled Commons; or, Parliamentary Biographer*, 1838. p. 84.
58 *BLG*.
59 BMD; *OA*.
60 CCEd; *CP*.
61 *DNB*.
62 BMD; PI: Martin Davis; *OA*.
63 Anc: beach Family Tree: Bertha Emmeline Wayatt; BMD; *B-1838*, vol. 4, p. 155, *DNB*; *OA*; thepeerage.com: person M, #233886, Edmund William Estcourt.
64 Anc: John Nicholson Family Tree: Edmund Hiley Estcourt; BMD; *OA*.
65 BMD; *OA*.
66 Anc: pole Family Tree: James Bucknall Estcourt; BMD; *B-1838*, vol. 4, p. 155, *DNB*; GA; *HP*; *OA*.
67 BMD; *DNB*; *HP*.
68 Anc: Bellville Family Tree: ingaltca
69 WFP F205.
70 GPA.
71 CCEd; *OA*.
72 CCEd, *DNB*; *OA*; Wikipedia: Arthur Benoni Evans.
73 Architects & Artists D-E, viewed 31 July 2019: <https://sussexparishchurches.org/architectsandartistsde/>
74 Calendars of Prisoners Berkeley, Cirencester, Northgate (Gloucester), Lawfords Gate (Bristol) and Winchcombe 1815–1840.
75 BMD; Evans, James Harington, *Memoir & Remains of the Rev. James Harington Evans*, 1855; *OA*.
76 Anc: Buckley/Ryan & O'Connell/Humphreys Family Tree; Anc: Packard Branches: Fitzwilliam Evans; BMD; c-1841; Tymms, Samuel, *The Family Topographer: The Oxford Circuit: Berkshire, Gloucestershire, Herefordshire, Monmouthshire, Oxfordshire, Shropshire, Staffordshire, Worcestershire*, 1834, p. 144.

77 *Hunt*; *The Lancet*, 1880, vol. IV, p. 127; Thomas Evans: Royal College of Physicians: Lives of the fellows, viewed 31 July 2019: <http://munksroll.rcplondon.ac.uk/Biography/Details/1467>.

78 c-1841.

79 BMD; c-1841–1861; GA. Harris & Angel: 'A History of Paper Making in and Around Winchcombe', *GSIA Journal* 1975.

80 BMD; c-1841; Thomas D. Eyre: Andrew Roberts: Lunacy Commission, Middlesex University.

81 CCEd; *OA*.

Letter F

1 BMD; *DNB*.

2 Anc: Morgan Family Tree: Sophie Morgan; BMD; CCEd; *DNB*.

3 BMD; c-1861; *OA*; Turrill, J., *The British Magazine and Monthly Register of Religious and Ecclesiastical Information, Parochial History, and Documents Respecting the State of the Poor, Progress of Education, &c.*, vol. 26, 1844, p. 475; thepeerage.com: person M, #385848.

4 *GM*, vol. 201, 1856, p. 258; Lieutenants in the Royal Navy—May 1805; Falconer, viewed 15 March 2019: <https://www.geni.com/people/Mary-Falconer/6000000009919639301 >; Lodge, Edmund, *The peerage of the British empire as at present existing. To which is added the baronetage*, 1832, pp. 237-8; Lodge, Edmund, *The Genealogy of the Existing British Peerage: With Sketches of the Family Histories of the Nobility*, 1838, p. 279.

5 *GM*, 1741, p. 88; *Lists of the Officers of His Majesty's, and the Hon. Company's Troops, Serving Under the Presidency of Bombay. Adjutant General's Office*, 1798, pp. xix & xx; *The Asiatic Journal and Monthly Register for British India and Its Dependencies*, vol. 10, 1820, p. 194; Registers of Employees of the East India Company and the India Office, 1746–1939; Fallon (Runnamoat), viewed 2 August 2019; <http://landedestates.nuigalway.ie/LandedEstates/jsp/estate-show.jsp?id=1293>.

6 BMD; *CA*; *MATB*.

7 Anc: Fane Matanle Family Tree: StephanieFane; *CA*; *HP*.

8 BMD; *Calcutta Magazine and Monthly Register*, vols III, 1830, p. 52; HP.

9 Anc: Newman McHaffie Tree: VickyNewman69; *CB*; *DNB*.

10 *GM*, vol. 22, 1825, p.190.

11 BMD; *OA*.

12 Anc: Grafton Pollard Extended Tree: cefyngrafton 13; BMD; CCEd; *OA*.

14 BMD; *Extract from the Report of the Committee of the London Society for Promoting Christianity amongst the Jews*, 1821, p. 7; Samuel Favell, viewed 2 August 2019: <http://www.gwydir.demon.co.uk/jo/genealogy/beddome/favell.htm>.

15 *DNB*.

16 E&W Wills—will of Frederick Lewis Ernest Baron De Feilitzsch; Essex Record Office; *Letters of Denization and Acts of Naturalization for Aliens in England & Ireland, 1701–1800*, 1923, p. 204; Office of Public Sector Information—Chronological Table of the Private and Personal Acts.

17 *Twigg's corrected list of the country-bankers of England and Wales*, 1830, p. 75.

18 BMD; *CA*; c-1851–1861; Sheepy Magna Burials, viewed 2 August 2019: <http://www.mdlp.co.uk/resources/Sheepy/Display%20Burials/Burials%20Frame.htm>.

19 Anc: Trie family, Hewitt Family Tree; BMD; *B-1835*; *CA*; CCEd, Fendall, C. P., Crutchley, E. A., *The Diary of Benjamin Newton*, 2013; *OA*.

20 Anc: Janes + Thickett FamiliesTree: Bob Janes; *The Athenaeum*, 1846, p. 138, 7 February; BMD.

21 Anc: Rathbone/Rooke/Fenton/Ford/Fussell/Agutter/Norton/Owen/families: Jane Chapman; BMD; *Campaigning in Spain and Belgium, The letters of Captain Thomas Charles Fenton, 4th Dragoons & the Scots Greys, 1809–15*; c-1861; Newton, Benjamin, *The Diary of Benjamin Newton: Rector of Wath, 1816-1818*, 1933.

22 NA: Northumberland Collections Service; A genealogy of the Selwyn family, viewed 2 June 2019: <https://www.selwyn-family.me.uk/genealogy/getperson.php?personID=I322&tree=CurtisHayward>.

23 Anc: Janes + Thickett Families: Bob Janes; BMD; c-1851–1871; *DNB*.

24 BMD; *Kent's Directory for the Year 1767*.

25 Anc: dacraig AQ Tree Jan 2019: dacraig5985; *Ars Quatuor Coronatorum*, vol. 37, 1924, p. 157; E&W Wills—will of Abrose Ferrell; *LG*, part 1, 1814, p.664; Roger Ferrall, viewed 2 August 2019: <https://www.danishfamilysearch.dk/cid14100975>; Markie Ferrall, viewed 2 August 2019: <https://sites.google.com/site/markoeoffshore/>; Ferrall, viewed 2 August 2019: <https://www.slaegtogdata.dk/forum/index.php?topic=79330.0>; WFP F200.

26 *Blackwood's Magazine*, vol. 24, 1828, p. 404; BMD; *CA*; c-1841; *DNB*; *The Genealogist*, 1911, p. 26; *LG*, part 1, 1834. p. 468; London, England, Stock Exchange Membership Applications, 1802–1924.

27 Anc: Howman Law Mc Pherson; BMD; c-1841; MI: Stow-on-the-Wold churchyard.

28 Anc: Bristow Family Tree; BMD; c-1871; *MATB*; *OA*.

29 *The Monthly Mirror*, 1802. BDA: Eagan to Garrett, 1978, p. 251; Piggott, Patrick, *The Life and Music of John Field, 1782–1837, Creator of the Nocturne*, 1973, pp. 8-9.

30 Anc: Jacob-Jacobs-Runions-Robar-Fountain Family Tree; Potts Family Tree; Articles of Clerkship, 1756–1874; *Reports of Cases Decided in the High Court of Chancery: By the Right Hon. Sir John Leach ... [et Al.] Vice-chancellors of England, 1826–1852*, vol. 5, 1835, pp. 14-18.

31 BMD; Piggott, Patrick, *The Life and Music of John Field, 1782–1837, Creator of the Nocturne*, 1973, pp. 8-9.

32 *Annual Report of the Committee of Management of the Art-Union of London, with List of Subscribers*, 1846, p. 60; BMD; c-1871–1881; Cumbria Archive and Local Studies Centre, Barrow: Reference BD HJ 77/22: Papers re. marriage settlement of George Fielder and Laura M. Sanders; *The List of the Queen's Scholars of St Peter's College, Westminster*, p. 561, *LG*, 10 August 1877, p. 4664.

33 Anc: KATH Chapman Family Tree, BMD; c-1841–1911; *Cheltenham Chronicle*, 11 August 1863; *Jacksons Oxford Journal*, 3 March 1821; Figgures, viewed 2 August 2019: <https://www.tribalpages.com/tribe/familytree?uid=firstfleet&surname=Figgures>.
34 *British Medical Journal*, 30 September 1871.
35 BMD; CCEd; *OA*.
36 Anc: Larry Tyrell; *BLG*; BMD; *CA*; c-1851; Centre for Buckinghamshire Studies—the Lee Papers of Hartwell; *HP*; London, England, Marriages and Banns, 1754–1921; Lipscomb, George, *The History and Antiquities of the County of Buckingham*, vol. 2, p. 309; *LG*, 1799; Lysons, *The Environs of London*, vol. 4: Counties of Herts, Essex & Kent (1796); Niles, William Ogden, *Niles' Weekly Register*, vol. 15, 17 October 1818; Pallot's Marriage Index for England: 1780–1837; *The Plantagenet Roll of the Blood Royal*: The Mortimer-Percy volume by Marquis of Ruvigny and Raineval; *VCH*, Buckinghamshire, vol. 2, 1908; WFP F176 & F187.
37 *BDA*: Habgood to Houbert, 1982, p. 112.
38 *Army List*, 1805; Durham University Library, Special Collections, Grey of Howick collection, 1794–1806: corresp with Lord Grey and others; Nelson, Paul David, *Sir Charles Grey, First Earl Grey: Royal Soldier, Family Patriarch*, 1996, p. 228; website: 60th Foot-British Regiments and the Men Who Led Them 1793–1815.
39 BMD; CCEd; *OA*.
40 *DNB*; *OA*.
41 BMD; Cobbett, R. S., *Memorials of Twickenham Parochial and Topographical*, 1872, p. 58; pp. 248-9; p. 385; *Copy of the Poll for the Election of Two Knights of the Shire, to Serve in Parliament for the County of Middlesex, July, 1802*, 1803, p. 90; *GM*, 1846, p. 555; WFP F201.
42 Anc: Roode Family Tree; BMD; c-1851; *Pigot's Directory*, 1830.
43 Richard Fitzmaurice, viewed 2 August 2019: <https://tunearch.org/wiki/Fitzmaurice%27s_Hornpipe>.
44 Eichstadius, H. C. A., *(Programma quo) Novi Prorectoratus auspicia die III. m. Febr. a. 1844 rite capienda Civibus indicit Academia Jenensis: Memorabilia Academia Jenens. II*, 1844, p. 32.
44 Andrew Fletcher, viewed 2 August 2019, https://www.clanmacfarlanegenealogy.info/genealogy/TNGWebsite/getperson.php?personID=I58317&tree=CC>.
45 *DNB*; WFP F199.
46 CCEd; E&W Wills—will of Henry Fletcher; *OA*; *Parliamentary Papers*, vol. 11, 1831, p. 389; Serle, viewed 2 August 2019: <http://www.twickenham-museum.org.uk/detail.php?aid=7&ctid=&cid=>; The Manor House, Twickenham.
47 Anc: Parker Family Tree; BMD; *BMJ*, 1851, p. 288; RCS: Plarr's Lives of the Fellows Online.
48 Anc: Powell/Williamson Family Tree; BMD; c-1851–1891.
49 Jackson's *Oxford Journal*, 24 March 1781.
50 *CB*.
51 *Allgemeine musikalische Zeitung*, vol. 4, 1801, p. 295; Sparr, Kenneth, 'The Guitar in Sweden until the Middle of the 19th Century', 23 April, 2012, viewed 2 August 2019: <http://www.tabulatura.com/SWEGUIT.htm>.
52 *Foster-1881*; *OA*; *VCH*, Worcestershire.
53 BMD; c-1851–1871; *GM*, vol. 165, 1839, p. 554; *OA*; Wikipedia: Edward Francis Walwyn Foley.
54 BMD; Burke, Edmund, *The Annual Register of World Events: A Review of the Year*, vol. 86, 1845, p. 187; *CP*; cracroftspeerage.co.uk.
55 Baring-Gould, Sabine, *Devonshire Characters and Strange Events*; *CP*; *DNB*; *Lodge-1833*, p. 217.
56 BMD; Duncan George Forbes, viewed 2 August 2019: <http://www.clanmacfarlanegenealogy.info/genealogy/TNGWebsite/getperson.php?personID=I58400&tree=CC>.
57 BMD; Gordon Forbes, viewed 2 August 2019: <http://www.worcestershireregiment.com/>.
58 *DNB*; Charles Forbes de Montalembert, viewed 2 August 2019: <https://fracademic.com/dic.nsf/frwiki/340443>.
59 BMD; c-1841–1861. Colvin, H. M., *A Biographical Dictionary of British Architects, 1600–1840*, 1997; Blake, Steven, 'John Forbes, the architect–a difficult man?' Viewed 2 June 2019: <http://pittvillehistory.org.uk/bios/Forbes.html>.
60 BMD; *CB*; *HP*; Mary Ford, née Anson, viewed 2 August 2019: <https://www.geni.com/people/Mary-Ford/6000000027036235997>; UCL–Slaves.
61 Anc: Rathbone/Fenton/Ford/Fussell/Owen/Norton/Agutter/Rooke families: Jane Chapman; BMD; *CA*; CCEd; c-1851–1901; *GM*, vol. 119, 1816, p. 562; *OA*, Descendants of John Kenrick, viewed 2 August 2019: <http://www.greywall.demon.co.uk/genealogy/woore.html>; State Library of Tasmania.
62 Anc: Blake Family Tree, Benjamin Ford Family Tree; BMD; c-1851–1871; GPA; Military Deserters, 1812–1927.
63 Anc: Foreshew EGF Family Tree; BMD; c-1841–1871; UK, Apprentices Indentured in Merchant Navy, 1824–1910.
64 BMD; c-1841–1871.
65 Anc: Norris tree 104505; Ayling, Geoffrey M., Haughton Forrest (1826–1925): *Biography, Catalogue and Gallery of Paintings*, 2013, p. 9; BMD; *CP*; *The London Chronicle*, vol. 71, 1792, 207; *MM*, vol. 3, 1821, p. 198; *Reports from Committees of the House of Commons which Have Been Printed by Order of the House: And are Not Inserted in the Journals [1715–1801]*, vol. 12, 1803, p. 169, p. 172.
66 CCEd; *VCH*, Gloucestershire; The Family of Col. Christopher Brooks, viewed 2 August 2019: <http://www.airgale.com.au/brooks/d3.htm>.
67 BMD; *B-1852*-1, p. 1053; c-1851–1871.
68 Anc: Hinxman of Andover; BMD; c-1851–1861.
69 BMD: Non-Conformist and Non-Parochial Registers, 1567–1970; *Preston Guardian*, May, 1876.
70 Anc: Genberg Family Tree, Hallowell Family Tree; BMD; c-1851–1871.
71 BMD; c-1851–1881.
72 Articles of Clerkship, 1756–1874; BMD; *OA*.
73 BMD; *CA*; *CP*; *DNB*; *HP*; *OA*.
74 BMD; *HP*.
75 c-1851–1861.

76 Anc: McClintock Family Tree: sylviawright54; BMD; *HP*.
77 Anc: cdo-atherton-gabriel-family-tree; CCEd, *OA*.
78 BMD; HEMBRY, Phyllis May, *The English Spa, 1560–1815: A Social History*, 1990, p. 237; *The Edinburgh Magazine, or Literary Miscellany*, vol. 14, 1791, p. 440; *GM*, vol. 90, part 1, 1820, p. 188; *Journals of the House of Commons*, vol. 62, 1807, p. 954; *The Scots Magazine*, vol. 53, 1791, p. 568; Masters of the Ceremonies in Cheltenham, viewed 2 August 2019: <https://btsarnia.org/2014/05/15/the-masters-of-the-ceremonies-in-cheltenham-an-essay/>.
79 Anc: Rowland Family(1); BMD; CCEd; Cheshire Archives and Local Studies: ref: DBC 1/9—Rev. Henry Foulkes of Oxford, marriage settlement; DAVIES, Henry, *A View of Cheltenham, in its Past and Present State,* 1843, p. 202.
80 Anc: Montagu Family Tree, Osbaldestons of Hunmanby and Hutton Buscel East Yorks to other aristocratic families; *B-1835*, vol. 2, p. 268; *CA*; *HP*.
81 BMD; *OA*.
82 Anc: Frustration; BMD; c-1841–1881; DOUGHTON, Daphne, *Journal of Medical Biography* 1998; 6: pp. 187-193. *LG*, 26 April 1870, p. 2303.
83 CAMPBELL, Rob, 'Clevedon: Medieval Manor to Victorian Resort', 2009, p. 202; *The Clevedonian*, August 2011, articles by Julia Elton.
84 Charles Richard Fox, viewed 2 August 2019: <https://www.findagrave.com/memorial/35773021/charles-richard-fox>.
85 Anc: Sequoia; *BLG*; BMD; *CA*.
86 CCEd, *OA*
87 BMD; c-1841–1871.
88 Anc: Cameron Family Tree, cdo-langford-family-tree, Dendy; BMD; CCEd; c-1841–1851; *OA*.
89 Anc: Victorians: MarchHare2; BMD; BUSH, Graham William Arthur, *Bristol and Its Municipal Government, 1820–185*, Bristol Record Society, 1976, p. 240; *GM*, vol. 93, part 1, 1823, p. 573; *GM*, 1840, p. 672.
90 BMD; *CA*; *DNB*.
91 CCEd; *OA*.
92 Anc: Crisp Family Tree: crispfamily1; BMD; *CA*; c-1851–1861.
93 Anc: COATES Family Tree: Diana COATES; Anc: Francis of Norfolk Family Tree: franciss70; BMD; c-1851–1861.
94 BMD; c-1841; *DNB*; thepeerage.com: person M, #389322.
95 Anc: BainSmith1: robbain; BMD; *B-1847*, p. 444; National Library of Scotland: History of the Clan Mackenzie, p. 437; *The Scots Magazine*, vol. 79, 1817, p. 319; thepeerage.com: person M, #81684.
96 CCEd; *OA*; *DNB*.
97 *DNB*.
98 *CB*.
99 Anc: Tommytree; Anc: Rowe Family Tree: Jane Roberts; BMD.
100 BMD; c-1841–1871; Mayors and Sheriffs of Bristol 1800–1899, viewed 17 March 2019: <http://www.davenapier.co.uk/mayors/mayors3.htm>; E&W Wills—will of William Fripp; The History of Broad Plain and the Soap Factory, viewed 17 March 2019: <https://www.gardinerhaskins.co.uk/the-history-of-broad-plain-and-the-soap-factory/> ; *Reports of Cases Argued and Determined in the Court of King's Bench: With Tables of the Names of the Cases and the Principal Matters*, vol. 1, 1823, pp. 126-134.
101 BMD; CCEd; Family of William Cokayne FRITH and Mary COX, viewed 17 March 2019: <http://www.firthworks.com/genealogy/Wallingford/fam481.html>; *A List of the Officers of the Army and of the Corps of Royal Marines*, 1821, p. 398; *OA*.
102 BMD; c-1861; CRAWFORD, Lieutenant-Colonel D. G., *Roll of the Indian Medical Service 1615–1930*, vol. 1, p. xi.
103 Anc: Gherashe/Uren/Waldeck/Pearson; BMD; British Library: India Office Records; c-1841–1861; *DNB*; *Lodge-1843*; *Walford-1893*; Juliana Rebecca Fuller, viewed 2 August 2019: <https://www.geni.com/people/Juliana-Fuller/6000000018971145024>.
104 *DNB*; *OA*; *United Service Magazine*, 1833.
105 CARNE, B. G. *Trans. BGAS*, 1995.
106 *B-1844*, p. 334.

Letter G

1 Anc: morgan 7-26-2010, Rowan Family Tree; BMD: *OA*.
2 *VCH*, Wiltshire: Stert.
3 Anc: Menes Family Tree; Anc: Scott Family Tree: peter scott; *ADB*.
4 *CA*; CCEd; c-1841–1851; *OA*.
5 *DNB*; *OA*.
6 Anc: Jacqueline Hull family tree; BMD; *B-1838*, p. 325; *CA*; GLASGOW G. H. H.: *Gloucestershire History* No. 14 'The Election of Gloucestershire County Coroners, 1800–1888 Part II', 2000, pp. 17-20; *OA*; *Slater's Directory*, 1850.
7 *VCH*, Wiltshire: Stert.
8 Anc: Moore 2015/06: mrbroddy; BMD; c-1851–1871; *The Court Magazine and Belle Assemblée*, 1847, p. 30; East Riding of Yorkshire Archives and Local Studies Service: Revd Timothy Francillon, Family Papers: reference: zDDX709/7: Letter to Mrs Francillon of Queens Square from Mrs Lillingstone; *The Law Times*, vol. 9, 1847, p. 364; *LG*, vol. 1, 1819, p 475; United Grand Lodge of England Freemason Membership Registers, 1751–1921; *Walford-1882*, p. 238.
9 Jean Galiffe, viewed 2 August 2019: <https://www.memorialatpeninsula.org/?p=15943>.
10 BMD; c-1851–1881; GPA.
11 BMD; c-1851; *OA*.
12 BMD; c-1841–1871; *Dictionary of British and Irish Botanists and Horticulturists: Including Plant Collectors, Flower Painter and Garden Designer*; *The Gardener's Magazine and Register of Rural & Domestic Improvement*, 1842.

13 BMD; c-1841–1861; *The Gentleman's and London Magazine: Or Monthly Chronologer, 1741–1794*, p. 616; *Journal of the Royal National Lifeboat Institution*; *OA*; Plymouth and West Devon Record Office: 460–Clark Estate Papers; *Walford-1882*, p. 60.
14 c-1841.
15 BMD; c-1841–1851; *LG*, part 1, 1845, p. 121.
16 Anc: gardner Family Tree: markarene; BMD; c-1851–1861.
17 BMD; c-1851.
18 BMD; c-1851.
19 BMD; c-1851; *GM*, vols 182-183, 1847, p. 423; *The Rugby Register, from the Year 1675 to the Present Time*, 1836, p. 168; Peter Garforth, viewed 2 August 2019: <https://www.findagrave.com/memorial/163137096/peter-garforth>; *GM*, Volume 182, 1847, p. 423.
20 Thomas Garnett, Royal Institution, viewed 2 August 2019: <https://www.rigb.org/whats-on/events-2014/june/fact--death-of-thomas-garnett>.
21 Anc: Garrard family tree: AlGarrard; BMD; CCEd; *OA*.
22 BMD; c-1851; *Pigot's Directory*, 1830.
23 *Cobbett's Political Register*, vol. 5, 1804, p. 177; *LM*, vol. 29, 1798, p. 480; E&W Wills—PROB 11/1628/417, will of Edward Garrow of Totteridge.
24 *DNB*; *HP*.
25 *American Migrations 1765–1799; South Carolina*; *England and Wales Visitation*, vol. I, III-XIV; *HP*; Slave Registers; UCL-Slaves; Charles Garth Colleton, viewed 2 August 2019: <https://www.bonhams.com/auctions/10168/lot/111/>.
26 BMD; c-1871; Clifton Gascoigne, viewed 2 August 2019: <https://www.geni.com/people/Lt-Col-Clifton-Gascoigne/6000000016917921544>.
27 BMD; *GM*, vols 181-182, 1847, p. 418; *OA*; The Descendants of Samuel Driver, viewed 2 August 2019: <http://www.pennyghael.org.uk/Driver.pdf>.
28 BMD; CCEd; *OA*; Wellcome Library.
29 Anc: Hyslop Family Tree: marianaholbrook; Humphry Family Tree: emmaeasterbrook; BMD; c-1841–1861.
30 Dressler, Roland & Jochen, Klauss, *Weimarer Friedhöfe*, 1996; *AGB*.
31 BMD; *LM*, vol. 18, 1787, p. 278.
32 c-1851, *Hunt*.
33 Anc: Dixon Family Tree: LoisMBrown48; Berrows' Index of Marriages; BMD; CCEd; Trouble House, viewed 3 August 2019: <https://www.thetroublehouse.co.uk/history>; c-1841–1871; *OA*.
34 Anc: Green/Richards/Lea 2012: MarianGreen758; BMD; c-1851, *Post Office Directory* 1860.
35 Anc: Taylor/French Tree: debbrady_1; BMD.
36 c-1841.
37 Gibson of Haddington, viewed 3 August 2019: <https://www.electricscotland.com/history/haddington/index.htm>.
38 BMD; CCEd; c-1851–1871; *OA*.
39 BMD; c-1861; *CL*; *OA*.
40 *B-1847-1*, p. 464; *GM*, vols. 182-183, 1847, p. 87; Hart, H. G., *The New Annual Army List*, 1845, p. 253; MI: Grasmere, Jane Elizabeth Gibson, viewed 7 July 2019: <https://www.northofthesands.org.uk/surnames/surname/36/Gibson>; *The Sydney Herald*, 1 May 1847.
41 BMD; Urchfont Church MI; *VCH*, Wiltshire, Urchfont.
42 BMD; *DNB*; Dorothy Gifford, memorial, viewed 3 August 2019: <http://www.edgt.org.uk/uploads/3/4/6/9/34695614/45_-_gifford_rev_jan_17.pdf>.
43 *DNB*.
44 BMD; c-1841–1851.
45 *DNB*; E&W Wills—will of Mary Gilbert; *HP*; Thomas Gilbert, viewed 3 August 2019: <natgould.org/thomas_gilbert_1720–1798.>.
46 BMD; *CA*; c-1841–1851.
47 *Dictionary of Ulster Biography*, viewed 15 May 2019: <http://www.newulsterbiography.co.uk/index.php/home/printPerson/2059>.
48 BMD; c-1871.
49 BMD; c-1851.
50 Anc: Bond Family Tree: Kim Bond; BMD; c-1841–1871.
51 Farrer, William, ed., *VCH*, Lancashire, vol. 6, 1911; *B-1848*, p. 438; Wilson, John, *Verses and Notes: Topographical, Historical, Antiquarian, Miscellaneous*, 1903; website: Marcella Gillibrand, viewed 3 August 2019: <https://www.geni.com/people/Marcella-Gillibrand/6000000020516510233>.
52 *DNB*.
53 c-1841.
54 Anc: Gilly family tree: B4A5L6E7Y; BMD; *CA*; CCEd; *The Baptismal, Marriage, and Burial Registers of the Cathedral Church of Christ and Blessed Mary the Virgin at Durham, 1609–1896*, 1897, p. 29.
55 Anc: Rankin tree: tobiasdr; Guthrie-Payne Family Tree: kelly11481; BMD; c-1841–1871; *The Jurist*, vol. 6, 1843, p. 21.
56 *Bath Chronicle* 30 July 1795; BMD.
57 *Grove*.
58 BMD; c-1841–1871; Farr, Grahame E.: *Records of Bristol Ships, 1800–1838* (vessels over 150 Tons), Bristol Record Society, 1950, p. 55; *Lodge-1832*, p. 344; Online Encyclopedia of Ohio History; Warwickshire County Record Office; Samuel Gist, viewed 3 August 2019: <https://texthistory.wordpress.com/2011/10/30/samuel-gist-an-enigma-of-manumission/>; Wormington MI.
59 *DNB*; *HP*.
60 Anc: Clemo Family Tree: Roseclemo; BMD; c-1841–1861; *OA*.
61 BMD; c-1841–1851; *OA*.
62 BMD; Bristol Obituaries, 1837; c-1841–1871; *DCB*; *Dover Telegraph*, 1850; Parish registers of Dover, Kent—Baptisms at St Peter and St Paul.

63 *AGB.*
64 BMD; CCEd; *OA*; Castle Eaton Family Notices 1800–1849, viewed 3 August 2019: <https://www.wiltshire-opc.org.uk/Items/Castle%20Eaton/Castle%20Eaton%20-%20Family%20Notices%201800-1849.pdf>.
65 Kane, John, & Askwith, William Harrison: *List of Officers of the Royal Regiment of Artillery from the Year 1716 to the Year 1899*, 1900, p. 204; *Malta Penny Magazine*, vol. 2, 1841. p. 3; *Proclami, notificazioni ed altri avvisi ufficiali, pubblicati dal governo dell'isola di Malta*. Dalli 5 ottobre 1813, 1830, p. xiii.
66 BMD; c-1841–1861; Iscoyd Park, viewed 3 August 2019: <https://iscoydpark.com/2018/10/the-history-of-iscoyd-park/>.
67 BMD; c-1861–1881; *The Post Office Directory of Gloucestershire, Herefordshire, Shropshire and the City of Bristol*, 1863, p. 354
68 BMD; Bristol University; c-1841–1851; *OA*.
69 BMD; *CA*; c-1841–1861; *OA*.
70 Anc: Graham-Bell Family Tree: tgbsquared; BMD; c-1851.
71 BMD; Robert Gomery, viewed 3 August 2019: <http://freepages.rootsweb.com/~gomery/genealogy/robgom.html>.
72 BMD; *British Medical Journal*, vol. 1859, p. 455; c-1841–1871; *Hunt*.
73 c-1841.
74 c-1841.
75 *DNB*; *OA*.
76 *BLG*; BMD; c-1841–1851; *Gloucestershire Notes and Queries*; MI: Swindon; *Journal of the House of Lords*: vol. 63: 1830–1831, pp. 795.
77 Anc: Goodlake Family Tree: Sarah Goodlake; *CA*; c-1841–1851.
78 Anc: Prothero Family Tree: kerrin65; BMD; Historic England: Oare House, Grade I List entry Number: 1001241.
79 Anc: Blomfield family tree: hugoblomfield; Anc: Newman McHaffie Tree: VickyNewman69; BMD; c-1841–1901; GA, Edwin Stephen Goodrich, viewed 3 August 2019: <https://embryo.asu.edu/pages/edwin-stephen-goodrich-1868-1946>.
80 B-1845; *Southern Reporter and Cork Commercial Courier*, 10 July 1823.
81 Anc: Slator/Watson/Lindsay/Johnson family tree: jaslator; BMD; c-1841–1851; *Examiner: A Weekly Paper on Politics, Literature, Music and the Fine Arts*, 1 January 1842, p. 14, *The London Chronicle*, vol. 105, 1809, p. 55; *The Spectator*, 22 January 1842, p. 19.
82 BMD; *OA*; *VCH*, Oxfordshire.
83 *CB*.
84 *The Edinburgh Review or Critical Journal*, 1817, p. 260; *Historical Memoirs of the Reign of Mary Queen of Scots: And a Portion of the Reign of King James the Sixth*, Abbotsford Club, 1836, pp. xix-xx; *MM*, vol. 18, 1804, p. 9; Rapport, Michael: *Nationality and Citizenship in Revolutionary France: The Treatment of Foreigners 1789-1799*, 2000.
85 *CP*.
86 Alger, John Goldworth: *Napoleon's British Visitors and Captives, 1801–1815*, 1904; *CP*; *CB*; *DNB*.
87 *HP*.
88 BMD; *CA*; CCEd; England & Wales, Criminal Registers, 1791–1892; *The Plantagenet Roll of the Blood Royal*, The Mortimer-Percy vol., p. 188.
89 Wikipedia.
90 BMD; Bruford, W. H., *Germany in the Eighteenth Century: The Social Background of the Literary Revival*, 1935, p. 34; *CP*; Ghibellino, Ettore, *Goethe and Anna Amalia: A Forbidden Love?*, 2007, p. 90; Mellish Family of Hodsock, Nottinghamshire, viewed 3 August 2019: <https://www.nottingham.ac.uk/manuscriptsandspecialcollections/collectionsindepth/family/mellish/mellishfamilyhistory.aspx>; Neubert, Franz, *Goethe und sein Kreis*, 1919, p. 199; *VCH*, Yorkshire; Wikipedia (German).
91 *HP*.
92 Anc: Ron Gould Family Tree: Kathryn Parker; BMD; GA: Land Tax Registers; E&W Wills—wills of various Gorges.
93 Jeffs, Julian, *Sherry*, 2016, p. 170.
94 BMD; c-1851–1861.
95 *HP*.
96 *CA*; *CP*.
97 BMD; c-1851–1861; *DNB*; *HP*.
98 BHO, *Survey of London*: vols 29 and 30, St James Westminster, part 1, 1960.
99 Anc: Goold Family Tree: phyllisgoold; Gould Family Tree: NDunkley50; BMD; CCEd; *OA*, c-1851–1861.
100 Anc: Gould Family Tree JsandonSkousgaard; Spencer/Lennon: i_spencer375; BMD; *DNB*.
101 BMD; Wikipedia (German).
102 *BLG*; National Library of Scotland; Thomas Graham Stirling, viewed 3 August 2019: <https://www.geni.com/people/Thomas-Graham-Stirling/6000000042939471938>.
103 BMD; *B-1898* p. 644; thepeerage.com: person M, #26122.
104 BMD; 'Mrs Graham's Balloon on Fire', *c*. 1850, viewed 3 August 2019: <https://www.scienceandsociety.co.uk/results.asp?image=10411166>.
105 *The Annual Register*, vol. 130, 1889, p. 150; BMD.
106 *DNB*; *OA*.
107 BMD; *OA*.
108 William L. Clements Library, University of Michigan, Manuscripts Division: Charles Grant, vicomte de Vaux Papers, 1756–1805.
109 *CA*; *DNB*.
110 *DNB*.
112 Anc: Blomfield family tree: hugoblomfield; BMD; *B-1836* p. 7; CCEd; c-1841–1851; Fortescue, Mary Teresa, *The History of Calwich Abbey*, 1915; *GM*, vol. 98, 1828, p. 570; Granville, Roger: *The History of the Granville Family: Traced Back to Rollo, First Duke of Normandy*, 1895; *OA*.

113 Anc: Dilts Family Tree: cherylmcmanus57, *B-1863-2*, p. 1317. *B-1838-4*, p. 165; BMD; *LG*, part 2, 1806, p. 1093; *Somerset Parish Registers*: Marriages, vol. 8, 1906, p. 83.
114 Anc: houben Family Tree: honey2b1; BMD; *Debrett 1822-II*, pp. 1238-9; *Lodge-1832*, p. 355; *GM*, vol. 218, 1865, p. 237.
115 Archives in London and the M25 area: Graves Scientific Papers; *DNB*; *OA*.
116 Temperley, Nicholas: 'Jonathan Gray and Church Music in York, 1770–1840', *Borthwick Papers*, issue 51, 1977.
117 Anc: Andrew Cook family tree: 1_andy984; BMD; c-1841–1891.; *LG*, part 2, 1810, p. 1792.
118 Anc: Gray Family Tree: NancyL41; *The Asiatic Journal and Monthly Miscellany*, 1845, p. 110; BMD; *CA*; c-1841–1891; *OA*
119 BMD; Hope-Jones, Arthur: *Income Tax in the Napoleonic Wars*, 2013.
120 *OA*.
121 *Debrett 1815*, p. 1119.
122 Anc: Strongitharm Family Tree; stephencordingley; BMD; *OA*.
123 *DNB*.
124 Anc: Townley Family Tree: ChrisRansome1.
125 Museums Sheffield, viewed 21 March 2019, http://www.sheffieldcutlerymap.org.uk/location/william-greaves-sons/>; William Greaves, viewed 21
126 BMD.
127 *B-1847*, p. 500; BMD; *CA*; c-1851; Gretton, Richard Henry: *The Burford Records: A Study in Minor Town Government*, 1920, p. 94; *Walford-1864*, p. 437.
128 Anc: Horton-Szar Family: danhortonszar; Anc: Tunbridge Wells Family Trees: sschibli; BMD; c-1851–1861.
129 Anc: Richardson Family Tree: suepiano162; Thomas Greg, of Belfast, viewed 21 March 2019: <https://www.geni.com/people/Thomas-Greg-of-Belfast/6000000027103766606>.
130 BMD; CCEd; *OA*; Phillimore, W. P. W.: 'Uley Registers', from: *Gloucestershire Notes and Queries*, vol. V. 1891–1893.
131 BMD; c-1841–1851.
132 BMD; c-1841.
133 *DNB*; WFP F187–F195.
134 Anc: Blomfield family tree: hugoblomfield; BMD; c-1841–1851.
135 *HP*.
136 BMD; *OA*; St Peter's, Netherseal, Leicestershire, Parish Register Notes.
137 BMD; *HP*; *OA*.
138 *DNB*; *HP*.
139 BMD; *CA*; *CP*; *HP*.
140 *BDA*, vol. 5, p. 359; *GM*, part 1; vol. 137, 1825, p. 650; *Grove*.
141 Bodleian Library: Catalogue of papers relating to the Cockerell (later Rushout) and Grieve families; BMD; *CA*; Anne Rushout, viewed 3 August 2019: <https://www.npg.org.uk/collections/search/person/mp85620/anne-rushout>; cracroftspeerage.
142 *DNB*.
143 Anc: Griffin Family Tree: peterwstevenson; BMD; c-1841–1851.
144 Anc: Drew Family Tree: lisa4134; BMD; c-1841–1861.
145 BMD; c-1841–1871.
146 BMD; *CA*; c-1851–1881.
147 BMD.
148 Anc: George Morgan Family Tree: George Morgan; Anc: Dilts Family Tree: cherylmcmanus57; Anc: Howard Charles King Family Tree: kgaum1984; BMD; Waters, Robert Edmond Chester, *Genealogical Memoirs of the Extinct Family of Chester of Chicheley: Their Ancestors and Descendants*, vol. 2, 1878, p. 730; Matthew Chitty Darby-Griffith, viewed 3 August 2019: <http://www.berkshirehistory.com/bios/mcdgriffith.html>; WFP-F205.
149 *DNB*.
150 Anc: Wilson/Brewster/Thring/Scrivens Family Tree: JanetWilson140; BMD; *GM*, vol. 71, 1792, p. 383; *GM*, vols 162-163, 1837, p. 438.
151 BMD; c-1851–1861; *OA*.
152 BMD; c-1841; *Pigot's Directory*, 1835; *The Bankrupt Directory; Being a Complete Register of All the Bankrupts from Dec. 1820 to Apr. 1843*, 1843, p. 174.
153 Fenner, Theodore: *Opera in London: Views of the Press, 1785–1830*; 1994, p. 334; *History of the Philharmonic Society of London 1813–1912*, 1912, p 555; Kassler, Michael, *Charles Edward Horn's Memoirs of His Father and Himself*, 2003, p. 1810; *The Musical Times*, January 1956; Miss Griglietti, viewed 22 March 2019: <http://www.urfm.braidense.it/risorse/prefemm_query_en.php?Nome1=Griglietti,Elizabeth%20Augusta>.
154 Anc: Giffen Family Tree: mgiffen1947; *Harper's Directory*, 1844.
155 BMD; *DNB*.
156 BMD; Daylesford House, viewed 3 August 2019: <https://historicengland.org.uk/listing/the-list/list-entry/1000760>.
157 *Grove*; Kaufman, Tom *Opera Today*, December 2005.
158 Anc: Donaldson Family Tree: James Donaldson; BMD; *HP*; *Royal military panorama, or, Officers' companion*, vol. 3; Slave Registers of former British Colonial Dependencies, 1812–1834.
159 BMD; c-1841–1871.
160 BMD; Buckinghamshire Archives; *CA*; c-1841–1871; *MATB*; Lysons; *OA*; John Grubb VI (1786–1846), viewed 3 August 2019: <https://www.genealogy.com/forum/surnames/topics/grubb/625/>; John Eustace Grubb, viewed 22 March 2019: <http://wyndhammarsh.co.uk/genealogy/getperson.php?personID=I8584&tree=CledwynMarsh>.
161 BMD; *OA*; Richard Gubbins, viewed 3 August 2019: <http://www.epsomandewellhistoryexplorer.org.uk/GubbinsRichard.html>.
162 Anc: Crump/Parker/Grampp/Joscher/Heede/Ochs Family Tree: AJoscher7504; Anc: Mills Roberts: Appledore5; BMD; c-1841–1861;

B-1914, p. 915; *CB*; Chick, Noah Alfred: *Annals of the Indian Rebellion, 1857-58*, p. 378; *DNB*; *HP*; *OA*.
163 *EB*.
164 BMD; c-1871.
165 Anc: Marshall-Brown Family Tree; Anc: KILGOUR-COOKE-Tree: j_l_kilgour; BMD; c-1841–1871.
166 BMD; c-1841; Jerdan, William: *Men I Have Known*, 1866, p. 106; GA; Hampshire Record Office: Knollis Family, Earls of Banbury; much additional information has come from the careful research into the Guydickens family by Linley Hooper.
167 WFP F200.
168 BMD; Articles of Clerkship; *LG*, 1813, page 2177.
169 BMD; GA; *Slater's Directory*, 1858.
170 Anc: middleton Family Tree: sarafox3; *The Army List*, 1805; *The Royal Military Calendar, Or Army Service and Commission Book*, 1820, pp. 347-8; *The Scots Magazine*, vol. 51, 1789, p. 156.
171 BMD; Articles of Clerkship; *The Court magazine and belle assemblée*, 1844, p. 19; *CA*; Gyde family of Gloucestershire, viewed 3 August 2019: <https://www.genealogy.com/forum/surnames/topics/gyde/1/>; thepeerage.com: person M, #302966.

Letter H

1 *DNB*.
2 Anc: Webster Family Tree: CarMauC; BMD; c-1871.
3 BMD; *BJU International*, vol. 95, Issue 9, 2005, p. 1193; MI: Coln St Dennis.
4 BMD; *CA*; *DNB*.
5 *AGB*; Johann Michael Friedrich Haide, viewed 3 August 2019: <https://www.carolineschelling.com/dramatis-personae/persons-h/>.
6 BMD; *CA*; CCEd.
7 *DNB*.
8 *DCB*.
9 Anc: Wilkins Family Tree: Robert Wilkins; BMD; c-1851–1861; *Pigot's Directory*, 1830.
10 Anc: Earls of Coventry Family Tree: Chris Wynne-Davies; BMD; *OA*.
11 BMD; *Bridgwater Times*, 1854; CCEd; *MM*, vol. 13, 1820; *OA*.
12 *DNB*.
13 *DNB*.
14 *DNB*.
15 *DNB*.
16 BMD; *OA*.
17 Anc: Toomey Family Tree: maxpax48; BMD; *OA*.
18 BMD; c-1841–1851.
19 BMD; *OA*.
20 BMD; *OA*; Frances Longley, viewed 3 August 2019: <https://www.werelate.org/wiki/Person:Frances_Longley_%281%29>.
21 BMD; c-1841–1891; Kent Archaeological Society: Hunton Index; *OA*.
22 BMD; c-1851; *CA*.
23 BMD; c-1851–1871; *Pigot's Directory*, 1830. *Transactions*, vol. 12 of the Royal Institution of Chartered Surveyors, 1880, p. 389.
24 BMD; c-1841–1851.
25 BMD; c-1851.
26 BMD; *CB*; *Debrett 1840*, p. 192; *DNB*.
27 BMD; *CA*; c-1841–1851; MI: Pitchcombe; *VCH*, Gloucestershire, vol. 11: Bisley and Longtree Hundreds.
28 Urchfont Church MI; *VCH*, Wiltshire, vol. 10; Wiltshire and Swindon Archives.
29 Anc: Julie Olsen Family Tree: Keith Olsen; Anc: Small-Begbie-Paul-Keirnan Family Tree: annep15; BMD; *OA*.
30 Anc: teresa1427: tjtree; BMD; c-1841–1851, England & Wales, Criminal Registers, 1791–1892; Tasmanian Archives: The National Archives (TNA): HO 11/17, p. 403.
31 Jagemann, Karoline, Emde, Ruth B., & von Heygendorff, Achim: *Selbstinszenierungen im klassischen Weimar: Caroline Jagemann*, p. 387-9.
32 Anc: hambidge: j5553; Anc: Davis Family Tree: alan_hadley; BMD; c-1841–1861; Gloucestershire Prison Records, 1728–1914.
33 *The Army List*, 1805; *The Scots Magazine, Or, General Repository of Literature, History, and Politics*, vol. 77, p. 554.
34 *CA*.
35 BMD; c-1841–1861; *Billings Directory of Worcestershire 1855*.
36 *CP*.
37 *CP*; *HP*.
38 Janet Hamilton-Dalrymple, viewed 3 August 2019: <https://www.clanmacfarlanegenealogy.info/genealogy/TNGWebsite/getperson.php?personID=I69897&tree=CC>.
39 *HP*; Hugh Hammersley, viewed 3 August 2019: <https://www.geni.com/people/Hugh-Hammersley/6000000006295413279>.
40 BMD; *DNB*; *OA*.
41 Anc: Danaher/Spiller Family Tree: bernicewhite154; Anc: Griffiths Family Tree: KimS512; GPA.
42 BMD; *B-1898*, p. 1396; MI: Westminster Abbey.
43 Spalding, Almut: *Elise Reimarus (1735–1805) The Muse of Hamburg: A Woman of the German Enlightenment*, 2005; John Hanbury, viewed 3 August 2019: <https://www.geni.com/people/John-Hanbury/6000000011832737200>.
44 BMD; *B-1898*, p. 1396; Neath Antiquarian Society: Gnoll Estate Papers.
45 Anc: JGAPUGH MOTHER Family Tree: eanpugh1; BMD; *B-1898*, p. 1396.

46 BMD; c-1871; Shakespeare Centre Library and Archives: Worcestershire Pages.
47 BMD; c-1841.
48 BMD.
49 Anc: BAKER/CROUCH/HANDY family tree: brillborrell.
50 BMD; *B-1864*, p. 362; *Country Life*, vol. 20, 1906, p. 272.
51 BMD; *B-1836*; E&W Wills—will of Louisa Darby Griffith; *A Record of the Parish of Padworth and Its Inhabitants*, 1911, p. 65; William Alers Hankey, viewed 3 August 2019: <https://www.fieldtrial.info/familytree/HTML/william-alers.html>.
52 BMD; *B-1836*; *CB*; *HP*; *OA*; RBS Heritage Online; thepeerage.com: person M, #233322.
53 BMD; CCEd; c-1851–1861; *OA*.
54 Anc: Stafford Family Tree2: blackfarmcat; BMD; c-1861.
55 BMD; c-1851, 1871.
56 Anc: CONNIFF NEE HARBIDGE Family Tree: rlrmcon; BMD; c-1861.
57 *CP*; *HP*.
58 *CP*.
59 c-1841.
60 BMD; c-1841–1861.
61 *Parliamentary Papers*, vol. 43, 1843, Northleach House of Correction, p. 17.
62 BMD; c-1841–1851.
63 *DNB*.
64 BMD; *OA*.
65 BMD; *OA*.
66 Anc: Dilts Family Tree: cherylmcmanus57, BMD; *DNB*.
67 Anc: Victorians: MarchHare2; BMD; c-1851–1871; Jordan, John Woolf: *Colonial families of Philadelphia.*
68 c-1841–1861; Kent Archaeological Society: MI: Footscray.
69 BMD; c-1841–1851.
70 Anc: Colin B Gurney (Coventry) Family Tree: COLINBGURNEY44; BMD; *DNB*; Harford, Alice: *Annals of the Harford Family*, 1909.
71 BMD; *DNB*.
72 *DNB*; *Grove*.
73 BMD; Boase, Frederic: *Modern English Biography: A–H*, column 1333, 1892; *A Roll of the Descendants Living or lately living in January, 1911, of Richard Garth, of Morden Park, Surrey*; Genealogy of Jack Fuller; *GM*; *Manchester Courier and Lancashire General Advertiser*, 13 May 1865; *Pigot's Directory*, 1835; *OA*.
74 Anc: Hartland Family Tree: marisadawn1; *Pigot's Directory*.
75 *Grove*.
76 BMD.
77 Anc: Gillette Family Tree Branches & Twigs: Andree99; BMD; c-1841.
78 Anc: Gillette Family Tree Branches & Twigs: Andree99; BMD; c-1841–1861.
79 BMD; c-1851.
80 Anc: Sandy (Scott)/Cooper: tskkj: BMD; c-1841–1881.
81 c-1851–1881.
82 BMD; c-1851–1861.
83 Anc: Lapp family tree: Dave Lapp; BMD; c-1851.
84 BMD; c-1851–1861.
85 *DNB*.
86 Anc: Rawson Family Tree: rawson2009; BMD; CCEd; *CL*; *OA*.
87 Anc: Hamblen Family Tree: SimonHamblen; BMD; Coote, Henry Charles, *The Practice of the Ecclesiastical Courts*, 1847, pp. 821-824; *GM*, vols 174-175, 1843, p. 313; Metcalfe, Walter Charles: *The Visitations of Essex by Hawley, 1552; Hervey, 1558; Cooke, 1570; Raven, 1612; and Owen and Lilly, 1634. To which are Added Miscellaneous Essex Pedigrees from Various Harleian Manuscripts*, part 2, 1879, p. 716.
88 *BDA*, vol. 7; *Grove*.
89 *DNB*.
90 BMD; *HP*.
91 BMD; c-1841–1851, 1861; *LG*; *Pigot's Directory*, Evesham, 1835; Shakespeare Centre Library and Archive; *Slater's Directory*.
92 Anc: Old Settle; BMD; H. L. Bradfer-Lawrence Collection; c-1841–1851; Whitaker, Thomas Dunham: *The History of Craven*, 1878; Yorkshire Archaeological Society.
93 BMD; c-1851–1881.
94 *CB*; *HP*.
95 Anc: Gardiner Family Tree: Anna Gardiner; Anc: Norton Family Tree: billshe169; BMD; c-1841–1861.
96 *HP*.
97 BMD; c-1841–1861; *LG*, 11 May 1858, p. 2397; *OA*.
98 *CA*; CCEd.
99 BMD; *OA*.
100 BMD; c-1841; HMS *Delphinen*, viewed 3 August 2019: <https://wrecksite.eu/wreck.aspx?16628>; Sailing Navies 1650–1850, [inactive 3 August 2019]; <http://www.sailingnavies.com/index.php>; Julia Pellew: thepeerage.com: person F, #402297.
101 Atkinson, David & Roud, Steve: *Street Literature of the Long Nineteenth Century: Producers, Sellers, Consumers*; 2017, p. 67; *Universal British Directory, for Cheltenham*, 1791.

102 Anc: Hayward Family Tree: jacky649; BMD; c-1851.
103 BMD; *OA*.
104 BMD; *OA*.
105 *DNB*.
106 *DNB*.
107 Collyer, William Bengo: *The Investigator*, 1823, p. 458; Lawson, Sir Charles: *The Private Life of Warren Hastings: First Govenor-general of India*, 1895, p. 5; *OA*; Hastings and Woodyatt families, viewed 3 August 2019: <http://www.woodyatt.bravehost.com/cradley/pafg13.htm>.
108 BMD; *CA*; CCEd.
109 BMD; Cobbett, Richard Stuteley: *Memorials of Twickenham: Parochial and Topographical*, 1872, p. 97; *Walford-1869*, p. 618.
110 BMD; c-1841–1871.
111 BMD; *MATB*; *OA*.
112 BMD; c-1841–1881; England & Wales, Criminal Registers, 1791–1892; Gloucestershire, England, Prison Records, 1728–1914.
113 *CA*; Catholic Encyclopedia.
114 CCEd; *OA*.
115 *Grove*.
116 *DNB*.
117 BMD; Royal College of Physicians: Munk's Roll: vol. III.
118 BMD; British Regiments and the Men Who Led Them 1793–1815, viewed 3 August 2019: <https://www.napoleon-series.org/military/organization/Britain/Infantry/Regiments/c_InfantryregimentsIntro.html>; GA; *VCH*, Gloucestershire.
119 BMD.
120 Arborfield Local History Society; BMD; *CB*; *OA*.
121 Anc: Haynes Family Tree: phaynes134; BMD; c-1851–1861.
122 BMD; c-1851.
123 BMD.
124 BMD; c-1841–1861; Cornwall Record Office; *VCH*, Worcestershire.
125 Anc: Hayward Family Tree: bruce Hayward; Isaac Johnson Thomas Hayward Esq Captain of the Royal Gloucestershire Militia, viewed 3 August 2019: <http://gallery.its.unimelb.edu.au/imu/imu.php?request=display&port=45208&id=b417&flag=start&offset=0&count=1&view=details&irn=14650&eparties=on>; Clyffe Hall, viewed 3 August 2019: <https://historicengland.org.uk/listing/the-list/list-entry/1284497>.
126 Anc: Gardiner Family Tree: Anna Gardiner; BMD; c-1841–1851.
127 BMD; c-1841–1861; Cornwall Record Office; *VCH*, Worcestershire.
128 Anc: Digby Family Tree: coshan64; BMD; *CA*; c-1891; *DNB*.
129 BMD; Brasenose College Register; CCEd; *OA*.
130 BMD; c-1851–1861; *Hunt*.
131 BMD; Paschaldi, Maria: *The Ionian Islands in British Official Discourse; 1815–1864*.
132 BMD; c-1841–1891: *CA*; MI: wall plaque, list of vicars, Isle of Grain Church.
133 Anc: Merged Pryce: Aaron Pryce; BMD; c-1841–1891.
134 *DNB*.
135 *DNB*.
136 BMD; *CA*; CCEd; c-1851–1871.
137 BMD; *CA*; c-1841.
138 BMD; c-1861; *The British Magazine and Monthly Register of Religious and Ecclesiastical Information, Parochial History, and Documents Respecting the State of the Poor, Progress of Education*, vol. 25, 1844, p. 588; *OA*.
139 Karl-Heinrich-Anton-von-Helldorff-auf-Schwersted, viewed 3 August 2019: <https://www.geni.com/people/Karl-Heinrich-Anton-von-Helldorff-auf-Schwerstedt-bei-Weimar/6000000041281945136>; <Zeno.org: Meine Bibliotek: Goethe, Johann Wolfgang; Gespräche; Personenverzeichnis>.
140 Anc: Ryrie/Oldfield/Elphinston/ Robertson: Marciacatsmo56; BMD; c-1851–1911.
141 Anc: Whitaker/Hamshaw Thomas Family Tree: Charlotte Martin; BMD; CCEd; *OA*.
142 Lucy Alleyne, viewed 3 August 2019: <http://www.alleynebarbados.org/>; CCEd; *Genealogies of Barbados Families: From Caribbeana and the Journal of the Barbados Museum and Historical Society*, 1983, p. 313; *OA*.
143 BMD; c-1841–1851, *GM*, vol. 171, 1842, p. 321.
144 WFP F198.
145 BMD; *CA*; CCEd.
146 Anc: Gorton Family Tree: Shibby_12; Anc: Mansfield Family Tree: suzywoopeterpat; BMD; c-1841–1871; *The Legal observer, or Journal of jurisprudence*, vol. 13 1837; UK, Articles of Clerkship, 1756–1874 for Frederick Herbert.
147 BMD; c-1841.
148 Anc: Hawkins Family Tree: ntiquvar2.
149 BMD; c-1841–1891.
150 BMD; Stanford Encyclopedia of Philosophy.
151 *DNB*.
152 B-1836; *DNB*.
153 *EB*.
154 BMD; *CA*; c-1841–1861.
155 Anc: Crutchley/Harvey/Cowan/Salkeld Family Tree: Martin Crutchley; BMD; c-1851–1861.
156 BMD; c-1851–1861, CCEd; *OA*.

157 *DNB*.
158 BMD; Munro Smith, G., *A History of the Bristol Royal Infirmary*, 1917; *The Registers of the Abbey Church of SS. Peter and Paul, Bath*, vol. 1, 1900, p. 279.
159 *CP*; *OA*.
160 BMD; Herbert, William: *The History of the Twelve Great Livery Companies of London*, 1836, p. 5; Rickerby, Joseph: *The City of London Poll-Book. Election 1837*, p. 53.
161 *CA*.
162 Berkeley Castle Muniments, Land at World's End Farm, Bevington, Reference: D4462/17/3; BMD; Davenport, Geoffrey, McDonald, Ian & Moss-Gibbons, Caroline: *The Royal College of Physicians and Its Collections: An Illustrated History*, 2001, p. 90; *MM*, vol. 26, 1808, p. 83.
163 Anc: Ritchie Family Tree: jenrit1; Anc: MACPHERSON Family Tree: martinmacp: Anc: RATHBONE Family Tree: pumaconcolor; BMD; *Bibliographer's Manual of Gloucestershire Literature*, 1891, p. 176; *Pigot's Directory*, 1830; *Reports of Cases Argued and Determined in the Court of King's Bench: With Tables of the Names of the Cases Argued and Cited, and the Principal Matters*, vol. 5, 1838, p. 11.
164 WFP F209.
165 *BMJ*; *Hunt*.
166 BMD; c-1851–1861; Haine, Colleen: *The Cloth Trade along the Painswick Stream*, GSIA, 1983; *VCH*, Gloucestershire.
167 Anc: The Austins of Bournstream: Clare Rees; Anc: Robins Family Tree: dradolphus; BMD; Fosbroke, Thomas Dudley: *Berkeley Manuscripts: Abstracts and Extracts of Smyth's Lives of the Berkeleys, Illustrative of Ancient Manners and the Constitution*, 1821, p. iv; Mills, Stephen: 'The Rise and Fall of Henry Hicks, Clothier of Eastington', reprinted from GSIA, 2002, pp. 19-28; Henry Hicks + A Note on the Family of the Reverend Edward Sparkes, Vicar of Clodock 1774-1813, viewed 3 August 2019: <http://www.ewyaslacy.org.uk/-/A-Note-on-the-Family-of-the-Reverend-Edward-Sparkes-Vicar-of-Clodock-1774-1813/1700s-1800s/nw_clo_1041>.
168 BMD; *Debrett 1840*; Hicks Beach, Mrs William: *A Cotswold Family—Hicks and Hicks Beach*; 1909.
169 BMD; *CB*; *GM*, vol. 157, 1835, p. 206.
170 Lewis/Hodek/Allen/Grisdale Family Tree: slewis571; BMD; *CA*; c-1851–1861.
171 BMD; Debrett 1840; Hicks Beach, Mrs William: *A Cotswold Family—Hicks and Hicks Beach*; 1909; *HP*.
172 BMD; Hicks Beach, Mrs William: *A Cotswold Family—Hicks and Hicks Beach*; 1909; *HP*.
173 *Ibid.*
174 *Ibid.*
175 BMD.
176 Anc: Parry-Fisher Family Tree: tlcompton; BMD; CCEd; *OA*; Wiltshire Archives.
177 Anc: Pope Family Tree: glennis thorpe; BMD; c-1841–1891.
178 Anc: Halford-Ashford Dynasty: Alison Ashford; BMD; c-1841–1881; *VCH*, Gloucester.
179 BMD; CCEd, *OA*.
180 Anc: Whole Family Tree: sales14536; Anc: Hillhouse and related Families: HRSatchel34; BMD; c-1841–1861; Hillhouse, Helen T. and Petigru, Laurens: *The Hillhouse Family* (South Carolina Branch), 1959; The Hilhouse Family of Bristol, viewed 3 August 2019: <http://onthetrailofhillhouse.blogspot.com/>; John Hilhouse, viewed 3 August 2019: <https://gw.geneanet.org/belfast8?lang=en&n=hillhouse&oc=0&p=john>.
181 *CP*.
182 BMD; *BMJ*; c-1841.
183 *BDA*, vol. 7, pp. 308-9; *CA*; *DNB*; Fenner, Theodore: *Opera in London: Views of the Press, 1785–1830*, 1994, p. 655.
184 *OA*; MI: St Edmund Hall Graveyard.
185 CCEd; *OA*.
186 *DNB*.
187 NA: 188—Shakespeare Birthplace Trust: Reference: ER 13/19/2.
188 *CP*.
189 *CA*, CCEd.
190 BMD; Bromsberrow Baptisms; CCEd; *CL*; c-1851–1861; *VCH*, Worcestershire.
191 Anc: COOPER Family Tree: domaco146; BMD; *Salisbury and Winchester Journal*, 14 September 1801.
192 BMD; *Hampshire Chronicle*, 1782; Mayo, Charles Herbert: *A Genealogical Account of the Mayo and Elton Families*, 1908.
193 Milhous, Judith: 'The Economics of Theatrical Dance in Eighteenth-Century London', *Theatre Journal*, vol. 55, 2003.
194 Devon Archives and Local Studies Service (South West Heritage Trust), Reference: Z1/44/22: Will (office copy) of John Hippisley; *OA*; *VCH*, Oxfordshire; Michael Allan Hippisley Matthews, the Hippisley family, viewed 3 August 2019: <http://www.boddyparts.co.uk/hippisleyfamily.htm>.
195 BMD; *CA*; *OA*, Michael Allan Hippisley Matthews, the Hippisley family, viewed 3 August 2019: <http://www.boddyparts.co.uk/hippisleyfamily.htm>.
196 *Ibid.*
197 *Ibid.*
198 BMD.
199 Bewley, Thomas: *Madness to Mental Illness: A History of the Royal College of Psychiatrists*, Online Archive 4; GA: Waller Family and Business Papers; *VCH*, Gloucestershire vol. 11.
200 Hitchman, Arthur F., and Starner, Delleen M.: *A History of Hitchman & Co. Limited 1796–1968*.
201 Wikipedia.
202 Wikipedia.
203 Wikipedia.
204 Anc: Caple/Campbell/Konopacky/ Fletcher: cjksr; BMD; c-1851–1861.
205 Anc: Williams Family Tree: mileham; BMD; c-1841–1851, 1861; London, Freedom of the City Admission Papers, 1681–1930.

206 BMD; *OA*.
207 BMD; *DNB*.
208 BMD; *OA*.
209 BMD; *CA*; Lancaster, B. (2004). 'Hodgson, Hodgson and Hodgson: clerical dynasties' *Bulletin Croydon Nat. Hist. Sci. Soc.*, 121: 2-4.
210 BMD; *OA*; *Slater's Directory*.
211 *LG*, part 2, 1827, p.2154; *The Legal Observer, Or, Journal of Jurisprudence*, vol. 8, 1834, p. 44; *Worcester Journal*, Thursday 25 October 1827.
212 BMD; *CA*; *OA*.
213 Wikipedia.
214 BMD; *CA*; *CL*.
215 BMD; British Museum: Worcester Porcelain Factory (Biographical details); *The European Magazine, and London Review*, vol. 76, 1819, p. 470; *LG*, vol. 2, 1820, p. 2177; Josiah Holdship, viewed 3 August 2019: <https://www.worcesterpeopleandplaces.org.uk/news/293/146/The-beginnings-of-the-Worcester-Porcelain-Company.html>.
216 Anc: Reinders Family Tree: michelle3990y7mailcom; Anc: Puflett Family Tree: lgilbert179; *CA*; *HP*; George Peter Holford, viewed 3 August 2019: <http://www.holfordtrust.com/the-holford-family/>.
217 *DNB*.
218 Anc: Ryrie/Oldfield/Elphinston/ Robertson: Marciacatsmo56; *HP*; *OA*; George Peter Holford, viewed 3 August 2019: <http://www.holfordtrust.com/the-holford-family/>.
219 BMD; *Liverpool Echo*, 8 May 2013; Malchow, Howard L.: *Gentlemen Capitalists: The Social and Political World of the Victorian Businessman*, 1992, p. 74; Gaskell, Elizabeth Cleghorn, Chapple, John, ed. & Wilson, Anita, ed., *Private Voices: The Diaries of Elizabeth Gaskell and Sophia Holland*, 1996.
220 BMD; c-1841–1871; *OA*.
221 *DNB*.
222 BMD; c-1851–1861; *Pigot's Directory to Cheltenham*, 1830.
223 Anc: Pigott Family Tree: RoyPigott900; BMD; c-1851; *OA*.
224 BMD; c-1851–1861; GA; *Hunt*.
225 BMD; *OA*; St Michael & All Angels, Tirley, viewed 3 August 2019: <http://places.wishful-thinking.org.uk/GLS/Tirley/StMichael6.html>.
226 BMD; thepeerage.com: person M, # 686549.
227 BMD; *HP*.
228 BMD; *OA*.
229 *DNB*.
230 *OA*.
231 CCEd; *OA*; West Sussex Record Office.
232 BMD; c-1841–1861.
233 BMD.
234 *CA*; *Williams*.
235 thepeerage.com: persons M, #480813 & 480814; WFP F196-F198.
236 BMD; *DNB*.
237 BMD; *BLG*.
238 *BLG*.
239 *DCB*.
240 BMD; *OA*.
241 BMD; CCEd, CL; *OA*.
242 BMD; thepeerage.com: person M, #683424; E&W Wills, NPC; *OA*; WFP F212, F220, F223.
243 Anc: George P. West and descendants: joycedrodgers; BMD; *Pigot's Directory*, 1830.
244 *CA*; *HP*.
245 *EB*.
246 BMD; CCEd, *OA*.
247 BMD.
248 *OA*.
249 *CP*.
250 BMD.
251 BMD; *OA*.
252 BMD; *CB*; CCEd; *OA*; thepeerage.com: person M, # 312798.
253 Anc: Hoskyns Family Tree: JanetHoskyns; BMD; *CB*; thepeerage.com: person M, # 312797.
254 BMD; *CP*.
255 BMD; Exeter working papers in British book trade history; 20: The British book trades 1784–1811: a tabulation of national directories; GA; *Hunt*; *OA*.
256 BMD; *The Christian's Monthly Magazine and Universal Review*, vol. 1, 1844, p. 489; *OA*; O'Hart, John: *The Irish Landed Gentry*, 1887, p. 641.
257 BMD; c-1851–1871.
258 Anc: Blackadder: shadow1984; Wikipedia: Sir William Houston, 1st baronet.
259 *CP*.
260 *CP*; *HP*.
261 *CP*.
262 *CP*.

263 GPA.
264 BMD; *Blackwood's Edinburgh Magazine*, vol. 2, 1818, p. 126; *Trans. BGAS*, vol. 7; *CA*; c-1851–1911; *AGB*; *DNB*; *GM*, vol. 182, 1847, p. 632; Macleod Genealogy; *OA*; *The Rifle Brigade Chronicle*, 1905; *The Spectator*, 6 October 1888, p. 23; UCL–Slaves: John Howell of Prinknash Park.
265 BMD; *DNB*.
266 BMD; *OA*; *VCH*, Warwickshire, vol. 5.
267 *DNB*.
268 *DNB*.
269 BMD; c-1841–1851; *VCH*, Worcestershire; *Worcestershire Chronicle*, Wednesday 10 May 1854.
270 Anc: Stafford Family Tree: davestafford165; BMD; c-1841–1861; *Parliamentary Papers*, vol. 20, 1846, p. 18.
271 *HP*; NPG.
272 *OA*.
273 Anc: Hughes Family Tree: Elisabeth Butcher; *DNB*; *OA*.
274 Anc: John Ashcroft Family Tree: John Ashcroft; *Minutes of Several Conversations at the ... Yearly Conference of the People Called Methodists* ..., 1843, p. 389.
275 *CB*.
276 BMD; c-1841–1861.
277 BMD; Bayley, Leslie W., 'Robert Hughes 1771–1827' (inaugural address to the Gloucestershire Masonic Society), 1952; Fosbroke, Thomas Dudley: *Abstracts of Records and Manuscripts Respecting the County of Gloucester*, 1807, p. 374; GA: Thomas and Robert Hughes, solicitors, of Cheltenham: Reference: D245; Hart, Gwen, *A History of Cheltenham*; Hembry, Phyllis May, *The English Spa, 1560–1815: A Social History*, 1990, pp. 182-90; *VCH*, Gloucestershire, Cheltenham; WFP F173–F176.
278 *DNB*.
279 *HP*; *VCH*, Oxfordshire.
280 *The British Critic, and Quarterly Theological Review*, 1827, p. 257; *MM*, vol. 36, 1832, p. 466; *OA*; *A Synopsis of the Members of the English Bar*, 1835, p. 27.
281 WFP F197.
282 BMD; *CP*; *The New Peerage; Or, Present State of the Nobility of England, Scotland, and Ireland*, 1769.
283 *HP*.
284 c-1851–1861.
285 *CA*; CCEd.
286 Anc: Jones/Stephens Family Tree: Stephen Jones; BMD; c-1841–1861.
287 BMD.
288 BMD; c-1841–1891.
289 BMD; c-1841–1891.
290 *CB*; *CP*; Wingerworth MI.
291 The Hunt family is dealt with extensively in vol. 1, *The Nomad*, pp. 133-142. The prime source was the website: Hunt of Boreatton, Released 28 January 2003, Hunt Family Records, but this website was not available when checked 3 August 2019. The records of the Hunt family of Boreatton are held at Shropshire Archives. A large variety of additional minor sources have been accessed but not catalogued, including BMD and census records.
292 Anc: Green/Ryan/Bodington Family Tree; GA—Gloucester City Deeds. Guildhall Library; Captains Register of Lloyds; Records of Sun Fire Office; Upton St Leonards Village History; Birchall, Dearman, Verey, David, ed.: *The Diary of a Victorian Squire*, 1983.
293 MI: Charlton Kings; *OA*.
294 Anc: Evans/White Family Tree: Anne Evans; BMD; c-1861–1891.
295 BMD; c-1851; *Pigot's Directory, Oxfordshire*, 1830.
296 *CB*; David Hunter-Blair, viewed 3 August 2019: <https://www.clanmacfarlanegenealogy.info/genealogy/TNGWebsite/getperson.php?personID=I37849&tree=CC>.
297 *CB*.
298 *DNB*; *OA*.
299 BMD; *OA*.
300 BMD; *OA*.
301 BMD; *OA*.
302 BMD; *OA*.
303 BMD; *CA*; CCEd; c-1841–1861, 1911.
304 WFP F199.
305 *AGB*.
306 *DNB*; *HP*.
307 BMD; Julius Hutchinson, viewed 3 August 2019: <https://www.werelate.org/wiki/Person:Julius_Hutchinson_(1)>.
308 BMD; *OA*.
309 BMD.
310 Anc: Morris Family Tree: Judith Morris; Anc: Mobey Family Tree: GaryJMobey; BMD; c-1841–1891, 1911; Huxley, Leonard, ed.: *Life and Letters of Thomas Henry Huxley*, 2011, p. 27; *Medical Times*, vol. 8, 1843, p. 118.
311 BMD; *CA*.
312 Anc: Hide family Draycott, Blockley, Stow: johnhyde193; BMD; c-1841–1871.
313 *OA*; *VCH*, Gloucestershire.
314 GA; *OA*; *VCH*, Gloucestershire; *Williams*.

Letter I

1 thepeerage.com: person M, # 241692; WFP F196.
2 Guildhall Library: Records of Sun Fire Office.
3 August Iffland, viewed 14 March 2020: <http://www.theatrehistory.com/german/iffland001.html>.
4 BMD; c-1851; E&W Wills—will of Alexander Iles; *VCH*, Gloucestershire, vol. 7, Fairford, 1981.
5 BMD; *CA*; c-1851.
6 BMD; c-1841.
7 BMD; c-1841.
8 BMD; c-1841.
9 BMD; Brendon, Vyvyen: *Children of the Raj*, 2015; Charles Imhoff: Lenckos, Elisabeth, East India Company at Home, 1757–1857, viewed 4 August 2019: <https://blogs.ucl.ac.uk/eicah/daylesford-case-study/>; *DNB*; Index of Irish Death Notices; *Notes & Queries*, 1936; Hawes, Christopher J.: *Poor Relations: The Making of a Eurasian Community in British India, 1773–1833*, 1996, p. 185; *VCH*, Gloucestershire.
10 *DNB*; Gleig, Revd G. R.: *Memoirs of the Life of Warren Hastings, first Governor-General of Bengal*, 1841.
11 *DNB*.
12 *DNB*.
13 BMD; *DNB*; *OA*.
14 Anc: Ryrie/Oldfield/Elphinston/Robertson: Marciacatsmo56; BMD; c-1841–1851; *OA*.
15 Anc: More/Taylor: suemore68; BMD; *CA*.
16 Anc: More/Taylor: suemore68; BMD; *CA*; c-1851–1861.
17 BMD; *OA*.
18 *Allgemeine musikalische Zeitung*, vol. 4, 1801, p. 295; Sparr, Kenneth, 'The Guitar in Sweden until the Middle of the 19th Century', viewed 4 August 2019.
19 BMD; CCEd; *CL*.
20 BMD; CCEd; *MM*, vol. 41; *OA*.
21 BMD; Charles Chamberlayne Irvine, viewed 4 August 2019: <https://gw.geneanet.org/ablondet?lang=en&n=irvine&oc=0&p=Laurence>; International Genealogical Index; *Royal Navy Officers* 1849.
22 Anc: Janes + Thickett Families: Bob Janes; BMD.
23 Anc: Ryrie/Oldfield/Elphinston/Robertson: Marciacatsmo56; BMD; CCEd; *OA*; Thomas Welch Hunt: Major, Joanne, viewed 4 August 2019: <https://georgianera.wordpress.com/tag/thomas-welch-hunt/>.

Letter J

1 BMD; c-1851–1861; *Hunt*.
2 Anc: Turner-Powell Family Tree: pdbruxner_randall; *OA*.
3 Mantzius, Karl: *A History of Theatrical Art in Ancient and Modern Time;* vol. VI *Classicism and Romanticism*, 1937.
4 BMD; *CA*; CCEd.
5 BMD; c-1841–1861.
6 Anc: German-Geach Family Tree: csgerman; Gloucestershire, England, Prison Records, 1728–1914.
7 BMD; *DNB*; *OA*.
8 *Hunt*.
9 BMD; c-1841–1851.
10 BMD; c-1841–1861.
11 BMD; *Cotswold Life*, January 2011.
12 BMD; *OA*; thepeerage.com: person F, #578786.
13 CCEd.
14 BMD; *CA*.
15 BMD; c-1841–1861.
16 BMD; c-1841–1861.
17 BMD; *CA*; CCEd; Jeaffreson, John Cordy: *A Book of Recollections*, 1894; *DNB*.
18 *CA*; Perry, Revd Frank: 'Chaplains in the HEIC 1805 to 1835', *The Church In Madras*, 1904.
19 c-1861; Catalogue of the library of St Bartholomew's Hospital and College, 1893.
20 *Littlebury's Directory and Gazetteer of Herefordshire*, 1876–77.
21 Wikipedia.
22 *DNB*.
23 Anc: Stratford Family Tree: Peter Stratford; BMD; c-1841–1851; *The Jurist*, vol. 6, 1843, p. 45.
24 *CA*; University of Hull, Landed Family and Estate Papers Subject Guide.
25 Murder Confessions 1715–1900: A Preliminary Typology, Watson, Cassie, viewed 4 August 2019: <https://legalhistorymiscellany.com/2018/06/07/murder-confessions-1730-1900-a-preliminary-typology/>.
26 BMD; c-1851–1861, 1881.
27 Anc: 2014-04-10: 1876win; BMD; *B-1838-4*; c-1851–1861; NPC.
28 Anc: Howman Law McPherson: ChristineParsons952; BMD; c-1851–1871; *Cheltenham Chronicle*, 17 Feb 1853.
29 CCEd; *OA*.
30 Anc: Garmston/Hughes of Worcester: Ken Gamston; CCEd, *OA*.

31 Anc: Ryrie/Oldfield/Elphinston/Robertson: Marciacatsmo56; *DNB*; thepeerage.com: person M, #170913.
32 *CA*; *CP*; *DNB*; *HP*.
33 Anc: Owen, Ginny: gowen160; BMD; CCEd; *OA*.
34 *DNB*.
35 BMD.
36 *CA*; PI: email information from Thomas Jenner-Fust; Waddams, S. M.: *Law, Politics and the Church of England* (the Career of Stephen Lushington 1782–1873), 1992.
37 Anc: Rule Family Tree: Stephen Rule; BMD: Non-Conformist and Non-Parochial Registers, 1567–1970; c-1851–1861, 1881; Melville's 1858 *Directory of Kent*.
38 Public Monument and Sculpture Association, National Recording Project.
39 Anc: Ingram and Morris big working tree: Angela Ingram; *CA*.
40 Anc: Newman McHaffie Tree: VickyNewman69; *OA*.
41 *CB*.
42 *DNB*.
43 Anc: Stouffer Family Tree: jdepatta1; BMD; c-1841; Green, Chris, ed., *The History of Alstone*, vol. 1; Jessop's Nursery, Cheltenham, viewed 4 August 2019: <http://xmera.co.uk/garden/nurseries/Jessops.html>.
44 CCEd; *OA*.
45 *DNB*.
46 *B-1838-4*.
47 BMD; c-1841–1901.
48 BMD; *B-1845*; *HP*; UCL–Slaves.
49 *GM*, 1828; *OA*.
50 *CA*; CCEd; *OA*; *VCH*, Gloucestershire, Lydney, Newnham-on-Severn; Edward Jones, Lydney, viewed 4 August 2019: <http://englishbuildings.blogspot.com/2012/10/lydney-gloucestershire.html>.
51 BMD.
52 BMD.
53 *The Annual Register*, 1807, p. 445; *CA*; CCEd; c-1841–1851; *GM*, vol. 75 part 1; *Sporting Magazine*, 1834; *VCH*, Gloucestershire, Lydney, Newnham-on-Severn.
54 *Universal British Directory*, Cheltenham, 1791; WFP F200.
55 BMd; *OA*.
56 *B-1836*; CCEd; *OA*.
57 BMD; c-1841–1851.
58 *The Court magazine and Belle Assemblée and Monthly Critic*, vol. 26, p. 36.
59 *CA*; CCEd; *GM*, vol. 119, 1816, p. 278.
60 *OA*.
61 BMD; c-1841–1891.
62 *OA*.
63 *OA*.
64 *OA*.
65 GPA.
66 GPA.
67 *CA*; *Williams*.
68 *DNB*.
69 BMD; c-1851; *Slater's Directory for Cheltenham*, 1859.

Letter K

1 *Grove*.
2 *DNB*.
3 BMD; Freemasons' United Grand Lodge of England 1813–1836, *Register of Admissions: Grand Stewards Lodge*-274 London 'A'; *The Foreign Office List, Forming a Complete British Diplomatic and Consular Handbook With Maps*, 1865.
4 *CA*.
5 BMD; c-1841–1861; *OA*.
6 BMD; *DNB*.
7 *B-1841*; p. 34; *B-1871-1*, p. 215; *GM*, vol. 84, 1814; *GM*, vol. 142, 1827, p. 283; Swanzy, Henry Biddall, *The Families of French of Belturbet and Nixon of Fermanagh, and their Descendants*, 1908.
8 BMD; c-1841–1851; *Pigot's Directory*, 1830; GA: Ref. Q/RID/2: Minutes of proceedings in cases of insolvent debtors under Acts of 5 George IV, c.61, and 7 George IV, c.57.
9 *DNB*.
10 *DNB*.
11 *DNB*.
12 BMD; c-1841–1851.
13 BMD; MI: Urchfont parish church; *Wiltshire Parish Registers*.
14 c-1841–1851; GPA.
15 *DNB*.

16 Anc: Sian Stephens Family Tree: Sian Stephens; BMD; *CA*; CCEd.
17 Anc: Brown Family Tree: davidbrown861; BMD; *DNB*; *The Belfast News Letter*, 3 September 1866; UCL–Slaves; *VCH*, Warwickshire, Austrey.
18 Anc: Franzitta Family Tree: scseke; BMD; c-1851–1891; *MM*, vol. 15, 1825, p. 189.
19 Gloucestershire, England, Prison Records, 1728–1914 for John Kendrick; *LG*, part 2, 1824, p. 1161.
20 Anc: LaurieFT290409: ElondonCricket; *CA*.
21 Anc: charles-pratt-kennedy; BMD; *Slater's Directory*.
22 *Debrett 1824-II*, p. 1013; GALLERY, Margaret, The Kenny Family of Treanmanagh, viewed 4 August 2019: <http://www.clarelibrary.ie/eolas/coclare/genealogy/don_tran/fam_his/kenny_family_treanmanagh_1650_1800.htm>.
23 Upton-upon-Severn, *Billings Directory*, 1855.
24 *CP*.
25 BMD; c-1851–1861.
26 *DNB*.
27 Anc: Keen Family Tree; CCEd, *GM*, vol. 93 part 2, 1823; vol. 27, 1829; Herefordshire Archive and Records Centre: Mortgages of Moreton Magna and Moreton Parva made by William Bird; *OA*.
28 BMD; CCEd; *OA*.
29 *DNB*; *OA*.
30 Anc: Temple Family Tree: lilianmidwinter1; BMD; c-1851–1891; Gloucestershire, England, Prison Records, 1728–1914 for Hannah Kilby: Registers of Prisoners the County Gaol 1854–1860.
31 BMD; c-1851.
32 BMD; Kimber family of Sapperton, viewed 4 August 2019: <https://www.rootschat.com/forum/index.php?topic=680491.0>; thepeerage.com: person F, #565752.
33 Anc: Painter family tree: mikepainter1949; BMD; c-1841.
34 *CP*.
35 *DNB*.
36 BMD; *CP*; thepeerage.com: person F, #117592; cracroftspeerage.co.uk: Lifford.
37 BMD; *CA*; CCEd; c-1851–1861.
38 MANDER, Charles Nicholas ed. *The Owlpen Papers*—'The Memoirs of Alan Cornwall'.
39 Anc: Ryrie/Oldfield/Elphinston/Robertson: Marciacatsmo56; *DNB*.
40 *DNB*; MANDER, Charles Nicholas ed. *The Owlpen Papers*—'The Memoirs of Alan Cornwall'.
41 *CB*.
42 *OA*.
43 MI: Leckhampton.
44 *Grove*; Maria Kirchgessner, viewed 4 August 2019: <https://www.sophie-drinker-institut.de/kirchgessner-marianne>.
45 *BLG*.
46 Luise Concordia Kloch, viewed 4 August 2019: <https://data.cerl.org/thesaurus/cnp01939802>.
47 *HP*.
48 BIEDRZYNSKI, Effi, *Goethe's Weimar*, 1994, p. 251.
49 BND.
50 BMD; *OA*.
51 Anc: Stewart Walters MacEachern Smith: SharonStewartDuff; *CA*.
52 *OA*.
53 BMD; c-1851–1891; *OA*.
54 Anc: harding Family Tree: superjan11; BMD; c-1851–1871; Shakespeare Centre Library and Archive.
55 *DNB*.
56 *DNB*.
57 *DNB*.
58 PERRY, Frank, *SPG Missionary: The Church in Madras*, 1904.
59 AGB.
60 *Grove*; MERCK, Johann Heinrich: *Ulrike Leuschner: Briefwechsel*, vol. 2.
61 *AGB*.
62 *AGB*.

Letter L

1 FELTHAM, John: *The Picture of London, for 1802*, 1807, p. 262; *Anecdotes of Music, Historical and Biographical: in a series of letters from a gentleman to his daughter*, 1814, p. 351.
2 All England & Wales, Criminal Registers, 1791–1892; Anc: The Tree of Life: peony15934; BMD.
3 WFP F188–F221; *Transactions of the Geological Society*, vols 1-2, 1814, p. 540.
4 Anc: Lait Family Tree: gpollard124; Anc: LAIT/GRAY Family Tree (www.yvonnereeds.com): moonbear_1; BMD.
5 *OA*.
6 Anc: Procter Family Tree: martinwolfgang1; *Antiques Trade Gazette*, lot 77, Dix Noonan Webb, 25 March 2015; BMD; c-1851–1861; *GM*, 1809; *MM*, vol. 27, 1809 & vol. 29, 1810.
7 BMD; *DNB*.
8 Wikipedia.

9 *DNB*.
10 Anc: Gange of Bickenhall Family Tree: jvg73; BMD; c-1841; UK, Poll Books and Electoral Registers, 1538–1893, Clifton 1830, p. 34.
11 BMD; c-1841; MI: parish church of St Peter and St Paul, Northleach.
12 Anc: Robson Family Tree: gompf1; BMD; CCEd; *OA*.
13 BMD; British Regimental Registers of Service, 1756–1900; *The India Office and Burma Office List*, 1842; *LG*, part 1, 1838, p. 1342; Stunt, Timothy C. F., *The Elusive Quest of the Spiritual Malcontent: Some Early Nineteenth-Century Ecclesiastical Mavericks*, 2015, p. 230.
14 Anc: Helen's Family Tree: Helen Evans; BMD; c-1841–1851.
15 Anc: Morgans Family Tree: Bobbie1959; BMD; *OA*.
16 BMD; c-1871– 1891; *OA*; Parker, J. H., *The Library of Anglo-Catholic Theology: Harmonia Apostolica, or, Two dissertations*, 1842, p. 11.
17 *DNB*.
18 BMD; c-1861.
19 BMD; *CP*; *HP*; *OA*; *The Register Book of Marriages belonging to the Parish St George, Hanover Square*, 1897; Sardsden House, viewed 4 August 2019: <https://historicengland.org.uk/listing/the-list/list-entry/1000503>.
20 BMD; *DNB*; WFP F234 8 April 1824: '...rec'd a strange Letter from Miss Jane Langton'.
21 Archives of Ontario; *CA*; Speight, Henry, *Upper Wharfedale*, 1900.
22 *Grove*.
23 BMD; c-1851.
24 Anc: Field Churchill Fletcher: Lavida85; BMD; c-1841–1891.
25 c-1851; *The American Farmer*, vol. 3, 1822, p. 148; *The Gardeners' Chronicle and Agricultural Gazette*, part 1, 1844, p. 516; *The Farmer's Magazine*, 1841, p. 129; *VCH*, Oxfordshire: Broadwell.
26 BMD; c-1841–1851; *DNB*; England & Wales, National Probate Calendar.
27 Freiherr von Lyncker, Karl Wilhelm Heinrich: *Ich diente am Weimarer Hof: Aufzeichnungen aus der Goethezeit*, 1997, p. 315.
28 BMD; *CP*.
29 Anc: Jasmine Holt: jazziholt; Anc: RJohnsonUKWilly: richardjohnson111; BMD; c-1841–1851; *Hunt*.
30 BM; Earwaker, J. P., *The History of The Ancient Parish of Sandbach*, 1890, p. 143; *GM*, vol. 193, 1853, p. 442; *OA*; Wikipedia—John Latham FRS MD.
31 Anc: Dorian Zanker Family Tree: Dorian Zanker; *HP*.
32 *OA*.
33 *CA*; *CP*; *DNB*; *HP*.
34 Anc: pole Family Tree: sheilathomas170; *CA*.
35 Anc: Thomas Lawler music career: posted 5 October 2012 by Mark Slater; BMD; c-1851–1891; Ganzl, Kurt: *Victorian Vocalists*, 2017, p. 532.
36 Anc: Lawley: Emma Marianne; *CB*.
37 *DNB*.
38 Anc: Charles Lawrence family tree: assemblyorder; BMD; *DNB*; UCL–Slaves; Watkins, John: *A Biographical Dictionary of the Living Authors of Great Britain and Ireland*, 1816, p. 198; WFP F197 & F198.
39 Anc: Mee/Muggeridge family tree: HillsForest; *OA*; *VCH*, Gloucestershire, Andoversford.
40 *DNB*.
41 Anc: Forsyth tomb: Peter Shirley; BMD; c-1841–1851; *GM*; GA; *OA*.
42 Agnew, David Carnegie A., *Protestant Exiles from France, Chiefly in the Reign of Louis XIV: Or, The Huguenot Refugees and Their Descendants in Great Britain and Ireland*, vol. 2, 1886, p. 456; Anc: Blomfield family tree: hugoblomfield; BMD; *CA*; Jenkins, Nicholas, W. H. Auden 'Family Ghosts', viewed 4 August 2019: <https://web.stanford.edu/~njenkins/archives/07commentary_w_h_auden_-_family_ghosts_website/index.html>.
43 Anc: Mick Dodge Family Tree: mickdodge1; BMD; thepeerage.com: person M, #533340.
44 *DNB*.
45 BMD; c-1871; *Dublin University Magazine*, vol. 5, 1835, p. 368; *Elizabeth College Magazine* (Guernsey), obituary, 1906; Ancestors of William Hirzel Le Marchant, viewed 4 August 2019: <http://fredric.co.nf/3576.htm>.
46 Anc: Blomfield family tree: hugoblomfield; BMD; c-1841–1901.
47 *Ibid*.
48 Anc: Duffell Family Tree: katys2004; BMD; *OA*.
49 *Ibid*.
50 *Ibid*.
51 BMD; *OA*; The John Rylands University Library; Wiltshire and Swindon Archives, Diocese of Salisbury.
52 *CB*.
53 Anc: Laura Kaatz's Genealogy Project; BMD; Hampshire Allegations for Marriage Licences vol. 1, p. 472; *OA*.
54 Oliver, George: *Collections, illustrating the history of the Catholic religion in the counties of Cornwall, Devon, Dorset, Somerset, Wilts, and Gloucester*, 1857.
55 *DNB*.
56 Austin, Roland: *Catalogue of the Gloucestershire Collection*, 1928; BMD; c-1841–1851.
57 Anc: Larry Tyrell; *BLG*; BMD; *CB*; Centre for Buckinghamshire Studies—Danesfield Estate, Medmenham & Centre for Buckinghamshire Studies—the Lee Papers of Hartwell; *Debrett 1835*; *The European Magazine, and London Review*, vol. 61, 1812, p. 498; *GM*, 1836; *HP*; Lipscomb, George, *The History and Antiquities of the County of Buckingham*, vol. 2, p. 309; Pallot's Marriage Index for England: 1780–1837; *VCH*, Buckinghamshire, vol. 2, 1908; WFP F176.

58 *Ibid.*
59 Roth, Cecil: article, *The Spectator*, 30 April 1937, Page 8.
60 Anc: Dilts Family Tree: cherylmcmanus57; *B-1838-4*, p. 552; BMD.
61 Anc: Stephen Tate Family Tree: sctate35; BMD.
62 BMD; c-1851; *CB*; Scotland, Select Marriages, 1561–1910; thepeerage.com: person F, #48847.
63 Anc: Lefever Family Tree: sallyewin51; BMD; c-1851.
64 Adam Leffler, viewed 4 August 2019: <operone.de>; Lysons, Daniel & Amott, John, *The Origin and Progress of the Meeting of the Three Choirs of Gloucester, Worcester & Hereford, and of the Charity Connected with It*, 1895.
65 BMD; GPA.
66 Market Lavington Museum; *VCH*, Wiltshire.
67 BMD; *OA*; Reeve, Henry, ed., *The Greville Memoirs*, 1874.
68 BMD; *OA*.
69 *CP*; *HP*.
70 Anc: Bruce Erickson Family Tree: Joyce Erickson; *BLG*; *CA*; *CB*; *DNB*.
71 Anc: Sally Scott Family Tree: sallyscott638; BMD; *B-1838-2*; *B-1846-1*; *CA*; Glanville-Richards, William Urmston Searle, *The Registers of Windlesham, Surrey, 1677–1793*, 1881, p. 57.
72 Anc: Moore family tree: mmijj60; BMD; *B-1838-2*; *B-1846-1*.
73 *Ibid.*; *DNB*.
74 BMD; c-1851–1861; GA; *LG*; *VCH*, Gloucestershire, vol. 6.
75 BMD; Combe Hay MI; *HP*; Shirley, E. P., *Stemmata Shirleiana*, 1873, p. 224; *VCH*, Somerset, vol. 1.
76 Adlestrop MI; Anc: Hoskyns Family Tree: JanetHoskyns; Jane Austen's Family, viewed 4 August 2019: <https://wc.rootsweb.com/cgi-bin/igm.cgi?op=GET&db=janeausten&id=I136>; BMD; Jones, John, *Balliol College: A History*, 1997; *OA*; WFP F173–F235.
77 BMD; *B-1847-2*, p. 1592; *CP*; Lodge, Edmund, *The Peerage of the British Empire*, 1855, p. 339; *OA*.
78 Anc: Fear & Gundry2: davrhifear; *LG*, 2 December 1853, p. 3569;
79 *Henry Harper's Cheltenham Directory & Guide*, 1844; *The Jurist*, vol. 11, part 2, 1848, p. 138; *The Spectator*, 21 November 1846, p. 19.
80 *CP*; WFP F192.
81 *B-1855*, p. 1653; *HP*; Public Record Office of Northern Ireland: Leslie Papers.
82 *Ibid.*; WFP F206.
83 BMD; c-1841, 1861; Fisher, Paul Hawkins, *Notes and Recollections of Stroud*, 1891; *MATB*, p. 276; MacLean, Lachlan, *An Historical and Genealogical Account of the Clan Maclean: From Its First Settlement at Castle Duart in the Isle of Mull, to the Present Period*, 1838, p. 279, *VCH*, Gloucestershire, vol. 11; Welch, R. Courtenay, *The Harrow School Register, 1801–1900*, 1894.
84 *CP; DNB*.
85 BMD; c-1841–1851; *MM*, vol. 9, 1825; *OA*.
86 BMD; CCEd; c-1841–1861; *OA*.
87 thepeerage.com: person M, #188637 and M, #188638.
88 BMD; c-1851–1861; *Slater's Cheltenham Directory*, 1858-59.
89 Archives Wales: Bangor University: Henllys Manuscripts; Griffith, John Edward, *Pedigrees of Angelsey and Caernarvonshire Families*, 1914.
90 *HP*.
91 CCEd; *OA*.
92 Anc: Drury Newnham(1)(1): jken49; *OA*; cracroftspeerage.co.uk.
93 BMD; c-1851–1861.
94 Anc: Rimell Family: Chastyn407; BMD.
95 *DNB*.
96 Anc: Henzey, Tyzack & Tittery: wrag44; BMD; c-1851–1861.
97 *B-1846-1*; CricketArchive Oracles; GA; Lancashire Record Office: Littledale Estate in Caton; Reminiscences of Miss Isabel Dobson (1806–1882).
98 BMD; c-1841–1851; CricketArchive Oracles; *LG*; *OA*.
99 Burgess, Geoffrey, and Hedrick, Peter 'The Oldest English Oboe Reeds? An Examination of Nineteen Surviving Examples', *The Galpin Society Journal*, vol. 42 (August, 1989), p. 34; Ennulat, Egbert M., 'William Ling, a Rediscovered English Mozart?' *Journal of Musicologi*, vol. 5, 1984.
100 *CB*; GA; Lippincott, James, *The Lippincotts in England and America*, 1909; Trinity College, Bristol.
101 *DNB*.
102 *Ibid.*
103 *CA*.
104 Anc: Avery Family Tree: Rosemary Avery; BMD; CCEd; *OA*; Juliet Louise Littlehales, viewed 4 August 2019: <http://www.thejenners.f2s.com/getperson.php?personID=I3514&tree=Littlehales>.
105 *Ibid.*; BMD; CCEd; *OA*.
106 *Hunt*.
107 Anc: Wilson Family Tree: RJordan79; *DNB*.
108 BMD; B-1846-1; GA; Mann, J. de L., *The Cloth Industry in the West of England from 1640 to 1880*, 1971; Pigot's Directory, 1842; Tann, Jennifer, *Gloucestershire Woollen Mills*, 1967.
109 *B-1838-4*, p. 678; *VCH*, Oxfordshire.
110 Anc: Jukes/Child Family Tree: KathrynJukes1; BMD;
111 Anc: Atkinson Taylor DNA Family Tree: Ross Buddle Atkinson; Anc: John Sharp Family Tree: howard_nicholson1; BMD; *B-1847-1*,

p. 47; *B-1875-1*, p. 159; *B-1885*, p. 642; *B-1898-1*, p. 57; c-1871; *Descent and Alliances of Croslegh: or Crossle, or Crossley, of Scaitcliffe; and Coddington of Oldbridge; and Evans, of Eyton Hall*, 1904, p. 363; Dixon, J. 'William Sharp, Surgeon' *Notes & Queries*, 22 June 1867; *DNB*: Thomas Barwick Lloyd Baker; GA: Reference: D3549, Personal and Estate Papers of the Lloyd-Baker Family of Hardwicke Court and their Predecessors; *Gloucestershire Echo*, 21 October 1915; Temple, Philip, *Northern Clerkenwell and Pentonville*, 2008, p. 267.

112 *DNB*.

113 *HP*.

114 Anc: Coulson Family Tree: Janda van der Veen; *CA*.

115 BMD; *OA*; website: Polly Holmes à Court.

116 Anc: holland Family Tree: Midwife79; BMD; *DNB*; Temperley, Nicholas, *Musicians of Bath and Beyond: Edward Loder (1809–1865) and His Family*, 2016.

117 BMD; c-1841–1861.

118 *HP*; Wikipedia.

119 BMD; *HP*.

120 BMD; c-1841–1851, 1861, 1871; *Pigot's Directory*, 1840.

121 BMD; c-1851–1891; *Pigot's Directory for Skipton*, 1829.

122 BMD; c-1851–1861.

123 *CA*.

124 *DNB*.

125 *EB*.

126 *Ibid.*

127 Anc: Our family Bolter, Melvin, Spinks and Mclaren: brendaannc; BMD; c-1841–1851; The Gloucestershire Lovegroves, viewed 4 August 2019: <http://lovegrove.one-name.net/famhiststemp/histories/family2temp/gloucstemp.html>; *VCH*, Gloucestershire, vol. 7, Cranham.

128 Anc: Our family Bolter, Melvin, Spinks and Mclaren: brendaannc; BMD; c-1841–1881.

129 *DNB*.

130 BMD; *MATB*.

131 Anc: melhuish of washfield: keithj146; *CA*; *The Bath and Cheltenham Gazette*, 29 January 1817; Curl, James Stevens, and Wilson, Susan, *The Oxford Dictionary of Architecture*, 2015, p. 558.

132 *Kelly's Titled, Landed & Official Classes*, 1890; Ruvigny de Raineval, Marquis, Melville Henry Massue, Plantagenet Roll of the Blood Royal: vol. 1.

133 Anc: Hewitt Family Tree: silversol; c-1841; *Pigot's Directory for Gloucester*, 1830.

134 Centre for Buckinghamshire Studies: solicitors' records relating to the estates of the Cavendish family of Thornton Hall, Bucks and Crakemarsh, Staffs; *HP*; *OA*.

135 *CA*; *HP*.

136 *CA*; *HP*.

137 Robison, John, *Proofs of a Conspiracy Against all the Religions and Governments of Europe Carried on in the Secret Meetings of Free Masons, Illuminati and Reading Societies. Collected from Good Authorities*, 1798.

138 CCEd; CERL Thesaurus: Charles Lucas; *DNB*; *OA*.

139 BMD; Blacker, Beaver H., *Gloucestershire Notes & Queries*, 1890; Crisp, Frederick Arthur, *Visitation of England and Wales*, 1921.

140 Anc: Walker Lean Family Tree: Patrick Walker; BMD; *DNB*.

141 BMD; c-1841–1851.

142 *CA*.

143 *BLG*; *OA*.

144 BMD; c-1841–1881; Gloucestershire, England, Prison Records, 1728–1914 for Charles Lupton, prisoners confined at Northleach House of Correction to 19 March 1847; NA, ADM 157/56/50: description: Folios 50-53. Heneage Lupton, born Sussex: Attestation papers to serve in the Royal Marines.

145 *OA*.

146 *CA*.

147 *CA*.

148 *HP*.

149 Anc: Karl Gumpper; BMD; *HP*; thepeerage.com: person M, #13087.

150 *Hunt*.

151 Anc: Calvert and Buxton 2014: gazetteer; *GM*, 1825; Blacker, Beaver H., *Gloucestershire Notes & Queries*; c-1841–1851; GA; Slyfield, Brian, *Aspects of Horsham's Past*; *VCH*, Gloucestershire.

152 *DNB*; Fleming, Lindsay, *Memoir and Select Letters of Samuel Lysons*, 1934.

153 Anc: Palfrey Family Tree: SusieBlackie56; BMD; *B-1871-1*; c-1841–1851, 1861, *DNB*; Fleming, Lindsay, *Memoir and Select Letters of Samuel Lysons*, 1934, *GM*, vol. 217, 1864; Pollock, Arthur William Alsager, *The United Service Magazine*, vol. 70, 1852.

154 BMD; *B-1898*; *CA*; *DNB*.

Letter M

1 Anc: Elliott Family Tree: AnneElliott27; BMD; *DNB*; WFP F208.

2 *B-1899*; Drenagh House, viewed 5 August 2019: <http://lordbelmontinnorthernireland.blogspot.com/2014/04/drenagh-house.html>.

3 BMD.

4 WFP F189.

5 Anc: Dightons of Clifford Chambers: John Cooper; *B-1847-2*, p. 803; *B-1898-1*, p. 966; Jon Hoyle, Gloucestershire County Council, Forest of Dean Archaeological Survey, 2008.

6 Duff Brown, James, and Stratton, Stephen Samuel, *British Musical Biography: a Dictionary of Musical Artists, Authors and Composers, born in Britain and its Colonies*, 1897.

7 GPA.

8 CA.

9 *DNB*.

10 William Lyon Mackenzie, The Canadian Encyclopedia, viewed 5 August 2019: <https://www.thecanadianencyclopedia.ca/en/article/mackenzie-william-lyon>.

11 BMD; c-1851, 1891; *London Standard*, Thursday, 8 June 1854, p. 2; Yorkshire Archaeological Society: H. L. Bradfer-Lawrence Collection.

12 *BDA*, vol. 10, 1984.

13 Neath Antiquarian Society.

14 BMD; c-1841–1851; *VCH*, Gloucestershire, vol. 10, King's Stanley.

15 *The Literary Gazette and Journal of the Belles Lettres, Arts, Sciences, &c.*, 1838; *OA*.

16 *Blackwood's Magazine*, vol. 1; Earl of Dunmore Published accounts, recited in *Gaelic Soup*, 17 February 2011; Knox, John, An Account of Harris, 1787; Mackenzie, Alexander, *History of the Macleods with Genealogies of the Principal Families of the Name*, 1889; Alexander Norman MacLeod, viewed 5 August 2019: <http://www.macleodgenealogy.com/ACMS/D0001/I2276.html>; *OA*.

17 *CA*.

18 BMD; c-1841–1851; Earl of Dunmore Published accounts, recited in *Gaelic Soup*, 17 February 2011; Knox, John, *An Account of Harris*, 1787; *The Naval and Military Magazine*, 1827.

19 *OA*.

20 *B-1899*, p. 288; Ryan, John, *The History and Antiquities of the County of Carlow*, 1833, p. 381; Charles Moore McMahon, viewed 5 August 2019: <http://www.genealogy.kirkpatrickaustralian.com/archives/getperson.php?personID=I14171&tree=TKA>.

21 *DNB*.

22 Anc: Goddard-Flicker-Mellish-Harvey: Chris Goddard; c-1841–1871; *OA*.

23 Public Record Office of Northern Ireland.

24 Anc: Grafton Pollard Extended Tree: cefyngrafton; *B-1898*; *CA*.

25 BMD; *GM*, 1834.

26 BMD; *The Law Advertiser*, vol. 8; *Pigot's Directory*, 1830.

27 *BLG*; Finley, Reginald Mainwaring, *Short history of the Mainwaring family*, 1890; *OA*.

28 *CA*.

29 Anc: Warren Lloyd Family Tree: warrenlloyd56; *B-1898*; Brock, Isaac, and Tupper, Ferdinand Brock, ed., *The Life and Correspondence of Sir Isaac Brock*, 1845, p. 263.

30 *CP*; *DNB*.

31 *DNB*.

32 Anc: Sandcraft Family Tree: jsandcraft; c-1841–1871; GPA.

33 Anc: Hookham Family Tree: Sue_Savidge; *CA*; c-1841–1871.

34 *DNB*.

35 Anc: jonas-malden_35678360; BMD.

36 *DNB*.

37 Brandt, George W., *German and Dutch Theatre, 1600–1848*, 1993; Von Küstner, Karl Theodor, *Album des Königl. Schauspiels und der Königl. Oper zu Berlin unter der Leitung von August Wilhelm Iffland, Karl Grafen von Brühl, Wilhelm Grafen von Redern und Karl Theodor von Küstner für die Zeit von 1796 bis 1851*, 1858.

38 BMD; c-1841–1861; Oxfordshire Health Archives.

39 BMD; British Isles theater playbills: outside London: Guide, Harvard Theatre Collection, Houghton Library, Harvard College Library; Burnim, Kalman A., *The Jewish Presence in the London Theatre, 1660–1800*; c-1841–1851; *The European Magazine, and London Review*, vols 59–60, July 1810, p. 233, and May 1811; *MM*, vol. 30, 1810, p. 286; Penley, Belville S., *The Bath Stage; a History of Dramatic Representations in Bath*; Philological Society: *Vauxhall Gardens 1661–1859*.

40 Anc: arnold wiggins tree 2016: karnold42; BMD; c-1841–1861; *Slater's Directory*, 1859.

41 Anc: Maltby and Family Tree: PhilipMann43; *CA*; CCEd; *DNB*.

42 BMD; *GM*, vol. 189, 1851; p. 451.

43 BMD; Petworth House of Correction, viewed 5 August 2019: <https://www.gravelroots.net/petworth/prison.html>.

44 Anc: Owen Family Tree: H_OWEN2; *B-1898*, p. 343; BMD; c-1861; Edward Mangin, viewed 5 August 2019: <https://www.findagrave.com/memorial/161975478/edward-mangin>; *OA*; *West Briton and Cornwall Advertiser*, 1852.

45 Anc: Owen Family Tree: H_OWEN2.

46 Anc: 1851 Millbrook Census: Hilary Kavanagh; BMD; Bromley, David and Janet, *Wellington's Men Remembered* vol. 2: A Register of Memorials to Soldiers who Fought in the Peninsular War and at Waterloo—vol. II: M to Z, 2015, p. 112; *Cobbett's Weekly Political Register*, vol. 2, 1802, p. 383; Brown, Steve, *British Regiments and the Men Who Led Them 1793–1815*: 74th Regiment of Foot; Burke, Edmund, *Annual Register*, vol. 38, 1796; *GM*, vol. 88; Guildhall Library: Records of Sun Fire Office [MS 11936/419]; *HP*; *A List of the Officers of the Army and of the Corps of Royal Marines*, 1839, p. 195; *The Scots magazine, or, General Repository of Literature, History and Politics*, vol. 57, 1795; *The Treble Almanack* for the year 1815; WFP F207.

47 *DNB*; *HP*; Lincolnshire Notes & Queries, vol. 22, 1932, p. 48; *The London Magazine, or, Gentleman's Monthly Intelligencer*, vol. 37, 1768, p. 118; Schellenberg, Betty A., *Literary Coteries and the Making of Modern Print Culture: 1740–1790*, 2016, p. 211.

48 *HP*.

49 *HP*.
50 *HP*; UCL–Slaves.
51 Anc: Ryan Family Tree: elricryan; c-1851.
52 c-1851; *Pigot's Directory*, 1830.
53 BMD; *CA*; c-1851–1881; *OA*.
54 Anc: Hacking Family Tree: penny_hacking; *DNB*; *OA*.
55 *EB*; *Grove*.
56 *London Gazette*, January 1849; *OA*; *The Spectator*, vol. 14, 1841, p. 589; UCL–Slaves.
57 Amott, John, *Origin and progress of the Meeting of the Three Choirs of Gloucester, Worcester, & Hereford*, 1865.
58 *HP*; Marjoribanks, Roger, 'Edinburgh Portrait, Sir John Marjoribanks, Bart, MP (1763–1833)', *The Book of the Old Edinburgh Club*, New Series, vol. 10, pp. 151-156, 2014.
59 Blacker, Beaver, *Gloucestershire Notes & Queries*, vol. IV, 1890: Charlton Kings Marriages 1538–1811; BMD; *B-1838-3*; Crisp, Frederick Arthur, *Visitation of England and Wales Notes*: vol. 4 1902, p. 26; Markham, Sir Clements R., *Markham Memorials* (2 vols); Nicholas, Thomas, *Annals and Antiquities of the Counties and County Families of Wales, 1991*; Register of Duties Paid for Apprentices' Indentures, 1710–1811; *Universal British Directory*, 1791; E&W Wills—will of Henry Markham; E&W Wills—will of Elizabeth Markham; WFP F173-F235.
60 Anc: Newman McHaffie Tree: VickyNewman69; BMD; c-1841–1861; *VCH*, Gloucestershire, vol. 11: Bisley and Longtree Hundreds, 1976.
61 BMD; Foster, Joseph, *Oxford Men and Their Colleges*, 1880–1892, p. 474; *OA*.
62 *BLG*; BMD; *CA*; c-1841–1861; *OA*.
63 BMD; *DNB*; *OA*.
64 Anc: McLeod Family Tree: aspenglow48jd *BLG*; *Debrett 1839*; Nottingham University Library, Department of Manuscripts and Special Collections: the Wright Papers, being the papers of the Marriot family of Yorkshire and Worcestershire, 1687–1908. Phyllis Shapiro—Muriel Moriarity—BettyLMarriott Ancestry.Com threads.
65 Ernst Friedrich, Baron von Brenn, viewed 5 August 2019: <https://gw.geneanet.org/genroy?lang=en&p=ernst+friedrich&n=von+brenn>.
66 Anc: Tree 2009: rex877; Anc: McKenzie/Walters Family: LouisePhilp; BMD; *CA*; CCEd; *GM*, vol. 196, 1854, p. 295; Pugin, A. W. N., *The Collected Letters of A. W. N. Pugin 1851–1852*, 2015, p. 420; Lancashire Archives: Hornby Castle Estate: Ref: DP 501.
67 Anc: Ganly Family Tree: Theresa Ganly; BMD; *CA*.
68 Anc: Alan Isaac Family Tree: arisaac; BMD; CCEd; *OA*.
69 BMD; c-1851; *Pigot's Directory*, 1830.
70 BMD; c-1841–1851; Hembry, Phyllis May, *The English Spa, 1560–1815: A Social History*, 1990, p. 150; Torode, Brian, The Masters of the Ceremonies in Cheltenham, viewed 5 August 2019: <https://btsarnia.org/2014/05/15/the-masters-of-the-ceremonies-in-cheltenham-an-essay/>.
71 BMD; *Edinburgh Gazette*, 15 March 1831.
72 Anc: Edwards-Hamilton Family Tree: medwards581; BMD; c-1841–1851.
73 BMD; c-1851.
74 *BDA*, vol. 10, 1984; BMD; Sainsbury & Company, *A Dictionary of Musicians, from the Earliest Ages to the Present Time*, 1827, pp. 121-2.
75 BMD; CCEd; c-1851; *OA*; Evesham MI.
76 Anc: Vick Family Tree: Billvick44; BMD; CCEd; c-1841; *OA*.
77 BMD; CCEd; *LM*, vol. 39, 1808 p.88; *OA*; MI: Widcomb.
78 Anc: Robert Bullock MarshamFamily Tree: assemblyorder; BMD; *OA*.
79 BMD; *CA*; *The Morning Chronicle*, Thursday, 21 October 1802; issue 10428.
80 *Slater & Co. Directory*, 1858.
81 BMD; CCEd; *OA*.
82 Samuel Favell, viewed 5 August 2019: <http://www.gwydir.demon.co.uk/jo/genealogy/beddome/favell.htm>; <https://www.wikitree.com/genealogy/Favel-Family-Tree-34>.
83 Kelley, Philip, and Hudson, Ronald, eds., *The Brownings' Correspondence*, vol. 2, pp. 342-343, 1984; WFP F195-F197.
84 BMD; *DNB*; *Williams*.
85 *DNB*.
86 *CA*; c-1861–1871; *An Inventory of the Historical Monuments in the County of Cambridgeshire*, vol. 1, West Cambridgeshire, 1968; *The Military [afterwards] Royal military panorama or Officer's companion*, 1814, p. 375.
87 Anc: Procter Family Tree: martinwolfgang1; BMD; c-1851; GA; *Reports of Cases Decided in the High Court of Chancery: With Notes and References to Both English and American Decisions*, vol. 2, 1843, pp. 502-513.
88 *HP*.
89 *GM*, 1837, p. 212, *A List of the Officers of the Army and of the Corps of Royal Marines*, vol. 48, 1800, p. 633; *The Royal Military Calendar*, etc., vol. 4, 1820, p. 316; George Henry Mason, viewed 5 August 2019: <magiminiland.org: Mason>; Young, Percy Marshall, *Alice Elgar: Enigma of a Victorian Lady*, 1978, p. 16.
90 Anc: Payne family tree: MarianneSibborn; BMD; c-1841–1871.
91 BMD; c-1851–1871.
92 *Pigot & Co.'s National Commercial Directory*, 1835; Smith, Brian, *A History of Malvern*, 1964.
93 Anc: Crowley Family Tree: HelenCrowley71; *CB*; *HP*.
94 BMD; *CA*; c-1841–1891; *OA*.
95 Masterman, Peters, Mildred, Masterman & Co., viewed 5 August 2019: <https://www.britishmuseum.org/research/search_the_collection_database/term_details.aspx?bioId=49151>
96 BMD; CCEd; *OA*.

97 *DNB*; WFP F199.
98 *Regestausgabe Briefe an Goethe (Biographische Informationen)*; SEIFERT, Siegfried, *Goethes Leben von Tag zu Tag: Generalregister: Namenregister—Register der Werke Goethes—Geographisches Register*, 2011, p. 263.
99 Anc: Matthews Family Tree: Ken Matthews; Family pedigree: kmatt20; BMD; *Pigot's Directory*, 1842.
100 *DNB*.
101 c-1841.
102 BMD; c-1841–1861.
103 *CA*; *DNB*.
104 BMD; c-1841–1861; *Hunt*.
105 MAYO, Charles Herbert, *A Genealogical Account of the Mayo & Elton Families*, 1908, p. 511; *VCH*, Wiltshire, vol. 10, Devizes, 1975; WFP F201-F209.
106 CCEd; MAYO, Charles Herbert, *A Genealogical Account of the Mayo & Elton Families*, 1908, pp. 144-193.
107 Anc: Clanwilliam Family Tree: Paddy Clanwilliam; *CP*; *OA*.
108 Anc: WIP-Hill, Wright, Mott, Point, Clubb, Clemons: tarynrh; BMD; CCEd; *OA*.
109 *EB*.
110 BMD; c-1861–1871; *CA*.
111 Anc: Riggs: my1972; Anc: Monteith FitzGibbon Family Tree: aneve67; Anc: Cruickshank Tree: davidcruickshank1; BRIDGEWATER, Patrick, *De Quincey's Gothic Masquerade*; *CA*; University of Nottingham: Manuscripts and Special Collections: Mellish.
112 *DNB*.
113 BMD.
114 BMD; *CB*; Cavalié Alexander Mercer, viewed 5 August 2019: <https://kirbyandhisworld.wordpress.com/tag/cavalie-mercer/>; UK Medical Registers, 1859–1959, 1875.
115 Anc: Henderson Family Tree: Marionpowell99; c-1841–1881; Samuel Mercer: RN Executive Officers 1790–1879, viewed 5 August 2019: <http://www.pbenyon.plus.com/Nbd/exec/M/Index.html>.
116 BMD; c-1841–1881.
117 Anc: Goldfinch: phil_goldfinch; *OA*.
118 Anc: Merewether Family Tree: AnnMerewether1; BMD; *CA*; *OA*.
119 Anc: Merewether Family Tree: AnnMerewether1; *OA*.
120 BMD; c-1841–1871; *Pigot*, Cheltenham 1830.
121 British Artist Index—Art of The Print; *AGB*; Johann Martin Metz, viewed 5 August 2019: <https://www.dorotheum.com/en/l/5590746/>; WFP F198.
122 Anc: Loree2: rwhite42; MI: Bath Abbey; HEMBRY, Phyllis May, *The English Spa, 1560–1815: A Social History*, 1990, p. 149; United Grand Lodge of England Freemason Membership Registers, 1751–1921.
123 Anc: Loree2: rwhite42; BMD; c-1841; *Hunt*.
124 *DNB*; Edward Thomas Michell, viewed 5 August 2019: <http://www.devon-mitchells.co.uk/getperson.php?personID=I3&tree=HuishSomerset>.
125 *Ibid.*; *OA*.
126 *Ibid.*
127 *Ibid.*; *DNB*; *OA*.
128 *Ibid.*; *CP*; *DNB*; *OA*.
129 BMD; *CA*; CCEd; *OA*.
130 Anc: Treanor Cullen Whanau: Ros Foster; BMD; c-1841–1861; National Maritime Museum.
131 Anc: Cullen Family Tree: Vanessa Tofield; *HP*; *OA*; UCL–Slaves; *Williams*.
132 Anc: Cullen Family Tree: Vanessa Tofield; BMD.
133 Scotland's first uilleann piper? viewed 5 August 2019: <https://thesession.org/discussions/27624>.
134 BURROWS, Jean, *Pennant*, The Local History Journal of Backwell, Nailsea, Tickenham and Wraxall, no. 8.
135 Anc: Ewing-Daniel: melissadaniel11; Essex Record Office, Archdeaconry Records, Marriage licences; *GM*, vol. 47, 1839, p. 97; *OA*.
136 Anc: Williamsonozterry: Terry Williamson; West Sussex Record Office: Petworth House Archives.
137 BMD; c-1841–1871.
138 Anc: Burleigh Family Tree: William Burleigh; *OA*; Henry Mills, viewed 5 August 2019: <http://www.boddyparts.co.uk/hippisley family.htm>; RUVIGNY and RANIEVAL, Marquis of, *The Plantagenet Roll of the Blood Royal:* The Mortimer-Percy vol., p. 146.
139 Anc: Martinson Family Tree: gip58; Gloucestershire, England, Prison Records, 1728–1914 for Mark Dyer and Job Mills, Registers of Prisoners The County Gaol 1825–1829.
140 Anc: Noah Huntley Family Tree: Noah Huntley; BMD; c-1851; *B-1871-2*, p. 924; *The Court Magazine, Lady's Magazine and Belle Assemblée*, vol. 23, p. 56; *The Jurist*, vol. 8, part 2, 1845, p. 439; *The Spectator*, 5 June 1847, p. 17; *Walford-1882*, p. 442; thepeerage.com: person M, #67735; WFP F196–198.
141 *OA*.
142 *DNB*.
143 BMD; c-1841–1871, thepeerage.com: person M, #363627.
144 c-1851–1861.
145 c-1841.
146 Anc: Sherrat-Dykes Family Tree Staffs-Yorkshire: TracyWaller211; *B-1898-2*; *DNB*; *Walford-1882*.
147 c-1851.
148 Anc: Baker and Green family tree: philandbel; BMD; *CA*; *Cambrian Quarterly Magazine and Celtic Repertory*, vol. 4, 1832.
149 *DNB*.
150 *DNB*.

151 BMD; c-1841–1871.
152 *DNB*.
153 *DNB*.
154 *DNB*.
155 Flekáček, Josef, *Small Story Histories/Nicholas Paganini*, published in Czech, in Prague, 1890, pp. 99-102; Goffrie, Charles, *The Violin, a Condensed History of the Violin: Its Perfection and Its Famous Makers*, 1878.
156 Durham Probate Records: pre-1858 original wills and inventories (1751–1775); MI: St Nicholas's church; Mackenzie, Eneas, *Historical Account of Newcastle-Upon-Tyne Including the Borough of Gateshead*, 1827; Elizabeth Moncaster, viewed 5 August 2019: <https://www.genuki.org.uk/big/eng/DEV/DevonWillsProject/DWP-Mon-My>; <https://www.rootschat.com/forum/index.php?topic=729018.0>; WFP F201-219.
157 Anc: Clyde Stewart Gillespie Scott Forsythe Mellon Hunter Coulter: heathermckinley30; CCEd; MI: Corston, viewed 17 March 2019: <https://www.batharchives.co.uk/sites/bath_record_office/files/COR%20MIs%20Issue%201.pdf>; *GM*, 1846, p. 550; *OA*.
158 *DNB*; *The Monthly Review*, vol. 97, 1822, page 187; WFP: F208, 10 June 1806.
159 *DNB*.
160 Anc: Theelke Family Tree: wilsonjosephine; *The Asiatic annual register or a view of the history of Hindustan and of the politics, commerce and literature of Asia*, vol. 8, for the year 1806, published 1809, p. 155; BMD; British Library: Asian and African Studies, Reference: IOR/J/1/19/259-62; c-1851; William Garrow Monk, viewed 5 August 2019: <https://garrowsociety.org/rootspersona-tree-2/monk-william-garrow/>.
161 BMD.
162 *CP*.
163 Anc: Clark_Freshwater 2016: Ian Clark; BMD; c-1841–1851; *LG*, part 1, 1838, p. 1071; Morris, Pat, 'John James, Iron Master', *Gloucestershire Society for Industrial Archaeology Journal* for 2011, pp. 33-44; *The Universal Magazine*, vol. 5, 1806, p. 91; *VCH*, Gloucester, 1988.
164 *EB*; de Norvins, Jacques Marquet (baron de Montbreton), *Souvenirs d'un historien de Napoléon: 1802–1810*, p. 136; Mathieu Paul Louis de Montmorency-Laval, viewed 5 August 2019: <https://gw.geneanet.org/skrebs1?lang=en&n=de+montmorency+laval&oc=0&p=mathieu+paul+louis>.
165 Anc: Urney Park and Beyond family tree: Perry Colin; BMD; CCEd; *Debrett 1840*; *OA*.
166 *ADB*; *HP*; George Ogle Moore, viewed 5 August 2019: <http://oglemoorefamilyhistory.blogspot.com/2009/09/>.
167 Anc: Ferris: Margi Couch; BMD; c-1851–1881.
168 Anc: Colles2018 2: colles2481; BMD; c-1841.
169 Anc: ej2b Birchall_Green Family Tree: ejbirchall; BMD; *CA*; CCEd; *OA*.
170 Anc: Condliff Family: SvitlanaCondliff; BMD; *OA*.
171 *DNB*; *The Literary Gazette and Journal of the Belles Lettres, Arts, Sciences, &c.*, 1842, p. 812.
172 BMD; c-1851–1861.
173 Anc: Cooke Barron worldwide: dec161; BMD; c-1841–1851; *OA*.
174 BMD; c-1841–1851, 1861; Hodgson-Hinde, John, Raine, James and Collingwood Bruce, John, *A History of Northumberland, in Three Parts: General history of the country*; Speight, Henry, *Upper Wharfedale*, 1900.
175 *DNB*.
176 Fenner, Theodore, *Opera in London: Views of the Press, 1785–1830*, 2003.
177 BMD; c-1861.
178 *CP*.
179 Anc: McClintock Family Tree: sylviawright54; *CP*.
180 *Ibid.*
181 Anc: Moore family tree: mmijj60; *CP*.
182 BMD; c-1841; *The Legal Observer, or, Journal of Jurisprudence*, vol. 15, 1838, p. 490.
183 BMD; c-1861; *OA*, *VCH*, Gloucestershire, Tidenham.
184 Anc: Byrt & Morgan Family Tree: Caroline Shepherd; CCEd; c-1851; *OA*; *MM*, vol. 14, 1820.
185 CCEd; c-1841.
186 *DNB*.
187 *GM*, 1815, p. 274; James Morley, viewed 5 August 2019: <https://www.mq.edu.au/macquarie-archive/lema/1792/>.
188 Anc: Prevost & related families: dolshouse; Charles Morris, viewed 5 August 2019: <http://www.the-malvern-hills.uk/other_history_charles_morris.htm>.
189 Griffith, J. K., *A General Cheltenham Guide*, 1816; *HP*; *Law Advertiser*, vol. 2, 1824; *VCH*, Gloucestershire.
190 Anc: 18C Fragments: dmelville62; BMD; c-1841–1861; CCEd; *The Guardian*, obituary 20 November 1895; *OA*; The Registers of Wadham College, Oxford.
191 *EB*; Jean Joseph Mounier, viewed 5 August 2019: <https://gw.geneanet.org/jm300974?lang=fr&n=mounier&oc=0&p=jean+joseph>; Archives nationales (France): ref: 234AP/1-234AP/2.
192 *DNB*.
193 *GM* 1839, p. 667; Pigot's Directory, 1830; The Legal Observer, or, Journal of Jurisprudence, vol. 15, 1837.
194 *DNB*.
195 Anc: Purvis Family Tree: Joseph Randolph Mullings; viewed 5 August 2019: <https://www.geni.com/people/Capt-Arthur-Randolph/6000000041345643674>; *Williams*.
196 *DNB*.
197 c-1841; *Pigot's Directory for Somerset*, 1844.
198 Anc: Smith Family Tree: SmithandHillTrees; BMD; UCL-Slaves: Thomas Townsend of Grenada; Philadelphia Jane Caroline Monro, viewed 5 August 2019: <http://www.clanmunrousa.org/gen/getperson.php?personID=I32399&tree=1>; WFP F206, F207.
199 BMD; c-1851; *DNB*; *GM*, 1846, p. 106; UCL–Slaves.

200 *DNB*.
201 *DNB*.
202 *The Edinburgh Almanack, or Universal Scots and Imperial Register*, 1828, p. 228; *The Edinburgh Magazine and Literary Miscellany*, vol. 85, 1820, p. 96; William Mure of Caldwell, viewed 5 August 2019: <https://universitystory.gla.ac.uk/biography/?id=WH1025&type=P>; <http://genealogy.kirkpatrickaustralian.com/archives/getperson.php?personID=I9529&tree=TKA>; WFP F188-F196.
203 Anc: Tulloch/Girma Family Tree: atgirma; CCEd; *OA*.
204 *DNB*.
205 *DNB*.
206 *CB*.
207 England & Wales Criminal Registers; Gloucestershire, England, Gaol Registers, 1815–1879: ref. Q/Gc6/1, and Q/Gc6/2.
208 BMD; CCEd; c-1841–1861; Gloucester FHS Marriage Index; *OA*.
209 Naphtali Hart Myers, viewed 5 August 2019: <https://jhse.org/articles/naphtali-hart-myers-1711-1788-new-yorker-and-londoner/>; <https://www.wikitree.com/genealogy/Myers-Family-Tree-8638>.
210 *CA*; *DNB*; *HP*.

Letter N

1 *Grove*; Baker, *Biographical Dictionary of Musicians*, 2001; Lister, Warwick, *Amico: The Life of Giovanni Battista Viotti*, 2009, p. 303; Radomski, James, *Manuel García (1775–1832): Chronicle of the Life of a Bel Canto Tenor at the Dawn of Romanticism*, 2000, p. 143.
2 BMD; MI: Cuckfield church; *HP*; *Meath Chronicle*.
3 *DNB*, Napier, William Francis Patrick, *The Life and Opinions of General Sir Charles James Napier, GCB*, 1857.
4 Anc: The Darby Sloan Connection: thegreatsloan; *DNB*, Napier, William Francis Patrick, *The Life and Opinions of General Sir Charles James Napier, GCB*, 1857; *The Literary Panorama, and National Register*, vol. 5, 1809, p. 1029; WFP F198.
5 Anc: Janes + Thickett Families: Bob Janes; *The European Magazine, and London Review*, vol. 81, 1822, p. 380; Pettigrew, Thomas Joseph, *Memoirs of the Life and Writings of the Late John Coakley Lettsom*, vol. 2, 1817.
6 Anc: Jackson Family Tree: annkrolzig; BMD; *DNB*; *OA*.
7 Anc: George Naylor Woods Laurie Family ancestral: kat7adelaide; BMD; Huntley Marriages 1790 to 1812; *The Monthly Review*, 1800, vol. 36; *MM*, 1816, vol. 1; Phillips: Sir Richard, *MM*, 1796, vol. 2.
8 Anc: Arthur Charles Burnaby Neate Family Tree: Winterstoke; *CA*.
9 *The Athenæum*; 1853. p. 191; BMD; c-1851; *Debrett 1840*, p. 400; *GM*, vol. 71, 1861, p. 468; Wikipedia: Sir Digby Neave, 3rd Baronet.
10 Bigland, Ralph etc. MI: St Mary's, Cheltenham; BMD; E&W Wills—will of Thomas Nettleship; *The London Magazine*, vol. 9, 1824 p. 111; *MM*, vol. 13, 1820; *Pigot's Directory*, 1830; Porter, Agnes, *A Governess in the Age of Jane Austen: The Journals and Letters of Agnes Porter*, 1998, pp. 341-2; Revd John Hunt, viewed 5 August 2019: <http://www.archerfamily.org.uk/family/>; Kingsley, Nicholas: landedfamilies.blogspot.com: angerstein of weeting hall; London, England, Freedom of the City Admission Papers, 1681–1930; WFP F173-F235.
11 WFP F188, F200–F201, F213 & F221.
12 BMD; c-1851, *CP*; *HP*.
13 *Blackwood's Edinburgh Magazine*, vol. 13, 1823, p. 736; vol. 19, 1826; *The Edinburgh Magazine and Literary Miscellany*, vol. 96, 1825; *The Edinburgh Annual Register*, 1814; *OA*; *The Scots Magazine and Edinburgh Literary Miscellany*, vol. 78, 1816, p. 156.
14 *B-1845*, p. 808; *Foster-1881*, p. 279; Catherine Newcombe, viewed 5 August 2019: <http://alison-stewart.blogspot.com/2014/04/the-newcombe-family-of-geashill.html> thepeerage.com: person: F, #428443; Revd Arthur Newcombe, viewed 5 August 2019: <https://gw.geneanet.org/wingers?lang=en&pz=alice+gwendolen&nz=wingfield&p=arthur&n=Newcombe>.
15 *GM*; NA; *OA*; Newdigate, viewed 5 August 2019: <https://www.geni.com/people/Lt-General-Sir-Edward-Newdegate/6000000028378549270>; WFP F181, F200.
16 *GM*, vol. 11, 1839, p. 554; vol. 161, 1837; Griffith, S. Y., *A New Historical Description of Cheltenham and its Vicinity*, 1826; *Pigot's Directory*, 1830.
17 BMD; c-1841–1861; *The European Magazine, and London Review*, vol. 72, 1817, p. 467; *OA*.
18 *Annual Register*, vol. 41, 1799, p. 5; Rutter, Owen, *A Brief History of the Firm of Messrs. Davison, Newman & Company*, 1938; Wikipedia.
19 BMD; GA; *Slater's Directory*, 1858.
20 GA; van Wyhe, John, editor 2002; The Complete Work of Charles Darwin Online.
21 *DNB*.
22 Anc: McIntyre Family Tree: pgic1; BMD; c-1851–1871.
23 BMD; c-1841–1871.
24 Anc: daldy Family Tree: Alan Daldy; BMD; Bayes, J. F. and Roberts, J., 'Turnpike Roads from Gloucester to Cheltenham', *GSIA*, 1971; *G&B*, p. 132; GA; *LG*, 1813, page 2177.
25 Anc: daldy Family Tree: Alan Daldy; *DNB*.
26 Anc: daldy Family Tree: Alan Daldy; BMD; c-1841–1851.
27 *Ibid*.
28 Anc: JadeBattye48, Johannesburg, Gauteng, South Africa family tree; BMD; *GM*, vol. 102, 1832; *OA*; Brayley, Edward Wedlake, *A Topographical History of Surrey*, vol. 1, part 2, 1841; WFP F206.
29 BMD; *CA*; c-1841–1851; *OA*.
30 BMD; c-1841–1871; *Debrett 1840*; *Reports of cases argued and determined in the Court of Queen's bench*; Augustus Newton, viewed 5 August 2019: <http://sites.rootsweb.com/~radfordfamily/findex1.htm>.
31 BMD; c-1841–1861; *Hunt*.
32 Anc: Ryrie/Oldfield/Elphinston/Robertson: Marciacatsmo56; BMD; *CA*; c-1841–1871.

33 *HP.*
34 *DNB.*
35 *DNB.*
36 Argent, Mark, *Recollections of R. J. S.Stevens: An Organist in Georgian London*, 1992, p. 135; Lister, Warwick, *Amico: The Life of Giovanni Battista Viotti*, 2009, p. 195; Lysons, Daniel, & Amott, John, (and others) *Origin and Progress of the Meeting of the Three Choirs of Gloucester, Worcester & Hereford, and of the Charity Connected with it*, 1895; Temperley, Nicholas, *The Music of the English Parish Church*, 1983, p. 199.
37 Anc: Bithell family tree: annetteraven; *Aris's Birmingham Gazette*, 6 March 1826; *B-1847-2*, p. 937, Gloucestershire, England, Prison Records, 1728–1914 for Benjamin Ireland Nind; *LG*, 1826, p. 1542.
38 Anc: Distaff Line Family Tree: judithpetheram; BMD; c-1851.
39 Anc: LeBoutillier Batiste (Payne): Bev Lang; BMD; c-1841–1861; UCL-Slaves; Marriages at Quedgeley 1813 to 1836.
40 *CA.*
41 *CP*; *HP*; Wikipedia.
42 *Ibid.*
43 *CA.*
44 *CA.*
45 *Ibid.*
46 *CA.*
47 BMD; *CA*; c-1851; *OA*.
48 BMD; c-1851.
49 Anc: Coulson Family Tree: j_vander_veen96; BMD; *OA*.
50 *Ibid.*; *DNB.*
51 Anc: Gigliucci Family Tree: Sylvia B. Hetzel; *DNB.*
52 BMD; *Pigot's Directory* 1842-4; *Hunt's Directory* (Cheltenham), 1847.
53 Wikipedia.
54 Anc: Brown Family Tree: davidbrown861; *The Belfast News Letter*, 3 September 1866; UCL–Slaves.

Letter O

1 Wikipedia.
2 Burke, Edmund, *Annual Register*, vol. 86, 1844, p. 184; *GM*, vol. 77, 1845, p. 197.
3 *CP.*
4 *DNB.*
5 *DNB.*
6 *ADB.*
7 Aspinall, Arthur, *The Later Correspondence of George III*; Boyer Lewis, Charlene M., *Elizabeth Patterson Bonaparte: An American Aristocrat in the Early Republic*, 2012, p. 128; *CB*; *GM*, vol. 80, part 1, 1810.
8 *DNB*; *OA.*
9 *Pigot*, 1830; *Hunt.*
10 BMD.
11 CCEd; *OA*; Waterford County Museum.
12 *Asiatic Journal and Monthly Miscellany*, 1832; BMD; Da Silva, Francisco Ribeiro (editor), *Estudos em homenagem a Luís António de Oliveira Ramos*, 2004, pp. 269-270, containing a paper by Bennett, Norman R., 'Notes on Offley, Forrester and the Forresters 1779–1861'; *GM*, 1830; *The London Magazine*, vol. 3, 1825; E&W-Wills—will of Charles Offley of Stroud; *Pigot*, 1830.
13 BMD; *DNB*; *OA.*
14 BMD; *A Collection of the Public General Statutes Passed in the Year 1836*; *VCH*, Wiltshire vol. 5.
15 *DNB.*
16 BMD; *OA.*
17 *The Post Office London Directory*, Kelly's Directories Limited, 1843, p. 312.
18 BMD; *Cobbett's Annual Register*, 1802, p. 1124; *GM*, vol. 42, 1836, p. 670; MI: Gloucester Cathedral, GA: D1018–Cambray Pavilion and Cambray Lodge Cheltenham; Gwent Archives: Records of the Rickards Family of Usk Priory: GB0218.D2570; *A List of the Officers of the Army and of the Corps of Royal Marines*; 1824, p. 532; *LG*, 1794.
19 BMD; c-1841–1861; *Pigot*, 1830, 1844.
20 Anc: Royalty & Peerage: Robert Candy; *GSIA*, 1879; *OA*; thepeerage.com: person: M, #668424.
21 Anc: Royalty & Peerage: Robert Candy; Anc: Janes + Thickett Families: Bob Janes; *OA*; thepeerage.com: person: M, #35375.
22 Anc: Macalister/Burgess/Hill/Aspinall/Lake etc.: Pat_Slay; *GM*, part 2, 1796, p. 879; *Hart's Annual Army List, Militia List, and Imperial Yeomanry List*, 1845, p. 343 & p. 358.
23 BMD; c-1841–1871; London Marriages and Banns, 1754–1921.
24 *DNB.*
25 Anc: Pyatt 1 Family Tree: pytc10; *B-1871-2*, p. 1035; *GM*, vol. 97, p. 485; *LG*, 1812; London, England, Marriages and Banns, 1754–1921; Muthu, Sankar, *Empire and Modern Political Thought*, 2012, p. 191; *Reports of Cases Heard and Decided in the House of Lords on Appeals and Writs of Error: During the Sessions 1831–1846*, vol. 8, 1843, pp. 657-8; Royle, Edward, *Bishop Bickersteth's visitation returns for the Archdeaconry of Craven*; Alexander Oswald Emmott, viewed 5 August 2019: <www.a-history-of-rawdon.co.uk>; <https://www.geni.com/people/Alexander-Oswald/6000000013199420026>.
26 Anc: Janes + Thickett Families: Bob Janes; *CA*; *DNB.*

27 Wikipedia.
28 Anc: Bowyer-Rice-Wood-Walker: LexieBowyer; BMD; c-1841–1871.
29 Anc: Kay Walker Family Tree: KableWalker; BMD; c-1841–1871; *DNB*.
30 Anc: Skliar-Ward Family Tree: bskliarward; BMD; Holyoake, George Jacob, *The History of the Last Trial by Jury for Atheism in England: A Fragment of Autobiography, Submitted for the Perusal of Her Majesty's Attorney-general and the British Clergy*, 1851, p. 9.
31 Wikipedia.

Letter P

1 *CP*; *DNB*; *HP*.
2 Anc: Kilby/Browne Family: jenniferkilby67; BMD; CCEd; *OA*.
3 Anc: clow & baines merge: David Clow; BMD; c-1841–1871, 1891; *The Universal Magazine of Knowledge and Pleasure*, 1805, p. 1891.
4 BMD; c-1851–1871
5 Anc: Peter R Plaichner Family Tree: Peter Plaichner; BMD; *CP*; Cracroft's Peerage.
6 Anc: Arthur Family Tree: Sydney Arthur; *CA*; *OA*.
7 *Ibid.*; *The Ecclesiastical Gazette, or, Monthly register of the affairs of the Church of England*, 1843, p. 273; *GM*, vol. 20, (vol. 174), 1843, p. 198.
8 Anc: Arthur Family Tree: Sydney Arthur; *CA*.
9 Anc: Day Family Tree: Peter Day; BMD; c-1841–1891.
10 Australian Convict Transportation Registers–Other Fleets & Ships, 1791–1868; Convict Record, Joseph Palmer, viewed 7 July 2019: <https://convictrecords.com.au/convicts/palmer/joseph/98421>; Gloucestershire, England, Gaol Registers, 1815–1879; England & Wales, Criminal Registers, 1791–1892; Medical journal of the *Adamant*, by James Hamilton, viewed 7 July 2019: <http://www.yearsleydna.com/convicts/convicts.html>.
11 *HP*.
12 BMD.
13 Anc: Riley Family Tree: DScott8021; Exton Family Tree: diyoung135; BMD; c-1841–1861; Chaceley, Worcestershire: vol. 5—Marriages & Banns 1813–1848, viewed 5 August 2019: <https://sites.rootsweb.com/~wrag44/chaceley/chaceleyvol5.htm>.
14 Anc: Palmer Family Tree: Ulick Palmer; *OA*.
15 BMD; CCEd; c-1841–1881; *DNB*; London, England, Marriages and Banns, 1754–1921; *OA*.
16 *DNB*; WFP-F201.
17 *DNB*.
18 BMD; *DNB*.
19 *DNB*.
20 *OA*.
21 *CP*.
22 Martin, Robert Montgomery, *History of the British Colonies: Possessions in Africa and Australia*, 1835, p. 406; *LG*, 1839; The register of admissions to Gray's inn, 1521–1889, together with the register of marriages in Gray's inn chapel, 1695–1754; South Australian Register, 1874.
23 Anc: parker 2018-03-28: edoni36; Anc: Flint Family Tree: janehickman49; BMD; Pallot's Marriage Index for England: 1780–1837; Upper Slaughter with Eyford Marriages 1813 to 1824.
24 Anc: Mellin family tree: andrew mellin; Anc: Mike Parker's Family Tree: Mike Parker; BMD; *CP*.
25 Curwen, Henry, *A History of Booksellers: The Old and the New*, 1873; *Studies in Newspaper and Periodical History*, vol. 2, Issue 1-2, 1994; Joseph and John Parker, booksellers, of Oxford, viewed 5 August 2019: <Oxford History: Stephanie Jenkins>.
26 Anc: Du Cane Family Tree: LeslieDuCane; *The Army List*, 1812, p. 76; *A List of the Officers of the Army and of the Corps of Royal Marines*, 1821, p. 278; *GM*, vol. 78, 1795, p. 790.
27 *DNB*.
28 BMD; c-1841; *LG*; London Metropolitan Archives.
29 *CA*; *DNB*.
30 *The European Magazine, and London Review*, vol. 56, 1809, p. 312; *The Literary Panorama*, vol. 12, 1813, p. 337; UCL-Slaves; University of Texas Libraries: OCLC Number: 62891329, Journal entries for the four Carrington sugar plantations (Chapel, Haggatt's, Valley and Harrison's plantations) of David Parris and his heirs, Anna Maria Carrington, wife of George Carrington, and Paul Carrington Parris; WFP F205-208.
31 BMD; c-1841–1861.
32 BMD; c-1841–1851; *GM*, vol. 102, p. 1180; Proceedings of the Old Bailey 16 August 1858; *Walford-1919*.
33 Anc: Blagden/Parry Family Tree: David Ditchfield; Anc: Eardley/Todd: malczwaby; BMD; c-1851–1861; *DNB*.
34 Anc: Royalty & Peerage: Robert Candy; BMD; *CA*; c-1841–1881; *DNB*; Farr, D., *Thomas Gambier Parry (1816–1888) as Artist and Collector*.
35 Anc: Blagden/Parry Family Tree: David Ditchfield; BMD; *DNB*; Welch, R. Courtenay, (comp. and ed. by) *The Harrow School register, 1800–1911*, 3rd ed. 1911.
36 Anc: Coulson Family Tree: j_vander_veen96; BMD; c-1851–1861; *OA*.
37 Anc: James Family Tree: ERD33; *OA*.
38 BMD; Burr, Daniel, *Memoir of the Life of Lieut. Gen. Daniel Burr. With a supplement*, 1821, pp. 94-97; c-1841; Fosbroke, Thomas Dudley, *Abstracts of Records and Manuscripts Respecting the County of Gloucester*, 1807, p. 140; *VCH*, Gloucestershire, vol. 4, 1988, Hempsted and vol. 6, 1965, Alderton with Dixton.

39 Anc: Coulson Family Tree: j_vander_veen96; BMD; CCEd; *OA*; Oxfordshire Record Office, Bradwell Grove Estate.
40 MI: Bath Abbey; Wikipedia: Partis College, Bath.
41 *CA*; CCEd.
42 *DNB*.
43 BMD; CCEd; c-1841; *DNB*–John Florio; London, England, Deaths and Burials, 1813–1980; *OA*; Oxfordshire Record Office, Bradwell Grove Estate; *The Times*, 30 August 1804.
44 Anc: Vickers (BarrieVickers68): BarrieVickers68; BMD; *CA*; c-1861; *DNB*.
45 *DNB*.
46 *Army List*, 1805; *DCB*.
47 *DNB*.
48 Anc: Research Tree: Reformers, Abolitionists, Suffragists and More: DawnMO83; *B-1885*; *The European Magazine, and London Review*, vol. 35, 1799, p. 285; *VCH*, Gloucestershire, Woodchester; thepeerage.com: person M, #82552, and M, #12866.
49 thepeerage.com: person M, #533257.
50 BMD; c-1841–1891.
51 Anc: Stretch Family Tree: medwards581; Anc: Chronicles from the Crypt: Cholmondeley/delaZouche; *B-1846-2*; *MM*, vol. 38, 1815. p. 579.
52 *The European Magazine and London Review*, vol. 9, 1786, p. 381; *OA*; WFP F131, F135–F136.
53 c-1841–1851.
54 CCEd; *OA*.
55 Anc: Edward Boulton of Sydney: gatp63; c-185, 1861; Massue, Melville Henry, Marquis de Ruvigny et Raineval, *The Clarence* volume, 1911.
56 BMD; c-1841.
57 Thomas Pearson, viewed 5 August 2019: <https://www.neh.gov/humanities/2011/septemberoctober/feature/forgotten-hero-in-forgotten-war>.
58 *HP*; *Lincolnshire Notes & Queries*, vol. 22, 1932, p. 48; *The London Magazine, or, Gentleman's Monthly Intelligencer*, vol. 37, 1768, p. 118; Schellenberg, Betty A., *Literary Coteries and the Making of Modern Print Culture: 1740–1790*, 2016, p. 211; The Peart Robinson Family, viewed 5 August 2019: <http://www.turtlebunbury.com/family/bunburyfamily_related/bunbury_family_related_peart_robinson.html>.
59 *CA*; CCEd.
60 Anc: Marshall & Thomas—Maynard & Beedle Tree: donalto1874; CCEd; MI: Church of St Matthew, Rushall; *OA*; Wiltshire and Swindon Archives: Wood Awdry: Wansbroughs, Solicitors, Chippenham.
61 Jagemann, Karoline, *Selbstinszenierungen im klassischen Weimar*, 2004, p. 814; Sofie Henriette Wilhelmine Peckelsheim, viewed 5 August 2019: <https://gw.geneanet.org/cvpolier?lang=en&n=von+seckendorff&oc=0&p=sofie+henriette+wilhelmine>.
62 Anc: Anderson/Pedder/Trevor Family Tree: hrhoward70; CCEd, *OA*.
63 Anc: Robert Peel 2nd Bt Family Tree: francesbragger; *GM*, 1841; *Williams*.
64 Anc: Robert Peel 2nd Bt Family Tree: francesbragger; *Williams*.
65 Anc: Robert Peel 2nd Bt Family Tree: francesbragger; *DNB*; *HP*.
66 BMD; *CA*; CCEd; c-1851–1861.
67 Anc: Parry Family Tree: MParry99Anc: Robert Peel 2nd Bt Family Tree: francesbragger; BMD; c-1841–1851.
68 *DNB*; *OA*.
69 Anc: Howman Law Mc Pherson: ChristineParsons952; BMD; c-1841–1861.
70 *Ibid.*
71 *CA*; *CP*.
72 *CB*; *CA*.
73 *CP*; *HP*.
74 *CP*.
75 Anc: Herron Family Tree: herronjk; *DNB*; Perry, Matthew C., *Narrative of the Expedition to the China Seas and Japan, 1852–1854*.
76 *DNB*.
77 Anc: Herron Family Tree: herronjk.
78 Anc: Brind Family Tree: robinbrind; BHO: *Survey of London*: vol. 24, the Parish of St Pancras part 4: King's Cross Neighbourhood: The Foundling Hospital and Doughty Estates; *Johnstone's London Commercial Guide, and Street Directory*, 1818, column 438.
79 Anc: Penfold Family Tree: David Haddon-Reece; *OA*.
80 *Universal British Directory*, 1791; Powell, William S., *Dictionary of North Carolina Biography*; William Pennington, viewed 29 June 2019: <http://www.onelibrary.com/genealogy/penningtonculmstock/pafc01.htm>.
81 Anc: Lady Gee and Me: anni3030; BMD; *GM*, vol. 98, part 2, 1828; *OA*; Francis Penyston, viewed 5 August 2019: <https://www.thornber.net/famhist/htmlfiles/ashton.html>; WFP F174-176.
82 Anc: fletcher Family Tree: francis fletcher; *DNB*.
83 Anc: Janes + Thickett Families: Bob Janes; McKenzie, Kirsten, *Imperial Underworld: An Escaped Convict and the Transformation of the British Colonial Order*, 2016, p. 80.
84 *CA*.
85 CCEd; *GM* 1837, p. 445; *The Christian's Monthly Magazine and Universal Review*, vol. 1, 1844, p. 245; NPC, PROB 11/2142/248; *OA*; Suffolk Marriage Strays, 1813-37.
86 Anc: Reese Family Tree: tcorbishley; *B-1847-1*, p. 1029; CCEd; *OA*.
87 Anc: Morison/Annatt Family Tree: Michael Morison; *OA*.
88 Personal information Hugo Simms—Perkins family bible.
89 BMD; c-1871; Personal information Hugo Simms.

90 BMD; c-1871–1881; William Francis Perkins, viewed 5 August 2019: <http://www.oxfordhistory.org.uk/holywell/south/061_062.html>.
91 BMD; Freedom of the City Admission Papers, 1681–1930; *GM*, 1846, p. 445; *The Legal Observer, or, Journal of Jurisprudence*, vol. 21, 1841, p. 56; *Post Office Directory*, 1845, p. 1481; *The Spectator*, 2 April 1842, p. 20.
92 Anc: DownloadGedcom.aspx: oadelong; BMD; *The European Magazine, and London Review*, vol. 55, 1809, p. 159; E&W Wills—will of George Wigley Perrott of Fladbury; *OA*; George Wigley Perrott, viewed 5 August 2019: <http://freepages.rootsweb.com/~parrott/genealogy/yorkshire.shtml>.
93 Berrington Estate Papers, viewed 14 February 2019: <https://wc.rootsweb.com/cgi-bin/igm.cgi?op=GET&db=willperf2&id=I482230>; BMD; Burke, Edmund, *Annual Register*, vol. 53, 1825, p. 148; *GM*, vol. 109, 1811, p. 288; *An Account of the Incorporated Society for clothing, maintaining, and educating Poor Orphans of Clergymen*, vol. 3, 1843, p. 38; E&W Wills—will of Thomas Perrott; Willian, Frank, *History of the Oxfordshire Regiment of Militia 1778–1900 including the Diary of the late Lt-Col. Thomas Mosley Crowder, 1852–1885*, 1900, p. 44.
94 BMD; c-1861; Obituary: *The Medical Times and Gazette*, 1870, p. 107.
95 Anc: Peters Family Tree: CaliforniaResearcher; BMD; *CA*; CCEd.
96 Anc: George Black Family: Winjin43; BMD; *OA*.
97 BMD; c-1841–1871; *OA*.
98 BMD; *VCH*, Gloucestershire vol. 7, Hatherop.
99 *LG*, part 1, 1829. p. 687; MI: Stonehouse Church, Gloucestershire.
100 *CP*; *HP*.
101 *OA*; The Roxburghe Club.
102 CCEd; *OA*; *VCH*, Wiltshire: Berwick St John.
103 Anc: Delyth Williams family tree: Delyth Williams; *OA*.
104 Anc: Fam11: MKelly9392; *GM*, vol. 155, 1834, p. 452; *Gloucestershire Chronicle*, 4 March 1843; John Hopkins University: *William Law Phelps papers: 1741–1840*.
105 *DNB*.
106 Anc: Okeover Family Tree: Bobbie1959; *CA*; *DNB*.
107 BMD; Wikipedia.
108 Anc: Royalty & Peerage: Robert Candy; *DNB*.
109 Anc: Royalty & Peerage: Robert Candy; *CA*; *DNB*; *HP*.
110 Anc: Dilts Family Tree: cherylmcmanus57.
111 *B-1845*; *DNB*.
112 *DNB*.
113 BMD; *DNB*; Sir Thomas Phillipps, viewed 13 March 2020 <https://www.wikitree.com/genealogy/Phillipps-Family-Tree-94>.
114 BMD; *CA*; c-1851–1871.
115 *DNB*.
116 BMD; c-1861; *DNB*.
117 Anc: Gibson and Rickards Family Tree: pe2662; BMD; *GM*, volume 89, part 1, 1819, p. 651; *GM* vol. 165, 1839, p. 666; *Repertorio di proclami, ordinanze, notificazioni ecc*, volumes 2-3, 1844, p. 160.
118 BMD; c-1841; *Pigot's Directory*, 1830.
119 *CA*; Bennett, James, *The Tewkesbury Yearly Register and Magazine*, 1837; *OA*.
120 Anc: Henry Phillpotts Bishop of Exeter: maureenq007; *OA*.
121 Anc: Henry Phillpotts Bishop of Exeter: maureenq007; *Williams*.
122 Anc: Henry Phillpotts Bishop of Exeter: maureenq007; *CA*.
123 *CA*; *DNB*; *HP*.
124 Anc: Herrington Henderson Ballantyne Scott family tree: ros196; website: Descendants of Richard Phipps.
125 BMD; c-1841–1851.
126 Anc: Taylor Family Tree: jillbuster; BMD; c-1841–1861.
127 Carlo Alfredo Piatti, viewed 13 March 2020: < http://www.alfredopiatti.com/>.
128 *OA*.
129 Anc: Davis Family Tree: laurhd; CCEd; c-1851; *OA*.
130 *The European Magazine, and London Review*, vols 57-58, 1810, p. 156; *OA*; Joe Bissett: Piggott of Somerset, viewed 6 August 2019: <https://lists.rootsweb.com/hyperkitty/list/piggott@rootsweb.com/thread/4878962/>.
131 *B-1885*; thepeerage.com: person M, #252211.
132 *DNB*; *HP*; UCL-Slaves.
133 Anc: The GOUGH family tree: andrew07; *DNB*.
134 BMD; c-1851–1871; *OA*.
135 Anc: MyFamily Tree: chrisfshore; BMD; Britain Express, Alton Priors White Horse, viewed 6 August 2019: <https://www.britainexpress.com/counties/wiltshire/ancient/alton-priors-white-horse.htm>.
136 BMD; c-1841–1851.
137 BMD; CCEd; *OA*, UCL-Slaves.
138 Anc: PITT Gloucestershire Cheltenham Family Tree: droylsden1; *OA*.
139 *Ibid*.; BMD; Graham, Sir Reginald, *Fox Hunting Recollections*; *GM*, vol. 13, 1840; vol. 169, 1841; *OA*; Vickery, Amanda, *The Gentleman's Daughter*; 2003.
140 Anc: PITT Gloucestershire Cheltenham Family Tree: droylsden1; BMD; *DNB*; *HP*.
141 BMD; Chamberlayne, Betty, *Gloucestershire History* No. 13 (1999) pp. 6-11, 'Maisemore Court and the Families Who Lived There', part II; *HP*; *MM*, vol. 11, 1801, p. 192.
142 *DNB*.

143 Anc: PITT Gloucestershire Cheltenham Family Tree: droylsden1; BMD.
144 BMD.
145 BMD; *CA*; *DNB*; Sir Thomas Joshua Platt, viewed 6 August 2019: <http://bloomsburypeople.blogspot.com/2011/02/sir-thomas-joshua-and-lady-augusta.html>.
146 *DNB*.
147 BMD; PI: Martin Playne.
148 Anc: Llewellyn Huth Meinertzhagen: chrisrooney46; BMD; PLAYNE, Arthur Twisden, *A History of the Parishes of Minchinhampton and Avening*, 1915; TANN, Jennifer, *Gloucestershire Woollen Mills*, 1967, MI: Bath Abbey Cemetery; Minchinhampton Marriages 1802–1812, viewed 6 August 2019: <http://www.glosgen.co.uk/records/minchmarr9.htm>.
149 Anc: Llewellyn Huth Meinertzhagen: chrisrooney46; BMD; PLAYNE, Arthur Twisden, *A History of the Parishes of Minchinhampton and Avening*, 1915.
150 *EB*.
151 BMD; *OA*.
152 BMD; *DNB*; *OA*.
153 *CA*.
154 BMD; *B-1838-3*.
155 *HP*.
156 CP; *The Edinburgh Annual Register*, vol. 10, 1821, p. 307.
157 Cracroft's Peerage.
158 Anc: Carlyle-Merrett Family Tree: CatherineCarlyle; *HP*.
159 c-1841.
160 Anc: Napper_Marsh_Rainone_Smith USE: louise2773; BMD; c-1841–1861; thepeerage.com: person M, #550953.
161 BMD; c-1861–1911.
162 BMD; c-1841; *OA*; thepeerage.com: person M, #550984.
163 Anc: Evesham Rudge Family Tree: Paula Howells; BMD; c-1861; thepeerage.com: person M, #551004.
164 BMD; thepeerage.com: person #550969.
165 Anc: Newman McHaffie Tree: VickyNewman69; Anc: Baker Family Tree 2013: igbaker; Anc: Weatherley of Middlesex/Herts Tree: Sam Ford; BMD; c-1851–1881; *Debrett 1840*, p. 444; *HP*.
166 BMD; c-1851–1891; *OA*; thepeerage.com: person M, #394392.
167 *OA*.
168 *OA*.
169 *Eton*, p. 71a; *OA*.
170 Anc: Gary Shaw 2: gary shaw; c-1841–1861; *The Topographer and Genealogist*, vol. 1, 1846, p. 192; *VCH*, Gloucestershire, vol. 6; BENNETT, R. G., *The Kentish Polhills*, 1958.
171 *Debrett 1824-II*; Clare County Library: GALLERY, Margaret, The Kenny Family of Treanmanagh from *c*. 1650 to the early 1900s; William Pollard, viewed 6 August 2019: <https://genealogy.links.org/links-cgi/readged?/home/ben/camilla-genealogy/current+!0:181083+5-9-0-1-0>.
172 *CA*; *HP*.
173 Anc: WISE BANBURY: banbury145; c-1851–1861; The Genealogical Society of South Africa, EGSSA Branch; *OA*; Plymouth and West Devon Record Office, Plympton Deeds.
174 *CP;* thepeerage.com: person M, #17339.
175 Anc: Hibberdpoole; BMD; c-1851–1871.
176 Anc: WOLLF Family Tree: FrançoiseDessertenne; Anc: [Montagu family] mclean Family Tree: lesleymclean47; *CB*; *Debrett 1835-II*, p. 269; Wiltshire and Swindon Archives, Burdett and Jones Families, Poore Family Papers.
177 Anc: pope Family Tree: andypope157; c-1891–1901; *DNB*; *OA*.
178 Anc: Blomfield family tree: hugoblomfield, Anc: de Loriol Chandieu Family Tree: Peter de LORIOL CHANDIEU; Anc: Hunter Derrick family tree: JuliaHunter52; BMD; BRADNEY, Joseph, *History of Monmouthshire*, vol. 1, 1904, p. 388; *DNB*: Bunsen; Granville Pedigree; National Library of Wales Journal, Cyf. 12, rh. 4 Gaeaf 1962, The Girlhood of Augusta Waddington (afterwards Lady Llanover)—1802-23; Reminiscences of Baroness Bunsen.
179 Wikipedia.
180 Anc: Sherman Family Tree: JerrySears85.
181 BMD; c-1861–1881; *GM*, vol. 161, 1837, p. 650.
182 Anc: Pole Family Tree: PaulKeen45; Anc: WILTSHIRE Burcombe Pitts Family Tree: droylsden1; *HP*; *OA*.
183 BMD; *CA*.
184 BMD; c-1851–1871; *CA*.
185 Anc: Victorians: MarchHare2; BMD; c-1841–1861; *CA*; KNOTT, John, *Popular Opposition to 1834 Poor Law*, 1986; ROMILLY, Joseph, *Romilly's Cambridge Diary 1832-42*, 1967, p. 250.
186 BMD; c-1841–1851; *Hunt*.
187 *CP*.
188 Anc: Poynder 2016: richendasc; BMD; c-1851–1871; *Eton*; *Social History of Medicine* vol. 21, No. 2 pp. 237–252, 2008: SMITH, Leonard, 'Your Very Thankful Inmate': Discovering the Patients of an Early County Lunatic Asylum.
189 Anc: Thomas Family Tree: janetjoybaxter; BMD; c-1841–1911.
190 Anc: Hallam Family Tree: helen_hallam88; *CA*.
191 BMD; *HP*.
192 *CP*; *HP*.
193 Anc: pratt Family Tree: davidnevilpratt; *DNB*.

194 Anc: Bowman Family Tree: cbnatch; *DNB*.

195 GA; *Hunt*; *VCH*, Gloucester.

196 Anc: Devine, Langsford, Hughes-Hallett, Lush Family Tree: Anne Varker; BMD: All Parish Records from 1558–1780 for the Parish of Westbury, Buckinghamshire; *The Court Magazine & Monthly Critic and Lady's Magazine*, vol. 13, 1844, p. 59; *GM*, vol. 60, part 1, 1790. p. 340; *GM*, vol. 186, 1849, p. 640; Lipscomb, George, *The History and Antiquities of the County of Buckingham*, vol. 3, 1847, p. 142; NA: Centre for Buckinghamshire Studies, Westbury estate: deeds and other documents relating to Barrington estate (Price estate to 1854), Reference: D169; *MM*, vol. 5, 1816, p. 84; Richards, J., *The Legal Guide*, vol. 7, 1842, p. 54; *VCH*, Buckingham: vol. 4, 1927: Westbury.

197 *OA*.

198 BMD; WFP: F203–F214.

199 *OA*.

200 c-1841–1861; GA; *LG*, 13 October 1876; *VCH*, Oxfordshire: Burford.

201 BMD; c-1841–1881.

202 *OA*.

203 Anc: BEAZLEY –CRISDALE Public Tree: aussiejeff; Anc: Money Family Tree 27 Apr 2015: stuartmoney; Anc: Goodlake Family Tree: Sarah Goodlake; BMD; CCEd; c-1841–1911; Cundee, J., *The Traveller's Guide: or, English Itinerary*, vol. 2, 1805, p. 631; Duncan, Leland L., *Inscriptions in the Churchyard of Stowting, Kent. Taken August 1890*; *Foster-1881*; p. 514; *GM*, 1840, p. 554; *OA*.

204 Anc: Shelton Family Tree: Grahamlsherwood; BMD; c-1841–1891; NA: GA: Price family of Tibberton Court: Reference: D2176; *Williams*.

205 BMD; c-1841–1851; Ellen Octavia Terry (Prichard), viewed 6 August 2019: <https://www.geni.com/people/Ellen-Terry/6000000012103634586>; Wikipedia.

206 CCEd; *OA*.

207 BMD; *DNB*–Sir William Russell; *GM*, vol. 11, 1839, p. 218; *LG*, part 2, 1836, p. 2238; Osborn, Bob, *The A-to-Z of Yeovil's History*, George Bragge Prowse, viewed 16 September 2018: <http://www.yeovilhistory.info/prowse-georgebragge.htm>

208 *OA*; *VCH*, Gloucestershire, vol. 11: Charlton.

209 Biber, George Edward, *The English Church on the Continent*, 1846, p. 79; Hartley, William, post: November 21, 2004, viewed 16 September 2018: <https://www.genealogy.com/forum/regional/countries/topics/englandcountry/88910/>; *OA*

210 BMD; c-1841.

211 Anc: Heather Fischer family tree: EcoMarie3; GPA.

212 *The Asiatic Journal and Monthly Miscellany*, vol. 17, 1835, p. 197; c-1841–1871 inc.; MI: Newland, Gloucestershire; *OA*.

213 c-1851; MI: Newland, Gloucestershire.

214 *OA*.

215 CCEd; *GM*, vol. 170, 1841; *OA*.

216 Burns, James, *Church of England Magazine*, 1838; *GM*, vol. 170, 1841; *OA*.

217 c-1841; *Reports of cases argued and determined in the English courts of Great Britain. Court of King's Bench, Bail Court, Court of Common Pleas*, 1838.

218 BMD; c-1841–1861.

219 *HP*.

220 BMD; *HP*; *OA*.

221 Anc: protheroe Family Tree: iankwright; Anc: Amanda Morrison Family Tree: AHatrick; BMD; *HP*.

222 BMD; c-1851; NA: GA: Reference: D3117/360; Stained Glass Windows at St Mary's, Purton, Wiltshire, viewed 22 September 2018: <https://www.myheritage.com/names/john_prower>.

223 BMD; c-1851.

224 Anc: Burrell Family Tree: cndyh1; BMD; *OA*.

225 Anc: Coulson Family Tree: j_vander_veen96; Anc: Tansey-Waldegrave: Sam Craig; Anc: gritten/steel Family Tree: speycaster66; BMD; Burke, Edmund, *The Annual Register of World Events: A Review of the Year*, vol. 68, 1827, p. 209; c-1841; Community Trees: An official Web site of The Church of Jesus Christ of Latter-day Saints; *CP*; *DNB*—La Touche; Metropolitan Museum of Art, New York; E&W Wills—will of John David Puget 1805; *The Royal Kalendar and Court and City Register for England, Scotland, Ireland and the Colonies*, 1833, p. 174; UCL–Slaves.

226 BMD; c-1841.

227 BMD; c-1841–1861.

228 Anc: Pine Grove Idaho Families family tree; BMD; c-1851.

229 Anc: PEARSON Family Tree 3rd try: Lynne Smith: BMD; *DNB*; *OA*.

230 *CA*; *OA*.

231 Anc: SPRIGGE Family Tree: John Sprigge; c-1851; *OA*.

232 Anc: SPRIGGE Family Tree: John Sprigge; Anc: Purnell Research tree: Lesley Rose; BMD; *B-1847-2*, p. 1085; c-1841–1891; *Debrett* 1840; supplement to *LG*, 23 March 1858; *MM*, vol. 19, 1805, p. 90; NA: GA Reference: D149/F61; *OA*; *Walford-1882*; p. 538.

233 Anc: A HARRISON Family Tree: AHARRISON19; Anc: Williams family tree: oswin1909; Blunt, John Henry, *Dursley and its Neighbourhood*, 1877, p. 201; BMD; *B-1847-2*, p. 1085; *LG*, number 12594, 9–13 November 1784; *LG*, 1826, p. 2064; E&W Wills—Will Registers 1802–1804 Piece 1375: Kenyon, Quire Numbers 383-433 (1802); Tann, Jennifer, *Gloucestershire Woollen Mills*, 1967, p. 141.

234 Anc: Williams family tree: oswin1909; *OA*.

235 Anc: Stone Family Tree: jillfara; BMD; *B-1847-2*, p. 1086.

236 Anc: Janes + Thickett FamiliesTree: Bob Janes; *DNB*.

237 Royal Academy of Music.

238 Anc: Joan Lesley Roberton Family Tree: joanroberton; BMD; CCEd; Howard, Joseph Jackson, and Crisp, Frederick Arthur, *Visitation of England and Wales Notes*, vol. 13, 1919, p. 146; *HP*; E&W Wills—will of Revd Henry Anthony Pye: Reference: PROB 11/1911/144; *OA*.

239 BMD; c-1841–1861, 1881; *OA*; *VCH*, Gloucestershire, vol. 11, Bisley and Longtree Hundreds: Sapperton: Church.

240 *CP*.
241 Anc: Gough/Douglas Family Tree: ydouglas15; *CA*.
242 Anc: Brooks-Hamilton_2010-05-22_January 2012: tonyahamilton1; Curteis, William Calverley, *Reports of Cases Argued and Determined in the Ecclesiastical Courts at Doctors' Commons*, 1844, pp. 1-15; United Grand Lodge of England Freemason Membership Registers, 1751–1921.
243 Anc: Pyrke 2013: gottschalk155; NPG: viewed 23 September 2018: <https://www.npg.org.uk/collections/search/portrait/mw254946/Octavius-Cobb-Rooke-Augusta-Harriet-Rooke-ne-Pyrke>; *OA*.
244 Anc: Pyrke 2013: gottschalk155; *OA*.
245 Anc: Hanks Family Tree: tonyhanks_1.

Letter Q

1 Anc: D.Tuttle Family Tree: David Tuttle; BMD; c-1861; Luc Frère, viewed 30 September 2018: <https://gw.geneanet.org/lfrlfr?lang=en&p=andrew&n=quicke>.

Letter R

1 BMD; *DNB*.
2 *CA*.
3 *OA*.
4 *OA*.
5 BMD; CCEd; c-1841–1861; *GM*, vol. 144 p. 270; E&W Wills—Will Registers 1829–1831 Piece 1767: Beard, Quire Numbers 101-150 (1830); *OA*; UK, Articles of Clerkship, 1756–1874 for James Ralfe, 1792.
6 *HP*; *OA*; WFP, F183-F201.
7 CCEd; *OA*.
8 Jenkins, Stephanie: viewed 23 September 2018: <http://www.oxfordhistory.org.uk/mayors/1836_1962/randall_thomas_1859.html>.
9 *DNB*; *OA*,
10 BMD; c-1841–1881; *DNB*.
11 BMD; c-1841–1851.
12 Anc: Lauzon Lindner Family Tree: Susan Lauzon; Anc: Newman-Knott Family Tree: SandraPatience; Anc: A5a(2): kim_andres; Anc: June 2018 Greenham and Thomas Family Lines: RGree56; Anc: Fisher Family Tree: fisherdavid1946; Anc: Gillespie_Thorburn Family Tree: beerwahhills; BMD; c-1841–1911.
13 Anc: Gilbert Family Tree: PaSmith44; Anc: Generations: sbestley1; Anc: firth_tree_for_mum: freda_dennis; CCEd; *OA*.
14 Anc: Wood/Nauss Family Tree: Sherrill Yates; Anc: Walker Family Tree: RubyGalili25; BMD; CCEd; *OA*.
15 *DNB*.
16 *CP*.
17 Anc: Henzey, Tyzack & Tittery: wrag44; BMD; c_1841–1871; NA: Lancashire Archives: Reference: DDX 243/6/11.
18 Anc: Harvey Family TreeFind: JoelleHarvey; Anc: View in TreeJanes + Thickett Families: Bob Janes; *DNB*; NA: Lancashire Record Office: Littledale Estate in Caton; Reminiscences of Miss Isabel Dobson (1806–1882).
19 *Blackwood's Lady's Magazine*, 1843, p. 308; BMD; *B-1847-2*; p. 1102; Jekyll Family History: viewed 23 September 2018: <http://www.archerfamily.org.uk/family/jekyll.htm>; WFP-F173-235.
20 Anc: McKay/Rich/Forsdyke/Bailey/Trimmer Tree: neilmckay21; BMD; c-1841.
21 Anc: Taylor: kekelu; *CA*; *Bath Chronicle and Weekly Gazette*, 4 June 1789; BMD; *B-1847-1*, vol. 1, p. 54; *btsarnia*: A tribute to the life and work of Brian Torode: viewed 28 September 2018: <https://btsarnia.org/2017/10/11/the-raymond-barkers-of-bisley-and-the-building-of-st-mary-of-the-angels/>; *CA*; CCEd; c-1851–1891; *Debrett 1839*, p. 196; *GM*, vol. 163, 1838, p. 444; *Hereford Journal*, 14 December 1796; *LG*, part 2, 1834. p. 2310; E&W Wills—will of John Raymond Barker of Fairford Park , Gloucestershire: Reference: PROB 11/1722/228; Nonconformist baptisms: Piece 4141: Carter Lane, Blackfriars (Presbyterian), 1760–1811; PI: June Lewis-Jones; Stone, Lawrence, *Broken Lives: Marital Separation and Divorce in England 1660–1857*; John Raymond-Barker, viewed 29 September 2018: <https://www.wikitree.com/wiki/Raymond-Barker-6>.
22 *Ibid*.
23 Anc: Read Family, Gillingham Dorset: aquaducks13; Anc: simpson gilman floyd: Anne1882; BMD; c-1851.
24 Anc: Hoskyns Family Tree: JanetHoskyns; Anc: Shipton Court Tree: Coorag02; BMD; *CB*; NPC: NA: PROB 11/2178/392; thepeerage.com: person M, #556987.
25 BMD; *The Colonial Journal*, vol. 1, Issues 1-2, 1816, p. 288; *Debrett 1832*, p. 199; *Foster-1881*, p. 524.
26 BMD; *CB*; *DNB*.
27 *EB*.
28 c-1841–1861; History of Taitlands, viewed 29 September 2018: <http://www.taitlands.co.uk/history>; St Peter's Church, Stainforth. MI.
29 BMD; c-1851.
30 *Pigot's Directory*, 1830 & 1842-4; The Royal Hotel, viewed 28 September 2018: <https://www.familytreehq.com/blog/>; The Royal Hotel, viewed 28 September 2018: <https://historicengland.org.uk/listing/the-list/list-entry/1320676>.
31 *DNB*.
32 Wikipedia; Everett, Andrew, *Josephine's Composer: The Life Times and Works of Gaspare Pacifico Luigi Spontini (1774–1851)*, 2013, p. 252; Wollenberg, Susan, *The Piano in Nineteenth-Century British Culture: Instruments, Performers and Repertoire*, 2017.

33 Anc: Reid of Jamaica Family Tree: Doug_Brough; *MM*, vol. 1, 1814, p. 97; UCL–Slaves; WFP F173–235.
34 *DNB*.
35 Complete Works of Carl Maria von Weber, Christiane Henriette von Reitzenstein, viewed 6 August 2019: <http://weber-gesamtausgabe.de/A00207A>.
36 *CA*; CCEd; *DNB*.
37 WFP-F207, 1 January 1805.
38 Anc: Sir John Rennie Family Tree: dwaynerennie1; *DNB*.
39 E&W Wills— Will of Francis James Rens: PROB 11/1840/251, 1 December 1834; Uncredited pedigree, viewed 6 October 2018: <https://www.genealogieonline.nl/stamboom-driessen/I7347801.php>.
40 Anc: Phipps Family Tree: SuzanneP17; BMD; c-1841–1861.
41 Anc: Pimblett Hughes Family Tree: Jan Pimblett; BMD; c-1851; London and Surrey, England, Marriage Bonds and Allegations, 1597–1921; London, England, Freedom of the City Admission Papers, 1681–1930 for George Reynell, 1829.
42 Anc: Tracey Family Tree: kossuth2; BMD; c-1841–1861.
43 Anc: Ricardo: Stephen Jemmett; BMD; *CA*; c-1851, *DNB*; *GM*, vol. 87, part 1, 1817.
44 *CP*; *OA*; Newell, Chris, viewed 6 October 2018: <http://www.wildot.co.uk/biogs/a_catley.htm>; thepeerage.com: person M, #394392.
45 Gloucestershire, England, Church of England Marriages and Banns, 1754–1938 for Frances Ingram; *The Register of Pennsylvania: devoted to the preservation of facts and documents and every other kind of useful information respecting the state of Pennsylvania*; 1832, p. 307; *Reports of Cases Argued and Determined in the High Court of Chancery: During the Time of Lord Chancellor Eldon*, vol. 1, 1821, p. 79; *VCH*, Gloucestershire, vol. 6, 1965: Bourton-on-the-Water.
46 Anc: Sammons Knapp Family Tree: esmeyer23; BMD; c-1851; *CP*; *HP*.
47 *CP*; *HP*; *OA*; thepeerage.com: person M, #16524.
48 BMD; *OA*; Newell, Chris, viewed 6 October 2018: <http://www.wildot.co.uk/biogs/a_catley.htm>; thepeerage.com: person M, #394392.
49 Anc: John and Sandra Bagnall Family Tree: Jwbagnall85; BMD; c-1851–1871; *OA*; *VCH*, Oxfordshire, Buscot.
50 *DNB*; *OA*.
51 Anc: Wilson Family Tree: Michael Wilson; CCEd; *DNB*; *OA*.
52 Anc: SMM: susanmacaskill; CCEd; *GM*, vol. 5, 1836; Newspaper Transcripts, Salisbury; *OA*.
53 Descendants of Ralph Richardson, viewed 6 October 2018: <https://www.theislandwiki.org/index.php/Descendants_of_Ralph_Richardson>; *OA*; Payne, James Bertrand, *Armorial of Jersey*, 1859, p. 328.
54 *Baines's Directory and Gazetteer Directory* of 1822.
55 Asher, Jean, and Warren, Sandra, MI: St Peter's Church, Stainforth, Settle, North Yorkshire, 2016; BMD; c-1851–1861.
56 Anc: Young Family Tree: lesleywilkins52; BMD; *CA*; c-1851–1891.
57 Day, Mark Trelawny, 19 November 2008, viewed 7 October 2018: <https://www.geni.com/people/Robert-Ricketts-Vice-Admiral-1st-Bt-Elms-Beaumont-Leys/6000000001781664411?through=6000000001781660784>; *Foster-1881*, p. 528; thepeerage.com: person M, #558817.
58 Anc: Milles Family Tree: Tempelburg; BMD; *B-1832-2*, p. 352; *CB*.
59 Anc: Milles Family Tree: Tempelburg; BMD; *CB*.
60 *CB*.
61 BMD; c-1841–1871.
62 BMD; c-1841–1861; *DNB*; *OA*.
63 Anc: Nigel Rideout Family Tree: nigelr1942; BMD; c-1841–1871.
64 Anc: Holland-2: GHolland98; *OA*.
65 *DNB*.
66 WFP F173-235.
67 Anc: Edwards-Hamilton Family Tree: medwards581; BMD; *CA*; c-1851.
68 BMD; *CA*; c-1851–1881.
69 Anc: Johnstone Family Tree: robjohnstone1; BMD.
70 Anc: You'll never know what you will find: RebeccaAnnBlyth; *CA*.
71 *DNB*; *HP*.
72 Anc: Robinson Family Tree: evelyn194861; BMD; c-1851–1861.
73 Anc: Broadbent Family Tree: shirlen_1; BMD; c-1871; Lancashire Record Office: DDCM 1/147 24 Mar. 1855.
74 Anc: Robinson of Chatburn: tomrobin29.
75 Anc: Robinson Family Tree: LorettaT41; *OA*.
76 Anc: Cottam Family Tree: Rosemary_Durham; Bedfordshire Archives Service Catalogue: reference: AL48/1-2, 1825; BMD; c-1841–1911 inc.; Bligh, Richard, *New reports of cases heard in the House of Lords*, 1822; *The Examiner*, issues 883-933, 1825 by Hunt, Leigh, Fonblanque, Albany William, and Forster, John.
77 BMD; c-1851.
78 BMD; c-1851; UK, Lunacy Patients Admission Registers, 1846–1912, County asylums and hospitals Piece 13: 1847 Jun–1849 Feb.
79 Anc: SMITH_ANDREWS TREE/28/12/17: iband60; BMD; c-1851.
80 Anc: McPhail Family Tree: L. McPhail; BMD; c-1851.
81 BMD; c-1871; *GM*, vol. 164, 1838, p. 666; *MM*, vol. 21, 1806, p. 377; *OA*.
82 BMD; *GM*, vol. 28, 1847, p. 549; Elizabeth Henville, viewed 13 October 2018: <https://www.myheritage.com/names/elizabeth_henville>; *OA*.
83 Anc: Skelton Family Tree: lilskelton; Seaver, J. Montgomery, *Rogers Family History.*
84 BMD; *OA*.
85 Anc: Rodocanachi (Chris Davies Greek Ancestry): Roydavies98; BMD; c-1841–1871.

86 Wikipedia.
87 BMD; c-1841–1851; Davenport, John Marriott, *Oxfordshire: Lords Lieutenant, High Sheriffs and Members of Parliament, &c.*, 1888, p. 86; *GM*, vol. 72, part 2, 1802; Hasted, Edward, *The History and Topographical Survey of the County of Kent*, vol. 4, 1798; NPC (Index of Wills and Administrations), 1858–1966; Shakespeare Centre Library and Archive: Oxfordshire Papers; WFP.
88 *CA*; CCEd; *OA*.
89 Anc: Wakefield Family Tree: aletanall; BMD; Dod, Charles Roger, *The Peerage Baronetage and Knightage of Great Britain and Ireland*, 1844, p. 323; *Notes and Queries*, 1863, pp. 118-9; Rooke family, viewed 20 October 2018: <https://www.ashefamily.info/ashefamily/6437.htm>.
90 Anc: Rathbone/Fenton/Ford/Fussell/Owen/Norton/Agutter / Rooke families: Jane Chapman; *Blackwood's Edinburgh Magazine*, vol. 25; *GM*, January 1856.
91 Anc: Fludyer Family Tree: wendy maul.
92 BMD; c-1841–1871.
93 BMD; c-1851; Gray, Denis, *Spencer Perceval: The Evangelical Prime Minister 1762–1812*, 1963.
94 Anc: Bridgitte's Branches: Bridgitte Allman; BMD; c-1851–1881; *OA*.
95 Anc: Family Tree: assemblyorder; *OA*.
96 Anc: Kunz Family Tree: noanoa1; Anc: Hersey Family Tree: handa175; BMD; *B-1898-2*, p. 1282; c-1851; *DNB*: John Horace Round; *MATB*, pp. 403-4; *GM*, 1842, p. 310; Howard, Joseph Jackson, and Crisp, Frederick Arthur, *Visitation of England and Wales*, vol. 13, 1905, p. 180; *OA*; thePeerage, person M, #687417; Thomas, William, *The Court Journal and Fashionable Gazette*, 1859, p. 164.
97 Anc: Varley Family Tree: ColinVarley; BMD; *B-1898-2*, p. 1282; *OA*.
98 *GM*, vol. 92, 1822, p. 476.
99 *DNB*.
100 Anc: Rowden Family Tree: bobfleetwood_1; *OA*.
101 *Ibid.*; baptism for Mary Ann Cooper at Langwm: viewed 21 October 2018: <http://www.rootschat.com/forum/index.php?topic=440219.0>.
102 Anc: Stretch Family Tree: medwards581; BMD.
103 *Allen's Indian Mail*, 1846, p. 738; *The Asiatic Journal*, 1842, p. 62; *The Indian News and Chronicle of Eastern Affaires: 1848*, 1848, p. 250; Registers of Employees of the East India Company and the India Office, 1746–1939.
104 BMD; c-1851–1891 inc.; BGAS *Newsletter*, August 2011; *OA*.
105 Anc: Nichols Family Tree: karenbillings1273; BMD; c-1851–1881.
106 BMD; c-1861.
107 Anc: Evesham Rudge Family Tree: Paula Howells; BMD; *DNB*; *OA*.
108 *Ibid.*, CA.
109 Anc: Williams: carranzoo; BMD; *OA*.
110 Anc: The Guy Tree: tilly1569; BMD; c-1851–1871 inc.; *Hunt*.
111 *CP*.
112 Anc: Coulson Family Tree: j_vander_veen96; Anc: Newman McHaffie Tree: VickyNewman69; BMD; Danley, Mark, Speelman, Patrick. *The Seven Years' War: Global Views*, 2012, p. 454; *GM*, 1760; Land Tax Records, 1692–1932 for Wager Russell, Tower, 1748; Matcham, Mary Eyre, *A Forgotten John Russell: being letters to a man of business, 1724–1751*, 1905.
113 Anc: bledington cooks: kimik4103; c-1841–1851; England & Wales, Criminal Registers, 1791–1892 for Hannah Russell.
114 *HP*.
115 c-1841.
116 *DNB*.
117 BMD–Scotland, Select Marriages, 1561–1910; Cowan, Samuel, *The Ruthven Family Papers*, 1912, p. 89, *CP*; Geni.UK, viewed 27 October 2018: <https://www.geni.com/people/Lady-Mary-Elizabeth-Leslie/>.
118 Anc: Jenna's Tree: snapdragon86; *DNB*.
119 Brahm, Felix, & Rosenhaft, Eve, *Slavery Hinterland: Transatlantic Slavery and Continental Europe, 1680–1850*, 2016, p. 146; Gould, Robert Freke, Yorston, John C., *A Library of Freemasonry*, vol. 4, 1906, p. 166; Hosack, David, and Francis, John W., *American Medical and Philosophical Register, or, Annals of Medicine, Natural History, Agriculture and the Arts*, vol. 2, 1814, p. 459; Linnean Society of London, *Charter and Bye-laws of the Linnean Society of London: Together with a Patent of Armorial Ensigns, and a List of the Society*, 1802, p. 48; Power, Orla, Thesis, *Irish planters, Atlantic merchants: the development of St. Croix, Danish West Indies, 1750–1766*, May 2011, viewed 27 October 2018: <https://aran.library.nuigalway.ie/handle/10379/6011>; Rodgers, N., *Ireland, Slavery and Anti-Slavery: 1612–1865*, 2007, pp. 61-64; Rodriguez, Pedro Acevedo (*et al.*), *Memoirs of the New York Botanical Garden*, vol. 78, 1996; The Royal Society, Repository GB 117, Ref No. EC/1797/20; Songhurst W. J., *Ars Quatuor Coronatorum*, vol. 37, 1924, pp. 145-147, p. 157; UCL-Slaves.
120 BMD; c-1851.
121 *The Annual Register*, vol. 88, 1847, p. 292; BMD; Sir Henry Rycroft, viewed 27 October 2018: <https://www.geni.com/people/Sir-Richard-Rycroft-1st-Baronet>; *Notes and Queries*, 1892, p. 477.
122 *Ibid.*; *CB*.
123 *CA*; *CP*; *DNB*; *HP*.
124 Anc: McLeod Family Tree: florabastin; *CA*; *DNB*.

Letter S

1 Anc: Ellen Margaret Bates: Hellen Trigg; BMD; Colville, Dorothy, *North Mymms–Parish and People*, 1972, chapter 23: The Sabine Family; Levere, Trevor Harvey, *Science and the Canadian Arctic: A Century of Exploration, 1818–1918*, 2003, p. 80; Sabine family,

viewed 27 October 2018: <https://www.findagrave.com/memorial/47522041/joseph-sabine>; Rowland Hunt, of Boreatton, viewed 27 October 2018: <http://www.william1.co.uk/e23.htm>; *Twelfth Meeting of the British Association; Held At Manchester In June 1842*, 1843, p. 6; *Walford-1864*, p. 51.

2 *DNB*.

3 MI: Leckhampton; *OA*.

4 Anc: ancestry_2014-04-10: 1876win; BMD; *OA*; *The Plantagenet Roll of the Blood Royal*, The Mortimer-Percy volume, by Marquis of Ruvigny and Rainevalf; Croftons Solicitors, viewed 27 October 2018: <https://www.croftons.co.uk/about-us/>.

5 BMD.

6 Anc: Underwood/Ashbury/Preest/Porter: Patricia Willmott; James Piers St Aubyn, viewed 27 October 2018: <http://www.scottisharchitects.org.uk/architect_full.php?id=203621>; Wikipedia.

7 Anc: St Clair Family Tree: HappyPanda67; *BLG*; BMD.

8 Anc: Howe Family Tree: rshowe1919; Anc: Clephane Family Tree: James Clephane; *B-1854*, p. 860; *CP*.

9 Anc: Brown Family Tree: Hurley90; *CP*; Wikipedia.

10 Anc: Green/Thorfinnson Family Tree: Christopher Green; Anc: Mackenzie, Cameron and Duncan Tree: jenniroseburke; BMD; c-1851; *The Ecclesiastical Gazette*, April 1840.

11 *BDA*, vol. 10, 1985, p. 53, Brown, James Duff, *Biographical Dictionary of Musicians*, 1886, p. 536; *DNB*; *Grove*, vol. 3, 1889, p. 220; London, Freedom of the City Admission Papers, 1681–1930 for James Salmon, 1780.

12 A History of Awdry Bailey and Douglas, viewed 28 October 2018: <https://www.awdrys.co.uk/assets/History/Legal%20Overview%20-%20A%20History%20of%20Awdry%20Bailey%20and%20Douglas.pdf>; BMD; c-1851.

13 Anc: Collingwood/Watson/Darling/Hopper/Byrne: amy Collingwood; BMD; Dodsley, J. *Annual Register*, 1830; *A Concise History of the City and Suburbs of Worcester*, 1816; *Reports of Cases Argued and Determined in the Court of King's Bench*, vol. 1, W. Clarke and Sons, 1806; Centre for Buckinghamshire Studies; *GM*, vol. 145, 1829, p. 462; *GM*, vol. 16, 1864, p. 539;Hasted, Edward, *The History and Topographical Survey of the County of Kent: Containing the Antient and Present State of It, Civil and Ecclesiastical*, vol. 6, 1798; Hughes, Stefan, *Catchers of the Light: The Forgotten Lives of the Men and Women Who First Photographed the Heavens*, 2012; *Journals of the House of Lords*, vol. 41, 1796, p. 83 (a petition to the House of Lords by Eliz. about the estate of the late Elliot Salter); Kingsley, Nicholas, viewed 28 October 2018: <http://landedfamilies.blogspot.com/2014/02/108-allhusen-of-stoke-court.html>; National Maritime Museum: Collections: Maria Pierrepont; O'Callaghan, Edmund Bailey, *Names of Persons for whom MARRIAGE LICENSES Were issued by the Secretary of the Province of New York Previous to 1784*. Printed by order of Gideon J. Ticker, Secretary of State. Albany: Weed, Parsons and Company, 1860, p. 206; Oliver, Vere Langford, *Caribbeana: being miscellaneous papers relating to the history, genealogy, topography, and antiquities of the British West Indies*,1914, p. 233; Royal Museums, Greenwich, viewed 28 October 2018: <http://collections.rmg.co.uk/collections/objects/204224.html#2Q6zpxpTR730C10A.99>, Salter, viewed 28 October 2018: <ttps://threedecks.org/index.php?display_type=show_crewman&id=12689>; *VCH*, Buckinghamshire: vol. 3, 1925; Winfield, R., *British Warships in the Age of Sail 1714–1792: Design, Construction, Careers and Fates*, 2007.

14 *B-1882-1*, p. 427, BMD; c-1841; *GM*, vol. 166, 1839, p. 566.

15 BMD; CCEd, *OA*.

16 *The Edinburgh Almanack, or Universal Scots and Imperial Register*, 1833, p. 147.

17 Anc: Janes + Thickett Families: Bob Janes; *DNB*; WFP F186-195.

18 *CA*; CCEd.

19 Anc: Mann Family Tree: Stuart Edward Tapley; *DNB*.

20 Anc: Family Tree: assemblyorder; *DNB*.

21 BMD; thePeerage, person M, #368822.

22 Anc: Royalty & Peerage: Robert Candy; *OA*.

23 Marshall, John, *Royal Navy Biography*, 1824; E&W Wills—will of Henry Savage, viewed 28 October 2018: <https://threedecks.org/index.php?display_type=show_crewman&id=12773>.

24 Anc: Schott Family Tree: RobertSchott1935; Beaven, Alfred B., *Bristol Lists: Municipal and Miscellaneous*, 1899; BMD; c-1841; UCL-Slaves.

25 Anc: Pearson Family Tree: bobfleetwood_1; BMD; c-1851.

26 Wikipedia.

27 *Ibid.*

28 *Ibid.*; *DNB*.

29 *Ibid.*

30 *Ibid.*

31 *Ibid.*

32 *Ibid.*; *Grove*.

33 *Ibid.*

34 Anc: Janes + Thickett Families: Bob Janes; BMD; CCEd; *OA*.

35 Anc: Newman McHaffie Tree: VickyNewman69; CCEd, *OA*.

36 *DNB*.

37 Anc: Scaysbrook 2018: Ian Scaysbrook; BMD; c-1841–1851.

38 Brandt, George W. (ed.), *German and Dutch Theatre, 1600–1848*, 2009.

39 *AGB*.

40 *EB*; Schiller, viewed 3 November 2018: <https://www.geni.com/people/Friedrich-von-Schiller/6000000022448861384?through=6000000000658145235>.

41 Schmieder, Heinrich Gottlieb, *Taschenbuch fürs Theater*, 1801, p. 200; von Goethe, Johann Wolfgang, Vulpius, Christiane, & Gräf, Hans Gerhard, *Goethes Briefwechsel mit seiner Frau*, vol. 1, 1916, p. 156, p. 162; Schmieder, Heinrich Gottlieb, *Journal für Theater u. andere schöne Künste*, 1797, pp. 74-5.

42 Gerard, Frances, *A Grand Duchess: The Life of Anna Amalia, Duchess of Saxe-Weimar-Eisenach*, 1902, p. 101, republished in a new edition by Fonthill Media, 2012; Biblioteca Virtual de la Filología Española, viewed 20 July 2019: <https://www.bvfe.es/autor/10676-schmid-ernst-august.html>.

43 Anc: Anthony Cryan Family Tree: cryanaj; BMD; CCEd; *OA*.

44 *EB*.

45 *EB*.

46 Kessler, Martin, *Johann Gottfried Herder, the Theologian Among the Classics: The Office of the General Superintendent of Saxonia Weimar*, works to the church history vol. 102, part 1, 2007, p. 42, n. 176; Bones of Contention: DNA Tests Reveal 'Schiller's' Skull Not His', *Der Spiegel*, 5 May 2008; Sautter, Ursula: 'Schiller Skull Mystery'. *Time*, 26 July 2007; Wilson, W. Daniel. (ed.) *Goethe's Weimar and the French Revolution: Documents of the Crisis Years*, 2004, p. 736.

47 *CP*; *DNB*.

48 Anc: McCombe/Clutterbuck Family Tree: johnmccombe2; BMD; c-1851; Church of St James, Longborough: viewed 4 November 2018: <https://historicengland.org.uk/listing/the-list/list-entry/1089762> E&W Wills—will of Elizabeth Scott; *GM*, vol. 182, 1847, p. 535; *The Sessional Papers printed by order of the House of Lords*, vol. IV, Public Bills, 1857, p. 11; Rudge, Thomas, *The History of the County of Gloucester*, 1803, p. 20.

49 Anc: Newman McHaffie Tree: VickyNewman69; BMD; *HP*.

50 *DNB*.

51 Anc: Oliver 6/2: Sylvia Harris; BMD; c-1841–1861 inclusive; Warwickshire County Record Office–Messrs. Stockton Sons and Fortescue of Banbury.

52 *B-1838-1*.

53 Anc: Ted & Betty Seaton: TedSeaton; Anc: *Hunt*; BMD; *CA*; Leech, Joseph, Sutton, Alan (ed.), *The Rural Rides of the Bristol Churchgoer*, 1981.

54 Catalogue of the German National Library, idn = 943332907; Wikipedia.

55 Anc: Lovett Family Tree: richardlovett57; BMD; c-1841–1891.

56 *EB*.

57 Anc: Branches Twigs & Stray Leaves: debbilm58; McLintock, Alexander Hare, (ed.), *An Encyclopedia of New Zealand*, 1966.

58 Anc: Selwyn: chris_selwyn; *OA*.

59 *CA*.

60 Anc: Hayes Family Tree: mmfhss; Anc: The Blake's tree: wendaherbert; Anc: Towe Family Tree: amtowe; BMD; sewell, viewed 5 November 2018: <https://www.geni.com/people/Francis-Warneford-Sewell/6000000015614712888>.

61 Anc: Bigtree: Msombre; BMD; *OA*.

62 Anc: Foster Family Tree: Joel Foster; *OA*.

63 Anc: FAMILY TREE: Brigitte Louise Theuma; *OA*.

64 Anc: Whitcombe Family Tree: Kate Whitcombe; Anc: Matthews Family Tree: saltheart; Seymour, viewed 5 November 2018: <https://www.findagrave.com/memorial/92119624>.

65 Anc: Newman McHaffie Tree: VickyNewman69; Anc: Wallace Family Tree: AlmaWallace43; BMD; CCEd; c-1861; *OA*.

66 *CP*; Wikipedia.

67 Anc: Owen, Ginny: gowen160; BMD; c-1851.

68 Lipscomb, George, *The History and Antiquities of the County of Buckingham*, vol. 2, 1847, p. 424; *The General Chronicle and Literary Magazine*, vol. 4, 1812, p. 445; *The New Lady's Magazine*, vol. 2, 1787, p. 112; E&W Wills—will of Sarah Shard; WFP.

69 *DNB*.

70 BMD; c-1851.

71 Anc: Eacret Emmigrants Ire-Aus Kensit-Kelly-Craig: margaret fry; BMD; c-1851; Crisp, Frederick Arthur, *Fragmenta Genealogica*, vol. 6, 1901, p. 43.

72 Anc: Ward Family Tree: librisilluminati; Anc: Michael George William Darlington: 1_MIKEDARLINGTON; *HP*; WFP-F185-195.

73 Anc: O'Neill-Pascoe-Woodcock-Harrup Tree: miconeill; c-1851; Shakespeare Centre Library and Archive.

74 Anc: Sheppard Family Tree: suerosss14; Anc: Duggan Family Tree: tephanieottawa; BMD; *B-1886-2*, p. 1659; WFP F180.

75 Anc: Selby-Lowndes Family Tree: DianeCoghlan; *Debrett 1840*, p. 497. Centre for Buckinghamshire Studies—Deeds and other documents relating to the estates of the Cavendish family of Thornton Hall, Bucks., and Crakemarsh, Staffs; Thornton Church Vault.

76 Anc: Sheptycki Family Tree: barry sheptycki; *DNB*.

77 *DNB*.

78 c-1851.

79 Anc: Ron Jockers Family Tree: travelers172; Anc: woolham Family Tree: sophiewoolham; CCEd; E&W—will of Reverend Samuel Shipley, Clerk of Ashbourne, Derbyshire, PROB 11/2113/368; *OA*.

80 Anc: Law Family Tree: John Harris; *GM*, vol. 215, 1863, p. 384.

81 *Slater's Directory*, 1858-59.

82 Anc: Lesley Wallace: mrsmegales.

83 *OA*.

84 *OA*.

85 Anc: Choat Family Tree: Malcolm Choat; BMD; c-1843; Original admin reference: 2015: website: The Jenner Connection. This does not exist 2018 and the exact reference has not been re-discovered; Fosbroke, Thomas Dudley, *Abstracts of Records and Manuscripts Respecting the County of Gloucester: Formed Into a History, Correcting the Very Erroneous Accounts, and Supplying Numerous Deficiencies in Sir Rob. Atkins, and Subsequent Writers*, vol. 1, 1807, p. 443.

86 Anc: Taylor/Ellett Family Tree: angela14788; BMD; c-1841–1901 inc.; *DNB*; GA: D134/F16: Marriage settlement of Hardwicke Shute, Esq., of Bristol and the Hon. Marianne Wolfe; Hardwicke, Robert, *Hardwicke's Annual Biography for 1856*, 1856, p. 374; *MM*, vol. 28, 1809, p. 117; *MM*, vol. 1, 1816, p. 553.

87 BMD; c-1851; *The Daily Telegraph*, 15 August 2010.
88 Anc: Wood Weldon Family Tree: JennyTidman; BMD; c-1851–1861.
89 *DNB*.
90 Anc: John Bird Monk: philmonk_1; BMD; CCEd; c-1851; *OA*.
91 Anc: White Family Tree: Anne Parratt; c-1841–1861.
92 *Ibid.*; c-1841–1891.
93 *Ibid.*; c-1841–1891.
94 BMD; *OA*.
95 *The Annual Register, Or, A View of the History, Politics etc.* vol. 63., Hare, Augustus J. C., *Story of My Life*, vols 1-3; Twickenham Museum, Houses of Local Interest & their Occupiers; F205-WFP.
96 Australian Convict Transportation Registers–Other Fleets & Ships, 1791–1868; England & Wales, Criminal Registers, 1791–1892.
97 BMD; Butler, Dugald, *The Tron Kirk of Edinburgh: Or Christ's Kirk at the Tron; a History*, 1906, p. 262; *DNB*; F186-WFP.
98 *HP*; Sinclair, viewed 10 November 2018: <http://www.clanmacfarlanegenealogy.info/genealogy/TNGWebsite/getperson.php?personID=I44614&tree=CC>.
99 Anc: Blaine Family Tree: malong; Anc: Lynch_2014_12: Phil Lynch; *Blackwood's Edinburgh Magazine*, vol. 15, 1824, p. 617; BMD; *B-1860*, p. 915; *HP*; thepeerage.com: person F, #201509; WFP F192.
100 *EB*.
101 BMD; c-1841, 1881; *Letter from the Secretary of State, with a Transcript of the List of Passengers who Arrived in the United States from the 1st October, 1819, to the 30th September, 1820*, 1821; *The Monthly Repository of Theology and General Literature*, vol. 15, 1820, p. 733; New Jersey, Deaths and Burials Index, 1798–1971; New York, Passenger and Crew Lists, 1820–1957; Obituary, Captain William Sketchley, viewed 10 November 2018: <http://www.limerickcity.ie/media/12%2018%2039.pdf>; *The New-Yorker*, vol. 8, 1839, p. 143.
102 BMD; *OA*.
103 Anc: Thomas Allen Descendents: tanyalang; *OA*.
104 Anc: Cruickshank Tree Version 2: davidcruickshank1; BMD; c-1841–1881; *OA*; Skinner, Thomas: *Fifty Years in Ceylon: An Autobiography*, 1891; Skinner, viewed 10 November 2018: <http://family.ray-jones.org.uk/rootspersona-tree/allan-maclean-skinner-q-c/>.
105 BMD; CCEd; *OA*.
106 Anc: Bowland/Bowen Family Tree: Kim Bowen; BMD; c-1841–1851.
107 Anc: Victorians: MarchHare2; BMD; *CA*; CCEd; My South African Ancestors, viewed 10 November 2018: <https://www.ballfamilyrecords.co.uk/dunn/I41.html>.
108 Anc: Edward Cooper family tree: ecooper981; E&W Wills—will of Doctor Fenwick Skrimshire, PROB 11/2218/285.
109 Anc: View in Tree7A.B. Middx.RV/8MiddxRVC/2V.B.Middx.Regiment: RobertJones1892; *DNB*.
110 Anc: Slaney Family Tree: toedwar; *HP*.
111 Anc: Gooch Family: KathleenMTaylor_1; *CA*; Slapp, viewed 10 November 2018: <http://hortonpallister.awardspace.com/b-2-9-joseph%20barnett.php>.
112 Anc: Macdonald Family Tree: LM_701_PJ; Anc: Kilbee Family Tree: Tom Spooner; BMD; CCEd, c-1851–1861, *OA*.
113 Anc: Slinger family tree: peter slinger; BMD; c-1861–1871; Tithe Survey 1841 Long Preston, viewed 10 November 2018: <http://www.longprestonheritage.org.uk/origins/Tithe%20Survey%20of%201841.pdf> Graves at St Oswald's, Horton-in-Ribblesdale, viewed 10 November 2018: <https://yorkshirechurchyards.files.wordpress.com/2015/03/a-horton-in-ribblesdale-mis-copy1.pdf>.
114 Anc: Sandra Gray Family Tree: Sandie Gray; Anc: Moore family tree: mmijj60; BMD; *B-1898-2*, p. 1391, c-1841–1911; *HP*.
115 Anc: Helps Family Tree: cgolowka; BMD; c-1841–1901; *Gloucester Journal*, 29 December 1923; *The Law Times*, vols 83–84, 1887, p. 301; *The Register, and Magazine of Biography: A Record of Births, Marriages, Deaths, and Other Genealogical and Personal Occurrences*, 1869, vol. 2, p. 84; *The Solicitors' Journal and Reporter*, vol. 12, 1868, p. 271.
116 BMD.
117 BMD; Stembridge, P. K., *The Goldney Family: A Bristol Merchant Dynasty*, 1998; WFP F200; *The Universal Magazine of Knowledge and Pleasure*, vol. 100, 1797; Younge, Edward; Collyer, John: *Reports of Cases Argued and Determined in the Court of Exchequer*, vol. 2, 1838 [the case of Smith v. Smith].
118 *DNB*.
119 Anc: McLennan Family Tree: nascentmc; BMD; c-1841–1881.
120 BMD; c-1841–1851.
121 Anc: Morway-Kelliher Family Tree: Valentina Espinola-McLaughlin; *CB*.
122 *CB*; thepeerage.com: person F, #48827.
123 *DNB*.
124 Anc: Kaye Tree West Yorkshire Aug 2018: kayegeoff2; *B-1845*; BMD; Cadwallader, viewed 17 November 2018: <http://www.keithblayney.com/Blayney/Cadwallader9.html>; *CB*; c-1841–1851, 1861; Henrietta Dodsworth, viewed 17 November 2018: <https://www.myheritage.com/names/henrietta_dodsworth>; *LG*, part 4, 1846, p. 3766; *The Parish Church of St Mary Alderbury and Whaddon: A short History*; *Salisbury and Winchester Journal*, March 1811.
125 Anc: Hubbard Family Tree: alihub50; BMD; c-1841–1891.
126 BMD; *CA*; CCEd; c-1851–1861; Haggard, John, *Reports of Cases Argued and Determined in the Ecclesiastical Courts at Doctors' Commons, and in the High Court of Delegates: Michaelmas term, 1827 to Trinity term, 1828*, 1829, p. 88.
127 CCEd; *OA*.
128 Anc: Clarke Walker Nicholson Murray- twigs and branches: Estellemur09; BMD; c-1851; Victoria, Australia, Assisted and Unassisted Passenger Lists, 1839–1923.
129 BMD; c-1841.
130 BMD; *B-1838-4*; *Lodge-1845*, p. 306; MI: Holy Trinity Church, Portland Street, Cheltenham; E&W Wills—will of John Carrington Smith, PROB 11/1988/349.

131 Anc: johnson–beale: DianeBeale1; BMD; c-1851.

132 Anc: Smith Family Tree: johncsharp_1; *HP*.

133 *CB*; Scotland, Select Marriages, 1561–1910.

134 Anc: Clarke Walker Nicholson Murray- twigs and branches: Estellemur09; BMD; c-1851; Anc: Farley Family Tree: Historycc; BMD; c-1841–1861; Victoria, Australia, Assisted and Unassisted Passenger Lists, 1839–1923.

135 BMD; c-1861.

136 c-1841; Laidlaw, Zoë, *Colonial Connections 1815–1845: Patronage, the Information Revolution and Colonial Government*, 2005; Shaw, William Arthur, *The Knights of England: A Complete Record from the Earliest Time*, vol. 2, 1906; Sutherland, Gillian, ed., *Studies in the Growth of Nineteenth Century Government*, 1972.

137 Anc: Bryan-Smith Family Tree: info6640; BMD; c-1851.

138 Anc: The Sainsbury Family: Martin Sainsbury; BMD.

139 *DNB*.

140 Anc: Murray/Gaughan Family Tree: Anneliese Wirth; *DNB*.

141 *DNB*.

142 BMD; c-1841.

143 BMD; c-1851–1871.

144 BMD; c-1851–1871.

145 *DCB*.

146 *CB*; Rae, Simon, *W. G. Grace: A Life*; Ashton Gate, viewed 18 November 2018: <https://www.ashtongatehouse.org/the-women>.

147 *CB*.

148 *Ibid., BLG*; *Debrett 1839*; Nottingham University Library, Department of Manuscripts and Special Collections: the Wright Papers, being the papers of the Marriot family of Yorkshire and Worcestershire, 1687–1908.

149 ANC [Montagu family] mclean Family Tree: Anc: Reinders Family Tree: michelle3990y7mailcom; lesleymclean47; *CA*; *CB*; CCEd; *GM*, vol. 181, 1811, p. 594; *GM*, 1837, part 1, p. 438; Montagu of Lackham, viewed 17 November 2018: <https://www.wiltshire.ac.uk/Portals/0/Lackham%20House%20History/Montagu%20Family.pdf?ver=2017-01-06-150017-697×tamp=1483715181916>.

150 BMD.

151 Anc: Boyd Family Tree: borthwick_kevin: Anc: Nigel Snow Family Tree, Anc: Kynaston Family Tree: Norman Scott; BMD; *Burke-1847-2*, p. 1314; Snow, Brentford, viewed 21 November 2018: <http://www.bhsproject.co.uk/families_clitherow.shtml>; Wikitree, viewed 21 November 2018: <https://www.wikitree.com/wiki/Malin-396>.

152 Anc: Seddon Family Tree: synthiabradley; c-1861–1871; Henry Snow, managed by Nigel Allen Snow, viewed 21 November 2018: <https://www.geni.com/people/henry-snow/6000000006563284542?through=6000000006563284507>.

153 *LG*, part 4, 1847, p. 4687.

154 Anc: Solly Squire Family Tree: robsolly; Knight, Roger, *Britain Against Napoleon: The Organization of Victory, 1793–1815*, 2013, p. xx; Wikipedia.

155 Anc: Lenas släktträd: Lena_Holmgren; Anc: Jane Bowden of Drogheda Family Tree: bpetty11; *DNB*; *HP*.

156 Anc: Royalty & Peerage: Robert Candy; *DNB*; *HP*.

157 Anc: Royalty & Peerage: Robert Candy; *CP*; *HP*.

158 *Ibid.*

159 *Ibid.*

160 *Ibid.*

161 *Ibid.*

162 *Ibid.*; *CA*; *CB*.

163 Anc: Bradley, Smith, Kerridge, Long Family Tree: Christine Bradley; BMD; *CP*; *HP*.

164 *DNB*.

165 *CP*.

166 Anc: View in TreeHerron Family Tree: herronjk; *The Athenaeum: A Magazine of Literary and Miscellaneous Information*, vol. 5, 1809; BMD; *B-1847-2*, p. 1534; Devizes marriages, viewed 24 November 2018: <https://www.wiltshire-opc.org.uk/Items/Devizes/Devizes%20-%20Marriages%201750-1837%20St.%20John%20The%20Baptist.pdf; Letters from the Past, viewed 24 November 2018: <http://www.earsathome.com/letters/Previctorian/turner1.html>; *GM*, vol. 109, 1811; *Wiltshire Archaeological Magazine*, vol. 97 2004.

167 BMD; Ettinger, *Theater-Kalender: auf das jahr 1796*, p. 199; Reinalter Helmut, *Freimaurerische Kunst–Kunst der Freimaurerei*; 2015; Spangler, viewed 25 November 2018: <https://ora-web.swkk.de//goe_reg_online/regest.vollanzeige_bio?id=41650&p_lfdnr=0&s_par=sp&n_par=1>; Spangler, viewed 25 November 2018: <http://www.archive-in-thueringen.de/de/findbuch/view/bestand/25949/systematik/65165.

168 HP; *The Edinburgh Directory for July 1797 to July 1798*; WFP F185-F196.

169 *OA*.

170 Anc: Marlow Family Tree: June Wilbur; BMD; c-1851–1861.

171 *CA*; *CP*; *HP*.

172 Deutsch, Otto Erich, *Mozart: A Documentary Biography*; Spitzeder, viewed 25 November 2018: <https://weber-gesamtausgabe.de/de/A009588.html>.

173 *OA*; *The British Magazine and Monthly Register of Religious and Ecclesiastical Information, Parochial History, and Documents Respecting the State of the Poor, Progress of Education, &c, vol. 21*, 1842.

174 BMD; c-1851; *OA*.

175 Anc: My Family File: PeterGoldhawk; BMD; *OA*.

176 *American Vital Records from the Gentleman's Magazine, 1731–1868*, 1987, p. 215; Brayley, E. W., *A Topographical History of Surrey*, 1841; *HP*; *The Town and Country Magazine or Universal Repository of Knowledge, Instruction and Entertainment, vol. V for the Year 1773*; UCL-Slaves.

177 Gurney, Joseph, *The trial (at large) of Joseph Stacpoole, Esq; William Gapper, ... and James Lagier: for wilfully and maliciously shooting at John Parker, Esq; tried ... at Maidstone, ... on Thursday, March 20, 1777*, 1777,
178 *OA*.
179 Anc: Hoskyns Family Tree: JanetHoskyns.
180 *Ibid.*, Innes, Ed. A., E. & M., *The Annual Peerage of the British Empire*, 1829.
181 Anc: Beech, Houghton, Ellis, Kerrison Saul and Howe Family Tree: rachbeech2; *CP*; *HP*.
182 Anc: Weids (e_t_weids): Edward Weids; c-1841; *Hunt*.
183 *Ibid.*
184 Bush, Graham William Arthur, *Bristol and Its Municipal Government, 1820–1851*, 1976.
185 *Williams*.
186 *AGB*: Josef Staudigl.
187 Anc: Stretch Family Tree: medwards581: BMD; c-1851; Kealy, Brian, *North Stainley—A Short History*.
188 Anc: Albrant Family Tree: albrantl; BMD; c-1851.
189 Anc: Woodward/Verity Family Tree: geewoodward; *CB*; *OA*.
190 Anc: Schneider Family Tree: Shirley Schneider; Anc: Anglo-Australian Burton family 29/12/2009: peterburton180; BMD; c-1841–1902 inc.; *Perth Gazette and W. A.*; *The Times*, 13 March 1802; WFP F175; WFP F268.
191 BMD; c-1841–1851.
192 Phillimore, W. P. W., & Blagg, Thomas M. eds., *Gloucestershire Parish Registers, Marriages*, vol. XVII.
193 *DNB*.
194 Anc: Brookes Family Tree: rbrookes59; Anc: Eggleston Family Tree: richmellie; George Hopewell Stephens, viewed 1 December 2018: <https://morethannelson.com/officer/george-hopewell-stephens/>.
195 The Townsend (Townshend) Family Records, viewed 1 December 2018: <http://www.astro.wisc.edu/~townsend/tree/record.php?ref=231>; *OA*.
196 *Annual Register*, vol. 78, 1837, p. 171; Cumria Archive Service Catalogue, viewed 1 December 2018: <http://www.archiveweb.cumbria.gov.uk/CalmView/Record.aspx?src=CalmView.Persons&id=NA976>.
197 *DNB*.
198 *LG*, part 2, 1846, p. 1602; *The Post Office London Directory*, Kelly's Directories Limited, 1843, p. 386.
199 BMD; *OA*.
200 Anc: Stevens Family Tree: Phillip Taylor; BMD; *OA*.
201 Articles of Clerkship, 1756–187; BMD; Exeter Working Papers in Book History; NA: GA, Messrs. Wilmot and Co., Solicitors, Reference: D1070; *Pigot's Directory*, 1830.
202 *CB*.
203 BMD; *CP*; thePeerage, person M, #10944.
204 Anc: Davies Family Tree_2014-10-21(1): marshrat7; Anc: Castle—Filleul Family Tree: Stephen Castle; BMD; *Slater's Directory*, 1850.
205 Anc: Worcester & Warwick Styles: peterstyles183; BMD; c-1841–1851.
206 *Grove*.
207 BMD; c-1851.
208 Anc: Stokey Family Tree: Chris Stokey; BMD; c-1841–1881; Alexander Stokey, viewed 1 December 2018: <https://www.myheritage.com/names/alexander_stokey>.
209 c-1841–1871.
210 Anc: WIP-Hill, Wright, Mott, Point, Clubb, Clemons: tarynrh; Anc: Meade Family Tree: hilbourne516; BMD; Anc: O'Connor–MeadeTree: Nancy O'Connor Evans; E&W Wills, WFP.
211 Anc: Family File 1: KarenD59; *Edinburgh Directory*, 1798.
212 Anc: Pearson Family Tree: Philip Pearson; BMD.
213 BMD; c-1841–1901; *OA*.
214 BMD; c-1851.
215 Anc: Smith/Minns/Steptoe: DISMITH4; BMD; c-1851.
216 Anc: John Phillip Binnie-Dawson Family Tree: pbd2001; Kitty Brewster, viewed 1 December 2018: <https://www.google.co.uk/search?q=http%3A%2F%2Fwww.kittybrewster.com%2C+the+Genealogy+of+the+Stratton+Family>.
217 Charles Spencer Van Straubenzee, viewed 2 December 2018: <https://gw.geneanet.org/frebault?lang=en&n=van+straubenzee&oc=0&p=charles+spencer>; thePeerage, person F, #626192.
218 BMD; c-1851, 1881, *CB*; *OA*.
219 BMD; CCEd; c-1841–1891 inc.; *OA*.
220 Anc: Jenkin Family Tree: Nicola Jenkin; Anc: Main Pye Family Tree: john pye; Anc:
Pamela Strong family tree: Pamstrong5; BMD; c-1851–1861.
221 *HP*.
222 BMD; c-1851–1861; *Slater's Directory*; William Francis Stucke, 2009, viewed 2 December 2018: <https://www.geni.com/people/Henry-Stucke/6000000004879094157?through=6000000004880716294>.
223 *DNB*; *HP*.
224 Anc: Paradise Family Tree: c_hall67; *NBD*, vol. 3, p. 1140.
225 Anc: Galinski Family Tree 2: cgalinski1961; *DNB*; *HP*.
226 Anc: Barker Doyle Dent Family Tree: Sue Williams Anc: Janes + Thickett Families: Bob Janes *The Atheneum*; BMD; c-1851–1861; Cotton Dent, viewed 20 July 2019: <https://www.myheritage.com/names/cotton_dent>; Geri H. Buurman-Dent, viewed 2 December 2018: <http://dentfamlinx.1apps.com/miscellany/sulivan_benjamin-sir.htm>; Sir Digby Dent, viewed 2 December 2018: <https://morethannelson.com/officer/sir-digby-dent/>; *GM*, 1842, p. 90; *The Law Times*, vol. 5, 1845, p. 15; *The Quarterly Review*, 1844, p. 60; *Salisbury and Winchester Journal*; thePeerage, person F, #588844.

227 *DNB*.
228 *BLG*; BMD; c-1841–1851; *Gloucestershire Notes and Queries*; MI: Swindon; *Journal of the House of Lords*: vol. 63: 1830–1831, pp. 795.
229 The Sutcliff Practice, viewed 2 December 2018: <http://www.northcravenheritage.org.uk/NCHTJ2017/2017/Medics/Medics.html>.
230 Anc: Faircloth Family Tree: trixiefaircloth; *CB*; *CP*.
231 Eleanor (Terrell) Hiley, viewed 2 December 2018: <https://www.wikitree.com/wiki/Terrell-18>; *CP*; *GM*, vol. 99, part 1, 1829, p. 650; *GM*, vol. 169, 1840, p. 221; *MM*, vol. 6, 1798, p. 396; Carter, Elizabeth, *Elizabeth Carter, 1717–1806: An Edition of Some Unpublished Letters*, 2005.
232 Anc: Old Settle: KenAndSarahLister; BMD; *OA*.
233 Burrows, Jean, Pennant: *The Local History Journal of Backwell, Nailsea, Tickenham and Wraxall*, no. 8.
234 Anc: gibsone: giblew.
235 *OA*.
236 *CA*; *DNB*.

Letter T

1 Anc: Pickett Family Tree: carl Hudson; BMD; c-1851, 1871–1881; *The Dublin Medical Press, a Weekly Journal of Medicine and Medical Affairs*, vol. III, no. CLXXXIII. July 1842.
2 Anc: Ganly Family Tree: Theresa Ganly; *OA*.
3 Anc: Karl Gumpper family tree: Karl Gumpper; Anc: CCEd; Brockhampton Family Tree No. 1–John Talbot Lutley's ancestry: geoffhicks1; Nicholas Fane de Salis, viewed 8 December 2018: <https://www.geni.com/people/Susan-Elwes/6000000011333422805?through=6000000013566036602>; *OA*.
4 Anc: Talbot Malahide Family Tree: colinjt182; Anc: Baron Talbot of Malahide Family Tree: maccormaic; Anc: Baggot Family Tree: Jennifer_Baggot; Catalogue of the papers of the Talbot family, Barons Talbot de Malahide, 13th–20th cent., viewed 6 August 2019: <http://www.bodley.ox.ac.uk/dept/scwmss/wmss/online/1500-1900/talbot/talbot.html>; WFP-F200.
5 Anc: Karl Gumpper family tree: Karl Gumpper.
6 Anc: The Harvey Family Tree: rwharvey19; *DNB*.
7 Anc: Oxford TALMAGE Family Tree: DavidNelson85; *OA*.
8 *EB*; Wikipedia.
9 Anc: Tancred Family Tree: lingfieldzoo; Encylopedia of New Zealand, viewed 8 December 2018: <https://teara.govt.nz/en/biographies/1t9/tancred-henry-john>; The Cyclopedia of New Zealand, viewed 8 December 2018: <http://nzetc.victoria.ac.nz/tm/scholarly/tei-Cyc03Cycl-t1-body1-d3-d57-d63.html>; WFP F196.
10 *ADB*.
11 BMD; c-1841–1851, 1861; Pallot's Marriage Index; *Pigot's Directory* for Stow-on-the-Wold, 1830.
12 *DNB*.
13 *GM*, vol. 109, 1811, p. 92; *OA*; *Oxford Journal*, March 1770; Chris Spensley, viewed 8 December 2018: <http://www.knightroots.co.uk/transcriptions/Parishes_B/Bishopstoke/Marriages/marriages.htm.
14 BMD; CCEd; *OA*.
15 Anc: Easten Family Tree: KarenEasten28; National Archives; Bristol Record Office; UCL-Slaves; WFP-F201; Wright, Nathalia, ed., *The Correspondence of Washington Allston*, 2014.
16 E&W Wills—will of Richard Taylor; WFP-F201.
17 BMD; c-1841–1851; England & Wales, Criminal Registers, 1791–1892.
18 BMD; c-1841–1861; Wikipedia.
19 Anc: Wood Family Tree: Tony Wood; BMD; c-1841–1871; Pocknell, Trevor, *Wadenhoe Villagers Through Time*.
20 *DNB*.
21 Brandt, George W., et al., *German and Dutch Theatre, 1600–1848*, 1993, p. 268; Douglas W. Stott, viewed 8 December 2018: <https://www.carolineschelling.com/dramatis-personae/persons-t/>; Henke, Burkhard, and Kord, Susanne, *Unwrapping Goethe's Weimar: Essays in Cultural Studies and Local Knowledge*, 2000; Krimmer, Elisabeth, *In the Company of Men: Cross-dressed Women Around 1800*, 2004, p. 192; Lohrer, Liselotte Bäuerle, *Goethe: Tagebücher, Johann Wolfgang von Goethe*.
22 *DNB*; *HP*.
23 *CP*; *HP*.
24 *OA*.
25 Anc: Terrot Family Tree: AnthonyTerrot; *DNB*.
26 Anc: Hewitt Woolsey Family Tree: silversol; BMD; c-1851–1901; *OA*.
27 c-1851.
28 BMD; (Upper Slaughter parish register).
29 Anc: Hutton Potts-Wallace_2017-03-06: Joanna Hammond; BMD; c-1911; thePeerage, person F, #636993.
30 Anc: Seddon Family Tree: synthiabradley; BMD; *CB*; *OA*.
31 Anc: Otto Family Tree: julie_h_otto; *CA*; *The Monthly Repository of Theology and General Literature*, vol. 15, 1820.
32 Anc: View in TreeDevers, Luttick, Scott, Taylor June 2014: neild144; BMD; Nichols, John Gough, *The Herald and Genealogist*, vol. 2, 1865.
33 Anc: Young-Thompson Family Tree_2011-05-30 r2: jythompson2; E&W Wills—will of Henry Thompson; WFP-F199; WFP-F224.
34 Anc: Kirby of Mayfield Family History Site: jvg73; *CB*.
35 Anc: Thompson Family Tree: excinders1; *CA*.
36 Anc: Young-Thompson Family Tree_2011-05-30 r2: jythompson2; The Makers of Cheltenham, viewed 9 December 2018: <https://cheltonia.wordpress.com/cheltenham-whos-who/>.

37 BMD; c-1851.
38 BMD; Criminal Records, Gloucester Sessions; England & Wales, Criminal Registers, 1791–1892; UK, Prison Hulk Registers and Letter Books, 1802–1849; New South Wales, Australia, Gaol Description and Entrance Books, 1818–1930; Australia, Convict Records Index, 1787–1867.
39 Anc: Anderson Family Tree: BarbaraBayle74; *CA*; *Hereford Journal*, 22 August 1855.
40 Anc: esdr family tree: edendy34; BMD; CCEd; c-1861; *OA*.
41 BMD; *CA*; c-1871.
42 Anc: R Alex Reed Family Tree: ralexreed; CCEd; *OA*.
43 Anc: Beresford Family Tree: Penny Beresford; BMD; c-1851; *OA*.
44 Anc: Sheridan Family Tree: goodsellannie; BMD; c-1851; *DNB*; *Survey of London*: vol. 40, the Grosvenor Estate in Mayfair, part 2 (The Buildings), 1980, pp. 176-184; Wikipedia: Thrupp & Maberley; WFP-F176 Diary of Agnes Witts.
45 BMD; c-1841–1851; *Slater's Directory*, 1858.
46 Anc: Chen Family Tree: Halima Chen; BMD; c-1851, GA.
47 BMD; c-1841–1851.
48 Anc: Davies-Steward-Rae-Ridgard: dalej72; *DNB*.
49 Anc: Corne/Roberts/Allman/St George Family Tree: geoffanddi; BMD; c-1851; *Johnstone's London Commercial Guide, and Street Directory*, 1818; *Colburn's New Monthly Magazine*, vol. 2, 1814; *The Spectator*, 1829; *The Post Office London Directory*, 1843; NA, Kew.
50 Articles of Clerkship, 1756–1874; BMD; c-1851–1881.
51 Anc: HEC Family Tree: eclarke164; BMD; *OA*.
52 Anc: Rimell Family: Chastyn407; BMD; *B-1847-2*, p. 1136; GA: Timbrell and Lightbourne vs. Croft, Hanbury Tracy, Williams, Burford, Burroughs, Delme...: Reference: D2153/1022.
53 Anc: Houchins/Mcintosh/Tocher: Mudhooks; BMD; *DNB*.
54 BMD; *MM*, vol. 23, 1807, p. 198; West Lavington burials, viewed 15 December 2018: <https://www.wiltshire-opc.org.uk/Items/West%20Lavington/West%20Lavington%20-%20Burials%201775-1799.pdf>.
55 Anc: TU Study: jhgtancestry; BMD; Games Licences, 1827; Selected Reports from the *Salisbury and Winchester Journal*.
56 BMD; c-1851–1881.
57 BMD; c-1851–1901; *LG*.
58 Anc: Phabayn Family Tree: suegudgeon; BMD; *CA*; c-1851–1891.
59 Anc: Victorians: MarchHare2; BMD; c-1851; *OA*.
60 *The Bankrupt Directory; Being a Complete Register of All the Bankrupts from Dec. 1820 to Apr. 1843*, 1843, p. 413; Davies, Henry, *The Stranger's Guide through Cheltenham*, 1834, p. 188; *London Robsons Street Directory*, 1832; ditto: 1843; E&W Wills—will of William Todd; *VCH*, Gloucestershire, vol. 7, Cranham, 1981, pp. 199-210; Swiss Cottages, Cranham Woods, RIBA, viewed 16 December 2018: <https://www.architecture.com/image-library/RIBApix/image-information/poster/swiss-cottages-cranham-woods-cranham-gloucestershire-perspective/posterid/RIBA83588.html>; 'William Thomas Todd', UCL-Slaves, viewed 16 December 2018: <http://wwwdepts-live.ucl.ac.uk/lbs/person/view/2146645707 >; Whitton, J. K., *A History of the Cotswold Sanatorium Company Ltd, Cranham*, 1998.
61 Anc: Lara Holman's Tree: lara136; *GM*, 1846, p. 538; *LM*, vol. 33, 1802, p. 560; *MM*, vol. 14, November, p. 356.
62 BMD; c-1851–1881; MI: Great Barrington.
63 Anc: Palmer Family Tree: Matthew Palmer; Clack, John Morley, *Select Remains of the Rev. J. M. Clack ... Also a brief memoir of the deceased, with a funeral oration and sermon*, 1817, p. 11; *GM*, vol. 100, part 1, 1830, p. 554; *The European Magazine, and London Review*, vol. 73, 1818, p. 541; E&W Wills—will of Benjamin Tomkins; St George in the East, viewed 9 December 2018: <https://www.british-history.ac.uk/london-environs/vol2/pp425-436>.
64 BMD; CCEd; c-1841; *OA*; *12th Report of Inspectors of Prisons—Southern & Western District*, 1847/48; *Parliamentary Papers*, vol. 45, 1835, p. 11, the PP definitely say 'F' but this was probably a transcription error.
65 Anc: Nigel Moss: Moss_Nigel; *DNB*.
66 Anc: Munn Family Tree; ElizabethMunn; *OA*.
67 BMD; c-1851.
68 Anc: Phipps Family Tree: barbarahenry25; *CA*.
69 c-1841; *Parliamentary Papers* (House of Commons and Command).
70 Anc: JadeBattye48, Johannesburg, Gauteng, South Africa family tree; BMD; Foster, Joseph, *Grantees of Arms*, vol. 2, 1916, p. 368; Fox, Robert, *The History of Godmanchester, in the County of Huntingdon, Etc.*, 1831, p. 302; Major, Joanne, and Murden, Sarah, *An Infamous Mistress: The Life, Loves and Family of the Celebrated Grace Dalrymple Elliot*, 2016 p. 45; E&W Wills; PRO, CO101/18: London, Thomas Townsend, —*A Plain Narrative of Sundry Facts and Consequences Which Have happened in the Island of Grenada Since its Submission to the British Arms in 1762, in Order to Shew What Were the Real Causes Which First Produced and Have Since Supported*, 23 July 1772; RCHM: The Manuscripts of the Earl of Dartmouth, 1972, p. 512; UCL–Slaves, viewed 9 December 2018: <'Thomas Townsend of Grenada', Legacies of British Slave-ownership database, http://wwwdepts-live.ucl.ac.uk/lbs/person/view/2146633025>.
71 Anc: Firkins & Shaw Family Tree: Stephen Rench; BMD; c-1851–1881; *GM*, vol. 154, 1833, p. 174; *OA*.
72 *DNB*.
73 Anc: Colman/Towse Family Tree: homeadccge; Towse, viewed 22 December 2018: <https://aim25.com/cgi-bin/vcdf/detail?coll_id=18249&inst_id=118&nv1=browse&nv2=repos>.
74 Anc: Robert Randall: Robert Randall; BMD.
75 Anc: Keld Family Tree: SuzieKeld5; Anc: Tracy Peerage Pedigree: WilliamBTracy; BMD, Lower Swell, Stanway and Swerford parish registers; *GM*, vol. 93, part 2; vol. 134, 1823, p. 380; *HP*; *VCH*, Gloucestershire, Sevenhampton, volume 9, Bradley Hundred, 2001, pp. 166-187; *VCH*, Gloucestershire, Whittington, volume 9, Bradley Hundred, 2001, pp. 233-248.

76 BMD; *Grove*.
77 Anc: Roy Family Tree: fsumom04; BMD; c-1851; Gloucestershire, England, Prison Records, 1728–1914 for Dennis Trenfield; *The Tewkesbury Yearly Register and Magazine, 1830–1850*; *The Spectator*, 10 April 1858, p. 3.
78 *CB*; *OA*.
79 Anc: Jenkin2012: Conan Jenkin; CCEd; *OA*.
80 BMD; c-1851–1861, 1891, 1901.
81 Anc: Burrell Family Tree: cndyh1; NA: Shropshire Archives: Reference SRO 1045/83-84 and SRO 1045/80-81; *OA*.
82 Anc: Sweet Family Tree: rjmsweet.
83 Anc: McKay/Rich/Forsdyke/Bailey/Trimmer Tree: neilmckay21; GPA.
84 Anc: Trye Family of Glos: PhilD19; BMD; *OA*.
85 Anc: Longworth Family Tree: LizzieAnn44; BMD; United Grand Lodge of England Freemason Membership Registers, 1751–1921.
86 Anc: Devers, Luttick, Scott, Taylor June 2014: neild144; *MM*, 1826.
87 *DNB*.
88 *Survey of London:* vol. 42, Kensington Square to Earl's Court, 1986.
89 Anc: BW 1: jaafton Anc: Mackintosh Family Tree: jackiecedwards; Anc: FORE and DILLON: Linda Lee Webb; *B-1847-1*, p. 242; *Blackwood's Lady Magazine*, 1857, p. 144; BMD; CCEd; Cole, viewed 24 December 2018: <http://www.twickenham-museum.org.uk/house-details.php?houseid=49&categoryid=1>; *Debrett 1840*, p. 174; St Giles Priory's Church burial ground, Little Malvern: viewed 23 December 2018: <https://www.gravestonephotos.com/public/cemeterylist.php?cemetery=3313>; *The Law Advertiser*, vol. 9, 1831, p. 231; E&W Wills—will of Stephen Cole; *Pigot & Co. South Wales Directory* for 1830, 1844; RCS: Plarr's Lives of the Fellows online, Identifier: RCS: E003313; Richmond, Lesley, Turton, Alison, *The Brewing Industry: A Guide to Historical Records*, 1990, p. 110.
90 Anc: Angela Glover Family Tree: Angela Glover; BMD; GA: Gloucestershire Quarter Sessions—Archives.
91 BMD; *DNB*.
92 *ADB*; Anc: Lucas/Allen Family Tree: anitalucas22.
93 Staff Medical Officers of the Malta Garrison, viewed 24 December 2018: <http://maltaramc.com/articles/contents/armymo.html>.
94 Anc: John Reynolds Scott #3: liviaurit; *OA*.
95 BMD; c-1851–1911.
96 c-1841.
97 Anc: Turner Family Tree: carolgardiner1.
98 Anc: WELCH-DORMAN-BUNT: John Welch; Anc: McKay/Rich/Forsdyke/Bailey/Trimmer Tree: neilmckay21; BMD; c-1841–1851.
99 Anc: David Holloway Family Tree: David Holloway; Gloucestershire, England, Prison Records, 1728–1914 for George Turner.
100 Timbs, John, *Anecdotes of the Lives of William Hogarth, Sir Joshua Reynolds, Thomas Gainsborough, Henry Fuseli, Sir Thomas Lawrence, and Turner*, 1881; *The Economist*, vol. 6, Issue 1, 1849, p. 82; *The Spectator*.
101 Anc: BMD; *OA*.
102 Anc: Bell/Murley/Lane: susiep93; CCEd; GA.
103 Anc: mcpherson Family Tree: jmcpherson979; Anc: Anne List (1949) Family Tree: Robert Meagher; BMD.
104 Anc: Dolman family 2: richarddolman59; BMD; c-1841; *Pigot's Directory* 1830.
105 Cameron, Percy B., Neill, Kenneth, *Shelley and His Circle, 1773–1822*, vols 1-2, 961; *CA*; *DNB*; Royal Asiatic Society, viewed 24 December 2018: <https://royalasiaticcollections.org/collection/tm-2-3_correspondence-with-sir-george-leman-tuthill-1772-1835/>.
106 *CP*; thePeerage, person # M, #33726.
107 Anc: Jennifer's Family Tree: Jennifer Bigger; *DNB*; *HP*.
108 BMD; c-1841–1851; *VCH*, Wiltshire, vol. 10 (1975), Devizes.
109 Anc: M-D MyH Backup: MacduffDuncan; Anc: GROVES: HelenLoisS; BMD; *B-1847-2*, p. 1274; Bristol MI: TYLER: Redland Parish Church, Redland Green, viewed 25 December 2018: <https://www.bristolinformation.co.uk/srch/srchit.asp?gdoc=gl&ref=271>; Colin CHATFIELD Worldwide, viewed 25 December 2018: <https://gw.geneanet.org/chatfhs?lang=en&pz=colin&nz=chatfield&ocz=1&p=john&n=tyler>, *MM*, vol. 42, 1816, p. 479.
110 *CP*; *DNB*—Chrles Tyler and George Tyler; BMD; Whittington Families, viewed 25 December 2018: <https://www.genealogieonline.nl/en/whittington-families/I14714.php>.
111 Anc: Seddon Family Tree: synthiabradley; Anc: owe/Dixon/Trenholme/Ingleby/Malcolm family tree: didesigns_1; Anc: Rowe/Trenholme/Malcolm/Stuart: mjsanford722; BM; c-1851; *B-1906*, p. 361; Family search: Schimelpenning, viewed 26 December 2018: <https://www.ancestry.co.uk/mediaui-viewer/tree/22758/person/-1119258758/media/e8bd466e-6c48-4f5e-83c9-e43fd7f45b31?_phsrc=MvT4242&_phstart=successSource>; *GM*, vol. 56, 1844, p. 646; *The Patrician*, vol. 3, 1847, p. 598; *The United Service Magazine*, 1830, p. 389.
112 Anc: JamesMichael White Family Tree: James Michael White; *OA*.
113 BMD; c-1851.

Letter U

1 Anc: Underwood/Kain Family Tree: Peter UNDERWOOD; Wikipedia.
2 BMD; censes 1841–1871; *OA*.
3 *The Original Bath Guide, Considerably Enlarged and Improved*, 1818, p. 128.
4 Glasgow Incunabula Project, viewed 26 December 2018: <https://www.gla.ac.uk/myglasgow/incunabula/provenancesbooksellers/>.
5 BMD; *CB*; *HP*.
6 BMD; c-1851–1871.

Letter V

1 Bartolommeo Valle, viewed 26 December 2018: <https://www.britishmuseum.org/research/search_the_collection_database/term_details.aspx?bioId=14493>.
2 Anc: Josh's Tree: angelaberger421; Anc: Family Tree: assemblyorder; BMD; Crofton Thomas Croasdaile Vandeleur, viewed 28 December 2018: <https://www.geni.com/people/Crofton-Croasdaile-Vandeleur/6000000014417103293?through=6000000014416693636>; thePeerage, person M, #148083.
3 Anc: Peterson/Baker/Green/Giblin: julia_giblin; Bristol Record Office.
4 Anc: Tracey West Family Tree: Tracey West; *B-1847-2*, p. 1316; BMD.
5 *CP*.
6 Bridgwater, Patrick, *De Quincey's Gothic Masquerade*, 2004, p. 33.
7 *HP*. *Survey of London*: vol. 14, St Margaret, Westminster, part III: Whitehall II No. 10, Downing Street.
8 Anc: Thanet Mayhews Family Tree: martinmayhew1; *OA*.
9 Anc: View in TreeHamm King Family Tree: David_W_King; *DNB*.
10 Anc: Earl Family Tree: LindaHolmes55; *DNB*.
11 *BDA*, vol. 14, p. 399; BMD; *DNB*.
12 BMD.
13 BMD.
14 BMD; c-1841–1881; *Debrett 1827-II*.
15 BMD; *CB*; Smiles, Samuel, *The Huguenots—Their Settlements, Churches and Industries in England and Ireland*, 1889.
16 BMD; *CB*; c-1841–1911; *CP*; *HP*.
17 BMD.
18 Anc: Corrigan Family Tree: eleanorjohnson209; BMD; CCEd; *OA*.
19 Anc: Murray Family Tree: johnmurray3131; The Aristocracy of London: part I: Kensington, 1863; Blacker, Beaver Henry, *Brief sketches of the parishes of Booterstown and Donnybrook*, 1860; BMD; *B-1852-2*, p. 1007; Casey, Christine, *Dublin: The Buildings of Ireland (Pevsner Architectural Guides: Buildings of Ireland*, 2005; c-1841–1891; *Debrett 1824-II*, p. 1013; *DCB*; *GM*, vol. 116, 1814; vol. 91, 1821; vol. 150, 1831, p. 379 Lodge, John, *The Peerage of Ireland, or, A Genealogical History of the Present Nobility of that Kingdom*, 1754; Notes on local history Written by the Rev. Mercer c.1948 [Rothwell and Oulton]; *The Treble Almanack for the Year*, 1804; *The Scots Magazine and Edinburgh Literary Miscellany*, vol. 68, 1806, p. 726; Mervin Vavasour, viewed 30 December 2018: <http://www.biographi.ca/en/bio/vavasour_mervin_9E.html>; www.findagrave.com.
20 BMD.
21 *The Annual Register*, vol. 83, 1842; BMD; c-1841–1851.
22 Anc: The Luth and Page Ancestors: caryn85; BMD; *HP*.
23 Anc: Venour: ursularuth; CCEd; *OA*.
24 *CP*.
25 BMD; Lady Henrietta Grosvenor, viewed 30 December 2018: <http://georgianaduchessofdevonshire.blogspot.com/2009/01/tart-of-week-lady-henrietta-grosvenor.html>.
26 *HP*.
27 Guarlford History Group.
28 Anc: Newman McHaffie Tree: VickyNewman69; *CP*.
29 *DNB*.
30 BDA, vol. 15, p. 162; Giuseppe VIGANONI, viewed 30 December 2018: <http://www.quellusignolo.fr/tenors/viganoni.html>.
31 Anc: Peel Family Tree: SharonCMaud; CCEd; *OA*.
32 Anc: Burrell Family Tree: cndyh1; BMD; *LG*, 2 December 1853, p. 3569.
33 Caroline Schelling, viewed 31 December 2018: <https://www.carolineschelling.com/dramatis-personae/persons-uv/>.
34 BMD; Geneall, Deutschland; *GM*, 1817; Landesarchiv Baden-Württemberg; Maria Caroline Rosalie van Chapuset, viewed 22 November 2018: <https://www.genealogieonline.nl/en/west-europese-adel/I339223.php>; Baron August Warren (Hastings) von Soden of Soden, viewed 22 November 2018: <https://worldconnect.rootsweb.ancestry.com/cgi-bin/igm.cgi?op=GET&db=kingsnkastles&id=I336501>.
35 Anc: irving Family Tree: Jintie Toovey; *OA*.
36 Anc: Lees Family Tree: ljleesedwinstowe; Wikipedia.

Letter W

1 Anc: Woodhouse Family(June 2010) tree: ronwoodhouse_1.
2 Anc: Turner Family Tree: RuthHTurner; thePeerage, person M, #558501; Sophia Margaret Vavasour Richardon and Ethel Frances Vavasour Kennard in the England & Wales, NPC (Index of Wills and administrations), 1858–1966, 1973–1995.
3 Anc: Bailey, Binns Etc: Martin Bailey; National Library of Wales, Bunsen and Waddington Letters.
4 England & Wales, Non-Conformist and Non-Parochial Registers, 1567–1970.
5 Chambers, John, *A General History of Malvern*, 1817; *Mary Barrett Browning's Correspondence*; Brayley, Edward Wedlake, *The Graphic and Historical Illustrator: an Original Miscellany of Literary, Antiquarian, and Topographical Information*, 1834; *VCH*, Worcestershire: vol. 3, 1913, Little Malvern, pp. 449-453.
6 Anc: Lynette Keen @Watkins Family Trees: Lynette Keen; MI: Beckford; *VCH*, Gloucestershire, Beckford, 1968, pp. 250-262.
7 Anc: Patrick/Heath Family Tree: CMCorns; UCL-Slaves.
8 Anc: glendakgardiner: glendakgardiner; Bullwinkle, Alan, Norman, Colin, MI: All Saints Church Little Shelford.

9 Australian Convict Transportation Registers—Other Fleets & Ships, 1791–1868; BMD; England & Wales, Criminal Registers, 1791–1892; Gloucestershire, England, Prison Records, 1728–1914.
10 *DNB*.
11 BMD; c-1841.
12 Anc: Walker Lean Family Tree: Patrick Walker; Farr, Grahame, *Records of Bristol Ships, 1800–1838 (vessels Over 150 Tons)*, Bristol Record Society, 1950, p. 97; *Railway practice: A collection of working plans and practical details of construction in the public works of the most celebrated engineers*, 1839.
13 Anc: Dennis Family Tree: RoseKempshall75.
14 *Ibid*.
15 *CB*; *CA*; WFP F95; *The Antijacobin Review: And Protestant Advocate: Or, Monthly Political and Literary Censor*, vol. 6, 1800.
16 BMD; CCEd; *OA*.
17 Anc: Lapointe Dumas: philip dumas; BMD; c-1851–1891.
18 Anc: View in Treestroud /leach/bray: Linda Long; BMD; *OA*.
19 BMD; *OA*.
20 *DNB*; BMD; *GM*, vol. 97, 1805, p. 83; *OA*.
21 Anc: Wallbank family tree: stevewallbank; BMD; CCEd; *GM*, vol. 163, 1838, p. 331; *OA*.
22 Anc: Wallbank family tree: stevewallbank; Anc: Victorians: MarchHare2; Anc: Smalley Family Tree: louisebatesbowman; Anc: Rathbone/Fenton/Ford/Fussell/Owen/Norton/Agutter/Rooke families: Jane Chapman; BMD; Edward William Boudier, viewed 3 January 2019: <https://www.npg.org.uk/collections/search/person/mp144034/edward-william-boudier>; *B-1847-2*, p. 1498; *B-1871-2*; p. 1594.
23 Anc: Burleigh Family Tree: William Burleigh; CCEd; *OA*; United Grand Lodge of England Freemason Membership Registers, 1751–1921.
24 Anc: The Romney Marsh Matrix: terrier781; The Camerons of Fassifern—and beyond; *OA*.
25 Anc: Bailes/Chick 30-03-16: Jessica Bailes; Wallington, viewed 3 January 2019: <https://www.geni.com/people/Col-Sir-John-Wallington-K-C-B/6000000028108670115?through=6000000028816709048>.
26 Birkett, viewed 3 January 2019: <https://www.geni.com/people/Charles-James-Nelson-Birkett/6000000000973971006>; BMD; *Cambrian Quarterly Magazine and Celtic Repertory*, vol. 5, 1833, p. 149; *DNB*—Bolton; GA: Price family of Tibberton Court: Reference: D2176; *GM*, vol. 86, part 1, 1816, p. 370 vol. 175, 1844, p. 111; *LG*, vol. 2, 1819, p. 1369; UCL-Slaves; Wallis, viewed 3 January 2019: <http://www.british-history.ac.uk/report.aspx?compid=16336#s5>; *House of Lords Journal*, vol. 62: 28 April 1830, pp. 247-257.
27 BMD, and interactions with the Arbuthnott, Burdett, Kirby, Smith, and Vavasour families.
28 BMD; c-1851–1891.
29 Anc: Walters_FamilyTree: tjwalters168; BMD; *CB*; c-1851; Painswick House, viewed 5 January 2019: <https://historicengland.org.uk/listing/the-list/list-entry/1000123>; *VCH*, Gloucestershire, Barnwood, 1988, pp. 410-420.
30 Anc: Ramstedt Sandholm Harris Johnson of England, Sweden: gregramstedt1; BMD; *The Legal Observer*, vol. 27, 1844, p. 26; *LG*, part 1, 1828, p. 244; Marriages from the Newcastle St Andrews Registers (1750–1799), viewed 5 January 2019: <https://www.genuki.org.uk/big/eng/NBL/Newcastle/StAndrews/ChurchRecords/NSA1750>; Richardson, Moses Aaron, *A Guide through Newcastle-upon-Tyne and its Vicinity*, 1846, p. 150.
31 Anc: Wansey: jenniferwansey80; *The New Monthly Magazine*, vol. 13, 1820, p. 755; *Second Annual Report of the Committee of the Bowyer Lane School Society, Camberwell: Submitted to the General Meeting Held at the Grove-House, Camberwell, on Monday, June 26th, 1815*, 1815, p. 27; Wansey, viewed 5 January 2019: <http://www.nickdelves.co.uk/wansey/wansey/1925_06Wansey_Family_Tree_Pages_23-34_transcribed.pdf>.
32 Anc: Beckford Family Tree: johnweekes1; Northwood House, viewed 5 January 2019: <https://www.northwoodhouse.org/charitable-trust/trust-history/>.
33 CCEd; *OA*; Wiltshire and Swindon History Centre: Ordinations: 1806: Reference: D/1/14/1/26.
34 *CP*; *DNB*; *HP*.
35 BMD; c-1841.
36 Anc: Wright Family Tree: sylviawright18; Angela Patricia Tugwell, viewed 5 January 2019: <https://www.geni.com/people/Mary/6000000011924087292?through=5608618647090048063>.
37 Anc: Combe Family Tree: broadbentcmf; BMD; *DNB*.
38 *DNB*; *OA*.
39 Anc: Royalty & Peerage: Robert Candy; *CP*.
40 Anc: WWFTR, WM Wadenhoe, Capt George Ward Hunt, Northants Regmt: trendier1; *DNB*.
41 Wright, Robert: *The Life of Major-General James Wolfe*, 1864; BMD; c-1851.
42 BMD; c-1841–1891; Gloucestershire, England, Prison Records, 1728–1914 for Jane Waring.
43 CCEd; *DNB*.
44 Anc: Boutcher: BoutcherofBermondsey; BMD; *B-1838-4*.
45 Anc: Alicia Warren family tree 23 mar 15: AliciaWarren12; Warren, viewed 5 January 2019: <https://ghgraham.org/charleswarren1798.html>.
46 Anc: Boardman Family Tree: tomboardman1; *DNB*.
47 *CB*; *HP*.
48 BMD.
49 Anc: Cresswell Main File 6: ccresswell390; *CA*.
50 Anc: Cresswell Main File 6: ccresswell390; BMD; c-1851; G&G Publishing The Past, viewed 5 January 2019: <https://ggbooks.wordpress.com/category/hanwood/>; *The Post Office London Directory*: Kelly's Directories Limited, 1843, p. 217.
51 BMD; *DNB*.
52 Anc: Mark Fagerburg Family: mfagerburg; *The British Friend*, vols 25-26, 1867, p. 234; c-1841–1851; *Pigot's Directory*, 1830.

53 Anc: Mary Calwell Family Tree: marycalwell; *B-1834*.
54 Anc: Clark-Kolb Family Tree: BarbaraClarkGoldberg; *MM*, 1805, p. 522; *LG*, 1813.
55 BMD; *MM*, vol. 29, 1810, p. 596; *OA*; *Walford-1882*, p. 90.
56 Anc: Colin B Gurney, (Coventry), Family Tree: COLINBGURNEY44; *Gloucestershire Chronicle*, 31 August 1833; *OA*.
57 Anc: Audrey scarlett: daviddilmore; BMD; *CA*; c-1841–1851; *OA*; UCL Joseph Watson, viewed 6 January 2019: <https://www.ucl.ac.uk/bslhistory/early-deaf-education/london-asylum>.
58 Anc: Royalty & Peerage: Robert Candy; *DNB*.
59 BMD; c-1841–1851.
60 BMD; c-1841–1891.
61 Anc: BREEZE family: USLimey; Newman, John Henry, Tracey, Gerard, ed., *The Letters and Diaries of John Henry Newman: Tract 90 and the Jerusalem Bishopric, January 1841–April 1842*, 1999. *The Annual Register, or, A View of the History and Politics of the Year 1842*, vol. 83.
62 *OA*.
63 Anc: BeaverKerry-Jan09: acclivity2; *OA*; *VCH*, Oxfordshire: vol. 11, Wootton Hundred (Northern Part), 1983.
64 Anc: Dyer Dec 2015: petalbo; BMD.
65 Anc: Wilson: c_c_wilson; BMD; c-1861.
66 *HP*; *Williams*.
67 Anc: Hatton Family Tree: SylviaHatton1; *OA*.
68 BMD; *Eton*; *MM*, vols 53-58, 1822, p. 85; E&W Wills—will of Richard Webb of Ham Common; the Peerage.com, person M, #116837, mistakenly referred to as 'Robert'; Richard Holden WEBB of London, viewed 5 January 2019: <https://www.ancestry.co.uk/boards/surnames.webb/5447/mb.ashx>; *VCH*, Berkshire: Bray with the borough of Maidenhead, 1923, pp. 93-107; WFP F209.
69 c-1841–1851.
70 CCEd; *OA*.
71 Wikipedia.
72 *OA*.
73 *CB*; *DNB*; Wikipedia; Sir John Wedderburn, viewed 6 January 2019: <https://www.clanmacfarlanegenealogy.info/genealogy/TNGWebsite/getperson.php?personID=I61231&tree=CC>; Joseph Knight, viewed 6 January 2019: <https://blackpresence.co.uk/joseph-knight/>.
74 Anc: MBLF Family Tree: lyndathecottagemb; Wikipedia.
75 Anc: MBLF Family Tree: lyndathecottagemb; *CA*.
76 *BDA*, vol. 13, p. 119; BMD; *Grove*; *MM*, vol. 21, 1806, p. 463.
77 Anc: Kasper-LoRe Family Tree: janicelore53 NPG, viewed 6 January 2019: <https://www.portrait.gov.au/people/henry-weigall-1829>; <http://familypedia.wikia.com/wiki/Henry_Weigall_(1829-1925)>.
78 Anc: Croser_Nutt Family 2014: Croserdavid; *BDA*, vol. 13, p. 337.
79 Anc: Harris Family Tree: pamelahetherington; *GM*, 1841, p. 206; NA: Nelson, viewed 6 January 2019: <http://www.nationalarchives.gov.uk/trafalgarancestors/details.asp?id=17849>.
80 BMD; c-1851.
81 *GM*, vol. 32, 1762; St James's Church, Hampstead Road, *Survey of London*: vol. 21: The parish of St Pancras part 3: Tottenham Court Road & neighbourhood (1949); Ross, Sir John: *Memoirs and correspondence of Admiral Lord De Saumarez: From original papers in possession of the family*, vol. 2, 1838; Raat, J. P.: *The Life of Governor Joan Gideon Loten (1710–1789)*, 2010; *Journals of the House of Lords*, vol. 30, 1760.
82 BMD; *The Quarterly Theological Review and Ecclesiastical Record*, vol. 2, 1825—Theology, p. 518; Francis Welles, Gwinnett, viewed 6 January 2019: <https://www.gwinnett.me.uk/characters/theodore-gwinnett-c-1773-1827>; Pittville: <http://pittvillehistory.org.uk/Pittville%20places/Blakebook.html>.
83 *DNB*.
84 BMD; CCEd; *OA*.
85 Anc: Bégin Earl Family Tree: LJ Bégin; *The Court Magazine & Monthly Critic and Lady's Magazine*, vol. 13, 1844, p. 59.
86 Anc: Newman McHaffie Tree: VickyNewman69; BMD; c-1841–1891.
87 BMD; c-1841–1861; *The Medico-chirurgical Review, and Journal of Medical Science. Analytical Series,* vol. 1, 1821. Mann, J. L., *Recollections of My Early and Professional Life*, 1887.
88 BMD; *DNB*; *Grove*; Alfredo Piatti, viewed 12 January 2019: <http://www.alfredopiatti.com/home/index.php?page=biography>.
89 BMD; *House of Commons Papers*, vol. 41, 1839; *OA*; *The Ecclesiastical Gazette, or, Monthly Register of the Affairs of the Church of England*, vols 5-6, 1843; UK, Lunacy Patients Admission Registers, 1846–1912.
90 Bruford, W. H., *Culture and Society in Classical Weimar 1775–1806*, 1962.
91 BMD; c-1841–1861.
92 *Ibid.*
93 Paget, J. W., *The Law Advertiser*, vol. 2, 1824; Gilbert, R. A., *William Wynn Westcott and the Esoteric School of Masonic Research.*
94 BMD; *CP*; *HP*; *Lodge-1832*, p. 344.
95 Anc: western2007: peterwestern1703; *OA*.
96 Anc: Caithness Family Tree: pdbruxner_randall; BMD; *CA*; CCEd; *DNB*.
97 Anc: Parsons Family Tree: rani4; Anc: Marshall Family Tree: bjmarshall143; BMD; c-1851–1881.
98 Anc: Sir Charles Wetherell Family Tree: jwitherel; *DNB*; *HP*; *OA*.
99 *OA*.
100 CCEd; *OA*.
101 Anc: Richardson Tree: Judith_Forster; *OA*; UCL-Slaves.
102 BMD; *OA*.

103 JAGEMANN, Caroline, *Selbstinszenierungen im Klassischen Weimar*; Weyrauch, viewed 13 January 2019: <https://www.hyperion-records.co.uk/c.asp?c=C1244>; Weber, viewed 13 January 2019: <https://weber-gesamtausgabe.de/de/A002129.html>; Weyrauch, viewed 13 January 2019: <https://www.geni.com/people/Wilhelmina-Sophia-Friederike-Weyrauch/6000000028661852871?through=6000000028661189525>.

104 Anc: Hardy Family Tree: hardy70; BMD; CCEd; Ecton Village, viewed 13 January 2019: <http://www.ectonvillage.co.uk/church/the-rectors-of-ecton/>; *OA*.

105 *Remains, Historical and Literary, Connected with the Palatine Counties of Lancaster and Chester*, 1843, p. 42; NA: GA: ref. D4582/4/3; NA: 160—Oxfordshire History Centre, Flick—Travell Family of Southrop, Flick/I/ii/11 17 August 1813 Limited Administration.

106 Anc: Gray Family Tree: Angela Gray; *The Bengal and Agra Annual Guide and Gazetteer, for 1841*, 1842, p. 242; BLUNT, Edward, *List of inscriptions on Christian tombs and tablets of historical interest in the United Provinces of Agra and Oudh*; BMD; Charles Whalley, viewed 13 January 2019: <https://www.thegazette.co.uk/London/issue/17253/page/1215/data.pdf>; *GM*, 1842, p. 540; *The India Office and Burma Office List*, 1828, p. 132; NA: GA: Deeds and other documents relating to messuages and land (field names given) in Evenlode... Reference: D6356/1-3.

107 BMD; c-1851; *OA*.

108 Anc: RFU 1895 Committee Robert Seymour Whalley Family Tree: Millerfiehn69; Anc: Payne Family Tree: henrylord65; August 19, viewed 15 January 2019: <http://www.limerickcity.ie/media/08%2019%2035.pdf> BMD; c-1851–1861, 1901; *The Gentleman and Citizen's Almanack*, 1815, p. 110; *The Royal Kalendar, and Court and City Register for England, Scotland, Ireland, and the Colonies*, 1822, p. 177; NA: Oxfordshire History Centre: Flick–Travell Family of Southrop: Assignment in trust to attend the reversion and inheritance: Reference: Flick/I/xvi/10; NA: Kew: Reference: WO 76/126/118; *The Analyst: A Quarterly Journal of Science, Literature, Natural History, and the Fine Arts*, vol. 1, 1834, p. 153.

109 BMD; c-1861; England & Wales, NPC (Index of Wills and Administrations), 1858–1966; *GM*, vol. 177, 1845, p. 644.

110 BMD; WFP—various.

111 *DNB*.

112 BMD; c-1841; *The Ecclesiastical gazette, or, Monthly register of the affairs of the Church of England, 1846. Remains, Historical and Literary, Connected with the Palatine Counties of Lancaster and Chester*, 1843; WFP—various.

113 Anc: Sawbridge Floaters: pennyharris56; *GM*, vol. 57, 1846, p. 197; *OA*.

114 BMD; *CA*; c-1841–1861.

115 Anc: Bates and Baker Family Tree 3: stevebates10; BMD; *GM*, vol. 165, 1838, p. 105; *OA*, The Wolfords in the County of Warwickshire, viewed 17 January 2019: <http://wolfordshistory.uk/church7.html>.

116 *OA*; *VCH*, Sussex, Bramber Rape (Southern Part). Originally published 1980.

117 BMD; CCEd; *OA*.

118 Anc: Pat Kemp tree: thekemper; *CB*; CARY, John: *Cary's New Itinerary: Or, An Accurate Delineation of the Great Roads, Both Direct and Cross Throughout England and Wales*, 1828. *GM*, vol. 76, part 2, 1806.

119 Anc: Carey Family Tree: RobertCarey31; *The Aberystwith Observer*, 20 May 1865; BMD; c-1841–1861.

120 BMD; *B-1847-2*, p. 1569, c-1851; *VCH*, Oxfordshire, vol. 10, Banbury Hundred, 1972.

121 Anc: Quinn: NickJQuinn; *CA*.

122 Anc: MAY and SIMONS Family: deborahmay125; BMD; *LG*, part 1, T. Neuman, 1840.

123 Anc: Scarlett Xara Small: david small; BMD; c-1841–1911; *London Magazine*, 1825; WHITCOMBE, Thomas Douglas, *Campaign of the Falieri and Piraeus in the Year 1827, Or, Journal of a Volunteer, Being the Personal Account of Captain Thomas Douglas Whitcombe*, 1992, appendix 1, p. 200.

124 *Ibid*., Anc: Martin_Voss Family Tree: Alison Smith BMD; *GM*, vols 174-175, 1843; *HP*; *OA*.

125 *Ibid*.; WHITCOMBE, Thomas Douglas, *Campaign* etc., pp. 36-37.

126 Thompson, Mark S., 'The Rise of the Scientific Soldier as seen through the Performance of the Corps of Royal Engineers During the early 19th Century', thesis, University of Sunderland February, 2009, appendix, viewed 19 January 2019: <https://sure.sunderland.ac.uk/3559/1/Mark_S_Thompson.pdf>; United Grand Lodge of England Freemason Membership Registers, 1751–1921; Andrew Douglas White, viewed 19 January 2019: <https://www.napoleon-series.org/research/biographies/GreatBritain/c_White.html>.

127 c-1841.

128 *DNB*.

129 Anc: Tim Greagsby Family Tree: TimGreagsby; *OA*.

130 BMD; CCEd; *OA*.

131 BMD; Dissenting Acadamies Online, viewed 19 January 2019: <https://dissacad.english.qmul.ac.uk/sample1.php?parameter=personretrieve&alpha=2056>; *VCH*, Essex: vol. 6, 1973.

132 *HP*: John Horrocks (1768–1804).

133 Anc: Glos Whittards (ANR) Family Tree: andyryyy; BMD; c-1841–1851, 1861; *Hunt*.

134 BMD; VICKERY, Amanda: *The Gentleman's Daughter*, 2003; Bukit Brown Trails, viewed 19 January 2019: <http://limsumin-bukitbrowntrails.blogspot.com/2011/12/at-fort-canning-in-search-of-john.html>.

135 Anc: Procter Family Tree: martinwolfgang1; Anc: Eacott/Woodcock Family Tree: susan lambert; *The Court Journal: Court Circular & Fashionable Gazette*, vol. 5, 1833, p. 574; *GM*, vol. 154, 1833, p. 174.

136 Anc: Sidney Carne Family Tree: Sidney Carne; BMD; c-1851–1891; Thomas Whitford at Brentor Village, viewed 26 August 2019: <http://www.brentorvillage.org/?page_id=7235>.

137 Anc: Brownrigg, Robt Family Tree: Elizabeth Goldthorpe; BMD; *CA*; c-1841–1881.

138 Anc: Adye-Brading family tree; BMD; c-1841–1861; JOHNSON, Joan: *The General*, 1987; thePeerage, person M, #37946; *VCH*, Gloucestershire, vol. 6, 1965, Lower Slaughter; *Dictionary of New Zealand National Biography*.

139 *HP*.

140 Anc: Jarrow Family Tree: hilaryjarrow; Anc: Molyneux-Kerr-Morehead Tree 2018-05-12_01: Suzanne Duggan; BMD; *B-1847-2*, p. 661; National Library of Ireland, Franks, viewed 20 January 2019: <http://sources.nli.ie/Record/MS_UR_033514>; National

Trust, Chastleton House; NUI Galway, viewed 20 January 2019: <http://landedestates.nuigalway.ie/LandedEstates/jsp/family-show.jsp?id=2430>; *OA*.

141 Anc: Whyte Family Tree: dianamorris6173; *B-1844-Enc*.; BMD.

142 Anc: van oppen Family Tree: Margaret Crowley; Betham, William, *The Baronetage of England, Or the History of the English Baronets, and Such Baronets of Scotland, as are of English Families: With Genealogical Tables, and Engravings of Their Armorial Bearings*, vol. 5, 1805, p. 456; *The Monthly Repository of Theology and General Literature*, vol. 9, 1814, p. 596; National Gallery, Lorne Campbell, viewed 20 January 2019: <https://www.nationalgallery.org.uk/media/15478/jean_gossart_an_elderly_couple.pdf>; NA: Staffordshire and Stoke-on-Trent Archive Service: Probate of Maria Louisa Whyte of Barrow Hill, Rocester, widow, Reference: D1134/14/14; E&W Wills—will of Gill Slater merchant of Liverpool proved 27/10/1802 PROB 11/1382/187; will of Thomas Slater of Liverpool proved 06/02/1818; David Purificato, Stony Brook University, viewed 20 January 2019: <https://pasttensejournal.files.wordpress.com/2016/05/purificato-well-worn-and-far-travelled.pdf>; Staffordshire Advertiser; 8 December 1855; UCL-Slaves; WFP F206, 26 February 1805; F212, Friday 13 October 1808; Whishaw, James, *A Synopsis of the members of the English Bar, etc.*, 1835, p. 153.

143 Anc: goodeve Family Tree: henry goodeve; Anc: descendant of john scarlett: mikescarlett167; BMD; c-1841–1891; Caroline & Martin Davis's families, viewed 21 January 2019: <http://archive.freerangephotography.co.uk/MDg3-o/p15.htm>.

144 BMD; *DNB*; *OA*.

145 Anc: jones/clarkson Family Tree: duchess363; *DNB*; *OA*.

146 *Ibid*.

147 BMD; c-1841; Fosbroke, Thomas Dudley, *Abstracts of Records and Manuscripts Respecting the County of Gloucester*, 1807, p. 404; *The Law Times*, 1845; *OA*; *VCH*, Gloucestershire, vol. 11, Bisley and Longtree Hundreds, 1976: Horsley: Education, pp. 183-184.

148 BMD.

149 BMD; Upper Slaughter Parish Registers.

150 BMD; c-1851.

151 BMD.

152 *DNB*.

153 Anc: Charles Rodrigues Family Tree: BONSAIACE; BMD; c-1851; *OA*; UCL-Slaves.

154 *DNB*.

155 Anc: Michael Moroni Hyatt, Hyatt Family Tree; Anc: Sandra Ellen Clarke and Rolland Fernand Joseph Junior Poirier Family Tree: sandrapoirier4; BMD; c-1841–1911.

156 Gloucestershire, England, Prison Records, 1728–1914 for Thomas Wilkins: Registers of Prisoners The County Gaol 1854–1860. England & Wales, Criminal Registers, 1791–1892.

157 WFP F08, F223, 26 May 1817.

158 Anc: Moore Family Tree: Kate_Davy, Wikipedia.

159 *LG*, part 3, 1843, p. 2648; *The Post Office London Directory*, Kelly's Directories Limited, 1843.

160 *LG*, part 3, 1845, p. 2679.

161 Anc: Roger Emery Family Tree: 1_rogeremery; NA: PROB 11/2020/228; NA: 182—West Sussex Record Office: The correspondence of the 5th Duke of Richmond.

162 *Hunt*.

163 WFP F175.

164 *Baily's Magazine of Sports & Pastimes*, vol. 28, 1876, pp. 84-85; BMD; Clifford, Naomi, *The Disappearance of Maria Glenn: A True Life Regency Mystery*, 2016; *GM*; vols 177–178, 1845, p. 315; National Trust, viewed 26 January 2019: <http://www.nationaltrustcollections.org.uk/object/1316178>; *OA*.

165 *OA*.

166 *CB*; *Dictionary of Welsh Biography*; *HP*.

167 *DNB*.

168 BMD; c-1851–1871. *The Asiatic Journal and Monthly Register for British and Foreign India, China, and Australia*, vol. 9, 1832, p. 51; *The Jurist*, vol. 6, part 2, 1843 p. 486; *The Railway Chronicle: Joint-stock Companies Journal. Register of Traffic, Shares, Engineering Improvements and All Matters Connected with Railways* ..., vol. 1, p. 706, 14 June 1845.

169 CCEd.

170 Fisher, Paul Hawkins, *Notes and Recollections of Stroud*, 1891; MI: Woodchester; *OA*.

171 Gloucestershire, Prison Records.

172 *Adelphi Calendar*, 20 March 1821; *The Literary Chronicle and Weekly review, for 1821-Forming an Analysis and General Repository of Literature, Philosophy, Science, Arts, History, Biography, The Drama, Morals, Manners, and Amusements, 14 April 1821*; Novello, J. Alfredo, *The Musical World*, vol. 8, 1838; *Hereford Times*, 27 February 1841; Rice, Albert R., *From the Clarinet D'Amour to the Contra Bass: A History of Large Size Clarinets, 1740–1860*, 2009.

173 Bennett, James: *The Tewkesbury Yearly Register and Magazine*, 1840; CCEd, *OA*.

174 BMD; c-1841–1851.

175 BMD; c-1851; *The Ecclesiastical Gazette*, vols 7-8, 1845, p. 78.

176 BMD.

177 *CB*; *HP*; Wikipedia.

178 Anc: Lewis Elliott Family Tree: julieandthomas1; *BLG*.

179 Orbell, John, *British Banking: A Guide to Historical Records*, 2017; Willis, Percival & Company records, viewed 27 January 2019: <https://archiveshub.jisc.ac.uk/search/archives/8e695e8d-4856-3d08-9536-397bc7136517>.

180 MI: All Saints Church Little Shelford; Anc: Urney Park and Beyond family tree: Perry_Colin; BMD; c-1851; Vignoles, viewed 27 January 2019: <https://gw.geneanet.org/elsa2002?lang=en&n=vignoles&oc=0&p=Margaret>.

181 *DNB*.

182 *DNB*; *OA*.
183 BMD; *B-1835-2*, p. 270; E&W Wills—will of Frances Wilson.
184 *OA*.
185 *OA*.
186 *DNB*.
187 Anc: E. J. Birchall family tree; *OA*.
188 BMD.
189 *ADB*, vol. 2, 1967; BMD.
190 BMD; c-1841–1911 inc.; *GM*, part 1, 1827; PI: additional information courtesy Marg Muntz.
191 Anc: Reid (Boolcunda) and Hack Family Tree; Articles of Clerkship, 1756–1874; *B-1871-2*; *GM*, part 1, 1807; *LG*, 11 July, 1826; *VCH*, Gloucestershire, vol. 4, the City of Gloucester, 1720–1835; Wilson, Erasmus: *The History of the Middlesex Hospital During the First Century of its Existence*, 1845.
192 *GM*, vol. 20, 1824; *Plarr's Lives of the Fellows of the Royal College of Surgeons of England*; *LG*, 20 April 1877; PI: additional information courtesy Marg Muntz.
193 BMD; PI: additional information courtesy Marg Muntz.
194 Anc: [Hampden] Cockayne Family Tree: florimell1919; Anc: [Macgrgor] Julie Avenell / Macdonald-Brown Family Tree: Julie Avenell; BMD; *GM*, vols 181-182, 1847, p. 196; *GM*, vol. 179 , 1846, p. 422; *OA*; Shockerwick House, viewed 27 January 2019: <http://www.bathfordsociety.org.uk/content/buildings/shockerwick_house_main.htm>.
195 *Figaro in London*, vol. 5, 1836, p. 123; *HP*; *OA*; Reverend William Winchester, viewed 27 January 2019: <https://www.dnw.co.uk/auction-archive/special-collections/lot.php?specialcollection_id=185&lot_id=89309>.
196 *HP*.
197 *Some Account of the English Stage, from the Restoration in 1660 to 1830*: In Ten vols, vol. 7, 1832, p. 678; Singers—Vauxhall Gardens, viewed 27 May 2019: <http://www.vauxhallgardens.com/vauxhall_gardens_singers_page.html>.
198 BMD; c-1851–1861; *The London Medical Directory*, 1846, p. 169.
199 Anc: Laws Family Tree: flissoh1; BMD; Roll of the Indian Medical Service, 1615–1930; Oxford Medical Men.
200 *CP*.
201 Anc: Nicholas_Thomas_3: debndave124; Anc: Badham Family Tree: jenniferturnbull1; Anc: Watton Bartholomew Tree 2015: gazetteer; BMD; thePeerage, person M, #31823.
202 BMD; c-1851–1871; Grier, Sydney C., introduced and annotated, *Letters of Warren Hastings to his Wife*, 1905; Marian Winter, viewed 28 January 2019: <https://www.findagrave.com/memorial/94646436>; *OA*.
203 BMD; c-1851–1861; Stroud Local History Society: *A Millennium Miscellany*, 2000.
204 Anc: Campbell Smith Forster Family Tree: ru_d_a_smith; Anc: Jacob's Ladder—Whole family: sammijohn; BMD; *B-1871-2*; c-1851–1871.
205 *OA*,
206 *Hunt*.
207 BMD; Crisp, Frederick Arthur, *Visitation of England and Wales*, vol. 10, 1902; Incoming Passenger Lists, 1878–1960; Gloucestershire, England, Electoral Registers, 1832–1974; Buchanan, viewed 31 January 2019: <http://www.ww2guards.com/ww2guards/Cemeteries_-_Scotland/Pages/BUCHANAN_CHURCHYARD_EXTENSION,_UK.html>; London, England, Electoral Registers, 1832–1965 for John Travell-J Witts; WWI Service Medal and Award Rolls, 1914–1920, Piece 2321: Voluntary Aid Detachment.
208 Bailey, Victor, *This Rash Act: Suicide Across the Life Cycle in the Victorian City*, 1998.
209 Anc: Lucas Family Tree: maryback_1; WFP.
210 Phillimore, W. P. W. (William Phillimore Watts), *Nottingham parish registers. Marriages* (vol. 3); BMD; c-1841–1911; *The Asiatic Journal and Monthly Miscellany*, vol. 38, 1842.
211 *Grove*.
212 *CP*.
213 *CA*.
214 Anc: Brown Family Tree: louby3; BMD; Anc: Samantha Swift family tree: Samantha Humphries; c-1841; Jackson, E., *Wedmore Parish Registers: Marriages, 1561–1839*, 1888, p. 106; *Pigot's Directory*.
215 *B-1832-2*, p. 641; BMD; Cracroft's Peerage.
216 *Historical Account of Newcastle-upon-Tyne Including the Borough of Gateshead*, published by Mackenzie and Dent, Newcastle-upon-Tyne, 1827.
217 c-1841–1881; Royal College of Surgeons: Plarr's Lives of the Fellows Online.
218 Wikipedia.
219 BMD; Clan Macfarlane, viewed 8 February 2019: <http://www.clanmacfarlanegenealogy.info/genealogy/TNGWebsite/getperson.php?personID=I84095&tree=CC>.
220 Wikipedia.
221 BMD; c-1851–1861; *Pigot's Directory*.
222 Doughton, Daphne, 'The Beginnings of the Cheltenham Dispensary', *Gloucestershire History* No. 5 (1991). *Pigot's Directory*, 1830.
223 *GM*, vol. 99, 1829, p. 649; Herefordshire Archive and Records Centre: Mostly mortgages of Moreton Magna and Moreton Parva made by William Bird, Elizabeth, etc.; *OA*; Phillimore, W. P. W., Gurney, Thomas, (ed.), *Middlesex Parish Registers*, vol. IV., 1912, p. 32.
224 *OA*.
225 Anc: Williams/Smith Family Tree: Julia Giffen; Anc: Donna's family tree: donnamaria ridler; BMD; c-1841–1861; Gloucestershire, England, Gaol Registers, 1815–1879; England & Wales, Criminal Registers, 1791–1892.
226 Anc: Horn Family Tree: nickhorn_1; BMD; *CA*; *Worcestershire Chronicle*, 10 August 1853.
227 Anc: Cruickshank Tree Version 2: davidcruickshank1; Anc: Taylor Family Tree: The Taylor Family; Anc: Family Tree: Coldrey, Abraham, Di Nallo, Tortolano: Marcel Di Nallo; BMD; c-1911; *Law Times, and Journal of Property*, vol. 33, 1859, p. 260; *Winchester*

Commoners. 1836–1890: A Register of Commoners who Have Entered Winchester College from the Commencement of Dr. Moberly's Headmastership, to the Present Time, 1891, p. 121.

228 Maritime Memorials, viewed 9 February 2019: <http://memorials.rmg.co.uk/m6482/>.

229 *DNB*.

230 Wordsworth, viewed 9 February 2019: <https://www.gracesguide.co.uk/Charles_Favell_Forth_Wordsworth>.

231 c-1851–1861; *LG*, part 2, 1839.

232 BMD; c-1851; *Asiatic Journal*, 1839.

233 BMD; *LG*, part 2, 1834; *LG*, part 2, 1840, p. 1904; E&W Wills—will of George Worrall; Frenchay Park House, viewed 29 May 2019: <https://www.facebook.com/StapletonandFrenchay/posts/frenchay-parkhousethe-cake-family-of-winterbourne-now-own-frenchay-park-house-fp/1754831424761830/>.

234 *OA*.

235 *CA*.

236 BMD; *GM*, vol. 70, 1791; vol. 91, part 2, 1821; Gye's *Bath directory*, 1819; WFP 220.

237 Anc: Good, Wheatley, Wratten & Blanch: wrag44; *Hunt*.

238 WFP 197.

239 c-1851–1871; Boyer, J. Patrick, *Another Country, Another Life: Calumny, Love, and the Secrets of Isaac Jelfs*, 2013.

240 *OA*.

241 Anc: Morison/Annatt Family Tree: Michael Morison; *Bulletins and Other State Intelligence*, part 2, 1855, p. 1985; *Hart's Annual Army List, Militia List, and Imperial Yeomanry List*, 1847, p. 93; NPC; *The United Service Magazine*, 1844, p. 159.

242 BMD; *OA*.

244 Anc: beach Family Tree: marietaylor55; *The Asiatic journal and monthly register for British and foreign India, China and Australasia*, vol. 14, 1834; *OA*.

244 CCEd; *OA*.

245 BMD; c-1841–1851; Deane and Wynch families of Ashen: papers 1773–1994, incl diaries and travel journals of Paul Marriot Wynch of the Bengal Civil Service, Essex Record Office, Chelmsford; *The Quarterly Oriental Magazine, Review and Register*, vol. 6, 1820; *GM*, vols 169-170, 1841.

246 BMD; *HP*.

247 Anc: Tonya Mae Wright Family Tree7.17.2017: Tonya Christman; Bucknall, viewed 27 January 2019: <https://www.wikitree.com/wiki/Dyot-Bucknall-2>; Wyndham, viewed 27 January 2019: <https://www.myheritage.com/names/george_wyndham>.

248 *HP*.

249 *Monthly Literary Register*, 1805; *OA*.

250 Anc: THOROLD Family Tree: MARCUS THOROLD; *B-1847-2*, p. 1658.

251 *Ibid*., Anc: Family Tree: assemblyorder; BMD; c-1841–1891.

252 *Ibid*.

253 *OA*.

254 *OA*; UK, Poll Books and Electoral Registers, 1538–1893.

255 *OA*.

256 Geneanet: Bradley's of South Derry.

Letter X

1 Ximenes, viewed 10 February 2019: <http://www.jewishencyclopedia.com/articles/15043-ximenes-sir-morris-moses>.

Letter Y

1 *CP*.

2 Anc: Dix Edgington Family Tree: elizabethgarner46BMD; BMD; c-1841–1891; UK, Lunacy Patients Admission Registers, 1846–1912.

3 BMD; c-1841–1881.

4 *OA*

5 BMD; c-1841–1851; *LG*, part 5, 1844.

6 *HP*.

7 BMD; c-1841–1851; Thrapston Bank, viewed 10 February 2019: <https://www.archive.barclays.com/items/show/5245>

8 *HP*.

9 thepeerage.com, person F, #170355.

10 thepeerage.com, person F, #616117.

11 BMD.

Letter Z

1 *Bye-gones: relating to Wales and the Border Countries*, 1887, p. 298; Förtsch, Epheuranken: *belletristische Beilage zum Würzburger Abendblatt*, vol. 23, 1863, p. 40; Zobel von Giebelstadt und Darstadt, die Freiherren, Genealogie.